THE NEW YORK PUBLIC LIBRARY
DESK REFERENCE

Fourth Edition

A STONESONG PRESS BOOK

HYPERION

New York

HYPERION
77 West 66th Street
New York, NY 10023-6298

 The New York Public Library

Library of Congress Cataloging-in-Publication Data

ISBN: 0-7868-6846-5

Printed in the United States of America on acid-free paper.

A Stonesong Press Book

Hyperion books are available for special promotions and premiums. For details contact Hyperion Special Markets, 77 West 66th Street, 11th Floor, New York, New York, 10023, or call 212-456-0100.

Fourth Edition

10 9 8 7 6 5 4 3 2 1

Typesetting by Brad Walrod, High Text Graphics, Inc.

Four-color maps created by Netmaps, S.A.

NEW YORK PUBLIC LIBRARY PROJECT SPONSOR

EDITORIAL DIRECTOR
Paul Fargis

EDITOR, FOURTH EDITION
Ellen Scordato

CONTRIBUTORS

Kenneth Anderson

Patricia Barnes-Svarney

Celia Bland

Eugene Brown

Bree Burns

Sheree Bykovsky

James Callan

Michelle Camardella

Melinda Corey

Susan Elliott

Alison Fargis

Paul Heacock

Lester Hoffman

Constance Jones

Karen Kniepp

Philip Koslow

Douglas Lancaster

Lawrence Lorimer

Bill McClain

Patricia Murphy

Andree Nolen

George Ochoa

Scott Prentzas

Louise Quayle

Akim Reinhardt

Sarah Scheffel

Thomas E. Svarney

Joanne Trestrail

Tad Tuleja

Craig Waff

To Alison

A Note from the Editors

Every attempt has been made to ensure that this publication is as accurate as possible and as comprehensive as space would allow. We are grateful to the many researchers, librarians, teachers, reference editors, and friends who contributed facts, figures, time, energy, ideas, and opinions. Our choice of what to include was aided by their advice and their voices of experience. The contents, however, remain subjective to some extent, because we could not possibly cover everything that one might look for in basic information. If errors or omissions are discovered, we would appreciate hearing from you, the user, as we prepare future editions. Please address suggestions and comments to The Stonesong Press, 11 East 47th Street, New York, NY 10017.

We hope you find our work useful.

CONTENTS

PREFACE

The New York Public Library, through its Research and Branch Libraries, provides free and open access to information on a scale unmatched by any other library in the world. Consisting of four major research libraries whose materials do not circulate and are used within their reading rooms—the Humanities and Social Sciences Library, The New York Public Library for the Performing Arts, the Schomburg Center for Research in Black Culture, and the Science, Industry and Business Library—and 85 neighborhood libraries with circulating collections throughout the Bronx, Manhattan, and Staten Island, it has more material than any other public library system in the nation.

The collections themselves reflect the profoundly democratic and all-encompassing nature of the Library. Numbering more than 50 million items, its holdings range from the most venerable monuments of human culture—such as the Gutenberg Bible and Jefferson's manuscript copy of the Declaration of Independence—to such icons of popular culture as 19th-century baseball cards, to the literary archives of Virginia Woolf, Jack Kerouac, and many others, to commonplace materials that document the everyday lives of otherwise anonymous people. The collections grow at a rate of approximately 10,000 items per week in dozens of languages. Over the years, the Library's holdings have played a vital role in the creation of innumerable works in the arts, science, literature, and history.

Founded in 1895, The New York Public Library officially opened the doors of its landmark building on Fifth Avenue on May 23, 1911, when on one day upwards of 50,000 visitors streamed past the guardian lions; today the Library system is visited and used annually by more than 15 million people, from neighborhood children and general readers to researchers and scholars from around the world. There are 1.7 million cardholders; over 6 million reference questions were answered last year, either in the libraries, by phone, or via the Internet. The Library's Telephone Reference service, augmented in 2002 by Ask Librarians Online, continues to provide quick, accurate information to thousands of users each year.

Today the global use of the Library's resources is dramatically increasing through access to catalogs and digitized collections via the Library's web site. An ongoing program to digitize primary source materials, both visual and textual, will make these unique items accessible from home. Additionally users have access to more than 300 electronic databases, some of which can also be used from home with a New York Public Library borrower's card.

Yet, as the Library embraces the technologies of the 21st century, the technology that has stood the test of time—the book—remains very much at the heart of what the Library does. Among these extraordinary collections are over 18 million books, a format that remains a convenient, easy-to-use tool for obtaining information. Back in 1989, when *The New York Public Library Desk Reference* was originally published, we felt that "a book fills a unique need for portability, individuality, and beauty." We still do. And it has been gratifying to find that this particular book seems to have filled the needs of our using public, as both a home and library reference.

Paul LeClerc
President, The New York Public Library

NOTE FROM THE NEW YORK PUBLIC LIBRARY

Like the first three editions, this fourth edition reflects the experience of librarians, professional researchers, and reference editors in handling a wide range of questions in many subject areas. It remains what it has been from its first publication—a compendium of basic information about a variety of subjects that allows readers to efficiently find answers to their questions. This edition has been thoroughly revised and updated to help the general reader handle the explosion of information that fills our 21st-century world. In response to many suggestions from users, and the impact of increased computer access to information, whole sections of the book have been rewritten and the popular easy-to-follow charts, graphs, and sidebars of the previous edition have been updated to include information through mid-2002. The index has been entirely reconceived, and hundreds of new text entries have been added to maintain the "browsabil-ity" factor that readers enjoy so much. Using as a criterion the works most likely to be available today in school and public libraries, all the bibliographies have been updated. Numerous web sites and phone numbers for further information are included. All of these tools can serve as a springboard for further inquiry by the reader.

Revising and updating a project such as this one is a major undertaking and has involved many people, including readers who have taken the time to write to us about omissions or errors in the earlier editions. Our special thanks to the staff of The Stonesong Press who have provided guidance and direction through all the editions.

Karen Van Westering
Director of the Publications Program
The New York Public Library

THE PHYSICAL WORLD

1

TIMES AND DATES

RECKONING DAYS AND HOURS

THE LENGTH OF THE DAY

The length of the *sidereal day* (Latin: *sider*—star) is determined by the rotation of the Earth, which causes the stars, to any observer, to appear to make one revolution each sidereal day from east to west. The length of a *true solar day* is determined by noting one passage of the Sun across the meridian of an observer and calculating the time that it takes for the Sun to cross the same point in the sky a second time. Because the Earth moves along its orbit around the Sun during the time it makes a single rotation, the solar day is slightly longer than the sidereal day (on average, by 3 minutes and 56 seconds of solar time).

The phrase "a red-letter day" dates from 1704, when holy days were marked in red letters on church calendars.

Over the course of a year (the time it takes the Earth to make one revolution around the Sun), the length of the true solar day varies because of (1) the eccentricity of the Earth's elliptical orbit and (2) the inclination of the equator (the plane running through the Earth's center and perpendicular to the Earth's axis of rotation) to the ecliptic (the plane of the Earth's orbit). The uniform length of our 24-hour calendar day, the *mean solar day*, is based on the average length of the true solar day over a year.

HOW IS THE DAY SUBDIVIDED?

The division of the day into hours is an arbitrary standard, as is the uniform length of the hour. Different cultures divided their days in different ways. The ancient Egyptians, Greeks, and Romans had a 24-hour day, but they divided it into 10 hours of light, 10 hours of dark, and 1 hour each of dawn and dusk (the twilight hours), which meant that the length of the hours depended on the seasons. Only after the invention of mechanical clocks in the late Middle Ages (see the sidebar "Clocks—Measuring Time") did a need develop for days, hours, and smaller units of time of uniform length. The mean solar day, under the common system of solar time, is thus divided as follows:

1 mean solar day = 24 mean solar hours
1 mean solar hour = 60 mean solar minutes
1 mean solar minute = 60 mean solar seconds

One mean solar day is thus equal to 86,400 (= 24 × 60 × 60) mean solar seconds.

For civil purposes, the time when the Sun crosses the local meridian is defined as noon, the midpoint between successive noons is defined as midnight, and the standard measurement of the day is from

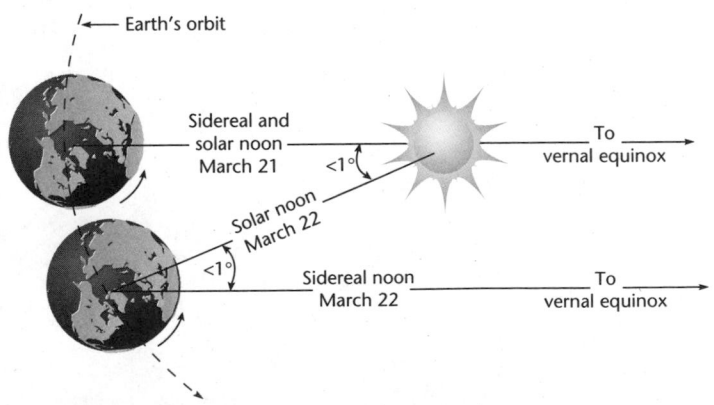

SIDEREAL AND SOLAR DAYS

midnight to midnight. (Some ancient peoples counted the day from dawn to dawn; others, such as the Jews, count their days from sunset to sunset.)

Under the 12-hour system of counting hours, the day is divided into two equal portions denoted by A.M. (before noon) and P.M. (after noon), derived from the Latin terms *ante meridiem* and *post meridiem.* The instant 4 hours and 15 minutes after midnight is designated 4:15 A.M.; the instant 5 hours and 23 minutes after noon is 5:23 P.M. According to the National Institute of Standards and Technology, confusion exists regarding 12 A.M., 12 P.M., noon, and midnight. The term *noon* is neither before or after noon—noon is noon; midnight is both 12 hours before noon and 12 hours after noon. It is best to refer to these times as noon and midnight instead of 12 A.M. and 12 P.M.

Clocks—Measuring Time

A Closer Look

The sundial may be the oldest device for measuring time, going back to the Fertile Crescent of about 2000 B.C. Its operation is based on the fact that the shadow of a fixed object will move around it from one side to the other as the Sun moves from east to west. Naturally, the duration of the hours marked off by a sundial changes according to the seasons of the year. Along with sundials, ancient peoples used water clocks that measured time by a constant rate of flow of water through a bowl-like device with an outlet. Sand flowing from one compartment into another also was used in late medieval Europe to measure time. These last two methods could be used at night; they also counted more uniform units of time.

With the invention of mechanical clocks, the hours became uniform. The first mechanical clocks appeared in Europe in the 14th century (mechanical timepieces existed in China at least two centuries earlier, though the Chinese never developed them highly). The earliest ones were driven by weights strung around a drum. As the weight fell, the mechanism was activated. Next came spring-driven clocks, although they had the disadvantage of running differently when the spring had just been wound and was in its most tense position and after it had unwound somewhat. The workings of all clocks depend on a motion or vibration that is constant and regular.

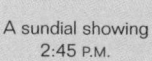

A sundial showing 2:45 P.M.

Circa 1581 the great Italian physicist Galileo (1564–1642) observed that the time it took for a pendulum to complete one total swing (called the period of oscillation) was almost independent of its magnitude—that is, how far it swung from side to side. He understood that this phenomenon could be used as a frequency mechanism for regulating a clock. In 1656, a Dutch physicist, Christian Huygens (1629–95), working independently, constructed the first pendulum clock. Pendulum clocks remained the most precise means of measuring time into the 20th century. Pendulums could be constructed to oscillate at specified frequencies once such factors as latitude, the pull of gravity, and weather and its effects on the materials used to make the clock had been compensated for.

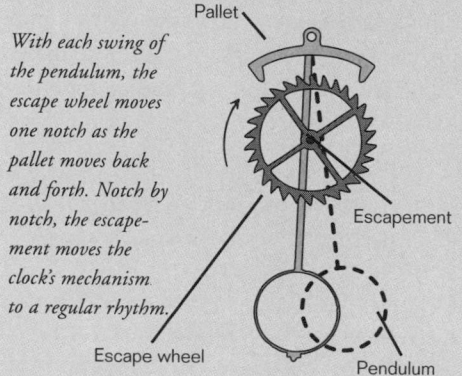

With each swing of the pendulum, the escape wheel moves one notch as the pallet moves back and forth. Notch by notch, the escapement moves the clock's mechanism to a regular rhythm.

Pallet
Escapement
Escape wheel
Pendulum

Quartz clocks, introduced in the 1930s, improved on the pendulum, though only after years of development. By controlling the frequency of an electric circuit through the regular mechanical vibration of the quartz crystal, high degrees of constancy in vibration can be achieved, making a quartz clock even more accurate than a pendulum.

In the 1940s, atomic clocks were introduced. Their frequencies are based on the vibrations of certain atoms and molecules that vibrate the same number of times per second. Atomic clocks are constant to within a few seconds every 100,000 years. The fundamental unit of atomic time is the SI second.

Ship's Bell Time Signals

On most ships, a day consists of six 4-hour watches. The watches change at 8 A.M., noon, 4 P.M., 8 P.M., midnight, and 4 A.M. A chime indicates each half hour. During a 4-hour watch, one bell chimes at the first half hour, two bells at the second, and so on, up to eight, when the next watch begins and the sequence starts over again.

1 bell	12:30 or	4:30 or	8:30 A.M. or P.M.
2 bells	1:00	5:00	9:00
3 bells	1:30	5:30	9:30
4 bells	2:00	6:00	10:00
5 bells	2:30	6:30	10:30
6 bells	3:00	7:00	11:00
7 bells	3:30	7:30	11:30
8 bells	4:00	8:00	12:00

On many vessels, the ship's whistle is blown at noon. On some ships, 1 lightly struck bell announces 15 minutes before the change of watch.

A 24-hour system, which avoids repeating numbers and clearly distinguishes between midnight and noon, is used by the U.S. military and throughout continental Europe. Under this system, midnight (the beginning of the day) is designated 0000, the following noon is 1200, and the following midnight is 2400. (The designation 2400 of one day is the same instant of time as that of 0000 of the following day.) The times 4:15 A.M. and 5:23 P.M. are designated as 0415 and 1723 under this counting system.

UNIVERSAL AND STANDARD TIME

The mean solar time determined by the meridian that runs through Greenwich, England (where that country's Royal Observatory was originally located), is referred to as *Greenwich Mean Time, Zulu Time,* or *Universal Time.* The *Coordinated Universal Time* (UTC) is an atomic scale kept in agreement with Universal Time and is also known as the world time standard. Such precise times are especially useful for marine and air navigation and tracking of artificial satellites and space probes.

From Greenwich, too, longitudes are measured around the world. Greenwich, having a 0° longitude, is called the *prime meridian.*

Standard time, which for most localities differs from universal time by an integral number of hours, was created by international agreement in 1883 to avoid the continuous changes in mean solar time with longitude. Lines at every 15° longitude were drawn down a map of the Earth to create 24 international time zones. Within each zone, all localities keep the same standard time (i.e., the same minutes and seconds). The time in each zone differs from that in each neighboring zone by exactly 1 hour. (Because of political boundaries, the boundary lines between time zones often zigzag.) A few areas keep time that differs from universal time by a nonintegral number of hours (such an area might have, for example, a 30-minute difference from an adjoining zone).

According to legend, in 1364, Charles V wrongly corrected a clockmaker and told him to use the Roman numeral IIII instead of IV for the number four. Rather than offend the king, the clockmaker obeyed. That tradition is still used for some clocks today.

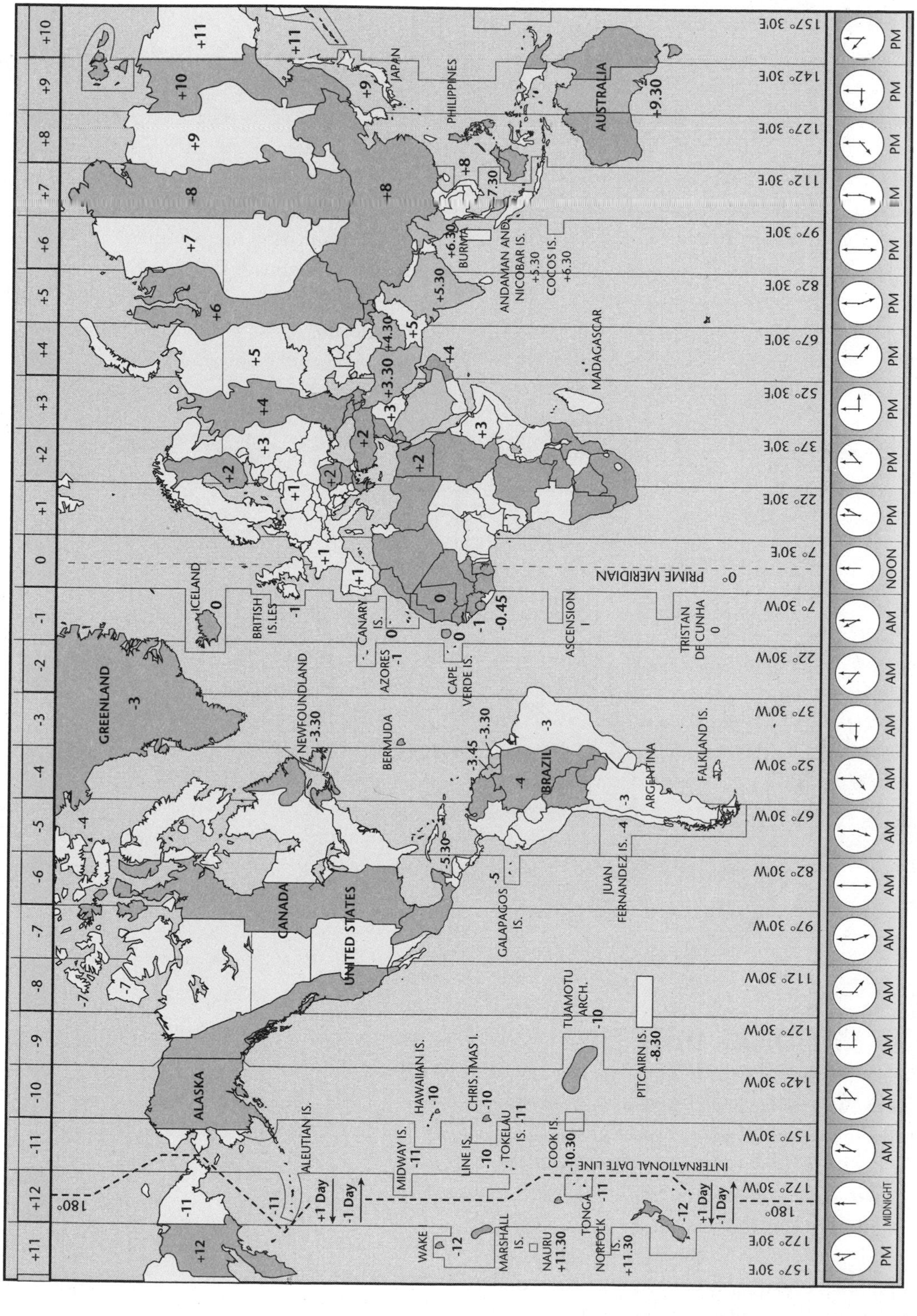

U.S. AND CANADIAN TIME ZONES

The continental United States has four standard time zones centered on the meridians 75° (Eastern Standard Time, or EST), 90° (Central Standard Time, or CST), 105° (Mountain Standard Time, or MST), and 120° (Pacific Standard Time, or PST) west of Greenwich; they are, respectively, 5, 6, 7, and 8 hours behind Universal Time. Alaska Standard Time is determined by the meridian at 135° west of Greenwich, and Hawaii-Aleutian Standard Time by the meridian at 150° west of Greenwich; they are 9 and 10 hours behind Universal Time. American Samoa and the Midway Islands use Samoan Standard Time, centered on the 165° W meridian and 11 hours behind Universal Time.

Canada has a total of six time zones: the four that apply to the continental United States and an additional two in the east. Atlantic Standard Time (which Puerto Rico and the U.S. Virgin Islands also keep) is determined by the meridian 60° west of Greenwich and is thus 4 hours behind Universal Time. Newfoundland Standard Time is determined by the meridian 52° 30′ west of Greenwich and is thus 3½ hours behind Universal Time.

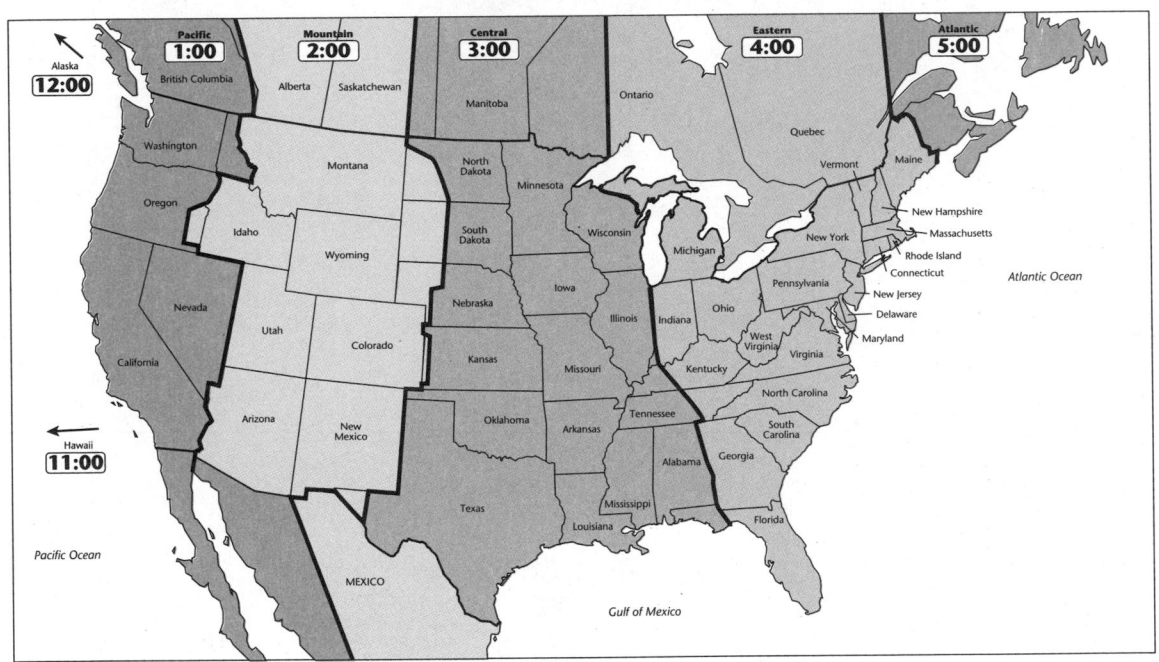

INTERNATIONAL DATE LINE

An imaginary line set at 180° longitude runs down the Earth. When someone crosses the line traveling to the west, one day is added—that is, Sunday on the east side of the line becomes Monday as one crosses westward. The line, of course, was fixed at the longitude exactly opposite Greenwich, England, on the other side of the Earth, but it zigzags for political reasons so that parts of countries do not find themselves on the wrong side—for instance, all of Siberia (west of the line), and all of Alaska (east of the line).

How does your Global Positioning Satellite (GPS) device work? Atomic clock timing signals from four or more Earth-orbiting satellites determine a user's position.

STANDARD TIME FOR MAJOR FOREIGN CITIES

The following list gives the time in cities around the world when it is noon Eastern Standard Time. An asterisk (*) indicates the morning of the following day.

Addis Ababa	8 P.M.	Geneva	6 P.M.	Ottawa	12 N
Alexandria	7 P.M.	Glasgow	5 P.M.	Panama	12 N
Amsterdam	6 P.M.	Halifax	1 P.M.	Paris	6 P.M.
Athens	7 P.M.	Hanoi	1 A.M.*	Prague	6 P.M.
Baghdad	8 P.M.	Havana	12 N	Quebec	12 N
Bangkok	12 M	Helsinki	7 P.M.	Rio de Janeiro	2 P.M.
Barcelona	6 P.M.	Ho Chi Minh City	1 A.M.*	Riyadh	8 P.M.
Beijing	1 A.M.*	Hong Kong	1 A.M.*	Rome	6 P.M.
Belfast	5 P.M.	Istanbul	7 P.M.	St. Petersburg	8 P.M.
Belgrade	6 P.M.	Jakarta	12 M	San Juan	1 P.M.
Berlin	6 P.M.	Jerusalem	7 P.M.	Santiago	1 P.M.
Bogotá	12 N	Johannesburg	7 P.M.	Seoul	2 A.M.*
Bombay	10:30 P.M.	Karachi	10 P.M.	Shanghai	1 A.M.*
Brasília	2 P.M.	Kuala Lumpur	1 A.M.*	Stockholm	6 P.M.
Brussels	6 P.M.	Lima	12 N	Sydney	4 A.M.*
Bucharest	7 P.M.	Lisbon	6 P.M.	Tangier	5 P.M.
Budapest	6 P.M.	Liverpool	4 P.M.	Teheran	8:30 P.M.
Buenos Aires	2 P.M.	London	5 P.M.	Tel Aviv	7 P.M.
Cairo	7 P.M.	Madrid	6 P.M.	Tokyo	2 A.M.*
Calcutta	10:30 P.M.	Managua	11 A.M.	Toronto	12 N
Calgary	10 A.M.	Manila	1 A.M.*	Tripoli	7 P.M.
Cape Town	7 P.M.	Marseilles	6 P.M.	Vancouver	9 A.M.
Caracas	1 P.M.	Mecca	8 P.M.	Venice	6 P.M.
Casablanca	5 P.M.	Melbourne	4 A.M.*	Vienna	6 P.M.
Copenhagen	6 P.M.	Mexico City	11 A.M.	Vladivostock	3 A.M.*
Delhi	10:30 P.M.	Montreal	12 N	Warsaw	6 P.M.
Dublin	5 P.M.	Moscow	8 P.M.	Winnipeg	11 A.M.
Edinburgh	5 P.M.	Munich	6 P.M.	Yangon	11:30 P.M.
Florence	6 P.M.	Naples	6 P.M.	Yokohama	2 A.M.*
Frankfurt	6 P.M.	Oslo	6 P.M.	Zurich	6 P.M.

TIME ADJUSTMENTS

DAYLIGHT SAVING TIME IN THE UNITED STATES

Daylight Saving Time is attained by advancing the clock 1 hour. In 1967, the Uniform Time Act went into effect in the United States. It proclaimed that all states, the District of Columbia, and U.S. possessions were to observe Daylight Saving Time starting at 2 A.M. on the last Sunday in April and ending at 2 A.M. on the last Sunday in October. Any state could exempt itself by law, and a 1972 amendment to the act authorized the states split by time zones to consider that split in exempting themselves. Non-Navaho sites in Arizona, Hawaii, part of Indiana, Puerto Rico, the Virgin Islands, Guam, and American Samoa are now exempt. (The Navaho Indian lands in Arizona do observe DST.) The Department of Transportation, which oversees the act, has modified some local zone boundaries in Alaska, Florida, Kansas, Michigan, and Texas over the past several years. Daylight Saving Time was extended by Congress during 1974 and 1975 to conserve energy, but the country then returned to the previous end-of-April to end-of-October system until 1987, when new legislation went into effect. The new bill, signed by President Ronald Reagan on July 8, 1986, moved the start of Daylight Saving Time up to the first

Sunday in April, but it did not change the end from the last Sunday in October.

INTERNATIONAL TIME ADJUSTMENTS

It is common throughout the world for clock time to be adjusted to use added daylight during summer.

Generally, Western Europe goes on daylight time on the last Sunday in March and changes back on the last Sunday in September. Most regions of the Commonwealth of Independent States stay on "advanced time" year-round. China, by government order, operates as one time zone even though it should, geographically, be in five different zones. For religious reasons, Israel is approximately 2 hours behind the rest of its time zone. Thus, the Sun may be setting there as early as 3:30 P.M.

Paraguay, Ireland, and the Dominican Republic adjust their clock time in winter instead of summer. Thus, their time is aptly known as winter time.

CALENDARS

NAMES OF THE DAYS

The names of the days in English derive from either ancient Latin or Saxon systems of naming days after gods or astrological planets.

English	Latin	Saxon
Sunday	Dies Solis (Sun)	Sun's Day
Monday	Dies Lunae (Moon)	Moon's Day
Tuesday	Dies Martis (Mars)	Tiw's Day
Wednesday	Dies Mercurii (Mercury)	Woden's Day
Thursday	Dies Jovis (Jupiter)	Thor's Day
Friday	Dies Veneris (Venus)	Frigg's Day
Saturday	Dies Saturni (Saturn)	Saterne's Day

DEFINITIONS OF A YEAR

A year can be defined in several ways.

The *tropical/equinoctial/solar/astronomical year* is the period (365 days, 5 hours, 48 minutes, and 46 seconds of mean solar time) spent by the Sun in making its apparent passage from vernal equinox to vernal equinox (defined in "The Seasons" section in this chapter).

The *sidereal year* is the period (365 days, 6 hours, 9 minutes, and 9.54 seconds) spent by the Sun in its apparent passage from a fixed star and back to the same position again. It is the true period of the Earth's revolution, and the difference in time between this and the tropical year is due to the precession of the equinoxes.

The *anomalistic year* is the period of time occupied by any planet in making one complete revolution from perihelion (the point in its orbit when it is closest to the Sun) to perihelion. For the Earth, this period is 365 days, 6 hours, 13 minutes, and 53 seconds. It is slightly longer than the sidereal year because of the extra time needed to reach an advancing perihelion, the lag being caused by the gravitational pull of the other planets.

Because the tropical year does not contain an integral number of days, the modern Gregorian *calendar year* (extending from January 1 to December 31) normally consists of 365 days (divided into 12 months). Because such a year is equivalent to 52 seven-day weeks plus one day, a given date normally advances by one day each year (for example, from Monday to Tuesday).

To avoid having the seasons move around the calendar, an extra leap day (February 29) is inserted in the calendar of a leap year, which thus has 366 days. A *leap year* is a year (e.g., 2004 and 2008) whose number is exactly divisible by 4, or, in case of the final year of a century, by 400. Thus, 1700, 1800, and 1900 were not leap years, but 2000 was.

A *fiscal year* is an accounting period of 12 months. The U.S. government's fiscal year (FY) ends on September 30; thus, its FY 2002 extends from October 1, 2001, to September 30, 2002. A business firm's fiscal year, however, may end on the last day of any month.

Some cultures have used or continue to use a *lunar year* (defined in "The Lunar Calendar" sidebar on the next page) of 12 lunar or synodic months.

The Lunar Calendar

Calendars based on the movements of the moon and Sun have been used since ancient times. Whereas today most calendars are based on the solar year of 365.25 days, in ancient times the lunar calendar was the one most commonly used. Notches in bones dating from 15,000 to 10,000 B.C. have been discovered in what are now Israel and Jordan; their recordings of number sequences are thought to be the first lunar calendars.

In the lunar system, time is based on the number of days between two moons, or 29.5306 days, resulting in a lunar year of 354.3672 days. The lunar year is thus approximately 11 days shorter than the solar year.

The ancient Chinese synchronized their lunar calendar with the solar year by intercalating, or adding, extra months at fixed intervals on a 60-year cycle. This calendar, along with the modern Western one, is still used today in China.

The ancient Hebrews also intercalated months into the lunar calendar to keep it in agreement with the solar year. This calendar of 12 lunar months, with an intercalary month added seven times in every 19-year cycle, is used today in Israel and by Jews throughout the world for religious purposes.

The traditional lunar calendar, without regard to the solar year, is still used today by Muslims. In order to establish agreement between lunar and civil, or calendar, months, they intercalate 11 days in each 30 years.

THE SEASONS

The beginnings of the four seasons occur when the Sun reaches certain points in its apparent path around the Earth.

Spring in the Northern Hemisphere (fall or autumn in the Southern Hemisphere) begins at the *vernal equinox* (about March 21), when the Sun crosses the equator as it ascends from a southerly to a northerly declination (its angular distance north or south of the celestial equator). On this day, the hours of daylight and darkness are equal in length (approximately 12 hours each) everywhere on Earth.

Summer in the Northern Hemisphere (winter in the Southern Hemisphere) begins at the *summer solstice* (about June 21), when the Sun reaches its most northerly declination (approximately 23.5° N). On this day, locations in the Northern (Southern) Hemisphere have their maximum (minimum) number of hours of daylight.

Fall or autumn in the Northern Hemisphere (spring in the Southern Hemisphere) begins at the *autumnal equinox* (about September 21), when the Sun crosses the equator as it descends from a northerly to a southerly declination. On this day, the hours of

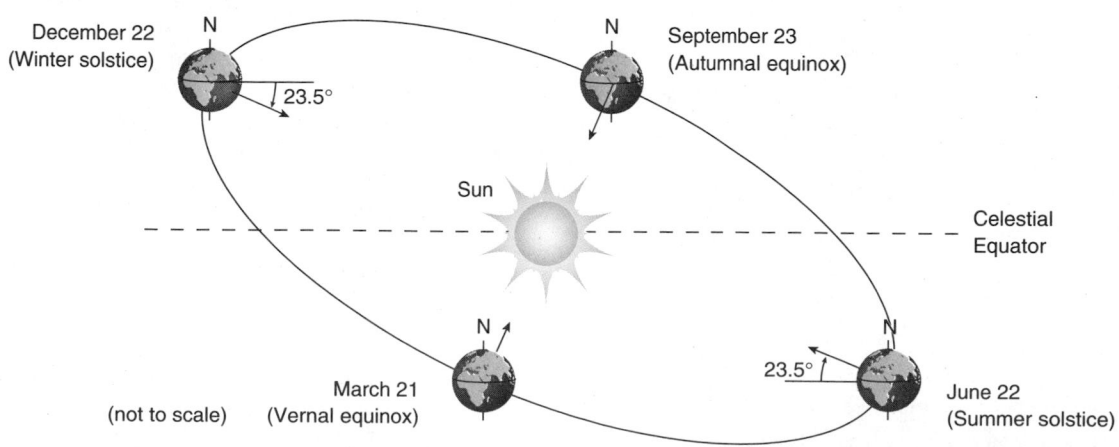

daylight and darkness are equal in length (approximately 12 hours each) everywhere on Earth.

Winter in the Northern Hemisphere (summer in the Southern Hemisphere) begins at the *winter solstice* (about December 21), when the Sun reaches its most southerly declination (approximately 23.5° S). On this day, locations in the Northern (Southern) Hemisphere have their minimum (maximum) number of hours of daylight.

THE DEVELOPMENT OF THE ROMAN/JULIAN/ GREGORIAN CALENDAR

According to legend, Romulus, one of the founders of the city of Rome, established the Roman calendar—most likely a version of the Greek lunar calendar—circa 738 B.C. King Numa Pompilius later added January at the beginning and February at the end to create a 12-month calendar year. In 46 B.C. Emperor Julius Caesar rejected the Roman lunar calendar in favor of a solar one, thus establishing a new dating system known as the Julian calendar. The solar year was made up of 365¼ days. A leap day was added every 4 years to maintain balance between the calendar and the seasons. However, because the Earth moves 11 minutes and 14 seconds faster every year than Caesar calculated, the calendar dates of the seasons regressed almost 1 day per century. In 1582 Pope Gregory XIII ordained that the calendar be decreased by 10 days that year and that no century year could be a leap year unless its date is evenly divisible by 400. (European nations adopted the Gregorian calendar at different dates, leading to some confusion regarding the 10 missing days in 1582.) See "Additional Sources of Information" at the end of this chapter to find out more about the development of the calendar.

Romulus 738 B.C.	King Numa Pompilius 713 B.C.	Council of Decemvirs 451 B.C.	Julius Caesar 47 B.C.	Augustus Caesar 8 B.C.	Gregory XIII Europe A.D. 1582 England A.D. 1752
Martius 31	Januarius 29	Januarius 29	Januarius 31	Januarius 31	January 31
Aprilis 30	Martius 31	Februarius 28	Februarius 29–30	Februarius 28–29	February 28–29
Maius 31	Aprilis 29	Martius 31	Martius 31	Martius 31	March 31
Junius 30	Maius 31	Aprilis 29	Aprilis 30	Aprilis 30	April 30
Quintilis 31	Junius 29	Maius 31	Maius 31	Maius 31	May 31
Sextilis 30	Quintilis 31	Junius 29	Junius 30	Junius 30	June 30
Septembris 31	Sextilis 29	Quintilis 31	Julius 31	Julius 31	July 31
Octobris 30	Septembris 29	Sextilis 29	Sextilis 30	Augustus 31	August 31
Novembris 31	Octobris 31	Septembris 29	Septembris 31	Septembris 30	September 30
Decembris 29	Novembris 29	Octobris 31	Octobris 30	Octobris 31	October 31
	Decembris 29	Novembris 29	Novembris 31	Novembris 30	November 30
	Februarius 28	Decembris 29	Decembris 30	Decembris 31	December 31
304 days	**355 days**	**355 days**	**348¼ days**	**365¼ days**	**365.2422 days**

PERPETUAL CALENDAR, 1775–2098

Look for the year you want in the following list. The number opposite each year is the number of the calendar on pages 14–17 to use for that year.

Year	No.	Year	No.	Year	No.	Year	No.	Year	No.
1775	1	1823	4	1871	1	1919	4	1967	1
1776	9	1824	12	1872	9	1920	12	1968	9
1777	4	1825	7	1873	4	1921	7	1969	4
1778	5	1826	1	1874	5	1922	1	1970	5
1779	6	1827	2	1875	6	1923	2	1971	6
1780	14	1828	10	1876	14	1924	10	1972	14
1781	2	1829	5	1877	2	1925	5	1973	2
1782	3	1830	6	1878	3	1926	6	1974	3
1783	4	1831	7	1879	4	1927	7	1975	4
1784	12	1832	8	1880	12	1928	8	1976	12
1785	7	1833	3	1881	7	1929	3	1977	7
1786	1	1834	4	1882	1	1930	4	1978	1
1787	2	1835	5	1883	2	1931	5	1979	2
1788	10	1836	13	1884	10	1932	13	1980	10
1789	5	1837	1	1885	5	1933	1	1981	5
1790	6	1838	2	1886	6	1934	2	1982	6
1791	7	1839	3	1887	7	1935	3	1983	7
1792	8	1840	11	1888	8	1936	11	1984	8
1793	3	1841	6	1889	3	1937	6	1985	3
1794	4	1842	7	1890	4	1938	7	1986	4
1795	5	1843	1	1891	5	1939	1	1987	5
1796	13	1844	9	1892	13	1940	9	1988	13
1797	1	1845	4	1893	1	1941	4	1989	1
1798	2	1846	5	1894	2	1942	5	1990	2
1799	3	1847	6	1895	3	1943	6	1991	3
1800	4	1848	14	1896	11	1944	14	1992	11
1801	5	1849	2	1897	6	1945	2	1993	6
1802	6	1850	3	1898	7	1946	3	1994	7
1803	7	1851	4	1899	1	1947	4	1995	1
1804	8	1852	12	1900	2	1948	12	1996	9
1805	3	1853	7	1901	3	1949	7	1997	4
1806	4	1854	1	1902	4	1950	1	1998	5
1807	5	1855	2	1903	5	1951	2	1999	6
1808	13	1856	10	1904	13	1952	10	2000	14
1809	1	1857	5	1905	1	1953	5	2001	2
1810	2	1858	6	1906	2	1954	6	2002	3
1811	3	1859	7	1907	3	1955	7	2003	4
1812	11	1860	8	1908	11	1956	8	2004	12
1813	6	1861	3	1909	6	1957	3	2005	7
1814	7	1862	4	1910	7	1958	4	2006	1
1815	1	1863	5	1911	1	1959	5	2007	2
1816	9	1864	13	1912	9	1960	13	2008	10
1817	4	1865	1	1913	4	1961	1	2009	5
1818	5	1866	2	1914	5	1962	2	2010	6
1819	6	1867	3	1915	6	1963	3	2011	7
1820	14	1868	11	1916	14	1964	11	2012	8
1821	2	1869	6	1917	2	1965	6	2013	3
1822	3	1870	7	1918	3	1966	7	2014	4

continues

Times and Dates

Perpetual Calendar, Continued

2015	5	2032	12	2049	6	2066	6	2083	6
2016	13	2033	7	2050	7	2067	7	2084	14
2017	1	2034	1	2051	1	2068	8	2085	2
2018	2	2035	2	2052	9	2069	3	2086	3
2019	3	2036	10	2053	4	2070	4	2087	4
2020	11	2037	5	2054	5	2071	5	2088	12
2021	6	2038	6	2055	6	2072	13	2089	7
2022	7	2039	7	2056	14	2073	1	2090	1
2023	1	2040	8	2057	2	2074	2	2091	2
2024	9	2041	3	2058	3	2075	3	2092	10
2025	4	2042	4	2059	4	2076	11	2093	5
2026	5	2043	5	2060	12	2077	6	2094	6
2027	6	2044	13	2061	7	2078	7	2095	7
2028	14	2045	1	2062	1	2079	1	2096	8
2029	2	2046	2	2063	2	2080	9	2097	3
2030	3	2047	3	2064	10	2081	4	2098	4
2031	4	2048	11	2065	5	2082	5		

Calendar 1

JANUARY

S	M	T	W	T	F	S
1	2	3	4	5	6	7
8	9	10	11	12	13	14
15	16	17	18	19	20	21
22	23	24	25	26	27	28
29	30	31				

FEBRUARY

S	M	T	W	T	F	S
				1	2	3
4	5	6	7	8	9	10
11	12	13	14	15	16	17
18	19	20	21	22	23	24
25	26	27	28			

(Full monthly calendar grids for January through December are shown for both Calendar 1 and Calendar 2.)

Calendar 2

Calendar 3

```
        JANUARY                      MAY                   SEPTEMBER
S  M  T  W  T  F  S       S  M  T  W  T  F  S       S  M  T  W  T  F  S
         1  2  3  4  5              1  2  3  4        1  2  3  4  5  6  7
6  7  8  9 10 11 12        5  6  7  8  9 10 11        8  9 10 11 12 13 14
13 14 15 16 17 18 19      12 13 14 15 16 17 18       15 16 17 18 19 20 21
20 21 22 23 24 25 26      19 20 21 22 23 24 25       22 23 24 25 26 27 28
27 28 29 30 31            26 27 28 29 30 31          29 30

        FEBRUARY                     JUNE                   OCTOBER
                  1  2                          1              1  2  3  4  5
3  4  5  6  7  8  9        2  3  4  5  6  7  8        6  7  8  9 10 11 12
10 11 12 13 14 15 16       9 10 11 12 13 14 15       13 14 15 16 17 18 19
17 18 19 20 21 22 23      16 17 18 19 20 21 22       20 21 22 23 24 25 26
24 25 26 27 28            23 24 25 26 27 28 29       27 28 29 30 31
                          30

        MARCH                        JULY                   NOVEMBER
                  1  2        1  2  3  4  5  6                       1  2
3  4  5  6  7  8  9        7  8  9 10 11 12 13        3  4  5  6  7  8  9
10 11 12 13 14 15 16      14 15 16 17 18 19 20       10 11 12 13 14 15 16
17 18 19 20 21 22 23      21 22 23 24 25 26 27       17 18 19 20 21 22 23
24 25 26 27 28 29 30      28 29 30 31                24 25 26 27 28 29 30
31

        APRIL                        AUGUST                 DECEMBER
   1  2  3  4  5  6                    1  2  3        1  2  3  4  5  6  7
7  8  9 10 11 12 13        4  5  6  7  8  9 10        8  9 10 11 12 13 14
14 15 16 17 18 19 20      11 12 13 14 15 16 17       15 16 17 18 19 20 21
21 22 23 24 25 26 27      18 19 20 21 22 23 24       22 23 24 25 26 27 28
28 29 30                  25 26 27 28 29 30 31       29 30 31
```

Calendar 4

```
        JANUARY                      MAY                   SEPTEMBER
S  M  T  W  T  F  S       S  M  T  W  T  F  S       S  M  T  W  T  F  S
            1  2  3  4              1  2  3           1  2  3  4  5  6
5  6  7  8  9 10 11        4  5  6  7  8  9 10        7  8  9 10 11 12 13
12 13 14 15 16 17 18      11 12 13 14 15 16 17       14 15 16 17 18 19 20
19 20 21 22 23 24 25      18 19 20 21 22 23 24       21 22 23 24 25 26 27
26 27 28 29 30 31         25 26 27 28 29 30 31       28 29 30

        FEBRUARY                     JUNE                   OCTOBER
                     1     1  2  3  4  5  6  7                 1  2  3  4
2  3  4  5  6  7  8        8  9 10 11 12 13 14        5  6  7  8  9 10 11
9 10 11 12 13 14 15       15 16 17 18 19 20 21       12 13 14 15 16 17 18
16 17 18 19 20 21 22      22 23 24 25 26 27 28       19 20 21 22 23 24 25
23 24 25 26 27 28         29 30                      26 27 28 29 30 31

        MARCH                        JULY                   NOVEMBER
                     1              1  2  3  4  5                          1
2  3  4  5  6  7  8        6  7  8  9 10 11 12        2  3  4  5  6  7  8
9 10 11 12 13 14 15       13 14 15 16 17 18 19        9 10 11 12 13 14 15
16 17 18 19 20 21 22      20 21 22 23 24 25 26       16 17 18 19 20 21 22
23 24 25 26 27 28 29      27 28 29 30 31             23 24 25 26 27 28 29
30 31                                                30

        APRIL                        AUGUST                 DECEMBER
      1  2  3  4  5                       1  2        1  2  3  4  5  6
6  7  8  9 10 11 12        3  4  5  6  7  8  9        7  8  9 10 11 12 13
13 14 15 16 17 18 19      10 11 12 13 14 15 16       14 15 16 17 18 19 20
20 21 22 23 24 25 26      17 18 19 20 21 22 23       21 22 23 24 25 26 27
27 28 29 30               24 25 26 27 28 29 30       28 29 30 31
                          31
```

Calendar 5

```
        JANUARY                      MAY                   SEPTEMBER
S  M  T  W  T  F  S       S  M  T  W  T  F  S       S  M  T  W  T  F  S
            1  2  3                    1  2           1  2  3  4  5
4  5  6  7  8  9 10        3  4  5  6  7  8  9        6  7  8  9 10 11 12
11 12 13 14 15 16 17      10 11 12 13 14 15 16       13 14 15 16 17 18 19
18 19 20 21 22 23 24      17 18 19 20 21 22 23       20 21 22 23 24 25 26
25 26 27 28 29 30 31      24 25 26 27 28 29 30       27 28 29 30
                          31

        FEBRUARY                     JUNE                   OCTOBER
1  2  3  4  5  6  7        1  2  3  4  5  6                    1  2  3
8  9 10 11 12 13 14        7  8  9 10 11 12 13        4  5  6  7  8  9 10
15 16 17 18 19 20 21      14 15 16 17 18 19 20       11 12 13 14 15 16 17
22 23 24 25 26 27 28      21 22 23 24 25 26 27       18 19 20 21 22 23 24
                          28 29 30                   25 26 27 28 29 30 31

        MARCH                        JULY                   NOVEMBER
1  2  3  4  5  6  7                 1  2  3  4        1  2  3  4  5  6  7
8  9 10 11 12 13 14        5  6  7  8  9 10 11        8  9 10 11 12 13 14
15 16 17 18 19 20 21      12 13 14 15 16 17 18       15 16 17 18 19 20 21
22 23 24 25 26 27 28      19 20 21 22 23 24 25       22 23 24 25 26 27 28
29 30 31                  26 27 28 29 30 31          29 30

        APRIL                        AUGUST                 DECEMBER
               1  2  3  4                       1        1  2  3  4  5
5  6  7  8  9 10 11        2  3  4  5  6  7  8        6  7  8  9 10 11 12
12 13 14 15 16 17 18       9 10 11 12 13 14 15       13 14 15 16 17 18 19
19 20 21 22 23 24 25      16 17 18 19 20 21 22       20 21 22 23 24 25 26
26 27 28 29 30            23 24 25 26 27 28 29       27 28 29 30 31
                          30 31
```

Calendar 6

```
        JANUARY                      MAY                   SEPTEMBER
S  M  T  W  T  F  S       S  M  T  W  T  F  S       S  M  T  W  T  F  S
               1  2                          1           1  2  3  4
3  4  5  6  7  8  9        2  3  4  5  6  7  8        5  6  7  8  9 10 11
10 11 12 13 14 15 16       9 10 11 12 13 14 15       12 13 14 15 16 17 18
17 18 19 20 21 22 23      16 17 18 19 20 21 22       19 20 21 22 23 24 25
24 25 26 27 28 29 30      23 24 25 26 27 28 29       26 27 28 29 30
31                        30 31

        FEBRUARY                     JUNE                   OCTOBER
      1  2  3  4  5  6              1  2  3  4  5                    1  2
7  8  9 10 11 12 13        6  7  8  9 10 11 12        3  4  5  6  7  8  9
14 15 16 17 18 19 20      13 14 15 16 17 18 19       10 11 12 13 14 15 16
21 22 23 24 25 26 27      20 21 22 23 24 25 26       17 18 19 20 21 22 23
28                        27 28 29 30               24 25 26 27 28 29 30
                                                     31

        MARCH                        JULY                   NOVEMBER
      1  2  3  4  5  6              1  2  3        1  2  3  4  5  6
7  8  9 10 11 12 13        4  5  6  7  8  9 10        7  8  9 10 11 12 13
14 15 16 17 18 19 20      11 12 13 14 15 16 17       14 15 16 17 18 19 20
21 22 23 24 25 26 27      18 19 20 21 22 23 24       21 22 23 24 25 26 27
28 29 30 31               25 26 27 28 29 30 31       28 29 30

        APRIL                        AUGUST                 DECEMBER
               1  2  3     1  2  3  4  5  6  7                 1  2  3  4
4  5  6  7  8  9 10        8  9 10 11 12 13 14        5  6  7  8  9 10 11
11 12 13 14 15 16 17      15 16 17 18 19 20 21       12 13 14 15 16 17 18
18 19 20 21 22 23 24      22 23 24 25 26 27 28       19 20 21 22 23 24 25
25 26 27 28 29 30         29 30 31                   26 27 28 29 30 31
```

Calendar 7

```
         JANUARY                    MAY                   SEPTEMBER
S  M  T  W  T  F  S     S  M  T  W  T  F  S     S  M  T  W  T  F  S
               1                 1  2  3  4  5  6  7                    1  2  3
2  3  4  5  6  7  8      8  9 10 11 12 13 14      4  5  6  7  8  9 10
9 10 11 12 13 14 15     15 16 17 18 19 20 21     11 12 13 14 15 16 17
16 17 18 19 20 21 22    22 23 24 25 26 27 28     18 19 20 21 22 23 24
23 24 25 26 27 28 29    29 30 31                 25 26 27 28 29 30
30 31

         FEBRUARY                  JUNE                    OCTOBER
   1  2  3  4  5                 1  2  3  4                             1
6  7  8  9 10 11 12      5  6  7  8  9 10 11      2  3  4  5  6  7  8
13 14 15 16 17 18 19    12 13 14 15 16 17 18      9 10 11 12 13 14 15
20 21 22 23 24 25 26    19 20 21 22 23 24 25     16 17 18 19 20 21 22
27 28                   26 27 28 29 30           23 24 25 26 27 28 29
                                                 30 31

          MARCH                    JULY                   NOVEMBER
   1  2  3  4  5                       1  2                 1  2  3  4  5
6  7  8  9 10 11 12      3  4  5  6  7  8  9      6  7  8  9 10 11 12
13 14 15 16 17 18 19    10 11 12 13 14 15 16     13 14 15 16 17 18 19
20 21 22 23 24 25 26    17 18 19 20 21 22 23     20 21 22 23 24 25 26
27 28 29 30 31          24 25 26 27 28 29 30     27 28 29 30
                        31

          APRIL                   AUGUST                  DECEMBER
                  1  2      1  2  3  4  5  6                    1  2  3
3  4  5  6  7  8  9      7  8  9 10 11 12 13      4  5  6  7  8  9 10
10 11 12 13 14 15 16    14 15 16 17 18 19 20     11 12 13 14 15 16 17
17 18 19 20 21 22 23    21 22 23 24 25 26 27     18 19 20 21 22 23 24
24 25 26 27 28 29 30    28 29 30 31              25 26 27 28 29 30 31
```

Calendar 8

```
         JANUARY                    MAY                   SEPTEMBER
S  M  T  W  T  F  S     S  M  T  W  T  F  S     S  M  T  W  T  F  S
1  2  3  4  5  6  7            1  2  3  4  5                          1
8  9 10 11 12 13 14      6  7  8  9 10 11 12      2  3  4  5  6  7  8
15 16 17 18 19 20 21    13 14 15 16 17 18 19      9 10 11 12 13 14 15
22 23 24 25 26 27 28    20 21 22 23 24 25 26     16 17 18 19 20 21 22
29 30 31                27 28 29 30 31           23 24 25 26 27 28 29
                                                 30

         FEBRUARY                  JUNE                    OCTOBER
         1  2  3  4              1  2               1  2  3  4  5  6
5  6  7  8  9 10 11      3  4  5  6  7  8  9      7  8  9 10 11 12 13
12 13 14 15 16 17 18    10 11 12 13 14 15 16     14 15 16 17 18 19 20
19 20 21 22 23 24 25    17 18 19 20 21 22 23     21 22 23 24 25 26 27
26 27 28 29             24 25 26 27 28 29 30     28 29 30 31

          MARCH                    JULY                   NOVEMBER
            1  2  3      1  2  3  4  5  6  7                 1  2  3
4  5  6  7  8  9 10      8  9 10 11 12 13 14      4  5  6  7  8  9 10
11 12 13 14 15 16 17    15 16 17 18 19 20 21     11 12 13 14 15 16 17
18 19 20 21 22 23 24    22 23 24 25 26 27 28     18 19 20 21 22 23 24
25 26 27 28 29 30 31    29 30 31                 25 26 27 28 29 30

          APRIL                   AUGUST                  DECEMBER
1  2  3  4  5  6  7            1  2  3  4                             1
8  9 10 11 12 13 14      5  6  7  8  9 10 11      2  3  4  5  6  7  8
15 16 17 18 19 20 21    12 13 14 15 16 17 18      9 10 11 12 13 14 15
22 23 24 25 26 27 28    19 20 21 22 23 24 25     16 17 18 19 20 21 22
29 30                   26 27 28 29 30 31        23 24 25 26 27 28 29
                                                 30 31
```

Calendar 9

```
         JANUARY                    MAY                   SEPTEMBER
S  M  T  W  T  F  S     S  M  T  W  T  F  S     S  M  T  W  T  F  S
   1  2  3  4  5  6            1  2  3  4        1  2  3  4  5  6  7
7  8  9 10 11 12 13      5  6  7  8  9 10 11      8  9 10 11 12 13 14
14 15 16 17 18 19 20    12 13 14 15 16 17 18     15 16 17 18 19 20 21
21 22 23 24 25 26 27    19 20 21 22 23 24 25     22 23 24 25 26 27 28
28 29 30 31             26 27 28 29 30 31        29 30

         FEBRUARY                  JUNE                    OCTOBER
         1  2  3                             1              1  2  3  4  5
4  5  6  7  8  9 10      2  3  4  5  6  7  8      6  7  8  9 10 11 12
11 12 13 14 15 16 17     9 10 11 12 13 14 15     13 14 15 16 17 18 19
18 19 20 21 22 23 24    16 17 18 19 20 21 22     20 21 22 23 24 25 26
25 26 27 28 29          23 24 25 26 27 28 29     27 28 29 30 31
                        30

          MARCH                    JULY                   NOVEMBER
                  1  2      1  2  3  4  5  6                    1  2
3  4  5  6  7  8  9      7  8  9 10 11 12 13      3  4  5  6  7  8  9
10 11 12 13 14 15 16    14 15 16 17 18 19 20     10 11 12 13 14 15 16
17 18 19 20 21 22 23    21 22 23 24 25 26 27     17 18 19 20 21 22 23
24 25 26 27 28 29 30    28 29 30 31              24 25 26 27 28 29 30
31

          APRIL                   AUGUST                  DECEMBER
   1  2  3  4  5  6              1  2  3        1  2  3  4  5  6  7
7  8  9 10 11 12 13      4  5  6  7  8  9 10      8  9 10 11 12 13 14
14 15 16 17 18 19 20    11 12 13 14 15 16 17     15 16 17 18 19 20 21
21 22 23 24 25 26 27    18 19 20 21 22 23 24     22 23 24 25 26 27 28
28 29 30                25 26 27 28 29 30 31     29 30 31
```

Calendar 10

```
         JANUARY                    MAY                   SEPTEMBER
S  M  T  W  T  F  S     S  M  T  W  T  F  S     S  M  T  W  T  F  S
         1  2  3  4  5            1  2  3           1  2  3  4  5  6
6  7  8  9 10 11 12      4  5  6  7  8  9 10      7  8  9 10 11 12 13
13 14 15 16 17 18 19    11 12 13 14 15 16 17     14 15 16 17 18 19 20
20 21 22 23 24 25 26    18 19 20 21 22 23 24     21 22 23 24 25 26 27
27 28 29 30 31          25 26 27 28 29 30 31     28 29 30

         FEBRUARY                  JUNE                    OCTOBER
                  1  2   1  2  3  4  5  6  7                 1  2  3  4
3  4  5  6  7  8  9      8  9 10 11 12 13 14      5  6  7  8  9 10 11
10 11 12 13 14 15 16    15 16 17 18 19 20 21     12 13 14 15 16 17 18
17 18 19 20 21 22 23    22 23 24 25 26 27 28     19 20 21 22 23 24 25
24 25 26 27 28 29       29 30                    26 27 28 29 30 31

          MARCH                    JULY                   NOVEMBER
                     1     1  2  3  4  5                             1
2  3  4  5  6  7  8      6  7  8  9 10 11 12      2  3  4  5  6  7  8
9 10 11 12 13 14 15     13 14 15 16 17 18 19      9 10 11 12 13 14 15
16 17 18 19 20 21 22    20 21 22 23 24 25 26     16 17 18 19 20 21 22
23 24 25 26 27 28 29    27 28 29 30 31           23 24 25 26 27 28 29
30 31                                            30

          APRIL                   AUGUST                  DECEMBER
         1  2  3  4  5                    1  2      1  2  3  4  5  6
6  7  8  9 10 11 12      3  4  5  6  7  8  9      7  8  9 10 11 12 13
13 14 15 16 17 18 19    10 11 12 13 14 15 16     14 15 16 17 18 19 20
20 21 22 23 24 25 26    17 18 19 20 21 22 23     21 22 23 24 25 26 27
27 28 29 30             24 25 26 27 28 29 30     28 29 30 31
                        31
```

Calendar 11

JANUARY

S	M	T	W	T	F	S
			1	2	3	4
5	6	7	8	9	10	11
12	13	14	15	16	17	18
19	20	21	22	23	24	25
26	27	28	29	30	31	

FEBRUARY

S	M	T	W	T	F	S
						1
2	3	4	5	6	7	8
9	10	11	12	13	14	15
16	17	18	19	20	21	22
23	24	25	26	27	28	29

MARCH

S	M	T	W	T	F	S
1	2	3	4	5	6	7
8	9	10	11	12	13	14
15	16	17	18	19	20	21
22	23	24	25	26	27	28
29	30	31				

APRIL

S	M	T	W	T	F	S
			1	2	3	4
5	6	7	8	9	10	11
12	13	14	15	16	17	18
19	20	21	22	23	24	25
26	27	28	29	30		

MAY

S	M	T	W	T	F	S
					1	2
3	4	5	6	7	8	9
10	11	12	13	14	15	16
17	18	19	20	21	22	23
24	25	26	27	28	29	30
31						

JUNE

S	M	T	W	T	F	S
	1	2	3	4	5	6
7	8	9	10	11	12	13
14	15	16	17	18	19	20
21	22	23	24	25	26	27
28	29	30				

JULY

S	M	T	W	T	F	S
			1	2	3	4
5	6	7	8	9	10	11
12	13	14	15	16	17	18
19	20	21	22	23	24	25
26	27	28	29	30	31	

AUGUST

S	M	T	W	T	F	S
						1
2	3	4	5	6	7	8
9	10	11	12	13	14	15
16	17	18	19	20	21	22
23	24	25	26	27	28	29
30	31					

SEPTEMBER

S	M	T	W	T	F	S
		1	2	3	4	5
6	7	8	9	10	11	12
13	14	15	16	17	18	19
20	21	22	23	24	25	26
27	28	29	30			

OCTOBER

S	M	T	W	T	F	S
				1	2	3
4	5	6	7	8	9	10
11	12	13	14	15	16	17
18	19	20	21	22	23	24
25	26	27	28	29	30	31

NOVEMBER

S	M	T	W	T	F	S
1	2	3	4	5	6	7
8	9	10	11	12	13	14
15	16	17	18	19	20	21
22	23	24	25	26	27	28
29	30					

DECEMBER

S	M	T	W	T	F	S
		1	2	3	4	5
6	7	8	9	10	11	12
13	14	15	16	17	18	19
20	21	22	23	24	25	26
27	28	29	30	31		

Calendar 12

JANUARY

S	M	T	W	T	F	S
				1	2	3
4	5	6	7	8	9	10
11	12	13	14	15	16	17
18	19	20	21	22	23	24
25	26	27	28	29	30	31

FEBRUARY

S	M	T	W	T	F	S
1	2	3	4	5	6	7
8	9	10	11	12	13	14
15	16	17	18	19	20	21
22	23	24	25	26	27	28
29						

MARCH

S	M	T	W	T	F	S
1	2	3	4	5	6	
7	8	9	10	11	12	13
14	15	16	17	18	19	20
21	22	23	24	25	26	27
28	29	30	31			

APRIL

S	M	T	W	T	F	S
				1	2	3
4	5	6	7	8	9	10
11	12	13	14	15	16	17
18	19	20	21	22	23	24
25	26	27	28	29	30	

MAY

S	M	T	W	T	F	S
						1
2	3	4	5	6	7	8
9	10	11	12	13	14	15
16	17	18	19	20	21	22
23	24	25	26	27	28	29
30	31					

JUNE

S	M	T	W	T	F	S
	1	2	3	4	5	
6	7	8	9	10	11	12
13	14	15	16	17	18	19
20	21	22	23	24	25	26
27	28	29	30			

JULY

S	M	T	W	T	F	S
				1	2	3
4	5	6	7	8	9	10
11	12	13	14	15	16	17
18	19	20	21	22	23	24
25	26	27	28	29	30	31

AUGUST

S	M	T	W	T	F	S
1	2	3	4	5	6	7
8	9	10	11	12	13	14
15	16	17	18	19	20	21
22	23	24	25	26	27	28
29	30	31				

SEPTEMBER

S	M	T	W	T	F	S
			1	2	3	4
5	6	7	8	9	10	11
12	13	14	15	16	17	18
19	20	21	22	23	24	25
26	27	28	29	30		

OCTOBER

S	M	T	W	T	F	S
					1	2
3	4	5	6	7	8	9
10	11	12	13	14	15	16
17	18	19	20	21	22	23
24	25	26	27	28	29	30
31						

NOVEMBER

S	M	T	W	T	F	S
	1	2	3	4	5	6
7	8	9	10	11	12	13
14	15	16	17	18	19	20
21	22	23	24	25	26	27
28	29	30				

DECEMBER

S	M	T	W	T	F	S
			1	2	3	4
5	6	7	8	9	10	11
12	13	14	15	16	17	18
19	20	21	22	23	24	25
26	27	28	29	30	31	

Calendar 13

JANUARY

S	M	T	W	T	F	S
					1	2
3	4	5	6	7	8	9
10	11	12	13	14	15	16
17	18	19	20	21	22	23
24	25	26	27	28	29	30
31						

FEBRUARY

S	M	T	W	T	F	S
	1	2	3	4	5	6
7	8	9	10	11	12	13
14	15	16	17	18	19	20
21	22	23	24	25	26	27
28	29					

MARCH

S	M	T	W	T	F	S
	1	2	3	4	5	
6	7	8	9	10	11	12
13	14	15	16	17	18	19
20	21	22	23	24	25	26
27	28	29	30	31		

APRIL

S	M	T	W	T	F	S
					1	2
3	4	5	6	7	8	9
10	11	12	13	14	15	16
17	18	19	20	21	22	23
24	25	26	27	28	29	30

MAY

S	M	T	W	T	F	S
1	2	3	4	5	6	7
8	9	10	11	12	13	14
15	16	17	18	19	20	21
22	23	24	25	26	27	28
29	30	31				

JUNE

S	M	T	W	T	F	S
			1	2	3	4
5	6	7	8	9	10	11
12	13	14	15	16	17	18
19	20	21	22	23	24	25
26	27	28	29	30		

JULY

S	M	T	W	T	F	S
					1	2
3	4	5	6	7	8	9
10	11	12	13	14	15	16
17	18	19	20	21	22	23
24	25	26	27	28	29	30
31						

AUGUST

S	M	T	W	T	F	S
	1	2	3	4	5	6
7	8	9	10	11	12	13
14	15	16	17	18	19	20
21	22	23	24	25	26	27
28	29	30	31			

SEPTEMBER

S	M	T	W	T	F	S
				1	2	3
4	5	6	7	8	9	10
11	12	13	14	15	16	17
18	19	20	21	22	23	24
25	26	27	28	29	30	

OCTOBER

S	M	T	W	T	F	S
						1
2	3	4	5	6	7	8
9	10	11	12	13	14	15
16	17	18	19	20	21	22
23	24	25	26	27	28	29
30	31					

NOVEMBER

S	M	T	W	T	F	S
	1	2	3	4	5	
6	7	8	9	10	11	12
13	14	15	16	17	18	19
20	21	22	23	24	25	26
27	28	29	30			

DECEMBER

S	M	T	W	T	F	S
			1	2	3	
4	5	6	7	8	9	10
11	12	13	14	15	16	17
18	19	20	21	22	23	24
25	26	27	28	29	30	31

Calendar 14

JANUARY

S	M	T	W	T	F	S
						1
2	3	4	5	6	7	8
9	10	11	12	13	14	15
16	17	18	19	20	21	22
23	24	25	26	27	28	29
30	31					

FEBRUARY

S	M	T	W	T	F	S
		1	2	3	4	5
6	7	8	9	10	11	12
13	14	15	16	17	18	19
20	21	22	23	24	25	26
27	28	29				

MARCH

S	M	T	W	T	F	S
		1	2	3	4	
5	6	7	8	9	10	11
12	13	14	15	16	17	18
19	20	21	22	23	24	25
26	27	28	29	30	31	

APRIL

S	M	T	W	T	F	S
						1
2	3	4	5	6	7	8
9	10	11	12	13	14	15
16	17	18	19	20	21	22
23	24	25	26	27	28	29
30						

MAY

S	M	T	W	T	F	S
	1	2	3	4	5	6
7	8	9	10	11	12	13
14	15	16	17	18	19	20
21	22	23	24	25	26	27
28	29	30	31			

JUNE

S	M	T	W	T	F	S
				1	2	3
4	5	6	7	8	9	10
11	12	13	14	15	16	17
18	19	20	21	22	23	24
25	26	27	28	29	30	

JULY

S	M	T	W	T	F	S
						1
2	3	4	5	6	7	8
9	10	11	12	13	14	15
16	17	18	19	20	21	22
23	24	25	26	27	28	29
30	31					

AUGUST

S	M	T	W	T	F	S
		1	2	3	4	5
6	7	8	9	10	11	12
13	14	15	16	17	18	19
20	21	22	23	24	25	26
27	28	29	30	31		

SEPTEMBER

S	M	T	W	T	F	S
					1	2
3	4	5	6	7	8	9
10	11	12	13	14	15	16
17	18	19	20	21	22	23
24	25	26	27	28	29	30

OCTOBER

S	M	T	W	T	F	S
1	2	3	4	5	6	7
8	9	10	11	12	13	14
15	16	17	18	19	20	21
22	23	24	25	26	27	28
29	30	31				

NOVEMBER

S	M	T	W	T	F	S
			1	2	3	4
5	6	7	8	9	10	11
12	13	14	15	16	17	18
19	20	21	22	23	24	25
26	27	28	29	30		

DECEMBER

S	M	T	W	T	F	S
					1	2
3	4	5	6	7	8	9
10	11	12	13	14	15	16
17	18	19	20	21	22	23
24	25	26	27	28	29	30
31						

WORDS DESCRIBING PERIODS OF TIME

annually	yearly; occurring once every 12 months
biannually	occurring twice a year (at unequally spaced intervals)
bicentennial	relating to a period of 200 years
biennial	relating to a period of 2 years
bimonthly	occurring once every 2 months
biweekly	occurring once every 2 weeks
centennial	relating to a period of 100 years (1 century)
daily	occurring once every 24 hours
decennial	relating to a period of 10 years (1 decade)
diurnal	daily; of a day
duodecennial	relating to a period of 12 years
fortnightly	occurring once every 2 weeks
millennial	relating to a period of 1,000 years (1 millennium)
monthly	occurring once every 30 days (approximately)
novennial	relating to a period of 9 years
octennial	relating to a period of 8 years
perennial	occurring year after year
quadrennial	relating to a period of 4 years (1 olympiad)
quadricentennial	relating to a period of 400 years
quincentennial	relating to a period of 500 years
quindecennial	relating to a period of 15 years
quinquennial	relating to a period of 5 years
semiannually	occurring once every 6 months (at equally spaced intervals)
semicentennial	relating to a period of 50 years
semidiurnal	occurring twice a day
semimonthly	occurring twice a month
semiweekly	occurring twice a week
septennial	relating to a period of 7 years
sesquicentennial	relating to a period of 150 years
sexennial	relating to a period of 6 years
thrice weekly	occurring three times a week
triennial	relating to a period of 3 years
trimonthly	occurring once every 3 months
triweekly	occurring once every 3 weeks
undecennial	relating to a period of 11 years
vicennial	relating to a period of 20 years
weekly	occurring once every 7 days

A "jiffy" is an actual unit of time. It is $\frac{1}{100}$ of a second.

MAJOR HOLIDAYS

AMERICAN

Dates marked with an asterisk (*) are the officially designated national holidays.

*January 1	New Year's Day
January 15	Martin Luther King Jr.'s Birthday
Third Monday in January	Martin Luther King Jr.'s Birthday (observed)
January 19	Robert E. Lee's Birthday (Southern states)
January 20	Inauguration Day
February 2	Groundhog Day
February 12	Lincoln's Birthday
February 14	Valentine's Day
February 22	Washington's Birthday
Third Monday in February	Washington's Birthday (observed as Presidents' Day)
March 17	St. Patrick's Day
March or April	Easter Sunday
April 1	April Fools' Day
April 14	Pan American Day
May 1	May Day
Second Sunday in May	Mother's Day
Third Saturday in May	Armed Forces Day
May 30	Memorial Day
*Last Monday in May	Memorial Day (observed)
June 3	Jefferson Davis's Birthday (Southern states)
June 14	Flag Day
Third Sunday in June	Father's Day
*July 4	Independence Day
*First Monday in September	Labor Day
September 17	Citizenship Day
Fourth Friday in September	Native American Day
October 12	Columbus Day
*Second Monday in October	Columbus Day (observed)
October 24	United Nations Day
October 31	Halloween
First Tuesday after the first Monday in November	Election Day
*November 11	Veterans' Day

*Fourth Thursday in November	Thanksgiving Day			Korea; Constitution Day in Panama
*December 25	Christmas Day		March 8	International Women's Day in UN member nations

CANADIAN

January 1	New Year's Day		March 17	St. Patrick's Day in Ireland and Northern Ireland
March or April	Good Friday		March 19	St. Joseph's Day in Colombia, Costa Rica, Italy, and Spain
	Easter Monday			
Last Monday before May 25	Victoria Day		March 21	Benito Juarez's Birthday in Mexico
July 1	Canada Day		March 22	Arab League Day in Arab League countries
First Monday in September	Labour Day		March 23	Pakistan Day in Pakistan
Second Monday in October	Thanksgiving Day		March 25	Independence Day in Greece; Lady Day (Quarter Day) in Great Britain
November 11	Remembrance Day		March 26	Fiesta del Arbol (Arbor Day) in Spain
December 25	Christmas Day			
December 26	Boxing Day		March 29	Youth and Martyrs' Day in Taiwan

OTHER

January	Australia Day on the last Monday in Australia		March 30	Muslim New Year in Indonesia
January 1	New Year's Day throughout the Western world and in India, Indonesia, Japan, Korea, the Philippines, Singapore, Taiwan, and Thailand; founding of Republic of China (Taiwan)		March–April	Carnival/Lent/Easter: The pre-Lenten celebration of Carnival (Mardi Gras) and the post-Lenten celebration of Easter are movable feasts widely observed in Christian countries.
January 2	Berchtoldstag in Switzerland		April 1	Victory Day in Spain; April Fools' Day (All Fools' Day) in Great Britain
January 3	Genshi-Sai (First Beginning) in Japan			
January 5	Twelfth Night (Wassail Eve or Eve of Epiphany) in England		April 5	Arbor Day in Korea
			April 6	Van Riebeeck Day in South Africa
January 6	Epiphany, observed by Catholics throughout Europe and Latin America		April 7	World Health Day in UN member nations
January 15	Adults' Day in Japan		April 8	Buddha's Birthday in Korea and Japan; Hana Matsuri (Flower Festival) in Japan
January 20	St. Agnes' Eve in Great Britain			
January 26	Republic Day in India			
January–February	Chinese New Year and Vietnamese New Year (Tet)		April 14	Pan American Day in the Americas
February	Hamstrom on the first Sunday in Switzerland		April 19	Declaration of Independence Day in Venezuela
February 3	Setsubun (Bean-throwing Festival) in Japan		April 22	Queen Isabella Day in Spain
			April 23	St. George's Day in England
February 5	Promulgation of the Constitution Day in Mexico		April 25	Liberation Day in Italy; ANZAC Day in Australia and New Zealand
February 6	New Zealand Day in New Zealand			
			April 26	Union Day in Tanzania
February 11	National Foundation Day in Japan		April 29	Emperor's Birthday in Japan
			April 30	Queen's Birthday in The Netherlands; Walpurgis Night in Germany and Scandinavia
February 27	Independence Day in the Dominican Republic			
March 1	Independence Movement Day in		April–May	Independence Day in Israel

continues

Other Holidays, continued

May	Constitution Day on first Monday in Japan
May 1	May Day–Labor Day in the Commonwealth of Independent States and most of Europe and Latin America
May 5	Children's Day in Japan and Korea; Victory of General Zaragosa Day in Mexico; Liberation Day in The Netherlands
May 8	V-E Day in Europe
May 9	Victory over Fascism Day in the Commonwealth of Independent States
May 14	Independence Day in Paraguay
May 31	Republic Day in South Africa
June 2	Founding of the Republic Day in Italy
June 5	Constitution Day in Denmark; World Environment Day in UN member nations
June 6	Memorial Day in Korea; Flag Day in Sweden
June 8	Muhammad's Birthday in Indonesia
June 10	Portugal Day in Portugal
June 12	Republic Day in the Commonwealth of Independent States; Independence Day in the Philippines
mid-June	Queen's Official Birthday on second Saturday in Great Britain; Midsummer Celebrations in Sweden
June 16	Soweto Day in U.N. member nations
June 20	Flag Day in Argentina
June 29	Feast of Saints Peter and Paul in Chile, Colombia, Costa Rica, Italy, Peru, Spain, Vatican City, and Venezuela
July 1	Half-year Holiday in Hong Kong; Bank Holiday in Taiwan; Dominion Day in Canada
July 5	Independence Day in Venezuela
July 9	Independence Day in Argentina
July 10	Bon (Feast of Fortune) in Japan
July 12	Orangemen's Day in Northern Ireland
July 14	Bastille Day in France
mid-July	Feria de San Fermin during second week in Spain

July 17	Constitution Day in Korea
July 18	National Day in Spain
July 20	Independence Day in Colombia
July 21–22	National Holiday in Belgium
July 22	National Liberation Day in Poland
July 24	Simon Bolivar's Birthday in Ecuador and Venezuela
July 25	St. James' Day in Spain
July 28–29	Independence Day in Peru
August	Bank Holiday on first Monday in Fiji, Grenada, Guyana, Hong Kong, Ireland, and Malawi; Discovery Day on first Monday in Trinidad and Tobago; Independence Day on first Tuesday in Jamaica
August 1	Lammas Day in England; National Day in Switzerland
August 9	National Day in Singapore
August 10	Independence Day in Ecuador
August 14	Independence Day in Pakistan
August 15	Independence Day in India and Korea; Assumption Day in Catholic countries
August 16	National Restoration Day in the Dominican Republic
August 17	Independence Day in Indonesia
August 31	Independence Day in Trinidad and Tobago
September	Rose of Tralee Festival in Ireland
September 7	Independence Day in Brazil
September 9	Choxo-no-Sekku (Chrysanthemum Day) in Japan
September 14	Battle of San Jacinto Day in Nicaragua
mid-September	Sherry Wine Harvest in Spain
September 15	Independence Day in Costa Rica, Guatemala, and Nicaragua; Respect for the Aged Day in Japan
September 16	Independence Day in Mexico and Papua New Guinea
September 18–19	Independence Day in Chile
September 28	Confucius' Birthday in Taiwan
October	Thanksgiving Day in Canada on second Monday; Kruger Day in South Africa during second week
October 1	National Day in People's Republic of China; Armed Forces Day in Korea; National Holiday in Nigeria

October 2	Mahatma Gandhi's Birthday in India
October 3	National Day in the Federal Republic of Germany; National Foundation Day in Korea
October 5	Republic Day in Portugal
October 9	Korean Alphabet Day in Korea
October 10	Founding of Republic of China in Taiwan
October 12	Columbus Day in Spain and widely throughout Latin America
October 19	Ascension of Muhammad Day in Indonesia
October 20	Revolution Day in Guatemala; Kenyatta Day in Kenya
October 24	United Nations Day in UN member nations
October 26	National Holiday in Australia
October 28	Greek National Day in Greece
November 1	All Saints' Day, observed by Catholics in most countries
November 2	All Souls' Day in Ecuador, El Salvador, Luxembourg, Macao, Mexico, San Marino, Uruguay, and Vatican City
November 3	Culture Day in Japan
November 4	National Unity Day in Italy
November 5	Guy Fawkes' Day in Great Britain
November 11	Armistice Day in Belgium, French Guiana, and Tahiti; Veterans' Day in France; Remembrance Day in Canada and Bermuda
November 12	Sun Yat-sen's Birthday in Taiwan
November 15	Proclamation of the Republic Day in Brazil
November 19	National Holiday in Monaco
November 20	Anniversary of the Revolution in Mexico
November 23	Kinro-Kansha-No-Hi (Labor/Thanksgiving Day) in Japan
November 30	National Heroes' Day in the Philippines
December 5	Discovery by Columbus Day in Haiti
December 6	Independence Day in Finland
December 8	Feast of the Immaculate Conception, widely observed in Catholic countries
December 10	Constitution Day in Thailand; Human Rights Day in UN member nations
mid-December	Nine Days of Posada during third week in Mexico
December 25	Christmas Day, widely observed in all Christian countries
December 26	St. Stephen's Day in Austria, Ireland, Italy, Liechtenstein, San Marino, and Switzerland; Boxing Day in Great Britain and Northern Ireland
December 28	National Day in Nepal
December 31	New Year's Eve throughout the world; Omisoka (Grand Last Day) in Japan; Hogmanay Day in Scotland

ADDITIONAL SOURCES OF INFORMATION

BOOKS

Barnett, Jo Ellen. *Time's Pendulum: From Sundials to Atomic Clocks, the Fascinating History of Timekeeping and How Our Discoveries Changed the World.* Harvest Books, 1999.

Blackburn, Bonnie, and Leofranc Holford-Strevens. *The Oxford Book of Days.* Oxford University Press, 2000.

Blaise, Clark. *Time Lord: Sir Sandford Fleming and the Creation of Standard Time.* Pantheon Books, 2001.

Chase, William D., and Helen M. Chase. *Chase's Annual Events.* Contemporary Books, annual.

Fitzpatrick, Gary L. *International Time Tables.* Scarecrow Press, 1990.

Landes, David S. *Revolution in Time: Clocks and the Making of the Modern World.* Harvard University Press, 1983.

Macey, Samuel L. *Encyclopedia of Time.* Garland, 1994.

————. *Time: A Bibliographic Guide.* Garland, 1991.

Mossman, Jennifer, ed. *Holidays and Anniversaries of the World.* Gale Research, 1990.

continues

Sobel, Dava. *Longitude: The True Story of a Lone Genius Who Solved the Greatest Scientific Problem of His Time*. Penguin, 1996.

Thompson, Sue Ellen, and Barbara W. Carlson. *Holidays, Festivals and Celebrations of the World Dictionary*. Omnigraphics, 1994.

Westrheim, Margo. *Calendars of the World*. Oneworld, 1993.

WEB SITES

http://timezoneconverter.com/
http://tycho.usno.navy.mil/tzones.html
(both give time around the world in various zones)

http://www.worldtime.com/
(interactive world atlas, information on local time)

http://www.time.gov
(to manually set your clock to the NIST's Universal Time Clock)

http://www.boulder.nist.gov/timefreq/service/time-computer.html
(to synchronize time on computers connected to the Internet, or via telephone for computers with analog modems)

2

WEIGHTS AND MEASURES

U.S. CUSTOMARY SYSTEM OF WEIGHTS AND MEASURES

The units of weights and measures commonly used today in the United States were derived during the colonial period from units used in Great Britain for many centuries.

LENGTH

1 nail (cloth)	=	2.25 inches		
1 palm	=	3 inches		
1 hand	=	4 inches		
1 span	=	6 inches		
1 quarter (cloth)	=	9 inches		
1 foot	=	12 inches		
1 pace	=	30 inches	=	2.5 feet
1 yard	=	36 inches	=	3 feet
1 fathom	=	6 feet	=	2 yards
1 rod	=	16.5 feet	=	5.5 yards
1 furlong	=	660 feet	=	220 yards
1 mile	=	5,280 feet	=	1,760 yards
1 nautical mile	=	6,076.1155 feet		

AREA

1 square foot	=	144 square inches		
1 square yard	=	9 square feet		
1 rood	=	10,890 square feet	=	40 square rods
1 acre	=	43,560 square feet	=	4 roods
1 square mile	=	640 acres		

VOLUME

1 cubic foot	=	1,728 cubic inches
1 cubic yard	=	27 cubic feet

CAPACITY (DRY MEASURE)

1 pint	=	33.6003125 cubic inches		
1 quart	=	67.200625 cubic inches	=	2 pints
1 gallon	=	268.8025 cubic inches	=	4 quarts
1 peck	=	537.605 cubic inches	=	2 gallons
1 bushel	=	2,150.42 cubic inches	=	4 pecks
1 cranberry barrel	=	5,876 cubic inches		
1 barrel	=	7,056 cubic inches		
1 cord-foot (wood)	=	16 cubic feet		
1 cord (wood)	=	128 cubic feet	=	8 cord-feet
1 freight ton	=	40 cubic feet		
1 register ton	=	100 cubic feet		

Go to "Chemistry," "Mathematics," and "Physics" in chapter 4; "Standard Sizes Chart" in chapter 19

Six Quick Ways to Measure When You Don't Have a Ruler

1. Most credit cards are $3^3/_8$ inches by $2^1/_8$ inches.
2. Standard business cards are printed $3^1/_2$ inches wide by 2 inches long.
3. Floor tiles are usually manufactured in 12-inch by 12-inch squares.
4. U.S. paper currency is $6^1/_8$ inches wide by $2^5/_8$ inches long.
5. The diameter of a quarter is approximately 1 inch, and the diameter of a penny is approximately $^3/_4$ inch.
6. A standard sheet of paper is $8^1/_2$ inches wide by 11 inches long.

CAPACITY (LIQUID MEASURE)

1 fluid dram	=	60 minims		
1 teaspoon	=	80 minims		
1 tablespoon	=	240 minims	=	3 teaspoons
1 fluid ounce	=	480 minims	=	2 tablespoons
1 gill	=	4 fluid ounces		
1 cup	=	8 fluid ounces	=	2 gills
1 pint	=	16 fluid ounces	=	2 cups
1 quart	=	32 fluid ounces	=	2 pints
1 gallon	=	128 fluid ounces	=	4 quarts
1 barrel	=	31.5 gallons	=	7,276.5 cubic inches
1 petroleum barrel	=	42 gallons	=	9,702 cubic inches

MASS (AVOIRDUPOIS)

1 dram	=	27.34375 grains		
1 ounce	=	16 drams		
1 pound	=	16 ounces		
1 hundredweight	=	100 pounds		
1 ton	=	2,000 pounds	=	20 hundredweights

MASS (TROY AND APOTHECARY)

1 scruple	=	20 grains	
1 pennyweight	=	24 grains	
1 dram	=	60 grains	= 3 scruples
1 ounce	=	480 grains	= 8 drams
1 pound	=	12 ounces	

ANGLE

1 minute	=	60 seconds
1 degree	=	60 minutes
1 sign	=	30 degrees
1 octant	=	45 degrees
1 sextant	=	60 degrees
1 quadrant	=	90 degrees
1 semicircle	=	180 degrees
1 circle	=	360 degrees

METRIC SYSTEM OF MEASUREMENT

The metric system is a system of weights and measures, based on decimals, or units of ten, that was developed in the 1790s in revolutionary France and revised and refined several times since that period. In 1960, an international conference gave it the official name *Système International d'Unités* (International System of Units, or SI). Virtually all countries except the United States use this system.

On December 23, 1975, President Gerald R. Ford signed the U.S. Metric Conversion Act, declaring a national policy of encouraging voluntary conversion to the metric system. Federal agencies have made a transition to the metric system, but adoption elsewhere in the country has been more gradual than anticipated in 1975.

The coldest temperature ever recorded was at Vostock II, Antarctica, −128.6°F on July 21, 1983.

BASIC UNITS

The metric system includes seven basic units for different types of measurement.

The basic unit of length is the *meter (m),* currently defined as the path traveled by light in a vacuum in $1/299,792.458$ of a second.

The basic unit of mass is the *kilogram (kg),* currently defined as the mass of a platinum-iridium cylinder preserved in a vault at Sèvres, near Paris, by the International Bureau of Weights and Measures.

The basic unit of time is the *second (sec),* currently defined as the duration of $9,192,631,770$ cycles of radiation given off by the element cesium 133 under certain conditions.

The basic unit of temperature is the *Kelvin (K),* which is the same size as a Celsius degree. The lowest temperature possible in theory (absolute zero) is 273.16 degrees below zero Celsius. Thus, $0 K = −273.16°C$. This unit is named after the British physicist Lord Kelvin (William Thomson; 1824–1907).

The basic unit of electric current is the *ampere (A),* defined as the current that, if maintained in two straight parallel wires of infinite length and negligible cross section, and placed in a vacuum, will produce between the wires a force of 0.0000002 newton (defined in the following section) per meter of length. This unit is named after the French physicist André M. Ampère (1775–1836).

The basic unit of luminosity intensity is the *candela (cd),* currently defined as the light given off by $1/600,000$ square meters of a black body (a perfect radiator) at the freezing point of platinum under a pressure of 101,325 newtons per square meter.

The basic unit of substance is the *mole (mol),* defined as the amount of substance equal to the molecular weight of that substance.

DERIVED UNITS

All other metric units are derived from the seven basic units defined in the preceding section.

One *newton (N)* is the force that imparts to a mass of one kilogram an acceleration of one meter per second. One *pascal (Pa),* the unit of pressure, is one newton per square meter. One *joule (J),* the unit of energy, is the work done by a force of one newton acting through a distance of one meter. These units are named after the English mathematician and philosopher Sir Isaac Newton (1642–1727); the French mathematician and philosopher Blaise Pascal (1623–62); and the English physicist James P. Joule (1818–89).

In electricity, one *coulomb (C)* is the electric charge transported through a conductor by a current of one ampere flowing for one second. One *volt (V)* is the electromotive force or difference in potential between two points in an electric field that requires one joule of work to move a positive charge of one coulomb from the point of lower potential to the point of higher potential. One *ohm* is the electrical resistance of a circuit in which an electromotive force of one volt maintains a current of one ampere. One *watt (W),* equal to one joule per second, is the electrical power developed in a circuit by a current of one ampere flowing through a potential difference of one volt. These units are named after the French physicist Charles A. Coulomb (1736–1806), the Italian physicist Count Alessandro Volta (1745–1827), the German physicist Georg Simon Ohm (1787–1854), and the Scottish engineer and inventor James Watt (1736–1819).

METRIC PREFIXES

The metric, or SI, system is based on the decimal system and follows a consistent name scheme using the prefixes listed below. Multiples and submultiples always related to the power of 10 are combined with the basic metric units to provide the multiples and submultiples in the metric or SI system. For example, centi + meter = centimeter, meaning one one-hundredth of a meter.

Prefix	Symbol	Multiples	Equivalent	Prefix	Symbol	Multiples	Equivalent
exa	E	10^{18}	quintillionfold	deci	d	10^{-1}	tenth part
peta	P	10^{15}	quadrillionfold	centi	c	10^{-2}	hundredth part
tera	T	10^{12}	trillionfold	milli	m	10^{-3}	thousandth part
giga	G	10^{9}	billionfold	micro	μ	10^{-6}	millionth part
mega	M	10^{6}	millionfold	nano	n	10^{-9}	billionth part
kilo	k	10^{5}	thousandfold	pico	p	10^{-12}	trillionth part
hecto	h	10^{2}	hundredfold	femto	f	10^{-15}	quadrillionth part
deka	da	10	tenfold	atto	a	10^{-18}	quintillionth part

TABLES OF METRIC WEIGHTS AND MEASURES

LENGTH
10 millimeters (mm) = 1 centimeter (cm)
10 centimeters = 1 decimeter (dm)
10 decimeters = 1 meter (m)
10 meters = 1 dekameter (dam)
10 dekameters = 1 hectometer (hm)
10 hectometers = 1 kilometer (km)

The highest temperature ever recorded on Earth was 136°F on September 13, 1992, in Al 'Azīzīyah, Libya

AREA
100 sq. millimeters (mm²) = 1 sq. centimeter (cm²)
10,000 sq. centimeters = 1 sq. meter (m²)
100 sq. meters = 1 are (a)
100 ares = 1 hectare (ha)
100 hectares = 1 sq. kilometer (km²)

VOLUME
1,000 cu. millimeters (mm³) = 1 cu. centimeter (cm³)
1,000 cu. centimeters = 1 cu. decimeter (dm³)
1,000 cu. decimeters = 1 cu. meter (m³)

CAPACITY (DRY AND LIQUID)
10 milliliters (ml) = 1 centiliter (cl)
10 centiliters = 1 deciliter (dl)
10 deciliters = 1 liter (l)
10 liters = 1 dekaliter (dal)
10 dekaliters = 1 hectoliter (hl)
10 hectoliters = 1 kiloliter (kl)

MASS
10 milligrams (mg) = 1 centigram (cg)
10 centigrams = 1 decigram (dg)
10 decigrams = 1 gram (g)
10 grams = 1 dekagram (dag)
10 dekagrams = 1 hectogram (hg)
10 hectograms = 1 kilogram (kg)
1,000 kilograms = 1 metric ton (t)

Go to "Cooking Equivalents and Substitutions" and "Champagne Bottle Sizes" in chapter 19

COMMON CONVERSION FACTORS

Weights/Measures

To Convert From	To	Multiply by	To Convert From	To	Multiply by
Acres	Hectares	0.40468586	Miles, square	Hectares	258.99881
Acres, square	Kilometers, square	0.004046856	Miles, square	Kilometers, square	2.5899881
Acres	Meters, square	4046.856	Miles, statute	Centimeters	160934.4
Centimeters	Meters	0.01	Miles, statute	Meters	1609.344
Centimeters, square	Meters, square	0.0001	Miles, statute	Kilometers	1.609344
Feet	Centimeters	30.48	Ounces, avoirdupois	Grams	28.349523
Feet	Meters	0.3048	Ounces, avoirdupois	Kilograms	0.028349523
Feet	Kilometers	0.0003048	Ounces, troy	Pounds, troy	0.083333
Feet, cubic	Liters	28.316847	Ounces, troy	Grams	31.10348
Feet, cubic	Meters, cubic	0.028316847	Pints, U.S. liquid	Millimeters	473.176473
Feet, square	Centimeters, square	929.0304	Pints, U.S. liquid	Liters	0.473176473
Feet, square	Meters, square	0.09290304	Pounds, avoirdupois	Grams	453.59237
Gallons, U.S. liquid	Liters	3.785412	Pounds, avoirdupois	Kilograms	0.45359237
Gallons, U.S. liquid	Meters, cubic	0.003785412	Pounds, avoirdupois	Quintals	0.0045359237
Grams	Ounces, troy	0.032151	Pounds, avoirdupois	Tons, metric	0.00045359237
Grams	Pounds, troy	0.002679	Pounds, troy	Ounces, troy	12
Hectares	Kilometers, square	0.01	Pounds, troy	Grams	373.2417216
Hectares	Meters, square	10,000	Quarts, dry	Liters	1.101221
Inches	Centimeters	2.54	Quarts, dry	Dekaliters	0.1101221
Inches	Meters	0.0254	Quarts, liquid	Milliliters	946.352946
Inches, cubic	Milliliters	16.387064	Quarts, liquid	Liters	0.946352946
Inches, cubic	Liters	0.016387064	Quintals	Tons, metric	0.1
Inches, cubic	Meters, cubic	0.000016387064	Ton-miles, long	Ton-kilometers, metric	1.635169
Inches, square	Centimeters, square	6.4516	Ton-miles, short	Ton-kilometers, metric	1.4359972
Inches, square	Meters, square	0.00064516	Tons, long	Kilograms	1016.047
Kilograms	Ounces, troy	32.15075	Tons, long	Tons, metric	1.016047
Kilograms	Pounds, troy	2.679229	Tons, metric	Quintals	10
Kilograms	Tons, metric	0.001	Tons, register	Meters, cubic	2.831685
Kilometers, square	Hectares	100	Tons, short	Kilograms	907.185
Kilometers, square	Miles, square	0.3861	Tons, short	Tons, metric	0.907185
Liters	Milliliters	1000	Yards	Centimeters	91.44
Liters	Meters, cubic	0.001	Yards	Meters	0.9144
Meters	Millimeters	1000	Yards, cubic	Liters	764.5549
Meters	Centimeters	100	Yards, cubic	Meters, cubic	0.7645549
Meters	Kilometers	0.001	Yards, square	Meters, square	0.836127
Meters, cubic	Liters	1000			
Meters, cubic	Tons, register	0.353147			
Miles, nautical	Kilometers	1.852			

Mile/Kilometer Conversions

Miles to Kilometers		Kilometers to Miles	
1	1.6	1	0.6
2	3.2	2	1.2
3	4.8	3	1.9
4	6.4	4	2.5
5	8.0	5	3.1
6	9.7	6	3.7
7	11.3	7	4.3
8	12.9	8	5.0
9	14.5	9	5.6
10	16.1	10	6.2
20	32.2	20	12.4
30	48.3	30	18.6
40	64.4	40	24.9
50	80.5	50	31.1
60	96.6	60	37.3
70	112.7	70	43.5
80	128.7	80	49.7
90	144.8	90	55.9
100	160.9	100	62.1
1,000	1,609.3	1,000	621.4

A Closer Look

TEMPERATURE CONVERSIONS

The following can be used as general guidelines to tell the temperature in both Celsius and Fahrenheit.

0°C	Freezing point of water (32°F)
10°C	A warm winter day (50°F)
20°C	A mild spring day (68°F)
30°C	Quite warm—almost hot (86°F)
37°C	Normal body temperature (98.6°F)
40°C	Heat wave conditions (104°F)
100°C	Boiling point of water (212°F)

To convert degrees Fahrenheit to degrees Celsius, subtract 32 from the Fahrenheit temperature, multiply the difference by 5, and then divide the product by 9. To convert degrees Celsius to degrees Fahrenheit, multiply the Celsius temperature by 1.8 and add 32.

Absolute zero, the theoretically lowest temperature possible, is equal to –273°C and –459.4°F.

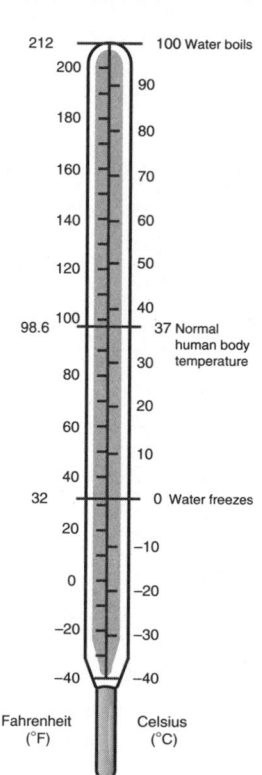

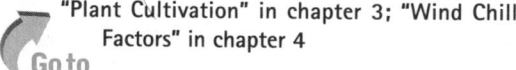

"Plant Cultivation" in chapter 3; "Wind Chill Factors" in chapter 4

Go to

Weights/Measures

SPECIAL WEIGHTS AND MEASURES

astronomical unit (AU)   The unit of length used in astronomy equal to the mean distance of Earth from the Sun, or about 93 million miles.

bale   A large bundle of goods. In the United States, the approximate weight of a bale of cotton is 500 pounds.

board foot (fbm)   A measurement used in lumber: 144 cubic inches (12 inches by 12 inches by 1 inch).

bolt   Used in measuring cloth: 40 yards.

British thermal unit (Btu)   A unit of heat energy measured as the amount of heat required to raise the temperature of 1 pound of water from 60° to 61°F at a constant pressure of 1 standard atmosphere (the weight of the atmosphere at mean sea level). One Btu is equal to 1054.5 joules in the meter-kilogram-second system of measurements.

bundle   Two reams of paper.

caliber   The diameter of a bore of a gun, usually expressed in modern U.S. and British usage in hundredths or thousandths of an inch and typically written as a decimal fraction.

Without using precision instruments, Eratosthenes measured the radius of the Earth in the 3rd century B.C. and came within 1% of the value determined by today's technology.

carat   Originally the weight of a seed of the carob tree in the Mediterranean region, today it has two separate meanings: (1) 200 milligrams, or 3.086 grains troy, used for measuring the weight of gemstones; and (2) a measure of the amount of gold per 24 parts of gold alloy; in this sense, it also spelled *karat*. Thus, 24-carat gold is pure, and 18-carat gold is ¾ gold and ¼ other metal.

case   Four bundles of paper.

chain (ch)   A unit of length equal to 66 feet and usually divided into 100 links. Used in surveying.

decibel   A unit of relative loudness. The smallest amount of change that can be detected by the human ear is 1 decibel. A 20-decibel sound is 10 times as loud as a 10-decibel sound; a 30-decibel sound is 100 times as loud.

10 decibels	A light whisper
20 decibels	Quiet conversation
30 decibels	Normal conversation
40 decibels	Light traffic
50 decibels	A typewriter; loud conversation
60 decibels	A noisy office
70 decibels	Normal traffic; a quiet train
80 decibels	Raucous music; the subway
90 decibels	Heavy traffic; thunder
100 decibels	A plane at takeoff

The speed of sound is usually placed at 1,088 feet per second at 32°F at sea level.

ell (English)   1¼ yards or ⅟₃₂ bolt. Used for measuring cloth.

em   A printer's measure designating the square width of any given type size. The em of 10-point type is 10 points. An en is one-half of an em.

freight ton (measurement ton)   40 cubic feet of merchandise. Used for cargo freight.

gauge   A measure of shotgun bore diameter. Gauge numbers originally referred to the number per pound of round lead balls of a diameter equal to that of the bore. Today, an international agreement assigns millimeter measures to each gauge.

Gauge	Bore Diameter in mm
6	23.34
10	19.67
12	18.52
14	17.60
16	16.81
20	15.90

Historic Weights and Measures

	Units	Location	Customary	Metric
Volume	amphora	Greece	10.3 gal.	38.8 l
		Rome	6.84 gal.	26 l
	bath	Israel	2.250 cu. in.	37 l
	ephah	Israel	1.1 bu.	40 l
	gallon, beer	England	282 cu. in.	4.62 l
	hekat	Israel	291 cu. in.	4.77 l
	tun	England	252 gal.	954 l
Weight	denarius	Rome	0.17 oz.	4.6 g
	dinar	Arabia	0.15 oz.	4.2 g
	drachma	Greece	0.154 oz.	4.36 g
	livre	France	1.08 lb.	490 g
	livre (demikilo)	France	1.10 lb.	500 g
	mite	England	0.05 grain	3.24 mg
	obol	Greece	11.2 grains	0.73 g
	pfund	Germany	1.1 lb.	500 g
	pound, tower:	England		
	12 oz.		5,400 grains	350 g
	15 oz.		6,750 grains	437 g
	16 oz.		7,200 grains	467 g
	shekel	Israel	0.5 oz.	14.1 g
	shekel, trade	Babylonia	0.3 oz.	8.37 g
Length	cubit	Greece	18.3 in.	46.5 cm
		Israel	21.8 in.	38.2 cm
		Rome	17.5 in.	44.4 cm
	hand	England U.S.	4 in.	10.2 cm
	stadion	Greece	622 ft.	190 m
	stadium	Rome	606 ft.	185 m

great gross   12 gross, or 1,728.

gross   12 dozen, or 144.

hand   A unit of measure equal to 4 inches. Used especially to measure the height of horses.

hertz   A unit of electromagnetic wave frequency equal to one cycle per second.

hogshead (hhd)   Two liquid barrels.

horsepower   The power needed to lift 33,000 pounds a distance of 1 foot in 1 minute (about 1½ times the power an average horse can exert) or to lift 550 pounds 1 foot in 1 second. Used to measure the power of steam engines, gasoline engines, etc.

Go to   "Words Describing Periods of Time" in chapter 1; "Food Weights and Measures" in chapter 19

knot   A unit for measuring the speed of ships. One knot is 1 nautical mile per hour, 10 knots is 10 nautical miles per hour, and so on.

league   Any of various units of distance from about 2.4 to 4.6 statute miles.

The length of the Mayflower *was measured in score-feet (1 score-foot is equal to 20 feet). After outliving its usefulness, the* Mayflower *was dismantled and rebuilt as a barn.*

light-year   A unit of length in interstellar astronomy equal to the distance that light travels in 1 year in a vacuum, or about 5,878,000,000,000 miles.

magnum   A large bottle of wine holding about ⅔ gallon.

parsec   The unit of measure for interstellar space equal to a distance having a heliocentric parallax of 1 second, or to 206,265 times the radius of Earth's orbit, or to 3.26 light-years, or to 19.2 trillion miles.

pica   One-sixth inch, or 12 points. Used to measure typographical material.

pipe   Two hogsheads. Used to measure wine and other liquids.

Early systems of measurement used body parts to calculate length. A cubit ran from elbow to middle fingertip. The distance from fingertip to fingertip of outstretched arms was a fathom.

point   0.013836 (approximately ½72) inch or ½12 pica. Used in printing to measure type size.

quintal   100,000 grams, or 220.46 pounds avoirdupois.

quire   24 or 25 sheets of paper.

ream   480 or 500 sheets of paper, or 20 quires.

ADDITIONAL SOURCES OF INFORMATION

ORGANIZATIONS AND SERVICES

National Institute of Standards and Technology
(formerly National Bureau of Standards)
Gaithersburg, MD, 20899
http://www.nist.gov

Standards Engineering Society
Miami, Florida 33176
http://www.ses-standards.org/

BOOKS

American Society for Testing and Materials. *Standard Practice for Use of International System of Units (SI): The Modernized Metric System.* ASTM, 1991.

Blocksma, Mary. *Reading the Numbers: A Survival Guide to the Measurements, Numbers, and Sizes Encountered in Daily Life.* Penguin, 1989.

Cook, James L. *Conversion Factors.* Oxford University Press, 1991.

Darton, Mike, and John Clark. *The Macmillan Dictionary of Measurement.* Macmillan, 1994.

The Economist Desk Companion: How to Measure, Convert, Calculate and Define Practically Anything. Henry Holt, 1994.

Fenna, Donald. *Elsevier's Encyclopedic Dictionary of Measures.* Elsevier, 1998.

Johnstone, William D. *For Good Measure.* NTC Publishing Group, 1996.

Sutcliffe, Andrea, ed. *Numbers: How Many, How Far, How Long, How Much.* HarperPerennial, 1996.

Weights/Measures

3

THE BIOLOGICAL WORLD

ANATOMICAL DRAWINGS OF THE HUMAN BODY

THE SKELETAL SYSTEM

FRONT VIEW

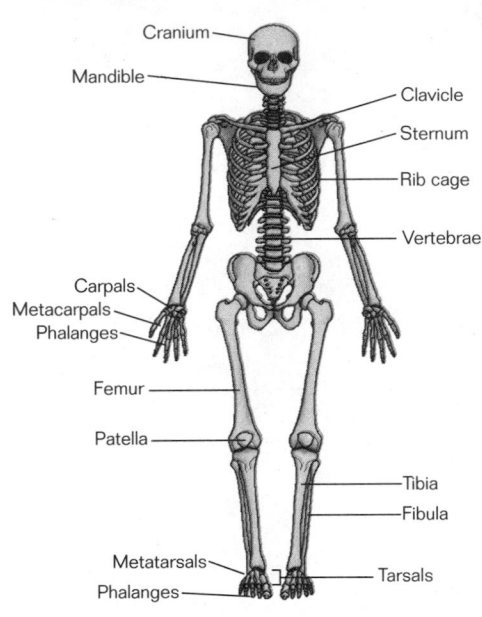

Cranium
Mandible
Clavicle
Sternum
Rib cage
Vertebrae
Carpals
Metacarpals
Phalanges
Femur
Patella
Tibia
Fibula
Metatarsals
Phalanges
Tarsals

REAR VIEW

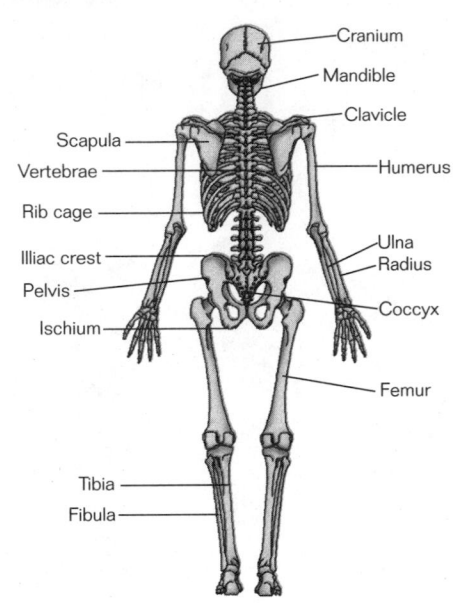

Cranium
Mandible
Clavicle
Scapula
Vertebrae
Humerus
Rib cage
Illiac crest
Ulna
Radius
Pelvis
Coccyx
Ischium
Femur
Tibia
Fibula

SKULL BONES

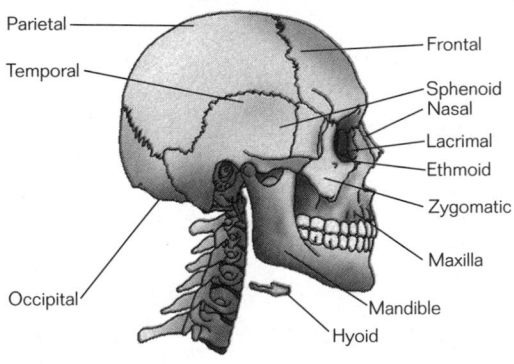

Parietal
Temporal
Frontal
Sphenoid
Nasal
Lacrimal
Ethmoid
Zygomatic
Maxilla
Mandible
Occipital
Hyoid

THE EYE

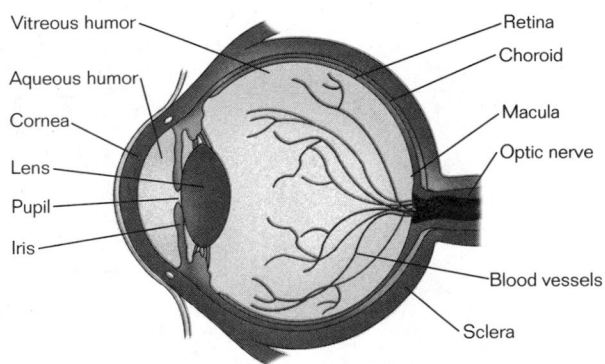

Vitreous humor
Aqueous humor
Cornea
Lens
Pupil
Iris
Retina
Choroid
Macula
Optic nerve
Blood vessels
Sclera

THE EAR

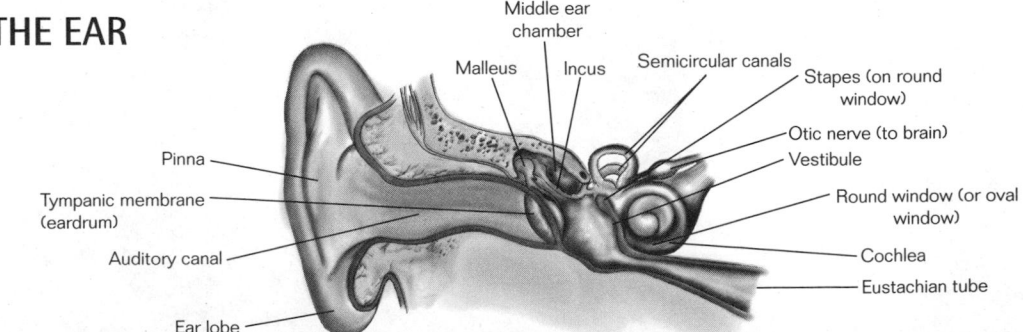

Middle ear chamber
Malleus
Incus
Semicircular canals
Stapes (on round window)
Otic nerve (to brain)
Vestibule
Round window (or oval window)
Cochlea
Eustachian tube
Pinna
Tympanic membrane (eardrum)
Auditory canal
Ear lobe

Biological World

THE BRAIN
PARTS

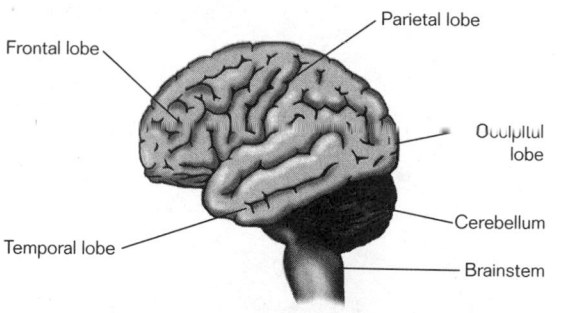

Frontal lobe

Parietal lobe

Occipital lobe

Temporal lobe

Cerebellum

Brainstem

FUNCTIONS

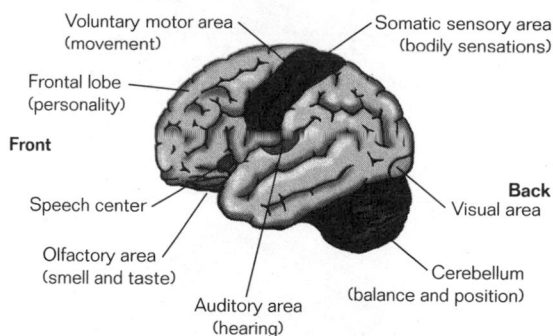

Voluntary motor area
(movement)

Frontal lobe
(personality)

Front

Somatic sensory area
(bodily sensations)

Back
Visual area

Speech center

Olfactory area
(smell and taste)

Auditory area
(hearing)

Cerebellum
(balance and position)

THE MUSCLE SYSTEM
FRONT VIEW

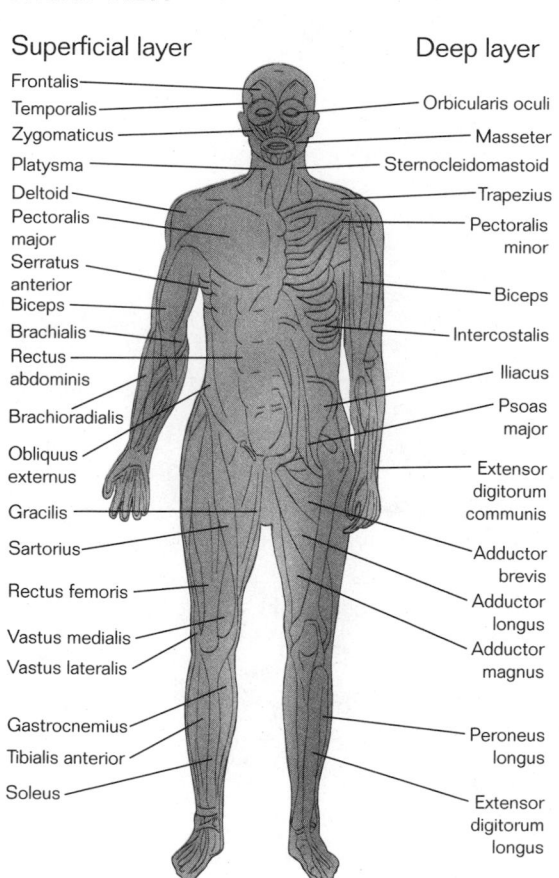

Superficial layer

Frontalis
Temporalis
Zygomaticus
Platysma
Deltoid
Pectoralis major
Serratus anterior
Biceps
Brachialis
Rectus abdominis
Brachioradialis
Obliquus externus
Gracilis
Sartorius
Rectus femoris
Vastus medialis
Vastus lateralis
Gastrocnemius
Tibialis anterior
Soleus

Deep layer

Orbicularis oculi
Masseter
Sternocleidomastoid
Trapezius
Pectoralis minor
Biceps
Intercostalis
Iliacus
Psoas major
Extensor digitorum communis
Adductor brevis
Adductor longus
Adductor magnus
Peroneus longus
Extensor digitorum longus

REAR VIEW

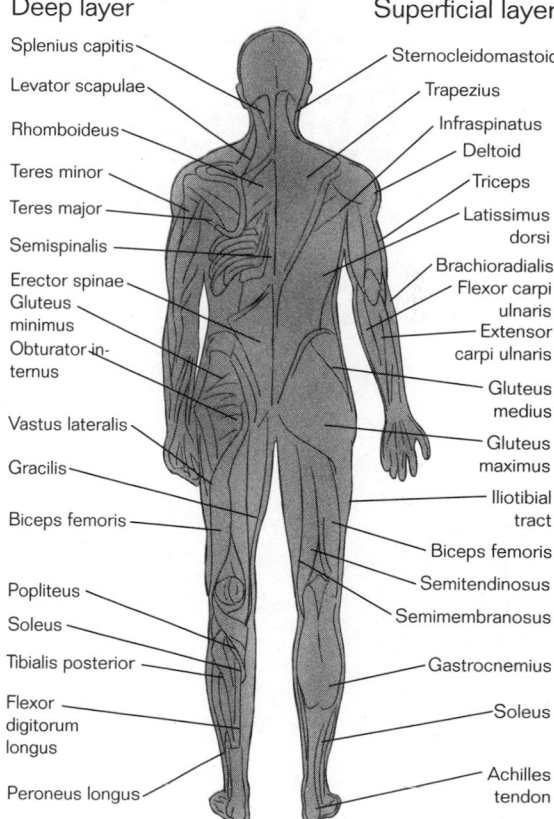

Deep layer

Splenius capitis
Levator scapulae
Rhomboideus
Teres minor
Teres major
Semispinalis
Erector spinae
Gluteus minimus
Obturator internus
Vastus lateralis
Gracilis
Biceps femoris
Popliteus
Soleus
Tibialis posterior
Flexor digitorum longus
Peroneus longus

Superficial layer

Sternocleidomastoid
Trapezius
Infraspinatus
Deltoid
Triceps
Latissimus dorsi
Brachioradialis
Flexor carpi ulnaris
Extensor carpi ulnaris
Gluteus medius
Gluteus maximus
Iliotibial tract
Biceps femoris
Semitendinosus
Semimembranosus
Gastrocnemius
Soleus
Achilles tendon

THE DIGESTIVE SYSTEM

THE RESPIRATORY SYSTEM

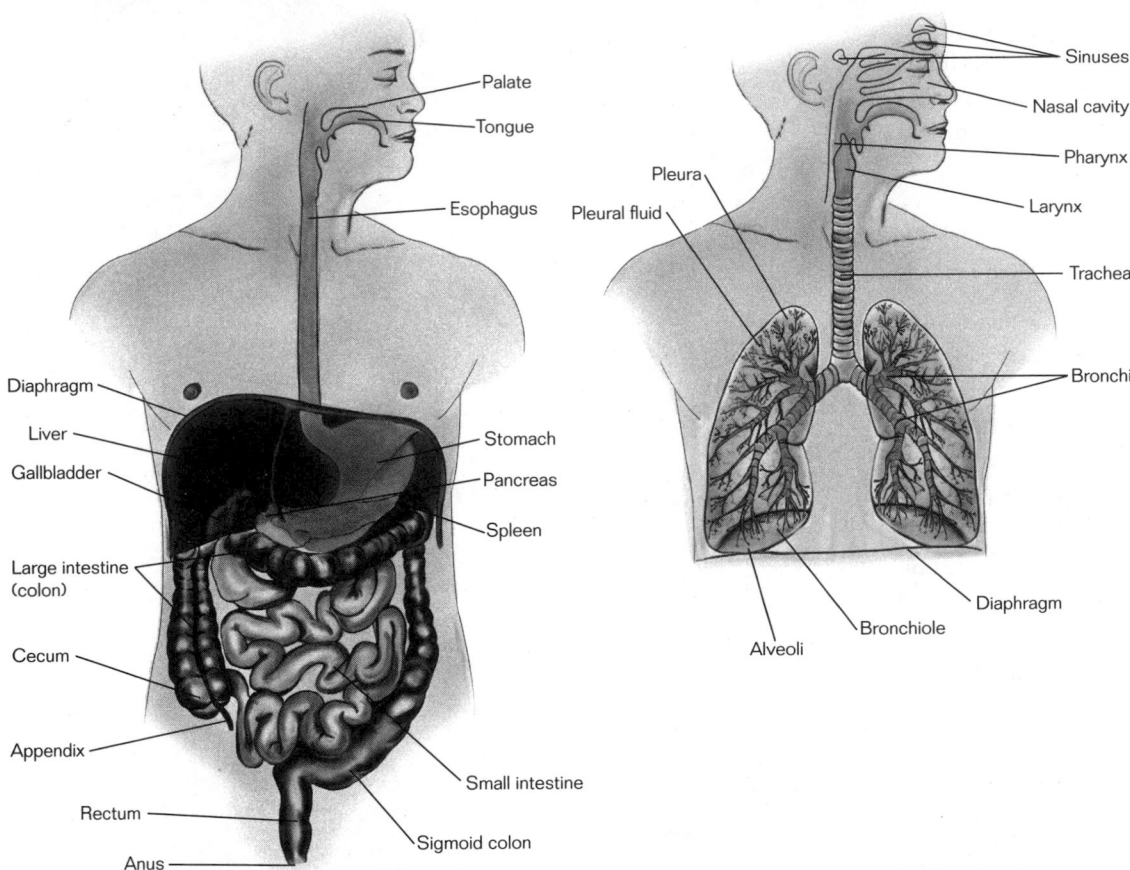

THE SCIENCE OF TAXONOMY

Taxonomy, or systematics, is the science of naming living organisms in a way that reflects their natural relationships. Taxonomic categories are arranged hierarchically, in a descending series of increasingly small ranks. The *taxa* (groups of related organisms; singular, *taxon*) most frequently used, from most to least in-

Taxonomic Level	Name	Distinguishing Feature
Kingdom	Animalia	Animal
Phylum	Chordata	Spinal cord
Subphylum	Vertebrata	Segmented backbone
Superclass	Tetrapoda	Four limbs
Class	Mammalia	Suckle young
Subclass	Theria	Live birth
Infraclass	Eutheria	Placenta
Order	Primates	Most highly developed
Superfamily	Hominoidea	Humanlike
Family	Hominidae	Two-legged
Genus	Homo	Human
Species	Sapiens	Modern human

clusive, are *kingdom, phylum* (plural, *phyla*), *class, order, family, genus* (plural, *genera*), and *species*; the names of plants often include *variety*. Although taxonomy dates from the days of Aristotle, in the 1700s Carolus Linnaeus developed the most familiar system: a binomial nomenclature assigning to each organism a two-word, always italicized Latin name designating its genus and species (for example, *Homo sapiens*). The table on page 36 shows the taxonomy of modern humans.

More recently, scientists are using classifications based on cladistics, which allows them to hypothesize relationships among organisms by examining their shared characteristics and evolutionary history. Simply put, cladistics groups together animals that share common traits and evolutionary history. However, not all scientists agree on cladistic classifications. Some do not agree with the interpretations of connections between groups; others believe multiple, new lineages can emerge from a single population at the same time. Thus, no universally accepted classification of life on Earth has emerged to date.

THE ANIMAL KINGDOM

The kingdoms of living organisms are divided into several phyla, classes, orders, and families. The examples below discuss vertebrates in terms of orders. Invertebrates are then discussed according to phyla.

THE ORDERS OF MAMMALS

More than one million different species of animals exist in the world. All animals with backbones, including humans, are chordates. That is, in the language of taxonomy, they belong to the phylum Chordata. Their subphylum is Vertebrata, meaning that their backbones are segmented. Mammals, members of the class Mammalia of vertebrate animals that includes humans, are the most highly advanced organisms on Earth. Warm-blooded and hairy, they have four-chambered hearts and relatively large brains. All but two species suckle their young.

The approximately 4,000 species of mammals are divided into 26 orders. Ten of these live in North America. Some orders include a wide range of animals; for example, shrews, lemurs, marmosets, monkeys, apes, and humans are all primates, one order of the class of mammals. Other orders are made up of only one sort of creature; order Chiroptera, for example, consists of 18 families of bats.

The Latin names of the orders of mammals given here are followed by their common names and the families that make up each order. Examples of the various types of animals included in each family also are given.

SUBCLASS PROTOTHERIA (MONOTREMES, OR EGG-LAYING ANIMALS)

Order Monotremata (egg-laying mammals)

These more primitive mammals make up the families *Tachyglossidae* (echidnas, also called spiny anteaters) and *Ornithorhynchidae* (platypuses).

SUBCLASS THERIA (ALL OTHER ORDERS OF LIVING MAMMALS)

INFRACLASS METATHERIA (MARSUPIALS)

Order Dasyuromorphia

This order has three families, two represented by a single living species. The Tasmanian tiger (family *Thylacinidae),* a larger carnivorous, wolflike animal, may in fact now be extinct. The numbat, or banded anteater (family *Myrmecobiidae)* feeds on ants and termites and has no pounch for carrying its young. The third family *(Dasyuridae)* are insectivorous and carnivorous marsupials, and include the marsupiak mice and the Tasmanian devil.

Order Didelphimorphia

This order includes the earliest marsupials known, dating from about 90 million years ago. Most are omnivorous (although some are fruit- or insect-eating) and most do not have pouches for carrying their young. Living forms include the Virginia opossum.

Order Diprotodontia

The families *Phascolarctidae* (koalas), *Vombatidae* (wombats), *Phalangeridae* (possums and cuscuses), *Petauridae* (gliders), and *Macropodidae* (kangaroo-like marsupials) are mainly herbivorous. The pygmy possums (family *Burramyidae*) and some gliders, on the other hand, are insectivorous. The honey possums (family *Tarsipedidae*), as their name implies, feed on pollen and nectar.

Order Microbiotheria (monito del monte)

This order has only one living species (family *Microbiotheridae*), a small pouched and insectivorous marsupial that constructs nests in thickets of bamboo in the beech forests of southern Chile and Argentina.

Order Notoryctemorphia (marsupial mole)

This order has only one living species (family *Notoryctidae*). Resembling the true moles and having large foreclaws and a tough leathery shield on its nose, it literally swims through Australian sand dunes.

Order Paucituberculata (shrew opossums)

There is only one family (*Caenolestidae*) of these small pouchless mammals, which are ground-dwelling and strongly insectivorous.

Koalas and humans are the only animals with unique prints. Koala prints cannot be distinguished from human fingerprints.

Order Peramelemorphia

This order includes the only marsupials—bandicoots (family *Peramelidae*) and the bilbies (family *Thylacomyidae*)—to have an advanced chorioallantoic placenta like those of the placental mammals. Small- to medium-sized, they use their elongate muzzles to feed chiefly on insects and other small animals.

INFRACLASS EUTHERIA (PLACENTALS)

Order Artiodactyla (even-toed hoofed animals)

Hoofed animals with an even number of toes include those that ruminate, or digest their food in four-chamber stomachs and chew cuds, and those that do not ruminate. Those that ruminate are the families *Girrafidae* (giraffes), *Cervidae* (deer, moose, reindeer, elk), *Antilocapridae* (pronghorn antelope), and *Bovidae* (cattle, bison, yaks, waterbucks, wildebeest, gazelles, springboks, sheep, musk oxen, goats). *Nonruminators* include the families Suidae (pigs), *Tayassuidae* (peccaries), *Hippopotamidae* (hippopotamuses), and *Camelidae* (camels, llamas).

Order Carnivora (meat eaters)

There are two suborders of these toe-footed creatures. They include the *Canidae* (wolves, dogs, jackals, foxes), *Ursidae* (bears, giant pandas), *Procyonidae* (coatis, raccoons, lesser pandas), and *Mustelidae* (martens, weasels, skunks, otters), which are all part of one superfamily characterized by long snouts and unretractable claws; and *Felidae* (cats, lions, cheetahs, leopards), *Hyaenidae* (hyenas), and *Viverridae* (mongooses, civets), all of which have retractable claws.

Order Cetacea (whales and porpoises)

Two suborders of order Cetacea are the toothed whales, which have regular conical teeth, and the baleen, or whalebone, whales, which have irregular whalebone surfaces instead of teeth. Toothed whales include the families *Physeteridae* (sperm whales), *Monodontidae* (narwhals, belugas), *Phocoenidae* (porpoises), and *Delphinidae* (dolphins, killer whales). Baleens are in the family *Eschrichtiidae* (gray whales), *Balaenidae* (right whales), or *Balaenoptridae* (fin-backed whales, humpback whales).

Order Chiroptera (bats)

There are two suborders of bats, the only mammals that can fly. Suborder *Megachiroptera* contains one family, the *Pteropodidae* (flying foxes, Old World fruit bats). Suborder *Microchiroptera* contains 17 families, including *Rhinopomatidae* (mouse-tailed bats), *Emballonuridae* (sheath-tailed bats), *Craseonycteridae* (hog-nosed or butterfly bats), *Noctilionidae* (bulldog or fisherman bats), *Nycteridae* (slit-faced bats), *Megadermatidae* (false vampire bats), and *Rhinolophidae* (horseshoe bats).

Order Dermoptera (colugos or flying lemurs)

These gliding tree mammals from Asia do not fly and are not lemurs, but they are known as flying lemurs, or family *Cynocephalidae*.

Order Hyracoidae (hyraxes, dassies)

Order Hyracoidae is one of three orders that has only one modern family remaining. *Procavia capensis* (the African rock hyrax) is one of nine living species in the family *Procaviidae*.

Order Insectivora (insect eaters)

The three members are the families *Talpidae* (moles), *Soricidae* (shrews), and *Erinaceidae* (hedgehogs).

Order Lagomorpha (pikas, hares, and rabbits)

Two families make up this order: *Ochotonidae* (pikas) and *Leporidae* (hares and rabbits of all sorts).

Order Macroscelidea (elephant shrews)

This order, represented by the family *Macroscelididae,* was once considered part of the order Insectivora. The elephant shrew has well-developed eyes and ears and a narrow, flexible, and elongate (but not retractable) trunklike snout that it uses to locate insect prey.

Order Perissodactyla (odd-toed hoofed animals)

The two suborders, Hippomorpha and Ceratomorpha, include creatures that have an odd number of toes. Families in this order are the *Equidae* (horses, donkeys, zebras), the *Tapiridae* (tapirs), and the *Rhinocerotidae* (rhinoceroses).

Order Pholidata (pangolins)

Family *Manidae* (pangolins) is the sole family in this order.

Order Pinnipedia (seals and walruses)

In the fin-footed order, there are *Otariidae* (eared seals, sea lions), *Odobenidae* (walruses), and *Phocidae* (earless seals).

Order Primates (primates)

The order to which people belong is divided into two suborders: the Prosimii, who have longer snouts than their relatives; and the Anthropoidae. The first group includes the families *Tupalidae* (tree shrew), *Lemuridae* (lemurs), *Daubentonlidae* (aye-ayes), *Lorisidae* (lorises, pottos), and *Tarsiidae* (tarsiers). The anthropoids include the families *Callitrichidae* (marmosets), *Cebidae* (New World monkeys), *Cercopithecidae* (baboons, Old World monkeys), *Hylobatidae* (gibbons), *Pongidae* (gorillas, chimpanzees, orangutans), and *Hominidae* (human beings).

Order Proboscidea (elephants)

Large enough to have an order all to itself is family *Elephantidae*.

Order Rodentia (gnawing mammals)

Order Rodentia, containing the most prolific mammals, includes three suborders. It takes in the families *Aplodontidae* (mountain beavers), *Sciuridae* (chipmunks, squirrels, marmots), *Cricetidae* (field mice, lemmings, muskrats, hamsters, gerbils), *Muridae* (Old World mice, rats), *Heteromyidae* (New World mice), *Geomyidae* (gophers), and *Dipodidae* (jerboas).

Order Scandentia (tree shrews)

This order, represented by the single family *Tupaiidae,* was once considered part of the order Insectivora. The squirrel-like tree shrew has a long snout and feeds mainly on insects and fruit.

Order Sirenia (dugongs and manatees)

The families *Trichechidae* (manatees) and *Dugongidae* (dugongs and other sea cows) make up the order Sirenia.

Order Tubulidentata (aardvarks)

Another mammal in an order by itself is family *Orycteropodidae*.

Order Xenarthra Edentata (toothless mammals)

Three families of mammals get by without teeth: *Dasypodidae* (armadillos), *Bradypodidae* (sloths), and *Myrmecophagidae* (hairy anteaters).

Biological World

Biological World

THE PHYLA OF INVERTEBRATES

Invertebrates are members of the animal kingdom with no spinal column, or backbone. They make up about 95 percent of all animal species. There are 20 phyla of invertebrates, the 2 largest being Arthropoda and Mollusca. Following are some of the phyla of invertebrates and descriptions of their members.

Phylum Annelida (segmented worms)

Also called annelid worms, this phylum includes earthworms, leeches, and marine worms. Annelid worms have soft bodies, are symmetrical, and can be anywhere from $\frac{1}{32}$ of an inch (half a millimeter) to 10 feet (3 meters) in length.

Phylum Arthropoda (arthropods)

This is the largest phylum of invertebrates, as well as the one with the most creatures; almost 80 percent of all animal species are arthropods. Arthropods have segmented bodies covered by external skeletons, called *exoskeletons,* which are molted from time to time to allow for growth. Their appendages ("arms" and "legs") are paired. Among the animals in this phylum are spiders, horseshoe crabs, crustaceans, insects, and centipedes.

Phylum Coelenterata (coelenterates)

Mostly marine invertebrates, coelenterates have three-layered body walls, tentacles, primitive nervous systems, and special stinger cells to protect themselves. Animals in this phylum include jellyfish, sea anemones, and corals.

Phylum Echinodermata (echinoderms)

Another marine invertebrate, the echinoderm, lives on the floor of the sea. Echinoderms are headless and have tube feet and external skeletons just below the surface of the skin. They can regenerate virtually any part of their bodies. Starfish, sea urchins, sand dollars, and sea cucumbers are some of the members of this phylum.

"Major Zoos and Aquariums" in chapter 11; **"Animal Highlights of the Most Popular National Wildlife Refuges"** in chapter 24

Go to

Phylum Platyhelminthes (flatworms)

As their name implies, these organisms are basically flat, soft-bodied, and symmetrical. These very primitive creatures come in two varieties: an aquatic group that includes planarians and a parasitic one that counts flukes and tapeworms among its members.

Phylum Mollusca (mollusks)

Most mollusks live inside shells and reside in the water. They have soft, unsegmented bodies and a powerful foot that enables them to move around. Clams, oysters, scallops, bivalves, octopuses, and squid are mollusks.

Phylum Nematoda (roundworms)

These wormlike animals have an outer coat made of noncellular material and a fluid-filled chamber that separates their body walls from their insides. They live both in water and on land. Among their number are rotifers, nematodes, and horsehair worms.

Phylum Porifera (sponges)

Porifera is the most primitive multicellular phylum. Sponges live mostly in colonies in the water, attached to rocks. They are basically sacs taking in water through small holes; their skeletons are formed from hard substances that become stuck in their body walls.

EXTINCT ANIMALS

Extinction has happened to species and subspecies throughout the time creatures have lived on this planet. The most well-known cases involved the "great dying" of the dinosaurs some 50 to 75 million years ago.

If creatures great and small have in fact been dying off throughout the ages, why is there suddenly concern about animals becoming extinct? Isn't extinction part of the natural order of things?

The answer is no, at least not on the scale it has occurred in recent times. Over most of the past 300 years, the rate of extinction of species was about one per year. At present, the rate of species extinction is at least a thousand times as great as that. This biodepletion is most rapid in tropical forests, which, though they cover only 6 percent of the Earth's land surface, shelter at least 50 percent of all species.

The two hemispheres of a dolphin's brain operate independently. For 8 hours, the entire brain is awake. The left side then sleeps for 8 hours. When it wakes up, the right side sleeps for 8 hours. Thus the dolphin gets 8 hours of sleep without ever having to stop physically.

The cause of this rapid acceleration in the rate of extinctions is human activity. With some species, like the dodo, the extinction was unintentional: people introduced predators to the dodo's island home where previously there had been none. Other creatures, such as the Eastern buffalo, were purposely killed off by human beings who wanted to "make room" for themselves.

In the late 20th century and beyond, extinctions are more likely to be a result of human activity. Rural landfills take in urban garbage, open land is blacktopped, factories produce toxins as by-products, and engineers alter waterways. These activities all have a direct impact on the ecosystems that support animal life.

A major cause of the extinction of species in tropical forests is the number of impoverished farmers who are moving into and clearing the forests. Species also suffer from climatic change—the planetary warming from the buildup of carbon dioxide and other greenhouse gases in the global atmosphere.

Increased awareness of the fragile links of interdependence among all of Earth's creatures, and of the impact that human activities can have on those creatures, have led some to hope that the latest era of "great dying" may soon stop. It remains to be seen, however, if the forces already in motion can be stopped in time to save the hundreds of species that teeter on the brink of extinction.

Listed here are the popular names of those animals thought to be endangered or extinct at the end of the 20th century. Exact figures are difficult to determine because endangered species often make the transition to extinction quickly and without notice. Occasionally populations of animals thought to be extinct are discovered to be extant (in existence). In these lists, the number of individual species is in parentheses. If no number appears, one of that species is extinct—i.e., not all beavers are extinct, but one species is.

MAMMALS

Anoa (2)
Antelope, giant sable
Argali
Armadillo (2)
Ass (2)
Avahi
Aye-aye
Babirusa
Baboon, gelada
Bandicoot (5)
Banteng
Bat (13)
Bear (6)

Beaver
Bison, wood
Bobcat, Mexican
Bontebok
Camel, Bactrian
Caribou, woodland
Cat (9)
Chamois, Apennine
Cheetah
Chimpanzee (2)
Chinchilla
Civet, Malabar large-spotted
Cochito
Deer (22)

Dhole
Dibbler
Dog, African wild
Dolphin (2)
Drill
Dugong
Duiker, Jentink's
Eland, western giant
Elephant (2)
Ferret, black-footed
Fox (3)
Gazelle (10)
Gibbons
Goral

continues

Gorilla
Hare, hispid
Hartebeest (2)
Hog, pygmy
Horse, Przewalski's
Huemul (2)
Hutia (4)
Hyena (2)
Ibex (2)
Impala, black-faced
Indri
Jaguar
Jaguarundi (4)
Kangaroo rat (6)
Kangaroo, Tasmanian forester
Koala
Kouprey
Langur (8)
Lechwe, red
Lemurs
Leopard (3)
Linsang, spotted
Lion, Asiatic
Loris, lesser slow
Lynx (2)
Macaque (5)
Manatee (3)
Mandrill
Mangabey (2)
Margay
Markhor (3)
Marmoset (4)
Marmot, Vancouver Island
Marsupial, eastern jerboa
Marsupial-mouse (2)
Marten, Formosian yellow-
   throated
Monkey (20)
Mountain Beaver, Point Arena
Mouse (19)
Muntjac, Fea's
Native-cat, eastern
Numbat
Ocelot
Orangutan
Oryx, Arabian
Otter (6)
Panda, giant

Pangolin, Temnick's ground
Panther, Florida
Planigale (2)
Porcupine, thin-spined
Possum (3)
Prairie Dog (2)
Pronghorn (2)
Pudu
Puma (3)
Quokka
Rabbit (4)
Rat (2)
Rat-kangaroo (5)
Rhinoceros (5)
Rice rat
Saiga, Mongolian
Saki (2)
Seal (5)
Sea-lion, Stellar
Seledang
Serow
Serval, Barbary
Shapo
Sheep, bighorn
Shou
Siamang
Sifakas
Sloth, Brazilian three-toed
Solenodon (2)
Squirrel (4)
Stag (2)
Suni, Zanzibar
Tahr, Arabian
Tamaraw
Tamarin (3)
Tapir (4)
Tarsier, Phillipine
Tiger (2)
Uakari
Urial
Vicuna
Vole (3)
Wallaby (6)
Whale (8)
Wolf (3)
Wombat, Queensland hairy-
   nosed

Woodrat (2)
Yak, wild
Zebra (3)

BIRDS

Akepa (2)
Akialoa (2)
Albatross (2)
Alethe, Thyolo
Blackbird, yellow-shouldered
Bobwhite, masked
Booby, Abbott's
Bristlebird (2)
Broadbill, Guam
Bulbul, Muritius olivaceous
Bullfinch, Sao Miguel
Bush-shrike, Ulugura
Bushwren, New Zealand
Bustard, great Indian
Cahow
Caracara, Audobon crested
Condor (2)
Coot, Hawaiian
Cotinga (2)
Crane (8)
Creeper (3)
Crow (3)
Cuckoo-shrike (2)
Curassow (3)
Curlew, Eskimo
Dove (2)
Duck (4)
Eagle (7)
Egret, Chinese
Eider, spectacled
Eider, Steller's
Elepaio, Oahu
Falcon (2)
Finch (2)
Flycatcher (4)
Fody (3)
Francolin, Djibouti
Freira
Frigatebird, Andrew's
Gnatcatcher, coastal California
Goose, Hawaiian
Goshawk, Christmas Island
Grackle, slender-billed

Grasswren, Eyrean
Grebe (2)
Greenshank, Nordmann's
Guan (2)
Guineafowl, white-breasted
Gull (2)
Hawk (4)
Hermit, hook-billed
Honeycreeper, crested
Honeyeater, helmeted
Hornbill, helmeted
Ibis (2)
Jay, Florida scrub
Kagu
Kakapo
Kestrel (2)
Kingfisher, Guam Micronesian
Kite (3)
Kokako
Lark, Raso
Macaw (3)
Magpie-robin, Seychelles
Malimbe, Ibadan
Malkoha, red-faced
Mallard, Mariana
Megapode (2)
Millerbird, Nihoa
Monarch, Tinian
Moorhen (2)
Murrelet, marbled
Nightjar, Puerto Rican
Nukupu'u
Nuthatch, Algerian
'O'o, Kauai
Ostrich (2)
'O'u
Owl (6)
Owlet, Morden's
Oystercatcher, Canarian black
Palila
Parakeet (10)
Parrot (15)
Parrotbill, Maui
Pelican, brown
Penguin, Galapagos
Petrel (2)
Pheasant (15)

Pigeon (6)
Piping-guan, black-fronted
Pitta, Koch's
Plover (3)
Pochard, Madagascar
Po'ouli
Prairie-chicken, Attwater's
   greater
Pygmy-owl, cactus ferruginous
Quail, Merriam's Montezuma
Quetzel, resplendent
Rail (6)
Rhea, lesser (incl. Darwin's)
Robin (3)
Rockfowl (2)
Roller, long-tailed ground
Scrub-bird, noisy
Shama, Cebu black
Shearwater, Newell's Townsend's
Shrike, San Clemente logger-
   head
Siskin, red
Sparrow (3)
Sparrowhawk, Anjouan Island
Starling (2)
Stilt, Hawaiian
Stork (2)
Sunbird, Marungu
Swiftlet, Mariana gray
Teal, Campbell Island flightless
Tern (3)
Thrasher, white-breasted
Thrush (5)
Tinamou, solitary
Towhee, Inyo California
Trembler, Martinique
Turaco, Bannerman's
Turtle dove, Seychelles
Vanga (2)
Vireo (2)
Wanderer, plain
Warbler (9)
Wattle-eye, banded
Weaver, Clarke's
Whipbird, western
White-eye (4)
Woodpecker (4)
Wren (2)

REPTILES

Alligator (2)
Anole, Culebra Island giant
Boa (6)
Caiman (6)
Chuckwalla, San Esteban Island
Crocodile (13)
Gavial
Gecko (4)
Iguana (17)
Lizard (7)
Monitor (4)
Python, Indian
Rattlesnake (2)
Sea turtle (6)
Skink (3)
Snake (8)
Tartaruga
Terrapin, river
Tomistoma
Tortoise (6)
Tracaja
Tuatara (2)
Turtle (22)
Viper, Lar Valley
Whipsnake, Alameda

AMPHIBIANS

Coqui, golden
Frog (5)
Guajon
Salamander (13)
Toad (7)

FISH

Ala balik
Ayumodoki
Blindcat, Mexican
Bonytongue, Asian
Catfish (3)
Cavefish (2)
Chub (14)
Cicek
Cui-ui
Dace (8)
Darter (17)
Gambusia (4)

Biological World

continues

Goby, tidewater
Logperch (2)
Madtom (5)
Minnow (3)
Nekogigi (catfish)
Pikeminnow, Colorado
Poolfish, Pahrump
Pupfish (7)
Salmon (4)
Sculpin, pygmy
Shiner (8)
Silverside, Waccamaw
Smelt, delta
Spikedace
Spinedace (3)
Splittail, Sacramento
Springfish (3)
Steelhead
Stickleback, unarmored three-
    spine
Sturgeon (5)
Sucker (7)
Tango, Miyako
Temoleh, Ikan
Topminnow, Gila
Totoaba
Trout (6)
Woundfin

MOLLUSKS

Ambersnail, Kanab
Acornshell, southern
Bankclimber, purple
Bean (2)

Blossom (4)
Campeloma, slender
Catspaw (2)
Clubshell (4)
Combshell (3)
Elimia, lacy
Elktoe (2)
Fanshell
Fatmucket, Arkansas
Heelsplitter (2)
Higgins eye
Kidneyshell, triangular
Lampmussel, Alabama
Lilliput, pale
Limpet, Banbury Springs
Lioplax, cylindrical
Mapleleaf, winged
Marstonia, royal
Moccasinshell (4)
Monkeyface (2)
Mucket (2)
Mussel, oyster
Pearlshell, Louisiana
Pearlymussel (7)
Pebblesnail, flat
Pigtoe (9)
Pimpleback, orangefoot
Pocketbook (5)
Rabbitsfoot, rough
Riffleshell (2)
Ring pink
Riversnail, Anthony's
Rocksnail (3)
Shagreen, Magazine Mountain

Slabshell, Chipola
Snail (16)
Spinymussel (2)
Springsnail (4)
Stirrupshell
Three-ridge, fat
Wartyback, white
Wedgemussel, dwarf

INSECTS

Beetle (10)
Butterfly (23)
Dragonfly, Hine's emerald
Fly, Delhi Sands flower-loving
Grasshopper, Zayante band-
    winged
Ground beetle (2)
Mold beetle, Helotes
Moth (2)
Naucorid, Ash Meadows
Skipper (2)
Tiger beetle (2)
Harvestman (3)
Pseudoscorpion, Tooth Cave
Spider (8)

CRUSTACEANS

Amphipod (4)
Crayfish (4)
Fairy shrimp (5)
Isopod (3)
Shrimp (4)
Tadpole shrimp, vernal pool

PETS

Though a wide variety of animals are kept as pets, the overwhelming majority are dogs and cats. Veterinarians and other animal-care experts suggest a number of basic rules to be considered by everyone contemplating pet ownership.

CHOOSING A PET

Do research on the kind of animal you want to get. Make sure you have the ability and finances to house and feed the animal (especially relevant with large dogs) and to pay for its medical care. Don't buy animals as gifts. If the recipient is not willing and able to care for the animal, it will be a disaster for all concerned.

When choosing a dog, don't base your choice on looks without considering the purpose for which it was bred (e.g., don't turn a hunting dog into a house dog). Make sure you have enough time to spend with a puppy. Puppies shouldn't be left alone for more than 3 or 4 hours. Make sure the puppy is bright and alert, though not hyperactive. Check for any signs of ill health and have the puppy examined by a veterinarian before accepting it. Don't separate a puppy from its mother and littermates before it is 6 weeks old.

"Traveling with Pets" in chapter 24   Go to

When choosing a kitten, try to see its parents and observe their temperament. If you get a kitten or cat from an animal shelter, ask the shelter staff about the animal's background. A kitten should respond to attention and not mind being held. It should have a healthy looking coat, pink gums, and no evidence of any discharge from its eyes or ears. Obtain a certificate of vaccinations and have the kitten examined by a veterinarian.

TRAINING

Never hit your dog or yell at it—such an action will only make the dog afraid or resentful. Because the dog craves affection and approval, a firm "No!" or "Bad dog!" is more than enough. A quick tug on your dog's leash or collar, however, is permissible to discourage unwanted behavior, especially with larger dogs. Using your leg to push your dog off balance is acceptable to teach it not to jump on people.

Issue reprimands immediately so that your dog associates your displeasure with a specific offense. Dragging your dog to the scene after the fact does no good.

When toilet training your dog, don't put down pieces of newspaper indoors, which will only make the dog think it's all right to eliminate in the house. Take your dog out first thing in the morning, 15 minutes after each meal, after vigorous play, and just before bedtime. Praise your dog for eliminating outside. Don't allow your dog access to the entire house until it is properly trained.

All dogs should be obedience-trained so that they respond to five basic commands: heel, sit, down, stay, and come. This is especially important with large aggressive breeds such as Dobermans, Rottweilers, and German shepherds. Dogs should be praised when they respond properly, and training should be incorporated into your dog's daily routine so that it remains effective. If you can't handle the job yourself, seek professional help. Options include group obe-dience lessons, a private trainer, and board and training kennels.

When disciplining a kitten, say "No!" in a deep voice. Holding your kitten gently by the scruff of the neck, as its mother would do, is permissible. Squirting your cat with a spritz of water can be effective in discouraging unwanted behavior, but it must be done while the offense is being committed.

Cats instinctively bury their stools; thus, getting your cat to use a litter box should not be hard. If your kitten eliminates outside the box, putting the stool in there will usually convey the message. Use absorbent clay litters and remove the stools every day with a slotted spoon. Replace the litter every third day and wash the pan with hot water, soap, and chlorine bleach. Keep on using the same type of litter once your cat is used to it.

SPAYING AND NEUTERING

Experts advise pet owners against breeding their animals at home because of the medical expenses involved (immunizations for the litter and possible health problems on the mother's part during or after pregnancy) and because of the possibility of not finding homes for the offspring. More than 15 million dogs and cats are put down every year because of overpopulation.

Neutering does not change a male dog's personality or his instinct to protect his home and those he loves. It simply makes him less aggressive toward other male dogs and stops him from marking his territory with urine.

Female cats will go into heat every 2 to 3 weeks if they are not mated. If they are going to be spayed, it should be done before the first onset of heat. The procedure should not be performed, however, before the cat is 5 or 6 months old; it can also be done after sexual maturity.

Neutering male cats will prevent roaming, spraying, and fighting. The operation can be performed either at 5–6 months old or after sexual maturity.

Biological World

PETS AND CHILDREN

Cats generally mix well with children and will tolerate treatment from a child that they would not accept from an adult. Experts recommend, however, that kittens not be introduced into a household where there are very young children who may frighten the cat with loud noise or rough handling. Parents should wait until the child is old enough to understand the animal's needs and play an active role in caring for it.

Relations between dogs and children should be carefully considered. For pet owners with young children, experts recommend a choice of breeds known for their gentle disposition and patience. These breeds include the basenji, bassett hound, beagle, boxer, bulldog, collie, Dalmatian, springer spaniel, German shepherd, golden retriever, Great Dane, Irish setter, Labrador retriever, and standard poodle. Less desirable breeds include the Afghan hound, Chow Chow, dachshund, Doberman, miniature schnauzer, Rottweiler, Weimaraner, and most varieties of terrier.

When a new baby is introduced into a household that already has a dog, a number of steps can be taken to prepare the pet for this dramatic change:

1. As the birth of your child approaches, prepare your dog gradually for the reduced attention that he or she is bound to receive by gradually modifying the amount of time you spend with the dog.
2. Bring home an article of your baby's clothing from the hospital and let your dog get used to the scent.
3. Praise your dog when the baby is around, so it associates good things with the baby.
4. Closely supervise your baby when it begins to crawl and interact with your dog. The dog will not necessarily recognize the baby as a human and may feel threatened.

NUTRITION

Allergies, gastrointestinal disorders, kidney disease, cancer, and other pet ailments can be linked to junk in pet foods. (Some dog foods, for example, contain grain hulls and peanut shells.) The best bet is to buy premium brands with meat-based protein sources.

Don't mix brands of pet food together, because each brand has its own balance of proteins, vitamins, and minerals.

Avoid low-quality foods, many of which contain materials that pets will be unable to digest. These undigestible materials will pass right through the system without providing any nutritional benefit.

Avoid soft, moist, processed foods wrapped in cellophane. They have little nutritional value and cause a disease of the red blood cells in cats.

Don't overfeed pets. Veterinarians estimate that three of five dogs are overweight. Dogs should not be more than 20 percent over the ideal weight for their particular breed. High-quality, low-calorie food can help in this area.

PET STAINS

In addition to removing the stain itself, remove any lingering odor so that your pet is not drawn back to the spot and prompted to urinate there again. To do this, it is necessary to use an enzyme odor remover, which breaks down urine molecules into carbon dioxide and water. Ordinary household cleaners will often leave enough traces of odor for your pet's sensitive olfactory organs to detect.

See also "Stain Removal: Urine" in chapter 19.

IMMUNIZATION
DOGS

5–8 weeks	Canine distemper-measles, CPI (parinfluenza)
8–16 weeks	DHLPP (distemper, hepatitis, leptospirosis, parainfluenza, parvovirus)
14–16 weeks	Rabies
12 months and then annually	DHLPP
12 months and then every three months	Rabies

Each locality may have specific requirements for immunizations and frequency of booster shots, and dog owners should check with their veterinarians. In some areas, for example, vaccination against Lyme disease, coronavirus, and kennel cough may also be necessary. In general, keep your dog away from strange dogs before the vaccination series is complete.

CATS

Any age	Upper respiratory infections (2–3 vaccinations 2–4 weeks apart)
8–12 weeks	Distemper (2–3 vaccinations 2–4 weeks apart)
	Rabies (2 vaccinations 2–4 weeks apart)
	Feline leukemia (2 vaccinations 2–4 weeks apart; 1 vaccination 2–4 months later)
12 weeks or older	Distemper (1 vaccination, then a yearly booster shot)
	Rabies (1 vaccination, then a yearly booster shot; also a 3-year booster is available)
	Feline leukemia (1 vaccination, then a yearly booster shot)
	Upper respiratory infections (1 vaccination, then a yearly booster shot)

A stool sample should be checked whenever shots are given.

ANIMAL FIRST AID

Animals, like people, suffer medical problems. Emergency and nonemergency ailments and traumas require quick attention to prevent serious situations from turning into life-threatening ones.

The meow of a cat is actually two distinct sounds. The "me" is a friendly greeting, but the "ow" means "I'm willing to defend myself." Although cats often meow at humans, they rarely meow at other cats.

Some problems—bleeding that cannot be stopped or convulsions, for instance—require the immediate attention of an expert in veterinary medicine. Many other problems, however, can be treated by the animal's owner.

The following are some common animal ailments and injuries. The symptoms and treatments for each are described. As with any medical condition, if the symptoms persist or the animal's owner is unsure about the nature of the problem, professional assistance should be sought.

BROKEN BONES

Symptoms   Some bone breaks show obvious symptoms: twisted or distorted limbs, or, in the case of a compound fracture, bone fragments sticking through the skin. Less apparent breaks cause great pain and discomfort. The animal will cry or bite when the affected area is touched; will lie around, often on the affected area; and will usually not walk, although in some cases it will walk despite the break, notably when the pelvis is broken. The fracture will not bear weight. Swelling of the affected area within 24 hours can be expected from any sort of fracture.

Treatment   Treatment of compound fractures by a veterinarian should be sought as soon as possible. Other breaks should be treated by a veterinarian within 24 hours. Apply an ice pack or cold wet compress to the affected area; change regularly. Protect the animal from further injury by confining it to a small room. Apply a temporary splint to broken limbs to avoid further dislocation.

See also "Treatment for Health Emergencies: Fractures, Dislocations, and Sprains" in chapter 17.

BURNS

Symptoms   All burns are painful to the touch. *Electrical burns* are the most serious and can cause heart attacks and death. The burned area will show seared flesh, reddened skin, lesions, and blisters. The animal may suffer respiratory distress; paleness or blueness, especially in lips, gums, and eyelid linings;

rigidity in limbs; glassy stare; collapse; and shock. *Thermal burns* cause a singed or charred area; the exposed skin is reddened or inflamed, and the wound is warm or hot to the touch. *Friction burns* are similar in appearance to thermal burns, but the skin is chafed or scraped and has bare spots; bare skin is rubbed raw, is reddish in color, and is irritated or inflamed. The trauma causing the friction burn may leave cuts, lacerations, or embedded foreign matter.

Treatment   Depending on the type and extent of the burn, it can often be treated at home. Electrical burns can stop an animal's heart and must be treated immediately by a veterinarian; if shock occurs, keep the animal warm with heating pads or hot water bottles and a blanket or heavy coat and seek veterinary treatment immediately. Thermal burns can be treated topically by applying the jellylike substance from an aloe plant, a solution made from Domeboro® (available at most pharmacies), or vitamin E oil. Friction burns can be treated in the same way as thermal burns; however, if foreign matter is embedded, or the burn does not respond to treatment, the animal should be taken to a veterinarian.

See also "Treatment for Health Emergencies: Burns" and "Electric Shock" in chapter 17 and "Home Remedies: Burns—First Degree" in chapter 18.

CAT DISEASES

Symptoms   Four major diseases affect the well-being of cats. *Cat distemper* induces high fever, lethargy, vomiting, and diarrhea; young kittens can develop distemper very quickly and will often die of it without exhibiting symptoms. *Rhinotracheitis* causes fever, sneezing, loss of appetite, and dehydration; additional symptoms can include discharge from eyes and nose, congestion, and swelling of membranes in the respiratory tract. *Calici virus* is characterized by sneezing and discharge from the eyes and nose; it may cause fever, lethargy, loss of appetite, dehydration, and ulcers on the tongue. *Pneumonitis* usually causes labored breathing, sneezing, coughing, snorting, wheezing, and listlessness; it

may induce a loss of body fluids and very high temperatures.

Treatment   Three of these diseases—cat distemper, rhinotracheitis, and calici virus—can be prevented by annual vaccinations. All four must be treated as quickly as possible by a veterinarian if symptoms are present. Professional treatment will, in most cases, effect a cure.

CONSTIPATION

Symptoms   The animal struggles or strains during a bowel movement without passing a stool, avoids food, and becomes nervous or irritated.

Treatment   Feed the animal brans, cereal foods, vegetables (peas, carrots, corn), or kibble; use infant-size glycerine suppositories or soap suppositories; give an enema if the animal will allow it; add a small amount of stool softener, such as Metamucil®, to food; give mineral oil or milk of magnesia, but dosages should depend on size and type of animal (consult a veterinarian).

See also "Home Remedies: Constipation" in chapter 18.

DENTAL DISORDERS

Symptoms   Tartar, a brown crust, appears on teeth, starting at the gum line; tooth enamel erodes, especially in cats; bone fragments, foreign matter, food particles, or hair accumulate on teeth; bad breath is present. *Throat* or *mouth infections* cause coughing and discharges from mouth or nose. *Gingivitis* develops when tartar or dirty teeth are untreated. *Uremia* can cause blackish tartar, bad breath, and extraordinary thirst.

Treatment   Clean the animal's teeth monthly with a mixture of one teaspoon salt or hydrogen peroxide to half a cup of water; apply to teeth with a cotton swab or soft toothbrush. Include hard food, such as kibble, in the animal's diet; provide hard things for the animal to chew on. Infections, gingivitis, or uremia should be treated by a veterinarian.

DIARRHEA

Symptoms   The animal passes liquid stool during bowel movement; there may be abnormal coloration of stool.

Treatment   Remove grease, oils, and milk from the animal's diet; avoid high-fiber foods, kibble, and dry catmeal (never give your cat any type of dog food). For dogs, feed the animal a mix of 1 part hamburger, drained of grease, and 1 part rice; cats digest 1 part cooked, minced chicken and 1 part rice best. If diarrhea results from ingestion of foreign matter (from teething or eating plants, soap, or other household materials), treat a dog with small doses of Kaopectate® or Pepto-Bismol®. (NEVER give a cat Pepto-Bismol or aspirin—both can be fatal.) If symptoms persist for more than 24 hours, or if blood is present in stool, consult a veterinarian.

DOG DISEASES

Symptoms   A number of conditions affect only dogs. *Canine distemper* causes severe diarrhea and may cause high fever, discharge from eyes and nose, thickening of foot pads, coughing, muscle contractions, convulsions, and pneumonia. *Infectious canine hepatitis* usually results in fever, lethargy, and congestion of the mucous membranes; it also can cause loss of appetite and insatiable thirst. *Leptospirosis* is characterized by high fever, lethargy, loss of appetite, congestion in the whites of the eyes, and possibly pain in walking, jaundice, vomiting, and diarrhea. *Infectious canine tracheobron-chitis (kennel cough)* causes high fever and severe dry coughing spasms.

Treatment   All four of these diseases can be prevented by annual vaccinations. If a dog is not vaccinated, early diagnosis of the symptoms of each disease is imperative. None of these diseases can be treated at home; take the dog to a veterinarian as soon as possible.

PARASITES, EXTERNAL

Symptoms   Fleas, ticks, lice, maggots, and mites are common external parasites that prey on animals. All cause animals to scratch excessively, which can lead to hair loss. *Fleas* are tiny brown insects that move through the animal's coat. *Ticks* are small, round, dark-colored insects with hard shells that attach themselves to an animal's skin. *Lice* are small, dark-gray insects that remain in one place on an animal's body. *Maggots* look like small worms. *Mites,* which are invisible to the unaided eye, characteristically cause skin and ear irritation.

Ringworm is a fungal disease that affects the outer layers of your pet's skin, nails, and hair. It gives off toxins that can damage the skin and hair and is highly contagious to pets and humans. Ringworm should be treated by a veterinarian.

Treatment   External parasites can be readily eliminated and controlled with commercially available powders, baths, sprays, and dips. Check the labels of such treatments carefully to be sure they are appropriate for use on your animal and that they will control the parasite in question. Fleas can be controlled with flea collars, sprays, powders, baths, or dips; treat animal and surrounding furniture and carpets to eliminate infestations. Ticks can be pulled off by hand; the animal should then be treated with spray, powder, or bath to eliminate unseen ticks; treat surrounding furniture and carpets to eliminate infestations. Lyme disease, which is spread by ticks, can be prevented by vaccination. Lice can be treated with the same potions that work on fleas and ticks. Maggots are an increasingly rare parasite that, if present, should be treated by a veterinarian. Mites can cause recurring mange in dogs, or other recurring skin conditions in other animals; any recurring condition should be treated by a veterinarian.

See also "Treatment for Health Emergencies: Insect Bites" in chapter 17.

PARASITES, INTERNAL

Symptoms   All internal parasites drain an animal's natural defenses, leaving it susceptible to infections and diseases. All are likely to cause loss of appetite and lethargy. *Tapeworms* leave visible, light-colored segments (that look like rice kernels in stools), around sleeping areas, under the animal's tail, or near its anus. *Roundworms* look like spaghetti; they are light yellow, 2 to 4 inches long, have slightly pointed ends, and can be seen in stools or vomit. *Hookworms* are almost invisible to the naked eye, but can cause diarrhea (often with blood present), cramps, pale gums and lips, a dry coat, a slight cough, and noticeable weight loss. *Whipworms* cause symptoms similar to those caused by hookworms, as well as possible inflammation of the colon. *Heartworms* block an animal's arteries, causing tiredness, listlessness, a poor coat, weight loss, and constant panting and coughing. *Coccidia* (one-celled protozoa) cause diarrhea, emaciation, and discharges from the animal's eyes and nose. *Toxoplasmosis* is a parasite that afflicts mostly cats; it frequently presents no symptoms at all.

Treatment   An infestation of internal parasites is a debilitating condition that should be dealt with by a veterinarian. Preventive medications for heartworm are available.

RABIES

Symptoms   Rabies—whose symptoms include fever, loss of appetite, and an inability to swallow that results in drooling—can cause encephalitis, convulsions, or paralysis. One type of rabies causes animals to attack anything that moves (cars, animals, people); another type causes only the other symptoms.

Treatment   Prevention of rabies is possible through regular vaccinations. Once contracted, however, there is no effective treatment for rabies, and the animal will have to be destroyed.

See also "Treatment for Health Emergencies: Animal Bites" in chapter 17.

RESPIRATORY INFECTIONS

Symptoms   Sneezing, coughing, runny eyes, swollen glands, difficulty swallowing, labored breathing, fever.

Treatment   If symptoms such as sneezing, coughing, and runny eyes are present but the animal re-

mains active and eats normally, the condition is probably not serious, and no treatment is needed. A veterinarian should examine the animal if symptoms continue for a while, if the animal becomes lethargic and loses appetite, if there are discharges of pus from its nose, if congestion becomes heavy or labored breathing is continued, or if fever of more than 102°F is present.

SHOCK

Symptoms   Weakness, collapse, pale or muddy-colored gums, fast heartbeat, difficulty breathing, no breathing, dilated pupils, low body temperature.

Treatment   Keep the animal warm by applying heating pads or hot water bottles and wrapping the animal in heavy blankets or coats. Take the animal to a veterinarian at once.

SKIN PROBLEMS

Symptoms   Localized skin conditions cause inflammation or irritation and may cause bald spots of red, raw, or discolored skin. More serious disorders such as moist eczema, wet dermatitis, or acute pruritis cause raw, oozing bald spots that may be damp to the touch or oozing pus. A lump on the animal's skin that does not go away within a few days may be a tumor. Other skin problems can cause dry, flaky skin; an oily coat; and constant biting, licking, or scratching. Symmetrical skin disorders affect both sides of an animal's body equally; a generalized condition affects the animal's whole body.

Treatment   Bald patches of red or raw skin and damp, oozing hot areas should be treated by a veterinarian. Localized inflammation can be treated with soothing topical sprays and lotions. Dry skin or coat can be soaked several times a day with water or a solution made from Domeboro® tablets (available at most pharmacies); small quantities of oil added to the animal's food also will help. Itchiness can be corrected with a solution of 1 part Alpha-Keri® (available from most pharmacies) to 20 or 30 parts water applied with a spray bottle; repeat as needed. A well-balanced diet, with appropriate levels of vitamins, can maintain healthy skin. Any skin condition that does not go away, or that reappears after treatment, should be treated by a veterinarian.

SPRAINS

Symptoms   Sprains usually occur in the joints of an animal's limbs, causing rapid swelling. The affected area will be hot to the touch. The animal will not walk normally, if it walks at all.

Treatment   Apply cold compresses or ice packs gently to the swollen area; keep the area cool for a day or two, changing the compress or ice when necessary. Wrap the affected area snugly with cloth, gauze, or athletic bandages; secure the wrapping to be sure the animal does not scratch or bite it off. Keep the animal quiet, discourage activity, and avoid stairs. For sprains that heal and recur, apply hot towels or compresses; keep the injured area moist and warm for several days. If a sprain does not heal, or pain and swelling continue or are severe, see a veterinarian.

See also "Treatment for Health Emergencies: Fractures, Dislocations, and Sprains" in chapter 17 and "Home Remedies: Sprains and Strains" in chapter 18.

WOUNDS

Symptoms   *Cuts* can be recognized by the presence of smoothly separated tissue and possible bleeding. *Lacerations* result in jaggedly torn skin, bleeding, swelling, irritation, and black or blue discoloration of the skin. *Abrasions* rub or scrape away the outer layers of skin, causing pain, swelling, redness, and heat. *Bruises* or *contusions* leave black-and-blue tissue and swelling.

Treatment   Any serious wound should be treated by a veterinarian if the bleeding will not stop, if blood is gushing out, or if shock is present. For cuts that are bleeding, apply a pressure bandage (clean gauze or cloth wrapped around some padding) pressed firmly but gently against the wound; an ice bag, pressed firmly but gently on the area; or a tourniquet. After the bleeding has been controlled, clean the wound with hydrogen peroxide or Bactine®

and then dry it. Keep skin from wrinkling or bunching and then apply an antiseptic or antibiotic to a gauze square and wrap snugly in place. Change the dressing daily and keep the animal from removing it. Lacerations can be treated in the same way as cuts, but an ice bag must be used to reduce swelling and prevent further inflammation. Abrasions require the application of a soothing cream, ointment, or lotion (Solarcaine®, Nupercainal®, Unguentine® ointment, or calamine lotion); a bandage is not needed, but the animal must be kept from licking the treated area. Bruises and contusions are best treated with cold compresses or ice packs.

See also "Treatment for Health Emergencies: Abrasions" and "Black Eyes and Bruises" in chapter 17.

THE PLANT KINGDOM

ORDERS OF PLANTS

There are more than 130 orders of plants. The following list includes some of the most common or important plant orders. The Latin names of the orders of plants given here are followed by their common names. Examples of the various types of plants included in each order are also given.

ORDER ASTERALES

The members of this order belong to a single large family consisting of some 15,000 to 20,000 species. Asterales includes many popular garden ornamentals, such as asters, mums, dahlias, daisies, marigolds, sunflowers, and zinnias. Other members are common weeds, such as dandelions, ragweeds, and thistles. Lettuce and safflower are among the economically important members of Asterales. Distribution is worldwide.

ORDER BEGONIALES (BEGONIAS)

This order of flowering plants consists of organisms ranging from small plants to relatively large shrubs. They are distributed mainly in the tropics around the world, but are popular cultivated plants in subtropical and temperate climates as well. There are about 1,000 species of the familiar begonia.

ORDER BETULALES (BIRCHES)

This order of flowering trees and shrubs are dominant in northern temperate and Arctic regions. Many of these plants are economically important. Birches are major sources of cabinet woods, and alders are important soil-builders. Other members of this order include ironwoods, hornbeams, and hazelnuts.

ORDER CACTALES (CACTI)

Cacti are often spiny, fleshy stemmed plants characteristically found in arid and semiarid regions. They are native to the Americas, but are cultivated worldwide for their unusual shapes and striking blossoms.

Some species are useful economically, especially in Mexico and Central and South America. Familiar members of the order include prickly pears, barrel cacti, saguaro, cereus, and opuntia.

ORDER CORNALES (DOGWOODS)

The more than 3,700 members of this order display considerable variety in form. Most of its 10 families are woody flowering plants, mainly shrubs, but several species, such as the ivy, are climbers. Other notable members of the order include dogwoods, sour gums, ginsengs, and parsleys. They are distributed worldwide, but are chiefly found in northern temperate zones.

The oldest living thing in the world was found in 1998 on Australia's island state of Tasmania—a naturally cloned king's holly shrub thought to be 43,000 years old.

ORDER FABALES

This order is second only to the grasses (Poales) in economic importance. It includes a variety of food products, including beans, peanuts, and peas. Other members, such as alfalfa and clover, provide grazing for animals. More than 20,000 species belong to this order, which can be found worldwide, especially in temperate regions.

ORDER FAGALES (BEECHES)

This order consists exclusively of deciduous or evergreen shrubs and trees, which often form forests that cover wide areas. They are mainly distributed over the Northern Hemisphere. Common members of this order include beeches, oaks, and chestnuts.

ORDER GERANIALES (GERANIUMS)

About 4,000 species make up this order of flowering plants, which are chiefly tropical in distribution. The order displays considerable variety in size and shape, from small annual plants to trees of the tropical rainforest. Although the order has some value as ornamental plants, it is generally not an economically important plant group. The major exception is flax, the source of a fiber that has been used by humans since prehistoric times.

ORDER JUGLANDES (WALNUTS)

The members of this order are generally large forest trees, found primarily in temperate areas but also in subtropical zones. They are distributed throughout eastern North America, Central America, western South America, and eastern Asia. Walnuts, hickories, and pecans are useful not only for their edible nuts, but for their valuable wood.

ORDER LAURALES (LAURELS)

Members of this order can be found worldwide, with the greatest concentration in the tropics. They are woody, with a simple, alternating leaf structure. Several members of this order are economically useful, such as the avocado, cinnamon, and sassafras trees.

ORDER MAGNOLIALES (MAGNOLIAS)

All members of this order are woody; most are small flowering trees, although the tulip tree can reach a height of 150 feet (46 meters). They are mainly distributed throughout wet, tropical regions, but some species survive in temperate climates. Besides the tulip tree, other common members of this order include magnolias and nutmegs.

ORDER NYMPHAEALES (WATER LILIES)

Not surprisingly, the members of this order are aquatic plants. They are cultivated worldwide for their beauty, but their natural habitats are temperate and tropical regions. Most are perennials.

ORDER OLEALES (OLIVES)

The members of this important order of small, woody flowering plants can be found throughout the world, except in the polar regions. Several families—especially the lilacs, jasmines, privets, and forsythia—are popular ornamental plants. Ashes are a notable source of hardwood timber, while the olive is widely cultivated as a source of olives and olive oil.

ORDER PRIMULALES (PRIMROSES)

This order contains nearly 2,000 species of flowering plants. Two of its three families are entirely com-posed of trees and shrubs; some of these are climbers or epiphytes (plants that grow on other plants, and are not rooted in soil). The order is important be-cause of its ornamental value. Representative mem-bers include cyclamen, primrose, and loosestrife.

ORDER ROSALES (ROSES)

Members of this order are among the most fre-quently encountered plants in temperate zones around the world. They are cultivated especially for their beauty and hardiness. Some of its members are valuable food plants, including apples, pears, peaches, apricots, and plums. Roses, flowering cher-ries, spirea, mountain ash, firethorn, and hawthorn are other familiar members of this order.

Go to "Major Botanical Gardens and Arboretums" in chapter 11

BOTANICAL NAMES OF PLANTS

The abbreviation "sp." following a genus indicates that the common name refers to all species of that genus.

Common Name	Botanical Name	Common Name	Botanical Name
Acacia, giraffe	*Acacia giraffae*	Asparagus, garden	*Asparagus officinalis*
Adder's-tongue	*Erythronium sibiricum*	Aspen, European	*Populus tremula*
	Ophioglossum vulgatum islandicum	quaking	*P. tremuloides*
		Aster	*Aster* sp.
Alder, European	*Alnus glutinosa*	Attalea	*Attalea funifera*
hazel	*A. rugosa*	Avocado, American	*Persea americana*
red	*A. ruba*	Balloon vine	*Cardiospermum halicacabum*
Alfalfa	*Medicago sativa*	Balsam, garden	*Impatiens balsamina*
Almond	*Prunus amygdalus*	Barley	*Hordeum vulgare*
Aloe	*Aloe* sp.	Bean, broad	*Vicia faba*
Amaryllis	*Amaryllis* sp.	kidney	*Phaseolus vulgaris*
Angelica	*Angelica polyclada*	sieva	*P. lunatus*
garden	*A. archangelica*	Beech, American	*Fagus grandifolia*
Apple	*Malus pumila*	European	*F. sylvatica*
	M. sylvestris	Beet, common	*Beta vulgaris*
Apricot	*Prunus armeniaca*	Birch, European white	*Betula pendula*
Arborvitae, eastern	*Thuja occidentalis*	paper	*B. papyrifera*
giant	*T. plicata*	sweet	*B. lenta*
Arum, East Asian	*Pinellia ternata*	white	*B. populifolia*
Ash, European	*Fraxinus excelsior*	yellow	*B. lutea*
green	*F. pennsylvanica*	Blackberry	*Rubus* sp.
white	*F. americana*	Bladderpod	*Lesquerella densipila*

continues

Biological World

Botanical Names of Plants, Continued

Common Name	Botanical Name	Common Name	Botanical Name
Blood-lily, Katharine	*Haemanthus katharinae*	Cocklebur, oriental	*Xanthium orientale*
Blueberry, highbush	*Vaccinium corymbosum*	Coconut	*Cocos nucifera*
Brake, sword	*Pteris ensiformis*	Coffee, Arabian	*Coffea arabica*
Bryony, white	*Bryonia alba*	Coneflower, pinewoods	*Rudbeckia bicolor*
Buckwheat	*Fagopyrum sagittatum*	Coreopsis, goldenwave	*Coreopsis drummondii*
Buttercup, creeping	*Ranunculus repens*	lance	*C. lanceolata*
Cabbage	*Brassica oleracea*	plains	*C. tinctoria*
	B. oleracea capitata	Corn	*Zea mays*
Kerguelen	*Pringlea antiscorbutica*	Cornflower	*Centaurea cyanus*
Cacao	*Theobroma cacao*	Coronilla, crownvetch	*Coronilla varia*
Calotrope, fantan	*Calotropis procera*	Cosmos	*Cosmos sp.*
Capeberry, South African	*Myrica cordifolia*	Cotton, Levant	*Gossypium herbaceum*
Carpotroche	*Carpotroche brasiliensis*	Sea Island	*G. barbadense*
Carrot	*Daucus carota*	upland	*G. hirsutum*
Cashew	*Anacardium occidentale*	Coventry bells	*Campanula trachelium*
Castor bean	*Ricinus communis*	Cowpea	*Vigna glabra*
Catalpa, Chinese	*Catalpa ovata*	yard-long	*V. sesquipedalis*
northern	*C. speciosa*	common	*V. sinensis*
Cedar	*Cedrus sp.*	Crotalaria	*Crotalaria vitellina*
California incense	*Libocedrus decurrens*	Croton, purging	*Croton tiglium*
Celery, garden	*Apium graveolens dulce*	Cucumber	*Cucumis sativus*
wild	*A. graveolens*	Currant, European black	*Ribes nigrum*
Chaulmoogra tree	*Gynocardia odorata*	red	*R. sativum*
common	*Hydnocarpus anthelmintica*	Cypress, Arizona	*Cupressus arizonica*
wight	*H. wightiana*	bald	*Taxodium distichum*
Cherry, black	*Prunus serotina*	Dahlia	*Dahlia sp.*
mazzard	*P. avium*	Dandelion	*Taraxacum officinale*
pin	*P. pennsylvanica*	Daphne	*Daphne sp.*
Chestnut, Chinese	*Castanea mollissima*	Date	*Phoenix dactylifera*
common horse-	*Aesculus hippocastanum*	Davallia, Fiji	*Davallia fejeensis*
Chickpea, gram	*Cicer arietinum*	Desert willow	*Chilopsis linearis*
Chinaberry	*Melia azedarach*	Dock, curly	*Rumex crispus*
Chrysanthemum, corn	*Chrysanthemum segetum*	Dogbane	*Apocynum sp.*
Pyrenees	*C. maximum*	Dogwood, cornelian cherry	*Cornus mas*
Cinchona, ledgerbark	*Cinchona ledgeriana*	flowering	*C. florida*
Clarkia, rose	*Clarkia elegans*	Dollar plant	*Lunaria annua*
Clover, alsike	*Trifolium hybridum*	Douglas fir	*Pseudotsuga menziesii*
burdock	*T. lappaceum*	common	*P. taxifolia*
crimson	*T. incarnatum*	Eggplant	*Solanum melongena*
Egyptian	*T. alexandrinum*	garden	*S. melongena esculentum*
Persian	*T. resupinatum*	Elm, American	*Ulmus americana*
red	*T. pratense*	Endive	*Cichorium endivia*
strawberry	*T. fragiferum*	Erysimum, plains	*Erysimum asperum*
subterranean	*T. subterraneum*	Eucalyptus	*Eucalyptus sp.*
uckling	*T. dubium*	Euphorbia, snow-on-	*Euphorbia marginata*
yellow sweet	*Melilotus officinalis*	the-mountain	
white	*Trifolium repens*	False-cypress, Lawson's	*Chamaecyparis lawsoniana*
white sweet	*Melilotus alba*	nootka	*C. nootkatensis*
Clubmoss, common	*Lycopodium clavatum*		

Biological World

Common Name	Botanical Name	Common Name	Botanical Name
Fern, common staghorn	*Platycerium bifurcatum*	reed canary	*Phalaris arundinacea*
common sword	*Nephrolepis exaltata*	Sudan	*Sorghum vulgare sudanense*
filmy	*Hymenophyllum atrovirens*	Hackberry, common	*Celtis occidentalis*
grape	*Botrychium virginianum*	Hart's-tongue	*Phyllitis scolopendrium*
holly	*Crytomium falcatum*	Hemlock, eastern	*Tsuga canadensis*
lady	*Athyrium filix-femina*	western	*T. heterophylla*
maidenhair	*Adiantum pedatum*	Hemp	*Cannabis sativa*
pine	*Anemia adiantifolia*	Hibiscus, kenaf	*Hibiscus cannabinus*
royal	*Osmunda regalis*	Hickory, shagbark	*Carya ovata*
tropical	*Gleichenia flabellata*	Holly, American	*Ilex opaca*
water	*Azolla pinnata*	English	*I. aquifolium*
wood	*Thelypteris normalis*	Hollyhock	*Althaea rosea*
Fescue, alta	*Festuca elatior arundinacea*	Horsetail, common	*Equisetum arvense*
meadow	*F. elatior*	Hyssop, hedge	*Gratiola* sp.
red	*F. rubra*	Indigo	*Indigofera* sp.
Fig	*Ficus carica*	Iris, blue flag	*Iris versicolor*
Filbert	*Corylus* sp.	German	*I. germanica*
Fir, cascades	*Abies amabilis*	grass	*I. graminea*
grand	*A. grandis*	Ironweed, kinka oil	*Vernonia anthelmintica*
noble	*A. procera*	Jacaranda	*Jacaranda* sp.
red	*A. magnifica*	Jimsonweed	*Datura stramonium*
white	*A. concolor*	Juniper, Savin	*Juniperus sabina*
Flax, common	*Linum usitatissimum*	Kale	*Brassica oleracea acephala*
Forget-me-not	*Myosotis* sp.	Kamala tree	*Mallotus philippinensis*
Foxglove, common	*Digitalis purpurea*	Knotweed, prostrate	*Polygonum aviculare*
Grecian	*D. lanata*	Lamb's quarter	*Chenopodium album*
Frenchweed	*Thlaspi arvense*	Larch, western	*Larix occidentalis*
Ginkgo	*Ginkgo biloba*	Larkspur, rocket	*Delphinium ajacis*
Gladiolus, common	*Gladiolus hortulanus*	Lemon	*Citrus limon*
horticultural		Lentil	*Lens culinaris*
Gooseberry, Chinese	*Actinidia chinensis*	Lespedeza, common	*Lespedeza striata*
Gourd, snake	*Trichosanthes* sp.	Korean	*L. stipulacea*
Grape, European	*Vitis vinifera*	wand	*L. intermedia*
fox	*V. labrusca*	Lettuce	*Lactuca sativa*
roundleaf	*Ribes rotundifolium*	Licania	*Licania rigida*
Grass, Bermuda	*Cynodon dactylon*	Lilac, common	*Syringa vulgaris*
buffalo	*Buchloe dactyloides*	Lily, regal	*Lilium regale*
Canada blue-	*Pao compressa*	Linden, American	*Tilia americana*
canary	*Phalaris canariensis*	Litsea	*Litsea* sp.
cocksfoot orchard	*Dactylis glomerata*	Locust, black	*Robinia pseudoacacia*
colonial bent-	*Argostis tenuis*	Lotus, East Indian	*Nelumbo nucifea*
common carpet-	*Axonopus affinis*	Lupine	*Lupinus arcticus*
crested wheat-	*Asgropyron cristatum*	tree	*L. angustifolius*
dallis	*Paspalum dilatatum*	Macadamia,	*Macadamia ternifolia*
desert wheat-	*Agropyron desertorum*	Queenslandnut	
Italian rye-	*Lolium multiflorum*	Magnolia, great-leaved	*Magnolia macrophylla*
Johnson	*Sorghum halepense*	southern	*M. grandiflora*
Kentucky blue-	*Poa pratensis*	Malope	*Malope trifida*
perennial rye-	*Lolium perenne*	Mango, common	*Mangifera indica*
quack	*Agropyron repens*		

continues

Biological World

Botanical Names of Plants, Continued

Common Name	Botanical Name	Common Name	Botanical Name
Maple, red	*Acer rubrum*	Pecan	*Carya illinoensis*
silver	*A. saccharinum*	Peony, fernleaf	*Paeonia tenuifolia*
sugar	*A. saccharum*	Pepper, bush red	*Capsicum frutescens*
Marattia	*Marattia salicina*	Pepperwort	*Marsilea minuta*
Marbleseed, western	*Onosmodium occidentale*	Perilla, common	*Pefrilla frutescens*
Marigold	*Tagetes* sp.	Persimmon, common	*Diospyros virginiana*
winter cape	*Dimorphoteca aurantiaca*	Petunia	*Petunia* sp.
Meadowrue, Sierra	*Thalictrum polycarpum*	Phlox, Drummond	*Phlox drummondii*
Milkweed, common	*Asclepias syriaca*	Pine, Austrian	*Pinus nigra*
Millet, pearl	*Pennisetum glaucum*	eastern white	*P. strobus*
Morning glory, common	*Ipomoea purpurea*	jack	*P. banksiana*
orizaba	*I. orizabensis*	loblolly	*P. taeda*
Muskmelon	*Cucumis melo*	longleaf	*P. palustris*
Mustard, black	*Brassica nigra*	ponderosa	*P. ponderosa*
white	*B. hirta*	shore	*P. contorta*
Nasturtium	*Tropaeolum* sp.	shortleaf	*P. echinata*
Niger seed	*Guizotia abyssinica*	slash	*P. caribea*
Oak, black	*Quercus velutina*	sugar	*P. lambertiana*
English	*Q. robur*	western white	*P. monticola*
scarlet	*Q. coccinea*	Pineapple	*Ananas comosus*
southern red	*Q. falcata*	Pink, clove	*Dianthus caryophyllus*
white	*Q. alba*	Pistachio	*Pistacia* sp.
Oat, common	*Avena sativa*	Plum, garden	*Prunus domestica*
Okra	*Hibiscus esculentus*	Japanese	*P. salicina*
Olive	*Olea europaea sativa*	Podocarpus	*Podocarpus* sp.
common	*O. europaea*	Polypody, rock	*Polypodium virginianum*
Oncoba, gorli	*Oncoba echinata*	Pomegranate, common	*Punica granatum*
Onion, garden	*Allium cepa*	Poplar, eastern	*Populus deltoides*
Orange, sweet	*Citrus sinensis*	Mongolian	*P. suaveolens*
trifoliate	*Poncirus trifoliata*	yellow, or tulip tree	*Liriodendron tulipfera*
Palm, African oil	*Elaeis guineensis*	Poppy, corn	*Papaver rhoeas*
Pansy, wild	*viola tricolor*	opium	*P. somniferum*
Parinarium	*Parinarium* sp.	oriental	*P. orientale*
Parsley	*Petroselinum crispum*	Portulaca, common	*Portulaca grandiflora*
common curly	*P. latifolium*	Potato	*Solanum tuberosum*
Parsnip	*Pastinaca sativa*	Primrose, evening	*Oenothera biennis*
Pea, field	*Pisum sativum arvense*	Lemarck	*O. lamarckiana*
garden	*P. sativum*	Pumpkin	*Cucurbita pepo*
sweet	*Lathyrus odoratus*	Purslane, common	*Portulaca oleracea*
Peach	*Prunus persica*	Pycnanthus, akomu	*Pycnanthus kambo*
Peanut	*Arachis hypogaea*	Quillwort	*Isoetes braunii*
Pear	*Pyrun communis*	Radish, garden	*Raphanus sativus*
Peavine, flat	*Lathyrus sylvestris*		

Biological World

Common Name	Botanical Name	Common Name	Botanical Name
Rape, bird	*Brassica campestris*	Sugarcane	*Saccharum officinarum*
winter	*B. napus*	Sumac	*Rhus* sp.
Red cedar, eastern	*Juniperus virginiana*	Sunflower, common	*Helianthus annuus*
Redtop	*Agrostis alba*	Sweetcane	*Saccharum spontaneum*
Redwood	*Sequoia sempervirens*	Sweetgum, American	*Liquidambar styraciflua*
Rhododendron, catawba	*Rhododendron catawbiense*	Sweet potato	*Ipomoea batatas*
Rhubarb, garden	*Rheum rhaponticum*	Sweet William	*Dianthus barbatus*
medicinal	*R. officinale*	Tallow wood	*Ximenia americana*
sorrel	*R. palmatum*		*X. caffra*
Rice	*Oryza sativa*	Tara vine	*Taraktogenos kurzii*
Rose, cabbage	*Rosa centifolia*	Tetradenia, Asian	*Tetradenia glauca*
Rubber, pará	*Hevea brasiliensis*	Timothy	*Phleum pratense*
Rutabaga	*Brassica napobrassica*	Tobacco	*Nicotiana glutinosa*
Rye	*Secale cereale*	common	*N. tabacum*
Safflower	*Carthamus tinctorius*	Tomato, common	*Lycopersicon esculentum*
Sage, garden	*Salvia officinalis*	Trefoil, bird's foot	*Lotus corniculatus*
scarlet	*S. splendens*	Tulip	*Tulipa* sp.
Salsify, vegetable-oyster	*Tragopogon porrifolius*	Tung oil tree	*Aleurites fordii*
Scammony, glorybind	*Convolvulus scammonia*	Tupelo, water	*Nyssa acquatica*
Scarlet runner	*Phaseolus coccineus*	Turnip	*Brassica rapa*
Sequoia, giant	*Sequoiadendron giganteum*	Vetch, common	*Vicia sativa*
	Sequoia gigantea	hairy	*V. villosa*
Sesame, oriental	*Sesamum indicum*	Hungarian	*V. pannonica*
Snapdragon, common	*Antirrhinum majus*	narrow leaf	*V. angustifolia*
Sorghum	*Sorghum bicolor*	one-flower	*V. articulata*
Soybean	*Glycine max*	purple	*V. benghalensis*
Spicebush, Japanese	*Lindera obtusiloba*	tiny	*V. hirsuta*
Spiderwort	*Tradescantia paludosa*	wooly pod	*V. dasycarpa*
Virginia	*T. virginiana*	Violet, field	*Viola arvensis*
Spikemoss	*Selaginella selaginoides*	Walnut, eastern black	*Juglans nigra*
Spinach	*Spinacia oleracea*	Waterlily	*Nymphaea alba*
Spruce, Norway	*Picea abies*	Watermelon	*Citrullus vulgaris*
red	*P. rubens*	Waterweed, Canadian	*Elodea canadensis*
Sitka	*P. sitchensis*	Wheat	*Triticum aestivum*
white	*P. glauca*	Willow, basket	*Salix viminalis*
Spurge, South American	*Sebastiania fruticosa*	big catkin	*S. gracilistyla*
Spurry, corn	*Spergula avensis*	black	*S. nigra*
Sterculia, hazel	*Sterculia foetida*	pussy	*S. discolor*
Stillingia	*Stillingia* sp.	white	*S. alba*
Stock, common	*Matthiola incana*	Yellow trumpet, Florida	*Stenolobium stans*
Strawberry, chiloe	*Fragaria chiloensis*	Yew, English	*Taxus baccata*
pine	*F. ananassa*	Pacific	*T. brevifolia*
Strophanthus	*Strophanthus glaber*	Yucca	*Yucca* sp.
arrow poison	*S. sarmentosus*	Zinnia, oblong leaf	*Zinnia angustifolia*

Biological World

GROUND COVERS

Common Name	Botanical Name
Sunlit Areas	
Pussytoes	*Antennaria neodioica* (1, 6)
Bearberry	*Arctostaphylos uva-ursi* (1, 2, 3, 6)
Cranberry cotoneaster	*Cotoneaster apiculata* (1)
Bearberry cotoneaster	*Cotoneaster dammeri* and *cultivars* (1)
Purpleleaf wintercreeper	*Euonymus colorata* (3, 4, 6)
Creeping juniper	*Juniperus horizontalis* and *cultivars* (6)
Japanese juniper	*Juniperus procumbens Nana* (4, 6)
Hall's honeysuckle	*Lonicera japonica Halliona* (3, 4, 6)
Pachistima	*Pachistima canbyi* (1, 2, 6)
Wineleaf cinquefoil	*Potentilla tridentata* (1, 2, 6)
Cinquefoil	*Potentilla verna Nana* (1, 5)
Stonecrop	*Sedum species* (5, 6)
Barren strawberry	*Waldsteinia ternata* (1, 3, 6)
Shade	
Carpet bugle	*Ajuga reptans* and *cultivars* (3, 4)
Lily of the valley	*Convallaria majalis* (4, 5)
Wintercreeper	*Euonymus fortunei* varieties (3, 4, 6)
English ivy	*Hedera helix* and *cultivars* (4, 6)
Plantain lily	*Hosta species* (5)
Lily turn	*Liriope spicata* (6)
Japanese spurge	*Pachysandra terminalis* (2, 6)
Periwinkle or myrtle	*Vinca minor* and *cultivars* (3, 6)

1. Requires well-drained soil
2. Requires acid soil
3. Good in sunlit areas or shade
4. Confine; may grow out of bounds
5. Herbaceous
6. Foliage retention in winter

VINES FOR SPECIAL USES

Common Name	Botanical Name
Five-leaf akebia	*Akebia quinata* (1, 2, 3, 4)
Virgin's-bower	*Clematis species* and *hybrids* (1, 2, 3, 4)
Wintercreeper	*Euonymus fortunei* (2, 3)
English ivy	*Hedera helix* and *cultivars* (2)
Climbing hydrangea	*Hydrangea petiolaris* (1, 2)
Boston ivy	*Parthenocissus tricuspidata* (2)
Japanese wisteria	*Wisteria floribunda* (1, 2, 3, 4)

1. Flowering
2. Wall cover
3. Screening
4. Trellis

Go to "Treatment for Health Emergencies: Poisoning: Plant Poisons" and "Poison Control Centers" in chapter 17

POISONOUS CULTIVATED AND WILD PLANTS

The following chart lists 50 poisonous plants. It tells which portions, or areas, of the plant are toxic, describes symptoms of the illnesses they cause, and indicates which plants are or may be fatal.

Plants	Toxic Portions	Symptoms of Illness; Degree of Toxicity
Autumn crocus	Bulbs	Nausea, vomiting, diarrhea; may be fatal.
Azalea	All parts	Nausea, vomiting, depression, breathing difficulty, prostration, coma; fatal.
Belladonna	Young plants, seeds	Nausea, twitching muscles, paralysis; fatal.
Bittersweet	Leaves, seeds, roots	Vomiting, diarrhea, chills, convulsions, coma.
Bleeding heart (Dutchman's-breeches)	Foliage, roots	Nervous symptoms, convulsions.
Buttercups	All parts	Digestive system injury.
Caladium	All parts	Intense burning and irritation of the tongue and mouth; can be fatal if the base of the tongue swells, blocking air passage of the throat.
Castorbean	Seeds, foliage	Burning in mouth, convulsions; fatal.
Cherry	Twigs, foliage	Gasping, excitement, prostration.
Daffodil	Bulbs	Nausea, vomiting, diarrhea; may be fatal.
Daphne	Berries (red or yellow)	Severe burns to mouth and digestive tract followed by coma; fatal.
Delphinium	Young plants, seeds	Nausea, twitching muscles, paralysis; fatal.
Dumbcane (Dieffenbachia)	All parts	Intense burning and irritation of the tongue and mouth; fatal if the base of the tongue swells, blocking air passage of the throat.
Elderberry	Roots	Nausea and digestive upset.
Elephant ear	All parts	Intense burning and irritation of the tongue and mouth; fatal if the base of the tongue swells, blocking air passage of the throat.
English holly	Berries	Severe gastroenteritis.
English ivy	Leaves, berries	Stomach pains, labored breathing, possible coma.
Foxglove	Leaves, seeds, flowers	Irregular heartbeat and pulse, usually accompanied by digestive upset and mental confusion; may be fatal.
Goldenchain	All parts, especially seeds	Excitement, staggering convulsions, coma; may be fatal.
Horse chestnut	All parts	Nausea, twitching muscles, sometimes paralysis.
Hyacinth	Bulbs	Nausea, vomiting, diarrhea; may be fatal.
Hydrangea	Buds, leaves, branches	Severe digestive upset, gasping, convulsions; may be fatal.
Iris	Freshly underground portions	Severe but not usually serious digestive upset.
Jack-in-the-pulpit	All parts, especially roots	Intense irritation and burning of the tongue and mouth.
Jimson weed (thorn apple; datura)	All parts	Abnormal thirst, distortion of vision, delirium, incoherence, coma; may be fatal.
Larkspur	Young plants, seeds	Nausea, twitching muscles, paralysis; fatal.
Laurel	All parts	Nausea, vomiting, depression, breathing difficulty, prostration, coma; fatal.
Lily of the valley	Leaves, flowers	Irregular heartbeat and pulse usually accompanied by digestive upset and mental confusion; may be fatal.
Mayapple	Unripe apples, leaves, and roots	Diarrhea, severe digestive upset.
Mistletoe	All parts, especially berries	Fatal
Monkshood	All parts, especially roots	Digestive upset and nervous excitement; juice in plant parts is fatal.

Biological World

continues

Poisonous Cultivated and Wild Plants, Continued

Plants	Toxic Portions	Symptoms of Illness; Degree of Toxicity
Morning glory	Seeds	Large amounts cause severe mental disturbances; fatal.
Mushrooms, wild	All parts of many varieties	Fatal.
Narcissus	Bulbs	Nausea, vomiting, diarrhea; may be fatal.
Nightshade	All parts, especially unripe berries	Intense digestive disturbances and nervous symptoms; often fatal.
Oak	Foliage, acorns	Gradual kidney failure.
Oleander	All parts	Severe digestive upset, heart trouble, contact dermatitis; fatal.
Philodendron	All parts	Intense burning and irritation of the tongue and mouth; fatal if the base of the tongue swells, blocking air passage of the throat.
Poinsettia	All parts	Severe digestive upset; fatal.
Poison hemlock	All parts	Stomach pains, vomiting, paralysis of the central nervous system; may be fatal.
Poison ivy and oak	All parts	Intense itching, watery blisters, red rash.
Poppy	Foliage, roots	Nervous symptoms, convulsions.
Potato	Foliage, green parts of vegetable	Intense digestive disturbances, nervous symptoms.
Privet	Berries, leaves	Mild to severe digestive disturbances; may be fatal.
Rhododendron	All parts	Nausea, vomiting, depression, breathing difficulty, prostration, coma; fatal.
Rhubarb	Leaf blade	Kidney disorder, convulsions, coma; fatal.
Rosary pea	Seeds, foliage	Burning in mouth, convulsions; fatal.
Rue	All parts	Skin irritation; if ingested, vomiting, convulsions, may be fatal
Snowdrop	Bulbs	Vomiting, nervous excitement.
Tomato	Vines	Digestive upset, nervous disorders.
Wisteria	Seeds, pods	Mild to severe digestive disturbances.

PLANT CULTIVATION

WHEN TO PLANT

Seeds, seedlings, and young plants should be planted outdoors according to the instructions specific to their variety. Here are general guidelines on when to plant what.

Plant Type	Variety	Warmer Zones	Cooler Zones
Vegetables	tender	spring, summer	late spring
	hardy	fall, winter	spring, summer
Flowers	perennials	fall, winter, spring	spring, late summer
	annuals	year-round	spring, summer
	bulbs, tender	spring	spring
	bulbs, hardy	fall	fall
Woody Plants	shrubs	fall, winter, spring	spring, fall
	trees	fall, winter, spring	spring, fall

USDA HARDINESS ZONES

ALASKA

HAWAII

Range Average Annual Minimum Temperatures for Each Zone	
Zone 1	Below -50˚F
Zone 2	-50˚ to -40˚F
Zone 3	-40˚ to -30˚F
Zone 4	-30˚ to -20˚F
Zone 5	-20˚ to -10˚F
Zone 6	-10˚ to 0˚F
Zone 7	0˚ to 10˚F
Zone 8	10˚ to 20˚F
Zone 9	20˚ to 30˚F
Zone 10	30˚ to 40˚F
Zone 11	Above 50˚F

FROST DATES

SPRING

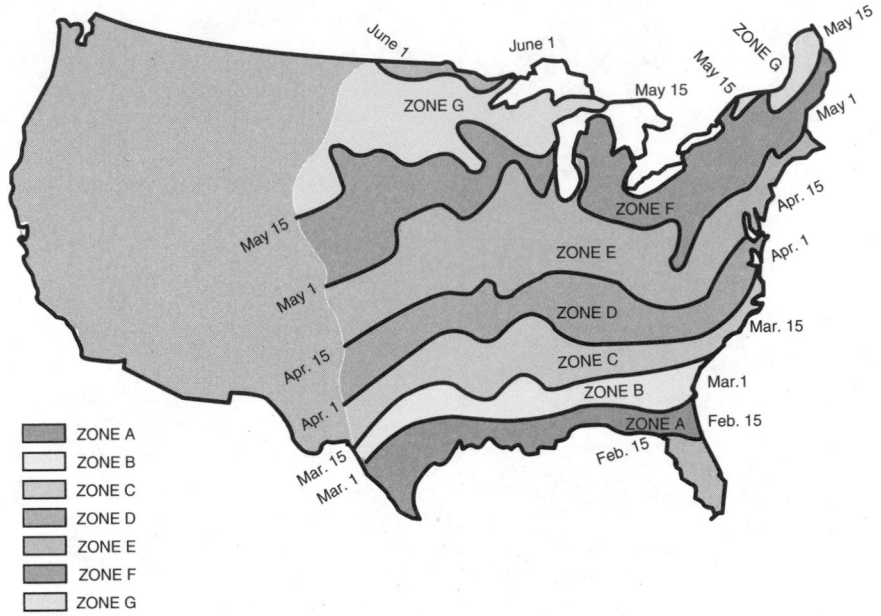

A zone map of the United States based on the average dates of the latest killing frost in spring east of the Rocky Mountains. Source: United States Department of Agriculture.

AUTUMN

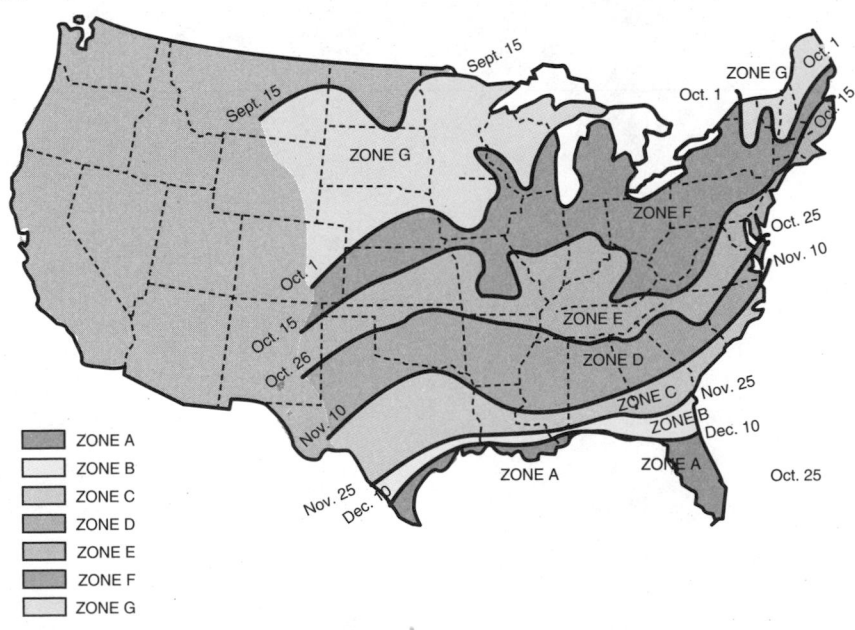

A zone map of the central and eastern part of the United States based on the average dates of the first killing frost in autumn. Source: United States Department of Agriculture.

GERMINATION TABLES

ANNUAL FLOWERS

Flower	Approximate Number of Days until Germination	Flower	Approximate Number of Days until Germination
Acrolinium	8–10	Gaillardia	12–15
Ageratum	7–11	Gomphrena	20–25
Alyssum, sweet	10–13	Helichrysum	5–10
Browallia	18–20	Larkspur	15–20
Cacalia	8–12	Lupine	25–30
Calendula	10–12	Marigold	5–8
California poppy	5–10	Nicotiana	20–25
Candytuft	6–9	Petunia	18–20
Canterbury bell	12–15	Phlox Drummondi	20–25
Celosia (coxcomb)	20–25	Pinks	5–8
Centaurea (ragged robin)	5–20	Portulaca	18–20
Chrysanthemum	6–8	Scabiosa	18–20
Cosmos	5–15	Snapdragon	20–25
Cynoglossum	11–15	Sweetpea	15–20
Flax	13–16	Verbena	8–10
Four-o'clock	12–15	Zinnia	5–8

VEGETABLE GARDEN PLANTS

Vegetable	Approximate Number of Days until Germination	Vegetable	Approximate Number of Days until Germination
Asparagus	21–28	Kohlrabi	6–8
Beans, bush	6–10	Lettuce	6–10
Beans, bush lima	6–10	Muskmelon	6–10
Beans, pole	6–10	Mustard	4–5
Beans, pole lima	7–12	Okra	15–20
Beets	7–10	Onion	8–12
Broccoli	6–10	Parsley	18–24
Brussels sprouts	6–10	Parsnip	12–18
Cabbage	6–10	Peas	6–10
Cabbage, Chinese	6–10	Pepper	10–14
Carrots	10–15	Pumpkin	6–10
Cauliflower	6–10	Radish	4–6
Celery	12–20	Rhubarb	12–14
Chard, Swiss	7–10	Rutabaga	4–7
Collards	6–10	Spinach	6–12
Corn, sweet	7–12	Squash, bush	6–10
Cress, garden	4–5	Squash, vine	6–10
Cucumber	6–8	Tomato	6–10
Eggplant	10–15	Turnip	4–7
Endive	8–12	Watermelon	8–12

Biological World

COMMON BIOLOGICAL TERMS

abaxial   Facing away from the stem or central axis of a plant or animal.

abiogenesis   A theory that living things can develop from nonliving material, as in spontaneous generation.

adaptation   The modification of an organism or part of an organism to adjust to new conditions or a new environment, as in adjustment of the eyes to bright light.

adenosine triphosphate (ATP)   A chemical compound present in all living cells that provides energy derived from food or sunlight for processes that require activity, such as contraction of a muscle or conduction of a nerve impulse.

The largest dinosaur egg ever discovered came from the Hypselosaurus. Measuring 1 foot by 10 inches, it had a liquid capacity of almost 6 pints.

appendage   A structure attached to a larger structure or part of an organism. Arms, legs, and other projections of body areas are examples of appendages.

ATP   *See* **adenosine triphosphate.**

bacteria   Tiny, one-celled plant organisms that are generally parasitic and lacking in chlorophyll. They are commonly involved in processes of fermentation and decay, and many species are the cause of diseases in humans and animals.

bladder   A saclike organ with a membranous wall that serves to collect or hold a fluid or gas. An example is the urinary bladder or the air bladder of marine animals.

blastula   A stage in the development of an embryo after the early phase of cell division when the cells form a hollow ball. The wall of the sphere is a single layer of cells, the blastoderm. The various organs, such as the gut, nervous system, and appendages, eventually evolve from cells of the blastula.

bud   An undeveloped appendage of an organism. A plant bud may develop into flowers or leaves while the bud of an animal embryo may become an arm, leg, or wing. Some bacteria and yeast cells reproduce by issuing buds, each of which becomes a new organism.

bug   Any of a large number of creeping or flying insects, mainly of the order Hemiptera. Examples of "true bugs" include bed bugs, cinch bugs, squash bugs, and giant water bugs.

calyx   A cuplike portion of a plant or animal organ. Examples include the sepals, or outermost parts of a flower, and the funnel-shaped part of a kidney that collects urine as it drains toward the bladder.

carnivore   Any meat-eating animal, particularly a member of the order Carnivora, which includes wolves, coyotes, bears, dogs, and cats.

cell   The basic structural unit of living things. It usually consists of a membranous wall containing protoplasm, a souplike mixture of proteins, enzymes, and other organic chemicals needed for survival and reproduction. Most cells also contain a nucleus that in turn holds the DNA molecules, or genetic material, that control the various cell functions.

chlorophyll   Any of nearly a dozen kinds of green pigments present in most plant cells. Chlorophylls are able to convert the energy from sunlight into carbohydrates, which plants form from carbon dioxide and water present in the environment. The carbohydrates in turn become a source of energy for animals and humans after the plant material is eaten.

chromosome   A rod-shaped unit of DNA present in the nucleus of a cell that is capable of reproducing itself. It contains a portion of the genetic or hereditary traits of the species it represents. The number of chromosomes and their shapes and sizes vary among different species and sexes within a species. Human males, for example, possess a Y-shaped chromosome that is not normally present in female cells and that governs masculine physical traits.

deoxyribonucleic acid (DNA)   A large molecule of nucleic acid found in the nuclei, usually in the chromosomes, of living cells. DNA controls such functions as the production of protein molecules in the cell and carries the template for reproduction of all the inherited characteristics of its particular species.

DNA   *See* **deoxyribonucleic acid.**

embryo   The young of a species at a very early stage of development, such as the rudimentary plant that bursts forth from a seed when it germinates, or the bird that has not yet hatched from its egg. In mammals, the embryo stage occurs after the cells of the blastula begin to specialize for the development of the fetus.

endogenous   Pertaining to factors influencing an organism that originate within that organism, as distinguished from *exogenous* factors, such as environmental influences, that originate on the outside.

evolution   The process by which a species of plants or animals gradually develops over a period of many generations from a simpler to a more complex form of organism. The traits of the simpler organism are often continued into the more complex form of the same organism, as can be observed in the brain and other structures of the human body.

exogenous   *See* **endogenous.**

fauna   The animal life of a region or period of history.

female   The sex of an animal that produces ova and bears offspring.

fermentation   A process whereby complex carbohydrates or other organic substances are converted to other chemicals by the action of enzymes produced by molds, yeasts, or bacteria. An example is the conversion of sugars to alcohol.

fertilization   The union of a male and a female reproductive cell resulting in the formation of a new organism. The term is also used to describe the process or enrichment of the soil for growing crops.

flora   The plant life of a region or period of history.

genitalia   The reproductive sex organs of a male or female of the species, particularly structures on the outside of the body.

genotype   *See* **phenotype.**

genus   A subdivision of a biological family. It is composed of a group of related species, such as the genus *Canis,* which includes various species of dogs.

gonads   The male and female reproductive organs.

haploid   Half the number of chromosomes ordinarily present in the nucleus of a cell. During reproduction, the offspring receives a haploid number of chromosomes from each parent, making a full, or diploid, set.

herbaceous   Herblike, usually used to describe a plant in which persistent woody tissue does not develop.

herbivore   An animal that feeds entirely or mainly on plant materials.

hormone   A chemical secretion of a gland or other tissue that triggers an action in another gland or tissue in a different part of the body.

immunity   A quality of being able to resist an infectious disease.

inbreeding   The mating of closely related individuals, as in self-pollinating plants or animals that are brothers and sisters.

joint   An area between two parts or segments of an organism, such as the junction of two separate bones of an animal or the node of a plant.

Biological World

karyotype   The general appearance of a set of chromosomes of an individual. Karyotype may be used to determine sex, genetic defects, and other chromosome-related factors.

kernel   The entire grain or seed of a cereal plant.

larva   The young, immature form of an organism that undergoes a change in structure to become an adult. The caterpillar and the maggot are examples of larvae.

leaf   An outgrowth of a stem of a plant, usually green, in which many living functions, such as photosynthesis, respiration, and food and water storage, take place.

lipid   Any of a group of fatty substances, including oils and waxes, produced by plant or animal tissues. Lipids generally are insoluble in water, but they can be dissolved in alcohol, benzene, or similar organic solvents.

male   The sex of an animal that produces spermatozoa or of a plant that produces pollen.

mammal   A warm-blooded, air-breathing vertebrate of the class Mammalia, possessing hair and mammary glands.

Mendel's laws   A series of natural principles of heredity discovered by Gregor Mendel. They govern such factors as dominant and recessive traits resulting from the interaction of genes that are inherited in pairs.

metabolism   The chemical and energy changes associated with the consumption of food and oxygen, the production of heat, and the calories used in physical activity.

natural selection   A principle proposed by Charles Darwin to explain the ability of various species to adapt to changes in the environment. Called "survival of the fittest," the theory offered an explanation for the survival of some species and extinction of others.

neuron   The structural and functional unit of a nerve, including the cell body and its axon and dendrite fibers.

nucleus   A structure present in most plant and animal cells. It contains the chromosomes and ribonucleic acid (RNA) molecules that direct the cell's life functions.

osmosis   The diffusion of water through a semipermeable membrane from the side with a greater concentration of a solution to the side with a lesser concentration.

osseous   Pertaining to bones, as something composed of bone or resembling bone.

phenotype   The physical features or appearance of an individual, as distinguished from the genotype, or genetic composition of his or her cells. Two or more people with the same physical appearance may belong to the same phenotype.

pistil   The female sex structure of a plant, usually containing the ovary.

Protozoa   A phylum, or large group, of one-celled animals.

receptor   Any cell or group of cells that is the target of a stimulus, such as the retina of the eye.

regeneration   The ability of some plants and animals to restore or replace lost tissues or structures, such as a claw or feather.

stamen   The pollen-producing structure of a plant. It usually consists of an anther, the actual pollen producer, on the tip of a flower filament.

stimulus   An environmental influence, such as a chemical or physical irritant, that induces or brings about a response in a cell or organism.

symbiosis   A relationship in which two organisms live together for the mutual benefit of each.

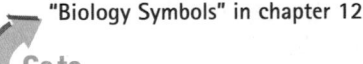

"Biology Symbols" in chapter 12

Go to

terrestrial Pertaining to plant or animal life on land rather than in water.

tissue A group of cells with similar structures and functions.

tropism The involuntary response of an organism to a stimulus, such as the response of a plant to gravity or sunlight.

vacuole Any of the spaces scattered about the protoplasm of a cell, usually containing fluid.

zygote The fertilized egg cell of a plant or animal.

ADDITIONAL SOURCES OF INFORMATION

ORGANIZATIONS AND SERVICES

American Horticultural Society
7931 E. Boulevard Dr.
Alexandria, VA 22308

American Society for the Prevention of Cruelty to Animals
424 E. 92nd St.
New York, NY 10028

American Veterinary Medical Association
1931 North Meacham Rd., Suite 100
Schaumburg, IL 60173-4360

Garden Club of America
598 Madison Ave.
New York, NY 10022

Men's Garden Clubs of America
5560 Merle Hay Rd.
Des Moines, IA 50323

National Wildlife Federation
1412 16th St., NW
Washington, DC 20036

The Nature Conservancy
4245 North Fairfax Drive, Suite 100
Arlington, VA 22203-1606

Sierra Club
85 Second St., 2nd Floor
San Francisco, CA 94105-3441

BOOKS

Ackerman, J. *Chance in the House of Fate: A Natural History of Heredity.* Houghton Mifflin, 2001.

American Kennel Club Staff. *The Complete Dog Book.* 18th ed. Howell, 1992.

Bell, P.R., and A.R. Hemsley. *Green Plants: Their Origin and Diversity.* Cambridge University Press, 2000.

Bondwell, Sally. *The American Animal Hospital Association of Dog Health and Care.* Quill, 1996.

Burton, M., and R. Burton. *International Wildlife Encyclopedia.* Marshall Cavendish, 2002.

Burton, R., and S.W. Kress. *The Audubon Backyard Birdwatcher: Birdfeeders and Bird Gardens.* Thunder Bay Press, 1999.

Carlson, D.G. *Cat Owner's Home Veterinary Handbook.* Hungry Minds, 1995.

Cutler, K.D., ed. *Burpee: The Complete Vegetable & Herb Gardener: A Guide to Growing Your Garden Organically.* Hungry Minds, 1997.

Day, David. *The Doomsday Book of Animals: A Natural History of Vanished Species.* Viking Penguin, 1983.

Diamond, Jared. *Guns, Germs, and Steel: The Fates of Human Societies.* Norton, 1999.

Ehrlich, Paul R., David S. Dobkin, and Darryl Wheye. *Birds In Jeopardy: The Imperiled and Extinct Birds of the United States and Canada, Including Hawaii and Puerto Rico.* Stanford University Press, 1992.

Forshaw, J., ed. *Encyclopedia of Birds.* 2nd ed. Academic Press, 1998.

Giffin, J.M., et al. *The Dog Owner's Home Veterinary Handbook.* Hungry Minds, 1999.

Gould, E., ed. *Encyclopedia of Mammals.* 2nd ed. Academic Press, 1998.

Biological World

Lane, D., and N. Ewart. *A–Z of Dog Diseases & Health Problems: Signs, Diagnoses, Causes, Treatment.* Hungry Minds, 1997.

Grizimek, Bernhard, ed. *Encyclopedia of Animals.* 15 vols. McGraw-Hill, 1990.

MacDonald, D.W., ed. *The Encyclopedia of Mammals.* Checkmark Books, 1995.

Mackey, Betty, et al. *The Gardener's Home Companion.* Macmillan, 1991.

Niklas, K.J. *The Evolutionary Biology of Plants.* University of Chicago Press, 1997.

Peterson, Roger T. *Peterson's First Guide to Wildflowers.* Houghton Mifflin, 1986.

Riley, Laura, and William Riley. *Guide to the National Wildlife Refuges.* Macmillan, 1992.

Sussman, Les. *The American Animal Hospital Association Encyclopedia of Cat Health and Care.* Quill, 1996.

Pollan, M. *The Botany of Desire: A Plant's-Eye View of the World.* Random House, 2001.

Raven, P.H., et al. *Biology of Plants.* W.H. Freeman, 1998.

Siegal, M., ed. *The Cornell Book of Cats: A Comprehensive and Authoritative Medical Reference for Every Cat and Kitten.* Villard Books, 1997.

Taylor, Norman. *Taylor's Master Guide to Gardening.* Houghton Mifflin, 1994.

Weiner, J. *The Beak of the Finch: The Story of Evolution in Our Time.* Vintage, 1995.

WEB SITES

American Veterinary Medical Association
http://www.avma.org

Academy of Natural Sciences of Philadelphia
http://www.acnatsci.org

American Museum of Natural History
http://www.amnh.org

Cornell Laboratory of Ornithology
http://www.birds.cornell.edu

National Audubon Society
http://www.audubon.org

National Museum of Natural History, Smithsonian
http://mnh.si.edu

Nature Conservancy
http://nature.org

Sierra Club
www.sierraclub.org

The World Conservation Union
http://www.iucn.org

4

THE PHYSICAL SCIENCES, MATH, AND TECHNOLOGY

ASTRONOMY

PHASES OF THE MOON

The Moon is the closest natural body to the Earth. Eight phases of the Moon are visible because the Moon has no light of its own. Its daylight side reflects the light of the Sun. As pictured below at the new moon, the dark side of the Moon is turned toward the Earth, and the Moon cannot be seen. The second phase is a waxing crescent moon, followed by a half moon, or first quarter. A waxing gibbous moon is then succeeded by a full moon. The Moon then begins to wane, through a waning gibbous moon, a third (or last) quarter moon, a waning crescent moon, and back to a new moon again. The cycle takes 27.3 days to complete.

LUNAR AND SOLAR ECLIPSES

An eclipse occurs when a celestial body, such as the Earth or Moon, casts a shadow so that another celestial body seems to dim or disappear. As each of the celestial bodies is in constant motion with respect to the others, the alignment of the bodies is not always perfect. Totality during an eclipse rarely lasts more than a few minutes.

An eclipse of the Moon (lunar eclipse) occurs when the Sun, Earth, and Moon are in a straight line so that the Moon is in the shadow of Earth. It is visible from any point on the Earth facing the Moon at the time of the eclipse.

A total solar eclipse takes place when the Earth, Moon, and Sun are in alignment in such a way that the umbra of the shadow of the Moon reaches the Earth. (The *umbra* is the dark central part of the cone-shaped shadow projecting from the Moon to Earth during this phenomenon.) All the light of the Sun is blocked or eclipsed because of the Moon's position. The *penumbra* (the lighter shadow) shows a partial solar eclipse.

In an annular solar eclipse, the alignment is just the same as in a total solar eclipse, but the Moon is too far away from the Earth at the time for the umbra of the shadow to reach Earth. The circle of the Moon is not large enough to block our seeing the Sun, so a ring of light from the corona, or outer fringe, of the Sun can be seen surrounding the moon's circle.

The shadow of the Moon during a solar eclipse is visible only along an arc-shaped path on a portion of the Earth, and the shadow moves at a speed between 1,060 and 2,100 miles per hour, depending on the latitude of the shadow, the rotation of the Earth, and the speed of the Moon through its own orbit.

Because the Sun, Earth, and Moon travel in relatively predictable orbits, astronomers since the days of ancient Babylonia (700 B.C.) have been able to calculate the future dates on which the Sun, Earth, and Moon will once again be in alignment. Therefore, astronomers can forecast the time and place of eclipses many years in advance. For example, at regular intervals of 18 years, 9 to 11 days (depending on leap years), and 8 hours (a period of one saros), the Sun and Moon will return to the same orbital node relative to Earth. During one saros, there are usually 41 total or partial solar eclipses and 29 lunar eclipses, or an average of about 4 eclipses a year. But each successive solar eclipse is observed about 120 degrees to

Total Lunar Eclipse

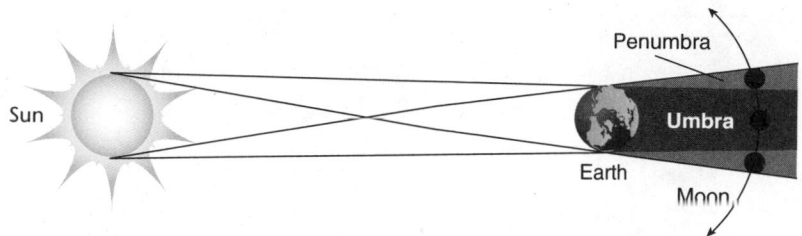

Annular Solar Eclipse

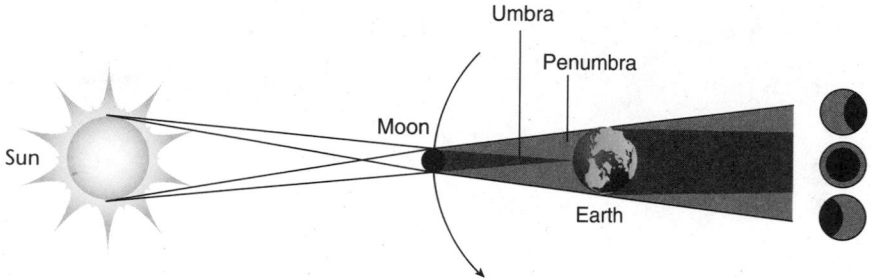

Total Solar Eclipse

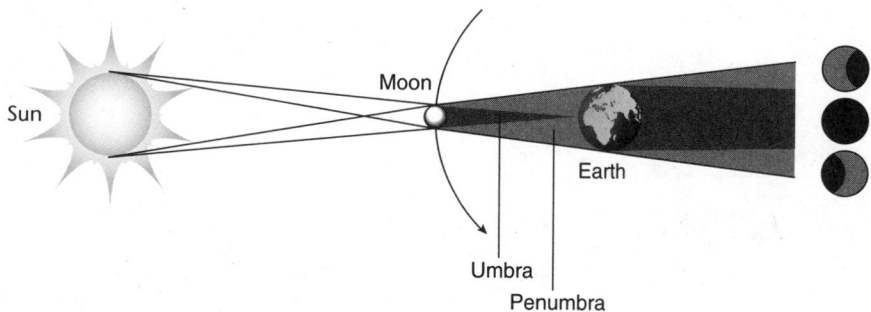

the west of the previous phenomenon and can be expected to recur at the same longitude on Earth after a period equivalent to three times the length of one saros. Each solar eclipse may affect an area only about 100 miles wide, and any given place on Earth can expect a total eclipse about once every 400 years.

"Reckoning Days and Hours" and "Calendars: The Seasons" in chapter 1

Go to

On rare occasions, sunlight can appear to be green. Known as a "green flash," this phenomenon occurs briefly when the Sun sets or rises on an extremely clear horizon. It is produced by the greater bending of green and blue rays as sunlight is refracted in the Earth's atmosphere.

ALL LUNAR ECLIPSES, 1999–2020

Date	Mid-eclipse (Universal Time)	Type	Date	Mid-eclipse (Universal Time)	Type
1999 January 31	16:17	Penumbral	2010 June 26	11:38	Umbral
1999 July 28	11:34	Umbral	2010 December 21	08:17	Total
2000 January 21	04:43	Total	2011 June 15	20:12	Total
2000 July 16	13:56	Total	2011 December 10	14:32	Total
2001 January 9	20:21	Total	2012 June 4	11:03	Umbral
2001 July 5	14:55	Umbral	2012 November 28	14:33	Penumbral
2001 December 30	10:29	Penumbral	2013 April 25	20:07	Umbral
2002 May 26	12:03	Penumbral	2013 May 25	04:10	Penumbral
2002 June 24	21:27	Penumbral	2013 October 18	23:50	Penumbral
2002 November 20	01:46	Penumbral	2014 April 15	07:45	Total
2003 May 16	03:40	Total	2014 October 8	10:54	Total
2003 November 9	01:18	Total	2015 April 4	12:00	Total
2004 May 4	20:30	Total	2015 September 28	02:47	Total
2004 October 28	03:04	Total	2016 March 23	11:47	Penumbral
2005 April 24	09:55	Penumbral	2016 September 16	18:54	Penumbral
2005 October 17	12:03	Umbral	2017 February 11	00:44	Penumbral
2006 March 14	23:47	Penumbral	2017 August 7	18:20	Umbral
2006 September 7	18:51	Umbral	2018 January 31	13:30	Total
2007 March 3	23:21	Total	2018 July 27	20:22	Total
2007 August 28	10:37	Total	2019 January 21	05:12	Total
2008 February 21	03:26	Total	2019 July 16	21:31	Umbral
2008 August 16	21:10	Umbral	2020 January 10	19:10	Penumbral
2009 February 9	14:38	Penumbral	2020 June 5	19:25	Penumbral
2009 July 7	09:38	Penumbral	2020 July 5	04:30	Penumbral
2009 August 6	00:39	Penumbral	2020 November 30	09:43	Penumbral
2009 December 31	19:23	Umbral			

ALL SOLAR ECLIPSES, 1999–2020

Date	Type	Date	Type	Date	Type
1999 February 16	annular	2006 September 22	annular	2014 April 29	annular
1999 August 11	total	2007 March 19	partial	2014 October 23	partial
2000 February 5	partial	2007 September 11	partial	2015 March 20	total
2000 July 1	partial	2008 February 7	annular	2015 September 13	partial
2000 July 31	partial	2008 August 1	total	2016 March 9	total
2000 December 25	partial	2009 January 26	annular	2016 September 1	annular
2001 June 21	total	2009 July 22	total	2017 February 26	annular
2001 December 14	annular	2010 January 15	annular	2017 August 21	total
2002 June 10	annular	2010 July 11	total	2018 February 15	partial
2002 December 4	total	2011 January 4	partial	2018 July 13	partial
2003 May 31	annular	2011 June 1	partial	2018 August 11	partial
2003 November 23	total	2011 July 1	partial	2019 January 6	partial
2004 April 19	partial	2011 November 25	partial	2019 July 2	total
2004 October 14	partial	2012 May 20	annular	2019 December 26	annular
2005 April 8	partial	2012 November 13	total	2020 June 21	annular
2005 October 3	annular	2013 May 10	annular	2020 December 14	total
2006 March 29	total	2013 November 3	partial		

TOTAL ECLIPSES OF THE SUN, 1900–2000

Date	Approximate Duration (min:sec)	Course of Central Line
1900 May 28	2:10	Mexico, United States, Spain, North Africa
1901 May 18	6:17	Indian Ocean, Sumatra, Borneo, New Guinea
1903 September 21	2:02	Antarctica
1904 September 9	6:19	Pacific Ocean
1905 August 30	3:46	Canada, Spain, North Africa, Arabia
1907 January 14	2:24	Soviet Union, China
1908 January 3	4:20	Pacific Ocean
1908 December 23	0:12	South America, Atlantic Ocean, Indian Ocean
1909 June 17	0:24	Greenland, Russia
1910 May 9	4:14	Antarctica
1911 April 28	4:58	Pacific Ocean
1912 April 17	0:02	Atlantic Ocean, Europe, Russia
1912 October 10	2:02	Brazil, South Atlantic Ocean
1914 August 21	2:15	Greenland, Europe, Middle East
1916 February 3	2:36	Pacific Ocean, South America, Atlantic Ocean
1918 June 8	2:23	Pacific Ocean, United States
1919 May 29	6:50	South America, Atlantic Ocean, Africa
1921 October 1	1:52	Antarctica
1922 September 21	5:59	Indian Ocean, Australia
1923 September 10	3:37	Pacific Ocean, Central America
1925 January 24	2:32	Northeast United States, Atlantic Ocean
1926 January 14	4:11	Africa, Indian Ocean, Borneo
1927 June 29	0:50	England, Scandinavia, Arctic Ocean, Soviet Union
1928 May 19	—	(Umbra barely touched Antarctica)
1929 May 9	5:07	Indian Ocean, Malaya, Philippines
1930 April 28	0:01	Pacific Ocean, United States, Canada
1930 October 21	1:55	South Pacific Ocean
1932 August 31	1:45	Arctic Ocean, East Canada
1934 February 14	2:53	Borneo, Pacific Ocean
1936 June 19	2:31	Greece, Turkey, Soviet Union, Pacific Ocean
1937 June 8	7:04	Pacific Ocean, Peru
1938 May 29	4:04	South Atlantic Ocean
1939 October 12	1:32	Antarctica
1940 October 1	5:35	South America, Atlantic Ocean, Africa
1941 September 21	3:22	Soviet Union, China, Pacific Ocean
1943 February 4	2:39	Japan, Pacific Ocean, Alaska
1944 January 25	4:09	South America, Atlantic Ocean, Africa
1945 July 9	1:15	Canada, Greenland, Scandinavia, Soviet Union
1947 May 20	5:14	Argentina, Brazil, Central Africa
1948 November 1	1:56	Africa, Indian Ocean
1950 September 12	1:13	Arctic Ocean, Soviet Union, Pacific Ocean
1952 February 25	3:05	Africa, Arabia, Iran, Soviet Union

Sciences

continues

Total Eclipses of the Sun, 1900–2000, Continued

Date	Approximate Duration (min:sec)	Course of Central Line
1954 June 30	2:35	United States, Canada, Scandinavia, Soviet Union
1955 June 20	7:08	Indian Ocean, Thailand, Pacific Ocean
1956 June 8	4:44	South Pacific Ocean
1957 October 23	—	(Umbra touched Antarctica)
1958 October 12	5:11	Pacific Ocean, Argentina
1959 October 2	3:01	Atlantic Ocean, Africa
1961 February 15	2:44	Europe, Soviet Union
1962 February 5	4:08	Borneo, New Guinea, Pacific Ocean
1963 July 20	1:40	Pacific Ocean, Alaska, Canada
1965 May 30	5:16	New Zealand, Pacific Ocean
1966 November 12	1:57	South America, Atlantic Ocean
1967 November 2	—	(Umbra touched Antarctica)
1968 September 22	0:40	Soviet Union
1970 March 7	3:28	Pacific Ocean, Mexico, Eastern United States
1972 July 10	2:36	Soviet Union, North Canada
1973 June 30	7:04	Atlantic Ocean, Central Africa, Indian Ocean
1974 June 20	5:08	Indian Ocean, Australia
1976 October 23	4:46	Africa, Indian Ocean, Australia
1977 October 12	2:37	Pacific Ocean, Colombia, Venezuela
1979 February 26	2:52	Northwest United States, Canada, Greenland
1980 February 16	4:08	Africa, Indian Ocean, India, China
1981 July 31	2:03	Soviet Union, Pacific Ocean
1983 June 11	5:11	Indian Ocean, New Guinea
1984 November 22	1:59	New Guinea, South Pacific Ocean
1985 November 12	1:59	Antarctica
1986 October 3	0:01	North Atlantic Ocean
1987 March 29	0:08	South Atlantic Ocean, Central Africa
1988 March 18	3:46	Sumatra, Borneo, Philippines
1990 July 22	2:33	Soviet Union, Pacific Ocean
1991 July 11	6:54	Hawaii, Mexico, South America
1992 June 30	5:20	South Atlantic Ocean
1994 November 3	4:15	Bolivia, Brazil, South Atlantic Ocean
1995 October 24	2:10	India, Southeast Asia, Indonesia
1997 March 9	2:50	Arctic Ocean, Russia
1998 February 26	4:08	Pacific Ocean, Venezuela, Atlantic Ocean
1999 August 11	2:23	Central Europe, Middle East, India

Visitation Rights

A Closer Look

When the Luna 2 spacecraft—launched by the then-Soviet Union (now Russia) in 1959—impacted the surface of the Moon, exploration of other planetary bodies in our solar system began. Since that time, unmanned craft have visited all the planets except Pluto—and that may change in the near future.

Here is a brief list of the more famous flybys and landings on other planetary bodies:

Mercury   Mariner 10 was the first spacecraft to visit Mercury, making three flybys in 1974 and 1975 before running out of fuel.

Venus   In1962, Mariner 2 became the first spacecraft to successfully fly by Venus. Twelve years later, Mariner 10 flew by Venus to gain a gravity assist to get to Mercury; on the way it took the first close-up images of cloud-shrouded Venus. Venera 7, launched by the Soviets, sent back surface data from Venus in 1970, becoming the first probe to do so; and by 1975, Venera 9 became the first spacecraft to land on the surface of another planet. (The spacecraft lasted only a few minutes, but was able to send back a few surface images). In 1978, Pioneer Venus made the first high-quality map of the planet. The Magellan spacecraft, launched in 1989, mapped 98 percent of the Venusian surface and 95 percent of the planet's gravity field. When its solar panels began to fail, engineers on Earth directed it into the Venusian atmosphere.

Mars   Mariner 4 took the first close-up images of the Martian surface in 1965. During a flyby of the planet in 1971, Mariner 9 became the first craft to orbit Mars and took the first close-up images of the Martian moons, Phobos and Deimos. Viking 1 was launched in 1975 and sent its lander to the Martian surface on July 20, 1976. Launched one month after Viking 1, Viking 2 released its lander to the surface in September 1976. Throughout the latter years of the twentieth-century, several Martian probes were lost, but the Mars Surveyor program, launched in 1996, successfully orbited Mars. The Mars Pathfinder (originally called the Mars Environmental Survey) was launched in 1996 and landed on the planet in July 1997. Renamed the Sagan Station after landing, the Pathfinder sent its surface rover, Sojourner, to record vital planetary data. Sojourner alllowed humans to have a mobile "telepresence" on the Martian surface.

Asteroids   The first close-up flyby of an asteroid occurred in 1991, when the Jupiter-bound Galileo spacecraft took images of asteroid Gaspra. In 1993, Galileo recorded the first images of a moon orbiting an asteroid when it showed Dactyl orbiting asteroid Ida. In 1996, the Near-Earth Asteroid Rendezvous (NEAR) spacecraft was launched. Renamed Shoemaker after geologist Eugene Shoemaker, it collected data for about a year, then was control-crashed into the asteroid.

Jupiter   Pioneer 10 was the first spacecraft to fly by Jupiter in 1973; Pioneer 11 followed a year later. (Pioneer 10 and 11 were also the first spacecraft to leave our solar system; both carrying a graphic message on a six-by-nine-inch gold anodized plaque.) Voyager 1, launched in 1977, flew past Jupiter in 1979; Voyager 2, launched a few weeks earlier than Voyager 1 in 1977, flew past the planet in 1979. (Both probes provided more data about the planets, moons, and rings of the visited planetary systems than ever before.) After its 1989 launch, the Galileo spacecraft reached Jupiter in 1995; it remains there through 2001 doing extensive study of the planet and its largest moons, Ganymede, Callisto, Europa, and Io.

Saturn   In 1979, Pioneer 11 became the first spacecraft to fly by Saturn. Voyager 1 flew past the planet in 1980; Voyager 2 flew by in 1981. Both probes revealed thousands of ringlets in Saturn's well-known rings, and seven additional satellites. NASA's Jet Propulsion lab could have directed Voyager 1 to Pluto but instead chose to send the probe to Titan, Saturn's largest moon. In 2004, the spacecraft Cassini—launched in 1977—is slated to orbit Saturn.

Uranus   Voyager 2 is the only spacecraft to fly by Uranus to date, doing so in 1986. It showed proof of rings around the planet and ten additional satellites. It also took close-up images of several moons, including Miranda, a satellite with a patchwork of various terrain.

Neptune   Voyager 2 flew by Neptune in 1989, the only probe to do so to date. It discovered active weather on the planet (including numerous large cloud features) and rings; it also recorded close-up images of Neptune's largest moon, Triton—a satellite complete with geysers.

Sciences

THE PLANETS

Planet	Mean Distance from Sun (millions of miles)	(millions of kilometers)	Sidereal Period of Revolution (years)	(days)	Moons	Diameter (miles)	(kilometers)	Period of Rotation (days)
Mercury	36	57.9	0.241	87.97	0	3,100	4,878	58.7
Venus	67	108.2	0.615	224.70	0	7,700	12,104	−243.0*
Earth	93	149.6	1.000	365.26	1	7,920	12,756	0.997
Mars	141	227.9	1.881	686.98	2	4,200	6,794	1.026
Jupiter	483	778.3	11.862		16	88,640	142,796	0.413
Saturn	886	1,427.0	29.46		18+	74,500	120,000	0.443
Uranus	1,782	2,869.6	84.01		21	32,000	52,400	−0.65*
Neptune	2,793	4,496.6	164.79		8	31,000	50,450	0.72
Pluto	3,670	5,913	247.7		1	1,500	2,400	6.387

*Both planets appear to have retrograde (opposite) rotation.

THE LIFE OF A STAR

A star begins its life by condensing out of the gases and dust that make up a nebula. Gravity causes the resulting globule to contract, thus heating up its center. When the temperature rises to a critical level, the mass starts to glow, becoming a protostar. The protostars with sufficient mass begin to convert hydrogen gas to helium by a nuclear reaction called fusion; those with insufficient mass become "failed stars," often called brown dwarf stars. If the star is successful at creating fusion, it enters its mature stages, in which it spends most of its life.

As the star ages, the core temperature rises enough so that the star becomes unstable. The core begins to deteriorate, while the outer layers swell out and cool, forming a red giant. At this stage, the typical star begins to shed its outer layers, creating a planetary nebula. When the outer layers have completely dissipated, only the tightly packed core, known as a white dwarf, remains.

If the star has a greater initial mass than an average star, however, the accelerated rate of core deterioration results in the star's sudden collapse, followed by a catastrophic explosion known as a supernova. Hypothetically, the superdense material forming at its core may not explode at all; instead, it could go on shrinking to form a black hole.

TYPES OF STARS

Not all stars are similar to our Sun. The differences are based on ages, size, formation, and structure of each star. The following is a brief list of the major stellar types.

black dwarfs   Stars in the latest stage of stellar life. After a star about the size of our Sun becomes a white dwarf, its energy is dissipated into space, and it is no longer luminous. Theoretically, the universe is not old enough to have formed any black dwarfs.

black holes   Theoretical regions of space that form when a massive star collapses. Because their gravitational field is so strong, light (photons) cannot escape—thus black holes can never really be seen. Black holes are inferred to exist by their gravitational effects on material falling into them. The binary star system Cygnus X-1 and the center of our own galaxy are thought to harbor black holes.

blue supergiants   The hottest, bluest, and most luminous stars. They are rare, and have large masses and low densities. Rigel in the constellation of Orion is a blue supergiant star.

hot subdwarfs   Stars with extremely high densities; they are also found at the center of most planetary nebulas, such as at the center of the Ring Nebula in the constellation Lyra.

Understanding the Invisible

A
Closer
Look

A black hole is a theoretical region of space in which the gravitational field is so strong that photon (light) particles cannot escape. To imitate a black hole's density, the Earth would have to be crushed to the size of a marble. Black holes are thought to be massive stars at the ends of their stellar lives. The problem with detecting a black hole is obvious. Because they don't produce or reflect light, seeing them in the inky black nighttime sky is impossible. Astronomers infer the presence of a black hole by the gravitational effects on the material falling into it.

J. Robert Oppenheimer and Hartland Snyder conceived the idea of a "black hole" in 1939 on the basis of Einstein's theory of general relativity. The idea was ignored, however, for several decades. One of the first possible black holes was found in the binary system Cygnus X-1, an X-ray source in the constellation of Cygnus. In 1994, astronomers using the Hubble Space Telescope noted that the region around the elliptical galaxy M87 in the Virgo Cluster was a possible black hole. In 1997, astronomers collected dramatic evidence for a supermassive black hole in NGC 4486B, a small elliptical satellite galaxy of M87. Many astronomers speculate that the core of our own Milky Way galaxy is a black hole. By the year 2001, astronomers claimed to have discovered more than 30 supermassive black holes in various galaxies. All the evidence is circumstantial; but if the effects in these regions are not caused by black holes, no alternative hypothesis is available.

neutron stars   The remains of a star with a mass between 1.4 and 3 solar masses. These stars collapse so violently that protons and electrons are rammed together to form neutrons. The mass of a neutron star is greater than the Sun, but a neutron star's size is only about 5 miles across *See also* **pulsars.**

novae   Usually associated with binary star systems, in which one of the stars is a white dwarf. As the mass from the companion star hits the white dwarf star, a fusion reaction occurs, and the star responds with a burst of brightness. Unlike the rare supernovae, novae appear once every few years.

pulsars   Thought to be rotating neutron stars. Their rotational speeds vary, from 642 times per second to once every 4 seconds. First discovered in 1967, pulsars send out radio waves in specific directions, much like a lighthouse beam of light sweeping around the sky.

red giants   Stars in the late stages of stellar life. They have low density and are brighter and larger than our Sun. Arcturus, in the constellation Boötes, is a red giant; it is predicted that our Sun will become a red giant at the end of its life, about 5 to 6 billion years from now.

red supergiants   The largest and brightest of stars, with a large mass and low density. Betelgeuse, in the constellation of Orion, is a red supergiant.

supernovae   Massive stars that undergo a gravitational collapse, then a gigantic explosion, blasting away the outer layers into space. The resulting gases spread out into space, with the core collapsing into a neutron star, or possibly a black hole. Seeing a supernova from Earth is rare. A supernova observed in the constellation of Taurus in 1054 produced the Crab Nebula; astronomer Johannes Kepler witnessed the last supernova seen in our Milky Way galaxy in 1604. Two more bright supernovae include one in 1987 in the Large Magellanic Cloud, a neighboring galaxy, and one in 1993 in the galaxy M81.

variable stars   Stars that change in brightness over time. There are numerous reasons for variability in stars: two stars eclipsing each other, explosions on the star, or a natural pulsation caused by an imbalance between the star's outer layer and core. Brightness can vary over the course of a day, a year, or several years.

white dwarfs   Stars at the end of stellar life. They form when a star depletes its thermonuclear energy, ceasing fusion. As the star collapses under its own weight, it becomes very dense. The gravitational energy is converted to heat, and the star continues to shine. The companion star of Sirius, in the constellation of Canis Major, is a white dwarf.

Sciences

white holes   Theoretical stars that have properties opposite from those of black holes. Instead of pulling matter into them, white holes are regions in which matter spontaneously appears.

CONSTELLATIONS

THE 12 ZODIACAL CONSTELLATIONS

Aquarius, the Water-Bearer
Aries, the Ram
Cancer, the Crab
Capricornus, the Goat
Gemini, the Twins
Leo, the Lion
Libra, the Balance or Scales
Pisces, the Fish
Sagittarius, the Archer
Scorpius, the Scorpion
Taurus, the Bull
Virgo, the Virgin

THE 28 CONSTELLATIONS NORTH OF THE ZODIAC

Andromeda, the Chained Lady
Aquila, the Eagle
Auriga, the Charioteer
Boötes, the Herdsman
Camelopardalis, the Giraffe
Canes Venatici, the Hunting Dogs
Cassiopeia, the Lady in the Chair
Cepheus, the King
Coma Berenices, Berenice's Hair
Corona Borealis, the Northern Crown
Cygnus, the Swan
Delphinus, the Dolphin
Draco, the Dragon
Equuleus, the Colt
Hercules (Kneeling)
Lacerta, the Lizard
Leo Minor, the Lesser Lion
Lynx, the Lynx
Lyra, the Lyre
Ophiuchus, the Serpent Holder
Pegasus, the Winged Horse
Perseus, the Hero
Sagitta, the Arrow
Serpens, the Serpent
Triangulum, the Triangle
Ursa Major, the Greater Bear
Ursa Minor, the Lesser Bear
Vulpecula, the Fox

THE 48 CONSTELLATIONS SOUTH OF THE ZODIAC

Antlia, the Air Pump
Apus, the Bird of Paradise
Ara, the Altar
Caelum, the Engraver's Chisel
Canis Major, the Greater Dog
Canis Minor, the Lesser Dog
Carina, the Keel
Centaurus, the Centaur
Cetus, the Whale
Chamaeleon, the Chameleon
Circinus, the Pair of Compasses
Columba, (Noah's) Dove
Corona Australis, the Southern Crown
Corvus, the Crow
Crater, the Bowl
Crux, the (Southern) Cross
Dorado, the Gilthead or Swordfish
Eridanus, the River
Fornax, the Furnace
Grus, the Crane
Horologium, the Clock
Hydra, the Water-Serpent or Hydra (fem.)
Hydrus, the Water-Snake or Sea-Serpent (masc.)
Indus, the Indian
Lepus, the Hare
Lupus, the Wolf
Mensa, the Table Mountain
Microscopium, the Microscope
Monoceros, the Unicorn
Musca, the Fly
Norma, the Square or Rule
Octans, the Octant
Orion, the Hunter
Pavo, the Peacock
Phoenix, the Fabulous Bird
Pictor, the Painter's Easel
Piscis Austrinus, the Southern Fish
Puppis, the Stern
Pyxis, the (Ship's) Compass
Reticulum, the Net
Sculptor, the Sculptor's Shop
Scutum, the Shield
Sextans, the Sextant
Telescopium, the Telescope
Triangulum Australe, the Southern Triangle
Tucana, the Toucan
Vela, the Sails
Volans, the Flying Fish

THE 25 NEAREST STAR SYSTEMS

Components in the following table are referred to as A, B, or C in the case of multiple-star systems.

A *light-year* is the distance light travels in a year, equal to 5.88 trillion miles (9.46 trillion kilometers).

Rank	Name	Components	Constellation	Distance from Sun (light-years)
1a	Proxima Centauri		Centaurus	1.23
1b	Rigil Kentaurus	A & B	Centaurus	4.35
2	Barnard's Star		Ophiuchus	5.98
3	Wolf 359		Leo	7.80
4	Lalande 21185		Ursa Major	8.23
5	L 726-8	A & B	Cetus	8.57
6	Sirius	A & B	Canis Major	8.57
7	Ross 154		Sagittarius	9.56
8	Ross 248		Andromeda	10.33
9	Epsilon Eridani		Eridanus	10.67
10	Ross 128		Virgo	10.83
11	L 789-6	A, B, & C	Aquarius	11.08
12	Groombridge 34	A & B	Andromeda	11.27
13	Epsilon Indi		Indus	11.29
14	61 Cygni	A & B	Cygnus	11.30
15	BD +59° 1915	A & B	Draco	11.40
16	Tau Ceti		Cetus	11.40
17	Procyon	A & B	Canis Minor	11.41
18	Lacaille 9352		Piscis Austrinus	11.47
19	GJ 111		Cancer	11.83
20	GJ 1061		Horologium	12.06
21	L 725-32		Cetus	12.20
22	BD +05° 1668		Canis Minor	12.34
23	Lacaille 8760		Microscopium	12.61
24	Kapteyn's Star		Pictor	12.63
25	Krüger 60	A & B	Cepheus	12.95

COMMON ASTRONOMY TERMS

Additional terms are defined in the preceding astronomy sections.

aberration The apparent displacement of a star owing to the orbital motion of Earth and the bending of light rays from the star. As the Earth travels around the Sun, the aberration causes the star to appear to trace an ellipse about its true position.

absorption nebula A nebula seen in silhouette because it is absorbing or blocking light from behind. It is also called a dark nebula.

accretion The process by which small particles coalesce by collisions or mutual gravitational pull, creating larger bodies. Accretion is suspected as a major process in the formation of the planets and satellites in any solar system.

albedo The proportion of light reflected from a celestial body. The Moon reflects only about 7 percent of the sunlight falling on it, whereas the albedo of Venus is more than 70 percent, owing to its heavy cloud cover, which reflects a greater proportion of light.

altitude Number of degrees above the horizon of an object on the celestial plane.

aphelion The point in an object's orbit that is farthest from the Sun. *See also* **perihelion.**

apogee The point in the Moon's orbit (or any other orbiting body, such as an artificial satellite) when it is farthest from the Earth. *See also* **perigee.**

asterism A pattern of stars that does not constitute one of the 88 official constellations. For example, the Big Dipper in the constellation of Ursa Major is an asterism.

The light that leaves the Sun takes 8 minutes to reach the Earth.

asteroid A small, rocky object or minor planet that orbits the Sun. Most asteroids have orbits in the asteroid belt, located between the orbits of Mars and Jupiter. Others can be found throughout the solar system, including those that come close to the Earth, called near-Earth asteroids. More than 8,000 asteroids have been discovered, and it is likely thousands more exist undetected throughout the solar system. Most asteroids are leftovers from the formation of the solar system; others are debris from collisions between larger planetary bodies or remnants of extinct comets.

astrometry The measure of the positions and apparent motions of celestial objects and the attempt to understand the factors that influence such movements.

astronomical unit An astronomical distance, equal to the average distance from the Earth to the Sun, or about 93,000,000 miles (150,000,000 kilometers).

big bang model A theory that describes the beginning of our universe as a titanic explosion. This explosion did not occur at a particular point in space, according to the theory, but rather was a transition from enormous density and temperature throughout all space to conditions of even lower density and lower temperature as space itself expanded. After the hypothetical explosion, the universe was swamped with energy in the form of radiant energy and various atomic particles. This phase was followed by a cooling and thinning out of the universe. It is believed that the universe is still expanding at this time.

binary star Two stars that are gravitationally attracted to each other. *See also* **double star.**

celestial sphere An imaginary sphere used to locate the positions and track the motions of all astronomical objects.

comet A small object composed of rock, ice, and gases moving about the Sun in an elliptical orbit. A comet has three distinct components: the *nucleus,* made up of rock and ice; the *coma,* consisting of gases and dust; and the *tail,* formed when gases and dust spread out from the nucleus or coma. Short-period comets complete their orbits in less than 200 years; long-period comets may take thousands of years to revolve around the Sun, or may never return at all (parabolic orbit). Some astronomers believe that comets originate in the Oort cloud, a hypothetical region of space that lies outside the solar system.

corona The outer envelope, or "atmosphere," of gas surrounding the Sun, possibly extending to the orbit of Earth. During an eclipse of the Sun, the corona may be visible around the edges of the Moon. It has a density that is about one-millionth that of the atmosphere of Earth.

cosmogony The study of how the universe was formed.

cosmology The study of the universe at large, of the distribution and behavior of the matter and energy in it, of the laws governing these factors, and of its origin and evolution.

dark matter Matter that is thought to exist in the universe but has not yet been observed. It is based on measurements of unexplained gravitational effects on visible matter.

declination On the celestial sphere, the coordinate analogous to latitude on the Earth. Declination is measured in degrees, minutes, and seconds of arc north (positive above the celestial equator) or south (negative below the celestial equator).

Doppler effect   The phenomenon in which, as a source of waves (e.g., sound or light) and the observer move relative to each other, the emitted wavelength appears to change. In astronomy, Doppler shifts are used to determine the velocity and direction of distant objects. For example, light from a galaxy shifts to the red on the electromagnetic spectrum if the galaxy is moving away from the observer (red shift) and to the blue if the galaxy is moving toward the observer (blue shift).

double star   Two stars that appear close together along a line of sight. Double stars may be an optical double, which are stars that just appear to be close as seen from Earth but are physically quite distant from one another; or true binaries, stars that are gravitationally bound to one another.

ecliptic   The apparent path of the Sun in the sky as seen from Earth.

fireball   A bright meteor, with an apparent magnitude ranging from about –5 to –20 (to compare, the Sun has an apparent magnitude of –26.7). Fireballs are sometimes seen during the day.

galaxy   A large system of stars, usually containing between 1 million and 1 trillion stars, along with clouds of gas and dust. Galaxies are sometimes classified according to their shapes as spiral, elliptical, or irregular.

globular cluster   A nearly spherical, dense cluster of hundreds of thousands to millions of stars.

gravitational collapse   The contraction of a star when the pressure of thermonuclear reactions can no longer sustain the force of self-gravitation. Collapse occurs at the end of a star's life when its fuel of hydrogen and other elements is depleted. Depending on its original mass, the star may evolve into a white dwarf, a neutron star, or a black hole, or it may explode as a supernova.

inferior conjunction   The passage of Mercury or Venus between the Earth and the Sun.

libration   The effect that allows an observer on Earth to see about 59 percent of the Moon's surface, slightly more than would otherwise be visible. Because the Moon's rotation and orbital period are equal (on average), the Moon always keeps the same face to the Earth. Libration occurs because the Moon's elliptical orbit speed is not constant and its orbit is slightly tilted.

meteor   A meteoroid that produces a streak of light as it enters the Earth's atmosphere and is vaporized by the resulting friction. This phenomenon is quite common when the Earth passes through swarms of meteoroids. The resulting meteor showers are usually associated with a specific constellation and time of year. Meteors are commonly called shooting or falling stars.

The Milky Way galaxy contains several hundred billion stars and is about 100,000 light-years across. Our solar system orbits the Milky Way once every 250 million years.

meteorite   A meteor that passes through the outer layers of the Earth's atmosphere and strikes the planet's surface. The resulting explosive impact buries or disperses the meteorite, leaving a crater behind. The largest meteorite to fall to Earth so far is the more than 60-ton Hoba West meteorite, discovered in 1920 in Namibia, Africa.

meteoroid   A small, solid particle of rock or other material that orbits the Sun, often along the same path as comets. Meteoroids form when a comet breaks up or leaves debris in its wake. Thousands of meteoroids traveling in closely grouped packs are called a swarm.

Milky Way   The spiral galaxy in which our solar system is located. It contains about 200 billion stars, has a diameter of about 100,000 light-years, and is about 12 to 14 billion years old.

Sciences

nadir   The point directly below the observer, or 90 degrees below the horizon. *See also* **zenith.**

nebula   A concentration of gas and dust in the galaxy.

oblate   The shape of a planet or natural satellite that is not completely spherical but bulges in the center and is flattened at the poles. The shape is usually caused by rapid spinning or the gravitational pull from an accompanying moon. For example, rapidly rotating Jupiter is an oblate spheroid.

occulation   The crossing of one body in front of another, such as the Moon in front of a star, relative to an observer.

opposition   The point in a planet's orbit when it is 180 degrees from the Sun, usually as observed from Earth.

orbit   The path of an object around a central body; gravitational attraction keeps the bodies in orbit.

parallax   The change in the relative position of an object when viewed from different places; in astronomy, the closer the object, the greater the parallax.

perigee   The point where the Moon (or any other orbiting body, such as an artificial satellite) is closest in its orbit to the Earth. *See also* **apogee.**

perihelion   The point in the orbit of an object when it is closest to the Sun. *See also* **aphelion.**

perturbation   A local gravitational disturbance in the uniform motion of a body because of the gravitational influence of another object. For example, a comet orbiting the Sun can be perturbed by a close encounter with Jupiter, the solar system's largest planet, which influences the orbit of the comet.

planetesimals   Large rocky bodies more than one mile in diameter thought to have formed in the early solar system. Scientists theorize that planetesimals later accreted to form the rocky cores of the planets.

plasma   Matter in the form of electrically charged particles; the state in which most of the universe exists.

proper motion   The apparent angular motion of an object across the sky, determined as change in position with respect to the background star; caused by the star's true motion and the relative motion of the solar system.

quasar   A contraction of the word *quasi-stellar,* used to describe celestial objects with a starlike appearance. Quasars are the most distant objects known. They have large red shifts indicating great recessional velocities and emit energy that is more than a thousand times that of an average galaxy.

About half of the stars we can see are actually two stars that orbit each other.

radio telescope   An astronomical instrument used to collect, detect, and analyze radio waves from cosmic sources, such as radio galaxies, pulsars, and quasars.

revolution   The movement of an object around a central body.

right ascension   The angle of an object eastward from the vernal equinox, along the celestial equator; right ascension is measured in hours, minutes, and seconds.

rotation   The movement of a body as it turns on its axis.

scintillation   The twinkling of a star, planet, or other bright object in the sky. The rapid variations in brightness are caused as turbulence in the Earth's atmospheric layers, which cause random refraction of the light from the celestial body.

solar wind   A stream of particles, primarily protons and electrons, that constantly flows outward from the Sun.

space-time   A four-dimensional way of describing events and locations with three units of distance and one of time. Under the influence of gravity, spacetime can actually warp and bend.

"Astronomers" in chapter 5; "Astronomy Symbols" in chapter 12

Go to

spectrum　Radiation (usually visible light) broken into its component wavelengths.

spectroscope　An instrument used to determine the spectrum or wavelength of a ray of light emanating from an object. A spectroscope is often used in astronomy.

star　A spherical celestial body consisting of a large mass of hot gas held together by its own gravity. It is self-luminating because of extensive internal nuclear reactions. Our Sun is a typical star.

superior conjunction　For a planet (Mercury or Venus) inside the Earth's orbit, the condition when the planet is behind the Sun, relative to the Earth.

syzygy　The condition when three celestial bodies are arranged in a straight line. Syzygy occurs during solar and lunar eclipses, when the Sun, Moon, and Earth are aligned.

terminator　The line separating sunlight and darkness on a planet or moon.

transit　The movement of a smaller object across the lighted face of a larger object, such as the movement of Mercury across the face of the Sun, or the moon Io across the face of the planet Jupiter.

universe　The entirety of all that is known to exist. The size of the observable universe is limited to the distance light has traveled since the Big Bang.

zenith　The point directly overhead from the observer, or 90 degrees above the horizon. *See also* **nadir.**

zodiacal light　A faint cone of light seen along the ecliptic at sunset, usually around the time of an equinox. It is caused by sunlight scattering small dust particles that possibly have an interplanetary origin.

CHEMISTRY

ELEMENTS AND THEIR SYMBOLS

Atomic Number	Symbol	Element	Atomic Number	Symbol	Element	Atomic Number	Symbol	Element
1	H	Hydrogen	22	Ti	Titanium	43	Tc	Technetium
2	He	Helium	23	V	Vanadium	44	Ru	Ruthenium
3	Li	Lithium	24	Cr	Chromium	45	Rh	Rhodium
4	Be	Beryllium	25	Mn	Manganese	46	Pd	Palladium
5	B	Boron	26	Fe	Iron	47	Ag	Silver
6	C	Carbon	27	Co	Cobalt	48	Cd	Cadmium
7	N	Nitrogen	28	Ni	Nickel	49	In	Indium
8	O	Oxygen	29	Cu	Copper	50	Sn	Tin
9	F	Fluorine	30	Zn	Zinc	51	Sb	Antimony
10	Ne	Neon	31	Ga	Gallium	52	Te	Tellurium
11	Na	Sodium	32	Ge	Germanium	53	I	Iodine
12	Mg	Magnesium	33	As	Arsenic	54	Xe	Xenon
13	Al	Aluminum	34	Se	Selenium	55	Cs	Cesium
14	Si	Silicon	35	Br	Bromine	56	Ba	Barium
15	P	Phosphorus	36	Kr	Krypton	57	La	Lanthanum
16	S	Sulfur	37	Rb	Rubidium	58	Ce	Cerium
17	Cl	Chlorine	38	Sr	Strontium	59	Pr	Praseodymium
18	Ar	Argon	39	Y	Yttrium	60	Nd	Neodymium
19	K	Potassium	40	Zr	Zirconium	61	Pm	Promethium
20	Ca	Calcium	41	Nb	Niobium	62	Sm	Samarium
21	Sc	Scandium	42	Mo	Molybdenum	63	Eu	Europium

continues

Elements and Their Symbols, Continued

Atomic Number	Symbol	Element	Atomic Number	Symbol	Element	Atomic Number	Symbol	Element
64	Gd	Gadolinium	80	Hg	Mercury	96	Cm	Curium
65	Tb	Terbium	81	Tl	Thallium	97	Bk	Berkelium
66	Dy	Dysprosium	82	Pb	Lead	98	Cf	Californium
67	Ho	Holmium	83	Bi	Bismuth	99	Es	Einsteinium
68	Er	Erbium	84	Po	Polonium	100	Fm	Ferium
69	Tm	Thulium	85	At	Astatine	101	Md	Mendelevium
70	Yb	Ytterbium	86	Rn	Radon	102	No	Nobelium
71	Lu	Lutetium	87	Fr	Francium	103	Lw	Lawrencium
72	Hf	Hafnium	88	Ra	Radium	104	Rf	Rutherfordium
73	Ta	Tantalum	89	Ac	Actinium	105	Db	Dubnium
74	W	Tungsten	90	Th	Thorium	106	Sg	Seaborgium
75	Re	Rhenium	91	Pa	Protactinium	107	Bh	Bohrium
76	Os	Osmium	92	U	Uranium	108	Hs	Hassium
77	Ir	Iridium	93	Np	Neptunium	109	Mt	Meitnerium
78	Pt	Platinum	94	Pu	Plutonium			
79	Au	Gold	95	Am	Americium			

The names of six recently created chemical elements, 104 through 109, were confirmed by the International Union of Pure and Applied Chemistry in 1998.

THE PERIODIC TABLE OF THE ELEMENTS

The Periodic Table of the Elements is a listing of the chemical symbols (and often many of their physical characteristics) of 109 elements. The first 92 elements occur in nature, with a few exceptions: astatine (atomic number 85), technetium (atomic number 43), and some other elements are artificial although their artificiality is debated. The remaining elements have been artificially created in laboratory particle accelerators. The chemical elements exist in a free state or combined with other elements.

In the Periodic Table, the elements are arranged in order of increasing atomic number from left to right and from top to bottom. The horizontal rows of elements are called *periods;* the vertical columns of related elements are called *groups*. Across the table, there is a general trend from metallic to nonmetallic elements; down a group, there is an increase in atomic size and in eletropositive behavior. The members of a group have similar behavior because of similarities in their electron configurations.

The first three periods are the short periods, containing elements with only *s* and *p* level electrons (the lowest energy levels) and having only up to 2 and 8 electrons, respectively. Period 1 consists of hydrogen (H) and helium (He) only, the two most abundant elements in the universe. Period 2 elements begin filling the second energy level, and the period ends with neon (Ne, atomic number 10). In Period 3, the third level is filled, ending with argon (Ar, atomic number 18).

Periods 4 and 5 are longer, each with 18 elements. Period 4 begins with potassium (K) followed by calcium (Ca). But after that, higher energy electrons (the *d* orbitals) begin to fill, giving the next elements in the center of the table characteristics unlike any of the previous elements. These elements, with their incomplete *d* subshell, are known as *transition* elements. This pattern repeats for Period 5 elements. Periods 6 and 7 contain 32 elements each. The Period 6 elements that follow lanthanum (La, atomic number 57) are called *lanthanoids*. This is also called the *rare earth series* and includes cerium (Ce) through lutetium (Lu). Period 7's transitional ele-

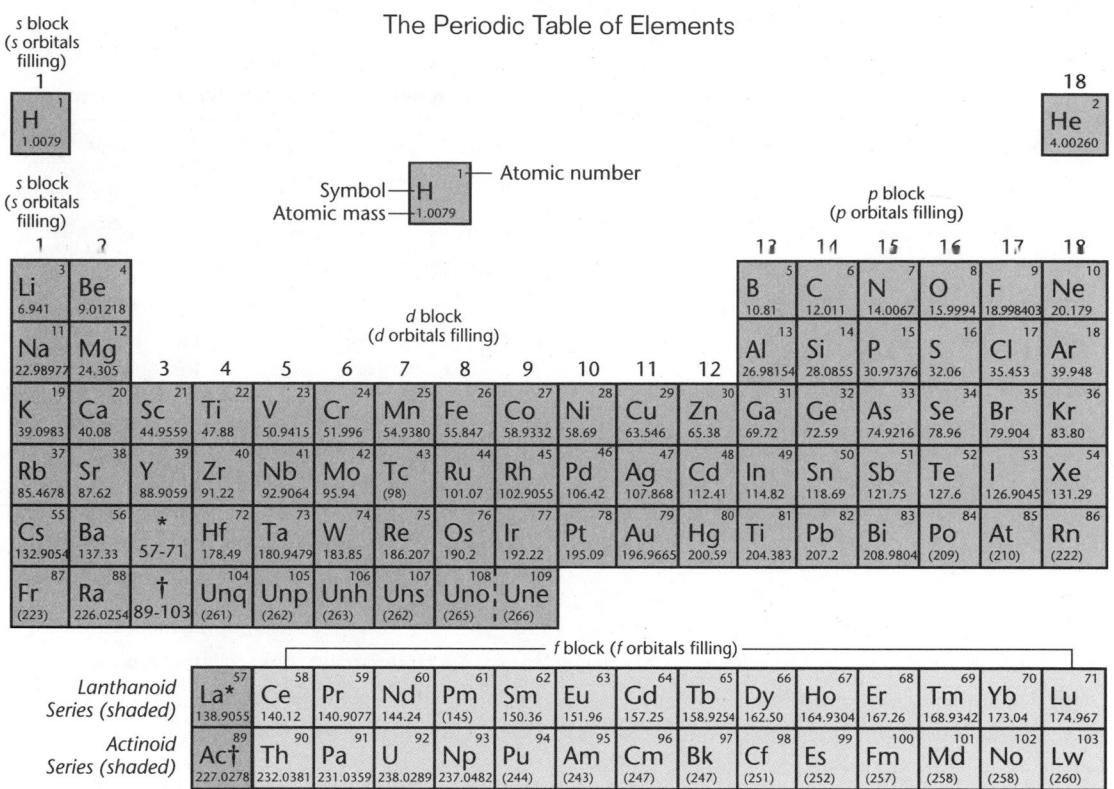

The Periodic Table of Elements

ments follow actinium (Ac, atomic number 89) and are called *actinoids*. This group includes thorium (Th) through lawrencium (Lw). Both of these groups are filling the *f* sublevel orbitals.

The Periodic Table can be divided into three basic groups: metals, nonmetals, and semimetals. In general, when you view the table, the metals are on the left, the nonmetals are on the extreme right, and the semimetals are in the center.

Metals make up the majority of the groups of elements. Most metals such as sodium (Na) are solid at room temperature, with mercury (Hg) being the only liquid metal. Metals have higher melting and boiling points because the atoms in the crystals are tightly packed together. In addition, their densities are high because the heavy nuclei are also tightly packed together. Metals have only a few (usually no more than four) valence electrons in the outermost shells. These are electrons that are often given up in a reaction, forming metallic, positive ions. Metals

(such as gold and copper) are generally good conductors of electricity. Elements of Group 1, including lithium, sodium, and potassium (but excluding hydrogen), are known as alkali metals; Group 2 metals, including magnesium and calcium, are the alkaline earth metals.

Nonmetals are usually dull in appearance, brittle, and not good electrical conductors. Many of the chemically active nonmetals are the halogens (Group 17), the group of elements that includes chlorine, bromine, and iodine. This group is highly reactive and electronegative and contains fluorine, the most highly electronegative element.

COMMON CHEMISTRY TERMS

Additional terms are defined in "Common Physics Terms" in this chapter.

acid   A substance that, in liquid form, will turn blue litmus paper red, react with alkalis (bases) to form salts, and dissolve metals to form salts. On the pH scale of 0 to 14, acids register in numbers less than 7.

alcohol   Any of a group of organic compounds that contains a hydroxyl (OH) group. A common example is ethyl alcohol (C_2H_5OH).

alkali   Any compound that has chemical qualities of a base, such as reacting with acids to form salts. On the pH scale, alkalis register in numbers larger than 7.

anion   An ion with a negative electric charge.

base   An alkaline substance, either in molecular or ionic form, that will accept or receive a proton from another chemical unit. An example is a hydroxyl ion.

benzene ring   A common organic molecule structure consisting of a ring of six carbon atoms with an equal number of attached hydrogen atoms (C_6H_6). Many organic chemicals occur in a benzene ring format with various atoms or radicals substituted for one or more hydrogen atoms, as in toluene and xylene as variations of benzene.

bond   A strong electric force that holds atoms together in molecules, crystals, and other combinations. A molecular bond may depend on the attractive force of an electron whose orbit spans the outer shells of two or more component atoms. In double bonds, two pairs of electrons may be shared equally by adjacent atoms.

catalyst   A substance that accelerates a chemical reaction without becoming a part of the end product of the reaction. A catalyst can generally be recovered in its original form following the reaction.

compound   A substance formed by the combination of two or more chemical elements that cannot be separated from the combination by physical means. The constituent atoms, however, can usually be separated by means of chemical reactions.

"Chemists" in chapter 5; "Chemistry Symbols" in chapter 12; "Chemical Additives" in **Go to** chapter 19

electrolyte   Any chemical, such as a mineral, that when melted or dissolved in water will show an electrical attraction or conduct an electric current.

electron   A negatively charged particle that moves in an orbit about the nucleus of an atom.

element   A substance composed of atoms with the same atomic number or the same number of protons in their nuclei. Examples include oxygen, hydrogen, carbon, and gold.

hydrocarbon   Any of a large group of chemical compounds consisting primarily of carbon and hydrogen atoms, usually associated with current or past life processes.

hydroxyl   Pertaining to the negatively charged OH (oxygen + hydrogen) radical in an organic compound.

inorganic chemistry   A branch of chemical science that deals primarily with elements and compounds that do not include hydrocarbons.

isotope   One of two or more atoms having the same atomic number but a different mass number due to the different number of neutrons in their nuclei. An example is zinc, which has isotopes with five different mass numbers ranging from 64 to 70. However, all of the isotopes have equal nuclear charges, orbital electrons, and chemical properties.

mass number   The atomic weight of an isotope, calculated from the numbers of protons and neutrons in the nucleus.

matter   Anything that has weight or fills space, such as a solid, liquid, or gas.

organic chemistry   A branch of chemistry that specializes in the composition, properties, and reactions of hydrocarbon compounds.

oxidation   Any chemical reaction that increases the number of oxygen atoms in a compound, or in which the positive valence is increased by a loss of electrons.

pH A symbol for hydrogen ion activity of a substance as an expression of the negative logarithm of the concentration of hydrogen ions in moles per liter. Values of pH range from 0 to 14, with a pH of 7 representing acid-base neutrality. The degree of acidity increases as the number progresses toward zero, while alkalinity increases as the pH number approaches 14.

polymer A huge molecule composed of repeating units of the same molecule. An example is polyethylene, formed by linking ethylene molecules into a giant chain.

reduction A chemical reaction in which a substance gains electrons or loses part of its positive valence. Reduction generally occurs in a reaction that also involves oxidation.

solute A substance that is dissolved in a solution.

solvent The substance that represents the greatest proportion of parts of a solution when two or more substances, such as a solid and liquid, are mixed.

valence A number that represents the combining power of an element, ion, or radical. The valence of hydrogen is +1, while the valence of oxygen is –2.

GEOLOGY AND GEOPHYSICS

LAYERS OF THE EARTH

Because the Earth's interior is inaccessible to observation, geologists have discerned its many layers by indirect methods. Earthquakes reveal the Earth's interior structure because certain seismic waves travel at varying speeds through materials of different densities. Other properties of the planet's interior can be inferred from magnetic, thermal, and gravitational characteristics.

CRUST

The Earth's outer solid *crust* surrounds the mantle. The crust makes up about 0.6 percent of the Earth's volume and 0.4 percent of its mass. Its overall thickness varies widely: beneath the oceans, the crust (mainly composed of basalt) ranges between 3 and 6.8 miles (5 to 11 kilometers) thick; beneath the continents, the crust (mostly light rocks such as granite) ranges between 12 and 40 miles (19 and 64 kilometers) thick.

The upper layer of the Earth is called the *lithosphere.* It includes the oceanic and continental crusts and part of the cooler, solid upper mantle.

MANTLE

The *mantle* makes up 84 percent of the Earth by volume and 67 percent by mass. It is about 1,802 miles (2,900 kilometers) thick and consists of silica, plus iron-, magnesium-, and other metal-rich minerals. The *Gutenberg discontinuity* separates the Earth's mantle from the outer core; the *Mohoovičić discontinuity* separates the uppermost portion of the mantle from the crust.

If the 4.6 billion years of Earth's existence were only a single day, the 40,000 years of human existence would cover only the last 2 seconds.

The hot plastic *asthenosphere,* part upper mantle and lower crust, separates the more brittle crust-mantle lithosphere above from the mesosphere below. Thought to be responsible for the movement of the lithospheric plates (crustal plates) that slowly "carry" the continents around the planet, the asthenosphere is about 186 miles (300 kilometers) thick. The more solid *mesosphere,* located below the asthenosphere, includes part of the upper mantle and all of the lower mantle.

CORE

The inner and outer *core* make up about 15 percent of the Earth by volume and 32 percent by mass. The *inner core* is about 800 miles (1,287 kilometers) thick; the *outer core* is about 1,400 miles (2,253 kilometers) thick. The inner core, thought to be solid, extends from the center of the Earth to the lower border of the outer core. The outer core, which appears to have characteristics of a liquid, extends to

Sciences

the Gutenberg discontinuity, the border between the mantle and outer core. Because of its extreme density, the entire core seems to be composed of mostly iron, with smaller amounts of other dense elements such as nickel. The pressure within the solid inner core reaches about 3 million atmospheres (1 atmosphere equals the atmospheric pressure at sea level); temperatures measure between 7,200 and 9,000°F (4,000 to 5,000°C)—nearly as hot as the Sun's surface. The heat is from the natural radioactive decay of uranium; it is also from dissipated heat from the Earth as it cooled after formation.

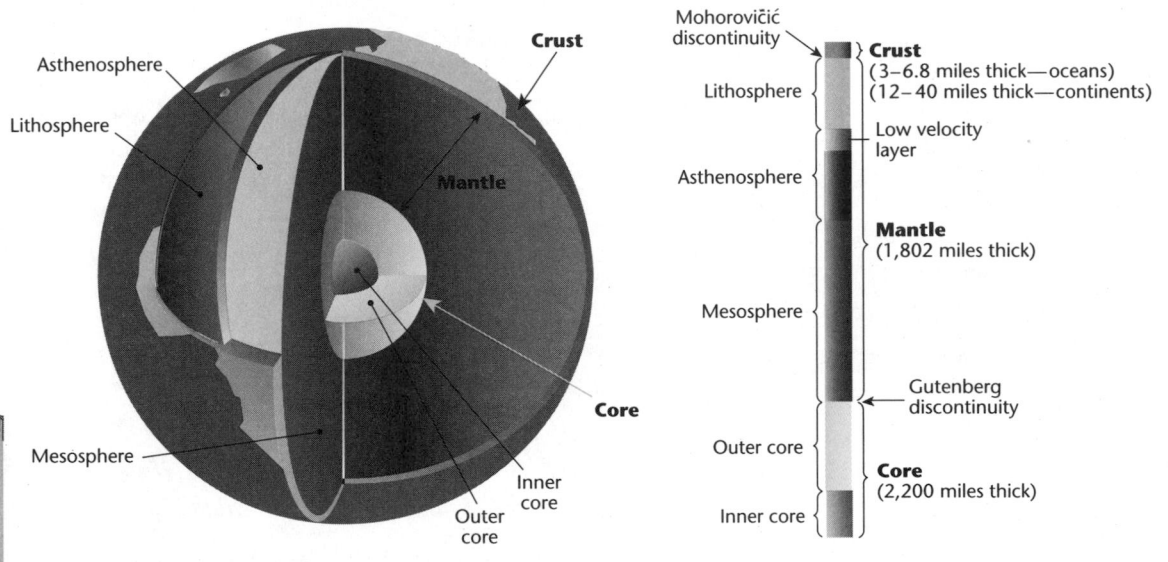

GEOLOGIC TIME SCALE

Age in Millions of Years	Era	Period or Epoch		Important Physical Events	Animal Life
		Quaternary	Holocene	Repeated extensions of ice caps in arctic and north temperate areas	Modern human beings
.01 ▶			Pleistocene	Continents generally elevated, mountains high, deserts widespread	Primitive man
±.5 ▶	CENOZOIC	Tertiary	Pliocene	Mountain building in northwestern North America. Deformation of Tethys geosyncline; Alps and Himalayas rise	Gorillas
13 ±1 ▶			Miocene	Extensive erosion surfaces cut on Appalachians and Rockies. Cool, dry climates over much of world	Whales, sabertooths
25 ±1 ▶			Oligocene	Initiation of mountain building in Tethys geosyncline. River and floodplain deposits begin on Great Plains	Apes, bats

MILLIONS OF YEARS BEFORE THE PRESENT

Age in Millions of Years	Era	Period or Epoch		Important Physical Events	Animal Life
36±2 ▶	CENOZOIC	Tertiary	Eocene	Climates warm and uniform; widespread jungles and forests	Alligators
58±2 ▶			Paleocene	Basins develop between ranges along Pacific Coast and Rockies	Kangaroos, birds, horses, camels, monkeys, elephants
65 ±2 ▶	MESOZOIC	Cretaceous		Mountain building in Rockies; seas invade much of western North America and cover Atlantic and Gulf coastal plains	Ancient birds, snakes, modern fish
135 ±5 ▶		Jurassic		Widespread mild, uniform climates Mountain building along Pacific Coast of North America Extensive marine invasions of southern and central Europe	Flying reptiles
180 ± ▶		Triassic		Fault basins in eastern North America Extensive deserts and dead seas develop in North America and Eurasia	Ichthyosaurs, tyrannosaurs
230 ±10 ▶	PALEOZOIC	Permian		Continents generally elevated Appalachian and Ural mountains complete their development Tethys geosyncline from Spain to India	Ammonites, finbacked reptiles
280 ±10 ▶		Carboniferous		Mountain building in southern North America and central Europe Extensive seas over much of interior North America	Amphibians, clams, lung fish
310 ±10 ▶		Devonian		Catskill delta built from New England mountains into New York and Pennsylvania Mountain building in northeastern North America Extensive submergence of geosynclines and interior of North America	Starfish
405 ±10 ▶		Silurian		Formation of Caledonian mountains in northwestern Europe Dead seas in Michigan, New York, Ohio, southeastern Canada Deltas and gravel beaches along eastern edge of Appalachian geosyncline	Sea scorpions, corals, sharks
425 ±10 ▶		Ordovician		Mountain building in northeastern North America Over 60 percent of North American continent covered by seas	Snails, jawless fish, echinoids
500 ±10 ▶		Cambrian		Climates generally mild and uniform Seas invade North American continent Geosynclines develop around edge of North America	Protozoans, trilobites

MILLIONS OF YEARS BEFORE THE PRESENT

Sciences

continues

Geologic Time Scale, Continued

Age in Millions of Years	Era	Period or Epoch	Important Physical Events	Animal Life
c. 600 ▶			Fault basins in Lake Superior region	Jellyfish, flagellates, amoebas, worms, sponges
1,000 ▶	PRECAMBRIAN		Deformation and mountain building through central North America	
2,000 ▶			Geosynclines develop throughout central North America	
3,000 ▶			Extensive mountain building in Lake Superior region Oldest dated rocks	
4,000 ▶			Probable origin of Earth from solar dust cloud	

This is only one interpretation of the geologic time scale. As scientists uncover more fossils and information about rock layers, the times, events, and animal life entries change.

PLATE TECTONICS

The theory of *plate tectonics* states that the lithosphere is divided into plates, or tabular blocks, that interact with each other over time. The crust and part of the solid upper mantle make up each crustal plate.

About 13 major crustal (lithospheric or tectonic) plates and many more small plates within the larger plates make up the Earth's crust, all moving in different directions and at various speeds (fractions of an inch per year). Most plates lie beneath a combination of ocean and continent; several lie only beneath ocean.

The true mechanism for the movement of the crustal plates is still unknown. Scientists theorize that convection in the upper mantle–lower crust, or asthenosphere, slowly "carries" the lithospheric plates around the planet; another theory states that convection in the mesosphere is transferred to the asthenosphere and moves the plates.

Crustal plates are created, are destroyed, and move past each other in a variety of ways.

Go to   "The Animal Kingdom" and "The Plant Kingdom" in chapter 3; "Major Zoos and Aquariums" and "Major Botanical Gardens and Arboretums" in chapter 11

Plate movement in ocean basins includes *seafloor spreading,* or diverging plates. A rift in the ocean floor constantly forms new crustal material—usually from volcanic action—and the ocean floor literally spreads apart. For example, the Mid-Atlantic Ridge is an area of seafloor spreading that splits the Atlantic Ocean; the plates move laterally about 1 inch (2.54 centimeters) per year. Shallow, substantial earthquakes are associated with diverging plates.

When one plate sinks under another, it is called *subduction,* with the subducting plate gradually breaking apart. The destructive plate margins where this occurs are called *subduction zones.* The surface expression of this activity takes the form of volcanic island areas associated with oceanic trenches, or a volcanic mountain region on an adjacent landmass. For example, the Japan Trench off the island of Honshu is the line where the Pacific plate subducts under the Eurasian plate. Some of the largest and deepest earthquakes are associated with subducting plates.

When two plates ram into one another, it is called *colliding plate boundaries,* causing the crust to buckle from intense pressure. For example, the Himalayas were formed by the collision of the Indo-Australian plate and the Eurasian plate. The Himalayas are still

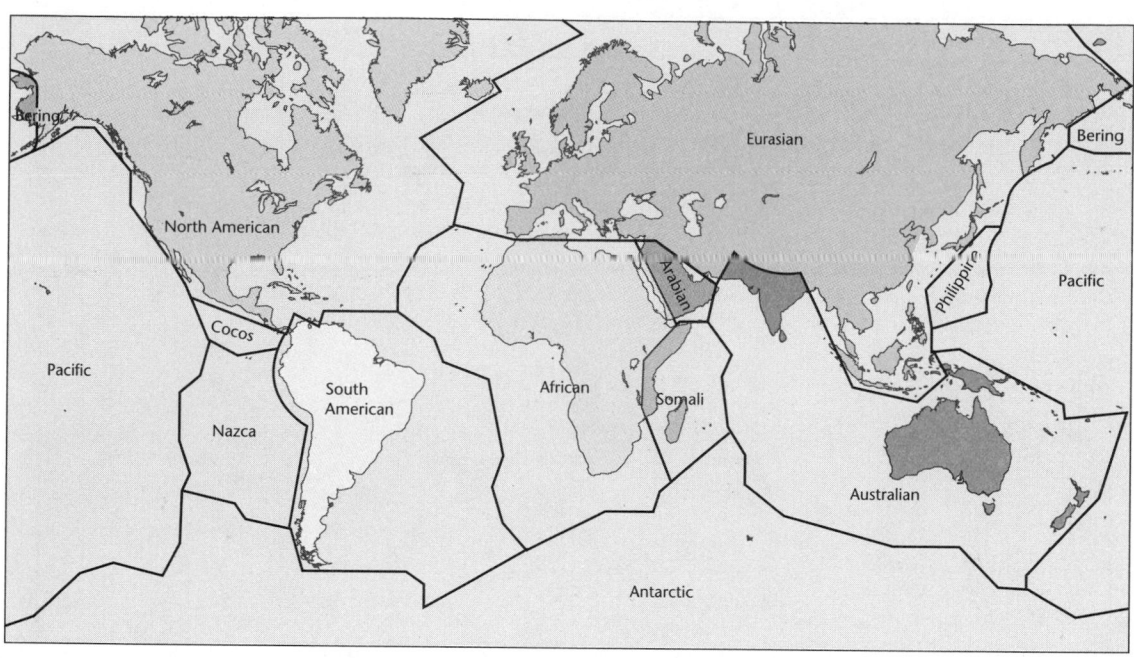

Crustal Plates Around the World (locations of crustal plates are approximate)

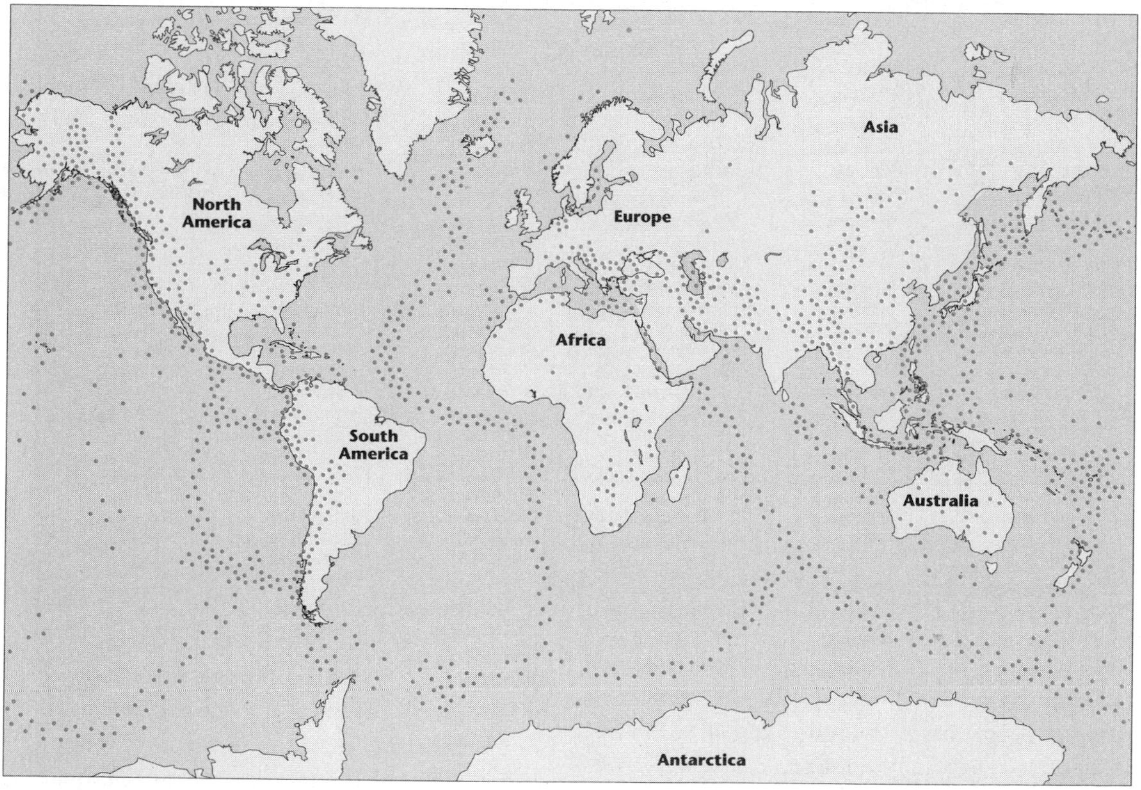

Major Earthquake and Volcanic Zones

Measuring an Earthquake

A Closer Look

Two scales have gained notoriety in the past decades: the Mercalli Earthquake Intensity Scale and the Richter Scale. The first, although now rarely used, was developed by Italian seismologist Giuseppe Mercalli in 1902 and measures an earthquake's destructiveness. The scale was modified by American seismologists in the 1930s and is known as the Modified Mercalli Scale.

Modern technology has made the Mercalli scale obsolete, although the method is often used to fill in "seismic blanks" when there is an insufficient number of seismic instruments—especially in remote areas. The more prominent scale is the Richter Scale, developed in 1935 by Charles Richter. The scale is logarithmic, which means that each successive whole number represents a 10-fold increase in power. Each magnitude number represents the maximum amplitude of a seismic wave at a distance of 62 miles (100 kilometers).

Richter Scale of Earthquake Magnitude

Magnitude	Energy equivalent in weight of TNT	Example
1.0	170 grams	
1.5	900 grams	
2.0	5.9 kilograms	
2.5	28 kilograms	
3.0	179 kilograms	
3.5	450 kilograms	
4.0	5.5 metric tons	
4.5	29 metric tons	Denver, Colorado (1965)
5.0	181 metric tons	
5.3	455 metric tons	San Francisco, California (1957)
5.5	910 metric tons	
6.0	5.7×10^3 metric tons	
6.3	14.4×10^3 metric tons	Long Beach, California (1933)
6.5	28.7×10^3 metric tons	San Fernando, California (1971)
7.0	181×10^3 metric tons	
7.1	228×10^3 metric tons	El Centro, California (1940)
7.5	910×10^3 metric tons	
7.7	1811×10^3 metric tons	Kern County, California (1962)
8.0	5706×10^3 metric tons	
8.2	$11,421 \times 10^3$ metric tons	San Francisco, California (1906)
8.5	$28,711 \times 10^3$ metric tons	Anchorage, Alaska (1964)
9.0	$181,999 \times 10^3$ metric tons	

Thanks to new techniques and more precise instrumentation, seismologists now use their own version of an earthquake scale to measure quakes. But the Richter Scale is still used by the popular press, because so many readers are familiar with it.

rising because of that collision—about ⅕ inch (5 millimeters) per year. Deep, substantial earthquakes are associated with colliding plates.

When plates slide by each other and no plate is created or destroyed, it is called a *strike-slip plate margin* (or *transform fault*). For example, along the San Andreas Fault in California, the Pacific plate slides northwest past the North American plate. Shallow, substantial earthquakes are associated with transform boundary plates.

Crustal plates have moved across the planet for at least the past 600 million years. Scientists believe that a supercontinent called *Pangaea,* first proposed by Alfred Wegener in 1915, existed about 250 million years ago. By 180 million years ago, the supercontinent had broken up into *Gondwanaland,* or Gondwana (a hypothetical continent formed by the union of South America, Africa, Australia, India, and Antarctica), and *Laurasia* (composed of North

Sciences

America and Eurasia). About 65 million years ago—at approximately the time of extinction of the dinosaurs—the two continents began to separate, slowly forming the familiar outlines of today's continents. Scientists estimate that in 50 million years, the west coast of North America will tear itself free from the mainland, Australia will move northward and collide with Indonesia, and Africa and Asia will split apart at the Red Sea.

See also "Earth's Layers" and "Earthquakes" in this chapter.

EARTHQUAKES

Earthquakes are considered one of the most deadly natural catastrophes that can affect human life. Most often, a quake occurs in an earthquake-prone zone where two tectonic plates meet, split, or slip by one another (*see* "Plate Tectonics," earlier in this chapter); the type of plate contact determines whether the earthquake will be shallow or deep. During the movement of these plates, intense forces overcome the friction between the plates. If the plates become "locked together," forces build up and eventually must give away—with the plates lurching into new positions and creating an earthquake. Other earthquakes form in association with volcanic regions, where the buildup of heat and pressure often triggers smaller tremors and localized quakes.

The *focus* is the point under the Earth's surface where the earthquake energy is released. The point on the surface just above the focus is called the *epicenter.* Most earthquake foci occur no more than 62 miles (100 kilometers) below the surface.

SOME IMPORTANT MINERALS AND THEIR USES

Mineral	Chemical Composition	Occurrence/ Important Producers	Uses
Arsenic	As	Chile, China, France, Sweden, Mexico, U.S.	Glassmaking, insecticides, preservatives
Beryl	$Be_3Al_{12}Si_6O_{18}$	Brazil, South Africa, U.S.	Beryllium ore, gemstones
Borax	$Na_2B_4O_7 10H_2O$	Tibet, U.S.	Antiseptic, disinfectant, flux, soap, water softener
Calcite	$CaCO_3$	Worldwide*	Building stones, portland cement, quicklime, soil conditioner
Chromite	$FeCr_2O_4$	Brazil, Philippines, South Africa, Turkey, former USSR	Chemicals, chromium ore, refractories
Chrysotile (serpentine)	$Mg_3Si_2O_5(OH)_4$	Canada, Russia, U.S.	Asbestos
Copper	Cu	Canada, Chile, Russia, U.S.	Chemicals, electronics, metal alloys, wire
Corundum	Al_2O_3	Greece, India, Myanmar, Sri Lanka, Thailand, U.S.	Abrasives, bearings, gemstones
Diamond	C	Australia, Brazil, South Africa, U.S.	Drills, gemstones, industrial abrasives, jewelry, tools and dies
Dolomite	$CaMg(CO_3)_2$	Worldwide†	Building stones, cement productions, magnesium source, refractories
Emerald	$Be_3Al_2Si_6O_{18}$	Australia, Columbia, Rhodesia, U.S., former USSR	Gemstones
Fluorite	CaF_2	Germany, Mexico, U.S.	Chemicals, metallurgy, optics
Gold	Au	Australia, Canada, South Africa, U.S.	Coins, dentistry, electronics, jewelry
Graphite	C	Madagascar, Mexico, Sri Lanka, U.S.	Brake linings, electronics, lubricants, pencils

* Usually mined as limestone or marble.   † Usually mined as the rock dolomite.

continues

Sciences

Some Important Minerals and Their Uses, Continued

Mineral	Chemical Composition	Occurrence/ Important Producers	Uses
Gypsum	$CaSO_4 \cdot 2H_2O$	Canada, France, Great Britain, Mexico, U.S.	Building materials, flux, plaster of paris, retardant (in cement)
Halite	$NaCl$	Worldwide	Chemical, rock salt
Hematite	Fe_2O_3	Brazil, Canada, U.S., Venezuela	Iron ore, pigment, polishing agent
Kaolinite	$Al_4Si_4O_{10}(OH)_2$	Worldwide/esp. England	Ceramics (esp. porcelain), paper (as coating)
Limonite	$Fe_2O_3 \cdot 3H_2O$	Worldwide/esp. U.S.	Iron ore, pigment
Magnesite	$MgCO_3$	Austria, China, U.S.	Cement production, chemicals, magnesium ore, refractories
Mercury	Hg	Mexico, Spain, U.S.	Barometers and thermometers, dentistry, electronics, lamps, medicines
Olivine	$(Mg,Fe)_2SiO_4$	Myanmar, U.S.	Gemstones, ornamental stone, refractories
Opal	SiO_2H_2O	Australia, Honduras, Mexico, U.S.	Gemstones
Platinum	Pt	Canada, South Africa, former USSR	Jewelry, catalytic converters, oil refining
Quartz	SiO	Worldwide	Building materials, electronics, gems, glass manufacture, jewelry, optics
Ruby	Al_2O_3	Myanmar, Sri Lanka, Thailand	Bearings, lasers, gemstones
Sapphire	Al_2O_3	Australia, Myanmar, Sri Lanka, Thailand, U.S.	Bearings, dies, gauges, gemstones
Siderite	$FeCO_3$	Germany, Great Britain	Iron ore
Silver	Ag	Canada, Mexico, Peru, U.S.	Coins, electronics, electroplating, jewelry, photography, silverware
Spinel	$MgAl_2O_4$	Myanmar, Sri Lanka, Thailand, U.S.	Gemstones
Sulfur	S	Worldwide/esp. Mexico, U.S.	Chemicals, explosives, fertilizers, sulfa drugs, sulfuric acid
Talc	$Mg_3Si_4O_{10}(OH)$	Brazil, France, Japan, U.S.	Ceramics, face powder, lubricants, paints, paper (as filler), sinks and countertops, talcum powder
Topaz	$Al_2SiO_4(F,OH)_2$	Brazil, Russia, U.S.	Gemstones
Uraninite	UO_2	Canada, South Africa, U.S.	Uranium ore (pitchblende)
Wolframite	$(Fe,Mn)WO_4$	Australia, England, Malay Peninsula, Myanmar, Portugal	Tungsten ore
Wollastonite	$CaSiO_3$	Finland, Italy, Romania, U.S.	Ceramics, paints (as filler)
Zircon	$ZrSiO_4$	Australia, Brazil, India, Sri Lanka, U.S.	Gemstones, zirconium ore

IGNEOUS, SEDIMENTARY, AND METAMORPHIC ROCKS

Igneous rocks are formed by the cooling and subsequent hardening of molten material. Intrusive igneous rocks are produced when magma hardens slowly underground. Extrusive igneous rocks result when lava, molten material that flows on the surface, solidifies quickly.

Sedimentary rocks form from the accumulation of eroded material that is transported and deposited by water, wind, or glaciers. Detrital sediments result when preexisting rock erodes; chemical sediments occur through precipitation in shallow marine environments.

Metamorphic rocks form when preexisting igneous or sedimentary rocks are transformed by external forces. Regional metamorphism alters rocks through heat and pressure. Contact metamorphism occurs when a magma intrusion heats the surrounding rock. Dynamic metamorphism is the product of tectonic forces, usually along thrust faults.

Sciences

IGNEOUS, SEDIMENTARY, AND METAMORPHIC ROCKS

Name	Type	Texture	Mineral Composition
Igneous			
Andesite	Extrusive	Coarse grains/crystalline	Feldspar, pyroxene, mica
Anorthosite	Intrusive	Coarse grains/crystalline	Feldspar; traces of iron oxides, pyroxene, olivine
Basalt	Extrusive	Fine grains/crystalline	Feldspar, pyroxene, usu. magnetite
Gabbro	Intrusive	Coarse grains/crystalline	Feldspar, pyroxene, olivine, magnetite
Granite	Intrusive	Coarse grains/crystalline	Quartz, feldspar; mica, hornblende, muscovite often present
Obsidian	Extrusive	Glassy/crystalline	Silicate minerals, often quartz and feldspar
Pegmatite	Intrusive	Coarse grains/crystalline	Quartz, feldspar; mica or pyroxene often present
Porphyry	Intrusive	Medium grains/crystalline	Feldspar, quartz, olivine, or pyroxene embedded in dark-colored groundmass
Pumice	Extrusive	Fine grains/crystalline	Quartz, feldspar
Rhyolite	Extrusive	Fine grains/often glassy/crystalline	Quarty, alkali feldspars, light-colored
Sedimentary			
Breccia	Detrital	Coarse, angular grains	Cemented rock fragments; calcite or silica
Chalk	Chemical	Fine, rounded grains	Calcite
Chert	Chemical	Fine grains/crystalline	Silica
Clay	Detrital	Fine, angular grains	Clay minerals, quartz, feldspar, mica
Coal	Chemical	Fine-medium grains	Organic matter (high carbon content)
Conglomerate	Detrital	Coarse, rounded grains	Cemented rock fragments; silica, iron oxides, or calcite
Dolomite	Chemical	Fine-coarse grains/crystalline	Dolomite
Flint	Chemical	Fine grains/crystalline	Silica
Gypsum	Chemical	Crystalline	Gypsum
Limestone	Chemical	Fine-coarse, angular, or rounded grains	Calcite; lesser amounts of quartz, organic matter, or fossils often present
Sandstone	Detrital	Medium, angular or rounded grains	Quartz; lesser amounts of calcite, silica, iron oxides, feldspar, or mica
Shale	Detrital	Fine, angular grains	Clay minerals, mica, usu. organic matter or fossils
Siltstone	Detrital	Fine, angular grains	Quartz, calcite
Metamorphic			
Gneiss	Regional	Coarse grains/foliated, crystalline	Quartz, feldspar; garnet, hornblende, mica may be present
Marble	Contact	Coarse-fine grains/crystalline	Calcite or dolomite
Quartzite	Contact	Coarse grains/nonfoliated	Quartz
Schist	Regional	Medium grains/foliated	Quartz, feldspar, mica
Slate	Regional	Fine grains/foliated	Quartz, feldspar, mica, clay minerals

COMMON GEOLOGY AND CARTOGRAPHY TERMS

Additional terms are defined in the preceding geology and geophysics sections.

abyssal zone A region of greatest ocean depth, generally greater than 328 feet (100 meters), including the deep-sea trenches. Biological activity is rare in the abyssal zone; light does not penetrate the water, as the depth and pressure are tremendous. The region represents about 96,525,000 square miles (250 million square kilometers) of Earth's surface.

age   An interval of geological time that indicates when a body of rock was formed in the surface of Earth. A group of ages forms an epoch.

alluvium   The sediment carried by rivers, including deposits from estuaries, lakes, and other freshwater bodies draining into a river. The particles of sediment are generally smaller than 0.000788 inch (0.02 millimeters), depending on such factors as valleyside slopes in the watershed, the distance carried downstream, and progressive wear on the particles as they move downstream.

barrier beach   An accumulation of sand, rock, and other material lying parallel to the coast but separated from it by a channel; a barrier beach measures from a few yards to a few miles in width. Large barrier beaches may be identified as barrier islands. They are formed by the action of waves but are usually vulnerable to overwashing or breaching during severe storms.

bathyal zone   A zone of ocean water ranging from about 656 to 3,281 feet (200 to 1,000 meters) in depth, generally located along continental slopes. Unlike the abyssal zone, light reaches the upper layer of the bathyal zone, and there is abundant biological activity in the water. The bathyal zone of the world covers a total of about 15,444,000 square miles (40 million square kilometers).

bed   The smallest division of stratified sedimentary rock, usually occurring as a relatively thin sheet of sedimentary material separating distinctively different layers above and below it. A bed often marks a particular event in geologic history, such as a volcanic eruption, and it may contain fossils that help identify its age.

Cambrian   The earliest period of the Paleozoic era, about 600 million years ago. Rocks formed at this period contain some of the earliest fossil remains of invertebrate animals.

"Major Science and Technology Museums and Their Special Collections" in chapter 11
Go to

continental drift   The shifting of continental landmasses from one location to another on the face of Earth, owing to seafloor spreading.

Coriolis effect   A force produced on objects moving on a north-south line on the surface of Earth because of the angular velocity of Earth as it rotates from west to east. Thus, a projectile fired directly southward from the North Pole would be deviated to the west. The Coriolis force affects mainly the flow of air in the atmosphere.

creep   The slowest mass movement of rock and soil on gentle slopes with angles of less than 20 degrees. The movement—usually fractions of an inch per year—is caused by freezing, thawing, wetting, drying, and the force of gravity. The effect can be observed in the tendency of telephone poles, tombstones, and other objects to change position (especially tilt) on gentle slopes over a period of years.

diagenesis   The process whereby sedimentary rock is formed from sediment because of compaction, reduced pore space between particles, and chemical reactions between molecules of the compressed particles and dissolved substances in moisture between the particles.

era   An interval of geological time composed of a group of periods.

estuary   The portion of a river that is affected by ocean tides above the mouth, with a resulting mixture of salt water and fresh water. Most estuaries are former valleys that were flooded by rising ocean levels after the last glacial event. The Hudson River is an example of an estuary.

fjord   A narrow sea inlet between mountain slopes. Most fjords were once glaciated valleys that became flooded by rising sea water after the last ice age. In some cases, the bottom of the fjord may be lower than the bottom of the sea at its opening into the fjord.

geology   The science of the structure and composition of Earth.

glacier   An accumulation of land ice that develops in the colder regions and higher latitudes of the Earth. It is formed by compaction of accumulated snow moving downslope from a source area because of the force of gravity. A glacier is usually confined within the limited space of a valley or basin. It may be gaining ice at the source but losing ice at a point where it melts while moving into warmer temperatures or a body of water.

intermittent stream   A stream, often in reference to desert areas, that carries water only part of the time, usually during a flash flood.

lava   *See* **magma.**

leaching   The action of water draining through soil layers carrying dissolved minerals or organic matter from the upper layers. Because leaching tends to remove alkaline substances, the soils eventually become acidic.

magma   Hot, molten material from deep underground, usually associated with volcanic eruptions. Magma that reaches the surface is called lava.

Mercator projection   A map in which the spherical Earth is projected as a cylinder onto a flat surface, resulting in straight-line bearings that are correct. Such a map is most commonly used for navigation charts, although the projection distorts the areas toward the North and South poles.

meridian   A line of longitude. It is formed by creating an imaginary line that approximates a semicircle around the Earth through both poles and at a right angle to the equator.

mesa   An isolated, flat-topped plateau with steep sides. Composed of limestone or hard sandstone, the mesa's top rock is usually more resistant to erosion than the underlying rock. Mesas eventually erode into buttes. Mesas are common in arid parts of the southwestern United States and Mexico.

metal   Any elementary substance, such as gold, copper, or silver, that is crystalline when solid and typically displays opacity, ductility, conductivity, and luster. Metals may be found in their natural state or in combination with other minerals, commonly called ores.

mid-ocean ridge   A ridge of volcanic mountains on the ocean floor, usually associated with seafloor spreading of crustal plates. These ridges occasionally rise above the surface and form volcanic islands such as Iceland, located on the Mid-Atlantic Ridge.

mineral   An inorganic compound naturally occurring in the Earth's crust and having a precise chemical formula and usually a crystalline structure. Minerals vary greatly in size, shape, color, and economic value. With the exception of natural glasses such as obsidian, they are the basic building blocks of rocks.

moraine   A mound or ridge of unstratified rock and dirt deposited by a glacier. Moraines may dam up melting glacier water, forming circular mountain lakes called tarns or long, narrow lakes such as those found in New York State's Finger Lakes region.

mountain   A naturally formed elevation that rises above the surrounding landmass and is higher than a hill, usually 2,000 feet (610 meters) or more. Mountains are formed by subduction (when a lithospheric plate dives under another plate) or by a collision between continental landmasses. The latter processes produced the Andes and the Himalayas, respectively. Volcanoes can also form singular or chains of mountains.

parallel   A line of latitude. It is formed by creating an imaginary line that runs parallel to the equator and connects places with the same latitude.

permafrost   A deep layer of soil that remains frozen during summer, despite the thawing of the ground above it. The result is in the poorly drained landscape typical of the arctic regions of Canada and northern Europe, especially the former Soviet Union.

plateau   A broad, flat land area raised sharply above the surrounding landscape on at least one side. They form where erosion-resistant rock rests on weaker rocks or soil.

Sciences

prime meridian   The line of zero degrees longitude that runs through Greenwich, England, and from which all other lines of longitude (meridians) are measured.

projection   In cartography, a systematic construction of intersecting coordinate lines on a flat surface, representing the meridians and parallels of the curved surface of the Earth. Each method of projection results in some distortion of the planet's features; *See* **Mercator projection** for an example.

relief   The variations in elevation and slope between the higher and lower parts of a given landscape. A map displaying these contour changes is called a relief map.

rock   an aggregate of minerals; generally classified as igneous, sedimentary, and metamorphic.

sand   Small, loose, granular substance formed by the disintegration of rock due to erosion. Consisting mostly of silicates, sand has a number of industrial uses, especially in abrasives and glassmaking.

scale   The ratio of the actual size of a place or region and its representation on a map.

seamount   An isolated submarine mountain that rises from the abyssal plain of the ocean floor but does not reach the surface of the water. Seamounts are volcanic in origin and may develop at points where the oceanic crustal plate passes over hot spots. Their existence may be an indirect proof of the theory of plate tectonics.

seismology   The study of the seismic waves generated by earthquakes or artificially produced vibrations of the Earth. Seismologists use these waves, measured on a seismograph, to locate petroleum reserves or to estimate the size and location of the Earth's plates.

soil   The layer of unconsolidated, fragmented, weathered rock mixed with organic material that makes up the topmost surface of the Earth.

stalactite   A columnar deposit, usually of calcium carbonate, hanging from the ceiling of a cave. It is formed by the precipitation of mineral-rich water and is often shaped like an icicle.

stalagmite   A columnar deposit, usually of calcium carbonate, that forms on a cavern floor. It is caused by the precipitation of mineral-rich water dripping from the ceiling.

stone   A concretion of mineral matter of indeterminate size and shape.

trench   A long, deep valley found on the ocean floor and bordering a subduction zone. Formed by the downward movement of one oceanic plate as it is consumed by another, a trench is associated with the creation of new oceanic crust. The Marianas Trench is the deepest in the world, measuring 36,201 feet (11,034 meters).

tundra   A vast, level, treeless plain characteristic of arctic and subarctic regions, especially in northern Europe, Asia, and North America. The top layer of the soil thaws each spring, while the base remains frozen, resulting in boggy areas. The dominant vegetation consists of mosses, lichens, and dwarf shrubs.

vent   An opening in the Earth's crust through which volcanic materials are violently expelled. Hydrothermal vents on ocean floors emit mineral-rich solutions that support a fantastic array of life, including tubeworms.

volcano   A vent in a mountain or the Earth's crust through which gases, rock fragments, and hot, molten lava are expelled from the Earth's interior. Volcanic eruptions usually occur along subduction zones or above hot spots, places where magma from the Earth's mantle upwells and melts through the crust.

water table   The irregular upper surface of underground water. It is usually highest beneath hills (though still farther below the surface) and about the same level as river channels in valleys.

weathering   The alteration or decomposition of rocks or soil by heat, cold, wind, precipitation, or chemical reactions, such as leaching, brought on by contact with the atmosphere.

METEOROLOGY

CLOUD TYPES

altocumulus (Ac)   Similar to cirrocumulus, with patches of small clouds occasionally separated by thin breaks. Although altocumulus clouds also may be identified by a "mackerel sky" pattern, they are lower, at around 10,000 feet, and the clumps of white or gray water droplets or ice crystals are larger. The clouds may develop directly overhead, depending on the temperature of the atmosphere, and may produce a shower.

altostratus (As)   Dull, drab gray or blue middle-level clouds that usually contain moisture in the form of water droplets. Altostratus clouds are often opaque, giving a "ground glass" view of the Sun or Moon behind them. They may be a source of virga, filaments of ice crystals or water droplets that fall toward Earth but evaporate before touching the ground.

cirrocumulus (Cc)   Loosely packed sheets of small white cloud segments at altitudes of around 18,000 to 20,000 feet, forming a "mackerel sky" resembling scales on a fish. The clouds may consist of ice crystals or water droplets or both. The patchy appearance is caused by vertical air currents at the cloud level, indicating a lack of stability and a possible approaching storm.

cirrostratus (Co)   Translucent veils of white fibrous cloud that tend to occur at altitudes of around 20,000 feet or more. Cirrostratus clouds often cover the entire sky and may cause the appearance of halos or reflected images of the Sun or Moon. These clouds may signal an approaching storm.

cirrus (Ci)   Generally, the highest clouds, forming "mares' tails" at altitudes from 20,000 to 40,000 feet. The clouds may appear as delicate white filaments, featherlike tufts, or fibrous bands of ice crystals.

cumulonimbus (Cb)   Thunderstorm clouds that may vary considerably in altitude from ominously dark lower portions below 5,000 feet to white anvil-shaped tops that may reach upward to 50,000 feet. They contain large amounts of moisture, some of which may be in the form of hail. The cumulonimbus

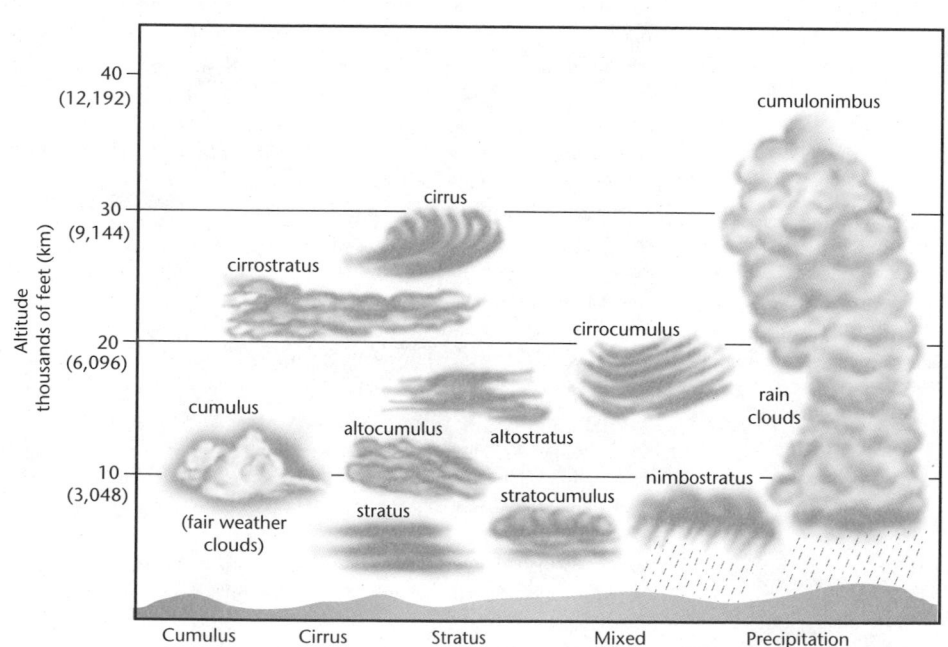

cloud may appear alone or as part of a wall of advancing storm clouds.

cumulus (Cu)   Low-level billowy clouds that are usually dark on the bottom while their tops resemble giant white cotton balls. A cumulus cloud may be relatively tall, extending from a base around 2,000 feet to a top near 10,000 feet above ground. It casts a dark shadow and may be a source of moisture but generally produces no more than a summer shower.

nimbostratus (Ns)   Low, dark rain clouds with ragged tops that have bottoms only a few hundred feet above ground and may range upward to an altitude of 3,000 feet. They obscure the Sun and are associated with continuous rain, sleet, or snow, but they are rarely accompanied by thunder or lightning.

stratocumulus (Sc)   Dark gray rolls of clouds that usually cover the entire sky at an altitude from 1,500 to 6,500 feet. The rounded segments may appear checkered or wavelike, and there may or may not be breaks of blue sky between segments. Stratocumulus clouds contain moisture but are usually not rain producers.

stratus (St)   Wispy foglike clouds that hover a few hundred feet above ground, sometimes obscuring hills or tall buildings. They may begin as ground fog and can be a source of drizzle.

BEAUFORT SCALE OF WIND FORCE

Beaufort Number	Knots	Description	Effect at Sea	Effect Ashore
0	Less than 1	Calm	Sea is like a mirror.	Smoke rises vertically.
1	1–3	Light air	Ripples with the appearance of a scale are formed but without foam crests.	Wind vanes are not moved, but wind direction is shown by smoke drift.
2	4–6	Light breeze	Small wavelets, still short but more pronounced, appear; crests have a glassy appearance but do not break.	Wind is felt on face; leaves rustle; ordinary vane is moved by wind.
3	7–10	Gentle breeze	Large wavelets appear; crests begin to break; foam is of glassy appearance, perhaps with scattered whitecaps.	Leaves and small twigs are in constant motion; wind extends light flag.
4	11–16	Moderate breeze	Small waves appear, becoming longer; there are fairly frequent whitecaps.	Dust and loose paper are raised; small branches are moved.
5	17–21	Fresh breeze	Moderate waves arise, taking a more pronounced long form; many whitecaps are formed (with chance of some spray).	Small trees in leaf begin to sway; crested wavelets form on island waters.
6	22–27	Strong breeze	Large waves begin to form; the white foam crests are more extensive everywhere (probably with some spray).	Large branches are in motion; whistling is heard in telegraph wires; umbrellas are used with difficulty.
7	28–33	Moderate gale (high wind)	Sea heaps up, and white foam from breaking waves begins to be blown in streaks along the direction of the wind; spindrift begins.	Whole trees are in motion; inconvenience is felt in walking against the wind.
8	34–40	Fresh gale	Moderately high waves of greater length appear; edges of crests break into spindrift. The foam is blown in well-marked streaks along the direction of the wind.	Twigs are broken off trees, and the wind generally impedes progress.

Beaufort Number	Knots	Description	Effect at Sea	Effect Ashore
9	41–47	Strong gale	High waves appear; dense streaks of foam arise along the direction of the wind; sea begins to roll; spray may affect visibility.	Slight structural damage occurs (chimney pots and slate removed).
10	48–55	Storm	Very high waves with long overhanging crests appear. The resulting foam in great patches is blown in dense white streaks along the direction of the wind. On the whole, the surface of the sea takes on a white appearance. The rolling of the sea becomes heavy and appears to come in shocks. Visibility is affected.	It is seldom experienced inland. Trees are uprooted; considerable structural damage occurs.
11	56–63	Violent storm	Exceptionally high waves appear. (Small and medium-size ships might for a long time be lost to view behind the waves.) The sea is completely covered with long white patches of foam lying along the direction of the wind. Everywhere the edges of the wave crests are blown into froth. Visibility is affected.	It is very rarely experienced and is accompanied by widespread damage.
12	Above 63 (above 72)	Hurricane	The air is filled with foam and spray. The sea is completely white with a driving spray; visibility is very seriously affected.	Devastation occurs.

WINDCHILL FACTOR

Windchill is based on the idea that moving air carries heat away from a warm body, making the temperature feel colder than the thermometer indicates. It was coined by Antarctic explorer Paul A. Siple in 1939, and the first windchill factor table was developed in 1945, measuring how long it would take water to freeze in a container 30 feet off the ground. In fall 2001, the National Weather Service issued a new windchill formula, based on experiments with humans and wind at about 5 feet off the ground. The new figures appear below, and the shaded area indicates temperatures that caused frostbite at exposures of 15 minutes or less.

Wind Speed (m.p.h.)	Thermometer Reading (°F)											
	30	25	20	15	10	5	0	−5	−10	−15	−20	−25
5	25	19	13	7	1	−5	−11	−16	−22	−28	−34	−40
10	21	15	9	3	−4	−10	−16	−22	−28	−35	−41	−47
15	19	13	6	0	−7	−13	−19	−26	−32	−39	−45	−51
20	17	11	4	−2	−9	−15	−22	−29	−35	−42	−48	−55
25	16	9	3	−4	−11	−17	−24	−31	−37	−44	−51	−58
30	15	8	1	−5	−12	−19	−26	−33	−39	−46	−53	−60
35	14	7	0	−7	−14	−21	−27	−34	−41	−48	−55	−62
40	13	6	−1	−8	−15	−22	−29	−36	−43	−50	−57	−64
45	12	5	−2	−9	−16	−23	−30	−37	−44	−51	−58	−65
50	12	4	−3	−10	−17	−24	−31	−38	−45	−52	−60	−67
55	11	4	−3	−11	−18	−25	−32	−39	−46	−54	−61	−68
60	10	3	−4	−11	−19	−26	−33	−40	−48	−55	−62	−69

PHYSICS

BASIC FORMULAS AND LAWS OF PHYSICS

acceleration $a = (v_f - v_0)/t$, where a represents acceleration, v_f represents the final velocity, v_0 represents the initial velocity, and t represents the time.

acceleration of gravity $W = mg$, where W represents the force of weight, m represents the mass of the object, and g represents acceleration due to gravity (32 ft/sec^2).

centrifugal force $F = mv^2/r$, where F represents force, m represents the mass of a moving object, v represents its velocity, and r represents the radius of the orbit of the mass.

Coulomb's law $F = kQ_aQ_b/d^2$, where F represents the electrostatic force, k represents a constant of proportionality, Q_a and Q_b represent quantities of electrostatic charge, and d represents the distance between the charges.

electrical power $P = IV$, where P represents power, I represents electrical current, and V represents electric potential.

energy-matter relationship $E = mc^2$, where E represents energy, m represents mass, and c represents the velocity of light.

gravity inverse-square law $F = g\,Mm/r^2$, where F represents force, g represents the acceleration due to gravity, M and m represent the masses of two objects, and r represents the distance between the masses.

kinetic energy $KE = \tfrac{1}{2}mv^2$, where KE represents kinetic energy, m represents the mass of a moving object, and v represents the velocity.

light inverse-square law $I_1/I_2 = (d_2/d_1)^2$, where I_1 represents the light intensity at distance d_1 from the source and I_2 represents the intensity of light at distance d_2 from the source.

mass and weight relationship $m_1/m_2 = W_1/W_2$, where m_1 and m_2 represent two masses and W_1 and W_2 represent their respective weights.

momentum $p = mv$, where p represents momentum, m represents the mass of the object, and v represents velocity.

Newton's second law $F = ma$, where F represents force, m represents mass of the object, and a represents the acceleration.

Ohm's law $R = V/I$, where R represents electrical resistance, V represents electrical potential, and I represents electrical current.

potential energy $E = mgh$, where E represents potential energy, m represents the mass of an object, g represents the acceleration due to gravity, and h represents the distance to be traveled by m.

power $P = W/t$, where P represents power, W represents work, and t represents the time required to perform the indicated work.

velocity $v = d/t$, where v represents the velocity and d represents the distance traveled in time t.

wave equation $V = f\lambda$, where V represents the velocity of the wave, f represents its frequency, and λ represents the wavelength.

weight   *See* **acceleration of gravity**.

work $W = Fd$, where W represents work, F represents the applied force, and d represents the distance over which it is applied.

COMMON PHYSICS TERMS

acceleration   The rate of change of velocity with respect to time. It is calculated by subtracting the initial or starting velocity from the final velocity and dividing the difference by the time required to reach that velocity.

achromatic   An optical system that will transmit light without breaking it down into its component colors.

acoustics   The science of the production, transmission, and effect of sound waves.

action   The effect produced by a force, such as the force of a hammer hitting a nail; the action of the force is its effect, and the nail is driven into the wood.

adhesion   The tendency of matter to cling to other types of matter, due to intermolecular forces.

adiabatic   Pertaining to any activity that is not accompanied by a gain or loss of heat.

anode   The positive terminal of an electrical current flow. In a vacuum tube, electrons flow from a cathode toward an anode.

Bohr theory   A commonly accepted concept of the atom introduced by Niels Bohr in 1913. It holds that each atom consists of a small, dense, positively charged nucleus surrounded by negatively charged electrons that move in fixed, defined orbits about the nucleus, the total number of electrons normally balancing the total positive charge of particles in the nucleus.

Boyle's law   The principle that the volume of a gas times its pressure is constant at a fixed temperature.

cathode   The negative terminal of an electric current system. In a vacuum tube, the filament serves as the cathode or source of electrons that are emitted.

conduction   The transfer of heat by molecular motion from a source of high temperature to a region of lower temperature, tending toward a result of equalized temperatures.

convection   The mechanical transfer of heated molecules of a gas or liquid from a source to another area, as when a room is warmed by the movement of air molecules heated by a radiator.

Coulomb's law   The principle that an electrostatic force of attraction or repulsion between electrical charges is directly proportional to the product of the electrical charges and inversely proportional to the square of the distance between them.

deceleration   The decrease in velocity per unit time. It is also called negative acceleration.

density   The mass per unit volume of a material. Every material has a characteristic density.

energy   The ability or capacity to do work. There are numerous types of energy, including potential (stored), kinetic (from motion), heat, light, electrical, chemical, and nuclear energy. One form of energy can be transformed into another form, but energy normally is not created or destroyed.

entropy   A physical quantity that is the measurement of the amount of disorder in a system.

equilibrium   A state of balance between opposing forces or effects.

force   The influence on a body that causes it to accelerate, as expressed by the formula $F = ma$, where F is force, m is mass, and a is acceleration.

friction   The resistance to motion between two surfaces moving over each other. It is usually measured in terms of force and velocity.

heat   A form of energy that results from the disordered motion of molecules. As the motion becomes more rapid and disordered, the amount of heat is increased.

kinetic energy   Energy that is associated with the motion of an object.

mass   The measured amount of a material. All materials possess mass, and that mass never changes no matter where it resides in the universe.

mechanics   A branch of physics that deals with the motion of objects.

medium   The matter through which a wave travels. Sound waves need a medium; light waves do not need a medium and can travel through a vacuum.

particle   Anything small and discrete, such as a proton, neutron, atom, or molecule.

Sciences

phase   The state of matter of a material—either solid, liquid, gas, or plasma.

physical law   A description of a certain behavior in nature; for example, the idea that an object does not change its position until it is acted on by an outside force is a physical law.

Planck's law   Relates temperature to wavelength, stating that hotter objects radiate most at shorter wavelengths.

It is rumored that in the late 19th century, Australian meteorologist Clemet Wragge gave tropical storms that hit his continent the names of politicians' wives and other people he didn't like.

plasma   A hot, ionized (electrically charged) gas.

potential energy   Energy that is stored because of position or configuration, such as the gravitational energy of a weight that is positioned on the roof of a building.

power   The rate at which work is performed.

pressure   The force acting on a per-unit area of a surface.

radiation   The emission and propagation of radiant energy—either atomic, by radioactive substances, or spectral, as in light.

reaction   The effect opposite of an action. A reaction is equal to an action but is in the opposite direction. For example, when a stone strikes a wall, the wall does not move or change shape—it pushes back with a reaction that is equal to the action.

resistance   A force that opposes a change in motion or shape.

speed   The distance traveled divided by the time it takes to travel the distance.

strain   The change in a shape or size of a body caused by pressure and movement.

stress   Tension forces exerted on a body that tend to produce a deformation of that body.

surface tension   The property of a liquid in which the surface molecules show a strong inward attraction, forming an apparent membrane across the surface of the liquid.

thermodynamics   The study of the movement of heat from one body to another and the relations between heat and other forms of energy.

vacuum   In theory, it is the absence of matter; in space, a vacuum is where air or other gases are almost exhausted.

velocity   The speed with which an object travels over a specified distance during a measured amount of time.

vibration   The regular oscillation, backward and forward, of a material. For example, elastic vibrates, as do most fluids.

viscosity   The property of a liquid that makes it resist flow or any change in the arrangement of its molecules. The higher the viscosity, the "thicker" a liquid seems.

weight   The force on a body produced by the downward pull of gravity on it.

work   The force applied to an object times the distance over which it is applied. Work may be independent of the energy expended.

Additional terms are defined in "Common Chemistry Terms" in this chapter.

"Symbols Used in Science, Mathematics, and Technology" in chapter 12
Go to

MATHEMATICS

BASIC RULES OF MATHEMATICS
ADDITION OF FRACTIONS

$$\frac{a}{b} + \frac{c}{d} = \frac{ad}{bd} + \frac{bc}{bd} = \frac{ad+bc}{bd}$$

$$\frac{2}{3} + \frac{4}{5} = \frac{2\times5}{3\times5} + \frac{3\times4}{3\times5} = \frac{10}{15} + \frac{12}{15} = \frac{10+12}{15} = \frac{22}{15} = 1\frac{7}{15}$$

SUBTRACTION OF FRACTIONS

$$\frac{a}{b} - \frac{c}{d} = \frac{ad}{bd} - \frac{bc}{bd} = \frac{ad-bc}{bd}$$

$$\frac{4}{5} - \frac{2}{3} = \frac{4\times3}{5\times3} - \frac{5\times2}{5\times3} = \frac{12}{15} - \frac{10}{15} = \frac{12-10}{15} = \frac{2}{15}$$

MULTIPLICATION OF FRACTIONS

$$\frac{a}{b} \times \frac{c}{d} = \frac{ac}{bd}$$

$$\frac{2}{5} \times \frac{7}{4} = \frac{2\times7}{5\times4} = \frac{14}{20} = \frac{14\div2}{20\div2} = \frac{7}{10}$$

DIVISION OF FRACTIONS

$$\frac{a}{b} \div \frac{c}{d} = \frac{a}{b} \times \frac{d}{c} = \frac{ad}{bc}$$

$$\frac{3}{4} \div \frac{2}{3} = \frac{3}{4} \times \frac{3}{2} = \frac{3\times3}{4\times2} = \frac{9}{8} = 1\frac{1}{8}$$

SOLVING FOR AN UNKNOWN NUMBER x, WHERE a, b, AND c ARE KNOWN NUMBERS
Unknown Multiplied by a Number

$$ax = b \qquad\qquad 5x = 10$$

$$\frac{ax}{a} = \frac{b}{a} \qquad\qquad \frac{5x}{5} = \frac{10}{5}$$

$$x = \frac{b}{a} \qquad\qquad x = 2$$

Number Added to an Unknown

$$x + a = b \qquad\qquad x + 7 = 10$$

$$x + a - a = b - a \qquad x + 7 - 7 = 10 - 7$$

$$x = b - a \qquad\qquad x = 3$$

Unknown in a Fraction

$$\frac{x}{a} = \frac{b}{c} \qquad\qquad \frac{x}{5} = \frac{3}{8}$$

$$xc = ab \qquad\qquad x \times 8 = 5 \times 3$$

$$x = \frac{ab}{c} \qquad\qquad x = \frac{5\times3}{8} = \frac{15}{8} = 1\frac{7}{8}$$

NUMBERS WITH EXPONENTS

$$a^1 = a$$

$$a^2 = a \times a$$

$$a^3 = a \times a \times a$$

$$a^n = a \times a \times \ldots \times a \ (n \text{ factors})$$

$$a^{-n} = \frac{1}{a^n}$$

$$a^x \times a^y = a^{x+y}$$

$$a^x \div a^y = a^{x-y}$$

Thus:

$$\frac{2^3}{3^2} = \frac{2\times2\times2}{3\times3} = \frac{8}{9}$$

$$10^{-3} = \frac{1}{10^3} = \frac{1}{1,000}$$

$$10^2 \times 10^3 = 10^{2+3} = 10^5 = 10 \times 10 \times 10 \times 10 \times 10 = 100,000$$

$$10^6 \div 10^4 = 10^{6-4} = 10^2 = 10 \times 10 = 100$$

If 111,111,111 is multiplied by itself, the result is all of the digits in ascending to descending order, or 12,345,678,987,654,321.

Sciences

DECIMAL AND PERCENT EQUIVALENTS OF COMMON FRACTIONS

A plus symbol (+) indicates that the decimal repeats.

Fraction	Decimal	Percent (%)	Fraction	Decimal	Percent (%)
1/64	0.015625	1.5625	1/2	0.5	50
1/32	0.3125	3.125	17/32	0.53125	53.125
1/16	0.0625	6.25	6/11	0.5454+	54.5454+
1/12	0.0833+	8.333+	5/9	0.5555+	55.5555+
1/11	0.0909+	9.0909+	9/16	0.5625	56.25
3/32	0.09375	9.375	4/7	0.571428+	57.1428+
1/10	0.1	10	7/12	0.5833+	58.3333+
1/9	0.1111+	11.1111+	19/32	0.59375	59.375
1/8	0.125	12.5	3/5	0.6	60
1/7	0.142857+	14.2857+	5/8	0.625	62.5
5/32	0.15625	15.625	7/11	0.6363+	63.6363+
1/6	0.1666+	16.6666+	21/32	0.65625	65.625
2/11	0.1818+	18.1818+	2/3	0.66666+	66.666+
3/16	0.1875	18.75	11/16	0.6875	68.75
1/5	0.2	20	7/10	0.7	70
7/32	0.21875	21.875	5/7	0.714285+	71.4285+
2/9	0.2222+	22.2222+	23/32	0.71875	71.875
1/4	0.25	25	8/11	0.7272+	72.7272+
3/11	0.2727+	27.2727+	3/4	0.75	75
9/32	0.28125	28.125	7/9	0.7777+	77.7777+
2/7	0.285714+	28.5714+	25/32	0.78125	78.125
3/10	0.3	30	4/5	0.8	80
5/16	0.3125	31.25	13/16	0.8125	81.25
1/3	0.33333+	33.333+	9/11	0.8181+	81.8181+
11/32	0.34375	34.375	5/6	0.8333+	83.3333+
4/11	0.3636+	36.3636+	27/32	0.84375	84.375
3/8	0.375	37.5	6/7	0.857142+	85.7142+
2/5	0.4	40	7/8	0.875	87.5
13/32	0.40625	40.625	8/9	0.8888+	88.8888+
5/12	0.4166+	41.6666+	9/10	0.9	90
3/7	0.428571+	42.8571+	29/32	0.90625	90.625
7/16	0.4375	43.75	10/11	0.9090+	90.9090+
4/9	0.4444+	44.4444+	11/12	0.9166+	91.6666+
5/11	0.4545+	45.4545+	15/16	0.9375	93.75
15/32	0.46875	46.875	31/32	0.96875	96.875

GEOMETRIC SHAPES AND THEIR AREA, CIRCUMFERENCE, AND VOLUME FORMULAS

In this section, π (pi) is the ratio of the circumference of a circle to its diameter. It is a transcendental number having a value to eight places of 3.14159265. For practical purposes, the value is 3.1416.

TWO-DIMENSIONAL SHAPES

circle   A continuous line or the plane bounded by such a line, in which every point of the line is equidistant from the central point lying on the plane. The complete distance along such a line is the circumference C of the circle. A circle is commonly described by its radius r—a straight line extending from the center of the circle to any point on the perimeter—and its diameter d—a straight line extending from a point on the perimeter, through the center, to a point on the perimeter on the other side of the circle (it is also expressed as twice the radius).

$$C = \pi d = 2\pi r \qquad \text{Area} = \pi r^2$$

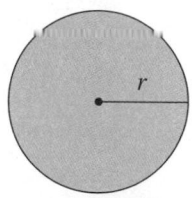

ellipse   The path of a point that moves so that the sum of its distances from two fixed points—the foci—is constant. An ellipse is commonly described by its semimajor axis *a* and its semiminor axis *b*.

Area = πab

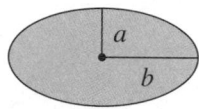

polygon   A closed plan figure bound by three or more straight lines.

rectangle   A four-sided polygon, bound by four straight lines at 90° angles, whose opposite sides are parallel to each other and are equal in length.

Area = (length)(width) = lw

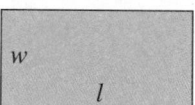

regular hexagon   A six-sided regular polygon.

Area = $2.59808a^2$

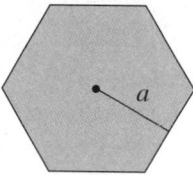

"Mathematics Symbols" in chapter 12; "Standard Sizes Chart" in chapter 19
Go to

regular octagon   An eight-sided regular polygon.

Area = $4.82843a^2$

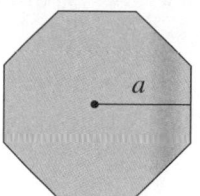

regular pentagon   A five-sided regular polygon.

Area = $1.72048a^2$

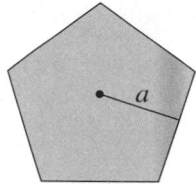

regular polygon   A polygon in which all sides are equal in length and all inside angles are equal.

square   A four-sided regular polygon. Its four inside angles are all 90°.

Area = a^2

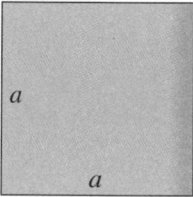

triangle   A three-sided polygon; its three inside angles always add up to 180°.

Area = ½(perpendicular height)(base) = ½ab

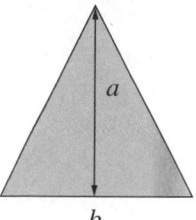

Sciences

THREE-DIMENSIONAL SHAPES

circular cylinder   A solid that has two equal-sided circular bases and a third side that joins the bases.

Volume = $\pi r^2 h$ Surface area = $2\pi rh + 2\pi r^2$

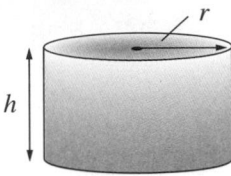

cube   A solid that has six square sides, with each at right angles to each adjacent side.

Volume = a^3 Surface area = $6a^2$

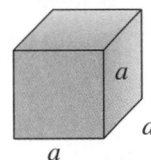

rectangular prism   A six-sided solid whose opposite sides are equal in length and parallel to each other. All junctions of its sides are at 90° angles.

Volume = lwh Surface area = $2hw + 2hl + 2lw$

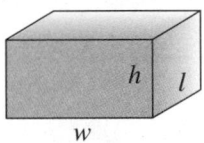

regular right pyramid   A solid figure having a polygonal base, the sides of which form the bases of triangular surfaces meeting at a common vertex point that is perpendicular to the center of the base and not in the same plane as the base.

Volume = $\frac{1}{3}h$(area of the base)

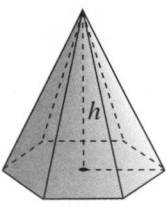

right circular cone   A flat-based, single-pointed solid formed by a rotating straight line that traces out a closed curve based from a fixed vertex point that is perpendicular to the center of the base and not in the same plane as the base.

Volume = $\frac{1}{3}\pi hr^2$ Surface area = $\pi r\sqrt{r^2 + h^2}$
(+ πr^2 if the base is added)

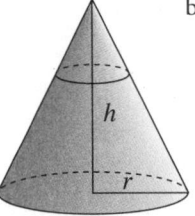

sphere   A solid that is bounded by a curved surface. Any point measured from the outside of the sphere to the center of the sphere is equal in distance.

Volume = $\frac{4}{3}\pi r^3$ Surface area = $4\pi r^2$

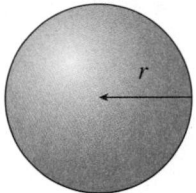

TRIANGLES

PYTHAGOREAN THEOREM

The square of the hypotenuse of a right-angled triangle is equal to the sum of the squares of the other two sides.

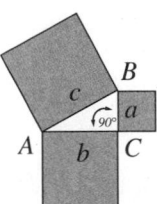

TRIGONOMETRIC FUNCTIONS

The standard abbreviation for each trigonometric function appears in parentheses after the name of the function.

cosecant (csc)   In a right triangle, the ratio of the length of the hypotenuse to the length of the side opposite to an acute angle (csc $A = c/a$); reciprocal of the sine function (csc $A = 1/\sin A$).

cosine (cos)   In a right triangle, the ratio of the length of the side adjacent to an acute angle to the length of the hypotenuse (cos $A = b/c$).

A googol is a 1 followed by 100 zeros. The name is said to have come from the 9-year-old nephew of the American mathematician Edward Kasner. A googolplex is the number 1 followed by a googol of zeros.

cotangent (cot or ctn)   In a right triangle, the ratio of the side adjacent to an acute angle to the length of the side opposite that angle (cot $A = b/a$); reciprocal of the tangent function (cot $A = 1/\tan A$).

secant (sec)   In a right triangle, the ratio of length of the hypotenuse to the length of the side adjacent to an acute angle (sec $A = c/b$); reciprocal of the cosine function (sec $A = 1/\cos A$).

sine (sin)   In a right triangle, the ratio of the length of the side opposite an acute angle to the length of the hypotenuse (sin $A = a/c$).

tangent (tan)   In a right triangle, the ratio of the length of the side opposite an acute angle to the length of the side adjacent to that angle (tan $A = a/b$).

TRIGONOMETRIC FORMULAS

Law of Sines

In any triangle, $a/\sin A = b/\sin B = c/\sin C$

Right Triangles

$a = c \sin A = b \tan A$
$b = c \cos A = a \cot A$
$c = a \operatorname{cosec} A = b \sec A$

For All Triangles

$A + B + C = 180°$

Given two angles (A and B) and one side (b):
$a = b \times \sin A/\sin B$
$c = b \times \sin C/\sin B$

Given two sides (b and c) and one angle (A):
$a = (b^2 + c^2 - 2bc \cos A)$
$\sin B = b/a \sin A$

Given three sides (a, b, and c):
$\cos A = (b^2 + c^2 - a^2)/2bc$
$\sin B = b/a \times \sin A$

The only number not found in the Roman numeral system is zero.

ROMAN NUMERALS

1	I	70	LXX	1,910	MCMX
2	II	80	LXXX	1,920	MCMXX
3	III	90	XC	1,930	MCMXXX
4	IV	100	C	1,940	MCMXL
5	V	150	CL	1,950	MCML
6	VI	200	CC	1,960	MCMLX
7	VII	300	CCC	1,970	MCMLXX
8	VIII	400	CD	1,980	MCMLXXX
9	IX	500	D	1,990	MCMXC
10	X	600	DC	2,000	MM
15	XV	700	DCC	3,000	MMM
20	XX	800	DCCC	4,000	MMMM OR M$\overline{\text{V}}$
25	XXV	900	CM	5,000	$\overline{\text{V}}$
30	XXX	1,000	M	10,000	$\overline{\text{X}}$
40	XL	1,500	MD	50,000	$\overline{\text{L}}$
50	L	1,900	MCM or	100,000	$\overline{\text{C}}$
60	LX		MDCCCC	1,000,000	$\overline{\text{M}}$

Sciences

COMPUTERS

PERSONAL COMPUTER COMPONENTS

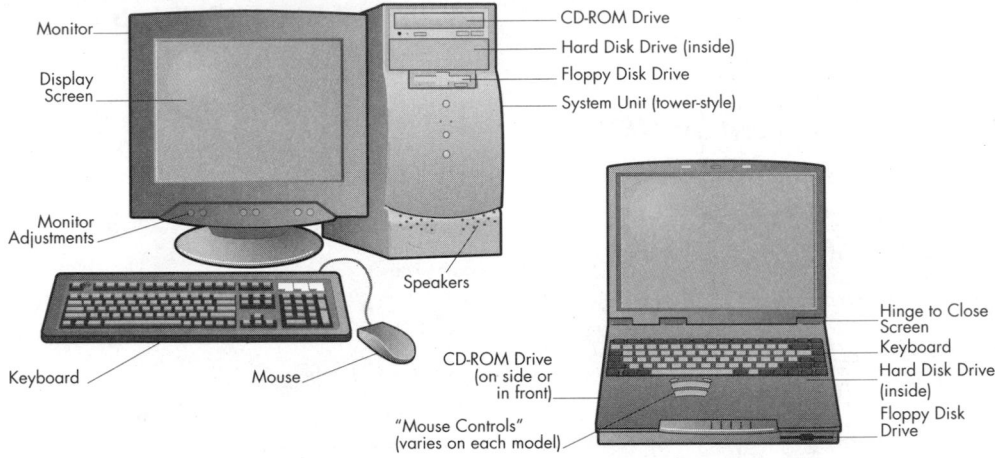

PERSONAL COMPUTER COMPONENTS

Monitor

Display Screen

Monitor Adjustments

Keyboard

Mouse

Speakers

CD-ROM Drive

Hard Disk Drive (inside)

Floppy Disk Drive

System Unit (tower-style)

CD-ROM Drive (on side or in front)

"Mouse Controls" (varies on each model)

Hinge to Close Screen

Keyboard

Hard Disk Drive (inside)

Floppy Disk Drive

NOTEBOOK COMPUTER COMPONENTS

MACs AND PCs

The computer market is now dominated by the PC (short for personal computer), which accounts for more than 90 percent of sales to homes and businesses. The first successful home computers, the PC and PC/XT models, were introduced in 1981 by the International Business Machines Corporation (IBM). In a short time, other manufacturers began marketing PCs. Known as IBM clones or IBM compatibles, these machines were powered by the same technology—the Intel microprocessor—as IBM's product. They could all use the same software and share the same data. Eventually, all IBM-compatible home computers became known as PCs, no matter which company manufactured them.

In 1984, Apple Computer added a new dimension to the home computer market when it introduced the Macintosh (Mac). Whereas PCs relied on complicated commands typed by the user, the Mac's operating system featured on-screen icons. Commands could be executed simply by positioning a pointer on an image and clicking a button. Because of this innovation, Macs were far less intimidating for novices and became extremely popular. Because Macs and PCs used different microprocessors and different file formats, they required different software and could not share data.

With the introduction of Microsoft's Windows and IBM's OS/2 during the 1990s, the difference between PCs and Macs diminished considerably (although IBM's OS/2 operating system is no longer popular). Both these operating systems (and their updated versions) use the same icon-based graphical user interface (GUI) and point-and-click technology as the Mac does. As a result, the Mac has lost some of its allure, and Apple's position in the computer industry has declined. Mac devotees maintain, however, that their computers are still easier to use than PCs; artists and designers tend to prefer the Mac because of its enhanced graphics capabilities. PC and Mac computers continue to be upgraded with additional speed and memory. For example, more than six generations of PC processors have been developed—such as those that include the Intel Pentium chips, which have allowed computers to be that much faster than the previous generations. Users of PCs and Macs have no problem exchanging e-mail because the messages are routed through providers' host computers.

Sciences

Growth of the Internet

A Closer Look

The Internet was originally a network of computers called the ARPnet (Advance Research Projects), a project managed by the United States Department of Defense's Advanced Research Project Agency (ARPA) for military and government purposes. Not long after its inception, various universities and other institutions with higher-end computers began their own networks and eventually merged with ARPnet to form the Internet.

The modern Internet is a huge network of electronic links between computers that span the world. Even though computers from all around the world use many different protocols (i.e., how a computer communicates with other computers), there is generally no problem with communication. The reason is that the connection between computers is processed through worldwide gateways that allow each protocol to be translated into a standard format. Thus, the computer user—with the right software and hardware—can receive text, and often sound and graphics, at his or her personal computer.

Because of the ease of use, millions of personal computer users are "on" the Internet, "surfing" for information from hundreds of thousands of university, library, commercial, and government databases (often using a connection called the World Wide Web, or WWW, that provides graphics, sound, and text to enhance the desired information); ordering items from online catalogs; sending electronic mail (e-mail); and creating their own home pages available for most Internet users to view. Even the most remote places can often connect to the Internet by using an Internet Service Provider (ISP), a link that usually provides a local access phone number to the Internet.

But the Internet is not infallible. It is often unable to handle a large number of users at once, creating a user bottleneck. For example, when the *Mars Pathfinder* space probe landed on Mars on July 4, 1997, millions of people tried to access the National Aeronautics and Space Administration's (NASA) server for images and information on the red planet. The system eventually overloaded, making it difficult to access NASA's home page and download information during the peak days of the Internet user activity.

INTERNET SEARCH ENGINES

With millions of Web sites in existence, finding information on the Internet would be a daunting task if not for the availability of search engines. A search engine is a Web site that uses special software (known as a robot) to comb the Internet and find nearly instantaneous matches for keywords typed by the searcher. (Yahoo! is sometimes referred to as a "links site" because it also provides a menu of hypertext links in a variety of broad categories, such as "Arts," "Education," "Science," and so on.) Each search engine has its own characteristics; a bit of experimentation will reveal which is best for a particular searcher's needs.

Alta Vista	http://www.altavista.digital.com
Excite	http://www.excite.com
Google	http://www.google.com
HotBot	http://www.hotbot.com
Infoseek	http://www.infoseek.com
Lycos	http://www.lycos.com
Northern Light	http://www.nlsearch.com
WebCrawler	http://www.webcrawler.com
Yahoo!	http://www.yahoo.com

NATIONAL INTERNET SERVICE PROVIDERS

National providers may offer a variety of services that include news, stock market updates, chat rooms, travel services, and online reference libraries. Some of the larger providers are listed here.

America Online	(800) 827-6364	http://www.aol.com
AT&T WorldNet	(800) 967-5363	http://www.att.com/worldnet
CompuServe	(800) 848-8199	http://www.compuserve.com
EarthLink	(800) 395-8425	http://www.earthlink.net
MCI Worldcom	(800) 550-0927	http://www.mci.com
Microsoft Network	(800) 373-3676	http://www.msn.com
Prodigy	800-776-3449	http://www.prodigy.com

National Internet service providers may or may not provide better connectivity and convenience than the numerous local providers throughout the country. (Check your local phone book's yellow pages for an ISP near you.) An online search for local providers can be conducted by using any search engine and the words "local ISPs."

Sciences

COMMON COMPUTER TERMS

address   A location in the computer memory where a particular unit of data is stored. The address may be in the form of an identifying label, name, or number.

algorithm   A defined set of instructions or procedural steps that will lead to a logical conclusion for a specific problem.

The first electronic computer was about 80 feet long, weighed 30 tons, and had 17,000 tubes.

analog computer   A computer that measures a function or behavior involving continuously variable signals, such as signals representing current, voltage, or other factors. An analog computer is also able to respond immediately to changes in input. The output may be presented in the form of a tracing on a graph or a design on a TV picture tube.

analog-to-digital computer   A device that is able to convert continuous analog signals into digital data, or discrete numbers.

architecture   The design of a computer so that hardware and software interface effectively.

arithmetic/logic unit   The part of a computer that performs calculations and comparisons.

array   An arrangement of data in which each item may be identified by a key or subscript so that a computer program can be designed to examine and extract specific data. An example is a calendar array in which a particular day of the year can be identified.

ASCII   Acronym for *A*merican *S*tandard *C*ode for *I*nformation *I*nterchange, a uniform character code used by many computer systems so that data can be exchanged directly between various types of central and remote units and peripheral devices. Each alphabetic and numeric character requires a full byte.

assembler   A computer program designed to assemble machine code from symbolic code or source language.

assembly language   A machine-oriented computer-programming language that can be translated directly into machine instructions.

bandwidth   The amount of data that can be transmitted in a certain amount of time. It is usually expressed in bits per second (bps) or bytes per second.

BASIC   Acronym for *B*eginner's *A*ll-purpose *Sym*bolic *I*nstruction *C*ode, a program that is a standard language for most personal computers. It is designed for developing programs in a "conversational mode" for online use.

baud rate   The rate at which information is transmitted serially from a computer. It is expressed in terms of bits per second.

BBS   *See* **bulletin board system.**

binary   A numbering system based on twos (2s) rather than decimals (10s). Each element has a digit value of either zero (0) or one (1) and is known as a bit.

bit   An acronym constructed from the words *bi*nary digi*t*. It refers to a single digit of a binary number.

bootstrap (boot)   The process of initializing or loading the basic operating instructions into a computer.

browser   Short for Web browser, a software application used to find and display Web pages on the Internet. The most popular graphical browsers are Netscape Navigator and Microsoft Internet Explorer. Mosaic was one of the very first browsers and is still occasionally encountered.

buffer   A temporary storage area for data that helps compensate for differences in the speed of operations of two or more parts of a computer system, such as the central processing unit and a printer.

Sciences

"Libraries Online" and "Data Banks Available **Go to** for Computer Research" in chapter 11

bug Any error or malfunction in a computer operation or program.

bulletin board system An electronic message center maintained by a newsgroup. Users can leave e-mail messages on the bulletin board and read messages left by others.

bus A group of wires through which data is sent from one part of the computer to another. Most personal computers have an internal bus that connects components to the Central Processing Unit (CPU) and main memory.

byte A set or unit of binary digits, usually eight bits, such as a division of a word. The storage capacity of a disk is usually given in megabytes.

cable modem A modem that operates over television coaxial cable lines. These lines offer a much wider bandwidth, allowing for faster access to the World Wide Web.

CD-ROM An abbreviation for *Compact Disk–Read Only Memory*. It is a large-storage compact disk that resembles a music CD and holds information that can be viewed on the computer screen but cannot be altered.

central processing unit (CPU) The part of the computer circuitry that actually handles the data processing and controls the storage, movement, and other basic computer functions. For personal computers, the terms *CPU* and *microprocessor* are used synonymously. A microprocessor is the single, large-scale integrated circuit on a fingernail-size silicon chip, and the heart of the CPU. *See* **microprocessor**.

character Any digit, letter, punctuation, or symbol, usually represented by a single byte of eight bits.

clock An electronic device that monitors, measures, or synchronizes various functions of a computer system.

COBOL An acronym formed from the words *CO*mmon *B*usiness *O*riented *L*anguage. A high-level programming language used for business applications.

command A part of a computer code that gives input/output instructions to the computer.

compiler A set of programs that compiles or converts a program into the machine language instructions used by a particular computer.

control data Computer information that helps organize data in key categories, such as sorting sequences.

control unit The part of the central processing unit that manipulates the sequences of operations according to the program instructions.

cookie A message sent from a Web server to a Web browser, usually to identify a user's preferences and requested pages.

CPU *See* **central processing unit.**

cursor A symbol appearing on a video display indicating the position where a user can add or delete characters.

cyberspace A slang term for the Internet and related spheres of digital communication. *See* **Internet.**

database A large file of organized information that may be updated and manipulated as needed.

data management system A set of commands used to search and retrieve content as well as to update and reference information from a database.

debug The process of removing errors or defects in software or hardware that cause malfunction of the computer.

diagnostic routine A program designed to trace the source of program errors or the cause of a computer malfunction.

Sciences

digital computer   A computer in which discrete numbers are used to express data and instructions.

direct access   *See* **random access.**

disk (diskette)   A circular plate coated with magnetic material that can be used to store computer data.

disk crash   The malfunction of a disk, either a floppy disk or a hard drive. Generally, floppy disks crash because of physical damage to the disk. Hard drives crash because of physical damage (lightning strikes or being dropped), contamination (dust or liquids), or an unaligned head.

disk drive   A device that is able to "read" data stored in magnetic material on a disk or to "write" data onto such a disk.

disk operating system   A program that controls how the various parts of a computer interact; also known by its acronym, DOS.

domain   The last part of a World Wide Web address that includes a main name and suffix. For example, "nypl.org" is a domain name. Standard top-level domains in the United States are *.com* (commercial), *.edu* (educational), *.gov* (government), *.mil* (military), *.org* (nonprofit organization), and *.net* (network). In 2000, seven new top-level domain names were added, the first since 1988. By 2002, *.aero* (air transportation industry), *.biz* (businesses), *.coop* (cooperatives), *.info* (information-based services), *.museum* (museums, archival institutions, and exhibitions), *.name* (individuals), *.pro* (accountants, lawyers, physicians, and other professionals) were operating or becoming operational. In addition, two-letter country code suffixes appear in some domain names.

DOS   *See* **disk operating system.**

download   To transfer a file from one computer to another.

DSL   An acronym for *Digital Subscriber Lines*. These technologies use various ways to pack data onto copper wires and are used only for connections from telephone switching stations to a home or office—not between switching stations.

e-book   an electronic version of a book. An e-book is a small computer—the size of a paperback or a notepad—with a screen that allows a user to read, save, highlight, bookmark, and annotate text.

e-mail   A computer application that enables users to send messages to other computers anywhere on the Internet.

error message   A message output by the computer, triggered by a program, indicating failure to follow a correct input/output routine, a hardware malfunction, or another problem that may cause the operation to discontinue.

execute   Performance of an operation specified by a program routine or instruction.

FAQ   Acronym for *Frequently Asked Questions*. A document that answers the most common queries about a particular subject. Almost all newsgroups post one or more FAQ lists.

fiber optic network   A technology that uses glass (or plastic) threads (fibers) to transmit data. A fiber optic cable consists of a bundle of glass threads, each of which is capable of transmitting messages modulated into light waves.

file   A collection of related data or information that is stored as a unit.

firewall   A combination of hardware and software that protects a computer or a system of computers from Internet hackers—users who access the computer or system via the Internet without permission.

flame   An insulting e-mail message or newsgroup posting. A series of flames and counterflames is often referred to as a flame war.

floppy disk   *See* **disk.**

FORTRAN   An acronym formed from the words *FOR*mula *TRAN*slator. It is a programming language used for mathematical and scientific operations.

FTP   An acronym for *File Transfer Protocol*, the basic function that allows a computer to transfer files back and forth between other computers over the Internet.

generation   Pertaining to a group of computers developed within the same time period and based on the model of an earlier product.

GIF   An acronym for *Graphics Interchange Format*. A GIF is a graphic image in a file format often used to display images on the computer screen or used on Web pages on the Internet. They most often are seen as gray-scale graphics. *See* **JPEG.**

gigabyte   A gigabyte is 1,024 megabytes; 1,024 gigabytes is a terabyte. Gigabytes are often used to measure the size (capacity) of a hard drive.

Gopher   A text-only Internet site that contains a series of menus organized by subject matter. Created before the advent of the World Wide Web, Gopher sites function as electronic libraries, providing access to documents such as research papers and periodical articles.

GUI   An acronym for *Graphical User Interface*, a system through which the user can interact with the computer by means of pictures and symbols called icons.

hard copy   A copy of the output of a computer that has been produced on paper, as distinguished from the electronic copy of the same data on disk or tape.

hardware   The physical equipment or devices, such as the central processing unit, of a computer system. *See also* **software.**

hexadecimal   A system of whole numbers with a base of 16 used in certain computer operations. Hexadecimal coding uses numerals 0 to 16 with the first 10 digits represented by 0 through 9 and the next 6 digits represented by the letters *A* through *F.*

high-level language   Any computer language in which each instruction corresponds to a group of machine code instructions. Examples include BASIC and COBOL.

home page   A term that applies both to the first page loaded by an Internet browser and the main document for an organization, newsgroup, or individual user.

housekeeping   Standard computer routines, such as deleting garbage or preliminary input/output functions, that are not directly related to a particular job.

HTML   An abbreviation for *Hypertext Markup Language*, which is used to create documents on the World Wide Web. Hypertext is a method of connecting sites through text-based links rather than the menu-oriented systems used by Gopher sites. Clicking on a link (typically an underlined word or phrase) automatically calls a new area of the current document or calls up a different website.

http   An abbreviation for *hypertext transfer protocol*, a common system for requesting and sending HTML documents on the Internet. It is the first element (http://) in all URL addresses on the World Wide Web.

hybrid computer   A computer that is able to perform both analog and digital computing functions.

icon   The graphic representation of a computer command.

input   The information a computer receives from a keyboard, tape, or disk.

input/output (I/O) terminal   A computer device that is capable of both receiving and retrieving data.

instruction   A part of a program that directs a computer to perform a single specific function as part of a sequence of functions.

interface   A device that serves as a link or common surface boundary between two different parts of a computer system.

Internet A cooperatively run global collection of computer networks with a common addressing scheme. First created during the 1970s as a channel for information sharing among scientists, it has now become a worldwide communications medium.

Internet service provider (ISP) A company that sells access to the Internet. In addition to the national online services, there are more than 100,000 local service providers in the United States.

interrupt A temporary suspension of processing by a computer, caused by input or other activity by another part of the system.

I/O terminal *See* **input/output (I/O) terminal.**

intranet private network inside a company or organization that uses the same kinds of software as does the public Internet. However, access to an intranet is limited—usually it is only for the internal use of the organization that created it.

Java A programming language that allows users to create applications, particularly multimedia applications that can run on several platforms without rewriting. Often used in Web sites.

joystick A lever that is connected to a computer for use in moving the cursor from one point to another on a video display terminal.

JPEG An acronym for *J*oint *P*hotographic *Ex*perts *G*roup. This is the name of the committee responsible for designing this photographic image-compression standard. JPEGs are usually photographs, stored as color or gray-scale digital images. *See* **GIF.**

K An abbreviation for kilo and a symbol for 1,000 (actually 2^{10}, or 1,024); it is commonly used to indicate the storage capacity of a computer's memory. For example, a 64K memory has a theoretical capacity of $64 \times 1,024$, or 65,536 bytes or data storage locations.

keyboard A device that encodes characters for a computer function by the pressing of keys. Pressing the keys formerly punched holes in cards that the computer read; now it more commonly provides a direct input of data to the computer.

label A group of computer characters used to identify a file, record, or memory storage area.

LAN *See* **network.**

language A set of characters that can be used to form a meaningful set of words and symbols in writing instructions for a computer. Examples include ALGOL, BASIC, COBOL, and FORTRAN.

laptop A small, portable computer that folds into a compact case. Laptop computers also frequently called notebook computers. Small size and light weight are priorities in laptop or notebook construction.

light pen A photoelectric device connected to the cathode-ray tube of a display unit. It can be used by the operator to activate the computer to change or modify an image displayed by touching the pen to the screen.

listserv An automated mailing list distribution system that allows a group of e-mail addresses to receive (and often send) e-mail to one another as a group.

local area network *See* **network.**

machine language A language composed of a set of numbers and symbols that can direct computer operations without the need for translation.

magnetic memory A memory device that uses magnetic fields for storing data.

mainframe computer A large professional computer system used by a major industry or government agency, as distinguished from a smaller minicomputer or microcomputer.

megabyte A megabyte is 1,024 kilobytes; 1,024 megabytes is a gigabyte. A computer's random-access memory (RAM) is usually measured in megabytes.

memory   The ability of a computer to store and retrieve data.

menu   A list of commands in a program from which the user can choose to initiate an action.

message   A combination of characters or symbols used to communicate information between points of a computer system. *See also* **error message.**

metadata   Descriptions of how, when, and by whom a particular set of data was collected, and how the data is formatted. Metadata is essential for understanding information stored in data warehouses.

microcomputer   A small personal computer.

microprocessor   *See* **Central Processing Unit.**

minicomputer   A computer that is larger in capacity, flexibility, and cost than a microcomputer. It may commonly be used to control industrial processes.

modem   An acronym formed from the words *mo*dulator *dem*odulator. It is an electronic device that allows computer data to be carried over telephone lines.

mouse   A movable device attached to a computer that permits the operator to reposition the cursor on the video display terminal.

multimedia   Software applications that incorporate sound, video, and animation with text and graphics.

netiquette   A set of informal rules promoted by newsgroups. Principles of netiquette discourage such practices as flaming, spamming, and overlong postings that hog Internet resources. *See also* "Network Etiquette (Netiquette)" in chapter 16.

network   A group of two or more computers hooked together. A local area network (LAN) is a network of computers connected together, usually within the same building; a wide area network (WAN) is a network of computers connected together, usually over long distances by telephone lines or radio waves.

newsgroup   A Usenet discussion group dedicated to a particular subject.

offline   Pertaining to computer functions that are not under the direct control of a central processing unit or computer operator. The term is sometimes applied to hard copy or stored data.

online   Computer operations that are under the direct control of the central processing unit or operator.

operating system (OS)   Any program that controls how the various parts of a computer interact.

optical scanner   An electronic device that scans direct or reflected light from a surface, such as a printed page, and converts the signals to machine-readable inputs.

OS   *See* **operating system.**

output   The results of a computer operation, which may appear in the form of a printout or visual display.

PalmPilot™   A specific brand of palmtop computer. A palmtop is a very small computer that literally fits in the palm of one's hand. Compared to full-size computers, the power of a palmtop is severely limited, but palmtops are practical for certain functions such as phone books and calendars. Palmtops that use a pen rather than a keyboard for input are often called handheld computers or PDAs.

peripheral   Any device that is separate from but connected to the computer for the purpose of supplying input or output functions, such as a modem or printer.

personal digital assistant (PDA)   A handheld device that combines computing, telephone/fax, and networking features. A typical PDA can function as a cellular phone, fax sender, and personal organizer. Unlike laptops, they use a stylus rather than a keyboard for input.

primary memory   The part of the computer used as the main storage area for data or programs.

Sciences

RAM   *See* **random-access memory.**

random access   The direct retrieval of data from a location in the computer memory without the need for sorting through sequential information.

Random-access memory (RAM)   A computer storage device that permits direct access to data independent of its location in the computer memory.

Read-only memory (ROM)   A type of computer memory that can be used to retrieve data for output only; new data cannot be written into it.

real time   Computer operations that permit rapid analyses of data so that decisions can be made immediately.

register   A part of the computer's central processing unit that stores information for future use. It may have specific uses, such as arithmetic functions or word processing. A computer may contain several different registers.

ROM   *See* **read-only memory.**

scanner   A device that scans a printed page and converts text and graphics into digital form. The data can then be incorporated into electronic documents.

serial processing   A type of computer function in which two or more programs are run in sequence rather than simultaneously.

server   A central computer that makes services available on a network.

Standard Generalized Markup Language (SGML)   A system for organizing and tagging elements of a document. SGML itself does not specify any particular formatting; rather, it specifies the rules for tagging elements. These tags can then be interpreted to format elements in different ways.

shareware   Copyrighted software programs that are distributed based on an honor system. Many shareware programs are free, but the author usually requests a small fee if the program is regularly used; the shareware can be copied for other computer users, but they too must pay a fee if the program is regularly used. Shareware cannot be sold by anyone but the author.

software   The programs or instructions used to operate a computer system, as distinguished from the hardware.

spam   In general, any unsolicited junk e-mail; or to use a newsgroup to send e-mail messages (typically advertisements) to a vast number of users without their permission.

storage capacity   The amount of data that can be stored in a computer memory. *See also* **K.**

surge protector   A device that protects software and hardware from sudden electrical surges. A surge protector is usually plugged into an electrical outlet; the computer is then plugged into the surge protector.

T-1 line   A dedicated phone connection supporting data rates of 1.544 Mbits per second. A T-1 line actually consists of 24 individual channels, each of which supports 64 Kbits per second. Each 64 Kbit/second channel can be configured to carry voice or data traffic.

terminal   An input/output device that allows an operator to control a computer. The terminal may consist of a keyboard and video display screen.

time sharing   A computer function of handling two or more tasks simultaneously, as when a mainframe computer is used to process operations of several remote terminals at the same time. Such a system depends on buffering and switching inputs and outputs for each terminal. This is done at such a high rate of speed that operators of individual terminals are unaware that others are sharing the same central processing unit.

track   A segment of a disk or other magnetic storage device that stores a fixed amount of data in a designated address for rapid retrieval.

Sciences

URL   Uniform Resource Locator. The addressing system for the World Wide Web. A typical URL would read http://www.nypl.org.

Usenet   A large, unedited Internet bulletin board that contains individual newsgroups.

virus   A destructive computer code inserted into an ordinary file or program. When downloaded, a virus will replicate itself within a user's computer system, often destroying data. As a protective measure, many computer users install antivirus software.

WAN (wide area network)   *See* **network.**

Web server   The outside computer that delivers Web pages to your computer. For example, if you entered the URL for the New York Public Library (http://www.nypl.org), the Web server for the library (nypl.org) would search for your query and send the requested page back to your browser.

Web site   A *Web site* is a location on the World Wide Web that contains a personal, commercial, or organizational home page.

word   A fixed number of bits processed by a computer as a single basic unit.

World Wide Web   The primary platform of the Internet. Created in 1989, the World Wide Web is a collection of files and databases linked by hypertext. It differs from older Internet applications in its ability to display graphics and multimedia in addition to text.

write   The process of recording data in a computer's memory.

write-protected disk   A computer disk designed to prevent altering the data stored on it.

SPACE EXPLORATION

MANNED SPACECRAFT

Apollo was the manned United States space program that eventually put 12 men on the Moon. The Apollo spacecraft included a command module for orbiting and a lunar module for landing on the Moon.

Gemini was the second series of United States manned missions, after the Mercury launches. The Gemini spacecraft seated two astronauts and was used to test rendezvous and docking maneuvers, human responses to weightlessness, extravehicular activity, and landing techniques.

Mercury was the first series of United States manned missions, including the first suborbital and orbital flights. These one-person crafts tested the feasibility of flight and monitored humans' reaction to space.

The *MIR* ("Peace") space station, built by the Soviet Union (now Russia), was the largest and longest-running permanent working space station. Launched in 1986, *MIR* was constructed of modules. It was used for extensive study of microgravity and other valuable space experiments. It was also the testing ground to determine the effects of the space environment on humans, and some cosmonauts stayed in the station for more than 400 days. Toward the end of its time in orbit, the station was host to an international crew of space travelers. Lack of funding, a host of technical problems, and a lowering orbit eventually caught up with the *MIR* project. In 2001, the Russian space agency officially closed the station, and sent the spacecraft plunging into the southern Pacific Ocean.

Skylab was the first and only United States space station, launched in 1973. It was not permanently manned but was visited by three separate crews of astronauts. In 1979, because of a technical problem, solar flares that caused atmospheric drag on the craft, and lack of funding (NASA was then concentrating on building a reusable shuttle), *Skylab* fell from orbit and burned up in the atmosphere.

Salyut was a series of seven Soviet space stations launched from 1971 to 1982. The addition of a second docking port—permitting the docking of a second *Soyuz* ferry, an unmanned *Progress* supply craft,

Sciences

and *Cosmos* modules—paved the way for the *MIR* space station.

The space shuttle is the reusable Earth-orbiting, manned vehicle used in the United States space program. There are four active shuttles (*Columbia, Discovery, Atlantis,* and *Endeavour*) in the fleet. Each shuttle can comfortably carry a crew of five to eight astronauts. Work done by the shuttle crews includes testing the reaction of humans in space, conducting Spacelab experiments, operating Earth-monitoring systems, and launching or capturing satellites into or from orbit. Currently, most space shuttle missions concentrate on ferrying astronauts, and shipping supplies and equipment to the Earth-orbiting International Space Station.

Voskhod, hastily developed by the Soviet Union, were actually *Vostok* craft modified to carry three persons. To make room, engineers removed the ejections that would be used in case of an aborted launch. The first extravehicular activity (EVA) was conducted during the second and last Voskhod mission in 1965.

Vostok ("east" in Russian) capsules, developed by the Soviet Union as their first manned spaceflight program, were one-person vehicles controlled from the ground.

HUMAN MISSIONS TO THE MOON

Mission	Launch Date	Crew	Comments
Apollo 8	December 21, 1968	Frank Borman James A. Lovell Jr. William A. Anders	First manned mission to orbit the Moon.
Apollo 10	May 18, 1969	Thomas P. Stafford John W. Young Eugene A. Cernan	Rehearsal for first landing; lunar module descended to within 2.2 miles (3.5 kilometers) of the Moon's surface.
Apollo 11	July 16, 1969	Neil A. Armstrong* Michael Collins† Edwin E. "Buzz" Aldrin Jr.*	First manned landing in Mare Tranquillitatis; Armstrong was the first human to walk on the Moon (July 20, 1969).
Apollo 12	November 14, 1969	Charles Conrad Jr.* Richard F. Gordon† Alan L. Bean*	Landed in Oceanus Procellarum.
Apollo 13	April 11, 1970	James A. Lovell Jr. John L. Swigert Jr. Fred W. Haise Jr	Never landed on the Moon; an accident en route required the craft to return after swinging around the far side of the Moon.
Apollo 14	January 31, 1971	Alan B. Shepard Jr.* Stuart A. Roosa† Edgar D. Mitchell*	Landed in Fra Mauro.
Apollo 15	July 26, 1971	David R. Scott* Alfred M. Worden† James B. Irwin*	Landed adjacent to the Imbrium Basin near Apennine Mountains.
Apollo 16	April 16, 1972	John W. Young* Thomas K. Mattingly II† Charles M. Duke Jr.*	Landed in highlands near Crater Descartes.
Apollo 17	December 7, 1972	Eugene A. Cernan* Ronald E. Evans† Harrison H. Schmitt*	Landed in Taurus Littrow Valley.

* Walked on Moon.   † Remained in command module, orbiting the Moon.

"Significant Inventions, Technological Advances, and Discoveries" Go to in chapter 5

COMMON ENGINEERING TERMS

aggregate   A mixture of several materials. For example, an aggregate of gravel, mud, natural sand, and crushed stone is used for making concrete.

alloy   A substance that has metallic properties and consists of two or more elements; usually at least one is a metal.

alternator   A type of alternating-current generator.

ammeter   An instrument that measures the strength of an electric current in amperes.

annealing   The process of making glass, metal, or an alloy less brittle by exposing it to heating and then cooling.

cantilever   A beam or other horizontal member supported on only one end.

cathode   The negative terminal of an electric current system. In a vacuum tube, the filament serves as the cathode or source of electrons that are emitted.

cathode-ray tube   A tube in which an electron beam is directed across a fluorescent tube in order to generate images. CRTs are used in oscilloscopes, radar, television sets, and computer monitors.

circuit   A line of conductors and other electrical devices along which an electrical current flows. A closed circuit allows the current to travel through all devices. If the circuit is broken at some point so that the current cannot flow, it is called an open circuit.

coil   A turned wire used to introduce inductance into an electrical circuit.

current   The flow of electricity. Metals are good conductors of electric current.

diode   A tube with two electrodes; the main use of diodes is to keep the electric current flowing in one direction.

dynamo   A type of generator; usually a direct-current generator. It converts energy of mechanical motion into electric current. *See also* **alternator.**

elasticity   The ability of an object or material to return to its original size and shape, after being pushed or pulled by an outside force. For example, rubber is elastic.

electrode   A rod, plate, or wire that is used to conduct electric current out of or into any device.

electromagnet   A coil with a soft iron core that acts as a magnet when an electric current is passed through it.

electromotive force   The force that moves an electric current around a circuit. For example, a generator produces an electromotive force.

engine   A machine that applies power to do work. It converts various forms of energy into mechanical force and motion.

expansion joint   A space left in structures or roads that allows for the expansion and contraction of the material, caused by heating and cooling of the surrounding environment.

filament   A metallic wire that is heated in an incandescent lamp in order to produce light.

fuse   A safety device that protects a circuit from receiving too much current. The fuse's wire melts in response to too much electric current passing through it, thus breaking the circuit.

galvanometer   An instrument that detects, measures, and determines the direction of a small electric current.

gasket   A deformable material, usually a ring of plastic or metal, that is used to make a pressure-tight joint between two (usually stationary) parts.

generator   A machine that converts mechanical energy into electrical energy.

"Major Scientists and Engineers" in chapter 5
Go to

Sciences

girder   A large beam of wood, metal, or concrete, usually found in skyscrapers and other large buildings. It is used for structural support.

insulator   A device with high resistance to heat, electricity, or sound; for example, an electrical insulator prevents electricity from sending current to other objects.

lubricant   A substance applied to a surface to reduce friction.

machine   A device that helps to do work. Most machines either overcome a force or change the direction of the applied force.

microphone   A device that acts as a transformer and amplifier of sound waves into electric currents.

motor   A machine that converts electrical energy into mechanical energy.

oscilliscope   An instrument that produces an image of varying electrical voltages on a cathode-ray tube.

polymer   Large molecules made up of a series of molecular units, similar to beads on a string. Natural polymers include rubber, wool, and cotton; synthetic polymers include nylon and polythene. Polymers are often called giant molecules.

pulley   A wheel over which a rope, chain, or wire passes. Pulleys are used to ease the pulling of objects or lifting of heavy weights.

pulley system   An arrangement of two or more pulleys that form a machine.

radar (*radio detection and ranging*)   An instrument in which a cathode-ray tube receives reflected radio waves to detect distant objects.

radio   A system of transmitting sound signals (as electric impulses) through the air using electromagnetic waves.

receiver   A device that transforms radio waves and translates them mainly into sounds or pictures.

relay   A device that controls a large electrical current along another circuit by switching on or off. The relay uses a small electric current to control the larger current.

resistor   A device that resists an electric current.

rheostat   *See* **variable resistor.**

stator   A stationary machine part about which a rotor turns.

switch   A device that is used to switch parts of a circuit on or off. When the switch is on, the electric current is flowing through; when the switch is off, the electric current is cut off.

television   A system for transmitting video and audio signals using electromagnetic waves. A television uses a cathode-ray tube to produce images built from 625 constantly changing lines, each of which contains 400 small dots of light.

thermocouple   Shortened term for thermoelectric couple.

thermoelectricity   The production of an electric current directly from heat, or the reverse.

transformer   A device that changes the voltage of an alternating current. Transformers are used to modify the high voltage received from power lines so that it can be used by homes that require lower voltage for electrical devices.

tube (or valve)   An electrical device that allows electric current to flow in only one direction. Such devices are also referred to as diodes, triodes, etc., depending on the number of electrodes present.

variable resistor (or rheostat)   A device that variably resists an electrical current. The resistance can be changed by varying the contacts, allowing the resistor to slide around a length of wire.

voltmeter   An instrument that measures electromotive force or potential difference between two points, usually in volts.

Sciences

ADDITIONAL SOURCES OF INFORMATION

ORGANIZATIONS AND SERVICES

American Association for the Advancement of Science
1200 New York Ave., NW
Washington, DC 20005
http://www.aaas.org

American Astronomical Society
200 Florida Ave., NW
Washington, DC 20009
http://www.aas.org

American Chemical Society
1155 16th St., NW
Washington, DC 20036
http://www.acs.org

American Geophysical Union
2000 Florida Ave., NW
Washington, DC 20009-1277
http://www.agu.org

American Institute of Physics
1 Physics Ellipse
College Park, MD 20740
http://www.aip.org

National Academy of Sciences
2101 Constitution Ave., NW
Washington, DC 20418
http://www.www4.nationalacademies.org/nas/nashome.nsf

National Aeronautics and Space Administration
300 E St., SW
Washington, DC 20546
http://www.nasa.gov

National Oceanic and Atmospheric Administration
14th St. and Constitution Ave., NW, Room 6013
Washington, DC 20230
http://www.noaa.gov

National Science Foundation
4201 Wilson Blvd.
Arlington, VA 22230
http://www.nsf.gov

National Technical Information Service
Department of Commerce
5285 Port Royal Rd.
Springfield, VA 22161
http://www.ntif.gov

National Weather Service Office of Public Affairs
1325 East-West Hwy.
Silver Spring Metro Center II
Silver Spring, MD 20910
http://www.nws.noaa.gov/pa

New York Academy of Sciences
2 E. 63rd St.
New York, NY 10021
http://www.nyas.org

Smithsonian Institution
1000 Jefferson Dr., SW
Washington, DC 20560
http://www.smithsonian.org/

MAGAZINES

Air & Space/Smithsonian
901 D Street, NW, 10th floor
Washington, DC 20024
http://www.airspacemag.com

Astronomy
21027 Crossroads Circle
P.O. Box 1612
Waukesha, WI 53187
http://www.astronomy.com

Discover Magazine
114 Fifth Ave.
New York, NY 10011
http://www.discover.com

Physics Today
One Physics Ellipse
College Park, MD 20740
http://www.aip.org/pt/

Popular Mechanics
224 W. 57th St.
New York, NY 10019
http://www.popularmechanics.com

Popular Science
2 Park Ave.
New York, NY 10016
http://www.popsci.com

Scientific American
415 Madison Ave.
New York, NY 10017
http://www.sciam.com

Sky & Telescope
P. O. Box 9111
Cambridge, MA 02178-9111
http://www.skypub.com

Sciences

Smithsonian Magazine
900 Jefferson Drive
Washington, DC 20560
http://www.smithsonianmag.si.edu

BOOKS

Abell, George O., et al. *Exploration of the Universe.* 6th ed. Saunders College, 1991.

Allaby, A., ed. *A Dictionary of Earth Sciences.* 2nd ed. Oxford University Press, 1999.

Beatty, J. Kelly, ed., et al. *The New Solar System.* 4th ed. Sky Publishing, 1999.

Clapham, Christopher. *The Concise Oxford Dictionary of Mathematics.* Oxford University Press, 1996.

Clarke, Donald, and Mark Dartford, eds. *The New Illustrated Science and Invention Encyclopedia: How It Works.* Marshall Cavendish, 1994.

Considine, Douglas, and Glenn D. Considine, eds. *Van Nostrand's Scientific Encyclopedia.* 8th ed., 2 vols. Van Nostrand Reinhold, 1997.

Curtis, Anthony R. *Space Almanac.* 2nd ed. Gulf, 1992.

Daintith, John, ed. *A Dictionary of Chemistry.* 3rd ed. Oxford University Press, 1996.

Dean, John A. *Lange's Handbook of Chemistry.* 14th ed. McGraw-Hill, 1996.

Dunlop, S. *A Dictionary of Weather.* Oxford University Press, 2001.

Hawking, Stephen. *A Brief History of Time: From the Big Bang to Black Holes.* Bantam, 1990.

Lambert, David, and the Diagram Group. *The Field Guide to Geology.* Facts on File, 1997.

Lide, David R., ed. *CRC Handbook of Chemistry and Physics: A Ready-Reference Book of Chemical and Physical Data.* 78th ed. CRC Press, 1997.

Ludlum, David, et al. *Clouds and Storms* (National Audubon Society Pocket Guide). Knopf, 1995.

Macaulay, David. *The Way Things Work.* Houghton-Mifflin, 1988.

McPhee, John. *Annals of the Former World.* Farrar, Straus & Giroux, 1998.

Parker, Sybil P., ed. *McGraw-Hill Encyclopedia of Science and Technology.* 8th ed. McGraw-Hill, 1997.

Pellant, Chris, *Rocks and Minerals.* Dorling Kindersley, 1992.

Pough, Frederick H. and Roger Tory Peterson. *Peterson's First Guide to Rocks and Minerals.* Houghton-Mifflin, 1991.

Ralston, Anthony, and Edwin D. Reilly, eds. *Encyclopedia of Computer Science.* 3rd ed. International Thompson, 1993.

Vernon, R.H. *The Rocks Beneath Our Feet.* Cambridge University Press, 2001.

Ward, P. D. *Rivers in Time: The Search for Clues to Earth's Mass Extinctions.* Columbia University Press, 2001.

Williams, Jack. *The Weather Book.* 2nd ed. Vintage, 1997.

Zukowsky, J., ed. *2001: Building for Space Travel.* Harry N. Abrams, 2001.

WEB SITES

Computer User High-Tech Dictionary
http://www.computeruser.com/resources/dictionary/dictionary.html

National Center for Atmospheric Research
http://www.ncar.ucar.edu/ncar/index.html

Natural Hazards Center
http://www.colorado.edu/hazards/

Online Encyclopedia Dedicated to Computer Technology
http://www.pcwebopedia.com

United States Army Corps of Engineers
http://www.usace.army.mil/

United States Geological Survey
http://www.usgs.gov

Sciences

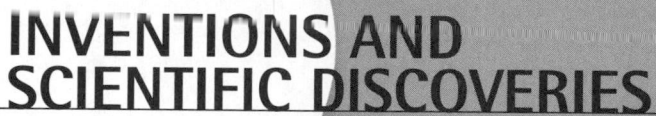

5

INVENTIONS AND
SCIENTIFIC DISCOVERIES

SIGNIFICANT INVENTIONS, TECHNOLOGICAL ADVANCES, AND SCIENTIFIC DISCOVERIES

Date	Invention/Advance/Discovery	Inventor/Origin
B.C.		
c. 12,000	Fire	Unknown
c. 5000	Woven cloth	Mesopotamia, Egypt
	Copper working	Rudna Glava, Yugoslavia
c. 3500	Wheeled vehicles	Sumeria, Syria
	Potter's wheel	Middle East
	Gold mining	Mesopotamia, Africa
	Sundial	Middle East
c. 3150	Irrigation	China, Egypt
c. 3000	Ox-drawn plow	Egypt
c. 2780	First step pyramid	Imhotep
c. 2700	Great Pyramid of Cheops	Cheops
c. 2640	Silk production	Si-ling Chi
c. 2500	Kite	China
	Cotton production	China, India
c. 1350	22-letter alphabet	Phoenicians
c. 1300	Musical notation	Ugarit, Syria
c. 700	First aqueduct	Sennacherib
570	Geographical and star charts	Anaximander of Miletus
430	Concept of atomic structure	Democritus
c. 400	Profession of medicine	Hippocrates
300	Deductive system of mathematics	Euclid
	Abacus	Asia, Middle East
c. 260	Theory that sun is the center of the solar system	Aristarchus
c. 250	Principles of the lever and other simple machines	Archimedes
c. 221	Beginning of the Great Wall of China	Shih Hwang-ti
c. 190	Ellipse and hyperbola	Appollonius
c. 140	Trigonometry	Hipparchus
	Wheel bearings	On a wagon found at Dejbjerg, Jutland
c. 85	Seed-planting machine	China
c. 40	Rotary winnowing machine	China

Inventions

A Closer Look

The Kite

The kite is not only the earliest form of flying machine, but also one of the few ancient technological objects to be used continuously into modern times. There is evidence that kites were known in China as early as 2500 B.C., and they eventually came to be used for recreational, religious, and military purposes throughout Asia and the Pacific islands. Kites served a ceremonial function, for example, in Polynesian myth, in which gods were personified in kite form.

One of the first references to kites in Europe is found in the 1300s: A German book contains an illustration of soldiers using a kite to drop a bomb over the walls of an enemy castle. By the 1600s, kites had lost their military overtones, growing popular as toys for children. In 1752, Benjamin Franklin used a kite to show the electrical nature of lightning. During the nineteenth century, kites saved lives—shipwrecked boats would use them to carry lines to potential rescuers onshore.

Also in the 1800s, kites were important in early studies of aeronautics. Lawrence Hargrave of Australia was one of the first to try to make the kite into a flying machine, a forerunner of our modern glider.

Leonardo da Vinci

A Closer Look

Modern science has its roots in the Italian Renaissance, and perhaps the most striking example of the "Renaissance Man" is Leonardo da Vinci (1452–1519). Although he is best known for his work as an artist, Leonardo's scientific contributions may rival his renowned *Mona Lisa*. In 1493, Leonardo sketched a design for a hovering machine that he called a "helix pteron," an early version of our modern helicopter. He designed and built the first swinging miter lock gates for canals. And he sketched the separation of traffic on two levels—a forerunner of modern road systems. In his scientific contributions, Leonardo was a precursor of two other Renaissance greats, Copernicus and Galileo.

Date	Invention/Advance/Discovery	Inventor/Origin
A.D.		
c. 80	Magnetism	China
c. 100	Paper making	China
c. 170	Function of the arteries	Galen
c. 180	Rotary fan	China
c. 230	Wheelbarrow	China
c. 500	Algebra	India
	Decimal system	India, Mesopotamia
c. 550	Water mill	Greece
580	Iron-chain suspension bridge	China
c. 600	Zero	India
640	Windmill	Persia
c. 700	Porcelain	T'ang dynasty
886	24-hour-day measurement system	Alfred the Great
c. 900	Moldboard plow	China
980	Canal locks	Ciao Wei-Yo
c. 1100	Rocket	China
1150	Paper mill	Spain
c. 1150	Gunpowder	China
1250	Magnifying glass	Roger Bacon
1260	Gun/cannon	Konstantin Anklitzen
1269	360° compass	Petrus Peregrinus de Maricourt
1280	Belt-driven spinning wheel	Hans Speyer
1285	Eyeglasses	Alessandro de Spina
1287	Nitric acid	Raymond Lully
1326	Metal cannon	Rinaldo di Villamagna
1335	Public striking clock	Palace Chapel of the Visconti, Milan, Italy
1360	Mechanical clock	Henri de Vick of Wurttemburg for King Charles V of France
1410	Wire	Rodolph of Nuremberg
1450	Printing press with movable type	Johann Gutenberg
1455	Cast-iron pipe	Castle of Dillenburgh, Germany
1474	Lunar nautical navigation	Regiomontanus
1489	Addition (+) and subtraction (–) signs in mathematics	Johann Widman
1493	Drawing of a flying machine	Leonardo da Vinci
1500	Portable clock	Peter Henlein
1520	Spirally grooved rifle barrel	August Kotter
1525	Portable shotgun (harquebus)	Marquis of Pescara

Inventions

continues

Significant Inventions, Technological Advances, and Scientific Discoveries, Continued

Date	Invention/Advance/Discovery	Inventor/Origin
c. 1535	Heliocentric planetary model	Copernicus
1538	Optic nerve	Constanzo Varolio
1540	Artificial limbs	Ambroise Parase
	Pistol	Camillo Vettelli
1550	Screwdriver	Gunsmiths and armorers (location unknown)
	Wrench	Unknown
	Ligature to stop bleeding during surgery	Ambroise Paré
1557	Enamel	Bernard Palissy
	Platinum	Julius Caesar Scaliger
1561	Dredger	Pieter Breughel
1565	Graphite pencil	Konrad Gesner
1569	Screw-cutting machine and ornamental turning lathe	Jacques Besson
1581	Pendulum motion	Galileo Galilei
1582	Modern calendar	Pope Gregory XIII and Christoph Clavius
1585	Time bomb	Dutch siege of Antwerp
1589	Hosiery-knitting machine	Rev. William Lee
1590	Compound microscope	Zacharias Jannsen
	Law of falling bodies	Galileo Galilei
1592	Wind-powered sawmill	Cornelius Corneliszoon
	Thermoscope (primitive thermometer)	Galileo Galilei
1597	Proportional compass (sector)	Galileo Galilei
1599	Silk-knitting machine	Rev. William Lee
1600	Wind-driven land vehicle	Simon Stevin
1603	Pantograph	Christoph Scheiner
1606	Surveying chain	Edmund Gunter
1609	Astronomical telescope	Galileo Galilei
	Laws of planetary motion	Johannes Kepler
1611	Coke (for iron)	Simon Sturtevant
	Rainbow theory	Johannes Kepler
1611	Double convex microscope	Johannes Kepler
1614	Logarithms	John Napier
1615	Solar-powered motor	Salomon de Caux
	Surveying by triangulation	Willebrord Snell von Roigen
1616	Function of the heart and complete circulation of the blood	William Harvey
	Medical thermometer	Santorio Santorii (Sanctorius)
1621	Rectilinear slide rule	William Oughtred
1630	Circular slide rule	Richard Delamain
1631	Multiplication ($\times$) sign	William Oughtred
	Vernier scale	Pierre Vernier
1637	Analytic geometry	René Descartes
1638	Micrometer	William Gascoigne
1642	Calculating machine	Blaise Pascal
1643	Barometer (Torricellian tube)	Evangelista Torricelli and Vincenzo Viviani
1647	Map of moon and star catalog	Helvius (Johannes Hewelcke)
1648	Hydrochloric acid	Johann Rudolph Glauber
	Concept of air pressure in barometers	Blaise Pascal
1650	Lymph glands	Olof Rudbeck

Inventions

Date	Invention/Advance/Discovery	Inventor/Origin
1654	Air vacuum pump	Otto von Guericke
	Basic laws of probability	Blaise Pascal and Pierre de Fermat
1656	Pendulum clock	Christiaan Huygens
1658	Clock balance spring	Robert Hooke
	Red blood cells	Jan Swammerdam
1661	Wood (methyl) alcohol	Robert Boyle
1662	Boyle's law/gas pressure laws	Robert Boyle
	Statistical mathematics	Sir William Petty
1664	Hygrometer	Francesco Folli
1666	Principles of integral calculus	Isaac Newton
1667	Blood transfusion (lamb to boy)	Jean-Baptiste Denis
	Wind gauge	Christian Forner
1668	Reflecting telescope	Isaac Newton
1669	Phosphorus	Hennig Brand
1671	Silk-spinning machine	Edmund Blood
	Binary number system	Gottfried Wilhelm Leibnitz
1674	Tourniquet	Morel, France
1675	Calibrated foot ruler	Unknown
	Speed of light	Ole Römer
1676	Artificial water filtration	William Woolcott
1679	Pressure cooker	Denis Papin
1682	Halley's comet	Edmond Halley
1683	Bacteria	Anton van Leeuwenhoek
	Spermatozoa	Anton van Leeuwenhoek
1684	Theory of gravity	Isaac Newton
	Foundations of integral and differential calculus	Gottfried Leibniz
1694	Plant pollen	Rudolph Jakob Camerarius
1695	Epsom salts	Nehemiah Grew
	Periodicity of comet orbit	Edmond Halley
1699	Portable fire pump	Dumaurier Duperrier
1701	Machine seed drill	Jethro Tull
1702	Tidal pump	George Sorocold
	Boron/borax	Guillaume Homberg
1709	Coke smelting (iron)	Abraham Derby
	Anemometer	Wolfius
	Alcohol thermometer	Gabriel Fahrenheit
1711	Tuning fork	John Shore
1712	Steam engine	Thomas Newcomen
1716	True porcelain (Meissen)	Johann Friedrich Bottger
1717	Fahrenheit temperature scale	Gabriel Fahrenheit
1718	Mercury thermometer	Gabriel Fahrenheit
1719	Color printing	Jakob Christof Le Blon
1729	Aberration of light	Rev. James Bradley
1731	Octant (Hadley's quadrant)	John Hadley
1732	Copper-zinc alloy	Christopher Pinchbeck
	Threshing machine	Michael Menzies
1733	Arsenic	George Brandt
	Flint-glass lens	Chester Moor Hall
	Fly shuttle (weaving)	John Kay
1735	Plant classification system	Carl von Linnè (Carolus Linnaeus)

Inventions

continues

Significant Inventions, Technological Advances, and Scientific Discoveries, Continued

Date	Invention/Advance/Discovery	Inventor/Origin
1736	Scarlet fever	William Douglass
1740	Curare (drug)	Charles Marie de Lacondamine
1742	Crucible steel production	Benjamin Huntsman
	Celsius temperature scale	Anders Celsius
1743	Wool carding machine	David Bourne
	Compound lever	John Wyatt
1746	Leyden jar (prototype of electrical condenser)	Pieter van Musschenbroeck and E. G. von Kleist
1747	Scurvy cure	James Lind
1748	Sea quadrant	B. Cole
1750	Dyanometer	Gaspard de Prony
1751	Nickel	Axel Frederik Cronstedt
1752	Lightning conductor	Benjamin Franklin
1755	Iron-girder bridge	M. Garvin
1756	Carbon dioxide	Joseph Black
1757	Sextant	John Campbell
1758	Achromatic lens (for eyeglasses)	John Dolland
	Refracting telescope	John Dolland
1760	Screw manufacturing machine	Job and William Wyatt
	Cast-iron cog wheel	Carron Iron Works, Scotland
1761	Mass production of steel scissors	Robert Hinchliffe
	Medical percussion method (diagnostic technique)	Joseph Leopold Avenbrugger
1762	Fire extinguisher	Ambrose Godfrey
1764	Spinning jenny	James Hargreaves
1766	Hydrogen	Henry Cavendish
1768	Aerometer	Antoine Baumé
1769	Steam automobile	Joseph Cugnot
	Steam tractor	Joseph Cugnot
	Hydraulic spinning machine	Richard Arkwright
1770	Sulfur dioxide	Joseph Priestley
	Electric battery	John Cuthbertson
1772	Nitrogen	Daniel Rutherford
1774	Oxygen	Karl Wilhelm Scheele, Joseph Priestley, and Antoine-Laurent Lavoisier
	Ammonia	Joseph Priestley
	Barium	Karl Wilhelm Scheele
	Chlorine	Karl Wilhelm Scheele
	Manganese	Karl Wilhelm Scheele
1775	Chain-driven machine	Crane (England)
	Digitalis (as drug)	William Withering
1776	One-person submarine	David Bushnell
1777	Circular saw	Samuel Miller
	Iron boat	Yorkshire, England
1778	Mortise tumbler (lock)	Robert Barron
	Flush toilet	Joseph Bramah
	Molybdenum	Karl Wilhelm Scheele
1779	Glycerine	Karl Wilhelm Scheele
1780	Artificial insemination	Lazzaro Spallanzani
1781	Uranus	William Herschel

Date	Invention/Advance/Discovery	Inventor/Origin
1782	Tellurium	Franz Joseph Müller
	Hot-air balloon	Joseph-Michel and Jacques-Étienne Montgolfier
1783	Hydrogen balloon	Jacques Alexandre Charles and the Robert brothers
	Tungsten	Don Fausto d'Elhuyar and Juan José d'Elhuyar
1784	Bifocal lenses	Benjamin Franklin
	Model helicopter	Launoy (France)
	Rope-spinning machine	Robert March
	Shrapnel shell	Henry Shrapnel
1785	Automatic gristmill	Oliver Evans
	Methane and ethylene	Claude Louis Berthollet
	Rule of electrical forces	Charles Coulomb
1786	Steamboat	John Fitch
1787	Roller bearings	John Garnett
	Power loom	Edmund Cartwright
1789	Uranium	Martin Heinrich Klaproth
	Zirconium	Martin Heinrich Klaproth
	Table of 31 chemical elements	Antoine Lavoisier
1790	Semaphore (visual telegraph)	Claude Chappé
	Cotton spinning and weaving machine (first U.S. patent)	William Pollard
1793	Cotton gin	Eli Whitney
	Astigmatism	Thomas Young
	Strontium	Thomas Charles Hope
	Daltonism (color blindness)	John Dalton
1794	Ball bearings	Philip Vaughan
1795	Hydraulic press	Joseph Bramah
1796	Lithography	Aloys Senefelder
	Smallpox vaccine	Edward Jenner
1797	Chromium	Louis Nicolas Vaquelin
	First parachute jump	André Jacques Garnerin
1798	Process of mass production	Eli Whitney
1799	Metric system	French Academy of Sciences
1800	Infrared light	William Herschel
	Method for storing electricity	Alessandro Volta
	Submarine (metal clad)	Robert Fulton
1801	Asteroid	Giuseppe Piazzi
	Niobium	Charles Hatchett
	Wave theory of light	Thomas Young
	Ultraviolet light	Johann Wilhelm Ritter (and William Hyde Wollaston)
1803	Modern atomic theory	John Dalton
	Iridium	Smithson Tennant
	Palladium and rhodium	William Hyde Wollaston
	Spray gun (aerosol medication)	Alan de Vilbiss
1804	Fishnet-making machine	Joseph Marie Charles Jacquard
	Food canning process	Nicolas Appert
1805	Mechanical silk loom	Joseph Marie Charles Jacquard
	Amphibious vehicle	Oliver Evans
	Morphine	Friedrich Wilhelm Adam Serturner

Inventions

continues

Significant Inventions, Technological Advances, and Scientific Discoveries, Continued

Date	Invention/Advance/Discovery	Inventor/Origin
1806	Beaufort wind scale	Francis Beaufort
	Carbon paper	Ralph Wedgwood
1807	Patent for gas-driven automobile	Isaac de Rivez
	Long-distance steamboat	Robert Fulton
	Potassium	Humphrey Davy
	Sodium	Humphrey Davy
	Sensory-motor nerve system	Charles Bell
1810	Homeopathy	Samuel Hahnemann
	Ammonia-soda reaction	Augustin Jean Fresnel
	Metronome	Dietrich Nikolaus Winkel
	Mowing machine	Peter Gaillard
1811	Avogadro's law	Amedeo Avogadro
	Iodine	Bernard Courteois
1813	Gun cartridge	Samuel Pauly
	Gas meter	Samuel Clegg
	Mine safety lamp	Humphrey Davy and George Stephenson
1814	Steam locomotive	George Stephenson
1816	Stethoscope	René Théophile and Hyacinthe Laënnec
	Phosphorus match	François Derosne
1817	Parkinson's disease	James Parkinson
	Lithium	John August Arfwedson
	Dental plate	Anthony A. Plantson
1818	Cadmium	Friedrich Strohmeyer
	Selenium	Johan Jakob Berzelius
	Hydrogen peroxide	Baron Louis-Jacques Thénard
	Strychnine	Pierre-Joseph Pelletier and Joseph-Bienaimé Caventou
	Geothermal energy experiment	F. de Larderel
1819	Dental amalgam	Charles Bell
	Dioptric system (for lighthouses)	Augustin Jean Fresnel
1820	Diphtheria	Pierre Fidèle Bretonneau
	Quinine	Pierre-Joseph Pelletier and Joseph-Bienaimé Caventou
	Electromagnetism	Hans Christian Oersted
1821	Caffeine	Pierre Joseph Pelletier
	Electric motor principle	Michael Faraday
	Heliotrope	Carl Friedrich Gauss
1822	Thermocouple	Thomas Johann Seebeck
1823	Electromagnet	William Sturgeon
1824	Galvanometer	André-Marie Ampère
	Magnetic pull	Dominique François Jean Arago
1825	Binocular telescope	J. P. Lemière
1826	Gas stove	James Sharp
1827	Aluminum	Friedrich Wohler
	Electrical resistance	George Simon Ohm
	Astigmatic lens	George Biddell Airy
	Microphone	Charles Wheatstone
	Trifocal lens	John Isaac Hawkins
	Water turbine	Benoît Fourneyron

Date	Invention/Advance/Discovery	Inventor/Origin
1828	First differential gear for four-wheeled vehicle	Onésiphore Pecqueur
	Stethoscope with earpiece	Pierre Adolphe Poirry
	Cocoa	Conrad van Houten
	Beryllium	Friedrich Wohler
	Thorium	Johan Jakob Berzelius
1830	Vanadium	Nils Gabriel Sefstrom
	Thermostat	André Ure
	Friction match	Charles Sauria
	Lawn mower	Edwin Beard Budding
	Paraffin	Karl, Baron von Reichenbach
1831	Electric bell	Joseph Henry
	Reaping machine	Cyrus McCormick
	Electromagnetic induction	Michael Faraday
	Electromagnetic balance	Antoine César Becquerel
	Magnetic north pole	James Clark Ross
	Chloroform	Samuel Guthrie
1833	Differential calculating machine	Charles Babbage
	Creosote	Karl, Baron von Reichenbach
	Nervous reflex	Marshall Hall
1834	Galvanic cells (continuous electric light)	James Bowman Lindsay
1835	Automatic revolver	Samuel Colt
1836	Steam shovel	William Smith Otis
	Stroboscope	Joseph Antoine Ferdinand Plateau
	Combine harvester	H. Hoare and J. Hascall
	Acetylene	Edmund Davy
1837	Braille reading system	Louis Braille
	Daguerreotype	Louis Jacques Mandé Daguerre
	Electric telegraph	William Fothergill Cooke and Charles Wheatstone
	Electric motor	Thomas Davenport
	Morse code	Samuel F. B. Morse
1838	Plant cells	Matthias Jakob Schleiden
	Stereoscope	Charles Wheatstone
1839	Animal cells	Theodore Schwann
	Protoplasm	Jan Evangelista Purkinje
	Vulcanization of rubber	Charles Goodyear
	First fuel cell	William Robert Grove
1840	Ozone	Christian Friedrich Schonbein
	Chronoscope	Charles Wheatstone
	Electroplating	John Wright
1841	Incandescent lamp	Frederick de Moleyne
1842	Carbon electrode battery	Robert Wilhelm Eberhard von Bunsen
	Underwater telegraph cable	Samuel F. B. Morse
	Ether anesthesia	Crawford Williamson Long
1844	Nitrous oxide anesthesia	Horace Wells and Gardner Q. Colton
1845	Rotary printing press	Richard M. Hoe
	Giant telescope	William Parsons
1846	Sewing machine	Elias Howe
	Use of anesthetic gases in surgery	William Morton
	Neptune	Johann Gottfield Galle and Heinrich Ludwig d'Arrest

Inventions

continues

Significant Inventions, Technological Advances, and Scientific Discoveries, Continued

Date	Invention/Advance/Discovery	Inventor/Origin
1847	Nitroglycerine	Ascanio Sobrero
	Chloroform anesthesia	Jacob Bell and James Young Simpson
1850	Foucault's pendulum (proving Earth's rotation)	Jean Bernard Léon Foucault
1851	Doppler principle	Christian Doppler
	Absolute zero	Lord Kelvin (William Thompson)
	Odometer	William Grayson
	Ophthalmoscope	Herman von Helmholtz
	Flash photography	Henry F. Talbot
1852	Steam-powered airship	Henri Giffard
	Piloted glider	George Cayley
	Microfilm	John Benjamin Dancer
	Fluorescence	George Gabriel Stokes
1853	Hypodermic syringe	Charles Gabriel Pravaz and Alexander Wood
1854	Paleozoic fossils	Adam Sedgwick
1855	Spinal anesthesia	J. L. Corning (U.S.)
	Bunsen burner	Robert Wilhelm Eberhard von Bunsen
	Stopwatch	Edward Daniel Johnson
	Safety match	Johan Edvard Lundstrom
	Battlefield nursing care	Florence Nightingale
1857	Passenger elevator	Elisha G. Otis
1858	Cell replication theory	Rudolf Virchow
	Mobius band	August Mobius
	Atomic and molecular weights	Stanislao Cannizzaro
1859	Cathode rays	Julius Plucker
	Theory of evolution through natural selection	Charles Darwin
	Internal combustion engine (coal gas)	Joseph-Etienne Lenoir
	Technique for drilling oil wells	Edwin Drake
	Ironclad ship	France (*La Gloire*)
1860	Linoleum	Frederick Walton
	Snap button	John Newnham
	Cesium	Robert Wilhelm Eberhard von Bunsen and Gustav Robert Kirchoff
1861	Pneumatic drill	Germain Sommelier
	Speech center of brain	Pierre Paul Broca
1862	Machine gun	Richard Jordan Gatling
1863	The word *Phonograph* first used in a British patent to describe a device to record a keyboard sequence on paper tape	F. B. Fenby
	TNT	J. Wilbrand
	Sodium carbonate process	Ernest Solvay
1864	Electromagnetic wave transmission	Mahlon Loomis
	Pasteurization	Louis Pasteur
	Refutation of spontaneous generation	Louis Pasteur
	Nitroglycerine and dynamite explosives	Alfred Nobel
	Railroad sleeping car	George Pullman
1865	Electric arc welding	Henry Wilde
	Reinforced concrete	W. B. Wilkinson
	Yale cylinder lock	Linus Yale, Jr.

Date	Invention/Advance/Discovery	Inventor/Origin
1865 (cont'd)	Offset printing (web press)	William Bullock
	Genetics	Gregor Johann Mendel
1866	Transatlantic cable	Cyrus West Field, Samuel Canning, and Daniel Gooch
	Lip reading	Alexander Melville Bell
1867	Formaldehyde	August Willichn von Hofmann
	Barbed wire	Lucien B. Smith
	Introduction of antiseptic practices in hospitals	Joseph Lister
	Bicycle	Ernest Michaux
	Typewriter	Christopher Latham Sholes
1868	Margarine	Hippolyte Megé-Mouries
	Stapler	Charles Henry Gould
	Plywood	John K. Mayo
	Helium (in Sun's chromosphere)	Edward Frankland and Joseph Normal Lockyer
1869	Periodic law	Dmitri Ivanovitch Mendeleyev
	Color photography	Charles Cros and Louis Ducos du Hauron
	Celluloid	John Wesley Hyatt and Isaiah Smith Hyatt
1871	Wind tunnel	Francis Herbert Wenham
1872	Hydroplane	Rev. Charles Meade Ramus
	Solar water distillation	Charles Wilson
1873	Direct current electric motor	Zénobe Théophile Gramme
	Electromagnetic radiation	James Clerk-Maxwell
1875	Mimeograph	Thomas Alva Edison
1876	Articulating telephone	Alexander Graham Bell
	Dewey decimal system	Melvil Dewey
	Carburetor (surface type)	Gottlieb Daimler
	Refrigerator	Karl Paul Gottfried von Linde
1877	Differential gear for tricycles	James Starley
	Switchboard	Edwin T. Holmes
	Four-cycle internal combustion engine	Nikolaus August Otto
	Phonograph	Thomas Alva Edison
	Liquid oxygen	Louis-Paul Cailletet and Raoul Pictet
1878	Cathode ray tube	William Crookes
	Milking machine	L. O. Colvin
	Electric alternator	Zénobe Théophile Gramme and Hippolyte Fontaine
	Carbon filament	Joseph Wilson Swann
1879	Arc lighting system	Edwin James Houston and Elihu Thomson
	Cash register	James J. Ritty
	Saccharin	Constantin Fahlberg and Ira Remsen
	Incandescent bulb patent	Thomas Alva Edison
1880	Hearing aid	R. G. Rhodes
	First successful roll film	George Eastman
	Inoculation	Louis Pasteur
1881	Interferometer	Albert A. Michelson
	Rechargeable battery	Camille Fauré
	Telephotography	Shelford Bidwell
1882	Induction coil	Lucien Gaulard and John Gibbs
	Commercial electric fan	Schuyler Skaats Wheeler
	Skyscraper	William Le Baron Jenny

Inventions

continues

Significant Inventions, Technological Advances, and Scientific Discoveries, Continued

Date	Invention/Advance/Discovery	Inventor/Origin
1882 (cont'd)	Three-wire system for transporting electrical power	Thomas Alva Edison
	Fountain pen	Lewis Edson Waterman
	Carburetor (float-feed spray)	Edward Butler
	Tuberculosis and cholera germs	Robert Koch
1883	Long-span suspension bridge (Brooklyn Bridge)	John Augustus Roebling
1884	Steam turbine	Charles Parsons
	Local anesthesia (cocaine)	K. Koller
	Gram bacteria test	Hans Christian Joachim Gram
1885	Ammonium picrate (explosive)	Eugène Turpin
	Gas-engine automobile	Gottlieb Daimler, Wilhelm Maybach, and Karl Friedrich Benz
1886	Aluminum electrolysis process	Paul Louis Toussaint Héroult and Charles Martin Hall
	Railway car brake	George Westinghouse
	Comptometer	Dorr Eugene Felt
	Linotype machine	Ottmar Mergenthaler
1887	Mach supersonic scale	Ernst Mach
	Contact lens	Eugen A. Frick
	Electrocardiogram	Augustus Desire Walker
1888	Alternating current motor	Nikola Tesla
	Cellulose photographic film	John Carbutt
	Monorail	Charles Lartigue
	Monotype	Tolbert Lanston
	Hand camera	George Eastman
	Gas-engine farm tractor	Charter Engine Co. (U.S.)
	Cotton picker	Angus Campbell
	Data-processing computer	Herman Hollerith
1889	Active molecules	Svante August Arrhenius
	Cordite	James Dewar and Frederick Augustus Abel
	Lysine (amino acid)	Edmund Drechsel
1890	Motion pictures	William Friese-Greene
	Electric subway train	London, England
1891	Electric motor car	William Morrison
	Silicon carbide	Eduard Goodrich Acheson
	Flashlight	Bristol Electric Lamp Co. (England)
	Aluminum boat	Escher Wyss & Co. (Switzerland)
	Zipper	Whitcomb L. Judson
	Diphtheria antitoxin	Emil Adolf von Behring and Shibasaburo Kitasato
1892	Cholera vaccine	Waldemar Mordecai Wolff Haffkine
	Phagocytes	Illya Mechnikov
	Vacuum flask (early thermos)	Sir James Dewar
	Viruses	Dmitri Iosifovich Ivanovsky
	Viscose rayon	C. F. Cross and E. J. Bevan
1893	Photoelectric cell	Julius Elster and Hans F. Geitel
	Electric toaster	Crompton & Co. (England)
	Diesel engine	Rudolf Diesel
1894	Argon gas	John William Strutt and William Ramsay
	Helium	William Ramsay
	Escalator	Jesse W. Reno

Date	Invention/Advance/Discovery	Inventor/Origin
1895	X rays	Wilhelm Konrad von Roentgen
	Electric hand drill	Wilhelm Fein
	Photographic typesetting	William Friese-Greene
	First public motion picture showing with on-screen projection	Louis Lumière and Auguste Lumière
	Wireless telegraph	Guglielmo Marconi
	Gas-engine motorcycle	Count Albert de Dion and Georges Bouton
1896	Electron	Joseph John Thomas
	Histidine (amino acid)	Albrecht Kossel and Sven A. Hedin
	Science of radioactivity	Henri Becquerel
1897	Conditioned reflexes	Ivan Petrovic Pavlov
	Cause of malaria (mosquito)	Ronald Ross
	Digestion physiology	Ivan Petrovic Pavlov
	Plasticine	William Harbutt
	Worm gear	Frederick W. Lanchester
1898	Antineuritic vitamin B	Christiaan Eijkman
	Krypton	William Ramsay and Morris William Travers
	Neon	William Ramsay and Morris William Travers
	Xenon	William Ramsay and Morris William Travers
	Vitamin-deficiency diseases	Christiaan Eijkman
	Loudspeaker	Horace Short
1899	Aspirin	Felix Hoffman
1900	Radon	Friedrich Ernst Dorn
	Tryptophan (amino acid)	Frederick Gowland Hopkins
	Paper clip	Johann Vaaler
	Alkaline battery	Thomas Alva Edison
	Tractor	Benjamin Holt
1901	Blood groups	Karl Landsteiner
	Valine and proline (amino acids)	Emil Hermann Fischer
	Electric typewriter	Thaddeus Cahill
	Vacuum cleaner	H. Cecil Booth
	Quantum theory	Max Karl Ernst Planck
1902	Hormones	William Maddock Bayliss and Ernest H. Starling
	Ionosphere	Arthur Edwin Kennelly and Oliver Heaviside
	Radium	Pierre Curie and Marie Curie
	Air conditioning	Willis H. Carrier
	Disc brakes	Frederick W. Lanchester
1903	First successful airplane flight	Orville Wright and Wilbur Wright
	Barbiturates	Emil Herman Fischer and Emil Adolf von Bering
1904	Diode vacuum tube	John Ambrose Fleming
1905	Theory of relativity	Albert Einstein
	Silicones	Frederic S. Kipping
	Chemical foam fire extinguisher	Alexander Laurent
	Hydraulic centrifugal clutch	Hermann Fottinger
1906	Crystal radio apparatus	H. H. C. Dunwoody
	Animated cartoon film	James S. Blackton and Walter Booth
	Motion-picture sound	Eugen Augustin Lauste
	Wasserman test (for syphilis)	August von Wasserman

Inventions

continues

Significant Inventions, Technological Advances, and Scientific Discoveries, Continued

Date	Invention/Advance/Discovery	Inventor/Origin
1907	Detergents (household)	Henkel et Cié (Germany)
	Upright vacuum cleaner (attached dust bag)	J. Murray Spangler
	Modern color photography	Louis Lumière
1908	Bakelite	Leo Henrik Baekeland
	Cellophane	Jacques E. Brandenberger
1909	Synthetic ammonia	Fritz Haber
	Typhus fever body louse	Charles Jules Henri Nicolle
	IUD (intrauterine device)	R. Richter
1910	Tumor virus	Francis Peyton Rous
	Gene theory of heredity	Thomas Morgan
	Neon lighting	Georges Claude
1911	Cosmic rays	Victor Franz Hess
	Theory of atomic structure	Ernest Rutherford and Niels Bohr
	Superconductivity	Heike Kamerlingh Onnes
	Binet intelligence test	Alfred Binet
	Calculating machine (full automatic multiplication and division)	Jay R. Monroe
	Monoplane	Léon Levasseur
1912	Diffraction of X rays	Max Theodor Felix von Laue
	Thiamine (vitamin B_1)	Casimir Funk
	Diesel locomotive	North British Locomotive Co. (England)
	Cabin biplane (airliner forerunner)	Igor Sikorsky
1913	Stainless steel	Harry Brearley
	Vitamin A	Thomas B. Osborne, Lafayette B. Mendel, Elmer V. McCollum, and M. Davis
	Isotope labeling	Georg von Hevesy and Friedrich A. Paneth
	Moving assembly line for mass production	Henry Ford
1914	Brassiere	Mary Phelps Jacob
	Leica 35mm camera	Oskar Barnack
	Tear gas	Dr. von Tappen
1915	Amplitude modulation (AM) radio	Hendrick Johannes van der Bijl and Raymond A. Heising
	British army tank	Walter Wilson and William Tritton
1917	VHF electromagnetic waves	Guglielmo Marconi
	SONAR detection system	Paul Langevin and Robert Boyle
1918	Vitamin D	Edward Mellanby
	Electric food mixer	Universal Co. (U.S.)
	Domestic refrigerator	Nathaniel Wales and E. J. Copeland
1920	Commercial radio broadcasts	Station KDKA, Pittsburgh, PA (U.S.)
1921	Insulin	Frederick G. Banting and Charles H. Best
	Hydraulic four-wheel brakes	Duesenberg Motor Co. (U.S.)
	Lie detector	John Larsen
	Wirephoto	Western Union Cables (U.S.)
1922	Vitamin E	Herbert McLean Evans
	Three-dimensional movies	Perfect Pictures (U.S.)
1924	Spin dryer	Savage Arms Corp.(U.S.)

Inventions

Date	Invention/Advance/Discovery	Inventor/Origin
1925	Quantum mechanics	Max Born and Werner Karl Heisenberg
	Technetium and rhenium	Ida Eva Noddack, Walter Karl, and Friedrich Noddack
	Wave mechanics	Erwin Schrödinger
	Hi-fi radio loudspeaker	C. W. Rice and E. W. Kellogg
1926	Aerosol can	Erik Rotheim
	Synthetic rubber	I. G. Farben (Germany)
	Liquid-fueled rocket	Robert H. Goddard
	Television	John Logie Baird, C. F. Jenkins, and D. Mihaly
1927	Iron lung	Philip Drinker and Louis Shaw
	Pop-up toaster	Charles Strite
	First solo, nonstop transatlantic flight	Charles Lindbergh
	Uncertainty principle in physics	Werner Heisenberg
	Sex hormones	Bernhard Zondek and Selmar Ascheim
1928	Penicillin	Alexander Fleming
	Vitamin C	Albert von Nagyrapolt Szent-Györgyi
	Particles in visible light	Chandrasekhara Raman
	Geiger counter	Hans Geiger
	Teletype	Edward Ernst Kleinschmidt
	PVC (polyvinylchloride)	Carbide Corp., Carbon Chemical Corp., and Du Pont (U.S.)
	Tomography	Andre Bocage
1929	Electron microscope	Max Knoll and Ernst Ruska
	Coaxial cable	Bell Telephone Laboratories (U.S.)
	Brain-wave electroencephalograph	Hans Berger
	Frozen food	Clarence Birdseye
	First color television image transmission	Bell Telephone Laboratories (U.S.)
1930	Pluto	Clyde Tombaugh
	Pepsin	John Howard Northrop
	Cyclotron	Ernest O. Lawrence and N. E. Edlesfsen
	Polystyrene	I. G. Farben (Germany)
	TV electronic scanning suitable for the home	Philo T. Pharnsworth
1931	Neutrino	Wolfgang Pauli
	Radio astronomy	Karl Jansky
	Photographic exposure meter	J. Thomas Rhamstine
	Fiberglass	Owens Illinois Glass Co. (U.S.)
	Blood bank	Sergei Sergeivitch
	TWX (teletypewriter exchange)	Bell Telephone & Telegraph (U.S.)
	Electric razor	Jacob Schick
	Cathode-ray tube for television transmission	Vladimir Zworykin
1932	Neutron	James Chadwick
	Proton bombardment (lithium disintegration)	John Douglas Cockcroft and Ernest Thomas Sinton Walton
	Positron	Carl David Anderson and Patrick M. Stuart Blackett
	Deuterium (heavy hydrogen)	Harold Urey
	Defibrillator	William Bennett Kouwenhoven
	Nylon and neoprene	Wallace Carothers and Arnold Collins

Inventions

continues

Significant Inventions, Technological Advances, and Scientific Discoveries, Continued

Date	Invention/Advance/Discovery	Inventor/Origin
1933	Riboflavin (vitamin B₂)	Richard Kuhn
	Pantothenic acid	Roger J. Williams
	Frequency modulation (FM)	Edwin H. Armstrong
	Polyethylene	Reginald Gibson and E. W. Fawcett
1934	Cerenkov effect	Pavel Alekseevich Cerenkov
	Vitamin K	Carl Peter Henrik Dam and Edward Adelbert Doisy
	Progesterone	Adolf Friedrich Johann Butenandt
	Vitamin B₆	Albert von Nagyrapolt Szent-Györgyi
1935	Meson	Hideki Yakawa
	Electronic hearing aid	Edwin A. Steven
	Richter earthquake scale	Charles Francis Richter
1936	Jet engine	Frank Whittle and Hans von Ohain
	Helicopter (contra-rotating rotors)	Henrich Focke
	Plexiglas	I. G. Farben (Germany)
1937	Citric acid cycle	Hans Adolf Krebs
	Niacin	Conrad A. Elvehjem
	Radio telescope	Grote Reber
1938	Cortisone	Edward C. Kendall, Philip S. Hench, and Tadeus Reichstein
	Folic acid	P. L. Day
	Teflon	Roy Plunkett
	LSD	Albert Hofman and Arthur Stoll
	Pressurized airplane cabin	Transcontinental Airways, Boeing 307 Stratoliner
	Ballpoint pen	Lázló J. Biro and Georg Biro
	Fluorescent lighting	Arthur H. Compton and George Inman
	Photocopy machine	Chester Carlson
	First all-plastic hard contact lenses	T. Obrig and F. Muller
1939	Jet aircraft	Hans von Ohain
	Binary calculator	John Atanasoff and George R. Stibitz
	DDT	Paul Hermann Müller
	Microfilm camera	Elgin G. Fassel
	Betatron	Donald W. Kerst
	Concept of black hole	J. Robert Oppenheimer and Hartland S. Snyder
1940	Plutonium	Glenn Theodore Seaborg and Edwin Mattison McMillan
	Radar	Robert M. Page (word coined by S. M. Tucker)
	Automatic transmission	General Motors (U.S.)
	Cavity magnetron (radar tube)	John Randall
1941	Microwave radar	U.S. Radiation Laboratory
	Dacron	John R. Whinfield
	First color television system	Peter Goldmark
1942	First sustained and controlled release of nuclear energy	Enrico Fermi and team
	Vitamin H (biotin)	Vincent du Vigneaud
1943	Streptomycin	Selman A. Waksman
	Electronic computer	Max Newman and T. H. Flowers

Inventions

Date	Invention/Advance/Discovery	Inventor/Origin
1944	Americium	Glenn T. Seaborg and Albert Ghiorso
	Curium	Glenn T. Seaborg and Albert Ghiorso
	Sequence-controlled calculator	Howard Aiken
1945	Artificial kidney	Willem J. Kolff
	Atomic bomb	J. Robert Oppenheimer and Manhattan Project team
	Tupperware	Earl W. Tupper
	Vinyl floor covering	Du Pont (U.S.)
1946	Electronic vacuum tube computer (ENIAC)	John W. Mauchly and J. Presper Eckert
1947	Coenzyme A	Fritz A. Lipman
	Vitamin B_{12} as cure for pernicious anemia	Karl A. Folkers
	Radiocarbon dating	Willard Frank Libby
	Holography	Dennis Gabor
	Supersonic aircraft	Bell XS-1 (U.S.)
	First supersonic flight	Chuck Yeager
1948	Transistor	William Shockley, John Bardeen, and Walter H. Brattain
	Atomic clock	William F. Libby
	Cybernetics	Norbert Wiener
	Long-playing phonographic record (microgroove record)	Peter Goldmark
	Solid electric guitar	Leo (Clarence) Fender, "Doc" Kauffman, and George Fullerton
	Velcro	Georges de Mestral
	Corneal contact lenses	Kevin Tuohy
1949	Berkelium	Glenn T. Seaborg and Stanley G. Thompson
	Jet airliner	R. E. Bishop and team
1950	Chlorpromazine (tranquilizer)	Paul Charpentier
	Radioimmunoassay	Rosalyn Sussman Yalow
	Xerographic copying machine	Haloid Co. (U.S.)
1951	Oral contraceptive pill	Gregory Goodwin Pincus, Min Chuch Chang, John Rock, and Carl Djerassi
1952	Artificial heart valve	Charles A. Hufnagel
	Hydrogen bomb	Edward Teller and team
	Experimental videotape	John Mullin and Wayne Johnson
	Transistor radio	Sony (Japan)
1953	DNA (deoxyribonucleic acid)	Francis H. Compton Crick and James D. Watson
	Fermium	Albert Ghiorso and Stanley G. Thompson
	Measles vaccine	John F. Enders and Thomas Peebles
	Reperine (antidepressant drug)	Nathan S. Kline
	Reserpine (antihypertensive)	Nathan S. Kline
	Heart-lung machine	John H. Gibbon
1954	Regular broadcast of color television	National Broadcasting Co. (U.S.)
1955	Fiber optics	Narinder S. Kapany
	Mendelevium	Albert Ghiorso
	RNA synthesis	Severo Ochoa
	Ultrasound (to observe heart)	Leskell (U.S.)
	Polio vaccine (killed-virus)	Jonas Salk
	Felt-tip pen	Esterbrook (England)
	Stereo tape recording	EMI Stereosonic Tapes
	Hovercraft	Christopher S. Cockerell

Inventions

continues

Significant Inventions, Technological Advances, and Scientific Discoveries, Continued

Date	Invention/Advance/Discovery	Inventor/Origin
1956	Amniocentesis	St. Mary's Hospital (England)
	Human growth hormone	Choh Hao Li
	DNA synthesis with enzymes, nucleotides	Arthur Kornberg
	Methacrylate corneal contact lenses	Norman Bier
1957	BCS theory (superconductivity)	John Bardeen, Leon N. Cooper, and J. Robert Schrieffer
	Interferon (protein)	Alick Isascs and Jean Lindeman
	Mossbauer effect (gamma radiation)	Rudolph Ludwig Mossbauer
	Polio vaccine (live virus)	Albert S. Sabin
	Artificial satellite	*Sputnik* (USSR)
	FORTRAN (computer language)	John Backus and team for IBM (U.S.)
	Intercontinental ballistic missile	USSR
	Laser theory	Gordon Gould
	Artificial-heart pacemaker	Clarence Lillehie
1958	Laser	Charles A. Townes and Arthur L. Schawlow
	Communications satellite	*SCORE* (U.S.)
	ALGOL computer language	Switzerland
	Nobelium	Albert Ghiorso
	Van Allen radiation belts	James A. Van Allen
	Integrated circuit	Jack S. Kilby, Texas Instruments (U.S.)
1959	Tunnel diode	Sony, Japan, based on work by Leo Esaki
	Microwave radio system	Pacific Great Eastern Railway between Vancouver and Dawson Creek–Fort St. John, British Columbia, Canada
	COBOL computer language	Grace Murray Hopper
	Ion engine	Alvin T. Forrester
1960	Argon ion laser	D. R. Herriott, A. Javan, and W. R. Bennett at Bell Laboratories (U.S.)
	Vertical takeoff and landing aircraft	Frank Taylor and team at Short Brothers & Harland (Northern Ireland)
	Weather satellite	*TIROS* (U.S.)
	Muonium	Vernon W. Hughes and coworkers
1961	Manned space flight	*Vostok 1* (U.S.S.R.)
	Stereophonic radio broadcast	Zenith and General Electric Companies (U.S.)
	Valium	Hoffman-LaRoche Laboratories (Switzerland)
	Kenyapithecus wickeri (hominid)	Louis S. B. Leakey
1962	Minicomputer	Digital Corp. (U.S.)
	Robotics	Rand Corp. and IBM (U.S.)
	X-ray astronomical sources	Riccardo Giacconi
	Muon neutrino	Leon Max Lederman, Melvin Schwartz, and Jack Steinberger
1963	Cassette tapes	Philips Co. (The Netherlands)
	Quarks	Murray Gell-Mann and George Zweig
	Quasars	Marten Schmidt
1964	BASIC computer language	Thomas E. Kurtz and John G. Kemeny
	Carbon fiber	RAF Farnborough (England)
	Home-use transistor videotape recorder	Sony (Japan)
	Laser eye surgery	H. Vernon Ingram

Quarks

Murray Gell-Mann and George Zweig formulated the concept of quarks in 1963 to explain the large variety of new elementary particles, called hadrons, that were being discovered. (Protons and neutrons are two types of hadrons.) Quarks are hypothetical particles presumed to be the basic constituents of hadrons. Quarks come in various "flavors," such as up, down, strange, and charmed.

But Gell-Mann and Zweig's theory left unanswered the question of why no one had ever observed isolated quarks. One theory stated that hadrons are composed of strings of quarks that are bound together so tightly that an infinite amount of energy would be required to break the bonds.

The search for quarks continued, and in 1969 strong evidence of their existence was discovered at the Stanford Linear Accelerator Center (SLAC). Richard E. Taylor of SLAC, Henry W. Kendall of MIT, and Jerome I. Friedman of MIT shared the 1990 Nobel prize for this work.

Date	Invention/Advance/Discovery	Inventor/Origin
1965	Word processor	IBM (U.S.)
	Rubella vaccine	Paul D. Parkman and Harry M. Meyer, Jr.
1966	Integrated radio circuit	Sony (Japan)
	Noise reduction system for audiotapes	Ray M. Dolby
1967	Bubble memory prototype (computers)	A. H. Bobeck and team at Bell Telephone Laboratories (U.S.)
	Pulsars	Jocelyn Bell Burnell
1968	Holographic storage technique	Bell Telephone Laboratories (U.S.)
	Hemoglobin molecule structure (complete)	Max Ferdinand Perutz
1969	Manned moon landing	*Apollo 11* (U.S.)
	PASCAL computer language	Niklaus Wirth
	Videotape cassette	Sony (Japan)
	Jumbo jet airliner	Joe Sutherland and team at Boeing (U.S.)
	Antibody chemical and molecular structure	Rodney Robert Porter
1970	Bar code system	Monarch Marking (U.S.) and Plessey Telecommunications (England)
	Computer floppy disk	IBM (U.S.)
	Remote-controlled lunar vehicle	*Lunokhod 1* (USSR)
1971	Earth-orbiting space station	*Salyut 1* (USSR)
	Liquid crystal display (LCD)	Hoffmann-LaRoche Laboratories (Switzerland)
	Quartz digital watch	George Theiss and Willy Crabtree
1972	Video disk	Philips Co. (The Netherlands)
	Video game	Noland Bushnel
	Artificial hip	John Charnley
	Enkephalin (brain chemical)	John Hughes
	Antimatter particles	Yuri Dmitriyevich Prokoshkin and coworkers
	Black holes	Robert L. F. Boyd
	MRI (magnetic resonance imaging)	Raymond Damadian
	Switching technology for cell phones	Amos E. Joel at Bell Laboratories
1973	Computerized axial tomography (CAT scan)	Allan Macleod Cormac and Godfrey N. Hounsfield
	Microcomputer	Trong Truong
	Recombinant DNA	Paul Berg
1974	Nonimpact printing	Honeywell (U.S.)
	J/psi atomic particle	Burton Richter and Samuel Chao Chung Ting

Inventions

continues

Significant Inventions, Technological Advances, and Scientific Discoveries, Continued

Date	Invention/Advance/Discovery	Inventor/Origin
1975	Hybrid cells	Jack Lucy and Ted Cocking
	Monoclonal antibodies	César Milstein
	Betamax videotaping system	Sony (Japan)
	Video home system (VHS)	Matsushita/JVC (Japan)
1976	Charm subatomic particle	Stanford Linear Accelerator Center (U.S.)
	Mars space probe landings	*Viking I* and *Viking II* (U.S.)
1977	Upsilon particle	Leon Lederman
	Neutron bomb	U.S. military
	Space shuttle	NASA (U.S.)
	Alkyd paint	Winsor & Newton Ltd. (England)
1978	Cyclosporin A	Tony Allison and Roy Calne
	Human insulin	Genentech (U.S.)
	Charon (Pluto's moon)	James Walter Christy and Robert S. Harrington
	Test-tube baby	Patrick C. Steptoe and Robert G. Edwards
1979	Single-cell protein process	ICI Agricultural Division (England)
1980	Solar-powered aircraft	Paul MacCready
1981	Anti-interferon	Medical Research Council's Molecular Biology Laboratory (England)
	First official recognition of AIDS	Centers for Disease Control (U.S.)
	Silicon 32-bit chip	Hewlett-Packard, U.S.
	Nuclear magnetic resonance (NMR) scanner	Thorn-EMI Research Laboratories and Nottingham University (England)
1982	Abnormal cancer-causing genes	Robert Weinberg and Mariano Barbacid
	Artificial heart	Robert Jarvik
	Airborne observatory	NASA (U.S.)
1983	W and Z particles	Carlo Rubbia and Simon van der Meer
	Biopol (biodegradable plastic)	ICI Agricultural Division (England)
	Biosensors	Cambridge Life Sciences (England)
	Carbon-fiber aircraft wing	Great Britain
	512K dynamic access memory chip	IBM (U.S.)
1984	Gene cloning	National Institutes of Health (U.S.); Transgene (France); and Otago University (New Zealand)
	Genetically engineered blood-clotting factor	Genentech (U.S.)
	Compact disk player	Sony and Fujitsu Companies (Japan) and Philips Co. (The Netherlands)
	Megabit computer chip	IBM (U.S.)
	Isolation of virus believed to cause AIDS	Robert C. Gallo (U.S. National Cancer Institute); Luc Montagnier (Pasteur Institute, France); and Myron Essex (Harvard School of Public Health, U.S.)
1985	Cloned leprosy genes (for vaccines)	Ron Davis and coworkers
	Anxiety chemical (human brain)	Alessandro Guidotti and Erminio Costa
	CD-ROM (compact disc read-only memory)	Hitachi (Japan)
	Image digitizer	Optronics (England)
	Polymer electric conductor	Terje Skotheim and team at Brookhaven National Laboratory (U.S.)
	Soft bifocal contact lens	Sofsite Contact Lens Laboratory (U.S.)

Inventions

Date	Invention/Advance/Discovery	Inventor/Origin
1985 *(cont'd)*	Positron emission tomography	Michael Phelps
	Publication of the first image from a positron transmission microscope	James Van House and Arthur Rich
	First baby born from frozen embryo	Australia
1986	DNA fingerprinting	Alec Jeffreys
	Diminished ozone shield	Susan Solomon at National Oceanic and Atmospheric Administration (U.S.)
	High-temperature superconductivity	Georg Bednorz and Karl Alex Müller
	Synthetic skin	G. Gregory Gallico, III
1987	Higher-temperature superconductivity	C. W. Chu, M. K. Wu, and coworkers
	Alzheimer's disease gene	National Institutes of Health (U.S.); University of Cologne (Germany)
	Gene-altered bacteria	Advanced Genetic Sciences (U.S.)
1988	Galaxy 12 billion light-years away	Simon J. Lilly
	Patented animal life	Philip Leder and Timothy Stewart
1989	Introduction of foreign gene into human patient	Steven A. Rosenberg and coworkers at National Institutes of Health (U.S.)
1991	Controlled nuclear fusion	Joint European Torus (Oxfordshire, England)
	X-ray research showing first photographs of the human brain recalling a word	Dr. Marcus Raichle and coworkers
1992	Fluctuations in cosmic background radiation	George Smoot
1994	Proof of Fermat's last theorem	Andrew John Wiles
1995	Decipherment of entire DNA sequence of living organism	Craig J. Venter and Hamilton Smith
1997	Cloning of adult animal	Ian Wilmut
	Atom laser	Wolfgang Ketterle
1998	Lunar Prospector discovers evidence of frozen water on the Moon	NASA
	Observations of supernovae suggest the expansion of the Universe is accelerating	Saul Perlmutter (Lawrence Berkeley National Lab) and Nicholar Suntzeff (Cerro Tololo Inter-American Observatory)
1999	Human stem cells found to have potential for treating incurable disease	James A. Thomson (University of Wisconsin), John D. Gearhart (Johns Hopkins University), Evan Y. Snyder (Harvard Medical School), Angelo L. Vescovi (National Neurological Institute), et al.
	Earliest life on Earth found to be 2.7 billion years old	Jochen Brocks, et. al. (University of Sydney)
	Cosmic ray bursts linked to collapse of massive stars	Shrinivas Kulkarni and Joshua Bloon (Caltech)
2000	Sequencing of the human genome accomplished	The Human Genome Project and Celera Genomics
	Potential first human ancestors to journey out of Africa found in Republic of Georgia	Reid Ferring, Carl Swisher, Susan Antòn, et al.
	NEAR Shoemaker spacecraft rendezvouses with the asteroid Eros	NASA
2001	First space "tourist" visits the International Space Station	Dennis Tito (U.S.)
	Sunken ancient Egyptian port city of Herakleion is rediscovered	Franck Goddio, leader of international mission

Inventions

MAJOR SCIENTISTS AND ENGINEERS

AEROSPACE ENGINEERS

Goddard, Robert Hutchings (1882–1945). American physicist who launched the first liquid-propellant rocket.

Sikorsky, Igor I. (1889–1972). Russian-born American aircraft designer responsible for the first multiengine airplane and the world's first true production helicopter.

Tsiolkovsky, Konstantin Eduardovich (1857–1935). Russian rocket pioneer and research scientist in aeronautics and astronautics who was one of the first to publish scientific papers about space flight.

The Wright brothers' historic flight covered a distance shorter than the length of today's space shuttle.

ASTRONOMERS

Aristotle (384–322 B.C.). Greek philosopher who developed many of the astronomical beliefs of his time, including the idea that the Earth was the center of the universe, into a cosmological system that dominated astronomy for nearly 1,800 years. He believed that everything in the universe was composed of four "basic elements"—earth, water, air, and fire.

Bode, Johann Elert (1747–1826). German astronomer who published the Titius-Bode Law in the late 1700s, a mathematical calculation that determines the distances to the planets in astronomical units.

Brahe, Tycho (1546–1601). Danish astronomer and one of the greatest astronomical observers before the advent of the telescope. His accurate measurements of planetary positions were the foundation for Johannes Kepler's formulation of the laws of planetary motion.

Cassini, Giovanni Domenico (1625–1712). Italian-born French astronomer who discovered several moons around Saturn and the dark division in Saturn's rings. He was the first of four generations of astronomers.

Copernicus, Nicolaus (1473–1543). Polish astronomer who revolutionized astronomy by proposing that the Sun, not the Earth, is the center of the solar system.

Eratosthenes of Cyrene (c. 276–c. 194 B.C.). Hellenic librarian and astronomer who was the first to estimate fairly accurately the circumference of the Earth.

Galileo Galilei (1564–1642). Italian astronomer and physicist who was the first to use a telescope for astronomical observations, discovering the moons around Jupiter and the phases of Venus.

Hale, George Ellery (1868–1938). American astrophysicist who discovered magnetic fields in sunspots and who secured funding for several large telescopes, including the 200-inch reflector on Palomar Mountain in California.

Halley, Edmond (1656–1742). British astronomer and physicist who determined the periodicity of the comet that bears his name.

Hawking, Stephen William (1942–). British theoretical physicist who is especially known for his theories on black holes and the origin and evolution of the universe.

Herschel, Sir John Frederick William (1792–1871). British astronomer, son of William Herschel, who made the first exhaustive study of the southern sky and made significant contributions to the development of photography.

Herschel, Sir William (1738–1822). German-born British astronomer who discovered the planet Uranus. He also founded modern stellar astronomy, discovered nearly 1,000 double stars, determined the general shape and size of the Milky Way, and published numerous catalogs of nebulae and clusters.

"Astronomy," "Meterology," and "Space Exploration" in chapter 4; "Astronomy Symbols" and "Weather Symbols" in chapter 12

Inventions

Hewish, Anthony (1924–). British radio astronomer whose work in radio scintillation led to the discovery of pulsars.

Hipparchus (c. 170–c. 120 B.C.). Greek astronomer and geographer who worked out the epicycle theory of the solar system, with the Earth at the center. He also discovered the precession of the equinox, calculated the length of a year within 6.5 minutes, and devised the first known star map.

Hoyle, Sir Fred (1915–). British astrophysicist who developed the steady-state hypothesis of the universe.

Hubble, Edwin Powell (1889–1953). American astronomer and cosmologist whose work demonstrated that the universe was expanding. He also formulated the Hubble constant, which measures the rate of expansion of the universe and is used to determine the age of the universe.

Jansky, Karl Guthe (1905–50). American radio engineer who, by discovering radio emissions from the Milky Way galaxy, founded the field of radio astronomy.

U.S. Army Lt. Thomas E. Selfridge was the first person to be killed in an airplane accident. The pilot of the flight was Orville Wright.

Jeans, Sir James Hopwood (1877–1946). British mathematician, astronomer, and physicist who was the first to propose that matter is continuously created throughout the universe. He also wrote numerous popular astronomy books.

Kepler, Johannes (1571–1630). German astronomer who formulated the three principal laws governing the motion and elliptical orbits of planetary bodies, thus eliminating the epicycle models that had governed astronomy for close to 2,000 years.

Kuiper, Gerard Peter (1905–73). Dutch-born American astronomer who studied lunar and planetary surface features. He discovered Mirända, a satellite of Uranus, and Nereid, a satellite of Neptune.

Laplace, Marquis Pierre Simon de (1749–1827). French mathematician, astronomer, and physicist who contributed extensively to celestial mechanics. Among other things, he established that the solar system has long-term stability. His nebular hypothesis postulated that the planets resulted from a primitive nebula that rotated around the sun.

Lowell, Percival (1855–1916). American astronomer who developed theories of life on Mars and predicted the existence of a ninth planet (Pluto, which would not be discovered until 1930).

Oort, Jan Hendrik (1900–92). Dutch astronomer who detected the rotation of the Milky Way galaxy and who postulated that a sphere of incipient cometary material, now called the Oort Cloud, surrounds the solar system far outside the orbit of Pluto.

Penzias, Arno (1933–). American astronomer who, with Robert Wilson (1936–), discovered the radio wave remnants of the Big Bang.

Piazzi, Giuseppe (1746–1826). Italian astronomer who discovered Ceres, the first asteroid (minor planet).

Ptolemy (Claudius Ptolemaeus) (c. A.D. 2nd century). Egyptian astronomer and encyclopedist who made extensive use of epicycles and other devices to achieve a fairly accurate match of observations with the idea that the Earth was the center of the universe. His achievement enabled the geocentric hypothesis to dominate astronomy for over a thousand years.

Sagan, Carl Edward (1934–96). American astronomer and exobiologist who increased public awareness and support of science through his popular writings and television presentations.

Schiaparelli, Giovanni Viginio (1835–1910). Italian astronomer who studied the planets and is known mostly for his report of *canali* (channels) on the planet Mars.

Shapley, Harlow (1885–1972). American astronomer who established the size and structure of our Milky Way galaxy.

Inventions

Shoemaker, Eugene (1928–97). American astrogeologist who established the meteoric nature of Meteor Crater in Arizona, helped map the Moon for the Apollo missions, and searched for asteroids that crossed the orbit of Earth.

Tombaugh, Clyde William (1906–97). American astronomer who discovered the planet Pluto in 1930.

Whipple, Fred Lawrence (1906–   ). American astronomer whose "dirty snowball" model of comet composition postulated that a cometary nuclei consists of a frozen mixture of water, carbon dioxide, ammonia, methane, and particles of dust, silicates, and other materials.

Wolszczan, Alex (1946–   ). Polish radio-astronomer, astrophysicist, and discoverer, along with Dale Frail of the National Radio Astronomy Observatory, of the first extrasolar planet, which was observed orbiting around pulsar PSR 1257+12 in the constellation Virgo.

BIOLOGISTS

Audubon, John James (1785–1851). French-American ornithologist and naturalist who is known for his bird drawings and paintings.

Bateson, William (1861–1926). British biologist who coined the term *genetics* (the causes and effects of heritable characteristics). He was a strong proponent of Gregor Mendel's work on heredity.

Borlaug, Norman Ernest (1914–   ). American agronomist and plant breeder who was one of the creators of the green revolution in agriculture. He won the Nobel Prize for peace in 1970 for his work on breeding "miracle" wheat for India and Mexico.

Burbank, Luther (1849–1926). American plant breeder who developed new varieties of many plants, including the Burbank potato, berries, and plums.

Carver, George Washington (c. 1860–1943). American agricultural researcher who developed new crop-rotation methods for conserving nutrients in soil and devised hundreds of new products from such crops as the peanut and sweet potato.

Cohen, Stanley H. (1922–   ). American biochemist who determined that DNA molecules could be cut, separated, and joined, thus paving the way for genetic engineering. He also worked on the mechanisms responsible for cell and organ growth.

Cuvier, Baron, Georges Léopold Chrétien Frédéric Dagobert (1769–1832). French comparative anatomist, paleontologist, and taxonomist who developed the first method of classifying mammals and founded the science of comparative anatomy. He was the first to propose that catastrophes were responsible for the extinction of species.

Darwin, Charles Robert (1809–82). British naturalist who revolutionized biology with his theory of evolution through the process of natural selection. He also provided geological evidence for evolution and made detailed observations of volcanoes and earthquakes.

de Vries, Hugo Marie (1848–1935). Dutch plant physiologist and geneticist who promoted the works of Gregor Mendel, which had been ignored for four decades. He also determined that mutations occur in organisms.

Lamarck, Jean Baptiste Pierre Antoine de Monet, Chevalier de (1744–1829). French naturalist who proposed an early theory of evolution. He was the first to distinguish between invertebrates and vertebrates, and he developed a classification system for invertebrates.

Leeuwenhoek, Anton van (1632–1723). Dutch microscopist who discovered numerous organisms, including protists, sperm (which he correctly assumed to be the source of reproduction), and bacteria.

Linnaeus, Carolus (Carl von Linné) (1707–78). Swedish naturalist who introduced certain classifications of organisms that are still in use today.

"Major Zoos and Aquariums" and "Major Botanical Gardens and Arboretums" in **Go to** chapter 11

Inventions

Mendel, Gregor Johann (1822–84). Austrian monk and botanist who discovered the basic laws of heredity, based on his studies of pea plants.

Miller, Stanley Lloyd (1930–   ). American chemist who created a primitive atmosphere that demonstrated how amino acids might have been generated in the oceans of a primitive Earth.

Sachs, Julius von (1832–97). German botanist who greatly developed the field of plant physiology. He was the first to demonstrate that photosynthesis occurs in chloroplasts.

Theophrastus (c. 372–c. 287 B.C.). Greek botanist and philosopher who described some 500 species of plants.

Tull, Jethro (1674–1741). British agriculturist, writer, and inventor who invented a machine for planting seeds. He is best known for his suggestions on plant cultivation, such as the use of manure and hoeing around crops to remove weeds.

von Frisch, Karl (1886–1982). Austrian entomologist, ethnologist, and zoologist who studied the dance of bees, recorded their detailed movements, and determined that they were actually communicating.

Wallace, Alfred Russel (1823–1913). British naturalist who formulated a theory of evolution by natural selection independently of Charles Darwin.

CHEMISTS

Arrhenius, Svante August (1859–1927). Swedish physical chemist whose work established the basis for modern electrochemistry. He also developed the theory of panspermia, in which bacterial spores were thought to travel from space to Earth. He won the Nobel Prize for chemistry in 1903.

Avogadro, Lorenzo Romano Amedeo Carlo, count of Quaregna and Cerreto (1776–1856). Italian physicist and chemist who expanded on Gay-Lussac's law of combining volumes and determined the formula for water. He differentiated molecules from atoms and was the first to use the word *molecule*. He developed Avogadro's constant and is considered one of the founders of modern physical chemistry.

Boltzmann, Ludwig (1844–1906). Austrian scientist and inventor of statistical mechanics and the concept of probability, concepts used to connect the behavior and properties of atoms and molecules with those of larger substances.

Boyle, Robert (1627–91). Irish-born chemist and physicist who explored the characteristics of gases and developed Boyle's law, which states that pressure and volume are inversely proportional for a fixed mass of gas at constant temperatures.

Cannizzaro, Stanislao (1826–1910). Italian chemist who established the use of atomic weights in chemical formulas and calculations.

Cavendish, Henry (1731–1810). English chemist and physicist who discovered hydrogen and determined the mass of the Earth.

Crookes, Sir William (1832–1919). British chemist and physicist who discovered the element thallium (using the then-new method of spectroscopy), invented the radiometer, and investigated radioactivity.

Curie, Marie Sklodowska (1867–1934). Polish-born French chemist who isolated the radioactive elements radium (with her husband Pierre Curie and Gustav Bemont) and polonium (with Pierre Curie) and was the first person to win two Nobel Prizes (for physics in 1903 and for chemistry in 1911).

Curie, Pierre (1859–1906). French physicist who codiscovered radium and polonium and shared the Nobel Prize for physics in 1903. He also discovered the piezoelectric effect, in which certain substances produce a current as the result of pressure.

Dalton, John (1766–1844). British chemist and physicist who determined the law of partial pressures and formulated an atomic theory of matter.

"The Animal Kingdom" and "The Plant Kingdom" in chapter 3
Go to

Davy, Sir Humphry (1778–1829). British chemist who established the important connection between electrochemistry and the elements, discovered the elements sodium and potassium, and invented a safety lamp for miners.

Hodgkin, Dorothy Crowfoot (1910–94). British chemist who determined the structure of vitamin B_{12} and analyzed the structure of penicillin. She won the Nobel Prize for chemistry in 1964.

Langmuir, Irving (1881–1957). American chemist who studied chemical reactions at high temperatures and low pressures, leading to the development of the gas-filled tungsten lamp. He also worked on thermal effects on gases, which led to using atomic hydrogen in welding torches. He won the Nobel Prize for chemistry in 1932.

An 11-year-old California boy mixed soda water powder with water, then accidentally left it on the back porch with the stirring stick still in it. The mixture froze during the night. His discovery later became known as the "popsicle."

Lavoisier, Antoine Laurent (1743–94). French chemist who was one of the first to quantify methods in chemistry. He determined the nature of combustion, noted the composition of the atmosphere, articulated the law of conservation of matter, and wrote the first modern chemistry book.

Mendeleev, Dmitri Ivanovich (1834–1907). Russian chemist who published the first periodic table of the elements in 1869.

Newlands, John Alexander Reina (1837–98). British chemist who was one of the first to determine periodicity in the properties of chemical elements.

Nobel, Alfred Bernhard (1833–96). Swedish chemist, engineer, and inventor of dynamite and several other explosives. His fortune endowed the Nobel Prizes.

Pauling, Linus Carl (1901–94). American chemist who applied quantum theory to molecular structures, establishing modern theoretical organic chemistry. He also determined the role of electrons in the formation of molecules and developed theories on ionic and covalent bonding, for which he won the Nobel Prize for chemistry in 1954. He was also awarded the Nobel Prize for peace in 1962 for his efforts to stop nuclear weapons testing.

Priestley, Joseph (1733–1804). British chemist and Presbyterian minister who first reported the discovery of oxygen. (Although Carl Scheele discovered the element earlier, he published his results after Priestley.)

Proust, Joseph Louis (1754–1826). French chemist who worked to measure the mass of each component of a compound. He formulated the law of constant proportions, which states that compounds always contain certain elements in the same proportion, regardless of the method of preparation.

Seaborg, Glenn Theodore (1912–99). American scientist. Codiscoverer of plutonium, he also discovered the transuranium elements through element 102 and identified more than 100 isotopes of a variety of elements.

Soddy, Frederick (1877–1966). English chemist who proposed the isotope theory of the elements and determined how radioactive elements break down. He won the Nobel Prize for chemistry in 1921.

Urey, Harold Clayton (1893–1981). American physical chemist whose pioneering isotope-separation methods enabled him to discover heavy water and deuterium (the heavy isotope of hydrogen). He also extensively studied the origin of the Earth and the other planets.

"Computers" in chapter 4; "Data Banks Available for Computer Research" in chapter 11

Go to

Inventions

COMPUTER SCIENTISTS

Babbage, Charles (1792–1871). British mathematician and inventor who developed one of the first early calculating machines, called the difference engine.

Hollerith, Herman (1860–1929). American inventor who developed the first electrically driven computer; it used punch cards to count the census.

Hopper, Grace Murray (1906–92). American computer programmer who helped invent COBOL, the computer language for business use.

Jacquard, Joseph Marie (1752–1834). French inventor who created the Jacquard loom; with this device, he programmed complicated carpet patterns onto punched cards.

Pascal, Blaise (1623–62). French mathematician, physicist, and religious philosopher who invented the first mechanical calculating machine and founded the modern theory of probabilities.

Turing, Alan Mathison (1912–54). British mathematician who developed the idea of a universal computer called the Turing machine, which could solve any type of mathematical problem by reducing it to coding in a given set of commands. (Bell Laboratories put his ideas into practice in 1939, by developing the first relay computer.)

Von Neumann, John (1903–57). Hungarian-born American mathematician who developed principles of design for digital computers and supervised the construction of the first stored-program computer.

EARTH SCIENTISTS AND ENVIRONMENTALISTS

Agassiz, Jean Louis Rodolphe (1807–73). Swiss-born American geologist and biologist who introduced the idea of the Ice Age, a period when ice sheets covered most of the Northern Hemisphere.

Agricola, Georgius (Georg Bauer) (1494–1555). German mineralogist who coined the word *fossil* but did not differentiate fossils from other types of rock.

Bjerknes, Vilhelm Friman Koren (1862–1951). Norwegian meteorologist who, with his son Jacob Aall Bonnevie Bjerknes (1897–1975), proved that the atmosphere was made up of air masses of different temperatures with sharp boundaries called fronts between them.

Today a desktop computer can store a million times more information than the first computer and is 50,000 times faster.

Brongniart, Alexandre (1770–1847). French geologist and paleontologist who pioneered the idea of using fossils to identify ages and layers of sedimentary rock.

Buys Ballot, Christoph Hendrik Diederik (1817–90). Dutch meteorologist who formulated the law for determining areas of low pressure based on observing the wind's direction.

Carson, Rachel Louise (1907–64). American ecologist and author of several scientific and popular publications concerning ecology and the environment, many of which inspired environmental protection policies.

Conybeare, William Daniel (1787–1857). British geologist and minister who synthesized the ideas of catastrophism (that geologic changes occur in brief bursts separated by long quiet periods) and progressivism (the biological theory that a series of creations yields organisms that are increasingly more complex).

Coriolis, Gustave-Gaspard (1792–1843). French physicist who, in 1835, first described the curving deflection of winds caused by the Earth's rotation, now called the Coriolis effect.

Cousteau, Jacques-Yves (1910–97). French oceanographer who developed the aqualung, underwater photography techniques, and the bathyscaph.

Inventions

He was also an author and filmmaker who increased public awareness of the diversity of ocean life and environmental problems of the oceans and the Earth.

Dana, James Dwight (1813–95). American geologist and mineralogist who wrote the first standard reference books in geology and mineralogy.

Drake, Edwin Laurentine (1819–80). American investor who drilled the world's first oil well in Titusville, Pennsylvania, in 1859. His work greatly advanced geological studies in the search for more oil.

Ewing, William Maurice (1913–74). American oceanographer who made detailed maps of the sea bottom using refraction of waves caused by explosions (similar to sonar). He helped describe the Mid-Atlantic Ridge, an area of seafloor spreading that cuts through the Atlantic Ocean.

Gilbert, Grove Karl (1843–1918). American geologist and geomorphologist who developed the foundations of 20th-century earth science. He contributed detailed descriptions of river and other geologic processes that became standards for his time.

Hadley, George (1685–1768). English lawyer and climatologist who suggested that the Earth's rotation from west to east caused the trade winds to blow from the northeast in the Northern Hemisphere and from the southeast in the Southern Hemisphere.

Hall, Sir James (1761–1832). British chemist and geologist who was one of the first scientists to use laboratory experiments to test geologic theories. He also showed that crystals form from melted rock.

Hess, Harry Hammond (1906–1969). American geologist and discoverer of the phenomena of seafloor spreading, which expanded the theory of plate tectonics.

Humboldt, (Friedrich Wilhelm Heinrich) Alexander, Baron von (1769–1859). Prussian scientific explorer who made detailed investigations of the Earth's magnetism, identified the Jurassic Period of geologic time, and explored the cold current running north along the Pacific coast of South America.

Hutton, James (1726–97). Scottish natural philosopher who was the founder of modern geology and geomorphology. He was the first to propose the idea of uniformitarianism—that is, that all geologic features can be explained by rocks from the past.

Leakey, Louis Seymour Bazett (1903–72) and **Leakey, Mary Nichol** (1913–96). British anthropologists and husband-and-wife team who found some of the oldest humanoid fossils in the Olduvai Gorge, Africa, including members of the Australopithecines. Mary later found a 3.75-million-year-old humanoid fossil at Laetoli, Africa.

Leakey, Richard Erskine Frere (1944–). Kenyan paleontologist, son of Louis and Mary Leakey. He found some of the oldest known humanoid fossils in Kenya, including a nearly complete fossil of a large *Homo erectus* (found with colleagues) in Kenya.

Leopold, Aldo (1886–1948). American naturalist who was one of the first scientists to arouse public interest in wilderness conservation. He wrote *A Sand County Almanac* (1949).

Lyell, Sir Charles (1797–1875). Scottish geologist whose *Principles of Geology* was one of the most influential works on geology. He shared James Hutton's belief that the present is the key to the past and held that fossils were the best guides to describing geologic rock layers. He was also one of the first to postulate that the Earth was millions of years old.

Maury, Matthew Fontaine (1806–73). American hydrologist and oceanographer who wrote the first text of modern oceanography, detailing the trade winds and ocean currents.

Mohs, Friedrich (1773–1839). German mineralogist who was the first to classify minerals based on hardness.

Muir, John (1838–1914). British-born American naturalist who is noted for his work to gain popular and federal support of forest conservation.

Playfair, John (1748–1819). Scottish mathematician, geologist, and philosopher who expanded on the work of his friend James Hutton. Playfair's law states that river tributaries are as deep as the surrounding major valley; he used this information to distinguish river valleys from glacial hanging valleys.

Pytheas (fl. 350 B.C.). Greek geographer and explorer who observed the strong Atlantic tides and correctly theorized that they were caused by the Moon.

Richter, Charles Francis (1900–85). American seismologist who developed a scale (the Richter scale) for measuring the intensity, or magnitude, of earthquakes.

Torricelli, Evangelista (1608–47). Italian mathematician and physicist who is considered the father of hydrodynamics. He proposed an experiment (later performed by his colleague Vincenzo Viviani) that demonstrated that atmospheric pressure determines the height a fluid will rise in a tube when it is inverted over a saucer of the same liquid. This idea led to the development of the barometer.

Wegener, Alfred Lothar (1880–1930). German geologist and meteorologist who suggested the idea of continental drift in 1912, noting that the coastlines of several continents fit roughly together into a supercontinent that he named Pangaea. His ideas were not accepted until the 1960s, when geomagnetic and oceanographic evidence established the theory of plate tectonics.

Werner, Abraham Gottlob (1750–1817). German mineralogist and geologist who developed the first systematic classification of minerals.

White, Gilbert (1720–93). British naturalist whose *Natural History and Antiquities of Selborne* was one of the first known works on ecology.

MATHEMATICIANS

Archimedes (c. 287–212 B.C.). Greek mathematician who is considered to be the greatest mathematician and engineer of ancient times. He derived the theory of the lever, discovered the principle of buoyancy, and developed methods for determining the volumes of geometric solids.

Bernoulli, Daniel (1700–82). Netherlands-born Swiss mathematician who is known for his pioneering work on hydrodynamics.

Cauchy, Baron Augustin Louis (1789–1857). French mathematician whose work concentrated on complex analysis. With the concepts of limit and continuity, he introduced rigor into the development of calculus.

Euclid (c. 330–c. 260 B.C.). Greek mathematician whose systematic proof of theorems in his *Elements of Geometry* formed the basis of most mathematical thought for the next 2,000 years.

Euler, Leonhard (1707–83). Swiss mathematician and physicist who was one of the founders of pure mathematics. The most prolific mathematician in history, he contributed to calculus, geometry, mechanics, and number theory.

Fermat, Pierre de (1601–65). French mathematician who helped lay the foundation for analytical geometry. He was also the founder of the modern theory of numbers.

Gauss, Karl Friedrich (1777–1855). German mathematician who worked on electricity and magnetism and on planetary orbits.

Hero of Alexandria (fl. 1st century A.D.). Greek mathematician and inventor who was best known for his formulation for the area of a triangle. He was also the inventor of the first known steam-powered engine.

Hypatia (c. 370–415). Egyptian mathematician and philosopher who was the first notable female mathematician.

Möbius, August Ferdinand (1790–1868). German mathematician who discovered the Möbius strip, a figure that has only one side and one edge. He also made major contributions to analytical geometry and topology.

"Geology and Geophysics" and "Mathematics" in chapter 4; "Symbols Used in Science, Mathematics, and Technology" in chapter 12

Inventions

Omar Khayya'm (1048–?). Best known for his *Rubaiyat* (a collection of poetical quatrains), he was a Persian mathematician and astronomer who was the first to demonstrate that a cubic equation might have two roots. His work was a step toward the unification of algebra and geometry.

Pappus of Alexandria (fl. 320 A.D.). Greek mathematician who wrote a compendium of eight books covering mathematical knowledge of his time.

The mother of Mike Nesmith (formerly of the rock group the Monkees) invented Liquid Paper.

Pythagoras (c. 580–c. 500 B.C.). Greek mathematician and philosopher who is credited with the theorem on right-angled triangles named after him and founding the science of acoustics.

Russell, Bertrand Arthur William, Earl (1872–1970). British philosopher and mathematician who had great influence in mathematical logic through the three-volume *Principia Mathematica* (1910, 1912, 1913) that he cowrote with Alfred North Whitehead.

Tartaglia (Niccolò Fontana) (1500–57). Italian mathematician, topographer, and military scientist who provided an algebraic solution to cubic equations and produced that first translation of Euclid's *Elements* into a modern language (Italian).

MEDICAL SCIENTISTS

Avicenna (980–1037). Persian physician whose encyclopedic *Canon of Medicine* was the authoritative treatise on medicine until the 17th century.

Banting, Sir Frederick Grant (1891–1941). Canadian medical scientist who, along with John Richard Macleod (1876–1935), discovered insulin.

Bernard, Claude (1813–78). French physiologist who introduced the concepts that the functions of the various organs within the body are closely interrelated and that the body maintains a constant internal environment despite external changes.

Blackwell, Elizabeth (1821–1910). The first female physician in the United States. Her small practice in New York expanded into the New York Infirmary for Women and Children, which had an all-female staff.

Bowman, Sir William (1816–92). British physician who founded histological anatomy and ophthalmic surgery. Working with a microscope, he made detailed descriptions of nerves, skin, and muscles. He also did major work on eye diseases.

Broca, Pierre Paul (1824–80). French physician, anthropologist, and surgeon who was the first to identify the speech center in the brain.

Crick, Francis Harry Compton (1916–). British molecular biologist who with James Watson discovered the double-helix structure of DNA, for which they shared the Nobel Prize for physiology or medicine in 1962.

Darwin, Erasmus (1731–1802). British physician who developed ideas on animal causation and classification of disease. He also worked out a theory of biological evolution somewhat similar to the one his grandson, Charles Darwin, developed years later.

Ehrlich, Paul (1854–1915). German physician, bacteriologist, and chemist who discovered numerous bacterial toxins and antitoxins; he was also the first to use chemotherapy in medicine. He shared the 1908 Nobel Prize for physiology or medicine with Ilja Mecnikov for their immunity studies.

Erasistratus of Chios (c. 276–c. 194 B.C.). Greek anatomist and physician whose work was the most respected of his time. Studies by Herophilus of Chalcedon and Erasistratus laid the foundation for anatomy and physiology. He also was one of the first to discover that the brain was the center of intelligence.

Fleming, Sir Alexander (1881–1955). British bacteriologist who discovered how the human body defends itself against bacterial infection. He also worked on eradicating syphilis. He shared the Nobel

Prize for physiology or medicine in 1945 with Sir Howard Florey and Ernst Chain for the discovery of penicillin.

Flourens, Jean Pierre Marie (1794–1867). French physician and anatomist who studied the physiology of the nervous system and the formation and growth of bones. He also discovered chloroform's anesthetic properties.

Franklin, Rosalind (1920–58). British crystallographer whose X-ray diffraction studies of DNA suggested a helical structure.

Freud, Sigmund (1856–1939). Austrian psychiatrist who laid the foundation for modern psychoanalysis. He introduced the concepts of ego, superego, and id and is known for his work on the interpretation of dreams.

Galen (c. 130–c. 200). Turkish-born physician who became one of the most famous and influential doctors of Rome. He developed a physiological model of the human body that was held as the standard for anatomy for centuries.

Harvey, William (1578–1657). British physician who discovered that heart pulsations caused blood to circulate around the body.

Hippocrates of Cos (c. 460–c. 370 B.C.). Greek physician who developed ideas that led to the Hippocratic oath. He started a school of medicine at Cos, where he encouraged the separation of medicine and religion.

Jenner, Edward (1749–1823). British physician who discovered the smallpox vaccine. He was also the founder of immunology and the pioneer of modern virology.

Jung, Carl Gustav (1875–1961). Swiss psychologist and psychiatrist who founded analytic psychology. His work contradicted many of the ideas of Sigmund Freud.

Koch, Robert (1843–1910). German physician, surgeon, and discoverer of the tuberculosis bacillus in 1882, and the cholera bacillus in 1883.

Pasteur, Louis (1822–95). French chemist and microbiologist who developed the germ theory of disease. He also developed the first vaccine against rabies and was the founder of microbiology.

Pavlov, Ivan Petrovich (1849–1936). Soviet physiologist who worked on blood circulation, digestion, and the physiology of the brain and nervous system. He is best known for his demonstration of the phenomenon of the conditioned reflex.

Ross, Sir Ronald (1857–1932). British physician responsible for discovering that malaria was transmitted by mosquitoes.

In 1809, Melitta Bentz invented the world's first drip coffeemaker by making a filter out of her son's notebook paper.

Sabin, Albert Bruce (1906–93). Polish-born American microbiologist who invented the first oral polio vaccine.

Salk, Jonas Edward (1914–95). American microbiologist who formulated the first successful polio vaccine, which was administrated by injection.

Stokes, William (1804–78). Irish physician who advanced the fields of cardiac and pulmonary disease.

Sydenham, Thomas (1624–89). English physician who was one of the founders of epidemiology. He was instrumental in describing numerous diseases, including measles and scarlet fever.

Watson, James Dewey (1928–   ). American biochemist who, with Francis Crick, discovered the double-helix structure of DNA, for which they shared the Nobel Prize for physiology or medicine in 1962.

Wilkins, Maurice (Hugh Frederick) (1916–   ). New Zealand–born British biophysicist who, with James Watson, Francis Crick, and Rosalind Franklin, discovered the structure of DNA. He shared the

Inventions

Schrödinger's Cat Paradox

A Closer Look

The theory of quantum mechanics states that for a specific event, there is not one but numerous possible states that may exist simultaneously at a microscopic level. When we observe the event—that is, make a measurement—one of the states becomes "real" on our (macroscopic) level.

In 1935, Erwin Schrödinger published an essay dealing with paradoxes that were occurring in the then-new field of quantum mechanics. He sought to explain the influence of measurement on an event by using his now famous Schrödinger's Cat paradox. In this imaginary setting, a cat is placed in a sealed box with a flask of poisonous gas. The decay of a radioactive atom "triggers" a mechanism that shatters the flask and kills the cat. In the course of an hour, the atom may decay, triggering the gas, but also, with equal probability, it may not.

We open the box after an hour and observe the radioactive atom. Until that measurement is made, the cat exists in our sealed box in two probable states, dead or alive, based on the equal probability of whether or not the atom has decayed. This question is resolved by our observation; that is, one of the states becomes "real," and the cat is either ready for some milk or needs to be buried.

Although this is a thought experiment, in the late 1990s physicists at the National Institute of Standards and Technology (NIST) in Boulder, Colorado, succeeded in creating a "Schrödinger-cat-like state of matter" in a single beryllium atom. The researchers trapped the atom with nonuniform electric fields and cooled it to near standstill. Then laser pulses were used to vibrate the atom's electrons, creating a dual presence, as if two atoms existed in distinct locations at the same time. The two states were separated by a distance larger than the normal area of the atom. For a brief period, the atom appeared to exist in two places, or states, similar to Schrödinger's cat.

1962 Nobel Prize with Watson and Crick (Franklin died before the award was presented).

PHYSICISTS

Alvarez, Luis Walter   (1911–88). American physicist who won the Nobel Prize for physics in 1968 for his work in advancing the field of high-energy-particle physics. He developed the practical linear accelerator. Alvarez and his son Walter, along with several others, first proposed the theory that massive extinctions around the time of the boundary between the Cretaceous and Tertiary periods were caused by the impact of a large meteorite or asteroid.

Ampere, Andre Marie   (1775–1836). French physicist and mathematician who laid the foundation of the science of electrodynamics and determined that electric currents produce magnetic fields.

Becquerel, Antoine Henri   (1852–1908). French physicist who discovered the natural radioactivity produced by uranium.

Bohr, Niels Hendrik David   (1885–1962). Danish physicist who was the first to apply quantum theory to atomic structure and to note the connection between spectral lines and the energy levels of elec-

trons. For his work with atoms, he was awarded the Nobel Prize for physics in 1922.

Celsius, Anders   (1701–44). Swedish astronomer who was the developer of the temperature scale that was named after him.

Chadwick, Sir James   (1891–1974). British physicist who discovered the neutron, for which he was awarded the Nobel Prize for physics in 1932.

Coriolis, Gaspard Gustave de   (1792–1843). French physicist who was first to coin the term *kinetic energy.* He was also the first to describe the effect (named after him) that deals with the apparent force on a moving object when observed from a rotating system. This Coriolis force governs the movement of atmospheric winds.

de Broglie, Prince Louis Victor Pierre Raymond (1892–1987). French physicist who discovered the wave nature of electrons and other particles. For this work, he won the Nobel Prize for physics in 1929.

Doppler, Christian Johann   (1803–53). Austrian physicist who discovered that a wave frequency changes when the source and observer are in motion relative to each other (the Doppler effect).

"Physics" in chapter 4; "Major Science and Technology Museums and Their Special Collections" in chapter 11   **Go to**

Dyson, Freeman (1923–). British physicist, educator, and author best known for his work on the possibility of extraterrestrial civilizations.

Einstein, Albert (1879–1955). German-born theoretical physicist who helped establish quantum theory (first put forth by Max Planck) by using it to describe photoelectric effects, work for which he was awarded the Nobel Prize for physics in 1921. He also developed the theories of special and general relativity.

Fahrenheit, Daniel Gabriel (1686–1736). Polish-born Dutch physicist who developed the temperature scale that was named after him. He invented a mercury thermometer.

Faraday, Michael (1791–1867). British physicist and chemist who proposed the idea of magnetic "lines of force," developed the first electric generator, and pioneered the study of low temperatures. He also discovered benzene.

Fermi, Enrico (1901–54). Italian-American physicist who produced the first controlled chain reaction in a nuclear reactor. He produced new radioactive isotopes by neutron bombardment, work for which he won the Nobel Prize for physics in 1938.

Feynman, Richard Phillips (1918–88). American theoretical physicist known for his work on the basic principles of quantum electrodynamics, for which he shared the Nobel Prize for physics in 1965.

Foucault, Jean Bernard Leon (1819–68). French physicist who invented the gyroscope, developed a method for demonstrating the rotation of the Earth (using a Foucault pendulum), and was the first to accurately determine the velocity of light.

Franklin, Benjamin (1706–90). American statesman and scientist who experimented with electricity and introduced the terms *positive* and *negative* to describe electric charge.

Gell-Mann, Murray (1929–). American physicist known for his work on the theory of elementary particles, including the postulation of fundamental building blocks he named "quarks."

Grimaldi, Francesco Maria (1618–63). Italian physicist who discovered optical diffraction and accepted the idea of waves of light. He also made one of the first lunar maps and started the tradition of naming the Moon's features after famous scientists.

Hertz, Heinrich Rudolf (1857–94). German physicist who discovered radio waves.

Joliot-Curie, Frédéric (1900–58) and **Irène** (1897–1956). French physicists who developed the first artificial radioactive substance, an isotope of phosphorus; for this work, they were awarded the Nobel Prize for chemistry in 1935. Irène was the daughter of chemists Marie and Pierre Curie.

Joule, James Prescott (1818–89). British physicist who measured the amount of heat produced by an electric current. He also determined that if a gas expands without performing work, its temperature falls.

Kelvin, Lord (William Thomson) (1824–1907). British theoretical and experimental physicist who proposed the absolute scale of temperature and the idea that mechanical energy tends to dissipate as heat, which Rudolf Clausius later developed into the concept of entropy.

Mach, Ernst (1838–1916). Austrian physicist who discovered that airflow becomes disturbed at the speed of sound. Mach numbers (which represent how fast a craft is traveling beyond the speed of sound) were named after him.

Maxwell, James Clerk (1831–79). British physicist who developed equations that served as a basis for the understanding of electromagnetism. He also determined that light is electromagnetic radiation, developed the kinetic theory of gases, and proved the particle nature of Saturn's rings.

Newton, Sir Isaac (1642–1727). English physicist and mathematician who invented calculus, determined the nature of white light, constructed the

Inventions

first reflecting telescope, and formulated the laws of motion and the theory of universal gravitation.

Ohm, Georg Simon (1789–1854). German physicist who determined the law (named after him) that states that electrical current is equal to the ratio of the voltage to the resistance.

Planck, Max Karl Ernst Ludwig (1858–1947). German physicist who developed the quantum theory to explain the nature of black-body radiation. He won the Nobel Prize for physics in 1918.

Roentgen, Wilhelm Conrad (1845–1923). German physicist who discovered X rays, for which he was awarded the Nobel Prize for physics in 1901.

Rutherford, Ernest, Lord (1871–1937). New Zealand–born British physicist who established the basic structure of the atom. He was also the first to change one element to another by an artificial nuclear reaction, for which he won the Nobel Prize for chemistry in 1908.

Schrödinger, Erwin (1887–1961). Austrian physicist who founded wave mechanics to describe the behavior of electrons in atoms. For this work, he shared the Nobel Prize for physics in 1933.

Tesla, Nikola (1856–1943). Serbian-American scientist and inventor responsible for the induction motor, rotating magnetic field principle, alternating-current power transmission, wireless communication, and numerous other electrical discoveries.

Thomson, William. *See* **Kelvin, Lord (William Thomson).**

Torricelli, Evangelista (1608–47). Italian physicist who used Galileo Galilei's ideas on the laws of motion to describe the motion of fluids.

Volta, Count Alessandro Giuseppe Antonio Anastasio (1745–1827). Italian physicist who built the first chemical battery and first produced electric current without using animal tissues.

Wilson, Charles Thomson Rees (1869–1959). British physicist who invented the Wilson Cloud Chamber, which revolutionized the study of particle

physics by allowing the tracks of subatomic particles to be easily viewed.

ADDITIONAL SOURCES OF INFORMATION

BOOKS

Ballard, Robert D., and W. Hively. *The Eternal Darkness.* Princeton University Press, 2000.

Biographical Dictionary of Mathematicians. Scribner, 1991.

Biographical Dictionary of Scientists. Scribner, 1981.

Boyer, Carl. *History of Mathematics.* Wiley, 1991.

James, Peter. *Ancient Inventions.* Ballantine Books, 1995.

Macaulay, David. *The Way Things Work.* Houghton-Mifflin, 1988.

McNeil, Ian. *Encyclopedia of the History of Technology.* Routledge, 1990.

Messadie, Gerald. *Dictionary of Inventions.* NTC Publishing Group, 1998.

Pacey, Arnold. *Technology in World Civilization: A Thousand-Year History.* M.I.T. Press, 1990.

Strandh, Sigvard. *The History of the Machine.* A&W Publishers Inc., 1979.

Van Dulken, S., and A. Phillips. *Inventing the 20th Century: 100 Inventions That Shaped the World.* New York University Press, 2000.

WEB SITES

Nobel e-Museum
http://www.nobel.se/

Nobel Prize Internet Archive
http://www.almaz.com/nobel/

ScienceDaily Magazine
http://www.sciencedaily.com/

Scientific American
http://www.sciam.com

II

THE WORLD OF IDEAS

6

PERFORMANCE AND ENTERTAINMENT ARTS

ILLUSTRATED LIST OF MUSICAL INSTRUMENTS

STRINGED INSTRUMENTS

The stringed instruments described below are divided into three classifications: plucked, hammered, and bowed. Other classifications are possible.

PLUCKED

guitar family   The guitar is a flat-backed stringed instrument of Spanish origin. It has a long, fretted neck and usually six strings, which are strummed or plucked with the fingers or a plectrum, or pick. Members of the guitar family include the banjo, which is strung with at least four but usually five strings and is generally played with the fingers, and the four-stringed ukulele, originally from Portugal but introduced into the Hawaiian Islands around 1879.

harp family   Originating in Mesopotamia and Egypt, the harp is an instrument with strings stretched vertically in an open triangular frame and played by plucking with the fingers. The modern harp usually has 46 strings and seven pedals that permit the playing of halftones.

harpsichord family   The harpsichord is a stringed instrument with one or more keyboards, also called manuals. The instrument has one or more strings for each key and produces tones when the strings are plucked with quills or leather points activated by the keys.

Guitar   Harp

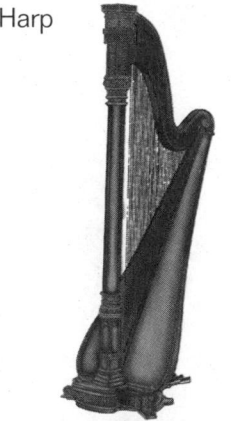

lute family   The lute is an ancient stringed instrument related to the guitar, with a large pear-shaped body, a fretted finger board, and a head with tuning pegs, which is often angled backward from the neck. The strings can be played with either a plectrum or the fingers.

Lute

lyre   Lyres come in many sizes. They are open, stringed instruments on a square or rectangular frame, played by plucking with the fingers. The lyre was used by the ancient Greeks to accompany singers and reciters.

zither   The zither is a flat-backed instrument usually having 30 to 40 strings stretched over a shallow horizontal soundboard. The instrument is played on a table or resting on the knees. It can be plucked with the fingers or played with a plectrum.

HAMMERED

clavichord   The clavichord, predecessor of the piano, is a stringed musical instrument with a rectangular keyboard. The strings are struck at various points from below by metal wedges, or tangents, attached directly to the key ends.

piano   This large keyboard instrument was introduced in Italy around 1700. Its steel wire strings sound when struck by covered hammers operated from the keyboard. In upright pianos, the strings are vertical; in wing-shaped pianos, they are horizontal.

BOWED

hurdy-gurdy This instrument of the Middle Ages is shaped like a lute or viol but played by turning a crank attached to a rosined wheel that causes the strings to vibrate. The hurdy-gurdy is most often associated with traveling musicians of the 17th century.

viol family Viols are stringed instruments played with a curved bow, characterized generally by six strings, frets, a flat back, and C-shaped sound holes. These instruments, used chiefly in the 16th and 17th centuries, vary in size from the treble viol to the bass viol.

violin family These instruments were developed in the 17th century but became popular around 1700. They are played with a straight bow, are characterized by a rounded back and F-shaped sound holes, and have fretless fingerboards. The violin is the highest pitched of the family. The viola, slightly larger than the violin, is tuned a fifth lower. The larger violoncello, or more commonly called the cello, is a rich-toned bass instrument. The largest and deepest-toned of all the violins is the double bass.

Violin Viola

Double Bass

Violoncello

WIND INSTRUMENTS

Wind instruments are divided into three classifications: open mouthpiece, reed type, and brass type.

OPEN MOUTHPIECE

flute family The flute is a high-pitched wind instrument consisting of a long slender tube, played by blowing across a hole near one end. The player can produce various tones by fingering the holes and keys along its length. Variations include the smaller piccolo and the larger alto flute and bass flute.

Flute

Piccolo

panpipes Primitive and varied in form, the panpipe is made of a row or rows of reeds or tubes of gradual length and bound together. The player blows across the open upper ends to produce sound.

pipe organ The pipe organ is a large wind instrument consisting of various sets of pipes. A keyboard controls the flow of air into the pipes, where sound is produced. Simple organs were widely used in religious services in 10th-century Europe. By the

Performance Arts

Middle Ages, portable and indoor tabletop organs were introduced.

recorder family   Unlike flutes, which are blown from the side, recorders are end blown. They have eight finger holes and a reedless mouthpiece. This instrument was popular from the Renaissance through the 18th century. Other members of the recorder family include the six-holed flagolet as well as the double and triple flagolets.

REED TYPE

bagpipe family   The bagpipe is a shrill-toned instrument with one double-reed pipe operated by finger stops and one or more drone pipes. The pipes are sounded by air forced with the arm from a leather bag, which is kept filled by the breath. The bagpipe is an ancient instrument, with Asian predecessors dating from the first millennium B.C.

bassoon family   This double-reed bass woodwind instrument dates from the Baroque musical period (1600–1750). It has a long, curved stem attached to the mouthpiece and is built in four joints: the wing, butt, long joint, and bell. The normal bassoon's range is two octaves lower than the oboe, and the contrabassoon sounds an octave further down.

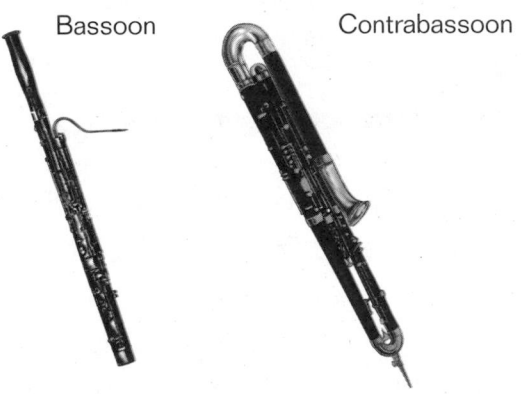

Bassoon   Contrabassoon

clarinet family   Clarinets are single-reed woodwind instruments with a long wooden or metal tube ending in a slightly flared bell. Orchestral types of clarinets have a variety of pitches, notably B-flat and A. The bass clarinet's tones are an octave lower than B-flat, and the E-flat clarinet is the sopranino.

A Clarinet   B-flat Clarinet

Bass Clarinet

oboe family   Oboes are double-reed orchestral instruments with a range of nearly three octaves and a high, penetrating, melancholy tone. The modern oboe has a flared bell. Another member of the oboe family is the English horn.

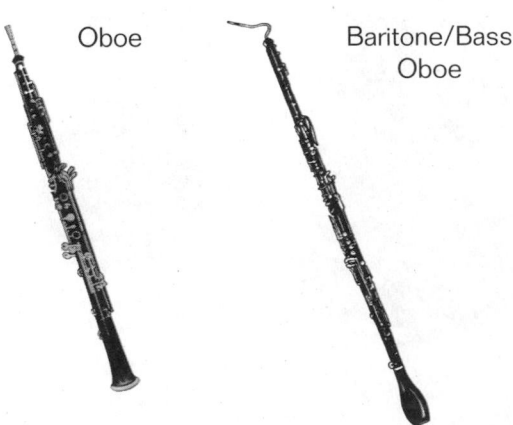

Oboe   Baritone/Bass Oboe

Performance Arts

reed-organ family   The reed organ differs from the pipe organ in that it produces the tones with a set of free metal reeds. Other members of the reed-organ family include the harmonica and the accordion.

saxophone family   The saxophone is a single-reed, keyed woodwind instrument with a conical bore and metal body. The two principal categories of saxophone are orchestral and band. The band, or military, saxophones are the type most commonly seen, particularly the alto and tenor.

Soprano Saxophone   Alto Saxophone

Tenor Saxophone   Baritone Saxophone

BRASS TYPE

horn family   The term *horn* commonly designates an orchestral valved instrument with a flared end. The French horn is a circular instrument with three valves and a funnel-shaped mouthpiece.

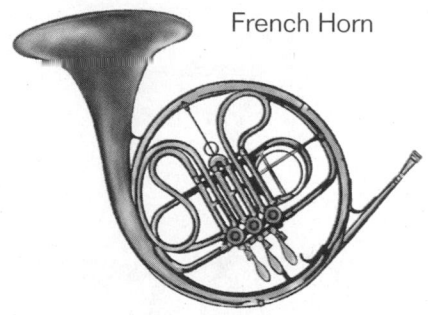

French Horn

saxhorn family   These valved brass-band instruments have a full, even tone and range in pitch from soprano to contrabass. Members of the saxhorn family include the alto horn, baritone, and euphonium.

trombone family   The trombone is a large brass wind instrument consisting of a long tube bent parallel to itself twice and ending in a bell mouth. The two types of trombones are the slide and the valve. The slide trombone produces different tones when the slide is moved in or out. The valve trombone is constructed, like the trumpet, with valves.

Tenor Trombone

Bass Trombone

Performance Arts

Modern nanotechnology has allowed scientists to produce a guitar no bigger than a blood cell. The guitar is 10 micrometers long with 6 strings.

trumpet family   The trumpet consists of a tube in an oblong loop or loops, with a flared bell and, in today's version, three valves for producing changes in pitch. Other members of the trumpet family include the cornet and the bugle.

Flügelhorn

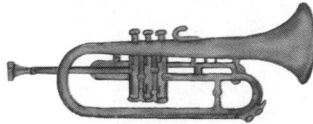

Cornet

Bugle

tuba family   This largest of the valved brass instruments has the lowest pitches in that group. The tuba consists of a conical bore and three to five valves. Various types of tubas include the sousaphone, double B-flat, double C, E-flat, and F.

Sousaphone   Tuba

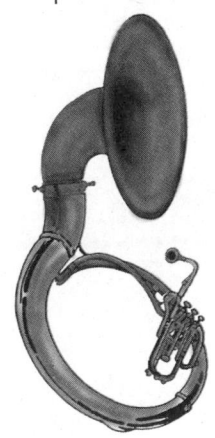

PERCUSSION INSTRUMENTS

Percussion instruments are divided into two classifications: definite pitch and indefinite pitch.

DEFINITE PITCH

glockenspiel   The glockenspiel consists of chromatically tuned, flat metal bars set in a frame. It is played with small hammers and produces bell-like tones.

kettledrum   Kettledrums consist of hollow hemispheres of copper or brass with a parchment head stretched across the top. The head can be tightened or loosened to change the pitch.

Kettledrum

tubular bells   An 18th-century invention, tubular bells are metal tubes of varying lengths hung vertically in a frame. They are struck with mallets and produce bell-like tones.

xylophone family   The xylophone consists of a series of wooden bars or other material graduated in length so that they sound the notes of the scale when struck with mallets.

INDEFINITE PITCH

bass drum   The bass drum is the largest and lowest-toned of the double-headed drums and lends itself to both marching bands and symphony orchestras.

castanets   These small, hollowed pieces of hard wood or ivory are held in the hand by a connecting cord and clicked together with the fingers to beat time to music.

cymbals Either handheld or mounted and struck with a stick, cymbals are circular, slightly concave brass plates that produce a variety of metallic sounds. Specific types of drum cymbals include the ride cymbal, hi-hats, and crash cymbals.

gong The gong is a slightly convex metallic disk that gives a loud resonant tone when struck with sticks or mallets. Flat gongs lack a definite pitch, but a knob, or boss, located at the gong's center lends it a specific pitch.

side drum or snare drum This instrument consists of a wooden or metal cylinder with two heads and wires, known as snares, strung across the bottom head for added vibration. The player strikes the upper head with sticks or wire brushes, which causes the snares to reverberate.

tambourine This instrument is a shallow, single-headed drum with jingling metal disks on the rim. The player shakes or hits the tambourine with the hand or sticks.

tenor drum This 19th-century invention is slightly deeper than the side drum and lacks snares. The tenor drum is a marching instrument usually played with felt-headed sticks.

triangle The triangle consists of a steel rod bent into a triangle shape, left open at one angle. It produces a high-pitched tinkling sound when struck with another steel rod.

ELECTRONIC INSTRUMENTS AND DEVICES

electric guitar The electric guitar's sounds are amplified by means of an electronic pickup that converts string vibrations into electric impulses. In the 1920s the body was hollow, but in the 1940s a solid body replaced the sound box with wood or fiber glass.

electronic organ The electronic organ consists of rotating tone wheels and fixed-pitch oscillators or vibrating reeds to generate sound like that of an acoustic organ.

Musical Instrument Digital Interface (MIDI) At its most basic form, the MIDI allows musicians to play multiple digital instruments from one mechanism. It transmits the information in a series of digital codes. The MIDI can be used for more complicated arrangements as well, such as connecting a variety of instruments to a master computer.

signal processor Electrified instruments transmit signal sounds to a number of devices (such as equalizers, pitch transposers, compressors, and limiters). These devices alter pitch, tone, and other components of the instrument, even making one musical instrument sound like another.

synthesizer This machine, equipped with a keyboard, contains filters, oscillators, and voltage-control amplifiers that are used to generate sounds

The Makeup of a Symphony Orchestra

A Closer Look

Strings	12 to 14 first violins, 10 to 12 second violins, 8 to 10 violas, 6 to 8 cellos, 4 to 6 double basses.
Woodwinds	2 flutes, 2 oboes, 2 clarinets, 2 bassoons.
Brass	2 trumpets, 2 or 4 horns, 2 or 3 trombones, 1 tuba.
Percussion	2 or 3 kettledrums and various instruments of definite pitch (glockenspiel, bells, xylophone) and indefinite pitch (snare drum, bass drum, cymbals, triangle).
Harps	1 or 2 (2 are called for more often than 1).

A larger orchestra would have this typical composition:

Strings	16 first violins, 14 second violins, 12 violas, 10 cellos, 8 double basses.
Woodwinds	2 flutes and piccolo, 2 oboes and English horn, 2 clarinets and bass clarinet, 2 bassoons and contrabassoon.
Brass	3 trumpets, 4 horns, 3 trombones, 1 tuba.
Percussion	As above.
Harps	As above.

Performance Arts

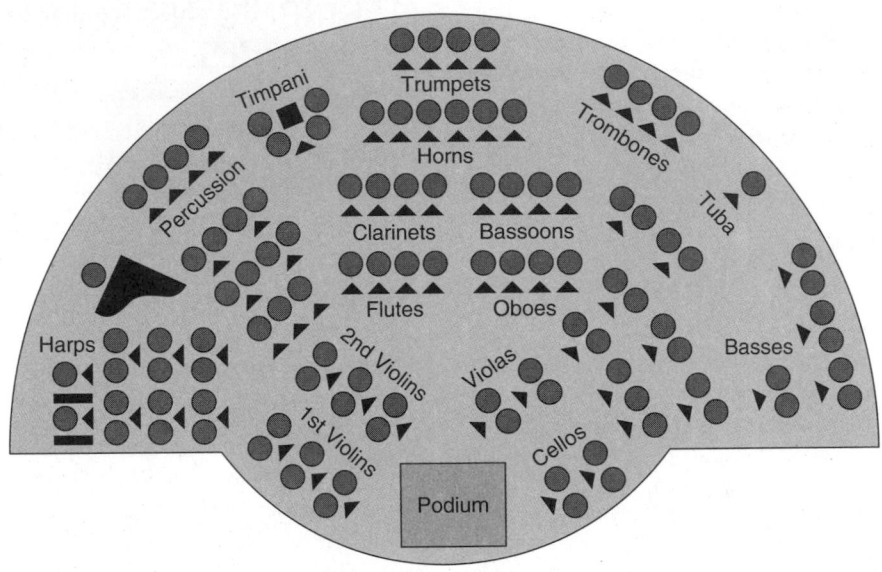

Instrument Positions in the Classic Orchestra

unobtainable from ordinary instruments or to imitate instruments and voices.

MAJOR COMPOSERS OF CLASSICAL MUSIC

AMERICAN

Amram, David (1930–   ), b. Pennsylvania. Composer and musical director of the New York Shakespeare Festival (1956–68) and the Lincoln Center Repertory Theater (1963–65). He has composed incidental music for plays, orchestra, opera, choral works, and jazz concerts.

Barber, Samuel (1910–81), b. Pennsylvania. Winner, two Pulitzer prizes, for the opera *Vanessa* (1958) and for *Piano Concerto No. 1* (1963). Known for their romantic style, his works also include two symphonies, the overture to *The School for Scandal* (1932) and the popular *Adagio for Strings* (1938).

Beach, Amy Marcy (1867–1944), b. New Hampshire. Composer whose symphonies, mass, and concerto were widely performed in the United States and abroad, particularly between 1893 and 1914. She was one of the first women composers in the United States to achieve wide respect and popularity. Her works include *Gaelic Symphony in E Minor,*

op. 32 (1896), *Piano Concerto in C Sharp Minor* (1899), and *Scottish Legend, op. 54* (1903).

Bernstein, Leonard (1918–90), b. Massachusetts. Conductor and music director of the New York Philharmonic (1958–69). He composed symphonies, songs, and ballets and is best known for his musicals, including *West Side Story* (1957). His world renown also stemmed from his ability to discuss music vividly and in a way intelligible to the musically uneducated person.

Blitzstein, Marc (1905–64), b. Pennsylvania. Pianist, composer, librettist. He was a student of Schoenberg. Among his most important works are orchestral variations; a piano concerto; operas, including the choral opera *The Cradle Will Rock* (1937); ballets; and film music.

Bloch, Ernest (1880–1959), b. Switzerland. Director of the Cleveland Institute of Music (1920–25) and the San Francisco Conservatory (1925–30). Influenced by his Jewish heritage, his works include symphonies, such as *Hivers-Printemps* (1905), *Israel* (1912–17), *America* (1926), *Voice in the Wilderness,* and *Evocations;* operas; chamber music; choral works; a piano sonata; songs; and *Avodath Hakodesh* (1933), a sacred service for Reform Judaism.

Cage, John   (1912–92), b. California. Originator of controversial and experimental theories, performances, and compositions. He is best known for his experiments with random-chance music and for introducing performances with prepared piano. His works include the *Music of Changes* for piano (1951), derived from the ideas of *I Ching; Imaginary Landscape No. 4* for 12 radios tuned randomly (1951); and *4'33"* (1952), in which no sound is called for. Cage collaborated with dancer Merce Cunningham, artist Marcel Duchamp, and others.

All popular songs can be accompanied on a guitar using only three chords. Typical chords are G, C, and D7.

Copland, Aaron   (1900–90), b. New York. Composer of three symphonies, a piano concerto, other orchestral works, chamber music, and ballets, including *Billy the Kid* (1938) and *Rodeo* (1942). The creator of a distinctly American music, Copland received the Pulitzer prize in 1945 for *Appalachian Spring* (1944).

Corigliano, John   (1938–   ), b. New York. Composer whose lyrical and rhythmical expression is in the tradition of Bartók and Prokofiev. His works include *Kaleidoscope* (1959) for two pianos, *Violin Sonata* (1963), the score for the film *Altered States* (1981), and the opera *The Ghosts of Versailles* (1991).

Cowell, Henry Dixon   (1897–1965), b. California. Pianist and composer of symphonies, an opera, and the piano concerto *Tales of Our Countryside* (1939). Cowell founded the New Musical Society (1927); he invented (with Leon Theremin) an electronic instrument called the "rhythmicon" and a method of playing the piano with forearm, elbow, and fist. His books on music include *New Musical Resources* (1930) and *Charles Ives and His Music* (1955).

Dello Joio, Norman   (1913–   ), b. New York. Concert pianist, organist, and award-winning composer whose style reflects the influence of American jazz, Italian opera, and the neoclassicism of the early 1900s. His works include piano sonatas, chamber music, orchestral and choral pieces, and ballets. He won the 1957 Pulitzer prize in music for his *Meditations on Ecclesiastes* for orchestra.

Gershwin, George   (1898–1937), b. New York. Composer of music in a distinct blend of classical, popular, and jazz styles. Gershwin's works include numerous popular songs and musical comedies and more ambitious concert pieces: *Rhapsody in Blue* (1924), *An American in Paris* (1928), and the jazz opera *Porgy and Bess* (1935).

Hanson, Howard   (1896–1981), b. Nebraska. Conductor and composer of romantic works, including symphonies, piano music, and the opera *Merry Mount* (1934). He served as director of the Eastman School of Music (1924–64) in Rochester, New York, and received the 1944 Pulitzer prize in music for his *Symphony No. 3, The Requiem* (1943).

Ives, Charles   (1874–1954), b. Connecticut. Composer of advanced and innovative works and winner of the Pulitzer prize in 1947 for his *Symphony No. 3*. His compositions—including four symphonies, chamber and choral music, songs, and piano works—stressed American folk and popular music, jazz, military marches, patriotic songs, and revival hymns.

MacDowell, Edward   (1860–1908), b. New York. Best known as a composer of piano works, MacDowell also wrote orchestral works, symphonic poems, and a suite that appropriates melodies of northern Native Americans. He was the first head of the department of music at Columbia University (1896–1904).

Menotti, Gian Carlo   (1911–   ), b. Italy. Composer of ballets, a piano concerto, and some of the most popular operas of the mid–20th century. He won the 1950 Pulitzer prize for *The Consul* and the 1955 Pulitzer prize for *The Saint of Bleecker Street*. He founded the Festival of Two Worlds in Spoleto, Italy.

Moore, Douglas   (1893–1969), b. New York. Composer of works noted for their use of the American vernacular, including the operas *The Devil and Daniel Webster* (1939) and *The Ballad of Baby Doe* (1956). He was the author of *Listening to Music* (1931) and *From Madrigal to Modern Music* (1942) and won the 1951 Pulitzer prize for *Giants of the Earth* (1951).

Performance Arts

Piston, Walter (1894–1976), b. Maine. Professor at Harvard and neoclassical composer of orchestral works, string quartets, sonatas, chamber music, and the ballet *The Incredible Flautist* (1938). Piston wrote studies of harmony and counterpoint. He won the Pulitzer prize in 1948 for his *Symphony No. 3* and in 1961 for his *Symphony No. 7.*

Schoenberg, Arnold (1874–1951), b. Austria. Originator of the revolutionary 12-tone system. The theory is exemplified in his works of 1921–33, including *Five Pieces* (1923) for piano and *Serenade* (1923) for seven instruments and bass baritone.

Schuman, William (1910–92), b. New York. President of the Juilliard School of Music (1945–61) and Lincoln Center (1962–69). Schuman composed ballets and concertos as well as chamber, orchestral, and choral works that featured energetic melodies, lively rhythms, and brilliant orchestrations. He was the winner of the first Pulitzer prize for music in 1943 for *A Free Song.*

Sessions, Roger (1896–1985), b. New York. Composer of intense, intellectual works, including eight symphonies, a violin concerto, piano works, organ pieces, and songs. His books include *Questions About Music* (1970). Sessions's most popular work is the orchestral suite *The Black Maskers* (1923), and he won the 1982 Pulitzer prize for *Concerto for Orchestra.*

Thomson, Virgil (1896–1989), b. Missouri. Music critic and composer. Based on early American hymns and folk songs, his works include two operas (with librettos by Gertrude Stein), a ballet, choral and chamber music, pieces for theater and film (among them *The River,* 1937), keyboard music, and songs. He wrote several books, including *The State of Music* (1939) and *Music, Right and Left* (1951). Thomson won the 1949 Pulitzer prize for the documentary *Louisiana Story.*

Varèse, Edgar (1883–1965), b. France. Founder and conductor of the New Symphony Orchestra, New York (1919), and founder of the International Composers Guild (1921). Varèse was a leading experimental composer of the early 1920s and wrote nontraditional works for orchestra with electronic music. His *Poème Electronique* (1958) is considered a major work in this field.

Zwilich, Ellen Taafe (1939–), b. Florida. Composer and first woman to receive the Pulitzer prize in music composition, in 1983, for her *Symphony No. 1.* Her works have been characterized as romantic with a lush Straussian flavor. Among her other works is *Trio for Piano, Violin, and Cello* (1987).

AUSTRIAN

Berg, Alban (1885–1935). Composer in Arnold Schoenberg's 12-tone system. Principal works are the opera *Wozzeck* (1925), the unfinished opera *Lulu* (1937), orchestral pieces, concertos, string quartets, *Lyric Suite* (1926–28), and a piano sonata.

Bruckner, Anton (1824–96). Organist and composer of romantic music. Much revised by his friends, his original compositions were published in 1929. Principal works include nine symphonies, choral works, and chamber music for string quintet.

The setting for the musical The Sound of Music is Salzburg, Austria, which is also Mozart's birthplace.

Czerny, Karl (1791–1857). Virtuoso pianist and composer of many works for piano. Best known for his technical studies, Czerny was a pupil of Beethoven and a teacher of Liszt.

Haydn, Franz Joseph (1732–1809). Consummate artist of the classical style in music, who has been called the "father of the symphony." Among his works are more than 100 symphonies, numerous concertos, 20 operas (five are lost), marionette operas, church music, string quartets, piano trios, keyboard sonatas and variations, songs, and 377 arrangements of Scottish and Welsh airs. His most famous works include *The Bird* quartet (1781), the oratorios *The Creation* (1798) and *The Seasons* (1801), and the *Surprise Symphony* (1791).

Haydn, Johann Michael (1737–1806). Brother of Franz Joseph Haydn and composer of oratorios and church music, symphonies, concertos, divertimenti, quintets, and other instrumental works.

Mahler, Gustav (1860–1911). Conductor of the Hamburg and Vienna operas and the Metropolitan Opera in New York. He composed nine symphonies, as well as songs, in a late Romantic style, including *Resurrection Symphony* (1894) and *Symphony of a Thousand* (1907).

Mozart, Wolfgang Amadeus (1756–91). Master of the classical style in all its forms of his time. Mozart began to compose and perform at age 6; at age 11 he had composed three symphonies and 30 other works and arranged some piano concertos of Johann Sebastian Bach. His principal works include the operas *The Marriage of Figaro* (1786), *Don Giovanni* (1787), and *The Magic Flute* (1791); chamber music; piano sonatas and fantasias; 50 symphonies; and church music, including the *Requiem* (1791). One of his most popular compositions is *A Little Night Music* (1787). Mozart's works are noted for their lyrical charm.

Schubert, Franz Seraph Peter (1797–1828). Composer of numerous symphonies, masses, quartets, and sonatas, but most notably of songs in the spirit of early romantic poetry. His works after 1823 consummate his lyrical, melodic style, as in the *No. 9 C Major Symphony* ("The Great") (1828); 22 piano sonatas, including the *Wanderer Fantasie* (1822); and the *Piano Trio in B-flat major* (1827) and *Piano Trio in E-flat major* (1827).

Strauss. Family of Viennese musicians. **Johann I** (1804–49) was the composer of waltzes famous throughout Europe. He was the father of **Johann II** (1825–99), who became his rival and who composed more than 400 waltzes, including *The Blue Danube* (1866) and *Tales from the Vienna Woods* (1868), as well as operettas. Johann II's brothers, **Josef** (1827–70) and **Eduard I** (1835–1916), were also successful composers and conductors.

Webern, Anton von (1883–1945). Editor, conductor, and composer in the 12-tone system of Arnold Schoenberg. Webern wrote a symphony for small orchestra, three cantatas, a string quartet, a concerto for nine instruments, songs, and other works. His major choral works include *Das Augenlicht* (1935), *First Cantata* (1939), and *Second Cantata* (1943).

BRITISH

Britten, (Edward) Benjamin (1913–76). Major 20th-century composer famous for his vocal music and operas. The latter include *Peter Grimes* (1945), *The Rape of Lucretia* (1946), *Billy Budd* (1951), *The Turn of the Screw* (1954), and *A Midsummer Night's Dream* (1960). Among his most popular works are *A Ceremony of Carols* (1942), *A Young Person's Guide to the Orchestra* (1945), and the *War Requiem* (1962).

Byrd, William (1543–1623). Organist and composer. A master of 16th-century polyphony, Byrd excelled in the composition of church music, including *Gradualia* (1605–07).

Delius, Frederick (1862–1934). Composer of orchestral works, including *Paris* (1899), *Appalachia* (1896), and *Brigg Fair* (1907); choral works, including *Sea Drift;* and the operas *A Village Romeo and Juliet* (1901) and *Fennimore and Gerda* (1910).

Dowland, John (c. 1563–1626). Lutenist and composer of the most important English collection of songs for the lute. His most famous work is *Lachrymae* (1605), a collection of dance pieces.

Elgar, Sir Edward (1857–1934). Composer best known for *Pomp and Circumstance,* a set of five marches; an adaptation of *Pomp and Circumstance* (1902) for the coronation of King Edward VII; *The Dream of Gerontius* (1900); *The Enigma Variations* (1899) for orchestra; and *Introduction and Allegro for Strings* (1905).

Gibbons, Orlando (1583–1625). Organist and composer of anthems, madrigals, chamber music, and keyboard pieces.

Holst, Gustav (1874–1934). Composer who combined an interest in folk music with a knowledge of Hindu scales and Sanskrit literature. His later music experimented with harmony and polytonality. Principal works include the operas *Savitri* (1908) and *The Perfect Fool* (1923); for orchestra, *The Planets* (1914–16) and *Egdon Heath* (1927); and for chorus, *Hymns from the Rig-Veda* (1910) and *Hymn for Jesus* (1917).

Morley, Thomas (1557–1602). Composer, theorist, and organist at St. Paul's Cathedral. Morley was

Performance Arts

granted a monopoly on music printing (1598) and wrote the first comprehensive treatise on composition in English (1597). He became known for his light songs, including canzonets, airs, and madrigals.

Purcell, Henry   (c. 1659–95). Organist at Westminster Abbey and composer of music for more than 40 plays, including the first important English opera, *Dido and Aeneas* (1689), and *The Fairy Queen* (1692), a masque. He also wrote odes, songs, cantatas, church music, chamber music, and keyboard works.

Sullivan, Sir Arthur   (1842–1900). Conductor, organist, and composer. His works include the grand opera *Ivanhoe* (1891); ballads; oratorios; cantatas, including *The Golden Legend;* church music; a symphony; songs; and works for piano. He is best known for light operas to librettos by W. S. Gilbert.

Tallis, Thomas   (c. 1505–85). Organist and composer. He was granted a monopoly in music printing with William Byrd (1575). Tallis's works include church music and secular pieces for vocals and keyboard.

Vaughan Williams, Ralph   (1872–1958). Composer noted for his adaptations of English folk music and Tudor church music. Principal compositions include *A London Symphony* (1913), *Norfolk Rhapsodies* (1906), and *The Lark Ascending* (1914), all for orchestra; *A Sea Symphony* (1910) and *Five Mystical Songs* (1911) for chorus; the operas *Hugh the Drover* (1914), *Riders to the Sea* (1937), and *The Pilgrim's Progress* (1951); and works for stage, chamber music, and songs.

FRENCH

Berlioz, Hector   (1803–69). Conductor and composer of romantic works. Berlioz is best known for his genius with orchestration and his way of relating musical works to story ideas, as in the *Symphonie Fantastique* (1830). He also wrote the symphonic work *Harold in Italy* (1834), the opera *Damnation of Faust* (1846), and the oratorio *Childhood of Christ* (1850–54).

Bizet, Georges   (1838–75). Composer best known for the operas *Carmen* (1875), *The Pearlfishers* (1863), *The Young Maid of Perth* (1867), and

Djmileh (1872). His *Symphony in C Major* (1868) is highly regarded. His music is melodic and tightly organized, with uncomplicated orchestral accompaniment.

Boulanger, Lili   (1893–1918). Composer in an impressionist style. She composed more than 50 works in the genres of secular and sacred music, chorus with and without orchestra, cantatas, chamber music, songs, and an uncompleted opera. Boulanger is best known for her cantata *Faust et Hélène* (1913), for which she was awarded the Prix de Rome.

Boulez, Pierre   (1925–   ). Composer of experimental works using the serial technique, including *Pli selon pli* (1962) and *Memoriales* (1975). Many of his compositions contain unusual rhythms with separate sounds. He served as music director of the New York Philharmonic (1971–77) and as director of L'Institut Recherche et Coordination Acoustique Musique until 1992.

Couperin, François   (1668–1733). Member of a family of distinguished organists. Organist to the king at Versailles, he composed music for organ and harpsichord, instrumental ensembles, secular songs, and church music. He wrote a well-known textbook, *The Art of Playing the Harpsichord.*

Debussy, Claude   (1862–1918). Composer noted for his impressionist style. Orchestral works include *La Mer* (1903–05) and *Nocturnes* (1893–99); piano works include *Clair de Lune* (1890), preludes, études, arabesques, and *The Children's Corner* (1906–08). Debussy also wrote choral works, an opera, and the well-known tone poem *Prelude to the Afternoon of a Faun* (1894).

Delibes, (Clément Philibert) Léo   (1836–91). Composer of operas, including *Le Roi l'a dit* (1873) and *Lakmé* (1883), and ballets, including *Coppélia* (1870) and *Sylvia* (1876).

Dukas, Paul   (1865–1935). Composer best known for the orchestral scherzo *Sorcerer's Apprentice* (1897), the opera *Ariane et barbe-Bleue* (1907), and the ballet *La Peri* (1912).

Fauré, Gabriel   (1845–1924). Organist and composer who excelled in songwriting and an adventurous use of harmony. He wrote the operas

Prométhée (1900) and *Pénélope* (1913), orchestral music, chamber works, and piano and church music. Fauré was the teacher of Maurice Ravel.

Franck, César (1822–90). A teacher who influenced an entire generation of composers. Distinctive compositions include *Symphony in D Minor* (1888), the *Symphonic Variations* (1885) for piano and orchestra, *Prelude, Chorale, and Fugue* (1884), and the opera *Hulda* (1894).

Gounod, Charles (1818–93). Composer of the operas *Faust* (1859) and *Romeo and Juliet* (1867). Gounod also wrote church music, symphonies, and cantatas. His music includes elements of seriousness, melodrama, and sentimentality.

Honegger, Arthur (1892–1955). Founding member of the Parisian group "The Six" in 1916 with Erik Satie, Darius Milhaud, and Jean Cocteau. Rejecting romanticism and impressionism, Honegger is best known for the oratorio *King David* (1921) and for *Pacific 231* (1923) and *Joan of Arc at the Stake* (1935), both for orchestra.

Ibert, Jacques François Antoine (1890–1962). Ibert's colorful works include a suite for orchestra, *Escales* (1922); *Divertissement* (1930); music for theater and film; chamber music; and works for piano and organ. He served as director of the Académie de France in Rome (1937) and the Paris Opera (1955).

Lully, Jean-Baptiste (orig. Lulli, Giambattista) (1632–87). Lully composed for the comedy ballets of Molière and was the founder of the French opera *(tragédie lyrique)*. He also composed court ballets, divertissements, church music, and two instrumental suites. His best-known works include *Cadmus and Hermione* (1673), *Amadis de Gaule* (1684), and *Roland* (1685).

Massenet, Jules Emile Frédéric (1842–1912). Best known for his pop operas *Le Roi de Lahore* (1877), *Manon* (1884), *Werther* (1892), and *Le Jongleur de Notre-Dame* (1902). Massenet also wrote oratorios, orchestral works, concertos, and songs.

Messiaen, Olivier Eugène Prosper Charles (1908–92). Organist and composer of symphonic poems and works for piano, organ, and vocals. He became known for using birdcalls, electronic sounds,

religious songs, and Oriental themes in his compositions. Messiaen helped form the group "Jeune France" in 1936 and wrote a treatise on composition. His works include the 10-movement symphony *Turangalila* (1949).

Milhaud, Darius (1892–1974). A member of the Parisian group "The Six," Milhaud composed works that combine jazz, polytonality, and Brazilian elements. He is well known for the opera *Christophe Colomb* (1930) and for ballets, including *Creation of the World* (1923).

Offenbach, Jacques (1819–80). Composer of 90 operettas, including the popular *Orpheus in the Underworld* (1858), *La Belle Hélène* (1864), and *La Vie Parisienne* (1866). His best work is thought to be *The Tales of Hoffmann,* which was unfinished at his death and later completed by Ernest Guiraud.

Poulenc, Francis (1899–1963). Member of the Parisian circle "The Six," Poulenc composed ballets, including *Les Biches* (1924); chamber music; a concerto for two pianos; songs; choral works; a cantata; and operas, among them *Dialogues of the Carmelites* (1957). He was noted for his vocal music featuring beautiful melodies and sensitive lyrics.

Rameau, Jean-Philippe (1683–1764). Theorist and important composer of French opera. His works include the operas *Castor et Pollux* (1737) and *Dardanus* (1739), the opera-ballet *Les Indes galantes* (1735), and the ballet-bouffon *Platée* (1745). His *Treatise of Harmony* (1722) laid the foundation for the modern theory of harmony.

Ravel, Maurice (1875–1937). Leading exponent of impressionism, who relied on the strong melodies and rich textures of 19th-century classical music. Ravel's principal works include *Rapsodie espagnole* (1908), *Daphnis and Chloe* (1912), and *Bolero* (1928), all for orchestra; and *Valses nobles et sentimentales* (1911) and *Gaspard de la nuit* (1908), both for piano.

Saint-Saëns, Charles Camille (1835–1921). Pianist and composer. Saint-Saëns began performing at age 10 and later composed symphonic poems under the influence of Franz Liszt; operas, including *Samson et Dalila* (1877); and concertos.

Satie, Erik (1866–1925). Composer noted for his ironic, humorous style and ranked as a leader in the development of modern music. Satie composed three ballets, including *Parade* (1917); operettas; a symphonic drama, *Socrates;* songs; and piano pieces.

GERMAN

Bach, Johann Sebastian (1685–1750). Baroque organist and composer; one of the greatest creators of Western music. Among his religious works are more than 200 cantatas, the *Mass in B Minor* (1733–49), and the *St. Matthew Passion* (1727). His other works include *The Well-Tempered Clavier* (1722), a collection of preludes and fugues; the Brandenburg concertos (1721); and many sonatas and suites. He had 20 children, 10 of whom survived, including **Wilhelm Friedemann** (1710–84), organist and composer; **Carl Philipp Emanuel** (1714–88), composer of religious music, symphonies, concertos, sonatas, and chamber music; **Johann Christoph Friedrich** (1732–95), composer; and **Johann Christian** (1735–82), composer of operas, chamber music, and church music.

Beethoven, Ludwig van (1770–1827). Considered one of the greatest composers of instrumental works, particularly symphonies, he is regarded as one of the founding fathers of musical romanticism. Beethoven was a student of Haydn, whose influence permeates his early works. By 1824 he had lost his hearing, but he continued to compose under the sponsorship of aristocratic patrons. His works include *Fidelio* (1805), an opera; a violin concerto and five piano concertos; the *Egmont* overture (1810); 32 piano sonatas, including the *Appassionata* (1804–05); 16 string quartets; the *Mass in D (Missa Solemnis)* (1818–23); and nine symphonies, the best known of which are the *Third (Eroica)* (1804), the *Fifth (Victory)* (1805), the *Sixth (Pastoral)* (1809), and the *Ninth (Choral)*. The *Ninth,* completed in 1823, is considered the greatest of his works.

Brahms, Johannes (1833–97). Developer of a romantic style that was both lyrical and classical. His principal works include four symphonies, two overtures, and two serenades for orchestra; two piano concertos, one violin concerto, and one concerto for violin and cello; *A German Requiem* (1857–68), his best-known choral work; piano solos, including variations on themes by Paganini, Handel, and Schumann; chamber music; rhapsodies; ballades; piano duets; waltzes; Hungarian dances; songs; folk song arrangements; and 11 choral preludes for organ.

Bruch, Max (1838–1920). Famous for his setting of the melody to the Jewish prayer *Kol Nidre* (1880) for cello and orchestra. His works also include three symphonies, three operas, an operetta, choral works, and chamber music.

Beethoven dedicated his third symphony, the Eroica, *to Napoleon but later tore it up when Napoleon crowned himself Emperor of France.*

Gluck, Christoph Willibald von (1714–87). Composer of more than 100 operas, among them *Orfeo ed Euridice* (1762) and *Alceste* (1767), which established a new style of Italian opera; 11 symphonies; instrumental trios; seven odes by Friedrich Klopstock for solo voice and keyboard; and a flute concerto.

Handel, George Frideric (1685–1759). Baroque composer most famous for the oratorio *Messiah* (1742). Trained in law and music in Germany, Handel produced his operas in Italy and London, incorporating German, Italian, and English styles. Among his works are many operas, including *Almira* (1705), *Ottone* (1723), and *Orlando* (1733); *Music for the Royal Fireworks* (1749) and *Water Music* (1717); suites for harpsichord; chamber music; and many Italian cantatas.

Hindemith, Paul (1895–1963). Composer, teacher, theorist, performer, and conductor who brought a neoclassical element to contemporary music. Early works, such as the opera *Murder, Hope of Women* (1921), reflect the expressionism of the period. Later works, including *Ludus Tonalis* (1942), exemplify his new theory of tonality expounded in *The Craft of Musical Composition* (1941, 1945). Hindemith was banned by the Nazis for his modernity. His best-known work is a symphony from his opera *Mathis the Painter* (1938).

Humperdinck, Engelbert (1854–1921). Composer of six operas, including the popular *Hansel and Gretel* (1893); incidental music; vocal works; and songs.

Mendelssohn, Felix (1809–47). Pianist, conductor, and composer of orchestral works, including five symphonies and the overture to *A Midsummer Night's Dream* (1826), choral works, including the oratorios *St. Paul* (1836) and *Elija* (1846); operas; incidental music; several collections of piano works; *Songs Without Words* (1832); and songs. His music contains smooth progressions in harmony accompanying melodies that are easy to sing.

Meyerbeer, Giacomo (1791–1864). Composer of operas in a spectacular style that influenced Richard Wagner. His works include *Robert le Diable* (1831), *Les Huguenots* (1836), and *Le Prophète* (1849).

Orff, Carl (1895–1982). Composer of stage works that combined instrumental singing, gestures, and dance, including the cantata *Carmina Burana* (1937); the opera *Der Mond* (1939); and musical plays. Orff developed a widely used system for teaching music to children.

Schumann, Clara Josephine Wieck (1819–96). Pianist and composer of piano works and songs. She was a renowned interpreter of music, particularly the works of her husband, Robert Schumann.

Schumann, Robert (1810–56). Composer of piano music, including sonatas and impromptus, and of orchestral works. His compositions include *Symphonic Études* (1834), *Fantasia in C Major* (1836), *Album for the Young* (1848), and *Piano Concerto in A Minor* (1845). The *Rhenish Symphony* (1850) combined classical and romantic elements.

Strauss, Richard (1864–1949). Composer of numerous operas, many with librettos by Hugo von Hofmannsthal, including the famous *Der Rosenkavalier* (1911); two ballets; tone poems for orchestra, including *Also Sprach Zarathustra* (1896); concertos; *Metamorphosen* (1945) for 23 solo strings; chamber music; songs; and piano works.

Wagner, Richard (1813–83). Composer of operas and architect of a theory of the "total" work of art, in which drama, spectacle, and music are fused.

Principal works include *Der Ring des Nibelungen* (1853–74), which was made up of four operas: *Das Rheingold* (1854), *Die Walküre* (1856), *Siegfried* (1857–69), and *Götterdämmerung* (1874); *Tristan and Isolde* (1859); and *Parsifal* (1882). Exiled for his role in the revolution of 1848, Wagner resettled in Bavaria in 1864, where he constructed his theater at Bayreuth.

Frideric Handel was known to have a fiery temper. During an argument with an opera singer, he picked her up by the waist and dangled her out of a two-story window.

Weber, Carl Maria von (1786–1826). Composer, conductor, pianist, critic, and virtual creator of romantic German opera. Principal works include the operas *Der Freischütz* (1821) and *Oberon* (1826), choral and orchestral pieces, piano sonatas, concertos, dances, and songs.

ITALIAN

Bellini, Vincenzo (1801–35). Composer of emotional and technically challenging operas, including *La Straniera* (1829), *La Sonnambula* (1831), *Norma* (1831), and *I Puritani* (1835).

Boccherini, Luigi (1743–1805). Cellist and composer. His principal compositions are for chamber music; he also wrote symphonies, concertos, and vocal music. His most popular works are his *Concerto in B-flat* (1770) for cello, and the minuet from his *String Quartet No. 3* (1771).

Boito, Arrigo (1842–1918). Poet and composer of operas, including *Mefistofele* (1868) and *Nerone* (1918). Boito is known chiefly for his librettos, notably for *Otello* (1887) and *Falstaff* (1893) by Giuseppe Verdi.

Cherubini, Maria Luigi (1760–1842). Composer of about 30 operas, among them the classic "rescue" opera *The Water Carrier* (1800); church music; string quartets; and piano sonatas. He served as director of the Paris Conservatory (1822).

Performance Arts

Clementi, Muzio (1752–1832). Pianist and composer of symphonies, piano sonatas, and piano studies, including *Gradus ad Parnassum* (1817).

Corelli, Arcangelo (1653–1713). Violinist and composer. His trio sonatas, solo violin sonatas, and concerti grossi established a style of composition for the violin.

Dallapiccola, Luigi (1904–75). Composer of 12-tone atonal music characterized by delicate counterpoint, lyrical line and textures, and subtle tone colors. He is most noted for his operas *The Prisoner* (1944) and *Odysseus* (1968), the oratorio *Job* (1950), and the *Christmas Concerto* (1956).

Donizetti, Gaetano (1797–1848). Prolific composer of operas. His best-known works included *Lucrezia Borgia* (1833), *La Favorite* (1840), and the comic operas *L'Elisir d'Amore* (1832) and *Don Pasquale* (1843).

Leoncavallo, Ruggiero (1858–1919). Composer of operas. His most successful was *Pagliacci* (1892). He wrote his own librettos, a ballet, and a symphonic poem.

Mascagni, Pietro (1863–1945). Opera composer and conductor. His most famous work is *Cavalleria Rusticana* (1890).

Monteverdi, Claudio (1567–1643). Ordained priest and composer of church music, including masses, vespers, and madrigals. He also wrote secular vocal music, at least 12 operas, and ballets. His works helped change the strict style of Renaissance music to the emotional style of the baroque movement. His *Orfeo* (1607) is called the first modern opera.

Palestrina, Giovanni Pierluigi da (Johannes Praenestinus) (c. 1525–94). Organist, choirmaster, and composer of church music, including masses, motets, and lamentations. He also wrote both sacred and secular madrigals.

Pergolesi, Giovanni Battista (1710–36). Composer of operas and comic intermezzos that became the prototype of the *opera buffa;* church music, including his renowned *Stabat Mater* (1736); and sonatas, which contributed to the development of the form.

Puccini, Giacomo (1858–1924). Composer of many operas with highly emotional melodies and orchestral brilliance. Best known are *La Bohème* (1896), *Tosca* (1900), and *Madame Butterfly* (1904). *Turandot* was completed after his death by Franco Alfano.

Respighi, Ottorino (1879–1936). Composer of operas, tone poems, and other orchestral works, chamber music, concertos, and songs. Among his most popular works are *The Fountains of Rome* (1917) and *The Pines of Rome* (1924), both symphonic poems.

Rossini, Gioacchino (1792–1868). Composer of operas. The best known are *William Tell* (1829) and *The Barber of Seville* (1816). Rossini also wrote cantatas, songs, piano pieces, and woodwind quintets.

Scarlatti, Alessandro (1660–1725). Conductor and the most prolific composer of Italian operas of his time. Besides composing about 80 operas, he wrote 20 oratorios, some 600 cantatas, 10 masses, a passion, motets, and other church music, chamber pieces, concertos, and works for harpsichord.

Scarlatti, (Giuseppe) Domenico (1685–1757). Son of Alessandro Scarlatti, and greatest Italian composer for harpsichord of his time. He wrote 550 pieces, now called sonatas, as well as concertos, operas, cantatas, masses, a *Stabat Mater,* and two *Salve Reginas.*

Tartini, Giuseppe (1692–1770). Violinist, teacher, composer, and theorist. He composed over 100 violin concertos and symphonies, solo sonatas, trio sonatas, and church music; published treatises on violin playing and acoustics; and established a violin school in Padua (1728).

Verdi, Giuseppe (1813–1901). Foremost composer of operas. His works are performed more often today than those of any other opera com-poser. They include *Rigoletto* (1851), *La Traviata* (1853), and the supreme *Otello* (1887) and *Falstaff* (1893). Verdi also composed church music, including the *Requiem* (1874), *Ave Maria* (1880), *Stabat Mater* (1898), and *Te Deum* (1898).

Vivaldi, Antonio (1678–1741). Violinist, composer, and ordained priest. Master of the Italian baroque, Vivaldi is best known for his instrumental music and the concertos *The Four Seasons* (1725). He also wrote church music, an oratorio, and nearly 50 operas.

RUSSIAN

Borodin, Aleksandr (1833–87). Composer and scientist. His works include three symphonies; *In the Steppes of Central Asia* (1880) for orchestra; string quartets; and the opera *Prince Igor* (1887), completed after his death by Nicolai Rimsky-Korsakov and Aleksandr Glazunov (1890).

Glinka, Mikhail (1804–57). Composer of two operas and other works. *A Life for the Czar* (1836) and *Ruslan and Ludmilla* (1842) established a Russian style against the conventions of Italian opera. Glinka introduced folk song into instrumental composition in the orchestral fantasia *Kamarinskaya*.

The Russian composer Aleksandr Borodin not only wrote the opera Prince Igor *but was also a professional chemist and the author of* On the Analogy of Arsenical with Phosphoric Acid.

Khachaturian, Aram (1903–78). Armenian composer whose works are distinguished for their incorporation of oriental folk elements. He is best known for the ballet *Gayane* (1942) and its popular "Sabre Dance" theme.

Mussorgsky, Modest (1839–81). Composer of operas and orchestral works. Mussorgsky is best known for his operas *Boris Godunov* (1868, 1874) and *Khovanschina* (1886), as well as for *Pictures at an Exhibition* (1874) for piano and *Night on Bald Mountain* (1860–66) for orchestra.

Prokofiev, Sergei (1891–1953). Composer, pianist, and conductor. His principal compositions are the operas *Love for Three Oranges* (1921) and *War and Peace* (1942); *Peter and the Wolf* (1936) and *Classical Symphony* (1918), both for orchestra and narrator; and seven symphonies, piano concertos, ballets, and piano sonatas.

Rachmaninoff, Sergei (1873–1943). Composer, pianist, and conductor whose works are filled with passion, power, and a feeling of melancholy. Rachmaninoff emigrated to the United States at age 17. His compositions include three operas; orchestral works, including the tone poem *Isle of the Dead* (1909); four concertos, including the *Second Piano Concerto* (1901); choral works, chamber music; and songs.

Rimsky-Korsakov, Nicolai (1844–1908). Composer of operas and orchestral works, including the popular symphonic suite *Scheherazade* (1888). His greatest works are the operas *Mlada* (1892), *Christmas Eve* (1895), *Sadko* (1898), and *The Golden Cockerel* (1907). His orchestration influenced the work of Igor Stravinsky and others.

Rubinstein, Anton (1829–94). Pianist and composer; founder of the Conservatory in St. Petersburg (1862). A representative of traditional Western ideas against the current of nationalism, he composed *Musical Portraits (Faust, Ivan the Terrible, Don Quixote)* for orchestra, 19 operas, 6 symphonies (including *The Ocean*), chamber music, 5 piano concertos, and other works.

Scriabin, Aleksandr (1872–1915). Composer and pianist. Scriabin experimented with esoteric harmonies related to theosophical ideas in *The Divine Poem* (1905) and *Poem of Ecstasy,* both for orchestra. He wrote sonatas, preludes, and *Prometheus* (1909–10), which includes the use of a "color organ" for slide projection.

Shostakovich, Dmitry (1906–75). Composer of chamber and symphonic works characterized by a bold, expressive modern style. Shostakovich alternated between political and satirical composition, later trying to bring his work closer to official prescriptions. His works include 15 symphonies, among them *May the First* (1930) and the outstanding *Ninth Symphony* (1940); operas; ballets, including *Lady Macbeth of Mtsensk* (1934) and revised in 1962 as *Katerina Ismailova;* piano works; sonatas; and 15 string quartets.

Stravinsky, Igor (1882–1971). Composer of the epochal ballets *The Firebird* (1910), *Petrouchka* (1911), and *Rite of Spring* (1913). Later works, such as *The Soldier's Tale* (1918), for narrator and instruments, and the ballet suite *Apollon Musagète* (1928) are more austere and neoclassical. Stravinsky settled in the United States in 1941, where he experimented with 12-tone composition, as in *Requiem Canticles* (1966).

Tchaikovsky, Peter Ilyich (1840–93). One of the most important Russian composers. His music is characterized by masterful orchestration and spirited yet often melancholy melodies. Tchaikovsky is best known for his ballet music, including *Swan Lake* (1876), *The Sleeping Beauty* (1889), and *The Nutcracker* (1892), and for his operas *Eugene Onegin* (1878) and *Queen of Spades* (1890). He also wrote symphonies, including the popular *Symphony No. 5* (1888), chamber music, and choral works, and he published books on harmony, autobiographical essays, and translations.

OTHER

Albéniz, Isaac (1860–1909). Spanish composer and pianist. Albéniz is known for his later piano works, notably *Iberia* (1906–09); he also wrote operas, including *The Magic Opal* (1893).

Bartók, Béla (1881–1945). Hungarian pianist and composer who studied and collected Hungarian folk music and developed a musical style that emphasized energetic rhythm, folk song scales, dissonance, and highly personal forms. His principal works include orchestral pieces; the opera *Duke Bluebeard's Castle* (1918); the ballet *The Wooden Prince* (1914–16); the pantomime *The Miraculous Mandarin* (1919, 1924, 1935); chamber music; piano works, including the *Mikrokosmos* (1926–37); and arrangements of folk songs. He emigrated to the United States in 1940.

Chávez, Carlos (1899–1978). Mexican composer of works using the idioms of Indian folk music, including *Xochipilli Macuilxochitl* (1940). Well-known works are the symphonic ode *Clio* (1969) and *Discovery* (1969).

Chopin, Frédéric François (1810–49). Polish composer and pianist. Called "the poet of the piano," he composed hundreds of pieces for that instrument, most notably two piano concertos and other pieces, including *Fantaisie-Impromptu* (1834).

Dvořák, Antonín (1841–1904). Czech composer of symphonies, operas, dances, and choral works in a nationalistic spirit and neoromantic style. His works include the *Symphonic Variations*, *Slavonic Rhapsodies*, and the opera *The Peasant Rogue* (1877). His best-known work, the *Symphony from the New World* (1893), contains elements of both Czech and American music.

Falla, Manuel de (1876–1946). Spanish composer and pianist. He published little but was the outstanding Spanish composer of his time. Principal works are the operas *La Vida Breve* (1905) and *El Retablo de Maese Pedro* (1923); the ballets *El Amor Brujo* (1915) and *The Three-Cornered Hat* (1919); and the *Fantasia Béticu* (1919) for piano.

Grainger, Percy Aldridge (1882–1961). Australian pianist and composer who settled in the United States in 1914. Head of the music department at New York University, he was known for his arrangements of traditional tunes from a variety of sources and for his interpretation of Edvard Grieg's piano music. His choral works include *Marching Song of Democracy* (1917) and *Tribute to Foster* (1930).

Granados, Enrique (1867–1916). Spanish pianist and composer, born in Cuba. Granados founded and directed the Academía Granados (1901) and composed seven operas, orchestral works, chamber music, a collection of *Tonadillas,* and *Goyescas* (1916), based on the paintings of Goya.

Grieg, Edvard (1843–1907). Norwegian composer, conductor, and pianist. Principal works include the overture *I Host* (1866), two suites from *Peer Gynt* (1876, 1888, 1891), *At a Southern Convent Gate* (1871) for chorus, and the 10-volume *Lyric Pieces* for piano.

Janáček, Leoš (1854–1928). Czech composer. Janáček wrote 10 operas, including *Jenufa* (1904); orchestral, choral, and piano works; chamber music; and songs. He published collections of Moravian folk music and a treatise on harmony.

Kodály, Zoltăn (1882–1967). Hungarian composer and music educator whose works are distinguished by the influence of native folk music. His best-known works are the suites from *Háry János* (1927) and *Psalmus Hungaricus* (1923). Kodály developed a widely used method of teaching music.

Lasso, Orlando di (Roland de Lassus) (1532–94). Belgian composer. Among his many works are masses, motets, magnificats, and other church music. The complete edition of his nearly 2,000 works consists of 60 volumes.

Liszt, Franz (1811–86). Hungarian composer who spent time in Paris and Rome and is credited with developing the rhapsody as a form of serious music and employing the term *symphonic poem* for a composition. He was an unsurpassed virtuoso pianist and a composer of symphonies, including *Faust* (1857); piano concertos, études, and 19 *Hungarian Rhapsodies* (1839–85); choral pieces; fantasia and fugues for organ; and songs.

Nielsen, Carl (1865–1931). Danish composer of operas, symphonies, string quartets, piano pieces, and songs, including *Hymns amoris* (1896). Nielsen served as director of the Copenhagen Conservatory (1915–27).

Paderewski, Ignace (1860–1941). Polish pianist and composer. One of the most renowned pianists of modern times, in 1919 Paderewski was prime minister of Poland. He composed many piano works, the opera *Manru* (1901), a symphony, a concerto, and songs.

Sibelius, Jean (1865–1957). Finnish composer. Sibelius attempted a national music, as in *En Saga* (1892) and *Lemminkäinen's Homecoming* (1895), based on the Finnish epic *The Kalevala*. Notable works include *The Swan of Tuonela* (1893), *Finlandia* (1900), and *The Oceanides* (1914).

Smetana, Bedřich (1824–84). Czech composer whose nationalist music was based on folk songs and dances, as in the opera *The Bartered Bride* (1866). Smetana wrote his best instrumental works despite deafness, especially *The Moldau,* which is part of *My Country* (1879), and the string quartet *From My Life* (1876).

Villa-Lobos, Heitor (1887–1959). Brazilian composer and educator. His works show the influence of Indian music and Brazilian folk songs; they include five operas, six symphonies, symphonic poems, serenades, choral music, piano solos, and songs.

Wieniawski, Henri (1835–80). Polish violinist and composer. Among Wieniawski's compositions are two concertos and popular pieces, including *Légende.*

MAJOR JAZZ COMPOSERS AND PERFORMERS

Armstrong, Louis "Satchmo" (c. 1890–1971), b. Louisiana. Trumpeter and singer; first internationally known jazz soloist. He introduced the music of New Orleans to the world, inaugurated the style of improvisation, and was the first to record scat singing. His most influential recording may be "West End Blues" (1939), but his most famous is "Hello, Dolly" (1969).

Basie, William "Count" (1904–84), b. New Jersey. Pianist and bandleader. His brand of Kansas City jazz became the classic swing-band style, featuring spare keyboard playing with a precise four-beat rhythm section. He started the Barons of Rhythm in Kansas City, Missouri, in 1935 and then moved to New York in 1936. His hits include "Jumpin' at the Woodside" (1938) and "Stay Cool" (1946).

Beiderbecke, Bix (1903–31), b. Iowa. Cornetist, pianist, and composer. Famous for his solos, he was known as the first great white jazz musician. He advanced simple jazz into a more complex form built around improvisation and extended chords. His improvisations on "Singin' the Blues" (1927) were much admired and imitated.

Carter, Betty (1930–98), b. Michigan. Vocalist noted for her scat singing, humming, moaning, and extraordinary technique. She performed with the bands of Max Roach, Charlie Parker, Miles Davis, and others from the late 1940s through the late 1950s.

Christian, Charlie (c. 1916–42), b. Texas. A major contributor to the bebop movement, he was also among the first to capitalize on the sound of the electric guitar. He was admired for his innovative use of harmonic inversions, dissonance, and long strings of uninflected eighth notes. Major works include "Seven Come Eleven" (1939), "Gone with What Wind" (1940), and "Breakfast Feud" (1941).

Coleman, Ornette   (1930–   ), b. Texas. Saxophonist and composer. He was a major influence on the avant-garde or "free-jazz" movement of the late 1950s and early 1960s, with a revolutionary style of breaking the restrictions of chords, ordinary harmony, bar lines, and tempered scales. Major recordings include "Something Else" (1958), "Congeniality" (1959), and "A Dedication to Poets and Writers" (1962).

Coltrane, John   (1926–67), b. North Carolina. Tenor/soprano saxophonist, composer, and bandleader. His explosive style and angular melodic lines have influenced jazz musicians. He is credited with developing polytonality in modern jazz, and his quartet, which performed from 1960 to 1965, ranks among the best. His masterworks include "Giant Steps" (1959) and "A Love Supreme" (1964).

Davis, Miles   (1926–91), b. Illinois. Trumpeter, composer, and bandleader. His lyrical and inventive playing made him a trendsetter for more than four decades. A major contributor to the bebop and cool forms of jazz, he pioneered the jazz-rock movement in the 1960s. His influential recordings include "Steamin'" (1956), "Kind of Blue" (1959), and "Bitches Brew" (1969).

Ellington, Edward Kennedy "Duke"   (1899–1974), b. Washington, D.C. Pianist, composer, and bandleader. Nominated for a Pulitzer prize, he is considered the most important composer of big-band music. He wrote and arranged many jazz classics, popular songs, and blues or "mood" pieces. "Mood Indigo" (1930), "It Don't Mean a Thing (If It Ain't Got That Swing)" (1932), "Sophisticated Lady" (1933), and "In a Sentimental Mood" (1935) are among his many great recordings.

Evans, Bill   (1929–80), b. New Jersey. Pianist, arranger, and composer whose soft harmonies, intricate voicing, and melodic improvising changed the sound of the piano in jazz. He earned national recognition for his playing in "Kind of Blue" (1959) with the Miles Davis Sextet.

Fitzgerald, Ella   (1918–96), b. Virginia. Vocalist acclaimed for her pure tone, voice control, improvisation, and interpretation of ballads. Her first hit was "A Tisket, A Tasket" (1938), and she became world famous in 1946 when she sang with the *Jazz at the Philharmonic* concert series.

Gillespie, John Birks "Dizzy"   (1917–93), b. South Carolina. Trumpeter and bandleader who pioneered the bebop movement in 1945 along with Charlie Parker. His Latin-influenced sound and virtuosity in upper-register playing are evident in his compositions "Salt Peanuts" (1945) and "A Night in Tunisia" (1946).

Goodman, Benny   (1909–86), b. Illinois. Clarinetist and bandleader known as the "Pied Piper of Swing." He played with symphony orchestras and pioneered interracial bands. His best-known recordings include "After You've Gone" (1935) and "Moonglow" (1936).

Hancock, Herbie   (1940–   ), b. Illinois. Pianist and composer whose highly individual keyboard style blends blues and bebop. He joined the Miles Davis Quintet in 1963 and helped expand the traditional jazz concept of the rhythm section and its relationship to the soloist. He contributed to the rock-jazz movement of the late 1960s and 1970s with his composition "Maiden Voyage" (1965).

Hawkins, Coleman   (1904–69), b. Missouri. His powerful, original style and rich tone made him the dominant tenor saxophonist during the late 1930s and early 1940s. He played with Fletcher Henderson's orchestra (1923–43). His most celebrated recording is "Body and Soul" (1939).

Henderson, Fletcher   (c. 1897–1952), b. Georgia. Bandleader, arranger, and trumpeter who pioneered the concept of the big band in the swing era. His best works include "Down South Camp Meeting" (1934), "Wrappin' It Up" (1934), and "King Porter Stomp" (1935).

Hines, Earl "Fatha"   (c. 1903–83), b. Pennsylvania. Pianist and bandleader. He is known for his innovative "trumpet-style" single-note solos coupled with powerful rhythm and bass patterns. His best recordings include "A Monday Date" (1928) and "Skip the Gutter" (1928) with Louis Armstrong.

Holiday, Billie "Lady Day"   (1915–59), b. Maryland. Vocalist famous for her melancholy improvisations of ballads and popular songs. She was discovered by record producer and critic John Hammond in 1933 and sang with Benny Goodman, Lester Young, Count Basie, and other great jazz musicians. She developed a large public following with her recordings of "Strange Fruit" (1939) and "Lover Man" (1944).

Joplin, Scott   (1868–1917), b. Texas. Composer and pianist who popularized the early jazz form of ragtime. His composition "The Maple Leaf Rag" (c. 1899) became an instant hit. His works include 33 rags, about two dozen songs, and a ragtime opera.

Lewis, John A.   (1920–2001), b. Illinois. Pianist and composer known for applying classical forms to jazz based on improvisation and carefully worked-out changes of tempo, key, meter, and instrumentation. He was one of the pioneers of cool jazz and founded the Modern Jazz Quartet. His noted works include "Bluesology" (1956) and "Between the Devil and the Deep Blue Sea" (1957).

Miller, Glenn   (1904–44), b. Iowa. Trombonist, arranger, and star bandleader during the big-band swing era. His distinctive sound combined a clarinet and four saxophones. "In the Mood" (1939) and "String of Pearls" (1941) were among his many hit songs.

Mingus, Charlie   (1922–79), b. Arizona. Double bassist, pianist, composer, arranger, and bandleader. He combined gospel and jazz forms to create a funky sound. He was the dominant bassist of the late 1950s and early 1960s. Best compositions include "Goodbye Pork Pie Hat" (1959) and "Better Git It in Your Soul" (1959).

Monk, Thelonious   (1917–82), b. North Carolina. Pianist and composer noted for his spare style, slow tempo, and distinctive phrasing. Monk was a major contributor to bebop. "'Round About Midnight" (1947) and "Criss Cross" (1951) are among his many important compositions.

Morton, Ferdinand "Jelly Roll"   (c. 1890–1941), b. Louisiana. Pianist, composer, and preeminent soloist who recorded about 175 sides and piano rolls between 1923 and 1929. Combining blues, rags, and marches, he is considered the first important jazz composer. His influential works included "The Pearls" (1919), "Wolverine Blues" (1923), "Grandpa's Spells" (1923), and "Smokehouse Blues" (1926).

Parker, Charlie "Bird"   (1920–55), b. Kansas. Alto saxophonist and composer whose virtuosity and inventive melodic lines made him a major influence in bebop. "Groovin' High" (1945) and "Out of Nowhere" (1948) are among his most innovative solos.

Reinhardt, Django   (1910–53), b. Belgium. Considered the most important jazz guitarist. His swing style of playing was characterized by a full sound, strong rhythms, salvos of sixteenth notes, vibrato, and surprising melodic lines. Notable works include "Tiger Rag" (1934) and "Stardust" (1935).

Smith, Bessie   (1894–1937), b. Tennessee. Vocalist considered the greatest of all the classic blues singers. She achieved the height of her fame in the 1920s pioneering jazz-oriented blues. Her best recordings include "Down-hearted Blues" (1923) and "Cold in Hand Blues" (1925).

Tatum, Art   (1910–56), b. Ohio. Pianist known for his dazzling high-speed arpeggios and elaborate runs stretching the length of the keyboard. Tatum was the premier pianist of New York's Swing Street clubs from the 1930s through the 1950s. "Tea for Two" (1923), "Tiger Rag" (1933), and "Stompin' at the Savoy" (1953) are among his many great recordings.

Vaughan, Sarah "Sassy"   (1924–90), b. New Jersey. Vocalist renowned for her operatic power, elegant phrasing, and extraordinarily wide range. She became popular while singing with Billy Eckstine's band in the mid-1940s. "Lover Man" (1945), recorded with Charlie Parker and Dizzy Gillespie, established her reputation.

Waller, Thomas "Fats"   (1904–43), b. New York. Pianist, songwriter, and entertainer. Waller's jazz ragtime style of playing in the 1920s and 1930s made many of his songs jazz standards. His notable works, "Honeysuckle Rose" (1929) and "Ain't Misbehavin'"

(1929), brought him fame as a satirical songwriter and entertainer.

Williams, Mary Lou   (1910–81), b. Georgia. Pianist, arranger, and composer. Known as "the first great female instrumentalist in jazz," she created harmonically innovative arrangements ranging from swing to avant-garde. She arranged scores for the bands of Earl Hines, Benny Goodman, and Duke Ellington. Her most famous composition is "Zodiac Suite" (1945).

Young, Lester "Prez"   (1909–59), b. Mississippi. Tenor saxophonist and premier soloist credited with transforming the "hot" jazz of the 1930s into the "cool" jazz of the 1940s and 1950s. His influential recordings include "Shoe Shine Boy" (1936), "Lady Be Good" (1936), and "Lester Leaps In" (1939).

COMMON MUSIC TERMS

a cappella   Choral music without accompaniment (literally, "in the church style").

accelerando   A direction to gradually increase the tempo.

accent   The emphasis given to one tone over another.

accidental   A sign used to indicate chromatic alteration; a sharp, double sharp, flat, double flat, or natural prefixed to a single note.

accompaniment   Secondary instrument or background vocal added to the principal instrument or soloist.

acoustics   The science of sound, which deals with intensity, quality, resonance, pitch, tone, and other qualities of sound.

adagietto   A direction to play slightly faster than adagio.

adagio   A direction to play slowly; between andante and largo.

adagissimo   A direction to play very slowly.

"Music" under "Reference Works for General Information" in chapter 11; "Music Symbols" in chapter 12

ad libitum   A direction to interpret, improvise, or omit, according to the player's preference.

affetuoso   A direction to play affectionately, with warmth.

agitato   A direction to play in an agitated, restless, hurried manner.

air   A tune or melody; the French 18th-century term for song; also, an instrumental piece whose melodic style is similar to that of a solo song.

alla breve   A direction to play twice as fast as the notation signifies; 2/2 instead of 4/4.

allargando   A direction to play slower, louder.

allegretto   A direction to play with moderately quick movement; between andante and allegro.

allegro   A direction to play quickly, briskly.

allemande   A moderately slow dance of German origin.

allentando   A direction to slow down.

alto   The highest adult male voice or lowest female voice; also, a tenor violin or viola.

andante   A direction to play in moderate tempo; "walking" speed; between allegretto and adagio.

andantino   A direction to play in tempo slightly quicker than andante.

animato   A direction to play with animation.

answer   In a fugue, the second or fourth statement of the subject.

anthem   A choral piece for use in church services.

appassionato   A direction to play passionately.

appoggiatura   An inharmonious note preceding a principal note, marked with a diagonal line through it, of short or long duration.

arabesque   A lyrical piece in a fanciful style; a term used first by Schumann and later by Debussy.

aria   An extended vocal solo in an opera or oratorio.

arioso   A piece of recitative song, but more song-like.

arpeggio   The technique of playing the notes of a chord successively rather than simultaneously.

ascending   Moving upward on a musical scale.

assai   A direction to play very quickly.

a tempo   A direction to play in time, following a deviation from the regular tempo.

atonal   Having no recognized tonal center or key.

aubade   Morning music, in contrast to *serenade,* or evening music.

augmentation   Presentation of a theme in notes of doubled value; the opposite of *diminution.*

auxiliary note   Usually, a grace note one degree above or below a principal note.

ballad   A narrative song, originally accompanied by dancing; also, an instrumental piece in ballad style.

bar line   A line drawn vertically across the staff to divide into measures.

baritone   The male voice between bass and tenor; also, any musical instrument intermediary between bass and tenor.

Baroque   A term signifying the music composed between 1600 and 1750, characterized by homophonic texture with the uppermost part carrying the melody over the bass line; a search for affective expression; the development of new styles for various functions and new techniques, such as dissonance and tonality.

bass   The lowest male voice, or lowest part in a musical composition; also, short for the double bass or bass tuba.

beat   A unit of rhythm or time in a composition as indicated by the conductor's gesture; each unit of a measure with respect to accent.

bebop (bop)   One of the principal styles of jazz developed in the early 1940s, characterized by complicated melody lines and chord patterns played at exceptional speed.

bel canto   The Italian vocal techniques of the 18th century with an emphasis on beauty of sound and brilliance of performance rather than dramatic expression or romantic emotion.

berceuse   A cradle song.

binary   Musical form in which both main sections are repeated and where the first section characteristically is tonally not self-contained but demands a resolution in the second part (AB).

bolero   A Spanish dance accompanied by castanets.

bowing   A method of using the bow on stringed instruments as indicated by signs for down bow (⊓) or up bow (V).

brace   A vertical line used to join two or more staves.

As estimated today, a compact disc may last around 150 years if handled carefully.

buffa   In the comic style.

buffo   The singer of a comic part.

cadence   A progression of chords that seems to move to a harmonic close or point of rest.

cadenza   An ornamental passage near the end of a composition.

canon   A contrapuntal composition in which the same melody is imitated by one or more voices overlapping in time in the same or related key.

cantata   A vocal form from the Baroque period that consists of arias, recitatives, duets, and choruses. The term now refers to secular or sacred choral works accompanied by orchestra, similar to the oratorio but shorter.

canticle   Religious song or chant.

canzona   A form of Italian lyric poetry corresponding to the ode, set to music in a style similar to a madrigal, though simpler; also, an instrumental piece in the style of a song.

canzonet   A vocal piece in a light vein, somewhat like a dance song, usually with instrumental accompaniment; a short instrumental piece.

capriccio   A short composition in free form.

castrato   A male singer castrated as a boy to maintain a soprano or alto voice range.

catch   A humorous round for three or more voices.

chaconne   A musical form based on a reiterated harmonic pattern.

chamber music   Instrumental compositions performed by a small ensemble, with one player for each part.

chanson   A song for solo voice or vocal ensemble; also, an instrumental piece of vocal character.

chant   A sacred song, usually monophonic and in free rhythm and used in accordance with prescribed ritual. The chant is the oldest form of choral music.

chorale   A psalm or hymn tune sung in church; also, a harmonization of a chorale melody.

chord   The combination of three or more tones played at once. A *diatonic chord* uses only notes proper to the key. A *triad* is a chord of three notes in which the lowest is combined with the third and fifth above it. A *common chord* is a triad in root position. A *dominant chord* is founded on the dominant of the key. An *inverted chord* uses a tone other than the root as its lowest tone.

chromatic scale   Consecutive series of notes that employ only a progression of semitones.

classical   Term for the period and style of music from about 1700 to about 1830, characterized by regular, short, clearly articulated phrases combined with symmetrical patterns and textures. Haydn, Mozart, and Beethoven are its chief representatives.

clef   A character that indicates the pitch of a particular line on a staff.

coda   A passage that brings a piece or movement to a conclusion.

comma   The small difference in pitch that occurs in the same note when obtained through different combinations of octaves, perfect fifths, and pure thirds.

common time   Four-four (⁴⁄₄) time—that is, four quarter notes to a measure.

compound interval   An interval that extends beyond an octave.

compound time   Time in which each beat of the bar is divisible into three, in contrast to *simple time,* in which each is divisible into two.

concertmaster   The leader of the first violins, next in rank to the conductor.

concerto   A composition for solo instrument, usually with orchestral accompaniment.

concerto grosso   A style of composition developed during the Baroque period (1600–1750) in which two groups of musicians, one large and one small, alternate in an echo effect.

concert pitch   Pitch at which the piano and other nontransposing instruments play.

console   The part of the organ from which the player controls the instrument—the keyboard, pedals, and so on—as distinguished from the pipes.

consonance   Combination of pitches that produce little tension and are generally considered pleasing; opposite of dissonance.

consort   A chamber ensemble; also, music written for such a group.

con spirito   A direction to play in a lively manner.

continuo   The bass, or lowest, line of a composition.

contralto   The range of a low female voice; alto.

cool   Style of modern jazz pioneered in the 1950s and 1960s, characterized by understated and emotionally subdued arrangements played by small ensembles.

counterpoint   Music consisting of two or more melodic lines played simultaneously.

countersubject   The contrasting motif to the subject of a fugue.

countertenor   The male alto voice.

couplet   Two lines having the same meter.

Performance Arts

courante   A lively dance in triple time; also, the second part of a suite.

crescendo   A direction to increase the volume.

cut time   Another term for 2/2 meter.

da capo   A direction to repeat from the beginning.

decrescendo   A direction to decrease the volume.

descant   A different melody sung in a higher pitch and simultaneously with the main melodic line. It is the earliest form of polyphony, with contrasting motions between the parts.

The first composer to have one of his works performed in space was Dmitry Shostakovich.

descending   Moving downward on a musical scale.

development   The extension of a theme through contrapuntal elaboration, modulation, rhythmical variation, etc.

diatonic   Referring to minor and major scales that employ a particular combination of whole tones and half tones; the harmony and melodies that use only the pitches of a particular diatonic scale.

diminished chord   A chord in which the highest and lowest tones form a diminished interval.

diminished interval   A perfect or minor interval reduced by a semitone.

diminuendo   Diminishing; getting softer.

diminution   The breaking up of the notes in a melody into quick figures, as is done in variations.

dissonance   A combination of tones that are unresolved, jarring.

divertimento   An 18th-century form of instrumental chamber music having several short movements.

divertissement   A fantasia on well-known tunes.

divisi   In orchestral music, an indication that a group of players who play the same parts are to play two or more separate parts.

do   The first tone of a diatonic scale.

dolce   A direction to play softly, sweetly.

dolente, doloroso   Sorrowful.

dominant   The fifth tone of the major or minor diatonic scale.

dominant chord   A chord with the fifth pitch of a scale as its root.

doppio movimento   Twice as fast.

Dorian mode   A church mode represented on the white keys of a keyboard instrument by an ascending scale from D to D.

dot   Written after a note, an indication of the prolongation of its length by one-half; the double dot indicates by three-fourths. Above or below the note, the dot indicates staccato.

double stop   A chord of two notes played on a bowed string instrument, obtaining a two-part harmony.

doxology   In Christian worship, a hymn of praise to God.

duet   A composition for two players or two voices, with or without accompaniment.

duple   Two units to the measure, such as 2/2, 2/4, or 2/8.

duration   The length of a tone.

dynamics   Varying and contrasting degrees of intensitiy or loudness.

eighth   A note whose value is one-eighth of a whole note.

enharmonic   Tones that have the same pitch when played on tempered instruments but that are different in notation, such as C (♯) and D (♭).

episode   The section of a fugue in which the main melody is not heard.

estinto   So soft that it can hardly be heard.

étude   A study; an exercise in technique.

exposition   The statement of the musical material on which a movement is based.

expression marks   Marks used to help the interpretation of a work; they are concerned with dynamics, tempo, and mood, and indicate forte, allegro, con spirito, etc.

fa   The fourth note of a diatonic scale.

falsetto   The false voice; an adult male voice in the alto and treble range.

fantasia   A piece in which the composition follows the fancy rather than any conventional form; of an improvisational character.

fermata   A symbol (⌒) placed over the note to show that it is to be played longer than its normal duration.

fifth   The interval between the tonic and the fifth tone above it. In the key of C major, C to G is a fifth.

figuration   The extended use of a particular melodic or harmonic figure; the ornamental treatment of a passage.

finale   The last movement of a work of several movements—for example, the conclusion of a concerto or the last act of an opera.

flat   A sign (♭) indicating that the pitch is to be lowered by one semitone.

form   The pattern of design of a work; its basic elements are repetition, variation, and contrast in the areas of harmony, rhythm, and tone.

forte   A direction to play loudly.

fortissimo   A direction to play very loudly.

forza   A direction to play with force.

forzando   Strongly accenting.

fourth   The interval between the tonic and the fourth diatonic tone above it; in the key of C major, C to F is a fourth.

fugue   A composition in which three or more voices enter at different times and imitate the main melody in different ways according to a set pattern.

fundamental   Also called the tonic; the lowest tone of a chord when the chord is founded on that tone; also, the lowest note in the harmonic series.

funk (funky)   Style of African American music popular in the mid-1960s that combines soul and jazz. It is characterized by complex interlocking syncopated rhythm patterns in duple meter.

galop   A quick dance in ¾ time popular in the 19th century.

giocoso   Jocose; merry.

glee   A simple part song, generally for male voices.

glissando   The execution of rapid scales by sliding the finger rapidly across keys or strings.

grace note   An ornamental note not essential to the melody and not counted as part of the measure.

grandezza   Grandeur.

grave   A direction to play slowly, solemnly.

grazioso   A direction to play gracefully.

Gregorian chant   A style of church music for unaccompanied voices, without definite rhythm, in one of the eight church modes.

half note   A note having half the time value of a whole note and twice that of a quarter note.

harmonic   A tone whose frequency is an integral multiple of a single frequency known as the fundamental tone.

harmony   The simultaneously sounded pitches, as in chords.

homophonic   Single-voiced; music in which one melody or part is supported by chords; the opposite of *polyphonic.*

imitation   The use of the same or similar melodic material in different voices successively.

impresario   The conductor or manager of an opera or concert company.

impromptu   An improvised composition without fixed form.

incidental music   Music for performance during the action of a play or film.

interlude   A short piece played between the acts of a drama; the verses of a song, parts of a church service, or sections of a cantata.

intermezzo   A play with music performed between the acts of an opera or drama that gave rise to opera buffa; an interlude; a short movement in a symphony.

interval   The distance in pitch between two notes, harmonic if they are played together, melodic if they are played in succession. *Perfect interval:* the prime, fourth, fifth, and octave. *Major interval:* the second, third, sixth, and seventh of the major scale. *Minor interval:* a chromatic half step smaller than a major interval. *Augmented interval:* a chromatic half step larger than perfect and major. *Diminished interval:* A chromatic half step smaller than perfect and minor.

intonation   The degree of accuracy with which pitches are produced.

inversion   The transposition of the lower and upper notes of an interval. In an inverted chord, the lowest tone is not its root; an inverted melody is one in which its intervals are inverted.

Ionian mode   A mode of church music represented on the white keys of a keyboard by an ascending scale from C to C.

key   The main pitch or tonal center to which all of the composition's pitches are related.

key signature   Sharps or flats placed at the beginning of a composition to indicate its key.

la   The sixth tone of a diatonic scale.

largo   A direction to play broadly, more slowly than adagio but not as slowly as grave.

leading tone   The seventh degree or tone of the scale; a semitone below the tonic.

legato   A direction to play smoothly and continuously.

lento   A direction to play slowly, but not as slowly as largo.

libretto   The text of an opera or oratorio.

litany   A song of invocation to God.

madrigal   An unaccompanied song for three or more voices using counterpoint and imitation.

maestoso   A direction to play in a majestic, stately manner.

magnificat   Canticle of the Virgin Mary sung as part of the evening service in Reformed churches and at vespers in the Catholic church.

major   Applied to chords, intervals, scales, and keys, a standard in contrast to diminished, augmented, or minor.

major scale   A diatonic scale in which the half steps occur between the third and fourth and the seventh and eighth tones.

march   A composition usually in duple meter and in simple, strongly marked rhythms and regular phrases for a procession or parade.

mass   A musical setting of the liturgy of the Eucharist.

mazurka   A polkalike Polish folk dance in triple time with strong accents on the normally weak second and third beats.

measure   A unit of rhythm or musical time, indicated by bar lines.

Mozart's full name was Johannes Chrysostomus Wolfgangus Theophilus Mozart, but he is often known as "Amadeus," which means "beloved of God."

mediant   The third tone of a diatonic scale.

melody   A rhythmically organized succession of single tones that form a musical idea.

mensural music   A medieval term for music with definite note values, as distinguished from plainsong.

meter   A scheme of accents; a grouping of beats into units of measure.

mezzo   Medium, half; moderate.

mezzo-forte   A direction to play moderately loudly.

mezzo-soprano   The female voice between soprano and alto.

Performance Arts

mi   The third tone in the diatonic scale.

middle C   The pitch represented by the first ledger line below the treble clef or the first above the bass clef.

minor   Intervals, scales, keys, and chords having intervals a semitone less than major.

minor scale   A diatonic scale having a minor third between the first and third tones and having several forms with different intervals above the fifth.

minuet   A slow, graceful dance of French origin in triple time; a composition in this rhythm.

mode   A selection of tones arranged in a scale that forms the basic tonal substance of a composition.

modulation   The change from one key to another through a succession of chords.

molto   Very.

monophony   Music consisting of a single melodic line without additional parts or accompaniment, as in plainsong or folk song.

mordent   An ornament played by quickly alternating a note with the note below it.

morendo   A fading away.

motet   An unaccompanied vocal composition with sacred lyrics from the 13th century.

motif   A short, significant melodic and/or rhythmic figure that recurs throughout a composition or section as a unifying element.

motion   The pattern of changing pitch levels in a melody.

natural   A musical symbol indicating the removal of a sharp or flat from a particular pitch.

nocturne   A musical composition in the romantic style, usually for piano, with an expressive melody over a broken-chord accompaniment.

note   A symbol used to express the relative time value of tones.

obbligato   An added melody, usually played by a solo instrument to enhance a vocal line.

octave   The distance between two pitches having the same name and located 12 half steps apart.

octet   A composition of eight parts or voices; also, the group of its performers.

opera   A drama set to music, in which words are sung in the form of recitatives, arias, and ensembles, usually accompanied by orchestra and generally performed with sets and costumes.

operetta   A light opera, usually humorous, with spoken dialogue, dances, and, almost unfailingly, a happy ending.

opus   A numbered musical work or composition.

oratorio   A musical setting of scriptural text set without costumes, scenery, or action.

orchestra   A large group of musicians who play together on various musical instruments, including strings, woodwinds, brass, and percussion.

overture   An introduction to a large composition such as an opera or oratorio; however, it can be independent or the predecessor of a symphonic poem.

parallel motion   The relative changes of pitches in two or more simultaneous voice-parts when the intervals separating them remain the same.

part   In orchestral or chamber music, the music or melodic line for a particular series of notes for voice or instrument.

partita   A set of related instrumental pieces; a series of variations or a suite.

part song   A 19th-century choral composition in the homophonic style in which the top part is the only carrier of the melody.

passion music   A musical setting for the story of the suffering and death of Christ.

pasticcio   An operatic medley of the 18th century made up of contributions of two or more composers.

pastorale   A musical composition suggestive of rural life.

pentatonic scale   A five-toned scale without semitones; the diatonic scale with fourth and seventh tones omitted.

phrase   A complete musical idea.

pianissimo   A direction to play very softly.

piano   A direction to play softly.

piano quartet   A term usually applied to quartets for piano, violin, viola, and cello.

piano quintet   A combination of piano with string quartet.

pitch   The perceived highness or lowness of a sound.

pizzicato   For violins and other bowed instruments, a direction that the string is to be picked with the finger.

plainsong   A nonmetrical chant in one of the church modes.

poco   Little.

polka   A lively dance in ¾ time that originated in Bohemia c. 1830.

polonaise   A Polish dance in ¾ time adopted as a musical form by Chopin.

polyphony   Contrapuntal music; a style in which two or more melodies are interwoven; the opposite of *homophony.*

prelude   An introductory movement complete in itself, as opposed to an introduction, which leads directly into the principal section; a short piano piece in one movement.

Roger Miller was inspired to write the classic song "King of the Road" when he saw a sign just west of Chicago that said, "Trailers for Sale or Rent."

program music   Music intended to depict a story or image.

progression   *Melodic:* the passage from tone to tone; *harmonic:* the passage from chord to chord.

quartet   A composition of four parts or voices; also, the performers of a four-part composition.

quintet   A composition of five voices or instruments; also, the performers of a five-part composition.

ragtime   Style of American music popular from about 1890 to the beginning of World War I, characterized by syncopated melodies set against a rhythmically strong bass.

re   The second tone of a diatonic scale.

recitative   A style of singing resembling dramatic speech.

refrain   Repeated lines that occur at the end of each stanza of a song or poem.

register   The range of a voice or instrument; a portion of the range of an instrument, as in upper register or lower register.

requiem   A mass for the dead; also, a musical setting for such a mass.

resolution   The progression from a dissonant tone or harmony to one that is consonant.

rest   A symbol indicating pause or silence.

rinforzando   A sudden accent on a single note or chord.

ritardando   A direction to slow the tempo gradually.

ritenuto   Immediate reduction in tempo.

romance   A short vocal or instrumental composition of a romantic character without fixed form.

rondo   A form of instrumental composition with a refrain that occurs at least three times in its original key between contrasting couplets.

root   The tonic of a triad or chord; the lowest tone, unless the chord is inverted.

round   A canon for three or more voices; the common name for a circle canon in which each singer returns from the conclusion of the melody to its beginning, repeating it.

scale   A series of tones arranged according to rising pitches.

scat   A technique of jazz singing that uses nonsense syllables for improvising vocal solos.

scherzo   A playful, humorous instrumental composition, usually in a rapid ¾ meter.

second   The interval between the tonic and the second tone of a diatonic scale; in the key of C major, C to D is a second.

semitone   One-half of a whole tone.

septet   A composition for seven voices or instruments.

sequence   Repetition of a short musical phrase at a different pitch.

serenade   An impromptu or unsolicited vocal or instrumental performance, often outdoors; an instrumental composition in several movements for a small group, between the symphony and the suite.

seventh   The interval between the tonic and the seventh tone of a diatonic scale; in the key of C major, C to B is a seventh.

sharp   A sign (♯) indicating that the pitch is to be raised by a half step.

si (or **ti**)   The seventh tone in a diatonic scale.

signature   A symbol placed on the staff at the beginning of a piece that shows the key and the meter.

sixth   The interval between the tonic and the sixth tone of a diatonic scale; in the key of C major, C to A is a sixth.

slur   A curved line over a series of notes that are to be played smoothly and continuously.

sol   The fifth tone of a diatonic scale.

solo   A piece performed either alone or with accompaniment.

sonata   An instrumental composition of three or four independent movements varying in mood, character, and tempo.

sonatina   A short, simple sonata.

soprano   The highest female or boy's voice; the treble.

sostenuto   Sustaining the tone to or beyond the nominal value.

sotto voce   In a low voice.

staccato   Direction to play notes in a distinct, detached manner.

staff   The five horizontal lines on and between which notes are written.

stretto   Compressed; in a fugue, the overlapping of subject and answer.

subdominant   The dominant below; the fourth tone of the diatonic scale, in the same relation to the key note from below as the dominant is from above.

subito   Suddenly.

subject   A melody or melody fragment that, because of its character, design, position, or treatment, is used in the basic musical form of a composition.

submediant   The sixth tone of a diatonic scale.

subtonic   The seventh tone of a diatonic scale; leading tone.

suite   An instrumental composition consisting of a series of movements or distinct compositions; originally, a cycle of dance tunes.

supertonic   The second tone of a diatonic scale.

symphonic poem   Originated by Franz Liszt, a large narrative orchestral work in one movement based on a nonmusical idea, either poetic or realistic.

symphony   A sonata for orchestra, usually in four contrasting movements.

syncopation   A rhythmic pattern that places emphasis on beats that are not normally accented, thus creating a catchy, lilting sound.

tempo   The speed at which a composition is played.

tenor   The highest natural adult male voice; also, the instrument of corresponding range.

ternary form   The form of a composition in three parts with repetition following one contrast (ABA).

texture   The way in which melody and harmony are combined to create layers of sound.

theme and variation   A musical form in which the theme is repeated and varied.

third   The interval between the tonic and the third tone of a diatonic scale; in the key of C major, C to E is a third.

ti (or **si**)   The seventh tone in a diatonic scale.

tie   A curved line that combines the duration of two notes of the same pitch.

time   Used synonymously with measure or rhythm.

time signature   The meter of a composition, shown by two numbers, one above the other; the lower tells the kind of note that represents one beat; the upper tells the number of these notes that make up a measure.

toccata   A composition popular in the 16th century, for organ or harpsichord, and resembling the capriccio.

tonal center   The tonic pitch around which a composition or scale is centered.

tone   A sound of definite duration and pitch; a note.

tone cluster   A group of notes played simultaneously with forearm, elbow, and fist in a method introduced by Henry Cowell.

tonic   The first tone of a diatonic scale; also called fundamental. In the key of C major, C is the tonic.

transposition   The rewriting or playing of a composition in a key other than the original one.

treble clef   G clef; indicates that the pitch G is located on the second line above middle C.

tremolo   Rapid repetition of a note to resemble trembling.

triad   A chord composed of a fundamental tone and the third and fifth above it.

trio   A composition for three parts or voices; the second part of a minuet or march.

triplet   A group of three notes played in the time value of two.

triple time   Time in which there are three beats to a measure.

Houseflies and car horns have something in common. Most American car horns beep in the key of F. The housefly also buzzes in the key of F.

turn   An embellishment consisting of a group of four or five notes that turn around the principal note.

tutti   Indications for passages for the whole orchestra as distinguished from those of the soloist.

twelve-tone music   A method of composition based on a chromatic scale of 12, rather than 8, tones, developed by Arnold Schoenberg.

unison   Equal pitch; performance of the same part by all voices.

variation   Development of a theme through a variety of forms; differences in rhythm, key, harmony, etc.

vivace   A direction to play in a lively manner.

voice   Vocal or instrumental part of a composition.

waltz   A dance in triple time performed by couples, which reached its peak of popularity during the 19th century; also, music in this rhythm.

whole note   The longest note in common use.

whole tone   An interval of a major second; the interval of two semitones.

Performance Arts

BASIC POSITIONS FOR BALLET

FEET

1st

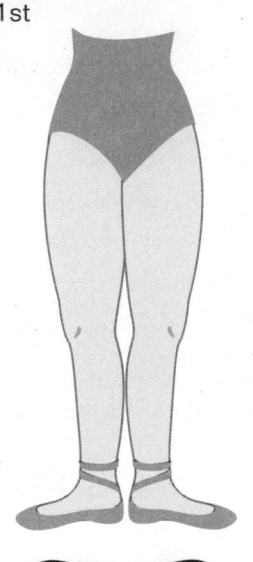

2nd

3rd

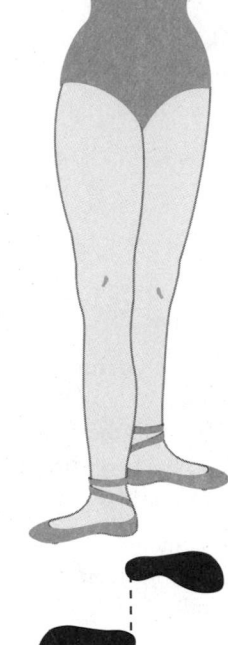

4th
open

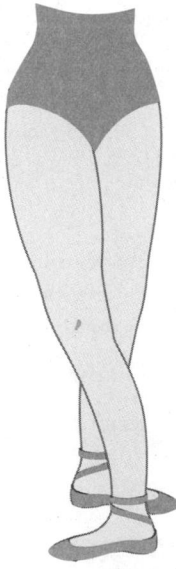

4th
crossed

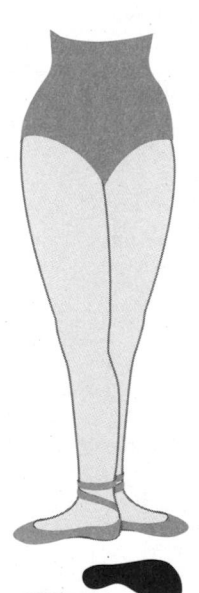

5th

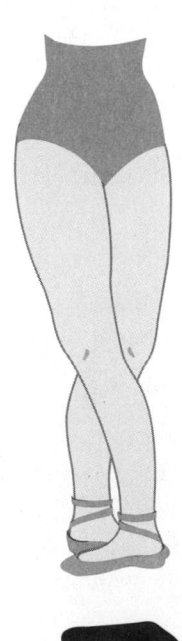

ARMS

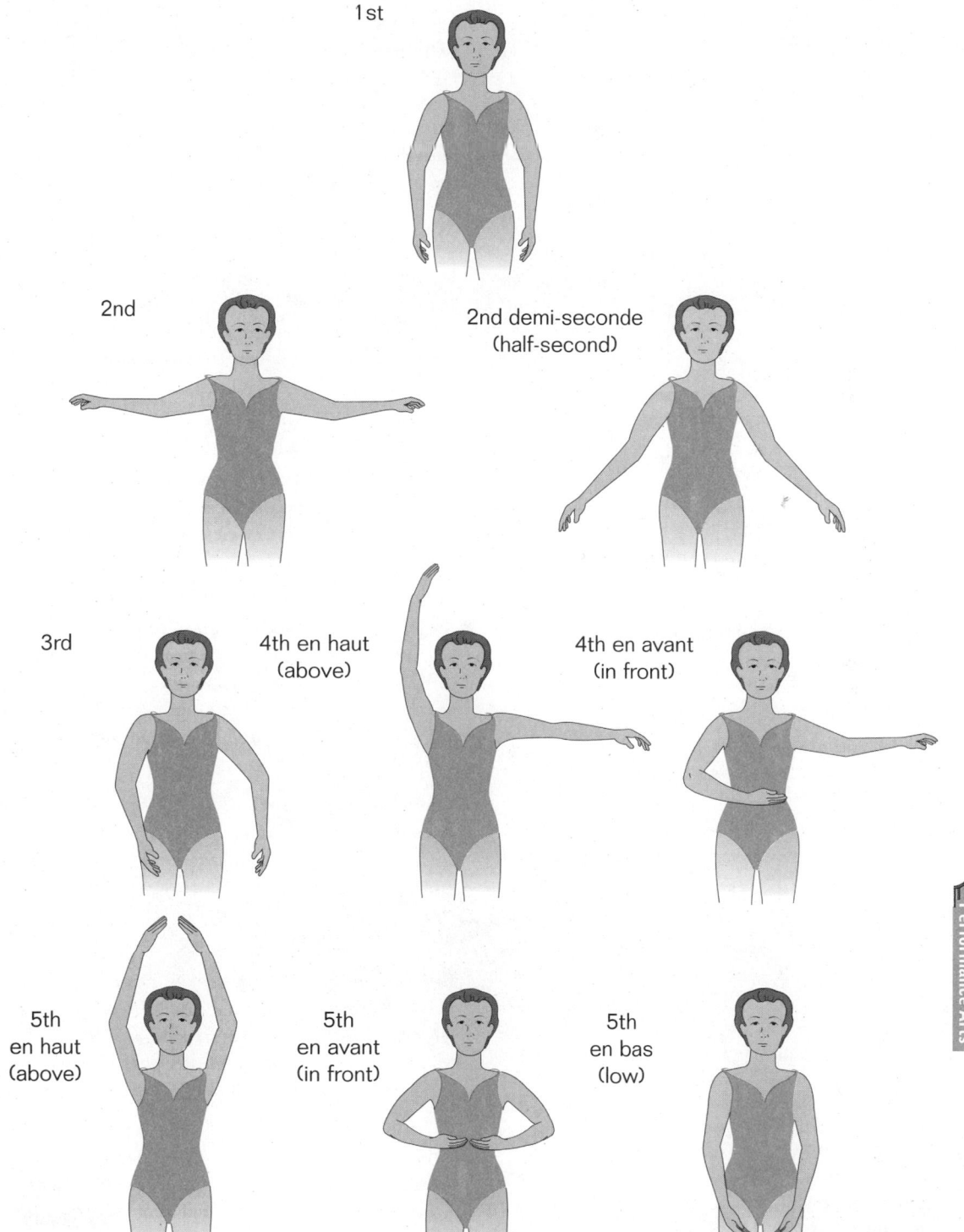

MAJOR DANCERS AND CHOREOGRAPHERS

AMERICAN

Ailey, Alvin (1931–89). Choreographer noted for blending African, modern, and jazz elements, as seen in works such as *Revelations* (1960) and *Cry* (1971). His Alvin Ailey American Dance Theater was formed in 1958.

Arpino, Gerald (1928–). Choreographer. Principal choreographer of the Joffrey Ballet, he became its artistic director in 1988. His sometimes trendy, energetic works include *Viva Vivaldi!* (1965) and *Trinity* (1970).

Astaire, Fred (1899–1987). Actor and dancer in musical comedies on Broadway, such as *The Band Wagon,* and films, including *Top Hat* (1935) and *Shall We Dance?* (1937). Having started in vaudeville with his sister, Adele, Astaire later costarred with Judy Garland, Rita Hayworth, and Ginger Rogers. He was distinguished by his original and graceful tap dancing.

Balanchine, George (1904–83). Russian-born American choreographer. Balanchine worked with Diaghilev's Ballets Russes (1924–29) and then came to America, founding the School of American Ballet in 1934. The New York City Ballet was created in 1948, with Balanchine as artistic director. He was an avatar of neoclassicism and the plotless ballet. Some of his major works, such as *Apollo* (1928) and *Agon* (1957), use the music of Stravinsky; other important works include *Serenade* (1934) and *Jewels* (1967).

Bujones, Fernando (1955–). One of the few American dancers to base his career primarily on classical ballets, Bujones starred with the American Ballet Theater from 1975 to 1985 and then embarked on a career as a guest artist and choreographer. He is best known for his performances in *Don Quixote, La Bayadère, Swan Lake, Giselle,* and *La Sylphide.*

Castle, Vernon (1887–1918) and **Irene** (1893–1969). Exhibition ballroom dancers whose elegance and style contributed to the spread of ballroom dancing before World War I. They created the Cas-tle Walk and popularized the tango and other dances.

Cunningham, Merce (1919–). Choreographer. He danced with Martha Graham's company, forming his own troupe in 1953, collaborating often with John Cage. His avant-garde and abstract works use isolated movements and the random ordering of dance movements. His works include *Summerspace* (1958) and the consecutively numbered *Events* (begun in 1964).

d'Amboise, Jacques (1934–). Dancer and leading interpreter of the works of Balanchine during his years with the New York City Ballet (1949–84). He founded the National Dance Institute, which brings dance to New York City schoolchildren.

de Mille, Agnes (1909–93). Choreographer. De Mille created ballets rooted in American folklore, such as *Rodeo* (1942) and *Fall River Legend* (1948). She also choreographed musicals for Broadway, including *Oklahoma!* (1943), and wrote *Dance to the Piper* (1952) and other books on dance.

Duncan, Isadora (1877–1927). Dancer; one of the first figures in modern dance. Turning to ancient Greece for inspiration, she rejected the rigid system of ballet and created an expressive form of dance, which she performed dressed in a flowing tunic. Her works include *Marseillaise* (1915) and *Marche Slave* (1917).

Dunham, Katherine (1912–). Choreographer and teacher. Through such works as the *Tropical Revues,* she was one of the first to bring African and Caribbean dance to the American stage. She also choreographed *Cabin in the Sky* (1940) for Broadway.

Farrell, Suzanne (1945–). Dancer with the New York City Ballet (1961–69, 1975–89) and Ballets of the 20th Century (1970–75). One of the leading interpreters of the works of Balanchine, Farrell created important roles in such ballets as *Don Quixote* (1965).

Feld, Eliot (1943–). Choreographer. He joined the American Ballet Theater in 1963, choreographing his first works, *Harbinger* and *At Mid-*

night (both 1967), there. In 1968, he formed the American Ballet company; and in 1974, the Feld Ballet.

Graham, Martha (1894–1991). Choreographer. A leader of modern dance, she created a rigorous technique, which includes the contraction, a dramatic percussive movement based on the body's movement during intake and release of breath. Her works such as *Appalachian Spring* (1944) explore American roots; others, such as *Night Journey* (1947) and *Clytemnestra* (1958), draw on Greek mythology, exploring the psychology and passions of their protagonists.

Gregory, Cynthia (1946–   ). Dancer. Noted for her virtuoso technique and majestic presence, she joined the San Francisco Ballet in 1961 and American Ballet Theater in 1965, where she was a principal dancer until 1991.

Holm, Hanya (1898–1992). German-born choreographer and teacher. A protégée of Mary Wigman, she started choreographing her own modern dance works in America, including *Trend* (1937). She also choreographed *Kiss Me Kate* (1948) and *My Fair Lady* (1956) for Broadway.

Horton, Lester (1906–53). Dancer, choreographer, and teacher. A leader in modern dance and influenced by Native American dance, he formed the Lester Horton Dancers in 1934. Among his notable students was Alvin Ailey.

Humphrey, Doris (1895–1958). A dancer with Denishawn, she left in 1927 to start a company with Charles Weidman. Her choreography is based on the principle of fall and recovery, which caters to the range of movement from balance to unbalance. Her works include *The Shakers* (1930) and *With My Red Fires* (1936).

Jamison, Judith (1944–   ). Jamison joined the Alvin Ailey American Dance Theater in 1965 and became artistic director following Ailey's death in 1989. She has starred in numerous Ailey ballets, including *Cry, Maskela Language, Choral Dances,* and *Revelations.*

Joffrey, Robert (1930–88). Choreographer. He formed his first company in 1954, and in 1956 he founded what became the Robert Joffrey Ballet. Joffrey's works include *Pas de Déesses* (1954) and *Astarte* (1967).

Jones, Bill T. (1952–   ). The recipient of a MacArthur Fellowship in 1993, Jones is a postmodernist who performs only in his own works and those of his collaborators. These include *Negroes for Sale* (1972), *Stories, Steps, and Stomps* (1978), *War Between the States* (1993), and *You Walk* (2000).

Kelly, Gene (1912–96). Actor, dancer, choreographer. In films such as *An American in Paris* (1952) and *Invitation to the Dance* (1956), he tried to make the choreography integral to the story and explored cinematic techniques for filming dance.

Kirkland, Gelsey (1953–   ). Kirkland achieved stardom as a principal dancer with both the New York City Ballet and the American Ballet Theater. She is best known for partnering Mikhail Baryshnikov in *Hamlet Connotations, Awakening,* and *Theme and Variations.*

Kirstein, Lincoln (1907–96). A promoter of American ballet, he brought George Balanchine to America and cofounded with him the School of American Ballet. He was general director of the New York City Ballet (1948–89) and wrote *Dance: A Short History of Classic Theatrical Dancing* (1935) and other books.

Limón, Jose (1908–72). Born in Mexico, Limón is regarded as the most electrifying performer in modern dance history. He performed with the Humphrey/Weidman Group from 1930 until 1945, when he founded the Jose Limón Dance Company.

Martins, Peter (1946–   ). Born in Denmark, he first danced with the Royal Danish Ballet (1965–1969). Martins then joined the New York City Ballet in 1970, becoming co–ballet master in chief in 1983 and ballet master in chief in 1990. Among his works, which follow in George Balanchine's neoclassical tradition, are *Calcium Night Light* (1977), *Eight Easy Pieces* (1979), *Ecstatic Orange* (1987), and *Jazz* (1993).

Mitchell, Arthur (1934–   ). Dancer with the New York City Ballet from 1955. In 1968, he founded the Dance Theater of Harlem, the first black classical dance company.

Nikolais, Alwin (1912–1993). Choreographer and founder of the Nikolais Dance Theater. His works, such as *Kaleidoscope* (1956), are theatrical productions in which dance, lighting, and sound play equal roles, forming abstract yet evocative patterns.

Robbins, Jerome (1918–98). Dancer and choreographer for the Ballet Theater (1941–44), where he choreographed *Fancy Free* (1944), and the New York City Ballet, where he was associate artistic director (1949–56) and later codirector (1983–90). His ballets combine the classical idiom with influences from jazz, modern, and social dance. Among his important works are *Goldberg Variations* (1971) and *Dances at a Gathering* (1969). His choreography for Broadway includes *West Side Story* (1957) and *Fiddler on the Roof* (1964).

Robinson, Bill (Bojangles) (1878–1949). Tap dancer who brought a new lightness to tap. Gaining renown with his appearance in the revue *Blackbirds* in 1928, he appeared in movies, including *The Little Colonel* with Shirley Temple.

St. Denis, Ruth (1879–1968). Dancer. Inspired by the Orient, her dances, such as *Radha* (1904) and *The Cobras* (1906), were both exotic and spiritual. In 1915, St. Denis founded Denishawn—the first school of modern dance—with her husband, Ted Shawn.

Shawn, Ted (1891–1972). Founder of Denishawn with Ruth St. Denis. In the 1930s, he started Men Dancers; with works such as *The Kinetic Molpai* (1935), he focused attention on male dancing. Shawn also founded the Jacob's Pillow Dance Festival.

Tallchief, Maria (1925–). Dancer with the Ballet Russe de Monte Carlo (1942–47) and the New York City Ballet (1948–1965). She founded the Chicago City Ballet and later was artistic director of the Lyric Opera of Chicago Ballet.

Taylor, Paul (1930–). Choreographer. He formed his own company in 1954, and his modern dance works are often characterized by humor. His works include *Arden Court* (1981), *Company B* (1991), *The Word* (1998), and *Dandelion Wine* (2000).

Tetley, Glen (1926–). At various times in his career, Tetley has danced and choreographed for Martha Graham, Jerome Robbins, and the American Ballet Theater. Among his best-known works are *Pierrot Lunaire* (1962), *Embrace Tiger and Return to Mountain* (1968), and *Sphinx* (1977).

Tharp, Twyla (1942–). Choreographer of idiosyncratic works that use ballet idiom to novel effect. She had her own modern dance company (1965–88) and then served as artistic associate with the American Ballet Theater (1988–91). Her works include *Deuce Coupe* (1973) and *Push Comes to Shove* (1976). She also choreographed the films *Hair* (1979) and *Amadeus* (1984). She founded the company Twyla Tharp Dance in 2000.

Villella, Edward (1936–). Dancer. As a member of the New York City Ballet (1957–79), he was noted for his virile dancing. He has been artistic director of the Miami City Ballet since 1985.

Weidman, Charles (1901–75). Dancer and choreographer. After dancing with Denishawn, he founded a company with Doris Humphrey in 1927 and later began his own company. His works, known for their humor, include *Flickers* and *And Daddy Was a Fireman*.

BRITISH

Ashton, Sir Frederick (1904–88). A pioneer of British ballet, he was chief choreographer of the Sadler's Wells (now Royal) Ballet from 1935, and its director from 1963 to 1970. His works, noted for their lyrical classicism, include *Symphonic Variations* (1946), *Les Patineurs* (1937), and *Ondine* (1958).

Dolin, Anton (1904–83). English dancer with Diaghilev's Ballets Russes (1924–29) and Ballet Theater. One of Britain's first danseurs nobles, in 1949 he founded the London Festival Ballet with Alicia Markova and served as artistic director.

Fonteyn, Dame Margot (1919–91). English dancer and prima ballerina assoluta of the Royal Ballet, which she joined in 1934 when it was the Vic Wells Ballet. Known for her musicality and refinement, she was the partner of Rudolf Nureyev after 1962; her major roles include Aurora in *Sleeping Beauty* and Juliet in *Romeo and Juliet*.

MacMillan, Kenneth (1929–92). The creator of more than 60 ballets, MacMillan was a bold innovator who expanded the dramatic and intellectual horizons of the dance, often grappling with social, psychological, and political themes. His masterworks include *The Burrow* (1958), *The Invitation* (1960), *Requiem* (1976), *Isadora* (1981), and *Valley of Shadows* (1983).

Markova, Dame Alicia (1910–). English dancer with the Ballets Russes (1925–29), Ballet Theater (1941–45), and other companies. Markova was one of the leading interpreters of *Giselle* and the first British ballerina of international renown.

Rambert, Dame Marie (1888–1982). Polish-born dancer, teacher, and ballet director. She advised Nijinsky on rhythm when he was choreographing *Le Sacre du Printemps* and later became one of the pioneers of modern British ballet, founding her Ballet Rambert in 1935.

Tudor, Antony (1908–87). English choreographer of ballets of psychological drama. He was associated with the American Ballet Theater (1939–49), then known as Ballet Theater, and later served as associate artistic director (1974–80). Among the ballets that exemplify his use of gesture to express character are *Lilac Garden* (1936) and *Pillar of Fire* (1942).

Valois, Dame Ninette de (1898–). A founder of modern British ballet. After dancing with the Ballets Russes (1923–26), she founded a school in London; and in 1931, a company, the Vic Wells Ballet, which became the Sadler's Wells Ballet and then the Royal Ballet. Her works include *The Rake's Progress* (1935) and *The Haunted Ballroom* (1934).

FRENCH

Béjart, Maurice (1927–). Choreographer. He founded the Ballet de l'Etoile in 1953, and later the Ballets of the 20th Century. In 1988, his troupe moved to Lausanne, Switzerland. Béjart's controversial works are highly theatrical and sometimes mystical; they include *Symphony for a Lonely Man* (1955) and *Ring Around the Ring* to Wagner (1991).

Camargo, Marie (1710–70). Dancer at the Paris Opera and rival of Marie Sallé, Camargo shortened the dancer's skirt to show her brilliant entrechats and other beats and eliminated the heels from her shoes for greater freedom of movement.

Noverre, Jean Georges (1727–1810). Choreographer and ballet reformer who tried with the *ballet d'action* to highlight the expressiveness of the ballet and integrate dance with drama. He wrote down his ideas in his *Letters sur la danse et sur les ballets.*

Perrot, Jules (1810–92). Dancer and ballet master of the Imperial Theater in St. Petersburg (1851–58). A leading dancer and choreographer of the Romantic era, he choreographed *La Esmeralda* and parts of *Giselle* (1841).

Petit, Roland (1924–). Founder of the Ballets de Paris de Roland Petit (1948) and director of the Ballet National de Marseilles since 1972. His story ballets combine high and popular art; his works include *Le Jeune homme et la mort* (1946) and *Le Loup* (1953).

Sallé, Marie (1707–56). Dancer with the Paris Opera (1727–40) and rival of Camargo. An advocate of the use of pantomime in ballet, Sallé was noted for her expressiveness and intelligence.

Vestris, Auguste (1760–1842). Dancer and teacher and illegitimate son of Gaetano. As premier danseur of the Paris Opera, he was noted for his exceptional elevation and virtuosity.

Vestris, Gaetano (1728–1808). Italian-born dancer and choreographer. Known as "the god of the dance," he became premier danseur of the Paris Opera in 1751 and cochoreographer in 1761. He was the first to discard the mask worn by dancers in performance.

RUSSIAN

Baryshnikov, Mikhail (1948–). A principal with the Kirov Ballet (1968–74), the Russian dancer defected to the West in 1974, joining the American Ballet Theater and serving as its director (1980–89). He then formed the White Oak Dance Project. His virtuosity and purity of classical style make him one of the leading male dancers of the period.

Danilova, Alexandra (1904–97). Russian-born dancer. Noted for her charm and elegance, she was a ballerina with the Ballets Russes (1927–29) and prima ballerina with the Ballet Russe de Monte Carlo (1938–52). She taught at the School of American Ballet (1964–89) and appeared in the film *The Turning Point* (1977).

Diaghilev, Sergei Pavlovich (1872–1929). Russian impresario and founder of the Ballets Russes (1909). He brought together leading choreographers, composers, and artists, from Fokine and Balanchine to Stravinsky and Picasso, whose collaborations revolutionized the ballet.

Eglevsky, Andre (1917–77). Russian-born dancer. A leading dancer with the Ballet Russe de Monte Carlo (1939–42), Ballet Theater (1942–43), and New York City Ballet (1951–58). He founded the Eglevsky Ballet Company in 1961.

Fokine, Michel (1880–1942). Russian-born choreographer for the Ballets Russes (1909–12, 1914–15). His emphasis on dramatic coherence and on the unity of the style of dance and decor with the subject matter revolutionized the ballet. His important works include *The Firebird* (1910) and *Petrouchka* (1911).

Ivanov, Lev (1834–1901). Russian choreographer. His most important ballets were *The Nutcracker* (1892) and the second and fourth acts of *Swan Lake* (1894).

Karsavina, Tamara (1885–1978). Russian dancer with the Ballets Russes and partner of Nijinsky. She created important roles in *The Firebird* and *Petrouchka* and wrote her autobiography, *Theatre Street*.

Lifar, Serge (1905–86). Russian dancer with the Ballets Russes (1923–29), where he created the title role in Balanchine's *Prodigal Son*. As director of the Paris Opera Ballet (1929–45, 1947–58), he reinvigorated French ballet, choreographing many works, including *Icare* (1935) and *Suite en blanc* (1943).

Makarova, Natalia (1940–   ). Russian dancer. A leading member of the Kirov Ballet (1959–70), she defected to the West, where she danced with the American Ballet Theater, the Royal Ballet, and other

companies. She won a Tony for her performance in the musical *On Your Toes*.

Massine, Léonide (1895–1979). Russian-born dancer and choreographer with the Ballets Russes (1914–21, 1925–28) and the Ballet Russe de Monte Carlo (1932–42). His works include *Parade* (1917) and *Gaîté, Parisienne* (1938).

Nijinska, Bronislava (1891–1972). The sister of Vaslav Nijinsky, she also worked with the Ballets Russes as a dancer and innovative choreographer, incorporating sport and satire into ballet. Among her important ballets are *Les Noces* (1923) and *Les Biches* (1924).

Nijinsky, Vaslav (1889–1950). Polish-Russian dancer and choreographer with the Ballets Russes, creating important roles in Fokine's ballets, such as *Petrouchka*. Considered by many to be the greatest dancer of the 20th century, he also choreographed works such as *L'Après-midi d'un faune* (1912) and *Le Sacre du printemps* (1913), which were radical breaks with ballet tradition.

Nureyev, Rudolf (1938–93). Russian dancer with the Kirov Ballet. He defected to the West in 1961, where he often partnered Dame Margot Fonteyn with the Royal Ballet. A leading dancer of his time, he was noted for his virtuosity and animal sensuality. He was director of the Paris Opera from 1983 to 1989.

Pavlova, Anna Matveyevna (1881–1931). Russian ballerina. She danced briefly with the Ballets Russes and then toured with her own company, introducing ballet to people all over the world. An outstanding ballerina, she was known for her grace and lightness and the spiritual quality of her dancing.

Petipa, Marius (1818–1910). French-born dancer who became first ballet master of the Imperial Theater of St. Petersburg in 1862. Russian ballet reached its apogee under his direction. He was one of the leading choreographers in ballet history, and his works include *La Bayadère* (1877) and *The Sleeping Beauty* (1890).

Plisetskaya, Maya (1925–   ). Leading Russian ballerina with the Bolshoi Ballet, which she joined in

1945. She is noted for her virtuosity and dramatic presence and for the pliancy of her arms.

Ulanova, Galina Sergeyevna (1910–   ). Russian dancer and teacher noted for her dramatic projection and lyricism. After joining the Kirov Ballet in 1928, she left to dance with the Bolshoi Ballet (1944–61), becoming the prima ballerina of Soviet ballet.

Youskevitch, Igor (1912–94). Russian-born dancer with the Ballet Russe de Monte Carlo (1938–44) and the Ballet Theater (1946–55). He was admired for his nobility and elegance and for his partnership with Alicia Alonso.

OTHER

Alonso, Alicia (1921–   ). Cuban dancer known for the purity of her classical style, particularly in the role of Giselle. After dancing with the American Ballet Theater and other companies, she founded the National Ballet of Cuba in 1959.

Bournonville, Auguste (1805–79). Danish choreographer. His Romantic works, such as *Napoli* (1842), form the core of the repertory of the Royal Danish Ballet.

Bruhn, Erik (1928–86). Danish-born dancer noted for his immaculate technique and nobility of style. After dancing with the American Ballet Theater and other companies, he was artistic director of the National Ballet of Canada (1983–86).

Cerrito, Fanny (1817–1909). Italian dancer, one of the leading ballerinas of the Romantic era. Noted for her strength and sensuous appeal, she created the leading role in *Ondine* (1843).

Elssler, Fanny (1810–84). Austrian daughter of an assistant to Franz Joseph Haydn, Elssler was one of the great ballerinas of the Romantic era, noted for her dramatic projection and earthiness. Her most famous dance was the Cachucha in *Le Diable boiteux* (1836).

Grisi, Carlotta (1819–99). Italian dancer with the Paris Opera. One of the great Romantic ballerinas, she created the title role in *Giselle*, whose libretto was written for her by Théophile Gautier.

Jooss, Kurt (1901–79). German choreographer whose theatrical works combined classical and modern modes of dance. His important works include *The Green Table,* a scathing indictment of war, and *Big City* (1932).

Taglioni, Marie (1804–84). Italian ballerina, the incarnation of the spiritual and lyrical ideal of the Romantic era. In the title role of *La Sylphide* (1832), she brought toe dancing to a new artistic level.

Wigman, Mary (1886–1973). German dancer and choreographer. The first major European modern dancer, Wigman choreographed somber works in an expressionist mode. Her works include *Totenmal* (1930).

COMMON DANCE TERMS

abstract dance   A plotless work composed of pure dance movements, although the composition may suggest a mood or subject.

adagio   Any dance to slow music; also, part of the classical pas de deux in ballet.

air, en l'   In ballet, a step done off the ground—for instance, tour en l'air, rond de jambe en l'air. It is the opposite of par terre.

allegro   A dance with a fast or moderate tempo.

allongé   In ballet, an elongated line; in particular, the horizontal line of an arabesque with one arm stretched front and the other back.

arabesque   In ballet, the extension of one leg straight in back at 90 degrees, with shoulders square; the position of the arms may vary.

assemblé   In ballet, a jump from one to both feet, usually landing in fifth position.

attitude   In ballet, a pose in which one leg is raised in back or in front with knee bent, usually with one arm raised.

balancé   A step that rocks from one foot to the other, usually in ¾ time.

ballet   From the Italian *balletto,* diminutive of *ballo,* "dance." Classical theatrical dancing based on the *danse d'école,* the rules and vocabulary that were codified around 1700 in France.

ballet blanc   A ballet in which the women wear white tutus, such as the second and fourth acts of *Swan Lake.*

ballet d'action   A ballet with a plot, usually tragic, advocated by reformer Jean Georges Noverre, ballet master of the Paris Opera, to bring dramatic coherence to the performance of ballet.

ballet de cour, le (court ballet)   Spectacles for entertainment, usually with allegorical or mythological themes, performed by the aristocracy in the 16th and 17th centuries, combining music, recitatives, and mime.

ballo   Standard Italian dances and their music of the 15th and 16th centuries.

ballon   In ballet, the ability of a dancer to remain suspended in air during a jump; elasticity in jumping.

ballroom dances   Social dances usually performed by couples, including the fox-trot, waltz, tango, rumba, and cha cha.

bas, en   In ballet, low, as in placement of arms.

basic movement   In ballroom dance, a characteristic figure that remains constant.

basse danse   A solemn court dance usually in duple time, popular in the 15th and 16th centuries.

battement   A beating movement of the legs.

bourrée, pas de   A series of small, fast steps executed with the feet very close together.

brisé   In ballet, a jump off one foot that is "broken" by a beating of the legs in the air.

cabriole   In ballet, a leap in which the lower leg beats against the upper one at an angle, before the dancer lands again on the lower leg.

cachucha   A Spanish dance in ¾ or ⅜ time with castanets.

cakewalk   An African American dance in which couples strut and compete with high kicks and fast steps.

cambré   In ballet, a bend from the waist to the side or to the back.

cancan   Originating around 1830 as a social dance, by 1844 it had become a raucous dance performed in French music halls.

chassé   A sliding step in which one foot "chases" and displaces the other.

chat, pas de   Catlike leap in which one foot follows the other into the air, knees bent; the landing is in the fifth position.

ciseaux   A jump in which the legs open in second position in the air, resembling a scissors.

coda   In ballet, the third and final part of the classical pas de deux.

contraction   A basic movement in the technique of Martha Graham, based on breath inhalation and exhalation.

contredanse   Popular social dance during the 18th century; done in rows or circles, it may have derived from English country dancing.

corps de ballet   The members of a ballet company who do not perform solo.

country dance   Traditional English dance in which dancers form two facing lines.

croisée   In ballet, a position with the body at an oblique angle and the working leg crossing the line of the body.

danseur noble   A male dancer who performs the "princely" roles of the classical ballet, such as the Prince in *Swan Lake.*

dégagé   In ballet, shifting weight from one foot to the other.

développé   In ballet, an unfolding of the leg in the air.

écarté   In ballet, a position with one leg extended at an oblique angle while the body is also at an oblique angle.

effacé   In ballet, a position of the body at an oblique angle and partly hidden.

entrechat   A ballet movement in which the dancer repeatedly crosses his or her legs in the air.

épaulement   In ballet, the position of the torso from the waist up.

fandango   A lively Spanish dance in triple time performed with castanets or tambourines.

fermé   In ballet, a closed position of the feet.

five positions   In ballet, the basic positions of the feet. *First position:* feet in a straight line, heels touching. *Second position:* feet in a straight line, heels apart. *Third position:* one foot in front of the other, parallel to it, with heel of front foot in hollow instep of back foot. *Fourth position:* one foot in front of the other, parallel, but apart. *Fifth position:* one foot in front of the other, parallel, with heel in front foot touching toe of back foot. See illustrations on page 192.

flamenco   A Sevillian gypsy dance, possibly originating in India, also with Moorish and Arabian influences, originally accompanied by songs and clapping and later by the guitar, and characterized by its heelwork *(taconeo).*

fondu   In ballet, a lowering of the body by bending the knee.

fouetté en tournant   A spectacular movement in which the dancer propels himself or herself around a supporting leg with rapid circular movements of the other leg while remaining in a fixed spot.

fox-trot   A social dance of American origin in duple time.

glissade   In ballet, a gliding step that usually connects two steps.

haut, en   In ballet, a position of the arms above the head.

jeté   In ballet, a leap from one leg to the other in which one leg is thrown to the side, front, or back. *Grand jeté:* a large leap forward.

jitterbug   A lively social dance popular during the 1930s; it originated at the Savoy Ballroom in Harlem in 1928, where it was known as the Lindy.

kabuki   A Japanese dance drama featuring stylized narrative choreographic movements.

mazurka   A Polish national dance in triple time with an accent on the second beat, characterized by proud bearing; clicking of heels; and *holubria,* a special turning step.

minuet   A slow and graceful dance, the most popular dance of the 18th century, characterized by symmetrical figures and elaborate curtsies and bows.

morris dance   An English folk dance that appeared in the 15th century, in which dancers wore bells on their legs and characters included a fool, a boy on a hobbyhorse, and a man in blackface.

ouvert   In ballet, an open position of the feet.

par terre   In ballet, steps performed on the floor. It is the opposite of en l'air.

pas de deux   A dance for two, usually a woman and a man. In its traditional form, it begins with an entrée and adagio, followed by solo variations for each dancer and a coda.

pavane   A grave, processional court dance popular in the 16th and 17th centuries.

penché   In ballet, leaning forward.

piqué   In ballet, stepping directly onto the point of a foot.

pirouette   A turn on one leg, with the toe of the other leg touching the knee of the turning leg.

plié   A bending of the knees in any of the five positions. *Demi plié:* a half bending of the knees, with heels on the floor. *Grand plié:* a full bending of the knees.

point   A position on the tip of the toes. *Demi-point:* a position on the balls of the feet.

polka   A Bohemian folk dance in duple time with a hop on the fourth beat. It became a popular ballroom dance in the mid–19th century.

port de bras   In ballet, the positions of the arms.

premier danseur   Principal male dancer.

promenade   In ballet, a slow turn of the body on the whole foot.

quadrille   A social dance popular in the 19th century. It was a square dance in five sections, each in a different time.

reel   Popular in Britain, Ireland, and Scotland, it is a lively dance for two or more couples; also, the second part of the Virginia reel. The Highland fling is a variant.

relevé   In ballet, a rising with a spring movement to point or demi-point.

révérence   A ballet bow or curtsy in which one foot is pointed in front and the body leans forward.

spotting   A fixing of the eyes on one spot as long as possible during turns to avoid dizziness and to keep one's orientation.

square dance   An American folk dance with an even number of couples forming a square, two lines, or a circle. The dance consists of figures announced by a caller.

tango   A social dance in ¾ time, which, after originating in Spain, developed in Argentina, where it was influenced by black dance style and rhythm.

tour en l'air   In ballet, a turn while jumping straight up in the air.

variation   Any solo performance in a ballet.

waltz   A social dance in ¾ time that became widely popular in the 19th century. It developed from the Landler, a German-Austrian turning dance.

MAJOR PLAYWRIGHTS

AMERICAN

Albee, Edward   (1928–   ). Playwright, producer, director. *Who's Afraid of Virginia Woolf?* (1962) made his reputation. Other works include *The Zoo Story* (1959), *A Delicate Balance* (1966), *Seascape* (1975), and *Three Tall Women* (1994).

Barry, Philip   (1896–1949). His most successful plays are witty and elegant comedies about the social elite. They deal with the true nature of love and marriage and with a quest for personal fulfillment. His works include *Holiday* (1929), *The Animal Kingdom* (1932), and *The Philadelphia Story* (1939).

Chayefsky, Paddy (Sidney)   (1923–81). Playwright and television writer and screenwriter. His most notable television plays, such as *Marty* (1953), and stage plays, such as *The Tenth Man* (1959), are about the search for love as a source of spiritual redemption. His screenplays include *Network* (1976).

Guare, John   (1938–   ). Playwright known for satires and black comedies that explore American society, often within the context of family relationships. In addition to writing stage works such as *The House of Blue Leaves* (1971) and *Six Degrees of Separation* (1990), he also wrote the screenplay for *Atlantic City* (1980).

Hellman, Lillian   (1905–84). Dramatist. Her tightly constructed plays skillfully depict human perversity and evil. Among her best are *The Children's Hour* (1934), *The Little Foxes* (1939), and *Watch on the Rhine* (1941).

Henley, Beth   (1952–   ). Her dark, comedic plays contain elements of the Southern Gothic tradition. She is best known for *Crimes of the Heart* (1981), which won the Pulitzer prize.

Inge, William   (1913–1973). Playwright. His tightly constructed realistic dramas deal with small-town life in the American Midwest, giving form to the yearnings and the guilt of simple people. Among his best plays are *Come Back, Little Sheba* (1950), *Picnic* (1953), *Bus Stop* (1955), and *Dark at the Top of the Stairs* (1957).

Mamet, David   (1947–   ). Dramatist known for *American Buffalo* (1975). He was awarded the 1984 Pulitzer prize for *Glengarry Glenn Ross*, for which he also wrote the screenplay. Other works include *Speed the Plow* (1988), *Oleanna* (1992), and the screenplay for *Wag the Dog* (1998).

Miller, Arthur   (1915–   ). Outstanding contemporary dramatist. His concern with the moral problems of American society led him to probe the psychological causes of behavior. His classic *Death of a Salesman* (1949) won the Pulitzer prize; other plays include *The Crucible* (1953) and *A View from the Bridge* (1955).

Odets, Clifford   (1906–63). Leading playwright of the Group Theatre and the most important of the American social dramatists of the 1930s. His plays of social and political protest include *Waiting for Lefty* (1935) and *Awake and Sing* (1935). Among his other works are *Golden Boy* (1937), *The Big Knife* (1949), and *The Country Girl* (1951).

Go to
"Important Authors" in chapter 8

O'Neill, Eugene (1888–1953). Probably the greatest American dramatist; also one of the bleakest and most pessimistic. He essayed almost every modern dramatic form. His later, naturalistic plays deal with the inevitability of fate: *The Iceman Cometh* (1939), *Long Day's Journey into Night* (1941), and *A Moon for the Misbegotten* (1943). Other significant works include *Anna Christie* (1920), *Desire Under the Elms* (1924), and *Ah, Wilderness!* (1933). He won the Pulitzer prize four times and, in 1936, the Nobel Prize for literature.

Rabe, David (1940–). Dramatist known for his harsh view of American society. His best-known plays are *The Basic Training of Pavlo Hummel* (1973), *Streamers* (1976), and *Hurlyburly* (1984).

Saroyan, William (1908–81). Playwright and novelist. His essential theme is the triumph of childlike goodness over the corruption of a materialistic society. He won the Pulitzer prize for his classic *The Time of Your Life* (1939) but refused the award.

Shepard, Sam (1943–). Playwright and actor. Myth and reality clash in his plays, which explore the disintegration of American values and the chaos beneath. His works include *Operation Sidewinder* (1970); *Buried Child* (1978), which won a Pulitzer prize; and *Fool for Love* (1984).

Sherwood, Robert (1896–1955). Dramatist and biographer. His plays deal with the conflict between man's civilized values and his frequent descent into savagery. Among his best works are *The Petrified Forest* (1935), *Idiot's Delight* (1936), and *There Shall Be No Night* (1940).

Simon, Neil (1927–). Playwright and screenwriter. He has had more Broadway comedy hits than any other playwright. Among his well-known plays and musicals are *Barefoot in the Park* (1963); *The Odd Couple* (1965); *Sweet Charity* (1966); *The Sunshine Boys* (1972); *Brighton Beach Memoirs* (1983); and *Lost in Yonkers* (1991), which won the Pulitzer prize and Tony award.

Wasserstein, Wendy (1950–). Awarded the Pulitzer prize in 1989 for *The Heidi Chronicles,* Wasserstein focuses on the lives of modern women, their search for identity, and their attitude to the traditional roles projected for them.

Wilder, Thornton (1897–1975). Playwright, novelist, and essayist. His work is a celebration of human existence; he sees man and the universe as intimately related. His major plays are *Our Town* (1938), *The Skin of Our Teeth* (1942), which both won Pulitzer prizes, and *The Matchmaker* (1953).

Williams, Tennessee (1911–83). Probably the greatest American dramatist since Eugene O'Neill. His essential theme is the vulnerability of beauty to time and to a society dominated by violence. Among his most significant plays are *The Glass Menagerie* (1945); *A Streetcar Named Desire* (1947), which won a Pulitzer prize; *Summer and Smoke* (1948), *Cat on a Hot Tin Roof* (1955), which also won a Pulitzer; and *Night of the Iguana* (1961).

Wilson, August (1945–). One of the most acclaimed American dramatists. Wilson has chronicled the African American experience through each decade of the 20th century. He has won the Pulitzer prize twice, for *Fences* in 1987 and *The Piano Lesson* in 1990.

Wilson, Lanford (1937–). Dramatist and screenwriter whose works explore the conflict between traditional values and modern life. Among his best plays are *The Hot L Baltimore* (1973) and *Talley's Folly*, which won the Pulitzer prize in 1980.

BRITISH

Beaumont, Francis (c. 1584–1616). Jacobean dramatist, best known for his collaborations with John Fletcher. They developed a new form called "tragicomedy," which allowed for the treatment of serious themes without a tragic resolution. Their works include *Philaster* (1610) and *The Maid's Tragedy* (c. 1611). Beaumont alone wrote *The Knight of the Burning Pestle* (c. 1607), a burlesque of the historical romances of the time.

Churchill, Caryl (1938–). Playwright. Known for using experimental techniques, she examines contemporary society from a feminist and socialist point of view. Among her works are *Light Shining in Buckinghamshire* (1976), *Cloud Nine* (1981), and *Serious Money* (1982).

Performance Arts

Coward, Noël (1899–1973). Playwright, actor, composer, and director. His comedies present witty, stylish people acting in accordance with their unconventional morality and in league against more banal types. His best plays are *Private Lives* (1930), *Design for Living* (1930), and *Blithe Spirit* (1933).

Dekker, Thomas (c. 1572–1632). Dramatist and pamphleteer. He centered his plays on contemporary life and merged Elizabethan romance with everyday realism, exhibiting sympathy for society's outcasts. His best plays are *The Shoemaker's Holiday* (1600), *The Honest Whore, Part I* (with Thomas Middleton, 1604; *Part II,* 1630), *Westward Ho!* (with John Webster, 1604), *The Roaring Girl* (with Middleton, 1607–08), and *The Witch of Edmonton* (with William Rowley and John Ford, 1621).

Eliot, Thomas Stearns (T. S.) (1888–1965). Poet, critic, and playwright, born in America. He spearheaded a new interest in formal verse drama. His most admired play, *Murder in the Cathedral* (1935), derived its form from Greek tragedy, medieval morality plays, and church ritual. Other plays include *The Cocktail Party* (1949).

Fletcher, John (1579–1625). Prolific and immensely popular playwright who collaborated with Francis Beaumont and many others, apparently including Shakespeare (*The Two Noble Kinsmen* [1613] and *Henry VIII* [1613]). Alone, Fletcher wrote two early tragedies, *Valentinian* (1610–14) and *Bonduca* (1609–14), and the comedies *Wit Without Money* (c. 1614) and *Rule a Wife and Have a Wife* (1624). He helped to lay the basis for the Restoration "comedy of manners."

Goldsmith, Oliver (c. 1728–74). Irish-born essayist, poet, novelist, and comic playwright. He ridiculed the sentimental comedy of the time and promoted what he called "laughing comedy," designed to make us smile at our own follies. His comic masterpiece is *She Stoops to Conquer* (1773).

Hare, David (1947–   ). Dramatist and screenwriter who often probes the political and moral condition of England and the world at large. In addition to writing plays such as *Slag* (1970), *Plenty* (1978), and *Pravda* (1985), he created the screen-play for *Strapless* (1990) and wrote *Licking Hitler* (1978) for British television.

Jonson, Ben (1572–1637). Dramatist, poet, and literary critic. He developed the "comedy of humours," which featured characters dominated by one overruling passion. His masterpieces are *Volpone* (1605–06), *Epicoene* (1610), *The Alchemist* (1610), and *Bartholomew Fair* (1614).

Kyd, Thomas (1558–94). Author of *The Spanish Tragedy* (1592), which introduced the theme of vengeance into Elizabethan drama; the "tragedy of revenge" became popular throughout the period. Kyd drew his inspiration from the Roman tragedies of Seneca.

Marlowe, Christopher (1564–93). Poet and playwright who ushered in the great age of Elizabethan drama. His distinctive blank verse—called "Marlowe's mighty line"—established this verse style as a basic tool of Elizabethan playwrights. His masterpieces are *Tamburlaine the Great: Part I* (c. 1586–87; *Part II,* 1587), *Dr. Faustus* (c. 1588), *The Jew of Malta* (c. 1589), and *Edward II* (1591). Marlowe, often in trouble with the law, was murdered in 1593.

Middleton, Thomas (c. 1570–1627). Jacobean dramatist with a dark and pessimistic vision of human corruption. In his comedies, the manners of the age are held up to scathing ridicule; his tragedies are remarkable for their penetrating psychological realism. His plays include *A Trick to Catch the Old One* (c. 1607), *A Chaste Maid in Cheapside* (1611), *The Changeling* (with William Rowley, 1622), and *Women Beware Women* (c. 1625).

Osborne, John (1929–94). His work was fueled by a disgust for the quality of life in contemporary Britain. In the opening of his most famous play, *Look Back in Anger* (1956), his protagonist, Jimmy Porter, a working-class intellectual rebel, opens fire on the establishment. Among Osborne's other works are *The Entertainer* (1957), *Luther* (1961), and *Inadmissible Evidence* (1964).

Pinter, Harold (1930–   ). Dramatist and actor. The motivation for the action in his plays is typically omitted; the characters evade real communication. The central motif is often two people in a room, involved in a seemingly commonplace situation that is gradually invested with menace, dread, and mystery. Pinter's language reproduces the inflections and rambling irrelevancy of everyday speech. His best plays include *The Birthday Party* (1958), *The Dumb Waiter* (1959), *The Homecoming* (1965), and *Betrayal* (1978).

Shakespeare, William (1564–1616). Elizabethan poet and dramatist. The most influential writer in English literature and perhaps the greatest dramatist of all time. His plays resonate with the full range of human emotion and experience. In his dramatic poetry, the English language reached perfection. As Ben Jonson wrote in his great tribute, "He was not of an age, but for all time!" Shakespeare wrote tragedies, comedies, and histories. His tragedies are *Titus Andronicus* (1594), *Romeo and Juliet* (c. 1595–96), *Julius Caesar* (1599), *Hamlet* (1602), *Othello* (1602–03), *Timon of Athens* (1604–05), *King Lear* (1605–06), *Macbeth* (1605–06), *Antony and Cleopatra* (1606–07), and *Coriolanus* (1607–10). His comedies are *The Comedy of Errors* (1591–94), *The Taming of the Shrew* (1593–94), *The Two Gentlemen of Verona* (1594–95), *Love's Labour's Lost* (1593–95), *A Midsummer Night's Dream* (1595–96), *The Merchant of Venice* (1596–97), *Much Ado About Nothing* (1598–99), *The Merry Wives of Windsor* (1598–99), *As You Like It* (1599–1600), *Twelfth Night* (1599–1600), *Troilus and Cressida* (1601–02), *All's Well That Ends Well* (1602–03), *Measure for Measure* (1603–04), *Pericles* (1606–08), *Cymbeline* (1609–10), *The Winter's Tale* (1610–11), and *The Tempest* (1611). The histories are *Henry VI: Part I* (1589–91), *Henry VI: Part II* (1590–91), *Henry VI: Part III* (1590–91), *Richard III* (1593), *Richard II* (1595), *King John* (1596–97), *Henry IV: Part I* (1597–98), *Henry IV: Part II* (1597–98), *Henry V* (1598–99), and *Henry VIII* (1613).

Shaw, George Bernard (1856–1950). Irish-born dramatist, journalist, critic, and Fabian socialist. His plays combine brilliant, incisive wit with a moral purpose: to expose the follies of the contemporary social order. He created a "drama of ideas," in which philosophical discussion becomes a theatrical event. Among his best-known works are *Arms and the Man* (1894), *Man and Superman* (1905), *Major Barbara* (1905), *Pygmalion* (1912), *Heartbreak House* (1913–19), and *Saint Joan* (1923).

Sheridan, Richard Brinsley (1751–1816). Irish-born comic playwright, theatrical manager, and politician. Sheridan sought to restore a comedy of wit to the post-Restoration theater, which had been engulfed by middle-class moralizing. His masterpieces are *The Rivals* (1775) and *The School for Scandal* (1777).

Stoppard, Tom (1937–). Playwright, born in Czechoslovakia. Heavily influenced by Beckett and the Theatre of the Absurd, he is best known for *Rosencrantz and Guildenstern Are Dead* (1967), *The Real Inspector Hound* (1968), *Arcadia* (1993), and *The Invention of Love* (1997).

Tourneur, Cyril (1575–1626). Jacobean dramatist, author of two famous tragedies of revenge, both based on Senecan drama: *The Revenger's Tragedy* (1606–07: the authorship of this play is in dispute but is generally ascribed to Tourneur) and *The Atheist's Tragedy* (1607–11).

Webster, John (c. 1580–1634). Jacobean dramatist and creator of two outstanding tragedies, *The White Devil* (1609–12) and *The Duchess of Malfi* (1613–14). His vision was one of dark, brooding pessimism.

Wilde, Oscar (1854–1900). Irish-born playwright, novelist, poet, and aesthete. Famous for his epigrammatic wit and for his eccentricity in dress and lifestyle, Wilde used his satirical gifts to expose the shallowness and hypocrisy of Victorian society. His comic masterpiece is *The Importance of Being Earnest* (1895).

FRENCH

Anouilh, Jean (1910–87). Dramatist and screenwriter. His plays, which are laced with humor, deal with the impossibility of purity surviving in a world dominated by compromise. Among his best-known works are *Thieves' Carnival* (1932), *Antigone* (1944), *The Waltz of the Toreadors* (1952), and *The Lark* (1953).

Beckett, Samuel (1906–89). Playwright and novelist, born in Ireland. One of the originators of the Theatre of the Absurd, he mixes comedy with existential anguish to express the dilemma of 20th-century man. His major works include *Waiting for Godot* (1952) and *Endgame* (1957). He was awarded the 1969 Nobel Prize for literature.

Corneille, Pierre   (1606–84). The first of the great French neoclassic dramatists. His early masterpiece, *Le Cid* (1637), was harshly criticized by the French Academy because it did not adhere to the "classical unities." All his later tragedies followed the rules. Other works include *Horace* (1640), *Cinna* (1640–41), and *Polyeuctes* (1641–42).

Genet, Jean   (1919–86). Novelist and preeminent dramatist of the Theatre of the Absurd. In the face of the void, his deeply alienated characters assume inauthentic roles, which become ritualized. Genet's best plays include *The Maids* (1947), *The Balcony* (1956), and *The Blacks* (1959).

Giraudoux, Jean   (1882–1944). Novelist and dramatist. Many of his plays are reinterpretations of Greek myth. Among his best works are *Tiger at the Gates* (1935) and *The Madwoman of Chaillot* (1946).

Hugo, Victor Marie   (1802–85). Poet, novelist, playwright, and politician; he was the acknowledged leader of French Romanticism. The famous "battle" that disrupted the premiere of his tragedy *Hernani* (1830) marked a watershed in the history of the Romantic movement. Other plays include *The King Amuses Himself* (1832—the source for Verdi's *Rigoletto*), *Ruy Blas* (1838), and *The Burgraves* (1843).

Ionesco, Eugene   (1912–94). Dramatist, born in Romania. One of the leading exponents of the Theatre of the Absurd. At the core of his work is the idea that human existence, language, and effort are essentially meaningless. His most famous plays are *The Bald Soprano* (1950), *The Lesson* (1951), and *Rhinoceros* (1959).

Molière (Jean Baptiste Poquelin)   (1622–73). Actor, director, and theater manager. He took the stylized comic archetypes of the commedia dell'arte and made them human, while retaining the "flaw" that always led them to folly. The result was a new genre, "character comedy." His satires caused great controversy. His greatest plays are *The School for Wives* (1662), *Tartuffe* (1664), *The Misanthrope*

(1666), *The Miser* (1668), and *The Bourgeois Gentleman* (1670).

Racine, Jean   (1639–99). Exemplar of French classicism and master of the Alexandrine line. The classical unities of time, place, and action provided an ideal framework for the concise action of his tragedies. His protagonists are usually driven by a single, dominant passion. His greatest works are *Andromache* (1667), *Bérénice* (1670), *Phèdre* (1676), and *Athalie* (1691).

Rostand, Edmund   (1868–1918). Poet and dramatist, responsible for the brief revival of the romantic spirit in the era of naturalism. His one masterpiece, *Cyrano de Bergerac* (1897), is a tour de force of dramatic poetry.

Sartre, Jean-Paul   (1905–80). Philosopher, novelist, essayist, and playwright. His dramas expound his existential philosophy: that man is essentially free, in a universe without God; and that he is defined by his own acts and is obliged to choose responsibly. Among his best-known works are *No Exit* (1944) and *Dirty Hands* (1948). Sartre won the Nobel Prize for literature in 1964.

GERMAN

Brecht, Bertolt   (1895–1956). Playwright, poet, stage director, and theorist. He created "epic theater," the purpose of which was to make people first *think,* and only later feel, about what they were seeing. The technique he used was alienation—the creation of emotional distance between the spectator and the event. Paradoxically, his ironic dramas are deeply moving. Among his greatest plays are *In the Jungle of Cities* (1923), *The Threepenny Opera* (1928), *Galileo* (1938–39), *Mother Courage and Her Children* (1941), and *The Good Woman of Setzuan* (1943).

Buchner, Georg   (1813–37). Three plays established Buchner as a seminal figure. His themes were distinctly modern: man's loneliness, his helplessness before the events of history and the conditions of society, and the absurdity of a world without God. Works by Buchner include *Danton's Death* (1835) and *Woyzeck* (1836).

GREEK

Aeschylus (525–456 B.C.). The originator of Greek tragedy as we know it. He added a second actor to the drama (thus making true stage dialogue possible), and he raised tragic diction to the level of grandeur. He explored themes of cosmic justice and the transmission of evil from generation to generation. He probably wrote some 90 plays, of which 7 survive complete, including *Prometheus Bound* (466–459 B.C.) and the trilogy *The Oresteia* (458 B.C.).

Aristophanes (c. 445–385 B.C.). The only surviving (and probably greatest) writer of Attic (ancient Athenian) old comedy. His freewheeling and joyous plays blend political satire, personal lampoon, portraits of domestic life, dance, music, and fantasy. Only 11 of his more than 40 plays survive, including *The Acharnians* (425 B.C.), *The Clouds* (423 B.C.), *The Wasps* (422 B.C.), *Peace* (422 B.C.), *The Birds* (414 B.C.), *Lysistrata* (411 B.C.), and *The Frogs* (405 B.C.).

Euripides (480–406 B.C.). Last of the great Greek tragedians. Influenced by the rationalism of the sophists, Euripides was distinctively modern. The depth of his characterization was new to the Attic stage, prefiguring psychological realism. His hatred of war was the mainspring of some of his best dramas. He wrote 92 plays, of which 19 survive, including *Alcestis* (438), *Medea* (431), *The Trojan Women* (415), *Electra* (413), *Iphegenia in Tauris* (412), *Orestes* (408), and *The Bacchae* (405).

Sophocles (c. 496–406 B.C.). The second of the great Greek tragedians. He introduced a third speaking actor, thus making possible more complex dramatic interactions. By creating self-contained works rather than the customary trilogies, he narrowed the focus to one solitary individual at the critical moment of his life, refusing to yield to time or circumstance. He wrote approximately 123 plays, of which 7 survive, including *Antigone* (c. 442–441 B.C.), *Oedipus Rex* (c. 430–426 B.C.), *Electra* (c. 409 B.C.), and *Oedipus at Colonus* (c. 404–401 B.C.).

IRISH

O'Casey, Sean (1880–1964). His plays present an antiheroic view of life, alternately tragic and comic. He mocked sentimental patriotism by looking at the brutality of war through the eyes of working-class Irish women. Among his best works are *The Shadow of a Gunman* (1923), *Juno and the Paycock* (1924), and *The Plough and the Stars* (1926).

Synge, John Millington (1871–1909). Poet and dramatist. His Irish peasant characters aspire to a wild life of freedom and fantasy, which they achieve in imagination as expressed through their powerful and poetic Irish idiom. Among his works are *In the Shadow of the Glen* (1903), *Riders to the Sea* (1904), and *The Playboy of the Western World* (1907). Synge was cofounder of the Abbey Theatre in Dublin, with William Butler Yeats and Lady Gregory.

ROMAN

Plautus (c. 251–184 B.C.). Popular comic playwright. His plays were based on Greek comedy and performed in Greek dress. A typical plot presents a young lover kept from his beloved by a stubborn father, a greedy pimp, or lack of money. A clever slave contrives an elaborate intrigue to unite the lovers, and the play follows the ups and downs of the scheme. Among his surviving works are *Pseudolus* (191 B.C.) and *The Menaechmi* (date unknown).

Seneca (4 B.C.–A.D. 65). Tragic playwright, stoic philosopher, and statesman. The form of his plays follows the conventions of Greek tragedy, but the content reflects his concern with the stoic absolutes of passion and reason. His plays deal with the triumph of evil in a single human soul and its devastating impact on the outer world. Nine of his plays survive, including *Agamemnon, Medea*, and *Phaedra* (dates unknown).

RUSSIAN

Chekhov, Anton Pavlovich (1860–1904). Great modern dramatist and short-story writer. He depicts the provincial aristocracy before the revolution, trapped in a stultifying environment and paralyzed by a lack of will. Stanislavsky's productions at the Moscow Art Theatre of Chekhov's greatest plays— *The Seagull* (1896), *Uncle Vanya* (1899), *The Three*

Sisters (1901), and *The Cherry Orchard* (1904)—made the Russian theater famous throughout the world.

Gorky, Maxim (Alexei Maximovich Peshkov) (1868–1936). Russian novelist, short-story writer, and playwright. Writing out of his own experience of poverty, he won international fame for his drama of the slums, *The Lower Depths* (1902).

SPANISH

Calderón de la Barca, Pedro (1600–81). Poet and last great playwright of the Spanish Golden Age. He wrote more than 200 full-length plays, as well as more than 70 one-act sacramental dramas, called "autos." In a time when the Spanish Empire was crumbling, his essential themes were faith and honor. Among his best-known plays are *The Phantom Lady* (1629), *Life Is a Dream* (1631–32), *Devotion to the Cross* (1633), *Secret Vengeance for Secret Insult* (1635), and *The Mayor of Zalamea* (1640–44).

García Lorca, Federico (1899–1936). Spanish poet and playwright, executed by Franco's soldiers soon after the outbreak of the Spanish Civil War. His poetic tragedies deal with the conflict between the individual and society—a conflict particularly bitter in Spain, where life was tightly regulated by an unyielding conservative moral code. His most famous plays are *Blood Wedding* (1933), *Yerma* (1934), and *The House of Bernarda Alba* (1936).

Molina, Tirso de (Gabriel Tellez) (c. 1571–1648). A disciple of Lope de Vega and the second great dramatist of the Spanish Golden Age. His most famous play is *The Trickster of Seville* (c. 1625), in which he created the great modern myth of Don Juan.

Vega Carpio, Lope de (1562–1635). Member of the Spanish Armada and the first great dramatist of the Spanish Golden Age. He established the *commedia* (new comedy) as the principal dramatic form in the Spain of his time. His works include *The Peasant in his Nook* (1611–15), *Fuenteovejuna* (1612), *The King's the Best Magistrate* (1620–23), and *The Knight from Olmedo* (1620–25).

OTHER

Ibsen, Henrik (1828–1906). Norwegian playwright. Generally credited with being the "father of modern drama," he demonstrated the power of psychological realism. His plays often present individuals in bitter conflict with the norms of society. His masterpieces include *Peer Gynt* (1867), *A Doll's House* (1879), *Ghosts* (1881), *An Enemy of the People* (1883), *The Wild Duck* (1884), and *Hedda Gabler* (1891).

Pirandello, Luigi (1867–1936). Italian dramatist and novelist, winner of the 1934 Nobel Prize for literature. The playwright par excellence of the conflict between illusion and reality, he depicts with eloquence the isolation of the individual from society and from himself. Among his best-known plays are *Right You Are—If You Think You Are* (1917), *Six Characters in Search of an Author* (1921), and *The Man with the Flower in His Mouth* (1923).

Strindberg, Johan August (1849–1912). Swedish playwright and seminal modern dramatist, best known for his intensely psychological plays about tormented male-female relationships. His later plays prefigure expressionism. Among his best-known works are *The Father* (1887), *Miss Julie* (1889), *The Dance of Death* (*Part I* and *Part II*—1900), and *A Dream Play* (1902).

MAJOR FILM DIRECTORS

AMERICAN

Capra, Frank (1897–1991), b. Sicily. A pioneer of screwball comedy with the Academy Award–winning *It Happened One Night* (1934), he is best known for fast-paced populist comedy-dramas such as *Mr. Deeds Goes to Town* (1936) and *Mr. Smith Goes to Washington* (1939) that show the triumph of the individual against the system. His Christmas fable *It's a Wonderful Life* (1946) is a television staple.

Coppola, Francis Ford (1939–   ), b. Michigan. In signature works *The Godfather* (1972) and *The Godfather, Part II* (1974), he fused his strengths—epic scale, operatic staging, and understanding of family conflict—into modern film tragedy. Other films, such as *Apocalypse Now* (1979), *Peggy Sue Got Married* (1986), and *The Godfather, Part III* (1990),

A Brief History of Film

Experiments in motion pictures began in the United States and Europe during the late 19th century. American inventor Thomas Alva Edison patented the first movie machine, the Kinetoscope, in 1891. Four years later, French inventors Louis and Auguste Lumière demonstrated the camera-projector called the *cinématographe*. American filmmaker Edwin S. Porter's eight-minute *The Great Train Robbery* (1903) launched the movies as mass entertainment.

American filmmakers soon became preeminent. Major studios were situated in New York, with D. W. Griffith the medium's most influential director. In dozens of films, he developed a grammar of shots and lighting effects to evoke audience emotion. His highly successful *The Birth of a Nation* (1915) pioneered the idea of film as art.

Between 1910 and 1920, American filmmaking shifted to Hollywood. Leading directors such as Cecil B. De Mille (*The Ten Commandments*, 1923), Ernst Lubitsch (*The Marriage Circle*, 1924), and John Ford (*The Iron Horse*, 1924) offered a variety of genres—epics, romantic comedies, and westerns. Mack Sennett pioneered film slapstick with the Keystone Cops and introduced English comic Charlie Chaplin. Portraying the forlorn "Tramp" in *The Kid* (1921), *The Gold Rush* (1925), and others, Chaplin became one of the first international movie stars.

Several other countries established themselves as filmmaking centers. Germany was the birthplace of the expressionist movement, embodied in Robert Weine's *The Cabinet of Dr. Caligari* (1919). In Russia, Sergei Eisenstein's *Potemkin* (1925) epitomized the idea of *montage*. France became a rich film source, with such humanistic directors as René Clair and Abel Gance.

The 1927 U.S. film *The Jazz Singer* introduced sound to movies, revolutionizing the industry worldwide. Genres requiring witty or action-oriented dialogue, such as gangster movies and screwball comedies, gained primacy, as did extravagant musicals. The American studios, including Metro-Goldwyn-Mayer, Paramount, and Warner Bros., honed a "studio system" that produced a steady stream of films and stars for Depression-era audiences seeking escape. American stars of the period included James Cagney, Bette Davis, Clark Gable, Cary Grant, and Katharine Hepburn. The system reached its apex in 1939, with dozens of now-classic films, including the Civil War epic *Gone with the Wind* (1939).

High artistic achievements marked European cinema during the years before WWII. Notable films included Jean Renoir's antiwar classic *Grand Illusion* (1937) and Leni Riefenstahl's Nazi paean *Triumph of the Will* (1935).

WWII and its aftermath also brought heightened realism to international filmmaking. Italian directors Roberto Rossellini and Vittorio De Sica ushered in neorealism with, respectively, *Open City* (1949) and *The Bicycle Thief* (1945). Countering the trend toward realism were such stylized, idiosyncratic filmmakers as Italy's Federico Fellini (*La Dolce Vita*, 1960) and Swedish psychological master Ingmar Bergman (*The Seventh Seal*, 1956).

In the 1950s and 1960s, a group of French directors (many of them film critics), initiated the *nouvelle vague* (new wave). This movement of quirky, original films included François Truffaut's *The Four Hundred Blows* (1959) and Jean-Luc Godard's *Breathless* (1960). German cinema reinvented itself after WWII with the varied social critiques of directors Werner Herzog, Wim Wenders, and Rainer Werner Fassbinder (*The Marriage of Maria Braun*, 1979).

Nonwestern cinema gained an international following after World War II through the works of Japanese directors Akira Kurosawa (*Rashomon*, 1950) and Yasujiro Ozu (*Tokyo Story*, 1953) and Indian filmmaker Satyajit Ray (*Pather Panchali*, 1955). National cinemas that have come to prominence since the 1970s include those of Australia and New Zealand, the former offering such filmmakers as Peter Weir and the latter, Jane Campion.

Changing tastes, decreasing film attendance, and corporate takeovers effectively destroyed the American studio system by the end of the 1960s. In its wake came increased experimentation and independence through filmmakers such as Stanley Kubrick, Robert Altman, Francis Ford Coppola (*The Godfather*, 1972) and Martin Scorsese (*Raging Bull*, 1980). In recent years, independent studios have grown in stature, becoming known for supporting high-quality original filmmaking such as Quentin Tarantino's *Pulp Fiction* (1994).

American films since the 1970s have been distinguished by the big-budget blockbuster. Primarily special-effects-laden fare, the blockbuster has been dominated by two directors: George Lucas and Steven Spielberg. Lucas's *Star Wars* (1977) and its sequels made hundreds of millions of dollars. With *Jaws* (1975) and *E.T.* (1982), Spielberg became the leading director of big-budget, high-tech films. However, director James Cameron's *Titanic* (1997) eclipsed all previous records for gross revenues and garnered 11 Academy Awards as well. Despite the success of blockbusters such as *The Matrix* (1999) and *Gladiator* (2000), small films like *Shakespeare in Love* (1998) and *Boys Don't Cry* (1999) surprised the industry by doing relatively well commercially.

have varied in subject matter but share Coppola's ambitiousness.

De Mille, Cecil B. (1881–1959), b. Massachusetts. Specializing at first in spicy modern narratives, he became known as the master of religious and historical epics such as *The Ten Commandments* (1923; remade 1956). He is credited with helping to establish Hollywood as a film capital. His sweeping entertainments include *The Sign of the Cross* (1932), *Samson and Delilah* (1949), and *The Greatest Show on Earth* (1952).

Ford, John   (1895–1973), b. Maine. The most celebrated and enduring American director, he combined strong storytelling and visual poetry in classic meditations on the country's conflict between frontier and civilization. Though successful in silents (*The Iron Horse,* 1924), he left his legacy in sound films. He won the Academy Award for best director for three films: *The Grapes of Wrath* (1940), *How Green Was My Valley* (1941), and *The Quiet Man* (1952). Other influential works include *Stagecoach* (1939), *My Darling Clementine* (1946), and *The Searchers* (1956).

Griffith, D. W.   (1875–1948), b. Kentucky. A pioneer in shaping the medium, and American cinema's standard bearer, he infused cinematic power into basic techniques of camera use, editing, and lighting. His Civil War epic *Birth of a Nation* (1915) is a hallmark in the development of film as art. Other major films from his hundreds of works include *Intolerance* (1916), *Broken Blossoms* (1919) and *Orphans of the Storm* (1922). His career ended soon after the advent of sound film.

Hawks, Howard   (1896–1977), b. Indiana. Prized for his storytelling ability and stylistic economy, he directed definitive works in several genres: gangster dramas (*Scarface,* 1932), screwball comedy (*Bringing Up Baby,* 1938; *His Girl Friday,* 1940), action films (*Only Angels Have Wings,* 1939), and westerns (*Red River,* 1948). He introduced actress Lauren Bacall in *To Have and Have Not* (1944), with Humphrey Bogart; insolent and fearless, the two actors embody the ideal Hawksian man and woman. He won an honorary Academy Award (1974).

Kubrick, Stanley   (1928–99), b. New York. He left a career as a still photographer to become a cool,

meticulous maker of visually stunning films. His sardonic, often pessimistic works include *Paths of Glory* (1957), *Dr. Strangelove* (1964), *2001: A Space Odyssey* (1968), *A Clockwork Orange* (1971), and *Full Metal Jacket* (1987). He resided in Britain from the 1960s until his death.

Lang, Fritz   (1890–1976), b. Austria. In Germany, his expressionist films *Dr. Mabuse* (1922), *Metropolis* (1927), and *M* (1931) conveyed tension and inexorable fate. He left Germany in 1933 after his film *The Testament of Dr. Mabuse* (1933) was banned by Nazis. He directed several films in Hollywood, many concerning injustice or corruption, including *Fury* (1936), *Hangmen Also Die* (1943), and *The Big Heat* (1953).

George Lucas was riding in a car with a friend when the car went over a bump. His friend said, "Oops, I just ran over a wookie back there." Thus was created the word that George later used in the Star Wars films.

Lubitsch, Ernst   (1892–1947), b. Germany. With the wit, visual brevity, and sexual polish known as "the Lubitsch Touch," he directed scores of sophisticated comedies, musicals, and dramas in Germany and America. Many remain classics: *The Marriage Circle* (1924), *The Love Parade* (1929), *Monte Carlo* (1930), *Trouble in Paradise* (1932), *Ninotchka* (1939). He received an honorary Academy Award in 1937.

Scorsese, Martin   (1942–   ), b. New York. Over decades of rough urban dramas, he has defined New York City as an underworld where denizens find resolution and redemption through violence. Notable New York films include *Mean Streets* (1973), *Taxi Driver* (1976), *GoodFellas* (1990), and *Raging Bull* (1980), hailed by some as the finest American film of the decade. Other films include *The Color of Money* (1986) and *The Age of Innocence* (1993). He is active in film preservation.

Soderbergh, Steven   (1963–   ), b. Atlanta. Soderbergh received acclaim for his first feature, the independent film *Sex, Lies, and Videotape* (1989), which he both wrote and directed. Nominated for an Academy Award for Best Director for both *Erin Brokovich* and *Traffic* in 2000, he won for the latter.

Spielberg, Steven (1947–), b. Ohio. One of the most commercially successful directors in film history, he specializes in big-budget adventure or science-fiction films that include *Jaws* (1975), *Close Encounters of the Third Kind* (1977), *Raiders of the Lost Ark* (1981), *E.T.* (1982), and *Jurassic Park* (1993). He gained respect with the Holocaust drama *Schindler's List* (1993), which won an Academy Award for best picture, and *Saving Private Ryan* (1998).

Welles, Orson (1915–85), b. Wisconsin. His stunning first film *Citizen Kane* (1941) influenced generations of filmmakers in its structure, composition, and cinematography—and the audacity of its maker, who became a lifelong boy wonder. Although later films were often compromised by studio intervention or self-indulgence, many are exceptional: *The Magnificent Ambersons* (1942), *The Lady From Shanghai* (1948), and *Touch of Evil* (1958).

Wilder, Billy (1906–2002), b. Austria. Blending masterful timing, wit, and worldliness, he created some of Hollywood's smartest comedies and most cynical dramas. Notable works include *Double Indemnity* (1944), *Sunset Boulevard* (1950), *Stalag 17* (1953), *Sabrina* (1954), and *Some Like It Hot* (1959). *The Lost Weekend* (1945) and *The Apartment* (1960) won Academy Awards for best picture and director.

ASIAN

Chen Kaige (1952–), b. China. A major presence in post–Cultural Revolution filmmaking, he is known for his mix of high drama and emotional subtlety in such films as *Yellow Earth* (1984), *King of Children* (1987), and *Farewell My Concubine* (1993). His early cinematographer, Zhang Yimou, also became a noted director.

Kurosawa, Akira (1910–98), b. Japan. The humanistic filmmaker's ability to convey universal messages in works like *Drunken Angel* (1948) and *Rashomon* (1950) has bridged cultures and brought decades of worldwide appeal. His samurai films have been influential: *The Seven Samurai* (1954) inspired *The Magnificent Seven* (1960); *Hidden Fortress* (1958) informed the *Star Wars* trilogy. Other notable films include *Yojimbo* (1961) and pioneering Shakespeare adaptations, *Throne of Blood* (1957) and *Ran* (1985).

Lee, Ang (1954–), b. Taiwan. Ang Lee's 1993 film *The Wedding Banquet* was the first film from Taiwan to earn an Academy Award nomination for Best Foreign Language Film, and his work *Crouching Tiger, Hidden Dragon* (2000) was the first Asian film to win in that category. Lee's other works include *Eat Drink Man Woman* (1994), *Sense and Sensibility* (1995), and *The Ice Storm* (1997).

Ozu, Yasujiro (1903–63), b. Japan. With films like *The Flavor of Green Tea over Rice* (1952) and *Tokyo Story* (1953), he is renowned for his simply filmed, delicate dramas of middle-class family life. He is also praised in his country for capturing Japan's national sensibility. Other representative films include *Early Spring* (1956) and *Late Autumn* (1961).

Ray, Satyajit (1921–92), b. Calcutta. Acclaimed for his humanity and subtle cinematic style, he gained early success with *Pather Panchali* (1955), the first entry in his "Apu Trilogy," about a Bengali child. Other parts are *The Unvanquished* (1957) and *The World of Apu* (1958). Later, more thematically and cinematically daring films include *The Lonely Wife* (1964) and *Distant Thunder* (1973). He won an honorary Academy Award (1992).

BRITISH

Chaplin, Charles (1889–1977), b. England. The preeminent director and star of silent film immortalized his "Tramp" character in films including *The Tramp* (1915) and *The Kid* (1921). Cofounding the studio United Artists, he directed some of his finest works for it: *The Gold Rush* (1925), *City Lights* (1931), and *Modern Times* (1936). His increasingly serious sound films include *The Great Dictator* (1940), *Monsieur Verdoux* (1947), and *Limelight* (1952). Accused of Communist affiliations, he was denied reentry to the United States in 1952 and did not return for 20 years. He won special Academy Awards in 1927–1928 and 1972. He was knighted in 1975.

Hitchcock, Alfred (1899–1980), b. England. Cinema's unmatched master of suspense built his international reputation in the 1930s with British thrillers *The Man Who Knew Too Much* (1934, remade 1956), *The 39 Steps* (1935), and *The Lady Vanishes* (1938). In Hollywood, his works became more lavish and cinematically refined, with top stars and crew. Some classic works include *Notorious* (1946), *Rear Window* (1954), *Vertigo* (1958), *North by Northwest* (1959), and *Psycho* (1960).

Lean, David (1908–91), b. England. He gained early notice with his literary adaptations *Brief Encounter* (1945) and *Great Expectations* (1946) but is most respected for his grand, ironic epics, notably *The Bridge on the River Kwai* (1957) and *Lawrence of Arabia* (1962). Blending human drama and 20th-century history, each won the Academy Award for best picture. Later films include *Doctor Zhivago* (1965) and *A Passage to India* (1984). He was knighted in 1984.

Powell, Michael (1905–90), b. England, and **Emeric Pressburger** (1902–88), b. Hungary. Successful filmmakers alone, they are renowned for their literate, visually stunning collaborations in the 1940s and 1950s. Among them are *The Life and Death of Colonel Blimp* (1943), *I Know Where I'm Going* (1945), *Black Narcissus* (1947), and the quintessential ballet film *The Red Shoes* (1948). Powell faced severe criticism following his study of a psychopath, *Peeping Tom* (1960).

FRENCH
Godard, Jean-Luc (1930–   ), b. France. Beginning with *Breathless* (1960), the former film critic influenced French New Wave and avant-garde filmmaking with his visually surprising, improvisational works. Acclaimed works of the period also include *The Little Soldier* (1960) and *Alphaville* (1965). By the late 1960s, he became more formless and didactic in works such as *Masculine Feminine* (1966) and *Weekend* (1968). After a hiatus, he turned to more humanistic filmmaking, with *First Name: Carmen* (1983) and others.

Renoir, Jean (1894–1979), b. France. Son of impressionist painter Auguste Renoir, he is unsurpassed at conveying the human condition through poetic, fluid filmmaking. The antiwar classic *Grand Illusion* (1937) and social meditation *The Rules of the Game* (1939) are considered his masterpieces. Other works include *Boudu Saved from Drowning* (1932), *Toni* (1935), and *The Crime of Monsieur Lange* (1936).

Truffaut, François (1932–84), b. France. Beginning with *The 400 Blows* (1959), he established himself as the central force of French New Wave. Tender and exuberant, his films are also renowned for their insight into human emotions. Among other major works are *Shoot the Piano Player* (1960), *Jules and Jim* (1961), and *The Wild Child* (1970). Notable books include *Hitchcock/Truffaut* (1983).

GERMAN
Fassbinder, Rainer Werner (1946–82), b. Germany. His spirited, iconoclastic dramas about modern German society made him a major force in rebuilding German cinema after World War II. A feverish worker, he made up to four films per year until his death at 36. Representative works include *Effi Briest* (1974), *Despair* (1978), *The Marriage of Maria Braun* (1979), and *Veronika Voss* (1982).

Murnau, F. W. (1888–1931), b. Germany. With *Nosferatu the Vampire* (1922) and *The Last Laugh* (1924), he refined a visually expressive style that influenced generations of filmmakers. His first U.S. work, *Sunrise* (1927), is considered one of the most beautiful works in film history. Other U.S. films include *Our Daily Bread* (1930) and *Tabu* (1931), codirected with Robert Flaherty.

Ophüls, Max (1902–57), b. Germany. Prizing *mise-en-scène* above plot, he was a master of fluid camera work and lush decor with an otherworldly, baroque quality that suited his often romantic tales. Among his most acclaimed works are *Letter from an Unknown Woman* (1948), *La Ronde* (1950), *The Earrings of Madame De* (1953), and *Lola Montez* (1955). His son is filmmaker Marcel Ophüls.

ITALIAN
Antonioni, Michelangelo (1912–   ), b. Italy. A major force in postwar Italian cinema, he is noted for conveying the emotional void of modern existence in such works as *The Red Desert* (1964), *L'Avventura* (1960), *Blow-Up* (1966), and *The Pas-*

senger (1975). He is expert in using the physical world to communicate metaphysical and psychological states.

De Sica, Vittorio (1902–74), b. Italy. With *Shoeshine* (1946) and *The Bicycle Thief* (1948), he made two pivotal (and Academy Award–winning) works of Italian neorealism. Other of his humane, varied works include *Umberto D* (1952); *The Condemned of Altona* (1962); *Yesterday Today and Tomorrow* (1963); and *The Garden of the Finzi-Continis* (1971); the last two winning foreign-film Academy Awards.

Fellini, Federico (1920–93), b. Italy. Humanistic, sharply observed, and sensual, he is Italy's most beloved and acclaimed filmmaker. He gained international fame with the autobiographical *I Vitelloni* (1953) and followed with *La Strada* (1954), which won the Academy Award for best foreign film. Other milestone films include *The Nights of Cabiria* (1957) and *8½* (1963), also Academy Award winners for best foreign film; *La Dolce Vita* (1960); the psychological study *Juliet of the Spirits* (1965); and the playful *Amarcord* (1973).

OTHER

Almodóvar, Pedro (1951–), b. Spain. Perhaps Spain's best-known modern filmmaker, Almodóvar's early films such as *Dark Habits* (1984) became cult hits. He gained international notoriety with *Women on the Verge of a Nervous Breakdown* (1988). *All About My Mother* (1999) won the Academy Award for Best Foreign Language Film.

Bergman, Ingmar (1918–), b. Sweden. Early films *Smiles of a Summer Night* (1955) and *The Seventh Seal* (1957) won prizes at the Cannes Film Festival and established his ability to portray human relationships and explore religious and philosophical concerns, often crises of faith and personal detachment. Other works include *Wild Strawberries* (1957), *Persona* (1966), *Cries and Whispers* (1972), and *Fanny and Alexander* (1983).

Buñuel, Luis (1900–83), b. Spain. A critical and cult favorite, he first demonstrated his outrageous visual style with the Surrealist classic *Un Chien andalou* (1928, with Salvador Dali). Later works incorporated fearless criticism of the Catholic church and other social institutions; among them are *L'Age d'or* (1930), *Los Olvidados* (1950), *Viridiana* (1961), and *That Obscure Object of Desire* (1977).

Eisenstein, Sergei (1898–1948), b. Latvia. A seminal voice in formulating film language, he developed the practice of *montage* in works including *The Battleship Potemkin* (1925), *October/Ten Days That Shook the World* (1928), and *The General Line* (1929). Later works, such as *Alexander Nevsky* (1938), further refined its use. A noted film theorist, he wrote such books as *Film Sense* (1942) and *Film Form* (1949).

Sembène, Ousmane (1923–), b. Senegal. The foremost filmmaker in sub-Saharan Africa, he established the region as a rich cinematic source from his first release, *Black Girl* (1966). It and other works, including *The Money Order* (1968), *The People* (1977), and *Camp de Thiaroye* (1988), explore conflicts between African and western cultures. From the 1960s, he has been a respected novelist and short story writer (*The Last of the Empire*, 1981).

THE ACADEMY AWARDS

The Academy Awards began in 1927. The awards for Best Supporting Actor and Best Supporting Actress were not included until 1936. The award for Best Foreign Film was added in 1956.

1927–28

Best Actor: Emil Jannings *(The Way of All Flesh)*
Best Actress: Janet Gaynor *(Seventh Heaven)*
Best Director: Frank Borzage *(Seventh Heaven)*; Lewis Milestone *(Two Arabian Knights)*
Best Picture: *Wings*

1928–29

Best Actor: Warner Baxter *(In Old Arizona)*
Best Actress: Mary Pickford *(Coquette)*
Best Director: Frank Lloyd *(The Divine Lady)*
Best Picture: *Broadway Melody*

1929–30

Best Actor: George Arliss *(Disraeli)*
Best Actress: Norma Shearer *(The Divorcee)*
Best Director: Lewis Milestone *(All Quiet on the Western Front)*
Best Picture: *All Quiet on the Western Front*

1930–31

Best Actor: Lionel Barrymore *(A Free Soul)*
Best Actress: Marie Dressler *(Min and Bill)*
Best Director: Norma Taurog *(Skippy)*
Best Picture: *Cimarron*

1931–32

Best Actor: Frederic March *(Dr. Jekyll and Mr. Hyde);* Wallace Berry *(The Champ)*
Best Actress: Helen Hayes *(The Sin of Madelon Claudet)*
Best Director: Frank Borzage *(Bad Girl)*
Best Picture: *Grand Hotel*

1932–33

Best Actor: Charles Laughton *(The Private Life of Henry VIII)*
Best Actress: Katharine Hepburn *(Morning Glory)*
Best Director: Frank Lloyd *(Cavalcade)*
Best Picture: *Cavalcade*

1934

Best Actor: Clark Gable *(It Happened One Night)*
Best Actress: Claudette Colbert *(It Happened One Night)*
Best Director: Frank Capra *(It Happened One Night)*
Best Picture: *It Happened One Night*

1935

Best Actor: Victor McLaglen *(The Informer)*
Best Actress: Bette Davis *(Dangerous)*
Best Director: John Ford *(The Informer)*
Best Picture: *Mutiny on the Bounty*

1936

Best Actor: Paul Muni *(The Story of Louis Pasteur)*
Best Actress: Luise Rainer *(The Great Ziegfeld)*
Best Supporting Actor: Walter Brennan *(Come and Get It)*
Best Supporting Actress: Gale Sondergard *(Anthony Adverse)*
Best Director: Frank Capra *(Mr. Deeds Goes to Town)*
Best Picture: *The Great Ziegfeld*

1937

Best Actor: Spencer Tracy *(Captains Courageous)*
Best Actress: Luise Rainer *(The Good Earth)*
Best Supporting Actor: Joseph Schildkraut *(The Life of Emile Zola)*
Best Supporting Actress: Alice Brady *(In Old Chicago)*
Best Director: Leo McCarey *(The Awful Truth)*
Best Picture: *The Life of Emile Zola*

1938

Best Actor: Spencer Tracy *(Boys Town)*
Best Actress: Bette Davis *(Jezebel)*
Best Supporting Actor: Walter Brennan *(Kentucky)*
Best Supporting Actress: Fay Bainter *(Jezebel)*
Best Director: Frank Capra *(You Can't Take It with You)*
Best Picture: *You Can't Take It with You*

1939

Best Actor: Robert Donat *(Goodbye Mr. Chips)*
Best Actress: Vivien Leigh *(Gone with the Wind)*
Best Supporting Actor: Thomas Mitchell *(Stagecoach)*
Best Supporting Actress: Hattie McDaniel *(Gone with the Wind)*
Best Director: Victor Fleming *(Gone with the Wind)*
Best Picture: *Gone with the Wind*

1940

Best Actor: James Stewart *(The Philadelphia Story)*
Best Actress: Ginger Rogers *(Kitty Foyle)*
Best Supporting Actor: Walter Brennan *(The Westerner)*
Best Supporting Actress: Jane Darwell *(The Grapes of Wrath)*
Best Director: John Ford *(The Grapes of Wrath)*
Best Picture: *Rebecca*

1941

Best Actor: Gary Cooper *(Sergeant York)*
Best Actress: Joan Fontaine *(Suspicion)*
Best Supporting Actor: Donald Crisp *(How Green Was My Valley)*
Best Supporting Actress: Mary Astor *(The Great Lie)*
Best Director: John Ford *(How Green Was My Valley)*
Best Picture: *How Green Was My Valley*

1942

Best Actor: James Cagney *(Yankee Doodle Dandy)*
Best Actress: Greer Garson *(Mrs. Miniver)*
Best Supporting Actor: Van Heflin *(Johnny Eager)*
Best Supporting Actress: Teresa Wright *(Mrs. Miniver)*
Best Director: William Wyler *(Mrs. Miniver)*
Best Picture: *Mrs. Miniver*

1943

Best Actor: Paul Lukas *(Watch on the Rhine)*
Best Actress: Jennifer Jones *(The Song of Bernadette)*
Best Supporting Actor: Charles Coburn *(The More the Merrier)*
Best Supporting Actress: Katina Paxinou *(For Whom the Bell Tolls)*
Best Director: Michael Curtiz *(Casablanca)*
Best Picture: *Casablanca*

1944

Best Actor: Bing Crosby *(Going My Way)*
Best Actress: Ingrid Bergman *(Gaslight)*
Best Supporting Actor: Barry Fitzgerald *(Going My Way)*
Best Supporting Actress: Ethel Barrymore *(None But the Lonely Heart)*

Best Director: Leo McCarey *(Going My Way)*
Best Picture: *Going My Way*

1945

Best Actor: Ray Milland *(The Lost Weekend)*
Best Actress: Joan Crawford *(Mildred Pierce)*
Best Supporting Actor: James Dunn *(A Tree Grows in Brooklyn)*
Best Supporting Actress: Anne Revere *(National Velvet)*
Best Director: Billy Wilder *(The Lost Weekend)*
Best Picture: *The Lost Weekend*

1946

Best Actor: Frederic March *(The Best Years of Our Lives)*
Best Actress: Olivia de Havilland *(To Each His Own)*
Best Supporting Actor: Harold Russell *(The Best Years of Our Lives)*
Best Supporting Actress: Anne Baxter *(The Razor's Edge)*
Best Director: William Wyler *(The Best Years of Our Lives)*
Best Picture: *The Best Years of Our Lives*

1947

Best Actor: Ronald Coleman *(A Double Life)*
Best Actress: Loretta Young *(The Farmer's Daughter)*
Best Supporting Actor: Edmund Gwenn *(Miracle on 34th Street)*
Best Supporting Actress: Celeste Holm *(Gentleman's Agreement)*
Best Director: Elia Kazan *(Gentleman's Agreement)*
Best Picture: *Gentleman's Agreement*

1948

Best Actor: Laurence Olivier *(Hamlet)*
Best Actress: Jane Wyman *(Johnny Belinda)*
Best Supporting Actor: Walter Huston *(Treasure of Sierra Madre)*
Best Supporting Actress: Claire Trevor *(Key Largo)*
Best Director: John Huston *(The Treasure of the Sierra Madre)*
Best Picture: *Hamlet*

1949

Best Actor: Broderick Crawford *(All the King's Men)*
Best Actress: Olivia de Havilland *(The Heiress)*
Best Supporting Actor: Dean Jagger *(Twelve O'Clock High)*
Best Supporting Actress: Mercedes McCambridge *(All the King's Men)*
Best Director: Joseph L. Mankiewicz *(A Letter to Three Wives)*
Best Picture: *All the King's Men*

1950

Best Actor: Jose Ferrer *(Cyrano de Bergerac)*
Best Actress: Judy Holliday *(Born Yesterday)*
Best Supporting Actor: George Sanders *(All About Eve)*
Best Supporting Actress: Josephine Hull *(Harvey)*
Best Director: Joseph L. Mankiewicz *(All About Eve)*
Best Picture: *All About Eve*

1951

Best Actor: Humphrey Bogart *(The African Queen)*
Best Actress: Vivien Leigh *(A Streetcar Named Desire)*
Best Supporting Actor: Karl Malden *(A Streetcar Named Desire)*
Best Supporting Actress: Kim Hunter *(A Streetcar Named Desire)*
Best Director: George Stevens *(A Place in the Sun)*
Best Picture: *An American in Paris*

1952

Best Actor: Gary Cooper *(High Noon)*
Best Actress: Shirley Booth *(Come Back, Little Sheba)*
Best Supporting Actor: Anthony Quinn *(Viva Zapata!)*
Best Supporting Actress: Gloria Grahame *(The Bad and the Beautiful)*
Best Director: John Ford *(The Quiet Man)*
Best Picture: *The Greatest Show on Earth*

1953

Best Actor: William Holden *(Stalag 17)*
Best Actress: Audrey Hepburn *(Roman Holiday)*
Best Supporting Actor: Frank Sinatra *(From Here to Eternity)*
Best Supporting Actress: Donna Reed *(From Here to Eternity)*
Best Director: Fred Zinnemann *(From Here to Eternity)*
Best Picture: *From Here to Eternity*

1954

Best Actor: Marlon Brando *(On the Waterfront)*
Best Actress: Grace Kelly *(The Country Girl)*
Best Supporting Actor: Edmond O'Brien *(The Barefoot Contessa)*
Best Supporting Actress: Eva Marie Saint *(On the Waterfront)*
Best Director: Elia Kazan *(On the Waterfront)*
Best Picture: *On the Waterfront*

1955

Best Actor: Ernest Borgnine *(Marty)*
Best Actress: Anna Magnani *(The Rose Tattoo)*
Best Supporting Actor: Jack Lemmon *(Mister Roberts)*
Best Supporting Actress: Jo Van Fleet *(East of Eden)*

Best Director: Delbert Mann *(Marty)*
Best Picture: *Marty*

1956

Best Actor: Yul Brynner *(The King and I)*
Best Actress: Ingrid Bergman *(Anastasia)*
Best Supporting Actor: Anthony Quinn *(Lust for Life)*
Best Supporting Actress: Dorothy Malone *(Written on the Wind)*
Best Director: George Stevens *(Giant)*
Best Picture: *Around the World in Eighty Days*
Best Foreign Film: *La Strada*

1957

Best Actor: Alec Guinness *(The Bridge on the River Kwai)*
Best Actress: Joanne Woodward *(The Three Faces of Eve)*
Best Supporting Actor: Red Buttons *(Sayonara)*
Best Supporting Actress: Miyoshi Umeki *(Sayonara)*
Best Director: David Lean *(The Bridge on the River Kwai)*
Best Picture: *The Bridge on the River Kwai*
Best Foreign Film: *The Nights of Cabiria*

1958

Best Actor: David Niven *(Separate Tables)*
Best Actress: Susan Hayward *(I Want to Live)*
Best Supporting Actor: Burl Ives *(The Big Country)*
Best Supporting Actress: Wendy Hiller *(Separate Tables)*
Best Director: Vincente Minnelli *(Gigi)*
Best Picture: *Gigi*
Best Foreign Film: *My Uncle*

1959

Best Actor: Charlton Heston *(Ben-Hur)*
Best Actress: Simone Signoret *(Room at the Top)*
Best Supporting Actor: Hugh Griffith *(Ben-Hur)*
Best Supporting Actress: Shelley Winters *(The Diary of Anne Frank)*
Best Director: William Wyler *(Ben-Hur)*
Best Picture: *Ben-Hur*
Best Foreign Film: *Black Orpheus*

1960

Best Actor: Burt Lancaster *(Elmer Gantry)*
Best Actress: Elizabeth Taylor *(Butterfield 8)*
Best Supporting Actor: Peter Ustinov *(Spartacus)*
Best Supporting Actress: Shirley Jones *(Elmer Gantry)*
Best Director: Billy Wilder *(The Apartment)*
Best Picture: *The Apartment*
Best Foreign Film: *The Virgin Spring*

1961

Best Actor: Maximillian Schell *(Judgment at Nuremberg)*
Best Actress: Sophia Loren *(Two Women)*
Best Supporting Actor: George Chakiris *(West Side Story)*
Best Supporting Actress: Rita Moreno *(West Side Story)*
Best Director: Jerome Robbins, Robert Wise *(West Side Story)*
Best Picture: *West Side Story*
Best Foreign Film: *Through a Glass Darkly*

1962

Best Actor: Gregory Peck *(To Kill a Mockingbird)*
Best Actress: Anne Bancroft *(The Miracle Worker)*
Best Supporting Actor: Ed Begley *(Sweet Bird of Youth)*
Best Supporting Actress: Patty Duke *(The Miracle Worker)*
Best Director: David Lean *(Lawrence of Arabia)*
Best Picture: *Lawrence of Arabia*
Best Foreign Film: *Sundays and Cybele*

1963

Best Actor: Sidney Poitier *(Lilies of the Field)*
Best Actress: Patricia Neal *(Hud)*
Best Supporting Actor: Melvyn Douglas *(Hud)*
Best Supporting Actress: Margaret Rutherford *(The V.I.P.s)*
Best Director: Tony Richardson *(Tom Jones)*
Best Picture: *Tom Jones*
Best Foreign Film: *8½*

1964

Best Actor: Rex Harrison *(My Fair Lady)*
Best Actress: Julie Andrews *(Mary Poppins)*
Best Supporting Actor: Peter Ustinov *(Topkapi)*
Best Supporting Actress: Lila Kedrova *(Zorba the Greek)*
Best Director: George Cukor *(My Fair Lady)*
Best Picture: *My Fair Lady*
Best Foreign Film: *Yesterday, Today and Tomorrow*

1965

Best Actor: Lee Marvin *(Cat Ballou)*
Best Actress: Julie Christie *(Darling)*
Best Supporting Actor: Martin Balsam *(A Thousand Clowns)*
Best Supporting Actress: Shelley Winters *(A Patch of Blue)*
Best Director: Robert Wise *(The Sound of Music)*
Best Picture: *The Sound of Music*
Best Foreign Film: *The Shop on Main Street*

1966

Best Actor: Paul Scofield *(A Man for All Seasons)*
Best Actress: Elizabeth Taylor *(Who's Afraid of Virginia Woolf?)*
Best Supporting Actor: Walter Matthau *(The Fortune Cookie)*
Best Supporting Actress: Sandy Dennis *(Who's Afraid of Virginia Woolf?)*
Best Director: Fred Zinnemann *(A Man for All Seasons)*
Best Picture: *A Man for All Seasons*
Best Foreign Film: *A Man and a Woman*

1967

Best Actor: Rod Steiger *(In the Heat of the Night)*
Best Actress: Katharine Hepburn *(Guess Who's Coming to Dinner)*
Best Supporting Actor: George Kennedy *(Cool Hand Luke)*
Best Supporting Actress: Estelle Parsons *(Bonnie and Clyde)*
Best Director: Mike Nichols *(The Graduate)*
Best Picture: *In the Heat of the Night*
Best Foreign Film: *Closely Watched Trains*

1968

Best Actor: Cliff Robertson *(Charly)*
Best Actress: Katharine Hepburn *(The Lion in Winter)*; Barbra Streisand *(Funny Girl)*
Best Supporting Actor: Jack Albertson *(The Subject Was Roses)*
Best Supporting Actress: Ruth Gordon *(Rosemary's Baby)*
Best Director: Sir Carol Reed *(Oliver!)*
Best Picture: *Oliver!*
Best Foreign Film: *War and Peace*

1969

Best Actor: John Wayne *(True Grit)*
Best Actress: Maggie Smith *(The Prime of Miss Jean Brodie)*
Best Supporting Actor: Gig Young *(They Shoot Horses Don't They?)*
Best Supporting Actress: Goldie Hawn *(Cactus Flower)*
Best Director: John Schlesinger *(Midnight Cowboy)*
Best Picture: *Midnight Cowboy*
Best Foreign Film: *Z*

1970

Best Actor: George C. Scott *(Patton;* refused*)*
Best Actress: Glenda Jackson *(Women in Love)*
Best Supporting Actor: John Mills *(Ryan's Daughter)*
Best Supporting Actress: Helen Hayes *(Airport)*
Best Director: Franklin Schaffner, Frank McCarthy *(Patton)*

Best Picture: *Patton*
Best Foreign Film: *Investigation of a Citizen Above Suspicion*

1971

Best Actor: Gene Hackman *(The French Connection)*
Best Actress: Jane Fonda *(Klute)*
Best Supporting Actor: Ben Johnson *(The Last Picture Show)*
Best Supporting Actress: Cloris Leachman *(The Last Picture Show)*
Best Director: William Friedkin *(The French Connection)*
Best Picture: *The French Connection*
Best Foreign Film: *The Garden of the Finzi-Continis*

1972

Best Actor: Marlon Brando *(The Godfather;* refused*)*
Best Actress: Liza Minnelli *(Cabaret)*
Best Supporting Actor: Joel Grey *(Cabaret)*
Best Supporting Actress: Eileen Heckart *(Butterflies Are Free)*
Best Director: Bob Fosse *(Cabaret)*
Best Picture: *The Godfather*
Best Foreign Film: *The Discreet Charm of the Bourgeoisie*

1973

Best Actor: Jack Lemmon *(Save the Tiger)*
Best Actress: Glenda Jackson *(A Touch of Class)*
Best Supporting Actor: John Houseman *(The Paper Chase)*
Best Supporting Actress: Tatum O'Neal *(Paper Moon)*
Best Director: George Roy Hill *(The Sting)*
Best Picture: *The Sting*
Best Foreign Film: *Day for Night*

1974

Best Actor: Art Carney *(Harry and Tonto)*
Best Actress: Ellen Burstyn *(Alice Doesn't Live Here Anymore)*
Best Supporting Actor: Robert De Niro *(The Godfather, Part II)*
Best Supporting Actress: Ingrid Bergman *(Murder on the Orient Express)*
Best Director: Francis Ford Coppola *(The Godfather, Part II)*
Best Picture: *The Godfather, Part II*
Best Foreign Film: *Amarcord*

1975

Best Actor: Jack Nicholson *(One Flew over the Cuckoo's Nest)*
Best Actress: Louise Fletcher *(One Flew over the Cuckoo's Nest)*
Best Supporting Actor: George Burns *(The Sunshine Boys)*

Performance Arts

Best Supporting Actress: Lee Grant *(Shampoo)*
Best Director: Milos Forman *(One Flew over the Cuckoo's Nest)*
Best Picture: *One Flew over the Cuckoo's Nest*
Best Foreign Film: *Dersu Uzala*

1976

Best Actor: Peter Finch *(Network)*
Best Actress: Faye Dunaway *(Network)*
Best Supporting Actor: Jason Robards *(All the President's Men)*
Best Supporting Actress: Beatrice Straight *(Network)*
Best Director: John G. Avildsen *(Rocky)*
Best Picture: *Rocky*
Best Foreign Film: *Black and White in Color*

1977

Best Actor: Richard Dreyfuss *(The Goodbye Girl)*
Best Actress: Diane Keaton *(Annie Hall)*
Best Supporting Actor: Jason Robards *(Julia)*
Best Supporting Actress: Vanessa Redgrave *(Julia)*
Best Director: Woody Allen *(Annie Hall)*
Best Picture: *Annie Hall*
Best Foreign Film: *Madame Rosa*

1978

Best Actor: Jon Voight *(Coming Home)*
Best Actress: Jane Fonda *(Coming Home)*
Best Supporting Actor: Christopher Walken *(The Deer Hunter)*
Best Supporting Actress: Maggie Smith *(California Suite)*
Best Director: Michael Cimino *(The Deer Hunter)*
Best Picture: *The Deer Hunter*
Best Foreign Film: *Get Out Your Handkerchiefs*

1979

Best Actor: Dustin Hoffman *(Kramer vs. Kramer)*
Best Actress: Sally Field *(Norma Rae)*
Best Supporting Actor: Melvyn Douglas *(Being There)*
Best Supporting Actress: Meryl Streep *(Kramer vs. Kramer)*
Best Director: Robert Benton *(Kramer vs. Kramer)*
Best Picture: *Kramer vs. Kramer*
Best Foreign Film: *The Tin Drum*

1980

Best Actor: Robert De Niro *(Raging Bull)*
Best Actress: Sissy Spacek *(Coal Miner's Daughter)*
Best Supporting Actor: Timothy Hutton *(Ordinary People)*
Best Supporting Actress: Mary Steenburgen *(Melvin and Howard)*
Best Director: Robert Redford *(Ordinary People)*
Best Picture: *Ordinary People*
Best Foreign Film: *Moscow Does Not Believe in Tears*

1981

Best Actor: Henry Fonda *(On Golden Pond)*
Best Actress: Katharine Hepburn *(On Golden Pond)*
Best Supporting Actor: John Gielgud *(Arthur)*
Best Supporting Actress: Maureen Stapleton *(Reds)*
Best Director: Warren Beatty *(Reds)*
Best Picture: *Chariots of Fire*
Best Foreign Film: *Memphisto*

1982

Best Actor: Ben Kingsley *(Gandhi)*
Best Actress: Meryl Streep *(Sophie's Choice)*
Best Supporting Actor: Louis Gossett, Jr. *(An Officer and a Gentleman)*
Best Supporting Actress: Jessica Lange *(Tootsie)*
Best Director: Richard Attenborough *(Gandhi)*
Best Picture: *Gandhi*
Best Foreign Film: *To Begin Again*

1983

Best Actor: Robert Duvall *(Tender Mercies)*
Best Actress: Shirley MacLaine *(Terms of Endearment)*
Best Supporting Actor: Jack Nicholson *(Terms of Endearment)*
Best Supporting Actress: Linda Hunt *(The Year of Living Dangerously)*
Best Director: James L. Brooks *(Terms of Endearment)*
Best Picture: *Terms of Endearment*
Best Foreign Film: *Fanny and Alexander*

1984

Best Actor: F. Murray Abraham *(Amadeus)*
Best Actress: Sally Field *(Places in the Heart)*
Best Supporting Actor: Haing S. Ngor *(The Killing Fields)*
Best Supporting Actress: Dame Peggy Ashcroft *(A Passage to India)*
Best Director: Milos Forman *(Amadeus)*
Best Picture: *Amadeus*
Best Foreign Film: *Dangerous Moves*

1985

Best Actor: William Hurt *(Kiss of the Spider Woman)*
Best Actress: Geraldine Page *(The Trip to Bountiful)*
Best Supporting Actor: Don Ameche *(Cocoon)*
Best Supporting Actress: Angelica Houston *(Prizzi's Honor)*
Best Director: Sydney Pollack *(Out of Africa)*
Best Picture: *Out of Africa*
Best Foreign Film: *The Official Story*

1986

Best Actor: Paul Newman *(The Color of Money)*
Best Actress: Marlee Matlin *(Children of a Lesser God)*
Best Supporting Actor: Michael Caine *(Hannah and Her Sisters)*

Performance Arts

Best Supporting Actress: Diane Wiest *(Hannah and Her Sisters)*
Best Director: Oliver Stone *(Platoon)*
Best Picture: *Platoon*
Best Foreign Film: *The Assault*

1987
Best Actor: Michael Douglas *(Wall Street)*
Best Actress: Cher *(Moonstruck)*
Best Supporting Actor: Sean Connery *(The Untouchables)*
Best Supporting Actress: Olympia Dukakis *Moonstruck)*
Best Director: Bernardo Bertolucci *(The Last Emperor)*
Best Picture: *The Last Emperor*
Best Foreign Film: *Babette's Feast*

1988
Best Actor: Dustin Hoffman *(Rain Man)*
Best Actress: Jodie Foster *(The Accused)*
Best Supporting Actor: Kevin Kline *(A Fish Called Wanda)*
Best Supporting Actress: Geena Davis *(The Accidental Tourist)*
Best Director: Barry Levinson *(Rain Man)*
Best Picture: *Rain Man*
Best Foreign Film: *Pelle the Conquerer*

1989
Best Actor: Daniel Day-Lewis *(My Left Foot)*
Best Actress: Jessica Tandy *(Driving Miss Daisy)*
Best Supporting Actor: Denzel Washington *(Glory)*
Best Supporting Actress: Brenda Fricker *(My Left Foot)*
Best Director: Oliver Stone *(Born on the Fourth of July)*
Best Picture: *Driving Miss Daisy*
Best Foreign Film: *Cinema Paradiso*

1990
Best Actor: Jeremy Irons *(Reversal of Fortune)*
Best Actress: Kathy Bates *(Misery)*
Best Supporting Actor: Joe Pesci *(GoodFellas)*
Best Supporting Actress: Whoopi Goldberg *(Ghost)*
Best Director: Kevin Costner *(Dances with Wolves)*
Best Picture: *Dances with Wolves*
Best Foreign Film: *Journey of Hope*

1991
Best Actor: Anthony Hopkins *(The Silence of the Lambs)*
Best Actress: Jodie Foster *(The Silence of the Lambs)*
Best Supporting Actor: Jack Palance *(City Slickers)*
Best Supporting Actress: Mercedes Ruehl *(The Fisher King)*

Best Director: Jonathan Demme *(The Silence of the Lambs)*
Best Picture: *The Silence of the Lambs*
Best Foreign Film: *Mediterraneo*

1992
Best Actor: Al Pacino *(Scent of a Women)*
Best Actress: Emma Thompson *(Howard's End)*
Best Supporting Actor: Gene Hackman *(Unforgiven)*
Best Supporting Actress: Marisa Tomei *(My Cousin Vinny)*
Best Director: Clint Eastwood *(Unforgiven)*
Best Picture: *Unforgiven*
Best Foreign Film: *Indochine*

1993
Best Actor: Tom Hanks *(Philadelphia)*
Best Actress: Holly Hunter *(The Piano)*
Best Supporting Actor: Tommy Lee Jones *(The Fugitive)*
Best Supporting Actress: Anna Paquin *(The Piano)*
Best Director: Steven Spielberg *(Schindler's List)*
Best Picture: *Schindler's List*
Best Foreign Film: *Belle Epoque*

1994
Best Actor: Tom Hanks *(Forrest Gump)*
Best Actress: Jessica Lange *(Blue Sky)*
Best Supporting Actor: Martin Landau *(Ed Wood)*
Best Supporting Actress: Diane Wiest *(Bullets over Broadway)*
Best Director: Robert Zemeckis *(Forrest Gump)*
Best Picture: *Forrest Gump*
Best Foreign Film: *Burnt by the Sun*

1995
Best Actor: Nicolas Cage *(Leaving Las Vegas)*
Best Actress: Susan Sarandon *(Dead Man Walking)*
Best Supporting Actor: Kevin Spacey *(The Usual Suspects)*
Best Supporting Actress: Mira Sorvino *(Mighty Aphrodite)*
Best Director: Mel Gibson *(Braveheart)*
Best Picture: *Braveheart*
Best Foreign Film: *Antonia's Line*

1996
Best Actor: Geoffrey Rush *(Shine)*
Best Actress: Frances McDormand *(Fargo)*
Best Supporting Actor: Cuba Gooding, Jr. *(Jerry Maguire)*
Best Supporting Actress: Juliette Binoche *(The English Patient)*
Best Director: Anthony Minghella *(The English Patient)*
Best Picture: *The English Patient*
Best Foreign Film: *Kolya*

Performance Arts

1997

Best Actor: Jack Nicolson (*As Good as It Gets*)
Best Actress: Helen Hunt (*As Good as It Gets*)
Supporting Actor: Robin Williams (*Good Will Hunting*)
Supporting Actress: Kim Basinger (*L.A. Confidential*)
Best Director: James Cameron (*Titanic*)
Best Picture: *Titanic*
Best Foreign Film: *Character*

1998

Best Actor: Roberto Benigni (*Life Is Beautiful*)
Best Actress: Gwyneth Paltrow (*Shakespeare in Love*)
Supporting Actor: James Coburn (*Affliction*)
Supporting Actress: Judi Dench (*Shakespeare in Love*)
Best Director: Steven Spielberg (*Saving Private Ryan*)
Best Picture: *Shakespeare in Love*
Best Foreign Film: *Life is Beautiful*

1999

Best Actor: Kevin Spacey (*American Beauty*)
Best Actress: Hilary Swank (*Boys Don't Cry*)
Supporting Actor: Michael Caine (*The Cider House Rules*)
Supporting Actress: Angelina Jolie (*Girl Interrupted*)
Best Director: Sam Mendes (*American Beauty*)
Best Picture: *American Beauty*
Best Foreign Film: *All About My Mother*

2000

Best Actor: Russell Crowe (*Gladiator*)
Best Actress: Julia Roberts (*Erin Brockovich*)
Supporting Actor: Benicio Del Toro (*Traffic*)
Supporting Actress: Marcia Gay Harden (*Pollock*)
Best Director: Steven Soderbergh (*Traffic*)
Best Picture: *Gladiator*
Best Foreign Film: *Crouching Tiger, Hidden Dragon*

2001

Best Actor: Denzel Washington (*Training Day*)
Best Actress: Halle Berry (*Monster's Ball*)
Supporting Actor: Jim Broadbent (*Iris*)
Supporting Actress: Jennifer Connelly (*A Beautiful Mind*)
Best Director: Ron Howard (*A Beautiful Mind*)
Best Picture: *A Beautiful Mind*
Best Foreign Film: *No Man's Land (Bosnia and Herzegovina)*

Go to "Book Awards and Their Recipients" in chapter 8

ADDITIONAL SOURCES OF INFORMATION

BOOKS

MUSIC

Arnold, Denis, ed. *The New Oxford Companion to Music.* 2 vols. Oxford University Press, 1988.

Grout, Donald, and Claude V. Palisca. *A History of Western Music.* Norton, 2000.

Kerfeld, Barry. *The New Grove Dictionary of Jazz.* St. Martin's Press, 1994.

Sadie, Stanley, ed. *The New Grove Dictionary of Opera.* 4 vols. Groves Dictionaries of Music, 1998.

DANCE

Bremser, Martha, ed. *International Dictionary of Ballet.* St. James Press, 2001.

Bremser, Martha. *Fifty Contemporary Choreographers.* Routledge, 2000.

Mazo, Joseph. *Prime Movers: The Makers of Modern Dance in America.* Princeton Book Co., 2000.

McQuade, *The Schirmer Biographical Dictionary of Dance.* Macmillan, 1998.

STAGE AND FILM

Corey, Melinda, and George Ochoa. *The American Film Institute Desk Reference.* Dorling Kindersley, 2002.

Hartnoll, Phyllis, and Peter Found, eds. *The Concise Oxford Companion to the Theatre.* 2nd ed. Oxford University Press, 1992.

Katz, Ephraim. *The Film Encyclopedia.* 3rd ed. HarperPerennial, 1998.

Riggs, Thomas. *Contemporary Dramatists.* 6th ed. St. James Press, 1998.

Rubin, Don, Ousmane Diakhate, and Hansel Ndumbe Eyoh, eds. *The World Encyclopedia of Contemporary Theatre.* Routledge, 2000.

Tibbetts, John C., and James M. Welsh. *The Encyclopedia of Stage Plays into Film.* Facts on File, 2001.

Performance Arts

7

THE VISUAL ARTS

MAJOR PAINTERS AND SCULPTORS

AMERICAN

Albers, Josef (1888–1976), b. Germany. Painter and designer, teacher at the Bauhaus, and director of the Yale School of Art. He is best known for his *Homage to the Square* series (begun 1949) and for his widely studied color theories.

Calder, Alexander (1898–1976), b. Pennsylvania. Sculptor best known for his mobiles and playful wire constructions of circuses, begun in 1926. Much of his later work is large, heavy sculpture, often for public areas.

Cassatt, Mary (1845–1926), b. Pennsylvania. Artist who spent much of her life in Paris, where she was allied with the Impressionists. She is best known for paintings of women with children, such as *The Bath* (1892), and for etchings, such as *The Letter* (1891).

Chicago, Judy (1939–   ), b. Chicago. A pioneer in feminist art and art education. Chicago's best-known work is *The Dinner Party* (1974–1979), a multimedia project dealing with women's history. Other important installations include *Womanhouse* (1971), *The Birth Project* (1984), and *The Holocaust Project* (1993).

Copley, John Singleton (1738–1815) b. Massachusetts. Painted portraits and historical subjects. His Boston portraits show a thorough knowledge of his New England models, and his talent as a draftsman and colorist produced pictures of aristocratic elegance and grace. His works include *Henry Pelham (Boy with a Squirrel)* (1765) and *Watson and the Shark* (1778).

Cornell, Joseph (1903–72), b. New York. His surrealist-influenced constructions are boxes filled with found objects and collaged images, arranged in privately symbolic ways. Some of the best-known examples are *Medici Slot Machine* (1942) and *Hôtel du Nord* (1953).

Davies, Arthur Bowen (1862–1928), b. New York. Member of The Eight and an organizer of the historic 1913 Armory Show. His symbolic, idyllic paintings include landscapes such as *Unicorns* (1906).

Davis, Stuart (1894–1964), b. Pennsylvania. Davis developed a distinctly American interpretation of cubism in his brightly colored paintings, such as *Hot Still-Scape for Six Colors* (1940) and *Colonial Cubism* (1954).

de Kooning, Willem (1904–97), b. The Netherlands. A leader of abstract expressionism in the United States, de Kooning is best known for his monumental, violently painted *Woman* series, begun in the early 1950s.

Demuth, Charles (1883–1935), b. Pennsylvania. One of the first to incorporate geometric shapes of modern technology into painting. His best-known work is *I Saw the Figure 5 in Gold* (1928).

Dove, Arthur Garfield (1880–1946), b. New York. In his paintings of abstracted natural forms, such as *Waterfall* (1925) and *Rise of the Full Moon* (1937), Dove was a forerunner of abstract expressionism.

Eakins, Thomas (1844–1916), b. Pennsylvania. An important portraitist, Eakins was criticized for innovations such as working from live nude models. His best-known works include *The Gross Clinic* (1875), which shows an operation in progress, and *Max Schmitt in a Single Scull* (1871).

Feininger, Lyonel (1871–1956), b. New York. Feininger, who taught at the Bauhaus (1919–32), developed a style of delicate architectural forms fractured by rays of light, as in *Church at Gelmeroda* (1936).

Frankenthaler, Helen (1928–   ), b. New York. Frankenthaler developed a technique of staining canvases with paint, creating sensuous abstract works such as *Mountains and Sea* (1952), a seminal work in this style, and *Arden* (1961).

Gorky, Arshile (1904–48), b. Armenia. An influence on abstract expressionism, Gorky painted abstract but often biomorphic forms in brilliant, glowing colors, as in *The Liver Is the Cock's Comb* (1944).

Henri, Robert (1865–1929), b. Ohio. Painter and influential teacher. As a member of The Eight, he was a leader in the rebellion against academic art. Henri is best known for his dramatic portraits, such as *Woman in Manteau* (1898), *Himself* (1913), and *Herself* (1913).

Holzer, Jenny (1950–), b. Ohio. A multi-media conceptual artist, Holzer brings provocative phrases to public attention via electronic message boards, posters, and web sites, among other things. Popular works include *Truisms* (1979–1983), *Survival Series* (1983–1985), and *Lustmord* (1997).

Hofmann, Hans (1880–1966), b. Germany. Founder of two U.S. art schools important in the development of abstract expressionism. Hofmann boldly manipulated violent, clashing colors, as in *Effervescence* (1944) and *The Gate* (1959).

Homer, Winslow (1836–1910), b. Massachusetts. One of the most prominent 19th-century American painters, Homer is best known for his dramatic seascapes, such as *West Point, Prout's Neck, Maine,* and *On a Lee Shore* (both 1900).

Hopper, Edward (1882–1967), b. New York. Hopper painted lonely street scenes, buildings, and interiors, giving careful attention to light and shade, as in *Nighthawks* (1942) and *Early Sunday Morning* (1930).

Indiana, Robert (1928–), b. Indiana. Pop artist best known for his bold and vivid signlike paintings and sculpture, such as the *Love* series (begun 1966).

Johns, Jasper (1930–), b. Georgia. A founder of pop art, Johns uses everyday signs, symbols, and objects—such as flags, targets, and beer cans—in his paintings and sculptures. An example is the painting *Three Flags* (1958).

Kline, Franz (1910–62), b. Pennsylvania. He painted large canvases with dynamic black and white brush strokes, as in *White Forms* (1955) and *Mahoning* (1956). His work exemplifies abstract expressionism.

Lichtenstein, Roy (1923–97), b. New York. Pop artist known for his paintings based on comic strips. Examples are *Masterpiece* (1962) and *Good Morning, Darling* (1964).

Louis, Morris (1912–62), b. Maryland. He used a technique of soaking poured paint through canvases, so that the canvas essentially became dyed by the paint. His work includes the *Veil* series (1954, 1958) and the *Unfurled* series (1960–61).

Moses, Grandma (Anna Mary Robertson Moses) (1860–1961), b. New York. A farmer's wife who began painting in her seventies. Her primitive, colorful works of farm life, such as *Sugaring-Off* (1943), achieved wide popularity.

Motherwell, Robert (1915–91), b. Washington. Painter, writer, and important theoretician of abstract expressionism. His works are characterized by amorphous shapes in austere colors; best known is the series *Elegy for the Spanish Republic,* begun in 1949.

Nevelson, Louise (1900–88), b. Russia. Sculptor known for her large works of painted wood, metal, and found objects. Examples are *Sky Cathedral* (1958) and *World* (1966).

If a statue of a horse has both front legs in the air, the rider died in battle. If the horse has one front leg in the air, the rider died as a result of battle. If the horse has all four legs on the ground, the rider died of natural causes.

Newman, Barnett (1905–71), b. New York. Painter whose works bridged abstract expressionism and the color field movement. His canvases are typically large planes of flat color with thin vertical stripes, such as *Onement I* (1948) and *Concord* (1949). He also produced sculpture.

Noguchi, Isamu (1904–88), b. California. Sculptor well known for his abstract works designed for architectural spaces, such as the sculpture garden for the UNESCO building in Paris (1958) and the entrance for the Museum of Modern Art in Tokyo (1969).

O'Keeffe, Georgia (1887–1986), b. Wisconsin. Painter whose most characteristic images are sculptural, organic forms such as bones and flowers. She lived in New Mexico and often used elements of the southwestern landscape, as in *Cow's Skull: Red, White, and Blue* (1931).

The Visual Arts

Oldenburg, Claes (1929–), b. Sweden. Leader of the pop-art movement, known for his giant sculptures of common objects, such as *Dual Hamburger* (1962) and *Lipstick* (1969).

Parrish, Maxfield (1870–1966), b. Pennsylvania. Creator of posters, magazine covers, and book illustrations in a distinctive, decorative style.

Pollock, Jackson (1912–56), b. Wyoming. A pioneer of abstract expressionism, Pollock developed a method called action painting. His canvases are typically large, with paint dripped, poured, and thrown in complex, dense rhythms, as in *Number 1* (1948), *Number 32* (1950), and *Blue Poles* (1953).

Prendergast, Maurice Brazil (1859–1924), b. Canada. Member of The Eight. He painted landscapes and figures in a colorful, decorative style influenced by the Nabis, as in *The Promenade* (1913).

Rauschenberg, Robert (1925–), b. Texas. His collagelike "combine paintings" appropriating everyday images and objects represent a transition between abstract expressionism and pop art. His work includes *Bed* (1955) and *Monogram* (1959).

Reinhardt, Ad (Adolph) (1913–67), b. New York. Associated with minimalism, Reinhardt began painting monochrome canvases by 1953. He is best known for his *Black Paintings,* begun in 1960.

Remington, Frederic (1861–1909), b. New York. Painter, sculptor, illustrator, and writer whose subject was life on the western plains. His works include the sculpture *Bronco Buster* (1895) and the painting *Evening on a Canadian Lake* (1905).

Rivers, Larry (1923–), b. New York. In his use of popular images from sources such as artworks and advertising, Rivers was a forerunner of pop art. His paintings include *Washington Crossing the Delaware* (1953) and the *Dutch Masters* series (1963). He has also done sculpture.

Rockwell, Norman (1894–1978), b. New York. Illustrator best known for his *Saturday Evening Post* covers (1916–63). His realistically drawn, popular works portray anecdotal scenes of small-town America. *The Four Freedoms* (1943) are among his most famous paintings.

Rothko, Mark (1903–70), b. Russia. Important figure in abstract expressionism. His canvases contain soft-edged, luminously colored rectangular forms. His work includes *No. 10* (1950) and a series of murals for an ecumenical chapel in Houston (1967–69).

Saint-Gaudens, Augustus (1848–1907) b. Ireland. A sculptor best known for his important public monuments and memorials, including the Adams Memorial in Washington, D.C.; several Lincoln sculptures in Chicago's Lincoln Park; the Shaw Memorial in Boston, Massachusetts; and the General Sherman, Peter Cooper, and Admiral Farragut monuments in New York City. He was active as a teacher throughout the 1890s and maintained a large studio in Cornish, New Hampshire.

Sargent, John Singer (1856–1925), b. Italy. Painter known for his vivid portraits of high society, such as *The Daughters of Edward D. Boit* (1882) and *Madame X* (1884). He also produced impressionistic watercolor landscapes.

Segal, George (1924–), b. New York. Sculptor known for his life-size plaster human figures in everyday environments, such as *Woman in Restaurant Booth* (1961) and *Cinema* (1963). Segal is associated with pop art.

Shahn, Ben (1898–1969), b. Lithuania. Versatile artist of social-realistic work that often tells a story without preaching. In the early 1930s, he did a series of 23 paintings based on the Sacco-Vanzetti trial.

Sheeler, Charles (1883–1965), b. Pennsylvania. Photographer and painter known for his depictions of industrial forms reduced to cool, formal simplification. His works include the paintings *Ballardvale Revisited* (1949) and *Steel-Croton* (1953).

Smith, David (1906–65), b. Indiana. Renowned abstract sculptor of welded metal forms. He worked on his large *Cubi* series from the late 1950s until his death.

Stella, Frank (1936–), b. Massachusetts. Abstract painter of large, colorful works on irregularly shaped canvases. Works such as *Empress of India* (1965) use series of angular stripes; later works such as *Guadalupe Island* (1979) exhibit sweeping arched forms and wildly exuberant colors.

Stuart, Gilbert (1775–1828) b. Rhode Island. Gilbert Stuart was America's leading portraitist of the Federal period, and he set a standard for portraiture. Best known for his portraits of George Washington, Stuart painted more than a thousand portraits of the next four presidents of the United States, governors, diplomats, merchants, and other leaders of the new nation, as well as their wives and children.

Sully, Thomas (1783–1872), b. England. A leading portraitist, especially of national figures. His most famous work is the historical painting *Washington's Passage of the Delaware* (1819).

Trumbull, John (1756–1843) b. Connecticut. John Trumbull's works include portraits, engravings, and historical paintings. He sought to capture the most important historical moments of the American Revolution. Among his many well-known works are *The Declaration of Independence* (1788) and the murals he painted for the rotunda of the Capitol (installed in 1826).

Warhol, Andy (1930–87), b. Pennsylvania. Leader of the pop art movement. His works are notable for the repetition of everyday images, such as Campbell's soup cans, and for figures from popular culture, such as Marilyn Monroe (both series begun 1962).

West, Benjamin (1738–1820), b. Pennsylvania. Working in both Neoclassical and Romantic styles, he produced paintings such as *The Death of General Wolfe* (1770) and *Death on a Pale Horse* (1802). West worked mainly in England and was a founder and president of the Royal Academy of Arts there.

Whistler, James Abbott McNeill (1834–1903), b. Massachusetts. Painter and graphic artist whose works show a brilliant sense of color and design. His paintings include *The White Girl: Symphony in White No. 1* (1862) and *The Artist's Mother: Arrangement in Gray and Black* (1871). His series of *Nocturnes* foreshadowed abstract art.

Wood, Grant (1891–1942), b. Iowa. Painter best known for his stern figures and stylized landscapes of the rural Midwest. *American Gothic* (1930) is a quintessential American work.

Wyeth, Andrew (1917–), b. Pennsylvania. Popular painter of rural landscapes and portraits in a meticulous, naturalistic style. His best-known work is *Christina's World* (1948). In 1986, Wyeth astonished the public with the appearance of a previously secret series, the *Helga* paintings.

BELGIAN/FLEMISH

Bruegel, Pieter, the Elder (c. 1525–69). Flemish painter of peasants at work and play, genre scenes, landscapes, and illustrations of proverbs. His paintings include *The Corn Harvest* (1565) and *The Peasant Wedding* (c. 1567).

Ensor, James (Baron) (1860–1949). Belgian painter and etcher. Ensor created innovative and grotesque compositions, such as *The Temptation of St. Anthony* (1887) and *The Entry of Christ into Brussels* (1888), opening the way for the surrealist movement.

Limbourg, Herman, Jean, and **Pol** (active 1380–1416). Flemish brothers who worked in France for the Duke of Berry. Their *Les Très Riches Heures du Duc de Berry* (1413–16) is an exquisite, colorful, illuminated manuscript, showing activities of daily life.

Magritte, René (1898–1967). A leading Belgian surrealist painter. His works, such as *The Key of Dreams* (1930) and *The Human Condition* (1934), are odd fantasies based on everyday situations, or plays on relationships between pictures and words.

Rubens, Peter Paul (1577–1640). The foremost Flemish artist and a major baroque figure. Working with great freedom and vitality, Rubens produced dynamic, monumental paintings. His works include *The Raising of the Cross* (1610–11), a series of allegorical paintings on the life of Marie de Médici (1622–25), and *The Judgment of Paris* (1638–39).

Van der Weyden, Rogier (c. 1400–64). Flemish painter. His religious works, such as *The Descent from the Cross* (1435) and *The Last Judgment* (c. 1450), combine monumentality with a profound sense of emotion. His penetrating portraits include *Francesco d'Este* (c. 1455).

The Visual Arts

Van Dyck, Sir Anthony   (1599–1641). A major Flemish baroque artist. Van Dyck's many portraits of the aristocracy include a number of Charles I of England (his royal patron from 1632 on) such as *Portrait of Charles I Hunting* (c. 1635). Van Dyck also painted religious works, such as *The Lamentation* (1634).

Van Eyck, Jan   (c. 1390–1441). A master of Flemish painting. In works such as the church altarpiece in Ghent (1426–32) and the *Arnolfini Wedding Portrait* (1434), Van Eyck achieved an unprecedented luminosity, intensity of color, and detail.

BRITISH

Bacon, Francis   (1909–92), b. Ireland. Painter of disturbing, hallucinatory images, as in *Three Studies at the Base of a Crucifixion* (1944) and his series based on Velázquez's *Pope Innocent X* portrait, begun in the 1950s.

Blake, William   (1757–1827). Painter, engraver, and poet. Blake, a mystic and visionary, created paintings and engravings for John Linnell's editions of the *Book of Job* (1821–26) and Dante's *Divine Comedy* (1824–27), and for his own poetic works in an unearthly, highly personal style.

Constable, John   (1776–1837). Leading English landscape painter. In works such as *The White Horse* (1819), *The Hay Wain* (1821), and *Salisbury Cathedral* (1827), he carefully observed natural phenomena and changes.

Gainsborough, Thomas   (1727–88). Portraitist and landscape painter. His well-known works include *Mr. and Mrs. Robert Andrews* (1748), *Mrs. Siddons* (1785), and his most famous painting, *The Blue Boy* (1770).

Hogarth, William   (1697–1764). Painter and engraver of satirical works, often on moral themes and told in a series of scenes, such as *The Rake's Progress* (1733–35) and *Marriage à la Mode* (1743–45).

Moore, Henry   (1898–1986). Sculptor whose abstract and figurative works are characterized by smooth organic shapes and hollows. His many public commissions include works for the Time-Life building in London (1952–53) and for Lincoln Center for the Performing Arts in New York City (1962–65).

Reynolds, Sir Joshua   (1723–92). Reynolds, first president of the Royal Academy of Arts, painted portraits of nearly every important figure of his day with great versatility. His works include *Commodore Keppel* (1753) and *Mrs. Siddons as the Tragic Muse* (1784).

Rossetti, Dante Gabriel   (1828–82). Painter and poet; one of the founders of the Pre-Raphaelite Brotherhood in 1848. His sensual and symbolic works include *The Annunciation* (1850) and *Beata Beatrix* (1864).

Turner, Joseph Mallord William   (1775–1851). The foremost English landscape painter. Turner depicted atmospheric effects with a style of shimmering light and luminous colors, as in *Calais Pier* (1803) and *The Grand Canal* (1835).

DUTCH

Bosch, Hieronymus (Jerom Bos)   (c. 1450–1516). Painter of bizarre and colorful religious allegories, filled with grotesque figures and animals and obscure symbolism. His works include *The Garden of Earthly Delights* (c. 1505–10) and *The Temptation of St. Anthony* (c. 1500).

The Dutch painter Rembrandt, often called the master of light and shade, painted almost 100 self-portraits.

Hals, Frans   (c. 1580–1666). He painted lively and naturalistic portraits and genre scenes in vivid, sparkling colors. His works include *The Banquet of the Officers of the St. George Militia* (1616) and *The Laughing Cavalier* (1624).

Mondrian, Piet   (1872–1944). A founder of the Stijl group and the magazine *Die Stijl*. Mondrian developed a geometric style known as "neoplasticism." Typical works consist of primary-color squares bounded by black outlines, as in *Composition in Yellow and Blue* (1929) and *Red, Yellow, and Blue Composition* (1930).

Rembrandt Harmenszoon van Rijn (1606–69). A master of the Dutch school, he produced some 600 paintings distinguished by their profound humanity, including *The Anatomy Lesson of Dr. Tulp* (1632), *The Blinding of Samson* (1636), and *The Night Watch* (1642). Rembrandt also painted nearly 100 self-portraits, dating from the 1620s to his last years.

Van Gogh, Vincent (1853–90). One of the most influential 19th-century artists. Many of van Gogh's vibrant, expressive paintings were produced in a 29-month period preceding his suicide. Among his most famous works are *The Potato Eaters* (1885), *The Night Café* (1888), *Starry Night* (1889), and a number of self-portraits.

Vermeer, Jan (Johannes) (1632–75). Vermeer mainly painted intimate interiors, often with solitary figures, depicting them with clarity and luminous, subtle colors. His work includes *Head of a Girl* (c. 1665), *Woman Weighing Pearls* (c. 1665), and *The Letter* (1666).

FLEMISH

See "Belgian/Flemish" above.

FRENCH

Arp, Jean (Hans) (1887–1966). Creator of abstract paintings, sculptures, and collages using organic forms, such as *Squares Arranged According to the Laws of Chance* (1916–17) and *Navel, Shirt, and Head* (1926). Arp was associated with dadaism and surrealism.

Bonnard, Pierre (1867–1947). A founder of the Nabis, Bonnard was a painter, lithographer, and illustrator. He excelled at domestic interiors with subtle lighting effects. His work includes *Bowl of Fruit* (1933).

Braque, Georges (1882–1963). A figure in fauvism and, with Picasso, a founder of cubism. Braque's works include the monumental *Nude* (1907–08) and *Woman with a Mandolin* (1937).

Cézanne, Paul (1839–1906). Postimpressionist painter. His works include *The Card Players* (1890–92), *Bathers* (1898–1905), and a series of increasingly abstracted, geometric landscapes of Mont Sainte-Victoire. Cézanne had a profound influence on modern art, especially cubism.

Chardin, Jean-Baptiste-Siméon (1699–1779). Painter of genre scenes and still lifes in a subtle, delicate, unsentimental style. His works include *Return from Market* (1739) and *Saying Grace* (c. 1740).

Corot, Jean-Baptiste Camille (1796–1875). Influential landscape painter whose delicately lit, carefully observed works include *View of the Forest of Fontainebleau* (1831) and *View of Avray* (c. 1840).

Courbet, Gustave (1819–77). The initiator of realism, Courbet was a revolutionary at odds with political authority and visual idealization. His paintings include *The Stone Breakers* (1849) and *The Artist's Studio* (1854–55).

Daumier, Honoré (1808–79). Painter, lithographer, and sculptor. A great social satirist, Daumier produced some 4,000 lithographs, such as *Rue Transnonain, 15 Avril, 1834* (1834) and *The Legislative Body* (1834).

David, Jacques-Louis (1748–1825). The leading neoclassical painter. David's work reflects his passion for the ideas of the French Revolution and for classical art. His paintings include *The Oath of the Horatii* (1784) and *The Death of Marat* (1793).

Degas, Edgar (1834–1917). Painter and sculptor. He exhibited with the impressionists, although his approach differed from theirs. His paintings, such as *The Bellini Family* (1858–59) and *The Glass of Absinthe* (1876), often use daring spatial innovations.

Delacroix, Eugène (1798–1863). The foremost French romantic painter. His exuberant, freely painted, and richly colored works include *The Death of Sardanapalus* (1827) and *Liberty Leading the People* (1830).

Dubuffet, Jean (1901–85). Painter and sculptor of semiabstract, primitive works. He often used mixed media such as asphalt, pebbles, and glass to enrich his paintings' surface. His works include the *Topographies* and *Texturologies* series (1957–59).

Duchamp, Marcel (1887–1968). Painter and sculptor. He created cubist works and also co-founded dadaism. His "ready-mades" are everyday objects exhibited as art. His works include the painting *Nude Descending a Staircase* (1912), the ready-made *Fountain* (1917), and the construction *The Bride Stripped Bare by Her Bachelors, Even* (1915–23).

Dufy, Raoul (1877–1953). Painter, illustrator, and decorator known for his fauvist landscapes, seascapes, and portraits of society, including *Riders in the Wood* (1931) and *Cowes Regatta* (1934).

Fragonard, Jean-Honoré (1732–1806). Rococo painter of playful, erotic scenes, done in delicate colors and free brushwork. His works include *The Swing* (1769) and four *Progress of Love* paintings (1771–73).

Gauguin, Paul (1848–1903). Postimpressionist painter. At age 35, he left his career and family to devote himself to painting; he developed a style called synthetism. His best-known works, using flat planes, solid figures, and bright colors, were done in Tahiti and include *Nevermore* (1897) and *Where Do We Come From? What Are We? Where Are We Going?* (1897).

Géricault, Théodore (Jean Louis André Théodore) (1791–1824). A founder of romanticism. His works, based on contemporary events, were done in a powerful, spontaneous style. They include *A Cavalry Officer* (1812) and *The Raft of the Medusa* (1819).

Ingres, Jean-Auguste-Dominique (1780–1867). A leading neoclassical painter, Ingres was also deeply influenced by Raphael. His works, including *La Grande Odalisque* (1814), *La Comtesse d'Haussonville* (1845), and *The Turkish Bath* (1859–62), are both rigidly academic and richly sensual.

Léger, Fernand (1881–1955). He created a distinctive style, characterized by flat planes of color and simplified forms based on the surfaces of machines. His paintings include *The City* (1919) and *Le Grand Déjeuner* (1921).

Lorrain, Claude (Claude Gellée, called Claude) (1600–82). In his influential landscape paintings, such as *The Embarkation of the Queen of Sheba* (1648) and *The Expulsion of Hagar* (1668), he depicted atmospheric and lighting variations in a lyrical, sensitive style.

Maillol, Aristide (1861–1944). Sculptor, painter, and woodcut artist. His best-known works are his calm, monumental female nudes, such as *The Mediterranean* (c. 1901).

Manet, Édouard (1832–83). He introduced extraordinary thematic and technical innovations. His *Luncheon on the Grass* and *Olympia* (both 1863), both paintings of contemporary women, nude and unidealized, shocked viewers of the time. His works also include *A Bar at the Folies-Bergères* (1881).

Matisse, Henri (1869–1954). Painter, sculptor, and lithographer. Matisse, a leader of the Fauves, was a master of vivid color and line used in decorative, sensual patterns. His paintings include *La Joie de Vivre* (1905–06) and *The Dance* (1910).

Millet, Jean-François (1814–75). Realist painter associated with the Barbizon School. His unidealized scenes of peasant life include *The Sower* (1850) and *The Angelus* (1855–57).

Monet, Claude (1840–1926). A founder of impressionism and a major landscape painter. His works include many series of the same subject seen under different atmospheric and lighting conditions, such as haystacks (1891), the Rouen Cathedral (1892–94), and water lilies (1899–1926).

Morisot, Berthe (1841–95). The first woman to join the Impressionists. Morisot's paintings have a delicate, luminous style and smooth brushwork. Her works include *The Cradle* (1873) and *Young Woman at the Dance* (1880).

Pissarro, Camille (1830–1903), b. Virgin Islands. Impressionist painter who was also influenced by pointillism. His works include *Red Roofs* (1877) and *The Boulevard Montmartre at Night* (1897).

Poussin, Nicolas (1594–1665). Painter who developed the standard for French classical art, though he spent most of his life in Italy. His contemplative, precise works include *The Rape of the Sabine Women* (1636–37) and *The Holy Family on the Steps* (1648).

Renoir, Pierre Auguste (1841–1919). Impressionist painter of sensuous, joyous, light-filled works, such as *Moulin de la Galette* (1876), *The Bathers* (1884–87), and *Luncheon of the Boating Party* (1881).

Rodin, Auguste (1840–1917). Sculptor of unusual power and expression. Many of his most famous works, such as *The Thinker* (1079–1900) and *The Kiss* (1886–98), are enlarged figures from his great unfinished *Gates of Hell* (begun 1880). Other well-known works include *The Burghers of Calais* (1884–86) and *Balzac* (1892–97).

Rouault, Georges (1871–1958). Expressionist; also associated with the Fauves. His subjects, in paintings such as *Little Olympia* (1906), *Three Judges* (1913), and *Christ Mocked* (1932), were prostitutes, corrupt judges, and Christ.

Rousseau, Henri (1844–1910). Self-taught painter of naive, stylized, colorful works, often of jungle scenes, including *Sleeping Gypsy* (1897) and *The Dream* (1910).

Rousseau, Théodore (1812–67). A leading figure of the Barbizon School. His landscapes, such as *Descent of the Cattle* (1835), are full of gravity and intensity.

Seurat, Georges (1859–91). Painter who developed the pointillist or neoimpressionist technique of using small dots of pure color. His works include *Bathing at Asnières* (1883–84) and *A Sunday Afternoon on the Island of La Grande Jatte* (1885–86).

Toulouse-Lautrec, Henri de (1864–1901). Painter and lithographer. He depicted music halls, cabarets, and brothels in an unidealized, vivid way, as in *At the Moulin de la Galette* (1892) and *In the Parlor at the Rue des Moulins* (1894).

Vuillard, Édouard (1868–1940). Painter, lithographer, and member of the Nabis, known for his intimate interiors and interest in flat patterns, as in *Mother and Sister of the Artist* (c. 1893) and *Sitting Room with Three Lamps* (1899).

Watteau, Jean-Antoine (1684–1721). Rococo painter. In works such as *A Pilgrimage to Cythera* (1717) and *La Toilette* (1720), he depicted delicate, sensuous scenes in an exquisitely colored, lyrical manner.

GERMAN

Beckmann, Max (1884–1950). Expressionist painter. His highly personal style reflected the misery of contemporary events in Germany. His works include *The Night* (1918–19) and a series of nine triptychs, including *Departure* (1932–35).

Dürer, Albrecht (1471–1528). Painter, engraver, and most influential artist of the German school. Dürer is known for his technical mastery and his adoption of the principles of the Italian Renaissance. His works include the *Apocalypse* woodcuts (1498), the engraving *St. Jerome in His Study* (1514), and the painting *Four Apostles* (1526).

Ernst, Max (1891–1976). A founder of dadaism and surrealism. His grotesque, sometimes whimsical paintings include *Two Children Are Threatened by a Nightingale* (1924) and *The Temptation of St. Anthony* (1945).

Grosz, George (1893–1959). Painter known for his savage caricatures of post–World War I bourgeois society, such as *The Suicide* (1916) and *Eclipse of the Sun* (1926). He left Germany for the United States in 1933.

Grünewald, Mathias (Mathis Gothardt Neithardt) (c. 1475–1528). Religious painter of unusually expressive works, most frequently of the crucifixion of Christ. His masterpiece is the Isenheim altarpiece (1515).

Holbein, Hans, the Younger (c. 1497–1543). Outstanding portrait and religious painter of the Northern Renaissance. His works include *Sir Thomas More* (1527) and the *Madonna of the Burgomeister Meyer* (c. 1528).

Kollwitz, Käthe Schmidt (1867–1945). Graphic artist and sculptor whose works reflect her socialist and pacifist views. They include the etching series *Peasants' War* (1902–08) and the lithography series *The War* (1923) and *Death* (1934–35).

ITALIAN

Angelico, Fra (Guido or **Guidolino di Pietro,** also known as **Giovanni da Fiesole)** (c. 1400–55). Religious painter of great expressiveness; a master of graceful line and color. Among his works are the frescoes for San Marco in Florence, including *The Annunciation* (c. 1447), and scenes from the lives of saints Stephen and Lawrence in the Vatican (c. 1447–49).

Bellini, family of Renaissance painters. **Jacopo** (c. 1400–70) ran a workshop in Venice with his sons **Gentile** (1429–1507) and **Giovanni** (c. 1430–1516). Jacopo's work includes *The Madonna and Child with Lionello d'Este* (c. 1441). Gentile excelled at depicting contemporary Venetian ceremonies, as in *The Procession in the Piazza San Marco* (1496). Giovanni, probably the most talented, produced expressive works such as *St. Francis in Ecstasy* (c. 1475) and the San Zaccaria altarpiece (1505).

> *The most looked-at painting in the Louvre is Leonardo da Vinci's* Mona Lisa.

Bernini, Giovanni Lorenzo (Gianlorenzo) (1598–1680). Sculptor, architect, painter, and leading baroque artist. His dramatic, masterful sculptures include *David* (1623) and *The Ecstasy of St. Theresa* (1645–52). Among his paintings is *Saints Andrew and Thomas* (1627).

Boccioni, Umberto (1882–1916). Painter, sculptor, and major figure of futurist art. His works include the painting *The City Rises* (1910) and the sculpture *Unique Forms of Continuity in Space* (1913).

Botticelli, Sandro (Alessandro di Mariano Filipepi) (c. 1444–1510). A favorite of the Medici, this Renaissance painter was a supreme colorist and master of the rhythmic line. He is known for his mythological scenes, such as *Primavera* (c. 1478) and *The Birth of Venus* (c. 1482). His religious works include *Madonna of the Magnificat* (c. 1485).

Canova, Antonio (1757–1822). Neoclassical sculptor. His graceful, polished works include the tomb of Pope Clement XIV (1783–87) and *Pauline Borghese as Venus* (1805–07).

Caravaggio, Michelangelo Merisi da (c. 1573–1610). An influential painter whose bold works are masterpieces of dramatic light and shadow, featuring figures with strong physical presence. They include *The Calling of St. Matthew* (c. 1598) and *The Conversion of St. Paul* (1600–01).

Carracci, family of painters. The brothers **Annibale** (1560–1609) and **Agostino** (1557–1602) and their cousin **Ludovico** (1555–1619) established an important academy of painting in Bologna. Annibale, the most talented, and Agostino painted richly sculptural, decorative frescoes for the Farnese Palace in Rome (1597–1600). Annibale also did landscape paintings, such as *Landscape with the Flight into Egypt* (1604).

Cellini, Benvenuto (1500–71). Sculptor, metalsmith, and author. His works include the gold and enamel saltcellar of Francis I (1540) and his masterpiece, the Mannerist *Perseus with the Head of Medusa* (1545–54).

Chirico, Giorgio de (1888–1978), b. Greece. Forerunner of surrealism. His best-known paintings are characterized by deep perspective, solitary figures, and objects used out of context. They include *Mystery and Melancholy of a Street* (1914) and *Disquieting Muses* (1916–17).

Correggio (Antonio Allegri) (c. 1494–1534). He painted graceful, delicately lit works, especially on mythological themes, such as *Jupiter and Io* (c. 1530), and illusionistic ceiling frescoes, such as *The Assumption of the Virgin* for the cathedral in Parma (1526–30).

da Vinci, Leonardo. *See* **Leonardo da Vinci.**

della Robbia, Florentine family of sculptors and ceramicists known for their enameled terra-cotta. **Luca** (c. 1400–82) founded a workshop; his works include *The Resurrection* and *The Ascension* (both late 1440s), for the Florence Cathedral. His nephew **Andrea** (1435–1525), best known for his medallions for the Foundling Hospital in Florence, continued the workshop with his sons, **Luca II, Giovanni,** and **Girolamo.**

Donatello (Donato di Niccolo di Betto Bardi) (c. 1386–1466). An innovative Renaissance artist, he developed a technique of shallow relief, *schiacciato*. Donatello's powerful and expressive sculptures include *David* (c. 1408), *St. George* (c. 1415), and *Mary Magdelene* (c. 1456).

Ghiberti, Lorenzo (1378–1455). Major early Renaissance sculptor. His two pairs of bronze doors for the Florence Baptistery, with their finely modeled scenes, are his masterpieces (1403–24 and 1425–52). His life-size bronzes include *St. John the Baptist* (1412–16) and *St. Matthew* (1419).

Giorgione (Giorgione da Castelfranco) (c. 1476–1510). His poetic and warmly colored works had a major influence on Venetian painting. They include *The Tempest* (c. 1500–10), *The Three Philosophers* (c. 1505–10), and *Sleeping Venus*, which was completed by Titian (c. 1510).

Giotto (Giotto di Bondone) (c. 1266–1337). Most important early Italian painter. His monumental figures and realistic treatment of pictorial space were major innovations. His works include the *Ognissanti Madonna* (c. 1310); frescoes in the Arena Chapel, Padua (finished 1313); and frescoes in the Bardi and Peruzzi chapels, Santa Croce, Florence (1320s).

Leonardo da Vinci (1425–1519). Painter, sculptor, architect, engineer, and scientist. His balanced, beautifully painted designs embody the High Renaissance; his studies of perspective and anatomy were also highly influential. His paintings include *The Virgin of the Rocks* (1483–85), *The Last Supper* (1495–98), and the *Mona Lisa* (1503–06).

Lippi. Family of Florentine painters. **Fra Filippo** (c. 1406–69) was an important early Renaissance artist whose works include *The Coronation of the Virgin* (1441) and the frescoes for the Prato cathedral (1452–65). His son, **Filippino** (c. 1457–1504), painted a fresco cycle for the Strozzi Chapel, Santa Maria Novella, Florence (1495–1502).

Mantegna, Andrea (1431–1506). Early Renaissance painter and engraver. His works show monumental forms and an interest in perspective. They include frescoes for the Ovetari Chapel in the Church of the Eremitani in Padua (1448–57), and the S. Zeno Altarpiece (1456–59).

Michelangelo Buonarroti (1475–1564). Sculptor, painter, architect, poet. The influence of this foremost Renaissance figure on Western art was supreme. His works, all in a heroic style, include the sculptures *Pietà* (1499), *David* (1501–04), *Moses* (1513–16), and the tombs of Lorenzo and Giuliano de Medici (1519–34). Also among his monumental works are the *Book of Genesis* frescoes (1508–12) on the Sistine Chapel's ceiling and the *Last Judgment* fresco (1534–41) on its altar wall.

When Michelangelo painted the scene of the last judgment in the Sistine Chapel, he put in hell those people he didn't like, including Pope Julius II, the man who forced him to paint the chapel.

Modigliani, Amedeo (1884–1920). Painter and sculptor. His style is characterized by an elongated, smooth line. Most of his works are portraits and female nudes, such as the paintings *Jeanne Hébuterne* (1919) and *Reclining Nude* (1919).

Piero della Francesca (c. 1420–92). Major Renaissance painter. His works are characterized by strong symmetricality and angularity and an interest in precise ratios of perspective. They include frescoes of *The Legend of the True Cross* in the Church of San Francesco, Arezzo (1452–64), and *The Flagellation of Christ* (c. 1456).

Pisano, family of sculptors. **Nicola** (c. 1220–84) worked in an elaborate, architectural style; his works include pulpits for the Pisa Baptistery (finished 1260) and Siena Cathedral (1265–68). His son, **Giovanni** (c. 1250–1314), created the decorative facade, Siena Cathedral (1284–96), and the pulpit, Pisa Cathedral (1302–10).

Raphael (Santi or **Sanzio)** (1483–1520). His exquisitely balanced paintings epitomize the High Renaissance. They include frescoes for the Vatican's Stanza della Segnatura, including *The School of*

The Visual Arts

Athens (finished 1511); *Galatea* (c. 1512); and *The Sistine Madonna* (1512).

Tintoretto (Jacopo Robusti) (1518–94). A great Venetian mannerist who employed dramatic lighting, coloring, and foreshortening. Among his paintings are a cycle in the Scuola di San Rocco in Venice, including an enormous *Crucifixion* (1564–87), and *The Last Supper* (1592–94).

Titian (Tiziano Vecellio) (c. 1490–1576). High Renaissance painter whose innovations, especially his expressive use of color, were influential. His works include *The Assumption of the Virgin* (1516–18), *Pope Paul III and His Grandsons* (1546), and the *Pietà* (1576).

Uccello, Paolo (c. 1396–1475). Florentine painter; early master of perspective. His colorful, decorative works, including three panels of *The Battle of San Romano* (c. 1455) and a cycle of frescoes for Santa Maria Novella, Florence (c. 1445), are notable for their foreshortening.

Veronese, Paolo (Paolo Caliari) (1528–88). Venetian painter whose large works depicting scenes of sumptuous ceremonies are distinguished by opulent colors. They include *The Marriage at Cana* (1562), *The Feast in the House of Levi* (1573), and decorative paintings for the Ducal Palace, Venice (1577–82).

Verrocchio, Andrea del (Andrea di Michele di Francesco di Cioni) (1435–88). Leading early Renaissance sculptor and painter. His sculptures include *The Doubting of Thomas* (1465); among his paintings is *The Baptism of Christ* (1472), in which he was assisted by his pupil, Leonardo da Vinci.

MEXICAN

Kahlo, Frida (1907–54). Painter of vivid works, especially self-portraits, conveying intense psychic and physical pain. They include *Frida and Diego Rivera* (1931) and *The Love Embrace of the Universe, the Earth (Mexico), Diego, Me and Señor Xolotl* (1949).

Orozco, José Clemente (1883–1949). Muralist whose monumental scenes contain humanitarian symbolism. His murals are in the New School for Social Research, New York City (1931), and Dartmouth College, New Hampshire (1932–34).

Rivera, Diego (1886–1957). A founder of the Mexican mural renaissance. His works pay homage to Mexico's history and workers. They include *The History of Mexico,* National Palace of Mexico City (1929–36), and a series at the Detroit Institute of Arts (1933).

Siqueiros, David Alfaro (1896–1974). One of the three great Mexican muralists. His dynamic brushwork reflects revolutionary themes. Siqueiros's murals include a series at the Plaza Art Center, Los Angeles (1932), and *The Liberation of Chile* at the Mexican School, Chillán, Chile (1942).

Tamayo, Rufino (1899–1991). A leading Mexican painter. His decorative works are influenced by cubism, fauvism, and themes from Mexican folklore. They include *Sleeping Musicians* (1950) and a series of murals at Smith College, Massachusetts (1943).

RUSSIAN

Chagall, Marc (1887–1985). Russian painter who lived mainly in France. His poetic, colorful, and symbolic works are often based on Jewish folklore. They include *I and the Village* (1911), *Self-Portrait with Seven Fingers* (1911), and murals for the Metropolitan Opera House, New York City (installed 1966).

Gabo, Naum (Naum Neemia Pevsner) (1890–1977). Russian-born American constructivist sculptor and theorist. His works include *Column* (1923) and *Kinetic Construction* (1920), a sculpture with a motor. In his *Realist Manifesto*, he proposed that concepts of time and space be included in art.

Kandinsky, Wassily (1866–1944). Russian painter, a founder of the avant-garde *Blaue Reiter* group, and a teacher at the Bauhaus. His series of *Compositions, Improvisations,* and *Impressions,* beginning in 1910, are often seen as the first purely abstract works.

Malevich, Kasimir Severinovich (1878–1935). Russian painter and founder of suprematism. He is known for his sparse geometric paintings, including

Black Square (1915) and the *White on White* series (c. 1918). He described his theories in the book *The Non-Objective World* (1915).

Tatlin, Vladimir Evgrafovich (1885–1953). Russian artist and a founder of constructivism. His works include the *Relief Constructions* series (begun 1913) and the *Corner Reliefs* (begun 1915).

SPANISH

Dalí, Salvador (1904–89). Surrealist painter who worked in a precise style. His hallucinatory images can be seen in *The Persistence of Memory* (1931), *Crucifixion* (1951), and *The Last Supper* (1955).

El Greco. *See* **Greco, El.**

Goya y Lucientes, Francisco Jose de (1746–1828). Highly original painter and graphic artist. His expressive works are often telling social satires. They include the paintings *Nude Maja* and *Clothed Maja* (both c. 1804) and *Charles IV and His Family* (1800); and etching series, such as *Los Caprichos* (1799) and *Disasters of War* (1810–14).

Greco, El (Domenikos Theotokopoulos) (1541–1614), b. Crete. Painter of dynamic scenes, often of religious ecstasy. His works, distinguished by elongated figures and vivid highlights, include *The Disrobing of Christ* (1577–79), *The Burial of Count Orgaz* (1586), and *View of Toledo* (1600).

Gris, Juan (José Victoriano González) (1887–1927). A developer of synthetic cubism, he used simple forms and a rhythmic style in his paintings and collages. His works include *Homage to Picasso* (1911–12), *The Violin* (1916), and *Violin and Fruit Dish* (1924).

Miró, Joan (1893–1983). Surrealist painter. He worked in a playful, lyrical style, with colorful, amoebic shapes. His works include *Harlequin's Carnival* (1924–25), *Dog Barking at the Moon* (1926), and ceramic murals for the UNESCO building, Paris (1955–58).

Murillo, Bartolemé Estéban (1618–82). Religious and portrait painter. Among his important works are a series for the Charity Hospital in Seville

(1671–73), portraits, and many depictions of the Immaculate Conception.

Picasso, Pablo (Pablo Ruiz y Picasso) (1881–1973). Painter, sculptor, graphic artist, ceramicist. He was an enormously versatile, original, and prolific artist. His *Les Desmoiselles d'Avignon* (1907) is a seminal cubist work. Other important paintings include *The Three Musicians* (1921) and *Guernica* (1937).

Ribera, Jusepe de (1591–1652). Baroque painter, mainly of religious scenes. His naturalistic yet mystical works include *The Martyrdom of St. Bartholomew* (c. 1630) and *The Mystic Marriage of St. Catherine* (1648).

Velázquez, Diego Rodríguez de Silva y (1599–1660). One of the greatest of Spanish painters. He was a master of shimmering tones and brilliant colors. His expressive works include *The Surrender of Breda* (1634–35), *Pope Innocent X* (1650), and *The Maids of Honor* (1656).

Zurbarán, Francisco de (1598–1664). Baroque painter. His works, mostly religious, combine severity with spiritual intensity. They include *The Apotheosis of St. Thomas Aquinas* (1631) and *St. Serapion* (1628).

OTHER

Brancusi, Constantin (1876–1957). Romanian sculptor whose economical, simple style was radically innovative. His works include *Bird in Space* (1919) and the immense *Endless Column,* erected in a park near his birthplace (1937).

Giacometti, Alberto (1901–66). Swiss sculptor and painter, known especially for his sculptures of elongated figures, such as *The Forest* (1950) and *Walking Man* (1960).

Klee, Paul (1879–1940). Swiss painter whose works, such as *Twittering Machine* (1922) and *Park Near L(ucerne)* (1938), combine theories of abstraction with playful childlike inventiveness. Klee was associated with the *Blaue Reiter* group.

Klimt, Gustav (1862–1918). Austrian painter; a founder of the Vienna Secession group and a figure of the art nouveau movement. His exotic, erotic, symbolic works include *Judith* (1909) and *The Kiss* (1907–08).

Kokoschka, Oskar (1886–1980). Austrian expressionist painter. He produced many portraits and landscapes, such as *Le Marquis de Montesquiou* (1909–10) and *Jerusalem* (1929–30), as well as a series of self-portraits.

Munch, Edvard (1863–1944). Leading Norwegian painter and graphic artist. He foreshadowed expressionism with his charged images of terror, despair, and isolation, as in the paintings *The Scream* (1893) and *Vampire* (1895).

Paik, Nam June (1932–   ), b. South Korea. A contemporary artist working primarily with video-related installations, sculptures, and performances. Paik has been instrumental in establishing video as an art form. As a student in Germany, Paik participated in the Fluxus Movement, combining music and performance. His video works include the installations and sculptures *TV Buddha* (1964), *Family of Robots* (1986), and *Megatron* (1995). He began experimenting with satellite technology in the late 1970s, as seen in *Wrap Around the World* (1988).

Phidias (Pheidias) (c. 500–432 B.C.). One of the greatest ancient Greek sculptors, although none of his original works survive. He sculpted the enormous *Athena Parthenos,* Athens (c. 447–439 B.C.); and the *Zeus,* Olympia, one of the Seven Wonders of the Ancient World (c. 435 B.C.).

Praxiteles (c. 370–330 B.C.). He was considered the greatest Greek sculptor of his time. His *Hermes with the Infant Dionysus* (c. 350–330 B.C.) is the only existing original work by an ancient master. He also sculpted the *Aphrodite of Cnidus* (c. 350–330 B.C.).

Schiele, Egon (1890–1918). Austrian expressionist painter and graphic artist who developed an angular, linear style. Many of his works are nudes, often in disturbing, erotic poses. His paintings include *The Embrace* (1917) and *Paris von Gütersloh* (1918).

ART MOVEMENTS AND STYLES

abstract expressionism Movement in painting, originating in New York City in the 1940s. It emphasized spontaneous personal expression, freedom from accepted artistic values, surface qualities of paint, and the act of painting itself. Jackson Pollock, Willem de Kooning, Robert Motherwell, and Franz Kline are important abstract expressionists.

art deco A design style prevalent during the 1920s and 1930s, characterized by a sleek use of straight lines and slender forms.

art nouveau A decorative art movement that emerged in the late 19th century. Characterized by dense asymmetrical ornamentation in sinuous forms, it is often symbolic and of an erotic nature. Gustav Klimt worked in an art-nouveau style.

Ash Can School Group of American artists active from 1908 to 1918. It included members of The Eight, such as Robert Henri and Arthur Davies; Edward Hopper was also part of the Ash Can group. Their work featured scenes of urban realism.

Barbizon School An association of French landscape painters, c. 1840–70, who lived in the village of Barbizon and who painted directly from nature. Théodore Rousseau was a leader; Jean-Baptiste Corot and Jean-François Millet were also associated with the group.

baroque A movement in European painting in the 17th and early 18th centuries, characterized by violent movement, strong emotion, and dramatic lighting and coloring. Giovanni Bernini, Michelangelo Caravaggio, and Peter Paul Rubens were among important baroque artists.

Byzantine A style of the Byzantine Empire and its provinces, c. 330–1450. Appearing mostly in religious mosaics, manuscript illuminations, and panel paintings, it is characterized by rigid, monumental, stylized forms with gold backgrounds.

"Major Art Museums and Their Special Collections" in chapter 11

Go to

classicism   Refers to the principles of Greek and Roman art of antiquity with its emphasis on harmony, proportion, balance, and simplicity. In a general sense, classicism refers to art based on accepted standards of beauty.

color field painting   A technique in abstract painting developed in the 1950s. It focuses on the lyrical effects of large areas of color, often poured or stained onto the canvas. Barnett Newman, Mark Rothko, and Helen Frankenthaler painted in this manner.

conceptual art   A movement of the 1960s and 1970s that emphasized the artistic idea over the art object. It attempted to free art from the confines of the gallery and the pedestal.

constructivism   A Russian abstract movement founded by Vladimir Tatlin, Naum Gabo, and Antoine Pevsner, c. 1915. It focused on art for the industrial age. Tatlin believed in art with a utilitarian purpose.

cubism   A revolutionary movement begun by Pablo Picasso and Georges Braque in the early 20th century. It employs an analytic vision based on fragmentation and multiple viewpoints.

dadaism   A movement, c. 1915–23, that rejected accepted aesthetic standards. It aimed to create antiart and nonart, often employing a sense of the absurd.

The Eight   A group of American painters who united out of opposition to academic standards in the early 20th century. Members of the group were Robert Henri, Arthur Davies, Maurice Prendergast, William James Glackens (1870–1938), Ernest Lawson (1873–1939), Everett Shinn (1876–1953), John Sloan (1871–1951), and George Luks (1867–1933).

expressionism   Refers to art that uses emphasis and distortion to communicate emotion. More specifically, it refers to early-20th-century northern European art, especially in Germany, c. 1905–25. Artists such as Georges Rouault, Oskar Kokoschka, and Egon Schiele painted in this manner.

"Literary Movements, Periods, and Styles" in chapter 8

Go to

fauvism   From the French word *fauve,* meaning "wild beast." A style adopted by artists associated with Henri Matisse, c. 1905–08. They painted in a spontaneous manner, using bold colors.

folk art   Works of a culturally homogeneous people without formal training, generally according to regional traditions and involving crafts.

futurism   An Italian movement, c. 1909–19, that attempted to integrate the dynamism of the machine age into art. Umberto Boccioni was a futurist artist.

Gothic   A European movement beginning in France. Gothic sculpture emerged c. 1200; Gothic painting appeared later in the 13th century. The artworks are characterized by a linear, graceful, elegant style more naturalistic than that which had existed previously in Europe.

impressionism   A late-19th-century French school of painting. It focused on transitory visual impressions, often painted directly from nature, with an emphasis on the changing effects of light and color. Claude Monet, Pierre Renoir, and Camille Pissarro were important Impressionists.

mannerism   A style, c. 1520–1600, that arose in reaction to the harmony and proportion of the High Renaissance. Mannerism featured elongated and contorted poses, crowded canvases, and harsh lighting and coloring.

minimalism   A movement in American painting and sculpture that originated in the late 1950s. It emphasized pure, reduced forms and strict, systematic compositions.

Nabis   From the Hebrew word for "prophet." A group of French painters active in the 1890s who worked in a subjective, sometimes mystical style, stressing flat areas of color and pattern. Pierre Bonnard and Édouard Vuillard were members.

naive art   Artwork, usually paintings, characterized by a simplified style, nonscientific perspective, and bold colors. The artists are generally not professionally trained. Henri Rousseau and Grandma Moses worked in this style.

neoclassicism A European style of the late 18th and early 19th centuries. Its elegant, balanced works revived the order and harmony of ancient Greek and Roman art. Jacques-Louis David and Antonio Canova are examples of neoclassicists.

op art An abstract movement in Europe and the United States, begun in the mid-1950s, based on the effects of optical patterns. Josef Albers worked in this style.

Al Capp, the creator of Li'l Abner, *once said, "Abstract art is a product of the untalented, sold by the unprincipled to the utterly bewildered."*

photorealism A figurative movement that emerged in the United States and Britain in the late 1960s and 1970s. The subject matter, usually everyday scenes, is portrayed in an extremely detailed, exacting style. It is also called superrealism, especially when referring to sculpture.

pointillism A method of painting developed by Georges Seurat and Paul Signac (1863–1935) in the 1880s. It used dabs of pure color that were intended to mix in the eyes of viewers rather than on the canvas. It is also called divisionism or neoimpressionism.

pop art A movement that began in Britain and the United States in the 1950s. It used the images and techniques of mass media, advertising, and popular culture, often in an ironic way. Works of Andy Warhol, Roy Lichtenstein, and Claes Oldenburg exemplify this style.

postimpressionism A term coined by British art critic Roger Fry to refer to a group of 19th-century painters, including Paul Cézanne, Paul Gauguin, and Vincent van Gogh, who were dissatisfied with the limitations of impressionism. The term has since been used to refer to various reactions against impressionism, such as fauvism and expressionism.

Pre-Raphaelite Brotherhood A group of English painters formed in 1848. These artists attempted to recapture the style of painting preceding the Italian artist Raphael. They rejected industrialized England and focused on painting from nature, producing detailed, colorful works. Dante Rossetti was a founding member.

realism In a general sense, refers to objective representation. More specifically, a 19th-century movement, especially in France, that rejected idealized academic styles in favor of everyday subjects. Honoré Daumier, Jean-François Millet, and Gustave Courbet were realists.

Renaissance Meaning "rebirth" in French. Refers to Europe, c. 1400–1600. Renaissance art, which began in Italy, stressed the forms of classical antiquity, a realistic representation of space based on scientific perspective, and secular subjects. The works of Leonardo da Vinci, Michelangelo, and Raphael exemplify the balance and harmony of the High Renaissance (c. 1495–1520).

rococo An 18th-century European style, originating in France. In reaction to the grandeur and massiveness of the baroque, rococo employed refined, elegant, highly decorative forms. Jean-Honoré Fragonard worked in this style.

Romanesque A European style developed in France in the late 11th century. Its sculpture is ornamental, stylized, and complex. Some Romanesque frescoes survive, painted in a monumental, active manner.

romanticism A European movement of the late 18th to mid–19th century. In reaction to neoclassicism, it focused on emotion over reason and on spontaneous expression. The subject matter was invested with drama and usually painted energetically in brilliant colors. Eugène Delacroix, Théodore Géricault, Joseph Turner, and William Blake were Romantic artists.

suprematism A Russian abstract movement originated by Kasimir Malevich, c. 1913. It was characterized by flat geometric shapes on plain backgrounds and emphasized the spiritual qualities of pure form.

surrealism   A movement of the 1920s and 1930s that began in France. It explored the unconscious, often using images from dreams. It used spontaneous techniques and featured unexpected juxtapositions of objects. René Magritte, Salvador Dalí, Joan Miró, and Max Ernst painted surrealist works.

symbolism   A painting movement that flourished in France in the 1880s and 1890s in which subject matter was suggested rather than directly presented. It featured decorative, stylized, and evocative images.

COMMON ART TERMS

acrylic   Water-soluble paint made from pigments and a plastic binder.

aquatint   An etching technique in which a solution of asphalt or resin is used on the plate. Aquatint produces prints with rich, gray tones.

caricature   An artwork humorously exaggerating the qualities, defects, or peculiarities of a person or idea.

cartoon   A humorous sketch or drawing usually telling a story or caricaturing some person or action. In fine arts, a preparatory sketch or design for a picture or ornamental motif to be transferred to a fresco or tapestry.

carving   In sculpture, the cutting of a form from a solid, hard material such as stone or wood, in contrast to the technique of modeling.

casting   In sculpture, a technique of reproducing a work by pouring into a mold a substance such as plaster or molten metal, which then hardens.

chiaroscuro   The rendering of light and shade in painting; the subtle gradations and marked variations of light and shade for dramatic effect.

collage   A composition made of cut and pasted pieces of materials, sometimes with images added by the artist.

colors, complementary   Two colors at opposite points on the color scale—for example, orange and blue, green and red.

colors, primary   Red, yellow, and blue, the mixture of which will yield all other colors in the spectrum but which themselves cannot be produced through a mixture of other colors.

colors, secondary   Orange, green, and purple—colors produced by mixing two primary colors.

composition   The organization of forms and colors within an artwork.

drypoint   A technique of engraving, using a sharp-pointed needle, that produces a furrowed edge resulting in a print with soft, velvety lines.

encaustic   A painting technique using pigments dissolved in hot wax.

engraving   The art of producing printed designs through various methods of incising on wood or metal blocks, which are then inked and printed.

etching   The technique of producing printed designs through incising on a coated metal plate, which is then bathed in corrosive acid, inked, and printed.

figure   A representation of a human or an animal form.

foreshortening   Reducing or distorting in order to represent three-dimensional space as perceived by the eye, according to the rules of perspective.

fresco   Meaning "fresh" in Italian. The technique of painting on moist lime plaster with colors ground in water.

frieze   A band of painted or sculpted decoration, often at the top of a wall.

genre painting   A realistic style of painting in which everyday life forms the subject matter, as distinguished from religious or historical painting.

gesso   Ground chalk or plaster mixed with glue, used as a base coat for tempera and oil painting.

gouache   A method of watercolor painting, but prepared with a more gluey base, producing a less transparent effect.

Go to   "Common Music Terms" and "Common Dance Terms" in chapter 6

highlight   On a represented form, a point of most intense light.

impasto   Paint applied very thickly. It often projects from the picture surface.

landscape   Painting in which natural scenery is the subject.

lithography   A printing process in which ink impressions are taken from a flat stone or metal plate prepared with a greasy substance, such as an oily crayon.

modeling   In sculpture, the building up of form using a soft medium such as clay or wax, as distinguished from carving. In painting and drawing, using color and lighting variations to produce a three-dimensional effect.

monochrome   A painting or drawing executed in a single color.

monotype   A single print made from a metal or glass plate on which an image has been represented in paint, ink, etc.

mural   A large painting or decoration done on a wall.

oil   A method of painting with pigments mixed with oil, producing a vast range of light and color effects.

palette   A flat board used by a painter to mix and hold colors, traditionally oblong, with a hole for the thumb; also, a range of colors used by a particular painter.

pastel   A soft, subdued color; also, a drawing stick made of ground pigments, chalk, and gum water.

perspective   A method of representing three-dimensional volumes and spatial relationships on a flat surface to produce an effect similar to what is seen by the eye.

polychrome   Of many or various colors.

polyptych   In painting, a work made of several panels or scenes joined together. A diptych has two panels; a triptych, three.

primary colors   *See* **colors, primary.**

relief   In sculpture, the projection of an image or form from its background. Sculpture formed in this manner is described as high relief or low relief (bas-relief), depending on the degree of projection. In painting or drawing, the apparent projection of parts conveying the illusion of three dimensions.

secondary colors   *See* **colors, secondary.**

stenciling   A method of producing images or letters from sheets of cardboard, metal, or other materials from which forms have been cut away.

still life   The representation of inanimate objects in painting, drawing, or photography.

tempera   A painting technique using pigments mixed with egg yolk and water. Tempera produces clear, pure colors.

texture   The visual and tactile quality of a work of art based on the particular way the materials are handled; also, the distribution of tones or shades of a single color.

tone   The effect of the harmony of color and values in a work.

trompe l'oeil   Meaning "fool the eye" in French. In painting, the fine, detailed rendering of objects to convey the illusion that the painted forms are real and three-dimensional.

value   In painting, the degree of lightness or darkness in a color.

wash   In painting, a thin layer of translucent color.

watercolor   Painting in pigments suspended in water. It can produce brilliant colors and transparent effects.

woodcut   A print made by carving on a wood block, which is then inked and printed.

MAJOR ARCHITECTS

AMERICAN

Bulfinch, Charles (1763–1844), b. Massachusetts. He designed the first theater in New England, the Federal Street Theater (1794); the Massachusetts State House (1795–97); and the Massachusetts General Hospital (1818–23), all in Boston. In his completion of the design of the Capitol building, Washington, D.C. (1818–30), he achieved a model for state capitols throughout the country.

Burnham, Daniel Hudson (1846–1912), b. New York. Architect and city planner. With his partner, John Root, he designed the first major skeleton skyscraper, the Masonic Temple Building, Chicago (1892). Alone, Burnham designed the Flatiron Building, New York City (1903), and Union Station, Washington, D.C. (1903–07).

Fuller, (Richard) Buckminster (1895–1983), b. Massachusetts. Architect and engineer. His revolutionary designs, such as the geodesic dome, aimed at achieving the maximum effect with a minimal investment of materials.

Gehry, Frank O. (1929–   ) b. Canada. Educated in the U.S.A. Postmodern architect and designer known for dramatic sculptural buildings such as the Vitra Design Museum, Weil am Rhein, Germany (1987), the Rasin ("Fred and Ginger") Building, Prague, Czech Republic (1996), and the Guggenheim Museum, Bilbao, Spain (1997), along with numerous private homes.

Graves, Michael (1934–   ), b. Indiana. Postmodern architect. His influences range from classical Greece and Rome to the work of Le Corbusier. Graves's designs are known for their use of color and mix of delicacy and strength. They include the Fargo-Moorhead Cultural Center Bridge, Fargo, North Dakota, and Moorhead, Minnesota (1977); and the Public Services Building, Portland, Oregon (1980–82).

Gropius, Walter (1883–1969), b. Germany. A great modern functionalist. In 1919, he reorganized the Weimar School of Art into the Bauhaus. He designed the glass Fagus Factory, Alfeld (1911–12), and the Bauhaus buildings, Dessau (1925–26). His U.S. work includes the Pan American Building, New York City (1957). In 1946, he and young associates formed The Architects Collaborative (TAC), working together on buildings such as the United States Embassy, Athens (1956).

Hunt, Richard Morris (1827–95), b. Vermont. Architect. His work, which closely follows historical styles, exemplifies 19th-century eclecticism. He designed the Lenox Library (1870–77) and the Tribune Building (1873–76), both in New York City; and various mansions, such as those for the Vanderbilts in New York City and Newport, Rhode Island.

Jefferson, Thomas (1743–1826), b. Virginia. President, statesman, architect, and scientist. Jefferson, a self-taught architect, designed Monticello, his house near Charlottesville, Virginia (1768–82); the Virginia State Capitol in Richmond (1785–99); and the University of Virginia, Charlottesville (1817–26).

Jenney, William Le Baron (1832–1907), b. Massachusetts. Architect and engineer. His 10-story-high Home Insurance Building in Chicago (1884–85) is often considered to have been the first skyscraper. It was the first steel-framed office building.

Johnson, Philip Cortelyou (1906–   ), b. Ohio. He is noted for his glass-walled house in New Canaan, Connecticut (1949), and for the New York State Theater at Lincoln Center (1964), his collaboration with Mies van der Rohe on the Seagram Building (1958), and the American Telephone and Telegraph Building (1978–84), all in New York City. Johnson's writings include *The International Style* (1932), which he coauthored.

Kahn, Louis Isadore (1901–74), b. Estonia. Kahn designed the Yale University Art Gallery, New Haven (1951–53); the Kimbell Art Museum, Fort Worth (1966–72); and many housing projects, such as Carver Court Housing, Coatesville, Pennsylvania

(1941–43). The Richards Medical Research Building, University of Pennsylvania (1957–64), has been admired for its integration of form and function.

Latrobe, Benjamin Henry   (1764–1820), b. England. Considered the first professional architect in the United States, Latrobe produced some of the best monumental architecture of his time in classic revival style. His works include the Bank of Pennsylvania, Philadelphia (1799); and the Roman Catholic Cathedral, Baltimore, the first cathedral built in the United States (1805–18). He also worked on the Capitol, Washington, D.C. (1803–17).

Mies van der Rohe, Ludwig   (1886–1969), b. Germany. A director of the Bauhaus (1930–33) and a founder of modern architecture. His U.S. buildings, mainly unornamented skyscrapers, include Chicago's Lake Shore Drive Apartments (1948–51); the Chicago Federal Center (1959–73); and, with Philip Johnson, the Seagram Building, New York City (1958).

Pei, I(eoh) M(ing)   (1917–   ), b. China. He carefully integrates his expressive works with their surrounding environment. His buildings include the Mile High Center, Denver (1955); the John Hancock Tower, Boston (1973); the East Wing of the National Gallery of Art, Washington, D.C. (1978); a pyramidal addition to the Louvre museum, Paris (1989); and the Rock and Roll Hall of Fame in Cleveland, Ohio (1998).

Richardson, Henry Hobson   (1838–86), b. Louisiana. His monumental building, Trinity Church, Boston (1872–77), exemplifies the "Richardson romanesque" style. His work also includes the Marshall Field store, Chicago (1885–87).

Mills, Robert   (1781–1855), b. South Carolina. Mills, a classic revivalist, was appointed architect of public buildings in Washington, D.C. There, he built the Patent Office (1836–40), the Treasury (1836–42), and the Post Office (1839–42). In 1833, he designed the Washington Monument (built 1848–84).

Saarinen, Eero   (1910–61), b. Finland. Son of Eliel. His works, especially his domed constructions,

are innovative. His projects include the Kresge Auditorium, Massachusetts Institute of Technology, Cambridge (1953–56); Dulles International Airport, Chantilly, Virginia (1958–62); and the Gateway Arch, St. Louis (1959–64). He also designed furniture, especially chairs.

Saarinen, (Gottlieb) Eliel   (1873–1950), b. Finland. Architect and city planner. He designed the National Museum (1902–04) in Helsinki, Finland. His work in the United States includes several buildings at the Cranbrook Foundation, where he was president of the Academy of Art; and, with his son, Eero, performance halls at the Berkshire Music Center in Tanglewood, Massachusetts (late 1930s–early 1940s). Saarinen's writings include *The City: Its Growth, Its Decay, Its Future* (1943).

Strickland, William   (1788–1854), b. New Jersey. Classic revivalist architect. His most original work is the Merchants' Exchange, Philadelphia (1832–34). Also in Philadelphia, he built the Second Bank of the United States (1818–24) and the U.S. Mint (1829–33). He was a founder and first president of the American Institution of Architects.

Sullivan, Louis Henry   (1856–1924), b. Massachusetts. Prominent in the development of modern architecture, Sullivan propounded the theory that form should follow function. He designed the Wainwright Building, St. Louis (1890–91); the Transportation Building at the World's Columbian Exposition, Chicago (1893); and the Stock Exchange in Chicago (1893–94).

Venturi, Robert   (1925–   ), b. Pennsylvania. Venturi uses architectural elements from popular culture in his work, which includes Guild House, Philadelphia (1962–66); the Humanities and Social Sciences Building, State University of New York, Purchase (1968–70); and the new building for the Seattle Art Museum (1991). His writings include *Complexity and Contradiction in Architecture* (1966).

Walter, Thomas Ustick   (1804–87), b. Pennsylvania. As government architect in Washington, D.C., from 1851 to 1865, he added the Senate and

The Visual Arts

House wings to the Capitol, built its central dome, and designed the interior of the Library of Congress. Walter was a founder and president of the American Institute of Architects.

White, Stanford (1853–1906), b. New York. Architect. He worked in partnership with Charles Follen McKim and William Rutherford Mead. White's accomplishments include the first Madison Square Garden (1887–91), the Washington Memorial Arch (1889–92), and the New York Herald Building (1890–95), all in New York City. White's buildings reflect his passion for graceful, decorative elements and rich ornamentation.

Wright, Frank Lloyd (1867–1959), b. Wisconsin. Architect. His innovative approach integrated modern technology into architectural aesthetics. He is especially known for his dramatic interior spaces. His buildings include the Larkin Building, Buffalo, New York (1904); the Imperial Hotel, Tokyo (1915–22); the Kaufmann house, "Fallingwater," Bear Run, Pennsylvania (1936–39); a Unitarian church, Madison, Wisconsin (1947); and the Guggenheim Museum, New York City (1959).

BRITISH

Adam, Robert (1728–92). Scottish architect. He designed, with his brother James, numerous public and private buildings in England and Scotland in a distinctive and decorative style that combines Palladian, Renaissance, and classical elements. Notable examples are Osterley Park (1761–80) and Syon House (1762–69), both in Middlesex, England.

Chambers, Sir William (1723–96), b. Sweden. His *Treatise on the Decorative Part of Civil Architecture* (1759) was a classic design text. He is known for Somerset House, London (begun 1776); and for decorative architecture in Kew Gardens, Surrey, England, especially the Chinese Pagoda (1763).

Jones, Inigo (1573–1652). One of the first great English architects. He broke from the Jacobean style, thus beginning the Renaissance and the Georgian periods in English architecture. His works include the Queen's House, Greenwich Palace, Kent (1616–35); and the royal banqueting hall, Whitehall Palace, London (1619–22). Both employ Palladian principles.

Lutyens, Sir Edwin Landseer (1869–1944). The leading English architect of his time, Lutyens combined romantic and classical styles. His outstanding achievement is the plan of New Delhi, India, centering on the Viceroy's House (1912–31). Other works include war memorials, such as the Cenotaph in London (1919–20), and the British Embassy in Washington, D.C. (1927–28).

Mackintosh, Charles Rennie (1868–1928). Scottish architect, artist, and furniture designer. His interiors, such as those for four Glasgow tearooms (1896–1919), display a sumptuous art nouveau style. His buildings, such as the Glasgow School of Art (1896–99), are subtly proportioned.

Paxton, Sir Joseph (1803–65). Architect and horticulturist. His Great Conservatory, a greenhouse in Chatsworth, England (1836–40), served as a model for the glass Crystal Palace, which he built for the Great Exhibition of 1851 in London. Paxton's use of glass and iron in this building was a great technological innovation.

Pugin, Augustus Welby Northmore (1812–52). Architect, designer, and author. Pugin, a Gothic revivalist, worked on the interior and ornamentation of the Houses of Parliament (1844–52) and designed more than 65 churches, including Saint George's, London (1840–48). His writings, however, were more influential than his buildings.

Nash, John (1752–1835). Architect and city planner. Nash, a leader in the neoclassic Regency style, planned the layout of Regent Street and Regent's Park in London (built c. 1818), remodeled Buckingham Palace (1824–30), and worked on the "Indian"-style Royal Pavilion in Brighton (1815–21).

Smirke, Sir Robert (1781–1867). Classic revivalist architect. His best-known work is the main facade of the British Museum, London (1823–47). Other achievements include the Royal College of

Physicians (1822–25) and the General Post Office (1823–29), also in London. Upon his retirement, his brother Sydney Smirke (1798–1877) continued work on the British Museum (1854–57).

Soane, Sir John   (1753–1837). Soane, a classic revivalist, developed a complicated and highly personal style. His works in London include the Bank of England (begun 1788), the Dulwich College Art Gallery (1811–14), and his own eccentric house at Lincoln's Inn Fields (1812–13), now a museum.

Vanbrugh, Sir John   (1664–1726). Architect and dramatist. His buildings include Blenheim Palace, Oxfordshire (1705–16), which epitomizes the English baroque; and the Queen's Theatre in the Haymarket, London (1704–05). He designed theatrical, picturesque country houses, such as Seaton Delaval, Northumberland (begun 1720).

Wren, Sir Christopher   (1632–1723). Astronomer, architect, and mathematician. His elegant and dignified designs were highly influential. He designed St. Paul's Cathedral, London (1675–1710), and 52 other London churches, including St. Mary-le-Bow (1671–80). Other works include the Sheldonian Theatre, Oxford (1664–69), and Trinity College Library, Cambridge (1679–84).

FRENCH

Garnier, Jean Louis Charles   (1825–98). His principal work is the ornate Opéra in Paris, with its grand staircase (1861–75). He also designed the Casino at Monte Carlo (1878–81) and Bischofsheim's Observatory, Nice (1880–88).

Hardouin Mansart, Jules   (1646–1708). Baroque architect. In 1699, he became chief architect of the royal buildings. Some of his major works are at the Palace of Versailles, including the Galerie des Glaces and the Grand Trianon (both 1678–89). In Paris, he designed the Church of the Invalides (1679–91) and the Place Vendôme (1698).

Labrouste, Henri (Pierre François Henri) (1801–75). He was one of the first to successfully use metal construction in architecture, as he did in the reading room of the Bibliothèque Sainte-Geneviève, Paris (1843–50). He also worked extensively on the Bibliothèque Nationale (1854–75).

Le Corbusier (Charles-Édouard Jeanneret) (1887–1965). b. Switzerland. His innovative buildings and writings express a revolutionary approach toward aesthetic and technological architectural problems. His works, reflecting industrial as well as sculptural influences, include the Villa Savoye, Poissy, France (1928–31); collaboration on the United Nations buildings, New York City (1947–53); and buildings for the new capital of the Punjab, Chandigarh, India (1951–65).

Ledoux, Claude Nicolas   (1736–1806). This imaginative neoclassicist's buildings include the Pavilion de Louveciennes and the theater at Besançon in France (both 1771–73). He is known for his architectural treatise of 1804 and for his plans for Chaux, an ideal city for the workers of the salt mines of Arc-et-Senans, France.

ITALIAN

Alberti, Leone Battista   (1404–72). Architect and painter. His treatise, *De Re Aedificatoria* (c. 1450), established architecture as an intellectual field. His works include the exteriors of the churches of San Francesco in Rimini (c. 1450–61) and Sant'Andrea in Mantua (c. 1470–72).

Bernini, Giovanni Lorenzo (Gian Lorenzo) (1598–1680). Major Italian baroque architect and sculptor. As architect of St. Peter's in Rome, he designed the ornate baldachin (canopy) under the dome (1624–33) and the monument for St. Peter's chair (1657–66). From 1656 to 1667, he worked on the piazza and colonnade in front of St. Peter's. His Cornaro Chapel, in the church of Santa Maria della Vittoria, Rome (1647–51), is a dynamic melding of sculpture and architecture.

Borromini, Francesco   (1599–1667). Italian baroque architect. His influential designs for churches and palaces were complex and extravagant. His works include the churches of San Carlo alle Quattro Fontane (1634–41) and Sant'Ivo alla Sapienza (1642–60) and the completion of the church of Sant'Agnese, Piazza Navona (1653–57), all in Rome.

Bramante (Donato di Angelo di Antonio) (1444–1514). Leading Italian High Renaissance architect. He designed much of the church of Santa Maria presso San Satiro (c. 1480) and the east end of Santa Maria delle Grazie (c. 1492), both in Milan. His plans for St. Peter's, Rome (1505–06), though not fully carried out, were influential.

Brunelleschi, Filippo (1377–1446). The first great architect of the Italian Renaissance. His masterpiece is the celebrated ribbed octagonal dome for the Florence Cathedral (1420–36). His other works include the Foundling Hospital (1419) and the churches of San Lorenzo (begun c. 1420) and Santo Spirito (begun 1436), all in Florence.

da Vinci, Leonardo. *See* **Leonardo da Vinci.**

Giotto (Giotto di Bondone) (c. 1266–1337). Florentine architect and painter. In 1334, he was appointed architect of the Florence Cathedral. His main accomplishment is the multicolored bell tower called Giotto's Tower (begun 1334).

Leonardo da Vinci (1452–1519). Painter, sculptor, architect, engineer, and scientist. Around 1488, Leonardo did architectural work for the Milan Cathedral; he later worked on the reconstructions of cathedrals in Pavia and Piacenza. Beginning in 1506, he served as architect and engineer in Milan for Louis XII. In Rome, from 1513 to about 1515, he worked on several projects for the Vatican. Although most of Leonardo's designs were not executed, his architectural studies are of great historic importance.

Michelangelo Buonarroti (1475–1564). Italian Renaissance sculptor, painter, architect, and poet. Michelangelo's designs include the Medici Chapel (1520–34), where he powerfully combined architecture and sculpture, and the Laurentian Library (begun 1524), both at San Lorenzo, Florence. His work includes designs for St. Peter's (1546–64); its monumental dome, completed after Michelangelo's death, is based largely on his ideas.

Palladio, Andrea (1508–80). Italian Renaissance architect; a leading figure in Western architecture. Classical models were of extreme importance to him. He published a famous treatise in 1570. His works include rebuilding the Basilica at Vicenza, Italy (1549–80); many houses, including the Villa Barbaro, Maser, Italy (1554–58); and the Villa Rotunda, Vicenza (1567–70). In Venice, he built the churches of San Giorgio Maggiore (1560–80) and Il Redentore (1576–80).

Piranesi, Giovanni Battista (1720–1778). Architect and designer. Although he constructed few buildings—among them, Santa Maria del Priorato (1764) in Rome—his imaginative designs and theoretical writings were a major influence on European neoclassicism. His *Antichità Romane* (1756) and *Parere su l'Architettura* presented classical Rome as the creative foundation for a contemporary architecture.

OTHER

Aalto, Alvar (1898–1976). Finnish architect and furniture designer. The works of this leading 20th-century architect combine Finnish building traditions with modern techniques. They include the Municipal Library, Viipuri, Finland (1933–35); the Finnish Pavilion for the World's Fair, New York City (1939); and the undulating Baker House, Massachusetts Institute of Technology, Cambridge, Massachusetts (1946–49).

Behrens, Peter (1868–1940). German architect and industrial designer. His factory buildings, such as the A. E. G. Turbine Factory, Berlin (1908–09), show a simple, utilitarian approach. He is also known for the German Embassy, Leningrad (1911–12). Le Corbusier, Ludwig Mies van der Rohe, and Walter Gropius were his students.

Berlage, Hendrik Petrus (1856–1934). Pioneering modern Dutch architect. He is known for the redbrick Stock Exchange (1897–1903) and the Diamond Workers' Union Building (1899–1901), both in Amsterdam. He was also active in urban planning and furniture design.

Gaudí y Cornet, Antonio (1852–1926). Spanish architect whose colorful, sculptural, undulating style has similarities to art nouveau as well as surrealism.

His masterpiece is the unfinished Expiatory Church of the Holy Family, Barcelona (begun 1883; work still in progress). Other examples of his work are Parc Güell (1900–14) and Casa Battló (1904–06) in Barcelona.

Hoffmann, Josef Franz Maria (1870–1956). Austrian architect and decorator; a leader of the early-20th-century Viennese style. He is known for his use of rectilinear forms with delicate ornamentation, as in the Palais Stoclet, Brussels (1905–11).

Loos, Adolf (1870–1933). Austrian architect. His purity of form influenced the development of the modern functional style. His best-known works include the office and store building on Michaelerplatz and the Steiner House, both in Vienna (both 1910).

Mendelsohn, Erich (1887–1953). German architect. In Germany, he built the Herman and Co. hat factory, Luckenwalde (1921–23), and the sculptural Einstein Tower Observatory, Potsdam (1919–24). He designed several buildings in Israel, including the Hebrew University on Mount Scopus, Jerusalem (1937–39), and four synagogues in the United States.

Niemeyer, Oscar (1907–   ). Brazilian architect. Influenced by Le Corbusier, Niemeyer is a daring and original designer. He collaborated on the United Nations buildings, New York City (1947–53); directed the building of Brazil's new capital, Brasília (1950–60); and designed the Mondadori Headquarters in Milan (1968–75).

Wagner, Otto (1841–1918). Austrian architect. The most significant work by this pioneer of modern architecture is the Postal Savings Bank Office, Vienna (1904–12). He also designed stations for the Vienna Municipal Railway (1894–1901) and the church at Steinhof (1905–07). His writings, including *Modern Architecture* (1895), were influential.

ARCHITECTURAL MOVEMENTS AND STYLES

baroque   A style that flourished in the 17th and early 18th centuries, characterized by exuberant decoration, curvaceous forms, and a grand scale generating a sense of movement; later developments within the movement show more restraint.

Bauhaus   The style of the Bauhaus School, founded in Germany by Walter Gropius in 1919, emphasizing simplicity, functionalism, and craftsmanship.

Byzantine   A style of the Byzantine Empire, dating from the 5th century. Its churches are characterized by masonry construction around a central plan, with domes, foliage patterns on stone capitals, and interiors decorated with mosaics and frescoes.

classical revival   A movement in England and the United States in the late 18th and 19th centuries that looked to the traditions of Greek and Roman antiquity. Robert Mills, William Strickland, Sir Robert Smirke, and Sir John Soane participated in this movement.

classicism   The architecture of Greek and Roman antiquity, distinguished by the qualities of simplicity, harmony, and balance; also, a later style that emphasizes these values.

Georgian   The prevailing style of English architecture during the reigns of George I, II, and III (1714–1820), based on the principles of the Italian Renaissance architect Andrea Palladio.

Gothic   A style employed in Europe during the 13th, 14th, and 15th centuries. It is characterized by the use of pointed arches and ribbed vaults, piers, and buttresses in the support of its stone construction. The style is exemplified in France by the Cathedral of Notre Dame in Paris and the cathedrals in Amiens and Chartres.

"Seven Wonders of the Ancient World" in chapter 26
Go to

Gothic revival A movement in the United States and Britain in the late 18th and 19th centuries that returned to building styles of the Gothic period.

international style A movement that developed in the 1920s, characterized by a regularized surface, a lightening of mass, and, often, large expanses of glass. Walter Gropius, Mies van der Rohe, and Le Corbusier worked in this style.

Norman A building style created by the Normans (1066–c. 1200) based on the Italian romanesque and characterized by sparsely decorated masonry and the use of the round arch. The style was used principally in castles, churches, and abbeys of massive proportions.

postmodernism A style that emerged in the 1970s characterized by references to and evocations of past architectural styles, particularly the classical tradition. It is frequently colorful and wittily ornamentative. Michael Graves works in this style.

Renaissance A European style of the 15th and 16th centuries, beginning in Italy. Ancient Roman elements were adapted to contemporary uses, with attention to the principles of the architect Vitruvius and to existing ruins. Symmetry, simplicity, and exact mathematical relationships were emphasized.

A Hindu temple represents a mountaintop or the abode of the gods, while the inner part of the temple is the "womb" chamber, representing birth.

rococo A style originating in France, c. 1720, developed out of baroque types and characterized by elegant, delicate ornamentation and refined use of different materials, such as stucco, metal, or wood, for an ethereal effect.

Romanesque A style developed in Europe, c. 1050, characterized by heavy masonry and the use of the round arch, barrel and groin vaults, narrow openings, the vaulting rib, the vaulting shaft, and central and western towers.

Tudor A style of English architecture prevalent during the reigns of the Tudors (1485–1558), transitional between Gothic and Palladian, with emphasis on country manors.

COMMON ARCHITECTURAL TERMS

abacus A stone slab at the top of a classical column aiding the support of the architrave.

acropolis The elevated stronghold in ancient Greek cities.

adobe Sun-dried brick used in places with warm, dry climates, such as Egypt and Mexico; also, the structures built out of adobe bricks.

aisle A passageway of a Christian church or a Roman basilica running parallel to the nave, separated from it by an arcade or colonnade.

ambulatory A continuous aisle in a building, especially around the apse in a church.

apse A semicircular area at the end of a church; in most churches it contains the altar.

arcade A series of arches supported by columns or piers, or a passageway formed by these arches.

arch A curved structure used to span an opening.

architrave The lowest part of an entablature resting on the capital of a column.

continued, p. 248

ILLUSTRATIONS OF ARCHITECTURAL ELEMENTS

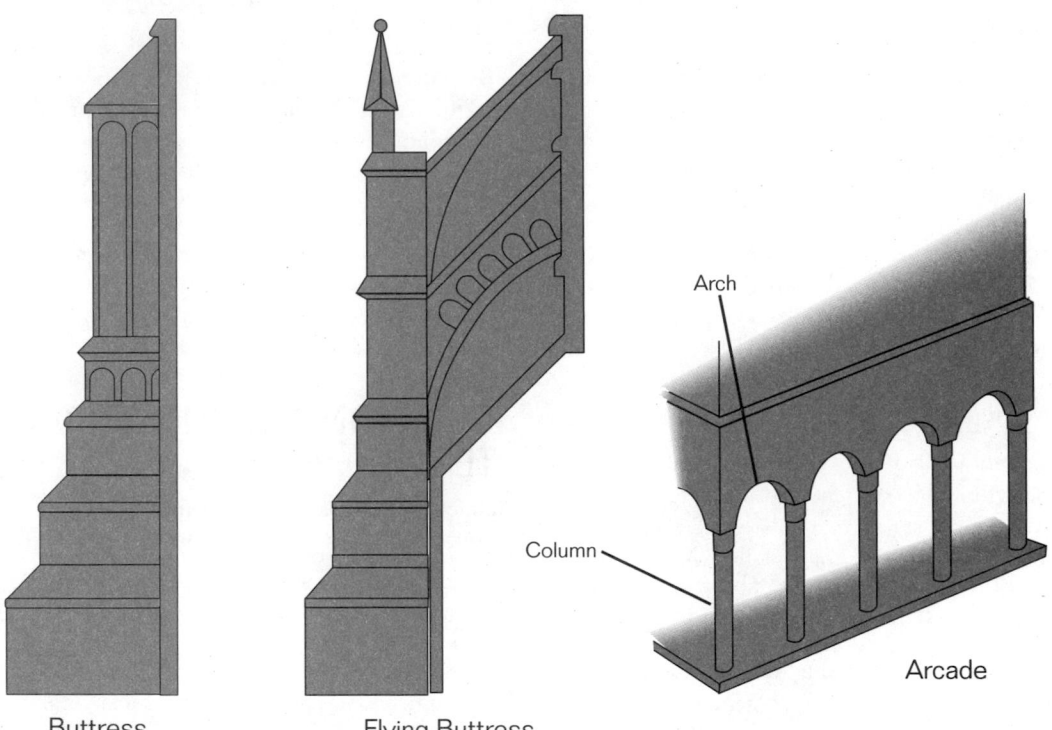

Buttress

Flying Buttress

Arch

Column

Arcade

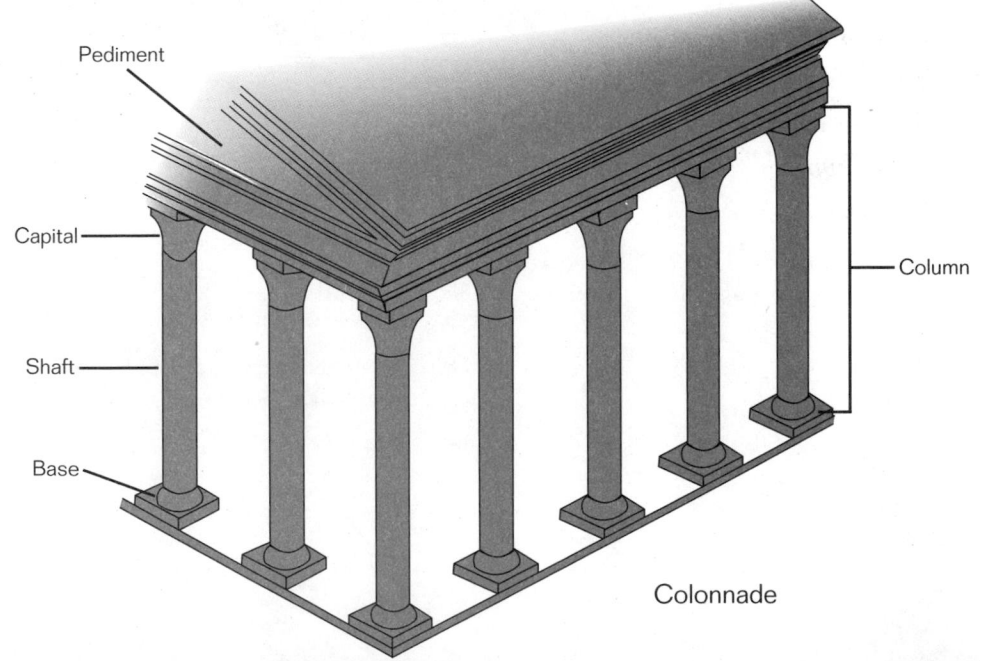

Pediment

Capital

Shaft

Base

Column

Colonnade

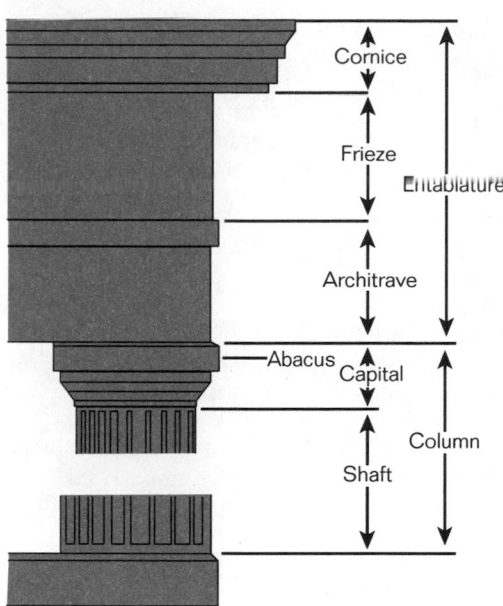

Column and Entablature

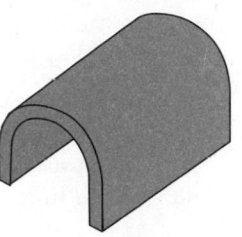

Barrel Vault

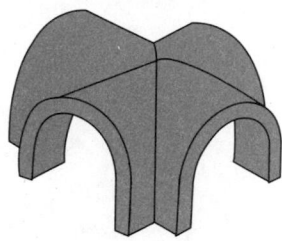

Groined Vault

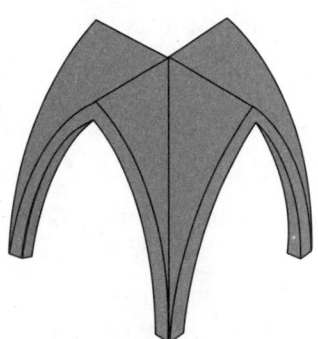

Ribbed Vault

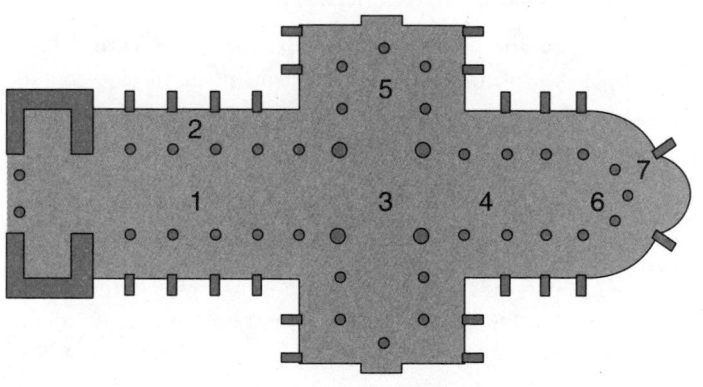

Church interior

1. Nave
2. Aisle
3. Crossing
4. Choir

5. Transept
6. Apse
7. Ambulatory

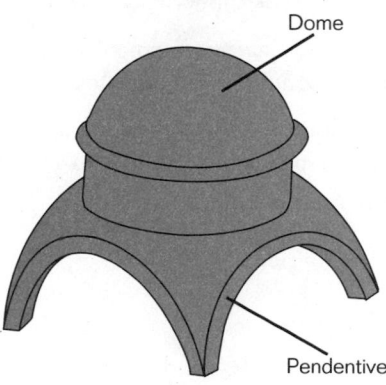

Vaulted Roof

ashlar   Stones hewn, squared, and smoothed for use in building, as distinguished from rough building stones.

atrium   In an ancient Roman house, a central room open to the sky, usually having a pool for the collection of rainwater. In churches, a front courtyard.

attic   The story above the cornice of a building.

baldachin   An ornamented canopy over an altar, tomb, or throne.

baptistery   A part of a church or a separate building, often octagonal or round, in which baptisms take place.

basilica   In ancient Roman architecture, a large oblong building, generally with double columns and a semicircular apse at one end. In Christian architecture, a church with a nave, apse, and aisles.

beam   A long piece of heavy wood, steel, etc., used as a horizontal support in construction.

buttress   A projecting support built into or against the external wall of a building, typically used in Gothic buildings. A flying buttress is an arch that transfers the thrust of a vault to a lower support.

campanile   A bell tower, especially one that stands apart from any other building.

cantilever   A horizontal projection, such as a balcony or beam, supported at one end only.

choir   A square or rectangular area in a church between the apse and the crossing.

clerestory   A row of windows in the upper part of a wall, especially in a church, to admit light below.

cloister   In religious institutions, a courtyard with covered walks.

colonnade   A row of columns, usually equidistant, supporting a beam or entablature.

column   A cylindrical vertical support usually consisting of a base, shaft, and capital.

Composite Order   A Roman order; its capital combines the Corinthian acanthus leaf decoration with volutes from the Ionic Order.

Corinthian Order   The latest of the three Greek orders, similar to the Ionic, but with the capital decorated with carvings of the acanthus leaf.

cornice   The upper part of an entablature, extending beyond the frieze; also, ornamental molding projecting along the top of a building or wall.

crossing   In a church, the area where the transept and the nave intersect, usually emphasized by a dome or tower.

dome   A vaulted roof of circular or polygonal shape.

Doric Order   The first and simplest of the three Greek orders and the only one that normally has no base.

entablature   The upper horizontal part of a classical order, between a capital and the roof; it consists of the architrave, frieze, and cornice.

facade   Any important face of a building, usually the principal front with the main entrance.

forum   The main public square of an ancient Roman city.

frieze   The middle part of an entablature, often decorated with sculpture.

gargoyle   A spout placed on the roof gutter of a Gothic building to carry away rainwater; usually carved in the shapes of fanciful animals and grotesque beasts.

Ionic Order   Second of the three Greek orders. Its capital is decorated with spiral scrolls (volutes).

lantern   A small structure on top of a dome, tower, or roof, often open to admit light below.

lintel   *See* **post and lintel.**

loggia   A roofed gallery with an open arcade or colonnade on at least one side.

minaret   A slender, lofty tower with balconies, attached to a Muslim mosque.

module   The measurement by which parts of a building are related to one another. An example is the diameter of a column.

narthex   The transverse entrance hall of a church.

nave   In a Roman basilica, the central aisle. In a church, the main section extending from the entrance to the crossing.

obelisk   A tall, tapering, four-sided stone shaft with a pyramidal top.

ogive   The pointed arch used in Gothic architecture.

order   A term applied to the three styles of Greek columns and entablatures (Doric, Ionic, and Corinthian) and to the Roman Composite and Tuscan orders, developed from the original three orders.

pagoda   A multistoried building, typically Asian, forming a tower with upward curving roofs over the individual stories.

pediment   In a classical building, the triangular gable between the horizontal entablature and the sloping roof; in general, an architectural feature over a door or window.

pendentive   A curved triangle at the corners of a square or polygonal room, used at the opening of a dome.

pier   An upright masonry support.

pilaster   A flattened, shallow column or pier projecting from a wall. It usually has a base, shaft, and capital but is decorative rather than structural.

portico   A structure usually attached to a building, such as a porch, consisting of a roof supported by piers or columns.

post and lintel   A method of construction in which vertical beams (posts) are used to support a horizontal beam (lintel).

pyramid   A quadrilateral masonry mass with steeply sloping sides meeting at an apex; in ancient Egypt, pyramids were used as royal tombs.

relief   Moldings and ornamentation projecting from the surface of a wall.

spandrel   The triangular area between the sides of two adjacent arches.

spire   A tall, tapering, pointed roof on a tower, as in the top of a steeple.

tracery   Ornament of ribs, bars, etc., in panels or screens, as in the upper part of a Gothic window.

transept   A structure that forms the arms of a cross-shaped church.

turret   A small tower, usually starting at some distance from the ground, attached to a building such as a castle or fortress.

Tuscan Order   A Roman order resembling the Doric, but with a base and an unfluted shaft.

vault   An arched brick or stone ceiling or roof. The simplest form is the **barrel vault,** a single continuous arch; the **groined vault** consists of two barrel vaults joined at right angles; a **ribbed vault** has a web of ribs added to the groins.

volute   A spiral scroll used on Ionic and Corinthian capitals.

westwork   In German Romanesque, a monumental entrance to a church consisting of towers, with a chapel above.

ziggurat   In ancient Assyria and Babylonia, a tower in the shape of a stepped pyramid. It formed the base of a temple.

ADDITIONAL SOURCES OF INFORMATION

Boorstin, Daniel J. *The Creators: A History of Heroes of the Imagination.* Random House, 1992.

Fleming, John, et al. *Penguin Dictionary of Architecture and Landscape.* 5th ed. Penguin, 2000.

Hunt, William D., Jr. *Encyclopedia of American Architects.* McGraw-Hill, 1980.

Janson, H. W., and Anthony Janson. *History of Art.* 6th ed. Abrams, 2001.

Kostof, Spiro. *A History of Architecture: Settings and Rituals.* 2nd ed. Oxford University Press, 1995.

Marks, Claude. *World Artists, 1950–1980.* H. W. Wilson Co., 1984.

_____. *World Artists, 1980–1990.* H. W. Wilson Co., 1991.

Musgrove, John, ed. *A History of Architecture: Sir Banister-Fletcher's.* 19th ed. Butterworth, 1987.

Phaidon Encyclopedia of Art and Artists. Phaidon Press Ltd., 1978.

Piper, David. *Random House Library of Painting and Sculpture.* Random House, 1981.

LITERATURE

Literature

IMPORTANT AUTHORS

Any list of "important" authors is subject to debate. The following list is not all-inclusive but does include many authors who have made a substantial contribution to literature.

The titles and years of first publication of each author's major works are given. In those instances where an author is known by a pseudonym, he or she is listed by that pseudonym with the real name in brackets.

A dagger (†) indicates that the author was awarded a Nobel Prize in literature. For American authors, an asterisk (*) designates a book that was awarded a Pulitzer prize in literature, and a plus sign (+) indicates that the work was awarded a National Book Award.

The shortest complete two-word sentence in the English language is "I am." One-word sentences include "Do." and "Go."

AMERICAN

Agee, James   (1909–55): *Let Us Now Praise Famous Men* (1941), **A Death in the Family* (1957), *Agee on Film* (1958, 1960)

Aiken, Conrad   (1889–1973): *The House of Dust: A Symphony* (1920), **Selected Poems* (1924), *Conversation; or, Pilgrim's Progress* (1940), *The Soldier* (1944), *The Kid* (1947), *Ushant: An Essay* (1952)

Alcott, Louisa May   (1832–88): *Little Women* (1868), *Little Men* (1871)

Algren, Nelson   (1909–81): *The Man with the Golden Arm* (1949), *A Walk on the Wild Side* (1956)

Anderson, Sherwood   (1876–1941): *Winesburg, Ohio* (1919), *The Triumph of the Egg* (1921)

Asimov, Isaac   (1920–92): *I, Robot* (1950), *Foundation* series (1951, 1952, 1953, 1982, 1986, 1988, 1993)

Auchincloss, Louis [Stanton]   (1917–   ): *Portrait in Brownstone* (1962), *Life, Law and Letters* (1979), *Diary of a Yuppie* (1987), *The Education of Oscar Fairfax* (1995)

Auden, W(ystan) H(ugh)   (1907–73): *Spain* (1937), *For the Time Being* (1944), **The Age of Anxiety: A Baroque Eclogue* (1947), *The Dyer's Hand* (1962)

Audubon, John James   (1785–1851): *The Birds of America* (1827–38)

Austin, Mary   (1868–1934): *A Woman of Genius* (1912), *Earth Horizon* (1932)

Baldwin, James   (1924–87): *Go Tell It on the Mountain* (1953), *Notes of a Native Son* (1955), *Nobody Knows My Name* (1961), *Another Country* (1962), *Just Above My Head* (1979)

Baraka, Imamu Amiri   (formerly LeRoi Jones, 1934–   ): *Preface to a Twenty Volume Suicide Note* (1961), *Dutchman* (1964), *The Slave* (1964), *The Toilet* (1964), *Black Music* (1967), *Eulogies* (1996)

Barth, John   (1930–   ): *The Sot-Weed Factor* (1960), *Giles Goat-Boy* (1966), *+Chimera* (1972)

Barthelme, Donald   (1931–89): *Come Back, Dr. Caligari* (1964), *Snow White* (1967), *City Life* (1970), *Sixty Stories* (1981)

Bartlett, John   (1820–1905): *Familiar Quotations* (1855)

Baum, L(yman) Frank   (1856–1919): *The Wonderful Wizard of Oz* (1900)

Beattie, Ann   (1947–   ): *Distortions* (1976), *Chilly Scenes of Winter* (1976), *Where You'll Find Me* (1986), *Picturing Will* (1989), *Perfect Recall: New Stories* (2001)

Bellow, Saul†   (1915–   ): *Dangling Man* (1944), *+The Adventures of Augie March* (1953), *Henderson, the Rain King* (1959), *+Herzog* (1964), *+Mr. Sammler's Planet* (1970), **Humboldt's Gift* (1975), *The Dean's December* (1982), *More Die of Heartbreak* (1987), *It All Adds Up* (1994), *Ravelstein* (2000)

Benchley, Robert   (1889–1945): *My Ten Years in a Quandary and How They Grew* (1936), *Benchley Beside Himself* (1943)

Go to   "Pseudonyms of Famous Authors" and "Book Awards and Their Recipients" in this chapter

Benét, Stephen Vincent (1898–1943): *John Brown's Body* (1928), *Western Star* (1943)

Benét, William Rose (1886–1950): *The Dust Which Is God* (1941)

Bierce, Ambrose (c. 1842–1914?): *Tales of Soldiers and Civilians* (1891), *Can Such Things Be?* (1893), *The Devil's Dictionary* (1911)

Bontemps, Arna (1902–73): *God Sends Sunday* (1931), *Sam Patch* (1951)

Boyle, Kay (1903–92): *Plagued by the Nightingale* (1931), *Death of a Man* (1936), *Thirty Stories* (1946), *The Underground Woman* (1975), *Fifty Stories* (1980)

Bradbury, Ray (1920–): *The Martian Chronicles* (1950), *The Illustrated Man* (1951), *Fahrenheit 451* (1953), *Something Wicked This Way Comes* (1962), *I Sing the Body Electric* (1969), *Green Shadows, White Whale* (1992)

Bradstreet, Anne (c. 1612–72): *The Tenth Muse Lately Sprung Up in America* (1650)

Brooks, Gwendolyn (1917–2000): *Annie Allen* (1949), *In the Mecca* (1968), *Family Pictures* (1970), *Children Coming Home* (1991)

Buck, Pearl S(ydenstricker)† (1892–1973): *The Good Earth* (1931), *My Several Worlds* (1954), *Imperial Woman* (1956)

Burroughs, Edgar Rice (1875–1950): *Tarzan of the Apes* (1914)

Burroughs, William S. (1914–97): *The Naked Lunch* (1959), *Cities of the Red Night* (1981)

Capote, Truman (1924–84): *Other Voices, Other Rooms* (1948), *The Grass Harp* (1951), *Breakfast at Tiffany's* (1958), *In Cold Blood* (1965)

Cather, Willa (1873–1947): *O Pioneers!* (1913), *The Song of the Lark* (1915), *My Ántonia* (1918), *One of Ours* (1922), *Shadows on the Rock* (1931)

Chandler, Raymond (1888–1959): *The Big Sleep* (1939), *Farewell, My Lovely* (1940), *The Long Goodbye* (1953)

Cheever, John (1912–82): *The Wapshot Chronicle* (1957), *The Wapshot Scandal* (1964), *Falconer* (1977), *The Stories of John Cheever* (1978)

Chopin, Kate (1851–1904): *Bayou Folk* (1894), *The Awakening* (1899)

Cooper, James Fenimore (1789–1851): *The Spy* (1821), *The Pioneers* (1823), *The Pilot* (1823), *The Last of the Mohicans* (1826), *The Prairie* (1827), *The American Democrat* (1838), *The Pathfinder* (1840), *The Deerslayer* (1841)

Crane, Stephen (1871–1900): *Maggie: A Girl of the Streets* (1893), *The Red Badge of Courage* (1895), *The Black Riders* (1895), *The Monster* (1899)

cummings, e.e. [Edward Estlin] (1894–1962): *The Enormous Room* (1922), *&* (1925), *is 5* (1926), *50 Poems* (1940), *I x I* (1944), *Ninety-five Poems* (1958), *Poems 1923–1954* (1955)

Dickinson, Emily (1830–86): *Poems* (1890), *Poems: Second Series* (1891), *Poems: Third Series* (1896), *The Single Hound* (1914)

Didion, Joan (1934–): *Slouching Towards Bethlehem* (1968), *The White Album* (1979), *Play It As It Lays* (1970), *Democracy* (1984), *The Last Thing He Wanted* (1996)

Dillard, Annie (1945–): *Pilgrim at Tinker Creek* (1974), *Teaching a Stone to Talk* (1982), *The Living* (1992), *Mornings Like This: Found Poems* (1995)

Doctorow, E(dgar) L(awrence) (1931–): *The Book of Daniel* (1971), *Ragtime* (1975), *Loon Lake* (1980), *World's Fair* (1985), *Billy Bathgate* (1989), *City of God* (2000)

Dos Passos, John (1896–1970): *Manhattan Transfer* (1925), *The 42nd Parallel* (1930), *1919* (1932), *The Big Money* (1936)

Dreiser, Theodore (1871–1945): *Sister Carrie* (1900), *The Financier* (1912), *The Titan* (1914), *The "Genius"* (1915), *An American Tragedy* (1925)

Edel, Leon (1907–1997): *Henry James: A Life* (5 vols., 1953–1972), *Bloomsbury: A House of Lions* (1979)

Eliot, T(homas) S(tearns)† (1888–1965): *Prufrock and Other Observations* (1917), *The Waste Land* (1922), *Murder in the Cathedral* (1935), *Four Quartets* (1943)

Ellison, Ralph (1914–94): +*Invisible Man* (1952), *Juneteenth* (1999)

Emerson, Ralph Waldo (1803–82): "Nature" (1836), "The American Scholar" (1837), *Essays: First Series* (1841), *Essays: Second Series* (1844), *The Conduct of Life* (1860)

Faulkner, William† (1897–1962): *Sartoris* (1929), *The Sound and the Fury* (1929), *As I Lay Dying* (1930), *Absalom, Absalom!* (1936), *The Hamlet* (1940), *Collected Stories* (1950), *+*A Fable* (1954), *The Reivers* (1962)

Fitzgerald, F(rancis) Scott (1896–1940): *Tales of the Jazz Age* (1922), *The Great Gatsby* (1925), *Tender Is the Night* (1933), *The Last Tycoon* (1941)

Franklin, Benjamin (1706–90): *Poor Richard's Almanack* (1733–58), *Autobiography* (1791)

Frost, Robert (1874–1963): *North of Boston* (1914), *Mountain Interval* (1916), **New Hampshire* (1923), **Collected Poems* (1930), **A Further Range* (1936), **A Witness Tree* (1942), *In the Clearing* (1962)

Gardner, John (1933–82): *Grendel* (1971), *October Light* (1976)

Ginsberg, Allen (1926–97): *Howl* (1956), *Kaddish and Other Poems* (1961), **The Fall of America* (1973)

Hammett, Dashiell (1894–1961): *The Maltese Falcon* (1930), *The Thin Man* (1934)

Hawkes, John Clendennin Burne, Jr. (1925–1998): *The Lime Twig* (1961), *The Blood Oranges* (1970), *Whistle Jacket* (1989), *An Irish Eye* (1997)

Hawthorne, Nathaniel (1804–64): *Twice-Told Tales* (1837; enlarged 1842), *The Scarlet Letter* (1850), *The House of the Seven Gables* (1851)

Heinlein, Robert A. (1907–88): *Stranger in a Strange Land* (1962)

Heller, Joseph (1923–1999): *Catch-22* (1961), *Something Happened* (1974), *Good as Gold* (1979), *Closing Time* (1994)

Hellman, Lillian (1905–84): *An Unfinished Woman* (1969), *Pentimento* (1973), *Scoundrel Time* (1976)

Hemingway, Ernest† (1899–1961): *The Sun Also Rises* (1926), *A Farewell to Arms* (1929), *For Whom the Bell Tolls* (1940), **The Old Man and the Sea* (1952), *A Moveable Feast* (1964)

Henry, O. [William Sydney Porter] (1862–1910): *The Four Million* (1906), *The Trimmed Lamp* (1907), *Whirligigs* (1910)

Hersey, John [Richard] (1914–93): **A Bell for Adano* (1944), *Hiroshima* (1946), *The Wall* (1950)

Howells, William Dean (1837–1920): *The Rise of Silas Lapham* (1885)

Hughes, Langston (1902–67): *The Weary Blues* (1926), *The Ways of White Folks* (1934), *Shakespeare in Harlem* (1942), *Ask Your Mama* (1961)

Hurston, Zora Neale (1903–1960): *Mules and Men* (1935), *Their Eyes Were Watching God* (1937), *Dust Tracks on a Road* (1942)

Irving, Washington (1783–1859): *History of New York* (1809), *The Sketch Book of Geoffrey Crayon, Gent.* (1819–20), *Legends of the Alhambra* (1832)

Jackson, Shirley (1919–65): "The Lottery" (1948), *The Bird's Nest* (1954), *The Haunting of Hill House* (1959), *We Have Always Lived in the Castle* (1962)

James, Henry (1843–1916): *The American* (1877), *The Europeans* (1879), *Daisy Miller* (1879), *The Portrait of a Lady* (1881), *The Bostonians* (1886), *Embarrassments* (1896), *The Two Magics* (1898), *The Awkward Age* (1899), *The Ambassadors* (1903), *The Golden Bowl* (1904)

Jarrell, Randall (1914–65): +*The Woman at the Washington Zoo* (1960), *No Other Books* (2000)

Jong, Erica (1942–   ): *Fear of Flying* (1973), *Fanny* (1980), *Fear of Fifty* (1994)

Kerouac, Jack (1922–69): *On the Road* (1957), *The Dharma Bums* (1958), *Desolation Angels* (1965)

Kosinski, Jerzy (1933–91): *The Painted Bird* (1965), +*Steps* (1968), *Being There* (1970), *Cockpit* (1975), *The Hermit of 69th Street* (1988)

Lardner, Ring(old) (1885–1933): *You Know Me, Al* (1916), *How to Write Short Stories* (1924), *The Love Nest and Other Stories* (1926)

Lewis, Sinclair† (1885–1951): *Main Street* (1920), *Babbitt* (1922), **Arrowsmith* (1925), *Dodsworth* (1929)

London, Jack (1876–1916): *The Call of the Wild* (1903), *The Sea-Wolf* (1904), *White Fang* (1906), *The Iron Heel* (1907), *Martin Eden* (1909)

Longfellow, Henry Wadsworth (1807–82): *Voices of the Night* (1839), *Ballads and Other Poems* (1841), *The Song of Hiawatha* (1855), *The Courtship of Miles Standish* (1858), *The Tales of a Wayside Inn* (1863)

Lowell, James Russell (1819–91): *A Fable for Critics* (1848)

Lowell, Robert (1917–77): *Land of Unlikeness* (1944), **Lord Weary's Castle* (1946), *Old Glory* (1964), **Dolphin* (1973)

Lowry, Malcolm (1909–57): *Ultramarine* (1933), *Under the Volcano* (1947), *Hear Us O Lord from Heaven Thy Dwelling Place* (1961)

Mailer, Norman (1923–): *The Naked and the Dead* (1948), *An American Dream* (1965), **The Armies of the Night* (1968), **The Executioner's Song* (1979), *Ancient Evenings* (1983), *Tough Guys Don't Dance* (1984), *Harlot's Ghost* (1991), *The Gospel According to the Son* (1997)

Malamud, Bernard (1914–86): *The Natural* (1952), +*The Magic Barrel* (1958), **+The Fixer* (1966), *The Tenants* (1971), *God's Grace* (1982)

McCarthy, Mary (1912–89): *The Groves of Academe* (1952), *Memories of a Catholic Girlhood* (1957), *The Group* (1963), *Intellectual Memoirs: New York, 1936–1938* (1992)

McCullers, Carson (1917–67): *The Heart Is a Lonely Hunter* (1940), *Member of the Wedding* (1946), *Clock Without Hands* (1961)

Melville, Herman (1819–91): *Typee* (1846), *Omoo* (1847), *White Jacket* (1850), *Moby-Dick* (1851)

Mencken, H(enry) L(ouis) (1880–1956): *The American Language* (1919, rev. 1921, 1923, 1936; suppl. 1945, 1948)

Michener, James (1907?–97): **Tales of the South Pacific* (1947), *Hawaii* (1959), *The Source* (1965), *The Drifters* (1971), *Chesapeake* (1978), *Mexico* (1992)

Miller, Henry (1891–1980): *Tropic of Cancer* (1934), *Tropic of Capricorn* (1939)

Mitchell, Margaret (1900–49): **Gone with the Wind* (1936)

Morrison, Toni [Chloe Anthony Wofford]† (1931–): *The Bluest Eye* (1970), *Sula* (1973), +*Song of Solomon* (1977), *Tar Baby* (1981), **Beloved* (1987), *Jazz* (1992), *Paradise* (1998)

Oates, Joyce Carol (1938–): +*Them* (1969), *Bellefleur* (1980), *Black Water* (1992), *Broke Heart Blues* (1999), *Blonde* (2000)

Paine, Thomas (1737–1809): *Common Sense* (1776), *The Age of Reason* (1794–95)

Parker, Dorothy (1893–1967): *Laments for the Living* (1930), *After Such Pleasures* (1933), *Here Lies* (1942)

Percy, Walker (1916–90): +*The Moviegoer* (1961), *The Last Gentleman* (1966), *Love in the Ruins* (1971), *The Thanatos Syndrome* (1987), *Signposts in a Strange Land* (1991)

Plath, Sylvia (1932–63): *The Colossus* (1960), *The Bell Jar* (1963), *Ariel* (1965), **Collected Poems* (1981)

Poe, Edgar Allan (1809–49): *Poems* (1831), *Tales of the Grotesque and Arabesque* (1840), *The Raven and Other Poems* (1845)

Porter, Katherine Anne (1890–1980): *Flowering Judas* (1930), *Pale Horse, Pale Rider* (1939), *Ship of Fools* (1962), **+Collected Stories* (1965)

Pound, Ezra (1885–1972): *Cantos* (1925–60)

Pynchon, Thomas (1937–): *V.* (1963), *The Crying of Lot 49* (1966), +*Gravity's Rainbow* (1973), *Vineland* (1990), *Mason & Dixon* (1997)

Rand, Ayn (1905–82): *The Fountainhead* (1943), *Atlas Shrugged* (1957)

Roth, Philip (1933–): +*Goodbye, Columbus* (1959), *Portnoy's Complaint* (1969), *The Ghost Writer* (1979), *The Counterlife* (1986), *Patrimony* (1991), +*Sabbath's Theater* (1995), *American Pastoral* (1997), *The Human Stain* (2000)

Salinger, J(erome) D(avid) (1919–): *The Catcher in the Rye* (1951), *Franny and Zooey* (1961)

Sandburg, Carl (1878–1967): *Chicago Poems* (1916), *Cornhuskers* (1918), *Complete Poems* (1950)

Saroyan, William (1908–81): *The Daring Young Man on the Flying Trapeze* (1934), *The Human Comedy* (1943)

Sexton, Anne (1928–74): *Live or Die* (1966), *Love Poems* (1969)

Singer, Isaac Bashevis† (1904–91): *Satan in Goray* (1935), *The Family Moskat* (1950), *Gimpel the Fool* (1957), *The Spinoza of Market Street* (1961), *A Crown of Feather* (1973)

Stein, Gertrude (1874–1946): *Three Lives* (1909), *The Autobiography of Alice B. Toklas* (1933), *Yes Is for a Very Young Man* (1946)

Steinbeck, John† (1902–68): *Tortilla Flat* (1935), *Of Mice and Men* (1937), *The Grapes of Wrath* (1939), *East of Eden* (1952)

Stowe, Harriet Beecher (1811–96): *Uncle Tom's Cabin* (1852)

Styron, William (1925–): *Lie Down in Darkness* (1951), *The Confessions of Nat Turner* (1967), +*Sophie's Choice* (1979), *A Tidewater Morning* (1993)

Thoreau, Henry David (1817–62): "Civil Disobedience" (1849), *Walden* (1854)

Twain, Mark [Samuel Langhorne Clemens] (1835–1910): *The Innocents Abroad* (1869), *Roughing It* (1872), *The Adventures of Tom Sawyer* (1876), *The Adventures of Huckleberry Finn* (1884)

Tyler, Anne (1941–): *Dinner at the Homesick Restaurant* (1982), *The Accidental Tourist* (1985), *Breathing Lessons* (1988), *Saint Maybe* (1991), *Ladder of Years* (1995), *Back When We Were Grownups* (2001)

Updike, John (1932–): *Rabbit, Run* (1960), *The Centaur* (1963), *Couples* (1968), *+Rabbit Is Rich* (1981), *The Witches of Eastwick* (1985), *Rabbit at Rest* (1990), *Brazil* (1994), *Licks of Love* (2000)

Vonnegut, Kurt Jr. (1922–): *Cat's Cradle* (1963), *Slaughterhouse-Five; or The Children's Crusade* (1969), *Breakfast of Champions* (1973), *Timequake* (1994)

Walker, Alice (1944–): *Meridian* (1976), *+The Color Purple* (1982), *The Temple of My Familiar* (1989), *The Way Forward Is with a Broken Heart* (2000)

Warren, Robert Penn (1905–89): *All the King's Men* (1946), *Promises* (1957)

Webster, Noah (1758–1843): *An American Dictionary of the English Language* (2 vols., 1828)

Welty, Eudora (1909–2000): *The Bride of the Innisfallen* (1955), *The Optimist's Daughter* (1972), *One Writer's Beginnings* (1984)

Wharton, Edith (1862–1937): *The House of Mirth* (1905), *Ethan Frome* (1911), *The Age of Innocence* (1920)

White, E(lwyn) B(rooks) (1899–1985): *One Man's Meat* (1942), *Here Is New York* (1949), *Charlotte's Web* (1952), *The Elements of Style* (1959)

Whitman, Walt (1819–92): *Leaves of Grass* (1855), *Drum Taps* (1865)

Wilson, Edmund (1895–1972): *Axel's Castle* (1931), *The Wound and the Bow* (1941), *Patriotic Gore* (1962)

Wolfe, Thomas (1900–38): *Look Homeward, Angel* (1929), *Of Time and the River* (1935), *The Web and the Rock* (1939)

Wolfe, Tom [Thomas Kennerly Wolfe, Jr.] (1931–): *The Pump House Gang* (1968), *The Electric Kool-Aid Acid Test* (1968), +*The Right Stuff* (1979), *The Bonfire of the Vanities* (1987), *A Man in Full* (1998)

Wouk, Herman (1915–): **The Caine Mutiny* (1951), *Marjorie Morningstar* (1955), *The Winds of War* (1971), *War and Remembrance* (1978)

Wright, Richard (1908–60): *Native Son* (1940), *Black Boy* (1945), *The Outsider* (1953)

AFRICAN

Armah, Ayi Kwei (Ghanaian, 1939–): *The Beautyful Ones Are Not Yet Born* (1968), *Why Are We So Blest?* (1972)

Beti, Mongo [Alexandre Biyidi] (Cameroonian, 1932–2001): *Le Pauvre Christ de Bomba* (1956), *Mission Terminée* (1957), *Le Roi Miraculé* (1958)

Cavafy, C(onstantine) P. (Egyptian, 1863–1933): *The Complete Poems of Cavafy* (1961)

Gordimer, Nadine† (South African, 1923–): *A Guest of Honour* (1970), *Burgher's Daughter* (1979), *My Son's Story* (1990), *The House Gun* (1998)

Laye, Camara (Guinean, 1928–80): *The Dark Child* (1953), *The Radiance of the King* (1954), *The Guardian of the Word* (1978)

Mahfouz, Naguib† (Egyptian, c. 1911–): *Midaq Alley* (1947), *Cairo Trilogy* (1956-57), *Children of Gelbewi* (1959), *Echoes of an Autobiography* (1995)

Paton, Alan Stewart (South African, 1903–88): *Cry the Beloved Country* (1948)

Sembene, Ousmane (Senegalese, 1923–): *The Black Docker* (1956), *God's Bits of Wood* (1960), *The Money Order* (1965)

Senghor, Léopold Sédar (Senegalese, 1906–): *Shadow Songs* (1945), *Nocturnes* (1961)

Soyinka, Wole† (Nigerian 1934–): *The Forest of a Thousand Daemons* (1968), *Aké: The Years of Childhood* (1981), *The Beatification of Area Boy* (1996)

ASIAN

Bashō, Matsuo [Matsuo Munefusa] (Japanese, 1644–94): *The Narrow Road to the Deep North* (1689)

Chatterji, Bankim Chandra (Indian, 1838–94): *The Chieftain's Daughter* (1865), *Krishna Kanta's Will* (1878)

Confucius (Chinese, c. 551–479 B.C.): *The Analects*

Kawabata, Yasunari† (Japanese, 1899–1972): *Snow Country* (1948), *Thousand Cranes* (1952), *Beauty and Sadness* (1965)

Lao-tzu (Chinese, c. 6th century B.C.): *Tao-te-ching*

Li Bo (Chinese, 701–762): *Complete Works*

Mishima, Yukio (Japanese, 1925–70): *Confessions of a Mask* (1949), *The Sailor Who Fell from Grace with the Sea* (1963), *The Sea of Fertility* (4 vols., 1965–70)

Murasaki, Shikibu (Japanese, c. 978–1015?): *The Tale of the Genji* (c. 1014)

Natsume, Sōseki (Japanese, 1867–1916): *I Am a Cat* (1905–07), *The Three-Cornered World* (1907), *And Then* (1910)

'Omar Khayyám (Persian, 1048–1131): *Rubáiyát* (1859)

Rushdie, Salman (Indian, 1947–): *Midnight's Children* (1981), *Shame* (1983), *The Satanic Verses* (1988), *Haroun and the Sea of Stories* (1990), *The Moor's Last Sigh* (1995)

Tagore, Rabindranath† (Indian, 1861–1941): *Gitāñjāli: Song Offerings* (1912)

Tanizaki, Jun'ichirō (Japanese, 1886–1965): "The Tattooer" (1911), *The Makioka Sisters* (1943–48), *Diary of a Mad Old Man* (1961)

Cao Zhan [T'sao Chan] (Chinese, c. 1715–63): *Dream the of Red Chamber* (c. 1763)

Literature

AUSTRALIAN

Clavell, James [du Maresq]   (1924–94): *King Rat* (1962), *Tai-Pan* (1966), *Shogun* (1975), *Noble House* (1981), *Gai-Jin* (1993)

Franklin, Miles [Stella Maria Sarah Miles] (1879–1954): *My Brilliant Career* (1901), *Some Everyday Folk and Dawn* (1909), *All That Swagger* (1936)

Greer, Germaine   (1939–   ): *The Female Eunuch* (1970)

Hospital, Janette Turner   (1942–   ): *The Ivory Swing* (1982), *Borderline* (1985), *Isobars* (1990)

Keneally, Thomas (Michael)   (1935–   ): *The Chant of Jimmie Blacksmith* (1972), *Confederates* (1979), *Schindler's List* (1982), *Women of the Inner Sea* (1992), *A River Town* (1995), *The Great Shame* (1998)

Malouf, David   (1934–   ): *Johnno* (1975), *An Imaginary Life* (1978), *Harland's Half Acre* (1984), *Remembering Babylon* (1993), *Conversations at Curlow Creek* (1996)

McCullough, Colleen   (1937–   ): *Tim* (1974), *The Thorn Birds* (1977), *The First Man in Rome* (1990)

Moorehead, Alan [McCrae]   (1910–83): *Gallipoli* (1956), *The White Nile* (1960), *The Blue Nile* (1962), *Cooper's Creek* (1963)

Richardson, Henry Handel [Ethel Florence Lindesay Richardson Robertson]   (1870–1946): *Maurice Guest* (1908), *The Getting of Wisdom* (1910), *The Fortunes of Richard Mahoney* (trilogy; 1917–29)

Shute, Nevil [Nevil Shute Norway]   (1899–1960): *A Town Like Alice* (1950), *On the Beach* (1957), *Trustee from the Toolroom* (1960)

West, Morris L(anglo)   (1916–1999): *The Devil's Advocate* (1959), *The Shoes of the Fisherman* (1963), *The Tower of Babel* (1967), *Harlequin* (1974), *The Clowns of God* (1981), *Lazarus* (1990), *Vanishing Point* (1996)

BRITISH

Amis, Sir Kingsley   (English, 1922–95): *Lucky Jim* (1954), *Jake's Thing* (1978), *Old Devils* (1986)

Austen, Jane   (English, 1775–1817): *Sense and Sensibility* (1811), *Pride and Prejudice* (1813), *Emma* (1816), *Persuasion* (1818)

Belloc, (Joseph) Hilaire   (English, 1870–1953): *The Bad Child's Book of Beasts* (1896), *On Nothing* (1908), *Cautionary Tales for Children* (1907)

Blake, William   (English, 1757–1827): *Poetical Sketches* (1783), *Songs of Innocence* (1789), *The Marriage of Heaven and Hell* (c. 1790), *Songs of Innocence and Experience* (1794), *Milton* (1804–8)

Boswell, James   (English, 1740–95): *The Life of Samuel Johnson* (1791)

Brontë, Charlotte   (English, 1816–55): *Jane Eyre* (1847)

Brontë, Emily   (English, 1818–48): *Wuthering Heights* (1847)

Browning, Elizabeth Barrett   (English, 1806–61): *Sonnets from the Portuguese* (1850), *Aurora Leigh* (1857), *Last Poems* (1862)

Browning, Robert   (English, 1812–89): *Bells and Pomegranates* (1841–46), *Dramatic Lyrics* (1842), *Men and Women* (1855), *Dramatis Personae* (1864)

Burgess, Anthony   (English, 1917–93): *A Clockwork Orange* (1962), *Earthly Powers* (1980)

Burns, Robert   (Scottish, 1759–96): *Poems, Chiefly in the Scottish Dialect* (1786)

Byron, Lord [George Gordon]   (English, 1788–1824): *Childe Harold's Pilgrimage* (1812–18), *The Prisoner of Chillon* (1816), *Manfred* (1817), *Don Juan* (1819–24)

Carroll, Lewis [Charles Lutwidge Dodgson] (English, 1832–98): *Alice's Adventures in Wonderland* (1865), *Through the Looking-Glass* (1871)

Chaucer, Geoffrey   (English, c. 1343–1400): *The Canterbury Tales* (c. 1387)

Christie, Agatha (English, 1890–1976): *The Murder of Roger Ackroyd* (1926), *Murder on the Orient Express* (1933), *Death on the Nile* (1937)

Clarke, Sir Arthur C(harles) (English, 1917–): *Childhood's End* (1953), *2001: A Space Odyssey* (1968), *Rendezvous with Rama* (1973), *3001: The Final Odyssey* (1997)

Coleridge, Samuel Taylor (English, 1772–1834): *Lyrical Ballads* (1798), *Sybilline Leaves* (1817), *Biographia Literaria* (1817)

Isaac Asimov was not only a highly prolific author; he was also extremely versatile. He wrote over 400 books and is the only author to have a book in every major Dewey-decimal category.

Conrad, Joseph (English, 1857–1924): *The Nigger of the "Narcissus"* (1897), *Lord Jim* (1900), *Typhoon* (1903), *Nostromo* (1904), *Chance* (1914)

Defoe, Daniel (English, 1660–1731): *Robinson Crusoe* (1719), *Moll Flanders* (1722), *Roxanna* (1724)

Dickens, Charles (English, 1812–70): *Oliver Twist* (1838), *Nicholas Nickleby* (1839), *A Christmas Carol* (1843), *David Copperfield* (1850), *Bleak House* (1853), *A Tale of Two Cities* (1859), *Great Expectations* (1861)

Donne, John (English, 1572–1631): *Songs and Sonnets* (1633)

Doyle, Sir Arthur Conan (English, 1859–1930): *Study in Scarlet* (1887), *The Sign of the Four* (1890), *The Adventures of Sherlock Holmes* (1892), *The Valley of Fear* (1915), *The Case-Book of Sherlock Holmes* (1927)

Dryden, John (English, 1631–1700): *All for Love* (1677), *Absalom and Achitophel* (1681), *Mac Flecknoe* (1682)

Durrell, Lawrence (English, 1912–90): *The Alexandria Quartet* (1957–60)

Eliot, George [Mary Ann Evans] (English, 1819–80): *Silas Marner* (1861), *Middlemarch* (1872)

Fielding, Henry (English, 1707–54): *Joseph Andrews* (1742), *Tom Jones* (1749)

Forster, E(dward) M(organ) (English, 1879–1970): *A Room with a View* (1908), *Howards End* (1910), *A Passage to India* (1924)

Golding, Sir William† (English, 1911–93): *Lord of the Flies* (1954), *Free Fall* (1959), *Rites of Passage* (1980)

Hardy, Thomas (English, 1840–1928): *Far from the Madding Crowd* (1874), *The Return of the Native* (1878), *Tess of the D'Urbervilles* (1891), *Jude the Obscure* (1895)

Hopkins, Gerard Manley (English, 1844–89): *Poems* (1918)

Johnson, Samuel (English, 1709–84): *A Dictionary of the English Language* (1755)

Keats, John (English, 1795–1821): *Poems* (1817), *Endymion* (1818), *Lamia, Isabella, and The Eve of St. Agnes and Other Poems* (1820)

Kipling, Rudyard† (English, 1865–1936): *The Jungle Book* (1894), *The Second Jungle Book* (1895), *Captains Courageous* (1897), *Kim* (1901), *Just So Stories* (1902)

Lawrence, D(avid) H(erbert) (English, 1885–1930): *Sons and Lovers* (1913), *Women in Love* (1921), *Lady Chatterley's Lover* (1928)

Lessing, Doris (English, 1919–): *The Grass Is Singing* (1950), *The Children of Violence* (1952–69), *The Golden Notebook* (1962), *Under My Skin* (1994), *Walking in the Shade* (1997)

Malory, Sir Thomas (English, c. 1408–c. 1471): *Le Morte d'Arthur* (1485)

Marvell, Andrew (English, 1621–78): *Miscellaneous Poems* (1681)

Maugham, W(illiam) Somerset (English, 1874–1965): *Of Human Bondage* (1915), *Cakes and Ale* (1930), *The Summing Up* (1938), *The Razor's Edge* (1944)

Milton, John (English, 1608–74): *Paradise Lost* (1667), *Paradise Regained* (1671)

Orwell, George [Eric Blair] (English, 1903–50): *Animal Farm* (1945), *Nineteen Eighty-four* (1949)

Pope, Alexander (English, 1688–1744): *An Essay on Criticism* (1711), "The Rape of the Lock" (1712)

Scott, Sir Walter (Scottish, 1771–1832): *The Bride of Lammermoor* (1819), *Ivanhoe* (1819), *Kenilworth* (1821)

Mark Twain's Tom Sawyer *(1876) was the first published novel ever written on a typewriter.*

Shelley, Mary [Mary Wollstonecraft] (English, 1797–1851): *Frankenstein, or the Modern Prometheus* (1818)

Shelley, Percy Bysshe (English, 1792–1822): *Prometheus Unbound* (1820), "Adonais" (1821)

Spenser, Edmund (English, c. 1552–99): *The Faerie Queene* (1590–96)

Stevenson, Robert Louis (Scottish, 1850–94): *Treasure Island* (1883), *The Strange Case of Dr. Jekyll and Mr. Hyde* (1886)

Swinburne, Algernon Charles (English, 1837–1909): *Atalanta in Calydon* (1865), *Poems and Ballads: First Series* (1866), *Poems and Ballads: Second Series* (1878)

Tennyson, Alfred (Lord) (English, 1809–92): *Poems, Chiefly Lyrical* (1830), *Poems* (1832), *In Memoriam* (1850), *Maud, and Other Poems* (1855), *Idylls of the King* (1859–85)

Thackeray, William Makepeace (English, 1811–63): *Vanity Fair* (1848), *Barry Lyndon* (1852)

Thomas, Dylan (English-Welsh, 1914–53): *Eighteen Poems* (1934), *Twenty-Five Poems* (1936), *A Child's Christmas in Wales* (1955), *Under Milk Wood* (1954), *Adventures in the Skin Trade* (1955)

Trollope, Anthony (English, 1815–82): *The Warden* (1855), *Barchester Towers* (1857)

Wells, H(erbert) G(eorge) (English, 1866–1946): *The Time Machine* (1895), *The Island of Dr. Moreau* (1886), *The Invisible Man* (1897), *The War of the Worlds* (1898), *Tono-Bungay* (1909)

Woolf, Virginia (English, 1882–1941): *Mrs. Dalloway* (1925), *To the Lighthouse* (1927), "A Room of One's Own" (1929)

Wordsworth, William (English, 1770–1850): *Lyrical Ballads* (1798)

CANADIAN

Atwood, Margaret (1939–   ): *The Circle Game* (1964), *Surfacing* (1972), *Life Before Man* (1979), *Bodily Harm* (1981), *The Handmaid's Tale* (1984), *Cat's Eye* (1988), *Alias Grace* (1996), *The Blind Assassin* (2000)

Connor, Ralph [Charles William Gordon] (1860–1937): *Black Rock* (1898), *The Sky Pilot* (1899), *The Men from Glengarry* (1901), *Glengarry School Days* (1902)

Davies, Robertson (1913–95): *A Mixture of Frailties* (1958), *Fifth Business* (1970), *The Rebel Angels* (1981), *What's Bred in the Bone* (1985), *The Lyre of Orpheus* (1988), *The Cunning Man* (1994)

Leacock, Stephen (1869–1944): *Literary Lapses* (1910), *Nonsense Novels* (1911), *My Discovery of the West* (1937)

Montgomery, Lucy Maude (1874–1942): *Anne of Green Gables* (1908), *Emily of New Moon* (1923), *The Blue Castle* (1926), *A Tangled Web* (1931), *Jane of Lantern Hill* (1937)

Munro, Alice (1931–   ): *Dance of the Happy Shades* (1968), *Who Do You Think You Are?* (1978), *The Progress of Love* (1986), *The Love of a Good Woman* (1998)

Pratt, E. J. (1882–1964): *The Witches' Brew* (1925), *Titans: Two Poems* (1926), *The Fable of the Goats and Other Poems* (1932), *The Titanic* (1935), *Brebeuf and His Brethren* (1940), *Towards the Last Spike* (1952)

Richler, Mordecai (1931–2001): *A Choice of Enemies* (1957), *The Apprenticeship of Duddy Kravitz*

(1959), *Cocksure* (1968), *St. Urbain's Horseman* (1971), *Barney's Version* (1997)

Roberts, Sir Charles G. D. (1860–1943): *Orion, and Other Poems* (1880), *In Divers Tones* (1887), *Songs of the Common Day* (1893), *Earth's Enigmas* (1896), *The Vagrant of Time* (1927), *The Iceberg, and Other Poems* (1934), *Further Animal Stories* (1936)

Ross, Sinclair (1908–1996): *As for Me and My House* (1941), *The Well* (1958), *The Lamp at Noon and Other Stories* (1968), *Whir of Gold* (1970), *Sawbones Memorial* (1974)

FRENCH

Balzac, Honoré de (1799–1850): *The Human Comedy* (1842–53)

Baudelaire, Charles Pierre (1821–67): *Les Fleurs du Mal* (1857), *Petits Poèmes en Prose* (1869)

Breton, André (1896–1966): *Nadja* (1928), *Les Vases Communicants* (1932), *L'Amour Fou* (1937)

Camus, Albert† (1913–60): *The Stranger* (1942, rev. 1953), *The Myth of Sisyphus and Other Essays* (1942), *Caligula* (1944), *The Plague* (1947), *The Rebel* (1951), *The Fall* (1956), *The First Man* (1994)

Colette [Sidonie-Gabrielle Colette] (1873–1954): *Claudine* (1900–03), *The Vagabond* (1910), *Mitsou* (1919), *Chéri* (1920)

Dumas, Alexandre, père (1802–70): *The Count of Monte Cristo* (1844–45), *The Three Musketeers* (1844)

Flaubert, Gustave (1821–80): *Madame Bovary* (1857), *Sentimental Education* (1869)

Gide, André† (1869–1951): *The Immoralist* (1902), *Straight Is the Gate* (1909), *The Pastoral Symphony* (1919), *The Counterfeiters* (1926)

Hugo, Victor (1802–85): *The Hunchback of Notre-Dame* (1831), *Les Misérables* (1862)

Malraux, André (1901–76): *Man's Fate* (1933), *Man's Hope* (1937)

Maupassant, [Henri René Albert] Guy de (1850–93): *Boule de Suif* (1880), "La Maison Tellier" (1881), *Bel-Ami* (1885), *Pierre et Jean* (1888)

Mauriac, François† (1885–1970): *Genetrix* (1923), *Thérèse Desqueyroux* (1927), *The Desert of Love* (1925), *A Woman of the Pharisees* (1941)

Montaigne, Michel de (1533–92): *Essais* (1580)

Proust, Marcel (1871–1922): *Remembrance of Things Past* (7 vols., 1913–27)

Rabelais, François (c. 1494–1553): *Gargantua and Pantagruel* (1532–64)

Rimbaud, Arthur (1854–91): *A Season in Hell* (1873), *Illuminations* (1886)

Rostand, Edmond (1868–1918): *Cyrano de Bergerac* (1897)

Sand, George [Amandine-Aurore Lucile Dupin] (1804–76): *Indiana* (1832), *Lélia* (1833), *She and He* (1859)

Sartre, Jean-Paul† (1905–80): *Nausea* (1938), *The Flies* (1943), *Being and Nothingness* (1943), *No Exit* (1945)

Stendhal [Marie Henri Beyle] (1783–1842): *The Red and the Black* (1830), *The Charterhouse of Parma* (1839)

Tocqueville, Alexis de (1805–59): *Democracy in America* (2 vols., 1835; 2 supplementary vols., 1840), *The Old Regime and the Revolution* (1856)

Valéry, Paul (1871–1945): *Charmes* (1922)

Verne, Jules (1828–1905): *A Journey to the Center of the Earth* (1864), *Twenty Thousand Leagues Under the Sea* (1870), *Around the World in Eighty Days* (1873)

Voltaire [François-Marie Arouet] (1694–1778): *Candide* (1759)

Zola, Émile (1840–1902): *Thérèse Raquin* (1867), *Nana* (1880), *Germinal* (1885)

GERMAN

Böll, Heinrich† (1917–85): *Billiards at Half-past Nine* (1959), *The Clown* (1963), *Group Portrait with Lady* (1971), *The Lost Honor of Katharina Blum* (1974)

Goethe, Johann Wolfgang von (1749–1832): *Wilhelm Meister's Apprenticeship* (1795–96), *Faust,* Part I (1808) and Part II (1832)

Grass, Günter (1927–): *The Tin Drum* (1959), *The Flounder* (1977)

Grimm, Jacob (1785–1863) and **Grimm, Wilhelm** (1786–1859): *Grimm's Fairy Tales* (1812–15)

Hesse, Hermann† (1877–1962): *Siddhartha* (1922), *Steppenwolf* (1927)

Kafka, Franz (1883–1924): *Metamorphosis* (1915), *In the Penal Colony* (1919), *The Trial* (1925), *The Castle* (1926), *Amerika* (1927)

Mann, Thomas† (1875–1955): *Buddenbrooks* (1903), *Death in Venice* (1912), *The Magic Mountain* (1924)

Rilke, Rainer Maria (1875–1926): *The Book of Hours* (1905), *New Poems* (2 vols., 1907–08), *Duino Elegies* (1923), *Sonnets to Orpheus* (1923)

ITALIAN

Boccaccio, Giovanni (1313–75): *Decameron* (1349–53)

Calvino, Italo (1923–85): *The Path to the Nest of Spiders* (1947), *Cosmicomics* (1965), *Invisible Cities* (1972), *If on a Winter's Night a Traveler* (1979), *Mr. Palomar* (1985)

Dante Alighieri (1265–1321): *Divine Comedy* (c. 1314–21)

Manzoni, Alessandro (1785–1873): *The Betrothed* (1825–26)

Petrarch [Francesco Petrarca] (1304–74): *Rimes* (1350–74)

LATIN AMERICAN

Borges, Jorge Luis (Argentine, 1899–1986): *Ficciones* (1944), *Labyrinthe* (1962), *The Book of Sand* (1975)

Césaire, Aimé (West Indian, 1913–): *Return to My Native Land* (1939), *The Tragedy of King Christophe* (1963)

Fuentes, Carlos (Mexican, 1928–): *The Death of Artemio Cruz* (1962), *Distant Relations* (1980), *The Old Gringo* (1985), *Myself with Others* (1998)

García Márquez, Gabriel† (Colombian, 1928–): *One Hundred Years of Solitude* (1967), *The Autumn of the Patriarch* (1975), *Love in the Time of Cholera* (1985), *The General in His Labyrinth* (1989), *Of Love and Other Demons* (1994)

Guzmán, Martín Luis (Mexican, 1887–1976): *The Eagle and the Serpent* (1928), *Memorias de Pancho Villa* (4 vols., 1938–40)

Machado de Assis, Joaquim Maria (Brazilian, 1839–1908): *Epitaph of a Small Winner* (1891), *Philosopher or Dog?* (1891), *Dom Casmurro* (1899)

Márquez, Gabriel García. See **García Márquez, Gabriel.**

Naipaul, Sir V(idiadhar) S(urajprasad)† (Trinidadian, 1932–): *The Mystic Masseur* (1957), *A House for Mr. Biswas* (1961), *In a Free State* (1971), *India: A Million Mutinies Now* (1990)

Neruda, Pablo [Neftalí Ricardo Reyes Basoalto]† (Chilean, 1904–73): *Twenty Love Poems and a Story of Despair* (1924), *The Heights of Macchu Picchu* (1947), *Canto General* (1950), *Odes to Common Things* (1954)

Paz, Octavio† (Mexican, 1914–1998): *The Labyrinth of Solitude* (1950), *Sun Stone* (1957), *Salamandra* (1962)

Vargas Llosa, Mario (Peruvian, 1936–): *The Green House* (1966), *Conversation in the Cathedral* (1969), *The War of the End of the World* (1981), *The Notebooks of Don Rigoberto* (1997)

RUSSIAN

Blok, Aleksandr (1880–1921): *Verses About a Beautiful Lady* (1905), *The Puppet Show* (1906), *The Twelve* (1918)

Bulgakov, Mikhail (1891–1940): *The Master and Margarita* (1973)

Chekhov, Anton   (1860–1904): *Uncle Vanya* (1897), *The Seagull* (1897), *The Three Sisters* (1901), *The Cherry Orchard* (1904)

Dostoyevsky, Fyodor   (1821–81): *Notes from the Underground* (1864), *Crime and Punishment* (1867), *The Idiot* (1874), *The Possessed* (1872), *The Brothers Karamazov* (1880)

Gogol, Nikolai   (1809–52): *Arabesques* (1835), *Mirgorod* (1835), *The Inspector General* (1836), *Dead Souls* (1842)

Gorky, Maxim   (1868–1936): *Foma Gordeev* (1899), *The Lower Depths* (1902), *Mother* (1906)

The Yongle Dadian (thesaurus of the Chinese Yongle reign) is the longest book ever written, containing 22,937 chapters in 11,095 volumes. More than 2,000 Chinese scholars worked for five years to complete the book.

Mandelshtam, Osip   (1891–1938): *Kameny* (1913), *Tristia* (1922)

Nabokov, Vladimir   (1899–1977): *Lolita* (1955), *Pale Fire* (1962), *Speak, Memory* (1966)

Pasternak, Boris†   (1890–1960): *My Sister—Life, Summer, 1917* (1922), *Doctor Zhivago* (1957)

Pushkin, Aleksandr   (1799–1837): *Eugene Onegin* (1833)

Solzhenitsyn, Aleksandr†   (1918–   ): *One Day in the Life of Ivan Denisovich* (1962), *The Cancer Ward* (1968), *The Gulag Archipelago* (1973)

Tolstoy, Leo [Count Lev]   (1828–1910): *War and Peace* (1868–69), *Anna Karenina* (1878)

Turgenev, Ivan   (1818–83): *A Month in the Country* (1855), *A Sportsman's Sketches* (1852), *A Nest of Gentlefolk* (1859), *On the Eve* (1860), *Fathers and Sons* (1862), *Smoke* (1867)

OTHER EUROPEAN

Andersen, Hans Christian   (Danish, 1805–75): *Fairy Tales for Children* (1835–42), *Tales and Stories* (1839), *New Fairy Tales* (1843–47), *New Tales and Stories* (1858–67)

Blasco Ibañez, Vicente   (Spanish, 1867–1928): *Blood and Sand* (1898), *The Cabin* (1898), *The Mayflower* (1895), *Reeds and Mud* (1902), *The Four Horsemen of the Apocalypse* (1916)

Canetti, Elias†   (1905–94): *Auto-da-Fé* (1935), *Crowds and Power* (1960)

Čapek, Karel   (Czech, 1890–1938): *R.U.R.: Rossum's Universal Robots* (1920), *Tales from Two Pockets* (1932), *Hordubal* (1933), *Meteor* (1934), *An Ordinary Life* (1934)

Catullus   (Roman, c. 84–54 B.C.): verse

Cervantes [y Saavedra], Miguel de   (Spanish, 1547–1616): *Don Quixote* (1605–15), *Exemplary Stories* (1613)

Dinesen, Isak [Karen Dinesen, Baroness Blixen-Finecke]   (Danish, 1885–1962): *Seven Gothic Tales* (1934), *Out of Africa* (1937), *Winter's Tales* (1942), *Last Tales* (1957)

García Lorca, Federico   (Spanish, 1898–1936): *The Gypsy Ballads* (1928), *The Poet in New York* (1940)

Gombrowicz, Witold   (Polish, 1904–69): *Ferdydurke* (1937), *Pornografia* (1960)

Hamsun, Knut†   (Norwegian, 1859–1952): *Mysteries* (1892), *Hunger* (1899), *Growth of the Soil* (1917)

Hašek, Jaroslav   (Czech, 1883–1923): *The Good Soldier Schweik* (4 vols., 1921–23)

Homer   (Greek, c. 700 B.C.): *The Iliad*, *The Odyssey*

Joyce, James   (Irish, 1882–1941): *Dubliners* (1914), *Portrait of the Artist as a Young Man* (1916), *Ulysses* (1922), *Finnegan's Wake* (1939)

Ovid   (Roman, 43 B.C.–A.D. 17?): *Amores* (c. 16 B.C.), *Heroines*, *Metamorphoses*

Petronius Arbiter   (Roman, ?–66): *Satyricon* (c. 50)

Plutarch   (Greek, c. 46–120): *Moralia, Parallel Lives*

Sappho   (Greek, c. 612–580 B.C.): verse

Swift, Jonathan   (Irish, 1667–1745): *Gulliver's Travels* (1726)

Undset, Sigrid†   (Norwegian, 1882–1949): *Kristin Lavransdatter* (1920–22), *The Master of Hestviken* (1925–27)

Vergil [Publius Vergilius Maro]   (Roman, 70–19 B.C.): *Georgics* (30 B.C.), *Eclogues* (37 B.C.), *Aeneid* (29–19 B.C.)

Wilde, Oscar   (Irish, 1854–1900): *The Picture of Dorian Gray* (1891), *The Importance of Being Earnest* (1895), *Salomé* (1896)

Yeats, William Butler†   (Irish, 1865–1939): *The Wind Among the Reeds* (1899), *The Wild Swans at Coole* (1917), *The Winding Stair* (1929)

LITERARY MOVEMENTS, PERIODS, AND STYLES

Aestheticism   A 19th-century European movement emphasizing aesthetic values over social or moral themes. Advocating "art for art's sake," leading aesthetes imbued their work with a flamboyant, nearly hedonistic quality. Charles Baudelaire and Oscar Wilde were among the movement's most notable figures.

Angry Young Men   A group of English writers, chiefly from the working or middle classes, who became prominent in the 1950s. Their work, characterized by a bitter disillusionment with traditional English society, produced the figure of the antihero, one who rebels against the Establishment. The group's leaders included Kingsley Amis and John Osborne.

baroque   Grandiose, ornate artistic style prevalent from the late 16th to the early 18th century. Initially associated with architectural forms, the term was later applied to the fine arts. In literature, the baroque style employed dramatic motifs and strong emotions in an attempt to expand the artistic vision.

Beat Generation   A group of American writers whose work expressed their alienation from middle-class society during the 1950s and 1960s. Led by Jack Kerouac and Allen Ginsberg, they disdained conventional values, focusing instead on self-discovery through drugs, sexual experience, and exotic travel.

Bloomsbury Group   A group of writers, artists, and intellectuals who held informal discussions in Bloomsbury, a section of London, throughout the early 20th century. Although individual members such as John Maynard Keynes (1883–1946), Lytton Strachey (1880–1932), and Virginia Woolf (1882–1941) were influential figures, the group produced no uniform moral or aesthetic principles.

The saying "The female of the species is more deadly than the male" comes from Rudyard Kipling's 1911 poem "The Female of the Species."

classical   The period in which Greek and Roman literature flourished. Classical writers in Greek include Sophocles, Aeschylus, and Herodotus; in Latin, Vergil, Ovid, and Cicero, among many others.

classicism   In a general sense, any literary style or movement that adheres to the principles of classical literature. In English literature, the term refers to the reaction of 18th- and 19th-century writers to romanticism. *See also* **Neoclassicism.**

Dadaism   A European movement founded during World War I and devoted to the negation of traditional artistic values. Dadaists embraced nihilism, irrationality, and the absurd, often shocking their audiences. The movement's leaders included André Breton (1896–1966) and Tristan Tzara (1896–1963). Breton later broke with Tzara and founded *surrealism.*

Décadents   A group originating in 19th-century France that emphasized the autonomy of art, the rejection of middle-class society, a sophisticated despair, and unconventional, often morbid experiences. Charles Baudelaire and Arthur Rimbaud were among the leading *décadents.*

Elizabethan   Pertaining to the drama and literature produced during the reign of Elizabeth I of England (1558–1603). The Elizabethan age saw the flowering of English literature, with its classical humanism and dazzling achievements in drama and verse forms. William Shakespeare, Christopher Marlowe, and Edmund Spenser were notable Elizabethans.

The Enlightenment   An intellectual movement in the late 17th and 18th centuries that sought the perfection of human society through applied reason. Rejecting conventional religious authority, its members postulated instead a rational unity of God, man, and nature. Jean-Jacques Rousseau and Voltaire were among its most influential thinkers.

Expressionism   An early-20th-century movement stressing individual expression and subjective truth as opposed to conventional forms and objective reality. Its followers used distorted imagery and narrative compression to depict violent emotions and the workings of the subconscious mind.

Futurism   A European movement (c. 1908–20) advocating the abandonment of conventional syntax and the uninhibited use of images drawn from the age of technology. Futurists exalted at the speed of modern life.

Gothic   In literature, the term applies to a specific form of the novel, popular in the late 18th and early 19th centuries, that featured supernatural horrors and violent events, often with a medieval setting.

Graveyard School   A preromantic movement of 18th-century British poets. Its members adopted a melancholy tone in their verses, which were usually set in graveyards or other gloomy locations.

Imagism   A movement in American and English poetry beginning around 1910. Borrowing freely from foreign verse techniques such as the *haiku* and *free verse,* it demanded precision in the use of imagery. Ezra Pound was influential within this movement.

Go to   "Art Movements and Styles" and "Architecture Styles and Movements" in chapter 7; "Philosophical Movements and Schools of Thought" in chapter 10

impressionism   In modern literature, the term refers especially to poems and novels that focus on the author's or character's inner life and subjective impressions. James Joyce, Thomas Mann, Marcel Proust, and Virginia Woolf employed impressionistic techniques, such as the stream of consciousness.

Irish Renaissance   A period of intense creative energy, beginning in the 19th century, aimed at the revival of Ireland's native culture. At the height of the movement, from 1900 to 1920, writers such as John Millington Synge and William Butler Yeats turned to traditional Irish folklore and themes for inspiration. The movement's influence continues to the present.

Jacobean   Pertaining to the literature produced during the reign of James I of England (1603–25). The period was one of great social upheaval. Reflecting the times, English literature rejected Elizabethan optimism for a darker, more cynical view of human affairs. William Shakespeare's greatest works were written in this period.

Lost Generation   A term coined by Gertrude Stein to describe a group of expatriate American writers who came into prominence after World War I (1914–18). Their work was characterized by disillusionment with postwar society. F. Scott Fitzgerald and Ernest Hemingway were among the group's notable figures.

metaphysical   Referring to a style of primarily 17th-century poetry emphasizing dramatic imagery, complex metaphors, and language in everyday use. John Donne is usually considered the greatest of the metaphysical poets.

modernism   A mid-20th-century (c. 1910–45) movement emphasizing a self-conscious break with past literary forms and the development of experimental techniques and fresh motifs. The Irish author James Joyce's use of interior monologue and myth as narrative structures typify modernism's concern with untried forms of expression.

naturalism   A late-19th-century and early-20th-century movement that rejected sentimentality, subjectivity, and preconceived notions of morality in art. Naturalist writers often chose their subjects from the

Literature

lower depths of society, viewing their characters' sordid lives or tragic fates with scientific detachment. Thomas Hardy, Émile Zola, and Theodore Dreiser were among the leading naturalists.

Neoclassicism   In European literature, the term refers to the emphasis placed on balance, restraint, clarity, and proportion in the works of late-17th-century and 18th-century writers such as Alexander Page, Jean Racine, Jonathan Swift, and Voltaire.

Parnassians   Late-19th-century school of French poets. Reacting against the emotionalism and subjectivity of romanticism, they attempted to replicate the precision of plastic arts such as sculpture in their work. The objective poetry thus created was a precursor of the realistic novel and drama.

Pre-Raphaelites   A group of poets and artists established in London in 1848. They asserted the superiority of nature in their work, rejecting formal or academic techniques in favor of sensual imagery and religious symbolism. Dante Gabriel Rossetti was one of its leaders.

realism   Movement originating in the late 19th century that portrayed the details of everyday life in factual, objective language and without idealization. The author sought to let the story tell itself, devoid of sentiment and thematic manipulation. Honoré de Balzac, Gustave Flaubert, and Henrik Ibsen wrote in this manner.

Renaissance   From the French word for "rebirth." It pertains to the literature produced in Europe from the mid–14th century to the end of the 16th century. Marked by a revival in classical values and learning, the period witnessed an outburst of creative activity unmatched in the history of western culture. Miguel de Cervantes, François Rabelais, and William Shakespeare were among the leading figures of the period.

Romanticism   Movement originating in 18th-century Europe as a reaction to Neoclassicism. Romantic works typically emphasized intense emotions, sensual imagery, and individualism and often featured lurid themes and sensational plots. Samuel Taylor Coleridge, Johann Goethe, and Jean-Jacques Rousseau are usually associated with this movement.

Socialist Realism   A state-mandated literary style that writers were obligated to follow in the former Soviet Union (c. 1932–90). Under this doctrine, all literary works were to display the steady progress of Soviet society toward achieving the goals of socialism. In practice, it was a tool by which the state could control freedom of expression.

Sturm und Drang   German phrase meaning "storm and stress." Nationalistic, late-18th-century German movement emphasizing dramatic story lines, turbulent emotions, and the individual's revolt against society. Johann Goethe's early work was written in this fashion.

Surrealism   A movement founded in France in the 1920s. It attempted to express the workings of the subconscious mind through automatic writing and irrational, often juxtaposed imagery. André Breton was the movement's principal architect.

Symbolism   A European movement originating with French poetry in the late 19th century. It sacrificed objective representation and realistic narrative techniques in favor of a pattern of images or symbols that conveyed the author's meaning. Joseph Conrad, Arthur Rimbaud, and Virginia Woolf employed symbolism in their writing.

Transcendentalism   A 19th-century American movement centered in New England. It advocated reliance on personal conscience over the dictates of external authority or moral conventions. Ralph Waldo Emerson and Henry David Thoreau were among its leaders.

Victorian   Pertaining to the drama and literature produced during the reign of Queen Victoria of England (1837–1901). Although associated with strict codes of moral conduct and social stagnation, the age witnessed a crisis in religious faith and growing social unrest. Joseph Conrad, Charles Dickens, George Eliot, George Bernard Shaw, and Oscar Wilde produced much of their greatest work during this period.

PSEUDONYMS OF FAMOUS AUTHORS

Real Name	Pseudonym or Pen Name
Brian W. Aldiss	Jael Cracken, Arch Mendicant, Peter Pica, John Runciman, C. C. Shackelton
Kingsley Amis	Robert Markham
Hans Christian Andersen	Villiam Christian Walter
Poul Anderson	A. A. Craig, Michael Karageorge, Winston P. Sanders
François-Marie Arouet	Voltaire
Isaac Asimov	Dr. A., Paul French, Dale F. George
Louis Auchincloss	Andrew Lee
Neftalí Ricardo Reyes Basoalto	Pablo Neruda
L. Frank Baum	Edith Van Dyne
Robert Benchley	Guy Fawkes
Marie Henri Beyle	Stendhal
Ambrose Bierce	Dod Grile
Eric Arthur Blair	George Orwell
Anne Brontë	Acton Bell, Lady Geralda, Olivia Vernon, Alexandria Zenobia
Charlotte Brontë	C. B., Currer Bell, Marquis of Douro, Genius, Lord Charles Wellesley
Emily Brontë	R. Acton, Ellis Bell
William S. Burroughs	William Lee
Barbara Cartland	Barbara Hamilton McCorquodale
Agatha Christie	Agatha Christie Mallowen, Mary Westmacott
Arthur C. Clarke	E. G. O'Brien, Charles Willis
Samuel Langhorne Clemens	Mark Twain
Michael Crichton	Jeffrey Hudson, John Lange
Edward Estlin Cummings	e. e. cummings
Karen Dinesen, Baroness Blixen-Finecke	Isak Dinesen
Charles Lutwidge Dodgson	Lewis Carroll
Amandine-Aurore-Lucile Dupin	George Sand
Mary Ann Evans	George Eliot
Howard Fast	E. V. Cunningham, Walter Ericson
Erle Stanley Gardner	A. A. Fair, Charles M. Green, Carleton Kendrake, Charles J. Kenny
Theodor Seuss Geisel	Theo Lesieg, Dr. Seuss
Edward St. John Gorey	Eduard Blutig, Mrs. Regera Dowdy, Redway Grode, O. Mude, Hyacinthe Phypps, Ogdred Weary, Dreary Wodge
Dashiell Hammett	Peter Collinson
Robert A. Heinlein	Anson MacDonald, Lyle Monroe, John Riverside, Caleb Saunders, Simon York
Eleanor Alice Burford Hibbert	Eleanor Burford, Philippa Carr, Elbur Ford, Victoria Holt, Kathleen Kellow, Jean Plaidy, Ellalice Tate
L. Ron Hubbard	Elron, Tom Esterbrook, Rene La Fayette, Capt. B. A. Northrop, Kurt von Rachen
Ford Herman Hueffer	Ford Madox Ford
E. Howard Hunt	John Baxter, Gordon Davis, Robert Dietrich, David St. John
LeRoi Jones	Imamu Amiri Baraka
Dean Koontz	David Axton, Brian Coffey, Deanna Dwyer, K. R. Dwyer, John Hill, Leigh Nichols, Andrew North, Richard Paige, Owen West, Aaron Wolfe
Józef Teodor Konrad Korzeniowski	Joseph Conrad
Louis LaMoore	Louis L'Amour, Tex Burns
T. E. Lawrence	J. H. Ross, T. E. Shaw
Manfred Lee and Frederic Dannay	Ellery Queen, Barnaby Ross
Salvatore A. Lombino	Hunt Collins, Evan Hunter, Richard Marsten, Ed McBain
Robert Ludlum	Jonathon Ryder, Michael Shepherd
James du Maresq	James Clavell
Alan McCrae	Alan Moorehead

continues

Literature

Real Name	Pseudonym or Pen Name
Kenneth Millar	John Ross Macdonald, Ross Macdonald
Edna St. Vincent Millay	Nancy Boyd
William Anthony Parker White	Theo Durrant
Nevil Shute Norway	Nevil Shute
Conor Cruise O'Brien	Donat O'Donnell
Dorothy Parker	Constant Reader
Eric Partridge	Vigilans
William Sydney Porter	O. Henry
William Saroyan	Sirak Goryan
Terry Southern	Maxwell Kenton
Irving Stone	Irving Tannenbaum
Gore Vidal	Edgar Box
Nathan Weinstein	Nathanael West
J. A. Wight	James Herriot
John Burgess Wilson	Anthony Burgess, Joseph Kell
Chloe Anthony Wofford	Toni Morrison
Willard Huntington Wright	S. S. Van Dine

POET LAUREATES

ENGLISH

In 1616, Ben Jonson was named England's first poet laureate; however, the title did not become an official royal office until 1668, when John Dryden assumed the honored post. Since that time, the office has been awarded for life. The poet laureate is responsible for composing poems for court and national occasions. At the time of each laureate's death, it is the duty of the prime minister to nominate successors from which the reigning sovereign will choose. It is the Lord Chamberlain who appoints the poet laureate by issuing a warrant to the laureate-elect. The life appointment is always announced in the *London Gazette*.

Laureateship	Poet	Birth and Death Dates
1668–88	John Dryden	1631–1700
1689–92	Thomas Shadwell	1643?–92
1692–1715	Nahum Tate	1652–1715
1715–18	Nicholas Rowe	1674–1718
1718–30	Laurence Eusden	1688–1730
1730–57	Colley Cibber	1671–1757
*1757–85	William Whitehead	1715–85
1785–90	Thomas Warton	1728–90
1790–1813	Henry James Pye	1745–1813
1813–43	Robert Southey	1774–1843
1843–50	William Wordsworth	1770–1850
†1850–92	Alfred, Lord Tennyson	1809–92
1896–1913	Alfred Austin	1835–1913
1913–30	Robert Bridges	1844–1930
1930–67	John Masefield	1878–1967
1968–72	Cecil Day-Lewis	1904–72
1972–84	Sir John Betjeman	1906–84
1984–98	Ted Hughes	1930–98
1999–	Andrew Motion	1952–

* The 1757 appointment was declined by Thomas Gray.   † The 1850 appointment was declined by Samuel Rogers.

AMERICAN

In 1986, Robert Penn Warren was named the first poet laureate of the United States. The American poet laureate is appointed annually by the Librarian of Congress.

Laureateship	Poet	Birth and Death Dates
1986–87	Robert Penn Warren	1905–89
1987–88	Richard Wilbur	1921–
1988–90	Howard Nemerov	1920–91
1990–91	Mark Strand	1934–
1991–92	Joseph Brodsky	1940–96
1992–93	Mona Van Duyn	1921–
1993–95	Rita Dove	1952–
1995–97	Robert Hass	1941–
1997–2000	Robert Pinsky	1940–
2001–	Billy Collins	1941–

BOOK AWARDS AND THEIR RECIPIENTS

NOBEL PRIZE FOR LITERATURE

The Swedish Academy in Stockholm annually awards this prize to a writer who "shall have produced in the field of literature the most outstanding work in an ideal direction." Recipients may be of any nationality.

2001 V. S. Naipaul, Great Britain
2000 Gao Xingjian, China
1999 Günter Grass, Germany
1998 José Saramago, Portugal
1997 Dario Fo, Italy
1996 Wisława Szymborska, Poland
1995 Seamus Heaney, Ireland
1994 Kenzaburo Oe, Japan
1993 Toni Morrison, U.S.
1992 Derek Walcott, West Indies
1991 Nadine Gordimer, South Africa
1990 Octavio Paz, Mexico
1989 Camilo José Cela, Spain
1988 Naguib Mahfouz, Egypt
1987 Joseph Brodsky, U.S.
1986 Wole Soyinka, Nigeria
1985 Claude Simon, France
1984 Jaroslav Seifert, Czechoslovakia
1983 William Golding, Great Britain
1982 Gabriel García Márquez, Colombia
1981 Elias Canetti, Bulgaria
1980 Czesław Miłosz, Poland–U.S.
1979 Odysseus Elytis, Greece
1978 Isaac Bashevis Singer, U.S.
1977 Vicente Aleixandre, Spain
1976 Saul Bellow, U.S.
1975 Eugenio Montale, Italy
1974 Eyvind Johnson, Sweden, and Harry Edmund Martinson, Sweden

1973 Patrick White, Australia
1972 Heinrich Böll, Federal Republic of Germany
1971 Pablo Neruda, Chile
1970 Aleksandr Solzhenitsyn, U.S.S.R.
1969 Samuel Beckett, Ireland
1968 Yasunari Kawabata, Japan
1967 Miguel Angel Asturias, Guatemala
1966 Samuel Joseph Agnon, Israel, and Nelly Sachs, Sweden
1965 Mikhail Sholokhov, U.S.S.R.
1964 Jean-Paul Sartre, France (declined the prize)
1963 Gorgios Seferis, Greece
1962 John Steinbeck, U.S.
1961 Ivo Andric, Yugoslavia
1960 Saint-John Perse, France
1959 Salvatore Quasimodo, Italy
1958 Boris Pasternak, U.S.S.R.
1957 Albert Camus, France
1956 Juan Ramón Jiménez, Spain
1955 Halldór Kiljian Laxness, Iceland
1954 Ernest Hemingway, U.S.
1953 Sir Winston Churchill, Great Britain
1952 François Mauriac, France
1951 Pär Lagerkvist, Sweden
1950 Bertrand Russell, Great Britain
1949 William Faulkner, U.S.
1948 T. S. Eliot, Great Britain
1947 André Gide, France
1946 Hermann Hesse, Germany *continues*

Nobel Prize for Literature *continued*

1945	Gabriela Mistral, Chile	1920	Knut Hamsun, Norway
1944	Johannes V. Jensen, Denmark	1919	Carl F. G. Spitteler, Switzerland
1943–	No Award	1918	No Award
1940		1917	Karl A. Gjellerup, Denmark, and Henrik Pontoppidan, Denmark
1939	Frans Eemil Sillanpää, Finland		
1938	Pearl S. Buck, U.S.	1916	Verner von Heidenstam, Sweden
1937	Robert Martin du Gard, France	1915	Romain Rolland, France
1936	Eugene O'Neill, U.S.	1914	No Award
1935	No Award	1913	Rabindranath Tagore, India
1934	Luigi Pirandello, Italy	1912	Gerhart Hauptmann, Germany
1933	Ivan A. Bunin, Russia	1911	Maurice Maeterlinck, Belgium
1932	John Galsworthy, Great Britain	1910	Paul J. L. Heyse, Germany
1931	Erik A. Karlfeldt, Sweden	1909	Selma Lagerlöf, Sweden
1930	Sinclair Lewis, U.S.	1908	Rudolf Eucken, Germany
1929	Thomas Mann, Germany	1907	Rudyard Kipling, Great Britain
1928	Sigrid Undset, Norway	1906	Giusuè Carducci, Italy
1927	Henri Bergson, France	1905	Henryk Sienkiewicz, Poland
1926	Grazia Deledda, Italy	1904	Frédéric Mistral, France, and José Echegaray, Spain
1925	George Bernard Shaw, Great Britain		
1924	Władysław S. Reymount, Poland	1903	Björnstjerne Björnson, Norway
1923	William Butler Yeats, Ireland	1902	Theodor Mommsen, Germany
1922	Jacinto Benavente, Spain	1901	René F. A. Sully-Prudhomme, France
1921	Anatole France, France		

PULITZER PRIZE IN LETTERS

Awarded by Columbia University in New York for distinguished work by an American author.

FICTION

2002	*Empire Falls* Richard Russo	1982	*Rabbit Is Rich* John Updike
2001	*The Amazing Adventures of Kavalier & Clay* Michael Chabon	1981	*A Confederacy of Dunces* John Kennedy Toole
		1980	*The Executioner's Song* Norman Mailer
2000	*Interpreter of Maladies* Jhumpa Lahiri	1979	*The Stories of John Cheever* John Cheever
1999	*The Hours* Michael Cunningham	1978	*Elbow Room* James Alan McPherson
1998	*American Pastoral* Philip Roth	1977	No Award
1997	*Martin Dressler: The Tale of an American Dreamer* Stephen Millhauser	1976	*Humboldt's Gift* Saul Bellow
		1975	*The Killer Angels* Michael Shaara
1996	*Independence Day* Richard Ford	1974	No Award
1995	*The Stone Diaries* Carol Shields	1973	*The Optimist's Daughter* Eudora Welty
1994	*The Shipping News* E. Annie Proulx	1972	*Angle of Repose* Wallace Stegner
1993	*A Good Scent from a Strange Mountain* Robert Olen Butler	1971	No Award
		1970	*Collected Stories* Jean Stafford
1992	*A Thousand Acres* Jane Smiley	1969	*House Made of Dawn* N. Scott Momaday
1991	*Rabbit at Rest* John Updike	1968	*The Confessions of Nat Turner* William Styron
1990	*The Mambo Kings Play Songs of Love* Oscar Hijuelos	1967	*The Fixer* Bernard Malamud
		1966	*The Collected Stories of Katherine Anne Porter* Katherine Anne Porter
1989	*Breathing Lessons* Anne Tyler		
1988	*Beloved* Toni Morrison	1965	*The Keepers of the House* Shirley Ann Grau
1987	*A Summons to Memphis* Peter Taylor	1964	No Award
1986	*Lonesome Dove* Larry McMurtry	1963	*The Reivers* William Faulkner
1985	*Foreign Affairs* Alison Lurie	1962	*The Edge of Sadness* Edwin O'Connor
1984	*Ironweed* William Kennedy	1961	*To Kill a Mockingbird* Harper Lee
1983	*The Color Purple* Alice Walker	1960	*Advise and Consent* Allen Drury

1959	*The Travels of Jaimie McPheeters* Robert Lewis Taylor	1939	*The Yearling* Marjorie Kinnan Rawlings
1958	*A Death in the Family* James Agee	1938	*The Late George Apley* John Phillips Marquand
1957	No Award	1937	*Gone with the Wind* Margaret Mitchell
1956	*Andersonville* MacKinlay Kantor	1936	*Honey in the Horn* Harold L. Davis
1955	*A Fable* William Faulkner	1935	*Now in November* Josephine Winslow Johnson
1954	No Award	1934	*Lamb in His Bosom* Caroline Miller
1953	*The Old Man and the Sea* Ernest Hemingway	1933	*The Store* T. S. Stribling
1952	*The Caine Mutiny* Herman Wouk	1932	*The Good Earth* Pearl S. Buck
1951	*The Town* Conrad Richter	1931	*Years of Grace* Margaret Ayer Barnes
1950	*The Way West* A. B. Guthrie, Jr.	1930	*Laughing Boy* Oliver LaFarge
1949	*Guard of Honor* James Gould Cozzens	1929	*Scarlet Sister Mary* Julia M. Peterkin
1948	*Tales of the South Pacific* James A. Michener	1928	*The Bridge of San Luis Rey* Thornton Wilder
1947	*All the King's Men* Robert Penn Warren	1927	*Early Autumn* Louis Bromfield
1946	No Award	1926	*Arrowsmith* Sinclair Lewis
1945	*A Bell for Adano* John Hersey	1925	*So Big* Edna Ferber
1944	*Journey in the Dark* Martin Flavin	1924	*The Able McLaughlins* Margaret Wilson
1943	*Dragon's Teeth* Upton Sinclair	1923	*One of Ours* Willa Cather
1942	*In This Our Life* Ellen Glasgow	1922	*Alice Adams* Booth Tarkington
1941	No Award	1921	*The Age of Innocence* Edith Wharton
1940	*The Grapes of Wrath* John Steinbeck	1920	No Award
		1919	*The Magnificent Ambersons* Booth Tarkington
		1918	*His Family* Ernest Poole

POETRY

2002	*Practical Gods* Carl Dennis	1974	*The Dolphin* Robert Lowell
2001	*Different Hours* Stephen Dunn	1973	*Up Country* Maxine Kumin
2000	*Repair* C. K. Williams	1972	*Collected Poems* James Wright
1999	*Blizzard of One* Mark Strand	1971	*The Carrier of Ladders* William S. Merwin
1998	*Black Zodiac* Charles Wright	1970	*Untitled Subjects* Richard Howard
1997	*Alive Together: New and Selected Poems* Lisel Mueller	1969	*Of Being Numerous* George Oppen
1996	*The Dream of the Unified Field* Jorie Graham	1968	*The Hard Hours* Anthony Hecht
1995	*Simple Truth* Philip Levine	1967	*Live or Die* Anne Sexton
1994	*Neon Vernacular* Yusef Komunyakaa	1966	*Selected Poems* Richard Eberhart
1993	*The Wild Iris* Louise Glück	1965	*77 Dream Songs* John Berryman
1992	*Selected Poems* James Tate	1964	*At the End of the Open Road* Louis Simpson
1991	*Near Changes* Mona Van Duyn	1963	*Pictures from Breughel* William Carlos Williams
1990	*The World Doesn't End* Charles Simic	1962	*Poems* Alan Dugan
1989	*New and Collected Poems* Richard Wilbur	1961	*Times Three: Selected Verse from Three Decades* Phyllis McGinley
1988	*Partial Accounts: New and Selected Poems* William Meredith	1960	*Heart's Needle* W. D. Snodgrass
1987	*Thomas and Beulah* Rita Dove	1959	*Selected Poems 1928–1958* Stanley Kunitz
1986	*The Flying Change* Henry Taylor	1958	*Promises: Poems 1954–1956* Robert Penn Warren
1985	*Yin* Carolyn Kizer	1957	*Things of This World* Richard Wilbur
1984	*American Primitive* Mary Oliver	1956	*Poems, North & South* Elizabeth Bishop
1983	*Selected Poems* Galway Kinnell	1955	*Collected Poems* Wallace Stevens
1982	*The Collected Poems* Sylvia Plath	1954	*The Waking* Theodore Roethke
1981	*The Morning of the Poem* James Schuyler	1953	*Collected Poems 1917–1952* Archibald MacLeish
1980	*Selected Poems* Donald Justice	1952	*Collected Poems* Marianne Moore
1979	*Now and Then: Poems 1976–1978* Robert Penn Warren	1951	*Complete Poems* Carl Sandburg
1978	*Collected Poems* Howard Nemerov	1950	*Annie Allen* Gwendolyn Brooks
1977	*Divine Comedies* James Merrill	1949	*Terror and Decorum* Peter Viereck
1976	*Self-Portrait in a Convex Mirror* John Ashbery	1948	*The Age of Anxiety* W. H. Auden
1975	*Turtle Island* Gary Snyder	1947	*Lord Weary's Castle* Robert Lowell
		1946	No Award

continues

Pulitzer Prize, Poetry *continued*

1945	*V-Letter and Other Poems* Karl Shapiro	1929	*John Brown's Body* Stephen Vincent Benét
1944	*Western Star* Stephen Vincent Benét	1928	*Tristram* Edwin Arlington Robinson
1943	*A Witness Tree* Robert Frost	1927	*Fiddler's Farewell* Leonora Speyer
1942	*The Dust Which Is God* William Rose Benét	1926	*What's O'Clock* Amy Lowell
1941	*Sunderland Capture* Leonard Bacon	1925	*The Man Who Died Twice* Edwin Arlington Robinson
1940	*Collected Poems* Mark Van Doren	1924	*New Hampshire: A Poem with Notes and Grace Notes* Robert Frost
1939	*Selected Poems* John Gould Fletcher		
1938	*Cold Morning Sky* Marya Zaturenska	1923	*The Ballad of the Harp-Weaver and Other Poems* Edna St. Vincent Millay
1937	*A Further Range* Robert Frost		
1936	*Strange Holiness* Robert P. T. Coffin	1922	*Collected Poems* Edwin Arlington Robinson
1935	*Bright Ambush* Audrey Wurdemann	1921	No Award
1934	*Collected Verse* Robert Hillyer	1920	No Award
1933	*Conquistador* Archibald MacLeish	1919	*Old Road to Paradise* Margaret Widdemer and *Corn Huskers* Carl Sandburg
1932	*The Flowering Stone* George Dillon		
1931	*Collected Poems* Robert Frost	1918	*Love Songs* Sara Teasdale
1930	*Selected Poems* Conrad Aiken		

DRAMA

2002	*Topdog/Underdog* Susan Lori-Parks	1974	No Award
2001	*Proof* David Auburn	1973	*That Championship Season* Jason Miller
2000	*Dinner with Friends* Donald Margulies	1972	No Award
1999	*Wit* Margaret Edson	1971	*The Effect of Gamma Rays on Man-in-the-Moon Marigolds* Paul Zindel
1998	*How I Learned to Drive* Paula Vogel		
1997	No Award	1970	*No Place to Be Somebody* Charles Gordone
1996	*Rent* Jonathan Larson	1969	*The Great White Hope* Howard Sackler
1995	*The Young Man from Atlanta* Horton Foote	1968	No Award
1994	*Three Tall Women* Edward Albee	1967	*A Delicate Balance* Edward Albee
1993	*Angels in America: Millenium Approaches* Tony Kushner	1966	No Award
		1965	*The Subject Was Roses* Frank D. Gilroy
1992	*The Kentucky Cycle* Robert Schenkkan	1964	No Award
1991	*Lost in Yonkers* Neil Simon	1963	No Award
1990	*The Piano Lesson* August Wilson	1962	*How to Succeed in Business Without Really Trying* music and lyrics by Frank Loesser and book by Abe Burrows
1989	*The Heidi Chronicles* Wendy Wasserstein		
1988	*Driving Miss Daisy* Alfred Uhry		
1987	*Fences* August Wilson	1961	*All the Way Home* Tad Mosel
1986	No Award	1960	*Fiorello!* book by Jerome Weidman and George Abbott; music by Jerry Bock; lyrics by Sheldon Harnick
1985	*Sunday in the Park with George* music and lyrics by Stephen Sondheim; book by James Lapine		
		1959	*J. B.* Archibald MacLeish
1984	*Glengarry Glen Ross* David Mamet	1958	*Look Homeward Angel* Ketti Frings
1983	*'night, Mother* Marsha Norman	1957	*Long Day's Journey Into Night* Eugene O'Neill
1982	*A Soldier's Play* Charles Fuller	1956	*The Diary of Anne Frank* Albert Hackett and Frances Goodrich
1981	*Crimes of the Heart* Beth Henley		
1980	*Talley's Folly* Lanford Wilson	1955	*Cat on a Hot Tin Roof* Tennessee Williams
1979	*Buried Child* Sam Shepard	1954	*The Teahouse of the August Moon* John Patrick
1978	*The Gin Game* Donald L. Coburn	1953	*Picnic* William Inge
1977	*The Shadow Box* Michael Cristofer	1952	*The Shrike* Joseph Kramm
1976	*A Chorus Line* conceived, choreographed, and directed by Michael Bennett; book by James Kirkwood and Nicholas Dante; music by Marvin Hamlisch and lyrics by Edward Kleban	1951	No Award
		1950	*South Pacific* Richard Rodgers, book by Oscar Hammerstein II and Joshua Logan; lyrics by Hammerstein
		1949	*Death of a Salesman* Arthur Miller
1975	*Seascape* Edward Albee	1948	*A Streetcar Named Desire* Tennessee Williams

1947	No Award	1933	*Both Your Houses* Maxwell Anderson
1946	*State of the Union* Russell Crouse and Howard Lindsay	1932	*Of Thee I Sing* book by George S. Kaufman and Morrie Ryskind; lyrics by Ira Gershwin
1945	*Harvey* Mary Chase	1931	*Alison's House* Susan Glaspell
1944	No Award	1930	*The Green Pastures* Marc Connelly
1943	*The Skin of Our Teeth* Thornton Wilder	1929	*Street Scene* Elmer L. Rice
1942	No Award	1928	*Strange Interlude* Eugene O'Neill
1941	*There Shall Be No Night* Robert E. Sherwood	1927	*In Abraham's Bosom* Paul Green
1940	*The Time of Your Life* William Saroyan	1926	*Craig's Wife* George Kelly
1939	*Abe Lincoln in Illinois* Robert E. Sherwood	1925	*They Knew What They Wanted* Sidney Howard
1938	*Our Town* Thornton Wilder	1924	*Hell-Bent fer Heaven* Hatcher Hughes
1937	*You Can't Take It with You* Moss Hart and George S. Kaufman	1923	*Icebound* Owen Davis
		1922	*Anna Christie* Eugene O'Neill
1936	*Idiot's Delight* Robert E. Sherwood	1921	*Miss Lulu Bett* Zona Gale
1935	*The Old Maid* Zoë Akins	1920	*Beyond the Horizon* Eugene O'Neill
1934	*Men in White* Sidney Kingsley	1919	No Award
		1918	*Why Marry?* Jesse Lynch Williams

NATIONAL BOOK AWARD

The National Book Award was known as the American Book Award from 1980 to 1986. The award reverted to its original name in 1987.

FICTION

2001	*The Corrections* Jonathan Franzen	1973	*Chimera* John Barth
2000	*In America* Susan Sontag	1972	*The Complete Stories of Flannery O'Connor* Flannery O'Connor
1999	*Waiting* Ha Jin		
1998	*Charming Billy* Alice McDermott	1971	*Mr. Sammler's Planet* Saul Bellow
1997	*Cold Mountain* Charles Frazier	1970	*Them* Joyce Carol Oates
1996	*Ship Fever and Other Stories* Andrea Barrett	1969	*Steps* Jerzy Kosinski
1995	*Sabbath's Theater* Philip Roth	1968	*The Eighth Day* Thornton Wilder
1994	*A Frolic of His Own* William Gaddis	1967	*The Fixer* Bernard Malamud
1993	*The Shipping News* E. Annie Proulx	1966	*The Collected Stories of Katherine Anne Porter* Katherine Anne Porter
1992	*All the Pretty Horses* Cormac McCarthy		
1991	*Mating* Norman Rush	1965	*Herzog* Saul Bellow
1990	*The Middle Passage* Charles Johnson	1964	*The Centaur* John Updike
1989	*Spartina* John Casey	1963	*Morte D'Urban* J. F. Powers
1988	*Paris Trout* Pete Dexter	1962	*The Moviegoer* Walker Percy
1987	*Paco's Story* Larry Heinemann	1961	*The Waters of Kronos* Conrad Richter
1986	*World's Fair* E. L. Doctorow	1960	*Goodbye, Columbus* Philip Roth
1985	*White Noise* Don DeLillo	1959	*The Magic Barrel* Bernard Malamud
1984	*Victory over Japan* Ellen Gilchrist	1958	*The Wapshot Chronicle* John Cheever
1983	*The Color Purple* Alice Walker	1957	*Field of Vision* Wright Morris
1982	*Rabbit Is Rich* John Updike	1956	*Ten North Frederick* John O'Hara
1981	*Plains Song* Wright Morris	1955	*A Fable* William Faulkner
1980	*Sophie's Choice* William Styron	1954	*The Adventures of Augie March* Saul Bellow
1979	*Going After Cacciato* Tim O'Brien	1953	*Invisible Man* Ralph Ellison
1978	*Blood Ties* Mary Lee Settle	1952	*From Here to Eternity* James Jones
1977	*The Spectator Bird* Wallace Stegner	1951	*The Collected Stories of William Faulkner* William Faulkner
1976	*J. R.* William Gaddis		
1975	*Dog Soldiers* Robert Stone and *The Hair of Harold Roux* Thomas Williams	1950	*The Man with the Golden Arm* Nelson Algren
1974	*Gravity's Rainbow* Thomas Pynchon and *A Crown of Feathers and Other Stories* Isaac Bashevis Singer		

continues

Literature

National Book Award *continued*

NONFICTION

From 1964 to 1979, the category of general nonfiction was eliminated. Prizes were given instead in specialized categories, such as history, contemporary affairs, the sciences, and biography.

2001   *The Noonday Demon: An Atlas of Depression* Andrew Solomon

2000   *In the Heart of the Sea: The Tragedy of the Whaleship Essex* Nathaniel Philbrick

1999   *Embracing Defeat: Japan in the Wake of World War II* John W. Dower

1998   *Slaves in the Family* Edward Ball

1997   *American Sphinx: The Character of Thomas Jefferson* Joseph Ellis

1996   *An American Requiem: God, My Father, and the War That Came Between Us* James Carroll

1995   *The Haunted Land: Facing Europe's Ghosts after Communism* Tina Rosenberg

1994   *How We Die: Reflections on Life's Final Chapter* Sherwin B. Nuland

1993   *United States: Essays 1952–1992* Gore Vidal

1992   *Becoming a Man: Half a Life Story* Paul Monette

1991   *Freedom* Orlando Patterson

1990   *The House of Morgan: An American Banking Dynasty and the Rise of Modern Finance* Ron Chernow

1989   *From Beirut to Jerusalem* Thomas L. Friedman

1988   *A Bright Shining Lie: John Paul Vann and America in Vietnam* Neil Sheehan

1987   *The Making of the Atom Bomb* Richard Rhodes

1986   *Arctic Dreams* Barry Lopez

1985   *Common Ground: A Turbulent Decade in the Lives of Three American Families* J. Anthony Lukas

1984   *Andrew Jackson and the Course of American Democracy, 1833–1845* Robert V. Remini

1983   *China: Alive in the Bitter Sea* Fox Butterfield

1982   *The Soul of a New Machine* Tracy Kidder

1981   *China Men* Maxine Hong Kingston

1980   *The Right Stuff* Tom Wolfe

1963   *Henry James, Vol. II: The Conquest of London; Henry James, Vol. III: The Middle Years* Leon Edel

1962   *The City in History: Its Origins, Its Transformations and Its Prospects* Lewis Mumford

1961   *The Rise and Fall of the Third Reich* William L. Shirer

1960   *James Joyce* Richard Ellmann

1959   *Mistress to an Age: A Life of Madame de Stael* J. Christopher Herold

1958   *The Lion and the Throne* Catherine Drinker Bowen

1957   *Russia Leaves the War* George F. Kennan

1956   *An American in Italy* Herbert Kubly

1955   *The Measure of Man* Joseph Wood Krutch

1954   *A Stillness at Appomattox* Bruce Catton

1953   *The Course of an Empire* Bernard A. DeVoto

1952   *The Sea Around Us* Rachel Carson

1951   *Herman Melville* Newton Arvin

1950   *Ralph Waldo Emerson* Ralph L. Rusk

THE GREAT BOOKS: A READING LIST

These books and writings about our civilization are recommended by the Great Books Foundation. They are listed in alphabetical order by author.

Adams, Henry	*The Education of Henry Adams* (1907)
Aeschylus	*Agamemnōn* (458 B.C.)
Aristotle (4th century B.C.)	*Politics*
	"On Happiness" (excerpt from *Nicomachean Ethics*)
	"On Tragedy"
Augustine, St.	*The City of God* (413–26)
Bible	*Genesis*
	Exodus
	Job
	Ecclesiastes
	The Gospel of Mark
Burke, Edmund	*Reflections on the Revolution in France* (1790)
Chaucer, Geoffrey	*The Canterbury Tales* (after 1387)

Chekhov, Anton	*Rothschild's Fiddle* (1894)
	Uncle Vanya (1897)
Clausewitz, Karl von	"What Is War?" [excerpt from *On War* (1833)]
Conrad, Joseph	"Heart of Darkness" [story in *Typhoon and Youth* (1902)]
Dante, Alighieri	"The Inferno" [canticle in *Divine Comedy* (c. 1314–21)]
Darwin, Charles	"The Moral Sense of Man and the Lower Animals" [excerpts from *On the Origin of Species* (1859) and *The Descent of Man* (1871)]
Dewey, John	"The Virtues" [excerpt from *Ethics* (1908)]
	"Habits and Will" [excerpt from *Human Nature and Conduct* (1922)]
Diderot, Denis	*Rameau's Nephew* (posthumously published in 1805)
Dostoevsky, Fyodor	*Notes from the Underground* (1864)
Euripides (5th century B.C.)	*Medea* (431 B.C.)
	Iphigeneia at Aulis
Flaubert, Gustave	"A Simple Heart" (short story, c. 1850)
Freud, Sigmund	"On Dreams" [excerpt from *The Interpretation of Dreams* (1899)]
Gibbon, Edward	*The History of the Decline and Fall of the Roman Empire* (1776, 1781, 1787–88)
Goethe, Johann Wolfgang von	*Faust,* Part I (1808)
Gogol, Nikolai	"The Overcoat" [First part of novel *Dead Souls* (1842)]
Hamilton, Alexander; Jay, John; Madison, James	The Federalist (1787–88)
Herodotus (5th century B.C.)	"The Persian Wars" (excerpt from his *History*)
Hobbes, Thomas	*Origin of Government*
Homer (8th century B.C.)	*The Iliad*
Hume, David	"Of Personal Identity" [excerpt from *A Treatise on Human Nature* (1739–40)]
	"Of Justice and Injustice" [excerpt from *Essays, Moral and Political* (1741–42)]
James, Henry	*The Beast in the Jungle* (1903)
Kafka, Franz	*The Metamorphosis* (1915)
Kant, Immanuel	*Conscience*
	"First Principles of Morals" [excerpt from *Fundamental Principles of the Metaphysic of Ethics* (1785)]
Kierkegaard, Søren	"The Knight of Faith" [excerpt from *Fear and Trembling* (1843)]
Locke, John	"Of Civil Government" [excerpt from the second of his *Two Treatises of Government* (1690)]
Machiavelli, Niccolò	*The Prince* (1513)
Maimonides (12th century)	"On Evil" [excerpt from *Guide for the Perplexed*]
Marx, Karl	"Alienated Labour" [excerpt from *Das Kapital* (1867)]
Melville, Herman	*Billy Budd, Sailor* (1924)
Mill, John Stuart	*On Liberty* (1859)
	Utilitarianism (1863)
Molière	*The Misanthrope* (1666)
Montaigne, Michel de	"Of Experience" [Book III, Chapter 13 (1588) of his *Essays*]
Montesquieu, Baron de	"Principles of Government" [excerpt from *The Spirit of the Laws* (1748)]
Nietzsche, Friedrich	*Thus Spake Zarathustra* (1883–85)
Plato (4th century B.C.)	*The Republic*
	Symposium
	The Crito
	The Apology
Rousseau, Jean-Jacques	*The Social Contract* (1762)
Schopenhauer, Arthur	"The Indestructibility of Our Inner Nature" [excerpt from *The World as Will and Representation* (1818)]
Shakespeare, William	*Hamlet* (1601)
	Othello (1604)
	King Lear (1605–6)
	Anthony and Cleopatra (1607)
	The Tempest (c. 1611)

continues

The Great Books: A Reading List *continued*

Shaw, George Bernard	*Caesar and Cleopatra* (1901)
Simmel, Georg	"Individual Freedom" [excerpt from *The Philosophy of Money* (1900)]
Smith, Adam	*Inquiry into the Nature and Causes of the Wealth of Nations* (1776)
Sophocles (5th century B.C.)	*Antigone*
	Oedipus the King
Swift, Jonathon	*Gulliver's Travels* (1726)
Thoreau, Henry David	*Civil Disobedience* (1849)
Thucydides (5th century B.C.)	*History of the Peloponnesian War*
Tocqueville, Alexis de	"The Power of the Majority" [excerpt from *Democracy in America* (1835, 1840)]
Tolstoy, Count Leo Nikolayevich	*The Death of Ivan Ilych* (1886)
Weber, Max	*The Protestant Ethic and the Spirit of Capitalism* (1920)

THE NEW YORK PUBLIC LIBRARY'S BOOKS OF THE CENTURY

To commemorate the New York Public Library's centennial, librarians identified the following books as ones that played defining roles in history and culture from 1895 to 1995—the Library's first one hundred years.

LANDMARKS OF MODERN LITERATURE

Anton Chekhov	*Tri Sestry [The Three Sisters]* (1901)
Marcel Proust	*À la Recherche du Temps Perdu [Remembrance of Things Past]* (3 vols., 1913–27)
Gertrude Stein	*Tender Buttons: Objects Food Rooms* (1914)
Franz Kafka	*Die Verwandlung [The Metamorphosis]* (1915)
Edna St. Vincent Millay	*Renascence and Other Poems* (1917)
William Butler Yeats	*The Wild Swans at Coole* (1917)
Luigi Pirandello	*Sei Personaggi in Cerce d'Autore [Six Characters in Search of an Author]* (1921)
T. S. Eliot	*The Waste Land* (1922)
James Joyce	*Ulysses* (1922)
Thomas Mann	*Der Zauberberg [The Magic Mountain]* (1924)
F. Scott Fitzgerald	*The Great Gatsby* (1925)
Virginia Woolf	*To the Lighthouse* (1927)
Federico García Lorca	*Primer Romancero Gitano [Gypsy Ballads]* (1928)
Richard Wright	*Native Son* (1940)
William Faulkner	*The Portable Faulkner* (1946)
W. H. Auden	*The Age of Anxiety: A Baroque Eclogue* (1947)
Samuel Beckett	*En Attendant Godot [Waiting for Godot; A Tragicomedy in Two Acts]* (1952)
Ralph Ellison	*Invisible Man* (1952)
Vladimir Nabokov	*Lolita* (1955)
Jorge Luis Borges	*Ficciones [Fictions]* (1944; 2nd augmented edition, 1956)
Jack Kerouac	*On the Road* (1957)
Gabriel García Márquez	*Cien Años de Soledad [One Hundred Years of Solitude]* (1967)
Philip Roth	*Portnoy's Complaint* (1969)
Toni Morrison	*Song of Solomon* (1977)

NATURE'S REALM

Maurice Maeterlinck	*La Vie des Abeilles [The Life of the Bee]* (1901)
Marie Sklodowska Curie	*Traité de Radioactivité [Treatise on Radioactivity]* (1910)
Albert Einstein	*The Meaning of Relativity* (1922)
Roger Tory Peterson	*A Field Guide to the Birds* (1934)
Aldo Leopold	*A Sand County Almanac* (1949)
Konrad Z. Lorenz	*Er Redete Mit dem Vieh, den Vögeln und den Fischen: [King Solomon's Ring: New Light on Animal Ways]* (1949)

Rachel Carson   *Silent Spring* (1962)
United States Surgeon General   *Smoking and Health* [known as *The Surgeon General's Report*] (1964)
James Watson   *The Double Helix: A Personal Account of the Discovery of the Structure of DNA*
                                               (1968)
Edward O. Wilson   *The Diversity of Life* (1992)

PROTEST AND PROGRESS

Jacob Riis   *The Battle with the Slum* (1902)
W. E. B. Du Bois   *The Souls of Black Folk* (1903)
Upton Sinclair   *The Jungle* (1906)
Jane Addams   *Twenty Years at Hull-House* (1910)
Lillian Wald   *The House on Henry Street* (1915)
Lincoln Steffens   *The Autobiography of Lincoln Steffens* (1931)
John Dos Passos   *U.S.A.* (1937)
John Steinbeck   *The Grapes of Wrath* (1939)
James Agee and Walker Evans   *Let Us Now Praise Famous Men* (1941)
Lillian Smith   *Strange Fruit* (1944)
Paul Goodman   *Growing Up Absurd* (1960)
James Baldwin   *The Fire Next Time* (1963)
Malcolm X   *The Autobiography of Malcolm X* (1965)
Randy Shilts   *And the Band Played On* (1987)
Alex Kotlowitz   *There Are No Children Here* (1991)

COLONIALISM AND ITS AFTERMATH

Joseph Conrad   *Lord Jim* (1900)
Rudyard Kipling   *Kim* (1901)
Mohandas K. Gandhi   *Satyagraha [Non-Violent Resistance]* (1921–40)
E. M. Forster   *A Passage to India* (1924)
Albert Camus   *L'Étranger [The Stranger]* (1942)
                                           United Nations Charter (1945)
Alan Paton   *Cry, the Beloved Country* (1948)
Edward Steichen   *The Family of Man: The Photographic Exhibition Created by Edward Steichen for*
                                               the Museum of Modern Art (1955)
Chinua Achebe   *Things Fall Apart* (1958)
Frantz Fanon   *Les Damnés de la Terre [The Wretched of the Earth]* (1961)
Jean Rhys   *Wide Sargasso Sea* (1966)
Tayeb el-Salih   *Mawsim al-Hijra ila al-Shamal [Season of Migration to the North]* (1969)
V. S. Naipaul   *Guerrillas* (1975)
Buchi Emecheta   *The Bride Price* (1976)
Ryszard Kapuscinski   *Cesarz [The Emperor]* (1978)
Rigoberta Menchú   *Me Llamo Rigoberta Menchú y Así me Nació Conciencia [I, Rigoberta Menchú]*
                                               (1983)
Marguerite Duras   *L'amant [The Lover]* (1984)

MIND AND SPIRIT

Emile Durkheim   *Le Suicide: Étude de Sociologie [Suicide: A Study in Sociology]* (1897)
Sigmund Freud   *Die Traumdeutung [The Interpretation of Dreams]* (1899)
Havelock Ellis   *Studies in the Psychology of Sex* (1901–28)
William James   *The Varieties of Religious Experience: A Study in Human Nature* (1902)
Kahlil Gibran   *The Prophet* (1923)
Bertrand Russell   *Why I Am Not a Christian* (1927)
Margaret Mead   *Coming of Age in Samoa* (1928)
Jean-Paul Sartre   *L'Être et le Néant [Being and Nothingness]* (1943)

continues

Literature

Mind and Spirit *continued*

Benjamin Spock	*The Common Sense Book of Baby and Child Care* (1946)
The Holy Bible	
Paul Tillich	*The Courage to Be* (1952)
Ken Kesey	*One Flew Over the Cuckoo's Nest* (1962)
Timothy Leary	*The Politics of Ecstasy* (1968)
Elisabeth Kübler-Ross	*On Death and Dying* (1969)
Bruno Bettelheim	*The Uses of Enchantment* (1976)

POPULAR CULTURE AND MASS ENTERTAINMENT

Bram Stoker	*Dracula* (1897)
Henry James	*The Turn of the Screw* (1898)
Arthur Conan Doyle	*The Hound of the Baskervilles* (1902)
Edgar Rice Burroughs	*Tarzan of the Apes* (1914)
Zane Grey	*Riders of the Purple Sage* (1912)
Agatha Christie	*The Mysterious Affair at Styles* (1920)
Dale Carnegie	*How to Win Friends and Influence People* (1936)
Margaret Mitchell	*Gone with the Wind* (1936)
Raymond Chandler	*The Big Sleep* (1939)
Nathanael West	*The Day of the Locust* (1939)
Grace Metalious	*Peyton Place* (1956)
Dr. Seuss	*The Cat in the Hat* (1957)
Robert A. Heinlein	*Stranger in a Strange Land* (1962)
Joseph Heller	*Catch-22* (1961)
Truman Capote	*In Cold Blood: A True Account of a Multiple Murder and Its Consequences* (1965)
Jim Bouton	*Ball Four: My Life and Hard Times Throwing the Knuckleball in the Big Leagues* (1970)
Stephen King	*Carrie* (1974)
Tom Wolfe	*The Bonfire of the Vanities* (1987)

WOMEN RISE

Edith Wharton	*The Age of Innocence* (1920)
Carrie Chapman Catt and Nettie Rogers Shuler	*Woman Suffrage and Politics: The Inner Story of the Suffrage Movement* (1923)
Margaret Sanger	*My Fight for Birth Control* (1931)
Zora Neale Hurston	*Dust Tracks on a Road* (1942)
Simone de Beauvoir	*Le Deuxième Sexe [The Second Sex]* (1949)
Doris Lessing	*The Golden Notebook* (1962)
Betty Friedan	*The Feminine Mystique* (1963)
Maya Angelou	*I Know Why the Caged Bird Sings* (1970)
Robin Morgan, editor	*Sisterhood Is Powerful: An Anthology of Writings from the Women's Liberation Movement* (1970)
Susan Brownmiller	*Against Our Will: Men, Women and Rape* (1975)
Alice Walker	*The Color Purple* (1982)

ECONOMICS AND TECHNOLOGY

Thorstein Veblen	*The Theory of the Leisure Class: An Economic Study of Institutions* (1899)
Max Weber	*Die protestantische Ethik und der Geist des Kapitalismus [The Protestant Ethic and the Spirit of Capitalism]* (1904)
Henry Adams	*The Education of Henry Adams* (1907)
John Maynard Keynes	*The General Theory of Employment, Interest and Money* (1936)
Friedrich A. von Hayek	*The Road to Serfdom* (1944)

Milton Friedman	*A Theory of the Consumption Function* (1957)
John Kenneth Galbraith	*The Affluent Society* (1958)
Jane Jacobs	*The Death and Life of Great American Cities* (1961)
Helen Leavitt	*Superhighway—Superhoax* (1970)
E. F. Schumacher	*Small Is Beautiful: A Study of Economics as if People Mattered* (1973)
Ed Krol	*The Whole Internet: User's Guide & Catalog* (1992)

UTOPIAS AND DYSTOPIAS

H. G. Wells	*The Time Machine* (1895)
Theodor Herzl	*Der Judenstaat [The Jewish State]* (1896)
L. Frank Baum	*The Wonderful Wizard of Oz* (1900)
J. M. Barrie	*Peter Pan* (1904)
Charlotte Perkins Gilman	*Herland* (1915)
Aldous Huxley	*Brave New World* (1932)
James Hilton	*Lost Horizon* (1933)
B. F. Skinner	*Walden Two* (1948)
George Orwell	*Nineteen Eighty-four* (1949)
Ray Bradbury	*Fahrenheit 451* (1953)
Ayn Rand	*Atlas Shrugged* (1957)
Anthony Burgess	*A Clockwork Orange* (1962)
Margaret Atwood	*The Handmaid's Tale* (1984)

WAR, HOLOCAUST, TOTALITARIANISM

Arnold Toynbee	*Armenian Atrocities: The Murder of a Nation* (1915)
John Reed	*Ten Days That Shook the World* (1919)
Siegfried Sassoon	*The War Poems* (1919)
Jaroslav Hašek	*Osudy Dobrého Vojáka Švejka za Světové Války [The Good Soldier Schweik]* (1921–23)
Adolf Hitler	*Mein Kampf* (1925–26)
Erich Maria Remarque	*Im Westen nichts Neues [All Quiet on the Western Front]* (1928)
Anna Akhmatova	*Rekviem [Requiem]* (1940)
Ernest Hemingway	*For Whom the Bell Tolls* (1940)
Arthur Koestler	*Darkness at Noon* (1940)
John Hersey	*Hiroshima* (1946)
Anne Frank	*Het Achterhuis [The Diary of a Young Girl]* (1947)
Winston Churchill	*The Gathering Storm* (1948)
Elie Wiesel	*La Nuit [Night]* (1958)
Mao Zedong	*Quotations from Chairman Mao* (1966)
Dee Alexander Brown	*Bury My Heart at Wounded Knee: An Indian History of the American West* (1970)
Aleksandr I. Solzhenitsyn	*Arkhipelag GULag, 1918–1956 [The Gulag Archipelago, 1918–1956: An Experiment in Literary Investigation]* (1973)
Michael Herr	*Dispatches* (1977)
Art Spiegelman	*Maus: A Survivor's Tale* (2 vols., 1986–91)

OPTIMISM, JOY, GENTILITY

Sarah Orne Jewett	*The Country of the Pointed Firs* (1896)
Helen Keller	*The Story of My Life* (1903)
G. K. Chesterton	*The Innocence of Father Brown* (1911)
Juan Ramón Jiménez	*Platero y yo [Platero and I]* (1917)
George Bernard Shaw	*Pygmalion* (1913)
Emily Post	*Etiquette in Society, in Business, in Politics, and at Home* (1922)
P. G. Wodehouse	*The Inimitable Jeeves* (1923)
A. A. Milne	*Winnie-the-Pooh* (1926)

continues

Optimism, Joy, Gentility *continued*

Willa Cather	*Shadows on the Rock* (1931)
Irma S. Rombauer	*The Joy of Cooking: A Compilation of Reliable Recipes with a Casual Culinary Chat* (1931)
J. R. R. Tolkien	*The Hobbit* (1937)
Margaret Wise Brown	*Goodnight Moon* (1947)
Harper Lee	*To Kill a Mockingbird* (1960)
Langston Hughes	*The Best of Simple* (1961)
Elizabeth Bishop	*The Complete Poems* (1969)

FAVORITES OF CHILDHOOD AND YOUTH

Beatrix Potter	*The Tale of Peter Rabbit* (1901)
Betty Smith	*A Tree Grows in Brooklyn* (1943)
C. S. Lewis	*The Lion, the Witch and the Wardrobe* (1950)
J. D. Salinger	*The Catcher in the Rye* (1951)
E. B. White	*Charlotte's Web* (1952)
Ezra Jack Keats	*The Snowy Day* (1962)
Maurice Sendak	*Where the Wild Things Are* (1963)
Patricia MacLachlan	*Sarah, Plain and Tall* (1985)

COMMON LITERARY TERMS

allegory   A story with an underlying meaning symbolized by the characters and action.

alliteration   The repetition of the same sounds—usually initial consonants of words or of stressed syllables—in any sequence of neighboring words.

allusion   A reference to a familiar person or event, often from literature.

anachronism   A chronological error in literature that places a person, event, or object in an impossible historical context.

anagram   A word or phrase created by transposing the letters of another word.

analogy   The relation of one thing to something familiar.

antagonist   The major character opposing a hero or a protagonist.

anthropomorphism   The assigning of human characteristics and feelings to animals and other nonhuman things.

anticlimax   Something that works against a climax, such as humor; a sudden descent from the lofty to the trivial.

antihero   A protagonist lacking in heroic qualities like courage, idealism, and honesty.

antithesis   A rhetorical figure in which sharply opposing ideas are expressed within a balanced grammatical structure.

assonance   The close repetition of similar vowel sounds.

autobiography   The story of one's life as written by oneself.

ballad   A poem, often meant to be sung, that tells a story.

bathos   A sudden descent from the lofty to the ordinary or ridiculous.

belles-lettres   Literature. Currently, lighter writings or appreciative essays on the beauties of literature.

bibliography   A list of books on a similar subject or by a given author or authors.

biography   The story of someone's life as written by another.

Literature

blank verse   Unrhymed poetry, especially poetry written in iambic pentameter.

cacophony   Discordant sounds, sometimes used in poetry for effect.

cadence   The natural rhythm of language determined by its inherent alternation of stressed and unstressed syllables.

caesura   A pause or break in a line of verse.

climax   The point of high emotional intensity at which a story or play reaches its peak.

conceit   A fanciful image, especially an elaborate or startling analogy.

couplet   Two successive lines of poetry, usually rhymed.

dénouement   Literally, the "unknotting": the final unraveling of the plot following the climax.

diction   The choice and arrangement of words in a literary work.

doggerel   Crudely written poetry.

elegy   A poetic lament.

epic   An extended narrative poem, exalted in style and heroic in theme.

epistolary novel   A novel written in the form of correspondence.

essay   A short written work of nonfiction, usually on one topic.

euphony   Harmonious sounds, often used in poetry for effect.

fable   A prose or poetic story that illustrates a moral.

fiction   Narrative writing drawn from the imagination of the author rather than from history or fact.

foot   A group of syllables forming a metrical unit.

free verse   A poem without regular meter or line length.

genre   A literary type or class.

haiku   An unrhymed poem form, originated by the Japanese, consisting of three lines of five, seven, and five syllables that record the essence of a moment.

hero   A character, often the protagonist, who exhibits qualities such as courage, idealism, and honesty.

high comedy   Comedy that is characterized by intellect or wit.

historical novel   A narrative that places fictional characters or events in historically accurate surroundings.

hyperbole   A deliberate overstatement.

iamb   A metrical foot that contains one short or unstressed syllable preceding one long or stressed syllable.

iambic pentameter   Poetry consisting of five parts per line, each part having one short or unstressed syllable and one long or stressed syllable.

imagery   Figurative language used to evoke particular mental pictures.

irony   An expression of a meaning that contradicts the literal meaning.

literature   Novels, stories, poems, and plays of high standards that entertain, inform, stimulate, or provide aesthetic pleasure.

low comedy   Humorous material that employs physical actions or jokes of questionable taste.

malapropism   A mistaken substitution of one word for another that sounds similar, generally with humorous effect.

metaphor   A figure of speech in which two unlikely objects are compared by identification or by the substitution of one for the other.

meter   The pattern of stressed and unstressed syllables in poetry.

motif   A theme, character, or verbal pattern that recurs in literature or folklore.

myth   A legend, usually made up in part of historical events, that helps define the beliefs of a people and that often has evolved as an explanation for rituals and natural phenomena.

nonfiction A historically accurate narrative.

novel A long work of fictional prose.

novella A short novel; also, the early tales or short stories of French and Italian writers.

ode A lyric poem marked by strong feelings and an involved style.

onomatopoeia Formation of a word by imitating the natural sound associated with the object or action involved; the use of words that are so named.

oxymoron A figure of speech that employs two contradictory terms. For examples, *see* "Oxymoron: Pairings of Contradictory or Incongruous Words" in chapter 13.

palindrome A word, a sentence, or a group of sentences (sometimes in verse) that reads the same backward and forward. For examples, *see* "Palindromes" in chapter 13.

parable A short story that illustrates a moral.

paradox An apparently contradictory statement that contains a truth that reconciles the contradiction.

parody A humorous, often exaggerated imitation of a serious literary work.

pathetic fallacy The assigning of human attributes to nature.

pathos An element that evokes feelings of pity, tenderness, and sympathy.

personification The assigning of human attributes to abstractions, objects, and other nonhuman things.

plot The organization of individual incidents in a narrative or play.

poem A rhythmic expression of feelings or ideas, often using metaphor, meter, and rhyme.

poetic license The practice of violating rules, expectations, or conventions to achieve a desired effect.

prologue An introductory speech or monologue, given by an actor or actress before a play, which helps to set the stage for what is to come.

prose Literary expression not marked by rhyme or metrical regularity.

prose poem A prose composition that exhibits the rhythms of verse

protagonist The main character of a play, novel, or story, usually the hero.

pun A humorous and often clever play on words in which one word evokes another with a similar sound but a different meaning.

refrain A phrase or verse that is repeated throughout a poem or song.

rhetorical question A question put forth to achieve an effect or make a point, to which an answer is not expected.

rhyme The repetition of similar or identical sounds at the ends of lines of verse.

rhythm The pattern of stressed and unstressed syllables in a line of poetry or prose.

satire Ridicule of human vice or folly; the work in which it is contained.

short story A brief work of narrative prose.

simile A comparison of two unlike things that usually employs *like* or *as*.

soliloquy A dramatic monologue meant to convey the thoughts of a character in a play.

sonnet A poem consisting of fourteen iambic pentameter lines with a rigidly prescribed rhyming scheme.

spondee A type of metrical foot with two stressed syllables.

spoonerism The transposition of the initial sounds of two or more words, often with humorous results. Named for a Professor Spooner of Oxford, who was famous for such transpositions.

style An author's individual method and tone.

subplot A secondary plot in a story.

symbol In literature, something that stands for, or means, something else.

theme The central idea or thesis of a work.

trochee   A metrical foot that contains one long or stressed syllable preceding one short or unstressed syllable.

verse   Lines of writing arranged in metrical patterns, or a single such line.

ADDITIONAL SOURCES OF INFORMATION

BOOKS

Andrews, William L., ed. *The Oxford Companion to African American Literature.* Oxford University Press, 1997.

Baldick, Chris. *The Concise Oxford Dictionary of Literary Terms.* Oxford University Press, 1991

Baldwin, Neil, and Diane Osen, eds. *The Writing Life: National Book Award Authors.* Random House, 1995

Bauer, Andrew. *The Hawthorn Dictionary of Pseudonyms.* Hawthorn Books, 1971.

Beckson, Karl, and Arthur Ganz. *Literary Terms: A Dictionary.* Farrar, Straus & Giroux, 1989.

Bede, Jean-Albert, and William B. Edgerton, eds. *Columbia Dictionary of Modern European Literature.* Columbia University Press, 1980.

Beetz, Kirk H., ed. *Beacham's Encyclopedia of Popular Fiction.* Beacham, 1996.

Benson, Eugene, and William Toye, eds. *The Oxford Companion to Canadian Literature.* 2nd ed. Oxford University Press, 1997.

Connolly, S. J., ed. *The Oxford Companion to Irish Literature.* Oxford University Press, 1999.

Contemporary Authors. 188 vols. Gale, 1962–2000.

Contemporary Authors: New Revision Series. 94 vols. Gale, 1962–2000.

Contemporary Literary Criticism. 137 vols. Gale, 1973–2000.

Cuddon, J. *A. Dictionary of Literary Terms and Literary Theory.* Blackwell, 1998.

Davidson, Cathy N., and Linda Wagner-Martin, eds. *The Oxford Companion to Women's Writing in the U.S.* Oxford University Press, 1995.

Drabble, Margaret, ed. *The Oxford Companion to English Literature.* Rev. 6th ed. Oxford University Press, 2000.

Frye, Northrop, Sheridan Baker, and George Perkins. *The Harper Handbook to Literature.* 2nd ed. HarperCollins, 1997.

Garland Henry and Mary, eds. *The Oxford Companion to German Literature.* 3rd ed., Oxford University Press, 1997.

Harmon, William, and Clarence Hugh Holman, *A Handbook to Literature.* 8th ed. Simon & Schuster, 1999.

Hart, James D. *The Oxford Companion to American Literature.* 6th ed. Oxford University Press, 1995.

Howatson, Margaret, and Ian Chilvers, eds. *The Oxford Companion to Classical Literature,* 3rd ed. Oxford University Press, 1993.

Levi, Anthony, ed. *Guide to French Literature.* 2 vols. St. James Press, 1994.

Moss, Joyce, and George Wilson, eds. *Literature and its Times.* 5 vols. Gale, 1997.

Murphy, Bruce, ed. *Benet's Readers Encyclopedia of American Literature.* 4th ed. HarperCollins, 1996.

National Book Foundation. *The National Book Awards: Forty-eight years of Literary Excellence: Winners and Finalists, 1950–1998.* National Book Foundation, 1998.

Ousby, Ian. *The Cambridge Guide to Literature in English,* 2nd ed. Cambridge University Press, 1994.

Padgett, Ron, ed. *World Poets.* 3 vols. Scribners, 2000.

Parini, Jay, et al. eds. *American Writers.* 4 vols. and 8 supplements. Scribners, 1974–2001.

Parini, Jay, et al. eds. *British Writers.* 8 vols. and 6 supplements. Scribners, 1974–2001.

Parker, Peter, ed. *A Reader's Guide to the 20th Century Novel.* Oxford University Press, 1995.

Preminger, Alex, and T. V. F. Brogan. *The New Princeton Encyclopedia of Poetry and Poetics.* Princeton University Press, 1996.

Serafin, Steven, ed. *The Encyclopedia of World Literature in the 20th Century.* 4 vols. St. James Press, 1999.

Skillion, Anne, ed. *The New York Public Library Literature Companion.* Free Press, 2001.

Sole Jr., Carlos A., and Maria I. Abreu, eds. *Latin American Writers.* 3 vols. Macmillan, 1989.

Stade, George, ed. *European Writers.* 3 vols. Scribners, 1992.

Wakeman, John, et al. eds. *World Authors.* 9 vols. H. W. Wilson, 1975–2000.

Wilde, William L., ed. *The Oxford Companion to Australian Literature*, 2nd ed. Oxford University Press, 1995.

WEB SITES
** Indicates subscription-based web sites

American National Biography**
http://www.anb.org

The American Verse Project
http://www.hti.umich.edu/a/amverse/

Bibliomania
http://www.bibliomania.com/

Electronic Poetry Center
http://www.epc.buffalo.edu/

Electronic Text Center, University of Virginia Library
http://etext.lib.virginia.edu

Literature Online
Bartleby.com

Literature Resource Center**
http://www.galenet.com/

MLA International Bibliography**
http://www.mla.org/publications/bibliography.htm

The On-Line Books Page
http://digital.library.upenn.edu/books/

Online Literary Criticism Collection
http://www.ipl.org/ref/litcrit

The Perseus Digital Library
http://www.perseus.tufts.edu

Project MUSE: Scholarly Journals Online**
http://muse.jhu.edu/

Virtual Reference Library
http://www.bl.uk/collections/resources/humanities/vrlnew.html

9  RELIGIONS

Religions

THE GREEK AND ROMAN DEITIES

The myths of the gods and goddesses of ancient Greece and Rome have had a lasting impact on Western thought. They have played an essential role in the development of the arts, philosophy, psychology, literature, and religion. The following list gives the names of these ancient deities as well as the spheres of influence ascribed to them.

Greek	Roman	Sphere of Influence
Adonis	———	Symbolizes the death of nature each autumn and its rebirth in the spring
Aeolus	———	God of the winds
Aphrodite	Venus	Goddess of love and beauty
Apollo	———	God of beauty, youth, poetry, music, prophecy, and archery
Ares	Mars	God of war
Artemis	Diana	Goddess of the hunt, moon, and nature
Asclepius	Aesculapius	God of medicine
Athena	Minerva	Goddess of wisdom
Chaos	———	God of the shapeless void that preceded creation of the Earth
Cronus	Saturn	Leader of the Titans who ruled the heavens after overthrowing his father, Uranus
Demeter	Ceres	Goddess of the earth, grain, and harvests
Dionysus	Bacchus (Liber)	God of wine
Dis (Hades)	Pluto	God of the underworld
Eos	Aurora	Goddess of dawn
Eris	Discordia	Goddess of strife and discord
Eros	Cupid (Amor)	God of love
Fates	Fates	Three sisters—Clotho, Lachesis, and Atropos (called Nona, Decuma, and Morta by the Romans)—who spun the thread of human destiny and cut it with their shears when they pleased
Flora	———	Goddess of flowers
Furies	Furies	Three goddesses, their heads (Eumenides) topped by serpents, who punished those who escaped human justice
Gorgons	———	Three winged sisters—Euryale, Medusa, and Stheno—the sight of whom turned mortals to stone
Graces	Graces	Three sisters—Aglaia, Euphrosyne, and Thalia—who were goddesses of banquets, dances, social enjoyments, and the arts
Hebe	Juventas	Goddess of youth
Hephaestus	Vulcan	God of fire
Hera	Juno	Sister and wife of Zeus; queen of the goddesses
Herakles	Hercules	Son of Zeus; greatest of Greek heroes, who performed 12 labors and was eventually granted immortality
Hermaphroditus	———	Son of Hermes and Aphrodite who was joined forever to the nymph of the fountain of Salmacis, creating one body with the sexual characteristics of both males and females
Hermes	Mercury	Messenger of the gods; patron of thieves
Hestia	Vesta	Goddess of the hearth
Hygeia	———	Goddess of health
Hymen	———	God of marriage
Hypnus	Somnus	God of sleep
———	Janus	Porter of heaven, who opens the year; also god of gates and doors, with two opposing faces
———	Lares	Spirits of ancestors who watch over homes and cities
———	Lemures	Spirits of the dead, both good and bad

Greek	Roman	Sphere of Influence
Metis	Prudence	First wife of Zeus, who helped him become king of gods; personification of prudence
Morpheus	———	God of dreams
Muses	Camenae	Nine sisters, daughters of Zeus, who are goddesses of the arts and sciences: Clio (history), Euterpe (lyric poetry), Thalia (comedy), Melpomene (tragedy), Terpsichore (dance), Erato (erotic poetry), Polyhymnia (sacred poetry), Urania (astronomy), and Calliope (epic poetry; chief of the Muses)
Nemesis	———	Goddess of vengeance
Nike	Victoria	Goddess of victory
Nymphs	———	Nature spirits who oversee water, trees, mountains, valleys, and particular locations
Nyx	Nox	Goddess of night
Pan	Faunus	God of flocks and shepherds
Persephone	Proserpine	Goddess of the underworld; symbol of the death of nature each autumn and its rebirth each spring
Plutus	———	God of wealth
———	Pomona	Goddess of fruit and gardens
Poseidon	Neptune	God of the oceans
Priapus	———	God of fertility
Psyche	Psyche	Goddess of the soul, who was united with Eros, or Cupid
Rhea	Ops	Goddess of fertility, wife of Cronus; mother of the Olympian gods and goddesses Demeter, Hades, Hera, Hestia, Poseidon, and Zeus
———	Romulus	Founder of the city of Rome; raised by a wolf with his twin brother, Remus
Satyrs	Satyrs	Field and forest gods with goats' feet and horns who represent nature's bounty and lust
Selene	Luna	Goddess of the moon
Sirens	———	Sea nymphs whose singing enchanted those who heard it
Thanatos	Mors	God of death
Titans	Titans	Sons and daughters of Uranus, who took power when Cronus overthrew their father: Atlas, Coeus, Crius, Dione, Epimetheus, Hyperion, Iapetus, Leto, Maia, Mnemosyne, Oceanus, Ophion, Pallas, Phoebe, Prometheus, Rhea, Tethys, Themis, and Thia
Tyche	Fortuna	Goddess of fortune or fate
Uranus	———	God of heaven; father of the Titans
Zeus	Jupiter (Jove)	Chief god of Olympus; ruler of heaven, who wielded thunder and lightning

——— indicates no corresponding deity in this culture.

THE WORLD'S MAJOR RELIGIONS

Religious beliefs are an intrinsic aspect of virtually every society that has ever existed. Many of these beliefs are organized and codified, often based on the teachings and writings of one or more founders. Other belief systems are less rigid in their external structures and may be transmitted orally from one generation to the next, either by family members or by religious leaders within the community.

While all religious beliefs are of vital importance to those who hold them, the less formalistic belief systems—variously referred to as animist or tribal religions, and adhered to by peoples all over the world—are not covered in this section.

BAHA'I

Baha'i has nearly 7 million followers worldwide and 750,000 followers in the United States. It was founded by Mirza Husayn 'Ali Nuri, who took the name Bahá'u'lláh (Glory of God) while in exile in Baghdad. Bahá'u'lláh's coming had been foretold by Mirza Ali Muhammad, known as al-Bab, who founded Babism in 1844, from which the Baha'i faith grew. The central tenets of the Baha'i faith are the oneness of God, the oneness of humanity, and the common foundation of all religion. Baha'ists also believe in the equality of men and women, universal education, world peace, and the creation of a world federal system of government.

BUDDHISM

Buddhism has 354 million followers worldwide and 2 million followers in the United States. It was founded by Siddhartha Gautama, known as the Buddha (Enlightened One), in southern Nepal in the 6th and 5th centuries B.C. The Buddha achieved enlightenment through meditation and gathered a community of monks to carry on his teachings. Buddhism teaches that meditation and the practice of virtuous and moral behavior can lead to Nirvana, the state of enlightenment. Before achieving Nirvana, however, one is subject to repeated lifetimes that are good or bad depending on one's actions *(karma)*. The doctrines of the Buddha describe temporal life as featuring "four noble truths": Existence is a realm of suffering; desire, along with the belief in the importance of one's self, causes suffering; achievement of Nirvana ends suffering; and Nirvana is attained only by meditation and by following the path of righteousness in action, thought, and attitude.

CONFUCIANISM

A faith with 6 million followers worldwide (the number of followers in the United States is uncertain), Confucianism was founded by Confucius, a Chinese philosopher, in the 6th and 5th centuries B.C. Confucius's sayings and dialogues, known collectively as the *Analects,* were written down by his followers. Confucianism, which grew out of a strife-ridden time in Chinese history, stresses the relationship between individuals, their families, and society, based on *li* (proper behavior) and *jen* (sympathetic attitude). Its practical, socially oriented philosophy was challenged by the more mystical precepts of Taoism and Buddhism, which were partially incorporated to create neo-Confucianism during the Sung dynasty (A.D. 960–1279). The overthrow of the Chinese monarchy and the Communist revolution during the 20th century have severely lessened the influence of Confucianism on modern Chinese culture.

HINDUISM

Hinduism has 760 million followers worldwide and 950,000 followers in the United States, Hinduism developed from indigenous religions of India in combination with Aryan religions brought to India c. 1500 B.C. and codified in the Veda and the Upanishads, the sacred scriptures of Hinduism. Hinduism is a term used broadly to describe a vast array of sects to which most Indians belong. Although many Hindus reject the caste system—in which people are born into a particular subgroup that determines their religious, social, and work-related duties—Hinduism classifies society at large into four groups: the Brahmins or priests, the rulers and warriors, the farmers and merchants, and the peasants and laborers. The goals of Hinduism are release from repeated reincarnation through the practice of yoga, adherence to Vedic scriptures, and devotion to a personal guru. Various Hindu deities are worshiped at shrines. The divine trinity, representing the cyclical nature of the universe, is made up of Brahma the creator, Vishnu the preserver, and Shiva the destroyer.

ISLAM

Islam has 1.1 billion followers worldwide and 5.6 million followers in the United States. It was founded by the prophet Muhammad, who received the holy scriptures of Islam, the Koran, from Allah (God) c. A.D. 610. Islam (Arabic for "submission to

God") maintains that Muhammad is the last in a long line of holy prophets, preceded by Adam, Abraham, Moses, and Jesus. In addition to being devoted to the Koran, followers of Islam (Muslims) are devoted to the worship of Allah through the Five Pillars: the statement "There is no god but God, and Muhammad is his prophet"; prayer, conducted five times a day while facing Mecca, the birthplace of Muhammad and the holy city of the Islamic world (Mecca is the capital of the Hejaz region of Saudi Arabia); the giving of alms; the keeping of the fast of Ramadan during the ninth month of the Muslim year; and the making of a pilgrimage to Mecca at least once, if possible. The two main divisions of Islam are the Sunni and the Shiite. The Wahabis are the most important Sunni sect; the Shiite sects include the Assassins, the Druses, and the Fatimids, among countless others.

JUDAISM

Stemming from the descendants of Judah in Judea, Judaism was founded c. 2000 B.C. by Abraham, Isaac, and Jacob. It has 14 million followers worldwide and 5.5 million followers in the United States. Judaism espouses belief in a monotheistic God, who is creator of the universe and who leads His people, the Jews, by speaking through prophets. His word is revealed in the Hebrew Bible (or Old Testament), especially in that part known as the Torah. The Torah also contains, according to rabbinic tradition, a total of 613 biblical commandments, including the Ten Commandments, which are explicated in the Talmud. Jews believe that the human condition can be improved, that the letter and the spirit of the Torah must be followed, and that a Messiah will eventually bring the world to a state of paradise. Judaism promotes community among all people of Jewish faith, dedication to a synagogue or temple (the basic social unit of a group of Jews, led by a rabbi), and the importance of family life. Religious observance takes place both at home and in the temple. Judaism is divided into three main groups who vary in their interpretation of those parts of the Torah that deal with personal, communal, international, and religious activities: the Orthodox community, which views the Torah as derived from God and therefore absolutely binding; the Reform movement, which follows primarily its ethical content; and the Conservative Jews, who follow most of the observances set out in the Torah but allow for change in the face of modern life. A fourth group, Reconstructionist Jews, rejects the concept of the Jews as God's chosen people, yet maintains rituals as part of the Judaic cultural heritage.

ORTHODOX CHURCH

With 214 million followers worldwide and over 4.2 million followers in the United States, the Orthodox Church is the third-largest Christian community in the world. It began its split from the Roman Catholic Church in the 5th century; the break was finalized in 1054. The followers of the Orthodox Church are in fact members of many different denominations, including the Church of Greece, the Church of Cyprus, and the Russian Orthodox Church. Orthodox religion holds biblical Scripture and tradition, guided by the Holy Spirit as expressed in the consciousness of the entire Orthodox community, to be the source of Christian truth. It rejects doctrine developed by the Western churches. Doctrine was established by seven ecumenical councils held between 325 and 787 and amended by other councils in the late Byzantine period. Relations between the Orthodox churches and Roman Catholicism have improved since Vatican Council II (1962–65).

PROTESTANTISM

Protestantism is a form of Christian faith. It includes any member of the various Christian churches established as a result of the Reformation, the 16th-century religious movement that aimed at reforming the Roman Catholic Church. The following is a list of major Protestant denominations and their beliefs.

"Holy Books of the World" in this chapter and "Religion Symbols" in chapter 12 Go to

Religions

MAJOR PROTESTANT DENOMINATIONS IN THE UNITED STATES

Denomination	Founder	Followers	Tenets
Amish Mennonites	Founded in Switzerland in the 1500s after secession from the Zurich state church; the followers of Jacob Ammann broke from the other Mennonites in Switzerland and Alsace in 1693; most Amish Mennonites emigrated to Pennsylvania in the 18th century when others rejoined the main Mennonite group.	80,000 Amish Mennonites; 200,000 Mennonites primarily located in the United States.	The Bible is the sole rule of faith; beliefs are outlined in the *Dordrecht Confession of Faith* (1632); Mennonites shun worldly ways and modern innovation (education and technology); the sacraments are adult baptism and communion.
Baptists	Founded by John Smyth in England in 1609 and Roger Williams in Rhode Island in 1638.	36 million in the United States; 38 million worldwide.	No creed; authority stems from the Bible; most Baptists oppose the use of alcohol and tobacco; baptism is by total immersion.
Church of Christ	Organized by Presbyterians in Kentucky in 1804 and in Pennsylvania in 1809.	1.6 million in the United States; 3 million worldwide.	The New Testament is believed in, and what is written in the Bible is followed without elaboration; rites are not ornate; baptism is of adults.
Church of England	King Henry VIII of England broke with the Roman Catholic Church; he issued the Act of Supremacy in 1534, which declared the king of England to be the head of the Church of England.	300,000 in the Anglican Orthodox Church in North America; 27 million worldwide.	Supremacy of the Bible is the test of doctrine; emphasis is on the most essential Christian doctrines and creeds; the *Book of Common Prayer* is used; the Church of England is part of the Anglican Communion, which is represented in the United States mainly by the Episcopal Church.
Disciples of Christ	Founded on the American frontier at the beginning of the 19th century as a means of cutting through doctrinal disputes to achieve Christian unity.	937,000, mostly in the United States.	Rigorous adherence to the New Testament as the basis of Christian faith; literal interpretation of the Bible; rejection of ecclesiastical institutions except for the congregation.

Denomination	Founder	Followers	Tenets
Episcopal Church	U.S. offshoot of the Church of England; it installed Samuel Seabury as its first bishop in 1784 and held its first General Convention in 1789, creating an independent church.	2.5 million in the United States; 70 million worldwide; 75 million worldwide are part of the Anglican Communion.	Worship is based on the *Book of Common Prayer* and interpretation of the Bible; services
Lutheran Church	Based on the writings of Martin Luther, who broke (1517–21) with the Roman Catholic Church and led the Protestant Reformation; the first Lutheran congregation in North America was founded in 1638 in Wilmington, Delaware; the first North American regional synod was founded in 1748 by Heinrich Melchior Mühlenberg.	9 million in the United States; 63 million worldwide.	Faith is based on the Bible and the Augsburg Confession (written in 1530); salvation comes through faith alone; services include the Lord's Supper communion; Lutherans are mostly conservative in religious and social ethics; infants are baptized; the church is organized in synods; the two largest synods in the United States are the Evangelical Lutheran Church in America and the Lutheran Church Missouri Synod.
Mennonites	*See* Amish Mennonites.		
Methodist Church	Reverend John Wesley began evangelistic preaching within the Church of England in 1738; a separate Wesleyan Methodist Church was established in 1791; the Methodist Episcopal Church was founded in the United States in 1784.	13.5 million in the United States; 26 million worldwide.	The name derives from the founders' desire to study religion "by rule and method" and follow the Bible interpreted by tradition and reason; worship varies by denomination within Methodism (the United Methodist Church is the largest congregation); the church is perfectionist in social dealings; communion and the baptism of infants and adults are practiced.

Religions

continues

Religions

Major Protestant Denominations in the United States, Continued

Denomination	Founder	Followers	Tenets
Pentecostal churches	The churches grew out of the "holiness movement" that developed among Methodists and other Protestants in the first decade of the 20th century.	10.6 million in the United States; 200 million worldwide.	Baptism in the Holy Spirit, speaking in tongues, faith healing, and the second coming of Jesus are believed in; of the various Pentecostal churches, the Assemblies of God is the largest; a perfectionist attitude toward secular affairs is common; services feature enthusiastic sermons and hymns; adult baptism and communion are practiced.
Presbyterian Church	Grew out of Calvinist churches of Switzerland and France; John Knox founded the first Presbyterian church in Scotland in 1557; the first presbytery in North America was established by Irish missionary Francis Makemie in 1706.	3.7 million in the United States; 50 million worldwide.	Faith is in the Bible; the sacraments are infant baptism and communion; the church is organized as a system of courts in which clergy and lay members (presbyters) participate at local, regional, and national levels; services are simple, with emphasis on the sermon.
Reformed churches	The churches trace their origin to the Swiss Reformation in the 16th century. The first Reformed church in the United States was founded by Alexander Whitaker in Virginia in 1611.	2 million in United States; number of followers worldwide is uncertain.	Confirmation of the Trinity and the humanity and divinity of Christ; belief in the justification of grace through faith.
Seventh-Day Adventist Church	Grew out of the teachings of William Miller in the 1840s; formally founded in North America in 1863.	775,000 in the United States; 8 million worldwide.	The Bible is the only creed; the second coming of Jesus is emphasized; members abstain from alcoholic beverages and tobacco; baptism and communion are practiced.
United Church of Christ	Formed in 1957 by the union of the General Council of Congregational Christian Churches with the Evangelical and Reformed Churches.	1.5 million, mostly in the United States.	Belief in the Bible is guided by the *Statement of Faith* (written in 1959); the church is organized by congregations, which are represented at a general synod that set policy; services are simple, with emphasis on the sermon; infant baptism and communion are practiced.

OTHER CHRISTIAN–BASED RELIGIONS AND ORGANIZATIONS

Religion/Org.	Founder	Followers	Tenets
The Church of Jesus Christ of Latter-Day Saints (Mormons)	Joseph Smith, in the 1820s, found golden tablets with *The Book of Mormon* inscribed on them; church headquarters were established in upstate New York in 1830, then in Ohio in 1831; after two more attempts to establish a permanent home for the church (the second resulting in Smith's death at the hands of a mob), Salt Lake City, Utah, was founded in 1847 under the leadership of Brigham Young.	4.7 million in the United States; 7.7 million worldwide.	Faith is based on the Bible, *The Book of Mormon, The Doctrine and Covenants,* and *The Pearl of Great Price,* all of which are considered scripture; stress is placed on revelation through the connection of spiritual and physical worlds and through proselytizing; members abstain from alcohol and tobacco and believe in community self-reliance; public services are conservative; there is baptism, laying on of hands, and communion; a secret temple holds other cermonies, including baptism for the dead.
Jehovah's Witnesses	Founded by Charles T. Russell in the United States in the late 19th century.	945,000 in the United States; 4 million worldwide.	Belief is in the imminent second coming of Christ and the potential salvation of mortal souls during the millennium; all members are ministers who proselytize their faith with door-to-door missionary work; members refuse service in the armed forces, will not salute national flags or participate in politics, will not accept blood transfusion (but will accept all other forms of medical treatment), and discourage smoking, drunkenness, and gambling.

continues

Religions

Other Christian–Based Religions and Organizations, Continued

Religion/Org.	Founder	Followers	Tenets
Religious Society of Friends (Quakers)	George Fox in England in the 17th century began preaching against organized churches, professing a doctrine of the Inner Light.	100,000 in the United States; 300,000 worldwide.	Reliance is on the Inner Light, the voice of God's Holy Spirit experienced within each person; meetings are characterized by quiet meditation without ritual or sermon; Quakers are active in peace, education, and social welfare movements; they refuse to bear arms or take oaths; earlier schisms are still reflected in three main affiliations of Friends.
Unitarian Universalist Association	The denomination resulted from the merger in 1961 of the Universalist Church of America (organized in 1779) and the American Unitarian Association (founded in 1825).	200,000 in the United States; 330,000 worldwide.	Members profess no creed; strong social, ethical, and humanitarian concerns are manifest in the search for religious truth through freedom of belief; theists, humanists, and agnostics are accepted in religious fellowship; efforts are aimed at the creation of a worldwide interfaith religious community; many members come from other denominations and religions.

ROMAN CATHOLICISM

The Roman Catholic Church, with 1.1 billion followers worldwide and 62 million followers in the United States, is the largest Christian church in the world. It claims direct historical descent from the church founded by the apostle Peter. The pope in Rome is the spiritual leader of all Roman Catholics. He administers church affairs through bishops and priests. Members accept the gospel of Jesus Christ and the teachings of the Bible, as well as the church's interpretations of these. God's grace is conveyed through the seven sacraments, especially the Eucharist or communion that is celebrated at mass, the regular service of worship. The other six sacraments are baptism, confirmation, penance, holy orders, matrimony, and anointing of the sick. Redemption through Jesus Christ is professed as the sole method of obtaining salvation, which is necessary to ensure a place in heaven after life on earth.

New York's Cathedral of St. John the Divine, begun in 1892, is only now nearing completion. Taking more than 100 years to construct, it will be the largest cathedral in the world when finished.

"Roman Catholic Patron Saints" and "The Roman Catholic Popes" in this chapter Go to

ROSICRUCIANISM

Rosicrucianism, a modern movement begun in 1868 by R. W. Little, claims ties to an older Society of the Rose and Cross that was founded in Germany in 1613 by Christian Rosencreuz. The number of its followers is uncertain. The Ancient Mystical Order Rosae Crusis (AMORC) was founded in San Jose, California, in 1915 by H. Spencer Lewis. The Rosicrucian Brotherhood was established in Quakertown, Pennsylvania, by Reuben Swinburne Clymer in 1902. Both sects could be classified as either fraternal or religious organizations, although they claim to empower members with cosmic forces by unveiling secret wisdom regarding the laws of nature.

SHINTO

Shinto, with 2.8 million followers worldwide (the number of followers in the United States is uncertain), is the ancient native religion of Japan, established long before the introduction of writing to Japan in the 5th century A.D. The origins of its beliefs and rituals are unknown. Shinto stresses belief in a great many spiritual beings and gods, known as *kami,* who are paid tribute at shrines and honored by festivals, and reverence for ancestors. Although Shinto has no overall dogma, adherents are expected to remember and celebrate the *kami,* support the societies of which the *kami* are patrons, remain pure and sincere, and enjoy life.

TAOISM

Both a philosophy and a religion, Taoism was founded in China by Lao-tzu, who is traditionally said to have been born in 604 B.C. Its number of followers is uncertain. It derives primarily from the *Tao-te-ching,* which claims that an ever-changing universe follows the Tao, or path. The Tao can be known only by emulating its quietude and effortless simplicity; Taoism prescribes that people live simply, spontaneously, and in close touch with nature and that they meditate to achieve contact with the Tao. Temples and monasteries, maintained by Taoist priests, are important in some Taoist sects. Since the Communist revolution, Taoism has been actively discouraged in the People's Republic of China, although it continues to flourish in Taiwan.

Madalyn Murray O'Hair, the renowned atheist who opposed prayer in schools, mysteriously disappeared on September 28, 1995, along with her son Jon Garth and adopted family member Robin Murray. In April 2001, David R. Waters was sentenced to 20 years in prison for his role in their abduction and murder.

ZOROASTRIANISM

An ancient religion that influenced both Judaism and Christianity, Zoroastrianism arose in Persia (modern-day Iran) as early as the 6th century B.C. Based mainly on a Persian text known as the *Avesta,* Zoroastrianism rejected the worship of multiple gods, adhering to belief only in Ahura Mazda, the "Wise Lord." With the advent of the Sasanid dynasty in the 3rd century A.D., Zoroastrianism became Persia's state religion, but it declined dramatically after the Islamic conquest of the 8th century. The remaining Zoroastrian believers eventually made their way to western India, where they are now known as Farsis, or Parsees. Numbering about 300,000 worldwide and 20,000 in the United States, they still adhere to tenets of the ancient religion. Among other beliefs, they revere the forces of nature, particularly fire, as expressions of Ahura Mazda's divine power.

SIGNIFICANT DATES IN THE HISTORY OF RELIGION

B.C.

c. 2000	Abraham, founder of Judaism, is alive.
c. 13th century	Moses, Hebrew lawgiver, is alive.
c. 1100–c. 500	The Vedas, sacred texts of the Hindus, are compiled.
604	Traditional birth date of Lao-tzu, founder of Taoism.
588	Traditional date of Zoroaster's revelation.
c. 563–c. 483	Buddha, founder of Buddhism, is alive.
551–479	Confucius, founder of Confucianism, is alive.
c. 200	The *Bhagavad Gita,* important Hindu text, is written.
6 or 4	Jesus of Nazareth, founder of Christianity, is born.

A.D.

33?	The Crucifixion and death of Jesus Christ.
64?	Peter, disciple of Jesus and, according to tradition, first bishop of Rome, dies.
c. 70–c. 100	First four books of the New Testament—Matthew, Mark, Luke, and John—are written.
5th century	Two Buddhist sects—Zen and Pure Land (or Amidism)—are established.
c. 570–632	Muhammad the prophet—whose teachings, recorded in the Koran, form the basis of Islam—is alive.
622	Muhammad flees persecution in Mecca and settles in Yathrib (later Medina); the first day of the lunar year in which this event, known as the Hegira, takes place marks the start of the Muslim era.

936	Traditional date of the arrival from Iran of the first Parsees (followers of Zoroastrianism) in India.
1054	Catholic Pope Leo IX condemns the patriarch of Constantinople, finalizing the split between the Orthodox Church and the Roman Catholic Church.
c. 1224–74	Saint Thomas Aquinas, Italian philosopher and Roman Catholic theologian, is alive.
1309–77	The Roman Catholic papacy is seated in Avignon, France.
1483–1546	Martin Luther, leader of the Protestant Reformation in Germany and author of "95 Theses" (1517) is alive.
1491–1556	Ignatius Loyola, founder of the Jesuit Order of Roman Catholic priests, is alive.
1509–64	John Calvin, leader of the Protestant Reformation in France, is alive.
1549	The first Christian mission in Japan is established.
1582	Jesuit Matteo Ricci is the first missionary to be sent to China.
1620	Plymouth Colony in North America is founded in December by 102 English Puritan separatists, known as Pilgrims.

One of the Dead Sea scrolls, the "Copper" scroll, lists 64 underground hiding places in Israel that supposedly contain gold, silver, aromatics, and manuscripts. These are believed to be treasures from the Temple at Jerusalem that were hidden for safekeeping.

1624–91	George Fox, English founder of the Protestant Society of Friends (the Quakers), is alive.
1703–91	John Wesley, English founder of the Protestant movement that later became the Methodist Church, is alive.
1869–70	The first Roman Catholic Vatican Council, at which the dogma of papal infallibility is promulgated, is convened by Pope Piux IX.
1869–1948	Mohandas K. Gandhi, Indian spiritual and political leader who helped his country achieve independence from Britain and sought rapprochement between Hindus and Muslims, is alive.
1933–45	The systematic persecution and attempted extermination of European Jews by Adolf Hitler's Nazi party, known as the Holocaust, takes place.
1948	The independent Jewish state of Israel is declared.
1962–65	The second Roman Catholic Vatican Council, at which changes were made in the liturgy and greater participation in services by lay church members was encouraged, is convened by Pope John XXIII and concluded by Pope Paul VI.

The Ten Commandments

A Closer Look

During their exodus from the land of Egypt, Moses led the people of Israel to Mount Sinai, where God issued to Moses the Ten Commandments. These commandments form the foundation of both Jewish and Christian morality. The following is from Exodus, chapter 20; the bold numbers indicate the verse number (the Ten Commandments also appear, with slightly different wording, in Deuteronomy 5:6–21).

1. **2** I am the Lord thy God, which have brought thee out of the land of Egypt, out of the house of bondage,

2. **3** Thou shalt have no other gods before me.

   4 Thou shalt not make unto thee any graven image, or any likeness of any thing that is in heaven above, or that is in the earth beneath, or that is in the water under the earth.

   5 Thou shalt not bow down thyself to them, nor serve them; for I the Lord thy God am a jealous God, visiting the iniquity of the fathers upon the Children unto the third and fourth generation of them that hate me; **6** And showing mercy unto thousands of them that love me, and keep my commandments.

3. **7** Thou shalt not take the name of the Lord thy God in vain; for the Lord will not hold him guiltless that taketh his name in vain.

4. **8** Remember the sabbath day, to keep it holy, **9** Six days shalt thou labor, and do all thy work; **10** But the seventh day is the sabbath of the Lord thy God; in it thou shalt not do any work, thou, nor thy son, nor thy daughter, nor thy manservant, nor thy maidservant, nor thy cattle, nor thy stranger that is within thy gates; **11** For in six days the Lord made heaven and earth, the sea, and all that in them is, and rested the seventh day; wherefore the Lord blessed the sabbath day, and hallowed it.

5. **12** Honor thy father and thy mother; that thy days may be long upon the land which the Lord thy God giveth thee.

6. **13** Thou shalt not kill.

7. **14** Thou shalt not commit adultery.

8. **15** Thou shalt not steal.

9. **16** Thou shalt not bear false witness against thy neighbor.

10. **17** Thou shalt not covet they neighbor's house, thou shalt not covet thy neighbor's wife, nor his manservant, nor his maidservant, nor his ox, nor his ass, nor anything that is thy neighbor's.

HOLY BOOKS OF THE WORLD

The Analects   A collection of Confucius's teachings thought to have been recorded by his students. They are considered the only sayings that can reliably be attributed to him.

Bhagavad Gita   A Sanskrit poem that is part of the Indian epic known as the *Mahabharata.* It describes, in a dialogue between Lord Krishna and Prince Arjuna, the Hindu path to spiritual wisdom and the unity with God that can be achieved through *karma* (action), *bhakti* (devotion), and *jnana* (knowledge). The *Bhagavad Gita* was probably written sometime between 200 B.C. and A.D. 200.

Five Classics   Five works traditionally attributed to Confucius that form the basic texts of Confucianism. They are the *Spring and Autumn Annals,* a history of Confucius's native district; the *I Ching* (or *Book of Changes*), a system of divining the future; the *Book of Rites,* which outlines ceremonies and describes the ideal government; the *Book of History;* and the *Book of Songs,* a collection of poetry. Together they promulgate a system of ethics for managing society based on sympathy for others, etiquette, and ritual. Although the dates of these books are uncertain, they were probably written before the 3rd century B.C.

Koran   (Arabic, **al-Qur'ân**) The primary holy book of Islam. It is made up of 114 *suras,* or chapters, which contain impassioned appeals for belief in God, encouragement to lead a moral life, portrayals of damnation and beatitude, stories of Islamic prophets, and rules governing the social and religious life of Muslims. Believers maintain that the Koran contains the verbatim word of God, revealed

The Seven Canonical Hours

A Closer Look

Psalms 118:164 states: "Seven times a day I praise you." These hours were designated as matins and lauds, prime, terce, sext, nones, vespers, and compline.

to the prophet Muhammad through the angel Gabriel. Some of the *suras* were written during Muhammad's lifetime, but an authoritative text was not produced until c. A.D. 650.

The shortest verse in the Bible is "Jesus wept" (John 11:35).

New Testament   The second portion of the Christian Bible, which contains 27 books that form the basis of Christian belief. These books include the sayings of Jesus; the story of his life and work; the death and resurrection of Jesus now celebrated as Easter; the teachings and writings of the apostles; and instruction for converting nonbelievers and for performing baptisms, blessings, and other rituals. The New Testament is believed to have been written c. A.D. 100, some 70 to 90 years after the death of Jesus.

Old Testament   The Christian name for the Hebrew Bible. It is the sacred scripture of Judaism and the first portion of the Christian Bible. According to Jewish teachings, it is made up of three parts: *the Law* (also known as the Torah or Pentateuch), consisting of the first five books (Genesis, Exodus, Leviticus, Numbers, and Deuteronomy), which de-

The Four Horsemen of the Apocalypse

A Closer Look

The Book of Revelation, attributed to John the Apostle, refers to four horsemen who will ride forth bringing hardships to the earth.

Pestilence	Rides a white horse and carries a bow and a crown
War	Rides a red horse and swings a great sword
Famine	Rides a black horse and carries scales
Death	Rides a pale horse and has Hades close behind

THE BOOKS OF THE BIBLE

The Old Testament

Genesis	Nahu
Exodus	Habakkuk
Leviticus	Zephaniah
Numbers	Haggai
Deuteronomy	Zachariah
Joshua	Malachi
Judges	Psalms
I Samuel	Proverbs
II Samuel	Job
I Kings	The Song of Songs
II Kings	Ruth
Isaiah	Lamentations
Jeremiah	Ecclesiastes
Ezekiel	Esther
Hosea	Daniel
Joel	Ezra
Amos	Nehemiah
Obadiah	I Chronicles
Jonah	II Chronicles
Micah	

The New Testament

Matthew	I Peter
Mark	II Peter
Luke	I John
John	II John
Acts	III John
Romans	Jude
I Corinthians	Revelation
II Corinthians	
Galatians	
Ephesians	
Philippians	
Colossians	
I Thessalonians	
II Thessalonians	
I Timothy	
II Timothy	
Titus	
Philemon	
Hebrew	
James	

scribes the origins of the world, the covenant between the Lord and Israel, the exodus and entry into the promised land, and the various rules governing social and religious behavior; *the Prophets*, including the former prophets (Joshua, Judges, I and II Samuel, I and II Kings) and the latter prophets (Isaiah, Jeremiah, Ezekiel, and the 12 minor prophets), which describes the history of the Israelites, the stories of heroes, kings, judges, and wars, and the choosing of David as leader of the Israelites; and *the Writings* (including Psalms, Job, Song of Solomon, and Ruth, among others), which describes the reactions of the people to the laws and covenants, as well as prayers and praises of the covenant. Some books of the Old Testament regarded as sacred by the Jews are not accepted as such by Christians; among Christians there are differences between Roman Catholics and Protestants about the inclusion of some books, the order of the books, and the original sources used in translating them. Scholars generally agree that the Old Testament was compiled from c. 1000 B.C. to c. 100 B.C.

Talmud   A compilation of Jewish oral law and rabbinical teachings that is separate from the scriptures of the Hebrew Bible, or Old Testament. The Talmud is made up of two parts: the *Mishna,* which is the oral law itself, and the *Gemara,* which is a commentary on the *Mishna.* The Talmud contains both a legal section (the *Halakah*) and a portion devoted to legends and stories (the *Aggada*). The authoritative Babylonian Talmud was compiled in the 6th century.

Tao-te-ching (The Way and Its Power)   The basic text of the Chinese philosophy and religion known as Taoism. It is made up of 81 short chapters or poems that describe a way of life marked by quiet effortlessness and freedom from desire. This state is thought to be achieved by following the creative, spontaneous life force of the universe, called the Tao. The book is attributed to Lao-tzu, but it was probably a compilation by a number of writers over a long period of time.

Upanishads   The basis of Hindu religion and philosophy that form the final portion of the *Veda.* The 112 Upanishads describe the relationship of the

Brahman, or universal soul, to the *atman,* or individual soul; they also provide information about Vedic sacrifice and yoga. The original texts of the Upanishads come from various sources and were written beginning c. 900 B.C.

Veda   The sacred scripture of Hinduism. Four Vedas make up the *Samhita,* a collection of prayers and hymns that are considered to be revelations of eternal truth written by seer-poets inspired by the gods. The *Rig-Veda,* the *Sama-Veda,* and the *Yajur-Veda* are books of hymns; the *Atharva-Veda* compiles magic spells. These writings maintain that the *Brahman,* or Absolute Self, underlies all reality and can be known by invoking gods through the use of hymns or mantras. The Vedic texts were compiled between c. 1000 B.C. and c. 500 B.C., making them the oldest known group of religious writings.

A Closer Look

The Twelve Apostles

The twelve men who were chosen to be the missionaries of Christ's word were Peter, Andrew, James (the Greater), John, Thomas, James (the Less), Jude (or Thaddaeus), Philip, Bartholomew, Matthew, Simon, and Judas Iscariot (who was replaced by Mathias). St. Paul is also considered an apostle.

ROMAN CATHOLIC PATRON SAINTS

Protector of	Saint(s)	Protector of	Saint(s)
Accountants	Matthew	Cripples	Giles
Actors	Genesius	Dancers	Vitus
Aviators	Joseph of Cupertino	Deaf	Francis de Sales
Altar boys	John Berchmans	Dentists	Apollonia
Architects	Thomas	Desperate situations	Jude
Art	Catherine of Bologna	Domestic animals	Antony
Artists	Luke	Dying	Joseph
Astronomers	Dominic	Ecologists	Francis of Assisi
Athletes	Sebastian	Editors	John Bosco
Authors	Francis de Sales	Emigrants	Frances Xavier Cabrini
Bakers	Elizabeth of Hungary	Eyes	Lucy and Odilia
Bankers	Matthew	Falsely accused	Raymund Nonnatus
Barren women	Antony of Padua	Farmers	Isidore the Farmer
Beggars	Martin of Tours	Fathers	Joseph
Blind	Raphael	Searchers for lost objects	Anthony
Bookbinders	Peter Celestine	Firefighters	Florian
Bookkeepers	Matthew	Fire prevention	Catherine of Siena
Booksellers	John of God	Fishermen	Andrew
Bowels	Erasmus		Peter
Boy Scouts	George	Foundlings	Holy Innocents
Bricklayers	Stephen	France	Joan of Arc
Brides	Nicholas of Myra	Funeral directors	Joseph of Arimathea
Broadcasters	Archangel Gabriel	Gardeners	Adelard
Builders	Vincent Ferrer	Girls	Agnes
Cabdrivers	Fiacre	Glassworkers	Luke
Cancer victims	Peregrine Laziosi	Gravediggers	Antony the Abbot
Carpenters	Joseph	Grocers	Michael
Charitable societies	Vincent de Paul	Hairdressers	Martin de Porres
Childbirth	Gerard Majella	Heart patients	John of God
Children	Nicholas of Myra	Homeless	Margaret of Cortona
Church	Joseph	Hospitals	Camillus de Lellis
Comedians	Vitus		John of God
Cooks	Martha	Hotel keepers	Amand

Protector of	Saint(s)	Protector of	Saint(s)
Hungary	Stephen	Printers	Augustine
Invalids	Roch		Genesius
Ireland	Patrick		John of God
Jewelers	Eligius	Prisoners	Dismas
Journalists	Francis de Sales	Radio workers	Gabriel
Laborers	Isidore	Rheumatism	James the Greater
Lawyers	Thomas More	Sailors	Brendan
	Yves		Erasmus
Learning	Ambrose	Scholars	Brigid
Librarians	Jerome	Scientists	Albert the Great
Lovers	Valentine	Sculptors	Four Crowned Martyrs
Mariners	Nicholas of Tolentine	Secretaries	Genesius
Married women	Monica	Servants	Martha
Mentally ill	Dympna	Sick	John of God
Messengers	Gabriel		Camillus de Lellis
Midwives	Raymund Nonnatus	Skaters	Lidwina
Missions	Francis Xavier	Skiers	Bernard
	Thérèse of Lisieux	Social justice	Joseph
	Leonard of Port Maurice	Social workers	Louise de Marillac
Mothers	Monica	Soldiers	George
Musicians	Cecelia		Martin of Tours
	Gregory		Michael the Archangel
Nurses	Agatha	Students	Catherine of Alexandria
	Camillus de Lellis		Thomas Aquinas
	John of God	Surgeons	Cosmas and Damian
Orators	John Chrysostom		Luke
Orphans	Jerome Emiliani	Tax collectors	Matthew
Painters	Luke	Teachers	Gregory
Pawnbrokers	Nicholas of Myra		John Baptist de la Salle
Philosophers	Justin	Television	Clare of Assisi
Physicians	Cosmas and Damian	Theologians	Alphonsus Liguori
	Luke		Augustine
Plasterers	Bartholomew	Throat	Blaise
Poets	David	Travelers	Christopher
Police officers	Michael	United States	The Immaculate
Poor	Antony of Padua		Conception
Postal workers	Gabriel	Vintners	Amand
Preachers	Catherine of		Urban
	Alexandria		Vincent
	John Chrysostom	Vocations	Alphonsus
Pregnant women	Gerard Majella	Widows	Paula
Priests	John Vianney	Women in labor	Anne
		Writers	Francis de Sales
		Youth	Aloysius Gonzaga

THE ROMAN CATHOLIC POPES

The religious head of the Roman Catholic Church is known as the pope or the bishop of Rome. He is elected by the College of Cardinals, who as a group rank next to the pope in ecclesiastical authority. New popes are elected upon the death or retirement of a current pope. To be elected, a new pope must be named on two-thirds of the ballots cast, and each member of the College of Cardinals must vote. Once elected, a pope must be asked by the dean of cardinals if he accepts the post. If he does, he is then asked to choose a name. The custom of a pope changing his name upon election originated shortly before the year 1000.

The following table includes all the popes of the Roman Catholic Church, beginning with St. Peter the Apostle, who is traditionally considered to be the first pope because of his appointment by Jesus and his role in organizing the church. Also included (in brackets) are the so-called antipopes, those who were elected or claimed to be pope at various times during church history but whose positions were later invalidated. The table gives the names of the popes, the years of their papacies, and the original names of those who changed their names upon election. Alternative spellings of names are given in parentheses.

ROMAN CATHOLIC POPES

Pope	Reign	Original Name
St. Peter the Apostle	died c. 64	Symeon (Simon)
St. Linus	c. 66–c. 78	
St. Anacletus (Cletus)	c. 79–c. 91	
St. Clement I	c. 91–c. 100	
St. Evaristus	c. 100–c. 109	
St. Alexander I	c. 109–c. 116	
St. Sixtus I	c. 116–c. 125	
St. Telesphorus	c. 125–c. 136	
St. Hyginus	c. 136–c. 142	
St. Pius I	c. 142–c. 155	
St. Anicetus	c. 155–c. 166	
St. Soter	c. 166–c. 174	
St. Eleutherius (Eleutherus)	c. 174–189	
St. Victor I	189–198	
St. Zephyrinus	198–217	
St. Callistus I (Calixtus)	217–222	
[St. Hippolytus]	217–235	
St. Urban I	222–230	
St. Pontianus (Pontian)	July 21, 230–September 29, 235	
St. Anterus	November 21, 235–January 3, 236	
St. Fabian	January 10, 236–January 20, 250	
St. Cornelius	March 251–June 253	
[Novatian]	March 251–c. 258	
St. Lucius I	June 25, 253–March 5, 254	
St. Stephen I	May 12, 254–August 2, 257	
St. Sixtus II	August 30, 257–August 6, 258	
St. Dionysius	July 22, 260–December 26, 268	
St. Felix I	January 3, 269–December 30, 274	
St. Eutychian	January 4, 275–December 7, 283	
St. Gaius (Caius)	December 17, 283–April 22, 296	
St. Marcellinus	June 30, 296–c. 304	
St. Marcellus I	November/December 306–January 16, 308	
St. Eusebius	April 18, 310–October 21, 310	
St. Miltiades (Melchiades)	July 2, 311–January 11, 314	
St. Silvester I	January 31, 314–December 31, 335	
St. Mark	January 18, 336–October 7, 336	
St. Julius I	February 6, 337–April 12, 352	
Liberius	May 17, 352–September 24, 366	
[Felix II]	c. 355–November 22, 365	
St. Damasus I	October 1, 366–December 11, 384	

Pope	Reign	Original Name
[Ursinus]	September 366–November 367	
St. Siricius	December 384–November 26, 399	
St. Anastasius I	November 27, 399–December 19, 401	
St. Innocent I	December 22, 401–March 12, 417	
St. Zosimus	March 18, 417–December 26, 418	
St. Boniface I	December 28, 418–September 4, 422	
[Eulalius]	December 27, 418–April 3, 419	
St. Celestine I	September 10, 422–July 27, 432	
St. Sixtus III	July 31, 432–August 19, 440	
St. Leo I	August/September 440–November 10, 461	
St. Hilary (Hilarus)	November 19, 461–February 29, 468	
St. Simplicius	March 3, 468–March 10, 483	
St. Felix III (II)	March 13, 483–March 1, 492	
St. Gelasius I	March 1, 492–November 21, 496	
Anastasius II	November 24, 496–November 19, 498	
St. Symmachus	November 22, 498–July 19, 514	
[Lawrence]	November 22, 498–February 499; 501–506	
St. Hormisdas	July 20, 514–August 6, 523	
St. John I	August 13, 523–May 18, 526	
St. Felix IV (III)	July 12, 526–September 22, 530	
Boniface II	September 22, 530–October 17, 532	
[Dioscorus]	September 22, 530–October 14, 530	
John II	January 2, 533–May 8, 535	Mercury
St. Agapitus I	May 13, 535–April 22, 536	
St. Silverius	June 8, 536–November 11, 537	
Vigilius	c. 538–June 7, 555	
Pelagius I	April 16, 556–March 3, 561	
John III	July 17, 561–July 13, 574	Catelinus
Benedict I	June 2, 575–July 30, 579	
Pelagius II	November 26, 579–February 7, 590	
St. Gregory I	September 3, 590–March 12, 604	
Sabinian	September 13, 604–February 22, 606	
Boniface III	February 19, 607–November 12, 607	
St. Boniface IV	September 15, 608–May 8, 615	
St. Deusdedit I (Adeodatus I)	October 19, 615–November 8, 618	
Boniface V	December 23, 619–October 25, 625	
Honorius I	October 27, 625–October 12, 638	
Severinus	May 28, 640–August 2, 640	
John IV	December 24, 640–October 12, 642	
Theodore I	November 24, 642–May 14, 649	
St. Martin I	July 5, 649–June 17, 653	
St. Eugene I	August 10, 654–June 2, 657	
St. Vitalian	July 30, 657–January 27, 672	
Adeodatus II	April 11, 672–June 17, 676	
Donus	November 2, 676–April 11, 678	
St. Agatho	June 27, 678–January 10, 681	
St. Leo II	August 17, 682–July 3, 683	
St. Benedict II	June 26, 684–May 8, 685	
John V	July 23, 685–August 2, 686	

continues

Religions

Roman Catholic Popes, Continued

Pope	Reign	Original Name
Conon	October 21, 686–September 21, 687	
[Theodore]	687	
[Paschal]	687	
St. Sergius I	December 15, 687–September 9, 701	
John VI	October 30, 701–January 11, 705	
John VII	March 1, 705–October 18, 707	
Sisinnius	January 15, 708–February 4, 708	
Constantine	March 25, 708–April 9, 715	
St. Gregory II	May 19, 715–February 11, 731	
St. Gregory III	March 18, 731–November 28, 741	
St. Zachary (St. Zacharius)	December 3, 741–March 15, 752	
Stephen (II) unconsecrated	March 22 or 23, 752–March 25 or 26, 752	
Stephen II (III)	March 26, 752–April 26, 757	
St. Paul I	May 29, 757–June 28, 767	
[Constantine]	July 5, 767–August 6, 768	
[Philip]	July 31, 768	
Stephen III (IV)	August 7, 768–January 24, 772	
Adrian I (Hadrian I)	February 1, 772–December 25, 795	
St. Leo III	December 26, 795–June 12, 816	
Stephen IV (V)	June 22, 816–January 24, 817	
St. Paschal I	January 24, 817–February 11, 824	
Eugene II	February 824–August 827	
Valentine	August 827–September 827	
Gregory IV	September 827–January 25, 844	
[John]	January 844	
Sergius II	January 844–January 27, 847	
St. Leo IV	April 10, 847–July 17, 855	
Benedict III	September 29, 855–April 17, 858	
[Anastasius (Bibliothecarius)]	August 855–September 855	
St. Nicholas I	April 24, 858–November 13, 867	
Adrian II (Hadrian II)	December 14, 867–November or December 872	
John VIII	December 14, 872–December 16, 882	
Marinus I	December 16, 882–May 15, 884	
St. Adrian III (St. Hadrian III)	May 17, 884–September 885	
Stephen V (VI)	September 885–September 14, 891	
Formosus	October 6, 891–April 4, 896	
Boniface VI	April 896	
Stephen VI (VII)	May 896–August 897	
Romanus	August 897–November 897	
Theodore II	November 897	
John IX	January 898–January 900	
Benedict IV	May/June 900–August 903	
Leo V	August 903–September 903	
[Christopher]	September 903–January 904	
Sergius III	January 29, 904–April 14, 911	
Anastasius III	c. June 911–c. August 913	
Lando	c. August 913–c. March 914	
John X	March 914–May 928	

Pope	Reign	Original Name
Leo VI	May 928–December 928	
Stephen VII (VIII)	December 928–February 931	
John XI	February or March 931–December 935 or January 936	
Leo VII	January 3, 936–July 13, 939	
Stephen VIII (IX)	July 14, 939–October 942	
Marinus II	October 30, 942–May 946	
Agapetus (Agapitus) II	May 10, 946–December 955	
John XII	December 16, 955–May 14, 964	Octavian
Leo VIII	December 4, 963–March 1, 965	
Benedict V	May 22, 964–June 23, 964	
John XIII	October 1, 965–September 6, 972	
Benedict VI	January 19, 973–July 974	
[Boniface VII]	June 974–July 974	Franco
	August 984–July 20, 985	
Benedict VII	October 974–July 10, 983	
John XIV	December 983–August 20, 984	Peter Canepanova
John XV	August 985–March 996	
Gregory V	May 3, 996–February 18, 999	Bruno
[John XVI]	February 997–May 998	John Philagathos
Silvester II	April 2, 999–May 12, 1003	Gerbert
John XVII	May 16, 1003–November 6, 1003	John Sicco
John XVIII	December 25, 1003–July 1009	John Fasanus
Sergius IV	July 31, 1009–May 12, 1012	Peter
Benedict VIII	May 17, 1012–April 9, 1024	Theophylact
[Gregory]	1012	
John XIX	April 19, 1024–October 20, 1032	Romanus
Benedict IX	October 21, 1032–September 1044	Theophylact
	March 10, 1045–May 1, 1045	
	November 8, 1047–July 16, 1048	
Silvester III	January 20, 1045–March 10, 1045	John of Sabina
Gregory VI	May 1, 1045–December 20, 1046	John Gratian
Clement II	December 24, 1046–October 9, 1047	Suidger
Damasus II	July 17, 1048–August 9, 1048	Poppo
St. Leo IX	February 12, 1049–April 19, 1054	Bruno
Victor II	April 13, 1055–July 28, 1057	Gebhard
Stephen IX (X)	August 2, 1057–March 29, 1058	Frederick of Lorraine
[Benedict X]	April 5, 1058–January 24, 1059	John Mincius
Nicholas II	December 6, 1058–July 19 or 26, 1061	Gerard
Alexander II	September 30, 1061–April 21, 1073	Anselm
[Honorius II]	October 28, 1061–May 31, 1064	Peter Cadalus
St. Gregory VII	April 22, 1073–May 25, 1085	Hildebrand
[Clement III]	June 25, 1080	Guibert
	March 24, 1084–September 8, 1100	
Victor III	May 24, 1086	Daufer (Daufari)
	May 9, 1087–September 16, 1087	
Urban II	March 12, 1088–July 29, 1099	Odo (Eudes)
Paschal II	August 13, 1099–January 21, 1118	Rainerius

continues

Religions

Roman Catholic Popes, Continued

Pope	Reign	Original Name
[Theodoric]	September 1100–January 1101	
[Albert (Adalbert)]	1101	
[Silvester IV]	November 18, 1105–April 12, 1111	Maginulf
Gelasius II	January 24, 1118–January 29, 1119	John of Gaeta
[Gregory VIII]	March 8, 1118–April 1121	Maurice Burdinus
Calistus II	February 2, 1119–December 14, 1124	Guido
Honorius II	December 21, 1124–February 13, 1130	Lamberto of Ostia
[Celestine II]	December 15–16, 1124	Teobaldo Boccapecci
Innocent II	February 14, 1130–September 24, 1143	Gregorio Papareschi
[Anacletus II]	February 14, 1130–January 25, 1138	Pietro Pierleoni
[Victor IV]	March 1138–May 29, 1138	Gregorio Conti
Celestine II	September 26, 1143–May 8, 1144	Guido of Citta di Castello
Lucius II	March 12, 1144–February 15, 1145	Gherardo Caccianemicic
Eugene III	February 15, 1145–July 8, 1153	Bernardo Pignatelli
Anastasius IV	July 8, 1153–December 3, 1154	Corrado
Adrian IV (Hadrian IV)	December 4, 1154–September 1, 1159	Nicholas Breakspear
Alexander III	September 7, 1159–August 30, 1181	Orlando (Roland) Bandinelli
[Victor IV]	September 7, 1159–April 20, 1164	Ottaviano
[Paschal III]	April 22, 1164–September 20, 1168	Guido of Crema
[Calistus III]	September 1168–August 29, 1178	Giovanni
[Innocent III]	September 29, 1179–January 1180	Lando
Luicius III	September 1, 1181–November 25, 1185	Ubaldo Allucingoli
Urban III	October 25, 1185–October 20, 1187	Umberto Crivelli
Gregory VIII	October 21, 1187–December 17, 1187	Alberto de Morra
Clement III	December 19, 1187–March 1191	Paolo Scolari
Celestine III	March/April 1191–January 8, 1198	Giacinto Bobo
Innocent III	January 8, 1198–July 16, 1216	Lotario
Honorius III	July 18, 1216–March 18, 1227	Cencio Savelli
Gregory IX	March 19, 1227–August 22, 1241	Ugo (Ugolino)
Celestine IV	October 25, 1241–November 10, 1241	Goffredo da Castiglione
Innocent IV	June 25, 1243–December 7, 1254	Sinibaldo Fieschi
Alexander IV	December 12, 1254–May 25, 1261	Rinaldo, Count of Segni
Urban IV	August 29, 1261–October 2, 1264	Jacques Pantaléon
Clement IV	February 5, 1265–November 29, 1268	Guy Foulques
Gregory X	September 1, 1271–January 10, 1276	Tedaldo Visconti
Innocent V	January 21, 1276–June 22, 1276	Pierre of Tarentaise
Adrian V (Hadrian V)	July 11, 1276–August 18, 1276	Ottobono Fieschi
John XXI	September 8, 1276–May 20, 1277	Pedro Juliñao (Peter of Spain)
Nicholas III	November 25, 1277–August 22, 1280	Giovanni Gaetano
Martin IV	February 22, 1281–March 28, 1285	Simon de Brie (Brion)
Honorius IV	April 2, 1285–April 3, 1287	Giacomo Savelli
Nicholas IV	February 22, 1288–April 4, 1292	Girolamo Masci
St. Celestine V	July 5, 1294–December 13, 1294	Pietro del Morrone
Boniface VIII	December 24, 1294–October 11, 1303	Benedetto Caetani
Benedict XI	October 22, 1303–July 7, 1304	Niccolò Boccasino
Clement V	June 5, 1305–April 20, 1314	Bertrand de Got
John XXII	August 7, 1316–December 4, 1334	Jacques Duèse
[Nicholas V]	May 12, 1328–July 25, 1330	Pietro Rainalducci

Pope	Reign	Original Name
Benedict XII	December 20, 1334–April 25, 1342	Jacques Fournier
Clement VI	May 7, 1342–December 6, 1352	Pierre of Rosier d'Engleton
Innocent VI	December 18, 1352–September 12, 1362	Étienne Aubert
Urban V	September 28, 1362–December 19, 1370f	Guillaume de Grimoard
Gregory XI	December 30, 1370–March 27, 1378	Pierre Roger de Beaufort
Urban VI	April 8, 1378–October 15, 1389	Bartolomeo Prignano
[Clement VII]	September 20, 1378–September 16, 1394	Robert of Cambrai
Boniface IX	November 2, 1389–October 1, 1404	Pietro Tomacelli
[Benedict XIII]	September 28, 1394–July 26, 1417	Pedro de Luna
Innocent VII	October 17, 1404–November 6, 1406	Cosimo Gentile de'Migliorati
Gregory XII	November 30, 1406–July 4, 1415	Angelo Correr
[Alexander V]	June 26, 1409–May 3, 1410	Pietro Philarghi (Peter of Candia)
[John XXIII]	May 17, 1410–May 29, 1415	Baldassare Cossa
Martin V	November 11, 1417–February 20, 1431	Oddo Colonna
[Clement VIII]	June 10, 1423–July 26, 1429	Gil Sanchez, Muñoz
[Benedict XIV]	November 12, 1425–?	Bernard Garnier
Eugene IV	March 3, 1431–February 23, 1447	Gabriele Condulmaro
[Felix V]	November 5, 1439–April 7, 1449	Amadeus VIII, Duke of Savoy
Nicholas V	March 6, 1447–March 24, 1455	Tommaso Parentucelli
Callistus III	April 8, 1455–August 6, 1458	Alfonso de Boria (Borgia)
Pius II	August 19, 1458–August 15, 1464	Enea Silvo Piccolomini
Paul II	August 30, 1464–July 26, 1471	Pietro Barbo
Sixtus IV	August 9, 1471–August 12, 1484	Francesco della Roverre
Innocent VIII	August 29, 1484–July 25, 1492	Giovanni Battista Cibò
Alexander VI	August 11, 1492–August 18, 1503	Rodrigo de Borja y Borja (Borgia)
Pius III	September 22, 1503–October 18, 1503	Francesco Todeschini
Julius II	November 1, 1503–February 21, 1513	Giuliano dell Rovere
Leo X	March 11, 1513–December 1, 1521	Giovanni de' Medici
Adrian VI (Hadrian VI)	January 9, 1522–September 14, 1523	Adrian Florensz Dedal
Clement VII	November 19, 1523–September 25, 1534	Giulio de' Medici
Paul III	October 13, 1534–November 10, 1549	Alessandro Farnese
Julius III	February 8, 1550–March 23, 1555	Giovanni Maria Ciocchi del Monte
Marcellus II	April 9, 1555–May 1, 1555	Marcello Cervini
Paul IV	May 23, 1555–August 18, 1559	Giampietro Carafa
Pius IV	December 25, 1559–December 9, 1565	Giovanni Angelo edici
St. Pius V	January 7, 1566–May 1, 1572	Michele Ghislieri
Gregory XIII	May 14, 1572–April 10, 1585	Ugo Boncompagni
Sixtus V	April 24, 1585–August 27, 1590	Felice Peretti
Urban VII	September 15, 1590–September 27, 1590	Giambattista Castagna
Gregory XIV	December 5, 1590–October 16, 1591	Niccolò Sfondrati
Innocent IX	October 29, 1591–December 30, 1591	Giovanni Antonio Achinetti
Clement VIII	January 30, 1592–March 5, 1605	Ippolito Aldobrandini
Leo XI	April 1, 1605–April 27, 1605	Alessandro Ottaviano de' Medici
Paul V	May 16, 1605–January 28, 1621	Camillo Borghese
Gregory XV	February 9, 1621–July 8, 1623	Alessandro Ludovisi
Urban VIII	August 6, 1623–July 29, 1644	Mafeo Barberini
Innocent X	September 15, 1644–January 1, 1655	Giambattista Pamfili
Alexander VII	April 7, 1655–May 22, 1667	Fabio Chigi
Clement IX	June 20, 1667–December 9, 1669	Giulio Rospigliosi

continues

Roman Catholic Popes, Continued

Pope	Reign	Original Name
Clement X	April 29, 1670–July 22, 1676	Emilio Altieri
Innocent XI	September 21, 1676–August 12, 1689	Benedetto Odescalchi
Alexander VIII	October 6, 1689–February 1, 1691	Pietro Ottoboni
Innocent XII	July 12, 1691–September 27, 1700	Antonio Pignatelli
Clement XI	November 23, 1700–March 19, 1721	Giovanni Francesco Albani
Innocent XIII	May 8, 1721–March 7, 1724	Michelangelo dei Conti
Benedict XIII	May 27, 1724–February 21, 1730	Pietro Francesco Orsini
Clement XII	July 12, 1730–February 6, 1740	Lorenzo Corsini
Benedict XIV	August 17, 1740–May 3, 1758	Prospero Lorenzo Lambertini
Clement XIII	July 6, 1758–February 2, 1769	Carlo della Torre Rezzonico
Clement XIV	May 18, 1769–September 22, 1774	Lorenzo Ganganelli
Pius VI	February 15, 1775–August 29, 1799	Giovanni Angelo Brachi
Pius VII	March 14, 1800–July 20, 1823	Luigi Barnab à Chiaramonte
Leo XII	September 28, 1823–February 10, 1829	Annibale Sermattei della Genga
Pius VIII	March 31, 1829–November 30, 1830	Francesco Saverio Castiglione
Gregory XVI	February 2, 1831–June 1, 1846	Bartolomeo Albert Cappellari
Pius IX	June 16, 1846–February 7, 1878	Giovanni Maria Mastai-Ferretti
Leo XIII	February 20, 1878–July 20, 1903	Gioacchino Vincenzo Pecci
St. Pius X	August 4, 1903–August 20, 1914	Giuseppe Melchiorre Sarto
Benedict XV	September 3, 1914–January 22, 1922	Giacomo Della Chiesa
Pius XI	February 6, 1922–February 10, 1939	Ambrogio Damiano Archille Ratti
Pius XII	March 2, 1939–October 9, 1958	Eugenio Maria Giuseppe Pacelli
John XXIII	October 28, 1958–June 3, 1963	Angelo Giuseppe Roncalli
Paul VI	June 21, 1963–August 6, 1978	Giovanni Battista Montini
John Paul I	August 26, 1978–September 28, 1978	Albino Luciani
John Paul II	October 16, 1978–	Karol Wojtyla

MAJOR RELIGIOUS HOLIDAYS IN THE UNITED STATES

January 6	*Feast of the Epiphany* (Christian) marks the arrival of the Three Wise Men who sought the newborn baby Jesus and the Twelfth Night, or end, of the Christmas season.
February 2	*Candlemas* (Christian) celebrates the presentation of the Christ child in the temple and the purification of the Blessed Virgin Mary 40 days after she gave birth to Jesus; mostly observed in Roman Catholic, Orthodox, and Anglican churches.
February or March	*Purim* (Jewish), the Feast of Lots, memorializes Queen Esther's prevention of the annihilation of the Persian Jews; it is a celebratory festival of food, entertainment, and costumes held on the 14th day of the lunar month of Adar or Adar II.
	Shrove Tuesday (Christian), or Mardi Gras, is the last day before Lent; it is celebrated by eating rich foods forbidden during Lent and by carnivals in such cities as New Orleans, Rio de Janeiro, and Nice.
February, March, or April	*Lent* (Christian) is a 40-day period of fasting and penitence in preparation for Easter. It begins on Ash Wednesday in Western churches and on the Monday 41 days before Easter in the Orthodox Church.

March or April	*Passover* (Jewish), or Pesach, commemorates the time when Moses led the Jews out of Egypt; it is celebrated for seven days by Reform and Israeli Jews and for eight days by Orthodox and Conservative Jews, starting on the 14th day of the lunar month Nisan with a meal of remembrance called a seder.
	Palm Sunday (Christian) celebrates Jesus' triumphal ride into Jerusalem and the start of Holy Week; it is observed the Sunday before Easter.
	Maundy Thursday (Christian), the Thursday before Easter, marks the Last Supper, the Agony in the Garden, and the arrest of Jesus.
	Good Friday (Christian), the Friday before Easter, commemorates Jesus' Crucifixion.
	Holy Saturday (Christian), the Saturday before Easter, is observed primarily in Roman Catholic, Orthodox Eastern, and Anglican churches.
	Easter Sunday (Christian) celebrates the day Jesus Christ rose from the dead.
May or June	*Ascension Day* (Christian) celebrates Christ's ascent to heaven; it is held 40 days after Easter.
	Shavuot (Jewish) celebrates the harvest of grain while also observing the receipt of the Ten Commandments by Israel; it is held for one day by Reform and Israeli Jews or for two days by Orthodox and Conservative Jews, starting the sixth day of the lunar month of Sivan.
	Pentecost (Christian), or Whitsunday, marks the descent of the Holy Spirit on the Apostles; it is held 50 days after Easter.
August 15	*The Assumption of the Blessed Virgin Mary* (Roman Catholic and Orthodox) is the principal feast day in honor of Mary, celebrating her assumption, body and soul, into heaven after her death.
September or October	*Rosh Hashanah* (Jewish) marks the start of the new year with solemn prayer and the blowing of the shofar, a ram's horn; it is observed for one day by Reform and Israeli Jews or for two days by Orthodox and Conservative Jews, starting the first day of the lunar month of Tishri.
	Yom Kippur (Jewish), the Day of Atonement, is a day of fasting and repentance for the previous year's sins; it concludes the 10 days of penitence that began on Rosh Hashanah; it is observed on the 10th day of the lunar month of Tishri.
	Sukkoth (Jewish), the Feast of the Tabernacles, is an autumn harvest festival that recalls the wandering of the Jews in the wilderness; it is celebrated for eight days (seven in Israel) starting on the 15th day of the lunar month of Tishri.
Sunday nearest October 31	*Reformation Sunday* (Protestant) celebrates the day Martin Luther nailed his "95 Theses" to a church door, heralding the start of the Protestant Reformation.

"Major Foreign Holidays" in chapter 1; "Seven Wonders of the Ancient World" in chapter 26

Go to

continues

Major Religious Holidays, continued

November 1	*All Saints' Day* (Christian) is the feast day honoring all martyrs and the Virgin Mary; it is celebrated by Roman Catholic, Orthodox, and Anglican churches; it is also known as All Hallow's Day and is preceded by Halloween on October 31.
Sunday nearest November 30	*Advent* (Christian) is the period of repentance through Christmas Eve preparation for the anniversary of the birth of Christ.
December	*Hanukkah* (Jewish), the Festival of Lights, is marked by the lighting of eight candles in a menorah; it commemorates the restoration of traditional worship and the rededication of the temple in Jerusalem after the victory of the Jews over the troops of the Syrian emperor Antiochus; it is held for eight days beginning on the 25th day of the lunar month of Kislev.
December 8	*Feast of the Immaculate Conception* (Roman Catholic) honors the Virgin Mary's state of freedom from original sin from the time of her conception.
December 9	*Feast of the Conception of St. Anne* (Orthodox) celebrates the conception of the Virgin Mary.
December 25	*Christmas Day* (Christian) celebrates the birth of Jesus Christ; in many Western countries, it has become a nonsectarian winter holiday.
_____*	First day of Muharram, the first month, (Islamic) celebrates the hegira of Muhammad to Medina. The beginning of the Islamic year.
_____*	*Ramadan* (Islamic) is a month of fasting to celebrate the revelation of the Koran. It is the ninth month of the Islamic calendar.
_____*	*Eid-al-Fitr* (Islamic) is one of the two main festivals of Islam; this holiday concludes the month of Ramadan and is a day of thanksgiving for the blessings of Ramadan. Large early-morning worship services are followed by small private celebrations. It is held on the first day of Shawwal, the tenth month.
_____*	*Eid-al Adha* (Islamic), the Feast of Sacrifice, is the second of the two main festivals of Islam; it follows the day of pilgramage, or Haj; it is traditionally celebrated with a large prayer services and commemorates Abraham's willingness to sacrifice his son Ismael to Allah. Because an animal was substituted for Ismael, animals are sometimes sacrificed and their meat given to the needy. It is held on the tenth day of the twelfth month, Thw al-Hijjah.

* The Islamic calendar works on a lunar cycle; annual holidays thus advance about 10 days a year on the solar calendar. It takes Ramadan, for example, 36 years to move around the entire solar year.

ADDITIONAL SOURCES OF INFORMATION

BOOKS

Achtemeier, Paul J., ed. *HarperCollins Bible Dictionary.* HarperCollins, 1996.

Armstrong, Karen, *A History of God, The 4000 Year Quest of Judaism, Christianity, and Islam.* Ballantine, 1994.

Cairns, Alan. *Dictionary of Theological Terms.* Evangelical Press, 1998.

Cavendish, Richard, ed. *Man, Myth and Magic: The Illustrated Encyclopedia of Mythology, Religion and the Unknown.* Rev. 94 ed. Marshall Cavendish, 1994.

Danielou, Alain. *The Myths and Gods of India.* Inner Traditions, 1992.

DuBois, Thomas, ed. *Encyclopedia of World Mythology.* 3 vols. ABC-CLIO, 2001.

Eliade, Mircea, ed. *The Encyclopedia of Religion.* 16 vols. Macmillan, 1993.

Esposito, John L., ed. *The Oxford History of Islam.* Oxford University Press, 2000.

Fisher-Schreiber, Ingrid, et al., eds. *The Encyclopedia of Eastern Philosophy and Religion.* Shambhala, 1994.

Freedman, David Noel, ed. *Eerdman's Dictionary of the Bible.* Eerdman's Publishing, 2000.

Johnston, Willim M., ed. *Encyclopedia of Monasticism.* Fitzroy, 2000.

Jordon, Michael. *The Encyclopedia of Gods.* Facts on File, 1993.

Kelly, J. N. D. *The Oxford Dictionary of Popes.* Oxford University Press, 1989.

Kolatch, Alfred J. *The Jewish Book of Why/The Second Jewish Book of Why.* Jonathan David Publications, 1989.

Melton, J. Gordon, ed. *The Encyclopedia of American Religions.* 6th ed. Gale, 1998.

Mercatante, Anthony S., ed. *The Encyclopedia of World Myth and Legend.* Facts on File, 1988.

Metzger, Bruce M., and Michael D. Coogan, eds. *The Oxford Companion to the Bible.* Oxford University Press, 1998.

Newsner, Jacob, et al., eds. *Encyclopedia of Judaism.* Continuum, 1998.

Parrinder, Geoffrey, ed. *World Religions: From Ancient History to the Present.* Facts On File, 1988.

Peters, F. E. *Judaism, Christianity, and Islam.* 3 vols. Kazi, 1996.

Queen, Edward L., et al., eds. *The Encyclopedia of American Religious History.* 2 vols. Facts on File, 1996.

Smart, Ninia. *Atlas of the World's Religions.* Oxford University Press, 1999.

Smith, Jonathan Z., ed. *The HarperCollins Dictionary of Religion.* HarperCollins, 1995.

Suzuki, Shunryu. *Zen Mind, Beginner's Mind.* John Weatherhill, 1986.

Telushkin, Joseph. *Jewish Literacy: The Most Important Things to Know About the Jewish Religion, Its People, Its History.* William Morrow, 1991.

Terry, Michael. *Reader's Guide to Judaism.* Fitzroy, 2000.

Ware, Timothy, and Kallistos Ware. *The Orthodox Church.* 2nd ed. Penguin, 1992.

WEB SITES

Comparative Analysis of Major World Religions
www.comparativereligion.com

Divine Digest
www.divinedigest.com

Adherents of World Religions
www.adherents.com

Religions

10

PHILOSOPHY

MAJOR WORLD PHILOSOPHERS

Abelard, Peter (1079–1142). French philosopher. One of the most influential medieval logicians and theologians. Around 1113, while teaching theology in Paris, Abelard fell in love with his student Heloise, whom he secretly married; he was condemned for heresy a few years later because of his nominalist views. He wrote *Sic et Non*.

Anaxagoras (c. 500–428 B.C.). Greek pre-Socratic philosopher who is said to have made Athens the center of philosophy and to have been Socrates's teacher; he rejected the four-elements theory of Empedocles and posited instead an infinite number of unique particles of which all objects are composed.

Anaximander (c. 611–547 B.C.). Greek pre-Socratic thinker who believed the universal substance to be "the boundless" or "the indefinite," rather than something resembling familiar objects. Unlike Thales (his teacher) and Anaximenes, he did not believe that a single element underlies all things.

Anaximenes (6th century B.C.). One of the pre-Socratics and an associate of Anaximander. He agreed with Thales that one type of substance underlies the diversity of observable things. Anaximenes believed that air was that universal substance and that all things are made of air in different degrees of density.

Anselm, St. (1033–1109). Italian monk and Scholastic theologian who became archbishop of Canterbury. St. Anselm founded Scholasticism, integrated Aristotelian logic into theology, and believed that reason and revelation are compatible. He is most famous for his influential ontological argument for God's existence.

Aquinas, St. Thomas (1225–74). The greatest thinker of the Scholastic School. His ideas, in 1879, were made the official Catholic philosophy. He incorporated Greek ideas into Christianity by showing Aristotle's thought to be compatible with church doctrine. In Aquinas's system, reason and faith (revelation) form two separate but harmonious realms whose truths complement rather than oppose one another. He presented influential philosophical proofs for the existence of God. His works include *Summa Theologica* (1267–1273) and *On Being and Essence*.

Aristotle (384–322 B.C.). Greek philosopher, scientist, logician, and student of many disciplines. Aristotle studied under Plato and became the tutor of Alexander the Great. In 335, Aristotle opened the Lyceum, a major philosophical and scientific school in Athens. He emphasized the observation of nature and analyzed all things in terms of "the four causes." In ethics, he stressed that virtue is a mean between extremes and that a person's highest goal should be the use of his or her intellect. Most of Aristotle's works were lost to Christian civilization from the 5th through the 12th centuries. Among his writings are *Metaphysics, Politics,* and *Rhetoric.*

Augustine of Hippo, St. (354–430). The greatest of the Latin church fathers and possibly the most influential Christian thinker after St. Paul. St. Augustine emphasized a person's need for grace. His *Confessions* and *The City of God* were highly influential.

Averroes (1126–98). Spanish-born Arabian philosopher, lawyer, and physician whose detailed commentaries on Aristotle were influential for over 300 years. He emphasized the compatibility of faith and reason but believed philosophical knowledge to be derived from reason. The church condemned his views.

Avicenna (980–1037). Islamic medieval philosopher born in Persia. His Neoplatonist interpretation of Aristotle greatly influenced medieval philosophers, including St. Thomas Aquinas. Avicenna was also a physician; his writings on medicine were important for nearly 500 years.

Ayer, Alfred Jules (1910–89). British proponent of logical positivism. Maintaining that philosophical arguments have no validity unless they can be verified by empirical means, Ayer proposed linguistic analysis as the essential method of philosophic investigation. His most influential work is *Language, Truth, and Logic* (1936).

Bacon, Sir Francis   (1561–1626). English statesman, essayist, and philosopher. He was one of the great precursors of the tradition of British empiricism and of belief in the importance of scientific method. He emphasized the use of inductive reasoning in the pursuit of knowledge.

Bentham, Jeremy   (1748–1832). English philosopher and lawyer and one of the founders of utilitarianism. Bentham was a highly influential reformer of the British legal, judicial, and prison systems. He is the author of *Introduction to the Principles of Morals and Legislation* (1789).

Berkeley, George   (1685–1753). Irish philosopher and an Anglican bishop; one of the British empiricists. Berkeley held to a "subjective idealism." He believed that everything that exists is dependent on being perceived by a mind. According to this view, material objects are simply collections of sensations or "ideas" in the mind of a person or of God. His works include *Essay Toward a New Theory of Vision* (1709) and *A Treatise Concerning the Principles of Human Knowledge* (1710).

Boethius   (c. 475–535). Roman statesman, philosopher, and translator of Aristotle, whose *Consolation of Philosophy* (written in prison) was widely read throughout the Middle Ages; it showed reason's role in the face of misfortune and was the link between the ancient philosophers and the Scholastics.

Buber, Martin   (1878–1965). German-Israeli philosopher influenced by Jewish mysticism and existentialism, a major force in 20th-century Jewish thought and philosophy of religion. His *I and Thou* (1923) held that God and man can have a direct and mutual "dialogue."

Comte, Auguste   (1798–1857). French founder of positivism and social reformer. Comte put forth a "religion of humanity" that replaced the notion of God with the notion of humankind as a whole. He invented the term *sociology.*

Democritus   (c. 460–370 B.C.). Greek philosopher who proposed a mechanistic theory of the world that required no supernatural forces, only the constant motion of the indestructible atoms of which everything is composed. He held that perception is an unreliable source of knowledge and that knowledge can be obtained through reason only.

Derrida, Jacques   (1930–   ). French philosopher and founder of deconstructionism, which challenges traditional Western concepts of meaning. In the view of deconstructionists, language refers only to language, and all written works may have innumerable meanings independent of the author's intention.

Descartes, René   (1596–1650). French philosopher and scientist, considered the father of modern philosophical inquiry. Descartes tried to extend mathematical method to all knowledge in his search for certainty. Discarding the medieval appeal to authority, he began with "universal doubt," finding that the only thing that could not be doubted was his own thinking. The result was his famous " *Cogito, ergo sum,*" or "I think, therefore I am." His major works are the *Discourse on Method* (1637) and *Meditations on First Philosophy* (1641).

Dewey, John   (1859–1952). Leading American philosopher, psychologist, and educational theorist. Dewey developed the views of Charles S. Peirce (1839–1914) and William James into his own version of pragmatism. He emphasized the importance of inquiry in gaining knowledge and attacked the view that knowledge is passive.

Diderot, Denis   (1713–84). Materialist thinker of the French Enlightenment and originator of the *Encyclopédie* (1751–72).

Diogenes   (c. 400–325 B.C.). Greek founder of cynicism who rejected social conventions and supposedly lived in a tub in defiance of conventional comforts.

Empedocles (c. 495–435 B.C.). Greek pre-Socratic philosopher who believed the universe to consist of four elements: air, fire, water, and earth. Empedocles held that the interaction between love and hate causes the mixing of the elements.

Engels, Friedrich (1820–95). German socialist thinker and historian and the cofounder of Marxism. He was Marx's lifelong collaborator and coauthor of the *Communist Manifesto* (1848) and an originator of the philosophy of dialectical materialism.

Epictetus (c. 50–138). Stoic moral philosopher who established a school of philosophy after being freed as a slave. His *Manual* teaches that only by detaching ourselves from what is not in our power can we attain inward freedom.

Epicurus (341–270 B.C.). Founder of the Epicurean philosophy and a follower of Democritus, the greatest ancient philosopher of atomism. Virtually all of Epicurus's writings are lost.

Foucault, Michel (1926–84). French philosopher and historian of ideas whose major works analyze the origin and growth of social institutions. In *Madness and Civilization* (1961), Foucault explores society's response to mental illness; *Discipline and Punish* (1975) examines the treatment of criminals.

Hegel, Georg Wilhelm Friedrich (1770–1831). German philosopher whose idealistic system of metaphysics was highly influential. It was based on a concept of the world as a single organism developing by its own inner logic through trios of stages called "thesis, antithesis, and synthesis" and gradually coming to embody reason. Hegel held the monarchy to be the highest development of the state. His works include *The Science of Logic* (1812, 1813, 1816) and *Phenomenology of Mind* (1807).

Heidegger, Martin (1889–1976). German philosopher who studied with Husserl. Heidegger's own philosophy, which was influenced by Kierkegaard, emphasized the need to understand "being," especially the unique ways that humans act in and relate to the world. He wrote *Being and Time* (1927).

Heraclitus (c. 535–475 B.C.). Pre-Socratic philosopher opposed to the idea of a single ultimate reality. Heraclitus believed that all things are in a constant state of change.

Hobbes, Thomas (1588–1679). English materialist and empiricist; one of the founders of modern political philosophy. In *Leviathan* (1651), Hobbes argued that because men are selfish by nature, a powerful absolute ruler is necessary. In a "social contract," men agree to give up many personal liberties and accept such rule.

Hume, David (1711–76). British empiricist whose arguments against the proofs for God's existence are still influential. In his *Treatise of Human Nature* (1739–40), Hume held that moral beliefs have no basis in reason, but are based solely on custom.

Husserl, Edmund (1859–1938). German philosopher who founded the phenomenology movement. He aimed at a completely accurate description of consciousness and conscious experience. His works include *Logical Investigations* (1900–01) and *Ideas Pertaining to a Pure Phenomenology and Phenomenological Philosophy* (1913).

James, William (1842–1910). American philosopher and psychologist, one of the founders of pragmatism, and one of the most influential thinkers of his era. James viewed consciousness as actively shaping reality, defined truth as "the expedient" way of thinking, and held that ideas are tools for guiding our future actions rather than reproductions of our past experiences. His writings include *The Will to Believe* (1897) and *Pragmatism* (1907).

Kant, Immanuel (1724–1804). German philosopher, possibly the most influential of modern times. He synthesized Leibniz's rationalism and Hume's skepticism into his "critical philosophy": in *The Critique of Pure Reason* (1781), Kant wrote that ideas do not conform to the external world, but rather the world can be known only insofar as it conforms to the mind's own structure. In *The Critique of Practical Reason* (1788), Kant claimed that morality requires a belief in God, freedom, and immortality,

Philosophy

How to Argue Logically

A Closer Look

We like to think that we speak logically all the time, but we are aware that we sometimes use illogical means to persuade others of our point of view. In the heat of an impassioned argument, or when we are afraid our disputant has a stronger case, or when we don't quite have all the facts we'd like to have, we are prone to engage in faulty processes of reasoning, using arguments we hope will appear sound.

Such defective arguments are called *fallacies* by philosophers who, starting with Aristotle, have cataloged and classified these fallacious arguments. There are now over 125 separate fallacies, most with their own impressive-sounding names, many of them in Latin.

Some arguments have easily recognizable defects. For instance, in the *argument ad hominem,* a person's views are criticized because of a logically irrelevant personal defect: "You can't take Smith's advice on the stock market; he's a known philanderer." In the *genetic fallacy,* something is mistakenly reduced to its origins: "We know that emotions are nothing more than physiology; after all, medical research has shown emotions involve the secretion of hormones." Another illogical argument is named for the erroneous thinking a wagering person may fall prey to, the *gambler's fallacy* (also called the *Monte Carlo fallacy*): "I'm betting on heads; it's got to come up since we've just had nine straight tails."

Some fallacies may not be recognized as erroneous reasoning because they are such commonly used forms of argument. For instance, if we say, "I'm sure my cold is due to the weather; I started sneezing right after it went from 60 degrees to 31 degrees in three hours," we are committing the fallacy with the Latin name of *post hoc ergo propter hoc* ("after this, therefore because of this"). Many a political argument exemplifies the fallacy of *arguing in a circle:* "Only wealthy men are capable of leading the country; after all, leadership can be learned only if you have had money to exercise power." Many prejudicial or stereotypical arguments commit the *fallacy of division,* or of applying to the part what may be true of the whole: "North Dakota has wide-open spaces; because Jack's farm is there, it must be quite large." The converse of this is the *fallacy of composition,* where properties of the parts are erroneously attributed to the whole: "Every apple on this tree is rotten; therefore, the tree itself is hopelessly diseased."

It may be a surprise to realize that some widely accepted forms of argument are just as fallacious as the most logically defective reasoning. When we appeal to the beliefs or behavior of the majority to prove the truth of something, we are committing the *fallacy of consensus gentium:* "Imbibing alcohol cannot be bad for people, because all cultures studied have used alcohol." Or consider the person who argues that "Tragedy is the highest form of literature; after all, didn't Aristotle consider it such?" This is a form of the *fallacy of arguing from authority.* There is also the *fallacy of ignoratio elenchus,* which has nothing to do with ignorance; its name means that the point made is irrelevant to the issue at hand, as in the untenable view of a lawyer who says, "Ladies and gentlemen of the jury, you cannot convict my client of manslaughter while driving under the influence; after all, advertisements for alcohol exist everywhere in our culture."

Philosophy

although these can be proved neither scientifically nor by metaphysics. Finally, in his *Foundations of the Metaphysic of Morals* (1785), he presented the concept of the categorical imperative.

Kierkegaard, Søren (1813–55). Danish philosopher, religious thinker, and extraordinarily influential founder of existentialism. Kierkegaard held that "truth is subjectivity," that religion is an individual matter, and that man's relationship to God requires suffering. He wrote *Either/Or* (1843) and *Fear and Trembling* (1843).

Leibniz, Gottfried Wilhelm (1646–1716). German philosopher, diplomat, and mathematician; one of the great minds of all time. Leibniz was an inventor (with Sir Isaac Newton) of calculus and a forefather of modern mathematical logic. He held that the entire universe is one large system expressing God's plan. His writings include *New Essays on Human Understanding* (1703–04).

Locke, John (1632–1704). Highly influential founder of British empiricism. In his *Essay Concerning Human Understanding* (1690), Locke wrote that all ideas come to mind from experience and that none are innate. He also held that authority derives solely from the consent of the governed, a view that deeply influenced the American Revolution and the writing of the U.S. Constitution. His *Two Treatises on Government* (1690) express his political thought.

Lucretius (c. 99–55 B.C.). Roman Epicurean philosopher and poet. In *De Rerum Natura* (On the Nature of Things), Lucretius depicted the entire world, including the soul, as composed of atoms.

Machiavelli, Niccolò (1469–1527). Italian Renaissance statesman and political writer. In *The Prince* (1513), one of the most influential political books of modern times, Machiavelli argues that any act of a ruler designed to gain and hold power is permissible. The term *Machiavellian* is used to refer to any political tactics that are cunning and power-oriented.

Maimonides (Moses ben Maimon) (1135–1204). Spanish-born medieval Jewish philosopher and thinker. Maimonides tried to synthesize Aristotelian and Judaic thought. His works, such as *Guide for the Perplexed,* had enormous influence on Jewish and Christian thought.

Marcus Aurelius (121–180). Roman emperor from A.D. 161 and a proponent of the Stoic philosophy. His *Meditations* held that death is as natural as birth and that the world is rational and orderly. Although a great humanitarian, Marcus Aurelius persecuted the Christians of his time.

Marx, Karl (1818–83). German revolutionary thinker, social philosopher, and economist. His ideas, formulated with Friedrich Engels, laid the foundation for 19th-century socialism and 20th-century communism. Although Marx was initially influenced by Georg Hegel, he soon rejected Hegel's idealism in favor of materialism. His *Communist Manifesto* (1848) and *Das Kapital* (1867) are among the most important writings of the last 200 years.

Mill, John Stuart (1806–73). English empiricist philosopher, logician, economist, and social reformer. His *System of Logic* (1843) described the basic rules for all scientific reasoning. As a student of Jeremy Bentham, he elaborated on utilitarian ethics; in *On Liberty* (1859), he presented a plea for the sanctity of individual rights against the power of any government.

Montesquieu, Baron de (Charles-Louis de Secondat) (1689–1755). French political philosopher, influenced by John Locke. In *Spirit of the Laws* (1748), Montesquieu put forth the theory of separation of powers that strongly influenced the writing of the U.S. Constitution.

Moore, G. E. (George Edward) (1873–1958). British philosopher who emphasized the "common sense" view of the reality of material objects. In ethics, Moore held that goodness is a quality known directly by moral intuition and that it is a fallacy to try to define it in terms of anything else.

More, Sir Thomas (1478–1535). A leading Renaissance humanist and statesman; Lord Chancellor of England. More was beheaded for refusing to accept the king as head of the church. Influenced by Greek thinking, he believed in social reform and drew a picture of an ideal peaceful state in his *Utopia* (1516).

Nietzsche, Friedrich Wilhelm (1844–1900). German philosopher, philologist, and poet. As a moralist, he rejected Christian values and championed a "Superman" who would create a new, life-affirming, heroic ethic by his "will to power." His works include *Thus Spake Zarathustra* (1883–85) and *Beyond Good and Evil* (1886).

Parmenides (fl. c. 500 B.C.). The founder of Western metaphysics. This pre-Socratic thinker held that "being" is the basic substance and ultimate reality of which all things are composed and that motion, change, time, difference, and reality are illusions of the senses.

The Greek philosopher Epicurus believed that the only evil in the world was pain.

Pascal, Blaise (1623–62). French philosopher, mathematician, scientist, and theologian. His posthumous *"Pensées"* ("Thoughts") argues that reason is by itself inadequate for man's spiritual needs and cannot bring man to God, who can be known only through mystic understanding.

Plato (c. 428–348 B.C.). Athenian father of Western philosophy and student of Socrates, after whose death he traveled widely. Upon returning to Athens, Plato founded an academy, where he taught until he died. His writings are in the form of dialogues between Socrates and other Athenians. Many of Plato's views are set forth in *The Republic* (c. 370 B.C.), where an ideal state postulates philosopher kings, specially trained at the highest levels of moral and mathematical knowledge. Plato's other works analyzed moral virtues, the nature of knowledge, and the immortality of the soul. His views on cosmology strongly influenced the next 2,000 years of scientific thinking.

Plotinus (205–270). Egyptian-born founder of Neoplatonism, who synthesized the ideas of Plato and other Greek philosophers. Plotinus believed all reality is caused by a series of outpourings (called emanations) from the divine source. Although not himself a Christian, he was a major influence on Christianity.

Pythagoras (c. 582–507 B.C.). Greek philosopher, mathematician, and mystic; founder of a religious brotherhood that believed in the immortality and the transmigration of the soul. Pythagoras may have been the first thinker to assert that numbers constitute the true nature of all things; he also may have coined the term *philosophy*.

Quine, Willard Van Orman (1908–   ). A leading American linguistic philosopher, Quine has explored the connections between language and logic and made important contributions to set theory.

Among his best-known works are *Word and Object* (1960) and *Theories and Things* (1981).

Rawls, John (1921–   ). American philosopher whose major work, *A Theory of Justice* (1971), revived interest in political theory. Rawls has attempted to provide a modern philosophical foundation for the idea of the social contract, first developed by John Locke and Jean Jacques Rousseau.

Rousseau, Jean-Jacques (1712–78). Swiss-French thinker, born in Geneva. Rousseau has been enormously influential in political philosophy, educational theory, and the romantic movement. In *The Social Contract* (1762), he viewed governments as being expressions of the people's "general will," or rational people's choice for the common good. Rousseau emphasized a person's natural goodness.

Russell, Bertrand (1872–1970). English philosopher and logician influential as an agnostic and a pacifist. Early work with Alfred North Whitehead gave birth to modern logic; they coauthored *Principia Mathematica* (3 vols., 1910–13). Russell changed his views numerous times but always sought to establish philosophy, especially epistemology, as a science.

Ryle, Gilbert (1900–76). British philosopher who was a leader in linguistic analysis. Ryle's work related grammar and word usage to the principles of logic. His main work, *The Concept of Mind* (1949), challenged Descartes's distinction between mind and body, arguing that the mind is a set of capacities belonging to the body.

Santayana, George (1863–1952). Spanish-born American philosopher and poet; a student of William James. Santayana attempted to reconcile Platonism and materialism, studied how reason works, and found "animal faith," or impulse, to be the basis of reason and belief. Among his works are *The Sense of Beauty* (1896) and *The Life of Reason* (5 vols., 1905–06).

Sartre, Jean-Paul (1905–80). French philosopher, novelist, and dramatist; one of the founders of existentialism. Sartre was a Marxist through much of his life. He held that man is "condemned to be free" and to bear the responsibility of making free choices. His primary philosophical work was *Being and Nothingness* (1943).

Schopenhauer, Arthur   (1788–1860). German post-Kantian philosopher who held that although irrational will is the driving force in human affairs, it is doomed not to be satisfied. He believed that only art and contemplation could offer escape from determinism and pessimism. Schopenhauer strongly influenced Friedrich Nietzsche, Sigmund Freud, Leo Tolstoy, Marcel Proust, and Thomas Mann. He wrote *The World as Will and Representation* (1818).

Scotus, John Duns   (c. 1266–1308). Scottish-born Scholastic philosopher who tried to integrate Aristotelian ideas into Christian theology. Scotus emphasized that all things depend not just on God's intellect but on divine will as well. He wrote *On the First Principle.*

Smith, Adam   (1723–90). Scottish philosopher and economist. The author of *An Inquiry into the Nature and Causes of the Wealth of Nations* (1776), he believed that if government left the marketplace to its own devices, an "invisible hand" would guarantee that the results would benefit the populace. Smith has had enormous influence on economists into the present day.

Socrates   (c. 470–399 B.C.). Athenian philosopher who allegedly wrote down none of his views, supposedly from his belief that writing distorts ideas. His chief student, Plato, is the major source of knowledge about his life. Socrates questioned Athenians about their moral, political, and religious beliefs, as depicted in Plato's dialogues; his questioning technique, called dialectic, has greatly influenced Western philosophy. In 399 B.C., he was brought to trial on charges of corrupting the youth and religious heresy. Sentenced to die, he drank poison.

Spinoza, Benedict (Baruch)   (1623–77). Dutch-born philosopher expelled from the Amsterdam Jewish community for heresy in 1656; he was attacked by Christian theologians 14 years later. In *Ethics Demonstrated in Geometrical Order* (1677), Spinoza

presents his views in a mathematical system of deductive reasoning. A proponent of monism, he held —in contrast to Descartes—that mind and body are aspects of a single substance, which he called God or nature.

Thales of Miletus   (c. 636–546 B.C.). Regarded as the first Western philosopher, this pre-Socratic monist thinker is said to have believed that the fundamental principle of all things, or universal substance, is water. All of his writings are lost.

Unamuno, Miguel de   (1864–1936). The major Spanish philosopher of his time. Unamuno criticized philosophic abstractions such as "man" for ignoring concrete men. He held that reason by itself is virtually useless and cannot reveal the basic fact of human immortality. He wrote *The Tragic Sense of Life in Men and Nations* (1913).

Voltaire (François Marie Arouet)   (1694–1778). French philosopher, essayist, and historian; one of the major thinkers of the Enlightenment. A Deist who was anti-Christian, Voltaire widely advocated tolerance of liberal ideas and called for positive social action. His novel *Candide* (1759) is a parody of the optimism of Gottfried Leibniz.

Whitehead, Alfred North   (1861–1947). British philosopher and mathematician who worked with Bertrand Russell. Whitehead tried to integrate 20th-century physics into a metaphysics of nature.

William of Ockham (Occam)   (c. 1285–1349). Franciscan monk and important English theologian and philosopher. In his nominalism, he opposed much of the thought of St. Thomas Aquinas and of medieval Aristotelianism; he also rejected the pope's power in the secular realm.

Wittgenstein, Ludwig   (1889–1951). Austrian-born philosopher who spent the last 20 years of his life in England. Wittgenstein was one of the most influential philosophers of the 20th century, primarily through his emphasis on the importance of the study of language. His *Tractatus Logico-Philosophicus* (1921) influenced analytic philosophy. His later views emphasized that philosophic problems are often caused by linguistic confusions.

Zeno of Elea (c. 490–430 B.C.). Pre-Socratic philosopher and disciple of Parmenides. Zeno argued that motion, change, and plurality are logical absurdities and that only an unchanging being is real. His four arguments against motion (Zeno's paradoxes) attempted to demonstrate logically that the notions of time and motion are erroneous.

Zeno (of Citium) the Stoic (c. 334–262 B.C.). Greek philosopher born in Cyprus; the founder of Stoicism.

PHILOSOPHICAL MOVEMENTS AND SCHOOLS OF THOUGHT

analytical philosophy An influential 20th-century movement whose major proponents include Bertrand Russell, Ludwig Wittgenstein, and such logical positivists as Rudolph Carnap (1891–1970) and Willard Van Orman Quine. This school of thought emphasizes restating philosophical problems in highly structured terms based on modern logic.

anthroposophy The philosophy of Rudolf Steiner (1861–1925), an Austrian-born thinker who held that cultivating man's spiritual development is humanity's most important task. His followers founded a large number of schools worldwide based on his philosophy.

Aristotelianism A system of thought originating with the teachings of Aristotle (4th century B.C.), who held that knowledge originates in experience and observation, from which comes an understanding of the universal. His teachings and writings were influential in the Western world until the fall of Rome, when all but his writings on logic were lost to Christian civilization in Europe. His empiricism was embraced by medieval thinkers, especially St. Thomas Aquinas. Aristotle's works were preserved in Syrian and Arabic cultures and were revived in the West at the end of the 12th century.

British empiricism The empiricism of John Locke, George Berkeley, and David Hume in the 17th and 18th centuries. They shared the axiom that our knowledge of the world derives from experience or sensation rather than from reason. This view was opposed to rationalism, as well as to the Platonic notion of Forms as the source of knowledge.

British idealism (neo-Hegelianism) The philosophy of Georg Hegel as followed in England and Scotland in the mid–19th century. The most prominent members of this school were Thomas Hill Green (1836–82), Bernard Bosanquet (1848–1923), and Francis Herbert Bradley (1846–1924). They were united in their opposition to empiricism and utilitarianism and in their emphasis on mind and spirit as primary.

Cambridge Platonists A group of 17th-century English philosophers and theologians who tried to provide Christian theology with a philosophical defense based on Platonic and Neoplatonic theories. Ralph Cudworth (1617–88) was the most prominent member.

Cartesianism The views of René Descartes as interpreted by 17th-century rationalistic, dualistic, and theistic philosophers. They held that the search for knowledge and certainty can be based on logical analysis and mathematical principles. Nicolas Malebranche (1638–1715) was the most prominent of Descartes's followers.

Cynics A school of Greek philosophers founded in the 4th century B.C. by Diogenes. According to legend, Diogenes walked around night and day with a lighted lantern seeking an honest man but could not find one. The Cynics held that virtue was the only good and that happiness was to be attained only by living in a simple state of nature with as few desires and needs as possible. They advocated moderation, self-discipline, and training of the mind as well as the body.

Cyrenaics A school of philosophy of the 4th century B.C. in Athens, founded by Cyrene, a disciple of

Socrates. Cyrenaics believed that only momentary feelings of pleasure or pain can be known; they held that the good life is one that maximizes pleasure derived from satisfying one's bodily desires. Unlike the Epicureans, the Cyrenaics focused on physical sensation and the primacy of personal experience. *See also* **hedonism.**

deism   A philosophical viewpoint appearing in England in the 17th and 18th centuries and in France in the 18th century. Deists held that although God created the universe and its laws, He then removed Himself from any ongoing interaction with the material world.

dialectical materialism   The philosophy of Karl Marx and many of his followers. It holds that matter is the primary reality and that it obeys the dynamic laws of change. The most fundamental of these laws is that progress occurs through conflict and struggle between opposing forces (thesis and antithesis), such as between different classes and between capitalism and communism. Essentially deterministic, this philosophy maintains that individuals have no influence over the course of history. *See also* **Marxism.**

Eleatics   A school of pre-Socratic philosophers (5th century B.C.) from Elea in southern Italy, of whom Parmenides and Zeno of Elea are the best known. The Eleatics denied the reality of what is known to the senses, holding that the ultimate reality is an undifferentiated and unchanging "being."

Encyclopedists   A group of 18th-century French writers who combined to produce an encyclopedia of philosophy, art, and science (1751–65), edited by Denis Diderot and Jean d'Alembert (1717–83). The work was skeptical about religion and advocated liberal, democratic political views. At the time, it was the largest compendium of human knowledge that had ever been produced.

Enlightenment (Age of Reason)   A mainly 18th-century European philosophical movement. Its thinkers strove to make reason the ruler of human life; they believed that all people could gain knowledge and liberation. They sought the perfection of human society through applied reason. Rejecting conventional religious and secular authority, this movement substituted tolerance, humanism, and positive social action by the state. Major Enlightenment figures include Voltaire, Jean-Jacques Rousseau, Denis Diderot, and Baron de Montesquieu in France; David Hume in England; and Gotthold Ephraim Lessing (1729–81) and Johann Gottfried von Herder (1744–1803) in Germany. *See also* **philosophes.**

Epicureanism   An ethical doctrine established in Greece in the 3rd century B.C. Based on the teachings of Epicurus, it maintained that pleasure is the highest good and that pleasure can only be attained through a life of virtuous conduct. Epicureans sought mental pleasures over bodily ones.

existentialism   A philosophy of the 19th and 20th centuries. The dogma holds that because there are no universal values, a person's essence is not predetermined but is based only on free choice; a person is in a state of anxiety because of his or her realization of free will; and there is no objective truth. Major existentialists were Søren Kierkegaard, Friedrich Nietzsche, Jean-Paul Sartre, Martin Heidegger, Karl Jaspers (1883–1969), and the religious existentialists Martin Buber and Gabriel Marcel (1889–1973).

hedonism   The ethical doctrine holding that pleasure is the highest or the only good in life, and that a person should strive for pleasure and the avoidance of pain. In ancient Greece, the Cyrenaics emphasized physical sensation, while the Epicureans stressed the importance of simple living and virtuous moral conduct. The utilitarians in the 19th century were also proponents of hedonism.

Hegelianism (neo-Hegelianism)   A school of thought associated with Georg Hegel in the 19th and early 20th centuries, especially in England, America, France, and Italy. Francis Herbert Bradley (1846–1924), Josiah Royce (1855–1916), and Benedetto Croce (1866–1952) were prominent members; they emphasized the importance of spirit and the belief that ideas and moral ideals are fundamental.

intuitionism   Any philosophy holding that intuition is the basis of knowledge or of philosophy. French philosopher Henri Bergson (1859–1941)

Famous Philosophical Quotes

A Closer Look

Aristotle	"Man is by nature a political animal."
Sir Francis Bacon	"Knowledge is power."
Jeremy Bentham	"The greatest happiness of the greatest number is the foundation of morals and legislation."
Confucius	"Hold faithfulness and sincerity as first principles."
René Descartes	"*Cogito, ergo sum*" (Latin for "I think, therefore I am").
Ralph Waldo Emerson	"Nature is a mutual cloud, which is always and never the same."
Friedrich Engels	"The state is not 'abolished,' it withers away."
Georg Hegel	"What experience and history teach us is this—that people and governments have never learned anything from history, or acted on principles deduced from it."
Thomas Hobbes	"The life of man [in a state of nature is], solitary, poor, nasty, brutish, and short."
Immanuel Kant	"Happiness is not an ideal of reason but of imagination."
John Locke	"No man's knowledge here can go beyond his experience."
Niccolò Machiavelli	"God is not willing to do everything, and thus take away our free will and that share of glory which belongs to us."
Karl Marx	"The proletarians have nothing to lose [in this revolution] but their chains. They have a world to win. Workers of the world, unite!"
	"Religion is the opium of the people."
	"The class struggle necessarily leads to the dictatorship of the proletariat."
John Stuart Mill	"Liberty consists in doing what one desires."
Friedrich Nietzsche	"I teach you the Superman. Man is something to be surpassed."
Thomas Paine	"Suspicion is the companion of mean souls, and the bane of all good society."
Plato	"The life which is unexamined is not worth living."
Jean-Jacques Rousseau	"Man was born free, and everywhere he is in chains."
Bertrand Russell	"It is undesirable to believe a proposition when there is no ground whatever for supposing it true."
Seneca	"Even while they teach, men learn."
Socrates	"There is only one good, knowledge, and one evil, ignorance."
Voltaire	"If God did not exist, it would be necessary to invent Him."

Philosophy

was a prominent advocate. In particular, intuitionism refers to a British school of thought that maintains that all ethical knowledge rests on moral intuition.

linguistic philosophy (linguistic analysis) The 20th-century school of thought whose key tenet is that philosophical problems are best approached by asking questions about the use of words and by analyzing how language works in specific social contexts.

logical positivism A 20th-century school founded in the 1920s in Europe that was extremely influential for American and English philosophers. It attempted to introduce mathematical and scientific methodology into philosophy. It rejected metaphysical speculation in favor of a vigorous analysis of experience and language, without which understanding is not possible. The school advocated the principle of verifiability, according to which all statements that could not be validated empirically were meaningless. Logical positivism held that this principle showed that all of metaphysics, religion, and ethics were incapable of being proved either true or false. *See also* **Vienna Circle.**

Manichaeanism A religious-philosophical doctrine that originated in Persia in the 3rd century A.D. and reappeared throughout the next 1,300 years. It holds that the entire universe, especially human life, is a struggle between the opposing forces of good and evil (light and darkness).

Bertrand Russell said, "The point of philosophy is to start with something so simple as not to seem worth stating, and to end with something so paradoxical that no one will believe it."

Marxism The political, economic, and philosophical theories developed by Karl Marx and Friedrich Engels in the second half of the 19th century. The philosophical side of Marxism is called dialectical materialism; it emphasizes economic determinism. *See also* **dialectical materialism.**

Miletian School The pre-Socratics from Miletus in Greece—Thales and his two best-known pupils, Anaximander and Anaximenes.

Neoplatonism A school of philosophy that flourished from the 2nd to the 5th centuries A.D. It was founded by Plotinus and was influential for the next thousand years.

nihilism An extremist movement in 19th-century Russia. *Ethical nihilism* is the theory that morality cannot be justified in any way and that all moral values are, therefore, meaningless and irrational. *Political nihilism* is the social philosophy that society and its social, political, and economic popularized institutions are so corrupt that their complete destruction is desirable. Nihilists may, therefore, advocate violence and even terrorism in the name of overthrowing what they believe to be a corrupt social order. The term *nihilism* was first popularized in *Fathers and Sons* (1862) by the Russian novelist Turgenev.

Ordinary Language Philosophy The 20th-century school advocating that we can best understand and resolve philosophic problems by analyzing how people other than philosophers ordinarily use language and the presuppositions underlying such use; the school holds that everyday language is adequate for philosophy. Ludwig Wittgenstein, Gilbert Ryle, and John L. Austin (1911–60) were the most influential members of this school.

personalism A term applied to any philosophy that makes personality (whether of people, God, or spirit) the supreme value or the source of reality. Personalism as a movement flourished in England and America in the 19th and 20th centuries. Personalists are usually idealists.

phenomenology A 20th-century school founded by Edmund Husserl and an important influence on existentialism. This school developed its own philosophical "method" of using intuition for describing consciousness and experience. Phenomenologists claim that this method can be used to study the inherent qualities of phenomena as they appear to the mind. They attempt to classify and describe all phenomena without resorting to universal concepts or preconceived notions of reality. The focus is on the phenomena, not on how it is perceived.

philosophes Term applied to 18th-century French Enlightenment thinkers such as Jean-Jacques Rousseau, Denis Diderot, and Voltaire.

Platonism Thoughts and writings developed in the 4th century B.C. in Athens by Plato, the greatest student of Socrates. Platonism's chief tenet is that the ultimate reality consists of unchanging, absolute, eternal entities called Ideas or Forms; all earthly physical objects are not truly real but merely partake in the Forms.

pragmatism An American philosophy developed in the 19th century by Charles Sanders Peirce (1839–1914) and William James and elaborated on in the 20th century by John Dewey. Its central precepts are that thinking is primarily a guide to action and that the truth of a concept or idea could be determined only by testing it against experimental results and practical consequences.

Pre-Socratics   Name given to all Greek "theorists of nature" or philosophers who lived before Socrates. Major pre-Socratics include Anaximander, Pythagoras, and Thales.

Pythagoreans   Followers of Pythagoras. The group flourished until about 400 B.C. and were influential in philosophy, religion, mathematics, and science. They strongly influenced the thinking of Plato and Neoplatonists.

Scholasticism   A movement (c. 9th century–17th century), especially at the medieval universities, that attempted to reconcile Christian dogma with the empiricism of Aristotle. Its adherents used highly analytical logical and linguistic methods of argumentation, especially with respect to the problem of universals. Aquinas, the movement's greatest thinker, demonstrated that faith and reason were separate but compatible ideas; his teachings were accepted by the Catholic church.

17th-century rationalists   A broad term referring to the rationalism shared by René Descartes, Gottfried Leibniz, and Benedict Spinoza. It held that reason and deduction could provide knowledge of the world independent of experience.

Sophists   Wandering teachers in the 4th and 5th centuries B.C. in ancient Greece who taught any subjects that their paying students wished to learn, from grammar to public speaking. They were strongly ridiculed by Plato, who held that they were less interested in truth than in pleasing their students for a fee.

Stoicism   A Greek school founded by Zeno in the 3rd century B.C. Stoics held that people should submit to natural law and that a person's chief duty is to conform to his destiny. They also believed the soul to be another form of matter, and thus not immortal. Stoics rejected material comfort and advocated freedom from earthly passions and desires. They

viewed reality as materialistic and defined the organizing principle of the universe as force, or God.

Thomism   The philosophical and theological system developed by St. Thomas Aquinas in the 13th century. Specifically, it refers to Aquinas's synthesis of philosophy and theology, in which reason seeks knowledge through experiment and observation, while faith seeks understanding through divine revelation. The two are thus never in conflict; rather, both come from God. Thomism is accepted as a vital doctrine in the Roman Catholic Church.

transcendentalism   A 19th-century movement developed in New England and expounded by Ralph Waldo Emerson (1803–82) and Henry David Thoreau (1817–62). It maintains that beyond our material world of experience is an ideal spiritual reality that can be grasped intuitively. It advocates a reliance on personal conscience, based on perception and experience, over the dictates of external authority or moral conventions.

utilitarianism   A theory of morality formulated in the 19th century and holding that all actions should be judged for rightness or wrongness in terms of their consequences; thus, the amount of pleasure people derive from those consequences becomes the measure of moral goodness. Jeremy Bentham believed that happiness was the sole consequence by which actions should be judged. John Stuart Mill equated morality with the attainment of the maximum good for the greatest number of people. *See also* **principle of utility** under "Common Philosophical Terms."

Vienna Circle   A major school of logical positivism founded by Moritz Schlick (1882–1936) in the 1920s. It was known for its hostility to metaphysics and theology and for its belief that physics is the model for all knowledge of the world. Other leading members of the school were Rudolph Carnap (1891–1970) and Otto Neurath (1882–1945).

Go to   "Major World Philosophers" and "Common Philosophical Terms" in this chapter

Young Hegelians A group of thinkers in Germany in the first half of the 19th century whose views strongly influenced Karl Marx. They were followers of Georg Hegel who believed that the political conditions under which they lived were irrational. They held that the goal of philosophy should be to promote a revolution of ideas and critical thinking about the world. Ludwig Feuerbach (1804–72) was the most important of the Young Hegelians.

COMMON PHILOSOPHICAL TERMS

Entries in this glossary include basic terms and concepts used by philosophers, branches of philosophy, and "isms" that describe various philosophical attitudes, beliefs, doctrines, positions, precepts, theories, and viewpoints.

absolutism The doctrine that there is one explanation of all reality—the absolute—that is unchanging and objectively true. Absolutists (such as G. W. F. Hegel) hold that this absolute, such as God or mind, is eternal and that in it all seeming differences are reconciled.

aesthetics (esthetics) The philosophical study of art, or of beauty in general. It attempts to systematically answer such questions as, What is beauty? How do we evaluate works of art? Are aesthetic judgments objective or subjective? How does art embody truth and convey knowledge? How does beauty in art relate to beauty in nature?

agnosticism The belief that it is impossible to know whether God exists, or to have any other theological knowledge. Thomas H. Huxley (1825–95) and Bertrand Russell were influential agnostics.

altruism The ethical theory that morality consists of concern for and the active promotion of the interests of others. Altruists strongly disagree with the doctrine of egoism, which states that individuals act only in their own self-interest.

analytic statement A statement true by definition, such as "All triangles have three sides."

anarchism A political philosophy that advocates the abolition of an organized state as the ruling government. Its advocates believe that individuals should be free to organize themselves in the ways that best enable them to fulfill their needs and ideals. The Russian thinker Mikhail Bakunin (1814–76) was an influential anarchist.

angst A German word meaning anxiety, anguish, or dread. The term was used by Martin Heidegger and other adherents of existentialism to express their belief that anxiety characterizes the human condition and that dread arises from our realization that we are totally responsible for all of our choices.

a posteriori knowledge Knowledge based on or derived from sensory experience.

a priori knowledge Knowledge acquired by the mind or reasoning alone, without any specific basis in experience—for instance, 2 + 2 = 4.

argument An attempt to relate one set of statements, called the premises or the starting point, to another set, called the conclusion or the end point, by valid means. Arguments are either inductive or deductive. *See also* **syllogism.**

asceticism The view that attention to the body's needs is evil, an obstacle to moral and spiritual development, and displeasing to God. According to this view, humans are urged to withdraw into an inner spiritual world to reach the good life.

associationism A philosophical theory of the mind that holds that all mental states can be analyzed as separate component items and that all mental activity can be explained by the combining and recombining of these items, often called ideas. David Hume and John Stuart Mill were prominent advocates of this view. *See also* **association of ideas.**

association of ideas (laws of association) The principles by which the mind connects ideas. Aristotle included similarity, contrast, and closeness; David Hume held the basic laws to be resemblance, closeness in time or place, and causality. Hume and

John Stuart Mill are the two most prominent philosophers who emphasized association as the basic principle of the mind. *See also* **associationism.**

Followers of conservative Franciscan philosopher Duns Scotus were called Dunsmen or Duncemen. Resisting more progressive forms of learning, they became regarded as dull or stupid. Hence, the term dunce.

atheism   The rejection of the belief in God. Some atheists have held that there is nothing in the world that requires a God in order to be explained. Atheism is not the same as agnosticism, which holds that we can have knowledge neither of the existence nor of the nonexistence of God.

atomism   The theory that reality is composed of simple and indivisible units (atoms) that are completely separate from and independent of one another. Philosophers have differed as to the nature of atoms; for instance, the Greek thinkers Leucippus and Democritus (5th century B.C.) held that the atoms are different-shaped bits of matter.

bad faith   Term used by Jean-Paul Sartre for self-deception and the deception of others caused by denying one's freedom of choice and one's responsibility for making decisions.

becoming   That which changes from one form to another, or, in Plato, that which is known only by experience and exists only temporarily. *See also* **being.**

being   Frequently used in metaphysics to contrast with appearance or nonexistence; often synonymous with unchanging substance, ultimate reality, God, infinity, or all that exists. Aristotle held that being is the subject matter of metaphysics. *See also* **becoming.**

Go to   "Philosophical Movements and Schools of Thought" and "Major World Philosophers" in this chapter

bioethics   A branch of philosophy that studies ethical issues that arise from conflicts between human rights and medical and biological research and the technology they use. Areas of concern are genetic manipulation, euthanasia, and brain control.

Buridan's ass   A story, falsely attributed to the 14th-century thinker John Buridan, in which an ass, faced with two equally desirable bales of hay, starves to death because he cannot find a good reason for preferring one bale to the other.

categorical imperative   Immanuel Kant's term for the binding moral law, which dictates that one should act only according to a maxim that could serve as a universal law—for instance, to treat humanity as an end and never only as a means.

cause   Whatever is responsible for change, action, or motion. Historically, Aristotle's analysis of cause falls into four types: material cause, the substance a thing is made of; formal cause, the design of the thing; efficient cause, the maker of the thing; and final cause, its purpose or function. David Hume argued that all knowledge of cause comes from our actual experience of observed regularities.

certainty   According to René Descartes, a condition of knowing that anything is true; various types of statements—for example, 1 + 1 = 2, or all widows are female—have certainty.

chain of being   An idea, originating with Plato and very influential in Western thought into the Renaissance, that all possible things are realized in the world in an ordered chain of diminishing complexity and richness, from God down to the tiniest, humblest bit of matter. The view captures the concept of the universe as an ordered hierarchy.

conceptualism   The doctrine, intermediate between nominalism and realism, that general ideas, such as the idea of man or of redness, exist explicitly in the human mind as concepts and implicitly in the minds of all people. These concepts are not arbitrary ideas, but reflect the similarities between particular things.

cosmogony   A theory or story about the origin of the universe, either scientific or mythological. Cosmogonies are also called creation myths.

cosmology   The systematic study of the origin and structure of the universe as a whole. Such philosophers as Plato, Aristotle, and Immanuel Kant considered cosmology to be a metaphysical speculation; today cosmology is a branch of the physical sciences.

counterexample   A specific fact that refutes or negates a generalization; for instance, a black swan is a counterexample to the statement "All swans are white."

deductive reasoning   Reasoning from a general statement to a particular or specific example; for example, "All cats are mortal; William is a cat; therefore, William is mortal." *See also* **syllogism.**

deontology   The ethical philosophy that makes duty the basis of all morality. According to deontological theorists, such as Immanuel Kant, some acts —such as keeping a promise or telling the truth— are moral obligations regardless of their consequences.

determinism   The view that every event has a cause and that everything in the universe is absolutely dependent on and governed by causal laws. Because determinists believe that all events, including human actions, are predetermined, determinism is typically thought to be incompatible with free will.

dialectic   A term with different meanings for different philosophers. It derives from the Greek word meaning "to converse" and is used to describe

More Than Just Philosophers

A Closer Look

Before knowledge was as specialized as it is today, many of the greatest philosophers followed their other interests while creating or studying philosophical systems. They did groundbreaking work in areas as far afield from philosophy proper as geometry, zoology, literary criticism, and calculus.

Perhaps Aristotle was the model for some of these thinkers, because he was regarded not only in his own time but also throughout most of the Middle Ages as a universal genius whose knowledge on any subject he had written on could hardly be questioned. His nonphilosophical writings were astonishingly broad; even a partial list of his subjects, which include physics, zoology, botany, sociology, political theory, and economics, is testimony to one of the greatest minds of all time.

Even medicine and the law were not too far afield for some of the great philosophers. Avicenna, Averroes, and John Locke were trained in medicine; Avicenna's *Canon of Medicine* was the most influential medieval medical treatise. And Jeremy Bentham, a founder of utilitarianism, was one of the most influential jurists and lawyers of the 19th century; his work deeply influenced reform of the British penal, judicial, and parliamentary systems.

History, too, is a philosopher's domain. *History of England,* not his philosophy books, brought David Hume success and renown in mid-18th-century England.

Both mathematics and logic were fruitfully developed by philosophers when they were not writing philosophical works. Gottfried Leibniz is the coinventor of calculus, along with Sir Isaac Newton; Blaise Pascal is one of the founders of the modern theory of probability; and Descartes invented analytical geometry almost single-handedly.

Logic, although now a separate discipline, was a part of philosophy until the late 19th century. Aristotle was the founder of logic, but many other philosophers have invented or organized entire sections of the field. John Stuart Mill formulated the "rules" of scientific experimentation that are now called Mill's methods; and Bertrand Russell and Alfred North Whitehead wrote *Principia Mathematica,* probably the most important work in modern logic.

The list of philosophers engaged in other fields is seemingly endless. Examples include Friedrich Nietzsche, whose *On the Birth of Tragedy* is a classic in Greek studies and literary criticism; William James, whose *Principles of Psychology* deeply influenced decades of thinking in that field; and John Dewey, the father of the American progressive education movement.

Socrates's method of teaching by question-and-answer technique. Plato used the word to mean the study of the Forms. To Immanuel Kant, it meant a method of criticizing claims of knowledge going beyond experience. Georg Hegel means by it the necessary pattern of thinking.

doubt According to René Descartes, the argument that nothing can be considered true unless it can never be doubted under any conditions. Descartes doubted everything "systematically" to find out if anything is indubitable; his "*Cogito, ergo sum*" ("I think, therefore I am") survived his test.

dualism Any philosophical theory holding that the universe consists of, or can only be explained by, two independent and separate forces, such as matter and spirit, the forces of good and evil, or the supernatural and natural. *See also* **mind-body problem.**

duty According to many ethical theories, the basis of the virtuous life. The Stoics held that man has a duty to live virtuously and according to reason; and Immanuel Kant held that his categorical imperative is the highest law of duty, no matter what the consequences.

egocentric predicament The belief that each of us is limited to, and by, our unique pattern of perceptions. Any knowledge of the world outside our minds would thus be colored by our perceptions. *See also* **solipsism.**

egoism The ethical theory that each person should forward his or her own self-interest. Egoists sometimes argue that this is not selfishness, but that self-interest is compatible with helping others as well. Some egoists also argue that, psychologically speaking, human beings always in fact seek their own well-being.

élan vital *See* **vitalism.**

empirical Based on experience, observation, or facts—in short, describing any knowledge derived from or validated by sensory experience.

empiricism The view that all knowledge of the world derives solely from sensory experience, using observation and experimentation if needed; empiricism also holds that reason on its own can never provide knowledge of reality unless it also utilizes experience. Empiricism suggests that any concept of the physical world is nothing more than a generalization derived from particular circumstances.

epistemology The branch of philosophy that studies how knowledge is gained, how much we can know, and what justification there is for what is known.

eschatology In theology, the study of "final things," such as death, resurrection, immortality, the second coming of Christ, and the day of judgment.

essence That which makes a specific thing what it is and not something else; its nature. While the Greek philosophers viewed essence and substance as basically the same, St. Thomas Aquinas and the philosophy of Scholasticism held that even nonexistent things have natures or essences distinguishable from the fact of their existence.

esthetics *See* **aesthetics.**

euthanasia The act of allowing a terminally ill person to freely choose when and how he or she will die; mercy killing.

fatalism The belief that "what will be will be," because all past, present, and future events have already been predetermined by God or another all-powerful force. In religion, this view may be called predestination; it holds that whether our souls go to heaven or hell is determined before we are born and is independent of our good deeds.

Forms According to Plato, the eternal, unchanging, immaterial, and perfect archetypes of which all existing things are merely imperfect copies; also called Ideas.

four elements According to many early Greek philosophers, the four basic constituents of the physical world: earth, air, fire, and water.

free will The theory that human beings have freedom of choice or self-determination; that is, that given a situation, a person could have done other than what he did. Philosophers have argued that free will is incompatible with determinism. *See also* **indeterminism.**

golden mean   The ethical doctrine, originating with Aristotle, that virtuous actions fall exactly between too much of some quality, such as impulsive behavior, and too little of it, such as timidity. It is associated with ethics calling for moderation.

"Peanuts" creator Charles M. Schulz once quipped, "There's a difference between a philosophy and a bumper sticker."

golden rule   The fundamental moral rule of most religions, especially Christianity, that states, "Do unto others as you would have others do unto you."

greatest happiness principle   *See* **principle of utility; utilitarianism** under "Philosophical Movements and Schools of Thought."

Hobson's choice   A choice offered without any real alternative—therefore, not really a choice at all.

humanism   Any philosophic view that holds that humankind's well-being and happiness in this lifetime are primary and that the good of all humanity is the highest ethical goal. Twentieth-century humanists tend to reject all beliefs in the supernatural, relying instead on scientific methods and reason. The term is also used to refer to Renaissance thinkers, especially in 15th-century Italy, who emphasized the revival of classical studies, or the humanities, and knowledge and learning not based on religious sources.

idealism   A term applied to any philosophy holding that mind or spiritual values, rather than material things or matter, are primary in the universe.

immortality   The view that the individual soul is eternal, and thus survives the death of the body it resides in. *See also* **transmigration of souls.**

indeterminism   The view that there are events that do not have any cause; many proponents of free will believe that acts of choice are capable of not being determined by any physiological or psychological cause.

inductive reasoning   Any process of reasoning from something particular to something general, or from a part to a whole. Inductive reasoning can be valid or invalid.

innate ideas   Ideas that are inborn and part of the mind at birth, rather than based on specific experiences. René Descartes believed there are "clear and distinct" ideas that are innate and that form the basis of all knowledge. Plato believed that knowledge of the Forms derives from innate ideas.

instrumentalism   A theory that holds that ideas and concepts should be regarded as tools or instruments to be used in specific situations. As such, they cannot be described as true or false, but only as effective or ineffective. This theory was first put forth by John Dewey.

justice   According to most philosophers, starting with Plato, the harmonious balance between the rights of the various members of a society. Justice is usually understood as including such social virtues as fairness, equality, and correct and impartial treatment.

language, philosophy of   *See* **philosophy of language.**

language game   A concept introduced by Ludwig Wittgenstein, who drew an analogy between how we use language and how we play games: Both have rules and moves that make sense only in the context of a particular game. Wittgenstein and his followers used this concept to point out that philosophers frequently try to make moves in one context that make sense only in another, as when they try to verify religious statements as if they were a part of science.

logic   The study of the rules and the nature of reasoning and of valid or sound patterns of thought. Aristotle classified many of the rules of reasoning. In the late 19th and early 20th centuries, logic was advanced into a branch of mathematics. Currently, mathematical logic is a growing field independent of philosophy. *See also* **syllogism.**

materialism   The theory that holds that the nature of the world is dependent on matter, or that matter is the only fundamental substance; thus, spirit and mind either do not exist or are manifestations of matter. Prevalent throughout the history of western civilization, this theory appeared as early as the 4th century B.C. in the teachings of Democritus, and it formed the basis for dialectical materialism, the philosophical doctrine underlying communism.

mathematical logic   *See* **logic.**

mathematics, philosophy of   *See* **philosophy of mathematics.**

mechanism   The philosophical theory that states that living organisms, including humans, are complex machines, because they are composed of matter.

metaethics   A branch of philosophy that analyzes ethics. It is concerned with such issues as, How are moral decisions justified? What is the foundation of any ethical view? What language is used to state moral beliefs?

metaphysics   The branch of philosophy concerned with the ultimate nature of reality and existence as a whole. Metaphysics also includes the study of cosmology and philosophical theology. Aristotle produced the first "system" of metaphysics.

metempsychosis   *See* **transmigration of souls.**

mind   *See* **philosophy of mind.**

mind-body problem   A central problem of modern philosophy that originated with René Descartes. It asks how the mind and the body are related.

monad   According to Leibniz, the ultimate and indivisible unit of all existence. Monads are not material, like atoms; each monad is self-activating, a unique center of force. All monads are in a "preestablished harmony" with each other and with God, the supreme monad.

monism   A term introduced in the 18th century to describe any theory that explains all phenomena by a single unifying principle or that reduces everything in the universe to one fundamental substance, energy, or force. In Georg Hegel, this concept can be seen in his vision of the world as a single organism, developing through a dialectical process. Benedict Spinoza held that mind and spirit are aspects of single entity, which he called God or nature.

mysticism   Any philosophy whose roots are in mystical experiences, intuitions, or direct experiences of the divine. In such experiences, the mystic believes that his or her soul has temporarily achieved union with God. Mystics believe reality can be known only in this manner, not through reasoning or everyday experience.

myth of Er   A parable at the end of Plato's *Republic* about the fate of souls after bodily death; according to Plato, the soul must choose wisdom in the afterlife to guarantee a good life in its next cycle of incarnation.

natural law   The theory that there is a higher law than the humanmade laws put forth by specific governments. This law is universal, unchanging, and a fundamental part of human nature. Advocates of this view believe that natural law can be discovered by reason alone. The theory originated with the Stoics and was elaborated on by St. Thomas Aquinas, among others.

natural rights   Certain freedoms or privileges that are held to be an innate part of the nature of being a human being and that cannot be denied by society. These are different from civil rights, which are granted by a specific nation or government. Philosophers have differed on which rights are natural, but usually included are life, liberty, equality, equal treatment under the law, the pursuit of happiness, and equality of opportunity. John Locke's influential views on natural rights inspired the writers of the U.S. Constitution.

God's Existence—Proofs For

A Closer Look

While theology may take God's existence as absolutely necessary on the basis of authority, faith, or revelation, many philosophers—and some theologians—have thought it possible to demonstrate by reason that there must be a God.

St. Thomas Aquinas, in the 13th century, formulated the famous "five ways" by which God's existence can be demonstrated philosophically:

1. *The "unmoved mover" argument.* We know that there is motion in the world; whatever is in motion is moved by another thing; this other thing also must be moved by something; to avoid an infinite regression, we must posit a "first mover," which is God.
2. *The "nothing is caused by itself" argument.* For example, a table is brought into being by a carpenter, who is caused by his parents. Again, we cannot go on to infinity, so there must be a first cause, which is God.
3. *The cosmological argument.* All physical things—even mountains, boulders, and rivers—come into being and go out of existence, no matter how long they last. Therefore, because time is infinite, there must be some time at which none of these things existed. But if there were nothing at that point in time, how could there be anything at all now, because nothing cannot cause anything? Thus, there must always have been at least one necessary thing that is eternal, which is God.
4. *Objects in the world have differing degrees of qualities such as goodness.* But speaking of more or less goodness makes sense only by comparison with what is the maximum goodness, which is God.
5. *The teleological argument (argument from design).* Things in the world move toward goals, just as the arrow does not move toward its goal except by the archer's directing it. Thus, there must be an intelligent designer who directs all things to their goals, and this is God.

Two other historically important "proofs" are the ontological argument and the moral argument. The former, made famous by St. Anselm in the 11th century and defended in another form by René Descartes, holds that it would be logically contradictory to deny God's existence. St. Anselm began by defining God as "that [being] than which nothing greater can be conceived." If God existed only in the mind, He then would not be the greatest conceivable being, for we could imagine another being that is greater because it would exist both in the mind and in reality, and that being would then be God. Therefore, to imagine God as existing only in the mind but not in reality leads to a logical contradiction; this proves the existence of God both in the mind and in reality.

Immanuel Kant rejected not only the ontological argument but the teleological and cosmological arguments as well, based on his theory that reason is too limited to know anything beyond human experience. He did argue, however, that religion could be established as presupposed by the workings of morality in the human mind ("practical reason"). God's existence is a necessary presupposition of there being any moral judgments that are objective, that go beyond mere relativistic moral preferences; such judgments require standards external to any human mind—that is, they presume God's mind.

naturalism   A philosophic view stating that all there is in reality is what the physical and human sciences (for example, physics or psychology) study and that there is no need to posit any supernatural forces or being, such as God, mind, or spirit.

naturalistic fallacy   A belief of many 20th-century philosophers in England and the United States that it is invalid to infer any statements of morality (for example, "Men ought to act kindly") from factual statements (for example, "Kindness is a natural quality"). The notion tries to derive *ought* from *is* and was first described by David Hume.

necessary and contingent truth   Terms used by philosophers to contrast two types of statements, such as "All widowers are male," which is necessarily true, and "All widowers are over 20 years old," which may be true but is not necessarily true.

nominalism   A doctrine, prevalent in the Middle Ages, that maintained that ideas and objects exist only in the particular instance, not as abstract concepts or forms. In opposition to realism, it held that all universals are merely names and have no existence of their own.

God's Existence—Arguments Against

A Closer Look

Arguments against God's existence have been given by philosophers, atheists, and agnostics. Some of these arguments find God's existence incompatible with observed facts; some are arguments that God does not exist because the concept of God is incoherent or confused. Others are criticisms of the proofs offered *for* God's existence.

One of the most influential and powerful "proofs" that there is no God proceeds from "The Problem from Evil." This argument claims that the following three statements cannot *all* be true: (a) evil exists; (b) God is omnipotent; and (c) God is all-loving. The argument is as follows:

- If God can prevent evil, but *doesn't*, then He isn't all-loving.
- If God intends to prevent evil, but *cannot*, then He isn't omnipotent.
- If God *both* intends to prevent evil and is capable of doing so, then how can evil exist?

Another argument claims that the existence of an all-knowing God is incompatible with the fact of free will—that humans do make choices. If God is omniscient, He must know beforehand exactly what a person will do in a given situation. In that case, a person is not in fact free to do the alternative to what God knows he or she will do, and free will must be an illusion. To take this one step further, if one chooses to commit a sin, how can it then be said that one sinned freely?

David Hume provided powerful critiques of the main arguments for God's existence. Against the cosmological argument (Aquinas's third argument), Hume argued that the idea of a necessarily existing being is absurd. He stated, "Whatever we can conceive as existent, we can also conceive as nonexistent." Hume also asked why the ultimate source of the universe could not be the entire universe itself, eternal and uncaused, without a God?

Hume also criticized the argument from design (Aquinas's fifth argument). In particular, he emphasized that there is no legitimate way we can infer the properties of God as the creator of the world from the qualities of His creation. For instance, Hume questioned how we can be sure that the world was not created by a team; or that this is not one of many attempts at creations, the first few having been botched; or, on the other hand, that our world is not a poor first attempt "of an infant deity who afterwards abandoned it, ashamed of his lame performance."

non sequitur   A Latin phrase meaning "it does not follow"; any argument where the conclusion drawn has not even the slightest connection to the premises offered.

objectivism   The view that there are moral truths that are valid universally and that it is wrong to knowingly gain pleasure from causing another pain.

obligation   In ethics, a moral necessity to do a specific deed. Some ethicists, following Immanuel Kant, hold that moral obligations are absolute. *See also* **categorical imperative.**

Ockham's razor   A principle attributed to the 14th-century English philosopher William of Ockham. It states that entities should not be mul-

tiplied beyond necessity, or that one should choose the simplest explanation, the one requiring the fewest assumptions and principles.

ontology   A branch of metaphysics that studies the nature of existence or reality, as such, as opposed to specific types of existing entities.

operationalism (operationism)   A philosophy of science according to which any scientific concept must be definable in terms of concrete, observable activities or the operations to which it refers.

optimism   The philosophic attitude that this is the best of all possible worlds, that hope and joy are justified, and that all things are ordered for the best. According to optimists, such as Gottfried Leibniz, evil either is an illusion or will be compensated for by an even greater good.

Philosophy

pantheism   The belief that God and the universe are identical; among modern philosophers, Benedict Spinoza is considered to be a pantheist.

particulars   *See* **universals.**

Pascal's wager   An argument made by Blaise Pascal for believing in God. Pascal said that either the tenets of Roman Catholicism are true or they are not. If they are true, and we wager that they are true, then we have won an eternity of bliss; if they are false, and death is final, what has the bettor lost? On the other hand, if one wagers against God's existence and turns out to be wrong, there is eternal damnation.

pessimism   The philosophic attitude holding that hope is unreasonable, that a person is born to sorrow, and that this is the worst of all possible worlds. Arthur Schopenhauer's philosophy is an example of extreme pessimism.

phenomenalism   The doctrine that the only knowledge we can ever have is of appearances, and thus that we can never know the nature of ultimate reality. Major adherents of the philosophy were John Stuart Mill and some members of the Vienna Circle.

philosopher king   In Plato's *Republic,* a philosopher trained by formal study in disciplines including mathematics and philosophy. Plato emphasized that philosopher kings' leadership would be shown by their ability to see the Forms, or universal ideals. *See also* **Forms.**

philosophy of language   The area of philosophic study whose subject matter is the nature and workings of language. Detailed discussions of such topics as meaning, reference, grammar, and symbols infuse this branch of philosophy.

philosophy of mathematics   A branch of philosophy that studies such questions as, What are mathematical statements about? Why is mathematics true? How do we come to have mathematical knowledge? Why is mathematics so useful in studying reality?

philosophy of mind   The area of philosophy that studies the mind, consciousness, and mental functions such as thinking, intention, imagination, and emotion. It is not one specific branch of philosophy, but rather an aspect of most traditional branches, such as metaphysics, epistemology, and aesthetics.

philosophy of religion   A branch of philosophy concerned with such questions as, What is religion? What is God? Can God's existence be proved? Is there immortality? What is the relationship between faith, reason, and revelation? Is there a divine purpose in the world?

philosophy of science   The branch of philosophy that studies the nature of science. It is particularly concerned with the methods, concepts, and assumptions of science, as well as with analyzing scientific concepts such as space, time, cause, scientific law, and verification.

physicalism   A theory about knowledge that originated within the Vienna Circle. It holds that all factual statements can be reduced to observations of physical objects and events. *See also* **operationalism.**

Plato's cave   An analogy in Plato's *Republic* between reality and illusion. The main image is of people who see on the walls of a cave only the shadows of the real objects moving around outside the cave. When these people leave the cave and see the real objects, they cannot, upon returning to the cave, convince those who have never left of the reality of the objects.

pluralism   The view that there are more than two kinds of fundamental, irreducible realities in the universe, or that there are many separate and independent levels of reality.

political philosophy   The branch of philosophy that studies a person as a political animal. It is concerned with such questions as, What obligations do I have to my government? How is political power justified? Under what conditions is war justified? It also studies the nature of property, justice, freedom, liberty, and political rights.

positivism   A theory originated by French philosopher Auguste Comte. It holds that all knowledge is defined by the limits of scientific investigation; thus, philosophy must abandon any quest for knowledge of an ultimate reality or any knowledge beyond that offered by science.

predestination   *See* **fatalism.**

premises   *See* **argument.**

principle (or law) of noncontradiction   Dating back to Aristotle, this universally accepted "law of thought" has two parts: A statement cannot be both true and false; nothing can both have a quality, like red, and not have it, at the same time.

The long sought-after philosopher's stone was believed by alchemists to have the power to change base metals into silver or gold.

principle of sufficient reason   The philosophical doctrine of Leibniz that asserts that for every fact there is a reason for its being the way it is rather than another way, even though we may not know that reason.

principle of utility (greatest happiness principle)   The basic tenet of utilitarianism. It states that the highest ethical good provides the greatest happiness for the greatest number of people.

psychologism   A view of philosophy holding that all philosophic concepts and problems are explainable based on psychological principles and that they should be treated by some form of psychological analysis. Advocates of this view may disagree on the type of psychological approach that is appropriate.

QED   Latin for *quod erat demonstrandum* ("that which was to be demonstrated"). This abbreviation is often used right before or after stating a conclusion, as a synonym for *therefore, thus,* or *as was to be shown.*

rationalism   A doctrine holding that reason or thinking alone, without recourse to observation or experience, can apprehend basic truths. The notion of innate, universal concepts is naturally associated with this theory. René Descartes, Gottfried Leibniz, Benedict Spinoza, and Georg Hegel were all essentially rationalists in their approach to the foundations of knowledge.

realism   The major medieval and modern view, other than nominalism, on the problem of universals. *Extreme realism,* which is close to Plato's theory of Forms, holds that universals exist independently of both particular things and the human mind; *moderate realism,* put forth by St. Thomas Aquinas, holds that universals exist as ideas in God's mind, through which He creates things.

reincarnation   *See* **transmigration of souls.**

relativism   The precept that people's ideas of right and wrong vary considerably from place to place and time to time; therefore, there are no universally valid ethical standards.

religion, philosophy of   *See* **philosophy of religion.**

science, philosophy of   *See* **philosophy of science.**

sensationalism   An empiricist theory of knowledge that holds that sensations are both the source of all knowledge and the ultimate verification of any statements. Thomas Hobbes originated the view; Étienne Condillac (1715–1880) and Ernst Mach (1838–1916) developed it.

sense data   The sensory qualities or feelings we experience directly, such as shapes, colors, and smells, without any interpretation of the material objects that may be causing them. Some empiricists and sensationalist philosophers make sense data the foundation of all factual knowledge.

skepticism   The philosophic theory that no certain knowledge can be attained by humans. Broadly speaking, skepticism states that all knowledge should be questioned and tested—for instance, by the scientific method.

Philosophy

social contract   That concept of an agreement between people, or between people and government or ruler, in which it is agreed that some personal liberties will be given up in exchange for the security of stable political rule. The term is used in the political philosophy of Thomas Hobbes, John Locke, and Jean-Jacques Rousseau to justify a form of political authority.

solipsism   The theory that one cannot know anything other than his or her own thoughts, feelings, or perceptions; therefore, other people and the real world must be projections of one's own mind with no existence in and of themselves. *See also* **egocentric predicament.**

spiritism   A term referring to the belief that spirits of the dead communicate with the living—for instance, at seances or through a medium.

spiritualism   The view that the ultimate reality in the universe is the spirit. Advocates of this view may disagree about the nature of the spirit.

state of nature   A term used by 17th- and 18th-century social philosophers such as Thomas Hobbes, John Locke, and Jean-Jacques Rousseau. It referred to the condition of humans without political organization, or before government.

subjectivism   The theory that all moral values are completely dependent on the personal tastes, feelings, or inclinations of the individual and have no source of validity outside such human subjective states of mind.

substance   A changeless, self-subsistent entity, not dependent on anything else, that underlies being in all its forms. It has been identified with God, mind, matter, and self-contained ultimate realities. *See also* **monad.**

supernaturalism   The belief that there are forces, energies, or beings beyond the material world—such as God, spirit, or occult forces—that affect events in our world.

syllogism   A kind of deductive reasoning or argument. As defined by Aristotle, it was considered the basis of reasoning for over two thousand years. In every syllogism, there are two statements (premises) from which a conclusion follows necessarily. Syllogisms are of three basic logical types, as illustrated by the following examples. *See also* **argument.**

1. If a broom is new, it sweeps clean; the broom is new; therefore, it sweeps clean.
2. Either the horse is male or female; the horse is not female; therefore, it is male.
3. All philosophers are men; all men are mortal; therefore, all philosophers are mortal.

synthetic statement   A factual statement describing a state of affairs, such as "Triangles are used in architectural studios."

tabula rasa   A Latin phrase meaning "blank slate," used by John Locke to describe the state of the human mind at birth. Locke believed there are no innate ideas and that the mind gets all of its ideas from experience.

tautology   Any statement that is necessarily true merely because of its meaning, such as "Bachelors are unmarried males" or "Every green object is colored." *See also* **necessary and contingent truth.**

teleological ethics   In contrast with deontological ethics, this moral theory holds that whether an action is morally right depends solely on its expected consequences.

transcendent   Beyond the realm of sense experience. In many religious views, God is held to be transcendent.

transmigration of souls (metempsychosis; reincarnation)   The belief that the same soul can, in different lifetimes (incarnations), reside in different bodies, human or animal. While typically a part of most Eastern religions, the doctrine came into Western philosophy from Pythagoras and his contemporaries in the 6th century B.C. and especially through Plato.

universals   The properties, or the abstract or general words, that apply to many individual things, called particulars. Redness, for instance, is a universal that applies to all red things.

utopianism The belief in the possibility or desirability of not just a better but a perfect society. The term derives from Sir Thomas More's *Utopia* (1516), which depicts an ideal state. Utopian states also appear in the writings of Plato and Sir Francis Bacon.

vitalism The theory that living organisms are inherently different from inanimate bodies; thus, life cannot be explained fully by materialistic theories as it is based on a vital force that is unlike other physical forces. Aristotle, Hans Driesch (1867–1941), and Henri Bergson (1859–1941) were prominent vitalists. In Bergson's view, the élan vital is the evolutionary force in organisms that propels life to achieve higher levels of structure.

will to believe A phrase made famous by William James. He held that in the absence of decisive evidence, the mind may create belief in order to act, often resulting in discovery. He also maintained that believing in such situations is a human right that should not be backed away from.

will to power The view, expounded by Friedrich Nietzsche, that power is the chief motivating force in human nature. The view was influential in 20th-century psychology and social science.

ADDITIONAL SOURCES OF INFORMATION

ORGANIZATIONS AND SERVICES

The Philosophy Documentation Center (P.O. Box 7147, Charlottesville, VA 22906) is a key source of information. Its publications include U.S. and international directories of philosophers, consciousness studies, and bibliographies. In conjunction with the InteLex Corporation, the PDC offers an online service that provides subscription-based access to dozens of philosophy journals. The PDC and InteLex currently operate Past Masters®, an online database containing the complete works of 30 philosophers ranging from Anselm to Wittgenstein. The PDC home page can be accessed at http://www.pdcnet.org.

BOOKS

Blackburn, Simon. *The Oxford Dictionary of Philosophy.* Oxford University Press, 1996.

Christian, James. *Philosophy: An Introduction to the Art of Wondering.* 7th ed. Harcourt Brace, 1998.

Collinson, Diane, ed. *Biographical Dictionary of 20th Century Philosophers.* Routledge, 1996.

The Concise Routledge Encyclopedia of Philosophy. Routledge, 2000.

Copleston, Frederick C. *History of Philosophy.* 9 vols. Image, 1994.

Craig, Edward. *The Routledge Encyclopedia of Philosophy.* 10 vols. Routledge, 1998.

Deutsch, Eliot, and Ron Bontekoe, eds. *A Companion Guide to World Philosophies.* Blackwell, 1997.

Durant, Will. *The Story of Philosophy.* Pocket Books, 1991.

Edwards, Paul, ed. *The Encyclopedia of Philosophy.* 4 vols. Free Press, 1973.

Ferm, Vergilius. *A History of Philosophical Systems.* Ayer, 1977.

Gregory, Richard L. *The Oxford Companion to the Mind.* Oxford University Press, 1987.

Jaspers, Karl. *The Great Philosophers.* 4 vols. Harcourt Brace, 1993.

Lacey, A. R. *A Dictionary of Philosophy.* 3rd ed. Routledge, 1996.

Lineback, Richard, ed. *The Philosopher's Index.* 34 vols. Philosopher's Information Center, 1967–2001.

Magill, Frank N., ed. *Masterpieces of World Philosophy.* HarperCollins, 1990.

O'Connor, D. J. *A Critical History of Western Philosophy.* Free Press, 1985.

Reese, William L., ed. *Dictionary of Philosophy and Religion: Eastern and Western Thought.* 2nd ed. Humanities Press, 1996.

Runes, Dagobert D., ed. *Dictionary of Philosophy.* Littlefield, 1984,

Philosophy

Russell, Bertrand. *A History of Western Philosophy.* Routledge, 1993.

Scharfstein, Ben-Ami. *A Comparative History of World Philosophy.* State University of New York Press, 1998.

Solomon, Robert C., and Kathleen M. Higgins. *A Short History of Philosophy.* Oxford University Press, 1996.

Urmson, James O. *A Concise Encyclopedia of Western Philosophy and Philosophers.* 3 rd ed. Hyman, 1990.

Warburton, Nigel. *Philosophy: Basic Readings.* Routledge, 1999.

Weiner, Philip P., ed. *Dictionary of the History of Ideas: Studies of Selected Pivotal Ideas.* 5 vols. Scribners, 1985.

WEB SITES

The Internet Encyclopedia of Philosophy
http://www.utm.edu/research/iep

Meta-Encyclopedia of Philosophy
http://www.ditext.com/encyc/frame.html

Philosophy in Cyberspace
http://www-personal.monash.edu.au/~dey/phil

Stanford Encyclopedia of Philosophy
http://plato.stanford.edu

Philosophy

11
LIBRARIES AND MUSEUMS

MAJOR LIBRARIES AND THEIR SPECIAL COLLECTIONS

UNITED STATES

Arizona

University of Arizona Library
P.O. Box 210055
1510 E. University
Tucson, AZ 85721
520-621-2101
http://www.library.arizona.edu/

Established in 1891, the University of Arizona has more than 3.7 million volumes, with special collections on photography as an art form, fine arts, drama, private presses, Southwestern Americana, Arizona, science history, science fiction, and Mexican colonial history.

American libraries are used by two-thirds of the population but are financed with less than 1% of tax dollars.

California

County of Los Angeles Public Library, Administration
7400 E. Imperial Hwy.
Downey, CA 90241
562-940-8415
http://www.colapublib.org/

Founded in 1912, this library system contains more than 5.5 million volumes, with special collections on Afro-American studies, Asian-Pacific studies, California, multimedia, mountaineering, Hispanic-Americans, Native Americans, and poetry. The collection is dispersed among 114 community, mobile, and institutional libraries.

Los Angeles Public Library System
630 W. Fifth St.
Los Angeles, CA 90071
213-228-7515
http://www.lapl.org/

Founded in 1872, this public library system has 62 branches with more than 6.1 million volumes. Its special collections are on California studies, children's literature, cooking, genealogy, Native American studies, modern languages, orchestral scores, U.S. patents, and standards and specifications.

Stanford University Libraries & Academic Information Resources
Green Library Information Center
557 Escondido Mall
Stanford, CA 94305
650-725-1064
http://www-sul.stanford.edu/

Founded in 1892, Stanford's libraries contain 5.4 million volumes. Its special collections cover transportation, music, science, California, Irish literature, engineering mechanics, children's literature, Chicano studies, theater, and Hebraica and Judaica.

University of California, Berkeley
245 Doe Library
Berkeley, CA 94720
510-642-3773
http://www.lib.berkeley.edu/

Founded in 1871, this library contains more than 8.1 million volumes. Special collections include the letters, literary manuscripts, and scrapbooks of Samuel Clemens (Mark Twain Collection) and Recollections of Persons Who Have Contributed to the Development of the West (Regional Oral History Office).

University of California Los Angeles Library
11334 University Research Library
P.O. Box 951575
Los Angeles, CA 90095
310-825-1201
http://www.library.ucla.edu/

Founded in 1919, the University of California Los Angeles Library has holdings of more than 6.4 million books. It has special collections on British Commonwealth history, contemporary Western writers, early English children's books, folklore, Latin American studies, Mazarinades, mountaineering, and Western Americana.

University of Southern California
Edward L. Doheny Memorial Library
University Park
3550 Trousdale Parkway
Los Angeles, CA 90089-0182
213-740-2543
http://www.usc.edu/library/

Founded in 1880, the University of Southern California has more than 2.7 million volumes, with a number of independent departmental libraries whose subject matter ranges from architecture and fine arts to gerontology. Its special collections include Native American ethnopharmacology, American literature, cinema, dentistry, international relations, Latin American studies, and philosophy.

Colorado

University of Colorado, Boulder
University Libraries Campus Box 184
Boulder, CO 80309-0184
303-492-7511
http://www.colorado.edu/

Founded in 1876, the University of Colorado maintains holdings of more than 2 million volumes, with special collections on juvenile literature, the history of silver, mountaineering, and Western U.S. history.

Connecticut

Yale University Library
120 High St.
P.O. Box 208240
New Haven, CT 06520
203-432-1818
http://www.library.yale.edu/

The second largest university library in the United States, Yale has 10.5 million volumes in its collection. Its rare books total more than 500,000. Yale's special collections are numerous; they include works by James Boswell, the Aaron Burr family, Daniel Defoe, John Dryden, James Joyce, D. H. Lawrence, the Lindbergh family, Marcus Aurelius, H. L. Mencken, Napoleon, Mark Twain, and Edith Wharton. Founded in 1701, the Yale Library has more than 50 subjects of special strength, including Babylonian tablets, futurism, legal thought, playing cards, sporting books, urban and regional planning, and Western Americana.

District of Columbia

Folger Shakespeare Library
201 E. Capitol St., SE
Washington, DC 20003-1094
202-544-4600
http://www.folger.edu/

Opened in 1932, the Folger Shakespeare Library houses the world's largest collection of Shakespeare's printed works. The collection includes approximately 280,000 books and manuscripts; 27,000 paintings, drawings, engravings and prints; and musical instruments, costumes, and films.

The Library of Congress
101 Independence Ave., SE
Washington, DC 20540
202-707-5000
http://lcweb.loc.gov/

The nation's largest single library, the Library of Congress, established in 1800, contains over 80 million

items, including about 20 million books and pamphlets. Its collections include over 1 million volumes on Hispanic and Portuguese culture, the largest collection of Russian literature outside Russia, and a collection from the Kennedy Center Performing Arts Library. Special collections include books for the blind and physically handicapped, cartography, folk music, law books, manuscripts, microforms, motion pictures, music, the Orient, prints and photographs, and more than half a million rare books. The library's first priority is service to the Congress of the United States. It also registers creative work for copyright and provides services to both the public and libraries throughout the country.

Florida

University of Florida Libraries
204 Library West
Gainesville, FL 32611
352-392-0342
http://www.uflib.ufl.edu/

Founded in 1905, this system contains more than 3 million volumes, with special collections on Florida history, Latin America, Judaica, aerial photographs, coastal engineering, New England literature, Brazilian law, and Florida newspapers.

Georgia

University of Georgia Libraries
Main Library
Jackson St.
University of Georgia
Athens, GA 30602
706-542-3251
http://www.libs.uga.edu/

Founded in 1800, this library system contains more than 3.3 million volumes, with special collections on music, theater, Georgia, Confederate imprints, Georgia authors, 19th- and 20th-century politics, and Georgia newspapers.

Hawaii

Hawaii State Library System
Office of the State Librarian
465 S. King St.
Honolulu, HI 96813
808-586-3704
http://www.hcc.hawaii.edu/hspls/hslov.html

Founded in 1852, Hawaii's libraries contain more than 3.4 million volumes, with a special collection devoted to Hawaiian history.

Illinois

Chicago Public Library
400 S. State St.
Chicago, IL 60605
312-747-4999
http://cpl.lib.uic.edu/CPL.html

Founded in 1872, Chicago's libraries offer more than 11.5 million volumes with special collections of national, U.S., foreign, and trade bibliographies; Chicago information; foreign-language encyclopedias; Abraham Lincoln papers; miniature books; early American newspapers; and World War I and II posters.

Northwestern University Library
1935 Sheridan Rd.
Evanston, IL 60208
847-491-7658
http://www.library.nwu.edu/

Founded in 1856, Northwestern holds more than 3 million volumes and bound periodicals, with special collections on Africa, architecture, contemporary music scores, feminism, German classics, Italian futurism, manuscripts, and printing.

University of Chicago Libraries
1100 E. 57th St.
Chicago, IL 60637
773-702-7874
http://www.lib.uchicago.edu/

The University of Chicago, founded in 1891, contains more than 5.8 million volumes. It maintains special collections of English Bibles, Lincolniana, modern poetry, anatomical illustrations, and Kentucky and Ohio River Valley history; children's books; early theology and Bible criticism; German fiction, 1790–1850; and books on ophthalmology.

University of Illinois Library at Urbana–Champaign
1408 W. Gregory Dr.
Urbana, IL 61801
217-333-0790
http://www.library.uiuc.edu/

This library's collection includes more than 8.1 million volumes, with special collections on American humor and folklore, freedom of expression, 16th- and 17th-century Italian drama, 19th-century publishing, Carl Sandburg, and H. G. Wells. Founded in 1868.

Indiana

Indiana University at Bloomington
Main Library
1320 East 10th St.
Bloomington, IN 47405
812-855-3403
http://www.indiana.edu/~libweb/index.php3

Founded in 1824, Indiana University has amassed a collection of more than 5.7 million volumes, with special collections of English and American literature, 19th-century British plays, English history, scientific and medical history, the works of Aristotle, and 19th-century French opera.

Iowa

University of Iowa Libraries
Main Library
100 Main Library
Iowa City, IA 52242
319-335-5299
http://www.lib/uiowa.edu/

Established in 1855, Iowa's libraries contain more than 3.6 million volumes, with special collections on Leigh Hunt and his friends, Abraham Lincoln, American Indians, Iowa authors, typography, the Union Pacific Railroad, editorial cartoons, the French Revolution, and the history of medicine.

Kansas

University of Kansas Libraries
Watson Library
1425 Jay Hack Blvd.
Lawrence, KS 66045
785-864-3956
http://www.lib.ukans.edu/

Established in 1866, the University of Kansas libraries contain in excess of 2.9 million volumes, with special collections on Anglo-Saxons, botany, children's books, Chinese classics, Colombia, the Continental Renaissance, economics, historical cartography, Irish history and literature, Kansas history, poetry, opera, ornithology, sound recordings, travel, and women.

Maryland

Enoch Pratt Free Library
400 Cathedral St.
Baltimore, MD 21201
410-396-5430
http://www.pratt.lib.md.us/

Founded in 1886, Enoch Pratt's collection of 2.3 million volumes has a special H. L. Mencken section and a Maryland history collection.

Johns Hopkins University
Milton S. Eisenhower Library
3400 N. Charles St.
Baltimore, MD 21218

410-516-8325
http://www.library.jhu.edu/

Established in 1876, Johns Hopkins has more than 2.4 million volumes, with special collections on economics, Lord Byron, French drama, modern German drama, German literature, sheet music, slavery, and trade unions.

Massachusetts

Boston Public Library
700 Boylston St.
Boston, MA 02116
617-536-5400
http://www.bpl.org/

Founded in 1852, the Boston library system is believed to be the oldest free municipal library system supported by taxation anywhere in the world. It has 6.3 million volumes, with the following special collections: the library of John Quincy Adams; military science, history, and the Civil War; astronomy, mathematics, and navigation; Robert and Elizabeth Browning; Daniel Defoe; drama; genealogy; government documents; heraldry; music; patents; Christian Science; the Sacco-Vanzetti papers; Walt Whitman; and World War I.

Harvard University Library
Wadsworth House
1341 Massachusetts Ave.
Cambridge, MA 02138
617-495-3650
http://hul.harvard.edu/

With more than 13 million volumes, the Harvard Library, founded in 1638, is the largest university library in the United States. Its special collections are numerous. They include the Trotsky archive; the Theodore Roosevelt Collection; and works by such authors as Dante, T. S. Eliot, Faulkner, Goethe, Kipling, Longfellow, Milton, Petrarch, Rousseau, Shakespeare, Steinbeck, and Thomas Wolfe. Some of its branches are located outside Massachusetts, such as the Harvard Library in New York and the Dumbarton Oaks Research Library and Collection in Washington, D.C. Others specialize in topics ranging from music to divinity and include Harvard's famed law library and the fine arts library at the Fogg Art Museum.

Massachusetts Institute of Technology (MIT) Libraries
Office of the Director
Room 14S-216
Cambridge, MA 02139-4307
617-253-5651
http://libraries.mit.edu

Founded in 1862, MIT's library holdings total approximately 2.4 million volumes, with special collections devoted to the early history of aeronautics, architecture and planning, civil engineering, 19th-century U.S. glass manufacturers, early works in mathematics and physics, shipbuilding and naval history, and spectroscopy.

University of Massachusetts at Amherst
W. E. B. DuBois Library
P.O. Box 34710
Amherst, MA 01003-4710
413-545-0284
http://www.library.umass.edu/

Founded in 1865, this university system maintains holdings in excess of 2.6 million volumes, with special collections on slavery and antislavery pamphlets; county atlases of New England, New York, and New Jersey; and the French Revolution.

Michigan

Detroit Public Library
5201 Woodward Ave.
Detroit, MI 48202
313-833-1000
http://www.detroit.lib.mi.us/

Founded in 1865, Detroit's library contains more than 2.7 million volumes, with special collections on automotive history, labor history, and black music, dance, and drama.

In the 10th century, the Grand Vizier of Persia took his entire library with him wherever he went. The 117,000-volume library was carried by camels trained to walk in alphabetical order.

Michigan State University Library
100 Library
East Lansing, MI 48824
517-353-8700
http://www.lib.msu.edu

Established in 1855, Michigan State has holdings of more than 3.9 million volumes, with special collections on American popular culture, American radical history, apiculture, cookery, criminology, fencing, illuminated manuscripts in facsimile, natural science, and veterinary history.

Library Administration
University of Michigan
818 Hatcher South
Ann Arbor, MI 48109-1205
734-764-9356
http://www.lib.umich.edu/

Founded in 1817, the University of Michigan's libraries contain nearly 6 million volumes, the fifth-largest collection in the country. The system consists of 18 collections located around campus. Major facilities include a medical and a fine-arts library. Separately administered are a library of Americana, a law library, a business-administration library, and the Gerald R. Ford Presidential Library.

Wayne State University Libraries
Dean of Libraries
3100 David Adamany
Undergraduate Library
5155 Gullen Mall
Detroit, MI 48202
313-577-4023
http://www.lib.wayne.edu/index.html

Wayne State has more than 2.9 million volumes, with special collections on 19th-century Spanish history, social studies, women and the law, law, and children and young people.

Minnesota

University of Minnesota Libraries–Twin Cities
499 O. Meredith Wilson Library
309 19th Ave. South
Minneapolis, MN 55455
612-624-4520
http://www.lib.umn.edu/

Founded in 1851, this university system contains more than 5.2 million volumes, with special collections on American and English literature, the history of quantum physics, ballooning, dime novels, information processing, Sherlock Holmes, children's literature, performing arts, private presses, August Strindberg, and the history of biology and medicine.

Missouri

Kansas City Public Library
311 E. 12th St.
Kansas City, MO 64106
816-701-3400
http://www.kcpl.lib.mo.us/

Founded in 1873, this library's collection numbers more than 2 million volumes, with special collections on black history and Missouri Valley history and genealogy.

Linda Hall Library of Science, Engineering and Technology
5109 Cherry St.
Kansas City, MO 64110-2498
816-363-4600
http://www.lhl.lib.mo.us/

Founded in 1946, the Linda Hall Library's holdings include more than 1 million volumes, with special collections in scientific journals; research monographs; conference and symposium proceedings; engineering standards and specifications; patent specifications and trademarks; unclassified NASA, Department of Energy, and government contractor reports; and geological maps.

St. Louis University Libraries
St. Louis University
3650 Lindell Blvd.
St. Louis, MO 63108
314-977-3100
http://www.slu.edu/libraries/

Founded in 1818, this system contains more than 1.2 million bound volumes and government documents. Libraries on campus include a divinity library, a library of the School of Social Service, a law library, and a medical library.

University of Missouri–Columbia
Administrative Offices
104 Ellis Library
Columbia, MO 65201-5149
573-882-4701
http://web.missouri.edu/~elliswww/

Established in 1839, this library holds more than 2.7 million volumes, with special collections devoted to American best-sellers, criminal law, philosophy, World War I and II posters, cartoons, and Fourth of July orations.

Washington University Libraries
P.O. Box 1061
One North Brookings Dr.
St. Louis, MO 63130
314-935-5400
http://library.wustl.edu/

Founded in 1853, this system maintains more than 3 million volumes, with special collections on German language and literature, Romance languages and literature, classical archeology and numismatics, architecture, musicology, history of the Russian Revolution and the Soviet Union, American and New York Stock Exchange reports, printing, and early history of communications-semantics.

Libraries

New Jersey

Princeton University Library
Firestone Library
One Washington Rd.
Princeton, NJ 08544
609-258-4820
http://libweb.princeton.edu

This university was founded as the College of New Jersey, Elizabeth, in 1746. The principal building in its library system is the Harvey S. Firestone Memorial Library, constructed in 1948. Princeton has approximately 4.7 million volumes, with special collections devoted to the Brontës, Disraeli, aeronautics, American historical manuscripts, chess, civil rights, coins, Emily Dickinson, emblem books, fishing and angling, graphic arts, Mormon history, mountaineering, papyrus manuscripts, publishing, sports, women, and famous individuals.

Rutgers, The State University of New Jersey
University Libraries
169 College Ave.
New Brunswick, NJ 08901
732-932-7505
http://www.libraries.rutgers.edu

Established in 1766, this venerable library contains more than 2.9 million volumes. It has a special collection of New Jersey public-sector collective-bargaining contracts.

New York

Brooklyn Public Library System
Grand Army Plaza
Brooklyn, NY 11238
718-230-2100
http://www.brooklynpubliclibrary.org/

Founded in 1896 and consolidated with the Brooklyn Library in 1902, the library system now has 58 branches with a total of more than 4.1 million books. Special collections cover Brooklyn history, chess and checkers, the Civil War, costumes, fire protection, and Walt Whitman.

Columbia University
University Libraries
535 W. 114th St.
New York, NY 10027
212-854-2247
http://www.columbia.edu/cu/lweb/

Founded in 1761, Columbia offers more than 6.9 million volumes, with special collections on anatomy, architecture, cancer research, fine arts, physiology, and plastic surgery.

Cornell University Libraries
201 Olin Library
Cornell University
Ithaca, NY 14853
607-255-3393
http://campusgw.library.cornell.edu/

With approximately 5.8 million volumes, the Cornell libraries include special collections on Southeast Asia, civil engineering, medical dissertations, field recordings, early-16th-century music, beekeeping, food and beverages, and labor history.

New York Public Library
Astor, Lenox & Tilden Foundations
476 Fifth Ave.
New York, NY 10018
212-930-0800
http://www.nypl.org

Established in 1895 by the consolidation of the Astor and Lenox libraries and the Tilden Trust, the New York Public Library, encompassing 85 neighborhood branches and 4 research centers with noncirculatory collections, contains more than 50 million cataloged items: books, manuscripts, microfilm, prints, maps, recordings, photographs, and sheet music. Among its special collections are ones on black history and culture; performing arts; English and American literature; bindings and illustrated books; Japanese prints; tobacco; early Bibles including the Gutenberg; maps, photographs and prints; Jewish, Oriental, Slavonic cultures, and U.S. history and genealogy.

New York State Library
State Education Department, Cultural Education
    Center
Empire State Plaza
Albany, NY 12230
518-474-5930
http://www.nysl.nysed.gov/

Founded in 1818, New York State's library contains more than 2.3 million volumes, with special collections on Dutch colonial records, New York State political and social history, and the Shakers.

New York University
Elmer Holmes Bobst Library
70 Washington Sq. South
New York, NY 10012
212-998-2505
http://www.nyu.edu/library/bobst

Established in 1831, New York University's holdings total approximately 4 million volumes, with special collections on Lewis Carroll, Robert Frost, rare Judaica and Hebraica, mathematics, and the history of dentistry.

Queens Borough Public Library System
89-11 Merrick Blvd.
Jamaica, NY 11432
718-990-0700
http://www.queenslibrary.org/

Organized in 1896, this library system contains more than 7.2 million books and has 62 branches. It maintains special collections of Long Island history and genealogy and a collection of over 1.5 million pictures.

State University of New York at Buffalo
University Libraries
433 Capen Hall
Buffalo, NY 14260
716-645-2967
http://ublib.buffalo.edu/libraries/

Founded in 1922, the State University libraries hold more than 2.3 million volumes, with special collections of poetry, the works of J. Frank Dobie, New York State governors' autographs, and books on science and engineering and the history of medicine.

Syracuse University Libraries
E. S. Bird Library
222 Waverly Ave.
Syracuse, NY 13244
315-443-2573
http://libwww.syr.edu/

Established in 1871, Syracuse University has holdings of more than 2.6 million volumes, with special collections on Stephen Crane, Loyalists in the American Revolution, economic history, Margaret Bourke-White, Rudyard Kipling, and cartoonists; science-fiction books and manuscripts; and the papers of Averell Harriman, Dorothy Thompson, and Benjamin Spock.

University of Rochester
Rush Rhees Library
Room 236
Rochester, NY 14627
716-275-4461
http://www.lib.rochester.edu/

Founded in 1850, the Rochester library's holdings include more than 2.3 million volumes, with special collections on 19th- and 20th-century public affairs, 19th-century botany and horticulture, American literature, regional history, and Leonardo da Vinci.

North Carolina

Duke University
William R. Perkins Library
P.O. Box 90193
Durham, NC 27708

919-660-5800
http://www.lib.duke.edu/reference/index.htm

Founded in 1838, Duke's library contains more than 4.5 million volumes, with special collections on American almanacs, architecture, city directories, Samuel Taylor Coleridge, Confederate imprints, Ralpho Waldo Emerson, Latin American history, manuscripts, the Methodist Church, newspapers, the Philippines, utopias, and Wesleyana.

University of North Carolina at Chapel Hill
Walter Royal Davis Library
Campus Box 3900
Chapel Hill, NC 27514
919-962-1301
http://www.lib.unc.edu/davis.html

Founded in 1795, North Carolina's library contains more than 4.2 million volumes, with special collections on North Carolina and Southern history.

Ohio

Cleveland Public Library
325 Superior Ave.
Cleveland, OH 44114
216-623-2800
http://www.cpl.org/

Founded in 1869, the Cleveland Public Library contains 2.5 million volumes. Its special collections are devoted to folklore, the Orient, and chess.

Ohio State University Libraries
William Oxley Thompson Memorial Library
1858 Neil Ave.
Columbus, OH 43210
614-292-6151
http://www.lib.ohio-state.edu

Established in 1873, Ohio State offers approximately 4 million volumes and bound periodicals. Special collections include those on the American Association of Editorial Cartoonists, American fiction to 1925, American sheet music, Australia, daguerreotypes and ambrotypes, dance notation, Reformation history, and science-fiction magazines.

Public Library of Cincinnati and Hamilton County
800 Vine St.
Library Square
Cincinnati, OH 45202
513-369-6900
http://www.cincinnatilibrary.org

Founded in 1853, Cincinnati's library has more than 3.5 million volumes, with 139,337 maps and special collections on local history, genealogy, theology, art, music, theater, and oral history.

Oklahoma

University of Oklahoma
University Libraries
410 W. Brooks St.
Room 212 NW
Norman, OK 73019-6030
405-325-2611
http://www.libraries.ou.edu

Founded in 1895, the University of Oklahoma's library holds more than 2.2 million volumes, with special collections devoted to early science, Western history, Native American papers, political speeches, theater, film, and dance.

Pennsylvania

Carnegie Library of Pittsburgh
4400 Forbes Ave.
Pittsburgh, PA 15213
412-622-3100
http://www.clpgh.org/clp/

Founded in 1895, the Carnegie Library collection contains more than 2.4 million volumes, with approximately 69,000 in foreign languages. It maintains special collections on architecture and design, the Atomic Energy Commission, cartoons, local history, U.S. patents, World War I, and 19th-century American and German music journals.

Free Library of Philadelphia
1901 Vine St.
Philadelphia, PA 19103
215-686-5322
http://www.library.phila.gov

Founded in 1891, the Free Library contains 6.7 million volumes and bound periodicals, with special collections on orchestral music, common law, automobile history, Americana, cuneiform tablets, Charles Dickens, Edgar Allan Poe, Beatrix Potter, Arthur Rackham, theater, and maps (including over 130,000 single-sheet maps, atlases, and geographies).

Pennsylvania State University
Dean's Office
Pattee/Paterno Library
510 Paterno Library
University Park, PA 16802
814-865-0401
http://www.libraries.psu.edu/

Established in 1857, Penn State's library has approximately 2 million volumes, with special collections on American sociology, anthropology, art, architecture, Australia, Bibles, black literature, the Columbus family papers, English literature, photography, Pennsylvania, science fiction, surrealism, and the United Steelworkers of America.

University of Pennsylvania Libraries
Van Pelt Library
3420 Walnut St.
Philadelphia, PA 19104-6206
215-898-7555
http://www.library.upenn.edu/vanpelt/

Founded in 1749, the University of Pennsylvania's libraries hold more than 4.2 million volumes, with special collections on church history, the Spanish Inquisition, canon law, witchcraft, Shakespeare, alchemy and chemistry, Aristotle, Bibles, Jonathan Swift, Sanskrit manuscripts, Theodore Dreiser, Washington Irving, and the Spanish Golden Age of literature, as well as Benjamin Franklin imprints.

University of Pittsburgh
University Libraries
3960 Forbes Ave.
Pittsburgh, PA 15260
412-648-7710
http://www.pitt.edu/NewPittInfo/libraries.html

Founded in 1873, the University of Pittsburgh has holdings of more than 3.3 million volumes, with special collections on ballet, 19th- and 20th-century American and English theater, popular culture, early history and travel, children's literature, "Mr. Rogers' Neighborhood" videos, and ethnic organizations.

South Carolina

University of South Carolina
Thomas Cooper Library
1322 Greene St.
Columbia, SC 29208
803-777-3142
http://www.sc.edu/library/

Founded in 1801, South Carolina's system contains more than 2.3 million volumes, with special collections on archeology, ornithology, aerial photography, and rare medical books.

Texas

Dallas Public Library
1515 Young St.
Dallas, TX 75201
214-670-1400
http://www.dallaslibrary.org

Founded in 1901, Dallas's library contains over 3 million volumes. Special collections cover business histories; children's literature; classical literature; classical recordings; Dallas black history; and diaries and manuscripts on dance, fashion, genealogy, grants, printing, and Texas.

Houston Public Library
500 McKinney Ave.
Houston, TX 77002
713-247-2700
http://www.hpl.lib.tx.us/hpl/index.html

Founded in 1901, the Houston Public Library has more than 4.1 million volumes, with special collections of Bibles; books on the Civil War, genealogy, Texas, and petroleum; Salvation Army posters; early Houston photographs; early printing and illuminated manuscripts; juvenile literature; and sheet music.

University of Texas at Austin
General Libraries
21st St. and Speedway St.
PCL 3.200
Austin, TX 78713
512-495-4350
http://www.lib.utexas.edu/

Founded in 1883, this university library system serves a student body of more than 46,000. With more than 7 million books and bound periodicals, its holdings are divided among individual libraries devoted to Asia; film; the Middle East; Latin America; public affairs; architecture and planning; chemistry; classics; engineering; fine arts; geology; physics, mathematics, and astronomy; science; business research; humanities; population research; and law. Its special collections cover Southern history, Canada, British Commonwealth literature, the U.S. Volleyball Association, and oral histories.

Utah

University of Utah
Marriott Library
295 South 1500 E.
Salt Lake City, UT 84112
801-581-8558
http://www.lib.utah.edu/

Founded in 1850, Utah's library contains in excess of 2 million volumes, with special collections on the Middle East, Western Americana, and the history of medicine.

Virginia

University of Virginia
Alderman Library
PO Box 400113
Charlottesville VA 22904-4113

804-924-3026
http://www.lib.virginia.edu/

Established in 1819, Virginia's library holds more than 4.1 million books and bound periodicals, with special collections devoted to American literature, the American Revolution, Americana, the Civil War and Reconstruction, political cartoons, Ceylon, classical studies, Stephen Crane, Oliver Cromwell, John Dos Passos, evolution, William Faulkner, finance, Robert Frost, Gothic novels, Bret Harte, Nathaniel Hawthorne, international law, Washington Irving, Thomas Jefferson, modern art, Mark Twain, typography and printing, Virginia, voyages and travels, and Walt Whitman.

Washington

University of Washington Libraries
Allen Library, Room 482
P.O. Box 352900
Seattle, WA 98195
206-543-1760
http://www.lib.washington.edu/

Founded in 1862, this university's holdings exceed 5.3 million volumes, with special collections devoted to East Asia, fisheries, forest resources, oceanography, and the Pacific Northwest.

Wisconsin

Milwaukee Public Library
814 W. Wisconsin Ave.
Milwaukee, WI 53233
414-286-3000
http://www.mpl.org/

Founded in 1878, the Milwaukee Public Library has more than 2.3 million volumes, with special collections on the Great Lakes, H. G. Wells, British and American authors, genealogy, and cookbooks.

University of Wisconsin–Madison
General Library System and Memorial Library
728 State St.
Madison, WI 53706
608-262-3193
http://www.library.wisc.edu/

The University of Wisconsin has amassed a collection of more than 4.5 million volumes since its founding in 1850. Special collections include those on alchemy, American gifts, bookplates, Brazilian positivism, Buddhism, children's literature, C. S. Lewis's letters, Calvinist theology and Dutch history, chess, Early American women authors, history of chemistry, medieval history, Mexican pamphlets, Polish literature and history, Tibetan studies, Mark Twain, and Welsh theology.

CANADA

Alberta

University of Alberta
5-02 Cameron Library
Edmonton, Alberta T6G 2J8
780-492-3790
http://libits.library.ualberta.ca/library.html

Established in 1909, Alberta's university system contains more than 3.7 million volumes, with special collections on literature, Native Americans, Victorian book arts, western Canada, and theology and canon law.

Ontario

University of Toronto Library System
130 Saint George St.
Toronto, Ontario M5S 1A5
416-978-8450
http://library.utoronto.ca/

Founded in 1827, the University of Toronto has holdings of more than 8 million volumes, with extensive sections of sheet music, films, slides, maps, and photographs. Its special collections include those on Shakespeare, the history of science, Darwin, Victorian natural history, ornithology, medical and related sciences, Italian plays, juvenile drama, Canada, and Canadian authors.

British Columbia

University of British Columbia Library
1956 Main Mall
Vancouver, British Columbia V6T 1Z1
604-822-3310
http://www.library.ubc.ca/

Established in 1915, British Columbia's library holds more than 3.5 million volumes, with special collections on Pacific Northwest history, Canada, the Orient, the history of science, English literature, and Canadian and Japanese maps.

Quebec

McGill University Libraries
3459 McTavish St.
Montreal, Quebec H3A 1Y1
514-398-4744
http://www.library.mcgill.ca/

Founded in 1821, this university system serves an enrollment of about 24,000 students and has holdings of 1.6 million volumes. Its special collections cover architecture, William Blake, Canada, entomology, early geology, the history of science and medicine, natural history and ornithology, printing, Shakespeare, and 16th- and 17th-century tracts.

THE DEWEY DECIMAL SYSTEM AND HOW TO USE IT

Melvil Dewey (1851–1931) believed in organization. Even as a child, he was busy devising a way to arrange his family's pantry to make it more efficient. Before his system of classifying library books was adopted, many libraries relied on systems that filed books by size or color—cumbersome and not very useful methods at best. While working as a librarian at Amherst College, Dewey developed a system that is used by most school and small public libraries today. Published anonymously in 1876, his classifications divide nonfiction books into 10 broad categories:

000–099	General works (encyclopedias and similar works)
100–199	Philosophy (how people think and what they believe)
200–299	Religion (including mythology and religions of the world)
300–399	Social sciences (folklore and legends, government, manners and customs, vocations)
400–499	Language (dictionaries, grammars)
500–599	Pure science (mathematics, astronomy, chemistry, nature study)
600–699	Technology (applied sciences—aviation, building, engineering, homemaking)
700–799	Arts (photography, drawing, painting, music, sports)
800–899	Literature (plays, poetry)
900–999	History (ancient and modern, geography, travel)

Each of these sections is further divided for accuracy in classification. For example, the numbers 500–599 cover the pure sciences, such as astronomy, chemistry, mathematics, paleontology, and physics. Each of these areas has its own division and section number. All books on mathematics are assigned numbers in the 510 to 519 range; mathematics is then broken down into types, such as algebra, arithmetic, and geometry. Geometry's specific number is 513, which can be subdivided through the use of decimal points to provide 10 basic categories. Additional digits can be added, creating an ever more precise categorization system.

Cataloging in Publication Data

On the copyright page of most books, under the heading "Cataloging in Publication Data," are numbers and abbreviations that help librarians index new acquisitions for the card catalog. These data can be helpful to readers as well. A typical entry is shown below with an explanation of each part of the entry:

Library of Congress Cataloging in Publication Data

[Author]	McLanathan, Richard B. K.
[Title]	World art in American museums.
[Possible subject card headings, in order of importance]	1. Art—United States—Guidebooks. 2. Art museums—United States—Guidebooks. 3. Museums—United States—Guidebooks. 4. Art—Canada—Guidebooks. 5. Art—museums—Guidebooks. 6. Museums—Canada—Guidebooks.
[Library of Congress No.]	1. Title.
	N510.M34 1983 708.13 *[Dewey Decimal No.]*
	ISBN 0-385-18515-4 *[International Standard Book Number: country number; publisher number; title number; and check digit. The ISBN was started by the British in 1967 and adopted in the United States a year later.]*

Books are arranged alphabetically within each classification by the first letters of the author's last name. Therefore, a library that has several books on American history of the colonial period will assign the same basic number (973.2) to all the books and shelve them alphabetically.

Dewey's aim was to create a system that would be simple enough for even casual users to understand, but complex enough to meet a library's expanding needs. His system was developed to meet the needs of many libraries. A second popular system was created to fit the requirements of a specific library, the Library of Congress. This system, now in wide use, is even more detailed and has the advantage of being able to accommodate growth of knowledge in unexpected areas.

THE LIBRARY OF CONGRESS SUBJECT HEADINGS

The Library of Congress Classification System is used in most large public and university libraries today. A Library of Congress (LC) number contains three lines: a letter at the top, a number in the middle, and a letter/number combination at the bottom.

The Library of Congress went through several systems before devising its own method. Because the Library of Congress contains almost every book ever published in the United States, as well as valuable tapes and research materials, it needs a highly flexi-

ble system. The Library of Congress Classification System contains 21 classes:

A	General works
B	Philosophy, psychology, and religion
C	Auxiliary sciences of history
D	History: general and outside the Americas
E	History: America (general) and United States (general)
F	History: United States (local), Canada, Central and South America, Caribbean
G	Geography, anthropology, recreation
H	Social sciences
J	Political science
K	Law
L	Education
M	Music
N	Fine arts
P	Language and literature
Q	Science
R	Medicine
S	Agriculture
T	Technology
U	Military science
V	Naval science
Z	Bibliography and library science

Each of these classes can be divided into a subclass with the addition of a second letter. With the addition of numbers, the category becomes even more specific. The flexibility of the system becomes apparent when one sees that the alphabet permits 26 subdivisions of any one class. Each of the subdivisions can be broken down further by using the numbers 1 to 9999.

Librarians recommend that researchers turn to Subject Headings Used in the Dictionary Catalog of the Library of Congress for assistance. Because the LC system groups related topics together, a researcher may discover unexpected, related avenues to pursue.

Cataloging in Publication Data might also include information on a book's illustrator, whether a book has an index or bibliography, and number of pages.

LIBRARIES ONLINE

Internet links to more than 2,000 libraries (as well as various information services) in more than 70 countries can be found on the Lib Web SunSITE (http://sunsite.berkeley.edu/Libweb). Especially noteworthy among library home pages is the Library of Congress site (http://www.loc.gov). The site provides access to the Library of Congress catalog and catalogs of other libraries, allows users to call up information on a wide variety of subjects, and contains links to other Internet sites. It also offers access to the American Memory collection, which contains both multimedia presentations and documents; THOMAS, a survey of all the legislation pending before Congress; and text and graphics from current and recent Library of Congress exhibitions.

In addition to the various libraries' home pages, the Internet also offers a number of virtual libraries—collections of electronic documents and hypertext links—that exist solely in cyberspace:

Internet Public Library
http://www.ipl.org

Carrie: A Full-Text Electronic Library
http://www.ukans.edu/carrie/carrie_main.html

CyberStacks
http://www.public.iastate.edu/~CYBERSTACKS

Library Gazebo Kiosk
http://www.netins.net/showcase/gazebo/kiosk.html

Public Libraries with Internet Services
http://sjcpl.lib.in.us

WebCATS: Library Catalogues on the Web
http://www.lights.com/webcats

The Virtual Library
http://thorplus.lib.purdue.edu/vlibrar/index.html

DATA BANKS AVAILABLE FOR COMPUTER RESEARCH

CompuServe Interactive Services, Inc.
Customer Service Department
P.O. Box 28650
Jacksonville, FL 32226-8650
800-848-8990
http://www.compuserve.com

This fee-based online system offers forums for users of various computers, with electronic editions of newspapers and computer magazines, an international newswire, conferences, and message boards. CompuServe provides remote computing services, a videotex information service, and a value-added network service, as well as games, entertainment, and personal finance services.

DIALOG Information Services, Inc.
Headquarters
11000 Regency Parkway
Suite 10
Cary, NC 27511

California Offices
3460 Hillview Ave.
Palo Alto, CA 94304

New York Offices
622 3rd Ave.
10th Floor
New York, NY 10017
800-334-2564
415-858-2700
http://www.dialog.com

This fee-based online system provides access to approximately 280 databases, making it possible to search through thousands of newspapers, general-interest and trade magazines, and other publications in seconds. It includes databases compiled by Dun & Bradstreet, Moody's Investor's Service, and Standard & Poor's.

Dow Jones News/Retrieval
P.O. Box 300
Princeton, NJ 08534-0300
609-520-4000
http://www.bis.dowjones.com

This fee-based online computer service offers an interactive information service with up-to-the-minute news and information to the business and financial community. Stories from the Wall Street Journal, Barron's, and the Dow Jones News Service appear as quickly as 90 seconds after filing and go back as far as 90 days. Dow Jones also offers online stock trading and portfolio management services.

Libraries

Getting Started in Genealogy

A Closer Look

The search for a greater understanding of our ancestors has boomed in the United States since the American Bicentennial celebration and the publication of Alex Haley's immensely popular *Roots*. Genealogists lament that too many of us live in historical vacuums, unable to name more than a generation or two of our closest relatives. To help you join this search for a history that extends beyond the last few generations, experts offer several tips:

1. Begin with your closest family members, recording basic information that is already known to you and working backward. This part of the investigation can be quite far-reaching if you contact distant relatives and check sources that they suggest. You may be fortunate enough to have access to family Bibles, letters, and diaries. Vital records such as birth and death certificates can yield a wealth of information at this stage.

2. Consult popular references for research techniques. Some of the best follow.
   - Andereck, Paul A., and Richard A. Pence. *Computer Genealogy: A Guide to Research Through High Technology.* Ancestry Publishing, 1991.
   - Beard Field, Timothy. *How to Find Your Family Roots.* McGraw-Hill, 1977.
   - Cerny, Johni, and Wendy Elliot. *The Library: A Guide to the LDS Family History Library.* Ancestry Publishing, 1988. The book is an explanatory guide to the largest single collection of genealogical works, run by the Church of Jesus Christ of Latter Day Saints.
   - Doane, Gilbert Harry, and James B. Bell. *Searching for Your Ancestors: The How and Why of Genealogy.* 6th ed. University of Minnesota Press, 1992. This introductory guide to genealogical research covers techniques and sources for locating genealogical data.
   - Eakle, Arlene, and Johni Cierny. *The Source: A Guidebook of American Genealogy.* Ancestry Publishing, 1984. The book is a compilation of resources, research techniques, and record sources.
   - Kurzweil, Arthur. *From Generation to Generation.* Schocken Books, 1982. This volume addresses genealogical techniques and subjects particular to Jewish family history, from locating information on European shtetls to Sephardic research.

3. Check out the libraries. Extensive genealogical collections exist at the Library of Congress, the New York Public Library, the Los Angeles Public Library, the Newberry Library in Chicago, and the Allen County Public Library in Fort Wayne, Indiana. Specialized libraries, such as the famed Genealogical Library of the Church of Jesus Christ of Latter-Day Saints in Salt Lake City, Utah, can be extremely helpful. This particular library offers more than 1.3 million reels of microfilm of all types of documents useful to genealogists. Also visit or contact local libraries in areas where your ancestors are known to have lived.

4. Consider contacting the following organizations, which have extensive genealogical records:

American Family Records Association
P.O. Box 15505
Kansas City, MO 64106
816-373-6570

Ellis Island
http://www.ellisisland.org

Genealogical Libraries on the WWW
http://genealogy.org

Federation of Genealogical Societies
http://www.fgs.org

Jewish Genealogical Society
P.O. Box 6398
New York, NY 10128
212-330-8257

Library of Congress
Local History and Genealogy Reading Room
1st Street and Independence Avenue
Washington, DC 20540
202-707-5000
http://leweb.loc.gov

National Archives and Records Administration
Consultant's Office
7th Street and Pennsylvania Avenue, NW
Washington, DC 20408
202-501-5402
http://www.nara.gov

National Genealogical Society
4527 17th St., N
Arlington, VA 22207
703-525-0050
http://www.genealogy.org/~ngs/

Libraries

Major Genealogical Libraries

Burton Collection, Detroit Public Library, 5201 Woodward Ave., Detroit, MI 48202

Dallas Public Library, 1515 Young St., Dallas, TX 75201

Daughters of the American Revolution Library, 1776 D St., NW, Washington, DC 20006 (to be used with the Library of Congress and National Genealogical Society Library, 4527 17th St. N, Arlington, VA 22207)

Genealogical Society Library, 50 E. N. Temple St., Salt Lake City, UT 84150

Los Angeles Public Library, 630 W. 5th St., Los Angeles, CA 90071

Newberry Library, 60 W. Walton St., Chicago, IL 60610

New England Genealogical Society, 101 Newbury St., Boston, MA 02116

New York Historic Genealogical and Biographical Society, 122–6 E. 58th St., New York, NY 10022

New York Public Library, 5th Avenue and 42nd Street, New York, NY 10018

Allen County Public Library, 301 W. Wayne St., Fort Wayne, IN 46802

State Historical Society of Wisconsin, 816 State St., Madison, WI 53706

Western Reserve Historical Society, 10825 East Blvd., Cleveland, OH 44106

Lexis-Nexis
9332 Springboro Pike
Miamisburg, OH 45342
800-444-3333
800-843-6476 (LEXIS-NEXIS EXPRESS)
http://www.lexisnexis.com

This legal, news, and business information service provides online access to more than 73,000 databases containing more than 1 billion separate documents. Areas covered include statutes, legal cases, and online law libraries; national and international news summaries from leading U.S. newspapers and magazines and worldwide wire services; company records and analysts' reports; and access to corporate financial data from the EDGAR system of the U.S. Securities and Exchange commission. Nonsubscribers can use LEXIS-NEXIS EXPRESS to conduct specific searches for a onetime fee.

Ovid Technologies
333 Seventh Ave.
New York, NY 10001
800-950-2035
212-563-3006
http://www.ovid.com

Ovid provides online access to bibliographic and full-text databases for academic, biomedical, and scientific research. Its clients represent Canada, Latin America, Europe, the Middle East, and Africa, as well as the United States.

Questel-Orbit
8000 Westpark Dr.
Suite 130
McLean, VA 22102
800-456-7248

703-442-0900
http://www.questel.orbit.com

This international online information company specializes in patent, trademark, scientific, chemical, and business information covering the United States and the world.

WILSONLINE
The H. W. Wilson Company
950 University Ave.
Bronx, NY 10452
800-367-6770
718-588-8400
http://www.hwwilson.com

WILSONLINE provides online access to The Readers' Guide to Periodical Literature, the Business Periodicals Index, the Index to Legal Periodicals, the Education Index, and numerous other periodical resources. It is used widely by corporations, government agencies, libraries, schools, and universities. Its database covers more than 3,000 periodicals and 500,000 books.

INFORMATION CENTERS

American Crafts Council Library
72 Spring St.
6th Floor
New York, NY 10012
212-274-0630
http://www.craftcouncil.org

Questions about the history of crafts or about learning how to pursue a particular craft, such as weaving or pottery, are answered. Calls may be made Tuesday through Friday between 10 A.M. and 5 P.M., EST.

Libraries

American Museum of Natural History Library
79th Street and Central Park West
New York, NY 10024
212-769-5400
http://library.amnh.org

Founded in 1869, this special library has 400,000 volumes devoted to subjects ranging from anthropology to travel and expedition, with sections on biology, ethnology, entomology, geology, herpetology, history of science, ichthyology, living and fossil invertebrates, mammalogy, mineralogy, museology, ornithology, and paleontology. Its special collections are devoted to astronomical instruments, rare books and manuscripts, rare films, and many other areas. The museum's librarians offer assistance in all areas.

Consumer Information Center
Pueblo, CO 81009
719-948-4000
http://www.pueblo.gsa.gov/

This federal government agency provides a wide selection of free publications such as its monthly National Consumer Buying Alert and guides to solar energy, tire buying, nutrition, budgeting, housing, and gardening. Write for a free catalog or specify your area of interest.

Educational Resources Information Center (ERIC)
AskERIC
2277 Research Blvd.
MS 4M
Rockville, MD 20850
800-LET-ERIC
202-219-2289
http://www.eric.ed.gov

The National Institute of Education within the U.S. Department of Education sponsors ERIC, the educational information system, to provide literature pertaining to various aspects of education. General questions about education are also answered. If a computer search is necessary, a charge will be imposed; otherwise, the information is free. ERIC also provides referrals to other organizations, including its own clearinghouses on adult, career, and vocational education; counseling and personnel services; educational management; elementary and early childhood education; handicapped and gifted children; higher education; information resources; junior colleges; languages and linguistics; reading and communications skills; rural education and small schools; science, mathematics, and environmental education; social studies/social science education; teacher education; tests, measurements, and evaluation; and urban education. Calls are accepted between 8 A.M. and 5:30 P.M., EST, weekdays.

"Federal Information Centers" in chapter 22   Go to

Museum of Television and Radio
25 W. 52nd St.
New York, NY 10019
Scheduled Activities: 212-621-6800
General: 212-621-6600
http://www.mtr.org
and
465 N. Beverly Dr.
Beverly Hills, CA 90210
Scheduled Activities: 310-786-1025

Founded in 1976, this museum has collected more than 10,000 radio and 8,000 TV tapes from the 1920s to the present and 2,400 radio scripts, with 1,600 available on microfiche. Its staff is knowledgeable about all aspects of broadcasting and has access to a thousand-volume library of books and magazines.

The National Archives and Records Administration
700 Pennsylvania Ave., NW
Washington, DC 20408-0001
202-501-5402
http://www.nara.gov

This federal government agency is responsible for keeping the permanent records of the U.S. government. Its holdings include maps, photographs, films, U.S. Census records, and all types of correspondence generated and received by government officials. The archives also contain ship passenger records dating as far back as 1820 and military records from the Revolutionary War. Some of its holdings occasionally overlap those of the Library of Congress. Call between 8:45 A.M. and 5:15 P.M., EST, weekdays.

United Nations Publications
2 United Nations Plaza, DC2-853
New York, NY 10017
800-253-9646
http://www.un.org/publications

This international organization's publications cover a wide range of topics, including human rights, public finance, atomic energy, treaties, and international statistics. The UN makes materials available in hardbound and paperback books, pamphlets, bulletins, periodicals, and official records—all in English, and frequently also in Spanish, French, and Russian. Write for a catalog and details of current offerings.

United States Military Academy Library
Bldg. 757
Corner of Thayer and Cullum
West Point, NY 10996-1711
914-938-3833
http://www.usma.edu

Founded in 1802, the academy's library contains 400,000 volumes pertaining to the history of the military as well as government documents.

REFERENCE WORKS FOR GENERAL INFORMATION

The following lists are not meant to be comprehensive but are intended to serve as wide-ranging sources for the subjects. A library will provide further reference materials and works on each of the subjects.

GENERAL REFERENCE WORKS

American Reference Books Annual. Libraries Unlimited, 1970–.

> This annual volume covers 1,300 to 1,800 new titles each year, reviewing about 300 categories of reference books. The most recent works in many disciplines are listed.

Bartlett's Familiar Quotations: A Collection of Passages, Phrases and Proverbs Traced to Their Sources in Ancient and Modern Literature. 16th ed. Little Brown, 1992.

> This work lists more than 22,500 familiar and world-famous quotations along with a 600-page keyword subject index.

Books in Print. Bowker, 1947–.

> This annual listing of books now in print or slated for publication by January 31 of the following year currently contains well over 700,000 titles.

Carruth, Gorton, ed. *The Volume Library.* The Southwestern Company, 1917–.

> This two-volume, 2.5-million-word family encyclopedia is revised annually. It covers subjects of interest to students and their families and is illustrated and thoroughly indexed.

Encyclopaedia Britannica. 15th ed. Encyclopaedia Britannica, 2002.

> A major comprehensive reference tool for any library.

Encyclopedia Britannica CD. Encyclopedia Britannica.

> An easily accessed CD reference with extensive cross-referencing and yearly updates.

Ethridge, James M., ed. *The Directory of Directories: An Annotated Guide to Business and Industrial Directories, Professional and Scientific Rosters, and Other Lists and Guides of All Kinds.* 2nd ed. Information Enterprises, 1982.

> The work lists 5,200 directories with categories such as business, education, and leisure, providing full details on each publication.

Garraty, John A., and Mark C. Carnes, eds. *American National Biography.* Oxford University Press, 1999.

> Expands on the coverage of the *Dictionary of American Biography.* Includes 17,450 scholarly essays on eminent Americans.

Guinness Book of Records. Bantam, 1955–; Facts On File, 1991–.

> An annual guide to "the biggest, largest, longest, most" all-time records.

Information Industry Market Place: An International Directory of Information Products and Services. Bowker, 1978.

> This international directory describes information collection centers, database and abstract publishers, information brokers, support services and suppliers, conferences, associations, periodicals, and reference books.

Parry, Melanie, ed. *Chambers' Biographical Dictionary.* 6th ed. Larousse, 1997.

> Introduced in 1897, Chambers' currently lists more than 17,500 biographies spanning the history of the world.

Readers' Guide to Periodical Literature. H. W. Wilson, 1900–.

> The Readers' Guide provides a quick overview of current events through indexing of 174 general-interest U.S. magazines in a range of subject areas.

Libraries

Sheehy, Eugene P., ed. *Guide to Reference Books.* American Library Association, 1986.

> Found on nearly every reference librarian's basic bookshelf, Sheehy's *Guide* is grouped into five main categories: general reference works; humanities; social and behavioral sciences; history and area studies; and science, technology, and medicine.

Who's Who in America. Marquis Who's Who, 1899–.

> The individuals listed in Who's Who provide the data to be included, so entries vary in completeness and accuracy. The work includes biographical details on approximately 72,000 Americans and others prominently linked to America.

World Almanac and Book of Facts. Newspaper Enterprise Association, 1868–.

> A handy and easy-to-use reference, the World Almanac is updated annually. It provides statistics and factual data on economic, educational, industrial, political, religious, and social issues.

ANTHROPOLOGY AND ETHNOLOGY

Ember, Melvin, and David Levinson, eds. *American Immigrant Cultures: Builders of a Nation.* Macmillan, 1997.

> Includes descriptive profiles and historical information on 161 ethnic groups of the United States. Covers cultural characteristics, detailed immigration and settlement histories, language, economic patterns, housing, religion, major holidays, marriage, family and kinship, relations with other ethnic groups, as well as discrimination. Maps and statistics.

Galens, Judy, Sheets, Anna J., and Young, Robyn V., eds. *Gale Encyclopedia of Multicultural America*, Gale, 1995.

> Informative and fascinating look at ethnic and racial populations of the United States, describing their history, assimilation, language, and religion, among other topics.

Glazer, Nathan, and Daniel P. Moynihan, eds. *Ethnicity: Theory and Experience.* Harvard University Press, January 1989.

> A classic collection of articles dealing with sociological theory as well as ethnic experience in the United States. First published 1975; updated.

Hunter, David E., and Philip Whitten, eds. *Encyclopedia of Anthropology.* Harper & Row, 1976.

> The first English-language encyclopedia in anthropological studies, this volume is compact, comprehensive, and accessible. It includes some 1,400 articles on pertinent topics, supplemented by generous illustrations, maps, diagrams, and photographs.

Lehman, Jeffrey, ed. *Gale Encyclopedia of Multicultural America: Primary Documents.* Gale 1999.

> Companion to the *Gale Encyclopedia of Multicultural America*, this volume is composed of 210 primary documents from 90 different U.S. groups, representing each ethnic group listed in the encyclopedia.

APPLIED ARTS

Boger, Louise A. *The Dictionary of Antiques and Decorative Arts.* Rev. ed. Scribner, 1979.

> This volume is international in scope, with short articles and illustrations covering furniture, glass, ceramics, styles, terms, and biographies.

Kovel, Ralph, and Terry Kovel. *Kovel's Antiques and Collectibles Price List.* Crown, annual.

> This book includes prices for more than 50,000 antiques and collectible items.

Kovel, Ralph, and Terry Kovel. *Kovel's Know Your Antiques.* Crown, 1990.

> This guide offers tips on how to recognize and evaluate any antique, large or small, like an expert. It covers pottery, porcelain, silver, pewter, furniture, pressed and cut glass, prints, bottles, ironware, tinware, letters, sheet music, autographs, books, magazines, and more. This volume also provides advice about caring for

antiques and recognizing frauds as well as bibliographies for each specialty.

Kovel, Ralph M., and Kovel, Terry. *Kovel's Know Your Collectibles.* Crown Publishing Group, May 1992.

This guide advises on what collectible objects are likely to increase in value and how to preserve, protect, and sell them. It covers ceramics, pottery, furniture, glass, toys, print advertisements, and many other items, with bibliographies for each major specialty.

Liman, Ellen. *The Collecting Book.* Penguin, 1980.

This book thoroughly describes individual collecting areas such as advertising memorabilia, comic books, tobacco items, clothing, boxes and tins, pottery, glass, and toys. It includes chapters on buying, preserving, and displaying collectibles, as well as numerous black-and-white photographs and extensive references to related publications and organizations.

ART AND ARCHITECTURE

American Art Directory. Bowker, 1898–.

A biennial guide to the thousands of art councils, museums, art libraries, and art schools in the United States, Canada, and abroad.

Artist's Market. Writer's Digest, 1974–.

This annual publication details names, addresses, contacts, payments, and other data for 4,000 purchasers of cartoons, illustrations, and photographs. It is considered a standard in its field.

Bell, Doris L. *Contemporary Art Trends: A Guide to Sources, 1960–1980.* Scarecrow Press, 1981.

This work identifies 41 contemporary art trends with listings of appropriate books and museum catalogs. It also contains a listing of 200 contemporary art journals and a bibliography.

Carley, Rachel. *The Visual Dictionary of American Domestic Architecture.* H. Holt & Co., 1994.

Chronologically presents the many styles of American houses, through clearly labeled black

and white illustrations of materials, structures, and design elements.

Hamlin, Talbot. *Architecture Through the Ages.* Putnam, 1953.

This excellent college text offers a survey history from the social point of view. Indexed and illustrated.

Mayer, Ralph. *The HarperCollins Dictionary of Art Terms and Techniques.* HarperCollins, 1992.

This book defines more than 3,200 terms used in the fields of ceramics, drawing, painting, printmaking, and sculpture.

Libraries in the U.S. issue more cards than VISA, have more children enrolled in summer programs than Little League, and have more visitors each week than all museums and zoos combined.

Musgrove, John, ed. *Sir Bannister Fletcher's A History of Architecture.* 19th ed. Butterworth, 1987.

This comprehensive view of architectural history has been revised and expanded to include worldwide coverage. It is extensively illustrated, with glossary, index, and bibliographies appended to each chapter.

Phaidon Dictionary of Twentieth-Century Art. 2nd ed. Dutton, 1977.

This concise and thorough survey covers international art movements and artists in depth from 1900.

Placzek, Adolph K., ed. *Macmillan Encyclopedia of Architects.* 4 vols. Free Press, 1982.

This volume offers a social and historical view of architecture through the ages, from ancient to modern times, in Europe, the Middle East, and North America.

Wilkes, Joseph A., and Robert T. Packard. *Encyclopedia of Architecture: Design, Engineering and Construction.* Wiley, 1990.

This five-volume work addresses the history of Western architecture over the past 200 years and covers 500 different topics, with 3,000 photographs. Each article was prepared by experts in the field.

ASTRONOMY

Eicher, David J. *The Universe from Your Backyard: A Guide to Deep Sky Objects from Astronomy Magazine.* Cambridge University Press, 1988.

A useful guide for all amateur astronomers.

Hoskin, Michael, ed. *The Cambridge Illustrated History of Astronomy.* Cambridge University Press, 1997.

Beautifully illustrated history of astronomy and astronomers.

Moore, Patrick, ed. *The International Encyclopedia of Astronomy.* Orion, 1987.

This popular reference work condenses difficult concepts into readable prose. No prior knowledge of astronomy is assumed. More than 2,500 entries include several major essays by experts in various fields as well as shorter articles. Illustrated in full color.

Muirden, James. *The Amateur Astronomer's Handbook.* 3rd ed. Harper, 1982.

This is an excellent guide for beginners who want to select equipment and set up their own observatories. It includes celestial charts and tables of eclipses and planetary positions.

Pasachoff, Jay M. *Contemporary Astronomy.* 4th ed. CBS College Publishing, 1989.

This textbook is perfect for beginners who have no background in mathematics or physics, presenting astronomical concepts in clear, colloquial English.

BUSINESS

Brownstone, David M., and Gorton Carruth. *Where to Find Business Information: A World Guide for Everyone Who Needs the Answers to Business Questions* (A Hudson Group Book). 2nd ed. Wiley, 1982.

More than 5,000 English-language publications from around the world are listed and briefly described, with concentration on current periodical publications and services, especially magazines, newsletters, computerized databases, printouts, and microforms. The compendium deals with all subjects of interest to business.

Business Periodicals Index: A Cumulative Subject Index to Periodicals in the Fields of Accounting, Advertising, Banking and Finance, General Business, Insurance, Labor and Management, Marketing and Purchasing, Office Management, Public Administra-tion, Taxation, Specific Businesses, Industries, and Trades. H. W. Wilson, 1958–.

This monthly index provides data on approximately 250 periodicals and certain U.S. government documents.

Consumers Index to Product Evaluations and Information Sources. Pierian Press, 1973–. Quarterly; annual cumulation.

A quarterly guide to consumer magazine articles in 14 subject areas.

Consumer Reports Buying Guide. Consumers Union, 1936–.

Issued annually as the December issue of Consumer Reports, this guide is a starting point for a comparative analysis of all types of products. It contains test results, brand and model ratings and rankings, and general buying advice on products as diverse as stereos and orange juice. It also provides a subject index to evaluations from the previous five years of Consumer Reports.

Dow Jones Irwin Business Almanac. Dow Jones-Irwin, 1977–.

This annual almanac provides business, financial, and tax statistics. It includes a short business directory and a review of the previous year's significant business news.

Dun and Bradstreet Million Dollar Directory. Dun and Bradstreet, 1959–.

This annual directory offers alphabetical listings of industries and businesses with a net worth of at least $1 million. It includes the name, address, corporate officers, Standard Industrial Classification (SIC) number, approximate sales, and number of employees for approximately 39,000 U.S. companies.

Dun and Bradstreet's Guide to Your Investments. Crowell, 1973–.

An introductory guide for amateur stock-market investors, this annual explains basic concepts for all types of investments: common and preferred stocks, bonds, real estate, stock options, small business investment companies, and formula investing.

Fortune World Business Directory. Time, Inc., 1957–.

Taken from the annual listing in the May issue of Fortune magazine ranking the 500 largest U.S. industrial corporations, this directory includes the "Fortune 500" plus the 50 largest banks.

Franchise Opportunities Handbook. U.S. Bureau of Industrial Economics and Minority Business Development Agency, 1972–.

One of the best publications on franchising, this annual guide provides details on equity capital needed to buy specific franchises, available training, and support services.

Help: (Washington): The Useful Almanac. Everest House, 1977–.

This annual almanac offers up-to-date information for consumers. It is arranged topically, with material on health, real estate, nutrition, energy, education, insurance, and numerous other subjects.

Moody's Handbook of Common Stocks. Moody's Investors Service, 1965–.

Described as a quick-reference tool, Moody's quarterly publishes data on approximately 1,000 stocks, outlining capitalization, earnings, and the projected outlook for each.

Standard and Poor's Register of Corporations, Directors and Executives. Standard and Poor's, 1928–.

A standard in the field, Standard and Poor's Register offers three volumes each year with current

information on about 46,000 U.S. and Canadian companies. The volumes include biographies of executives as well as separate listings of newly added individuals and companies, obituaries for the previous year, and complete data on each company.

Standard Directory of Advertisers. National Register Publishing, 1907–.

This annual directory lists over 17,000 companies that advertise nationally through various media. The directory provides details on officers and sales personnel, product lines, advertising agencies, and media.

Thomas Register of American Manufacturers and Thomas Register Catalog File. Thomas Publications, 1905–.

This annual authoritative listing of manufacturers is grouped by more than 70,000 product classifications. Its 17 volumes contain lists of products and services; company names, addresses, and phone numbers; names of executives; and ratings. Also included are a brand-name index and company catalogs.

U.S. Master Tax Guide. Commerce Clearing House, 1917–.

Using information on the Internal Revenue Code regulations and court and tax court decisions, this annual handbook covers all aspects of preparing federal income taxes for corporations, estates and trusts, individuals, and partnerships. It is considered a standard in its field.

COMMUNICATIONS

Barnouw, Eric, ed. *International Encyclopedia of Communications.* 4 vols. Oxford University Press, 1989.

This comprehensive, illustrated four-volume encyclopedia covers the entire spectrum of communications studies. Most articles are followed by brief bibliographies, and the work is extensively cross-referenced.

Brown, Les. *Les Brown's Encyclopedia of Television.* Visible Ink Press, 1992.

> This reference work covers television terminology, notable television programs, and profiles of important television personalities, including actors, directors, producers, and writers.

Representative American Speeches Series. H. W. Wilson, 1967–.

> This annual publication includes selected major speeches with biographical notes on the speaker.

Writers Market: Where to Sell What You Write. Writer's Digest, 1929–.

> An essential annual reference for freelance writers that gives the pertinent data on more than 4,500 publishers of books, periodicals, audiovisual materials, greeting cards, plays, and other materials. It includes basics of copyright law and authors' rights.

EDUCATION

American Universities and Colleges. Walter de Gruyter, 2001.

> This comprehensive directory provides information about the structure of higher education in the United States, as well as complete details on each of the more than 1,700 institutions granting baccalaureate or higher degrees.

Durnin, Richard G. *American Education: A Guide to Information Sources.* Gale, 1982.

> This bibliography covers books relating to American education, with 107 topical chapters listing works on childhood through higher education. Most works included are recent publications, but classic works also are described.

Passow, Harry A., ed. *Dictionary of Education.* Greenwood, 2002.

> This volume offers definitions of technical and professional terms and concepts in all areas of education.

The World of Learning. Europa Publications, 1947–.

> This annual directory of international institutions includes educational and scientific institutions and organizations listed by country.

ETHNIC STUDIES
See **Anthropology and Ethnology.**

FILM

Halliwell, Leslie, and John Walker, eds. *Halliwell's Film and Video Guide.* HarperCollins (published annually).

> This regularly revised comprehensive work covers a wide range of popular film lore.

Katz, Ephraim. *The Film Encyclopedia.* 4th ed. HarperInformation, 2001.

> This volume covers directors, producers, actors, composers, and screenwriters, as well as major studios and film centers; it does not list individual movies.

GEOGRAPHY AND TRAVEL GUIDES

Rand McNally Comprehensive World Atlas. 2nd ed. Rand McNally, 1991.

> This atlas includes 350 color maps and map inserts, with individual maps of each U.S. state and Canadian province. It also provides a list of 1980 census totals for about 20,000 U.S. political subdivisions. The main index contains 82,000 entries.

Rand McNally Road Atlas, latest edition. United States, Canada, and Mexico. Rand McNally.

> This annual publication offers maps of all 50 states, each Canadian province, Central America, Mexico, and Puerto Rico, plus a 23,000-item place-name index. It also includes information on population, national park areas, mileage, recreational and historical sites, area codes, time zones, and how to compute miles per gallon.

Libraries

Merrian-Webster's Geographical Dictionary. 3rd ed. Merriam-Webster, 1997.

> This work presents basic geographic, demographic, economic, and historical notes on world countries, regions, cities, and natural features, with maps.

HISTORY

Barraclough, Geoffrey, ed. *The Times Concise Atlas of World History.* 4th ed. Hammond, 1995.

> Seven sections detail the history of the world, beginning with "The World of Early Man" and concluding with "The Age of Global Civilizations." This work contains approximately 600 maps and illustrations depicting the rise and fall of major civilizations, as well as significant religious and historical events.

Barzun, Jacques, and Henry F. Graff. *The Modern Researcher.* 6th ed. Harcourt Brace, 2002.

> This essential reference stresses historical research and provides methodologies useful to those in the humanities and social sciences.

Carruth, Gorton. *The Encyclopedia of American Facts & Dates.* 10th ed. HarperCollins, 1997.

> This chronologically arranged encyclopedia of American history has become a standard reference book for students and others seeking basic information. It covers explorations, treaties, battles, politics, literature, and science, among other topics.

LAW

Black, Henry Campbell, and Bryan Garner, eds. *Black's Law Dictionary,* 7th ed. West Group, 1999.

> A standard reference in the field, Black's gives detailed definitions in all aspects of law, including criminal procedure, estate planning, accounting, taxes, and commercial transactions.

Cohen, Morris L., and Robert C. Berring. *How to Find the Law.* 9th ed. West, 1989.

> A basic text for law students, as well as a helpful tool for the layman investigating resources and methodologies of legal research.

LINGUISTICS

Guinagh, Kevin, ed. *Dictionary of Foreign Phrases and Abbreviations.* 3rd ed. H. W. Wilson, 1982,

> This dictionary contains definitions for more than 5,000 French, German, Greek, Italian, Latin, and Spanish abbreviations, phrases, quotations, and proverbs that appear in the English language. Similar expressions are cross-referenced.

Merriam-Webster's Collegiate Dictionary. 10th ed. Merriam-Webster, 1998.

> Almost 160,000 entries are offered, with pronunciations, functional labels, inflected forms, word histories, usage, and word divisions. Also included is the first known date of use for each word. The dictionary contains sections with biographical and geographical entries, foreign words and phrases, degree-granting colleges and universities, signs and symbols, and a style manual.

Roget's International Thesaurus. 6th ed. HarperInformation, 2001.

> Topical listings of more than 250,000 words are provided, with an alphabetical index for easy use.

Strunk, William, and E. B. White. *The Elements of Style.* 4th ed. Macmillan, 1999.

> A classic book noted for its simplicity and directness, *Elements* consists of only five chapters: "Elementary Rules of Usage," "Elementary Principles of Composition," "A Few Matters of Form," "Words and Expressions Commonly Misused," and "An Approach to Style."

Webster's New World College Dictionary. 4th ed. Wiley, 1999.

> This authoritative dictionary provides over 150,000 entries, with in-depth etymologies, pronunciations, foreign expressions, a syllabification system, and over 11,000 Americanisms.

Libraries

LITERATURE

Drabble, Margaret, ed. *The Oxford Companion to English Literature.* 6th ed. Oxford University Press, 2000.

> Entries on English fiction, authors, and literary schools and movements are presented.

France, Peter, ed. *The New Oxford Companion to Literature in French.* Oxford University Press, 1995.

> *The New Oxford Companion to Literature in French* is a new work rather than a revision of the old *Companion to French Literature.* Coverage is extended to francophone writing throughout the world.

Garland, Henry, and Mary Garland. *The Oxford Companion to German Literature.* 3rd ed. Oxford University Press, 1997.

> German writers and their works, with cultural and historical background, are provided.

Gassner, John, and Edward Quinn, eds. *The Readers' Encyclopedia of World Drama.* Dover Publications, 2002.

> The book has entries on playwrights, critics, national dramatic literatures, and histories. Emphasis is on drama as literature.

Granger, Edith. *The Columbia Granger's Index to Poetry in Anthologies. 12th ed.* Columbia University Press, 2002.

> This standard work is indexed by title, first line, author, and subject.

Hart, James D. *Oxford Companion to American Literature.* 6th ed. Oxford University Press, 1995.

> This volume has entries on American fiction, authors, and literary schools and movements.

Harvey, Paul, and J. E. Heseltine. *The Oxford Companion to French Literature.* Oxford University Press, 1969.

> This volume covers authors and their works, with survey articles, terms, and movements from the Middle Ages to 1939.

Howatson, Margaret C., and Ian Chilvers. *Concise Oxford Companion to Classical Literature.* Oxford University Press, 1993.

> This comprehensive guide has entries on authors, characters, plots, literary forms, and cultural and historical background. A chronological table and maps are included.

MLA International Bibliography of Books and Articles on the Modern Languages and Literatures. Modern Language Association of America, 1921–. Annual.

> This useful reference covers articles and books in English, French, German, Spanish, Italian, Portuguese, Rumanian, and other languages.

Sader, Marion, ed. *The Reader's Adviser 6 Vol. Set.* 14th ed. Greenwood, 1993.

> This basic guide to literature covers the best in English and American fiction, poetry, essays, biographies, and other areas in the fields of reference, history, philosophy, and science.

MEDICAL SCIENCE

American Medical Association Family Medical Guide. 3rd ed. Charles R. Clayman, ed. 1994.

> This layperson's handbook features articles on diseases and disorders, diagnostic charts, and an index of drugs and medications.

Berkow, Robert, ed. *The Merck Manual of Medical Information.* Merck & Company, 1997.

> Written for the general reader, this version of *The Merck Manual of Diagnosis and Therapy* is comprehensive and easy-to-use.

Komaroff, Anthony, and Harvard Medical School. *The Harvard Medical School Family Health Guide.* Simon & Schuster, 1999.

> This family health guide covers symptoms, disorders, diseases, health maintenance, and information about the U.S. health care system. Includes more than 900 illustrations and full-color photographs.

Physicians' Desk Reference to Pharmaceutical Specialties and Biologicals. Medical Economics, 1947–.

This compendium, commonly referred to as the PDR, is a standard reference work for physicians and other health professionals. It offers details on dosage, contraindications, side effects, precautions, and undesirable interactions of pharmaceutical products.

The New Wellness Encyclopedia. Staff of the University of California, Berkeley, Wellness Letter, eds. Houghton Mifflin, 1995.

This comprehensive guide focuses on preventive health through good eating, exercise, and risk reduction for disease.

MUSIC

Abraham, Gerald. *The Concise Oxford History of Music.* Oxford University Press, 1985.

This scholarly survey of Western music from ancient to modern times is presented chronologically. It describes the musical styles of each period and region, with extensive bibliographies.

Garland Encyclopedia of World Music. Garland Publishing, 1998.

Sweeping overview of the indigenous musical forms of the world's peoples, described in essay-style articles.

Grout, Donald J. *A History of Western Music.* 5th ed. Norton, 1996.

This standard one-volume history of music is used in thousands of colleges and graduate schools. This illustrated volume contains a bibliography, chronology, and glossary.

Havlice, Patricia Pate. *Popular Song Index.* 3rd ed. Scarecrow Press, 1989.

Hundreds of songbooks from the second half of the 20th century, including children's songs, folk songs, hymns, and popular music, are anthologized.

Sadie, Stanley, ed. *The New Grove Dictionary of Music and Musicians.* Reprint ed. 20 vols. Grove's Dictionaries of Music, 1995.

This comprehensive dictionary includes entries and articles on composers, performers, theorists, music publishers, scholars, terminology, genres, and orchestras, with exhaustive bibliographies.

MYTHOLOGY, FOLKLORE, AND POPULAR CUSTOMS

Bulfinch, Thomas. Illustrated by Giovannie Caselli. *The Illustrated Bulfinch's Mythology: The Age of Fable, the Age of Chivalry, and the Legends of Charlemagne.* Hungry Minds, 1997.

The classic work on mythology, Bulfinch's summarizes Greek, Roman, Norse, Arthurian, and other myths, with notes on the Iliad, the Odyssey, and the Aeneid.

Mercatante, Anthony. *The Facts On File Encyclopedia of World Mythology and Legend.* Facts On File, 1988.

This comprehensive reference covers world mythologies in thematic, biographical, and narrative essays.

Thompson, Stith. *The Folktale.* University of California Press, 1977.

Considered a standard in the field, this work discusses the form and development of folk stories, with summaries of the most popular folktales of Europe, western Asia, and the Native North Americans. It also covers various methods of researching and studying folktales and folklore.

PHILOSOPHY

Borchert, Donald M. *Encyclopedia of Philosophy (Supplement).* Gale, 1996.

A companion to the eight-volume *Encyclopedia of Philosophy* published by Macmillan.

Encyclopedia of Philosophy, 8 vols. Macmillan, 1973.

An excellent scholarly reference, this eight-volume encyclopedia contains hundreds of articles relevant to political science as well as philosophy and biographies of scores of key figures such as Aristotle, Darwin, Hobbes, Jefferson, Locke, Machiavelli, Malthus, Marx, Mill, Plato, and Rousseau.

Libraries

Magill, Frank N., ed. *Masterpieces of World Philosophy: More Than 100 Classics of the World's Greatest Philosophers Analyzed and Explained.* HarperCollins, 1990.

This book contains more than 100 synopses and commentaries on key figures in Eastern and Western philosophy, including analyses of important influences on their development.

POLITICAL SCIENCE

Andriot, Laurie. *Internet Blue Pages: The Guide to Federal Government Web Sites.* 2nd ed. Information Today, 2000.

This wide-ranging guide to online information from the U.S. federal government is organized by agency. Comprehensive entries describe and list the function or purpose of each agency, its URLs, and links from various agency home pages.

Baum, Lawrence. *The Supreme Court.* 7th ed. Congressional Quarterly, 2000.

This overview of the Supreme Court explains its processes and discusses the justices, as well as examining policy-making influence and impact on government and individuals.

Congressional Quarterly's Guide to Congress. Latest ed. Congressional Quarterly.

This accurate, nonpartisan guide to the history, power, structure, and workings of Congress includes the texts of the Articles of Confederation, Constitution, Declaration of Independence, and important preconstitutional documents.

Klingemann, Hans-Dieter, and Robert E. Goodin, eds. *A New Handbook of Political Science.* Oxford University Press, 1998.

Containing contributions from 42 internationally known political scientists, this handbook covers the development of political science in the last quarter of the 20th century.

Roberts, Henry M., and William J. Evans, Daniel H. Honemann, and Thomas J. Balch. *Robert's Rules of Order: Newly Revised.* 10th ed. Perseus Publishing, 2000.

This completely revised edition provides the authoritative guide to parliamentary procedure.

Washington Information Directory. Congressional Quarterly, 1975–.

This annual publication describes 5,000 congressional, executive, and nongovernmental agencies, committees, and organizations. It is considered an indispensable guide to both official and unofficial Washington.

RECREATION AND SPORTS

Fortin, Francois, ed. *Sports: The Complete Visual References.* Firefly Books, 2000.

Illustrates and describes approximately 120 sports, including new sports. Summarizes history, equipment, playing fields, and techniques of each sport covered.

Levinson, David, and Karen Christensen, eds. *Encyclopedia of World Sport: From Ancient Times to the Present.* 3 vols. ABC-CLIO, 1996.

Comprehensive set covering the history of sport.

Robert, Markel, ed. *Women's Sports Encyclopedia.* Holt, 1997.

A comprehensive history of women in sports, including hundreds of biographies, world records to 1997, and a timeline dating from Ancient Greece.

RELIGION

Adams, Charles J., ed. *A Reader's Guide to the Great Religions.* 2nd ed. The Free Press, 1977.

Through bibliographic essays, this work covers major religions as well as ancient beliefs, religions of Mexico and Central and South America, the Sikh religion, and the Jains. It includes a subject index and an index of authors, compilers, translators, and editors for the serious researcher.

Attwater, Donald, and Catherine R. John. *Penguin Dictionary of Saints.* 3rd ed. Penguin, 1996.

This book provides brief biographical sketches of the best-known saints. The selections are worldwide but emphasize those in Great Britain.

Brandon, S. G. F., ed. *Dictionary of Comparative Religions.* Macmillan, 1978.

Thorough and concise, this volume defines anthropology, iconography, philosophy, and the psychology of primitive, ancient, Asian, and Western religions. Articles describe practices and philosophies of specific religions, with terminology for each and pertinent bibliographies.

The Illustrated Bible Dictionary. 3 vols. Tyndale House, 1980.

Comprehensive and well organized, this dictionary is based on the revised standard version. It offers definitions from all aspects of books of the Bible; major works and doctrines; and history, geography, customs, and cultures of biblical times. Extensive photographs, charts, diagrams, cross-references, and a useful index are included.

Kohlenberger, John R., and Richard E. Whitaker. *The Analytical Concordance to the New Revised Standard Version of the New Testament.* William B. Eerdmans Publishing, 1997.

This massive work contains both a concordance and an index-lexicon. Entries give the English word followed by a subtitle line with three elements: definition, Greek word, and an English transliteration of the Greek word. Included are complete listings of each passage in which the subject word appears, with an explanation of its use in context.

SCIENCE AND TECHNOLOGY

Allin, Craig W. ed. *Encyclopedia of Environmental Issues.* 3 vols. Salem Press, 2000.

Covers a wide range of environmental issues in 475 articles.

Chen, Ching-Chih. *Scientific and Technical Information Sources.* 2nd ed. MIT, 1986.

Although the book is primarily a guide for science and technology librarians, it is a useful guide to relevant sources for the layperson.

The Cutting Edge: An Encyclopedia of Advanced Technologies. Oxford University Press, 2000.

This volume contains 102 signed, cross-referenced entries, describing each technology's development and direction, as well as the opinions it provokes.

McGraw-Hill Encyclopedia of Science and Technology. 7th ed. McGraw-Hill, 1996.

This 20-volume compendium continues to be the basic reference source covering important topics from earliest times to the present. Annual updates are available.

Walker, Peter, ed. *Chambers Dictionary of Science and Technology.* Larousse Kingfisher Chambers, 1999.

A revision and expansion of a classic work, the *Chambers Dictionary* provides 45,000 understandable, alphabetical definitions of terms used in a variety of scientific disciplines.

SOCIAL SCIENCE

Baltes, Paul B., and Neil J. Smelser, eds. *International Encyclopedia of the Social and Behavioral Sciences.* Elsevier Science, 2001.

This scholarly summary of the social sciences includes signed articles on numerous specific topics, as well as hundreds of biographies.

Calhoun, Craig J. ed. *Dictionary of the Social Sciences.* Oxford University Press, February 2001.

Includes terms from anthropology, sociology, political science, economics, human geography, and cultural studies.

See also **Anthropology and Ethnology; Political Science;** and **Sociology.**

SOCIOLOGY

Barnes, Harry Elmer, and Howard Becker. *Social Thought from Lore to Science.* 3rd ed. Peter Smith, 1990.

This is a three-volume encyclopedic inventory of the history of sociology.

Directory of Counseling Services. International Association of Counseling Services, 1969–.

This annual publication lists members of the American Personnel and Guidance Association who offer public and private counseling dealing with education, family, marriage, personal problems, rehabilitation, and vocational guidance.

STATISTICS AND DEMOGRAPHY

Bureau of the Census Catalog. U.S. Bureau of the Census, 1946–.

This catalog provides listings of all published and unpublished material (tape, cards, or microform) created by the Census Bureau during the period covered.

Kotz, Samuel, and Normal L. Johnson, eds. *Encyclopedia of Statistical Sciences,* 9 vols. Wiley, 1982–1988; updates 1997-8.

Information on many topics in statistical his-tory and application of statistical methods is presented in this nine-volume work, intended primarily for readers who seek more information than general references can offer.

United Nations Statistical Yearbook. United Nations, 1949–.

This annual publication is considered the best source for international statistics. It offers data on such topics as agriculture, balance of payments, communications, construction, energy, population, transport, and wages and prices in 150 countries and territories.

THEATER AND PERFORMING ARTS

Cohen, Selma, ed. *International Encyclopedia of Dance.* 6 vols. Oxford University Press, 1998.

Scholarly and groundbreaking work on dance around the world.

Hatnoll, Phyllis, ed. *The Oxford Companion Guide to World Theatre.* 4th ed. Oxford University Press, 1983.

Articles on all aspects of theater are included, from history to theater architecture, technical the-ater, terminology, and experimental theater. Also included are articles on national dramatic literature, plays, actors, playwrights, and teachers.

Hughes, Catherine. *American Theater Annual.* Gale Research, 1976–.

All plays opening on and off Broadway during the year are listed, with details of cast members, opening and closing dates, plot summaries, and review excerpts.

Koegler, Horst. *The Concise Oxford Dictionary of Ballet.* 2nd ed. Oxford University Press, 1982.

This book contains more than 5,000 alphabetically arranged entries covering all areas of ballet: choreographers, composers, dancers, history, schools and companies, and basic definitions.

Notable Names in the American Theater. James T. White, 1976.

This major work is divided into nine sections covering administrators, agents, archivists, authors, casting directors, composers, conductors, critics, designers, directors, educators, historians, lyricists, performers, playwrights, producers, and teachers.

Theatre World. Crown, annual.

This theater yearbook gives a complete pictorial and statistical record of each Broadway season from 1944–45 to the present.

MAJOR ART MUSEUMS AND THEIR SPECIAL COLLECTIONS

Internet links to numerous museums can be found on the Virtual Library Museums Pages, supported by the International Council of Museums. The organization's home page can be accessed at http://icom.org/vlmp.

UNITED STATES

Arizona
University Art Museum
Arizona State University Art Collections
Nelson Fine Arts Center and Matthews Center
Arizona State University
P.O. Box 872911
Tempe, AZ 85287-2911

480-965-2787 (ARTS)
http://asuartmuseum.asu.edu

Founded in 1950, Arizona State's collection includes American paintings of the 18th and 19th centuries; a fine print collection with Rembrandts, Whistlers, and Dürers; fine Americana and decorative arts, particularly pottery; European painting and sculpture; Latin American arts; and crafts.

California

California Palace of the Legion of Honor
100 34th Ave.
San Francisco, CA 94121
415-750-3600

M. H. deYoung Museum
75 Tea Garden Dr.
Golden Gate Park
San Francisco, CA 94118
415-750-3600

These museums are run by a joint administration, although they are not located near each other. Founded in 1924 and 1895, respectively, each museum has extensive collections. The deYoung includes the Hearst collection of Flemish Gothic tapestries; fine primitive pre-Columbian artifacts; Northwest Coast Native American, African, and Oceanic arts collections; and Renaissance and Baroque art. The California Palace is noted for its 18th-century French furniture and decorative arts; its French paintings, including those of Monet, Renoir, Fragonard, Boucher, Manet, and Corot; Rodin sculptures; and an extraordinary collection of prints and drawings of all periods.

J. Paul Getty Museum
1200 Getty Center Dr.
Los Angeles, CA 90049
310-440-7300

The world's best-endowed museum, the Getty was created in 1953. This popular museum is housed in a recreation of the 1st century B.C. Villa dei Paryri at Herculaneum, complete with elaborate gardens. The Getty has acquired extraordinary classical collections, including illuminated manuscripts and French decorative arts.

Huntington Library, Art Collections, and Botanical Garden
1151 Oxford Rd.
San Marino, CA 91108
626-405-2100
http://www.huntington.org

In the Huntington complex, established in 1919, a beautiful garden setting enhances the extraordinary

collections of 18th-century British paintings, including Gainsborough's Blue Boy and Lawrence's Pinkie; Renaissance bronzes and 18th-century marbles; early editions of Shakespeare and Chaucer in the extensive library; and prints and drawings. The setting includes a Japanese garden and 16th-century samurai's house.

Los Angeles County Museum of Art
5905 Wilshire Blvd.
Los Angeles, CA 90036
323-857-6111
http:// www.lacma.org/

Established in 1910, this museum houses a general collection in three pavilions surrounded by a sculpture garden with works from Rodin's time to the present. Its acquisitions include early Near and Middle Eastern antiquities; Roman, Greek, Western, and modern art; Far Eastern collections; textiles; costumes; Indian arts; pottery; Italian mosaics; pre-Columbian, African, and Oceanic arts; and 19th- and 20th-century American and European paintings.

A researcher at the Smithsonian Museum removed a lens from the compound eye of a half-billion-year-old trilobite (a marine invertebrate animal), attached it to a microscope, and took a photograph of a building.

Norton Simon Museum
411 W. Colorado Blvd.
Pasadena, CA 91105
646-449-6840
http://nortonsimon.org

Established in 1924 as the Pasadena Museum of Modern Art, this museum has developed worldwide prominence through the loans of collector Norton Simon. His collections include European art from the Renaissance to recent times, with Old Masters of the highest quality.

Colorado

The Denver Art Museum
100 W. 14th Avenue Pkwy.
Denver, CO 80204-2788
720-865-5000
http://www.denverartmuseum.org

The Denver Art Museum is noted for its collection of primitive African, Oceanic, American, Native American, and Northwest Indian arts; its Peruvian art; its collection of the arts of China, Japan, Korea, India, Southeast Asia, Tibet, and the Middle and Near East; period rooms; Impressionist, post-Impressionist, and modern paintings; prints, drawings, and photographs; and the Neusteter Institute of Fashion, Costume, and Textiles.

Connecticut

The New Britain Museum of American Art
56 Lexington St.
New Britain, CT 06052-1412
860-229-0257
www.nbmaa.org

The New Britain Collection, established in 1903, focuses on outstanding American paintings from colonial times to the present. It includes Hudson River School painters and the Low memorial collection of American illustration, with N. C. Wyeth classics.

Yale Center for British Art
P.O. Box 208280
New Haven, CT 06520
203-432-2800

This collection of British watercolors, drawings, paintings, books, and prints is the largest of its kind outside Great Britain. Established in 1977, the center was the gift of Paul Mellon, a lifelong collector of British art.

Yale University Art Gallery
P.O. Box 208271
New Haven, CT 06520-8271
203-432-0600
http://www.yale.edu/artgallery

This outstanding world art collection has been built up since the gallery's founding in 1832. It includes the Jarves collection of early Italian paintings; collections of American silver, painting, and decorative arts; modern art; Greek and Roman vases; manuscripts; prints and drawings; and primitive arts.

Delaware

Delaware Art Museum
2301 Kentmere Pkwy.
Wilmington, DE 19806
302-571-9590
http://www.delart.org

The Delaware Art Museum, founded in 1912, specializes in American paintings, with examples by Hudson River School painters such as John Sloan, Howard Pyle, and the Wyeth family. There is an extensive collection of English pre-Raphaelites, a research library on American arts, and prints and drawings.

Henry Francis Du Pont Winterthur Museum
Route 52
Winterthur, DE 19735
302-888-4600

Founded in 1930, Winterthur has an outstanding collection of American furniture, furnishings, and decorative arts from the colonial period to the mid–19th century. Period rooms display extensive collections of ceramics, glass, Chinese porcelain, fabrics, lighting fixtures, and carpets.

District of Columbia

Arthur M. Sackler Gallery, Smithsonian Institution
1050 Independence Ave., SW
Washington, DC 20560
202-357-4880
http://www.asia.si.edu

This gallery contains a permanent collection of Asian art, including ancient works from China, the Indian subcontinent, and Southeast Asia as well as scrolls and other work by notable 20th-century painters.

Freer Gallery of Art, Smithsonian Institution
1050 Independence Ave., SW
Washington, DC 20560
202-357-4880
http://www.asia.si.edu

Established in 1906, the Freer has one of the world's best collections of Oriental art and a comprehensive collection of Whistler paintings (his close friend Charles Freer gathered the collection and donated it).

Hirshhorn Museum and Sculpture Garden, Smithsonian Institution
P.O. Box 37012
Hirshhorn Museum and Sculpture Garden
MRC Code 350
Washington, DC 20013-7012
202-357-3091
http://www.hirshhorn.si.edu

Created in 1966 to specialize in modern art, the Hirshhorn's collection is so vast that only a small portion can be displayed at any time.

National Gallery of Art
6 Constitution Ave.
Washington, DC 20565
202-737-4215
http://www.nga.gov

The National Gallery was endowed by Andrew Mellon in 1937 and continues to benefit from his children's donations. It includes paintings and sculptures of all schools of Western art, decorative arts, and drawings and prints, with all the classic masters represented.

Smithsonian American Art Museum, Smithsonian Institution
Washington, DC 20560-0970
202-275-1500
http://www.nmaa.si.edu

Housed in the historic Greek Revival Old Patent Office, the museum has a definitive collection of American arts, including graphic and decorative arts, from colonial times to the present.

The J. Paul Getty museum is the richest in the world. It paid $22 million for Fra Bartolommeo's The Rest on the Flight Into Egypt with Saint John the Baptist.

Hawaii

Honolulu Academy of Arts
900 S. Beretania St.
Honolulu, HI 96814
808-532-8787
http://www.honoluluacademy.org

The academy, founded in 1927, has a general collection representing everything from ancient Near Eastern and Mediterranean arts to European and American arts. Medieval art, the Michener Collection of Japanese prints, Monet's Water Lilies, and the arts of Africa, Oceania, and the Americas are also included.

Illinois

The Art Institute of Chicago
11 South Michigan Ave.
Chicago, IL 60603
312-443-3600
http://www.artic.edu

Founded in 1879, the Art Institute of Chicago has excellent collections in all areas of art. It is noted for the works of Old Masters, Impressionists, and American and Far Eastern artists; graphics; and Thorne miniature rooms. Famed works include Seurat's *Sunday Afternoon on the Island of la Grande Jatte,* Rembrandt's *Young Girl at an Open Half-Door,* and Mary Cassatt's *The Bath.*

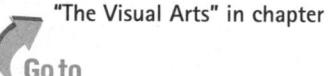

"The Visual Arts" in chapter 7

Go to

Oriental Institute Museum
University of Chicago
1155 E. 58th St.
Chicago, IL 60637
Museum Office: 773-702-9502
http://www-oi.uchicago.edu

Founded in 1919, the Oriental Institute houses a top collection of archeology and art of the ancient Near East, Babylonia, Egypt, early Christian cultures, and Islamic civilization.

Indiana

Indianapolis Museum of Art
1200 W. 38th St.
Indianapolis, IN 46208
317-923-1331
http://www.ima-art.org

Noted for its Chinese, primitive, and American art, this museum, founded in 1883, has an outstanding general collection of Old Masters, Turner watercolors, and European and American decorative arts.

Kansas

Wichita Art Museum
619 Stackman Dr.
Wichita, KS 67203
316-268-4921
http://www.wichitaartmuseum.org

Established in 1935, this museum's outstanding collection is noted for its American paintings, sculptures, prints, and drawings.

Kentucky

J. B. Speed Art Museum
2035 S. Third St.
Louisville, KY 40208
502-634-2700
http://www.speedmuseum.org

This extensive collection, founded in 1925, includes European painting, sculpture, and decorative arts from the Middle Ages to the present; French and Flemish tapestries; and Kentuckiana.

Maryland

The Baltimore Museum of Art
10 Art Museum Dr.
Baltimore, MD 21218
410-396-6300
http://www.artbma.org

Best known for its classic modern collections, this outstanding museum, established in 1914, displays contemporary drawings, period rooms illustrating stylistic development in Maryland, Old Masters paintings, and Far Eastern art.

Walters Art Gallery
600 N. Charles St.
Baltimore, MD 21201
410-547-9000
http://www.thewalters.org

Assembled by father and son, the Walters Art Gallery opened in 1931 with exquisite medieval treasures and Byzantine and Islamic art; early Christian liturgical vessels, Renaissance enamels, and jewelry; paintings from various periods; and Greek, Roman, and Etruscan art.

Massachusetts

Fogg Art Museum
32 Quincy St.
Harvard University
Cambridge, MA 02138
617-495-9400

With the largest and most extensive art collection of any university in the United States, the Fogg, opened in 1895, is particularly noted for its drawings and prints of all periods. It also has a fine collection of Chinese sculptures, stones and bronzes, jades, and ceramics.

Isabella Stewart Gardner Museum
280 The Fenway
Boston, MA 02115
617-566-1401
http://www.gardnermuseum.org

This personal collection, founded in 1900, covers a wide range of world art, with masterpieces such as Titian's *The Rape of Europa,* Giotto's *Presentation of the Child Jesus in the Temple,* and Botticelli's *Madonna of the Eucharist.*

Museum of Fine Arts
465 Huntington Ave.
Boston, MA 02115
617-267-9300
http://www.mfa.org

This collection, founded in 1870, includes masterpieces from around the world. It is noted for its Far Eastern, ancient, Egyptian, Greek, and Roman collections; its Old Masters, Impressionist, and post-Impressionist works; and its American paintings and decorative arts. It also has American silver, prints and drawings, ancient musical instruments, and ship models. Famed works include Paul Revere's Liberty Bowl,

Renoir's *Le Bal... Bougival,* and a Greek marble *Head of Aphrodite.*

Michigan

The Detroit Institute of Arts
5200 Woodward Ave.
Detroit, MI 48202
313-833-7900
http://www.dia.org

Founded in 1885, this institute is renowned for its comprehensive collection of world arts, especially its Old Master paintings of northern Europe, French 18th-century decorative arts, art of the ancient world, period rooms, prints and drawings, and American arts since colonial times.

Henry Ford Museum and Greenfield Village
20900 Oakwood Blvd.
Dearborn, MI 48124
313-271-1620
http://www.hfmgv.org

Described as a "Disneyland of Americana," the indoor/outdoor facilities, established in 1929, of the museum and village offer demonstrations of crafts and manufacturing techniques that complement its extensive collections of arts, crafts, artifacts, and technology. Activities include everything from antique car rallies to country fairs on its 14 acres.

Minnesota

The Minneapolis Institute of Arts
2400 Third Ave. S.
South Minneapolis, MN 55404
612-870-3000
http://www.artsmia.org

This outstanding general collection is strongest in European paintings from Old Masters to the present. Founded in 1912, the institute also houses the Pillsbury Collection of Chinese bronzes, Japanese prints and paintings, textiles, and photographs.

Walker Art Center
725 Vineland Pl.
Minneapolis, MN 55403
612-375-7600
http://www.walkerart.org

Founded in 1879, this museum contains contemporary art, including paintings, sculpture, drawings, and prints. Its renowned Minneapolis Sculpture Garden is a 7½-acre urban garden featuring 40 sculptures and a conservatory with horticultural displays.

Libraries

Missouri

Nelson-Atkins Museum of Art
4525 Oak St.
Kansas City, MO 64111
816-561-4000
http://www.Nelson-Atkins.org

This museum contains prestigious collections of European and American art as well as a renowned Oriental Collection.

The St. Louis Art Museum
One Fine Arts Dr.
St. Louis, MO 63110
314-721-0067
http://www.slam.org

Founded in 1881, the St. Louis Art Museum contains a comprehensive collection of art. Among its more than 35,000 works are important pre-Columbian and German Expressionist collections.

New Jersey

Princeton University Art Museum
Princeton, NJ 08544
609-258-3788
http://www.princetonartmuseum.org/

Opened in 1882, this comprehensive collection contains a wide spectrum of world art, including Chinese paintings and bronzes, classical antiquities, and French paintings and sculptures.

New Mexico

The University of New Mexico
Center for the Arts
University Art Museum
Room 1017
Albuquerque, NM 87131
505-277-4001
http://unmartmuseum.unm.edu

Established in 1963, the museum has important collections of 19th- and 20th-century prints and photographs and American paintings of the 20th century, with emphasis on artists who worked in New Mexico.

New York

Albany Institute of History and Art
125 Washington Ave.
Albany, NY 12210
518-463-4478
http://www.albanyinstitute.org

Founded in 1791, the institute's collection focuses on the fine and decorative arts of Albany and Hudson River artists, with portraits, silver, furniture, and period rooms.

The Brooklyn Museum of Art
200 Eastern Pkwy.
Brooklyn, NY 11238
718-638-5000
http://www.brooklynart.org

The Brooklyn Museum was founded in 1023 and has amassed comprehensive collections of Egyptian and classical arts; American arts; European and American graphics; and pre-Columbian, African, Native American, and other primitive arts.

The Cloisters
799 Fort Washington Ave.
Fort Tryon Park, NY 10040
212-923-3700
http://www.metmuseum.org

A branch of the Metropolitan Museum devoted exclusively to medieval art, the Cloisters opened in 1938 and incorporates four medieval cloisters, an arcade, a chapel, and exhibition rooms. The museum features 12th- and 13th-century Byzantine and Romanesque art from France and Spain.

Cooper-Hewitt, National Design Museum, Smithsonian Institution
2 E. 91st St.
New York, NY 10128
212-849-8300
http://ndm.si.edu/

Established in 1897, the Cooper-Hewitt is housed in the Carnegie mansion. Its excellent collection of decorative arts includes furniture, fabrics, wallpaper, ceramics, drawings, prints, architecture and design publications, and metalwork. It boasts the world's largest collection of Winslow Homer drawings and sketches by other late-19th-century artists.

The Frick Collection
One E. 70th St.
New York, NY 10021
212-288-0700
http://www.frick.org

The former home of Henry Clay Frick, built in 1914 as an 18th-century model, still has most of its original furnishings intact, including excellent European paintings from the 14th through the 18th centuries.

Guggenheim Museum
See **Solomon R. Guggenheim Museum.**

The Jewish Museum
1109 Fifth Ave.
New York, NY 10128
212-423-3200
http://www.jewishmuseum.org

This preeminent U.S. collection numbers over 23,000 objects spanning 4 millennia, ranging from ancient Eastern Mediterranean archeological artifacts to contemporary art and including paintings, sculpture, ceramics, textiles, wood, metalwork, photography, drawings, prints, coins, medals, and broadcast materials. A permanent exhibit, The Jewish Experience, spans 4,000 years of history and culture.

The Metropolitan Museum of Art
1000 Fifth Ave.
New York, NY 10028
212-879-5500
http://www.metmuseum.org

One of the world's major museums, founded in 1870, the Metropolitan houses definitive collections covering about 5,000 years of art. A few of the highlights include medieval armor collections, Tiffany stained-glass windows, the complete Temple of Dendur, extensive painting collections, sculpture, decorative arts, and a re-creation of a classic Ming dynasty Chinese garden court.

The Museum of Modern Art
11 W. 53rd St.
New York, NY 10019
212-708-9480
http://www.moma.org

Begun in 1929, this exceptional collection traces the evolution of art from the Impressionist period forward. It represents a variety of disciplines, including drawings and prints, industrial design, architecture, paintings, sculpture, and decorative arts.

The Solomon R. Guggenheim Museum
1071 Fifth Ave.
New York, NY 10128
212-423-3500
http://www.guggenheim.org

Founded in 1937, this excellent collection of modern drawings, prints, paintings, and sculpture emphasizes abstract and nonobjective subjects. It is housed in a stunning Frank Lloyd Wright building.

Whitney Museum of American Art
945 Madison Ave.
New York, NY 10021
212-570-3600
http://www.whitney.org/index.shtml

Opened in 1966, the Whitney houses New York's largest collection of 20th-century art, with changing exhibitions of drawings, paintings, sculpture, and architecture. It shows contemporary avant-garde film and video and holds the Biennial of Contemporary American Art, a showcase of the best recent work.

Ohio
Cincinnati Art Museum
953 Eden Park Dr.
Cincinnati, OH 45202
513-721-5204
http://www.cincinnatiartmuseum.org

Founded in 1886, this major museum has an excellent, comprehensive general collection noted for its Near Eastern and American arts, Old Masters, medieval art, musical instruments, and drawings and prints.

Cleveland Museum of Art
11150 East Blvd.
Cleveland, OH 44106
216-421-7340
http://www.clevelandart.org

This excellent museum, founded in 1913, has a wide-ranging collection representing the artistic accomplishments of cultures throughout the world. It is recognized for one of the best Far Eastern collections and for its medieval art, Old Masters, classical antiquities, and American arts from the colonial time forward.

The Toledo Museum of Art
2445 Monroe St.
Toledo, OH 43620
and
P.O. Box 1013
Toledo, OH 43697
419-255-8000
http://www.toledomuseum.org

This museum is a renowned cultural center for art and music, featuring extensive collections of glass, European and American paintings, sculpture, and decorative arts. Collections range from ancient Egypt, Greece, and Rome through the Middle Ages and the Renaissance to contemporary Europe and America.

Oklahoma
Gilcrease Museum
1400 Gilcrease Museum Rd.
Tulsa, OK 74127
918-596-2700
http://www.gilcrease.org

This exceptional art collection, founded in 1942, captures the saga of America from prehistoric to modern times; the Gilcrease's art of the Old West is rivaled only by that of the Smithsonian. The institute also has maps, books, documents, artifacts, and manuscripts.

Oregon

Portland Art Museum
1219 SW Park Ave.
Portland, OR 97205
503-226-2811
http://www.portlandartmuseum.org

The Portland, founded in 1892, focuses on Native American arts of the Northwest. It also includes a unique collection of Cameroon art, pre-Columbian arts, Renaissance painting and sculpture, Ethiopian crosses, and European and American painting and sculpture.

Pennsylvania

The Carnegie Museum of Art
4400 Forbes Ave.
Pittsburgh, PA 15213
412-622-3131
http://www.cmoa.org/

This museum, founded in 1896, displays art from around the world, including American art since the colonial period; ancient and classical art; African, pre-Columbian, and Native American art; and European painting, sculpture, and decorative arts from the Renaissance forward. Works by Van Gogh, Cézanne, and Monet are included.

Pennsylvania Academy of the Fine Arts
118 N. Broad St.
Philadelphia, PA 19102
215-972-7600
http://www.pafa.org

Founded in 1805, the Pennsylvania Academy offers an excellent collection of American art from the 18th century to the present, with major works by Thomas Eakins, Charles Willson Peale, and William Rush.

Philadelphia Museum of Art
P.O. Box 7646
Philadelphia, PA 19101
215-763-8100
http://www.philamuseum.org

This museum, established in 1876, is noted for its masterpieces from the 12th to the 19th centuries; Barberini tapestries designed by Rubens; arms and armor; glass; European and American period rooms; folk, decorative, and primitive art; and the Stieglitz Center collection of photographs.

The University Museum of Archaeology and Anthropology, University of Pennsylvania
33rd and Spruce Sts.
Philadelphia, PA 19104
215-898-4000
http://www.museum.upenn.edu/

Founded in 1887, the museum is renowned for its worldwide acquisitions of ancient and primitive art, its collection of Native American gold, and the largest grouping of West African art in the Americas. It has sponsored more than 275 expeditions to gather outstanding artifacts from the ancient Near, Middle, and Far East; Southeast Asia; the Mediterranean; the Pacific; Europe; Africa; and the Americas.

Texas

Amon Carter Museum
3501 Camp Bowie Blvd.
Fort Worth, TX 76107
817-738-1933
http://www.cartermuseum.org

Housed since its founding in 1961 in an impressive building designed by Philip Johnson, this museum concentrates on American paintings and sculptures from the 19th century forward, specializing in the works of the Old West. It also has a fine print collection and excellent Remingtons and Russells.

Kimbell Art Museum
3333 Camp Bowie Blvd.
Fort Worth, TX 76107
817-332-8451
http://www.kimbellart.org

Noted for its masterpieces from around the world, this collection, founded in 1972, ranges from 12th-century panel paintings to J. M. W. Turner landscapes, Gainsboroughs, and Goyas.

The Museum of Fine Arts
1001 Bissonet
P.O. Box 6826
Houston, TX 77265-6826
713-639-7300
http://www.mfah.org

This wide-ranging collection of world art, established in 1900, is especially strong in contemporary art; pre-Columbian and Native American art; Old Masters; and later European and American paintings and sculptures.

Virginia

Virginia Museum of Fine Arts
2800 Grove Ave.
Richmond, VA 23221-2466
804-340-1400
http://www.vmfa.state.va.us

This museum, which opened its doors in 1936, features important collections of British sporting art and French Impressionist and post-Impressionist art, American paintings since World War II, and art nouveau and art deco objects; a collection of Russian imperial Easter eggs by Fabergé; and one of the nation's leading collections of art from India, Nepal, and Tibet.

Wisconsin

Elvehjem Museum of Art, University of Wisconsin
800 University Ave.
Madison, WI 53706
608-263-2246
http://www.lvm.wisc.edu

Established in 1962, this is one of the three largest university museums in the United States. Its wide-ranging collection of world art dates back to ancient times, with fine examples of classical coins and marbles; American painting, sculpture, and decorative arts from the 18th century forward; Indian miniatures; and Socialist Realist (propagandist) paintings from Russia.

CANADA

Alberta

The Glenbow Museum
130 9th Ave., SE
Calgary, Alberta T2G 0P3
403-268-4100
http://www.glenbow.org

This museum features exhibits on military history, mineralogy, and western Canadian history. These include artifacts from Indian and Inuit peoples as well as the Hudson Bay Company and the Canadian Pacific Railroad. The art gallery features works by historical and contemporary western Canadian artists, including Francis N. Hopkins, Emily Carr, John Hall, Ron Moppett, and Chris Cran.

BRITISH COLUMBIA

The Royal British Columbia Museum of Anthropology
675 Belleville St.
Victoria, British Columbia V8W 9W2
250-356-7226
http://www.royalbcmuseum.bc.ca

The Royal British Columbia Museum displays a range of exhibitions depicting the accomplishments of native peoples, the achievements of early explorers and settlers, and British Columbia's natural heritage and archeological past. It includes a 14-foot-high woolly mammoth and a native Indian penitentiary.

Ontario

Art Gallery of Hamilton
123 King St. West
Hamilton, Ontario L8P 4S8
905-527-6610
http://www.artgalleryofhamilton.com

A major North American museum, this gallery was established in 1914. It is noted for its collection of Canadian art; 20th-century British and American painting, sculpture, drawings, and prints; and French Impressionist works.

Museum of Civilization
100 Laurier Street
P.O. Box 3100, Station B
Gatineau, Quebec J8X 4H2
817-776-7000
http://www.civilization.ca

Opened in 1845, this museum specializes in history and folk culture, with excellent collections of the arts and crafts of Native Americans, particularly Eskimos and Northwest Coast Indians.

Museum of Nature
Victoria Memorial Museum Building
240 McLeod St.
P.O. Box 3443, Station D
Ottawa, Ontario K1P 6P4
613-556-4700
http://www.nature.ca

Formerly part of the Museum of Civilization, the Museum of Nature contains one of the world's largest and finest natural history collections. Comprised of 24 major science collections of more than 10 million specimens, the museum's holdings cover four billion years of Earth history.

National Gallery of Canada
P.O. Box 427, Station A
Ottawa, Ontario K1N 9N4
613-990-1985
http://www.national.gallery.ca

With more than 40,000 works, this museum contains the largest collection of Canadian art in the world and includes painting, sculpture, prints, drawings, photographs, video, film, and Inuit art.

Royal Ontario Museum
100 Queens Park Crescent
Toronto, Ontario M5S 2C6
416-586-5549
http://www.rom.on.ca

From suits of armor to suits by Chanel, from totem poles to monstrous dinosaurs, the ROM is the largest museum in Canada. It is one of the world's few multi-disciplinary museums combining art, archeology, and science. The museum features a planetarium, as well as a prominent display of historical and contemporary ceramic art.

MAJOR SCIENCE AND TECHNOLOGY MUSEUMS AND THEIR SPECIAL COLLECTIONS

American Museum of Natural History
Central Park West at 79th St.
New York, NY 10024
212-769-5000
http://www.amnh.org

One of the world's largest natural history museums, opened in 1869, it has exceptional collections on Native Americans, Eskimos, dinosaurs, wildlife, minerals, and fossil specimens.

The Field Museum of Natural History
1400 South Lake Shore Dr.
Chicago, IL 60605
312-922-9410
http://www.fieldmuseum.org

Founded in 1893, the Field Museum contains definitive collections on anatomy, anthropology, costumes, ethnology, geology, Native American artifacts, science, textiles, and zoology. Among its highlights is Sue, the world's largest and most complete *Tyrannosaurus Rex* skeleton.

Franklin Institute Science Museum and Planetarium
222 North 20th St.
Philadelphia, PA 19103
215-448-1200
http://www.fi.edu

Founded in 1824, this comprehensive museum offers collections featuring science, history, industry, technology, aeronautics, astronomy, space exploration, and stamps and coins.

"The Physical Sciences, Mathematics, and **Go to** Technology" in chapter 4

Museum of Science
Science Park
Boston, MA 02114
617-589-0100
http://www.mos.org

Founded in 1030, this science and technology museum includes collections of mineral and plant specimens, mounted animals, and exhibits on human physiology. Interactive exhibits demonstrate the principles of electricity as well as the inner workings of computers. The planetarium features rotating shows relating to space.

National Air and Space Museum, Smithsonian Institution
Seventh St. and Independence Ave., SW
Washington, DC 20560
202-357-2700
http:// www.nasm.si.edu

Founded in 1946, this museum houses a definitive collection of aeronautical and astronautical items; aircraft and spacecraft; and instruments, equipment, art, uniforms, and personal memorabilia related to air and space.

The Royal Tyrrell Museum
P.O. Box 7500
Drumheller, Alberta T0J 0Y0
Canada
403-823-7707
http://www.tyrrellmuseum.com

Canada's only museum devoted to paleontology features hands-on displays and computer simulations covering 4.5 billion years of Earth's history. Forty full dinosaur skeletons make up the world's largest exhibit of complete dinosaurs.

CHILDREN'S MUSEUMS

There are more than 90 museums located throughout the United States devoted to children. Although most museums offer at least a few special programs for children, those listed here focus almost exclusively on young visitors. For additional information, see the listing "Children's and Junior Museums" in The Official Museum Directory, published annually by the American Association of Museums.

Brooklyn Children's Museum
145 Brooklyn Ave.
Brooklyn, NY 11213
718-735-4400
http://www.brooklynkids.org

Founded in 1899, this was the world's first children's museum. Its teaching collection includes more than 50,000 items, with exhibits on cultural history, natural history, and technology. It houses a greenhouse, a steam engine, and a gristmill. Children may attend workshops in school classes or groups. A portable loan collection and children's resource library is also available.

Capital Children's Museum
800 Third St., NE
Washington, DC 20002
202-675-4120
http://www.ccm.org

Founded in 1974, Capital Children's International Hall has a hands-on exhibit on Mexico where children learn to make their own tortillas, weave, and do other Mexican arts and crafts. Additional facilities include a living room, metric exhibit, simple machines display, communications exhibit, and futuristic center.

Children's Museum
300 Congress St.
Boston, MA 02210
617-426-6500
http://www.bostonkids.org

Located on Boston's picturesque waterfront, Children's Museum was founded in 1913. It offers special collections of Native American and Japanese art; Americana; games, toys, dolls, and dollhouses; and bird, insect, shell, and mineral specimens. The Exhibit Center presents participatory and cased exhibitions on child development, natural history, science and technology, careers, handicaps, and cross-cultural understanding. Its Resource Center makes available over 10,000 books, games, and other items.

Children's Museum of Manhattan
The Tisch Building
212 W. 83rd St.
New York, NY 10024
(212) 721-1234
http://www.cmom.org

Founded in 1979, this museum features hands-on, participatory exhibits related to science, nature, and art. A center for media and performing arts includes a television production and editing studio where children create their own television programs. Children contribute

their art, toys, and found objects to the museum's rotating exhibits.

The Eugene Field House and St. Louis Toy Museum
634 S. Broadway
St. Louis, MO 63102
314-421-4689
http://www.eugenefieldhouse.org

Founded in 1936, this museum is housed in the birthplace of Eugene Field. It contains a collection of antique toys and dolls, along with a library on the works of Field.

The Exploratorium
3601 Lyon St.
San Francisco, CA 94123
415-563-7337
http://www.exploratorium.edu

Housed in the Palace of Fine Arts, this science museum offers 500 participatory exhibits and artworks illustrating the physical nature of the world and the sensory mechanisms through which we perceive it. Founded in 1969, it hosts field trips, concerts, lectures, and school groups.

Children's Museum of Los Angeles
205 S. Broadway
Suite 608
Los Angeles, CA 90012
213-687-8801
http://www.childrensmuseumla.org

Children participate in a variety of activities at this museum in such places as Sticky City, with giant foam blocks for construction fun; City Streets, with city vehicles and street signs; TV Studios, where children create their own news broadcasts; and Workshop Place, which fosters creativity in arts and crafts.

Please Touch Museum
210 N. 21st St.
Philadelphia, PA 19103
215-963-0667
http://www.pleasetouchmuseum.org

Founded in 1976, the Please Touch Museum issues a children's newspaper and offers special exhibits on cultural artifacts of daily life, folk art and sculpture, natural science, technology, musical instruments, games, registered toys, costumes, masks, foot gear, and hats.

MAJOR ZOOS AND AQUARIUMS

Zoos, or zoological gardens, are private or public parks where animals of all sorts are exhibited and studied.

Most major cities throughout the world have zoos. Zoos vary widely in scale and type, from petting zoos that allow contact between children and animals to primate research centers to amusement parks that put on shows with trained animals.

Aquariums are facilities with tanks (usually with glass sides) and pools for keeping live water animals and plants.

The following list of major zoos and aquariums in the United States and Canada is arranged by state and province. The name, address, phone number, and Web site of each are given, and, where available, the facility's specialty.

Links to Web sites for many other U.S. zoos and aquariums are provided at

http://www.mindspring.com/~zoonet/www_virtual_
  lib/zoos.html

UNITED STATES

Alabama
Birmingham Zoo
2630 Cahaba Rd.
Birmingham, AL 35223
205-879-0409
http://www.birminghamzoo.com/

Arizona
Arizona-Sonora Desert Museum
2021 N. Kinney Rd.
Tucson, AZ 85743
520-883-1380
http://www.desertmuseum.org
Specialty: natural history of the Arizona-Sonora desert

Phoenix Zoo
455 N. Galvin Pkwy.
Phoenix, AZ 85008
602-273-1341
http://www.phoenixzoo.org

Arkansas
Little Rock Zoo
1 Jonesboro Dr.
Little Rock, AR 72205
501-666-2406
http://www.littlerockzoo.com/

California
Chaffee Zoo (formerly Fresno Zoo)
894 West Belmont Ave.
Fresno, CA 93728
559-498-2671
http://www.chaffeezoo.org

The Los Angeles Zoo
5333 Zoo Dr.
Los Angeles, CA 90027-1498
213-666-4650
http://www.lazoo.org/

Marine World Six Flags
2001 Marine World Pkwy.
Vallejo, CA 94589
707-643-ORCA
http://www.sixflags.com

Oakland Zoo
9777 Golf Links Rd.
P.O. Box 5238
Oakland, CA 94605
510-632-9525
http://www.oaklandzoo.org/

San Diego Zoo
P.O. Box 120551
San Diego, CA 92112
619-234-3153
http://www.sandiegozoo.org/

San Francisco Zoo
1 Zoo Rd.
San Francisco, CA 94132-1098
415-753-7080
http://www.sfzoo.org
Specialties: primates, cats, endangered species

Santa Ana Zoo
1801 E. Chestnut Ave.
Santa Ana, CA 92701
714-836-4000
http://santaanazoo.org/
Specialty: primates

Sea World San Diego
Sea World of California
500 Sea World Dr.
San Diego, CA 92109
619-226-3901
http://www.seaworld.com
Specialties: trained marine mammals, waterfowl, fish

Steinhart Aquarium at California Academy of Sciences
Golden Gate Park
San Francisco, CA 94118
415-750-7145
http://www.calacademy.org

Birch Aquarium
Scripps Institute of Oceanography
University of California
9500 Gilman Dr., 0207
La Jolla, CA 92093
858-534-FISH
http://www.aquarium.ucsd.edu
Specialties: marine fish and invertebrates of southern California

Colorado
Cheyenne Mountain Zoological Park
4250 Cheyenne Mountain Zoo Rd.
Colorado Springs, CO 80906
719-475-9555
http://www.cmzoo.org
Specialties: primates, large felids (giraffes), hoofed mammals

Denver Zoo
2300 Steele St.
Denver, CO 80205
303-376-4800
http://www.denverzoo.org/
Specialties: waterfowl, North American hoofed mammals

Connecticut
Beardsley Zoo
1875 Noble Ave.
Bridgeport, CT 06610
203-394-6565
http://www.beardsley.zoo.com
Specialty: fauna of North and South America

Mystic Aquarium/Institute for Exploration
55 Coogan Blvd.
Mystic, CT 06355-1997
860-572-5955
http://www.mysticaquarium.org

District of Columbia
National Zoological Park
Smithsonian Institution
3001 Connecticut Ave., NW
Washington, DC 20008
202-673-4800
http://www.natzoo.si.edu/

Florida
Busch Gardens
P.O. Box 9158
Tampa, FL 33674
813-987-4800
http://www.buschgardens.com
Specialties: African hoofed mammals, parrots

Palm Beach Zoo at Dreher Park
1301 Summit Blvd.
West Palm Beach, FL 33405-2494
561-547-WILD
http://www.palmbeachzoo.org
Specialties: South American and South Floridian animals

Jacksonville Zoological Park
8605 Zoo Parkway
Jacksonville, FL 32218
904-757-4463
http://www.jaxzoo.org

Marineland of Florida
9600 Ocean Shore Blvd.
St. Augustine, FL 32080-8613
904-460-1275
http://www.marineland.net
Specialties: marine mammals, marine theme displays

Miami Metrozoo
12400 SW 152nd St.
Miami, FL 33177-1499
305-251-0400
http://www.zsf.org

Georgia
Zoo Atlanta
800 Cherokee Ave.
Atlanta, GA 30315
404-624-5600
http://www.zooatlanta.org
Specialties: amphibians, reptiles, giant apes

Hawaii
Honolulu Zoo
151 Kapahulu Ave.
Honolulu, HI 96815-4096

808-971-7171
808-926-3191
http://www.honoluluzoo.org
Specialty: Galapagos tortoise

Waikiki Aquarium
University of Hawaii
2777 Kalakaua Ave.
Honolulu, HI 96815
808-923-9741
http://waquarium.otted.hawaii.edu/
Specialty: aquatic life of Hawaii and the tropical Pacific

Illinois

**Chicago Zoological Park
(Brookfield Zoo)**
3300 Golf Rd.
Brookfield, IL 60513
708-485-0263
800-201-0784
http://www.brookfieldzoo.org
Specialties: Tropic World, Seven Seas

John G. Shedd Aquarium
1200 S. Lake Shore Dr.
Chicago, IL 60605
312-939-2435
http://www.sheddnet.org

Lincoln Park Zoological Gardens
2201 N. Clark St.
Chicago, IL 60614
312-742-2000
http://www.lpzoo.com/
Specialties: primates, South American mammals

Indiana

Fort Wayne Children's Zoo
3411 Sherman Blvd.
Fort Wayne, IN 46808
260-427-6800
http://www.kidszoo.com/

Indianapolis Zoo
1200 W. Washington St.
Indianapolis, IN 46222
317-630-2001
http://www.indyzoo.com

Mesker Park Zoo
2421 Bement Ave.
Evansville, IN 47712
812-428-0715
Specialty: large geographic exhibits

Kansas

Topeka Zoological Park
635 SW Gage Blvd.
Topeka, KS 66606-2066
785-272-5821
785-272-7042
http://www.topekazoo.org

Kentucky

Louisville Zoological Garden
1100 Trevilian Way
P.O. Box 37250
Louisville, KY 40213
502-459-2181
http://www.louisvillezoo.org

Louisiana

Audubon Aquarium of the Americas
P.O. Box 4327
New Orleans, LA 70178
800-774-7394
http://www.audoboninstitute.org/aoa/

Audubon Park & Zoological Garden
P.O. Box 4327
New Orleans, LA 70178
866-IT'S-A-ZOO
http://www.audoboninstitute.org/zoo/

BREC's Baton Rouge Zoo
3601 Thomas Rd.
Baker, LA 70807
504-775-3877
http://www.brzoo.org

Maryland

Baltimore Zoo
Druid Hill Park
Baltimore, MD 21217
410-366-LION
410-396-7102
http://www.baltimorezoo.org

National Aquarium in Baltimore
Pier 3, 501 E. Pratt St.
Baltimore, MD 21202
410-576-3800
http://www.aqua.org

Massachusetts

New England Aquarium
Central Wharf
Boston, MA 02110
617-973-5200

http://www.neaq.org/
Specialties: marine fish, invertebrates of the world

Zoo New England
Franklin Park Zoo
One Franklin Park Rd.
Boston, MA 02121
617-541-5466
http://www.zoonewengland.com/

Michigan
Detroit Zoological Park
8450 West Ten Mile Rd.
P.O. Box 39
Royal Oak, MI 48068-0039
248-398-0900
http://www.detroitzoo.org/
Specialties: polar bears, penguins

Potter Park Zoological Gardens
1301 S. Pennsylvania Ave.
Lansing, MI 48912
517-483-4221
517-483-4074
http://www.potterparkzoo.org

Minnesota
Lake Superior Zoological Gardens
7210 Fremont St.
Duluth, MN 55807
218-733-3777
http://www.lszoo.org

Minnesota Zoo
13000 Zoo Blvd.
Apple Valley, MN 55124
952-431-9200
952-431-9500
http://www.mnzoo.com/

St. Paul's Como Zoo
1250 Kaufman Drive North
St. Paul, MN 55103-1060
651-645-1014
651-487-8200
http://www.stpaul.gov/depts/parks/comopark/index.
   html/html
Specialties: large mammals

Mississippi
Jackson Zoological Park
2918 W. Capitol St.
Jackson, MS 39209
601-352-2585
http://techlink.net/jacksonzoo/

Missouri
Kansas City Zoological Gardens
6800 Zoo Dr.
Kansas City, MO 64132
816-513-5700
http://www.kansascityzoo.org

St. Louis Zoo
One Government Dr.
St. Louis, MO 63110-1935
314-781-0900
http://www.stlzoo.org/

Nebraska
Folsom Children's Zoo
1222 South 27th St.
Lincoln, NE 86502
402-475-6741
http://www.lincolnzoo.org

Omaha's Henry Doorly Zoo
3701 S. 10th St.
Omaha, NE 68107
402-773-8401
http://www.omahazoo.org
Specialties: largest cat complex in North America

New Jersey
Turtle Back Zoo
560 Northfield Ave.
West Orange, NJ 07052
973-731-5800
http://www.turtlebackzoo.com
Specialty: turtles

New Mexico
Rio Grande Zoological Park
903 10th St., SW
Albuquerque, NM 87102
505-764-6200
http://www.cabq.gov/biopark/zoo
Specialty: hoofed mammals

New York
Buffalo Zoological Gardens
300 Parkside Ave.
Buffalo, NY 14214-1999
716-837-3900
http://www.buffalozoo.org

**Central Park Wildlife Conservation Center
(formerly Central Park Zoo)**
830 Fifth Avenue
New York, NY 10021

212-861-6030
http://www.wcs.org/home/zoos/centralpark

**Aquarium for Wildlife Conservation
(formerly New York Aquarium)**
West 8th St. and Surf Ave.
Brooklyn, NY 11224
718-265-FISH
http://www.wcs.org/home/zoos/nyaquarium

**International Wildlife Conservation Park
(formerly Bronx Zoo)**
185th St. and Southern Blvd.
Bronx, NY 10460
718-367-1010
http://www.wcs.org/home/zoos/bronxzoo

Staten Island Zoo
614 Broadway
Staten Island, NY 10310
718-442-3100
http://www.statenislandzoo.org
Specialty: reptiles

North Carolina

North Carolina Zoological Park
4401 Zoo Parkway
Asheboro, NC 27203
800-488-0444
910-879-7000
http://www.nczoo.org/
Specialty: African wildlife

North Dakota

Dakota Zoo
Dakota Zoological Society
P.O. Box 711
Bismarck, ND 58502
701-223-7543
http://www.dakotazoo.org
Specialty: North American fauna

Ohio

Cincinnati Zoo & Botanical Garden
3400 Vine St.
Cincinnati, OH 45220
513-281-4700
http://www.cincyzoo.org/
Specialties: insects, amphibians, great apes, cats

Cleveland Metroparks Zoo
3900 Wildlife Way
Cleveland, OH 44109
216-661-6500
http://clemetzoo.com/
Specialties: Geoffroy's tamarin, white stork

Columbus Zoo and Aquarium
9990 Riverside Dr.
Powell, OH 43065
http://www.colszoo.org/
Specialties: gorillas, reptiles, cichlids

Toledo Zoo
P.O. Box 140130
Toledo, OH 43614-0001
419-385-5721
http://www.toledozoo.org/

Oklahoma

Oklahoma City Zoological Park
2101 NE 50th St.
Oklahoma City, OK 73111
405-424-3344
http://www.okczoo.com

Tulsa Zoo and Living Museum
6421 E. 36th St. North
Tulsa, OK 74115-2121
918-669-6600
Specialties: North American animals, plants, earth
    sciences

Oregon

Oregon Zoo
4001 SW Canyon Rd.
Portland, OR 97221
503-226-1561
http://www.zooregon.org/
Specialties: elephants, chimpanzees

Pennsylvania

Philadelphia Zoological Garden
3400 W. Girard Ave.
Philadelphia, PA 19104-1196
215-243-1100
http://www.phillyzoo.org/
Specialties: waterfowl, great apes, reptiles

Pittsburgh Zoo & Aquarium
One Wild Place
Pittsburgh, PA 15206
412-665-3640
800-474-4966
http://zoo.pgh.pa.us

Rhode Island

Roger Williams Park Zoo
1000 Elmwood Ave.
Providence, RI 02907-3600
410-785-3510
http://www.rwpzoo.org

South Carolina
Riverbanks Zoological Park and Botanical Gardens
500 Wildlife Pkwy.
P.O. Box 1060
Columbia, SC 29202
803-779-8717
http://www.riverbanks.org/

South Dakota
Great Plains Zoo and Delbridge Museum
805 S. Kiwanis Ave.
Sioux Falls, SD 57104
605-367-7003
http://www.gpzoo.org
Specialty: animals of the North American Great Plains

Tennessee
Knoxville Zoological Gardens
P.O. Box 6040-3500
Knoxville, TN 37914-0040
865-637-5331
http://www.knoxville-zoo.org/
Specialties: large cats, African elephants, red pandas, Southern white rhinoceros

Memphis Zoo
2000 Prentiss Place
Memphis, TN 38112
901-276-WILD
http://www.memphiszoo.org/
Specialties: aquatic animals, rare ruminants

Texas
Abilene Zoological Gardens
2070 Zoo Lane
Nelson Park
Abilene, TX 79602
915-676-6085
http://www.abilenetx.com/zoo/zoo.htm

Caldwell Zoo
2203 Martin Luther King Blvd.
Tyler, TX 75710
903-593-0121

Dallas Aquarium
P.O. Box 150113
Dallas, TX 75315-0113
214-670-8443
http://www.dallas-zoo.org

Dallas Zoo
Fair Park
650 South R.L.Thornton Fwy.

Dallas, TX 75203
214-670-5656
http://www.dallas-zoo.org

Fort Worth Zoo
1989 Colonial Pkwy.
Fort Worth, TX 76110
817-871-7050
http://www.fortworthzoo.com

Gladys Porter Zoo
500 Ringgold St.
Brownsville, TX 78520
956-546-7187
http://www.gpz.org/

Houston Zoological Gardens
1513 N. MacGregor
Houston, TX 77030
713-523-5888
http://www.houstonzoo.org

San Antonio Zoological Garden and Aquarium
3903 N. St. Mary's St.
San Antonio, TX 78212
210-734-7184
http://www.sazoo-aq.org/
Specialties: antelope, waterfowl, whooping cranes

Utah
Utah's Hogle Zoo
2600 E. Sunnyside Ave.
Salt Lake City, UT 84108
801-582-1631
http://www.xmission.com/~hoglezoo/

Virginia
Virginia Zoo
3500 Granby St.
Norfolk, VA 23504
757-624-9937
http://www.virginiazoo.org

Washington
Seattle Aquarium
1483 Alaskan Way, on Pier 59
Seattle, WA 98010
206-386-4300
http://www.seattleaquarium.org

Woodland Park Zoological Gardens
601 North 59th St.
Seattle, WA 98103
206-684-4880
http://www.zoo.org/

Wisconsin
Henry Vilas Zoo
702 S. Randall Ave.
Madison, WI 53715-1665
608-266-4732
http://www.vilaszoo.org/

Milwaukee County Zoological Gardens
10001 W. Blue Mound Rd
Milwaukee, WI 53226
414-771-5500
http://www.milwaukeezoo.org/

Racine Zoological Garden
2131 N. Main St.
Racine, WI 53402
626-636-9189
http://www.racinezoo.org

CANADA

Alberta
Calgary Zoo, Botanical Garden & Prehistoric Park
1300 Zoo Road NE
Calgary, Alberta Canada T2E 7V6
403-232-9300
http://www.calgaryzoo.ab.ca/

British Columbia
Stanley Park Zoological Gardens
Stanley Park
Vancouver, British Columbia V6G 1Z4
604-257-8400
http://www.city.vancouver.bc.ca/parks/3.htm

Vancouver Public Aquarium
Stanley Park
P.O. Box 3232
Vancouver, British Columbia V6B 3X8
604-659-3474
http://www.vanaqua.org
Specialties: marine mammals, fishes and invertebrates of the Northeast Pacific

Manitoba
Assiniboine Park Zoo
The Zoological Society of Manitoba
54 Zoo Drive
Winnipeg, Manitoba R3P 2N8
204-982-0660 (Zoological Society)
204-986-2327 (Zoo info)
http://www.zoosociety.com
Specialty: Nearctic animals

Ontario
Toronto Zoo
361A Old Finch Ave.
Scarborough, Ontario M1B 5K7
416-392-5900
http://www.torontozoo.com/

Quebec
Biodôme de Montréal
4777, Pierre de Coubertin
Montréal, Québec H1V 1B3
514-868-3000
http://www.biodome.qc.ca

Jardin Zoologique de Quebec and Aquarium de Quebec
8173 avenue du Zoo
Charlesbourg, Québec G1G 4G4
418-622-0313
http://www.aquarium.qc.ca/

Société Zoologique de Granby
Horace Boivin Pavilion
525, rue St-Hubert
Granby, Québec J2G 5P3
401-372-9113
877-GRANBY-ZOO
http://www.zoodegranby.com

MAJOR BOTANICAL GARDENS AND ARBORETUMS

Botanical gardens are places where collections of plants and trees are kept for exhibition and scientific study. Arboretums are places where many kinds of trees and shrubs are grown for exhibition or study.

The following list of major botanical gardens and arboretums in the United States is arranged by state.

Addresses, phone numbers, and Web sites of numerous other botanical gardens and arboreta that are members of the American Association of Botanical Gardens and Arboreta are listed at http://www.mobot.org/AAGBA/member-list.html.

Alabama
Birmingham Botanical Gardens
2612 Lane Park Rd.
Birmingham, AL 35523
205-414-3900
http://www.bbgardens.org/

Arizona

Desert Botanical Garden
1201 N. Galvin Pkwy.
Papago Park
Phoenix, AZ 85008
480-941-1225
http://www.dbg.org

California

Balboa Park
1549 El Prado
San Diego, CA 92101
619-239-0512
http://www.balboapark.org

**Huntington Library, Art Collections, and
  Botanical Gardens**
1151 Oxford Rd.
San Marino, CA 91108
626-405-2100
http://www.huntington.org/

J. Paul Getty Museum and Gardens
The Getty Center
1200 Getty Center Drive
310-440-7300
http://www.getty.edu

Strybing Arboretum and Botanical Gardens
9th Ave. at Lincoln Way
Golden Gate Park
San Francisco, CA 94122
415-661-1316
http://www.strybing.org/

Villa Montalvo Arboretum
15400 Montalvo Rd.
Saratoga, CA 95070
408-961-5800
http://www.willamontalvo.org

Colorado

Denver Botanic Gardens
909 York St.
Denver, CO 80206
303-331-4000
http://www.botanicgardens.org/

Connecticut

Glebe House Museum and Gertrude Jekyll Garden
Hollow Rd.
Woodbury, CT 06798
203-263-2855

Harkness Memorial State Park
275 Great Neck Rd.
Waterford, CT 06385
860-443-5725
http://dep.state.ct.us/rec/parks/harkhist.htm

Delaware

Nemours Mansion and Gardens
P.O. Box 109
1600 Rockland Rd.
Wilmington, DE 19899
302-651-6912
http://www.nemours.org

Henry Francis du Pont Winterthur Museum
Rte. 52
Winterthur, DE 19735
800-448-3883
http://www.winterthur.org

District of Columbia

Dumbarton Oaks
1703 32nd St., NW
Washington, DC 20007
202-339-6410
http://www.doaks.com

Gardens of the Washington National Cathedral
Massachusetts and Wisconsin aves.
Washington, DC 20016-5098
202-537-6200
http://www.cathedral.org

United States Botanical Garden
245 First St., SW
Washington, DC 20024-3021
202-226-4082
202-225-8333 (information recording)
http://www.nationalgarden.org

United States National Arboretum
3501 New York Ave., NE
Washington, DC 20002-1958
202-245-2726
http://www.usna.usda.gov

Florida

Edison and Ford Winter Estates
2350 McGregor Blvd.
Ft. Myers, FL 33901
941-334-3614
http://www.edison-ford-estate.com

Fairchild Tropical Garden
10901 Old Cutler Rd.
Miami, FL 33156-4299
305-667-1651
http://www.fairchildgarden.org

Cypress Gardens
2641 South Lake Summit Drive
Winter Haven, FL 33884
863-324-2111
http://www.cypressgardens.com

Alfred B. Maclay State Gardens
3540 Thomasville Rd.
Tallahassee, FL 32308
850-487-4115
http://www.floridastateparks.org

Georgia

Atlanta Botanical Garden
1345 Piedmont Ave.
Atlanta, GA 30309
404-876-5859
http://www.atlantabotanicalgarden.org

Callaway Gardens
U.S. Highway 27
P.O. Box 2000
Pine Mountain, GA 31822-2000
706-663-2281
800-255-5292
http://www.callawaygardens.com

The State Botanical Garden of Georgia
2450 S. Milledge Ave.
Athens, GA 30605
706-542-1244
http://www.uga.edu/botgarden

Hawaii

Foster Botanic Garden
180 N. Vineyard Blvd.
Honolulu, HI 96817
808-522-7066
http://www.co.honolulu.hi.us/parks/hbg/fbg.htm

Hoomaluhia Botanical Garden
45-680 Luluku Road
Kaneohe, HI 96744
808-233-7323
http://www.co.honolulu.hi.us/parks/hbg/hmbg.htm

Wahiawa Botanical Garden
1396 California Avenue
Wahiawa, HI 96786
808-621-7321
http://www.co.honolulu.hi.us/parks/hbg/wbg.htm

Idaho

Idaho Botanical Gardens
2355 N. Penitentiary Rd.
P.O. Box 2140
Boise, ID 83701
208-343-8649
http://www.idahobotanicalgarden.org/

Illinois

Garfield Park Conservatory
300 N. Central Park Ave.
Chicago, IL 60624-1996
312-746-5100
http://www.garfield-conservatory.org/

Lincoln Park Conservatory
2391 N. Stockton Dr.
Chicago, IL 60614-3419
312-742-7736
http://chicagoparkdistrict.com

Indiana

Indianapolis Museum of Art Gardens
1200 W. 38th St.
Indianapolis, IN 46208
317-920-2660
http://www.ima-art.org/

Iowa

Des Moines Botanical Center
909 E. River Dr.
Des Moines, IA 50316
515-323-8900
http://www.botanicalcenter.com/

Kansas

Botanica
The Wichita Gardens
701 Amidon
Wichita, KS 67203
316-264-0448
http://www.botanica.com

Louisiana

Audubon Louisiana Nature Center
P.O. Box 4327
5700 Read Blvd.
New Orleans, LA 70178
504-246-5672
http://www.auduboninstitute.org/lnc/index.htm

Maine

Asticou Azalea Garden
Asticou Way
Mount Desert Island
Northeast Harbor, ME 04662
207-276-5040
http://www.acadiamagic.com/Asticou2.html

Maryland

Hampton National Historic Site
535 Hampton Lane
Towson, MD 21286
410-823-1309 x226
http://www.nps.gov/hamp/index.htm

Massachusetts

Arnold Arboretum
125 Arborway
Jamaica Plain, MA 02130-3519
617-524-1718
http://www.arboretum.harvard.edu

Berkshire Botanical Garden
P.O. Box 826
Intersection Routes 102 and 183
Stockbridge, MA 01262
413-298-3926
http://www.berkshirebotanical.org/

Stanley Park
400 Western Ave.
Westfield, MA 01086
413-568-9312
http://www.stanleypark.org

Michigan

Anna Scripps Whitcomb Conservatory
Belle Island Botanical Society
Belle Isle Greenhouse
Detroit, MI 48207
313-852-4064
hhtp://www.bibsociety.org

Matthaei Botanical Garden
University of Michigan
1800 Dixboro Rd.
Ann Arbor, MI 48105-9406
313-998-7061
http://www.lsa.umich.edu/mbg

Missouri

Missouri Botanical Garden
P.O. Box 299
St. Louis, MO 63166-0299
800-642-8842
http://www.mobot.org/welcome.html

New Hampshire

Aspet
Saint-Gaudens National Historic Site
R.R. 3, P.O. Box 73
Cornish, NH 03745
603-675-2175

New Jersey

Deep Cut Park Horticultural Center
352 Red Hill Rd.
Middletown, NJ 07748
732-842-4000
http://www.monmouthcountyparks.com/parks/deepcut/
  horticultural_center.html

Frelinhuysen Arboretum
53 E. Hanover Ave.
Morristown, NJ 07962-1295
201-326-7600
http://www.morrisig.com/vgreen/arbor.htm

The Rutgers Gardens
Cook College, Rutgers University
122 Ryders Lane
New Brunswick, NJ 08901
732-932-8451
http://aesop.rutgers.edu/~rugardens/

New Jersey Botanical Garden
Morris Rd.
Ringwood, NJ 07458
973-962-7527
http://www.state.nj.us/travel/virtual/gardens/botanical.
  html

New Mexico

Living Desert Zoo and Gardens
P.O. Box 100
Carlsbad, NM 88221
505-887-5516
http://www.emnrd.state.nm.us/nmparks/PAGES/parks/
  desert/desert.htm

New York

Brooklyn Botanic Garden
1000 Washington Ave.
Brooklyn, NY 11225-1099

718-623-7200
http://www.bbg.org/

New York Botanical Garden
Bronx River Parkway @ Fordham Road
200th St. and Kazimiroff Blvd.
Bronx, NY 10458-5126
718-817-8700
http://www.nybg.org

Vanderbilt Mansion National Historic Site
4097 Albany Post Rd.
Hyde Park, NY 12538
845-229-9115
http://www.nps.gov/vama

North Carolina

Botanical Gardens at Asheville
151 W. T. Weaver Blvd.
Asheville, NC 28804
828-252-5190
http://www.ahevillbotanicalgardens.org

Sarah P. Duke Memorial Gardens
418 Anderson Street
P.O. Box 90341 Duke University
Durham, NC 27708-0341
919-684-3698
http://www.hr.duke.edu/dukegardens/dukegardens.html

North Carolina Botanical Garden
CB 3375, Totten Center
University of North Carolina at Chapel Hill
Chapel Hill, NC 27599-3375
919-962-0522
http://www.unc.edu/depts/ncbg

North Dakota

International Peace Garden
R.R. 1, Box 116
Dunseith, ND 58329
701-263-4390
http://www.peacegarden.com

Ohio

Dawes Arboretum
7770 Jacksontown Rd., SE
Newark, OH 43056-9380
800-44DAWES
740-323-2355
http://www.dawesarb.org

Cleveland Botanical Garden
11030 East Blvd.
Cleveland, OH 44106

216-721-1600
http://cbgarden.org/

Holden Arboretum
9500 Sperry Rd.
Kirtland, OH 44094-5172
440-946-4400
http://www.holdenarb.org

Oklahoma

Will Rogers Garden Exhibition Building
3400 NW 36th St.
Oklahoma City, OK 73112
405-943-0827

Oregon

Berry Botanic Garden
11505 SW Summerville Ave.
Portland, OR 97219
503-636-4112
http://www.berrybot.org/

Pennsylvania

Historic Bartram's Garden
54th Street and Lindbergh Boulevard
Philadelphia, PA 19143
215-729-5281
http://www.bartramsgarden/index.html

Longwood Gardens
Route 1
P.O. Box 501
Kennet Square, PA 19348-0501
610-388-1000
http://www.longwoodgardens.org/

Morris Arboretum of the University of Pennsylvania
100 Northwestern Avenue
Philadelphia, PA 19118
215-247-5777
http://upenn.edu/arboretum/

Phipps Conservatory and Botanical Gardens
One Schenley Park
Pittsburgh, PA 15213-3830
(412) 622-6914
http://www.phipps.conservatory.org/

Tyler Arboretum
515 Painter Rd.
Media, PA 19063
610-566-5431
http://www.tylerarboretum.org

Libraries

Rhode Island

Hammersmith Farm
Bellevue Ave.
Newport, RI 02840
401-846-7346

South Carolina

Brookgreen Gardens
P.O. Box 3368
Pawleys Island, SC 29585-3368
843-235-6000
800-849-1931
http://www.brookgreen.com

Magnolia Plantation and Gardens
3550 Ashley River Rd.
Charleston, SC 29414
843-571-1266
800-367-3517
http://magnoliaplantation.com

Tennessee

Memphis Botanic Garden
750 Cherry Rd.
Memphis, TN 38117
901-685-1566
http://www.memphisbotanicgarden.com

Rock City Gardens
See Rock City, Inc.
1400 Patten Rd.
Lookout Mountain, GA 30750
706-820-2531
http://www.seerockcity.com/

Texas

Dallas Arboretum and Botanical Garden
8525 Garland Rd.
Dallas, TX 75218
214-327-8263
http://www.dallasarboretum.org/

Fort Worth Botanic Garden
3220 Botanic Garden Blvd.
Fort Worth, TX 76107
817-871-7686
http://www.fortworthgov.org/pacs/botgarden/

Samuel Grand Park Garden
6200 E. Grand Ave.
Dallas, TX 75223
214-670-1383

Virginia

Monticello
Home of Thomas Jefferson
P.O. Box 316
Charlottesville, VA 22902
434-984-9800
434-984-9822
http://www.monticello.org/

Mount Vernon Estate and Gardens
P.O. Box 110
Mount Vernon, VA 22121
703-780-2000
http://www.mountvernon.org/

Pavillion Gardens
University of Virginia
P.O. Box 400305
Charlottesville, VA 22903
434-924-7969
http://www.virginia.edu/uvatours/gardens/

Washington

Washington Park Arboretum
University of Washington
P.O. Box 358010
Seattle, WA 98195-8010
206-543-8800
http://depts.washington.edu/wpa/

Wisconsin

Mitchell Park Horticultural Conservatory
"The Domes"
524 S. Layton Blvd.
Milwaukee, WI 53215
414-649-9800
http://www.countyparks.com/horticulture/

Olbrich Botanical Gardens
3330 Atwood Ave.
Madison, WI 53704
608-246-4550
http://www.olbrich.org

III

THE WAY WE COMMUNICATE

12

SYMBOLS AND SIGNS

SYMBOLS USED IN SCIENCE, MATHEMATICS, AND TECHNOLOGY

ASTRONOMY SYMBOLS

SOLAR SYSTEM OBJECTS

⊙	the Sun
☾, ☽	the Moon
☿	Mercury
♀	Venus
⊕, ♁	Earth
♂	Mars
♃	Jupiter
♄	Saturn
♅, ♅	Uranus
♆	Neptune
♇	Pluto
☄	comet
①, ②, ③, etc.	asteroids in the order of their discovery

PHASES OF THE MOON

●	new moon
☽, ☽	first quarter
○	full moon
☾, ☾	last quarter

STELLAR OBJECTS

*	fixed star
α, β, γ, etc.	stars (of a constellation) in the order of their brightness: the Greek letter is followed by the Latin genitive of the name of the constellation

ASPECTS AND NODES

☌	conjunction: with reference to bodies having the same longitude, or right ascension
☐	quadrature: being 90° apart in longitude, or right ascension
☍	opposition: being 180° apart in longitude, or right ascension
☊	ascending node
☋	descending node

PHYSICAL CHARACTERS

A	albedo
D	diameter
M	mass
R	radius

"Astronomy" in chapter 4

Go to

UNITS OF MEASUREMENT

A.U.	astronomical unit
l.y.	light-year
pc	parsec
h, ʰ	hours [5h *or* 5ʰ]
m, ᵐ	minutes of time [5m *or* 5ᵐ]
s, ˢ	seconds of time [16s *or* 16ˢ]
°	degrees of arc
′	minutes of arc
″	seconds of arc

DIRECTIONS

+	toward the zenith; toward the north celestial, ecliptic, or galactic pole
−	toward the nadir; toward the south celestial, ecliptic, or galactic pole
γ	vernal equinox

ORBITAL ELEMENTS

a	mean distance, semimajor axis
e	eccentricity of orbit
i	inclination to the ecliptic
P	sidereal period of revolution or rotation
Ω	longitude of ascending node
ω	argument of perihelion

COORDINATES

h	altitude
A	azimuth
δ	declination
α, R.A.	right ascension
β	celestial latitude
λ	celestial longitude
b	galactic latitude
l	galactic longitude

OTHER SYMBOLS

Δ	distance from earth
π	parallax
ø	geographical or astronomical latitude

Although the @ has no name in the United States (it's just called the "at symbol"), other countries call it "monkey's tail," "little snail," "cat's tail," or "spider monkey."

Symbols/Signs

BIOLOGY SYMBOLS

♃	perennial herb
♂, ♂	male organism or cell; staminate plant or flower
♀	female organism or cell; pistillate plant or flower
☿	perfect, or hermaphroditic, plant, or flower
○	individual, especially **female**, organism

□	individual, especially male, organism
×	crossed with; hybrid
+	wild type
P	parental generation
F	filial generation; offspring
F₁, F₂, F₃, etc.	offspring of the first, second, third, etc., filial generation

Go to
"The Biological World" in chapter 3

CHEMISTRY SYMBOLS

+	"and," "plus," or "together with," used between the symbols of reacting substances in chemical equations; when placed above a symbol or to its right as a superscript, the plus sign indicates a unit charge of positive electricity; the sign also indicates dextrorotation
—	single bond, used between the symbols of elements or groups that form a compound; when placed above a symbol or to its right as a superscript, the dash indicates a unit charge of negative electricity; it also signifies levorotation or the removal of a part from a compound
•	separates parts of a compound considered loosely joined (free radical)
⬡	benzene ring
=	"forms" or "results in," used between the symbols of reacting substances in chemical equations; a double bond; two unit charges of negative electricity when placed above a symbol or to its right as a superscript

≡	triple bond or triple negative charge
:	unshared pair of electrons; sometimes a double bond
⋮	triple bond
( )	groups or radicals within a compound
[ ]	with parentheses, shows certain radicals; in coordination formulas, shows relationship to the central atom
⌒ or ⌣	unites attached atoms or groups in structural formulas for cyclic compounds
→	gives, passes over to, or leads to; reaction direction
⇌	is in equilibrium with; forms and is formed from; reversible reaction
↓	precipitation of a substance
↑	gas expelled
≡, ⇌	is equivalent to; used in equations to show how much of one substance will react with a given amount of another so that no excess of either remains
<	bivalent element
>	bivalent radical

Go to
"Chemistry" in chapter 4

Symbols/Signs

ELECTRONICS SYMBOLS

BATTERIES

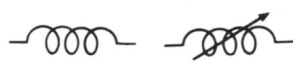

Single Cell   Multicell

CAPACITORS

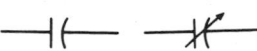

Fixed   Variable

HEADSETS

Single   Double

INDUCTORS

Fixed   Variable

INSTRUMENTS

  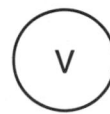 

Ammeter   Ohmeter   Voltmeter   Wattmeter

LAMPS

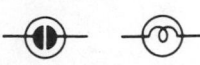

Neon   Filament

RECTIFIERS

Half Wave   Full Wave

RESISTORS

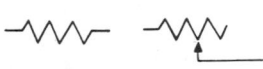

Fixed   Variable

TRANSFORMERS

Air Core   Iron Core

VACUUM-TUBE TRIODES

Directly Heated   Indirectly Heated
Cathode   Cathode

WIRES

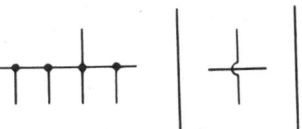

Connected   Not Connected

OTHER SYMBOLS

    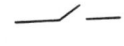

Alternating Cur-   Antenna   Ground   Spark Gap   Single Throw
rent Source   Switch

MATHEMATICS SYMBOLS

"Special Units of Measurement" in **Go to** chapter 2

OPERATION

+	plus; positive
−	minus; negative
∼	difference
×	multiplied by
÷	divided by
±	plus or minus
∓	minus or plus
!	factorial
Σ	summation of
Π	product
√	square root
∛	cube root
∜	fourth root
ⁿ√	nth root
$\|b\|$	absolute value of b, magnitude of b

GROUPING

( )	parentheses	
[ ]	brackets	indicate that the quantities enclosed by them are to be taken together
{ }	braces	

RELATION

=	equal to
≠	not equal to
≡	identical with; congruent to (in number theory)
≈	nearly equal to
>	greater than
>>	much greater than
<	less than
<<	much less than
≧ *or* ≥	greater than or equal to
≦ *or* ≤	less than or equal to
≯	not greater than
≮	not less than
∝	varies directly as; is proportional to
:	is to; the ratio of
::	proportion
∺	geometrical proportion

FUNCTIONS

$f(x)$	function
log	logarithm
ln	natural logarithm

CONSTANTS

e	base (2.718) of natural logarithms
π	pi (3.1416)
∞	infinity
i	imaginary unit ($\sqrt{-1}$)

GEOMETRY

$\angle$	angle
$\llcorner$	right angle
$\perp$	perpendicular
$\parallel$	parallel
$\bigcirc$ *or* $\odot$	circle
$\frown$	arc of a circle
$\bigcirc$	ellipse
$\varnothing$	diameter
$\triangle$	triangle
$\square$	square
$\square$	rectangle
$\boxplus$	cube
$\square$	rhomboid
°	degree
$'$	minute
$''$	second
$\simeq$	congruent to (in geometry)
m	slope
r	radius
d	diameter

SET THEORY AND LOGIC

$\cup$	union
$\cap$	intersection
Λ *or* ϕ	empty set; null set
$\in$	is an element of
$\notin$	is not an element of
$\therefore$	therefore
$\because$	since
$\mid$	is deducible from

CALCULUS

d	differential of
∂	partial differential
$\int$	integral
$\oint$	contour integral
lim	limit

Fractions and Decimals

%	percent

"Mathematics" in chapter 4; "First Aid" **Go to** (chapter 17); "Heath and Nutrition" (chapter 18)

MEDICINE AND PHARMACOLOGY SYMBOLS

Å	angstrom unit		in d.	daily
Ā,ĀĀ, āā, āa	of each		lot.	a lotion
a.c.	before meals		ⓜ	heart murmur
ad	up to; so as to make		♏, ♏	minim
add.	let there be added; add		μ	micron
ad lib.	at pleasure; as needed or desired		μμ	micromicron
agit.	shake		mod. praesc.	in the manner prescribed
aq.	water		O., o.	a pint
b. (i.) d.	twice daily		ol.	oil
c̄	with		oz.	ounce
cap.	take; capsule		p.c.	after meals
coch.	a spoonful		pil.	pill(s)
d.	give		p.r.n.	as circumstances may require
dil.	dilute *or* dissolve		pulv.	powder
Dx	diagnosis		Px	past history
fldxt.	fluid extract		q. (i.) d.	four times daily
ft.	make		q.l.	as much as you please
ft. mist.	let a mixture be made		q.s.	as much as will suffice
ft. pulv.	let a powder be made		q.v.	as much as you like
gr.	a grain		℞	take: used at the beginning of a prescription
gtt.	drops		rep.	let it be repeated
H.	hour		Rh+	positive blood factor
haust.	a draft		RH-	negative blood factor
Hx	history		♂	$\frac{1}{1000}$ of a second

continues

s̄	without
S, Sig.	write: used in prescriptions to indicate the directions to be placed on the label of the medicine
sol.	solution
s.o.s.	if necessary
s̄s̄	one half
tab.	tablet

t. (i.) d.	three times daily
ut dict.	as directed
w/v	weight in volume
℥	ounce
f ℥	fluidounce
ʒ	dram
f ʒ	fluidram
℈	scruple

PHYSICS SYMBOLS

α	alpha particle
Å	angstrom unit
β	beta ray
γ	gamma radiation
ε	electromotive force
η	efficiency
Λ	equivalent conductivity; permeance
λ	wavelength
μ	magnetic moment
ν	frequency
ρ	density; specific resistance
σ	conductivity
φ	luminous flux; magnetic flux
φ	fluidity
Ω	ohm
B	magnetic induction; magnetic field
c	speed of light

e	electronic charge of electron
E	electric field
G	conductance; weight
h	Planck's constant
H	enthalpy
L	inductance
n	index of refraction
P	momentum of a particle
R	universal gas constant
S	entropy
T	absolute temperature; period
V	electrical potential; frequency
W	energy
X	magnification; reactance
Y	admittance
Z	impedance

Go to "Physics" and "Meteorology" in chapter 4

WEATHER SYMBOLS

FRONTS

Warm   Cold   Occluded   Stationary

GROUND VISIBILITY

Fog (Light)   Fog (Heavy)   Haze   Visibility Reduced by Smoke

PRECIPITATION

Drizzle   Rain Showers   Hail Showers   Sleet   Snow   Snow (Drifting, Slight to Moderate)

SKY CONDITIONS

Clear Sky

Cloudy (Partly)

Cloudy (Completely Overcast)

STORMS

Lightning

Thunderstorm

Tornado

Tropical Storm

Hurricane

Sandstorm or Dust Storm

WIND SPEEDS

Calm

Approx. 1 mph (1 knot)

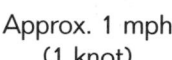
Approx. 6 mph (5 knots)

Approx. 12 mph (10 knots)

Approx. 58 mph (50 knots)

CULTURAL SYMBOLS

MUSIC SYMBOLS

Symbol	Meaning	Symbol	Meaning	Symbol	Meaning
𝅝	whole note	𝄾	eighth rest	¢	[²⁄₂] time
𝅗𝅥	half note	𝄿	sixteenth rest	$\frac{6}{8}$	[⁶⁄₈] time
𝅗𝅥.	dotted half note	𝅀	thirty-second rest	𝄞	treble, or G, clef
𝅘𝅥	quarter note	𝅁	sixty-fourth rest	𝄢	bass, or F, clef
𝅘𝅥𝅮	eighth note	♯	sharp	𝄡	alto, or C, clef
𝅘𝅥𝅯	sixteenth note	X	double sharp		measure
𝅘𝅥𝅰	thirty-second note	♭	flat		final bar
𝅘𝅥𝅱	sixty-fourth note	♭♭	double flat		repeat
	whole rest	♮	natural		repeat measure
	half rest	$\frac{3}{4}$	¾ time	D.C.	repeat from the beginning
𝄼	quarter rest	C	⁴⁄₄ time		

p	piano (soft)	*ff*	fortissimo (very loud)	tie
pp	pianissimo (very soft)	< crescendo	trill
f	forte (loud)	> decrescendo	

"Common Music Terms" in chapter 6; "Major World Religions" in chapter 9   **Go to**

RELIGION SYMBOLS

BUDDHISM

Buddha

Lotus

The Wheel

CHRISTIANITY

Celtic Cross

Latin Cross

Orthodox Cross

Agnus Dei

Chi Rho

Descending Dove; Holy Spirit

HINDUISM

Mandala

Om

Shiva

ISLAM

Star and Crescent

JUDAISM

Menorah

Star of David

Ten Commandments

SHINTO

Torii

TAOISM

Water: Life-Giving Source

Yin-Yang

ZODIAC SIGNS

Symbols		Sign	Planet	Element	Personality Traits
		Aries The Ram Mar. 21–Apr. 19	Mars	fire	bold, impulsive, confident, independent
		Taurus The Bull Apr. 20–May 20	Venus	earth	patient, determined, stubborn, devoted
		Gemini The Twins May 21–June 21	Mercury	air	ambitious, alert, intelligent, temperamental
		Cancer The Crab June 22–July 22	Moon	water	moody, sensitive, impressionable, sympathetic
		Leo The Lion July 23–Aug. 22	Sun	fire	noble, generous, enthusiastic, temperamental
		Virgo The Virgin Aug. 23–Sept. 22	Mercury	earth	intellectual, methodical, placid, tactless
		Libra The Scales Sept. 23–Oct. 23	Venus	air	just, sympathetic, orderly, persuasive, sociable
		Scorpio The Scorpion Oct. 24–Nov. 21	Mars	water	loyal, philosophical, willful, domineering
		Sagittarius The Archer Nov. 22–Dec. 21	Jupiter	fire	practical, imaginative, mature, just
		Capricorn The Goat Dec. 22–Jan. 19	Saturn	earth	ambitious, blunt, loyal, persistent
		Aquarius The Water Carrier Jan. 20–Feb. 18	Uranus	air	unselfish, generous, idealistic, original
		Pisces The Fishes Feb. 19–Mar. 20	Neptune	water	sympathetic, sensitive, timid, methodical

 "Astronomy: Constellations" in chapter 4

Go to

The swastika predates Hinduism and is considered an auspicious sign in India. It is the symbol painted on each toe in drawings of Buddha's footprint. It was also used by Native Americans.

Symbols/Signs

BIRTHSTONES AND FLOWERS

Month	Birthstone	Flower
January	garnet	snowdrop
February	amethyst	primrose
March	aquamarine or bloodstone	violet
April	diamond	daisy
May	emerald	hawthorn
June	pearl, alexandrite, or moonstone	rose
July	ruby	water lily
August	sardonyx or peridot	poppy
September	sapphire	morning glory
October	opal or tourmaline	hops
November	topaz	chrysanthemum
December	turquoise or lapis lazuli	holly

"Botanical Names of Plants" in chapter 3; "Some Important Minerals and Their Uses" in chapter 4   **Go to**

SYMBOLS TO GUIDE THE TRAVELER

MAP AND CHART SYMBOLS

BOUNDARIES

International   Provincial or State   County   Township   Incorporated Village

CITIES AND TOWNS

Capital City   Urban Area   Town or Village

CULTURAL, HISTORICAL, AND RECREATIONAL SYMBOLS

Point of Interest   Campsite   Winter Sports Area   State Monuments, Memorials, and Historical Sites   Ruins   National Wildlife Refuge   Ranger Station

Symbols/Signs

HYDROGRAPHIC FEATURES

 Intermittent River
 Intermittent Lake
 Freshwater Lake: Reservoir
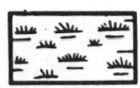 Marsh: Swamp
 Dams / Falls

NATURAL FEATURES

 Glaciers and Ice Shelves
 Passes
 Elevation Above Sea Level

ROADS AND RAILROADS

 Superhighway

Superhighway Under Construction
Dual Highway
Main Road
Secondary Road

 Bridge and Road
 Drawbridge and Road
 Tunnel and Road
 Railroad Track, Single
 Railroad Tracks, Two or More
Railroad Station

DISTRESS SIGNALS

The symbols below, used for ground-to-air communication, may be made of strips of fabric or parachutes, pieces of wood, tree branches, stones, or any other material.

I Need Doctor   **II** Need Medicine   **X** Cannot Proceed   **F** Need Food and Water   **≽** Need Weapons   **K** Indicate Direction

↑ Going This Way   **▷** Aircraft Damaged   Attempting Take Off   **△** Safe to Land   **LL** All Well   **L** Need Fuel and Oil

N No   **Y** Yes   **JL** Don't Understand   **W** Need Engineer   **□** Need Compass and Map   **⋮** Need Signal Lamp

Symbols/Signs

INTERNATIONAL ROAD SIGNS

 Curve

 Intersection

 Opening Bridge

 Road Works

 Tunnel

 Pedestrian Crossing

 Watch Out for Children

 Animals Crossing

 Road Narrows

 Slippery Road

 Danger

 No Entry

 Road Closed

 Closed to Motor Vehicles

 Closed to Motorcycles

 Closed to Pedestrians

 No Left Turns

 No U-Turns

 Overtaking Prohibited

 Speed Limit

 End of All Restrictions

 Yield

 Stop

 Direction to Follow

 Traffic Circle

 Parking

 Hospital

 Mechanical Help

 Telephone

 Filling Station

 Camping Site

 Caravan Site

 Youth Hostel

SYMBOLIC ALPHABETS

SEMAPHORE CODE

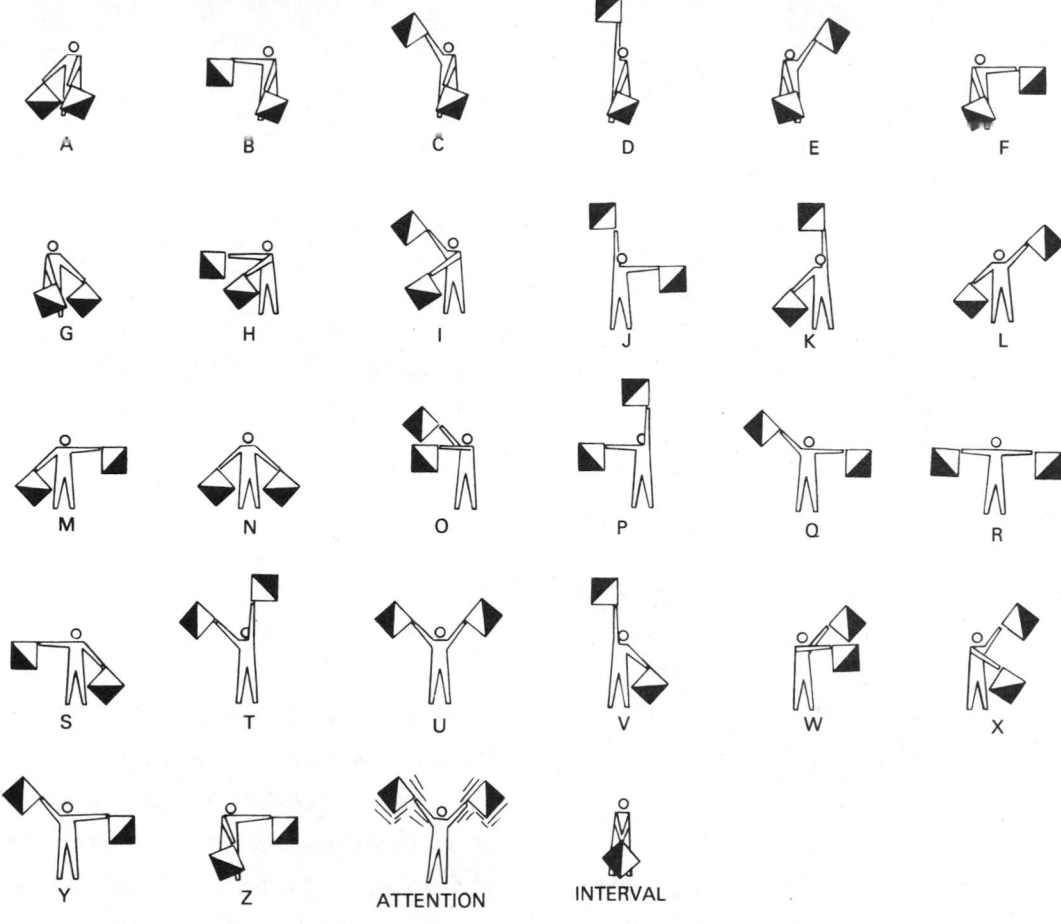

INTERNATIONAL RADIO ALPHABET AND MORSE CODE

A	Alpha	· —	P	Papa	· — — ·
B	Bravo	— · · ·	Q	Quebec	— — · —
C	Charlie	— · — ·		(kaybec)	
D	Delta	— · ·	R	Romeo	· — ·
E	Echo	·	S	Sierra	· · ·
F	Foxtrot	· · — ·	T	Tango	—
G	Golf	— — ·	U	Uniform	· · —
H	Hotel	· · · ·	V	Victor	· · · —
I	India	· ·	W	Whiskey	· — —
J	Juliet	· — — —	X	X ray	— · · —
K	Kilo	— · —	Y	Yankee	— · — —
L	Lima	· — · ·	Z	Zulu	— — · ·
	(leema)		1	one	· — — — —
M	Mike	— —	2	two	· · — — —
N	November	— ·	3	three	· · · — —
O	Oscar	— — —			

4	four	· · · · —
5	five	· · · · ·
6	six	— · · · ·
7	seven	— — · · ·
8	eight	— — — · ·
9	nine	— — — — ·
10	ten	— — — — —
.	period	· — · — · —
,	comma	— — · · — —
?	question	· · — — · ·
	mark	
;	semicolon	— · — · — ·
:	colon	— — — · · ·
-	hyphen	— · · · · —
'	apostrophe	· — — — — ·

SIGN LANGUAGE

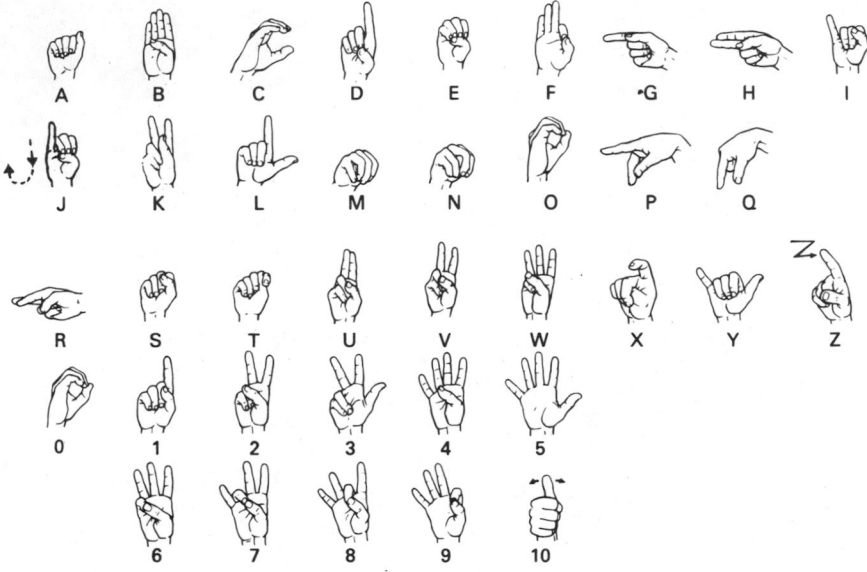

BRAILLE ALPHABET, NUMBERS, AND PUNCTUATION

Between 1826 and 1837, Louis Braille, a blind Frenchman, developed a system of printing and writing for the blind that uses raised dots representing letters, numbers, and punctuation.

The six dots of the Braille cell are arranged and numbered:

```
1 • • 4
2 • • 5
3 • • 6
```

The capital sign, dot 6,

```
1 • • 4
2 • • 5
3 • ● 6
```

placed before a letter makes a capital letter.

The number sign, dots 3, 4, 5, 6,

```
1 • ● 4
2 • ● 5
3 ● ● 6
```

placed before the characters a–j, makes the numbers 1 through 0. For example: <u>a</u> preceded by the number sign is 1, <u>b</u> is 2, etc.

George Washington was a Freemason and adopted the pyramid (a symbol of knowledge and wisdom) and the all-seeing eye of God as national emblems. They are still found on dollar bills.

The system illustrated on the next page is Standard English Braille—Grade 1 (letters, numerals, and punctuation). Grade 2 Braille additionally makes use of approximately 300 contractions (combinations of cells to shorten the lengths of a word). Grade 3 Braille, rarely used, employs additional contractions.

Go to "Telecommunications Device for the Deaf (TDD)" and "Books for Blind and Physically Handicapped Persons" in chapter 22

a	b	c	d	e	f	g	h	i	j
1	2	3	4	5	6	7	8	9	0

k	l	m	n	o	p	q	r	s	t

u	v	w	x	y	z

comma	colon	semicolon	period	exclamation point	parenthesis
,	:	;	.	!	( )

question mark	hyphen	apostrophe	left quotation mark	right quotation mark
?	–	'	"	"

BUSINESS AND MONETARY SYMBOLS

A/C, a/c	account; account current	P/A	power of attorney
A/O, a/o	account of	P/C, p/c	prices current; petty cash
B/D	bank draft	P/N	promissory note
B/E	bill of exchange	w/	with
B/L	bill of lading	W/B	waybill
B/P	bills payable	w/o	without
B/R	bills receivable	@	at/per/priced at
B/V	book value	#	number, pounds
C/D	carried down; certificate of deposit	%	percent/per hundred
C/N	circular note; credit note	¢	cent
C/O	care of; carried over; cash order	$	dollar
d/d	delivered	DM	deutsche mark
D/O	delivery order	€	euro
G/A	general average	F	franc
L/C, l/c	letter of credit	L	lira
M/D, m/d	month's date	£	pound
N/S, n/s	not sufficient funds	R	ruble
o/c	overcharge	R̶	rupee
O/S	out of stock	Y, ¥	yen

Symbols/Signs

PROOFREADERS' MARKS

∧	Insert material as indicated in margin
ℒ	Delete
stet	Restore deleted material; let it stand (in text, use dots to indicate what is to be restored)
⌒	Close up; print as one word
⌒ℒ	Delete and close up
tr	Transpose (in text, indicate how to change order of)
ⓢⓟ	Spell out
#	Insert space
eq #	Space evenly
hr #	Insert hair space
⎕	Insert or indent one em space
⊓	Move up
⊔	Move down
⊐	Move to the right
⊏	Move to the left
⊐⊏	Center
‖	Align vertically
=	Align horizontally; straighten type
9	Turn over inverted letter
wf	Wrong font
✕	Broken type; reset
¶	Begin a new paragraph
no ¶	Do not begin a new paragraph; run paragraphs together
(⁄)	Insert parentheses
[⁄]	Insert brackets
⌃	Insert comma
⁒⁄	Insert semicolon
:⁄	Insert colon
⊙	Insert period
?	Insert question mark
|·|·|	Insert ellipses
⌄	Insert apostrophe (or single quotation mark)
❦ ❧	Insert quotation marks
|=|	Insert hyphen
⅃ₘ	Insert em dash
⅃ₙ	Insert en dash
⌄	Insert superscript or superior
∧	Insert subscript or inferior
cap	Capitalize lowercase letter
lc	Lowercase capital letter
s.c.	Set in SMALL CAPITALS (in text, indicate by double underline)
rom	Set in roman type
bf	Set in **boldface** type
ital	Set in *italic* type

Go to   "Diacritical Marks" in chapter 13; "Grammar and Punctuation" (chapter 14); and "Network Etiquette (Netiquette)" in chapter 16

SMILEYS

Smileys, also known as emoticons, or emotional icons, are faces viewed sideways that are added to online messages in order to convey feelings.

:-)	Happy	8-|	In suspense
:-(	Sad	|-|	Asleep (indicates boredom)
;-)	Winking	:-&	Tongue-tied
:-t	Cross	:-#	Lips are sealed
:-o	Surprised	:-\	Undecided

ADDITIONAL SOURCES OF INFORMATION

BOOKS

Becker, Udo, ed. *The Continuum Encyclopedia of Symbols.* Continuum International, 2000.

Biedermann, Hans. *Dictionary of Symbolism.* Peter Smith, 1990.

Chevalier, Jean, et al., eds. *A Dictionary of Symbols.* Penguin, 1997.

Dreyfuss, Henry, ed. *Symbol Sourcebook: An Authoritative Guide to International Graphic Symbols.* Van Nostrand Reinhold, 1984.

Jean, Georges. *Signs, Symbols, and Ciphers.* Abrams, 1998.

Juliann, Nadia. *The Mammoth Dictionary of Symbols.* Carroll & Graf, 1995.

Lehner, Ernst. *Symbols, Signs, and Signets.* Peter Smith, 1990.

Mattia, Fioretta. *Elsevier's Dictionary of Acronyms, Initialisms, Abbreviations and Symbols.* Elsevier, 1997.

Tresidder, Jack. *Symbols and Their Meanings.* Friedman/Fairfax, 2000.

WEB SITES

The American Sign Language Browser
http://commtechlab.msu.edu/sites/aslweb

Encyclopedia of Symbols
http://www.symbols.com

National Federation for the Blind's Braille Page
http://www.nfb.org/brailco.htm

Symbols/Signs

13

ALPHABETS AND WORDS

ALPHABETIZATION

There are two ways of alphabetizing a list of words, terms, or names. In both cases, the compiler of the list compares the first letters of the entries, then the second letters, and so forth. In a word-by-word list, the first word of each entry is considered, then the second, and third if necessary; hyphens are ignored. A letter-by-letter list is considered without regard for whether the entry consists of one word or more than one; spaces and hyphens are ignored.

The following list is arranged according to the word-by-word system:

> sea
> Sea Side Heights
> seafood
> seagull
> seal
> seaside
> season ticket
> seasoning
> second best
> second name
> secondary

Here is the same list compiled under the letter-by-letter system:

> sea
> seafood
> seagull
> seal
> seaside
> Sea Side Heights
> seasoning
> season ticket
> secondary
> second best
> second name

Either method of alphabetization is acceptable, as long as it is scrupulously adhered to. Although some lists may be better served by one approach or the other, neither is considered more correct.

ACRONYMS

Acronyms are pronounceable formations made by combining the initial letters or syllables of a string of words. Some abbreviations look like acronyms but are listed as abbreviations because they are not pro-

nounced as words; for example, CIA (usually pronounced "C-I-A") and DAR (usually pronounced "D-A-R"). A few acronyms may be pronounced either as words ("REM") or as abbreviations ("R-E-M"). Acronyms marked with an asterisk (*) have been generally accepted and used as common words.

Acronym	Stands for
ABEND	abnormal end
ACE	American Council on Education
ACTION	American Council to Improve Our Neighborhoods
AFTRA	American Federation of Television and Radio Artists
AID	Agency for International Development
AID	American Institute of Decorators
AID	Army Intelligence Department
AIDS	acquired immune deficiency syndrome
AIIM	Association for Information and Image Management
ALCOA	Aluminum Company of America
ALGOL	algorithmic oriented language
ALIBI	adaptive location of internetworked bases of information
ALINK	active link
AMEX	American Express Company
AMEX	American Stock Exchange
AMVETS	American Veterans of World War II
ANSI	American National Standards Institute
ARC	AIDS-related complex
ARCO	Atlantic Richfield Company
ASCAP	American Society of Composers, Authors, and Publishers
ASCII	American Standard Code for Information Interchange
AWACS	airborne warning and control system
AWOL, awol*	absent without leave
BAM	Brooklyn Academy of Music
BAM	basic access method
BART	Bay Area Rapid Transit
BASIC	Beginner's All-purpose Symbolic Instruction Code (computer language)
BASS	Bass Anglers Sportsman Society
BIB	Bureau of International Broadcasting
BIOS	basic input/output system
bit*	binary digit
BIZNET	American Business Network (database)
BOLD	bibliographic on-line display (document retrieval system)
CAB	Civil Aeronautics Board
CAD	computer-aided design
CARE	Cooperative for American Relief Everywhere

Acronym	Stands for
CAT (scan)	computerized axial tomography
CD-ROM	compact disk–read only memory
CLASSMATE	Computer Language to Aid and Stimulate Scientific, Mathematical and Technical Education
CODEC	coder/decoder
COMSAT	Communications Satellite Corporation
CONOCO	Continental Oil Company
CONUS	Continental United States
CORE	Congress of Racial Equality
COSMIC	Computer Software Management and Information Center
CURE	Citizens United for Racial Equality
DAM	Dayton Art Museum
DAM	Denver Art Museum
DELCO	Dayton Engineering Laboratory Company
DEW	distant early warning
DISCO	Defense Industrial Security Clearing Office
DOS	disk operating system
EARS	Electronic Airborne Reaction System
EARS	Electronically Agile Radar System
EARS	Emergency Airborne Reaction System
ELECTRA	Electrical, Electronics and Communications Trade Association
ENDEX	Environmental Data Index
EPCOT®	Experimental Prototype Community of Tomorrow
EXIMBANK	Export-Import Bank of the United States
FAQ	frequently asked questions
FEDLINK	Federal Library Information Network
FEW	Federally Employed Women
FICA	Federal Insurance Contributions Act (Social Security)
FLIP	Flexible Loan Insurance Program
FLIP	floating instrument platform
GAAP	generally accepted accounting principles
GAG	Graphic Arts Guild
GARB	Garment and Allied Industries Requirements Board
GATT	General Agreement on Tariffs and Trade
GENIE	General Electric Network for Information Exchange
GEO	Geostationary Earth Orbit
GEOS	graphic environment operating system
GILS	Government Information Locator Service
GIPSY	general information processing system

Acronym	Stands for
GLAAD	Gay and Lesbian Alliance Against Defamation
GOES	Geostationary Operational Environmental Satellite
GRAD	graduate resume accumulation and distribution
GUPCO	Gulf Petroleum Corporation
HALF	Human Animal Liberation Front
HART	Honolulu Area Rapid Transit
HEAL	Health Education Assistance Loans
HUD	(Department of) Housing and Urban Development
IMAX®	Maximum Image
INLAW	infantry laser weapon
INTELSAT	International Telecommunications Satellite Consortium
INTERMARC	International Machine-Readable Catalog
INTERPOL	International Criminal Police Organization
INTERTELL	International Intelligence Legion
JAG	judge advocate general
JOBS	Job Opportunities in the Business Sector
JUMPS	Joint Uniform Military Pay System
LAN	local area network
laser*	light amplification by stimulated emission of radiation
LEAP	Loan and Educational Aid Program
LEM	lunar excursion module
LILCO	Long Island Lighting Company
LORAN	Long-range Navigation
MACOM	major army command
MAD	mutually assured destruction
MADD	Mothers Against Drunk Driving
MARC	machine-readable cataloging
maser*	microwave amplification stimulated emission of radiation
MASH	mobile army surgical hospital
MOMA	Museum of Modern Art (New York)
NAFTA	North American Free Trade Agreement
NAM	network access machine
NAM	National Association of Manufacturers
NAPA	National Automotive Parts Association

A Closer Look

Recurrent Letters of the Alphabet

The letters of the alphabet in the order of their normal recurrence from most frequent to least frequent: E, T, A, O, I, N, S, H, R, D, L, U, C, M, P, F, Y, W, G, B, V, K, J, X, Z, Q.

Alphabets

Acronym	Stands for
NAPA	National Police Officers' Association of America
NARAD	Navy Research and Development
NARCO	United National Narcotics Commission
NASA	National Aeronautics and Space Administration
NASCAR	National Association of Stock Car Auto Racing
NASDAQ	National Association of Securities Dealers Automatic Quotation
NATO	North Atlantic Treaty Organization
NECCO	New England Confectionery Company
NOAA	National Oceanographic and Atmospheric Administration
NOMAD	navy oceanographic and meteorological device
NORAD	North American Defense Command
NOW	National Organization for Women
NOW	negotiable order of withdrawal (a NOW account is a savings account on which checks can be drawn)
OASIS	Overseas Access Service for Information Systems
ODECO	Ocean Drilling and Exploration Company
ODESY	On-Line Data Entry System
OPEC	Organization of Petroleum Exporting Countries
OSHA	Occupational Safety and Health Administration
OXFAM	Oxford Famine Relief
PAC	Pacific Air Command
PAC	political action committee
PATCO	Port Authority Transit Corporation
PATH	Port Authority Trans-Hudson
PEN	Poets, Playwrights, Editors, Essayists, and Novelists
PEST	People for Environmentally Sustainable Transport
PET	parent effectiveness training
PET	positron emission tomography
PIN	personal identification number
PIN	Police Information Network
PIM	personal information manager
PIRG	public interest research group
POSIX	Portable Operating System Interface for Computer Environments
PUSH	People United to Serve Humanity
radar*	radio detecting and ranging
RAM	random access memory
READ	real-time electronic access and display

Acronym	Stands for
RIF	Reading Is Fundamental
ROM	read-only memory
SAC	Strategic Air Command
SADD	Students Against Drunk Driving
SAFE	system for automated flight efficiency
SAG	Screen Actors Guild
SALT	Strategic Arms Limitation Talks
SAM	surface-to-air missile
SAP	system access protocol
SARA	Superfund Amendments and Reauthorization Act (1986)
SCOPE	Scientific Committee on Problems of the Environment
SCOR	Scientific Committee on Oceanic Research
SCOSTEP	Scientific Committee on Solar-Terrestrial Physics
scuba*	self-contained underwater breathing apparatus
SEATO	Southeast Asia Treaty Organization
SEP	simplified employee pension
snafu*	situation normal—all fouled up
sonar*	sound navigation ranging
START	Strategic Arms Reduction Talks
SUNOCO	Sun Oil Company
SWAK	sealed with a kiss
SWAT	Special Weapons and Tactics
TAC	Tactical Air Command
TIROS	Television and Infra-Red Observation Satellite
UNESCO	United Nations Educational, Social, and Cultural Organization
UNICEF	United Nations International Children's Emergency Fund
VISTA	Volunteers in Service to America
WAC	Women's Army Corps
WAIS	wide area information server
WAN	wide area network
WARMER	World Action for Recycled Material and Energy from Rubbish
WASP	white Anglo-Saxon Protestant
WATS	Wide Area Telecommunications Service
WAVES	Women Accepted for Volunteer Emergency Service (navy)
WHO	World Health Organization
WISE	World Information Systems Exchange
WORM	write once–read many
WUDO	Western European Defense Organization
yuppie*	young urban professional
zip*	zone improvement plan (code)

Alphabets

COMMON ABBREVIATIONS

An abbreviation is a shortened form of a word or phrase. Some abbreviations, such as Mr. and Mrs., always substitute for the longer form. Abbreviations are not limited to, but frequently are used for, titles, academic degrees, organizations, measurements, and scientific words. An asterisk (*) indicates a frequently used abbreviation that is incorrect according to the scientific metric notation system.

Abbr.	Stands for
1GL	first-generation language
2DR	two-door
2GL	second-generation language
2WD	two-wheel drive
3GL	third-generation language
4DR	four-door
4GL	fourth-generation language
4WD	four-wheel drive
a	acre
AA	Alcoholics Anonymous
AAA	American Automobile Association
ABC	American Broadcasting Company
ABM	antiballistic missile
AC	alternating current
ACLU	American Civil Liberties Union
ACT	American College Test
AD, A.D.	*anno domini* (Latin, in the year of our Lord)
A/D	analog to digital
ADA	American Dental Association
addn.	addition
addnl.	additional
adm.	administration, administrative
AEC	Atomic Energy Commission
AEF	American Expeditionary Force (World War I)
aet.	*aetatis* (Latin, of age, aged)
AF	air force
AFB	air force base
AFC	American Football Conference
AFDC	Aid to Families with Dependent Children
AFL	American Football League
AFL-CIO	American Federation of Labor and Congress of Industrial Organizations
Afr.	Africa, African
AFT	American Federation of Teachers
AFTP	Anonymous File Transfer Protocol
agcy.	agency
agt.	agent
AH, A.H.	*anno Hegirae/anno Hebraico* (Latin, in the year of the Hegira/Latin, in the Hebrew year)

Abbr.	Stands for
AHL	American Hockey League
AI	artificial intelligence
AIA	American Institute of Architects
aka, a.k.a.	also known as
AKC	American Kennel Club
AL	American League
AM	amplitude modulation
A.M.	*anno mundi* (Latin, in the year of the world)
A.M., AM, a.m.	*ante meridiem* (Latin, before noon)
AMA	American Medical Association
AMU	atomic mass unit
anon.	anonymous
AP	Associated Press
A/P	accounts payable
APA	American Psychological Association
APB	all points bulletin
APO	army post office (overseas)
appl.	applied
approx.	approximately
appt.	appointment
Apr.	April
APR	annual percentage rate
apt.	apartment
A/R	accounts receivable
ARV	American Revised Version
ASAP	as soon as possible (pronounced "A-S-A-P" or "A-SAP")
assn.	association
asoc.	associate
asst.	assistant
AST	Alaska Standard Time
AT&T	American Telephone and Telegraph Company
ATM	automated/automatic teller machine
ATTN, attn.	attention
atty.	attorney
ATV	all-terrain vehicle
Aug.	August
AV	audiovisual
AV	Authorized Version
AVR	automatic voice recognition
b.	born
B and B, B&B	bed and breakfast
B and E	breaking and entering
BBB	Better Business Bureau

"Weights and Measures" in chapter 2; "Symbols and Signs" in chapter 12; "Abbreviated Titles That Follow Names" in chapter 15

Alphabets

Abbr.	Stands for
BBC	British Broadcasting Corporation
bbl.	barrel(s)
BC, B.C.	before Christ
BC, B.C.E.	before the Christian era
bef.	before
bf, b.f.	boldface
BLT	bacon, lettuce, and tomato
BMOC	big man on campus
BP	blood pressure
B.P.O.E.	Benevolent and Protective Order of Elks
BR	bedroom
BSA	Boy Scouts of America
bu.	bushel
BV, BVM	Blessed Virgin, Blessed Virgin Mary
b/w	black and white
BX	base exchange (commissary)
BYOB	bring your own beer/ booze/bottle
C	centigrade, Celsius
c., ca.	*circa* (Latin, about)
calc.	calculate, calculated
Cantab.	*Cantabrigiensis* (Latin, of Cambridge)
caps	capital letters
CATV	community antenna television, *now called* cable television
CBS	Columbia Broadcasting System
cc	cubic centimeter
cc, CC	carbon copy
CCC	Civilian Conservation Corps
CCU	cardiac/coronary/critical care unit
CD	certificate of deposit
CDC	Centers for Disease Control
CDT	Central Daylight Time
CEO	chief executive officer
cf.	*confer* (Latin, compare)
CFO	chief financial officer
CIA	Central Intelligence Agency
cm	centimeter
c/o	in care of
COD	cash on delivery
COO	chief operating officer
CP	Communist Party
CPA	certified public accountant
cpi	characters per inch
CPI	consumer price index
CPR	cardiopulmonary resuscitation
CPU	central processing unit
CSA	Confederate States of America
CST	Central Standard Time
cu.	cubic
DAR	Daughters of the American Revolution
dB	decibel
DB	database
d/b/a	doing business as

Abbr.	Stands for
DC	District of Columbia
DC	direct current
Dec.	December
dept.	department
dist.	district
div.	division
DMV	Department (Division) of Motor Vehicles
DMZ	demilitarized zone
DNA	deoxyribonucleic acid
DOA	dead on arrival
DOB	date of birth
doz.	dozen
Dr.	Doctor
D.S.M.	Distinguished Service Medal
D.S.O.	Distinguished Service Order
DST	Daylight Saving Time
DTs	*delerium tremens* (Latin, trembling delirium)
DUI	driving under the influence
DVD	digital video disc
DWI	driving while intoxicated
ED	emotional disability, emotionally disabled
EDS	Electronic Data Systems
EEO	equal employment opportunity
e.g.	*exempli gratia* (Latin, for example)
eng.	engineering
Eng.	English
engr.	engineer
engr.	engraved
EPA	Environmental Protection Agency
ERA	earned run average
ESP	extrasensory perception
esp.	especially
EST	Eastern Standard Time
et al.	*et alii, et aliae, et alia* (Latin, and others)
etc.	*et cetera* (Latin, and others of the same kind; and so forth)
ex.	example
exch.	exchange
ext.	extension
f., F	female, feminine
f., ff.	and following
F	Fahrenheit
FAA	Federal Aviation Administration
fax	facsimile
FBI	Federal Bureau of Investigation
FCC	Federal Communications Commission
FDA	Food and Drug Administration
FDIC	Federal Deposit Insurance Corporation
Feb.	February

Alphabets

"Cooking Measurement Abbreviations" in chapter 19; **"Airline Codes, Toll-Free Numbers, and Web Sites"** and **"Airport Codes"** in chapter 24

Abbr.	Stands for
fed.	federal
FHA	Federal Housing Administration
fig.	figure
FM	frequency modulation
f.o.b., FOB	free on board
fr.	from
Fr.	French
Fri.	Friday
FRM	fixed rate mortgage
FRS	Federal Reserve System
ft.	foot
f/t	full time
FTC	Federal Trade Commission
f/x	special effects
FWD	front-wheel drive
FYI	for your information
G	giga (metric prefix meaning 1,000,000,000)
GAO	General Accounting Office
G.A.R.	Grand Army of the Republic
GED	General Educational Development (tests)
GED	general equivalency diploma
Gk.	Greek
GMAT	Graduate Management Admission Test
GMT	Greenwich Mean Time
GNP	gross national product
GOP	Grand Old Party (Republican party)
gov., govt.	government
G.P.	general practitioner
GPA	grade point average
GPO	Government Printing Office
GRE	Graduate Record Examination
GSA	General Services Administration
GSA	Girl Scouts of America
GSO	general staff officer
GUI	graphical user interface
HEW	(Department of) Health, Education, and Welfare
H.M.S.	His/Her Majesty's Ship
hp	horsepower
HQ	headquarters
hr.	hour
HR	home run
H.R.	House of Representatives
H.R.H.	His/Her Royal Highness
HS	high school
ht., hgt.	height
HTML, html	hypertext markup language
HVAC	heating, ventilating, and air conditioning
ibid.	*ibidem* (Latin, in the same place)
I.B.M.	International Business Machines Corporation

Abbr.	Stands for
ICBM	intercontinental ballistic missile
ICC	Interstate Commerce Commission
ICF	intermediate care facility
ICU	intensive care unit
i.e.	*id est* (Latin, that is)
IGY	International Geophysical Year
IHS	Jesus (Greek contraction)
ILGWU	International Ladies' Garment Workers' Union
IMO	in my opinion
in.	inch
INRI	*Iesus Nazarenus Rex Iudaeorum* (Latin, Jesus of Nazareth, King of the Jews)
INS	Immigration and Naturalization Service
I.O.U.	I owe you
I.Q.	intelligence quotient
IRA	individual retirement account
IRA	Irish Republican Army
IRS	Internal Revenue Service
ISBN	international standard book number
ISO	International Organization for Standardization
Jan.	January
Jr.	Junior
k	karat
k	kilo (metric prefix meaning 1,000)
K	Kelvin
kb (K*, KB*)	kilobyte
kbps (KBps*)	kilobytes per second
kg	kilogram
KGB	*Komitet Gosudarstvennoi Bezopasnosti* (Russian, State Security Committee)
kHz	kilohertz
KJV	King James Version
km	kilometer
kW (kw*)	kilowatt
kWh (kwh*)	kilowatt-hour
l	liter
lat.	latitude
Lat.	Latin
lb.	pound
lc, l.c.	lowercase
L.C.	Library of Congress
LCD	liquid crystal display
LD	learning disability, learning disabled
LDS	Latter-Day Saints
LED	light-emitting diode
LMT	Local Mean Time
long.	longitude
LSAT	Law School Admission Test

Abbr.	Stands for
ltr.	letter
m	meter
m., M	male, masculine
M	mega (metric prefix meaning 1,000,000)
Mac	Macintosh computer
Mar.	March
max.	maximum
MB	megabyte (1,024 kilobytes)
MBps	megabytes per second
MC, emcee	master of ceremonies
mg	milligram
mgr.	manager
MHz	megahertz
mi.	mile
min.	minimum, minute
ml	milliliter
mm	millimeter
mo.	month
M.O.	money order
M.O.	*modus operandi* (Latin, mode of operation)
Mon.	Monday
MP, M.P.	Military Police
mph	miles per hour
MRI	magnetic resonance imaging
ms., mss.	manuscript, manuscripts
MSG	monosodium glutamate
MVP	most valuable player
MYOB	mind your own business
N/A	not applicable
NAACP	National Association for the Advancement of Colored People
N.B.	*nota bene* (Latin, note well)
NBA	National Basketball Association
NBC	National Broadcasting Company
NCAA	National Collegiate Athletic Association
NCO	noncommissioned officer
NEA	National Education Association
NEA	National Endowment for the Arts
NFL	National Football League
NHL	National Hockey League
NIH	National Institutes of Health
NL	National League
NLRB	National Labor Relations Board
NMHA	National Mental Health Association
non seq.	*non sequitur* (Latin, it does not follow)
NOS	not otherwise specified
Nov.	November
NR	not rated

Abbr.	Stands for
NRA	National Recovery Administration
NRA	National Rifle Association
NRC	National Research Council
NRC	Nuclear Regulatory Commission
N.S.	New Style
NSA	National Security Agency
NSC	National Security Council
NSF	National Science Foundation
NSF	not sufficient funds
NTSB	National Transportation Safety Board
Oct.	October
OCR	optical character recognition
op. cit.	*opere citato* (Latin, in the work cited)
O.S.	Old Style
OT	occupational therapy
OT, o/t	overtime
OTC	over-the-counter (non-prescription)
Oxon.	*Oxoniensis* (Latin, of Oxford)
oz.	ounce
PA (system)	public address (system)
p and h	postage and handling
P&I	principal and interest
P&L	profit and loss
PB&J	peanut butter and jelly
PBS	Public Broadcasting Service
PC	personal computer
PCB	polychlorinated biphenyl
PDA	public display of affection
PDR	*Physicians Desk Reference*
PDT	Pacific Daylight Time
PE	physical education
perp.	perpetrator
pk.	peck
P.M., PM, p.m.	*post meridiem* (Latin, after noon)
P.M.	prime minister
PMS	premenstrual syndrome
pmt.	payment
PO	post office
POB	post office box
POE	place of employment
POV	point of view
POW, PW	prisoner of war
ppb	parts per billion
ppm	parts per million
ppt	parts per thousand
prep., prep	preparatory
Pres.	President
prev.	previous
PRN	*pro re nata* (Latin, for an occasion that has written—as needed)
pro tem.	*pro tempore* (Latin, for the time being)
P.S., PS	postscript

Go to "Two-Letter State and Territory Abbreviations," "Geographic Directional Abbreviations," and "Street Designators (Street Suffixes)" in chapter 25

Abbr.	Stands for	Abbr.	Stands for
PSA	public service announcement	SOS	international Morse code distress signal (dot dot dot dash dash dash dot dot dot), often wrongly thought to stand for "Save Our Ship"; however, the letters do not stand for words
psi	pounds per square inch		
PST	Pacific Standard Time		
psych	psychology		
pt.	pint		
p/t	part-time	SPCA	Society for the Prevention of Cruelty to Animals
PTA	Parent-Teacher Association		
PX	post exchange (commissary)	SPQR	*senatus populusque romanus* (Latin, the Senate and the Roman people)
QA	quality assurance		
Q&A	questions and answers	sq.	square
Q.E.D.	*quod erat demonstrandum* (Latin, which was to be demonstrated)	Sr.	Senior
		SRO	standing room only
QMHP	qualified mental health professional	SSA	Social Security Administration
qt.	quart	SSN	Social Security number
qty.	quantity	Sun.	Sunday
q.v.	*quod vide* (Latin, which see)	SUV	sport utility vehicle
R&B	rhythm and blues	T	ton
R&D	research and development	TA	teaching assistant
RBC	red blood cells, red blood cell count	TA	transactional analysis
rbi	run batted in	TB	tuberculosis
RDA	recommended daily allowance	TBA, tba	to be announced
REM	rapid eye movement (pronounced "R-E-M" or "REM")	TD	touchdown
		TDD	telecommunications device for the deaf
RFD	rural free delivery	temp.	temporary
RIP, R.I.P.	*requiescat in pace* (Latin, rest in peace)	TF	task force
RNA	ribonucleic acid	TGIF	thank God it's Friday
ROTC	Reserve Officers' Training Corps (pronounced "R-O-T-C" or "ROTC")	Thurs.	Thursday
		TIA	transient ischemic attack
rpm	revolutions per minute	TLC	tender loving care
RR	railroad	TM	trademark
R and R	rest and relaxation	TM	transcendental meditation
RSV	Revised Standard Version	TMJ	temporomandibular joint
R.S.V.P., RSVP	*repondez s'il vous plait* (French, respond if you please)	TNT	trinitrotoluene
		TOEFL	Test of English as a Foreign Language
rtw	ready to wear	TSS	toxic shock syndrome
Rx	prescription	TTY	teletypewriter
S&H	shipping and handling	Tues.	Tuesday
S-M, S and M	sadism and masochism	TVA	Tennessee Valley Authority
		uc, u.c.	uppercase
SASE	self-addressed stamped envelope	UFO	unidentified flying object
SAT	Scholastic Aptitude Test	UHF	ultra high frequency
Sat.	Saturday	UK	United Kingdom
SBA	Small Business Administration	UN	United Nations
SBS	sick building syndrome	UPI	United Press International
sc, s.c.	small capitals	US, USA	United States, United States of America
SCLC	Southern Christian Leadership Conference	USA	United States Army
SDI	Strategic Defense Initiative	USAF	United States Air Force
SDS	Students for a Democratic Society	USCG	United States Coast Guard
sec.	seconds	USDA	United States Department of Agriculture
SEC	Securities and Exchange Commission	USIA	United States Information Agency
Sen.	Senate	USMC	United States Marine Corps
Sept.	September	USN	United States Navy
seq.	*sequentes* (Latin, the following)	USO	United Service Organization
SNF	skilled nursing facility		

Alphabets

Abbr.	Stands for
USS	United States Ship
USSR	Union of Soviet Socialist Republics
v., vs.	versus
VA	Veterans Administration
VCR	video cassette recorder
VD	venereal disease
VFW	Veterans of Foreign Wars
VHF	very high frequency
VIP	very important person
viz.	*videlicet* (Latin, namely)
VP	Vice President
W	watt
WB	World Bank
WBC	white blood cells/white blood cell count
WC	water closet (toilet)
WCTU	Women's Christian Temperance Union
Wed.	Wednesday
wk.	week
WNBA	Women's National Basketball Association
WP	word processing
WPA	Works Progress Administration
WTO	World Trade Organization
WWW	World Wide Web
WYSIWYG	what you see is what you get
Xmas	Christmas
XO	executive officer
yd.	yard
YTD	year to date
YMCA	Young Men's Christian Association
YMHA	Young Men's Hebrew Association
YWCA	Young Women's Christian Association
YWHA	Young Women's Hebrew Association
yr.	year

COMMONLY MISUSED WORDS

accept	to receive; to answer affirmatively
except	to leave out (verb); with the exclusion of (preposition)
affect	to influence; to pretend
effect	a result, an influence, an impression (noun); to bring about (verb)
antagonist	an adversary
protagonist	the leading character
anxious	worried, uneasy
eager	impatiently desirous
bathos	triteness, sentimentality
pathos	sympathy
brake	to reduce speed
break	to separate; to collapse; to destroy

capital	a city that is a seat of government; money; an uppercase letter
capitol	the building in which a legislature meets
compare	to examine differences and similarities
contrast	to examine differences
diagnosis	the identification of a disease or situation
prognosis	a prediction of the likely course of a disease or situation
dinner	the main meal of the day, at noontime or in the evening
supper	the evening meal
dyeing	coloring with dye
dying	ceasing to live
emigrate	to leave a country to live elsewhere
immigrate	to enter a country to live there
flair	skill, talent
flare	a bright light; an outburst
gorilla	an ape
guerrilla	a member of an irregular military force
hole	a space, a void
whole	complete, intact
illegible	cannot be read because of bad printing or handwriting
unreadable	uninteresting, not worth reading
ingenious	brilliant, clever
ingenuous	simple, naive
its	belonging to it
it's	it is
lay	to put; to set down
lie	to rest in a horizontal position; to make an untrue statement
liable	responsible; likely
libel	a defamatory statement
majority	more than half
plurality	more votes than any other candidate; the margin of victory
notable	worthy, impressive
notorious	widely known and ill-regarded
peace	harmony; the absence of war
piece	part of a whole
personal	intimate; having to do with a specific person
personnel	the employees of a company or organization

pray	to address a deity; to implore
prey	a victim
principal	main (adjective); the person in charge (noun)
principle	a moral rule; a law
put (someone) down	to criticize or disparage someone
put (someone) on	to mislead someone, especially in a joking way
recollect	to remember
re-collect	to collect again
sail	fabric that catches the wind to propel a boat (noun); to ride in a boat, especially one that is wind-powered (verb)
sale	a discounted offering; the act of selling
stationary	not moving
stationery	writing materials
talk to	to address others
talk with	to converse together
viral	having to do with a virus
virile	manly
whose	of which; of who
who's	who is
your	belonging to you
you're	you are

SPELLING GUIDELINES

Many words in American English are spelled just as they sound. That is, a long *a* sound is often spelled with an *a*. Aside from the old saw "*i* before *e* except after *c*, unless sounded as *a* as in *neighbor* and *weigh*," there are few easy ways of remembering the intricacies of correct spelling. The following table shows the ways in which various sounds common in English words can be spelled.

Sound	Spellings
a	sat, meringue, salmon, laugh
ah	father, aunt, calm, sergeant, Afrikaans
aw	saw, caught, order, ought, walk
ay	fade, aerobic, plain, cay, break, neigh, whey, regime
ch	cello, chip, question, nature
e	any, guess, leopard, friend, bread
ee	me, see, lea, ski, either, Aesop, very, believe, phoenix
er	earth, jerk, stir, turn, author, martyr
f	fall, telephone, rough
ih	hit, English, women, busy, cabbage, build, carriage, sieve
i	ice, sly, geyser, high, buy, die, papaya, eye
j	jam, ledge, tragedy
k	kelp, character, slack, acre, aqua, account
n	nap, know, pneumonia, gnaw
oh	bone, oat, soul, oh, folk, brooch, crow, though, bureau, load
oo	do, loo, blew, sue, you, cruise
ow	cow, bough, sauerkraut, found
sh	push, ocean, chauffeur, special, fascist, tissue, compulsion, nation, vicious, noxious, nauseous, sure
uh	up, oven, trouble, was, does
v	love, of
z	xylophone, zebra, visible
zh	regime, division, brazier

COMMONLY MISSPELLED WORDS

abscess
accept/except
accessory
accidentally
accommodate
accompany
accrue
acknowledgment
acquaintance
acquire
address
affect/effect
aisle/isle
allege

all right
already
amateur
analogous
antarctic
antecedent
apparent
appearance
arctic
argument
arithmetic
asparagus
asthma
athletic

attendance
attorney
auxiliary

banana
baptize
bargain
battalion
bazaar
beginning
believe
benign
biscuit
bizarre
bookkeeper

buoyant
bureau
burglar

calendar
cantaloupe
capital/capitol
cashmere
caterpillar
ceiling
cellar
cemetery
cereal/serial
chamois
chandelier

changeable
chaperon(e)
chauffeur
chief
cinnamon
circuit
circumference
cocoa
colonel/kernel
commitment
committee
compliment/
    complement
comptroller

concede
conceive
conscientious
conscious
consensus
consignment
convenient
coquette
corduroy
correspondent
cough
counterfeit
crucifixion

debt
definite
dependent
design
desirable
desperately
dessert/desert
devise
diaphragm
diarrhea
dictionary
diphtheria
disappear
disappoint
dispel
dissatisfied

effect/affect
eighth
embarrass
embezzle
environment
equipped
erroneous
especially
etiquette
exaggerate
exceed
excel
existence
expense

familiar
fascinate

fatigue
February
fiancé
fiancée
financier
foreclosure
forehead
foreign
foreword/forward
formerly/formally
forth/fourth
forty
fragile
freight

gauge
gingham
glacier
government
grammar
grease
guarantee
guess
guest

handkerchief
harass
height
heir
hemorrhage
hygiene
hypocrisy

idol/idle
incite/insight
independence
indict
indispensable
infinitesimal
irresistible
isthmus
its/it's

judgment

khaki

laboratory
larynx

laugh
league
library
license
licorice
literature
lose/loose
lying

mackerel
maintenance
malign
maneuver
manual
mathematics
mattress
medicine
minuscule
mischief
missionary
misspell
misstate
molasses
mortgage
mosquitoes

necessary
neighbor
niece
noticeable
nuisance

obedience
occasion
occur
occurred
occurrence
o'clock
offense
omitted

parallel
parliament
perseverance
phenomenon
physician
plaid
pneumonia

politically
porcelain
possess
potatoes
prairie
precede/proceed
preferred
principle/principal
privilege
probably
protégé
protégée
pseudonym
psychology
ptomaine

quiet/quite

rarefy
raspberry
receipt
receive
recess
recognize
recommend
reference
remittance
rendezvous
repellent
repentance
reservoir
résumé
reverence
rhythm
ridiculous

sacrilege
sacrilegious
sandwich
satire/satyr
scissors
secretary
seize
separately
siege
sieve
similar
sincerely

soliloquy
special
squirrel
stationary/
    stationery
straight/strait
strengthen
succeed
success
suit/suite
superintendent
supersede
susceptible
synagogue
syringe

tariff
temperance
tenement
than/then
their/there/they're
threshold
to/too/two
tobacco
tomatoes
tragedy
transferred
truly
Tuesday

usually

vaccinate
vacuum
villain
vinegar

warrant
Wednesday
weird
wholly
whose/who's
withhold

yolk
your/you're

zephyr

No other words in the English language rhyme with the words month, orange, silver, *or* purple.

Go to "American English and British English: Punctuation Differences" in chapter 14

Alphabets

PHONETIC SYMBOLS

VOWELS

iy	beat	ʌ	but	
ɪ	bit	ə	banana, sister	
ɛ	bet	aɪ	by	
æ	bat	aʊ	bound	
ɑ	box, car	ɔɪ	boy	
ɔ	bought, horse	ɝ	burn	
oʷ	bone	ɪər	beer	
ʊ	book	ɛər	bare	
uʷ	boot	ʊər	tour	

CONSONANTS

ŋ	velar nasal—si**ng**
θ	dental fricative—**th**ing
ð	dental fricative—**th**is
ʃ	postalveolar fricative—**sh**ort
ʒ	postalveolar fricative—mea**s**ure
tʃ	palatal fricative—it**ch**
dʒ	palatal fricative—**j**ust
ɹ	dental/alveolar/postalveolar approximant—bi**r**d
ɺ	retroflex tap (or flap)—wri**t**er
ʔ	glottal plosive—pause between vowels in co**op**erate

AMERICAN ENGLISH AND BRITISH ENGLISH: SPELLING AND NAME DIFFERENCES

It has been said that the United States and Great Britain are two nations divided by a single language. This is true in a number of ways. In the first place, spellings of the same words can be decidedly different. The following list shows some common examples of the variances between American and British spellings.

American	British
center	centre
check (money)	cheque
color	colour
curb	kerb
defense	defence
gray	grey
honor	honour
inquire	enquire
jail	gaol
jewelry	jewellery
labor	labour
organization	organisation
pajamas	pyjamas
peddler	pedlar

American	British
pretense	pretence
program	programme
realize	realise
recognize	recognise
theater	theatre

The two versions of the English language also diverge when it comes to the names for many everyday objects and events. It is easy for a visitor from across the Atlantic to provoke amusement from the natives by calling a cloth used to wipe one's mouth a *napkin* in England, or by asking an American waiter for the *W.C.* The following is a list of some common American terms and their counterparts in the United Kingdom.

American	British
apartment	flat
bathroom	toilet, W.C., or loo
Big Dipper	the Plough
candy	sweets
checkers	draughts
closet	cupboard
corn	maize
cracker	biscuit
diaper	nappy
drugstore	chemist's
elevator	lift
faucet	tap
gas, gasoline	petrol
hood (of car)	bonnet
line	queue
napkin	serviette
oven	cooker
round-trip ticket	return ticket
suspenders	braces
truck	lorry
trunk (of car)	boot
underpass	subway
undershirt	vest
vacation	holiday

DIACRITICAL MARKS

´	acute accent (as in *café*)
˘	breve (pronunciation symbol that indicates a short vowel)
¸	cedilla (as in (*François*)
^	circumflex (as in *château*)
¨	diaeresis or umlaut (as in *Köln*)
`	grave accent (as in *à la carte*)
¯	macron (pronunciation symbol that indicates a long vowel)
˜	tilde (as in *São Tomé*)

THE INDO-EUROPEAN FAMILY OF LANGUAGES

"CENTUM" LANGUAGES

"SATEM" LANGUAGES

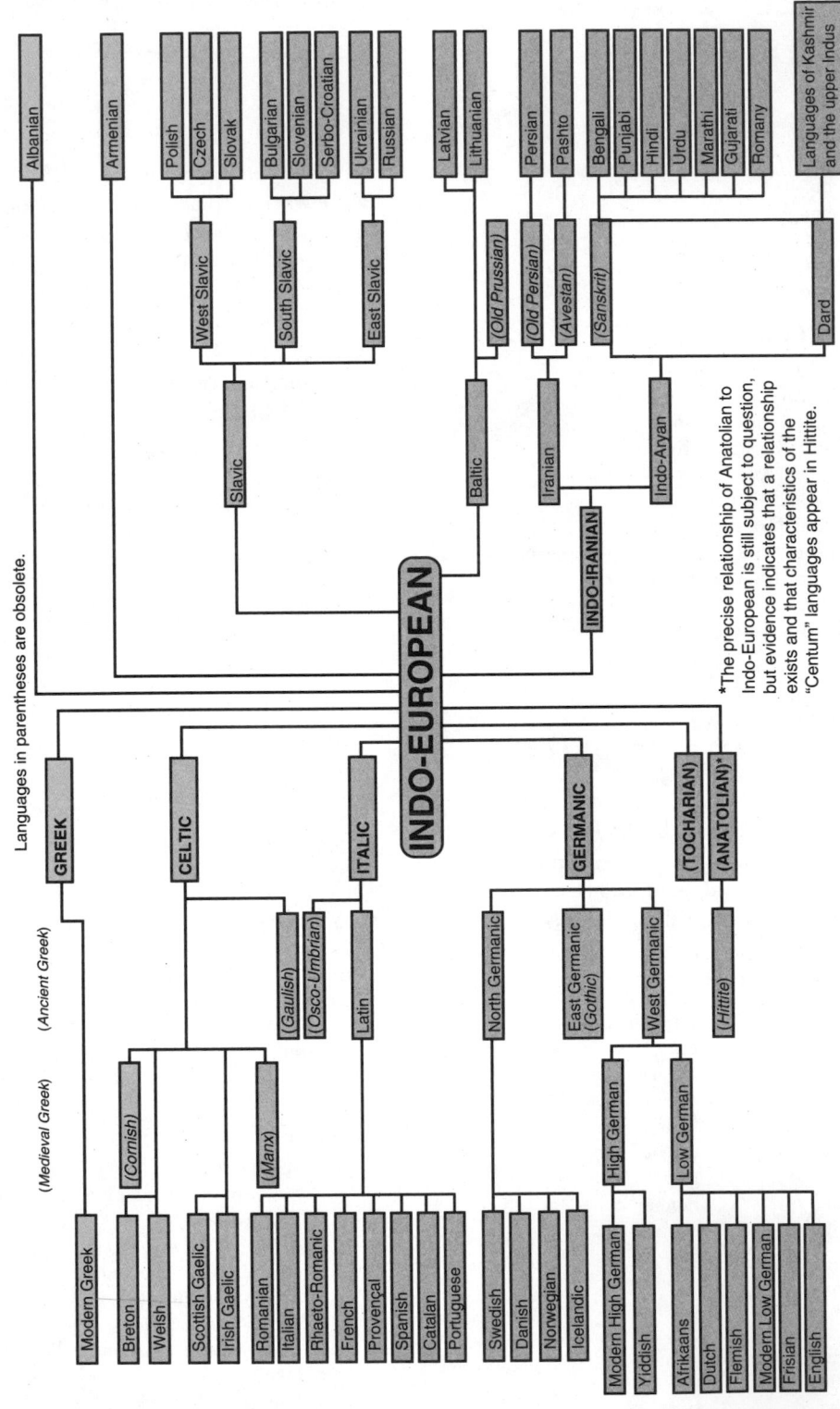

Languages in parentheses are obsolete.

*The precise relationship of Anatolian to Indo-European is still subject to question, but evidence indicates that a relationship exists and that characteristics of the "Centum" languages appear in Hittite.

Alphabets

FREQUENTLY USED FOREIGN WORDS AND PHRASES

KEY TO ABBREVIATIONS

A	Arabic	Gr	German	It	Italian	Sp	Spanish
Fr	French	H	Hebrew	L	Latin	R	Russian
Gk	Greek	Hw	Hawaiian	lit.	literally	Y	Yiddish

Word/Phrase	Meaning
à bas (Fr)	down with
ab initio (L)	from the beginning
ab ovo usque ad mala (L)	from soup to nuts (lit., "from the egg to the apples")
ab urbe condita (L)	from the founding of the city (Rome, 753 B.C.)
a cappella (It)	in the church style (vocally)
adagio (It)	slowly
ad astra per aspera (L)	to the stars through difficulties
ad eundum (L)	to the same degree
ad hoc (L)	for a particular purpose (lit., "to this")
ad infinitum (L)	without end
ad libitum (L)	ad lib, freely (lit., "to pleasure")
ad nauseam (L)	to the point of disgust
aere perennius (L)	more durable than bronze
aficionado (Sp)	enthusiast, fan
alea jacta est (L)	the die is cast
alfresco (It)	in the open air
allegro (L)	fast, lively
alma mater (L)	old school (lit., "fostering mother")
aloha (Hw)	greeting or farewell
amor con amor se paga (Sp)	one good turn deserves another (lit., "love is repaid with love")
amor vincit omnia (L)	love conquers all
ancien régime (Fr)	the old regime (pre–French revolution)
anno domini; A.D. (L)	in the year of the Lord
annus mirabilis (L)	wonderful year
a posteriori (L)	inductive (lit. "from what comes after")
après moi, le déluge (Fr)	after me, the deluge
a priori (L)	deductive (lit., "from what comes before")
arma virumque cano (L)	I sing of arms and the man (Virgil)
ars gratia artis (L)	art for art's sake
ars longa, vita brevis (L)	art is long, life is short
au contraire (Fr)	on the contrary
au courant (Fr)	up to date, contemporary
au naturel (Fr)	nude, plain
aurea mediocritas (L)	golden mean
autre temps, autre mœurs (Fr)	other times, other customs
avant-garde (Fr)	forward, advanced; vanguard
ave atque vale (L)	hail and farewell
beau geste (Fr)	noble gesture
beau idéal (Fr)	highest ideal
bête noire (Fr)	someone or something strongly detested (lit., "black beast")
billet doux (Fr)	love letter
Blitzkrieg (Gr)	lightning war
bon marché (Fr)	inexpensive (lit., "good market")
bon mot (Fr)	clever turn of phrase
bonne chance (Fr)	good luck

Word/Phrase	Meaning
bon vivant (Fr)	partygoer; one who enjoys life
bon voyage (Fr)	good journey
campesino (Sp)	peasant, farmer
canard (Fr)	insult, hoax (lit., "duck")
carpe diem (L)	seize the day
carte blanche (Fr)	free hand, no restrictions (lit., "white card")
cause célèbre (Fr)	scandal; notorious incident
caveat emptor (L)	let the buyer beware
c'est la vie (Fr)	that's life
ceteris paribus (L)	other things being equal
chacun á son gout (Fr)	each to his own taste
chef d'œuvre (Fr)	masterpiece
cherchez la femme (Fr)	look for the woman
chutzpah (Y)	gall, daring
ciao (It)	good-bye, so long
circa (c., ca.) (L)	about, approximately
cogito ergo sum (L)	I think, therefore I am
cognoscenti (It)	intellectuals; those in the know
comédie de mœurs (Fr)	comedy of manners
comme ci comme ça (Fr)	so-so, neither good nor bad
comme il faut (Fr)	proper, appropriate
con mucho gusto (Sp)	with pleasure
corpus delicti (L)	evidence (lit., "body of the crime")
coup de grâce (Fr)	final blow
coup d'état (Fr)	overthrow of government
cui bono? (L)	to whose benefit?
cul de sac (Fr)	dead end (lit., "end of the bag")
cum grano salis (L)	with a grain of salt
de capo (It)	from the top
déclassé (Fr)	fallen in social standing
décolletage (Fr)	low-cut style
de facto (L)	in fact
de gustibus non est disputandum (L)	there is no arguing about taste
de jure (L)	in law
demimonde (Fr)	underworld; other side of the tracks
de mortuis nil nisi bonum (L)	of the dead [say nothing] but good
Deo gratias (L)	thanks be to God
Deo volente (L)	God willing
dernier cri (Fr)	the last word
déshabillé (Fr)	carelessly or scantily dressed
deus ex machina (L)	desperate or contrived solution (lit., "god from the machine")
dolce far niente (It)	sweet idleness
Doppelgänger (Gr)	phantom double
Drang nach Osten (Gr)	drive toward the east
dum spiro spero (L)	while there's life, there's hope
élan vital (Fr)	vital force
embarras de richesses (Fr)	embarrassment of riches
enfant terrible (Fr)	prodigy
en passant (Fr)	in passing; by the way
entre nous (Fr)	privately, between us
épater le bourgeois (Fr)	shock the middle class
e pluribus unum (L)	from many, one
ersatz (Gr)	fake, imitation
et cetera (etc.) (L)	and others

Word/Phrase	Meaning
Eureka! (Gk)	I've found it!
ex cathedra (L)	with high authority (lit., "from the chair")
exempli gratia (e.g.) (L)	by way of example
ex post facto (L)	after the fact
fait accompli (Fr)	accomplished fact
faute de mieux (Fr)	for want of something better
faux pas (Fr)	social error (lit., "false step")
femme fatale (Fr)	alluring, dangerous woman
fin de siècle (Fr)	end of century; decadent
flagrante delicto (L)	caught in the act (lit., "with the crime blazing")
gaudeamus igitur (L)	let us therefore rejoice
glasnost (R)	openness
gnothi seauton (Gk)	know yourself
gonif (Y)	thief
goy (Y)	gentile
habeas corpus (L)	writ requiring a court appearance (lit., "[that] you have the body")
haut monde (Fr)	high society
hoi polloi (Gk)	common people, mob
homo lupus homini (L)	man is a wolf to man
honi soi qui mal y pense (Fr)	shame to him who thinks evil of it
hubris (Gk)	overweening pride, arrogance
idée fixe (Fr)	fixed idea, obsession
id est (i.e.) (L)	that is
infra dignitatem (infra dig.) (L)	beneath one's dignity
in loco parentis (L)	in the place of parents
in medias res (L)	in the middle of things
in vino veritas (L)	in wine, truth
ipso facto (L)	by the fact itself
joie de vivre (Fr)	good spirits, exuberance (lit., "joy of living")
jus gentium (L)	law of nations
kamikaze (J)	suicide pilot (lit., "divine wind")
klutz (Y)	clumsy person
kvetch (Y)	complain, carp
la belle dame sans merci (Fr)	the beautiful woman without mercy
laissez-faire (Fr)	noninterference (lit., "let [people] do [as they wish]")
lapsus linguae (L)	slip of the tongue
Lebensraum (Gr)	living room; elbow room
lèse majesté (Fr)	treason
l'état, c'est moi (Fr)	I am the state
lingua franca (L)	common language (lit., "French tongue")
macher (Y)	big shot
magnum opus (L)	major work
mañana (Sp)	tomorrow
manqué (Fr)	failed
maven (Y)	expert, authority
mazel tov (Y)	congratulations
mea culpa (L)	my fault
memento mori (L)	reminder of death
mens sana in corpore sano (L)	a sound mind in a sound body
meshuggah (Y)	crazy
mirabile dictu (L)	amazingly (lit., "remarkable to say")
modus operandi (M.O.) (L)	method of operation
morituri te salutamus (L)	we who are about to die salute you
mutatis mutandis (L)	with the needed changes made

Alphabets

Word/Phrase	Meaning
ne plus ultra (L)	the best
n'est-ce pas? (Fr)	isn't that true?
noblesse oblige (Fr)	the responsibility of noble birth
nom de plume (Fr)	pen name
non sequitur (L)	something that does not follow
nosh (Y)	nibble, eat
nota bene (N.B.) (L)	note well
nunc aut nunquam (L)	now or never
obiter dictum (L)	something said in passing; a peripheral comment
o tempora, o mores! (L)	o the times, o the customs!
panem et circenses (L)	bread and circuses
par excellence (Fr)	above all, preeminently
par exemple (Fr)	for example
pari passu (L)	at an equal pace
parvenu (Fr)	newcomer, upstart; noveau riche
passim (L)	here and there
per diem (L)	by the day
per favore (It)	please
persona non grata (L)	unwanted person
pièce de résistance (Fr)	showpiece item
pied à terre (Fr)	in-town apartment; temporary lodging
plus ça change, plus c'est la même chose (Fr)	the more things change, the more they are the same
pons asinorum (L)	insoluble problem (lit., "bridge of asses")
por favor (Sp)	please
prego (It)	please; you're welcome
prima facie (L)	on the face of it; at first sight
primus inter pares (L)	first among equals
prix fixe (Fr)	fixed price
pro bono publico (L)	for the public good
que será será (Sp)	what will be will be
quid pro quo (L)	fair exchange; tit for tat
quién sabe? (Sp)	who knows?
quod erat demonstrandum (Q.E.D.) (L)	as has been demonstrated
quod vide (q.v.) (L)	which see (used as cross-reference)
raison d'être (Fr)	reason for being
rara avis (L)	rarity (lit., "rare bird")
reductio ad absurdum (L)	reduction to absurdity (in logical argument)
répondez s'il vous plaît (R.S.V.P.) (Fr)	respond if you please
requiescat in pace (R.I.P.) (L)	rest in peace
salaam aleicham (A)	peace
sancta sanctorum (L)	holy of holies
sangfroid (Fr)	aplomb; composure
savoir faire (Fr)	social savvy (lit., "to know what to do")
schadenfreude	pleasure taken in problems of others
schlemiel (Y)	unlucky person, loser
schmaltz (Y)	excessive sentimentality
schtick (Y)	gimmick; a performer's idiosyncracy
semper fidelis (L)	always faithful
shalom (H)	greeting or farewell (lit., "peace")
sic (L)	thus
sic semper tyrannis (L)	thus always to tyrants
sic transit gloria mundi (L)	thus passes the glory of the world

Alphabets

Word/Phrase	Meaning
sine qua non (L)	something indispensable (lit., "without which not")
sotto voce (It)	softly (lit., "in a soft voice")
status quo (L)	current state of affairs
Sturm und Drang (Gr)	storm and stress
sui generis (L)	one of a kind, unique
tabula rasa (L)	clean slate (lit., "erased tablet")
tant mieux (Fr)	all the better
tant pis (Fr)	all the worse
tempus fugit (L)	time flies
terra firma (L)	solid ground
terra incognita (L)	unknown territory
tête-à-tête (Fr)	intimate conversation (lit., "head to head")
tout de suite (Fr)	immediately
tout le monde (Fr)	everyone
tovarish (R)	comrade
trompe l'œil (Fr)	illusionary art or decor (lit., "fool the eye")
vade mecum (L)	handbook, guide (lit., "go with me")
vaya con Dios (Sp)	go with God
veni, vedi, vici (L)	I came, I saw, I conquered
verboten (Gr)	forbidden
verbum sapienti sat (L)	a word to the wise is enough
volte-face (Fr)	about-face, reversal
vox clamantis in deserto (L)	a voice crying in the desert
vox populi, vox Dei (L)	the voice of the people is the voice of God
Wanderjahr (Gr)	year of travel
Wanderlust (Gr)	desire to travel
Weltanschauung (Gr)	philosophy, outlook
Weltschmerz (Gr)	world-weariness (lit., "world pain")
Wunderkind (Gr)	prodigy
yenta (Y)	gossip or busybody
Zeitgeist (Gr)	spirit of the times

A Closer Look

Common Phrases in Major World Languages

English	French	German	Italian	Spanish	Chinese	Japanese
Hello/ good day	Bonjour	Guten Tag	Buon giorno	Hola/ Buenos días	Ni hao	Kon-nichiwa
Please	S'il vous plaît	Bitte	Per favore	Con su permiso/ por favor	Qíng	Douzo
Thank you	Merci	Danke	Grazie	Gracias	Xie xìe	Arigatou
Excuse me/ pardon me	Excusez-moi/ pardon	Entschuldigen Sie	Mi scusi	Discúlpeme	Qíng ràng	Gomennasai/ shitsurei shimasu
Yes	Oui	Ja	Sì	Sí	Shì	Hai
No	Non	Nein	No	No	Bú shì	Iie
Good-bye/ so long	Au revoir/ à bientôt	Auf Wiedersehen	Arrivederci	Adiós/ hasta la vista	Zài jiàn	Sayounara

Alphabets

GREEK PREFIXES AND SUFFIXES

PREFIXES

Prefix	Meaning in English	Prefix	Meaning in English	Prefix	Meaning in English
a	not	chole, cholo	bile	ergo	work
acantho	spiny, thorny	chondro	cartilage	erythro	red
acous	hearing	choreo	dance	ethno	race, nation
acro	top, tip	choro	country	eu	good
adeno	gland	chrom(at)o	color	ex	out
aero	air, gas	chrono	time	exo	outside, external
allo	other	chryso	gold	galacto	milk
amphi	both, around	cleisto	closed	gam(o)	copulation, together
amylo	starch	clino	slope	gastro	stomach
an	not	cocci	berry-shaped	geo	earth, land
ana	again, thorough, thoroughly	coela	stomach	geronto	old age
		conio	dust	glosso	tongue
andro	man	copro	excrement	gluc, glyc	sweet
anem(o)	wind	cosmo	universe	glypto,	carving
anthropo	man	cranio	skull	glyph	
anti	against	cryo	cold	gnath(o)	jaw
apo	away	crypto	hidden	gon(o)	reproduction (sexual)
arch(i)	chief	cteno	comb, rake		
arche(o), archae(o)	old, ancient	cymo	wave	grapho	writing
		cysto	bladder	gymno	nude, naked
arthro	joint	cyto	cell	gynec(o), gynaec(o)	woman
aster, astro	star	dactylo	finger		
atmo	vapor	deca	ten	haemato	blood
auto	self	dendro	tree	hagio	holy
azo	nitrogen	dermo, dermato	skin	halo	salt, sea
baro	weight			haplo	simple
batho, bathy	deep	deutero	second	hecto	hundred
		di(s)	apart	helico	spiral
biblio	book	dia	through	helio	sun
bio	life	dino	terrible	hema	blood
blepharo	eyelid	diplo	double	hemi	half
bracchio	arm	dodeca	twelve	hepato	liver
brachy	short	dyna, dynamo	force, power	hepta	seven
branchio	gills			hetero	different
broncho	throat	dys	evil, difficult	hexa	six
caco	evil	echino	spiny	histo	tissue
cardio	heart	ecto	outside, external	hodo	path, way
carpo	fruit	ef	out	holo	whole, complete
cath, cato	down, thorough, thoroughly	ele, em, en	in, into	homeo	similar, like
		encephalo	brain	homo	same
ceno	common	ennea	nine	hydro	water
cephalo	head	entero	gut	hyeto	rain
cero	wax	ento	inside, interior	hygro	wet
chilo	lip	entomo	insect	hylo	matter
chiro	hand	eo	dawn, early	hymeno	membrane
chloro	green	eph, epi	on	hyper	above

Prefix	Meaning in English	Prefix	Meaning in English	Prefix	Meaning in English
hypno	sleep	onto	being	pyo	pus
hypo	under	oo	egg	pyro	fire
hypso	high	ophio	snake	rheo	flow
hystero	womb	opthalm(o)	eye	rhino	nose
iatro	medicine	ornitho	bird	rhizo	root
ichthyo	fish	oro	mouth	sacchro	sugar
iso	equal	ortho	straight	sapro	decompose
kerato	horn	osteo	bone	sarco	flesh
kinesi,	movement	oto	ear	scato	excrement
kineto		oxy	sharp	schisto,	split
lepto	slender	pachy	thick	schizo	
leuko	white	paleo,	ancient, old	sclero	hard
litho	stone	palaeo		seleno	moon
logo	word, oral	pan	all	sidero	iron
lyo, lysi	dissolving	para	close, beside	somato	body
macro	large	patho	suffering, disease	speleo	cave
malaco	soft	pedo	child	spermato	seed
mega,	great	penta	five	sphygmo	pulse
megalo		peri	around, very	splanchno	guts
melano	black	petro	stone	stato	position
mero	part	phago	eating	stauro	cross
meso	middle	phlebo	vein	steno	short, narrow
meta	beyond, after,	phono	sound	stereo	solid
	changed	photo	light	stomato	mouth
metro	measure	phreno	brain	stylo	pillar
micro	small	phyco	seaweed	sy, syl,	with
miso	hatred	phyllo	leaf	sym, syn	
mono	one, single	phylo	species	tachy	rapid
morpho	shape	physio	nature	tauto	same
myelo	spinal cord	phyto	plant	tele	distant
mylo	fungus	picro	bitter	teleo	final
myo	muscle	piezo	pressure	telo	distant, final
necro	dead body	pleuro	side (of body)	thalasso	sea
neo	new	pluto	riches	thanato	death
nepho	cloud	pneumato	breath, spirit	theo	god
nephro	kidney	pneumo	lung	thermo	heat
neuro	nerve	polio	gray matter	thio	sulfur
noso	sickness	poly	many	toco	child, birth
noto	back (of body)	pro	before, forward	topo	place
nycto	night	proto	first	toxico	poison
octa, octo	eight	pseudo	false	trachy	rough
odonto	tooth	psycho	mind, spirit, soul	xeno	foreign
oligo	few	psychro	cold	zoo	living
ombro	rain	ptero	wing	zygo	double
oneiro	dream				

The Hawaiian alphabet has only 12 letters: the five vowels and the consonants H, K, L, M, N, P, *and* W.

SUFFIXES

Suffix	Meaning in English	Suffix	Meaning in English	Suffix	Meaning in English
algia	pain	iasis	disease	phany	manifestation
androus	man	iatrics, iatry	medical treatment	phobe, phobia	fear
archy	rule, government	itis	inflammation		
biosis	life	kinesis	movement	phone, phony	sound
blast	bud	lepsy	seizure, fit		
branch	gills	lith	stone	phyllous	leaf
carpous	fruit	logy	science of, list	phyte	plant
cele	hollow	lysise, lyte	dissolving	plasia, plasis	growth
cephalic, cephalous	head	machy	battle, fight		
		mancy, mantic	foretelling	plasm	matter
chrome	color			plast	cell
coccous	berry-shaped	mania(c)	craving	plegia	paralysis
cracy, crat	rule, government	mere, merous	part	plerous	wing
dendron	tree			rrhagia, rrhagic, rrhea	flow
derm	skin	meter, metry	measure		
drome, dromous	run (race)	morphic, morphous	shape	saur	lizard
emia	blood	mycete	fungus	scope, scopy	observation
gamy	marriage	nomy	science of, law of	sect, section	cutting
gen(ous), geny, gony	giving birth to, bearing	odont	tooth	soma, some	body
		odynia	pain	sophy	wisdom
gnathous	jaw	oid	like, similar	sperm, spermous	seed
gnomy, gnosis	knowledge	oma	tumor		
		opia	eye, sight	stichous	row
gon	angle	opsia	sight	stome, stomous	mouth
gonium	seed	opsis	appearance		
gram, graph(y)	writing	pathy	suffering, disease	taxis, taxy	order
		phage, phagous	eating	tomy	cutting
hedral, hedron	side, sided			trophy	feed
				tropous, tropy	turned

LATIN PREFIXES AND SUFFIXES

PREFIXES

Prefix	Meaning in English	Prefix	Meaning in English	Prefix	Meaning in English
a, abs	from	brevi	short	cruci	cross
ac, ad, af, ag, al, an, ap, as, at	to, toward	calci	lime	cupro	copper, bronze
		centi	hundred	de	not, down
		cerebro	brain	deci	tenth
alti, alto	high	cervico	neck	demi	half
ambi	both	circum	around	denti	tooth
ante	before	cirro	curl	di(s)	apart
api	bee	cis	near, on the near side of	digit(i)	finger
aqui	water	co, col, com, con,	with, thorough, thoroughly	dorsi, dorso	back (of body)
arbori	tree			e, ec, ef	out
audio	hearing	cor		equi	equal
avi	bird	contra	against	ex	out
bacci	berry	costo	rib	extra	outside, external

Prefix	Meaning in English	Prefix	Meaning in English	Prefix	Meaning in English
febri	fever	ob, oc	against	re	again
ferri, ferro	iron	octa, octo	eight	recti	straight
fissi	split	oculo	eye	reni	kidney
fluvio	river	of, op	against	retro	backward
gemmi	bud	oleo	oil	sacro	dedicated
igni	fire	omni	all	sangui	blood
il, im, in	not, against, in, into, on	oro	mouth	se	apart
		ossi	bone	sebi, sebo	fatty
inguino	groin	ovi, ovo	egg	septi	seven
inter	between	pari	equal	sidero	star
intra, intro	inside, interior	per	through, very	somni	sleep
ir	not, against, in, into, on	pinni	fin, web	spiro	breath
		pisci	fish	stelli	star
juxta	close, near, beside	plano	flat	sub, suc, suf, sum, sup	under
labio	lip	plumbo	lead (metal)		
lacto	milk	pluvio	rain		
ligni	wood	post	after	super, supra	above
luni	moon	pre	before	terri	land, earth
magni	great	preter	beyond	trans	through, on the far side of
mal(e)	bad, evil	primi	first		
multi	many	pro	for, forward	ultra	beyond
naso	nose	pulmo	lung	uni	one, single
nati	birth	quadri	four	vari(o)	different
nocti	night	quinque	five		

SUFFIXES

Suffix	Meaning in English	Suffix	Meaning in English	Suffix	Meaning in English
cidal, cide	kill	fugal, fuge	run away from	pennale	wing
fid	split	grade	walking	vorous	eating

COMMON CROSSWORD-PUZZLE WORDS

Certain words frequently appear in crossword puzzles. Following is a list of such words, particularly ones not used regularly in everyday speech. Many of these words will be recognized by avid crossword-puzzle solvers. People new to crosswords will find familiarity with the list helpful in checking and building a crossword vocabulary.

Word	Meaning	Word	Meaning	Word	Meaning
aalii	tree; wood	adit	mine entrance	Aire	French river
Aare	Swiss river	adze	shaping tool	ait	river island
abbé	monk; cleric	Aeolus	Greek god of wind	alae	winglike part
abele	white poplar	aga	Muslim chief	alar	winged
abet	aid; assist	agar	moss; culture medium	alef	Hebrew letter
abou	father (Arabic)	agee	awry; askew	alen	Danish length
acer	maple genus	agha	Muslim leader	Aleut	Alaskan Indian
Acre	Israeli city	agora	assembly	Alma	Crimean river
acta	deeds	Agra	site of Taj Mahal	aloe	bitter herb; lily
Adah	wife of Lamech	aile	winged (heraldry)	alop	askew
Adak	Alaskan island	Aino,	Japanese aborigine	ama	cup; candlenut
Adar	Jewish month	Ainu		amah	Oriental nurse

continues

Alphabets

Common Crossword–Puzzle Words, Continued

Word	Meaning	Word	Meaning	Word	Meaning
ameer	Arab chieftain	axil	leaf angle	cava	pepper shrub; vein
amir	Arab chieftain	axon	nerve-cell process	Cayuga	Iroquoian tribe
Amos	biblical prophet	Baal	god; idol	cere	wax; wrap
ana	collection; anthology	baft	astern	Ceres	grain goddess
anas	duck genus	Bahia	Brazilian state; bay	Clare	Irish county
ani	blackbird; cuckoo	baht	Siamese coin	Clio	muse of history
anil	indigo shrub	Baku	Caspian harbor	Comus	god of mirth
anile	old-womanish; feeble	Bali	Indonesian island	Coos	Oregon tribe
anion	ion; particle	Balt	Lett; Lithuanian	copa	Spanish measure
anise	fragrant seed	banc	judge's bench	cor	heart; brightest star
anoa	wild Celebes ox	bane	evil; scourge	corium	dermis; layer
ans	Belgian commune	bani	Romanian money	cos	lettuce
ansa	loop; handle	Bann	Irish river	Cree	Indian tribe
ante	poker stake; before	Barre	Vermont city	Crimea	Russian peninsula
anti	opposed	Baya	Bantu tribe	cuir	leather (French)
A one	first-rate; tops	Beda	Arabian city	cull	choose; assort
apa	wallaba tree	beka	biblical money;	cuya	Cuban timber tree
apis	bee; Egyptian sacred		Hebrew weight	dace	carplike fish
	bull	Belem	Brazilian city	Dade	Florida county
apod	footless	Benares	Indian city	dado	groove
Apollo	sun god	Bera	Arabian city	Dail	Irish parliament
Aral	Soviet sea	berm	bank; lodge	daler	Dutch money
Aran	Irish island	Berne	Swiss city	Davos	Swiss resort
Ares	Greek god of war	bes	ancient Roman weight	Dee	English river
aria	opera solo	besa	Abyssianian money	dhai	midwife
aril	seed covering	besant	old French money	dhak	East Indian dye tree
artel	union; cooperative	bezant	circle (heraldry)	dhal	lentil
arum	cuckoopint; flowerin	bhar	Indian weight	dhan	cattle; property
	plant	bilk	cheat	dhow	Oriental sailing ship
Asgard	abode of Norse gods	binh	Annam weight	dinar	Bulgarian or Yugoslav
Astarte	Phoenician love goddess	bisse	snake (heraldry)		money
atap	palm; nipa	Blanc	peak in Alps	dop	diamond holder
ates	sweetsop	boa	feathered scarf; con-	dopp	dip
Atka	Aleutian tribe		strictor	Duma	Russian council
atle	Tamarisk salt tree	bole	friable clay	durn	gatepost
Atli	Norse king	bolo	knife; machete	dyad	pair
Aton	Egyptian solar deity	Bonn	West German city	Dyak	Borneo tribe
atri	Italian commune	brae	Scottish hillside	dyne	unit of force
Attica	Greek district; New	brut	dry wine	ebon	black
	York State prison	cabal	secret group; junta	Edda	Icelandic saga; Norse
Attu	Alaskan island	Caen	French city		prose
Aude	French river	Caddo	Indian tribe	ede	Dutch commune
Auk	diving bird	cadi	Muslim judge	Eder	German river
aune	French length	Cain	Abel's brother	Edo	Tokyo
aux	French commune	calp	limestone	Eger	German river
avav	pepper shrub; hum-	cam	gear	Ela	highest note; Guido's
	mingbird	Carib	South American		note
avocet	bird; plover		Indian	Elam	biblical kingdom
awn	beard on grain	carr	pool	élan	dash; ardor

A Closer Look

Oxymoron: A Pairing of Contradictory or Incongruous Words

bittersweet	home office	passive aggressive
clearly confused	jumbo shrimp	randomly organized
cruel kindness	linear curve	same difference
definite maybe	liquid gas	sweet sorrow
eloquent silence	nonalcoholic beer	taped live
idiot savant	nondairy creamer	war games
genuine imitation	old news	working vacation
good grief	open secret	

Word	Meaning	Word	Meaning	Word	Meaning
Elbe	German river	Faroe	Danish islands	grao	Portuguese weight
Elia	Lamb pen name; Kazan	fass	Austrian measure	gulden	Dutch money
		faun	satyr; Roman half goat	Hades	Greek underworld
Elul	Jewish month	Faunus	rural deity	hadj	pilgrimage
emir	Muslim chieftain	fels	Indian money	haft	handle
emu	ostrichlike bird	fete	festival	ha ha	laugh; sunken fence
Enna	Sicilian city	fiat	command; decree	haka	dance
Enns	Austrian river	fief	feudal estate	Hamar	city in Norway
Enos	Seth's son	fils	son (French)	Hamite	biblical tribe
ente	grafted (heraldry)	flak	antiaircraft bursts	Han	river in China
ento	inner (prefix)	flan	custard	hart	stag
Enyo	Ares' mother	flay	skin	hemo	blood (prefix)
Eolus	Colorado mountain	fosse	moat; pit	Hera	queen goddess
epee	fencing blade	Frey	Norse god	Herat	Afghanistan city
ephah	Hebrew measure	Frigg	Odin's wife	Hermes	Greek god
epi	finial; spire	gad	rove	Herod	biblical ruler
Erda	Norse earth goddess	Gael	Celt	Herr	Mister (German)
eri	silkworm	gam	mouth; leg	Hesse	German state
Eris	goddess of discord	gaol	prison	Hilo	Hawaiian city
Erlau	Hungarian commune	gar	needle fish	hin	Hebrew measure
ern	sea eagle	gard	French department	Hiram	biblical ruler
erne	sea eagle; Irish river	gare	railway station (French)	hiro	Japanese length
Erse	Gaelic			Hler	Norse god
esker	glacial ridge	Gaspé	Canadian peninsula	hoar	frost
esne	serf	gata	shark	hod	brick tray; coal scuttle
esse	existence; abstract being	Gaza	biblical city	Hood	Oregon mountain
		Gerd	Frey's wife	hora	Israeli dance
Este	Italian commune	Geri	Odin's wolf	Horeb	biblical mountain
Estes	Colorado park	ghat	range; pass	Hosea	biblical prophet
estop	prevent by law	gila	lizard	Hoth	Norse god
et al.	and others (Latin abbreviation)	Gilead	biblical mountain	huk	Philippine guerrilla
		gnu	antelope; wildebeest	hula	Hawaiian dance
etui	vanity case; needle case	Goa	former Portuguese colony	Hun	barbarian; vandal
evoe	bacchanals' cry			Hydra	nine-headed monster
ewer	pitcher	Golo	Bantu tribe	iamb	verse foot
exe	English river	Goshen	biblical land of plenty	ibex	wild goat
fane	temple	gowl	monster	ibid.	same place (abbreviation)
fanon	cape; orale	gradus	ancient Roman length		
faro	card game	graf	German count	ibis	wading bird

Alphabets

continues

A
Closer
Look

Palindromes

A palindrome can be a single word, a verse, a sentence, a series of sentences, or a number that reads the same forward and backward. People have been creating palindromes in all languages since at least as early as the third century B.C. Palindromic sentences often become jokes when meanings are ascribed to them and when punctuation is added. For example, the two best-known English palindromes are "Able was I ere I saw Elba," which was not written by but could have been uttered by Napoleon, and "Madam, I'm Adam," which is fun to think of as the first introduction. Note that "madam" alone is a palindromic word, but sentences are more amusing:

Enid and Edna dine.
A man, a plan, a canal, Panama!
Draw, O Caesar, erase a coward.

Al lets Dell call Ed Stella.
Dennis sinned.
Ma is a nun, as I am.

Naomi, did I moan?
Niagara, O roar again!
He lived as a devil, eh?

And here is a palindromic conversation between two owls:

"Too hot to hoot!"
"Too hot to woo!"
"Too wot?"
"Too hot to hoot!"
"To woo!"
"Too wot?"
"To hoot! Too hot to hoot!"

Common Crossword–Puzzle Words, Continued

Word	Meaning	Word	Meaning	Word	Meaning
Ibo	West African tribe	itea	Virginia willow	Kano	Nigerian walled city
ici	here (French)	ixia	iris	kaph	Hebrew letter
icon	religious image	jako	parrot	Kara	Arabian sea
Ida	Asia Minor range; Crete mountain	jama	tunic	kava	Polynesian beverage
		jami	mosque	kawa	Pepper shrub
Idas	killer of Castor	jann	genie	kela	Arabian weight
ideo	idea (prefix)	jara	palm	keno	lotto; bingolike game
ides	Roman date	Jebu	West African tribe	Kent	English county
iglu	Eskimo hut	Jehu	biblical ruler	kepi	military cap
ilex	holly	Jena	German city	kerf	notch
ilia	hipbones	jeté	ballet jump	khat	Turkish length
imam	caliph	jhow	Tamarisk shrub	Kiel	German canal
immi	Swiss measure	jib	triangular sail	Kiev	Russian city
Indus	Indian river	jilt	cheat; reject	kil	monk's cell; Irish church; kilometer (abbreviation)
inee	arrow poison	jinn	demon		
Inez	Don Juan's mother	Joad	English philosopher		
Inga	shrub genus	Joshua	biblical ruler	kiln	oven
Iole	Hercules' captive	Jove	chief Roman god	Kiowa	Indian tribe
Iona	Scottish isle	juba	African dance	kipe	basket
Ionia	Asia Minor district	Jung	psychiatrist	kiri	Kaffir war club
iota	Greek letter; bit	Juno	Roman queen of gods	kiwi	flightless bird
Irra	Babylonian god	junu	charm	Kobe	Honshu port
Isar	Bavarian river	jura	French department	Koko	Lord High Executioner
Iser	Czech river	kabul	Indian river	kola	nut
Isere	French river	kadi	judge	kopek	Russian money
Isis	Egyptian goddess; sister and wife of Osiris	Kafir	Bantu tribe	koss	Indian length
		kana	Japanese writing	kraal	enclosure

Alphabets

Word	Meaning	Word	Meaning	Word	Meaning
kris	dagger	marl	clay-filled soil	nipa	drink; East Indian palm
Krishna	Hindu god	Maui	Hawaiian island		
krona	Icelandic money	Mayo	Irish county; mayonnaise	oast	kiln; oven
Kronos	Titan			obi	Oriental sash
kudu	African antelope	Mede	ancient Persian	obit	death notice
Kurd	Turkish tribe	Medusa	Gorgon	oca	edible tuber
kvas	Russian sour beer	mega	great (prefix)	octo	eight (prefix)
lac	resin	meld	declare, in cards	oda	harem room
lact	milk (prefix)	Melos	Aegean island	odea	music hall
Lagos	capital of Nigeria	merl	blackbird	Order	Baltic river
lait	milk (French)	Metz	French city	oeuf	egg (French)
lama	Buddhist monk; Tibetan priest	mil	wire measure	ogee	arch; molding
		Milo	Greek Island	okie	migratory worker
Lamech	biblical patriarch	Minos	Greek king	okra	gumbo
lar	gibbon	moa	flightless bird; ostrich	ola	palm leaf
lath	strip of wood	Moab	biblical tribe	olay	palm leaf
lave	bathe	moho	honey-eating bird	olio	medley
lea	meadow	mohr	gazelle	olla	jar; meat dish
Leda	Castor's mother; swan	mojo	voodoo charm	Olor	swan genus
lees	dregs	moki	New Zealand raft	Omei	China mountains
Lena	Asian river	Moro	Philippine Muslim	omni	all (prefix); Atlanta arena
Lenape	Indian tribe	Mors	Roman god of death		
Leto	Apollo's mother	Morta	goddess of fate	Omsk	Russian city
Levi	Jacob's son; Hebrew tribe	Muir	Alaska glacier	oner	individual; corker
		mumm	disguise	onus	burden
Leyte	Pacific island	nacre	mother-of-pearl	opah	colorful fish
libra	Mexican weight	nae	no (Scottish)	ope	unlock (poetic)
Lido	Adriatic resort	Nahor	biblical patriarch	orca	killer whale
limn	portray	naif	lustrous	Orel	Russian port
limu	edible seaweed	Namur	Belgian commune	orle	heraldic bearing
Linz	Austrian city	nard	anoint; spice	Orly	French airport
liss	fleur-de-lis	neap	tide	orne	French department
lobo	timber wolf	neb	beak; nose	ort	morsel; leftover
loch	Scottish lake	Nebo	biblical mountain	osier	willow tree
Loki	Norse god	née	born (French)	Ossa	Greek mountain
loup	half-mask (French)	Nene	English river; Hawaiian bird	otic	pertaining to the ear
luff	sail into wind			Otoe	Oklahoma tribe
Luna	moon goddess	nep	catnip	oyez	attention; court cry
Lys	Belgian river	Nereid	sea nymph	paal	Javanese length
Maas	Dutch river	ness	promontory	pac	boot, moccasin
mage	magician	Nestor	Greek king	paca	rodent
Maia	Hermes' mother	neve	glacier; snow	padre	priest; cleric
Main	German river	newt	eft	pala	Indian weight
mani	peanut	nez	nose (French)	palp	tentacle; feeler
mano	hand grinding stone	nimb	halo	Panay	Philippine island

continues

The word posh *is supposedly an acronym for "port outward, starboard home." The term was coined to describe how rich people, traveling by sea to the Indies, avoided getting the morning sun on their side of the ship.*

Alphabets

Common Crossword-Puzzle Words, Continued

Word	Meaning	Word	Meaning	Word	Meaning
pard	leopard	sari	Indian dress	tapa	bark cloth
parr	young fish	sego	edible bulb	Tara	Irish capital; plantation in *Gone With the Wind*
pas	dance step	sera	antitoxins; evening (Italian)		
pavis	shield; cover			tare	biblical weed; allowance
Pelée	Martinique volcano	serac	glacial ridge; white cheese	tarn	lake; pool
pelu	hardwood tree			taro	edible root
peri	fairy	sere	dry; parched	tat	make lace; crochet
phon	loudness	serif	part of printer's letter	tec	detective
phot	light unit	seta	bristle	tela	membrane; tissue
pica	type measure	Seth	biblical patriarch; Adam's son	tele	from a distance (prefix)
Pico	Azores volcano			tern	gull
rale	rattle; breathing noise	shay	carriage	Terra	earth goddess
Rama	incarnation of Vishnu	Shem	biblical patriarch	Thalia	one of the Graces
rame	branch	shiv	knife	Thetis	Achilles' mother
rana	Indian prince	Sikh	Hindu soldier	tia	aunt (Spanish)
rani	Indian queen	sine	trigonometry function	tic	spasm
rati	Indian weight	sire	lord; father; beget	tio	uncle (Spanish)
Remi	ancient people of Gaul	Siva	Hindu god	Tioga	New York county
rena	rockfish	skag	part of a ship's keel	toga	Roman cloak
ret	soak flax	skew	twist	tole	lacquered metalware
rete	network	Skye	Hebrides island	Toltec	Mexican tribe
Rhea	Titan; Cronus's wife	sloe	plum; blackthorn	tome	large volume
Rhus	sumac genus	Smee	Captain Hook's assistant; pintail duck	tong	Chinese secret society
ria	narrow inlet; estuary			tor	craggy hill; pea
rial	Iranian coin	snee	dirk; knife	tort	civil wrong
rien	nothing (French)	soir	evening (French)	torte	rich cake
Riga	Baltic city	Sol	sun god	tret	waste allowance
rime	frost	sora	marsh bird	Triton	Greek god of sea
ripa	riverbank	Spad	biplane; nail	Truk	Island in Carolines
rom	gypsy husband	Spes	Roman goddess of hope	tsar	Russian despot
rood	crucifix			tsun	Chinese length
Rosa	shrub genus	Sri	Hindu goddess	tun	vat; cask
Ross	Antarctic sea	SRO	box-office sign	tutu	New Zealand shrub, ballet skirt
roti	roasted (French)	stere	dry measure		
rotl	Muslim weight	stet	let it stand	tyro	novice
Ruhr	German river; industrial area	stile	wall step; set of steps	über	over (German)
		stoa	portico	uca	crab
rune	mysterious sign; old alphabet character	suet	hard fat	uke	ukulele
		Suva	Fiji capital	ule	rubber tree
rupee	Indian money	Taal	Afrikaans	ulex	spine shrub
Saar	European river	Tabor	biblical mountain	Ulm	German city
Sac	Algonquin Indian; pouch	tabu	forbidden	ulna	elbow bone
		tace	body armor	unde	wavy; lined (heraldry)
sago	starch; pudding	tael	Oriental weight	ungula	hoof; claw
samp	cereal; maize; pudding	tamp	pack; ram	Ural	Russian river; range
sans	without (French)	Taos	New Mexico town	Urd	Norse goddess of destiny

The word dude *was coined by Oscar Wilde and his friends. It is a combination of the words* duds *and* attitude.

Word	Meaning	Word	Meaning	Word	Meaning
urde	key-shaped (heraldry)	vivo	lively (music)	yaba	cabbage tree
Uri	Swiss commune	viz	namely	yak	ox
Uria	Bathsheba's husband	voce	voice (Italian)	Yalu	Korean river
ursa	bear	vole	rodent	yamp	tuber
urus	ox; aurochs	WAC	female GI	yapa	palm-leaf mat
Ute	Colorado Indian	Waco	Texas city	yegg	burglar
Utu	Babylonian god	wadd	black ocher	Yemen	Arabian state
uvea	iris layer	wadi	dry riverbed	yen	Japanese money; urge
uvic	grapelike	wale	cloth ridge	yin	Chinese weight
Vaal	South African river	wang	Dutch East Indies weight	Ymir	Norse giant
vair	heraldic tincture	weft	web; yarn	Yser	Belgian river
vale	valley; glen; farewell	weir	fish trap	zak	Dutch measure
vari	diverse (prefix)	wen	cyst; old English letter	zany	nutty; crazy
vasa	ducts	woad	dyestuff	Zara	Italian province
Veda	Hindu bible	Wodan	Norse god	zee	final letter; zed
vega	meadow	Woden	Norse god	Zen	Buddhist sect
veld	South African grassland	Wotan	Norse god	zero	nothing; cipher
Venus	Roman goddess of love	xema	Arctic gull	zeta	Greek letter
vert	green	Xenia	Ohio city	Zeus	chief Olympian god
Vesta	goddess of hearth	xeno	foreign (prefix)	Zion	hill; heaven
Vishnu	Hindu god	xeres	wine; sherry	Zulu	Bantu tribe
vita	life (Latin)	Xosa	Kaffir tribe	Zuni	Pueblo Indian
vite	quick (French)	Xtian	Christian	zwei	two (German)

There are nine different ways to pronounce the letters ough. *All are contained in the sentence "A rough-coated, dough-faced, thoughtful ploughman strode through the streets of Scarborough; after falling into a slough, he coughed and hiccoughed."*

Go to "94 Acceptable Two–Letter Scrabble® Words" in chapter 23

Alphabets

FOREIGN ALPHABETS

GREEK			ARABIC			HEBREW			CYRILLIC	
Forms	Name	Latin†	Form	Name	Latin†	Forms	Name	Latin†	Forms	Latin†
A α	alpha	a (ā)	ا	alif		א	aleph		А а	a
B β	beta	b	ب	bā	b	ב	beth	b	Б б	b
									В в	v
Γ γ	gamma	g, n	ت	tā	t	ג	gimel	g	Г г	g
Δ δ	delta	d	ث	thā	th	ד	daleth	d	Д д	d
E ε	epsilon	e	ج	jīm	j	ה	he	h	Е е	(y) e
Z ζ	zeta	zd, z	ح	ḥā	ḥ	ו	vav	v	Ж ж	zh
H η	eta	ē	خ	khā	kh	ז	zayin	z	З з	z
Θ θ	theta	th*	د	dāl	d	ח	het	ch (H)	И и Й й	j (i, ī)
I ι	iota	i	ذ	dhāl	dh	ט	teth	ṭ	К к	k
K κ	kappa	k	ر	rā	r	י	yod	y	Л л	l
Λ λ	lambda	l	ز	zāy	z	כ ך	kaf	k, ch	М м	m
M μ	mu	m	س	sīn	s	ל	lamed	l	Н н	n
N ν	nu	n	ش	shīn	sh	מ ם	mem	m	О о	o
Ξ ξ	xi	x	ص	sād	ṣ	נ ן	nun	n	П п	p
O o	omicron	o	ض	dād	ḍ	ס	samekh	s	Р р	r
Π π	pi	p	ط	tā	ṭ	ע	ayin	'	С с	s
P ρ	rho	r, hr	ظ	zā	ẓ	פ ף	pe	p, f	Т т	t
Σ σ ς	sigma	s	ع	'ayn	'	צ ץ	sadhe	ts	У у	u
T τ	tau	t	غ	ghayn	gh	ק	koph	q	Ф ф	f
Υ υ	upsilon	u (u, ü)	ف	fā	f	ר	resh	r	Х х	kh
Φ φ	phi	ph*	ق	qāf	q	שׂ	sin	ś	Ц ц	ts
X χ	chi	ch*	ك	kāf	k	שׁ	shin	sh	Ч ч	ch
Ψ ψ	psi	ps	ل	lām	l	ת	tav	t	Ш ш	sh
Ω ω	omega	ō	م	mīm	m				Щ щ	shch
			ن	nūn	n				Ъ ъ	"
			ه	hā	h				Ы ы	y
			و	wāw	w				Ь ь	'
			ي	yā	y				Э э	e
									Ю ю	yu
									Я я	ya

Gamma is transliterated as *n* when it precedes *kappa, xi, chi,* or another *gamma; upsilon* is transliterated as *u* when it is the final element in a diphthong. The *sigma* form ς is used only in final position.

*The letters *th, ph,* and *ch* represent strongly aspirated stops, *t, p,* and *k,* respectively.

The forms shown are of the letters in isolation. They may vary when used in words. The letter *alif* does not have a sound.

Pronunciation of vowels in letter names: *ā = a* in *father, ī = i* in *machine, ū = u* in *rule.*

The second form (and the second transliteration) of a letter when shown is used at the end of a word only. Vowels are shown by a system of subscript and superscript dots; the symbols shown are consonants. The letter *aleph* does not have a sound.

The Cyrillic alphabet is used for writing various Slavic languages, including Russian.

† The columns headed "Latin" show the letters used when these alphabets are transliterated into the Latin alphabet. The sounds represented by these letters are similar to the standard sounds in English. Diacritics indicate that the sound is somewhat different from the English sound represented by the letter shown; for any great difference the sound is shown in parentheses after the letter.

ADDITIONAL SOURCES OF INFORMATION

BOOKS

The American Heritage Book of English Usage. Houghton Mifflin, 1996.

Axtell, Roger E. *Dos and Taboos of Using English Around the World.* Wiley, 1995.

Ayto, John. *The Oxford Dictionary of Slang.* Oxford University Press, 2000.

Bonk, Mary Rose. *Acronyms, Initialisms, and Abbreviations Dictionary.* 27th ed. 3 vols. Gale, 2000.

Chapman, Robert L., et al., eds. *Dictionary of American Slang.* HarperCollins, 1998.

Chapman, Robert L., ed. *Roget's International Thesaurus.* 5th ed. HarperCollins, 1992.

The Chicago Manual of Style. 14th ed. University of Chicago Press, 1993.

Donadio, Stephen, et al., eds. *The New York Public Library Book of 20th Century American Quotations.* The Stonesong Press/Warner Books, 1992.

Edmunds, David. *The Oxford Reverse Dictionary.* Oxford University Press, 1999.

Ehrlich, Eugene. *The Highly Selective Dictionary for the Extraordinarily Literate.* HarperCollins, 1997.

———. *The Highly Selective Thesaurus for the Extraordinarily Literate.* HarperCollins, 1994.

———. *Veni Vidi Vici: Conquer Your Enemies, Impress Your Friends with Everyday Latin.* HarperPerennial, 1995.

Firmage, Richard. *Alphabet: The Story of One of Civilization's Greatest Inventions.* Bloomsbury, 2000.

Funk, Charles Earle. *A Hog on Ice and Other Curious Expressions.* HarperCollins, 1985.

Glazier, Stephen. *Word Menu.* Random House, 1998.

Heifetz, Josefa. *The Word Lover's Dictionary: Unusual, Obscure, and Preposterous Words.* Carol Publishing, 1996.

Hoad, T. F. *The Concise Oxford Dictionary of English Etymology.* Oxford University Press, 1993.

Jones, Daniel. *English Pronouncing Dictionary.* 15th ed. Cambridge University Press, 1997.

Kemp, Peter, consultant ed. *The Oxford Dictionary of Literary Quotations.* Oxford University Press, 2000.

Knowles, Elizabeth M., ed. *The Oxford Dictionary of Phrase, Proverb, and Quotation.* Oxford University Press, 1997.

Knowles, Elizabeth, and Julia Eliot. *The Oxford Dictionary of New Words.* Oxford University Press, 1999.

> *The word* facetiously *has all the vowels, including* y, *in order.*

Laird, Charlton, and the editors of Webster's New World dictionaries. *Webster's New World Thesaurus.* Macmillan, 1997.

Lighter, J. E. *Random House Dictionary of American Slang.* 2 vols. Random House, 1997.

McArthur, Tom. *The Concise Oxford Companion to the English Language.* Oxford University Press, 1998.

McCutcheon, Marc. *Descriptionary: A Thematic Dictionary.* 2nd ed. Facts on File, 2000.

Preston, Charles, and Barbara Ann Kipfer. *The USA Today Crossword Puzzle Dictionary.* The Stonesong Press/Hyperion, 1996.

Pulliam, Tom. *The New York Times Crossword Puzzle Dictionary.* Times Books, 1997.

Robinson, Andrew. *The Story of Writing.* Thames and Hudson, 1999.

Room, Adrian. *The Cassell Dictionary of Word Histories.* Cassell, 2000.

Strunk, William, Jr., and E. B. White. *The Elements of Style.* 4th ed. Macmillan, 1999.

Sutcliffe, Andrea, ed. *The New York Public Library Writer's Guide to Style and Usage.* The Stonesong Press/HarperCollins, 1994.

Alphabets

Urdang, Laurence. *The New York Times Dictionary of Misunderstood, Misused, and Mispronounced Words.* Black Dog and Leventhal, 2001.

Webster's New World College Dictionary. 4th ed. Simon & Schuster, 1999.

Zinsser, William. *On Writing Well: An Informal Guide to Writing Nonfiction.* 6th rev. ed. Harper-Collins, 1998.

WEB SITES

The CMU Pronouncing Dictionary
Maintained by Kevin Lonzo, Robotics Institute, Carnegie Mellon University.
http://www.speech.cs.cmu.edu/cgi-bin/cmudict

Evolution of Alphabets
The development of alphabets in animation.
http://www.wam.umd.edu/~rfradkin/alphapage.html

The Evolution of Languages
Exploratorium magazine site explains where languages come from.
http://www.exploratorium.edu/exploring/language

The King's English
Online edition (copyright by the Trustees of Columbia University) of the 2nd edition of the book by Henry Watson Fowler and Francis George Fowler (copyright 1908 by the Clarendon Press).
http://www.bartleby.com/116/101.html

Merriam-Webster Online
Includes a searchable dictionary and thesaurus and other helpful language information links (copyright Merriam-Webster).
http://www.m-w.com/

The World Wide Web Acronym and Abbreviation Server
A searchable database of acronyms and abbreviations.
http://www.ucc.ie/info/net/acronyms/acro.html

Yahoo!—Reference: Dictionaries: Language
List of links to online dictionaries in many languages (copyright by Yahoo! Inc.).
http://www.yahoo.com/Reference/Dictionaries/Language/

Alphabets

14

GRAMMAR AND PUNCTUATION

Writing is a slow, painstaking process, and like playing tennis or the violin, it requires practice, practice, practice. The purpose of writing—and this is obviously true of language itself—is to communicate ideas. To communicate effectively, writers follow the general concepts of grammar, putting words and sentences together in a customary manner so that they can be readily understood. A person can be a good writer without being an expert in grammar, but some knowledge of the rules of language usage can promote confidence in speech and writing and a better understanding of language as a tool for imparting information.

This is not to say that everyone must write the same sentence to communicate the same concept. On the contrary, American English is so varied that it is possible to express the same basic idea in any number of ways. And each of those ways can be equally correct.

A very difficult sentence to punctuate is That that is is that that is not is not. *The correct punctuation is:* That that is, is; that that is not, is not.

What makes a variety of different sentences equally valid is grammar. Grammar is a set of rules that defines the ways words can and cannot be used. These rules are not arbitrarily imposed on the language by English teachers or grammarians; they have, instead, grown out of the language itself and can be observed in action in the everyday speech and writing of those who grew up speaking and writing it.

Much of grammar is intuitive and can be understood by anyone who has spoken American English for any length of time, even without a knowledge of the rules. For instance, the sentence *You be not home go yet* is readily recognized as incorrect even without knowledge of the rules of word order.

But because American English is a complex and difficult language, it is sometimes helpful to have the rules at hand in case logic and intuition fail. What

follows, then, are the basics of grammar, spelling, punctuation, and alphabetization for American English. The information presented here is by no means exhaustive, and because language is a constantly changing thing, there can never be a "final word" as to what is correct and what is incorrect. As E.B. White wrote in his classic guide to writing well, *The Elements of Style*, "Writing is an act of faith, not a trick of grammar." Still, this guide should help provide a start in understanding grammar, usage, and punctuation.

THE PARTS OF SPEECH

The parts of speech define the ways words can be used in various contexts. Every word in the English language functions as at least one part of speech; many words can serve, at different times, as two or more parts of speech, depending on the context.

adjective   A word or combination of words that modifies a noun *(blue-green, central, half-baked, temporary).*

adverb   A word that modifies a verb, an adjective, or another adverb *(slowly, obstinately, much).*

article   Any of three words used to signal the presence of a noun. *A* and *an* are known as indefinite articles; *the* is the definite article.

conjunction   A word that connects other words, phrases, or sentences *(and, but, or, because).*

interjection   A word, phrase, or sound used as an exclamation and capable of standing by itself *(oh, Lord, damn, my goodness).*

noun   A word or phrase that names a person, place, thing, quality, or act *(Fred, New York, table, beauty, execution).* A noun may be used as the subject of a verb, the object of a verb, an identifying noun, the object of a preposition, or an appositive (an explanatory phrase coupled with a subject or object).

preposition   A word or phrase that shows the relationship of a noun to another noun *(at, by, in, to, from, with).*

pronoun   A word that substitutes for a noun and refers to a person, place, thing, idea, or act that was mentioned previously or that can be inferred from the context of the sentence *(he, she, it, that)*.

verb   A word or phrase that expresses action, existence, or occurrence *(throw, be, happen)*. Verbs can be transitive, requiring an object *(her* in *I met her)*, or intransitive, requiring only a subject *(The sun rises)*. Some verbs, like *feel,* are both transitive *(Feel the fabric)* and intransitive *(I feel cold,* in which *cold* is an adjective and not an object).

MODIFIERS

There are two basic types of modifiers: single-word modifiers, which are generally adverbs or adjectives; and phrases, which are usually introduced by prepositions. Modifiers should be placed as close as possible to the words they modify to ensure clarity.

Adjectives, which modify nouns, often precede the nouns they modify. They serve to restrict, characterize, or further define the nouns immediately following. Thus, *great* in the sentence *You did a great job* is an adjective modifying the noun *job*.

Nouns can also be used to modify nouns. They, too, appear immediately before the noun being modified, and only their position in the sentence indicates that they are acting as modifiers rather than nouns. The noun *telephone* works as a modifier of the noun *booth* when it appears in the phrase *a telephone booth*.

When two or more adjectives each modify the noun independently, they are separated by commas *(a silly, cheerful mood)*. When the first adjective modifies an idea expressed by the combination of the second adjective and the noun, no comma is used *(a pretty oil painting)*. In some cases, two or more adjectives are combined, often with a hyphen, so that they function as a single adjective. In these compound adjectives, the first term modifies the second, which modifies the noun *(a high-flying airplane)*.

Adverbs modify verbs, adjectives, or other adverbs or phrases. They can often be recognized by their characteristic *-ly* ending. When modifying verbs, adverbs generally appear immediately after the verbs *(quickly* in the sentence *He walked quickly through*

the room). When used to modify an adjective, the adverb will immediately precede the adjective *(a swiftly moving deer);* such compounds are not hyphenated.

In ancient Rome, authors did not punctuate their writing. It was up to the reader to insert the punctuation he felt was proper.

Phrases that modify nouns are often introduced by prepositions and immediately follow the nouns they modify. An example of a modifying phrase is *in the corner* in the sentence *The dog in the corner wagged her tail*. While useful in defining the nouns to which they are attached, modifying phrases are not as important to the sentence in the way a subject, verb, and object are. Such phrases can be essential or nonessential. In the sentence *The dog in the corner wagged her tail,* the phrase *in the corner* is essential because it identifies *which* dog wagged her tail. Clauses that modify nouns or pronouns contain a subject and a verb and can be either essential or nonessential. When they are introduced by relative pronouns (such as *who, what, that, which,* and *whose)*, they are known as relative clauses. An example is *who wants to know* in the sentence *Anyone who wants to know can get the information*. Relative clauses are also known as dependent clauses because they cannot stand alone.

SENTENCE STRUCTURE

Individual words, even once their parts of speech are identified, do not communicate very much by themselves. They must be combined in such a way that they can convey meaning. This is done by forming sentences that combine words that have meaning in and of themselves (nouns, verbs, adjectives, adverbs, and pronouns) with those that are solely functional (conjunctions, prepositions, interjections, and articles).

Three main types of sentences can be constructed from these parts. Statements are sentences that tell of a fact, an occurrence, or an opinion; they provide information *(My daughter is almost three years old)*. Questions are sentences that seek out information *(How old is your daughter?)*. Commands are sentences that make a demand *(Tell your daughter to keep her hands off the cookies)*. In addition, there are exclamations *(You're a fool!)*, answers to questions *(Fine, thank you)*, sounds or cries *(Yipes!)*, and calls to others *(Yoo-hoo, Buzzy!)*.

SIMPLE SENTENCES

Every sentence includes two basic components, the subject and the predicate. The subject is what the sentence is about, and the predicate is what the sentence says about the subject:

The car (subject)	*has a flat tire.* (predicate)

Often, the subject performs an action upon the predicate *(Herb kicked the ball)*. A sentence may have a compound subject *(**Ducks and geese** fly south for the winter)*, a compound predicate *(We **had dinner and went dancing**)*, or both.

The predicate contains at least one verb and sometimes one or more objects; the verb expresses the action of the sentence, and the object is the recipient of the action. Two types of sentences, however, do not contain objects. In sentences that have linking verbs (whose sole function is to connect subject and predicate), the predicate describes the subject with a predicate (identifying) noun or a predicate adjective *(My favorite food is **spinach**; I feel **happy**)*. When the verb is intransitive (it does not act upon anything), it takes no object, and the predicate consists solely of action *(The coyotes **howled**)*.

Transitive verbs, however, take one of two types of objects. Direct objects are the recipients of the verb's action *(Mary scrambled **eggs**)*, and indirect objects describe to or for whom the action occurs *(I loaned **Jackie** my sweater)*. Indirect objects always precede direct objects in a sentence.

COMPOUND, COMPLEX, AND COMPOUND–COMPLEX SENTENCES

These three types of sentences are made up of two or more clauses, each of which contains a subject and a predicate. An independent, or main, clause can stand on its own as a complete sentence, but a dependent, or subordinate, clause cannot. A compound sentence consists of two or more independent clauses *(Jane enjoyed scuba diving, but her husband preferred golf)*. A complex sentence has one independent clause and one or more dependent clauses:

When I arrived at the office, (dependent)	*I found the memo on my desk.* (independent)

Compound-complex sentences combine the two:

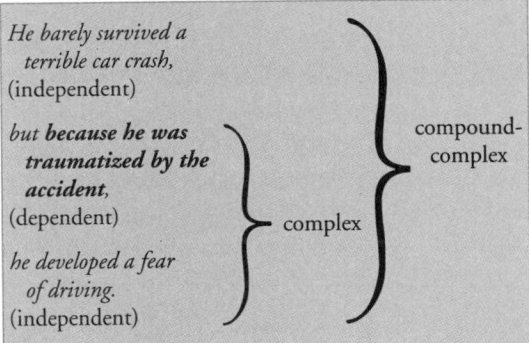

Dependent clauses may function as adjectives *(The woman **who gave the speech** was a famous athlete)*, as adverbs *(We walked along the beach **as the sun was setting**)*, or as nouns *(She was disappointed **that she could not attend the party**)*. Dependent clauses that are essential to the meaning of a sentence are called restrictive clauses *(The tree **that grew in the courtyard** was planted a century ago)*. Those that are not essential are called nonrestrictive clauses *(His mother, **who recently had a face-lift**, is quite vain)*.

Sentences may also use prepositional phrases in the role of adjectives *(The machine **in the factory** ran day and night)* or adverbs *(**After several years**

abroad, *Chris was ready to come home).* A prepositional phrase is made up of a preposition *(over, at, with, during)* and its object *(Meet me* **in St. Louis***).*

See also "Modifiers" earlier in this chapter.

SUBJECT–VERB AGREEMENT

The verb generally follows the subject in statements *(We* **are** *happy).* It is often the first word in commands (**Come** *over here,* in which the subject *You* is understood, though not written). The verb precedes the subject in questions (**Am** *I blue?).* The verb and the subject must agree in number if the verb is one that can show number. Verbs that show number are the conjugations of *to be* and the third-person singular present tense form of verbs, which usually end in *-s* (*he* **shops,** but *they* **shop** for plural form). Both the subject and verb must be either singular *(I am)* or plural *(we are).*

A few subjects pose particularly tricky problems of subject-verb agreement. *Either* and *neither* are frequently misconstrued as plural subjects, although they should always be paired with singular verbs *(Neither of us is ready).* Other subjects, such as *none* and *pair,* can be used in singular or plural constructions, depending on their meaning. For instance, when *none* means "not one," it is singular *(None of the guests is here);* when it means "not any," it is plural *(None are more beautiful than a rose).*

Compound subjects can also pose agreement difficulties. Most of the time, a compound subject is plural *(Paul and Carol are ready for vacation).* But when a compound subject expresses a thought or concept that is definitely singular, it should be followed by a singular verb *(Hitting a ball and driving it over the outfield wall is a skill few can master).*

TENSE, VOICE, AND MOOD

Verbs not only define the action of a sentence but also describe the nature of that action through tense, voice, and mood.

Verbs have six tenses that characterize the timing of the action. The present tense indicates an action as now taking place *(I* **see***; She* **goes***)* or a state or condition as now existing *(The plums* **are** *ripe);* an action that is habitual *(He* **speaks** *with an accent);* or an action that is always the same *(The clock* **strikes** *twelve at noon).* The past tense indicates an action completed or in progress in the past but not continuing into the present *(I* **saw***; She* **went***; He* **spoke***)* or a state or condition in existence at a former time *(The plums* **were** *ripe).* The future tense, always formed with *shall* or *will,* indicates an action that will occur in the future *(I* **shall see***; She* **will go***; He* **will speak***)* or a state that will exist in the future *(The plums* **will be** *ripe).*

The present perfect tense, always formed with *have* or *has,* indicates an action or state as completed at the time of speaking but not at any definite time in the past *(I* **have seen** *him many times; She* **has gone** *to the conference; He* **has spoken** *often before)* or an action or state that occurred in the past and continues in the present *(The plums* **have been** *ripe for days).* The past perfect, always formed with *had,* indicates an action or state as completed before a specified or implied time in the past *(I* **had seen** *the movie before it was reviewed; She* **had gone** *home before the announcement was made; He* **had spoken** *before the bell rang; The plums* **had been** *ripe long before they were picked).* The future perfect tense, always formed with *shall have* or *will have,* indicates an action as completed or a state as having ended in relation to a specified time in the future *(I* **shall have seen** *the video before it must be returned; She* **will have gone** *before her brother arrives; He* **will have spoken** *before the break for lunch; By the time they are picked, the plums* **will have been** *ripe for several days).* Each tense has a progressive form, formed by combining with verb *to be* and adding the *-ing* suffix, which is used to indicate that the action or state expressed by the verb is continuing *(I* **have been walking** *for hours).*

Most verbs are made into past tense by adding the *-ed* suffix, regardless of whether the verb's action is performed by the subject *(I* **walked** *to the store)* or on the subject *(My dog* **was walked***).* But as the examples in the preceding paragraph indicate, a number of verbs are made into other tense forms in ways that follow no general rule at all. The only rule that can be applied is the age-old maxim "When in doubt, consult a dictionary."

In every tense, verbs take one of two voices—active or passive—that indicate whether the subject of a sentence is the doer or receiver of the action. The active voice makes the subject the doer *(The children saw everything in the museum);* the passive voice makes the subject the recipient of the action *(The children will be seen by a doctor).*

F. Scott Fitzgerald once said, "Cut out all those exclamation marks. An exclamation mark is like laughing at your own jokes."

Likewise, in every tense, verbs also have one of three moods. A verb's indicative mood is used to make a statement or ask a question *(I see every one of his movies; Did you see his latest film?).* The imperative mood makes a request or command *(See if you can*

fix this; See here!). In the subjunctive mood, a verb expresses a thought that is not fact at the time the sentence is spoken or written *(If they could see me now, they'd be amazed; It remains to be seen if the business will be a success).*

VERBALS

In the form of verbals, verbs function not only as words of action but also as adjectives, nouns, or adverbs. Verbals cannot serve as the verb in the predicate of a sentence because they are incomplete forms of the verb. They can, however, be modified by adverbs just as verbs are. There are three types of verbals: participles, gerunds, and infinitives.

Participles combine the work of a verb and an adjective and end with the *-ing* or *-ed* suffix. Present participles, which express present or continuing action or state of being, end with *-ing* and take the active voice *(The boy is **growing**; It turned into an **exciting** game).* Past participles, which express completed action or a time or state gone by, end

---

Four Common Grammatical Problems

A Closer Look

Double Negative   Do not use two negative words to express a single negative statement.

WRONG:	*I **don't** owe Amy **no** money.*
RIGHT:	*I **don't** owe Amy any money.*
RIGHT:	*I owe Amy **no** money.*

Dangling Participial Phrase   A participial phrase modifies the first noun or pronoun following the comma that ends the participial phrase.

WRONG:	*Sitting in the living room, a loud **knock** on the door was heard by Ellen.*
RIGHT:	*Sitting in the living room, **Ellen** heard a loud knock on the door.*

Split Infinitive   Do not place an adverb between the parts of an infinitive.

WRONG:	*I try **to** often **visit** Laura.*
RIGHT:	*I try **to visit** Laura often.*

Parallel Structure   When parts of a sentence are parallel in meaning, place them in parallel or similar constructions.

WRONG:	*Her morning consisted of a leisurely breakfast and strolling downtown.*
RIGHT:	*Her morning consisted of **a** leisurely breakfast and **a** stroll downtown.*

Or:

WRONG:	*We are responsible for choosing the costumes and that they should all be the correct size.*
RIGHT:	*We are responsible for **choosing** the costumes and **making sure** that they are all the correct size.*

with *-ed* and take the passive voice (*He was **thrilled** to be there; She admired the **polished** brass*). The perfect participle links the present participle with the word *having* and takes the active voice (***Having worn out their welcome,** our houseguests finally left*).

Gerunds function as nouns and end with *-ing.* They may be used and modified just like ordinary nouns in simple and complex grammatical structures (***Eating** all those nachos was not a good idea; The dog's **barking** kept me awake all night; She loved nothing more than **throwing** a party*).

Almost always accompanied by the word *to,* the infinitive may be used as a noun, an adjective, or an adverb. In its noun form, the infinitive resembles the gerund (*Mark liked **to work** alone*). As an adjective, it modifies a noun (*It was her dream **to visit** Borneo*); and as an adverb, it modifies a verb (*The engine struggled **to turn** over*). For the sake of style, the *to* is sometimes dropped from the infinitive (*I feel the earth [to] **move** under my feet*).

PUNCTUATION

Punctuation helps to make sense of the various parts constituting a sentence. It shows where to pause or stop, defines possession and contraction, sets off nonessential modifiers and asides, indicates excitement or interrogation, clarifies incompletion or continuation, and denotes dialogue and special terms.

TERMINATING PUNCTUATION

Four punctuation marks that can signal the end of a sentence are the period (.), the question mark (?), the exclamation point (!), and the ellipsis (. . .).

The **period** is used at the end of any sentence that is not a question or an exclamation. It shows that a sentence is finished and is followed by a space and a capital letter beginning the next sentence.

The **question mark** is used to terminate a sentence that is a question (*How much do you think this is worth?*), to terminate a question within quoted dialogue (*"Do you like my haircut?" he asked*), or to ter-minate a question within a sentence (*Will the Orioles lose every game this year? is the question on the minds of fans everywhere*). The question mark is not used to set off indirect questions (*Everyone wants to know whether the Orioles will continue losing*).

The **exclamation point** terminates sentences that convey excitement (*What a finish that play has!*) or are emphatic (*Leave me alone!*). It can also be used to terminate individual words used as interjections (*You'll get here today? Terrific!*), even when an interjection is within a sentence (*Take four parts gin, add one part vermouth, and, behold! you have a martini*).

Ancient Greek texts had no punctuation and no spaces between words.

The **ellipsis** indicates that one or more words are missing. When used at the end of a complete sentence, an ellipsis is made up of four dots (*I had hoped to go. . . .*). Four dots indicate that although what's there makes a complete sentence, one or more words have been omitted from the end of the sentence. A four-dot ellipsis can also indicate the omission of one or more sentences. When the middle portion of a sentence has been omitted, a three-dot ellipsis is used.

PAUSE PUNCTUATION

The punctuation marks that can indicate a pause are the comma (,), the semicolon (;), the colon (:), the dash (—), and the ellipsis (. . .).

Commas are used to separate two main clauses set apart by a conjunction, such as *and, but,* or *or* (*I'd hoped to be done this afternoon, but I'm not sure that's possible*). Commas can separate shorter clauses that do not have a conjunction between them (*I work, I sleep, I work some more*). They are also used to set off all manner of words and phrases, such as adverbial clauses (*When he was finished, he set down his knife*); transitional expressions (*Her remarks, on the other hand, were uncalled for*); conjunctions (*We are often late; however, we must be back by five o'clock*); illustrative expressions (*They were confused; that is, they felt bewildered and afraid); and nonrestrictive clauses (*Your writing, although it is quite good, is not what we're looking for*).

In addition, commas are used to separate a series of words or phrases (*Hope, charity, and faith were not enough to sustain her*); to set off direct address (*You know, son, that's a good idea*); to set a direct quotation apart from the speaker (*"Don't quote me," he said*); and to set off a question being asked about the previous part of the sentence (*It was fun, wasn't it?*).

Finally, commas indicate the inference of a word not stated, especially one used earlier in the sentence (*For us it's money; for them, food*); set off the parts of an address, place name, or date (*They went to London, England, to conduct research; She arrived on Monday 25, 1998*); and separate a name from a title following it (*Paul Fargis, President*).

The **semicolon** signals a more complete stop than is indicated by the comma. It is used to separate parts of a sentence that contain commas (*Our organization runs on the dedication, concern, and compassion of its staff; the generosity, moral support, and wisdom of its directors; and the gratitude, hope, and joy expressed by those it serves*). A semicolon can also join clauses that are not connected by a coordinating conjunction (*They left for London yesterday; I am leaving today*) as well as those joined by conjunctive adverbs (*It's easy to lie; however, lying is a bad habit to get into*).

The **colon** represents the closest thing to the full stop indicated by a period. It can mark the separation of an enumerated list or extract from the rest of a text (*The Ten Commandments:*) or can introduce an appositive (*She wanted only one thing: sleep*) or series (*It's easy to list the things money won't buy: love, health, happiness, and peace*). The colon also precedes an illustrative or explanatory phrase; many style guides recommend beginning such phrases with capital letters if they can function as sentences in and of themselves (*His Excellency demands satisfaction: He will expect you on the dueling field at dawn*).

Colons are frequently used in contexts other than sentences. They can separate book titles from their subtitles (*Curious Customs: The Stories Behind 296 Popular American Rituals*); set off the salutation in business correspondence (*Dear Mr. President:*) and the labels in memoranda (*To:*); and separate the elements of time (*8:45*), ratios (*3:5 mix of boys to girls*), and biblical references (*Deuteronomy 1:5*).

Watch out for spell checkers! If you ran the following sentence through your computer's spell checker, it would tell you that nothing was wrong: I have bin trying too improve my spelling for sum time now cents my secretary always says that it isn't two grate.

The **dash,** known as the em dash to compositors and editors, represents an abrupt shift within a sentence. It separates a clause or phrase from the rest of the sentence, whether for emphasis (*You want—my god, you need—an expert*) or to introduce a parenthetical remark (*He hopes to turn a profit—something I can't see happening anytime soon—within six months*). Dashes also are used to separate quoted material from its author (*"I still find the Strunkian wisdom a comfort"—E. B. White*).

The **ellipsis** is used in dialogue to indicate faltering speech (*"We want . . . that is . . . "*).

BRACKETS AND PARENTHESES

Brackets [ ] are specialized tools for setting off material from the rest of the text. They can be used with editorial comments: The *main point [emphasis mine] has been missed;* or as parentheses within parentheses: *It is hoped (some might say prayed [even atheists pray sometimes]) that she will pull through.* Brackets should not be used when simple paren-theses will do.

Parentheses ( ) are used to set off explanatory words and phrases that demand more of a break than is shown by commas and less than that indicated by dashes: *We can't bear it (or so we believe)*; to surround numbers when enumerating points in a sentence: *He hopes (1) to be employed and (2) to make lots of money*; to give abbreviations: *American Telephone & Telegraph (AT&T)*; and to indicate potential plurals or other alternatives: *Please tell us which course(s) of action you wish to take.*

APOSTROPHES, SINGLE QUOTATION MARKS, AND DOUBLE QUOTATION MARKS

Apostrophes are used to indicate a contraction *(didn't)* or a possessive by adding *'s* to most words *(Mr. Marx's humor)*; an apostrophe alone is added to form the possessive of plurals *(the kittens' tails)*. Apostrophes also appear in shortened forms of the year *(the '80s)* and for plurals of numbers, letters, and terms *(She received two A's and three B's)*.

Single quotation marks are used for quotes within quotes *("'I'm not sure,' is what I think he said," she responded)* and for titles and special terms mentioned in dialogue *("She said she doesn't read the 'His' column anymore," he told his buddy)*.

Charlotte Brontë and William Wordsworth asked their publishers to correct the punctuation in their manuscripts.

Double quotation marks are used for direct quotations and dialogue *("What was she up to?" he asked)*; to set off special terms *(soldiers are sometimes called "grunts")*; and to indicate the titles of stories, articles, songs, book chapters, radio shows, poems, and lectures.

Punctuating a sentence that contains quotation marks can be tricky. Commas used to set off quoted material from the speaker are placed within the quotation marks *("I hope it's finished," she said)*. A period is also placed within the quotation marks *("We're done.")*. A question mark or exclamation point end-

ing a sentence that ends in a quotation mark is placed within the quotation marks too *("Will you marry me?")*. However, when quoted material is used in a question, but is not itself a question, the question mark is placed outside *(Do you think he really meant "till death do us part"?)*.

AMERICAN ENGLISH AND BRITISH ENGLISH: PUNCTUATION DIFFERENCES

As if confusion about spelling and word choice were not enough, (see "American English and British English: Spelling and Name Differences" in Chapter 13), there are also punctuation differences between American and British English. Although American English always uses double quotation marks to indicate speech, British English, especially in older texts, usually uses single quotation marks. A few more recent British publications use double quotation marks.

In both American and British English, periods and commas at the end of a quote come before the closing quotation marks when the quote is a full sentence (or a full sentence broken up by a connecting phrase such as *he said*):

> *"When you come to meet me," she explained hastily, "please bring the blue folders."*

In American English, the placement of periods and commas remains the same even when the quote is a sentence fragment. But in British English, periods and commas punctuating sentence fragments are placed outside quotation marks.

AMERICAN ENGLISH:	*She described the party as "a sumptuous affair," and said that she arrived home "long after midnight."*
BRITISH ENGLISH:	*She described the party as "a sumptuous affair", and said that she arrived home "long after midnight".*

ADDITIONAL SOURCES OF INFORMATION

The American Heritage Book of English Usage. Houghton Mifflin, 1996.

Castle, Lana R. *Style Meister: The Quick-Reference Custom Style Guide.* Castle Communications, 1999.

The Chicago Manual of Style. 14th ed. University of Chicago Press, 1993.

Fowler, H. W. *Dictionary of Modern English Usage.* 3rd ed. Rev. by R. W. Burchfeld. Wordsworth Editions, 1997.

Garner, Bryan A. *A Dictionary of Modern American Usage.* Oxford University Press, 1998.

Greenbaum, Sidney. *The Oxford English Grammar.* Oxford University Press, 1996.

Kramer, Melinda G., et al. *Prentice-Hall Handbook for Writers.* Prentice-Hall, 1995.

Maggio, Rosalie. *Talking About People: A Guide to Fair and Accurate Language.* Oryx Press, 1997.

Martin, Phyllis. *Word Watcher's Handbook: A Deletionary of the Most Abused and Misused Words.* iUniverse.com, 2000.

MLA Handbook for Writers of Research Papers. 4th ed. Modern Language Association, 1999.

The New York Public Library Writer's Guide to Style and Usage. HarperCollins, 1994.

Strunk, William, Jr., and E. B. White. *The Elements of Style.* 4th ed. Allyn & Bacon, 2000.

Words into Type. 3rd ed. Prentice-Hall, 1986.

Zinsser, William. *On Writing Well: An Informal Guide to Writing Nonfiction.* Rev. ed. HarperReference, 1998.

15

LETTERS AND
FORMS OF ADDRESS

PERSONAL LETTERS

The popularity of electronic mail has reversed the slow demise of letter writing in the United States. Many people who never write personal letters email friends and associates on a daily basis. Email can be used to invite friends or coworkers to a casual gathering, such as an office picnic or a drinks party. Birthday and holiday cards can be emailed, as can thank-you notes and casual correspondence. There are, however, several situations in which a personal letter or announcement mailed in the traditional way is expected or required. Birth or death announcements, wedding invitations, and thank-you notes for wedding, christening, and bar or bat mitzvah presents require a more formal presentation than email can provide. Thank-you notes to the host or hostess of a party or to someone who has done a favor are not required, but they will make the writer's gratitude clear and warm the heart of the person who gets them.

Other occasions demand notes or letters as well. The death of someone in a friend's family is one such event, especially if you cannot express your condolences personally at a wake or during *shiva*. A letter of condolence need not be long and involved, but it should be a personal, handwritten note, not just a printed sympathy card.

Every time you lick a stamp, you consume $^1/_{10}$ calorie.

Formal invitations require a written response. Wedding invitations are the most common kind of formal invitation that people receive. While response cards are frequently included with wedding invitations, a personal response in addition to or in place of the response card will be greatly appreciated.

When a friend or family member has something important to celebrate—a promotion or graduation, or receipt of an award or other honor—a congratulatory note will make the celebration even happier. Even the briefest of notes adds a warmth that cannot be conveyed by a phone call.

Personal letter writing can also be done for no good reason at all. Or, rather, you may write letters to friends and family simply to keep in touch with them and to let them know that you are thinking of them. These are perhaps the most enjoyable letters to receive.

The U.S. Postal Service delivers mail to 134 million addresses, including 20 million post office boxes. About 1 million new addresses are added each year.

Personal letters, while not requiring a strict format, do have a few guidelines. The date should be written at the top, either in the center or the right-hand corner. The salutation, which may be a bit warmer than it would for a business letter ("My dearest Jeanne,"), should be followed by a comma instead of a colon.

The body or text of a personal letter is, of course, a highly personal matter. It should be written with less of an eye to what would be stylistically or grammatically correct and more of an eye to expressing feelings and thoughts. A personal letter should sound like you, and techniques that would be out of place in a business letter, such as using dashes, ellipses, and sentence fragments, can be employed in personal correspondence.

Closings for personal letters are also a matter of choice. "Love," is appropriate for those you do love; "Fondly," or "All my best," or "Affectionately," might be right for friends. As with the rest of the letter, the closing should express your own feelings.

BUSINESS PROTOCOL AND FORMS OF ADDRESS

BUSINESS LETTERS

Like business phone calls, business letters should be brief and to the point. The first line below the letterhead should include the date, with the name, company, and address of the recipient appearing two lines below it at the left margin. Two lines below the address, the salutation is given.

Go to
"Business Etiquette" in chapter 16; "U.S. Postal Service" in chapter 25

If the recipient is known personally, he or she can be greeted by first name ("Dear Fred:"). If the recipient is known casually or not at all, use Mr. or Ms. ("Dear Mr. Burrows:" or "Dear Ms. Johnston:"). When the addressee is unknown, "Dear Sir or Madam:" or something like "Dear Sales Manager:" can be used

The first paragraph of a business letter should clearly explain the purpose of writing. It should be straightforward and concise. If the letter is being written at the suggestion of someone else, this should be stated in the first paragraph along with the reason for writing.

The length of a business letter is determined by what needs to be said. If a reply is desired, the last paragraph should simply state, "I look forward to hearing from you at your earliest convenience." A response by a specific date should not be demanded unless there is a good reason for doing so.

Appropriate closings for a business letter include "Best wishes," "Sincerely," "Sincerely yours," or "Yours truly." Informal closings like "Yours," or "Cheers," should not be used. The signature can be either your full name ("Henry Wiggins") or, if the writer and the recipient are well acquainted, a first name alone ("Henry"). The writer's full name and company title should be typed below the signature unless they appear at the top of the letterhead.

HOW TO PREPARE A RÉSUMÉ

Along with a cover letter, a résumé is the first impression a prospective employee makes on a potential employer. Therefore, it is important that the résumé provide as much relevant information as possible about the person being described in it: you. Send a cover letter and résumé to a specific person. The correct spelling of their name is imperative. Close the cover letter by requesting an interview and state the intention to call in a week or two. It is also important that the résumé be kept brief—no more than one full side of a sheet of 8½-by-11-inch paper.

A résumé must be neatly typed, with at least a ¾-inch margin on both sides, top, and bottom. Single-space all information in the résumé, leaving one line of space between blocks of information. Use underlining, capital letters, small capitals, bold or italic type, and bullets or asterisks to highlight important information.

Begin a résumé with your name, address, and home and business telephone numbers. They can be laid out on the page in any way you find visually pleasing, so far as space allows. Do not include your age, marital status, or other personal facts.

Many résumés then list a career goal, such as "Career goal: Systems engineer responsible for monitoring, maintaining, and improving plant facilities" or "Objective: Position as illustrator/designer with opportunity to create book jackets from concept through mechanicals." Including a career goal is a good tactic if you are looking for a specific type of job; however, job hunters who would consider any of several possible careers are better off omitting any specific career goal.

The glue on Israeli postage stamps is certified kosher.

Most résumés then present a chronological outline of work experience, starting with one's current or most recent job and working backward. For each job listed, the important duties and skills involved should be outlined or described. Depending on how much "real world" experience you have, relevant high school or college employment, internships, and part-time work can be included. Such a portion of a typical résumé might look like the one on page 452.

This section is followed by one outlining your educational background, again from your most recent experience backward. List the date, school or course attended, and certificate or diploma obtained. Depending on the extent of your work experience, you may want to give a more detailed description of your

Work Experience

1999–present	Vice President, Marketing, *eTech.com*
	Responsible for developing, implementing, and overseeing marketing of all services provided by this Internet technology company.
	—Created company's first five-year marketing plan
	—Developed continuing training program for sales force
	—Increased client billings by 25 percent
1996–1999	Marketing Director, *Numbercrunch, Inc.*

higher education. If you are a college student, you may want to list your high school and any pertinent coursework or special achievements.

In the last part of your résumé, list any work you have done with civic or charitable organizations and any awards or certificates of recognition you have received. Place these under an appropriate heading, such as "COMMUNITY SERVICE." If you have no such background, leave this section out of your résumé.

Finally, it is unnecessary to write "References available upon request" at the bottom of a résumé. Anyone looking at it will assume you can provide references and will ask for them if and when they are needed.

When submitting an electronic résumé, preserve formatting by sending it as an Adobe .pdf (portable document file), which is the standard for sharing electronic documents. The recipient will need the Acrobat Reader to view it, but it is freely available from Adobe and widely used. When emailing a résumé to a career-placement site or a company's web site, be sure to list computer skills, and to include an email address and/or Web address.

SPOKEN AND WRITTEN FORMS OF ADDRESS

This section gives the correct forms of address for U.S. government officials, diplomats, UN officers, religious leaders, royalty, the British peerage, and military personnel. For each personage, the table on pages 453–457 gives the appropriate form or forms to be used in letter addresses, in letter salutations, in direct conversation, and in more formal introductions.

In Elizabethan England, a person of higher social standing was addressed as Goodman or Goodwife. A lower member of a clerical order was called Sir Priest.

In diplomatic and other public circles, "Sir" is generally considered an acceptable alternative to the formal address in both written and spoken greetings; this greeting does not apply to religious or titled persons. The use of "Madam" or "Ma'am" for a female addressee is less customary but still acceptable, especially for high officeholders ("Madam Governor"). This rule also holds for high officials of foreign countries.

For greetings in which "Mr." is used, the feminine equivalent may be "Madam" or, less formally, "Mrs.," "Miss," or "Ms."

Go to "American English and British English: Spelling and Name Differences" in chapter 13; "American English and British English: Punctuation Differences" in chapter 14

Forms of Address

Person	Letter Address	Letter Greeting	Spoken Greeting	Formal Introduction
Government Officials—Federal				
President of the United States	The President The White House 1600 Pennsylvania Avenue, NW Washington, DC 20500 president@whitehouse.gov	Dear Mr. (*or* Madam) President	Mr. (*or* Madam) President	The president *or* the President of the United States *or* President Jones
Former President	The Honorable John J. Jones Address	Dear Mr. (*or* Mrs., Ms.) Jones	Mr. (*or* Mrs., Ms.) Jones	Former president John J. Jones
Vice President	The Vice President Executive Office Building Washington, DC 20501 vice.president@whitehouse.gov	Dear Mr. (*or* Madam) Vice President	Mr. (*or* Madam) vice president	The vice president *or* the vice president of the United States *or* Vice President Jones
Cabinet members	The Honorable John (*or* Jane) Jones The Secretary of ____	Dear Mr. (*or* Madam) Secretary	Mr. (*or* Madam) secretary	The secretary of ____, John (*or* Jane) J. Jones
Attorney General	The Honorable John (*or* Jane) Jones The Attorney General U.S. Department of Justice 950 Pennsylvania Avenue, NW Washington, DC 20530-0001 AskDOJ@usdoj.gov	Dear Mr. (*or* Madam) Attorney General	Mr. (*or* Madam) attorney general	The attorney general, John (*or* Jane) J. Jones
Chief Justice	The Chief Justice The Supreme Court One First Street, NE Washington, DC 20543	Dear Mr. (*or* Madam) Justice *or* Dear Mr. (*or* Madam) Chief Justice	Mr. (*or* Madam) chief justice	The chief justice *or* Chief Justice Jones
Associate Justice	Mr. Justice Jones *or* Madam Justice Jones The Supreme Court One First Street, NE Washington, DC 20543	Dear Mr. (*or* Madam) Justice	Mr. (*or* Madam)	Mr. (*or* Madam) Justice Jones *or* Justice Jones
Senator	The Honorable John (*or* Jane) Jones United States Senate Washington, DC 20510	Dear Senator Jones	Senator Jones	Senator Jones from Montana
Speaker of the House	The Honorable John (*or* Jane) Jones Speaker of the House of Representatives United States House of Representatives Washington, DC 20515	Dear Mr. (*or* Madam) Speaker	Mr. (*or* Madam) speaker	The speaker of the House of Representatives

continues

Continued

Person	Letter Address	Letter Greeting	Spoken Greeting	Formal Introduction
Representative	The Honorable John (or Jane) Jones United States House of Representatives Washington, DC 20515	Dear Mr. (or Mrs., Ms.) Jones	Mr. (or Mrs., Ms.) Jones	Representative Jones from New Jersey
Diplomats and Consuls				
U.S. Ambassador	The Honorable John (or Jane) Jones Ambassador of the United States American Embassy Address	Dear Mr. (or Madam) Ambassador	Mr. (or Madam) ambassador	The American ambassador or The ambassador of the United States of America
Consul	John (or Jane) Jones, Esq. American Consul Address	Dear Mr. (or Mrs., Ms.) Jones	Mr. (or Mrs., Ms.) Jones	Mr. (or Mrs., Ms.) Jones
Foreign Ambassador	His (or Her) Excellency John (or Jane) Johnson Ambassador of _____ Address	Excellency or Dear Mr. (or Madam)	Mr. (or Madam) ambassador	The Ambassador of _____ Ambassador
United Nations Officials				
Secretary-General of the United Nations	His Excellency Milo Jones Secretary-General of the United Nations United Nations Plaza New York, NY 10017	Excellency or Dear Mr. Secretary-General	Mr. Jones or the secretary-general	The secretary-general of the United Nations
U.S. Representative to the United Nations	The Honorable John (or Jane) Jones United States Permanent Representative to the United Nations United Nations Plaza New York, NY 10017	Dear Mr. (or Madam) Ambassador	Mr. (or Madam) ambassador	The United States representative to the United Nations
Foreign Heads of State				
Premier	His (or Her) Excellency John (or Amelia) Smith Premier of _____	Excellency or Dear Mr. (or Madam) Premier	Your excellency	The premier of _____

Person	Letter Address	Letter Greeting	Spoken Greeting	Formal Introduction
President of a republic	His (*or* Her) Excellency John (*or* Amelia) Smith President of ___	Excellency *or* Dear Mr. (*or* Madam) President	Your Excellency	President Smith
Prime minister	His (*or* Her) Excellency John (*or* Amelia) Smith	Excellency *or* Dear Mr. (*or* Madam) Prime Minister	Mr. (*or* Madame) prime minister	The prime minister of ___

Government Officials—State and Local

Person	Letter Address	Letter Greeting	Spoken Greeting	Formal Introduction
Governor	The Honorable John (*or* Jane) Jones Governor of ___ State Capitol Address	Dear Governor Jones	Governor *or* Governor Jones	Governor Jones *or* The governor of ___ (only used outside his or her state)
State representative (includes assembly person, delegate)	The Honorable John (*or* Jane) Jones Address	Dear Mr. (*or* Mrs., Ms.) Jones	Mr. (*or* Mrs., Ms.) Jones	Mr. (*or* Mrs., Ms.) Jones
State senator	The Honorable John (*or* Jane) Jones Address	Dear Senator Jones	Senator Jones	Senator Jones
Justice of State Supreme Court	The Honorable John (*or* Jane) Jones Justice Division Supreme Court of the State of ___ Address	Dear Justice Jones	Mr. *or* Madam Justice Jones *or* Justice Jones	Mr. (*or* Madam) Justice Jones *or* Justice Jones
Mayor	The Honorable John (*or* Jane) Jones His (*or* Her) Honor the Mayor City Hall Address	Dear Mayor Jones	Mayor Jones *or* Mr. (*or* Madam) Mayor *or* Your Honor	Mayor Jones *or* The Mayor

Religious Officials*

Person	Letter Address	Letter Greeting	Spoken Greeting	Formal Introduction
The Pope	His Holiness the Pope *or* His Holiness Pope John XII Vatican City Rome, Italy	Your Holiness *or* Most Holy Father	Your Holiness *or* Most Holy Father	His Holiness the Holy Father *or* the Pope *or* the Pontiff
Cardinal	His Eminence John Cardinal Jones, Archbishop of ___ Address	Your Eminence *or* Dear Cardinal Jones	Your Eminence *or* Cardinal Jones	His Eminence Cardinal Jones

* If the cleric holds a doctorate in divinity, it is customary to add the designation D.D. after his or her name in the letter address.

continues

Forms of Address

Continued

Person	Letter Address	Letter Greeting	Spoken Greeting	Formal Introduction
Bishop (Catholic)	The Most Reverend John Jones, Bishop (or Archbishop) of ____ Address	Your Excellency or Dear Bishop (Archbishop) Jones	Your Excellency or Bishop (Archbishop) Jones	Bishop (Archbishop) Jones
Monsignor	The Reverend Monsignor James Harding Address	Right Reverend and dear Monsignor or Dear Monsignor Harding	Monsignor Harding or Monsignor	Monsignor Harding
Priest	The Reverend John Jones Address	Reverend Father or Dear Father Jones	Father or Father Jones	Father Jones
Brother	Brother John or Brother John Jones	Dear Brother John or Dear Brother	Brother or Brother John	Brother John
Sister	Sister Mary Luke Address	Dear Sister Mary Luke or Dear Sister	Sister Mary Luke or Sister	Sister Mary Luke
Protestant Clergy	The Reverend John (or Jane) Jones	Dear Reverend Jones	Reverend Jones	The Reverend John Jones
Bishop (Episcopal)	The Right Reverend John Jones Bishop of ____ Address	Dear Bishop Jones	Bishop Jones	The Right Reverend John Jones, Bishop of Detroit
Rabbi	Rabbi Arthur (or Anne) Milgrom Address	Dear Rabbi Milgrom	Rabbi Milgrom or Rabbi	Rabbi Arthur Milgrom
Foreign Royalty and Nobility				
King or Queen	His (Her) Majesty King (Queen) ____ Address (letters traditionally are sent to reigning monarchs not directly but via the private secretary)	Your Majesty	Your Majesty or Sir or Madam	Varies depending on titles, holdings, etc.
Other royalty	His (Her) Royal Highness, the Prince (Princess) of ____ Address	Your Royal Highness or	Your Royal Highness or Sir Madam	His (Her) Royal Highness, the Duke (Duchess) of Gloucester
Duke/Duchess	His/Her Grace, the Duke/Duchess of ____	My Lord Duke/Madam or Dear Duke/Duchess of ____	Your Grace or Duke/Duchess	His/Her Grace, the Duke/Duchess of Bridgeport
Marquess/Marchioness	The Most Honorable the Marquess/Marchioness of Bridgeport	My Lord/Madam or Dear Lord/Lady Bridgeport	Lord/Lady Bridgeport	Lord/Lady Bridgeport
Earl	The Right Honorable the Earl of Franklin	My Lord or Dear Lord Franklin	Lord Franklin	Lord Franklin

Person	Letter Address	Letter Greeting	Spoken Greeting	Formal Introduction
Countess (wife of an earl)	The Right Honorable the Countess of Franklin	Madam *or* Dear Lady Franklin	Lady Franklin	Lady Franklin
Viscount/ Viscountess	The Right Honorable the Viscount/Viscountess Tyburn	My Lord/Lady *or* Dear Lord/Lady Tyburn	Lord/Lady Tyburn	Lord/Lady Tyburn
Baron/Baroness	The Right Honorable Lord/ Lady Austin	My Lord/Madam *or* Dear Lord/Lady Austin	Lord/Lady Austin	Lord/Lady Austin
Baronet	Sir John Jones, Bt.	Dear Sir *or* Dear Sir John	Sir John	Sir John Jones
Wife of Baronet	Lady Jones	Dear Madam *or* Dear Lady Jones	Lady Jones	Lady Jones
Knight	Sir John Jones	Dear Sir *or* Dear Sir John	Sir John	Sir John Jones
Wife of knight	Dear Madam or Dear Lady Jones	Dear Lady Jones	Lady Jones	Lady Jones

Military Personnel

For commissioned officers in the U.S. armed services, the full rank is used as a title only in addressing letters and in formal introductions: one writes to Major General Ann Jones, U.S. Army, and introduces her as Major General Jones. In greetings, the full rank is shortened to General: "Dear General Jones." Similar acceptable shortened greetings follow.

For enlisted personnel, a similar principle applies. Sergeants—whether staff sergeants, gunnery sergeants, or first sergeants—are greeted simply as "Sergeant"; privates first class are referred to as "Private"; and, in the navy and Coast Guard, chief petty officers are referred to as "Chief." Other noncommissioned officers are greeted by their ranks although, informally, lower grades may be referred to generically as "Soldier" or "Sailor."

The universal terms of respect that lower ranks must use when addressing senior officers are "Sir" and "Madam." These terms are not applied to noncommissioned officers, however; the appropriate affirmative response to a sergeant, for example, is "Yes, Sergeant."

Service	Full Rank	Greetings
Army, Air Force, Marines	General of the army	General
	Lieutenant General	General
	Brigadier General	General
	Lieutenant Colonel	Colonel
	First Lieutenant	Lieutenant
	Second Lieutenant	Lieutenant
Navy, Coast Guard	Fleet Admiral	Admiral
	Vice Admiral	Admiral
	Rear Admiral	Admiral
	Lieutenant Commander	Commander
	Lieutenant, Junior Grade	Lieutenant

GRADES AND RANKS FOR U.S. MILITARY PERSONNEL
COMMISSIONED OFFICERS

Grade	Air Force, Army, and Marine Corps	Navy and Coast Guard
O–10	General	Admiral
O–9	Lieutenant general	Vice admiral
O–8	Major general	Rear admiral (upper half)
O–7	Brigadier general	Rear admiral (lower half)
O–6	Colonel	Captain
O–5	Lieutenant colonel	Commander
O–4	Major	Lieutenant commander
O–3	Captain	Lieutenant
O–2	First lieutenant	Lieutenant (junior grade)
O–1	Second lieutenant	Ensign
Special grades[1]	General of the air force	Fleet admiral
	General of the army	

[1] Five-star commissioned officers. The marine corps does not have a special grade for commissioned officers. No five-star generals are living at this time.

WARRANT OFFICERS

Grade	All Services
W-5	Chief warrant officer
W-4	Chief warrant officer
W-3	Chief warrant officer
W-2	Chief warrant officer
W-1	Warrant officer

Roman Catholic cardinals place the word Cardinal *between their first and last names to show humility; for example, Timothy Cardinal Manning.*

ENLISTED PERSONNEL

Grade	Air Force	Army	Marine Corps	Navy and Coast Guard
E-9	Chief master sergeant	Sergeant major	Sergeant major Master gunnery sergeant	Master chief petty officer
E-8	Senior master sergeant	First sergeant Master sergeant	First sergeant Master sergeant	Senior chief petty officer
E-7	Master sergeant	Sergeant first class	Gunnery sergeant	Chief petty officer
E-6	Technical sergeant	Staff sergeant	Staff sergeant	Petty officer first class
E-5	Staff sergeant	Sergeant	Sergeant	Petty officer second class
E-4	Senior airman	Corporal	Corporal	Petty officer third class
E-3	Airman first class	Private first class	Lance corporal	Seaman
E-2	Airman	Private	Private first class	Seaman apprentice
E-1	Airman basic	Private	Private	Seaman recruit
Special grades[1]	Chief master sergeant of the air force	Sergeant major of the army	Sergeant major of the marine corps	Master chief petty officer of the navy

[1] Senior enlisted advisers. Each branch of service has only one adviser.

ABBREVIATED TITLES THAT FOLLOW NAMES

An abbreviated title can tell more about a person than his or her name. It identifies a rank or position, membership in a monastic or secular order, academic degree, or military or civil honor. The following list includes some familiar as well as some obscure abbreviated titles.

Abbreviation	Title
A.B.	*Artium Baccalaureus* (Latin, Bachelor of Arts)
A.M.	*Artium Magister* (Latin, Master of Arts)
A.R.A.	Associate of the Royal Academy
A.S.	Associate of Science
B.A.	Bachelor of Arts
Bart., Bt.	Baronet
B.C.S.W.	Board-Certified Social Worker
B.D.	Bachelor of Divinity
B.S.	Bachelor of Science
B.S.S.	Bachelor of Social Science
C.P.A.	Certified Public Accountant
C.S.W.	Certified Social Worker
D.A.	District Attorney
D.B.	*Divinitatis Baccalaureus* (Latin, Bachelor of Divinity)
D.C.	Doctor of Chiropractic
D.D.	*Divinitatis Doctor* (Latin, Doctor of Divinity)
D.D.S.	Doctor of Dental Surgery
D.O.	Doctor of Osteopathy
D.S.O.	Distinguished Service Order
D.V.M.	Doctor of Veterinary Medicine
Esq.	Esquire
F.R.S.	Fellow of the Royal Society
J.D.	*Juris Doctor* (Latin, Doctor of Law, Doctor of Jurisprudence), *Jurum Doctor* (Latin, Doctor of Laws)
J.P.	Justice of the Peace
Kt.	Knight
L.H.D.	*Litterarum Humaniorum Doctor* (Latin, Doctor of Humanities)
Litt.D.	*Litterarum Doctor* (Latin, Doctor of Letters)
LL.B.	*Legum Baccalaureus* (Latin, Bachelor of Laws)
LL.D.	*Legum Doctor* (Latin, Doctor of Laws)

"Acronyms" and **"Common Abbreviations"** in chapter 13

Go to

L.P.N.	Licensed Practical Nurse
M.A.	Master of Arts
M.B.A.	Master of Business Administration
M.D.	*Medicinae Doctor* (Latin, Doctor of Medicine)
M.Div.	Master of Divinity
M.Ed.	Master of Education
M.P.	Member of Parliament
M.S.	Master of Science
M.S.W.	Master of Social Work
N.P.	Notary Public
Ph.B.	*Philosophiae Baccalaureus* (Latin, Bachelor of Philosophy)
Ph.D.	*Philosophiae Doctor* (Latin, Doctor of Philosophy)
Ph.G.	Graduate in Pharmacy
Psy.D.	Doctor of Psychology
R.	*Rex, Regina* (Latin, King, Queen)
R.N.	Registered Nurse
R.Ph.	Registered Pharmacist
S.B.	Bachelor of Science
S.J.	Society of Jesus
S.M.	Master of Science
S.T.B.	*Sacrae Theologiae Baccalaureus* (Latin, Bachelor of Sacred Theology)

ADDITIONAL SOURCES OF INFORMATION

Blumenthal, Lassor A. *The Art of Letter Writing.* Perigee, 1986.

Bly, Robert W. *The Encyclopedia of Business Letters, Fax Memos, and E-Mail.* Career Press, 1999.

Booher, Dianna. *E-Writing: 21st Century Tools for Effective Communication.* Pocket Books, 2001.

De Vries, Mary A. *The New American Handbook of Letter Writing.* Signet, 2000.

Holberg, Andrea, ed. *Forms of Address: A Guide for Business and Social Use.* Rice University Press, 1994.

McCaffree, Maryjane, and Pauline Innis. *Protocol: The Complete Handbook of Diplomatic, Official and Social Usage.* Rev. ed. Devon, 1999.

Swartz, Oretha D. *Service Etiquette.* 4th ed. Naval Institute Press, 1988.

IV

DAILY LIFE

16

ETIQUETTE

Images of raised pinkies and white gloves may come readily to mind, but etiquette is as much a system of ethics as it is one of manners. All the niceties of social intercourse can be reduced down to the Golden Rule: "Do unto others as you would have others do unto you." (In her 1922 classic primer on etiquette, Emily Post redefined this dictum as "Keep your hands to yourself.") Courtesy is essential in any social situation, be it a business meeting, a lunch with co-workers, or a family reunion and, once learned, good manners can become so thoroughly ingrained that their observance becomes a matter of instinct rather than a conscious duty.

The Chinese philosopher Confucius taught his disciples that courtesies "when they are practiced with all the heart" lead to moral excellence.

This chapter details the basic rules for smoothing personal contacts and developing tact and good manners. It is hardly exhaustive—a great many books have been written on planning and organizing a wedding, for instance—and it does not cover the moral, psychological, or social implications of etiquette. But the chapter does describe what can be expected to occur when one participates in certain social activities and what is expected of those who participate.

WEDDING ETIQUETTE

Because weddings vary greatly in their level of formality and style, each component of a wedding—from the invitations to the reception—is flexible. The rule of thumb is that the various elements that make up a wedding should be compatible. That is, if a formal, evening church wedding is held, it should be preceded by formal, engraved invitations and followed by a formal, sit-down dinner; likewise, a wedding held in an open field in the countryside would call for an informal dining arrangement, perhaps a buffet.

INVITATIONS AND ANNOUNCEMENTS

Wedding invitations, like weddings themselves, come in two basic varieties: formal and informal. A formal, traditional invitation is engraved or printed in black ink on high-quality white or ivory paper. The size of the paper is either 5-by-7 inches, folded in half before being put in an envelope, or 4-by-5 inches, inserted into an envelope without folding.

The wording of a formal wedding invitation is written in the third person, and the date and time are written out in full. A typical example might read:

Mr. and Mrs. Henry Appleton
request the honor of your presence
at the marriage of their daughter
Carol June
to
Mr. Alan Hart
Saturday, the fourth of February
at eleven o'clock
St. Albert's Church
Bayonne, New Jersey

The invitation to the wedding ceremony itself can also invite the recipient to a reception afterward. If all those receiving invitations to the reception are not invited to the ceremony, or vice versa, a separate invitation to the reception is printed and, for those invited to both events, included with the wedding invitation. The reception invitation or the combined invitation should include the instructions "R.S.V.P."

Traditionally, the invitation is covered with a piece of tissue paper and enclosed with the reception invitation (and a response card and its envelope, if desired) in an inner envelope. The names of those invited, including a couple's children if they are also invited, are written out in full on the inner envelope. This inner envelope is then enclosed in an outer envelope that bears the handwritten names of all invited and their address, without abbreviations. Modern custom allows the bride's parents to forgo using an inner envelope altogether when sending out invitations.

Other enclosures that may be sent with the wedding invitation include cards designating reserved pews, "At-Home" cards that announce when the bride and groom will return from their honeymoon and where they will reside, and maps or other travel information.

Nontraditional, informal invitations can be designed and printed or handwritten in whatever style or form the bride and groom desire. African traditions, for instance, can be integrated into African American weddings by including Kinte colors and Adrinke symbols on the invitations.

Wedding announcements usually are sent to people who would like to know about the wedding but who would not be expected to attend. They use the same paper and printing as the invitations. The wording is also similar, although the parents of both the bride and the groom are often mentioned and the words *announce the marriage of* replace *request the honor of your presence at the marriage of.* Wedding announcements are sent out the day of, or shortly after, the wedding.

Response to a wedding invitation is dictated by the type of invitation. A formal invitation traditionally is answered with a third-person, handwritten note that might read:

> Mr. and Mrs. Harold Sloane
> accept with pleasure (or regret they will be
> unable to attend)
> Mr. and Mrs. Appleton's
> kind invitation for
> Saturday, the fourth of February.

Of course, if a response card is enclosed, it may simply be filled out and returned. If the invitation is less formal, a handwritten response in more standard, informal English is correct.

SHOWERS

Bridal or wedding showers can be given by any close friend of the bride. They should not be given by a member of the bride's immediate family.

There is no set rule for the number of showers that can be held before a wedding, although only members of the wedding party are invited to more than one shower. Nor is there a hard-and-fast rule for the types of parties they should be; serving anything from coffee and cake to cocktails to a light supper is appropriate.

Unless it is a surprise shower, the guest list is drawn up by the bride (or the bride and groom if both are to be present). The host for the party should set the limit on the number of guests. Guests invited to the shower should also be invited to the wedding, unless the wedding is to be very small.

"Etiquette" means, literally, "warning sign" as in "Keep off the Grass." When Louis XIV's gardener complained that the nobles were ignoring such warnings, the king ordered them to observe "the etiquettes." This term soon meant the rules for deportment at court.

Everyone attending a shower is expected to bring a present, which is opened at the party. The host or another friend of the bride should keep a list of who gave what, so that thank-you notes can be sent later on.

BACHELOR DINNER

Several days before the wedding, a bachelor dinner can be given for the groom. It is usually held in a private room of a restaurant and hosted by the best man or the ushers, although a groom may give his own bachelor dinner.

Generally, the men drink and eat a great deal. At some point in the evening, the groom toasts his bride-to-be. It is rarely appropriate to break the glasses after such a toast, although this was once the custom. The only important rule regarding bachelor dinners is that they should not be held the night before the wedding, so that there is adequate time for the groom to recover from the festivities.

REHEARSAL DINNER

The wedding rehearsal takes place the day before the wedding and is usually followed by a dinner party, or "rehearsal dinner." Customarily, the groom's parents host this dinner party, but it can be given by the bride's family or a close friend of the couple. Those invited include the members of the bridal party, immediate family, out-of-town family members who have been invited to the wedding, and the person performing the ceremony. Seating for rehearsal dinners may be arranged at one long table or, to fit more guests, at a U-shaped table. (See illustrations on next page.)

Best man   Bride   Groom   Maid of honor

Groom's father

Groom's mother

Bride's mother   Honored guest   Clergy or person performing service   Bride's father

Rehearsal Dinner—Seating Arrangement at One Long Table

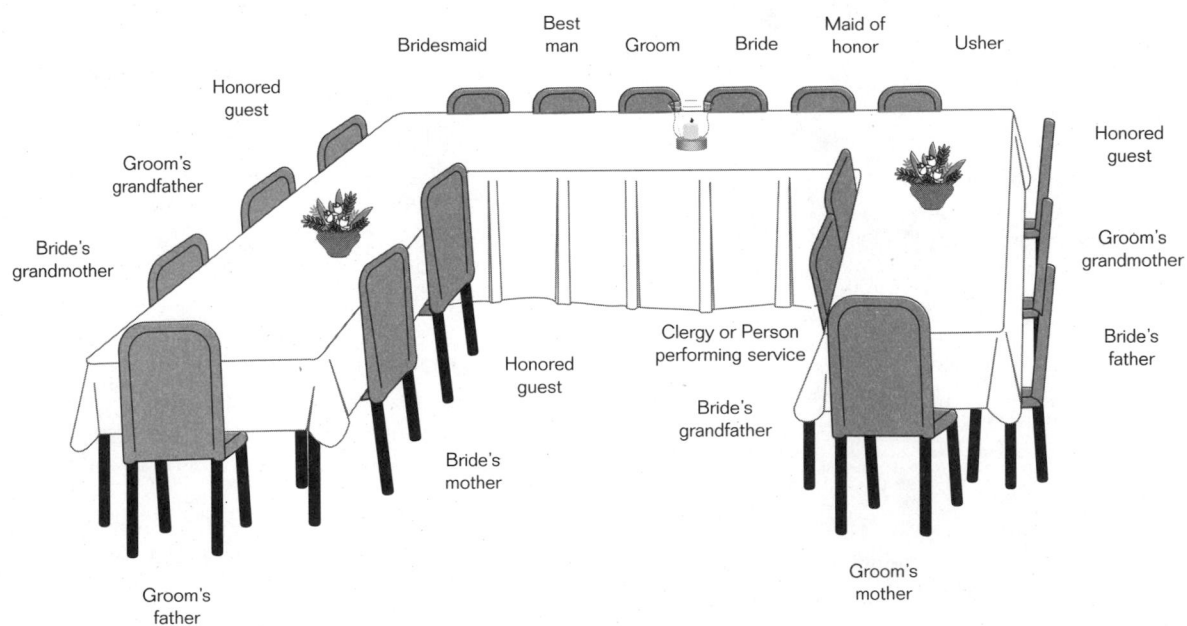

Bridesmaid   Best man   Groom   Bride   Maid of honor   Usher

Honored guest

Groom's grandfather

Bride's grandmother

Honored guest

Groom's grandmother

Bride's father

Clergy or Person performing service

Honored guest

Bride's grandfather

Bride's mother

Groom's father

Groom's mother

Rehearsal Dinner—Seating Arrangement at a U-shaped Table

CEREMONY

The wedding ceremony itself can be as formal or informal as the bride and groom wish it to be. For most weddings to which guests are invited, and especially church and synagogue weddings, a prescribed series of events will take place.

First comes the processional. In Christian and Reform Jewish weddings, the ushers come down the aisle first, arranged in height order, followed by any junior ushers. They are followed by junior bridesmaids, then bridesmaids, in height order, with the shortest first. Then comes the maid or matron of honor, the flower girls, the ring bearer, and, finally, the bride, holding the right arm of her father. The groom and the best man wait at the front of the room with the clergy.

Orthodox and Conservative Jewish processionals are led by the ushers, who are followed by the bridesmaids. Next come the rabbi and cantor followed by the best man and then the groom, accompanied by his mother and father. The maid of honor is next; she is followed by the bride, who walks between her mother and father.

The guests stand during the processional and remain standing until the clergy has asked them to sit, usually after opening remarks or a prayer. Once at the front of the room, the bride's father (or parents) steps back or to one side, and the groom steps forward to meet his bride. Bride and groom stand next to each other holding hands or with her hand on his arm, if they wish.

In Protestant ceremonies, the father of the bride gives her away before sitting down in the first pew. In Roman Catholic ceremonies, the father of the bride sits with his wife as soon as the bride is delivered to the groom. Orthodox and Conservative Jewish ceremonies require that the parents of the bride and groom remain at the front of the room; if there is space, they stand under the marriage canopy, known as a *chuppah*.

The actual events of the wedding ceremony differ widely among various denominations. African American couples sometimes include a symbolic jumping-of-the-broom in the ceremony in remembrance of enslaved African men and women jumping over a broomstick to symbolize their commitment during a time when they were forbidden by law to marry. Most Christian services include a blessing of the ring or rings. (If the bride is wearing an engagement ring, she should put it on her right hand for the service and then place it outside the wedding band afterward.) Orthodox Jewish services are mostly in Hebrew, and two glasses of wine are shared by the couple before the groom breaks the goblet at the end of the ceremony.

The recessional for Christian and Reform Jewish weddings is led by the bride and groom. They are followed by the flower girl, the best man and maid or matron of honor, and the ushers and bridesmaids; a line of bridesmaids follows the bride and a line of ushers follows the groom. Orthodox and Conservative Jewish recessionals are led by the bride and groom, followed by the bride's parents, the groom's parents, the maid of honor with the best man, the flower girl, and the rabbi and cantor. Bridesmaids and ushers bring up the rear. In Orthodox ceremonies, all the men are on one side, and all the women on the other.

RECEPTION

The style of the reception will follow the style of the rest of the wedding. Ordinarily, photographs are taken immediately after the ceremony; they are ordered and paid for by the bride's family.

A receiving line greets guests as they come into the room. The line consists of the mothers of the bride and groom, the wedded couple, the maid of honor, and, at the discretion of those involved, the fathers of the couple, the bridesmaids, the best man, and the ushers.

Formal receptions have assigned tables for those attending. The bridal party will generally be at the head table, and a parents' table will be nearby. Other guests should be assigned to tables with people whose company they will enjoy.

Almost all receptions include a toast to the bride and groom, which is proposed by the best man. The groom should reply with thanks after the toast has

Etiquette

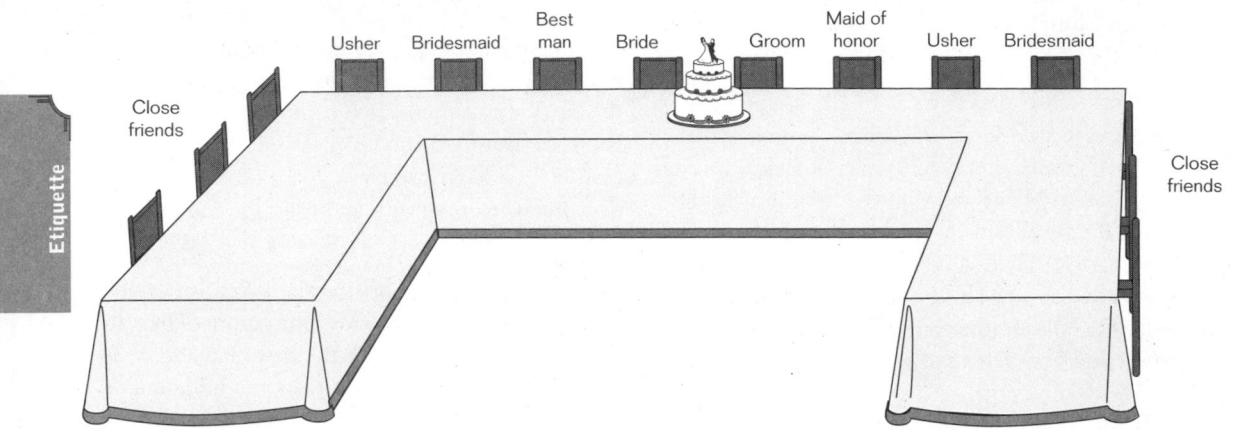

Reception—Seating Arrangement at Head Table

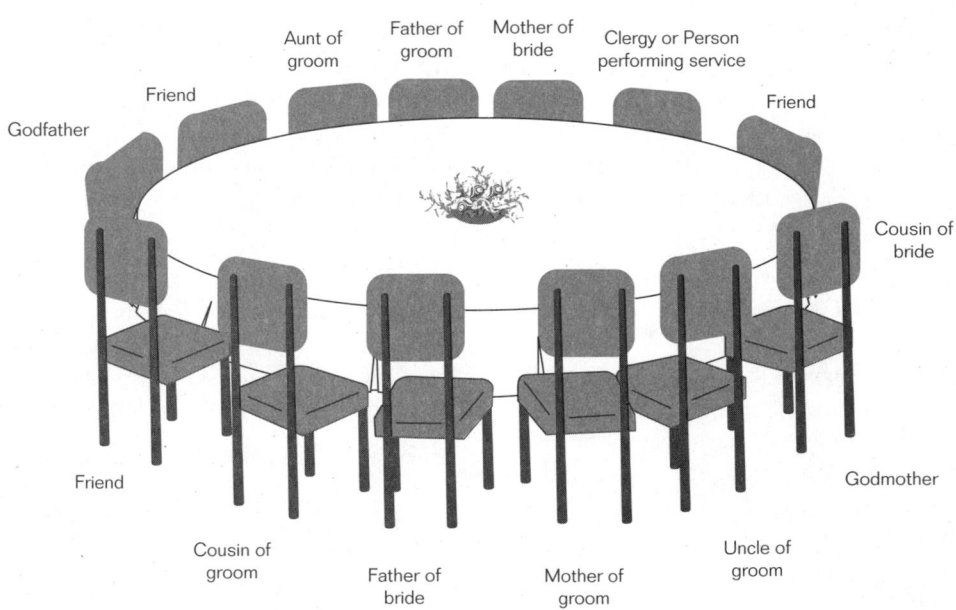

Reception—Seating Arrangement at Parents' Table

been drunk and offer a toast to his bride; other toasts may be offered as well. The toasts can be followed by dancing or a meal, if one is to be served. The wedding cake is cut just before dessert, or shortly before the bride and groom leave the reception if it is not a formal dinner. The bride cuts the first slice, with the help of her new husband, from the bottom tier of the cake, and the couple offer each other a bite. The top layer of the cake, with its decorations, is removed and saved for the bride and groom, while the remainder is cut up and served to the guests.

At the reception's end, the bride usually will toss her bouquet from stairs or a landing, turning her back and throwing it over her shoulder to her bridesmaids or other female friends; the one who catches it is supposed to marry next. Then the newlyweds change clothes, say good-bye to their families, and, led by the best man, leave in a shower of confetti, rose petals, rice, or birdseed.

GIFTS AND THANK-YOU NOTES

Gifts can be sent to the address on the At-Home card, if one is enclosed with the invitation, or to the home of the bride's mother. They also can be brought to the reception. Custom dictates that a wedding gift can be given to the bride and groom within the first year of their marriage. A note should be included explaining why the gift was delayed. Among some people, money is an appropriate wedding gift; it is usually presented to the bride in an

---

Division of Wedding Expenses

A Closer Look

Today, the groom and his family often offer to share some of the wedding expenses that traditionally have been borne by the bride's family. This is a significant change of custom, as the costs of traditional weddings have become too prohibitive for many families to absorb. If the groom's family does not offer to share expenses, however, the bride's family should plan a wedding in accordance with their means.

The traditional division of expenses is listed below. In addition to the change noted above, it should be kept in mind that there are numerous exceptions and variations depending on religion, ethnicity, or local custom. Many items may be omitted without diminishing the ceremony in any way.

Expenses Paid by Bride's Family
Bridal consultant, if needed
Invitations and announcements
Flowers for the church and receptions, bouquets for
   the bridesmaids, bouquet for bride (sometimes given
   by groom)
Music for the ceremony, including organist or choir fee
Transportation of bridal party to church or synagogue
   and reception
Bride's presents to her bridesmaids
Bride's present to groom (optional)
Groom's wedding ring
Sexton's fee (church fee)
Accommodations for out-of-town bridesmaids
All expenses of reception, including music

Expenses Paid by Bridesmaids
Dress and accessories
Transportation to and from town of wedding
Gift to the couple and contribution to a gift from all
   bridesmaids to the bride

Expenses Paid by Groom's Family
Bride's rings, both engagement and wedding
Groom's present to bride (optional)
Groom's presents to ushers and best man
Groom's boutonniere and boutonnieres for ushers
Ties and gloves for the ushers
Clergy member's fee; tips to altar boys
Corsages for immediate members of both families and
   bride's going-away corsage
Accommodations for out-of-town ushers
Bachelor dinner (optional, and often given by ushers)
Rehearsal dinner (optional, but becoming more
   standard)
Honeymoon

Expenses Paid by Ushers
Transportation to and from town of wedding
Rental of wedding attire
Gift to the couple and contribution to a gift from all
   ushers to the groom
Bachelor dinner (optional, and often given by groom)

Expenses Paid by Out-of-Town Guests
Transportation and accommodations
Gift to the couple

envelope, which she will place in a special purse or in a box or basket put out for this purpose. Envelopes, and usually gifts as well, are not opened until after the reception.

Thank-you notes should be handwritten and should mention the gift that was given. They should be sent shortly after the couple's honeymoon is over.

ANNIVERSARY GIFTS

Etiquette authorities differ on the appropriate gifts to be presented on the occasion of individual wedding anniversaries. The following list represents a modern consensus, with the eight oldest and most traditional gifts indicated in *italic*.

1	*Paper* or plastic
2	Cotton or calico
3	Leather
4	Linen, silk, or synthetics (rayon, nylon)
5	*Wood*
6	Iron
7	Copper, wool, or brass
8	Bronze or electrical appliances
9	Pottery
10	*Tin* or aluminum
11	Steel
12	Silk or linen
13	Lace
14	Ivory
15	*Crystal* or glass
20	*China*
25	*Silver*
30	Pearls
35	Coral or jade
40	Rubies or garnets
45	Sapphires or tourmalines
50	*Gold*
55	Emeralds or turquoise
60	*Diamonds* or gold
75	Diamonds or gold

BUSINESS ETIQUETTE

The business world is extraordinarily demanding and extremely competitive. In it, there are really only a few criteria on which members will be judged: competence, initiative, leadership, and how well one gets along with others. In this last area, manners play a crucial role, for individuals must be able to present themselves well and deal well with others if they wish to succeed in business.

APPOINTMENTS

Business life requires that people meet each other face-to-face to conduct transactions or exchange information. To do so, they schedule appointments. The first rule regarding business appointments is that they should be kept if at all possible; failing to show up for an appointment will be taken as a sign of uninterest, carelessness, and lack of professionalism. If an appointment cannot be kept, it should be canceled as far in advance as possible. If an individual is unavoidably delayed, he or she should telephone the host or have someone else make the call.

When greeting a person who has a severe loss of vision, always identify yourself. When talking to a person in a wheelchair, try to sit down so that you are at eye level. Never shout at a person with a hearing impairment; shouting inhibits lip reading and distorts the sounds amplified by hearing aids.

When guests are shown into the office where the appointment will take place, the host should rise from his or her desk, shake hands, and greet them; if the host and guests have not met before, they should introduce themselves. The guests should be offered seats, and the host should either sit back down at the desk or sit with the visitors. Coffee or tea may be offered by the host but should not be requested by the guests.

Any business meeting should get to the business at hand as quickly as possible. It is just as important to listen as it is to talk, not simply to be polite but to get the most out of the meeting. It is also important not to interrupt others during meetings. Taking notes during a business meeting is acceptable.

The host usually will conclude a business meeting, either by making remarks that sum up the discussion or by suggesting outright that everything pertinent has now been discussed. It is important for guests to pick up on such cues, gather their belongings, thank the host, shake hands, and leave. A follow-up letter, thanking the host for the meeting and outlining whatever was agreed upon at the meeting, should be sent by the next business day.

ENTERTAINMENT

Business entertaining generally takes place in an office; over breakfast, lunch, or dinner at a restaurant; or over drinks after work. The purpose of business entertaining is to conduct business in a congenial setting that is less formal than an office.

The person initiating business entertainment acts as the host. That person is responsible for deciding on the setting, making reservations, and paying the bill. The site chosen for entertaining a client or colleague should be appropriate to the person being invited and the nature of the business relationship; a prestigious restaurant would be right for entertaining a major client, while drinks at a clubby bar might be a good choice for entertaining a vendor who regularly sells supplies to the company.

Regardless of the setting, it should be kept in mind that business is the main purpose of the get-together. The host should endeavor to bring up the business at hand before the guest becomes impatient. However, business discussions should not interfere with the pleasure of enjoying the meal.

In 1907, President Theodore Roosevelt set a world record for handshaking by shaking hands with 8,513 people at a New Year's Day White House presentation.

The host should pick up the check when it is brought to the table, look it over, and pay it. Because business entertaining should give both parties more or less equal status, it makes no difference whether the host is a man or a woman. There is no reason for a guest even to show a pretense of wanting to pick up the check; the guest can express his or her thanks to the host as she or he is leaving.

GIFTS

Gift giving is not at all unusual among people who work together. Bosses often give gifts to employees for birthdays, Christmas, or Secretaries' Day; staff members may give the boss a present for holidays or birthdays; office colleagues sometimes give each other gifts; and executives can give presents to clients or vendors.

Such gifts are generally not lavish, although the type of gift is dictated by the nature of the relationship. Bosses tend to give larger presents to their employees than staff members give to the boss. Gifts to colleagues reflect the degree of friendship between them. Clients or vendors give and receive gifts appropriate to the amount of business transacted and the longevity of the relationship.

Business gifts should be less personal than gifts for a friend. A date book or similar office accessory, costume jewelry, a tie, or a bottle of wine makes a good, inexpensive business gift. More lavish presents, like theater tickets, food baskets, or a case of wine, can be given to long-standing clients or employees.

THE TELEPHONE

For many companies, the telephone is an essential tool for conducting business. Proper telephone manners can make it an effective tool.

Many people think that having a secretary or assistant place calls will enhance the image of an executive. In fact, having others place calls for oneself is an inconvenience, both for the secretary or assistant who must place the call and for the person receiving the call, who must wait for the executive to get on the line. People in business should place their own phone calls.

When the call goes through, the caller should identify himself or herself by name and company; if the nature of the call is not readily apparent, the caller should volunteer this information. With some companies, this process will have to be repeated two or three times—with the switchboard operator, a secretary, and the person being called.

Go to

"Business Letters" in chapter 15

A caller should not take offense if asked to identify the reason for the call, although this type of questioning is often a thinly disguised way of keeping a boss insulated from people he or she does not want to receive calls from. Screening phone calls is acceptable, but not if the caller is then asked to hold the line and finally is told that the person being called is not available. As with placing calls, the most convenient and polite way of dealing with incoming calls is to answer them yourself; if you are too busy to answer the phone yourself, a secretary should keep the interrogation of a caller to a minimum.

People answering business phones should identify themselves and ask if they can help the caller. They should be attentive, organized, and unhurried. If answering someone else's phone, they should be ready to take a message.

Business phones should not be used for personal calls. If a personal call must be made, or if one is received, it should be kept as brief as possible. Similarly, business calls should be kept brief and to the point. Chattiness and rudeness are always to be avoided in business telephone calls.

NETWORK ETIQUETTE (NETIQUETTE)

Just as social and business etiquette involves the use of good manners and consideration for others, network etiquette, or "netiquette," follows conventions on how people should conduct themselves when using a computer network or the Internet. Here are a few tips to keep in mind once you're online and surfing the Internet.

- When composing electronic mail, you must choose words carefully. Sending e-mail is not a secure procedure; because there is no control over where e-mail goes after it's sent, anyone could be reading your message.
- Unlike face-to-face or telephone conversations, computer communications make facial expressions or verbal emphasis difficult to convey. In addition, type styles are not transmitted well— if at all. If used for emphasis, they will some-

times produce an unreadable garbled message on the recipient's end. Instead of using italic or boldface to add emphasis, you can use *asterisks* or write in UPPERCASE. Avoid using uppercase too often in messages you send on the Internet because it is the equivalent of shouting. "Smileys" or "emoticons" are faces viewed sideways that are added to online messages to convey feelings: :) stands for a smile, :(stands for a frown, and ;) stands for a wink. "Smileys" are discussed in Chapter 12.

- While surfing the Net, a person cannot be judged by his age, weight, sex, or color, but a person can and will be judged by the quality of his or her writing. Correct spelling and grammar count.
- You may never see or meet the people you communicate with, so it's easy to be rude. Remember that you are interacting with other people, not simply with a computer screen.

PARTIES

GENERAL ASPECTS

Parties come in all shapes and sizes. They can be held for holidays, anniversaries, housewarmings, birthdays, weddings, or farewells, or just to have some friends over. Parties range from sit-down dinners in banquet halls to tea and cookies in living rooms. But whatever the size or style of the party, certain aspects need to be tended to make it a success.

INVITATIONS

Invitations can be given in writing, in person, or by telephone, or e-mail depending on the sort of party they are for. Engraved invitations are sent for formal parties, such as weddings and anniversary parties. Less formal events require less formal invitations; handwritten notes on personal stationery or printed invitation cards with blanks that can be filled in can be used. Invitations to small informal parties can be issued by telephone or by e-mail. Invitations should be sent out about three weeks before a party.

R.S.V.P.s

Your invitation should include a request that guests respond if you want to know in advance who will be coming. A formal invitation can include a response card or just "R.S.V.P." Informal invitations can include a statement like "Unless we hear otherwise, we'll expect you on the third" or "Please let us know if you can make it." Telephone invitations will usually get immediate responses; however, if you are invited by telephone and do not know whether you can attend, it is acceptable to put off a response. In any case, it is important to respond to an invitation as quickly as possible so that the hosts can plan accordingly.

ATTIRE

Formal events call for certain types of attire, especially for men. *White tie* is the most formal evening attire and includes a white tie, wing collar, and tailcoat. *Black tie* is the more common evening wear and includes a tuxedo, a bow tie, and a white, soft shirt. When the occasion calls for *semiformal* attire, that usually means a sport coat, shirt, tie, and nice slacks for men, and a dress or pantsuit for women.

Every aspect of a Japanese tea ceremony, from the tea bowls to the flowers and food, is carefully chosen by the host and should be complimented by his or her guests.

FORMAL DINNER PARTIES

SEATING ARRANGEMENTS

The host and hostess, as well as any guests of honor, are the people around whom seating arrangements are set at more formal dinner parties. The host and hostess will usually sit at either end of the table; a male guest of honor sits at the hostess's right and a female guest of honor at the host's right. Other guests are told where to sit by the host and hostess,

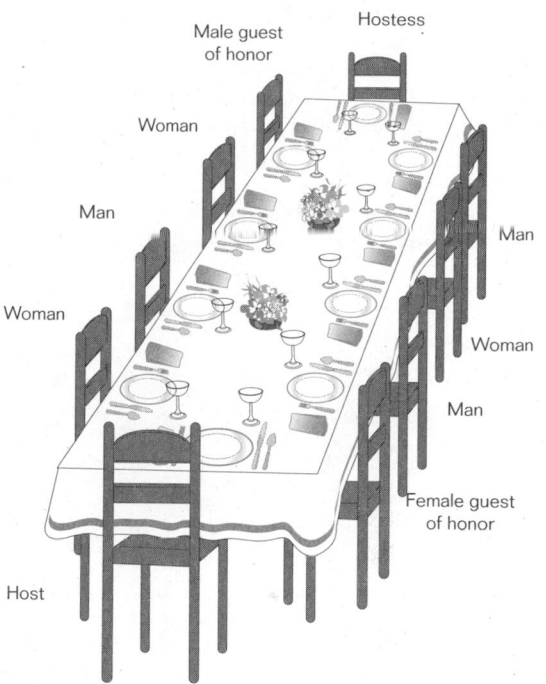

Formal Dinner Party—Seating Arrangement

either personally or by using place cards. Although it is customary to alternate men and women at a sit-down dinner, this practice can be ignored if there are more members of one sex than of the other. Husbands and wives can be seated together or separated. Obviously, buffet dinner parties, cocktail parties, and other informal get-togethers do not require any sort of specific seating arrangement; guests can be expected to fend for themselves.

TABLEWARE

A place setting at a formal dinner party can be somewhat intimidating to guests unfamiliar with such events. The arrangement of plates, glasses, and utensils is fairly standard, however, and fairly easy to deal with, as illustrated on the next page.

The basic setting should be in place when the guests sit down. A service plate is in the center, usually with the napkin on top of it. Flanking the plate will be the flatware: a dessert or salad fork to the immediate

a Oyster or shellfish fork	**e** Fork and knife for salad and cheese	**i** Water goblet
b Soup spoon	**f** Sherry glass (with soup)	**j** Champagne glass (with dessert)
c Fork and knife for fish	**g** White wineglass (with fish)	**k** Butter plate and knife
d Fork and knife for meat	**h** Red wineglass (with meat)	

Formal Dinner Party—Place Setting

a Water goblet	**e** Soup spoon	**i** Dinner fork
b Wine glass	**f** Dessert spoon	**j** Salad plate
c Coffee cup and saucer	**g** Knife	**k** Butter plate and knife
d Coffee spoon	**h** Dessert or salad fork	

Informal Dinner Party—Place Setting

left of the plate; a dinner fork to the left of it; and a fish fork, if needed, on the outside. To the right of the plate are, from closest to farthest, the salad knife; the meat knife; the fish knife; a soup or fruit spoon (or both); and, if shellfish is being served, a shellfish fork. Utensils are used in order from the outside in.

Glasses are placed above the knives to the right of the plate. There will be a water goblet and, extending to the right from there, a champagne glass, one or two wineglasses, and a sherry glass.

In addition to the service plate, a butter plate is placed above the forks, to the left of the service plate. The butter knife is set across the butter plate.

Formal etiquette dictates that a soup bowl must always be tipped away from, never toward, the diner.

SERVING

Food at a formal dinner party is usually served by hired help. Guests are served from the left, and plates are cleared from the right. The female guest of honor is served first; if there is no guest of honor, women are served before men or, if this is hard to manage, a woman is served the first plate with the other guests served in order. The hostess is served last. Warmed dinner plates are usually brought out just before the entree is served. A clean service plate should be brought out for each of the other courses.

INFORMAL DINNER PARTIES

If the dinner party is less formal and fewer courses are served, the basic place setting is arranged with fewer utensils. (See illustration on preceeding page.)

DEATHS AND FUNERALS

Plans for death should be discussed with family and loved ones before such plans are likely to be needed. A person's desires regarding the sort of funeral held, disposal of the body by burial or cremation, and donation of organs need to be known. Practical matters—where to find insurance papers, the will, bills, bank accounts, safety deposit boxes, or investment holdings—also should be dealt with in advance.

FUNERAL ARRANGEMENTS

Funeral directors provide a variety of services and handle the details of funeral arrangements, such as placement of a death notice in the newspaper; selection of a coffin; and travel to church, synagogue, and graveyard. Many of these arrangements can be made in advance or at the time of death. The death notice includes the deceased's name and date of death, the names of immediate family members who survive, and the place and time of the wake and funeral if the funeral is not private.

WAKES

Traditionally, wakes were held at the dead person's home, but today wakes are usually held at a funeral home. They are strictly a Christian phenomenon; Jews sit *shiva* during a seven-day period of mourning and remembrance immediately after burial. Anyone may attend a wake, unless it is kept private. The hours and days are set and usually appear in the death notice in the newspaper. Nonfamily members should sign the guest book provided at the funeral home, stay just long enough to express sympathy to the bereaved family, and then leave. Expressions of sympathy are best if they come from the heart; when at a loss for what to say, a simple "I'm sorry" is enough. Standing, kneeling, or praying at the coffin is optional.

FLOWERS

Sending flowers is a customary way of expressing sympathy, especially if attendance at the wake or funeral is not possible. They can be sent to the funeral home or the church along with a card. Flowers are not appropriate for Jewish funerals or if the death notice requests donations to charity instead.

FUNERAL SERVICES

Unless specified as private in the death notice, funeral services can be attended by anyone. They should be viewed not as an obligation but as an opportunity to publicly bid farewell to the person who died and to show concern for the survivors. Religious affiliation is unimportant; one may attend a funeral service regardless of faith. It is important to speak to the bereaved family at the funeral service; if sympathy has already been expressed at the wake, a positive comment about the service, the eulogy, or the church or synagogue would be appropriate.

BURIAL

For Jews, burial takes place within 24 hours, or as quickly as possible. Christians are buried two or more days after death. Close friends and family members are generally the only people expected to attend the actual interment.

A reception generally is held after the burial. The funeral director or a family member will invite those present to attend. It can be held at the home of a relative or at a catering hall or restaurant. Food and drink are provided by the bereaved family or arranged for by them.

LETTERS OR CALLS OF CONDOLENCE

Letters or calls of condolence are appropriate in lieu of attendance at a wake or funeral service. They should be brief and should focus on memories of the dead person, sympathy for the survivors, and offers of help to the survivors. Avoid pity in such communications or visits, and make clear that a response is not expected soon.

AFTER BURIAL

It is important to be available to the grieving family after all ceremonies are over. If the family is Jewish, they will sit *shiva* for seven days; it is appropriate to drop by and bring food but not flowers. If the family is Christian, stop by a few days later to listen and talk. Whatever the religious affiliation, friends who are willing to listen and talk to bereaved family members are highly valued at this time.

ADDITIONAL SOURCES OF INFORMATION

Ford, Charlotte, and Jacqueline Demontravel. *21st-Century Etiquette.* Lyons Press, 2001.

Lauter, Peter. *Wireless Etiquette: A Guide to the Changing World of Instant Communication.* Omnipoint Communications, 1999.

Martin, Judith. *Miss Manners' Guide to Domestic Tranquillity: The Authoritative Manual for Every Civilized Household, However Harried.* Three Rivers Press, 2000.

Miller, Samantha. *E-Mail Etiquette.* Warner Books, 2000.

Pincus, Marilyn, and Letitia Baldrige. *Everyday Business Etiquette.* Barrons, 1996.

Post, Elizabeth. *Emily Post's Etiquette.* 16th ed. HarperCollins, 1997.

Post, Peggy. *Emily Post's Entertaining: A Classic Guide to Adding Elegance and Ease to Any Festive Occasion.* HarperReference, 1998.

_____. *Emily Post's Wedding Etiquette.* Harper Information, 2000.

Spizman, Robyn Freedman. *The Perfect Present: The Ultimate Gift Guide for Every Occasion.* Crown, 1998.

Stewart, Marjabelle Young. *Commonsense Etiquette: A Guide to Gracious, Simple Manners for the Twenty-First Century.* Griffin, 1999.

Tuckerman, Nancy, and Nancy Dunnan. *The Amy Vanderbuilt Complete Book of Etiquette.* 1st ed. Doubleday, 1995.

Von Drachenfels, Suzanne. *The Art of the Table: A Complete Guide to Table Setting, Table Manners and Tableware.* Simon & Schuster, 2000.

Woodward, Chiquita, *It's Just What I Always Wanted! More than 2,000 Imaginative and Unique Gifts.* Hyperion, 1999.

17

FIRST AID

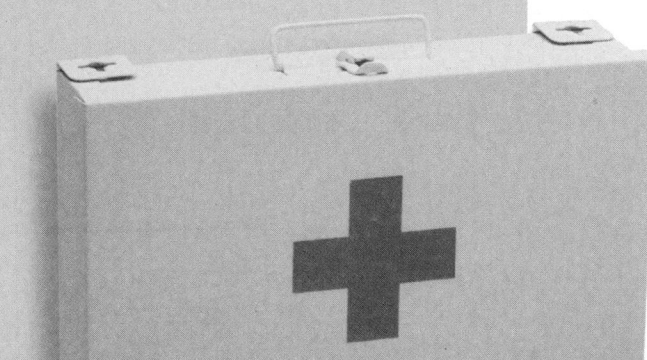

LIFESAVING PROCEDURES

The American Medical Association recommends that when a person is injured or becomes suddenly ill one should ***immediately call for medical help.*** After help is summoned, priority should be given to these objectives:

1. Maintain breathing and circulation
2. Prevent loss of blood
3. Prevent further injury
4. Prevent shock

MAINTAINING BREATHING AND CIRCULATION

When breathing stops, the victim has enough oxygen in the blood and other tissues to sustain life for only a few minutes. Any delay in restoring the flow of oxygen to the brain and other body organs can result in death or permanent damage. Start artificial respiration and manual external cardiac massage immediately if the person is not breathing. Basic cardiopulmonary resuscitation (CPR)—mouth-to-mouth breathing and external cardiac massage—does not require equipment. It can be done by only one or two rescuers, but having more rescuers increases the chances for success.

If you are not directly involved in the rescue effort, you can help by calling a doctor, an emergency medical service (EMS), or the police or fire department. But rescuers should not wait for professional support to arrive. Seconds count. Rescue may involve

---

A Closer Look

Methods of Cardiopulmonary Resuscitation (CPR)

Mouth-to-Mouth Breathing

Step 1: If there are no signs of breathing or there is no significant pulse, place one hand under the victim's neck and gently lift. At the same time, push with the other hand on the victim's forehead. This will move the tongue away from the back of the throat to open the airway. If available, a plastic "stoma," or oropharyngeal airway device, should be inserted now.

Step 2: While maintaining the backward head tilt position, place your cheek and ear close to the victim's mouth and nose. Look for the chest to rise and fall while you listen and feel for breathing. Check for about 5 seconds.

Step 3: Next, while maintaining the backward head tilt, pinch the victim's nose with the hand that is on the victim's forehead to prevent leakage of air, open your mouth wide, take a deep breath, seal your mouth around the victim's mouth, and blow into the victim's mouth with four quick but full breaths. For an infant, give gentle puffs and blow through the mouth *and* nose and do not tilt the head back as far as for an adult.

If you do not get an air exchange when you blow, it may help to reposition the head and try again.

If there is still no breathing, give one breath every 5 seconds for an adult and one gentle puff every 3 seconds for an infant until breathing resumes.

If the victim's chest fails to expand, the problem may be an airway obstruction. Mouth-to-mouth respiration should be interrupted briefly to apply first aid for choking. See the "Choking" subsection in "Treatment for Health Emergencies."

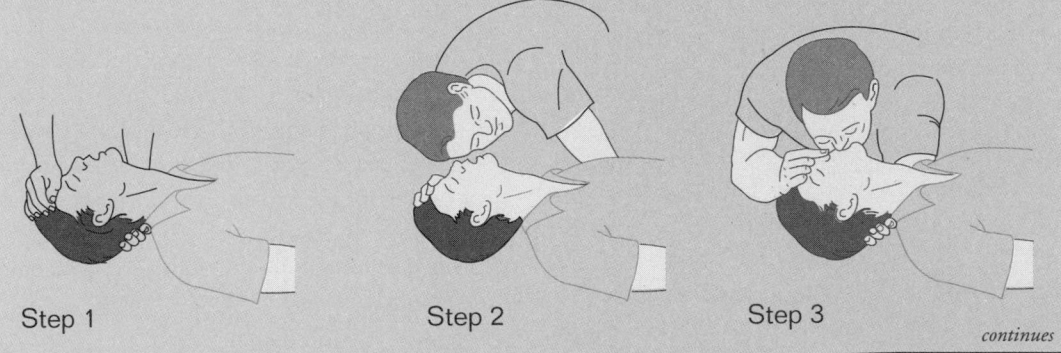

Step 1   Step 2   Step 3

continues

Methods of Cardiopulmonary Resuscitation (CPR), continued

Cardiac Massage

Check the carotid artery pulse. If there is no pulse, begin external cardiac massage by squeezing the heart between the sternum (breastbone) and the spinal column. To begin external cardiac massage, take a position facing the victim and uncover his or her chest. Find the bottom (xiphoid process) of the breastbone and place your index and middle fingers next to it to mark the location. Next, place the heel of your other hand on the sternum, just above the xiphoid process. Remove your first hand and place it on the second, interlocking the fingers. Holding your arms straight, rock back and forth from the hips and press downward so the sternum is depressed between one and two inches. Do not press on the xiphoid process and do not exert enough pressure to cause internal injuries to the liver or other organs in the area.

If possible, mouth-to-mouth breathing and external cardiac massage should be combined at a rate of 12 breath cycles and 60 chest compressions per minute. If at least two rescuers are available, one should perform mouth-to-mouth breathing while the other does chest compressions.

Check frequently for signs of a carotid artery pulse, a return of normal skin coloring, or signs of spontaneous breathing. Even if normal breathing returns, remain ready to resume CPR if necessary and until a doctor or other professional medical help arrives.

Mouth-to-Nose Breathing

When mouth-to-mouth breathing is not feasible, mouth-to-nose breathing can be performed in a similar manner by placing your mouth over the victim's nose and holding his or her lips closed between the thumb and forefinger.

For Small Children

If the victim is a small child, your mouth can be placed over both the nose and mouth. Be careful about extending the neck of an infant because soft tissues in the neck may obstruct the upper airway if the head is tilted too far.

External cardiac massage for a small child should be done with the pressure of two thumbs or two fingers, and compression should be limited to a depth of only one-half to one inch, depending on the size of the child.

For Drowning Victims

If drowning is the cause, do not wait until the victim can be transported to shore or placed on a flat surface to begin CPR. Mouth-to-mouth artificial respiration can be started while the victim is in a boat or is floating in the water. See the "Choking" and "Drowning" subsections in "Treatment for Health Emergencies" later in this chapter.

First Aid

three related actions: opening an airway to the lungs, restoring breathing, and restoring circulation.

First, place the victim on his or her back on a hard, flat surface, such as the floor. If breathing has stopped because of poisonous gas or lack of oxygen, move the victim quickly to fresh air before beginning CPR.

Second, examine the victim closely for possible injuries or other obstacles that would interfere with CPR action. Check for a pulse in the carotid artery, on either side of the neck beneath the chin. Try to get the attention of the victim by talking, pinching, or tapping. If there is no response, assume that the person is unconscious. Look, listen, and feel for any signs of air moving in or out of the victim's lungs.

PREVENTING LOSS OF BLOOD

Heavy bleeding, or hemorrhaging, is a life-threatening emergency. Bleeding from a large artery can result in death in less than five minutes. As with maintaining breathing and circulation, immediate action is needed. Notify a doctor, an emergency medical service (EMS), the police, or the fire department. If the victim can be moved safely and quickly, take him or her to a nearby hospital emergency room.

First Aid

COVERING THE WOUND

Unless there are injuries or other conditions that might interfere, keep the victim lying down with the bleeding part of the body raised higher than the rest of the body. If the bleeding is external, as from an open wound, place a clean cloth, handkerchief, pad, or similar object directly over the wound and press firmly, with both hands if necessary.

If blood soaks through the cloth, add more cloth and keep pressing, but do not take off the original pad or cloth until the bleeding is under control. Ice placed directly over the wound may help reduce the blood flow by causing constriction of the blood vessel that is the source of blood loss.

There are four basic blood types: A, B, O, and AB. The most common is type O, present in 40% to 60% of the population.

Apply firm pressure to the pressure point (see **Pressure Points** below) to control blood flow to the wound. If possible, apply pressure to the pressure point with one hand while your other hand presses a pad over the wound. Do not apply a tourniquet unless there is no other way to stop the loss of blood. A tourniquet can result in the death of tissues in an arm, leg, hand, or foot and may lead to amputation.

A
Closer
Look

Pressure Points

Fingers usually can be applied without worsening a victim's condition to control bleeding at a pressure point. There are a half-dozen pressure points where bleeding from an artery can be stopped or reduced by pressing the artery against a bone located next to it.

Neck, Mouth, or Throat

To stop bleeding from the neck, mouth, or throat area, apply pressure at a point near the base of the neck where an artery passes alongside the trachea, or windpipe. Place the thumb of the hand against the back of the victim's neck and the fingers on the neck just below the larynx, or Adam's apple. Then push the fingers against the artery.

Lower Arm

An artery supplying the lower arm passes by the bone of the upper arm about halfway along the upper arm. Pressing the artery against the arm bone can stop bleeding from nearly any point beyond.

Upper Arm

A pressure point for controlling the loss of blood in the area of the upper arm, shoulder, or armpit should be found where an artery passes over the outer surface of the top rib. Place the thumb in the position shown (the top rib is indicated in the drawing) and the fingers over the shoulder so that they press against the area behind the collarbone. Apply pressure to the artery crossing the top rib.

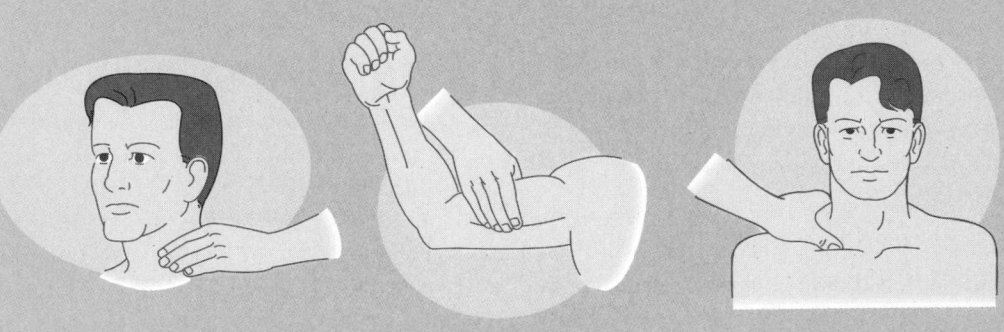

Neck, Mouth, or Throat   Lower Arm   Upper Arm

continues

Pressure Points, continued

Head Below Eye and Above Jawbone

Bleeding from an artery supplying the area of the face below the level of the eye usually can be controlled by finding the pressure point on the artery that crosses the edge of the jawbone.

Head Above Eye Level

For bleeding above the level of the eye, the rescuer should be able to find a pressure point where an artery passes over one of the skull bones in front of the upper portion of the ear, as shown in the drawing.

Leg or Foot

To stop bleeding from a leg or foot, apply pressure at a point in the area of the groin where the femoral artery passes over one of the bones of the pelvis, as shown in the drawing. If the blood flow slackens or stops, you can assume you have found the pressure point.

If at first you do not find the exact pressure point location, try again. The locations may vary somewhat with different body builds. You will know when you find the correct place, because bleeding will diminish or stop. As when a tourniquet is used, remember to release pressure at intervals to allow some blood to flow to deprived tissues. Do not continue compressing an artery if bleeding stops.

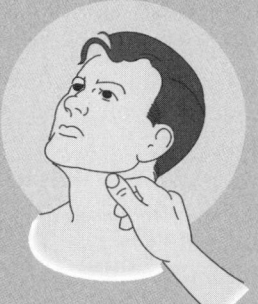

Head Below Eye and
Above Jawbone

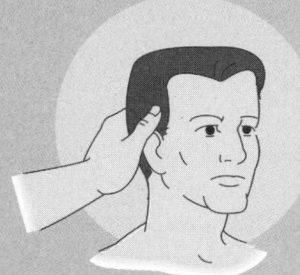

Head Above Eye Level

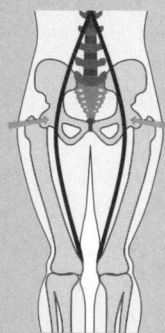

Leg or Foot

First Aid

GENERAL CARE OF THE VICTIM

Heavy bleeding leads to symptoms of shock: thirst, cold and clammy skin, dizziness, and falling blood pressure. Keep the victim flat and covered with a blanket or coat. Also, maintain body temperature by making sure the victim is not lying on a cold or damp surface. Do not use the shock position if you suspect the victim has a head, neck, or back injury and cannot be moved.

> **Go to** "Anatomical Drawings of the Human Body" in chapter 3; "Medicine and Pharmacology Symbols" in chapter 12

Unless the victim is unconscious or suffering from an abdominal wound, allow him or her to drink water or other beverages as needed; blood loss requires replacement of fluids. Do not give a wounded person alcoholic beverages, which would have the effect of increasing fluid depletion.

If the victim has suffered an open abdominal or chest wound and professional medical help is not immediately available, cover any protruding organs with a clean damp cloth held in place with a bandage or by hand pressure.

An open chest wound may result in a lung collapse unless the wound can be covered quickly with a gauze or cloth pad held in place by a firm bandage to prevent air from moving in or out of the lung. If a gauze pad is not available, make a pad from plastic sheeting, aluminum foil, or other clean material to form an airtight seal. If a bandage is not available, use a belt to hold the pad in place. Do not touch an open wound except as necessary to apply pressure or a pad or other dressing. Never try to explore a wound to locate fragments of metal, glass, or other debris that may have caused the injury.

An ice-cream headache is triggered when cold food or drink hits the roof of the mouth. The pain peaks in about 25 to 60 seconds, and skin temperature on the forehead falls almost 2 degrees Fahrenheit.

ADVISING DOCTORS AND EMS PERSONNEL

If a tourniquet is applied to stop the loss of blood from an arm or leg so seriously damaged that it may have to be amputated, be sure to advise the doctor or emergency medical service (EMS) personnel who will eventually take charge. Better yet, attach a note or write a message with lipstick on the victim's forehead that a tourniquet has been used. Do not assume that a hospital emergency-room doctor or intern many miles away will be aware that a tourniquet or any other special first-aid measures may have been applied at the scene of the accident.

PREVENTING FURTHER INJURY

First aid in an emergency should be limited to no more than is necessary to save a life or prevent further injury. In most cases, do not move an injured person from an accident site before a doctor, emergency personnel, or police or fire personnel arrive. An exception is a situation, such as a building fire or potential explosion, in which the lives of the rescuers as well as the victims could be in danger. If there is an injury to the neck or spine, a victim should not be moved until a stretcher or other carrying device that provides firm support is available. Improper

movement of the victim could cause a broken or dislocated bone that may damage an internal organ or pinch or sever a vital nerve trunk and result in death or permanent disability.

If the victim appears to have a head injury, movement should be delayed until a doctor has examined the person. Even then, any movement should be supervised by a physician. Do not move the head, or other body parts, if there is bleeding from the nose, mouth, or ears. If the victim is unconscious, you must assume that he or she has a head injury.

Never assume that an unconscious, disoriented, or apparently incoherent person is drunk. The victim may have suffered a head injury in a fall, a physical assault, or an accident. There are numerous causes of impaired consciousness, including brain hemorrhage, concussion, carbon-monoxide poisoning, epilepsy, encephalitis, diabetic coma, hypoglycemia, heart trouble, psychiatric disorders, and barbiturates or other medications. Never give alcoholic beverages to an accident victim, and never offer fluids of any kind to a person who is unconscious or semiconscious or who has internal injuries.

PREVENTING SHOCK

Shock can be expected at any accident scene. It is a common, natural reaction to any severe physical or psychological injury. Generally, shock results from an automatic change in a person's blood circulation, as nature suddenly diverts blood to the vital organs in an effort to ensure the victim's survival. This natural reaction, however, can lead to death through circulatory collapse.

Shock prevention is next in priority to maintaining respiration and control of bleeding. Watch for—but do not wait for—the common shock signs: (1) a weak, rapid pulse, (2) skin that is cold and moist with "cold sweat," (3) dilated pupils or eyes that appear "vacant," (4) restless or abnormally anxious behavior, (5) nausea or thirst, (6) faintness and weakness. If the person becomes quiet and slips into unconsciousness, shock has already progressed beyond the first stages.

First Aid

First-Aid Kits

A Closer Look

Many people are confused about the meanings of terms, such as bandages and dressings, used by health professionals. Dressings are held in place by bandages. A *dressing* can be anything placed over an open wound to control bleeding, absorb blood or secretions, and prevent infectious agents from entering the body through the wound. The best kind of dressing is a piece of sterile gauze, but in an emergency, any clean material may become a dressing—even a sheet, a piece of plastic, or a newspaper. Fluffy materials, such as cotton wool, however, should not be used because the loose fibers will stick to body tissues.

A *bandage* is a strip of muslin, gauze, or other material used to hold a compress or dressing in place. A *roller bandage* is a long strip of cloth that can be used as a dressing or compress as well as a bandage. A *triangular bandage* is one cut from a square of cloth along a diagonal line. A *compress* is a square of fabric, generally of flannel or wool, used to apply heat, cold, or medications to the skin.

An ideal family first aid kit should contain the following:

12 4-by-4-inch sterile dressings in sealed envelopes	1 pair of needle-nose pliers
12 2-by-2-inch sterile dressings in sealed envelopes	1 eyedropper
2 15-foot-long roller bandages, 1 inch wide	1 set of measuring spoons
	12 wooden tongue blades (for finger splints)
2 15-foot-long roller bandages, 2 inches wide	12 wood splints, 12–18 inches long
1 roll of adhesive tape	1 bar of antiseptic soap
4 triangular bandages with safety pins	1 package of salt
1 clean bedsheet	1 package of baking soda
2 small bath towels	1 package of aspirin tablets
2 large bath towels	1 package of antihistamine tablets
1 pair of blunt-nose scissors	1 package of anti-motion-sickness tablets
1 pair of tweezers	1 large package of adhesive bandages, assorted sizes
	1 package of paper cups

A usual first-aid measure for shock is to position the victim so that the head is lower than the rest of the body, thus allowing gravity to pull blood toward the brain. An exception may be necessary if the victim has a head injury and cannot be moved.

Keep the victim warm and protected from the weather. Providing too much warmth, however, can lead to sweating with loss of vital body fluids and redirection of the blood flow from the vital organs to the surface of the body. Fluids may be given to a shock victim under certain circumstances—if the person is conscious, does not have internal injuries, and can swallow. Fluids can be vital for the survival of a victim who has suffered burns. It is better to give fluids in the early stages of shock, because fluids may not be absorbed from the digestive system later. If the accident site is some distance from the nearest

hospital or doctor's office, small amounts of warm water or tea may be offered. But do not offer fluids if emergency service personnel or other professional help are nearby and the victim is likely to be anesthetized for surgery. If a physician is available, by telephone or otherwise, let the doctor make the final decision about fluids for accident victims.

Some persons at an accident scene may suffer only minor cuts and bruises but experience psychological shock. The signs and symptoms are the same as for victims with serious physical injuries. Time and personnel permitting, psychological shock cases should receive the same care for their shock symptoms as the severely injured. If those with psychological shock are allowed to slip into unconsciousness with possible circulatory failure, their condition will obviously complicate the overall rescue effort.

First Aid

TREATMENT FOR HEALTH EMERGENCIES

ABRASIONS

A minor break in the skin, such as one caused by scraping or rubbing against a rough surface, should be washed with soap and water and treated with mild antiseptic, such as hydrogen peroxide. Then cover the abrasion with a sterile gauze dressing held in place with a bandage. If signs of infection appear, consult a doctor.

ANIMAL BITES

Animal bites, whether from a pet or a wild animal, can cause a puncture wound, a laceration, or an avulsion, in which part of the flesh is torn away. First aid should be directed toward control of bleeding and protecting the wound from infection until it can be examined by a doctor. Unless the wound is extremely painful or bleeding profusely, clean it with soap and water and cover it with a sterile dressing before taking the victim to a doctor's office or hospital emergency room.

Many animal bites require a tetanus shot and, if the animal is identified as being rabid, additional protection against rabies. In most communities, local health authorities require notification of any serious animal bite.

BLACK EYES AND BRUISES

Black eyes and bruises are actually a type of closed wound in which blood from a damaged vessel in the soft tissues has leaked into a space beneath the skin. Apply ice or a cold compress to reduce the swelling and control the further loss of blood under the skin. In most cases, the pool of blood will be reabsorbed and the skin color will return to normal.

BOILS AND BLISTERS

A *boil* is a tender, often painful, pus-filled swelling of the skin. A boil is also known as a *furuncle*, and a group of furuncles is a *carbuncle*. Boils should be treated quickly and carefully to prevent the spread of a more serious infection and the formation of a scar. A boil around the nose or face can be particularly serious and should be treated with antibiotics by a doctor. Most other boils should be treated with moist heat to cause spontaneous rupture and drainage. The pus contains staphylococcus bacteria and should not be allowed to spread the infection.

Blisters are fluid-filled skin eruptions that may be caused by allergy, injury, sunburn, insect bites, infection, friction, irritation, or drug reaction. Correcting the cause is important if the cause is an infection, allergy, or drug reaction. Most ordinary blisters can be treated with a mild antiseptic and a protective dressing. Do not puncture a blister. If the blister is accidentally broken, treat it as a wound.

BURNS

Burns can be caused by contact with heat, chemicals, electricity, or radiation. One of the effects is "burn shock," in which body fluid is diverted from normal blood flow to the brain, heart, and other vital organs to the burned area of the body. Burn shock is the same as physical or psychological shock and can even follow severe sunburn. Small thermal burns, as those caused from fire, steam, or touching a hot object, usually result in pain, a reddened skin area, and blisters. In many cases, the burn can be treated with ice or cold water. Do not try to open a blister. It can be protected by a pad held in place with a loose bandage.

In addition to all of the riches found in King Tut's tomb, archaeologists also found a personal first-aid kit that included bandages and a finger sling.

Never apply ointments or grease, including butter or margarine, baking soda, or other household substances, to a burned skin area.

A severe or extensive thermal burn requires professional care in a hospital. A doctor and/or emergency personnel should be summoned. While waiting for professional medical care, the victim should be made to lie down with the head and chest lower than the legs (shock position). Cover the burned area with a clean cloth to exclude air. Infection is a common complication if the skin is broken. If the victim is conscious and can swallow, provide adequate non-alcoholic liquids to drink. Because of burn shock, body tissues require fluid replacement. See "Lifesaving Procedures: Preventing Shock" earlier in this chapter.

FIRST- AND SECOND-DEGREE BURNS

First-degree burns are marked by redness or other skin discoloration, pain, and swelling. An ordinary sunburn is typical of a first-degree burn. These burns generally are treated as small thermal burns and usually will heal with the application of cold water followed by a dry dressing.

Second-degree burns are often the result of exposure to flame, scalding liquids, or a very severe sunburn. The skin is usually reddish, mottled, and damaged, with signs of body fluid loss. These burns are treated as extensive thermal burns, requiring professional medical care.

THIRD-DEGREE BURNS

Third-degree burns are marked by damage to tissues beneath the skin. The area may resemble a second-degree burn at first, but it quickly progresses to a whitish or charred coloration. Third-degree burns often result from contact with high-voltage electricity, steam, or boiling water, or from an accident in which the person is trapped in burning clothing. A third-degree burn is a true medical emergency. While ice or cold water may be used as a first-aid measure for first- or second-degree burns, nothing should be applied to a third-degree burn. Do not even remove clothing from burn areas. Burn areas can be covered temporarily, however, with sterile dressings, clean sheets, or even plastic garment bags. Do not put plastic materials over facial burns.

If the third-degree burn victim is conscious and not vomiting, small amounts of fluid should be offered.

The recommended beverage is lukewarm water containing a teaspoon of salt and one-half teaspoon of baking soda per quart of liquid, to be sipped at a rate of one ounce every four or five minutes while waiting for professional medical help.

The first known dentists were the Etruscans, who in 700 B.C. carved false teeth from mammals' teeth and created partial bridges that could be used to eat.

CHEMICAL BURNS

Chemical burns, either acid or alkali, are generally corrosive reactions that tend to affect the skin, eyes, and digestive tract. They usually result from spills, leaks, and splashes. A strong acid or alkali can cause permanent tissue damage. An alkali burn may be more serious than an acid burn because an acid usually is neutralized by contact with body tissues, whereas an alkali can continue causing damage until it is neutralized by another substance or washed away with copious amounts of water.

As a result, all chemical burns should be flooded—not merely rinsed—with water. It is usually important to remove contaminated clothing, which tends to absorb the chemical and hold it next to the skin, exacerbating the damage. Water flooding should continue while clothing is being removed. If possible, insert a hose under the clothing to inject water between the skin and the contaminated fabric.

CHOKING

Obstruction of the airways leading to the lungs can be caused by food, candy, chewing gum, or other objects accidentally inhaled. If air is unable to reach the lungs, the body's oxygen supply can become exhausted in a few minutes, resulting in death.

(*Note:* A person whose windpipe [trachea] is blocked cannot talk but must make those around aware that he or she is choking, using sign language or any other means so that first aid can be given immediately.)

There are two accepted ways of giving first aid to a choking person.

1. The Heimlich maneuver, which consists of a series of thrusts to the upper abdomen. Stand behind the victim and put your arms around his or her upper abdomen so that your hands can be clasped in a fist at the bottom of the victim's breastbone. Then quickly push your fist upward into the victim's chest, putting pressure on the lungs so that any air in them will be squeezed backward up into the windpipe, pushing the obstruction into the mouth. The Heimlich maneuver may have to be repeated six or more times to dislodge a foreign body in the throat. If the victim is pregnant or very obese, the rescue pressure should be directed through the chest rather than the abdomen.

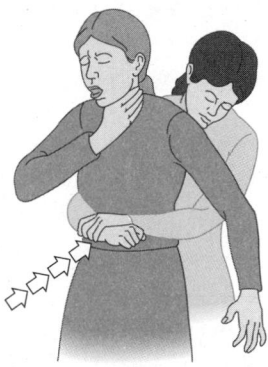

2. Firm blows over the spinal column between the shoulder blades. Stand behind the choking person and help him or her lean over, using one hand on the victim's chest to lend support.

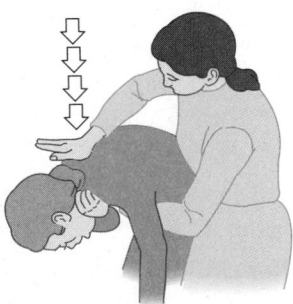

Then hit high on the back with the heel of your hand. Four or more back blows may be needed to dislodge the object in the windpipe.

CONCUSSIONS

A concussion can result from a head injury and may be accompanied by a brief or longer period of unconsciousness. The victim may experience headache, blurred vision, or other signs of nervous system damage and may lapse into a coma. The victim, even if conscious, should be treated as an unconscious person. Keep the person quiet and warm, watch for signs of shock, and help maintain breathing if necessary while awaiting arrival of a doctor or emergency medical service (EMS) personnel.

CONVULSIONS

A convulsion, or seizure, involves a disturbance of the nervous system that affects the muscles of movement. The person experiencing a convulsive seizure will lose consciousness and may have uncontrollable twitching of the muscles, or the muscles may become rigidly contracted. There are different kinds of seizures and many possible causes. In general, however, first aid should be aimed at keeping the victim safe until the seizure ends naturally. Keep calm and reassure other people who may be nearby. Clear the area of anything hard or sharp to lessen the chance of the victim hurting themselves. Remove glasses, if any, and loosen any tight neckware. Cushion the head and turn the person gently onto their side to help keep the airway open. You should not place anything in the victim's mouth, or restrain their movements, during or after the seizure. Meanwhile, keep track of the time; if the seizure lasts more than five minutes, or if the person has more than one seizure after another, summon a doctor or EMS personnel.

DROWNING

Drowning is a form of asphyxiation due to an inability of the victim to get oxygen into the lungs. It may also be complicated by inhalation of fluid into the lungs. First aid for a drowning victim requires

CPR procedures to maintain breathing and circulation. Do not waste time trying to squeeze water out of the lungs, particularly if the accident occurred in freshwater. If the victim has been in seawater, try to keep the body positioned with the head and chest lower than the abdomen and legs to assist fluid drainage from the lungs. See the "Methods of Cardiopulmonary Resuscitation (CPR)" sidebar earlier in this chapter.

ELECTRIC SHOCK

Severe electric shock can be caused by contact with ordinary electric lines in a home, office, or factory, as well as by high-voltage lines or a lightning bolt. An electric charge can have a number of effects on the body, including muscular contractions or seizures, paralysis of the lungs, abnormal heart function, bone fractures, thermal burns, and changes in blood chemistry.

Saving a person from further injury or death by electrocution should be done carefully so that the rescuer does not also become a victim. The electric shock victim first must be safely separated from contact with the electricity by turning the electricity off or by removing a wire or electric appliance with an insulated tool, such as a dry stick. In some cases, it may be easier to throw a loop of rope or cloth about the victim's arm or leg and drag him or her away from the source of electricity. However, do not go within 20 feet of a person who is being electrocuted by high-voltage electrical currents until the power is turned off. If the victim is alive but unconscious, summon a doctor or EMS personnel. If breathing has stopped or there is no pulse, begin CPR immediately while awaiting the arrival of medical professionals.

FRACTURES, DISLOCATIONS, AND SPRAINS

Fractures, dislocations, and sprains generally will require the use of splints and, for arm injuries, slings to prevent movement. Splints can be made with wood, pillows, or rolled-up newspaper, if necessary. See illustrations on page 488.

A *fracture* is a broken bone. If medical help is not available, these emergency treatment methods should be followed:

- Call an ambulance
- While waiting for professional medical help, prevent movement by splinting the injury in the position in which you found it. No attempt should be made to try to reset a broken bone.
- If the broken bone punctures the skin, control the bleeding with direct pressure. Cover the wound with sterile dressing and secure it in place. See the "Pressure Points" sidebar under "Preventing Loss of Blood" earlier in the chapter.
- Keep the person warm and watch closely for signs of shock.

A *dislocation* is an injury in which a bone is displaced from its proper position at a joint. Suspect a dislocation if the injured part is swollen or visibly out of shape, or if the person is in intense pain and cannot put weight on the injured part. If medical help is not available, these emergency methods should be followed:

- Without an X ray, it is difficult to tell whether a bone is dislocated or fractured, so treat the injury as if a fracture has occurred. To prevent movement, splint the joint in the position in which you found it. Do not try to correct the dislocation yourself. See "Preventing Shock" earlier in the chapter.
- Take the person to an emergency room for an X ray and examination.

"Health and Nutrition" in chapter 18

Go to

First Aid

Leg Splint

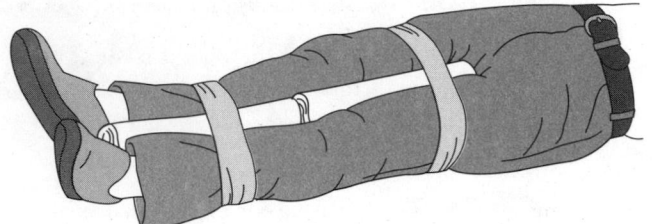

Arm Splint

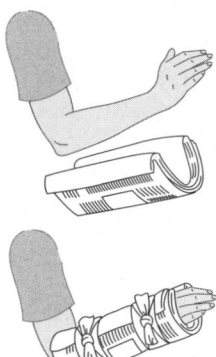

Splint and Sling Combinations

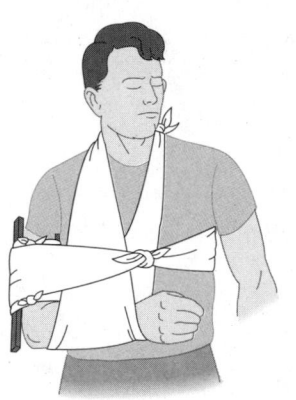  

Sprain Treatment

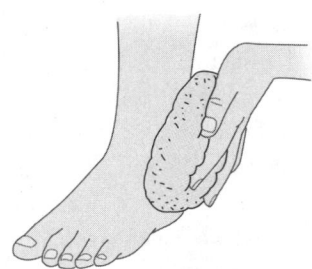 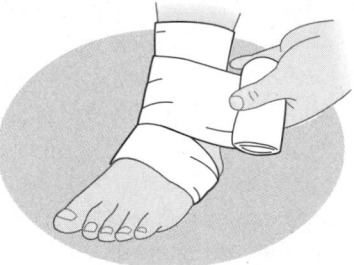

TREATMENT OF SPRAINS

A *sprain* is an injury to the ligaments. It occurs when a ligament or muscle is wrenched or twisted outside its normal range of movement and ligaments are torn. For a serious sprain, which may be indistinguishable from a fracture, treat the injury as if a fracture has occurred. For less severe, less painful sprains, follow these emergency methods:

- Do not let the person stand on or use the injured body part.
- Apply ice and compress the injury to decrease swelling.
- Support and immobilize the sprain with an elastic bandage.
- Keep the sprain elevated with either a pillow or sling.

FROSTBITE

The most common cold-weather injury is frostbite. Severe cold can constrict the blood vessels, thereby reducing the normal flow of warm blood to the exposed tissues. The symptoms usually include a very cold feeling in the exposed skin area followed by a loss of feeling. The skin may appear flushed or red at first, but later it becomes white or a grayish yellow. Because of the loss of feeling, the victim is often unaware of the danger of frostbite.

The victim should be taken into a warm environment, and all tight or wet clothing in the affected body area should be removed. The frostbitten area should be immersed in warm—but not extremely hot—water (experts recommend a water temperature of around 105°F).

You can offer the victim hot coffee, tea, cocoa, or soup, but smoking should be avoided because it has an effect similar to that of cold, causing constriction of blood vessels. Do not rub the frostbitten tissues. If bleeding, swelling from fluid accumulation, or other complications develop after the exposed areas have thawed, notify a doctor immediately.

HEAT CRAMPS, HEAT EXHAUSTION, HEATSTROKE

Prolonged exposure to high temperatures can lead to several life-threatening health problems. The most serious effects are heat exhaustion and heatstroke. *Heat cramps* are usually in the form of painful muscle spasms caused by excessive sweating and loss of body salt. The skin may be hot and dry or cool and clammy. In most cases, heat cramps can be treated with food and liquid containing sodium chloride (ordinary table salt).

Heat exhaustion, or heat prostration, is due to loss of body fluid. It is marked by nausea, weakness, excessive sweating, and faintness. The skin is pale and clammy, the pulse is weak, and the victim may show signs of shock. The loss of body fluid results in loss of blood volume and, in turn, a deficiency of oxygenated blood reaching the brain. Have the victim lie flat with the head down and give him or her small sips of cool, slightly salted liquids every few minutes. Do not give the victim too much fluid too rapidly.

Heatstroke, or sunstroke, is the most serious type of heat injury. It may begin suddenly with headache, dizziness, and fatigue. The skin is hot, dry, and flushed, and the pulse is extremely rapid. The victim can develop a very high fever of around 105°F, experience convulsions, or become unconscious. Unless first aid is given immediately, the person may suffer circulatory collapse and die. Cool the body by wrapping the victim in wet clothing or bedding. Use snow or ice, if available, or immerse the person in cool water while awaiting the arrival of an emergency medical service (EMS) crew or a physician. Check the victim's temperature every 10 minutes to make sure the body temperature does not fall too rapidly. Hypothermia, or excessively cold body temperature, could complicate the condition.

INSECT BITES

Bites or stings of ants, bees, hornets, wasps, yellow jackets, mosquitoes, and other insects usually result in the injection of substances under the skin of the person attacked. The body's reaction may vary from mild itching to a severe form of shock, depending on the venom or other foreign protein injected and the sensitivity of the person to the substance. Some hypersensitive persons can experience an extreme allergic reaction, known as *anaphylactic shock*, marked by breathing difficulty or circulatory failure within a few minutes after a bite or sting. Such individuals require special prescription drugs that should be carried when they expect to be near stinging or biting insects.

For most people who experience insect bites and stings, first aid may require only the application of ice or a cold compress to slow the rate of venom absorption. If the insect leaves its stinger in the skin, remove it with care, as the venom sac usually is still attached and should not be squeezed.

First Aid

Ticks and other insects that may cling to the skin may require application of a petroleum product or similar irritant in order to remove them. In addition to causing local pain, swelling, and irritation, bites of ticks and other insects can result in serious infections requiring hospitalization.

NOSEBLEEDS

Nosebleeds are usually caused by rupture of the numerous capillaries in the soft tissues near the tip of the nose. A nosebleed may be started by an injury, high blood pressure, physical activity, or sudden change in atmospheric pressure, as may occur in traveling from sea level to a mountaintop. First aid requires keeping the victim quiet and in a seated position with the head leaning forward. Apply pressure to the outside of the bleeding nostril, or insert gauze pads in one or both nostrils and squeeze the outside of the nose toward the midline. Also, apply ice or a cold compress to the nose and surrounding areas of the face. If the nose continues to bleed, notify a doctor.

POISONING

A poison is anything that may be injurious to health or dangerous to life if it is swallowed, inhaled, or touched by the skin. Common sources of poisons include contaminated foods, carbon-monoxide gas, cleaning products and solvents, certain household plants, pesticides, and medicines.

In any case of a swallowed poison, the container of food or other substance should be saved, with the label and any remaining contents, so that doctors or poison control center personnel can recommend the most rapid and effective treatment.

First aid for most cases of swallowed poisons depends on the type of substance involved and the condition of the victim. Do not try to induce vomiting in any poisoning victim if he or she is unconscious or having convulsions.

Go to "Directory of Poison Control Centers" in this chapter; "Poisonous Cultivated and Wild Plants" in chapter 3; "Disposal of Hazardous Household Chemicals" in chapter 19

CORROSIVE POISONS

Do not induce vomiting if the victim may have swallowed a corrosive substance, such as an acid or alkali, or has a burning pain in the mouth or throat. Examples of corrosive substances are toilet-bowl cleaners, drain cleaners, lye, washing soda, and chlorine bleach.

- Do not attempt to "neutralize" swallowed acids or alkalis.
- Do not use activated charcoal for swallowed corrosive poisons.
- Do give the victim adequate amounts of milk or water.
- Do begin CPR if breathing stops.

FOOD POISONING

Food poisoning may be caused by enterotoxins, or poisons produced by bacteria that may or may not still be in the food. Symptoms usually include nausea and vomiting, cramps, diarrhea, fever, and headache, which may begin minutes to hours after the food has been eaten.

First aid in most cases includes bed rest, preferably close to a bathroom, and avoidance of any food or beverage until vomiting has stopped. When vomiting has ended, the victim should be offered sweetened tea or soft drinks and strained broth or bouillon with a little salt added. It is important to replace the body fluids and electrolytes (minerals) lost in vomiting or diarrhea.

In addition to vomiting, cramps, or diarrhea, symptoms of poisoning may include loss of consciousness, confusion or disorientation, an unusual odor on the breath, pain or a burning sensation in the mouth or throat, and stains or discoloration in or about the mouth from the leaves or berries of poisonous plants.

If the symptoms are severe, with signs of shock or the presence of blood or mucus in the diarrhea, a doctor should be notified.

A potentially fatal form of food poisoning that does not always cause vomiting or diarrhea is botulism. It is caused by a bacteria-produced poison, usually found in home-canned or processed foods. Botulism attacks the nervous system. The victim may feel no symptoms for a day or two and then experience visual problems, dry mouth and swallowing difficulty, and constipation as the poison gradually paralyzes various organ systems. Immediate hospitalization is needed to prevent the spread of the paralyzing effects to the respiratory system.

INHALED POISONS

A common type of inhaled poison is carbon-monoxide gas, as produced by a car or truck engine in a confined area or by a faulty furnace or fireplace. The first symptoms are usually headache, yawning, breathing difficulty, dilated pupils, dizziness, faintness, ringing in the ears (tinnitus), nausea, and heart palpitations, followed by loss of consciousness. A distinctive sign is a cherry-red coloring of the mucous membranes. Persons with a light complexion may show a similar bright red coloring of the skin.

In the 16th century, people believed that a piece of red coral would stop bleeding, cure madness, and protect against curses.

First aid requires fresh air and oxygen. Give mouth-to-mouth resuscitation until an emergency medical service (EMS) unit can arrive to provide 100-percent oxygen by mask. Do not give any stimulants, but keep the victim warm and as quiet as possible.

In rescuing a person from an inhaled poison, such as smoke or carbon monoxide, protect yourself against becoming a victim of the same dangerous situation. Be sure that oxygen is available by opening doors or windows of an enclosed space. If possible, carry an independent air supply if you must enter a confined or overheated area to rescue a victim of inhaled poisons. Alternatively, place a wet cloth over your nose and mouth. When a second res-

cuer is present, tie a rope around your waist and give the other end to the second rescuer, who can pull you to safety if you also are overcome by poisonous fumes.

NONCORROSIVE POISONS

Most medicines, such as aspirin, may be noncorrosive poisons. Generally, the doctor may recommend that you try to induce vomiting if the person has swallowed a noncorrosive poison that is not a petroleum distillate product. If you do not know whether the swallowed substance is corrosive or noncorrosive—or even if it is actually poisonous—call a poison control center.

To induce vomiting, use syrup of ipecac (1 tablespoon for a child; 2 tablespoons for an adult) when it is available. The syrup of ipecac should be followed with one or more 8-ounce glasses of water.

If the person does not vomit within 15 minutes after one dose of syrup of ipecac, repeat the dose.

If syrup of ipecac is not available, use soapy water or a handwashing liquid detergent dissolved in water, or place the handle of a spoon or your finger at the back of the victim's throat. If the victim is a child, hold the child with the head lower than the hips while you induce vomiting. This position will reduce the chance of vomit entering the lungs.

Save a sample of the vomit so that it can be analyzed in a medical laboratory.

PETROLEUM DISTILLATES

For swallowed petroleum distillates, such as gasoline, kerosene, lighter fluid, paint thinner, or furniture polish, call the nearest poison control center or hospital emergency room immediately for specific instructions. The exact type and amount of the poison may determine the treatment. Some products contain more than one kind of poison.

Symptoms may include coughing, choking, cyanosis (blue skin), breath holding, a burning sensation in the stomach, lethargy, coma, convulsions, and spontaneous vomiting.

- Do not induce vomiting. There is a great risk that some of the vomited poison may enter the lungs; some hydrocarbon products are more than a hundred times as poisonous in the lungs as in the digestive tract.
- Do, if recommended by a doctor, give the person a glass of milk to dilute the poison and reduce stomach irritation.

PLANT POISONS

The major contact poison plants in North America are poison ivy, poison oak, and poison sumac. They are usually identified by their clusters of three shiny leaflets. Signs and symptoms of contact with these plants include itching skin and blisters. These are effects of a poisonous resin in the leaves. Some first-aid relief can be had by diluting and washing away the resin with a strong laundry soap and water. Follow-up treatments can include moistened dressings, starch baths, or oatmeal baths to relieve the itching. Do not break the blisters. If the blisters are oozing and crusting, exposing them to dry air may give some relief. More serious adverse effects can result from chewing the leaves of poison ivy or inhaling the smoke of plants being burned. Swallowing or inhaling the resin causes painful swelling of the lining of the throat, accompanied by fever and weakness. The symptoms may require professional medical treatment.

A study of American coins and currency revealed the presence of bacteria, including staphylococcus, E. coli, and klebsiella, on 18% of the coins and 7% of the bills.

SNAKEBITES

Most snakebites should be treated like those of any wild animal. If the bite is from a poisonous snake, the symptoms may vary according to the type of snake and its venom. But most poisonous snake bites will be followed immediately by an intense pain and a feeling of numbness in the bite area. The bite of a pit viper, such as a rattlesnake, cottonmouth, or copperhead, is often identified by fang punctures about one-half inch apart. Such a bite may also produce swelling. Other snakebites may or may not leave fang marks. A wound from the bite of a coral snake may show a chewing action of the snake's jaws.

In general, a snakebite victim should remain still. Any body movement will tend to increase the spread of venom. If the bite is in an arm or leg, the limb should be immobilized and kept lower than the level of the heart. If a hospital or other medical facility is less than 30 to 40 minutes away, the victim should be delivered there for professional care as quickly as possible. Other first-aid measures are suggested only for cases in which a doctor or hospital is not easily available.

A constriction band should be tied around the arm or leg a few inches above the bite and between the bite and the heart. The bite may be washed with soap and water and covered with a sterile dressing. Ice or a cold compress can be applied, but not directly over the bite. As in any other serious injury, the victim should be monitored closely for signs of shock. In some cases, an incision can be made in the bite area for removal of some of the venom by suction. Incision and suction, however, should be performed only if a doctor is not available and immediately after the bite has been inflicted. The person making the incision should be aware that when cutting into an arm or leg, there is a high risk of causing permanent damage to nerves, blood vessels, muscles, or other tissue.

DIRECTORY OF POISON CONTROL CENTERS

Following is a list of poison control centers and state offices that can refer you to local poison control centers. Also, check your local phone directory for nearby centers or call 800-222-1222, a national poison control number that will route your call to the nearest available center in the United States.

UNITED STATES

Alabama
Alabama Poison Center
205-345-0600
800-462-0800 (Alabama only)

Regional Poison Control Center
The Children's Hospital of Alabama
205-939-9201
205-933-4050
800-292-6678 (Alabama only)

Alaska
Anchorage Poison Center
Providence Hospital Pharmacy
907-261-3193
800-478-3193 (Alaska only)

Arizona
Arizona Poison and Drug Information Center
Arizona Health Sciences Center
520-626-6016
800-362-0101 (Arizona only)

Samaritan Regional Poison Center
Good Samaritan Regional Medical Center
602-253-3334
800-362-0101 (Arizona only)

Arkansas
Arkansas Poison and Drug Information Center
University of Arkansas for Medical Sciences
501-686-5540
800-376-4766 (Arkansas only)

California
California Poison Control System
800-876-4766 (800-8-POISON) (California only)

Colorado
Rocky Mountain Poison and Drug Center
303-629-1123

Connecticut
University of Connecticut Health Center
203-674-3056
800-343-2722 (Connecticut only)

Delaware
The Poison Control Center
215-386-2100

District of Columbia
National Capital Poison Center
202-625-3333

Florida
The Florida Poison Information Center
Tampa General Hospital
813-256-4444
800-282-3171 (Florida only)

Georgia
Georgia Poison Center
Hughes Spalding Children's Hospital
404-616-9000
800-282-5846 (Georgia only)

Hawaii
Hawaii Poison Center
808-941-4411

Idaho
Idaho Poison Center
208-334-4570
800-632-8000 (Idaho only)

Illinois
BroMenn Poison Control Center
BroMenn Regional Medical Center
309-454-6666

Regional Poison Control Center
Rush-Presbyterian-St. Luke's Medical Center
312-942-5969
800-942-5969

Indiana
Indiana Poison Center
317-929-2323
800-382-9097 (Indiana only)

Iowa
Poison Information Center
515-241-6254
800-362-2327 (Iowa only)

Kansas
Mid-American Poison Control Center
University of Kansas Medical Center
913-588-6633
800-332-6633 (Kansas only)

First Aid

First Aid

Kentucky
Kentucky Regional Poison Center
Kosair Children's Hospital
502-589-8222
800-722-5725 (Kentucky only)

Louisiana
Louisiana Drug and Poison Information Center
Northeast Louisiana University
318-362-5393
800-256-9822 (Louisiana only)

Maine
Maine Poison Control Center
207-871-2950
800-442-6305 (Maine only)

Maryland
Maryland Poison Center
410-528-7701
800-492-2414 (Maryland only)
    For DC suburbs, see **District of Columbia**

Massachusetts
Massachusetts Poison Control System
617-232-2120
800-682-9211

Michigan
Blodgett Regional Poison Center
800-632-2727 (Michigan only)

Poison Control Center
Children's Hospital of Michigan
313-745-5711
800-764-7661

Minnesota
Hennepin Regional Poison Center
Hennepin County Medical Center
612-347-3141
Pet line: 612-337-7387

Minnesota Regional Poison Center
St. Paul-Ramsey Medical Center
612-221-2113

Mississippi
Mississippi Regional Poison Control Center
University of Mississippi Medical Center
601-354-7660

Missouri
Regional Poison Center
Cardinal Glennon Children's Hospital
314-772-5200
800-366-8888

Montana
Rocky Mountain Poison and Drug Center
303-629-1123

Nebraska
The Poison Center
402-390-5555
800-955-9119 (Nebraska and Wyoming only)

Nevada
Rocky Mountain Poison and Drug Center
303-629-1123 (Southern Nevada)

Washoe Medical Center
702-328-4129 (Northern Nevada)

New Hampshire
New Hampshire Poison Information Center
Dartmouth Hitchcock Medical Center
603-650-8000
800-562-8236 (New Hampshire only)

New Jersey
New Jersey Poison Information and Education System
800-764-7661

New Mexico
New Mexico Poison and Drug Information Center
University of New Mexico
505-843-2551
800-432-6866 (New Mexico only)

New York
Central New York Poison Control Center
SUNY Health Science Center
315-476-4766
800-252-5655

Finger Lakes Regional Poison Center
University of Rochester Medical Center
716-275-5151
800-333-0542

Hudson Valley Poison Center
Phelps Memorial Hospital Center
914-336-3030
800-336-6997

New York City Poison Control Center
N.Y.C. Department of Health
212-340-4494

Western New York Regional Poison Control Center
Children's Hospital of Buffalo
716-878-7654, 7655, 7856, 7857

North Carolina

Carolinas Poison Center
704-355-4000
800-848-6946

Duke Poison Control Center
North Carolina Regional Center
919-684-8111
800-672-1697 (North Carolina only)

North Dakota

North Dakota Poison Information Center
701-234-5575
800-732-2200 (North Dakota, Minnesota and South
   Dakota only)

Ohio

Central Ohio Poison Center
614-228-1323
800-682-7625

Cincinnati Drug & Poison Information Center
   and Regional Poison Control System
513-558-5111
800-872-5111 (Ohio only)

Oklahoma

Oklahoma Poison Control Center
405-271-5454
800-522-4611 (Oklahoma only)

Oregon

Oregon Poison Center
Oregon Health Sciences University
503-494-8968
800-452-7165 (Oregon only)

First Aid

A Closer Look

The Signs and Signals of Heart Attacks and Strokes

Heart-Attack Warning Signs

- Uncomfortable pressure, fullness, squeezing, or pain in the center of the chest lasting two minutes or more
- Spreading of pain to shoulders, neck, or arms
- Severe pain, dizziness, fainting, sweating, nausea, or shortness of breath

Not all of these signals are always present. Don't wait! Get help immediately.

Stroke Warning Signs

- Sudden, temporary weakness or numbness of the face, arm, and leg on one side of the body
- Temporary loss of speech, or trouble speaking or understanding speech
- Temporary dimness or loss of vision, particularly in one eye
- Unexplained dizziness, unsteadiness, or sudden falls

Many major strokes are preceded by "little strokes," warning signals, like the above, experienced days, weeks, or months before the more severe event.

In Case of Emergency

- If you are having chest discomfort that lasts for two minutes or more, call the emergency medical service (EMS) in your area.
- If you can get to a hospital faster by car, have someone drive you.

Before an Emergency

- Find out which hospitals in your area offer 24-hour emergency cardiac care.
- Select in advance the facility nearest your home and office, and tell your family and friends so that they will know what to do.
- Keep a list of emergency rescue service numbers next to your telephone and in a prominent place in your pocket, wallet, or purse.

Pennsylvania
Central Pennsylvania Poison Center
University Hospital
717-531-6111
800-521-6110

Pittsburgh Poison Center
412-681-6669

The Poison Control Center (greater Philadelphia
   metropolitan area)
215-386-2100
800-722-7112

Rhode Island
Rhode Island Poison Center
401-444-5727

South Carolina
Palmetto Poison Center
College of Pharmacy
University of South Carolina
803-765-7359
800-922-1117 (South Carolina only)

South Dakota
McKennan Poison Control
605-336-3894
800-952-0123 (South Dakota only)

Tennessee
Middle Tennessee Regional Poison Center
Vanderbilt University Medical Center
615-936-2034
800-288-9999

Texas
North Texas Poison Center
800-746-7661

Texas Poison Control Network at Galveston
The University of Texas Medical Branch
409-765-1420 (Galveston)
713-654-1701 (Houston)
800-764-7661 (Texas only)

Utah
Utah Poison Control Center
801-581-2151
800-456-7707 (Utah only)

Vermont
Vermont Poison Center
802-658-3456

Virginia
Blue Ridge Poison Center
University of Virginia
804-924-5543
800-451-1428

Georgetown University Hospital
202-625-3333

Virginia Poison Center
Virginia Commonwealth University
804-828-9123
800-552-6337 (Virginia only)

Washington
Washington Poison Center
Children's Hospital and Medical Center
206-526-2121
800-732-6985 (Washington only)

West Virginia
West Virginia Poison Center
304-348-4211
800-642-3625 (West Virginia only)

Wisconsin
Poison Center
Children's Hospital of Wisconsin
414-266-2222
800-815-8855 (Wisconsin only)

Poison Center
University Hospital
608-262-3702
800-815-8855 (Wisconsin only)

Wyoming
The Poison Center
402-390-5555
800-955-9119 (Wyoming and Nebraska only)

First Aid

CANADA

British Columbia
B. C. Drug and Poison Information Centre
604-682-5050
800-567-8911

Ontario
Ontario Regional Poison Control Centre
The Hospital for Sick Children
416-813-5900
800-268-9017 (Ontario only)

Nova Scotia and Prince Edward Island
Poison Information Centre
902-428-8161 (Nova Scotia)
800-565-8161 (Prince Edward Island)

Quebec
Quebec Poison Control Center
418-656-8090

ADDITIONAL SOURCES OF INFORMATION

ORGANIZATIONS AND SERVICES

American College of Emergency Physicians
P.O. Box 619911
Dallas, TX 75261-9911
800-798-1822
http://www.acep.org

American Medical Association
515 N. State St.
Chicago, IL 60610
312-464-5000
http://www.ama-assn.org

American National Red Cross
17th and D Sts., NW
Washington, DC 20006
703-206-6000
http://www.redcross.org/index.html

National Association of Emergency Medical Technicians
102 W. Leake St.
Clinton, MS 39056-4252
800-346-2368
http://www.naemt.org

National Safety Council First Aid Institute
1121 Spring Lake Drive
Itasca, IL 60143
800-621-6244
http://www.nsc.org

BOOKS

Brown, Andrew J. *First Aid: Principles and Practices.* Macmillan, 1987.

Clayman, Charles. *The American Medical Association Family Medical Guide.* 3rd ed. Random House, 1994.

Handal, Kathleen. *The American Red Cross First Aid and Safety Handbook.* Little Brown, 1992.

Jagoda, Andy, *The Good Housekeeping Family First Aid Book.* ACMD Publishing Book, Hearst Books, 2000.

Thygerson, Alton L. *National Safety Council First Aid Handbook.* Jones and Bartlett Publishers, 1995.

Zydio, Stanley, and James A. Hill. *The American Medical Association Handbook of First Aid and Emergency Care.* Random House, 1990.

First Aid

18

HEALTH AND NUTRITION

QUESTIONS TO ASK YOUR DOCTOR

"I wish I'd asked the doctor about that" is a common lament after routine checkups and more serious consultations as well. Ambiguous symptoms that may indicate illness, such as pain, changes in emotional stability, or changes in eating or sleeping habits, should be reported. Your physician may need to be reminded of important facts about your family history, previous health problems, and other factors that can affect diagnosis and treatment. Many professionals suggest making a list of health-related questions/concerns before seeing the doctor. Consider the following for inclusion in your list.

At routine checkups—individual concerns related to problems experienced since the last visit:

- I have been experiencing _____ [headaches, back pain, unexplained drowsiness, trouble sleeping, dizziness, etc.]. What could that mean? What do you recommend?
- I have a family history of _____ [heart disease, diabetes, high blood pressure, breast cancer, etc.]. Could my symptoms indicate that I am developing a problem?

Other general areas of concern:

- What are my cholesterol levels? What should they be? What do my numbers mean?
- What is my blood pressure? What should it be? What do my numbers mean?
- Do I need medication? How long will I need to take it?
- Do I need to make any major lifestyle changes [stop smoking, modify activities, stop/start/change exercise program, change diet, etc.]?

When X rays, blood tests, or other types of tests are recommended:

- Why do I need to have this test? What will the results tell you?
- Are there any risks involved in having this test performed?

- When and how will I get the results? Depending on the results, what treatment or other tests may be recommended?
- Will the test be painful? How long will it take?
- How should I prepare for the test? Can it be scheduled early in the morning if overnight fasting is required? What about other medications I am taking? Should I take them while fasting for the test? Can I drink water to swallow my pills? [If you are diabetic or take any medication that must be taken with food or liquid, remind the doctor of your situation and get specific instructions, especially when consulting a specialist who is not your regular physician.]
- How much will the test cost?

When immunization or nonsurgical treatment is recommended:

- What are the benefits of this treatment?
- Are there any risks involved with this treatment? What physical or emotional side effects can I expect?
- Are there other treatments with fewer side effects or risks that I should consider?
- What will this treatment cost?
- How can I tell if the treatment is working?

About medication:

- What are the risks/benefits associated with this medication?
- How will this medication interact with prescriptions I am already taking? Should I avoid alcohol or certain foods?
- Please explain exactly how this medication is to be taken. In the morning or night? With food or milk, or on an empty stomach? What if I forget to take it?
- Is this medication expensive? Would a generic prescription be as effective?
- How will I know if the medication is working? What problems should I call you about?

"Anatomical Drawings of the Human Body" in chapter 3; "Health Insurance" in Chapter 20; and "Medicare" in chapter 25

Health/Nutrition

Shelf Life of Medicine

A
Closer
Look

Pharmacists generally do not mark containers with expiration dates, although the containers usually show the dates of the original prescriptions. If a prescription drug is more than one year old but is not in its original container clearly showing the expiration date, it should be replaced. First-aid creams in tubes usually have expiration dates marked on the tubes, but the dates are generally hard to see. After the components separate, the creams should not be used. Vitamins and minerals will keep for a long time if protected from heat, moisture, and light. A good rule of thumb about the shelf life of drugs is "When in doubt, throw it out." Following is a list of the shelf life of some common drugs.

Cold tablets	1–2 years
Laxatives	2–3 years
Minerals	6 years or more
Nonprescription painkiller tablets	1–4 years
Prescription antibiotics	2–3 years
Prescription antihypertension tablets	2–4 years
Travel sickness tablets	2 years
Vitamins	6 years or more

If surgery is recommended:

- What procedure are you recommending? [Ask for details about the procedure.]
- Why do I need this operation?
- Are there other types of treatment available? If so, what are they?
- What are the benefits of having the procedure?
- What are the risks involved in this procedure?
- What is the prognosis if I choose not to have surgery?
- Who will perform the operation? What experience do you (does she/he) have with this type of procedure?
- I'd like to get a second opinion. Is there someone you'd recommend that I see?
- What type of anesthesia will be used? What are the risks involved? Are there alternatives?
- Will this be performed as inpatient or outpatient surgery? [If what seems to be a major procedure will be performed on an outpatient basis, ask further questions.] How long will I be in the hospital?
- Where will the procedure be performed? Is there a good success rate for this operation at that hospital? [A hospital may have high success rates with a procedure performed there frequently, whereas another medical center nearby

has less success because that type of surgery is not often scheduled.]
- How much will the surgery cost? What is your fee? [Also check with your insurance company to see how much of the cost will be covered and how much your own cost will be.]
- How should I prepare for the surgery? Can it be scheduled early in the morning if overnight fasting is required?
- What about regular medications I am taking? Should I take them before surgery? Can I drink water to swallow my pills? What about after surgery? Will I take my regular medications as usual? Should I bring my prescriptions to the hospital with me? [If you take medication for chronic conditions such as diabetes or mental/emotional illness, be sure to discuss these issues with both the surgeon and your regular physician. If new orders for your regular medications are to be written in the hospital and you will be there for an extended stay, take a list of your prescriptions with you. Once there, ask what you are being given. If the amounts or medications are unfamiliar, check with your doctor.]
- How much pain can I expect after the operation? How long will it last? Will I need medication for pain during the recovery period?

Health/Nutrition

- How long will my recovery period be? Will I need special care at home after I leave the hospital?
- Should I expect to have an emotional reaction following my surgery? What support groups or coping methods do you recommend?
- After I leave the hospital, what symptoms should I call to report? When will a follow-up visit be scheduled?
- Will there be any restrictions on my activities [driving, climbing stairs, lifting, bending, sexual intercourse, etc.]? How long will it be before I can return to work?
- What should I tell my family about the surgery?

THE PATIENT'S BILL OF RIGHTS

The provision of a written statement of patient rights has become standard practice in many health-care in-

stitutions in recent years. Such documents typically emphasize the health provider's intention to treat each patient with respect, to acknowledge the patient's right to refuse treatment/make decisions concerning treatment, to provide the best available treatment regardless of an individual's ability to pay for care, and to keep each patient's medical information confidential. The issues of a person's right to self-determination (decisions concerning treatment and the right to refuse treatment) and the protection of confidential medical records are usually central. A list of the patient's responsibilities concerning care usually follows the enumeration of rights.

An example of a typical patient's bill of rights is the following document that is now law in Florida.

Go to "First Aid" in chapter 17; "Insurance" in chapter 20; "Forms and Contracts" in chapter 21; "Disabilities" in chapter 22

The Patient's Bill of Rights

Each health-care facility or provider shall observe the following standards:

Individual Dignity

1. The individual dignity of a patient must be respected at all times and upon all occasions.
2. Every patient who is provided health-care services retains certain rights to privacy, which must be respected without regard to the patient's economic status or source of payment for his care. This patient's rights to privacy must be respected to the extent consistent with providing adequate medical care to the patient and with the efficient administration of the health-care facility or provider's office. However, this subparagraph does not preclude necessary and discreet discussion of a patient's case of examination by appropriate medical personnel.
3. A patient has the right to a prompt and reasonable response to a question or request. A health-care facility shall respond in a reasonable manner to the request of a patient's health-care provider for medical services to the patient. The health-care facility shall also respond in a reasonable manner to the patient's request for other services customarily rendered by the health-care facility to the extent such services do not require the approval of the patient's health-care provider or are not inconsistent with the patient's treatment.
4. A patient in a health-care facility has the right to retain and use personal clothing or possessions as space permits, unless for him to do so would infringe upon the right of another patient or is medically or programmatically contraindicated for documented medical, safety, or programmatic reasons.

Information

1. A patient has the right to know the name, function, and qualifications of each health-care provider who is providing medical services to the patient. A patient may request such information from his responsible provider or the health-care facility in which he is receiving medical services.
2. A patient in a health-care facility has the right to know what patient support services are available in the facility.
3. A patient has the right to be given by his health-care provider information concerning diagnosis, planned course of treatment, alternatives, risks, and prognosis, unless it is medically inadvisable or impossible to give this information to the patient, in which case the information must be given to the patient's guardian or a person designated as the patient's representative. A patient has the right to refuse this information.
4. A patient has the right to refuse any treatment based on information required by this paragraph, except as otherwise provided by law. The responsible provider shall document any such refusal.
5. A patient in a health-care facility has the right to know what facility rules and regulations apply to patient conduct.
6. A patient has the right to express grievances to a health-care provider, a health-care facility, or the appropriate state licensing agency regarding alleged violations of patients' rights. A patient has the right to know the health-care provider's or health-care facility's procedures for expressing a grievance.
7. A patient in a health-care facility who does not speak English has the right to be provided an interpreter when receiving medical services if the facility has a person readily available who can interpret on behalf of the patient.

Financial Information and Disclosure

1. A patient has the right to be given, upon request, by the responsible provider, his designee, or a representative of the health-care facility full information and necessary counseling on the availability of known financial resources for the patient's health care.
2. A health-care provider or a health-care facility shall, upon request, disclose to each patient who is eligible for Medicare, in advance of treatment, whether the health-care provider or the health-care facility in which the patient is receiving medical services accepts assignment under Medicare reimbursement as payment in full for medical services and treatment rendered in the health-care provider's office or health-care facility.
3. A health-care provider or a health-care facility shall, upon request, furnish a patient, prior to provision of medical services, a reasonable estimate of charges for such services. Such reasonable estimate shall not preclude the health-care provider or health-care facility from exceeding the estimate or making additional charges based upon changes in the patient's condition or treatment needs.
4. A patient has the right to receive a copy of an itemized bill upon request. A patient has a right to be given an explanation of charges upon request.

Access to Health Care

1. A patient has the right to impartial access to medical treatment or accommodations, regardless of race, national origin, religion, physical handicap, or source of payment.
2. A patient has the right to treatment for any emergency medical condition that will deteriorate from failure to provide such treatment.

continues

The Patient's Bill of Rights, Continued

Experimental Research

In addition to the provisions of s. 766.103, a patient has the right to know if medical treatment is for purposes of experimental research and to consent prior to participation in such experimental research. For any patient, regardless of ability to pay or source of payment for his care, participation must be a voluntary matter; and a patient has the right to refuse to participate. The patient's consent or refusal must be documented in the patient's care record. [Florida statutes chapter 381 (026).]

APPROXIMATE DATES OF CHILDBIRTH

Find the date of the last menstrual period in the top line (lightface type) of the pair of lines. The dark number (boldface type) in the line below will be the expected day of delivery.

Jan 1 2 3 4 5 6 7 8 9 10 11 12 13 14 15 16 17 18 19 20 21 22 23 24 25 26 27 28 29 30 31	
Oct 8 9 10 11 12 13 14 15 16 17 18 19 20 21 22 23 24 25 26 27 28 29 30 31 [1 2 3 4 5 6 7	**Nov**
Feb 1 2 3 4 5 6 7 8 9 10 11 12 13 14 15 16 17 18 19 20 21 22 23 24 25 26 27 28	
Nov 8 9 10 11 12 13 14 15 16 17 18 19 20 21 22 23 24 25 26 27 28 29 30 [1 2 3 4 5	**Dec**
Mar 1 2 3 4 5 6 7 8 9 10 11 12 13 14 15 16 17 18 19 20 21 22 23 24 25 26 27 28 29 30 31	
Dec 6 7 8 9 10 11 12 13 14 15 16 17 18 19 20 21 22 23 24 25 26 27 28 29 30 31 [1 2 3 4 5	**Jan**
Apr 1 2 3 4 5 6 7 8 9 10 11 12 13 14 15 16 17 18 19 20 21 22 23 24 25 26 27 28 29 30	
Jan 6 7 8 9 10 11 12 13 14 15 16 17 18 19 20 21 22 23 24 25 26 27 28 29 30 31 [1 2 3 4	**Feb**
May 1 2 3 4 5 6 7 8 9 10 11 12 13 14 15 16 17 18 19 20 21 22 23 24 25 26 27 28 29 30 31	
Feb 5 6 7 8 9 10 11 12 13 14 15 16 17 18 19 20 21 22 23 24 25 26 27 28 [1 2 3 4 5 6 7	**Mar**
June 1 2 3 4 5 6 7 8 9 10 11 12 13 14 15 16 17 18 19 20 21 22 23 24 25 26 27 28 29 30	
Mar 8 9 10 11 12 13 14 15 16 17 18 19 20 21 22 23 24 25 26 27 28 29 30 31 [1 2 3 4 5 6	**Apr**
July 1 2 3 4 5 6 7 8 9 10 11 12 13 14 15 16 17 18 19 20 21 22 23 24 25 26 27 28 29 30 31	
Apr 7 8 9 10 11 12 13 14 15 16 17 18 19 20 21 22 23 24 25 26 27 28 29 30 [1 2 3 4 5 6 7	**May**
Aug 1 2 3 4 5 6 7 8 9 10 11 12 13 14 15 16 17 18 19 20 21 22 23 24 25 26 27 28 29 30 31	
May 8 9 10 11 12 13 14 15 16 17 18 19 20 21 22 23 24 25 26 27 28 29 30 31 [1 2 3 4 5 6 7	**June**
Sept 1 2 3 4 5 6 7 8 9 10 11 12 13 14 15 16 17 18 19 20 21 22 23 24 25 26 27 28 29 30	
June 8 9 10 11 12 13 14 15 16 17 18 19 20 21 22 23 24 25 26 27 28 29 30 [1 2 3 4 5 6 7	**July**
Oct 1 2 3 4 5 6 7 8 9 10 11 12 13 14 15 16 17 18 19 20 21 22 23 24 25 26 27 28 29 30 31	
July 8 9 10 11 12 13 14 15 16 17 18 19 20 21 22 23 24 25 26 27 28 29 30 31 [1 2 3 4 5 6 7	**Aug**
Nov 1 2 3 4 5 6 7 8 9 10 11 12 13 14 15 16 17 18 19 20 21 22 23 24 25 26 27 28 29 30	
Aug 8 9 10 11 12 13 14 15 16 17 18 19 20 21 22 23 24 25 26 27 28 29 30 31 [1 2 3 4 5 6	**Sept**
Dec 1 2 3 4 5 6 7 8 9 10 11 12 13 14 15 16 17 18 19 20 21 22 23 24 25 26 27 28 29 30 31	
Sept 7 8 9 10 11 12 13 14 15 16 17 18 19 20 21 22 23 24 25 26 27 28 29 30 [1 2 3 4 5 6 7	**Oct**

PRECAUTIONS DURING PREGNANCY

Good nutrition and prenatal medical care are essentials for maternal well-being and delivery of a healthy baby. It is also important to be aware of lifestyle habits, environmental hazards, and communicable diseases that may adversely affect the developing child. The following is a list of known risk factors for pregnancy. Consult your doctor for specifics if you are pregnant and have been exposed to one of these hazards.

ALCOHOL

Research has shown that heavy drinking during pregnancy leads to greatly increased chances of a child with fetal alcohol syndrome or some other

Health/Nutrition

birth defect. It is not known whether occasional social drinking is harmful to a developing fetus, so most doctors recommend against any alcohol consumption during pregnancy.

CAFFEINE

Excessive use during pregnancy may cause a baby's birth weight to be a little lower than average. Low birth weight is associated with increased vulnerability to infection and disease. Caffeine is found in tea, coffee, chocolate, some cola drinks, and some over-the-counter medications.

CHEMICALS

Prolonged exposure to lead, arsenic, formaldehyde, mercury, benzene, or ethylene oxide (or inhalation of their fumes) may increase the chances of having a miscarriage.

CHICKEN POX (VARICELLA)

When a pregnant mother develops chicken pox, the fetus has a 25 percent chance of also becoming infected. A small number of infants affected develop birth defects, including scars, eye problems, poor growth, an underdeveloped limb, small head size, delayed development, and/or mental retardation. The fetus is most at risk if the mother develops chicken pox between the eighth and twentieth weeks of pregnancy. Infection shortly before delivery can cause serious problems for the newborn, but the baby can be treated with a vaccine to prevent/lessen chicken pox's effects. The vaccine is not recommended during pregnancy, however, as its effects on the developing fetus are not yet clear.

DRUGS AND MEDICATIONS

Drug use during pregnancy can result in addicted infants who experience painful, life-threatening withdrawal symptoms after birth. In addition, some drugs and prescription and nonprescription medications may cause birth defects or complications during pregnancy and childbirth. Always consult your physician regarding pregnancy and medication usage.

"Disposal of Hazardous Household **Go to** Chemicals" in chapter 19; "Average Cost of Raising a Child" in chapter 20; and "Family Planning in chapter 22

FIFTH DISEASE (ERYTHEMA INFECTIOSUM)

Fifth disease is caused by a virus and occurs most often in children from ages 4 to 14. Symptoms include a mild fever, sore throat, flulike aches or pains, a bright red rash on the face, and a bumpy rash on other parts of the body. Adults often have no noticeable symptoms and children may not show symptoms until several weeks after infection. Contracting fifth disease in pregnancy (especially during the first half) can cause miscarriage, stillbirth, or heart problems if the fetus is also infected.

HOT TUBS, SAUNAS, AND STEAM BATHS

Research indicates that an increase in the mother's core body temperature may cause developmental abnormalities in the fetus, premature labor, or both. Hot showers or baths at home are okay, but saunas, steam baths, and immersion above the hips in hot tubs should be avoided.

MEASLES

Pregnant women who contract red measles (rubella) may have an increased risk of miscarriage or delivering an infant with low birth weight. Infection with German measles during pregnancy is known to put the fetus at risk for development of birth defects.

RADIATION

Avoid X rays of the abdomen whenever possible during pregnancy. X rays of the head, mouth, and extremities are permissible if medical staff are aware of your condition and take proper precautions. Also avoid environmental areas where excess radiation may be present, as prenatal exposure to radiation can cause birth defects.

Health/Nutrition

SMOKING

Research has shown that heavy smoking (more than a pack of cigarettes per day) results in smaller babies with increased vulnerability to infection and illness. Smoking during pregnancy also increases the risk of miscarriage or stillbirth. As with the use of alcohol, it is not known whether any level of smoking is completely safe for the developing fetus, so it is best to stop smoking completely before becoming pregnant.

TOXOPLASMOSIS

Toxoplasmosis is a parasitic infection usually contracted by eating undercooked infected meat, raw eggs, or unpasturized milk; handling infected soil; or handling cat litter from an outdoor cat that is infected. About 40 percent of women who become infected during pregnancy will pass the infection on to their unborn infants. Fetal infections may interfere with development of the brain, eyes, heart, kidneys, blood, liver, or spleen.

IMMUNIZATION SCHEDULE FOR INFANTS, CHILDREN, AND ADULTS

The following information is based on U.S. Preventive Services Task Force Recommendations.

Children Under 10 Years Old

Immunizations	Frequency
DTaP or DTP (Diptheria/ tetanus/pertussis[1])	5 immunizations: at 2, 4, and 6 mos., between 12–18 mos.; and once between 4–6 yrs.
Polio	4 immunizations: at 2, 4, between 6–18 mos., 4–6 yrs.
MMR (Measles, mumps, rubella)	2 immunizations: between 12–15 mos. and 4–6 yrs. If missed, give by ages 11–12.
H. influenzae[2] type B (hib)	3 or 4 immunizations, depending on the vaccine: at 2, 4, and 6 mos. and between 12–15 mos.
Hepatitis B	3 or 4 immunizations: at birth, 1, 2, and 12 mos.; or between 0–2 mos., 1–2 mos. later, and between 6–18 mos.
Varicella[3]	1 immunization: between 12–18 mos., or anytime for older children with no previous immunization and no history of chicken pox

A Closer Look

Flu Shots

Influenza, or flu, is a viral disease, thought to be spread by airborne particles from an infected person's respiratory tract. Risk of transmission is especially high in winter, when people tend to stay indoors and when temperature and humidity are low. Vaccines against influenza are available; however, because the flu virus mutates rapidly, new strains appear each year, rendering immunizations against previous years' strains ineffective. Vaccines are administered as an injection in the upper arm.

Who should get a flu shot every year?

- People over the age of 65
- Residents of long-term care facilities
- People with serious illnesses, especially chronic respiratory disease, cardiopulmonary disease, kidney disease, diabetes, or anemia
- Medical and nursing home personnel

Ages 11 to 24

Immunizations	Frequency
Tetanus-diphtheria (Td)	1 booster between 11–16 yrs. and then periodically[4]
Hepatitis B	If not previously immunized, 3 immunizations: at current (next) visit, 1 mo. later, and 6 mos. later
MMR	1 immunization: between 11–12 yrs. if second dose was not received at 4–6 yrs.
Varicella	1 immunization: between 11–12 yrs. if susceptible to chicken pox
Rubella	1 immunization: after 12 yrs. for females who are not pregnant

Ages 25 to 64

Rubella	1 immunization: recommended for all females of childbearing age vaccination history
Tetanus-diphtheria (Td)	1 booster every 10 yrs., or as recommended[4]

Ages 65 and Older

Tetanus-diphtheria (Td)	1 booster every 10 yrs., or as recommended[4]
Pneumonia	1 immunization: administered one time to all people whose immune systems have not been compromised[4]
Influenza	1 immunization: annually

[1] Whooping cough   [2] Influenza (the flu)   [3] Chicken pox   [4] Discuss with your physician

For more information, call the Centers for Disease Control's National Immunization Information Hot Line at 800-232-2522 (English) or 800-232-0233 (Spanish), or visit the Web site at http://www.cdc.gov/nip.

EXPECTED NUMBER OF DEATHS AT GIVEN PERIODS OF LIFE PER 100,000 INFANTS BORN ALIVE

Period of Life (Birthday to Birthday)	Number of Deaths During Interval	Number of Persons Remaining (Alive) at End of Interval
At birth	N/A	100,000
Birth to age 1	721	99,279
1 to 5	138	99,141
5 to 10	88	99,053
10 to 15	109	98,944
15 to 20	349	98,595
20 to 25	469	98,126
25 to 30	478	97,648
30 to 35	586	97,062
35 to 40	795	96,267
40 to 45	1,132	95,135
45 to 50	1,644	93,491
50 to 55	2,397	91,094
55 to 60	3,652	87,442
60 to 65	5,511	81,931
65 to 70	7,732	74,199
70 to 75	10,565	63,634
75 to 80	13,111	50,523
80 to 85	15,986	34,537
85 and above	34,537	0

Source: U.S. National Center for Health Statistics, *National Vital Statistical Report* (Vol. 48, No. 11, July 24, 2000).

LIFE EXPECTANCY BY RACE, SEX, AND AGE

EXPECTATION OF LIFE IN YEARS

Exact Age in Years	All Races			White			Black		
	Both Sexes	Male	Female	Both Sexes	Male	Female	Both Sexes	Male	Female
0	76.7	73.8	79.5	77.3	74.5	80.0	71.3	67.6	74.8
1	76.3	73.4	79.0	76.8	74.0	79.4	71.4	67.7	74.8
5	72.4	69.5	75.1	72.9	70.1	75.5	67.6	63.9	70.9
10	67.4	64.6	70.2	67.9	65.2	70.6	62.6	59.0	66.0
15	62.5	59.7	65.2	63.0	60.2	65.6	57.7	54.1	61.1
20	57.7	55.0	60.3	58.2	55.5	60.8	53.0	49.5	56.2
25	53.0	50.3	55.5	53.4	50.8	55.9	48.4	45.1	51.4
30	48.2	45.7	50.6	48.6	46.1	51.0	43.8	40.6	46.7
35	43.5	41.0	45.8	43.9	41.5	46.2	39.3	36.2	42.0
40	38.8	36.4	41.1	39.2	36.8	41.4	34.9	31.9	37.5
45	34.3	31.9	36.4	34.6	32.3	36.7	30.6	27.7	33.1
50	29.8	27.6	31.8	30.1	27.9	32.0	26.6	23.9	28.8
55	25.5	23.5	27.4	25.7	23.7	27.6	22.8	20.4	24.8
60	21.5	19.6	23.2	21.6	19.7	23.3	19.3	17.1	21.0
65	17.8	16.0	19.2	17.8	16.1	19.3	16.1	14.3	17.4
70	14.3	12.8	15.5	14.4	12.8	15.6	13.0	11.5	14.1
75	11.3	10.0	12.2	11.3	10.0	12.2	10.5	9.2	11.3
80	8.6	7.5	9.2	8.5	7.5	9.1	8.2	7.1	8.7
85	6.3	5.5	6.7	6.3	5.4	6.6	6.3	5.5	6.6
90	4.7	4.1	4.9	4.5	4.0	4.7	4.8	4.3	4.9
95	3.5	3.0	3.6	3.3	2.9	3.4	3.7	3.4	3.7
100	2.6	2.3	2.7	2.4	2.2	2.4	2.8	2.7	2.8

RECOMMENDED WEIGHTS

DETERMINING YOUR BODY MASS INDEX (BMI)

Height	Weight															
	100	110	120	130	140	150	160	170	180	190	200	210	220	230	240	250
5'0"	20	21	23	25	27	29	31	33	35	37	39	41	43	45	47	49
5'1"	19	21	23	25	26	28	30	32	34	36	38	40	42	43	45	47
5'2"	18	20	22	24	26	27	29	31	33	35	37	38	40	42	44	46
5'3"	18	19	21	23	25	27	28	30	32	34	35	37	39	41	43	44
5'4"	17	19	21	22	24	26	27	29	31	33	34	36	38	39	41	43
5'5"	17	18	20	22	23	25	27	28	30	32	33	35	37	38	40	42
5'6"	16	18	19	21	23	24	26	27	29	31	32	34	36	37	39	40
5'7"	16	17	19	20	22	23	25	27	28	30	31	33	34	36	38	39
5'8"	15	17	18	20	21	23	24	26	27	29	30	32	33	35	36	38
5'9"	15	16	18	19	21	22	24	25	27	28	30	31	32	34	35	37
5'10"	14	16	17	19	20	22	23	24	26	27	29	30	32	33	34	36
5'11"	14	15	17	18	20	21	22	24	25	26	28	29	31	32	33	35
6'0"	14	15	16	18	19	20	22	23	24	26	27	28	30	31	33	34
6'1"	13	15	16	17	18	20	21	22	24	25	26	28	29	30	32	33
6'2"	13	14	15	17	18	19	21	22	23	24	26	27	28	30	31	32
6'3"	12	14	15	16	17	19	20	21	22	24	25	26	27	29	30	31
6'4"	12	13	15	16	17	18	19	21	22	23	24	26	27	28	29	30

Interpretation   Under 18.5 = Underweight; 18.5–24 = Normal; 25–29 = Overweight; 30 and over = Obese

Health/Nutrition

To estimate your body mass index (BMI), first identify your weight (to the nearest 10 pounds) in one of the columns across the top. Then move your finger down the column until you come to the row that represents your height. Inside the square where your weight and height meet is a number that is an estimate of your BMI. For example, if you weigh 160 pounds and are 5'7", your BMI is 25.

HEIGHT AND WEIGHT CHARTS FOR CHILDREN

DESIRABLE WEIGHTS IN POUNDS FOR BOYS 5 TO 18 YEARS OLD

Height (in inches)	Age (in years)													
	5	6	7	8	9	10	11	12	13	14	15	16	17	18
38	34	34												
39	35	35												
40	36	36												
41	38	38	38											
42	39	39	39	39										
43	41	41	41	41										
44	44	44	44	44										
45	46	46	46	46	46									
46	47	48	48	48	48									
47	49	50	50	50	50	50								
48		52	53	53	53	53								
49		55	55	55	55	55	55							
50		57	58	58	58	58	58	58						
51			61	61	61	61	61	61	61					
52			63	64	64	64	64	64	64					
53			66	67	67	67	67	68	68					
54				70	70	70	70	71	71	72				
55				72	72	73	73	74	74	74				
56				75	76	77	77	77	78	78	80			
57					79	80	81	81	82	83	83			
58					83	84	84	85	85	86	87			
59						87	88	89	89	90	90	90		
60						91	92	92	93	94	95	96		
61							95	96	97	99	100	103	106	
62							100	101	102	103	104	107	111	116
63							105	106	107	108	110	113	118	123
64								109	111	113	115	117	121	126
65								114	117	118	120	122	127	131
66									119	122	125	128	132	136
67									124	128	130	134	136	139
68										134	134	137	141	143
69										137	139	143	146	149
70										143	144	145	148	151
71										148	150	151	152	154
72											153	155	156	158
73											157	160	162	164
74											160	164	168	170

Go to "Deaths and Funerals" in chapter 16; "U.S. Population" in chapter 25

Go to "Children" in chapter 22; "Parenting" in chapter 22

DESIRABLE WEIGHTS IN POUNDS FOR GIRLS 5 TO 18 YEARS OLD

Height (in inches)	5	6	7	8	9	10	11	12	13	14	15	16	17	18
38	33	33												
39	34	34												
40	36	36	36											
41	37	37	37											
42	39	39	39											
43	41	41	41	41										
44	42	42	42	42										
45	45	45	45	45	45									
46	47	47	47	48	48									
47	49	50	50	50	50	50								
48		52	52	52	52	53	53							
49			54	55	55	56	56							
50			56	57	58	59	61	62						
51			59	60	61	61	63	65						
52			63	64	64	64	65	67						
53			66	67	67	68	68	69	71					
54				69	70	70	71	71	73					
55				72	74	74	74	75	77	78				
56					76	78	78	79	81	83				
57					80	82	82	82	84	88	92			
58						84	86	86	88	93	96	101		
59						87	90	90	92	96	100	103	104	
60						91	95	95	97	101	105	108	109	111
61							99	100	101	105	108	112	113	116
62							104	105	106	109	113	115	117	118
63								110	110	112	116	117	119	120
64								114	115	117	119	120	122	123
65								118	120	121	122	123	125	126
66									124	124	125	128	129	130
67									128	130	131	133	133	135
68									131	133	135	136	138	138
69										135	137	138	140	142
70										136	138	140	142	144
71										138	140	142	144	145

Age (in years)

Health/Nutrition

HOME REMEDIES

The following should not be considered medical advice and is prepared for informational purposes only. Always consult a professional health-care practitioner for medical problems. Do not give aspirin to children under the age of 15 unless directed by a physician.

"Treatment for Health Emergencies" and "Directory of Poison Control Centers" in chapter
Go to 17

ALLERGIES, SEASONAL

Symptoms   Watery eyes, stuffy nose, coughing. *Asthma* symptoms include a wheezing/hacking cough that may get worse at night, causes a tight feeling in the chest, and is often accompanied by panicky feelings of being unable to breathe. See your doctor if you experience these symptoms.

Remedies   Drink plenty of fluids to flush your system of allergens. Avoid strenuous exercise, especially if it causes asthmatic wheezing (see your doctor). Sleep with your head/chest elevated to facilitate breathing. Don't smoke or wear cologne, and avoid others who do. Keep your home and office dust-free (vacuum with a special filter, if necessary). Stay away from known irritants, such as smoke, perfumes, animals, and outdoor activities. Over-the-counter antihistamines and analgesics usually provide some relief, but remember that antihistamines cause drowsiness, and follow package directions carefully. Decongestants can provide temporary relief, but nasal congestion may return when use is discontinued. Horseradish and red/cayenne pepper can also be used as decongestants, either by adding them to food or by placing a small pinch under the nostrils or on the tongue. Get plenty of rest, and see your doctor if symptoms persist.

BACK PAIN FROM MUSCLE STRAIN

Symptoms   Pain that occurs when you move the affected portion of your back, which may ache and be sore to the touch; swelling and bruising may be present in severe cases. (Always call your doctor about sudden, unexpected back pain that occurs for no reason or about pain that moves from one body part to another, is severe, lasts more than 2 to 3 days, or is accompanied by fever or vomiting.)

Remedies   Rest in bed to take pressure off the back and allow it to heal. Take analgesics, such as aspirin, ibuprofen, naproxen sodium, or acetaminophen. If there is swelling or bruising, apply a cold pack (ice in a plastic bag wrapped in a towel) for 20 minutes and then remove the pack for 20 minutes, repeating this process for 2 to 3 hours.

BURNS, FIRST-DEGREE

Symptoms   A feeling of heat with pain and reddening but no blistering. If signs of infection (fever, chills, swelling, increased redness, or pus in the burned area) develop, seek medical attention. (Always see a doctor for more serious burns or any that cover a large area of the body.)

Remedies   Hold the burned area under cold tap water for 5 to 10 minutes to stop the burn process and reduce the amount of skin damage. (Don't apply ice or ice water, which can further damage the skin.) Leave the burn uncovered and keep it elevated, if possible. Use a dry, sterile dressing if necessary. Do not rub butter or salve onto the burn, as this can cause more damage. Analgesics may be taken orally to relieve pain, but experts advise against using local anesthetic sprays or ointments, as these can slow the healing process and may cause allergic reactions. *See also* "Treatment for Health Emergencies: Burns" in chapter 17.

COLDS, SORE THROATS, AND COUGHS DUE TO COLDS

Symptoms   Sneezing, runny nose, slight fever (101°F or less). Call a doctor if any of the following symptoms develop: a bright red sore throat; wheezing or difficulty breathing; irritability; lethargy; confusion/delirium; earache; visible pus deposits in the throat; enlarged/tender neck glands; persistent dry cough; cough that produces thick yellow-green or gray phlegm; a bad odor from the throat, nose, or ears; or a fever of over 103°F (104°F in a child under 12, 100.5°F in an infant less than two months old, or 102°F in an adult over 60).

Remedies   Bed rest if feverish; plenty of fluids; analgesics for aches and pains; chicken soup; foods and drinks rich in vitamin C.

Influenza was so named by 15th-century Italians because they thought the disease was caused by the influence of the stars and planets.

CONSTIPATION

Symptoms   Hard, small, dry bowel movements (usually fewer than three times a week); pain and difficulty having bowel movements; feeling bloated and uncomfortable; an urge to defecate but inability to do so.

Remedies Drink plenty of water (8 to 10 glasses per day) and exercise regularly. Eat foods containing plenty of fiber, such as beans, whole grain and bran cereals, fresh fruits, and vegetables (such as asparagus, brussels sprouts, cabbage, and carrots). Respond immediately to the urge to have a bowel movement—putting it off is one of the major causes of constipation, especially in busy, stressed people. Adults and children may become constipated from a reluctance to defecate in public bathrooms (at school or work) because of lack of privacy or time constraints. If this is a problem, try eating fruit or cereal an hour before bedtime and setting the alarm to rise 30 minutes earlier than usual. Eat a high-fiber breakfast soon after getting out of bed. Then shower, dress, and prepare for the day. The extra fiber, early breakfast, and morning time to spare will facilitate the occurrence of bowel movements before leaving home for the day. Keep in mind that bowel movements are a very individual matter; some people normally have more than one a day, but for others, three or four times a week is the norm. Laxatives, stool softeners, and enemas should be used rarely and with great caution, as they are habit-forming. If you become dependent on such products, gradually reduce the amount used while making healthy lifestyle changes; abrupt withdrawal can cause serious problems. Extreme constipation can result in intestinal blockage—a very serious matter—so it is important to check with your doctor if constipation is a long-standing problem or causes major discomfort.

FLU (INFLUENZA)

Symptoms Headache, general aches and pains, fatigue, chills, fever up to 104°F, burning sensation in the eyes, dry cough. Symptoms may resemble a cold but are more severe and develop faster; the person seems to get sick very quickly. People over age 65 and those with chronic illnesses should receive annual influenza immunizations, as complications from the flu can be severe.

Remedies Bed rest, analgesics for aches and pains, and warm fluids. Use over-the-counter medications

to reduce symptoms if desired, but be sure to follow directions carefully. Decongestants can provide temporary relief, but nasal congestion may return when use is discontinued. Horseradish and red/cayenne pepper can also be used as decongestants, either by adding them to food or placing a small pinch under the nostrils or on the tongue.

HEADACHES

Symptoms Generalized pain in the head or neck area. (Seek medical attention for pain that is localized on one side of the face or head; sudden, severe headaches of any type; persistent pain accompanied by nausea, high fever, or other symptoms; pain resulting from an injury or blow to the head or face; or pain accompanied by disorientation, drowsiness, or confusion.)

Remedies Relax in a quiet area. Eat a nutritious meal if your stomach is empty. Take analgesics to relieve pain. Apply heat to relax tense muscles in the neck and shoulders. Use ice packs on the head itself. Wipe the brow and neck with vinegar. Some headaches respond well to aspirin and hot coffee; others are made worse by caffeine. If headaches are frequent, try to identify their cause (stress, hunger, menstrual cycle, certain foods) and work to remove it.

HICCUPS

Symptoms Quick, jerky inhalations accompanied by a peculiar noise, caused by a spasmodic jerking of the diaphragm muscle. Hiccups usually stop within a few minutes but can continue for hours, days, or weeks. Sometimes the condition even requires hospitalization because they disturb sleep and preclude normal respiration. Call your health-care provider if hiccups continue more than 1 day.

Remedies Regular, rhythmic breathing. The diaphragm muscle is not under voluntary control, but forcing yourself to breathe in a very regular pattern should get it back into a normal rhythm. Take deep enough breaths so that the diaphragm area (center of the lower rib cage down to the waist) moves in and

Health/Nutrition

out; quick shallow breaths that move only the upper chest will not solve the problem. (Avoid very deep, too-slow breaths, as these may cause hyperventilation.) If the hiccups do not respond within a minute or two, wait 5 minutes and try again. If you still have no success, try holding your breath. Breathe out until you have emptied your lungs as much as possible and then hold it as long as you can without becoming really uncomfortable. Then take a deep breath and hold it (again, only until you begin to feel uncomfortable). Breathe normally for a few minutes to see if the hiccups subside; then repeat.

HYPERVENTILATION

Symptoms Dizziness, shortness of breath, chest pain or tightness, numbness/tingling of the extremities or around the mouth. In most cases, there is no obvious breathing irregularity—that is, one cannot tell that the hyperventilating person is breathing too deeply or too fast.

Remedies Until medical attention is available, hold a paper bag over the mouth and nose, crumpling the edges so that little air can escape. Exhale into the bag and then inhale while still holding it over the mouth and nose. Repeat this procedure until symptoms subside (sometimes it takes several minutes).

(*Note:* The symptoms of hyperventilation are also symptoms of some life-threatening medical conditions. Also, frequent/chronic hyperventilation can cause serious complications. Therefore, it is recommended that you seek medical attention immediately if any of the symptoms described here are present, even if hyperventilation is suspected.)

INDIGESTION

Symptoms Mild abdominal discomfort soon after eating; feeling "too full" after a heavy meal.

Remedies Drink ½ cup of tepid water mixed with 1 tablespoon of vinegar, 1 tablespoon of lemon juice, or the juice of one freshly squeezed lime.

INSECT BITES

Symptoms Localized pain, itching, swelling. (If allergic symptoms such as all-over itching, a rash, or breathing difficulties occur, seek emergency medical attention immediately.)

Remedies For bee stings, a drop of ammonia applied directly to the wound will often stop the pain and prevent swelling; alternatively, use an antihistamine gel or ointment. If bites are numerous, you may want to take an over-the-counter antihistamine orally to reduce discomfort, but remember that such products usually make you drowsy. *See also* "Treatment for Health Emergencies: Insect Bites" in chapter 17.

On his first voyage to the South Pacific, Captain Cook lost almost half of his crew to scurvy (caused by lack of vitamin C). Once the cause of scurvy was discovered, lemon juice was issued on all British navy ships.

INSOMNIA

Symptoms Inability to fall or stay asleep at night despite feeling tired and in need of rest, resulting in daytime drowsiness and fatigue. Symptoms may include feelings of anxiety, obsessive thinking or planning, or excessive worrying when trying to fall asleep.

Remedies Get plenty of exercise in the late afternoon or early evening, but avoid strenuous workouts just before bedtime. Don't take naps during the day. Set a regular bedtime and stick to it (at least until difficulties are resolved), and also set a regular time to wake up. A light snack before bedtime may be helpful, but don't overdo it. Try wheat germ, brown rice, celery, milk, turkey, bananas, figs, yogurt, or tuna snacks because they are rich in tryptophan, an amino acid that promotes sleep. Avoid potatoes, cheese, chocolate, tomatoes, and spinach, all of which contain tryamine, a stimulant. If you smoke, try to cut down—nicotine is a powerful stimulant. Work to reduce other chemical/nutritional stimulants, too, such as iced tea, colas, and coffee. Decrease alcohol consumption and review all medications (prescription and over-the-counter) for their side effects. If you have been taking any form of sleep aid, your body needs time to adjust to falling asleep on its own. If anxiety or stress is keeping you awake, spend time relaxing before going to bed. Soak in a warm bath, gaze into the fireplace, or listen to music by candlelight (gazing at a lighted candle can actually make you sleepy). Once in bed, try not to dwell on your problems. Take some deep, slow breaths, and think soothing thoughts. If you do not fall asleep within 15 or 20 minutes, get out of bed and go into another room. Engage in a relaxing activity until you feel sleepy, and then go back to bed and try again.

PREMENSTRUAL SYNDROME (PMS)

Symptoms   Feeling bloated, out of sorts, irritable, and/or depressed.

Remedies   Make a calendar charting menstrual periods and PMS symptoms over several months and use it to predict the next episode. Cut down on salty foods, chocolate, and caffeine for a day or two prior to anticipated onset. Try to reschedule stressful events that occur during periods of PMS; avoid highly emotional situations and postpone major decisions until hormone levels return to normal. Get plenty of rest, exercise, and good nutrition. When PMS symptoms occur, drink plenty of water to reduce water retention and flush impurities from the system. Take diuretics only on the advice of a physician, as overuse can cause serious medical problems.

RASHES, PLANT-ALLERGY

Symptoms   Redness and/or small bumps accompanied by itching, usually after contact with plants such as poison oak or poison ivy.

Remedies   Calamine lotion may provide some relief, but an over-the-counter antihistamine gel or

ointment will work better. Taking oral antihistamines may be necessary, especially at bedtime, to avoid scratching and infecting the area. Rashes due to contact with such plants may persist for weeks, are easily spread and infected by scratching, and are difficult to cure at home. If symptoms are still present in 2 to 3 days, see your doctor. *See also* "Poisonous Cultivated and Wild Plants" in chapter 3; "Treatment for Health Emergencies: Poisoning: Plant Poisons" in chapter 17.

RASHES, HEAT

Symptoms   Redness and a burning sensation when skin is touched.

Remedies   Take a cool (not cold) bath; apply cool compresses wet with a solution of baking soda and water, or apply calamine lotion. Leave the area open to the air if possible to avoid irritation, and stay out of the heat. If rash persists, see your doctor.

(*Note:* Some rashes are symptoms of illnesses such as infection or food allergies. If you do not know what may have caused a rash, see your doctor, especially if symptoms persist.)

If you burn your mouth when eating spicy foods, instead of reaching for water, eat something sweet.

SPRAINS AND STRAINS OF THE ANKLE, FOOT, HAND, WRIST, OR ELBOW

Symptoms   Pain and swelling of the injured limb (full range of motion still present; limb still capable of bearing weight). Seek medical attention if the skin is broken, the limb cannot move normally in all directions, numbness/blue discoloration occurs, or bones seem out of place and are painful when pressed.

Remedies   Elevate the injured limb to reduce swelling. Apply an ice pack to the injured area for

20 minutes; then remove the pack for 20 minutes. Repeat this cycle until swelling stops or improves. Rest the limb as much as possible to prevent further injury, and keep it elevated. After the first few days, applying heat to the area will promote healing, but do not apply heat initially as this can make swelling worse. You may wrap the injured limb loosely in a stretch bandage for support and comfort. Analgesics may be taken for the pain. See your doctor if symptoms are still present after 5 days. *See also* "Treatment for Health Emergencies: Fractures, Dislocations, and Sprains" in chapter 17.

STREP THROAT

Symptoms Redness and pain or burning sensation when swallowing. If neck glands are swollen or tender, see your doctor. Strep throat symptoms include white pus areas in the back of the throat; fever; sometimes headaches, stomach pain, or a rash on the body. (However, these symptoms do not always indicate strep throat, and one may have strep throat without experiencing these symptoms.) Consult your physician if symptoms of strep throat appear, if pain is severe, or if a sore throat persists more than 2 to 3 days.

Remedies Cut down on smoking, rest your voice, and use a humidifier or vaporizer to moisten the air. (Smoking, excessive vocalizing, and too-low humidity can cause or aggravate coughs and sore throats.) Throat soothers include gargling with salt water several times a day (½ to 1 teaspoon of salt in a cup of warm water), hot tea with lemon and honey, and medicated throat lozenges. (Plain lemon drops work well, too; the sourness stimulates the production of saliva to moisten your throat.) Analgesics may be taken to relieve pain.

LOOKING FOR SIGNS OF BREAST CANCER

It is important for you to know the signs of breast cancer, because most breast cancers are discovered by women themselves, not their doctors. If you dis-

cover any of the signs of breast cancer, see your doctor immediately. It is a frightening experience to find a lump or another possible cancer sign, but you should know that 8 of 10 lumps are *not* cancerous. Many women have naturally lumpy breasts. But your doctor should determine whether a lump or other sign is actually cancer or a harmless condition.

To find out how many calories it takes to maintain your current weight, multiply your weight by 15.

ASK FOR A BREAST EXAM

Don't be embarrassed. Asking your doctor or nurse for a breast examination as part of an office visit is one good way to learn what is normal for your breasts. But examination by a doctor is not enough —you, too, should examine your breasts monthly. Ask your doctor or nurse to teach you breast self-examination to be sure you are practicing it correctly.

PRACTICE BREAST SELF-EXAMINATION

Breast self-examination is an important key to early diagnosis. Along with regular examination by your physician, monthly self-examination can give you peace of mind because it helps you know how your breasts normally feel.

Knowing the normal feel of your breasts makes it easier to notice any changes early, when treatment is most effective. To examine your breasts correctly, you should follow the six steps described page 516.

WHEN TO EXAMINE YOUR BREASTS

Every month! If you menstruate, the best time to practice breast self-examination is 2 or 3 days after the end of your period, when your breasts are least likely to be tender or swollen. If you no longer menstruate, choose a day such as your birth date. That way, you will remember to do it every month.

HOW TO PERFORM A BREAST SELF-EXAMINATION

1. Stand before a mirror. Inspect both breasts for anything unusual, such as any discharge from the nipples or puckering, dimpling, or scaling of the skin.

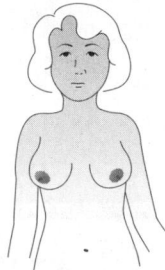

2. Watching closely in the mirror, clasp hands behind your head and press hands forward. This step and step 3 are designed to emphasize any changes in the shape or contour of your breasts. As you do them, you should be able to feel your chest muscles tighten.

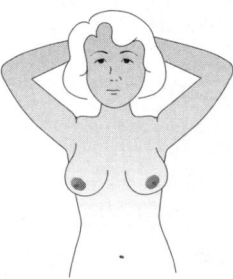

3. Press hands firmly on hips and bow slightly toward the mirror as you pull your shoulders and elbows forward.

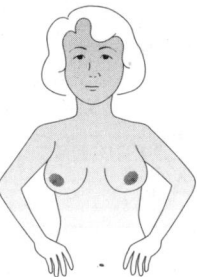

Note: Some women do the next part of the exam in the shower: Fingers glide over soapy skin, making it easy to concentrate on the texture underneath.

4. Raise your left arm. Use a few fingers of your right hand to explore your left breast firmly, carefully, and thoroughly. Beginning at the outer edge, press the flat part of your fingers in small circles, moving the circles slowly around the breast. Gradually work toward the nipple. Be sure to cover the entire breast. Pay special attention to the area between the breast and the armpit, including the armpit itself. Feel for any unusual lump or mass under the skin.

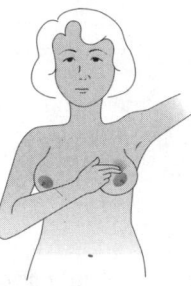

5. Gently squeeze the nipple and look for a discharge. Repeat the exam on your right breast.

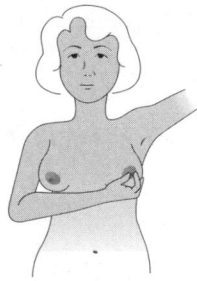

6. Repeat steps 4 and 5 lying down. Lie flat on your back with your left arm over your head and a pillow or folded towel under your left shoulder. This position flattens the breast and makes it easier to examine. Use the same circular motion described earlier. Repeat on your right breast.

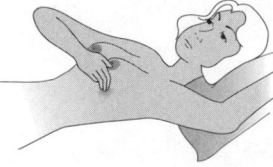

WHEN TO GET A MAMMOGRAM

The National Cancer Institute, the American College of Radiology, and the American Cancer Society recommend regular mammograms for women over 40, either annually, or once every 2 years, depending on a woman's age and medical history. Detection through mammography screening can lead to early treatment, adding years to the lives of women receiving such treatment.

Unfortunately, only a little more than a third of American women follow these guidelines. Of the 34 million women who do not get mammograms as recommended, about 4 million are expected to contract breast cancer at some point.

The ventriloquist Paul Winchell was not only the voice of Tigger in the Winnie the Pooh films, he also invented an early form of the artificial heart. He donated the patent for his life-saving device to the University of Utah.

Consult your physician for more information about whether it is time for you to get a mammogram.

INFECTIOUS DISEASES AND HOW THEY ARE SPREAD

Disease	Agent	Transmission
AIDS (acquired immune deficiency syndrome)	Virus	Contact of body fluid (semen, blood, vaginal secretions) with that of an infected person. Sexual contact and sharing of unclean paraphernalia for intravenous drugs are the most common means of transmission.
Blastomycosis	Fungus	Inhaling contaminated dust
Botulism	Bacteria	Consuming contaminated food
Chicken pox	Virus	Direct or indirect contact with infected person
Common cold	Virus	Direct or indirect contact with infected person
Diphtheria	Bacteria	Direct contact with infected person
Encephalitis	Virus	Mosquito bite
Gonorrhea	Bacteria	Sexual contact
Hepatitis	Virus	Direct or indirect contact with infected person
Herpes simplex	Virus	Direct contact with infected person
Histoplasmosis	Fungus	Inhaling contaminated dust
Hookworm	Nematode	Contact with contaminated soil
Infectious mononucleosis	Virus	Direct or indirect contact with infected person
Influenza	Virus	Direct or indirect contact with infected person
Lyme disease	Bacteria	Deer tick bite
Malaria	Protozoa	Mosquito bite
Measles	Virus	Direct or indirect contact with infected person
Mumps	Virus	Direct or indirect contact with infected person
Pertussis (whooping cough)	Bacteria	Direct or indirect contact with infected person
Poliomyelitis	Virus	Direct contact with infected person
Rubella (German measles)	Virus	Direct or indirect contact with infected person
Scarlet fever	Bacteria	Direct or indirect contact with infected person
Spotted fever	Rickettsia	Tick bite
Syphilis	Bacteria	Sexual contact
Tapeworm	Nematode	Consuming infected meat or fish
Toxoplasmosis	Protozoa	Consuming raw meat; contact with contaminated soil
Trichomoniasis	Protozoa	Sexual contact
Typhus	Rickettsia	Lice, flea, tick bite
Yellow fever	Virus	Mosquito bite

Health/Nutrition

DENTAL CARE

Dental-care professionals offer the following advice to maintain healthy teeth that will last a lifetime:

1. Have regular dental checkups.
2. Limit the amount of sugary foods you eat, and brush teeth immediately after eating sweets.
3. Brush teeth at least twice daily with a fluoride toothpaste.
4. Use a toothbrush with rounded bristles and be sure it is not too hard. Look for one that has American Dental Association (ADA) approval. And get a new toothbrush every 3 to 4 months—worn-down bristles do not clean your teeth well.
5. Floss regularly—at least once per day.
6. Drink fluoridated water (available in about half of the cities and towns in the United States). For added protection, especially if fluoridated water is not available, your dentist may prescribe a fluoridated gel, rinse, or tablet. Fluoride drops can be used for infants.
7. Follow other recommendations from your dentist concerning tooth and gum care.

Chiropractic

A Closer Look

Chiropractic is based on the idea that the structure of the human body, particularly the spinal column, has a profound effect on the functioning of all systems and organs of the body. Manipulation of the spine is perhaps the best-known type of chiropractic treatment. Its purpose is to align misplaced vertebrae to relieve unhealthy pressure on the nerves connecting the brain and body, thus restoring all functions to health. Doctors of Chiropractic (D.C.s) base their diagnoses on information collected via physical examination, patient history, X rays, magnetic resonance imagings (MRIs), laboratory tests, and other traditional diagnostic tools. Their whole-person approach may include physiological therapeutics—such as heat or massage, acupuncture, trigger point therapy, and counseling on stress management and lifestyle issues—as well as spinal and extravertebral manipulations. Treatment does not include pharmaceutical or surgical interventions, but nutritional counseling is often provided, as chiropractic doctors receive intensive education in all aspects of healthy nutrition.

For more information, contact the American Chiropractic Association, 1701 Clarendon Blvd., Arlington, VA 22209 (telephone: 800-986-4636; fax: 703-243-2593), or stop by the Chiropractic Online service at Web site http://www.amerchiro.org/.

Osteopathy

A Closer Look

Osteopathic physicians (D.O.s) are licensed to perform surgery, prescribe medication, and specialize in all areas of medicine from neurosurgery to psychiatry. Their approach to treatment emphasizes the importance of body mechanics and manipulative methods to detect and correct faulty structure and function. Noninvasive therapies are used whenever possible, with the goal of restoring the body to health by freeing it to heal itself. Osteopaths are specially trained in manual treatment of musculoskeletal disorders. They can specialize in sports medicine as well as pediatrics, general practice, or obstetrics/gynecology. They utilize generally accepted physical, pharmacological, and surgical methods of diagnosis.

For more information, contact the American Osteopathic Association's Public Relations Department, 142 E. Ontario St., Chicago, IL 60611 (telephone: 800-621-1773 or 312-280-5800), or see its Web site at http://www.aoa-net.org

Fluoride is a mineral that is present in most water to some extent. The water-fluoridation process used in the United States since 1945 is a means of ensuring that everyone receives the benefits of enough fluoride to prevent the tooth decay that seemed inevitable before its implementation. Fluoride is important to oral health for several reasons:

- It helps to deactivate the bacteria that cause tooth decay.
- It is an essential part of the repair process as tooth enamel rebuilds small areas of decay before large cavities form.
- It makes tooth enamel more resistant to the acid formed by bacteria.

Fluoride is most effective on the smooth surfaces of the teeth and least effective on the chewing surfaces on the back teeth (molars). Regular brushing and

Homeopathy

A Closer Look

The homeopathic approach to health care treats the whole person—body, mind, and spirit. One of its basic principles is the Law of Similars, which advocates stimulation of the body's own defense system by ingesting minute amounts of a substance that produces the same symptoms as the illness. (Homeopathic physicians point out that this approach is similar to the process of immunization used in conventional medicine.) The second basic principle is the use of minimum dosage to produce effective results. This concept is based on many practitioners' experience that use of an extreme dilution of the required substance (reducing the amount of substance to 1 part in 10,000 or even 100,000) produces better results than a stronger dosage. In addition to these foundations for treatment, homeopathic practitioners believe that symptoms of illness are often the body's own defense at work, and that treatment based on suppressing symptoms may interfere with the body's own healing process.

Health-care providers who practice homeopathy may be identified by one or more of these sets of initials:

RSHom (NA)   Member of the Registered Society of Homeopaths in North America
DHANP   Diplomate of the Homeopathic Association of Naturopathic Physicians
DHt   Diplomate of Homeotheraputics
CCH   Certified in Classical Homeopathy

For more information, contact The National Center for Homeopathy, 801 N. Fairfax St., Ste. 306, Alexandria, VA 22314 (telephone: 703-548-7790; fax: 703-548-7792; e-mail: info@homeopathic.org), or visit the center's Web site at http://www.homeopathic.org

flossing also help to prevent tooth decay by removing bacteria-containing plaque (an invisible sticky coating on teeth) that produces cavity-causing acid.

To protect teeth further against decay, plastic sealants are now widely used and recommended. The application is a simple one: the teeth are cleaned and wiped completely dry, and the substance is painted onto the tooth surface. The resulting coating (which may be clear or tinted) can last as long as 10 years, protecting teeth from the bacteria that cause decay. Many dentists now recommend that a sealant be applied to children's teeth immediately after the adult teeth appear, before any decay begins to occur.

For detailed information on preventive dental care and specific problems, see your dentist. Or contact the American Dental Association, 211 E. Chicago Ave., Chicago, IL 60611 (telephone: 312-440-2500; fax: 312-440-2800), or visit the ADA's Web site at http://www.ada.org/.

Go to "Living Will" in chapter 20; "Aging" in chapter 22; "Social Security" in chapter 25

LIVING WILLS

One of the most controversial issues in society today is a person's right to decide whether to live or die. With the enormous advances in medical care during recent decades, many more families are being asked to make difficult choices about life-sustaining measures for loved ones who are critically ill and unable to make their own decisions. Senior citizens, nursing-home patients, those who are seriously ill, and members of the public at large are now encouraged to record their thoughts by executing living wills. When properly prepared and executed, a living will can speak for someone who no longer has the ability to speak for herself.

Many states have legislation in place regarding the right of terminally ill persons or family members to decide to withhold life-sustaining measures, and the law in your state may not be as conservative or liberal as you would prefer. But laws are changing constantly in this field. Experts in the field suggest executing a living will that not only conforms to state legislative guidelines, but also includes information that may be of value in the future if state laws change.

There are numerous resources available for anyone desiring to create a living will. Check the reference section of your public library for handbooks containing sample living wills for every state with current legislation, and generic forms for states without such laws. Or contact one of the organizations listed below for information on creating living wills and related legal issues.

Choice in Dying
1035 30th Street, NW
Washington, DC 20007
202-338-9790
Fax: 202-338-0242
http://www.choices.org

Death with Dignity National Center
11 Dupont Circle, NW, Suite 202
Washington, DC 20036
202-969-1669
Fax: 202-969-1668
http://www.deathwithdignity.org

Euthanasia Research & Guidance Organization (ERGO)
24829 Norris Lane
Junction City, OR 97448-9559
Messages and Fax: 541-998-1873
e-mail: ergo@efn.org
http://www.finalexit.org

TEN LEADING CAUSES OF DEATH

The table at right ranks the causes of death by age group according to mortality rates. Cause of death corresponds to classifications in the *International Classification of Diseases*; however, abbreviated forms have been used for reasons of space.

Go to "Statistics and Demography" under "Reference Works for General Information" in chapter 11

Rank	Age Groups		
	<1	1–4	5–9
1	Congenital Anomalies (6,212)	Unintentional Injury & Adverse Effects (1,935)	Unintentional Injury & Adverse Effects (1,544)
2	Short Gestation (4,101)	Congenital Anomalies (564)	Malignant Neoplasms (487)
3	SIDS (2,822)	Homicide & Legal Intervention (399)	Congenital Anomalies (198)
4	Maternal Complications (1,343)	Malignant Neoplasms (365)	Homicide & Legal Intervention (170)
5	Respiratory Distress Syndrome (1,295)	Heart Disease (214)	Heart Disease (156)
6	Placenta Cord Membranes (961)	Pneumonia & Influenza (146)	Pneumonia & Influenza (70)
7	Perinatal Infections (815)	Septicemia (89)	Chronic Lower Respiratory Disease* (54)
8	Unintentional Injury & Adverse Effects (754)	Perinatal Period (75)	Benign Neoplasms (52)
9	Intrauterine Hypoxia (461)	Cerebro-vascular (57)	Cerebro-vascular (35)
10	Pneumonia & Influenza (441)	Benign Neoplasms (53)	HIV (29)

* Bronchitis, Emphysema, Asthma

| Age Groups | | | | | | | |
10–14	15–24	25–34	35–44	45–54	55–64	65+	All Ages
Unintentional Injury & Adverse Effects (1,710)	Unintentional Injury & Adverse Effects (13,349)	Unintentional Injury & Adverse Effects (12,045)	Malignant Neoplasms (17,022)	Malignant Neoplasms (45,747)	Malignant Neoplasms (87,024)	Heart Disease (605,673)	Heart Disease (724,859)
Malignant Neoplasms (526)	Homicide & Legal Intervention (5,506)	Suicide (5,365)	Unintentional Injury & Adverse Effects (15,127)	Heart Disease (35,056)	Heart Disease (65,068)	Malignant Neoplasms (384,186)	Malignant Neoplasms (541,532)
Suicide (317)	Suicide (4,135)	Homicide & Legal Intervention (4,565)	Heart Disease (13,593)	Unintentional Injury & Adverse Effects (10,946)	Chronic Lower Respiratory Disease* (10,162)	Cerebro-vascular (139,144)	Cerebro-vascular (158,448)
Homicide & Legal Intervention (290)	Malignant Neoplasms (1,699)	Malignant Neoplasms (4,385)	Suicide (6,837)	Liver Disease (5,744)	Cerebro-vascular (9,653)	Chronic Lower Respiratory Disease* (97,896)	Chronic Lower Respiratory Disease* (112,584)
Congenital Anomalies (173)	Heart Disease (1,057)	Heart Disease (3,207)	HIV (5,746)	Cerebro-vascular (5,709)	Diabetes (8,705)	Pneumonia & Influenza (82,989)	Unintentional Injury & Adverse Effects (97,835)
Heart Disease (170)	Congenital Anomalies (450)	HIV (2,912)	Homicide & Legal Intervention (3,567)	Suicide (5,131)	Unintentional Injury & Adverse Effects (7,340)	Diabetes (48,974)	Pneumonia & Influenza (91,871)
Chronic Lower Respiratory Disease* (98)	Chronic Lower Respiratory Disease* (239)	Cerebro-vascular (670)	Liver Disease (3,370)	Diabetes (4,386)	Liver Disease (5,279)	Unintentional Injury & Adverse Effects (32,975)	Diabetes (64,751)
Pneumonia & Influenza (51)	Pneumonia & Influenza (215)	Diabetes (636)	Cerebro-vascular (2,650)	HIV (3,120)	Pneumonia & Influenza (3,856)	Nephritis (22,640)	Suicide (30,575)
Cerebro-vascular (47)	HIV (194)	Pneumonia & Influenza (531)	Diabetes (1,885)	Chronic Lower Respiratory Disease* (2,828)	Suicide (2,963)	Alzheimer Disease (22,416)	Nephritis (26,182)
Benign Neoplasms (32)	Cerebro-vascular (178)	Liver Disease (506)	Pneumonia & Influenza (1,400)	Pneumonia & Influenza (2,167)	Septicemia (2,093)	Septicemia (19,012)	Liver Disease (25,192)

Source: Centers for Disease Control

COMBINING FORMS OF MEDICAL TERMS

Prefix	Meaning of Prefix	Example	Prefix	Meaning of Prefix	Example
a-, ab-, an-	away, lack of, without	astigmatism	galact-	milk	galactose
acro-	extremity, end	acroparesthesia	gastro-	stomach	gastroenteric
adeno-	gland	adenous	gloss-	tongue	glossitis
adreno-	adrenal gland	adrenocortex	hemi-	half	hemiplegic
aero-	gas, air	aerophagia	hepato-	liver	hepatocolic
allo-	different, another	allorhythmia	hydro-	water	hydrocephalic
ambi-	both, both sides	ambidextrous	hyper-	above, beyond	hyperacidity
antero-	before, in front of	anterograde	hypo-	below, less	hypoglycemia
anti-	against	antiseptic	ileo-	end of small intestine	ileocolic
arterio-	artery	arteriospasm	ilio-	flank, upper hip bone	iliopelvic
arthro-, arthr-	joint	arthritis	infra-	below, inferior	infraorbital
bacterio-	bacteria	bacteriological	inter-	between	interdigital
blephari-	eyelash, eyelid	blepharitis	intra-	within	intrauterine
brady-	slow	bradycardia	kerat-	cornea, hard tissue	keratoid
broncho-	windpipe	bronchospasm	laryngo-, larying-	voice box	laryngitis
cardio-	heart, heart region	cardiovascular			
cephalo-	head	cephalometry	leuko-, leuk-	white	leukocyte
cerebro-	brain	cerebrovascular	mega-	abnormally large	megacolon
cervico-	neck	cervicobrachial	mela-	black	melanin
chole-	bile	cholecystis	myelo-, myel-	marrow, nerve sheath	myelination
chondro-	cartilage	chondroblastoma	myo-	muscle	myospasm
chromo-	color	chromogen	neo-	new	neoplasm
chylo-	lymph	chylomicron	nephro-, nephr-	kidney	nephritis
contra-	against, opposite	contraindication	neuro-, neuri-, neur-	nerve	neuritis
costo-	rib	costochondral			
cyst-	bladder, sac	cystitis	osteo-	bone	osteoarthritis
dacryo-	tears	dacryocystitis	peri-, pneumo-	around or about the lungs or air	pericardial pneumonia
derma-	skin	dermatitis			
dextro-	right side	dextromanual	sacro-	sacrum (triangular bone above tailbone)	sacroiliac
dys-	abnormal, bad, painful	dysentery			
encephalo-, encephal-	brain	encephalitis	sero-	serum, blood	serofibrous
			tachy-	rapid	tachycardia
endo-	inside	endocardium	thrombo-	blood clot	thrombosis
entero-	intestines	enterospasm	tracheo-	windpipe	tracheotomy
ep-, epi-	at, over, upon	epiglottis	utero-	uterus, womb	uterotomy
ex-, exo-	out, outside	excrement	vaso-	blood vessel	vasodilator
fibrino-	threadlike	fibrinogen	ventro-	belly, abdominal	ventroptosia
fibro-	fiber, fibrous	fibrocystic	zymo-	enzyme, fermentation	zymocide

"Common Biological Terms" in chapter 3; "Medical Science" under "Reference Works for General Information" in chapter 11; "Medicine and Pharmacology Symbols" in chapter 12

Go to

Health/Nutrition

RECOMMENDED DAILY (OR DIETARY) ALLOWANCES

In the following tables, heights and weights are medians of the U.S. population and are not meant to suggest ideal height-to-weight ratios.

PROTEINS

	Age (years)	Weight (pounds)	Heights (inches)	Protein (grams)
Males	11–14	99	62	45
	15–18	145	69	59
	19–24	160	70	58
	25–50	174	70	63
	51+	170	68	63
Females	11–14	101	62	46
	15–18	120	64	44
	19–24	128	65	46
	25–50	138	64	50
	51+	143	63	50
Pregnant				65
Nursing				62–65

FAT-SOLUBLE VITAMINS

	Age (years)	Weight (pounds)	Height (inches)	Vitamin A (IUs*)	Vitamin D (IUs)	Vitamin E (IUs)
Males	11–14	99	62	1,000	10	10
	15–18	145	69	1,000	10	10
	19–24	160	70	1,000	10	10
	25–50	174	70	1,000	5	10
	51+	170	68	1,000	5	10
Females	11–14	101	62	800	10	8
	15–18	120	64	800	10	8
	19–24	128	65	800	10	8
	25–50	138	64	800	5	8
	51+	143	63	800	5	8
Pregnant				800	10	10
Nursing				1,200–1,300	10	11–12

*IUs = International Units

"Cooking Equivalents and Substitutions," "Cooking Times and Serving Sizes," "Chemical Additives," and "Beverages" in chapter 19

Go to

Health/Nutrition

WATER-SOLUBLE VITAMINS

	Age (years)	Weight (pounds)	Height (inches)	Vitamin C (mg*)	Folate (mcg)	Niacin (mg)	Riboflavin (mg)	Thiamin (mg)	Vitamin B6 (mg)	Vitamin B12 (mg)
Males	11–14	99	62	50	150	17	1.5	1.3	1.7	2.0
	15–18	145	69	60	200	20	1.8	1.5	2.0	2.0
	19–24	160	70	60	200	19	1.7	1.5	2.0	2.0
	25–50	174	70	60	200	19	1.7	1.5	2.0	2.0
	51+	170	78	60	200	15	1.4	1.2	2.0	2.0
Females	11–14	101	62	50	150	15	1.3	1.1	1.4	2.0
	15–18	120	64	60	180	15	1.3	1.1	1.5	2.0
	19–24	128	65	60	180	15	1.3	1.1	1.6	2.0
	25–50	138	64	60	180	15	1.3	1.1	1.6	2.0
	51+	143	63	60	180	13	1.2	1.0	1.6	2.0
Pregnant				70	400	17	1.6	1.5	2.2	2.2
Nursing				90–95	260–280	20	1.7–1.8	1.6	2.1	2.6

*mg = milligrams

MINERALS

	Age (years)	Weight (pounds)	Height (inches)	Calcium (mg)	Phosphorus (mg)	Iodine (mg)	Iron (mg)	Magnesium (mg)	Zinc (mg)
Males	11–14	99	62	1,200	1,200	150	12	270	15
	15–18	145	69	1,200	1,200	150	12	400	15
	19–24	160	70	1,200	1,200	150	10	350	15
	25–50	174	70	800	800	150	10	350	15
	51+	170	68	800	800	150	10	350	15
Females	11–14	101	62	1,200	1,200	150	15	280	12
	15–18	120	64	1,200	1,200	150	15	300	12
	19–24	128	65	1,200	1,200	150	15	280	12
	25–50	138	64	800	800	150	15	280	12
	51+	143	63	800	800	150	10	280	12
Pregnant				1,200	1,200	175	30*	320	15
				1,200	1,200	200	15	355	16–19

*A pregnant woman often requires iron supplement tablets because of the difficulty of providing an adequate iron intake in an otherwise balanced diet.

ACTIVITIES AND THE CALORIES THEY CONSUME

Activity		100 lbs.	125 lbs.	150 lbs.**	175 lbs.	200 lbs.
		Calories Expended per Hour*				
		Person weighing:				
Rest and light activity	Lying down or sleeping	53	67	80	93	107
	Sitting	67	83	100	117	133
	Typing	73	92	110	128	147
	Driving	80	100	120	140	160
	Standing	93	117	140	163	187
	Housework	120	150	180	210	240
	Shining shoes	123	154	185	216	247
Moderate activity	Bicycling (5½ mph)	140	175	210	245	280
	Walking (2½ mph)	140	175	210	245	280
	Gardening	147	183	220	257	293
	Canoeing (2½ mph)	153	192	230	268	307
	Golf (foursome)	167	208	250	292	333
	Lawn mowing (power mower)	167	208	250	292	333
	Fencing	200	250	300	350	400
	Rowing a boat (2½ mph)	200	250	300	350	400
	Swimming (¼ mph)	200	250	300	350	400
	Calisthenics	200	250	300	350	400
	Walking (3¼ mph)	200	250	300	350	400
	Badminton	200	250	350	350	400
	Horseback riding (trotting)	200	250	350	350	400
	Square dancing	200	250	350	350	400
	Volleyball	233	250	350	350	400
	Roller skating	233	292	350	408	467
	Stacking heavy objects (boxes, logs)	233	292	350	408	467
Vigorous activity	Baseball pitching	240	300	360	420	480
	Ditch digging (hand shovel)	267	333	400	467	533
	Ice-skating (10 mph)	267	333	400	467	533
	Chopping or sawing wood	267	333	400	467	533
	Bowling (continuous)	267	333	400	467	533
	Tennis	280	350	420	490	560
	Aerobic dancing	300	375	450	525	600
	Waterskiing	320	400	480	560	640
	Hill climbing (100 feet per hour)	327	408	490	572	653
	Basketball	333	417	500	583	667
	Football	333	417	500	583	667
	Jogging (5 mph)	367	458	550	642	733
	Skiing (10 mph)	400	500	600	700	800
	Squash and handball	400	500	600	700	800
	Bicycling (13 mph)	440	550	660	770	880
	Rowing (machine)	480	600	720	840	960
	Scull rowing (race)	560	700	840	980	1,120
	Running (10 mph)	600	750	900	1,050	1,200

* All figures are approximate, as individual differences in metabolism and how activities are performed affect energy expenditure.

** To approximate your own caloric usage, divide the figure under the "Person weighing 150 pounds" column by 150 to get the approximate caloric expenditure per pound, and then multiply the result by your own body weight.

VITAMIN/MINERAL FOOD CHART (BEST FOOD SOURCES FOR EACH VITAMIN AND MINERAL)

Consult your physician before taking vitamin or mineral dietary supplements or giving them to children. Follow medical advice and label directions carefully, and keep both prescription and nonprescription supplements out of the reach of children. Overdoses can be harmful or fatal.

VITAMINS

Vitamin	Chief Functions	Results of Deficiency	Characteristics
Vitamin A Provitamin, carotene	Essential for maintaining the integrity of epithelial membranes; helps maintain resistance to infections; necessary for the formation of rhodopsin and prevention of night blindness	**Mild:** Retarded growth; increased susceptibility to infection; abnormal function of gastro intestinal, genitourinary, and respiratory tracts due to altered epithelial membranes; dry, shriveled, thickened skin, sometimes pustule formation; night blindness **Severe:** Xerophthalmia, a characteristic eye disease, and other local infections	Fat-soluble; not destroyed by ordinary cooking temperatures; destroyed by high temperatures when oxygen is present; marked capacity for storage in liver *Note:* Excessive intake of carotene, from which vitamin A is formed, may produce yellow discoloration of the skin (carotenemia).
Thiamin **Vitamin B$_1$**	Important role in carbohydrate metabolism; essential for maintenance of normal digestion and appetite; essential for normal functioning of nervous tissue	**Mild:** Loss of appetite; impaired digestion of starches and sugars; colitis, constipation, or diarrhea; emaciation **Severe:** Nervous disorders of various types; loss of coordinating power of muscles; beriberi; paralysis	Water-soluble; not readily destroyed by ordinary cooking temperature; destroyed by exposure to heat, alkali, or sulfites; not stored in body
Riboflavin **Vitamin B$_2$**	Important in formation of certain enzymes and in cellular oxidation; normal growth; prevention of cheilosis and glossitis	Impaired growth; lassitude and weakness; cheilosis; glossitis, atrophy of skin; anemia; photophobia; cataracts	Water-soluble; alcohol-soluble; not destroyed by heat in cooking unless with alkali; unstable in light, especially in presence of alkali
Niacin Nicotinic acid Nicotinamide Antipellagra vitamin	As the component of two important enzymes, it is important in glycolysis, tissue respiration, and fat synthesis; nicotinic acid but not nicotinamide causes vasodilation and flushing; prevents pellagra	Pellagra; gastrointestinal disturbances; mental disturbances	Soluble in hot water and alcohol; not destroyed by heat, light, air, or alkali; not destroyed in ordinary cooking
Vitamin B$_{12}$ Cyanoco-balamin	Produces remission in pernicious anemia; essential for normal development of red blood cells	Pernicious anemia	Soluble in water or alcohol; unstable in hot alkaline or acid solutions

Good Sources	Recommended Daily Allowances	
Natural: Animal fats (butter, cheese, cream, egg yolk, whole milk); fish liver oil; liver; vegetables (green leafy, especially escarole, kale, and parsley; and yellow, especially carrots) **Artificial:** Concentrates in several forms; irradiated fish oils	Males 11 yrs. and older Females 11 yrs. and older Pregnant females Lactating females Children Infants	1,000mg retinol equivalents 800mg retinol equivalents 1,000mg retinol equivalents 1,200mg retinol equivalents 400–700mg retinol equivalents 400mg retinol equivalents
Natural: Widely distributed in plant and animal tissues but seldom occurs in high concentration, except in brewer's yeast; other good sources are whole-grain cereals, peas, beans, peanuts, oranges, heart, liver, kidney, many vegetables and fruits, and nuts **Artificial:** Concentrates from yeast; rice polishings; wheat germ	Males 11 yrs. and older Females 11 yrs. and older Pregnant females Lactating females Children Infants	1.2–1.5mg 1.0–1.1mg 1.4–1.6mg 1.5–1.7mg 0.7–1.2mg 0.3–0.5mg
Eggs, green vegetables, liver, kidney, lean meat, milk, wheat germ, dried yeast, enriched foods	Males 11 yrs. and older Females 11 yrs. and older Pregnant females Lactating females Children Infants	1.4–1.8mg 1.2–1.3mg 1.6mg 1.7–1.8mg 0.8–1.2mg 0.4–0.5mg
Yeast, lean meat, fish, legumes, whole-grain cereals and peanuts, enriched foods	Males 11 yrs. and older Females 11 yrs. and older Pregnant females Lactating females Children Infants	16–19 mg 13–15 mg 17 mg 20 mg 9–16 mg 6–8 mg
Liver, kidney, dairy products; most of vitamin required by humans is synthesized by intestinal bacteria	Males 11 yrs. and older Females 11 yrs. and older Pregnant females Lactating females Children Infants	3 mcg 3 mcg 4 mcg 5 mcg 2–5mcg 1–2mcg

Health/Nutrition

continues

Vitamins, Continued

Vitamin	Chief Functions	Results of Deficiency	Characteristics
Vitamin C Ascorbic acid	Essential to formation of intracellular cement substances in a variety of tissues including skin, dentin, cartilage, and bone matrix; important in healing of wounds and fractures of bones; prevents scurvy; facilitates absorption of iron	**Mild:** Lowered resistance to infections; joint tenderness; susceptibility to dental caries, pyorrhea, and bleeding gums **Severe:** Hemorrhage; anemia; scurvy	Soluble in water; easily destroyed by oxidation, and heat hastens the process; lost in cooking, particularly if water in which food was cooked is discarded; loss is greater if cooked in iron or copper utensils; quick-frozen foods lose little; stored in the body to a limited extent
Vitamin D	Regulates absorption of calcium and phosphorus from the intestinal tract; antirachitic	**Mild:** Interferes with utilization of calcium and phosphorus in bone and teeth formation; irritability; weakness **Severe:** Rickets may be common in young children; osteomalacia in adults	Soluble in fats and organic solvents; relatively stable under refrigeration; stored in liver; often associated with vitamin A
Vitamin E Alpha tocopherol	Normal reproduction in rats; prevention of muscular dystrophy in rabbits and sheep	Red blood cell resistance to rupture is decreased	Fat soluble; stable to heat in absence of oxygen
Vitamin B₆ Pyridoxine	Essential for metabolism of tryptophan; needed for utilization of certain other amino acids	Dermatitis around eyes and mouth; neuritis; anorexia; nausea and vomiting	Soluble in water and alcohol; rapidly inactivated in presence of heat, sunlight, or air
Folate (Folic acid)	Essential for normal functioning of hematopoietic system	Anemia	Slightly soluble in water; easily destroyed by heat in presence of acid; decreases when food is stored at room temperature *Note:* A large dose may prevent the appearance of anemia in a case of pernicious anemia but still permits neurological symptoms to develop.

* IUs = International Units

Good Sources	Recommended Daily Allowances	
Natural: Abundant in most fresh fruits and vegetables, especially citrus fruit and juices and tomatoes **Artificial:** Ascorbic acid; cevitamic acid	Males 11 yrs. and older	50–60mg
	Females 11 yrs. and older	50–60mg
	Pregnant females	80 mg
	Lactating females	100mg
	Children	15mg
	Infants	35mg
	The infant diet is likely to be deficient in vitamin C unless orange or tomato juice or another form is added.	
Butter, egg yolks, fish liver oils, fish having fat distributed through the flesh, (such as salmon, tuna fish, herring) sardines, liver, oysters, yeast, and foods irradiated with ultraviolet light; formed in the skin by exposure to sunlight; artificially prepared forms exist	Males 11 yrs. and older	200–400 IU*
	Females 11 yrs. and older	200–400 IU*; after age 22, none except during pregnancy or lactation
	Pregnant females	400–600 IU*
	Lactating females	400–600 IU*
	Children	400 IU*
	Infants	400 IU*
Lettuce and other green, leafy vegetables, wheat germ oil, margarine, rice	Males 11 yrs. and older	8–10mg
	Females 11 yrs. and older	8mg
	Pregnant females	10mg
	Lactating females	11mg
	Children	10–15 IU*
	Infants	5 IU*
Blackstrap molasses, meat, cereal grains, wheat germ	Males 11 yrs. and older	1.8–2.2mg
	Females 11 yrs. and older	1.8–2.2mg
	Pregnant females	2.6mg
	Lactating females	2.5mg
	Children	0.9–1.6mg
	Infants	0.3–0.6mg
Glandular meats; yeast; green, leafy vegetables	Males 11 yrs. and older	400mcg
	Females 11 yrs. and older	400mcg
	Pregnant females	800mcg
	Lactating females	500mcg
	Children	100–300mcg
	Infants	30–45mcg

Health/Nutrition

MINERALS

Mineral	Chief Functions	Results of Deficiency
Calcium (Ca++)	Necessary for formation of bones and teeth; functioning of nerves and muscles; blood clotting; activation of enzymes that convert food to energy	Rickets (soft, deformed bones) and poor growth in children; osteoporosis in adults; muscle cramps
Iodine (I-)	Necessary for normal thyroid function; regulates oxidation in cells	Disturbance in thyroid function (hypothyroidism); in infants, stunting and mental retardation (cretinism)
Iron* (Fe++)	Necessary for production of hemoglobin and myoglobin (structures that enable oxygen to be carried in blood and stored in muscles)	Fatigue; weakness; headaches; shortness of breath; iron-deficiency anemia
Phosphorus (PO₄)	Necessary for formation of bones and teeth; activation of enzymes that convert food to energy; maintenance of body's proper chemical balance; nerve/muscle function	Weakness; pain in bones (deficiency is rare)
Magnesium (Mg++)	Essential to bone growth and production of cells and genetic material; cofactor in enzymatic release of energy; regulates neuromuscular sensitivity	Muscle cramps and weakness; twitching; confusion; (deficiency most often seen in alcoholics and people taking diuretics or dehydrated from prolonged diarrhea)

*At least 110,000 cases of accidental overdose of iron pills in children under 6 have been reported. Some were hospitalized and at least 35 died. From 1988 to 1992, children's deaths due to iron poisoning accounted for almost ⅙ of all children's poisoning deaths reported to poison control centers. (The number/percentage is increasing, probably due to the increased use of iron supplements among

Good Sources	Recommended Daily Allowances		
Milk and milk products; dark-green, leafy vegetables; broccoli; oysters; tofu; bone meal	Males and females	11–24 yrs.	1,200mg
		21 yrs. and older	800mg
	Pregnant/Lactating females		1,200mg
	Children	1–10 yrs.	800mg
	Infants	birth–6 mos.	400mg
		7 mos.–1 yr.	600mg
Seafood, iodized salt (in micrograms)	Males and females	11 yrs. and older	150mcg
	Pregnant females		25mcg
	Lactating females		50mcg
	Children	1–3 yrs.	70mcg
		4–6 yrs.	90mcg
		7–10 yrs.	120mcg
	Infants	birth–6 mos.	40mcg
		7 mos.–1 yr.	50mcg
Red meat and liver; egg yolks; green leafy vegetables; dried apricots; acidic foods prepared in cast-iron pots; whole-grain breads and cereals	Males	11–18 yrs.	12mg
		19 yrs. and older	10mg
	Females	11–50 yrs.	15mg
		51+ yrs.	10mg
	Pregnant females		30mg
	Lactating females		15mg
	Children	1–10 yrs.*	10mg
	Infants	birth–6 mos.*	6mg
		7 mos.–1 yrs.*	10mg
Milk and milk products; egg yolks; meat, poultry, and fish; whole-grain breads and cereals; beans; nuts	Males and females	11–24 yrs.	1,200mg
		25–51+ yrs.	800mg
	Pregnant/lactating females		1,200mg
	Children	1–10 yrs.	800mg
	Infants	birth–6 mos.	300mg
		7 mos.–1 yr.	500mg
Green, leafy vegetables; nuts; beans; whole-grain breads and cereals; oysters; scallops	Males	11–14 yrs.	270mg
		15–18 yrs.	400mg
		19 yrs. and older	350mg
	Females	11–14 yrs.	280mg
		15–18 yrs.	300mg
		19 yrs. and older	280mg
	Pregnant females		320mg
	Lactating females with infants	1–6 mos.	355mg
		7 mos.–1 yr.	340mg
	Children	1–3 yrs.	80mg
		4–6 yrs.	120mg
		7–10 yrs.	170mg
	Infants	birth–6 mos.	40mg
		7 mos.–1 yr.	60mg

Health/Nutrition

adults.) New federal labeling/packaging regulations went into effect in July 1997 to address the issue; however, parents must be aware of this danger. Ingestion of as few as five tablets/200mg has caused death in children; immediate medical attention is required for any incident of known or possible overdose. Iron poisoning can also be harmful to adults.

continues

Minerals, Continued

Mineral	Chief Functions	Results of Deficiency
Potassium (K+)	Essential to regulation of fluid balance; aids in natural impulse transmission and muscle contraction	Muscle weakness; cardiac arrest; kidney damage (deficiency most often seen in people taking diuretics or dehydrated from prolonged diarrhea)
Selenium (Se)	Necessary for prevention of fat and body chemical breakdown	Deficiency almost unknown in humans, can cause cardiomyopathy
Sodium (Na+)	Necessary to maintenance of fluid balance	Deficiency rare in U.S.; sodium loss due to extremely heavy perspiration (usually in athletes) can cause muscle cramps, weakness, headache
Zinc (Zn++)	Essential element in enzymes necessary for digestion	Wounds slow to heal; loss of taste/appetite; stunted growth and sexual development in children

Health/Nutrition

Good Sources	Recommended Daily Allowances		
Bananas, citrus fruits, dried fruits; deep yellow vegetables; potatoes; beans; milk; whole grain breads and cereals	Males and females (including pregnant or lactating)	19–51+ yrs.	2,000mg
	Children	1 yr.	1,000mg
		2–5 yrs.	1,400mg
		6–9 yrs.	1,600mg
		10–18 yrs.	2,000mg
	Infants	birth–6 mos.	500mg
		7 mos.–1 yr.	700mg
Chicken; egg yolks; seafood; whole-grain breads and cereals; mushrooms, onions, and garlic	Males	11–14 yrs.	40 mcg
		15–18 yrs.	50 mcg
		19–51+ yrs.	70 mcg
	Females	11–14 yrs.	45 mcg
		15–18 yrs.	50 mcg
		19–51+ yrs.	65 mcg
	Pregnant females		65 mcg
	Lactating females		75 mcg
	Children	1–6 yrs.	20 mcg
		7–10 yrs.	30 mcg
	Infants	birth–6 mos.	10 mcg
		7 mos.–1 yr.	15 mcg
Table salt; processed foods; milk; drinking water (some locations)	Males and females	19–51+ yrs.	500mg
	Children	1 yr.	225mg
		2–5 yrs.	300mg
		6–9 yrs.	400mg
		10–18 yrs.	500mg
	Infants	birth–6 mos.	120mg
		7 mos.–1 yr.	200mg
Beef, liver; oysters/shellfish; yogurt; wheat germ; beans; fortified cereals	Males	11 yrs. and older	15mg
	Females	11 yrs. and older	12mg
	Pregnant females		30mg
	Lactating females		15mg
	Children 1–10 yrs.		10mg
	Infants birth–1 yr.		5mg

Health/Nutrition

ALCOHOL CONSUMPTION

The effects of drinking alcoholic beverages depend in part on the amount of actual ethyl alcohol consumed and one's body weight. The level of alcohol in the blood is calculated in terms of milligrams (1 milligram = $\frac{1}{28,350}$ of an ounce) of pure alcohol per deciliter (1 deciliter = 3.5 fluid ounces) of blood. This is usually expressed as mg/dl. Twelve ounces of beer, 4 ounces of wine, or a 1.5-ounce shot of 80-proof whiskey, gin, or vodka contain approximately the same amount of ethyl alcohol: 8 grams, or 8,000 mg.

Blood alcohol concentrations often are expressed as a percentage of blood, as 0.05 percent for 50 milligrams of alcohol per deciliters of blood. It is recommended that drinkers keep their blood alcohol concentration (BAC) below 0.04 percent.

Depending on body weight and other factors, it takes the average adult nearly 1 hour for his or her liver to metabolize (break down) 8 grams of alcohol. Alcohol tends to accumulate in the blood because it is absorbed faster than it is metabolized.

Alcohol is absorbed through the membranes of the mouth and esophagus, from the stomach, and from the intestines. The rate of absorption is affected by proteins, fats, and carbohydrates in the digestive tract, which can slow absorption; by carbonation in drink mixers, which increases absorption; by the amount of water added to dilute the alcoholic beverage or the water or soft drinks consumed between alcoholic beverages; and by the presence of congeners (chemicals such as methyl alcohol, tannins, and histamines) present in the type of alcoholic beverage being consumed. The health of the drinker is also important, as a healthy liver metabolizes alcohol more efficiently.

"Precautions During Pregnancy: Alcohol" in this chapter; "Beverages" in chapter 19
Go to

A blood level of 20 to 30 mg/dl (the equivalent of 0.02 to 0.03 percent, or one or two drinks for an average adult) causes central nervous system changes in behavior, coordination, and ability to think clearly. Because alcohol is an anesthetic, the drinker may not notice the changes in his or her own behavior.

At a blood level of 50 mg/dl (0.05 percent), the drinker may experience sedation or a tranquilized feeling. Between 50 and 150 mg/dl (0.05 to 0.15 percent), there is a definite loss of coordination.

A concentration of 80 to 100 mg/dl (0.08 to 0.10 percent) is considered evidence of "legal intoxication" in many states, even though the alcohol level may be estimated by a breath test rather than actual blood analysis.

At blood levels between 150 and 200 mg/dl (0.15 and 0.20 percent), a person is obviously intoxicated and may show signs of delirium.

At levels between 300 and 400 mg/dl (0.30 and 0.40 percent), the drinker usually loses consciousness.

At levels above 500 mg/dl (0.50 percent), the heart and respiration become so depressed that they cease to function, and death follows.

DRINKING AND DRIVING

It is unsafe to drink and drive; in addition, many states have very strict driving-while-intoxicated (DWI) laws. The table on the next page is intended as a general guideline of at least how long to wait after imbibing before driving a motor vehicle. Note that it may take more than a night's sleep; a 115-pound person who has had 5 drinks in one evening may still be impaired the next morning, 13 hours later. The time varies, however, from person to person, and the best rule is "Don't drink and drive."

In the table, one drink equals 1½ ounces of liquor (86 proof), or 4 ounces of wine or champagne, or 12 ounces of beer.

WAITING PERIOD BEFORE DRIVING AFTER DRINKING

Body Weight	1 Drink	2 Drinks	3 Drinks	4 Drinks	5 Drinks	6 Drinks
100–119 pounds	0 hours	3 hours	6 hours	10 hours	13 hours	16 hours
120–139 pounds	0 hours	2 hours	5 hours	8 hours	10 hours	12 hours
140–159 pounds	0 hours	2 hours	4 hours	6 hours	8 hours	10 hours
160–179 pounds	0 hours	1 hour	3 hours	5 hours	7 hours	9 hours
180–199 pounds	0 hours	0 hours	2 hours	4 hours	6 hours	7 hours
200–219 pounds	0 hours	0 hours	2 hours	3 hours	5 hours	6 hours
Over 219 pounds	0 hours	0 hours	1 hour	3 hours	4 hours	6 hours

ADDITIONAL SOURCES OF INFORMATION

ORGANIZATIONS AND SERVICES

Alcoholics Anonymous
General Service Office
P.O. Box 459 Grand Central Station
New York, NY 10163
212-870-3400
http://www.alcoholics-anonymous.org

Alzheimer's Association
919 N. Michigan Ave., Ste. 1100
Chicago, IL 60611-1676
800-272-3900 (24-hour line) or 312-335-8700
http://www.alz.org/

The American Academy of Allergy, Asthma, & Immunology
611 E. Wells St.
Milwaukee, WI 53202
800-822-2762 (24-hour referral line)
http://www.aaaai.org

American Academy of Neurology
1080 Montreal Ave.
St. Paul, MN 55116
651-695-1940
http://www.aan.com

American Academy of Ophthalmology
655 Beach St.
San Francisco, CA 94109
415-561-8500
http://www.eyenet.org

American Cancer Society
1599 Clifton Rd., NE
Atlanta, GA 30329-4251
800-227-2345
http://www.cancer.org

American Chronic Pain Association
P.O. Box 850
Rocklin, CA 95677
916-632-0922
Fax: 916-632-3208

American Diabetes Association
1701 N. Beauregard St.
Alexandria, VA 22311
800-232-3472
Fax: 703-549-6995
http://www.diabetes.org

American Heart Association
Nation's Capital Affiliate
5535 Wisconsin Ave., NW, Ste. 940
Washington, DC 20015-2030
202-686-6888
Fax: 202-686-6162
http://americanheart.org

American Lung Association
1740 Broadway
New York, NY 10019-4374
212-315-8700
http://www.lungusa.org

American Medical Association
515 N. State St.
Chicago, IL 60610
312-464-5000
http://www.ama-assn.org/

American Optometric Association
243 N. Lindbergh Blvd.
St. Louis, MO 63141
314-991-4100
http://www.aoanet.org

American Speech-Language-Hearing Association
10801 Rockville Pike
Rockville, MD 20852
800-498-2071
TTY: 301-897-0157
Fax: 301-897-7355
http://www.asha.org

Health/Nutrition

Hot Lines and Information Services

A Closer Look

AIDS Hot Line	800-342-AIDS
Alzheimer's Disease and Related Disorders Association	800-621-0379
Cancer Hot Line	800-4-CANCER
Depression Hot Line	800-551-0008
Dial-a-hearing screening test	800-222-EARS
Medicare Hot Line	800-638-6833
Shriner's Hospital free children's hospital care referral line	800-237-5055

Arthritis Foundation
1330 W. Peachtree St.
Atlanta, GA 30309
800-283-7800 (24-hour recording) or 404-872-7100
http://www.arthritis.org

The Center for Nutrition Policy and Promotion
U.S. Department of Agriculture
1120 20th St., NW, Ste. 200, North Lobby
Washington, DC 20036
202-418-2312
Fax: 202-208-2321
http://www.usda.gov/cnpp

Center for Science in the Public Interest
Nutrition Action Healthletter
1875 Connecticut Ave., NW, Ste. 300
Washington, DC 20009
202-332-9110
Fax: 202-265-4954
http://www.cspinet.org

Centers for Disease Control and Prevention (CDC)
1600 Clifton Rd., NE
Atlanta, GA 30333
404-639-3311
http://www.cdc.gov/

CDC National Prevention Information Network
P.O. Box 6003
Rockville, MD 20849-6003
800-458-5231
TTY: 800-243-7012
e-mail: info@cdcnpin.org
http://www.cdcnpin.org

National Association of People With AIDS (NAPWA)
1413 K St., NW, Ste. 700
Washington, DC 20005
202-898-0414
Fax: 202-898-0435
http://www.napwa.org

National Cancer Institute
Public Inquiries Office
Bldg. 31, Room 10A03
31 Center Drive, MSC 2580
Bethesda, MD 20892
301-435-3848
http://www.nci.nih.gov/
http://www.cancernet.nci.nih.gov/

National Council on Alcoholism and
Drug Dependence
20 Exchange Place, Suite 2902
New York, NY 10005
800-622-2255 or 212-269-7797
Fax: 212-269-7510
http://www.ncadd.org/

National Institute of Child Health and
Human Development
Public Information and Communications Branch
Bldg. 31, Room 2A-32
31 Center Dr., MSC 2425
Bethesda, MD 20892-2425
301-496-5133
http://www.nichd.niv.gov/

National Institutes of Health
Bethesda, MD 20892
301-496-1776
Fax: 301-402-0601
http://www.nih.gov/

National Library of Medicine
8600 Rockville Pike
Bethesda, MD 20894
888-346-3656 or 301-594-5983
DOCLINE Service Desk: 800-633-5666
http://www.nlm.nih.gov/

National Women's Health Network
514 10th St., NW, Ste. 400
Washington, DC 20004
202-347-1140
http://www.womenshealthnetwork.org/

Health/Nutrition

The President's Council on Physical Fitness and Sports
200 Independence Ave., SW, Ste. 738-H
Washington, DC 20201
202-690-9000
http://www.fitness.gov/

SMOKENDERS, Inc.
901 NW 133rd St., #A
Vancouver, WA 98685
800-828-4357

MAGAZINES

Natural Health
Box 1200
Brookline Village, MA 02147
http://www.naturalhealthmagazine.com

Prevention
Men's Health
33 E. Minor St.
Emmaus, PA 18098
http://www.prevention.com

Weight Watchers Magazine
360 Lexington Ave.
New York, NY 10017
http://www.weight-watchers.com

BOOKS

Alcoholics Anonymous. Alcoholics Anonymous World Services, 2001.

Cancer Research Institute HelpBook: What to Do When Cancer Strikes. (To order, send $2 postage and handling to Cancer Research Institute HelpBook, P.O. Box 5199, FDR Station, New York, NY 10150-5199, or call 800-992-2623.)

The Complete Food Count Guide. Editors of *Consumer Guide* with the Nutrient Analysis Center, Chicago Center for Clinical Research. Publications International, 1996.

Dupont, Robert L., and John P. McGovern. *A Bridge to Recovery: An Introduction to 12-Step Programs.* American Psychiatric Press, 1994.

Fries, James F., M.D. *Arthritis: A Comprehensive Guide to Understanding Your Arthritis.* 3rd ed. Addison-Wesley, 1990.

Garrison, Robert H., Jr., and Elizabeth Somer. *The Nutrition Desk Reference.* 3rd ed. Keats, 1997.

Greif, Judith, and Beth Ann Golden. *AIDS Care at Home: A Guide for Caregivers, Loved Ones, and People with AIDS.* Wiley, 1994.

Herbert, Victor, and Genell J. Subak-Sharpe, eds. *The Mount Sinai School of Medicine Complete Book of Nutrition.* St. Martin's Press, 1990.

Klesges, Robert C., and Margaret DeBon. *How Women Can Finally Stop Smoking.* Hunter House, 1994.

Komaroff, Anthony L., ed. *Harvard Medical School Family Health Guide.* Simon & Schuster, 1999.

Larson, David E., ed. *The Mayo Clinic Family Health Book.* 2nd ed. William Morrow, 1996.

Morgentaler, Abraham. *The Male Body: A Physician's Guide to What Every Man Should Know About His Sexual Health.* Fireside, 1993.

Northrup, Christiane. *Women's Bodies, Women's Wisdom: Creating Physical and Emotional Health and Healing.* Bantam Books, 1994.

Wexler, Nancy, Wesley J. Smith, and Ron Normon. *Mama Can't Remember Anymore: How to Manage the Care of Aging Parents.* Partners Publishing, 1997.

Yudofsky, Stuart C., Robert E. Hales, and Tom Ferguson. *What You Need to Know About Psychiatric Drugs.* American Psychiatric Press, 1991.

Health/Nutrition

19

HOUSEHOLD TIPS

FOOD

Properly preparing, storing, and cooking food is vital to a healthy, well-run household. The tips below provide information commonly needed in the kitchen.

COOKING EQUIVALENTS AND SUBSTITUTIONS

COMMON KITCHEN MEASURES

pinch (a few grains) = less than ⅛ teaspoon
3 teaspoons = 1 tablespoon
2 tablespoons = 1 fluid ounce
4 tablespoons = ¼ cup
5 tablespoons + 1 teaspoon = ⅓ cup
16 tablespoons = 1 cup
1 cup = ½ pint or 8 fluid ounces
2 cups = 1 pint
2 pints = 1 quart
4 quarts = 1 gallon
2 dry pints = 1 dry quart
8 dry quarts = 1 peck
4 pecks = 1 bushel

COOKING MEASUREMENT ABBREVIATIONS

Measure	Abbreviation
degrees Celsius	°C
degrees Fahrenheit	°F
fluid ounce	fl. oz.
gram	g
kilogram	kg
liter	l
milligram	mg
milliliter	ml
ounce	oz.
pint	pt.
pound	lb.
quart	qt.
tablespoon	tbsp.
teaspoon	tsp.

Go to "Recommended Daily (or Dietary) Allowances" and "Activities and the Calories They Con–sume" in chapter 18

METRIC COOKING MEASURE EQUIVALENTS

Customary	Metric
1 teaspoon	4.9 milliliters
1 tablespoon	14.8 milliliters
1 ounce (dry)	28.35 grams
1 fluid ounce	29.57 milliliters
1 cup	236.6 milliliters
1 pint	473.2 milliliters
1 quart	946.4 milliliters
0.9 quart (dry)	1 liter
1.06 quarts (liquid)	1 liter
1 pound	454 grams
2.2 pounds	1 kilogram
32° Fahrenheit (freezing point)	0° Celsius
212° Fahrenheit (boiling point)	100° Celsius

FOOD WEIGHTS AND MEASURES

Bread

1-pound loaf	12 to 16 slices
1 slice	½ cup soft or ¼ cup dry bread crumbs

Dairy

1 pound cheese	4 to 5 cups, shredded
1 pound cottage cheese	2 cups
3 ounces cream cheese	6 tablespoons
8 ounces cream cheese	1 cup
1 pound butter	2 cups (4 sticks)
1 quart milk	4 cups
1 pound instant nonfat dry milk	5 quarts liquid skim milk
13-ounce can evaporated milk	1⅔ cups
½ pint cream	1 cup
1 cup heavy cream	2 cups, whipped

Eggs

3 to 4	1 cup
8 to 10 whites	1 cup
12 to 14 yolks	1 cup
1 yolk	2 tablespoons

Flour

1 pound all-purpose flour	4 cups, sifted
1 pound cake flour	4¾ to 5 cups, sifted
1 pound whole-wheat flour	3½ to 3¾ cups, unsifted
1 pound cornmeal	3 cups

Go to
"U.S. Customary System of Weights and Measures" and "Metric System of Measurements" in chapter 2

Fruit

juice of 1 medium lemon	2 to 3 tablespoons
juice of 1 medium orange	⅓ to ½ cup
grated rind of medium orange	1 tablespoon
1 apple	1 cup, sliced
1 pound apples	3 cups, pared and sliced
3 to 4 bananas (1 pound)	1¾ cups, mashed
1 pound cherries	2 cups, pitted
1 pound cranberries	2 cups
1 pound grapes	2½ cups, seeded
1 pound raisins	2½ cups
1 pound cut candied fruit	3 cups
1 pound finely cut dates	1½ cups

Meat and Poultry

1 pound ground cooked meat	5 cups
1 pound diced cooked meat	5 cups
3½-pound chicken	3 cups diced, cooked

Nuts

1 pound almonds in shell	1¼ cups, shelled
1 pound pecans in shell	2 cups, chopped
1 pound walnuts in shell	1½ to 1¾ cups, chopped
¼ pound chopped nuts	about 1 cup

Sweeteners and Flavorings

1 pound confectioners' sugar	3½ cups
1 pound brown sugar	2¼ to 2½ cups, firmly packed
1 pound granulated sugar	2 cups
1 pound honey, molasses, or syrup	1⅓ cups or syrup
1 pound cocoa	4 cups
1 ounce unsweetened chocolate	1 square
6-ounce package chocolate chips	1 cup

Vegetables

1 whole bay leaf	¼ teaspoon, crushed
1 pound split peas	2½ cups
1 large green pepper	1 cup, diced
¼ pound sliced mushrooms (1¼ cups)	¼ to ½ cup, cooked
1 medium onion	½ cup, chopped
1 pound potatoes (3 medium)	2½ cups, sliced
1 pound green beans (3 cups)	2½ cups, cooked
1 pound cabbage	2½ cups, cooked
1 pound carrots	2½ cups, diced, or 2 cups, cooked
1 medium bunch celery	4½ cups, chopped
1 pound tomatoes (3 medium)	1½ cups, cooked

FOOD SUBSTITUTIONS

Ingredient	Substitution
Baking powder (1 teaspoon)	¼ teaspoon baking soda + ½ teaspoon cream of tartar
Baking powder (1¼ teaspoons)	½ teaspoon baking soda + 2 tablespoons vinegar
Black pepper	White pepper or paprika
Bouillon (1 cup)	1 bouillon cube dissolved in 1 cup hot water
Bread crumbs (1 cup)	¾ cup cracker crumbs
Butter (1 cup)	1 cup margarine *or* 1 cup vegetable shortening *or* ⅞ cup lard
Buttermilk or sour milk (1 cup)	1 cup yogurt *or* 1 cup whole milk + 1 tablespoon lemon juice *or* 1 tablespoon vinegar *or* 1¾ teaspoons cream of tartar
Carrots	Parsnips *or* baby white turnips
Chocolate Semisweet (1⅔ ounces)	1 ounce unsweetened chocolate + 4 teaspoons sugar
Unsweetened (1 ounce—1 square)	3 tablespoons cocoa powder + 1 tablespoon shortening
Cream, heavy (1 cup)	⅞ cup buttermilk *or* yogurt + 3 tablespoons butter
Croutons	Cubes of crustless white bread sautéed in butter
Curry powder	Turmeric plus cardamom, ginger powder, and cumin
Dry mustard	Prepared mustard
Egg, for thickening or baking	2 egg yolks

continues

Ingredient	Substitution
Flour	
All-purpose, for thickening (1 tablespoon)	1½ teaspoons cornstarch *or* 1½ teaspoons arrowroot *or* 1 tablespoon quick-cooking tapioca
All-purpose, for bread baking (1 cup)	Up to ½ cup bran, whole-wheat flour, *or* cornmeal + enough all-purpose flour to fill cup
Cake (1 cup sifted)	1 cup minus 2 tablespoons all-purpose flour
Fresh herbs (1 tablespoon)	⅓ to ½ teaspoon dried herbs
Honey (1 cup)	1¼ cups sugar + ¼ cup liquid, *or* 1 cup molasses
Lemon juice	Vinegar *or* lime juice *or* white wine
Mushrooms, fresh (1 pound)	6 oz. canned
Olive oil	Vegetable oil
Onion, chopped (1 cup)	1 tablespoon instant minced onion, reconstituted
Parsley	Chervil
Scallions	Green or white onions, *or* onion powder to taste
Shallots	2 parts onion + 1 part garlic
Sugar, brown (1 cup)	1 cup granulated sugar + 1 tablespoon molasses
Sugar, granulated (1 cup)	1¾ cups confectioners' sugar *or* 1 cup molasses + ½ teaspoon baking soda
Tomato sauce (2 cups)	¾ cup tomato paste + 1 cup water
Wine vinegar	Cider vinegar with a little red wine or white distilled vinegar with a little white wine
Yeast, active dry (1 tablespoon— 1 package)	1⅗-ounce cake yeast

KOSHER SUBSTITUTIONS

According to Jewish dietary laws, certain food items, such as pork products, shellfish, and some cuts of beef, are not allowed to be eaten. Also, meat and dairy products are not to be eaten at the same time. Below is a list of ingredients that may be problematic in preparing a kosher dish. On the right are acceptable replacements for these items.

Ingredient	Substitution
Butter	In pastry: all-vegetable margarine or vegetable shortening
	To sauté vegetables: all-vegetable margarine
	To fry meat or poultry: equal parts rendered chicken fat and oil; oil; equal parts oil and all-vegetable margarine
Ham or bacon	Used as flavoring: an equal quantity of anchovies, mushrooms, or pungent vegetables
Milk or cream	In chicken stew, soup, or sauce: for each ½ cup, ½ cup chicken stock mixed with 1 egg yolk and 1 teaspoon cornstarch
	In pancakes: an equal quantity of water, 1 tablespoon oil for each cup of flour, and twice as many eggs
Shellfish	An equal amount of firm fish that has both fins and scales

LOW-FAT SUBSTITUTIONS

Without changing your diet, you can significantly reduce your intake of fat by making the following substitutions for basic ingredients:

Ingredient	Substitution
Baker's chocolate, unsweetened	For each ounce, ¼ cup cocoa powder + 2 tsp. margarine
Butter	On vegetables and popcorn: butter substitute such as Butter Buds
	For sautéeing onions and garlic: nonstick cooking spray and broth in a nonstick pan
	To prevent burning: chicken broth
Crème fraiche	Plain low-fat yogurt

Ingredient	Substitution
Eggs	For scrambled eggs and omelettes: egg substitute such as Egg Beaters
	For baking: 2 egg whites for 1 egg; 3 egg whites *or* 1 egg and 1 white for 2 eggs
Heavy cream	For whipped cream: substitute Cool Whip *or* low-fat whipped cream in a spray can
	For cooking: replace ½ cup cream with 1 tbsp. Butter Buds combined with ⅓ cup skim milk
Roux	Use cornstarch, arrowroot, or pureed vegetables, *or* make the roux with 1 tbsp. Butter Buds and ⅓ cup skim milk instead of the butter
Sour cream	Plain low-fat yogurt *or* 1 cup low-fat cottage cheese combined with 2 tbsp. skim milk and 1 tbsp. lemon juice in the blender
Whole milk	Skim *or* low-fat milk

Only tom (male) turkeys gobble. Hen turkeys make a clicking noise.

COOKING TIMES AND SERVING SIZES

When cooking meat, poultry, fish, and shellfish, the oven temperatures and cooking time used depends on the size of the serving.

OVEN TEMPERATURE SETTINGS

175° to 225°F	Warm
250° to 275°F	Very slow
300° to 325°F	Slow
350° to 375°F	Moderate
400° to 425°F	Hot
450° to 475°F	Very hot

ROASTING MEAT AND POULTRY

Recommended oven temperatures are given in parentheses. Use a meat thermometer to monitor internal temperatures.

To Roast Chicken (375°F)

Chickens weighing between 2 and 4 pounds can be roasted for 30 minutes per pound. Add 15 minutes to the total roasting time if the chicken is stuffed. When the chicken is done, a meat thermometer inserted in the thickest part of the thigh will read 190°F; a thermometer inserted in the stuffing will read 165°F. Estimate ½ pound per serving.

Household Tips

To Roast Beef (325°F)

Cut	Weight in Pounds	Minutes per Pound	Internal Temperature (°F)
Standing rib	4–8		
rare		20–25	140
medium		25–30	160
well-done		30–35	170
Rolled rib	5–7		
rare		30–35	140
medium		35–40	160
well-done		40–45	170
Rib eye	4–6		
rare		20	140
medium		22	160
well-done		24	170
Sirloin tip	3½–4	35–40	160
Tenderloin (roast at 425°F)			
whole	4–6	10	140
half	2–3	20	140

To Roast Lamb (325°F)

Cut	Weight in Pounds	Minutes per Pound	Internal Temperature (°F)
Leg	5–8	30–35	175–180
Shoulder	4–6	30–35	175–180
Cushion shoulder	3–5	30–35	175–180
Rib (rack)	4–5	40–45	175–180
Rolled shoulder	3–5	40–45	175–180
Crown roast	4–6	40–45	175–180

To Roast Pork (350°F)

Although human cases of trichinosis have greatly declined since 1950, pork should always be cooked to an internal temperature of at least 160° F, the temperature at which trichinosis parasites are killed.

Cut	Weight in Pounds	Minutes per Pound	Internal Temperature (°F)
Loin, center	3–5	20–22	160–170
Loin, half	5–7	22–25	160–170
Loin, rolled	3–5	25–30	160–170
Sirloin	3–4	25–30	160–170
Crown	4–6	20–22	160–170
Picnic shoulder	5–8	20–22	160–170
Rolled shoulder	3–5	22–25	160–170
Fresh ham (leg)			
whole	10–14	20–22	160–170
half	5–7	22–25	160–170
Spareribs	3	30	160–170

To Roast Ham and Other Cured Pork (325°F)

Cut	Weight in Pounds	Minutes per Pound	Internal Temperature (°F)
Whole ham	10–14		
uncooked		20	160
fully cooked		10	130
Half ham	5–7		
uncooked		25	160
fully cooked		15	130
Picnic shoulder	5–8	30	170
Rolled shoulder	2–4	40	170

To Roast Veal (325°F)

Cut	Weight in Pounds	Minutes per Pound	Internal Temperature (°F)
Leg	5–8	25–30	170
Loin	4–6	30–35	170
Rib (rack)	3–5	35–40	170
Rolled rump	3–5	40–45	170
Rolled shoulder	4–6	40–45	170

To Roast Duck or Goose (325°F)

Roast duck or goose about 30 minutes per pound. Estimate 1 pound per serving.

To Roast Turkey (325°F)

Turkey is done when a meat thermometer inserted in the thickest part of the thigh reads 185°F, or when a thermometer inserted in the stuffing reads 165°F. Plan on ½ pound per serving.

Ready-to-Cook Weight in Pounds	Total Number of Hours
4–8	3–4
8–12	4–4½
12–16	4½–5
16–20	6–7½
20–24	7½–9

BROILING MEAT AND POULTRY

To Broil Steak (place 2 inches from preheated oven broiler)

For a 1-inch-thick sirloin, porterhouse, T-bone, or ribeye:

Rare	5 minutes each side
Medium	7 minutes each side
Well-done	10 minutes each side

For a 1½-inch-thick sirloin, porterhouse, T-bone, or ribeye:

Rare	6 minutes each side
Medium	8 minutes each side
Well-done	12 minutes each side

For filet mignon, decrease the cooking time by 1 minute on each side. When grilling steak over hot charcoals, have the grill 3 inches from the fire and cook the meat 1 minute less on each side.

To Broil Lamb (place 2 inches from preheated oven broiler)

1-inch chops or patties	about 6 minutes on each side
1½-inch chops	9 minutes on each side
2-inch chops	11 minutes on each side

To Broil Pork (place 2 inches from preheated oven broiler)

Chops (¾ to 1 inch thick), shoulder steaks (½ to ¾ inch thick), and patties (1 inch thick) should be broiled about 11 minutes on each side.

For all boneless meat, allow ⅓ to ½ pound per serving; if the meat contains bone, estimate ½ to ¾ pound per serving.

A Closer Look

Carving a Turkey

Before carving a turkey or other whole bird, allow it to rest breast side up on a platter outside the oven for 10 to 20 minutes, depending on size. This allows the juices to settle into the meat. While the bird is resting, make sure your carving knife (not serrated) is very sharp, and assemble a second large platter and a long two-tined carving fork.

1. Pierce the knee joint with the fork and bend the leg away from the body. Slice between the thigh and body to expose the hip joint, and then work the knife between the ball and socket to cut the leg from the body. Separate the thigh from the drumstick, slice the meat from each, and arrange on the serving platter. Repeat for the other leg.
2. Pierce the meaty part of the wing with the fork and pull the wing away from the body. Cut between the body and the wing, then through the wing joint to remove the wing from the body. Cut the wing in half at the joint and add the pieces to the serving platter, or remove the meat from the wing and arrange for serving.
3. Starting near the neck, slice the breast lengthwise across the grain of the meat. Continue removing slices until you reach the breastbone, and then turn the bird around and repeat for the second breast. Place the slices on the serving platter and enjoy.

COOKING FISH AND SHELLFISH

To Cook Fish

Fish can be cooked at either a very high temperature for a short time or a low temperature for a longer period. Following are general guidelines:

Baked	10 minutes at 500°F
Broiled	15 minutes
Deep-fried	2 minutes at 370°F
Pan-fried	10 minutes
Poached	10 minutes per pound
or steamed	

Allow ¾ to 1 pound of whole fish per serving, ½ pound per serving of dressed fish, fillets, and steaks.

To Cook Shellfish

There are many ways to cook shellfish. Here are just a few.

Starting with boiling water, drop in seafood and let it simmer as follows:

Shrimp	5 minutes
Crab	20 minutes
Lobster	20 to 40 minutes

Clams and mussels can be steamed until their shells just open.

Shrimp, scallops, clams, and oysters can be deep-fried at 370°F for about 3 minutes.

Allow the following quantities per serving:

1 quart unshelled soft-shell clams
1 to 2 crabs
1 small lobster or 1 pound unshelled lobster
6 to 8 oysters
⅔ cup or ⅓ pound shelled scallops
¼ pound unshelled shrimp

COOKING TIMES FOR FRESH VEGETABLES

Vegetable	Amount per Serving	Cooking Time (in minutes)*
Artichoke	1 whole	30–40
Asparagus	5–7 stalks	10–15
Beans (green and wax)	⅓ pound	5–10
Beans (lima)	¾ pound	20–25
Beets	⅓ pound	35–45, whole
Broccoli	½ pound	10–15
Brussels sprouts	⅓ pound	5–10
Cabbage	⅓ pound	5
Carrots	⅓ pound	10–15
Cauliflower	⅓ pound	20–25, whole; 10–15, flowerets
Corn	1–2 ears	5
Eggplant	¼ medium, sliced, broiled, or sautéed	5–10
Mushrooms	¼ pound, caps or sliced and sautéed	5
Onions	⅓ pound	20–30, whole
Peas	½ pound	5–10
Peppers (green)	1 medium, sliced sautéed	3–5
Potatoes	1 medium	20–25, sliced; 90, baked, 350°F
	3 small new	20–25, whole
Potatoes (sweet) or yams	1 medium, sliced	30–35
Spinach	½ pound	5
Squash (summer) or zucchini	½ pound, sliced, boiled, or sautéed	5–10
Tomatoes	½ pound, sliced	5–10 (without water)
Turnips	⅓ pound, cubed	25–30

* Boiled or steamed unless otherwise noted.

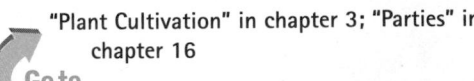

"Plant Cultivation" in chapter 3; "Parties" in chapter 16

Go to

COOKING FRESH FRUIT

To cook any of the fruits below, prepare the fruit according to the directions and add to the proper amount of boiling water. Add sugar and cook for the appropriate time.

Fruit	Amount[1]	How to Prepare	Amount of Boiling Water (cups)	Amount of Sugar (cups)	Cooking Time After Adding Fruit (in minutes)
Apples	8 medium	Pare and slice	½	¼	8 to 10 (slices) / 12 to 15 (sauce)
Apricots	15	Halve; pit and peel if desired	½	¾	5
Cherries	1 quart	Remove pits	1	⅔	5
Cranberries	1 pound	Sort	1 or 2, as desired[2]	2	5
Peaches	6 medium	Pare, pit, and halve or slice	¾	¾	5
Pears	6 medium	Pare, core, and halve or slice	⅔	⅓	10 (soft varieties); 20 to 25 (firm varieties)
Plums	8 large	Halve, pit	½	⅔	5
Rhubarb	1½ pounds	Slice	¾	⅔	2 to 5

[1] Makes 6 servings, about ½ cup each.   [2] Cranberries make 6 servings with 1 cup water; 8 servings with 2 cups water.

SERVING LARGER GROUPS

Here's how much to buy when you need to feed a crowd.

Type	8 Servings	12 Servings	16 Servings
Meat/Poultry/Fish			
Boneless	2–3 lbs.	3–4 lbs.	5–6 lbs.
Chops, roasts	3–5 lbs.	5–7 lbs.	7–9 lbs.
Ribs	6–8 lbs.	9–12 lbs.	12–15 lbs.
Whole birds	8–10 lbs.	12–14 lbs.	16–20 lbs.
Greens			
Lettuce	1–2 heads	2–3 heads	4–5 heads
Cooked leafy greens, peas	4 lbs.	6 lbs.	8 lbs.
Other vegetables	2 lbs.	3 lbs.	4 lbs.
Frozen, in 1-lb. bags	2 bags	3 bags	4 bags
Starches			
Potatoes	2–3 lbs.	4–5 lbs.	6–7 lbs.
Rice (uncooked)	3 cups	4½ cups	6 cups
Pasta (uncooked)	1 lb.	1½ lbs.	2 lbs.
Potato or pasta salad	1 quart	2 quarts	3 quarts
Dessert			
Cakes	1	1	2
Pies	1	2	3
Ice cream	2 pints	4 pints	6 pints
Drinks			
Iced drinks	2 liters	4 liters	6 liters
Coffee (ground)	¼ lb.	½ lb.	1 lb.

Recommended Maximum Food Storage Times

Food	Maximum	Type of Storage	Food	Maximum	Type of Storage
Beef	1–3 days	Refrigerator	Flour	8 months	Pantry
Butter	2 weeks	Refrigerator	Ground meat	1–2 days	Refrigerator
Canned goods	1 year	Pantry	Milk	1 week	Refrigerator
Cereal	2–3 months	Pantry	Dried pasta	2 years	Pantry
Cheese	1–3 weeks	Refrigerator	Poultry	1–2 days	Refrigerator
Eggs	1–2 weeks	Refrigerator	Rice	2 years	Pantry
Fish	1 day	Refrigerator			

Temperature of Food for Control of Bacteria

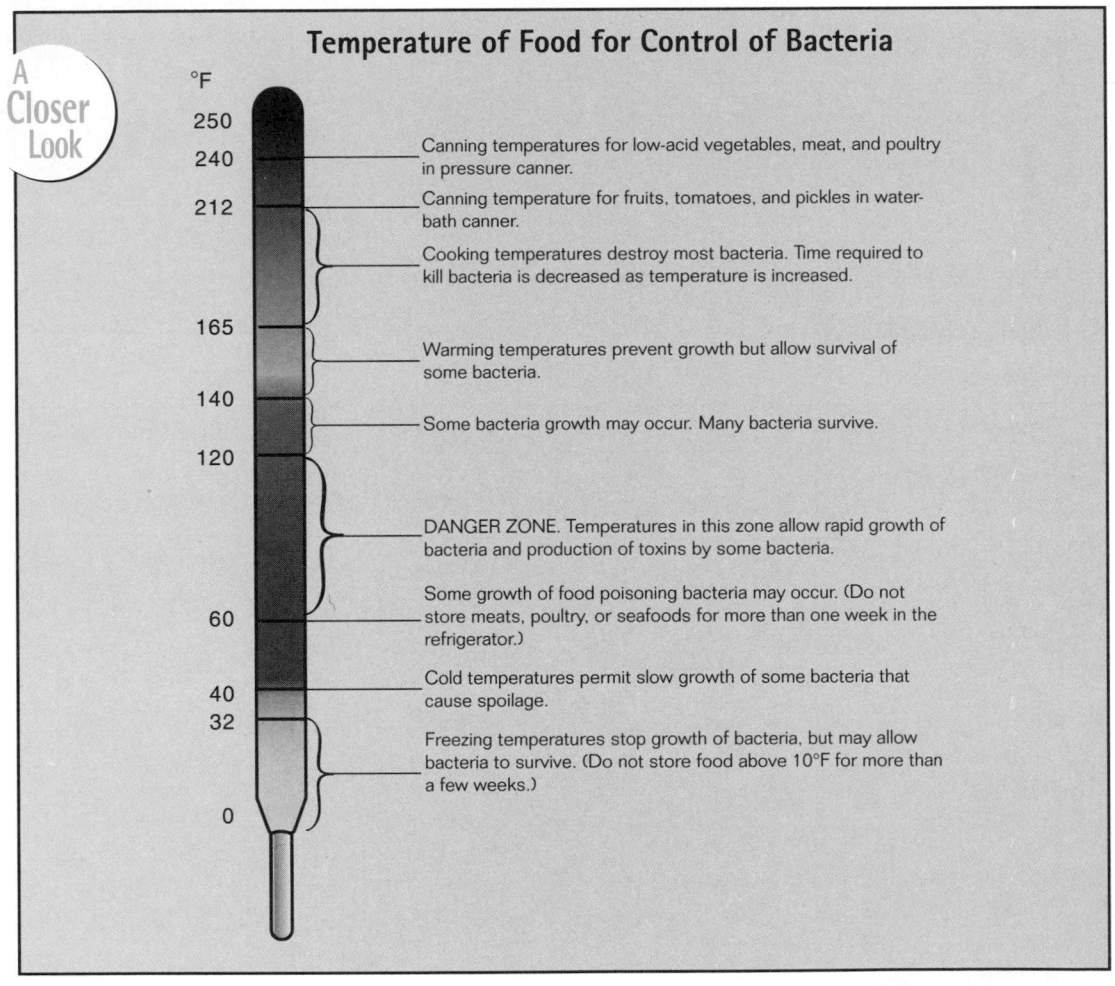

°F

250
240 — Canning temperatures for low-acid vegetables, meat, and poultry in pressure canner.

212 — Canning temperature for fruits, tomatoes, and pickles in water-bath canner.

Cooking temperatures destroy most bacteria. Time required to kill bacteria is decreased as temperature is increased.

165 — Warming temperatures prevent growth but allow survival of some bacteria.

140 — Some bacteria growth may occur. Many bacteria survive.

120

DANGER ZONE. Temperatures in this zone allow rapid growth of bacteria and production of toxins by some bacteria.

Some growth of food poisoning bacteria may occur. (Do not store meats, poultry, or seafoods for more than one week in the refrigerator.)

60

40 — Cold temperatures permit slow growth of some bacteria that cause spoilage.

32 — Freezing temperatures stop growth of bacteria, but may allow bacteria to survive. (Do not store food above 10°F for more than a few weeks.)

0

Go to "Temperature Conversions" in chapter 12

FOOD HOT LINES

To provide consumers with information on cooking, health, and nutrition, several organizations have established toll-free telephone services.

Nutrition Hot Line
American Institute for Cancer Research
800-843-8114
e-mail: aicrweb@aicr.org

Center for Food Safety and Applied Nutrition
888-723-3366

Turkey Talk-Line
Butterball
800-323-4848 (November–December only)

Meat and Poultry Hot Line
Department of Agriculture
800-535-4555
800-256-7072 (TDD/TTY)

Holiday Bake-Line
Land-O-Lakes
800-782-9606 (November–December only)

Nutrition Information Line
American Dietetic Association
800-366-1655

PANTRY BASICS

Certain ingredients are used so frequently by the typical home cook that they should always be ready. Keep the following basics on hand at all times to simplify weekly and daily shopping and cooking.

Canned goods   fruit juice, soft drinks, tomato sauce, soups, canned beans, peanut butter, tuna fish

Condiments   ketchup, prepared mustard, mayonnaise, maple syrup, Tabasco® sauce, soy sauce, Worcestershire sauce®, horseradish, salad dressing, tahini

Dry goods   coffee, tea, breakfast cereal, rice, pasta, dried beans, flour, bread crumbs, baking soda, baking powder, yeast, cornstarch, cream of tartar

Fats and oils   butter, olive oil, vegetable oil

Fresh foods   bread, milk, eggs, cheese, yogurt, celery, carrots, potatoes, garlic, onions, lemons, limes

Seasonings   sugar, salt, black pepper, paprika, oregano, basil, bay leaves, cayenne pepper, dry mustard, curry powder, chili powder, cumin, coriander, thyme, sage, rosemary, dill, tarragon, ginger, cinnamon, nutmeg, cloves, cocoa, vanilla extract, honey, wine vinegar, balsamic vinegar

HERBS AND SPICES

Herbs can provide creative, flavorful alternatives to salt for seasoning foods. Through the skillful use of herbs and spices, you can create imaginative flavors and turn simple foods into gourmet delights.

Employees at the Ivory Soap company overmixed a batch of soap, causing it to be filled with excess bubbles. As a result, the soap floated. Customers loved it, and Ivory soap has been floating ever since.

Herbs and spices differ only in that most herbs grow in temperate areas while most spices grow in tropical regions. Many people like to grow their own herbs in order to have a fresh supply throughout the growing season. Professional cooks also prefer fresh herbs. Because fresh herbs are less concentrated, two to three times as much of them should be used if a recipe calls for dried herbs.

Here are some tips for cooking with herbs and spices.

- In general, the weaker the flavor of the main staple item, the lower the level of added seasoning required to achieve a satisfactory balance of flavor in the end product.
- Dried herbs are stronger than fresh, and powdered herbs are stronger than crumbled. A useful formula is ¼ teaspoon powdered herb = ¾ to 1 teaspoon crumbled = 2 teaspoons fresh.

Household Tips

- Leaves should be finely chopped because the more cut surface exposed, the more flavor will be absorbed.
- A mortar and pestle can be used to powder dry herbs when necessary.
- Scissors are often the best utensil for cutting fresh herbs.
- Be conservative with amounts until you are familiar with the strength of an herb. The aromatic oils can be too strong if a great deal is used.
- The flavoring of herbs is lost by extended cooking. Add herbs to soups or stews about 45 minutes before completing the cooking. For cold foods such as dips, cheeses, vegetables, and dressings, herbs should be added several hours, or even overnight, before using.
- For casseroles and hot sauces, add finely chopped fresh or dried herbs directly to the mixture.
- To become familiar with the specific flavor of an herb, try mixing it with butter and/or cream cheese, letting it set for at least an hour, and then spreading it on a plain cracker.
- Dried herbs should be stored in plastic bags, boxes, or tins rather than cardboard containers. They should be out of direct sunlight and away from the stove.

As a world commodity, coffee is second only to crude oil.

SELECTING HERBS AND SPICES TO GO WITH FOODS

Food	Herbs and Spices
Beef	Bay leaf, chives, cloves, cumin, garlic, hot pepper, marjoram, rosemary, savory
Bread	Allspice, caraway, cardamom, curry powder, marjoram, oregano, poppy seed, rosemary, thyme
Cakes	Allspice, cardamom, ginger
Cheese	Anise, basil, chervil, chives, curry, dill, fennel, garlic, marjoram, oregano, parsley, sage, thyme
Fish	Sweet basil, chervil, dill, fennel, French tarragon, garlic, parsley, thyme
Fruit	Anise, cinnamon, coriander, cloves, ginger, lemon verbena, mint, rose geranium, sweet cicely
Lamb	Garlic, marjoram, oregano, rosemary, thyme
Pork	Coriander, cumin, garlic, ginger, hot pepper, pepper sage, savory, thyme
Poultry	Garlic, oregano, rosemary, sage, savory
Salads	Anise, basil, chives, dill, French tarragon, garlic chives, marjoram, mint, oregano, parsley, savory, sorrel, tarragon (many are best used fresh or added to salad dressing; otherwise, use herb vinegars for extra flavor)
Sauces	Allspice, basil, cardamom, chili powder, chives, cumin, curry, fennel, ginger, marjoram, oregano, parsley, rosemary
Soups	Bay leaf, chervil, French tarragon, marjoram, parsley, savory, rosemary
Stews	Allspice, basil, cardamom, chili powder, curry, dill, ginger, parsley, sage
Vegetables	Basil, chervil, chives, dill, French tarragon, marjoram, mint, parsley, pepper, thyme

Herbal Salt Substitutes

These can be placed in shakers and used instead of salt.

Basic salt substitute   Use 2 teaspoons garlic powder and 1 teaspoon each of basil, oregano, and powdered lemon rind (or dehydrated lemon juice). Put ingredients into a blender and mix well. Store in a glass container and add rice to prevent caking.

Tangy salt substitute   Mix well 3 teaspoons basil; 2 teaspoons each of savory (summer is best), celery seed, ground cumin seed, sage, and marjoram; and 1 teaspoon lemon thyme. Powder with a mortar and pestle.

Spicy seasoning   Mix in a blender 1 teaspoon each of cloves, pepper, and coriander seed (crushed); 2 teaspoons paprika; and 1 tablespoon rosemary. Store in an airtight container.

CHEMICAL ADDITIVES

Additives are substances not naturally found in foods that are introduced during processing to improve flavor, appearance, or consistency or to preserve freshness.

COMMON ADDITIVE TERMS

Antioxidants retard the oxidation of unsaturated fats and oils, colorings, and flavorings. Oxidation leads to rancidity, flavor changes, and loss of color. Most of these effects are caused by the reaction of oxygen in the air with fats.

Chelating agents trap trace amounts of metal atoms that would otherwise cause food to discolor or go rancid.

Emulsifiers keep oil and water mixed together.

Flavor enhancers contribute little or no flavor of their own, but accentuate the natural flavor of foods. They are most often used when very little of a natural ingredient is present.

Thickening agents are natural or chemically modified carbohydrates that absorb some of the water present in food, thereby making the food thicker. Thickening agents "stabilize" factory-made foods by keeping the complex mixtures of oils, water, acids, and solids well mixed.

TYPES OF ADDITIVES

The information on the following pages comes from the Center for Science in the Public Interest and is available from the organization as a color chart entitled "Chemical Cuisine." The address is 1875 Connecticut Ave., NW, Suite 300, Washington, DC 20009-5728 or call 202-332-9110.

Following each entry is a letter that corresponds to one these three categories:

(A) *Avoid.* The additive is unsafe in the amounts normally consumed or is poorly tested.

(C) *Caution.* The additive may be unsafe, is poorly tested, or is used in foods that people tend to eat too much of.

(S) *Safe.* The additive appears to be safe.

CHEMICAL ADDITIVES

ALGINATE; PROPYLENE GLYCOL ALGINATE Thickening agent, foam stabilizer *Ice cream, cheese, candy, yogurt*	Alginate, an apparently safe derivative of seaweed (kelp), maintains the desired texture in dairy products, canned frosting, and other factory-made foods. Propylene glycol alginate, a chemically modified algin, thickens acidic foods (soda pop, salad dressing) and stabilizes the foam in beer. (S)
ALPHA TOCOPHEROL (vitamin E) Antioxidant, nutrient *Vegetable oil*	Vitamin E is abundant in whole wheat, rice germ, and vegetable oils. It is destroyed by the refining and bleaching of flour. Vitamin E prevents oils from turning rancid. (S)
ARTIFICIAL COLORINGS	Most artificial colorings are synthetic chemicals that do not occur in nature. Though some are safer than others, colorings are not listed by name on labels. Colorings are used almost solely in foods of low nutritional value (candy, soda pop, gelatin desserts, etc.). Several dyes have caused allergic reactions (Yellow No. 5) or promoted cancer, and there is evidence that colorings may cause hyperactivity in some sensitive children. The use of coloring usually indicates that fruit or other natural ingredients have not been used. (A)
ARTIFICIAL FLAVORINGS *Soft drinks, candy, breakfast cereals, gelatin desserts, other food items.*	Hundreds of chemicals are used to create flavors; many may be used in a single flavoring, as in cherry soda pop. Most flavoring chemicals also occur in nature and are probably safe, but they may cause hyperactivity in some children. (A)

continues

Household Tips

Chemical Additives, Continued

ASCORBIC ACID (vitamin C); ERYTHORBIC ACID Antioxidant, nutrient, color stabilizer *Oily foods, cereals, soft drinks, cured meats*	Ascorbic acid helps maintain the red color of cured meats and prevents the formation of nitrosamines (see also SODIUM NITRITE). It helps prevent loss of color and flavor by reacting with unwanted oxygen. It is used as a nutrient additive in drinks and breakfast cereals. Sodium ascorbate is a more soluble form of ascorbic acid. Erythorbic acid (sodium erythorbate) serves the same functions as ascorbic acid but has no value as a vitamin. (S)
ASPARTAME Artificial sweetener *Drink mixes, gelatin, desserts, other foods*	Aspartame, made up of two amino acids, was thought to be the perfect artificial sweetener, but questions have arisen about the quality of the cancer tests done on it. In addition, some individuals have reported severe behavioral effects after drinking diet soda. People with PKU should avoid it. (C)
BETA CAROTENE Coloring, nutrient *Margarine, shortening, non-dairy whiteners, butter*	Beta carotene is used as an artificial coloring and a nutrient supplement. The body converts it to vitamin A, which is part of the light-detection mechanism of the eye. (S)
BROMINATED VEGETABLE OIL (BVO) Emulsifier, clouding agent *Soft drinks*	BVO keeps flavor oils in suspension and gives a cloudy appearance to citrus-flavored soft drinks. The residues of BVO found in body fat are cause for concern. Safer substitutes are available. (A)
BUTYLATED HYDROXYANISOLE (BHA) Antioxidant *Cereals, chewing gum, potato chips, vegetable oil*	BHA retards rancidity in fats, oils, and oil-containing foods. While most studies indicate it is safe, a 1982 Japanese study demonstrated that it causes cancer in rats. This synthetic chemical often can be replaced by safer chemicals. (A)
BUTYLATED HYDROXYTOLUENE (BHT) Antioxidant *Cereals, chewing gum, potato chips, oils, other edibles*	BHT retards rancidity in oils. It both increased and decreased the risk of cancer in various animal studies. Residues of BHT occur in human fat. BHT is unnecessary or is easily replaced by safe substitutes. (A)
CAFFEINE Stimulant *Coffee, tea, cocoa (natural), soft drinks (additive)*	Caffeine may cause miscarriages or birth defects and should be avoided by pregnant women. It also keeps many people from sleeping. New evidence indicates that caffeine may cause fibrocystic breast disease in some women. (A)
CALCIUM (OR SODIUM) PROPIONATE Preservative *Bread, rolls, pies, cakes*	Calcium propionate prevents mold on bread and rolls. The calcium is a beneficial mineral; the propionate is safe. Sodium propionate is used in pies and cakes because calcium alters the action of chemical leavening agents. (S)
CALCIUM (OR SODIUM) STEAROLYL LACTYLATE Dough conditioner, whipping agent *Bread dough, cake fillings, artificial whipped cream, processed egg white*	This additive strengthens bread dough so that it can be used in bread-making machinery for more uniform grain and volume. It acts as a whipping agent in dried, liquid, or frozen egg white and artificial whipped cream. Sodium stearoyl fumerate serves the same purpose. (S)
CARRAGEENAN Thickening and stabilizing agent *Ice cream, jelly, chocolate milk, infant formula*	Carrageenan is obtained from seaweed. Large amounts of carrageenan have harmed test animals' colons; the small amounts in food are probably safe. Better tests are needed. (C)

"Vitamin/Mineral Food Chart" in chapter 18

Go to

CASEIN; SODIUM CASEINATE Thickening and whitening agent *Ice cream, ice milk, sherbet, coffee creamers*	Casein, the principal protein in milk, is a nutritious protein that contains adequate amounts of all the essential amino acids. (S)
CITRIC ACID; SODIUM CITRATE Acid flavoring, chelating agent *Ice cream, sherbet, fruit drinks, candy, carbonated beverages, instant potatoes*	Citric acid is versatile, widely used, cheap, and safe. It is an important metabolite in virtually all living organisms and is especially abundant in citrus fruits and berries. It is used as a strong acid, a tart flavoring, and an antioxidant. Sodium citrate, also safe, is a buffer that controls the acidity of gelatin desserts, jam, ice cream, candy, and other foods. (S)
CORN SYRUP Sweetener, thickener *Candy, toppings, syrups, snack foods, imitation dairy foods*	Corn syrup is a sweet, thick liquid made by treating cornstarch with acids or enzymes. It may be dried and used as corn syrup solids in coffee whiteners and other dry products. Corn syrup contains no nutritional value other than calories, promotes tooth decay, and is used mainly in low-nutrition foods. (C)
DEXTROSE (GLUCOSE, CORN SUGAR) Sweetener, coloring agent *Bread, caramel, soda pop, cookies, other foods*	Dextrose is an important chemical in every living organism. A sugar, it is a source of sweetness in fruits and honey. Added to foods as a sweetener, it represents empty calories and contributes to tooth decay. Dextrose turns brown when heated and contributes to the color of bread crust and toast. (C)
DIGLYCERIDES	*See* MONOGLYCERIDES and DIGLYCERIDES.
ETHYLENEDIAMINE TETRA-ACETIC ACID (EDTA) Chelating agent *Salad dressing, margarine, sandwich spreads, mayonnaise, processed fruits and vegetables, canned shellfish, soft drinks*	Modern food-manufacturing technology, which involves metal rollers, blenders, and containers, results in trace amounts of metal contamination in food. EDTA traps metal impurities, which would otherwise promote rancidity and the breakdown of artificial colors. (S)
FERROUS GLUCONATE Coloring, nutrient *Black olives, vitamin pills*	Used by the olive industry to generate a uniform jet-black color and in pills as a source of iron, this substance is safe. (S)
FUMARIC ACID Tartness agent *Powdered drinks, pudding, pie, fillings, gelatin desserts*	A solid at room temperature, inexpensive, and highly acidic, fumaric acid is the ideal source of tartness and acidity in dry food products. However, it dissolves slowly in cold water, a drawback cured by adding dioctyl sodium sulfosuccinate (DSS), a poorly tested, detergentlike additive. (S)
GELATIN Thickening and gelling agent *Powdered dessert mix, yogurt, ice cream, cheese spreads, beverages*	Gelatin is a protein obtained from animal bones, hooves, and other parts. It has little nutritional value because it contains little or none of several essential amino acids. (S)
GLYCERIN (GLYCEROL) Maintainer of water content *Marshmallows, candy, fudge, baked goods*	Glycerin forms the backbone of fat and oil molecules and is quite safe. The body uses it as a source of energy or as a starting material in making more complex molecules. (S)
GUMS (ARABIC, FURCELLERAN, GHATTI, GUAR, KARAYA, LOCUST BEAN, TRAGACANTH) Thickening agents, stabilizers *Beverages, ice cream, frozen puddings, salad dressings, dough, cottage cheese, candy, drink mixes*	Gums derive from natural sources (bushes, trees, or seaweed) and are poorly tested. They are used to thicken foods, prevent sugar crystals from forming in candy, stabilize beer foam (arabic), form gel in pudding (furcelleran), encapsulate flavor oils in powdered drink mixes, and keep oil and water mixed in salad dressings. Tragacanth sometimes causes severe allergic reactions. (S)

Household Tips

continues

Chemical Additives, Continued

HEPTYL PARABEN Preservative *Beer, noncarbonated soft drinks*	Heptyl paraben—short for the heptyl ester of parahydroxybenzoic acid—is a preservative. Studies suggest that this chemical is safe, but, like other additives in alcoholic beverages, it has never been tested in the presence of alcohol. (C)
HYDROGENATED VEGETABLE OIL Source of oil or fat *Margarine, processed foods*	Vegetable oil, usually a liquid, can be made into a semisolid by treating it with hydrogen. Hydrogenation reduces levels of polyunsaturated oils. Many people eat too much oil and fat of all kinds, natural and hydrogenated. High-fat diets promote obesity, heart disease, and possibly cancer. (C)
HYDROLYZED VEGETABLE PROTEIN (HVP) Flavor enhancer *Instant soups, frankfurters, sauce mixes, beef stew*	HVP consists of vegetable (usually soybean) protein that has been chemically broken down into the amino acids of which it is composed. HVP is used to bring out the natural flavor of food. (S)
INVERT SUGAR Sweetener *Candy, soft drinks, many other foods*	Invert sugar, an even mixture of dextrose and fructose (two sugars), is sweeter and more soluble than sucrose (table sugar). Invert sugar forms when sucrose is split in two by an enzyme or acid. It contributes to tooth decay. (C)
LACTIC ACID Acidity regulator *Spanish olives, cheese, frozen desserts, carbonated beverages*	This safe acid occurs in almost all living organisms. It inhibits spoilage in Spanish-type olives, balances the acidity in cheese making, and adds tartness to frozen desserts, carbonated fruit-flavored drinks, and other goods. (S)
LACTOSE Sweetener *Whipped topping mix, breakfast pastry*	Lactose is a carbohydrate found only in milk. One-sixth as sweet as table sugar, it is added to food as a slightly sweet source of carbohydrate. Milk turns sour when bacteria convert lactose to lactic acid. Worldwide, more people are lactose-intolerant than tolerant. Many people not of northern European descent have trouble digesting lactose. (S)
LECITHIN Emulsifier, antioxidant *Baked goods, margarine, chocolate, ice cream*	A common constituent of animal and tissues, lecithin is a source of the nutrient choline. It keeps oil and water from separating, retards rancidity, reduces spattering in a frying pan, and leads to fluffier cakes. Major sources are egg yolks and soybeans. (S)
MANNITOL Sweetener, other uses *Chewing gum, low-calorie foods*	Not quite as sweet as sugar and poorly absorbed by the body, mannitol contributes only half as many calories as sugar. Used as the "dust" on chewing gum, it prevents gum from absorbing moisture and becoming sticky. (S)
MONOGLYCERIDES and DIGLYCERIDES Emulsifiers *Baked goods, margarine, candy, peanut butter*	These substances make bread softer, improve the stability of margarine, and make caramel less sticky. They prevent staleness and keep the oil in peanut butter from separating. Monoglycerides and diglycerides are safe, though most foods they are used in are high in refined flour, sugar, or fat. (S)
MONOSODIUM GLUTAMATE (MSG) Flavor enhancer *Soup, seafood, poultry, cheese, sauces, stews, other foods*	This amino acid brings out the flavor of protein-containing foods. Large amounts of MSG fed to infant mice destroyed nerve cells in the brain. Public pressure forced baby food companies to stop using MSG. MSG can cause a burning sensation in the back of the neck and forearms, tightness of the chest, and headaches in some people. (C)
PHOSPHORIC ACID; PHOSPHATES Acidulant, chelating agent, buffer, emulsifier, nutrient, discoloration inhibitor *Baked goods, cheese, powdered foods, cured meats, soft drinks, cereals, dehydrated potatoes*	Phosphoric acid acidifies and flavors cola beverages. Phosphate salts are in hundreds of processed foods for many purposes. Calcium and iron phosphates act as mineral supplements. Sodium aluminum phosphate is a leavening agent. Calcium and ammonium phosphates serve as food for yeast in bread. Sodium acid pyrophosphate prevents discoloration. Phosphates are not toxic, but their widespread use has led to dietary imbalances that may contribute to osteoporosis. (C)

POLYSORBATE 60 Emulsifier *Baked goods, frozen desserts, imitation dairy products*	Polysorbate 60 is short for polyoxyethylene-(20)-sorbitan monostearate. Like its close relatives polysorbate 65 and 80, it works the same way that diglycerides do, but smaller amounts are needed. They keep baked goods from going stale, keep dill oil dissolved in bottled dill pickles, help coffee whiteners dissolve in coffee, and prevent oil from separating out of artificial whipped cream. (S)

PROPYL GALLATE
Antioxidant
*Vegetable oils, meat products,
  potato sticks, chicken soup
  base, chewing gum*
	This substance retards the spoilage of fats and oils and is often used with BHA and BHT because of the synergistic effect these additives have. The best long-term feeding study on this additive was peppered with suggestions but not proof of cancer. (A)

QUININE Flavoring *Tonic water, quinine water, bitter lemon*	This drug can cure malaria and is used as a bitter flavoring in a few soft drinks. There is a slight chance that quinine may cause birth defects, so pregnant women should avoid quinine-containing beverages and drugs. It has been very poorly tested. (A)
SACCHARIN Synthetic sweetener *Diet products*	Saccharin is 350 times sweeter than sugar. Studies have not shown that saccharin helps people lose weight. In 1977, the FDA proposed that saccharin be banned because of repeated evidence that it causes cancer. It is gradually being replaced by aspartame. (A)
SALT (SODIUM CHLORIDE) Flavoring *Most processed foods*	Salt is used liberally in many processed foods. Other additives contribute additional sodium. A diet high in sodium may cause high blood pressure, which increases the risk of heart attack and stroke. (A)
SODIUM BENZOATE Preservative *Fruit juices, carbonated drinks, pickles, preserves*	Manufacturers have used sodium for over 70 years to prevent the growth of microorganisms in acidic foods. (S)

SODIUM CARBOXY-
  METHYL-CELLULOSE
  (CMC)
Thickening and stabilizing agent
*Ice cream, beer, pie fillings, icings,
  diet foods, candy*
	CMC is made by reacting cellulose with derivative of acetic acid. Studies indicate that CMC is safe. (S)

SODIUM NITRITE;
  SODIUM NITRATE
Preservative, coloring, flavoring
*Bacon, ham, frankfurters,
  luncheon meats, smoked fish,
  corned beef*
	Nitrite can lead to the formation of small amounts of potent cancer-causing chemicals (nitrosamines), particularly in fried bacon. Nitrite is tolerated in foods because it can prevent the growth of bacteria that cause botulism poisoning. Nitrite also stabilizes the red color in cured meats and gives a characteristic flavor. Companies should find safer methods of preventing botulism. Sodium nitrate is used in dry-cured meats because it slowly breaks down into nitrite. (A)

SORBIC ACID;
  POTASSIUM SORBATE
Prevents growth of mold
*Cheese, syrup, jelly, cakes,
  wines, dry fruits*
	These additives occur naturally in many plants and are safe under normal circumstances. (S)

SORBITAN
  MONOSTEARATE
Emulsifier
*Cakes, candy, frozen desserts,
  puddings, icings*
	Like monoglycerides, diglycerides, and polysorbates, this additive keeps oil and water mixed. In chocolate candy, it prevents the discoloration that occurs when the candy is warmed up, then cooled down. (S)

Household Tips

continues

Chemical Additives, Continued

SORBITOL Sweetener, thickening agent, maintainer of moisture *Dietetic drinks and foods, candy, shredded coconut, chewing gum*	Sorbitol occurs naturally in fruits and berries and is a close relative of the sugars; however, it is half as sweet as sugar. It is used in noncariogenic chewing gum because oral bacteria do not metabolize it well. Large amounts of sorbitol (2 ounces for adults) have a laxative effect, but otherwise it is safe. Diabetics use sorbitol because it is absorbed slowly and does not cause blood sugar to increase rapidly. (S)
STARCH; MODIFIED STARCH Thickening agent *Soups, gravies, baby foods*	Starch, the major component of flour, potatoes, and corn, is used as a thickening agent. It does not, however, dissolve in cold water. Chemists have solved this problem by reacting starch with various chemicals. These modified starches are added to some foods to improve their consistencies and to keep the solids suspended. Starch and modified starches make foods look thicker and richer than they really are. (S)
SUGAR (SUCROSE) Sweetener *Table sugar, sweetened foods*	Sucrose, ordinary table sugar, occurs naturally in fruit, sugar cane, and sugar beets. Americans consume about 65 pounds of refined sugar per person per year. Sugar, corn syrup, and other refined sweeteners make up about one-eighth of the average diet, but they contain no vitamins, minerals, or protein. (A)
SULFUR DIOXIDE; SODIUM BISULFITE Preservative, bleach *Dried fruits, wines, processed potatoes*	Sulfiting agents prevent discoloration (in dried fruits, some "fresh" shrimp, and some dried, fried, and frozen potatoes) and bacterial growth (in wines). They also destroy vitamin B₁ and can cause severe reactions in asthmatics. This additive has caused at least seven deaths. (A)
VANILLIN; ETHYL VANILLIN Substitute for vanilla *Ice cream, baked goods, beverages, chocolate, candy, gelatin desserts*	Vanilla flavoring is derived from a bean, but vanillin, the major flavor component of vanilla, is cheaper to produce in a factory. A derivative, ethyl vanillin, comes closer to matching the taste of real vanilla. Both chemicals are safe. (S)

OUTLAWED ADDITIVES

Name	Year Outlawed	Use
Cobalt salts	1966	Beer foam stabilizer
Cyclamate	1960	Artificial sweetener
Dulcin	1950	Artificial sweetener
Green No. 1	1965	Coloring agent
Orange B	1978	Coloring agent
Red No. 2	1976	Coloring agent
Safrole	1960	Root beer flavoring
Violet No. 1	1973	Coloring agent

Go to "Consumer Information and Protection" in chapter 22; "Treatment for Health Emergencies" in chapter 17; "Home Remedies" in chapter 18

BEVERAGES

Selecting and serving beverages, especially alcoholic beverages, can often be confusing. The information below is intended to aid hosts and hostesses serve their guests responsibly and pleasurably.

AMOUNT OF LIQUOR NEEDED FOR NUMBER OF DRINKS SERVED

Liquor is commonly sold in 750-milliliter and 1-liter bottles. A 750-milliliter bottle is equivalent to 25.4 fluid ounces. One liter is equivalent to 33.8 fluid ounces.

A Closer Look

Champagne Bottle Sizes

Name	Capacity	Bottles
Bottle	0.75 liter	1
Magnum	1.5 liters	2
Jeroboam	3 liters	4
Rehoboam	4.5 liters	6
Methuselah	6 liters	8
Salmanazar	9 liters	12
Balthazar	12 liters	16
Nebuchadnezzar	15 liters	20

Number of People	Number of Drinks	Amount Needed
For cocktails		
4	10 to 16	one 750-ml bottle
6	15 to 22	two 750-ml bottles
8	18 to 24	two 750-ml bottles
12	20 to 40	three 750-ml bottles
20	40 to 65	three 1-liter bottles
For buffet or dinner		
4	8 cocktails	one 750-ml bottle
	8 glasses of wine	two 1-liter bottles
	4 liqueurs	one 750-ml bottle
	10 highballs	one 750-ml bottle
6	12 cocktails	one 750-ml bottle
	12 glasses of wine	three 1-liter bottles
	8 liqueurs	one 750-ml bottle
	16 highballs	two 750-ml bottles
8	16 cocktails	one 750-ml bottle
	16 glasses of wine	three 1-liter bottles
	16 liqueurs	one 750-ml bottle
	18 highballs	two 750-ml bottles
20	40 cocktails	three 750-ml bottles
	40 glasses of wine	seven 1-liter bottles
	25 liqueurs	two 750-ml bottles
	50 highballs	three 1-liter bottles
For after-dinner party		
4	12 to 16	one 750-ml bottle
6	18 to 26	two 750-ml bottles
8	20 to 34	two 750-ml bottles
12	25 to 45	three 750-ml bottles
20	45 to 75	three 1-liter bottles plus one 750-ml bottle

Household Tips

MIXING DRINKS

Always be sure of your ingredients and measure them accurately. A jigger is 1½ ounces; a pony, ¾ ounce; a bar spoon, ½ teaspoon; and a dash, 7 to 10 drops.

Ice should always be the first ingredient that goes into the glass. Use new ice for every drink and do not let drinks stand too long before serving. The best bartenders chill cocktail glasses in the refrigerator before serving.

Drinks containing fruit juices, eggs, or other dissimilar ingredients should always be shaken fast and vigorously. The ingredients will mix more readily and completely in a shaker or an electric blender. Never shake drinks mixed with carbonated water or ginger ale. Stir them smoothly and not too vigorously for about half a minute. This will keep the drink sparkling and prevent a flat taste. It also will chill the drink properly and thoroughly.

When a drink calls for fruit juice, use fresh juice if possible. The juice is put into the mixing glass with the proper amount of sugar or other sweetener before the liquor.

Fine granulated sugar can be used for sweetening in most cases. Many people prefer simple syrup, which can easily be made by dissolving 2 cups of granulated sugar in 1 cup of boiling water. One teaspoon of simple syrup is equivalent to one teaspoon of sugar.

For drinks requiring a twist of lemon, orange, or lime, use a piece of peel about 1½ inches long and ¼ inch wide. Twist this over the drink to extract a bit of oil, and then drop in the peel.

ALCOHOLIC DRINK RECIPES

Except where otherwise indicated, *shake* means to shake with cracked ice and then strain into a glass; *stir* means to stir over ice in the glass; and *straight up* means served without ice.

"Alcohol Consumption" and "Precautions During Pregnancy" in chapter 18
Go to

Alexander   Shake 1 oz. brandy, 1 oz. crème de cacao, and 1 oz. cream.

B & B   Stir ½ oz. benedictine and ½ oz. brandy (or cognac); B & B may also be served straight up.

Black Russian   Stir 1½ oz. vodka and ¾ oz. Kahlua®.

Black Velvet   Pour equal parts Guinness® stout and champagne over ice in a tall glass.

Bloody Mary   Shake or stir 1½ oz. vodka, 3 oz. tomato juice, the juice of ½ lemon, a dash each of Worcestershire® and Tabasco® sauce, and a pinch each of salt, pepper, and celery salt.

Bronx Cocktail   Shake 1 oz. gin, ½ oz. dry vermouth, ½ oz. sweet vermouth, and ½ oz. orange juice.

Bullshot   Substitute consommé for tomato juice and follow the directions for Bloody Mary.

Champagne Cocktail   Mix 1 lump sugar, 2 dashes angostura bitters, and 1 oz. brandy; top with chilled champagne.

Cosmopolitan   Shake 1¼ oz. Absolut Citron®, ¼ oz. Rose's® lime juice, ¼ oz. Cointreau® or triple sec, ¼ cup cranberry juice, 1 cup ice cubes; garnish with lime.

Cuba Libre (Rum and Coke®)   Over ice in a tall glass, pour 1 oz. light rum and the juice of ½ lime; top with cola.

Daiquiri   Shake 1½ oz. light rum, the juice of 1 lime, and 1 teaspoon powdered sugar (often served with the addition of crushed fruit or fruit juice as strawberry daiquiri, peach daiquiri, etc.; blended with crushed ice, it becomes a frozen daiquiri).

Gibson   A martini with the addition of a pearl onion instead of the traditional olive.

Gimlet   Shake 1 oz. gin and 1 oz. Rose's® lime juice or the juice of 1 lime.

Gin and Tonic   Pour 2 oz. gin over ice in a tall glass; top with tonic water.

Gin Fizz   Shake 2 oz. gin, the juice of ½ lemon, and 1 teaspoon powdered sugar; top with soda water in a tall glass.

Grasshopper   Shake ½ oz. crème de menthe, ½ oz. white crème de cacao, and ½ oz. cream.

Harvey Wallbanger   Add 1 oz. Galliano® to a Screwdriver.

Jack Rose   Shake 1½ oz. apple brandy, the juice of ½ lime, and 1 teaspoon grenadine.

Kir   To a glass of chilled white wine, add 1 teaspoon crème de cassis.

Mai Tai   Shake 2 oz. rum, 1 oz. curaçao, the juice of ½ lime, ½ oz. grenadine, ½ oz. almond-flavored syrup, and ½ teaspoon powdered sugar; serve over crushed ice.

Manhattan   Stir with cracked ice 1½ oz. whiskey, ¾ oz. sweet vermouth, and a dash of angostura bitters; serve over ice or straight up with a maraschino cherry.

Margarita   Shake 1½ oz. tequila, ½ oz. Cointreau® or triple sec, and the juice of ½ lime; serve in a chilled, salt-rimmed glass.

Martini   Stir gin and dry vermouth; strain into a chilled glass. The original ratio of gin to vermouth was 2:1, but contemporary tastes tend toward "drier" ratios of 3:1, 5:1, and even 7:1. Serve straight up with an olive or, less traditionally, over ice or with a lemon twist. Made with a pearl onion, it is called a Gibson; with vodka, a vodka martini or Vodkatini.

Mint Julep   Mix in a tall glass 1 lump sugar, 1 tablespoon water, and 4 sprigs of mint; fill the glass with crushed ice; add 2 oz. bourbon, and serve with straws, without stirring.

Old-Fashioned   Mix in a short glass ½ lump sugar, 2 dashes angostura bitters, and 1 dash water; stir in ice cubes and 2 oz. whiskey.

Orange Blossom   Shake 1 oz. gin and 1 oz. orange juice.

Pimm's Cup   Over ice in a tall glass, pour 1 oz. Pimm's No. 1 Cup®; top with lemonade, 7-Up®, or ginger ale.

Piña Colada   Over crushed ice in a tall glass, pour ½ oz. light rum; ½ oz. dark rum; 1 oz. each of orange, lime, and pineapple juice; and 1 dash of grenadine. Top with coconut milk.

Before refrigerators, ice was cut from frozen lakes in the winter, put aboard ships, and transported around the world.

Pink Gin   Add 1 dash angostura bitters to 2 oz. gin. Pink Gin may be served straight up or with water or soda and ice.

Planter's Punch   Over crushed ice in a tall glass, pour 2 oz. soda water, the juice of 2 limes, and 2 teaspoons powdered sugar; stir to frost glass; add 2 dashes angostura bitters and 2 oz. rum.

Rickey   Over cracked ice, pour 2 oz. gin and the juice of ½ lime; top with soda water. This traditional gin rickey is often modified by substituting other spirits—hence, Scotch rickey, Irish rickey, etc.

Rob Roy   Using Scotch whiskey, follow the directions for a Manhattan.

Rusty Nail   Stir 2 oz. Scotch whiskey with 1 oz. Drambuie®.

Salty Dog   Stir 2 oz. gin, 2 oz. grapefruit juice, and ¼ teaspoon salt.

Sangre   A Bloody Mary made with tequila instead of vodka.

Screwdriver   Over ice in a tall glass, pour 2 oz. vodka; top with orange juice.

7 & 7   Over ice, pour 1½ oz. Seagram's® whiskey; top with 7-Up.®

Sidecar   Shake 1 oz. brandy, ½ oz. Cointreau® or triple sec, and the juice of ½ lemon.

Household Tips

Singapore Sling   Shake 2 oz. gin, ½ oz. cherry brandy, the juice of ½ lemon, and 1 teaspoon powdered sugar; pour over ice cubes in a tall glass and top with soda water.

Stinger   Shake or stir 1 oz. brandy and 1 oz. white crème de menthe.

Tequila Sunrise   Shake or stir in a tall glass 1½ oz. tequila and 3 oz. orange juice; add 1 oz. grenadine; do not stir.

Toddy   Dissolve 1 lump sugar in a little water in a short glass; add 2 oz. spirits (brandy, gin, rum, or whiskey) and top with water (with boiling water, the drink is a hot toddy).

Tom Collins   Shake 2 oz. gin, the juice of ½ lemon, and 1 teaspoon powdered sugar; pour over ice cubes in a tall glass and top with soda water (made with vodka in place of gin, this is a Vodka Collins).

Whiskey Sour   Shake 2 oz. whiskey, the juice of ½ lemon, and ½ teaspoon powdered sugar.

White Lady   Shake 1½ oz. gin, 1 teaspoon powdered sugar, 1 teaspoon cream, and 1 egg white.

Zombie   Blend with cracked ice 3 oz. rum, ½ oz. apricot brandy, 1 oz. pineapple juice, the juice of 1 lime and 1 orange, and 1 teaspoon powdered sugar. Strain into a tall frosted glass; float ½ oz. rum (151 proof) on top before serving with straws.

WINES AND THEIR SERVICE

Red table wines should be served cool or at room temperature. Room temperature means about 65 to 68°F, so some cooling may be necessary. Red wines go well with all foods with the possible exception of seafood. White table wines, rosé wines, and all sparkling wines—both red and white—should be served well chilled. Dry wines should not be served with sweet dishes.

So that corks stay moist and tight, store wines on their sides. If the cork is removed an hour or two before serving, red wines will expand a bit and give off a delightful scent. Smell the cork to see if it is sour-smelling; if so, the wine has started to turn to vinegar and should not be served; it can, however, be kept for cooking.

Many good wines will contain a small amount of sediment. This is harmless and will settle on the bottom of the bottle if it is stood upright for about two hours before serving. When serving champagne, hold the bottle at a slight angle for a few seconds after the cork is removed. This reduces the amount of frothing and maintains a maximum amount of sparkle.

Wineglasses should be placed to the right of the water goblet; they are arranged according to their use, the first wineglass being closest to the water goblet. If more than one wine is served, the glasses used first are removed when the course is through.

The person serving should fill his or her own glass one-quarter full and then taste the wine to check the quality and flavor. Then the other glasses should be filled half to three-quarters full but never to the very top. Wine is poured as soon as a course is served. The person pouring should not lift the glasses from the table.

When more than one wine is served, remember that light wine comes before heavy or full wine, dry white wine precedes sweet red wine, and dry red wine is served before white sweet wine. The "correct" wine is always the one you like best; however, certain wines complement certain foods. The following wine and food list is a guide to what people generally like. One's own taste should be the final judge.

SELECTING WINES TO GO WITH FOODS

After Dinner   Brandy, Cointreau, benedictine, crème de menthe.

Canapés, Crackers, Olives, Cheese Dips, Other Hors d'Oeuvres   Sherry, vermouth, or champagne.

Cheese or Nuts   Port, sherry, red Burgundy, muscatel, zinfandel, Barbera.

How to Store Coffee

Bean form	Room temperature	4–5 weeks
	Freeze	5–6 months (grind amount needed only)
	Refrigerator	Avoid
Ground	Room temperature	7–10 days
	Freezer	5–6 weeks
	Refrigerator	Up to 3 weeks

Desserts   Sweet sauterne, champagne, port, muscatel, Tokay.

Fowl   Rhine wine, dry sauterne, champagne, Bordeaux, white or red Burgundy (with game).

Meats   Claret, red Burgundy, rosé (with cold cuts).

Seafood   Chablis, Rhine wine, Moselle, dry sauterne, white Burgundy.

Soups   Sherry or Madeira.

PRIME WINE VINTAGES BY REGION/VARIETY

The years of prime wine vintages are given in descending order of quality.

Australia
Coonawarra: 1990, 1997, 1991, 1998/99
Hunter Valley: 1991, 1998, 1999, 1996

Chile
1999, 1997, 1996, 1994

California
Cabernet Sauvignon: 1994, 1997, 1991, 1992
Chardonnay: 1997, 1995, 1992, 1991
Pinot Noir: 1997, 1994, 1991, 1999
Zinfandel: 1994, 1996, 1993, 1991

France
Alsace: 1997, 1990, 1996, 1998
Bordeaux, red: 1990, 1995, 1998, 1994
Bordeaux, white: 1990, 1999, 1997, 1998
Burgundy, red: 1990, 1996, 1995, 1997
Burgundy, white: 1990, 1996, 1995, 1992
Loire: 1996, 1995, 1990, 1999
Rhone: 1998, 1990, 1995, 1999

Germany
Mosel: 1990, 1996, 1995, 1994
Rhine: 1996, 1990, 1994, 1999

Italy
Piedmont: 1990, 1998, 1996, 1997
Tuscany: 1997, 1990, 1995, 1999
Veneto/Amarone: 1997, 1990, 1995, 1998

Spain
Ribera del Duero: 1996, 1995, 1991, 1994
Rioja: 1995, 1994, 1999, 1990

CLOTHING

The following section contains instructions about properly washing clothing, removing stains, and choosing the right size.

WASHING INSTRUCTIONS FOR DIFFERENT FABRIC TYPES

Cottons and Linens   Separate whites and colors. Pretreat and soak heavily soiled articles. Load washer about 3 pounds lighter than manufacturer's recommendation. Wash whites and colorfast items in very hot water with all-purpose detergent for a full washer cycle. Extremely dirty articles should be washed separately. Use cool water for colors that are likely to bleed, with a shorter cycle for lightly soiled loads. For lightweight and sheer cottons, wash whites in warm water and colors in cool water with an all-purpose detergent for a shortened washing cycle.

Synthetics   Wash white nylon separately from other synthetics, as it picks up color easily. A 3- or 4-pound load of easy-care fabrics washes and dries with fewer wrinkles than a capacity load. Wash in warm

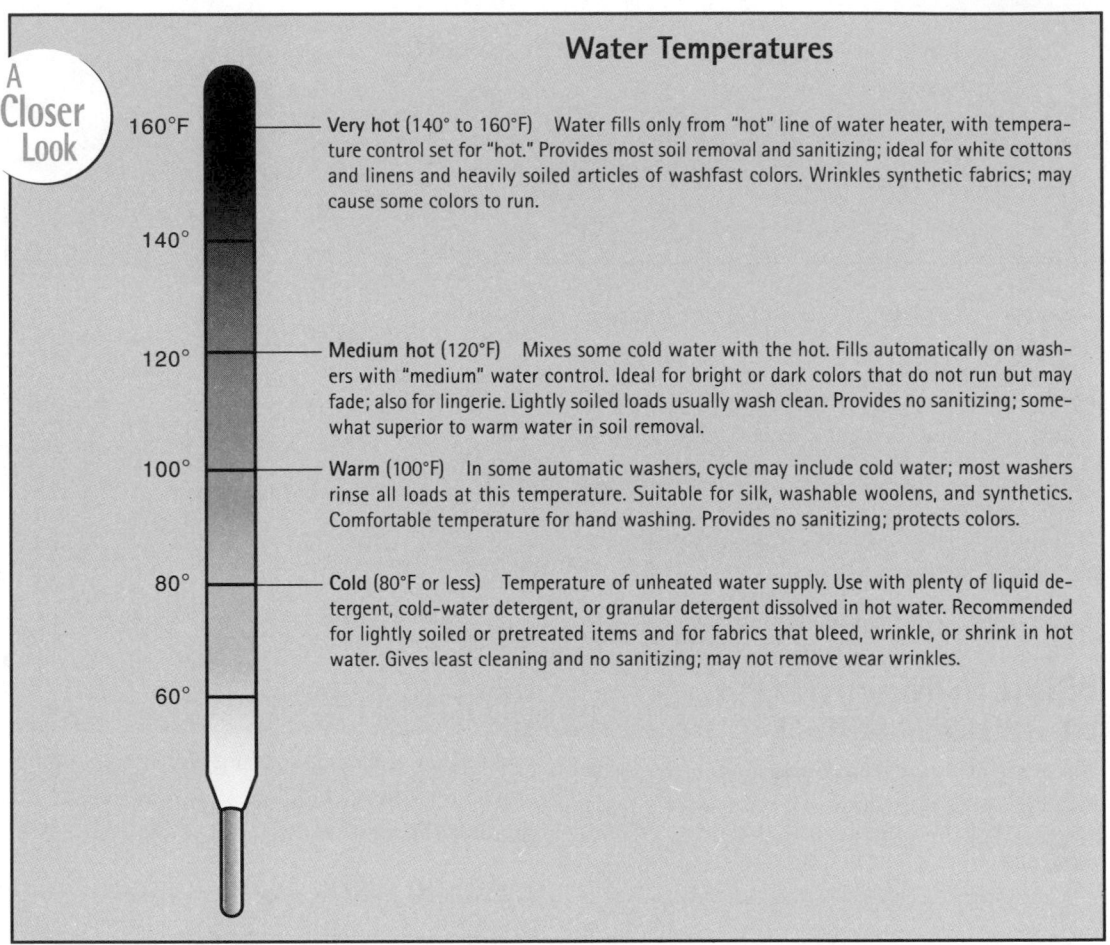

Water Temperatures

A Closer Look

160°F — **Very hot (140° to 160°F)** Water fills only from "hot" line of water heater, with temperature control set for "hot." Provides most soil removal and sanitizing; ideal for white cottons and linens and heavily soiled articles of washfast colors. Wrinkles synthetic fabrics; may cause some colors to run.

140°

120° — **Medium hot (120°F)** Mixes some cold water with the hot. Fills automatically on washers with "medium" water control. Ideal for bright or dark colors that do not run but may fade; also for lingerie. Lightly soiled loads usually wash clean. Provides no sanitizing; somewhat superior to warm water in soil removal.

100° — **Warm (100°F)** In some automatic washers, cycle may include cold water; most washers rinse all loads at this temperature. Suitable for silk, washable woolens, and synthetics. Comfortable temperature for hand washing. Provides no sanitizing; protects colors.

80° — **Cold (80°F or less)** Temperature of unheated water supply. Use with plenty of liquid detergent, cold-water detergent, or granular detergent dissolved in hot water. Recommended for lightly soiled or pretreated items and for fabrics that bleed, wrinkle, or shrink in hot water. Gives least cleaning and no sanitizing; may not remove wear wrinkles.

60°

Household Tips

or cool water with an all-purpose detergent and a shortened washing cycle. Use hot water for badly soiled articles.

Woolens and Delicates   Hand wash in cold water with Woolite® or a similar detergent and rinse thoroughly. Roll woolens tightly in a towel to remove excess water (do not wring) and dry flat on a drying rack. Allow delicates to drip-dry. Follow manufacturer's instructions when "dry clean only" appears on the care label.

TECHNIQUES FOR WASHING FABRICS

Soaking   To help loosen stains and dirt, soak heavily soiled articles, dusty curtains and draperies, and certain stained fabrics before washing. Agitate the items for a few minutes in the washer with warm

water and detergent, using about half the detergent needed for washing. Extract the water before washing as usual. If you have to soak only a few items, use a small container such as a bucket. Submerge the fabric in a warm detergent solution for 15 minutes or until stains diminish. Agitate with your hands and extract excess water before washing as usual.

Loading   A washer load made up of two large sheets or tablecloths with a variety of smaller articles washes more effectively than one made up of all large articles. Bulky pieces such as blankets, bedspreads, and throw rugs should be washed individually.

Rinsing   To maximize effective rinsing, do not overload your washer or add more detergent than recommended by the manufacturer. If the machine does not extract water efficiently, have its spinning mechanism checked.

To reach out-of-the-way places with your vacuum cleaner, use an empty wrapping paper tube as an extension. Flatten the end of the tube to reach into tight crevices.

Using Fabric Softener Fabric softeners make textiles softer and fluffier while minimizing wrinkles and deep creases. Softeners also reduce the static electricity that builds up on some fabrics when they rub against each other. Add fabric softener to the final rinse water in proportion to the weight of the clothes rather than the volume of water. Some softeners come in sheets that you can add to the dryer. To keep fabrics soft, use a softener each time you wash, as washing removes any softener added to previous loads.

STAIN REMOVAL

Many common stains fall into one of three categories: greasy, nongreasy, and combination. These stains can be removed by following the appropriate method for each given below. When necessary, separate directions are given for washable and nonwashable articles. Directions for nonwashables are for articles made of fabrics that are not damaged by the application of small amounts of water.

GREASY STAINS

Washable Articles Regular washing, either by hand or by machine, removes some greasy stains. Some stains can be removed by rubbing soap or detergent into the stain and then rinsing with warm water. On some wash-and-wear or permanent-press fabrics, it may be necessary to rub soap or detergent thoroughly into the stain and allow it to stand for several hours, or overnight, before rinsing. Often, however, a grease solvent is necessary; this is effective even after an article has been washed. Sponge the

stain thoroughly with the grease solvent and dry. Repeat if necessary. It often takes extra time to remove greasy stains from a fabric with a special finish.

A yellow stain may remain after a solvent treatment if the stain has been set by age or heat. To remove a yellow stain, use a chlorine or peroxygen bleach. If it is safe for the fabric, a strong sodium perborate treatment is usually the most effective.

Nonwashable Articles Sponge stains well with grease solvent and dry. Repeat if necessary. It may take extra time to remove greasy stains from fabrics with a special finish.

A yellow stain may remain after a solvent treatment if the stain has been set by age or heat. To remove a yellow stain, use a chlorine or peroxygen bleach. If safe for the fabric, a strong sodium perborate treatment is usually the most effective.

NONGREASY STAINS

Many fresh stains can be removed by simple treatments. Stains set by heat or age may be difficult or impossible to remove.

Washable Articles Sometimes, regular laundry methods will remove nongreasy stains; in other cases, laundering will actually set the stains. Sponge the stain with cool water or soak it in cool water for 30 minutes or longer; some stains require an overnight soak. If the stain persists after sponging or soaking, work a soap or detergent into it and then rinse. If the stain remains after detergent treatment, use a chlorine or peroxygen bleach.

Nonwashable Articles Sponge the stain with cool water. If it remains, rub soap or detergent on the stain and work it into the fabric. Rinse. A final sponging with rubbing alcohol helps to remove the soap or detergent and to dry the fabric more quickly. Test alcohol on the fabric first to be sure it does not affect the dye. Dilute the alcohol with 2 parts of water before using it on acetate. If the stain remains after rinsing, use a chlorine or peroxygen bleach.

COMBINATION STAINS

Combination stains are caused by materials that contain both greasy and nongreasy substances.

Washable Articles   Sponge the stain with cool water or soak in cool water for 30 minutes or longer. If the stain persists, work soap or detergent into it and then rinse thoroughly. Allow the article to dry. If a greasy stain remains, sponge with a grease solvent. Allow the article to dry. Repeat if necessary. If a colored stain remains after the fabric dries, use a chlorine or peroxygen bleach.

Nonwashable Articles   Sponge the stain with cool water. If it remains, rub soap or detergent on the stain and work it into the fabric. Rinse the spot well with water. Allow the article to dry. If a greasy stain remains, sponge with a grease solvent. Allow to dry. Repeat if necessary. If a colored stain remains after the fabric dries, use a chlorine or peroxygen bleach.

SPECIFIC STAINS

Adhesive Tape   Scrape gummy matter from stains carefully with a dull table knife; avoid damaging fabric. Sponge with a grease solvent.

Early mattresses were filled with straw and held up with a rope stretched across the bed frame. If the rope was tight, sleep was comfortable. Hence the phrase, "sleep tight."

Alcoholic Beverages   Follow directions for nongreasy stains. An alternative method, if alcohol does not affect the color of the fabric, is to sponge the stain with rubbing alcohol. Dilute alcohol with 2 parts of water before using on acetate. If a stain remains, use a chlorine or peroxygen bleach.

The alcohol in alcoholic beverages will cause bleeding of some dyes, which results in loss of color or formation of a dye ring around the edge of the stain. When either change occurs, the original appearance of the fabric cannot be restored.

Antiperspirants and Deodorants   Wash or sponge the stain thoroughly with soap or detergent and warm water. Rinse. If the stain is not removed, use a chlorine or peroxygen bleach. Antiperspirants that contain such substances as aluminum chloride are acid; they may cause fabric damage and change the color of some dyes. Fabric color may be restored by sponging with ammonia. Dilute ammonia with an equal volume of water for use on wool or silk. Rinse.

Blood   Follow directions for nongreasy stains, with one variation. If the stain is not removed by soap or detergent, put a few drops of ammonia on it and repeat the treatment with detergent. Rinse. Follow with a bleach treatment if necessary. Bloodstains that have been set by heat will be difficult to remove.

Candy and Syrup   For chocolate candy and syrup, follow directions for combination stains. For other candy and syrup, follow directions for nongreasy stains.

Carbon Paper   Work soap or detergent into the stain; rinse well. If the stain is not removed, put a few drops of ammonia on it and repeat the treatment; rinse well. Repeat again if necessary.

Chewing Gum   Scrape gum off without damaging fabric. The gum can be scraped off more easily if it is first hardened by rubbing it with ice. If a stain remains, sponge thoroughly with a grease solvent.

Chlorine Bleach   Use one of the following treatments to remove yellow chlorine bleach stains from fabrics with resin finishes, or to prevent such stains from appearing. Always treat the fabric before ironing it. On some fabrics, the yellow stains form before ironing; on others, after ironing. In either case, ironing before the chlorine is removed weakens the fibers.

Yellow stains caused by the use of chlorine bleach on wool and silk cannot be removed. White or faded spots caused by use of chlorine bleach on colored fabrics cannot be restored to the original color.

Treatment for any fabric: Rinse fabric thoroughly with water. Then soak for 30 minutes or longer in a solution containing 1 teaspoon of sodium thiosulfate to each quart of warm water. Rinse thoroughly. To strengthen the treatment, make the sodium thiosulfate solution as hot as is safe for the fabric.

Treatment for white or colorfast fabrics: Rinse the fabric thoroughly with water. Then use a color remover, following the directions given on the package for removing stains.

Coffee and Tea   *With cream:* Follow directions for combination stains.

Without cream: Follow directions for nongreasy stains.

Alternatively, for both types of stains, and if safe for the fabric, pour boiling water through the spot from a height of 1 to 3 feet.

Correction Fluid   Sponge the stain with acetone or amyl acetate. Use amyl acetate on acetate, Arnel®, Dynel®, and Verel®; use acetone on other fabrics.

Cosmetics and Crayon   *Washable articles:* Apply undiluted liquid detergent to the stain, or dampen the stain and rub in soap or detergent until thick suds are formed. Work in until the outline of the stain is gone; then rinse well. Repeat if necessary. It may help to dry the fabric between treatments.

Nonwashable articles: Sponge with a grease solvent until no more color is removed. If the stain is not removed, use the method given for washable articles.

Dyes   Follow directions for nongreasy stains; if bleach is needed, use chlorine bleach or color remover. A long soak in sudsy water often is effective on fresh dye stains.

Fish Slime, Mucus, Vomit   Follow directions for nongreasy stains or treat the stain with a lukewarm solution of salt and water—¼ cup salt to each quart of water. Sponge the stain with the solution or soak the stain in it. Rinse well.

Fruit, Fruit Juices   Follow directions for nongreasy stains or, if it is safe for the fabric, pour boiling water through the spot from a height of 1 to 3 feet. When any fruit juice is spilled on a fabric, it is a good idea to sponge the spot immediately with cool water. Some fruit juices, citrus among them, are invisible on the fabric after they dry but turn yellow on aging or heating. This yellow stain may be difficult to remove.

Furniture Polish   Follow directions for greasy stains or, if the polish contains wood stain, follow directions given for paint.

Glue and Mucilage   *Airplane glue, household cement:* Follow directions for correction fluid.

Casein glue: Follow directions for nongreasy stains.

Plastic glue: Wash the stain with soap or detergent and water before the glue hardens; some types of glues cannot be removed after they have hardened.

To remove some dried plastic glue stains, immerse the stain in a hot 10-percent acetic acid solution or hot vinegar. Keep acid or vinegar at or near the boiling point until the stain is removed. This may take 15 minutes or longer. Rinse with water.

Other types of glues and mucilage: Follow directions for nongreasy stains, but soak the stain in hot water instead of cool.

Grass, Flowers, Foliage   *Washable articles:* Work soap or detergent into the stain; then rinse. If it is safe for the dye, sponge the stain with alcohol. Dilute the alcohol with 2 parts of water for use on acetate. If the stain remains, use a chlorine or peroxygen bleach.

Nonwashable articles: Use the methods for washable articles, but try alcohol first if it is safe for the dye.

Ink, Ballpoint   Sponge the stain repeatedly with acetone or amyl acetate, or spray it with hair spray. This will remove fresh stains. Old stains may also require bleaching. Washing removes some types of ballpoint ink stains but sets other types. To see whether the stain will wash out, mark a scrap of similar material with the ink and wash it.

Ink, Black (India ink)   Treat the stain as soon as possible. These stains are very hard to remove if dry.

Washable articles: Force water through the stain until all loose pigment is removed; otherwise, the stain will spread when treated. Wash with soap or detergent, several times if necessary. Then soak the stain in warm suds containing 1 to 4 tablespoons of ammonia to a quart of water. Dried stains may need to be soaked overnight. An alternative method is to force water through the stain until all loose pigment is removed, wet the spot with ammonia, and then work soap or detergent into it. Rinse. Repeat if necessary.

The first vacuum cleaner was so large it had to be drawn by horses and required a team of men to use it.

Nonwashable articles: Force water through the stain until all loose pigment is removed; otherwise, the stain will spread when you treat it. Sponge stain with a solution of water and ammonia (1 tablespoon of ammonia per 1 cup of water). Rinse with water. If stain remains, moisten it with ammonia and then work soap or detergent into it. Rinse. Repeat if necessary. If ammonia changes the color of the fabric, sponge first with water and then moisten with vinegar. Rinse well.

Ink, Drawing (colors other than black)   Follow directions for nongreasy stains. If bleach is needed, use a color remover if it is safe for the dye. If a color remover is not safe, try other bleaches.

Ink, Writing   *Washable articles.* Follow directions for nongreasy stains. Because writing inks vary greatly in composition, it may be necessary to try more than one kind of bleach. Try a chlorine bleach on all fabrics for which it is safe. For other fabrics, try peroxygen bleach. A few types of inks require treatment with color removers. A strong bleach treatment may be needed. A strong bleach, however, may leave a faded spot on some colored fabrics. If a yellow stain remains after bleaching, treat it as a rust stain.

Nonwashable articles: If possible, use a blotter (for small stains) or absorbent powder to remove excess ink before it soaks into the fabric. Then follow directions for washable articles.

Iodine   *Washable articles:* Three methods for removing iodine stains are given below. If the method you try first does not remove the stain, try another.

Water: Soak in cool water until the stain is removed; some stains require soaking overnight. If the stain remains, rub it with soap or detergent and wash it in warm suds. If the stain is not removed, soak the fabric in a solution containing 1 tablespoon of sodium thiosulfate to each pint of warm water, or sprinkle the crystals on the dampened stain. Rinse well as soon as the stain is removed.

Steam: Moisten the stain with water; then hold it in the steam from a boiling teakettle.

Rubbing alcohol: If alcohol is safe for the dye, cover the stain with a pad of cotton soaked in it. If necessary, keep the pad wet for several hours. Dilute with 2 parts water for use on acetate.

Nonwashable articles: Try the steam or alcohol methods given above.

Mildew   *Washable articles:* Treat mildew spots while they are fresh, before the mold growth has a chance to weaken the fabric. Wash the mildewed article thoroughly and dry it in the sun. If the stain remains, treat it with a chlorine or peroxygen bleach.

Nonwashable articles: Send the article to a dry cleaner promptly.

Mud   Let the stain dry; then brush well. If the stain remains, follow directions for nongreasy stains. Stains from iron-rich clays not removed by this method should be treated as rust stains.

Mustard   *Washable articles:* Rub soap or detergent into the dampened stain; rinse. If the stain is not removed, soak the article in a hot detergent solution for several hours, or overnight if necessary. If the stain remains, use a bleach.

Nonwashable articles: If alcohol is safe for the dye, sponge the stain with it. Dilute the alcohol with 2 parts of water for use on acetate. If alcohol cannot be used, or if it does not remove the stain completely, follow the treatment for washable articles but omit the soaking.

Nail Polish   Follow directions for correction fluid. Nail polish removers also can be used to remove stains. Before using nail polish remover on acetate, Arnel®, Dynel®, or Verel®, test it on a scrap of material to make sure it will not damage the fabric.

Computer printer toner powder should be wiped off fabric with a clean, dry cloth, then rinsed out with cold water.

Paint, Varnish   Treat stains promptly, as they are always harder—and sometimes impossible—to remove after they have dried on fabric. Because there are so many different kinds of paints and varnishes, no one method will remove all stains. Read the label on the container; if a certain solvent is recommended as a thinner, it may be more effective in removing stains than the other solvents recommended.

Washable articles: To remove fresh stains, rub soap or detergent into the stain and wash. If the stain has dried or is only partially removed by washing, sponge it with turpentine until no more paint or varnish is removed (for aluminum paint stains, dry cleaning may be more effective than turpentine). While the stain is still wet with the solvent, work soap or detergent into it, put the article in hot water, and soak it overnight. Thorough washing will remove most types of paint stains. If the stain remains, repeat the treatment.

Nonwashable articles: Sponge fresh stains with turpentine until no more paint is removed (for aluminum paint stains, dry cleaning may be more effective than turpentine). If the stain remains, put a drop of liquid detergent on it and work it into the fabric with the edge of the bowl or a spoon. Alternatively, sponge the stain with turpentine and treat with detergent as many times as necessary. If alcohol is safe for the dye, sponge the stain with it to remove turpentine and detergent. Dilute the alcohol with 2 parts of water for use on acetate. If alcohol is not safe for the dye, sponge the stain first with warm soap or detergent solution, then with water.

Pencil   A soft eraser will remove pencil marks from some fabrics. If the marks cannot be erased, follow directions for carbon paper.

Perfume   Follow directions for alcoholic beverages.

Perspiration   Wash or sponge the stain thoroughly with soap or detergent and warm water. Work carefully because some fabrics are weakened by perspiration; silk is the fiber most easily damaged. If perspiration has changed the color of the fabric, try to restore it by treating it with ammonia or vinegar. Apply ammonia to fresh stains and apply vinegar to old stains; rinse with water.

If an oily stain remains, follow directions for greasy stains. Remove any yellow discoloration with a chlorine or peroxygen bleach. If it is safe for the fabric, the strong sodium perborate treatment recommended for greasy-stain removal is often the most effective for these stains.

Rust   *Oxalic-acid method:* PRECAUTION: OXALIC ACID IS POISONOUS IF SWALLOWED. Moisten the stain with oxalic-acid solution (1 tablespoon of oxalic-acid crystals in 1 cup warm water). If the stain is not removed by a single treatment, heat the solution and repeat. If the stain is stubborn, place oxalic-acid crystals directly on it. Moisten the stain with water as hot as is safe for the fabric; allow it to stand a few minutes, or dip it in hot water. Repeat if necessary. Do not use this method on nylon. Rinse the article thoroughly. If it is allowed to dry in the fabric, oxalic acid will cause damage.

Cream-of-tartar method: If the treatment is safe for the fabric, boil the stained article in a solution containing 4 teaspoons of cream of tartar to each pint of water. Boil until the stain is removed. Rinse thoroughly.

Lemon-juice method: Spread the stained portion over a pan of boiling water and squeeze lemon juice on it; or sprinkle salt on the stain, squeeze lemon juice on it, and spread the fabric in the sun to dry. Rinse thoroughly. Repeat if necessary.

Color removers can be used to remove rust stains from white fabrics.

Scorch Stains   If the article is washable, follow the directions for nongreasy stains. To remove light scorch stains from an article that is nonwashable, apply hydrogen peroxide. The strong treatment may be needed to remove the stains. Repeat if necessary. Severe scorch stains cannot be removed, however, because the fabric already has been damaged.

Shellac   Using alcohol, sponge or soak the stain. Dilute the alcohol with 2 parts water for use on acetate. If alcohol bleeds the dye, try turpentine.

Shoe Polish   Because there are many different kinds of shoe polish, no one method will remove all stains. It may be necessary to try more than one of the methods given below.

1. Follow directions for cosmetics.
2. Sponge the stain with alcohol if it is safe for the dye in the fabric. Dilute the alcohol with 2 parts water for use on acetate.
3. Sponge the stain with grease solvent or turpentine. If turpentine is used, remove it by sponging with a warm soap or detergent solution or with alcohol.

If the stain is not removed by any of these methods, use a chlorine or peroxygen bleach. If safe for the fabric, the strong sodium perborate treatment

recommended for greasy-stain removal is often the most effective.

Soft Drinks   Follow directions for nongreasy stains. When any soft drink is spilled on a fabric, sponge the spot immediately with cool water. Some soft drinks are invisible after they dry but turn yellow on aging or heating. The yellow stain may be difficult to remove.

Natural gas is naturally odorless. The odor is added to make its fumes detectable.

Soot, Smoke   Follow directions for cosmetics.

Tar   Follow directions for greasy stains. If the stain is not removed by this method, sponge it with turpentine.

Urine   To remove stains caused by normal urine, follow directions for nongreasy stains. If the color of the fabric has been changed, sponge the stain with ammonia. If this treatment does not restore the color, sponging with acetic acid or vinegar may help. If the stain is not removed by one or both of these methods, see directions for medicines and yellowing.

Yellowing, Brown Stains   To remove storage stains—or unknown yellow or yellow-brown stains—from fabrics, use as many of the following treatments as necessary, if safe for the fabric, in the order given.

1. Wash.
2. Use a mild treatment of a chlorine or peroxygen bleach.
3. Use the oxalic-acid method for treating rust stains.
4. Use a strong treatment of a chlorine or per-oxygen bleach.

CLOTHING SIZE CONVERSION TABLES

WOMEN

Blouses and sweaters

U.S.	32	34	36	38	40	42	44
British	34	36	38	40	42	44	46
European	38	40	42	44	46	48	50

Coats and dresses

U.S.	4	6	8	10	12	14	16	18
British	6	8	10	12	14	16	18	20
European	34	36	38	40	42	44	46	48

Shoes

U.S.	5–5½	6–6½	7–7½	8–8½	9
British	3½–4	4½–5	5½–6	6½–7	7½
European	37	38	39	40	41

Stockings

U.S. and British	8	8½	9	9½	10	10½
European	0	1	2	3	4	5

MEN

Hats

U.S.	6⅝	6¾	6⅞	7	7⅛	7¼	7⅜	7½
British	6½	6⅝	6¾	6⅞	7	7⅛	7¼	7⅜
European/Japanese	53	54	55	56	57	58	59	60

Shirts

U.S. and British	14	14½	15	15½	16	16½	17
European/Japanese	36	37	38	39	41	42	43

Shoes

U.S.	7	7½	8	8½	9	9½	10	10½	11
British	5½	6	6½	7	7½	8	8½	9	9½
European	39	40	41	42	43	43	44	44	45

Socks

U.S. and British	9½	10	10½	11	11½	12	12½
European	39	40	41	42	43	44	45

Suits and coats

U.S. and British	34	36	38	40	42	44	46
European	44	46	48	50	52	54	56

STANDARD SIZES OF MATERIALS AND TOOLS

Most materials and tools used in household repairs and improvements are sold in standardized sizes. The charts below list sizes commonly encountered in hardware and home supply stores.

INTERIOR MATERIALS

WALLS

Type	Thicknesses	Lengths	Widths
Decorative hardboard (embossed surface)	1/4″	4′ to 16′	4′
Fiberboard (burlap or cork-surfaced)	15/32″	8′, 10′, 12′, 14′	4′
Gypsum board (plain or vinyl-surfaced)	1/4″, 3/8″, 1/2″	6′ to 16′	2′, 4′
Hardboard (tempered or untempered)	3/8″, 3/16″, 1/4″, 5/16″	6′ to 16′	4′
Hardwood plywood (prefinished)	5/32″, 3/16″, 1/4″, 7/16″	7′, 8′	4′
Hardwood plywood (veneered paneling)	1/8″ to 3/4″	7′, 8′, 9′, 10′	4′
Particle-core plywood	3/4″, 7/16″	7′, 8′, 9′, 10′	4′
Plastic-surfaced hardboard	1/8″, 3/16″, 1/4″	6′, 7′, 8′, 10′	16″, 4′
Prefinished hardboard	1/8″, 3/16″, 1/4″	6′ to 16′	16″, 4′
Textured plywood (rough-sawn, brushed, grooved)	3/8″, 5/8″	8′, 9′, 10′	4
Unfinished plywood	3/4″ to 1 7/8″	8′, 9′, 10′	4′
Vinyl-surfaced plywood	3/16″, 1/4″, 5/16″	7′, 8′	4′
Wood-grained hardboard	3/16″, 1/4″	7′, 8′, 9′, 10′	4′

CEILINGS

Type	Thicknesses	Lengths	Widths
Acoustical panels	1/2″, 3/4″, 1″	2′, 8′, 10′, 12′, 14′	2′, 4′
Acoustical tiles	1/2″	12″	12″
Decorative acoustical tile (embossed, textured, etc.)	1/2″	12″, 2′, 4′	12″, 2′
Fiberglass acoustical panels	2″	8′, 10 1/2′, 12 1/2′, 14′, 16′	4′
Plastic-surfaced hardboard blocks	1/4″	16″	16″
Wood-grained planks	1/2″	4′	5 3/16″, 6 3/8″, 8 3/16″

FLOORS

Type	Thicknesses	Lengths	Widths
Asphalt (or asphalt-asbestos) tile	1/8″, 3/16″	9″	9″
Ceramic-tile sheets	1/8″, 1/4″	12″	12″
Indoor-outdoor carpet	N/A	As desired	3′, 6′, 9′, 12′, 15′
Indoor-outdoor carpet tile	N/A	9″, 12″	9″, 12″
Sheet vinyl	N/A	As desired	6′, 9′, 12′
Vinyl and vinyl-asbestos tile	1/2″ to 1/8″	9″, 12″, 18″, 36″	4″, 9″, 12″, 18″, 36″
Wood parquet blocks	5/16″, 7/16″	9″, 10″	9″, 10″
Wood strips	3/8″	2″	1′ to 8′

BATHROOM FIXTURES

Types	Lengths	Depths	Heights
Bathtubs	4'6", 5', 5'6"	2', 2'6", 2'7", 2'8"	1'2", 1'3", 1'4"
Compact corner tubs	3'2", 3'6", 4'	3'3", 3'10", 4'1½"	12"
One-piece fiberglass recessed shower units	3', 4', 5'	3'	6'1½"
One-piece fiberglass tub/shower units	5'	2'8⅞"	6'1½"
Shower stalls	2'6" to 3'6"	2'6" to 3'6"	6'3" to 6'5"
Sinks	19" to 30"	16" to 20"	2'7" (counter height)
Toilets (tank size)	18" to 23½"	25" to 30"	18½" to 40"

KITCHEN EQUIPMENT

Type	Widths	Depths	Heights
Built-in ovens (set in cabinet)	23¾" to 36"	23½"	29¾"
Built-in ranges (set in countertop)	12" to 42"	19" to 22"	34" to 36"
Dishwashers	24"	24¼" to 30"	34" to 36"
Double sinks (set in counters)	32"	20"	2'7"
Drop-in ranges and ovens (recessed into base cabinets)	30"	24" to 27¼"	34" to 36"
Freestanding ranges and ovens	20" to 42"	24¾" to 26⅝"	35" to 36"
Freezers (chest)	46½" to 72"	29", 32"	36", 37"
Freezers (upright)	24" to 32"	26" to 32"	57" to 71"
Ranges and eye-level ovens	30"	27⅛" to 28¾"	59⅛", 64⅛"
Refrigerators	28" to 35"	25" to 30"	61" to 36"
Single sinks (set in counters)	24", 30"	21"	2'7"
Slide-in ranges and ovens (set between base cabinets)	20" to 36"	24" to 26⅞"	34" to 36"
Triple sinks (set in counters)	42", 45"	21", 22"	2'7"

EXTERIOR MATERIALS

SIDING

Type	Thicknesses	Lengths	Widths
Aluminum (horizontal)	N/A	9'4½", 10', 12'6", 16'	8", 10"
Hardboard lap (horizontal)	⅜", ⁷⁄₁₆"	12', 16'	6", 8", 9", 10", 12"
Hardboard panels (vertical)	¼", ⁵⁄₁₆", ⅜", ⁷⁄₁₆"	6', 7', 8', 9', 10', 16'	4'
Plywood panels	⅜", ½", ⅝"	8', 9', 10', 12'	4'
Prefinished steel (horizontal)	N/A	12'6"	8", 9½"
Vinyl lap (horizontal)	N/A	12½"	8", 12"
Vinyl V-grooved (vertical)	N/A	10'	10"
Wood lap (horizontal)	½", ⅝", ¾"	3' to 20'	6", 8", 10", 12"

continues

Exterior Materials, Continued

DOORS AND WINDOWS

Type	Thicknesses	Heights	Widths
Bifold, 2-door units	1⅛″, 1⅜″	6′8″	2′, 2′8″, 3′
Bifold, 4-door units	1⅛″, 1⅜″	6′8″	3′, 4′, 5′, 6′
Flush (hollow, solid)	1⅜″, 1¾″, 2¼″	6′8″, 7′	6″
Louvered	1⅛″, 1⅜″	6′6″, 6′8″, 7′	1′3″ to 3′
Panel	1⅜″, 1¾″	6′8″, 7′	1′2″ to 3′4″
Sash (with one or more glass panels)	1⅜″, 1¾″	6′8″, 7′	2′ to 3′6″
Sliding glass, 2-panel units	N/A	6′8″	5′, 6′, 6′2¼″, 8′8¼″
Sliding glass, 3-panel units	N/A	6′8″	9′, 9′¾″, 12′, 12′2¾″
Steel entry (single, double, sidelight)	1¾″	6′8″	2′8″, 3′

DISPOSAL OF HAZARDOUS HOUSEHOLD CHEMICALS

Many of the ordinary household cleaners and other materials we use every day must be disposed of properly to avoid endangering ourselves, our pets, and our environment. Never throw containers of flammable, reactive, or corrosive liquids such as paint, solvents, or automotive fluid in the trash, where they might leak or evaporate dangerously. Read the label for disposal information and adhere to community regulations regarding the disposal of these substances. The following methods are recommended for the safe disposal of toxic household waste.

Method A   For small amounts, dilute with lots of water and pour down the drain. For large amounts, use method D.

Method B   In a well-ventilated place away from pets and people, allow to evaporate, or combine it with an absorbent material such as cat litter and

Material	Method A	Method B	Method C	Method D
Antifreeze	■			
Brake fluid			■	■
Car batteries			■	■
Contact cement		■		
Degreasers			■	
Diesel fuel			■	■
Furniture polish				■
Kerosene			■	
Motor oil			■	■
Paint—latex		■		
Paint—oil base				■
Paint stripper	■			
Paint thinner				■
Paintbrush cleaner—phosphate	■			
Paintbrush cleaner—solvent				■
Power-steering fluid			■	■
Rust remover	■			
Solvent-based glue, adhesive, sealant				■
Transmission fluid			■	■
Water-based glue, adhesive, sealant		■		
Wood finish				■
Wood preservative				■

Household Tips

Indoor Light Bulbs

A Closer Look

Lumens measure how much light a bulb puts out. Watts measure the amount of power a bulb uses. Both measurements appear on light bulb packaging. Use the chart below to find right bulb for the purpose.

Type	Watts	Lumens	Hours
Soft white incandescent	40	445	750–1,500
	100	1,710	
Halogen spot or floodlight	50	600	2,500–3,000
	90	1,300	
Halogen bulb	60	960	2,250–3,000
	100	1,850	
Compact fluorescent	11	600	8,000–10,000
	15	925	
	23	1,580	
Compact fluorescent reflector	15	725	10,000
	20	1,000	

allow to solidify. Wrap thoroughly in plastic and discard in trash.

Method C   Recycle at a local center set up for this purpose, or use method D.

Method D   Save for special collection by local authorities or call your local health department, cooperative extension service, or environmental protection agency for instructions.

RECYCLING

You can help protect the environment by taking three steps to limit the amount of garbage sent to landfills and incinerators:

1. Reduce the amount of disposable material you use in the form of shopping bags, paper towels, product packaging, and so on.
2. Reuse as many items as possible (such as coffee cans to hold nails, newspaper as packing material, old sheets as drop cloths).
3. Recycle as much of the rest as possible.

Many organic materials, such as food and yard waste, can go into a compost pile (see next section), and a growing number of other items are now recycled through community programs. Follow your city's recycling laws and make the most of voluntary

recycling centers that take up the slack. To make recycling easier, post a list of recyclables in your kitchen or garage and set up separate containers to sort them according to local regulations. Rinse out containers before discarding and, where applicable, return deposit cans and bottles. Most municipalities have facilities to recycle the following items.

Paper	Newspaper, magazines, catalogs, corrugated cardboard, smooth (gray) cardboard, egg and produce cartons, beverage cartons, paper bags, wrapping paper, office paper, junk mail, paperback books, telephone books
Plastic	Bottles and jugs
Glass	Bottles and jars
Metal	Cans, aluminum foil and trays, utensils, pots and pans, appliances, furniture, machine parts, tools, nuts and bolts

COMPOSTING

Composting is a great way to recycle certain biodegradable materials to the benefit of your yard and garden. In a compost heap, you may dispose of fruit and vegetable peels, stems, leaves and cores, pulp from your juicing machine, crushed egg-shells, coffee grounds, cut flowers, woodstove ashes, sawdust,

Household Tips

A Closer Look

Stop Blowing Fuses!

Electrical overloads—trying to draw too much electricity through a circuit—causes fuses to blow and circuit breakers to trip. To prevent this, be aware of how much electricity common appliances use and avoid having too many on at one time on one circuit. Two or more of the following appliances will overload a 15-amp circuit.

Appliance	Amps
Clothes washer	10
Hair dryer	10
Iron	9
Microwave	6–12
Portable heater	10
Refrigerator	6–15
Table saw	13–15
Toaster	7–10
Window air conditioner	8–16

chicken and rabbit droppings, grass clippings, hedge trimmings, small wood chips, leaves, pine needles, sod, and dirt. Finished compost can be worked into yard and garden soil to enrich it and make your plantings thrive. Here's how to make compost:

1. Collect equal parts wet or green material and dried or brown material, making sure both have been reduced to fairly small pieces.
2. Using alternating layers of green and brown, build a pile roughly 3′ × 3′ × 3′. This pile can be freestanding, or you can use one of the many compost containers on the market. Dampen the pile as you build, and sprinkle in some fresh soil or compost starter (available at garden stores) as a catalyst.
3. For the first month, turn the pile once a week to aerate and to blend decomposed material with fresh material. Use a pitchfork for this job and wet the compost if necessary.
4. After the first month, insert a compost thermometer into the pile to monitor its temperature. Decomposing compost will heat up to the 120° to 160°F range; turn the pile whenever it cools below this temperature. The compost is ready to use when it no longer heats up.

HOW TO BUILD A FIRE

Before starting a fire in your fireplace, make sure you have a screen to keep sparks and coals inside. For best results, use a rack to elevate the fire and allow air to flow underneath. Keep fireplace tools handy for tending the fire as it burns.

1. Remove most of the soot and ashes from previous fires, leaving larger coals and charred logs.
2. Crumple or loosely roll several sheets of newspaper and arrange on top of the coals.
3. Lay short, dry kindling over the newspaper in a crisscross or side-by-side pattern. If the logs or wood pieces you will use are damp or green, place fire-starters beneath the kindling.
4. Put a few small to medium logs atop the kindling. Larger pieces can be added after the fire has established itself.
5. Open the flue. Use long fireplace matches to light the fire in several places, from below.

BABY-SITTER CHECKLIST

Whenever you leave your children with a baby-sitter, it is important to provide the sitter with the basic information he or she will need to care for your children and to handle any emergencies. Show the sitter around your home, explaining door locks, alarm systems, and fire extinguishers; point out first-aid supplies and telephones; and indicate the location of your children's toys, clothing, and food. In addition, leave the following list of phone numbers and vital data by the telephone.

Your home address and phone number(s)
Children's names, ages, heights, and weights
Mother's name, location, and phone number(s)
Father's name, location, and phone number(s)
Fire department/paramedics phone number(s)
Police department phone number(s)
Poison-control center phone number(s)
Children's doctor's name, address, and phone number
Nearest hospital/emergency room, address, and phone number
Taxi or car service name and phone number(s)
Nearest reliable neighbor's name, address, and phone number

Household Tips

Reliable friends/relatives' names, addresses, and phone numbers
Children's school name(s) and phone number(s):
Children's health-insurance-plan number and insurer's phone number(s)
Children's health problems (allergies, asthma, etc.)
Mealtimes and bedtimes
Children's duties
Children's food and play preferences
Baby-sitter's duties

CAR-MAINTENANCE CHECKLIST

You can keep your car running longer and better by following a few simple maintenance routines. Your owner's manual indicates how often you should change fluids, tune the engine, rotate the tires, etc. Follow the manufacturer's recommendations, increasing the frequency of maintenance for cars that see heavy use or lots of stop-and-go driving. If you or your car's monitoring systems detect problems, maintenance should be performed as needed. Your maintenance schedule should include a number of basic procedures.

Fluids

Change motor oil and filter
Replace antifreeze/coolant
Replace automatic-transmission fluid and filter
Refill windshield-washer fluid and change blades

Engine

Change spark plugs
Check alternator and starter
Clean battery and terminals
Clean/replace air filter
Check timing
Check intake manifold
Check/replace PCV (positive crankcase ventilation)
Check/replace belts

Tires

Check air pressure
Check treads, replace tire if less than 1/16″
Rotate tires
Check brakes/pads
Check wheel alignment

ADDITIONAL SOURCES OF INFORMATION

ORGANIZATIONS AND SERVICES

Auto Safety Hot Line
U.S. Department of Transportation
400 7th St., SW, Room 5326
Washington, DC 20580
800-424-9393
http://www.nhtsa.dot.gov

This hot line provides information on air bags, seat belts, child seats, auto recalls, and other safety issues. Open 8 A.M. to 10 P.M. EST.

Genova Plumbers Hot Line
7034 E. Court St.
Davison, MI 48423
800-521-7488

The staff can suggest solutions to plumbing problems involving gutters and plastic fittings as well as more technical problems. The hotline operates weekdays between 8 A.M. and 5 P.M., EST.

Major Appliance Consumer Action Panel (MACAP)
20 N. Wacker Dr.
Chicago, IL 60606
312-984-5858

MACAP responds to inquiries about problems with major appliances. Call for further instructions. It is open weekdays from 8:30 A.M. to 5 P.M., CST.

Shopsmith, Inc.
6530 Poe Ave.
Dayton, OH 45414
800-543-7586

Shopsmith answers questions related to woodworking. If they cannot answer your question, they will research the information and call back. Call weekdays between 8 A.M. and 9 P.M. and Saturdays between 9 A.M. and 1 P.M., EST.

Soap and Detergent Association
1500 K Street, NW, Ste. 300
Washington, DC 20005
202-347-2900
E-mail: info@sdahq.org

This association answers questions on all aspects of soaps and detergents. They also have free publications. Call Monday through Friday from 9 A.M. to 4:45 P.M., EST.

Household Tips

MAGAZINES

COOKING AND DINING

Bon Appetit
6300 Wilshire Blvd.
Los Angeles, CA 90048
http://www.bonappetit.com

Food and Wine
1120 Avenue of the Americas
New York, NY 10036
http://www.foodandwine.com

Gourmet
4 Times Square
New York, NY 10036
http://eat.epicurious.com/gourmet

HOME AND GARDENING

Architectural Digest
6300 Wilshire Blvd.
Los Angeles, CA 90048
http://www.archdigest.com

Better Homes and Gardens
1716 Locust St.
Des Moines, IA 50309
http://www.bhglive.com

Country Living
P.O. Box 7138
Red Oak, IA 51591
http://www.countryliving.com

The Family Handyman
2915 Commerce Drive
Eagen, MN 55121
http://www.familyhandyman.com

Horticulture
98 N. Washington St.
Boston, MA 02114

House Beautiful
1700 Broadway, 36th floor
New York, NY 10019
http://homearts.com

Metropolitan Home
1633 Broadway
New York, NY 10019
http://www.methome.com

Southern Living
2100 Lakeshore Dr.
Birmingham, AL 35209
http://www.southernliving.com

BOOKS

Bernstein, Peter, and Christopher Ma. *The Practical Guide to Practically Everything*. Random House, 1998.

Brody, Jane. *Jane Brody's Good Food Book*. Bantam, 1987.

Bykofsky, Sheree, and Paul Fargis, eds. *The Big Book of Life's Instructions*. Galahad Books, 1999.

Cunningham, Marion, et al. *Fannie Farmer Cookbook*. Knopf, 1996.

Dadd, Debra Lynn. *Home Safe Home*. Tarcher/Putnam, 1997.

Family Circle editors. *The Family Circle Good Cook's Book*. Simon & Schuster, 1993.

Green, Mark. *The Consumer Bible*. Workman, 1998.

Heloise. *All-New Hints from Heloise*. Perigee, 1989.

Hufnagel, James A., et al. *The Stanley Complete Step-by-Step Book of Home Repair and Improvement*. Simon & Schuster, 2000.

Johnson, Hugh. *Hugh Johnson's Pocket Encyclopedia of Wine 2001*. Fireside/Simon & Schuster, 2000.

Kaplan, Leon. *Keep This Book in Your Glove Compartment*. Berkley Books, 1997.

Mendelson, Cheryl. *Home Comforts: The Art and Science of Keeping House*. Scribner, 1999.

Mr. Boston Official Bartender's and Party Guide. Warner, 2000.

Reader's Digest Association. *Ask the Family Handyman*. Reader's Digest Association, 1999.

Rombauer, Irma S., et al. *The Joy of Cooking*. Rev. ed. Simon & Schuster, 1997.

Rosso, Julee, and Sheila Lukins. *The New Basics Cookbook*. Workman, 1989.

Satin, Morton. *Food Alert! The Ultimate Sourcebook for Food Safety*. Facts on File, 1999.

Household Tips

PERSONAL FINANCES

Personal finances are often a mystifying subject. The objective of making more from your income than just enough to live on is shared by many. But faced with a huge assortment of possible investments, insurance plans, real-estate ventures, and retirement plans, how can you, as an individual, decide on the best course of action?

This chapter provides a starting point. It contains information on making a budget, the types of insurance available, loans, real estate, and mortgages. Social Security and retirement planning are covered, and glossaries of financial and real-estate terms are included. You should consult some of the many reputable sources on the World Wide Web, books and periodicals devoted to financial planning, or professional financial planners, however, before you create a master plan for your personal finances.

> *The most fortunate 1% of households have accumulated more wealth than the bottom 95%.*

TABLES OF COMMON INTEREST

SIMPLE INTEREST

Simple interest is computed on the amount of the principal (total amount borrowed) of a loan. To calculate simple interest: Dollar amount × Interest rate × Length of time (in years) = Amount of Interest.

SIMPLE INTEREST ON A $100 LOAN

Time	Annual Rate							
	5%	6%	7%	8%	9%	10%	15%	20%
1 month	.4167	.5000	.5833	.6667	.7500	.8333	1.2500	1.6667
6 months	2.5000	3.0000	3.5000	4.0000	4.5000	5.0000	7.5000	10.0000
12 months	5.0000	6.0000	7.0000	8.0000	9.0000	10.0000	15.0000	20.0000
24 months	10.0000	12.0000	14.0000	16.0000	18.0000	20.0000	30.0000	40.0000
36 months	15.0000	18.0000	21.0000	24.0000	27.0000	30.0000	45.0000	60.0000

COMPOUND INTEREST

Compound interest means earning interest on the interest in addition to interest on the principal. To calculate compound interest: (Original dollar amount + Earned interest) × Interest rate × Length of time = Amount of Compound Interest. To determine the approximate number of years it will take for the principal to double, divide the interest rate percent into 72.

COMPOUND INTEREST ON $100 PRINCIPAL, COMPOUNDED ANNUALLY

Time	Annual Rate					
	5%	6%	7%	8%	9%	10%
6 months	2.50	3.00	3.50	4.00	4.50	5.00
1 year	5.00	6.00	7.00	8.00	9.00	10.00
2 years	10.25	12.36	14.49	16.64	18.81	21.00
3 years	15.76	19.10	22.50	25.97	29.50	33.10
4 years	21.55	26.25	31.08	36.05	41.16	46.41
5 years	27.63	33.82	40.26	46.93	53.86	61.05

MORTGAGE AMORTIZATION FACTORS

Monthly mortgage payments include a percentage of the principal plus interest on the principal. The size of the monthly payment reflects the amount of the loan, the term of the loan, and the interest rate that applies—whether fixed or variable.

MONTHLY PRINCIPAL + INTEREST PAYMENT ON A $100,000 LOAN

Term	Interest rate							
	4%	5%	6%	7%	8%	9%	10%	15%
5 years	1841.65	1887.12	1933.28	1980.12	2027.64	2075.84	2124.71	2379.00
10 years	1012.45	1060.66	1110.21	1161.08	1213.28	1266.76	1321.51	1613.35
15 years	739.69	790.79	843.86	898.83	955.65	1014.27	1074.61	1399.59
20 years	605.98	659.96	716.43	775.30	836.44	899.72	965.03	1316.79
25 years	527.84	584.59	644.30	706.80	771.82	839.20	908.71	1280.84
30 years	477.42	536.82	599.55	665.30	733.76	804.62	877.58	1264.45
35 years	442.77	504.69	570.19	638.86	710.26	783.99	859.67	1256.81
40 years	417.94	482.20	550.21	621.43	695.31	771.36	849.16	1253.22

MAKING A BUDGET

The first step in personal financial planning is to get a clear picture of where you currently stand. An inventory of expected income and expenses projected on both a monthly and an annual basis will allow individuals and families to create a budget. A budget helps to keep expenses within the boundaries of income while also showing what amount, if any, is available for investments.

Following are outlines of income and expense categories that you should include in any personal budget. Note that expenses include fixed obligations and flexible or discretionary outlays, which you can change as circumstances and objectives change.

Income

Salaries (total in household) _____

Bonuses, tips _____

Investments (interest, dividends, capital gains, real-estate income) _____

TOTAL INCOME _____

Expenses

Housing (rent or mortgage payments) _____

Utilities (gas, electric, water, telephone) _____

Taxes (federal, state, and local income; local real estate; Social Security) _____

Interest payments (car, bank loan, credit card, other loans) _____

Principal payments (amount of borrowed principal repaid) _____

Insurance (health, life, property) _____

Education (tuition, supplies, room and board) _____

Personal expenses _____

Contributions _____

Food _____

Transportation _____

TOTAL FIXED OUTLAYS _____

Clothing   _____
Entertainment   _____
Vacations and recreation   _____
Furniture, appliances, and home improvements   _____
Health and beauty   _____
Savings (general or specific for future purchases or objectives) _____
Miscellaneous   _____
    TOTAL VARIABLE OUTLAYS   _____

TOTAL EXPENSES   _____

    AMOUNT AVAILABLE FOR INVESTING   _____
    (total income minus total expenses)

Budgets are useful only when the amounts specified in each category are not regularly exceeded. If you have trouble keeping a budget, you should make sure that your spending targets reflect your actual expenses and that the members of your household understand the ultimate benefits of budgeting income and expenses. Many software tools, such as Quicken and Microsoft Money, can help make budgeting easier. These programs will help identify the gaps between what the dollars budgeted and actual spending. With these programs, you can also evaluate how and why your spending changes over time. Putting your information into a spreadsheet will save you time re-keying and recalculating should any of your expenses change.

On the World Wide Web, Money.com offers an instant budget maker that can help you judge your spending in comparison to people in similar income situations and with similar expenses, showing whether or not you are spending more or less than people of similar means for each expense item.

Here are some additional guidelines for spending that you may want to evaluate against your own:

Average % of Gross Income

Housing & Utilities	25 to 40%	Savings	10% plus
Taxes	20%	Entertainment & Vacations	5%
Transportation	15%	Debt (credit cards, personal loans)	5%
Food	10%	Other expenses	5%
Clothing	5%		

HOW MUCH CAN YOU SPEND ON HOUSING?

To figure out how much you can afford in monthly rent or mortgage payments, first calculate your total monthly income. If you rent, the total of your rent plus other debt outlays (for credit cards, school loans, etc.) should not exceed 36 percent of your income. If you own your home, the total of your mortgage principal, mortgage interest, real-estate taxes, and homeowner's insurance should not exceed 28 percent of your income. *See also* "Real Estate and Mortgages," later in this chapter.

AVERAGE COST OF RAISING A CHILD

The Agricultural Research Service of the U.S. Department of Agriculture calculates that it costs a two-parent, two-child family $121,230–$241,770 to raise a child to the age of 18. The cost per child increases by a factor of 1.26 for a family with only one child, while it decreases by a factor of 0.78 for a family with three children.

TOTAL SPENDING IN DOLLARS FOR CHILD REARING OVER 18 YEARS

Yearly Income	Yearly Expense (0–2 years)	Housing	Food	Transport	Clothes	Health Care	Education & Child Care	Misc.	Total Expenditures
$38,000 or less	$ 6,280	$39,900	$17,550	$ 9,120	$ 8,970	$ 9,480	$12,390	$17,540	$121,230
$38,000–$64,000	8,740	55,170	28,650	24,420	10,680	11,640	16,560	18,510	165,630
More than $64,000	13,000	89,580	35,670	32,760	13,770	13,380	26,250	30,090	241,770

If you plan on sending that child to a 4-year private college, in 2002 it will cost you about $30,000 a year. If your child is an infant in 2002, by the time he or she reaches 18 the cost is projected to reach $75,000 a year.

CALCULATING YOUR NET WORTH

Use the following chart to calculate your current net worth. Be sure to include amounts held individually and jointly to evaluate your family's net worth.

Assets

Cash on hand and liquid assets
    Checking and savings accounts _____
    Cash value of life insurance _____
    U.S. savings bonds _____
    Equity in pension funds _____
    Money-market funds _____
    Brokerage funds _____
    Trusts _____
    Debts owed you _____
    Other _____
    TOTAL _____

Personal Holdings

    Car(s) (current value) _____
    Home(s) _____
    Boat(s) _____
    Major appliances _____
    Furs and jewelry _____
    Antiques and collectibles _____
    Art _____
    Other _____
    TOTAL _____

Investments

    Common stocks _____
    Preferred stocks _____
    Corporate and municipal bonds _____
    Mutual funds _____
    Certificates of deposit _____
    Business investments _____
    Real-estate investments _____

Personal Finances

IRAs   _____
Other   _____
TOTAL   _____

TOTAL ASSETS   _____

Liabilities

Bills due   _____
Revolving charge and bank-card debts   _____
Taxes due   _____
Outstanding mortgage   _____
Outstanding loans (bank, insurance, etc.)   _____
Stock margin accounts payable   _____
Other debts   _____

TOTAL LIABILITIES   _____

NET WORTH (Assets minus liabilities)   _____

INSURANCE

Life is full of risks. One way you can minimize the effects of these risks is to obtain insurance. By insuring your health, your life, your property, and your car, as well as getting coverage for loss of income in the event of a disability, you can ensure that you and your family remain financially stable even if catastrophe strikes. Additionally, you can use some types of insurance to further your personal financial goals.

HEALTH INSURANCE

Health insurance covers the costs of medical care. It is available to individuals and families through private insurers, health maintenance organizations (HMOs), and preferred provider organizations (PPOs). Although many Americans are covered by one of these plans (paid for by or organized through employers, unions, or other groups), you can buy individual policies to provide additional coverage or to replace the group benefits. For the self-employed, individual policies are often the only choice available.

PRIVATE INSURANCE

Health insurance obtained from a private company can cover a wide variety of services and may pay for these services directly or through reimbursements to the insured individual. Patients are free to select their own doctors under these plans.

FEE FOR SERVICE

Under fee-for-service plans, the individual pays a percentage of medical costs, called coinsurance, usually around 20 percent, and the insurance company pays the rest, usually 80 percent. With fee-for-service insurance, a patient sees a doctor of his or her choice, then the patient or medical care provider submits a claim to the insurance company for reimbursement. Such plans frequently pay according to a predetermined fee schedule. Any amounts in excess of the scheduled fee are considered to be over the limits of reasonable expenses and will not be reimbursed. In addition, fee-for-service plans include deductibles normally ranging from $100 to $500 annually. The insured is responsible for paying all medical costs up to the deductible; then insurance pays 80 percent of covered expenses. Fee-for-service policies usually have an annual out-of-pocket maximum, meaning that once the maximum expense limit is reached, the insured is responsible for paying the rest of the medical expenses for that year. These policies may also have lifetime benefit maximums to protect themselves against severe loss should an insured become very ill and need expensive treatment. It is best to choose a policy with a lifetime limit of $1 million or more, to protect yourself in the event of catastrophic injury.

The manual for IRS employees includes provisions for collecting taxes after a nuclear war.

MANAGED CARE

The three major types of managed care plans are HMOs, PPOs, and POS plans. Managed care plans generally provide comprehensive health benefits to members and often offer incentives to patients to use the providers within their network. Instead of paying separately for each service rendered, coverage is paid for in advance. These plans minimize out-of-pocket medical expenses when you receive coverage from providers within the plan.

HEALTH MAINTENANCE ORGANIZATIONS (HMOs)

HMOs provide medical care to those who pay a quarterly or monthly fee. HMOs are oriented toward preventive health care, and people who pay the premium are entitled to medical, surgical, and hospital care. Some plans also cover the costs of some prescription medicines and provide partial coverage of dental services. Some HMOs provide the services of several doctors at a single location connected with a hospital. Others allow subscribers to receive care from doctors in their individual offices; the doctors then are reimbursed by the HMO on a fee-for-service basis. Important aspects of an HMO that you should scrutinize are the patient-to-physician ratio, the services for which deductibles or additional fees are charged, the availability of maternity benefits, and the relationship of the HMO or participating doctor to a hospital.

PREFERRED PROVIDER ORGANIZATIONS (PPOs)

PPOs resemble HMOs in most respects, cutting the cost of health care by negotiating lower rates with selected providers. But you have more freedom of choice with a PPO, because it covers care not only by selected providers but by professionals outside the network. Some plans, however, require that you apply for preapproval of treatment by nonnetwork providers. Even when treatment is pre-approved, a lower percentage of your costs is reimbursed than for care by preferred providers. You generally must pay out-of-network providers up front and submit a claim to the PPO to get your money back. They offer more flexibility than an HMO, however, the premiums are higher and, as with fee-for-service plans, you may have to pay coinsurance when selecting doctors outside of the network.

POINT-OF-SERVICE (POS)

Point-of-service coverage is similar to PPO, however, with this type of plan you usually select a primary care physician who coordinates all of your medical care.

MEDICARE

Medicare is the federal program of hospital and medical insurance primarily for those over 65 years of age and who are no longer covered by an employer's plan. With the high cost of healthcare these days, many elderly people have to purchase supplemental insurance to cover expenses that Medicare does not cover. These programs, called Medigap or MedSup, are private insurance policies that help cover the gaps in Medicare coverage.

LONG-TERM HEALTH CARE INSURANCE

This type of insurance is a must today for anyone nearing or in retirement. People are living longer and their needs, as they age, are greater. This type of insurance can help protect the assets that you have accumulated over your lifetime should you require long-term healthcare, such as going into a nursing home. A long-term care policy can cover the medical care, nursing care, and other assistance that you may need if you have a chronic illness or disability, when you are not well enough to care for yourself over an extended period of time. Long-term care can be expensive but, with life expectancy on the rise, it can be well worth the expense.

Personal Finances

LIFE INSURANCE

The purpose of life insurance is to provide future financial security for your family. Life insurance provides an immediate estate that will enable your family to maintain the household after you die. You also can use life insurance to build up cash reserves for future expenses, such as retirement or college tuition.

By purchasing a life-insurance policy, you are buying into a risk-sharing group. Although no one can predict with any reliability when any individual is going to die, it is possible to predict with great accuracy the number of nonsmoking 32-year-old women who exercise regularly and are not overweight who will die at any given point over the next 40 years. The costs of premiums for people of different ages in various risk categories then can be calculated on the basis of how much the insurance company will pay in benefits to each group's beneficiaries. Buy when you are young and healthy and when you have dependents. Older people and those not in the best of health pay much higher rates.

You have six types of life insurance to choose from, all but one of which (term insurance) fall into the category of cash-value insurance. Term insurance works the same way automobile or homeowner's insurance works—the insured item being your life. Cash-value plans add investment to the picture, crediting a portion of your premiums to an interest-bearing account. You can borrow against the account while you are alive, and the cash value is paid out tax-free to your beneficiaries upon your death.

term insurance   Provides a death benefit to beneficiaries for a specified period of time. It can be renewable or convertible to whole life and features a low initial premium that rises with each new term. Term life typically has no cash value.

whole life insurance   Offers protection for life at a fixed premium. It provides a fixed death benefit and a cash value that can be borrowed against and increases over the years. These policies are more expensive.

Go to "Life Expectancy in 1995 by Race, Sex, and Age" in chapter 18; "Government Benefits" in chapter 25

universal life insurance   Offers permanent protection, flexible premiums and death benefits, and a cash value based on premiums paid to date and current interest rates. They usually have higher yields than plain whole life but they generally don't guarantee a certain rate.

excess interest whole life insurance   Provides permanent protection, a fixed premium that the insurer may adjust after the policy is issued, a fixed death benefit, a cash value that grows depending on market conditions, and the possibility that premiums may be reduced or dispensed with for one or more years if investments are sufficiently profitable.

variable life insurance   Offers permanent protection; fixed or flexible premiums; policyholder control over the investment of the policy's cash value; and variable death benefits and cash values, depending on the investment performance of the underlying assets in the account. Policy owners can choose among several investment options for these assets, mainly among bond and stock funds.

adjustable life insurance   Gives permanent protection that can be reduced to a shorter term if desired, a death benefit that can be raised or lowered, and premiums that can be increased or decreased.

The American Council of Life Insurance recommends that you evaluate your life-insurance needs, buy from a company licensed in your state, select a trustworthy insurance agent, compare costs of similar policies, ask about lower premium rates for nonsmokers, and read your policies and understand them. After selecting coverage that is right for you, inform your beneficiaries about the kind and amount of life insurance you own, keep your policy in a safe place at home, keep the company's name and policy number in a safe deposit box, and check your coverage periodically to be sure it meets your current needs.

DISABILITY INSURANCE

Disability insurance provides coverage for loss of income when an illness or injury prevents you from working. Compulsory temporary disability insurance is provided in California, Hawaii, New Jersey, New York, Rhode Island, and Puerto Rico. Social Security also provides disability coverage at varying levels, depending on family size and the recipient's age and usually only to those who are severely disabled.

Long-term disability insurance usually covers between 50 to 70 percent of your income. In addition, three types of disability insurance are available through private companies:

noncancelable Policies that protect your income as long as you continue to make premium payments. Coverage may be increased as income increases.

guaranteed renewable Policies that are less expensive than noncancellable ones, because insurers can increase premium rates. The insurer is not permitted to cancel or amend the policy benefits during the period that the policy is guaranteed renewable.

optionally or conditionally renewable Policies that can be renewed or not renewed each year, for reasons stated in the policy, with variable premium rates. They are the least expensive private option.

More information about disability insurance can be obtained from the Health Insurance Association of America, 555 13th Street NW, Suite 600 East, Washington, D.C. 20004.

PROPERTY AND LIABILITY INSURANCE

The purchase of a home is the largest investment most individuals will make in their lifetimes. The home also represents the largest portion of their total financial worth. It therefore makes sense to insure against its possible damage or loss. Even renters stand to lose a substantial amount of money if the uninsured contents of their apartments or houses are destroyed. Determining the cost of rebuilding or refurnishing your home will enable you to properly select the amount of coverage you will need.

A wide array of homeowner's insurance policies is available, including coverage for renters and apartment dwellers. The type of coverage most appropriate for you depends on the sort of risks your property is exposed to and the value of the property. Some policies cover only specific causes of damage or loss, while others provide "all-risk" coverage that pays for any loss or damage except that specifically excluded by the policy. Available homeowner's policies follow:

homeowner's 1 Covers damage caused by fire, lightning, extended perils (such as windstorms, hail, smoke damage, explosions, riots, and vehicular and aircraft damage), vandalism, malicious mischief, theft, and personal liability. This very limited policy is seldom sold or purchased.

homeowner's 2 Adds extended coverage for a variety of other potential problems—such as broken water pipes, freezing of plumbing fixtures, and building collapse—to the coverage offered in homeowner's 1.

homeowner's 3 An "all risks" policy for buildings that is more extensive than either 1 or 2. It also can cover personal property to a limited extent. The only events it excludes are flood, earthquake, war, and nuclear accident.

homeowner's 4 Covers personal property only. The extent of coverage is generally the same as in 2, but the policy is designed for renters.

homeowner's 5 Provides the most comprehensive "all risks" coverage for homes and personal property.

homeowner's 6 Designed for condominium owners. It covers loss of personal property and loss of use of the dwelling.

homeowner's 8 More limited than homeowner's 1. Homeowner's 8 is a named-perils policy designed for owners of older homes where the cost of reconstructing the home in the event of a catastrophic loss exceeds the market value of the home.

Ask for replacement cost coverage, which will help you replace what you lost even if the value of those items has risen. Otherwise, the insurer will pay you only the depreciated value. You can also purchase an inflation guard, which increases your premium with the rate of building cost inflation.

Homeowner's policies cover more than just a home and its contents. Most types include the main dwelling, any other structures on the property, personal belongings that are kept in the dwelling or elsewhere, costs of additional living expenses, and comprehensive personal liability—including medical payments and damage to others' property.

Comprehensive personal liability insurance protects against the loss of your home or property in the event that someone is injured accidentally, whether the injury occurs at the home or elsewhere (such as on a golf course or during a softball game). This type of insurance pays up to a set amount for each occurrence of personal liability (injury and property damage) and up to set amounts for medical payments to others and damage to others' property. Excluded from the comprehensive personal liability insurance provisions of most homeowner's policies are losses resulting from business or professional activities; use of boats, ships, and planes; intentional injury or damage; acts of war or nuclear accidents; and liabilities covered by other insurance policies, such as workers' compensation. Additional liability insurance is available for some of these situations. If you are looking for a comprehensive plan, umbrella liability coverage, for those with substantial net worth, covers both auto and homeowner's liability limits above the underlying coverage.

AUTOMOBILE INSURANCE

When you are evaluating the risks to which you are regularly exposed, driving a car is one risk you must consider. The possibility of an accident involving your car is so great that most states have made at least limited automobile insurance mandatory.

Automobile insurance covers three broad risk categories:

liability insurance   Covers personal injuries and property damage resulting from ownership, maintenance, or use of a vehicle. Separate limits for payments apply to each person involved in an accident and to the property damage incurred.

medical insurance   Covers the medical costs incurred in an accident up to a set amount per person per accident.

collision insurance   Pays the costs of having a car repaired after it has been damaged in an accident.

Additional automobile insurance, such as comprehensive insurance, also is available to pay for damages resulting from fire or theft. Insurance also is available for damages resulting from an uninsured driver, towing and labor, and transportation needed while a damaged car is repaired. Many states mandate the inclusion of no-fault personal injury insurance in any automobile insurance policy; this provides benefits for those injured in an accident, regardless of who was responsible for the accident.

The types of coverage and the monetary limits of the policy, the driver's age, the frequency of use of the vehicle, the driver's accident history, and the place where the vehicle is kept are considered in determining the cost of liability insurance. Costs for coverage of damage to a vehicle are calculated on the purchase price of the vehicle and its age. When evaluating insurance policies, it is important to compare what is *not* covered by a given policy—its exclusions—as well as what *is* covered and how much it will cost. Comparative shopping and a trustworthy insurance agent can help you choose wisely when buying insurance for your vehicles.

CREDIT AND LOANS

One key to enhancing personal finances is credit. With loans, credit cards, revolving-charge plans at department stores, and other methods of delaying payment, people obtain goods and services for which they otherwise would have to wait. Of course, use of credit results in debts and interest charges that must be paid to maintain a good credit rating and ensure the availability of more credit.

Getting credit is a fairly straightforward procedure. You can apply to a bank for a loan or a bank credit card—such as VISA® or MasterCard®—or to a department store or gasoline company for a revolving charge account by filling out an application form. These companies will ask about your income, employment history, length and type of residence, credit history, and major assets (car, home, etc.) to determine your creditworthiness.

As of 1998, 44 percent of families in America had credit card balances, holding a median balance of $1,700, paying a median interest rate of 15 percent.

A positive credit history—meaning that you have received credit and made payments on time—is one of the strongest recommendations for further credit. If you have never had credit before, a good first step is to obtain a department-store or gasoline-company credit card (these types of cards are often easier to get than bank credit cards) or to take out a small loan at a bank where you keep a savings and/or checking account. Having a reasonably large amount of money in the bank also can help persuade issuers to provide you with credit.

When you want to obtain credit, especially once you have established creditworthiness, comparison shopping is very important. Different states have different limits on the amount of interest that can be charged on consumer loans and bank cards. Interest rates on loans can range from less than 2 percent per month to 36 percent per year or more. Credit-card rates range from less than 11 percent to 22 percent or more per year. You do not need to be a resident of a state to get credit from lending institutions headquartered there, and you can apply by mail.

The amount of indebtedness you should assume is not easy to calculate. Credit-granting institutions base their decisions on your gross income and expenses. Your own decision about how much credit you should use is harder to evaluate. Calculating the amount of money you have available from your income after deducting monthly expenses will give you some idea of what you can afford, although other factors—such as ever-decreasing balances in your

checking and savings accounts, use of overdrafts or credit to cover regular expenses, and difficulty making payments on credit lines you already have—may suggest that additional credit is not a good idea.

If you find yourself overwhelmed with debt and getting into trouble with too many outstanding credit card bills, you may wish to consolidate your debt. By obtaining a consolidation loan, you can pay off several bills with the proceeds from the loan and then make one payment a month instead of several to various creditors. This is also advantageous if the interest rate on the loan is less than the interest rates of your other bills.

Consumer credit counseling services are good sources of advice. These organizations help consumers find a way to repay debts through careful budgeting and management of funds. Often, these nonprofit organizations are funded by creditors. The counseling services can sometimes negotiate with your creditors to get them to accept a longer pay-off period.

If you own a home you may be able to obtain a home equity loan to use for various purposes, including paying down your debt. A home equity loan is based on the difference between the amount of equity paid on a home and its current market value.

Problems that can arise from credit, such as billing errors or unfair denial of credit, can be remedied under federal regulations. The Fair Credit Billing Act requires that, if you notify a creditor in writing about an error on a bill, your complaint must be acknowledged within 30 days and resolved within 90 days. The Equal Credit Opportunity Act requires creditors to give you a reason if you are denied credit and prohibits discrimination based on race, gender, age, marital status, religion, national origin, or receipt of public assistance.

If you are denied credit on the basis of a negative report from a credit bureau, you can obtain the information that agency supplied to the creditor free of charge if you request it within 30 days of being turned down, or for a small fee at any time. You can

Personal Finances

challenge the accuracy of any item in your credit file; this forces the credit bureau to investigate the item and remove it if it cannot be substantiated. If there is negative information on your credit report that is factual, you can take certain steps to help your situation, such as paying any balances due and having the creditors update your file. In seven years, negative information, except for bankruptcies (which may take ten years), will be removed from your report. Any item in your file also can be amended at your request to include a 100-word explanation that will be added to your file. For assistance in dealing with credit problems, contact the nonprofit National Foundation for Credit Counseling, 800-388-CCCS (2227), http://www.nfcc.org

Many banks now issue debit cards. (Increasingly, ATM cards can function as debit cards as well.) Usually, the only requirement for obtaining a debit card is a checking account. Be aware that the cost of any item that you purchase with a debit card will be automatically deducted from your checking account immediately. It is easy to confuse debit and credit cards because they look alike. However, if you use a debit card and do not realize that the money is being withdrawn automatically from your checking account you may lose track off how much money you have in your account to pay your bills. Immediately keep track of all withdrawals made with your debit card in order to keep your checkbook balanced.

Hundreds of credit bureaus exist throughout the United States, but three companies predominate nationally. Contact one of the following for information on your credit rating:

Equifax Inc.
P.O. Box 105873
Atlanta, GA 30348
800-233-7654 for Maryland residents
800-548-4548 for Vermont residents
800-997-2493 for all 50 states
http://www.equifax.com

TransUnion LLC
Consumer Disclosure Center
P.O. Box 1000
Chester, PA 19022

800-888-4213
800-916-8800
http://www.transunion.com

Experian Credit Bureau, Inc.
Attn: Consumer Assistance Department
P.O. Box 596
Pittsburgh, PA 15230
888-EXPERIAN
888-397-3742
http://www.experian.com

REAL ESTATE AND MORTGAGES

American society is geared toward home ownership. The desire to own a home, and the labyrinthine process of purchasing one, can have a tremendous impact on an individual's or a family's finances. A home represents the single largest financial commitment most people will make in their lifetimes. It therefore requires a careful, reasoned decision based on a thorough examination of the steps involved in the purchase. What follows are some of the basics involved in buying a home and obtaining a mortgage. Potential home buyers are cautioned to seek out as much additional information as is practical from specialized books, real-estate professionals, and friends who have made similar purchases.

THE DECISION TO BUY A HOME

Owning their own home is something most people believe to be desirable regardless of their financial circumstances. They think that owning a home is a perfect investment and that renting is akin to throwing money away. This is not always the case. Home ownership often includes a great many hidden expenses, while renters take care of the basic need for shelter at a set monthly cost without having to deal with headaches such as various taxes, sewage disposal, or sidewalk repairs.

You need to consider a number of factors when deciding whether to buy your own home. First among these should be the way you lead your life. Home ownership can provide greater space, a chance to set down roots, the option to make any alterations you choose, the possibility of providing yard space and better schools for your children, and the pride of having a home of your own. Renters have greater flexibility about when they can move, generally pay less of their income for shelter, avoid the ancillary costs and added work of maintaining a residence, and can use any excess funds for investments that offer a guaranteed rate of return.

Also of great importance in the decision to buy a home is your current financial situation. Home ownership requires enough money to make a down payment (generally at least 10 percent of the purchase price, and often 20 or 25 percent) to obtain a mortgage and to make payments on that mortgage for many years to come. Renters need to have enough money to make some sort of security deposit and to pay the rent each month.

AFFORDABILITY

It is best to shop for a mortgage before you shop for a home so that you know how much money is available to you. A long-standing rule of thumb is that the annual cost of a home should not exceed 25 percent of your gross annual income. If you can manage monthly payments that do not exceed 25 percent of your income, you will probably have little trouble obtaining a mortgage or making the payments.

A penny minted in 1727 was the first U.S. coin to have the words "United States of America." It also bore the motto, "Mind Your Own Business."

But even if mortgage payments come to 25 percent of your income, the cost of a home will be substantially more. You will need funds to cover utilities, water and sewage costs, various taxes, repairs, improvements, and even garbage cans and yard equipment. Additional costs may include commuting expenses. It is wise to set aside an additional 10 percent of the basic annual costs for unseen expenses.

A careful evaluation of present and projected income and expenses—including money spent on nonessen-tial interests, hobbies, and pastimes—will give you some idea of what you can afford to pay for a home on a monthly basis. From there, you can look at mortgage-payment schedules to find out how much of a mortgage you can afford.

One thing to keep in mind when deciding what you can afford is that many experts advise against buying the most expensive house in a given neighborhood. A lower-priced home in a higher-priced neighborhood offers greater security and a better likelihood of seeing the property value increase.

See also "How Much Can You Spend on Housing?", earlier in this chapter.

AN OLD HOME OR A NEW ONE?

If you have a choice between buying a new home or one that has been occupied, you must weigh the pluses and minuses of each. The value of similar new and used homes in similar neighborhoods will go up about equally, but other aspects of each type of home may make you choose one over the other.

New homes have more modern amenities, are often less likely to suffer system breakdowns (that is, plumbing, heating, and water supply), should not require much upkeep or many repairs, and often can be mortgaged for a greater percentage of the price over a longer term. Older homes frequently are less expensive, have larger rooms, are better built, have finished landscaping, and are closer to the center of town. The individual merits of the actual houses you look at will guide you in making a final choice.

THE DOWN PAYMENT

Among the many decisions to be made in the home-buying process is whether to make a large or small down payment.

While a higher down payment can reduce your monthly payments or the term of the mortgage, there are a number of advantages in making as small a down payment as possible: You retain access to your money; the money you pay in later years will be less valuable, because of inflation, than money spent now; and the interest included in your mortgage payments is tax deductible, so the more you borrow, the more you can deduct. However, with a down payment of less than 20 percent, the lender may require you to purchase private mortgage insurance (PMI), which protects the bank should you default.

THE MORTGAGE

At one time, the only mortgages widely available in the United States were fixed-rate mortgages that required fixed monthly payments for a specific period, usually 25 or 30 years. Recently, however, a wide variety of mortgage options has become available. A hybrid loan, for instance, offers a fixed rate initially for the first 5 to 7 years and then converts to an adjusted rate for the rest of the term. Here are some others:

graduated payment mortgage (GPM)   Has a fixed rate of interest but varying payments. Payments begin at a low amount and are increased at a fixed rate each year, rising to a level higher than on a fixed-rate mortgage. Initial payments may be lower than the cost of interest, in which case the unpaid interest is added to the principal. This type of mortgage is good for first-time buyers who expect their incomes to rise during the course of the mortgage. These loans are available in 15- and 30-year amortization schedules. They work well in markets where real estate appreciation is expected to be rapid.

pledged-account mortgage (PAM)   A variation of the GPM based on the difference between payments and the accrued interest from a savings account pledged to that purpose by the borrower. A pledged account mortgage allows the borrower to obtain 100 percent financing if a relative agrees to pledge a savings account or a certificate of deposit as collateral for the loan. The pledged money continues to earn interest, eventually payable to the person who pledged the money. When the borrower has sufficient equity in the property, the pledge money is returned.

adjustable-rate mortgage (ARM)   Has a flexible interest rate that varies according to a selected interest-rate index. The rate may go up when the

index goes up, and most rates go down when the index goes down. This type of mortgage may contain limitations on the maximum and minimum rates. The changing rate can affect the monthly payment, the term, or the outstanding principal. Some plans change the rate more frequently than they change the payments. This can result in underpayments on interest that then are added to the outstanding balance.

balloon mortgage   Requires that the loan be paid off in full or refinanced at the end of the mortgage term, usually 5 to 7 years. The advantage of the balloon mortgage is that monthly payments during the term are generally lower than they would be for a traditional 30-year mortgage. These are good for first or starter homebuyers.

convertible ARM   A combination of both fixed rate and adjustable rate mortgages, allowing the borrower to convert to a fixed rate mortgage after a set period of time.

graduated-payment adjustable-rate mortgage (GPARM)   Combines features of GPMs and ARMs. Some plans defer interest in the early years, others set rising payments during the first several years, and still others fix low payments early on. Countless variations are possible.

wraparound mortgage   Allows the buyer to assume the balance of a lower-rate mortgage from the seller, making payments to amortize both that original mortgage and the additional amount being borrowed at prevailing rates. This mortgage reduces the overall interest rate on the total amount. Wraparound mortgages are very rare and allow buyers to purchase a home without qualifying for a loan or paying closing costs.

shared-appreciation mortgage (SAM)   In return for a reduced interest rate for the borrower, the lender receives a set portion of the amount by which the home has appreciated when it is sold or the loan is paid. Because the final value of the home cannot be determined in advance, additional interest can be due if the value has not appreciated sufficiently. Be aware, however, that should your home appreciate significantly, the lender may benefit more than you do. You should make sure that this type of arrangement is in your best interest.

Federal Housing Administration Loans These loans are insured by the U.S. Department of Housing and Urban Development. They are designed to make housing affordable for those with low to moderate incomes. Offered at both fixed and adjustable rates, they may require down payments of as little as 3 percent.

reverse mortgage Really not a mortgage at all, but a way of getting monthly payments in return for some of the equity in a house. It is advantageous for people over the age of 75 with significant equity and insufficient cash.

points Charged by many lenders in addition to the mortgage payments themselves. These additional amounts—each point is equal to 1 percent of the loan—are paid by the buyer at the time the mortgage goes into effect (at the closing). They represent a portion of the interest that you pay up front in exchange for a lower rate later. The longer you plan on staying in the house, the more points you should consider paying.

See also "Mortgage Amortization Factors," earlier in this chapter.

GOING TO CONTRACT

Anything and everything can and possibly will go wrong when it comes time to draw up a contract and close the deal to buy a home. No list of potential pitfalls could be considered all-inclusive. The best advice is to obtain a lawyer who is familiar with the kind of property purchase you are making and to read every word in every document presented to you with your lawyer.

COMMON REAL-ESTATE TERMS

amortization A gradual paying off of a mortgage by periodic installments.

appraisal An estimation of a property's value, often made by lenders before deciding the amount of a mortgage.

assessed valuation A value placed on a property as a basis for taxation.

assumable mortgage A mortgage taken over from the seller of a property by the buyer.

balloon payment The final payment on a loan or mortgage, usually larger than the previous payments.

binder An agreement by the buyer to cover the down payment on the purchase of real estate before a final contract is drawn up.

broker Usually a licensed agent who acts on behalf of the seller of a property, making arrangements for the sale.

closing The meeting of a buyer, a seller, a banker, and attorneys for all parties at which a real-estate sale is completed with the writing of checks. It usually takes place 30 to 60 days after the signing of the contract.

commission The amount paid to a real-estate broker for services rendered.

condominium A multiple-unit dwelling, townhouse, or detached house; the owner buys a title to a single unit and an undivided interest in common areas (the land, roof, elevator, etc.).

contract A binding agreement between parties to transact real estate under agreed-upon terms.

cooperative apartment A multiple-unit dwelling; buyers purchase individual shares in a cooperative corporation that owns the building. Each share entitles the holder to a proprietary lease on an apartment in the building.

deed A written document that conveys ownership of real property.

equity The value of an owner's real property after deducting mortgages and liens.

escrow   A written agreement or something of value placed in the care of someone else and, once conditions are met, delivered to a designated party. Often used for payment of taxes along with mortgage payments.

Fannie Mae   The Federal National Mortgage Association—the largest secondary mortgage agency.

Federal Housing Administration (FHA)   A division of the federal government's Department of Housing and Urban Development that insures mortgages.

foreclosure   A legal procedure in which real estate is sold by the lender to pay a defaulting borrower's debt.

Freddie Mac   The Federal Home Loan Mortgage Corporation, which buys mortgages from lenders, allowing the lenders to make new mortgages.

Ginnie Mae   The Government National Mortgage Association (GNMA), which buys FHA-insured loans from lenders.

indexing   A means of adjusting the interest rate on a loan or mortgage according to an agreed-upon index or indicator.

interest   Money paid to a lender for use of borrowed principal.

LIBOR   An average of rate quotes from five major international banks. Fannie Mae and Freddie Mac use LIBOR as an index of loans they purchase.

lien   A claim on the property of another granted as security for the payment of a loan or mortgage.

lock   The commitment of a borrower to a mortgage rate some time between the application and the closing date; obtaining a lock may require a payment by the borrower.

mortgage   A written instrument that creates a lien on a given property in return for a loan.

mortgage insurance (MI)   Also called Private Mortgage Insurance (PMI), typically required by the lender when the loan-to-value ratio is above 80 per-

cent on a conforming loan. FHA loans always require mortgage insurance.

point   An amount equal to 1 percent of a loan, charged to the borrower by the lender.

prepayment penalty   An additional fee charged for paying off a mortgage before it is due.

principal   The amount of money borrowed from a lender for a mortgage, upon which interest is computed.

qualifying ratio   The ratio of the borrower's fixed monthly expenses to his or her gross monthly income. Conforming ratios are often expressed as two numbers such as 28/36 where 28 would be the gross debt service ratio and 36 would be the total debt service ratio. These ratios help lenders determine a potential borrower's creditworthiness.

title   A written document that gives evidence of property ownership.

title insurance   Insurance against loss resulting from defects of title to a specifically described parcel of real estate.

INVESTMENTS AND RETIREMENT

If you are like most people, your main source of income for the greater part of your life is the salary or fees you earn from working. This income may or may not be adequate to support the lifestyle you want to maintain. If you would like to increase your income, you might consider making investments. Even if your earned income is enough for the present, you might want to invest now to plan for a secure retirement.

SETTING GOALS

There is little point in considering investments without developing the goals you hope to reach by making those investments. Investing is a means to an end. That end generally can be described as financial security—having enough income to live on after you retire. But a more specific set of goals is essential.

You must develop short-term and long-term strategies. Calculate the amounts you have available to invest now and those you can make available in the future. Then figure the rate of return you require from your investments, taking into account the amount of income you will need those investments to produce in the future after factoring in inflation. You also need to evaluate your need for access to the principal or profit on short notice, along with whether you are willing to take greater risks for a potentially higher return or will accept lower profits in return for greater security.

France had the first supermarket in the world. It was started by relatives of the people who started the Texas Big Bear supermarket chain.

Other aspects you should consider when creating short- and long-term goals are diversification of your investments to reduce risks, the tax status of the income your investments will produce, and the availability of loans using your investments as collateral.

Setting goals is a continual process. Your current goals should be based on how you envision your future.

CHOOSING YOUR INVESTMENTS

Once you have decided on your investment goals, you must answer the most difficult question of all: What should you invest in? The possibilities are almost limitless.

It is unwise to select an investment without close scrutiny. Selecting a stock because someone—even a stockbroker—tells you "it's a good bet" is not a good way to handle your money. You can select the types of investments you believe will be most effective in helping you reach your short- and long-term goals. But you then should seek professional assistance from an appropriate source: bankers for information about money-market accounts, individual retirement accounts (IRAs), or certificates of deposit (CDs); or stockbrokers for information about stocks and bonds.

Be aware, however, that these investment professionals stand to profit from the advice they give. The less ethical may try to steer you toward investments that are not ideal for you.

The first and best investment you can make, one that guarantees a return and does not put your money at risk, is to pay off your debts. Investing $2,000 in a mutual fund that pays 10 percent does not make sense if you are paying 18 percent interest on a $2,000 credit-card balance. Using the money to pay off the debt will put you 8 percent ahead of the game.

Here are the most widely used investment vehicles:

bank accounts These investments involve virtually no risk (they are insured by the federal government up to $100,000) and are very liquid (they allow for easy access to your money), but they offer low returns. Checking and savings accounts usually require a minimum balance if you want to avoid fees. Keep enough money in your accounts to avoid fees, and if the account does not pay interest, put the remainder in a savings account that does. Bank accounts are good short-term investments for money that you need to keep on hand. Banks have different rates of interest and fees. Shop around for the bank that requires the lowest minimums, charges the lowest fees, and yields the highest rates of interest.

life insurance Cash-value life-insurance policies invest a portion of your premiums in an account that bears interest at a moderate rate and grows over time. While low-risk, this investment is relatively expensive when you consider the unspectacular rate of return. You can borrow against the value of your policy while you are alive, but you cannot withdraw funds or the interest you earn. Cash-value life insurance does pay a tax-free death benefit to your heirs when you die, but that savings is minimal unless you are in a high tax bracket. A better choice for low-risk investing would be bonds, and for long-term investing, stocks.

annuities   Offered by insurance companies, annuities resemble a combination of cash-value life insurance and individual retirement accounts (IRAs). You contribute to the plan during the accumulation phase, it grows and compounds without taxation, and you receive distributions after age 59½. Penalties apply for early withdrawal, and if you die before the pay-out phase begins, your beneficiaries receive a sum equal to your investment. Although they are tax-deferred, annuities include high fees to make up for high operating expenses. Annuities can provide peace of mind, guaranteeing an income stream in retirement that continues throughout a lifetime. You pay more for this insurance, but, for some, the benefits are well worth the extra cost. A fixed annuity pays out fixed installments, whereas a variable annuity can allow the investor to capture market returns by varying the payment with the investment value of the account. (See "Planning for Retirement," later in this chapter, for more viable investments.)

bonds   When you purchase a bond, you lend money to the issuer of the bond. Bonds are safe investments—you get back your investment plus interest when the bond matures—but lose value relative to other investments when interest rates rise. Depending on the type of bond, this investment can tie up your money for one week to 30 years. Bonds offer a moderate return on your investment, which in some cases will be tax-free. The different types of bonds are issued by banks (certificates of deposit), state governments (municipal bonds), the federal government (treasuries), mortgage holders (Ginnie Maes), and corporations (corporate bonds). Bank CDs generally require a minimum $500 investment and mature in one week to five years, penalizing early withdrawal of your money. Municipal bonds and treasuries may require as little as $25 to invest and mature in an average of 10 years. Treasury bills, one type of U.S. bond, are six-month instruments in $10,000 denominations. These bills offer market interest rates with high security, can easily be sold, and are not subject to state and local income taxes. A minimum investment of $500 or more is required by various Ginnie Maes, which mature after a period of up to 30 years. Corporate bonds may require a minimum deposit of $1,000 and mature in one to 30 years, but they can be cashed in easily before they mature. Bonds represent a stable vehicle for the short- to long-term investment of money that you will not need in the interim. You can purchase bonds individually or through diversified bond funds (see "Mutual Funds," later in this chapter).

stocks   A share of stock is a small piece of a publicly held company, so its performance as an investment depends on the fortunes of that company. Some stocks pay dividends that reflect the company's profitability, and they grow or decline in capital value according to the financial health of the company. As a result, stocks may fluctuate greatly in value and yield unreliable dividends, making them a poor short-term investment choice. And because companies may fail at any time, the funds you invest in stocks may disappear completely. Thus, you should not invest in stocks unless you can afford to lose the money you put into them, you have the stomach to ride out the company's hard times, and you can stand to put your money at risk. In return for your patience and intestinal fortitude, however, stocks can offer phenomenal returns over the long run, making them an excellent way to build wealth for the future. Investing in individual stocks requires time-consuming research into companies, detailed reporting to the IRS, and the payment of transaction fees to a broker. To avoid these drawbacks, as well as to minimize risk through diversification, invest in a stock fund that consists of a portfolio of various stocks and is managed by an investment professional (see "Mutual Funds," later in this chapter). Stocks are a good way to invest disposable income for the long term.

real estate   In terms of risk and return, real estate is comparable to stock as an investment. The value of real estate goes up and down with the local economy, and the capital investment is substantial, but in the long term, owning real estate is a superb way to build wealth. If you own your home, you build equity as you pay off your mortgage, which increases your net worth (you also may borrow against your equity if necessary). You will pay real-estate taxes and the various expenses of home ownership, but you also will receive tax breaks to offset that expense. You can achieve the same results and bring in rent money by investing in real estate other than your home, but being a landlord brings many headaches. Only the very wealthy can afford to hold nonrental property other than their primary residence, because they pay taxes on it, tie up large sums of capital, and do not see a penny of profit until they sell (and profit is not guaranteed). Real-estate oddities such as limited partnerships and time shares most often offer high risk without high returns while they tie up your money. But owning your home is a very worthwhile long-term investment if you buy wisely. Another way to invest in real estate without owning property is to invest in real estate investment trust (REIT) mutual funds. This strategy enables you to capture the returns of the real estate market without the hassle of taking care of the property or putting up a large down payment. It also helps to lessen the risk by spreading your investment across a number of different properties held within the portfolio.

small business   Given the rate at which small businesses fail, investing in a small business is not for the faint of heart. The returns, however, can be staggering if careful research and management combine with good luck. You can minimize your risk by starting your own business instead of buying out someone or investing in an ongoing enterprise. That way, you have complete control over your investment, even if you do have to put in long hours to make it pay off. As with stock, you should be prepared to lose your money, and as with real estate, you should view a small business as a long-term investment.

miscellaneous   Precious metal received a lot of attention as an investment in the 1970s and 1980s, but the rapid growth in value of precious metals at that time is uncharacteristic. More typically, precious metals represent a hedge against inflation, but they do not outpace inflation as an investment. Collectibles such as coins, stamps, antiques, or wine are not good

investments. The risk is very high, and the potential returns are disproportionately mediocre; it is also quite difficult to turn these investments into cash.

WORTH THE RISK?

All investments involve risk. As you plan your investment strategy, you must decide what kinds of risks you are willing to take. The rule of thumb is that lower-risk investments yield lower returns and higher-risk investments yield higher returns, but this oversimplifies the picture. In addition to weighing the historical performance of a potential investment, you must consider your investment goals and timeline.

If you want to make long-term investments to finance your retirement, for instance, you will do better putting money into a volatile vehicle like stocks than into a stable but low-yielding one like a money-market account. When all is said and done, your investment probably will grow more over the years—despite the risks. Nevertheless, it is unwise to put your entire nest egg into one volatile basket. Always keep a portion of your investments in lower-risk vehicles such as bonds, and diversify your high-risk investments across several different vehicles. That way, if one investment collapses, you won't go broke.

You can put about $50 in pennies in a half-gallon milk container.

For shorter-term goals like saving up for a new car, you are better off with lower-risk investments that are unlikely to lose value in the near future. Emergency money or money you will need within the next five years should not go into risky investments.

Who you are should come into play as well. If you like to play it safe with your money, accept that your investment results will be solid but not spectacular. If you are attracted by the prospect of big money, accept that you will have to take some risks. Older investors, those with limited funds to invest, or people

Personal Finances

with greater financial and family commitments should take fewer risks; while younger, wealthier, and unmarried investors can afford to venture into the unknown.

MUTUAL FUNDS

Mutual funds are professionally managed portfolios of investment vehicles like stocks and bonds. When you invest in a mutual fund, your money goes into a large pool with that of many other investors. With that large pool of cash, money managers can invest in a portfolio geared to meet specific goals, such as stability or growth. Many investors find mutual funds an attractive way to go, because the legwork is done by a professional, they can achieve diversification even with a small investment, and their transaction costs are reduced.

When choosing a mutual fund, consider the individual fund's historical performance as well as the performance of other, similar funds managed by the same firm. You should choose a fund that fits in with your financial picture and investment goals and consider the possible tax impact of its dividends and capital-gains distributions. And don't forget to figure in the cost of the fund—both the up-front load, or commission, charged by the broker (many no-load funds are available) and the ongoing operating fees charged by the fund. Operating fees can take a significant bite out of your returns.

Mutual funds fall into several categories based on the types of investments you make:

money-market funds   The safest type of fund, money-market accounts are virtually identical to bank savings accounts from the investor's standpoint, except they require a minimum deposit to open ($1,000–$25,000) and they offer check-writing privileges. Money-market funds also pay higher interest, yet they keep your money as safe as money in savings accounts by investing it in conservative vehicles such as short-term bank certificates of deposit (CDs), U.S. Treasury bonds, and corporate bonds. The interest on some funds is tax-free.

Money-market funds are good short-term investments for funds that you need to keep liquid.

bond funds   The manager of a bond fund assembles a portfolio of bonds that mature at about the same rate. Short-term funds feature bonds with a maturity cycle of 2 to 3 years, intermediate-term funds focus on bonds that mature in 7 to 10 years, and long-term funds include 20-year instruments. As the bonds come due, managers reinvest in similar bonds. Bond funds emphasize dividends, or income, over capital growth and are reasonably safe.

stock funds   Specializing in small, medium, or large companies, stock funds may focus on capital growth or value. **Value-oriented funds** are portfolios of stocks that are well priced in relation to the size and profitability of the company. **Growth-oriented funds** feature companies whose revenues and profits are growing quickly. Growth and small-company orientation translate into higher risk and return, while value and large-company orientation make a fund safer relative to other stock investments. Stock funds may specialize in overseas companies, in certain industries, or in socially responsible or environmentally conscious companies. **Index funds** select a portfolio meant to mirror the performance of a stock-market index, such as the *Standard and Poor's 500* (an index of the stocks of America's 500 largest corporations). Index funds often outperform the market, because they cost less to manage, using computers rather than people to select stocks.

hybrid funds   These mutual funds combine investment in a variety of vehicles, usually stocks and bonds. They are safer and slower growing than stock funds, but riskier and higher yielding than bond funds. If your investment strategy is middle-of-the-road, but you don't have enough money to invest in separate stock funds and bond funds, a hybrid fund offers a good alternative.

funds of funds   Investment companies sell mutual-fund packages that consist of funds that invest in other funds. This can simplify your investment strategy even further than conventional mutual funds, allowing you to buy into a diversified portfolio that includes both stock funds and bond funds. It is essential to shop carefully to find a high-quality fund of funds, or the benefits of simplicity may be canceled out by poor performance.

MAJOR MUTUAL FUND COMPANIES

American Century
800-345-6488
http://www.americancentury.com

Charles Schwab & Company
800-526-8600
http://www.schwab.com

Dreyfus Service Corp.
800-443-9792
http://www.dreyfus.com

Fidelity Investments
800-544-6666
http://www.fidelity.com

Franklin Templeton Investments
800-342-5236
http://www.franklintempleton.com

Janus
888-223-0351
http://www.janus.com

Scudder Investments
800-SCUDDER
http://www.myscudder.com

Strong Funds
800-368-1480
http://www.estrong.com

T. Rowe Price
800-638-5660
http://www.troweprice.com

Transamerica
800-89-ASK-US
http://www.transamerica.com

Vanguard Group
800-662-7447
http://www.vanguard.com

PLANNING FOR RETIREMENT

Although few working people require income from their investments to meet routine expenses, most people will require income from outside sources in order to retire in security and comfort. There are three potential providers of retirement income: pension plans funded by an employer, government retirement funds, and an individual's own retirement fund. The best way to ensure your financial security after retirement is to arrange for retirement income from at least two or even all three of these sources. With life expectancy on the increase, retirees today are living a lot longer and are staying active, thus spending more money in retirement. Today, you must plan on having your retirement savings last 30 years or more.

employer-funded retirement plans   Can be pension plans, profit-sharing plans, or a combination of the two. Most pension plans define the benefits due and eligibility qualifications required of each employee in advance. They are designed to provide employees with a guaranteed income after they reach a certain age, generally 65, and retire. Some plans allow for early retirement at reduced benefits. In addition to providing income after retirement, many plans also provide vested benefits for employees who stop working for the company before they reach the minimum retirement age, death benefits, medical benefits, and a pension for surviving spouses.

employer-sponsored plans   Include 401(k) plans, in which you contribute a percentage of your paycheck before taxes and reduce your taxable income (and sometimes the employer matches your contribution), and 403(b) plans, which are like 401(k)s but are available to employees of not-for-profit and public-sector organizations. Many financial advisors recommend contributing the maximum allowed to these accounts, if you can afford to do so. You save on your taxes and benefit more from compounding returns.

profit-sharing plans   Differ from pension plans in that an employer's contributions to the fund are dependent on company profits. Profit-sharing plans also may have provisions for vesting at an earlier age and withdrawal and loan privileges.

If you are self-employed or own a small business with fewer than 20 employees, you have two options

Personal Finances

for setting up a retirement plan for your business. **Simplified employee pension individual retirement accounts** (SEP-IRAs) let you save up to 13.05 percent of pretax income, up to $24,000 a year. **Keogh plans** allow for the contribution of up to 20 percent of pretax income, to a maximum of $30,000 annually. Under a Keogh, you can establish a vesting schedule that requires employees to remain with the company a certain number of years before they are entitled to their entire savings.

Social Security   The basic retirement plan provided by the government. More than 90 percent of the workers in the United States are earning benefits under Social Security through contributions they and their employers make in the form of Social Security taxes. Social Security provides monthly payments to qualified workers who retire at age 62 or older; health insurance for the elderly under Medicare; and monthly payments to disabled workers and to spouses and children of workers who retire, become disabled, or die. However, if you retire at 62 you will receive a smaller amount of Social Security then if you wait until full retirement age at 65—or 67, for those born in 1960 or later. If you put off retirement until age 70, you stand to benefit even more with special credits you receive from Social Security for delaying your retirement. The dollar amount of benefits is dependent on the rate set by the government as well as on other sources of income the retiree has available. People qualify for Social Security benefits on the basis of "quarters of coverage." Workers earn one credit toward coverage for a set amount of income they earn, up to four credits each calendar year. A worker is eligible for retirement benefits if he or she has earned as many credits as the number of calendar years between age 21 (or since 1950) and retirement. Visit the Social Security Administration at www.ssa.gov to calculate your future benefits.

The future of Social Security, however, is uncertain. By 2013, benefits will start to exceed payroll revenues as millions of baby boomers start retiring. By 2030, every two people working will have to produce enough tax revenue to support one retiree. This imbalance will make it impossible for such a small work force to support the current Social Security system. Securing your own financial retirement by investing wisely may not only be your best bet but also your only bet toward a secure retirement.

individual retirement plans   Can be created according to needs and financial resources using many of the investments outlined above. The most popular individual plan, the **individual retirement account** (IRA), allows some individuals to deduct contributions of up to $2,000 a year from their income taxes. Married couples who file taxes jointly can take the full deduction if their adjusted gross income (AGI) is less than $40,000 or if one or both spouses are not covered by an employer-sponsored retirement plan. A single taxpayer with an income of less than $25,000 also is eligible for the full deduction. Single taxpayers earning between $25,000 and $40,000 and married joint-filers earning between $40,000 and $60,000 can take a partial deduction, depending on their income. If you are investing for the long term, it may make sense to maintain an IRA even if you cannot deduct your contributions. Many IRAs are simply mutual funds tailored to the needs of retirement-minded investors, so they can be used in much the same way and may better meet your retirement investing goals than other funds. In addition, conventional IRAs are tax-free until they pay out in your retirement years. A Roth IRA, which allows for contributions of up to $2,000 a year as long as your income is less than $110,000 (for singles) or $160,000 (for couples), is a nondeductible IRA in which your money grows tax free. You pay income on your money up front but when you withdraw the money in retirement those withdrawals are not taxed.

Several online tools can help you determine what you need to do now to secure your financial future. You can also opt to seek the advice of a financial planner, who for a fee or a commission can aid you in building a solid financial future.

COMMON INVESTMENT TERMS

accrued interest　Interest earned by a bond since the last payment was made.

Alternative Trading System (ATS)　An electronic system that allows securities to be traded even after the markets have closed, often for a more reasonable price than attainable by trading on an exchange. Some ATSs are also called electronic communication networks or ECNs.

AMEX　The American Stock Exchange.

appreciation　The increase in value of an investment.

asset　Something you own or that is owed to you.

bear market　A declining stock market.

bid and asked price　The highest price offered for a security at a given time *(bid)* and the lowest price accepted for that security at that time *(asked).*

Big Board　The New York Stock Exchange.

blue chip　The stock of a top-rated company known for the quality of its products and the security and return on investment of its stock; also the company itself.

bond　A corporation's note acknowledging indebtedness for a certain amount and promising to pay interest at a given rate on that amount as well as to pay back the principal on a certain date. *See also* **junk bond; Treasury bond.**

book value　The theoretical worth of a share of stock as shown on a company's balance sheet. This has little relationship to the stock's market value.

bull market　A rising stock market.

capital gain or capital loss　The gain or loss resulting from the sale of an asset.

capital stock　All shares of stock in a company, both common and preferred.

capitalization　All securities issued by a company, including bonds, common and preferred stock, and debentures.

collateral　Property or securities used by a borrower to secure a loan.

convertible securities　Securities that can be exchanged by the holder for common stock or another security.

coupon bond　A bond with coupons attached that are clipped by the holder and presented for payment of interest due.

current assets　The total amount of cash, securities, inventory, and receivables expected during the normal business cycle of a company, usually one year.

current liabilities　The total amount of debt and other payments that will be due during the normal business cycle of a company, usually one year.

debenture　An unsecured promissory note backed by a company's general credit.

discount　The amount of money below the issuing price of a stock or bond at which it sells.

discretionary account　A securities account that leaves some or all decisions about purchases and sales to the discretion of a broker.

dividend　A payment by a company equally divided among its stockholders. *See also* **stock dividend.**

Dow Jones average　The average price of selected stocks, used as an indicator of the stock market's performance.

equity　The interest stockholders have in a company, or the amount of property a property holder actually has paid for as opposed to the portion held by a mortgage.

ex-dividend　A stock that does not pay a recently declared dividend to its new purchaser.

Federal Deposit Insurance Corporation (FDIC)　The federal agency that insures amounts of up to $100,000 deposited in qualified banks.

fiduciary　Someone who acts on behalf of another in financial matters.

gilt-edged security   A high-grade preferred stock or bond issued by a company with a strong performance record.

income fund   A mutual fund designed to provide current income.

individual retirement account (IRA)   A tax-sheltered and sometimes tax-deductible retirement plan.

interest   The money paid by a borrower to a lender for the use of the borrowed money.

investment   The use of money to make more money.

junk bond   A high-risk, high-yielding corporate bond.

Keogh plan   A tax-sheltered retirement plan for self-employed people with no pension plans.

liabilities   All claims against and amounts owed by a person or company.

listed stock   Stock traded on a securities exchange.

margin   The portion of a stock's price paid by the buyer when the broker arranges for the remainder to be purchased on credit.

market order   An order to buy or sell at the current market price of a security.

maturity   The date on which a bond or loan is to be paid off.

money-market fund   A mutual fund that invests in short-term financial securities.

municipal bond   A bond issued by a local government.

mutual fund   An investment company that continually offers new stock and redeems outstanding shares on demand.

Nasdaq   The electronic market for trading over-the-counter securities. Companies on Nasdaq are predominately growth-oriented securities, many of which are technology stocks.

odd lot   An amount of stock bought or sold in units other than 10 shares or 100 shares.

offer   The price at which someone is willing to sell.

over-the-counter market   The arena in which stocks not listed on exchanges are bought and sold.

par   The issuing value of a share of common stock.

preferred stock   Stock that must receive its share of earnings before payment is made on common stock.

premium   The amount over par value by which a preferred stock is sold.

puts and calls   Options that give the right to sell or buy a specified number of shares of stock at a specified price within a specified time.

red herring   A preliminary prospectus issued to gauge interest in a new stock issue.

Securities and Exchange Commission (SEC)   The federal agency that oversees securities trading.

stock   Ownership shares in a company.

stock dividend   Shares distributed to current shareholders in a company in proportion to those they hold.

stock split   The division of currently outstanding shares into a larger number of shares.

tax shelter   A way in which taxes on income may be legally decreased, eliminated, or deferred.

tender offer   An offer by one company to purchase shares of stock in another company directly from its stockholders.

Treasury bill   A short-term U.S. government security sold at a discount in competitive bidding.

Treasury bond   A long-term U.S. government bond issued in $1,000 denominations.

yield   The amount of dividend or interest expressed as a percentage of the selling price.

zero-coupon bonds   Bonds that are sold at a discount from their face value but do not pay interest.

Personal Finances

TIPPING

"Domestic Travel" and "Foreign Travel" in chapter 24 **Go to**

The following list suggests what are generally considered to be adequate amounts to tip various people for services rendered. Keep in mind that tips are a way of expressing satisfaction. Larger tips should be given to those who provide extraordinarily good service; smaller tips or no tip at all should be given when service is poor.

Location	Person	Amount
Airport	Skycap	$1–$2 per bag
	In-flight personnel	None
Barbershop	Haircutter	15% of the cost, generally a minimum of $1
Beauty shop	One operator	15% of bill
	Person who washes hair	$2 or more depending on bill
	Manicurist	$2–3 or more depending on cost
	Spa services	15–20% of bill
Cruise ship	Staff	Expect to spend between $65 and $100 per person, per week on gratuities.
	Cabin Steward	$3–3.50 per person, per day
	Dining Room Waiter	$3–3.50 per person, per day
	Dining Room Busboy	$1.50–2.00 per day
	Wine Steward	$1.50 per person, per day of wine service
	Maitre d'/Head Waiter	$5.00 per person for entire cruise if exceptional service
	Room Service Waiter	$1–2 per order
	Bar Tab	On most cruise ships a 15% gratuity is automatically added to your bill at the end of the cruise
Deliveries	Pizza	$1–2 if short distance, $2–3 for longer distance or $5 or more for large delivery.
	Furniture	$5–10 per person, perhaps $20 if it is heavy or requires assembly
Driver	Taxi	15–20% of fare
	Limousine	20% of fare
Hotel	Housekeeping	$2–5 a night, consider more if you stay longer than one week
	Bellhop	$1–2 per bag, an additional $1 or more for showing the room
	Concierge	$5–10 (for restaurant reservations, theater tickets, etc.)
	Room-service waiter	15% of bill
	Lobby attendant	None for opening door or calling taxi from stand; $1 or more for help with luggage or finding a taxi on the street
	Desk clerk	None unless special service is given during long stay; then, $5
Restaurant	Waiter	15–20% of bill
	Headwaiter/maitre d'	None, unless special services are provided; then, about $5
	Wine steward	15% of wine bill
	Bartender	10–15% of bar bill
	Busperson	None
	Server at counter	15% of bill
	Coat check	$1–2 per coat
	Rest-room attendant	50 cents if provided with a handtowel only. $1 or more if special services are provided
	Car-park attendant	$1–2 given when car is brought to you
Sports arena	Usher	$1 per party if shown to your seat
Tour	Guide	$1–2 per day/per person
	Driver	$1–2 per day/per person
Train	Dining-car waiter	15% of bill
	Steward/bar-car waiter	15% of bar bill
	Redcap or porter	Posted rate plus 50¢

ADDITIONAL SOURCES OF INFORMATION

ORGANIZATIONS AND SERVICES

Consult the following organization for referrals to reputable planners:

Financial Planning Association
Atlanta—Denver—Washington D.C.
800-322-4237
404-845-0011
Fax: 404-845-3660
http://www.fpanet.org

MAGAZINES AND NEWSPAPERS

The following publications offer substantial coverage of events and trends that affect personal finances. Addresses and phone numbers are for subscriptions.

Barron's National Business Weekly
200 Burnett Rd.
Chicopee, MA 01020
800-544-0422
www.barrons.com

Business Week
1221 Avenue of the Americas
New York, NY 10020
800-635-1200
http://www.businessweek.com

Forbes
60 Fifth Ave.
New York, NY 10011
800-888-9896
http://www.forbes.com

Fortune
Time Life Building
Rockefeller Center
New York, NY 10020
800-621-8000
http://www.fortune.com

Kiplinger's Personal Finance Magazine
The Kiplinger Washington Editors, Inc.
1729 H St., NW
Washington, DC 20006
800-544-0155
http://kiplinger.com

Money
Time Life Building
Rockefeller Center
New York, NY 10020
http://www.money.com

The Wall Street Journal
84 2nd Ave
Chicopee, MA 01020
800-568-7625
http://www.wsj.com

BOOKS

Chilton, David. *The Wealthy Barber*, 3rd ed. Prima Publishing, 1998.

Clifford, Denis, and Cora Johnson. *Plan Your Estate*, 5th ed. Nolo Press, 2000.

Dunnan, Nancy. *Dun and Bradstreet Guide to Your Investments 1999*. HarperCollins, 1999.

Eisenberg, Richard. *The Money Book of Personal Finance*. Warner, 1998.

Garner, Robert J., et al. *Ernst & Young's Personal Financial Planning Guide*, 3rd ed. Wiley, 1999.

Good-Garton, Julie. *All About Mortgages: Insider Tips for Financing Your Home*, 2nd ed. Dearborn Publishing, 1999.

Hunt, Mary. *The Complete Cheapskate: How to Get Out of Debt, Stay Out and Break Free from Money Worries Forever*. Broadman & Holman, 1998.

Kiplinger's Buying & Selling a Home, 6th ed. Kiplinger Books, 1999.

Patterson, Martha P. *The New Working Woman's Guide to Retirement Planning: Saving and Investing Now for a Secure Future*, 2nd ed. University of Pennsylvania Press, 1999.

Rowland, Mary. *The New Commonsense Guide to Mutual Funds,* revised. Bloomberg Press, 1998.

Siegel, Alan M., et al. *The Wall Street Journal Guide to Planning Your Financial Future: The Easy-To-Read Guide to Planning for Retirement*. Fireside, 1998.

Tyson, Eric. *Personal Finances for Dummies*, 3rd ed. Hungry Minds, Inc., 2000.

Tyson, Eric, and Ray Brown. *Mortgages for Dummies*. Hungry Minds, Inc., 1999.

21

LEGAL INFORMATION

FORMS AND CONTRACTS

The documents in the following sections are fairly standard versions of simple agreements, requests, or statements. They are meant to demonstrate the basic content of similar documents. Because laws vary from state to state (and because agreements can have their own special circumstances, terms, or other complexities), it is always a good idea to consult with a lawyer before drawing up or signing a contract. For additional legal forms and contracts, consult the Internet Legal Resource Guide: http://www.ilrg.com/forms.

BILL OF SALE

Bill of Sale
of

_____

STATE OF   )
)   ss:

COUNTY OF   )

KNOW YE ALL MEN BY THESE PRESENTS,

That I, _____ , of

_____ ,

       Street Address   *City*   *State*   *Zip*

for and in consideration of payment of the sum of $ _____ , the receipt of which is hereby acknowledged, do hereby grant, bargain, sell, and convey to:

_____ , of

_____ ,

       Street Address   *City*   *State*   *Zip*

and his/her heirs, executors, administrators, successors, and assigns the following property:

_____

_____

_____

_____

      I hereby warrant that I am the lawful owner of said property and that I have full legal right, power, and authority to sell said property. I further warrant said property to be free of all encumbrances and that I will warrant and defend said property hereby sold against any and all persons whomsoever.

      IN WITNESS WHEREOF, I, the seller, have hereto set my hand and seal this _____ day of _____ , 20_____ .

                                       (Signed) _____

                                                    Seller

Legal Information

CERTIFICATE OF NOTARY

A certificate of notary often accompanies agreements or statements; it may be required in some localities. A certificate of notary might be useful with the following documents in this section:

- Bill of Sale
- Declaration of Gift
- Living Will
- Power of Attorney
- Privacy Act/Freedom of Information Act Request
- Request for Reason for Adverse Credit Action

Certificate of Notary

STATE OF)

) ss:

COUNTY OF)

On this _____ day of _____ , 20___ , before me personally came and appeared _____ , known, and known to me, to be the individual described in and who executed the foregoing instrument, and who duly acknowledged to me that he/she executed same for the purpose therein contained.

IN WITNESS WHEREOF, I hereunto set my hand and official seal.

_____

Notary Public

My commission expires:_____

CONTRACT

Agreement Between Owner and Contractor

THIS AGREEMENT is hereby entered into this _____ day of _____ , 20_____ , between _____ , of

_____

| *Street Address* | *City* | *Street* | *Zip* | *Phone* |

hereinafter called Owner, and _____ , of

_____

| *Street Address* | *City* | *Street* | *Zip* | *Phone* |

hereinafter called the Contractor.

The said parties, for the considerations hereinafter mentioned, hereby agree to the following:

Description of the Work

1. The Contractor shall provide all materials and labor required to perform all of the work for:

as shown on the drawing(s), and set forth in the specifications and/or description(s) prepared by _____ , which drawing(s) and specifications and/or description(s) are identified by the signatures of the parties to this agreement, and which form a part of this agreement and are incorporated by reference herein for all purposes.

Payment

2. Under the terms of this agreement, the Owner agrees to pay the Contractor, for materials to be furnished and work to be done, the sum of _____ ($ _____), subject to any additions or deductions as hereinafter provided for in this agreement, and to make the following payments:

_____

_____

_____

and that the final payment shall be made subject to the hereinafter stated conditions of this agreement.

It is agreed that no payment made under this agreement shall be considered conclusive evidence of full performance of this contract, either wholly or in part by the Contractor, and that acceptance of payment shall not be considered by the Contractor to be acceptance by the Owner of any defective materials or workmanship.

Liens

3. Final payment shall not be due until such time as the Contractor has provided the Owner with a release of any liens arising from this agreement; or receipts for payment in full for all materials and labor

for which a lien could be filed; or a bond satisfactory to the Owner indemnifying the Owner against any lien.

Timely Completion of the Work

4. The Contractor agrees that the various portions of the work shall be completed on or before the following dates:

_____

_____

_____

and the entire work shall be completed on or before the _____ day of _____ , 20_____.

In the event the work is not completed by the aforementioned date, the Owner shall be entitled to receive as damages from the Contractor, the sum of _____ ($ _____) per _____ , it being agreed that the aforementioned sum is reasonable, taking into account the difficulty in determining the exact amount of damages the Owner would sustain in the event of said delay, and that the agreed sum shall be considered as liquidated damages.

If the Contractor is delayed in the completion of the work by any changes ordered in the work, by acts of God, fire, flood, or any other unavoidable casualties; or by labor strikes, late delivery of materials; or by neglect of the Owner, his agents or representatives; or by any subcontractor employed by the Contractor; the time for completion of the work shall be extended for the same period as the delay occasioned by any of the aforementioned causes.

Surveys and Easements

5. The Owner shall provide and pay for all surveys. All easements for access across the property of another, and for permanent changes, and for the construction or erection of structures shall also be obtained and paid for by the Owner.

Licenses, Permits, and Building Codes

6. The Contractor shall obtain and pay for all permits and licenses required for the prosecution and timely completion of the work. The Contractor shall comply with all appropriate regulations relating to the conduct of the work and shall advise the Owner of any specifications or drawings which are at variance therewith.

Materials and Equipment

7. The Contractor shall provide and pay for all materials, tools, and equipment required for the prosecution and timely completion of the work. Unless otherwise specified in writing, all materials shall be new and of good quality.

Samples

8. Whenever the Owner may require, the Contractor will furnish for approval all samples as directed, and the work shall be in accordance with approved samples.

Labor and Supervision

9. In the prosecution of the work the Contractor shall at all times keep a competent foreman and a sufficient number of workers skilled in their trades to suitably perform the work.

continues

Agreement Between Owner and Contractor, Continued

The foreman shall represent the Contractor and, in the absence of the Contractor, all instructions given by the Owner to the foreman shall be binding upon the Contractor as though given to the Contractor. Upon request of the foreman, instructions shall be in writing.

Alterations and Changes

10. All changes and deviations in the work ordered by the Owner must be in writing, the contract sum being increased or decreased accordingly by the Contractor. Any claims for increases in the cost of the work must be presented by the Contractor to the Owner in writing, and written approval of the Owner shall be obtained by the Contractor before proceeding with the ordered change or revision.

In the event that additional work, not shown on the drawings and/or not described in the specifications, is required to comply with laws, regulations, or building codes, such additional work shall be considered as done under the terms of this agreement.

Correction of Deficiencies

11. The Contractor agrees to reexecute any work that does not conform to the drawings and specifications, warrants the work performed, and further agrees that he shall remedy any defects resulting from faulty materials or workmanship that shall become evident during a period of one year after completion of the work. This provision shall apply with equal force to all work performed by subcontractors as to work that is performed by direct employees of the Contractor.

Protection of the Work

12. It shall be the responsibility of the Contractor to reasonably protect the work, the property of the Owner, and adjacent property and the public; and the Contractor shall be responsible for any damage, injury, or death resulting from his negligence or from any intentional act of the Contractor or the Contractor's employees, agents, or subcontractors.

Cleaning Up

13. The Contractor shall keep the premises free from the accumulation of waste and, upon completion of the work, shall remove all waste, equipment, and other materials and leave the premises in broom-clean condition.

Contractor's Liability Insurance

14. The Contractor shall obtain insurance to protect himself against claims for property damage arising out of his or any subcontractor's performance of this contract; and to protect himself against claims under provisions of Workman's Compensation and any similar employee benefit acts, and from claims for bodily injury, including death, due to performance of this contract by the Contractor or any subcontractor employed for the performance of this contract.

Owner's Liability Insurance

15. It shall be the responsibility of the Owner, at the Owner's option, to obtain insurance to protect himself from the contingent liability of claims for property damage and bodily injury, including death, that may arise from the performance of this contract.

Fire Insurance with Extended Coverage

16. The Owner shall obtain fire insurance with extended coverage at 100 percent of the value of the entire structure, including materials and labor related to the work described in this agreement. Certificates of insurance shall be filed with the Contractor if he so requests. The aforesaid fire insurance need

not include tools, equipment, scaffolding, or forms owned or rented by the Contractor, any subcontractor, or their respective employees.

Owner's Right to Terminate the Agreement

17. In the event the Contractor shall fail to meet the provisions of this agreement, the Owner shall, after seven (7) days' written notice to the Contractor and his surety, have the right to take possession of the premises in order to complete the work as specified in the agreement. The Owner may deduct the cost thereof from any payment then and thereafter due to the Contractor or may, at his option, terminate the agreement, take possession of any materials, and complete the work as he deems appropriate. If the unpaid balance of the contracted sum exceeds the Owner's expenses of completing the work, such excess shall be paid to the Contractor. If such expense shall exceed the unpaid balance, the Contractor shall pay the difference to the Owner.

Contractor's Right to Terminate the Agreement

18. In the event the Owner shall fail to pay the Contractor within seven (7) days after the date upon which payment shall become due, the Contractor shall have the right, after seven (7) days' written notice to the Owner, to stop work and may, at his option, terminate the agreement and recover from the Owner payment for all work executed, plus any loss sustained, plus a reasonable profit, plus damages.

In the event the work is stopped by any court or other public authority for a period of thirty (30) days through no fault of the Contractor, the Contractor shall have the right to stop work and may, at his option, terminate the agreement and recover from the Owner payment for all work executed, plus any loss sustained, plus a reasonable profit, plus damages.

Assignment of Rights

19. Neither the Owner nor Contractor shall have the right to assign any rights or interest occurring under this agreement without the written consent of the other; nor shall the Contractor assign any sums due, or to become due, to him under the provisions of this agreement.

Access and Inspection

20. The Owner, Owner's representative, and public authorities shall at all times have access to the work.

An appropriately licensed representative of the Owner, whose authority shall be set forth in writing by the Owner, shall have the authority to direct the removal of any materials and the taking down of any portions of the work failing to meet drawings, specifications, laws, regulations, or building codes; the reexecution of said work deemed as being done under the provisions of Article 11 of this agreement.

Any other removal of materials or taking down of any portions of the work as directed by the Owner's representative shall be in writing and at the sole expense of the Owner.

Attorney Fees

21. Attorney fees and court costs shall be paid by the defendant in the event that judgment must be obtained, and is, to enforce this agreement or any breach thereof.

IN WITNESS WHEREOF, the parties hereto set their hands and seals the day and year written above.

_____   _____
Witness as to Owner   *Owner*

_____   _____
Witness as to Contractor   *Contractor*

Legal Information

DECLARATION OF GIFT

Declaration of Gift

TO ALL TO WHOM THESE PRESENTS SHALL COME OR MAY CONCERN, KNOW THAT on this _____ day of _____ , 20___ , I, _____ , of _____ ,

Street	_City_	_State_	_Zip_

being of sound and disposing mind and memory, do hereby irrevocably give, bestow, and deliver up

to _____ ,

of _____ ,

Street	_City_	_State_	_Zip_

all of my right, title, and interest in the following described property valued at _____ _____ ($ _____):

_____

_____

_____

_____

_____

_____

_____

_____

IN WITNESS WHEREOF, I hereunto set my hand and seal on the date above mentioned.

_____

LEASES

"Open" Rental Agreement

THIS AGREEMENT is made this _____ day of _____ , 20_____ ,
between _____ , of

_____
| Street Address | City | State | Zip |

hereinafter called "Owner," and _____ , of

_____
| Street Address | City | State | Zip |

hereinafter called "Renter."

Property

_____

_____

_____

_____

_____
| Year | Make | Model/Type |

_____
| Capacity | Horsepower | Serial No. |

The Owner warrants that to the best of his/her knowledge and belief, the aforesaid property is free of any known faults or deficiencies which would affect its safe and dependable operation under normal and prudent usage.

Rental Period

The Owner agrees to rent the above-described property to the Renter for a period of _____
beginning _____ and ending _____ .

Use of Property

_____

_____

_____

_____

_____

The Renter further agrees that the rented property (A) shall not be used beyond any rated capacity; (B) shall not be used for any illegal purpose; (C) shall not be used in any manner for which it was not designed, built, or designated by the manufacturer; (D) will not be used in a negligent manner; (E) will not be

continues

Open Rental Agreement, Continued

operated by any other person without the written permission of the Owner; and (F) will not be removed from the designated area of use or operation.

Area of Use or Operation

The Renter agrees to operate/use the above-described property only at the following location or within the following described area(s):

_____

_____

_____

Insurance

The Renter hereby agrees that he/she shall fully indemnify the Owner for any and all damage to or loss of the rented property and any accessories or related equipment during the term of this Agreement whether caused by fire, theft, flood, vandalism, or any other cause, except that which shall be determined to have been caused by a fault or deficiency of the rented property, accessories, or equipment.

Rental Rate

The Renter hereby agrees to pay the Owner at the rate of $ _____ per _____ for the use of said property and any accessories/equipment. Any fuel used shall be paid for by the Renter.

Deposit

The Renter further agrees to make a deposit of $ _____ with the Owner, said deposit to be used, in the event of loss of or damage to the rented property and any accessories/equipment during the term of this Agreement, to defray fully or partially the cost of necessary repairs or replacement. In the absence of any damage or loss, said deposit shall be credited toward payment of the rental fee, and any excess shall be returned to the Renter.

Return of Property to Owner

The Renter hereby agrees to return the rented property and any accessories/equipment to the Owner at _____ no later than

_____ .

Termination of Agreement

It is mutually agreed that the Renter shall have the right to terminate this Agreement at any time by payment of one full day's rental for each 24-hour period or any part thereof, during which the Renter has retained possession of the property and any accessories/equipment during the term of this Agreement.

IN WITNESS WHEREOF, the parties hereto hereby execute this Agreement.

(Signed) _____
                                                                 Renter

(Signed) _____
                                                                 Owner

Seasonal Lease Agreement—Furnished Country/Seashore House

Landlord_____

                                           Address   *Phone*

Managing Agent _____

_____

                                         Address   *Phone*

Premises _____

_____

Tenant _____

_____

                                         Address   *Phone*

Tenant _____

_____

                                         Address   *Phone*

1. The LANDLORD hereby leases to _____ (and) _____ , hereinafter termed TENANT, the premises described above for a term of _____ beginning _____ and ending _____ , at a monthly rate of $_____ , making a total rental amount payable under this lease of $_____ .

2. The tenant agrees to pay the rent in the following manner:_____ (Landlord specify if payments are to be made by mail, and if so, to what address. If payments are to be made to the landlord or his agent in person, state the place where, and the person to whom, payments should be made.)

3. The tenant, in addition to rent, agrees to pay all charges for water, gas, fuel oil, and electricity used during the term of the lease, such charges to be paid monthly in addition to rent.

4. Upon receipt of any payment for rent or utilities in cash, the landlord agrees to issue a receipt stating the tenant's name, a description of the premises, the amount paid, the date paid, and the period for which rent or utilities is paid.

5. The tenant agrees to place a security deposit of $ _____ , to be used by the landlord at the termination of this lease for the cost of replacing or repairing damage, if any, to the premises or furnishings caused by the intentional or negligent acts of the tenant.

6. The landlord agrees to return said security deposit to the tenant upon the tenant's vacating the premises subject to the terms and conditions herein.

7. The tenant agrees to take good care of the premises and of the furnishings therein, and at the end of the term of this lease to deliver up to the landlord the premises and furnishings in good order, normal wear and tear excepted.

8. The landlord covenants that the leased premises are, to the best of his or her knowledge, clean, safe, sound, and healthful and that there exists no violation of any applicable housing code, law, or

Legal Information

continues

Seasonal Lease Agreement, Continued

regulation of which he or she is aware, and that no such violation will be permitted to exist during the term of this lease or any extension thereof.

9. The tenant shall promptly comply with all laws, orders, ordinances, and regulations pertaining to his or her use of the premises, and the tenant shall not keep therein any article or thing of a dangerous, flammable, or explosive nature that might be pronounced "hazardous" or "extra hazardous" by any responsible insurance company.

10. The tenant shall, in case of fire, give immediate notice to the proper authorities and to the landlord, who will cause the damage to be promptly repaired; but if the premises be so damaged that the landlord shall decide to terminate this lease, then upon 10 days' personal or written notice to the tenant, this lease shall terminate and the accrued rent shall be paid up to the time of the fire.

11. The tenant shall do no cooking in any room used for sleeping purposes, but shall have the right to use jointly with any other tenants a room set aside by the landlord for that purpose.

12. The tenant shall, at reasonable times, give access to the landlord or his agents for any reasonable and lawful purpose. Except in situations of compelling emergency, the landlord shall give the tenant at least 24 hours' notice of intention to seek access, the date and time at which access will be sought, and the reason therefor.

13. In the event of default by the tenant, the tenant shall remain liable for all rent due or to become due during the term of this lease. The landlord shall have the obligation to relet the premises in the landlord's name for the balance of the term, or longer, and will apply proceeds of such reletting toward the reduction of the tenant's obligations enumerated herein.

14. The tenant shall permit the landlord or his agents to show the premises at reasonable hours, to persons desiring to rent or purchase same, 30 days prior to the expiration of this lease, and will permit the notice "To Let" or "For Sale" to be placed on said premises and remain thereon without hindrance or molestation after said date.

15. The tenant shall not assign this lease, nor underlet or underlease the premises, or any part thereof, nor make any alterations to the premises, nor permit same to be used at any time during the term of this lease for any other purpose than a private residence.

16. This lease, and any attached List of Furnishings signed by both parties and dated, and incorporated herein by reference for all purposes, constitutes the entire agreement between the parties hereto. No changes shall be made herein except by writing, signed by each party and dated.

17. In the event legal action is required to enforce any provision of this agreement, the prevailing party shall be entitled to recover reasonable attorney's fees and costs.

18. This lease, when filled out and signed, is a binding legal obligation.

IN WITNESS WHEREOF, the parties hereto have executed this agreement.

_____   _____
Witness as to landlord   *Landlord*
                                                   By _____

_____   _____
Witness as to landlord   *Landlord*

                                                   _____
                                                              Tenant

_____   Dated this _____ day of _____ , 20_____ .
Witness as to landlord

Lease Agreement—Unfurnished Apartment

Landlord _____

_____
       Address   *Phone*

Managing Agent _____

_____
       Address   *Phone*

Premises _____

       Address   *Apt. No.*

Tenant _____

Tenant _____

1. The LANDLORD hereby leases to _____ (and) _____ , hereinafter termed TENANT, the premises described above for a term of beginning and ending _____ , at a monthly rate of $ _____ , making a total rental amount payable under this lease of $ _____ .

2. The tenant agrees to pay the rent herein provided subject to the terms and conditions set forth herein.

3. Rent shall be payable in equal monthly installments to be paid in advance on the _____ day of each month.

4. Rent shall be payable in the following manner:
(Specify above if payments are to be made by mail, and if so, to what address. If payments are to be made to the landlord or the landlord's agent in person, state the place where, and the person to whom, payments are to be made.)

5. Upon receiving any payment of rent in cash, the landlord agrees to issue a receipt stating the tenant's name, a description of the premises, the amount of rent paid, the date paid, and the period for which rent is paid.

6. The landlord covenants that the leased premises are, to the best of his or her knowledge, clean, safe, sound, and healthful and that there exists no violation of any applicable housing code, law, or regulation of which he or she is aware.

7. The tenant agrees to comply with all sanitary laws, ordinances, and rules, and all orders of the Board of Health or other authorities affecting the cleanliness, occupancy, and preservation of the premises during the term of this lease.

8. The tenant shall use the leased premises exclusively as a private residence for no more than _____ persons, and the tenant will not make alterations therein without the written consent of the landlord.

9. The tenant shall keep fixtures in said apartment in good order and repair, and the tenant shall cause to be made, at the tenant's expense, all required repairs to heating and air-conditioning apparatus, refrigerator, range, electric and gas fixtures, and plumbing work whenever such damage shall have resulted from misuse, waste, or neglect, it being understood that the landlord is to have same in good order and repair when giving possession.

Legal Information

continues

Lease Agreement—Unfurnished Apartment, Continued

10. The tenant shall not keep or have in the leased premises any article or thing of a dangerous, flammable, or explosive nature that might be pronounced "hazardous" or "extra hazardous" by any responsible insurance company.

11. The tenant shall give prompt notice to the landlord of any dangerous, defective, unsafe, or emergency condition in the leased premises, said notice being given by any suitable means. The landlord shall repair and correct said conditions promptly upon receiving notice thereof from the tenant.

12. The landlord covenants that all essential services are now provided and shall be provided at all times during the term of this lease and any extension, renewal, or continuation thereof, except where any interruption of essential services shall be for maintenance or for cause beyond control of the landlord such as strike, storm, civil insurrection, fire, or acts of God. "Essential services" hereunder are defined as heat, hot and cold running water, a properly functioning toilet, light in public areas, and suitable building security.

13. The _____ shall pay for gas and electricity except to the extent otherwise set forth herein.

14. The landlord covenants that consumption of electricity for the public halls and other common areas and use and consumption of gas for heat or hot water in public areas are recorded on separate meters, and that said electricity and gas are and will at all times be billed to and paid by the landlord.

15. The tenant covenants that during the last 30 days of this lease, or any renewal thereof, the landlord or his agents, with reasonable notice, and at reasonable hours, have the privilege of showing the premises to prospective buyers or tenants.

16. The tenant shall, at reasonable times, give access to the landlord or his agents for any reasonable and lawful purpose. Except in situations of compelling emergency, or to show the premises for rental or sale, the landlord agrees to give the tenant 24 hours' notice, stating the time and date when access will be sought, and the reason therefor.

17. The landlord covenants that the tenant and the tenant's family shall have, hold, and enjoy the leased premises for the term of this lease, subject to the provisions and conditions set forth herein.

18. The tenant covenants that he shall not commit nor permit a nuisance in or upon the premises, that he shall not maliciously or by reason of gross negligence damage the premises, and that he shall not engage in conduct so as to interfere substantially with the comfort and safety of occupants of adjacent apartments or buildings.

19. The tenant agrees to place a security deposit with the landlord in the amount of $ _____ , to be used by the landlord for the cost of replacing and/or repairing damage, if any, to the premises caused by the intentional or negligent acts of the tenant.

20. The landlord agrees, within 10 days of receiving said security deposit, to deposit same in an interest-bearing account in a banking organization, in which said deposit shall earn interest at a rate which shall be the prevailing rate earned by other such deposits made with banking organizations in such circumstances.

21. The landlord agrees, within 10 days of making such deposit, to notify the tenant, in writing, of the name and address of the banking organization in which the deposit of security money has been made.

22. The landlord shall be entitled to receive, as administrative expenses, an amount equal to 1 percent per annum upon the security payment so deposited, which shall be in lieu of all other administrative and custodial expenses. The balance of the interest paid by the banking organization shall be the money of

the tenant and shall be paid to the tenant on each anniversary of this lease or any extension or renewal thereof.

23. The landlord agrees to return said security deposit to the tenant within 10 days of the tenant's vacating the leased premises subject to the terms and conditions set forth herein.

24. In the event of any breach by the tenant of any of the tenant's covenants or agreements herein, the landlord may give the tenant five days' notice to cure said breach, setting forth in writing which covenants or agreements have been breached. If any breach is not cured within said five-day period, or reasonable steps to effectuate said cure are not commenced and diligently pursued within said five-day period and thereafter until said breach has been cured, the landlord may terminate this lease upon five days' additional notice to the tenant, with said notice being in lieu of a Notice to Quit, which tenant hereby waives. The tenant shall then become liable for the cost of landlord's normal redecorating and cleaning expenses related to preparation of the premises for rental to a succeeding tenant.

Said termination shall be ineffective if the tenant cures said breach or commences and diligently pursues reasonable steps to effectuate such cure at any time prior to the expiration of said five-day termination. Upon terminating this lease as provided herein, the landlord or his agent may commence proceedings against the tenant for his removal as provided for by law.

25. In the event of any breach by the landlord of any of the landlord's covenants or agreements herein, the tenant may give the landlord 10 days' notice to cure said breach, setting forth in writing the manner in which said covenants and agreements have been breached. If said breach is not cured within said 10-day period, or reasonable steps to effectuate said cure are not commenced and diligently pursued within said 10-day period and thereafter until said breach has been cured, rent hereunder shall be fully abated from the time at which said 10 days' notice expired until such time as the landlord has fully cured the breach set forth in the notice provided for in this paragraph.

26. In no case shall any abatement of rent hereunder be effected where the condition set forth in the notice provided for herein was created by the intentional or negligent act of the tenant, but the landlord shall have the burden of proving that rent abatement may not be effected for the foregoing reason.

27. The landlord agrees to deliver possession of the leased premises at the beginning of the term provided for herein. In the event of the landlord's failure to deliver possession at the beginning of said term, the tenant shall have the right to rescind this lease and to recover any consideration paid under terms of this agreement.

28. The tenant agrees that this lease shall be subject to and subordinate to any mortgage or mortgages now on said premises or which any owner of said premises may hereafter at any time elect to place on said premises.

29. Unless otherwise provided for elsewhere in this lease, any notice required or authorized herein shall be given in writing, one copy of said notice mailed via U.S. certified mail, return receipt requested, and one copy of said notice mailed via U.S. first-class mail.

Notice to the tenant shall be mailed to him at the leased premises. Notice to the landlord shall be mailed to him, or to the managing agent, at their respective addresses as set forth herein, or at such new address as to which the tenant has been duly notified.

30. This lease constitutes the entire agreement between the parties hereto. No changes shall be made herein except by writing, signed by each party and dated. The failure to enforce any right or remedy

continues

Lease Agreement—Unfurnished Apartment, Continued

hereunder, and the payment and acceptance of rent hereunder, shall not be deemed a waiver by either party of such right or remedy in the absence of a writing as provided for herein.

31. In the event legal action is required to enforce any provision of this agreement, the prevailing party shall be entitled to recover reasonable attorney's fees and costs.

32. The landlord and tenant agree that this apartment lease, when filled out and signed, is a binding legal obligation.

IN WITNESS WHEREOF, the parties hereto have executed this agreement.

_____

Landlord

By _____

_____
Witness as to landlord

_____
Witness as to landlord

_____

Tenant

_____
Witness as to tenant

_____
Witness as to tenant

_____

Tenant

_____
Witness as to tenant

_____
Witness as to tenant

Dated this _____ day of _____ , 20____ .

LIVING WILL

Living Will

Directive to Physicians:

I, _____ , of

_____ ,

| Street Address | Apt. No. | City | State | Zip |

being of sound mind, do hereby willfully and voluntarily make known my desire that my life not be prolonged under any of the following conditions, and do hereby further declare:

1. If I should, at any time, have an incurable condition caused by any disease or illness, or by any accident or injury, and be determined by any two or more physicians to be in a terminal condition whereby the use of "heroic measures" or the application of life-sustaining procedures would only serve to delay the moment of my death, and where my attending physician has determined that my death is imminent whether or not such "heroic measures" or life-sustaining measures are employed, I direct that such measures and procedures be withheld or withdrawn and that I be permitted to die naturally.

2. In the event of my inability to give directions regarding the application of life-sustaining procedures or the use of "heroic measures," it is my intention that this directive shall be honored by my family and physicians as my final expression of my right to refuse medical and surgical treatment, and my acceptance of the consequences of such refusal.

3. I am mentally, emotionally, and legally competent to make this directive and I fully understand its import.

4. I reserve the right to revoke this directive at any time.

5. This directive shall remain in force until revoked.

IN WITNESS WHEREOF, I have hereunto set my hand and seal this _____ day of _____ , 20_____ .

(Signed) _____

Declaration of Witness:

The declarant is personally known to me and I believe him/her to be of sound mind and emotionally and legally competent to make the herein-contained **Directive to Physicians**. I am not related to the declarant by blood or marriage, nor would I be entitled to any portion of the declarant's estate upon his/her decease, nor am I an attending physician of the declarant, nor an employee of the attending physician, nor an employee of a health-care facility in which the declarant is a patient, nor a patient in a health-care facility in which the declarant is a patient, nor am I a person who has any claim against any portion of the estate of the declarant upon his/her decease.

(Signed) _____   (Signed) _____

Witness   *Witness*

_____   _____

Address   *Address*

Legal Information

POWER OF ATTORNEY

Power of Attorney

STATE OF   )
)   ss:

COUNTY OF   )

KNOW YE ALL MEN BY THESE PRESENTS,

That I, _____ , of

_____ ,

      Street Address   *Apt. No.*   *City*   *State*   *Zip*

do hereby make, constitute, and appoint _____ , of

_____ ,

      Street Address   *Apt. No.*   *City*   *State*   *Zip*

as my true and lawful Attorney-in-Fact, for me and in my name, place, and stead to:

_____

_____

_____

_____

_____

     I further give and grant to my said Attorney-in-Fact full power and authority to do and perform every act necessary and proper to be done in the exercise of any of the foregoing powers as fully as I might or could do if personally present, with full power of substitution and revocation, hereby ratifying and confirming all that my said Attorney-in-Fact shall lawfully do, or cause to be done by virtue hereof.

     This instrument may not be changed orally.

     IN WITNESS WHEREOF, I have hereunto set my hand and seal this day of _____ , 20__ .

                                (Signed) _____

PRIVACY ACT/FREEDOM OF INFORMATION ACT REQUEST

Attn: _____

    This is a request under provisions of Title 5 USC, Sec. 552, the Freedom of Information Act, and Title 5 USC, Sec. 552a, the Privacy Act.

    Please furnish me with copies of all records on me retrievable by the use of an individual identifier and by the use of any combination of identifiers (e.g., name + date of birth + Social Security number, etc.) that are contained in the following systems of records:

_____

_____

_____

_____

    In order to identify myself and to facilitate your search of records systems, I provide the following information:

_____

    Last Name   *First*   *Middle*

_____

    Street   *City*   *State*   *Zip*

_____

    Date of Birth   *Place of Birth*   *Sex*   *Social Security Number*

    In the event that any part or all of my records are withheld, I request a complete list of all records being withheld and the specific exemption being claimed for the withholding of each.

    In the event that search and copying fees are estimated to exceed $ _____ , I request an opportunity to review such records, or to have a duly authorized representative review such records, in order to select those to be copied.

    If you have any questions regarding this request, please telephone me at _____ weekdays between _____ and _____ or write to me at the above address.

    As provided for by Sec. 552(a)(6)(i) of the Freedom of Information Act, I shall expect to receive a reply within twenty (20) business days.

                           Sincerely,

                         _____

Legal Information

PROMISSORY NOTE

Promissory Note

$ _____

Date _____

_____ after the above date I promise to pay to the order of _____
(number of days)

the sum of _____ ($ _____),
together with interest at _____ percent per annum, payable at
_____.

The maker and endorser of this note further agree to waive demand, notice of nonpayment and protest, and in case suit shall be brought for the collection hereof, or the same has to be collected upon demand of an attorney, to pay reasonable attorney's fees for making such collection. Deferred interest payments to bear interest from maturity at _____ percent per annum, payable semiannually.

(Signed) _____
Maker

(Signed) _____
Endorser

Due _____

REQUEST FOR REASON FOR ADVERSE CREDIT ACTION

Request for Reason for Adverse Credit Action

Date: _____

Dear _____

On _____ , I was notified that my application for credit dated _____ was denied based upon information received by you from a source other than a consumer credit reporting agency.

Pursuant to my right under the Fair Credit Reporting Act, Title 15 USC, Sec. 1681m(b), I hereby request that the nature of the information received by you be disclosed to me.

Please forward such information to me at the above address.

Thank you for your prompt attention to this matter.

Sincerely,

_____

SECURITY AGREEMENT

Security Agreement

STATE OF   )

)   ss:

COUNTY OF   )

KNOW YE ALL MEN BY THESE PRESENTS,

That I, _____ , of

_____ ,

   Street Address   *Apt. No.*   *City*   *State*   *Zip*

hereinafter called "Debtor," hereby grant to _____ , of

_____ ,

   Street Address   *Apt. No.*   *City*   *State*   *Zip*

hereinafter called the "Secured Party," a security interest in the following described property as collateral to secure payment of the obligation described herein.

Collateral

_____

_____

_____

_____

Obligation

_____

_____

_____

_____

    Default in the payment of all or any part of the obligation described is a default under this Agreement. Upon such default, the Secured Party may declare all of the above-described obligation(s) immediately due and payable and shall have the remedies of a secured party under provisions of the Uniform Commercial Code. In the event legal action is required to enforce any provision of this Agreement, the prevailing party shall be entitled to recover reasonable attorney's fees and costs.

    The Debtor hereby agrees to exercise reasonable caution and care in use of the herein-described collateral; to adequately insure or keep insured the described collateral; not to attempt to sell, assign, or dispose of said collateral or his/her interest therein; not to encumber nor to permit any encumbrance against same; and not to remove said collateral from the county where the Debtor resides without written permission of the Secured Party.

Legal Information

continues

Security Agreement, Continued

EXECUTED this _____ day of _____ , 20___ .

(Signed) _____
Debtor

(Signed) _____
Secured Party

STATUTE OF LIMITATIONS

A statute of limitations defines the time span after an alleged offense during which legal action may be brought. After that time has elapsed, legal proceedings cannot be initiated, regardless of a case's merits.

If you angrily shake your fist at someone, it's legally considered "assault." If you follow up your actions by punching the person in the nose, the offense is "assault and battery."

FEDERAL STATUTE OF LIMITATIONS

CAPITAL OFFENSES

There is no limitation on prosecution in cases punishable by death and in the crime of murder, even when the death penalty is not prescribed.

NONCAPITAL OFFENSES

The limitation on noncapital offenses is five years, although Congress may make specific exceptions.

STATE STATUTE OF LIMITATIONS

This varies by crime and by state. On the World Wide Web, check http://www.findlaw.com/11stategov/ for links to Web pages for all 50 states. Each state Web page has extensive links to legal resources within that state, including legislative information, state constitution, statutes, and court opinions.

COPYRIGHTS

The copyright law protects works of authorship, published or unpublished, in any tangible medium of expression. Under this law, creators of—among other things—books, theatrical works, computer programs, videotapes, movies, music, lyrics, choreography, pantomimes, and recordings can secure exclusive rights to perform, display, or reproduce their works. These individuals have a property right for their work and may license it for reproduction or other use.

However, anyone may make "fair use" of copyrighted material. The definition of this term depends on who is using the material, how much is used, the percentage of the entire work that the excerpt used constitutes, the purpose of the use, and the effect such use may have on the ability of the copyright holder to derive income from his or her creation. For example, a teacher may be able to photocopy a few pages of a book for use in a classroom, but an advertising firm may be entitled to quote no more than a few lines from the same book in an ad without obtaining permission from the copyright holder. And while it may be lawful to quote 200 words from a novel without asking permission, the same would not be true in the case of a poem if the 200 words constituted the whole poem.

The term of copyright for a work depends on when it was created. Works created on or after January 1, 1978, are protected as soon as the work is fixed in a tangible means of expression, for the life of the author plus 70 years. In cases of joint authorship, the term is measured by the life of the longest surviving author, plus 70 years. If the work is of corporate au-

The Death Penalty

A Closer Look

States That Have Capital Punishment			States and Districts That Do Not Have Capital Punishment
Alabama	Kentucky	Ohio	Alaska
Arizona	Louisiana	Oklahoma	District of Columbia
Arkansas	Maryland	Oregon	Hawaii
California	Mississippi	Pennsylvania	Iowa
Colorado	Missouri	South Carolina	Maine
Connecticut	Montana	South Dakota	Massachusetts
Delaware	Nebraska	Tennessee	Michigan
Florida	Nevada	Texas	Minnesota
Georgia	New Hampshire	Utah	North Dakota
Idaho	New Jersey	Virginia	Rhode Island
Illinois	New Mexico	Washington	Vermont
Indiana	New York	Wyoming	West Virginia
Kansas	North Carolina		Wisconsin

thorship, a work for hire, anonymous or pseudonymous, it is protected for 95 years after publication or 120 years after creation, whichever is shorter. Works created before January 1, 1978, but not published, are protected from January 1, 1978 through the life of the author plus 70 years or until December 31, 2002, whichever is longer. Works created before January 1, 1978, but published between January 1, 1978 and December 31, 2002, are protected for the life of the author plus 70 years or December 31, 2047, whichever is longer.

Works published before 1923 are in the public domain; they are no longer protected by copyright. Works published with an effective copyright notice between 1923 and 1963 were protected for 28 years. If their copyright was renewed, they were protected for 47 additional years. Later legislation added an automatic 20 years to this term; thus, they could be protected for 28 years plus 67 years. If the copyright was not renewed, they are in the public domain. Works published from 1964 through 1977, when published with a copyright notice, are protected for 28 years, with an automatic extension of 67 years for a second term.

On March 1, 1989, the United States joined the Berne Convention for the Protection of Literary and Artistic Works, an international copyright treaty.

Under this convention, works are copyrighted from the moment they are fixed, or notated in some tangible form, such as in writing or on audiotape.

Under the 1909 Copyright Act, works published without notice went into the public domain upon publication. Works published without a copyright notice between January 1, 1978, and March 1, 1989, effective date of the Berne Convention Implementation Act, retained copyright only if copyright registration was made within five years of publication. A copyright notice is not required for works published as of March 1, 1989, but it is still recommended.

A copyright notice includes the word "Copyright" or the abbreviation "Copr." the year the work was first published, and the name of the owner of the copyright. The copyright symbol, a "C" in a circle (except for recordings, which use a circled "P"), also must be displayed.

Displaying the notice of copyright is sufficient to establish exclusive rights to an original work. In many cases, however, formal registration of a copyright claim is a prerequisite for filing suit for infringement for works whose country of origin is the United States. In addition, subject to certain exceptions, the remedies of statutory damages and attorneys' fees are not available for those infringements occurring before registration.

In 1992, Congress passed legislation that applies the same principles of fair use governing published works to unpublished works created between 1964 and 1977 (inclusive). The legislation also prescribes more stringent criminal sanctions for copyright infringement, designating certain violations as felonies.

A copy of any work registered for copyright must be deposited with the Library of Congress. Works that are not registered for copyright also may need to be deposited there.

In addition to the Berne Convention, the United States is a member of the Universal Copyright Convention, another multilateral agreement. Most countries of the world belong to one or both of these conventions, offering international copyright protection to all authors' registered works. The basic feature of this protection is "national treatment," under which the alien author is treated by a country in the same manner that it treats its own authors.

The international implementation of *General Agreement on Tariffs and Trade* (GATT) restored copyright protection to certain foreign works that had entered the public domain in the U.S. GATT also criminalized the production and distribution of pirated sound recordings and music videos.

The Digital Millennium Copyright Act of 1998 sought to update U.S. copyright law for the digital age. The Act makes it a crime under most circumstances for an individual to circumvent access-protection technology built into software or other media or for an individual to manufacture, sell, or distribute code-cracking devices used to illegally copy software or other media.

Currently, filing for copyright registration costs $30. For more information and application forms, write to

Register of Copyrights
The Library of Congress
101 Independence Ave.
Washington, DC 20559
http://lcweb.loc.gov/copyright

PATENTS

Congressional grants of patents and copyrights are based on Article I, Section 8 of the Constitution, which states that "Congress shall have power . . . to promote the progress of science and useful arts, by securing for limited times to authors and inventors the exclusive rights to their respective writings and discoveries."

A patent is the grant of a property right to an inventor, excluding others from making, using, or selling his or her invention. The invention may consist of "any new and useful process, machine, manufacture, or composition of matter, or any new and useful improvements thereof . . ." This patent law also covers ornamental designs, plants, and new forms of animal life. But no one can patent printed matter or a way of doing business.

In addition to being useful, the invention must be new. If the inventor describes the invention in a printed publication, uses the invention publicly, or places it on sale, he or she must apply for a patent before one year goes by; otherwise, any right to a patent is lost.

The Patent and Trademark Office currently receives more than 150,000 applications for patents each year, and it has granted more than 5 million patents since 1790. The agency grants new patents only after a diligent search of the records to make sure that the patent is original. Inventors may use the agency's Search Room (patent-research library) in Washington or any of the many patent-depository libraries throughout the United States to conduct their own searches before filing.

Although inventors can handle their own applications, the agency advises that the process is complex enough to require a patent attorney—a lawyer who also has a degree in engineering or physical science.

Only the inventor may apply for a patent. If the inventor is dead or incapacitated, a legal representative or guardian may apply. If two or more persons shared the ideas for the invention, they may apply jointly. But if one person had the idea and the other financed its development, only the person with the original idea may apply.

The application consists of a written description of the invention, with "claims" relating its distinguishing features—ways in which it does things in an entirely novel manner or improves significantly on previous inventions. If applicable, diagrams must accompany the description. Models usually are unnecessary. The Patent Office keeps all documents submitted in application for a patent strictly confidential during the process.

It is not uncommon for some or all of the claims to be rejected on the first action by the patent examiner; relatively few applications are allowed as filed. The applicant responds to the examiner's objections with clarification and explanation. If the Patent Office finally rejects the application, the inventor can take the case to the Board of Patent Appeals and Interferences. If the board turns down the application, the inventor has recourse through the Court of Appeals for the Federal Circuit or a civil suit in U.S. District Court in Washington, D.C.

About 1 percent of all patent applications encounter a problem because two or more applications are filed by different inventors claiming substantially the same patentable invention. Only one of the inventors can receive a patent, and the procedure to determine that one is called an *interference*. Each party to such a proceeding must submit evidence proving when the invention was made. As in the case of the rejection of any other patent, the decision of the examiners can be appealed.

If a patent applied for before June 8, 1995, is granted, it is good for 17 years. Under the terms of the GATT international treaty, most patents applied for after that date have a term of 20 years if granted (patents on ornamental designs have a term of 14 years).

Small entities—individual inventors, small businesses, and not-for-profit organizations—pay a filing fee of $370 for most patents and an additional fee of $640 if the patent is issued. For ornamental designs, the fees are $165 (filing fee) and $460 (upon issue of patent), and for plant varieties, the

fees are $255 and $310. Large entities such as corporations pay twice these amounts. Inventors also must pay maintenance fees after 3½, 7½, and 11½ years. Currently, these fees for small entities are $440, $1,010, and $1,550. For large entities, fees are $880, $2,020, and $3,100.

Once a patent is granted, all documents relating to it become available for public inspection. The Patent Office can keep such information secret, however, if its commissioner decides that such information is vital to the national security.

As with any other property, patents may be sold or assigned in whole or in part to someone else. The patent holder also may license others to use the process or produce the product under specific conditions. The Patent Office cautions that a part owner of a patent—no matter how small his or her interest—may make, use, and sell the invention for his or her own profit without regard to the other owner. He or she also may sell the interest (or any part of it) or license others to use or make it. Therefore, inventors should be very careful when agreeing to sell a part interest in their patent.

Patented articles must be marked with the word "Patent" and the number of the patent. Some people use "Patent Pending" or "Patent Applied For" to inform others of the status of a patent claim, but such words have no legal effect. To combat infringement of a patent, the person holding the patent may bring a civil suit.

Patents granted by the Patent and Trademark Office protect inventions in the United States only. However, the United States is a signatory of several treaties that facilitate applications for patent protection in other countries. For further information, write to

Patent Assistance Center
Crystal Plaza 3
Washington, D.C. 20231
800-786-9199
http://www.uspto.gov

"Significant Inventions, Technological **Go to** Advances, and Scientific Discoveries" in chapter 5

Legal Information

FEDERAL JUDICIAL SYSTEM

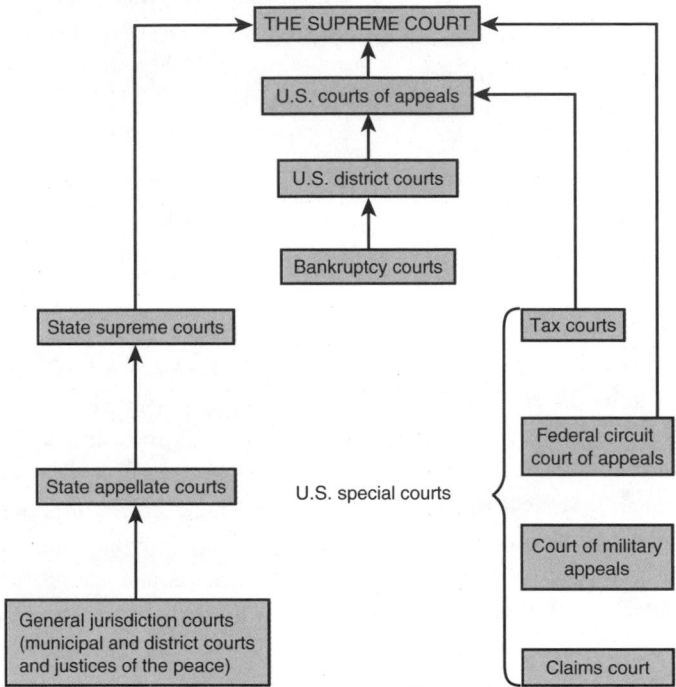

SUPREME COURT JUSTICES

This section lists all the Supreme Court justices in U.S. history. The first date for each justice is the year when the justice took the oath of office. The second date is the last year the person served as a Supreme Court justice. Some justices were appointed in the preceding year but actually assumed office during the first year listed.

Justice	Term	Justice	Term	Justice	Term
John Jay*	1789–95	Alfred Moore	1800–04	James M. Wayne	1835–67
James Wilson	1789–98	John Marshall*	1801–35	Roger B. Taney*	1836–64
John Blair, Jr.	1790–96	William Johnson	1804–34	Philip P. Barbour	1836–41
William Cushing	1790–1810	Henry Brockholst	1807–23	John Catron	1837–65
John Rutledge	1790–91	Livingston		John McKinley	1838–52
James Iredell	1790–99	Thomas Todd	1807–26	Peter V. Daniel	1842–60
Thomas Johnson	1792–93	Gabriel Duval	1811–35	Samuel Nelson	1845–72
William Paterson	1793–1806	Joseph Story	1812–45	Levi Woodbury	1845–51
John Rutledge*	†1795	Smith Thompson	1823–43	Robert C. Grier	1846–70
Oliver Ellsworth*	1796–1800	Robert Trimble	1826–28	Benjamin R. Curtis	1851–57
Samuel Chase	1796–1811	John McLean	1830–61	John A. Campbell	1853–61
Bushrod Washington	1798–1829	Henry Baldwin	1830–44	Nathan Clifford	1858–81

*   Chief Justice

†   John Rutledge took the oath of office as Chief Justice in 1795 as a recess appointee. However, the Senate rejected his appointment later that year.

Justice	Term	Justice	Term	Justice	Term
David Davis	1862–77	Charles E. Hughes	1910–16	Fred M. Vinson*	1946–53
Samuel F. Miller	1862–90	Horace H. Lurton	1910–14	Thomas C. Clark	1949–67
Noah H. Swayne	1862–81	Joseph R. Lamar	1911–16	Sherman Minton	1949–56
Stephen J. Field	1863–97	Willis Van Devanter	1911–37	Earl Warren*	1953–69
Salmon P. Chase*	1864–73	Mahlon Pitney	1912–22	John Marshall	1955–71
Joseph P. Bradley	1870–92	James C. McReynolds	1914–41	Harlan II	
William Strong	1870–80	Louis D. Brandeis	1916–39	William J. Brennan, Jr.	1956–90
Ward Hunt	1873–82	John H. Clarke	1916–22	Charles E. Whittaker	1957–62
Morrison R. Waite*	1874–88	William H. Taft*	1921–30	Potter Stewart	1958–81
John M. Harlan	1877–1911	George Sutherland	1922–38	Byron R. White	1962–93
William B. Woods	1881–87	Pierce Butler	1923–39	Arthur J. Goldberg	1962–65
Stanley Matthews	1881–89	Edward T. Sanford	1923–30	Abe Fortas	1965–69
Samuel Blatchford	1882–93	Harlan F. Stone	1925–41	Thurgood Marshall	1967–91
Horace Gray	1882–1902	Charles E. Hughes*	1930–41	Warren E. Burger*	1969–86
Melville W. Fuller*	1888–1910	Owen J. Roberts	1930–45	Harry A. Blackmun	1970–94
Lucius Q. C. Lamar	1888–93	Benjamin N. Cardozo	1932–38	Lewis F. Powell, Jr.	1972–87
David J. Brewer	1890–1910	Hugo L. Black	1937–71	William H. Rehnquist	1972–86
Henry B. Brown	1891–1906	Stanley F. Reed	1938–57	John Paul Stevens	1975–
George Shiras, Jr.	1892–1903	Felix Frankfurter	1939–62	Sandra Day O'Connor	1981–
Howell E. Jackson	1893–95	William O. Douglas	1939–75	William H. Rehnquist*	1986–
Edward D. White	1894–1910	Frank Murphy	1940–49	Antonin Scalia	1986–
Rufus W. Peckham	1896–1909	Harlan F. Stone*	1941–46	Anthony M. Kennedy	1988–
Joseph McKenna	1898–1925	James F. Byrnes	1941–42	David H. Souter	1990–
Oliver W. Holmes	1902–32	Robert H. Jackson	1941–54	Clarence Thomas	1991–
William R. Day	1903–22	Wiley B. Rutledge	1943–49	Ruth Bader Ginsburg	1993–
William H. Moody	1906–10	Harold H. Burton	1945–58	Stephen Gerald Breyer	1994–
Edward D. White*	1910–21				

*Chief Justice

SUPREME COURT DECISIONS

The following Supreme Court decisions are among the most significant in the 19th and 20th centuries.

1803 *Marbury v. Madison.* For the first time, the Court ruled an act of Congress unconstitutional, establishing the principle of judicial review.

1819 *McCullock v. Maryland.* The Court's ruling upheld the constitutionality of the creation of the Bank of the United States and denied to the states the power to tax such an institution because, as Justice John Marshall put it, "the power to tax is the power to destroy."

1819 *Trustees of Dartmouth College v. Woodward.* The Court ruled that a state could not arbitrarily alter the terms of a contract. Although this case applied to a college, its implications widened in later years when the same principle was used to limit the ability of states to interfere with business contracts.

1857 *Dred Scott v. Sanford.* The Missouri Compromise was declared unconstitutional because it deprived a person (a slave) of his property without due process of law. This was only the second time the Court had asserted the power of judicial review. The decision also stated that slaves are not citizens of any state or of the United States.

1877 *Munn v. Illinois.* States were allowed to regulate businesses when "a public interest" was involved. This principle was weakened by rulings in other cases in the late 19th century.

Legal Information

1896 *Plessy v. Ferguson.* The Court ruled that state laws enforcing segregation by race are constitutional if accommodations are equal as well as separate. This ruling was overturned by the Court's 1954 *Brown v. Board of Education of Topeka* decision.

1904 *Northern Securities Co. v. U.S.* The Court backed government action against big businesses that restrained trade, in effect putting teeth in the Sherman Act.

1908 *Muller v. Oregon.* The Court ruled that a state could legislate maximum working hours based on evidence compiled by future Supreme Court Justice Louis D. Brandeis.

1911 *Standard Oil Co. of New Jersey et al. v. U.S.* The Court dissolved the Standard Oil Trust—not because of its size, but because of its unreasonable restraint of trade. The principle involved is called "the rule of reason."

1919 *Schenck v. U.S.* The Court upheld the World War I Espionage Act. In a landmark decision dealing with free speech, Justice Oliver W. Holmes said that a person who encourages draft resistance during a war is a "clear and present danger."

1935 *Schechter v. U.S.* Invalidating the National Industrial Recovery Act of the New Deal, the Court declared that Congress could not delegate its powers to the president.

1951 *Dennis et al. v. U.S.* The Court ruled the 1946 Smith Act constitutional. The act made it a crime to advocate the overthrow of the government by force. In its 1957 *Yates v. U.S.* decision, the Court tempered this ruling by permitting such advocacy in the abstract if it is not connected to action to achieve the goal.

1954 *Brown v. Board of Education of Topeka.* In an example of sociological jurisprudence, the Court held that laws enforcing segregated schools were unconstitutional. It called for desegregation of schools "with all deliberate speed."

1957 *Roth v. U.S.* This ruling based obscenity decisions on whether a publication appeals to "prurient interests." The Court also said that obscene material is that which lacks any "redeeming social importance."

1961 *Mapp v. Ohio.* The Court extended the federal exclusionary rule to the states. This rule prevented prosecutors from using illegally obtained evidence in a criminal trial.

1962 *Baker v. Carr.* The Court held that state legislatures must be apportioned to provide equal protection under the law (14th Amendment). A follow-up decision applied the same principle to the size of congressional districts, insisting that they be approximately equal in population.

1966 *Miranda v. Arizona.* The Court declared that before questioning suspects, police must inform them of their right to remain silent; that any statements they make can be used against them; and that they have the right to remain silent until they have an attorney, which the state will provide if they cannot afford one.

1972 *Furman v. Georgia.* The Court found unconstitutional all death-penalty statutes then in force in the states. However, it held out the possibility that if these statutes were rewritten to be less subjective and randomly imposed, they might be constitutional (as the Court has subsequently held in many instances).

1973 *Roe v. Wade.* The Court ruled state laws prohibiting abortion unconstitutional, except as they apply to the last trimester of pregnancy, on the basis that the 14th Amendment provides for a woman's freedom to make a private decision about her reproductive practices.

1978 *University of California v. Bakke.* The ruling allowed a university to admit students on the basis of race if the school's goal is to combat discrimination. Subsequent decisions of the Court have filled in the details of how government and business may use quotas to make up for racism in the past.

1986 Bowers v. Hardwick. In a case involving the enforcement of Georgia's law against sodomy, the Court ruled that states have the power to regulate sexual relations in private between consenting adults.

The U.S. Supreme Court traditionally begins its sessions on the first Monday in October.

1989 Webster v. Reproductive Health Services. The Court upheld a Missouri law forbidding public employees to perform most abortions, prohibiting the use of public buildings for abortions, and requiring a fetal-viability test prior to abortions after the 20th week of pregnancy. This case set a precedent allowing other states to restrict access to abortions.

1993 Harris v. Forklift Systems, Inc. In a suit brought by a Tennessee woman against her former employer, the Court found that workers may claim sexual harassment even when severe economic or emotional damage does not result. The decision broadened Title VII civil-rights protections against sexual discrimination in the workplace and enlarged the legal definition of sexual harassment.

1996 Romer v. Evans The Court struck down an amendment to Colorado's state constitution that barred homosexuals from seeking civil-rights protection against discrimination.

1999 Reno v. ACLU The Court struck down two provisions of the Communications Decency Act of 1996 that criminalized the "knowing" transmission of "obscene or indecent" messages on the Internet to any recipient under 18 years of age, ruling that the statute abridged the First Amendment guarantee of freedom of speech.

2000 Bush v. Gore In a 5–4 decision in a suit arising out of the disputed 2000 presidential election results in Florida, brought by George W. Bush against Albert Gore, Jr., the court ruled that the manual recounts ordered by the Florida Supreme Court violated the U.S. Constitution's equal protection and due process clauses.

COMMON LEGAL TERMS

accessory An accessory *before* the fact helps another person commit or try to commit a crime but is not present at the commission of the crime. An accessory *during* the fact witnesses a crime but does not do what he or she could do to prevent it. An accessory *after* the fact helps another avoid arrest for the commission of a crime.

accomplice An individual who joins with another to commit a crime. The accomplice bears equal responsibility under the law.

actus reus A wrongful act, as opposed to *mens rea*—thoughts and intentions behind the act. For example, in a murder, *homicide* is the *actus reus,* and *malice aforethought* is the *mens rea.*

adjudication A final judgment in a legal proceeding.

affidavit A written statement sworn or affirmed to be true before a person legally authorized to administer an oath.

age of consent The minimum age for marrying without parental consent; also, the minimum age for consensual sexual relations. Sexual intercourse with someone below the age of consent can result in a charge of assault or statutory rape, even if both people participate willingly.

alibi An assertion or fact placing the defendant at the time of the crime in another location than the scene of that crime.

amicus curiae Latin for "friend of the court." A person or organization not party to a case who submits information useful to the court in that proceeding. Amicus curiae briefs generally are submitted when the suit involves matters of wide public interest.

amnesty An act of government forgiving members of a group, such as unregistered gun owners or illegal aliens, who normally would be subject to prosecution.

appeal   A request to a superior court to reverse the decision of a lower court or government agency or to grant a new trial.

appellate court   A court whose jurisdiction is confined to reviewing decisions of lower courts or agencies.

arraignment   A court procedure in which formal charges are brought against a defendant, who is advised of his or her constitutional rights and may have the opportunity to offer a plea.

assault   A threatened or attempted physical attack in which the attacker appears to have the ability to bring about bodily harm if not stopped. *Aggravated assault* involves an attack perpetrated with recklessness and intent to injure seriously or an assault with a deadly weapon. *Battery* is an assault in which the assailant makes physical contact with the victim.

attachment   A court writ authorizing legal authorities to seize property that may be needed for the payment of a judgment in a judicial proceeding. *See also* **writ.**

bail   Security provided to ensure the presence of a defendant in court during the course of a case. Defendants raising this security are said to "make bail"; those fleeing and forfeiting the security have "jumped bail." The actual document securing the defendant's release is the "bail bond."

bar   A collective term for all lawyers practicing in a particular court system.

battery   *See* **assault.**

bench warrant   A court order authorizing a public official to arrest a person and bring that individual to court.

bequest   Personal property bequeathed (given as a gift) in a will. *Devise* is the term for handing down real property (land and what is built upon it or affixed to it) through a will.

beyond a reasonable doubt   The degree to which jurors must be convinced before they may convict a person of a crime. The jurors must find the prosecution's case proven beyond the point at which a reasonable, average, prudent person would be convinced before returning a verdict of guilty.

bill of particulars   The specific events to be dealt with in a criminal trial, presented to the defendant so that he or she may effectively prepare a defense.

binding over   The action of a lower court shifting a case to a grand jury or superior court when the inferior court believes that a crime has been committed. Also, a court order to jail a defendant during the course of a proceeding.

boilerplate   Language uniformly found in certain types of documents—for instance, the "small print" in a contract that people often neglect to read.

breach of contract   Failure to do something required in a contract. *See also* **contract.**

breaking and entering   The illegal entrance into premises with criminal intent. Simply pushing a door open and walking in may constitute breaking and entering.

brief   A document in which a lawyer makes his or her client's case by raising legal points and citing authorities.

burden of proof   In a civil case, the requirement that a plaintiff or defendant must show that the majority of evidence is on his or her side in order to win a suit. In a criminal case, the prosecutor's burden of proof is to prove every fact involved in a charge.

burglary   Unlawful presence in a building with the intent of committing a felony or taking something of value. *See also* **robbery.**

capacity   The ability to understand the facts and significance of one's behavior. A defendant cannot be convicted of a crime in which he or she did not have the legal capacity to comprehend it.

cease and desist order   A legal order preventing a person or organization from continuing a specific activity. A *mandatory injunction,* on the other hand, orders the performance of a specified act.

certiorari   A writ in which a superior court commands an inferior court to deliver the records of a proceeding to the superior body so that it may decide whether there is basis for appeal.

The guarantee that each state will have an equal number of votes in the Senate is the only provision in the Constitution that cannot be amended. (Article V.)

character witness   *See* **witness.**

chattel   Personal, rather than real, property. A *chattel mortgage,* for example, is a loan to buy an expensive item, such as a car, in which the item, or chattel, is security for the debt.

circumstantial evidence   Evidence based not on direct observation or knowledge but implied from things already known.

civil contempt   *See* **contempt of court.**

class action   A lawsuit brought by a group of people with a shared purpose.

clemency   A reduction of criminal punishment, often granted to prevent the execution of a prisoner.

codicil   An addition to a will altering it.

common-law marriage   A relationship in which two people live together as husband and wife without formally getting married.

community property   Property owned by a husband and wife jointly.

competency hearing   A procedure to determine legal capacity (for example, of a defendant in a criminal case), understand the charges, and cooperate with a lawyer in preparing a defense. *Compos mentis* is a finding of competence to stand trial; *non compos mentis* is the finding of a lack of competence to go to trial.

complaint   The first statement of facts (in a civil proceeding) or accusation (in a criminal case).

compos mentis   *See* **competency hearing.**

consent decree   An agreement between two parties sanctioned by the court—for example, between a company and the government, involving allegations of violations of antitrust laws. In the consent decree, the company would agree to cease such practices without formally admitting guilt.

conspiracy   The plotting by two or more people to break the law.

contempt of court   Anything done to hinder the work of the court. *Civil contempt* involves failure to follow a court order benefiting another party in a case, as in the failure to pay court-ordered damages; *criminal contempt* consists of the obstruction of justice.

contract   A commitment between two or more parties, enforceable by law.

corpus delicti   The object upon which a crime has been committed. The term does not necessarily refer to a body, although a corpse with a knife in its back would be an example in a homicide.

corroborating evidence   Additional evidence of a different character to the same point that backs up proof already offered in a proceeding.

criminal contempt   *See* **contempt of court.**

criminal negligence   *See* **negligence.**

cross-examination   The interrogation of a witness to discredit or show in a new light testimony that was offered by that person during direct examination.

custody   In a divorce case, the right to house, care for, and discipline a child.

damages   A court-ordered monetary award to someone who has suffered loss or injury by another.

de facto   Actually exercising power though not legally or officially established. A practice sanctioned by custom, as opposed to *de jure,* a practice formally backed by law.

de jure   *See* **de facto.**

decree   A court's decision in a case; its judgment.

defamation   The damaging of another person's reputation through writing (*libel*) or speech (*slander*).

default judgment   A court determination made against a defendant who fails to show up in court or fails to take some other court-required action.

defendant   A person or institution being sued or accused in a legal proceeding.

deposition   A pretrial interrogation of a witness, usually in a lawyer's office.

devise   *See* **bequest.**

directed verdict   A verdict declared by the court in a civil trial before the jury gets the case. Judges render this verdict when the facts and the law in a case point to a definite conclusion. There cannot be a directed verdict of guilty in a criminal trial, since that would violate a defendant's right to trial by jury.

discovery   A pretrial process that enables one side in a litigation to elicit information from the other side relating to the facts in the case.

disorderly conduct   A broad spectrum of offenses, such as drunkenness or fighting, that disturb the public peace.

district attorney   *See* **prosecutor.**

docket   A list of cases to be tried by a court—its calendar. Also, a summary of a court's activities.

double jeopardy   The condition of being tried a second time for a crime after the first case has been decided. Double jeopardy is prohibited by the 5th Amendment of the U.S. Constitution.

due process   The general doctrine that legislation must promote the legitimate aims of government (*substantive due process*) and that nobody can be deprived of liberty or property through unfair procedures (*procedural due process*).

easement   The right to use another person's land.

emancipation   The parental yielding of authority over, control over, and responsibility for a minor.

eminent domain   The right of the state to convert private property to public property.

entrapment   A defense by which a defendant seeks to show that he or she would not have committed an unlawful act if not tricked into doing it by law-enforcement officials.

equal protection   The 14th-Amendment requirement that all groups of people be treated equally by the legal system.

estate   Everything an individual owns.

eviction   The dispossessing of a tenant from land or premises he or she has occupied.

evidence   Testimony, documents, and objects used to prove matters of fact at a trial.

exclusionary rule   A rule preventing introduction at a criminal trial of evidence obtained in violation of the 4th Amendment's prohibition against unreasonable searches and seizures, even if that evidence otherwise would be admissible. *See also* **search and seizure.**

executor/executrix   A man or woman, respectively, appointed to administer the provisions of a will.

eyewitness   A person who can testify as to what happened because he or she was there when it happened and saw it. Technically, a person who offers testimony of something overheard is an *earwitness*.

fair hearing   A special administrative procedure set up to ensure that a person will not be harmed or denied his or her rights without due process of law before a court can intervene. Examples of extraordinary circumstances calling for a fair hearing include loss of welfare benefits and deportation.

fair use   The conditions under which a person can use material copyrighted by another.

false imprisonment   *See* **kidnapping.**

false pretenses   The means to take another's property through trickery. This crime involves the intent to secure the title to the property through some seemingly legal transaction. *See also* **larceny.**

fee   An interest in which land is or may become possessory; *freehold* is land held in fee.

felony   A serious crime, as opposed to a *misdemeanor.* The distinction often is made in terms of the applicable punishment; felonies are punishable by a certain minimum prison term—under federal law, one year.

felony murder   A homicide committed in the course of another crime, such as a burglary.

fiduciary   A person in a position of trust who acts for the benefit of another person. Examples are executors, corporate directors, and infant guardians.

finding   The basis in fact or law for a judgment. *See also* **judgment.**

fraud   The injury of a person or group of persons through deceit.

freehold   *See* **fee.**

frisk   *See* **stop and frisk.**

garnishment   The legal impoundment of funds by which a creditor sends notices through the court to the debtor's employer, thus seizing the debtor's salary to pay off the debt owed to the creditor.

grand jury   A jury of from 12 to 23 people empowered to look into possible criminal activity in an area, report on it, and indict individuals when it finds evidence that they have committed a crime.

grand larceny   *See* **larceny.**

grandfather clause   A provision in some laws allowing people who had legally engaged in an activity prior to its restriction by law to continue to engage in that activity.

guardian   A person entrusted to look out for the interests of a minor or an incompetent person. The specific fiduciary relationship is defined by law and court orders.

habeas corpus   The order by a judge to have a prisoner brought to court to determine the legality of the imprisonment.

harmless error   An error in a trial that had no effect on the outcome of the case. An appeals court will not overturn a judgment if it determines that errors made in the original trial were unimportant.

hearsay evidence   Statements made outside of court attesting to some fact; therefore the person making the statements may not be cross-examined or otherwise scrutinized. For example, if A testifies in court that he heard B say something, in most cases, B's statement will not be admissible as evidence.

homicide   An act in which one person causes the death of another. *See also* **manslaughter; murder.**

hung jury   A jury that is unable to reach a verdict.

immunity from prosecution   The exemption of a witness from prosecution to thwart a refusal to testify based on constitutional rights. The witness cannot be prosecuted on the basis of anything he or she says while testifying under such immunity.

impanel   To select a jury.

in camera   A judicial proceeding from which the public is excluded. Although the term literally means "in chambers," the proceeding can be held anywhere outside of open court.

in loco parentis   A person or institution acting toward a minor "in place of parents" without a formal adoption procedure—for example, the relationship between a school and a student.

in rem A proceeding involving property without reference to the claims of people on that property.

indictment A document delivered to a grand jury in which a public prosecutor accuses one or more persons of committing a crime. If the grand jury thinks the evidence submitted is sufficient to warrant a trial, it endorses the indictment as a true bill.

infant A person who has not reached the age of majority (usually 18), at which he or she enjoys the full rights of citizenship and is legally responsible for his or her acts.

information A prosecuting attorney's written accusation of criminal activity, similar to an indictment but not presented to a grand jury. Information may be used to initiate proceedings against defendants in state, but not federal, courts.

infringement A violation of a law or right.

injunction A court order preventing someone from doing a specific act.

injury The violation of a person's rights to the point where he or she suffers any kind of damage, including financial.

inquest A coroner's investigation into the cause of death.

insanity A mental state in which a person lacks legal responsibility.

intestate Without a will.

judgment A court's final decision in a case. *See also* **verdict.**

jury A representative group of people who determine issues of fact at a trial. The Constitution guarantees the right to trial by jury for all crimes punishable by imprisonment for more than six months. In civil trials, juries range in number from 6 to 12 people. State trial juries do not need a unanimous vote to convict (with the exception of six-person juries), but federal juries do.

kidnapping The illegal seizure and removal of a person without his or her consent. *False imprisonment* involves illegally confining a person against his or her will without moving that person and may be committed by police officers who fail to make arrests properly.

larceny The act of gaining the use or possession of property through an overtly illegal act, as in stealing a car. *Grand larceny* involves the theft of an object worth more than a specified amount. *See also* **robbery.**

leading question A lawyer's question to a witness that predetermines the answer, thus putting words in the witness's mouth. Such questions are legitimate during cross-examination but not during direct examination.

libel *See* **defamation.**

magistrate An official, such as a justice of the peace, who performs low-level judicial functions.

majority, age of *See* **infant.**

malfeasance Wrongful conduct by a public official. *Misfeasance* is the misperforming of a proper act. *Nonfeasance* is the nonperformance of an act that a person has agreed to or is duty-bound to do.

malice aforethought An antisocial state of mind, often at issue in a murder trial, marked by cruelty and recklessness for which there is no justification. *See also* **manslaughter.**

malpractice Wrongful conduct by a professional, either through negligence or lack of ethics.

mandamus A writ commanding someone, often a public official, to perform some act. Mandamus frequently is issued when time is of the essence. *See also* **writ.**

mandatory injunction *See* **cease and desist order.**

manslaughter Homicide without malice aforethought. *Voluntary manslaughter* is homicide with mitigating circumstances—for example, a fight in which one person kills another. *Involuntary manslaughter* is killing through criminal negligence, as in drunk driving.

material witness *See* **witness.**

mens rea *See* **actus reus.**

Miranda rule The obligation of the police, when interrogating someone after an arrest, to read to that person his or her constitutional rights. These rights include the right to a lawyer, to remain silent until advised by counsel, and to know that anything he or she say may be used as evidence.

misdemeanor *See* **felony.**

misfeasance *See* **malfeasance.**

mistrial The ending of a trial before the rendering of a verdict. Possible causes include a hung jury or the incapacity of the judge, jurors, or attorneys.

mitigating circumstances Conditions under which a crime was committed that tend to reduce the punishment in a case—for example, the circumstances leading to a crime of passion.

moral turpitude Baseness, depravity, vileness, or extreme antisocial behavior. A person's moral turpitude is sometimes taken into account by a judge when sentencing.

murder Homicide with malice aforethought. Murder in the second degree generally involves less premeditation than the same crime in the first degree. *See also* **malice aforethought; premeditation.**

negligence Carelessness, acting without reasonable caution, putting another person at risk of injury, or not performing an act that one is obliged to do, with the same consequences. In *criminal negligence,* there is the added element of recklessness.

next of kin Closest blood relatives or, lacking them, the next closest relations, even if they are related only by marriage.

nolo contendere A defendant's statement that the charges in a case will not be contested.

non compos mentis *See* **competency hearing.**

nonfeasance *See* **malfeasance.**

notary public A person with the authority to administer oaths, witness documents, and accept depositions.

on the merits A court judgment resting on the facts in the case rather than on a legal technicality.

open court Judicial proceedings fully accessible to the public.

pardon An act by which a governor or the president can excuse a person from punishment and restore his or her civil rights; however, a pardon usually does not wipe out a conviction.

parole The release of a person from prison under controlled conditions. The parolee must fulfill certain requirements, such as reporting regularly to a parole officer.

perjury The act of lying while under oath.

plaintiff The person who initiates a lawsuit.

plea A defendant's answer to a complaint.

Bexley, Ohio's Ordinance No. 223 (1919) prohibits the installation and usage of slot machines in outhouses.

plea bargain A deal between the prosecutor and the accused, in which the accused pleads guilty in return for lesser punishment than might be received at the end of a trial.

polling the jury A proceeding in which the judge asks each juror, after the verdict has been rendered, to restate his or her decision in the case.

power of attorney A document in which one person authorizes another to act as an agent on his or her behalf.

preliminary hearing A proceeding held after an arrest but before an indictment to see whether there is sufficient evidence to continue holding the prisoner and proceed with a case. *See also* **indictment.**

premeditation   The degree of planning and forethought sufficient to show intent to commit an act—often a factor in determining the degree of guilt in a murder case.

preponderance of evidence   The standard of proof used to settle civil lawsuits—determining which side's evidence has greater weight.

presentment   A grand jury's accusation, based not on material presented to it by a prosecutor, but on its own investigation.

preventive detention   The holding of a prisoner without bail; also accomplished by setting bail so high that the prisoner cannot meet it.

In Hartford, Connecticut, you can be arrested for walking across a street on your hands.

pro bono   Meaning "for the good"—the taking of a case by an attorney without a fee. Pro bono cases often are defended on behalf of groups backing important causes.

probable cause   The rule under which police need to have a reasonable belief that someone has committed a crime before making an arrest, or that the object for which they are searching in connection with a crime is at a specific location before they search for and seize it. *See also* **search and seizure.**

probate   The process by which the legitimacy of a will is established.

probation   The suspension of a person's sentence, leaving that individual at liberty but under court supervision.

process   A writ requiring that a person appear in court.

prosecutor   The person responsible for bringing the accused to justice. Depending on the level on which he or she functions, the prosecutor usually is

called a *district attorney, county prosecutor, federal prosecutor*, or, if appointed by a legislature to conduct an investigation, a *special prosecutor.*

protective custody   The imprisonment of an individual for his or her own protection.

public defender   A lawyer provided by the state to an accused person who cannot afford or refuses counsel.

punitive damages   An award to a plaintiff in a civil suit that exceeds actual losses, thereby punishing the defendant for his actions.

real property   Land and what is built on it, growing upon it, and affixed to it.

reasonable doubt   *See* **beyond a reasonable doubt.**

release on one's own recognizance   To free the accused on a promise to appear in court rather than on bail.

resident alien   A foreign citizen who intends to live in the United States permanently. Immigration authorities must approve the status of a resident alien.

restraining order   A temporary order granted to prevent some action until a hearing can be held on that action.

robbery   The use of violence or intimidation to seize another person's property. *See also* **burglary.**

search and seizure   A law-enforcement procedure involving the search of a person or premises when police have probable cause to suspect they will find and be able to seize criminal evidence. *See also* **probable cause; search warrant.**

search warrant   A court order authorizing law-enforcement officials to look for objects or people involved in the commission of a crime and to produce them in court. The order stipulates the places that the officials may search.

self-defense   A plea by which a person may justify the use of force to ward off an attack if the attack was unprovoked, retreat was impossible, and the threat of harm seemed imminent.

self-incrimination   An act in a legal proceeding by which a person says something that causes him or her to appear guilty of some type of crime. Under the 5th Amendment, a person cannot be forced to make such a statement.

sequester   To prevent a jury from having outside contacts until a trial is finished.

show cause order   A court order, issued at the request of one party, requiring a second party to convince the court, usually within a matter of days, that a specific act should not be carried out or allowed.

slander   *See* **defamation.**

statute of limitations   The period of time during which a person may initiate a legal action. See "Statute of Limitations," earlier in this chapter.

statutory rape   A criminal offense involving sex with a boy or girl under the age of consent; the age differs in various states.

stay   A court order preventing some act or proceeding until a specific condition is met or the stay is lifted.

stop and frisk   A procedure in which police who believe a suspect may be carrying a weapon with the intent to use it can stop that person and search the suspect's outer layer of clothing for a weapon.

subpoena   A court writ requiring a person to appear to testify at a judicial proceeding at a specific time and place under penalty of law.

Celebrated attorney Clarence Darrow (1857–1938) spent only one year in law school, opting to learn the law at a Youngstown, Ohio, law office.

summary judgment   A procedure by which a party in a civil dispute, if it believes that the other side's argument is without merit, can move to have a case resolved before going to trial.

summons   A notice to appear in court as a defendant in a suit.

testament   *See* **will.**

tort   A violation of legal duty, not involving a contract, that results in harm to another person or another person's property—for example, an act of libel that damages a person's reputation.

true bill   *See* **indictment.**

venue, change of   The transfer of a trial to another location, usually on the grounds that a fair trial is improbable in the original jurisdiction.

verdict   A judge or jury's finding of fact. The *judgment*, not the verdict, is the final determination in a case. For example, a judge can declare a jury's verdict *false*—that is, invalid—because it is not based on the evidence.

voir dire   A term usually applied to the interrogation of people to determine their competency as jurors. The term, which is French for "speak the truth," also describes a trial hearing without the jury present to determine a matter of fact or law, such as the validity of a confession.

waiver   The conscious forgoing of a legal right.

warrant   A court writ directing a public employee to do something—for example, to make an arrest.

will   A document specifying the disposition of a person's property after his or her death. Most states require two or three people to witness a will. Although *will* generally means the same thing as *testament*, the latter applies only to the distribution of personal property, as opposed to real property.

witness   A person who testifies in court under oath. A *material witness* is one whose testimony is central to a case; a *character witness* testifies to the character of an individual.

Legal Information

writ A written order from a judicial body commanding a law-enforcement officer to do something specified.

wrongful death statute A law that enables survivors or the person administering an estate to sue for monetary compensation for a death caused by some person or persons. The law is based on the fact that the death deprives survivors or the estate of the services or income of the deceased.

youthful offender One who, at a judge's discretion, may be sentenced with special consideration given to his or her age. The category applies to defendants older than juveniles (no longer minors) but not yet, in the opinion of the judge, adults. Offender is usually between the ages of 18 and 25.

ADDITIONAL SOURCES OF INFORMATION

ORGANIZATIONS AND SERVICES

American Bar Association (ABA)
541 N. Fairbanks St.
Chicago, IL 60611
312-988-5522
http://www.abanet.org

The ABA publishes the *Directory of Lawyer Referral Services*, which lists services located throughout the United States and covers a range of general and special-interest needs. The office is open from 9 A.M. to 5 P.M., CST.

American Civil Liberties Union (ACLU)
125 Broad St.
New York, NY 10004
212-549-2500
http://www.aclu.org

The ACLU monitors civil-rights issues and incidents across the country and files lawsuits against parties whose actions violate the U.S. Constitution. Through a variety of publications and ac-

tivities, its educational arm seeks to raise the public's awareness of constitutional topics. The office is open weekdays from 9 A.M. to 5:30 P.M., EST.

Lamba Legal Defense and Education Fund
120 Wall Street
Suite 1500
New York, NY 10005
212-809-8585
http://www.lambdalegal.org

This is the nation's oldest and largest organization working for the civil rights of gay men, lesbians, and people with HIV/AIDS. For the telephone numbers and hours of operation of Lamda's regional legal help desks, consult the website or call the general telephone number above.

NAACP Legal Defense and Education Fund
99 Hudson St.
16th Floor
New York, NY 10013
212-219-1900

The staff at the NAACP Legal Defense Fund will put individuals or groups who feel that they have been discriminated against in touch with an attorney who can help. The office is open weekdays from 9:30 A.M. to 5 P.M., EST.

National Center for Youth Law
405 14th St.
15th Floor
Oakland, CA 94612
510-835-8098
http://www.youthlaw.org

This organization provides counseling and referrals related to legal matters affecting young people, including juvenile justice and child welfare. The office is open from 9 A.M. to 5 P.M., PST.

National Legal Aid & Defender Association
1625 K St., NW
Suite 800
Washington, DC 20006
202-452-0620
http://www.nlada.org

This association acts as a clearinghouse of organizations providing legal services for those without the means to pay. The office is open from 9 A.M. to 5:30 P.M., EST.

NOW Legal Defense and Education Fund
395 Hudson St.
New York, NY 10014
212-925-6635
http://www.nowldef.org

This organization provides referrals for legal issues related to women's rights, such as economic inequality, pregnancy discrimination, and problems with changing one's surname. The office is open weekdays from 9:30 A.M. to 1:00 P.M., EST.

BOOKS

American Bar Association. *Consumers' Guide to Getting Legal Help.* ABA, nd.

Belli, Melvin, and Allen P. Wilkinson. *Everybody's Guide to the Law.* Harper Perennial, 1987.

Black, Henry C. *Black's Law Dictionary,* 7th ed. West, 1999.

Bove, Alexander A., Jr. *The Complete Book of Wills and Estates,* 2nd ed. Henry Holt, 2000.

Coughlin, George Gordon, Jr. *Your Handbook of Everyday Law.* HarperCollins, 1993.

Elias, Stephen, and Susan Levinkind. *Legal Research: How to Find and Understand the Law,* 9th ed. Nolo Press, 2001.

Feinman, Jay M. *Law 101: Everything You Need to Know about the American Legal System.* Oxford, 2000.

Gifis, Steven H. *Law Dictionary.* Barron's, 1996.

Hall, Kermit L., ed. *The Oxford Companion to the Supreme Court.* Oxford, 1992.

Hall, Kermit L., ed. *The Oxford Guide to United States Supreme Court Decisions.* Oxford, 2001.

Jordan, Cora. *Neighbor Law: Fences, Trees, Boundaries & Noise.* Nolo, 2001.

Pressman, David. *Patent It Yourself,* 8th ed. Nolo Press, 2000.

Ventura, John. *Law for Dummies,* IDG Books, 1996.

Wilson, Lee. *The Copyright Guide, Revised.* Allworth Press, 2000.

WEB SITES

http://www.findlaw.com
Provides a comprehensive listing of legal resources.

http://www.ilrg.com
Provides a categorized index of legal websites

http://www.lawyers.com
Provides legal information and resources, such as a lawyer locator.

http://www.law.cornell.edu/lii.html
Provides a starting point for finding legal information online; maintained by the Legal Information Institute at Cornell Law School.

http://www.lectlaw.com/inll/1.htm
Provides links to a large number of topics of legal issues for federal, state, and foreign laws.

Legal Information

22

USEFUL ADDRESSES AND PHONE NUMBERS

AGING

PRIVATE ORGANIZATIONS

American Association of Retired Persons
601 E St. NW
Washington, DC 20049
800-424-3410
http://www.aarp.org

American Society on Aging
833 Market St., Suite 511
San Francisco, CA 94103
415-974-9600
http://www.asaging.org

Andrus Gerontology Center
University of Southern California
Ethel Percy Andrus Gerontology Center
3715 McClintock Ave.
Los Angeles, CA 90089-0191
213-740-6060
http://www.usc.edu/dept/gero

Associacion Nacional por Personas Mayores
(National Association for Hispanic Elderly)
234 E. Colorado Blvd.
Suite 300
Pasadena, CA 91101
626-564-1988
http://www.aoa.gov/directory/139.html

Associacion Nacional por Personas Mayores
(National Association for Hispanic Elderly)
Job Placement Center
1452 West Temple St.
Suite 100
Los Angeles, CA 90026
213-202-5900

National Senior Citizens Law Center
1101 14th St., NW, Suite 400
Washington, DC 20005
202-289-6976
http://www.nsclc.org

Self-Help for the Elderly
407 Sansome St.
San Francisco, CA 94111-3112
415-982-9171
http://www.selfhelpfortheelderly.com

STATE COMMISSIONS AND OFFICES

State commissions and offices on aging are responsible for coordinating services for older Americans.

They can provide information on programs, services, and opportunities for the aging.

Alabama

Department of Senior Services
770 Washington Ave.
RSA Plaza, Suite 470
Montgomery, AL 36130
334-242-5743
877-425-2243
800-243-5463 (Alabama only)
http://adss.state.al.us

Alaska

Commission on Aging
Division of Senior Services
Department of Administration
P.O. Box 110209
Juneau, AK 99811-0209
907-465-3250
907-465-2205 (TTY)
http://www.alaskaaging.org

Arizona

Aging and Adult Administration
Department of Economic Security
1789 W. Jefferson, 950A
Phoenix, AZ 85007
602-542-4446
http://www.de.state.az.us.aaa

Arkansas

Division of Aging and Adult Services
Department of Human Services
P.O. Box 1437, Slot S-530
Little Rock, AR 72203-1437
501-682-2441
800-482-8049 (Arkansas only)
http://www.state.ar.us/dhs/aging

California

Department of Aging
1600 K St.
Sacramento, CA 95814
916-322-3887
800-510-2020 (Information line)
800-735-2929 (TDD)
http://www.aging.ca.gov

 "Investments and Retirement" in chapter 20

Go to

Colorado

Division of Aging and Adult Services
Office of Adult and Veterans Services
Colorado Department of Human Services
1575 Sherman St.
Denver, CO 80203-1714
303-866-2800
http://www.cdhs.state.co.us/oss/aas

Connecticut

Elderly Services Division
Department of Social Services
25 Sigourney St., 10th Floor
Hartford, CT 06106-5033
860-424-5277
800-994-9422
http://www.stelderlyservices.state.ct.us

Delaware

**Division of Services for Aging and Adults with
    Physical Disabilities**
1901 N. DuPont Highway
1st Floor Annex
New Castle, DE 19720
302-577-4791
800-223-9074 (Delaware only)
http://dsaapd.com

District of Columbia

D.C. Office on Aging
441 4th St., NW, Suite 900 South
One Judiciary Sq.
Washington, DC 20001
202-724-5622
http://www.dcoa.dc.gov

Florida

Department of Elder Affairs
4040 Esplanade Way, Suite 315
Tallahassee, FL 32399-7000
850-414-2000
http://elderaffairs.state.fl.us

Georgia

Office of Aging Services
2 Peachtree St., NW, 9th Fl.
Atlanta, GA 30303
404-657-5258
http://www2.state.ga.us/departments/dhr/aging.html

Hawaii

Executive Office on Aging
250 South Hotel, Room 406
Honolulu, HI 96813
808-586-0100
http://www.state.hi.us/eoa

Idaho

Idaho Commission on Aging
3380 Americana Terrace
Suite 120
Boise, ID 83706
208-334-3833
http://www.idahoaging.com

Illinois

Department on Aging
421 E. Capitol Ave., #100
Springfield, IL 62701-1789
217-785-2870
800-252-8966 (voice/TDD inside Illinois)
http://www.state.il.us/aging

Indiana

Bureau of Aging/In-Home Care Services Division
Department of Human Services
P.O. Box 7083, MS-21
Indianapolis, IN 46207-7083
317-232-7020
800-986-3505
800-532-3213 (Inside Iowa only)
http://www.in.gov/fssa/elderly/aging

Iowa

Department of Elder Affairs
200 10th St., 3rd Fl.
Des Moines, IA 50309-3609
515-281-5187
800-532-3213 (Iowa only)
http://www.state.ia.us/elderaffairs

Kansas

Department on Aging
New England Building
503 S. Kansas Ave.
Topeka, KS 66603-3404
785-296-4986
785-291-3167 (TTY)
800-432-3535 (Kansas only)
http://www.agingkansas.org/kdoa

Kentucky

Office of Aging Services
Department for Social Services
275 E. Main St., 5C-D
Frankfort, KY 40601
502-564-6930
http://chs.state.ky.us/aging/

Louisiana

Governors Office of Elder Affairs
P.O. Box 80374
Baton Rouge, LA 70898-0374
225-342-7100
http://www.gov.state.la.us/depts/elderly/htm

Maine

Bureau of Elder and Adult Services
11 Statehouse Station
35 Anthony Ave.
Augusta, ME 04333-0011
207-624-5335
800-262-2232
207-624-5442 (TTY)
888-720-1925 (TTY)
http://www.state.me.us/dhs/beas/welcome.htm

Maryland

Office on Aging
301 W. Preston St., Suite 1007
Baltimore, MD 21201
410-767-1100
410-767-1083 (TDD)
800-243-3425 (Maryland only)
http://www.mdoa.state.md.us/

Massachusetts

Executive Office of Elder Affairs
1 Ashburton Pl., 5th Floor
Boston, MA 02111
617-727-7750
800-882-2003 (Massachusetts only)
800-872-0166 (TDD Massachusetts only)
http://www.state.ma.us/elder

Michigan

Office of Services to the Aging
P.O. Box 30676
Lansing, MI 48909
517-373-8230
http://www.miseniors.net

Minnesota

Minnesota Board on Aging
444 Lafayette Rd.
St. Paul, MN 55155-3843
651-296-2770
800-882-6262
800-652-9747 (Minnesota only)
http://www.mnaging.org

Mississippi

Council on Aging
Division of Aging and Adult Services
750 N. State St.
Jackson, MS 39202
601-359-4929
800-948-3090 (Mississippi only)
http://www.mdhs.state.ms.us/aas.html

Missouri

Department of Health and Senior Services
P.O. Box 570
Jefferson City, MO 65102
573-751-6400
800-235-5503
http://www.health.state.mo.us/

Montana

Senior and Long Term Care Division
Bureau of Aging Services
Department f Health and Human Services
P.O. Box 4210
Helena, MT 59604
406-444-4077
800-332-2272 (Montana only)
http://www.dphhs.state.mt.us/sltc

Nebraska

Nebraska Department on Aging
Department of Health and Human Services
P.O. Box 95044
Lincoln, NE 68509
402-471-2306
http://www.hhs.state.ne.us/ags/agsindex.htm

Nevada

Division for Aging Services
Department of Human Resources
3100 West Sahara Avenue, Suite 103
Las Vegas, NV 89102
702-486-3545
http://www.nvaging.net

New Hampshire

Division of Elderly and Adult Services
Brown Building
129 Pleasant St.
Concord, NH 03301
603-271-4680
800-351-1888 (New Hampshire only)
http://www.dhhs.state.nh.us

New Jersey

Division of Senior Affairs
Department of Health and Senior Services
P.O. Box 807
Trenton, NJ 08625-0807
609-943-3437
800-792-8820 (New Jersey only)
http://www.state.nj.us/health/senior/sraffair.htm

New Mexico

State Agency on Aging
228 E. Palace Ave.
Santa Fe, NM 87501
505-827-7640
800-432-2080 (New Mexico only)
http://www.nmaging.state.nm.us

New York

New York State Office for the Aging
2 Empire State Plaza
Albany, NY 12223-1251
518-474-5731
800-342-9871 (New York only)
http://aging.state.ny.us/

North Carolina

Division of Aging
Department of Human Resources
2101 Mail Service Center
Raleigh, NC 27699-2101
919-733-3983
800-662-7030 (voice/TDD in North Carolina only)
http://www.dhhs.state.nc.us/aging/home.htm

North Dakota

Department of Human Service
Aging Services Division
600 South 2nd Street, Suite 1C
Bismarck, ND 5854-5729
701-328-8910
701-328-8968 (TDD)
800-451-8693
http://lnotes.state.nd.us/dhs/dhsweb.nsf/ServicePages/
AgingServices

Ohio

Ohio Department of Aging
50 W. Broad St., 9th Floor
Columbus, OH 43215
614-466-5500
614-466-6191 (TDD)
800-282-1206 (Ohio only—nursing home information)
http://www.state.oh.us/age/

Oklahoma

Aging Services
312 NE 28th Street
Oklahoma City, OK 3105
405-521-2281
405-236-5513 (TDD)
http://www.okdhs.org/aging/index.html

Oregon

Seniors and People with Disabilities
Department of Human Services
500 Summer St., NE 97301
Salem, OR 97310-0105
503-945-5811
800-232-3020 (voice/TDD in Oregon)
http://www.sdsd.hr.state.or.us

Pennsylvania

Department of Aging
555 Walnut St., 5th Fl.
400 Market St., 7th Floor
Harrisburg, PA 17101-1919
717-783-1549
http://www.aging.state.pa.us/aging/site/default.asp

Rhode Island

Department of Elderly Affairs
160 Pine St.
Providence, RI 02903
401-222-2858
800-322-2880 (Rhode Island only)
http://www.dea.state.ri.us

South Carolina

Division on Aging
Office of the Governor
202 Arbor Lake Dr., #301
Columbia, SC 29223-4535
803-898-2850
800-868-9095
http://www.state.sc.us/dss

South Dakota
Office of Adult Services and Aging
700 Governors Dr.
Pierre, SD 57501
605-773-3656
http://www.state.sd.us

Tennessee
Commission on Aging
Andrew Jackson Bldg.
500 Deaderick St., 9th Floor
Nashville, TN 37243-0860
615-741-2056
http://www.state.tn.us

Texas
Texas Department on Aging
4900 N. Lamar Blvd.
P.O. Box 12786, Capitol Station
Austin, TX 78751
512-424-6840
http://www.tdoa.state.tx.us

Utah
Division of Aging and Adult Services
P.O. Box 45500
Salt Lake City, UT 84145-0500
801-538-3910
http://www.hsdaas.state.ut.us

Vermont
Department of Aging and Disabilities
103 S. Main St.
Waterbury, VT 05671-2301
802-241-2400 (voice/TDD)
http://www.dad.state.vt.us

Virginia
Department for the Aging
1600 Forest Ave., Suite 102
Richmond, VA 23229
804-662-9333
800-552-4464 (Virginia only)
800-552-3402 (Virginia only—Ombudsman Hotline)
http://www.aging.state.va.us

Washington
Aging and Adult Services Administration
P.O. Box 45050
Olympia, WA 98504-5050
800-422-3263
800-737-7931 (TDD)
http://www.aasa.dshs.wa.gov/

West Virginia
Commission on Aging
Holly Grove Capitol Complex
1900 Kanawha Blvd. East
Charleston, WV 25305-0160
304-558-3317
http://www.state.wv.us

Wisconsin
Bureau of Aging and Long Term Care Resources
1 West Wilson St., Room 450
P.O. Box 7851
Madison, WI 53707-7851
608-266-2536
http://www.dhfs.state.wi.us/aging/

Wyoming
Division on Aging
6101 Yellowstone Road, Room 259B
Cheyenne, WY 82002-0480
307-777-7986
800-442-2766 (Wyoming only)
http://wdhfs.state.wy.us/aging/index.htm

American Samoa
Territorial Administration on Aging
Government of American Samoa
Pago Pago, AS 96799
011-684-633-1251
http://www.government.as/aging.htm

Guam
Division of Senior Citizens
Department of Public Health and Social Services
Government of Guam
P.O. Box 2816
Agana, GU 96910
011-671-475-0263
http://ns.gov.gu/government.html

Puerto Rico
Oficina para los Asuntos de la Vejez
Comisión de Derechos Ciudadanos (CODECI)
PO Box 50063
Cobians Plaza Piso U M Ofic C
Ave. Ponce de León
Puerto Rico
787-721-6121
http://www.gobierno.pr

Virgin Islands
Virgin Islands: Senior Citizens Affairs
Department of Human Services
Knud Hansen Complex
Building A 1303 Hospital Ground
St. Thomas, VI 00840
340-774-0930
http://www.usvi.gov/humanservices/

ALCOHOLISM AND DRUG ABUSE

Al-Anon Family Group Headquarters
1600 Corporate Landing Parkway
Virginia Beach, VA 23454-5617
757-563-1600
http://www.al-anon.alateen.org

Alcohol and Drug Problems Association of North America
307 North Main
St. Charles, MO 63301
314-589-6702
http://www.adpana.com

Substance Abuse and Mental Health Service Administration
U.S. Department of Health and Human Services
Center for Substance Abuse Prevention
5600 Fishers Lane
Rockville, MD 20857
301-443-0365
http://www.os.dhhs.gov

Alcoholics Anonymous World Services
475 Riverside Dr.
New York, NY 10115
212-870-3400
http://www.aa.org

American Council on Alcoholism
3900 North Fairfax Drive
Suite 401
Arlington, VA 22203
703-248-9005
http://www.aca-usa.org

American Council on Alcohol Problems
2376 Lakeside Dr.
Birmingham, AL 35244
205-989-8177
http://www.american councilonalcoholproblems.com

"Safe Alcohol Consumption" in chapter 18

Go to

Association of Halfway House Alcoholism Programs of North America
5 Ridgeview Road
P.O. Box 610
Kerhonkson, NY 12446
845-626-2684
http://www.ahhap.org

BACCHUS and GAMMA
Peer Education Network
P.O. Box 100430
Denver, CO 80250-0430
303-871-0901
http://www.bacchusgamma.org

Cocaine Helpline
800-COCAINE

Do It Now Foundation
P.O. Box 27568
Tempe, AZ 85285-7568
480-736-0599
http://www.doitnow.org

Families Anonymous
P.O. Box 3475
Culver City, CA 90231-3475
800-736-9805
http://www.familiesanonymous.org

Narcotics Anonymous
P.O. Box 9999
Van Nuys, CA 94109
818-773-9999
http://www.na.com

National Association for Children of Alcoholics
11426 Rockville Pike, Suite 100
Rockville, MD 20852
301-468-0985
888-554-COAS (888-554-2627)
http://www.nacoa.org

National Association of Alcoholism and Drug Abuse Counselors
901 N. Washington St.
Suite 600
Alexandria, VA 22314
703-741-7686
800-548-0497
http://www.naadac.org

National Association on Drug Abuse Problems
355 Lexington Ave.
New York, NY 10017
212-986-1170
http://www.nadap.com

National Cocaine Hotline
800-992-9239

National Council on Alcoholism and Drug Dependence
20 Exchange Place
Suite 2902
New York, NY 10005
212-269-7797
800-NCA-CALL (800-622-2255)
http://www.ncadd.org

National Families in Action
2957 Clairmont Rd.
Suite 150
Atlanta, GA 30345
770-934-6364
http://www.nationalfamilies.org

National Family Partnership
(formerly National Federation of Parents for Drug-Free Youth)
2490 Coral Way
Suite 501
Miami, FL 33145
305-856-4886
800-705-8997
http://www.nfp.org

National Parents Resource Institute for Drug Education
166 St. Charles St.
Bowling Green, KY 42101
800-279-6361
http://www.prideusa.org

Odyssey Center
Substance Abuse Training For Professionals
7475 Dakin St.
Suite 601
Denver, CO 80221
303-657-0996

Women in Need, Inc.
115 W. 31st St.
New York, NY 10001
212-695-7330
http://women-in-need.org/

CHILDREN

CHILD ABUSE

American Association for Protecting Children
c/o American Humane Association
63 Inverness Dr. East
Englewood, CO 80112

800-227-4645
http://www.americanhumane.org

American Professional Society on the Abuse of Children
National Office
P.O. Box 26901
CHO 3B-3406
Oklahoma City, OK   73190
405-271-8202
http://www.apsac.org

Child Welfare League of America
Headquarters
440 First St. NW, 3rd Fl.
Washington, DC 20001-2085
202-638-2952
http://www.cwla.org/

The Children's Defense Fund
25 E Street NW
Washington, DC 20001
202-628-8787
cdfinfo@childrensdefense.org

Clearinghouse on Child Abuse and Neglect Information
330 C Street SW
Washington, DC 20447
703-385-7656
800-FYI-3366
http://www.calib.com/nccanch

Klaas Kids Foundation
P.O. Box 925
Sausalito, CA 94966
415-331-6867
http://www.klaaskids.org/

National Association of Child Advocates
1522 K Street NW
Suite 600
Washington, DC 20005-1202
http://www.childadvocacy.org

National Children's Alliance
1612 K Street, NW, Suite 500
Washington, DC 20006
202-452-6001
800-239-9950
http://www.nncac.org/

Parents Anonymous
675 W. Foothill Blvd., Suite 220
Claremont, CA 91711
909-621-6184
http://www.parentsanonymous.org

"Traveling Tips for the Disabled" in chapter 24 **Go to**

Prevent Child Abuse America
200 S. Michigan Ave., 17th Fl.
Chicago, IL 60604
312-663-3520
800-CHILDREN (800-244-5373)
http://www.preventchildabuse.org

DISABLED CHILDREN

**Association for Children with Retarded Mental
  Development/Lifespire**
345 Hudson St., 3rd Fl.
New York, NY 10014
212-741-0100
http://www.acrmd.com

**ERIC Clearinghouse of Disabilities and Gifted
  Education**
Department of Education
1110 N. Glebe Rd.
Arlington, VA 22201-5704
800-328-0272
http://www.ericec.org

National Center for Learning Disabilities
381 Park Ave. South, Suite 1401
New York, NY 10016
212-545-7510
888-575-7373
http://www.ld.org

**National Information Center for Children and Youth
  with Handicaps**
P.O. Box 1492
Washington, DC 20013
202-884-8200
800-695-0285
http://www.nichcy.org

RUNAWAYS

American Youth Work Center & Youth Today
1200 17th St., NW, 4th Fl.
Washington, DC 20036
202-785-0764
800-599-2455
http://www.youthtoday.org

Focus Adolescent Services
1-877-FOCUS
http://www.focusas.com/

National Center for Missing and Exploited Children
Charles B. Wang International Children's Bureau
699 Prince Street
Alexandria, VA 22314-3175

703-274-3900
800-THE-LOST
http://www.missingkids.com/

National Network for Youth
1319 F St., NW, 4th Fl.
Washington, DC 20004
202-783-7949
http://www.nn4youth.org

National Runaway Switchboard
3080 N. Lincoln Ave.
Chicago, IL 60657
800-621-4000
http://www.nrscrisisline.org

CONSUMER INFORMATION AND PROTECTION

BETTER BUSINESS BUREAUS

Some locations are serviced by local bureaus in adjoining states. To locate the bureau nearest you, use the zip code search or state directory at http://www.bbb.org/bureaus/index.html.

UNITED STATES—NATIONAL HEADQUARTERS

Council of Better Business Bureaus
4200 Wilson Blvd., Suite 800
Arlington, VA 22203
703-276-0100
http://www.bbb.org

STATE, COUNTY, AND CITY GOVERNMENT CONSUMER PROTECTION OFFICES

Listed below are consumer protection offices that are part of state, county, and city governments. Some are located in governors' offices, state attorney generals' offices, or mayors' offices. Check in your state to see which office can help resolve complaints, furnish information or helpful publications, or provide other services. As a general rule, the first place to go for help with a consumer problem is the local office nearest your home. If you are having a problem with a business outside your state, however, contact the consumer office in the state in which you made the purchase. Because most offices require that complaints be in writing, you might save time by writing, rather than calling, with your initial complaint.

Alabama—State Office

Director
Consumer Protection Division
Office of the Attorney General
11 S. Union St.
Montgomery, AL 36130
334-242-7334
800-392-5658 (Alabama only)
http://www.ago.state.al.us/consumer.cfm

Alaska

Attorney General's Office
1031 W. 4th Ave.
Suite 200
Anchorage, AK 99501
907-465-2133
http://www.law.state.ak.us/consumer/

Arizona—State Offices

Consumer Protection Office of the Attorney General
1275 W. Washington St., Room 259
Phoenix, AZ 85007
602-542-3702
602-542-5763
800-352-8431 (Arizona only)
http://ag.state.az.us/consumer/index.html

Assistant Attorney General
Consumer Protection Office of the Attorney General
402 W. Congress St., Suite 315
Tucson, AZ 85701
520-628-6504
800-352-8431

Arizona—SELECTED County Offices

County Attorney
Apache County Attorney's Office
P.O. Box 637
St. Johns, AZ 85936
520-337-4364

County Attorney
Cochise County Attorney's Office
P.O. Drawer CA
Bisbee, AZ 85603
520-432-9377

County Attorney
Coconino County Attorney's Office
Coconino County Courthouse

100 E. Birch
Flagstaff, AZ 86001
520-779-6518

County Attorney
Gila County Attorney's Office
1400 E. Ash St.
Globe, AZ 85501
520-425-3231

County Attorney
Graham County Attorney's Office
Graham County Courthouse
800 W. Main
Safford, AZ 85546
520-428-3620

County Attorney
Greenlee County Attorney's Office
P.O. Box 1717
Clifton, AZ 85533
520-865-4108

County Attorney
La Paz County Attorney's Office
1320 Kofa Avenue
P.O. Box 709
Parker, AZ 85344
520-669-6118

County Attorney
Mohave County Attorney's Office
P.O. Box 7000
Kingman, AZ 86402
520-753-0719

County Attorney
Navajo County Attorney's Office
P.O. Box 668
Holbrook, AZ 86025
520-524-4026

County Attorney
Pima County Attorney's Office
1400 Legal Services Building
32 N. Stone
Tucson, AZ 85701
520-740-5600

County Attorney
Pinal County Attorney's Office
P.O. Box 887
Florence, AZ 85232
520-868-6271

County Attorney
Santa Cruz County Attorney's Office
2100 N. Congress Dr., Suite 201

Nogales, AZ 85621
520-761-7800 x3121

County Attorney
Yavapai County Attorney's Office
Yavapai County Courthouse
255 E. Gurley
Prescott, AZ 86301
520-771-3344

County Attorney
Yuma County Attorney's Office
168 S. Second Ave.
Yuma, AZ 85364
520-329-2270

Arizona—City Office

Consumer Affairs Division
Tucson City Attorney's Office
1501 N. Oracle Annex
Tucson, AZ 85705
520-791-4886

Arkansas—State Office

Consumer Protection Division
Office of Attorney General
200 Tower Bldg.
323 Center St.
Little Rock, AR 72201
501-682-2341 (voice/TDD)
800-482-8982 (voice/TDD in Arkansas)

California—State Offices

California Department of Consumer Affairs
400 R St., Suite 1080
Sacramento, CA 95814
916-445-1254 (consumer information)
916-522-1700 (TDD)

Office of the Attorney General
Public Inquiry Unit
P.O. Box 944255
Sacramento, CA 94244-2550
916-322-3360

Bureau of Automotive Repair
California Department of Consumer Affairs
10220 Systems Parkway
Sacramento, CA 95827
916-255-4200

California—SELECTED County Offices

District Attorney
Alameda County District Attorney's Office
1225 Fallon St., Room 900

Oakland, CA 94612
510-272-6222

District Attorney
Contra Costa County District Attorney's Office
725 Court St., 4th Floor
Martinez, CA 94553
925-646-4500

Business Affairs
Fresno County District Attorney's Office
2220 Tulare St., Suite 1000
Fresno, CA 93721
559-488-3133

Consumer and Major Business Fraud Section
Kern County District Attorney's Office
1215 Truxtun Ave.
Bakersfield, CA 93301
661-868-2340

Los Angeles County Department of Consumer Affairs
500 W. Temple St.
Room B-96
Los Angeles, CA 90012-2706
213-974-1452

Consumer and Environmental Protection Unit
Marin County District Attorney's Office
3501 Civic Center Dr., Room 130
San Rafael, CA 94903
415-499-6450

District Attorney
Mendocino County District Attorney's Office
P.O. Box 1000
Uklah, CA 95482
707-463-4211

Consumer Protection Division
Monterey County District Attorney's Office
P.O. Box 1131
Salinas, CA 93902
831-755-5073
831-647-7773

Consumer Affairs Division
Napa County District Attorney's Office
931 Parkway Mall
Napa, CA 94559
707-253-4211

Consumer Protection Division
Orange County District Attorney's Office
401 Civic Center Dr. West, Suite 120
Santa Ana, CA 92701
714-834-3600

Economic Crime Division
Riverside County District Attorney's Office
4075 Main St.
Riverside, CA 92501
909-955-5400

Consumer and Environmental Protection Division
Sacramento County District Attorney's Office
901 G Street
Sacramento, CA 95814
916-874-6218

Consumer Fraud Division
San Diego County District Attorney's Office
Hall of Justice
330 West Broadway
San Diego, CA 92101
619-531-4040

Consumer and Environmental Protection Unit
San Francisco County District Attorney's Office
880 Bryant Street
San Francisco, CA 94103
415-552-6400
415-553-1752

If you want to send a letter to the North Pole, the correct address is North Pole, AK 99705.

Consumer and Business Affairs Division
San Joaquin County District Attorney's Office
Courthouse
Stockton, CA 95202
209-468-2400

Consumer Fraud Department
San Luis Obispo County District Attorney's Office
County Government Center
1050 Monterey St., Room 450
San Luis Obispo, CA 93408
805-781-5800

Consumer Fraud and Environmental Protection Unit
San Mateo County District Attorney's Office
401 Marshall St.
Hall of Justice and Records
Redwood City, CA 94063
650-363-4636

Consumer Mediation Program
Santa Barbara County District Attorney's Office
1105 Santa Barbara St.
Santa Barbara, CA 93101
805-568-2390

Consumer Fraud Unit
Santa Clara County District Attorney's Office
70 W. Hedding St., West Wing
San Jose, CA 95110
408-299-7400

Division of Consumer Affairs
Santa Cruz County District Attorney's Office
701 Ocean St., Room 200
Santa Cruz, CA 95060
831-424-2050

Consumer Affairs Unit
Solano County District Attorney's Office
600 Union Ave.
Fairfield, CA 94533
707-421-6859

Consumer Fraud Unit
Stanislaus County District Attorney's Office
800 11th Street, Room 200
Modesto, CA 95354
209-525-5550

Consumer and Environmental Protection Division
Ventura County District Attorney's Office
800 S. Victoria Ave.
Ventura, CA 93009
805-654-3110

Special Services Unit—Consumer/Environmental
Yolo County District Attorney's Office
301 Second Street
Woodland, CA 95695
530-666-8180

California—City Offices
Consumer Protection Division
Los Angeles City Attorney's Office
200 N. Main St.
1600 City Hall East
Los Angeles, CA 90012
213-485-4515

Consumer Division
Santa Monica City Attorney's Office
1685 Main St., Room 310
Santa Monica, CA 90401
310-458-8336

Colorado—State Offices
Consumer Protection Unit
Office of the Attorney General
1525 Sherman St., 7th Fl.
Denver, CO 80203
303-866-4500

Inspection and Consumer Services
Department of Agriculture
Main Offices
2331 West 31st Ave.
Denver, Colorado 80211
303-477-0093

Colorado—County Offices

District Attorney
Archuleta, LaPlata, and San Juan Counties District
Attorney's Office
1060 East 2nd Ave.
Durango, CO 81301
970-247-8850

District Attorney
Boulder County District Attorney's Office
P.O. Box 471
Boulder, CO 80306
303-441-3700

Denver County District Attorney's Economic Crime
and Fraud Office
Second Judicial District
303 W. Colfax Ave., Suite 1300
Denver, CO 80204
720-913-9179

Economic Crime Division
El Paso and Teller Counties District Attorney's Office
105 East Vermijo
Colorado Springs, CO 80903
719-520-6002

District Attorney
Pueblo County District Attorney's Office
201 W. 8th St., Suite 801
Pueblo, CO 81003
719-583-6030

Consumer Fraud Investigator
Weld County District Attorney's Consumer Office
P.O. Box 1167
Greeley, CO 80632
970-356-4010

Connecticut—State Offices

Department of Consumer Protection
State Office Bldg.
165 Capitol Ave.
Hartford, CT 06106
860-713-6300
800-842-2649

Antitrust/Consumer Protection
Office of Attorney General
55 Elm St.
Hartford, CT 06106
860-808-5318

Connecticut—City Office

Middletown Office of Consumer Protection
243 deKoran Dr.
Middletown, CT 06457
860-344-3491

Delaware—State Offices

Consumer Protection Unit
Office of Attorney General
Carvel State Building, 5th Fl.
820 N. French St.
Wilmington, DE 19801
302-577-8600

District of Columbia

Department of Consumer and Regulatory Affairs
941 North Capital St. NE
Washington, DC 20002
202-282-DCRA

Florida—State Offices

Department of Agriculture and Consumer Services
Division of Consumer Services
407 South Calhoun St.
Mayo Building
Tallahassee, FL 32399-0800
850-488-2221
800-435-7352 (Florida only)
800-352-9832 (in Spanish)

Consumer Division
Office of the Attorney General
The Capital, Suite PL01
Hollywood, FL 32399-1050
850-487-1963

Florida—SELECTED County Offices

Broward County Consumer Affairs Division
115 S. Andrews Ave., Room A-460
Fort Lauderdale, FL 33301
954-765-5350

Consumer Advocate
Metropolitan Dade County Consumer Protection
Division
140 W. Flagler St., 9th Floor
Miami, FL 33130
305-375-4222

Dade County Economic Crime Unit
Office of the State Attorney
1469 Northwest 13th Terrace, Room 600
Miami, FL 33125
305-324-3030

**Hillsborough County Department of Consumer
Affairs**
8900 N. Armenia Ave., Suite 222
Tampa, FL 33602
813-272-6750

Orange County Consumer Fraud Unit
415 N. Orange Ave.
P.O. Box 1673
Orlando, FL 32802
407-836-2490

Citizens Intake
Palm Beach County Office of State Attorney
401 North Dixie Highway
West Palm Beach, FL 33401
561-355-7100

Palm Beach County Division of Consumer Affairs
50 South Military Trail, Suite 201
West Palm Beach, FL 33405
561-712-6600

Pasco County Consumer Affairs Division
West Pasco Government Center
7530 Little Rd., Suite 140
New Port Richey, FL 34654
727-847-8110

Pinellas County Office of Consumer Affairs
15251 Roosevelt Boulevard, Suite 209
Clearwater, FL 33760
727-464-6200

Florida—City Offices

Chief of Consumer Affairs
City of Jacksonville Division of Consumer Affairs
117 W. Duval St.
Jacksonville, FL 32202
904-630-1212 Ext. 4090

Tamarac Board of Consumer Affairs
7525 NW 88th Ave.
Tamarac, FL 33321
954-724-1346

Georgia—State Office

Governors Office of Consumer Affairs
2 Martin Luther King, Jr. Dr., Suite 356
Atlanta, GA 30334

404-651-8600
404-656-3790
800-869-1123 (Georgia only)

Hawaii—State Offices

Office of Consumer Protection
Department of Commerce and Consumer Affairs
Honolulu Office
Leiopapa A. Kamehama Building
235 S. Beretania St., Suite 801
Honolulu, HI 96813
808-586-2630

Office of Consumer Protection
Department of Commerce and Consumer Affairs
Hilo Office
345 Kekuanaoa St., Suite 12
75 Aupuni St.
Hilo, HI 96720
808-933-0910

Office of Consumer Protection
Department of Commerce and Consumer Affairs
Wailuku Office
1063 Lower Main St.
Suite c-216
Wailuku, HI 96793
808-984-8244

Idaho—State Office

Office of the Attorney General
Consumer Protection Unit
700 W. Jefferson St.
P.O. Box 83720
Boise, ID 83720
208-334-2424
800-432-3545 (Idaho only)

Illinois—State Offices

Governors Office of Citizens Assistance
222 S. College
Springfield, IL 62706
217-782-0244
800-252-8666 (Illinois only)

Consumer Protection Division
Office of the Attorney General
100 W. Randolph, 12th Floor
Chicago, IL 60601
312-814-3000
800-386-5438 (Illinois only)

Consumer Protection Division
Office of the Attorney General
500 S. Second St.
Springfield, IL 62706
217-782-9011
800-243-0618 (Illinois only)

Illinois—Regional Offices
Assistant Attorney General
Carbondale Regional Office
Office of the Attorney General
1001 East Main St.
Carbondale, IL 62901
618-529-6400
800-243-0607 (Illinois only)

Assistant Attorney General
East Central Regional Office
Office of the Attorney General
1776 E. Washington St.
Urbana, IL 61802
217-278-3366

Assistant Attorney General
Kankakee Regional Office
Office of the Attorney General
1012 N. 5th Ave.
Kankakee, IL 60901
815-935-8500

Assistant Attorney General
Metro–East Illinois
201 West Pointe Dr., Suite 7
Belleville, IL 62226
618-236-8616
618-236-8619 (TTY)

Assistant Attorney General
Northern Illinois Regional Office
7230 Argus Drive
Rockford, IL 61107
815-484-8100
815-484-8113 (TTY)

Assistant Attorney General
Peoria County
Office of the State's Attorney
324 Main St., Room 111
Peoria County Courthouse
Peoria, IL 61602
309-672-6900

Assistant Attorney General
Quincy Regional Office
Office of the Attorney General
628 Main St.
Quincy, IL 62301

217-223-2221 (voice/TDD)
217-223-2254 (TTY)

Illinois—SELECTED County Offices
Adams County Office of the State's Attorney
521 Vermont St.
Quincy, IL 62301
217-277-2225

Calhoun County Office of the State's Attorney
County Courthouse
P.O. Box 187
Hardin, IL 62047
618-576-9013

Clark County Office of the State's Attorney
2nd Floor Courthouse
501 Archer
Marshall, IL 62441
217-826-6142

You can have a birthday greeting sent from the President of the United States to anyone 80-years-old or older. Send your request a few months in advance to your local congressman or senator.

Consumer Fraud Division
Cook County Office of the State's Attorney
303 Daley Center
Chicago, IL 60602
312-603-5440
312-603-7605 (TDD)

State's Attorney
Madison County Office of the State's Attorney
Madison County Administration Building
157 N. Main St., Suite 402
Edwardsville, IL 62025
618-692-6280

Director
Consumer Protection Division
Rock Island County Office of the State's Attorney
County Courthouse
210 15th St.
Rock Island, IL 61201
309-786-4451, ext. 229

Illinois—City Offices

Chicago Department of Consumer Services
121 N. LaSalle St., Room 808
Chicago, IL 60602
312-744-4006
312-744-9385 (TTY)
312-744-9400 (complaint line)

Des Plaines Consumer Protection Commission
1420 Miner St., 6th Fl.
Des Plaines, IL 60016
847-391-5300

Indiana—State Office

Consumer Protection Division
Office of the Attorney General
Indiana Government Center South, 5th Fl.
402 W. Washington St.
Indianapolis, IN 46204
317-232-6330
800-382-5516 (Indiana only)

Indiana—SELECTED County Offices

Consumer Protection Division
Lake County Prosecutor's Office
2293 N. Main St.
Crown Point, IN 46307
219-755-3300

Marion County Prosecuting Attorney
560 City-County Bldg.
200 E. Washington St.
Indianapolis, IN 46204-3363
317-327-3522

Vanderburgh County Prosecuting Attorney
Administration Bldg., Room 108
Civic Center Complex
Evansville, IN 47708
812-435-5150

Indiana—City Office

Director
Gary Office of Consumer Affairs
401 Broadway B2
Gary, IN 46402
219-881-5297

Iowa—State Office

Consumer Protection Division
Office of the Attorney General
1305 E. Walnut St., 2nd Floor
Des Moines, IA 50319
515-281-5926

Kansas—State Office

Consumer Protection Division
Office of the Attorney General
120 SW 10th Ave., 2nd Fl.
Kansas Judicial Center
Topeka, KS 66612-3751
785-296-3751
800-432-2310 (Kansas only)

Kansas—SELECTED County Offices

Consumer Fraud Division
Johnson County District Attorney's Office
Johnson County Courthouse
P.O. Box 728
Olathe, KS 66051
913-715-3000

Consumer Fraud and Economic Crime Division
Sedgwick County District Attorney's Office
535 North Main
Wichita, KS 67203
316-383-7921

Assistant District Attorney
Shawnee County District Attorney's Office
200 SE 7th St.
Topeka, KS 66603
785-233-8200 Ext. 4330

Kentucky—State Offices

Consumer Protection Division
Office of the Attorney General
The Capitol, Suite 118
700 Capitol Avenue
Frankfort, KY 40601
502-696-5389

Consumer Protection and Education Division
Kentucky Department of Insurance
P.O. Box 517
Louisville, KY 40602
502-564-6034
800-432-9257 (Kentucky only)

Louisiana—State Office

Office of the Attorney General
One American Place
301 Main St., 12th Fl.
P.O. Box 94095
Baton Rouge, LA 70804-9005
225-342-7900
800-351-4889 (consumer hotline)

Louisiana—SELECTED County Office

Consumer Protection Division
Jefferson Parish District Attorney's Office
Gretna Courthouse
Annex Building, 5th Fl.
Gretna, LA 70053
504-368-1020

Maine—State Offices

Department of Financial and Professional Regulation
Bureau of Consumer Credit Protection
State House Station No. 35
Augusta, ME 04333-0035
207-624-8527
800-965-5235

Department of the Attorney General
Public Protection Division
Consumer Information and Mediation Service
6 State House Station
Augusta, ME 04333-0006
207-626-8849

Number 10 Downing Street in London still has the 23 chairs used by Gladstone and Disraeli during Queen Victoria's reign. Only one of the chairs has arms.

Maryland—State Offices

Consumer Protection Division
Office of the Attorney General
200 St. Paul Pl.
Baltimore, MD 21202
410-528-8662
410-576-6550
888-743-0023

Licensing & Consumer Services
Motor Vehicle Administration
6601 Ritchie Highway, NE
Glen Burnie, MD 21062
410-768-7536

Consumer Affairs Specialist
Eastern Shore Branch Office
Consumer Protection Division
Office of the Attorney General
Salisbury District Court/Multiservice Center
201 Baptist St., Suite 30
Salisbury, MD 21801-4976
301-543-6620

Maryland—SELECTED County Offices

Howard County Office of Consumer Affairs
6751 Gateway Drive, 2nd fl.
Columbia, MD 21046
410-313-6420
410-313-6401

Montgomery County Division of Consumer Affairs
100 Maryland Ave., 3rd Floor
Rockville, MD 20850
240-7773636

Massachusetts—State Offices

Consumer Protection Division
Department of the Attorney General
200 Portland St.
Boston, MA 02114
617-727-8400 (consumer hotline)

New Bedford Office of the Attorney General
105 William St., 1st fl.
New Bedford, MA 02740
508-990-9700

Fair Labor and Business Practices
Pittsfield Office of the Attorney General
160 North St.
Pittsfield, MA 01201
413-447-7324 ext. 218

Worcester Office of the Attorney
One Exchange Place
Worcester, MA 01608
508-792-7600

Western Massachusetts Consumer Protection Division
Department of the Attorney General
1350 Main St., 4th Fl.
Springfield, MA 01103
413-784-1240

Massachusetts—SELECTED County Offices

Consumer Fraud Prevention
Franklin County District Attorney's Office
238 Main St.
Greenfield, MA 01301
413-774-5102 Ext. 226

Consumer Protection
Northwestern District Attorney's Office
1 Gleason Plaza
Northhampton, MA 01060
413-586-9225

City Offices
Mayor's Office of Consumer Affairs and Licensing
Boston City Hall, Room 817
Boston, MA 02201
617-635-3834

Michigan—State Offices

Consumer Protection Division
Office of the Attorney General
P.O. Box 30213
Lansing, MI 48909
517-373-1140
517-335-1935

Bureau of Automotive Regulation
Michigan Department of State
Mutual Building, 2nd Fl.
208 N. Capitol Ave.
Lansing, MI 48918
517-373-0964

Michigan—SELECTED County Offices

Bay County Consumer Protection Unit
1230 Washington Ave.
Suite 768
Bay City, MI 48708
989-895-4185

Consumer Protection Department
Macomb County Office of the Prosecuting Attorney
One South Main
Mt. Clemens, MI 48043
586-469-5350

Michigan—City Office

City of Detroit
Consumer Affairs Department
65 Cadillac Square
Suite 1600
Detroit, MI 48226
313-224-6995

Minnesota—State Offices

Office of Consumer Services
Office of the Attorney General
1400 NCL Tower
445 Minnesota St.
St. Paul, MN 55101
651-296-3353
800-657-3787
651-297-7206 (TTY)
800-366-4812 (TTY)

Minnesota—SELECTED County Office

Citizen Protection Unit
Hennepin County Attorney's Office
C-2000 County Government Center
Minneapolis, MN 55487
612-348-5550

Minnesota—City Office

Consumer Affairs Division
Minneapolis Department of Licenses & Consumer Services
City Hall, Room 1C
350 S. Fifth St.
Minneapolis, MN 55415
612-673-2080

Mississippi—State Offices

Office of the Secretary Of State
Regulation and Enforcement Division
P.O. Box 136
Jackson, MS 34205-0136
601-359-1350

Office of the Attorney General
Consumer Protection Division
P.O. Box 220
Jackson, MS 39205-0220
601-359-3680

Missouri

Office of the Attorney General
Consumer Protection Division
Supreme Court Building
P.O. Box 899
207 West High Street
Jefferson City, MO 65102
573-751-3321

Montana-State Offices

Department of Justice
Office of Attorney General
Consumer Protection Division
P.O. Box 201401
Helena, MT 59620-1401
406-444-2026

Montana Department of Commerce
Consumer Affairs Unit
P.O. Box 200501
Helena, MT 59620-0501
406-444-3797

Nebraska—State Office

Office of the Attorney General
Consumer Protection Division
2115 State Capitol
Lincoln, NE 68509
402-471-2682
800-727-6432

Nevada

Nevada Attorney General
Consumer Affairs Division
Carson City Office
100 North Carson Street
Carson City, NV 89701-4717
775-684-1100

Telemarketing, Securities and Deceptive Trade Practices
Consumer Affairs Division
555 East Washington St., Suite 3900
Las Vegas, NV 89101
702-486-3777

Bureau of Consumer Protection
Office of the Attorney General
1000 East William St., Suite 200
Carson City, NV 89710
775-687-6300

New Hampshire—State Office

Chief Consumer Protection and Antitrust Bureau
Office of the Attorney General
33 Capital St.
State House Annex
Concord, NH 03301
603-271-3591

New Jersey—State Offices

Division of Consumer Affairs
Office of Consumer Protection
124 Halsey St.
Newark, NJ 07101
973-504-6200
800-242-5846
973-504-6588 (TDD)

Office of the Attorney General
Division of Consumer Affairs
P.O. Box 080
Trenton, NJ 08625-0080
609-292-4925

New Jersey—Selected County Offices

Atlantic County Division of Consumer Affairs
Department of Law
1333 Atlantic Avenue
Atlantic City, NJ 08401
609-343-2376

Burlington County Department of Consumer Affairs
County Office Building
3rd Floor, Room 354
49 Rancocas Road
PO Box 6000
Mount Holly, NJ 08060-6000
609-265-5054

Camden City Attorney
Office of the City Attorney
Suite 419—City Hall
P.O. Box 95120
Camden, NJ 08101
856-757-7170

Cape May County Consumer Affairs
4 Moore Rd.
Cape May Courthouse, NJ 08210-1601
609-463-6475

Cumberland County Consumer Affairs
788 E. Commerce St.
Bridgeton, NJ 08302
856-453-2203

Essex County
Division of Community Action/Consumer Services
50 South Clinton St., 3rd floor
East Orange, NJ 07018
973-395-8350

Gloucester County
Department of Consumer Protection/Weights & Measures
152 N. Broad St.
Woodbury, NJ 08096
856-853-3349

Hudson County Consumer Affairs
Administration Bldg.
595 Newark Ave.
4th floor, Room 407
Jersey City, NJ 07306
201-795-6295

Hunterdon County Consumer Affairs
P.O. Box 2900
Flemington, NJ 08822
908-806-5174

Livingston Division of Consumer Affairs
357 S. Livingston Ave.
Livingston, NJ 07039
973-535-7976

Mercer County
Office of Consumer Affairs
640 S. Broad St., Rm. 404
Trenton, NJ 08650-0068
609-989-6671

Middlesex County
Consumer Affairs
Middlesex County Administration Bldg.
J.F.K. Square, 2nd floor, Suite 290
New Brunswick, NJ 08901
732-745-3875

Monmouth County
Department of Consumer Affairs
50 E. Main St.
P.O. Box 1255
Freehold, NJ 07728
732-431-7900

North Bergen Consumer Affairs
Municipal Bldg.
4233 Kennedy Blvd.
North Bergen, NJ 07047
201-330-7292

Ocean County Consumer Affairs
1027 Hooper Ave. Bldg. 2
P.O. Box 2191
Toms River, NJ 08754
732-929-2105

Passaic County Department of Law and Public Safety
Division of Weights and Measures
Consumer Protection
1310 Route 23, North
Wayne, NJ 07470
973-305-5881

Perth Amboy Division of Consumer Affairs
City Hall
260 High St,
Perth Amboy, NJ 08861
732-826-0290

Secaucus Department of Consumer Affairs
203 Patterson Plank Road
Secaucus, NJ 07091
201-330-2008

Somerset County Consumer Affairs
Administration Bldg.
20 Grove Street

P.O. Box 3000
Somerville, NJ 08876-1262
908-231-7000

Union County Consumer Affairs
300 North Ave., East
P.O. Box 186
Westfield, NJ 07091
908-654-9840

Wayne Township Division of Consumer Affairs
475 Valley Road
Wayne, NJ 07470
973-694-1800

New Mexico—State Office

Santa Fe Office of Attorney General
Consumer Protection Division
407 Galisteo St.
Bataan Memorial Building, Rm. 260
P.O. Drawer 1508
Santa Fe, NM 87501
505-827-6060
800-678-1508

New Mexico
Albuquerque Regional Office
Consumer Protection Division
111 Lomas NW, Suite 300
Albuquerque, NM 87102
505-222-9000
800-300-2020

New York—State Offices

Office of the Attorney General
Albany Executive Offices
State Capitol, Room 220
Albany, NY 12224-0341
518-474-7330

Consumer Fraud Bureau
Office of the Attorney General
New York Executive Offices
120 Broadway
New York, NY 10271
212-416-8345
800-771-7755

New York State Consumer Protection Board
5 Empire State Plaza, Suite 2101
Albany, NY 12223-1556
518-474-8583

Department of Insurance
Consumer Services Bureau
25 Beaver St.
New York, NY 10004

212-480-6400
800-342-3736

Department of Law
Office of the Attorney General
Bureau of Investor Protection and Securities
120 Broadway, 23rd Fl.
New York, NY 10271
212-416-8200

Bureau of Weights and Measures
Department of Agriculture and Markets
1 Winners Circle
Albany, NY 12235
518-457-3452

New York—Regional Offices

Buffalo Regional Office
Office of Attorney General
Consumer Affairs Division
107 Delaware Ave. 4th Fl.
Buffalo, NY 14202
800-771-7755 (toll free in NY)

Office Wagon Number 123 was the address for the Ringling Brothers and Barnum and Bailey Circus main office and ticket wagon.

Poughkeepsie Regional Office
Office of Attorney General
Consumer Affairs Division
235 Main St. 3rd Fl.
Poughkeepsie, NY 12601
800-771-7755 (toll free in NY)

Rochester Regional Office
Office of Attorney General
Consumer Affairs Division
144 Exchange Blvd.
Rochester, NY 14614-2175
716-546-7430
800-771-7755 (toll free in NY)
716-327-3249 (TDD)

Suffolk Regional Office
Office of the Attorney General
300 Motor Parkway
Hauppauge, NY 11788-5127
631-231-2401

Syracuse Regional Office
Office of Attorney General
Consumer Affairs Division
615 Erie Blvd. West, Ste. 102

Syracuse, NY 13210-2339
315-448-4848
800-771-7755 (toll free in NY)

Utica Regional Office
Office of Attorney General
Consumer Affairs Division
207 Genesee St. Rm. 504
Utica, NY 13501
315-793-2225
800-771-7755 (toll free in NY)

New York—SELECTED County Offices

Broome County District Attorney's Office
The Press Building, 7th Fl.
19 Chenango St.
Binghamton, NY 13901
607-778-8000

Dutchess County Department of Consumer Affairs
98 Peach Road
Poughkeepsie, NY 12601
845-486-2949

Erie County District Attorney's Office
Consumer Fraud Bureau
25 Delaware Ave.
Buffalo, NY 14202
716-858-2424

Nassau County Office of Consumer Affairs
160 Old Country Rd.
Mineola, NY 11501
516-571-2600

Orange County District Attorney's Office
255 Main St.
Goshen, NY 10924
845-291-2050

Orange County Department of Weights and Measures
County Government Center
255 Main St.
Goshen, NY 10924
845-291-2400

Putnam County Department of Consumer Affairs
110 Old Route 6, Building 3
Carmel, NY 10512
845-225-2039

Rockland County Office of Consumer Protection
50 Sanitarium Road
Pomona, NY 10970
845-364-2680

Steuben County Department of Weights, Measures, and Consumer Affairs
3 E. Pulteney Square
Bath, NY 14810
607-776-9631

Suffolk County Department of Consumer Affairs
North County Complex, Building 340
Hauppauge, NY 11788
631-853-4600

Ulster County Consumer Fraud Bureau
20 Lucas Avenue
Kingston, NY 12401
845-340-3260

Westchester County District Attorney's Office
111 Dr. Martin Luther King, Jr. Blvd.
White Plains, NY 10601
914-285-3303

Westchester County Department of Consumer Protection
112 East Post Road, 4th Fl.
White Plains, NY 10601
914-995-2155

New York—City Offices

Babylon Consumer Protection Board
Town Hall
200 East Sunrise Highway
Lindenhurst, NY 11757
631-957-3005

Town of Colonie Consumer Protection Board
Memorial Town Hall
Newtonville, NY 12128
518-783-2704

Mt. Vernon Office of Consumer Affairs
City Hall, 11th Fl.
Mt. Vernon, NY 10550
914-665-2433

New York City Department of Consumer Affairs
42 Broadway
New York, NY 10004
212-487-4444

Queens Neighborhood Office
New York City Department of Consumer Affairs
120-55 Queens Blvd., Room 301A
Kew Gardens, NY 11424
718-286-2990

Staten Island Neighborhood Office
New York City Department of Consumer Affairs
Staten Island Borough Hall, Room 422

Staten Island, NY 10301
212-487-4444

City of Oswego Office of Consumer Affairs
City Hall
West Oneida St.
Oswego, NY 13126
315-342-7245

Ramapo Consumer Protection Board
Ramapo Town Hall
237 Route 59
Suffern, NY 10901-5399
845-357-5100

Schenectady Bureau of Consumer Protection
City Hall
Jay St., Room 204
Schenectady, NY 12305
518-382-5061

Yonkers Office of Consumer Protection,
Weights and Measures
87 Nepperhan Ave.Yonkers, NY 10703
914-377-6807

North Carolina—State Office

Consumer Protection Section
Office of the Attorney General
North Carolina Department of Justice
P.O. Box 629
Raleigh, NC 27602
919-716-6400

North Dakota—State Offices

Office of the Attorney General
State Capitol Bldg.
Bismarck, ND 58505
701-328-2210
800-472-2600 (North Dakota only)

North Dakota—SELECTED County Offices

Quad County Community Action Agency
27½ South Third Street
Grand Forks, ND 58201
701-746-5431

Ohio—State Offices

Consumer Protection Section
Ohio Attorney General
30 E. Broad St., 25th Floor
Columbus, OH 43215-3428
614-466-4320
800-282-0515 (toll free in Ohio)

Office of Consumers' Counsel
10 West Broad Street, Suite 1800
Columbus, OH 43215-3485
614-466-9467
877-742-5622 (toll-free in Ohio)

Ohio–SELECTED County Offices

Economic Crime Division
Franklin County Office of Prosecuting Attorney
369 South High Street
Columbus, OH 43215
614-462-3555.

Montgomery County Fraud and Economic Crimes Division
Dayton Montgomery County Fraud Section
301 West 3rd Street
Dayton, OH 45402
513-225-4747

Portage County Office of Prosecuting Attorney
466 South Chestnut Street
Ravenna, OH 44266-3000
330-296-4593

Summit County Office of Prosecuting Attorney
53 University Avenue
Akron, OH 44308-1680
330-643-2800
330-643-8277 (TDD/TTY)

Ohio–City Office

Neighborhood Services Department
Cincinnati Office of Consumer Affairs
Division of Human Services
City Hall, Room 126
Cincinnati, OH 45202
513-352-6146

Oklahoma–State Offices

Consumer Protection Unit
Office of the Attorney General
4545 N. Lincoln Blvd., #260
Oklahoma City, OK 73105
(405) 521-3921

Department of Consumer Credit
4545 N. Lincoln Blvd., Suite 260
Oklahoma City, OK 73105
405-521-3653

Oregon–State Offices

Financial Fraud Section
Department of Justice
1162 Court St. NE

Salem, OR 97310
503-378-4732
503-378-4320 (hotline)
503-229-5576 (in Portland only)

Pennsylvania–State Offices

Office of Attorney General
Strawberry Square, 14th Floor
Harrisburg, PA 17120
717-787-9707
800-441-2555 (toll free in PA)

Office of Consumer Advocate
Office of Attorney General
Forum Place, 5th Floor
555 Walnut Street
Harrisburg, PA 17101-1921
717-783-5048 (for utilities only)

Pennsylvania–Branch Offices

Bureau of Consumer Services
Pennsylvania Public Utility Commission
PO Box 3265
Harrisburg, PA 17105-3265
717-783-1740
800-782-1110 (general complaints)

Bureau of Consumer Protection
Office of Attorney General
1001 State Street, 1009
Erie, PA 16501
814-871-4371
800-441-2555 (toll free in PA)

Bureau of Consumer Protection
Office of Attorney General
301 Chestnut Street, Suit 105
Harrisburg, PA 17101
717-787-7109
800-441-2555 (toll free in PA)

Bureau of Consumer Protection
Office of Attorney General
171 Lovell Avenue, Suite 202
Ebensburg, PA 15931
814-471-1831
800-441-2555 (toll free in PA)

Bureau of Consumer Protection
Office of Attorney General
21 South 12th Street, 2nd Floor
Philadelphia, PA 19107
215-560-2414
800-441-2555 (toll free in PA)

Bureau of Consumer Protection
Office of Attorney General
Manor Complex, 6th Floor
564 Forbes Avenue
Pittsburgh, PA 15219
412-565-5135
800-441-2555 (toll free in PA)

Bureau of Consumer Protection
Office of Attorney General
Samter Building, Room 214
101 Penn Avenue
Scranton, PA 18503-2025
570-963-4913
800-441-2555 (toll free in PA)

Pennsylvania—SELECTED County Offices

Bucks County Consumer Protection/Weights and
Measures
50 North Main Street
Doylestown, PA 18901
215-348-7442
Toll free in PA: 1-800-441-2555

Chester County Weights and Measures/
Consumer Affairs
Government Services Center, Suite 390
601 Westtown Road
West Chester, PA 19382-4547
610-344-6150
800-441-2555 (toll free in PA)

Cumberland County Consumer Affairs
Weights and Measures
One Courthouse Square
Carlisle, PA 17013-3330
717-240-6180
800-441-2555 (toll free in PA)

Delaware County Office of Consumer Affairs
Media Courthouse
201 West Front Street
Media, PA 19063
610-891-4865
800-441-2555 (toll free in PA)

Montgomery County Department of Consumer
Affairs
Human Services Center
1430 Dekalb Street, P.O. Box 311
Norristown, PA 19404-0311
610 2783565
717-963-4913
800-441-2555 (toll free in PA)

Economic Crime Unit
Philadelphia District Attorney's Office
1421 Arch Street
Philadelphia, PA 19102
215-686-8750

Rhode Island—State Offices

Attorney General
Consumer Protection Unit
150 South Main Street
Providence, RI 02903
401-274-4400

South Carolina—State Offices

Consumer Protection Office
Office of the Attorney General
P.O. Box 11549
Columbia, SC 29211
888-95-FRAUD (Insurance fraud)
888-662-4328 (Medicaid fraud)
877-BE-ALERT (Securities Fraud)

State Ombudsman Office of Executive Policy and
Program
1205 Pendleton Street, Room 308
Columbia, South Carolina 29201
803-734-0457

South Dakota—State Offices

Office of The Attorney General
Division of Consumer Protection
500 East Capitol Ave
Pierre, SD 57501-5070
605-773-4400
800-300-1986 (South Dakota only)

Tennessee—State Offices

Office of the Attorney General
Consumer Protection Division
425 5th Ave. North, 2nd Floor
Nashville, TN 37243
615-741-4737
800-342-8385

Division of Consumer Affairs
Department of Commerce and Insurance
500 James Robertson Parkway
Nashville, TN 37243-0600
800-342-8385 (inside Tennessee)
615-741-4737

Texas—State Offices

Consumer Protection Division
Office of Attorney General
1600 Pacific Ave., Ste. 1700
Dallas, TX 75201
214-742-8944

Consumer Protection Division
Office of Attorney General
310 N. Mesa, Ste. 900
El Paso, TX 79901-1301
915-542-4800/1596

Consumer Protection Division
Office of Attorney General
808 Travis, Ste. 812
Houston, TX 77002
713-223-5886
713-223-5821

Consumer Protection Division
Office of Attorney General
916 Main St., Ste. 806
Lubbock, TX 79401-2905
806-747-5238

Consumer Protection Division
Office of Attorney General
3201 North McColl Rd., Ste. B
McAllen, TX 78501
956-682-4547

Consumer Protection Division
Office of Attorney General
115 East Travis St., Ste. 925
San Antonio, TX 78205-1607
210-225-4191

25 Main St. in Cooperstown, New York, is the site of the famous National Baseball Hall of Fame.

Office of Consumer Credit Commissioner
2601 N. Lamar Blvd.
Austin, Texas 78705
512-936-7600
800-538-1579

Texas—SELECTED County Offices

Dallas County District Attorney's Office
Specialized Crime Division
133 North Industrial Blvd., LB 19
Dallas, TX 75207-4399
214-653-3820

Harris County Consumer Fraud Division
Office of District Attorney
1201 Franklin, Ste. 600
Houston, TX 77002
713-755-5836

Utah—State Office

Division of Consumer Protection
Department of Commerce
160 East 300 South
Box 146704
Salt Lake City, UT 84114-6704
801-530-6601
800-721-7233 (toll free in Utah)

Consumer Protection Division
Office of the Attorney General
Utah State Capitol Office
111 State Capitol
Salt Lake City, UT 84114
801-530-6601

Vermont—State Offices

Public Protection Division
Office of the Attorney General
109 State Street
Montpelier, VT 05602
802-828 3171

Consumer Assurance Section
Department of Agriculture, Food and Market
116 State Street
Montpelier, VT 05602
802-828-3456

Virginia—State Offices

Antitrust and Consumer Litigation Section
Office of the Attorney General
900 East Main Street
Richmond, VA 23219
804-786-2116
804-786-0122

Office of Consumer Affairs
Department of Agriculture and Consumer Services
Washington Building, Suite 100
P.O. Box 1163
Richmond, VA 23219
804-786-2042
800-552-9963 (Toll free in VA)
804-371-6344 (TDD)

Virginia—SELECTED County Offices

Office of Citizen and Consumer Affairs
2100 Clarendon Blvd, Suite 314
Arlington, VA 22201
703-228-3260
703-228-4611 (TTY)

**Fairfax County Department of Cable
  Communications and Consumer Protection**
12000 Government Center Parkway, Suite 433
Fairfax, VA 22035
703-324-5949

**Prince William County
Office of Consumer Affairs**
1 County Complex Court
Prince William, Virginia 22192
703-792-4660

Virginia—City Offices

**Carmen Gonzales, Consumer Affairs Administrator
Alexandria Office of Consumer Affairs**
City Hall
301 King Street, room 1900
P.O. Box 178
Alexandria, VA 22313
703-838-4350
703-838-5056 (TDD)

**Consumer Affairs Division
Virginia Beach Office of the Commonwealth
  Attorney
Consumer Affairs Division**
2425 Nimmo Parkway
Virginia Beach, VA 23456-9060
757-426-5836

Washington—State Offices

**Consumer and Business Fair Practices Division
Office of the Attorney General**
900 Fourth Ave. Suite 2000
Seattle, WA 98164-1012
206-464-6684
800-551-4636 (toll free in Washington)

**Consumer and Business Fair Practices Division
Office of the Attorney General**
West 1116 Riverside
Spokane, WA 99201-1194
509-456-3123

**Consumer and Business Fair Practices Division
Office of the Attorney General**
1019 Pacific Ave S. 3rd Floor
Tacoma, WA 98402-4411
253-593-2904

Washington—City Offices

**Chief Deputy Prosecuting Attorney
Fraud Division**
900 4th Ave., #1002
Seattle, WA 98164
206-296-9010

**Revenue and Consumer Affairs Division
Department of Finance**
Key Tower
700 5th Avenue, Room 4250
Seattle, WA 98104
206-684-8484

West Virginia—State Offices

**Consumer Protection Division
Office of the Attorney General**
812 Quarrier Street, 6th Floor
P.O. Box 1789
Charleston, WV 25326-1789
304-558-8986
800-368-8808 (in WV only)

**Divisions of Weights and Measures
Department of Labor**
570 McCorkle Ave.
St. Albans, WV 25177
304-722-0602

**City of Charleston
Department of Consumer Protection**
P.O. Box 2749
Charleston, WV 25330
304-348-6439

Wisconsin—State Offices

**Director, Consumer Protection
Department of Agriculture, Trade and Consumer
  Protection**
2811 Agriculture Dr.
P.O. Box 8911
Madison, WI 53708
608-224-4921
800-422-7128 (toll free in WI)

**Director, Consumer Protection
Department of Agriculture, Trade and Consumer
  Protection**
3610 Oakwood Hills Parkway
Eau Claire, WI 53701-7754
715-839-3848

**Director, Consumer Protection
Department of Agriculture, Trade and Consumer
  Protection**
200 N. Jefferson Street, Suite 146-A

Green Bay, WI 54301
920-448-5110

Director, Consumer Protection
Department of Agriculture, Trade and Consumer
  Protection
10930 W. Potter Road, Suite C
Milwaukee, WI 53226-3450
414-266-1231

Wyoming—State Offices

Office of the Attorney General
123 Capitol Building
200 W. 24th Street
Cheyenne, WY 82002
307-777-7841
307-777-5351 (TDD)

Office of Consumer Protection and Citizen Advocacy
Department of Justice
Office of the Attorney General
P.O. Box 7857
Madison, WI 53707-7857
608-266-1221
800-422-7128 (in WI)

Wisconsin—SELECTED County Offices

District Attorney
Marathon County District Attorney's Office
Marathon County Courthouse
Wausau, WI 54401
715-847-5555

Assistant District Attorney
Milwaukee County District Attorney's Office
Consumer Fraud Unit
821 West State Street, Room 412
Milwaukee, WI 53233-2485
414-278-4585

Consumer Fraud Investigator
Racine County Sheriff's Department
717 Wisconsin Avenue
Racine, WI 53403
414-636-3125
800-242-4202, ext. 3125 (Toll free)

American Samoa

Assistant Attorney General
Consumer Protection Bureau
Office of the Attorney General
Executive Office Building, Utulei
P. O. Box 7
Pago Pago, AS 96799
684- 633-4163

Puerto Rico

Secretary
Department of Justice
Apartado 9020192
San Juan, Puerto Rico 00902
787-721-2900

Virgin Islands

Department of Licensing and Consumer Affairs
Property & Procurement Bldg.,
1 Sub Base, Rm 205
St. Thomas, USVI 00802
340-774-3130
809-721-2900

DISABILITIES

TELECOMMUNICATIONS DEVICE FOR THE DEAF

Hearing- and speech-impaired people who use a telecommunications device for the deaf (known as TDD or TTY) can get help with calls made from a TDD to a TDD by using the following service:

> **TDD/TTY Operator Services**
> 800-855-1155

The TDD operator can help you if you have telecommunications devices for the deaf to make:

- Credit card calls (if you have a telephone credit card)
- Collect calls (calls paid for by the person you are calling)
- Third-number telephone calls (calls billed to a number other than the one you are calling to or from)
- Person-to-person calls (calls to a specific person)
- Calls from a hotel or motel
- Calls from a coin phone (credit card, collect, or bill to third-number calls only)

The TDD operator can also help you:

- Get the number if you have a problem with a call
- Get assistance for problems with calls

"Sign Language" and "Braille Alphabet, Numbers, and Punctuation" in chapter 12

Go to

- Get telephone numbers that you cannot find in the telephone book
- Report problems with your telephone

The TDD operator cannot interpret voice to TDD or TDD to voice.

Remember, most calls made with the help of an operator are more expensive, so dial calls yourself when you can to save money.

BOOKS FOR BLIND AND PHYSICALLY HANDICAPPED PERSONS

The Library of Congress has a free reading program for blind and physically handicapped individuals and offers publications in Braille and recorded books and magazines to persons who cannot hold a book or see well enough to read regular print. Special playback equipment is available on a loan basis from the Library of Congress, and cassettes and recordings on discs can be ordered from about 158 cooperating libraries. Anyone who is medically certified as unable to hold a book or read ordinary print because of a visual handicap can borrow these materials postage-free and return them in the same manner. For more information, contact:

>   **National Library Service for the Blind and Physically Handicapped**
>   The Library of Congress
>   Washington, DC 20542
>   202-707-5100
>   800-424-9100

Recording for the Blind and Dyslexic (RFB) is a national nonprofit service organization that provides free cassettes of educational textbooks and other resources to medically certified individuals. Eligibility extends to visually, physically, and perceptually handicapped individuals. One of RFB's special services is a collection of cassettes of a wide variety of consumer publications from the federal government. There is a one-time registration fee. For more information and an application, contact:

Recording for the Blind and Dyslexic
20 Roszel Rd.
Princeton, NJ 08540
609-452-0606
800-221-4792 (toll free outside New Jersey)
http://www.rfbd.org

DOMESTIC VIOLENCE RESOURCES

Below is a partial listing of domestic violence resources in the United States. Where possible, a statewide, toll-free hot line is listed; for states that do not have one, there is an organization that can refer you to legal assistance, crisis counseling, and shelters in your area.

National
Domestic Violence Resource Center
National Criminal Justice Resource Center
Box 6000-AIQ
Rockville, MD 20850
301-251-5063
800-627-6872
http://www.ncjrs.org

National Coalition Against Domestic Violence
P.O. Box 18749
Denver, CO 80218
303-839-1852
http://www.ncadv.org

National Coalition Against Domestic Violence Public Policy Office
1532 16th Street, NW
Washington, DC 20036
202-745-1211
http://www.ncadv.org

National Coalition on Child Abuse and Family Violence
800-222-2000

National Domestic Violence Hot Line
800-799-7233

Alabama
Alabama Coalition Against Domestic Violence
334-832-4842

Alaska

Alaska Network on Domestic Violence and Sexual Assault
907-586-3650

Arizona

Arizona Coalition Against Domestic Violence
602-279-2900

Arkansas

Arkansas Coalition Against Violence to Women and Children
501-812-0571

California

California Alliance Against Domestic Violence
916-444-7163
800-524-4765

California Alliance Against Domestic Violence-Southern Office
310-649-2479

Statewide California Coalition for Battered Women
562-981-1202
888-722-2952

Colorado

Colorado Coalition Against Domestic Violence
303-831-9632

Connecticut

Connecticut Coalition Against Domestic Violence
860-282-7892
800-281-1481 (in CT)
888-774-2900 (in-state Hotline)

Delaware

Family Violence Program
Battered Women's Hot Line
302-762-6110

Delaware Coalition Against Domestic Violence
302-658-2958

District of Columbia

DC Coalition Against Domestic Violence
202-299-1181

Domestic Violence Clinic
International Woman's Human Rights Clinic
At Georgetown Law Center
202-662-9640

Florida

Florida Coalition Against Domestic Violence
850-425-2749
800-500-1199 (in FL)

Georgia

Georgia Coalition on Family Violence
770-984-0085
800-334-2836 (in GA)

Hawaii

Hawaii State Coalition Against Domestic Violence
808-486-5072

Idaho

Idaho Coalition Against Sexual and Domestic Violence
208-384-0419

Illinois

Illinois Coalition Against Domestic Violence
217-789-2830 (9 A.M.–5 P.M.)

Indiana

Indiana Coalition Against Domestic Violence
317-543-3908
800-332-7385

Iowa

Iowa Coalition Against Domestic Violence
515-244-8028
800-942-0333 (in IA)

Kansas

Safe House
620-231-8251

Kansas Coalition Against Sexual and Domestic Violence
785-232-9784

Kentucky

Kentucky Domestic Violence Association
502-695-2444

Lincoln Trail Domestic Violence Program
(Elizabethtown County)
800-767-5838

Louisiana

Louisiana Coalition Against Domestic Violence
225-752-1296

Maine
Maine Coalition to End Domestic Violence
207-941-1194

Caring Unlimited
207-324-1802
800-239-7298

Maryland
Maryland Network Against Domestic Violence
301-352-4574
800-MD-HELPS

Massachusetts
Battered Women Fight Back, Inc.
617-971-0131

Battered Women's Hotline
617-661-7203

Domestic Violence Initiative
617-424-6456

Massachusetts Coalition of Battered Women's Services
617-248-0922

Michigan
Michigan Coalition Against Domestic and Sexual Violence
517-347-7000

Minnesota
Minnesota Coalition for Battered Women
651-646-6177
651-646-0994 (emergency hot line, call collect 24 hours)

Mississippi
Mississippi State Coalition Against Domestic Violence
601-981-9196
800-898-3234

Missouri
Missouri Coalition Against Domestic Violence
573-634-4161

Montana
Montana Network Against Domestic Violence and Sexual Assault
406-586-0263
406-586-4111
800-655-7867

Nebraska
Nebraska Domestic Violence and Sexual Assault Coalition
402-476-6256
800-876-6238 (in Nebraska)

Nevada
Nevada Network Against Domestic Violence
775-828-1115
800-230-1955

New Hampshire
New Hampshire Coalition Against Domestic and Sexual Violence
603-224-8893
800-852-3388 (in NH)

New Jersey
New Jersey Coalition for Battered Women
609-584-8107
800-572-7233

New Mexico
New Mexico State Coalition Against Domestic Violence
505-246-9240
800-773-3645 (state hot line)

Women's Community Association
505-247-4219 (24 hours)

New York
New York State Coalition Against Domestic Violence
518-432-4864
800-942-6906

Poder
800-942-6908 (Spanish)

North Carolina
North Carolina Coalition Against Domestic Violence
919-956-9124

North Dakota
North Dakota Council on Abused Women's Services
701-255-6240
800-472-2911 (in ND)

Ohio
Ohio Domestic Violence Network
614-784-0023
800-934-9840

Oklahoma

Oklahoma Coalition on Domestic Violence and Sexual Assault
405-848-1815
800-522-7233

Oregon

Oregon Coalition Against Domestic and Sexual Violence
503-365-9644

Pennsylvania

Pennsylvania Coalition Against Domestic Violence
717-545-6400
800-932-4632

Rhode Island

Rhode Island Council on Domestic Violence
401-467-9940
800-494-8100 (in RI)

South Carolina

South Carolina Coalition Against Domestic Violence and Sexual Assault
803-750-1222
800-260-9293

South Dakota

South Dakota Coalition Against Domestic Violence and Sexual Assault
605-945-0869
800-572-9196

Tennessee

Tennessee Coalition Against Domestic and Sexual Violence
615-386-9406
800-289-9018 (info line)

Statewide Domestic Violence and Child Abuse Hotline
800-356-6767

Texas

Council On Family Violence
512-794-1133

Utah

Domestic Violence Advisory Council
801-538-4635
800-897-5465 (in UT)

Vermont

Vermont Network Against Domestic Violence and Sexual Assault
802-223-1302 (weekdays, daytime)

Virginia

Virginians Against Domestic Violence
757-221-0990
800-838-VADV

Washington

Washington State Domestic Violence Hot Line
800-562-6025

Washington State Coalition Against Domestic Violence
360-407-0756

West Virginia

West Virginia Coalition Against Domestic Violence
304-965-3552

Wisconsin

Wisconsin Coalition Against Domestic Violence
608-255-0539 (9 A.M.–5 P.M. weekdays)

Wyoming

Wyoming Coalition Against Domestic Violence and Sexual Assault
307-755-5481

FAMILY PLANNING

Family Planning Council
260 S. Broad St., Suite 1000
Philadelphia, PA 19102
215-985-2600
http://www.familyplanning.org

International Planned Parenthood Federation
Western Hemisphere Region
120 Wall St., 9th Fl.
New York, NY 10005
212-248-6400
http://www.ippf.org/

National Family Planning and Reproductive Health Association
1627 K St. NW, 12th Fl.
Washington, DC 20006
202-293-3114
http://www.nfprha.org

"Precautions During Pregnancy" in chapter 18; "Average Cost of Raising a Child" in chapter 20

Go to

Planned Parenthood Federation of America
810 Seventh Ave.
New York, NY 10019
212-541-7800
http://www.plannedparenthood.org

Population Institute
107 2nd St., NE
Washington, DC 20002
202-544-3300
http://www.populationinstitute.org

Resolve: The National Infertility Association
1310 Broadway
Somerville, MA 02144-1779
617-643-2424
http://www.resolve.org

FEDERAL GOVERNMENT AGENCIES AND BUREAUS

Here is a selection of federal agencies that offer a wide range of information, enforcement, and/or complaint-handling services for products and services used by the general public. Many offices also have telecommunications devices for the deaf (TDDs). Voice users can call 800-877-8339 for the help of a relay operator from the Federal Information Relay Service.

Agriculture Department
Consumer and Community Affairs Director
Park Center, Rm. 912
Park Center Drive
Alexandria, VA 22302
703-305-2000
http://www.usda.gov

Civil Rights Commission
Congressional Affairs Unit
624 9th St. NW
Washington, DC 20425
202-376-8317
http://www.usccr.gov

Commerce Department
Public Affairs
1401 Constitution Ave., NW
Washington, DC 20230
202-482-5151
http://www.doc.gov

Commodity Futures Trading Commission
Office of Governmental Affairs
Headquarters Office
Three Lafayette Centre
1155 21st Street, NW
Washington DC 20581
Phone: (202) 418-5000
http://www.cftc.gov

Federal Consumer Information Center
Pueblo, CO 81009
800-FED-INFO
http://www.pueblo.gsa.gov/

Education Department
U.S. Department of Education
Consumer Affairs Staff
400 Maryland Avenue, SW
Washington, DC 20202-0498
800-USA-LEARN (1-800-872-5327)
http://www.ed.gov/index.jsp

U.S. Department of Energy
Office of Consumer and Public Liaison
1000 Independence Ave., SW
Washington, DC 20585
800-dial-DOE
http://www.energy.gov/

Environmental Protection Agency
Public Information Center
US EPA Headquarters
Ariel Rios Building
1200 Pennsylvania Ave., N.W.
Washington, DC 20460
212-637-3660
212-637-3675 (community relations)
212-637-3671 (environmental education)
http://www.epa.gov

Environmental Protection Agency
Main Regional Office
290 Broadway
New York, NY 10007-1866
212-637-5000
http://www.epa.gov

Environmental Protection Agency
Edison Laboratories
2890 Woodbridge Ave.
Edison, NJ 08837-3679
732-321-6754
http://www.epa.gov

Environmental Protection Agency
Niagara Falls Public Information Center
345 Third Street, Suite 530

Niagara Falls, NY 14303
716-285-8842
http://www.epa.gov

Federal Communications Commission
Consumer Assistance and Small Business Office
445 12th Street SW
Washington, DC 20554
888-CALL-FCC (225-3522)
888-TELL-FCC (835-5322) (TYY)
http://www.fcc.gov

Federal Deposit Insurance Corporation
Division of Finance
550 17th Street, NW
Washington, DC 20429-9990
800-759-6596
202-736-0000
Call Center Numbers:
877-ASKFDIC (877-275-3342)
800-925- 4618 (TDD)

Federal Housing Finance Board
1777 F Street, NW
Washington, DC 20006-5210
202-408-2500
http://www.fhfb.gov/

Federal Maritime Commission
Office of Informal Inquiries and Complaints
Main Offices
800 North Capitol Street, N.W.
Washington, D.C. 20573
202-523-5807
http://www.fmc.gov

Federal Maritime Commission
Los Angeles Area Representative
P.O. Box 230
839 South Beacon Street, Room 320
San Pedro, CA 90733-0230
310-514-4905

Federal Maritime Commission
Miami Area Representative
Customs Management Center
909 S.E., 1st Avenue, Room 705
Miami, Florida 33131
305-536-4316

Federal Maritime Commission
New Orleans Area Representative
U.S. Customs House
423 Canal Street, Room 309B
New Orleans, Louisiana 70130
504-589-6662

Federal Maritime Commission
New York Area Representative
Federal Maritime Commission
Building No. 75, Room 205B
JFK International Airport
Jamaica, NY 11430
718-553-2228

Federal Maritime Commission
Seattle Area Representative
c/o U.S. Customs
7 South Nevada Street, Suite 100
Seattle, Washington 98134
206-553-0221

Federal Reserve
Board of Governors
Division of Consumer and Community Affairs
20th Street and Constitution Avenue, NW,
Washington, DC 20551
202-452-3819
202-452-3102
http://www.federalreserve.gov/

Health and Human Services Department
Consumer Affairs and Information
200 Independence Avenue, SW
Washington, DC 20201
877-696-6775
http://www.hhs.gov/

Health and Human Services Department
Food and Drug Administration
5600 Fishers Lane
Rockville, MD 20857-0001
888-INFO-FDA (888-463-6332)
http://www.fda.gov/

Department of Health and Human Services
National Health Information Center
P.O. Box 1133
Washington, DC 20013-1133
800-336-4797 (toll-free) or
301-565-4167 (in the Washington, D.C., area)
http://www.health.gov/nhic/

Office of Inspector General
Small Business Administration
Investigations Division
Mail Code: 4113
409 Third Street, SW
Washington, DC 20416
OIG Fraud Line
800-767-0385
202-205-7151
http://www.sba.gov/ig/

U.S. Department of Housing and Urban Development
451 7th Street S.W.
Washington, DC 20410
202-708-1112
202-708-1455 (TTY)
http://www.hud.gov

U.S. Department of the Interior
Consumer Affairs Administrator
1849 C. Street N.W.
Washington, DC 20240
202-208-3100
http://www.doi.gov/

U.S. Department of Transportation
400 7th Street, S.W.
Washington D.C. 20590
202-366-4000
http://www.dot.gov/

Department of Labor
Consumer Affairs Department
200 Constitution Avenue, NW
Washington, DC 20210
866-4-USA-DOL
877-889-5627 (TTY)
http://www.dol.gov

National Credit Union Administration
1775 Duke Street
Alexandria VA 22314
703-518-6300
http://www.ncua.gov

National Institute of Standards and Technology
100 Bureau Drive, Stop 3460
Gaithersburg, MD 20899-3460
301-975-NIST (6478)
301-975-8295 (TTY)
http://www.nist.gov/

National Labor Relations Board
1099 14th Street
Washington, D.C. 20570-0001
202-273-1770
http://www.nlrb.gov/

U.S. Nuclear Regulatory Commission
Office of Public Affairs (OPA)
Washington, D.C. 20555
800-368-5642 (toll free)
301-415-8200
301-415-5575 (TDD)
http://www.nrc.gov/

"Federal Judicial System" in chapter 21; "Federal Government" in chapter 25

Go to

Peace Corps
The Paul D. Coverdell Peace Corps Headquarters
1111 20th Street NW
Washington, D.C. 20526
800-424-8580 or
202-695-1857 (TTY)
http://www.peacecorps.gov/

Postal Rate Commission
Office of the Consumer Advocate
1333 H Street, NW
Suite 300
Washington, DC   20268-0001
202-789-6800
202-789-6881 (TTY)
http://www.prc.gov/

Security and Exchange Commission
SEC Headquarters
450 Fifth Street, NW
Washington, DC 20549
Office of Education and Assistance
800-SEC-0330
202-942-8088
202-942-7114 (TTY)
202-942-9634 (complaint center)
http://www.sec.gov/

Security and Exchange Commission
Northeast Regional Office
233 Broadway
New York, NY 10279
646-428-1500

Security and Exchange Commission
Southeast Regional Office
1401 Brickell Avenue, Suite 200
Miami, FL 33131
305-536-4700

Security and Exchange Commission
Midwest Regional Office
175 W. Jackson Boulevard
Suite 900
Chicago, IL 60604
312-353-7390

Security and Exchange Commission
Central Regional Office
1801 California Street, Suite 4800
Denver, CO 80202-2648
303-844-1000

Security and Exchange Commission
Pacific Regional Office
5670 Wilshire Boulevard, 11th Floor
Los Angeles, CA 90036-3648
323-965-3998

Hot Lines and Information Services

A Closer Look

Air safety hot line	800-FAA-SURE (800-322-7873)
Auto safety hot line	800-424-9393
Child abuse hot line	800-4-A-CHILD (800-422-4453)
Domestic violence hot line	800-799-SAFE (800-799-7233)
Drug hot line	800-662-HELP (800-662-4357)
Gay/lesbian youth hotline	800-347-TEEN (800-347-8336)
National Center for Missing and Exploited Children	800-843-LOST (800-843-5678)
National Organization for Victim Assistance (NOVA)	800-879-NOVA (800-879-6682)
National Runaway Switchboard	800-621-4000
Parents who have kidnapped their children hot line	800-A-WAY-OUT (800-292-9688)
Product safety hot line	800-638-2772

Social Security Administration
Office of Public Inquiries
Windsor Park Building
6401 Security Blvd.
Baltimore, MD 21235
800-772-1213
410-965-8882 (HQ only)
800-325-0778 (TTY)
http://www.ssa.gov/

U.S. Small Business Administration
SBA Answer Desk
6302 Fairview Road, Suite 300
Charlotte, North Carolina 28210
800-UASK-SBA (1-800-827-5722)
704-344-6640 (TTY)
hhtp://www.sba.gov

U.S. Small Business Administration
Office of Advocacy
409 3rd St., SW
Washington, DC 20416
202-205-6533
http://www.sba.gov/ADVO/

United States Postal Service
Office of Inspector General
ATTN: HOTLINE
1735 N. Lynn Street
Arlington, VA 22209-2020
888-USPS-OIG
888-877-7644
866-OIG-TEXT (TTY)
888-644-8398 (TTY)
http://www.uspsoig.gov/
http://www.usps.com/

Veterans Health Administration
810 Vermont Ave. NW
Washington, DC 20420
202-273-5400
http://www.va.gov/

FEDERAL INFORMATION CENTERS

The Federal Information Center (FIC) offers information about federal government services, programs, and regulations. The FIC can also tell you which federal agency to contact for help with specific problems.

Their toll-free number is 800-688-9889 (800-326-2996 for TDD users). The FIC is open for public inquiries from 9:00 A.M. to 8:00 P.M., Eastern time, Monday through Friday, except federal holidays. They can also be reached on the World Wide Web at http://fic.info.gov/.

PARENTING

ADOPTION
Adoptive Families of America
3333 Highway 100 North
Minneapolis, MN 55422
612-535-4829
http://www.adoptivefam.org

National Adoption Center
1500 Walnut St., Suite 701
Philadelphia, PA 19102
215-735-9988
800-TO-ADOPT
http://www.adopt.org

National Adoption Information Clearinghouse
330 C St. SW
Washington, DC 20447
703-352-3488
http://www.calib.com/naic

North American Council on Adoptable Children
970 Raymond Ave., Suite 106
St. Paul, MN 55114
612-644-3036
http://www.ncac.org

Orphan Voyage
1122 Marco Place
Jacksonville, FL 32207
904-398-4269

Orphan Voyage
Gay Swearington
13906 Pepperrell Drive
Tampa, FL 33624
904-468-2622

SINGLE-PARENT FAMILIES

Big Brothers/Big Sisters of America
230 N. 13th St.
Philadelphia, PA 19107
215-567-7000
http://www.bbbsa.org

Parents Without Partners
1650 South Dixie Highway, Suite 510
Boca Raton, FL 33432
561-391-8833
http://www.parentswithoutpartners.org

Single Mothers By Choice
P.O. Box 1642
New York, NY 10028
212-988-0993

RADIO AND TELEVISION NETWORKS

ABC, Inc.
77 W. 66th St.
New York, NY 10023
212-456-7777
http://www.abc.com

ABC, Inc.
500 S. Buena Vista St.
Burbank, CA 91521-4551
818-560-1000

American Movie Classics (AMC)
530 Fifth Ave., 6th Fl.
New York, NY 10036
212-382-5200

American Movie Classics (AMC)
Viewer Mail
200 Jericho Quadrangle
Jericho, NY 11753
516-803-3000
http://www.amctv.com

Arts & Entertainment Television Network (A&E)
235 E. 45th St.
New York, NY 10017
212-210-1400
http://www.AandE.com

Associated Press Broadcast Services
1825 K St., NW, Suite 800
Washington, DC 20006
800-821-4747
202-736-1105 or 800-527-7234 (Radio Division)
202-736-1155 (Television Division)
202-736-9500 (Broadcast News Center)
202-736-1116 or 800-342-5147 (Customer Service)
http://www.apbroadcast.com

Black Entertainment Television (BET)
2000 M St. NW
Washington, DC 20036
202-533-1990
http://www.bet.com

Black Entertainment Television (BET)
West Coast Headquarters
1840 Century Park E. #600
Los Angeles, CA 90067
310-552-8400
http://www.bet.com

Bravo Networks
200 Jericho Quadrangle
Jericho, NY 11753
800-531-0002
516-803-3000
http://www.bravotv.com

Cable News Network (CNN)
One CNN Center
Box 105366
Atlanta, GA 30348-5366
404-827-1700
http://www.cnn.com

Cable News Network (CNN)
New York Office
5 Penn Plaza, 20th Floor
New York, NY 10001
212-714-7800
http://www.cnn.com

Cable News Network Financial News (CNNFN)
Cable News Network (CNN)
5 Penn Plaza, 20th Floor
New York, NY 10001
800-959-4228
212-714-7800
http://www.cnnfn.com

Cable Satellite Public Affairs Network (C-Span)
400 N. Capitol St., NW, Suite 650
Washington, DC 20001
202-737-3220-765-464-3080 (viewer services)
http://www.c-span.org

Cartoon Network
1050 Techwood Dr., NW
Atlanta, GA 30318
4040-885-4390
http://cartoonnetwork.com

CBS Corporation
51 W. 52nd St.
New York, NY 10019-6188
212-975-4321
http://www.cbs.com

CBS Corporation
7800 Beverly Blvd.
Los Angeles, CA 90036
323-575-2345
http://www.cbs.com

Cinemax
1100 Avenue of the Americas
New York, NY 10036
212-512-1000
http://www.cinemax.com

Comedy Central
1775 Broadway
New York, NY 10019
212-767-8600
http://www.comcentral.com

Consumer News and Business Channel (CNBC)
2200 Fletcher Ave.
Fort Lee, NJ 07024
800-788-2622
877-251-5685 (viewer services)
http://www.cnbc.com

Consumer News and Business Channel (CNBC)
3000 W. Alameda Ave. #C296
Burbank, CA 91523
818-840-3214

Court TV
600 Third Ave.
New York, NY 10016
212-973-2800
http://www.courtv.com

The Discovery Channel
641 Lexington Ave., 8th Fl.
New York, NY 10022
212-751-2220
859-342-8439 (viewer relations)
http://www.discovery.com

Every year, thousands of people visit 12305 Fifth Helena Dr. in Brentwood, California. It's the first house that Marilyn Monroe owned and the house where she died.

The Disney Channel
3800 W. Alameda Ave.
Burbank, CA 91505
818-569-7500
http://disneychannel.disney.go.com/disneychannel

The Disney Channel
500 Park Ave., 7th Fl
New York, NY 10022
212-735-5380
http://disneychannel.disney.go.com/disneychannel

E! Entertainment Television, Inc.
11 W. 42nd St., 19th Floor
New York, NY 10036
212-852-5100
and
5750 Wilshire Blvd.
Los Angeles, CA 90036
323-954-2400
http://www.eonline.com

Entertainment and Sports Programming Network (ESPN)
935 Middle St.
Bristol, CT 06010
860-766-2000
http://www.espn.com

Fox Broadcasting Company
10201 W. Pico Blvd.
Los Angeles, CA 90035
310-369-1000
http://www.fox.com

Fox Broadcasting Company
P.O. Box 900
Beverly Hills, CA 90213
310-369-1000
http://www.fox.com

fX Network
10000 Santa Monica Boulevard
Los Angeles, CA 90067
310-286-3800
http://www.fxnetworks.com

fX Network
P.O. Box 900
Beverly Hills, CA 90213
http://www.fxnetworks.com

Game Show Network
550 Madison Ave.
New York, NY 10022
212-833-8500
http://www.gameshownetwork.com

The Golf Channel
90 Park Ave., #1700
New York, NY 10016
212-984-1056
http://www.golf.com/golfchannel

Home Box Office, Inc. (HBO)
1100 Avenue of the Americas
New York, NY 10036
212-512-1000
http://www.hbo.com

Home and Garden TV
9721 Sherrill Blvd.
Knoxville, TN 37932
865-694-2700 (corporate headquarters)
865-694-7879 (consumer questions)
http://www.hgtv.com

Home Shopping Networks
1 HSN Drive
St. Petersburg, FL 33729
727-872-1000
http://www.hsn.com

Independent Film Channel
11 Penn Plaza
New York, NY 10001
646-273-7200
http://www.ifctv.com

Independent Film Channel
Rainbow Media Holdings, Inc.
200 Jericho Quadrangle
Jericho, NY 11753

516-803-3000
http://www.ifctv.com

The Learning Channel
7700 Wisconsin Ave.
Bethesda, MD 20814-3522
301-986-1999
http://www.tlc.discovery.com

Lifetime Television
309 W. 49th St.
New York, NY 10019
212-474-7000
http://www.lifetimetv.com

Madison Square Garden Network (MSG)
Two Pennsylvania Plaza
New York, NY 10021
212-465-5926
http://www.msgnetwork.com

MSNBC
MSNBC TV
One MSNBC Plaza
Secaucus, NJ 07094
201-583-5000
201-583-5012 (MSNBC Cable)
http://www.msnbc.com

MTV Networks
MTV Studios
1515 Broadway
New York, NY 10036
212-258-8000
http://www.mtv.com/

MTV Networks
2600 Colorado Avenue
Santa Monica, CA 90404
310-752-8000
http://www.mtv.com/

TNN Networks
(The National Network, formerly The Nashville Network)
1515 Broadway #4228
New York, New York 10036
212-846-2566
888-POP-1090 (toll-free)
http://www.thenewtnn.com/

National Public Radio (NPR)
635 Massachusetts Avenue N.W.
Washington, D.C. 20001
202-513-2000
http://www.npr.org

NBC Cable Networks
2200 Fletcher Avenue
Fort Lee, NJ 07024
201-346-2314
http://www.nbc.com

NBC Studios/NBC News
30 Rockefeller Plaza
New York, N.Y. 10112
212-664-4444
212-664-3700 (tours)
http://www.nbc.com

NBC Entertainment
3000 West Alameda Avenue
Burbank, CA 91523
818-840-4444
http://www.nbc.com/

Nickelodeon/Nick at Night
1515 Broadway
New York City, NY 10036
212-258-7500
212-258-8000
800-NICK-NET
http://nick.com

Nickelodeon/Nick at Night
231 West Olive Ave.
Burbank, CA 91502
818-736-3000
http://nick.com

Hallmark Channel
12700 Ventura Blvd.
Studio City, CA 91604
212-930-1947
http://www.hallmarkchannel.com

OVATION—The Arts Network
5801 Duke Street
Suite D-112
Alexandria, VA 22304
800-OVATION
http://www.ovationtv.com/

The Playboy Channel
Corporate Headquarters
680 North Lake Shore Drive
Chicago, Illinois 60611
312-751-8000
http://www.playboy.com/

The Playboy Channel
New York Office
730 Fifth Avenue
New York, New York 10019

212-261-5000
http://www.playboy.com/

The Playboy Channel
Playboy Enterprises International, Inc.
9242 Beverly Boulevard
Beverly Hills, California 90210
310-246-4000
http://www.playboy.com/

Public Broadcasting Service (PBS)
Public Broadcasting Service
1320 Braddock Place
Alexandria, Virginia 22314
703-739-5000
http://www.pbs.org/

QVC
1200 Wilson Drive
West Chester, PA
888-81LOCAL
http://qvc.com

Reuters Information Services, Inc.
1700 Broadway
New York, NY 10019
212-273-1700

Reuters America
3 Times Sq.
New York, NY 10036
646-223-4000

The SciFi Channel
USA Networks
1230 Avenue of the Americas, 18th Floor
New York, NY 10020
212-413-5000
http://www.scifi.com/

Sheridan Broadcasting Corporation and American Urban Radio Network
960 Penn. Ave. #200
Pittsburgh, PA 15222
412-456-4000

Showtime
1633 Broadway, 17th Floor
NY, NY 10019
212-708-1275
http://www.sho.com/

The Travel Channel
7700 Wisconsin Avenue
Bethesda, MD 20814-3522
888-892-3484
http://travel.discovery.com/

Turner Classic Movies (TCM)
1050 Techwood Dr.
Atlanta, GA 30318.
404-827-1500
http://www.turnerclassicmovies.com

Turner Network Television (TNT)
One CNN Center
Box 105366
Atlanta, GA 30348-5366
404-827-1500
http://www.tnt.tv/

TV Food Network
1180 Avenue of the Americas, 12th Fl.
New York, NY 10036
212-398-8836
http://www.foodtv.com/

United Paramount Network (UPN)
11800 Wilshire Blvd
Los Angeles, CA 90025-6602
310-575-7000
http://www.upn.com/

United Press International (UPI)
World Headquarters
1510 H St.
Washington, DC 20005
202-898-8000
http://www.upi.com/

USA Network
1230 6th Ave
New York, NY 10020
212-408-9100
http://www.usanetwork.com/

VH1
1515 Broadway, 12th Floor
New York, NY 10036
212-258-8000
http://www.vh1.com/

Viewer's Choice
18 Bay St.
Box 787, Suite 100
Toronto, Ontario
M5J 2T3
416-965-2010
800-565-MOVIE (6684)
416-956-2083 (TTY/TDD)
800-661-6674 (TTY/TDD)

Warner Brothers Network
411 Hollywood Blvd.
Burbank, CA 91505

818-977-5000
http://wb.com

The Weather Channel
300 Interstate North Pkwy.
Atlanta, GA 30339-2404
800-471-5544
770-226-0000
http://www.weather.com/

Westwood One Inc.
9540 Washington Boulevard
Culver City, CA 90232
310-840-4000
http://www.westwoodone.com/

UNITED STATES SERVICE ACADEMIES

The Air Force Academy
Colorado Springs, CO 80840
719-333-3070 (Admissions)
719-472-0102 (Visitors Center)
http://www.usafa.af.mil/

The Merchant Marine Academy
300 Steamboat Rd
Kings Point, NY 11024
516-773-5000
http://www.usmma.edu/

US Military Academy
West Point, N.Y. 10996
Phone: (845) 938-4011
http://www.usma.edu/

US Naval Academy
121 Blake Road Annapolis,
Maryland 21402-5000
410-293-1000
410-236-6933 (Information and Tours)
800-778-4260 (Visitor Center)
http://www.usna.edu

ADDITIONAL SOURCES OF INFORMATION

MAGAZINES

AFRICAN AMERICAN INTEREST

Ebony
820 S. Michigan Ave.
Chicago, IL 60605
312-322-9200
http://ebony.com

"Newspapers" in chapter 25

Essence
1500 Broadway
New York, NY 10036
212-642-0600
http://www.essence.com

Jet
820 S. Michigan Ave.
Chicago, IL 60605-2103
312-322-9200
http://www.jetmag.com

Upscale
P.O. Box 10798
Atlanta, GA 30310
404-758-7467
http://www.upscalemagazine.com

AGING

Modern Maturity
American Association of Retired Persons
601 E St. NW
Washington, DC 20049-0001
202-434-6880
http://www.modernmaturity.org
http://www.aarp.org

My Generation
780 Third Ave.
New York, NY 10017
212-826-8877
http://www.mygeneration.org

New Choices
Reader's Digest Road
Pleasantlville, NY 10570-7000
914-238-1000
http://www.newchoices.com

CONSUMER INFORMATION AND PROTECTION

Consumer Reports
Consumers Union of the U.S., Inc.
101 Truman Ave.
Yonkers, NY 10703-1044
914-378-2200
http://www.consumerreports.org

GAY/LESBIAN

The Advocate
P.O. Box 4371
Los Angeles, CA 90078-4371

323-871-1225
http://www.advocate.com

Out Magazine
80 8th Ave., Suite 315
New York, NY 10011
http://www.out.com

GENERAL INTEREST

American Heritage
90 Fifth Ave,
New York, NY 10011
212-367-3100
http://www.americanheritage.com

The Atlantic Monthly
77 N. Washington St., Ste. 5
Boston, MA 02117
617-854-7700
http://www.theatlantic.com

Harpers
666 Broadway
New York, NY 10012
212-420-5720
http://www.harpers.org

National Geographic
1145 17th St., NW
Washington, DC 20036
202-857-7000
http://www.nationalgeographic.com

The New Yorker
4 Times Square
New York, NY 10036
212-286-2860
http://www.newyorker.com

People
1271 Avenue of the Americas
New York, NY 10020
212-522-1212
http://www.people.com

Reader's Digest
Reader's Digest Rd.
Pleasantville, NY 10570
914-238-1000
http://www.readersdigest.com

Smithsonian
750 9th St. NW
Suite 710MRC
Washington, DC 20560
202-275-2000
http://www.smithsonianmag.com

Utne Reader
1624 Harmon Place
Suite 330
Minneapolis, MN 55403
612-338-5040
http://www.utne.com

Vanity Fair
4 Times Square
New York, NY 10036
212-286-8180
http://www.vanityfair.com

HISPANIC AMERICAN INTEREST

Latina Magazine
1500 Broadway, 7th Fl.
New York, NY 10036
212-642-0200
http://www.latina.com

MEN'S INTERESTS

Details
7 West 34th St., 4th Fl.
New York, NY 10001
212-630-4000
http://www.details.com

Esquire
250 West 55th St., 7th Fl.
New York, NY 10019
212-649-4020
http://www.esquire.com

FHM—For Him Magazine
110 Fifth Ave.
New York, NY 10011
212-886-3600
http://www.fhmus.com

Gear
450 West 15th St.
New York, NY 10011
212-771-7000

GQ
4 Times Square
New York, NY 10036
212-286-2860
http://www.qc.com

Maxim
1040 Avenue of the Americas, 14th Fl.
New York, NY 10018
212-302-2626
http://www.maximonline.com

Men's Health
733 Third Ave., 15th Fl.
New York, NY 10017
212-697-2040
http://www.menshealth.com

Men's Journal
1290 Avenue of the Americas
New York, NY 10104
212-484-1616
http://www.mensjournal.com

Penthouse
11 Penn Plaza
New York, NY 10001
212-702-6000
http://www.penthouse.com

Playboy
680 N. Lake Shore Dr.
Chicago, IL 60611
312-751-8000
http://www.playboy.com

Stuff Magazine
1040 Avenue of the Americas
New York, NY 10018
212-372-3889
http://www.stuff-mag.com

PARENTING AND FAMILY

American Baby
1440 Broadway, 14th Fl.
New York, NY 10018
212-204-4200
http://www.americanbaby.com

Baby Talk
530 Fifth Ave.
New York, NY 10036
212-522-8989
http://www.parenting.com

Child Magazine
375 Lexington Ave.
New York, NY 10017
212-499-2000
http://www.child.com

Family
51 Atlantic Ave., Ste. 200
Floral Park, NY 11001
516-616-1930
http://www.familymedia.com

Family Digest
P.O. Box 3368
Danville, CA 94526-9568

925-838-4800
http://www.familydigest.com

Healthy Kids
1440 Broadway
New York, NY 10018
212-204-4200
http://www.healthykids.com

Lamaze Parents Magazine
9 Old Kings Highway S.
Darien, CT 06820-4505
203-656-3600
http://www.lamaze.com

Parenting Magazine
530 Fifth Ave.
New York, NY 10036
212-522-8989
http://www.parenting.com

Parents Magazine
375 Lexington Ave.
New York, NY 10017
212-499-2000
http://www.parents.com

Working Mother
135 West 50th St., 6th Fl.
New York, NY 10020-1208
212-445-6100
http://www.workingmother.com

WOMEN'S INTERESTS

Allure
4 Times Square
New York, NY 10036
212-286-7441
http://www.allure.com

Cosmopolitan
224 W. 57th St.
New York, NY 10019
212-649-3570
http://www.cosmomag.com

Elle
1633 Broadway
New York, NY 10019
212-767-5800
http://www.elle.com

Family Circle
375 Lexington Ave.
New York, NY 10017
212-499-2000
http://www.familycircle.com

Good Housekeeping
959 8th Ave.
New York, NY 10019
212-649-2200
http://www.goodhousekeeping.com

Harpers Bazaar
1700 Broadway
New York, NY 10019
212-903-5000
http://www.harpersbazaar.com

InStyle
1271 Avenue of the Americas
New York, NY 10020
212-522-1212
http://www.instyle.com

Jane
7 West 34th St.
New York, NY 10001
212-630-3900
http://www.janemag.com

Marie Claire
1790 Broadway
New York, NY 10019
212-649-5000
http://www.marieclaire.com

More
125 Park Ave.
New York, NY 10017
212-557-6600
http://www.more.com

Ms.
20 Exchange Place, 22nd Fl.
New York, NY 10005-509-2092
212-509-2092
http://www.msmagazine.com

O, The Oprah Magazine
1700 Broadway
New York, NY 10019
212-903-5000
http://www.oprah.com

Rosie
375 Lexington Ave.
New York, NY 10017
212-499-1772
http://www.rosie.com

Seventeen
850 Third Ave., 9th Fl.
New York, NY 10022
212-407-9700
http://www.seventeen .com

Vogue
4 Times Square
New York, NY 10036
212-286-286
http://www.vogue.com

W
7 West 34th St.
New York, NY 10001
212-630-4000
http://www.wmagazine.com

Woman's Day
1633 Broadway
New York, NY 10019
212-767-6000
http://www.womansday.com

Woman's World
270 Sylvan Ave.
Englewood Cliffs, NJ 07632
201-569-6699

YM
15 East 26th St.
New York, NY 10010
646-758-0555
http://www.ym.com

BOOKS

AGING

Beers, Mark & Steven Urice. *Aging in Good Health: A Complete Essential Medical Guide for Men and Women over Fifty and their Families.* Pocket Books, 1992.

Binstock, Robert H. and Linda K. George, eds. *Handbook of Aging and the Social Sciences,* 4th ed. Academic Press, 1995.

ALCOHOLISM AND DRUG ABUSE

Evans, Glen, et al. *The Encyclopedia of Alcoholism.* 2nd ed. Facts on File, 1991.

National Directory of Drug Abuse and Alcoholism Treatment and Prevention Programs. Gordon Press, 1991.

Sabroe, Knud-Erik. *Alcohol and Society: Patterns and Attitudes.* Coronet Books, 1994.

CONSUMER INFORMATION AND PROTECTION

Consumer Reports Buying Guide. Consumer Reports, annual.

Consumer Resource Handbook. U.S. Office of Consumer Affairs, annual.

DISABILITIES

Bondo, Bruce E. *Tax Options & Strategies: A State by State Guide for Persons with Disabilities, Senior Citizens, Veterans and their Families.* Demos Vermande, 1995.

Doyle, Brian. *Disability, Discrimination and Equal Opportunities: A Comparative Study of the Employment Rights of Disabled Persons.* Mansell, 1995.

Witt, Melanie A. *Job Strategies for People with Disabilities: Enable Yourself for Today's Job Market.* Peterson's Guides, 1992.

DOMESTIC VIOLENCE

Berry, Dawn Bradley. *Domestic Violence Sourcebook: Everything You Need to Know.* Lowell House, 1996.

FAMILY PLANNING

Freeman, Sarah and Vern Bullough. *The Complete Guide to Fertility and Family Planning.* Prometheus Books, 1992.

Pocket Guide for Family Planning Service Providers. J. H. Piego, 1995.

PARENTING

Casey, Eileen. *Maternity Leave: The Working Woman's Guide to Combining Pregnancy, Motherhood and Career.* Avon, 1995.

Starer, Dan. *Who to Call: The Parent's Sourcebook.* Quill, 1992.

GENERAL

Berkman, Robert L. *Find It Fast.* HarperPerennial, 1997.

The World Almanac and Book of Facts. World Almanac Books, annual.

V

RECREATION

23

SPORTS AND GAMES

Sports/Games

AUTO RACING

Track races are held on oval asphalt tracks that are rectangular in shape with straightaways and banked (curved and sloped upward) corners. Road races are held on courses that include straight sections, hills, and various types of turns, such as hairpins and doglegs. Drag races are held on a drag strip, a straight paved track usually about 440 yards long.

Stock cars are late-model American-made production sedans (with front-mounted engines, doors, fenders, and a windshield) that have been modified to increase their power and speed. They typically race 200 to 600 miles on oval tracks.

Formula 1 cars are custom-built according to specifications that govern such elements as body design and engine size. The basic vehicle has a smooth contour to decrease air resistance, a low driver's seat in an open cockpit, no fenders, a spoiler near the back to hold the car to the road, and a rear-mounted engine. Formula 1 cars are used in Grand Prix races that are held on road courses up to 200 miles long.

When Barney Oldfield became the first man to drive a car 60 mph, most doctors claimed that such speed would cause deafness.

Indy cars are similar to Formula 1 cars but have different engine sizes, chassis (frame) formats, and transmission configurations. Such cars race on oval tracks for 150 miles or longer.

Drag-racing vehicles include *pro stock* (modified production cars) and *dragsters* (long, narrow-framed single seaters with large rear wheels).

AUTO RACING FLAGS

Flag	Message
Solid green	Indicates the start of an event: a race, a practice, etc. Signals that laps are being counted
Red and yellow, divided diagonally	Indicates the race must be restarted; usually shown after a yellow flag if the first lap has not been completed.
Blue with diagonal orange stripe	Signals a driver to let a faster driver overtake. Also called the "move over" flag.
Solid yellow	Signals drivers to proceed with caution; usually indicates an accident or debris on the track. In certain shorter races the lap count is suspended, in others such as NASCAR, Formula I, and Indy car, the laps are still counted
Solid red	Indicates danger. The race must stop and all drivers should turn off their engines. The lap count is suspended.
Solid black	Indicates a penalty on a particular car, which must leave the track. If the driver has broken a rule, a penalty is assessed. If the car is unfit to race, repairs must be made before the car can return to the track.
Solid white	Signals one lap remaining in a race. Displayed when the race leader crosses the finish line at the beginning of the final lap, and to all remaining cars until the leader again crosses the finish line
Black and white checkered	Signals the finish of the event: a race, a practice, etc. Waved when the leader passes the finish line.

INDIANAPOLIS 500

A major auto race in the United States for many years has been the Indianapolis 500, which consists of 250 laps around the 2½-mile-long oval track at the Indianapolis Motor Speedway in Indiana. The winners since 1911 follow.

Date	Driver	Car	Average m.p.h.
1911	Ray Harroun	Marmon	74.602
1912	Joe Dawson	National	78.719
1913	Jules Goux	Peugeot	75.933
1914	Rene Thomas	Delage	82.474
1915	Ralph DePalma	Mercedes	89.840
1916	Dario Resta	Peugeot	84.001[1]
1917	No race held		
1918	No race held		
1919	Howard Wilcox	Peugeot	85.050
1920	Gaston Chevrolet	Monroe	88.618
1921	Tommy Milton	Frontenac	89.621
1922	Jimmy Murphy	Murphy Special	94.484
1923	Tommy Milton	H.C.S. Special	90.954
1924	L. L. Corum–Joe Boyer	Duesenberg Special	98.234
1925	Peter DePaolo	Duesenberg Special	101.127
1926	Frank Lockhart	Miller Special	95.904[2]
1927	George Souders	Duesenberg Special	97.545
1928	Louis Meyer	Miller Special	99.482
1929	Ray Keech	Simplex Piston Ring Special	97.585
1930	Billy Arnold	Harry Hartz Special	100.448
1931	Louis Schneider	Bowes Seal Fast Special	96.629
1932	Fred Frame	Miller-Hartz Special	104.144
1933	Louis Meyer	Tydol Special	104.162
1934	William Cummings	Boyle Products Special	104.863
1935	Kelly Petillo	Gilmore Speedway Special	106.240
1936	Louis Meyer	Ring Free Special	109.069
1937	Wilbur Shaw	Shaw-Gilmore Special	113.580
1938	Floyd Roberts	Burd Piston Ring Special	117.200
1939	Wilbur Shaw	Bolye Special	115.035
1940	Wilbur Shaw	Bolye Special	114.277
1941	Floyd Davis–Mauri Rose	Noc-Out Hose Clamp Special	115.117
1942	No race held		
1943	No race held		
1944	No race held		
1945	No race held		
1946	George Robson	Thorne Engineering Special	114.820
1947	Mauri Rose	Blue Crown Spark Plug Special	116.338
1948	Mauri Rose	Blue Crown Spark Plug Special	119.814
1949	Bill Holland	Blue Crown Spark Plug Special	121.327
1950	Johnny Parsons	Kurtiss-Kraft Wynns Special	124.001[3]
1951	Lee Wallard	Belanger Special	126.244
1952	Troy Ruttman	Agajanian Special	128.922
1953	William Vukovich	Fuel Injection Special	128.740
1954	William Vukovich	Fuel Injection Special	130.840
1955	Robert Sweikert	Zink Special	128.209
1956	Pat Flaherty	Zink Special	128.490
1957	Sam Hanks	Belond Exhaust Special	135.601
1958	Jimmy Bryan	Belond Special	133.791
1959	Rodger Ward	Leader CARD Special	135.856
1960	Jim Rathmann	Ken-Paul Special	138.767
1961	A. J. Foyt	Bowes Special	139.130
1962	Rodger Ward	Leader Card Special	140.292

[1] 300 miles   [2] 400 miles   [3] 345 miles

continues

Sports/Games

Indianapolis 500 Winners, Continued

Date	Driver	Car	Average m.p.h.
1963	Parnelli Jones	Agajanian Special	143.137
1964	A. J. Foyt	Sheraton-Thompson Special	147.350
1965	Jim Clark	Lotus-Ford	150.686
1966	Graham Hill	Lola-Ford	144.317
1967	A. J. Foyt	Coyote Ford	151.207
1968	Bobby Unser	Offenhauser-Eagle	152.882
1969	Mario Andretti	Hawk-Ford	156.867
1970	Al Unser	P. J. Colt-Ford	155.749
1971	Al Unser	Johnny Lightning Special	157.735
1972	Mark Donohue	Sunoco McLaren-Offy	162.962
1973	Gordon Johncock	Eagle-Offenhauser	159.036[4]
1974	Johnny Rutherford	McLaren-Offenhauser	158.589
1975	Bobby Unser	Eagle-Offenhauser	149.213[5]
1976	Johnny Rutherford	McLaren-Offenhauser	148.725[6]
1977	A. J. Foyt	Coyote-Foyt	161.331
1978	Al Unser	Lola-Cosworth	161.363
1979	Rick Mears	Penske-Cosworth	158.899
1980	Johnny Rutherford	Chaparral	142.862
1981	Bobby Unser	Penske-Cosworth	138.085
1982	Gordon Johncock	Wildcat-Cosworth	162.026
1983	Tom Sneva	March-Cosworth	162.117
1984	Rick Mears	March-Cosworth	163.612
1985	Danny Sullivan	March-Cosworth	152.982
1986	Bobby Rahal	March-Cosworth	170.722
1987	Al Unser	March-Cosworth	162.175
1988	Rick Mears	Penske-Chevrolet	149.809
1989	Emerson Fittipaldi	Penske-Chevrolet	167.581
1990	Arie Luyendyk	Lola-Chevrolet	185.981
1991	Rick Mears	Penske-Chevrolet	176.460
1992	Al Unser, Jr.	Galmer-Chevrolet	134.479
1993	Emerson Fittipaldi	Penske-Chevrolet	157.207
1994	Al Unser, Jr.	Penske-Ilmor Mercedes	160.872
1995	Jacques Villeneuve	Reynard-Ford Cosworth	153.616
1996	Buddy Lazier	Reynard-Ford Cosworth	147.956
1997	Arie Luyendyk	G-Force Aurora	145.827
1998	Eddie Cheever Jr.	Dallara-Aurora	145.155
1999	Kenny Brack	Dallara-Aurora	153.176
2000	Juan Montoya	G. Force-Aurora	167.607
2001	Helio Castroneves	Dallara-Aurora	153.601

[4] 332.5 miles   [5] 435 miles   [6] 255 miles

BASEBALL

Baseball, named for the three bases and home plate that are parts of the playing field, has 9 or 10 players on each side. The offensive team sends to home plate one batter at a time, who uses a wooden or metal bat to try to hit a small cowhide-covered ball thrown from the pitcher to the catcher, two members of the defensive team. The defensive team also consists of four infielders and three outfielders. If the batter hits the ball on the ground, he must run to-

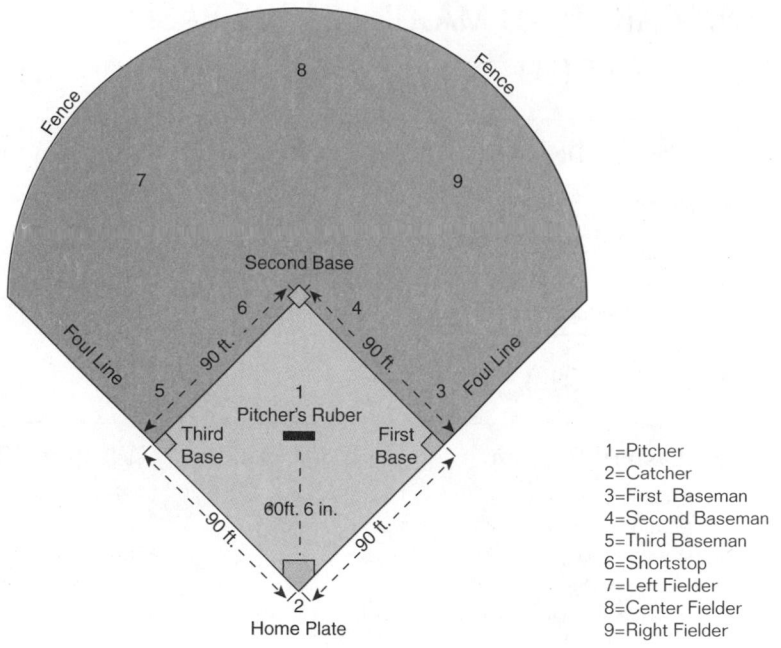

1=Pitcher
2=Catcher
3=First Baseman
4=Second Baseman
5=Third Baseman
6=Shortstop
7=Left Fielder
8=Center Fielder
9=Right Fielder

Baseball Field

ward first base; he is out if a defensive player throws the ball to a teammate standing on first base before the runner reaches the base. The batter is also out if the ball he hits is caught by a defensive player before it hits the ground. A strike is called if the batter in a swing fails to strike the pitched ball, fails to swing at a pitch determined by the umpire to be a strike, or hits the ball into foul territory. Three strikes put the batter out (a strikeout). Outs may also be made when a defensive player who has the ball tags a base runner when the runner is between bases, or when a defensive player who has the ball steps on second base, third base, or home plate if the runner is forced to move to that base because the batter or another base runner is moving to occupy the preceding base.

The offensive team attempts to score runs by causing offensive base runners to go around all four bases and cross home plate safely. The offensive team scores runs by accumulating hits, which are balls hit between the two foul lines that go uncaught, allowing a batter to safely reach first base (a single), second base (a double), or third base (a triple), thus driving

runners ahead of him to circle the bases. Batters can also reach base and move the runners ahead a base by obtaining a walk, four pitches that the batter does not swing at and that are determined by the umpire not to be strikes. Runs also can be scored with a home run, whereby a batter hits the ball over the outfield fence or far enough that he can circle the bases. The game is divided into nine innings, with three outs for each team in each inning. The batting, or offensive, team takes the field (defensive positions) after making three outs, when the opponents become batters. At the end of nine innings, the team that has accumulated the most runs is the winner. If both teams have scored the same number of runs at the end of nine innings, extra innings are played until the tie is broken.

Cleveland Indians star Lou Boudreau blew his nose and blew a game. He forgot that putting a towel to his face was the "steal" sign.

U.S. AND CANADIAN MAJOR LEAGUE BASEBALL TEAMS

AMERICAN LEAGUE (AL)

Eastern Division	Central Division	Western Division
Baltimore Orioles	Chicago White Sox	Anaheim Angels
Boston Red Sox	Cleveland Indians	Oakland Athletics
New York Yankees	Detroit Tigers	Seattle Mariners
Tampa Bay Devil Rays	Kansas City Royals	Texas Rangers
Toronto Blue Jays	Minnesota Twins	

NATIONAL LEAGUE (NL)

Eastern Division	Central Division	Western Division
Atlanta Braves	Chicago Cubs	Arizona Diamondbacks
Florida Marlins	Cincinnati Reds	Colorado Rockies
Montreal Expos	Houston Astros	Los Angeles Dodgers
New York Mets	Milwaukee Brewers	San Diego Padres
Philadelphia Phillies	Pittsburgh Pirates	San Francisco Giants
	St. Louis Cardinals	

WORLD SERIES

After each major league team plays a regular-season schedule of 162 games, the three division winners in each league plus a wild-card team (the second-place division team with the best won-lost record) meet in a series of playoffs to determine the league pennant winner. The American League pennant winner then meets the National League pennant winner in October in a best-of-seven-games World Series for the major league championship that has been played since 1903 (except for the years 1904 and 1994). A best-of-nine-games World Series was played in 1903, 1919, 1920, and 1921. Tied games were played in 1907 and 1912. Winners and losers of the World Series follow.

Year	Winner	League	Loser	League	Games
1903	Boston Red Sox	AL	Pittsburgh Pirates	NL	5–3
1904	No series				
1905	New York Giants	NL	Philadelphia Athletics	AL	4–1
1906	Chicago White Sox	AL	Chicago Cubs	NL	4–2
1907	Chicago Cubs	NL	Detroit Tigers	AL	4–0–1
1908	Chicago Cubs	NL	Detroit Tigers	AL	4–1
1909	Pittsburgh Pirates	NL	Detroit Tigers	AL	4–3
1910	Philadelphia Athletics	AL	Chicago Cubs	NL	4–1
1911	Philadelphia Athletics	AL	New York Giants	NL	4–2
1912	Boston Red Sox	AL	New York Giants	NL	4–3–1
1913	Philadelphia Athletics	AL	New York Giants	NL	4–1
1914	Boston Braves	NL	Philadelphia Athletics	AL	4–0
1915	Boston Red Sox	AL	Philadelphia Phillies	NL	4–1
1916	Boston Red Sox	AL	Brooklyn Dodgers	NL	4–1
1917	Chicago White Sox	AL	New York Giants	NL	4–2
1918	Boston Red Sox	AL	Chicago Cubs	NL	4–2
1919	Cincinnati Reds	NL	Chicago White Sox	AL	5–3

Year	Winner	League	Loser	League	Games
1920	Cleveland Indians	AL	Brooklyn Dodgers	NL	5–2
1921	New York Giants	NL	New York Yankees	AL	5–3
1922	New York Giants	NL	New York Yankees	AL	4–0
1923	New York Yankees	AL	New York Giants	NL	4–2
1924	Washington Senators	AL	New York Giants	NL	4–3
1925	Pittsburgh Pirates	NL	Washington Senators	AL	4–3
1926	St. Louis Cardinals	NL	New York Yankees	AL	4–3
1927	New York Yankees	AL	Pittsburgh Pirates	NL	4–0
1928	New York Yankees	AL	St. Louis Cardinals	NL	4–0
1929	Philadelphia Athletics	AL	Chicago Cubs	NL	4–1
1930	Philadelphia Athletics	AL	St. Louis Cardinals	NL	4–2
1931	St. Louis Cardinals	NL	Philadelphia Athletics	AL	4–3
1932	New York Yankees	AL	Chicago Cubs	NL	4–0
1933	New York Giants	NL	Washington Senators	AL	4–1
1934	St. Louis Cardinals	NL	Detroit Tigers	AL	4–3
1935	Detroit Tigers	AL	Chicago Cubs	NL	4–2
1936	New York Yankees	AL	New York Giants	NL	4–2
1937	New York Yankees	AL	New York Giants	NL	4–1
1938	New York Yankees	AL	Chicago Cubs	NL	4–0
1939	New York Yankees	AL	Cincinnati Reds	NL	4–0
1940	Cincinnati Reds	NL	Detroit Tigers	AL	4–3
1941	New York Yankees	AL	Brooklyn Dodgers	NL	4–1
1942	St. Louis Cardinals	NL	New York Yankees	AL	4–1
1943	New York Yankees	AL	St. Louis Cardinals	NL	4–1
1944	St. Louis Cardinals	NL	St. Louis Browns	AL	4–2
1945	Detroit Tigers	AL	Chicago Cubs	NL	4–3
1946	St. Louis Cardinals	NL	Boston Red Sox	AL	4–3
1947	New York Yankees	AL	Brooklyn Dodgers	NL	4–3
1948	Cleveland Indians	AL	Boston Braves	NL	4–2
1949	New York Yankees	AL	Brooklyn Dodgers	NL	4–1
1950	New York Yankees	AL	Philadelphia Phillies	NL	4–0
1951	New York Yankees	AL	New York Giants	NL	4–2
1952	New York Yankees	AL	Brooklyn Dodgers	NL	4–3
1953	New York Yankees	AL	Brooklyn Dodgers	NL	4–2
1954	New York Giants	NL	Cleveland Indians	AL	4–0
1955	Brooklyn Dodgers	NL	New York Yankees	AL	4–3
1956	New York Yankees	AL	Brooklyn Dodgers	NL	4–3
1957	Milwaukee Braves	NL	New York Yankees	AL	4–3
1958	New York Yankees	AL	Milwaukee Braves	NL	4–3
1959	Los Angeles Dodgers	NL	Chicago White Sox	AL	4–2
1960	Pittsburgh Pirates	NL	New York Yankees	AL	4–3
1961	New York Yankees	AL	Cincinnati Reds	NL	4–1
1962	New York Yankees	AL	San Francisco Giants	NL	4–3
1963	Los Angeles Dodgers	NL	New York Yankees	AL	4–0
1964	St. Louis Cardinals	NL	New York Yankees	AL	4–3
1965	Los Angeles Dodgers	NL	Minnesota Twins	AL	4–3
1966	Baltimore Orioles	AL	Los Angeles Dodgers	NL	4–0
1967	St. Louis Cardinals	NL	Boston Red Sox	AL	4–3
1968	Detroit Tigers	AL	St. Louis Cardinals	NL	4–3
1969	New York Mets	NL	Baltimore Orioles	AL	4–1
1970	Baltimore Orioles	AL	Cincinnati Reds	NL	4–1
1971	Pittsburgh Pirates	NL	Baltimore Orioles	AL	4–3

continues

World Series Winners, Continued

Year	Winner	League	Loser	League	Games
1972	Oakland Athletics	AL	Cincinnati Reds	NL	4–3
1973	Oakland Athletics	AL	New York Mets	NL	4–3
1974	Oakland Athletics	AL	Los Angeles Dodgers	NL	4–1
1975	Cincinnati Reds	NL	Boston Red Sox	AL	4–3
1976	Cincinnati Reds	NL	New York Yankees	AL	4–0
1977	New York Yankees	AL	Los Angeles Dodgers	NL	4–2
1978	New York Yankees	AL	Los Angeles Dodgers	NL	4–2
1979	Pittsburgh Pirates	NL	Baltimore Orioles	AL	4–3
1980	Philadelphia Phillies	NL	Kansas City Royals	AL	4–2
1981	Los Angeles Dodgers	NL	New York Yankees	AL	4–2
1982	St. Louis Cardinals	NL	Milwaukee Brewers	AL	4–3
1983	Baltimore Orioles	AL	Philadelphia Phillies	NL	4–1
1984	Detroit Tigers	AL	San Diego Padres	NL	4–1
1985	Kansas City Royals	AL	St. Louis Cardinals	NL	4–3
1986	New York Mets	NL	Boston Red Sox	AL	4–3
1987	Minnesota Twins	AL	St. Louis Cardinals	NL	4–3
1988	Los Angeles Dodgers	NL	Oakland Athletics	AL	4–1
1989	Oakland Athletics	AL	San Francisco Giants	NL	4–0
1990	Cincinnati Reds	NL	Oakland Athletics	AL	4–1
1991	Minnesota Twins	AL	Atlanta Braves	NL	4–3
1992	Toronto Blue Jays	AL	Atlanta Braves	NL	4–3
1993	Toronto Blue Jays	AL	Philadelphia Phillies	NL	4–2
1994	No series				
1995	Atlanta Braves	NL	Cleveland Indians	AL	4–2
1996	New York Yankees	AL	Atlanta Braves	NL	4–2
1997	Florida Marlins	NL	Cleveland Indians	AL	4–3
1998	New York Yankees	AL	San Diego Padres	NL	4–0
1999	New York Yankees	AL	Atlanta Braves	NL	4–0
2000	New York Yankees	AL	New York Mets	NL	4–1
2001	Arizona Diamondbacks	NL	New York Yankees	AL	4–3

BASKETBALL

Basketball usually is played indoors on a rectangular wooden court by two teams, each with five players. At both ends of the court are suspended two goals, or baskets (18 inches in diameter), consisting of a circular metal rim 10 feet above the floor attached to a square backboard made of wood, plastic, or fiberglass. A cord net is hung below the rim. The object is to shoot the ball so that it goes through the basket from above and to prevent your opponents from doing the same. Basketball uses a large rubber ball covered with leather.

Play begins with a jump ball. The official throws the ball upward at the center circle between two opposing players. The two players try to tip or slap the ball to a teammate and thus gain possession of the ball. Each team defends one goal. There are offensive and defensive halves of the court for each team, divided by the midcourt line. A player advances the ball down the court by passing to a teammate, dribbling (bouncing the ball while walking or running), or shooting the ball at the basket. Running or walking while holding the ball is not permitted. If a shot goes in the basket, two points are awarded to the shooting team. If a shot is missed (usually hitting the rim or backboard), a defensive player may rebound the ball (catch it as it bounces away from the basket). He then may begin to advance the ball to the other end of the court in preparation for a shot by his team. An offensive player may also rebound a missed shot and shoot again. A shot made from beyond the three-point line (22 feet from the center of the basket on NBA courts) scores three points instead of the usual two.

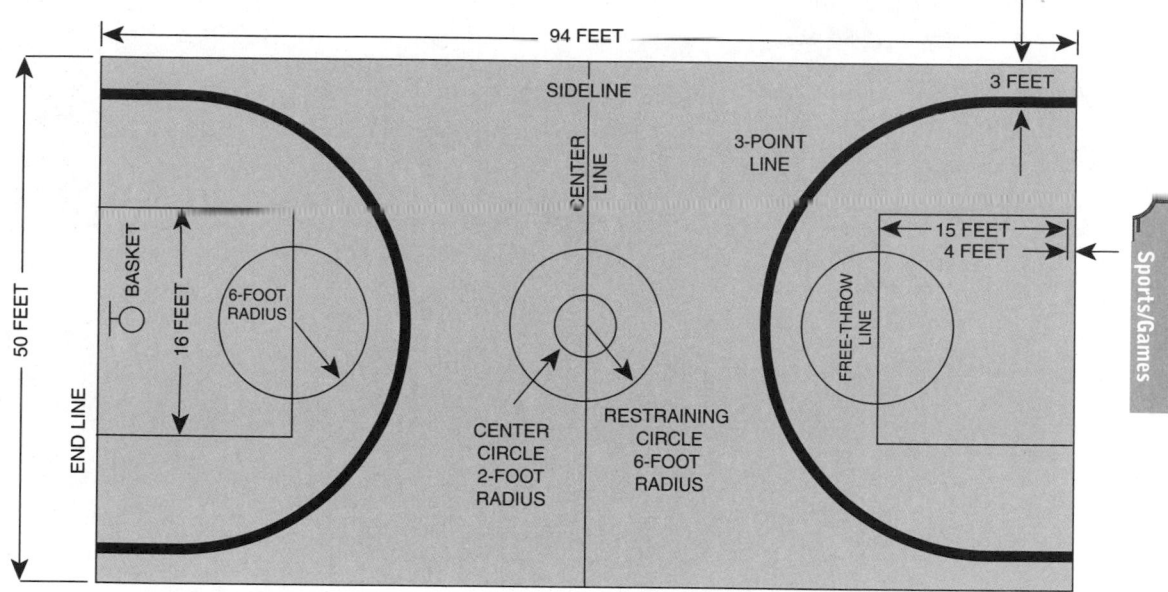

Basketball Court

Holding, pushing, grabbing, and similar types of body contact are not permitted; these are called fouls. They may result in a foul shot or free throw, an unimpeded shot taken by the offended player from a line on the court 15 feet from the basket. A successful free throw scores one point.

Professional basketball games are divided into four 12-minute quarters; the team with more points at the end of that time wins the game.

NATIONAL BASKETBALL ASSOCIATION (NBA) TEAMS

EASTERN CONFERENCE

Atlantic Division	Central Division
Boston Celtics	Atlanta Hawks
Miami Heat	Chicago Bulls
New Jersey Nets	Cleveland Cavaliers
New York Knicks	Detroit Pistons
Orlando Magic	Indiana Pacers
Philadelphia 76ers	Milwaukee Bucks
Washington Wizards	New Orleans Hornets
	Toronto Raptors

WESTERN CONFERENCE

Midwest Division	Pacific Division
Dallas Mavericks	Golden State Warriors
Denver Nuggets	Los Angeles Clippers
Houston Rockets	Los Angeles Lakers
Minnesota Timberwolves	Phoenix Suns
San Antonio Spurs	Portland Trail Blazers
Utah Jazz	Sacramento Kings
Vancouver Grizzlies	Seattle SuperSonics

NATIONAL BASKETBALL ASSOCIATION CHAMPIONS

After each National Basketball Association (NBA) team plays a regular-season schedule of 82 games, the eight teams in each conference with the best won-lost records meet in a series of play-offs to determine the conference champion. The Eastern Conference champion then meets the Western Conference champion in the spring in a best-of-seven-games series for the NBA championship. Winners and losers of the NBA championship series are listed on the next page.

Year	NBA Winners	Conference	Losers	Conference	Games
1947	Philadelphia Warriors	E	Chicago Stags	W	4–1
1948	Baltimore Bullets	W	Philadelphia Warriors	E	4–2
1949	Minneapolis Lakers	W	Washington Capitols	E	4–2
1950	Minneapolis Lakers	W	Syracuse Nationals	E	4–2
1951	Rochester Royals	W	New York Knickerbockers	E	4–3
1952	Minneapolis Lakers	W	New York Knickerbockers	E	4–3
1953	Minneapolis Lakers	W	New York Knickerbockers	E	4–1
1954	Minneapolis Lakers	W	Syracuse Nationals	E	4–3
1955	Syracuse Nationals	E	Fort Wayne Pistons	W	4–3
1956	Philadelphia Warriors	E	Fort Wayne Pistons	W	4–1
1957	Boston Celtics	E	St. Louis Hawks	W	4–3
1958	St. Louis Hawks	W	Boston Celtics	E	4–2
1959	Boston Celtics	E	Minneapolis Lakers	W	4–0
1960	Boston Celtics	E	St. Louis Hawks	W	4–3
1961	Boston Celtics	E	St. Louis Hawks	W	4–1
1962	Boston Celtics	E	Los Angeles Lakers	W	4–3
1963	Boston Celtics	E	Los Angeles Lakers	W	4–2
1964	Boston Celtics	E	San Francisco Warriors	W	4–1
1965	Boston Celtics	E	Los Angeles Lakers	W	4–1
1966	Boston Celtics	E	Los Angeles Lakers	W	4–3
1967	Philadelphia 76ers	E	San Francisco Warriors	W	4–2
1968	Boston Celtics	E	Los Angeles Lakers	W	4–2
1969	Boston Celtics	E	Los Angeles Lakers	W	4–3
1970	New York Knickerbockers	E	Los Angeles Lakers	W	4–3
1971	Milwaukee Bucks	W	Baltimore Bullets	E	4–0
1972	Los Angeles Lakers	W	New York Knickerbockers	E	4–1
1973	New York Knickerbockers	E	Los Angeles Lakers	W	4–1
1974	Boston Celtics	E	Milwaukee Bucks	W	4–3
1975	Golden State Warriors	W	Washington Bullets	E	4–0
1976	Boston Celtics	E	Phoenix Suns	W	4–2
1977	Portland Trail Blazers	W	Philadelphia 76ers	E	4–2
1978	Washington Bullets	E	Seattle Supersonics	W	4–3
1979	Seattle Supersonics	W	Washington Bullets	E	4–1
1980	Los Angeles Lakers	W	Philadelphia 76ers	E	4–2
1981	Boston Celtics	E	Houston Rockets	W	4–2
1982	Los Angeles Lakers	W	Philadelphia 76ers	E	4–2
1983	Philadelphia 76ers	E	Los Angeles Lakers	W	4–0
1984	Boston Celtics	E	Los Angeles Lakers	W	4–3
1985	Los Angeles Lakers	W	Boston Celtics	E	4–2
1986	Boston Celtics	E	Houston Rockets	W	4–2
1987	Los Angeles Lakers	W	Boston Celtics	E	4–2
1988	Los Angeles Lakers	W	Detroit Pistons	E	4–3
1989	Detroit Pistons	E	Los Angeles Lakers	W	4–0
1990	Detroit Pistons	E	Portland Trail Blazers	W	4–1
1991	Chicago Bulls	E	Los Angeles Lakers	W	4–1
1992	Chicago Bulls	E	Portland Trail Blazers	W	4–2
1993	Chicago Bulls	E	Phoenix Suns	W	4–2
1994	Houston Rockets	W	New York Knickerbockers	E	4–3
1995	Houston Rockets	W	Orlando Magic	W	4–0
1996	Chicago Bulls	E	Seattle Supersonics	W	4–2
1997	Chicago Bulls	E	Utah Jazz	W	4–2
1998	Chicago Bulls	E	Utah Jazz	W	4–2
1999	San Antonio Spurs	W	New York Knicks	E	4–1
2000	Los Angeles Lakers	W	Indiana Pacers	E	4–2
2001	Los Angles Lakers	W	Philadelphia 76ers	E	4–1

Sports/Games

BICYCLE RACING

Road-racing bicycles have a free front wheel, multiple gears on the rear wheel, and a brake for each wheel. Track-racing bicycles have a single fixed gear on the rear wheel and no brakes. Cyclo-cross bicycles have typical road gears but have stronger rims and fatter tires.

The basic types of road races are (1) *time trials,* in which cyclists start at intervals and race either over a fixed distance (generally between 10 and 100 miles) to achieve the fastest time, or for a fixed time (generally 12 or 24 hours) to achieve the longest distance; (2) *criteriums,* in which cyclists ride a predetermined number of laps (covering a total distance ranging from 10 to 60 miles) on a closed circuit of 1 to 3 miles; (3) *road races,* in which cyclists ride from point to point, around several long circuits, or complete a combination of the two over a course that features long, steep climbs; and (4) *multiday stage races,* lasting from three days to three weeks, that include a combination of time trials, criteriums, and road races and whose winner is the cyclist with the lowest accumulated time for all stages.

Track races are held on steeply banked tracks either outdoors or inside buildings called *velodromes.* The basic types of track races are (1) *sprints,* in which two or more cyclists compete over a short distance (generally 1,000 meters for men and 500 meters for women); (2) *handicaps,* a massed-start event where the order in which each cyclist starts is determined by past proven speed; and (3) *pursuits,* in which two cyclists or teams start directly opposite from each other and then try to catch up to one another (over a distance of 4 to 5 kilometers) before reaching the finish.

In cyclo-cross races (generally 1 to 15 kilometers long), cyclists race off-road and encounter such obstacles as fences, streams, mud, sand, forests, ditches, fallen trees, gates, creek beds, and artificial hurdles, forcing them to dismount occasionally and carry their bicycles.

TOUR DE FRANCE

The most famous stage race is the Tour de France, a three-week event held annually in France and portions of other European countries in late June and early July and ranging in length from 2,500 to 3,000 miles. The course is changed each year and includes steep mountain climbs. Winners of the Tour de France follow.

Year	Cyclist	Home Country
1903	Maurice Garin	France
1904	Henri Cornet	France
1905	Louis Trousselier	France
1906	Rene Pottier	France
1907	Lucien Petit-Breton	France
1908	Lucien Petit-Breton	France
1909	Francois Faber	France
1910	Octave Lapize	France
1911	Gustave Garrigou	France
1912	Odile Defraye	Belgium
1913	Phillippe Thys	Belgium
1914	Phillippe Thys	Belgium
1915	*Race not held*	
1916	*Race not held*	
1917	*Race not held*	
1918	*Race not held*	
1919	Firmin Lambot	Belgium
1920	Phillippe Thys	Belgium
1921	Leon Scieur	Belgium

Year	Cyclist	Home Country
1922	Firmin Lambot	Belgium
1923	Henri Pelissier	France
1924	Ottavio Bottecchia	Italy
1925	Ottavio Bottecchia	Italy
1926	Lucien Buysse	Belgium
1927	Nicolas Frantz	Luxembourg
1928	Nicolas Frantz	Luxembourg
1929	Maurice Dewaele	Belgium
1930	Andre Leducq	France
1931	Antonin Magne	Italy
1932	Andre Leducq	France
1933	Georges Speicher	France
1934	Antonin Magne	Italy
1935	Romain Maes	Belgium
1936	Sylvere Maes	Belgium
1937	Roger Lapebie	France
1938	Gino Bartali	Italy
1939	Sylvere Maes	Belgium
1940	*Race not held*	

continues

Tour de France Winners, Continued

Year	Cyclist	Home Country
1941	*Race not held*	
1942	*Race not held*	
1943	*Race not held*	
1944	*Race not held*	
1945	*Race not held*	
1946	*Race not held*	
1947	Jean Robic	France
1948	Gino Bartali	Italy
1949	Fausto Coppi	Italy
1950	Fredi Kubler	Switzerland
1951	Hugo Koblet	Switzerland
1952	Fausto Coppi	Italy
1953	Louison Bobet	France
1954	Louison Bobet	France
1955	Louison Bobet	France
1956	Roger Walkowiak	France
1957	Jacques Anquetil	France
1958	Charly Gaul	Luxembourg
1959	Fredrico Bahamontes	Spain
1960	Gastone Nencimi	Italy
1961	Jacques Anquetil	France
1962	Jacques Anquetil	France
1963	Jacques Anquetil	France
1964	Jacques Anquetil	France
1965	Felice Gimondi	Italy
1966	Lucien Aimar	France
1967	Roger Pingeon	France
1968	Jan Janssen	Holland
1969	Eddy Merckx	Belgium
1970	Eddy Merckx	Belgium
1971	Eddy Merckx	Belgium

Year	Cyclist	Home Country
1972	Eddy Merckx	Belgium
1973	Luis Ocana	Spain
1974	Eddy Merckx	Belgium
1975	Bernard Thevenet	France
1976	Lucien Van Impe	Belgium
1977	Baernard Thevenet	France
1978	Bernard Hinault	France
1979	Bernard Hinault	France
1980	Joop Zoetemelk	Holland
1981	Bernard Hinault	France
1982	Bernard Hinault	France
1983	Laurent Fignon	France
1984	Laurent Fignon	France
1985	Bernard Hinault	France
1986	Greg LeMond	United States
1987	Stephen Roche	Ireland
1988	Pedro Delgado	Spain
1989	Greg LeMond	United States
1990	Greg LeMond	United States
1991	Miguel Indurain	Spain
1992	Miguel Indurain	Spain
1993	Miguel Indurain	Spain
1994	Miguel Indurain	Spain
1995	Miguel Indurain	Spain
1996	Bjarne Riis	Denmark
1997	Jan Ullrich	Germany
1998	Marco Pantani	Italy
1999	Lance Armstrong	United States
2000	Lance Armstrong	United States
2001	Lance Armstrong	United States

BOWLING

Bowling, or tenpins, is an indoor sport in which a player attempts to knock down 10 wooden pins that are arranged in a triangular formation. The player accomplishes this by rolling a ball down a wooden lane, or alley. The ball, which weighs at most about 16 pounds, is fitted with three holes for thumb and finger grips. Each game is divided into 10 frames, and the bowler is allowed a maximum of two rolls per frame, except for the last frame, where he is allowed three. If a player knocks down all 10 pins with one roll, it is called a strike; the second roll of the frame is not used, except for the 10th frame, where three strikes are possible. If a player knocks down all 10 pins using both rolls of the frame, it is called a spare. The number of pins knocked down by the end of the game determines the score, with spares scoring 10 plus the number of pins knocked down on the next roll, and strikes scoring 10 plus the number of pins knocked down on the next two rolls. A perfect game of 12 consecutive strikes scores 300.

FOOTBALL

American football has 11 players on each team and is played on a large rectangular field. At each end of the field is an end zone, where the goalposts are placed. The object is to gain possession of an inflated leather or pigskin ball and move it across the opponents' goal line by running or passing, thus scoring a touchdown, which is worth six points.

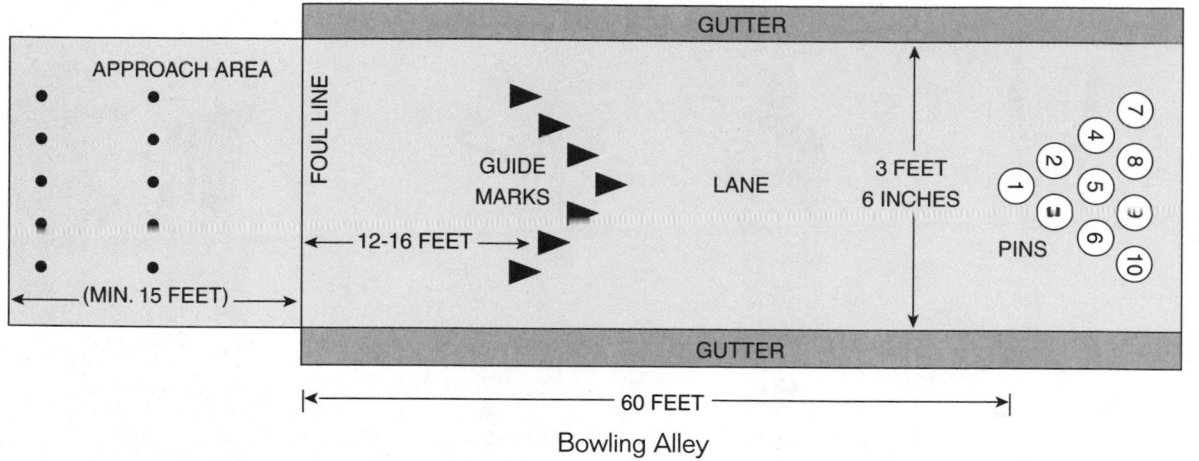

Bowling Alley

Passing the ball is usually done by the quarterback. Players also score points by kicking the ball through the goalposts. This opportunity is given automatically after a touchdown; the point is called a point after touchdown, or extra point. A field goal scores three points. The defensive team can score by downing an offensive player in his own end zone. This is called a safety and scores two points.

The term "down" in football has been used since the late 19th century. When a ball carrier was tackled, he would yell "down" to keep opponents from piling on top of him.

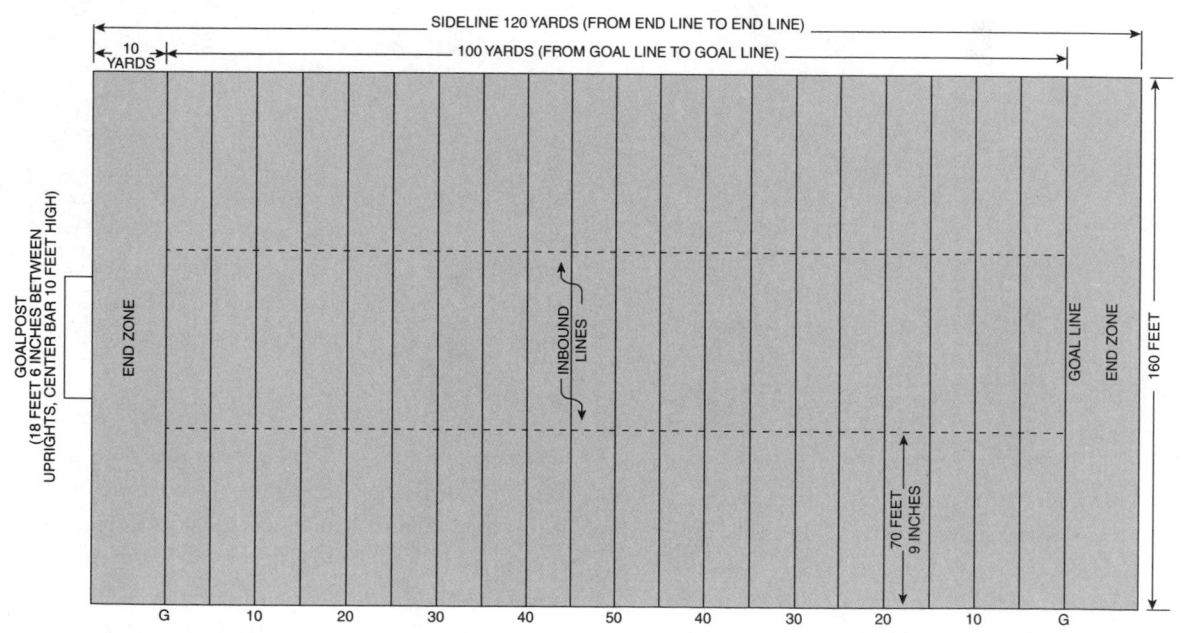

Football Field

Official Football Signals

TOUCHDOWN, FIELD GOAL, or SUCCESSFUL TRY

ILLEGAL FORWARD PASS
If followed by raised hand flung downward: INTENTIONAL GROUNDING OF PASS.

FIRST DOWN

DEAD BALL or NEUTRAL ZONE ESTABLISHED
With raised fist closed: FOURTH DOWN.

LOSS OF DOWN

ILLEGAL CHUCKING

NO TIME-OUT or TIME-IN WITH WHISTLE

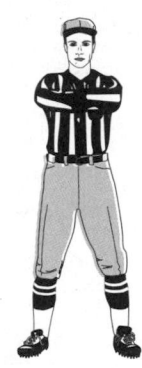

DELAY OF GAME or EXCESS TIME-OUT
If followed by forearms rotated over and over in front of body: ILLEGAL FORMATION.

PERSONAL FOUL

HOLDING

ILLEGAL USE OF HANDS

PENALTY REFUSED, INCOMPLETE PASS, PLAY OVER, or MISSED GOAL

Sports/Games

DOUBLE TOUCH

PASS JUGGLED IN-
BOUNDS AND CAUGHT
OUT OF BOUNDS

SAFETY

INTERFERENCE WITH
FORWARD PASS or
FAIR CATCH

INVALID FAIR
CATCH SIGNAL

INELIGIBLE RECEIVER, or IN-
ELIGIBLE MEMBER OF KICK-
ING TEAM DOWNFIELD

TIME-OUT
If followed by placing one hand on
top of cap: REFEREE'S TIME-
OUT; if followed by arm swung at
side: TOUCHBACK.

OFFSIDE, ENCROACHING,
or FREE KICK VIOLATION

ILLEGAL MOTION AT SNAP

CRAWLING, PUSHING, or
HELPING RUNNER

UNSPORTSMANLIKE
CONDUCT

ILLEGAL CUT

The offensive team must gain 10 yards in four tries, called downs, or give up possession of the ball. If 10 or more yards are gained, the offense has four more downs to advance the ball. If on the fourth down (or, rarely, before) it seems unlikely that the 10-yard minimum will be reached, the offense has the option of kicking the ball to the opponents. This is called a punt, and the defensive team, after catching the ball, goes on offense. The defensive team may also gain possession of the ball, and thus become the offense, by catching a ball passed by the quarterback that was intended for a teammate (interception), or by recovering the ball after it has been dropped by an offensive player (fumble). The defense hinders the attempts of the offense to gain yardage by tackling the ball carrier and pulling him to the ground. Because blocking and tackling can be very rough, football players wear protective helmets and substantial padding.

In 1950 the Los Angeles Rams were the first professional football team to put an insignia on their helmets. They painted yellow horns on their blue leather helmets.

The game is divided into four 15-minute periods; the team with the most points after the end of that time is the winner.

NATIONAL FOOTBALL LEAGUE (NFL) TEAMS

NATIONAL FOOTBALL CONFERENCE (NFC)

Eastern Division	Central Division	Western Division
Arizona Cardinals	Chicago Bears	Atlanta Falcons
Dallas Cowboys	Detroit Lions	Carolina Panthers
New York Giants	Green Bay Packers	New Orleans Saints
Philadelphia Eagles	Minnesota Vikings	San Francisco 49ers
Washington Redskins	Tampa Bay Buccaneers	St. Louis Rams

AMERICAN FOOTBALL CONFERENCE (AFC)

Eastern Division	Central Division	Western Division
Buffalo Bills	Baltimore Ravens	Denver Broncos
Indianapolis Colts	Cincinnati Bengals	Kansas City Chiefs
Miami Dolphins	Cleveland Browns	Oakland Raiders
New England Patriots	Jacksonville Jaguars	San Diego Chargers
New York Jets	Pittsburgh Steelers	Seattle Seahawks
	Tennessee Titans	

THE SUPER BOWL

After each National Football League (NFL) team plays a regular-season schedule of 16 games, the three division winners in each conference plus wild-card teams (the three teams with the best won-lost records in the rest of the conference) meet in a series of playoff games to determine the conference champion. The National Football Conference (NFC) champion then meets the American Football Conference (AFC) champion in January in the Super Bowl game for the NFL championship. The first four Super Bowls were played between the champions of the National Football League and the American Football League (AFL); the leagues then merged. Winners and losers of the Super Bowl are listed on the next page.

SUPER BOWL WINNERS

Bowl	Year	Winner	Conference	Loser	Conference	Score
I	1967	Green Bay Packers	NFL	Kansas City Chiefs	AFL	35–10
II	1968	Green Bay Packers	NFL	Oakland Raiders	AFL	33–14
III	1969	New York Jets	AFL	Baltimore Colts	NFL	16–7
IV	1970	Kansas City Chiefs	AFL	Minnesota Vikings	NFL	23–7
V	1971	Baltimore Colts	AFC	Dallas Cowboys	NFC	16–13
VI	1972	Dallas Cowboys	NFC	Miami Dolphins	AFC	24–3
VII	1973	Miami Dolphins	AFC	Washington Redskins	NFC	14–7
VIII	1974	Miami Dolphins	AFC	Minnesota Vikings	NFC	24–7
IX	1975	Pittsburgh Steelers	AFC	Minnesota Vikings	NFC	16–6
X	1976	Pittsburgh Steelers	AFC	Dallas Cowboys	NFC	21–17
XI	1977	Oakland Raiders	AFC	Minnesota Vikings	NFC	32–14
XII	1978	Dallas Cowboys	NFC	Denver Broncos	AFC	27–10
XIII	1979	Pittsburgh Steelers	AFC	Dallas Cowboys	NFC	35–31
XIV	1980	Pittsburgh Steelers	AFC	Los Angeles Rams	NFC	31–19
XV	1981	Oakland Raiders	AFC	Philadelphia Eagles	NFC	27–10
XVI	1982	San Francisco 49ers	NFC	Cincinnati Bengals	AFC	26–21
XVII	1983	Washington Redskins	NFC	Miami Dolphins	AFC	27–17
XVIII	1984	Los Angeles Raiders	AFC	Washington Redskins	NFC	38–9
XIX	1985	San Francisco 49ers	NFC	Miami Dolphins	AFC	38–16
XX	1986	Chicago Bears	NFC	New England Patriots	AFC	46–10
XXI	1987	New York Giants	NFC	Denver Broncos	AFC	39–20
XXII	1988	Washington Redskins	NFC	Denver Broncos	AFC	42–10
XXIII	1989	San Francisco 49ers	NFC	Cincinnati Bengals	AFC	20–16
XXIV	1990	San Francisco 49ers	NFC	Denver Broncos	AFC	55–10
XXV	1991	New York Giants	NFC	Buffalo Bills	AFC	20–19
XXVI	1992	Washington Redskins	NFC	Buffalo Bills	AFC	37–24
XXVII	1993	Dallas Cowboys	NFC	Buffalo Bills	AFC	52–17
XXVIII	1994	Dallas Cowboys	NFC	Buffalo Bills	AFC	30–13
XXIX	1995	San Francisco 49ers	NFC	San Diego Chargers	AFC	49–26
XXX	1996	Dallas Cowboys	NFC	Pittsburgh Steelers	AFC	27–17
XXXI	1997	Green Bay Packers	NFC	New England Patriots	AFC	35–21
XXXII	1998	Denver Broncos	AFC	Green Bay Packers	NFC	31–24
XXXIII	1999	Denver Broncos	AFC	Atlanta Falcons	NFC	34–19
XXXIV	2000	St. Louis Browns	AFC	Tennessee Titans	AFC	23–16
XXXV	2001	Baltimore Ravens	AFC	New York Giants	NFC	34–7
XXXVI	2002	New England Patriots	AFC	St. Louis Rams	NFC	20–17

GOLF

Golf is an outdoor game in which players hit a small hard ball with specially designed clubs that consist of a metal shaft and a wooden or metal club head. The object is to strike the ball with the club so that the ball goes into a cup that is sunk in the ground and marked with a flag. A standard golf course is divided into 18 holes, each with a tee, where the initial stroke is made; a grass fairway; and a green, a smooth grass surface where the cup is located. Each player attempts to reach the green and hit the ball into the cup using as few strokes as possible. Obstacles—such as water,

tall grass called rough, or traps filled with sand—may be found near the green or fairway. As many as 14 different types of clubs may be used depending on the length of shot required or the terrain. The distance from tee to cup varies greatly, but generally the distance is from 100 to 600 yards. The length and difficulty of the hole determine the par, the number of strokes that a good golfer would need to put the ball into the cup. After 18 holes, the player with the lowest number of strokes is the winner of that round. Golf tournaments are typically won by the player with the best (lowest) cumulative score after four rounds.

THE MASTERS

Four major golf tournaments carry the most important titles in professional golf. They are the Masters, the Professional Golfer's Association (PGA) Tournament, the U.S. Open, and the British Open. The Masters, played at the Augusta National Golf Club in Augusta, Georgia, is the title most sought in professional golf. The winners of the Masters Tournament follow.

Year	Winner	Score	Year	Winner	Score
1934	Horton Smith	284	1969	George Archer	281
1935	Gene Sarazen*	282	1970	Billy Casper*	279
1936	Horton Smith	285	1971	Charles Coody	279
1937	Byron Nelson	283	1972	Jack Nicklaus	286
1938	Henry Picard	285	1973	Tommy Aaron	283
1939	Ralph Guldahl	279	1974	Gary Player	278
1940	Jimmy Demaret	280	1975	Jack Nicklaus	276
1941	Craig Wood	280	1976	Ray Floyd	271
1942	Byron Nelson*	280	1977	Tom Watson	276
1943	No tournament held		1978	Gary Player	277
1944	No tournament held		1979	Fuzzy Zoeller*	280
1945	No tournament held		1980	Severiano Ballesteros	275
1946	Herman Keiser	282	1981	Tom Watson	280
1947	Jimmy Demaret	281	1982	Craig Stadler*	284
1948	Claude Harmon	279	1983	Severiano Ballesteros	280
1949	Sam Snead	282	1984	Ben Crenshaw	277
1950	Jimmy Demaret	283	1985	Bernhard Langer	282
1951	Ben Hogan	280	1986	Jack Nicklaus	279
1952	Sam Snead	286	1987	Larry Mize*	285
1953	Ben Hogan	274	1988	Sandy Lyle	281
1954	Sam Snead*	289	1989	Nick Faldo	283
1955	Cary Middlecoff	279	1990	Nick Faldo	278
1956	Jack Burke	289	1991	Ian Woosnam	277
1957	Doug Ford	283	1992	Fred Couples	275
1958	Arnold Palmer	284	1993	Bernhard Langer	277
1959	Art Wall, Jr.	284	1994	Jose Maria Olazabal	279
1960	Arnold Palmer	282	1995	Ben Crenshaw	274
1961	Gary Player	280	1996	Nick Faldo	276
1962	Arnold Palmer*	280	1997	Tiger Woods	270
1963	Jack Nicklaus	286	1998	Mark O'Meara	279
1964	Arnold Palmer	276	1999	Jose Maria Olazabal	280
1965	Jack Nicklaus	271	2000	Vijay Singh	278
1966	Jack Nicklaus*	288	2001	Tiger Woods	272
1967	Gay Brewer	280	2002	Tiger Woods	276
1968	Bob Goalby	277			

*Won in a playoff.

HORSE RACING

Horses are raced either under saddle (by a jockey) or in harness (with a driver). Saddle racing occurs either on flat courses or involves jumping over artificial obstructions such as ditches, hedges, and walls (steeplechases) or framelike barriers (hurdles). In harness races, a horse trained as a trotter or pacer is driven from a small two-wheeled vehicle called a sulky.

Thoroughbred saddle racing, run on flat courses, involves purebred (pedigreed) horses bred especially for racing. Thoroughbred horses originated from a cross between Arabian stallions and English mares. Competitions differ according to distance, horse age, weight to be carried, and other considerations. In *sweepstakes,* owners pay a stake (fee) for their horses to be eligible. In *handicaps,* horses are given different weights, based on their past performance, to equalize their chances to win. Top weights are assigned to better horses; lesser weights are assigned to those horses considered inferior.

A horse's age is established by January 1st in the year in which it is born. Horses must be at least two years old to run in flats, three years old to run in steeple-chases, and four years old to run in hurdles.

Flat races are run counterclockwise on oval tracks; thus the horses turn left. Distances are measured in furlongs (1 furlong = ⅛ mile = 220 yards).

THE TRIPLE CROWN

The best-known horse races in the United States are the Kentucky Derby (1¼ miles; at Churchill Downs in Louisville, KY), the Preakness Stakes (1¹³⁄₁₆ miles; at Pimlico Race Course in Baltimore, MD), and the Belmont Stakes (1½ miles; at Belmont Park in El-mont, NY). These three races for three-year-olds make up horse racing's Triple Crown. Eleven horses have won all three events.

Year	Horse	Year	Horse
1919	Sir Barton	1946	Assault
1930	Gallant Fox	1948	Citation
1935	Omaha	1973	Secretariat
1937	War Admiral	1977	Seattle Slew
1941	Whirlaway	1978	Affirmed
1943	Count Fleet		

WINNING HORSES IN THE KENTUCKY DERBY

Year	Horse	Year	Horse	Year	Horse
1875	Aristides	1901	His Eminence	1927	Whiskery
1876	Vagrant	1902	Alan-a-Dale	1928	Reigh Count
1877	Baden Baden	1903	Judge Himes	1929	Clyde Van Dusen
1878	Day Star	1904	Elwood	1930	Gallant Fox
1879	Lord Murphy	1905	Agile	1931	Twenty Grand
1880	Fonso	1906	Sir Huon	1932	Burgoo King
1881	Hindoo	1907	Pink Star	1933	Brokers Tip
1882	Apollo	1908	Stone Street	1934	Cavalcade
1883	Leonatus	1909	Wintergreen	1935	Omaha
1884	Buchanan	1910	Donau	1936	Bold Venture
1885	Joe Cotton	1911	Meridian	1937	War Admiral
1886	Ben Ali	1912	Worth	1938	Lawrin
1887	Montrose	1913	Donerail	1939	Johnstown
1888	Macbeth II	1914	Old Rosebud	1940	Gallahadion
1889	Spokane	1915	Regret	1941	Whirlaway
1890	Riley	1916	George Smith	1942	Shut Out
1891	Kingman	1917	Omar Khayyam	1943	Count Fleet
1892	Azra	1918	Exterminator	1944	Pensive
1893	Lookout	1919	Sir Barton	1945	Hoop Jr.
1894	Chant	1920	Paul Jones	1946	Assault
1895	Halma	1921	Behave Yourself	1947	Jet Pilot
1896	Ben Brush	1922	Morvich	1948	Citation
1897	Typhoon II	1923	Zev	1949	Ponder
1898	Plaudit	1924	Black Gold	1950	Middleground
1899	Manuel	1925	Flying Ebony	1951	Count Turf
1900	Lieutenant Gibson	1926	Bubbling Over	1952	Hill Gail

continues

Winning Horses in the Kentucky Derby, Continued

Year	Horse
1953	Dark Star
1954	Determine
1955	Swaps
1956	Needles
1957	Iron Liege
1958	Tim Tam
1959	Tomy Lee
1960	Venetian Way
1961	Carry Back
1962	Decidedly
1963	Chateauguay
1964	Northern Dancer
1965	Lucky Debonair
1966	Kauai King
1967	Proud Clarion
1968	Forward Pass*
1969	Majestic Prince

Year	Horse
1970	Dust Commander
1971	Canonero II
1972	Riva Ridge
1973	Secretariat
1974	Cannonade
1975	Foolish Pleasure
1976	Bold Forbes
1977	Seattle Slew
1978	Affirmed
1979	Spectacular Bid
1980	Genuine Risk
1981	Pleasant Colony
1982	Gato del Sol
1983	Sunny's Halo
1984	Swale
1985	Spend a Buck
1986	Ferdinand

Year	Horse
1987	Alysheba
1988	Winning Colors
1989	Sunday Silence
1990	Unbridled
1991	Strike the Gold
1992	Lil E. Tee
1993	Sea Hero
1994	Go for Gin
1995	Thunder Gulch
1996	Grindstone
1997	Silver Charm
1998	Real Quiet
1999	Charismatic
2000	Fusaichi Pegasus
2001	Monarchos
2002	War Emblem

*In 1968, Dancer's Image finished first but was disqualified.

ICE HOCKEY

Ice hockey is played on a rectangular rink that is surrounded by a wooden wall. At each end of the ice is placed a netted goal. Six skaters make up each team, including the goalie, whose job it is to protect the goal. By using wooden sticks, the players attempt to propel a rubber disc, called the puck, across the ice and into the opponents' goal. This scores a point.

The game begins with a faceoff in the center of the ice. The official drops the puck between two players, one from each team. Both teams try to gain control of the puck and to advance it toward the opponent's goal by skating with the puck, passing it to a teammate, or shooting it directly toward the goal. The defense tries to hinder this advance by deflecting or intercepting a pass or shot or by bodychecking an opposing player. This is physically blocking an opponent with a hip or shoulder.

There is a wide range of penalties for which an offending player may be removed from the ice for a stated number of minutes. During this time, the penalized team plays with one fewer player than its opponents, giving a power play to the fully manned team. Penalty times range from two minutes for minor violations to ejection from the game for the most serious fouls. Holding on to the puck or to an opponent, checking from behind, tripping, using the stick illegally, and fighting all normally result in penalties. The offensive player in control of the puck must cross his own blue line before any of his teammates. In moving down the ice and attacking the opponent's end, if an attacking player without the puck crosses that line first, he is offside. This is a violation, leading to a resetting of the puck and a new faceoff.

There are only 2 days in the entire year without games played in one of the 4 major professional sports (football, hockey, basketball, and baseball)—the day before and the day after the Major League All-Star game.

Hockey is a rough sport and players wear hip pads, shoulder pads, padded gloves, and helmets. The game consists of three 20-minute periods with rest periods in between. The team with more goals at the end of that time wins the game.

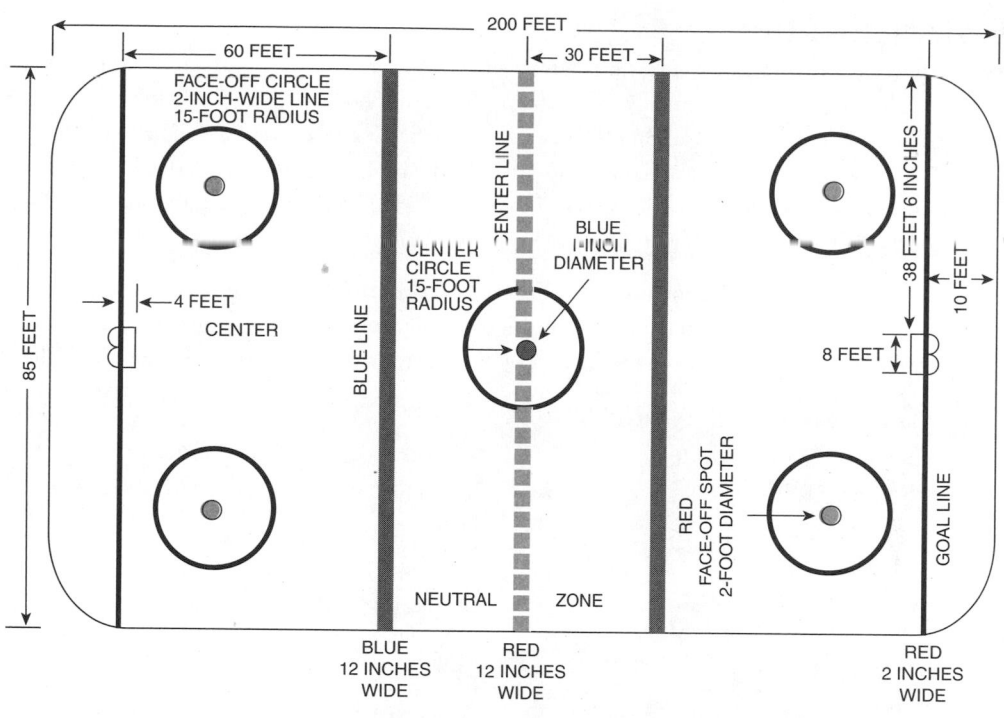

Ice Hockey Rink

NATIONAL HOCKEY LEAGUE (NHL) TEAMS

WESTERN CONFERENCE

Pacific Division

Anaheim Mighty Ducks
Dallas Stars
Los Angeles Kings
Phoenix Coyotes
San Jose Sharks

Northwest Division

Calgary Flames
Colorado Avalanche
Edmonton Oilers
Minnesota Wild
Vancouver Canucks

Central Division

Chicago Blackhawks
Columbus Blue Jackets
Detroit Red Wings
Nashville Predators
St. Louis Blues

EASTERN CONFERENCE

Northeast Division

Boston Bruins
Buffalo Sabres
Montreal Canadiens
Ottawa Senators
Toronto Maple Leafs

Southeast Division

Atlanta Thrashers
Carolina Hurricanes
Florida Panthers
Tampa Bay Lightning
Washington Capitals

Atlantic Division

New Jersey Devils
New York Islanders
New York Rangers
Philadelphia Flyers
Pittsburgh Penguins

Sports/Games

THE STANLEY CUP

In 1893 the governor-general of Canada, Lord Stanley of Preston, presented a cup (then called the Dominion Challenge Trophy) to be awarded annually to the country's amateur hockey champion. After two professional leagues, the National Hockey Association (NHA) and the Pacific Coast Hockey Association (PCHA), began a playoff in 1911, the winner was awarded the cup. In 1917 the NHA disbanded, and the NHL was formed. From 1923 to 1926 the Western Canada Hockey League (WCHL) champion also participated in the Stanley Cup playoffs. After 1926 the Stanley Cup has been awarded exclusively to the NHL champion.

Under the present system each National Hockey League (NHL) team plays a regular-season schedule of 82 games. The eight teams in each conference with the highest point total (two points are awarded for each win, and one point for each tie) then meet in a series of playoffs to determine the conference champion. The West-

THE STANLEY CUP WINNERS

Season	Winner	Loser	Games
1926–27	Ottawa Senators	Boston Bruins	2–0
1927–28	New York Rangers	Montreal Maroons	3–2
1928–29	Boston Bruins	New York Rangers	2–0
1929–30	Montreal Canadiens	Boston Bruins	2–0
1930–31	Montreal Canadiens	Chicago Black Hawks	3–2
1931–32	Toronto Maple Leafs	New York Rangers	3–0
1932–33	New York Rangers	Toronto Maple Leafs	3–1
1933–34	Chicago Black Hawks	Detroit Red Wings	3–1
1934–35	Montreal Maroons	Toronto Maple Leafs	3–0
1935–36	Detroit Red Wings	Toronto Maple Leafs	3–1
1936–37	Detroit Red Wings	New York Rangers	3–2
1937–38	Chicago Black Hawks	Toronto Maple Leafs	3–1
1938–39	Boston Bruins	Toronto Maple Leafs	4–1
1939–40	New York Rangers	Toronto Maple Leafs	4–2
1940–41	Boston Bruins	Detroit Red Wings	4–0
1941–42	Toronto Maple Leafs	Detroit Red Wings	4–3
1942–43	Detroit Red Wings	Boston Bruins	4–0
1943–44	Montreal Canadiens	Chicago Black Hawks	4–0
1944–45	Toronto Maple Leafs	Detroit Red Wings	4–3
1945–46	Montreal Canadiens	Boston Bruins	4–1
1946–47	Toronto Maple Leafs	Montreal Canadiens	4–2
1947–48	Toronto Maple Leafs	Detroit Red Wings	4–0
1948–49	Toronto Maple Leafs	Detroit Red Wings	4–0
1949–50	Detroit Red Wings	New York Rangers	4–3
1950–51	Toronto Maple Leafs	Montreal Canadiens	4–1
1951–52	Detroit Red Wings	Montreal Canadiens	4–0
1952–53	Montreal Canadiens	Boston Bruins	4–1
1953–54	Detroit Red Wings	Montreal Canadiens	4–3
1954–55	Detroit Red Wings	Montreal Canadiens	4–3
1955–56	Montreal Canadiens	Detroit Red Wings	4–1
1956–57	Montreal Canadiens	Boston Bruins	4–1
1957–58	Montreal Canadiens	Boston Bruins	4–2
1958–59	Montreal Canadiens	Toronto Maple Leafs	4–1
1959–60	Montreal Canadiens	Toronto Maple Leafs	4–0
1960–61	Chicago Black Hawks	Detroit Red Wings	4–2
1961–62	Toronto Maple Leafs	Chicago Black Hawks	4–2
1962–63	Toronto Maple Leafs	Detroit Red Wings	4–1
1963–64	Toronto Maple Leafs	Detroit Red Wings	4–3
1964–65	Montreal Canadiens	Chicago Black Hawks	4–3

Season	Winner	Loser	Games
1965–66	Montreal Canadiens	Detroit Red Wings	4–2
1966–67	Toronto Maple Leafs	Montreal Canadiens	4–2
1967–68	Montreal Canadiens	St. Louis Blues	4–0
1968–69	Montreal Canadiens	St. Louis Blues	4–0
1969–70	Boston Bruins	St. Louis Blues	4–0
1970–71	Montreal Canadiens	Chicago Black Hawks	4–3
1971–72	Boston Bruins	New York Rangers	4–2
1972–73	Montreal Canadiens	Chicago Black Hawks	4–2
1973–74	Philadelphia Flyers	Boston Bruins	4–2
1974–75	Philadelphia Flyers	Buffalo Sabres	4–2
1975–76	Montreal Canadiens	Philadelphia Flyers	4–0
1976–77	Montreal Canadiens	Boston Bruins	4–0
1977–78	Montreal Canadiens	Boston Bruins	4–2
1978–79	Montreal Canadiens	New York Rangers	4–1
1979–80	New York Islanders	Philadelphia Flyers	4–2
1980–81	New York Islanders	Minnesota North Stars	4–1
1981–82	New York Islanders	Vancouver Canucks	4–0
1982–83	New York Islanders	Edmonton Oilers	4–0
1983–84	Edmonton Oilers	New York Islanders	4–1
1984–85	Edmonton Oilers	Philadelphia Flyers	4–1
1985–86	Montreal Canadiens	Calgary Flames	4–1
1986–87	Edmonton Oilers	Philadelphia Flyers	4–3
1987–88	Edmonton Oilers	Boston Bruins	4–0
1988–89	Calgary Flames	Montreal Canadiens	4–2
1989–90	Edmonton Oilers	Boston Bruins	4–1
1990–91	Pittsburgh Penguins	Minnesota North Stars	4–2
1991–92	Pittsburgh Penguins	Chicago Black Hawks	4–0
1992–93	Montreal Canadiens	Los Angeles Kings	4–1
1993–94	New York Rangers	Vancouver Canucks	4–3
1994–95	New Jersey Devils	Detroit Red Wings	4–0
1995–96	Colorado Avalanche	Florida Panthers	4–0
1996–97	Detroit Red Wings	Philadelphia Flyers	4–0
1997–98	Detroit Red Wings	Washington Capitals	4–1
1998–99	Dallas Stars	Buffalo Sabres	4–2
1999–2000	New Jersey Devils	Dallas Stars	4–2
2001–2002	Detroit Red Wings	Carolina Hurricanes	4–1

ern Conference champion then meets with the Eastern Conference champion in the spring in a best-of-seven-games series for the NHL championship.

SOCCER

Soccer, often referred to as "football" outside the United States, is played by two opposing teams of 11 players each on a rectangular field. At either end of the field is a goal, constructed of a pair of upright 8-foot-high posts with a 24-foot-long crossbar. The object of the game is for one set of players to force the ball into the goal defended by the opposing team.

At the beginning of a game, the choice of field ends and the opportunity to kick off are decided by a coin toss. Once play has started, players may not touch the ball with their hands with two exceptions: Goalkeepers within their areas may touch the ball with their hands, and when the ball goes out of bounds by crossing the touch lines, it is thrown back by hand. The team in possession of the ball is the offensive team. By kicking the ball or using their heads, members of the offensive team try to move the ball down the field until one of its members is in a position to shoot the ball into the goal of the opposing team.

The defending team may gain possession of the ball by intercepting passes or by tackling opposing play-

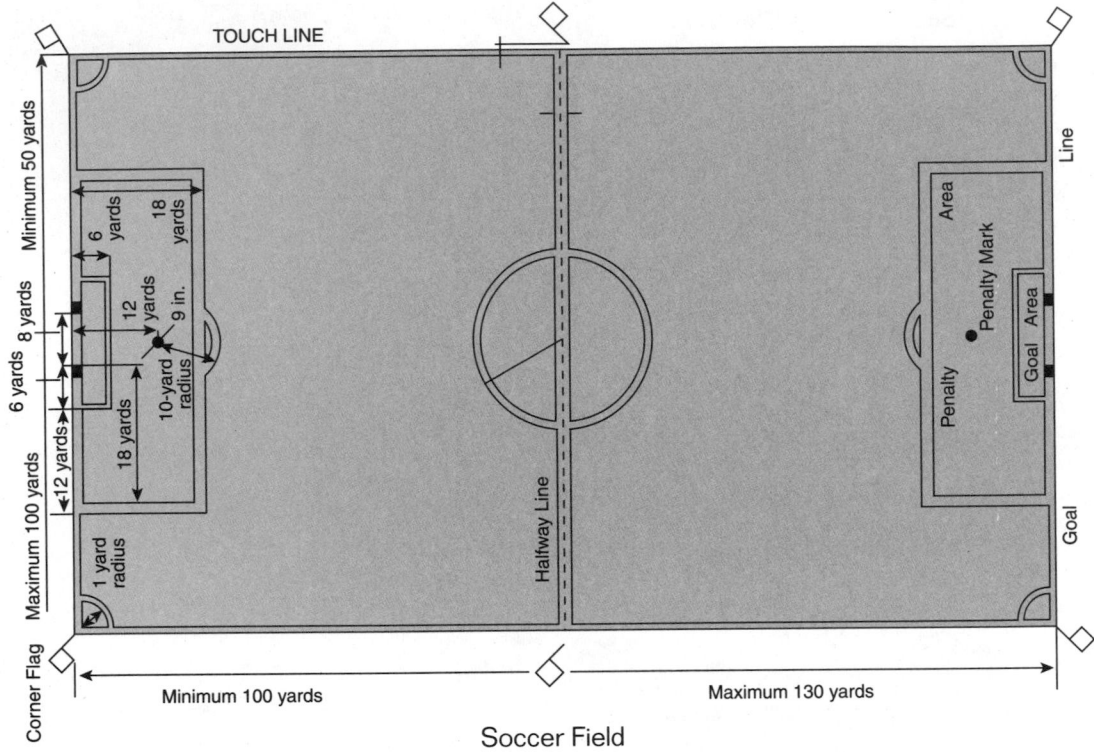

Soccer Field

ers. A tackle can be either a use of the feet or a charge against an opponent's shoulder. The penalty for a violent or dangerous tackle is a direct free kick at the ball by the opposing side.

When the ball goes out of play by passing over the goal line beyond the goalposts, it is restarted by the opposing team. The defending team kicks the ball back into play from within that half of the goal area nearest to where the ball crossed the line; the offensive team kicks it back from the corner circle at the nearest corner flag. As with free kicks, generally, the ball may not be touched again by the kicker until it has been touched by another player. A goal may be scored from a direct corner kick.

When a goal is scored, the game is restarted with a kickoff by the team conceding the goal. A match consists of two 45-minute periods. At the end of the match, the team scoring the greater number of goals is the winner. If no goals are scored, or an equal number of goals is scored by both teams, the game is considered a draw.

THE WORLD CUP

The World Cup championship, the contest for international soccer supremacy, is played every four years at different locations throughout the world.

WORLD CUP WINNERS		
Year	Winner	Loser
1930	Uruguay	Argentina
1934	Italy	Czechoslovakia
1938	Italy	Hungary
1942	*No competition*	
1946	*No competition*	
1950	Uruguay	Brazil
1954	West Germany	Hungary
1958	Brazil	Sweden
1962	Brazil	Czechoslovakia
1966	England	West Germany
1970	Brazil	Italy
1974	West Germany	Netherlands
1978	Argentina	Netherlands
1982	Italy	West Germany
1986	Argentina	West Germany
1990	West Germany	Argentina
1994	Brazil	Italy
1998	France	Brazil
2002	Brazil	Germany

TENNIS

Tennis is played either indoors or outdoors on a rectangular court, which may be grass, clay, or synthetic. A small felt-covered rubber ball is hit back and forth over a net with wooden or metal rackets, which are fitted with strings made of lamb's gut, nylon, or synthetic material. The net, which is 3 feet above the court's surface at its midpoint, is stretched across the court. Tennis may be played either as singles, with one player on each side, or as doubles, with two players on each side. In doubles, the court is 9 feet wider than in singles, because of the addition of two doubles alleys.

To initiate play, the server stands behind the baseline and to the right of the center mark and hits the ball with the racket so that the ball lands in the diagonally opposite service court of the opponent. If this first serve does not land in this service area because it is hit too long or too wide, or hits the net, the server may try again with a second serve. If this second serve is not a legal serve, the receiver scores a point. At each point, the serve alternates left to right, with the server always serving from behind the baseline to the diagonally opposite service court. The receiver attempts to return a legal serve by hitting the ball anywhere into the opponent's court, which in-cludes the alleys in doubles. Play continues until one player (or one team, in doubles) fails to make a legal return. A point is then scored by the opponent.

Four points, designated as 15, 30, 40, and game, constitute a game; a player must win each game by at least two points. Thus, if after six points in any game, each player has scored three, the score is 40–40 (this is called deuce). One player must then score two consecutive points to win the game; this player has the advantage after winning the first of these two points. Having the advantage, if the player wins the second consecutive point, he or she wins the game; but if the opponent wins that point, the score goes back to 40–40, or deuce. Play then continues until one player wins the game by scoring two consecutive points.

Each player (or team, in doubles) alternates by serving one game and receiving the next. The first to win six games wins a set, provided the margin of victory is two games or more. Thus, if the score reaches six games to four, the set is over, but at six to five, play continues. If the score reaches six to six, a tiebreaker is usually employed. A match consists of the best two out of three sets in women's play and usually the best three out of five in men's play.

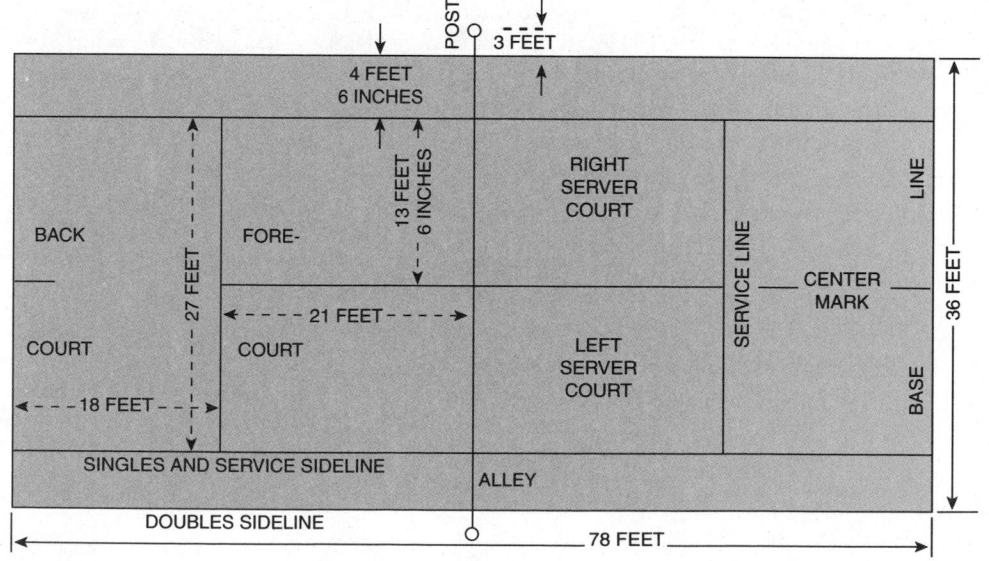

Tennis Court

WIMBLEDON

There are four major championships in professional tennis that make up the Grand Slam: the French Open; the Australian Open; the U.S. Open; and the All-England Lawn Tennis Championships, better known as Wimbledon. Wimbledon is the oldest and most prestigious tournament of the four. The winners since 1877 follow.

MEN'S SINGLES CHAMPIONS

1877	Spencer W. Gore	1919	Gerald Patterson	1961	Rod Laver
1878	P. F. Hadow	1920	Bill Tilden	1962	Rod Laver
1879	J. T. Hartley	1921	Bill Tilden	1963	Chuck McKinley
1880	J. T. Hartley	1922	Gerald Patterson	1964	Roy Emerson
1881	William Renshaw	1923	William Johnston	1965	Roy Emerson
1882	William Renshaw	1924	Jean Borotra	1966	Manuel Santana
1883	William Renshaw	1925	Jean Rene Lacoste	1967	John Newcombe
1884	William Renshaw	1926	Jean Borotra	1968	Rod Laver
1885	William Renshaw	1927	Henri Cochet	1969	Rod Laver
1886	William Renshaw	1928	Jean Rene Lacoste	1970	John Newcombe
1887	Herbert Lawford	1929	Henri Cochet	1971	John Newcombe
1888	Ernest Renshaw	1930	Bill Tilden	1972	Stan Smith
1889	William Renshaw	1931	Sidney Wood	1973	Jan Kodes
1890	Willoughby Hamilton	1932	Ellsworth Vines	1974	Jimmy Connors
1891	Wilfred Baddeley	1933	Jack Crawford	1975	Arthur Ashe
1892	Wilfred Baddeley	1934	Fred Perry	1976	Bjorn Borg
1893	Joshua Pim	1935	Fred Perry	1977	Bjorn Borg
1894	Joshua Pim	1936	Fred Perry	1978	Bjorn Borg
1895	Wilfred Baddeley	1937	Donald Budge	1979	Bjorn Borg
1896	Harold Mahoney	1938	Donald Budge	1980	Bjorn Borg
1897	Reginald Doherty	1939	Bobby Riggs	1981	John McEnroe
1898	Reginald Doherty	1940	No tournament held	1982	Jimmy Connors
1899	Reginald Doherty	1941	No tournament held	1983	John McEnroe
1900	Reginald Doherty	1942	No tournament held	1984	John McEnroe
1901	Arthur Gore	1943	No tournament held	1985	Boris Becker
1902	H. Laurence Doherty	1944	No tournament held	1986	Boris Becker
1903	H. Laurence Doherty	1945	No tournament held	1987	Pat Cash
1904	H. Laurence Doherty	1946	Yvon Petra	1988	Stefan Edberg
1905	H. Laurence Doherty	1947	Jack Kramer	1989	Boris Becker
1906	H. Laurence Doherty	1948	Bob Falkenburg	1990	Stefan Edberg
1907	Norman Brookes	1949	Ted Schroeder	1991	Michael Stich
1908	Arthur Gore	1950	Budge Patty	1992	Andre Agassi
1909	Arthur Gore	1951	Dick Savitt	1993	Pete Sampras
1910	Anthony F. Wilding	1952	Frank Sedgman	1994	Pete Sampras
1911	Anthony F. Wilding	1953	Vic Seixas	1995	Pete Sampras
1912	Anthony F. Wilding	1954	Jaroslav Drobny	1996	Richard Krajicek
1913	Anthony F. Wilding	1955	Tony Trabert	1997	Pete Sampras
1914	Norman Brookes	1956	Lew Hoad	1998	Pete Sampras
1915	No tournament held	1957	Lew Hoad	1999	Pete Sampras
1916	No tournament held	1958	Ashley Cooper	2000	Pete Sampras
1917	No tournament held	1959	Alex Olmedo	2001	Goran Ivanisevic
1918	No tournament held	1960	Neale Fraser	2002	Lleyton Hewitt

WOMEN'S SINGLES CHAMPIONS

1884	Maud Watson	1921	Suzanne Lenglen	1962	Karen Susman
1885	Maud Watson	1922	Suzanne Lenglen	1963	Margaret Smith
1886	Blanche Bingley	1923	Suzanne Lenglen	1964	Maria Bueno
1887	Lottie Dod	1924	Kitty McKane	1965	Margaret Smith
1888	Lottie Dod	1925	Suzanne Lenglen	1966	Billie Jean King
1889	Blanche Bingley Hillyard	1926	Kitty McKane Godfree	1967	Billie Jean King
1890	L. Rice	1927	Helen Wills	1968	Billie Jean King
1891	Lottie Dod	1928	Helen Wills	1969	Ann Jones
1892	Lottie Dod	1929	Helen Wills	1970	Margaret Smith Court
1893	Lottie Dod	1930	Helen Wills Moody	1971	Evonne Goolagong
1894	Blanche Bingley Hillyard	1931	Cilly Aussem	1972	Billie Jean King
1895	Charlotte Cooper	1932	Helen Wills Moody	1973	Billie Jean King
1896	Charlotte Cooper	1933	Helen Wills Moody	1974	Chris Evert
1897	Blanche Bingley Hillyard	1934	Dorothy Round	1975	Billie Jean King
1898	Charlotte Cooper	1935	Helen Wills Moody	1976	Chris Evert
1899	Blanche Bingley Hillyard	1936	Helen Jacobs	1977	Virginia Wade
1900	Blanche Bingley Hillyard	1937	Dorothy Round	1978	Martina Navratilova
1901	Charlotte Cooper Sterry	1938	Helen Wills Moody	1979	Martina Navratilova
1902	Muriel Robb	1939	Alice Marble	1980	Evonne Goolagong
1903	Dorothea Douglass	1940	No tournament held	1981	Chris Evert Lloyd
1904	Dorothea Douglass	1941	No tournament held	1982	Martina Navratilova
1905	May Sutton	1942	No tournament held	1983	Martina Navratilova
1906	Dorothea Douglass	1943	No tournament held	1984	Martina Navratilova
1907	May Sutton	1944	No tournament held	1985	Martina Navratilova
1908	Charlotte Cooper Sterry	1945	No tournament held	1986	Martina Navratilova
1909	Dora Boothby	1946	Pauline Betz	1987	Martina Navratilova
1910	Dorothea Douglass Chambers	1947	Margaret Osborne	1988	Steffi Graf
		1948	A. Louise Brough	1989	Steffi Graf
1911	Dorothea Douglass Chambers	1949	A. Louise Brough	1990	Martina Navratilova
		1950	A. Louise Brough	1991	Steffi Graf
1912	Ethel Larcombe	1951	Doris Hart	1992	Steffi Graf
1913	Dorothea Douglass Chambers	1952	Maureen Connolly	1993	Steffi Graf
		1953	Maureen Connolly	1994	Conchita Martinez
1914	Dorothea Douglass Chambers	1954	Maureen Connolly	1995	Steffi Graf
		1955	A. Louise Brough	1996	Steffi Graf
1915	No tournament held	1956	Shirley Fry	1997	Martina Hingis
1916	No tournament held	1957	Althea Gibson	1998	Jana Novotna
1917	No tournament held	1958	Althea Gibson	1999	Lindsay Davenport
1918	No tournament held	1959	Maria Bueno	2000	Venus Williams
1919	Suzanne Lenglen	1960	Maria Bueno	2001	Venus Williams
1920	Suzanne Lenglen	1961	Angela Mortimer	2002	Serena Williams

VOLLEYBALL

Volleyball is played either outdoors or indoors on a rectangular court, with six players to a side. An inflated ball is hit back and forth over a net; the players try to prevent the ball from hitting the court on their own side. The net's top is 8 feet above the floor (7½ feet in women's play). To initiate play, a player serves the ball by hitting it with the hand or fist and thereby sending it over the net toward the opponent's court. After the serve, the ball may be hit with any part of the body. The ball may be hit a maximum of three times by each team, the final hit sending the ball over the net. Catching or holding the ball is not permitted.

If the receiving team allows the ball to hit the floor on its side, or hits the ball out of bounds, the serving team scores a point and serves again. If the serving team allows the ball to hit the floor, hits it out of bounds, or fails to make a legal serve, the serve is transferred to the opponents, but no point is scored. The first team to reach 15 points wins the game, provided the margin of victory is at least two points. In championship play, a match is won by winning three out of five games.

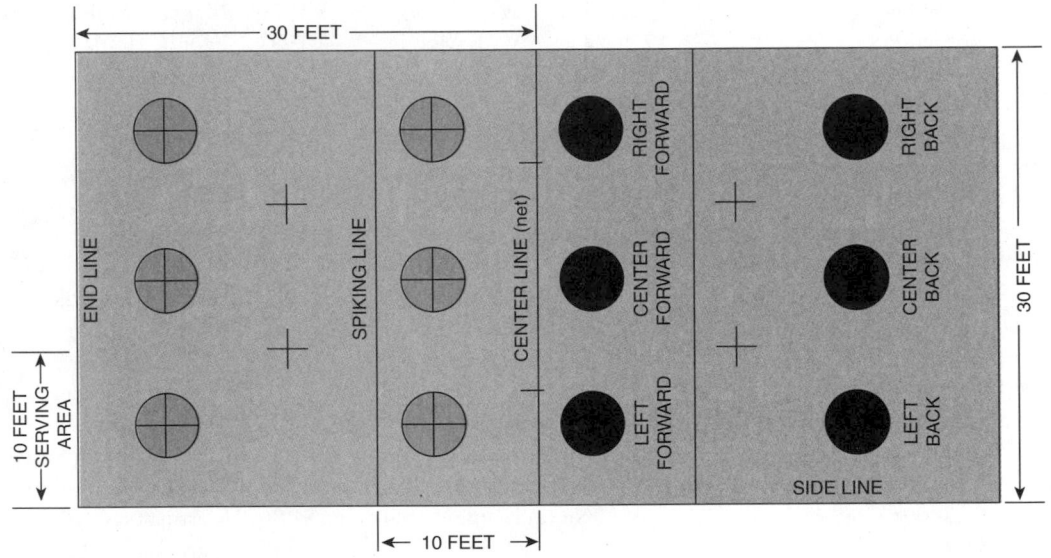

Volleyball Court

OLYMPIC GAMES

The modern Olympic Games began in Athens in 1896, to promote greater international understanding through athletics. The games originated in ancient Greece sometime prior to 776 B.C., but were discontinued after 392 A.D. The Olympic Games competition is held every four years at different locations throughout the world. Since 1994 winter and summer games have been played in alternating four-year cycles. Winter games occurred in 1994, 1998, and so on; summer games occurred in 1996, 2000, and so on.

LOCATIONS

SUMMER GAMES

1896	Athens, Greece	1932	Los Angeles, California
1900	Paris, France	1936	Berlin, Germany
1904	St. Louis, Missouri	1940	No games held
1908	London, England	1944	No games held
1912	Stockholm, Sweden	1948	London, England
1920	Antwerp, Belgium	1952	Helsinki, Finland
1924	Paris, France	1956	Melbourne, Australia
1928	Amsterdam, The Netherlands	1960	Rome, Italy

1964	Tokyo, Japan
1968	Mexico City, Mexico
1972	Munich, West Germany
1976	Montreal, Canada
1980	Moscow, USSR
1984	Los Angeles, California

1988	Seoul, South Korea
1992	Barcelona, Spain
1996	Atlanta, Georgia
2000	Sydney, Australia
2004	Athens, Greece

WINTER GAMES

1924	Chamonix, France
1928	St. Moritz, Switzerland
1932	Lake Placid, New York
1936	Garmisch-Partenkirchen, Germany
1940	No games held
1944	No games held
1948	St. Moritz, Switzerland
1952	Oslo, Norway
1956	Cortina, Italy
1960	Squaw Valley, California

1964	Innsbruck, Austria
1968	Grenoble, France
1972	Sapporo, Japan
1976	Innsbruck, Austria
1980	Lake Placid, New York
1984	Sarajevo, Yugoslavia
1988	Calgary, Canada
1992	Albertville, France
1994	Lillehammer, Norway
1998	Nagano, Japan
2002	Salt Lake City, Utah

2000 SUMMER OLYMPIC EVENTS

Men and Women		Men	Women
Archery	Modern pentathlon	Baseball (team)	Rhythmic gymnastics
Badminton	Rowing	Boxing	Softball (team)
Basketball (team)	Shooting	Wrestling—Freestyle	Synchronized swimming (team)
Beach volleyball	Soccer (team)	Wrestling—Greco-Roman	
Canoeing/Kayaking	Table tennis		
Cycling	Taekwando		
Diving	Tennis		
Equestrian*	Triathlon		
Fencing	Volleyball		
Field hockey (team)	Water polo (team)		
Gymnastics	Weight lifting		
Handball (team)	Yachting		
Judo			

Men's Swimming	Women's Swimming
50m, 100m, 200m, 400m, 1,500m freestyle	50 m, 100m, 200m, 400m, 800m freestyle
100m, 200m backstroke	100m, 200m backstroke
100m, 200m breaststroke	100m, 200m breaststroke
100m, 200m butterfly	100m, 200m butterfly
200m, 400m individual medley	200m, 400m individual medley
400m, 800m freestyle relay	400m, 800m freestyle relay
400m medley relay	400m medley relay

continues

2000 Summer Olympic Events, Continued

Men's Track and Field	Women's Track and Field
100m, 200m, 400m dash	100m, 200m, 400m dash
800m, 1,500m, 5,000m, 10,000m run	800m, 1,500m, 5,000m, 10,000m run
110m, 400m hurdles	100m, 400m hurdles
400m relay (4 × 100)	400m relay (4 × 100)
1,600m relay (4 × 400)	1,600m relay (4 × 400)
3,000m steeplechase	20km walk
20km, 50km walk	Marathon
Marathon	High jump
High jump	Long jump
Long jump	Triple jump
Triple jump	Discus
Discus	Hammer throw
Hammer throw	Javelin
Javelin	Pole vault
Pole vault	Shot put
Shot put	Heptathlon
Decathlon	

* In equestrian events, men and women competed against one another; in shooting, they competed separately, as well as against one another.

2002 WINTER OLYMPIC GAMES

Except for ski jumping, all winter sports at the 2002 Olympic games were divided into two classes, one for men and the other for women. Only men competed in ski jumping events. In pairs figure skating and ice dancing, men and women performed together.

Alpine skiing
Downhill
Slalom
Giant slalom
Super giant slalom
Combined

Biathlon
Men: 20km individual, 10km sprint, 12.5km pursuit, 30km relay (4 × 7.5)
Women: 15km individual, 7.5km sprint, 10km pursuit, 30km relay (4 × 7.5)

Bobsledding
Men: 2-man, 4-man
Women: 2-woman

Cross-country skiing
Men: 15km and 50km classic, combined pursuit start, 30km freestyle, 40km relay (4 × 10), 1.5km sprint
Women: 10km and 30km classic, combined pursuit, 15km freestyle, 20km relay (4 × 5) 1.5km sprint

Curling

Figure skating
Men's singles
Women's singles
Pairs
Ice dancing

Freestyle skiing
Moguls
Aerials

Ice hockey (team)

Luge
Singles
Doubles (one competition, open to men and women)

Nordic combined
Individual
Sprint
Team

Ski jumping
90m, 120m (individual)
120m (team)

Snowboarding
Parallel giant slalom
Halfpipe

Short track speed skating
Men: 500m, 1,000m, 1,500m, 5,000m relay
Women: 500m, 1,000m, 1,500m, 3,000m relay

Skeleton speed skating
Men: 500m, 1,000m, 1,500m, 5,000m, 10,000m
Women: 500m, 1,000m, 1,500m, 3,000m, 5,000m

MAJOR SPORTS FIGURES

The following list of leading sports personalities is not meant to be comprehensive. The athletes selected have made notable contributions to their respective sports or the world of sports at large. Many are popular contemporary figures whose current accomplishments only hint at their long-term potential, or who have achieved a measure of notoriety through their individual style. Every effort has been made to include American and international athletes, men and women, and figures from as wide a variety of sports as possible.

Each figure is an American unless otherwise noted. All are listed by the name under which they are best known; bracketed names indicate that the athlete began his or her career under that name. If an individual was or is involved in a team sport, the team or teams with which that person is most closely associated are included as well.

Aaron, Henry (Hank) (1934–). Baseball player (outfielder); Milwaukee-Atlanta Braves, Milwaukee Brewers. He holds numerous major league records, including career home runs (755) and runs batted in (2,297).

Abdul-Jabbar, Kareem [Lew Alcindor] (1947–). Basketball player (center); Milwaukee Bucks, Los Angeles Lakers. The NBA's all-time leading scorer (38,387 points), he won most valuable player honors six times.

Ali, Muhammed [Cassius Clay] (1942–). Boxer, noted for his wit. Ali won the heavyweight championship three times. During the Vietnam War, he refused induction into the military and was suspended and stripped of his title.

Ashe, Arthur (1943–93). Tennis player. He won the U.S. Open (1968) and Wimbledon (1975) singles championships. After contracting AIDS, he became a leading spokesperson in the fight against that disease.

Bannister, Roger (1929–). British middle-distance runner. He was the first person to run a mile in under 4 minutes (May 6, 1954).

Blair, Bonnie (1964–). Speed skater. She won gold medals in three consecutive Olympics (1988, 1992, 1994) and was the recipient of the 1992 Sullivan Award.

The University of Alabama football team was originally called the Red Elephants. After they won the 1920 Rose Bowl, a sportswriter said, "they washed over their opponents like a crimson tide." The team has been known as the Crimson Tide ever since.

Bird, Larry (1956–). Basketball player (forward); Boston Celtics. A three-time NBA most valuable player (1984–86), he is credited (with Magic Johnson) for the sharp increase in the sport's popularity in the mid-1980s.

Borg, Bjorn (1956–). Swedish tennis player. A five-time Wimbledon singles champion, he led Sweden to its first Davis Cup title (1975). He was noted for his strong base-line play and dazzling shots.

Brown, Jim (1936–). Football player (fullback); Cleveland Browns. During his career, he gained 12,312 yards and was named the NFL's most valuable player three times. He retired after the 1965 season to become an actor.

Bryant, Paul ("Bear") (1913–83). College football coach; various universities. He led Alabama to 25 winning seasons and 6 national championships. His career total of 323 victories is third on the all-time list.

Bubka, Sergei (1963–). Ukrainian pole vaulter. The first to clear the 20-foot barrier (both indoors and outdoors), he holds the world record in this event. He won a gold medal at the 1988 Olympics.

Butkus, Dick (1942–). Football player (linebacker); Chicago Bears. An eight-time NFL Pro

Bowl selection, he was noted for his aggressive, relentless style of play and bruising tackles.

Button, Dick (1929–   ). Figure skater. Twice an Olympic gold medalist (1948, 1952), he won the world championship five consecutive years (1948–52). He later became famous for his commentary during televised skating events.

Chamberlain, Wilt (1936–99). Basketball player (center); Philadelphia–San Francisco Warriors, Philadelphia 76ers, Los Angeles Lakers. He led the NBA in scoring seven times, setting a single-game record with 100 points (1962).

Cobb, Ty (1886–1961). Baseball player (outfielder); Detroit Tigers. Cobb won 12 batting titles during his 24-year career, and his lifetime batting average of .367 is the highest in major league history.

Comaneci, Nadia (1961–   ). Romanian gymnast. She achieved seven perfect scores while winning gold medals in the all-around, balance-beam, and uneven-bar competitions at the 1976 Olympics.

Connors, Jimmy (1952–   ). Tennis player. Noted for his on-court tantrums and powerful service, he is the all-time leader among men, with 109 tournament titles, including five U.S. Open and two Wimbledon championships.

Cooper, Cynthia (1963–   ). Basketball player (forward). A two-time WNBA MVP (1997–98) and three-time scoring leader (1997–99), she led the Houston Comets to the first four WNBA championships (1997–2000).

Corbett, James J. ("Gentleman Jim") (1866–1933). Boxer. Considered to have been the first "scientific" fighter, Corbett was heavyweight champion from 1892 to 1897. His 1891 bout with Peter Jackson went 61 rounds, ending in a draw.

DiMaggio, Joe (1914–99). Baseball player (outfielder); New York Yankees. He hit safely in a major league record 56 consecutive games (1941). Known as the "Yankee Clipper" for his graceful style, he won

the American League most valuable player award three times.

Earnhardt, Dale (1952–2001). Race car driver. A seven-time NASCAR national champion (1980, 1986–87, 1990–91, 1993–94), Earnhardt died in a final-lap crash at the 2001 Daytona 500.

Ederle, Gertrude (1906–   ). Swimmer. In 1926, she became the first woman to swim the English Channel, breaking the existing men's record for the crossing.

Evert, Chris (1954–   ). Tennis player. Second among women in all-time tournament victories with 157, she captured six U.S. Open championships and three Wimbledon titles. She was noted for her cool, unflappable on-court demeanor.

Faldo, Nick (1957–   ). British golfer. Winner of the Masters tournament in 1989, 1990, and 1996, he also won three British Open titles (1987, 1990, 1992) and led the European team to victory in the 1995 Ryder Cup.

Fleming, Peggy (1948–   ). Figure skater. She was U.S. champion for five consecutive years (1964–68) and also captured three straight world titles (1966–68). After winning a gold medal in the 1968 Winter Olympics, she starred with the Ice Follies and Holiday on Ice.

Foreman, George (1948–   ). Boxer. He twice held a heavyweight title (1973–74, 1994–95). At 45, he was the oldest fighter ever to win a championship bout.

Fosbury, Dick (1947–   ). High jumper. A gold medalist in the 1968 Olympics, he invented the technique known as the "Fosbury flop."

Foyt, A. J. (1935–   ). Race car driver. A four-time winner of the Indianapolis 500, he also captured seven U.S. Auto Club championships. His 67 lifetime victories in Indy car racing are a record.

Gehrig, Lou (1903–41). Baseball player (first baseman); New York Yankees. He set the major league record for consecutive games played (2,130;

broken, 1995) and career grand-slam home runs (23), and he still holds the American League single-season record for runs batted in (184; set 1931). His career was prematurely ended by amyotrophic lateral sclerosis (ALS), now widely known as Lou Gehrig's disease.

Gibson, Althea (1927–   ). Tennis player. She won both the U.S. Open and Wimbledon singles championships in consecutive years (1957–58). She was the first African American to compete in either event and the first to be named Associated Press female athlete of the year.

Graf, Steffi (1969–   ). German tennis player. In 1988, at the age of 19, she won the coveted Grand Slam of tennis (Australian, French, U.S. Open, Wimbledon). She has captured five U.S. Open and seven Wimbledon championships.

Gretzky, Wayne (1961–   ). Canadian hockey player (center); Edmonton Oilers, other teams. The leading scorer in NHL history, he received the Hart Trophy as the league's most valuable player nine times (1980–87, 1989). His smooth, dominant ice style earned him the nickname "The Great One."

Griffey, Ken, Jr. (1969–   ). Baseball player (outfielder); Seattle Mariners, Cincinnati Reds. Noted for his charismatic personality and acrobatic fielding, Griffey twice led the American League in home runs (1994, 1997).

Halas, George ("Papa Bear") (1895–1983). Football executive and coach. He founded the Chicago Bears in 1920 and led the team to five NFL championships during his 40 years as its head coach. His 324 career victories are second on the all-time list.

Hamilton, Scott (1958–   ). Figure skater. He reigned as U.S. and world champion four consecutive years (1981–84) and won an Olympic gold medal in 1984.

Hamm, Mia (1972–   ). Soccer player. The all-time leading scorer in women's international soccer (81 goals), she starred on two World Cup champions

(1991, 1999) and two U.S. Olympic teams (gold medal, 1996; silver medal, 2000).

Heiden, Eric (1958–   ). Speed skater. He won all five gold medals in men's events at the 1980 Olympics and was world champion three consecutive years (1977–79). He was the 1980 Sullivan Award winner.

Henderson, Rickey (1958–   ). Baseball player (outfielder); Oakland A's, New York Yankees, other teams. He holds the major league single-season record for stolen bases (130), set in 1982, and is the all-time career stolen-base leader (still active).

Henie, Sonja (1912–69). Norwegian figure skater. She won 10 consecutive world championships (1927–36) and earned 3 Olympic gold medals (1928, 1932, 1936). Henie transformed the sport by introducing ballet movements into her routines.

Hogan, Ben (1912–97). Golfer. He won four U.S. Open titles and captured both the PGA and the Masters championships twice. He survived serious injuries sustained in a 1949 car crash and returned to win the 1950 U.S. Open.

Jackson, Reggie (1946–   ). Baseball player (outfielder); Oakland A's, New York Yankees, other teams. Noted for his flamboyant style, he led the American League in home runs four times, and hit five round-trippers (including three in the final game) in the 1977 World Series. His many World Series heroics earned him the nickname "Mr. October."

Johnson, Earvin ("Magic") (1959–   ). Basketball player (guard); Los Angeles Lakers. With Larry Bird, he helped bring the sport to a new level of popularity in the mid-1980s. He won NBA most valuable player honors three times and ranks second in career assists. He retired after announcing that he had contracted the HIV virus but returned to lead the "Dream Team" to a gold medal in the 1992 Olympics.

Johnson, Randy (1963–   ). Baseball player (pitcher); Seattle Mariners, Arizona Diamondbacks

He led the American League in strikeouts four consecutive seasons (1992–95). At 6′10″, his imposing mound presence has earned him the nickname "Big Unit."

Jones, Marion (1975–   ). Track and field competitor. A two-time world champion in the 100m dash (1997, 1999), she won five medals (3 gold, 2 bronze) at the 2000 Olympics.

Jordan, Michael (1963–   ). Basketball player (guard); Chicago Bulls. A ten-time NBA leading scorer (1987–93, 1996–98) and five-time winner of the league's most-valuable-player award, Jordan led the Bulls to six championships in eight seasons (1991–93, 1996–98). He is regarded by many as the greatest player in the history of the game for his dazzling moves and clutch performances.

Joyner-Kersee, Jackie (1962–   ). Track and field performer. Twice an Olympic gold-medal winner in the heptathlon (1988, 1992), she is widely considered to be one of world's greatest female athletes.

Killy, Jean Claude (1943–   ). French skier. He won three gold medals in Alpine events (downhill, slalom, giant slalom) in the 1968 Olympics and twice took the World Cup overall championship (1967, 1968).

King, Billie Jean (1943–   ). Tennis player. King won the U.S. Open singles championship 4 times and captured 6 Wimbledon titles. Her 39 Grand Slam titles (including doubles and mixed-doubles play) is third on the all-time list. In 1973 she defeated Bobby Riggs in the "Battle of the Sexes" tennis exhibition.

Kiraly, Karch (1960–   ). Volleyball player. He led the U.S. Olympic team to two gold medals (1984, 1988) and won the gold medal in the first Olympic beach volleyball competition (1996).

Laver, Rod (1938–   ). Australian tennis player. He twice won tennis's Grand Slam (1962, 1969) and earned four Wimbledon titles (1961–62, 1968–69).

Lemieux, Mario (1965–   ). Canadian hockey player; Pittsburgh Penguins. He led the NHL in scoring five times (1988–89, 1992–93, 1996) and earned the league's most valuable player award three times (1988, 1993, 1996). Despite recuperating from Hodgkin's disease, he was the NHL's scoring champ in 1993.

Leonard, Sugar Ray (1956–   ). Boxer. He held titles in five different weight classes (welterweight, junior middleweight, middleweight, light heavyweight, super middleweight) over his 14-year career.

Lewis, Carl (1961–   ). Track and field performer. He won nine gold medals in running events (4 × 100m relay; 100m and 200m dashes) and the long jump in the 1988 and 1992 Olympics.

Lombardi, Vince (1913–70). Football coach; Green Bay Packers, Washington Redskins. He led the Packers to five NFL championships and victories in Super Bowls I and II. The trophy awarded to the Super Bowl champion is named in his honor.

Louganis, Greg (1960–   ). Diver. He twice won Olympic gold medals in springboard and platform diving (1984, 1988). He remained competitive despite having contracted the HIV virus.

Louis, Joe (1914–81). Boxer. Nicknamed the "Brown Bomber," he held the world heavyweight championship from 1937 to 1949.

Mantle, Mickey (1931–95). Baseball player (outfielder); New York Yankees. He won the American League triple crown in 1956 and hit a record 18 World Series home runs. He was named the AL's most-valuable-player three times.

Marciano, Rocky (1923–69). Boxer. The world heavyweight champion from 1952 to 1956, he retired undefeated with 49 victories (43 by knockouts).

Marino, Dan (1961–   ). Football player (quarterback); Miami Dolphins. Among the NFL's all-time leading quarterbacks, he is third in passing efficiency and first in both touchdown passes and passing yardage. He is considered one of the greatest passers in league history, despite never having won a Super Bowl.

Mays, Willie (1931–　). Baseball player (outfielder); New York–San Francisco Giants, New York Mets. Third on the all-time career home-run list (660), his enthusiastic play and effervescent personality led to his nickname "Say Hey Kid."

McEnroe, John (1959–　). Tennis player. Third on the all-time tournament victory list with 77, he won four U.S. Open singles championships (1979–81, 1984) and three Wimbledon singles titles (1981, 1983–84). He was noted for his short temper on court.

McGwire, Mark (1963–　). Baseball player (first baseman); Oakland Athletics, St. Louis Cardinals. He hit 70 home runs in 1998, breaking Roger Maris's season home-run record (61).

Messier, Mark (1961–　). Canadian hockey player (center); Edmonton Oilers, New York Rangers. Twice chosen the NHL's most valuable player (1990, 1992), he led the Rangers to the team's first Stanley Cup championship in 54 years (1994).

Montana, Joe (1956–　). Football player (quarterback); San Francisco 49ers, Kansas City Chiefs. Montana ranks in the top ten in career passing percentage, yardage, completions, and touchdowns. He is the only player to win the Super Bowl MVP award three times (1982, 1985, 1990).

Morceli, Noureddine (1970–　). Algerian middle-distance runner. He held world records in four events (1,500 meter, mile, 2,000 meter, and 3,000 meter).

Moser-Proll, Annemarie (1953–　). Austrian skier. She won six World Cup Alpine overall championships (1971–75, 1979) and took the gold medal in the women's downhill at the 1980 Olympics.

Namath, Joe (1943–　). Football player (quarterback); New York Jets. He led the Jets to victory over the heavily favored Baltimore Colts in Super Bowl III after guaranteeing a win, putting the upstart AFL on an equal footing with the older, established NFL. His flamboyant off-field personality led to his nickname "Broadway Joe."

Navratilova, Martina (1956–　). Tennis player (born Czechoslovakia). She won nine Wimbledon championships and four U.S. Open titles (1983–84, 1986–87) on her way to 56 career Grand Slam titles (singles and doubles) and a record 161 victories in all.

Nicklaus, Jack ("Golden Bear") (1940–　). Golfer. The leading money winner on the PGA tour eight times, he captured six Masters tournaments among his 70 career wins, second on the all-time list.

Nurmi, Paavo (1897–1973). Finnish distance runner. He won six Olympic gold medals (1920, 1924, 1928) and broke numerous world records in the 1,500m, 5,000m, and cross-country events.

Owens, Jesse (1913–80). Track and field competitor. He broke four world records in one afternoon of competition (May 25, 1935) and won four gold medals in the 1936 Olympics.

Palmer, Arnold (1929–　). Golfer. In 1968 he became the first to earn $1 million on the PGA tour. He captured four Masters (1958, 1960, 1962, 1964) and two British Opens (1961–62) on his way to over 70 career tournament wins.

Payton, Walter (1954–99). Football player (running back); Chicago Bears. The NFL's career rushing leader (16,726 yards), he led the league five consecutive seasons (1976–80).

Pelé [Edson Arantes do Nascimento] (1940–　). Brazilian soccer player. He scored 1,281 goals during his 22-year career, and led Brazil to three World Cup championships (1958, 1962, 1970). His speed and acrobatic skills earned him an international following.

Petty, Richard (1937–　). Race car driver. The winner of seven NASCAR national championships,

Petty achieved seven Daytona 500 victories and a record 200 career wins.

Plante, Jacques (1929–86). Canadian hockey player (goalie); Montreal Canadiens. He won the Vezina Trophy (awarded to the NHL's top goalie) seven times. He was the first goalie to wear a protective mask in a game (1959).

Rice, Jerry (1962–). Football player (receiver); San Francisco 49ers. He holds NFL records for career touchdowns (156) and receptions (942). Rice was the most valuable player in Super Bowl XXIII (1989).

Richard, Maurice ("Rocket") (1921–2000). Canadian hockey player (right wing); Montreal Canadiens. He scored 544 regular-season and 82 playoff goals and starred on eight Stanley Cup champions.

Rickey, Branch (1881–1965). Baseball executive; St. Louis Cardinals, Brooklyn Dodgers, Pittsburgh Pirates. Known for his innovative ideas, he signed Jackie Robinson to a major league contract with the Dodgers, thus breaking baseball's so-called color barrier (1947). He also established the sport's first farm system (Cardinals, 1919).

Ripken, Cal, Jr. (1960–). Baseball player (infielder); Baltimore Orioles. Twice the American League's most valuable player (1983, 1991), he broke Lou Gehrig's record for consecutive games played in 1995.

Robinson, Jackie (1919–72). Baseball player (infielder); Brooklyn Dodgers. The first African American to play in the major leagues (1947), he was selected the National League's most valuable player in 1949.

Rockne, Knute (1888–1931). Football coach; Notre Dame (college). Rockne helped to modernize the game by introducing the platoon system and stressing the forward pass. He built Notre Dame into a perennial college-football powerhouse.

Roy, Patrick (1965–). Canadian hockey player (goalie); Montreal Canadiens; Colorado Avalanche. He holds several major NHL records, including career regular-season victories and career playoff victories.

Ruth, Babe [George Herman] (1895–1948). Baseball player (outfielder, pitcher); Boston Red Sox, New York Yankees. Ruth set major league records for home runs in a season (60, in 1927) and career (714); both were later eclipsed.

Ryan, Nolan (1947–). Baseball player (pitcher); various teams. He holds numerous major league records, including strikeouts in a season (383, in 1973), career strikeouts (5,714), and career no-hit games (7).

Rudolph, Wilma (1940–94). Sprinter. She took three gold medals in the 1960 Olympics (100m and 200m dashes, 4 x 10m relay). She was the Sullivan Award winner in 1961.

Sampras, Pete (1971–). Tennis player. He has won more Grand Slam singles titles (13), including four at the U.S. Open and seven at Wimbledon, than any other male player.

Secretariat (1970–1989). Race horse. He captured horse racing's coveted Triple Crown in 1973, winning the Belmont Stakes by an astounding 31 lengths. He sired and grandsired notable thoroughbreds (Risen Star, Charismatic).

Shoemaker, Willie (1931–). Jockey. He rode four Kentucky Derby and five Belmont Stakes champions and retired as horse racing's leading career money winner.

Shula, Don (1930–). Football coach; Baltimore Colts, Miami Dolphins. He led six teams to the Super Bowl, winning twice (with the Dolphins). His 1972 Miami team went 17–0. He retired as the NFL's all-time leader in victories (347).

Simpson, O(renthal) J(ames) (1947–). Football player (running back); Buffalo Bills. Simpson set the NFL single-season rushing record with 2,003 yards (1974; broken 1984) and led the league in rushing four times. In his 1995 criminal trial, Simpson was found not guilty of the murders of his ex-wife, Nicole Brown Simpson and her friend, Ronald Goldman. In 1997 he was found liable for the murders in a subsequent civil trial.

Smith, Dean (1931–). Basketball coach; North Carolina (college). He led his teams to 25 NCAA tournament appearances and won national championships in 1982 and 1993. He is college basketball's all-time "winningest" coach.

Spitz, Mark (1950–). Swimmer. Spitz won seven gold medals in the 1972 Olympics, setting world records in each event. His 11 career medals (9 gold, 1 silver, 1 bronze) in two Olympic appearances (1968, 1972) are the most by an American (tied with Matt Biondi).

Stengel, Casey [Charles Dillon] (1890–1975). Baseball manager; various teams. He led the New York Yankees to 10 American League pennants (1949–53, 1955–58, 1960) and 7 World Series titles (1949–53, 1956, 1958) and was the first manager of the expansion New York Mets (1962). He was famous for his eccentric use of language, termed "Stengelese."

Summitt, Pat (1952–). Women's basketball coach. Tennessee (college). She has led the Lady Vols to 6 NCAA championships (1987, 1989, 1991, 1996–98) and ranks second in career victories.

Thorpe, Jim (1888–1953). Multisport athlete. He won both the pentathlon and the decathlon in the 1912 Olympics but was later disqualified for a prior loss of his amateur status. His medals were restored in 1982. He also played professional baseball (1913–19) and football (1919–26). Thorpe is considered the greatest Native American athlete of all time.

Tyson, Mike (1966–). Boxer. At 19, he became the youngest fighter to win a heavyweight championship (1986). The undisputed champion from 1987 to 1990, he was stripped of his crown after a felony rape conviction (1992). He regained the title in 1996 but lost it to Evander Holyfield in 1997.

Weissmuller, Johnny (1904–84). Swimmer. He won 52 national championships and 5 Olympic gold medals and set 67 world records. After retiring, he earned fame as the lead actor in a series of Tarzan films.

Williams, Venus (1980–). Tennis player. She won two Grand Slam tournaments in 2000 (Wimbledon, U.S. Open) and captured gold medals in singles and doubles (with sister Serena) at the 2000 Olympics.

Witt, Katarina (1965–). German figure skater. She twice won Olympic gold medals (1984, 1988) and captured four world championships (1984–85, 1987–88).

Wooden, John (1910–). Basketball coach; UCLA (college). He won a record 10 national championships (1964–65, 1967–73, 1975). His UCLA team set an NCAA record with 88 consecutive wins (1971–74).

Woods, Tiger (1975–). Golfer. He was the first player to win three consecutive U.S. Amateur titles (1994–96) and the youngest golfer to win the Masters (1997, with a record low score of 270 and a record margin of 12 strokes). His early professional successes and enthusiastic followers have created a popular phenomenon known as "Tigermania."

Young, Cy (1867–1955). Baseball player (pitcher); various teams. He holds the major league records for career wins (511) and losses (316). The annual award given to the best pitcher in each league is named in his honor.

Zaharias, Babe Didrikson (1914–56). Multisport athlete. She captured two gold medals in the 1932 Olympics (80m hurdles, javelin), earned All-America honors in basketball (1930–32), and won numerous amateur and professional golf tournaments (in the 1940s and 1950s). She is considered one of the greatest female athletes of all time.

BOARD GAMES

BACKGAMMON

Backgammon is a board game played by two players, each with 15 markers, or stones, which at the beginning of the game are placed in a standard initial configuration (see diagram) on the board. The board is divided into two tables, each with 12 triangular spaces, or points. Each player rolls two dice to determine the number of points moved by the stones, with black moving around the board in one direction and white moving in the opposite direction. The numbers on each die can be combined to move one stone the total amount indicated, or each die's value can be applied separately to single stones. If "doubles" are thrown (such as two 6s), the player can move twice as many points as are shown on the dice—in this case, four stones can move 6 spaces each, one can move 6 spaces and one 18 spaces, two can move 12 spaces each, or one stone can move 24 spaces. The object of the game is to be the first person to move his or her stones around the board and then off, called bearing off. A player may begin bearing off only when all of his or her stones are on the table opposite his or her beginning table. Each number on the die must correspond exactly with the number of the point a stone is on in order to bear the stone off. However, when all the stones are off

the six point, a roll of 6 may bear off a stone on the five point; when all stones are off the six and five points, a roll of 6 or 5 may bear off a stone on the four point, and so on.

A university study found that people spend more on refreshments at tractor pulls than they do at football games.

Any number of stones of the same color may stay on one point, but stones of the opposite color may not occupy the same point. A point occupied by two or more stones of the same color is said to be closed; it prevents the opponent from landing there. A point occupied by one marker (or none) is open. A single stone on any point is called a blot, and the opponent may land there with a hit. The opponent then places the blot on the bar, thereby sending it back to the owner's beginning table. The blot can reenter the game only when the owner rolls a number on one of the dice corresponding to an open point or one occupied by stones of the owner's color on his or her beginning table. All blots on the bar must reenter the table before the owner makes another move.

Backgammon depends on the roll of the dice and is therefore partially a game of chance, but it can also involve complex strategy and tactics. The game may

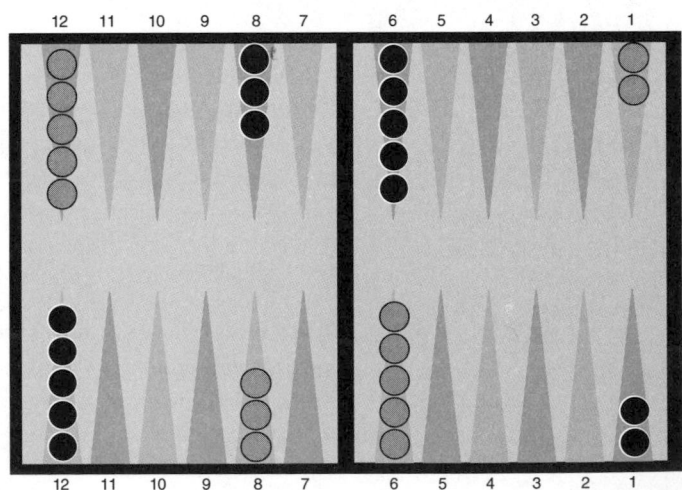

Backgammon Starting Position

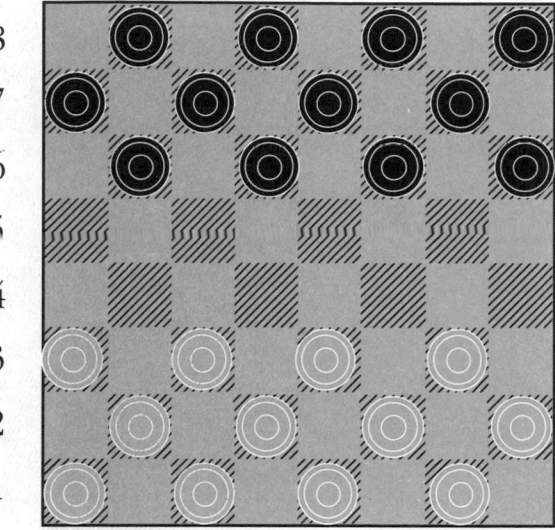

Checkers Starting Position

make use of the doubling cube, which is a die with a number on each face (2, 4, 8, 16, 32, 64). Using this cube, either player can at any point in the game double the stakes, whether they be points, as in tournament play, or money, as in the gambling version.

CHECKERS

Checkers is played by two players on a board with 64 squares alternating light and dark. Only the dark squares of the board are used. The board is eight squares wide and eight squares long. Each player uses 12 wooden discs called checkers, usually red for one player and black for the other. The pieces are set up on the dark squares of the first three ranks, four in each rank. Black moves first, and the players alternate turns by moving one checker forward diagonally toward the opposing player's checkers. The object is to jump over the opponent's pieces, which are then removed from play. A player wins when all the opponent's pieces have been removed. If a player manages to advance a piece to the last rank on the opposite end of the board, that piece becomes a king and thereby acquires the capability of moving backward as well as forward.

CHESS

Chess is a game for two players, one directing the white pieces and one directing the black pieces. It is played on a board with 64 squares of alternating colors, black and white. The board is eight squares wide and eight long. Squares on the board are normally referred to by coordinates, using numbered ranks and lettered files. (See illustration, p. 728.) Each player has 16 pieces: eight pawns, two rooks, two knights, two bishops, a queen, and a king. To start the game, the pieces are set up using the 32 spaces of ranks 1 and 2 (for one color) and 7 and 8 (for the other color). Rooks occupy the outermost files (a and h), with knights placed next to them (b and g); next to them are the bishops (c and f). Toward the center of the board (d and e) the king and queen are placed, with the white queen on a white square and the black queen on a black square. The pawns are placed in front of these pieces, using ranks 2 and 7.

The object of the game is to capture the opponent's king by placing him in checkmate. In this position, the king is under attack by an opposing piece (check), and wherever the king moves, it remains under attack by that or another opposing piece. The attacking side thus wins the game. If a player feels

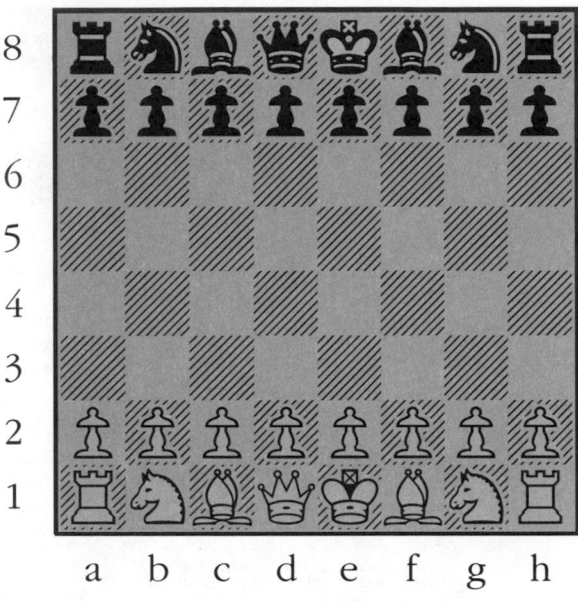

Chess Starting Position

that checkmate is unavoidable, he or she may give up, or resign. If neither white nor black is able to checkmate the opponent or force resignation, a draw may be agreed upon. If the king is not in check and if a player can make no moves, or if all otherwise legal moves would expose his king to check, the game ends in a stalemate.

Any piece may capture, or take, an opponent's piece by landing on the square occupied by that piece. The king, however, cannot be captured and is instead put into check when attacked. If a piece is captured, it is removed from the board. If a pawn reaches the last rank (1 or 8), it is immediately "promoted" to a queen, rook, bishop, or knight at its owner's wish, without regard to the number of them the owner already has.

Each type of piece moves in a prescribed way. A rook moves forward or back, left or right as many squares in one direction as is desired. Knights move two squares in one direction (forward, back, left, or right) and one square at right angles to the first direction—or one square in one direction and two squares at right angles to the first move—resulting in an L-shaped move. The knight is the only piece that

may jump over another piece. Bishops move diagonally any number of spaces in one direction. The queen moves forward, back, left, right, or diagonally any number of spaces in one direction. The king moves as the queen does, but one space at a time. Pawns move forward only, one space at a time, except for the first move, which may be two spaces. Pawns capture pieces by moving diagonally. There are only two instances in which pieces may move in other than these prescribed ways:

1. *Castling* is a two-part move involving the king and a rook. If neither of these pieces has moved previously, if there are no pieces between them, and if the king is neither in check nor would move through or to a guarded square, the king may move two spaces toward the rook, and the rook may move to the square on the other side of the king.

2. If, by moving ahead two squares on its first move, a black pawn lands next to a white pawn on the same rank, the white pawn may capture the black pawn by moving diagonally to the square immediately behind the black pawn. This is called taking *en passant*, or capturing in

passing. Of course, a black pawn may capture a white pawn in the same way.

MONOPOLY®

Monopoly® uses a board with 40 spaces around the perimeter. Players, starting with a fixed amount of money, roll two dice and, in turn, advance their tokens around the board the number of spaces indicated by the dice. If a player lands on any of 22 properties, that player may buy it at a stated price. This money goes into the bank. The player then receives a deed for that property, which states the rent that an opposing player must pay the owner if the player lands on it. The object of the game is to accumulate the properties and, by charging rent when an opponent lands there, to drive opposing players into bankruptcy. Properties are grouped by colors, with two or three to a group. If a player acquires all the properties within a single color, that player may develop those properties by purchasing houses and hotels. These dramatically increase the rent.

In addition to the color-coded properties, which are given street names, there are also four railroads and

---

A Closer Look

The Most Landed–On Spaces on the Monopoly® Game Board

According to Irvin R. Hertzel of Iowa State University, there are 10 spaces on the Monopoly® game board you can count on landing on more than the others. Using a computer, Hertzel, a mathematician, was able to figure out the overall probability of landing on each square. The following are the 10 most landed-on spaces.

1. Illinois Avenue
2. Go
3. B. & O. Railroad
4. Free Parking
5. Tennessee Avenue
6. New York Avenue
7. Reading Railroad
8. St. James Place
9. Water Works
10. Pennsylvania Railroad

---

two utility companies that may be purchased. These also carry rents, but they may not be developed. If a player lands on any of six spaces, three called "Chance" and three "Community Chest," that player must pick up a card from two piles placed in the center of the board and follow its instructions. These involve monetary transactions either beneficial or harmful to the player. There is a neutral space called "Free Parking," a "Jail" space, two tax spaces, and a space called "Go." Play begins on the Go space, and the players collect $200 each time they circle the board and pass it.

In informal play, Monopoly® may involve considerable negotiation and trading among players. The game ends when all but one player has gone bankrupt; the remaining player is the winner.

SCRABBLE®

Scrabble® is a word game for two, three, or four players. The game uses a Scrabble® board with 225 spaces, 100 lettered tiles, 2 blank tiles, and a tile rack for each player. Each player, starting with seven letters, attempts to form words on the board using letters from his or her own hand and from words on the board. Words may read from left to right or from top to bottom. Usually a new word uses one letter from a word already on the board, with which it interlocks at right angles, as in a crossword. Letters may be added to an existing word to form a new one.

Each player, after using some or all of his or her tiles to form a word on the board, replenishes the playing hand from the pool of remaining tiles, which are facedown. Thus, each player always has seven tiles with which to form words, except toward the end of the game, when the pool runs out.

Each letter has a numerical value associated with it; this number is marked on the tile. Players score for each word formed, based on the value of each letter in the word. Scores are recorded with pencil and paper. Players may augment scores by using certain

A Closer Look

94 Acceptable Two-Letter Scrabble® Words

aa	be	fa	lo	om	ti
ad	bi	go	ma	on	to
ae	bo	ha	me	op	uh
ag	by	he	mi	or	um
ah	da	hi	mm	os	un
ai	de	hm	mo	ow	up
al	do	ho	mu	ox	us
am	ef	id	my	oy	ut
an	eh	if	na	pa	we
ar	el	in	ne	pe	wo
as	em	is	no	pi	xi
at	en	it	nu	re	xu
aw	er	jo	od	sh	ya
ax	es	ka	oe	si	ye
ay	et	la	of	so	
ba	ex	li	oh	ta	

premium spaces on the board. These special spaces result in doubling or tripling the values of single letters or complete words. When no player is able to form additional words, each player's score is tallied. Values of unplayed letters for each player are subtracted. The highest score wins the game.

CARD GAMES

BLACKJACK

Blackjack is a gambling game that uses a standard 52-card deck. Ace counts as 1 or 11 points; king, queen, jack, and 10 count as 10 each; all other cards count as their face number. The object is to hold two or more cards totaling 21 or as close to 21 as possible without going over. Cards are dealt one at a time, clockwise, starting with the player at the dealer's left. Each player receives one card facedown and one card faceup. After this initial deal, each player may stand and refuse more cards or take additional cards faceup. For example, having been dealt a king down and a 6 up (totaling 16), if the player chooses to take an additional card and receives another 6, that player is out with 22. An ace and a picture card or a 10 is called blackjack; it totals 21 and beats all other hands.

Various betting methods are used, but usually bets are made before and after the initial deal and after each subsequent deal. All players play against the dealer, and bets are settled depending on which hands are closest to but not over 21; if the dealer has the same count as a given player, the hand is considered a standoff.

BRIDGE

Contract bridge uses a standard 52-card deck and is a game for four players, in partnerships of two. The teams are designated North–South and East–West. Cards in each suit rank ace (high), king, queen, jack, 10, 9, . . . 2 (low); and suits rank spades (high), hearts, diamonds, and clubs (low). Each player receives cards, dealt one at a time clockwise, starting at the dealer's left.

Each player in turn gets a chance to make a bid, which is a statement of the intention to win more than six tricks. At the same time, the player either declares a high-ranking suit (trump) or declares no trump. If a player chooses not to bid, he or she may pass. Bids go around the table in clockwise rotation, with each bid being higher than any preceding bid. A bid may be doubled by an opponent or redoubled by a partner. These double the scoring value of a bid if it is played. This bidding segment of the game is called the auction, and the highest bid becomes the contract. One member of the contracting team declares the trump and becomes the declarer. That person's partner spreads his or her hand faceup on the table and becomes the dummy.

The object of the game is to win tricks in order to fulfill the contract or to defeat the opponent's attempt to fulfill it. The player to the declarer's left leads, and all players must follow suit if possible. A trick is won by the highest card of the suit led if no trump is played, or by the highest trump played.

When all 13 tricks have been taken, the result is scored. There is a complicated scoring system depending primarily on whether the contract was made and by how much. The two members of a partnership score their combined tricks as a single unit. Extra points may be scored in several ways. A bonus is scored if a doubled or redoubled bid is made. One of two types of slams is scored if the contracting team wins 12 tricks or all 13. Honor points are scored when a player receives certain cards in the deal (ace, king, queen, jack, 10 of trump, or the four aces if no trump has been declared).

When a side accumulates 100 or more points in trick scores, the game is over. The side that first wins two out of three games wins a rubber. After each rubber, partnerships may change and play may begin again.

PINOCHLE

Pinochle is played by two to four players and uses a 48-card deck, which includes two of each rank from 9 to ace in all four suits. The rank of cards in each suit is ace (high), 10, king, queen, jack, 9. Cards are dealt three at a time, clockwise, starting to the dealer's left. In two-hand pinochle, both players receive 12 cards; in three-hand (auction pinochle), each receives 15; and in four-hand (partnership pinochle), each receives 12 cards. The remaining cards, if any, form the stock. After an ad hoc high-ranking suit, called trump, has been determined, the

player to the left of the dealer leads by placing a card in the middle, followed by each player in rotation. Tricks are won by the high trump or by the higher card of the suit led if no trump is played. The winner of the trick leads for the next trick. Except in two-hand pinochle, a player must always follow the suit that is led, if possible.

Cards taken in tricks determine the scoring, with each ace counting 11, each ten 10, each king 4, each queen 3, and each jack 2. Nines do not score. A player can also score points by winning the last trick. In addition, certain combinations of cards, called melds, have scoring value. These include the flush (ace, 10, king, queen, jack in the same suit); the marriage (king and queen in the same suit); groups of cards of the same rank (four aces, four kings, etc.); and two special melds, the nine of trump and the pinochle (queen of spades and jack of diamonds).

Points taken in tricks are added to those accumulated by melding. Usually the player or team that first reaches 1,000 points wins the game.

POKER

Poker is a popular card game that uses a standard 52-card deck, with cards ranking ace (high), king, queen, jack, 10, 9, … 2 (low). The ace can also rank low if used as part of ace-2-3-4-5. Jokers are sometimes used as wild cards, which can stand for any card the holder chooses. There are hundreds of forms of poker, but invariably the cards are dealt clockwise, one at a time, starting with the player to the dealer's left. Usually each player receives five cards facedown, but depending on the type of poker, more cards may be dealt, or some may be dealt faceup.

Poker is a gambling game that uses chips of different monetary value. Bets by players go into a pile of chips called the pot. The object is to win the pot, either by showing the best hand or by making a bet that no one is willing to match. The rank of poker hands without wild cards is as follows. The top six hands are illustrated on the next page.

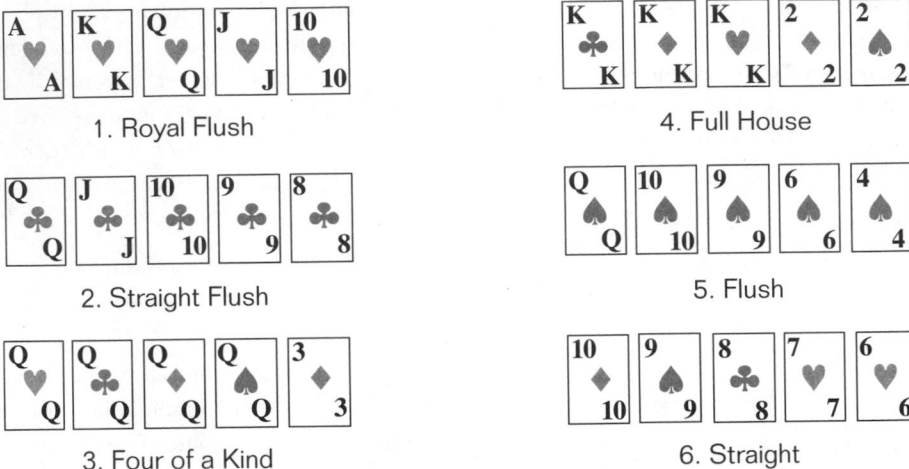

1. Royal Flush

2. Straight Flush

3. Four of a Kind

4. Full House

5. Flush

6. Straight

Top Six Winning Poker Hands

1. *Royal flush:* a sequence of ace, king, queen, jack, 10 of the same suit
2. *Straight flush:* five cards in sequence in the same suit
3. *Four of a kind:* four cards of the same rank
4. *Full house:* three of a kind and a pair
5. *Flush:* five cards of the same suit
6. *Straight:* five cards in sequence, regardless of suit
7. *Three of a kind:* three cards of the same rank
8. *Two pair:* two cards of the same rank and two others of a different rank
9. *One pair:* two cards of the same rank
10. *High card:* five unmatched cards, one with the highest rank of the five

RUMMY

Rummy uses a regular deck of 52 cards. The cards rank king (high), queen, jack, 10, . . . 2, ace (low). Cards are dealt one at a time, clockwise, starting at the dealer's left. The number of cards dealt to each player depends on the number of players in the game: with two players, 10 cards each; with three or four players, 7 cards each; with five or six players, 6 cards each. The undealt remainder of the deck is placed facedown, forming the stock. Its top card is turned up next to the stock, forming the discard pile. The object is to form groups (three or more cards of the same rank) or sequences (three or more cards of

the same suit in sequence of rank). Forming groups or sequences is called melding.

One at a time and proceeding clockwise, players draw one card from the top of the stack or the top of the discard pile. If melding is possible, groups or sequences are placed faceup in front of the player. A player may also lay off, or add to his or her own or an opponent's melds. A player's turn ends by his placing one card faceup on the discard pile. When one player melds all the cards remaining in a hand, that player goes out, thus ending that deal, which is then scored. The player going out scores his or her own melds plus the points left in the opponents' hands. The other players score just their own melds. Aces count as 1; all picture cards count as 10; and the rest of the cards count as their face number. High score wins.

Except when going out, a player must discard one card after each play, whether or not that player has melded or laid off.

SOLITAIRE

Solitaire, or Patience, refers to a group of card games played by one person. The most popular and best known of these games is Klondike. Using a standard 52-card deck, the player deals a tableau or layout, consisting of seven piles of cards. The first pile on the far left has one card, the second pile two, and so on to the far right pile, which has seven cards. These cards are dealt facedown except for the top card in each pile. On these piles, descending sequences are built in alternating colors. For example, a red 9 may be placed on a black 10. Entire sequences or individual cards may be moved from pile to pile, provided correct colors and sequences are maintained. If a down card in a pile is revealed, it is turned faceup and may then become part of a sequence. When a pile is exhausted, a king may replace it.

When they become available, aces are placed above the original layout. The object is to build sequences in suit from the four aces (the foundations) up to the four kings, thus using all cards of the original layout as well as the remaining cards, which form the stock. From the stock, the player turns up one card at a time, forming a waste pile. The top card of the waste pile is available for play on the layout or foundations. The player goes through the stock only once and wins the game if he or she successfully places the entire deck on the foundations. Many players employ alternative, more liberal methods of dealing the stock.

ADDITIONAL SOURCES OF INFORMATION

ORGANIZATIONS AND SERVICES

GENERAL

Amateur Athletic Union of the U.S.
c/o The Walt Disney World Resort
P.O. Box 10000
Lake Buena Vista, FL 32830-1000
407-934-7200
http://aausports.org

National Collegiate Athletic Association (NCAA)
700 W. Washington Street
P.O. Box 6222
Indianapolis, IN 46206-6222
http://www.ncaa.org

AUTO RACING

American Hot Rod Association (AHRA)
N. 101 Hayford Rd.
Spokane, WA 99204
509-244-2372

Championship Auto Racing Teams (CART)
755 W. Big Beaver, Ste. 00
Bloomfield Hills, MI 40084
248-362-8800
http://www.cart.com

National Association for Stock Car Racing
http://www.nascar.com/index.html

National Hot Rod Association (NHRA)
2035 Financial Way
Glendora, CA 91740
626-914-4761
http://www.nhra.com

BASEBALL

American League (AL)
245 Park Ave.
New York, NY 10022
212-931-7600
http://www.majorleaguebaseball.com/al/

Baseball Hall of Fame
P.O. Box 590
Cooperstown, NY 13326
607-547-7200
http://www.baseballhalloffame.org

Major League Baseball Commissioner's Office
245 Park Ave.
New York, NY 10022
212-931-7800
http://www.majorleaguebaseball.com

National Association of Professional Baseball Leagues
(minor league clubs)
P.O. Box A
St. Petersburg, FL 33731
727-822-6937
http://www.minorleaguebaseball.com

National League (NL)
245 Park Ave.
New York, NY 10022
212-931-7700
http://www.majorleaguebaseball.com/nl/

Sports/Games

BASKETBALL

Basketball Hall of Fame
P.O. Box 179
1150 West Columbus Ave.
Springfield, MA 01101-0179
413-781-6500
http://www.hoophall.com

National Basketball Association (NBA)
645 Fifth Ave.
New York, NY 10022
212-826-7000
http://www.nba.com

BICYCLE RACING

United States Cycling Federation (USCF)
(amateur)
c/o USOC
1 Olympic Plaza
Colorado Springs, CO 80909
719-578-4581

BOWLING

National Bowling Association
377 Park Ave. South
7th Floor
New York, NY 10016
212-689-8308
http://www.tnbainc.org

Professional Bowler's Association of America (PBA)
1720 Merriman Rd.
P.O. Box 5118
Akron, OH 44334-0118
330-836-5568
http://www.pba.org

FOOTBALL

National Football Foundation and College Hall of Fame
22 Maple Ave.
Morristown, NJ 07960
973-829-1933
http://www.footballfoundation.com

National Football League (NFL)
280 Park Ave.
New York, NY 10017
212-450-2000
http://www.nfl.com

Pro Football Hall of Fame
2121 George Halas Dr., NW
Canton, OH 44708
330-456-8207
http://www.profootballhof.com

GOLF

Ladies Professional Golf Association (LPGA)
100 International Golf Dr.
Daytona Beach, FL 32124-1092
904-274-6200
http://www.lpga.com

Professional Golfer's Association of America (PGA)
100 Avenue of the Champions
P.O. Box 109601
Palm Beach Gardens, FL 33410-9601
561-624-8400
http://www.pga.com

U.S. Golf Association (USGA)
Liberty Corner Rd.
P.O. Box 708
Far Hills, NJ 07931-0708
908-234-2300
http://www.usga.org

U.S. Golf Association Museum and Library
Golf House
Far Hills, NJ 07931-0708
908-234-2300
http://www.usga.org/golfhouse/index.html

HORSE RACING

National Museum of Racing and Hall of Fame
191 Union Ave.
Saratoga Springs, NY 12866-3566
518-584-0400
http://www.racingmuseum.org

U.S. Trotting Association
750 Michigan Ave.
Columbus, OH 43215-1191
614-224-2291
http://www.ustrotting.com

Sports/Games

ICE HOCKEY

American Hockey League (AHL)
1 Monarch Place
Suite 2400
Springfield, MA 01103
413-781-2030
http://www.canoe.ca/AHL/home.html

Hockey Hall of Fame
BCE Place
30 Yonge St.
Toronto, Ontario MSE 1X8
Canada
416-360-7735
http://www.hhof.com

National Hockey League (NHL)
1251 Avenue of the Americas
New York, NY 10020
212-789-2000
http://www.nhl.com

SOCCER

U.S. Soccer Federation
1801 South Prairie Ave.
Chicago, IL 60616
312-808-1300
http://www.US-Soccer.com/

TENNIS

International Tennis Hall of Fame and Museum
Newport Casino
194 Bellevue Ave.
Newport, RI 02840
401-849-3990
800-457-1144
http://www.tennisfame.org

U.S. Tennis Association (USTA)
70 West Red Oak Ln.
White Plains, NY 10604
914-696-7000
http://www.usta.com

TRACK AND FIELD

Intercollegiate Association of Amateur Athletes of America (IC4A)
P.O. Box 3
Centerville, MA 02632
508-771-5060

International Amateur Athletics Federation
17 rue Princesse Florestine
BP 359
MC 98007 Monaco Cedex
(011) 33 377 93 10 88 88
http://www.iaaf.org

USA Track and Field
P.O. Box 120
Indianapolis, IN 46206-0120
317-261-0500
http://www.usatf.org

VOLLEYBALL

USA Volleyball
715 S. Circle Road
Colorado Springs, CO 80910
719-228-6800
http://www.usavolleyball.org

OLYMPIC GAMES

United States Olympic Committee (USOC)
Olympic Plaza
Colorado Springs, CO 80909-5760
719-632-5551
http://www.usoc.org

BOARD AND CARD GAMES

American Contract Bridge League (ACBL)
2990 Airways Blvd.
Memphis, TN 38116-3847
901-332-5586
http://www. acbl.org

National Scrabble Association (NSA)
c/o Williams & Co.
P.O. Box 700
Greenport, NY 11944
631-477-0033
http://www. scrabble-assoc.com

United States Chess Federation (US Chess)
3054 NYS Route 9W
New Windsor, NY 12553
845-562-8350
http://www.uschess.org

MAGAZINES

ESPN: The Magazine
19 E. 34th Street
New York, NY 10016

The Sporting News
P.O. 51575
Boulder, CO 80323

Sports Illustrated
1271 Avenue of the Americas
New York, NY 10020

BOOKS

GENERAL

Diagram Group. *Rules of the Game: The Complete Illustrated Encyclopedia of All the Sports of the World.* Rev ed. St. Martin's, 1995.

Donavan, Michael Leo. *The Name Game: Football, Baseball, Hockey & Basketball——How Your Favorite Sports Teams Were Named.* Warwick, 1997.

Kent, Michael, ed. *The Oxford Dictionary of Sports Science and Medicine.* Oxford University Press, 1998.

Palmatier, Robert S., and Harold L. Ray. *Dictionary of Sports Idioms.* NTC, 1993.

Porter, David L., ed. *Biographical Dictionary of American Sports.* 4 vols. Greenwood, 1987–89.

AUTO RACING

Golenbock, Peter, and Greg Fielden. *The Stock Car Racing Encyclopedia.* Hungry Minds, 1997.

Gunnell, John A., ed. *Race Car Flashback: A Celebration of America's Affair with Auto Racing from 1900 to the 1980s.* Krause Publications, 1994.

Popely, Rick, and L. Spencer Riggs. *Indianapolis 500 Chronicle.* Publications International, 1998.

BASEBALL

The Baseball Encyclopedia: The Complete and Definitive Record of Major League Baseball. 10th ed. Macmillan General Reference, 1996.

Bjarkman, Peter C., ed. *Encyclopedia of Major League Baseball: American League Team Histories.* Carroll & Graf, 1993.

Bjarkman, Peter C., ed. *Encyclopedia of Major League Baseball: National League Team Histories.* Carroll & Graf, 1993.

Dewey, Donald, et al. *Encyclopedia of Major League Baseball Teams.* HarperCollins, 1993.

Dickson, Paul. *The New Dickson Baseball Dictionary.* Harcourt Brace, 1999.

Lorimer, Lawrence. *The National Baseball Hall of Fame Baseball Desk Reference.* Dorling Kindersley, 2002.

Neft, David S., Richard M. Cohen, and Michael L. Neft. *The Sports Encyclopedia: Baseball.* 21st ed. St. Martin's, 2001.

Nemec, David. *The Great Encyclopedia of 19th Century Major League Baseball.* Donald I. Fine, 1997.

Pietrusza, David. *Major Leagues: The Formation, Sometimes Absorption and Mostly Inevitable Demise of 18 Professional Baseball Organizations, 1871 to Present.* McFarland, 1991.

Riley, James A. *The Biographical Encyclopedia of the Negro Baseball Leagues.* Carroll & Graf, 1994.

Solomon, Burt. *The Baseball Timeline.* Dorling Kindersley, 2001.

Thorn, John, et al., eds. *Total Baseball: The Official Encyclopedia of Major League Baseball.* 7th ed. Total Sports, 2001.

Ward, Geoffrey C., and Ken Burns. *Baseball: An Illustrated History.* Knopf, 1994.

BASKETBALL

Douchant, Mike. *Encyclopedia of College Basketball.* Gale Research, 1994.

Hubbard, Jan, ed. *The Official NBA Basketball Encyclopedia.* 3rd ed. Doubleday, 2000.

Neft, David S., and Richard M. Cohen. *The Sports Encyclopedia: Pro Basketball.* St. Martin's, 1992.

Savage, Jim. *Encyclopedia of the NCAA Basketball Tournament: The Complete Independent Guide to College Basketball's Championship Event.* Dell, 1990.

Vancil, Mark. *The NBA at Fifty.* Park Lane, 1996.

BICYCLE RACING

Abt, Samuel. *Pedaling for Glory: Victory and Drama in Professional Bicycle Racing.* Motorbooks International, 1997.

Nye, Peter. *Heart of Lions: The History of American Bicycle Racing.* W. W. Norton, 1989.

Ritchie, Andrew. *Bicycle Racing Record Book.* Motorbooks International, 1998.

Sutherland, Sandra W. *No Brakes!: Bicycle Track Racing in the United States.* Iris, 1996.

BOWLING

Allen, George, and Dick Ritger. *Complete Guide to Bowling Principles: The Encyclopedia.* Technical Education, 1994.

FOOTBALL

Carroll, Bob, et al., eds. *Total Football II: The Official Encyclopedia of the National Football League.* HarperCollins, 1999.

Maher, Tod, and Bob Gill, eds. *The Pro Football Encyclopedia: The Complete and Definitive Record of Professional Football.* Hungry Minds, 1997.

Neft, David S., Richard M. Cohen, and Rich Korch. *The Sports Encyclopedia: Pro Football.* 17th ed. St. Martin's, 1999.

Ours, Robert. *College Football Encyclopedia: The Authoritative Guide to 124 Years of College Football.* Prima, 1993.

GOLF

Campbell, Malcolm. *Random House International Encyclopedia of Golf: The Definitive Guide to the Game.* Random House, 1991.

Glenn, Rhonda. *The Illustrated History of Women's Golf.* Taylor, 1991.

Peper, George. *Golf Magazine's Encyclopedia of Golf: The Complete Reference.* HarperCollins, 1993.

United States Golf Association. *The Official Rules of Golf.* Triumph Books, 2000.

HORSE RACING

Ainslie, Tom. *Ainslie's Complete Guide to Thoroughbred Racing.* Fireside, 1988.

Bowen, Edward L. *The Jockey Club's Illustrated History of Thoroughbred Racing in America.* Bullfinch, 1994.

Stout, Nancy. *Homestretch: A Celebration of America's Greatest Tracks.* Running Press, 2000.

ICE HOCKEY

Diamond Dan, et al. eds. *Total Hockey: The Official Encyclopedia of the National Hockey League.* Total Sports, 2000.

Fischler, Stan. *Fischler's Illustrated History of Hockey.* Warwick, 1993.

SOCCER

Lablanc, Michael L., and Richard Henshaw. *The World Encyclopedia of Soccer.* Gale Research, 1993.

Murray, Bill. *The World's Game: A History of Soccer.* University of Illinois Press, 1998.

Pickering, David. *Cassell Soccer Companion: History, Facts, and Anecdotes.* Continuum, 1999.

Radnedge, Keir. *The Complete Encyclopedia of Soccer 2000–2001.* Carleton Books, 2000.

Sports/Games

TENNIS

Collins, Bud, and Zander Hollander, eds. *Bud Collins's Tennis Encyclopedia*. 3rd ed. Visible Ink Press, 1997.

Gillmeister, Heiner. *Tennis: A Cultural History*. Cassell Academic, 1997.

Savage. Jim. *The Grand Slam Tennis Encyclopedia: The Definitive Record of Wimbledon, the Australian Open, the French Open, and the U.S. Open*. Macmillan General Reference, 1996.

TRACK AND FIELD

Lawson, Gerald. *World Record Breakers in Track & Field Athletics*. Human Kinetics, 1997.

VOLLEYBALL

Kessel, John. *Volleyball Encyclopedia*. Sports Support Syndicate, 1996.

Shewman, Byron. *Volleyball Centennial: The First 100 Years*. Masters, 1996.

OLYMPIC GAMES

Wise, Michael T., et al., eds. *Chronicle of the Olympics, 1896–1996*. Dorling-Kindersley, 1996.

Young, David C. *The Modern Olympics: A Struggle for Revival*. Johns Hopkins University Press, 1996.

BOARD AND CARD GAMES

Mohr, Merilyn Simonds. *The New Games Treasury: More Than 500 Indoor and Outdoor Favorites with Strategies, Rules and Traditions*. Houghton Mifflin, 1997.

WEB SITES

CBS SportsLine
A major online sports information network
www.cbs.sportsline.com

CNN/SI
Comprehensive online site from Cable News Network and Sports Illustrated
sportsillustrated.cnn.com

ESPN SportsZone
The online site of the cable sports giant
www.espn.go.com

Sporting News
Online counterpart to the long-running print publication
www.sportingnews.com

USA Today
Online site of the nationwide daily newspaper
www.usatoday.com

TRAVEL

BASIC INFORMATION

Whether you're planning a weekend getaway nearby or an extended stay on another continent, careful preparation is essential for a safe and successful trip.

Airline security and increased antiterrorism procedures after September 11, 2001, created tight carry-on restrictions and longer delays at airports. Air travelers are advised to call their airline carrier or check up-to-date web sites before traveling to stay informed about the latest alerts and procedures.

TRAVELERS' CHECKLIST

Things to Do

✓ Arrange for the post office to hold your mail, or have someone collect it daily.

✓ Stop all deliveries to your home.

✓ Arrange for the care of your animals, plants, and lawn.

✓ Put your valuables in a safety-deposit box.

✓ Notify your neighbors and the police of absence and let them know how you can be reached.

✓ Leave a key with a neighbor.

✓ Arrange for travelers' insurance coverage, if needed.

✓ Notify your travel agent of any special needs you might have, such as the use of an airport wheelchair.

✓ Reconfirm your airline ticket and other reservations.

✓ Tag your luggage for easy identification.

✓ Set timers or leave a light on.

✓ Empty the refrigerator and turn it on low.

✓ Turn off the hot water.

✓ Lock all doors and windows.

Things to Bring

✓ Government-issued photo I.D.

✓ Airline or other tickets and travel documents.

✓ Auto registration, if driving.

✓ Passport, visas, and health certificates.

✓ Medical information and doctor's name and telephone number.

Travelers' First–Aid Kit

A Closer Look

Antiseptic lotion or ointment
Aspirin or acetaminophen
Cold and cough remedies
Gauze bandages and adhesive tape, elastic bandages
Heating pad
Ice pack
Identification bracelet
Insect repellent and insect-bite medication
Medical information regarding condition, allergies, medications, blood type, and special needs
Milk of magnesia and diarrhea medication
Moleskin for blisters and calluses
Physician's name, address, and telephone number
Prescription medications and refills
Sunscreen and sunburn-relief lotion
Telephone numbers of emergency contacts
Thermometer
Throat lozenges
Vitamins

✓ Special over-the-counter or prescription medications.

✓ Insurance papers.

✓ Credit cards.

✓ Travelers' checks and personal checks.

✓ Cash, including some in the currency of the country to which you are traveling.

✓ Names and addresses of people to contact in an emergency.

✓ Names, addresses, phone numbers, reservation numbers, and dates for places where you will be staying.

✓ Lightweight fold-up tote bag for purchases.

✓ Addresses of friends and family to whom to send mail.

✓ Extra pair of eyeglasses (or contacts) and your eyeglass (or contact) prescription.

TIPS FOR TRAVELERS WITH DISABILITIES

Good planning is key to enjoyable travel by people with disabilities. Since the passage of the Americans with Disabilities Act in 1990, travel in the United States is much more accessible for those with disabilities. Airports, railroads, and public and private transportation systems all must provide access for the disabled. Cruise ships have increasing numbers of cabins and ramps designed for disabled travelers. However, it is still advisable to consult with a travel agent who specializes in handling travelers with disabilities or to research facilities beforehand by calling the carrier or via the Internet, especially when traveling outside the United States.

FURTHER INFORMATION

Access-Able Travel Source
http://www.access-able.com/

Mobility International
541-343-1284
Fax 541-343-6812

National Park Service
(for information on U.S. highway rest areas)
202-208-6843

Society for the Advancement of Travel for the Handicapped (SATH)
212-447-7284
Fax 212-725-8253

CAR-RENTAL AGENCY TOLL-FREE NUMBERS AND WEB SITES

Alamo
(U.S. and international)
800-462-5266
800-522-9292 TDD
http://www.goalamo.com

AutoEurope
(U.S. and Europe)
800-223-5555
http://www.auto-europe.com/

Avis
(U.S. and international)
800-331-1212 domestic
800-331-1084 international
800-331-2323 TDD
http://www.avis.com/

Budget
(U.S. and international)
800-527-0700 domestic
800-472-3325 international
800-826-5510 TDD
http://www.budgetrentacar.com/

Dollar/EuroDollar
(U.S. and international)
800-800-4000 domestic
800-800-6000 international
800-232-3301 TDD
http://www.dollarcar.com/

Enterprise
(U.S. and Canada)
800-736-8227
http://www.pickenterprise.com/

Europe by Car
(Europe)
800-223-1516
http://www.europebycar.com/

Hertz
(U.S. and international)
800-654-3131 domestic
800-654-3001 international
800-654-2280 TDD
http://www.hertz.com/

Kemwel Holiday Autos
(U.S. and international)
800-678-0678
http://www.kemwel.com/

National
(U.S. and international)
800-227-7368 domestic
800-227-3876 international
800-328-6323 TDD
http://www.nationalcar.com/

Many businesses provide TDD lines, which are telecommunication devices for the deaf.

Payless
(U.S. and international)
800-729-5377
http://www.paylesscar.com/

Rent-a-Wreck
(U.S. and international)
800-535-1391
http://rentawreck.com/raw/

Thrifty
(U.S. and international)
800-847-4389
http://www.thrifty.com/

"Symbols to Guide the Traveler" in chapter 12

Go to

Traveling with Pets

Although most travelers leave home without them, vacationing with pets is possible; if you plan carefully, taking your pet along can save on guilt, worry, and even money. It's easier to leave the goldfish in the care of friends, but the family dog can go with you almost anywhere. Information and suggestions to make this easier appear below.

Travel Checklist

✓ Proper identification (name and address tag)
✓ Thermos of water
✓ Plastic bowls
✓ Proof of up-to-date immunizations
✓ Pet carrier
✓ First-aid kit, including bandages, antiseptic, and medications (including tranquilizers) prescribed by your veterinarian

✓ Food (and can opener, if needed)
✓ Certificate of good health signed by your veterinarian
✓ Leash and muzzle
✓ Flea powder or flea collar
✓ Blanket
✓ Pet toys
✓ Grooming tools

Pretravel Suggestions

Introduce your pet to car travel with trial runs.

Allow your pet to become familiar with the pet carrier before your trip.

Do not feed your pet for several hours before the trip.

Exercise your pet right before leaving.

Travel Restrictions

Automobile No restrictions.

Bus Except for Seeing Eye dogs, pets are prohibited on buses in interstate travel.

Train Pets may be taken only in private compartments or in the baggage car.

Airplane Pets can come on board in pet carriers or can remain in the baggage compartment. Restrictions vary, so inquire of individual airlines in advance.

National park Pets are allowed on leashes except in bathing areas.

State and private parks Restrictions vary, so check with the individual facility.

Hotel, motel, and campground Most do accept pets; notify the owner ahead of time.

International Travel (Including Hawaii)

Most countries require a recent certificate of good health and proof of immunizations. In addition, the following places may require a quarantine (at the owner's expense) for the number of days indicated. The number of days in quarantine may vary according to the type of pet and its state of health. Check with individual embassies or consulates for specific requirements.

Hawaii	180	Norway	120
Hong Kong	180	Panama	180
Jamaica	180	Singapore	30
Jordan	42	Sweden	120
Korea	21	Trinidad and Tobago	180
Malta	180	United Kingdom	180
Mauritius	180		

Returning Home

Upon your return, a quarantine officer at customs will check documents and inspect your animal. The official may require confinement of any animal that you have purchased abroad; typically confinement is in your own home rather than in an official quarantine. Pets purchased abroad also will require proof of immunization, certificates of good health, and payment of an import duty.

HOTEL/MOTEL CHAIN TOLL-FREE NUMBERS AND WEB SITES

American Historic Inns, Inc.
(U.S.) 800-379-4887
http://www.bnbinns.com

Best Western
(U.S. and international)
800-780-7234
800-528-2222 TDD
http://www.bestwestern.com/

Clarion
(U.S. and international)
800-252-7466
800-228-3323 TDD
http://www.clarioninn.com/

Comfort Inn
(U.S. and international)
800-228-5150
800-228-3323 TDD
http://www.comfortinn.com/

Days Inn
(U.S. and international)
800-329-7155
800-228-3323 TDD
http://www.daysinn.com/

Delta
(U.S. and international)
800-268-1133
http://www.deltahotels.com/

Doubletree
(U.S. and Mexico)
800-222-8733
800-528-9898 TDD
http://www.hilton.com/doubletree

EconoLodge
(U.S. and Canada)
800-553-2666
800-228-3323 TDD
http://www.econolodge.com

Embassy Suites
(U.S. and international)
800-362-2779
http://www.embassy-suites.com/

Hampton Inn
(U.S. and international)
800-426-7866
http://www.hampton-inn.com/

Hilton
(U.S. and international)
800-445-8667
http://www.hilton.com/

Holiday Inn
(U.S. and international)
800-465-4329
http://www.holiday-inn.com/

Howard Johnson
(U.S. and international)
800-446-4656
800-654-8442 TDD
http://hojo.com/

Hyatt
(U.S. and international)
800-233-1234
http://www.hyatt.com/

LaQuinta
(U.S.)
800-531-5900
800-426-3101 TDD
http://www.laquinta.com/

Marriott
(Includes Marriott Hotels, Renaissance, Courtyard Marriott, Residence Inn, Fairfield Inn, TownPlace Suites, Spring Hill Suites)
(U.S. and international)
888-236-2427
http://www.marriott.com/

Quality Inn
(U.S. and international)
800-228-5151
800-228-3323 TDD
http://www.qualityinn.com

Radisson
(U.S. and international)
800-333-3333
800-906-2200 TDD
http://www.radisson.com/

Ramada Inn
(U.S. and Canada)
800-272-6232
800-228-3232 TDD
http://www.ramada.com/

Red Lion
(U.S. and Mexico)
800-733-5466
800-528-9898 TDD
http://www.redlion.com

Travel

Rodeway Inn
(U.S. and international)
800-228-2000
800-228-3323 TDD
http://www.rodeway.com

Sheraton
(U.S. and international)
800-325-3535
http://www.sheraton.com/

Sleep Inn
(U.S. and international)
800-753-3746
800-228-3323 TDD
http://www.hotelchoice.com

Summit International
(U.S. and international)
800-457-4000
http://www.summithotels.com/

Westin
(U.S. and international)
800-228-3000
800-325-1717 TDD
http://www.westin.com/

AIRLINE CODES, TOLL-FREE NUMBERS, AND WEB SITES

Airline (Home Country)	Code	Toll-Free Number(s)	Web Site
ACES (Colombia)	VX	800-846-2237	http://www.aces.com.co/index2.htm
Aer Lingus (Ireland)	EI	800-223-6537	http://www.aerlingus.ie/
Adria Airways (Slovenia)	JP		http://www.adria.si/eng/index.htm
Aeroflot Russian International Airlines (Russia)	SU	800-995-5555	http://www.aeroflot.com/
Aerolineas Argentinas (Argentina)	AR	800-333-0276	http://www.aerolineas.com.ar/english
Aeromexico (Mexico)	AM	800-237-6639	http://www.aeromexico.com/
Aeroperu (Peru)	PL	800-777-7717	http://www.travelx.com/aeroperu.html
Air Afrique (Côte d'Ivoire)	RK	800-456-9192	http://www.sinergia.it/airafrique.htm
Air Caledonie/Air Calin (New Caledonia)	SB	800-677-4277	http://www.pacificislands.com/airlines/caledonie.html
Air Canada (Canada)	AC	800-776-3000 800-361-8071 TDD	http://www.aircanada.ca/
Air China (China)	CA	800-882-8122	http://www.airchina.org.cn/english/index.htm
Air Fiji (Fiji Islands)	PC	800-677-4277	http://www.airfiji.net
Air France/Air Inter Europe (France)	AF	800-237-2747	http://www.airfrance.fr/
Air India (India)	AI	800-223-2250	http://www.airindia.com/
Air Jamaica (Jamaica)	JM	800-523-5585	http://www.airjamaica.com
Air Madagascar (Madagascar)	MD	800-821-3388	http://www.air-mad.com
Air Malawi			http://www.africaonline.co.ke/airmalawi/
Air Malta	KM		http://www.airmalta.com
Air Mauritius (Mauritius)	MK	800-537-1182	http://www.airmauritius.int.en/
Air Nauru (Nauru)	ON	800-677-4277	http://www.pacificislands.com/airlines/nauru.html
Air New Zealand (New Zealand)	NZ	800-926-7255	http://www.airnewzealand.com
Air Seychelles (Seychelles)	HM	800-677-4277	http://www.airseychelles.net
Air Slovenia			http://www.adria.si/eng/index.htm
Air Ukraine (Ukraine)	6U		http://www.airukraine.com
Air Vanuatu (Micronesia)	NF	800-677-4277	http://www.pacificislands.com/airlines/vanuatu.html
Air Zimbabwe (Zimbabwe)	UM	800-742-3006	http://www.airzimbabwe.com

Airline (Home Country)	Code	Toll–Free Number(s)	Web Site
Air Tran Airways (U.S.)	J7	800-247-8726	http://www.airtran.com/
Alaska Airlines (U.S.)	AS	800-252-7522	http://www.alaska-air.com/
Alitalia (Italy)	AZ	800-223-5730	http://www.alitalia.it/english/index.html
All Nippon Airways/ANA (Japan)	NH	800-235-9262	http://www.metrotel.co.uk/travlog/ana.html
Aloha Airlines (U.S.)	AQ	800-367-5250 800-334-4833 TDD	http://www.alohaair.com/
American Airlines (U.S.)	AA	800-433-7300 800-543-1586 TDD	http://www.aa.com
American Trans Air/ATA (U.S.)	TZ	800-225-2995 800-293-6194 TDD	http://www.ata.com
American West Airlines (U.S.)	HP	800-235-9292 800-526-8077 TDD	http://www.americanwest.com
Ansett Australia (Australia)	AN	800-366-1300	http://www.ansett.com.au/
Asiana Airlines (South Korea)	OZ	800-227-4262	http://www.us.flyasia.com
Austrian Airlines (Austria)	OS	800-843-0002	http://www.aua.com/
Avianca Colombia (Colombia)	AV	800-284-2622	http://www.avianca.com/
Aviateca (Guatemala)	GU	800-327-9832	http://www.grupotaca.com
Bahamasair (Bahamas)	UP		http://www.bahamasair.com
Balkan Bulgarian Airlines (Bulgaria)	LZ	800-852-0944	http://www.balkan-air.com/
Bangkok Airways	PG		http://www.bkkair.co.th
British Airways (United Kingdom)	BA	800-247-9297	http://www.us.british-airways.com/
British Midland (United Kingdom)	BD	800-788-0555	http://www.flybmi.com
BWIA International (Trinidad and Tobago)	BW	800-538-2942	http://www.bwee.com/caribbean
Cathay Pacific Airways (Hong Kong)	CX	800-233-2742	http://www.cathay-usa.com/
Cayman Airways	KX	800-422-9626	http://www.caymanairways.com
China Airlines (Taiwan)	CI	800-227-5118	http://www.china-airlines.com/
China Eastern Air (China)	MU	800-200-5118	http://www.cea.online.sh.cn/html/enindex.html
Comair—a subsidiary of Delta Airlines (U.S.)	DL	800-354-9822	http://www.fly-comair.com/
Continental Airlines (U.S.)	CO	800-525-0280 (domestic) 800-231-0856 (international)	http://www.continental.com/
Copa (Panama)	CM	800-892-2672	http://www.copaair.com/
Croatia Airlines (Croatia)	OU	800-247-5353	http://www.croatiaairlines.com
Cyprus Airways (Cyprus)	CY	800-333-2977	http://www.cyprusairways.com
Czech Airlines/CSA (Czech Republic)	OK	800-223-2365	http://www.csa.cz/
Delta Airlines (U.S.)	DL	800-221-1212	http://www.delta-air.com/
Egypt Air (Egypt)	MS	800-334-6787	http://www.egyptair.com.eg/dos/home.asp
El Al Israel Airlines (Israel)	LY	800-223-6700	http://www.elal.com
Emirates Air (United Arab Emirates)	EK	800-777-3999	http://www.emiratesairline.com
Ethiopian Airlines (Ethiopia)	ET	800-445-2733 (Eastern U.S.) 800-433-9677 (Midwestern and Western U.S.)	http://www.ethiopianairlines.com
EVA Airways (Taiwan)	BR	800-695-1188	http://www.evaair.com

continues

Airline Codes, Toll-Free Numbers, and Web Sites, Continued

Airline (Home Country)	Code	Toll-Free Number(s)	Web Site
Finnair (Finland)	AY	800-950-5000	http://www.finnair.fi
Frontier Airlines (U.S.)	F9	800-432-1359	http://www.flyfrontier.com/
Garuda Indonesia (Indonesia)	GA	800-342-7832	http://garudaindonesia.com
Greenlandair			http://www.greenland-guide.dk/gla/default.htm
Gulf Air (Persian Gulf)	GF	888-359-4853	http://www.gulfairco.com/
Guyana Airways (Guyana)	GY	800-242-4210	http://www.turq.com/guyana/guyana.html
Hawaiian Airlines (U.S.)	HA	800-367-5320	http://www.hawaiianair.com/
Horizon Air—a subsidiary of Alaska Airlines (U.S.)	AS	800-547-9308	http://www.horizonair.com/
Iberia Airlines (Spain)	IB	800-772-4642	http://www.iberia.com
Icelandair (Iceland)	FI	800-223-5500	http://www.icelandair.com/
Japan Airlines/JAL (Japan)	JL	800-525-3663	http://www.japanairlines.com
Kenya Airways (Kenya)	KQ	800-343-2506	http://www.kenya-airways.com
KLM Royal Dutch Airlines (The Netherlands)	KL	800-374-7747	http://www.klm.nl/
Korean Air (South Korea)	KE	800-438-5000	http://www.koreanair.com
Kuwait Airways (Kuwait)	KU	800-424-1128	http://www.kuwait-airways.com
LACSA Airlines (Costa Rica)	LR	800-225-2272	http://www.lacsa.com
Lan Chile (Chile)	LA	800-735-5526	http://www.lanchile.com/
Lauda Air (Austria)	NG	800-645-3880	http://www.laudaair.com
LOT Polish Airlines (Poland)	LO	800-223-0593	http://www.lot.com
LTU International Airways (Germany)	LT	800-888-0200	http://www.ltu.de/
Lufthansa Airlines (Germany)	LH	800-645-3880	http://www.lufthansa.com/
Malaysia Airlines		888-359-8655	http://www.malaysiaair.com
MALEV Hungarian Airlines (Hungary)	MA	800-223-6884	http://www.malev.hu/ew/angol/default.asp
Martinair Holland (The Netherlands)	MP	800-627-8462	http://www.martinair.com
Mesa Airlines (U.S.)	YV	800-637-2247	http://www.mesa_air.com/
Mexicana Airlines (Mexico)	MX	800-531-7921	http://www.mexicana.com.mx/mxz/english/home.asp
Midway Airlines (U.S.)	JI	800-446-4392 or 888-226-4392	http://www.midwayair.com
Midwest Express Airlines (U.S.)	YX	800-452-2022	http://www.midwestexpress.com/
New England Airlines (U.S.)	EJ	800-243-2460	http://www.ids.net/flybi/nea/
Nica Airlines (Nicaragua)	6Y	800-831-6422	http://www.grupotaca.com
Northwest Airlines (U.S.)	NW	800-225-2525 (domestic) 800-447-4747 (international)	http://www.nwa.com/
Olympic Airways (Greece)	OA	800-223-1226	http://www.olympic-airways.gr
Pacific Coastal Airlines (U.S.)	8P	800-663-2872	http://www.pacific-coastal.com/
Peninsula Airways/Penair (U.S.)	KS	800-448-4226	http://www.penair.com/
Philippine Airlines (The Philippines)	PR	800-435-9725	http://www.philippinesair.com
Polynesian Airlines (Western Samoa)	PH	800-677-4277	http://www.polynesianair.com

Airline (Home Country)	Code	Toll–Free Number(s)	Web Site
Qantas Airways (Australia)	QF	800-227-4500	http://www.qantas.com/au/index.html
Reno Air (U.S.)	QQ	800-736-6247	http://www.renoair.com/
Royal Air Maroc (Morocco)	AT	800-344-6726	http://www.royalairmaroc.com
Royal Jordanian Airlines (Jordan)	RJ	800-223-0470	http://www.rja.com.jo/
Royal Nepal Airlines (Nepal)	RA	800-266-3725	http://www.royalnepal.com
Royal Tonga Airline (Tonga)	WR	800-486-6426	http://www.tongatapu.net.to/tonga/islands/royalt/default.htm
Sabena Belgian World Airlines (Belgium)	SN	800-950-1000	http://www.sabena.com/
Saudi Arabian Airlines (Saudi Arabia)	SV	800-472-8342	http://www.saudiairlines.com
Scandinavian Airlines/SAS (Scandinavia)	SK	800-221-2350	http://www.sas.se/
Singapore Airlines (Singapore)	SQ	800-742-3333	http://www.singaporeair.com/
Solomon Airlines (Solomon Islands)	IE	800-677-4277	http://www.solomonairlines.com/english/
South African Airways/SAA (South Africa)	SA	800-722-9675	http://www.saa.co.za/1024.html
Southwest Airlines (U.S.)	WN	800-435-9792	http://www.iflyswa.com/
Sun Air			http://www.fiji.to/
Sunflower Airlines (Fiji Islands)	PI	800-707-3454	http://www.fijiguide.com/Sunflower/sunad.html
SWISS (Switzerland)	SR	877-359-7947	http://www.swiss.com/
TACA International Airlines (El Salvador)	TA	800-535-8780	http://www.grupotaca.com
TAP Air Portugal (Portugal)	TP	800-221-7370	http://www.tap-airportugal.pt/en/index1.html
Thai Airways International (Thailand)	TG	800-221-2500	http://www/thaiair.com
Transbrasil Airlines (Brazil)	TR	800-872-3153	http://www.transbrasil.com.br/
Travel Air (Costa Rica)	8T	800-924-2727	http://www.centralamerica.com/cr/tran/travlair.htm
Turkish Airlines/THY/Turk Hava Yollari (Turkey)	TK	800-874-8875	http://www.turkishairlines.com/
Trans World Airlines/TWA (U.S.)	TW	800-221-2000 (domestic) 800-892-4141 (international)	http://www.twa.com/
United Airlines (U.S.)	UA	800-241-6522	http://www.ual.com/
Ukraine International Airlines (Ukraine)	PS	800-876-0114	http://www.ukraine-international.com/eng/index.html
USAirways/USAir (U.S.)	US	800-428-4322	http://www.usairways.com/
Varig Brazilian Airlines (Brazil)	RG	800-468-2744 or 800-262-1706	http://www.varig.com.br
VASP Brazilian Airlines (Brazil)	VP	800-732-8277	http://www.vasp.com.br/
Virgin Atlantic Airways (U.K.)	VS	800-862-8621	http://www.virgin-atlantic.com
WestJet Airlines (Canada)	WJ	800-538-5696	http://www.westjet.com/
World Airways (U.S.)	WO	800-967-5350	http://www.worldair.com/

Travel

AIRPORT CODES, NAMES, AND LOCATIONS

UNITED STATES AIRPORTS

Code	U.S. Airport	Location
ABQ	Albuquerque International Airport	Albuquerque, NM
ACY	Atlantic City International Airport	Atlantic City, NJ
ANC	Anchorage International Airport	Anchorage, AK
ATL	Hartsfield International Airport	Atlanta, GA
AUS	Robert Mueller/Bergstrom International Airport	Austin, TX
BDL	Bradley International Airport	Hartford, CT
BHM	Birmingham International Airport	Birmingham, AL
BNA	Nashville International Airport	Nashville, TN
BOS	Logan International Airport	Boston, MA
BRO	Brownsville/South Padre Island International Airport	Brownsville, TX
BUR	Burbank/Pasadena/Glendale Airport	Burbank, CA
BWI	Baltimore/Washington International Airport	Baltimore, MD
CAE	Columbia Metropolitan Airport	Columbia, SC
CHS	Charleston International Airport	Charleston, SC
CLE	Hopkins International Airport	Cleveland, OH
CLT	Charlotte/Douglas International Airport	Charlotte, NC
CMH	Port Columbus International Airport	Columbus, OH
CVG	Greater Cincinnati International Airport	Covington, KY/Cincinnati, OH
DCA	Ronald Reagan Washington National Airport	Washington, DC
DEN	Denver International Airport	Denver, CO
DFW	Dallas/Ft. Worth International Airport	Dallas, TX
DTW	Detroit Metropolitan Airport	Detroit, MI
EWR	Newark International Airport	Newark, NJ
FLL	Ft. Lauderdale/Hollywood International Airport	Ft. Lauderdale, FL
GPT	Gulfport/Biloxi Regional Airport	Biloxi, MS
HNL	Honolulu International Airport	Honolulu, HI
HOU	William P. Hobby Airport	Houston, TX
HSV	Huntsville International Airport	Huntsville, AL
IAD	Dulles International Airport	Washington, DC
IAH	Houston Intercontinental Airport	Houston, TX
JAN	Jackson International Airport	Jackson, MS
JAX	Jacksonville International Airport	Jacksonville, FL
JFK	John F. Kennedy International Airport	New York, NY
LAS	McCarran International Airport	Las Vegas, NV
LAX	Los Angeles International Airport	Los Angeles, CA
LGA	La Guardia Airport	New York, NY
MCI	Kansas City International Airport	Kansas City, MO
MCO	Orlando International Airport	Orlando, FL
MEM	Memphis International Airport	Memphis, TN
MIA	Miami International Airport	Miami, FL
MKE	General Mitchell International Airport	Milwaukee, WI
MOB	Mobile Regional Airport	Mobile, AL
MSP	Minneapolis/St. Paul International Airport	Minneapolis, MN
MSY	Moisant International Airport	New Orleans, LA
MYR	Myrtle Beach International Airport	Myrtle Beach, SC
OAK	Metropolitan Oakland International Airport	Oakland, CA

Travel

Code	U.S. Airport	Location
OKC	Will Rogers World Airport	Oklahoma City, OK
ORD	O'Hare International Airport	Chicago, IL
PDX	Portland International Airport	Portland, OR
PHL	Philadelphia International Airport	Philadelphia, PA
PHX	Sky Harbor International Airport	Phoenix, AR
PIT	Greater Pittsburgh International Airport	Pittsburgh, PA
RDU	Raleigh-Durham International Airport	Raleigh, NC
RIC	Richmond International Airport	Richmond, VA
RNO	Reno-Cannon International Airport	Reno, NV
SAN	San Diego International Airport	San Diego, CA
SAT	San Antonio International Airport	San Antonio, TX
SAV	Savannah International Airport	Savannah, GA
SDF	Standiford Field	Louisville, KY
SEA	Seattle/Tacoma International Airport	Seattle, WA
SFO	San Francisco International Airport	San Francisco, CA
SJC	San Jose International Airport	San Jose, CA
SLC	Salt Lake City International Airport	Salt Lake City, UT
SMF	Sacramento Metropolitan Airport	Sacramento, CA
SRQ	Sarasota/Bradenton International Airport	Sarasota, FL
STL	Lambert–St. Louis International Airport	St. Louis, MO
TPA	Tampa International Airport	Tampa, FL
TUL	Tulsa International Airport	Tulsa, OK

INTERNATIONAL AIRPORTS

Code	International Airport	Location
ACA	General Juan N. Alvarez Airport	Acapulco, Mexico
AEP	Jorge Newbery Airpark	Buenos Aires, Argentina
AKL	Auckland International Airport	Auckland, New Zealand
ALA	Almaty International Airport	Almaty, Kazakhstan
AMS	Schiphol International Airport	Amsterdam, The Netherlands
ANR	Deurne Airport	Antwerp, Belgium
ANU	V. C. Bird/Coolidge International Airport	Antigua Island, Antigua
ARN	Arlanda International Airport	Stockholm, Sweden
ASU	Silvio Pettirossi Airport	Asuncion, Paraguay
ATH	Hellinikon International Airport	Athens, Greece
AUA	Queen Beatrix International Airport	Oranjestad, Aruba
AUH	Abu Dhabi International Airport	Abu Dhabi, United Arab Emirates
BAH	Bahrain International Airport	Bahrain, Bahrain
BAK	Baku Bina International Airport	Baku Bina, Azerbaijan
BBU	Baneasa Airport	Bucharest, Romania
BCN	Barcelona Transoceanic Airport	Barcelona, Spain
BDA	Kindley Field	Bermuda
BEY	Beirut International Airport	Beirut, Lebanon
BFN	JBM Hertzog Airport	Bloemfontein, South Africa
BFS	Belfast International Airport	Belfast (Northern Ireland), United Kingdom
BGI	Grantley Adams International Airport	Bridgetown, Barbados
BIM	South Bimini International Airport	Bimini, Bahamas

continues

Travel

Airport Codes, Names, and Locations, Continued

Code	International Airport	Location
BJS	Beijing International Airport	Beijing, China
BJX	Leon International Airport	Leon, Mexico
BKK	Don Muang International Airport	Bangkok, Thailand
BNE	Brisbane International Airport	Brisbane (Queensland), Australia
BOG	Eldorado Airport	Bogotá, Colombia
BOM	Bombay International Airport	Bombay, India
BRU	Brussels Airport	Brussels, Belgium
BSL	Basel/Mulhouse EuroAirport	Basel, Switzerland
BUD	Budapest Ferihegyi Airport	Budapest, Hungary
BZE	Belize International Airport	Belize City, Belize
CAI	Cairo International Airport	Cairo, Egypt
CAN	Baiyun Airport	Guangzhou, China
CAS	Casablanca Airport	Casablanca, Morocco
CCS	Simon Bolivar Airport	Caracas, Venezuela
CCU	Dum Dum International Airport	Calcutta, India
CDG	Charles de Gaulle Airport	Paris (Roissy), France
CGH	São Paulo Congonhas Airport	São Paulo, Brazil
CGK	Joekarno-Hatta International Airport	Jakarta, Indonesia
CGN	Cologne/Bonn Airport	Cologne, Germany
CHC	Christchurch International Airport	Christchurch, New Zealand
CJU	Cheju International Airport	Cheju, South Korea
CPH	Copenhagen International Airport	Copenhagen, Denmark
CPT	Capetown International Airport	Capetown, South Africa
CRL	Charleroi Brussels South Airport	Brussels, Belgium
CUN	Cancun International Airport	Cancun, Mexico
CUR	Hato Airport	Curacao, Netherlands Antilles
DBV	Hrvastka Airport	Dubrovnik, Croatia
DEL	Delhi International Airport	New Delhi, India
DOH	Doha Airport	Doha, Qatar
DUB	Dublin Airport	Dublin, Ireland
DUR	Louis Botha International Airport	Durban, South Africa
DUS	Dusseldorf Airport	Dusseldorf, Germany
EBB	Entebbe International Airport	Entebbe, Uganda
EZE	Ezeiza International Airport	Buenos Aires, Argentina
FCO	Fiumicino (Leonardo da Vinci) Airport	Rome, Italy
FLR	Peretola Airport	Florence, Italy
FPO	Freeport International Airport	Freeport, Bahamas
FRA	Frankfurt International Airport	Frankfurt, Germany
FRU	Bishkek/Frunze Manas International Airport	Bishkek (Chuy), Kyrgyzstan
GCM	Owen Roberts International Airport	Grand Cayman, Cayman Islands
GDL	Miguel Hidalgo y Costilla Airport	Guadalajara, Mexico
GEN	Gardermoen Airport	Oslo, Norway
GIG	Rio de Janeiro/Galeao International Airport	Rio de Janeiro, Brazil
GLA	Glasgow Airport	Glasgow (Scotland), United Kingdom
GND	PT Saline Airport	Grenville, Grenada
GVA	Geneva International Airport	Geneva, Switzerland
GYE	Simon Bolivar Airport	Guayaquil, Ecuador
HAM	Fuhlsbuttel International Airport	Hamburg, Germany

Code	International Airport	Location
HEL	Helsinki-Vantaa International Airport	Helsinki, Finland
HIJ	Hiroshima Airport	Hiroshima, Japan
HKG	Kai Tek (Chek Lap Kok) International Airport	Hong Kong, China
HND	Haneda International Airport	Tokyo, Japan
INN	Kranebitten Airport	Innsbruck, Austria
IST	Ataturk/Yesilkov International Airport	Istanbul, Turkey
JAV	Ilulissat Airport	Jakobshavn, Greenland
JCN	Inchon International Airport	Inchon, South Korea
JFJ	Kangerlussuaq (Sondre Stromfjord) Airport	Kangerslussuaq, Greenland
JNB	Johannesburg/Grand Central International Airport	Johannesburg, South Africa
JRS	Atarot Airport	Jerusalem, Israel
KBL	Kabul Airport	Kabul, Afghanistan
KDL	Kärdla Airport	Kärdla, Estonia
KHI	Quaid-e-Azam International Airport	Karachi, Pakistan
KIN	Norman Manley Airport	Kingston, Jamaica
KIX	Kansai International Airport	Osaka, Japan
KTP	Kingston Airport	Kingston, Jamaica
KUL	Sultan Abdul Aziz Shah, Subang International Airport	Kuala Lumpur, Malaysia
KWI	Kuwait Airport	Kuwait
LED	Pulkovo II International Airport	St. Petersburg (Leningrad), Russia
LGW	Gatwick Airport	London (England), United Kingdom
LHR	Heathrow International Airport	London (England), United Kingdom
LIM	Jorge Chavez International Airport	Lima, Peru
LIS	Lisbon Airport	Lisbon, Portugal
LPA	Las Palmas/Gran Canaria Airport	Las Palmas/Gran Canaria (Canary Islands), Spain
LPB	J. F. Kennedy/El Alto Airport	La Paz, Bolivia
LUX	Findel Airport	Luxembourg
MAD	Madrid Barajas Airport	Madrid, Spain
MAN	Ringway International Airport	Manchester (England), United Kingdom
MBJ	Sangster Airport	Montego Bay, Jamaica
MCT	Seeb Airport	Muscat, Oman
MEL	Tullamarine International Airport	Melbourne (Victoria), Australia
MEX	Benito Juarez International Airport	Mexico City, Mexico
MFM	Macau International Airport	Macau, Macao
MGA	A. C. Sandino Airport	Managua, Nicaragua
MLA	Malta International Airport	Malta
MLE	Hulele International Airport	Malé, Maldives
MNL	Ninoy Aquino International Airport	Manila, Philippines
MRX	Caribe Santiago Mariño International Airport	Margarita Island, Venezuela
MUC	Strauss International Airport	Munich, Germany
MVD	Carrasco Airport	Montevideo, Uruguay
MXP	Milano-Malpensa International Airport	Milan, Italy
NAP	Capodichino International Airport	Naples, Italy
NAS	Nassau International Airport	Nassau, Bahamas
NBO	Jomo Kenyatta International Airport	Nairobi, Kenya
NEV	Nevis Airport	Charlestown, Nevis
NRT	Narita International Airport	Tokyo, Japan

continues

Airport Codes, Names, and Locations, Continued

Code	International Airport	Location
OHD	Ohrid Airport	Ohrid, Republic of Macedonia
ORY	Orly Airport	Paris (Orly), France
OST	Ostend Airport	Oostende, Belgium
OTP	Otopeni International Airport	Bucharest, Romania
PAP	Mais Gate Airport	Port-au-Prince, Haiti
PEK	Beijing (Peking) Capital Airport	Beijing (Peking), China
PER	Perth International Airport	Perth (Western Australia), Australia
PMI	Palma de Mallorca Airport	Balearic Islands, Spain
POP	La Union Airport	Puerto Plata, Dominican Republic
POS	Piarco International Airport	Port of Spain (Trinidad Island), Trinidad
PRG	Ruzyne Airport	Prague, Czech Republic
PTP	Le Raizet Airport	Pointe-a-Pitre, Guadeloupe
PTY	Tocumen Airport	Panama City, Panama
PVR	Ordaz International Airport	Puerto Vallarta, Mexico
QCA	Makkah Airport	Mecca (Makkah), Morocco
RAD	Beef Island Airport	Tortola, British Virgin Islands
REK	Reykjavik Airport	Reykjavik, Iceland
RIX	Riga International Airport	Riga, Latvia
RUH	King Khalid Airport	Riyadh, Saudi Arabia
SAL	San Salvador International Airport	San Salvador, El Salvador
SCL	Comodoro Arturo Merino Benite Airport	Santiago, Chile
SDA	Saddam International Airport	Baghdad, Iraq
SDQ	Airport of the Americas	Santo Domingo, Dominican Republic
SEL	Kimpo International Airport	Seoul, South Korea
SHA	Hongqiao Airport	Shanghai, China
SHJ	Sharjah International Airport	Sharjah, United Arab Emirates
SIN	Changi International Airport	Singapore
SIP	Simferopol International Airport	Adygea, Ukraine
SJO	Juan Santamaria International Airport	San Jose, Costa Rica
SJU	Marin International Airport	San Juan, Puerto Rico
SKB	Golden Rock Airport	Basseterre, St. Kitts
SLL	Salalah International Airport	Salalah, Oman
SLU	Vigie Airport	Castries, St. Lucia
SOF	Sofia Airport	Sofia, Bulgaria
STT	Cyril E. King Airport	Charlotte Amalie (St. Thomas), U.S. Virgin Islands
STX	Alexander Hamilton Airport	Christensted (St. Croix), U.S. Virgin Islands
SVO	Sheremetyevo International Airport	Moscow, Russia
SXF	Schönefeld Airport	Berlin, Germany
SXM	Princess Juliana Airport	Philipsburg (St. Martin), Netherlands Antilles
SYD	Kingsford-Smith International Airport	Sydney (New South Wales), Australia
TAS	Tashkent International Airport	Tashkent, Uzbekistan
TLV	Ben Gurion Airport	Tel Aviv, Israel
TPE	Chiang Kai Shek Airport	Taipei, Taiwan
TRN	Caselle International Airport	Turin, Italy
TXL	Tegel Airport	Berlin, Germany
UIO	Mariscal Airport	Quito, Ecuador
ULN	Ulan Bator Airport	Ulan Bator, Mongolia

Code	International Airport	Location
VIE	Wien-Schwechat International Airport	Vienna, Austria
VNO	Vilnius International Airport	Vilnius, Lithuania
VVI	Viru Viru International Airport	Santa Cruz, Bolivia
WAW	Okçecie Airport	Warsaw, Poland
WQX	Gander International Airport	Gander (Newfoundland), Canada
XPL	Comayagua Airport	Comayagua, Honduras
YAP	Yap International Airport	Yap Island, Micronesia
YEG	Edmonton International Airport	Edmonton (Alberta), Canada
YHZ	Halifax International Airport	Halifax (Nova Scotia), Canada
YOW	Ottawa International Airport	Ottawa (Ontario), Canada
YUL	Dorval International Airport	Montreal (Quebec), Canada
YVR	Vancouver International Airport	Vancouver (British Columbia), Canada
YWG	Winnipeg International Airport	Winnipeg (Manitoba), Canada
YXU	Greater London International Airport	London (Ontario), Canada
YYC	Calgary International Airport	Calgary (Alberta), Canada
YYJ	Victoria International Airport	Victoria (British Columbia), Canada
YYZ	Pearson International Airport	Toronto (Ontario), Canada
ZAG	Zagreb Airport	Zagreb, Croatia
ZAZ	Zaragoza International Airport	Zaragoza, Spain
ZRH	Zurich-Kloten Airport	Zurich, Switzerland

Travel

DOMESTIC TRAVEL

STATE TOURISM OFFICES

Alabama Bureau of Tourism and Travel
P.O. Box 492
401 Adams Ave.
Montgomery, AL 36103-4927
800-252-2262 or 334-242-4169
http://www.touralabama.org

Alaska Tourism Division
2600 Cordova St., Ste. 201
Anchorage, AK 99503-2745
907-929-2200
http://www.travelalaska.com

Arizona Office of Tourism
2702 N. 3rd St., Ste. 4015
Phoenix, AZ 85004
888-520-3433
http://www.arizonaguide.com

Arkansas Department of Parks and Tourism
One Capitol Mall
Little Rock, AR 72201
800-628-8725 or 501-682-7777
http://arkansas.com

California Office of Tourism
P.O. Box 1499
Sacramento, CA 95812-1499
800-862-2543
http://gocalif.ca.gov

Colorado Tourism Office
1625 Broadway, Ste. 1700
Denver, CO 80202
800-265-6723
http://colorado.com

The Boston University Bridge is the only place in the world where it is possible for a boat to sail under a train running under a car driving under an airplane.

Connecticut Office of Tourism
Department of Economic and Community
   Development
505 Hudson St.
Hartford, CT 06106
800-282-6863 or 860-270-8080
http://www.tourism.state.ct.us

Delaware Tourism Office
99 Kings Hwy.
Dover, DE 19901
866-284-7483 or 302-739-4271
http://www.visitdelaware.net

Visit Florida
661 E. Jefferson St., Ste. 300
Tallahassee, FL 32301
888-737-2872 or 941-922-3575
http://www.flausa.com

**Georgia Department of Industry,
   Trade and Tourism**
P.O. Box 1776
Atlanta, GA 30301
800-847-4842 or 404-656-3590
http://www.georgia.org

Hawaii Visitors and Convention Bureau
2270 Kalakaua Ave., Ste. 801
Honolulu, HI 96815
800-GO-HAWAII or 808-923-1811
http://www.visithawaii.org

Idaho Department of Commerce
Tourism Division
700 West State St.
P.O. Box 83720
Boise, ID 83720-0093
800-842-5858 or 208-334-2470
http://www.visitid.org

Illinois Bureau of Tourism
100 W. Randolph St., Suite 3-400
Chicago, IL 60601
800-226-6632 or 217-785-6334
http://www.enjoyillinois.com

Indiana Tourism Department
One N. Capitol Ave., Ste. 700
Indianapolis, IN 46204-2288
800-289-6646 or 317-232-4685
http://www.in.gov/tourism/

Iowa Division of Tourism
200 E. Grand Ave.
Des Moines, IA 50309
888-472-6035 or 515-242-4705
http://www.traveliowa.com/index.htm

Kansas Department of Commerce and Housing
Division of Travel and Tourism
700 SW Harrison St., Ste. 1300
Topeka, KS 66603-3712
800-252-6727 or 785-296-2009
http://www.travelks.com

Kentucky Department of Travel Development
500 Mero St., Ste. 2200
Frankfort, KY 40601
800-225-8747 (TDD equipped) or 502-564-4930
http://www.kytourism.com

Louisiana Office of Tourism
P.O. Box 94291
Baton Rouge, LA 70804-9291
800-677-4082 or 225-342-8119
http://www.crt.state.la.us/crt/tourism.htm

Maine Office of Tourism
29 State House Station
Augusta, ME 04330
888-624-6345 or 207-287-5711
http://www.visitmaine.com

Maryland Office of Tourist Development
217 E. Redwood St., 9th Fl.
Baltimore, MD 21202
800-543-1036 or 800-634-7386
http://www.mdisfun.org

Massachusetts Office of Travel and Tourism
10 Park Plaza, Ste. 4510
Boston, MA 02116
800-227-6277 or 617-973-8500
http://www.mass-vacation.com

Travel Michigan
4225 Miller Rd., Ste. 4
Flint, MI 48507-9821
888-784-7328 or 517-373-0670
http://travel.michigan.org

Minnesota Travel Information Center
100 Metro Square
121 7th Pl. East
St. Paul, MN 55101
800-657-3700 or 651-296-5029
http://www.exploreminnesota.com

Mississippi Development Authority
Division of Tourism
P.O. Box 849
Jackson, MS 39205
800-927-6378 or 610-359-3297
http://www.visitmississippi.org

Missouri Division of Tourism
P.O. Box 1055
Jefferson City, MO 65102
800-877-1234 or 573-751-4133
http://www.missouritourism.com

Travel Montana
Department of Commerce
1424 9th Ave.
P.O. Box 200533
Helena, MT 59620-0533
800-847-4868 or 406-444-2654
http://travelmontana.state.mt.us

Nebraska Division of Travel and Tourism
P.O. Box 98907
Lincoln, NE 68509-9807
800-228-4307
http://www.visitnebraska.org

Nevada Commission on Tourism
401 North Carson St.
Carson City, NV 89701
800-638-2328 or 775-687-4322
http://www.travelnevada.com

**New Hampshire Division of Travel and
    Tourism Development**
172 Pembroke Rd.
P.O. Box 1856
Concord, NH 03302-1856
800-386-4664
http://www.visitnh.gov

**New Jersey Commerce and Economic
    Growth Commission**
Division of Travel and Tourism
P.O. Box 820
20 W. State St.
Trenton, NJ 08625
800-847-4865 or 609-777-0885
http://www.state.nj.us/travel

New Mexico Department of Tourism
491 Old Santa Fe Trail
Santa Fe, NM 87503
800-733-6396 (ext. 0643) or 505-827-7400
http://www.newmexico.org

New York Division of Tourism
30 S. Pearl St., 2nd Fl.
Albany, NY 12245
800-225-5697 or 518-474-4116
http://iloveny.state.ny.us

**North Carolina Division of Tourism,
    Film and Sports Development**
4324 Mail Service Center
Raleigh, NC 27699-4324
800-847-4862 or 919-715-5900
http://www.visitnc.com

North Dakota Tourism
Liberty Memorial Bldg.
604 East Blvd.
Bismarck, ND 58505-0825
800-435-5663 or 701-328-2525
http://www.ndtourism.com

Ohio Division of Travel and Tourism
P.O. Box 1001
Columbus, OH 43216-0101
800-282-5393
http://www.ohiotourism.com

Oklahoma Tourism and Recreation Department
15 N. Robinson, Ste. 100
Oklahoma City, OK 73102
800-652-6552 or 405-521-2406
http://www.otrd.state.ok.us

Oregon Tourism Commission
775 Summer St., NE
Salem, OR 97310
800-547-7842
http://www.traveloregon.com

*The interstate highway system
requires that one mile in every five
be straight. These sections can be
used as airstrips in time of war or
other emergencies.*

Pennsylvania Office of Tourism
Commonwealth Keystone Bldg.
400 North St., 4th Fl.
Harrisburg, PA 17120-0225
800-847-4872 or 717-232-8880
http://www.experiencepa.com

Rhode Island Tourism Division
One W. Exchange St.
Providence, RI 02903
800-556-2484 or 401-222-2601
http://visitrhodeisland.com

**South Carolina Department of Parks,
    Recreation, and Tourism**
1205 Pendleton St., Ste. 106
Columbia, SC 29201
800-868-2492 or 803-734-1700
http://www.travelsc.com

South Dakota Department of Tourism
Capitol Lake Plaza
711 E. Wells Ave.
c/o 500 E. Capitol Ave.
Pierre, SD 57501-5070
800-732-5682 or 605-773-3301
http://www.travelsd.com

"States and Territories" in chapter 25; "United
    States" in the atlas
Go to

Travel

Tennessee Department of Tourist Development
Rachel Jackson Bldg., 5th Fl.
320 6th Ave. N
Nashville, TN 37202-3170
800-836-6200 or 615-741-2159
http://www.state.tn.us/tourdev/

Texas Department of Economic Development
Tourism Division
P.O. Box 141009
Austin, TX 78714
800-888-8839 or 512-478-0098
http://traveltex.com

Utah Travel Council
P.O. Box 147420
Salt Lake City, UT 84114-7420
800-200-1160 or 801-538-1030
http://www.utah.com

Vermont Department of Tourism and Marketing
6 Baldwin St., Drawer 33
Montpelier, VT 05633-1301
800-837-6668 or 802-828-3237
http://www.1-800-vermont.com

Virginia Tourism Corporation
901 E. Byrd St.
Richmond, VA 23219-2048
800-847-4882 or 800-326-3244
http://www.virginia.org

Washington Department of Tourism
P.O. Box 42500
Olympia, WA 98504
800-544-1800 or 360-725-5050
http://www.tourism.wa.gov

Washington, D.C., Convention and Visitors Association
1212 New York Ave. NW, Ste. 600
Washington, DC 20005
800-422-8644 or 202-789-7000
http://www.washington.org

West Virginia Division of Tourism
2101 Washington St. E
Charleston, WV 25305
800-225-5982 or 304-558-2200
http://www.state.wv.us/tourism/

Wisconsin Department of Tourism
201 W. Washington
P.O. Box 7976
Madison, WI 53707-7976
800-432-8747 or 608-266-2161
http://www.travelwisconsin.com

Wyoming Business Council—Tourism
Interstate 25 at College Dr.
Cheyenne, WY 82002
800-225-5996 or 307-777-7777
http://www.wyomingtourism.org

Go to "Time Adjustments: Daylight Savings Time in the United States" in chapter 1

PRECIPITATION CHART

AVERAGE PRECIPITATION FOR SELECTED STATES AND CITIES (IN INCHES)

State	City	Jan/Feb	Mar/Apr	May/Jun	Jul/Aug	Sep/Oct	Nov/Dec
Alabama	Mobile	5.1	5.4	5.4	6.9	4.4	4.7
Alaska	Juneau	4.1	3.0	3.3	4.7	7.3	4.7
Arizona	Phoenix	0.7	0.6	0.1	0.9	0.8	0.8
California	Los Angeles	2.5	1.4	0.1	0.1	0.3	1.7
	San Francisco	3.8	2.2	0.1	0.04	0.7	3.0
Colorado	Denver	0.6	1.5	2.1	1.7	1.1	0.8
Connecticut	Hartford	3.3	3.7	3.9	3.4	3.7	4.0
Delaware	Wilmington	3.0	3.4	3.7	3.8	3.2	3.4
District of Columbia	Washington	2.7	2.9	3.5	3.9	3.2	3.1
Florida	Jacksonville	3.6	3.2	4.6	6.8	5.0	2.5
	Miami	2.0	2.6	7.7	6.6	6.6	2.2
Georgia	Atlanta	4.8	5.0	3.9	4.3	3.2	4.1

AVERAGE PRECIPITATION FOR SELECTED STATES AND CITIES (IN INCHES)

State	City	Jan/Feb	Mar/Apr	May/Jun	Jul/Aug	Sep/Oct	Nov/Dec
Hawaii	Honolulu	2.9	1.9	0.8	0.5	1.5	3.4
Idaho	Boise	1.3	1.3	0.9	0.4	0.8	1.4
Illinois	Chicago	1.4	3.2	3.6	3.9	3.1	2.7
Indiana	Indianapolis	2.4	3.4	3.7	4.0	2.8	3.3
Iowa	Des Moines	1.0	2.8	4.1	4.0	3.1	1.6
Kansas	Dodge City	0.5	1.7	3.2	2.8	1.6	0.7
Kentucky	Louisville	3.1	4.4	4.0	4.0	2.9	3.7
Louisiana	New Orleans	5.5	4.7	5.2	6.1	4.3	5.1
Maine	Portland	3.4	3.9	3.5	3.0	3.5	4.7
Massachusetts	Boston	3.6	3.6	3.2	3.0	3.2	4.1
Michigan	Detroit	1.8	2.8	3.3	3.3	2.5	2.7
Minnesota	Duluth	1.0	2.1	3.4	3.8	3.2	1.5
	Minneapolis	0.9	2.2	3.7	3.6	2.5	1.3
Mississippi	Jackson	5.0	5.7	4.1	4.1	3.4	5.4
Missouri	Kansas City	1.1	2.8	4.9	4.2	4.1	1.8
	St. Louis	2.0	3.5	3.8	3.4	2.9	3.2
Montana	Helena	0.6	0.9	1.9	1.1	0.8	0.6
Nebraska	Omaha	0.8	2.4	4.2	3.4	3.0	1.3
Nevada	Reno	1.0	0.5	0.6	0.3	0.4	0.9
New Jersey	Atlantic City	3.3	3.6	3.0	4.0	2.9	3.5
New Mexico	Albuquerque	0.5	0.5	0.6	1.5	0.9	0.5
New York	Albany	2.3	3.0	3.5	3.3	2.9	3.1
	Buffalo	2.5	2.8	3.3	3.6	3.3	3.8
	New York	3.3	4.0	4.0	4.2	3.7	4.2
North Carolina	Raleigh	3.6	3.2	3.8	4.0	3.0	3.1
North Dakota	Bismarck	0.4	1.2	2.5	1.9	1.2	0.5
Ohio	Cleveland	2.1	3.0	3.6	3.5	3.0	3.1
	Columbus	2.2	3.2	4.0	4.0	2.6	3.0
Oklahoma	Oklahoma City	1.3	2.7	4.8	2.6	3.5	1.7
Oregon	Portland	4.6	3.0	1.8	0.9	2.2	5.7
Pennsylvania	Philadelphia	3.0	3.5	3.7	4.0	3.0	3.4
	Pittsburgh	2.5	3.3	3.7	3.5	2.7	2.9
Rhode Island	Providence	3.7	4.1	3.5	3.4	3.6	4.4
South Carolina	Charleston	3.4	3.5	5.5	6.9	3.9	2.7
South Dakota	Huron	0.6	1.6	3.0	2.2	1.4	0.6
Tennessee	Memphis	4.0	5.4	4.3	3.6	3.3	5.4
	Nashville	3.7	4.6	4.2	3.7	3.0	4.4
Texas	Dallas–Ft. Worth	2.0	3.1	3.9	2.3	3.5	2.1
	Houston	3.1	3.1	5.1	3.5	4.6	3.6
Utah	Salt Lake City	1.2	2.0	1.4	0.8	1.4	1.3
Vermont	Burlington	1.7	2.5	3.3	3.9	3.1	2.8
Virginia	Norfolk	3.6	3.4	3.8	4.0	3.5	3.0
	Richmond	3.2	3.3	3.7	4.7	3.4	3.2
Washington	Seattle-Tacoma	4.7	2.9	1.6	1.0	2.6	5.9
Wisconsin	Milwaukee	1.5	3.1	3.0	3.5	2.9	2.4
Wyoming	Lander	0.6	1.4	2.1	0.6	1.1	0.7

Travel

AIR MILEAGE FROM NEW YORK CITY—DOMESTIC

Albuquerque	1,810
Atlanta	747
Baltimore	170
Boston	188
Chicago	711
Denver	1,628
Detroit	483
Kansas City, MO	1,097
Los Angeles	2,446
Memphis	953
Miami	1,095
Nashville	758
New Orleans	1,173
Omaha	1,144
Philadelphia	83
Phoenix	2,142
Portland, OR	2,455
St. Louis	873
Salt Lake City	1,972
San Francisco	2,568
Seattle	2,419
Washington, D.C.	204

NATIONAL PARK DIRECTORY

For detailed information on the National Parks, write to the Superintendent of Documents at the Government Printing Office in Washington, D.C., 20402, or call 202-512-1800. The GPO's *The National Parks: Index* describes each park. Or go to http://www.nps.gov for online information about National Parks.

Acadia National Park, Bar Harbor, Maine
Area: 47,633 acres
Open: Year-round
Major attractions: Mountains (highest point on Atlantic coast) showing marine erosion and glaciation, lakes, forests, marine life
Activities: Camping, fishing, hiking, biking, horseback riding, cross-country skiing, swimming, nature walks

Arches National Park, Moab, Utah
Area: 76,519 acres
Open: Year-round
Major attractions: Huge rock formations caused by erosion, mountains, Colorado River gorge
Activities: Camping, climbing, hiking, nature walks

Badlands National Park, Interior, South Dakota
Area: 242,755 acres
Open: Year-round
Major attractions: Multicolored peaks and spires caused by erosion, fossil sites, wildlife, Pine Ridge Indian Reservation near site of Wounded Knee battleground.
Activities: Camping, fishing, hiking, biking, bird watching, horseback riding, cross-country skiing

Big Bend National Park, Big Bend National Park, Texas
Area: 801,163 acres
Open: Year-round
Major attractions: Mountains, canyons, desert, U.S. and Mexican flowers, trees, wildlife.
Activities: Camping, boating, fishing, hiking, horseback riding, biking, stargazing, whitewater rafting

Biscayne National Park, Homestead, Florida
Area: 172,924 acres
Open: Year-round
Major attractions: Underwater coral reefs, marine life.
Activities: Boating, snorkeling, scuba diving, camping, kayaking, swimming, wildlife viewing

Black Canyon of the Gunnison National Park, Montrose, Colorado
Area: 27,705 acres
Open: Year-round
Major attractions: Monolithic rock walls rising 2,000 feet above the Gunnison River.
Activities: Camping, boating, climbing, fishing, hiking, stargazing, mountaineering, snowshoeing, skiing, kayaking

Bryce Canyon National Park, Bryce Canyon, Utah
Area: 35,836 acres
Open: Year-round
Major attractions: Multi-colored rock erosions.
Activities: Camping, hiking, horseback riding, biking, museum tours, cross country skiing

Canyonlands National Park, Moab, Utah
Area: 337,570 acres
Open: Year-round
Major attractions: Rock formations, ancient cliff dwellings, Green River and Colorado River canyons.
Activities: Camping, boating, climbing, fishing, hiking, stargazing, white-water rafting, nature walks

Capitol Reef National Park, Torrey, Utah
Area: 241,905 acres
Open: Year-round
Major attractions: Colorful rock formations, desert plays and wildlife, pioneer exhibits (including a one-room schoolhouse).

Activities: Camping, boating, climbing, fishing, hiking, stargazing, mountaineering, nature walks, horseback riding

Carlsbad Caverns National Park, Carlsbad, New Mexico
Area: 46,775 acres
Open: Year-round
Major attractions: Nation's deepest limestone cavern with spectacular underground formations, above-ground desert plants, rock formations
Activities: Cavern tours, hiking, wildlife viewing

Channel Islands National Park, Ventura, California
Area: 249,561 acres
Open: Year-round
Major attractions: Marine life, sea birds
Activities: Boating, hiking, fishing, scuba diving, snorkeling, camping, kayaking, nature walks

Crater Lake National Park, Crater Lake, Oregon
Area: 183,224 acres
Open: Year-round
Major attractions: Deepest lake in the United States (2,000 feet) in crater of extinct volcano, multicolored rocks, forests, mountain flowers, wildlife
Activities: Camping, boating, fishing, hiking, stargazing, biking, nature walks, snowshoeing, bird-watching

Death Valley National Park, Death Valley, California
Area: 3,367,627 acres
Open: Year-round
Major attractions: Spectacular desert scenery, rare desert wildlife, historical sites and remnants of mining.
Activities: Biking, bird-watching, camping, hiking, swimming, nature walks, horseback riding

Denali National Park and Preserve, Denali, Alaska
Area: 4,740,912 acres
Open: Year-round
Major attractions: Peaks of Alaska Range, including Mount McKinley (20,320 feet—highest point in North America), rare wildlife and subarctic plant life, huge Denali fault, break in earth's crust.
Activities: Camping, dogsledding, fishing, hiking, stargazing, mountaineering, snowshoeing, snowmobiling, cross-country skiing, nature walks

Everglades National Park, Homestead, Florida
Area: 1,399,078 acres
Open: Year-round
Major attractions: Immense subtropical wilderness, mangrove swamps, wild animals, rare birds
Activities: Camping, boating, fishing, hiking, nature walks, biking

Gates of the Arctic National Park and Preserve, Fairbanks, Alaska
Area: 7,523,898 acres
Open: Year-round
Major attractions: Snow-covered peaks of Brooks Range north of the Arctic Circle, tundra wilderness, wildlife
Activities: Hunting, camping, fishing, hiking, mountaineering, snowshoeing, dogsledding, cross-country skiing

Glacier Bay National Park, Gustavus, Alaska
Area: 3,224,840 acres
Open: Year-round (Visitor center open only during the summer months)
Major attractions: Great Mendenhall Glacier, iceberg formations from glaciers, dense coastal rain forests, wildlife, nearby, Mount Logan, highest point in Canada (19,850 feet)
Activities: Camping, hiking, hunting, fishing, kayaking, boating

Gateway National Recreation Area New York City, New York (Brooklyn, Queens, and Staten Island), and Monmouth County, New Jersey
Area: 26,600 acres
Open: Year-round; several visitor centers
Major attractions: Jamaica Bay Wildlife Refuge, Jacob Riis and Sandy Hook beaches, Floyd Bennett Field Campground
Activities: Auto touring, biking, bird-watching, boating, camping, fishing, hiking, horseback riding, nature walks, stargazing, swimming, wildlife viewing

Glacier National Park, West Glacier, Montana
Area: 1,013,572 acres
Open: Year-round (Most park services and facilities are available from late May through October. In late fall, winter, and spring there are very limited services available in the park.)
Major attractions: Rugged mountain peaks of Continental Divide, glaciers, numerous alpine lakes and streams, rare wildflowers, wildlife, ancient Blackfoot hunting grounds
Activities: Hiking, horseback riding, camping, fishing, cross-country skiing, boating

Grand Canyon National Park, Grand Canyon, Arizona
Area: 1,217,403 acres
Open: Year-round
Major attractions: Mile-deep, 1.5-billion-year-old canyon of Colorado River, showing geologic features with fossil plants and animals, multicolored rocks, wide range of plants and animals, Havasupai Indian reservation

continues

Activities: Camping, horseback riding, hiking, boating, nature walks, white-water rafting

Grand Teton National Park, Moose, Wyoming
Area: 309,994 acres
Open: Year-round
Major attractions: Mountains, trails of famous early explorers, perennial snowfields, wild plants, animals, and birds
Activities: Camping, boating, fishing, hiking, snowshoeing, horseback riding, snowmobiling

Great Basin National Park, Baker, Nevada
Area: 77,180 acres
Open: Year-round
Major attractions: The South Snake Range (example of a desert mountain island), Wheeler Peak (13,063 feet), Lehman Caves, alpine lakes, ancient bristlecone-pine groves
Activities: Camping, biking, hiking, snowshoeing, horseback riding, caving

Great Smoky Mountains National Park, Gatlinburg, Tennessee
Area: 521,621 acres
Open: Year-round
Major attractions: Highest mountains in the eastern United States (6,500 feet), wide range of plants, wildlife
Activities: Camping, fishing, hiking, nature walks, biking, horseback riding

Guadalupe Mountains National Park, Salt Flat, Texas
Area: 86,416 acres
Open: Year-round
Major attractions: Desert wilderness, limestone fossil reef, wildlife, highest point in Texas (8,749 feet)
Activities: Camping, hiking, nature walks, bird-watching

Haleakala National Park, Makawao, Maui, Hawaii
Area: 29,824 acres
Open: Year-round
Major attractions: Haleakala crater, scenic pools, rare wildlife, semitropical vegetation
Activities: Camping, hiking, nature walks, horseback riding, swimming, stargazing

Hawaii Volcanoes National Park, Hawaii National Park, Hawaii
Area: 209,695 acres
Open: Year-round
Major attractions: Volcano activity, semitropical plants, birds
Activities: Camping, hiking, nature walks, bird-watching, hunting, museums, stargazing

Hot Springs National Park, Hot Springs, Arkansas
Area: 5,550 acres
Open: Year-round
Major attractions: Ancient hot springs for bathing with reputed therapeutic benefits
Activities: Camping, hiking, bathing, museums, bird-watching

Isle Royale National Park, Houghton, Michigan
Area: 571,790 acres
Open: April through October
Major attractions: Historic fisheries, hardwood and evergreen forests, pre-Columbian copper mines, wildlife, lighthouses, shipwrecks
Activities: Camping, hiking, fishing, kayaking, boating, swimming, scuba diving, stargazing

Joshua Tree National Park, Twentynine Palms, California
Area: 1,017,748 acres
Open: Year-round
Major attractions: Meeting point of the Colorado and Mojave Deserts, natural oases, Joshua tree forests, geological formations
Activities: Camping, hiking, nature walks, biking, bird-watching, horseback riding

Katmai National Park, King Salmon, Alaska
Area: 3,674,530 acres
Open: June through September
Major attractions: Varied subarctic environment, Alagnak Wild River, Valley of 10,000 Smokes, wildlife
Activities: Camping, hiking, mountaineering, fishing, kayaking, wildlife viewing

Kenai Fjords National Park, Seward, Alaska
Area: 670,000 acres
Open: Year-round
Major attractions: Mountains, ice fields, fjord system, varied marine life
Activities: Camping, hiking, fishing, boating, kayaking, wildlife viewing

Kings Canyon National Park, Three Rivers, California
Area: 461,901 acres
Open: May through October
Major attractions: High Sierra peaks, giant sequoia trees, mile-deep canyon, alpine lakes, glaciers and snowfields, wildlife
Activities: Camping, hiking, horseback riding, fishing, cross-country skiing, mountaineering

Kobuk Valley National Park, Kotzbue, Alaska
Area: 1,750,737 acres
Open: Year-round

Major attractions: Baird Mountain peaks, forests, tundra, great sand dunes, prehistoric archaeological sites, arctic wildlife

Activities: Camping, hiking, boating, fishing, dogsledding, cross-country skiing

Lake Clark National Park and Preserve, Anchorage, Alaska

Area: 2,619,733 acres

Open: Year-round

Major attractions: Aleutian Range peaks, Cook Inlet, live volcanoes, fossils, forests, wildlife

Activities: Camping, hiking, boating, fishing, hunting, bird-watching, white-water rafting, kayaking, mountaineering

Lassen Volcanic National Park, Mineral, California

Area: 106,372 acres

Open: Year-round (Access is difficult in winter and spring.)

Major attractions: Live volcano (intermittent eruptions from 1914 to 1921), hot springs

Activities: Camping, hiking, boating, fishing, snowshoeing, cross-country skiing

Mammoth Cave National Park, Mammoth Cave, Kentucky

Area: 52,830 acres

Open: Year-round

Major attractions: Large cavern (330 miles of passageways), underground river

Activities: Camping, hiking, boating, fishing, nature walks, cave tours, horseback riding

Mesa Verde National Park, Mesa Verde National Park, Colorado

Area: 52,122 acres

Open: May through October

Major attractions: Pre-Colombian cliff dwellings, lookout showing six mountain ranges in four states

Activities: Camping, hiking, cliff-dwelling tours, stargazing, bird-watching

Mount Rainier National Park, Ashford, Washington

Area: 235,625 acres

Open: Year-round

Major attractions: Mountain terrain (summit is 14,400 feet) featuring glaciers, forests, and subalpine meadows

Activities: Hiking, camping, guided climbs, horseback riding, snowshoeing, skiing, wildlife viewing

North Cascades National Park, Marblemount, Washington

Area: 504,781 acres

Open: Year-round

Major attractions: Alpine wilderness area featuring mountains, lakes, forests, glaciers, wildlife

Activities: Camping, hiking, boating, fishing, horseback riding, kayaking, mountaineering, white-water rafting

Olympic National Park, Port Angeles, Washington

Area: 922,651 acres

Open: Year-round

Major attractions: Rain forests of giant evergreens, mountains (including Hurricane Ridge), rocky beaches on peninsula between Pacific Ocean and Puget Sound, indigenous plants and wildlife

Activities: Camping, hiking, boating, fishing, bird watching, stargazing, mountaineering, kayaking

Petrified Forest National Park, Petrified Forest National Park, Arizona

Area: 93,533 acres

Open: Year-round

Major attractions: Petrified logs now in form of multicolored quartz, prehistoric Native American rock carvings, part of the Painted Desert

Activities: Hiking, nature walks, biking, horseback riding, museums

Redwood National Park, Crescent City, California

Area: 112,598 acres

Open: Year-round

Major attractions: Redwood forests, including tallest known tree in the world, Pacific Ocean coastline

Activities: Camping, hiking, fishing, white-water rafting, kayaking, biking, scuba diving, snorkeling

Rocky Mountain National Park, Crescent City, California

Area: 265,723 acres

Open: Year-round

Major attractions: Mountains, lakes, streams, forests, wildflower meadows, wild animals

Activities: Camping, hiking, fishing, horseback riding, cross-country skiing, mountaineering, snowshoeing

Saguaro National Park, Tucson, Arizona

Area: 91,446 acres

Open: Year-round

Major attractions: Giant Saguaro cacti, wildlife

Activities: Hiking, nature walks, wildlife viewing

Sequoia National Park, Three Rivers, California

Area: 402,510 acres

Open: Year-round

Major attractions: High Sierra peaks, including Mount Whitney (14,494 feet), sequoia forests, wildlife

continues

Activities: Camping, hiking, fishing, caving, horseback riding, climbing, mountaineering, wildlife viewing

Shenandoah National Park, Luray, Virginia
Area: 199,014 acres
Open: Year-round
Major attractions: Blue Ridge Mountains, hardwood forests, wildflowers
Activities: Camping, hiking, horseback riding, nature walks, biking, climbing

Theodore Roosevelt Memorial National Park, Medora, North Dakota
Area: 70,447 acres
Open: Year-round
Major attractions: Little Missouri River badlands, site of former President Theodore Roosevelt's ranch, wildlife
Activities: Camping, hiking, kayaking, horseback riding, bird-watching, nature walks

Virgin Islands National Park, St. John, U.S. Virgin Islands
Area: 14,689 acres
Open: Year-round
Major attractions: Tropical plant and animal life, marine life, sandy beaches, colonial plantations, early Carib relics
Activities: Camping, hiking, fishing, nature walks, swimming, diving, kayaking, snorkeling

Voyageurs National Park, International Falls, Minnesota
Area: 218,200 acres
Open: Year-round
Major attractions: Evergreen forests, ancient rock outcroppings, bogs, glacial lakes, wildlife
Activities: Boating (access to interior is mainly by boat), camping, fishing, hiking, swimming, skiing

Wind Cave National Park, Hot Springs, South Dakota
Area: 28,295 acres
Open: Year-round
Major attractions: Limestone caverns, bison herds, wildlife
Activities: Camping, hiking, nature walks, caving, horseback riding, stargazing

Wrangell-St.Elias National Park and Preserve, Glennallen, Alaska
Area: 8,323,618 acres
Open: Year-round
Major attractions: Largest U.S. national park, greatest concentration of peaks over 14,000 feet in North America, rugged coastline, boreal forests, alpine tundra, wildlife

Activities: Climbing, hunting, fishing, mountaineering, camping, boating, kayaking, wildlife viewing, white-water rafting, horseback riding

Yellowstone National Park, Yellowstone National Park, Wyoming
Area: 2,219,791 acres
Open: Year-round
Major attractions: Oldest national park, spectacular wilderness, Old Faithful geyser, hot springs, lakes, streams, and waterfalls, wildlife, the Grand Canyon of the Yellowstone
Activities: Camping, hiking, fishing, cross-country skiing, boating, nature walks, horseback riding

Yosemite National Park, Yosemite National Park, California
Area: 761,266 acres
Open: Year-round
Major attractions: Mountain peaks over 10,000 feet, spectacular granite domes and monoliths, highest waterfall in the United States, sequoia groves, wildlife
Activities: Camping, hiking, rock climbing, mountaineering, fishing, horseback riding, biking, nature walks, swimming, skiing

Zion National Park, Springdale, Utah
Area: 146,592 acres
Open: Year-round (Visitor center open from Memorial Day through Labor Day)
Major attractions: Huge canyons and gorges carved by mountain rivers, colorful rock cliffs, wildlife
Activities: Camping, hiking, horseback riding, climbing, skiing

NATIONAL WILDLIFE REFUGES LOCATIONS AND FACILITIES

This is not a listing of the entire Refuge System, but of only those refuges that offer visitor centers or visitor contact stations. The address given is that of the office that administers the refuge; it does not necessarily reflect the location of the refuge.

Refuge conditions, regulations, and activities are varied and subject to change. Please check with the refuge manager regarding conditions, regulations, and facilities for persons with disabilities before taking a trip to a refuge. Check http://refuges.fws.gov for more information.

"The Animal Kingdom" and "The Plant Kingdom" in chapter 3
Go to

continues

Travel

	Food/lodging nearby	Hunting	Fishing	Nonmotorized boating	Motorized boating	Archaeological sites	Auto-tour route	Hiking trails	Wildlife viewing sites	Educational programs	Visitor contact station	Visitor center	Winter	Fall	Summer	Spring
Alabama																
Bon Secour NWR, 12295 State Hwy. 180, Gulf Shores, AL 36542	●			●			●	●			●			●		●
Choctaw NWR, P.O. Box 808, Jackson, AL 36545	●	●	●				●				●		●	●		●
Eufaula NWR, 509 Old Hwy. 165, Eufaula, AL 36027	●	●	●	●	●		●	●			●	●	●	●		●
Wheeler NWR, 2700 Refuge Hq. Rd., Decatur, AL 35603	●	●	●		●	●					●	●	●	●		
Alaska																
Alaska Maritime NWR, 2355 Kachemak Bay Dr, Suite 101, Homer, AK 99603	●					●					●	●			●	●
Aleutian Islands Unit, PCS 486, Box 5251, FPO AP, Adak, AK 96506-5251		●	●		●	●									●	●
Alaska Peninsula NWR, P.O. Box 277, King Salmon, AK 99613		●	●	●	●											
Arctic NWR, 101 12th Ave.,, Box 20, Fairbanks, AK 99701		●	●	●	●							●			●	
Becharof NWR, P.O. Box 277, King Salmon, AK 99613		●	●	●	●			●				●				
Innoko NWR, P.O. Box 69, McGrath, AK, 99627		●	●	●	●											
Izembek NWR, #1 Izembek Dr., P.O. Box 127, Cold Bay, AK 99571		●	●	●	●											
Kanuti NWR, 101 12th Ave., Box 11, Room 262, Fairbanks, AK 99701		●	●	●	●							●			●	●
Kenai NWR, P.O. Box 2139, Soldotna, AK 99669-2139	●	●	●	●	●					●		●		●		
Kodiak NWR, 1390 Buskin River Rd., Kodiak, AK 99615		●	●	●	●							●				
Koyukuk NWR, P.O. Box 287, Galena, AK 99741		●	●	●	●											
Nowitna NWR, P.O. Box 287, Galena, AK 99742		●	●	●	●											
Tetlin NWR, P.O. Box 779, Tok, AK 99780	●	●	●	●	●	●	●	●		●	●	●		●		●
Togiak NWR, P.O. Box 270, Dillingham, AK 99576		●	●	●	●									●	●	●
Yukon Delta NWR, P.O. Box 346, Bethel, AK 99559-0346		●	●	●	●							●				
Yukon Flats NWR, 101 12th Ave., Room 264, Fairbanks, AK 99701	●	●	●	●	●			●						●	●	

Travel

National Wildlife Refuges Locations and Facilities, Continued

	Food/lodging nearby	Hunting	Fishing	Nonmotorized boating	Motorized boating	Archaeological sites	Auto-tour route	Hiking trails	Wildlife viewing sites	Educational programs	Visitor contact station	Visitor center	Winter	Fall	Summer	Spring
Arizona																
Bill Williams NWR, 60911 Hwy. 95, Parker, AZ 85344		■	■				■	■	■	■	■		■	■		■
Buenos Aires, NWR, P.O. Box 109, Sasabe, AZ 85633	■	■				■	■		■	■	■	■	■	■	■	■
Cabeza Prieta NWR, 1611 North Second Ave., Ajo, AZ 85321		■									■					
Cibola NWR, Route 2, Box 138, Cibola, AZ 85328-9609	■			■	■				■	■	■	■	■			
Imperial NWR, P.O. Box 72217, Yuma, AZ 85365		■		■	■	■		■	■	■			■	■		■
Kofa NWR, 356 W. 1st St., P.O. Box 6290, Yuma, AZ 85366-6290		■						■			■		■			
Arkansas																
Big Lake NWR, P.O. Box 67, Manila, AR 72006		■	■	■			■		■	■	■	■	■	■		■
Felsenthal NWR, P.O. Box 1157, Crossett, AR 71635	■	■	■	■	■		■	■	■	■	■	■	■	■		■
Holla Bend NWR, Rt. 1, Box 59, Dardanelle, AR 72834-9704		■	■	■	■		■	■	■	■	■	■	■	■		■
Wapanocca NWR, P.O. Box 279, Turrell, AR 72384-0279		■	■	■			■		■	■	■	■	■	■		■
White River NWR, 321 West 7th St., P.O. Box 308, DeWitt, AR 72042-0308									■						■	
California																
Don Edwards San Francisco Bay NWR, P.O. Box 524, Newark, CA 94560-0524	■								■	■	■	■	■	■		■
Havasu NWR, P.O. Box 3009, Needles, CA 92363	■	■	■	■	■	■			■	■	■		■	■		■
Humbolt Bay NWR, 1020 Ranch Rd., Loleta, CA 95551-9633	■			■		■			■	■	■		■	■		■
Kern NWR, P.O. Box 670, Delano, CA 93216-0670	■	■	■	■			■		■	■	■		■	■		■
Lower Klamath NWR, Rt. 1, Box 74, Tulelake, CA 96134-9715	■	■		■					■	■	■		■	■	■	■
Modoc NWR, P.O. Box 1610, Alturas, CA 96101-1610	■	■		■	■		■		■	■	■		■	■		■
Sacramento NWR, 752 County Rd. 99W, Willows, CA 95988-9639	■		■	■			■		■	■	■		■	■		■
Salton Sea NWR, 906 W. Sinclair Rd., Calipatria, CA 92233-0120	■	■							■	■	■		■	■		■

Sweetwater Marsh NWR, 301 Caspian Way, Imperial Beach, CA 91932-3149

Tijuana Slough NWR, 301 Caspian Way, Imperial Beach, CA 91932-3149

Tule Lake NWR, Rt. 1, Box 74, Tulelake, CA 96134-9715

Colorado

Alamosa NWR, 9383 El Rancho Ln., Alamosa, CO 81101-9003

Arapaho NWR, P.O. Box 457, Walden, CO 80480-0457

Browns Park NWR, 1319 Hwy. 318, Maybell, CO 81640

Rocky Mountain Arsenal NWR, Bldg. 111, Commerce City, CO 80022-1748

Connecticut

Stewart B. McKinney NWR, 730 Old Clinton Rd., P.O. Box 1030, Westbrook, CT 06498-1030

Delaware

Bombay Hook NWR, 2591 Whitehall Neck Rd., Smyrna, DE 19977-9764

Prime Hook NWR, RD 3, Box 195, Milton, DE 19968-9751

Florida

Arthur R. Marshall Loxahatchee NWR, 10216 Lee Road, Boynton Beach, FL 33437-4796

Cedar Keys NWR, 16450 NW 31st Pl., Chiefland, FL 32626

Chassahowitzka NWR, 1502 S.E. Kings Bay Dr., Crystal River, FL 34429

Crystal River NWR, 1502 S.E. Kings Bay Dr., Crystal River, FL 34429

Egmont Key NWR, 1502 S.E. Kings Bay Dr., Crystal River, FL 34429

Great White Heron NWR, P.O. Box 430510, Big Pine Key, FL, 33043-0510

Hobe Sound NWR, P.O. Box 645, Hobe Sound, FL 33475-0645

J.N. "Ding" Darling NWR, 1 Wildlife Dr., Sanibel, FL 33957

Key West NWR, P.O. Box 430510, Big Pine Key, FL 33043-0510

Lake Woodruff NWR, 4490 Grand Ave., P.O. Box 488, DeLeon Springs, FL 32130-0488

Lower Suwannee NWR, 16450 NW 31st Pl., Chiefland, FL 32626

Merritt Island NWR, P.O. Box 6504, Titusville, FL 32782

National Key Deer Refuge, P.O. Box 430510, Big Pine Key, FL 33043-0510

St. Marks NWR, P.O. Box 68, St. Marks, FL 32355

St. Vincent NWR, 479 Market St., P.O. Box 447, Apalachicola, FL 32329-0447

continues

Travel

Travel

National Wildlife Refuges Locations and Facilities, Continued

Location	Food/lodging nearby	Hunting	Fishing	Nonmotorized boating	Motorized boating	Archaeological sites	Auto-tour route	Hiking trails	Wildlife viewing sites	Educational programs	Visitor contact station	Visitor center	Winter	Fall	Summer	Spring
Georgia																
Banks Lake NWR, Route 2, Box 3330, Folkson, GA 31537			●	●	●				●		●			●		●
Harris Neck NWR, 1000 Business Center Dr., Suite 10, Savannah, GA 31405	●	●	●	●				●	●	●	●			●	●	●
Okefenokee NWR, Route 2, Box 3330, Folkson, GA 31405	●		●	●	●			●	●	●	●	●		●		●
Piedmont NWR, Route 1, Box 670, Juliette Rd., Round Oak, GA 31038	●	●	●		●	●		●	●	●		●		●		●
Hawaii																
Hakalau Forest NWR, 32 Kinoole St., Suite 101, Hilo, HI 96720-2469		●						●	●		●		●	●	●	●
Kealia Pond NWR, P.O. Box 1042, Kihei, HI 96753-1042									●							
Kilauea Point NWR, P.O. Box 1128, Kilauea, Kauai, HI 96754-1128						●		●	●	●		●	●	●	●	●
Midway Atoll NWR, P.O. Box 29460, Midway Island Station #4, Lihue, HI 96820-1860			●			●			●		●		●	●		●
Idaho																
Bear Lake NWR, 370 Webster, P.O. Box 9, Montpelier, ID 83254-1019	●	●	●	●			●	●	●	●	●		●	●	●	●
Camas NWR, 2150 East 2350 North, Hamer, ID 83425-5030		●														
Deer Flat NWR, 13751 Upper Embankment Rd., Nampa, ID 83686-8046		●	●	●	●	●	●	●	●	●	●		●	●	●	●
Grays Lake NWR, 74 Grays Lake Rd., Wayan, ID 83285-5006	●		●						●							
Kootenai NWR, HCR 60, Box 283 (Westside Rd.) Bonners Ferry, ID 83805-9518																
Minidoka NWR, 961 E. Minidoka Dam, Rupert, ID 83350-9414	●	●	●	●	●		●	●	●	●	●		●	●	●	●
Illinois																
Brussels District, HCR, Box 107, Brussels, IL 62013-0107			●	●	●			●	●	●	●	●	●	●		●
Chautauqua NWR, 19031 E. County Rd. 2015 N, Havana, IL, 62644				●					●						●	
Clarence Cannon NWR, 1704 North 24th St., Quincy, IL 62301	●	●	●	●	●		●	●	●		●					

Crab Orchard NWR, 8588 Rte. 148, Marion, IL, 62959

Cypress Creek NWR, 0137 Rustic Campus Dr., Ullin, IL 62992

Mark Twain NWR Complex, 1704 N. 24th St., Quincy, IL 62301

Savanna District, P.O. Box 336, Savanna, IL 61074

Indiana

Muscatatuck NWR, 12985 E. U.S. Hwy. 50, Seymour, IN 47274

Iowa

DeSoto NWR, 1434 316th Ln., Missouri Valley, IA 51555-7033

McGregor District, P.O. Box 460, McGregor, IA 52157

Neal Smith NWR, P.O. Box 399, Prairie City, IA 50228

Union Slough NWR, 1710 360th St., Titonka, IA 50480

Wapello District, 10728 County Rd. X61, Wapello, IA 52653-9477

Kansas

Flint Hills NWR, P.O. Box 128, 530 West Maple, Hartford, KS 66854

Kirwin NWR, R.R. 1, Box 103, Kirwin, KS 67644

Quivira NWR, R.R. #3, Box 48A, Stafford, KS 67578

Louisiana

Atchafalaya NWR, 1010 Gause Blvd., Bldg. 936, Slidell, LA 70458

Cameron Prairie NWR, 1428 Hwy. 27, Bell City, LA 70630

Catahoula NWR, P.O. Drawer Z, Rhinehart, LA 71363-0201

D'Arbonne NWR, Route 2, Box 401-A, Farmerville, LA 71241

Delta NWR, 1010 Gause Blvd., Bldg. 936, Slidell, LA 70458

Grande Cote NWR, 401 Island Rd., Marksville, LA 71351

Lacassine NWR, 209 Nature Rd., Lake Arthur, LA 70549

Lake Ophelia NWR, 401 Island Rd., Marksville, LA 71351

Sabine NWR, 3000 Holly Beach Hwy., Hackberry, LA 70645

Tensas River NWR, Route 2, Box 295, Tallulah, LA 71282

Upper Ouachita NWR, Route 2, Box 401-A, Farmerville, LA 71241

Maine

Moosehorn NWR, RR 1, Box 202, Ste. 1, Baring, ME 04694-9703

Petit Manan NWR, P.O. Box 279, Millbridge, ME 04658-0279

continues

National Wildlife Refuges Locations and Facilities, *Continued*

	Food/lodging nearby	Hunting	Fishing	Nonmotorized boating	Motorized boating	Archaeological sites	Auto-tour route	Hiking trails	Wildlife viewing sites	Educational programs	Visitor contact station	Visitor center	Winter	Fall	Summer	Spring
Maine, continued																
Rachel Carson NWR, 321 Port Rd., Wells, ME 04090	■	■							■		■			■	■	■
Sunhaze Meadows NWR, 1033 S. Main St., Old Town, ME 04468-2023		■	■	■	■								■	■	■	■
Maryland																
Blackwater NWR, 2145 Key Wallace Dr., Cambridge, MD 21613-9536	■	■	■	■	■		■	■	■	■	■	■	■	■	■	■
Eastern Neck NWR, 1730 Eastern Neck Rd., Rock Hall, MD 21661-1815	■	■	■	■			■		■		■		■	■	■	
Patuxent Research Refuge, 12100 Beech Forest Rd., Suite 138, Laurel, MD 20708-4036		■						■			■	■			■	■
Massachusetts																
Great Meadows NWR, Weir Hill Rd., Sudbury, MA 01776-1427	■	■	■					■	■	■	■			■	■	■
Monomoy NWR, Wikis Way, Morris Island, Chatham, MA 02633-2556	■		■						■		■			■	■	
Parker River NWR, 261 Northern Blvd., Plum Island, Newburyport, MA 01950-4315	■	■	■	■	■		■	■	■		■		■	■	■	■
Silvio O. Conte National Fish and Wildlife Refuge, 28 Avenue A, Turner Falls, MA 01376											■		■		■	■
Michigan																
Seney NWR, HCR #2, Box 1, Seney, MI 49883	■	■	■	■	■		■	■	■	■	■	■	■	■	■	■
Shiawassee NWR, 6975 Mower Rd., Saginaw, MI 48601	■	■	■						■		■			■		■
Minnesota																
Agassiz NWR, Route 1, Box 74, Middle River, MN 56737	■	■					■			■	■		■	■	■	■
Big Stone NWR, RR 1, Box 25, Odessa, MN 56276	■	■					■				■		■	■	■	■
Fergus Falls WMD, Route 1, Box 76, Fergus Falls, MN 56537		■									■	■	■	■	■	■
Hamden Slough NWR, Route 1, Box 32, Audubon, MN 56511-9713	■	■	■	■			■		■		■				■	■
Litchfield WMD, 971 East Frontage Rd., Litchfield, MN 55355	■													■	■	■

Minnesota Valley NWR, 3815 East 80th St., Bloomington, MN 55425-1600

Morris WMD, Route 1, Box 877, Morris, MN 56267

Rice Lake NWR, Route 2, Box 67, McGregor, MN 55760

Rydell NWR, Route 3, Box 105, Erskine, MN 56535

Tamarac NWR, HC 10, Box 145, Rochert, MN 56578-9735

Upper Mississippi River Wildlife & Fish Refuge, 51 E. 4th St., Rm. 1010, Winona, MN 55987

Winona District, 51 E. 4th St., Room 203, Winona, MN 55987

Mississippi

Mississippi Sandhill Crane NWR, 7200 Crane Ln., Gautier, MS 39553-2500

Mississippi WMD, P.O. Box 1070, 16736 Highway 8 West, Grenada, MS 38902-1070

Noxubee NWR, Route #1, Box 142, Brooksville, MS 39739

St. Catherine Creek NWR, P.O. Box 117, Sibley, MS 39165

Yazoo NWR, Route 1, Box 286, 728 Yazoo Refuge Rd., Hollandale, MS 38748

Missouri

Annada District, P.O. Box 88, Annada, MO 63330-0088

Mingo NWR, 24279 State Hwy 51, Puxico, MO 63960

Squaw Creek NWR, P.O. Box 158, Mound City, MO 64470

Swan Lake NWR, Route 1, Box 29A, Summer, MO 64681-0068

Montana

Benton Lake NWR, 922 Bootlegger Tr., Great Falls, MT 59404-6133

Bowdoin NWR, HC 65 Box 570, Malta, MT 59538

Charles M. Russell NWR, P.O. Box 110, Lewistown, MT 59457-0110

Lee Metcalf NWR, P.O. Box 247, Stevensville, MT 59870

Medicine Lake NWR, 223 North Shore Rd., Medicine Lake, MT 59247-9600

National Bison Range, 132 Bison Range Rd., Moiese, MT 59824

Red Rock Lakes NWR, Monida Star Route, Box 15, Lima, MT 59739

Nebraska

Fort Niobrara NWR, HC 14, Box 67, Valentine, NE 69201

Rainwater Basin WMD, P.O. Box 1686, Kearney, NE 68848-1686

Nevada

Ash Meadows NWR, P.O. Box 115, Amargosa Valley, NV 89020

Ruby Lake NWR, HC 60, Box 860, Ruby Valley, NV 89833-9802

continues

Travel

Travel

National Wildlife Refuges Locations and Facilities, Continued

Refuge key:

New Hampshire
- R1 — Great Bay NWR, 336 Nimble Hill Rd., Newington, NH 03801
- R2 — Lake Umbagog NWR, P.O. Box 240, Errol, NH 03579
- R3 — Wapack NWR, Weir Hill Rd., Sudbury, MA 01776-1427

New Jersey
- R4 — Cape May NWR, 24 Kimbles Beach Rd., Cape May Courthouse, NJ 08210-4207
- R5 — Edwin B. Forsythe NWR-Barnegat, 70 Collingstown Rd., P.O. Box 544, Barnegat, NJ 08005-0544
- R6 — Edwin B. Forsythe NWR-Brigantine, P.O. Box 72, Great Creek Rd., Oceanville, NJ 08231-0072
- R7 — Great Swamp NWR, 152 Pleasant Plains Rd., Basking Ridge, NJ 07920
- R8 — Wallkill River NWR, P.O. Box 383, Sussex, NJ 07461-0383

New Mexico
- R9 — Bitter Lake NWR, P.O. Box 7, Roswell, NM 88202-0007
- R10 — Bosque del Apache NWR, P.O. Box 1246, Socorro, NM 87801-1246
- R11 — Las Vegas NWR, Route 1, Box 399, Las Vegas, NM 87701
- R12 — Maxwell NWR, P.O. Box 276, Maxwell, NM 87728-0276

New York
- R13 — Jamaica Bay WR, Public Affairs Office, 210 New York Avenue, Staten Island, NY 10305
- R14 — Iroquois NWR, P.O. Box 517, 1101 Casey Rd., Alabama, NY 14003-0517
- R15 — Montezuma NWR, 3395 Routes 5/20 East, Seneca Falls, NY 13148-9778
- R16 — Wertheim NWR, P.O. Box 21, Smith Rd., Shirley, NY 11967-0021

ACTIVITIES / WILDLIFE VIEWING SEASONS	R1	R2	R3	R4	R5	R6	R7	R8	R9	R10	R11	R12	R13	R14	R15	R16
Food/lodging nearby			■	■		■		■		■	■	■	■	■		■
Hunting	■			■	■			■		■	■			■	■	
Fishing		■		■		■		■	■		■			■	■	■
Nonmotorized boating		■		■		■			■		■			■		■
Motorized boating		■				■			■							■
Archaeological sites																
Auto-tour route						■			■	■			■		■	
Hiking trails	■			■		■			■	■			■		■	
Wildlife viewing sites		■		■		■		■	■	■	■		■	■	■	■
Educational programs						■			■	■			■		■	
Visitor contact station	■	■				■		■	■	■	■			■		■
Visitor center									■	■			■		■	
Winter									■	■	■		■	■	■	■
Fall	■	■	■	■		■		■	■	■	■		■	■	■	■
Summer		■	■						■	■						
Spring			■	■	■	■		■	■	■			■	■	■	■

North Carolina

Mackay Island NWR, P.O. Box 39, Knotts Island, NC 27950-0039

Mattamuskeet NWR, Route 1, Box N-2, Swan Quarter, NC 27885

Pea Island NWR, P.O. Box 1969, Manteo, NC 27954-1969

Pee Dee NWR, Rt. 1, Box 92, Wadesboro, NC 28170

Roanoke River NWR, P.O. Box 430, Windsor, NC 27983

North Dakota

Arrowwood NWR, 7745 11th St. SE, Pingree, ND 58476-8308

Arrowwood WMD, 7745 11th St. SE, Pingree, ND 58476-8308

Audubon NWR, RR 1, P.O. Box 16, Coleharbor, ND 58531

Chase Lake Prairie Project WMD, 5924 19th St. SE, Woodworth, ND 58496

Des Lacs NWR, P.O. Box 578, Kenmare, ND 58746-0578

Devils Lake WMD, P.O. Box 908, Devils Lake, ND 58301-0908

J. Clark Sayler NWR, P.O. Box 66, Upham, ND 58789

Kulm WMD, P.O. Box E, Kulm, ND 58456-0170

Lake Ilo NWR, P.O. Box 127, Dunn Center, ND, 58626-0127

Long Lake NWR, 12000 353rd St. SE, Moffitt, ND 58560-9740

Sullys Hill National Game Preserve, P.O. Box 908. Devils Lake, ND 58301-0908

Tewaukon NWR, 9754 143½ Ave. SE. Cayuga, ND 58013

Upper Souris NWR, 17705 212th Ave. NW, Berthold, ND 58718-9666

Valley City WMD, 11515 River Rd., Valley City, ND 58072-9619

Ohio

Ottawa NWR, 14000 West State Rt. 2, Oak Harbor, OH 43449

Oklahoma

Salt Plains NWR, Route 1, Box 76, Jet, OK 73749-9722

Sequoyah NWR, Route 1, Box 18A, Vian, OK 74962

Tishomingo NWR, Route 1, Box 151, Tishomingo, OK 73460

Washita NWR, Route 1, Box 68, Butler, OK 73625-9744

Wichita Mountains Wildlife Refuge, RR 1, Box 448, Indiahoma, OK 73552

Oregon

Ankeny NWR, 2301 Wintel Rd., Jefferson, OR 97352-9758

Hart Mountain National Antelope Refuge, P.O. Box 111, Lakeview, OR 97630-0107

Klamath Forest NWR, HC 63, Box 303, Chiloquin, OR 97624-9616

Malheur NWR, HC 72, Box 245, Princeton, OR 97721-9505

continues

Travel

National Wildlife Refuges Locations and Facilities, Continued

Travel

Refuge	Food/lodging nearby	Hunting	Fishing	Nonmotorized boating	Motorized boating	Archaeological sites	Auto-tour route	Hiking trails	Wildlife viewing sites	Educational programs	Visitor contact station	Visitor center	Winter	Fall	Summer	Spring
Oregon, continued																
McNary NWR, P.O. Box 1700, Umatilla, OR 97882-0700		■	■					■	■	■	■	■		■		■
Sheldon, NWR, P.O. Box 111, Lakeview, OR 97630-0107		■	■							■	■				■	■
Umatilla NWR, P.O. Box 700, Umatilla, OR 97882-0700	■	■	■	■	■	■	■		■	■	■		■	■	■	■
William L. Finley NWR, 26208 Finley Refuge Rd., Corvallis, OR 97333-9533	■	■	■			■	■	■	■	■	■	■	■	■		■
Pennsylvania																
Erie NWR, 11296 Wood Duck Ln., Guys Mills, PA 16327		■	■						■	■	■			■		■
John Heinz NWR at Tinicum, Ste. 104, Scott Plaza 2, Philadelphia, PA 19113	■							■	■	■	■	■			■	■
Rhode Island																
Ninigret NWR, P.O. Box 307, Shoreline Plaza, Rte. 1A, Charlestown, RI 02813-0317	■		■					■	■	■	■	■	■	■	■	■
Sachuest Point NWR, P.O. Box 307, Shoreline Plaza, Rte. 1A, Charlestown, RI 02813-0317	■		■						■				■	■	■	■
South Carolina																
ACE Basin NWR, P.O. Box 848, Hollywood, SC 29449-0848		■	■			■			■	■	■		■	■	■	■
Cape Romain NWR, 5801 Hwy. 17 North, Awendaw, SC 29429	■	■		■	■		■		■	■	■	■	■		■	■
Carolina Sandhills NWR, Rte. 2, Box 100, McBee, SC 29101	■	■	■	■	■		■	■	■	■	■		■		■	■
Santee NWR, Rte. 2, Box 370, Summerton, SC 29148	■	■							■	■	■			■		■
South Dakota																
Lacreek NWR, HC 5, Box 114, Martin, SD 57551	■	■	■	■	■		■	■	■	■	■	■	■	■	■	■
Lake Andes NWR, 38672 291st St., Lake Andes, SD 57356-6838	■	■	■	■	■				■	■	■					■

Madison WMD, P.O. Box 48, Madison, SD 57042-0048

Sand Lake NWR, 39650 Sand Lake Dr., Columbia, SD 57433

Waubay NWR, RR1, Box 39, Waubay, SD 57273-9910

Tennessee

Chickasaw NWR, 1505 Sand Bluff Rd., Ripley, TN 38063

Cross Creeks NWR, 643 Wildlife Rd., Dover, TN 37058

Hatchie NWR, 4172 Hwy. 76 South, Brownsville, TN 38012-8332

Reelfoot NWR, 4343 Hwy. 157, Union City, TN 38261

Tennessee NWR, P.O. Box 849, 810 East Wood St., Paris, TN 38242-0849

Texas

Anahuac NWR, P.O. Box 278, Anahuac, TX 77514-0278

Aransas NWR, P.O. Box 100, Austwell, TX 77950-0100

Atwater Prairie Chicken NWR, P.O. Box 519, Eagle Lake, TX 77434-0519

Brazoria NWR, 1212 North Velasco, Ste. 200, Angleton, TX 77515

Buffalo Lake NWR, P.O. Box 179, Umbarger, TX 79091-0179

Hagerman NWR, 6465 Refuge Rd., Sherman, TX 75092-5817

Laguna Atascosa NWR, P.O. Box 450, Rio Hondo, TX 78583-0450

McFaddin NWR, P.O. Box 609, Sabine Pass, TX 77655-0609

Muleshoe NWR, P.O. Box 549, Muleshoe, TX 79347-0549

San Bernard NWR, 1212 North Velasco, Ste. 200, Angleton, TX 77515

Santa Ana NWR, Rte. 2, Box 202A, Alamo, TX 78516

Utah

Bear River Migratory Bird Refuge, 58 South 950 West, Brigham City, UT 84302

Fish Springs NWR, P.O. Box 568, Dugway, UT 84022-0568

Ouray NWR, 266 West 100 North, Ste. 2, Vernal, UT 84078

Vermont

Missisquoi NWR, P.O. Box 163, Swanton, VT 05488-0163

Virginia

Back Bay NWR, 4005 Sandpiper Rd., Virginia Beach, VA 23456-2412

Chincoteague NWR, P.O. Box 62, Chincoteague, VA 23336-0062

Eastern Shore of Virginia NWR, 5003 Hallett Circle, Cape Charles, VA 23310

Presquile NWR, P.O. Box 189, Prince George, VA 23875

continues

Travel

National Wildlife Refuges Locations and Facilities, Continued

	Food/lodging nearby	Hunting	Fishing	Nonmotorized boating	Motorized boating	Archaeological sites	Auto-tour route	Hiking trails	Wildlife viewing sites	Educational programs	Visitor contact station	Visitor center	Winter	Fall	Summer	Spring
Washington																
Columbia NWR, P.O. Drawer F, 735 E. Main St., Othello, WA 99344-0227	■	■	■	■	■		■	■	■	■	■			■		■
Conboy Lake NWR, Box 5, 100 Wildlife Refuge Rd., Glenwood, WA 98619-0005	■	■						■	■	■	■					■
Little Pend Oreille NWR, 1310 Bear Creek Rd., Colville, WA 99114-9713		■	■						■		■				■	■
McNary NWR, P.O. Box 1700, Umatilla, OR 97882-0700	■	■														
Nisqually NWR, 100 Brown Farm Rd., Olympia, WA 98516-2302		■	■				■	■	■	■	■		■	■		■
Ridgefield NWR, P.O. Box 457, 301 N. Thrid St., Ridgefield, WA 98642-0457		■	■		■		■		■	■	■		■		■	
Turnbull NWR, 26010 South Smith Rd., Cheney, WA 99004-9326		■		■	■		■	■	■	■	■		■	■	■	■
West Virginia																
Ohio River Islands NWR, P.O. Box 1811, Parkersburg, WV 26102-1811		■														
Wisconsin																
Horicon NWR, W4279 Headquarters Rd., Mayville, WI 53050	■	■	■	■			■	■	■	■	■		■	■	■	
Leopold WMD, W4279 Headquarters Rd., Mayville, WI 53050		■	■	■											■	
Necedah NWR, W7996 20th St. West, Necedah, WI 54646-7531		■	■				■	■	■	■	■					
St. Croix WMD, 1764 95th St., New Richmond, WI 54017									■		■					
Trempealeau NWR, W28488 Refuge Rd., Trempealeau, WI 54661-8272																
Wyoming																
National Elk Refuge, 675 E. Broadway, P.O. Box C, Jackson, WY 83001	■	■	■	■			■	■	■	■	■		■	■	■	■
Seedskadee NWR, P.O. Box 700, Green River, WY 82935-0700		■	■						■	■					■	■
Puerto Rico																
Cabo Rojo NWR, P.O. Box 510, Boqueron, PR 00622-0510	■							■	■	■	■		■	■	■	■
Culebra NWR, P.O. Box 190, Culebra, PR 00775	■	■	■	■				■			■		■	■	■	

ACTIVITIES

WILDLIFE VIEWING SEASONS

ANIMAL HIGHLIGHTS OF SOME POPULAR NATIONAL WILDLIFE REFUGES

State	Refuge	Wildlife
Alabama	Wheeler	Ducks, geese, alligators
Alaska	Kenai	Moose, wolf, bear, swan, caribou
Arizona	Imperial	Yuma clapperrail, bald eagle
Arkansas	Felsenthal	American alligator, eagle, red-cockaded woodpecker, waterfowl
California	San Francisco Bay	Waterfowl, harbor seals
Colorado	Brown's Park	Antelope, mule deer, elk, waterfowl
Florida	St. Mark's	Alligator, otter, various toads, black bear, woodpecker, gopher tortoise
Georgia	Okefenokee	Alligator, sandhill crane, owl, woodstork
Idaho	Bear Lake	White-faced ibis
Illinois	Crab Orchard	Beaver, deer, bald eagle, wild turkey, Canadian geese
Iowa	De Soto	Snow and Canadian geese, eagles, many duck species
Kansas	Kirwin	Deer, quail, wild turkey, river otter
Louisiana	Tensas River	Deer, black bears, waterfowl, raptors
Maine	Moosehorn	Black bear, beaver, porcupine, American woodcock, bald eagle, waterfowl
Maryland	Blackwater	Deer, waterfowl, Delmarva fox squirrel, bald eagles
Massachusetts	Monomoy	Shorebird, waterfowl, harbor and gray seals
Michigan	Sency	Black bear, beaver, white-tailed deer, eagle, osprey, otter
Minnesota	Tamarac	White-tailed deer, black bear, river otter, moose, eagle, waterfowl, wild turkey, porcupine, beaver
Mississippi	Noxubee	White-tailed deer, alligator, red-cockaded woodpecker, wild turkey
Missouri	Mingo	White-tailed deer, coyote, fox, weasel, bobcat, waterfowl
Montana	Charles M. Russell	Antelope, bighorn sheep, sharp-tailed grouse, bobcat, coyote
Nebraska	Fort Niobrara	Buffalo, elk, Texas longhorn, white-tailed deer, sharp-tailed grouse, prairie chicken, meadowlark, sandpiper
Nevada	Stillwater	Long-billed dowitcher, black-necked stilt, American white pelican, double-crested cormorant, white-faced ibis
New Jersey	Forsythe (Brigantine Division)	Otter, red fox, bald eagle, peregrine falcon, hawk, owl, snowgeese
New Mexico	Bosque del Apache	Coyote, snow geese, sandhill and white whooping crane, mule deer, porcupine, badger, mountain lion
New York	Iroquois	White-tailed deer, beaver, muskrat, fox, mink, raccoon, turkey, waterfowl, eagle
North Carolina	Alligator River	Waterfowl, American woodcock, raptors, black bears, American alligators, white-tailed deer, raccoons, rabbits, quail, river otters, red wolves, red-cockaded woodpeckers
North Dakota	Des Lacs	Snow geese, ducks, sparrow
Oklahoma	Wichita Mountains	Bison, elk, buffalo, deer, longhorn cattle, coyote, red-tailed hawk, prairie dog
Oregon	Malheur	Tundra swan, sandhill crane, owl, hawk, egret, heron
Pennsylvania	Erie	Eagle, owl, sandpiper, beaver
Rhode Island	Ninigret	Raptors, waterfowl, songbirds, osprey, coyote, white-tailed deer, opossum, hawk
South Carolina	Cape Romain	Alligator, raccoon, loggerhead sea turtle, deer, waterfowl, shorebirds
South Dakota	Lacreek	Eagle, falcon, whooping crane, owl, hawk, trumpeter swans, geese
Tennessee	Reelfoot	Ducks, geese, raptors, wading birds, shorebirds, bald eagle, osprey
Texas	Hagerman	Bobwhite quail, mourning dove, white-tailed deer, bobcat, geese, ducks
Utah	Fish Springs	Heron, egret, white-faced ibis, coyote, raven, gopher snake

continues

State	Refuge	Wildlife
Vermont	Missisquoi	Deer, raccoon, muskrat, waterfowl
Virginia	Chinocteague	Wild pony, deer, more than 100 species of birds
Washington	Columbia	Coyote, hawk, owl, duck, geese
Wisconsin	Horicon	Mink, raccoon, coyote, red fox, white-tailed deer, crane, heron, ducks
Wyoming	National Elk	Elk, moose, bighorn sheep, mule deer, coyote, badger, porcupine, weasel

---

A
Closer
Look

Best Theme Parks

Although the traditional American tourist attractions—from Mount Rushmore to the Grand Canyon to the Statue of Liberty to the Golden Gate Bridge—are still high on many travelers' itineraries, since the 1950s the greatest volume of visitors has been seen at "theme" amusement parks modeled on the pioneering, enormously successful Disneyland. U.S. amusement parks entertain more than 170 million visitors a year. These are the top 10 according to *Amusement Business Magazine*.

1. **Magic Kingdom, Walt Disney World, Buena Vista, Florida**
   http://disneyworld.disney.go.com/waltdisneyworld/parksandmore/parkindex?id=TPMagicKingdomPrk
2. **Disneyland, Anaheim, California**
   http://www.disneyland.disney.go.com/disneylandresort/disneyland/index?id=227
3. **Epcot Center, Walt Disney World, Buena Vista, Florida**
   http://disneyworld.disney.go.com/waltdisneyworld/parksandmore/parkindex?id=TPEpcotPrk
4. **Disney MGM Studios, Walt Disney World, Buena Vista, Florida**
   http://disneyworld.disney.go.com/waltdisneyworld/parksandmore/parkindex?id=TPDisneyMGMStudiosPrk
5. **Animal Kingdom, Disney–MGM–Studios, Walt Disney World, Buena Vista, Florida**
   http://disneyworld.disney.go.com/waltdisneyworld/parksandmore/parkindex?id=TPAnimalKingdomPrk/
6. **Universal Studios, Orlando, Florida**
   http://www.universalstudios.com/themeparks/html/orlando/univstudios/sfamily/
7. **Universal Islands of Adventure, Orlando, Florida**
   http://www.universalstudios.com/themeparks/html/orlando/islands/
8. **Universal Studios, Hollywood, California**
   http://www.universalstudios.com/themeparks/html/hollywood/main.html
9. **Sea World, Orlando, Florida**
   http://www.seaworld.com/seaworld/sw_florida/swfframe.html
10. **Busch Gardens, Tampa Bay, Florida**
    http://www.4adventure.com/buschgardens/bg_tampa/frame.html

---

INTERNATIONAL TRAVEL

GOVERNMENT TOURIST INFORMATION CENTERS

The following list includes the U.S. locations (and/or English-language web sites when available) for official tourist information centers of other nations. Tourist information also may be obtained by contacting the appropriate embassy (*see* "Requirements Before Proceeding Abroad: Individual Country Requirements," later in this chapter, for embassy addresses, telephone numbers, and web sites).

Additional information for certain countries may be obtained from the following regional associations:

European Travel Commission
(Members: Austria, Belgium, Croatia, Cyprus, Czech Republic, Denmark, Estonia, Finland, France, Germany, Great Britain, Greece, Hungary, Iceland, Ireland, Italy, Luxembourg, Malta, Monaco, Netherlands, Norway, Poland, Portugal, Romania, Slovenia, Spain, Sweden, Switzerland, and Turkey)
One Rockefeller Plaza, Suite 214
New York, NY 10020
212-218-1200
http://www.visiteurope.com

Scandinavian Tourist Board
(Members: Denmark, Finland, Iceland, Norway,
and Sweden)
655 Third Ave.
New York, NY 10017
800-346-4636 or 212-885-9700
http://www.goscandinavia.com

The following list includes national tourist offices
and associated web sites:

Anguilla Tourist Board
http://www.net.ai

Antigua and Barbuda Department of Tourism
610 Fifth Ave., Suite 311
New York, NY 10020
888-268-4227 or 212-541-4117
http://www.antigua-barbuda.org/

Argentina National Tourist Council
12 W. 56th St.
New York, NY 10019
212-603-0443
http://www.sectur.gov.ar/homepage.htm

Aruba Tourism Authority
1000 Harbor Blvd.
Weehawken, NJ 07087
800-862-7822 or 201-330-0800
http://www.interknowledge.com/aruba/index.html

Australian Tourist Commission
2049 Century Park East, Suite 1920
Los Angeles, CA 90067
310-229-4870
http://www.atc.net.au

Austrian National Tourist Office
P.O. Box 1142
New York, NY 10108-1142
212-944-6880
http://www.anto.com/

Bahamas Ministry of Tourism
150 E. 52nd St., 28th Floor North
New York, NY 10022
800-327-7678 or 212-758-2777
http://www.bahamas.com

Consulate General of Bangladesh
10850 Wilshire Blvd., Suite 1250
Los Angeles, CA 90024
310-441-9399
http://www.bangladeshconsulatela.com

Barbados Tourism Authority
800 Second Ave., 2nd Floor
New York, NY 10017
800-221-9831 or 212-986-6516
http://www.barbados.org/

Belgian National Tourist Office
780 Third Ave., Suite 1501
New York, NY 10017
212-758-8130
http://www.visitbelgium.com

Belize Tourist Board
800-624-0686
http://www.travelbelize.org

Bermuda Department of Tourism
205 E. 42nd St., 16th Floor
New York, NY 10017
800-223-6106 or 212-818-9800
http://www.bermudatourism.com/

Bhutan
Far Fung Places
1914 Fell St.
San Francisco, CA 94117
415-386-8306
http://www.farfungplaces.com

If you walked the entire length of China's Great Wall, you would be walking farther than the distance between New York City and Miami, Florida.

Tourism Corporation of Bonaire
10 Rockefeller Plaza, Suite 900
New York, NY 10020
800-266-2473 or 212-956-5912
http://www.infobonaire.com

Brazilian Tourism Center
16 W. 46th St.
New York, NY 10036
212-730-0515

British Virgin Islands Tourist Board
370 Lexington Ave., Suite 1605
New York, NY 10017
800-835-8530 or 212-696-0400
http://www.bviwelcome.com

"Major Zoos and Aquariums" and "Major Botanical Gardens and Arboretums" in chapter 11
Go to

Travel

Canadian Tourism Commission
http://www.canadatourism.com

Cayman Islands Department of Tourism
420 Lexington Ave., Suite 2733
New York, NY 10170
212-682-5582
http://www.caymanislands.ky

Chilean National Tourism Board
800-244-5366
http://www.visit-chile.org

China National Tourist Office
350 Fifth Ave., Suite 6413
New York, NY 10118
212-760-8218
http://www.cnto.org

Cook Islands Tourism Corporation
http://www.cook-islands.com

Costa Rican National Tourist Board
800-343-6332
http://www.tourism-costarica.com

Curaçao Tourist Board
475 Park Ave. South, Suite 2000
New York, NY 10016
800-270-3350 or 212-683-7660
http://www.curacao-tourism.com

Cyprus Tourism Organization
13 E. 40th St.
New York, NY 10016
212-683-5280
http://www.cyprustourism.org/

Czech Center New York
1109 Madison Ave.
New York, NY 10028
212-288-0971
http://www.czech.cz/new_york/

The Danish Tourist Board
655 Third Ave., 18th Floor
New York, NY 10017
212-885-9700
http://www.dt.dk/

Dominica Tourist Office
800 Second Ave., Suite 1802
New York, NY 10017
212-949-1711
http://www.dominica.dm/tourism.htm

Dominican Republic Tourist Office
136 E. 57th St., Suite 803
New York, NY 10022
888-358-9599 or 888-374-6361 or 212-575-4966

Egyptian Tourist Authority
630 Fifth Ave., Suite 1706
New York, NY 10111
212-332-2570
http://touregypt.net/

Estonian Tourist Board
http://www.tourism.ee

Fiji Visitors Bureau
5777 W. Century Blvd., Suite 220
Los Angeles, CA 90045
800-932-3454 or 310-568-1616
http://www.bulafiji.com

Finnish Tourist Board
655 Third Ave.
New York, NY 10017
800-346-4636 or 212-885-9700
http://www.finland-tourism.com

French Government Tourist Office
44 Madison Ave., 16th Floor
New York, NY 10022
212-838-7800
http://www.francetourism.com

French Polynesia
Tahiti Tourist Promotion Board
300 Continental Blvd., Suite 160
El Segundo, CA 90245
900-365-4949 or 310-414-8484
http://www.gototahiti.com

German National Tourist Office
122 E. 42nd St., 52nd Floor
New York, NY 10168-0072
212-661-7200
http://www.visits-to-germany.com

Gibraltar Tourist Board
http://www.gibraltar.gi/tourism/

Greek National Tourism Organization
Olympic Tower
645 Fifth Ave.
New York, NY 10022
212-421-5777
http://www.gnto.gr/

"The Atlas" on pages 945–952

Go to

Greenland
http://www.greenland-guide.gl/

Grenada Board of Tourism
800 Second Ave., Suite 400-K
New York, NY 10017
800-927-9554 or 212-687-9554
http://www.grenada.org

Guam Visitors Bureau
1336-C Park St.
Alameda, CA 94501
800-873-4826 or 510-865-0366
http://www.visitguam.org

Guatemala Tourist Commission
300 Sevilla Ave., Suite 210-A
Coral Gables, FL 33134
305-443-0343
http://www.inguat.net/indexe.html

Haiti
http://www.haititourisme.org

Honduras Tourism Institute
299 Alhambra Circle
Coral Gables, FL 33114
305-461-0600
http://www.turq.com/honduras.html

Hong Kong Tourism Board
115 E. 54th St., 2nd Floor
New York, NY 10022-4512
800-282-4582 or 212-421-3382
http://www.hkta.org

Hungarian National Tourist Office
150 E. 58th St.
New York, NY 10155-3398
212-355-0240
http://www.gotohungary.com

Icelandic Tourist Board
655 Third Ave.
New York, NY 10017
212-949-9700
http://www.goiceland.org

Government of India Tourist Office
1270 Avenue of the Americas, Suite 1808
New York, NY 10020
212-586-4901
http://www.tourindia.com/

Indonesian Council of Tourism Partners
22660 Pacific Coast Highway #108
Malibu, CA 90265
866-INDONESIA or 877-717-7700 or
    808-638-8500 or 310-338-2217
http://www.ictpindonesia.com

Irish Tourist Board
345 Park Ave.
New York, NY 10154
800-223-6470 or 212-418-0800
http://www.irelandvacations.com

Israel Ministry of Tourism Information Center
800 Second Ave., 16th Floor
New York, NY 10017
888-774-7723 or 212-499-5650
http://www.goisrael.com/

Italian Government Tourist Board
630 Fifth Ave., Suite 1565
New York, NY 10111
212-245-5618 or 212-245-4822
http://www.italiantourism.com/html/welcome.html

Jamaica Tourist Board
801 Second Ave., 20th Floor
New York, NY 10017
800-233-4582 or 212-856-9727
http://www.jamaicatravel.com/

Japanese National Tourist Organization
One Rockefeller Plaza, Suite 1250
New York, NY 10020
212-757-5640
http://www.jnto.go.jp/

Jordan Tourism Board
Court House Place
2000 N. 14th St., Suite 770
Arlington, VA 22201
877-SEE-JORDAN or 703-243-7404
http://www.tourism.com.jo

Kenya Tourist Office/Consulate
424 Madison Ave.
New York, NY 10017
212-486-1300
http://www.kenyatourism.org

**Korea, Republic of (South Korea)
    Korea National Tourism Office**
One Executive Dr., Suite 100
Fort Lee, NJ 07024
800-868-7567 or 201-585-0909
http://www.knto.or.kr/english/index.html

Lebanon Ministry of Tourism
http://www.lebanon-tourism.gov.lb/main.htm

Lithuania Department of Tourism
C/o Vytis Tours
40-24 235th St.
Douglaston, NY 11363
718-423-6161
http://www.tourism.lt

Luxembourg National Tourist Office
17 Beekman Pl.
New York, NY 10022
212-935-8888
http://www.ont.lu/address.htm

Macau Government Tourist Office
Integrated Travel Resources, Inc.
5757 W. Century Blvd., Suite 660
Los Angeles, CA 90045-6407
310-568-0009
http://www.macautourism.gov.mo

Malaysia Tourism Promotion Board
120 E. 56th St., Suite 804
New York, NY 10022
800-558-6787 or 212-754-1113
http://tourism.gov.my/

Maldives Tourist Promotion Board
http://www.visitmaldives.com

Malta Tourist Office
300, Lanidex Plaza
Parsippany, NJ 07054
887-466-2582 or 973-884-0899
http://visitmalta.com

Mauritius Tourism Promotion Authority
http://www.mauritius.net

Mexican Government Tourist Office
1911 Pennsylvania Ave.
Washington, DC 20006
800-446-3942 or 202-728-1750
http://mexico-travel.com

Federated States of Micronesia Visitors Board
http://www.visit-fsm.org

**Monaco Government Tourist and
   Convention Bureau**
565 Fifth Ave., 23rd Floor
New York, NY 10017
800-753-9696 or 212-286-3330
http://www.monaco-tourism.com

Moroccan National Tourist Office
20 E. 46th St., Suite 120
New York, NY 10017
212-557-2520
http://www.tourism-in-morocco.com

Nepal Tourism Board
http://www.welcomenepal.com

The Netherlands Board of Tourism
355 Lexington Ave.
New York, NY 10017
888-464-6552 or 212-370-7360
http://www.holland.com/us/

New Zealand Tourism Board
501 Santa Monica Blvd., Suite 300
Santa Monica, CA 90401
800-388-5494 or 310-395-7480
http://www.nztb.org.nz

Niue Tourism Office
http://www.niueisland.com

Norfolk Island Tourism
http://www.norfolkisland.com.au

Northern Ireland Tourist Board
551 Fifth Ave., Suite 701
New York, NY 10176
212-922-0101
http://www.ni-tourism.com

Norwegian Tourist Board
655 Third Ave., Suite 1810
New York, NY 10022
212-885-9700
http://www.visitnorway.com

Palau Visitors Authority
http://www.visit-palau.com

Papua New Guinea Tourism Promotion Authority
Los Angeles, CA
949-752-5440
http://www.paradiselive.org.pg

Philippine Tourism Center
556 Fifth Ave.
New York, NY 10036
212-575-7915

Polish National Tourist Office
275 Madison Ave., Suite 1711
New York, NY 10016
212-338-9412
http://www.polandtour.org/

ICEP—Portuguese Trade & Investment Commission
590 Fifth Ave., 3rd Floor
New York, NY 10036
800-767-8842 or 212-354-4610
http://www.portugal.org/tourism/index.html

Puerto Rico Tourism Company
666 Fifth Ave., 15th Floor
New York, NY 10103
800-866-7827 or 212-586-6262
http://www.prtourism.com

Romania National Tourist Office
342 Madison Ave., Suite 210
New York, NY 10173
800-621-8687 or 212-545-7118
http://www.romaniatouristoffice.com

Russian National Tourist Office
130 W. 42nd St., Suite 412
New York, NY 10036
877-221-7120 or 212-575-3431
http://www.russia-travel.com

Rwandan Office of Tourism and National Parks
http://usembkigali.net/pas/tourism.htm

Saba Tourist Office
http://www.sabatourism.com

St. Eustatias Tourist Office
http://www.turq.com/statia

St. Kitts and Nevis Department of Tourism
414 E. 75th St., Suite 5
New York, NY 10021
800-582-6208 or 212-535-1234
http://www.interknowledge.com/stkitts-nevis/knacc01.htm

St. Lucia Tourist Board
820 Second Ave., 9th Floor
New York, NY 10017
800-456-3984 or 212-867-2950
http://www.interknowledge.com/st-lucia/index.html

St. Maarten Tourist Office
675 Third Ave., Suite 1806
New York, NY 10017
800-786-2278 or 212-953-2084
http://www.st-maarten.com

"Foreign Dialing Codes" in chapter 26

Go to

St. Martin Tourist Office
French West Indies Tourist Board
444 Madison Ave.
New York, NY 10022
900-990-0040 (95 cents per minute)
http://www.interknowledge.com/st-martin/index.html

St. Vincent and the Grenadines Tourist Office
801 Second Ave.
New York, NY 10017
800-729-1726 or 212-687-4981
http://www.turq.com/stvincent/

Scottish Tourist Board (*See also* United Kingdom—British Tourist Authority)
http://www.visitscotland.com

Senegal Tourism Office
http://www.senegal-tourism.com

National Tourism Organization of Serbia
http://www.serbia-tourism.org/

Seychelles Tourist Office
235 E. 40th St., Suite 24A
New York, NY 10016
212-687-9766

Singapore Tourism Board
590 Fifth Ave., 12th Floor
New York, NY 10036
212-302-4861
http://www.singapore-usa.com

Slovak Tourist Board
345 E. 12th St.
New York, NY 10003
212-358-9686
http://www.sacr.sk/

Slovenian Travel Inc.
345 E. 12th St.
New York, NY 10003
212-358-9024
http://www.sloveniatravel.com/

South African Tourism Board
500 Fifth Ave., 20th Floor, Suite 2040
New York, NY 10110
800-822-5368 or 212-730-2929
http://www.satour.org

Tourist Office of Spain
666 Fifth Ave., 35th Floor
New York, NY 10103
212-265-8822
http://www.okspain.org/

Travel

Sri Lanka Tourist Board
111 Wood Avenue South
Iselin, NJ 08830
732-516-9800
http://www.lanka.net/ctb/

Swedish Travel and Tourism Council
P.O. Box 4649, Grand Central Station
New York, NY 10163-4649
212-885-9700
http://www.gosweden.org

Switzerland Tourism
Swiss Center
608 Fifth Ave.
New York, NY 10020
800-794-7795
http://www.myswitzerland.com

Taiwan Visitors Association
405 Lexington Ave., 37th Floor
New York, NY 10174
212-867-1632
http://www.tva.org.tw/

Tanzania Tourist Board
http://www.tanzania-web.com

Tourism Authority of Thailand
351 E. 52nd St.
New York, NY 10222
212-754-1770
http://www.tat.or.th/

Tonga Visitors Bureau
4805 Driftwood Ct.
El Sobrante, CA 94803-1805
510-233-1381 or 510-768-6227

Trinidad and Tobago Tourism Development Authority
25 W. 43rd St., Suite 1508
New York, NY 10036
800-748-4224 or 888-595-4868 or 212-719-0540
http://www.visittnt.com

Tunisian Tourism Office
1575 Massachusetts Ave., NW
Washington, DC 20005
202-466-2546
http://tourismtunisia.com

Turkish Tourism and Information Office
821 United Nations Plaza
New York, NY 10017
212-687-2194
http://www.turkey.org

Turks and Caicos Tourist Office
1146 Biscayne Blvd., Suite 302
North Miami, FL 33181
305-891-4117
http://www.turksandcaicostourism.com

Uganda Tourist Board
http://www.visituganda.com

United Kingdom—British Tourist Authority
551 Fifth Ave., 7th Floor
New York, NY 10176
800-462-2748
http://www.travelbritain.org

U.S. Virgin Islands, Divisions of Tourism (St. Croix, St. John, St. Thomas)
http://www.usvi.net

Vanuatu National Tourism Office
http://www.vanuatutourism.com/intro.htm

Venezuelan Tourism Association
P.O. Box 3010
Sausalito, CA 94966
800-331-0100 or 415-331-0100

Wales Tourist Board (*See also* United Kingdom-British Tourist Authority)
http://www.visitwales.com

Zambia National Tourist Board
237 E. 52nd St.
New York, NY 10022
212-308-2155
http://www.zamnet.zm/zamnet/zntb/zntb.html

INTERNATIONAL AUTO REGISTRATION MARKS

Abu Dhabi	UAE	Fiji	FJI	Mexico	MEX
Afghanistan	AFG	Finland	FIN	Moldova	MD
Albania	AL	France	F	Monaco	MC
Alderney	GBA	Gambia	WAG	Mongolia	MGL
(Channel Islands)		Georgia	GE	Morocco	MA
Algeria	DZ	Germany, Federal	D	Mozambique	MOC
Andorra	AND	Republic of		Myanmar	BUR
Argentina	RA	Ghana	GH	Namibia	NAM
Australia	AUS	Gibraltar	GBZ	Nauru	NAU
Austria	A	Great Britain	GB	Nepal	NEP
Bahamas	BS	Greece	GR	Netherlands	NL
Bahrain	BRN	Grenada	WG	Netherlands Antilles	NA
Bangladesh	BD	Guatemala	GCA	New Zealand	NZ
Barbados	BDS	Guernsey	GBG	Nicaragua	NIC
Belarus	BY	Guyana	GUY	Niger	RN
Belgium	B	Haiti	RH	Nigeria	WAN
Belize	BZ	Hong Kong	HK	Norway	N
Benin	DY	Hungary	H	Pakistan	PK
Bolivia	BL	Iceland	IS	Panama	PA
Bosnia	BIH	India	IND	Papua New Guinea	PNG
Botswana	RB	Indonesia	RI	Paraguay	PY
Brazil	BR	Iran	IR	Peru	PE
Brunei	BRU	Iraq	IRQ	Philippines	RP
Bulgaria	BG	Ireland	IRL	Poland	PL
Burkina Faso	BF	Isle of Man	GBM	Portugal	P
Burundi	RU	Israel	IL	Qatar	Q
Cambodia	K	Italy	I	Romania	RO
Cameroon	RVC	Ivory Coast	CI	Russian Federation	RUS
Canada	CDN	Jamaica	JA	Rwanda	RWA
Central African	RCA	Japan	J	St. Lucia	WL
Republic		Jersey	GBJ	St. Vincent	WV
Chad	TCH	Jordan	HKJ	Samoa	WS
Chile	RCH	Kazakhstan	KZ	San Marino	RSM
Colombia	CO	Kenya	EAK	Saudi Arabia	SA
Congo, Republic	RCB	Krygyzstan	KS	Senegal	SN
of the		Kuwait	KWT	Seychelles	SY
Congo, Democratic	ZRE	Laos	LAO	Sierra Leone	WAL
Republic of		Latvia	LV	Singapore	SGP
Costa Rica	CR	Lebanon	RL	Slovakia	SK
Croatia	HR	Lesotho	LS	Slovenia	SLO
Cuba	C	Liberia	LB	Somalia	SO
Curaçao	NA	Libya	LAR	South Africa	ZA
Cyprus	CY	Liechtenstein	FL	South Korea	ROK
Czech Republic	CZ	Lithuania	LT	Spain	E
Denmark	DK	Luxembourg	L	Sri Lanka	CL
Dominican Republic	DOM	Macedonia	MK	Sudan	SUD
Ecuador	EC	Madagascar	RM	Suriname	SME
Egypt	ET	Malawi	MW	Swaziland	SD
El Salvador	ES	Malaysia	MAL	Sweden	S
Eritrea	ER	Mali	RMM	Switzerland	CH
Estonia	EST	Malta	M	Syria	SYR
Ethiopia	ETH	Mauritania	RIM	Taiwan	RC
Faroe Islands	FO	Mauritius	MS	Tajikistan	TJ

continues

International Auto Registration Marks Continued

Tanzania	EAT	Turkmenistan	TM	Venezuela	YV
Thailand	T	Uganda	EAU	Vietnam	VN
Togo	TG	Ukraine	UA	Yemen	AND
Trinidad and Tobago	TT	United States	USA	Zambia	Z
Tunisia	TN	Uruguay	ROU	Zimbabwe	ZW
Turkey	TR	Vatican City	SCV		

AIR MILEAGE FROM NEW YORK CITY—INTERNATIONAL

Acapulco	2,260
Amsterdam	3,639
Antigua	1,783
Aruba	1,963
Athens	4,927
Barbados	2,100
Beijing	6,844
Bermuda	771
Bogotá	2,487
Bombay	7,808
Brussels	3,662
Buenos Aires	5,302
Caracas	2,123
Copenhagen	3,849
Curaçao	1,993
Frankfurt	3,851
Geneva	3,859
Glasgow	3,211
Hamburg	3,806
Hong Kong	8,095
Johannesburg	7,964
Kingston	1,583
Kuwait City	6,366
Lima	3,651
Lisbon	3,366
London	3,456
Madrid	3,588
Manchester	3,336
Mexico City	2,086
Milan	4,004
Moscow	4,680
Nassau	1,101
Oslo	3,671
Paris	3,628
Reykjavík	2,600
Rio de Janeiro	4,816
Rome	4,280
St. Croix	1,680
San Juan	1,609
Santo Domingo	1,560
Sydney	9,932
Tel Aviv	5,672
Tokyo	6,755
Zurich	3,926

INTERNATIONAL CURRENCIES

The table on the opposite page lists the official names for selected currencies around the world. Colonial legacies have made certain names—dollar, peso, franc, and pound, for example—widespread. The traveler should not assume equivalency in value, or transferability, among units sharing a name; that is, one cannot spend Central African francs in France or Turkish lira in Rome.

The column titled "Smaller Monetary Unit" lists the anglicized form of the plural—e.g., Czech 100 halers—followed by the native language plural in parentheses (haleru). When no smaller unit is given, the traveler may assume none exists. Where more than one term is used locally for the same unit, both names are given, separated by *or*. Units of measurement with the word *new* preceding them are the current international exchange unit. There may be an older unit of currency still in circulation that is not to be confused with the new unit.

The abbreviations used are as follows:

CFA   Communauté financieére africaine (African Financial Community)

CFP   Communauté financieére pacific (Pacific Financial Community)

European currency changed on January 1, 2002, when Austria, Belgium, Finland, France, Germany, Greece, Ireland, Italy, Luxembourg, the Netherlands, Portugal, and Spain—12 of the 15 nations of the European Union—began using the euro throughout their economies. (The other three EU members, the United Kingdom, Sweden, and Denmark, re-

Travel

tained their own currency.) Old national currencies appear in ( ) for the 12 euro nations. Old currencies were in use alongside the euro for two months, until February 28, 2002. After that date, commercial banks can continue to accept the old currencies in exchange for euros, but other businesses do not.

INTERNATIONAL CURRENCIES

Location	Currency	Smaller Monetary Unit
Albania	lek	100 qindarka
Angola	kwanza	100 lwei
Argentina	peso	10,000 australes
Armenia	dram	100 louma
Australia	Australian dollar	100 cents
Austria	euro (schilling)	100 cents (100 groschen)
Bahamas	Bahamian dollar	100 cents
Bahrain	Bahraini dinar	1,000 fils
Barbados	Barbadian dollar	100 cents
Belarus	rouble	100 kopeks (rarely used)
Belgium	euro (Belgian franc)	100 cents (100 centimes)
Belize	Belize dollar	100 cents
Bermuda	Bermudan dollar	100 cents
Bosnia and Herzegovina	convertible marka	——
Burundi	Burundi franc	100 centimes
Canada	Canadian dollar	100 cents
Cape Verde	Escudo caboverdiano	100 centavos
Cayman Islands	Cayman dollar	100 cents
Chile	Chilean peso	100 centavos
China	renminbi yuan	10 jiao or 100 fen
Comoros	Comorian franc	100 centimes
Congo, Democratic Republic of (formerly Zaire)	Congolese franc	100 centimes
Costa Rica	colon	100 céntimos
Czech Republic	koruna	100 haléū
Denmark	Danish kroner	100 øre
Dijbouti	Dijbouti franc	100 centimes
Egypt	pound	100 piastres
Eritrea	nafka	100 cents
Estonia	kroon	100 sents
Ethiopia	Ethiopian birr	100 cents
Faroe Islands	Denmark krone	100 øre
Fiji	Fiji dollar	100 cents
Finland	euro (markka)	100 cents (100 penniä)
France	euro (French franc)	100 centimes
Georgia	lari	100 tetri
Germany	euro (Deutsche mark)	100 cents (100 pfennig)
Ghana	Cedi	100 pesewas
Greece	euro (Drachma)	100 cents (100 leptae)
Greenland	Denmark krone	100 øre
Guinea	Guinea franc	100 centimes
Guyana	Guyana dollar	100 cents
Hungary	Forint	100 fillér

continues

International Currencies, Continued

Location	Currency	Smaller Monetary Unit
Iceland	Icelandic króna	100 aurar
India	Indian rupee	100 paisa
Indonesia	rupiah	100 sen
Iran	rial	——
Ireland	euro (punt or pound)	100 cents (100 puigin or pence)
Israel	shekel	100 agora
Italy	euro (lira)	100 cents (100 centesimi)
Jamaica	Jamaican dollar	100 cents
Japan	yen	——
Kenya	Kenyan shilling	100 cents
Kuwait	Kuwaiti dinar	1,000 fils
Laos	kip	100 at
Lebanon	Lebanese pound	100 piastres
Liberia	Liberian dollar	100 cents
Libya	Libyan dinar	1,000 dirhams
Liechtenstein	Swiss franc	100 rappen or centimes
Lithuania	lita	100 centu
Luxembourg	euro (Luxembourg franc)	100 cents (100 centimes)
Macedonia	dinar	100 paras
Madagascar	Franc Malgache	100 centimes
Malaysia	Malaysia dollar or ringitt	100 sen
Maldives	rufiyaa	100 laaris
Malta	Maltese lira	100 cents or 1,000 mils
Mexico	peso	100 centavos
Moldova	lei	——
Mongolia	tughrik	100 möngö
Namibia	Namibian dollar	100 cents
Nepal	Nepalese rupee	100 paisa
Netherlands	euro (guilder or florin)	100 cents (100 cents)
New Zealand	New Zealand dollar	100 cents
Nicaragua	córdoba	100 centavos
Oman	rial Omani	1,000 baisas
Pakistan	Pakistani rupee	100 paisa
Panama	balboa	100 centésimos
Paraguay	guaraní	100 céntimos
Peru	new sol	100 cénts
Philippines	Philippines peso	100 centavos
Poland	zlory	100 groszy
Portugal	euro (escudo)	100 cents (100 centavos)
Russia	new rouble	100 kopeks
Rwanda	Rwanda franc	100 centimes
St. Helena	St. Helena pound	100 pence
São Tomé and Princípe	dobra	100 centavos
Saudi Arabia	Saudi Arabian riyal	100 halala
Seychelles	Seychelles rupee	100 cents
Singapore	Singapore dollar	100 cents
Slovakia	koruna	100 halierov
Slovenia	tolar	100 stotins
Solomon Islands	Solomon Island dollar	100 cents

Location	Currency	Smaller Monetary Unit
Somalia	Somali shilling	100 cents
Spain	euro (peseta)	100 cents (100 céntimos)
Sri Lanka	Sri Lanka rupee	100 cents
Sudan	Sudanese dinar	10 pounds
Suriname	Suriname guilder	100 cents
Swaziland	Lilangeni	100 cents
Sweden	Swedish krona	100 öre
Switzerland	Swiss franc	100 centimes or rappen
Syria	Syrian pound	100 piastres
Taiwan	new Taiwan dollar	100 cents
Tajikistan	Tajikistan rouble	100 tanga
Tanzania	Tanzanian shilling	100 cents
Thailand	baht	100 satang
Togo	franc CFA	100 centimes
Trinidad and Tobago	Trinidad dollar	100 cents
Tunisia	Tunisian dinar	1,000 millimes
Turkey	Turkish lira	100 kurus
Ukraine	hryvna	100 kopiykas
United Arab Emirates	UAE dirham	100 fils
United States	U.S. dollar	100 cents
Uzbekistan	sum	100 tiyin
Venzuela	bolívar	100 céntimos
Vietnam	dông	10 hào or 100 xu
Yemen	riyal	100 fils
Zimbabwe	Zimbabwe dollar	100 cents

REQUIREMENTS BEFORE PROCEEDING ABROAD

This listing is prepared solely for the information of U.S. citizens traveling as tourists and does not apply to persons planning to immigrate to foreign countries. A visa is generally an endorsement or stamp placed by officials of a foreign country on a U.S. passport that allows the bearer to visit that country.

PASSPORTS

Persons who travel to a country where a U.S. passport is not required should have documentary evidence of their U.S. citizenship and identity to facilitate reentry into the United States. Countries that do not require a passport to enter or depart frequently require this evidence. Documentary evidence of U.S. citizenship may be an expired passport, a certified birth certificate, a certificate of naturalization, a certificate of citizenship, or a report of birth abroad of a citizen of the United States.

IMPORTANT

Travelers should check passport and visa requirements with the consular officials of the countries to be visited well in advance of their departure dates, because such information is subject to change.

Documentary evidence of identity may be a valid driver's license or government identification provided they identify you by physical description or photograph.

Some Arab and African countries will not issue visas or allow entry if your passport gives evidence of travel to Israel. If this applies to you, consult the nearest U.S. passport agency for guidance.

In addition to the passport agencies listed below, passport applications and information are available at approximately 4,500 public facilities in the United States. If an automated appointment number is listed, please call that number in advance to make an appointment. Have your Social Security number available when calling.

"Countries of the World" in chapter 26

Boston Passport Agency
Thomas P. O'Neill Federal Bldg.
10 Causeway St., Suite 247
Boston, MA 02222-1094
Automated appointment #: 617-878-0900
Services provided to Maine, Massachusetts, New Hampshire, Rhode Island, upstate New York, and Vermont

Chicago Passport Agency
Kluczynski Federal Bldg.
230 S. Dearborn St., Suite 380
Chicago, IL 60604-1564
Automated appointment #: 312-341-6020
Services provided to Illinois and Michigan

Honolulu Passport Agency
Prince Kuhio Federal Bldg.
300 Ala Moana Blvd., Suite 1-330
Honolulu, HI 96850
Recorded information #: 808-522-8283
Services provided to American Samoa, the Federated States of Micronesia, Guam, Hawaii, and the Northern Mariana Islands

Houston Passport Agency
Mickey Leland Federal Bldg.
1919 Smith St., Suite 1400
Houston, TX 77002-8049
Automated appointment #: 713-751-0294
Services provided to Kansas, Oklahoma, New Mexico, and Texas

Los Angeles Passport Agency
Federal Bldg.
11000 Wilshire Blvd., Suite 1000
Los Angeles, CA 90024-3615
Automated appointment #: 310-575-5700
Services provided to southern California (all counties south of and including San Luis Obispo, Kern and San Bernardino) and Nevada (Clark County only)

Miami Passport Agency
Claude Pepper Federal Office Bldg.
51 SW First Ave., 3rd Floor
Miami, FL 33130
Automated appointment #: 305-539-3600
Services provided to Florida, South Carolina, and the U.S. Virgin Islands

National Passport Center
31 Rochester Avenue
Portsmouth, NY 03801-2900
Services provided: Passport by mail (Form DSP-82) applications accepted

New Orleans Passport Agency
One Canal Place
365 Canal St., Suite 1300
New Orleans, LA 70130-6508
Automated appointment #: 504-412-2600
Services provided to Alabama, Arkansas, Georgia, Iowa, Indiana, Kentucky, Louisiana, Mississippi, Missouri, North Carolina, Ohio, Puerto Rico, Tennessee, Virginia, (except District of Columbia suburbs), and Wisconsin

New York Passport Agency
376 Hudson St.
New York, NY 10014-3621
Automated appointment #: 212-206-3500
Services provided to New York City and Long Island

Philadelphia Passport Agency
U.S. Custom House
200 Chestnut St., Room 103
Philadelphia, PA 19106-2970
Automated appointment #: 215-418-5937
Services provided to Delaware, New Jersey, Pennsylvania, and West Virginia

San Francisco Passport Agency
95 Hawthorne St., 5th Floor
San Francisco, CA 94105-3901
Automated appointment #: 415-538-2700
Services provided to Arizona, northern California (all counties north of and including Monterey, Kings, Tulare, and Mono), Nevada (except Clark County), and Utah

Seattle Passport Agency
Henry Jackson Federal Bldg.
915 Second Ave., Suite 992
Seattle, WA 98174-1091
Automated appointment #: 206-808-5700
Services provided to Alaska, Colorado, Idaho, Minnesota, Montana, Nebraska, North Dakota, Oregon, South Dakota, Washington, and Wyoming

Stamford Passport Agency
One Landmark Square
Broad and Atlantic Sts.
Stamford, CT 06901-2667
Automated appointment #: 203-969-9000
Services provided to Connecticut and New York (Westchester County only)

Washington Passport Agency
1111 19th St. NW
Washington, DC 20524

Automated appointment #: 202-647-0578
Services provided to Maryland, northern Virginia
  (including Alexandria and Arlington, Fairfax,
  Loudon, Stafford, and Prince William Counties)

Special Issuance Agency
1111 19th St., NW Room 350
Washington, DC 20524
Services provided: Applications accepted for
  diplomatic, official, and no-fee passports

Call the National Passport Information Center's passport information number 900-225-5674 (TDD 900-225-7778) (charges incurred per minute) or 888-362-8668 (TDD 888-498-3648) (flat rate charge) to obtain more information, to request a passport application or to check on the status of a passport application. Automated information is available 24 hours a day, 7 days a week. Operators can be reached Monday through Friday (excluding federal holidays) from 8:00 A.M. to 8:00 P.M. Eastern standard time. Services are provided in English and Spanish.

Visit the U.S. State Department at its web site for information about Passport Services: http://travel.state.gov/passport_services.html

VISAS

> **IMPORTANT**
>
> It is the responsibility of the traveler to obtain a visa, where required, from the appropriate embassy or nearest consulate of the country to be visited before proceeding abroad.

Allow sufficient time for processing your visa application, especially if you apply by mail. Most foreign consular representatives are located in principal cities, particularly Chicago, New Orleans, New York, San Francisco, and Washington, D.C. In many instances, a traveler may be required to obtain visas from the consular office in the area of his or her residence. You can obtain addresses of foreign consular offices in the United States by consulting the *Congressional Directory* (available in most libraries), by accessing the U.S. State Department's online list of foreign consular offices in the U.S. (http://www.state.gov/www/travel/consular_offices/fco_index.html), or by visiting the web sites listed below and in the "Government Tourist Information Centers" and "Additional Sources of Information" sections of this chapter.

For further assistance, you can also contact travel agents and visa information services such as World Wide Visa Services (800-527-1861), World Travel Guide Online Services (http://www.wtgonline.com), and Travel Document Systems (800-874-5100; Washington, D.C., local number 202-638-3800; fax 202-638-4674; http://www.traveldocs.com). In addition, the U.S. State Department's Bureau of Consular Affairs (http://travel.state.gov) offers a wealth of information for travelers, including health and safety advisories.

IMMUNIZATIONS

Under the International Health Regulations adopted by the World Health Organization, a country may require certificates of immunization against yellow fever. A few countries still require a cholera immunization as well. Check with health-care providers or your records to ensure other immunizations (for example, tetanus and polio) are up to date. Prophylactic medication for malaria and certain other preventive measures are advisable for some travelers. No immunizations are required to return to the United States. Pertinent information is included in Health Information for International Travel (the "Yellow Book"), available from the U.S. Government Printing Office, Washington, DC 20402, http://www.bookstore.gpo.gov, or you can obtain it from your local health department or physician, or by contacting the Public Health Foundation at http://bookstore.phf.org.

An increasing number of countries have established regulations regarding AIDS testing, particularly for long-term visitors. Check with the embassy or consulate of the country you plan to visit for the latest information on whether this is a requirement for entry.

CONTACT INFORMATION FOR INDIVIDUAL COUNTRIES—ONLINE SOURCES

Country	Supplemental Web Site
Afghanistan, Islamic State of	http://www.afghan-web.com
Albania, Republic of	http://www.albinfo.com
Algeria, Democratic and Popular Republic of	http://www.algeria-tourism.org
Andorra	http://www.andorra.com
Angola, Republic of	http://www.africavacationguide.com/travel/Angola_Practical_Info.html
Anguilla	http://www.travelnotes.org/LatinAmerica/Anguilla/anguilla_tourism.htm
Antigua and Barbuda	http://www.travelnotes.org/LatinAmerica/Antigua/antigua_tourism.htm
Argentina	http://www.consuladoargentino-losangeles.org/argentina_tourism_online.htm
Armenia, Republic of	http://www.tourismarmenia.com
Aruba	http://www.aruba.com
Australia	http://www.australia.com
Austria	http://www.touristnet.at/englisch/index.htm
Azerbaijan, Republic of	http://www.friends-partners.org/oldfriends/azerbaijan
Bahamas, Commonwealth of	http://www.bahamatravelnet.com/home.html
Bahrain, State of	http://www.bahraintourism.com
Bangladesh, People's Republic of	http://www.bangladesh.com/travel/
Barbados	http://www.funbarbados.com
Belarus, Republic of	http://www.belarusguide.com
Belgium	http://www.trabel.com
Belize	http://www.belize.com
Benin, Republic of	http://www.sas.upenn.edu/African_Studies/Country_Specific/Benin.html
Bermuda	http://www.bermuda.com
Bhutan	http://www.bhutan-info.org
Bolivia	http://www.boliviaweb.com
Bosnia and Herzegovina, Republic of	http://www.bosnet.org/bosnia/
Botswana, Republic of	http://www.botswana-online.com
Brazil	http://www.lonelyplanet.com/destinations/south_america/brazil/
British Virgin Islands (includes Anegarda, Jost van Dyke, Tortola, and Virgin Gorda)	http://www.britishvirginislands.com
Brunei Darussalam, State of	http://www.brunei.bn
Bulgaria, Republic of	http://www.travel-bulgaria.com
Burkina Faso	http://www.worldskip.com/burkinafaso/
Burundi, Republic of	http://www.burundi.org
Cambodia, Kingdom of	http://www.cambodia-web.net
Cameroon, Republic of	http://www.adminet.com/world/cm/
Canada	http://canada.worldweb.com
Cape Verde, Republic of	http://www.traveldocs.com/cv/
Cayman Islands	http://cayman.com.ky
Central African Republic	http://www.africaguide.com/country/car/
Chad, Republic of	http://www.africavacationguide.com/travel/Chad_Practical_Info.html
Chile	http://www.lonelyplanet.com/destinations/south_america/chile_and_easter_island/
China, People's Republic of China	http://www.chinasite.com
Colombia	http://www.drcomputer.com/colombia/guide01.htm
Comoros Islands (Federal Islamic Republic of the Comoros)	http://www.ksu.edu/sasw/comoros/comoros.html

Country	Supplemental Web Site
Congo, Democratic Republic of (formerly Zaire)	http://www.africaguide.com/country/zaire
Congo, Republic of the	http://www.sas.upenn.edu/African_Studies/Country_Specific/Congo.html
Cook Islands	http://cookpages.com
Costa Rica	http://www.amerisol.com
Côte d'Ivoire, Republic of (Ivory Coast)	http://www.africaguide.com/country/ivoryc/
Croatia	http://www.hr/
Cuba	http://lonelyplanet.com/destinations/caribbean/cuba/
Curaçao	http://www.curacao.com
Cyprus, Republic of	http://www.windowoncyprus.com
Czech Republic	http://czech-tourism.com
Denmark, Kingdom of (including Greenland and the Faroe Islands)	http://www.alltraveldenmark.com
Dijbouti, Republic of	http://www.tuttinsieme.it/tutti/tut/af/djibouti/djidir.htm
Dominica, Commonwealth of	http://www.delphis.dm/basics.htm
Dominican Republic	http://www.dr1.com
Ecuador (including Galapagos Islands)	http://www.tuttinsieme.it/tutti/tut/souame/ecuador/eqdir.htm
Egypt, Arab Republic of	http://www.tourism.egnet.net/culture.htm
El Salvador	http://www.latinworld.com/centro/elsalvador/index.html
Equatorial Guinea, Republic of	http://www.lonelyplanet.com/destinations/africa/equatorial_guinea/
Eritrea	http://www.africavacationguide.com/travel/Eritrea_Practical_Info.html
Estonia	http://www.tuttinsieme.it/tutti/tut/eur/estonia/tourism.htm
Ethiopia, Federal Democratic Republic of	http://tour.ethiopiaonline.net
European Union	http://europa.eu.int/index_en.htm
Fiji	http://www.fijivision.com/tourist.html
Finland	http://www.travelmad.com/html/finland.htm
Former Yugolsav Republic of Macedonia (FYROM)	http://www.middleeastnews.com/Macedonia.html
France	http://www.franceway.com/welcome.htm
French Guiana	http://www.lonelyplanet.com/destinations/south_america/french_guiana/
French Polynesia	http://www.tahiti-explorer.com
French West Indies	http://www.cieux.com/fwi.html
Gabonese Republic (Gabon)	http://dmoz.org/Regional/Africa/Gabon/Travel_and_Tourism/
Gambia	http://www.gambia.com
Georgia, Republic of	http://dmoz.org/Regional/Asia/Georgia/Travel_and_Tourism/Lodging/
Germany, Federal Republic of	http://www.deutschland-tourismus.de/e/dest_con_main_e.html
Ghana	http://www.ghana.com/republic/tourism
Greece	http://www.greek-tourism.gr
Greenland	http://www.lonelyplanet.com/destinations/europe/greenland/
Grenada	http://www.turq.com/grenada.html
Guam	http://www.guam.net/home/bjohns/guamlinks.html
Guatemala	http://www.lonelyplanet.com/destinations/central_america/guatemala/
Guinea, Republic of	http://www.ware.it/Africa/Guinea/1guinea.htm
Guinea-Bissau, Republic of	http://www.west-africa.com/Guinea-Bissau/Guinea-Bissau.htm
Guyana, Co-operative Republic of	http://www.turq.com/guyana.html
Haiti	http://www.haititourisme.org
Holy See, Apostolic Nunciature of the (the Vatican)	http://www.vatican.va

continues

Contact Information, Continued

Country	Supplemental Web Site
Honduras	http://www.latinworld.com/centro/honduras/index.html
Hong Kong (Special Administrative Region of the People's Republic of China)	http://www.e-hongkong.com
Hungary, Republic of	http://www.miwo.hu/index-en.phtml
Iceland	http://www.travelnet.is/
India	http://india-tourism.de/english/
Indonesia, Republic of	http://www.indonesiatourism.com
Iran	http://www.salamiran.org
Iraq	http://www.undp.org/missions/iraq
Ireland	http://www.goireland.com
Israel and the Occupied Territories (Jerusalem, Gaza, Golan Heights, and the West Bank)	http://www.infotour.co.il
Italy	http://www.italytourism.it
Jamaica	http://www.jamaica-irie.com
Japan	http://www.japan-guide.com
Jordan, Hashemite Kingdom of	http://www.seejordan.org
Kazakstan	http://www.asiatour.org
Kenya	http://www.seekenya.com
Kiribati, Republic of (formerly Gilbert Islands)	http://www.tskl.net.ki/kiribati/
Korea, Democratic People's Republic of (North Korea)	http://www.lonelyplanet.com/destinations/north_east_asia/north_korea/
Korea, Republic of (South Korea)	http://www.lonelyplanet.com/destinations/north_east_asia/south_korea/
Kuwait, State of	http://www.undp.org/missions/kuwait
Kyrgyz Republic (Kyrgyzstan)	http://www.bishkek.su/KyrgyzstanTourism/
Laos (Lao People's Democratic Republic)	http://www.visit-laos.com
Latvia	http://www.tvnet.lv/en/
Lebanon	http://www.lol.com.lb/tourism/index.shtml
Lesotho, Kingdom of	http://www.undp.org/missions/lesotho/
Liberia, Republic of	http://www.liberia.net
Liechtenstein	http://www.tourismus.li/
Lithuania	http://www.baltic.ws/lithuania/tourism.html
Luxembourg, Grand Duchy of	http://www.alltravelluxembourg.com
Macau	http://www.macau.gov.mo
Madagascar, Democratic Republic of	http://www.madagascar-guide.com/top/HP_Fr1Eng.html
Malawi	http://malawi.tripod.com/
Malaysia (and the Borneo States, Sarawak, and Sabah)	http://www.interknowledge.com/malaysia/index.html
Maldives	http://www.tuttinsieme.it/tutti/tut/as/maldives/tourism.htm
Mali, Republic of	http://www.traveldocs.com/ml
Malta	http://visitmalta.com
Marshall Islands, Republic of the	http://travel.state.gov/marshall_islands.html
Mauritania, Republic of	http://www.arab.net/mauritania/mauritania_contents.html
Mauritius	http://www.mauritius-info.com
Mexico	http://www.go2mexico.com

Country	Supplemental Web Site
Micronesia, Federated States of (Kosrae, Yap, Pohnpei, and Chuuk)	http://www.lonelyplanet.com/destinations/pacific/federated_states_of_micronesia/
Moldova, Republic of	http://www.net.md/tourism/
Monaco, Principality of	http://www.monte-carlo.mc/
Mongolia	http://www.mol.mn
Morocco	http://www.arab.net/morocco/morocco_contents.html
Mozambique, Republic of	http://www.mozambique.mz
Myanmar, Union of	http://www.myanmar.com
Namibia	http://www.iwwn.com.na/namtour/
Naura, Republic of	http://www.traveldocs.com/nr/
Nepal, Kingdom of	http://www.undp.org/missions/nepal
Netherlands	http://www.goholland.com
Netherlands Antilles	http://www.islandconnoisseur.com/abc/
New Zealand	http://www.tourism.net.nz
Nicaragua	http://www.latinworld.com/centro/nicaragua/index.html
Niger, Republic of	http://www.txdirect.net/~jmayer/fon.html#LiNiger
Nigeria, Republic of	http://www.nigeria.com
Niue	http://www.hideawayholidays.com.au/niue_.htm
Norfolk Island	http://www.ni.net.nf/
Northern Mariana Islands, Commonwealth of the	http://www.mariana-islands.gov.mp/
Norway, Kingdom of	http://www.alltravelnorway.com
Oman, Sultanate of	http://www.omanet.com/back.htm
Pakistan	http://www.pak.gov.pk
Palau, Republic of	www.lonelyplanet.com/destinations/pacific/palau/
Panama	http://www.panamainfo.com
Papua New Guinea	http://lonelyplanet.com/destinations/australasia/papua_new_guinea/
Paraguay	http://www.latinworld.com/sur/paraguay/index.html
Peru	http://www.peru-explorer.com
Philippines	http://www.tourism.gov.ph
Poland, Republic of	http://www.pl-info.net/en/tourism/index.shtml
Portugal (including Azores and the Madeira Islands)	http://portugal-info.net
Qatar, State of	http://www.arab.net/qatar/qatar_contents.html
Romania	http://www.ici.ro/romania/tourism/index.html
Russia	http://russia-tourism.com
Rwanda, Republic of	http://www.bcr-rwanda.com/index1024.html
Saba	http://www.reefrainfrst.com/saba.htm
St. Eustatius	http://travel.discovery.com/dest/weisdb/caribbean/saba/over.html
St. Kitts and Nevis	http://www.geographia.com/stkitts-nevis/index.htm
St. Lucia	http://www.turq.com/stlucia.html
St. Marteen	http://www.gobeach.com/page3.htm
St. Martin	http://www.gobeach.com/page3.htm
St. Vincent and the Grenadines	http://www.turq.com/stvincent/
San Marino, Republic of	http://inthenet.sm/rsm/intro.htm
São Tome and Principé	http://www.traveldocs.com/st/
Saudi Arabia, Kingdom of	http://www.arabia.com
Scotland	http://www.electricscotland.com/tourist/
Senegal, Republic of	http://www.senegal-tourism.com

continues

Contact Information, Continued

Country	Supplemental Web Site
Serbia and Montenegro ("Federal Republic of Yugoslavia")	http://www.travelnotes.org/Europe/serbia.htm
Seychelles	http://www.sey.net
Sierra Leone	http://www.sierra-leone.org
Singapore	http://www.newasia-singapore.com
Slovak Republic	http://www.slovakia.org/tourism/
Slovenia, Republic of	http://www.ntz-nta.si/
Solomon Islands	http://www.commerce.gov.sb/
Somali Democratic Republic (Somalia)	http://www.arab.net/somalia/somalia_contents.html
South Africa	http://www.southafrica.net
Spain	http://www.tourspain.es/turespai/marcoi.htm
Sri Lanka	http://www.lonelyplanet.com/destinations/indian_subcontinent/sri_lanka/
Sudan, Republic of	http://www.sudan.net/tourism.shtml
Suriname, Republic of	http://www.surinam.net
Swaziland, Kingdom of	http://www.swazi.com
Sweden	http://www.europeanvacationguide.com/travel/Sweden_Practical_Info.html
Switzerland	http://www.traveling.ch/
Syrian Arab Republic	http://www.arab.net/syria/syria_contents.html
Taiwan, Republic of China on	http://www.taipei.org
Tajikistan	http://www.lonelyplanet.com/destinations/central_asia/tajikistan/
Tanzania, United Republic of (Zanzibar)	http://www.newafrica.com/travel/highlights/details.asp?countryid=49
Thailand, Kingdom of	http://www.thailandtravelsearch.com/thailand/tourism_travel_directory/index.shtml
Togo, Republic of	http://www.republicoftogo.com
Tonga	http://www.tongaonline.com
Trinidad and Tobago	http://discovertrinidad.com
Tunisia	http://www.arab.net/tunisia/tunisia_contents.html
Turkey, Republic of	http://www.exploreturkey.com
Turkmenistan	http://www.turkmenistan.com
Tuvalu Island	http://www.emulateme.com/tuvalu.htm
Uganda, Republic of	http://www.africa-insites.com/uganda/default.htm
Ukraine	http://www.un.int/ukraine/
United Arab Emirates (UAE) (Abu Dabi, Dubai, Sharjah, Ras Al Khaimah, Fujairah, Ajman, and Umm Al Quwain)	http://www.emirates.org
United Kingdom (England, Northern Ireland, Scotland, and Wales)	http://www.great-britain.org
Uruguay	http://www.visit-uruguay.com/colonia.htm
U.S. Virgin Islands	http://www.virginisles.com/facts/tourism.html
Uzbekistan, Republic of	http://www.tourism.uz
Vanuatu	http://www.tourismvanuatu.com/welcome.htm
Venezuela	http://www.lonelyplanet.com/destinations/south_america/venezuela/
Vietnam	http://www.gocvietnam.com
Western Samoa	http://public-www.pi.se/~orbit/samoa/welcome.html
Yemen, Republic of	http://www.al-bab.com/yemen
Zambia, Republic of	http://www.zambia.co.zm/
Zimbabwe	http://www.travelnotes.org/Africa/Zimbabwe/zimbabwe_tourism.htm

CONTACT INFORMATION FOR INDIVIDUAL COUNTRIES

The following lists contact information for embassies and consulates of individual countries in the United States. Wherever possible, the contact information provided is for the Consular Division of the embassy, which is the division handling visas, passports, and other such services. Contact information for United Nations Missions in the United States is provided for countries that do not have an embassy or a consulate in America.

Afghanistan, Islamic State of   Inquiries should be addressed to the Permanent Mission of the Islamic State of Afghanistan to the United Nations, 360 Lexington Ave., 11th Fl., New York, NY 10017 (212-972-1212) or the Consulate General in New York at 212-972-2276.

Albania, Republic of   Contact the Embassy of the Republic of Albania, 2100 S St. NW, Washington, DC 20005 (202-223-4942, fax 202-628-7342) or the Permanent Mission of the Republic of Albania to the United Nations at 212-249-2059.

Algeria, Democratic and Popular Republic of Contact the Embassy of the Democratic and Popular Republic of Algeria, Consular Section, 2118 Kalorama Rd. NW, Washington, DC 20008 (202-265-2800, fax 202-667-2174), http://www.algeria-us.org, or the Permanent Mission of the Democratic and Popular Republic of Algeria to the United Nations at 212-750-1960.

Andorra   Contact the Permanent Mission of Andorra to the United Nations, Two United Nations Plaza, 25th Fl., New York, NY 10017 (212-750-8064, fax 212-750-6630).

Angola, Republic of   Contact the Embassy of the Republic of Angola, Consular Section, 1615 M St. NW, Suite 900, Washington, DC 20036 (202-785-1156, fax 202-785-1258), http://www.angola.org or the Permanent Mission of the Republic of Angola to the United Nations at 212-861-5656.

Anguilla. *See* **British West Indies.**

Antigua and Barbuda   Contact the Embassy of Antigua and Barbuda, 3216 New Mexico Ave. NW, Washington, DC 20016 (202-362-5122, fax 202-362-5225) or the Consulate General in Miami at 305-381-6762.

Argentina   Contact the Embassy of Argentina, Consular Section, 1811 Q St. NW, Washington, DC 20009 (202-238-6460, fax 202-332-3171), http://embajadaargentina-usa.org or the nearest Consulate General: Atlanta (404-880-0805), Chicago (312-819-2606), Houston (713-871-8935), Los Angeles (323-954-9155), Miami (305-373-7794), or New York (212-603-0400).

Armenia, Republic of   Contact the Embassy of the Republic of Armenia, 2225 R St., NW, Washington, DC 20008 (202-319-1976, fax 203-319-2982), http://www.armeniaemb.org or the Consulate General in Los Angeles at 310-657-3817.

Aruba   Contact the Embassy of the Netherlands, 4200 Linnean Ave. NW, Washington, DC 20008 (202-244-5300, fax 202-362-3430), http://www.netherlands-embassy.org or the nearest Consulate General: Chicago (312-856-0110), Houston (713-622-8000), Los Angeles (310-268-1598), or New York (212-246-1429). *See also* **Netherlands.**

Australia   Contact the Embassy of Australia, 1601 Massachusetts Ave., NW, Washington, DC 20036 (202-797-3000, fax 202-797-3168), http://www.austemb.org or the nearest Consulate General: Atlanta (404-760-3400), Honolulu (808-524-5050),

Los Angeles (310-229-4800), New York (212-351-6500), or San Francisco (415-536-1970).

Austria   Contact the Embassy of Austria, Consular Section, 3524 International Ct. NW, Washington, DC 20008 (202-895-6767, fax 202-895-6773), http://www.austria.org or the nearest Consulate General: Chicago (312-222-1515), Los Angeles (310-444-9310), or New York (212-737-6400).

Azerbaijan, Republic of   Contact the Embassy of the Republic of Azerbaijan, 927 15th St. NW, Suite 700, Washington, DC 20005 (202-842-0001, fax 202-842-0004), http://www.azembassy.com or to the Permanent Mission of the Republic of Azerbaijan to the United Nations at 212-371-2559.

Azores. *See* **Portugal.**

Bahamas, Commonwealth of   Contact the Embassy of the Commonwealth of the Bahamas, 2220 Massachusetts Ave. NW, Washington, DC 20008 (202-319-2660, fax 202-319-2668) or the nearest Consulate General: Miami (305-373-6295) or New York (212-421-6420).

Bahrain, State of   Contact the Embassy of the State of Bahrain, 3502 International Dr. NW, Washington, DC 20008 (202-342-0741, fax 202-362-2192), http://www.bahrainembassy.org or the Consulate General in New York at 212-223-6200.

Bangladesh, People's Republic of   Contact the Embassy of the People's Republic of Bangladesh, 3510 International Dr., NW, Washington, DC 20007 (202-244-2745, fax 202-244-5366), http://www.bangladoot.org or the Consulate General in Los Angeles (310-441-9399) or New York (212-599-6767).

Barbados   Contact the Embassy of Barbados, 2144 Wyoming Ave. NW, Washington, DC 20008 (202-939-9200, fax 202-332-7467) or the Consulate General: Miami (305-442-1994) or New York (212-867-8435).

Belarus, Republic of   Contact the Embassy of the Republic of Belarus, 1619 New Hampshire Ave. NW, Washington, DC 20008 (202-986-1606, fax 202-986-1805).

Belgium   Contact the Embassy of Belgium, 3330 Garfield St., NW, Washington, DC 20008 (202-333-6900, fax 202-333-3079), http://www.diplobel.org/usa or the nearest Consulate General: Atlanta (404-659-2150), Chicago (312-263-6624), Los Angeles (323-857-1244), or New York (212-586-5110).

Belize   Contact the Embassy of Belize, 2535 Massachusetts Ave. NW, Washington, DC 20008 (202-332-9636, fax 202-332-6888) or the Consulate General in Hollywood, CA at 213-469-7343.

Benin, Republic of   Contact the Embassy of the Republic of Benin, 2124 Kalorama Rd. NW, Washington, DC 20008 (202-232-6656, fax 202-265-1996) or the Permanent Mission of the Republic of Benin to the United Nations at 212-249-6014.

Bermuda. *See* **United Kingdom.**

Bhutan, Kingdom of   Contact the Permanent Mission of the Kingdom of Bhutan to the United Nations, Two United Nations Plaza, 27th Floor, New York, NY 10017 (212-826-1919, fax 212-826-2998).

Bolivia   Contact the Embassy of the Republic of Bolivia, Consular Division, 1819 H St. NW, Suite 240, Washington, DC 20006 (202-232-4827, fax 202-232-8017), http://www.bolivia-usa.org or the nearest Consulate General: Miami (305-358-3450), New York (212-687-0530), or San Francisco (415-495-5173).

Bonaire. *See* **Netherlands Antilles.**

Bosnia and Herzegovina, Republic of   Contact the Embassy of Bosnia and Herzegovina, 2109 E St. NW, Washington, DC 20037 (202-337-1500, fax 202-337-1502), http://www.bosnianembassy.org or the Consulate General in New York at 212-593-1042.

Botswana, Republic of Contact the Embassy of the Republic of Botswana, 1531–1533 New Hampshire Ave. NW, Washington, DC 20036 (202-244-4990, fax 202-244-4164) or the Permanent Mission of the Republic of Botswana to the United Nations at 212-889-2277.

Brazil Contact the Embassy of Brazil Consular Services, 3009 Whitehaven St. NW, Washington, DC 20008 (202-338-2828, fax 202-238-2818), http://www.brasilemb.org or the nearest Consulate General: Boston (617-542-4000), Chicago (312-464-0244), Houston (713-961-3063), Los Angeles (323-651-2664), Miami (305-285-6200), New York (917-777-7777), or San Francisco (415-981-8170).

British Virgin Islands (including **Anegarda, Jost van Dyke, Tortola,** and **Virgin Gorda**). *See* **United Kingdom.**

British West Indies (including **Anguilla, Cayman Islands, Montserrat,** and **Turks and Caicos Islands**). *See* **United Kingdom.**

Brunei Darussalam, State of Contact the Embassy of the State of Brunei Darussalam, 3520 International Ct. NW, Washington, DC 20008 (202-237-1838, fax 202-885-0560), http://www.bruneiembassy.org or the Permanent Mission of the State of Brunei Darussalam to the United Nations at 212-697-3465.

Bulgaria, Republic of Contact the Embassy of the Republic of Bulgaria, 1621 22nd St. NW, Washington, DC 20008 (202-387-0174, fax 202-234-7973), http://www.bulgaria-embassy.org or the Consulate General in New York at 212-935-4646.

Burkina Faso Contact the Embassy of Burkina Faso, 2340 Massachusetts Ave. NW, Washington, DC 20008 (202-332-5577, fax 202-667-1882), http://www.burkinaembassy-usa.org or the Permanent Mission of Burkina Faso to the United Nations at 212-288-7515.

Burundi, Republic of Contact the Embassy of the Republic of Burundi, 2233 Wisconsin Ave. NW, Suite 212, Washington, DC 20007 (202-342-2574, fax 202-342-2578) or the Permanent Mission of the Republic of Burundi to the United Nations at 212-499-0001.

Cambodia, Kingdom of Contact the Royal Embassy of Cambodia, 4500 16th St. NW, Washington, DC 20011 (202-276-7742, fax 202-726-8381) or the Permanent Mission of the Kingdom of Cambodia to the United Nations at 212-223-0676.

Cameroon, Republic of Contact the Embassy of the Republic of Cameroon, 2349 Massachusetts Ave. NW, Washington, DC 20008 (202-265-8790, fax 202-387-3826) or the Honorary Consulate in Houston at 713-774-7693.

Canada Contact the Embassy of Canada 501 Pennsylvania Ave. NW, Washington, DC 20001 (202-682-1740, fax 202-682-7726), http://www.canadianembassy.org or the nearest Consulate General: Atlanta (404-532-2000), Boston (617-262-3760), Buffalo (716-858-9500), Chicago (312-616-1860), Dallas (214-922-9806), Detroit (313-567-2340), Los Angeles (213-346-2700), Miami (305-579-1600), Minneapolis (612-332-7486), New York (212-596-1628), or Seattle (206-443-1777).

Cape Verde, Republic of Contact the Embassy of the Republic of Cape Verde, 3415 Massachusetts Ave. NW, Washington, DC 20007 (202-965-6820, fax 202-965-1207) or the Consulate General in Boston at 617-353-0014.

Cayman Islands. *See* **British West Indies.**

Central African Republic Contact the Embassy of the Central African Republic, 1618 22nd St. NW, Washington, DC 20008 (202-483-7800, fax 202-332-9893) or the Honorary Consulate in New York at 212-983-0330.

Chad, Republic of Contact the Embassy of the Republic of Chad, 2002 R St. NW, Washington, DC 20009 (202-462-4009, fax 202-265-1937), http://www.chadembassy.org or the Permanent Mission of the Republic of Chad to the United Nations at 212-986-0980.

Chile Contact the Embassy of Chile, 1732 Massachusetts Ave. NW, Washington, DC 20036 (202-785-1746, fax 202-887-5579), http://www.chile-usa.org or the nearest Consulate General: Chicago (312-654-8780), Houston (713-621-5853), Los Angeles (310-785-0047), Miami (305-373-8623), New York (212-355-0612), or San Francisco (415-982-7662).

China, People's Republic of Contact the Embassy of the People's Republic of China, 2300 Connecticut Ave. NW, Washington, DC 20008 (202-328-2500, fax 202-588-0032), http://www.china-embassy.org or the nearest Consulate General: Chicago (312-803-0098), Houston (713-524-0780), Los Angeles (213-807-8088), New York (212-330-7400), or San Francisco (415-674-2900).

China, Republic of. *See* **Taiwan.**

Colombia Contact the Embassy of Colombia, Consular Division, 1857 Connecticut Ave. NW, Suite 524, Washington, DC 20008 (202-332-7476, fax 202-332-7180), http://www.colombiaemb.org or the nearest Consulate General: Atlanta (404-255-3038), Boston (617-536-6222), Chicago (312-923-1196), Houston (713-527-8919), Los Angeles (323-653-4299), Miami (305-448-5558), New Orleans (504-525-5580), New York (212-949-9898), San Francisco (415-495-7195), San Juan, PR (787-754-6885), or Seattle (202-332-7476).

Comoros Islands (Federal Islamic Republic of the Comoros) Contact the Embassy of the Federal Islamic Republic of Comoros, 420 E. 50th St., New York, NY 10022 (212-972-8010, fax 212-983-4712).

Congo, Democratic Republic of (formerly Zaire) Contact the Zairian Embassy, 1800 New Hampshire Ave. NW, Washington, DC 20009 (202-234-7690, fax 202-237-0748) or the Permanent Mission of the Democratic Republic of Congo to the United Nations at 201-812-1636.

Congo, Republic of the Contact the Embassy of the Republic of the Congo, 4891 Colorado Ave. NW, Washington, DC 20011 (202-726-5500, fax 202-726-1860) or the Permanent Mission of the Republic of Congo to the United Nations at 212-744-7840.

Cook Islands Contact the Embassy of New Zealand, 37 Observatory Circle NW, Washington, DC 20008 (202-328-4800, fax 202-667-5227), http://www.nzemb.org, the Consulate General in Los Angeles (310-207-1605) or New York (212-832-4038).

Costa Rica Contact the Embassy of Costa Rica, Consular Division, 2114 S St. NW, Washington, DC 20008 (202-234-2945), http://www.costarica-embassy.org or the nearest Consulate General: Atlanta (770-951-7025), Chicago (312-263-2772), Fremont, CA (510-790-0785), Houston (713-266-1527), Los Angeles (213-380-7915), Miami (305-871-7485), New Orleans (504-581-6800), New York (212-509-3066), or San Juan, PR (787-723-6227).

Côte d'Ivoire, Republic of (Ivory Coast) Contact the Embassy of the Republic of Côte d'Ivoire, 2424 Massachusetts Ave. NW, Washington, DC 20008 (202-797-0300) or the Honorary Consulate in San Francisco at 415-391-0176.

Croatia, Republic of Contact the Embassy of the Republic of Croatia, 2343 Massachusetts Ave. NE, Washington, DC 20008 (202-588-5899, fax 202-588-8936), http://www.croatiaemb.org or the nearest Consulate General: Chicago (312-482-9902), Los Angeles (310-477-1009), or New York (212-599-3066).

Cuba   Travel to Cuba is restricted by U.S. Department of Treasury regulations requiring that citizens obtain a license to visit Cuba. Contact the Licensing Division, Office of Foreign Assets Control, U.S. Department of the Treasury, 1500 Pennsylvania Ave. NW, Treasury Annex, Washington, DC 20220 (202-622-2480, fax 202-622-1657, info-by-fax service 202-622-0077). There is no Cuban embassy in the United States, as the U.S. does not maintain diplomatic relations with Cuba. For more information about entry requirements and visas, contact the Embassy of Switzerland, Cuban Interests Section, 2360 16th St. NW, Washington, DC 20009 (202-797-8518, fax 202-797-8521).

Curaçao. *See* **Netherlands Antilles.**

Cyprus, Republic of   Contact the Embassy of the Republic of Cyprus, 2211 R St. NW, Washington, DC 20008 (202-462-5772, fax 202-483-6710) or the Consulate General in New York at 212-686-6016.

Czech Republic   Contact the Embassy of the Czech Republic, Consular Department, 3900 Spring of Freedom St. NW, Washington, DC 20008 (202-274-9121, fax 202-363-6308), http://www.mzv.cz/washington/ or the Consulate General in Los Angeles (310-473-0889) or New York (212-717-5643).

Denmark, Kingdom of (including **Greenland** and the **Faroe Islands**) Contact the Royal Danish Embassy, 3200 Whitehaven St. NW, Washington, DC 20008 (202-234-4300, fax 202-328-1470), http://www.denmarkemb.org or the nearest Consulate General: Chicago (312-787-8780), Los Angeles (310-443-2090), or New York (212-223-4545).

Dijbouti, Republic of   Contact the Embassy of the Republic of Dijbouti, 1156 15th St. NW, Suite 515, Washington, DC 20005 (202-331-0270, fax 202-331-0302) or the Permanent Mission of the Republic of Dijbouti to the United Nations at 212-753-3163.

Dominica, Commonwealth of   Contact the Embassy of the Commonwealth of Dominica, 3216 New Mexico Ave. NW, Washington, DC 20016 (202-364-6781, fax 202-364-6791) or the Consulate General in New York at 212-599-8478.

Dominican Republic   Contact the Embassy of the Dominican Republic, 1715 22nd St. NW, Washington, DC 20008 (202-332-6280, fax 202-265-8057), http://www.domrep.org or the nearest Consulate General: Baltimore (410-719-8788), Boston (617-482-8121), Chicago (312-486-8400), Houston (713-266-0165), Miami (305-358-3220), New Orleans (504-522-1843), New York (212-768-2480), Philadelphia (215-923-3006), or San Francisco (415-982-5144).

Ecuador (including the **Galapagos Islands**)   Contact the Embassy of Ecuador, Consular Section, 2535 15th St. NW, Washington, DC 20009 (202-234-7166, fax 202-265-9325), http://www.ecuador.org or the nearest Consulate General: Jersey City, NJ (201-985-1700), New Orleans (504-523-3229), New York (212-808-0170), or San Francisco (415-957-5921).

Egypt, Arab Republic of   Contact the Embassy of the Arab Republic of Egypt, 3521 International Ct. NW, Washington, DC 20008 (202-895-5400, fax 202-244-4319), http://www.embassyofegypt washingtondc.org or the nearest Consulate General: Chicago (312-828-9162), Houston (713-961-4915), New York (212-759-7120), or San Francisco (419-346-9700).

El Salvador   Contact the Embassy of El Salvador, Consular Affairs, 1424 16th St. NW, 2nd Floor, Washington, DC 20036 (202-331-4032) or the nearest Consulate General: Boston (617-577-9111), Chicago (312-322-1393), Houston (713-270-6239), Dallas (214-637-0732), Los Angeles (213-383-5776), Miami (305-371-8850), New York (212-889-5608), or San Francisco (415-781-7924).

England. *See* **United Kingdom.**

Equatorial Guinea, Republic of   Contact the Embassy of the Republic of Equatorial Guinea, 2020 16th St. NW, Washington, DC 20009 (202-518-5700, fax 202-518-5252) or the Permanent Mission to the Republic of Equatorial Guinea to the United Nations at 914-664-1882.

Eritrea   Contact the Embassy of Eritrea, 1708 New Hampshire Ave. NW, Washington, DC 20009 (203-319-1991, fax 202-319-1304) or the Permanent Mission of Eritrea to the United Nations at 212-687-3390.

Estonia   Contact the Embassy of Estonia, 2131 Massachusetts Ave. NW, Washington, DC 20008 (202-588-0101, fax 202-588-0108), http://www.estemb.org or the Consulate General in New York at 212-883-0636.

Ethiopia, Federal Democratic Republic of   Contact the Embassy of Ethiopia, Consular Affairs, 3506 International Dr. NW, Washington, DC 20008 (202-274-4555), http://www.ethiopianembassy.org or the Permanent Mission of Ethiopia to the United Nations at 212-421-1830.

European Union (**Belgium, Denmark, Finland, France, Germany, Greece, Ireland, Italy, Luxembourg, the Netherlands, Portugal, Spain, Sweden** and **the United Kingdom**)   Established to promote cooperation between the United States and the member states of the Union, the European Union's Delegation of the European Commission to the United States offers helpful information on trade agreements, international policies, justice matters, and many other topics of interest to prospective travelers in Europe. For more information, contact the European Union, Delegation of the European Commission to the United States, 2300 M St., NW, Washington, DC 20007 (202-862-9500, fax 202-429-1766), http://www.eurunion.org.

Faroe Islands. *See* **Denmark.**

Federal Republic of Yugoslavia. *See* **Serbia and Montenegro.**

Fiji   Contact the Embassy of Fiji, 2233 Wisconsin Ave. NW, Suite 240, Washington, DC 20007 (202-337-8320, fax 202-337-1996) or the Permanent Mission of Fiji to the United Nations at 212-687-4130.

Finland   Contact the Embassy of Finland, 3301 Massachusetts Ave. NW, Washington, DC 20008 (202-298-5800, fax 202-298-6030), http://www.finland.org or the Consulate General in Los Angeles (310-203-9903) or New York (212-750-4400).

Former Yugoslav Republic of Macedonia (FYROM)   Contact the Embassy of the Former Yugoslav Republic of Macedonia, 3050 K St. NW, Washington, DC 20007 (202-337-3063, fax 202-337-3093) or the Consulate General in New York at 212-317-1727.

France (including **French Guiana, French Polynesia,** and **French West Indies**)   Contact the Embassy of France, 4101 Reservoir Rd. NW, Washington, DC 20007 (202-944-6000, fax 202-944-6148), http://www.info-france-usa.org or the nearest Consulate General: Atlanta (404-495-1660), Boston (617-542-7374), Chicago (312-787-5359), Houston (713-572-2799), Los Angeles (310-235-3200), Miami (305-372-9799), New Orleans (504-523-5772), New York (212-606-3689), or San Francisco (415-397-4330).

French Guiana. *See* **France.**

French Polynesia (including **Society Islands, French Southern** and **Antarctic Lands, Tuamotu, Gambier, French Austral, Marquesas, Kerguelen, Crozet, New Caldeonia, Tahiti,** and **Wallis** and **Futuna Islands**). *See* **France.**

French West Indies (including **Guadeloupe, Isles des Saintes, La Desirade, Marie Galante, Martinique, St. Barthelemy,** and **St. Martin**). *See* **France.**

Gabonese Republic (Gabon)   Contact the Embassy of the Gabonese Republic, 2034 20th St. NW, Washington, DC 20009 (202-797-1000, fax 202-332-0668) or the Permanent Mission of the Gabonese Republic to the United Nations at 212-686-9720.

Galapagos Islands. *See* **Ecuador.**

Gambia   Contact the Embassy of Gambia, 1155 15th St. NW, Washington, DC 20005 (202-785-1399, fax 202-785-1430) or the Honorary Consulate in Beverly Hills, CA at 310-274-5084.

Georgia, Republic of   Contact the Embassy of the Republic of Georgia, Consular Office, 1615 New Hampshire Ave. NW, Suite 300, Washington, DC 20009 (202-393-6060, fax 202-393-4537), http://www.georgiaemb.org or the nearest Honorary Consulate: Boston (617-492-0727), Houston (281-633-3500), or San Juan, PR (787-724-8070).

Germany, Federal Republic of   Contact the German Consulate at the Embassy of the Federal Republic of Germany, 4645 Reservoir Rd. NW, Washington, DC 20007 (202-298-4393, fax 202-471-5558), http://www.germany-info.org or the nearest Consulate General: Atlanta (404-659-4760), Boston (617-536-4414), Chicago (312-580-1199), Houston (713-627-7770), Los Angeles (323-930-2703), Miami (305-358-0290), New York (212-610-9700), or San Francisco (415-775-1061).

Ghana   Contact the Embassy of Ghana, 3512 International Dr., NW, Washington, DC 20008 (202-686-4520, fax 202-686-4527), http://www.ghanaembassy.org or the Consulate General in New York at 212-832-1300.

Gibraltar. *See* **United Kingdom.**

Great Britain. *See* **United Kingdom.**

Greece   Contact the Embassy of Greece, Consular Section, Massachusetts Ave. NW, Washington, DC 20008 (202-939-5818, fax 202-234-2803), http://www.greekembassy.org or the nearest Consulate General: Boston (617-543-0100), Chicago (312-

225-3915), Los Angeles (310-826-5555), New York (212-988-5500), or San Francisco (415-775-2102).

Greenland. *See* **Denmark.**

Grenada   Contact the Embassy of Grenada, 1701 New Hampshire Ave. NW, Washington, DC 20009 (202-265-2561) or the Consulate General in New York at 212-599-0301.

Guadeloupe (French West Indies). *See* **France.**

Guatemala   Contact the Embassy of Guatemala, Consular Section, 2220 R St. NW, Washington, DC 20008 (202-745-4952, fax 202-745-1908), http://www.guatemala-embassy.org or the nearest Consulate General: Chicago (312-332-1587), Houston (713-953-9531), Los Angeles (213-365-9251), Miami (305-679-9945), New York (212-686-3837), or San Francisco (415-788-5651).

Guinea, Republic of   Contact the Embassy of the Republic of Guinea, 2112 Leroy Pl. NW, Washington, DC 20008 (202-483-9420, fax 202-483-8688) or the Permanent Mission of the Republic of Guinea to the United Nations at 212-687-8115.

Guinea-Bissau, Republic of   Contact the Embassy of the Republic of Guinea-Bissau, 15929 Yukon Lane, Rockville, MD 20855 (301-947-3958) or the Permanent Mission of the Republic of Guinea-Bissau to the United Nations at 212-338-9380.

Guyana, Republic of   Contact the Embassy of the Republic of Guyana, 2490 Tracy Pl. NW, Washington, DC 20008 (202-265-6900, fax 202-232-1297), http://www.guyana.org/govt/embassy.html or the Consulate General in New York at 212-527-3215.

Haiti, Republic of   Contact the Embassy of the Republic of Haiti, 2311 Massachusetts Ave. NW, Washington, DC 20008 (202-332-4090, fax 202-745-7215), http://www.haiti.org or the nearest Consulate General: Boston (617-266-3660), Chicago (312-922-4004), Miami (305-859-2003), or New York (212-697-9767).

Holy See, Apostolic Nunciature of the (the Vatican) Contact the Holy See Nunciature, 3339 Massachusetts Ave. NW, Washington, DC 20008 (202-333-7121) or the Permanent Observer Mission of the Holy See to the United Nations at 212-370-7885. *See also* **Italy.**

Honduras Contact the Embassy of Honduras, Consular Section, 1528 K St. NW, 2nd Floor, Washington, DC 20005 (202-737-2972, fax 202-737-2907) or the nearest Consulate General: Chicago (773-342-8281), Houston (713-622-7911), Los Angeles (213-383-9244), Miami (305-447-8927), New York (212-269-3611), San Francisco (315-392-0076), or Tampa (813-209-3249).

Point Roberts, Washington, is cut off from the rest of the state by British Columbia, Canada. To travel between Point Roberts and the rest of the state, you must pass through both Canadian and U.S. customs.

Hong Kong (Special Administrative Region of the People's Republic of China). *See* **China, People's Republic of.**

Hungary, Republic of Contact the Embassy of the Republic of Hungary, 3910 Shoemaker St. NW, Washington, DC 20008 (202-362-6730, fax 202-966-8135), http://www.hungaryemb.org or the Consulate General in Los Angeles (310-473-9344) or New York (212-752-0669).

Iceland Contact the Embassy of Iceland, 1156 15th St. NW, Suite 1200, Washington, DC 20005 (202-265-6653, fax 202-265-6656), http://www.iceland.org or the Consulate General in New York at 212-593-2700.

India Contact the Embassy of India, Consular Wing, 2536 Massachusetts Ave. NW, Washington, DC 20008 (202-939-9806, fax 202-797-4693), http://www.indianembassy.org or the nearest Consulate General: Chicago (312-595-0405), Houston (713-626-2148), New York (212-774-0600), or San Francisco (415-668-0662).

Indonesia, Republic of Contact the Embassy of the Republic of Indonesia, 2020 Massachusetts Ave. NW, Washington, DC 20036 (202-775-5200, fax 202-775-5365) or the nearest Consulate General: Chicago (312-345-9300), Houston (713-785-1691), Los Angeles (213-383-5126), New York (212-879-0600), or San Francisco (415-474-9571).

Iran, Islamic Republic of The United States does not maintain diplomatic or consular relations with Iran. Inquiries should be addressed to the Embassy of Pakistan, Interest Section of the Islamic Republic of Iran, 2209 Wisconsin Ave. NW, Washington, DC 20007 (202-965-4990, fax 202-965-1073) or to the Permanent Mission of the Islamic Republic of Iran to the United Nations at 212-682-2020.

Iraq The United States suspended diplomatic and consular operations in Iraq in 1990. Since February 1991, U.S. passports are not valid for travel in, to, or through Iraq without authorization from the Department of State. Passport validation requests should be forwarded in writing to Deputy Assistant Secretary for Passport Services, Office of Passport Policy and Advisory Services—US Dept. of State, 2401 E St. NW, 9th Floor, Washington, DC 20522. For more information, contact the Embassy of Algeria, Iraqi Interests Section, 1801 P St. NW, Washington, DC 20036 (202-483-7500, fax 202-462-5066).

Ireland Contact the Embassy of Ireland, 2234 Massachusetts Ave. NW, Washington, DC 20008 (202-462-3939, fax 202-232-5993), http://www.irelandemb.org or the nearest Consulate General: Boston (617-267-9330), Chicago (312-337-1868), New York (212-319-2555), or San Francisco (415-392-4214).

Israel and the Occupied Territories (Jerusalem, Gaza, Golan Heights, and the **West Bank)** Contact the Embassy of Israel, Consular Section, 3514

International Dr. NW, Washington, DC 20008 (202-364-5557, fax 202-364-5429), http://www.israelemb.org or the nearest Consulate General: Atlanta (404-487-6500), Boston (617-535-0200), Chicago (312-297-4800), Houston (713-627-3780), Los Angeles (323-852-5500), Miami (305-925-9400), New York (212-499-5410), Philadelphia (215-546 5556), or San Francisco (415-844-7500).

Italy Contact the Embassy of Italy, 3000 Whitehaven St. NW, Washington, DC 20008 (202-612-4400, fax 202-518-2154), http://www.italyemb.org or the nearest Consulate General: Boston (617-542-0483), Chicago (312-467-1550), Houston (713-850-7520), Los Angeles (310-820-0622), Miami (305-374-6322), New York (212-737-9100), Philadelphia (215-592-7329), or San Francisco (415-292-9210).

Ivory Coast. *See* **Côte d'Ivoire.**

Jamaica Contact the Embassy of Jamaica, 1520 New Hampshire Ave. NW, Washington, DC 20036 (202-452-0660, fax 202-452-0081), http://www.emjam-usa.org or the Consulate General in Miami (305-374-8431) or New York (212-935-9000).

Japan Contact the Embassy of Japan, 2520 Massachusetts Ave. NW, Washington, DC 20008 (202-238-6700, fax 202-328-2187), http://www.embjapan.org or the nearest Consulate General: Anchorage (907-562-8424), Atlanta (404-892-2700), Boston (617-973-9772), Chicago (312-280-0400), Denver (305-534-1151), Detroit (313-567-0120), Guam (671-646-1290), Honolulu (808-543-3111), Houston (713-652-2977), Kansas City, MO (816-471-0111), Los Angeles (213-617-6700), Miami (305-530-9090), New Orleans (504-529-2101), New York (212-371-8222), Portland, OR (503-221-1811), San Francisco (415-777-3533), or Seattle (206-682-9107).

Jordan, Hashemite Kingdom of Contact the Embassy of the Hashemite Kingdom of Jordan, Consular Section, 3504 International Dr. NW, Washington, DC 20008 (202-966-2861, fax 202-686-4491), http://www.jordanembassyus.org or the Consulate in New York at 212-832-0119.

Kazakhstan, Republic of Contact the Embassy of the Republic of Kazakhstan, 1401 16th St. NW, Washington, DC 20008 (202-387-6101, fax 202-462-3829), http://www.president.kz or the Consulate in New York at 212-888-3024.

Kenya Contact the Embassy of Kenya, 2249 R St. NW, Washington, DC 20008 (202-387-6101, fax 202-462-3829), http://www.kenyaembassy.com or the Permanent Mission of Kenya to the United Nations at 212-486-1985.

Kiribati, Republic of (formerly **Gilbert Islands**) Contact the British Embassy, Consular Section, 3100 Massachusetts Ave. NW, Washington, DC 20008 (202-588-7800, fax 202-588-7850).

Korea, Democratic People's Republic of (North Korea) The United States currently does not maintain diplomatic or consular relations with North Korea. The Swedish Embassy in Cambodia is acting as the consular protecting power for the U.S. government in North Korea. A U.S. Treasury Department license must be obtained for any U.S. citizen to engage in any travel-related transaction, whether travel will be to or within North Korea. Before planning any travel to North Korea, contact the Licensing Division, Office of Foreign Assets Control, U.S. Department of the Treasury, 1500 Pennsylvania Ave. NW, Treasury Annex, Washington, DC 20220 (202-622-2480, fax 202-622-1657, info-by-fax service 202-622-0077). Visa information must be obtained from a consulate in a country that maintains diplomatic relations with North Korea, such as France.

Korea, Republic of (South Korea) Contact the Embassy of Korea, Consular Division, 2320 Massachusetts Ave. NW, Washington, DC 20008 (202-939-5663, fax 202-342-1597), http://emb.dsdn.net or the nearest Consulate General: Atlanta (404-522-1611), Boston (617-641-2830), Chicago (312-822-9485), Honolulu (808-595-6109), Houston (713-961-0186), Los Angeles (213-385-9300), New York

Travel

(646-674-6000), San Francisco (415-921-2251), or Seattle (206-441-1011).

Kuwait, State of   Contact the Embassy of the State of Kuwait, 2940 Tilden St. NW, Washington, DC 20008 (202-966-0702, fax 202-966-0517) or the Permanent Mission of the State of Kuwait to the United Nations at 212-973-4300.

Kyrgyz Republic (Kyrgyzstan)   Contact the Embassy of the Kyrgyz Republic, 1732 Wisconsin Ave. NW, Washington, DC 20007 (202-338-5141, fax 202-338-5139), http://www.kyrgyzstan.org or the Consulate General in New York at 212-319-2836.

Laos (Lao People's Democratic Republic)   Contact the Embassy of Lao People's Democratic Republic, Consular Section, 2222 S St. NW, Washington, DC 20008 (202-332-6416, fax 202-332-4923), http://www.laoembassy.com or the Permanent Mission of the Lao People's Democratic Republic to the United Nations at 212-832-2734.

Latvia   Contact the Embassy of Latvia, 4325 17th St. NW, Washington, DC 20011 (202-726-8213, fax 202-726-6785), http://www.latvia-usa.org or the nearest Honorary Consulate: Houston (713-888-0404), Palos Verdes, CA (310-377-1784), or Willoughby, OH (216-951-6665).

Lebanon   Contact the Embassy of Lebanon, 2560 28th St. NW, Washington, DC 20008 (202-939-6300, fax 202-939-6324), http://www.lebanonembassy.org or the nearest Consulate General: Detroit (313-567-0233), Los Angeles (323-467-1253), or New York (212-744-7905).

Lesotho, Kingdom of   Contact the Embassy of the Kingdom of Lesotho, 2511 Massachusetts Ave. NW, Washington, DC 20008 (202-797-5533, fax 202-234-6815) or the Honorary Consulate in New Orleans at 504-524-6908.

Liberia, Republic of   Contact the Embassy of the Republic of Liberia, 5201 16th St. NW, Washington, DC 20011 (202-723-0437, fax 202-723-0436),

http://www.liberiaemb.org or the Consulate General in New York (212-687-1025).

Libya   Since December 1981, U.S. passports are not valid for travel in, to, or through Libya without authorization from the Department of State. Application for exemption to this restriction should be submitted in writing to Passport Services, U.S. Department of State, 1111 19th St. NW, Washington, DC 20524, Attn: CA/PPT/PAS. In addition, U.S. citizens need a Treasury Department license in order to engage in any transactions related to travel to and within Libya. Before planning any travel to Libya, U.S. citizens should contact the Licensing Division, Office of Foreign Assets Control, U.S. Department of the Treasury, 1500 Pennsylvania Ave. NW, Treasury Annex, Washington, DC 20220 (202-622-2480, fax 202-622-1657, info-by-fax service 202-622-0077). Application and inquiries for visas must be made through a country that maintains diplomatic relations with Libya.

Liechtenstein   Contact the Embassy of Switzerland, 2900 Cathedral Ave. NW, Washington, DC 20008 (202-745-7900, fax 202-387-2564), http://www.swissemb.org or the nearest Consulate General: Atlanta (404-870-2000), Chicago (312-915-0061), Houston (713-650-0000), Los Angeles (310-575-1145), New York (212-758-2560), or San Francisco (415-788-2272).

Lithuania   Contact the Embassy of Lithuania, 2622 16th St. NW, Washington, DC 20009 (202-234-5860, fax 202-328-0466), http://www.ltembassyus.org or the Consulate General in Chicago (312-397-0382) or New York (212-354-7849).

Luxembourg, Grand Duchy   Contact the Embassy of the Grand Duchy of Luxembourg, 2200 Massachusetts Ave. NW, Washington, DC 20008 (202-265-4171, fax 202-328-8270), http://www.luxembourg-usa.org or the Consulate General in New York (212-888-6664) or San Francisco (415-788-0816).

Macau (Macau became a Special Administrative Region of the People's Republic of China in December 1999.) Contact the Embassy of the People's Republic of China, 2300 Connecticut Ave. NW, Washington, DC 20008 (202-328-2500, fax 202-588-0032) or the nearest Consulate General of China: Chicago (312-803-0098), Houston (713-524-0780), Los Angeles (213-807-0088), New York (212-330-7400), or San Francisco (415-674-2900). Or contact the American Consulate General in Hong Kong (852-2523-9011).

Macedonia. *See* **Former Yugoslav Republic of Macedonia (FYROM).**

Madagascar, Republic of Contact the Embassy of the Republic of Madagascar, 2374 Massachusetts Ave. NW, Washington, DC 20008 (202-265-5525, fax 202-265-3034), http://www.embassy.org/madagascar.

Malawi Contact the Embassy of Malawi, 2408 Massachusetts Ave. NW, Washington, DC 20008 (202-797-1007) or the Honorary Consulate in Vista, CA (760-598-1836).

Malaysia (and the **Borneo States, Sarawak,** and **Sabah**) Contact the Embassy of Malaysia, Consular Division, 1900 24th St. NW, Washington, DC 20008 (202-328-2700, fax 202-483-7669) or the Consulate General in Los Angeles (213-892-1238) or New York (212-490-2722).

Maldives Contact the Permanent Mission of the Republic of Maldives to the United Nations, 800 2nd Ave., Suite 400E, New York, NY 10017 (212-599-6195).

Mali, Republic of Contact the Embassy of the Republic of Mali, 2130 R St. NW, Washington, DC 20008 (202-332-2249, fax 202-332-6603), http://www.maliembassy.org or the Permanent Mission of the Republic of Mali to the United Nations at 212-737-4150.

Malta Contact the Embassy of Malta, 2017 Connecticut Ave. NW, Washington, DC 20008 (202-462-3611), http://www.magnet.mt or the Consulate in New York at 212-725-2345.

Marshall Islands, Republic of Contact the Embassy of Marshall Islands, 2433 Massachusetts Ave. NW, Washington, DC 20008 (202-234-5414, fax 202-232-3236), http://www.rmiembassyus.org or the Consulate General in Honolulu at 808-545-7767).

Martinique (French West Indies). *See* **France.**

Santa Fe, New Mexico, founded in 1607, is the oldest continuously occupied state capital. It has no regularly scheduled airline service and no passenger train service.

Mauritania, Republic of Contact the Embassy of the Republic of Mauritania, 2129 Leroy Pl. NW, Washington, DC 20008 (202-232-5700, fax 202-319-2623) or the Permanent Mission of the Republic of Mauritania to the United Nations at 212-986-7963.

Mauritius Contact the Embassy of Mauritius, 4301 Connecticut Ave. NW, Suite 441, Washington, DC 20008 (202-244-1491, fax 202-966-0983), http://www.idsonline.com/usa/embassydc.html or the nearest Honorary Consulate: Atlanta (404-264-1700), Los Angeles (310-557-2009), or San Francisco (415-693-9233).

Mayotte Island. *See* **France.**

Mexico Contact the Embassy of Mexico, Consular Division, 2827 16th St. NW, Washington, DC 20009 (202-736-1000, fax 202-797-8458), http://www.embassyofmexico.org or contact the nearest Consulate General: Albuquerque (505-247-2147), Atlanta (404-266-2233), Austin, TX (512-478-2866), Boston (617-426-4181), Calexico, CA (760-357-3863), Chicago (312-855-0066), Dallas (214-630-7341), Denver (303-331-1110), El Paso,

TX (915-533-3644), Fresno, CA (559-233-9770), Houston (713-271-6800), Los Angeles (213-351-6800), Miami (305-716-4977), New Orleans (504-522-3698), New York (212-217-6400), Philadelphia (215-922-3834), Phoenix (602-242-7398), Portland, OR (503-274-1442), Sacramento, CA (916-441-3287), San Antonio, TX (210-227-1085), San Bernardino, CA (909-889-9836), San Diego, CA (619-231-8414), San Jose, CA (408-294-3414), or Santa Ana, CA (714-835-3069).

Micronesia, Federated States of (Kosrae, Yap, Panape, and Truk)   Contact the Embassy of the Federated States of Micronesia, 1725 N St. NW, Washington, DC 20036 (202-223-4383, fax 202-223-4391), http://www.fsmembassy.org or the nearest Consulate General: Guam (671-646-9154) or Honolulu (808-836-4775).

Miquelon Island. *See* **France.**

Moldova, Republic of   Contact the Embassy of the Republic of Moldova, 2101 S St. NW, Washington, DC 20008 (202-667-1130, fax 202-667-1204), http://www.moldova.org or the Permanent Mission of the Republic of Moldova to the United Nations at 212-682-3523.

Monaco, Principality of   Contact the Consulate General of Monaco, 565 Fifth Ave., New York, NY 10017 (212-759-5227) or the nearest Honorary Consulate: Chicago (312-642-1242), Los Angeles (213-655-8970), New Orleans (504-522-5700), New York (212-759-5227), San Francisco (415-362-5050), or San Juan, PR (787-721-4215).

Mongolia   All foreigners are required to be registered with the police at the Citizen's Information and Registration Center in Mongolia upon arrival and are warned to do so in order to avoid being denied exit and/or fined upon departure. Contact the Embassy of Mongolia, 2833 M St. NW, Washington, DC 20007 (202-333-7117, fax 202-298-7117), http://www.monemb.org or the Permanent Mission of Mongolia to the United Nations at 212-861-9460.

Montenegro. *See* **Serbia and Montenegro.**

Montserrat. *See* **British West Indies.**

Morocco, Kingdom of   Contact the Embassy of the Kingdom of Morocco, 1601 21st St. NW, Washington, DC 20009 (202-462-7979, fax 202-265-0161) or the Consulate General in New York at 212-758-2625.

Mozambique, Republic of   Contact the Embassy of the Republic of Mozambique, 1990 M St. NW, Suite 570, Washington, DC 20036 (202-293-7146, fax 202-835-0245), http://www.embamoc-usa.org or the Permanent Mission of the Republic of Mozambique to the United Nations at 212-644-5965.

Myanmar, Union of   Contact the Embassy of the Union of Myanmar, 2300 S St. NW, Washington, DC 20008 (202-332-9044, fax 202-332-9046) or the Permanent Mission of the Union of Myanmar to the United Nations at 212-535-1310.

Namibia   Contact the Embassy of Namibia, 1605 New Hampshire Ave. NW, Washington, DC 20009 (202-986-0540, fax 202-986-0443) or the Honorary Consulate in Detroit at 313-259-0054.

Nepal, Kingdom of   Contact the Royal Nepalese Embassy, 2131 Leroy Pl. NW, Washington, DC 20008 (202-667-4550, fax 202-667-5534), http://www.newweb.net/nepal_embassy or the Consulate General in New York at 212-370-3988.

Netherlands, the, and **Netherlands Antilles** (including **Bonaire, Curaçao, Saba, St. Maarten,** and **Statia [St. Eustatius]**)   Contact the Embassy of the Netherlands, 4200 Linnean Ave. NW, Washington, DC 20008 (202-244-5300, fax 202-362-3430), http://www.netherlands-embassy.org or the nearest Consulate General: Chicago (312-856-0110), Houston (713-622-8000), Los Angeles (310-268-1598), or New York (212-246-1429).

New Caledonia (French Polynesia). *See* **France.**

New Zealand Contact the Embassy of New Zealand, 37 Observatory Circle NW, Washington, DC 20008 (202-328-4800, fax 202-667-5227), http://www.nzemb.org or the Consulate General in Los Angeles (310-207-1605) or New York (212-832-4038).

Nicaragua Contact the Embassy of Nicaragua, 1627 New Hampshire Ave. NW, Washington, DC 20009 (202-939-6531, fax 202-939-6574) or the nearest Consulate General: Houston (713-272-9628), Los Angeles (213-252-1170), Miami (305-220-6900), New Orleans (504-523-1507), New York (212-986-6562), or San Francisco (415-765-6821).

Niger, Republic of Contact the Embassy of the Republic of Niger, 2204 R St. NW, Washington, DC 20008 (202-483-4224, fax 202-683-3169) or the Permanent Mission of the Republic of Niger to the United Nations at 212-421-3260.

Nigeria, Republic of The U.S. State Department has issued the following entry-requirement-related information for Nigeria: "A visa is required and must be obtained in advance; airport visas are not available. Promises of entry into Nigeria without a visa are credible indicators of a fraudulent commercial scheme in which the perpetrators seek to exploit the foreign traveler's illegal presence in Nigeria with threats of extortion or bodily harm. U.S. citizens cannot legally depart Nigeria unless they can prove, by presenting their entry visas, that they entered Nigeria legally." Contact the Embassy of the Federal Republic of Nigeria, 1333 16th St. NW, Washington, DC 20036 (202-986-8400, fax 202-775-1385), http://www.nigeria-government.com/faqframe.html or the Consulate General in New York at 212-808-0301.

Niue. *See* **New Zealand.**

Norfolk Island. *See* **Australia.**

Northern Ireland. *See* **United Kingdom.**

Northern Mariana Islands, Commonwealth of the Self-governing commonwealth in political union with the U.S.; no restrictions on entry or travel for U.S. citizens.

North Korea. *See* **Korea, Democratic People's Republic of.**

Norway, Kingdom of Contact the Royal Norwegian Embassy, 2720 34th St. NW, Washington, DC 20008 (202-333-6000, fax 202-337-0870), http://www.norway.org or contact the nearest Consulate General: Houston (713-521-2900), Miami (305-358-4386), Minneapolis (612-332-3338), New York (212-421-7333), or San Francisco (415-986-0766).

Oman, Sultanate of Contact the Embassy of the Sultanate of Oman, 2535 Belmont Rd. NW, Washington, DC 20008 (202-387-1980, fax 202-745-4933) or the Permanent Mission of the Sultanate of Oman to the United Nations at 212-355-3505.

Pakistan, Islamic Republic of Contact the Embassy of the Islamic Republic of Pakistan, 2315 Massachusetts Ave. NW, Washington, DC 20008 (202-939-6200, fax 202-387-0484), http://www.pakistan-embassy.com or the Consulate General in Los Angeles (310-441-5114) or New York (212-879-5800).

Palau, Republic of Contact the Embassy of the Republic of Palau, 1150 18th St. NW, Suite 750, Washington, DC 20036 (202-452-6814, fax 202-452-6281), http://www.ropembassy.org or the Consulate in Guam (671-646-9281).

Panama Contact the Embassy of Panama, 2862 McGill Terrace NW, Washington, DC 20008 (202-483-1407, fax 202-387-6141) or the nearest Consulate General: Atlanta (404-522-4114), Coral Gables, FL (305-447-3700), Houston (713-622-4451), New Orleans (504-525-3458), New York (212-840-2450), Philadelphia (215-574-2994), San Francisco (415-391-4268), or Tampa, FL (305-447-3700).

Papua New Guinea   Contact the Embassy of Papua New Guinea, 1779 Massachusetts Ave. NW, Suite 805, Washington, DC 20036 (202-745-3680, fax 202-745-3679), http://www.pngembassy.org or contact the Consulate General in Honolulu (808-623-8144).

Paraguay   Contact the Embassy of Paraguay, 2400 Massachusetts Ave. NW, Washington, DC 20008 (202-483-6960, fax 202-234-4508) or the Consulate General in Miami (305-374-9090) or New York (212-682-9441).

Charles Lindbergh was not the first person to fly across the Atlantic. Eight years before Lindbergh's flight, two men copiloted a twin-engine plane from Newfoundland to Ireland. Lindbergh's achievement was doing it alone.

Peru   Contact the Embassy of Peru, 1700 Massachusetts Ave. NW, Washington, DC 20036 (202-833-9860, fax 202-659-8124), http://www.peruemb.org or the nearest Consulate General: Chicago (312-782-1599), Houston (713-781-5000), Los Angeles (213-252-5910), Miami (305-374-1305), Paterson, NJ (973-278-3324), New York (212-481-7410), or San Francisco (415-362-5185).

Philippines   Contact the Embassy of the Philippines, 1600 Massachusetts Ave. NW, Washington, DC 20036 (202-467-9300, fax 202-467-9417), http://www.embassyonline.com or the nearest Consulate General: Chicago (312-332-6458), Guam (671-646-4620), Honolulu (808-595-6316), Los Angeles (213-639-0980), New York (212-764-1330), or San Francisco (415-433-6666).

Poland, Republic of   Contact the Consular Division of the Embassy of the Republic of Poland, 2224 Wyoming Ave. NW, Washington, DC 20008 (202-234-3800, fax 202-328-2152), http://www.polishworld.com/polemb or the nearest Consulate

General: Boston (617-357-1980), Chicago (312-337-8166), Los Angeles (310-442-8500), New York (646-237-2100), or San Juan, PR (809-721-0495).

Portugal (including **Azores and the Madeira Islands**)   Contact the Embassy of Portugal at 2125 Kalorama Rd. NW, Washington, DC 20008 (202-328-8610, fax 202-462-3726), http://www.portugalemb.org or the nearest Consulate General: Boston (617-536-8740), Newark (973-643-4200), New York (212-246-4580), or San Francisco (415-346-3400).

Qatar, State of   Contact the Embassy of the State of Qatar, 4200 Wisconsin Ave. NW, Suite 200, Washington, DC 20016 (202-274-1600, fax 202-237-0061) or the Consulate General in Houston at 713-355-8221.

Reunion Island. *See* **France.**

Romania   Contact the Embassy of Romania, Consular Section, 1607 23rd St. NW, Washington, DC 20008 (202-332-2879, fax 202-232-4748), http://www.roembus.org or the nearest Consulate General: Chicago (312-573-1315), Los Angeles (310-444-0043), or New York (212-682-9122).

Russian Federation   Contact the Embassy of the Russian Federation, Consular Division, 2641 Tunlaw Rd. NW, Washington, DC 20007 (202-939-8907, fax 202-483-7579), http://www.russianembassy.org or the nearest Consulate General: New York (212-348-0926), San Francisco (415-928-6878), or Seattle (206-728-1910).

Rwanda, Republic of   Contact the Embassy of the Republic of Rwanda, 1714 New Hampshire Ave. NW, Washington, DC 20009 (202-232-2882, fax 202-232-4544), http://www.rwandemb.org or the Consulate General in San Francisco at 415-772-9181.

Saba. *See* **Netherlands Antilles.**

St. Barthelemy (French West Indies). *See* **France.**

St. Eustatius (Statia). *See* **Netherlands Antilles.**

St. Kitts and Nevis   Contact the Embassy of St. Kitts and Nevis, 3216 New Mexico Ave. NW, Washington, DC 20016 (202-686-2636, fax 202-686-5740) or the Permanent Mission of St. Kitts and Nevis to the United Nations at 212-535-1234.

St. Lucia   Contact the Embassy of St. Lucia, 3216 New Mexico Ave., Washington, DC 20016 (202-364-6792, fax 202-364-6723) or the Consulate in New York at 212-697-9360.

St. Maarten. *See* **Netherlands Antilles.**

St. Martin (French West Indies). *See* **France.**

St. Pierre. *See* **France.**

St. Vincent and the Grenadines   Contact the Embassy of St. Vincent and the Grenadines, 3216 New Mexico Ave., Washington, DC 20016 (202-364-6730, fax 202-364-6736) or the Honorary Consulate in Malibu, CA (310-457-8111) or New Orleans (504-523-1385).

Samoa, Independent State of   Contact the Embassy to the United States and Permanent Mission of the Independent State of Samoa to the United Nations, 800 Second Ave., Suite 400J, New York, NY 10017 (212-599-6196, fax 212-599-0797) or the Honorary Consulate in Honolulu at 808-677-7197.

San Marino, Republic of   Contact the Permanent Mission of the Republic of San Marino to the United Nations, 327 East 50th St., New York, NY 10022 (212-751-1234, fax 212-751-1436).

São Tomé and Príncipé   Contact the Permanent Mission of São Tomé and Príncipé to the United Nations, 400 Park Ave., 7th Floor, New York, NY 10022 (212-317-0533, fax 212-317-0580).

Saudi Arabia, Kingdom of   Contact the Royal Embassy of Saudi Arabia, 601 New Hampshire Ave. NW, Washington, DC 20037 (202-342-3800), http://www.saudiembassy.net or the nearest Consulate General: Houston (713-785-5577), Los Angeles (310-479-6000), or New York (212-752-2740).

Scotland. *See* **United Kingdom.**

Senegal, Republic of   Contact the Embassy of the Republic of Senegal, 2112 Wyoming Ave. NW, Washington, DC 20008 (202-234-0450, fax 202-332-6315) or the Honorary Consulate General in Miami (305-371-4286) or Newton, MA (617-964-9641).

Serbia and Montenegro (Federal Republic of Yugoslavia)   The Federal Republic of Yugoslavia currently has no consular office issuing visas in the United States. The Embassy of Yugoslavia in Ottawa, Canada, will accept applications from the U.S. (613-233-6289).

Seychelles   Contact the Embassy and Permanent Mission of Seychelles to the United Nations, 800 Second Ave., Suite 400C, New York, NY 10017 (212-972-0785, fax 212-972-1786).

Sierra Leone   Contact the Embassy of Sierra Leone, 1701 19th St. NW, Washington, DC 20009 (202-939-9261, fax 202-483-1793) or the Permanent Mission of Sierra Leone to the United Nations at 212-688-1656.

Singapore, Republic of   Contact the Embassy of the Republic of Singapore, 3501 International Pl. NW, Washington, DC 20008 (202-537-3100, fax 212-537-0876).

Slovak Republic   Contact the Embassy of the Slovak Republic, 2201 Wisconsin Ave. NW, Suite 250, Washington, DC 20007 (202-965-5160, fax 202-965-5166), http://www.slovakemb.com or the nearest Honorary Consulate: Broadview Heights, OH (440-838-4949), Chicago (630-548-1944), Denver (303-692-8833), Eden Prairie, MN (612-937-9006), or Pittsburgh (412-531-2990).

Slovenia, Republic of   Contact the Embassy of the Republic of Slovenia, 1525 New Hampshire Ave. NW, Washington, DC 20036 (202-667-5363, fax 202-667-4563), http://www.embassy.org/slovenia or the Consulate General in New York at 212-370-3006).

Travel

Solomon Islands   Contact the Embassy to the United States and Permanent Mission of the Solomon Islands to the United Nations, 800 Second Ave., Suite 400L, New York, NY 10017 (212-599-6192, fax 212-661-8925).

Somali Democratic Republic (Somalia)   Contact the Consulate of the Somali Democratic Republic in New York (212-688-9410).

South Africa   Contact the Embassy of South Africa, Consular Section, Suite 220, Van Ness Center, 4301 Connecticut Ave. NW, Washington, DC 20008 (202-232-4400, fax 202-244-9417), http://usaembassy.southafrica.net or the Consulate General in Los Angeles (323-651-0902) or New York (212-213-4880).

South Korea. *See* **Korea, Republic of.**

Spain   Contact the Embassy of Spain, Consulate General, 2375 Pennsylvania Ave. NW, Washington, DC 20037 (202-728-2330, fax 202-728-2302), http://www.spainemb.org or the nearest Consulate General: Boston (617-536-2506), Chicago (312-782-4588), Houston (713-783-6200), Los Angeles (323-938-0158), Coral Gables, FL (305-446-5511), New Orleans (504-525-4951), New York (212-355-4080), San Juan, PR (787-758-6090), or San Francisco (415-922-2995).

Sri Lanka   Contact the Embassy of Sri Lanka, 2148 Wyoming Ave. NW, Washington, DC 20008 (202-483-4025, fax 202-232-7181), or the Consulate General in Los Angeles at 323-624-0479.

Statia (St. Eustatius). *See* **Netherlands Antilles.**

Sudan, Republic of the   Contact the Embassy of the Republic of the Sudan, 2210 Massachusetts Ave. NW, Washington, DC 20008 (202-338-8565, fax 202-667-2406), http://www.sudanembassyus.org or the Consulate General in New York at 212-573-6033.

Suriname, Republic of   Contact the Embassy of the Republic of Suriname, 4301 Connecticut Ave. NW, Suite 460, Washington, DC 20008 (202-244-

7488, fax 202-244-5878) or the Consulate in Miami at 305-593-2697.

Swaziland, Kingdom of   Contact the Embassy of the Kingdom of Swaziland, 3400 International Dr. NW, Washington, DC 20008 (202-362-6683, fax 202-244-8059) or the Permanent Mission of the Kingdom of Swaziland to the United Nations at 212-371-8910.

Sweden   Contact the Embassy of Sweden, 1501 M St. NW, Washington, DC 20005 (202-467-2600, fax 202-467-2699), http://www.swedenemb.org or the nearest Consulate General: Chicago (312-781-6262), Los Angeles (310-445-4008), New York (212-583-2550), or San Francisco (415-788-2631).

Switzerland   Contact the Embassy of Switzerland, 2900 Cathedral Ave. NW, Washington, DC 20008 (202-745-7900, fax 202-387-2564), http://www.swissemb.org or the nearest Consulate General: Atlanta (404-870-2000), Chicago (312-915-0061), Houston (713-650-0000), Los Angeles (310-575-1145), New York (212-599-5700), or San Francisco (415-788-2272).

Syrian Arab Republic (Syria)   The U.S. State Department cautions travelers that "Entry to Syria is not granted to persons with passports bearing an Israeli visa or entry/exit stamps, or to persons born in the Gaza region or of Gazan descent. Foreigners who wish to stay 15 days or more in Syria must register with Syrian Immigration by their fifteenth day in Syria. Americans between the ages of 18 and 45 who are of Syrian birth or recent descent are subject to the Syrian compulsory military service requirement, unless they receive an exemption from the Syrian Embassy in the United States prior to their entry into Syria." Contact the Embassy of the Syrian Arab Republic, 2215 Wyoming Ave. NW, Washington, DC 20008 (202-232-6313, fax 202-234-9548), http://www.embassyofsyria-usa.org or the Honorary Consulate General in Houston (713-622-8860) or Newport Beach, CA (949-640-9888).

Tahiti (French Polynesia). *See* **France.**

Taiwan, Republic of China on Contact the Taipei Economic and Cultural Representative Office (TECRO), 4201 Wisconsin Ave. NW, Washington, DC 20016 (202-895-1800, fax 202-966-0825) or the Representative Office in New York at 212-486-0088.

Tajikistan Contact the Embassy of the Russian Federation, Consular Division, 2641 Tunlaw Rd. NW, Washington, DC 20007 (202-939-8907, fax 202-483-7579), http://www.russianembassy.org or the nearest Consulate General: New York (212-348-0926), San Francisco (415-928-6878), or Seattle (206-728-1910).

Tanzania, United Republic of (Zanzibar) Contact the Embassy of the United Republic of Tanzania, 2139 R St. NW, Washington, DC 20008 (202-939-6125, fax 202-797-7408) or the Permanent Mission of the United Republic of Tanzania to the United Nations at 212-972-9160.

Thailand, Kingdom of Contact the Royal Thai Embassy, 1024 Wisconsin Ave. NW, Washington, DC 20007 (202-944-3600, fax 202-944-3611), http://www.thaiembdc.org or the nearest Consulate General: Chicago (312-236-2447), Los Angeles (213-962-9574), or New York (212-754-1770).

Togo, Republic of Contact the Embassy of the Republic of Togo, 2208 Massachusetts Ave. NW, Washington, DC 20008 (202-234-4212, fax 202-232-3190) or the Honorary Consulate in Miami at 305-371-4286.

Tonga Contact the Consulate General of Tonga, 360 Post St., Suite 604, San Francisco, CA 94108 (415-781-0365, fax 415-781-3964).

Trinidad and Tobago Contact the Embassy of Trinidad and Tobago, 1708 Massachusetts Ave. NW, Washington, DC 20036 (202-467-6490, fax 202-785-3130), http://tradepoint.tidco.co.tt/trade mission/washington.html or the Consulate in Miami (305-374-2199) or New York (212-682-7272).

Tunisia The U.S. State Department cautions travelers that "Americans born in the Middle East or with Arabic names have experienced delays in clearing Immigration at airports upon arrival. American citizens of Tunisian origin are expected to enter Tunisia as Tunisians, on their Tunisian passports. If the Tunisian/American succeeds in entering on an American passport, there is a high probability that a Tunisian passport will be required before exiting the country." Contact the Embassy of Tunisia, 1515 Massachusetts Ave. NW, Washington, DC 20005 (202-862-1850, fax 202-862-1858) or the nearest Honorary Consulate: Miami (305-375-6195), New York (212-272-6962), or San Francisco (415-922-9222).

Japan's New Tokyo International Airport is only 40 miles from Tokyo; however, due to traffic, it typically takes four hours or more to catch a flight.

Turkey, Republic of Contact the Embassy of the Republic of Turkey, Consular Section, 2525 Massachusetts Ave. NW, Washington, DC 20008 (202-612-6740, fax 202-319-1639), http://www.turkey.org or the nearest Consulate General: Chicago (312-263-0644, ext. 28), Houston (713-622-5849), Los Angeles (323-937-0118), or New York (212-949-0160).

Turkmenistan Contact the Embassy of Turkmenistan, 2207 Massachusetts Ave. NW, Washington, DC 20008 (202-588-1500, fax 202-588-0697), http://www.turkmenistanembassy.org or the Permanent Mission of Turkmenistan to the United Nations at 212-486-8908.

Turks and Caicos Islands. *See* **British West Indies.**

Tuvalu Island Contact the British Embassy, 3100 Massachusetts Ave. NW, Washington, DC 20008 (202-588-6500, fax 202-588-7870).

Travel

Uganda, Republic of   Contact the Embassy of the Republic of Uganda, 5911 16th St. NW, Washington, DC 20011 (202-726-7100, fax 202-726-1727), http://ugandaweb.com/ugaembassy/ or the Permanent Mission of the Republic of Uganda to the United Nations at 212-949-0110.

Ukraine   Contact the Embassy of Ukraine, 3350 M St. NW, Washington, DC (202-333-0606, fax 202-333-0817), http://www.ukremb.com or the Consulate General in Chicago (312-642-4388) or New York (212-371-5690).

United Arab Emirates (UAE) (Abu Dabi, Dubai, Sharjah, Ras Al Khaimah, Fujairah, Ajman, and **Umm Al Quwain)**   Contact the Embassy of the United Arab Emirates, 1255 W. 22nd St. NW, Washington, DC 20037 (202-955-7999) or the Permanent Mission of the United Arab Emirates to the United Nations at 212-371-0480.

United Kingdom (England, Northern Ireland, Scotland, and **Wales)**   Contact the British Embassy, 3100 Massachusetts Ave. NW, Washington, DC 20008 (202-588-6500, fax 202-588-7870), http://www.britainusa.com or the nearest Consulate General: Atlanta (404-954-7700), Boston (617-248-9555), Chicago (415-617-1300), Houston (713-659-6270), Los Angeles (310-477-3322), New York (212-745-0200), or San Francisco (415-981-3030).

Uruguay   Contact the Embassy of Uruguay, Consular Office, 2715 M St., 3rd Floor NW, Washington, DC 20007 (202-331-4219, fax 202-331-8142) or the nearest Consulate General: Chicago (312-867-3893), Los Angeles (310-394-5777), Miami (305-443-9764), or New York (212-753-8581).

Uzbekistan, Republic of   Contact the Embassy of the Republic of Uzbekistan, Consular Section, 1746 Massachusetts Ave. NW, Washington, DC 20036 (202-530-7291, fax 202-293-6804), http://www.uzbekistan.org or the Consulate General in New York at 212-754-7403.

Vanuatu, Republic of   Contact the British Embassy, Consular Section, 3100 Massachusetts Ave.

NW, Washington, DC 20008 (202-588-6500, fax 202-588-7870) or the Permanent Mission of the Republic of Vanuatu to the United Nations at 212-593-0144.

Vatican. *See* **Holy See, Apostolic Nunciature of the.**

Venezuela   Contact the Embassy of Venezuela, 1099 30th St. NW, Washington, DC 20007 (202-342-2214, fax 202-342-6820), http://www.embavenez-us.org or the nearest Consulate General: Boston (617-266-9475), Chicago (312-236-9655), Houston (713-974-0028), Miami (305-577-4214), New Orleans (504-522-3284), New York (212-826-1660), San Francisco (415-955-1982), or San Juan, PR (787-766-4250).

Vietnam   Contact the Embassy of Vietnam, 1233 20th St. NW, Suite 400, Washington, DC 20037 (202-861-0737, fax 202-861-0917), http://www.vietnamembassy-usa.org or the Consulate in San Francisco at 415-922-1577.

Wales. *See* **United Kingdom.**

Yemen, Republic of   Contact the Embassy of the Republic of Yemen, 2600 Virginia Ave. NW, Washington, DC 20037 (202-965-4760, fax 202-337-2017), http://www.nusacc.org/yemen or the Permanent Mission of the Republic of Yemen to the United Nations at 212-355-1730.

Zaire. *See* **Congo, Democratic Republic of.**

Zambia, Republic of   Contact the Embassy of the Republic of Zambia, 2419 Massachusetts Ave. NW, Washington, DC 20008 (202-265-9717, fax 202-332-0876) or the Permanent Mission of the Republic of Zambia to the United Nations at 212-972-7200.

Zanzibar. *See* **Tanzania.**

Zimbabwe   Contact the Embassy of Zimbabwe, 1608 New Hampshire Ave. NW, Washington, DC 20009 (202-332-7100, fax 202-483-9326) or the Permanent Mission of Zimbabwe to the United Nations at 212-980-9511.

CUSTOMS INFORMATION

At reentry into the United States, you must declare all articles in your possession that you have acquired abroad, stating their actual purchase price or, if they were not purchased, their market value in the country where you acquired them. You must fill out a declaration form before reaching customs to show to U.S. customs inspectors.

If you were out of the country for 48 hours or more, you will be exempt from paying duty and federal tax on the first $400 worth of goods. Generally, values above that amount are subject to duty at a straight 10 percent. For example, if you bring in $600 worth of goods, you will pay about $20 in duty. If you are traveling with your family, remember that each family member is allowed the same $400 exemption.

The items brought into the United States must be for your own use or for personal gifts. You may not resell them for profit.

If you leave the United States with foreign-made goods already in your possession, be sure to register them, using their serial numbers, with the customs office *before* leaving, or bring proof (sales slips, for example) with you that you bought them in the United States. If you lack proof of domestic purchase or registration, you may be charged duty upon reentry.

There are customs restrictions on bringing in certain plants, animals, medications, and foods, and children may not bring in alcohol. You can get a list of restricted items from the U.S. Department of Agriculture, Washington, DC 20205.

For further information, contact the local office of the Treasury Department or the U.S. Customs Service, P.O. Box 7407, Washington, DC 20004, 202-566-8195, http://www.customs.ustreas.gov/travel/index.html (a comprehensive web site that may answer all your questions).

ADDITIONAL SOURCES OF INFORMATION

WEB SITES

Access-Able Travel
http://www.access-able.com/
Especially for travelers with disabilities, contains links to many other helpful sites

All of the Embassies of Washington, D.C.
TeleDiplomacy, Inc.
http://www.embassy.org/embassies.index.html
Contact information for foreign government offices in the United States

All the Hotels on the Web
Internet Marketing Service, Ltd.
http://www.all-hotels.com

Breezner's Guide to Airport Rental Cars
http://www.bnm.com/rcar.htm

The Centers for Disease Control
Home Travel Information Page
http://www.cdc.gov/travel/index.htm

How Far Is It?
Bali Online
http://www.indo.com/distance/

National Park Service
http://www.nps.gov

Travel Document Systems
http://www.traveldocs.com/
Country-by-country information plus downloadable passport and visa applications and services online

Travelocity
http://www.travelocity.com
Information about destinations and booking travel

U.S.-based Embassies and Consulates
InfoCatch
http://www.embassyweb.com
Links to foreign embassies on-line

The U.S. State Department's Travel Warnings Site
http://travel.state.gov/travel_warnings.html

Washington Post's International Information Online
The Washington Post Company
http://www.washingtonpost.com/wp-srv/inatl/front.htm

World Travel Guide Online Services
Columbus Group
http://www.wtgonline.com/

MAGAZINES

Condé Nast Traveler
4 Times Square
New York, NY 10036
http://www.condenast.co.uk

Travel & Leisure
1120 Avenue of the Americas
New York, NY 10036
http://www.traveleisure.com

BOOKS

Audubon Guide to the National Wildlife Refuges (series). Griffin, 2000.

Axtell, Roger E. *Do's and Taboo's of Using English Around the World.* Wiley, 1995.

Berlitz Pocket Guides (series). Berlitz Travel Guides. See most recent editions.

Birnbaum, Stephen. *Birnbaum's Travel Guides* (series). Houghton-Mifflin. See most recent editions.

Colwell, Stephen D., and Ann R. Shulman. *Trouble-Free Travel: And What to Do When Things Go Wrong.* Nolo Press, 1996.

Fodor's Guides (series). See most recent editions. Prentice-Hall.

Goode, J. Paul. *Goode's World Atlas.* 20th ed. Rand McNally, 1999.

Hostelling International Guidebook (series). International Youth Hostel Federation. See most recent editions.

Hostelling Experience: North America 2001. America Youth Hostels, 2001.

Lonely Planet Guides (series). Lonely Planet. See most recent editions.

Mobil Travel Guides (series). Fodor's Travel Publications. See most recent editions.

National Geographic's Guide to the Interstates: Crossing America. National Geographic Society, 2001.

National Geographic's Guide to the National Parks of the United States. National Geographic Association, 2001.

Nwanna, Gladson I., Ph.D. *Americans Traveling Abroad: What You Should Know Before You Go.* 2nd ed. World Travel Institute Press, 1995.

Safro, Jill, ed. *Birnbaum's Walt Disney World for Kids, by Kids.* Hyperion, 2001.

Sakach, Deborah. *Bed & Breakfasts and Country Inns.* 12th ed. American Historic Inns, Inc., 2001.

Simony, Maggy, ed. *The Traveler's Reading Guide: Ready-Made Reading Lists for the Armchair Traveler.* Facts on File, 1993.

Traveling with Your Pet—The AAA Petbook. AAA Publishing, 2001.

Wade, Betsy. *The New York Times Practical Traveler Handbook: An A–Z Guide to Getting There and Back.* Times Books, 1994.

VI

THE POLITICAL WORLD

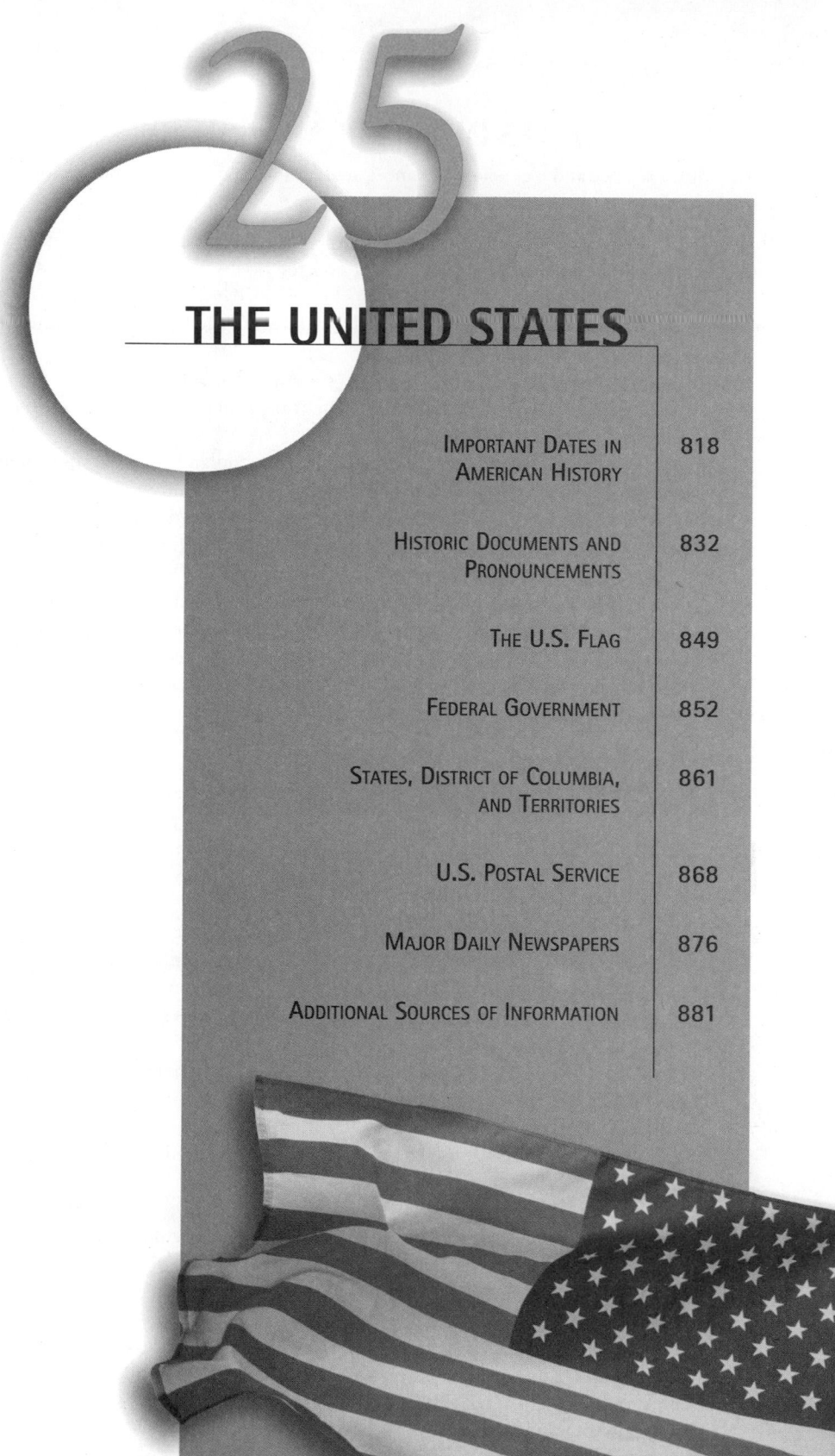

25

THE UNITED STATES

IMPORTANT DATES IN AMERICAN HISTORY

For significant science and technology advances, refer to the time line in chapter 5; for important dates and events in sports, refer to chapter 23.

20,000 B.C.E.	*Homo sapiens* first appears in the Americas (soon after its appearance in Europe). Archaeologists theorize that Asians migrate to America over the Bering Strait land bridge during the next ten millennia (Beringian Theory).
7000 B.C.E.	Native Americans develop agriculture independent of the Eastern Hemisphere.
700s	First Puebloan towns (Pueblos) appear in the American Southwest.
985	Bjarni Hejolfsson is the first European to sight the Americas from his boat in the North Atlantic.
1000	Leif Erikson explores Labrador.
1004	Norse settlements founded in Labrador and Newfoundland. Internal squabbling and conflicts with Skraelings (Native Americans) lead to their disappearance.
1150	Hopi Pueblo of Oraibi founded in what is now northeastern Arizona. Keresan Pueblo of Akoma (Acoma) is founded in what is now western New Mexico. They are the oldest continuously inhabited communities in the modern United States.
1350	Mohawk Hiawatha ("He Makes Rivers") and Huron Deganawidah ("Two River Currents Flowing Together") establish the Iroquois League of Nations. It is the oldest functioning government still in existence in North America.
1470s	English fishermen begin working off the northeastern Canadian coast.
1492	In the name of Spain, Italian Cristobal Colon (Christopher Columbus) lands on a Caribbean island (exact location unknown). Columbus makes three more voyages to the Americas.
1497	Italian Giovanni Caboto (John Cabot) explores the Canadian coast in the name of England.
1499	Italian Amerigo Vespucci sails to South America. A cartographer calls the continents of the New World "America," based on Vespucci's first name.
1513	Spain's Juan Ponce de Leon searches for the Fountain of Youth in Florida.
1524	Italian Giovanni de Verrazano maps the Atlantic coast from Maine to South Carolina in the name of France.
1534	Spain's Cabeza de Vaca ventures from Florida to Texas over a two-year period.
1534	France's Jacques Cartier explores the St. Lawrence River and Canada over a seven-year period.
1539	Spain's Hernan de Soto explores the South from the Carolinas to Mississippi.
1540	Spain's Francisco Vasquez de Coronado pillages the southwestern Pueblos, venturing as far as the southern Great Plains.
1542	Spain's Juan Rodriguez de Cabrillo sails up the California coast to Oregon.
1565	Spain establishes the colony of San Agustin (St. Augustine) in Florida.
1576	Martin Frobisher explores Canada on behalf of England.
1585	Sir Walter Raleigh establishes the Roanoke colony in Virginia in the name of England; the colonists return to England by year's end.
1587	Second Roanoke colony established in Virginia. Virginia Dare becomes the first baby born in North America to English parents, but soon afterward the colony disappears.
1598	Don Juan de Onate conquers the Pueblos of the Southwest in the name of Spain.
1500s	European, African, and Asian diseases and Spanish conquests kill more than 90 percent of all indigenous peoples in the Western Hemisphere.
1600	France establishes small, short-lived settlements along the St. Lawrence River.
1602	France's Samuel de Champlain begins explorations of New England and the St. Lawrence River.
1607	The Virginia Company of Plymouth establishes the colony of Sagadahoc, on the Kennebec River of Maine; it lasts less than a year.

1607	The Virginia Company of London establishes a colony at Jamestown, Virginia.
1608	France's first successful colony is established at Quebec.
1609	Englishman Henry Hudson explores Canada and New York for the Netherlands.
1610	Spain establishes Santa Fe, New Mexico.
1613	Holland's Dutch East India Company establishes New Amsterdam (later New York).
1614	In Virginia, Indian chief Powhatan forges an alliance with the English by marrying his daughter Pocahontas to colonist John Rolfe.
1617	Pocahontas dies of disease during a trip to England; Powhatan dies the next year.
1619	First meeting of the Virginia Assembly (House of Burgesses). Twenty indentured servants are the first black Africans sold in Britain's North American colonies.
1620	The Virginia Company of Plymouth establishes the Plymouth colony in present-day Massachusetts; settlers sign the Mayflower Compact establishing their local government.
1620	New Amsterdam is named the capital of New Netherlands.
1628	The Company of New France builds a fur trading network with Algonquin and Cree peoples that stretches from the Great Lakes to the Mississippi Valley.
1630	The Massachusetts Bay Colony is established.
1634	Lord Baltimore establishes Maryland colony, which permits the practice of Catholicism.
1636	Roger Williams is expelled from Massachusetts and founds Rhode Island colony. Harvard University is founded to train Christian ministers.
1637	In the Pequot War (begun 1636), New England colonists massacre Native American women and children and sell the survivors into slavery in the Caribbean.
1639	The Fundamental Order of Connecticut is the first written constitution in the British colonies.
1640	The New Netherlands Charter of Freedoms and Exemptions is written.
1654	Spanish Sephardim arriving in New Amsterdam are the first Jews in America.
1651	England passes the first Navigation Act affecting the colonial economy.
1663	England establishes colonies in the Carolinas and New Jersey.
1664	England captures New Amsterdam, renaming it New York.
1676	New England colonists win King Philip's War against Native Americans. Twenty-five percent of New England's Native Americans are dead.
1680	Pueblos revolt and drive the Spanish from the Southwest.
1681	William Penn establishes Pennsylvania colony.
1682	La Salle explores the Mississippi River from Minnesota to the Gulf of Mexico for France.
1689	The English reform their colonial policy after colonial rebellions in Massachusetts, New York, and Maryland.
1689	The French establish colonies at Mobile, New Orleans, and Pensacola.
1692	Spain reconquers the Pueblos of the Southwest.
1692	In Salem, Massachusetts, 19 people are convicted of witchcraft and executed.
1701	The French establish Fort Detroit.
1712	After a slave rebellion in New York City, 21 Africans are executed and 6 more commit suicide.
1718	The Spanish establish San Antonio, Texas.
1723	Abenaki (Indian) Wars rage in Maine and Vermont for more than four years.
1731	The first American circulating library is founded in Philadelphia.
1732	James Oglethorpe establishes the colony of Georgia.
1732	Benjamin Franklin publishes the first *Poor Richard's Almanac*.
1739	The religious revival known as the Great Awakening begins.
1741	After another slave rebellion in New York City, 26 Africans are publicly executed and another 71 are sold and deported.

United States

1754	The French establish Fort Duquesne near present-day Pittsburgh. They defeat a force from British Virginia led by George Washington, beginning the French and Indian War.
1756	England and France declare war.
1757	French troops capture Fort William Henry in New York.
1758	British and American troops capture Fort Duquesne, rename it Fort Pitt.
1759	British troops capture Quebec City, the French capital in Canada, in the last major battle of the war.
1763	The Treaty of Paris ends the French and Indian War; France gives up nearly all its American territories. Spain cedes Florida to the British.
1764	Britain imposes the Revenue Act taxes (the Sugar Act) on the colonies to pay for the French and Indian War.
1765	Britain passes the Stamp Act tax and the Quartering (British troops) Act; colonists organize the Sons of Liberty and the Stamp Act Congress in opposition.
1766	The Stamp Act is repealed, but the Declaratory Act affirms the King's power over the colonies.
1767	The Townshend Acts impose British duties on many goods imported to the colonies.
1768	England closes the Massachusetts Assembly and the British Army occupies Boston. The colonists resist by agreeing not to buy or import items that are taxed.
1770	The Townshend Acts are repealed, but England taxes tea. Five Americans are killed by British soldiers in the Boston Massacre.
1770	Spain establishes Monterey, California.
1773	Americans dump $10,000 worth of tea into Boston Harbor in the Boston Tea Party.
1774	The Coercive (Intolerable) Acts close Boston Harbor and bring trade to a standstill.
1774	The first Continental Congress meets in Philadelphia and draws up a Declaration of Rights and Grievances.
1775	"The shot heard 'round the world" at the Battle of Lexington and Concord begins the Revolutionary War.
1775	The Second Continental Congress meets and raises an army, appointing George Washington as its commander. King George III declares the colonies to be in rebellion.
1776	Thomas Paine publishes *Common Sense*; the British Army evacuates Boston; the Continental Congress signs the Declaration of Independence on July 4.
1776	The British Army captures New York City; the British execute Nathan Hale for spying; the Continental Army attacks British forces in New Jersey at Princeton and Trenton.
1777	The British Army occupies Philadelphia. Americans stop British general Burgoyne's southward march through New York at Saratoga and win a resounding victory. The American Army winters at Valley Forge.
1777	Continental Congress drafts the Articles of Confederation, a plan for a united government after independence.
1778	France sends military aid to the colonies; the British Army evacuates Philadelphia.
1778	Britain's Captain James Cook sails to Alaska and Hawaii.
1779	The British Army captures Savannah.
1780	British capture Charleston and defeat Americans at Camden, South Carolina. American traitor Benedict Arnold escapes to England.
1781	American and French troops and the French fleet surround the British army of General Cornwallis at Yorktown, Virginia. Cornwallis surrenders, ending Britain's hopes for victory.
1781	Maryland is the 13th state to ratify the Articles of Confederation, establishing an independent confederacy of American states.
1783	In the Treaty of Paris, Britain recognizes American independence and cedes Florida back to Spain. George Washington resigns as commander of the Continental Army.
1787	Congress passes the Northwest Ordinance, organizing territories in the Great Lakes region.

United States

Admission of 13 Original States

State	Date of Admission	State	Date of Admission
1. Delaware	December 7, 1787	8. South Carolina	May 23, 1788
2. Pennsylvania	December 12, 1787	9. New Hampshire	June 21, 1788
3. New Jersey	December 18, 1787	10. Virginia	June 25, 1788
4. Georgia	January 2, 1788	11. New York	July 26, 1788
5. Connecticut	January 9, 1788	12. North Carolina	November 21, 1789
6. Massachusetts	February 6, 1788	13. Rhode Island	May 29, 1790
7. Maryland	April 28, 1788		

A Closer Look

1787   A constitutional convention meets in Philadelphia to discuss revisions to the Articles of Confederation. Instead it writes a new Constitution establishing a more powerful central government, subject to acceptance by 9 of the 13 colonies.

1787   The new Constitution is fiercely debated; Delaware is the first state to ratify.

1788   New Hampshire is the ninth state to ratify the constitution, putting it into effect. Three other states ratify in 1788, and Rhode Island—after 12 "no" votes—ratifies in 1790.

1789   First federal elections: George Washington is elected president and inaugurated in the federal capital, New York City. John Adams is elected vice president.

1790   Congress approves the first ten amendments to the Constitution, the Bill of Rights, and submits them to the states for ratification.

1790   Congress selects a site between northern and southern states, on the Potomac River, for the new national capital, to be called the District of Columbia.

1791   The Bill of Rights is ratified; Vermont becomes the 14th state, splitting off from New York State.

1792   George Washington is elected to a second term as president.

1793   Eli Whitney and others invent the cotton gin, increasing cotton production and the demand for slaves in the South; the Fugitive Slave Act makes it illegal to harbor escaped slaves.

1793   Captain Robert Gray establishes the U.S. claim to the Columbia River in the wilderness of the Northwest.

1794   Washington uses federal troops to crush the Whiskey Rebellion in Pennsylvania.

1796   Washington refuses to run for a third term and publishes his farewell address. John Adams is elected president. Thomas Jefferson is vice president.

1798   President Adams signs the Alien and Sedition Acts, which impose harsh restrictions on non-citizens and curtail freedom of the press. Thomas Jefferson leads opposition to the acts, and all expire or are repealed by 1802.

1799   George Washington dies at his home in Mount Vernon.

1800   Thomas Jefferson wins the presidential election and is inaugurated in the new capital, which has been named for George Washington, already considered "the father of his country."

1801   John Marshall is appointed Chief Justice of the Untied States Supreme Court, which he will help make into an important branch of the federal government.

1801   Spain, which gained the Louisiana Territory from France in 1763, cedes it back to France.

1803   The Supreme Court, in *Marbury v. Madison*, overturns a congressional act because it violates the Constitution.

1803   Thomas Jefferson agrees to buy the Louisiana Territory from France, nearly doubling the area of the United States.

1804   Jefferson supports the Lewis and Clark expedition to explore the vast northern reaches of the Louisiana Purchase.

United States

1804	Bitter rivals Aaron Burr and Alexander Hamilton fight a duel; Hamilton, the architect of early U.S. economic policy, dies of his wounds.
1806	Lewis and Clark return to St. Louis after traveling overland to the Pacific and back, bringing descriptions of the native peoples, rugged landscape, and wildlife of the West.
1807	Robert Fulton invents the first practical steamboat.
1808	In accordance with the Constitution, the importation of slaves becomes illegal.
1811	American troops attack and defeat Shawnee Indians at Tippacanoe in Indiana. The Shawnee will fight for Britain in the War of 1812, which begins next year.
1812	The U.S. declares war on Britain, beginning the War of 1812.
1813	U.S. Captain Oliver Hazard Perry wins the naval Battle of Lake Erie, then writes his superior: "We have met the enemy and they are ours."
1814	British forces capture Washington, D.C., and burn down the White House, the Capitol, and the Library of Congress. Americans defeat the British on Lake Champlain, however, ending the British threat of an invasion from Canada.
1815	The War of 1812 ends in December 1814; before word reaches America, General Andrew Jackson routs the British in the Battle of New Orleans—with the help of pirate Jean Laffitte.
1816	Efforts begin to repatriate free African-Americans to Liberia, West Africa. Some 22,000 will return to Africa over the next 45 years.
1817	New York begins building the Erie Canal.
1818	The 49th parallel becomes the U.S.-Canadian border from Minnesota to the Rocky Mountains; England and the U.S. occupy Oregon Territory jointly.
1819	Spain sells Florida to the U.S.
1820	The Missouri Compromise mandates that states enter the union in pairs, one slave and one free, to maintain the political balance between slave states and free states.
1821	Sequoia creates a written syllabary for the Cherokee language; Emma Willard founds the first American college for women.
1823	President James Monroe issues the Monroe Doctrine, declaring the preeminence of the United States in the Western Hemisphere.
1825	The Erie Canal is completed, providing rapid transport of Midwestern goods to the Atlantic through the port of New York City.
1825	Andrew Jackson receives the most popular votes in the presidential election but lacks a majority in the electoral college; the House of Representatives elects John Quincy Adams.
1826	The American Temperance Society is founded, devoted to outlawing the manufacture and sale of alcoholic beverages.
1827	The Cherokee Nation adopts a written constitution. The governor of Georgia vows to seize all Cherokee lands by 1830.
1828	The Baltimore-Ohio Railroad begins passenger service.
1830	The United States Postal Service is the nation's single largest employer, with one post office per 1,500 Americans nationwide.
1830	The Mexican government tries but fails to stem the flood of U.S. immigrants to Texas.
1830	The Indian Removal Act authorizes the removal of Native Americans from the South.
1831	Cyrus McCormick's invention of the automatic reaper for harvesting wheat is the first of many labor-saving devices that will revolutionize farming.
1831	William Lloyd Garrison begins publishing the abolitionist newspaper *The Liberator*.
1831	The religious movement known as the Second Great Awakening begins.
1831	Nat Turner leads a slave rebellion in Virginia; he is eventually caught and executed. The price of cotton triples in the next five years, further entrenching slavery in the South.
1832	The Supreme Court upholds Cherokee land claims, but Georgia sells the land anyway.

United States

1835	President Andrew Jackson signs a treaty justifying the removal of Cherokees from the South; the Second Seminole War begins in Florida.
1835	American immigrants in Texas begin war to secede from Mexico; the Mexican army crushes rebel forces at the Alamo and Goliad.
1836	Sam Houston's rebel army defeats the Mexican army at the San Jacinto River. The Republic of Texas becomes an independent nation.
1837	The first modern public school system is created in Massachusetts.
1838	The U.S. Army begins the removal of Cherokees. The journey to Indian Territory west of the Mississippi is known as the Trail of Tears. A third of Cherokees die on the way.
1840	The Whig Party elects its first presidential candidate, William Henry Harrison.
1841	Harrison catches pneumonia at his inauguration and dies after one month in office.
1843	Former slave Sojourner Truth begins giving abolitionist lectures.
1844	Mormon leader Joseph Smith is killed by a lynch mob in Carthage, Illinois. Mormons are driven out of nearby Nauvoo, Illinois, and begin migrating to Utah.
1844	Three days of anti-immigrant riots erupt in Philadelphia.
1844	The anti-immigrant, anti-Catholic American Republican Party (the Know Nothings) is founded in New York City.
1844	Samuel F. B. Morse invents the telegraph.
1845	Former slave Frederick Douglass publishes "Narrative" of his life.
1845	Congress annexes Texas; Mexico severs diplomatic ties to the U.S.
1846	Hostilities break out between the U.S. and Mexico; Congress declares war.
1846	A treaty with Britain sets the U.S.-Canadian border from the Rockies to the Pacific.
1847	A potato famine in Ireland results in large waves of Irish immigrants to the U.S.
1847	Mormon leader Brigham Young establishes Salt Lake City.
1847	American troops capture Mexico City. In a treaty ending the war, Mexico cedes vast territories in present-day southwestern U.S.
1848	The Seneca Falls (NY) Convention on women's rights is held.
1849	Thousands of gold seekers known as 49ers rush to California by land and sea after reports of a gold strike the previous year. The territory becomes a state in 1850.
1850	The Compromise of 1850 provides that new states south of the 36'30" line of latitude will be slave states; former slave Harriet Tubman begins helping fugitive slaves escape to Canada on her "Underground Railroad."
1852	*Uncle Tom's Cabin* by Harriet Beecher Stowe gains huge popularity in the North, sensitizing millions to the evils of slavery.
1854	The Kansas-Nebraska Act overturns the Compromise of 1850 and provides that Kansas will determine its stance on slavery by popular vote.
1854	The Republican Party is founded to oppose extension of slavery to western territories.
1856	Kansas Territory has competing proslavery and antislavery governments. More than 200 die in the ensuing violence known as Bleeding Kansas.
1857	In the Dred Scott case, the Supreme Court declares that slaves are property with no citizenship rights.
1858	Senate candidates Abraham Lincoln and Stephen Douglas debate slavery in Illinois. Douglas wins the Senate campaign; Lincoln will run for president in 1860.
1859	Antislavery fanatic John Brown raids the U.S. armory at Harper's Ferry, Virginia. He is convicted of treason and executed, but antislavery activists consider him a hero.
1859	The Comstock Lode silver-mining boom begins in Nevada.
1860	Republican candidate Abraham Lincoln is elected president. South Carolina secedes from the U.S. State militia forces seize federal armories throughout the South.

Secession of American States

	State	Date of Secession		State	Date of Secession
1.	South Carolina	December 20, 1860	7.	Texas	February 1, 1861
2.	Mississippi	January 9, 1861	8.	Virginia	April 17, 1861
3.	Florida	January 10, 1861	9.	Arkansas	May 6, 1861
4.	Alabama	January 11, 1861	10.	North Carolina	May 20, 1861
5.	Georgia	January 19, 1861	11.	Tennessee	June 8, 1861
6.	Louisiana	January 26, 1861			

1860   The short-lived Pony Express begins delivering mail between Missouri and California.

1861   Ten more Southern states secede and form the Confederate States of America. Confederate troops fire on Ft. Sumter in Charleston Bay; Congress (now without all its Southern representatives) declares war.

1861   Bull Run (Manassas), the first pitched battle of the war, is a Confederate victory.

1861   The transcontinental telegraph is completed, ending operation of the Pony Express.

1862   In major battles at Shiloh (TN), Second Bull Run (VA), Antietam (MD), and Fredericksburg (VA), both armies sustain huge losses. Confederate armies, undermanned and undersupplied, fight the Union to a standstill.

1862   An Indian uprising in Minnesota leads to 1,000 dead on both sides; 38 Dakota Sioux are hanged. In Colorado, U.S. militias massacre 300 Cheyenne at Sand Creek.

1863   President Lincoln issues the Emancipation Proclamation, declaring all slaves in the Confederacy free. Union armies win major battles at Gettysburg (PA) and Vicksburg (MS). Hundreds die in draft riots and race riots in Northern cities.

1864   Union General Grant drives through Confederate lines in northern Virginia and besieges Richmond (the Confederate capital). General Sherman captures Atlanta, then marches across Georgia to the sea.

1865   Grant's army captures Richmond and forces the surrender of the Confederate army at Appomattox, Virginia, ending the war. Days later, Southern patriot John Wilkes Booth assassinates President Lincoln in Washington.

1865   Congress passes the 13th Amendment, outlawing slavery.

1866   Congress passes the 14th Amendment, giving citizenship rights to former slaves.

1867   The Reconstruction Act establishes a federal military presence in the Southern states.

1868   Lieutenant Colonel George Custer's 7th Cavalry massacres Cheyenne civilians at the Washita River.

1868   Hard-line Republicans in Congress impeach (accuse) President Johnson. In his trial, the Senate is one vote short of removing him from office.

1869   The first transcontinental railroad is linked at Promontory Point, Utah.

1869   Elizabeth Cady Stanton and Susan B. Anthony establish the National Women's Suffrage Association.

1872   John D. Rockefeller founds Standard Oil, which extracts and refines oil; its first major product is kerosene for home lighting.

1876   Custer and his 7th Cavalry, on a mission to attack Native Americans in the Dakota Territory, are wiped out in a surprise counterattack, later known as Custer's Last Stand.

1876   Alexander Graham Bell invents the telephone.

1876   In the presidential election, neither Rutherford Hayes nor Samuel Tilden gains an electoral college majority, leaving the election to be decided by Congress.

Readmission of American States

A Closer Look

State	Date of Readmission	State	Date of Readmission
1. Tennessee	July 24, 1866	7. North Carolina	June 25, 1868
2. Arkansas	June 22, 1868	8. South Carolina	June 25, 1868
3. Alabama	June 25, 1868	9. Virginia	January 26, 1870
4. Florida	June 25, 1868	10. Mississippi	February 23, 1870
5. Georgia	June 25, 1868*	11. Texas	March 30, 1870
6. Louisiana	June 25, 1868		

*Readmitted a second time on July 15, 1870

1877	Southern congressmen help elect Hayes in return for promises that he will end Reconstruction. Federal troops are withdrawn from the South.
1877	The Great Railroad Strike of 1877 sparks widespread sympathy strikes across the nation, but President Hayes uses federal troops to crush the strike.
1878	New Haven, Connecticut, is the site of the first working telephone system.
1879	The first electric lighting system is installed in Cleveland, Ohio.
1880	Large waves of immigrants begin arriving from Eastern Europe.
1881	The Federation of Organized Trades and Labor Unions (later the American Federation of Labor) is founded.
1882	The first Chinese Exclusion Act, banning Chinese immigrants, is passed.
1883	The Pendleton Act creates the federal civil service system.
1884	The first skyscraper is designed in Chicago by architect Louis Sullivan.
1886	Police in Chicago fire into a group of strikers. During a protest demonstration three days later, a bomb kills policemen and many demonstrators are killed in the Haymarket Riot.
1886	The last major Indian war ends with the surrender of chief Geronimo in Arizona.
1889	Jane Addams opens Hull House in Chicago, a "settlement house" where immigrants and the poor can receive education and emergency assistance.
1890	Indian reservation police capture and kill chief Sitting Bull; two weeks later, army cavalry massacre 300 Lakotas at Wounded Knee Creek, South Dakota.
1890	The Sherman Anti-Trust Act is passed to restrain the power of business trusts and monopolies.
1890	The Mississippi legislature establishes a literacy test to keep African-Americans from voting. Other Southern states follow suit.
1892	Telephone lines between New York and Chicago are completed.
1892	The federal government establishes Ellis Island as its official immigration arrival site.
1893	A financial panic brings widespread business failure and unemployment.
1894	Federal troops are sent to Illinois to force an end to railway workers' strike against wage cuts at the Pullman Car Co.
1895	Once numbering more than 40,000,000, there are now fewer than 1,000 bison in the world.
1896	The Supreme Court rules in *Plessy v. Ferguson* that racial segregation is constitutional if facilities (such as schools) are "separate but equal."
1898	The U.S. battleship *Maine* is destroyed by explosions in Havana in January; the U.S. soon declares war on Spain. Fighting ends in August; the U.S. gains possession of Cuba, Puerto Rico, the Philippine Islands, and Guam.
1898	The U.S. annexes the Hawaiian Islands.
1900	The U.S. becomes the world's leading industrial nation in terms of population involved in industry, industrial output, and percentage of gross national product.

United States

1901   U.S. Steel is founded by Andrew Carnegie.

1901   President McKinley is assassinated; Vice President Theodore Roosevelt is sworn in, becoming the youngest president to serve. Theodore Roosevelt establishes the national parks system during his presidency.

1903   The Wright brothers fly the first power-driven airplane in Kitty Hawk, North Carolina.

1904   The U.S. begins building the Panama Canal.

1906   A major earthquake and fire devastate San Francisco.

1908   Henry Ford produces the first Model T automobile.

1910   The National Association for the Advancement of Colored People (NAACP) is founded.

1911   The Triangle Shirt Waist Company fire in New York City kills 146 workers.

1913   The Ford Motor Company uses the first moving assembly line.

1913   The 17th Amendment provides for direct election of Senators (previously chosen by state legislatures.

1914   World War I begins in Europe; the U.S. remains neutral.

1914   The National Guard kills families of striking coal miners in Ludlow, Colorado. The miners take over the coal fields until driven out by federal troops.

1915   The ocean liner *Lusitania* is sunk by a German submarine; nearly 1,200 people die, including 128 Americans. The U.S. moves toward aiding Allied nations.

1916   Mexican general Pancho Villa raids New Mexico settlements; U.S. forces pursue him into Mexico.

1916   Jeanette Rankin of Montana is the first woman elected to the House of Representatives.

1917   The U.S. enters World War I on April 4; U.S. forces begin arriving in France.

1918   U.S. forces see heavy fighting; World War I ends with an armistice in November.

1919   President Wilson urges U.S. Senate to ratify the Treaty of Versailles, ending the world war, and join the League of Nations; the Senate refuses. Wilson suffers a stroke and is disabled.

1920   The 18th Amendment prohibits manufacture or sale of alcoholic beverages (Prohibition); it will be repealed in 1933. The 19th Amendment gives women the right to vote.

1920   The first commercial radio station, KDKA in Pittsburgh, reports the results of the presidential election: Warren Harding will be the new president.

1921   Margaret Sanger founds the American Birth Control League (later Planned Parenthood).

1923   President Harding, whose administration has been tarnished by rumors of corruption, dies unexpectedly; straight arrow Vice President Calvin Coolidge is sworn in.

1924   Congress establishes quotas to limit immigration, especially from Asia, Latin America, and Africa.

1925   The sensational Scopes Monkey Trial in Dayton, Tennessee, tests a state law banning the teaching of evolution. Famed attorney Clarence Darrow defends Scopes; the prosecution is led by William Jennings Bryan, a three-time candidate for president.

1925   Nellie Tayloe Ross of Wyoming becomes the first female governor.

1927   Charles Lindbergh makes the first solo nonstop trans-Atlantic flight, from New York to Paris.

1927   The first Academy Awards are presented.

1927   *The Jazz Singer*, the first motion picture with synchronized sound, is released.

1927   Anarchists Nicola Sacco and Bartolomeo Vanzetti, convicted as "radicals" for murders in a 1920 shoe factory robbery, are executed despite international pleas claiming their innocence.

1928   Amelia Earhart is the first woman to fly solo across the Atlantic.

1929   The stock market crashes, marking the beginning of the Great Depression.

1931   More than one-quarter of all Americans are unemployed. Another quarter have only part-time work.

1931   The Empire State Building in New York opens; it is the tallest structure in the world.

1932	Thousands of World War I veterans march on Washington, demanding early payment of a bonus voted by Congress. The U.S. Army disperses the marchers, using tanks and cavalry.
1932	Franklin Roosevelt is elected president in a landslide, promising "a new deal for the American people," who are suffering from the deepening Depression.
1933	During his first 100 days in office, President Roosevelt and Congress enact a wide range of economic recovery programs.
1935	The Social Security Act creates a federal system to provide support for retired and unemployed workers through taxes paid by employers and employees.
1936	The Great Sit Down Strike against General Motors in Flint, Michigan, leads to the recognition of the United Auto Workers union by GM.
1936	African-American track star Jesse Owens wins four gold medals at the summer Olympics in Adolf Hitler's Berlin, calling Nazi beliefs of racial superiority into question.
1938	The first federal minimum wage is implemented.
1939	Germany invades Poland, beginning World War II in Europe; the U.S. is officially neutral but secretly provides assistance to the Allies.
1940	The U.S. rapidly increases aid to Britain and introduces the first peacetime draft.
1941	Japan attacks the Pearl Harbor naval base in Hawaii on December 7; the U.S. declares war on Japan and Germany, entering World War II.
1942	In the Philippines, 10,000 Allied troops surrender to the Japanese. U.S. Naval forces defeat the Japanese fleet in the battles of the Coral Sea and Midway. Allies invade North Africa.
1943	The Allies invade Italy, capture Guadalcanal from Japan, and begin sustained bombing of German cities.
1944	The Allies invade the Normandy coast of France, liberate Paris, and drive the German army back toward its borders. In the Pacific, forces win naval battle of the Philippine Sea and capture Guam and Saipan.
1945	President Roosevelt dies in April; Harry Truman becomes president.
1945	Germany surrenders as Soviet and U.S. troops converge on Berlin; Hitler commits suicide.
1945	The U.S. captures Iwo Jima and Okinawa from Japan and firebombs Tokyo. In August, the first atomic bombs are dropped on cities of Hiroshima and Nagasaki. Japan surrenders, ending World War II.
1945	Nazi leaders are put on trial by the Allies in the Nuremberg Tribunal. Allied nations approve the charter of the United Nations.
1946	A Cold War between superpowers—the U.S. and the Soviet Union—begins.
1947	The U.S. appropriates billions under the Marshall Plan to help its European allies rebuild and to limit the spread of Communism.
1947	African-American Jackie Robinson plays for the Brooklyn Dodgers, becoming the first of his race to play in major league baseball since before 1900.
1948	President Truman ends desegregation in the U.S. armed forces by executive order.
1949	The North Atlantic Treaty Organization (NATO) is established.
1950	Communist-led North Korea invades U.S. ally South Korea. U.S. and other United Nations troops intervene, beginning the Korean Conflict.
1950	Former State Department official Alger Hiss, suspected of sending secrets to the Soviet Union, is convicted of perjury. Senator Joseph McCarthy of Wisconsin claims to have lists of other Communists in the government.
1951	Julius and Ethel Rosenberg are convicted of treason for giving the USSR atomic secrets during World War II and are sentenced to death.
1951	The first nuclear power plant is built in the U.S.

United States

1952   Former general Dwight Eisenhower is elected president on the Republican ticket, ending 20 years of Democratic presidents.

1952   The U.S. detonates the first hydrogen bomb at Eniwetok Atoll in the mid-Pacific.

1953   An armistice agreement ends the Korean conflict; North and South Korea remain divided.

1954   In *Brown v. Board of Education*, the Supreme Court declares "separate but equal" schools for white and black students unconstitutional.

1954   Congress censures Senator McCarthy, ending his "witch-hunt" for Communists in the government.

1955   African-American Rosa Parks is arrested in Montgomery, Alabama, for refusing to give up her seat to a white person; next year, local minister Martin Luther King, Jr. helps organize a boycott of buses, beginning a new era of civil rights demonstrations.

1956   USSR premier Nikita Khruschev tells Western ambassadors, "We will bury you!"; the Cold War intensifies.

1956   Passage of the Federal Aid Highway Act inaugurates the first interstate highway system.

1957   Federal troops enforce the desegregation of Little Rock Central High School in Arkansas.

1957   The USSR launches *Sputnik,* the first man-made satellite, shocking Americans and beginning the "Space Race"; the U.S. launches its first satellite the following year.

1959   Alaska and Hawaii become the 49th and 50th states.

1959   USSR premier Khrushchev visits the U.S.

1960   Cuban leader Fidel Castro expropriates U.S.-owned businesses, begins creating a communist regime, and accepts aid from the USSR.

1960   An American U-2 spy plane is shot down over the USSR.

1960   Civil rights demonstrators sit in at lunch counters in Greensboro, North Carolina, to force integration of public accommodations.

1960   Presidential candidates John Kennedy and Richard Nixon appear in the first televised presidential debates; Kennedy wins a close election.

1961   U.S.-supported fighters invade Cuba at the Bay of Pigs; they are defeated and captured.

1961   Civil rights workers begin Freedom Rides to integrate interstate buses in the South.

1961   Alan Shepard is the first American astronaut in space.

1962   The U.S. detects Soviet nuclear missiles in Cuba and demands their removal; after tense discussions, the Soviets dismantle the missiles and remove them.

1962   James Meredith is the first African-American to register at the University of Mississippi.

1962   John Glenn is the first American astronaut to orbit the earth.

1962   Rachel Carson publishes *Silent Spring,* about chemical pollution in the environment.

1963   Martin Luther King, Jr. is jailed in Birmingham, Alabama, for civil rights activity; King gives his "I Have a Dream" speech before 250,000 civil rights marchers in Washington, D.C.

1963   President Kennedy is assassinated in Dallas, Texas; Lyndon Johnson becomes president.

1964   Congress passes the Gulf of Tonkin Resolution, escalating the Vietnam War.

1964   Congress passes the Civil Rights Act, challenging racial segregation and discrimination in the public sector.

1965   The U.S. begins bombing of North Vietnam as involvement in war escalates.

1965   Congress passes the Voting Rights Act, striking down restrictions faced by African-Americans in the South. Black leader Malcolm X is assassinated in New York's Harlem.

1965   President Johnson announces new Great Society programs to help the poor.

1965   Riots in the Watts section of Los Angeles begin years of racial violence in cities, including Cleveland and Chicago (1966) and Newark and Detroit (1967).

1966   The National Organization for Women is founded.

1966	U.S. troops in Vietnam approach 400,000.
1966	In *Miranda v. Arizona,* the U.S. Supreme Court requires that suspects be read their rights to remain silent and to have legal counsel.
1967	Hundreds of thousands oppose the Vietnam War in demonstrations around the country.
1967	Hippie culture in San Francisco flowers during the "Summer of Love."
1967	Boxing champion Muhammad Ali refuses induction into the army; his title is taken away.
1968	A major offensive by Vietcong during the Tet holiday shakes public confidence in the war.
1968	Martin Luther King Jr. is assassinated in Memphis.
1968	President Johnson decides not to run for reelection; Democratic presidential hopeful Robert Kennedy is assassinated; protesters and police clash violently at the Democratic convention in Chicago; Vice President Humphrey is nominated.
1968	Republican Richard Nixon is elected president.
1969	The U.S. bombs Vietcong strongholds in Cambodia; U.S. troop strength reaches 534,000.
1969	U.S. astronauts land on the moon; millions watch on television as Neil Armstrong is the first human being to walk on its surface.
1970	U.S. and South Vietnamese troops invade Cambodia, setting off hundreds of antiwar demonstrations; at Kent State University in Ohio, four demonstrators are killed by National Guard.
1970	Earth Day is celebrated for the first time; President Nixon signs the Clean Air Act.
1971	The *New York Times* publishes the Pentagon Papers, government documents that reveal official disagreement about the Vietnam War in the 1960s.
1971	The 26th Amendment lowers the voting age from 21 to 18.
1972	President Nixon visits China and meets with Mao Zedong.
1972	As U.S. troops leave Vietnam, North Vietnamese troops advance; the U.S. resumes the bombing of North Vietnam's cities.
1972	Men paid by Nixon's reelection campaign are caught after breaking into Democratic Party offices in the Watergate apartment complex. The White House denies any involvement.
1973	A cease-fire is concluded in Vietnam, but the U.S. continues bombing.
1973	In *Roe v. Wade,* the Supreme Court establishes the right of women to abortion.
1973	Nixon's staff is implicated in the Watergate burglary and cover-up in Senate hearings; secret taping of White House conversations is revealed.
1974	The Supreme Court orders Nixon to give tapes to the prosecutors; the tapes reveal Nixon's involvement in Watergate scandal. Faced with impeachment, he resigns August 9.
1974	President Gerald Ford pardons Nixon for any crimes he may have committed in office.
1974	Oil prices skyrocket; the cost of living rises rapidly.
1975	The North Vietnamese capture Saigon as last Americans evacuate; Vietnam is unified under a Communist government.
1975	Teamsters leader James Hoffa, suspected of ties with organized crime, disappears and is presumed dead. His body is never found.
1976	Georgia Democrat Jimmy Carter defeats Gerald Ford for the presidency; he is the first southerner elected since before the Civil War.
1977	President Carter pardons 10,000 draft resisters from the Vietnam era.
1977	The Alaska oil pipeline opens, carrying oil nearly 800 miles from Prudhoe Bay to Valdez.
1978	The U.S. agrees to return the Panama Canal to Panama in December 1999.
1978	Residents evacuate Love Canal, near Niagara Falls, New York, because the landfill on which their houses are built is filled with toxic wastes.
1979	President Carter negotiates the Camp David Accords, a peace treaty between Israel and Egypt.

1979   A nuclear accident at Three Mile Island, Pennsylvania, causes little damage but prompts concern about the safety of nuclear power plants.

1979   Militant nationalists in Iran take 66 hostages at the U.S. embassy in Tehran.

1980   The U.S. boycotts the summer Olympics in Moscow because Soviets have invaded Afghanistan.

1980   An attempt by U.S. forces to rescue the hostages in Iran ends in disaster.

1980   Conservative Ronald Reagan wins the Republican presidential nomination and defeats Jimmy Carter in the general election.

1980   Mount Saint Helens, a volcano in Washington State, erupts continuously for nine hours on May 18, killing 57 and causing billions of dollars of property damage

1981   U.S. hostages are released by Iran soon after President Reagan's inauguration.

1981   Reagan is seriously wounded in an assassination attempt.

1981   Sandra Day O'Connor becomes the first woman appointed to the Supreme Court.

1982   The Equal Rights Amendment to the Constitution, approved by Congress in 1972, fails to gain ratification by two-thirds of the states.

1982   Federal antitrust action breaks up AT&T, which controls most local telephone systems.

1982   The Vietnam War Memorial is dedicated in Washington.

1983   President Reagan proposes the Strategic Defense Initiative, a plan to shoot down incoming long-range missiles.

1983   A suicide bomber kills 246 at a U.S. Marines barracks in Lebanon; U.S. troops invade Grenada.

1984   The U.S. mines harbors in Nicaragua to pressure its leftist government; Congress votes to cut off funds aimed at toppling the Nicaraguan government.

1984   President Reagan is reelected; Democratic nominee Geraldine Ferraro is the first woman nominated for vice president by a major party.

1985   President Reagan meets with new Soviet leader Mikhail Gorbachev; they agree to pursue talks on arms control.

1986   The space shuttle *Challenger* explodes after liftoff, killing seven.

1986   White House aides resign in the Iran-Contra affair; it is revealed they secretly sold weapons to Iran and used the proceeds to support opposition Contras in Nicaragua.

1987   After congressional hearings, Reagan admits that "policy went astray" in Iran-Contra.

1987   The Dow Jones stock average loses nearly a quarter of its value in one day, October 19.

1987   President Reagan's nomination of conservative Robert Bork to the Supreme Court is defeated by a 58–42 vote in the Senate after bruising confirmation hearings.

1988   Vice President George Bush is elected president, carrying 40 states.

1989   The USSR begins to break apart, as many of its republics declare independence; these changes end the Cold War and leave the U.S. as the single world superpower.

1989   The oil tanker *Exxon-Valdez* runs aground and spills 11 million gallons of oil into Prince William Sound, Alaska, causing widespread environmental damage.

1989   Chinese soldiers massacre student demonstrators in Beijing's Tiananmen Square; relations between the U.S. and China are strained.

1989   The U.S invades Panama and arrests President Manuel Noriega; he is later tried and convicted for his role in international smuggling of cocaine.

1990   The Americans with Disabilities Act offers new protections for the disabled.

1990   Iraq attacks neighboring Kuwait; with U.N. support, the U.S. plans a military response.

1991   U.S.-dominated United Nations forces defeat Iraq in the Persian Gulf War.

1991   Los Angeles police are videotaped beating African-American suspect Rodney King.

1991   Conservative Clarence Thomas is named to the Supreme Court after contentious confirmation hearings.

1992   Police are acquitted in the Rodney King beating, setting off the city's worst riots in history.

United States

1992	Hurricane Andrew strikes south Florida, leaving 250,000 homeless and $20 billion in damage.
1992	Democrat Bill Clinton is elected president, defeating President Bush's run for reelection.
1993	Federal agents attack the Branch Davidian cult complex near Waco, Texas; a fire kills leader David Koresh and at least 70 others, including women and children.
1993	A bomb explodes under the World Trade Center in New York, killing six and injuring hundreds. Islamic militants are caught and later convicted.
1993	Massive flooding of the Mississippi River and its tributaries causes $10 billion in damage.
1993	The North American Free Trade Agreement, sponsored by the Clinton administration, passes in Congress.
1994	A major earthquake kills 50 and causes widespread damage northeast of Los Angeles.
1994	Republicans gain control of the House of Representatives for the first time since 1952 and the Senate for the first time since 1986; Newt Gingrich is named Speaker of the House.
1995	Republicans propose conservative Contract with America legislation.
1995	A federal office building in Oklahoma City is blown up, killing 169; Timothy McVeigh and Terry Nichols are arrested and later convicted.
1995	Congress forces a shutdown of federal offices in a budget dispute with the Clinton administration.
1996	Unabomber Theodore Kaczinski, who mailed lethal bombs to victims, is arrested.
1996	Congress reforms the federal welfare system; Clinton signs the changes into law.
1996	President Clinton is elected to a second term; Republicans keep control of Congress.
1997	The House of Representatives fines Speaker Newt Gingrich $300,000 for ethics violations.
1997	Tobacco companies agree to pay states for medical costs of some tobacco-related illnesses.
1998	Bill Clinton is accused of an improper relationship with a White House intern; he denies, then later admits indiscretion. The House impeaches (charges) him with perjury and obstruction of justice.
1998	U.S. Embassies in Tanzania and Kenya are bombed by terrorists.
1999	The Senate acquits President Clinton of impeachment charges.
1999	Serbian troops invade Kosovo. The U.S. leads NATO bombing of Serbia; after 11 weeks, Serbia agrees to withdraw.
2000	After reaching historic highs, the stock market begins a long decline as investors lose faith in dot-com and high-tech companies.
2000	Republican George W. Bush wins the presidency; the election is decided by results in Florida, where vote-counting disputes are ultimately resolved by the Supreme Court.
2000	In congressional elections, Republicans have a slim lead in the House; the Senate is divided 50–50. First Lady Hillary Clinton is elected senator from New York.
2001	Timothy McVeigh is executed for the Oklahoma City bombing.
2001	On September 11, terrorist hijackers crash airliners into New York's World Trade Center and the Pentagon in Washington. Nearly 3,000 are killed, including hundreds of police and firemen, when the Trade Center towers collapse.
2001	Letters containing deadly anthrax are received by news organizations and by U.S. senators, causing five deaths. The source of the letters cannot be determined.
2001	The U.S. identifies Islamic militant Osama bin Laden's terrorist organization as the culprit in the September 11 attacks. President Bush declares a "War on Terror," and the U.S. begins bombing in Afghanistan, where bin Laden is in hiding.
2001	The Taliban regime in Afghanistan collapses; U.S. troops and Afghan allies carry out search-and-destroy missions against the terrorists, but do not find bin Laden.
2002	The Enron corporation declares bankruptcy, the largest in U.S. history. Revelations of accounting improprieties prompt congressional investigation.

United States

HISTORIC DOCUMENTS AND PRONOUNCEMENTS

THE DECLARATION OF INDEPENDENCE

IN CONGRESS, JULY 4, 1776

The unanimous Declaration of the thirteen united States of America

When in the Course of human events, it becomes necessary for one people to dissolve the political bands which have connected them with another, and to assume among the powers of the earth, the separate and equal station to which the Laws of Nature and of Nature's God entitle them, a decent respect to the opinions of mankind requires that they should declare the causes which impel them to the separation.

We hold these truths to be self-evident, that all men are created equal, that they are endowed by their Creator with certain unalienable rights, that among these are life, liberty and the pursuit of happiness. That to secure these rights, governments are instituted among men, deriving their just powers from the consent of the governed,—That whenever any form of government becomes destructive of these ends, it is the Right of the People to alter or to abolish it, and to institute a new government, laying its foundation on such principles and organizing its powers in such form, as to them shall seem most likely to effect their safety and happiness. Prudence, indeed, will dictate that governments long established should not be changed for light and transient causes; and accordingly all experience hath shown, that mankind are more disposed to suffer, while evils are sufferable, than to right themselves by abolishing the forms to which they are accustomed. But when a long train of abuses and usurpations, pursuing invariably the same object evinces a design to reduce them under absolute despotism, it is their right, it is their duty, to throw off such government, and to provide new guards for their future security.—Such has been the patient sufferance of government. The history of the present King of Great Britain is a history of repeated injuries and usurpations, all having in direct object the establishment of an absolute tyranny over these States. To prove this, let facts be submitted to a candid world.

He has refused his assent to laws, the most wholesome and necessary for the public good.

He has forbidden his Governors to pass laws of immediate and pressing importance, unless suspended in their operation till his assent should be obtained; and when so suspended, he has utterly neglected to attend to them.

He has refused to pass other laws for the accommodation of large districts of people, unless those people would relinquish the right representation in the legislature, a right inestimable to them and formidable to tyrants only.

He has called together legislative bodies at places unusual, uncomfortable, and distant from the depository of their public records, for the sole purpose of fatiguing them into compliance with his measures.

He has dissolved Representative Houses repeatedly, for opposing with manly firmness his invasions on the rights of the people.

He has refused for a long time, after such dissolutions, to cause others to be elected; whereby the legislative powers, incapable of annihilation, have returned to the people at large for their exercise; the State remaining in the mean time exposed to all the dangers of invasion from without, and convulsions within.

He has endeavoured to prevent the population of these States; for that purpose obstructing the laws for naturalization of foreigners; refusing to pass others to encourage their migrations hither, and raising the conditions of new appropriations of lands.

He has obstructed the administration of justice, by refusing his assent to laws for establishing judiciary powers.

He has made judges dependent on his will alone, for the tenure of their offices, and the amount and payment of their salaries.

He has erected a multitude of new offices, and sent hither swarms of officers to harass our people, and eat out their substance.

He has kept among us, in times of peace, standing armies without the consent of our legislatures.

He has affected to render the military independent of and superior to the civil power.

He has combined with others to subject us to a jurisdiction foreign to our constitution, and unacknowledged by our laws; giving his assent to their acts of pretended legislation:

For quartering large bodies of armed troops among us:

For protecting them, by a mock trial, from punishment for any murders which they should commit on the inhabitants of these States:

For cutting off our trade with all parts of the world:

For imposing taxes on us without our consent:

For depriving us in many cases, of the benefits of trial by jury:

For transporting us beyond seas to be tried for pretended offenses:

For abolishing the free system of English laws in a neighbouring province, establishing therein an arbitrary government, and enlarging its boundaries so as to render it at once an example and fit instrument for introducing the same absolute rule into these colonies:

For taking away our charters, abolishing our most valuable laws, and altering fundamentally the forms of our governments:

For suspending our own legislatures, and declaring themselves invested with power to legislate for us in all cases whatsoever.

He has abdicated government here, by declaring us out of his protection and waging war against us.

He has plundered our seas, ravaged our coasts, burnt our towns, and destroyed the lives of our people.

He is at this time transporting large armies of foreign mercenaries to complete the works of death, desolation and tyranny, already begun with circumstances of cruelty and perfidy scarcely paralleled in the most barbarous ages, and totally unworthy of the head of a civilized nation.

He has constrained our fellow citizens taken captive on the high seas to bear arms against their country, to become the executioners of their friends and brethren, or to fall themselves by their hands.

United States

The Declaration of Independence, Continued

He has excited domestic insurrections amongst us, and has endeavoured to bring on the inhabitants of our frontiers, the merciless Indian savages, whose known rule of warfare is an undistinguished destruction of all ages, sexes and conditions.

In every stage of these oppressions we have petitioned for redress in the most humble terms: Our repeated petitions have been answered only by repeated injury. A prince, whose character is thus marked by every act which may define a tyrant, is unfit to be the ruler of a free people.

Nor have we been wanting in attentions to our British brethren. We have warned them from time to time of attempts by their legislature to extend an unwarrantable jurisdiction over us. We have reminded them of the circumstances of our emigration and settlement here. We have appealed to their native justice and magnanimity, and we have conjured them by the ties of our common kindred to disavow these usurpations, which, would inevitably interrupt our connections and correspondence. They too have been deaf to the voice of justice and of consanguinity. We must, therefore, acquiesce in the necessity which denounces our separation, and hold them, as we hold the rest of mankind, enemies in war, in peace friends.

WE, THEREFORE, the Representatives of the United States of America, in General Congress, Assembled, appealing to the Supreme Judge of the world for the rectitude of our intentions, do, in the name, and by authority of the good people of these Colonies, solemnly publish and declare, That these United Colonies of the British Crown, and that all political connection between them and the State of Great Britain, is and ought to be totally dissolved; and that as free and independent States, they have full power to levy war, conclude peace, contract alliances, establish commerce, and to do all other acts and things which independent States may of right do. And for the support of this Declaration, with a firm reliance on the protection of Divine Providence, we mutually pledge to each other our lives, our fortunes and our sacred honor.

Georgia

BUTTON GWINNETT	GEO. WALTON
LYMAN HALL	

North Carolina

WM. HOOPER	JOHN PENN
JOSEPH HEWES	

South Carolina

EDWARD RUTLEDGE	THOMAS LYNCH JUNR.
THOS. HEYWARD JUNR.	ARTHUR MIDDLETON

Maryland

SAMUEL CHASE	CHARLES CARROLL
WM. PACA	OF CARROLLTON
THOS. STONE	

Virginia

George Wythe
Richard Henry Lee
Th. Jefferson
Benja. Harrison

Thos. Nelson Jr.
Francis Lightfoot Lee
Carter Braxton

Pennsylvania

Robt. Morris
Benjamin Rush
Benja. Franklin
John Morton
Geo. Clymer

Jas. Smith
Geo. Taylor
James Wilson
Geo. Ross

Delaware

Caesar Rodney
Geo. Read

Tho. M'Kean

New York

Wm. Floyd
Phil. Livingston

Frans. Lewis
Lewis Morris

New Jersey

Richd. Stockton
Jno. Witherspoon
Fras. Hopkinson

John Hart
Abra Clark

New Hampshire

Josiah Bartlett
Wm. Whipple

Matthew Thornton

Massachusetts Bay

John Hancock
Saml. Adams
John Adams

Robt. Treat Paine
Elbridge Gerry

Rhode Island

Step. Hopkins

William Ellery

Connecticut

Roger Sherman
Saml. Huntington

Wm. Williams
Oliver Wolcott

THE CONSTITUTION OF THE UNITED STATES OF AMERICA

PREAMBLE

WE THE PEOPLE of the United States, in order to form a more perfect Union, establish justice, insure domestic tranquility, provide for the common defense, promote the general welfare, and secure the blessings of liberty to ourselves and our posterity, do ordain and establish this Constitution for the United States of America.

ARTICLE I

SECTION 1. All legislative powers herein granted shall be vested in a Congress of the United States, which shall consist of a Senate and House of Representatives.

SECTION 2. The House of Representatives shall be composed of members chosen every second year by the people of the several States, and the electors in each State shall have the qualifications requisite for electors of the most numerous branch of the State Legislature.

No person shall be a Representative who shall not have attained to the age of twenty-five years, and been seven years a citizen of the United States, and who shall not, when elected, be an inhabitant of that State in which he shall be chosen.

Representatives and direct taxes shall be apportioned among the several States which may be included within this Union, according to their respective numbers, which shall be determined by adding to the whole number of free persons, including those bound to service for a term of years, and excluding Indians not taxed, three-fifths of all other persons. The actual enumeration shall be made within three years after the first meeting of the Congress of the United States, and within every subsequent term of ten years, in such manner as they shall by law direct. The number of representatives shall not exceed one for every thirty thousand, but each State shall have at least one Representative; and until such enumeration shall be made, the State of New Hampshire shall be entitled to choose three, Massachusetts eight, Rhode Island and Providence Plantations one, Connecticut five, New York six, New Jersey four, Pennsylvania eight, Delaware one, Maryland six, Virginia ten, North Carolina five, South Carolina five, and Georgia three.

When vacancies happen in the representation from any State, the executive authority thereof shall issue writs of election to fill such vacancies.

The House of Representatives shall choose their Speaker and other officers; and shall have the sole power of impeachment.

SECTION 3. The Senate of the United States shall be composed of two Senators from each State, chosen by the legislature thereof, for six years and each Senator shall have one vote.

Immediately after they shall be assembled in consequence of the first election, they shall be divided as equally as may be into three classes. The seats of the Senators of the first class shall be vacated at the expiration of the second year, of the second class at the expiration of the fourth year, and of the third class at the expiration of the sixth year, so that one-third may be chosen every second year; and if vacancies happen by resignation, or otherwise, during the recess of the legislature of any State, the executive thereof may make temporary appointments until the next meeting of the legislature, which shall then fill such vacancies.

No person shall be a Senator who shall not have attained to the age of thirty years, and been nine years a citizen of the United States, and who shall not, when elected, be an inhabitant of that State for which he shall be chosen.

The Vice President of the United States shall be President of the Senate, but shall have no vote, unless they be equally divided.

The Senate shall choose their other officers, and also a President pro tempore, in the absence of the Vice President, or when he shall exercise the office of President of the United States.

The Senate shall have the sole power to try all impeachments. When sitting for that purpose, they shall be on oath or affirmation. When the President of the United States is tried, the Chief Justice shall preside: and no person shall be convicted without the concurrence of two thirds of the members present.

Judgment in cases of impeachment shall not extend further than to removal from office, and disqualification to hold and enjoy any office of honor, trust or profit under the United States: but the party convicted shall nevertheless be liable and subject to indictment, trial, judgment and punishment, according to law.

SECTION 4. The times, places and manner of holding elections for Senators and Representatives, shall be prescribed in each State by the legislature thereof; but the Congress may at any time by law make or alter such regulations, except as to the places of choosing Senators.

The Congress shall assemble at least once in every year, and such meeting shall be on the first Monday in December, unless they shall by law appoint a different day.

SECTION 5. Each House shall be the judge of the elections, returns and qualifications of its own members, and a majority of each shall constitute a quorum to do business; but a smaller number may adjourn from day to day, and may be authorized to compel the attendance of absent members, in such manner, and under such penalties as each House may provide.

Each House may determine the rules of its proceedings, punish its members for disorderly behavior, and, with the concurrence of two-thirds, expel a member.

Each House shall keep a journal of its proceedings, and from time to time publish the same, excepting such parts as may in their judgment require secrecy; and the yeas and the nays of the members of either house on any question shall, at the desire of one-fifth of those present, be entered on the journal.

Neither House, during the session of Congress, shall, without the consent of the other, adjourn for more than three days, nor to any other place than that in which the two Houses shall be sitting.

SECTION 6. The Senators and Representatives shall receive a compensation for their services, to be ascertained by law, and paid out of the Treasury of the United States. They shall in all cases, except treason, felony and breach of the peace, be privileged from arrest during their attendance at the session of their respective Houses, and in going to and returning from the same; and for any speech or debate in either House, they shall not be questioned in any other place.

No Senator or Representative shall, during the time for which he was elected, be appointed to any civil office under the authority of the United States, which shall have been created, or the emoluments whereof shall have been increased during such time; and no person holding any office under the United States, shall be a member of either House during his continuance in office.

SECTION 7. All bills for raising revenue shall originate in the House of Representatives; but the Senate may propose or concur with amendments as on other bills.

Every bill which shall have passed the House of Representatives and the Senate, shall, before it becomes a law, be presented to the President of the United States; if he approves he shall sign it, but if not he shall return it, with his objections to that House in which it shall have originated, who shall enter the objections at large on their journal, and proceed to reconsider it. If after such reconsideration two thirds of that House shall agree to pass the bill, it shall be sent, together with the objections, to the other House, by which it shall likewise be reconsidered, and if approved by two thirds of that House, it shall become a law. But in all such cases the votes of both Houses shall be determined by yeas and nays, and the names of the persons voting for and against the bill shall be entered on the journal of each House respectively. If any bill shall not be returned by the President within ten days (Sundays excepted) after it shall have been presented to him, the same shall be a law, in like manner as if he had signed it, unless the Congress by their adjournment prevent its return, in which case it shall not be a law.

United States

Every order, resolution, or vote to which the concurrence of the Senate and House of Representatives may be necessary (except on a question of adjournment) shall be presented to the President of the United States; and before the same shall take effect, shall be approved by him, or being disapproved by him, shall be repassed by two thirds of the Senate and House of Representatives, according to the rules and limitations prescribed in the case of a bill.

SECTION 8. The Congress shall have power to lay and collect taxes, duties, imposts and excises, to pay the debts and provide for the common defense and general welfare of the United States; but all duties, imposts and excises shall be uniform throughout the United States;

To borrow money on the credit of the United States;

To regulate commerce with foreign nations, and among the several States, and with the Indian tribes;

To establish a uniform rule of naturalization, and uniform laws on the subject of bankruptcies throughout the United States;

To coin money, regulate the value thereof, and of foreign coin, and fix the standard of weights and measures;

To provide for the punishment of counterfeiting the securities and current coin of the United States;

To establish post offices and post roads;

To promote the progress of science and useful arts, by securing for limited times to authors and inventors the exclusive right to their respective writings and discoveries;

To constitute tribunals inferior to the Supreme Court;

To define and punish piracies and felonies committed on the high seas, and offenses against the law of nations;

To declare war, grant letters of marque and reprisal, and make rules concerning captures on land and water;

To raise and support armies, but no appropriation of money to that use shall be for a longer term than two years;

To provide and maintain a navy;

To make rules for the government and regulation of the land and naval forces;

To provide for calling forth the militia to execute the laws of the Union, suppress insurrections and repel invasions;

To provide for organizing, arming, and disciplining the militia, and for governing such part of them as may be employed in the service of the United States, reserving to the States respectively, the appointment of the officers, and the authority of training the militia according to the discipline prescribed by Congress;

To exercise exclusive legislation in all cases whatsoever, over such district (not exceeding ten miles square) as may, by cession of particular States, and the acceptance of Congress, become the seat of the Government of the United States, and to exercise like authority over all places purchased by the consent of the legislature of the State in which the same shall be, for the erection of forts, magazines, arsenals, dock-yards, and other needful buildings;—And

To make all laws which shall be necessary and proper for carrying into execution the foregoing powers, and all other powers vested by this Constitution in the Government of the United States, or in any department or officer thereof.

SECTION 9. The migration or importation of such persons as any of the States now existing shall think proper to admit, shall not be prohibited by the Congress prior to the year one thousand eight hundred and eight, but a tax or duty may be imposed on such importation, not exceeding ten dollars for each person.

The privilege of the writ of habeas corpus shall not be suspended, unless when in cases of rebellion or invasion the public safety may require it.

No bill of attainder or ex post facto law shall be passed.

United States

No capitation, or other direct, tax shall be laid, unless in proportion to the census or enumeration herein before directed to be taken.

No tax or duty shall be laid on articles exported from any State.

No preference shall be given by any regulation of commerce or revenue to the ports of one State over those of another: nor shall vessels bound to, or from, one State, be obliged to enter, clear, or pay duties in another.

No money shall be drawn from the Treasury, but in consequence of appropriations made by law; and a regular statement and account of the receipts and expenditures of all public money shall be published from time to time.

No title of nobility shall be granted by the United States: And no person holding any office of profit or trust under them, shall, without the consent of the Congress, accept of any present, emolument, office, or title, of any kind whatever, from any King, Prince, or foreign State.

SECTION 10. No State shall enter into any treaty, alliance, or confederation; grant letters of marque and reprisal; coin money; emit bills of credit; make any thing but gold and silver coin a tender in payment of debts; pass any bill of attainder, ex post facto law, or law impairing the obligation of contracts, or grant any title of nobility.

No State shall, without the consent of the Congress, lay any imposts or duties on imports or exports, except what may be absolutely necessary for executing its inspection laws: and the net produce of all duties and imposts, laid by any state on imports or exports, shall be for the use of the Treasury of the United States; and all such laws shall be subject to the revision and control of the Congress.

No State shall, without the consent of Congress, lay any duty of tonnage, keep troops, or ships of war in time of peace, enter into any agreement or compact with another State, or with a foreign power, or engage in war, unless actually invaded, or in such imminent danger as will not admit of delay.

ARTICLE II

SECTION 1. The executive power shall be vested in a President of the United States of America. He shall hold his office during the term of four years, and together with the Vice President, chosen for the same term, be elected, as follows:

Each State, shall appoint, in such manner as the legislature thereof may direct, a number of electors, equal to the whole number of Senators and Representatives to which the State may be entitled in the Congress; but no Senator or Representative, or person holding an office of trust or profit under the United States, shall be appointed an elector.

The electors shall meet in their respective States, and vote by ballot for two persons, of whom one at least shall not be an inhabitant of the same State with themselves. And they shall make a list of all the persons voted for, and of the number of votes for each; which list they shall sign and certify, and transmit sealed to the seat of the Government of the United States, directed to the President of the Senate. The President of the Senate shall, in the presence of the Senate and House of Representatives, open all the certificates, and the votes shall then be counted. The person having the greatest number of votes shall be the President, if such number be a majority of the whole number of electors appointed; and if there be more than one who have such majority, and have an equal number of votes, then the House of Representatives shall immediately choose by ballot one of them for President; and if no persons have a majority, then from the five highest on the list the said House shall in like manner choose the President. But in choosing the President, the votes shall be taken by States, the representation from each State having one vote; a quorum for this purpose shall consist of a member or members from two-thirds of the States, and a majority of all the States shall be necessary to a choice. In every case, after the choice of the President, the person having the greatest number of votes of the electors shall be the Vice President. But if there should remain two or more who have equal votes, the Senate shall choose from them by ballot the Vice President.

The Congress may determine the time of choosing the electors, and the day on which they shall give their votes; which day shall be the same throughout the United States.

No person except a natural born citizen, or a citizen of the United States, at the time of the adoption of this Constitution, shall be eligible to the office of President; neither shall any person be eligible to that office who shall not have attained to the age of thirty-five years, and been fourteen years a resident within the United States.

In case of the removal of the President from office, or of his death, resignation, or inability to discharge the powers and duties of the said office, the same shall devolve on the Vice President, and the Congress may by law provide for the case of removal, death, resignation, or inability, both of the President and Vice President, declaring what officer shall then act as President, and such officer shall act accordingly, until the disability be removed, or a President be elected.

The President shall, at stated times, receive for his services, a compensation, which shall neither be increased nor diminished during the period for which he shall have been elected, and he shall not receive within that period any other emolument from the United States, or any of them.

Before he enter on the execution of his office, he shall take the following oath or affirmation:—"I do solemnly swear (or affirm) that I will faithfully execute the office of President of the United States, and will to the best of my ability, preserve, protect and defend the Constitution of the United States."

SECTION 2. The President shall be Commander in Chief of the Army and Navy of the United States, and of the militia of the several States, when called into the actual service of the United States; he may require the opinion, in writing, of the principal officer in each of the executive departments, upon any subject relating to the duties of their respective offices, and he shall have power to grant reprieves and pardons for offenses against the United States, except in cases of impeachment.

He shall have power, by and with the advice and consent of the Senate, to make treaties, provided

two-thirds of the Senators present concur; and he shall nominate, and by and with the advice and consent of the Senate, shall appoint ambassadors, other public ministers and consuls, Judges of the Supreme Court, and all other officers of the United States, whose appointments are not herein otherwise provided for, and which shall be established by law: but the Congress may by law vest the appointment of such inferior officers, as they think proper, in the President alone, in the courts of law, or in the heads of departments.

The President shall have power to fill up all vacancies that may happen during the recess of the Senate, by granting commissions which shall expire at the end of their next session.

SECTION 3. He shall from time to time give to the Congress information of the State of the Union, and recommend to their consideration such measures as he shall judge necessary and expedient; he may, on extraordinary occasions, convene both Houses, or either of them, and in case of disagreement between them, with respect to the time of adjournment, he may adjourn them to such time as he shall think proper; he shall receive ambassadors and other public ministers; he shall take care that the laws be faithfully executed, and shall commission all the officers of the United States.

SECTION 4. The President, Vice President and all civil officers of the United States, shall be removed from office on impeachment for, and conviction of, treason, bribery, or other high crimes and misdemeanors.

ARTICLE III

SECTION 1. The judicial power of the United States, shall be vested in one Supreme Court, and in such inferior courts as the Congress may from time to time ordain and establish. The judges, both of the Supreme and inferior Courts, shall hold their offices during good behavior, and shall, at stated times, receive for their services, a compensation, which shall not be diminished during their continuance in office.

SECTION 2. The judicial power shall extend to all cases, in law and equity, arising under this Constitution, the laws of the United States, and

United States

treaties made, or which shall be made, under their authority;—to all cases affecting ambassadors, other public ministers and consuls;—to all cases of admiralty and maritime jurisdiction;—to controversies to which the United States shall be a party;—to controversies between two or more States;—between a State and citizens of another State;—between citizens of different States,—between citizens of the same State claiming lands under grants of different States, and between a State, or the citizens thereof, and foreign States, citizens or subjects.

In all cases affecting ambassadors, other public ministers and consuls, and those in which a State shall be a party, the Supreme Court shall have original jurisdiction. In all the other cases before mentioned, the Supreme Court shall have appellate jurisdiction, both as to law and fact, with such exceptions, and under such regulations as the Congress shall make.

The trial of all crimes, except in cases of impeachment, shall be by jury; and such trial shall be held in the State where the said crimes shall have been committed; but when not committed within any State, the trial shall be at such place or places as the Congress may by law have directed.

SECTION 3. Treason against the United States, shall consist only in levying war against them, or in adhering to their enemies, giving them aid and comfort. No person shall be convicted of treason unless on the testimony of two witnesses to the same overt act, or on confession in open court.

The Congress shall have power to declare the punishment of treason, but no attainder of treason shall work corruption of blood, or forfeiture except during the life of the person attainted.

ARTICLE IV

SECTION 1. Full faith and credit shall be given in each State to the public acts, records, and judicial proceedings of every other State. And the Congress may by general laws prescribe the manner in which such acts, records, and proceedings shall be proved, and the effect thereof.

SECTION 2. The citizens of each State shall be entitled to all privileges and immunities of citizens in the several States.

A person charged in any State with treason, felony, or other crime, who shall flee from justice, and be found in another State, shall on demand of the executive authority of the State from which he fled, be delivered up, to be removed to the State having jurisdiction of the crime.

No person held to service or labor in one State, under the laws thereof, escaping into another, shall, in consequence of any law or regulation therein, be discharged from such service or labor, but shall be delivered up on claim of the party to whom such service or labor may be due.

SECTION 3. New States may be admitted by the Congress into this Union; but no new State shall be formed or erected within the jurisdiction of any other State; nor any State be formed by the junction of two or more States, or parts of States, without the consent of the legislatures of the States concerned as well as of the Congress.

The Congress shall have power to dispose of and make all needful rules and regulations respecting the Territory or other property belonging to the United States; and nothing in this Constitution shall be so construed as to prejudice any claims of the United States, or of any particular State.

SECTION 4. The United States shall guarantee to every State in this Union a republican form of Government, and shall protect each of them against invasion; and on application of the legislature, or of the executive (when the legislature cannot be convened) against domestic violence.

ARTICLE V

The Congress, whenever two thirds of both Houses shall deem it necessary, shall propose amendments to this Constitution, or on the application of the legislatures of two thirds of the several States, shall call a convention for proposing amendments, which, in either case, shall be valid to all intents and purposes, as part of this Constitution, when ratified by the legislatures of three fourths of the several States, or by conventions in three fourths thereof, as the one or the other mode of ratification may be proposed by the Congress; provided that no amendment which may be made prior to the year one thousand eight hundred and eight shall in any manner affect the first and fourth clauses in the Ninth Section of the First Article; and that no State, without its consent, shall be deprived of its equal suffrage in the Senate.

George Washington was not the first president of the United States. In 1781 John Hanson of Maryland was named the first "president of the United States in Congress assembled," and seven others followed.

Article VI

All debts contracted and engagements entered into, before the adoption of this Constitution, shall be as valid against the United States under this Constitution, as under the Confederation.

This Constitution, and the laws of the United States which shall be made in pursuance thereof; and all treaties made, or which shall be made, under the authority of the United States, shall be the supreme law of the land; and the judges in every State shall be bound thereby, any thing in the Constitution or laws of any State to the contrary notwithstanding.

The Senators and Representatives before mentioned, and the members of the several State legislatures, and all executive and judicial officers, both of the United States and of the several States, shall be bound by oath or affirmation, to support this Constitution; but no religious test shall ever be required as a qualification to any office or public trust under the United States.

Article VII

The ratification of the conventions of nine States shall be sufficient for the establishment of this Constitution between the States so ratifying the same.

Done in convention by the unanimous consent of the States present the seventeenth day of September in the year of our Lord one thousand seven hundred and eighty seven and of the independence of the United States of America the twelfth. In witness whereof we have hereunto subscribed our names,

Geo. Washington—*President* and deputy from Virginia

Attest William Jackson *Secretary*

New Hampshire

John Langdon	Nicholas Gilman

Massachusetts

Nathaniel Gorham	Rufus King

Connecticut

Wm. Saml. Johnson	Roger Sherman

New York

Alexander Hamilton

New Jersey

Wil. Livingston	Wm. Paterson
David Brearley	Jona. Dayton

Pennsylvania

B. Franklin	Thos. FitzSimons
Thomas Mifflin	Jared Ingersoll
Robt Morris	James Wilson
Geo. Clymer	Gouv. Morris

Delaware

Geo. Read	Richard Bassett
Gunning Bedfordjun	Jaco. Broom
John Dickinson	

Maryland

James McHenry	Danl. Carroll
Dan of St. Thos. Jenifer	

Virginia

John Blair	James Madison Jr.

North Carolina

Wm. Blount	Hu. Williamson
Richd. Dobbs Spaight	

South Carolina

J. Rutledge	Charles Pinckney
Charles Cotesworth Pinckney	Pierce Butler

Georgia

William Few	Abr. Baldwin

Amendments

[The first ten amendments to the Constitution are called the *Bill of Rights*.]

AMENDMENT I (1791)

Congress shall make no law respecting an establishment of religion, or prohibiting the free exercise thereof; or abridging the freedom of speech, or of the press; or the right of the people peaceably to assemble, and to petition the Government for a redress of grievances.

AMENDMENT II (1791)

A well regulated militia, being necessary to the security of a free State, the right of the people to keep and bear arms, shall not be infringed.

AMENDMENT III (1791)

No soldier shall, in time of peace be quartered in any house, without the consent of the owner, nor in time of war, but in a manner to be prescribed by law.

AMENDMENT IV (1791)

The right of the people to be secure in their persons, houses, papers, and effects, against unreasonable searches and seizures, shall not be violated, and no warrants shall issue, but upon probable cause, supported by oath or affirmation, and particularly describing the place to be searched, and the persons or things to be seized.

AMENDMENT V (1791)

No person shall be held to answer for a capital, or otherwise infamous crime, unless on a presentment or indictment of a Grand Jury, except in cases arising in the land or naval forces, or in the militia, when in actual service in time of war or public danger; nor shall any person be subject for the same offense to be twice put in jeopardy of life or limb; nor shall be compelled in any criminal case to be a witness against himself, nor be deprived of life, liberty, or property, without due process of law; nor shall private property be taken for public use, without just compensation.

AMENDMENT VI (1791)

In all criminal prosecutions, the accused shall enjoy the right to a speedy and public trial, by an impartial jury of the State and district wherein the crime shall have been committed, which district shall have been previously ascertained by law, and to be informed of the nature and cause of the accusation; to be confronted with the witnesses against him; to have compulsory process for obtaining witnesses in his favor, and to have the assistance of counsel for his defense.

AMENDMENT VII (1791)

In suits at common law, where the value in controversy shall exceed twenty dollars, the right of trial by jury shall be preserved, and no fact tried by a jury, shall be otherwise reexamined in any Court of the United States, than according to the rules of the common law.

AMENDMENT VIII (1791)

Excessive bail shall not be required, nor excessive fines imposed, nor cruel and unusual punishments inflicted.

AMENDMENT IX (1791)

The enumeration in the Constitution, of certain rights, shall not be construed to deny or disparage others retained by the people.

AMENDMENT X (1791)

The powers not delegated to the United States by the Constitution, nor prohibited by it to the States, are reserved to the States respectively, or to the people.

AMENDMENT XI (1798)

The judicial power of the United States shall not be construed to extend to any suit in law or equity, commenced or prosecuted against one of the United States by citizens of another State, or by citizens or subjects of any foreign State.

United States

AMENDMENT **XII** (1804)

The electors shall meet in their respective States, and vote by ballot for President and Vice President, one of whom, at least, shall not be an inhabitant of the same State with themselves; they shall name in their ballots the person voted for as President, and in distinct ballots the person voted for as Vice President, and they shall make distinct lists of all persons voted for as President, and of all persons voted for as Vice President, and of the number of votes for each, which lists they shall sign and certify, and transmit sealed to the seat of the government of the United States, directed to the President of the Senate;—The President of the Senate shall, in the presence of the Senate and House of Representatives, open all the certificates and the votes shall then be counted;—The person having the greatest number of votes for President, shall be the President, if such number be a majority of the whole number of electors appointed; and if no person have such majority, then from the persons having the highest numbers not exceeding three on the list of those voted for as President, the House of Representatives shall choose immediately, by ballot, the President. But in choosing the President, the votes shall be taken by States, the representation from each State having one vote; a quorum for this purpose shall consist of a member or members from two-thirds of the States, and a majority of all the States shall be necessary to a choice. And if the House of Representatives shall not choose a President whenever the right of choice shall devolve upon them, before the fourth day of March next following, then the Vice President shall act as President, as in the case of the death or other constitutional disability of the President.—The person having the greatest number of votes as Vice President, shall be the Vice President, if such number be a majority of the whole number of electors appointed, and if no person have a majority, then from the two highest numbers on the list, the Senate shall choose the Vice President; a quorum for the purpose shall consist of two-thirds of the whole number of Senators, and a majority of the whole number shall be necessary to a choice. But no person constitu-

tionally ineligible to the office of President shall be eligible to that of Vice President of the United States.

AMENDMENT **XIII** (1865)

SECTION 1. Neither slavery nor involuntary servitude, except as a punishment for crime whereof the party shall have been duly convicted, shall exist within the United States, or any place subject to their jurisdiction.

SECTION 2. Congress shall have power to enforce this article by appropriate legislation.

AMENDMENT **XIV** (1868)

SECTION 1. All persons born or naturalized in the United States, and subject to the jurisdiction thereof, are citizens of the United States and of the State wherein they reside. No State shall make or enforce any law which shall abridge the privileges or immunities of citizens of the United States; nor shall any State deprive any person of life, liberty, or property, without due process of law; nor deny to any person within its jurisdiction the equal protection of the laws.

SECTION 2. Representatives shall be apportioned among the several States according to their respective numbers, counting the whole number of persons in each State, excluding Indians not taxed. But when the right to vote at any election for the choice of electors for President and Vice President of the United States, Representatives in Congress, the executive and judicial officers of a State, or the members of the legislature thereof, is denied to any of the male inhabitants of such State, being twenty-one years of age, and citizens of the United States, or in any way abridged, except for participation in rebellion, or other crime, the basis of representation therein shall be reduced in the proportion which the number of such male citizens shall bear to the whole number of male citizens twenty-one years of age in such State.

SECTION 3. No person shall be a Senator or Representative in Congress, or elector of President and Vice President, or hold any office, civil or military, under the United States, or under any State, who, having previously taken an oath, as a member of

Congress, or as an officer of the United States, or as a member of any State legislature, or as an executive or judicial officer of any State, to support the Constitution of the United States, shall have engaged in insurrection or rebellion against the same, or given aid or comfort to the enemies thereof. But Congress may by a vote of two-thirds of each house, remove such disability.

SECTION 4. The validity of the public debt of the United States, authorized by law, including debts incurred for payment of pensions and bounties for services in suppressing insurrection or rebellion, shall not be questioned. But neither the United States nor any State shall assume or pay any debt or obligation incurred in aid of insurrection or rebellion against the United States, or any claim for the loss or emancipation of any slave; but all such debts, obligations and claims shall be held illegal and void.

SECTION 5. The Congress shall have power to enforce, by appropriate legislation, the provisions of this article.

AMENDMENT XV (1870)

SECTION 1. The right of citizens of the United States to vote shall not be denied or abridged by the United States or by any State on account of race, color, or previous condition of servitude.

SECTION 2. The Congress shall have power to enforce this article by appropriate legislation.

AMENDMENT XVI (1913)

The Congress shall have power to lay and collect taxes on incomes, from whatever source derived, without apportionment among the several States, and without regard to any census or enumeration.

AMENDMENT XVII (1913)

SECTION 1. The Senate of the United States shall be composed of two Senators from each State, elected by the people thereof, for six years; and each Senator shall have one vote. The electors in each State shall have the qualifications requisite for electors of the most numerous branch of the State legislatures.

SECTION 2. When vacancies happen in the representation of any State in the Senate, the executive authority of such State shall issue writs of election to fill such vacancies: *Provided,* that the legislature of any State may empower the executive thereof to make temporary appointments until the people fill the vacancies by election as the legislature may direct.

SECTION 3. This amendment shall not be so construed as to affect the election or term of any Senator chosen before it becomes valid as part of the Constitution.

AMENDMENT XVIII (1919)

SECTION 1. After one year from the ratification of this article the manufacture, sale, or transportation of intoxicating liquors within, the importation thereof into, or the exportation thereof from the United States and all territory subject to the jurisdiction thereof for beverage purposes is hereby prohibited.

SECTION 2. The Congress and the several States shall have concurrent power to enforce this article by appropriate legislation.

SECTION 3. This article shall be inoperative unless it shall have been ratified as an amendment to the Constitution by the legislatures of the several States, as provided in the Constitution, within seven years from the date of the submission hereof to the States by the Congress.

AMENDMENT XIX (1920)

SECTION 1. The right of citizens of the United States to vote shall not be denied or abridged by the United States or by any State on account of sex.

SECTION 2. Congress shall have power to enforce this article by appropriate legislation.

AMENDMENT XX (1933)

SECTION 1. The terms of the President and Vice President shall end at noon on the 20th day of January, and the terms of Senators and Representatives at noon on the 3d day of January, of the years in which such terms would have ended if this article had not been ratified; and the terms of their successors shall then begin.

SECTION 2. The Congress shall assemble at least once in every year, and such meeting shall begin at noon on the 3d day of January, unless they shall by law appoint a different day.

SECTION 3. If, at the time fixed for the beginning of the term of the President, the President elect shall have died, the Vice President elect shall become President. If a President shall not have been chosen before the time fixed for the beginning of his term, or if the President elect shall have failed to qualify, then the Vice President elect shall act as President until a President shall have qualified; and the Congress may by law provide for the case wherein neither a President elect nor a Vice President elect shall have qualified, declaring who shall then act as President, or the manner in which one who is to act shall be selected, and such person shall act accordingly until a President or Vice President shall have qualified.

SECTION 4. The Congress may by law provide for the case of the death of any of the persons from whom the House of Representatives may choose a President whenever the right of choice shall have devolved upon them, and for the case of the death of any of the persons from whom the Senate may choose a Vice President whenever the right of choice shall have devolved upon them.

SECTION 5. Sections 1 and 2 shall take effect on the 15th day of October following the ratification of this article.

SECTION 6. This article shall be inoperative unless it shall have been ratified as an amendment to the Constitution by the legislatures of three-fourths of the several States within seven years from the date of its submission.

AMENDMENT XXI (1933)

SECTION 1. The eighteenth article of amendment to the Constitution of the United States is hereby repealed.

SECTION 2. The transportation or importation into any State, Territory, or possession of the United States for delivery or use therein of intoxicating liquors, in violation of the laws thereof, is hereby prohibited.

SECTION 3. This article shall be inoperative unless it shall have been ratified as an amendment to the Constitution by conventions in the several States, as provided in the Constitution, within seven years from the date of the submission hereof to the States by the Congress.

AMENDMENT XXII (1951)

SECTION 1. No person shall be elected to the office of the President more than twice, and no person who has held the office of President, or acted as President, for more than two years of a term to which some other person was elected President shall be elected to the office of the President more than once. But this article shall not apply to any person holding the office of President when this article was proposed by the Congress, and shall not prevent any person who may be holding the office of President, or acting as President, during the term within which this article becomes operative from holding the office of President or acting as President during the remainder of such term.

SECTION 2. This article shall be inoperative unless it shall have been ratified as an amendment to the Constitution by the legislatures of three-fourths of the several States within seven years from the date of its submission to the States by the Congress.

AMENDMENT XXIII (1961)

SECTION 1. The District constituting the seat of Government of the United States shall appoint in such manner as the Congress may direct:

A number of electors of President and Vice President equal to the whole number of Senators and Representatives in Congress to which the District would be entitled if it were a State, but in no event more than the least populous State; they shall be in addition to those appointed by the States, but they shall be considered, for the purposes of the election of President and Vice President, to be electors appointed by a State; and they shall meet in the District and perform such duties as provided by the twelfth article of amendment.

SECTION 2. The Congress shall have power to enforce this article by appropriate legislation.

AMENDMENT XXIV (1964)

SECTION 1. The right of citizens of the United States to vote in any primary or other election for President or Vice President, for electors for President or Vice President, or for Senator or Representative in Congress, shall not be denied or abridged by the United States or any State by reason of failure to pay any poll tax or other tax.

SECTION 2. The Congress shall have power to enforce this article by appropriate legislation.

AMENDMENT XXV (1967)

SECTION 1. In case of the removal of the President from office or of his death or resignation, the Vice President shall become President.

SECTION 2. Whenever there is a vacancy in the office of the Vice President, the President shall nominate a Vice President who shall take office upon confirmation by a majority vote of both Houses of Congress.

SECTION 3. Whenever the President transmits to the President pro tempore of the Senate and the Speaker of the House of Representatives his written declaration that he is unable to discharge the powers and duties of his office, and until he transmits to them a written declaration to the contrary, such powers and duties shall be discharged by the Vice President as Acting President.

SECTION 4. Whenever the Vice President and a majority of either the principal officers of the executive departments or of such other body as Congress may by law provide, transmit to the President pro tempore of the Senate and the Speaker of the House of Representatives their written declaration that the President is unable to discharge the powers and duties of his office, the Vice President shall immediately assume the powers and duties of the office as Acting President.

Thereafter, when the President transmits to the President pro tempore of the Senate and the Speaker of the House of Representatives his written declaration that no inability exists, he shall resume the powers and duties of his office unless the Vice President and a majority of either the principal officers of the executive department or of such other body as Congress may by law provide, transmit within four days to the President pro tempore of the Senate and the Speaker of the House of Representatives their written declaration that the President is unable to discharge the powers and duties of his office. Thereupon Congress shall decide the issue, assembling within forty-eight hours for that purpose if not in session. If the Congress, within twenty-one days after receipt of the latter written declaration, or, if Congress is not in session, within twenty-one days after Congress is required to assemble, determines by two-thirds vote of both Houses that the President is unable to discharge the powers and duties of his office, the Vice President shall continue to discharge the same as Acting President; otherwise, the President shall resume the powers and duties of his office.

AMENDMENT XXVI (1971)

SECTION 1. The right of citizens of the United States who are eighteen years of age or older, to vote shall not be denied or abridged by the United States or by any State on account of age.

SECTION 2. The Congress shall have power to enforce this article by appropriate legislation.

AMENDMENT XXVII (1992)

No law, varying the compensation for the services of the Senators and Representatives, shall take effect, until an election of Representatives shall have intervened.

> *The U.S. has signed more than 300 treaties with Native American nations. According to U.S. Constitution Article VI, such treaties "shall be the supreme law of the land."*

THE EMANCIPATION PROCLAMATION

President Abraham Lincoln's Emancipation Proclamation took effect on January 1, 1863. Although it did not actually free any slaves, it made clear for the first time that slavery would be abolished when the Union won the Civil War.

By the President of the United States of America:

A Proclamation.

Whereas on the 22d day of September, A.D. 1862, a proclamation was issued by the President of the United States, containing, among other things, the following, to wit:

"That on the 1st day of January, A.D. 1863, all persons held as slaves within any State or designated part of a State the people whereof shall then be in rebellion against the United States shall be then, thenceforward, and forever free; and the executive government of the United States, including the military and naval authority thereof, will recognize and maintain the freedom of such persons and will do no act or acts to repress such persons, or any of them, in any efforts they may make for their actual freedom.

"That the executive will on the 1st day of January aforesaid, by proclamation, designate the States and parts of States, if any, in which the people thereof, respectively, shall then be in rebellion against the United States; and the fact that any State or the people thereof shall on that day be in good faith represented in the Congress of the United States by members chosen thereto at elections wherein a majority of the qualified voters of such States shall have participated shall, in the absence of strong countervailing testimony, be deemed conclusive evidence that such State and the people thereof are not then in rebellion against the United States."

Now, therefore, I, Abraham Lincoln, President of the United States, by virtue of the power in me vested as Commander-in-Chief of the Army and Navy of the United States in time of actual armed rebellion against the authority and government of the United States, and as a fit and necessary war measure for suppressing said rebellion, do, on this 1st day of January, A.D. 1863, and in accordance with my purpose so to do, publicly proclaimed for the full period of one hundred days from the first day above mentioned, order and designate as the States and parts of States wherein the people thereof, respectively, are this day in rebellion against the United States the following, to wit:

Arkansas, Texas, Louisiana (except the parishes of St. Bernard, Plaquemines, Jefferson, St. John, St. Charles, St. James, Ascension, Assumption, Terrebonne, Lafourche, St. Mary, St. Martin, and Orleans, including the city of New Orleans), Mississippi, Alabama, Florida, Georgia, South Carolina, North Carolina, and Virginia (except the forty-eight counties designated as West Virginia, and also the counties of Berkeley, Accomac, Northampton, Elizabeth City, York, Princess Anne, and Norfolk, including the cities of Norfolk and Portsmouth), and which excepted parts are for the present left precisely as if this proclamation were not issued.

And by virtue of the power and for the purpose aforesaid, I do order and declare that all persons held as slaves within said designated States and parts of States are, and henceforward shall be, free; and that the Executive Government of the United States, including the military and naval authorities thereof, will recognize and maintain the freedom of said persons.

And I hereby enjoin upon the people so declared to be free to abstain from all violence, unless in necessary self-defense; and I recommend to them that, in all cases when allowed, they labor faithfully for reasonable wages.

And I further declare and make known that such persons of suitable condition will be received into the armed service of the United States to garrison forts, positions, stations, and other places, and to man vessels of all sorts in said service.

And upon this act, sincerely believed to be an act of justice, warranted by the Constitution upon military necessity, I invoke the considerate judgment of mankind and the gracious favor of Almighty God.

THE GETTYSBURG ADDRESS

President Abraham Lincoln wrote the Gettysburg Address on the back of an envelope during a train ride from Washington, D.C., to Pennsylvania. The event of its presentation was the dedication of the battlefield as a memorial. Several longer speeches preceded Lincoln's, and were much better received by the crowd, although now long forgotten. Upon delivering the Gettysburg Address, President Lincoln received a polite response. Few present at the time realized they had just heard what many now consider the greatest presidential address of all time. The following is the Nicolay draft from the Library of Congress, thought to be the earliest surviving copy of the speech.

Four score and seven years ago our fathers brought forth, upon this continent, a new nation, conceived in liberty, and dedicated to the proposition that "all men are created equal"

Now we are engaged in a great civil war, testing whether that nation, or any nation so conceived, and so dedicated, can long endure. We are met on a great battle field of that war. We come to dedicate a portion of it, as a final resting place for those who died here, that the nation might live. This we may, in all propriety do. But, in a larger sense, we can not dedicate—we can not consecrate—we can not hallow, this ground—The brave men, living and dead, who struggled here, have hallowed it, far above our poor power to add or detract. The world will little note, nor long remember what we say here; while it can never forget what they did here.

It is rather for us, the living, we here be dedicated to the great task remaining before us—that, from these honored dead we take increased devotion to that cause for which they here, gave the last full measure of devotion—that we here highly resolve these dead shall not have died in vain; that the nation, shall have a new birth of freedom, and that government of the people, by the people, for the people, shall not perish from the earth.

THE U.S. FLAG

As English settlers populated the colonies, each territory adopted a flag. By 1707, each colony had its own flag, the forerunners of the individual state flags today. The first colonial flag representing all the colonies, however, was believed to have been raised on Prospect Hill in Boston at the Battle of Bunker Hill in 1775. The "Continental Colors" bore the cross of the British flag in the upper left corner with 13 alternating red and white stripes extending horizontally to represent the 13 colonies. In 1777, the first Continental Congress "Resolved, that the Flag of the United States be thirteen stripes alternate red and white, that the Union be thirteen stars white on a blue field, representing a constellation."

This flag was flown at Fort McHenry, Maryland, during the War of 1812 and was the inspiration for Francis Scott Key's "Star-Spangled Banner." By 1818, five more states had joined, and on April 4, Congress voted to keep the number of stripes at 13 and to add a star to the field for every new state, the stars for the new states being added on July 4 after each state's admission to the Union.

The table on page 850 shows the order in which states joined the Union and the number of revisions the flag went through before arriving at its current design. *See also* "Admission of the 13 Original States" in this chapter.

THE PLEDGE OF ALLEGIANCE

"I pledge allegiance to the flag of the United States of America, and to the Republic for which it stands, one nation under God, indivisible, with liberty and justice for all."

The phrase "under God" was added to the pledge by an Act of Congress in 1954. The original pledge, written in 1892 by Francis Bellamy, contained the phrase "my flag."

United States

THE U.S. FLAG: 1777–1960

Date Introduced	Number of Stars	Design Number	New States
June 14, 1777	13	1	Original 13 colonies
May 1, 1795	15	2	Vermont, Kentucky
July 4, 1818	20	3	Tennessee, Ohio, Louisiana, Indiana, Mississippi
July 4, 1819	21	4	Illinois
July 4, 1820	23	5	Alabama, Maine
July 4, 1822	24	6	Missouri
July 4, 1836	25	7	Arkansas
July 4, 1837	26	8	Michigan
July 4, 1845	27	9	Florida
July 4, 1846	28	10	Texas
July 4, 1847	29	11	Iowa
July 4, 1848	30	12	Wisconsin
July 4, 1851	31	13	California
July 4, 1858	32	14	Minnesota
July 4, 1859	33	15	Oregon
July 4, 1861	34	16	Kansas
July 4, 1863	35	17	West Virginia
July 4, 1865	36	18	Nevada
July 4, 1867	37	19	Nebraska
July 4, 1877	38	20	Colorado
July 4, 1890	43	21	North Dakota, South Dakota, Montana, Washington, Idaho
July 4, 1891	44	22	Wyoming
July 4, 1896	45	23	Utah
July 4, 1908	46	24	Oklahoma
July 4, 1912	48	25	New Mexico, Arizona
July 4, 1959	49	26	Alaska
July 4, 1960	50	27	Hawaii

CARE AND USE

Many Americans see the flag as a sacred article representing their devotion to the nation. On the other end of the spectrum, the U.S. Supreme Court has upheld flag burning as a constitutionally protected right. The following conventions concern the care and use of flags.

The U.S. flag should be flown on holidays and special occasions, but only in good weather. The flag is flown from sunrise to sunset, and at night only if well lit. The flag is flown at half-mast to commemorate the deaths of state officials and until noon on Memorial Day. The flag should not touch the ground while being handled, and it should be hoisted and lowered during the playing of "Taps." It should appear prominently above any other flags and be to its own right (stars to the left). In a group of flags, it should be in the center. The United Nations flag and the Navy Chaplain church pennant may fly above it.

If the flag is hung on a pole extending from a building, the union (the field of stars) should be away from the building; when the flag is hung over the center of a street, the union should be to the north in an east-west street and to the east in a north-south street.

On a platform, the flag may be hung flat against the wall behind and above the speaker with the field of stars to the audience's left. In a church or public auditorium, the flag on its staff should be to the speaker's right as he or she faces the audience and all other flags to the speaker's left. If the flag is flown anywhere else in the chancel or on a platform, it should be to the right of the audience as they face the platform.

Salute when the flag passes in a parade or review, is being raised or lowered, is present at the playing of the national anthem, or is present at the saying of the Pledge of Allegiance.

Civilians should salute the flag by standing at attention and placing their right hands over their hearts. Men should remove their hats and hold them over their left shoulders with their right hands. Military personnel in uniform should give the military salute. Noncitizens should stand at attention.

The flag at the White House is flown only when the president is in residence and only from sunrise to sunset. At the Capitol building, the flag flies over the appropriate wing when the House or Senate is in session. The flag is flown all night long and is lit by lights from the Capitol dome. Other special national monuments also fly the flag at night, notably Fort McHenry National Monument in Baltimore, Maryland, where Francis Scott Key was inspired to write "The Star-Spangled Banner."

The United States is the only country that does not tip its flag to honor the host nation during the opening ceremonies of the Olympics.

United States

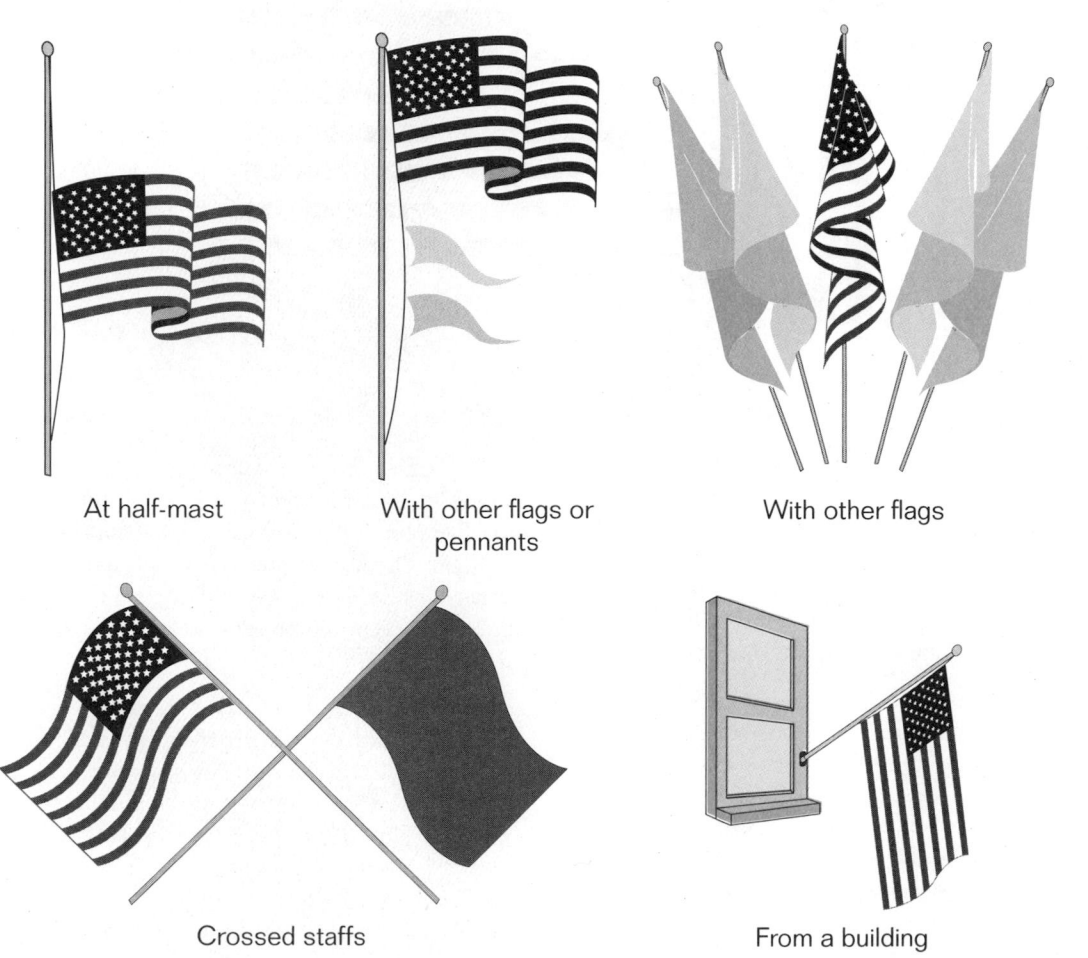

At half-mast

With other flags or pennants

With other flags

Crossed staffs

From a building

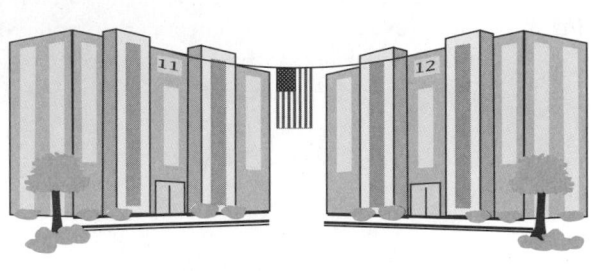

Over a street

On a platform

Against a wall

FEDERAL GOVERNMENT

While the total size of the federal government has grown considerably since 1789, its relationship to the size of the country has actually decreased during that time, employing a smaller percentage of the nation's workers and constituting a smaller percentage of the economy.

The chart on p. 853 shows the structure of the U.S. government, along with its departments and agencies. The tripartite system of government features checks and balances. The president must sign all congressional legislation, unless Congress overrides his veto. Congress may impeach and remove the president. The senate must approve presidential ap-

pointees (including U.S. Supreme Court Justices) and ratify all treaties signed by the president. Although appointed by the president and approved by the senate, the U.S. Supreme Court may overturn any federal legislation it deems unconstitutional and rule against unconstitutional actions or inactions by the executive branch.

Croatia was the first country to recognize the United States as an independent country in 1776.

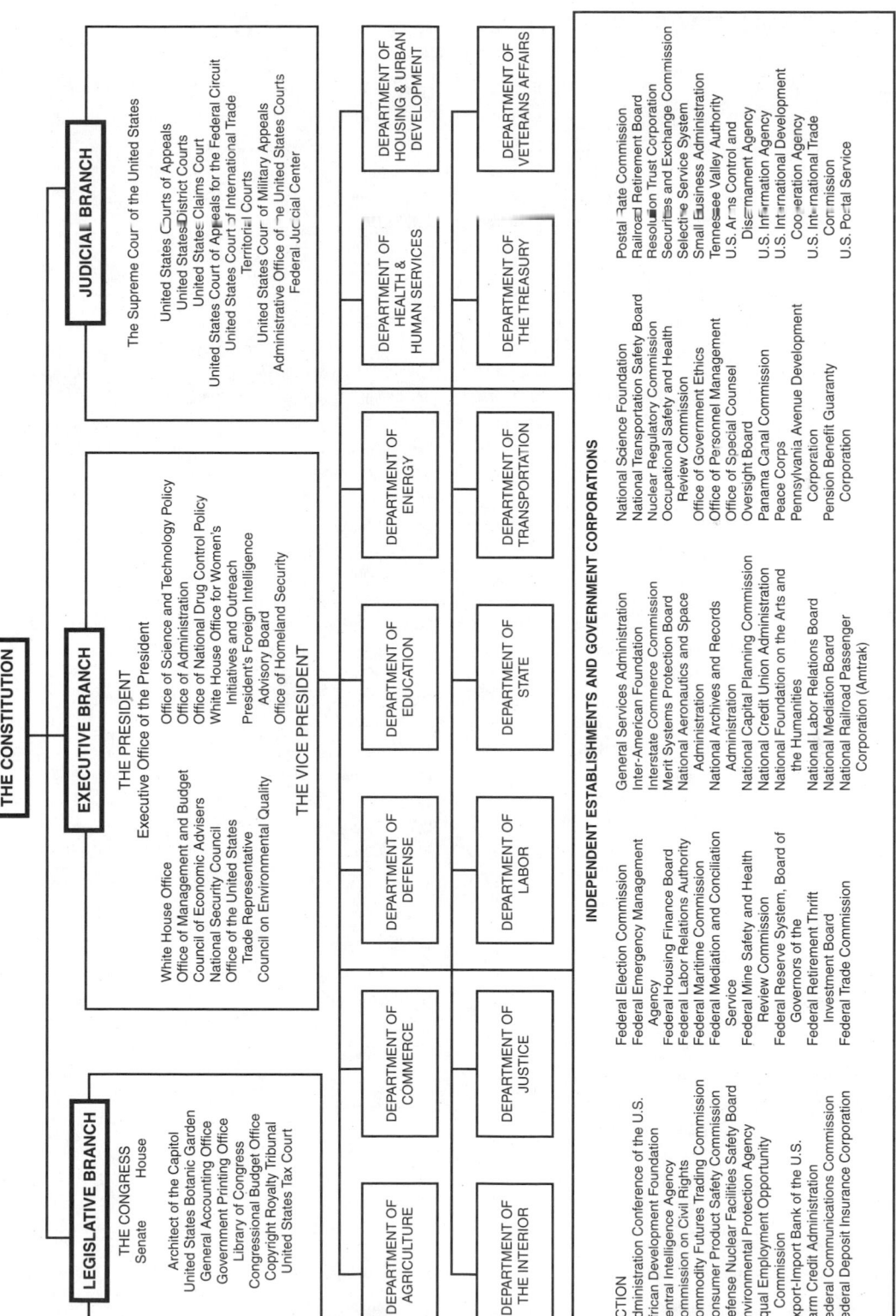

Federal Government Structure

PRESIDENTS AND VICE PRESIDENTS OF THE UNITED STATES

President	Term	Year of Birth–Death	Party	Vice President	Year of Birth–Death	Congresses
1. George Washington	4/30/1789–3/3/1797	1732–1799	I	John Adams	1735–1826	1, 2, 3, 4
2. John Adams	3/4/1797–3/3/1801	1735–1826	F	Thomas Jefferson	1743–1826	5, 6
3. Thomas Jefferson	3/4/1801–3/3/1805	1743–1826	D-R	Aaron Burr	1756–1836	7, 8
	3/4/1805–3/3/1809			George Clinton	1739–1812	9, 10
4. James Madison	3/4/1809–3/3/1813	1751–1836	D-R	George Clinton	1739–1812	11, 12
	3/4/1813–3/3/1817			Elbridge Gerry	1744–1814	13, 14
5. James Monroe	3/4/1817–3/3/1825	1758–1835	D-R	Daniel D. Tompkins	1774–1825	15, 16, 17, 18
6. John Quincy Adams	3/4/1825–3/3/1829	1767–1848	D-R	John C. Calhoun	1782–1850	19, 20
7. Andrew Jackson	3/4/1829–3/3/1833	1767–1845	D	John C. Calhoun	1782–1850	21, 22
	3/4/1833–3/3/1837			Martin Van Buren	1782–1862	23, 24
8. Martin Van Buren	3/4/1837–3/3/1841	1782–1862	D	Richard M. Johnson	1780–1850	25, 26
9. William Henry Harrison	3/4/1841–4/4/1841	1773–1841	W	John Tyler	1790–1862	27
10. John Tyler	4/6/1841–3/3/1845	1790–1862	W	—	—	27, 28
11. James K. Polk	3/4/1845–3/3/1849	1795–1849	D	George M. Dallas	1792–1864	29, 30
12. Zachary Taylor	3/4/1849–7/9/1850	1784–1850	W	Millard Fillmore	1800–1874	31
13. Millard Fillmore	7/10/1850–3/3/1853	1800–1874	W	—	—	31, 32
14. Franklin Pierce	3/4/1853–3/3/1857	1804–1869	D	William R. King	1786–1853	33, 34
15. James Buchanan	3/4/1857–3/3/1861	1791–1868	D	John C. Breckinridge	1821–1875	35, 36
16. Abraham Lincoln	3/4/1861–3/3/1865	1809–1865	R	Hannibal Hamlin	1809–1891	37, 38
	3/4/1865–4/15/1865			Andrew Johnson	1808–1875	39
17. Andrew Johnson	4/15/1865–3/3/1869	1808–1875	NU	—	—	39, 40
18. Ulysses S. Grant	3/4/1869–3/3/1873	1822–1885	R	Schuyler Colfax	1823–1885	41, 42
	3/4/1873–3/3/1877			Henry Wilson	1812–1875	43, 44
19. Rutherford B. Hayes	3/4/1877–3/3/1881	1822–1893	R	William A. Wheeler	1819–1887	45, 46
20. James Garfield	3/4/1881–9/19/1881	1831–1881	R	Chester A. Arthur	1829–1886	47
21. Chester A. Arthur	9/20/1881–3/3/1885	1829–1886	R	—	—	47, 48
22. Grover Cleveland	3/4/1885–3/3/1889	1837–1908	D	Thomas A. Hendricks	1819–1885	49, 50
23. Benjamin Harrison	3/4/1889–3/3/1893	1833–1901	R	Levi P. Morton	1824–1920	51, 52
24. Grover Cleveland	3/4/1893–3/3/1897	1837–1908	D	Adlai E. Stevenson	1835–1914	53, 54
25. William McKinley	3/4/1897–3/3/1901	1843–1901	R	Garret A. Hobart	1844–1899	55, 56
	3/4/1901–9/14/1901			Theodore Roosevelt	1858–1919	57
26. Theodore Roosevelt	9/14/1901–3/3/1905	1858–1919	R	—	—	57, 58
	3/4/1905–3/3/1909			Charles W. Fairbanks	1852–1918	59, 60
27. William H. Taft	3/4/1909–3/3/1913	1857–1930	R	James S. Sherman	1855–1912	61, 62
28. Woodrow Wilson	3/4/1913–3/3/1921	1856–1924	D	Thomas R. Marshall	1854–1925	63, 64, 65, 66
29. Warren G. Harding	3/4/1921–8/2/1923	1865–1923	R	Calvin Coolidge	1872–1933	67, 68
30. Calvin Coolidge	8/3/1923–3/3/1925	1872–1933	R	—	—	68
	3/4/1925–3/3/1929			Charles G. Dawes	1865–1951	69, 70
31. Herbert C. Hoover	3/4/1929–3/3/1933	1874–1964	R	Charles Curtis	1860–1936	71, 72
32. Franklin D.Roosevelt	3/4/1933–1/20/1941	1882–1945	D	John N. Garner	1868–1967	73, 74, 75, 76
	1/20/1941–1/20/1945			Henry A. Wallace	1888–1965	77, 78
	1/20/1945–4/12/1945			Harry S Truman	1884–1972	79
33. Harry S Truman	4/12/1945–1/20/1949	1884–1972	D	—	—	79, 80
	1/20/1949–1/20/1953			Alben W. Barkley	1877–1956	81, 82
34. Dwight D. Eisenhower	1/20/1953–1/20/1961	1890–1969	R	Richard M. Nixon	1913–1994	83, 84, 85, 86

F = Federalist; D-R = Democratic-Republican; D = Democrat; W = Whig; R = Republican; NU = National Union Party, a coalition of Republicans and War Democrats (Andrew Johnson was a Democrat); I = Independent

President	Term	Year of Birth–Death	Party	Vice President	Year of Birth–Death	Congresses
35. John F. Kennedy	1/20/1961–11/22/1963	1917–1963	D	Lyndon B. Johnson	1908–1973	87, 88
36. Lyndon B. Johnson	11/22/1963–1/20/1965	1908–1973	D	—	—	88
	1/20/1965–1/20/1969			Hubert H. Humphrey	1911–1978	89, 90
37. Richard M. Nixon	1/20/1969–1/20/1973	1913–1994	R	Spiro T. Agnew*	1918–1996	91, 92
	1/20/1973–8/9/1974			Gerald R. Ford	1913–	93
38. Gerald R. Ford	8/9/1974–1/20/1977	1913–	R	Nelson A. Rockefeller	1908–1979	93, 94
39. James (Jimmy) Carter	1/20/1977–1/20/1981	1924–	D	Walter F. Mondale	1928–	95, 96
40. Ronald Reagan	1/20/1981–1/20/1989	1911–	R	George Bush	1924–	97, 98, 99, 100
41. George H. W. Bush	1/20/1989–1/20/1993	1924–	R	J. Danforth Quayle	1947–	101, 102
42. William Clinton	1/20/1993–1/20/2001	1946–	D	Albert A. Gore, Jr.	1948–	103, 104, 105
43. George W. Bush	1/20/2001–	1946–	R	Richard B. Cheney	1941–	106

* Spiro T. Agnew resigned on October 10, 1973. Gerald R. Ford was inaugurated December 6, 1973.

UNITED STATES SUPREME COURT JUSTICES

Justices to the U.S. Supreme Court are nominated by the president, subject to hearings by the senate judiciary committee, and confirmed by a majority vote of the senate. In the following chart, Chief Justices are italicized.

Justice	Term	Justice	Term	Justice	Term
John Jay	1789–1795	Robert C. Grier	1846–1870	Horace H. Lurton	1910–1914
John Rutledge	1789–1791	Benjamin R. Curtis	1851–1857	Charles E. Hughes	1910–1916
William Cushing	1789–1810	John A. Cambell	1853–1861	Willis Van Devanter	1911–1937
James Wilson	1789–1798	Nathan Clifford	1858–1881	Joseph R. Lamar	1911–1916
John Blair	1789–1796	Noah H. Swayne	1862–1881	*Edward D. White*	1910–1921
Robert H. Harrison	1789–1790	Samuel F. Miller	1862–1890	Mahlon Pitney	1912–1922
James Iredell	1790–1799	David Davis	1862–1877	James C. McReynolds	1914–1941
*John Rutledge**	1795	Stephen J. Field	1863–1897	Louis D. Brandeis	1916–1939
Samuel Chase	1796–1811	*Salmon P. Chase*	1864–1873	John H. Clarke	1916–1922
Oliver Ellsworth	1796–1800	William Strong	1870–1880	*William H. Taft*	1921–1930
Bushrod Washington	1798–1829	Joseph P. Bradley	1870–1892	George Sutherland	1922–1938
Alfred Moore	1799–1804	Ward Hunt	1873–1882	Pierce Butler	1922–1939
John Marshall	1801–1835	*Morrison R. Waite*	1874–1888	Edward T. Sanford	1923–1930
William Johnson	1804–1834	John M. Harlan	1877–1911	Harlan F. Stone	1925–1941
H. Brockholst Livingston	1806–1833	William B. Woods	1880–1887	*Charles E. Hughes*	1930–1941
Thomas Todd	1807–1826	Stanley Mathews	1881–1889	Owen J. Roberts	1930–1945
Joseph Story	1811–1845	Horace Gray	1882–1902	Benjamin N Cardozo	1932–1938
Gabriel Duval	1811–1835	Samuel Blatchford	1882–1893	Hugo L. Black	1937–1951
Smith Thompson	1823–1843	Lucius Q. C. Lamar	1888–1893	Stanley F. Reed	1938–1957
Robert Trimble	1826–1828	*Melville Fuller*	1888–1910	Felix Frankfurter	1939–1962
John McClean	1829–1861	David J. Brewer	1890–1910	William O. Douglas	1939–1975
Henry Baldwin	1830–1844	Henry B. Brown	1890–1906	Frank Murphy	1940–1949
James M. Wayne	1835–1867	George Shiras, Jr.	1892–1903	*Harlan F. Stone*	1941–1946
Roger B. Taney	1836–1864	Howell E. Jackson	1893–1895	James F. Byrnes	1941–1942
Philip P. Barbour	1836–1841	Edward D. White	1894–1910	Robert H. Jackson	1941–1954
John Catron	1837–1865	Rufus W. Peckham	1895–1909	Wiley B. Rutledge	1943–1949
John McKinley	1837–1852	Joseph McKenna	1898–1925	Harold H. Burton	1945–1958
Peter V. Daniel	1841–1860	Oliver W. Holmes	1902–1932	*Fred M. Vison*	1946–1953
Samuel Nelson	1845–1872	William D. Day	1903–1922	Tom C. Clark	1949–4967
Levi Woodbury	1845–1851	William H. Moody	1906–1910	Sherman Minton	1949–1956

*Rutledge was appointed Chief Justice and served one term, but he was not confirmed in that position by the Senate.

continues

United States Supreme Court Justices, Continued

Justice	Term	Justice	Term	Justice	Term
Earl Warren	1953–1969	Abe Fortas	1965–1969	Sandra Day O'Connor	1981–
John Marshall Harlan	1955–1971	Thurgood Marshall	1967–1991	Antonin Scalia	1986–
William J. Brennan, Jr.	1956–1990	*Warren C. Burger*	1967–1986	Anthony M. Kennedy	1988–
Charles E. Whitaker	1957–1962	Harry A. Blackmun	1970–1994	David H. Souter	1990–
Potter Stewart	1958–1981	Lewis F. Powell, Jr.	1972–1987	Clarence Thomas	1991–
Byron R. White	1962–1993	*William H. Rehnquist*	1972–	Ruth Bader Ginsberg	1993–
Arthur J. Goldberg	1962–1965	John P. Stevens III	1975–	Stephen Breyer	1994–

WHERE TO WRITE YOUR SENATORS AND REPRESENTATIVES

Constituents can write to their senators and representatives at the following addresses:

Senator's name
United States Senate
Washington, DC 20510

Representative's name
United States House of Representatives
Washington, DC 20515

Listings of specific addresses of members of Congress are in the most current edition of *The Congressional Staff Directory* or *Congressional Quarterly's Washington Directory,* both of which are available in local libraries. These books also list the home offices of members of Congress. Local telephone directories may also be consulted.

Both the Senate and the House have offices in the Capitol Building, and additional offices are housed at the following buildings:

SENATE OFFICES

Dirksen Senate Office Building
Constitution Avenue between 1st and
2nd Streets, NE

Hart Senate Office Building
2nd Street and Constitution Avenue, NE

Russell Senate Office Building
Constitution Avenue between Delaware Avenue and
1st Street, NE

HOUSE OFFICES

Cannon House Office Building
Independence Avenue between C and
1st Streets, SE

Longworth House Office Building
Independence Avenue between C and South
Capitol Streets, SE

Rayburn House Office Building
Independence Avenue between South Capitol and
1st Streets, SE

Four pairs of U.S. presidents have been related: John and John Quincy Adams (father/son), Benjamin and William Henry Harrison (grandfather/grandson), Theodore and Franklin Delano Roosevelt (cousins), and George H. W. Bush and George W. Bush (father/son).

COMMON LEGISLATIVE TERMS

Many terms below are defined in the context of the U.S. Congress. Some of the terms may be applicable as well, with some variation, to state legislatures.

act A bill that has been approved by both the Senate and the House of Representatives and has been signed by the president or passed over his veto, thus becoming law. Acts are sometimes reviewed by the Supreme Court to determine their constitutionality.

"Business Protocols and Forms of Address" in chapter 15

Go to

United States

The Electoral College

A Closer Look

The president and vice president of the United States are elected not by popular vote but by the Electoral College, as stipulated in Article II, Section 1, of the U.S. Constitution. On Election Day, each state selects a number of electors equal to that of its U.S. senators and representatives; these electors are all affiliated with the party that has received the highest popular vote in their districts. Including the District of Columbia's three electoral votes, the total is 538, with a majority of 270 votes needed to win. The votes are counted in a joint session of Congress on January 6. If no candidate for president has won a majority, the House selects one of the three leading candidates, with all members from a state voting in a bloc; if no vice presidential candidate has a majority, the Senate, voting as individuals, choose one from the top two candidates.

In four presidential elections, the winners of the largest number of popular votes failed to win the presidency:

1824 None of the four major Democratic candidates (John Quincy Adams, Andrew Jackson, Henry Clay, William H. Crawford) received a majority of electoral votes, thereby sending the election to the House of Representatives. Despite his overwhelming advantage in the popular vote (43.1%), Andrew Jackson was bypassed by the House in favor of John Quincy Adams, the second highest recipient of popular votes (30.5%). John C. Calhoun was chosen Vice President by the Electoral College.

1876 The Democratic presidential nominee Samuel J. Tilden (NY) initially led in both popular votes (4,284,020–4,036,572) and electoral votes (184–165) over Republican Rutherford B. Hayes (OH). However, this did not include the electoral tallies of Florida, South Carolina, and Louisiana. Their combined 20 electoral votes could swing the election either way. Early indications gave these states to Tilden. Republicans challenged on the grounds of corrupt balloting procedures. Two sets of electors from each of the states emerged, one from each party. A 15-member commission of 8 Republicans and 7 Democrats (5 senators, 5 representatives, 5 Supreme Court justices) negotiated the infamous Compromise of 1877. Democrats agreed to accept the Republican electors from the three states, thereby giving Hayes the presidency 185–184. In return, the Republicans agreed to withdraw all union troops from the South and put an end to Reconstruction. As a result, the federal government would no longer attempt to guarantee the civil, legal, or human rights of African-Americans, and the South would soon witness the rise of a de facto state of apartheid known as Jim Crow.

1888 Democrat Grover Cleveland won the popular vote, 5,540,050–5,444,337, but lost the electoral vote (233–168) and presidency to Republican Benjamin Harrison.

2000 Democrat Al Gore won the popular vote, 50,996,582–50,456,062, but lost the electoral vote (271–266) and presidency to Republican George Bush, Jr.

amendment A change or revision in the wording of a pending bill or other measure by striking out existing language, by inserting new language, or both.

appropriate act A legislative act authorizing the expenditure of federal funds for a specific purpose or purposes.

bill A measure proposing legislation to create a new act or to amend or repeal existing law.

budget A statement of future federal-government expenses and revenues initially formulated by the president and the executive branch. Congress considers the proposed budget in a series of appropriation acts initially introduced in the House of Representatives.

caucus An informal group of legislators that exists to promote issues of common interest (based, for example, on regional, political, ideological, ethnic, or economic concerns) and that possibly shares research staff.

cloture A parliamentary maneuver in the Senate to force the end of a filibuster, thus permitting a measure, amendment, or motion to come to a vote. Cloture, which limits consideration of a pending matter to an additional 30 hours, can be invoked only by an affirmative vote of three-fifths (normally 60 members) of the full Senate.

coalition   A combination of individuals or parties, usually needed to gain a majority vote.

committee of the whole   The legislative forum in which the entire membership of the House of Representatives meets under special rules of procedure (most notably limiting individual debate to five minutes instead of the usual hour) in order to expedite their deliberations on particular categories of legislation.

George Washington is the only Independent president: he never belonged to a political party.

committee   A legislative group in either house of Congress that considers bills, resolutions, and other legislative matters over which the committee has jurisdiction. Committees are fact-finding bodies that hold hearings and listen to witnesses as well as investigate and debate issues, and then prepare a piece of legislation or a bill to present to the whole body for debate. *See also* **conference committee; joint committee; standing committee.**

conference committee   A temporary group of members of both houses of Congress assigned to reconcile differing versions of the same bill passed in the House and Senate. *See also* **joint committee.**

Congressional Record   A substantially verbatim account of the daily proceedings of Congress, kept since 1873.

deficit   The amount by which expenditures (outlays) exceed revenues (receipts) in a given fiscal period. Deficit spending occurs when the government borrows money to cover the difference between income and spending. *See also* **surplus.**

filibuster   A procedural strategy by which a senator controls the floor and debates a bill at length in order to block or delay Senate action on it. *See also* **cloture.**

impeachment   The formal presentation of charges against a public official accused of misconduct in order to bring about his or her trial and removal from office, if convicted. The House of Representatives can vote for impeachment of federal officials; the Senate is responsible for trying them.

initiative   The procedure by which voters petition a state legislature for a new law. Typically, the legislature rejects the initiative and puts it out to a referendum by the voters. *See also* **referendum.**

joint committee   A committee that includes members of both the Senate and the House and that can publish studies and background reports within its specified jurisdictions, but normally lacks authority to report legislation.

line-item veto   The power of a chief executive to veto particular parts of a bill rather than reject the bill as a whole.

lobbyist   A person representing a special interest who seeks to influence lawmakers or a regulatory agency by pressing the views of a group, organization, or industry on issues under consideration.

majority leader   The leader of the party holding the majority of members in the House or Senate. The majority leader plans strategy, guides debate, maintains party discipline, and speaks for the party either in support of or in criticism of the president. The Senate majority leader also leads the Senate as a whole and must negotiate the agenda with the minority party.

majority party   The party holding the majority of the seats in a legislative body.

mandate   A vote of confidence from the people, often used loosely to indicate broad support for a party's policy initiative.

minority leader   The leader of the party holding a minority of seats in a legislative body, who serves as the party's principal spokesperson and strategist.

minority party   The party holding a minority of seats in a legislative body.

override   Congress's negation of a president's vote by voting for a bill with a two-thirds majority.

pocket veto   The indirect veto of a bill by the president. A pocket veto occurs when the president has not signed a bill within ten days of its presentation to him and Congress has adjourned within those ten days.

political action committee (PAC) A group formed outside of political parties in order to raise money for donation to lawmakers who support the group's policies and aims.

president pro tempore The constitutionally recognized officer of the Senate who presides over the chamber when the vice president of the United States, who also functions as president of the Senate, is absent. Normally, however, the president pro tempore appoints a succession of other senators to serve as the presiding officer.

quorum A predetermined minimum number of members of a legislative assembly who must be present in order for the assembly to conduct business.

reapportionment A change or adjustment in the size or boundaries of legislative districts based on population increases or decreases.

recall A special popular vote held in order to consider removing an elected official before he or she has completed his or her term of office.

referendum A legislative issue on which voters can vote directly, usually at the time of an election. *See also* **initiative.**

representative Any elected official who represents voters in a legislative body; the term most often refers to a member of the House of Representatives, the lower house of Congress. States elect differing numbers of representatives to Congress, depending on their population as determined by the federal census. Representatives serve two-year terms.

rider An attempt to secure passage of a controversial proposal by attaching it as an amendment to a nonrelated bill whose passage is otherwise considered essential.

senator A member of the Senate, the upper house of Congress. Each state elects two senators, who serve overlapping terms of six years.

Speaker of the House The presiding officer in the House, elected by the consensus of the majority party.

standing committee A permanent committee in either the House or the Senate that is assigned jurisdiction over particular issues.

surplus The amount by which revenues (receipts) exceed expenditures (outlays) in a given fiscal period. *See also* **deficit.**

veto The power given to the president under the Constitution to refuse to sign a bill and so prevent it from becoming law. The president may return it to the Congress with notes on his objections. *See also* **line-item veto; override; pocket veto.**

whip An elected representative who serves as an assistant to the majority or minority leader and who is responsible for gathering members of his or her party and making sure they are present when a crucial partisan vote occurs.

HOW A BILL BECOMES LAW

FIRST READING

To become law, a bill is introduced by a senator or representative in the Senate or House and is assigned a number or title by the clerk of the House. The bill is then assigned to the committee of the Senate or House that is responsible for the particular area the bill relates to (for example, a bill providing aid to farmers would go to the Committee on Agriculture). The committee debates the bill, listens to the opinions of interested people and members of Congress, and sometimes offers amendments to the bill. The bill is then voted on by the committee and, if passed, is sent back to the clerk of the House. If the bill is unacceptable to the committee when they receive it, they may table it, killing consideration of the bill. This process is called the first reading of the bill.

SECOND AND THIRD READINGS

In the second reading, the clerk of the House reads the bill to the House, which then debates it and suggests amendments. At the third reading, after the bill is debated, a vote is called for and the title of the bill is read before the vote.

PASSAGE

If the bill passes, it is sent to the other house, where it is again debated, amendments are added, and a vote is taken. If it passes with amendments, a joint congressional committee (composed of members of both the House and the Senate) tries to reach a compromise between the two versions of the bill. If not passed by the second house, the bill dies.

Only four women have appeared on U.S. currency: Martha Washington, Pocahontas, Susan B. Anthony, and Sacagawea.

PRESIDENTIAL ACTION

When the bill is passed, it is sent to the president. If he signs it, it becomes law. If he holds the bill for ten days (not including Sundays), it automatically becomes law without his signature, unless Congress has adjourned during that time, in which case the bill is automatically killed in a process known as a *pocket veto*. If the president disapproves of the bill, he vetoes it, sending it back to the house that originally produced it, along with his objections.

Once back in the house, the bill is debated again in light of the president's comments and a roll-call vote is taken. To remain an active bill, it must receive at least a two-thirds vote from that house. If it does not, it is defeated. If the bill does get the support of two-thirds of that house, it is sent to the other house, where it again must receive a vote of two-thirds to override a presidential veto.

FEDERAL SPENDING AS A PERCENTAGE OF THE BUDGET

As the U.S. government has grown in size over the years, so has its spending and its accumulation of debt. The following chart outlines that growth and the directions it has taken since 1790.

Year	Defense	Veterans Benefits	Social Security	Health/ Medicare	Education	Interest on Debt	Federal Debt in Millions
1790	14.9	4.1	N/A	N/A	N/A	55.0	75.463
1800	55.7	0.6	N/A	N/A	N/A	31.3	82.976
1810	48.4 (1814 = 79.9)	1.0	N/A	N/A	N/A	34.9	53.173
1820	38.4	17.6	N/A	N/A	N/A	28.1	91.016
1830	52.9	9.0	N/A	N/A	N/A	12.6	48.565
1840	54.3 (1847 = 80.7)	10.7	N/A	N/A	N/A	0.7	3.573
1850	43.8	4.7	N/A	N/A	N/A	1.0	63.543
1860	44.2 (1865 = 88.9)	1.7	N/A	N/A	N/A	5.0	64.844
1870	25.7	9.2	N/A	N/A	N/A	41.7	2,436.453
1880	19.3	21.2	N/A	N/A	N/A	35.8	2,090.909
1890	20.9 (1899 = 48.6)	33.6	N/A	N/A	N/A	11.4	1,222.397
1900	36.6	27.0	N/A	N/A	N/A	7.7	1,263.417
1910	45.1 (1919 = 59.5)	23.2	N/A	N/A	N/A	3.1	1,146.940
1920	37.1	3.4	N/A	N/A	N/A	16.0	24,299.321
1930	25.3	6.6	N/A	N/A	N/A	19.9	16,185.310
1940	17.5 (1945 = 89.4)	6.0	0.3	0.5	20.8	9.4	42,967.531
1950	32.2	20.3	1.8	0.6	0.6	11.3	256,853.0
1960	52.2	5.9	12.6	0.9	1.0	7.5	290,525.0
1970	41.8	4.4	15.5	6.2	4.4	7.3	308,927.0
1980	22.7	3.6	20.1	9.4	5.4	8.9	909,050.0
1990	23.9	2.3	19.8	12.4	3.1	14.7	3,266,073.0
2000	16.2	2.5	22.9	19.6	3.3	14.7	5,686,000.0

United States

STATES, DISTRICT OF COLUMBIA, AND TERRITORIES

America comprises 50 states, the District of Columbia, and 9 territories. State and territorial governments are independent of each other but subordinate to the federal government. The following chart provides basic information concerning all of them.

State	Entry Date (Rank)	Capital	Flower	Bird	Motto	Nickname
Alabama	12/14/1819 (22)	Montgomery	Camellia	Yellow Hammer	We dare defend our rights	Heart of Dixie; Camelia State
Alaska	1/3/1959 (49)	Juneau	Forget-me-not	Willow Ptarmigan	North to the future	The Last Frontier
Arizona	2/14/1912 (48)	Phoenix	Saguaro	Cactus Wren	*Diat Deus* (God enriches)	Grand Canyon State
Arkansas	6/16/1836 (25)	Little Rock	Apple Blossom	Mockingbird	*Regnat populus* (The people rule)	Land of Opportunity
California	9/9/1850 (31)	Sacramento	Golden Poppy	California Valley Quail	*Eureka!* (I found it)	Golden State
Colorado	8/1/1876 (38)	Denver	Blue Columbine	Lark Bunting	*Nil sine numine* (Nothing without providence)	Centennial State
Connecticut	1/9/1788 (5)	Hartford	Mountain Laurel	American Robin	*Qui transtulet sustinet* (He who transplanted still sustains)	Constitution State; Nutmeg State
Delaware	12/7/1787 (1)	Dover	Peach Blossom	Blue Hen Chicken	Liberty and independence	First State; Diamond State
District of Columbia	U.S Capital 12/1/1800	Washington	American Beauty Rose	Wood Thrush	*Justia Omnibus* (Justice for all)	Capital City
Florida	3/3/1845 (27)	Tallahassee	Orange Blossom	Mockingbird	In God we trust	Sunshine State
Georgia	1/2/1788 (4)	Atlanta	Cherokee Rose	Brown Thrasher	Wisdom, justice, and moderation	Empire State of the South; Peach Tree State
Hawaii	8/21/1959 (50)	Honolulu	Hibiscus	Nene Goose	The life of the land is perpetuated in righteousness	Aloha State
Idaho	7/3/1890 (43)	Boise	Syringa	Mountain Bluebird	*Esto perpetua* (It is eternal)	Gem State
Illinois	12/3/1818 (21)	Springfield	Native Violet	Cardinal	State sovereignty— national union	Prairie State; Land of Lincoln
Indiana	12/11/1816 (19)	Indianapolis	Peony	Cardinal	Crossroads of America	Hossier State
Iowa	12/28/1846 (29)	Des Moines	Wild Rose	Goldfinch	Our liberties we prize and our rights we will maintain	Hawkeye State
Kansas	1/29/1861 (34)	Topeka	Sun Flower	Western Meadowlark	*Ad astr per aspera* (To the stars through difficulties)	Sunflower State
Kentucky	6/1/1792 (15)	Frankfort	Goldenrod	Kentucky Cardinal	United we stand, divided we fall	Bluegrass State
Louisiana	4/30/1812 (18)	Baton Rouge	Magnolia	Eastern Brown Pelican	Union, justice, and confidence	Pelican State

States, District of Columbia, and Territories, Continued

State	Entry Date (Rank)	Capital	Flower	Bird	Motto	Nickname
Maine	3/15/1820 (23)	Augusta	Pine Cone and Tassel	Chickadee	*Dirgo* (I Direct)	Pine Tree State
Maryland	4/28/1788 (7)	Annapolis	Black-eyed Susan	Baltimore Oriole	*Fati maschii, parole femine* (Manly deeds, womanly words)	Old Line State; Free State
Massachusetts	2/6/1788 (6)	Boston	Mayflower	Chickadee	*Ense petit placidam sub liberate quietem* (By the sword we seek peace but peace only under liberty)	Bay State; Colony State
Michigan	1/26/1837 (26)	Lansing	Apple Blossom	Robin	*Si quaeris peninulam amoenam circumspice* (If you seek a pleasant peninsula, look about you)	Great Lakes State; Wolverine State
Minnesota	5/11/1858 (32)	St. Paul	Showy Lady Slipper	Common Loon	*L'etoile du nord* (Star of the north)	North Star State
Mississippi	12/10/1817 (20)	Jackson	Magnolia	Mockingbird	*Virtute et armis* (By valor and arms)	Magnolia State
Missouri	8/10/1821 (24)	Jefferson City	Hawthorn	Bluebird	*Salus populi suprema lex esto* (The welfare of the people shall be the supreme law)	Show-Me State
Montana	11/8/1889 (41)	Helena	Bitterroot	Western Meadowlark	*Oro y plata* (Gold and silver)	Treasure State
Nebraska	3/1/1867 (37)	Lincoln	Goldenrod	Meadowlark	Equality before the law	Cornhusker State
Nevada	10/3/1864 (36)	Carson City	Sagebrush	Mountain Bluebird	All for our country	Sagebrush State; Battle Born State
New Hampshire	6/21/1788 (9)	Concord	Purple Lilac	Purple Finch	Live free or die	Granite State
New Jersey	12/18/1787 (3)	Trenton	Purple Violet	Eastern Goldfinch	Liberty and prosperity	Garden State
New Mexico	1/6/1912 (47)	Santa Fe	Yucca	Roadrunner	*Crescit eundo* (It grows as it goes)	Land of Enhancement
New York	7/26/1788 (11)	Albany	Rose (any color)	Bluebird	*Excelsior* (Ever upward)	Empire State
North Carolina	11/21/1789 (12)	Raleigh	Dogwood	Cardinal	*Esse quam videri* (To be rather than to seem)	Tar Heel State; Old North State
North Dakota	11/2/1889 (39)	Bismark	Wild Prairie Rose	Western Meadowlark	Liberty and union, now and forever one and inseparable	Peace Garden State
Ohio	3/1/1803 (17)	Columbus	Scarlet Carnation	Cardinal	With God, all things are possible	Buckeye State
Oklahoma	11/16/1907 (46)	Oklahoma City	Mistletoe	Scissor-tailed Flycatcher	*Labor omnia vincit* (Labor conquers all things)	Sooner State

State	Entry Date (Rank)	Capital	Flower	Bird	Motto	Nickname
Oregon	2/14/1859 (33)	Salem	Oregon Grape	Western Meadowlark	The union	Beaver State
Pennsylvania	12/12/1787 (2)	Harrisburg	Mountain Laurel	Ruffed Grouse	Virtue, liberty, and independence	Keystone State
Rhode Island	5/29/1790 (13)	Providence	Violet	Rhode Island Hen	Hope	Little Rhody; Ocean State
South Carolina	5/23/1788 (8)	Columbia	Carolina Jessamine	Carolina Wren	*Dum spiro spero* (While I breath, I hope)	Palmetto State
South Dakota	11/2/1889 (40)	Pierre	Pasque Flower	Pheasant	Under God, the people rule	Coyote State; Sunshine State
Tennessee	6/1/1796 (16)	Nashville	Iris	Mockingbird	Agriculture and commerce	Volunteer State
Texas	12/29/1845 (28)	Austin	Blue Bonnet	Mockingbird	Friendship	Lone Star State
Utah	1/4/1896 (45)	Salt Lake City	Sego Lily	Seagull	Industry	Beehive State
Vermont	3/4/1791 (14)	Montpelier	Red Clover	Thrush	Freedom and unity	Green Mountain State
Virginia	6/25/1788 (10)	Richmond	Flowering Dogwood	Cardinal	*Sic semper tyrannis* (Thus always to tyrants)	Old Dominion
Washington	11/11/1889 (42)	Olympia	Rhododendron	Willow Goldfinch	*Alki* (By and by)	Evergreen State
West Virginia	6/20/1863 (35)	Charleston	Big Rhododendron	Cardinal	*Montani semper liberi* (Mountaineers are always free)	Mountain State
Wisconsin	5/29/1848 (30)	Madison	Wood Violet	Robin	Forward	Badger State
Wyoming	7/0/1890 (44)	Cheyenne	Indian Paintbrush	Meadowlark	Equal Rights	Equality State

Territories	Year Acquired	Capital	Flower	Bird	Motto
American Samoa	1899	Pago Pago	Paog (Ua-Fla)	—	*Samoa Muamua le Atua* (In Samoa God is first)
Federated States of Micronesia	1947	Pohnpei	—	—	—
Guam	1950	Agana	Puti Tai Nobio (Bougainvillea)	Toto (Fruit Dove)	Where America's day begins
Marshall Islands	1947	Majuro	—	—	Joannes est monem eius (John is his name)
Midway Islands	1867	N/A	—	—	—
Northern Mariana Islands	1947	Saipan	—	—	—
Palu	1947	Koror	—	—	—
Puerto Rico	1898	San Juan	Mega	Reinita	—
Virgin Islands	1927	Charlotte Amalie	Yellow Elder	Yellow Breast	—

STATE NAME ORIGINS

The etymologies of some state names are more well established than others.

Alabama   From the Muskogee Indian language, perhaps meaning "town."

Alaska   A Russian corruption of the Aleutian word *alashak,* meaning "mainland."

Arizona   Origin unknown; perhaps a Spanish corruption of either the Pima word *arizonac,* meaning "small spring," or the Aztec word *arizuma,* meaning "silver-bearing."

Arkansas   A French corruption of *Quapaw,* the name of the people indigenous to the region.

Nebraska is the only state in the nation with a unicameral (one-house) state legislature.

California   The name of a fictitious earthly paradise in the 16th-century Spanish romance *Las Serged de Explandian* by Montalvo.

Colorado   Spanish for "red."

Connecticut   English corruption of *Quinnehtukqut,* the name of the people indigenous to the region.

Delaware   Corruption of the nickname of a former English governor of Virginia, Lord de La Warr.

Washington, District of Columbia   named for George Washington and Christopher Columbus.

Florida   Spanish for "flowery Easter."

Georgia   Named for King George II of England.

Hawaii   English corruption of *owhyhee* or *awaiki,* indigenous words meaning "homeland."

Idaho   Origin unknown; possibly an English corruption of *idahi,* the Na-i-shan Dine (a.k.a Plains Apache, Lipan Apache, or Kiowa-Apache) name for the Comanche people. Possibly a fabricated word.

Illinois   From *Illini,* the French corruption of the Piwarea (a.k.a Peoria) word for "men."

Indiana   English place name reflective of the word "Indian."

Iowa   English corruption of the name of the Paxoje (a.k.a Ioway) people who are indigenous to the region.

Kansas   English corruption of the name of the Kaw (a.k.a Kansa) people who are indigenous to the region.

Kentucky   Origin unknown; perhaps from the Haudenosaunee (a.k.a Iroquois) word *ken-ta-ten,* meaning "meadow."

Louisiana   Named for King Louis XIV of France.

Maine   Origin unknown; perhaps archaic French term meaning "province," or named for the French province of Mayne.

Maryland   Named for Queen Henrietta Maria of England, wife of King Charles I.

Massachusetts   The name of the people indigenous to the region.

Michigan   French corruption of the Anishinabe (a.k.a Ojibwa or Chippewa) word *micigama,* meaning "great water."

Minnesota   English corruption of the Dakota (a.k.a Sioux) words *mni sosha,* meaning "muddy water."

Montana   The Latin word for "mountainous."

Nebraska   English corruption of the UmoN'hoN (a.k.a Omaha) word for "flat water."

Lake Superior is the second-largest freshwater lake in the world.

Nevada   Spanish for "snow-clad."

New Hampshire   Named for the English county of Hampshire.

New Jersey   Named for the Isle of Jersey off the coast of England.

New Mexico   Named for the Spanish territory of northern Mexico, originally a Spanish corruption of *Mexika*, a Nauhuatl-speaking nation indigenous to the region.

New York   Originally New Netherlands, named for England's Duke of York after English conquest.

North Carolina   Named for King Charles I of England, from the Latin *Carolus* meaning "Charles."

North Dakota   The name of the people indigenous to the region (a.k.a Lakota, Nakota, and Sioux).

Ohio   Origin unknown; perhaps an English corruption of a Haudenosuanee (a.k.a Iroquois) word meaning "great water."

Oklahoma   A word coined in the 19th century to mean "Indian" by Choctaw-speaking Reverend Allen Wright.

Oregon   Origin unknown; perhaps an English corruption of an unknown indigenous word.

Pennsylvania   Named for the colony's founder, Sir William Penn, and the English word "sylvan," an adjective referring to forests.

Rhode Island   Origin unknown; perhaps an English corruption of an earlier Dutch name, *Roode Elandt*, meaning "red island," or named by the English for the Greek island of Rhodes.

South Carolina   see North Carolina.

South Dakota   see North Dakota.

Tennessee   Originally the state of Franklin, in honor of Benjamin Franklin. Renamed in 1788, an English corruption of *Tanasi,* the name of a Cherokee town.

Texas   English corruption of the Spanish name *Tejas,* itself a corruption of the name of peoples indigenous to the region who spoke a language in the Caddoan family.

"North America" and "United States" in the atlas
Go to

Utah   English corruption of *Ute,* the collective name of several peoples indigenous to the region who speak dialects of the Numic language, which is part of the Uto-Aztecan family.

Vermont   English corruption of the French *vert,* meaning "green," and *mont,* meaning "mountains."

Virginia   Named for Queen Elizabeth I of England, also known as the Virgin Queen.

Washington   Named for George Washington.

West Virginia   See Virginia.

Wisconsin   English corruption of *ouisconsin,* an Anishinabe (a.k.a Ojibwa or Chippewa) word meaning "grassy place."

The Mississippi River is the world's third longest (behind the Amazon and the Nile). However, the Missouri River from its mouth to the Gulf of Mexico is the world's longest unbroken riverine waterway.

Wyoming   From the Wyoming Valley in Pennsylvania. Origin unknown, perhaps an English corruption of a word from one of the languages in the Algonquin family, spoken by the peoples indigenous to Pennsylvania.

TERRITORIAL ACQUISITION

The United States' territorial expansion across the American continent involved two processes: gaining recognition of exclusive rights to land from the its imperial rivals (mostly European), and then seizing actual control of the land in question from its indigenous inhabitants, the various Native nations who lived there. Both processes involved negotiations and occasionally open wars of aggression instigated by the U.S. The following chart reflects the various phases by which the U.S. gained the rights to its present territory exclusive from other imperial rivals.

United States

Territory	Date Acquired	Sq. Miles	How Acquired
Original 13 States	1783	888,685	Treaty of Paris with Great Britain
Louisiana Purchase	1803	827,192	Purchase from France
Florida	1819	72,003	Adams-Onis Treaty with Spain
Texas	1845	390,143	Annexation of Independent Texas
Oregon Territory	1846	285,580	Oregon Boundary Treaty with Great Britain
Mexican Cession	1848	529,017	Conquest of Mexico/Treaty of Guadalupe-Hidalgo
Gadsden Purchase	1853	29,640	Purchase from Mexico
Midway Islands	1867	2	Annexed Uninhabited Islands
Alaska	1867	589,757	Purchase from Russia
Wake Island	1898	3	Annexed Uninhabited Island
Hawaii	1898	6,450	Conquest of Independent nation
The Philippines	1899	115,600	Conquest of Spain/Treaty of Paris (independent 1946)
Puerto Rico	1899	3,435	Conquest of Spain/Treaty of Paris
Guam	1899	212	Conquest of Spain/Treaty of Paris
American Samoa	1900	76	Treaty with Germany, Great Britain
Panama Canal Zone	1904	553	Hay-Nunau-Varilla Treaty with Panama (Returned 1978)
Corn Islands	1914	4	Treaty with Nicaragua (Returned 1978)
Virgin Islands	1917	133	Purchase from Denmark
Trust Territory of Pacific Islands	1947	717	United Nations Trusteeship. Now independent: Federated States of Micronesia (1990), Marshall Islands (1991), and Palau (1994)

THE AMERICAN PEOPLE

The population of the United States has grown and its demographic composition has changed much since the republic's inception. The following chart traces that growth and dynamic change since 1790.

Year	No. of States	Population	Percent Increase	Percent Urban/Rural	Percent White/Non–White	Persons per Household	Birth Rate per 1,000 people	Death Rate per 1,000 people
1790	13	3,929,214	—	5.1/94.9	80.7/19.3	5.79	N/A	N/A
1800	16	5,308,483	35.1	6.1/93.9	81.1/18.9	N/A	55.0	N/A
1810	17	7,239,881	36.4	7.3/92.7	81.0/19.0	N/A	54.3	N/A
1820	23	9,638,543	33.1	7.2/92.8	81.6/18.4	N/A	55.2	N/A
1830	24	12,866,020	33.5	8.8/91.2	81.9/18.1	N/A	51.4	N/A
1840	26	17,069,543	32.7	10.8/89.2	83.2/16.8	N/A	51.8	N/A
1850	31	23,191,876	35.9	15.3/84.7	84.3/15.7	5.5	43.3	N/A
1860	33	31,443,321	35.6	19.8/80.2	85.6/14.4	5.28	44.3	N/A
1870	37	39,818,449	26.6	25.7/74.3	86.2/13.8	5.09	38.3	N/A
1880	38	50,155,783	26.0	28.2/71.8	86.5/13.5	5.04	39.8	N/A
1890	44	62,947,714	25.5	35.1/64.9	87.5/12.5	4.93	31.5	N/A
1900	45	75,994,575	20.7	39.6/60.4	87.9/12.1	4.76	32.3	17.2
1910	46	91,972,266	21.0	45.6/54.4	88.9/11.1	4.54	30.1	14.7
1920	48	105,710,620	14.9	51.2/48.8	89.7/10.3	4.34	27.7	13.0
1930	48	122,755,046	16.1	56.1/43.9	89.8/10.2	4.11	21.3	11.3
1940	48	131,669,275	7.2	56.5/43.5	89.8/10.2	3.76	19.4	10.8
1950	48	150,697,361	14.5	64.0/36.0	89.5/10.5	3.37	24.1	9.6
1960	50	179,323,175	18.5	69.9/31.1	88.6/11.4	3.33	23.7	9.5
1970	50	203,302,031	13.4	73.6/26.4	87.6/12.4	3.14	18.4	9.5
1980	50	226,542,199	11.4	73.7/26.3	85.9/14.1	2.75	15.9	8.8
1990	50	248,718,301	9.8	75.2/24.8	83.9/16.1	2.63	16.6	8.6
2000	50	281,421,906	13.2	80.2/19.8	75.1/24.9	2.59	14.4	8.5

U.S. POPULATION BY STATE: 2000

State	Population	% change since 1990	Persons per sq. mile	State	Population	% change since 1990	Persons per sq. mile
Alabama	4,447,100	10.1	87.6	Montana	902,195	12.9	6.2
Alaska	626,932	14.0	1.1	Nebraska	1,711,263	8.4	22.3
Arkansas	2,673,400	13.7	51.3	Nevada	1,998,257	66.3	18.2
California	33,871,648	13.6	217.1	New Hampshire	1,235,786	11.4	137.8
Colorado	4,301,261	30.6	41.5	New Jersey	8,414,350	8.6	1,134.5
Connecticut	3,405,565	03.6	702.9	New Mexico	1,819,046	20.1	15.0
Delaware	783,600	17.6	401.0	New York	18,976,457	5.5	401.9
District of Columbia	572,059	−5.7	9,378.0	North Carolina	8,049,313	21.4	165.2
Florida	15,982,378	23.5	296.4	North Dakota	642,200	0.5	9.3
Georgia	8,186,453	26.4	141.4	Ohio	11,353,140	4.7	277.3
Hawaii	1,211,537	9.9	188.6	Oklahoma	3,450,654	9.7	50.3
Idaho	1,293,953	28.5	15.6	Oregon	3,421,399	20.4	35.6
Illinois	12,419,293	8.6	223.4	Pennsylvania	12,281,054	3.4	274.0
Indiana	6,080,485	9.7	169.5	Rhode Island	1,048,319	4.5	1,003.2
Iowa	2,926,324	5.4	52.4	South Carolina	4,012,012	15.1	133.2
Kansas	2,688,418	8.5	32.9	South Dakota	754,844	8.5	9.9
Kentucky	4,041,769	9.6	101.7	Tennessee	5,689,283	16.7	138.0
Louisiana	4,468,976	5.9	102.6	Texas	20,851,820	22.8	79.6
Maine	1,274,923	3.8	41.3	Utah	2,233,169	29.6	27.2
Maryland	5,296,486	10.8	541.9	Vermont	608,827	8.2	65.8
Massachusetts	6,349,097	5.5	809.8	Virginia	7,078,515	14.4	178.8
Michigan	9,938,444	6.9	175.0	Washington	5,894,121	21.1	88.6
Minnesota	4,919,479	12.4	61.8	West Virginia	1,808,344	0.8	75.1
Mississippi	2,844,658	10.5	60.6	Wisconsin	5,363,675	9.6	98.8
Missouri	5,595,211	9.3	81.2	Wyoming	493,782	8.9	5.1
				United States	**281,421,906**	**13.1**	**79.6**

IMMIGRATION TO THE UNITED STATES

Immigration has played an integral role in the expansion of the United States since its inception. During the antebellum era, there were no restrictions on immigration. By the end of the 19th century, restrictive legislation such as the Chinese Exclusion Act (1882) affected various sources of immigration. Today, individual nations are assigned quotas for the number of legal emigrants they may send to the U.S. (Note: not all nations have the same quotas.) Immigrants who can prove political persecution should they be returned to their home country are not counted in their country's quotas. The sole exception is Cuba, whose refugees do not have to prove political persecution. The following chart shows the broad geographic sources of U.S. immigrants in millions.

Decade	Europe	Americas	Asia
1820s	0.106	0.012	N/A
1830s	0.496	0.033	N/A
1840s	1.597	0.062	N/A
1850s	2.453	0.075	0.042
1860s	2.065	0.167	0.065
1870s	2.272	0.404	0.070
1880s	4.735	0.427	0.070
1890s	3.555	0.039	0.075
1900s	8.065	0.362	0.324
1910s	4.332	1.144	0.247
1920s	2.463	1.517	0.112
1930s	0.348	0.160	0.016
1940s	0.621	0.355	0.032
1950s	1.326	0.997	0.150
1960s	1.123	1.716	0.590
1970s	0.800	1.983	1.588
1980s	0.762	3.616	2.738
1990s	1.291	4.530	5.547

AMERICAN WORKERS

As the historical processes of urbanization, immigration, and the Industrial Revolution steadily expanded during the 19th century, the face of the American workforce began to change. The following numbers chart many of those changes.

Year	No. of workers in millions	Male percent of workers	Female percent of workers	Percent of married females working	Percent unemployed	Farmers as a percent of workers	Percent of workers in unions
1810	2.330	N/A	N/A	N/A	N/A	84	N/A
1840	5.660	N/A	N/A	N/A	N/A	75	N/A
1860	11.110	N/A	N/A	N/A	N/A	53	N/A
1870	12.506	85	15	N/A	N/A	53	N/A
1880	17.392	85	15	N/A	N/A	52	N/A
1890	23.318	83	17	19	4 (1894 = 18)	43	N/A
1900	19.073	82	18	21	5	40	3
1910	38.167	79	21	25	6	31	6
1920	41.614	79	21	24	5 (1921 = 12)	26	12
1930	48.830	78	22	25	9 (1933 = 25)	22	7
1940	53.011	76	24	27	15 (1944 = 1)	17	27
1950	62.208	72	28	31	5.3	12	25
1960	69.628	67	33	38	5.5	8	26
1970	82.771	62	38	43	4.9	4	25
1980	106.940	58	42	52	7.1	3	23
1990	125.840	55	45	58	5.6	3	16
2000	137.673	54	46	60	4.5	3	15

U.S. POSTAL SERVICE

ZIP CODES

Five-digit ZIP (Zone Improvement Plan) codes were introduced in 1964 to identify each postal delivery area in the United States. In some areas, two cities may share a ZIP code; in others, such as New York City, one geographic area may have many ZIP codes, including separate ZIP codes for each major office building. In this book, the Zip codes are representative rather than specific for the larger cities. In New York City, for example, the indicated ZIP code is 10199, which is the ZIP code for the Manhattan borough postmaster. In 1983, the USPS introduced the ZIP +4 code, an expanded version of ZIP codes. Use of the four-digit add-on is voluntary, and it is primarily intended for the use of businesses and bulk mailers. For the ZIP code for a specific address in any area served by the U.S. Postal Service, the reader should consult a copy of the *U.S. Postal Service National Five-Digit ZIP Code & Post Office Directory,* available at any local post office and revised yearly, or use the U.S. Postal Service online ZIP code service at http://www.usps.gov/ncsc.

Aberdeen, SD	57401	Allentown, PA	18101	Anniston, AL	36201
Abilene, TX	79604	Alton, IL	62002	Antioch, CA	94509
Addison, IL	60101	Altoona, PA	16601	Appleton, WI	54911
Akron, OH	44309	Amarillo, TX	79120	Arcadia, CA	91006
Alameda, CA	94501	Ames, IA	50010	Arlington, TX	76010
Albany, GA	31706	Anaheim, CA	92803	Arlington Heights, IL	60004
Albuquerque, NM	87101	Anchorage, AK	99501	Artesia, CA	90701
Alexandria, LA	71301	Anderson, IN	46011	Arvada, CO	80004
Alexandria, VA	22313	Anderson, SC	29621	Asheville, NC	28810
Alhambra, CA	91802	Annapolis, MD	21401	Ashland, KY	41101
Allen Park, MI	48101	Ann Arbor, MI	48106	Aspen, CO	81611

Crystal, MN	55428	Elmira, NY	14901	Galesburg, IL	61401
Culver City, CA	90230	El Monte, CA	91731	Galveston, TX	77550
Cumberland, MD	21502	El Paso, TX	79910	Gardena, CA	90247
Cupertino, CA	95014	Elyria, OH	44035	Garden City, MI	48135
Cuyahoga Falls, OH	44222	Emporia, KS	66801	Garden Grove, CA	92642
Cypress, CA	90630	Englewood, CO	80110	Garfield, NJ	07026
Dallas, TX	75260	Enid, OK	73701	Garfield Heights, OH	44125
Daly City, CA	94015	Erie, PA	16515	Garland, TX	75040
Danbury, CT	06810	Escondido, CA	92025	Gary, IN	46401
Danville, IL	61832	Euclid, OH	44112	Gastonia, NC	28052
Danville, VA	24541	Eugene, OR	97401	Glendale, AZ	85301
Davenport, IA	52802	Evanston, IL	60201	Glendale, CA	91209
Davis, CA	95616	Evansville, IN	47708	Glendora, CA	91740
Dayton, OH	45401	Everett, MA	02149	Glenview, IL	60025
Daytona Beach, FL	32114	Everett, WA	98203	Gloucester, MA	01930
Dearborn, MI	48120	Fairborn, OH	45324	Goldsboro, NC	27530
Dearborn Heights, MI	48127	Fairfield, CA	94533	Grand Forks, ND	58201
Decatur, AL	35602	Fairfield, OH	45014	Grand Island, NE	68802
Decatur, IL	62521	Fair Lawn, NJ	07410	Grand Junction, CO	81501
Deerfield Beach, FL	33441	Fall River, MA	02720	Grand Prairie, TX	75051
De Kalb, IL	60115	Fargo, ND	58102	Grand Rapids, MI	49501
Delray Beach, FL	33444	Farmington, NM	87401	Granite City, IL	62040
Del Rio, TX	78840	Fayetteville, AR	72701	Great Falls, MT	59401
Denton, TX	76201	Fayetteville, NC	28302	Greeley, CO	80631
Denver, CO	80201	Ferndale, MI	48220	Green Bay, WI	54303
Des Moines, IA	50318	Findlay, OH	45839	Greenfield, WI	53220
Des Plaines, IL	60018	Fitchburg, MA	01420	Greensboro, NC	27420
Detroit, MI	48233	Flagstaff, AZ	86001	Greenville, MS	38701
Dothan, AL	36303	Flint, MI	48502	Greenville, NC	27834
Downers Grove, IL	60515	Florence, AL	35631	Greenville, SC	29602
Downey, CA	90241	Florence, SC	29501	Gresham, OR	97030
Dubuque, IA	52001	Florissant, MO	63033	Grosse Pointe, MI	48230
Duluth, MN	55806	Fond du Lac, WI	54935	Gulfport, MS	39503
Duncanville, TX	75138	Fontana, CA	92335	Hackensack, NJ	07602
Dunedin, FL	32132	Fort Collins, CO	80521	Hagerstown, MD	21740
Durham, NC	27701	Fort Dodge, IA	50501	Hallandale, FL	33009
East Chicago, IN	46312	Fort Lauderdale, FL	33110	Haltom City, TX	76117
East Cleveland, OH	44112	Fort Lee, NJ	07024	Hamilton, OH	45011
East Detroit, MI	48021	Fort Myers, FL	33906	Hammond, IN	46320
East Lansing, MI	48823	Fort Pierce, FL	34981	Hampton, VA	23670
Easton, PA	18042	Fort Smith, AR	72901	Hanover Park, IL	60103
East Orange, NJ	07019	Fort Wayne, IN	46802	Harlingen, TX	78550
East Providence, RI	02914	Fort Worth, TX	76161	Harrisburg, PA	17107
East St. Louis, IL	62201	Frankfort, KY	40601	Hartford, CT	06101
Eau Claire, WI	54703	Frederick, MD	21701	Harvey, IL	60426
Edina, MN	55424	Fredericksburg, VA	22404	Hattiesburg, MS	39402
Edmond, OK	73034	Freeport, IL	61032	Haverhill, MA	01831
Edmonds, WA	98020	Freeport, NY	11520	Hawthorne, CA	90250
El Cajon, CA	92020	Fremont, CA	94538	Hayward, CA	94544
El Dorado, AR	71730	Fresno, CA	93706	Hazleton, PA	18201
Elgin, IL	60120	Fridley, MN	55432	Hempstead, NY	11551
Elizabeth, NJ	07207	Fullerton, CA	92634	Hialeah, FL	33010
Elk Grove, IL	60007	Gadsden, AL	35901	Highland, IN	46322
Elkhart, IN	46515	Gainesville, FL	32608	Highland Park, IL	60035
Elmhurst, IL	60126	Gaithersburg, MD	20877	Highland Park, MI	48203

High Point, NC	27260	Killeen, TX	76541	Long Branch, NJ	07740
Hillsboro, OR	97123	Kingsport, TN	37660	Longmont, CO	80501
Hilo, HI	96720	Kingston, NC	38501	Longview, TX	75602
Hobbs, NM	88240	Kingsville, TX	78363	Longview, WA	98632
Hoboken, NJ	07030	Kirkwood, MO	63122	Lorain, OH	44052
Hoffman Estates, IL	60195	Knoxville, TN	37950	Los Altos, CA	94022
Holland, MI	49423	Kokomo, IN	46902	Los Angeles, CA	90052
Hollywood, FL	33022	La Crosse, WI	54601	Los Gatos, CA	95030
Holyoke, MA	01040	Lafayette, IN	47901	Louisville, KY	40231
Honolulu, HI	96820	Lafayette, LA	70501	Loveland, CO	80538
Hopkinsville, KY	42240	La Habra, CA	90631	Lowell, MA	01853
Hot Springs, AR	71901	Lake Charles, LA	70601	Lubbock, TX	79402
Houma, LA	70360	Lakeland, FL	33805	Lufkin, TX	75901
Houston, TX	77201	Lakewood, CA	90714	Lynchburg, VA	24506
Huber Heights, OH	45424	Lakewood, CO	80215	Lynn, MA	01901
Huntington, WV	25704	Lakewood, OH	44107	Lynwood, CA	90262
Huntington Beach, CA	92647	Lake Worth, FL	33461	Macon, GA	31213
		La Mesa, CA	91941	Madison, WI	53714
Huntington Park, CA	90255	La Mirada, CA	90638	Madison Heights, MI	48071
Huntsville, AL	35813	Lancaster, CA	93534	Malden, MA	02148
Hurst, TX	76053	Lancaster, OH	43130	Manchester, NH	03103
Hutchinson, KS	67501	Lancaster, PA	17604	Manhattan, KS	66502
Idaho Falls, ID	83401	Lansing, IL	60438	Manhattan Beach, CA	90266
Independence, MO	64050	Lansing, MI	48924	Manitowoc, WI	54220
Indianapolis, IN	46206	La Puente, CA	91747	Mankato, MN	56001
Inglewood, CA	90311	Laredo, TX	78041	Mansfield, OH	44901
Inkster, MI	48141	Largo, FL	34640	Maple Heights, OH	44137
Iowa City, IA	52240	Las Cruces, NM	88001	Maplewood, MN	55109
Irvine, CA	92713	Las Vegas, NV	89199	Marietta, GA	30060
Irving, TX	75015	Lawrence, IN	46226	Marion, IN	46952
Irvington, NJ	07111	Lawrence, KS	66044	Marion, OH	43302
Ithaca, NY	14850	Lawrence, MA	04842	Marlborough, MA	01752
Jackson, MI	49201	Lawton, OK	73501	Marshalltown, IA	50158
Jackson, MS	39205	Leavenworth, KS	66048	Mason City, IA	50401
Jackson, TN	38301	Lebanon, PA	17042	Massillon, OH	44646
Jacksonville, FL	32203	Lee's Summit, MO	64063	Maywood, IL	60153
Jamestown, NY	14701	Leominster, MA	01453	McAllen, TX	78501
Janesville, WI	53545	Lewiston, ID	83501	McKeesport, PA	15134
Jefferson City, MO	65101	Lewiston, ME	04240	Medford, MA	02155
Jersey City, NJ	07303	Lexington, KY	40511	Medford, OR	97501
Johnson City, TN	37601	Lima, OH	45802	Melbourne, FL	32901
Johnstown, PA	15901	Lincoln, NE	68501	Melrose, MA	02176
Joliet, IL	60436	Lincoln Park, MI	48146	Memphis, TN	38101
Jonesboro, AR	72401	Linden, NJ	07036	Menlo Park, CA	94025
Joplin, MO	64801	Lindenhurst, NY	11757	Menomonee Falls, WI	53051
Kalamazoo, MI	49001	Little Rock, AR	72231	Mentor, OH	44060
Kankakee, IL	60901	Littleton, CO	70220	Merced, CA	95340
Kansas City, KS	66106	Livermore, CA	94550	Meriden, CT	06450
Kansas City, MO	64108	Livonia, MI	48150	Meridian, MS	39301
Kearny, NJ	07032	Lodi, CA	95240	Merrillville, IN	46410
Kenner, LA	70062	Logan, UT	84321	Mesa, AZ	85201
Kennewick, WA	99336	Lombard, IL	60148	Mesquite, TX	75149
Kenosha, WI	53140	Lompoc, CA	93436	Miami, FL	33152
Kent, OH	44240	Long Beach, CA	90809	Miami Beach, FL	33139
Kettering, OH	45429	Long Beach, NY	11561	Middletown, CT	06457

Middletown, OH	45042	New Orleans, LA	70113	Oxnard, CA	93030
Midland, MI	48640	Newport, RI	02840	Pacifica, CA	94044
Midland, TX	79711	Newport Beach, CA	92660	Paducah, KY	42001
Midwest City, OK	73130	Newport News, VA	23607	Palatine, IL	66067
Milford, CT	06460	New Rochelle, NY	10802	Palm Springs, CA	92263
Milpitas, CA	95035	Newton, MA	02158	Palo Alto, CA	94303
Milwaukee, WI	53203	New York, NY	10199	Panama City, FL	32401
Minneapolis, MN	55401	Niagara Falls, NY	14302	Paramount, CA	90723
Minnetonka, MN	55345	Niles, IL	60648	Paramus, NJ	07652
Minot, ND	58701	Norfolk, VA	23501	Paris, TX	75460
Mishawaka, IN	46544	Normal, IL	61761	Parkersburg, WV	26101
Missoula, MT	59801	Norman, OK	73069	Park Ridge, IL	60068
Mobile, AL	36601	Norristown, PA	19401	Parma, OH	44129
Modesto, CA	95350	Northampton, MA	01060	Pasadena, CA	91109
Moline, IL	61265	Northbrook, IL	60062	Pasadena, TX	77501
Monroe, LA	71203	North Charleston, SC	29406	Pascagoula, MS	39567
Monroeville, PA	15146	North Chicago, IL	60064	Passaic, NJ	07055
Monrovia, CA	91016	North Las Vegas, NV	89030	Paterson, NJ	07510
Montclair, NJ	07042	North Little Rock, AR	72114	Pawtucket, RI	02860
Montebello, CA	90640	North Miami, FL	33261	Peabody, MA	01960
Monterey, CA	93940	North Miami Beach, FL	33160	Pembroke Pines, FL	33024
Monterey Park, CA	91754			Pensacola, FL	32501
Montgomery, AL	36119	North Olmsted, OH	44070	Peoria, IL	61601
Moore, OK	73160	North Richland Hills, TX	76180	Perth Amboy, NJ	08861
Moorhead, MN	56560			Petaluma, CA	94952
Morgantown, WV	26505	North Tonawanda, NY	14120	Petersburg, VA	23804
Mountainview, CA	94042	Norwalk, CA	90650	Phenix City, AL	36867
Mount Prospect, IL	60056	Norwalk, CT	06856	Philadelphia, PA	19104
Mount Vernon, NY	10551	Norwich, CT	06360	Phoenix, AZ	85027
Muncie, IN	47302	Norwood, OH	45212	Pico Rivera, CA	90660
Murfreesboro, TN	37130	Novato, CA	94947	Pine Bluff, AR	71601
Murray, UT	84107	Nutley, NJ	07110	Pinellas Park, FL	34665
Muskegon, MI	49440	Oak Forest, IL	60452	Pittsburg, CA	94565
Muskogee, OK	74401	Oaklando, CA	94615	Pittsburgh, PA	15290
Nacogdoches, TX	75961	Oak Lawn, IL	60455	Pittsfield, MA	01201
Nampa, ID	83651	Oak Park, IL	60301	Placentia, CA	92670
Napa, CA	94558	Oak Park, MI	48237	Plainfield, NJ	07061
Naperville, IL	60540	Oak Ridge, TN	37830	Plano, TX	75074
Nashua, NH	03060	Ocala, FL	32678	Plantation, FL	33318
Nashville, TN	37229	Oceanside, CA	92054	Pleasant Hill, CA	94523
National City, CA	91950	Odessa, TX	79761	Pleasanton, CA	94566
Naugatuck, CT	06770	Ogden, UT	84401	Plum, PA	15239
New Albany, IN	47150	Oklahoma City, OK	73125	Plymouth, MN	55447
Newark, CA	94560	Olathe, KS	66061	Pocatello, ID	83201
Newark, DE	19711	Olympia, WA	98501	Pomona, CA	91766
Newark, NJ	07102	Omaha, NE	68108	Pompano Beach, FL	33060
Newark, OH	43055	Ontario, CA	91761	Ponca City, OK	74601
New Bedford, MA	02740	Orange, CA	92613	Pontiac, MI	48343
New Berlin, WI	53151	Orange, NJ	07051	Portage, IN	46368
New Britain, CT	06050	Orem, UT	84057	Port Arthur, TX	77640
New Brunswick, NJ	08901	Orlando, FL	32802	Port Huron, MI	48060
New Castle, PA	16108	Oshkosh, WI	54901	Portland, ME	04101
New Haven, CT	06511	Ottumwa, IA	52501	Portland, OR	97208
New Iberia, LA	70560	Overland Park, KS	66204	Portsmouth, NH	03801
New London, CT	06320	Owensboro, KY	43201	Portsmouth, OH	45662

Portsmouth, VA	23707	St. Cloud, MN	56301	Silver Springs, MD	20907
Poughkeepsie, NY	12601	St. Joseph, MO	64501	Simi Valley, CA	93065
Providence, RI	02904	St. Louis, MO	63155	Sioux City, IA	51101
Provo, UT	84601	St. Louis Park, MN	55426	Sioux Falls, SD	57101
Pueblo, CO	81003	St. Paul, MN	55101	Skokie, IL	60076
Quincy, IL	62301	St. Petersburg, FL	33730	Slidell, LA	70458
Quincy, MA	02269	Salem, MA	01970	Somerville, MA	02143
Racine, WI	53403	Salem, OR	97301	Somerville, NJ	08876
Rahway, NJ	07065	Salina, KS	67401	South Bend, IN	46624
Raleigh, NC	27611	Salinas, CA	93907	South Euclid, OH	44121
Rancho Cucamonga, CA	91730	Salt Lake City, UT	84199	Southfield, MI	48037
		San Angelo, TX	76902	South Gate, CA	90280
Rancho Palos Verdes, CA	90274	San Antonio, TX	78284	Southgate, MI	48195
		San Bernardino, CA	92403	South San Francisco, CA	94080
Rapid City, SD	57701	San Bruno, CA	94066		
Raytown, MO	64133	San Buenaventura (Ventura), CA	93001	Sparks, NV	89431
Reading, PA	19612			Spartanburg, SC	29301
Redding, CA	96001	San Clemente, CA	92672	Spokane, WA	99210
Redlands, CA	92373	San Diego, CA	92199	Springfield, IL	62703
Redondo Beach, CA	90277	Sandusky, OH	44870	Springfield, MA	01101
Redwood City, CA	94064	Sandy, UT	84070	Springfield, MO	65801
Reno, NV	89510	San Francisco, CA	94188	Springfield, OH	45501
Renton, WA	98058	San Gabriel, CA	91776	Springfield, OR	97477
Revere, MA	02151	San Jose, CA	95101	Stamford, CT	06904
Rialto, CA	92376	San Leandro, CA	94577	State College, PA	16801
Richardson, TX	75080	San Luis Obispo, CA	93401	Sterling Heights, MI	48311
Richfield, MN	55423	San Mateo, CA	94402	Steubenville, OH	43952
Richland, WA	99352	San Rafael, CA	94901	Stillwater, OK	74074
Richmond, CA	94802	Santa Ana, CA	92799	Stockton, CA	95208
Richmond, IN	47374	Santa Barbara, CA	93102	Stow, OH	44224
Richmond, VA	23232	Santa Clara, CA	95051	Strongsville, OH	44136
Ridgewood, NJ	07450	Santa Cruz, CA	95060	Suffolk, VA	23434
Riverside, CA	92507	Santa Fe, NM	87501	Sunnyvale, CA	94086
Riviera Beach, FL	33404	Santa Maria, CA	93454	Sunrise, FL	33345
Roanoke, VA	24022	Santa Monica, CA	90406	Superior, WI	54880
Rochester, MI	48308	Santa Rosa, CA	95402	Syracuse, NY	13220
Rochester, MN	55901	Sarasota, FL	34230	Tacoma, WA	98413
Rochester, NY	14692	Saratoga, CA	95070	Tallahassee, FL	32301
Rockford, IL	61125	Savannah, GA	31402	Tamarac, FL	33320
Rock Hill, SC	29730	Sayreville, NJ	08872	Tampa, FL	33630
Rock Island, IL	61201	Schaumburg, IL	60194	Taunton, MA	02780
Rockville, MD	20850	Schenectady, NY	12305	Taylor, MI	48180
Rockville Center, NY	11570	Scottsdale, AZ	85251	Tempe, AZ	85282
Rocky Mount, NC	27801	Scranton, PA	18505	Temple, TX	76501
Rome, GA	30161	Seal Beach, CA	90740	Terre Haute, IN	47808
Rome, NY	13440	Seaside, CA	93955	Texarkana, TX	75501
Rosemead, CA	91770	Seattle, WA	98109	Texas City, TX	75590
Roseville, MI	48066	Selma, AL	36701	Thornton, CO	80229
Roseville, MN	55113	Shaker Heights, OH	44120	Thousand Oaks, CA	91360
Roswell, NM	88201	Shawnee Mission, KS	66202	Tinley Park, IL	60477
Royal Oak, MI	48068	Shawnee, OK	74801	Titusville, FL	32780
Sacramento, CA	95813	Sheboygan, WI	53081	Toledo, OH	43601
Saginaw, MI	48065	Shelton, CT	06484	Topeka, KS	66603
St. Charles, MO	63301	Sherman, TX	75090	Torrance, CA	90510
St. Clair Shores, MI	48080	Shreveport, LA	71102	Torrington, CT	06790

Trenton, NJ	08650	Walnut Creek, CA	94596	Wheaton, IL	60187
Troy, MI	48099	Waltham, MA	02154	Wheat Ridge, CO	80033
Troy, NY	12180	Warner Robins, GA	31093	Wheeling, WV	26003
Tucson, AZ	85726	Warren, MI	48090	White Plains, NY	10602
Tulsa, OK	74103	Warren, OH	44481	Whittier, CA	90605
Turlock, CA	95380	Warwick, RI	02886	Wichita, KS	67276
Tuscaloosa, AL	35401	Washington, DC	20013	Wichita Falls, TX	76307
Tustin, CA	92680	Waterbury, CT	06701	Wilkes-Barre, PA	18701
Twin Falls, ID	83301	Waterloo, IA	50701	Williamsport, PA	17701
Tyler, TX	75712	Watertown, NY	13601	Wilmette, IL	60091
Union City, CA	94587	Waukegan, IL	60085	Wilmington, DE	19850
Union City, NJ	07087	Waukesha, WI	53186	Wilmington, NC	28402
University City, MO	63130	Wausau, WI	54401	Wilson, NC	27893
Upland, CA	91786	Wauwatosa, WI	53213	Winona, MN	55987
Upper Arlington, OH	43221	Weirton, WV	26062	Winston-Salem, NC	27102
Urbana, IL	61801	West Allis, WI	53214	Woburn, MA	01801
Utica, NY	13504	West Covina, CA	91793	Woodland, CA	95695
Vacaville, CA	95688	Westfield, MA	01085	Woonsocket, RI	02895
Valdosta, GA	31601	Westfield, NJ	07090	Worcester, MA	01613
Vallejo, CA	94590	West Haven, CT	06516	Wyandotte, MI	48192
Valley Stream, NY	11580	West Jordan, UT	84084	Wyoming, MI	49509
Vancouver, WA	98661	Westland, MI	48185	Yakima, WA	98903
Vicksburg, MS	39180	West Lafayette, IN	47906	Yonkers, NY	10702
Victoria, TX	77901	West Memphis, AR	72301	Yorba Linda, CA	92686
Vineland, NJ	08360	West Mifflin, PA	15122	York, PA	17405
Virginia Beach, VA	23450	Westminster, CA	92683	Youngstown, OH	44501
Visalia, CA	93277	Westminster, CO	80030	Ypsilanti, MI	48197
Vista, CA	92083	West New York, NJ	07093	Yuma, AZ	85364
Waco, TX	76702	West Orange, NJ	07052	Zanesville, OH	43701
Walla Walla, WA	99362	West Palm Beach, FL	33406		

TWO-LETTER STATE AND TERRITORY ABBREVIATIONS

Alabama	AL	Kentucky	KY	Ohio	OH
Alaska	AK	Louisiana	LA	Oklahoma	OK
American Samoa	AS	Maine	ME	Oregon	OR
Arizona	AZ	Marshall Islands	MH	Palau	PW
Arkansas	AR	Maryland	MD	Pennsylvania	PA
California	CA	Massachusetts	MA	Puerto Rico	PR
Colorado	CO	Michigan	MI	Rhode Island	RI
Connecticut	CT	Minnesota	MN	South Carolina	SC
Delaware	DE	Mississippi	MS	South Dakota	SD
District of Columbia	DC	Missouri	MO	Tennessee	TN
Federated States of	FM	Montana	MT	Texas	TX
Micronesia		Nebraska	NE	Utah	UT
Florida	FL	Nevada	NV	Vermont	VT
Georgia	GA	New Hampshire	NH	Virginia	VA
Guam	GU	New Jersey	NJ	Virgin Islands	VI
Hawaii	HI	New Mexico	NM	Washington	WA
Idaho	ID	New York	NY	West Virginia	WV
Illinois	IL	North Carolina	NC	Wisconsin	WI
Indiana	IN	North Dakota	ND	Wyoming	WY
Iowa	IA	Northern Mariana	MP		
Kansas	KS	Islands			

GEOGRAPHIC DIRECTIONAL ABBREVIATIONS

North	N	West	W	Southwest	SW
East	E	Northeast	NE	Northwest	NW
South	S	Southeast	SE		

STREET DESIGNATORS (STREET SUFFIXES)

Alley	ALY	Forge	FRG	Path	PATH
Annex	ANX	Fork	FRK	Pike	PIKE
Arcade	ARC	Forks	FRKS	Pines	PNES
Avenue	AVE	Fort	FT	Place	PL
Bayou	BYU	Freeway	FWY	Plains	PLNS
Beach	BCH	Gardens	GDNS	Plaza	PLZ
Bend	BND	Gateway	GTWY	Point	PT
Bluff	BLF	Glen	GLN	Port	PRT
Bottom	BTM	Green	GRN	Prairie	PR
Boulevard	BLVD	Grove	GRV	Radial	RADL
Branch	BR	Harbor	HBR	Ranch	RNCH
Bridge	BRG	Haven	HVN	Rapids	RPDS
Brook	BRK	Heights	HTS	Rest	RST
Burg	BG	Highway	HWY	Ridge	RDG
Bypass	BYP	Hill	HL	River	RIV
Camp	CP	Hills	HLS	Road	RD
Canyon	CYN	Hollow	HOLW	Row	ROW
Cape	CPE	Inlet	INLT	Run	RUN
Causeway	CSWY	Island	IS	Shoal	SHL
Center	CTR	Islands	ISS	Shoals	SHLS
Circle	CIR	Isle	ISLE	Shore	SHR
Cliffs	CLFS	Junction	JCT	Shores	SHRS
Club	CLB	Key	KY	Spring	SPG
Corner	COR	Knolls	KNLS	Springs	SPGS
Corners	CORS	Lake	LK	Spur	SPUR
Course	CRSE	Lakes	LKS	Square	SQ
Court	CT	Landing	LNDG	Station	STA
Courts	CTS	Lane	LN	Stream	STRM
Cove	CV	Light	LGT	Street	ST
Creek	CRK	Loaf	LF	Summit	SMT
Crescent	CRES	Locks	LCKS	Terrace	TER
Crossing	XING	Lodge	LDG	Trace	TRCE
Dale	DL	Loop	LOOP	Track	TRAK
Dam	DM	Mall	MALL	Trail	TRL
Divide	DV	Manor	MNR	Trailer	TRLR
Drive	DR	Meadows	MDWS	Tunnel	TUNL
Estates	EST	Mill	ML	Turnpike	TPKE
Expressway	EXPY	Mills	MLS	Union	UN
Extension	EXT	Mission	MSN	Valley	VLY
Fall	FL	Mount	MT	Viaduct	VIA
Falls	FLS	Mountain	MTN	View	VW
Ferry	FRY	Neck	NCK	Village	VLG
Field	FLD	Orchard	ORCH	Ville	VL
Fields	FLDS	Oval	OVAL	Vista	VIS
Flats	FLT	Park	PARK	Walk	WALK
Ford	FRD	Parkway	PKY	Way	WAY
Forest	FRST	Pass	PASS	Wells	WLS

MAJOR DAILY NEWSPAPERS

NATIONAL

Christian Science Monitor
One Norway St.
Boston, MA 02115-3195
http://www.csmonitor.com

USA Today
1000 Wilson Blvd.
Arlington, VA 22209
http://www.usatoday.com

Wall Street Journal
200 Liberty St.
New York, NY 10281
http://www.wsj.com

LOCAL (BY STATE)

Alabama

Birmingham News
2200 4th Ave. N.
Birmingham, AL 35203

Birmingham Post-Herald
P.O. Box 2553
Birmingham, AL 35202-2553

Montgomery Advertiser
P.O. Box 1000
Montgomery, AL 36101-1000

Alaska

Anchorage Daily News
P.O. Box 149001
Anchorage, AK 99514-9001

Arizona

Arizona Republic
P.O. Box 1950
Phoenix, AZ 85001-1950

Arizona Daily Star
P.O. Box 26807
Tucson, AZ 85726-6807

Phoenix Gazette
P.O. Box 1950
Phoenix, AZ 85001-1950

Arkansas

Arkansas Democrat-Gazette
Capitol Avenue and Scott
P.O. Box 2221
Little Rock, AR 72203

California

Fresno Bee
3425 N. 1st St.
Fresno, CA 93726-6819

Los Angeles Times
Times Mirror Square
Los Angeles, CA 90012

Sacramento Bee
2100 Q St.
P.O. Box 15779
Sacramento, CA 95852

San Diego Union-Tribune
350 Camino de la Reina
San Diego, CA 92108

San Francisco Chronicle
901 Mission St.
San Francisco, CA 94103

San Francisco Examiner
110 Fifth St.
San Francisco, CA 94103

Colorado

Denver Post
1560 Broadway
Denver, CO 80202

Rocky Mountain News
400 West Colfax Ave.
Denver, CO 80201

Connecticut

Hartford Courant
285 Broad St.
Hartford, CT 06115-2510

New Haven Register
40 Sargent Dr.
New Haven, CT 06511

Delaware

News-Journal
P.O. Box 19850
Wilmington, DE 19850

District of Columbia

Washington Post
1150 15th St., NW
Washington, DC 20071

Florida

Florida Times Union
One Riverside Ave.
Jacksonville, FL 32202-4924

Fort Lauderdale Sun-Sentinel
200 E. Las Olas Blvd.
Ft. Lauderdale, FL 33301-2293

Miami Herald
One Herald Plaza
Miami, FL 33132-1693

Orlando Sentinel
633 N. Orange Ave.
Orlando, FL 32801

St. Petersburg Times
P.O. Box 1121
St. Petersburg, FL 33701

Georgia

Atlanta Journal and Constitution
72 Marietta St., NW
Atlanta, GA 30303

Hawaii

Honolulu Advertiser
605 Kapiolani Blvd.
Honolulu, HI 96813

Honolulu Star Bulletin
P.O. Box 3080
Honolulu, HI 96802

Idaho

Idaho Statesman
1200 N. Curtis Rd.
Boise, ID 83707

Illinois

Chicago Sun-Times
401 N. Wabash Ave.
Chicago, IL 60611

Chicago Tribune
435 N. Michigan Ave.
Chicago, IL 60611

Indiana

Indianapolis Star News
307 N. Pennsylvania St.
Indianapolis, IN 46204-1811

Post-Tribune
1065 Broadway St.
Gary, IN 46402-2998

South Bend Tribune
225 W. Colfax Ave.
South Bend, IN 46626-0001

Iowa

Des Moines Register
P.O. Box 957
Des Moines, IA 50304

Kansas

Topeka Capital-Journal
616 Jefferson St.
Topeka, KS 66607-1197

Wichita Eagle
825 E. Douglas St.
Wichita, KS 67201

Kentucky

Courier-Journal
525 W. Broadway
Louisville, KY 40202-2137

Herald-Leader
100 Midland Ave.
Lexington, KY 40508

Louisiana

The Advocate
525 Lafayette St.
Baton Rouge, LA 70821

Times-Picayune
3800 Howard Ave.
New Orleans, LA 0140

Maine

Daily News
491 Main St.
Bangor, ME 04402

United States

Portland Press Herald
P.O. Box 1460
390 Congress St.
Portland, ME 04101

Maryland

The Baltimore Sun
501 N. Calvert St.
Baltimore, MD 21278-0001

Massachusetts

Boston Globe
135 Morrissey Blvd.
Boston, MA 02107

Boston Herald
1 Herald Square
Boston, MA 02106

Michigan

Detroit Free Press
321 W. Lafayette Blvd.
Detroit, MI 48226

Detroit News
615 W. Lafayette Blvd.
Detroit, MI 48226

Republican Gerald Ford is the only unelected president. President Nixon appointed him vice president after Spiro Agnew resigned. Ford then assumed the presidency after Nixon's resignation.

Minnesota

St. Paul Pioneer Press
345 Cedar St.
St. Paul, MN 55101-1057

Star Tribune
425 Portland Ave.
Minneapolis, MN 55488-0001

Mississippi

Clarion Ledger
311 E. Pearl St.
Jackson, MS 39205

Missouri

Kansas City Star
1729 Grand Ave.
Kansas City, MO 64108

Post-Dispatch
900 N. Tucker Blvd.
St. Louis, MO 63101

Montana

Billings Gazette
401 N. Broadway
Billings, MT 59101-1243

Great Falls Tribune
P.O. Box 5468
Great Falls, MT 59403

Nebraska

Lincoln Journal
926 P St.
Lincoln, NE 68501

Lincoln Star
926 P St.
Lincoln, NE 68508

World-Herald
World-Herald Square
Omaha, NE 68102

Nevada

Las Vegas Review-Journal
1111 W. Bonanza
Las Vegas, NV 89125

Las Vegas Sun
800 S. Valley View
Box 4275
Las Vegas, NV 89127

Reno Gazette Journal
P.O. Box 22000
Reno, NV 89520-2000

New Hampshire

Union-Leader
P.O. Box 9555
Manchester, NH 03108

New Jersey

Asbury Park Press
3601 Hwy. 66
Neptune, NJ 07754

Record
150 River St.
Hackensack, NJ 07601

Star-Ledger
Star-Ledger Plaza
Newark, NJ 07102-1200

Why is American paper currency known as "greenbacks"? During the Civil War, the cash-strapped federal government selected the distinctive green color in use today because it was cheapest ink available.

New Mexico

Albuquerque Journal
7777 Jefferson NE
Albuquerque, NM 87109

Albuquerque Tribune
7777 Jefferson NE
Albuquerque, NM 87109

New York

Buffalo News
One News Plaza
P.O. Box 100
Buffalo, NY 14240

Newsday
235 Pinelawn Rd.
Melville, NY 11747-4250

New York Daily News
450 W. 33rd St.
New York, NY 10001

New York Post
1211 Sixth Ave.
New York, NY 10036

New York Times
229 W. 43rd St.
New York, NY 10036-3913

North Carolina

Observer
P.O. Box 32188-28232
Charlotte, NC 28232

News & Observer
215 S. McDowell St.
Raleigh, NC 27602

North Dakota

Bismark Tribune
P.O. Box 1498
707 E. Front Ave.
Bismark, ND 58502-1498

Ohio

Akron Beacon Journal
44 E. Exchange St.
Akron, OH 44328-0001

Blade
541 Superior St.
Toledo, OH 43660-0001

Cincinnati Enquirer
312 Elm St.
Cincinnati, OH 45202-2410

Cincinnati Post
125 E. Court St.
Cincinnati, OH 45202-1211

Cleveland Plain Dealer
1801 Superior Ave.
Cleveland, OH 44114-2198

Columbus Dispatch
34 S. Third St.
Columbus, OH 43215

Daily News
Fourth and Ludlow Sts.
Dayton, OH 45401

Oklahoma

Oklahoman
9000 N. Broadway
Oklahoma City, OK 73114

Tulsa World
P.O. Box 1770
Tulsa, OK 74102

United States

Oregon

The Oregonian
1320 SW Broadway
Portland, OR 97201-3469

Pennsylvania

Philadelphia Daily News
400 N. Broad St.
Philadelphia, PA 19101

Philadelphia Inquirer
400 N. Broad St.
Philadelphia, PA 19101

Pittsburgh Post-Gazette
P.O. Box 957
50 Boulevard of Allies
Pittsburgh, PA 15222

Pittsburgh Press
34 Boulevard of Allies
Pittsburgh, PA 15230

Rhode Island

Journal-Bulletin
75 Fountain St.
Providence, RI 02902

South Carolina

Post & Courier
134 Columbus St.
Charleston, SC 29403-4800

The State
P.O. Box 1333
Columbia, SC 29202

South Dakota

Argus Leader
P.O. Box 5034
Sioux Falls, SD 57117-5034

Tennessee

Commercial Appeal
495 Union Ave.
Memphis, TN 38103-3221

Nashville Banner
1100 Broadway
Nashville, TN 37203-3116

News-Sentinel
204 W. Church Ave.
Knoxville, TN 37902-1612

Tennessean
1100 Broadway
Nashville, TN 37203-3116

Texas

Austin American-Statesman
P.O. Box 670
Austin, TX 78767

Dallas Morning News
Communications Center
Dallas, TX 75265

Express-News
P.O. Box 2171
San Antonio, TX 78297

Fort Worth Star-Telegram
400 W. 7th St.
Fort Worth, TX 76102

Houston Chronicle
801 Texas Ave.
Houston, TX 7700

Houston Post
4747 Southwest Fwy.
Houston, TX 77027

Utah

Deseret News
30 E. First St.
Salt Lake City, UT 84110

Salt Lake Tribune
143 S. Main St.
Salt Lake City, UT 84111

Vermont

Free Press
191 College St.
Burlington, VT 05401

Virginia

Virginian-Pilot
150 W. Brambleton Ave.
Norfolk, VA 23510

Richmond Times-Dispatch
P.O. Box 85333
Richmond, VA 23293-1000

United States

Washington

Seattle Post-Intelligencer
101 Elliott Ave., W
Seattle, WA 98119

Seattle Times
P.O. Box 70
Seattle, WA 98111-1070

West Virginia

Herald Dispatch
P.O. Box 2017
946 Fifth Ave.
Huntington, WV 25720

News-Register
1500 Main St.
Wheeling, WV 26003

Wisconsin

Milwaukee Journal Sentinel
333 W. State St.
Milwaukee, WI 53203-1305

State Journal
P.O. Box 8058
Madison, WI 53708

Wyoming

Wyoming Tribune-Eagle
702 W. Lincolnway
Cheyenne, WY 82001

ADDITIONAL SOURCES OF INFORMATION

MAGAZINES

NEWSMAGAZINES

Newsweek
251 W. 57th St.
New York, NY 10019
http://www.newsweek.com

Time
1271 Avenue of the Americas
New York, NY 10020
http://www.pathfinder.com

U.S. News & World Report
2400 N St., NW
Washington, DC 20037
http://www.usnews.com

Harper's Magazine
666 Broadway, 11th Floor
New York, NY 10012
http://www.harpers.org

PUBLIC, SOCIAL, AND POLITICAL AFFAIRS

Mother Jones
731 Mission St.
San Francisco, CA 94103
http://www.motherjones.com

The Nation
72 Fifth Ave.
New York, NY 10011
http://www.thenation.com

The New Republic
1220 19th St., NW
Washington, DC 20036
http://www.enews.com/magazines/tnr

BOOKS

Ayers, Edward L., et al. *American Passages: The History of the United States,* 2 vols. New York: Harcourt Inc., 2000.

Barone, Michael, Grant Ujifusa, and Richard E. Cohen. *The Almanac of American Politics 1998.* Times Books, 1997.

Congress and the Nation. Congressional Quarterly, published every four years.

Congressional Quarterly Almanac. Congressional Quarterly, annual.

Congressional Quarterly Weekly. Congressional Quarterly, weekly.

Consumer's Resource Handbook. U.S. Office of Consumer Affairs, latest edition.

Flags of America. 2nd ed. National Flag Foundation, 1994.

United States

Foner, Eric, and John A. Garraty, eds. *The Reader's Companion to American History.* Houghton Mifflin, 1991.

Garwood, Alfred N. *Almanac of the Fifty States.* Information Publication, 1987.

Hatch, Jane M. *The American Book of Days.* 3rd ed. H. W. Wilson, 1978.

Henretta, James A., et al. *America's History,* 4th edition, 2 vols. New York: Bedford/St. Martin's, 2000.

Kane, Joseph Nathan. *Nicknames and Sobriquets of U.S. Cities, States, and Countries.* 3rd ed. Scarecrow Press, 1979.

Lesko, Matthew. *Information U.S.A.* Viking, 1986.

Norton, Mary Beth, et al. *A People and a Nation,* 6th edition, 2 vols. New York: Houghton Mifflin, 2001.

Schlesinger, Arthur M., Jr., ed. *The Almanac of American History.* Putnam, 1984.

Shearer, Benjamin F., and Barbara S. Shearer. *State Names, Seals, Flags and Symbols: A Historical Guide.* Greenwood, 1994.

Statistical Abstract of the United States. U.S. Bureau of the Census, annual.

Urdang, Laurence, ed. *The Timetables of American History.* Touchstone, 1996.

26

THE WORLD

COUNTRIES OF THE WORLD

Afghanistan
Area: 647,500 km² (249,999 mi²)
Capital: Kabul
Government: In transition
Population: 25,888,797
Languages: Pushtu, Afghan Persian, Turkic
Religions: Sunni Muslim, Shi'a Muslim

Albania
Area: 28,750 km² (11,100 mi²)
Capital: Tirana
Government: Republic
Population: 3,490,435
Languages: Albanian, Greek
Religions: Muslim, Albanian Orthodox, Roman
  Catholic

Algeria
Area: 2,381,740 km² (919,590 mi²)
Capital: Algiers
Government: Republic
Population: 31,193,917
Languages: Arabic, French, Berber dialects
Religion: Sunni Muslim

Andorra
Area: 450 km² (174 mi²)
Capital: Andorra la Vella
Government: Coprincipality of France and Spain
Population: 66,824
Languages: Catalan, French, Castilian
Religion: Roman Catholic

Angola
Area: 1,246,700 km² (481,351 mi²)
Capital: Luanda
Government: Republic
Population: 10,145,267
Languages: Portuguese, Bantu dialects
Religions: Indigenous beliefs, Roman Catholic,
  Protestant

Anguilla
Area: 91 km² (35 mi²)
Capital: The Valley
Government: Dependent territory of United Kingdom
Population: 11,797
Language: English
Religions: Anglican, Methodist

Antarctica
Area: 14,000,000 km² (5,500,000 mi²)
Capital: None
Government: Various nations—including Argentina,
  Australia, Chile, France, New Zealand, Norway, and

United Kingdom—claim areas of the continent;
  Antarctic Treaty of 1959, signed by 42 nations, places
  these claims in abeyance and stipulates peaceful uses
  of Antarctica.
Population: No indigenous inhabitants; seasonal
  population of researchers averages about 4,000 in
  summer and 1,000 in winter.

Antigua and Barbuda
Area: 440 km² (170 mi²)
Capital: Saint John's
Government: Parliamentary democracy affiliated with
  United Kingdom
Population: 66,464
Languages: English, local dialects
Religions: Anglican, Methodist, Roman Catholic

Argentina
Area: 2,766,890 km² (1,068,296 mi²)
Capital: Buenos Aires
Government: Republic
Population: 36,955,182
Languages: Spanish, English, Italian
Religions: Roman Catholic, Protestant, Jewish

Armenia
Area: 29,283 km² (11,306 mi²)
Capital: Yerevan
Government: Presidential republic
Population: 3,344,336
Languages: Armenian, Russian
Religion: Armenian Orthodox

Aruba
Area: 193 km² (75 mi²)
Capital: Oranjestad
Government: Independent territory of the Netherlands
Population: 69,539
Languages: Dutch, Papiamento, Spanish, English
Religions: Roman Catholic, Protestant

Australia
Area: 7,686,850 km² (2,967,893 mi²)
Capital: Canberra
Government: Federal parliamentary state affiliated with
  Great Britain
Population: 19,164,620
Languages: English, aboriginal languages
Religions: Anglican, Roman Catholic, other Protestant
  faiths

Austria
Area: 83,850 km² (32,374 mi²)
Capital: Vienna
Government: Federal republic
Population: 8,131,111
Language: German
Religions: Roman Catholic, Protestant

Azerbaijan
Area: 86,506 km² (33,400 mi²)
Capital: Baku
Government: Parliamentary republic
Population: 7,748,163
Languages: Azeri, Russian
Religions: Muslim, Orthodox

If there were only 100 people in the world, half would live in just 5 countries: 21 in China, 15 in India, 5 in the former Soviet Union, 5 in the United States, and 4 in Indonesia.

Bahamas
Area: 13,940 km² (5,382 mi²)
Capital: Nassau
Government: Independent commonwealth affiliated with United Kingdom
Population: 294,982
Languages: English, Creole
Religions: Baptist, Anglican, Roman Catholic, other Protestant faiths

Bahrain
Area: 620 km² (239 mi²)
Capital: Manama
Government: Monarchy
Population: 634,137
Languages: Arabic, English, Farsi, Urdu
Religions: Shi'a Muslim, Sunni Muslim

Bangladesh
Area: 144,000 km² (55,598 mi²)
Capital: Dhaka
Government: Republic
Population: 129,194,224
Languages: Bangla, English
Religions: Muslim, Hindu

Barbados
Area: 460 km² (166 mi²)
Capital: Bridgetown
Government: Parliamentary democracy affiliated with United Kingdom
Population: 274,059
Language: English
Religions: Anglican, Pentecostal, Methodist, Roman Catholic

Barbuda
See **Antigua and Barbuda.**

Belarus
Area: 207,718 km² (80,200 mi²)
Capital: Minsk
Government: Constitutional republic
Population: 10,366,719
Languages: Byelorussian, Russian
Religions: Russian Orthodox, Baptist

Belgium
Area: 30,520 km² (11,784 mi²)
Capital: Brussels
Government: Constitutional monarchy
Population: 10,241,506
Languages: Flemish, French
Religions: Roman Catholic, Protestant

Belize
Area: 22,960 km² (8,865 mi²)
Capital: Belmopan
Government: Parliamentary democracy affiliated with United Kingdom
Population: 249,183
Languages: English, Spanish, Maya, Garifuna
Religions: Roman Catholic, Anglican, Methodist

Benin
Area: 112,620 km² (43,483 mi²)
Capital: Porto-Novo
Government: Multiparty democracy
Population: 6,395,919
Languages: French, Fon, Yoruba, tribal dialects
Religions: Indigenous beliefs, Muslim, Christian

Bermuda
Area: 50 km² (19 mi²)
Capital: Hamilton
Government: Dependent territory of United Kingdom
Population: 63,022
Language: English
Religions: Anglican, Roman Catholic, African Methodist

Bhutan
Area: 47,000 km² (18,147 mi²)
Capital: Thimphu
Government: Monarchy
Population: 2,005,222
Languages: Dzongkha, other Tibetan dialects, Nepalese dialects
Religions: Lamaistic Buddhist, Hindu

Bolivia
Area: 1,098,580 km² (424,162 mi²)
Capitals: La Paz and Sucre
Government: Republic
Population: 8,152,620
Languages: Spanish, Quechua, Aymara
Religions: Roman Catholic, Protestant

Bosnia and Herzegovina
Area: 51,129 km² (19,741 mi²)
Capital: Sarajevo
Government: Republic
Population: 3,835,777
Languages: Serbo-Croatian
Religions: Muslim, Serbian Orthodox, Roman Catholic

Botswana
Area: 600,370 km² (231,803 mi²)
Capital: Gaborone
Government: Parliamentary republic
Population: 1,576,470
Languages: English, Setswana
Religions: Indigenous beliefs, Christian

Brazil
Area: 8,511,970 km² (3,286,472 mi²)
Capital: Brasília
Government: Federal republic
Population: 172,860,370
Languages: Portuguese, Spanish, English, French
Religion: Roman Catholic

British Virgin Islands
Area: 150 km² (58 mi²)
Capital: Road Town
Government: Dependent territory of United Kingdom
Population: 20,353
Language: English
Religions: Methodist, Anglican, other Protestant faiths, Roman Catholic

Brunei
Area: 5,770 km² (2,228 mi²)
Capital: Bandar Seri Begawan
Government: Constitutional sultanate
Population: 336,376
Languages: Malay, English, Chinese
Religions: Muslim, Buddhist, Christian, indigenous beliefs

Bulgaria
Area: 110,910 km² (42,822 mi²)
Capital: Sofia
Government: Emerging democracy
Population: 7,796,694
Language: Bulgarian
Religions: Bulgarian Orthodox, Muslim, Jewish, Roman Catholic

Burkina Faso
Area: 274,200 km² (105,869 mi²)
Capital: Ouagadougou
Government: Parliamentary republic
Population: 11,946,065

Languages: French, Sudanic tribal dialects
Religions: Muslim, indigenous beliefs, Christian

Burma
See **Myanmar.**

Burundi
Area: 27,830 km² (10,745 mi²)
Capital: Bujumbura
Government: Republic
Population: 6,054,714
Languages: Kirundi, French, Swahili
Religions: Roman Catholic, indigenous beliefs, Protestant, Muslim

Cambodia
Area: 181,040 km² (69,900 mi²)
Capital: Phnom Penh
Government: Constitutional monarchy
Population: 12,212,306
Languages: Khmer, French
Religions: Theravada Buddhist

Cameroon
Area: 475,440 km² (183,567 mi²)
Capital: Yaoundé
Government: Unitary republic
Population: 15,421,937
Languages: English, French, African languages
Religions: Indigenous beliefs, Christian, Muslim

Canada
Area: 9,976,140 km² (3,851,788 mi²)
Capital: Ottawa
Government: Confederation, with parliamentary democracy
Population: 31,278,097
Languages: English, French
Religions: Roman Catholic, United Church, Anglican

Cape Verde
Area: 4,030 km² (1,556 mi²)
Capital: Praia
Government: Republic
Population: 401,343
Languages: Portuguese, Crioulo
Religions: Roman Catholic and indigenous beliefs

Cayman Islands
Area: 260 km² (100 mi²)
Capital: George Town
Government: Dependent territory of United Kingdom
Population: 34,763
Language: English
Religions: United Church, Anglican, Baptist, Roman Catholic

Central African Republic
Area: 622,980 km² (240,533 mi²)
Capital: Bangui
Government: Military republic
Population: 3,512,751
Languages: French, Sangho, Arabic, Hunsa, Swahili
Religions: Christian (with animist beliefs), indigenous beliefs, Muslim

Chad
Area: 1,284,000 km² (495,752 mi²)
Capital: N'Djamena
Government: Republic
Population: 8,824,504
Languages: French, Arabic, Sara, Sango
Religions: Muslim, Christian, indigenous beliefs/animism

Chile
Area: 756,950 km² (292,258 mi²)
Capital: Santiago
Government: Republic
Population: 15,152,797
Language: Spanish
Religions: Roman Catholic, Protestant

China
Area: 9,596,960 km² (3,705,386 mi²)
Capital: Beijing
Government: Communist
Population: 1,261,832,482
Languages: Mandarin, Yue, Wu, Minbei, Minnan, Xiang, Gan, Hakka dialects, minority languages
Religions: Officially atheist; Confucianist, Taoist, Buddhist, Muslim, Christian

Christmas Island
Area: 135 km² (52 mi²)
Capital: The Settlement
Government: Territory of Australia
Population: 2,195
Language: English
Religions: Buddhist, Muslim, Christian

Colombia
Area: 1,138,910 km² (439,733 mi²)
Capital: Bogotá
Government: Republic
Population: 39,685,655
Language: Spanish
Religion: Roman Catholic

Comoros
Area: 2,170 km² (838 mi²)
Capital: Moroni
Government: Independent republic
Population: 578,400
Languages: Arabic, French, Cormorian
Religions: Sunni Muslim, Roman Catholic

Congo, Democratic Republic of (formerly Zaire)
Area: 2,345,410 km² (905,563 mi²)
Capital: Kinshasa
Government: Republic
Population: 51,964,999
Languages: French, Lingala, Swahili, Kingwana, Kikongo, Tshiluba
Religions: Roman Catholic, Protestant, Kimbanguist, Muslim, indigenous beliefs

Congo, Republic of the
Area: 342,000 km² (132,046 mi²)
Capital: Brazzaville
Government: Republic
Population: 2,830,961
Languages: French, Lingala, Kikongo
Religions: Christian, animist, Muslim

Cook Islands
Area: 240 km² (93 mi²)
Capital: Avarua
Government: Self-governing in association with New Zealand
Population: 19,989
Language: English
Religion: Cook Islands Christian Church

Costa Rica
Area: 51,100 km² (19,730 mi²)
Capital: San José
Government: Democratic republic
Population: 3,710,558
Languages: Spanish, English
Religion: Roman Catholic

Croatia
Area: 56,524 km² (21,824 mi²)
Capital: Zagreb
Government: Republic
Population: 4,282,216
Language: Serbo-Croatian
Religion: Roman Catholic

Cuba
Area: 110,860 km² (42,803 mi²)
Capital: Havana
Government: Communist
Population: 11,141,997
Language: Spanish
Religions: Roman Catholic, Orthodox

Cyprus
Area: 9,250 km² (3,571 mi²)
Capital: Nicosia

The World

Government: Republic; northern part administered
by Turkey
Population: 758,363
Languages: Greek, Turkish, English
Religions: Greek Orthodox, Muslim, Armenian,
Maronite

The Czech Republic
Area: 78,864 km² (30,342 mi²)
Capital: Prague
Government: Parliamentary democracy
Population: 10,272,179
Languages: Czech, Slovak
Religions: Roman Catholic, Czech Brethren

Denmark
Area: 43,070 km² (16,629 mi²)
Capital: Copenhagen
Government: Constitutional monarchy
Population: 5,336,394
Languages: Danish, Faroese, Greenlandic, German
Religions: Evangelical Lutheran, other Protestant faiths,
Roman Catholic

Djibouti
Area: 22,000 km² (8,494 mi²)
Capital: Djibouti
Government: Republic
Population: 451,442
Languages: French, Arabic, Somali, Afar
Religions: Muslim, Christian

Dominica
Area: 750 km² (290 mi²)
Capital: Roseau
Government: Parliamentary democracy
Population: 71,540
Languages: English, French patois
Religions: Roman Catholic, Methodist, Pentecostal,
Seventh-Day Adventist, Baptist

Dominican Republic
Area: 48,730 km² (18,815 mi²)
Capital: Santo Domingo
Government: Republic
Population: 8,442,533
Language: Spanish
Religion: Roman Catholic

Ecuador
Area: 283,560 km² (109,483 mi²)
Capital: Quito
Government: Republic
Population: 12,920,092
Languages: Spanish, Indian languages (especially
Quechua)
Religion: Roman Catholic

Egypt
Area: 1,001,450 km² (386,660 mi²)
Capital: Cairo
Government: Republic
Population: 68,359,979
Languages: Arabic, English, French
Religions: Muslim, Coptic Christian

El Salvador
Area: 21,040 km² (8,124 mi²)
Capital: San Salvador
Government: Republic
Population: 6,122,515
Languages: Spanish, Nahua
Religions: Roman Catholic, Protestant Evangelical

Equatorial Guinea
Area: 28,050 km² (10,830 mi²)
Capital: Malabo
Government: Republic
Population: 474,214
Languages: Spanish, French, Fang, Bubi, Ibo
Religion: Roman Catholic

Eritrea
Area: 123,300 km² (45,754 mi²)
Capital: Asmara
Government: In transition
Population: 4,135,933
Languages: Afar, Bilen, Kunama, Nara, Arabic,
Tobedawi, Saho, Tigre, Tigrinya
Religions: Muslim, Eritrean Orthodox Christian

Estonia
Area: 45,100 km² (17,413 mi²)
Capital: Tallinn
Government: Republic
Population: 1,431,471
Languages: Estonian, Russian
Religions: Lutheran, Russian Orthodox

Ethiopia
Area: 1,133,380 km² (437,600 mi²)
Capital: Addis Ababa
Government: Constitutional republic
Population: 64,117,452
Languages: Amharic, Tigrinya, Orominga, Guaraginga,
Somali, Arabic, English
Religions: Muslim, Ethiopian Orthodox, animist

Falkland Islands
Area: 12,170 km² (4,699 mi²)
Capital: Stanley
Government: Dependent territory of United Kingdom
Population: 2,805
Language: English
Religions: Anglican, Roman Catholic

Faroe Islands
Area: 1,400 km² (541 mi²)
Capital: Tórshavn
Government: Self-governing overseas administrative
    division of Denmark
Population: 45,296
Languages: Faroese, Danish
Religion: Evangelical Lutheran

Fiji
Area: 18,270 km² (7,054 mi²)
Capital: Suva
Government: Military republic
Population: 832,494
Languages: English, Fijian, Hindustani
Religions: Christian, Hindu, Muslim

Finland
Area: 337,030 km² (130,127 mi²)
Capital: Helsinki
Government: Republic
Population: 5,167,486
Languages: Finnish, Swedish, Lapp, Russian
Religions: Evangelical Lutheran, Greek Orthodox

France
Area: 547,030 km² (211,208 mi²)
Capital: Paris
Government: Republic
Population: 59,329,691
Languages: French, regional dialects
Religions: Roman Catholic, Protestant, Jewish, Muslim

French Guiana
Area: 83,534 km² (32,253 mi²)
Capital: Cayenne
Government: Overseas department of France
Population: 172,605
Language: French
Religion: Roman Catholic

French Polynesia
Area: 4,000 km² (1,544 mi²)
Capital: Papeete
Government: Overseas territory of France
Population: 249,110
Languages: French, Tahitian
Religions: Protestant, Roman Catholic

Gabon
Area: 267,670 km² (103,347 mi²)
Capital: Libreville
Government: Republic
Population: 1,208,436
Languages: French, Fang, Myene, Bateke,
    Bapounou/Eschira, Bandjabi
Religions: Christian, animist, Muslim

The Gambia
Area: 11,300 km² (4,363 mi²)
Capital: Banjul
Government: Republic
Population: 1,367,124
Languages: English, Mandinka, Wolof, Fula, local
    dialects
Religions: Muslim, Christian, indigenous beliefs

Georgia
Area: 69,699 km² (26,911 mi²)
Capital: Tbilisi
Government: Republic
Population: 5,019,538
Languages: Georgian, Russian
Religions: Georgian Orthodox

Germany
Area: 356,910 km² (137,803 mi²)
Capital: Berlin
Government: Federal republic
Population: 82,797,408
Language: German
Religions: Protestant, Roman Catholic

Ghana
Area: 238,540 km² (92,100 mi²)
Capital: Accra
Government: Republic
Population: 19,533,560
Languages: English, Akan, Moshi-Dagomba, Ewe,
    Ga-Adangbe
Religions: Indigenous beliefs, Muslim, Christian

Gibraltar
Area: 6.5 km² (2.5 mi²)
Capital: Gibraltar
Government: Dependent territory of United Kingdom
Population: 27,578
Languages: English, Spanish, Italian, Portuguese,
    Russian
Religions: Roman Catholic, Anglican, Muslim, Jewish

Greece
Area: 131,940 km² (50,942 mi²)
Capital: Athens
Government: Presidential parliamentary
Population: 10,601,527
Languages: Greek, English, French
Religions: Greek Orthodox, Muslim

Greenland
Area: 2,175,600 km² (839,999 mi²)
Capital: Nuuk (Godthåb)
Government: Self-governing overseas administrative
    division of Denmark
Population: 56,309

The World

Languages: Eskimo dialects, Danish
Religion: Evangelical Lutheran

Grenada
Area: 340 km² (131 mi²)
Capital: St. George's
Government: Parliamentary democracy affiliated with
  United Kingdom
Population: 89,312
Languages: English, French patois
Religions: Roman Catholic, Anglican, other Protestant
  faiths

Guadeloupe
Area: 1,780 km² (687 mi²)
Capital: Basse-Terre
Government: Overseas department of France
Population: 426,493
Languages: French, Creole
Religions: Roman Catholic, Hindu, pagan African

Guatemala
Area: 108,890 km² (42,042 mi²)
Capital: Guatemala City
Government: Republic
Population: 12,639,939
Languages: Spanish, Quiche, Cakchiquel, Kekchi, other
  Indian dialects
Religions: Roman Catholic, Protestant, traditional
  Mayan

Guernsey
Area: 64 km² (25 mi²)
Capital: St. Peter Port
Government: British crown dependency
Population: 65,386
Languages: English, French, Norman-French
Religions: Anglican, Roman Catholic, other Protestant
  faiths

Guinea
Area: 245,860 km² (94,927 mi²)
Capital: Conakry
Government: Republic
Population: 7,466,200
Languages: French, tribal languages
Religions: Muslim, Christian, indigenous beliefs

Guinea-Bissau
Area: 36,120 km² (13,948 mi²)
Capital: Bissau
Government: Republic
Population: 1,285,715
Languages: Portuguese, Criolo, African languages
Religions: Indigenous beliefs, Muslim, Christian

Guyana
Area: 214,970 km² (83,000 mi²)
Capital: Georgetown
Government: Republic
Population: 697,286
Languages: English, Amerindian dialects
Religions: Christian, Hindu, Muslim

Haiti
Area: 27,750 km² (10,714 mi²)
Capital: Port-au-Prince
Government: Republic
Population: 6,867,995
Languages: French, Creole
Religions: Roman Catholic/voodoo, Protestant

Honduras
Area: 112,090 km² (43,278 mi²)
Capital: Tegucigalpa
Government: Republic
Population: 6,249,598
Languages: Spanish, Amerindian dialects
Religions: Roman Catholic, Protestant

Hong Kong
Area: 1,077 km² (416 mi²)
Capital: None
Government: Special administrative region of China
Population: 7,120,000
Languages: Cantonese, English
Religions: Local religions, Christian

Hungary
Area: 93,030 km² (35,919 mi²)
Capital: Budapest
Government: Republic
Population: 10,138,844
Language: Hungarian (Magyar)
Religions: Roman Catholic, Calvinist, Lutheran

Iceland
Area: 103,000 km² (39,768 mi²)
Capital: Reykjavík
Government: Republic
Population: 276,365
Languages: Icelandic
Religions: Evangelical Lutheran, other Protestant faiths,
  Roman Catholic

India
Area: 3,287,590 km² (1,269,338 mi²)
Capital: New Delhi
Government: Federal republic
Population: 1,014,003,817
Languages: Hindi, English, Bengali, Telugu, Marathi,
  Tamil, Urdu, Gujarati, Malayalan, Kannada, Oriya,

Punjabi, Assamese, Kashmiri, Sindhi, Sanskrit, Hindustani
Religions: Hindu, Muslim, Christian, Sikh, Buddhist, Jains

Indonesia
Area: 1,904,570 km² (735,272 mi²)
Capital: Jakarta
Government: Republic
Population: 224,784,210
Languages: Bahasa Indonesian, Javanese, English, Dutch
Religions: Muslim, Protestant, Roman Catholic, Hindu, Buddhist

Iran
Area: 1,648,000 km² (636,293 mi²)
Capital: Teheran
Government: Theocratic republic
Population: 65,619,636
Languages: Farsi, Turk, Kurdish, Arabic, Luri, Baloch
Religions: Shi'a Muslim, Sunni Muslim, Zoroastrian, Jewish, Christian, Baha'i

Iraq
Area: 434,920 km² (167,923 mi²)
Capital: Baghdad
Government: Republic
Population: 22,675,617
Languages: Arabic, Kurdish, Assyrian, Armenian
Religions: Shi'a Muslim, Sunni Muslim, Christian

Ireland
Area: 70,280 km² (27,135 mi²)
Capital: Dublin
Government: Republic
Population: 3,797,257
Languages: English, Irish (Gaelic)
Religions: Roman Catholic, Anglican

Israel
Area (excluding occupied territories): 20,770 km² (8,019 mi²)
Capital: Jerusalem
Government: Parliamentary democracy
Population: 5,842,454 (excluding occupied territories)
Languages: Hebrew, Arabic, English
Religions: Jewish, Muslim, Christian, Druze
See also **West Bank and Gaza Strip.**

Italy
Area: 301,230 km² (116,305 mi²)
Capital: Rome
Government: Republic
Population: 57,634,827
Languages: Italian, German, French, Slovene
Religion: Roman Catholic

Ivory Coast
Area: 322,460 km² (124,502 mi²)
Capital: Abidjan (also Yamoussoukro)
Government: Republic
Population: 15,980,950
Languages: French, Dioula, tribal languages
Religions: Muslim, indigenous beliefs, Christian

Jamaica
Area: 10,990 km² (4,243 mi²)
Capital: Kingston
Government: Parliamentary democracy affiliated with United Kingdom
Population: 2,652,689
Languages: English, Creole
Religions: Protestant, Roman Catholic, spiritualist cults

Japan
Area: 377,835 km² (145,882 mi²)
Capital: Tokyo
Government: Constitutional monarchy
Population: 126,549,976
Language: Japanese
Religions: Shinto, Buddhist, Christian

Jersey
Area: 117 km² (45 mi²)
Capital: Saint Helier
Government: British crown dependency
Population: 89,721
Languages: English, French, Norman-French
Religions: Anglican, other Protestant faiths, Roman Catholic

Jordan
Area: 91,880 km² (35,475 mi²) (excluding West Bank)
Capital: Amman
Government: Constitutional monarchy
Population: 4,998,564 (excluding West Bank)
Languages: Arabic, English
Religions: Sunni Muslim, Christian

Kazakhstan
Area: 2,717,428 km² (1,049,200 mi²)
Capital: Alma Alta
Government: Constitutional republic
Population: 16,733,227
Languages: Kazakh, Russian
Religions: Muslim, Russian Orthodox

Kenya
Area: 582,650 km² (224,961 mi²)
Capital: Nairobi
Government: Republic
Population: 30,339,770
Languages: English, Swahili, local languages
Religions: Protestant, Roman Catholic, indigenous beliefs, Muslim

Kiribati
Area: 710 km² (274 mi²)
Capital: Tarawa
Government: Republic
Population: 91,985
Languages: English, Gilbertese
Religions: Roman Catholic, Protestant, Seventh-Day
  Adventist, Baha'i

*There are two independent nations
smaller than New York City's
Central Park: Vatican City and
Monaco. Each is less than one
square mile.*

**Korea, Democratic People's Republic of
  (North Korea)**
Area: 120,540 km² (46,540 mi²)
Capital: Pyongyang
Government: Communist
Population: 21,687,550
Language: Korean
Religions: Buddhist, Confucianist, Ch'ondogyo

Korea, Republic of (South Korea)
Area: 98,480 km² (38,023 mi²)
Capital: Seoul
Government: Republic
Population: 47,470,969
Language: Korean
Religions: Confucianist, Christian, Buddhist, Shamanist,
  Ch'ondogyo

Kuwait
Area: 17,820 km² (6,880 mi²)
Capital: Kuwait City
Government: Nominal constitutional monarchy
Population: 1,973,572
Languages: Arabic, English
Religions: Sunni Muslim, Shi'a Muslim, Christian,
  Hindu, Parsi

Kyrgyzstan
Area: 198,509 km² (76,642 mi²)
Capital: Bishkek
Government: Constitutional republic
Population: 4,685,230
Languages: Kirghiz, Russian
Religions: Muslim, Russian Orthodox

Laos
Area: 236,800 km² (91,428 mi²)
Capital: Vientiane
Government: Communist

Population: 5,497,459
Languages: Lao, French, English
Religions: Buddhist, animist

Latvia
Area: 63,701 km² (24,595 mi²)
Capital: Riga
Government: Republic
Population: 2,404,926
Languages: Lettish, Lithuanian, Russian
Religions: Lutheran, Russian Orthodox, Catholic

Lebanon
Area: 10,400 km² (4,015 mi²)
Capital: Beirut
Government: Republic
Population: 3,578,036
Languages: Arabic, French, Armenian, English
Religions: Muslim and Christian, each divided into sects
  (17 in all)

Lesotho
Area: 30,350 km² (11,718 mi²)
Capital: Maseru
Government: Modified constitutional monarchy
Population: 2,143,141
Languages: Sesotho, English, Zulu, Xhosa
Religions: Christian, indigenous beliefs

Liberia
Area: 111,370 km² (43,000 mi²)
Capital: Monrovia
Government: Republic
Population: 3,164,156
Languages: English, Niger-Congo languages
Religions: Indigenous beliefs, Christian, Muslim

Libya
Area: 1,759,540 km² (679,358 mi²)
Capital: Tripoli
Government: Military dictatorship
Population: 5,115,450
Languages: Arabic, Italian, English
Religion: Sunni Muslim

Liechtenstein
Area: 160 km² (62 mi²)
Capital: Vaduz
Government: Constitutional monarchy
Population: 32,204
Languages: German, Alemannic
Religions: Roman Catholic, Protestant

Lithuania
Area: 65,190 km² (25,170 mi²)
Capital: Vilnius
Government: Republic

Population: 3,620,756
Languages: Lithuanian, Polish, Russian
Religions: Roman Catholic

Luxembourg
Area: 2,586 km² (998 mi²)
Capital: Luxembourg
Government: Constitutional monarchy
Population: 437,389
Languages: Luxembourgish, German, French, English
Religions: Roman Catholic, Protestant

Macau
Area: 16 km² (6 mi²)
Capital: Macau
Government: Overseas territory of Portugal until 1999
Population: 496,837
Languages: Portuguese, Cantonese
Religions: Buddhist, Roman Catholic

Macedonia
Area: 25,713 km² (9,928 mi²)
Capital: Skopje
Government: Republic
Population: 2,041,467
Languages: Macedonian, Albanian, Serbo-Croatian
Religions: Eastern Orthodox, Muslim

Madagascar
Area: 587,040 km² (226,656 mi²)
Capital: Antananarivo
Government: Republic
Population: 15,506,472
Languages: French, Malagasy
Religions: Indigenous beliefs, Christian, Muslim

Malawi
Area: 118,480 km² (45,745 mi²)
Capital: Lilongwe
Government: Constitutional republic
Population: 10,385,849
Languages: English, Chichewa, Tombuka
Religions: Protestant, Roman Catholic, Muslim, indigenous beliefs

Malaysia
Area: 329,750 km² (127,316 mi²)
Capital: Kuala Lumpur
Government: Constitutional monarchy with hereditary rulers in peninsular states
Population: 21,793,293
Languages: Malay, English, Chinese dialects, Tamil, Hakka dialects, tribal languages
Religions: Muslim, Buddhist, Hindu, Confucianist, Christian

Maldives
Area: 300 km² (116 mi²)
Capital: Male
Government: Republic
Population: 301,475
Languages: Divehi, English
Religion: Sunni Muslim

Mali
Area: 1,240,000 km² (478,764 mi²)
Capital: Bamako
Government: Republic
Population: 10,685,948
Languages: French, Bambara
Religions: Muslim, indigenous beliefs, Christian

Malta
Area: 320 km² (124 mi²)
Capital: Valletta
Government: Parliamentary democracy
Population: 391,670
Languages: Maltese, English
Religion: Roman Catholic

Man, Isle of
Area: 588 km² (227 mi²)
Capital: Douglas
Government: British crown dependency
Population: 73,112
Languages: English, Manx Gaelic
Religions: Anglican, other Protestant faiths, Roman Catholic

Martinique
Area: 1,100 km² (425 mi²)
Capital: Fort-de-France
Government: Overseas department of France
Population: 414,516
Languages: French, Creole patois
Religions: Roman Catholic, Hindu, pagan African

Mauritania
Area: 1,030,700 km² (397,953 mi²)
Capital: Nouakchott
Government: Republic
Population: 2,667,859
Languages: Hasaniya Arabic, French, Toucouleur, Fula, Sarakole, Wolof
Religion: Muslim

Mauritius
Area: 1,860 km² (718 mi²)
Capital: Port Louis
Government: Parliamentary democracy affiliated with United Kingdom
Population: 1,179,368

Languages: English, Creole, French, Hindi, Urdu, Hakka, Bojpoori
Religions: Hindu, Roman Catholic, Anglican, Muslim

Mayotte
Area: 375 km² (145 mi²)
Capital: Dzaoudzi
Government: Territorial collectivity of France
Population: 155,911
Languages: Mahorian, French
Religions: Muslim, Christian

Mexico
Area: 1,972,550 km² (761,602 mi²)
Capital: Mexico City
Government: Federal republic
Population: 100,349,766
Language: Spanish, Mayan dialects
Religions: Roman Catholic, Protestant

Moldova
Area: 33,701 km² (13,012 mi²)
Capital: Kishinev
Government: Republic
Population: 4,430,654
Languages: Romanian, Russian
Religions: Russian Orthodox, Seventh-Day Adventist

Monaco
Area: 1.9 km² (.7 mi²)
Capital: Monaco
Government: Constitutional monarchy
Population: 31,693
Languages: French, English, Italian, Monegasque
Religion: Roman Catholic

Mongolia
Area: 1,565,000 km² (604,247 mi²)
Capital: Ulaanbaatar
Government: Republic
Population: 2,616,383
Languages: Khalkha Mongol, Turkic, Russian, Chinese
Religions: Tibetan Buddhist, Muslim

Montserrat
Area: 100 km² (39 mi²)
Capital: Plymouth
Government: Dependent territory of United Kingdom
Population: 6,409
Language: English
Religions: Anglican, other Protestant faiths, Roman Catholic

Morocco
Area: 446,550 km² (172,413 mi²)
Capital: Rabat
Government: Constitutional monarchy

Population: 30,122,350
Languages: Arabic, French, Berber dialects
Religions: Muslim, Christian, Jewish

Mozambique
Area: 801,950 km² (309,633 mi²)
Capital: Maputo
Government: Republic
Population: 19,104,696
Languages: Portuguese, indigenous languages
Religions: Indigenous beliefs, Christian, Muslim

Myanmar (formerly Burma)
Area: 676,550 km² (261,216 mi²)
Capital: Yangon (Rangoon)
Government: Military
Population: 41,734,853
Languages: Burmese, ethnic languages
Religions: Buddhist, Christian, Muslim, animist beliefs

Namibia
Area: 824,290 km² (318,258 mi²)
Capital: Windhoek
Government: Republic
Population: 1,771,327
Languages: Afrikaans, German, English, indigenous languages
Religions: Christian, indigenous beliefs

Nauru
Area: 20 km² (8 mi²)
Capital: Yaren
Government: Republic
Population: 11,845
Languages: Nauruan, English
Religions: Protestant, Roman Catholic

Nepal
Area: 140,800 km² (54,363 mi²)
Capital: Kathmandu
Government: Constitutional monarchy
Population: 24,702,119
Languages: Nepali, local languages
Religions: Hindu, Buddhist, Muslim

The Netherlands
Area: 41,526 km² (16,033 mi²)
Capital: Amsterdam and The Hague
Government: Constitutional monarchy
Population: 15,892,237
Language: Dutch
Religions: Roman Catholic, Protestant

Netherlands Antilles
Area: 800 km² (313 mi²)
Capital: Willemstad (on Curacao)
Government: Autonomous territory of the Netherlands

Population: 207,827
Languages: Dutch, Papiamento, English, Spanish
Religions: Roman Catholic, Protestant, Jewish, Seventh-Day Adventist

New Caledonia
Area: 19,060 km² (7,359 mi²)
Capital: Nouméa
Government: Overseas territory of France
Population: 201,816
Languages: French, Melanesian-Polynesian dialects
Religions: Roman Catholic, Protestant

New Zealand
Area: 268,680 km² (103,737 mi²)
Capital: Wellington
Government: Parliamentary democracy affiliated with United Kingdom
Population: 3,819,762
Languages: English, Maori
Religions: Anglican, Presbyterian, Roman Catholic

Nicaragua
Area: 129,494 km² (49,998 mi²)
Capital: Managua
Government: Republic
Population: 4,812,569
Languages: Spanish, English, Amerindian dialects
Religion: Roman Catholic

Niger
Area: 1,267,000 km² (489,189 mi²)
Capital: Niamey
Government: Republic (under military control)
Population: 10,075,571
Languages: French, Hausa, Djerma
Religions: Muslim, indigenous beliefs, Christian

Nigeria
Area: 923,770 km² (356,668 mi²)
Capital: Lagos
Government: Republic
Population: 123,337,822
Languages: English, Hausa, Yoruba, Ibo, Fulani
Religions: Muslim, Christian, indigenous beliefs

Niue
Area: 260 km² (100 mi²)
Capital: Alofi
Government: Self-governing territory affiliated with New Zealand
Population: 1,837
Languages: Polynesian (Tongan-Samoan dialect), English
Religions: Ekalesia Nieu, Mormon

Norfolk Island
Area: 36 km² (13 mi²)
Capital: Kingston
Government: Territory of Australia
Population: 2,285
Languages: English, Norfolk
Religions: Anglican, other Protestant faiths, Roman Catholic, Seventh-Day Adventist

Norway
Area: 324,220 km² (125,181 mi²)
Capital: Oslo
Government: Constitutional monarchy
Population: 4,481,162
Languages: Norwegian, Lapp, Finnish
Religions: Evangelical Lutheran, other Protestant faiths, Roman Catholic

Oman
Area: 212,460 km² (82,031 mi²)
Capital: Muscat
Government: Absolute monarchy
Population: 2,533,389
Languages: Arabic, English, Baluchi, Urdu
Religions: Ibadhi Muslim, Sunni Muslim, Shi'a Muslim, Hindu

Pakistan
Area: 803,940 km² (310,401 mi²)
Capital: Islamabad
Government: Federal republic
Population: 141,553,775
Languages: Urdu, English, Punjabi, Sindhi, Pushtu, Baluchi
Religions: Muslim, Christian, Hindu

Palau
Area: 458 km² (177 mi²)
Capital: Koror
Population: 18,766
Government: Parliamentary republic
Languages: English, Palauan
Religions: Christian, Modekngei

Panama
Area: 78,200 km² (30,193 mi²)
Capital: Panama City
Government: Centralized republic
Population: 2,808,268
Languages: Spanish, English
Religions: Roman Catholic, Protestant

Papua New Guinea
Area: 461,690 km² (178,259 mi²)
Capital: Port Moresby
Government: Parliamentary democracy affiliated with United Kingdom

Population: 4,926,984
Languages: English, Motu, local dialects
Religions: Roman Catholic, Protestant, indigenous
  beliefs

Paraguay
Area: 406,750 km² (157,046 mi²)
Capital: Asunción
Government: Republic
Population: 5,585,828
Languages: Spanish, Guarani
Religions: Roman Catholic, Mennonite, other
  Protestant faiths

Peru
Area: 1,285,220 km² (496,223 mi²)
Capital: Lima
Government: Republic
Population: 27,012,899
Languages: Spanish, Quechua, Aymara
Religion: Roman Catholic

Philippines
Area: 300,000 km² (115,830 mi²)
Capital: Manila
Government: Republic
Population: 81,159,644
Languages: Philipino (Tagalog), English
Religions: Roman Catholic, Muslim, Buddhist

Poland
Area: 312,680 km² (120,727 mi²)
Capital: Warsaw
Government: Democratic state
Population: 36,646,023
Language: Polish
Religions: Roman Catholic, Russian Orthodox, Catholic

Portugal
Area: 92,080 km² (35,552 mi²)
Capital: Lisbon
Government: Republic
Population: 10,048,232
Language: Portuguese
Religions: Roman Catholic, Protestant

Qatar
Area: 11,000 km² (4,247 mi²)
Capital: Doha
Government: Traditional monarchy
Population: 744,483
Languages: Arabic, English
Religion: Muslim

Réunion
Area: 2,510 km² (969 mi²)
Capital: Saint-Denis

Government: Overseas department of France
Population: 720,934
Languages: French, Creole
Religion: Roman Catholic

Romania
Area: 237,500 km² (91,699 mi²)
Capital: Bucharest
Government: Republic
Population: 22,411,121
Languages: Romanian, Hungarian, German
Religions: Romanian Orthodox, Roman Catholic,
  Protestant, Muslim, Jewish

Russia
Area: 17,075,352 km² (6,592,800 mi²)
Capital: Moscow
Government: Constitutional republic
Population: 146,001,176
Language: Russian
Religions: Russian Orthodox, Baptist, Jewish, Muslim

Rwanda
Area: 26,340 km² (10,170 mi²)
Capital: Kigali
Government: Republic (under military control)
Population: 7,229,129
Languages: Kinyarwanda, French, Kiswahili, English
Religions: Roman Catholic, Protestant, indigenous
  beliefs, Muslim

St. Helena
Area: 122 km² (47 mi²)
Capital: Jamestown
Government: Dependent territory of the United
  Kingdom
Population: 7,197
Language: English
Religions: Anglican, other Protestant faiths, Roman
  Catholic

St. Kitts and Nevis
Area: 269 km² (104 mi²)
Capital: Basseterre
Government: Constitutional monarchy affiliated with
  United Kingdom
Population: 38,819
Language: English
Religions: Anglican, other Protestant faiths, Roman
  Catholic

St. Lucia
Area: 620 km² (239 mi²)
Capital: Castries
Government: Parliamentary democracy affiliated with
  United Kingdom
Population: 156,260

The World

Languages: English, French patois
Religions: Roman Catholic, Protestant, Anglican

St. Pierre and Miquelon
Area: 242 km² (93 mi²)
Capital: Saint-Pierre
Government: Territorial collectivity of France
Population: 6,896
Language: French
Religion: Roman Catholic

St. Vincent and the Grenadines
Area: 340 km² (131 mi²)
Capital: Kingstown
Government: Constitutional monarchy affiliated with
    United Kingdom
Population: 115,461
Languages: English, French patois
Religions: Anglican, other Protestant faiths, Roman
    Catholic, Seventh-Day Adventist

Samoa
Area: 2,860 km² (1,104 mi²)
Capital: Apia
Government: Constitutional monarchy
Population: 179,466
Languages: Samoan, English
Religions: Congregational, Roman Catholic, other
    Protestant faiths

San Marino
Area: 60 km² (23 mi²)
Capital: San Marino
Government: Republic
Population: 26,937
Language: Italian
Religion: Roman Catholic

São Tome and Principé
Area: 960 km² (371 mi²)
Capital: São Tome and Principé
Government: Republic
Population: 159,883
Language: Portuguese, Fang
Religions: Roman Catholic, Evangelical Protestant,
    Seventh-Day Adventist

Saudi Arabia
Area: 2,149,690 km² (829,995 mi²)
Capital: Riyadh
Government: Monarchy
Population: 22,023,506
Language: Arabic
Religion: Muslim

"The World's Major Religions" in chapter 9;
"Frequently Used Foreign Words and
Phrases" in chapter 13
Go to

Senegal
Area: 196,190 km² (75,748 mi²)
Capital: Dakar
Government: Republic
Population: 9,987,494
Languages: French, Wolof, Pulaar, Diola, Mandingo
Religions: Muslim, indigenous beliefs, Christian

Seychelles
Area: 455 km² (176 mi²)
Capital: Victoria
Government: Republic
Population: 79,326
Languages: English, French, Creole
Religions: Roman Catholic, Anglican

Sierra Leone
Area: 71,740 km² (27,699 mi²)
Capital: Freetown
Government: Republic
Population: 5,232,624
Languages: English, Mende, Krio, Temne
Religions: Muslim, indigenous beliefs, Christian

Singapore
Area: 633 km² (244 mi²)
Capital: Singapore
Government: Republic
Population: 4,151,720
Languages: Chinese, Tamil, Malay, English
Religions: Buddhist, Muslim, Christian, Hindu, Sikh,
    Taoist Confucianist

Slovakia
Area: 49,035 km² (18,928 mi²)
Capital: Bratislava
Government: Parliamentary democracy
Population: 5,407,956
Languages: Slovak, Hungarian
Religions: Roman Catholic, Protestant, Orthodox,
    Uniate

Slovenia
Area: 20,246 km² (7,817 mi²)
Capital: Ljubljana
Government: Republic
Population: 1,927,593
Languages: Slovene, Serbo-Croatian
Religions: Roman Catholic, Protestant

Solomon Islands
Area: 28,450 km² (10,985 mi²)
Capital: Honiara
Government: Independent parliamentary state within
    British Commonwealth
Population: 466,194

Languages: Melanesian, English, local dialects
Religions: Anglican, Roman Catholic, other Protestant
  faiths

Somalia
Area: 637,660 km² (246,201 mi²)
Capital: Mogadishu
Government: In transition
Population: 7,253,137
Languages: Somali, Arabic, Italian, English
Religion: Sunni Muslim

South Africa
Area: 1,221,040 km² (471,444 mi²)
Capital: Pretoria, Cape Town, and Bloemfontein
Government: Republic
Population: 42,421,021
Languages: Afrikaans, English, Zulu, Xhosa, Tswana
Religions: Christian, Hindu, Muslim

Spain
Area: 504,750 km² (194,884 mi²)
Capital: Madrid
Government: Parliamentary monarchy
Population: 39,996,671
Languages: Castilian Spanish, Catalan, Galician, Basque
Religion: Roman Catholic

Sri Lanka
Area: 65,610 km² (25,332 mi²)
Capital: Colombo
Government: Republic
Population: 19,238,575
Languages: Sinhala, Tamil, English
Religions: Buddhist, Hindu, Christian, Muslim

Sudan
Area: 2,505,810 km² (967,493 mi²)
Capital: Khartoum
Government: Republic, with military
Population: 35,079,814
Languages: Arabic, Nubian, Ta Bedawie, Nilotic and
  Nilo-Hamitic dialects, Sudanic dialects, English
Religions: Sunni Muslim, indigenous beliefs, Christian

Suriname
Area: 163,270 km² (63,039 mi²)
Capital: Paramaribo
Government: Republic
Population: 431,303
Languages: Dutch, English, Sranan Tongo, Javanese
Religions: Hindu, Muslim, Roman Catholic, Protestant

Svalbard
Area: 62,049 km² (23,597 mi²)
Capital: Longyearbyen
Government: Territory of Norway

Population: 3,231
Languages: Russian, Norwegian
Religion: Evangelical Lutheran

Swaziland
Area: 17,360 km² (6,703 mi²)
Capital: Mbabane
Government: Independent monarchy within British
  commonwealth
Population: 1,083,289
Languages: English, siSwati
Religions: Christian, indigenous beliefs

Sweden
Area: 449,960 km² (173,729 mi²)
Capital: Stockholm
Government: Constitutional monarchy
Population: 8,873,052
Languages: Swedish, Lapp, Finnish
Religions: Evangelical Lutheran, Roman Catholic

Switzerland
Area: 41,290 km² (15,942 mi²)
Capital: Bern
Government: Federal republic
Population: 7,262,372
Languages: German, French, Italian, Romansch
Religions: Roman Catholic, Protestant, Jewish

Syria
Area: 185,180 km² (71,498 mi²)
Capital: Damascus
Government: Military republic
Population: 16,305,659
Languages: Arabic, Kurdish, Armenian, Aramaic,
  Circassian, French
Religions: Sunni Muslim, Alawite, Druze, other Muslim
  sects, Christian

Taiwan
Area: 35,980 km² (13,892 mi²)
Capital: Taipei
Government: Republic
Population: 22,191,087
Languages: Mandarin Chinese, Taiwanese and Hakka
  dialects
Religions: Buddhist, Confucianist, Taoist, Christian

Tajikistan
Area: 139,909 km² (54,019 mi²)
Capital: Dushanbe
Government: Republic
Population: 6,440,732
Languages: Tadzhik, Russian
Religion: Muslim

Tanzania
Area: 945,090 km² (364,899 mi²)
Capital: Dar es Salaam (scheduled to move to Dodoma, 2005)
Government: Republic
Population: 35,306,126
Languages: Swahili, English
Religions: Christian, Muslim, indigenous beliefs

Thailand
Area: 514,000 km² (198,455 mi²)
Capital: Bangkok
Government: Constitutional monarchy
Population: 61,230,874
Languages: Thai, English, local dialects
Religions: Buddhist, Muslim

Togo
Area: 56,790 km² (21,927 mi²)
Capital: Lomé
Government: One-party republic
Population: 5,018,502
Languages: French, Ewe, Mina, Dagomba, Kabyè
Religions: Indigenous beliefs, Christian, Muslim

Tokelau
Area: 10 km² (4 mi²)
Capital: None (various local government agencies)
Government: Territory of New Zealand
Population: 1,503
Languages: Tokelauan, English
Religions: Congregational Christian Church, Roman Catholic

Tonga
Area: 748 km² (289 mi²)
Capital: Nuku'alofa
Government: Constitutional monarchy
Population: 102,321
Languages: Tongan, English
Religions: Free Wesleyan, Roman Catholic, Mormon

Trinidad and Tobago
Area: 5,130 km² (1,981 mi²)
Capital: Port-of-Spain
Government: Parliamentary democracy
Population: 1,175,523
Languages: English, Hindi, French, Spanish
Religions: Roman Catholic, Hindu, Protestant, Muslim

Tunisia
Area: 163,610 km² (63,170 mi²)
Capital: Tunis
Government: Republic
Population: 9,593,402
Languages: Arabic, French
Religions: Muslim, Christian, Jewish

Turkey
Area: 780,580 km² (301,382 mi²)
Capital: Ankara
Government: Republican parliamentary democracy
Population: 65,666,677
Languages: Turkish, Kurdish, Arabic
Religion: Muslim (mostly Sunni)

Turkmenistan
Area: 488,000 km² (188,417 mi²)
Capital: Ashkhabad
Government: Republic
Population: 4,518,268
Languages: Turkmen, Russian
Religion: Sunni Muslim, Eastern Orthodox

Turks and Caicos Islands
Area: 500 km² (193 mi²)
Capital: Grand Turk (Cockburn Town)
Government: Dependent territory of United Kingdom
Population: 17,502
Language: English
Religions: Baptist, Methodist, Anglican, Seventh-Day Adventist

Tuvalu
Area: 26 km² (10 mi²)
Capital: Funafuti
Government: Democracy affiliated with United Kingdom
Population: 10,838
Languages: Tuvaluan, English
Religion: Protestant

Uganda
Area: 236,040 km² (91,135 mi²)
Capital: Kampala
Government: One-party republic
Population: 23,317,560
Languages: English, Luganda, Swahili, Bantu and Nilotic languages
Religions: Roman Catholic, Protestant, Muslim, indigenous beliefs

Ukraine
Area: 603,729 km² (233,100 mi²)
Capital: Kiev
Government: Republic
Population: 49,153,027
Languages: Ukrainian, Russian
Religions: Russian Orthodox, Baptist, Roman Catholic, Jewish

United Arab Emirates
Area: 83,600 km² (32,278 mi²)
Capital: Abu Dhabi
Government: Federation of seven emirates

The World

Population: 2,369,153
Languages: Arabic, Farsi, English, Hindi, Urdu
Religions: Muslim, Christian, Hindu

United Kingdom
Area: 244,820 km² (94,525 mi²)
Capital: London
Government: Constitutional monarchy
Population: 59,508,382
Languages: English, Welsh, Scottish Gaelic
Religions: Anglican, other Protestant faiths, Roman
   Catholic, Jewish, Muslim

United States
Area: 9,629,046 km² (3,717,796 mi²)
Capital: Washington, D.C.
Government: Federal republic
Population: 275,562,673
Languages: English, Spanish
Religions: Protestant, Roman Catholic, Jewish

Uruguay
Area: 176,220 km² (68,039 mi²)
Capital: Montevideo
Government: Republic
Population: 3,334,074
Language: Spanish
Religions: Roman Catholic, Protestant, Jewish

Uzbekistan
Area: 447,293 km² (172,700 mi²)
Capital: Tashkent
Government: Republic
Population: 24,755,519
Languages: Uzbek, Russian
Religions: Muslim, Eastern Orthodox

Vanuatu
Area: 14,760 km² (5,699 mi²)
Capital: Port-Vila
Government: Republic
Population: 189,618
Languages: English, French, Bislama
Religions: Protestant, Roman Catholic, indigenous
   beliefs

Vatican City
Area: 0.438 km² (108.7 acres)
Capital: Vatican City
Government: Independent papal state
Population: 870
Languages: Italian, Latin
Religion: Roman Catholic

Venezuela
Area: 912,050 km² (352,143 mi²)
Capital: Caracas

Government: Republic
Population: 23,542,649
Languages: Spanish, Amerindian dialects, Portugeuse,
   Italian
Religion: Roman Catholic

Vietnam
Area: 329,560 km² (127,243 mi²)
Capital: Hanoi
Government: Communist
Population: 78,773,873
Languages: Vietnamese, French, Chinese, English,
   Khmer, tribal dialects
Religions: Buddhist, Confucianist, Taoist, Roman
   Catholic, indigenous beliefs, Muslim, Protestant

Wallis and Futuna
Area: 274 km² (106 mi²)
Capital: Mata-Utu
Government: Overseas territory of France
Population: 15,283
Languages: French, Wallisian
Religion: Roman Catholic

West Bank and Gaza Strip
Area: 6,240 km² (2,410 mi²)
Capital: None
Government: Israeli military rule
Population: 1,427,741 (excluding Israeli settlers)
Languages: Arabic, Hebrew, English
Religions: Muslim, Jewish, Christian

Western Sahara
Area: 2,860 km² (1,097 mi²)
Capital: None
Government: Moroccan administrative protectorate
Population: 222,631
Languages: Hassaniya Arabic, Moroccan Arabic
Religion: Muslim

Yemen
Area: 527,970 km² (203,849 mi²)
Capital: Sanaa
Government: Republic
Population: 17,479,206
Language: Arabic
Religions: Muslim, Christian, Hindu

Yugoslavia, Federal Republic of
(Consists of Serbia, the largest republic of
   preindependence Yugoslavia, and Montenegro, the
   smallest republic) This country has not been
   recognized by the United States.
Area: 102,173 km² (39,449 mi²)
Capital: Belgrade
Government: Federal republic

The World

Population: 10,662,087
Languages: Serbo-Croatian, Hungarian (Vojvodina), Albanian (Kosovo), Montenegrin
Religions: Serbian Orthodox, Muslim, Roman Catholic

Zambia
Area: 752,610 km² (290,583 mi²)
Capital: Lusaka
Government: Multiparty state
Population: 9,582,418
Languages: English, indigenous languages and dialects
Religions: Christian, Muslim, Hindu, indigenous beliefs

Zimbabwe
Area: 390,580 km² (150,803 mi²)
Capital: Harare
Government: Parliamentary democracy
Population: 11,342,521
Languages: English, Shona, Sindebele
Religions: Indigenous/Christian beliefs, Christian, indigenous beliefs, Muslim

GREAT EVENTS IN WORLD HISTORY

Throughout prehistory, antiquity, and the early Middle Ages, it is often difficult to place exact dates. Therefore, most of the dates in this time line up to the year A.D. 1000 should be considered approximate.

1,600,000 B.C. Earliest humanlike ancestors.
250,000 B.C. Earliest Homo sapiens.
70,000 B.C. Neanderthals use stone tools and fire.
40,000 B.C. Ice Age ends; Cro-Magnons migrate into Europe.
30,000 B.C. Neanderthals disappear.
28,000 B.C. Asians cross land bridge between Asia and America.
20,000 B.C. European cave art exists.
12,000 B.C. Dog domesticated from Asian wolf.
8000 B.C. Agriculture develops in Near East.
6500 B.C. Wheel invented by Sumerians.
6000 B.C. First true pottery made.
5000 B.C. Copper, first shapable metal, smelted in Persia.
4236 B.C. Earliest date on Egyptian calendar.
3760 B.C. Earliest date on Jewish calendar.
3600 B.C. Bronze made in southwestern Asia.
3100 B.C. Egypt united under first dynasty.

3000 B.C. Phoenicians migrate to eastern Mediterranean.
2780 B.C. First Egyptian pyramid built.
2700 B.C. Cheops builds Great Pyramid at Giza.
2697 B.C. Huang-ti becomes "Yellow Emperor" of China.
2640 B.C. Legendary Empress Si Ling-chi introduces silk production in China.
2340 B.C. Sargon establishes Semitic and Sumerian civilizations.
2150 B.C. Aryans invade Indus Valley.
2000 B.C. Bronze Age begins in Europe.
1760 B.C. Shang dynasty is founded in China.
1750 B.C. Hammurabi, Babylonian king, issues code of laws.
1400 B.C. Iron Age begins in Asia.
1250 B.C. Exodus of Israelites from Egypt.
1193 B.C. Greeks destroy city of Troy.
1100 B.C. Pa-out-She, Chinese scholar, compiles first dictionary.
1000 B.C. Hebrews establish Jerusalem as capital of Israel.
994 B.C. Teutons migrate to Rhine River area.
850 B.C. Epic poems of the Greek poet Homer are the first great works of Western literature.
815 B.C. Carthage is founded by Phoenicians.
776 B.C. First Olympic Games are held in Greece.
753 B.C. Rome is founded.
580 B.C. King Nebuchadnezzar builds Hanging Gardens of Babylon.
563 B.C. Buddha is born.
559 B.C. Cyrus establishes Persian Empire.
551 B.C. Confucius is born.
460 B.C. Pericles establishes democracy in Athens, beginning a golden age that will make Greek culture a predominant influence in the Mediterranean for 1,000 years.
450 B.C. Herodotus' *History* surveys the known world; he is later called "the father of history."
426 B.C. Demosthenes leads Athenians to victories in the Peloponnesian War.
424 B.C. Sophocles' play *Oedipus Rex* is performed in Athens.

399 B.C.   Athenian philosopher Socrates is put to death for his teachings. His students Plato and Aristotle are the first great Western philosophers.

336 B.C.   Alexander III, king of Macedonia, begins conquests that will include Egypt, the Mediterranean, and the Middle East by his death in 323 B.C.

300 B.C.   Meng-Tse spreads the philosophy of Confucius in Orient.

270 B.C.   Rome conquers the Italian peninsula.

236 B.C.   Asoka, emperor of India, becomes a Buddhist missionary.

218 B.C.   North African city-state Carthage sends Hannibal through Spain and over the Alps to attack Rome; he retreats in 207 B.C.

215 B.C.   China builds Great Wall to protect against invasions from central Asia.

201 B.C.   Carthage surrenders to Rome.

146 B.C.   Greece becomes a Roman province.

64 B.C.   Rome captures Jerusalem.

54 B.C.   Roman general Julius Caesar conquers Gaul (France), invades Britain.

48 B.C.   Caesar returns to Rome, becomes Dictator for Life; is assassinated in 44 B.C.

28 B.C.   Octavian defeats rivals and becomes the first Roman emperor under the name Caesar Augustus.

5 B.C.   Jesus Christ is born.

A.D. 30   Jesus is executed.

A.D. 32   Saul of Tarsus (Paul) begins early Christian missionary work.

A.D. 64   Rome under Nero is partly destroyed by fire.

A.D. 70   A Roman force destroys the great Jewish Temple in Jerusalem.

A.D. 79   Eruption of Vesuvius destroys Pompeii.

A.D. 135   The Romans destroy Jerusalem, scatter Jews to the four corners of the empire.

A.D. 177   Persecution drives Christians in Rome to worship in catacombs.

A.D. 268   Goths, tribes from northern Europe, invade Greece.

A.D. 312   Constantine becomes first Christian emperor of Rome.

A.D. 330   Constantine moves the capital of the empire from Rome to Constantinople (present-day Istanbul, Turkey).

"Significant Dates in the History of Religion" in chapter 9; "Philosophical Movements and Schools of Thought" in chapter 10

A.D. 370   Asian Huns invade Europe.

A.D. 395   The Roman Empire divides into two—East and West.

A.D. 399   *Confessions* by the North African bishop Augustine tells the story of his conversion to Christianity.

A.D. 406   Vandals from central Europe invade Gaul (France); Romans leave Britain.

A.D. 410   Goths sack Rome.

A.D. 425   Germanic tribes including Angles and Saxons invade Britain.

A.D. 433   Mongol leader Attila the Hun begins conquests in Asia and Europe.

A.D. 476   The Goths depose Western Roman emperor, the Western Roman Empire comes to an end.

A.D. 550   Eastern emperor Justinian codifies Roman law in Corpus Juris Civilis.

A.D. 570   Muhammad is born at Mecca.

A.D. 627   Emperor Tai Zong of Tang Dynasty begins a golden age in China.

A.D. 632   Muhammad dies, having established the Muslim faith, which will grow to be a major world religion.

A.D. 634   Muslims begin conquest of Near East and Africa.

A.D. 711   Moors (Muslims from North Africa) invade Spain from North Africa.

A.D. 768   Charlemagne (Charles the Great), becomes king of the Franks. He will be crowned Holy Roman Emperor in 800.

A.D. 862   Vikings, tribes originating in Scandinavia, seize control of northern Russia, raid France.

A.D. 874   Vikings settle Iceland.

A.D. 900   Spain begins to drive out Moors.

A.D. 932   Printed books from woodblocks are developed in China.

A.D. 936   German Otto I becomes Holy Roman Emperor.

A.D. 995   Fugiware Michiaga founds Japanese golden age.

A.D. 1000   Vikings begin exploration of North America.

1054 Eastern (Byzantine) and Western (Roman) churches separate. Muslim (Islamic) culture spreads in Africa.

1066 Normans, Viking tribe settled in western France, conquer Britain.

1096 Pope and European kings launch First Crusade to oust Muslims from Holy Land.

1148 Second Crusade begins.

1156 Civil wars are fought in Japan.

1161 Chinese use explosives in warfare.

1162 Thomas á Becket becomes archbishop of Canterbury. He is murdered in 1170.

1189 Last recorded Viking voyage to North America.

1190 Genghis Khan begins conquest of Asia.

1192 Crusaders reach Jerusalem but fail to capture the city.

1202 Arabic numerals introduced to Europe.

1204 Crusaders capture and sack Constantinople.

1210 Mongol leader Genghis Khan invades China.

1210 Francis of Assisi founds Franciscan religious order.

1215 The Magna Carta, limiting royal power, is signed by England's King John.

1228 Sixth Crusade results in capture of Jerusalem.

1240 Mongols capture Moscow, destroy Kiev.

1244 Muslim forces recapture Jerusalem.

1259 Thomas Aquinas develops a systematic theology that will prevail in the Western (Roman) Church.

1260 Kublai Khan, grandson of Genghis Khan, founds Yuan dynasty in China.

1271 Venetian Marco Polo travels to China; he returns in 1295.

1274 Mongols' invasion of Japan fails.

1291 Crusades end as Muslims rout Christians in Palestine.

1295 King Edward I summons first representative English Parliament.

1336 Civil war lasting until 1392 begins in Japan.

1337 Hundred Years' War between England and France begins.

1347 Plague spreads from China to Cyprus.

1348 Plague spreads to England.

1351 Plague reaches Russia; more than 25 million Europeans die.

1363 Tamerlane, leader of a Mongol tribe, begins conquest of western Asia.

1368 Mongol dynasty ends in China; Ming dynasty begins.

1402 Tamerlane conquers Ottoman Empire centered in Turkey.

1419 Henry the Navigator of Portugal begins period of African explorations.

1429 Joan of Arc leads a victorious French army against the English at Orleans; she is executed as a witch in 1431.

1453 Ottoman Turks conquer Constantinople, ending the Byzantine Empire.

1453 The Hundred Years' War ends; England loses all territories in France.

1454 Printing press using movable metal type is introduced.

1455 England's Wars of the Roses begin.

1478 Spanish Inquisition to punish heretics (especially Muslims and Jews) begins.

1482 Portuguese colonize African Gold Coast.

1492 Christopher Columbus discovers "the Indies," actually islands in the unknown Western Hemisphere.

1507 First world map showing "America."

1517 German monk Martin Luther protests against Church abuses, beginning the Protestant Reformation in northern Europe.

1519 Hernan Cortés conquers Aztecs and claims Mexico for Spain.

1522 Crew under Ferdinand Magellan circumnavigates the world.

1531 Francisco Pizarro begins conquest of Peru for Spain.

1534 Henry VIII is excommunicated and declares himself head of the Church of England. Ignatius Loyola founds the Jesuits, a monastic order opposing the Reformation.

1542 French theologian John Calvin establishes Protestant government in Geneva.

1547 Ivan IV becomes first czar of united Russia.

1557 Portuguese establish colony at Macao.

1558 Elizabeth I becomes queen of England.

1582 More accurate Gregorian calendar is introduced in western Europe.

Go to "Art Movements and Styles" and "Architectural Styles and Movements" in chapter 7; "Literary Movements, Periods, and Styles" in chapter 8

1588 An armada of Spanish warships attacks England, is defeated by the English fleet.

1603 England's Queen Elizabeth dies; her reign has been a golden age for British arts and letters.

1604 Russia begins settlement in Siberia.

1607 English found North American colony of Virginia.

1618 Thirty Years' War begins as a conflict between Europe's Protestants and Catholics.

1620 English Pilgrims reach Cape Cod, found Plymouth Colony.

1626 Dutch found New Amsterdam (New York).

1637 Russian explorers reach Pacific coast of Siberia.

1642 English Puritans under Oliver Cromwell wage war against King Charles I; Charles is captured and beheaded in 1649.

1654 Portuguese take Brazil from Dutch.

1660 England's monarchy is restored.

1661 English take control of Bombay in India.

1664 Manchu dynasty is founded in China.

1683 Turkish army overruns Vienna.

1696 Peter the Great leads Russian modernization program.

1715 French king Louis XIV, the Sun King, dies; during his long reign, French manners and styles have been admired and imitated throughout Europe.

1733 English weaver John Kay invents the flying sewing shuttle, an early advance in the Industrial Revolution.

1763 British defeat French in North America, gain control of Canada.

1775 American colonists revolt against the British government, beginning the American Revolution.

1776 Colonists publish the Declaration of Independence.

1781 British army surrenders to Americans and French at Yorktown, Virginia.

1783 Treaty of Paris recognizes independence of American colonies.

1788 First English convicts are transported to Australia.

1789 French Revolution begins.

1789 U.S. Constitution takes effect; George Washington is elected first president.

"Significant Inventions, Technological Advances, and Scientific Discoveries" Go to in chapter 5

1792 France is declared a republic.

1793 France's King Louis XVI is beheaded. A Reign of Terror leads to many executions.

1793 Toussaint L'Ouverture leads a revolt, ending slavery in French Haiti.

1793 First free settlers migrate to Australia.

1796 French commander Napoleon Bonaparte invades Italy.

1798 Napoleon occupies Rome and invades Egypt but is defeated in the Battle of the Nile by British admiral Horatio Nelson.

1799 Napoleon become first consul of France.

1803 France, in need of money, sells Louisiana territory to the United States.

1804 Bonaparte becomes Napoleon I, emperor of France; the Napoleonic Code establishes a new legal framework for all territories controlled by France.

1805 The French lose the naval battle of Trafalgar to Britain but win on land at Austerlitz against Austria and Russia.

1806 Napoleon dissolves Holy Roman Empire.

1807 England abolishes slave trade.

1808 Napoleon overruns Spain.

1812 Napoleon invades Russia and occupies Moscow but is forced to retreat, losing most of his army to cold and starvation.

1812 The U.S. declares war on Britain.

1813 French armies suffer losses in Germany and Spain; in 1814, Napoleon abdicates.

1815 Napoleon returns to power; British and Prussian armies defeat him decisively at Waterloo, ending the Napoleonic wars.

1819 Spain cedes Florida to the United States.

1821 Mexico, together with many South and Central American countries, declares independence from Spain.

1823 U.S. President Monroe issues the Monroe Doctrine, a warning against European colonization in the Americas.

1830 Revolutions depose the French king, gain Belgium's independence from the Netherlands.

1833 England bans slavery and child labor in factories.

The World

1836 Texas secedes from Mexico, declares independence as the Republic of Texas.

1837 Queen Victoria succeeds to the British throne at age 18.

1846 Famines begin in Ireland. More than 1 million die; many emigrate to the U.S.

1848 Mexico cedes California and New Mexico territories to the U.S. after defeat in the Mexican-American War.

1848 *The Communist Manifesto* by Marx and Engels helps fan revolutions in France, Belgium, Austria, and Poland.

1849 A gold strike in California attracts thousands of adventurers from around the world.

1851 Louis Napoleon declares himself emperor of France.

1854 Britain and France begin Crimean War against Russia; treaty in 1856 guarantees free access to the Black Sea.

1854 Japan ends isolation, signs commercial treaty with the U.S.

1858 Czar Alexander begins emancipating the serfs in Russia.

1861 U.S. Civil War begins.

1861 A unified Kingdom of Italy is established.

1865 Northern states win U.S. Civil War, abolish slavery; President Lincoln is assassinated.

1867 United States acquires Alaska from Russia; Dominion of Canada gains independence from Britain.

1868 Japan ends 700-year shogun rule, begins modernization.

1869 Suez Canal is completed, shortening trade routes between Asia and Europe; the first transcontinental railroad is completed across the U.S.

1870 Prussia invades France and captures Paris; the French government of Louis Napoleon falls.

1871 Germany is united under Kaiser Wilhelm of Prussia.

1881 Russia's Czar Alexander is assassinated by terrorists.

1894 Sun Yat-sen begins move to end Manchu dynasty in China.

1895 European nations complete colonization of Africa, extend colonies and commercial concessions in Asia.

1898 Spain cedes Cuba, Puerto Rico, the Philippines, and Guam to the U.S. after defeat in the Spanish-American War.

1899 Occupying U.S. forces begin a three-year war against insurgents in the Philippines.

1899 Britain defeats Dutch settlers in South Africa.

1900 In China, the Boxer Rebellion against European traders, is put down by an international (European) force.

1901 U.S. President McKinley is assassinated. Theodore Roosevelt becomes president.

1903 Panama secedes from Colombia, agrees with U.S. plan to build Panama Canal.

1903 Americans Orville and Wilbur Wright make the first powered heavier-than-air flight.

1905 Japan gains concessions from Russia in Asia after victories in Russo-Japanese War.

1905 Russian protests against repressive government lead to violence; put down by the czarist government in 1906.

1906 Mohandas Gandhi begins nonviolent protests in South Africa against segregation of East Indians.

1908 William d'Arcy discovers oil in Persian Gulf region.

1908 Japan begins long occupation of Korea.

1909 The first moving assembly line is introduced at a Ford Motor plant in Detroit.

1910 South Africa gains independence from Britain.

1910 Chinese revolution ends Manchu dynasty, and republic is formed under president Sun Yat-Sen.

1912 Passenger ship *Titanic* sinks; 1,513 lives are lost.

1914 Germany and Austria declare war on France, Britain, and Russia (the Allied Powers) and invade Belgium, beginning the Great War (later called World War I).

1914 The Panama Canal opens.

1915 German submarines disrupt shipping in the Atlantic. Germans use poison gas on the battlefield.

1916   England uses tanks for first time. Battle of the Somme (July–November) causes more than 1.3 million casualties.

1917   The United States declares war on Germany and Austria, joins the Allied Powers (Allies).

1917   In Russia, revolutionaries overthrow the czar; Bolsheviks seize power; Russia withdraws from the war.

1918   The Allies drive Germans back. Kaiser Wilhelm of Germany abdicates; Germany signs armistice ending World War I.

1919   Allies impose heavy penalties on Germany in the Treaty of Versailles and form the League of Nations.

1919   Sinn Fein declares independence for Ireland; civil war against British rule begins, leading to independent Irish state declared in 1921.

1922   Union of Soviet Socialist Republics (USSR) is established; Fascist Benito Mussolini gains power in Italy.

1923   Adolf Hitler forms National Socialist (Nazi) Party in Germany. Turkey becomes a republic, ending the 600-year-old Ottoman Empire.

1924   Joseph Stalin succeeds Lenin as leader of USSR.

1927   Leader Chiang Kai-shek purges Communists in Chinese government, beginning a long civil war.

1929   A worldwide depression begins; the U.S. stock market crashes in October.

1929   Fighting begins between Jews and Arabs in Palestine.

1930   Mohandas Gandhi begins civil disobedience campaign, protesting British political and commercial control in India.

1931   The Great Depression deepens; banks fail, millions in Europe and U.S. are unemployed.

1931   The Japanese occupy Manchuria.

1932   Franklin Roosevelt is elected U.S. president.

1933   Nazi Adolf Hitler is named chancellor of Germany, purges opposition; Great Purges begin in USSR.

1934   Chinese Nationalist armies drive Communists, led by Mao Zedong, on 6,000-mile "Long March" to remote Yunan Province.

1935   Italy invades Ethiopia. Hitler begins open rearmament; German Jews lose citizenship, civil rights.

1936   Germany makes alliances with Italy and Japan; Spanish Fascist leader Franco begins Spanish Civil War.

1936   Britain's King Edward VIII abdicates to marry an American divorcee.

1937   Japanese invade China, capturing Peking and Shanghai; German aircraft bomb Spain in support of Franco.

1938   Germany annexes Austria; Munich Pact grants Czechoslovakia's Sudentenland to Germany.

1939   Franco captures Madrid, ending the Spanish Civil War; Italy invades Albania; Germany invades Poland September 1; Britain and France (the Allies) declare war, beginning World War II.

1940   German armies overrun France, Belgium, Denmark, and Norway; British pilots defeat German bombers in the Battle of Britain. Japan and Italy join war against Britain and France.

1941   Germany invades Russia; Italy and Germany invade Egypt; Japanese attack Pearl Harbor in Hawaii; U.S. declares war, joins Allies.

1942   Japanese capture Philippines and most of Southeast Asia; U.S. defeats Japan in the naval Battle of Midway. Allies invade North Africa.

1943   Allies invade Italy; Italian government surrenders; USSR defeats Germans at Stalingrad; Allied bombing raids devastate German cities. Allies begin recapture of Japanese Pacific bases.

1944   Allies invade France, liberate Paris, Brussels, and Rome; Allies defeat Japanese in Philippine Sea and Saipan. Germans bombard London with V-2's, first long-range missiles.

1945   Allies close in on Berlin; Hitler commits suicide; Germany surrenders.

1945   U.S. drops atom bombs on Japanese cities Hiroshima and Nagasaki; Japan surrenders, ending the war.

The World

"Supreme Court Decisions" in chapter 21; **Go to**
"Important Dates in American History"
in chapter 25

1946 The United Nations is established.

1946 German war crime trials are held in Nuremburg.

1946 The Philippines become independent after 48 years as a U.S. possession.

1947 Marshall Plan provides U.S. aid for European war recovery.

1947 Britain grants independence to Indian subcontinent, forming nations of India and Pakistan.

1948 Nation of Israel is established; war begins between Israel and Arab League.

1948 Gandhi is assassinated by a Hindu extremist.

1948 Communists gain control of Czechoslovakia; Korea is divided into communist North and capitalist South; the USSR blockades Berlin; Allies defeat blockade by airlifting food to Berlin.

1949 Mao Zedong's communists gain control of China; defeated Nationalists set up government on island of Taiwan.

1949 Germany is divided into Communist East Germany and capitalist West; U.S. and its allies form the North Atlantic Treaty Organization (NATO).

1950 North Korean troops, supported by USSR and China, invade South Korea. U.S.-led UN troops are sent to defend South Korea.

1951 Chinese Communists occupy Tibet.

1952 Jawaharlal Nehru is elected first prime minister of India; Elizabeth II ascends to the British throne; World War II general Eisenhower is elected U.S. president.

1953 USSR leader Josef Stalin dies; USSR announces development of hydrogen bomb.

1953 An armistice ends Korean War, leaving borders between North and South unchanged.

1954 Vietnamese defeat French at Dien Bien Phu, French withdraw; Vietnam is divided into communist North Vietnam and capitalist South Vietnam. Algeria begins war against French colonial rule.

1955 European communist states sign Warsaw Pact in opposition to NATO.

1956 Soviets crush anti-Russian uprising in Hungary; Egypt nationalizes Suez Canal, and British withdraw; Israel invades Egypt.

1957 Russia launches first artificial satellite, *Sputnik 1*; U.S. launches *Explorer 1* the next year.

1957 European Common Market is formed.

1958 Army overthrows French government over Algerian war; General de Gaulle becomes premier.

1959 Revolutionary Fidel Castro overthrows Cuban government, becomes premier.

1960 First sub-Saharan African colonies become independent.

1960 Castro aligns Cuba with the USSR.

1961 U.S.-supported invasion of Cuba at Bay of Pigs fails. U.S. sends military advisers to South Vietnam.

1961 USSR sends first human, Yuri Gagarin, into space. The U.S. puts John Glenn into orbit the next year.

1961 East Germany builds the Berlin Wall to prevent East Germans from escaping to the west.

1962 Discovery of Soviet missiles in Cuba and U.S. blockade threaten nuclear war; Soviets agree to remove missiles.

1962 Nelson Mandela is imprisoned for activities against South Africa's apartheid (racial separation) laws.

1962 Algeria gains independence from France.

1963 U.S. President Kennedy is assassinated.

1963 The United States, Great Britain, and Soviet Union sign nuclear test ban treaty.

1963 The U.S. sends military advisers to South Vietnam to resist guerrilla attacks from communist North.

1964 The U.S. begins bombing of North Vietnam.

1965 The U.S. sends combat troops to Vietnam. Antiwar protests begin.

1966 China undergoes "Cultural Revolution."

1967 In Six-Day War, Israel occupies Jerusalem and West Bank of Jordan River.

The World

1968 North Vietnam launches Tet offensive against South Vietnam; U.S. troop deployment in Vietnam passes 500,000. Soviets crush Czech uprising.

1968 Martin Luther King, Jr., and U.S. presidential candidate Robert Kennedy are assassinated; Richard Nixon is elected president.

1968 Student demonstrations close universities in France and U.S.; Mexican police fire on student protesters.

1969 U.S. astronauts land on the moon.

1969 Peace talks to end Vietnam War begin in Paris; the U.S. begins gradual reduction of troop strength.

1970 U.S. troops invade Cambodia.

1971 Communist China replaces Taiwan in United Nations.

1972 U.S. president Nixon travels to China to renew relations.

In Paraguay, dueling is legal provided both parties are registered blood donors.

1973 A U.S.-supported coup overthrows Chile's elected Marxist government; General Augusto Pinochet becomes president.

1973 Syria and Egypt attack Israel in October War.

1973 A cease-fire in Vietnam ends involvement of U.S. ground troops.

1974 Accused of serious crimes in the Watergate scandal, U.S. president Nixon resigns to avoid impeachment.

1975 North Vietnamese troops storm Saigon, last Americans are evacuated. Vietnam is unified under communist government.

1976 Mao Zedong, chairman of the People's Republic of China, dies.

1976 Riots in Soweto township increase racial tensions in South Africa.

1978 U.S. president Carter helps negotiate the Camp David Accords, a peace treaty between Israel and Egypt.

1979 Muslim leader Ayatollah Khomeini gains control of Iran; Iranians seize U.S. Embassy in Tehran and hold hostages until early 1980.

1979 Soviet Union invades Afghanistan, beginning a nine-year war.

1979 Nicaraguan dictator Somoza is driven into exile; the leftist Sandinista party takes power.

1980 Iraq invades Iran, beginning an eight-year war. The Solidarity trade union confronts communists in Poland.

1981 Ronald Reagan takes office as U.S. president; he is wounded by an assassination attempt but recovers.

1981 Egyptian president Sadat is assassinated.

1983 Soviets shoot down South Korean airliner, and 269 are killed.

1983 Terrorists in Lebanon destroy U.S. embassy, bomb U.S. and French military barracks; more than 350 are killed.

1984 Peacekeepers withdraw from Lebanon; Indian prime minister Indira Gandhi is assassinated.

1985 Mikhail Gorbachev becomes leader of the USSR.

1986 Corazon Aquino is elected president of Philippines, replacing longtime dictator Ferdinand Marcos.

1986 U.S. space shuttle *Challenger* explodes in flight, killing crew of seven.

1986 U.S. aircraft raid Libya in retaliation for terrorist bombing in Germany.

1986 A nuclear accident at Chernobyl near Kiev in the Ukraine causes widespread damage and injury.

1987 Gorbachev introduces economic and social reforms in the USSR; U.S. and USSR agree to reduce nuclear arms.

1988 USSR begins withdrawal from Afghanistan. Iran and Iraq sign a cease-fire. Jordan's King Hussein cedes land and authority to Palestine Liberation Organization (PLO).

1989 Chinese massacre protesters in Beijing's Tiananmen Square.

1989 U.S. troops invade Panama and take General Manuel Noriega into custody.

1989 The Berlin Wall is opened; Czechoslovakia elects a noncommunist government; Romanian leader Nicolae Ceaùsescu is overthrown and executed; Pinochet regime ends in Chile.

1990 Black leader Nelson Mandela is released from South African prison after 27 years.

1990 Iraq invades Kuwait; UN approves military action against Iraq.

1990 East German regime falls, Germany reunites; Poland elects Solidarity leader Lech Walesa president.

1991 A U.N. force led by the U.S. drives Iraqis from Kuwait in 100-hour Operation Desert Storm.

1991 Soviet communist coup fails; the Soviet Union is dissolved; Boris Yeltsin becomes Russian president.

1991 Croatia and Slovenia declare independence from Yugoslavia; communist government of Albania falls.

1992 South African whites vote to end white minority rule.

1992 Serbian nationalists begin "ethnic cleansing" of Muslims in Bosnia.

1992 Hindu extremists destroy a mosque in Ayodhya, India.

1993 South Africa adopts a constitution providing equal rights for black citizens.

1993 Maastricht Treaty and North American Free Trade Agreement (NAFTA) establish free trade blocs in Europe and North America.

1993 World Trade Center in New York is evacuated after terrorist bomb explodes in underground garage; six are killed.

1994 Nelson Mandela is elected first black president of South Africa.

1994 The Hutu majority kill more than 500,000 Tutsi in Rwanda.

1994 Israel signs peace treaty with Jordan, extends Palestinian self-rule.

1994 Russian forces invade the breakaway republic of Chechnya.

1995 Earthquake in Kobe, Japan, kills 5,000.

1995 NATO forces bomb Serb positions in Bosnia; a peace treaty ends the fighting in December.

1995 Israeli prime minister Itzhak Rabin is assassinated.

1996 Israel cracks down on terrorists in response to suicide bombings.

1996 UN tribunal indicts Serbs and Croats for war crimes.

1996 Russians and Chechens sign peace treaty.

1997 Insurgents in Zaire overturn dictator, change country name to Democratic Republic of Congo.

1997 Hong Kong reverts to Chinese control after 156 years as British colony.

1998 Peace treaty signed between Ireland and Northern Ireland.

1998 Indonesian riots overthrow longtime President Suharto.

1998 India and Pakistan test nuclear weapons for the first time.

1998 Serb forces massacre civilians in Kosovo.

1999 U.S. president Clinton is acquitted of impeachment charges.

1999 NATO bombs Serbia; Serbs agree to withdraw troops from Kosovo.

1999 Russia troops reenter Chechnya.

2000 Vladimir Putin is elected Russian president.

2000 Israel withdraws troops from Lebanon, ending long occupation.

2000 Yugoslav president Slobodan Milosevic loses election, is driven from office by mass protests.

2001 Israeli-Palestinian violence increases; Ariel Sharon becomes Israeli prime minister.

2001 Terrorists highjack passenger jets in U.S., crash them into World Trade Center in New York, Pentagon in Washington; almost 3,000 are killed.

2001 U.S. and Britain bomb Afghanistan, where Osama bin Laden, presumed leader of terrorists, is in hiding.

2001 Muslim fundamentalist regime in Afghanistan collapses; U.S. ground troops continue search for bin Laden.

2002 Israel invades the West Bank and Gaza Strip; Palestinian suicide bombings intensify.

MAJOR WARS, BATTLES, AND OTHER ARMED CONFLICTS

Simultaneous wars that were part of one general conflict but that had different names depending on the continent where they were fought are grouped together.

War, Battle, or Conflict	Date
Trojan War (Achaeans and other Greek peoples)	12th century B.C.
Persian Wars (Persians vs. Greek city-states)	499–494, 490, 480–479 B.C.
Marathon, Battle of	490 B.C.
Salamis, Battle of (naval)	480 B.C.
Thermopylae, Battle of	480 B.C.
Plataea, Battle of	479 B.C.
Pelopennesian War (Athens vs. Sparta)	431–404 B.C.
Sparta-Thebes conflict in Greece	
Leuctra, Battle of	371 B.C.
Greece vs. Macedonia	
Chaeronea, Battle of	338 B.C.
Alexander the Great, conquests of	334–323 B.C.
Wars between Alexander's successors	315–280 B.C.
Punic Wars (Carthage vs. Rome)	
First	264–241 B.C.
Second (Hannibalic)	218–201 B.C.
Third	149–146 B.C.
Social War (Marsic or Marsian War) (Rome vs. Samnites and Marsi)	90–88 B.C.
Mithridatic Wars (Rome vs. Pontus)	88–84, 82–81, 74–63 B.C.
Gallic Wars (Julius Caesar's conquest of Gaul for Rome)	58–51 B.C.
Roman civil wars	49–31 B.C.
Pharsalus, Battle of	48 B.C.
Philippi, Battle of	42 B.C.
Actium, Battle of (naval)	Sept. 2, 31 B.C.
Rome vs. Germans (under Arminius)	
Teutoburg Forest, Battle of	A.D. 9
Rome vs. Visigoths	
Adrianople, Battle of	378
Rome vs. Franks	
Soissons, Battle of	486
Franks (under Charles Martel) vs. Saracen Muslims	
Tours, Battle of	Oct. 732
Normans (under William the Conqueror) vs. Saxons	
Hastings, Battle of	Oct. 14, 1066
Crusades (attempts by Western Christians to free Holy Land from Muslims)	
First	1096–99
Second	1147–49
Third	1187–92
Fourth	1202–04
Fifth	1217–21
Sixth (Diplomatic)	1228–29
Seventh	1248–50
Eighth	1270
Genghis Khan, conquests of	1198–1227

War, Battle, or Conflict	Date
Scottish struggle for independence from England	
Bannockburn, Battle of	June 24, 1314
Hundred Years' War (France vs. England)	1337–1453
Crécy, Battle of	Aug. 26, 1346
Calais, Siege of	1346–47
Poitiers, Battle of	1356
Agincourt, Battle of	Oct. 25, 1415
Orléans, Siege of	1428–May 1429
Roses, Wars of the (English civil wars)	1455–99
Bosworth Field, Battle of	Aug. 22, 1485
Scotland and France vs. England	
Flodden Field, Battle of	Sept. 9, 1513
Spain and Venice vs. Turkey	
Lepanto, Battle of (naval)	Oct. 7, 1571
Spain vs. England	
Armada, the Spanish, defeat of (naval)	July 31–Aug. 8, 1588
Catholic League vs. France	
Ivry, Battle of	Mar. 14, 1590
Thirty Years' War (conflict among various European countries)	1618–48
English Civil War	1642–52
Edgehill, Battle of	Oct. 23, 1642
Marston Moor, Battle of	July 2, 1644
Dunbar, Battle of	Sept. 3, 1650
England vs. the Netherlands	1652–54, 1665–67
Devolution, War of (France vs. Spain)	1667–68
Dutch War (France and England vs. the Netherlands)	1672–78
King Philip's War (New England colonies vs. Wampanoag, Narragansett, and Nipmuck Indians)	July 4, 1675–Aug. 12, 1676
English Civil War	
Monmouth Rebellion	1685
Grand Alliance, War of the (War of the League of Augsburg) (France vs. England, Holy Roman Empire, Germany, Austria, Spain, Sweden, the Netherlands, and Brandenburg)	1688–97
King William's War (French vs. English colonies in America)	1689–97
Great Northern War (Sweden vs. Russia, Poland, and Denmark)	1700–21
Spanish Succession, War of the (France vs. England, Holland, Austria, Prussia, Portugal, and Savoy)	1701–14
Queen Anne's War (French vs. English colonies in America)	1702–13
Jenkins' Ear, War of (Great Britain vs. Spain)	Oct. 1739–41
Austrian Succession, War of the (Austria, England, the Netherlands, and Saxony vs. Prussia, Spain, France, and Bavaria)	1740–48
King George's War (British vs. French colonies in North America)	1744–48
Stuart attempt to regain the British throne	
Culloden Moor, Battle of	April 16, 1746
Seven Years' War (Prussia and Great Britain vs. Austria, France, Sweden, Russia, Saxony, Spain, and Kingdom of the Two Sicilies)	1756–63
French and Indian War (British vs. French colonies in North America)	1756–63
Cherokee War (Cherokee Indians vs. settlers on the western borders of Virginia and the Carolinas)	1759–61

continues

The World

Major Wars, Battles, and Other Armed Conflicts, Continued

War, Battle, or Conflict	Date
American Revolution	1775–81
Lexington and Concord, Battles of	Apr. 19, 1775
Fort Ticonderoga, Battle of	May 10, 1775
Bunker Hill, Battle of	June 17, 1775
Canada Expedition	Sept. 1775–June 1776
Long Island, Battle of	Aug. 27, 1776
Trenton, Battle of	Dec. 26, 1776
Princeton, Battle of	Jan. 2–3, 1777
Bennington, Battle of	Aug. 15, 1777
Saratoga, Battle of	Oct. 7, 1777
Brandywine, Battle of the	Sept. 11, 1777
Germantown, Battle of	Oct. 4, 1977
Monmouth, Battle of	June 28, 1778
Wyoming Valley Massacre	Summer 1778
Savannah, Battle of	Dec. 23–29, 1778
Bonhomme Richard and *Serapis,* naval battle between	Sept. 23, 1779
Savannah, Siege of	Sept.–Oct. 1779
Charleston, Siege of	Feb.–May 1780
Camden, Battle of	Aug. 16, 1780
Kings Mountains, Battle of	Oct. 7, 1780
Cowpens, Battle of	Jan. 17, 1781
Yorktown, Siege of	Sept.–Oct. 19, 1781
French Revolution (French civil war and war against most European countries)	1789–99
Bastille, storming of the	July 14, 1789
Reign of Terror	Sept. 1793–July 1794
Franco-American Naval War	1798–1800
Napoleon I, campaigns of and wars against	1796–1815
(France vs. various European countries)	
Italian campaign	Mar. 1796–Apr. 1797
Nile, Battle of the (naval)	Aug. 1, 1798
Marengo, Battle of	June 14, 1800
Hohenlinden, Battle of	Dec. 3, 1800
Copenhagen, Battle of (naval)	Apr. 2, 1801
Trafalgar, Battle of (naval)	Oct. 21, 1805
Austerlitz, Battle of	Dec. 2, 1805
Jena and Auerstädt, Battles of	Oct. 14, 1806
Eylau, Battle of	Feb. 8, 1807
Friedland, Battle of	June 14, 1807
Aspern, Battle of	1809
Wagram, Battle of	1809
Borodino, Battle of	Sept. 7, 1812
Leipzig, Battle of	Oct. 16–19, 1813
Waterloo, Battle of	June 18, 1815
Barbary Wars (United States vs. Morocco, Algiers, Tunis, and Tripoli)	1801–05, 1815
War of 1812 (United States vs. Great Britain)	1812–15
Detroit, Surrender of	Aug. 18, 1812
Frenchtown, Battle of	Jan. 22, 1813
Lake Erie, Battle of (naval)	Sept. 10, 1813
Thames, Battle of the	Oct. 5, 1813

The World

War, Battle, or Conflict	Date
War of 1812 (United States vs. Great Britain), *cont.*	
Chippewa, Battle of	July 5, 1814
Bladensburg, Battle of	Aug. 24, 1814
Lake Champlain, Battle of (naval)	Sept. 11, 1814
New Orleans, Battle of	Jan. 8, 1815
Creek War (United States vs. Creek Indians)	1813–14
Greek War of Independence (from Turkey)	1821–29
Navarino, Battle of (naval)	Oct. 20, 1827
Anglo-Burman Wars	1824–26, 1852–53, 1885
Java War (Java vs. the Netherlands)	1825–30
Russo-Turkish Wars	1828–29, 1853–56, 1877–78
Texas struggle for independence from Mexico	1836
Alamo, Siege of the	Feb. 23–Mar. 6, 1836
San Jacinto, Battle of	Apr. 21, 1836
Anglo-Chinese (Opium) War	1839–42
Anglo-Afghan Wars	1839, 1878–79
Sikh Wars (Great Britain vs. India)	1845, 1849
Mexican War (United States vs. Mexico)	1846–48
Taiping Rebellion (Chinese rising against Manchu Dynasty)	1850–64
Crimean War (Russia vs. Ottoman Empire, Great Britain, France, and Sardinia)	1853–56
Sevastopol, Siege of	Sept. 14, 1854–Sept. 9, 1855
Second Opium War (Great Britain and France vs. China)	1856–60
Sepoy Mutiny (revolt of Indian soldiers against British rule)	1857–59
Austro-Sardinian War (War of Italian Liberation) (Austria vs. France and Sardinia)	1859
Magenta, Battle of	June 4, 1859
Solferino, Battle of	June 24, 1859
Civil War, U.S.	1861–1865
Eastern Theater	
Fort Sumter, attack on	Apr. 12–14, 1861
Bull Run (Manassas), First Battle of	July 21, 1861
Ball's Bluff, Battle of	Oct. 21, 1861
Monitor and *Merrimack*, naval battle between	Mar. 9, 1862
Fair Oaks (Seven Pines), Battle of	May 31–June 1, 1862
Seven Days' Battles	June 25–July 1, 1862
Cedar Mountain, Battle of	Aug, 9, 1862
Bull Run (Manassas), Second Battle of	Aug. 29–30, 1862
Antietam, Battle of	Sept. 17, 1862
Fredericksburg, Battle of	Dec. 13, 1862
Chancellorsville, Battle of	May 1–5, 1863
Gettysburg, Battle of	July 1–3, 1863
Charleston, Sieges of	July–Aug. 1863
Fort Pillow Massacre	Apr. 12, 1864
Wilderness, Battle of the	May 5–6, 1864
Spotsylvania, Battle of	May 8–18, 1864
Cold Harbor, Battle of	June 1–3, 1864
Petersburg, Siege of	June 1864–Apr. 2, 1865
Cedar Creek, Battle of	Oct. 19, 1864
Sherman's March to the Sea	Nov. 15–Dec. 25, 1864

continues

Major Wars, Battles, and Other Armed Conflicts, Continued

War, Battle, or Conflict	Date
Civil War, U.S., *cont.*	
Fort Fisher, Battle of	Jan. 15, 1865
Five Forks, Battle of	Apr. 1, 1865
Appomattox Court House	Apr. 9, 1865
Western Theater	
Boonville, Battle of	June 17, 1861
Fort Henry, Battle of	Feb. 6, 1862
Fort Donelson, Battle of	Feb. 13–16, 1862
Shiloh (Pittsburg Landing), Battle of	Apr. 6–7, 1862
Island No. 10, Battle of	Apr. 7–8, 1862
Corinth, Battle of	Oct. 3–4, 1862
Murfreesboro (Stones River), Battle of	Dec. 31, 1862–Jan. 2, 1863
Vicksburg, Siege of	May 19–July 3, 1863
Chickamauga, Battle of	Sept. 19–20, 1863
Chattanooga, Battle of	Nov. 23–25, 1863
Lookout Mountain, Battle of	Nov. 24, 1863
Missionary Ridge, Battle of	Nov. 24–25, 1863
Kennesaw Mountain, Battle of	June 27, 1864
Atlanta, Siege of	July 20–Sept. 2, 1864
Franklin, Battle of	Nov. 30, 1864
Nashville, Battle of	Dec. 15–16, 1864
Off Cherbourg, France	
Alabama and *Kearsarge*, naval battle between	June 19, 1864
War of the Triple Alliance (Brazil, Argentina, and Uruguay vs. Paraguay)	1864–70
Seven Weeks' War (Prussia vs. Austria)	June 14–July 1866
Ten Years' War (Cuba vs. Spain)	1868–78
Franco-Prussian War	July 19, 1870–Feb. 1, 1871
Gravelotte, Battle of	Aug. 18, 1870
Metz, Siege of	Aug. 19–Oct. 27, 1870
Sedan, Battle of	Sept. 1, 1970
Russo-Turkish War	1877–78
Zulu War (Great Britain vs. Zulus)	1879
First South African War (Great Britain vs. Transvaal)	1881
War of the Pacific (Chile vs. Peru and Bolivia)	1879–84
Mahdist War (revolt of followers of the Mahdi against Egyptian rule)	1881–90
Khartoum, Siege of	Jan. 1885
Sino-French War	1884–85
Sino-Japanese War	1894–95
Spanish-American War	1898
Manila Bay, Battle of (naval)	May 1, 1898
San Juan Hill, Battle of	July 1, 1898
Santiago, Battle of (naval)	July 3, 1898
Boer War (South African War, Anglo-Boer War, or Second War of Freedom) (Great Britain vs. Transvaal and Orange Free State)	1899–1902
Boxer Rebellion (China vs. foreign powers involved in the country)	1900–01
Russo-Japanese War	Feb. 5, 1904–Sept. 5, 1905
Japan Sea (Tsushima), Battle of the (naval)	May 27, 1905
Mexican Civil War	1910–20

The World

War, Battle, or Conflict	Date
Balkan Wars	
First (Turkey vs. Serbia, Montenegro, Greece, and Bulgaria)	Oct. 8, 1912–May 30, 1913
Second (Bulgaria vs. Serbia, Greece, Turkey, Montenegro, and Romania)	June 29–Aug. 10, 1913
World War I (Austria, Germany, Turkey, and Bulgaria vs. Russia, France, Great Britain, Serbia, Italy, and United States)	July 28, 1914–Nov. 11, 1918
Charleroi, Battle of	Aug. 22–23, 1914
Tannenberg, Battle of	Aug. 26–30, 1914
Marne, First Battle of the	Sept. 5–14, 1914
Ypres, First Battle of	Oct. 20 and 31, Nov. 11, 1914
Coronel, Battle of (naval)	Nov. 1, 1914
Falklands, Battle of the (naval)	Dec. 8, 1914
Dogger Bank, Battle of (naval)	Jan. 24, 1915
Ypres, Second Battle of	Apr. 22–May 24, 1915
Gallipoli Expedition (Dardanelles Campaign)	Apr. 25, 1915–Jan. 9, 1916
Verdun, Siege of	Feb. 21–Dec. 1916
Kut al Imara, Battle of	Apr. 1916
Asiago, Battle of	May 14–June 1916
Jutland, Battle of (naval)	May 31–June 1, 1916
Somme, Battle of the	July–Nov. 1916
Arras, Battle of	Apr. 4–May 4, 1917
Ypres (Passchendaele), Third Battle of	July 31–Nov. 10, 1917
Caporetto, Battle of	Oct.–Dec. 1917
Cambrai, Battle of	Nov. 20–Dec. 7, 1917
St. Quentin, Battle of	Mar. 21, 1918
Belleau Wood, Battle of	June 3–9, 1918
Chateau-Thierry, Battle of	July 15–21, 1918
Marne, Second Battle of the	July 18–Aug. 7, 1918
Amiens, Battle of	Aug. 8, 1918
St. Mihiel, Battle of	Sept. 12–21, 1918
Argonne, Battle of the	Sept. 26–Nov. 11, 1918
Vittorio Veneto, Battle of	Oct. 1918
October (Bolshevik) Revolution and counterrevolutionary movements (Russian civil war)	1917–20
Polish-Soviet War	1920–21
Greco-Turkish War	1921–22
Chinese Civil War	1927–36, 1946–50
Chaco War (Paraguay-Bolivia)	Dec. 1928–Nov. 1935
Japanese invasion of Manchuria and other parts of China	1931–37
Italian invasion of Ethiopia	Oct. 3, 1935–May 5, 1936
Spanish Civil War	1936–39
World War II (Germany, Italy, and Japan vs. United States, England, France, Russia, and other countries)	1939–45
Western European Theater	
Poland, German conquest of	Sept. 1–17, 1939
Norway and Denmark, fall of	Apr.–June 1940
Western Europe, German conquest of	May–June 1940
Britain, Battle of (air)	June 19–Oct. 12, 1940
Bismarck, sinking of the (naval)	May 1941
Normandy invasion	June 6, 1944
Rhine River, Allied advance toward the (Operation Market Garden)	Fall 1944
Bulge, Battle of the	Dec. 16, 1944–Jan. 21, 1945

continues

The World

Major Wars, Battles, and Other Armed Conflicts, Continued

War, Battle, or Conflict	Date
World War II (Germany, Italy, and Japan vs. United States, England, France, Russia, and other countries), *cont.*	
Russian Front	
Finland, Soviet attack on	Nov. 30, 1939–Mar. 13, 1940
Soviet Union, initiation of German attack on	June 22, 1941
Stalingrad, Siege of	July 1942–Feb. 2, 1943
Kursk, Battle of	July 12–19, 1943
Dniepr River, Soviet offensive across the	Summer–fall 1943
Ukraine, Soviet liberation of	Winter 1944
Berlin, fall of	Apr. 16–May 2, 1945
Mediterranean Theater	
Tobruk, Battles of	Dec. 1940, June and Nov. 1942
Greece, German conquest of	Apr.–May 1941
El Alamein, First Battle of	July 2–4, 1942
El Alamein, Second Battle of	Aug. 30–Nov. 4, 1942
North Africa, Allied invasion of (Operation Torch)	Nov. 8, 1942–May 11, 1943
Sicily, Allied invasion of	July 10–Aug. 16, 1943
Italy, Allied invasion of	Sept.–Oct. 1943
Anzio, operation at	Jan.–June 1944
Pacific Theater	
Pearl Harbor, bombing of (air/naval)	Dec. 7, 1941
Malaya and Dutch East Indies, Japanese conquest of	Dec. 7, 1941–Feb. 15, 1942
Philippines, Japanese conquest of the	Dec. 22, 1941–May 6, 1942
Burma, Japanese invasion of	Jan.–May 1942
Lombok Strait, Battle of (naval)	Feb. 19–20, 1942
Java Sea, Battle of the (naval)	Feb. 27, 1942
Tokyo, Doolittle bombing of	Apr. 18, 1942
Coral Sea, Battle of the (naval)	May 7–8, 1942
Midway, Battle of (naval)	June 4–5, 1942
Savo Sea, Battle of the (naval)	Aug. 1942
Guadalcanal, Battle of (land/naval)	Aug. 7, 1942–Feb. 7, 1943
Eastern Solomons, Battle of the (naval)	Aug. 23–25, 1942
Santa Cruz Island, Battle of (naval)	Oct. 26, 1942
Gilbert Islands, conquest of the	Nov. 1943
Marshall Islands, invasion of the	Jan. 1944
New Guinea, conquest of	Apr.–July 1944
Leyte Gulf, Battle of (naval)	Oct. 24, 1944
Iwo Jima, conquest of	Feb. 19–Mar. 16, 1945
Okinawa, invasion of	Mar. 31, 1945
Hiroshima and Nagasaki, atomic bombing of	Aug. 6 and 9, 1945
Algerian war for independence from France	1945–62
Indonesian war for independence from the Netherlands	1945–49
Vietnamese war for independence from France	1946–54
Dien Bien Phu, fall of	May 7, 1954
Arab-Israeli War	1948–49
Korean War (North Korea and Communist China vs. South Korea and United Nations forces)	1950–53
38th parallel, initial North Korean attack across the	June 25, 1950
Inchon, UN landing at	Sept. 15, 1950
Manchurian border, Chinese Communist crossing of	Nov. 26, 1950

War, Battle, or Conflict	Date
Hungary, uprising in and Soviet invasion of	Oct. 23–Nov. 1956
Suez War (Israel, Great Britain, and France vs. Egypt)	Oct. 29–Dec. 1956
Revolutionary guerrilla warfare in Cuba (against Batista regime)	1956–59
Vietnam War (South Viet Nam and United States vs. North Vietnam)	1960–75
Tet Offensive, beginning of	Jan. 31, 1968
Bay of Pigs invasion (United States vs. Cuba)	Apr. 17–19, 1961
India-Pakistan war	1965
Six Day War (Israel vs. Egypt, Jordan, and Syria)	June 5–10, 1967
Nigerian civil war	1967–70
Bangladesh war (India vs. Pakistan)	1971–72
Yom Kippur War (Israel vs. Egypt and Syria)	Oct. 1973
Lebanon, civil war and Syrian and Israeli occupation of	1973–85
Soviet intervention in Afghanistan	1979–89
Persian Gulf War (Iran vs. Iraq)	1980–88
Salvadoran civil war	1980–92
Falklands War (Argentina vs. Great Britain)	Apr. 2–June 14, 1982
Grenada, United States intervention in	Oct. 25–27, 1983
Yugoslavian civil war	1987–99
Panama, United States invasion of	1989
Persian Gulf War (Iraq vs. United States and coalition of numerous countries)	1990–91
Rwandan civil war	1994
Chechnya, Russian invasion of	1994–96
Yugoslavia, NATO intervention in	1999
Afghanistan, intervention in	2001–2002

WORLD EXPLORATION AND DISCOVERY

40,000 B.C. Cro-Magnons migrate to Europe from Near East.

28,000 B.C. Humans migrate from Asia to Americas over land bridge.

5000 B.C. Sumerians migrate to Mesopotamia.

2300 B.C. Semites migrate from Arabia to Mesopotamia.

2000 B.C. Israelites migrate from Euphrates Valley to Canaan.

1000 B.C. Phoenician sailors explore Britain and western Africa.

700 B.C. Central Asian tribes migrate to Persia.

640 B.C. Greek explorer Colaeus reaches Gibraltar and Spain.

600 B.C. Egyptian pharaoh Necho circumnavigates Africa; Greek explorer Midacritus finds tin in England or Brittany.

510 B.C. Greek traveler Scylax explores Indus River, Red Sea, and Arabia.

500 B.C. Bantu tribes migrate through eastern Africa; Greek explorer Hekataios travels to Spain and North Africa; Carthaginian explorer Himlico visits French Atlantic Coast.

480 B.C. Carthaginian admiral Hanno explores west coast of Africa.

424 B.C. Greek traveler Herodotus visits North Africa, Italy, and Arabia.

400 B.C. Greek explorer Ctesias travels to Ganges River in India.

345 B.C. Greek explorer Pythias explores northwest European coastline.

327 B.C. Alexander the Great leads army to Indus Valley of India.

325 B.C. Greek admiral Nearchus attempts to circumnavigate Arabia.

302 B.C. Greek traveler Megasthenes visits India, Tibet, and Ceylon.

218 B.C. Hannibal leads army with elephants from Spain to Italy.

138 B.C. Decimus Brutus becomes first Roman to reach west coast of Spain.

128 B.C.   Chinese explorer of central Asia has contact with Greeks.

112 B.C.   Greek explorer Eudoxus sails to India and western Africa.

100 B.C.   Greek explorer Hippalus finds direct ocean route to India.

55 B.C.   Julius Caesar leads Roman army to Britain.

A.D. 20   King Juba of Morocco explores Canary Islands.

Cleopatra was part Macedonian, part Greek, and part Iranian. She was not an Egyptian.

A.D. 80   Gnaeus Agricola explores Atlantic coast of Britain.

A.D. 100   Roman explorer Julius Maternus crosses Sahara to Sudan; Alexander, Greek trader, sails to Vietnam and Cambodia; Chinese explorer Kan Ying reaches Black Sea.

A.D. 370   Huns, nomadic Mongols, invade Europe and reach Gaul.

A.D. 400   Chinese monk Fa Hsien visits India, Ceylon, and Java.

A.D. 407   Northern European Goths and Vandals spread to Mediterranean.

A.D. 431   Gunavarman, prince of Kashmir, travels to Java and China.

A.D. 570   Brendan, Irish monk, reportedly discovers America.

A.D. 620   Vikings explore Ireland.

A.D. 645   Chinese monk Yuan Chuang travels overland to India and returns.

A.D. 861   Vikings discover Iceland.

A.D. 872   Iraqi traveler Ibn Wahab visits China.

A.D. 900   Mayans migrate from Central America to Yucatan Peninsula; Arab traveler Ibn Rosteh explores Malay Peninsula and Java.

A.D. 921   Arabian diplomat Ahmad Ibn Fodhlan explores Russia and Poland.

A.D. 950   Maori sailors discover New Zealand.

A.D. 980   Arabs migrate to east coast of Africa.

A.D. 981   Eric the Red discovers Greenland.

A.D. 986   Viking sailor Bjarne Herjulfsson sights North America.

A.D. 1000   Leif Ericsson explores Atlantic coast of North America.

1002   Thorwald Ericsson explores American coast below New England.

1007   Viking Thorfinn Karlsefni establishes North American colony.

1150   Polynesian Toi Kai Rakan opens settlement of New Zealand.

1165   Spanish rabbi Benjamin visits synagogues of Asia and Near East.

1245   Franciscan monk Giovanni Carpini travels to Mongol capital.

1271   Marco Polo begins 24-year journey to Orient and Near East.

1291   Vivaldi brothers try sailing Atlantic from Genoa to India; Italian explorer Malocello discovers Canary Islands.

1337   Josef Faquin circumnavigates known world of 14th century.

1350   Polynesian chief Marutuahu establishes colony in New Zealand.

1419   Portuguese King Henry begins African exploration.

1431   Portuguese explorer discovers Azores.

1440   Italian explorer Niccolò Conti travels in Indonesia and Malaya.

1446   Portuguese explorer Nuno Tristao is lost on second trip to Africa.

1455   Venetian sailor Cadamosto discovers Cape Verde Islands.

1482   Portuguese navigator Diego Cao explores Congo River; Portugal establishes African Gold Coast settlements.

1488   Portuguese explorer Bartholomeu Dias sails around Cape of Good Hope.

1492   Christopher Columbus discovers the West Indies; German navigator Martin Behaim shows Earth is spherical.

1493   Pope Alexander VI divides New World between Spain and Portugal.

1494   Bartolome Colon, brother of Columbus, explores Haiti.

1495   Francisco de Almeida establishes Portuguese naval bases in eastern Africa.

1497   Italian John Cabot discovers Newfoundland for England.

1498   Columbus discovers South America and Trinidad; Portuguese navigator Vasco da Gama finds sea route to India.

1499   Spanish explorer Vincent Yañez Pinzon discovers mouth of Amazon River.

1500   Portuguese explorer Pedro Cabral discovers Brazil.

1501   Amerigo Vespucci explores coast of Brazil; Spanish explorer Rodrigo Bastidas discovers Colombia.

1502   Columbus discovers Nicaragua; Spaniard Alonso de Ojeda explores Haiti, Guiana, and Venezuela.

1504   Portuguese explorer Pacheco Pereira visits India.

1505   Portuguese establish settlements in Mozambique; Portuguese nobleman Tristão da Cunha leads expedition to India.

1507   German maps by Martin Waldseemuller identify New World as "America."

1510   Afonso de Albuquerque establishes Portuguese base in India at Goa.

1512   Spanish priest Bartolomé Las Casas is missionary to Cuban Indians.

1513   Balboa, in Panama, discovers Pacific Ocean; Ponce de Leon explores Florida and West Indies; Portuguese reach Canton, China.

1514   Spanish explorer Francisco de Montejo travels to West Indies.

1516   Spanish explorer Juan Diaz de Solís discovers Rio de la Plata, Uruguay.

1517   Spanish explorer Fernandez de Cordoba discovers Mayan ruins.

1518   Pedro Alvarado explores Southeast Mexico for Spain; Spanish conquistador Juan de Grijalva discovers Aztec Empire.

1519   Hernán Cortés conquers Mexico for Spain.

1521   Ferdinand Magellan dies in an attempt to circumnavigate Earth.

1522   Spanish navigator Juan Sebastián del Cano is first to circumnavigate Earth.

1524   Italian explorer Giovanni da Verrazano discovers New York harbor; Francisco Pizarro explores the west coasts of Panama and Peru.

1526   Italian Sebastian Cabot explores Rio de la Plata, Uruguay.

1527   Cabeza de Vaca begins trek from Florida to Mexican west coast.

1528   Spanish explorer Panfilo de Narvaez dies near mouth of Mississippi.

1530   German adventurer Nikolaus Federmann explores Venezuela, Colombia, and the Andes.

1533   Spanish conquistador Francisco Pizarro conquers Peru; Spanish conquistador Sebastián de Benalcázar conquers Ecuador.

1535   Jacques Cartier explores Saint Lawrence River; Spanish explore Chile; Spanish explorer Don Pedro de Mendoza establishes settlement of Buenos Aires.

1536   Spaniard Jimánez de Quesada explores Colombia and Orinoco River; Spanish conquistador Domingo de Irala explores Parana and Paraguay rivers.

1540   Vásquez de Coronado explores Arizona and New Mexico; Spanish monk Andres Urdaneta explores Philippine Islands.

1541   Hernando de Soto discovers Mississippi River; Francisco de Orellana travels Amazon River from source in Peru to mouth; Gonzalo Pizarro crosses the Andes from Ecuador to the Amazon River.

1542   Portuguese explorer Mendes Pinto is first European in Japan.

1544   Spanish conquistadors explore coast of Oregon.

1553   English explorer Richard Chancellor establishes Russian trade route.

1554   English explorer Sir Hugh Willoughby dies seeking Northeast Passage.

1557   Portuguese establish Chinese base at Macao.

1562   French explorer Jan Ribault establishes colony in South Carolina.

1564   Miguel López de Legazpi claims Marianas and Philippines for Spain and founds Manila.

1569   Spanish explorer Alvaro Bazan crosses Chaco of South America.

1576   English explorer Sir Martin Frobisher searches for Northwest Passage.

1581   Cossack Timofeevich extends Russian territory into Siberia.

1582   Cossack Koltso aids Timofeevich in exploration of Siberia; Spanish explorer Berrio navigates Orinoco River.

1584   Sir Walter Raleigh explores Virginia and North Carolina.

1592   Explorer Cornelis de Houtman discovers Dutch route to East Indies.

1594   Dutch explorer Willem Barents searches for Northeast Passage.

1595 Dutch establish settlements on Guinea Coast.

1598 Van Neck leads second Dutch expedition to East Indies; English explorer Will Adams travels to Japan.

1602 Englishman Bartholomew Gosnold explores New England coast.

1603 Samuel de Champlain explores Saint Lawrence River as "route to China."

1607 Englishman John Smith helps establish Jamestown, Virginia.

1608 Champlain founds city of Quebec; John Smith explores Cape Cod and Chesapeake Bay.

1610 Henry Hudson discovers Hudson Bay and River; Dutch navigator Willem Schouten sails around Cape Horn.

1613 Dutch colonist Jan Coen establishes factories in Indonesia; English explorer William Baffin discovers Baffin Bay and Island.

1614 Dutch captain Christianssen establishes fort at Albany, New York.

1615 Champlain explores lakes Huron and Ontario.

1617 Dutch explorers Jakob LeMaire and Willem Schouten start trip around world.

1618 French explorer Imbert discovers Timbuktu in Africa.

1620 English Pilgrims reach Cape Cod.

1626 French establish settlements in Madagascar; Dutch settle New Amsterdam in North America; French missionary Jean de Brébeuf explores Lake Huron region.

1631 English captain Thomas James explores James Bay in Canada.

1637 Russian explorers reach Pacific coast of Siberia.

1642 French explorer Sieur de Maisonneuve founds city of Montreal; Dutch explorer Abel Tasman discovers Van Dieman's Land (Tasmania).

1645 Capuchin monks explore Congo River.

1646 French missionary Isaac Jogues discovers Lake George.

1649 Cossack Dezhnev explores Siberia and Alaska for Russia; Cossack Stadukhin explores the Lena and Kolyma rivers in Siberia.

1652 Dutch colonist Jan van Riebeek founds Cape of Good Hope settlement.

1659 French fur trader Pierre Radisson explores Minnesota.

1670 French fur trader Perrot explores upper Mississippi region.

1673 French explorers Louis Joliet and Jacques Marquette navigate the length of the Mississippi.

1675 Belgian explorer Louis Hennepin discovers Niagara Falls and Mississippi River source.

1679 Frenchman Daniel Duluth explores Minnesota and Great Lakes.

1681 Sieur de La Salle explores Mississippi and names delta area Louisiana; English buccaneer William Dampier explores South Pacific islands.

1682 Buero da Silva explores Central Mountains region of Brazil; Pieres de Campos explores rivers of South America.

1683 Dutch explorer Aerssen establishes colony of Suriname; German naturalist Kaempfer visits Java, Thailand, and Japan.

1685 French missionary Claude Allouez explores western Lake Superior.

1697 Cossack Atlasov explores Kamchatka Peninsula for Russia.

1699 William Dampier explores northwest coast of Australia.

1721 Norwegian missionary Hans Egede is first European in Greenland in 200 years.

1723 Russian adventurer Fedorov explores northwest coast of America.

1732 Gvozdev explores Bering Sea and Alaska coastline for Russia.

1741 Russian explorer Chrikov discovers some Aleutian Islands.

1744 Frenchman Charles La Condamine measures arc of meridian in Andes.

1745 Basov explores Aleutian Islands for Russia.

1770 English navigator James Cook explores east coast of Australia.

1772 English explorer Samuel Hearne is first European to reach Arctic Ocean; Frenchman Yves Kerguélen-Trémarec discovers Antarctic islands; James Cook searches for possible continent of Antarctica.

1776 Cook searches for possible Atlantic–Pacific maritime passage.

1784 Daniel Boone explores Appalachian and Ozark areas.

1789 Scottish fur trader Sir Alexander Mackenzie explores western Canada.

Guam has no sand, only ground coral, which is used to make its roads.

1790 Russian fur trader Aleksandr Baranov explores Alaska; American explorer Robert Gray discovers Columbia River.

1797 German adventurer Hornemann explores caravan routes of Sahara Desert.

1798 British explorer George Bass circumnavigates Tasmania.

1799 German explorer Alexander von Humboldt tours North and South America.

1802 English explorer Matthew Flinders circumnavigates Australia; Portuguese explorers cross Africa.

1804 Lewis and Clark begin exploration of Louisiana Purchase; Russian Lisyanskii explores Pacific from Hawaii to Alaska.

1805 Canadian Fraser explores Canada west of Rocky Mountains; Russian navigator Adam Krusenstern maps Sakhalin, discovers mouth of Amur River.

1815 Russian navigator Otto Kotzebue discovers many Pacific islands.

1818 French explorer René Caillé crosses Sahara, reaching Timbuktu.

1819 English explorer Sir William Parry finds Northwest Passage in Arctic.

1820 American Nathaniel Palmer discovers Palmer Peninsula of Antarctica.

1821 Russian Fabian Bellinghausen leads South Pole expedition.

1825 British explorer Sir John Franklin surveys Canadian Arctic region.

1828 German physicist Georg Erman circumnavigates Earth, studying magnetic fields.

1829 English explorer Freemantle founds West Australia colony.

1830 British Lander brothers explore Niger River and Delta.

1831 American Benjamin Bonneville explores Rocky Mountains and California; British explorer James Ross finds North Magnetic Pole.

1835 British colonist Bourke explores new areas of Australia; American pioneer Jim Bowie explores U.S. Southwest.

1837 American trapper Joseph Walker explores Sierra Mountains.

1840 Frenchman Dumont d'Urville discovers Antarctic islands.

1842 John Fremont begins exploration west of Rockies.

1843 British colonist Edward Eyre explores South and West Australia; Scottish explorer Sir James Ross proves Antarctica has ice barrier.

1846 German explorer Friedrich Leichhardt disappears crossing Australia.

1847 French naturalist Comte de Castelnau crosses South America west to east.

1848 American explorer Elisha Kane surveys Gulf of Mexico.

1850 English naval officer Sir Robert McClure discovers Northwest Passage.

1851 German explorer Heinrich Barth crosses Sahara Desert twice; American explorer Savage rediscovers Yosemite Valley.

1853 Englishman Sir Richard Burton is first non-Muslim to visit Mecca and Medina; American explorer Elisha Kane leads Arctic expedition.

1854 U.S. Commodore Matthew Perry ends isolation of Japan; German Schlagintweit brothers explore Central Asia; Portuguese explorer Silva Porto crosses South Africa, west to east.

1855 Russian adventurer Nevelskoi explores Amur and proves Sakhalin is an island.

1856 Scottish missionary David Livingstone explores Africa; English explorers Richard Burton and John Speke discover Lake Tanganyika; English explorer Gregory crosses Australia east to west.

1857 English explorer John Speke discovers Lake Victoria.

1860   Irish explorer Robert Burke is first to cross Australia south to north; German explorer Karl Decken leads Kilimanjaro Mountain expedition; John Speke and James Grant prove Lake Victoria is source of Nile; American Isaac Hayes searches for "open sea" above Arctic Circle.

1863   Frenchman Louis Faidherbe explores Senegal and Niger River in Africa.

1864   Hermann Schlagintweit is first European to cross Kuenlun range.

1866   Doudart explores Mekong River route to source for France.

1871   Russian naturalist Aleksi Fedchenko explores Asian mountain ranges; British journalist Henry Stanley finds missing Livingstone; American Charles Hall is first to explore above 82 degrees north latitude.

1872   French colonist Francis Garnier searches for China–Tibet river route.

1874   John and Alexander Forrest survey western Australia.

1878   German Eduard Schnitzer (Emin Pasha) explores African lake country; English explorer Sir George Nares surveys Magellan Strait; Russian Grigori Potanin explores Gobi Desert of Mongolia.

1879   Swedish explorer Nils Nordenskjöld discovers Northeast Passage; Russian Nikolai Przhevalski is first to cross Tibet's Humboldt Mountains; Joseph Thompson explores Great Rift Valley of Africa.

1880   French colonist Pierre Brazza explores African river routes to sea.

1882   French explorer Pierre Bonvalot discovers ancient cities of Asia.

1883   French officer Foucauld explores Algerian oases and Morocco.

1885   Portuguese explorer Capelo crosses South Africa.

1888   Norwegian Fridtjof Nansen explores Greenland ice cap; French explorer Louis Binger leads African scientific expedition.

1889   German explorer Hans Meyer is first to scale Kilimanjaro peak; Austrian Oskar Baumann explores African rivers and lakes.

1891   German Erich von Drygalski explores West Greenland.

1892   Scottish oceanographer William Bruce explores Antarctic coastline; Englishman William Conway is first to scale 23,000-foot Himalayan peaks; American Robert Peary explores Greenland and proves it is an island.

1893   Swedish engineer Andre explores Arctic by balloon; German explorer Goetzen crosses Africa east to west.

1894   Englishwoman Mary Kingsley explores Ogowe River in Africa.

1895   French explorer Charles Bonin crosses Tibet and Mongolia; Englishman Frederick Jackson explores Franz Josef Land in Arctic.

1897   Gerlache de Gomery leads Belgian Antarctic expedition.

1899   Sweden's Sven Hedin finds sources of Bramaputra and Indus rivers.

1900   Norwegian Carsten Borchgrevink is early Antarctic explorer.

1906   Norwegian Roald Amundsen is first to navigate Northwest Passage.

1908   British explorer Sir Ernest Shackleton nearly reaches South Pole.

1909   American explorer Robert Peary is first to reach North Pole.

1910   Bavarian officer Wilhelm Filchner leads German Antarctic expedition.

1911   Norwegian explorer Roald Amundsen reaches South Pole; American explorer Bingham discovers Machu Picchu in Peru; British explorer Sir Douglas Mawson leads Antarctic expedition.

1912   British explorer Robert Scott reaches South Pole.

1913   Theodore Roosevelt explores central Brazilian rivers.

1926   Americans Floyd Bennett and Richard Byrd fly over North Pole; American Lincoln Ellsworth flies over North Pole; Italian engineer Umberto Nobile flies over North Pole, from Norway to Alaska.

1927   American Charles Lindbergh is first to fly solo across Atlantic Ocean.

1929   American explorer Richard Byrd is first to fly over South Pole; German Hugo Eckener makes round-the-world flight.

1931   Eckener flies over North Pole.

1932   British explorer St. John Philby crosses Arabia's Rub-al-Kali Desert; French explorer Jean Piccard explores stratosphere in balloon gondola.

1935   Lincoln Ellsworth flies over South Pole.

1937   Russian aviator Valeri Chkalov is first to fly from USSR to America over North Pole.

1947   Norwegian Thor Heyerdahl sails balsa raft from Peru to Polynesia.

1953   British mountaineer Sir Edmund Hillary and Tenzing Norgay of Nepal scale Mount Everest.

1956   Heyerdahl explores Easter Island and eastern Pacific.

1957   (July 1957–Dec. 1958) As part of the International Geophysical Year, 67 nations cooperate in scientific exploration of the Earth and its environment.

1957   Soviet Union launches *Sputnik 1,* the world's first artificial earth satellite.

1958   *Explorer 1,* first U.S. satellite, is launched and discovers Van Allen radiation belts around Earth; U.S. nuclear submarine *Nautilus* passes under ice cap at North Pole.

1959   Soviet probes *Lunas 1, 2, and 3,* respectively, fly by, impact, and photograph the moon.

1960   U.S. submarine *Triton* completes first circumnavigation of the globe under water; U.S. Navy Lieutenant Don Walsh and French explorer Jacques Piccard dive in the bathyscaphe *Trieste* to a record 35,000 feet to the floor of the Mariana Trench, the deepest point in the Pacific Ocean; NASA weather satellite *TIROS 1* transmits television pictures of cloud cover.

1961   Soviet cosmonaut Yuri Gagarin, in *Vostok 1,* is first person to orbit Earth.

1962   John Glenn, in *Freedom 7,* is first U.S. astronaut to orbit around the Earth; NASA's *Mariner 2* becomes first space probe to fly by another planet (Venus).

1964   NASA's *Ranger 7* returns close-up photographs of the Moon just prior to impacting the lunar surface.

1965   NASA's *Mariner 4* space probe, as it flies by the planet Mars, transmits first close-up pictures of the planet's surface.

1966   Soviet Union's *Luna 9* and NASA's *Surveyor 1* make first soft landings on lunar surface.

1968   U.S. astronauts Frank Borman, James Lovell, and William Anders, in *Apollo 8,* are first persons to orbit the moon.

1969   U.S. astronauts Neil Armstrong and Edwin "Buzz" Aldrin, in *Apollo 11*'s lunar landing module *Eagle,* are first persons to step onto the lunar surface.

1970   Soviet Union's unmanned probe *Luna 16* returns from the Moon with rock samples; its *Luna 17* mission lands a self-propelled vehicle on the Moon; its *Venera 7* space probe lands on Venus.

1971   NASA's *Mariner 9* becomes first space probe to orbit another planet (Mars).

1973   NASA's *Pioneer 10* becomes first space probe to fly by the planet Jupiter.

1974   NASA's *Mariner 10* space probes takes first close-up photographs of the planets Venus and Mercury.

1976   NASA's *Vikings 1* and *2* become first spacecraft to land on surface of Mars.

1978   Italian Reinhold Messner and Austrian Peter Habeler make the first conquest of Mount Everest without artificial oxygen supplies; Japanese explorer Naomi Uemura becomes the first person to make a solo journey to the North Pole.

1979   NASA's *Voyager 1,* during flyby of Jupiter, discovers ring, erupting volcanoes on the Jovian satellite Io, and three new satellites; NASA's *Pioneer 11,* becomes first space probe to fly by the planet Saturn.

1980   During flyby of the planet Saturn, *Voyager 1* discovers six new satellites.

1981   NASA scientists report that two meteorites found in the Antarctic may have originated on the planet Mars.

1982   Soviet space probes *Veneras 13* and *14* land on Venus and transmit first color photos.

1983   *Pioneer 10* becomes first spacecraft to leave solar system.

1984   Soviet engineers drill 7.5 miles to reach the Earth's lower crust.

1985   Deep oceanic vents are found in the Mid-Atlantic Ridge; U.S. oceanographer Robert Ballard leads French-American team, using sonar and a robot submarine, that discovers wreck of British ocean liner *Titanic* .

The World

1986   NASA's *Voyager 2* space probe flies by the planet Uranus and discovers ten new satellites; European Space Agency's *Giotto* space probe photographs nucleus of Halley's comet.

1989   *Voyager 2* flies by the planet Neptune and discovers six new satellites and five rings.

1995   NASA's *Galileo* space probe releases entry probe into Jupiter's atmosphere and becomes first craft to orbit the planet.

1997   NASA's *Pathfinder* space probe lands on the surface of Mars, and its *Sojourner* rover carries out first mobile exploration of another planet.

1998   Former *Mercury* astronaut Senator John Glenn (77) becomes the oldest person ever to fly in space; assembly of International Space Station begins; *Lunar Prospector* becomes first NASA moon launch in 25 years.

1999   Bertrand Picard and Brian Jones become the first people to circumnavigate Earth nonstop in a balloon; Air Force Lieutenant Colonel Eileen Collins becomes the first woman to command a NASA space shuttle mission; spacecraft *Stardust* is launched to gather dust samples from Comet Wild-2 and return them to Earth.

2000   The first cargo ship docks with the International Space Station; the first official crew reaches the station. Rendezvous spacecraft reaches the asteroid Eros, the first spacecraft to orbit an asteroid.

2001   The *Mir* space station—the largest manmade object in space—falls into the South Pacific Ocean; the first citizen "space tourist," Dennis Tito, visits the International Space Station; Claudie Haigneré becomes the first European woman astronaut to visit the International Space Station.

2002   Mark Shuttleworth becomes the second space tourist to visit the International Space Station; Mars Odyssey, which reached Mars in 2001, begins its science mapping mission at the red planet; scientists are still able to contact *Pioneer 10,* a spacecraft launched 30 years ago.

POPULATION OF MAJOR WORLD CITIES

An asterisk (*) indicates that the population figure is for the metropolitan area.

City	Description	Population
Addis Ababa, Ethiopia	Capital since 1896	2,639,000
Ahmedabad, India	Founded in 1411	3,298,000
Alexandria, Egypt	Founded by Alexander the Great, 332 B.C.	3,431,000
Algiers, Algeria	Founded in 10th century on Roman site	1,885,000
Amman, Jordan	Site of biblical city of Ammonites	1,300,000
Amsterdam, the Netherlands	Founded in 1300	1,101,000
Ankara, Turkey	Capital of Galacia around 300 B.C.	3,028,000
Athens, Greece	Ancient Greek city-state in 700 B.C.	772,000
Auckland, New Zealand	Founded in 1840, original capital	346,000
Baghdad, Iraq	Center of Islamic culture since 813	4,797,000
Baku, Azerbaijan	Founded in 9th century	1,149,000
Bandung, Indonesia	Founded in 1810	2,368,000
Bangalore, India	Founded in 16th century	4,087,000*
Bangkok, Thailand	Capital since 1782	5,876,000
Barcelona, Spain	Founded by Carthaginians around 300 B.C.	2,819,000*
Barranquilla, Colombia	Inland seaport since 1935	1,157,000
Beijing, China	Founded around 1122 B.C. as Peking; renamed in 1949	10,839,000
Beirut, Lebanon	Site of ancient Phoenician settlement	1,900,000*
Belgrade, Serbia	Site of Singidunum, ancient Roman camp	1,555,000
Belo Horizonte, Brazil	Cattle and cotton-trading center	4,170,000*

City	Description	Population
Berlin, Germany	Founded in 13th century; capital of Germany 1871–1945, of United Germany since 1990	3,471,000*
Birmingham, England	Market town since before 13th century	1,020,000
Bogotá, Colombia	Founded by conquistadors in 1538	5,699,000
Bombay, India	Established in early Christian era	12,572,000*
Brisbane, Australia	Founded in 1824 as a penal colony	1,146,000
Brussels, Belgium	Capital since 1530	948,000
Bucharest, Romania	Capital since 1861	2,054,000
Budapest, Hungary	Site of Aquincum, 2nd-century Roman camp	2,011,000
Buenos Aires, Argentina	Settled by conquistadors in 1536	2,961,000
Cairo, Egypt	Site of 7th-century Arab military camp	6,790,000
Calcutta, India	Developed from 1690 English factory site	4,400,000
Calgary, Alberta, Canada	Originally (1875) Northwest Mounted Police post	899,000*
Cali, Colombia	Founded by conquistadors in 1536	2,710,000*
Cape Town, South Africa	Founded in 1652 as Dutch naval base	855,000
Caracas, Venezuela	Founded by conquistadors in 1567	3,153,000*
Casablanca, Morocco	Site of ancient city of Anfa	3,541,000*
Chicago, Illinois, United States	Originally portage site for fur traders	2,896,000
Chittagong, Bangladesh	Portuguese trading post in 1600s	2,041,000*
Chongqing, China	Former capital of Nationalist China	3,870,000
Cologne, Germany	Site of Roman (A.D. 50) Colonia Agrippina	964,000
Copenhagen, Denmark	Capital since 1443	1,338,000*
Córdoba, Argentina	Founded in 1573; university founded in 1613	1,434,000*
Damascus, Syria	City of Egyptians and Hittites before 1000 B.C.	2,335,000*
Delhi, India	Capital of northern India in 13th century	7,207,000
Dhaka, Bangladesh	Capital since 1971 secession from Pakistan	6,105,000*
Dnepropetrovsk, Ukraine	Founded in 1787 at Cossack village site	1,190,000
Donetsk, Ukraine	Founded in 1870, called Stalino until 1961	1,121,000
Dresden, Germany	Originally (A.D. 922) a Slavonic settlement	491,000
Dublin, Ireland	Originally a 9th-century Viking base	985,000*
Düsseldorf, Germany	Rhine River port since 11th century	576,000
Edmonton, Alberta, Canada	Originally (1795) Hudson Bay trading post	617,000
Essen, Germany	Ruhr Valley city founded in 9th century	627,000
Frankfurt, Germany	Site of ancient Roman military camp	651,000
Fukuoka, Japan	Seaport on Hakata Bay founded in 13th century	1,285,000
Genoa, Italy	Roman settlement in 3rd century B.C.	678,000
Glasgow, Scotland	Founded by 6th-century missionaries	663,000
Guadalajara, Mexico	Originally founded in 1530	1,646,000
Guangzhou, China	Inland seaport since 3rd century B.C.	3,114,000
Guatemala City, Guatemala	Founded as capital in 1776	1,167,000
Guayaquil, Ecuador	Founded by conquistadors in 1535	1,877,000
Hamburg, Germany	Founded in 9th century by Charlemagne	1,707,000
Harbin, China	Village until linked by railroad in 1898	2,505,000
Havana, Cuba	Founded in 1519 as Spanish navy base	2,256,000
Ho Chi Minh City, Vietnam	Formerly Saigon, ancient Khmer village	4,322,000*
Hyderabad, India	Founded as Golconda; capital in 1589	3,045,000
Hyderabad, Pakistan	Founded in 1768 as capital of Sind	1,151,000*
Ibadan, Nigeria	Founded around 1830 as military camp	1,731,000
Istanbul, Turkey	Until A.D. 300, Byzantium; until 1930, Constantinople	7,490,000
Jakarta, Indonesia	Founded in 1619 as Batavia; renamed 1971	8,228,000

continues

The World

Population of Major World Cities, Continued

City	Description	Population
Jerusalem, Israel	Capital of ancient kingdoms of Israel and Judah	592,000
Johannesburg, South Africa	Founded as gold-mining camp in 1886	1,196,000
Kanpur, India	Village until ceded to British in 1801	2,111,000
Karachi, Pakistan	Founded in 1725 as Hindu trading center	11,794,000*
Kharkov, Ukraine	Founded in 1654 as outpost of Moscow	1,555,000
Kiev, Ukraine	"Mother of Russian Cities," founded in A.D. 882	2,670,000
Kinshasa, Democratic Republic of Congo	Founded in 1881 as Leopoldville; renamed 1966	5,064,000
Kobe, Japan	Ancient fishing village until 1868	1,477,000
Kuala Lumpur, Malaysia	Founded as tin-mining settlement in 1857	1,378,000
Lagos, Nigeria	Former slave trading center; now the capital	5,195,000*
Lahore, Pakistan	Capital of Mogul sultans in 11th century	6,040,000*
La Paz, Bolivia	Founded in 1548; capital since 1898	1,001,000
Leipzig, Germany	Founded in 11th century; Bach was organist here	511,000
Lima, Peru	Site of oldest university in Americas (1551)	7,443,000*
Lisbon, Portugal	Ancient Phoenician, Carthaginian trading center	818,000
Liverpool, England	Chartered in 1207 by King John	482,000
Lodz, Poland	Founded in 1423; belonged to Russia until 1919	849,000
London, England	Established in A.D. 43 as Roman town of Londinium	7,074,000
Los Angeles, California, United States	Founded in 1781 as capital of Spanish colony	3,598,000
Madras, India	Founded in 1640 as British outpost	5,361,000*
Madrid, Spain	A Moorish fortress until 932	3,029,000
Managua, Nicaragua	Established as capital in 1855 to end feud	959,000
Manila, Philippines	Founded by Spanish in 1571	1,655,000
Marseilles, France	Originally Massilia, Ionian Greek colony, in 600 B.C.	1,087,000
Mecca, Saudi Arabia	Birthplace of Muhammad in 570	630,000
Medellín, Colombia	Coffee, drugs, mining center founded in 1675	1,970,000*
Melbourne, Australia	Founded 1835 by Tasmanian settlers	3,217,000
Mexico City, Mexico	Aztec capital until captured by Cortés in 1521	8,605,000
Milan, Italy	Ancient Celtic town captured by Romans in 222 B.C.	1,371,000
Minsk, Belarus	City on Moscow-Warsaw rail link founded in 11th century	1,772,000
Monterrey, Mexico	Founded in 1579; invaded by U.S. troops in 1846	1,110,000
Montevideo, Uruguay	Settled by Spanish in 1726; capital since 1828	1,378,000
Montreal, Quebec, Canada	Site of Indian encampment, founded by French in 1642	3,337,000
Moscow, Russia	Founded in 1147; became capital around 1340	9,233,000
Munich, Germany	Founded in 1158; birthplace of Nazi movement, 1923	1,240,000
Nagoya, Japan	Buddhist temple site in 2nd century; now an industrial city	2,155,000
Nanjing, China	Founded in 1368; twice capital in 20th century	2,211,000
Naples, Italy	Named Neapolis (New City) by Greek settlers around 600 B.C.	1,369,000
New York City, New York, United States	Founded in 1609 as New Amsterdam by Dutch; renamed 1664	7,420,000
Nizhni Novgorod, Russia	Founded in 1221; called Gorky after Maxim Gorky during Soviet era	1,458,000
Novosibirsk, Russia	"Chicago of Siberia," founded in 1893 on Trans-Siberian Railway	1,478,000
Odessa, Ukraine	Founded by Tartars in 14th century	1,096,000

City	Description	Population
Osaka, Japan	Founded in 16th century as capital city	2,624,000
Ottawa, Ontario, Canada	Selected as capital in 1858 by Queen Victoria	323,000
Palermo, Italy	Founded by Phoenicians in 8th century B.C.	698,000
Paris, France	Grew from pre-Roman settlement named Lutetia Parisiorum	2,152,000
Port-au-Prince, Haiti	Founded by sugar planters in 1749; capital since 1804	917,000
Pôrto Alegre, Brazil	Founded in 1742 by settlers from Azores	1,288,000*
Prague, Czech Republic	Grew from 10th-century trading center	1,226,000
Pusan, South Korea	Originally a fishing village; opened to trade in 1443	3,830,000
Pyongyang, North Korea	Existed as Heijo, Korean cultural center, in 1100 B.C.	2,639,000
Quebec City, Quebec, Canada	Site of Indian settlement visited by Cartier in 1535	168,000
Quezon City, Philippines	Founded in 1940 as site of future capital	1,989,000
Quito, Ecuador	Originally Quito Indian camp; captured by Incas in 1470	1,487,000
Recife, Brazil	Settled by Portuguese in 1535	1,346,000
Rio de Janeiro, Brazil	Founded by Portuguese in 1502; capital since 1889	5,851,000
Riyadh, Saudi Arabia	Onetime center of classic Arabic architecture	2,776,000*
Rome, Italy	According to legend, founded in 753 B.C. by Romulus	2,775,000
Rosario, Argentina	City in La Pampa region; founded in 1730	1,118,000
Rotterdam, the Netherlands	North Sea port chartered in 1328	593,000
St. Petersburg, Russia	Founded in 1703; named Leningrad from 1924 to 1991	5,113,000
Salvador, Brazil	Founded in 1549 as Bahia	2,211,000
Samara, Russia	Founded in 1586; formerly Kuibyshev	1,232,000
Santiago, Chile	Founded in 1541 by conquistadors	5,067,000
Santo Domingo, Dominican Republic	Oldest continuous European settlement in Americas, founded in 1496	2,135,000
São Paulo, Brazil	Founded in 1554 by Jesuit missionaries on Indian campsite	9,786,000
Sapporo, Japan	Founded in 1869 in government plan to develop Hokkaido Island	1,774,000
Seoul, South Korea	Originally named Keijo, a Korean capital since 1392	10,776,000
Seville, Spain	Originally Hispalis, a Phoenician trading center	719,000
Shanghai, China	Existed as Hu-tsen in Sung dynasty, 11th century	7,551,000
Shenyang, China	Formerly Mukden, capital city of 12th-century Tartars	3,860,000
Singapore, Singapore	Originally Singhapura, destroyed in 1365; refounded in 1819	3,462,000
Sofia, Bulgaria	Founded as Sardica by 2nd-century Romans; capital since 1879	1,192,000
Stockholm, Sweden	Originally a fishing village, founded in 13th century	736,000
Surabaja, Indonesia	Grew from 17th-century Javanese trading post	2,701,000
Sydney, Australia	First British settlement in Australia, 1788	3,770,000
Taipei, Taiwan	Settled in 18th century by Chinese mainland immigrants	2,596,000
Tashkent, Uzbekistan	Ancient central Asian city; existed in 1st century B.C.	2,148,000
Tbilisi, Georgia	Also called Tiflis; settled in 4th century B.C.	1,310,000
Tehran, Iran	Settled in 13th century by refugees from Mongol invasion	6,750,000
Tianjin, China	Also called Tientsin, ancient trading center	4,575,000
Tokyo, Japan	Founded in 12th century as fortress for warlord	8,164,000
Toronto, Ontario, Canada	Originally Fort Rouille, 1749; York, 1793; renamed 1834	4,344,000*
Tripoli, Libya	Founded as Oea by Phoenicians in 7th century B.C.	591,000
Tunis, Tunisia	Pre-Carthaginian city with access to Mediterranean	1,897,000*
Turin, Italy	Ancient Roman city of Augusta Taurinorum	962,000

continues

The World

Population of Major World Cities, Continued

City	Description	Population
Valencia, Spain	Former city of Romans, Visigoths, Moors	764,000
Vancouver, British Columbia, Canada	Originally settled in 1875 as Granville; renamed 1886	1,831,000*
Vienna, Austria	Capital of the Austro-Hungarian Empire 1278–1918; now capital of the Austrian republic	1,595,000
Volgograd, Russia	Founded in 1589 as Tsaritsyn; later Stalingrad; renamed Volgograd in 1961	1,003,000
Warsaw, Poland	Settled in 11th century; capital since 1596	1,651,000
Washington, District of Columbia, United States	Founded in 1790 on site selected by George Washington	607,000
Wellington, New Zealand	Founded in 1840; replaced Auckland as capital in 1865	166,000
Yangon, Myanmar	Existed as fishing village in 6th century	4,196,000
Yekaterinburg, Russia	Founded in 1721; called Sverdlovsk during Soviet era	1,351,000
Yokohama, Japan	Feudal fishing village until opened to foreign trade in 1859	3,307,000

THE UNITED NATIONS

The United Nations organization was established during World War II as an outgrowth of an agreement among 26 countries fighting the Germany-Italy-Japan Axis. It replaced the League of Nations as an instrument for the promotion of international peace and security.

The name was suggested by U.S. President Franklin D. Roosevelt in 1941 and was officially adopted the following year. The United Nations was formally organized on June 26, 1945, following an initial San Francisco conference to draft a charter.

The basic charter contains 19 chapters, divided into 111 articles, and provides for the support of a number of international organs and agencies (see chart).

THE SIX OFFICIAL LANGUAGES OF THE UNITED NATIONS

Arabic   French
Chinese   Russian
English   Spanish

SECRETARIES-GENERAL OF THE UNITED NATIONS

Name	Trygve Lie
Country	Norway
Term of Office	1946–1952
Name	Dag Hammarskjöld
Country	Sweden
Term of Office	1953–1961
Name	U Thant
Country	Myanmar (formerly Burma)
Term of Office	1961–1971
Name	Kurt Waldheim
Country	Austria
Term of Office	1972–1981
Name	Javier Pérez de Cuellar
Country	Peru
Term of Office	1982–1991
Name	Boutros Boutros-Ghali
Country	Egypt
Term of Office	1992–1996
Name	Kofi Annan
Country	Ghana
Term of Office	1997–

THE UNITED NATIONS SYSTEM

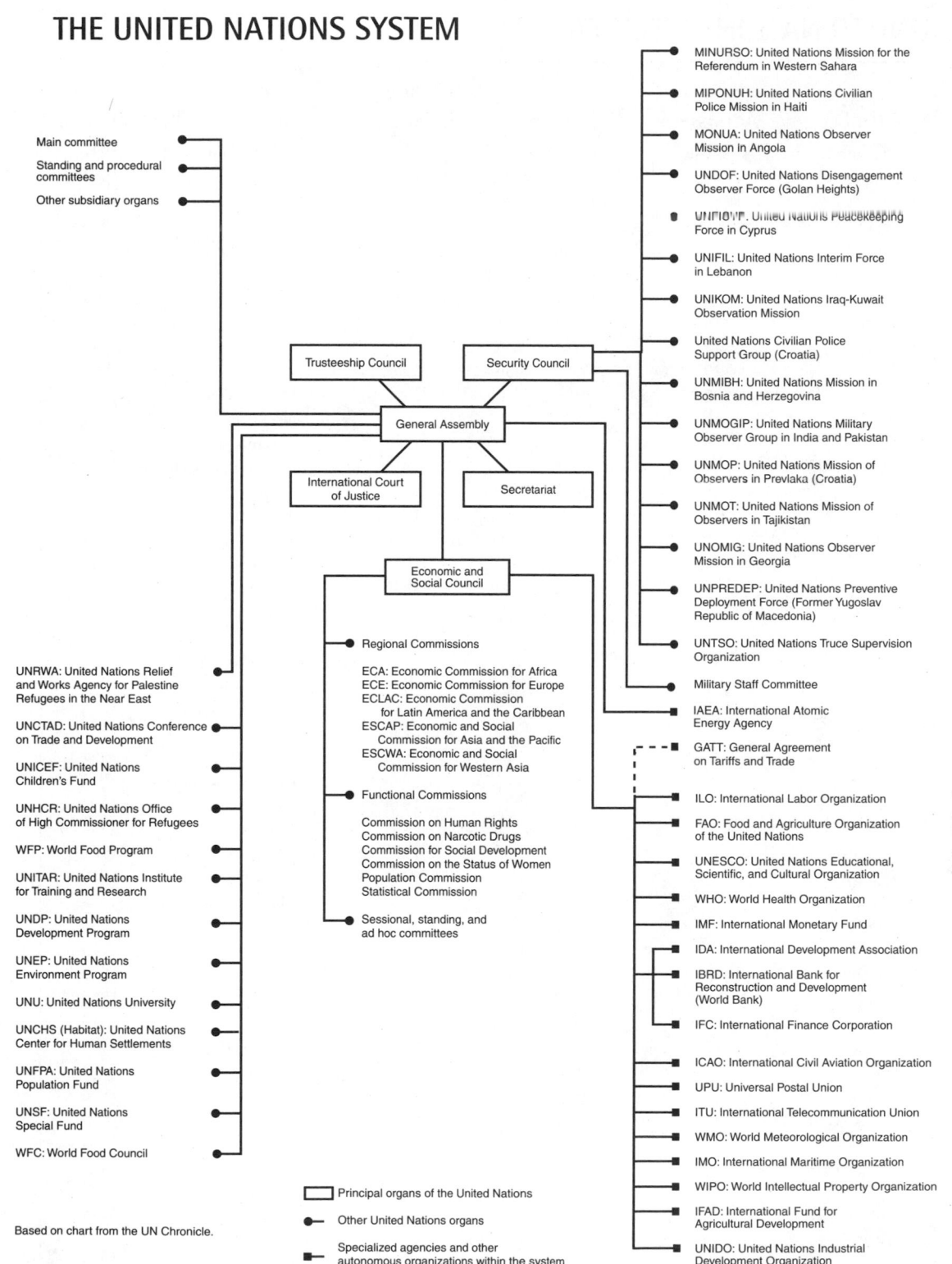

Main committee

Standing and procedural committees

Other subsidiary organs

Trusteeship Council

Security Council

General Assembly

International Court of Justice

Secretariat

Economic and Social Council

MINURSO: United Nations Mission for the Referendum in Western Sahara

MIPONUH: United Nations Civilian Police Mission in Haiti

MONUA: United Nations Observer Mission In Angola

UNDOF: United Nations Disengagement Observer Force (Golan Heights)

UNFICYP: United Nations Peacekeeping Force in Cyprus

UNIFIL: United Nations Interim Force in Lebanon

UNIKOM: United Nations Iraq-Kuwait Observation Mission

United Nations Civilian Police Support Group (Croatia)

UNMIBH: United Nations Mission in Bosnia and Herzegovina

UNMOGIP: United Nations Military Observer Group in India and Pakistan

UNMOP: United Nations Mission of Observers in Prevlaka (Croatia)

UNMOT: United Nations Mission of Observers in Tajikistan

UNOMIG: United Nations Observer Mission in Georgia

UNPREDEP: United Nations Preventive Deployment Force (Former Yugoslav Republic of Macedonia)

UNTSO: United Nations Truce Supervision Organization

Military Staff Committee

IAEA: International Atomic Energy Agency

GATT: General Agreement on Tariffs and Trade

ILO: International Labor Organization

FAO: Food and Agriculture Organization of the United Nations

UNESCO: United Nations Educational, Scientific, and Cultural Organization

WHO: World Health Organization

IMF: International Monetary Fund

IDA: International Development Association

IBRD: International Bank for Reconstruction and Development (World Bank)

IFC: International Finance Corporation

ICAO: International Civil Aviation Organization

UPU: Universal Postal Union

ITU: International Telecommunication Union

WMO: World Meteorological Organization

IMO: International Maritime Organization

WIPO: World Intellectual Property Organization

IFAD: International Fund for Agricultural Development

UNIDO: United Nations Industrial Development Organization

UNRWA: United Nations Relief and Works Agency for Palestine Refugees in the Near East

UNCTAD: United Nations Conference on Trade and Development

UNICEF: United Nations Children's Fund

UNHCR: United Nations Office of High Commissioner for Refugees

WFP: World Food Program

UNITAR: United Nations Institute for Training and Research

UNDP: United Nations Development Program

UNEP: United Nations Environment Program

UNU: United Nations University

UNCHS (Habitat): United Nations Center for Human Settlements

UNFPA: United Nations Population Fund

UNSF: United Nations Special Fund

WFC: World Food Council

Regional Commissions

ECA: Economic Commission for Africa
ECE: Economic Commission for Europe
ECLAC: Economic Commission for Latin America and the Caribbean
ESCAP: Economic and Social Commission for Asia and the Pacific
ESCWA: Economic and Social Commission for Western Asia

Functional Commissions

Commission on Human Rights
Commission on Narcotic Drugs
Commission for Social Development
Commission on the Status of Women
Population Commission
Statistical Commission

Sessional, standing, and ad hoc committees

Based on chart from the UN Chronicle.

☐ Principal organs of the United Nations

● Other United Nations organs

■ Specialized agencies and other autonomous organizations within the system

The World

UNITED NATIONS MEMBER STATES

Member	Year of Admission	Member	Year of Admission	Member	Year of Admission
Afghanistan	1946	Cyprus	1960	Korea, Republic of	1991
Albania	1955	Czech Republic	1993	Kuwait	1963
Algeria	1962	Denmark	1945	Kyrgyzstan	1992
Andorra	1993	Djibouti	1977	Lao People's	1955
Angola	1976	Dominica	1978	Democratic Republic	
Antigua and Barbuda	1981	Dominican Republic	1945	Latvia	1991
Argentina	1945	Ecuador	1945	Lebanon	1945
Armenia	1992	Egypt	1945	Lesotho	1966
Australia	1945	El Salvador	1945	Liberia	1945
Austria	1955	Equatorial Guinea	1968	Libyan Arab Jamahiriya	1955
Azerbaijan	1992	Eritrea	1993	Liechtenstein	1990
Bahamas	1973	Estonia	1991	Lithuania	1991
Bahrain	1971	Ethiopia	1945	Luxembourg	1945
Bangladesh	1974	Fiji	1970	Macedonia (the former	1993
Barbados	1966	Finland	1955	Yugoslav Republic of)	
Belarus	1945	France	1945	Madagascar	1960
Belgium	1945	Gabon	1960	Malawi	1964
Belize	1981	Gambia	1965	Malaysia	1957
Benin	1960	Georgia	1992	Maldives	1965
Bhutan	1971	Germany	1973	Mali	1960
Bolivia	1945	Ghana	1957	Malta	1964
Bosnia and	1992	Greece	1945	Marshall Islands	1991
Herzegovina		Grenada	1974	Mauritania	1961
Botswana	1966	Guatemala	1945	Mauritius	1968
Brazil	1945	Guinea	1958	Mexico	1945
Brunei Darussalam	1984	Guinea-Bissau	1974	Micronesia	1991
Bulgaria	1955	Guyana	1966	(Federated States of)	
Burkina Faso	1960	Haiti	1945	Moldova	1992
Burundi	1962	Honduras	1945	Monaco	1993
Cambodia	1955	Hungary	1955	Mongolia	1961
Cameroon	1960	Iceland	1946	Morocco	1956
Canada	1945	India	1945	Mozambique	1975
Cape Verde	1975	Indonesia	1950	Myanmar	1948
Central African	1960	Iran (Islamic	1945	Namibia	1990
Republic		Republic of)		Nauru	1999
Chad	1960	Iraq	1945	Nepal	1955
Chile	1945	Ireland	1955	Netherlands	1945
China	1945	Israel	1949	New Zealand	1945
Colombia	1945	Italy	1955	Nicaragua	1945
Comoros	1975	Jamaica	1962	Niger	1960
Congo, Democratic	1960	Japan	1956	Nigeria	1960
Republic of		Jordan	1955	Norway	1945
Congo, Republic of the	1960	Kazakhstan	1992	Oman	1971
Costa Rica	1945	Kenya	1963	Pakistan	1947
Côte d'Ivoire	1960	Kiribati	1999	Palau	1994
Croatia	1992	Korea, Democratic	1991	Panama	1945
Cuba	1945	People's Republic of		Papua New Guinea	1975

Member	Year of Admission	Member	Year of Admission	Member	Year of Admission
Paraguay	1945	Slovakia	1993	Uganda	1962
Peru	1945	Slovenia	1992	Ukraine	1945
Philippines	1945	Solomon Islands	1978	United Arab Emirates	1971
Poland	1945	Somalia	1960	United Kingdom of	1945
Portugal	1955	South Africa	1945	Great Britain and	
Qatar	1971	Spain	1955	Northern Ireland	
Romania	1955	Sri Lanka	1955	United Republic of	1961
Russian Federation	1945	Sudan	1956	Tanzania	
Rwanda	1962	Suriname	1975	United States of	1945
Saint Kitts and Nevis	1983	Swaziland	1968	America	
Saint Lucia	1979	Sweden	1946	Uruguay	1945
Saint Vincent and	1980	Syrian Arab Republic	1945	Uzbekistan	1992
the Grenadines		Tajikistan	1992	Vanuatu	1981
Samoa	1976	Thailand	1946	Venezuela	1945
San Marino	1992	Togo	1960	Viet Nam	1977
São Tomé and Principe	1975	Tonga	1999	Yemen	1947
Saudi Arabia	1945	Trinidad and Tobago	1962	Yugoslavia	1945
Senegal	1960	Tunisia	1956	Zambia	1964
Seychelles	1976	Turkey	1945	Zimbabwe	1980
Sierra Leone	1961	Turkmenistan	1992		
Singapore	1965	Tuvalu	2000		

INTERNATIONAL ORGANIZATIONS

ADB	African Development Bank
AL	Arab League (League of Arab States)
ANZUS	ANZUS Council; treaty signed by Australia, New Zealand, and the United States
APC	African Peanut (Groundnut) Council
AsDB	Asian Development Bank
ASEAN	Association of Southeast Asian Nations
BENELUX	Belgium, Netherlands, Luxembourg Economic Union
CACM	Central American Common Market
CARICOM	Caribbean Community and Common Market
CCC	Customs Cooperation Council
CDB	Caribbean Development Bank
CE	Council of Europe
CEAO	West African Economic Community
CENTO	Central Treaty Organization
CFA	African Financial Community
CE	Council of Europe
CIS	Commonweath of Independent States (12 members of former Soviet Union)
CP	Colombo Plan
EC	European Community
ECA	Economic Commission for Africa (UN)
ECE	Economic Commission for Europe (UN)
ECLAC	Economic Commission for Latin America and the Caribbean (UN)
ECOSOC	Economic and Social Council (UN)
ECOWAS	Economic Community of West African States
ESCWA	Economic and Social Commission for Western Asia (UN)
EFTA	European Free Trade Association
EIB	European Investment Bank
ENTENTE	Political-Economic Association of Ivory Coast, Benin, Niger, Burkina Faso, and Togo
ESA	European Space Agency
ESCAP	Economic and Social Commission for Asia and the Pacific (UN)
EU	European Union
FAO	Food and Agriculture Organization (UN)
G-77	Group of 77
GA	General Assembly (UN)
GCC	Gulf Cooperation Council

IAEA	International Atomic Energy Agency (UN)
IBEC	International Bank for Economic Cooperation
IBRD	International Bank for Reconstruction and Development ("World Bank," UN)
ICAO	International Civil Aviation Organization (UN)
ICJ	International Court of Justice (UN)
IDA	International Development Association (IBRD affiliate, UN)
IDB	Inter-American Development Bank
IDB	Islamic Development Bank
IEA	International Energy Agency (associated with OECD)
IFAD	International Fund for Agricultural Development (UN)
IFC	International Finance Corporation (IBRD affiliate, UN)
IIB	International Investment Bank
ILO	International Labor Organization (UN)
IMF	International Monetary Fund (UN)
IMO	International Maritime Organization (UN)
INTELSAT	International Telecommunications Satellite Organization
INTERPOL	International Criminal Police Organization
IOC	International Olympic Committee
IOM	International Organization for Migration
ITU	International Telecommunications Union (UN)
LAIA	Latin American Integration Association
NAFTA	North American Free Trade Agreement
NAM	Nonaligned Movement
NATO	North Atlantic Treaty Organization
OAPEC	Organization of Arab Petroleum Exporting Countries
OAS	Organization of American States
OAU	Organization of African Unity
ODECA	Organization of Central American States

OECD	Organization for Economic Cooperation and Development
OIC	Organization of the Islamic Conference
OIEC	Organization for International Economic Cooperation
OPEC	Organization of Petroleum Exporting Countries
PAHO	Pan American Health Organization
SAARC	South Asian Association for Regional Cooperation
SADC	Southern African Development Community
SC	Security Council (UN)
SELA	Latin American Economic System
SPC	South Pacific Commission
SPF	South Pacific Forum
TC	Trusteeship Council (UN)
TDB	Trade and Development Board (UN)
UDEAC	Economic and Customs Union of Central Africa
UEAC	Union of Central African States
UNCTAD	UN Conference on Trade and Development
UNDP	UN Development Program
UNESCO	UN Educational, Scientific, and Cultural Organization
UNICEF	UN Children's Fund
UNIDO	UN Industrial Development Organization
UPU	Universal Postal Union (UN)
WEU	Western European Union
WFC	World Food Council (UN)
WFTU	World Federation of Trade Unions
WHO	World Health Organization (UN)
WIPO	World Intellectual Property Organization (UN)
WMO	World Meteorological Organization (UN)
WTO	World Tourism Organization
WTO	World Trade Organization

SEVEN WONDERS OF THE ANCIENT WORLD

Artemision at Ephesus   This temple of the Greek goddess Artemis (also the Roman goddess Diana) was begun in 541 B.C. at Ephesus (now a site in Turkey) and completed 220 years later. The temple was 425 feet long and 220 feet wide with 127 marble columns, each 60 feet tall. The gates were made of cypress and the ceiling of cedar. The temple was destroyed by the Goths in A.D. 262.

The Colossus of Rhodes   This 100-foot-tall bronze statue of the sun god Helios was erected between 292 and 280 B.C. in the harbor at Rhodes. According to legend, it appeared to stand astride the harbor but was actually on a promontory overlooking it. The statue was toppled by an earthquake around 224 B.C. and lay in ruins until A.D. 653, when the remains were sold as scrap metal.

The Hanging Gardens of Babylon   This series of five terraces of glazed brick, each 50 feet above the next, was erected by King Nebuchadnezzar for his wife, Amytis, in 562 B.C. The terraces, featuring rare and exotic plants, were connected by a winding stairway. A pumping device supplied water so the gardens could be irrigated by fountains.

The Mausoleum at Halicarnassus This 140-foot-high white marble structure was built in 352 B.C. at Halicarnassus (now a site in Turkey) in memory of King Mausolus of Caria. Its massive base contained the sarcophagus and supported 36 columns crowned with a stepped pyramid on which was constructed a marble chariot. It was destroyed for the use of stone to build a castle for the Knights of Saint John in 1402.

Olympian Zeus This statue of the supreme god in Greek mythology was executed in gold and ivory for the temple at Olympia. The figure of the seated Zeus was 40 feet tall and rested on a base that was 12 feet high. The portions of the statue representing the flesh of the god were covered with marble, and his cloak was made of gold. Golden lions rested near his feet.

"Major World Philosophers" in chapter 10; Go to "Cultural Symbols" in chapter 12

The Pyramids of Egypt These were started by Khufu (Cheops) around 2700 B.C. as tombs for the ancient kings. The three largest and finest were erected during the 4th dynasty at Gizeh, near Cairo. The largest of the group is the Khufu Pyramid, built of limestone blocks from a base 756 feet wide on each side and covering an area of 13 acres. It is 482 feet high. Smaller pyramids were built for wives and other members of the royal families.

The Tower of Pharos This was a great lighthouse built on the island of Pharos, at Alexandria, Egypt, during the reign of Ptolemy Philadelphus, 285 B.C. Also called the Pharos, it was 500 feet tall with a ramp leading to the top. Light was produced with a fire and reflectors and could be seen from a distance of 42 miles.

ROYAL RULERS OF EUROPE AND ASIA

CHINA

Major Chinese Dynasties

Hsia	c.1994–c.1523 B.C.
Shang	c.1523–c.1027 B.C.
Zhou	c.1027–256 B.C.
Western Zhou	c.1027–771 B.C.
Eastern Zhou	770–256 B.C.
Spring and Autumn Period	722–481 B.C.
Warring States Period	403–222 B.C.
Qin	221–206 B.C.
Han, Former (Western)	202 B.C.–A.D. 8
Hsin	A.D. 9–23
Han, Later (Eastern)	25–220
Period of Disunion	220–589
Three Kingdoms Period	220–265
Wei	220–265
Shu	221–263
Wu	222–280
Jin	265–420
Western Jin	265–317
Eastern Jin	317–420
Northern Dynasties	386–581
Northern Wei	386–534
Eastern Wei	534–550
Northern Ch'i	550–577
Western Wei	535–557
Northern Zhou	557–581
Southern Dynasties	420–589
Song	420–479
Ch'i	479–502
Liang	502–557
Ch'en	557–589
Sui	581–618
Tang	618–906
Five Dynasties (Wu Tai)	907–960
Later Liang	907–923
Later Tang	923–936
Later Jin	936–946
Later Han	947–950
Later Zhou	951–960
Ten Kingdoms	902–979
Liao	947–1125
Western Xia	990–1227
Jin	1115–1234

The World

Major Chinese Dynasties, *continued*

Sung	960–1279
Northern Sung	960–1127
Southern Sung	1127–1279
Yüan (Mongol)	1260–1368
Ming	1368–1644

Qing (Manchu) Dynasty Rulers

Shun Chih	1644–1661
K'ang Hsi	1661–1722
Yung Cheng	1722–1735
Ch'ien Lung	1735–1796
Chia Ch'ing	1796–1820
Tao Kuang	1820–1851
Hsien Feng	1851–1861
T'ung Chi	1861–1875
Kuang Hsu	1875–1898
Tzu Hsi (empress dowager)	1898–1908
Hsiian T'ung	1908–1912

ENGLAND/GREAT BRITAIN

Saxon

Egbert	829–839
Ethelwulf	839–858
Ethelbald	858–860
Ethelbert	860–866
Ethelred I	866–871
Alfred	871–899
Edward (the Elder)	899–924
Athelstan	924–940
Edmund I	940–946
Edred	946–955
Edwy	955–959
Edgar	959–975
Edward (the Martyr)	975–978
Ethelred II	978–1016
Edmund II	1016

Danish

Canute	1017–1035
Harold I	1035–1040
Hardicanute	1040–1042

Saxon

Edward (the Confessor)	1042–1066
Harold II	1066

Norman

William I (the Conqueror)	1066–1087
William II (Rufus)	1087–1100
Henry I (Beauclerc)	1100–1135
Stephen	1135–1154

Plantagenet

Henry II	1154–1189
Richard I (Coeur de Lion)	1189–1199
John (Lackland)	1199–1216
Henry III	1216–1272
Edward I	1272–1307
Edward II	1307–1327
Edward III	1327–1377
Richard II	1377–1399

Lancaster

Henry IV (Bolingbroke)	1399–1413
Henry V	1413–1422
Henry VI	1422–1461

York

Edward IV	1461–1470

Lancaster

Henry VI (restored)	1470–1471

York

Edward IV (restored)	1471–1483
Edward V	1483
Richard III	1483–1485

Tudor

Henry VII	1485–1509
Henry VIII	1509–1547
Edward VI	1547–1553
Mary I	1553–1558
Elizabeth	1558–1603

Stuart

James I	1603–1625
Charles I	1625–1649
[Commonwealth	1649–1653;
Oliver Cromwell, Lord	
Protector, 1653–1658;	
Richard Cromwell, Lord	
Protector, 1658–1659;	
military rule until the	
Restoration]	

Charles II	1660–1685
James II	1685–1688
William III and Mary II	1689–1702
Anne	1702–1714

Hanover

George I	1714–1727
George II	1727–1760
George III	1760–1820
George IV	1820–1830
William IV	1830–1837
Victoria	1837–1901

Saxe-Coburg

Edward VII	1901–1910

Windsor

George V	1910–1936
Edward VIII	1936
George VI	1936–1952
Elizabeth II	1952–

FRANCE

Henri I	1031–1060
Philip I	1060–1108
Louis VI	1108–1137
Louis VII	1137–1180
Philip II	1180–1223
Louis VIII	1223–1226
Louis IX	1226–1270
Philip III	1270–1285
Philip IV	1285–1314
Louis X	1314–1316
John I	1316
Philip V	1316–1322
Charles IV	1322–1328
Philip VI	1328–1350
John II	1350–1364
Charles V	1364–1380
Charles VI	1380–1422
Charles VII	1422–1461
Louis XI	1461–1483
Charles VIII	1483–1498
Louis XII	1498–1515
François I	1515–1547
Henri II	1547–1559
François II	1559–1560
Charles IX	1560–1574

Henri III	1574–1589
Henri IV	1589–1610
Louis XIII	1610–1643
Louis XIV	1643–1715
Louis XV	1715–1774
Louis XVI	1774–1792
(First Republic)	1792–1804
Napoleon I	1804–1814
Louis XVIII	1814–1824
Charles X	1824–1830
Louis Philippe	1830–1848
(Second Republic)	1848–1852
Napoleon III	1852–1870

GERMANY

Frederick I	1701–1713
Frederick William I	1713–1740
Frederick II	1740–1786
Frederick William II	1786–1797
Frederick William III	1797–1840
Frederick William IV	1840–1861
William I	1861–1888
Frederick III	1888
William II	1888–1918

JAPAN

Tokugawa Shogun rule	1603–1868
(Meiji) Mutsuhito	1868–1912
Taisho (Yoshihito)	1912–1926
Shōwa (Hirohito)	1926–1989
Heisei (Akihito)	1989–

RUSSIA

Ivan III	1462–1505
Vasilly III	1505–1533
Ivan IV	1533–1584
Theodore I	1584–1598
Boris Godunov	1598–1605
Theodore II	1605
Demetrius I	1605–1606
Basil IV	1606–1610
Wladyslaw (Polish Prince)	1610–1613
Mikhail Romanov	1613–1645
Alexis I	1645–1676
Theodore III	1676–1682
Ivan V and Peter I	1682–1689
Peter I (alone)	1689–1725

The World

Russia, *cont.*			Catherine II	1762–1796
Catherine I	1725–1727		Paul I	1796–1801
Peter II	1727–1730		Alexander I	1801–1825
Anna	1730–1740		Nicholas I	1825–1855
Ivan VI	1740–1741		Alexander II	1855–1881
Elizabeth	1741–1762		Alexander III	1881–1894
Peter III	1762		Nicholas II	1894–1917

ORDER OF BRITISH PEERAGE

Titles of nobility, or peerages, are granted by the king or queen of Great Britain upon the recommendation of the prime minister. In most *hereditary peerages,* the title passes on to a peer's eldest son, or to his closest male heir if the peer has no son (the other children are considered commoners). The title becomes extinct if there is no male heir. There are some ancient peerages that allow the title to be passed to a daughter if the holder leaves no male descendant. The last hereditary peerage was granted in 1964.

Life peerages are created each year by the British monarch for several distinguished persons. Life peers hold the rank for their own lives only; the titles do not pass on to their children. Both men and women may be granted life peerages, and the titles given to them are baron or baroness.

The following are the five grades of peers, ranked from the highest to the lowest, and the dates they were created. (Duke is the highest hereditary rank below that of prince.)

1. duke   *or*   duchess (1337)
2. marquess,   *or*   marchioness (1385)
   marquis
3. earl   *or*   countess (c. 800–1000)
4. viscount   *or*   viscountess (1440)
5. baron   *or*   baroness (c. 1066)

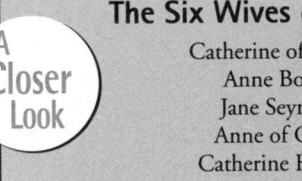

A Closer Look

The Six Wives of Henry VIII

Catherine of Aragon
Anne Boleyn
Jane Seymour
Anne of Cleves
Catherine Howard
Catherine Parr

GENEALOGY CHARTS OF THE BRITISH MONARCHY

Before the Conquest (827–1066)

Symbols

=	Marriage
│	Offspring
—	Siblings
Numerals	Order of rule

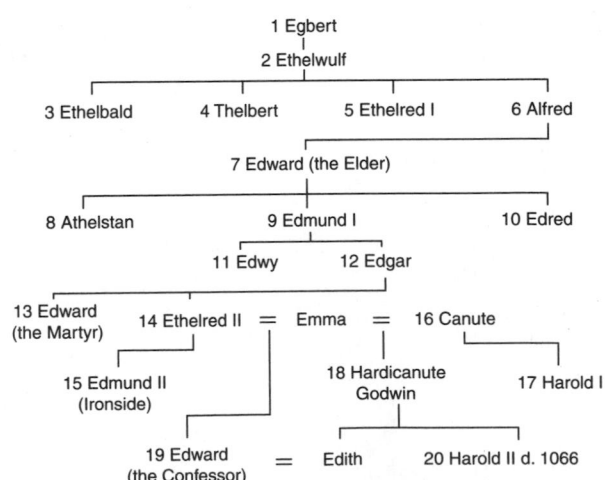

Norman Line (1066–1154)
Union of English and Norman
Lines in Henry II

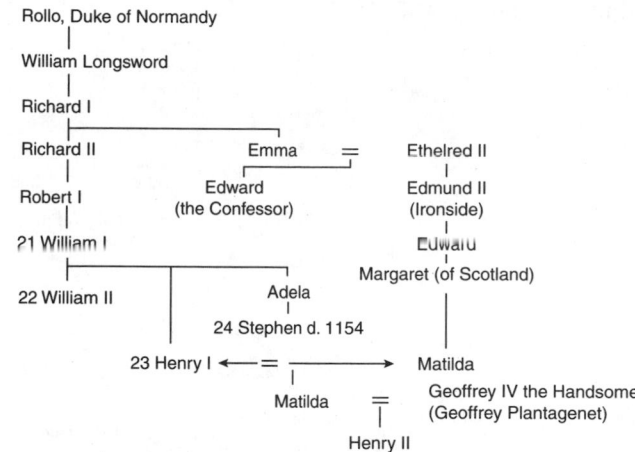

Plantagenet Line (1154–1399)

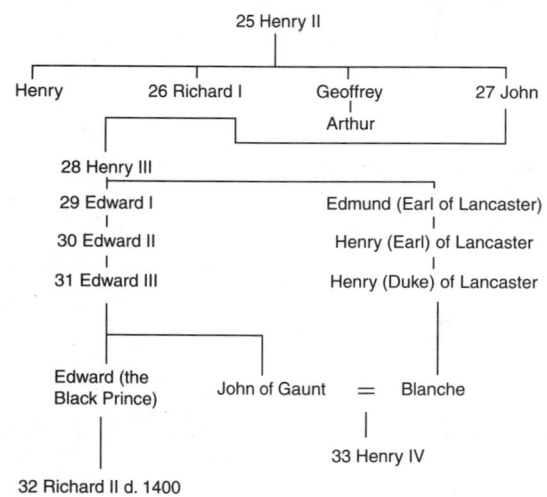

House of Lancaster (1399–1461)
House of York (1461–1485)

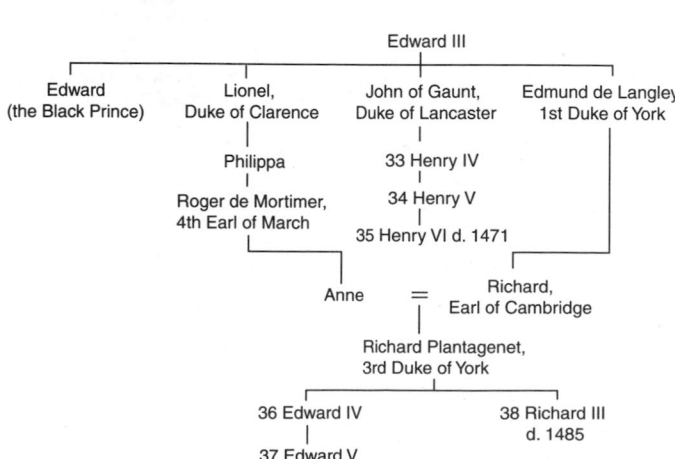

The World

House of Tudor (1485–1603)

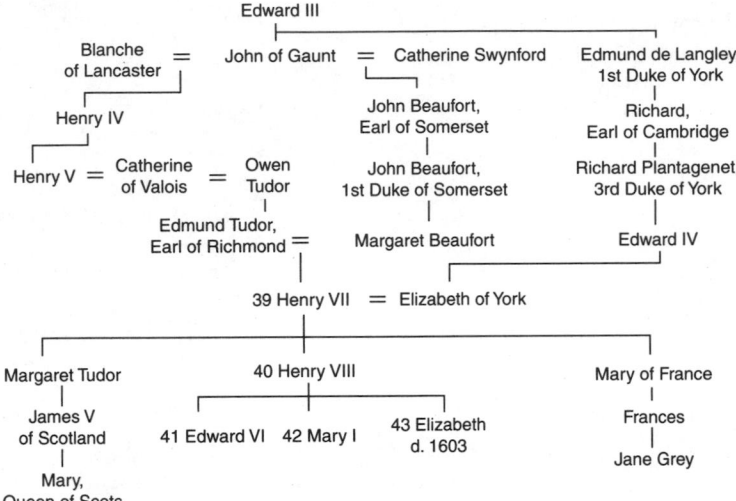

House of Stuart (1603–1714)

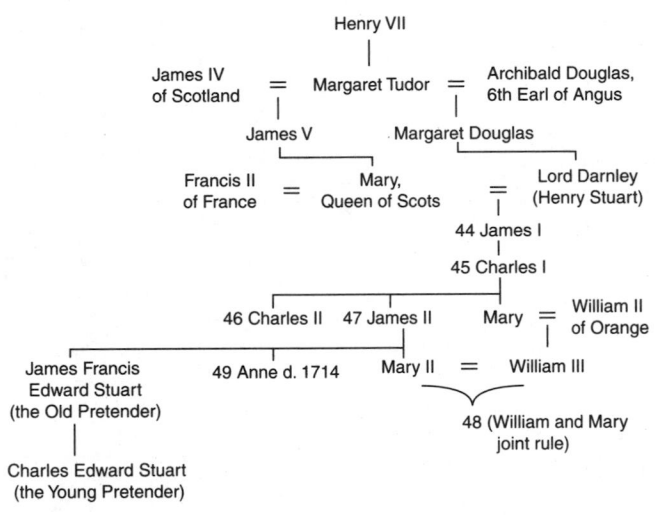

Houses of Hanover, Saxe-Coburg, and Windsor (1714–

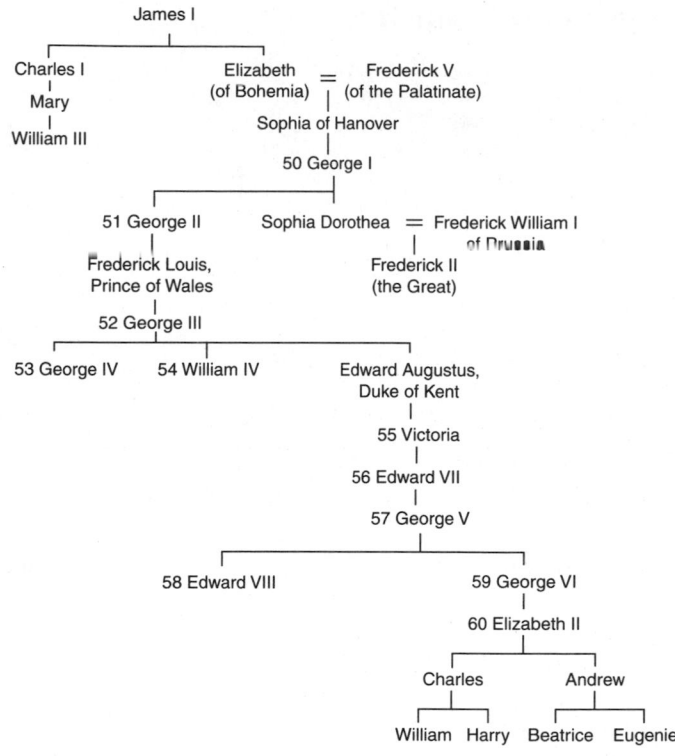

CONNECTIONS BETWEEN ROYAL FAMILIES

In the following charts, the notations (V1), (V2), and so on indicate the first, second, etc., child of Victoria, Queen of England.

ENGLAND, DENMARK, AND RUSSIA

Connections Between the Royal Families of England, Denmark, and Russia

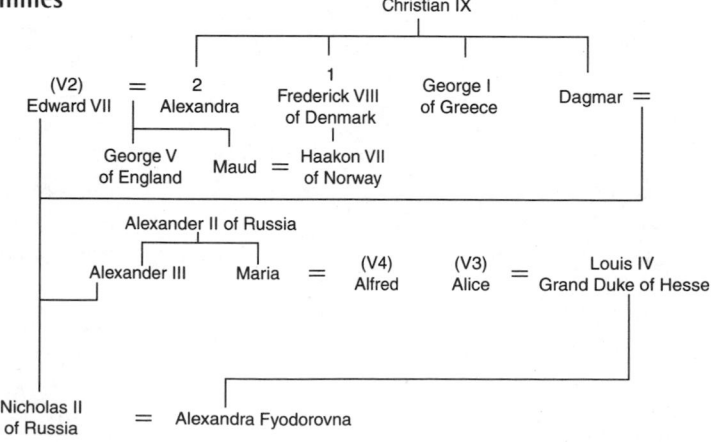

ENGLAND, GERMANY, AND SPAIN

Connections Between the Royal Families
of England, Germany, and Spain

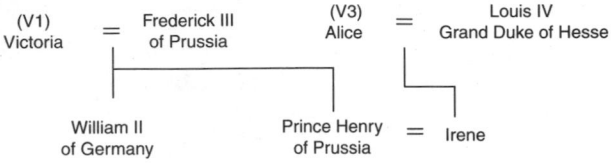

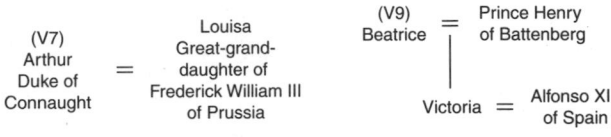

PRIME MINISTERS

AUSTRALIA

Sir Edmund Barton	1901–1903
Alfred Deakin	1903–1904
John Christian Watson	1904
George Houston Reid	1904–1905
Alfred Deakin	1905–1908
Andrew Fisher	1908–1909
Alfred Deakin	1909–1910
Andrew Fisher	1910–1913
Sir Joseph Cook	1913–1914
Andrew Fisher	1914–1915
William Morris Hughes	1915–1923
Stanley Melbourne Bruce	1923–1929
James Henry Scullin	1929–1932
Joseph Aloysius Lyons	1932–1939
Earle Page	1939
Robert Gordon Menzies	1939–1941
Arthur William Fadden	1941
John Curtin	1941–1945
Francis M. Forde (served 6 days)	1945
Joseph Benedict Chifley	1945–1949
Robert Gordon Menzies	1949–1966
Harold E. Holt	1966–1967
John McEwan (served 22 days)	1967–1968
John G. Gorton	1968–1971
William McMahon	1971–1972
(Edward) Gough Whitlam	1972–1975
Malcolm Fraser	1975–1983
Bob Hawke	1983–1991
Paul Keating	1991–1996
John Winston Howard	1996–

CANADA

John Alexander Macdonald	1867–1873
Alexander Mackenzie	1873–1878
John Alexander Macdonald	1878–1891
Sir John J. Abbott	1891–1892
Sir John S. D. Thompson	1892–1894
Sir Mackenzie Bowell	1894–1896
Sir Charles Tupper	1896
Sir Wilfrid Laurier	1896–1911
Sir Robert Laird Borden	1911–1920
Arthur Meighen	1920–1921
W. L. Mackenzie King	1921–1926
Arthur Meighen	1926
W. L. Mackenzie King	1926–1930
Richard Bedford Bennett	1930–1935
W. L. Mackenzie King	1935–1948
Louis Stephen Saint Laurent	1948–1957
John George Diefenbaker	1957–1963
Lester Bowles Pearson	1963–1968
Pierre Elliott Trudeau	1968–1979
Charles Joseph (Joe) Clark	1979–1980
Pierre Elliott Trudeau	1980–1984
John Napier Turner	1984
Brian Mulroney	1984–1993
Kim Campbell	1993
Jean Chretien	1993–

ENGLAND/GREAT BRITAIN

Sidney Godolphin (Earl of Godolphin)	1700–1701
Charles Howard (Earl of Carlisle)	1701–1702
Sidney Godolphin (Earl of Godolphin)	1702–1710

John Poulett (Earl Poulett)	1710–1711	Duke of Wellington (Arthur Wellesley)	1828–1830
Robert Harley (Earl of Oxford)	1711–1714	Charles Grey (Earl Grey)	1830–1834
Charles Talbot (Duke of Shrewsbury)	1714	William Lamb (Viscount Melbourne)	1834
Charles Montagu (Earl of Halifax)	1714–1715	Sir Robert Peel	1834–1835
Charles Howard (Earl of Carlisle)	1715	William Lamb (Viscount Melbourne)	1835–1841
Robert Walpole (Earl of Oxford)	1715–1717	Sir Robert Peel	1841–1846
James Stanhope (Earl Stanhope)	1717–1718	Lord John Russell	1846–1852
Charles Spencer (3rd Earl of Sunderland)	1718–1721	Edward George Geoffrey Smith Stanley (Earl of Derby)	1852
Robert Walpole (Earl of Oxford)	1721–1742	George Hamilton Gordon (Earl of Aberdeen)	1852–1855
Spencer Compton (Earl of Wilmington)	1742–1743	Viscount Palmerston (Henry John Temple)	1855–1858
Henry Pelham	1743–1754	Edward George Geoffrey Smith Stanley (Earl of Derby)	1858–1859
Duke of Newcastle (Thomas Pelham-Holles)	1754–1756	Viscount Palmerston (Henry John Temple)	1859–1865
William Cavendish (Duke of Devonshire)	1756–1757	Earl (formerly Lord John) Russell	1865–1866
Duke of Newcastle (Thomas Pelham-Holles)	1757–1762	Edward George Geoffrey Smith Stanley (Earl of Derby)	1866–1868
John Stuart (Earl of Bute)	1762–1763	Benjamin Disraeli (Earl of Beaconsfield)	1868
George Grenville	1763–1765	William Ewart Gladstone	1868–1874
Marquis of Rockingham (Charles Watson-Wentworth)	1765–1766	Benjamin Disraeli (Earl of Beaconsfield)	1874–1880
William Pitt (Earl of Chatham)	1766–1768	William Ewart Gladstone	1880–1885
Augustus Henry Fitzroy (Duke of Grafton)	1768–1770	Robert Arthur Talbot Gascoyner-Cecil (Marquis of Salisbury)	1885–1886
Frederick North (Earl of Guilford)	1770–1782	William Ewart Gladstone	1886
Marquis of Rockingham (Charles Watson-Wentworth)	1782	Robert Arthur Talbot Gascoyner-Cecil (Marquis of Salisbury)	1886–1892
Earl of Shelburne (William Petty)	1782–1783	William Ewart Gladstone	1892–1894
William Henry Cavendish Bentinck (Duke of Portland)	1783	Earl of Rosebery (Archibald Philip Primrose)	1894–1895
William Pitt	1783–1801	Robert Arthur Talbot Gascoyner-Cecil (Marquis of Salisbury)	1895–1902
Henry Addington (Viscount Sidmouth)	1801–1804	Arthur James Balfour	1902–1905
William Pitt	1804–1806	Sir Henry Campbell-Bannerman	1905–1908
William Wyndham Grenville (Baron Grenville)	1806–1807	Herbert Henry Asquith (Earl of Oxford and Asquith)	1908–1916
William Henry Cavendish Bentinck (Duke of Portland)	1807–1809	David Lloyd George (Earl of Dwyfor)	1916–1922
Spencer Perceval	1809–1812	Andrew Bonar Law	1922–1923
Robert Banks Jenkinson (Earl of Liverpool)	1812–1827	Stanley Baldwin (Earl Baldwin of Bewdley)	1923–1924
George Canning	1827		
Frederick John Robinson (Viscount Goderich)	1827–1828		

James Ramsay MacDonald	1924	Sir Anthony Eden	1955–1957
Stanley Baldwin (Earl Baldwin of Bewdley)	1924–1929	Harold Macmillan	1957–1963
		Sir Alec Douglas-Home	1963–1964
James Ramsay MacDonald	1929–1935	Harold Wilson	1964–1970
Stanley Baldwin (Earl Baldwin of Bewdley)	1935–1937	Edward Heath	1970–1974
		Harold Wilson	1974–1976
Neville Chamberlain	1937–1940	James Callaghan	1976–1979
Winston Churchill	1940–1945	Margaret Thatcher	1979–1990
Clement Attlee	1945–1951	John Major	1990–1997
Winston Churchill	1951–1955	Tony Blair	1997–

FOREIGN DIALING CODES

Note: For international telephone calls automatically routed through AT&T, dial 011 and then dial the code for that country, the city code if one is indicated, and the subscriber telephone number to be reached. Other long-distance telephone services may have other procedures and should be consulted for their specific instructions.

Algeria	213	Denmark	45	Guantanamo Bay	
American Samoa	684	(Copenhagen 1 or 2)		U.S. naval base	53
Andorra	376	Ecuador	593	(all points 99)	
(all points 628)		(Guayaquil 4)		Guatemala	502
Argentina	54	(Quito 2)		(Guatemala City 2)	
(Buenos Aires 1)		Egypt	20	Guyana	592
Australia	61	(Alexandria 3)		(Georgetown 2)	
(Melbourne 39)		(Cairo 2)		Haiti	509
(Sydney 2)		El Salvador	503	(Port-au-Prince 1)	
Austria	43	England. *See* United		Honduras	504
(Vienna 1)		Kingdom.		Hong Kong	852
Bahrain	973	Ethiopia	251	(Hong Kong 9)	
Bangladesh	880	(Addis Ababa 1)		Hungary	36
Belgium	32	Fiji	679	(Budapest 1)	
(Brussels 2)		Finland	358	Iceland	354
(Antwerp 3)		(Helsinki 9)		(Akureyri 6)	
Belize	501	France	33	(Reykjavík 1)	
Bolivia	591	(Marseille 491)		India	91
(La Paz 2)		(Nice 492 or 493)		(Bombay 22)	
Brazil	55	(Paris 1)		(Calcutta 33)	
(Brasília 61)		French Antilles	596	(New Delhi 11)	
(Rio de Janeiro 21)		French Antilles-	590	Indonesia	62
Cameroon	237	Guadeloupe		(Jakarta 21)	
Chile	56	French Polynesia	689	Iran	98
(Santiago 2)		Gabon	241	(Teheran 21)	
China	86	Germany	49	Iraq	964
(Beijing 10)		(Frankfurt 69)		(Baghdad 1)	
(Shanghai 21)		(Munich 89)		Ireland	353
Colombia	57	(Berlin 30)		(Dublin 1)	
(Bogotá 1)		(other areas of former		(Galway 91)	
Costa Rica	506	East Germany 37)		Israel	972
Cyprus	357	Greece	30	(Haifa 4)	
Czech Republic	42	(Athens 1)		(Jerusalem 2)	
(Prague 2)		Guam	671	(Tel Aviv 3)	

Italy	39	New Zealand	64	Spain	34
(Florence 55)		(Auckland 9)		(Barcelona 3)	
(Rome 6)		(Wellington 4)		(Madrid 1)	
(Venice 41)		Nicaragua	505	(Seville 54)	
Ivory Coast	225	(Managua 2)		Sri Lanka	94
Japan	81	Nigeria	234	(Columbo 1)	
(Tokyo 3)		(Lagos 1)		Suriname	597
(Osaka 6)		Norway	47	Sweden	46
(Yokohama 45)		(Bergen 5)		(Goteborg 51)	
Jordan	962	(Oslo 2)		(Stockholm 8)	
(Amman 6)		Oman	968	Switzerland	41
Kenya	254	Pakistan	92	(Geneva 22)	
Korea, South	82	(Islamabad 51)		(Bern 31)	
(Pusan 51)		(Karachi 21)		(Zurich 1)	
(Seoul 2)		Panama	507	Taiwan	886
Kuwait	965	Papua New Guinea	675	(Tainan 6)	
Liberia	231	Paraguay	595	(Taipei 2)	
Libya	218	(Asuncion 21)		Thailand	66
(Tripoli 21)		Peru	51	(Bangkok 2)	
Liechtenstein	423	(Lima 1)		Tunisia	216
(all points 75)		Philippines	63	(Tunis 1)	
Luxembourg	352	(Manila 2)		Turkey	90
Malawi	265	Poland	48	(Istanbul 1)	
(Domasi 531)		(Warsaw 22)		United Arab Emirates	971
Malaysia	60	Portugal	351	(Abu Dhabi 2)	
(Kuala Lumpur 3)		(Lisbon 1)		(Dubai 4)	
Mexico	52	Qatar	974	United Kingdom	44
(Mexico City 5)		Romania	40	(Belfast 1232)	
(Guadalajara 3)		(Bucharest 1)		(Glasgow 141)	
Monaco	377	Russia	7	(London 207 or 208)	
(Casablanca 2)		(Moscow 095)		Uruguay	598
Morocco	212	Saipan	670	(Montevideo 2)	
(Agadir 8)		San Marino	39	Vatican City	39
Namibia	264	(all points 541)		(all points 6)	
Netherlands	31	Saudi Arabia	966	Venezuela	58
(Amsterdam 20)		(Riyadh 1)		(Caracas 2)	
(Rotterdam 10)		Senegal	221	(Maracaibo 61)	
(The Hague 70)		Singapore	65	Yemen Arab Republic	967
Netherlands Antilles	599	South Africa	27	Yugoslavia	381
Netherlands Antilles-Aruba	297	(Cape Town 21)		(Belgrade 11)	
(Aruba 8)		(Johannesburg 11)			
New Caledonia	687	(Pretoria 12)			

ADDITIONAL SOURCES OF INFORMATION

ORGANIZATIONS AND SERVICES

The Asia Foundation
465 California St., 14th Fl.
San Francisco, CA 94104

Bureau of Public Affairs
U.S. Department of State
2201 C St., NW
Washington, DC 20520

Carnegie Endowment for International Peace
1779 Massachusetts Ave. NW
Washington, DC 20036

Central Intelligence Agency
Public Affairs Director
Washington, DC 20505

European Union Office of Press and Public Affairs
2300 M St., NW
Washington, DC 20037

Middle East Institute
1761 N St., NW
Washington, DC 20036

Organization of American States
17th Street and Constitution Avenue, NW
Washington, DC 20006

United Nations Headquarters
United Nations Plaza
New York, NY 10017

United Nations Information Center
1775 K St., Suite 400
Washington, DC 20006

United States Mission to the United Nations
799 United Nations Plaza
New York, NY 10017

BOOKS

Banks, Arthur S., and Muller, Thomas C., eds. *Political Handbook of the World, 2000*, CSA, 2000.

Barzun, Jacques, *From Dawn to Decadence, 500 Years of Western Cultural Life*, HarperPerennial, 2001.

Black, Jeremy, ed. *The DK Atlas of World History*, DK Publishers, 2000.

Central Intelligence Agency, *The World Factbook*, U.S. Government Printing Office, annual.

Chandler, David. *Macmillan Encyclopedia of Military History*. 2 vols, Macmillan, 1996.

Clements, John, ed. *Clements' Encyclopedia of World Government*, Political Research, 2000.

Commire, Anne, ed. *Women in World History*, 11 vols. Gale, 2000.

DK Publishing Staff, *World Desk Reference*, DK Publishers, 2000.

Hammond staff, *Hammond World Atlas*, 3rd ed. Hammond, 2000.

Hulme, F. Edward. *Flags of the World: Their History, Blazonry, and Associations*. Gordon Press, 1977.

Krieger, Joel, ed. *The Oxford Companion to Politics of the World*, Oxford, 2001

Maps on File 2000. Facts on File, 2000.

Oxford staff, *Oxford Desk Reference Atlas*, 3rd ed. Oxford, 2000.

Schraepler, Hans-Albrecht. *Dictionary of International Economic Organizations*. Georgetown University Press, 1999.

Simony, Maggy. *The Traveler's Reading Guide: Ready-Made Reading Lists for the Armchair Traveler*. Rev. ed. Holt, Rinehart and Winston, 1994.

Wetterau, Bruce. *The New York Public Library Book of Chronologies*. Prentice Hall, 1994.

Williamson, David. *The Kings and Queens of England*, Lund Humphries, 1998.

World Almanac Staff. *The World Almanac and Book of Facts*. Pharo Books, annual.

WEB SITES

Comparative Analysis of Major World Religions
www.comparativereligion.com

Atlapedia—Key facts and statistics on all countries of the world as well as physical and political maps.
http://www.atlapedia.com

The CIA World Factbook—Comprehensive facts about the world's countries complied by the CIA (see book listed above).
http://www.cia.gov/cia/publications/factbook

Ragz International World History—Covers wide variety of topics from prehistory through World War II.
http://www.ragz-international.com/index1.htm

World History—E-texts, maps, and links on a variety of history topics from antiquity to the twentieth century.
http://www.fsmitha.com

City Population—Statistics and maps about the population of the major agglomerations of the world.
http://www.citypopulation.de

The World

ATLAS

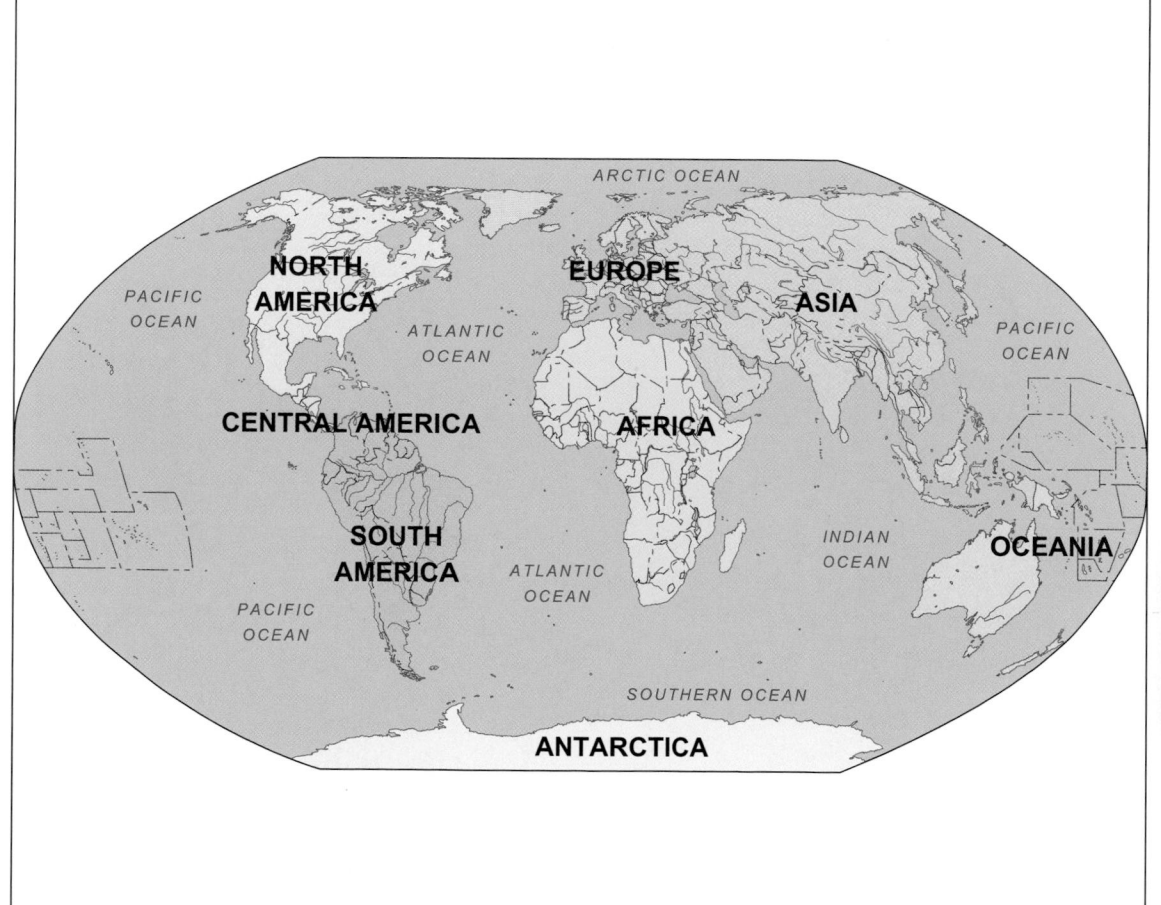

ATLANTIC
OCEAN

Gulf of
Biscay

EUROPE

ASIA

MEDITERRANEAN SEA

Black Sea

Aral
Sea

Caspian Sea

Sardinia I.

Sicily I.

Crete I.

Cyprus I.

Algiers   Tunis
Oran   C. Bon
Str. of Gibraltar   Melilla (Sp.)
Ceuta (Sp.)   TUNISIA
Rabat   Gulf of Gabès
Casablanca   Tripoli   Bengasi
MOROCCO   Alexandria
Agadir   Marrakech   Cairo
El-Gîza

Madeira Islands (Por.)
Canary Islands (Sp.)
El Aaiún
Western Sahara

ALGERIA

LIBYA

Waha

EGYPT

Aswân

Tamanrasset

Port Sudan

Ras Nouâdhibou
MAURITANIA
Nouakchott
MALI
Tombouctou

Djado

Zouar

Omdurmân   Asmera
Khartoum   ERITREA

SENEGAL
C. Vert   Dakar
GAMBIA   Banjul   Bamako
GUINEA-BISSAU   Bissau
GUINEA
Conakry   Freetown
SIERRA LEONE
Monrovia
LIBERIA   Abidjan

NIGER

BURKINA FASO
Niamey
Ouagadougou
Bobo
Dioulasso
Kumasi
GHANA
Accra   Lomé

Kano

CHAD

Ndjamena

L. Chad

SUDAN

White Nile
Blue Nile

Djibouti
DJIBOUTI

Gulf of Aden

Socotra I. (Yemen)
Ras Asir

BENIN
TOGO
Abuja
NIGERIA
Porto Novo
Lagos

Abidjan

IVORY COAST

CENTRAL AFRICAN REPUBLIC

ETHIOPIA
Addis Ababa

SOMALI REPUBLIC

Gulf of Guinea

Malabo
Bioko I.
EQUATORIAL GUINEA
SÃO TOMÉ & PRINCIPE
São Tomé
Pagalu I. (Ec. G.)

CAMEROON
Douala
Yaoundé

Bangui

Libreville
CONGO
GABON
Brazzaville
Pointe-Noire   Kinshasa

Isiro   L. Albert
Juba   UGANDA
Kampala   Mogadishu
KENYA
RWANDA   Nairobi
Kigali
Bujumbura   L. Victoria
BURUNDI
L. Tanganyika   Mombasa
Pemba I.
Zanzibar I.
Dar es Salaam
Mafia I.

Ascension I. (U.K.)

Luanda

TANZANIA

Cosmoledo Islands (Sey.)

St. Helena I. (U.K.)

ANGOLA

ZAMBIA
Lusaka

L. Malawi

MALAWI
Lilongwe

COMOROS
Moroni   Mayotte I. (Fr.)

ATLANTIC

OCEAN

NAMIBIA

Windhoek

ZIMBABWE
Harare
Bulawayo

BOTSWANA

Gaborone   Pretoria
Johannesburg   Mbabane
Vereeniging   SWAZILAND
LESOTHO   Maputo
Maseru   Durban
SOUTH AFRICA
Cape Town
C. of Good Hope   Port Elizabeth

MOZAMBIQUE

Mozambique Channel

Antananarivo

MADAGASCAR

MAURITIUS
Porto Luis
Réunion Is. (Fr.)

INDIAN

OCEAN

Population:

ANGOLA   Country
● **Luanda**   Capital
• Pointe Noire   Other cities
———— -----   Natinal Border

Scale: 1:40.000.000
0   300   600   900 km

CAPE VERDE
Praia

SEYCHELLES
Victoria

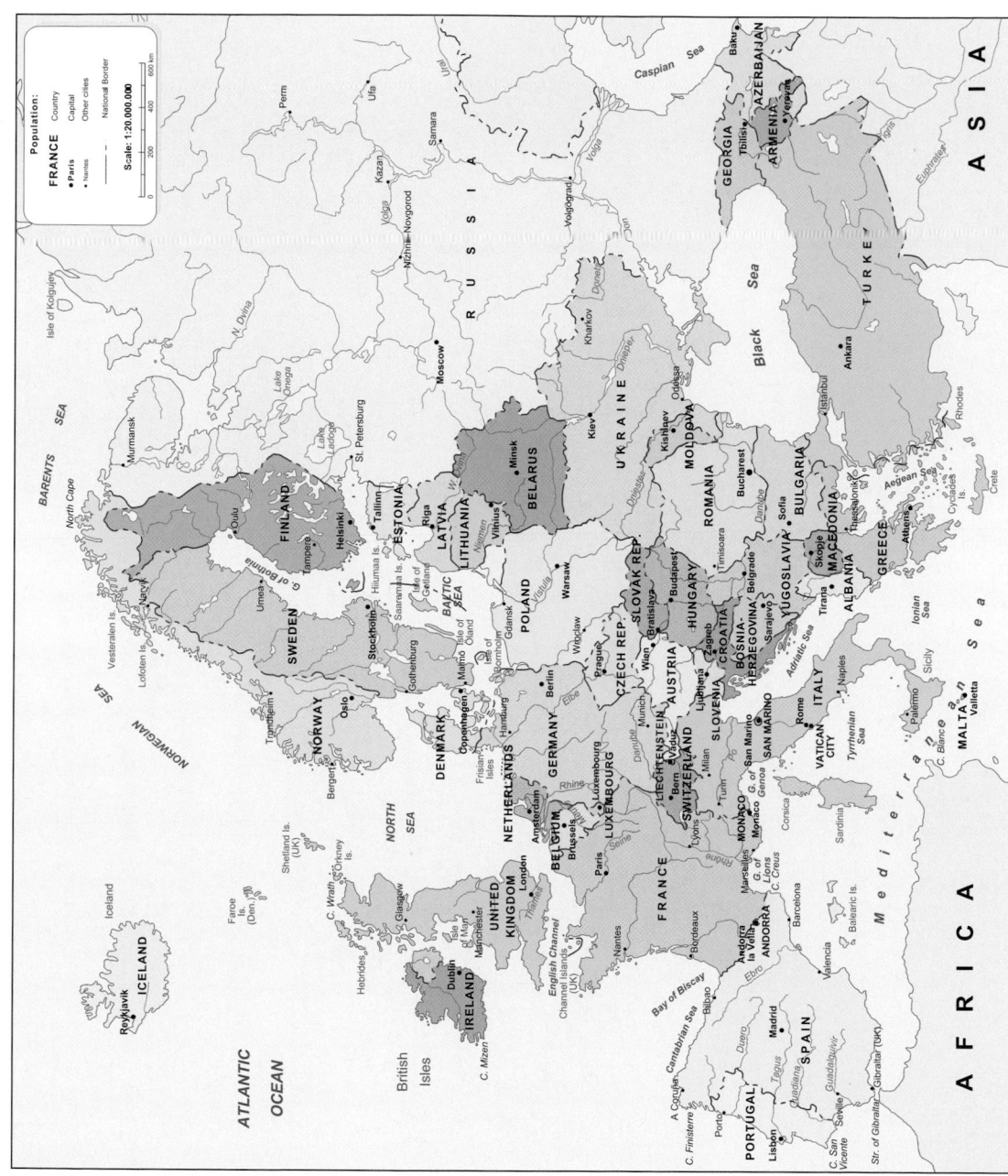

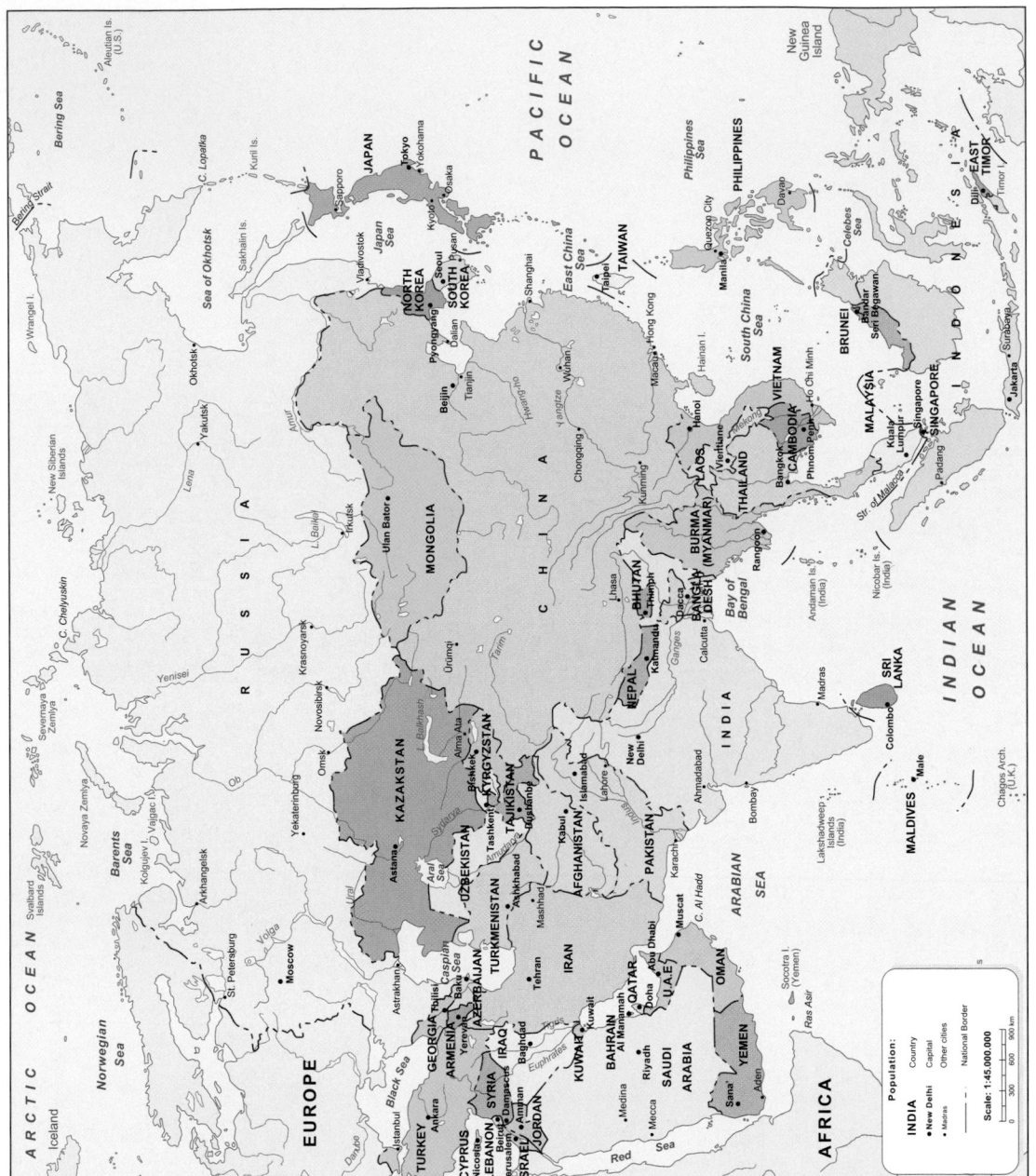

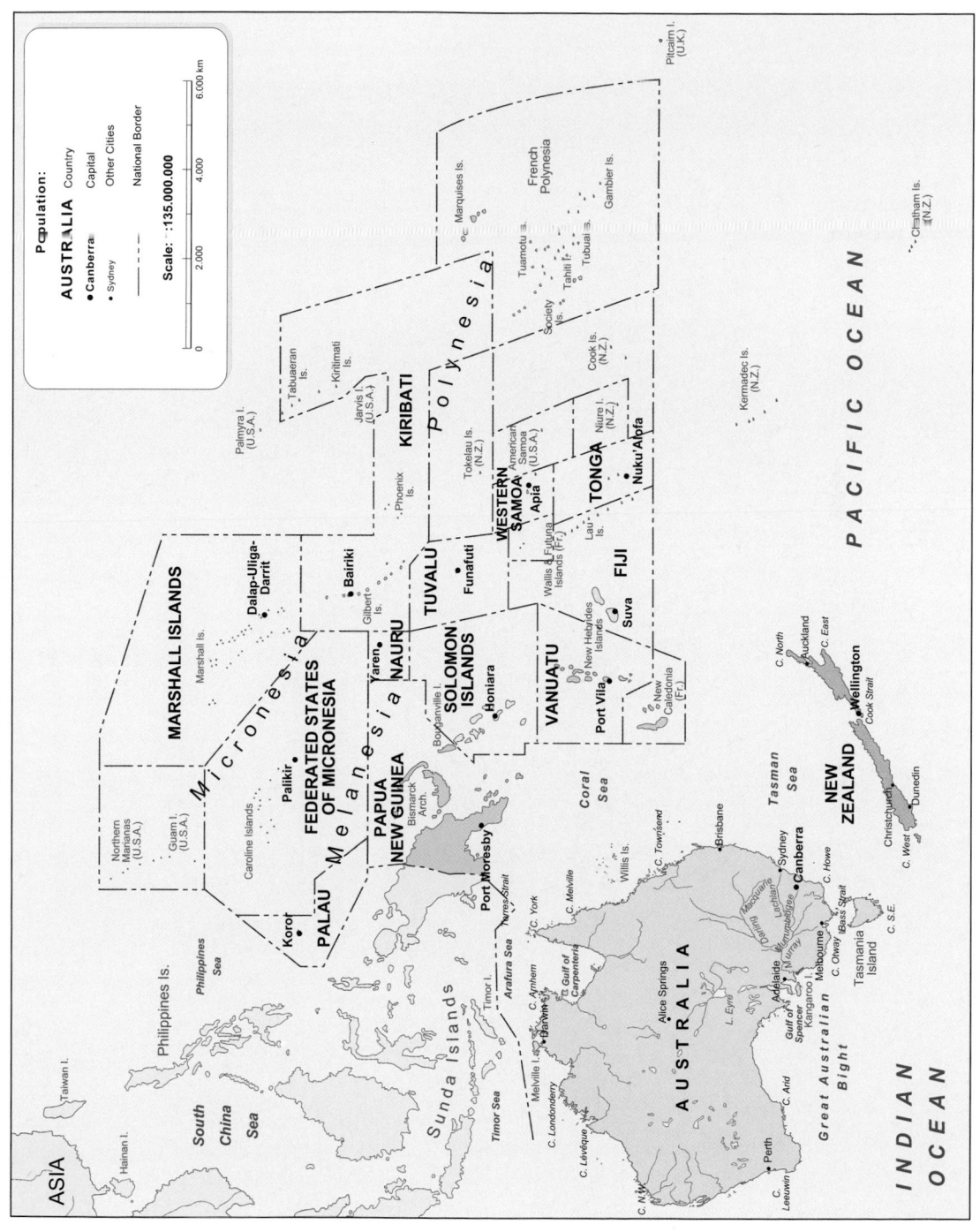

Population:

AUSTRALIA Country
● Canberra Capital
● Sydney Other Cities
—·—·— National Border

Scale: 1:135.000.000

0   2.000   4.000   6.000 km

ASIA

Taiwan I.
Hainan I.

Philippines Is.

South
China
Sea

*Philippine
Sea*

Northern
Marianas
(U.S.A.)

Guam I.
(U.S.A.)

Caroline Islands

Palmyra I.
(U.S.A.)

Tabuaeran
Is.

Kiritimati
Is.

Jarvis I.
(U.S.A.)

KIRIBATI

MARSHALL ISLANDS

Marshall Is.

Dalap-Uliga-
Darrit

Bairiki

Gilbert
Is.

NAURU

Yaren

M i c r o n e s i a

**FEDERATED STATES
OF MICRONESIA**

Palikir

PALAU

Korot

Phoenix
Is.

Tokelau Is.
(N.Z.)

American
Samoa
(U.S.A.)

**WESTERN
SAMOA**
Apia

Niue I.
(N.Z.)

Tuamotu Is.

Marquises Is.

French
Polynesia

Gambier Is.

Tahiti I.
Tubuai Is.

Society
Is.

P o l y n e s i a

Pitcairn I.
(U.K.)

TUVALU
Funafuti

TONGA
Nuku'Alofa

Wallis & Futuna
Islands (Fr.)

Lau
Is.

FIJI
Suva

Cook Is.
(N.Z.)

Kermadec Is.
(N.Z.)

P A C I F I C   O C E A N

Chatham Is.
(N.Z.)

**SOLOMON
ISLANDS**
Honiara

Bougainville I.

VANUATU
Port Vila

New Hebrides
Islands

New
Caledonia
(Fr.)

**PAPUA
NEW GUINEA**

Bismarck
Arch.

Port Moresby

Torres Strait

Timor I.

Sunda Islands

Melanesia

C. York

C. Melville

Willis Is.

*Coral
Sea*

C. Townsend

Brisbane

Sydney
Canberra

C. Howe

C. North
Auckland

C. East

**NEW
ZEALAND**
Wellington

Cook Strait

Christchurch
C. West
Dunedin

*Tasman
Sea*

Bass Strait

C. S.E.

Tasmania
Island

*Philippines
Sea*

Melville I.
Darwin
C. Arnhem

Gulf of
Carpentaria

Arafura Sea

C. Londonderry

C. Lévêque

C.N.W.

Alice Springs

A U S T R A L I A

Darling
Macquarie
Lachlan
Murrumbidgee
Murray

Adelaide
Gulf of
Spencer
Kangaroo I.

L. Eyre

Melbourne

C. Otway

*Great Australian
Bight*

C. Arid

Perth

C.
Leeuwin

*I N D I A N
O C E A N*

Gulf of
México

Yucatan
Channel

Gulf of
Honduras

Greater   Antilles

Lesser Antilles

Caribbean Sea

CENTRAL

AMERICA

Nicaragua

Coco I.
(C. Rica)

C. de la Aguja
Cartagena
Maracaibo

Gulf of Venezuela
L. Maracaibo

Margarita I.

Caracas

VENEZUELA

Orinoco

Georgetown

GUYANA   Paramaribo   Cayenne

SURINAM   C. Orange

FRENCH
GUIANA

Gulf of
Darien

Medellin

Magdalena

•Bogotá

Cali

COLOMBIA

Malpelo I.
(Colombia)

C. San Francisco

•Quito

ECUADOR

Gulf of
Guayaquil   Guayaquil

Galapagos
Islands
(Ec.)

Pto.
Baquerizo
Moreno

Marañón

Pta. Negra

Trujillo

PERU

•Lima

Callao

Amazon
River Delta
Marajó I.

Belém

Manaus

Amazon

B   R   A   Z   I   L

Fortaleza

Fernando de
Noronha I.

C. San Roque

Recife

Titicaca

•La Paz

BOLIVIA

•Sucre

Potosí

Grande

Brasília

Salvador

Todos
los Santos
Bay

Iquique

Gulf
of
Arica

PARAGUAY

Grande

Belo Horizonte

Rio de Janeiro

C. Frio

Trinidad I.

San Félix I.
San
Ambrosio I.

Asunción

Paraná

São Paulo

Sao Francisco I.

Sta. Catarina I.

CHILE

Juan Fernández
Arch.
(Chile)

Salado

•Santiago

Córdoba

Santa Fe

Rosario

Uruguay

Pôrto
Alegre

URUGUAY

Buenos
Aires

Montevideo

La Plata

Rio de la Plata

Paraná

ARGENTINA

C. San Antonio

Pta. Lavapie

Blanca Bay

Gulf of San Matías

Chiloé I.

Chonos Arch.

Gulf of San Jorge

C. Tres Puntas

Gulf of Penas

Falkland I.
(U.K.)

Magellan's Str.

C. San Diego

C. Horn

Drake Str.

South
Georgia I.
(U.K.)

PACIFIC

OCEAN

ATLANTIC

OCEAN

ATLANTIC

OCEAN

Population:

PERU   Country

• Lima   Capital

• Callao   Other Cities

National Border

Scale: 1:35.000.000

0   300   600   900 km

Atlas

ASIA

ARCTIC OCEAN

Greenland Island

Iceland

Bering Sea

Wrangel I.

St. Lawrence I.

Bering Strait

Barrow Pt.

Ellesmere Island

Nunivak I.

ALASKA (U.S.A.)

Yukon

Fairbanks

C. Bathurst

Queen Elizabeth Islands

Melville I.

Banks I.

Devon I.

Baffin Bay

Anchorage

Kodiak I.

C. Amundsen

Prince of Wales

Victoria I.

Gulf of Boothia

Baffin Land

Davis Strait

Labrador Sea

Gulf of Alaska

Great Bear Lake

Mackenzie

Southampton I.

Hudson Strait

C. Wolstenholme

C. Chidley

C. Charles

Newfoundland Island

Alexander Arch.

Great Slave Lake

Lake Athabasca

Hudson Bay

Belcher Is.

C. Henrietta Maria

James Bay

C. Race

Gulf of St. Lawrence

St-Pierre et Miquelon (Fr.)

Queen Charlotte Islands

Edmonton

Reindeer Lake

Nelson

Eastmain

Vancouver Island

Vancouver

Calgary

Lake Winnipeg

C. Flattery

Seattle

Regina

Winnipeg

Lake Superior

Lake Huron

Ottawa

Montreal

St. John

Québec

C. Sable

Bay of Fundy

Portland

Columbia

UNITED

Minneapolis

Lake Michigan

Toronto

Lake Ontario

Boston

C. Cod

Long I.

C. Blanco

STATES OF

Detroit

Lake Erie

Cleveland

New York

Philadelphia

C. Mendocino

Pt. Arena

AMERICA

Denver

Missouri

Chicago

Ohio

Washington

Chesapeake Bay

Bermuda I. (U.K.)

San Francisco

Sacramento

Kansas City

St. Louis

C. Hatteras

ATLANTIC

Las Vegas

Colorado

Arkansas

Tennessee

Memphis

Atlanta

OCEAN

Pt. Concepción

Los Angeles

Phoenix

Gila

Dallas

Mississippi

Alabama

PACIFIC

Houston

New Orleans

Miami

Rio Grande

Mississippi River Delta

C. Sable

Straits of Florida

OCEAN

Gulf of California

Monterrey

Gulf of Mexico

Yucatan Channel

C. San Lucas

MEXICO

C. Catoche

Greater Antillas

C. Corrientes

Guadalajara

Gulf of Campeche

Gulf of Honduras

Revilla Gigedo Is.

México

L. Maracaibo

Gulf of Tehuantepec

Gulf of Mosquitos

Caribbean Sea

C. Gracias a Dios

CENTRAL AMERICA

L. Nicaragua

Population:

CANADA   Country

● **Ottawa**   Capital

• Calgary   Other cities

—— – –   National Border

Scale: 1:37.500.000

0   300   600   900 km

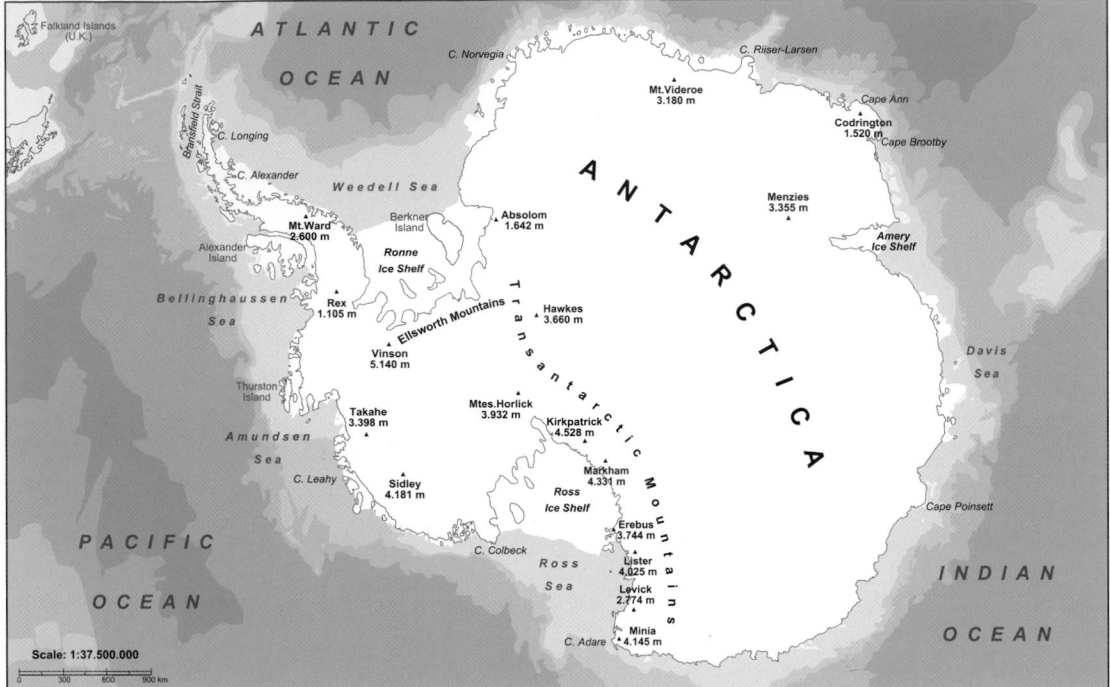

Scale: 1:37.500.000

ATLANTIC OCEAN

PACIFIC OCEAN

INDIAN OCEAN

Falkland Islands (U.K.)

C. Norvegia

C. Riiser-Larsen

Mt.Videroe 3.180 m

Cape Ann

Codrington 1.520 m

Cape Brootby

ANTARCTICA

Menzies 3.355 m

Amery Ice Shelf

Weedell Sea

Bransfield Strait

C. Longing

C. Alexander

Berkner Island

Absolom 1.642 m

Ronne Ice Shelf

Mt.Ward 2.600 m

Alexander Island

Bellinghaussen Sea

Rex 1.105 m

Ellsworth Mountains

Hawkes 3.660 m

Davis Sea

Vinson 5.140 m

Transantarctic Mountains

Thurston Island

Mtes.Horlick 3.932 m

Kirkpatrick 4.528 m

Takahe 3.398 m

Amundsen Sea

Markham 4.331 m

C. Leahy

Sidley 4.181 m

Ross Ice Shelf

Erebus 3.744 m

Lister 4.025 m

C. Colbeck

Ross Sea

Levick 2.774 m

Minia 4.145 m

C. Adare

Cape Poinsett

0   300   600   900 km

INDEX

Index

The Sonata Since Beethoven

Franz Liszt's dedication of his Sonata in B Minor to Robert
Schumann in 1853 (facs. after Bory/LISZT 158; cf. SSB X)

THE SONATA

SINCE

BEETHOVEN

The Third and Final Volume of
A History of the Sonata Idea

By WILLIAM S. NEWMAN

Chapel Hill
The University of North Carolina Press

PRINTED BY THE COLONIAL PRESS INC., CLINTON, MASS.

To Claire
who has seen through all three volumes with me

Preface

As with its two predecessors, this third and final volume in *A History of the Sonata Idea* has benefitted substantially from the expert help of colleagues, librarians, and research assistants, far and near. Especially during the past thirty months of final writing, it has benefitted from uncommonly generous responses to unconscionably urgent requests for particular advices, materials, and aids. When such help can be identified with specific discussions in the text, I have acknowledged it in footnotes. But I have also wanted to acknowledge that and other help collectively, in this Preface.

For critical readings and evaluations of entire sections and chapters, I am grateful to Professor Roger Hannay at The University of North Carolina at Chapel Hill (with regard to 20th-c. dilemmas, ssb I), to Professor Martin Chusid at New York University (Schubert, ssb VII), to Professor Edward A. Lippmann at Columbia University (Schumann, ssb VIII), to Professor Eric Werner at Tel Aviv University in Ramat Aviv, Israel (Mendelssohn, ssb VIII), to Professor Karl Geiringer at the University of California in Santa Barbara (Brahms, ssb IX), to Mr. Edward Waters at The Library of Congress (Liszt, ssb X), to Professor Nicholas Temperley at the University of Illinois in Urbana (19th-c. England, ssb XIV), and to Professors Erna F. Novikova and Aleksandr Dmitrievich Alekseev of Moscow (19th-c. Russia, ssb XVIII).

For more specific advices and/or making valued materials available, I am likewise grateful to Dr. Birgitte Moyer of Menlo Park, Calif. (Reicha, Czerny, and A. B. Marx on "sonata form," ssb II), Professor Rey M. Longyear at the University of Kentucky (German literary references, ssb II), Dr. Harry Bergholz at The University of North Carolina at Chapel Hill (Strindberg's *Spöksonaten*, ssb II), Mrs. Alice (William J.) Mitchell of New York City (Czerny, ssb VII), Dr. Ingeborg Heussner of Marburg, West Germany (Moscheles, ssb VII), Dr. Marc-André Souchay of Hannover-Kleefeld, West Germany (Schubert, ssb VII), Mr. Arthur Hedley of London (Liszt and Chopin, ssb X and

XII), Miss Friedelind Wagner of Bayreuth (Wagner, ssb X), Dr. Rita
Benton at the State University of Iowa in Iowa City (Wagner and
Pleyel, ssb X), the late Mr. Arthur Loesser of Cleveland (Wagner and
Hallé, ssb X), Mr. Clarence Adler of New York City (Godowsky, ssb
XI), Dr. Stephen Young at Meredith College in Raleigh (Karg-Elert,
ssb XI), Professor Alexander Ringer at the University of Illinois in
Urbana (Gernsheim, ssb XI, and constructive evaluations throughout
ssb), Professor Ronald E. Booth, Jr., at The University of North Caro-
lina at Charlotte (Heller, ssb XII), Mr. Joseph Bloch at the Juilliard
School of Music and Mr. Raymond Lewenthal of New York City (Alkan,
ssb XII), Professors Aloys Fleischman at University College in Cork and
Brian Boydell at the University of Dublin (Irish sons., ssb XV), Pro-
fessor Ingmar Bengtsson of Uppsala (Swedish sons., ssb XV), Professor
Howard Allen Craw at Loma Linda University in Riverside (Dussek,
ssb XVII), Dr. Elod J. Juhász of Radio Budapest, the late Dr. József
Gát at the Budapest Academy of Music, and Professor Béla Böszörmeny-
Nagy of Boston University (Hungarian sons., ssb XVII), Mr. James F.
Jones at Florida State University in Tallahassee (Dohnányi, ssb XVII),
Miss Carol Greene at the University of Indiana in Bloomington (Aliabiev, ssb XVIII), Mr. Vladimir Horowitz of New York City (Rach-
maninoff, ssb XVIII), and Professor Delmer D. Rogers at the University
of Texas in Austin (Bristow, ssb XIX).

   For still other advices and/or materials I am indebted to Dr.
Rudolph Kremer at The University of North Carolina at Chapel Hill
(19th-c. organ sons.), Dr. Fritz Oberdoerffer and Mr. Joe W. Bratcher
at the University of Texas in Austin (rare sons. in their private collections), and Mr. Harold Schonberg of the *New York Times* (spot
questions on past pianists).

   Much of the searching through periodicals, in several other lan-
guages as well as English, and much of the statistical work for the
present volume were accomplished by able graduate assistants at The
University of North Carolina at Chapel Hill. For these contributions
it is a pleasure to thank the (then) Misses Katherine Ruth Boardman,
Anne Chan, Marcia Judith Citron, Gloria Merle Huffman, Sophie
Morgan, and Mary Vinquist. It is also a pleasure to thank certain other
Chapel Hillians in and around the University, including Mr. Rudi
Schnitzler for two proofreadings of the entire volume, Mrs. Hilde
(Alfred T.) Brauer for providing or checking many of the German
translations, Professor Alfred Engstrom for an extended French translation, Mr. John J. Bobkoff and Mrs. Angele Avizonis for Russian trans-
lations, Mrs. Helen (William E.) Jenner for "autographing" the 115
music examples that are not facsimiles, and Mrs. Jeanne D. Hudson for

drawing the chart of "Regions and Production Spans" (ssв IV). (In defense of the translators, I should add that I assume full responsibility
for the individual translations not otherwise credited. An average, not
exceptional, sample of the translation problem is provided in the midst
of the Wagner discussion, ssв X.) A particular pleasure has been the
reading of many of the duo sonatas under examination with interested
colleagues and students, among whom I should like especially to thank
Professor Edgar Alden, Mrs. Jeanine Zenge, and Miss Ivy Geoghegan,
violinists; Miss Ann Woodward, violist; and Mr. Charles Griffith and
Miss Kathryn Logan, cellists.

Many of those "unconscionably urgent requests" have been directed
to music librarians in numerous countries, among whom, at this point,
I should like to thank especially Dr. James Pruett, Mr. Nyal Williams,
and Miss Thelma Thompson of The University of North Carolina at
Chapel Hill, Mr. William Lichtenwanger at the Library of Congress,
Mr. Gordon Mapes at the Curtis Institute of Music in Philadelphia,
Mr. Frank C. Campbell, Mr. Neil Ratliff, and Mr. Richard Jackson at
the Library & Museum of the Performing Arts in New York, Mr. Neil
K. Moran at the Boston Public Library, Mr. Donald W. Krummel at
the Newberry Library in Chicago, Mr. A. Hyatt King at the British
Museum in London, Dr. Imogen Fellinger at the Zentralstelle für
Musikbibliographie des 19. Jahrhunderts in Köln, and Dr. Leopold
Nowak at the Österreichische Nationalbibliothek in Vienna.

The kind permissions granted by numerous publishers or their U.S.
agents to quote sentences or music examples from copyrighted publications that they control are acknowledged separately wherever the
quotations occur in the present volume.

Finally, I should like to express my gratitude to the University Research Council of The University of North Carolina at Chapel Hill,
the American Council of Learned Societies, and the National Endowment for the Humanities for the grants and their renewals that have
provided the free time and the assistance so essential to a project of
this sort. And at the same time I should like to express my gratitude to
Chairman Wilton Mason and my other colleagues in the Music Department for co-operating so generously during two semesters of reduced schedules.

Some Abbreviations and Editorial Policies

All the short titles used throughout the present volume are listed in
one alphabetical sequence and amplified in full in the concluding

Bibliography. A hyphenated, lowercase "-m" at the end (as in Brahms/WERKE-m) continues to indicate a source consisting primarily of music. Articles in reference works, reviews in periodicals, and prefaces in music editions are not given separate short titles, ordinarily, but the first time such an item is cited in any one discussion its author is added in parentheses (if known). Cross references to the previous two volumes in the present set, SBE and SCE, include page numbers. However, for familiar reasons of cost and accuracy, the many cross references within the present volume, SSB, give only the chapter number (or merely *supra* and *infra* within the same chapter). But knowing the chapter, the reader should then be able to locate the exact page(s) readily enough through the detailed Index. In Chapter VI only, as explained therein, each cross reference after a composer's name can be expected to lead to a music example by that composer as well as to a discussion of his music.

As in the two previous volumes, no attempt has been made here to use a parenthetical *sic* after every apparent error in a quoted source, or to apply one policy consistently to all uses of suffixes (e.g., biographic or biographical), or prefixes (La Laurencie or Laurencie), or spellings (catalog or catalogue), or transliteration (Handoshkin or Khandochkine). In each such alternative, common usage and the original or "best" available sources have had to be the prime determinants. (One is fortunate if only each alternative can be treated consistently within itself!) A main reason for supplying what must seem like excessive documentation to some readers—for example, page numbers (in fact, inclusive page numbers) for articles in reference works—has been to spare the reader the vexatious searching that can be brought on by just such alternatives, if not by an unfamiliar alphabetical order (as that of Swedish will be to some), or a variable alphabetical order (as results from the different handling of the German umlaut), or multiple divisions of a book (as in the 8 "Registers" of the *American Supplement* to GROVE, 3d ed.), or a listing under another heading (such as Calvocoressi's views on "cyclic devices" under "d'Indy" in Cobbett/CHAMBER II 3).

Quotation marks are used again around "sonata form" to distinguish the textbook concept or mold from other uses of the term form, and around "sonata" alone to indicate that a certain work is actually so called. Italics are used for a title that is quoted in full or up to a logical stopping point in its original language, wording, and spelling, whereas quotation marks are used for freer, translated, and/or partial references to a title. Abbreviated references to a particular passage in a music score—for example, Dussek's Op. 35/3/ii/1-7—follow the order of opus number (if any), other number (if any), movement (lowercase roman numeral), and measure(s). The measure numbering, which is absent, alas, from nearly all 19th-century publications, starts in ssb with the first full measure, starts anew in each movement, and includes no repeated sections except those only indicated by da capo signs. Often, when a systematic catalogue exists for a composer's works, the catalogue reference (as doubly abbreviated below) and its pertinent number replace the opus and/or other number—for example, C. 151/ii/1–7 for the Dussek passage just cited.

Major and minor keys continue to be indicated, respectively, by uppercase and lowercase letters only. And the optional accompaniments still specified in the early 19th century continue to be indicated by the plus-or-minus symbol, ±, with the plus sign reserved for obligatory (*obbligato*) accompaniments and the ampersand, &, for the simple fact of an accompaniment (as in P & Vn ± Vc). The order of P & Vn or Vn & P (etc.) depends on the earliest available source. An arrow (→) is used in the abbreviated graphs of structural designs to indicate a transition (within a movement) or *attacca* (between movements).

The abbreviations for musical terms in ssb are confined largely to the documentary apparatus. Most if not all of them should be self-evident in context. They include the following:

acc'd.	accompanied
aug.	augmented
B.	referring to a work as indexed in Brown/CHOPIN
Bn	bassoon
C.	referring to a work as indexed in Craw/DUSSEK
Cl	clarinet
D.	referring to a work indexed in Deutsch/SCHUBERT-I.
ded.	dedicated
dim.	diminished
dom.	dominant
ed.	edited, edition, editor
ex(x).	example(s)
F	fast, as the tempo of one movement in a cycle
facs.	facsimile
Fl	flute
H	harpsichord
Hn	horn
In	introduction, as the starting section of a movement in a cycle
J.	referring to a work as indexed in Jähns/WEBER

Ju.	referring to a work as indexed in Jurgenson/TSCHAÏKOWSKY
M	moderate, as the tempo of one movement in a cycle
Mi	minuet, as one movement in a cycle
mod.	modern
ms(s).	measure(s)
MS(S)	manuscript(s)
Ob	oboe
P	pianoforte
2 Ps	two pianos, four hands
P-duet	one piano, four hands
pub.	publication, published, publisher
Ro	rondo, as one movement in a cycle
S	slow, as the tempo of one movement in a cycle
Sc	scherzo
trans.	translated, translation, translator
Va	variations; viola
Vc	(violon)cello
Vn	violin
WoO	referring to a work without opus number as indexed in Kinsky & Halm/BEETHOVEN

W. S. N.

Contents

Music Examples

Tables and Charts

The Sonata Since Beethoven

Chapter I

The Scope and Gist of the Problem

The Terminal Point Reassessed

The Sonata Since Beethoven becomes the third and, contrary to earlier plans, the final volume in *A History of the Sonata Idea*. As explained at the outset (SBE 3), the over-all study had been projected originally in a single volume, then was reprojected in four volumes when the first of the sonata's four main eras alone required a full volume to cover its hypothetical minimum of detail.[1] That now only a third rather than a fourth volume completes the set needs explaining, even though the third, like the second, has grown to fully twice the length of the first volume. In other words, and as one pertinent way of getting into the scope and nature of the problem, it is necessary to explain why "The Sonata in the Romantic Era" and "The Sonata in the Modern Era" that were to complete the projected four-volume set have had to give way to this single volume with its changed title and its conclusion in late Romanticism.

Mainly, as the over-all study has come closer and closer to the Modern sonata, one realization has forced itself on me increasingly. It is that that most recent manifestation of the "sonata" cannot yet—if, indeed, it can ever—be subjected to the methods and treatment, nor adequately related to either the historical or the musical goals, that have governed the project thus far. In fact, whereas it had still seemed possible thirty years ago, in my own dissertation on "The Present Trend of the Sonata Idea" (SBE 4), to arrive at a neatly rational disposition of "Modern" trends and styles, now it no longer seems possible to arrive at any perspective whatsoever that is either clear or comprehensive. (Right away we run onto dangerous ground that is itself symptomatic of the problem!) Up to the late 1930's one could still treat "Modern" music primarily as a tonal phenomenon or departure.

---

1. The 4-vol. plan was still announced and assumed in the 2d, revised, 1966 ed. of SBE (p. 3).

And even up to the early 1950's one could still treat it rationally, in established terms, although by then less as a tonal than as a textural and syntactic problem.[2] But since the early 1950's, at least for those not to be hoodwinked here and there by the "emperor's clothes," what positive, genuinely musical tangibles have remained that are still capable of generalization?

To be sure, the term "sonata" itself continues to be applied, though less often, as a title—for example, by yesterday's avant-gardists Boulez and Henze. This fact means that we still could continue at least with our "semantic approach" (ssʙ 5–7) the tracing of what the word has meant and how it has been used. However, at once the crucial question follows as to whether the over-all definition that helped to buttress that approach still has force. "The sonata is a solo or chamber instrumental cycle of aesthetic or diversional purpose, consisting of several contrasting movements that are based on relatively extended designs in 'absolute' music" (sʙᴇ 7). On the surface, this definition still should have some validity, even in today's newest music. But in fact it no longer makes sense at all. After some three and one-half centuries, "sonata" has come full circle back to its original use "merely as the general term for any music to be played on instruments" (sʙᴇ 6). Whatever more constructive forces may have moved in in its place, the "sonata" in our definition has been undermined at its core by the dissolution of music's very building blocks and by the abandonment, destruction, or exhaustion, whether deliberate or unwitting, of nearly everything that previously had determined the sonata's styles and forms.

Such heretical statements could bring countercharges—for example, that our once flexible definition of the sonata idea now has rigidified into a Procrustean standard; or that the era designations originally accepted here mainly as customary, convenient, man-made delimitations (sʙᴇ 3 and 7) now have graduated into historical determinants in their own right. But rather than get involved in the aesthetics and dilemma of Modern music it is more direct and pertinent here to opine that by now the intriguing yet nervously unstable, newest "music" has simply left the field of music and gone into some other field, whether it be the mathematics of chance and permutations, the acoustics and exploration of raw sound, or the science of electronics. If "extended designs in 'absolute' music" (rather than calculated disunity, discontinuity, and nihilism) are actually still a main goal in the newest medium, then, in any case, their cohesive forces are no longer those that have unified the sonata throughout its more than

2. In 1953 it was "explained" primarily as a return from "phrase grouping" to "motivic play" (Newman/ᴜɴᴅᴇʀsᴛᴀɴᴅɪɴɢ 152–54).

three centuries of changing styles and forms. They are no longer over-all tonality, nor structural rhythm, nor thematic integration through melodic recurrences, interrelationships, and development.

But then, it might well be asked, at least could not this history of the sonata idea have been extended just up to the period when these newest trends began to dominate? Thus, one might find justifications in William Austin's recent, stimulating book on *Music in the 20th Century* for stretching the concept of the "Romantic Era" so as to include much of the music composed since World War I and right up to World War II.[3] After all, not a few of the "late-Romantics" whom we do include in the present volume continued to compose through most or all of that period if not longer—for example, Strauss, d'Indy, Elgar, Nielsen, Rachmaninoff, and D. G. Mason. Indeed, every pair of music's adjacent eras has shared a substantial overlap that similarly exhibits, side by side, both the old and the new. And Austin himself devotes the first third of his book to re-evaluations of the late Romantics. Yet it is also Austin who argues convincingly for the firm establishment of "the new styles" before World War I (while, understandably for his purposes, eschewing such labels as "Romanticism" and "Modernism").[4] In particular, he attributes the "remarkably sudden" contrast and the "great dividing line" to the introduction in 1911–12 of one of the most representative works each by his three central figures of 20th-century music, Bartók, Stravinsky, and Schoenberg; and of New Orleans jazz in New York.

In the present study we have to depend less objectively on any such tangible dividing line and more subjectively on overlapping but increasingly divergent views that began at least a half generation earlier. Those divergent views chiefly concerned the structural functions of tonality. Thus, we retain in this study composers who continued to employ tonality as a prime agent of larger forms, even those like Reger, Nielsen, Strauss, and d'Indy, who exploited its subtleties to the point where it almost contradicted itself, and even those whose later works occasionally take us well beyond World War I. And we exclude in this study, though sometimes on scarcely more tangible grounds than personal intuition, composers who seem to have contributed principally if not deliberately to undermining the structural functions of tonality. This delimitation means excluding even those like Busoni, Joseph Haas, Debussy, Scriabin, Ives, and, for that matter, Delius (!), Janáček, Ropartz, Thirion, Bréville, and Pâque, who had all begun in the most traditional manner before World War I, and who nearly all had

3. Austin/20TH 2, 30, 179.
4. Austin/20TH 179, 24–32.

demonstrated this manner in early, traditional sonatas. Only occasionally have confirmed Romantics been rejected because they came *too* late—for example, Somervell, Boughton, F. C. Nicholls, Gretchaninov, and Harold Morris. But the sonatas of these men have seemed so outmoded in style as to be anachronistic. In any case, for all the overlapping of old and new, it is pertinent to note that this final volume generally stops with composers born before 1880.

But to continue with the question raised above, there are two other reasons besides the beginnings of the Modern Era for stopping this volume generally by World War I rather than World War II. In the first place, the newest trends are not only incompatible with past trends and indigestible as actual music; they are too close to be viewed other than myopically. Until larger views are possible, any attempts to categorize or judge those newest trends (including the attempts already made here) must remain contentious at best. Up to now, it has been hard enough to see the preceding, Romantic Era in sufficient perspective, let alone the Modern Era. Who can know yet where time will put the dividing lines, or what trends and styles will prove to be significant, or which names will plunge abruptly into obscurity and which will live on? In the second place, the 20th century still lacks many of the archival, bibliographic, biographic, and critical checks and balances that have proved so essential as starting points and controls in the previous two volumes of the present study. With such aids the approach can be historical. Without them it can only be journalistic or reportorial, however detailed.

The Starting Point

The start of the Romantic Era poses no similar problem of scope for us but is even harder to delimit than the end.[5] In fact, it is the least delimitable of any of the era divisions encountered in all three of our volumes, for it offers nothing quite so tangible as the assault on tonality and the return of motivic play that characterize that onset of the Modern Era, or the *basso continuo* practice that helps to delimit the Baroque Era (SBE 8), or the change-over from that practice to Alberti bass that marks the early phase of the Classic Era (SCE 3–5). Certain style innovations—especially the more forthright, extended melodies, the "um-pah-pah" bass, the increasingly chromatic harmony, the new, nationalistically flavored dance rhythms, the squarer phrase-and-period

5. Delimiting the start is the subject of an interesting recent article, Engel/ ROMANTISCHEN, with special reference to Mendelssohn (as also in Werner/MENDELS-SOHN 47–51). Cf., too, cols. 785–86 in F. Blume's valuable survey of the Romantic Era (MGG XI 785–845); Bücken/19. 1–2; Dannreuther/ROMANTIC 3–4.

syntax, the wider-spaced scoring, the richer and more varied textures, the more personal, subjective inscriptions, and a more formalistic or self-conscious approach to form—all these do characterize the early (and much of the later) Romantic music (ssr VI). But no one of them ever permeates or brackets the era quite so inclusively as either the *basso continuo* or the Alberti bass in its respective era. And deciding on which side of the fence to place sonata composers during the Classic-Romantic overlap has had to depend often on subjective opinion again (cf. sce 4–5)—perhaps more often than before—chiefly as to whether they have seemed to be looking backward or forward with respect to those same or related traits.

Clementi and Beethoven were still writing sonatas in the early 1820's; yet, in spite of increasing signs of those Romantic style innovations in their later music, they remained largely oriented toward Classic sonata styles (cf. sce 130, 542, 753). On the other hand, Dussek (ssB XVII), who had already died in 1812, belonged unequivocally with the future as one of the most stylistically precocious of all early Romantic sonata composers, along with Field and his obscure, short-lived companion Pinto (both ssB XIV). Even Weber completed his sonatas no later than Beethoven's. Yet who would question his just classification among the Romantics (ssB VIII)? Schubert raises more of a problem because his sonatas relate so closely to Beethoven's. Both men were great and different enough to create distinctive spurs of their own in the mountainous course of music history. But, granted that both hovered right over that Classic-Romantic fence, Schubert must still be put on the opposite side from Beethoven (as any comparative reading of their last sonatas should confirm; ssB VI and VII). Ries, Czerny, and Moscheles (ssB VII), Cramer (ssB XIV), and, to some extent Hummel (ssB VIII), might all have been put (and, indeed, kept turning up) in the preceding era, mainly for their academicisms and their epigonic imitations of the great Classic masters. But their chief service to the 19th century was as immediate transmitters of Beethoven's music throughout Europe, and in that capacity they belong with the Romantics.

Paradoxically, in the absence of a clear enough dividing line, music historians have tended to emphasize the style innovations while maintaining that the Romantic Era is only an extension, outgrowth, or exaggeration of the Classic Era.[6] Yet the name itself for the era came

6. Cf. Blume in MGG XI 802–6, with references to Lang/WESTERN 740, 741, and 816 (cf., also, pp. 817–25); Einstein/ROMANTIC 4; Bücken/19. (especially 17–20); Handschin (*Musikgeschichte* [Basel, 1948] 355). Cf., also, Nagel/ROMANTISCHEN 268–69, 272.

at least loosely into use sooner, more generally, and less self-consciously than that for any other main era of music or the other arts. Of course, "Romance" (or "Romanza") as a music title (e.g., in Mozart's K. 466/ii and K. 525/ii) and as a type of novel had been employed well before the start of the 19th century.[7] Goethe's several early 19th-century mentions of "romantic," especially in reference to literature, are well known, including his preference for the objective or "classical" as against Schiller's subjective or "romantic"; and his designation of classic as healthy and romantic as sickly.[8] Jean Paul's and E. T. A. Hoffmann's interest in promoting a subjective romantic ideal as against antiquated, prosaic classicism[9] strongly influenced Schumann. Wrote Hoffmann, music "is the most romantic of all arts—one might almost say, the only purely romantic [art]." [10]

As early as 1836, Moscheles dubbed Schumann a "romantic musician" in a highly pertinent review (ssb VIII) of Schumann's Sonata in f♯, Op. 11.[11] Schumann himself wrote of musical romanticism on numerous occasions around 1840, although not altogether specifically or consistently.[12] (By the early 1840's can be found titles like "Sonate romantique," as in Op. 5 by L. Ehlert [ssb VIII], or descriptions like Schumann's own term "a big romantic sonata," for his *Faschingsschwank*, Op. 26 [ssb VIII]). Schumann got closest to our present concept when he wrote that Beethoven's "Ninth Symphony" was "the turning point from the classical to the romantic period." [13]

Main Themes (German Hegemony)

Between the early, precocious Romanticisms of Dussek, starting before 1800, and the near exhaustion of Romantic music, around World War I, the course of sonata history may be previewed by summarizing briefly its most central and frequently recurring themes. Its background is a complex of sociopolitical history that touches and even parallels music history from time to time to a surprising degree (as in the series of revolutions, monarchies, and republics that coincided almost to the year with fairly distinct episodes of sonata history in France; cf. the

7. Cf. Nagel/ROMANTISCHEN 261–62.
8. Cf. Dannreuther/ROMANTIC 3; MGG XI 791–92. In Longyear/SCHILLER "romantic" seems nowhere to be identified with Schiller and music.
9. Cf. MGG XI 792–93; Lang/WESTERN 743–44.
10. Quoted with more, in Nagel/ROMANTISCHEN 262.
11. NZM V (1836) 135–37; cf., also, RGM for June 21, 1840, p. 346 (referring to Moscheles' use of the term as the first from Leipzig and as a pedantry!).
12. His uses of the term are collected and compared in Boetticher/SCHUMANN 352–54; cf., also, pp. 394–96 (tracing other contemporary uses).
13. As quoted in Shedlock/SONATA 207.

start of ssb XII). This background begins with the convulsions of the French Revolution and continues with their aftermath in the Napoleonic empire, followed by the international revolutions of 1830 and 1848. It includes the ties, rivalries, alliances, intrigues, and eventual separation of Austria and Prussia as major powers. It includes the long-sought unification of Germany and of Italy, as well as the humiliation of France in the Franco-Prussian War, all in the early 1870's. It includes the widening and deepening relationships, intercourse, and frictions between these countries and the relatively more stable, liberal country of England as well as what are, from our viewpoint, the outlying, increasingly important countries comprehended under Scandinavia, East Europe, Russia, and the Americas. And it includes those rapid advances in industry, agriculture, communication, transportation, science, and education that benefitted society quite as much as they contributed to the causes of World War I (and II).

The course of sonata history during this same century and a quarter may be divided into three progressively shorter phases.[14] Each phase occurred much the same in time and kind throughout the regions where the sonata flourished, although without any obvious parallels to the two categories of Romantic music that clearly dominated public taste—opera and light diversional pieces. From before 1800 to about 1850 (or around the revolutions of 1848), occurred the early phase, which began in the Classic-Romantic borderland already noted (with its five Beethoven transmitters) and included the most distinguished composers of early Romantic sonatas (Dussek, Weber, Schubert, and Mendelssohn).[15] From about 1840 to 1885, an overlapping middle phase can be defined, starting with a widely alleged slump in the quantity and quality of sonata production (ssb II) that was partly belied, however, by the composition and/or publication around that time of some of the first main sonatas by Schumann, Chopin, and Liszt. Within little more than a decade this phase began to show a revival of interest, which was furthered by the first sonatas of Brahms. From the mid 1870's to World War I, a third, final, overlapping phase can be defined. It is marked at its start, concurrent with the epochal political events just noted, by a conspicuous spurt of interest almost everywhere, especially in the duo sonata (and other chamber music). Its composers include such important contributors to the sonata as the later Brahms, Richard Strauss, and Reger in Austro-Germany; Franck, Fauré, Saint-

14. Cf. Westerly/PIANOFORTE 183–86 for a chap. in 4 pp. that synopsizes what might be called the standard view (in 1924) of "The Sonata Since Beethoven."
15. The pat labels for Schubert and Mendelssohn, respectively, in Einstein/ROMANTIC 89–91 and 124–26 are "Romantic Classic" and "Romantic Classicist."

Saëns, and d'Indy in France; Grieg in Norway; Medtner and Rachmaninoff in (and out of) Russia; and MacDowell in the United States. But its composers also include a whole class of Romantic epigones, such as Dubois, d'Albert, Sinding, and Bortkiewicz—all men with much skill, yet too derivative and formulized in their music to survive.

Like the sonatas of Corelli in the Baroque Era (SBE 9–10) or of Haydn, Mozart, and Beethoven in the Classic Era (SCE 5–6, 454), those of four composers—Schubert, Schumann, Chopin, and Brahms—are singled out in the present volume as main cornerstones of the Romantic sonata. In particular (and as before) they comprise the reference framework for Chapter VI on "Styles and Forms," leaving only their background, circumstances, and cultivation to be discussed in the later, pertinent composer chapters. If in turn, any one of these four composers is to be singled out as the one most important and central contributor to the sonata since Beethoven, the choice clearly must be Brahms. Certainly Brahms was the most sonata-minded among them, both in the proportion of his attention and the nature of his musical thinking (SSB IX). In this respect at least, Brahms deserved to be called the third "B" by Bülow.[16] If, furthermore, any one axis of composers is to be singled out as defining opposing trends of the Romantic sonata it just as clearly must be that represented by Liszt (SSB X) and Brahms, whose antipodes of style and form still contrasted sharply in the sonatas —progressive and conservative, respectively—of their second-generation followers.

And, finally, if there is any one nationality or region that is to be singled out as the most germinal and central to the Romantic sonata it is no longer Italy, as it had been at least in the earlier phases of the Baroque and Classic eras (SBE 39–40 and SCE 64–65). Rather it is (Austro-)Germany from start to finish. (It would be appropriate to say Austro-Germany, without the parentheses, except that Schubert's sonatas did not gain recognition for almost a half-century after his death [SSB VII] and Brahms wrote several of his sonatas before he moved to Vienna.)

The same three phases of Romantic sonata history stand out within this German hegemony. First, following the incomparable heritage from the Classic Viennese masters, the compositions of Mendelssohn and Schumann became the loosely axial, or conservative and more progressive, reference standards, respectively, for the sonatas of a whole, mid-19th-century generation of composers.[17] Then, as was just

16. Cf. May/BRAHMS II 528–29; Cobbett/CHAMBER I 160–61 and 327 (both D. Tovey).

17. Cf. Maclean/RUBINSTEIN 139, 148, and 150 on the continuing tendency to relate all music to Mendelssohn.

observed, the music of Brahms and Liszt similarly governed the next generation. (Wagner's overpowering influence would be included here, too, except that it touched the sonata much less significantly [ssʙ X] apart from a few notable consequences at the end of the era, like Op. 63 by d'Indy [ssʙ XIII].) And finally, certain men hardly so well remembered today, especially Rheinberger in Munich and Kiel in Berlin (both ssʙ X), continued to maintain the German hegemony at the end of the era. But now it was not so much the surprisingly strong compositions by these men, thoroughly steeped in the previous German styles, as their high reputations as teachers that kept the German influence dominant.

Indeed, right from the start of the era, the main Austro-German centers—notably Vienna, Leipzig, and Berlin—became the international meccas for all students aspiring to the best, with the notable exception of the most important French-born composers, who trained in their own country. For example, among other outlanders of the sonata who polished their training in Germany, there were Bennett and Stanford in England, Albéniz in Spain, Grieg and Sinding in Norway, Sibelius in Finland, Rubinstein in Russia, and MacDowell (as well as most of the "Boston Classicists") in the United States. Furthermore, few of the sonata composers who did not train in Austro-German centers failed to come under the profound influence of the German masters, including even such ardent native Frenchmen as Saint-Saëns and d'Indy, as well as Franck in France, Elgar in England, Nielsen in Denmark, Martucci in Italy, and Medtner (of German descent) in Russia and elsewhere.

The Mainest Theme—Beethoven's Influence

The foregoing remarks on German hegemony in the Romantic sonata lead to what is at once the most important of these main themes and the justification for the present volume's title. That theme is the all-pervasive influence of Beethoven's sonatas throughout the era and wherever the sonata was cultivated. (Of course, their influence has extended beyond the Romantic Era, too, although it has dropped off necessarily in the same degree as have those previously mentioned forces—tonal, melodic, rhythmic—on which the Beethoven sonata thrives.) It is perhaps hard to realize now that the strongest early Romantics, including Schubert, Mendelssohn, and Weber, had to resist being swallowed up in the maelstrom of Beethovenism (the less strong did not resist) quite as Verdi and Debussy had to resist Wagnerism seventy-five years later.

The devotion to, even idolatry of, Beethoven's sonatas was extraordinary throughout the era.[18] It began as early as 1800, in his own lifetime, with the transmitters mentioned earlier, and soon spread to France, England, and other countries by way of the publishers, though not yet the public performers.[19] We see this devotion or idolatry in slavish imitations like a "Sonate pathétique" in c by L. Berger and another by Lauska published early in the century (both SSB VIII), or in such a collection, published late in the century, as John Petzler's *Twelve Sonatas for the Pianoforte, Composed in Imitation of Some of the Works of Beethoven.*[20] We see it in the articles, reviews, lectures, and whole books on Beethoven's sonatas that were published or reported frequently in every main music periodical of the era, culminating in such widely divergent studies as the multivolume sets by Rolland and Riemann.[21] We see it in the essential place given to Beethoven's solo sonatas in 19th-century piano pedagogy, as by Liszt[22] and in Wagner's proposals for an ideal music education.[23] And we see it, above all, in the public performances of Beethoven's sonatas, which occurred only sporadically before the middle of the century, then began to multiply and soon to snowball as they became general fare wherever recitals were given.[24]

To judge by contemporary reviews of those recitals and by the nature of surviving 19th-century editions of Beethoven's sonatas (such as the still ubiquitous ed. by Bülow & Lebert), the licenses taken in performance would shock present-day purists (e.g., the trills and tremolos Liszt is supposed to have added in the first mvt. when he in-

18. The cultivation of Beethoven's music has not been investigated with regard to his sons. so thoroughly or illuminatingly as it has in Mahaim/BEETHOVEN for his late quartets. But there is considerable information about this aspect of the solo sons. in Prod'homme/BEETHOVEN, and of the duo sons. in Müller-Reuter/LEXIKON II *passim.* Cf., also, SCE 542. Boyer/BEETHOVEN and Schrade/BEETHOVEN are broader studies of the developing and changing attitudes toward Beethoven in the 19th c. (the latter in France).

19. Cf. Favre/FRANÇAISE 103–4; SSB XII and XIV (opening pp.).

20. Cf. MMR XVII (1886) 39 (criticizing the composer for having to copy the masters).

21. For samples and further references, cf. SCE 503–42 *passim.* Typical of many such contributions not yet noted in the Beethoven literature are the articles in RGM for 1846 *passim;* DWIGHT'S X–XVI (1856–60) *passim;* SMZ XVII (1877) 45 ff.; MT XXIV (1883) 206 (report of lectures at the London Institution). Cf., further, the reviews cited in Boyer/BEETHOVEN 202–65 *passim.*

22. Cf. BÜLOW BRIEFE I 343; Fay/GERMANY 229–30, 237–38.

23. Cf. WAGNER PROSE IV 198 and V 59–126 *passim* (especially 81–84).

24. Cf. under Cramer, Pinto, and Potter in SSB XIV and the introduction to SSB XII. A check through RGM for 1834–50 *passim* suggests that the largest number of performances before 1850 of Beethoven sons. occurred in Paris, being almost half the number of performances of sons. by all composers that occurred then and there.

troduced Op. 27/2 in Paris in 1832[25]). But we have the great pianists of the century—Liszt and Clara Schumann at first,[26] then Bülow and Rubinstein[27]—to thank for taking the lead in making Beethoven's sonatas so popular. In 1873 Rubinstein still doubted the advisability of including more than one Beethoven sonata in a recital[28] and in London five years later Bülow was censured for playing an all-Beethoven recital, for choosing the last five solo sonatas, at that, and worse still, for doing them all from memory.[29] Yet by 1861 complete cycles of the "thirty-two" were being played, soon from memory.[30]

Of course, today's favorites were yesterday's, too, and a good share of the Beethoven performances were confined to Opp. 13, 27/1, 31/2, 53, and 57, as well as the "Kreutzer Sonata," Op. 47 (played for the 48th time "at these concerts" in London, March 3, 1883[31] and played often by Clara Schumann and Joachim,[32] among other duo teams). But by the 1870's most audiences were getting ample exposure to the other and later sonatas, too.[33] Exceptional is the awe and fascination with which Op. 106 in B♭ was regarded almost from its first publication in 1819, much as it still is today.[34] There were the deliberate imitations of it in Mendelssohn's own Op. 106 in B♭ (SSB VIII), the allusion to it in Brahms's Op. 1 in C (SSB IX), the special notices of it taken by Schumann and Wagner,[35] Marxsen's orchestration of its "Scherzo" in 1835,[36] and such amusing incidents as Potter's instruction to Bennett to ask the dealer "for the Sonata that nobody plays."[37] And there were the early performances, first in Paris by Liszt in 1836 (if what Berlioz

25. Cf. Prod'homme/BEETHOVEN 125–27; Fay/GERMANY 168 (on Bülow).
26. Cf. Hanslick/WIEN I 333–36; Litzmann/SCHUMANN III 617–24.
27. Cf. Mason/MEMORIES 226–27.
28. Mason/MEMORIES 226–27.
29. MT XIX (1878) 665. Cf., also, MT XXI (1880) 351–52 (on 3 all-Beethoven recitals by "Herr Bonawitz"). Sietz/HILLER II 80 reports all-Beethoven recitals of 4 or 5 sons. each, including one in which the audience yelled for his "Sonata in F Flat"! Cf. Pleasants/HANSLICK 185.
30. Cf. SCE 527 and the introduction to SSB XIX.
31. MT XXIV (1883) 193.
32. E.g., cf. Fay/GERMANY 162, 27.
33. E.g., a surprising representation can be found in MMR II and III (1872–73) *passim* (especially Clara Schumann) and SMZ XVI and XVII (1876–77). As early as 1833 in London Moscheles gave private performances of Opp. 109 and 111 (MO-SCHELES I 288–89).
34. On the 19th-century career of this work, cf. Newman/Op. 106 (originally read at the Annual Meeting of the American Musicological Society in 1968 [New Haven]) cf. also, SCE 530–32.
35. Cf. Schumann/SCHRIFTEN I 453; NZM XLVI (1857) 158; Prod'homme/BEETHOVEN 249.
36. Müller-Reuter/LEXIKON II 138.
37. Cf. Bennett/BENNETT 33–34 and 400; SSB XIV.

praised was actually Op. 106);[38] then in Germany, Vienna, and Russia, in 1843, 1847, and 1853, respectively, by Mortier de Fontaine;[39] in London by Moscheles (privately?) in 1845,[40] Alexandre Billet in 1850, and Arabella Goddard (from memory, in her debut) in 1853;[41] and again in Germany by Franz Wüllner in 1854 and earlier[42] and in Vienna by Clara Schumann in 1856.[43] No doubt a little of the exceptional interest in Op. 106 relates to the growing historical interest among pianists (and other musicians) throughout the century (ssb II). Thus, in 1837 Moscheles pioneered not only the idea of the solo recital but a return, that soon, to the harpsichord for the playing of Scarlatti's sonatas.[44] And by 1885–86, Anton Rubinstein brought the interest to a peak with his celebrated "seven historical concerts," ranging in content from mid-16th- to mid-19th-century music (with many sons.) and given throughout Europe.[45]

Subordinate Themes (the Great and the Small)

Along with the main themes just introduced, certain subordinate themes in the present volume may be pointed out in advance. Most of these themes, apart from the question of great and small composers that is raised below, need only to be identified here, in the interest of an introductory overview, since they all figure in the succeeding, five survey chapters of Part One. First, Beethoven's unsurpassed example and an increasing tendency to value originality for its own sake in the arts help to explain a new, elevated attitude toward the sonata as one of the loftiest and most challenging of musical forms, especially after its supposed slump around 1840 (supra) and equally in the minds of composer, performer, and perceiver (ssb II). Second, as already implied, the Romantic sonata becomes more and more of a main staple in piano solo and ensemble recitals alike (ssb III). Third, its spread comes to depend at least as much on its popularization by travelling recitalists as its propagation by publishers and its enjoyment by students or amateur groups (ssb III and IV). Fourth, its vehicle par excellence is the vehicle par excellence of Romantic instrumental music in general

38. Cf. Prod'homme/BEETHOVEN 248–49 (referring also to Liszt's later recollection of playing Op. 106 at age 10 [1821!], "very badly, undoubtedly, but with feeling").
39. Prod'homme/BEETHOVEN 247; Pleasants/HANSLICK 185 (but read B♭ for B).
40. MOSCHELES II 138 (but read B♭ for B).
41. Schonberg/PIANISTS 238; HALLÉ 26–27; MUSICAL WORLD for April, 1853, p. 243 (review of Goddard); Bache/BACHE 227, 255.
42. Kämper/WÜLLNER 8–12; BRAHMS BRIEFWECHSEL XIV 9, XV 37.
43. Litzmann/SCHUMANN III 621.
44. Cf. MOSCHELES II 22–23, 35–36 ("old masters"), 45, 224–25.
45. Cf. Rubinstein/ERINNERUNGEN 111–14, including the complete programs.

—that is, the piano, whether in solos or in duos with some other instrument (ssв V). And fifth, the most progressive Romantic sonatas aim at, and sometimes achieve, a new over-all dynamism through more complete integration of their several movements and more broadly planned climax structures (ssв VI). In fact, "over-all dynamism" would belong in our repeated definition of "sonata" (*supra*) if that definition were confined to the more progressive sonata since Beethoven.

The question of great and small composers brings up the hard judgments of time—scarcely a new question, but one that recurs with special meaning, as in our previous two volumes, every time a comprehensive survey of individual composers is made. In nearly all instances the judgments have seemed just. Often they are harsh, sometimes they are unpredictable, but only rarely do they seem wrong. Part Two of the present volume takes up over 625 individual composers, as against slightly over 400 in the Classic and 300 in the Baroque volume. (Among apparent explanations for the increase are the greater number of countries participating, the larger populations in those countries, the larger proportions of composers and music lovers interested in the sonata, the increased publication of new sonatas, and the greater number of sonata advertisements, reviews, and performance announcements supplied in music journals, especially in Germany and England.) Most of the principal Romantic composers contributed at least one or two sonatas over and above their early training exercises. Even most of the notable exceptions—among them, Verdi, Meyerbeer, Bizet, Gounod, Bruckner, and Mahler—wrote instrumental works akin to the sonata. Aside from Brahms, those who did pay more attention to our genre may not have devoted as big a share of their total outputs as their Baroque or Classic predecessors. Yet apparently more of them, proportionally as well as absolutely, left sonatas that are still heard today in the concert hall, in the studio, and in recordings.[46]

In any case, our concern at this point is not with that proportion that does survive, which still adds up to only about fifteen composers. It is with that considerably larger portion of once-great composers, whose sonatas, like those by the huge majority of small composers, no longer get heard at all. One is surprised to discover, especially among the late Romantics, how many are the once mighty and how hard they have fallen, leaving their conspicuous marks only in the historical records.[47] Such are Raff in Wiesbaden, Rheinberger in Munich,

---

46. Partial confirmation for this generalization can be found in the current program listings of the *New York Times*, catalogues of the chief publishers of practical performing eds., and the *Schwann Long Playing Record Catalog*.

47. They all still get full attention in MGG.

A. G. Ritter in Magdeburg, and Grädener in Hamburg (all in ssb X); or Kiel (ssb X), Gernsheim, Wilhelm Berger, Kaun, Kahn, and Juon (the last 5 in ssb XI), all in Berlin; or Rubinstein in St. Petersburg and Medtner in Moscow and elsewhere (both in ssb XVIII); or Stanford in London (ssb XIV) and D. G. Mason in New York (ssb XIX).

Nearly all of these men have in common an undeniable mastery of their craft, a conservative orientation to German music, and a debilitating tendency to prolificity, beyond which their harsh dismissals by time may have different (if any) explanations. Thus, Grädener, Kiel, and Berger may have followed too closely in Brahms's footsteps to survive independently. Rheinberger and Medtner may have deliberated and philosophized too much in their music for the more intensive, streamlined tastes of a later generation. Rubinstein may have won more enthusiasm for his compositions than they deserved, through his sensational successes as a pianist. Ritter actually may have won less interest in his compositions than they deserve, through the mere circumstances of chance.

But to the question that is raised almost invariably in such instances, "Why has this music been neglected or overlooked?" [48] there has to be one further, more general answer. The number of topflight sonatas alone (or quartets, or songs, and so on) that has accumulated over some three centuries has far surpassed both the occasions and the outlets, public or private, for hearing them. The same question of neglect keeps coming up even for sonatas that do survive, at least to a degree, such as those by Schubert and Schumann (ssb VI–VIII). Whatever more inherent reasons may exist in such works, when they do get "neglected" the answer ordinarily is that they are not being killed by time but inundated or buried alive by music's own population explosion!

A different question arises with the many smaller Romantics—with those who won less if any significant recognition in their own day for their sonatas and usually deserved no more, nor any perpetuation of their works through new efforts to bring these back to life. Should those men have been allowed to rest in peace, with their names rapidly ceasing to clutter the pages of music histories and dictionaries? Here once more, as in the previous two volumes, the answer has to be "no." Those men need to be included in order to balance and round out the total environments within which the greats or the once-greats have predominated. Sometimes a composer needs to be included merely to preserve his name on the chance that some further, more localized

48. E.g., cf. Cobbett/CHAMBER I 27 on A. Ashton and I 566 on J. Holbrooke; or GROVE V 466–68 on J. B. McEwen; or MMR I (1871) 24 on opportunities to hear sons.

study will uncover more of his sonatas and/or more significance than has been credited to them.

Again as in our previous two volumes, the obscure composers have been brought back to light chiefly by systematic combings of the principal music encyclopedias, periodicals, catalogues, and locale or composer monographs.[49] And again (cf. sce 8–9) the aim has been to include every composer whose sonatas reveal at least some musical or historical distinction, or have attracted at least some attention in reviews, performances, or special studies. These generally obscure composers, plus a few others included with even less apparent reason, do figure here mostly as statistical support for trends or as fillers in the over-all picture. Yet it has not seemed sufficient to bunch them into statistical, space-saving tables (except for about 60 of some 110 Americans merely tabulated in ssb XIX because too little is known about them to write more). The tables not only would sacrifice the prose continuity and condemn some to anonymity who deserve better. They would emphasize the ordinary and typical rather than whatever might distinguish any individuals. On the other hand nothing is gained by supplying more than essential orientation, sonata output, and bibliography for run-of-the-mill composers whose sonatas are remembered by nothing more than a neutral review, or even a negative one (such as the 10-page [!], partly satirical disparagement of a thoroughly unpromising Op. 1, ded. to Meyerbeer by one Maurice Levy, otherwise unknown here[50]).

The obscure composers we have been considering are not the kind implied in E. J. Dent's assertion that the history of music is written in bad music.[51] We have been thinking generally of musical conservatives who are competent but inconsequential, whereas Dent implies that it is the innovators, often rash and not necessarily conservative, who produce the historically progressive, "bad music." Even the most interesting of our more obscure composers were conservatives in the sense that they were direct disciples and not leaders—for example, Draeseke, Viole, and Reubke (all ssb X), three talented imitators of Liszt. The least interesting of our obscure composers are those who are not only conservative among their contemporaries but in relation to the whole

49. Contemporary (19th-c.) sources have been of increased value in the present vol., including especially AMZ, NZM, MW, SMW, SMZ, RGM, and MT, among periodicals, and Schilling/LEXICON, Mendel/LEXICON, Fétis/BU, BROWN & STRATTON, and GROVE Am. Suppl., among encyclopedias. The fullest recent source for names has continued to be MGG (of which only Vol. XIV was still not available at press time, mid 1968, for ssb).

50. CAECILIA XXVI (1847) 242–51. The same opinion is expressed more briefly in NZM XXVI (1847) 141–42.

51. Cf. Howes/ENGLISH 12, 27–28.

era. Thus, Sinding as an epigone arouses less historical interest here than Ries as an early-Romantic. Somewhat related is the obscure composer who has aroused no interest because he fits in no national pattern. Thus, perhaps one Otto Schweizer got in no German dictionaries because he moved to London, where Novello published his Sonata for P & Vc in 1887,[52] and in no English dictionaries because he was not native born.

Methods, Policies, and Sources

As with its two predecessors, the present volume divides into two complementary but asymmetrical parts (cf. SBE 9–10 and SCE 7–8). Part One, in six chapters, provides the over-all view, surveying successively the problem, meaning, use, spread, scoring, and form of the sonata since Beethoven. Part Two, in more than twice as many chapters and nearly four times as many pages, provides the more detailed views. It takes up the individual composers and their sonatas, region by region according to early, middle, and late phases (with 1850 and 1885 being the approximate, most frequent inner dividing lines for the era). A certain minimum of overlapping and repetition is unavoidable between and within the two parts—in fact, necessary. As before, our semantic approach gives preference to works actually called "sonata," although, naturally, taking related works into consideration when they do relate (SCE 6–7). And as before, each composer is identified primarily with the region where he lived, composed his sonatas, and exerted his chief influence, rather than the land of his birth when there is a difference.[53] Thus, Chopin is identified with Paris rather than Warsaw. But in that age of rapidly improving travel and more frequent changes of residence, a composer must often be located more arbitrarily, or merely returned to his birthplace, anyway. Chronologically, each composer is introduced around the time of his chief or only sonata(s), which may or may not be the time when he "flourished" in terms of any better known or more significant works by him in other categories. Thus, Mussorgsky is introduced with other composers around 1860 rather than a half generation later, when his chief operas began to appear. Also, the amount of space allocated to each composer depends first here on the artistic worth and historical significance of his sonata writing—which are largely matters of personal evaluation, in any case —and only secondly on the over-all importance generally credited to

52. Reviewed in NZM LXXXIII/2 (1887) 466.
53. " 'Made in England' was Walker's definition of English music, and it avoids difficulties raised by blood and birthplace" (Howes/ENGLISH 21).

him. Mussorgsky may be cited to illustrate that policy, too, in view of the relatively short space allocated to him here.

The literature on Romantic music is vast and mushrooming, as is suggested by the nearly 850 entries pertinent to the present study alone, in the Bibliography. But much of it still needs assimilating, consolidating, and re-organizing. A notable step in that direction has been the establishment in Köln of a Zentralstelle für Musikbibliographie des 19. Jahrhunderts.[54] Among over-all treatments of Romantic music, those by Bücken and Einstein have been utilized most here,[55] along with the first two of the three promised volumes in the Marxist-oriented survey by Knepler and the admirably planned article by Blume (MGG XI 785–845).

There are no previous, over-all studies of the Romantic sonata.[56] But there are numerous studies that concentrate wholly or partly on that topic within particular regions, periods, and/or scorings. Such are the studies by Egert on the early-Romantic (mainly German) piano sonata, Favre on French piano music up to 1830, Alekseev on Russian piano music up to recent times, Asaf'ev on Russian music of all types since about 1800, Reeser similarly on Dutch music, Szabolcsi on Hungarian music history, Lissa on Romantic Polish music, Closson and Borren on Belgian music history, Temperley on early-Romantic music in England, Sloan on the American violin sonata, Wolverton on American piano music up to 1830, Shand on the violin sonata from 1851 to 1917, and still others, to be cited where they apply. Needless to say, the widened regions of the 19th-century sonata and the increasing studies from those regions, rarely translated, present the researcher with increasing problems, at times nearly insurmountable problems, in Slavic and other exotic languages.

Much richer, although still hit-or-miss, are the studies on individual composers. Schubert fares best, thanks especially to the fundamental studies by the late O. E. Deutsch, and including monographs on the sonatas by Költzsch and others (SSB VII). Brahms fares second best (SSB IX), although apart from a very few peripheral studies like

54. Warm thanks are owing to the Director, Dr. Imogen Fellinger, for several advices by correspondence. Cf., also, DMf XIX (1966) 172–76, regarding a symposium on 19th-c. "Unterhaltungs- und Gebrauchsmusik" in Coburg in 1965.

55. In this discussion of sources, when only the author's name is given, the full title of the book in question is self-evident in the Bibliography.

56. A recent one-vol. survey of all son. history, in Rumanian (Nicolescu/SONATA—recall the 2 previous over-all accounts, by Klauwell and Borrel, as cited in SBE 12, 426, 411)—includes a short chap. on the Romantic son. And there are pertinent sections in my own survey articles in MGG XII 868–910, RICORDI ENCICLOPEDIA IV 243–49, and Gatti & Basso/LA MUSICA IV 429–43 (all pub. since SCE appeared in 1963).

Mitschka's, his sonatas still offer a major, open topic for prospective and prospecting dissertationists. (So, for that matter, do the sonatas of nearly every other important Romantic composer, including Dussek, Weber, Mendelssohn, Schumann, Chopin, Liszt, Fauré, Saint-Saëns, and Grieg, there being thus far chiefly a few studies on the sonatas of minor figures like Loewe [SSB VIII] or on separate categories like Rheinberger's organ sonatas [SSB X].) Among these front-rankers of the Romantic sonata, Schumann, Chopin, and Liszt have all engendered substantial bodies of music literature, but this literature, especially on Liszt (SSB X), is in serious need of re-evaluation, revision, clarification, re-organization, and amplification. It should be added that even when a special study does exist on a Romantic composer's sonatas it is likely to be usable (with all due credit) almost exclusively for its factual information rather than its musical analysis. An initiated reader can better his understanding from another's intelligent analysis. But the writer is in a different position, still more so when confronted by the complexities of Romantic as against Baroque and Classic traits of style and form (cf. SBE 67–68 and SCE 113). He must see the score for himself and go one big step further by making his own analysis, both because the most objective style-critical approach still depends heavily on subjective opinion and because each writer needs to maintain his own consistent, personal slant.[57]

The pertinent literature on Romantic music is further enriched by the many publications of memoirs, diaries, letters, travel reports, and intimate first-hand biographies by and about musicians. Among the most useful sources of this sort in the present study are those by or about Moscheles, Spohr, Mendelssohn, both Schumanns, Weber, Brahms, Joachim, Chorley, Hallé, Chopin (in Sydow & Hedley), Bülow, and both W. and D. G. Mason. Contemporary accounts of concert life have contributed much, too, especially the large number in the several collections by Hanslick in Vienna.

But more fruitful than any other of our contemporary sources for new and more detailed information have been the periodicals, the chief of which have been searched in detail here, throughout the portions of the Romantic Era (up to 1915) in which they appeared.[58] In

---

57. A significant dichotomy of old and new approaches, especially to "sonata form," is presented in W. J. Mitchell's thorough, enlightening review of *The Beethoven Quartets* by Joseph Kerman, in MQ LIII (1967) 421–34. Note also, with regard to Schubert, how, for example, Egert/FRÜHROMANTIKER 74–91 disagrees with Költzsch, and Truscott/UNITY with Brown.

58. These are AMZ, CAECILIA, NZM, MW, SMW, DM, DMZ, SMZ, MT, HARMONICON, QUARTERLY, RGM, and DWIGHT'S. Besides their general superiority for our purposes, these periodicals nearly all have the advantage of a full table of contents in each

order of value, these have provided many reviews of new publications, reports of concerts, announcements of publications and concerts, and larger, more general articles. In particular, the many reviews cited throughout the present volume—undoubtedly too many for some readers[59]—have provided us often with the best, if not the only, facts we have about a sonata's title, movements, keys, style traits (when the specific comments do not reduce to generalities), and "faults" in composition or scoring; about its publisher, quality of publication, and date (at least as a *terminus ad quem,* since the review might be delayed as much as several years); and even about the composer himself. Not seldom they include from one to several short or long music examples (though rarely a complete movement or complete sonata as a supplement), which may well prove to be the only actual taste we can still get of a sonata no longer locatable. In their typically discursive manner of leading from the general to the specific, the reviews frequently open with choice, quotable generalizations about the sonata's current status and function in the world of music (ssb II). The length and number of reviews (in different periodicals) give at least a statistical hint of the interest the sonata and its composer were arousing at the time of publication, especially when compared with the response to previous or subsequent sonata publications from the same man.

Moreover, the evaluations themselves in the reviews, although generally superseded by the evaluations of time (and placed last, not first, in importance here), do give at least a choice sampling of contemporary opinion and at most some eloquent, discerning critiques that still seem as valid as ever.[60] To be sure, excessive praise was likely to be lavished on the more competent but conservative, readily fathomed works, much, conversely, as undue faults and confusion were likely to be charged to the more innovative, less readily fathomed works. And the critics frequently disagreed (as on A. B. Marx's Op. 16, ssb VIII). Moreover, every significant composer from Beethoven on (sce 539) suffered at least one nemesis among his reviewers. Reger and Grieg were plagued with exceptional virulence (ssb XI and XIV). Brahms was contemptuous of his reviewers' understanding (ssb IX) and Liszt expressed hostility toward his reviewers, including the many who

---

vol., though not cumulative indexes except for a few runs (especially AMZ from 1798–1848). A few vols. in the runs could not be found. Numerous other periodicals, as well as a few newspapers, were of occasional help, as cited in later chaps.

59. But references to such reviews are otherwise scarce, being seldom included in any but the most detailed composer bibliographies.

60. That 19th-c. writers were alert to the problems of music criticism is suggested in repeated references to these problems, such as that in MT XXIII (1882) 337 on the misuse of critical adjectives.

hid behind initials and more cryptic signatures (e.g., numbers and Greek letters) or simply remained anonymous.[61] Yet by and large, the reviews seem about as fair in their evaluations as reviews ever do.

Certainly, Schumann left a rich legacy of reviews that have come to rank among the valued 19th-century commentaries on early 19th-century music (and the most quoted throughout much of ssb; cf. ssb VIII, including special references to Plantinga/SCHUMANN). These reviews appeared mostly during the decade after he founded the important *Neue Zeitschrift für Musik* (NZM, from 1834) and centered often around a special interest in new piano sonatas (ssb VIII). They could be ecstatic in their enthusiasms for the best (as in the encomiums of Schubert's and Mendelssohn's sons., ssb VII and VIII, or the "Hat's off!" articles that heralded both Chopin and Brahms, ssb XII and IX), although occasionally they could go overboard, too (as in the reviews that saw promise, not to be fulfilled, in D. F. E. Wilsing; ssb VIII [62]). On the other hand, over his various noms de plume, Schumann's reviews could be unqualifiedly negative, seldom miscalculating and often indulging in witty, gentle, or harsh sarcasm (as in those of sons. or related pieces by one J. Nisle,[63] by Anton Halm, ssb VII, and by Czerny, ssb VII). Whatever their direction and tone, these reviews usually start with or branch off into broader discussions that include, along with much else, significant commentaries on the history, nationalism, quality versus quantity, career values, deterioration, excessive virtuosity, surfeit of motivic play, and conservatism of the sonata.[64]

With regard to sources for dating Romantic music, it has proved possible—more so than anticipated—to arrive at the year of publication for the large majority of the sonatas under discussion and nearly that close for most of the others. Relatively few of the Romantic sonatas are dated in MGG, GROVE, or other main dictionaries, past and present, when, indeed, they are itemized and not simply lumped under "considerable piano music" or "several sonatas." Pazdírek's *Universal-Handbuch* supplies only a rough, late *terminus ad quem* (1904–10) with regard to dates, although it is invaluable as a nearly exhaustive list of all 19th-century publications. And American copyrights do not begin to help substantially until the end of the century (ssb XIX, introduction). But when a sonata cannot be found in the remarkable cumulative, annual, or even monthly volumes issued on a more or less

61. Cf. LISZT LETTERS I 328.

62. Cf. the enthusiastic review by Bülow of Viole's Op. 1 (ssb X).

63. Johann Friedrich Nisle? Cf. Schumann/SCHRIFTEN I 306–7; Schilling/LEXICON V 176–77; MGG IX 1537–38; ssb VIII.

64. Cf. Schumann/SCHRIFTEN I 59, 92–93 and 452, 123 and 306–7, 395–96, 453; II 10, 11, 118, 80–81; also, ssb II and III.

international basis since 1815 by Whistling and Hofmeister, then it is likely to turn up in a periodical announcement or review, in somebody's letters, diary, or memoirs, or in a present-day study. And if all these fail, one of the fine publishing or plate-number indexes such as those by Deutsch, Hopkinson, Weinmann, or Tyson is likely to solve the problem. The few Italian and Spanish publications that have come up here have posed the chief problems.

In any case, as before (scɛ 13–14), accurate dating is essential to any discussion of influences and of which way they flowed in the tightly packed Romantic Era. Unfortunately, library catalogues that go beyond 1800, much less dated catalogues, are still few and limited. The new, 33-volume catalogue of the New York Public Library (with supplements; Cat. nypl) is the notable exception on both counts. Cobbett's anthological *Cyclopedic Survey of Chamber Music* (including many general as well as composer articles), Altmann's *Kammermusik-Katalog,* and the Müller-Reuter *Lexikon* are indispensable tools that add some dates of published music to the majority they derive from hofmeister. Although the publishers seldom dated their 19th-century editions, the composers helped as the century wore on by becoming increasingly disposed to observe a single, correct sequence of opus numbers. Modern "complete" editions, which usually cope with the dating as well as the editorial problems, exist only for the most important of the Romantics who wrote sonatas and but few others. (Otherwise, present-day reprints of Romantic sonatas are rare.)

The Pleasures of Musical Romanticism

This introductory chapter should not be concluded without at least a mention of the pleasures experienced in working on the Romantic sonata, which have been at least the equal of those experienced in working on the Baroque and on the Classic sonata. For every pianist there is, of course, the lure of the music produced by some of the foremost masters of the piano, from Dussek to Rachmaninoff, during this greatest century in the piano's development as an instrument.[65] For every devotee of good literature there is the frequent association, even through so absolute a musical genre as the sonata, with notable men of letters at every turn, not to mention the numerous composers who themselves were capable writers in this century of hybrid arts.

65. Although the 128 music exx. in ssB can only hint, long as many of them are, at the nature of the sons. they illustrate, they do give a broad view of advances in Romantic piano writing, including 14 facs. of autographs or first eds. (most of them not hitherto pub.).

For the historically-minded researcher there is the excitement of a century that saw precipitous advances in government, transportation, communications, industry, capital-labor relations, and science. And for the would-be humanitarian there is the idealism of noble, staunch, warm friendships, exemplified above all by the triangular interrelationships of Robert and Clara Schumann and Brahms.

Only at the end of the era does the spirit of brotherly love become distorted and sidetracked into the ominous private hates and prejudices of a Pfitzner or a d'Indy, breeding the kind of poison that eventually sickens studies such as Boetticher's immense monograph on Schumann (SSB VIII). But delving into the Romantic era before that miscarriage of brotherly love is likely to evoke much the same nostalgic feelings that are evoked today by viewing reruns of the best movies from that relative, more recent age of innocence, the decade before World War II.

Part One

The Nature of the Romantic Sonata

Chapter II

Romantic Concepts of the Sonata

The Word Itself

This chapter concerns the views that the Romantics themselves held of the sonata, whether as a title, as a particular form, as an aesthetic problem, or as a historical phenomenon of varying significance. In all these views the single most important consideration is the transition, by mid-century, from a loose, casual concept of a free, even a fantasy, form (cf. SCE 28) to a tight, fixed concept of a highly specific form, specific enough to crystalize in the textbooks and even to become a criterion by which sonatas soon were evaluated.

Throughout the 19th century occasional uses of the word "sonata" still occurred in its generic sense, merely as an instrumental piece. Thus, in a collection published by Bacon in Philadelphia about 1815, "Twenty four sonatas for the piano forte," the two "sonatas" by Beethoven prove to be simply one piece each from his "Contretänze" and his "Ländlerische Tänze." [1] In 1860 Bülow was still asking—rhetorically, to be sure—"What is a sonata? Isn't any instrumental music a sonata?" [2]

A generic concept is also implied when "sonata" is equated with other instrumental titles. Thus, it is equated with symphony by Mendelssohn, T. Kullak, and Rheinberger;[3] with suite by Speidel (SSB X), Penfield (SSB XIX), Daneau (SSB XIII), and Kiel;[4] with the passacaglia by Moulaert (SSB XIII); with piano quintet by Brahms (SSB IX), viola concerto by Paganini (SSB XVI), and string quartet by Rode (Op. 24),[5] Paganini, and Rossini (SSB XVI); and with fantasy by many an admirer of the two sonatas "quasi una fantasia," Op. 27/1

1. Cf. LC MUSIC 206–7.
2. BÜLOW BRIEFE IV 368–69.
3. As in Rheinberger's *Symphonische Sonate*, Op. 47 (cf. MW II [1871] 389–91 and 406–7 for a discussion of this equation by A. Maczewski); also, MGG IX 62 (E. Werner) on Mendelssohn and NZM XXIV (1846) 149–50 on Kullak.
4. Cf. Egert/FRÜHROMANTIKER 157. Cf., also, MGG VI 221.
5. Cf. Bachmann/VIOLINISTES 260.

and 2, and later precedents set by Beethoven, including Schubert, Schumann, Mendelssohn, and Liszt (ssb VII, VIII, and X).[6]

Yet in far more instances there were deliberate efforts to keep "sonata" and related terms delimited and separate. Thus, "sonata" was distinguished variously, and more or less precisely, from "symphony" and "fantasy," by Schumann;[7] from (organ) "voluntary," by both Mendelssohn and his publisher;[8] from "concerto," by Moscheles, Schumann, and Liszt;[9] and from both "suite" and "programme music," by A. Spanuth.[10] Furthermore, not a few writers had sufficiently fixed concepts of what a sonata should be to rule out works called by that name when they did not conform. Thus, as late as 1906 a French audience was disturbed by Liszt's use of the title for a work in one movement,[11] and in 1929 the dissertationist Paul Egert still declared that L. Berger's Op. 18 "is no sonata" because only one and the same motive recurs throughout all three movements.[12]

"Sonatina" as the diminutive of "sonata" appears far more often in the Romantic than in the preceding eras—in fact, about as often as "sonata," though largely over short, light pedagogic sonatas in Clementi's style. Richard Strauss used the term more in the generic sense when he applied it to his two late wind ensembles (ssb XI). There are also variants or expansions of the term, like "sonatilles" (as by Raff, ssb X) or "sonatina concertante" (as by Julius Weismann, for Vc & P; ssb XI). "Grande" appears as a qualifier in sonata titles too often and variously to have any one connotation. A reviewer in 1812 (J. F. Rochlitz?) thought it should apply to a "dreadfully long" work.[13] And perhaps it was also the same reviewer who, on the basis of content as well as length, wondered both at the failure to add "grande" to the title of a large-scale sonata by Czerny and at the error of adding it to one small-scale sonata each by Kuhlau and G. Schuberth.[14] A Berlin reviewer congratulated Mendelssohn for not calling his Op. 4 "Grande Sonate" or even "Grande Sonate pathétique et mélancolique" in line with the tendency to make "everything big, big. . . ."[15] By

6. Among several references to this last equation, cf. AMZ XXVIII (1826) 137–40, Shedlock/SONATA 195, GROVE IX 217 (P. Spitta).

7. Schumann/SCHRIFTEN I 329 and 70 (partially contradicting Vol. I, p. 395). Cf. SCE 32–34.

8. Cf. Edwards/MENDELSSOHN 2, 15–16; ZIMG III (1901–2) 337–38 (C. Maclean).

9. Cf. NZM VI (1837) 65; Storck/SCHUMANN 67; Wasielewski/SCHUMANN 279–80.

10. MW VIII (1877) 77–78 and 93–94.

11. MDC IV (1906) xxvi.

12. Cf. L. Berger in ssb VIII; also, SCE 117 on Beethoven.

13. AMZ XIV (1812) 393.

14. AMZ XXIV (1822) 382, XXVIII (1826) 708, XXIX (1827) 99.

15. Jacob/MENDELSSOHN 48–50.

1830 one A. Devaux's term "Grand Sonata" was regarded as a "nearly obsolete title [that] . . . conjures up in our memory all those past glories [Beethoven, Mozart, Clementi, and Steibelt] that triumphant fashion has so long covered with dust . . . [Devaux] has some formi dable skips; introduced, perhaps, by the author to save himself from the danger of having a perriwig placed on his head by the ultra-moderns." [16] But in 1861 Henri Herz's addition of "di bravura" to the same title was regarded as new to the "Classic tradition." [17] "Sonate brillante" had been used at least a few times (as in 1834 by Loewe; ssb VIII). Numerous other, more expressive qualifiers also occur in the Romantic sonata titles, such as "dramatique," [18] "sentimentale" (A. M. Nava; ssb XVI); "agréable," "pastorale," or "caractéristique." [19]

Explanations by Theorists

Apparently it was by or before 1837 that the industrious Carl Czerny (ssb VII) made an interesting claim by implication. In the preface to his Op. 600 he implied that he was the first to describe the sonata in any basic detail, although not until 1848 did this three-volume treatise on composition appear in print (in an English trans. of the original German, which did not appear for another year):[20]

16. HARMONICON VIII/1 (1830) 33–34.
17. DMZ II (1861) 229; but cf. HOFMEISTER 1828 (Whistling) 602.
18. MGG VIII 464 (J. Bonfils).
19. The last 3 are among a variety of titles to be found in HOFMEISTER 1828 (Whistling) 577–606.
20. Czerny/COMPOSITION I iii; cf. Newman/THEORISTS (with errors) and Newman/CZERNY (but add that, thanks to word from Mr. Neil Ratliff of the New York Public Library, the issues of the Hofmeister *Monatsbericht* in question may be found in that institution and at the University of Illinois). Warm thanks are owing to Dr. Hedwig Mitringer at the Gesellschaft der Musikfreunde in Vienna and Dr. Imogen Fellinger at the Zentralstelle für Musikbibliographie des 19. Jahrhunderts in Köln for help in dating the rare German ed. (of which Vol. I, at least, is in Vienna); also, to Mrs. Birgitte Moyer of Menlo Park, Calif., for correspondence regarding Czerny's claim and Reicha's possible priority. Mrs. Moyer is currently completing a Ph.D. diss., "Concepts of Musical Form in the 19th Century, With Special Reference to A. B. Marx and Sonata Form" (Stanford University).
While the present volume was going to press a new, thorough, and enlightening diss. on the theoretical recognition of "son. form" *ca.* 1700–1850, Ritzel/SONATEN-FORM (1968), was received (thanks to the kindness of Dr. Lothar Hoffmann-Erbrecht in Frankfurt/M). It has been possible here to incorporate references to the most essential points pertinent to the following discussion.
And further contributions keep coming! Still more recently, Churgin/SONATA has found another important link in a description of "son. form" (not so called) by Francesco Galeazzi in 1796 that anticipates Reicha's description of 1826 (*infra*); also in JAMS XXI/2 (summer 1968), Pierro Weiss of Columbia University is able to show (pp. 233–34) that as early as 1814 Reicha had anticipated his own description.

By the phrase *doctrine of composition,* has hitherto been understood only the instruction in thorough bass and counterpoint. These sciences are indisputably as essential to the composer, as orthography and grammar to him who desires to become a poet and author. But, even with the best-grounded knowledge of harmony and pure composition, the pupil is still ignorant of the *forms* which the different pieces must assume, and which, in music in general, and in that for single instruments in particular, are practicable and usual; and in no treatise on thorough bass which has yet appeared, has the manner of constructing a sonata, a variation, a quartett, a symphony, or even a waltz, been fundamentally described.

Then, Czerny went on to "describe" in detail, in the forty-nine pages of his sixth chapter,[21] what "must" go into each of the four movements (allegro, adagio or andante, scherzo or minuet, and finale or [i.e., especially] rondo). In connection with the first movement (and with a proscription against returning to the "original key" in the development section), he cautioned that "we must always proceed in a settled form. For, if this order were evaded or arbitrarily changed, the composition would no longer be a regular Sonata" (p. 35). He still viewed the first movement, at least nominally, as being in "two parts." Its first part (not called "exposition" by the translator) consists of the "principal subject," its extension and a modulation to "the nearest related key," a "middle subject" and its extension in the related key, and a "final melody" that closes in that key at the repeat sign. Its second part divides into two sections, a modulatory "development" (the translator's word) of any of those ideas or a new one, ending back in the original key; and a recapitulation (not so called by the translator) that restates the first part except for abridgments and adjustments needed to remain in the original key. In the further discussions of the first and succeeding movements Czerny showed how Mozart might have expanded one of his "sonata forms" (not the translator's term; Son. in D for P-duet, K. 123a/i) and he quoted other examples from successful sonatas for P solo by Haydn, Clementi, Mozart, Beethoven (as well as Beethoven's Rondo in C, Op. 51/1), and Dussek.

In terms of detail and clarity, Czerny seems to have been justified in claiming by implication that when he wrote Op. 600, sonata form was for the first time being "fundamentally described."[22] The point is

---

21. Czerny/COMPOSITION I 33–81.

22. But Ritzel/SONATENFORM 213–23, 228, 233, 272–73, and 274 credits significant priority to 2 articles totalling nearly 30 pp., by Heinrich Birnbach, in the 1827–28 vols. of the Berlin *Allgemeine musikalische Zeitung*. Ritzel points to Birnbach's ternary concept and his derivation of the principles from the actual literature rather than the a priori postulation of a theory, with exx. to fit, by the subsequent "pragmatists" (p. 214), Czerny, Marx, *et al.* Birnbach did not use the term "sonata form." On the inadequacy of the pragmatic approach as a source of musicological information, cf. W. F. Korte in AfMW XXI (1964) 9–10.

well worth emphasizing because to the extent that his textbook description was a fair abstraction of the still fluid Classic forms (SCE 115–17), it provided an astonishing illustration of the degree to which theory can trail practice.[23] Not until as much as sixty years after some of the masterworks of Haydn, Mozart, Beethoven, and Clementi had appeared, and not even until well after the entire sonatas of Dussek and Weber and the first of Schumann and Chopin had been composed did anyone write an explicit description of what happens in a sonata.

However, in 1845, three years before Czerny's Op. 600 finally was published, a still more explicit description appeared, nearly three times as detailed. It is a 137-page section in the first edition of the third of the four highly influential, often reprinted volumes in *Die Lehre von der musikalischen Komposition* by Adolph Bernhard Marx.[24] Marx devoted much attention to details of phrase-and-period syntax, he preferred a ternary to a binary concept of "sonata form," and he included among the other movements the overlapping types like the "sonata rondo" and the "fugal sonata." In the preface to this volume (p. v), he said that its publication was only made possible by improvements in the methods and quality of teaching over the previous few years. Actually, Marx's second volume, which had already appeared in 1838 and presumably was written about the same time as Czerny's discussion, incorporated a preliminary statement that summarizes the same basic points in five pages and even seems to assume a general knowledge of the information on the reader's part.[25] Included, at least in brief, are the distinctions between "sonata form" and the sonata cycle in several movements, "sonata form" and the rondo principle, "sonata form" as a two- and as a three-part concept, the tonal course of major and of minor "sonata forms," and variants in the thematic design of "sonata form."

The theorists' treatment of the sonata has always given the lion's share of attention to the first fast movement, sometimes to the almost total neglect of the other movements. As discussed in our previous volume (SCE 26–35), few theorists had shown more than a hazy recognition of "sonata form" during the Classic Era and up to the late 1830's. H. C. Koch was seen to come closest to such recognition in his explanation of the first movement of a symphony, with, however, an implication that the sonata was less classifiable and somewhat different (more intimate) in style (SCE 32–34). Between Koch and the clear,

23. D. F. Tovey comments aptly on this discrepancy in BRITANNICA XVI 11–12.
24. Marx/LEHRE III 194–330. Cf. MGG VIII 1734–38 (K. Hahn); Ritzel/SONATEN-FORM 228–36.
25. Marx/LEHRE II 497–501.

precise explanations of Czerny and Marx, a significant missing link can be found in an eight-page discussion of "fully-developed binary design" in the final volume, published in Paris in 1826,[26] of Anton Reicha's notable *Traité de haute composition musicale*. Although this discussion does not mention the word "sonata" and does not quite recognize the ternary implications of the design, it does cover the essentials (including the terms "exposition" and "development"), as the chart reproduced in Ex. 1 illustrates. It should be added that Czerny had known this chart well, since it was he who translated Reicha's work, along with two earlier treatises by Reicha, for the bilingual edition published in Vienna in 1832 (not 1834).[27]

Descriptions in Other Writings

In general, other 19th-century writers on music, even the lexicographers, were slower than these enterprising theorists to arrive at explicit statements about design in the sonata. Among representative samples of what they did have to say,[28] the description of the symphony and sonata by Friedrich Schneider (SSB VIII) in the earliest editions, 1820 and 1827, of his treatise on harmony and composition failed to disclose any structural principles.[29] F.-H.-J. Blaze wrote even less on these two genres in his dictionary of 1821, his remarks being merely paraphrased in Peter Lichtenthal's dictionary of 1826.[30] Fétis in 1830 simply likened the sonata, for one, two, or three instruments, to chamber music for more instruments, as being "a sort of symphony" in miniature, though, he said in effect, it rarely included the minuet (or scherzo) that the symphony's perfecters, from Vanhal to Beethoven, had added to the cycle of a binary quick movement ("en deux parties"), a slower movement, and a rondo.[31] Gustav Schilling, editor of the valuable, six-volume *Universal-Lexicon*, disregarded structural principles, concentrating only on the scoring and the deleterious effect of specific programmes (cf. *infra*), in his article of 1838 on the sonata.[32] The brothers Escudier dealt mainly with the cycle, values,

26. Not 1824 for Vol. II (as in MGG XI 148 and Ritzel/SONATENFORM 280); cf. GROVE VII 107 and Cat. NYPL XXV 412.
27. Reicha & Czerny/COMPOSITION, from which our Ex. 1 comes. Although Czerny did add some comments of his own, Mrs. Birgitte Moyer (*supra*) confirms that the discussion and chart in question are unaltered from the original French ed. (which is at the Library of Congress). Cf., also, Ritzel/SONATENFORM 249–57, 271–72.
28. Cf. Newman/THEORISTS for further citations; also, SCE 116 for a typical, concise summary by a theorist after Marx (Ernst Pauer, 1878).
29. Schneider/ELEMENTS 120–21.
30. CASTIL-BLAZE (1825 ed.) 287, 271–72; LICHTENTHAL 197–98, 208–9.
31. Fétis/MUSIQUE 224–30.
32. Schilling/LEXICON VI 418–20.

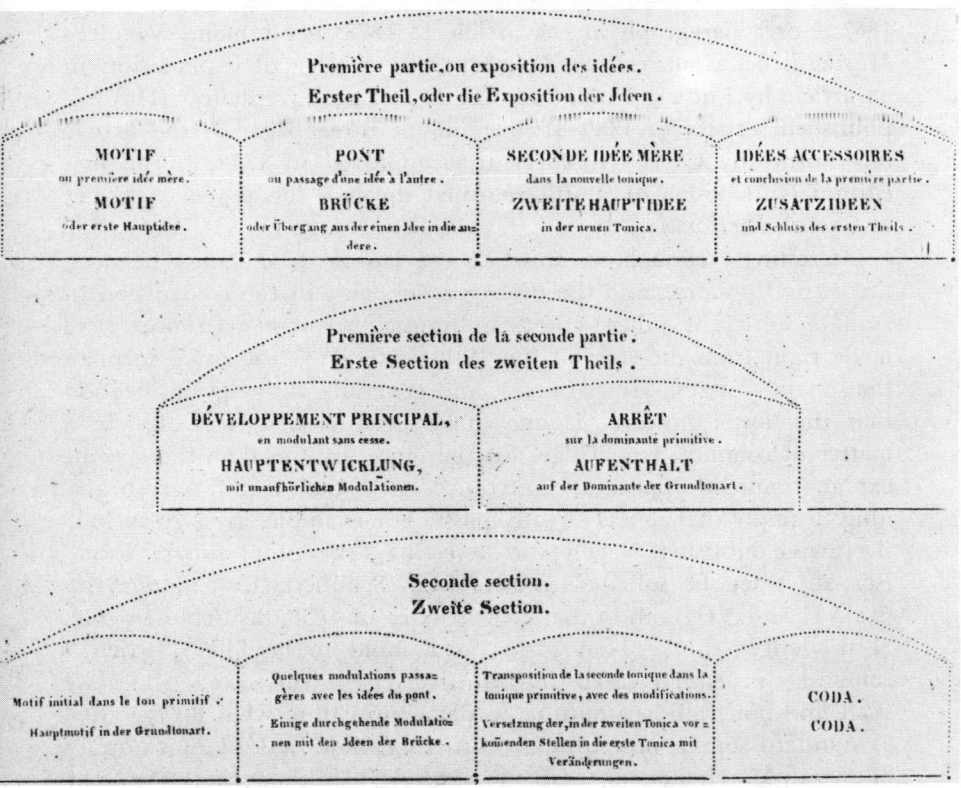

Ex. 1. "La grande coupe binaire," facs. of Anton Reicha's
chart in Reicha & Czerny/COMPOSITION IV 1165.

performance, and composers of the sonata, but not its forms, in their
music dictionary of 1844.[33] Except for names of more recent composers, F. S. Gassner did not go beyond the generalities of most 18th-
century definitions of "sonata" in his 1849 abridgment of Schilling/
LEXICON.[34] In fact, not until 1865 do we find a clear, full dictionary
summary of the principles detailed by Czerny and Marx, and then
it occurs in Arrey von Dommer's complete revision of Koch's *Musikalisches Lexikon* of 1802.[35] Even after 1865 such detailed explanations remained infrequent. Mainly, there appeared relatively brief
explanations like a pamphlet, "On the Structure of a Sonata," by
G. A. Macfarren (SSB XIV), which was published in London about

33. ESCUDIER II 87–88.
34. GASSNER 790.
35. DOMMER & KOCH 779–89 (plus pp. 789–91 on "die ältere Sonate").

1867;[36] or a paragraph in the article of 1878 in Hermann Mendel's *Musikalisches Conversations-Lexikon*;[37] or a page of explanation in an article by Ludwig Nohl, "The Father of the Symphony" (Haydn), published serially in 1880–81;[38] or about three pages in the article on "Form" by C. H. H. Parry that appeared in 1879 in the first edition (with much of it still retained through the present 5th ed.) of *Grove's Dictionary*.[39]

Interestingly enough, in spite of the lag we have noted between theory and practice, and the even greater delay in the recognition of "sonata form" by other writers on music, frequent references were made right from the start of the 19th century to "the usual form of the sonata" (or some such words), and generally with the implication that this form, however it may have been viewed, was already a matter of common knowledge. Furthermore, by the time the specific explanations did appear, the references to "sonata form" were beginning to imply that it was already passé. For example, as early as 1803 the Swiss publisher Nägeli was rejecting "the usual sonata form" (SCE 26) when he solicited sonatas from Schubert, Liste, Hoffmann (SSB VII and VIII), and others. In a letter of 1838, Schumann wrote, "I no longer think about form [as a mold to be filled?] when I compose; [instead] I create it [intuitively?]." [40] Yet several times we shall find him calling attention to departures from what he regarded as standard sonata procedures, as in his review in 1841 of Chopin's "Funeral March Sonata," Op. 35 (SSB XII). Although in 1837 the first historian of the sonata, C. F. Becker, did not refer to any standard form,[41] six years later the second such historian did, even to summarizing the three divisions of "sonata form" in one sentence.[42] In 1849 the organ sonata was described as being less well defined (in its form) than the piano sonata.[43]

By 1862 Selmar Bagge was assuring his readers that although exact "sonata form" was not observed in Schubert's Op. 78/i, it did not have to be.[44] In 1868 a reviewer of the posthumous editions of Mendelssohn's Opp. 105 and 106 described as "obsolete" the requirement to repeat the "second part" of a "sonata form," at the same time adher-

---

36. Cf. the review of it in MT XV (1871) 282.
37. Mendel/LEXIKON IX 299–306 (chiefly p. 303).
38. Nohl/SYMPHONY, especially pp. 597–98.
39. GROVE 1st ed., I 548–49 and 550–51; references to this explanation suffice in Parry's article on the "Sonata," which first appeared in 1883 in Vol. III, pp. 554–84.
40. Gertler/SCHUMANN 111 fn.
41. Becker/KLAVIERSONATE. Cf. *infra*.
42. Faisst/CLAVIERSONATE 22 and 55.
43. NZM XXX (1849) 186.
44. Bagge/SCHUBERT 34.

ing to tradition by singling out the development as "that crucial test of a composer's power." [45] In 1875, a reviewer of one Gustav Wolff's "Four Sonatinas" for P solo objected to the lack of any attribute but the routine "classical mould." [46] And in 1882 a reviewer expressed disappointment in new sonatas by W. Berger (ssb XI), H. Franke (ssb XVII), F. Hummel (ssb X), and P. Rüfer (ssb XII), because they did not advance beyond traditional forms. As he put it, in scarcely one out of a hundred such works, sight unseen, would he err by starting his review, "With regard to the form, the gentlemen X, Y, and Z have in their newest works kept faithfully to the norms established by our predecessors and have strictly avoided any arbitrary deviation from the holy rules." [47]

Moreover, the same reviewer found that all but one of the composers (F. Hummel) failed to achieve what became almost a *sine qua non* of the late-Romantic Era—that is, cyclical unity, chiefly through thematic interrelationships of the movements. Elisabeth von Herzogenberg had such interrelationships in mind within a single movement when she wrote to Brahms of her delight in discovering how the coda of his Op. 108/i confirms the organism of the "sonata form." [48] We shall see in later chapters how many late-Romantics emphasized this aspect of the sonata cycle and "sonata form," among them d'Indy (ssb XIII) and MacDowell (ssb XIX), who not only exploited but wrote about it.

Meanwhile, the resistance to, and concern with, textbook "sonata form" as a musical law or standard continued to rise. In a letter of 1888 to Bülow, Richard Strauss explained his growing interest in programme music by declaring,

From the F minor symphony [1884] onwards I have found myself in a gradually ever increasing contradiction between the musical-poetic content that I want to convey a[nd] the ternary sonata form that has come down to us from the classical composers. In the case of Beethoven the musical-poetic content was for the most part completely covered by this very '*Sonata form*,' which he raised to its highest point, wholly expressing in it what he felt and wanted to say. Yet already there are to be found works of his (the last movement of the A flat major sonata, Adagio of the A minor quartet, etc.), where for a new content he had to devise a new form. Now, what was for Beethoven a 'form' absolutely in congruity with the highest, most glorious content, is now, after 60 years, used as a formula inseparable from our instrumental music (which I strongly dispute), simply to accommodate and enclose a 'pure musical' (in the strictest and narrowest meaning of the word) content, or

45. MT XIII (1868) 382 and 387. Cf. *infra*, on the question of originality.
46. MT XVII (1875) 275.
47. MW XIII (1882) 555–56.
48. BRAHMS BRIEFWECHSEL II 211.

worse, to stuff and expand a content with which it does not correspond. . . .
Of course, purely formalistic, Hanslickian music-making will no longer be
possible, and we cannot have any more random patterns, that mean nothing
either to the composer or the listener, and no symphonies (Brahms excepted,
of course) that always give me the impression of being giant's clothes, made
to fit a Hercules, in which a thin tailor is trying to comport himself
elegantly.[49]

But whereas Strauss sought to escape the rigidity of the form itself,
others sought to escape the rigidity of form classifications. Bernard
Shaw as music critic wrote in 1891 regarding a new biography of
Chopin,

I am made somewhat restive by such passages as:
"In the Concerto, Chopin's subordination to, and inability to cope with,
form was as conspicuous as was his superiority and independence of it in his
smaller works."
This implies that form means sonata form and nothing else, an unwarranted piece of pedantry, which one remembers as common enough in the
most incompetent and old-fashioned criticisms of Chopin's ballades, Liszt's
symphonic poems, and Wagner's work generally, but which is now totally
out of countenance.[50]

C. H. H. Parry argued about 1900 that the "sonata form" that had
once served an aristocratic, conventional, complexly organized society
so well was by now too formal and inflexible to be adapted to the
newer poetic and spiritual content.

Others preferred to delve deeper into the meaning of "sonata
form"—for instance, Otto Klauwell in 1897 (2 years before his short
son. history appeared; cf. *infra*). Klauwell explained its "higher" significance, in the absence of a poetic text or any practical function,
as a dramatic, dualistic conflict followed by its resolution.[51] Then
there was the Russian theorist and composer S. I. Taneyev, who excelled in his imaginative, resourceful teaching of the principles of
"sonata form," as reported by a former student during 1905–6.[52] And
there was August Halm, who in 1913 published his study, "On Two
Cultures of Music." In this study Halm saw the contrast of monistic
and dualistic (sonata) principles as the essential distinction between
Baroque and Classic music.[53]

49. As trans. in BÜLOW-STRAUSS 82–83. Cf., also, Ernest Newman's hope in 1908
that someone would get rid of "this system of Chinese compression" by writing a
monograph "On Sonata Form, Its Cause and Cure," as quoted in Finck/GRIEG 231;
and further comments in H. T. Finck's previous book on Grieg (New York: John
Lane, 1906), pp. 102–3.
50. Shaw/LONDON II 209; cf., also, II 305, 306, 307.
51. Klauwell/ÄSTHETISCHE.
52. TEMPO XXXIX (1956) 14–15 (T. de Hartmann).
53. Halm/KULTUREN, especially pp. 7–143.

Pessimistic and Optimistic Views

Throughout the Romantic Era there was a steady stream of pessimistic opinions to the effect that the sonata had already or would soon come to its end, recalling similar statements encountered in both the Baroque and Classic Eras (cf. SBE 26, 31; SCE 37, 47). That there actually was something of a slump in sonata production and a turn to trivial music, especially in the 1830's (cf. SSB I), is borne out by statistics in Chapter IV. There also was a steady stream of optimistic opinions about the sonata's status and prognosis. But, true to form, the pessimists outnumbered the optimists. A sampling of these conflicting opinions, unavoidably repetitious at times, follows in one separate chronology each for the pessimists and the optimists.

To start with some negative opinions on the sonata's status, we find W. J. Tomaschek (SSB XVII) recalling in his autobiography of 1846 how even before 1810 "a strange disinterest in the sonata for piano and the symphony for orchestra had become evident. Innumerable [sets of] variations were expected to do in place of the pianist's sonatas, and overtures in place of the orchestra's symphonies." [54] The American church composer Thomas Hastings wrote briefly of the symphony and somewhat disparagingly of the extravagance and display in etudes, concertos, and variations, disregarding the sonata entirely, in his book of 1822 on musical taste.[55] With reference to three piano sonatas by Charles Ambrose (SSB XIV), an English reviewer noted in 1825 that the sonata had become unfamiliar and its style outmoded.[56] In Paris by 1830 Fétis asserted,

In the last several years the sonata has fallen into discredit. A certain futility of taste, which has contaminated music, has replaced the serious forms of this sort with kinds of lighter works that are called fantasias, *airs variés,* capriccios, etc.[57]

In 1832 a London review of Pio Cianchettini's Op. 26 began, shrewdly enough,

A *sonata* once more!—The newest fashions after all are but old ones forgotten and revived. . . . But has the sonata been defunct long enough to have slipped clean out of memory?—Hardly; and Mr. Cianchettini may have performed the operation of resuscitation rather too soon. At all events, we are quite sure that his sonata is too good, and, we must add, too difficult, to become popular just now, or to rekindle a passion for the old title.[58]

54. Trans. from the German in Kahl/LYRISCHE 61.
55. Hastings/TASTE 148–53.
56. HARMONICON III/1 (1825) 139.
57. Fétis/MUSIQUE 230.
58. HARMONICON X/1 (1832) 256.

In Germany in 1833, the lexicographer Carl Gollnick said again that sonatas had given way to potpourris and the like,[59] and in 1838 the conservative lexicographer Gustav Schilling said the sonata had become a "mere jangle." [60] Also in 1838, a reviewer (of C. Decker's Op. 10, ssb VIII) wished that the time for the sonata were more appropriate so that the considerable values it did have would not be neglected.[61] A year later, in the most extended discussion of the problem encountered here,[62] G. W. Fink attributed this neglect not to the younger composers, as was being charged by the professional pianists, but to the current taste of the public and the dilettante pianists, which was discouraging publishers from printing more than a few out of a substantial number of sonatas actually being created. It is true, he added, that the younger composer was less interested in following the past masters and was writing mainly patchwork music. But he should not be judged on his Op. 1 alone and the sonata should not be viewed as dead, merely asleep.

Schumann, though barely through composing his own three important piano sonatas, wrote similarly, in 1839 and 1841, about the decline of the sonata:

Strange [it is] that suddenly there are mostly unknowns who are writing sonatas; [and] further, that it is precisely the older composers still living amongst us—those who grew up in the sonata's heyday and from whom admittedly only Cramer and Moscheles could be named as most outstanding— who [now] cultivate the genre least. It is easy to guess what moves the former, mostly young[er] artists [i.e., the unknowns]. There is no worthier form by which they might introduce and ingratiate themselves [better] in the eyes of the finer critics. But in consequence most sonatas of this sort can be considered only as a kind of testing grounds, as studies in form. They are scarcely born out of a strong inner compulsion. . . . Occasional lovely manifestations of this sort are sure to appear here and there, and [some] already have done so. But otherwise it seems the form has run its course, and this [drop-off] is certainly in the order of things, and [what is more] we should not have to repeat the same [form] year after year and at the same time deliberate over the new. So one writes sonatas or fantasias (what matters the name!); let one not forget music and the rest will succeed through our good genius. . . .

[The sonata is] but smiled at with pity in France and scarcely more than tolerated even in Germany. . . .[63]

In 1843 a German reviewer argued that the orchestral symphony was

59. Gollnick/TERMINOLOGIE 136.
60. Schilling/LEXICON VI 418.
61. AMZ XL (1838) 160.
62. AMZ XLI (1839) 181–84.
63. Trans. from Schumann/SCHRIFTEN I 394–95, 452.

likely to retain its popularity indefinitely and unchallenged.[64] But he still felt that, with only a few exceptions, the sonata, like the fugue, was giving way to those variations, rondos, capriccios, etudes, and other types that the dilettantes, afraid of the sonata's old-fashioned name and formalism, found more suitable to the (now) favorite instrument, the pianoforte, and to helping their own popularity. It was in 1843, too, that the Leipzig publisher C. A. Klemm preferred to issue Schubert's Sonata in E, D. 459, as *Fünf Klavierstücke*, apparently because the title "sonata" had become old-fashioned.[65] Bearing out one of Schumann's remarks (*supra*), a Parisian review of 1845 began by saying the sonata had been unpopular in France for thirty years.[66] In 1852 Bülow could find nothing of value in the sonata since Beethoven except Hummel's Op. 81 in f$\sharp$ (ssb VIII) and the contributions of Schumann and Chopin.[67] In 1855 the French lexicographer Charles Soullier persisted in regarding the sonata as having "died with the 18th century that produced it so abundantly." [68] And when Rubinstein came to London in 1856, Edward Bache reported that "the publishers won't bite" on his sonatas and that in another year or so it would be "a good time [instead] for simple musical music again." [69]

Indeed, in spite of the succession of masterworks from Schubert to Reger, a decline in the sonata continued to be remarked and lamented right through the Romantic Era, and still longer. Thus, in 1871 a reviewer saw this decline in the scholasticism of the current sonata, but now he advanced its former heyday, like the symphony's, to include Schumann among its onetime masters. By 1895 Shedlock advanced the heyday another generation to include Brahms among its masters. But near the end of his pioneer sonata history he still wondered whether time would include Liszt. "Is Liszt's sonata [in b] a Phoenix rising from its ashes? Shall we be able to say 'La sonata est morte! Vive la sonate!' Time will tell. Hitherto Liszt's work has not borne fruit." [70] In 1901 in Paris the music critic Camille Bellaigue proclaimed the end of the sonata, that "admirable, vanished species." [71] In America one early writer on MacDowell said "sonata

64. AMZ XLV (1843) 453.

65. Cf. Brown/SCHUBERT 57. Schubert's *Grand Duo* in C, D. 812, was also originally called "Sonata" (ssb VII).

66. RGM, March 3, 1845, p. 68.

67. BÜLOW BRIEFE III 50; originally in NZM XXXVI (1852) 234.

68. Quoted in Shedlock/SONATA 220 from Soullier/DICTIONNAIRE.

69. Bache/BACHE 77.

70. Shedlock/SONATA 220. The answer in 1903 in Schüz/SONATE was that Liszt's Son. in b does promise to be "the sonata of the future."

71. *Guide musical* (Brussels) XLVII (1901) 99–101.

form" in particular was "consigned to hopeless antiquity" and another to "perdition." [72] And in 1920 the Swiss historian Karl Nef concluded—quite unjustly, it is felt here—that the 19th century "was unable to maintain itself on the lofty plane of the sonata." [73]

Among the fewer, more optimistic views of the 19th-century sonata's trends, one might cite, from 1840, a reviewer who indicated full respect for the Classic masterworks but urged more respect for the newer, more brilliant, fuller-textured sonata styles, too.[74] Or one might cite, from 1845, another reviewer (F. Brendel?), who acknowledged a low ebb of interest, but now found sonatas stirring everywhere again, most of them better than expected. "Flügel, Chopin, Winterle, Evers, even Thalberg and Kalkbrenner have composed and published them, . . . some at their own expense and others, who had better luck or better known names, at other people's expense." [75] In the following year the same reviewer rejoiced that the quality and public interest were keeping pace with the quantity in the revival.[76] The entertaining English writer H. F. Chorley was able to acknowledge in 1860 that the thirty-year period that "has seen the return (after a season of eclipse) to the noble but grave [?] sonatas of Clementi and Dussek has also seen the establishment of the wayward, incomplete, fantastic, yet most fascinating Chopin, on a pedestal of his own." [77] The periodicals of the 1860's and 1870's do reflect a growing interest in sonatas and chamber music[78] as against the variations and potpourris of the previous generation that Schumann had opposed in his idealistic, imaginary "League of David" (SSB VIII) but that other writers and countries had accepted with much less question.[79] A German writer in 1873, exactly contradicting contemporary views by the pessimists (*supra*), attributed the sonata's improved status over the past thirty years to greater interest on the part of amateurs in a territory previously ruled by the aristocracy and the professionals, to increased popularity and sales of pianos, and to more frequent publications of sonatas.[80]

72. As quoted in Eagle/MACDOWELL 17.
73. Nef/HISTORY 301. Steger/CZERNY 74–77 continued in 1924 to reflect the idea that Schubert was too lyrical, Schumann too impassioned, and Chopin too confined to small forms to write fully valid (?) sons.
74. AMZ XLII (1840) 824–25.
75. NZM XXIII (1845) 177.
76. NZM XXIV (1846) 146.
77. Chorley/RECOLLECTIONS 398.
78. Cf. DMZ I–III (1860–62) *passim* (e.g., II [1861] 76 on music in Paris).
79. E.g., cf. RGM and HARMONICON, both *passim*, in the 1830's.
80. NZM LXIX/2 (1873) 493–94.

Standards and Tastes

Besides the conflicting opinions just quoted on falls and rises in the sonata's status, there were certain views or attitudes that remained more constant throughout the Romantic Era. One view was that of the sonata as an, if not *the*, ideal of both technical and musical achievement to which a composer might aspire—usually an ideal that related to Beethoven's image and one that could not be approached other than with the highest standards and greatest sincerity. Of course, especially during the sonata's slump in the second quarter of the 19th century, it is not hard to understand that almost any sonata would be likely to command high respect alongside the kinds of pieces on which the publishers were thriving. In any music catalogue or periodical of the time the sonatas appear only infrequently among long lists of pieces with titles such as those of the following piano solos: *Grand Military Divertimento,* by F. Ries (ssb VII); *A Favourite Air, from the Ballet of Nina, with Variations by Mayseder,* arranged by F. Ries; *"Cherry Ripe," composed by E. Horn, and arranged as a Rondo . . . ,* by T. Valentine; *La Salle d'Apollon, a collection of German Waltzes.*[81]

As a sample of respect for the sonata in that same early phase of the Romantic Era, a paragraph may be quoted from a letter of 1829 in which Karl Loewe (ssb VIII) offered four sonatas to the publisher T. Trautwein:

Don't be misled by the usual cries of unintelligent players and little informed publishers who think the sonata as such doesn't make a hit or do well; and that it would need a special title or the issuing of single movements from sonatas in order to provide a market for them, which (as one certainly sees) go as fast as they come—no; on the contrary, the sonata is for all times, and, especially for a productive composer, the most basic form, scarcely to be improved upon, [and] by [means of] which he often has the opportunity to show what he can do. And just so will the sonata always remain at the summit for unspoiled players (the Beethoven and Weber [sonatas] still demonstrate this [truth] every day). . . .[82]

In spite (or because?) of his pessimisms (*supra*), Schumann referred to the sonata as "this noble musical form" and cited a Sonata for P-duet by one G. Adler as worth mentioning only because it was cast in that "valued, distinguished form." [83] Two reviews, in 1844

81. These particular titles come from HARMONICON IV/1 (1826) 74–78; cf., also, the pieces pub. in Vol. IV/2.
82. Trans. from La Mara/MUSIKERBRIEFE II 131.
83. Schumann/SCHRIFTEN II 319, 320.

and 1855, of sonatas by C. Gurlitt (Opp. 3 and 16; ssв X) begin with these related statements:

Under the pressing flood of worthless trivialities, rhapsodic ideas, pleasant nothings, [and] rehashing of foreign ideas, it is truly pleasant to find now and then the higher aspiration to, and the concentrated strength for, more important accomplishments; [and] even more pleasant to find a young aspiring artist in the beginning of his career who scorns a cheap attempt [to win] audience approval and [who] endeavors [instead] to win entrance to the temple of honor by greater and more art-worthy creations [i.e., sonatas]. . . .

If a composer puts himself to the test with one of the greatest and most important art forms, which the sonata is, the highest demands will be made of him, because not only are an honorable endeavor [and] an artistic conviction required, but after such great examples [as those of the Classic masters] there must be, besides strong talent, a perfect mastery of form and, generally speaking, the technical wherewithal—in short, a superior grade of artistic maturity.[84]

Musical standards would be raised, said a reviewer in 1872, if more sonatas were still being written.[85] One M. E. Doorley was advised in 1874 to write smaller pieces rather than his Sonata in G, for P solo, under review, for the composing of sonatas presupposed "high[er] standards" of art and craft.[86] And in a typical discussion of the same question, a reviewer of a Sonata in D by J. Edwards (ssв XIV) concluded that the "higher standard of art" demanded by the sonata made it beyond the grasp of a "new" composer.[87] Two acrid reviews, in 1875 and 1879, rejected the title "sonata" for works by L. Tarnowski and A. W. Dreszer (both ssв XVII) because of low standards as well as excessive freedoms.[88]

The two reviews just mentioned bring up a special aspect of the Romantic sonata's association with high ideals, which is the constant quest for originality, almost as though originality were an aesthetic fact in itself. We saw this quest develop in the Classic Era (e.g., sce 41–42, 383–84). It was already present in the early 19th century when, for example, a reviewer wrote that a sonata cannot be a mere routine; there must be some caprice, exploration, and originality, if not excessive.[89] It reappeared endlessly in what we shall find to be the most frequent and pat expression in neutral or less favorable reviews of sonatas—"good craftsmanship, but lacking in originality." And it nettled a composer like Rubinstein who complained that "the minute

84. nzm XX (1844) 115 and XLIII (1855) 278.
85. mmr II (1872) 93.
86. mt XVI (1874) 585.
87. mt XVII (1875) 533.
88. mw VI (1875) 513 and X (1879) 366.
89. amz XIV (1812) 392.

a musician leans in his style upon Schumann, Chopin, Mendelssohn, Wagner, [or] Liszt, he is harshly reproached for it [the derivation] and it is cited as [evidence for] a lack of originality—which [inequity] leads the [musical] young to the quest for originality [for its own sake], and how often to the unbeautiful!" [90]

To be sure, originality did often lack in the many sonatas that conformed to a traditional or textbook routine. And it did lack (as too often in Rubinstein's own sons.) in the many sonatas with weak ideas—that is, without melodic distinction. But that phrase "originality, if not excessive" rightly suggests conservative limitations in the quest for originality. In most instances the reviewers' "originality" or "creative spark" could be translated as melodic distinction alone—an essential though hardly an all-inclusive trait. It will be recalled that Beethoven's originality became "bizarre" in the eyes and ears of his reviewers (e.g., SCE 512–13). As the 19th century wore on not many reviewers could greet genuine experimentation with the sympathy and understanding that Schumann's own "originality," rare musicianship, and exceptional literary background permitted. And even Schumann revealed puzzlement over a work like Chopin's Sonata in bb, Op. 35 (ssb XII).

An incidental facet of the quest for originality is the persistent emphasis in the later 19th century (after "sonata form" had spread through the textbooks) on the development section as the main outlet for originality. Thus, we read in a review of Benjamin Dale's notable Sonata in d, ". . . we pass on to the development, in which the composer shows us of what stuff he is made of [!]." [91] Originality in that sense simply means freedom from more specific textbook stipulations. That the development section has no monopoly on originality in masterworks of the Romantic sonata hardly needs any special defense here.

Orientations, Chiefly Historical

Certain currents and conflicts within Romantic musical thought may be touched on now as they bore on the larger orientations of the Romantic sonata—that is, on its relations to other times, other music, and other art. There was, for example, the moot question as to whether the sonata was essentially an academicism in the 19th century, because of its derivation from the masterworks of musical classicism, or was actually a valid manifestation of musical Romanti-

90. Extracted from a longer statement trans. in ssb XVIII.
91. mt LIX (1918) 165.

cism. We have seen that Reicha advanced the understanding of the sonata in 1824 (*supra*). Yet his own outlook, like that of the two other main theorists in the early century, S. Sechter and M. Hauptmann, was based on the past and was anti-Romantic.[92] The writer Rochlitz was more on the fence. In a review of two sonatas by Weber, in 1818 (ssb VIII), he wondered how to treat the new phenomenon, which had expanded so greatly in size and content that all was changed but the terminology.[93] Should he measure it against past criteria and censure it accordingly, or recognize the disparity between theory and practice and view it for what it is? Schumann became an anti-Classic when he reviewed new sonatas:

> There is one group of sonatas that are most difficult to discuss. They are those correctly written, honest, well-intended ones such as the Mozart-Haydn school produced by the hundreds [and] from which examples still appear here and there. To fault them one would have to fault the sound human mind that created them. They have natural continuity, dignified bearing. . . . However, to draw attention nowadays, or merely to please, it takes more than simply being honest. And did Beethoven then live in vain? . . . In brief, the sonata style of 1790 is not that of 1840. The demands of form and content have increased in all respects.[94]

A second not quite answerable question was that of how importantly the Romantic sonata rated in the total panorama of Romantic music. Of course, its relative importance varied from country to country, as will be seen in Chapter IV, on the spread of the Romantic sonata. And that importance can be documented at least roughly by publication statistics, which also are to be found in Chapter IV. But in any case there is good reason to argue that instrumental music in general, and piano music in particular, achieved new importance in the 19th century—in fact, became the predominant "voice" of musical Romanticism.[95] To be sure, at the start of the era, much of the orientation was still toward opera or church music. Thus, Schubert was unable to get help from his teacher Salieri in the how of constructing a sonata, for "Salieri understood singing and the older operatic form but of instrumental music (sonata, quartet, symphony) he had as little idea as he had of true church music." [96]

Furthermore, some of the 18th-century suspicion of absolute, purely instrumental music still persisted in the 19th century. One reads, for

92. Cf. Werner/MENDELSSOHN 52.
93. AMZ XX (1818) 681–83.
94. Trans. from Schumann/SCHRIFTEN II 11; among several similar statements, cf. Vols. II 307, and I 276–77, 363.
95. Cf. Einstein/ROMANTIC 32–37, 198–200.
96. Deutsch/SCHUBERT–M 112 (L. von Sonnleithner).

example, continuing references to that celebrated quip attributed to Fontenelle at least since 1755, "Sonata, what good are you to me?" [97] But these references now turn less on the broad question of the validity of absolute music than on the specific one of the validity of a sonata tied to a programme. No student of Romanticism in the arts will be surprised at the frequency with which that specific question arises in Part Two of the present volume. But he may well be surprised at how rarely the association is more than skin deep between a sonata, even the most poetic sort, and any verbal, titular, visual, or mood-type programme. Schilling ridiculed programmatic sonata titles in 1838, suggesting, for example, that "Departure from London" could just as well be "Departure from Frankfurt." [98] But he did grant that there might be a valid analogy between poetic and musical mood in such a sonata title as that of Dussek's *Élégie harmonique*. Although Schumann ridiculed such titles, too, as well as programmatic inscriptions,[99] his numerous references in his reviews and his approaches to his own sonatas show him to have been at least ambivalent, if not on the other side, on the question of sonata programmes (as discussed, with further references and sources, in ssb VIII).

With further regard to programmatic influences, a typical discussion in 1860 centered around doubts that the listener would enjoy, say, Mendelssohn's "Calm Sea" (Overture, Op. 27) any less if he did not know the title, since "Every art work is beautiful through what it is, not through what it means." [100] Yet in the same periodical, two years later, is a statement to the effect that Schubert's Sonata in a, Op. 143 (D. 784), appeals primarily to our sense of imagery.[101] A writer in 1868 distinguished the sonata and symphony from "descriptive music," but still managed to find extramusical functions for them, the sonata being the place where "a mental problem is clearly worked out," and the symphony where a "profound system of philosophy [is] developed." [102] In 1892 Bernard Shaw as music critic wrote of a programmatic overture that it was "a predestined failure, since it is impossible to tell a story in sonata form, because the end of a story is not a recapitulation of the beginning, and the end of a move-

---

97. Cf. SBE 353, SCE 36–37 and 605; also, Egert/FRÜHROMANTIKER 43 (citing a reference in 1800), CASTIL-BLAZE 272 (questioning its significance, in 1821), ESCUDIER II 88 (citing, in 1844, a parody by Fétis), NZM XLVIII (1858) 103 (Bülow).
98. Schilling/LEXICON VI 419.
99. E.g., Schumann/SCHRIFTEN I 91, 92, 306.
100. DMZ I (1860) 153–56 (W. Wauer).
101. DMZ III (1862) 41.
102. MT XIII (1868) 599.

ment in sonata form is." [103] But one is then reminded of H. G. Sear's efforts to show that Strindberg called his play *Spöksonaten* (*Ghost Sonata*; 1907) because (and only because) he was actually organizing the scenes into the sections of "sonata form." [104] One is also reminded of J. Todhunter's poem called *Beethoven's* "Sonata *Appassionata*," which literally parallels the themes and sections in all three movements of the music, as quoted and described by Calvin S. Brown.[105] In his letter of 1888 to Bülow (quoted *supra*) Strauss, like Shaw, found "sonata form" to be an unsatisfactory vehicle for the expression of an extramusical idea. But he added, on the other hand, that unity of mood and consistency of structure are "only possible through the inspiration by a poetical idea, whether or not it be introduced as a programme." [106]

Turning to another aspect of Romanticism, we find that the well-known, newly developed consciousness of history in the 19th century touched the sonata quite as much as other music and other arts. Interest in the sonatas of past eras is evidenced both by recitals and by editions of early music, and by writers, too, whose historical accounts range from single paragraphs to full studies. It is true that today we find faults in every aspect of those pioneer efforts. Yet without them, faulty or not, the present knowledge of sonata history could hardly have been won.

Among historical accounts, there is a vague outline made in 1808 by E. T. A. Hoffmann for a projected article, never written, on the sonata.[107] This was followed in 1837 by what might be called the first historical account, C. F. Becker's short sketch of the keyboard sonata in Germany, centering around Kuhnau's supposed priority.[108] Then in 1845 came Imanuel Faisst's enterprising doctoral dissertation (79

103. Shaw/LONDON 82.

104. Sear/SPOOK. But Dr. Harry Bergholz, Chief Bibliographer of the Wilson Library at the University of North Carolina, has kindly called to my attention Strindberg's letter of April 1, 1907, to Emil Schering, in which he relates the title specifically to Beethoven's Op. 31/2 (known as the "Specter Sonata" on the continent), probably having in mind the same passage (iii/96–107) that he had cited earlier, in the stage directions to Act II/i in *Brott och Brott*.

105. Brown/TONES 56, 63, 120–28. Brown also refers to poems that describe sons. (Chopin's Op. 35, pp. 35–36; Schumann's Op. 105, p. 76) and poems that convey their feel (p. 140). Dr. Rey Longyear at the University of Kentucky kindly has called attention, by correspondence, to what he regards as a strained effort by W. F. Mainland to find a literal "sonata form" in F. von Matthison's poem "Abendlandschaft" because Schiller said the poet "made a lovely sonata of it"; cf., also, Longyear/SCHILLER 106, 128, 173.

106. BÜLOW-STRAUSS 82–83.

107. Hoffmann/SCHRIFTEN 16; trans. in full in SSB VIII.

108. Becker/KLAVIERSONATE; revised in 1840, with exx., in Becker/HAUSMUSIK 33–39. Cf. SBE 11–12, 240.

pp. in print) on the keyboard sonata up to Emanuel Bach.[109] Along with several more short sketches,[110] the chief further contributions up to World War I were C. H. H. Parry's 31-page article of 1883 in the first edition of *Grove's Dictionary* (still largely intact in the 5th ed.); Shedlock's valued book of 1895 on the piano sonata;[111] Klauwell's book of 1899 on the sonata over all, incorporating chiefly Shedlock's findings and the special researches of Wasielewski;[112] and Selva's book of 1913 on the sonata in general, largely based on d'Indy's writings.[113]

As discussed earlier,[114] two interdependent currents of thought dominate these accounts, both founded by Faisst on a philosophy of historical evolution.[115] One is the idea that all sonata history falls into one continuous chain of progressive events, especially the "evolution," bit by bit, of "sonata form." The other is the related or derived idea that in particular the keyboard sonatas of Kuhnau, Scarlatti, and Emanuel Bach fall into one "single chronological line leading directly to full-fledged 'sonata form' " (SBE 11). Before the end of the era these ideas hardened into standard history-book explanations such as are still repeated in many recent summary accounts of the sonata.[116] Representative of the last is this statement published in 1964, with its traditional but actually untenable explanation of Emanuel Bach's historical significance: J. S. Bach's son "Carl Philip Emanuel, who counts for less in artistic interest and merit, is much more important historically, for the part he played in the evolution of sonata form, one of the most fertile discoveries of the human brain, makes him historically one of the most important composers who have ever lived." [117]

The Romantic historical consciousness touched the sonata in further ways. It showed up in archaic titles such as "Sonata da camera" (as by A. L. Peace; SSB XIV) or "Trio Sonate" (as by A. Sandberger; SSB

109. Faisst/CLAVIERSONATE.
110. Riehl/CHARAKTERKÖPFE 222–26; a "Historical Sketch of the Sonata," from Biber to Schubert, in MMR I (1871) 100–102; a sketch by Otto Kade, in NZM LXXI/1 (1876) 257–59 and 265–67; Bagge/SONATE; Eitner/SONATE (on early exx. of "son. form"); Goldschmidt/SONATENFORM; Pougin/SONATE; Schüz/SONATE; Michel/SONATE (collected lectures); Gascue/SONATA (collected lectures). Attention to son. history is also paid in WAGNER PROSE V 81–85 *passim*.
111. Shedlock/SONATA; cf. the evaluative Foreword, pp. v–x, in the Da Capo reprint of 1964 (W. S. Newman).
112. Klauwell/SONATE.
113. Selva/SONATE.
114. SBE 5–6, 240; SCE 15–16, 117–18, 261.
115. E.g., cf. Faisst/CLAVIERSONATE 7, 51 fn.
116. E.g., cf. Shedlock/SONATA 11–12, 125–26; Bie/PIANOFORTE 69, 86–90, 110, 168; Pougin/SONATE; Emmanuel/FRANCK 55–63; and Emmanuel/DUKAS 71; also, Allen/PHILOSOPHIES 156, 291, 300–301 (with further exx.).
117. Howes/ENGLISH 11. Cf. SCE 429–30.

XI). It permeated the writings of musicians not especially concerned with the historical outlook. Thus, Moscheles (SSB VII), although he found Corelli's "trio" sonatas antiquated, showed an interest in early keyboard sonatas, especially in conjunction with his pioneer historical recitals.[118] Schumann even poked fun at historical interest in the sonata —"In short, one sought to introduce historical interest (laugh not, Eusebius!)"; yet he showed a curiosity about the genesis of its movements and, of course, a strong absorption in its Classic styles as demonstrated by the past, great masters, in spite of his objections to perpetuating these styles in the mid 19th century (as quoted *supra*).[119] But near the end of the era, when MacDowell showed an interest in sonata history as it had come to him through his German training, he supplied one example of how Schumann's objections had developed into blind spots. In particular, he voiced, to an extreme degree, the late-19th-century depreciations of Mozart's piano sonatas.[120]

The increasing number of historical recitals in the 19th century (cf. SSB I and III) introduced not only the sonatas of the greatest masters but of some of the lesser ones, too—for example, sonatas by Kuhnau (SBE 239–42), Paradisi (or Paradies; SCE 686–92), D. Scarlatti (SCE 261–73), S. Arnold (SCE 765), and Porpora (SBE 258–59).[121] With the recitals came the increasing number of editions of "old masters," edited by Bülow, Ernst Pauer, Köhler, and others. We think of these as infamous editions, today, because of the undeniable violence they did to the original text and contemporary performance practices. Yet they, too, contributed essentially, albeit narrowly and one-sidedly, to the foundations of sonata history.[122]

Finally, mention should be made of the pronounced rise of nationalistic feelings in the 19th century as these touched the sonata. Such feelings comprised one more concomitant of the Romantic historical consciousness (as well as the new and changing political forces; SSB I). Even at the start of the century Rochlitz felt compelled to ask why a German, F. Ries (SSB VII), should write his sonata dedication in French to another German, Beethoven.[123] Schumann, too, showed occa-

118. E.g., cf. MOSCHELES I 261, 304–10 (regarding a Handel festival he helped to organize); II 35–36.
119. E.g., Schumann/SCHRIFTEN I 59, II 11.
120. Cf. MacDowell/ESSAYS 193, 194, 200, 239, 253; SCE 500; SSB XIX.
121. Cf. the reports of such sons. being performed, in MT XVIII (1878) 161, XX (1879) 166, XXIII (1882) 661, XXIV (1882) 20 and 229, XXV (1884) 103; MERCURE II (Jan.–June, 1906) 526–31 (an article on current performances illustrating the "evolution" of the son. since the 18th century).
122. Cf. SCE 15.
123. AMZ IX (1806–7) 365. Recall Beethoven's own preference for German as against French or Italian titles and inscriptions in his late sons. (SCE 525, 529, 531).

sional prejudices against the French and Italians when he disparaged the recollections of their styles in certain weak German sonatas.[124] In 1855 his successor (as editor of NZM), Brendel, set the pattern for claiming the priority and superiority of the German sonata,[125] a pattern that was to arouse the ire of the equally chauvinistic Italian, Torrefranca (SCE 172–74). On the other hand, a French reviewer in 1843 already lamented the infiltration of new styles and resultant deterioration after "a century of French dominance in the sonata." [126] Outlying countries, much newer to the sonata, quickly showed their own nationalistic zeal, producing sonatas "in Hungarian style," "in Russian style," and so on (SSB XVII and XVIII). Only the English and Americans seemed to welcome—in fact, sometimes prefer—foreign influences. Thus, an English reviewer, writing on a Sonata, Op. 20, by Stanford, made passing mention of those "leading German musicians, whose utterances always awaken interest and expectation" (SSB XIV).

124. E.g., cf. Schumann/SCHRIFTEN I 92 and 452.
125. E.g., Brendel/GESCHICHTE I 193, 299.
126. RGM for Dec. 10, 1843, pp. 419–20.

Chapter III

The Sonata in Romantic Society

Sources and Functions

How did the sonata figure in Romantic society? Answers to that question are no readier at hand nor easier to assemble than they were for the corresponding questions in our previous two volumes. The surprisingly few books that take a sociological view of all music history are too broad to allow appreciable space to any single instrumental genre like the sonata.[1] But the source materials that would be essential to a full account of the sonata's place in society do prove to be more abundant for the Romantic than for the Baroque or Classic Era (cf. SBE 33–34; SCE 43–44). They include all those memoirs, diaries, letters, travel reports, intimate biographies, and periodical notices or reviews that were mentioned earlier (SSB I). From such sources and from an occasional survey already done in the 19th century like Hanslick's on Vienna concert life (Hanslick/WIEN), rich studies wait to be prepared on Romantic concert life (to put the most needed topic first) and on the pursuit of music in the Romantic Era, whether as a profession, as an avocation, or in education. Clearly, any such study would be of immediate value, as in the present chapter.

In the Classic Era the three main functions of Baroque music still carried over—that is, music at court, in church, and in the theater (SBE 33–34, SCE 43–44). But the Classic sonata profited extensively only from the first of these functions, at court. Furthermore, it fulfilled two other functions increasingly, that of diversion for the middle-class amateur and that of pedagogic material for teachers and students. In

1. One does find a briefly pertinent section on the Beethoven son. in the Marxist-oriented study Knepler/XIX (Vol. II, Chap. V, *passim*), and on the instrumental soloist in Engel/GESELLSCHAFT 149. And as in both SBE and SCE, there are numerous occasions throughout SSB to cite findings on musicians, pubs., and instruments, in the excellent, more specialized study Loesser/PIANOS (cf. SCE 43–44).

the Romantic Era, all three Baroque functions ceased to concern the sonata to any important extent. No use of the sonata in the theater has turned up here. The only appreciable use in church was that of the organ sonata, mainly during the Offertory and to supply informal preludes and postludes in the Protestant service.[2] Intended for such use (according to dedications, titles, chorale themes, etc.) were numerous organ sonatas that we shall meet in later chapters, by Mendelssohn, Merkel, Reubke, Karg-Elert, Rheinberger, and several British and American composers. The sonata's use at court, especially during the earlier 19th century, was more extensive than in church—in fact, still considerable. But rarely does the court connection seem to have been the prime stimulus for any significant output of Romantic sonatas. When Schubert dedicated his Op. 42 (D. 845) to Archduke Rudolph of Austria (Beethoven's most honored dedicatee) or Weber and Loewe their Opp. 24 and 32, respectively, to Grand Duchess Maria Paulowna at Weimar, they were not serving at court but simply currying ducal favor.

In any case, of more importance to the Romantic sonata were its increasing functions as diversional and as pedagogic material, and now more than ever as solid fare in public and private recitals. Since the sonata as recital fare seems to have been a primary goal of the principal sonata composers, its function in that capacity is considered first and foremost here. After all, most Romantic sonatas are difficult to play, both artistically and athletically. Only highly trained performers could hope to project them satisfactorily. The German writer W. H. von Riehl may have been understating the abilities of not a few serious, enthusiastic, middle-class avocationalists when he wrote in 1853, "Since Beethoven the quartets and trios have become concert music, only [professional] virtuosos can still play the [music written for] piano, and the comfortable, genial, instrumental domestic music [by the Vienna Classic masters] exists not at all anymore." [3] But in the century before the widespread development of phonographs, player pianos, radio, and television, each sonata had to be performed anew and by an advanced performer every time it was to be heard. And it was the recital, public or private, that provided the chief opportunities. Our interest at the moment is in who gave these recitals and what they played.

2. A MS, incomplete "Sonata para Ofertorio" for orchestra, dated 1882, is listed in the *Catalogo de musica de los archivos de la Catedral de Santiago de Cuba y del Museo Bacardi* (Havana: Biblioteca nacional Jose Marti, 1961), p. 59.
3. Riehl/CHARAKTERKÖPFE I 208.

The Recitalists

Most of the leading 19th-century recitalists who gave prominence to the sonata in their programs were cited earlier in connection with Beethoven's all-pervasive influence and with historical recitals (SSB I). Liszt, "Klara" (Schumann, née Wieck), and Moscheles were the pioneer piano recitalists in the 1830's, with Clara continuing for more than a half century. Anton Rubinstein and Bülow followed in the 1840's and 1850's, both continuing for more than forty years. And Paderewski, d'Albert, Rachmaninoff, and Hofmann were among the leaders around the end of the era.[4] Chopin was one great pianist who, in his remarkably few public recitals, played little but his own music, apart from joining in occasional duets and larger ensembles. Even among his own sonatas Chopin seems to have played only Op. 65, for Vc & P, in public (with Franchomme; SSB XII). Some of the pianists who did much for the sonata did most of their playing on their home ground rather than internationally. Such, for example, were Charles Hallé, Arabella Goddard, and Agnes Zimmerman in London; or Raoul Pugno and Blanche Selva in Paris; or Golinelli, Martucci, and Longo in Italy. Other celebrated pianists, like Field, Steibelt, Kalkbrenner, Thalberg, Henselt, Gottschalk, and Tausig, appear to have given less place to the sonata, largely because nearly all of them flourished during the sonata's slump, in the second quarter of the century (SSB I, II, IV).

Among violinists who did much for the sonata, Joachim must be named first. Certainly, his closeness to the Schumanns and Brahms and his more than sixty years of performing in all the main centers made him one of the most important of Romantic musicians. Before him Spohr deserves first mention and near the end of his career Ysaÿe and Kreisler. Paganini seems to have played only his own unorthodox sonatas at his recitals. Other important violin virtuosos, like Kreutzer, Rode, Vieuxtemps, Wieniawski, Sarasate, and Wilhelmj, seem to have made less use of sonatas, no doubt partly because the accompanied keyboard sonatas still being published in the first half-century offered no opportunities for virtuosity and the genuine duos too few. Among cellists Piatti was the nearest equivalent to Joachim.

As one description of what must have been some of the fine recital playing of the century, in typical programs that include sonatas, a review in *The Musical Times* may be quoted almost in full of four

4. Cf. the vivid individual accounts of these and other contemporary pianists and their almost legendary careers in Loesser/PIANOS and Schonberg/PIANISTS.

out of five recitals given within less than four weeks in 1876 by Rubinstein:[5]

The visit of Herr Rubinstein to this country, after an absence of several years, has most undoubtedly been the event of the musical season. No such excitement has been produced within our recollection by the performances of any artist in London, as by those of this great pianist. He has already given four recitals at St. James's Hall, and a fifth and last is announced to take place on May 29th, after our going to press. The programmes of the recitals are worth giving, as showing the versatility of Herr Rubinstein, and his complete command of every style of playing.

FIRST RECITAL, May 3.—Preludes and Fugues, J. S. Bach; Rondo in A minor, Mozart; Gigue in A major, Handel; Sonata in F minor, Op. 57, Beethoven; Kreisleriana, Schumann; Sonata in B flat minor, Chopin; Etudes, Chopin; Miniatures, Caprice, Barcarolle, and Valse Caprice, Rubinstein.

SECOND RECITAL, May 10.—Variations, Handel; Sonata in E, Op. 109, Beethoven; Etudes Symphoniques, Schumann; Momens Musicales, Schubert; Scherzo à Capriccio, Mendelssohn; Nocturne, Field; Polacca, Weber; Preludes, Ballades and Etudes, Chopin; Leonore, 5th Barcarolle, and Tarantelle, Rubinstein.

THIRD RECITAL, May 16.—Fantasia, Op. 15, Schubert; Sonata (Moonlight), Beethoven; Variations Sérieuses, Mendelssohn; Nocturnes and Polonaises, Chopin; Carnaval, Schumann; Suite, Romance, and Etudes, Rubinstein.

FOURTH RECITAL, May 25.—Preludes and Fugue, Rubinstein; Sonata in A flat, Weber; "Warum," "Vogel als Prophet," "Abends," and "Traumeswirren," Schumann; Sonata in C minor, Op. 111, Beethoven; Nocturne, Field; Etude, Thalberg; "Chanson d'Amour," and "Si oiseau j'étais," Henselt; Nocturne, Mazurka, Valse, and Etudes, Chopin; Barcarolle and "Erl-König," Schubert-Liszt; Rhapsodie Hongroise, Liszt.

It is almost impossible to convey in words to those who have not heard it, any idea of Rubinstein's truly astounding playing. His execution is enormous, and under his fingers the greatest difficulties seem like mere child's-play. But it is not his almost unequalled command of the keyboard which rivets the attention and enlists the sympathies of his audiences, but the wonderful depth of his expression. His touch combines the extremes of power and delicacy; his *fortissimo,* while most sonorous, is free from the least trace of thumping, while in more tender passages, his *cantabile* is most exquisite. In nothing is he so great as in the delivery of a simple melody; in this his style is so absolutely unaffected and so full of charm and feeling that it goes straight to the heart of the hearer. Such playing as that of Mozart's Rondo and the slower numbers of Schumann's "Kreisleriana" at the first recital, or of the first movement of the "Moonlight" Sonata at the third, will not soon be forgotten by those who were present. On the other hand, it must be confessed that there is one drawback to the perfect enjoyment of his performances. As will be inferred from what we have said, Rubinstein is an impulsive player, and therefore to some extent unequal. At times he appears

5. MT XVII (1876) 500–501.

to let himself be fairly carried away by his music, and to lose all self-control. Hence his Allegros are too often hurried into Prestos; and, though his execution is equal to all the demands made upon it, the music suffers in consequence.

We are inclined to think Rubinstein greatest of all in his rendering of Chopin. The dreamy and romantic music of the Polish composer finds in him a most congenial exponent, and the exquisite delicacy with which what have been called Chopin's "filagree-work passages" are given is unsurpassable.

In addition to his recitals, Herr Rubinstein has also been heard in the Concert given by M. Wieniawski at St. James's Hall on the 20th ult. The performance on that occasion by these two great artists of Beethoven's celebrated "Kreutzer" sonata was the most magnificent within our recollection, alike in the vigour and passion of the Allegros, and in the exquisite taste and delicacy with which the well-known variations were given. Herr Rubinstein was in this work heard at his best, and was most admirably seconded by M. Wieniawski, who appears to be playing more finely than ever.

Concerts, Private and Public

The sample programs just listed bring us to a further consideration of the 19th-century recitals in which sonatas figured, which is their content. Our references necessarily must be confined mostly to public recitals. Programs seem to have been printed but rarely for private recitals. Nor were there any advertisements nor more than an occasional review from which we still might get information. In letters and memoirs we do find not infrequent mentions of sonatas being played at private gatherings, but seldom with any indication of what else may have been played or sung, let alone any complete program. Most of the occasions seem to have been too informal and spontaneous for set programs, anyway. Of one thing we can be sure—that private music-making of a high order constituted a favorite, "postman's" recreation for the professionals and a main indulgence for the dilettantes. That much the records do reveal, starting from the "Schubertiaden" in early-19th-century Vienna, where Schubert himself seems to have given the only, few lifetime performances of his own sonatas.[6] Moscheles "never wearied of making music with his brother artists," as in a private concert in 1839 for the French royal family at which he played his own four-hand Sonata in E♭ with Chopin.[7] Carl Friedberg has told of the indelible impressions made on him and his excitement when he was allowed to turn pages around 1887 for Brahms in music-making

6. More information than usual is given in a diary entry of 1827 reporting a "Schubertiad" at which he participated in his own "Grand Duo," as trans. in Deutsch/SCHUBERT-D 590–92 (cf., also, pp. 568, 571, 680 on the Son. in G, D. 894).

7. Cf. MOSCHELES I 251–52 and II 57–60, SSB VII; also, Schlesinger/CRAMER 74 for the banquet concert he and Cramer gave in honor of Clementi in 1827 (including 3 Clementi sons.).

shared by Clara Schumann, Joachim, and others, music-making that included late violin sonatas by both Brahms and Beethoven.[8] Amy Fay related in 1873 how extraordinarily Liszt would play for informal gatherings of his pupils, a quarter century after he had discontinued his public concert tours, one work he played being Chopin's Sonata in b, Op. 58.[9]

Of course, sonatas were by no means the main ingredient in the private music-making, especially before 1850. And the standards and interest could hardly be expected to be so high in most instances. The same Moscheles also reported boredom and poor manners at private concerts, as in London in 1832.[10] Yet, in 1828 the discriminating English author Edward Holmes expressed agreeable surprise at the good quality of much of the music, including private and dilettante performances, that he had been hearing in his travels in Vienna, Berlin, St. Petersburg, and other centers.[11]

Up to the mid 1850's the majority of public concerts consisted not only of a variety of compositions by a variety of composers, as is still true today, but of a variety of ensembles played by a variety of performers, as had been true throughout the previous century. On such a program it was unusual to include ensemble sonatas.[12] Their lack of sufficient color or display to counterbalance their length, their continued identification with more intimate or dilettantish music (especially in the accompanied keyboard settings, earlier in the century), and their connotations of obsolescence and academicism as the century advanced (ssb II)—these were the likely reasons for excluding them. Moreover, on such a variegated program it was still more unusual to include a solo—that is, piano—sonata, especially a Romantic rather than a Classic sonata. As late as 1848, when Charles Hallé performed Beethoven's Sonata in E♭, Op. 31/3 in London, he was told by the director of the Musical Union (predecessor of the Popular Concerts) that sonatas "were not works to be played in public" and that "no solo sonatas had ever before been included in any [London] concert programme." [13] Yet within eight years the respected William Henry Holmes would be announcing piano recitals that included one sonata each by J. W. Davison, G. A. Macfarren, Brahms, and Rubinstein, and

8. Smith/FRIEDBERG 13–14, 25–26.

9. Fay/GERMANY 211–14.

10. E.g., MOSCHELES 278–79.

11. E.g., Holmes/RAMBLE 125–27, 157–58, 236–37, 265–66, 282–83.

12. For 2 typical programs, without any sons., cf. MOSCHELES I 123 and Schlesinger/CRAMER 81. The sources for specific 19th-c. programs are many but scattered. As usual, the periodicals are especially helpful, including MDC at the end of the century.

13. HALLÉ 103.

two sonatas by Schumann.[14] And actually, at least a trickle of solo sonata performances in public can be found in one center or another from the start of the century, including those of Clara Schumann from 1835 and of Moscheles from 1837 (right in London; *infra*).

If much the same near exclusion of sonatas in public concerts of the first half-century can be surmised for Germany and certainly for regions more distant from the sonata's home centers, it does not quite apply to public concerts in Paris. There the ensemble and even the solo sonata seem to have fared somewhat better. A typical program, with typically incomplete listings, was one given in La Salle Chantereine on April 1, 1838. It included a first performance in Paris of a Moscheles Septet, a *Fantaisie concertante* in which Osborne and Bériot collaborated (as composers and/or performers?), a Sonata for P & Cl (by whom?), some airs or duos by Rossini and Mercadante, a Fantaisie (played and/or composed?) by Thalberg, a Trio for P, Vn, & Vc by Franck, "played for the first time," and "still some other works." [15] But a search through the periodical *Revue et gazette musicale de Paris* from its start in 1834 to 1850, during the concert heyday of Liszt, Chopin, Kalkbrenner, Thalberg, and Herz, has hardly borne out a statement in the issue for February 8, 1835 (p. 50) that concerts in that day rarely failed to include quintets, quartets, and sonatas, as well as the names of Boccherini, Haydn, Mozart, and Bach. Mozart's and Haydn's sonatas rarely turned up. Beethoven's appeared occasionally on the programs, though not nearly so often as his symphonies nor as other composers' fantasias and opera transcriptions for piano, songs, and various instrumental chamber groups.

The first recitals performed entirely by one pianist occurred in the later 1830's. In 1837, wrote Charlotte Moscheles,

. . . there had been no recitals for pianoforte music, and these were introduced by Moscheles [in London]. Many of his colleagues called this a venturous undertaking. Moscheles, however, held to his purpose, taking the precaution to interweave a little vocal music with the instrumental, so as to relieve the monotony which people warned him against. . . . The newspapers were loud in their praises of the new scheme, but censured the introduction of vocal music, adding that it was an interruption, and the one blot in an otherwise perfect entertainment. On three occasions Moscheles played some music of Scarlatti and his contemporaries on a harpsichord, built in the year 1771. . . .[16]

Moscheles' first "soirée," on February 18, 1837, consisted of the follow-

14. MT VII (1856) 177. Cf. GROVE IV 330 (G. Grove).
15. Vallas/FRANCK 38–39.
16. MOSCHELES II 22–23.

ing program, interspersed with "a little vocal music," as listed in a favorable review six days later:

Part I. Grande Sonate brillante (C major, in four movements [Op. 24]) Piano-forte, Mr. Moscheles; Weber.—Cantata, Miss Birch, 'Mad Bess;' Purcell. —Three preludes and Fugues (C sharp major, C sharp minor, and D major) P[iano]. F[orte]. Mr. Moscheles; S. Bach.—German Song, Miss Masson, 'Das erste Veilchen,' (The first violet) Mendelssohn.—Sonate Dramatique (D minor, Op. 29 [31/2!], in three movements) P. F. Mr. Moscheles; Beethoven. Part II. A selection from the Suites of Lessons (including the celebrated Cat's Fugue), as originally written for the harpsichord, and, by desire, performed on that instrument by Mr. Moscheles, D. Scarlatti.—The Harmonious Black-smith, with Handel's Variations, Mr. Moscheles; Handel.—Duet, Miss Birch and Miss Masson, (Cosi fan Tutte) Mozart.—Les Adieux, l'Absence, et le Retour, sonate charactéristique [Op. 81a], P. F. Mr. Moscheles; Beethoven.— Glee, Miss Birch, Miss Masson, Messrs. Vaughan and Bradbury, 'Go, feeble tyrant;' Jackson.—A selection of new MS Studies, P. F. Mr. Moscheles; Moscheles. Conductor of the Vocal Music, Sir George Smart.[17]

In the very same month Clara Wieck began a series of eight recitals in Berlin that also consisted "purely of pieces for solo pianoforte and songs with pianoforte" (or P & Vn), including Beethoven's sonatas Opp. 47 and 57.[18] She played only the last two movements of Op. 57 on the first recital and then the whole of it, "by request," at a later one.

In early 1839 in Rome Liszt took the one further step by playing the whole program himself, although not including any sonatas. Referring to one of the recent, variegated concerts in Paris, he wrote in June of that year,

What a contrast to the tiresome *musical soliloquies* (I do not know what other name to give this invention of mine) with which I contrived to gratify the Romans, and which I am quite capable of importing to Paris, so un-bounded does my impudence become! Imagine that, wearied with warfare, not being able to compose a programme which would have common sense, I have ventured to give a series of concerts all by myself, affecting the Louis XIV style, and saying cavalierly to the public, "The concert is—myself." For the curiosity of the thing I copy one of the programmes of the soliloquies for you:—
    1. Overture to William Tell, performed by M[onsieur]. L[iszt].
    2. Reminiscences of the *Puritani*. Fantaisie composed and performed by the above-mentioned!
    3. Etudes and fragments by the same to the same!
    4. Improvisation on themes given—still by the same.

17. MUSICAL WORLD IV (1836–37) 155–56; on p. 184 the program of the 2d "soirée" (Mar. 4, 1837) is given, including Beethoven's sons. Opp. 17, 26, and 28, but none by Moscheles himself.
18. AMZ XXXIX (1837) 193, 194, 196, 257–58. Cf., also, NZM VII (1837) 87 ("Florestan und Eusebius"); AMZ XL (1838) 164–65 and 369 (in Vienna); Hanslick/WIEN I 332–33.

And that was all; neither more nor less, except lively conversation during the intervals, and enthusiasm if there was room for it.[19]

The Make-Up of the Recitals

Ferdinand Hiller praised Liszt as one of the first front-rank composers to play the music of others,[20] which praise Liszt richly deserved throughout his career as a performer. His introduction of Beethoven's Op. 106 to Paris—in fact, to the musical world—in 1836, as described by Berlioz,[21] is sufficient indication of his enterprise as regards the sonata.[22] Of course, the pianists who composed less, or less successfully, had more reason to play the music of other composers. Clara Schumann's large repertoire, during the long career that saw over 2,000 recitals, included at least 51 sonatas—28 for P solo, 4 for P-duet or 2 Ps, 16 for P & Vn, and 3 for P & Vc. The composers of these sonatas, listed in the order in which she first took them up, are Czerny, Mozart (including 7 for P & Vn), Pleyel, Vanhal, Hummel, Beethoven (9 for P solo, 4 for P & Vn, one for P & Vc), Schumann (3 for P solo, 2 for P & Vn), Moscheles, Brahms (Op. 5 for P solo and all 3 Vn sons.), Mendelssohn, Scarlatti, Haydn (one), Clementi (one), and Schubert (2 for P solo and one for arpeggione).[23] It is evident that her tastes became increasingly conservative as she aged.

An exceptional set of statistics has been prepared [24] on about 285 known public performances of solo and duo sonatas in England during the first half of the 19th century and all in London except 22 in Manchester, 2 in Cambridge, and one each in Liverpool, Brighton, Reading, Norwich, and Bury St. Edmunds. The sonatas of one composer, Beethoven (especially Opp. 47, 30, 27/2, and 31/2, in that order), account for 153, or nearly 54 per cent, of the performances, with Mozart (16 performances, especially K. 497), Weber, Dussek, G. A. Macfarren, Clementi, Mendelssohn, Spohr, and perhaps a dozen others trailing far behind. Between 1801 and 1813 about 20 performances are known, 7 for P solo and the rest for H solo or for duo (P & one other instrument). Between 1814 and 1836 none are known. Between 1837 (when Moscheles began his "soirées," *supra*) and 1850, about 265 per-

---

19. As trans. in LISZT LETTERS I 31–32. Our present word "recital" was not introduced until Liszt played a year later in London (cf. Loesser/PIANOS 371).

20. Gertler/SCHUMANN 35 fn. 90.

21. RGM for June 12, 1836, p. 200.

22. But the samples of his programs in 1837–38 that are summarized in Romann/LISZT I 419 and 426–27, and II/1 428 do not happen to specify sons.

23. The foregoing information, from Litzmann/SCHUMANN III 615–24, is not likely to be complete.

24. Temperley/CORRESPONDENCE.

formances are known, including 140 (53%) duos (90 for P & Vn, 37 for P & Vc, 13 other), 12 (4%) for P-duet (9 of Mozart sons.), and 113 (43%) P solos.

One begins to wonder that the pianists played as many sonatas as they did, bearing in mind not only the recurring predictions of the sonata's downfall (ssb II) but the considerable length of the Romantic sonatas in particular. Like Beethoven's Op. 106, Schubert's posthumous Sonata in A, Brahms's Op. 34b, and especially the longest sonatas of later Romantics like Raff, Rheinberger, Reger, d'Indy, Dukas, Medtner, Godowsky, and Dale, all last closer to forty than thirty minutes, and some more than an hour (cf. ssb VI). A partial answer to the length was the considerable length of the recitals themselves, as must be evident already from the programs of Rubinstein and others that have been quoted here. Clearly the audiences were less in a hurry than their present-day descendants. "A little under two hours" was given as the average length in a series of chamber music programs (including sons.) in 1880.[25] But two hours would hardly be sufficient for a solo piano recital by Oscar Beringer the following year that included Beethoven's Op. 106, Weber's Op. 39, Brahms's Op. 5, and Liszt's Sonata in b! [26] The eccentric French virtuoso Alkan (ssb XII) had the goodness to put the exact timings beside each work on the printed programs of his long piano recitals, supposedly so that his audiences would not be taken by surprise.[27]

Among related questions that the recitals raised, one was the advisability of encores. Bülow extended one of his long recitals to a considerably greater length by repeating the fugue finale of Beethoven's Op. 106.[28] Rubinstein extended one of his still more by playing the whole of Chopin's Sonata in b, Op. 58, as his "first" encore.[29] Francis Hueffer, lecturing in London in 1880, presumably would have preferred Rubinstein's way of meeting the "encore nuisance," because, he said, playing only one movement destroys the complete organism that a sonata or symphony must be.[30] Yet playing one or two movements from a sonata was common practice throughout the Romantic Era.[31] The first public exposure of Brahms's Op. 1 came when Bülow played the opening movement, only, in 1854, and of his

25. mt XXI (1880) 354.
26. mt XXII (1881) 138–39. Cf. Müller-Reuter/lexikon I 425 for an exceptionally long program, including Bülow playing the Liszt Son. in b.
27. Bloch/alkan 2.
28. Cf. bülow briefe IV 291, 292, 579, 582.
29. Friedheim/liszt 195.
30. mt XXI (1880) 344.
31. E.g., cf. the mention of this practice in Bennett/bennett 148–49.

Op. 5 when Clara Schumann played the second and third movements, only, also in 1854 (ssb IX). Not infrequently, one of the movements from a sonata has had a life of its own, anyway, like the finale, "Perpetuum mobile," from Weber's Op. 24, or the slow movement, "March funèbre," from Chopin's Op. 35.

In any case, as against that variegated type of program that had prevailed earlier, there was some effort to make a single organism of the whole recital, including not a few all-Beethoven programs (ssb I). In 1860 a reviewer even questioned the equating of different styles and the levelling effect that resulted when Bülow played Bach, Mozart, Beethoven, Wagner, Chopin, Bülow, and Liszt "all in one breath" in a solo recital.[32] Such a reviewer had little patience with the stunts and novelties that still beset many a program on which sonatas figured, usually by way of bait for the audience. For example, one George Fox, eight years old, doing an "Improvisation in Sonata Form" was the bait that was cast out to lure a full audience to a benefit recital in 1878,[33] providing but a single instance of the endless, usually vain attempts to discover prodigies in the 19th century.[34] Another method of arousing curiosity that became fashionable for a time was that of withholding the composer's name on the program, leaving the audience and reviewer to guess. This method perplexed one reviewer in 1881, as he frankly confessed, after Bülow and Wilhelmj played an anonymous, well-liked duo for P & Vn that proved to be Ferdinand Hummel's Op. 24 in c.[35]

The Sonata and the Professional

The sonata could figure in several ways in the Romantic musician's career. For one thing, as in the two previous eras (sbe 30, sce 46–47), it seems to have made an ideal Op. 1 by which aspiring, serious-minded composers could introduce themselves in print, even though no Op. 2 might ever follow or the direction of interest might be changed entirely. Loewe stressed this advantage in a letter to his publisher quoted previously (ssb II). In 1853 the English pianist Edward Bache considered launching his career with a published sonata, although

32. dmz I (1860) 119.
33. mt XIX (1878) 663.
34. Cf. Holmes/ramble 157–58: "We have so much of child's play lately in England [1830], that it is to be hoped the fashion is on the decline; for if extremes be good, how much better it would be to employ those whose tops are bald with dry antiquity. . . ."
35. smw XXXIX (1881) 1107.

the challenge to create so imposing a form worried him.[36] We are reminded of the ideal achievement that the sonata represented to Romantic composers and critics (ssb II). Wrote Schumann, in 1844, too involutely,

A sonata as an Op. 1 has a twofold claim on our sympathies. Since, in any case, the fullest concentration of the creative powers demands attention to compositions of larger, artistically worthier designs than fantasias [and] transcriptions (whose production today is, in a double sense [the original and its adaptation?], no longer art), then such is all the more true when an artist, instead of pouring out a few borrowed ideas in a slovenly, worn-out form flooded with passagework, introduces himself in public with a work that requires the declaration of his own ideas in a refined, noble form and hence [that requires] both capability of effort and artistic experience.[37]

Schumann seems to have taken special note of "prize sonatas" that were introductory works by neophytes, although he did not always approve of the reward.[38] Not a few other and later reviewers paid special attention to introductory sonatas, prize-winning or not, sometimes spending as much as the first half of the review repeating much the same thoughts on the significance of an Op. 1.[39]

Composing sonatas could be advantageous to the performers, too, who knew better than any other, as Biber, Tartini, Scarlatti, and other virtuosos had known in previous centuries, what to write that would show their performance skills to best advantage. The sonatas of Kalkbrenner and Thalberg were justified chiefly in that sense (ssb XII). Hanslick praised Clara Wieck (who was also a composer in her own right) for playing Beethoven's sonatas in Vienna in 1837 and for not being one of those numerous performers—including three in Vienna in 1845, Thalberg, Evers, and Willmers—who wrote sonatas as vehicles for their display "but were no Beethovens." [40] A performer had a particular chance to ingratiate himself if he introduced in his sonata some tune that was then in favor, perhaps locally. Usually he treated the tune as a subject for variations in the slow movement or for more brilliant variations in the finale. This procedure obtained especially in

36. Bache/BACHE 15–17.
37. Trans. from Schumann/SCHRIFTEN II 348. Bülow noted that a Son. as an Op. 1 permitted the composer to see his progress in perspective (NZM XLV [1856] 21–22). Cf., also, the statement of 1799 trans. in SCE 47.
38. E.g., cf. his review in 1842 of "Drei Preissonaten," in Schumann/SCHRIFTEN II 79–83.
39. For 2 later samples, cf. NZM XXV (1864) 112 (prize son.) and LXVI/2 (1870) 369–71.
40. Hanslick/WIEN I 333.

the early 19th century, as in sonatas by Wölfl (SCE 564), Moscheles (SSB VII), and Ries (SSB VII).[41]

Although composing sonatas might have the foregoing advantages for the Romantic musician, one advantage it was less likely to have was immediate financial profit. Wagner undoubtedly was recounting his own experiences when he had his imaginary pilgrim to Beethoven tell of rebuffed efforts to make money from the sale of sonatas and how the prospective publishers advised writing "galops and pot-pourris," instead.[42] Fauré found the French publishers afraid to invest in his Op. 13 and had to accept the "honor" alone of having it published by Breitkopf & Härtel in Leipzig in 1877 (SSB XIII). An article of 1889 on Algernon Ashton began,

> It is said that none but the most enthusiastic musicians in the present day devote their talents to such complicated and learned labours as are necessary to the production of sonatas and the higher forms of musical art. . . . *The answer is that they are not produced because they are not profitable.*[43]

In their way, of course, the sonata composers had to struggle with the same problems that confronted any other artist, or any other entrepreneur, for that matter. They lived ceaselessly active, hectic, exhausting lives between their composing, teaching, performing, rehearsing, hearing, and writing about music.[44] They fought to establish and preserve some scale of fair compensation for their sonatas and like products.[45] And they faced the familiar maze of charges and regulations for the rental of concert halls, use of instruments, special privileges, and so on.[46] To be sure, the few most successful composers made substantial incomes. Mendelssohn, for example, could afford the luxury of withholding his MSS from publication for considerable periods, both because he liked the prolonged opportunity to touch them up here and there and simply because in his fastidiousness he disliked

41. In 1824 Czerny wrote Liszt's father offering to write variations for young Liszt to play, on some tune currently popular in Paris (cf. Stegner/CZERNY 21). Cf., also, MOSCHELES I 201–2.

42. WAGNER PROSE VII 23.

43. MT XXX (1889) 616 (italics original). Ashton himself became cynical about music pub. (cf. MGG I 750 [G. Abraham]).

44. Cf. the descriptions of daily life in MOSCHELES I 211–12, 301, 314–15 and II 20–21, 168; Stanford/BENNETT 645–46.

45. For sample fees asked by representative composers (although without translation into real money), cf. Hanslick/WIEN I 279 (on Beethoven's charges); MOSCHELES I 222; MENDELSSOHN/Moscheles 273 (on Mendelssohn's charges); Jansen/SCHUMANN II 273–74 (on Schumann expecting twice what he suggested for Brahms in 1853); May/BRAHMS 134; BRAHMS BRIEFWECHSEL XII 20 and XIV no. 12; MT XV (1872) 418, 446–47, 510, 541 (only indirectly related, on church organists' salaries).

46. Cf. the list of charges and restrictions for the use of a hall, in MT XV (1872) 364.

seeing "such nice, clean manuscript pass into the dirty hands of engravers, customers and the public." [47]

Two other classes of sonata composers had less to do with these professional problems. There were the promising, short-lived composers—among them Pinto, Schunke, Reubke, and Lekeu—who barely completed their training and entered their twenties before they died or could become involved with the exigencies of a professional career. And there were the not few women who composed sonatas—among them, Emilie Meyer, Johanna Müller-Hermann, Elizabeth Kuyper, Luise Adolpha Le Beau, Cécile Chaminade, Agnes Zimmerman, Ethel Smyth, Amy Marcy Beach, Clara Anna Korn, and Clara Kathleen Rogers (not to mention the numerous other women who figure indirectly here as performers, counselors, and benefactors of some of the main champions of the sonata, including George Sand, Pauline Viardot-García, Jenny Lind, Jane Sterling, Henriette Sontag, Clara Schumann, Elisabeth von Herzogenberg, W. M. F. Neruda, Blanche Selva, and Claire Murray Newman).[48] Intentionally or not, these women were put in a class of their own by the reviewers, who were invariably well-meaning but invariably cavalier, too, and who seldom completed a review without at least implying that the sonata was "surprisingly good for a woman" and showed "fine skill if not much inspiration." This class of composer had fewer struggles with professional problems both because there were usually other sources of income and because there were generally fewer opportunities for publication and other advancements, anyway (perhaps providing one reason why Dame Ethel Smyth became such a stalwart champion of woman suffrage).

Amateurs and Students

The amateurs or dilettantes who played sonatas in the earlier 19th century were direct descendants of the later 18th-century type, who mostly preferred the lightest, frothiest examples (SCE 44–46). Living at "the time when the word 'brilliant' came into fashion" and "legions of girls had fallen in love with Czerny," [49] they became the consumers of publications like F. W. Grund's *Trois Sonatines . . . aux amateurs,* Schubert's *Sonatas faciles* and *Grande Sonate agréable* (SSB VIII), or Steibelt's *Two Sonatas . . . Dedicated to the fair sex.*[50] After the mid-

47. Cf. his letter of June 12, 1843, to K. Klingmann, as trans. in Selden-Goth/ MENDELSSOHN 325.

48. Among special sources on women composers are Elson/WOMAN and Cobbett/ CHAMBER II 591–92 (M. Drake-Brockman) and I 185 (W. W. Cobbett).

49. Schumann/SCHRIFTEN I 162.

50. WOLFE II 842.

dle of the 19th century and the sonata's slump period, these amateurs or dilettantes seem to have branched off in three main directions. The most serious-minded and capable of them, like Brahms's surgeon friend Theodor Billroth, sought as nearly as possible to keep up with the Romantic sonata in all its structural, emotional, and athletic expansions, and with the professional masters who created and played it. The less capable amateurs, though sometimes quite as serious-minded, tended of necessity to remain or become diligent students, having to content themselves more or less with pedagogic compromises, as noted below. And the least serious-minded of the amateurs largely must have turned away to other genres for want of up-to-date sonata novelties light enough for their superficial grasp.

Closely related to these different directions taken by the amateur, is the distinct dichotomy that developed in the 19th century between sonatas designed for the concert hall and those designed for teaching. One would be tempted to oversimplify this dichotomy by calling it art versus pedagogy. But, of course, art and pedagogy should never be mutually exclusive and, for the most part, do not prove to be in the Romantic sonata. One might come closer to the dichotomy by calling it "grande sonate" versus "petite sonatine," or large-scale and difficult versus diminutive and easy, notwithstanding such exceptions, respectively, as the five sensitive, technically easy little "sonatinas," Op. 70, by Theodor Kirchner (ssʙ X) and the lengthy, difficult *Grande Sonate d'Étude, doigtée pour faire atteindre l'habilité supérieure du mécanisme dans plusieurs nouvelles formes de passages,* Op. 268, by Czerny (ssʙ VII, with exx.). But the real dichotomy is one more of kind than of degree. It is the dichotomy of new style versus old style. When Clementi wrote his delightful sonatinas (sᴄᴇ 751), their lightness, efficiency, naivety, and characteristic idioms were inherent in the current Classic language. When the Romantic composers continued to employ the same styles, with little or no modernization, in their teaching sonatas or sonatinas, all the way from Kuhlau to Nicolai von Wilm, they were perpetuating a language and idioms that were no longer current at all.

So well recognized was this dichotomy that it is not surprising to find one and the same composer—for example, Kuhlau (ssʙ XV) or Reinecke (ssʙ X)—using the current style for his concert sonatas and the old style for his teaching sonatas. Reviewers frequently took note of the dichotomy, as we shall discover in later chapters. Schumann generally fought the persistence of the old style in whatever sonatas came his way (". . . the sonata style of 1790 is not that of 1840," as trans. in ssʙ II). Yet he could recommend a thorough grounding in the old style of writing sonatas as a prerequisite to the "free [newer] style" for aspiring composers.[51] With Bülow it was not a question of a dichotomy but of the validity of any sonatas at all after Beethoven's except Chopin's, Schumann's, and Hummel's Op. 81 in f♯, and apart from his concession that "for exercise in private it [a post-Beethoven sonata] may always be accepted." [52] But he made that gloomy statement in 1852 when he was only twenty-two and before he was playing many Romantic sonatas.

In 1828 J. A. G. Heinroth began a long review of Jakob Schmitt's *Sonate à l'usage des Élèves avancés* with some specific ideas about the pedagogic values of the sonata:[53]

> In each *Messkatalog* [Leipzig book fair catalog; ʜᴏꜰᴍᴇɪꜱᴛᴇʀ 1828 (Whistling)?] appear music items written now for this, now for that purpose, designated to satisfy now this, now that stated need. They sprout from the fantasy of composers like mushrooms out of the ground. And although their titles tell in what category they belong, they still have this in common with the mushrooms, that one cannot distinguish the edible from the inedible or even [the] dangerous at first glance.
>
> A lot of sonatas *à l'usage des élèves avancés* are offered to us that by no means accomplish what one rightly expects of them. Thus, when the student is tired and worn out with his *Exercices* and *Etudes* by Cramer, Müller, Clementi, etc., the teacher may give him a little [musical] relaxation. But this relaxation must always contain something whereby he [the student] is brought closer to his goal. Therefore a good teacher gives sonatas to him based on ideas that are lovely, melodious, and fluent, but not trifling, wooden, and clumsy, and whose treatment is good and intelligible; sonatas that present no mere chain of modulations and do not go astray constantly into the most outlandish keys; [and] sonatas in which natural voice-leading prevails and which are orthographically written with regard to rhythm as well as harmony. If the teacher is concerned especially with attack, fingering, and clarity in the exercises and studies, then [by contrast] he calls the student's attention in the sonatas to the theme, to the treatment of the same, [to] how it appears now in the soprano, now in the bass, etc. In this manner the student learns something useful while he relaxes.

The titles of the teaching sonatas often specify their particular values for students, thereby pleasing the reviewers. These last characteristically sought, as Spitta sought in so many of Bach's works, to find some value, whether moral, pedagogic, recreational, or concert,

---

51. Cf. Jansen/ꜱᴄʜᴜᴍᴀɴɴ II 206; also, p. 70 for further advices by him on writing sons.
52. ɴᴢᴍ XXXVI (1852) 234.
53. ᴄᴀᴇᴄɪʟɪᴀ IX (1828) 193–96.

in every work under examination.[54] Thus, we find "Easy and Pleasing Sonatas With Fingering and Interpretation Indicated" (H. Wohlfahrt, ssb IX);[55] or Sonata in F "written expressly for small hands" (E. M. Lott);[56] or, recalling Czerny's equation above, "Etudes ou Sonates" (A. Romberg, ssb VIII);[57] or "Three Sonatas in [an] Easy, Pleasing Style of Playing and [arranged in] Progressive Steps" (by the pedagogue K. R. Hennig). Series of "progressive sonatas" account for a large number of the countless teaching sonatas published in the 19th century, filling many pages of PAZDÍREK (but represented by only a fraction of their number in the present volume).

54. Schumann emphasized such values only infrequently (as in Schumann/ SCHRIFTEN I 91), preferring to concentrate on aspects of the music itself. Unfortunately, conceding that a son. would serve well for teaching purposes could be as damning as calling one of the "fair sex's" sons. "well done for a woman"!
55. Cf. the typical review in NZM LXI/2 (1865) 343.
56. MT XXIV (1883) 300.
57. Cf. AMZ XV (1813) 839–40, reviewing only the etude aspects.

Chapter IV

The Spread of the Romantic Sonata

Trends in Space and Time

The general regions, main centers, and particular institutions where the Romantic sonata was introduced, composed, published, and enjoyed; the policies and practices by which its publication was affected; and the relative importance attached to it in the larger musical scene —these are the topics that now come up, under "The Spread of the Romantic Sonata." We come shortly to a survey of the main centers where the composers wrote their sonatas, the performers played them, the patrons heard and subsidized them, the publishers issued them, the consumers bought them, the critics reviewed them, and the teachers guided their students through them. By way of preliminary overviews, two charts of geographic spread and related time spans are offered. The first shows the distribution, by countries or larger regions, of the 629 composers who are at least touched on individually in the present volume, subdivided into early-, middle-, and late-Romantic groups (cf. ssb I). To the uncertain extent that our selection is equally representative for the several regions, it helps to confirm the hegemony in Austro-Germany and the continuing, strong sonata activities in France

The Distribution of 629 Romantic Sonata Composers by Regions and Era Phases

	Austria	Germany & Switz.	France & Low Countries	Great Britain	Scandi- navia	Italy & Iberia	East- ern Europe	Russia	The Amer- icas	Totals
Early-Rom. (1800–1850)	15	57	21	23	11	12	8	9	5	161
Mid-Rom. (1840–1885)	11	59	24	34	9		11	10	21	179
Late-Rom. (1875–1915)	17	73	45	36	21	12	31	23	31	289
TOTALS	43	189	90	93	41	24	50	42	57	629

and Great Britain during the Romantic Era. It shows the sharp increase of interest almost everywhere in the late-Romantic Era. And it also shows that the sharp drop in sonata production in Italy during the late-Classic Era continues throughout the Romantic Era, but that new interest begins to develop in regions that had been "outlying" from the standpoint of the sonata. As the standard music history books make clear enough, Italy was too preoccupied with opera throughout the era, and the "outlying" regions with national or folk interests up to the mid-century, to pay more attention than they did to the sonata.

The second geographic-time chart is more specific and more limited. Paralleling two maps and a chart of distribution in our two previous volumes (SBE 96; SCE 62–63), this chart shows the seventeen countries or regions in which, and the time spans during which, sixty-eight of the chief composers of Romantic sonatas wrote their sonatas. The countries or regions can no longer be narrowed down to cities because so often the composers moved about too much (which is why they keep reappearing in the summaries of individual city centers, *infra*). At the very least, composers had always managed to move back and forth across Europe at an astonishing rate, in spite of the most harrowing travel conditions (cf. SCE 164). But especially after the rapid development of railroads, steamships, and telegraphy, all well before the mid-century,[1] the composers seemed to become an even more peripatetic lot. And itinerant performers at the era's end, like Rachmaninoff and Kreisler, became virtual world citizens. In further regard to the second chart, the time spans must be read with latitude because publication, not composition, dates have had to suffice in most instances, and because the composer's main sonata output may have fallen within or at either end of the extremes. Like the statistics later in this chapter, this chart helps to confirm that the alleged slump in sonata output during the second quarter of the century (SSB II) was partly imagined and only partly real.

As suggested on these two geographic-time charts (and discussed in SSB I), the Austro-German hegemony with respect to the sonata constituted the main hub from which this form type fanned out during the Romantic Era, spreading as far east as Russia, as far west as the Americas, and eventually to all world centers where Western music

1. The excitement of a first train ride, in 1831, is reported in MOSCHELES I 249–50, after numerous unfortunate travel experiences (e.g., pp. 115–18 and 230–34). Schumann compared Beethoven's and Liszt's mode of travel (Boetticher/SCHUMANN 618). Chopin showed much interest, in 1844, in the telegraphic service established between Baltimore and Washington (Sydow & Hedley/CHOPIN 250).

Regions and Production Spans of
Some Main Romantic Sonata Composers

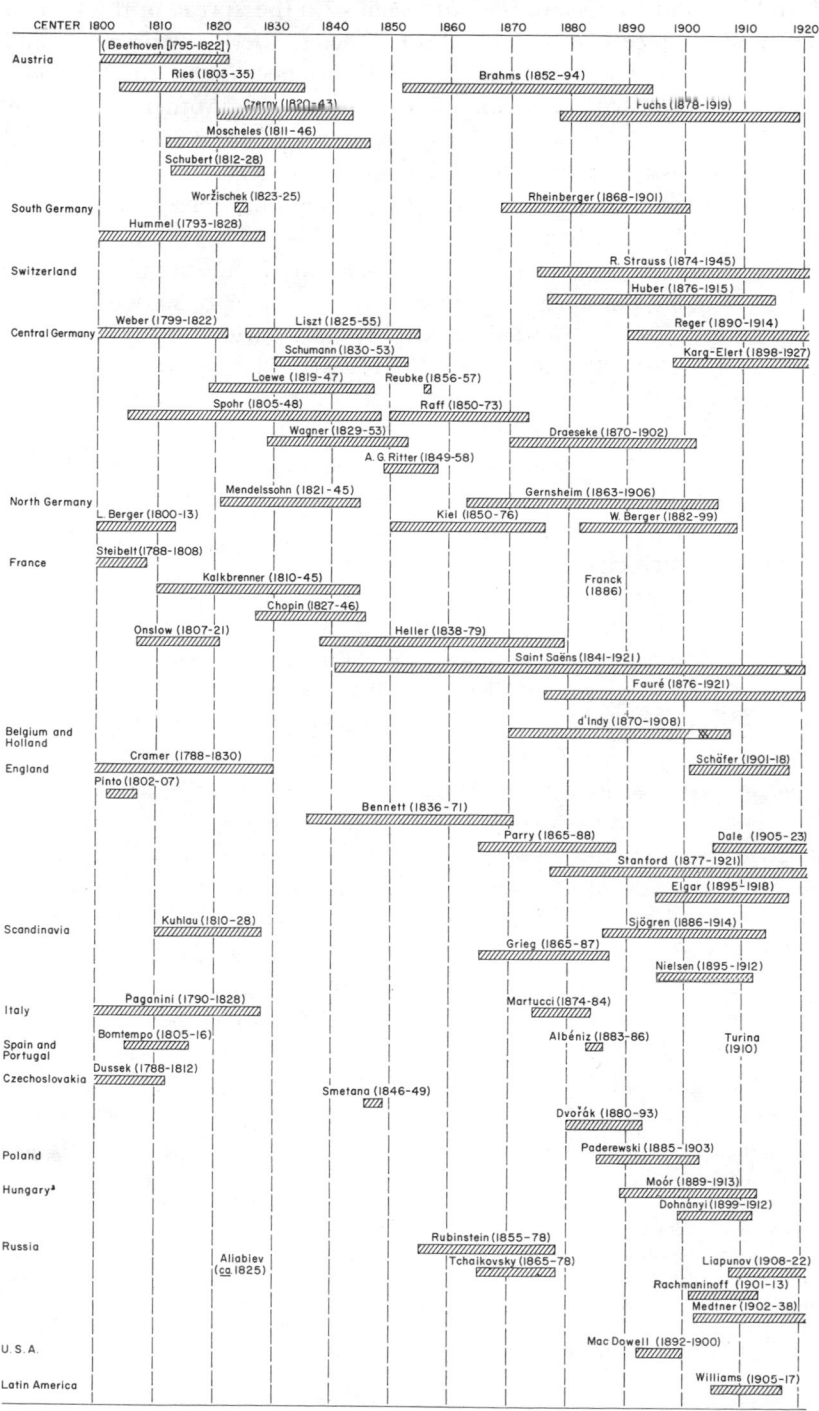

| CENTER | 1800 | 1810 | 1820 | 1830 | 1840 | 1850 | 1860 | 1870 | 1880 | 1890 | 1900 | 1910 | 1920 |

Austria
(Beethoven [1795-1822])
Ries (1803-35)
Brahms (1852-94)
Czerny (1820-43)
Fuchs (1878-1919)
Moscheles (1811-46)
Schubert (1812-28)

South Germany
Woržischek (1823-25)
Rheinberger (1868-1901)
Hummel (1793-1828)

Switzerland
R. Strauss (1874-1945)
Huber (1876-1915)

Central Germany
Weber (1799-1822)
Liszt (1825-55)
Reger (1890-1914)
Schumann (1830-53)
Karg-Elert (1898-1927)
Loewe (1819-47)
Reubke (1856-57)
Spohr (1805-48)
Raff (1850-73)
Wagner (1829-53)
Draeseke (1870-1902)
A. G. Ritter (1849-58)

North Germany
Mendelssohn (1821-45)
Gernsheim (1863-1906)
L. Berger (1800-13)
Kiel (1850-76)
W. Berger (1882-99)

France
Steibelt (1788-1808)
Kalkbrenner (1810-45)
Franck (1886)
Chopin (1827-46)
Onslow (1807-21)
Heller (1838-79)
Saint Saëns (1841-1921)
Fauré (1876-1921)

Belgium and Holland
d'Indy (1870-1908)

England
Cramer (1788-1830)
Schäfer (1901-18)
Pinto (1802-07)
Bennett (1836-71)
Parry (1865-88)
Dale (1905-23)
Stanford (1877-1921)
Elgar (1895-1918)

Scandinavia
Kuhlau (1810-28)
Sjögren (1886-1914)
Grieg (1865-87)
Nielsen (1895-1912)

Italy
Paganini (1790-1828)
Martucci (1874-84)

Spain and Portugal
Bomtempo (1805-16)
Albéniz (1883-86)
Turina (1910)

Czechoslovakia
Dussek (1788-1812)
Smetana (1846-49)
Dvořák (1880-93)

Poland
Paderewski (1885-1903)

Hungary[a]
Moór (1889-1913)
Dohnányi (1899-1912)

Russia
Rubinstein (1855-78)
Aliabiev (ca 1825)
Tchaikovsky (1865-78)
Liapunov (1908-22)
Rachmaninoff (1901-13)
Medtner (1902-38)

U.S.A.
MacDowell (1892-1900)

Latin America
Williams (1905-17)

was taking hold.[2] This fanning out began with the spread of the Vienna Classic masterpieces, especially through Ries, Czerny, Moscheles, and other "Beethoven transmitters" (ssb VII). It became an international Romantic force with the spread of sonatas (and other music) by Dussek,[3] Hummel, Weber, Schubert, Mendelssohn, and Schumann; and after them, Liszt,[4] Brahms, Rheinberger, Kiel, Reger, and others. And it operated increasingly in the larger international senses that a good majority of the Romantic sonata composers in other regions got their advanced training in Austria and/or Germany before launching their careers at home (ssb I), and a considerable number of native German composers of sonatas settled down to their careers in those other regions—especially England, Scandinavia, Russia, and the Americas— but only *after* they had completed their training in the fatherland. If there was less of this personal interchange with the French, especially following the Franco-Prussian War of 1870–71, there was certainly no less influence exercised by Austro-German music on the French sonata (and other music)—hardly so, in a country where both Brahms and Wagner left such clear stamps, not to be erased prior to the sophistications and iconoclasms of Satie and others.

As always, the immediate incentives to compose sonatas in the Romantic Era were local—a conservatory prize, a concert opportunity, the invitation of a sympathetic publisher, the interests of a particular recitalist, the challenge to a particular student. Such incentives abound first of all in city centers. In the Baroque and Classic eras the separate cities or related communities proved to be tantamount to schools, each dominated by its leading composer, especially in Italy and Germany. In the Romantic Era the separate city centers continued to be the prime breeding grounds of the sonata. One might suppose that after the epochal advances in transportation and communication and after the unification of all Germany in 1871, the artistic individualities of the cities would be submerged in the newly heightened spirit of nationalism. (The significant production in France and England has always concentrated almost exclusively in the one government capital of each country, Paris and London.) But one can sense quite as much difference of style and import between the sonatas produced in, say,

2. In Lochner/KREISLER 93 it was still most unexpected as late as 1923 to find the Japanese ambassador organizing 8 recitals to be played by Fritz Kreisler and his pianist in Tokyo, and specifying nearly all the duo sons. in the standard repertoire as items to be included.

3. This remarkably precocious Romantic (1760–1812!) is placed in his Czech homeland in ssb XVII because he moved around too much to be placed in any one other region. But his own background and experiences were primarily German.

4. Liszt is put in Germany in ssb X not only because he spent so many years there but because he wrote his most important son., Son. in b, during that time.

Vienna, Munich, Leipzig, and Berlin, at the end of the era as at the start. It should be possible here at least to summarize the local circumstances that made these differences in the most active centers of the sonata.[5] A separate list showing the main publishers in most of these centers appears later in this chapter.

The Main City Centers

In **Vienna** the great Classic masters had brought independent instrumental music almost up to a par with opera in popular interest. From Schubert on, the cultivation of serious music became chiefly the province of the middle classes rather than the nobility. The once high-toned Augarten concerts (where Beethoven and Bridgetower had introduced the "Kreutzer Sonata" in 1803), depreciated in quality in the early 19th century below what might be called "the sonata level," [6] and sonatas virtually disappeared from public performances until the mid 1830's. But this genre was furthered in private, largely dilettante groups like the "Schubertiaden" (ssb III) or, later, the circle of performing and other friends around Brahms. The concerts of the Wiener Philharmonische orchestra and the Gesellschaft der Musikfreunde;[7] the outstanding chamber groups, including the Joachim Quartet; the presence of Schubert, Brahms, and Bruckner, among other composers; the fine teaching, from Sechter and Czerny to R. Fuchs;[8] and the residence or visits of nearly every important concert artist of the century[9]—all these contributed to an appropriate atmosphere for the sonata.

The musical life of **Munich** continued to be identified with that of the Bavarian court throughout the Romantic Era, opera being the first interest right through the association of Wagner with King Ludwig II and the opera conducting of Richard Strauss. Almost the sole institution open to public concerts was the Musikalische Akademie der Hofkapelle; but chamber music seems to have flourished only in private.[10] The main training ground was the Königliche Musikschule, founded in 1846, reorganized in 1867 by Bülow, and honored by the

5. The sources of information most utilized here are the city articles in MGG and GROVE, with further references; the articles on chamber organizations indexed country by country in Cobbett/CHAMBER; and the bibliography up to 1947 in Schaal/LOKALGESCHICHTS.

6. Cf. Hanslick/WIEN I 70–75.

7. The extensive (but inadequately cat.) collection in this society's "Archiv" is evidence of more interest in the son. than is generally realized.

8. Cf. MGG XIV 612 (A. Orel).

9. E.g., cf. Hanslick/WIEN I 328–45, II 167–71.

10. Cf. MGG IX 891, 895 (O. Kaul).

influential teaching of Rheinberger (from 1859), L. Thuille, F. Wüllner, and others.

Weimar continued to shine musically in the Romantic Era under the patronage of the Grand Dukes of Saxe-Weimar-Eisenach, as it had shone since before Bach's service there. Among leading onetime residents pertinent to the Romantic sonata were Hummel and Liszt, the latter attracting Bülow, Raff, and Joachim to his circle, each for a short time. But opera was again the reigning interest. Of chief bearing on our topic after Liszt's stay, 1848–61, was the establishment of a music school in 1872 and Richard Strauss's orchestral conductorship as Hofkapellmeister from 1889 to 1894.

Leipzig, whose musical glories also go back before Bach's service, became one of the Romantic sonata's principal centers, partly for the very reason that Leipzig had only rarely placed prime emphasis on opera. More important, it provided some of the sonata's richest if more conservative nourishments, influenced to a considerable degree by veneration of Beethoven's music. Thus, it provided numerous sympathetic publishers (*infra*), topped by Breitkopf & Härtel, which firm traces back to Bach's lifetime. It provided the celebrated Gewandhaus concerts, similarly venerable, and headed successively, between 1835 and 1895, by five important musicians of varying significance in their sonatas, Mendelssohn, F. Hiller, Gade, Rietz, and Reinecke.[11] It provided one of the most widely attended conservatories, founded by Mendelssohn in 1843 and further enhanced by the teaching of Schumann, Moscheles, Hauptmann, Ferdinand David, Reinecke, and others. And it fostered the two leading music periodicals of the time in German, the conservative *Allgemeine musikalische Zeitung* (1798–1848 under Rochlitz, G. W. Fink, and others) and the progressive *Neue Zeitschrift für Musik* (from 1834, under Schumann, Brendel, and others).

The royal court of Saxony was still the main sponsor of music in 19th-century **Dresden,** with opera—especially the German opera introduced by Weber and Wagner—and the state orchestra being the stronger, most continuous currents. But chamber music flowed strongly, too, abetted by fine instrumentalists like Karol Lipiński and Clara Schumann, by composers like Robert Schumann and Volkmann, and by the founding of the Dresden Conservatory in 1856.[12]

Like Leipzig, **Berlin** became one of the Romantic sonata's principal

11. Werner/MENDELSSOHN 311–23 recalls Schumann's statistics on composers performed in Leipzig in 1837–38 (quoted in part near the end of the present chap.) and discusses the content of 8 Leipzig concerts between 1837 and 1841 (not including sons.); cf. Schumann/SCHRIFTEN I 373–80 and 501–11.

12. Cf. MGG III 778–79 (H. Schnoor & K. Laux).

though more conservative centers, again with Beethoven as the catalyst, but this time in spite of the predominance of opera, song, and choral music. The factors conducive to composing and playing sonatas (and other instrumental music) in Berlin were various and the list of participants notable and long.[13] The royal patronage that had provided the 18th-century court of Frederick the Great with the services of Emanuel Bach, Quantz, the Graun brothers, and the Benda brothers (SBE 297–300, SCE 412–40) sponsored only occasional instrumental concerts in the 19th century, sometimes only single pieces as opera entr'actes. In its place, first the dilettantes became the patrons of instrumental music, in their private homes, then the middle classes, in the "garden" or other public concert series and in the halls, large and small, that began to multiply before the mid century. The concerts by a continuous parade of visiting virtuosos included at least twenty by Liszt alone in 1841. Among numerous music schools founded in 19th-century Berlin, three turn up most often in the sonata annals. A Hochschule für Musik that Friedrich Wilhelm IV had wanted Mendelssohn to establish in 1840 did not become a reality until the appointment of Joachim in 1869, with Kiel and Bargiel being two of the teachers most sought after. The Sternsche Konservatorium, founded in 1850, included A. B. Marx, Theodor Kullak, Gernsheim, and Pfitzner on its faculty. And the amalgamated Konservatorium Klindworth-Scharwenka (from 1893) had its beginnings in 1866 in the Klavier-Schule Tausig. Robert Kahn, Hugo Kaun, Wilhelm Berger, and Paul Juon were among other late Romantics in Berlin (Busoni being classified here as a Modern). Berlin also fostered important publishers (e.g., Bote & Bock) and periodicals (e.g., *Berliner Allgemeine Musikzeitung* from 1824, and its successors), though not so important as Leipzig's.

Hamburg was a merchant trading city, yet somewhat apart from the mainstream of European Romantic music.[14] A principal 19th-century dividing line in all its activities was its devastating fire of 1842. Brahms was Hamburg's most distinguished, if belatedly recognized, citizen, by birth and training, and by residence most of his years before he settled in Vienna (1863). Liszt and Joachim were among the most influential visiting performers, again. A Hamburg Konservatorium was founded in 1873, with Karl Grädener among its faculty. Before then an active series of chamber music programs had been instituted by the violinist Karl Rose. Julius Schuberth was a main publisher (from 1826).

Paris and London continued to be two of the most active and, at least in the first half of the century, most cosmopolitan centers of the

13. Cf. MGG I 1714, 1721–27, 1729–33, 1738, 1741 (D. Sasse).
14. Cf. MGG V 1401–10 (K. Stephenson).

sonata. In **Paris** the long established Concert spirituel had been a main musical casualty of the French Revolution, but there was an increasing number of public concert series to take its place in the 19th century, including that, from 1828, of the Conservatoire de Musique, which had been founded during the Revolution, in 1795.[15] Among these series and notwithstanding the major French preoccupation with opera, there were several devoted to chamber music, starting with the establishment of Baillot's quartet in 1814 but dating chiefly from about 1850 and later.[16] The Conservatoire, by virtue of its age and national control, tended to be the most conservative of the music schools. Among musicians variously associated with it who are close to our topic may be named Reicha, Fétis, Berlioz, L. Adam (sce 655–58), Dubois, Widor, Fauré, M. Emmanuel, Dukas, and d'Indy. More liberal were the École Niedermeyer (from 1853; attended by Fauré) and the Schola cantorum (founded by d'Indy and others in 1894). Whereas the first half-century had seen the shorter or longer residences of Steibelt, Kalkbrenner, Liszt, Chopin, Thalberg, and other foreigners in Paris (much as in the later 18th century), the later 19th century saw a growing resistance to foreigners, as in the Société Nationale de Musique (which Saint-Saëns helped to found in 1871) and its offshoots (ssb XIII). This Société, which did much to promote the sonata and other chamber music, aimed first of all at "bringing to light all musical strivings, whatever their form, provided they reveal elevated and truly artistic aspirations in their authors." [17] Among 19th-century French periodicals, the *Revue et gazette musicale de Paris* (rgm) and the later, short runs of *La Musique de chambre* (mdc) and *Le Mercure musical* (mercure) paid considerable attention to the sonata, as did important publishers like Costallat, Hamelle, Rouart-Lerolle, and Durand.

London was the patron of patrons in 19th-century music.[18] Although no front-rank sonata composers can be cited among native Britishers, the sonata activities, like nearly all other musical activities, were at least as rich in that city as in any other. There were the dizzying successions of concert series, each with its particular hall, emphasis, and flavor, yet almost all touching the sonata in some way—the Promenade Concerts, the Popular Concerts, the Ancient Concerts, the so-called King's Concerts, and all the others, which occurred in the mornings,

15. Cf. the convenient lists of Parisian concert series and educational organizations in grove VI 550–52 (various authors); also, II 408–11 (M. L. Pereyra) on the Conservatoire.

16. Cf. grove VI 551 and mgg X 779 (G. Ferchault).

17. Trans. from the French quotation in mgg X 780.

18. "In Germany music is treated as an *art;* in this country [England] it is chiefly looked on as a *business*" (mmr I [1871] 39).

afternoons, or evenings, by subscriptions, for benefits, or according to some other plan, and in the Hanover Square Rooms, Argyle Rooms, St. James Hall, or some other building.[19] There were the many music societies, each with its special goals, its own concert series, and sometimes its own hall—the Society of British Musicians, the Philharmonic Society, the New Philharmonic Society, the Royal Philharmonic Society, the Queen Square Select Society, the People's Concert Society, and so on. There were the music education institutions, headed by British composers we shall be meeting later (ssb XIV), notably the Royal Academy of Music (from 1822) and the Royal College of Music (tracing back to 1873). And there were the numerous active publishers listed later in this chapter, as well as excellent periodicals that include *The Quarterly Musical Magazine and Review* (QUARTERLY), *The Harmonicon* (HARMONICON), *The Musical World* (MUSICAL WORLD), and *The Musical Times* (MT). In the early 19th century the concerts were of the older, variegated type,[20] but, as we have seen (ssb III), the newer, single-purpose type began as soon in London as elsewhere. Moreover, the tastes, originally oriented fully to Baroque and Classic music, became increasingly tolerant, even receptive, to more up-to-date music. As in Paris and Berlin, there was scarcely a major soloist or ensemble group that did not visit London.[21]

Pertinent circumstances may be noted more briefly in other important music centers that, however, contributed less to the sonata. A potential environment for this genre was created by the 19th-century activities of the Toonkunst and the Concertgebouw societies in **Amsterdam,** the Conservatoire royal de Musique and the Société philharmonique in **Brussels,** the Kammermusikforeningen and Royal Danish Conservatory in **Copenhagen,** and the government operated Academy of Music and Conservatory in **Stockholm.** In **Prague,** the Union of Musical Artists dated from 1803 and the Prague Conservatory (where Dvořák served in 1901–4) traced back to 1810. But not until the 1860's, when Germany's domination lessened and Smetana came to the fore, did the musical climate favor the eventual founding of the Czech Philharmonic Orchestra, the Chamber Music Union (from 1876; pro-German), and the Czech Chamber Music Union (from 1894). In **Warsaw** the most pertinent institutions were the Warsaw Conservatory,

19. Cf. the detailed articles on London in GROVE V, especially 368–69, 375–87 (K. Dale & others), and MGG VIII, especially 1158–69 (N. Temperley). As a sample, the weekly schedule, Monday through Saturday, of the Royal Albert Hall Concerts, called, respectively, for a "Ballad," "English," "Classical," "Oratorio," "Wagner," and "Popular" night (MT XVI [1874] 1).

20. For sample programs, without sons., cf. HARMONICON IV/1 (1826) 104–5, 126–30.

21. Cf. MGG VIII 1165 for a list of main visiting soloists.

opened in 1821 (at Elsner's urging) but closed during 1831–61 by the Russians, and the Chopin School, from 1861. In **Budapest** there were the Philharmonic Society, from 1853, the National Conservatory, which traces back to 1836, and the Academy of Music, from 1875 (under Liszt's aegis).

In Russia both private and public concerts go back well before the 19th century, two leading institutions being the Music Academy in **Moscow,** from 1800, and the Philharmonic Society in **Saint Petersburg,** from 1802.[22] Along with nationalistic endeavors (under five successive Czars), the German influences were strong in Russia throughout the century, especially Schumann's and Wagner's. In the United States, where German influences were all-pervasive,[23] one may recall the founding of the Handel & Haydn Society in 1815, the Harvard Musical Association in 1837, the Mendelssohn Quintette Club (for chamber music), in 1849, and a music education curriculum at Harvard University under J. K. Paine in 1861, all in **Boston;** a Euterpean orchestra dating from the 18th century and the Philharmonic Symphony Society in **New York** in 1842; and a Philadelphia Conservatory of Music in **Philadelphia** (from 1877), where numerous private chamber groups were active throughout the century.

The Publishers and Their Policies

No one circumstance helped more to spread the sonata, of course, than its publication, especially when the publisher was enterprising enough to list and advertise it adequately. In conjunction with the city centers just noted, the most active publishers of Classic and Romantic sonatas between 1800 and 1915 may be tabulated by cities, with those listed first that issued the most sonatas.[24] Publishers who moved are listed in both cities, but not their agents in other cities (such as Breitkopf & Härtel, Simrock, Schott, and Ricordi, among other agents in London).

The Most Active Publishers of Sonatas Between 1800 and 1915
Vienna: Artaria, Haslinger, Diabelli, Mechetti, Bureau des Arts et d'Industrie, Mollo, Pennauer, Traeg
Leipzig: Breitkopf & Härtel, Kistner, Peters, Schott, Zimmermann,

22. MGG XI 1154, 1160–68 (K. Laux).
23. A typical season of U.S. programs and performances is described in MT XXV (1884) 91–92.
24. Based on statistics compiled from sons. listed in Cobbett/CHAMBER and Cat. NYPL, and from work lists of the solo and ensemble sons. at the Library of Congress.

Jurgenson, Cranz, Hofmeister, Rieter-Biedermann, Siegel, Kahnt, Rahter, J. Schuberth, Senff

Berlin: Simrock, Bote & Bock, Fürstner

Paris: Durand, Richault, Costellat, Rouart-Lerolle, Schlesinger, Heugel, Eschig, Hamelle, Leduc, Mathot, Senart, Hayet, Lemoine, Durdilly

London: Novello, Augener, Cramer, Joseph Williams, Chappell, Cocks, Curwen, Forsyth, Birchall, Oxford University Press

Other of the most active sonata publishers included André in Offenbach and Frankfurt, F. W. Schuberth in Hamburg, Hansen in Copenhagen, Ricordi in Milan, Urbánek in Prague, Gebethner & Wolff in Warsaw, Rozsavolgyi in Budapest, Jurgenson in Moscow, Schmidt in Boston, G. Schirmer in New York, and Presser in Philadelphia. Although not all of these publishers were in the sonata's main centers, Leipzig, one of those centers, held a clear lead in sonata publications (especially through Breitkopf & Härtel), with Paris and London following next. Neither in Vienna nor Berlin did the publishing of sonatas keep pace with their composition.

The statistics later in this chapter indicate a healthy number of sonatas published throughout the 19th century. Yet, one gets the frequent impression, especially during that alleged slump of the second quarter-century, that publishers generally were loathe to invest in the printing of something so extended, elaborate, and precious or outmoded as a sonata (SSB II). In his letter of 1829 quoted earlier (SSB II), Loewe seemed to be arguing against this kind of resistance on his publisher's part. Most of the publishers' rejections encountered in the present study include a fear of the modern and the unfamiliar, probably explaining André's enigmatic rejection of Weber's set of accompanied sonatas Op. 10 in 1810 for no other reason than that they "are too good!" [25]

Sometimes sonatas were sold in advance on a subcription basis to eliminate the risk for the publisher.[26] Naturally, the publisher saw no risk when the composer's reputation insured success. Coventry and Hollier were only too glad to solicit the six organ sonatas Mendelssohn wrote for them in 1844–45.[27] But, like the Nürnberg publisher J. U. Haffner about a half-century earlier (SCE 71–72, 812), the Swiss pub-

---

25. Nohl/GLUCK & WEBER 102–3; cf. SSB VIII on Weber.

26. Cf. Vogel/SCHUBERT 493–94, explaining why so few of Schubert's sons. had been pub.; MT LIX (1918) 164 (F. Corder), on how the Society of British Composers enabled Dale's 62-p. Son. in d to be pub.

27. Cf. Edwards/MENDELSSOHN 15; SSB VIII.

lisher J. G. Nägeli followed an unusual course when he made up whole anthologies of solo sonatas by both personal and published solicitation. Advertising in August of 1803 after at least six of the seventeen volumes in his first collection (Anth. NÄGELI-m) had appeared, he explained:

> It is known that the most remarkable and consequential epoch of this art form [i.e., keyboard compositions, "sonata form" being specified later] dates from Clementi. My next purpose is therefore this—to bring to light the best works of that composer and those others who align themselves with him in matters both aesthetic and historical, thereby expanding materially the arts of keyboard composition and performance. . . . I have corresponded for a long time with many excellent artists to that purpose . . . the justly important Herr von Beethoven has already sent me important tidings and Herr Abt Vogler permits me to hope of such. . . . I will add all the other keyboard composers to the list when I conquer them with the confidence of knowing the renowned composers have been won.[28]

This first of Nägeli's sonata anthologies by solicitation and commission included not only the Classic names he mentioned but several of our early-Romantics—Cramer, Dussek, Liste, and Steibelt (E. T. A. Hoffmann's several contributions being rejected; SSB VIII). His other, similar but smaller, anthology, *Die musikalische Ehrenpforte* (1827), included sonatas by Ries and Czerny (SSB VII) but not those Nägeli sought in vain from Schubert, Weber, Mendelssohn, Spohr, Hummel, Moscheles, and several others.[29]

Probably Nägeli was not publishing those sonatas simply, in modern parlance, to decorate his catalogue. Yet just that reason for publishing sonatas was given in a prolix review of 1839 by Fink (summarized in SSB II):

> Only the smallest number of new sonatas find a publisher nowadays, and even those that still manage to get published owe their desired appearance in public to a certain generosity on the part of well-known music publishers who want to show to the world that they are in a position to dare to bring out publications that at best will prove not to be advantageous but to be disadvantageous financially; [in short,] they want to prove that they are willing to sacrifice for true art. [Etc.] [30]

28. Trans. from AMZ V (1802–3) Intelligenz-Blatt 97–100; cf. SCE 26 for the continuation of this extract with some curious stipulations regarding the solicited sons. Periodic progress reports also appeared throughout 1803 and 1804 in *Zeitung für die elegante Welt* and *Wiener Zeitung*.

29. Cf. Deutsch/SCHUBERT-D 541; also, MOSCHELES I 120, in which Charlotte Moscheles writes her husband in 1826: ". . . old Nägeli, of Zurich, asks you to compose a Sonata for his periodical, but you are to avoid all repeating notes, all tenths, and all the usual signs used to indicate the expression."

30. Trans. from AMZ XLI (1839) 181–84.

Fink concluded by noting how few copies were sold when a sonata did get published. It must have been a rare edition that reached the 1,150 copies made when Lamborn Cock issued W. S. Bennett's Sonata in A♭, Op. 16, *The Maid of Orleans* (reissued only 3 years later by Kistner of Leipzig).[31]

With further regard to the publication of Romantic sonatas, reviewers helped to maintain or raise the quality of the edition itself by almost always ending their longer pieces with some comment on the format, the engraving, its accuracy, the quality of paper, and perhaps the cost. Thus, Rochlitz ended with unfavorable comments on these aspects after a favorable review of two of Weber's piano sonatas, in 1818.[32] In that same letter of 1829 by Loewe to his publisher (SSB II), cited several times already, the composer said he would welcome a new cover for his sonatas, "provided I [myself] don't find it superficial or even unacceptable." But he doubted the need for "a special title or the issuing of single movements from sonatas in order to provide a market for them."

Intriguing covers and special titles, original or acquired, did indeed help to make a sonata better known and, even, more popular, sometimes distinguishing it undeservedly from its fellows. They have always helped in this way, as with Purcell's "Golden Sonata," or Tartini's "Devil's Trill," or Clementi's "Didone abbandonata." But they helped especially in the programmatically minded Romantic Era, even when there was no more of a "programme" than the title itself, as in Beethoven's "Moonlight Sonata," Moscheles' "Sonata mélancolique," or Medtner's "Sonate orageuse." [33] Of course, no programmatic title was involved, but rather a question of current taste, when, according to Schumann, Schubert (too hopefully) foresaw better publication prospects for his so-called "Grand Duo," D. 812, by entitling it "Sonata" instead of "Symphony" on the autograph.[34]

The publication of separate sonata movements came up earlier in connection with the programming of separate movements in recitals (SSB III). Such publications occurred often. For example, each of the four movements of Spohr's Op. 125 appeared separately[35] as did those

31. Cf. Bennett/BENNETT 442. In 1882, 1,000 was given as the number of copies in a choral ed. (MT XXIII [1882] 117). No study of 19th-c. son. eds. is known here comparable to the new study by K. Hortschansky for the 18th century, in AM XL (1968) 154–74.

32. AMZ XX (1818) 687–88.

33. Recall that the validity of such titles was questioned by contemporary reviewers (SSB II). Cf., also, the review in MMR III (1873) 104–5 of W. S. Bennett's, *The Maid of Orleans,* Op. 46.

34. Schumann/SCHRIFTEN I 329–30.

35. PAZDÍREK XIII 915.

of M. Labey's Sonata "en 4 parties" (ssb XIII) and S. N. Penfield's *Poem of Life*, subtitled *Four Characteristic Pieces in the Form of a Sonata* (ssb XIX). The Spohr and Labey sonatas were each published in their entirety, too. But in most instances of separate publications only one movement from a sonata was so treated, as with the favorite movements of British organ sonatas by E. Silas and W. T. Best (ssb XIV).[36] A reviewer even asked in 1875, now that a performer was no longer "mad" if he played a whole sonata at one sitting, why was it not possible to publish the whole of a "Sonata No. 1" for P solo by one E. A. Sydenham instead of merely its "Andante"? [37]

The use of opus numbers continued to be as erratic for Cramer, Dussek, and Schubert as it had been for Haydn, Mozart, and Clementi, typically with each publisher starting his own sequence, sometimes a separate sequence for each category of a composer's works (cf. sce 78–79). But after the reasonably satisfactory sequence of Beethoven's opus numbers and the apparently meticulous sequence of Czerny's 861 opus numbers (in the approximately two-thirds of his published works to which op. nos. were assigned! ssb VII), composers seem to have paid more attention to this organizational aspect of their output and taken more control of it. Ries (ssb VII) and Czerny were among those composers who assigned further, separate sequences of numbers to their sonatas,[38] thus not only confirming the chronological orders but indicating which out of a still larger number of sonatas by them they themselves regarded as important enough to go into these specially numbered lists. One effect of the composer's assigning his own opus numbers was to include MS sonatas in the sequence—an effect evident especially in the designations of many a late-Romantic's sonatas that got only partially into print (e.g., those of C. V. Stanford). The publication of sonatas in sets under single opus numbers largely disappeared in the Romantic Era except for the diminutive pedagogic types and the shorter examples of a prolific composer like Raff (ssb X) or Reger (ssb XI). Most of the serious Romantic sonatas—for instance, Schumann's or Chopin's—were too long and too individual to be levelled in this manner. Toward the end of the era some composers began to discard opus numbers entirely, as did Strauss, in his later years, and Dukas.

The accompanied sonatas of the early Romantic Era such as Dussek, Cramer, and Ries still wrote, continued to be published in separate

36. For an extreme example, cf. the long list of separate eds. of the finale from Weber's Op. 24 ("Perpetuum mobile"), in pazdírek XV 182–83.

37. mt XVII (1875) 245.

38. Cf. Czerny's letter of 1823 to C. F. Peters as quoted in ssb VII.

parts for the keyboard and for the violin or other accompanying instrument. At most, a more soloistic passage in the "accompaniment" might be cued into the piano part (as in the finale of Ries's Op. 76/1). As this kind of ensemble became more of a true duo (SSB V), the pianist's score began to include the other part in full.

Plagiarism seems to have been much less of a problem in the Romantic than in the Baroque and Classic sonata (cf. SBE 44–45 and SCE 75–76). It may have been discouraged not only by the steps taken toward better protection of creative property, including the gradually firmer and more specific U.S. provisions after the first copyright law was enacted in 1831 (SSB XIX), but by the greater emphasis on artistic individuality, originality, and self-identity that was characteristic of all Romantic art (SSB II). When the plagiarism of a sonata did occur it was less likely to be a direct steal [39] than one of the countless arrangements that were constantly being made of the most successful sonata movements, especially in the first half-century, whether for P-duet, 2 Ps, various other ensembles, large or small, or full orchestra. As but one example, Chopin's "Marche funèbre," composed in 1837 and incorporated in 1839 as the third movement of Op. 35, was arranged once or more for P & organ, harmonium, mandolin or Vn, zither, 2 Ps, harmonium & Vn-or-Vc, mandolin & P, Vn & P, Vn-or-Fl & P, P & Vc, Fl & P, 2 Vns, Fl & Vn, cornet & P, harmonium & P & Vn, and many more combinations up to full orchestra.[40]

Some Quantitative Aspects of Publication

Like the sociological approach to sonata history (SSB III) and closely related to it, the quantitative approach remains one of the most promising facets awaiting further investigation. As any trained researcher knows only too well, the statistics of quantity can be not only colorless but risky, as when they are not representative enough or are interpreted either too stiffly or too loosely. Yet, without them as one foundation, it is impossible to make safe generalizations about distributions, proportions, or trends. Thus, in our discussion earlier of the content of programs in which sonatas figured (SSB III), statistics were available for only one aspect—the sonata in England in the first

39. Brahms presumably was joking when he asked Simrock whether a theme in his "Regenlied" Sonata, Op. 78, could be regarded as a plagiarism of his song by that name, pub. by Rieter-Biedermann (BRAHMS BRIEFWECHSEL XVI 218; SSB IX).

40. PAZDÍREK III 291–92. PAZDÍREK is the most convenient and one of the most thorough listings of these arrangements, which represent a broad tangential extension of the Romantic son. that can get no more than passing mentions here except as scoring variants (SSB V).

half-century; but these provided the firmest basis we have thus far for any generalizations that could be made about the types of sonatas preferred in programs. In the present chapter statistics have already helped to illustrate the geographical spread of the Romantic sonata composers and in the remainder they will give some idea both of the quantity of published sonatas by those composers and of their quantitative relationship to other categories of Romantic music. Furthermore, quantitative statistics will be offered in Chapter V regarding the most popular settings of the Romantic sonata, and in Chapter VI regarding some of their most prevalent style and structural traits.

These statistical applications should at least suggest a few of the many further and more thorough applications that await the necessary investigations. For example, it would illuminate the topics in all four chapters (ssb III–VII on use, spread, scoring, and form) to find a better basis than chance observation for rating the sonata composers according to the contemporary popularity of their sonatas. If the proof of that popularity lies mainly in the number of sales and performances, then some sort of statistical formula would have to be worked out that might add, say, the sizes of the editions of the composer's published sonatas to the number of reprints, the number of arrangements, the number and extent (if not the consensus) of the reviews, and the number of performances, all divided by the number of the composer's published sonatas. In this way, Franck, with one sonata, would not necessarily be rated below Rheinberger, with twenty-nine sonatas. The main sources for such an investigation would be, once more, those essential bibliographic tools—the chief periodicals, plus HOFMEISTER, plus PAZDÍREK. If these tools have any main shortcoming it is their understandably strong German orientation.[41]

Unfortunately, there was nothing in the 19th century quite like our present-day *Schwann Long-Playing Record Catalog* to reflect public tastes and preferences; or, on a more systematic basis, like the periodic polls taken by the Stanford University psychologist Paul R. Farnsworth, which most recently (1964) rated Brahms, Schubert, Chopin, Schumann, R. Strauss, Mendelssohn, Tchaikovsky, and Liszt in that order of "eminence" (picking out here only Romantics who contributed consequentially to the son. out of the first 28 of 103 composers of all time rated by 853 members of the American Musicological Society).[42]

41. In MT XXIV (1883) 295–303, "The Music Publishers' Association's Catalogue" apparently was the first of its kind in England.
42. The findings of the poll were circulated by mail in 1965. Cf. Farnsworth/ TASTE 39–47, 68–80. In Fuchs/CRITIQUE, 50,000 (!) compositions and their 2,576 composers are rated as to quality (and difficulty of the music), with Schubert the only Romantic in the first class (after Bach, Beethoven, Handel, and Mozart).

At most, 19th-century writers seem to have left only brief tabulations that throw light on musical taste or popularity, and none of these found here happens to focus on the sonata. At least pertinent, however, are Schumann's counts of composers performed at the Gewandhaus and other concerts in Leipzig during the winter of 1837–38 (in the first of 2 articles on music in Leipzig during that and the next winter).[43] He found 17 performances of works by Mozart, 15 by Beethoven, 7 by Weber, 5 by Haydn, 3–5 each by Cherubini, Spohr, Mendelssohn (who was then conducting the Gewandhaus Orchestra), and Rossini, 2 each by Handel, Bach, Vogler, Cimarosa, Méhul, Onslow, and Moscheles, and one each by several others.

As to some rough idea of how many sonatas the Romantics wrote, we can start with the total of their published sonatas listed in the cumulative volumes of HOFMEISTER from 1828 (Whistling's cumulative list going back to at least 1800) to 1913, which in round numbers is about 7,475.[44] The rounding out of the numbers is necessary, at best, because it is not always possible to tell sonatas by the Romantics from those by the Classics (the latter being about twice as many in the same vols.), or reprints from first editions, or arrangements from original scorings, or one method of listing from another. Moreover, although HOFMEISTER has usually covered publications in Austro-Germany quite thoroughly, it has varied greatly in its coverage of those in other countries. Thus, probably most of at least 190 sonatas by British composers known to have been published between 1801 and 1850 [45] can be found in the early volumes of HOFMEISTER. But more and more publications outside of Germany cannot be found in the later volumes as the rising spirit of nationalism and the sheer bulk of the publications limited the coverage increasingly to Austro-Germany. An educated guess might then bring the total of published sonatas in the Romantic Era up to about 10,000, or the grand total of sonatas composed during that time to as many as 30,000, since in the experience of the present study, at least twice as many sonatas remained in MS. This conjecture of 30,000 sonatas is like the total of more than 625 composers noted in the present volume in being not less, as might be supposed on first thought, but well over a third higher than the corresponding figures for the Classic Era (sce 68 and 8). One can only assume, again (ssb I),

---

43. Schumann/SCHRIFTEN I 373–80, 501–11 (less specific, but with similar conclusions). Cf. Werner/MENDELSSOHN 311–12.

44. The dates of each cumulative vol. up to 1897 and the total no. of its son. listings may be seen in our next tabulation (infra).

45. Temperley/CORRESPONDENCE. Cf. their analysis by decades and scoring types in ssb V.

that larger populations, more countries, and more participation by the middle classes largely account for the differences.

In connection with quantities, the alleged slump in sonata output during the second quarter-century gets some support from HOFMEISTER, though less than is suggested by the following breakdown for most of the 19th century:

The Number of Sonatas Listed in the Cumulative Volumes of HOFMEISTER *during the 19th Century*

Inclusive years	Number of sonatas (rounded to nearest 5)
(*ca.* 1800–)1828 (Whistling)	1,800
1829–33	130
1834–38	145
(*ca.* 1815–)43	1,886
1844–51	170
1852–59	285
1860–67	320
1868–73	310
1874–79	435
1880–85	390
1886–91	365
1892–97	260

The two large numbers actually represent much larger cumulations than the other figures, the first from at least 1800 (including HOF-MEISTER 1815 [Whistling]), the second from at least 1815 (meaning a considerable overlap). In any case, the spans of lowest output, 1829–33 and 1834–38, are hardly late enough nor the numbers of sonatas for those years small enough to bear out a statement by Kretzschmar in 1910 that in 1850 only three sonatas were published! [46] The larger figures in the second half-century represent, apart from longer cumulations, the rise of interest in the sonata especially around 1870. This rise actually lasted longer than it appears to, since allowance has to be made for that increasing tendency to exclude non-German publishers in HOFMEISTER.

Our last quantitative tabulation here gives some hint of the sonata's relative cultivation among all categories of 19th-century music, although mainly only through the critical period of the slump and, again, only insofar as this information can be culled from and is

46. Kretzschmar/AUFSÄTZE I 163.

representative in the publications listed in HOFMEISTER. This time the numbers are only systematic estimates translated into percentages of the total publications rather than exact counts rounded out. Furthermore, they include all publications between about 1800 and 1851, Classic or earlier as well as Romantic, plus a late-Romantic span, 1904–8, for comparison. The heading "Other categories," by far the most numerous, covers from 20 to 25 types of settings, including miscellaneous instrumental combinations, church music, other vocal music, and arrangements. The first and fourth totals are much the largest again, for the reasons given above. Even though they are only rough estimates, these percentages give a better idea of the sonata's

Percentages of Sonatas and Other Categories in
HOFMEISTER *up to 1908*

Categories	Percentages					
	(*ca.* 1800–)1828	1829–33	1834–38	(*ca.* 1815–)43	1844–51	1904–8
Orchestra: symphonies, overtures, marches, fantasias	1.5	1.5	1.0	1.5	1.0	6.5
Orchestra & voice: operas & extracts, other nonchurch music	2.5	1.0	1.5	1.5	.05	4.0
Piano solo: rondos, variations, fantasias, dances	21.0	32.0	27.0	25.0	29.0	8.5
Chamber music for 3 or more instruments	10.0	8.5	5.0	7.0	8.0	8.5
Other categories (see text)	56.5	55.5	64.0	61.0	57.0	68.5
SONATAS	8.5	1.5	1.5	4.0	4.5	4.0
TOTAL LISTINGS (= 100%)	44,000	8,900	9,500	55,000	19,510	26,000

relative slump in the second quarter-century than the absolute figures in the previous tabulation. Moreover, they relate the sonata to other categories and its slump to other trends. They indicate that the slump was well on the way toward ending by the early 1840's. At the same time they show, to a lesser degree, a corresponding slump and restoration in chamber music, and, in an approximate way, a compensatory rise and decline in light piano music, a fact noted by nearly all those who commented on the sonata's slump during its occurrence. However, a strong word of caution is needed when this last tabulation is used to relate the sonata to categories more remote from it. The sonata has always been one of the easier genres to print because so few instruments have been involved. Naturally, the larger the ensemble the costlier is the publication, the fewer are its public sales, and the more are the compositions that remain in MS. Opera, for example, must be vastly underrated in its popularity by this tabulation. But not until there are catalogues that list the 19th-century holdings of the largest libraries, both MSS and publications, will it be possible to do any more than guess at such a rating. All that can be added here beyond the guesses is the estimate that by the 1850's the sonata returned to only about half of the relative position it had held among all music publications early in the century, during the overlap with the late-Classic Era. From the 1850's to the end of the Romantic Era, the sonata appears to have accounted for not quite a twentieth of all music publications.

Chapter V

Instruments, Settings, and Performance Practices

The Piano as the Voice of Romanticism

The alternative of piano-or-harpsichord that prevailed in the high-Classic Era (SCE 84–89) ended with the piano's full victory around the turn of the century. From then on, as Einstein has emphasized so tellingly, the "pianoforte" became the focal instrument of musical Romanticism. It provided the most direct and universal answer to the Romantic penchant for "sheer sound" as an aesthetic fact in itself— for the mystical depths and highs of new sonorities, for a mysterious "withdrawal" from the specific "word" of a text into the greater but more occult truth of "wordless music." [1] Cortot has seen the new intimacy and techniques of the piano as opening the way to the Romantic sonata after Beethoven.[2] A eulogy on the piano credited to Liszt in 1837 amplifies its values in ways that he must have endorsed even if he was not the actual author:

My piano is to me what his boat is to the seaman, what his horse is to the Arab: nay, more, it has been till now my eye, my speech, my life. Its strings have vibrated under my passions, and its yielding keys have obeyed my every caprice. Perhaps the secret tie which holds me so closely to it is a delusion; but I hold the piano very high. In my view it takes the first place in the hierarchy of instruments; it is the oftenest used and the widest spread. . . . In the circumference of its seven octaves it embraces the whole circumference of an orchestra; and a man's ten fingers are enough to render the harmonies which in an orchestra are only brought out by the combination of hundreds of musicians. . . . We can give broken chords like the harp, long sustained tones like the wind, staccati and a thousand passages which before it seemed only possible to produce on this or that instrument. . . . The piano has on the one side the capacity of assimilation; the capacity of taking into itself the

1. Cf. Einstein/ROMANTIC 6–8, 33–35, 198–200.
2. Cortot/INTERPRÉTATION 140–41.

life of all (instruments); on the other it has its own life, its own growth, its individual development. . . . It is a microcosm, a micro-theus. . . .[3]

In less mystical terms, the piano became the most useful, the most versatile, the most characteristic of all instruments. It could sing, as Schubert rejoiced to discover,[4] and almost as the clavichord had sung for Emanuel Bach (SCE 428). It could be infinitely poetic, as Schumann reveals in his oft-quoted description in 1834 of Chopin playing his "Aeolian Harp Étude."[5] And it could be brilliant, stentorian, daemonic, overpowering, as the many descriptions of Liszt's playing make abundantly clear.[6] It became by all odds the favorite solo instrument in recitals, the indispensable instrument in most chamber music, and the standard instrument in the home. Indeed, as E.-L. F. Fétis (son of François-Joseph) observed in 1847, the piano's popularity, especially in Paris, was making the violin, flute, cello, harp, and other instruments obsolete, as well as "large amounts of music . . .—overtures and entire opera scores—arranged for two flutes, [or] two violins, [or] two guitars, [or] two flageolets."[7] There was not even a mention of the cello part when "Moscheles himself plays Beethoven's" Sonata in D, Op. 102/1, nor either the cellist or violinist when "Madame Schumann played" trios by Moscheles and Mendelssohn.[8]

The first half of the 19th century saw most of the basic improvements in pianos as we know them today.[9] The range was gradually increased to seven octaves and more; heavier, tenser strings were introduced to provide fuller tones that lasted longer and carried better; metal braces were added to resist both the greater tension of more and heavier strings and the effect of changing temperature and humidity on the strings and wood frame; and these braces were then united in a single cast-iron frame. At the same time the strings were fixed better through improved bridging; the principle of cross- or over-stringing was introduced as a means of freeing the strings from their metallic environment and improving the resonance of the sounding board, which was

3. As trans. from RGM for 1837, in Bie/PIANOFORTE 281–82. On the doubtful authorship cf. SSB X on Liszt. Cf., also, Thalberg's statement on the social value of the piano, as trans. in Rimbault/PIANOFORTE 159–61.
    4. Deutsch/SCHUBERT-D 436.
    5. Schumann/SCHRIFTEN I 234–35.
    6. Cf. Loesser/PIANOS 365–71; Schonberg/PIANISTS 151–71.
    7. As introduced and trans. in Loesser/PIANOS 413.
    8. MOSCHELES II 45 and 78.
    9. Cf. GROVE VI 733–44 and 606–7 (A. J. Hipkins & R. E. M. Harding), with further bibliography; also, Rimbault/PIANOFORTE 148–59 (interesting especially as a pioneer account). Further, cf. Loesser/PIANOS 301–4, 397–411, 458–65, 509–15, 518–36, 549–60, 566–74, 586–613, with much new information; Bie/PIANOFORTE 309–16.

itself improved; the hammers were covered better and more heavily, with specially prepared felt; the action was enlivened, particularly by the repetition device in the double-escapement; and both the soft or shifting pedal and the damper pedal were perfected.[10] Square and upright pianos in the home underwent similar improvements. There was also considerable experimentation, notably Paul von Janko's promising but unsuccessful redesign of the piano keyboard, in 1882–84, in favor of greater facility and stretches.[11] Broadwood, Érard, Clementi, Pleyel, Stodart, Bösendorfer, Chickering, Steinway, and Bechstein (in that approximate order) were among the leaders in the development and manufacture of pianos. The Bechstein piano was first played in recital by Bülow, in January, 1857, in Berlin, on which occasion Bülow also introduced Liszt's Sonata in b to the public.[12]

In the vanguard among proponents of these piano improvements were the composers, performers, and appreciators, themselves. Thus, right at the start of the era, Dussek, as one of his striking, prescient Romanticisms (ssb XVII), took a special interest in the piano's development. From 1793 on, he repeatedly persuaded Broadwood to extend the range of his pianos (up to 6 octaves) and in his sonata titles and scores he repeatedly specified "additional keys"; he indicated the use of the pedal for particular effects as early as 1799 and often thereafter in his sonatas; he achieved extraordinary success when he played Érard's first piano with the new repetition action in Paris in 1808; and he continued to struggle courageously with inadequate instruments up to his death in 1812.[13] In the last regard, a reviewer ended a favorable report in 1813 of a Sonata Op. 27 by Friedrich Schneider with this typical reminder:

> That the work demands a well-rehearsed, solid player has already been indicated. But it also demands an effective instrument, capable of many graduations from delicate to robust, as well as expressive legato.[14]

Hummel preferred the light, clean, yet solid touch of the Streicher-Graf piano made in Vienna, for his concert playing.[15] Moscheles was another early Romantic who took a keen and continuing interest in the piano's development. In the 1820's and 1830's he preferred the lightness of touch, clarity of tone, and "more supple mechanism for my repeating notes, skips, and full chords" on the Clementi piano as

10. Cf. the pedal instruction under the first Schumann ex. in ssb VIII.
11. Cf. Loesser/PIANOS 566–69.
12. Raabe/LISZT II 250.
13. Cf. ssb XVII; Craw/DUSSEK 53–54, 75, 171, 175, 468–71.
14. AMZ XV (1813) 178–79 (Rochlitz).
15. Egert/FRÜHROMANTIKER 10–11. Cf. Hummel/ANWEISUNG 426–28.

against the heavier touch, yet fuller, more resonant tone of the Broadwood. The Érard's repetition also appealed to him, but not its tone at first.[16] Chopin seems to have been satisfied with the piano as he found it, regarding the still delicate, wood-frame Pleyel as "perfection," and always preferring it to the Érard (which Thalberg and Liszt used) or the Broadwood.[17]

The Organ as the Voice of the Church

In sonata history the organ has followed a rather well-defined, somewhat independent course of its own, partly because of the nature of the instrument and partly because of its primary dedication to church service (cf. SBE 36, 56–57; SCE 89–91). During the 19th century, the organ, like the piano, went through its own epochal "improvements," although not without sacrificing the ensemble of the former, "classic" organ.[18] Mainly it increased in size, power, complexity, and expressive range. Fundamental were the developments of a pneumatically assisted action, by the early 1840's, and of the application of electric power, within the next generation. Electro-pneumatic action was perfected by the turn of this century. In the words of Willi Apel,

Organists [inclined toward these "improvements"] naturally boast of, and revel in, that multiplicity of devices: couplers, swells, pistons, crescendo pedal, combination pedals, etc., which, in connection with overpowering or sentimental stops (Trumpet, Stentorphone, Tuba mirabilis, Vox angelica, Unda maris, Tremulant), enable them to pass instantly from the softest whisper to a roar far surpassing the *fff*-effects of the biggest orchestra, to imitate all conceivable colors of the orchestra, and to produce a great variety of sensational effects.[19]

The mid- to late-Romantic Era contributed more to the organ sonata than the Classic Era, with Mendelssohn's *Six Grand Sonatas for the Organ*, Op. 65 (1844–45) at the start and the peak, and further successful examples by Merkel, Reubke, A. G. Ritter, Rheinberger, Reger, Karg-Elert (who also wrote sons. for his version of the harmonium; SSB XI), Widor, Vierne, Guilmant, Lemmens, and still others.[20] The organ sonata usually differed from the piano sonata, when it was not

16. MOSCHELES I 65, 106–7, 109, 111, 219, 245–47; II 15, 29, 168 (on a piano with octave coupler), 230–32.
17. Cf. Sydow & Hedley/CHOPIN 101, 305, 315, 317; CONGRESS CHOPIN 456 (J. Urbański).
18. Cf. GROVE VI 303–18 (R. Whitworth).
19. Apel/DICTIONARY 532.
20. Kremer/ORGAN includes a full bibliography of organ sonatas since 1845.

simply an arrangement of the latter (*infra*), in its greater solemnity, often being adapted to or even designated for church use (ssb III); in its frequent use of chorales, variations, fantasias, and fugal or related contrapuntal movements; in its somewhat more conservative idioms; and, of course, in its exploitation of the most widely divergent orchestral colors.[21] In 1849 a reviewer, though recognizing the piano sonata's greater definition since Mozart and Beethoven, found identifiable traits in the organ sonata, too. He found the extremes of its best styles in the logical, serious Sonata in d, Op. 11, by A. G. Ritter (ssb X), but not in the sentimental disorganized *Phantasie-Sonate*, Op. 83, by A. Hesse (ssb XVII).[22]

In 1871, while defending church organists' salaries as the equal of piano teachers', an English churchman derided the "average Organist of the provinces" who plays pieces "of the light, unorganlike character" and who "is fond of [appropriating] movements from the piano sonatas, and always the most unsuitable of these unsuitables." To which, one of those provincial organists rejoined, "I only get 7s. 6d. for giving a lesson on one of Beethoven's Sonatas; therefore I am amply paid if I play that same sonata to the public for 7s. 6d!" [23] Occasionally one finds piano sonatas that sound as though they should have been scored for organ and designated for church use in the first place, such as Lekeu's Sonata in g, with two fugues and three free movements (ssb XIII). Reger is known to have endorsed an article of 1899 by Riemann urging that the tendency toward archaic, salon lyricism and the adaptation of the "old" piano sonata in the organ sonatas from Mendelssohn to Rheinberger be abandoned for the variations, fugues, chorales, and fantasias, and a genuine return to the "Bachian spirit." [24]

Other Instruments of the Romantic Sonata

Unlike the keyboard instruments, the violin, viola, and cello had attained nearly their full developments before the Romantic Era (sbe 54, sce 91–92) and underwent no such epochal changes in the 19th century. There were no advances in instrument construction beyond the perfection of the Tourte bow. And even the extreme virtuosity introduced by Paganini in his violin sonatas (and other Vn music)

21. Cf. Frotscher/ORGELSPIEL II 1150–51, 1164–65, 1204–11 (distinguishing between fantasy, motto [or programmatically associative], and chorale sonatas); also, the ex. by D. Buck in ssb XIX.
22. nzm XXX (1849) 185–86, with exx. (G. Siebeck).
23. mt XV (1871) 283 and 315.
24. Barker/REGER 170. Cf., also, zimg III (1901–2) 337–38 (chiefly on Mendelssohn).

did not surpass that in the Baroque Era, from Biber's to Locatelli's sonatas, as much as might be supposed (cf. SBE 146–47). There was important new literature for all three instruments, of course.[25] It includes, for example, the sonatas for Va & P by J. N. Hummel, Onslow (as alternatives to Vc & P), Rubinstein, Brahms (as alternatives to Cl & P), Bowen, and Dale; and those for Vc & P by Mendelssohn, Chopin, Brahms, Gernsheim, Kiel, Lalo, Grädener, Saint-Saëns, Hiller, Rubinstein, F. Hummel, Moór, Draeseke, Reger, Nicodé, Kahn, Rachmaninoff, Juon, Vierne, Holbrooke, and Fauré. The sonatas for Vn and P were far too numerous to summarize in any similar manner except for the observation that so few of them—chiefly those by Schumann, Brahms, Franck, Fauré, and Strauss—survive as first-class masterpieces still played today.[26] There was an occasional new stringed instrument, too—notably, H. Ritter's large, more sonorous but somewhat unmanageable "viola alta," [27] used (not in its 5-string extension) in two sonatas by Draeseke (SSB X).

The Spanish guitar and its ancestors had been the vehicle of a special branch of the sonata ever since the sonata's origins (cf. SBE 18, 65–66; SCE 92–93). It still survived as such in the early, though not the later, 19th century. Sor, Giuliani, Spohr, Paganini, and Nava were among its chief exponents, both as performers and sonata composers.[28] Spohr also left harp sonatas.

The wind instruments underwent significant changes and experiments in the 19th century with respect to materials, size and range, bore, placing of holes, and perfection of the mechanical keys. Only the clarinet and flute were used to any appreciable extent in sonatas, and relatively little at that.[29] Thus, among composers of sonatas for Cl & P, chiefly in the mid- and late-Romantic Era, might be named Brahms, Draeseke, Rheinberger (as an alternative to Vn & P; SSB X, with ex.), Jenner, Reger, Stanford (SSB XIV, with ex.), and Saint-Saëns (SSB XIII, with ex. and with mentions of almost the only noteworthy examples for Ob & P and for Bn & P). Composers of sonatas for Fl & P include Kuhlau (SSB XV, with ex.), Barnett, G. A. Macfarren, Reinecke, and Widor. Both F. Hummel and Rheinberger left sonatas for Hn & P, and Nisle for P & "cor de chasse." Under wind instruments may also be

25. Cf. Cobbett/CHAMBER II 536–53.
26. Eligible for more consideration from the later Romantic Era are sons. by R. Fuchs, Reger, Kahn, Rheinberger, Gernsheim, Saint-Saëns, and Witkowski (all discussed in SSB).
27. Cf. MGG XIII 1687–88 (A. Berner).
28. Cf. SCE 663–64 and 569–70; SSB VIII and XVI, respectively.
29. Cf. Cobbett/CHAMBER I 65, 280, 401–3, 572, and II 194; the separate listings for each instrument with P in Altmann/KAMMERMUSIK; also, Tuthill/CLARINET.

noted the "sonatas" for voice & P by Spohr (with text) and Medtner (on vowels only).[30]

Settings, Favorite and Less Favorite

To explore the Romantic settings of the sonata we need to start with some idea of what the settings were and which were most used. A tabulation follows that analyzes, by settings and in order of preference, the quantitative statistics derived from HOFMEISTER, in the penultimate tabulation of the previous chapter. Although exact figures, not rounded off, are given this time, they must still be regarded only as rough approximations. Those same variables, uncertainties, and possible contradictions or overlaps again stand in the way of greater precision. Recall, also, that the HOFMEISTER volumes terminating in 1828 and 1843 represent much larger, overlapping cumulations—at least a quarter-century each—than the other volumes. The headings for P-duet and 2Ps include one example each with string accompaniment. The "trios" of the earlier decades are included not only because the title "sonata" admits them in our semantic approach (SSB I) but because the genesis of the piano trio lay so clearly in the accompanied sonata. Most of these "trios" are not broken down by setting in HOFMEISTER but may be assumed, in fact, to consist largely of "sonatas" for $P \pm Vn \pm Vc$, the few others being for P with Vn & Hn, or Va & Vc, or Fl & Vn (several), or Fl & Va, or Fl & Vc (several). Also, HOFMEISTER does not distinguish between accompanied piano sonatas and true duos in the listings for P & Vn, again a problem only for the earlier decades.

The tabulation of settings happens to give us another view of the second-quarter-century slump in sonata output (SSB II and IV), once more suggesting that its significance and extent were exaggerated by contemporaries. The conspicuous absence of any 19th-century organ sonatas prior to Mendelssohn's in 1844–45 does not mean any special drop in organ publications then (preludes, fugues, chorale arrangements, etc.), but rather no inclination to adapt the sonata idea to organ use until a relative universalist like Mendelssohn set the example.[31] Above all, the tabulation brings out the strong preference for the solo piano setting in the 19th century, nearly twice (41% as against 21%) what

30. For further exx., cf. T. Kewitsch in SSB XI (on 3 poems for 3 mvts.) and C. Fowler in MT XXVII (1886) 109 (for voice, P, & Vn).

31. HOFMEISTER (ca. 1815–)43, p. 325 does list organ sons. by one Möller and by "Gio. Morandi," but if these men are the same that are mentioned in Frotscher/ORGELSPIEL 1080 and 799–800, respectively, their sons. probably were too early for our tabulation.

The 19th-Century Sonata Settings, in Order of Preference, in the Cumulative Volumes of HOFMEISTER

Settings	(ca. 1800–)1828	1829–33	1834–38	(ca. 1815–)43	1844–51	1852–59	1860–67	1868–73	1874–79	1880–85	1886–91	1892–97	Totals/%
P solo	701	83	75	777	71	138	114	167	180	151	115	62	2,634/41
P & Vn	381	16	25	333	33	53	71	58	107	79	112	108	1,376/21
P-duet	149	13	27	202	39	51	71	44	35	40	7	8	686/11
P & Fl	155	5	9	157	3		8		2	13	13		365/6
P & Vc	23	5	6	41	10	16	17	20	57	52	37	38	322/5
Trios	154		1	139									294/5
Organ solo				49	10	16	25	17	13	27	36	23	167/3
Duos, mixed, without P	51	2		72	3	2	2	1	12		1		115/2
Duos, unmixed, without P	3			13			3		16	3	7	1	113/2
Harp solo	54	1		4	1		1	1	2	1	27	7	75/1
2 Ps	4			31			1						42/1
Guitar solo	9			17			1						41/
Guitar & Vn	24	1		11				1					41/
Harp & Vn	29	4		9		3	2		4	3	3	2	41/
Vn solo	9			4		4	2		4	4	2	7	40/
P & Va	4			10			1			3	3	1	31/
Other duos, with P	11	1	1	5			4		2	3	1	2	30/
P & Cl	4			9						7			25/
Guitar duos	9			3									18/
Fl solo	10												13/
Cl solo	9												9/
Vc solo	6									5			6/
Zither solo													5/
TOTALS	1,799	130	145	1,886	170	283	322	309	434	388	364	259	6,489/100

(←------ less than one per cent ------→)

is indicated for the next most numerous setting, P & Vn. However, it is interesting to note the latter catching up near the end of the era, a trend that tallies with the output we shall be observing especially in Germany, France, and England (ssb XI, XIII, and XIV).[32] The sonata for Vc & P showed an almost equally healthy rise. It is interesting to notice, too, how much more appeal the sonata for P-duet had for composers (and performers) than that for 2 Ps, this time a trend that every present-day, two-piano team in search of original literature must have lamented. Of course, the problem of having two approximately equal pianos at hand has always been a practical deterrent. The virtual disappearance of the guitar sonata has already been mentioned.

It is possible to add one further, shorter tabulation, of some 340 19th-century sonata settings in order of preference, limited in this instance to those supposedly dating from 1801 to 1850 by composers in England from their infancy (or later if Irish).[33] Parentheses are used to indicate additional, unpublished settings. The "uncertain" settings, which cannot be ascribed to a particular decade, even include

English Sonata Settings from 1801 to 1850, in Order of Preference

Settings	1801–10	1811–20	1821–30	1831–40	1841–50	Uncertain	Totals/%
P solo	83	35	4	2	5 (3)	70	202/59
P acc'd. by 1 or more strings or winds	38 (3)	9	1			36	87/25
Duo (P + 1 other instrument)			1		8 (9)	22	40/12
Organ	3					6	9/3
P-duet	1				(2)		3/1
TOTALS	128	44	6	2	27	134	341/100

some that may not belong to the first half-century at all. They are based on indirect information and represent sonatas that may or may not have been published. Although it is not possible to relate the two tabulations any more closely and although the totals would not be proportional, anyway, since the larger tabulation includes the more chamber-music-minded, second half-century, there still is a rough concordance in the highest preferences. The chief differences are the much

32. Unperceptive is a statement in NZM LXVIII/2 (1872) 377 that nobody was writing or pub. sons. for Vn & P anymore (or trios).
33. From Temperley/CORRESPONDENCE.

greater evidence of the slump and the lesser interest in the P-duet that are shown in the English tabulation. There is actually less concordance between the latter and the summary of public sonata performances, also in England, during the same period, as given in connection with recital content in Chapter III. In the performances the settings for P & Vn slightly topped those for P solo (53% as against 49%). But this difference may well be explained by the relative infrequency of *all* solo performances during that period.

The Nature of the Settings

By virtue of its position as the most favored type, the sonata's setting for P solo deserves first attention here. Schumann summed up three main styles of piano writing with his usual astuteness (in the course of his review of a Sonata in E♭ by Loewe; ssв VIII):

The older I get, the more I realize that the piano communicates basically and idiomatically chiefly in three ways—through full texture and harmonic variety (as by Beethoven, [or] Franz Schubert), through use of the pedal (as by Field), or through volubility (as by Czerny, [or] Herz). In the first category one finds the heavy-set player, in the second the fantasying [sort], and in the third the [sort with] the pearly [touch]. Many-sided, cultivated composer-virtuosos, like Hummel, Moscheles, and, most recently, Chopin, unite all three means and therefore become most loved by the performers. . . .[34]

Further discussion of these and other treatments of the piano in the Romantic sonata would take us into problems of style that are better deferred to the next chapter. But it is worth noting here that already in 1821 the French music lexicographer F.-H.-J. Blaze had written "The sonata is most appropriate [when scored] for piano [solo, rather than the outmoded setting of Vn-or-Fl/bass], on which one can play three or four, or even more, distinct parts at once. It is also on this instrument that it [the sonata] has advanced the furthest in its astonishing progress." [35]

In 1838, Schilling also recognized that the piano rather than the violin had become the primary vehicle of the sonata. Yet he was falling behind the times in still not dissociating the piano from its traditional, often optional "accompaniment" of Vn, Fl, &/or Vc.[36] That that most characteristic Classic setting (sce 98–105) was disappearing in the early-Romantic Era is symptomized by a change of heading in

34. Schumann/schriften I 58.
35. castil-blaze II 272.
36. Schilling/lexicon VI 418.

the pertinent category in HOFMEISTER. In 1815 the heading that included accompanied-keyboard sonatas merely read "Duetten für das Pianoforte." [37] In 1828 it read "Duetten für Pianoforte und Violine etc.," already taking cognizance of the violin's rise toward equality in true duos.[38] Although many of the "accompaniments" actually continued to be subordinate under the latter heading, they were no longer qualified as optional ("ad libitum," etc.) in succeeding volumes of HOFMEISTER. On the other hand, the concept of the violin as an accompanying instrument continued to reveal itself throughout the era, long after the violin achieved full partnership. In 1844 Mendelssohn still spoke of "accompanying sonatas" when he praised the violin playing of the thirteen-year-old Joachim.[39] And ten years later Brahms still spoke of wanting "to accompany Frau Schumann" (if he could learn the flute part in Kuhlau's sonatas [SSB XV]).[40] Throughout his life, except in his Op. 120/1 and 2, Brahms was one of the large majority of composers who continued to place the piano before its partner in the titles of his duo sonatas.[41]

Of course, even in the true duos for P & Vn (or other instrument) from the Romantic Era, the piano part usually dominates, at least to the extent that it includes the bass and most of the harmonic support, it has more notes to play, and its performer can keep track of both parts in his score. Yet the custom no longer prevails of listing only the chief luminary and his part in an ensemble sonata when that luminary is the pianist (as with Moscheles and Clara Schumann, *supra*), whereas the custom does often persist when he is the violinist or other instrumentalist.[42] Certainly, piano parts that were actually subordinated to the other part, like the one by Viotti singled out in the Classic Era (SCE 676), were infrequent, apart from pedagogic examples. Gade's *Sonate Nr. 2, D moll, für Pianoforte und Violine* (1850; SSB XV) has such a part, in spite of the order of its title. Saint-Saëns' *Sonate pour clarinette, avec accompagnement*

---

37. In AMZ XX (1818) 632 Rochlitz reviewed Ries's Son. Op. 76 for P ± Fl with the sarcastic remark that "The flute cannot be dispensed with entirely, as the title says; it actually takes the theme alone once, in the second movement, [with] the piano [getting] nothing but mere accompaniment!" For late exx. of the acc'd. P son., cf. Ries in SSB VII and Ladurner in SSB XII.

38. HOFMEISTER 1815 (Whistling), 297–320, and 1828 (Whistling), 470–514.

39. Bennett/BENNETT 157.

40. Joachim/LETTERS 78.

41. Cf. Geiringer/BRAHMS 26. In the present vol. an effort has been made to retain the order of the original title, although contradictory listings often leave that order uncertain.

42. E.g., cf. Lochner/KREISLER 93.

de piano, Op. 167 (1921; ssв XIII) has one, too, in full agreement with its title.[43] Stanford was aiming at a return to Baroque styles when he used a like title (ssв XIV). A sonata by Paul Caro (ssв XVII), Op. 42 for Vc & P (in that order), was reviewed sarcastically because of its "humble" piano part:

> And the composer said: There are enough sonatas in which the cello fights a losing battle against the piano. Therefore, friends, let's do something else! I shall write you a sonata in which the pianist must humble himself and leave the Word to the cellist. And so he did.[44]

In a true duo with piano, the piano does have most of the responsibility for the harmony and all of it for the bass, unless its partner has a low enough range to share the responsibility, as the cello has. But the greater expressive and color range of the violin or other instrument may counteract this domination by the piano to a considerable degree. Apart from these considerations, in thematic, rhythmic, figural, and other textural activity the two instruments are likely to contribute about equally and in a variety of ways. For instance, each of the two instruments may accompany the other in turn. They may engage in a dialog of the same or contrasting ideas, at close or distant intervals. Or they may perform distinctly different lines simultaneously, in a counterpoint governed by rhythmic conjunction or rhythmic opposition. They may reinforce each other at the unison or one or more octaves apart, in the same note values or with either part decorating or outlining the other. Or either instrument may simply play alone for a time, with the other waiting to re-enter. At least some of these procedures are illustrated in a passage from a work (Ex. 2) by the expert, post-Brahmsian composer, Daniel Gregory Mason of Boston and New York (ssв XIX).

The setting for P-duet is well represented throughout much of the 19th century on our tabulation of settings (*supra*), although most of the best examples and most of the interest on the part of significant sonata composers seem to have come in the first half of the century. After substantial contributions only by Mozart and Clementi among the chief Classics, Schubert led the way in the 19th century with some of the greatest masterpieces in that category (ssв VII). Most of these, however, were not made known until the second half-century.[45] Weber, Ries, Moscheles, Cramer, Hummel, and Onslow were other

43. A similar title was used by F. W. Langhans in his Op. 11 (with comments to that effect in ммʀ XIX [1889] 87).
44. Trans. from ᴅм X/4 (1910–11) 189.
45. Cf. ɴᴢм LXIX/2 (1873) 505–7 (A. B. Vogel).

Ex. 2. From the first movement of Daniel Gregory Mason's Sonata in g, Op. 5 (after the original ed. of 1913, by kind permission of G. Schirmer, Inc.).

substantial contributors early in the century, Hummel's Op. 92 (ssb VIII) and Onslow's Op. 22 being outstanding examples of the genre. Furthermore, Cramer and Hummel, Moscheles and Mendelssohn, Moscheles and Chopin, Cramer and Herz, Cramer and Liszt, and Chopin and Liszt were among the many pairs we find performing duets in the first half-century.[46]

A reviewer in 1847 noted—too negatively, as our tabulation suggests—that few (original) duets were being written any more, regretting the shortage as the loss of a treasured domestic pleasure.[47] His explanation was that the new virtuoso piano writing, with its octaves, arpeggios, and pedal effects, already sounded like two players, but was better left to the virtuoso soloists. It is interesting that Brahms saw fit to arrange or have arranged for P-duet much of his chamber music, chiefly so that he could try it over with Clara Schumann and other intimates.[48] An original, exceptionally attractive Sonata for P-duet from the second half-century is Op. 17 in g (composed in 1865–66) by the Swiss composer Hermann Goetz (ssb X). In Ex. 3 is quoted

46. Cf. MOSCHELES I 23, 64–65, 74, 77, 274; Schlesinger/CRAMER 71–72, 77–79.
47. NZM XXVI (1847) 41–42.
48. Cf. Altmann/KAMMERMUSIK 309–10.

Ex. 3. From the first movement of Hermann Goetz's Sonata in g, Op. 17 (after the original Kistner ed. of 1878 at the New York Public Library).

the start of the second theme in the first movement, illustrating the balance, clean texture, and melodic interchanges that the most skillful writers in this idiom could achieve.[49]

As mentioned earlier, the setting for 2 Ps fared much less well than that for P-duet. A reviewer in 1845, finding reason to praise an Op. 1 for 2 Ps by A. Bergt (ssb VIII), discussed the dearth in his opening paragraph.[50] He thought the difficulty of finding two instruments, together and sufficiently matched, had been exaggerated and that prospects for a rise in output were now good. But one still can name only two composers who left examples of some renown, these being Brahms and the prolific late Swiss Romantic, Hans Huber. And even their contributions are seldom played today. Brahms's Sonata in f, Op. 34b, is preferred, instead, in its final form as the piano Quintet in f (ssb IX) and Huber's three contributions qualify

49. Cf., also, the ex. from the start of Op. 17 in Georgii/KLAVIERMUSIK 578.
50. NZM XXIII (1845) 53.

as something short of masterpieces (ssb XI). Dussek had left several effective "Duos" or "Duos concertants," mostly still in the Classic idiom and intended for harp & P as well as 2 Ps.[51] The few further contributions, including those by Onslow (ssb XII, with ex.), H. Grädener, and Reinecke,[52] would hardly pass muster among today's performers. Rare in this general category is Smetana's one-movement Sonata in e for eight hands at 2 Ps.[53]

In the select category of sonata for unaccompanied violin,[54] inevitably under the strong influence of the styles and techniques in J. S. Bach's precedent (sbe 269–70), are late-Romantic examples of more or less distinction by Karg-Elert, J. Weismann, J. Röntgen, Ysaÿe, and, especially, Reger. Karg-Elert also left one or two sonatas each for unaccompanied Va, Fl, Cl, Bn, and saxophone (ssb XI). Earlier in the century L. Jansa had provided a "Sonate brillante" for Vn alone with an optional accompaniment by a second Vn (1828; ssb VII). And A. Romberg left three "Etudes ou sonates" for Vn alone that were reviewed as having more value in the former sense (ca. 1813; ssb VIII). Two piano sonatas in a similarly select category, for left hand alone, may be cited, by Zichy and Reinecke, but not one by Kalkbrenner usually cited as the pioneer in this setting, since it actually requires two hands (ssb XII).

Transcriptions and Arrangements

The transcribing or arranging of sonatas (and other music) in the 19th century is a major topic in itself, and one that throws considerable light on Romantic attitudes toward music. It is also a topic with its own sources, bibliography, and history. Not seldom it raises questions of stylistic and even functional propriety, such as the questions brought up earlier regarding the adaptation of piano sonatas to the organ. Indirectly and conversely, it sometimes raises the question of whether a work has been scored for its best medium in the first place—such as the solo piano sonatas of R. Fuchs, Sibelius, and Tchaikovsky (ssb XI, XV, and XVIII, with exx.), whose frequent piano writing in block chords suggests orchestration as the better mode of expression (ssb XI and XVII). Although this topic of arranging must be regarded as only tangential to the basic questions of the sonata, it comes up repeatedly, if only incidentally, throughout the present

51. Cf. Craw/DUSSEK 406.
52. Cf. Altmann/KAMMERMUSIK 285–92.
53. Cf. ssb XVII. The same setting was employed by H. Mohr in a Sonatine in G, pub. by Breitkopf & Härtel in 1894.
54. Cf. Gates/SOLO 179–214, with exx.

study and needs at least this separate notice here. We are interested not so much in the wide variety of settings that is involved as in the half-dozen or so ways those settings pertain to the sonata.

The simplest or least arranging was ordinarily that kind done to provide an alternative part in a duo. In the sonatas for Vn & P by Franck (ssb XIII) and Grieg (Op. 13, ssb XV) surprisingly little was done (by the composers or whom?) beyond adjustments of range to convert the Vn into Vc parts. In Brahms's two Sonatas for Cl & P, Op. 120, the composer also changed details of slurring and rests in deference to the unlike idioms when he himself made the Va (though not the Vn) parts out of the clarinet parts.[55] Such alternative parts can be found throughout the Romantic duo literature[56] for the obvious reasons that they widened the market for publication sales and permitted that many more musicians, especially the dilettantes, to have at least a go at the music. Reviewers generally reflected the public interest in such matters. For instance,

This [Son. in B♭, Op. 2/1, by J. N. Hummel] was originally written for a violoncello accompaniment [actually H-or-P & Vn-or-Fl & Vc; ssb VIII], the latter now being altered for a [2d?] flute, at some expense of effect, of course, yet very pleasing in its new state. It is so arranged that it may be played without the accompaniment, which is printed in small notes over the regular piano-forte part, whenever essential.[57]

Another kind of a sonata arrangement was that that occurred during the evolution of a particular work, whether as the final setting or an earlier one. The most renowned example, among several examples that we shall be encountering in Part Two, was Brahms's Sonata in f, Op. 34b, mentioned above under settings for 2 Ps, as the forerunner of his piano Quintet in f, Op. 34. Later (ssb IX) the valuable lesson in scoring to be derived from this final arrangement will be discussed and illustrated. But the Sonata was not published until after the Quintet. F. W. Grund's *Grande Sonate* in g, Op. 27, for P solo, was also first published in a different version, as a *Trio de salon* for P-duet & Va-or-Vc-or-Hn, yet it won its successes, including Schumann's praise in 1839, only in the solo version (ssb VIII). The final published version was also the more successful one with regard to the three sonatas each, Opp. 38 and 43, for Vc & P, by B. H. Romberg (ssb VIII). These had been arranged, although whether by him is not clear) from three trios for 2 Vcs & Va and three "Sonatas faciles" for Vc and string bass that had been published in 1825 and 1826, respectively. Of course, no ques-

55. Cf. ssb IX; Cobbett/CHAMBER I 182 (D. F. Tovey).
56. Cf. Altmann/KAMMERMUSIK *passim*.
57. HARMONICON VI/1 (1828) 108.

tion of which version fared best is involved in the sort of P-duet mentioned earlier that Brahms made or had made from his larger ensembles for informal trial and demonstration.

Still another kind of an arrangement was that of a favorite sonata movement. In Chapter IV some of the incredibly many and varied settings of the "Marche funèbre" from Chopin's Op. 35 were listed, and nearly the same could have been done for certain other favorites, like Weber's "Perpetuum mobile" (finale of Op. 24).[58] Highly published pianist-composers like Ries, Moscheles, and Czerny seem to have done almost as much arranging as original composing, including sonata movements and whole sonatas by themselves and others, among a much larger quantity of lighter things.[59] As but one sample, Moscheles arranged his own "Sextuor" in E♭, Op. 35 (for P, Vn, Fl, 2 Hns, & Vc) as a *Grande Sonate* for P solo, for P-duet, and for 2 Ps.[60]

There was also the arranging done to popularize (or Romanticize) favorite sonatas from the past. In some of this arranging, parts were added without changing the original. After a Gewandhaus concert in Leipzig in the winter of 1839–40, Schumann wrote,

. . . and Herr Concertmaster [Ferdinand] David, accompanied by Mendelssohn, [played] in an outstanding manner two movements—priceless compositions—from the sonatas for violin alone by Bach, the same of which it was asserted formerly that "it would be unthinkable to add any other part to them," which [assertion] Mendelssohn thereupon contradicted in the loveliest style, enriching the original with all sorts of lines, so that it was a treat to hear.[61]

Schumann himself added accompaniments in his last years to all six of Bach's unaccompanied violin Partitas and Sonatas (ssb VIII). Grieg's four volumes of "freely composed" accompaniments to be played on a second piano with Mozart's solo piano sonatas are still used by teachers today.[62] Among the countless other 19th-century arrangements of sonata movements by the Classic masters, and as examples of the kind that did change the original, we might cite Elgar's arrangement of the "Allegro" from Mozart's K. 547 in F, for P & Vn, as a choral "Gloria" (!) and the finale from Beethoven's Op. 23 in a, for P & Vn, as a wind quintet.[63]

Finally, among categories of arranging there is the sort that makes "sonatas" out of medleys of popular tunes and the like. Such would

58. Cf. ssb VIII; pazdírek XV 182–83.
59. Cf. their long entries in pazdírek.
60. pazdírek X 827.
61. Schumann/schriften I 511.
62. Cf. their listing in pazdírek VI 567.
63. Cf. Young/elgar 402–3.

be Czerny's fifteen *Sonatine[s] facile[s] e progressive[s] sopra i piu accredidati motive d'opere. . . .*[64] In the many potpourris of this sort "sonata" is reduced to its original meaning merely of "instrumental piece."

Some Aspects of Performance Practices

Like the topic of arrangements (*supra*), that of performance practices represents a major field in itself. It, too, must be regarded as only tangential to sonata history, yet frequently comes up in passing in the present volume and requires at least this special mention here. Oddly enough, although the Romantic Era is closest in time to our own era and should be, one would assume, that much more familiar to us, it actually has been about as little known or explored for performance practices as the Renaissance Era. Since 1963 many musicians have been shocked into an awareness of their unfamiliarity with 19th-century practices by the recordings of the Edwin Welte piano rolls that had been made about 1905.[65] They have heard how, only that recently, Carreño, Leschetizky, d'Albert, de Pachmann, and numerous other greats among both performers and composer-performers were taking liberties, especially with the tempo but also with the notes themselves, that would fail a college freshman today. (Xaver Scharwenka's playing of Beethoven's Op. 90/i is representative. Interesting is the fact that Debussy, Grieg, and the other composer-performers take decidedly fewer liberties with their own music.) Studies on 19th-century performance practices are much to be desired.[66] Bach, of course, has always drawn most of the attention, with the centuries before and after him receiving successively less attention.

It is not that the 19th-century musicians and writers themselves failed to take an interest in performance practices. A considerable interest developed early as one facet of the new interest in music history (SSB II). In the last chapters of Hummel's epochal treatise on piano playing (Hummel/ANWEISUNG), first published in 1827, the cultivated pianist made several remarks about the differing styles of past and contemporary musicians, including the ability of Mozart and Clementi to excel as performers without use of the pedal (p. 152 [452!]); the approximate metronome speeds that Beethoven, Clementi, Cramer, and numerous others intended with certain tempo markings

---

64. Cf. PAZDÍREK III 687.

65. *Legendary Masters of the Keyboard*, pub. by The Classics Record Library as album WV 6633/1–3.

66. Memoirs, letters, and periodicals are the main sources, again, along with the original MSS and eds. Cf. the interesting chap. on this topic in Schonberg/PIANISTS 119–33.

(p. 457); and the preference for uniformity of style in the music of past masters, including J. S. Bach, Handel, Scarlatti, Emanuel Bach (!), and Mozart (!), as against sharp contrasts in that of the contemporaries, especially Beethoven (p. 466). Naturally, the playing of Beethoven's sonatas became a primary topic for writers on performance practices. Pioneer landmarks were certain sections in the writings of Czerny between 1842 and 1852,[67] in which every sonata movement (among many other of Beethoven's works) is given a metronome mark and discussed briefly, too often superficially, from the standpoints of character, style, and, occasionally, specific problems.

But in the editing of past masterworks throughout the 19th century there was a remarkable difference between an avowed reverence for the authenticity of the *Urtext* and the actual policies that editors chose to follow. The typical explanation, offered time after time, can be found as recently as 1945, in the preface to editions of Schumann's sonatas Opp. 105 and 121, for Vn & P:

> The present revision has been undertaken in the hope of restoring their popularity. It will be disapproved by those who are accustomed to regard an original musical text in all its details less as a guide for interpretation than as a sacred document which must never be tampered with—even if it can be irrefutably shown that this text, instead of revealing the composer's intentions, has unfortunately had the result of obscuring them.[68]

As was also typical, these editions gave no clue as to what was original and what was changed. Clara Schumann and Max Vogrich, although they came to many different conclusions, did much better in their respective editions of Robert Schumann's collected works. Otherwise, going back in time, one must report much the same of the now infamous sonata editions that Epstein did of Mozart, Bülow and Lebert of Beethoven, Bülow of Scarlatti and Emanuel Bach, and Czerny himself of Beethoven in contradictions of his own writings. According to its subtitle, Tausig's edition of five Scarlatti sonatas (Edition Peters 3014) might be exempted here as belonging in the realm of "concert transcriptions," including, for example, the unacknowledged change from d to e, articulation marks, fuller chords, double-notes, terms of expression, and tempo inflections in the much played "Pastorale." Yet there were still those astonishing, elaborate changes, not under the heading of transcriptions, that the Bach-Gesellschaft editor Wilhelm Rust made, again without acknowledgment, in and around his grandfather's sonatas, by way of fully Romanticizing or Wagnerizing them (SCE 583–89, with exx.).

67. Assembled in Badura-Skoda/CZERNY.
68. (G.) *Schirmer's Library of Musical Classics*, Vols. 1696 and 1699 (H. Bauer).

At the start of the era Dussek specified that no ornaments should be added in one of his most important sonatas, "Elégie harmonique" (C. 211). Many another musician after him showed a similar desire to adhere to the letter of the score, as did one who argued in 1877 for playing the "small notes" before the beat, as they were engraved, and not on the beat, in the subordinate theme of Beethoven's Op. 27/2/iii.[69] But the need to enrich the texture, free the rhythm, and intensify the expression was too strong for the best of the Romantics. What is most surprising is that the Romantics "improved" not only on the alleged thin scoring and strait-laced quality of "old music" (as we saw Mendelssohn and Schumann do with Bach, or Grieg with Mozart; *supra*) but on the music written by earlier Romantics. That is, we not only find, for example, defenses for editorial extensions and octave doublings in the sonatas Mozart and Beethoven had written for keyboards with only five octaves,[70] or for Bülow's alterations by way of solving technical problems in Beethoven's sonatas,[71] or for changes in the notation in order to make the rhythmic organization clearer.[72] But we also find no less a master than Liszt writing to Sigmund Lebert in 1868–70 regarding editions of Weber and Schubert,

In the *various readings* you will probably find some things not inappropriate; —I flatter myself that I have thus given performers greater licence, and have increased the effect without damaging or overloading Weber's style. . . . In the [Schubert] Sonatas you will find some various readings, which appear to me tolerably *appropriate*. Several passages, and the whole of the conclusion of the C major Fantasia, I have re-written in modern pianoforte form, and I flatter myself that Schubert would not be displeased with it. . . . My endeavor with this work is to avoid quibbling and pretentiousness, and to make the edition a practical one for teachers and players. And for this reason at the very last I added a goodly amount of fingering and pedal marks. . . . With regard to the deceptive *Tempo rubato,* I have settled the matter provisionally in a brief note (in the finale of Weber's A♭ major Sonata); other occurrences of the *rubato* may be left to the taste and momentary feeling of gifted players. A metronomical performance is certainly tiresome and nonsensical; time and rhythm must be adapted to and identified with the melody, the harmony, the accent and the poetry. . . . But how indicate all this? I shudder at the thought of it.[73]

69. MT XVIII (1877) 135 ("Allegro").
70. Cf. DMZ III (1862) 153–55, with exx.
71. Cf. MMR III (1873) 2–5 and 42–43 (E. Dannreuther), 113–16, 128–30.
72. Cf. MW XIV (1883) 397–401 (R. Westphal).
73. LISZT LETTERS II 160–61, 165, 194. Cf. the serial review article in MMR III 69–70, 84–85, 91–101, 113–16, 128–30, and especially 154–57 (with exx.); MMR IV (1874) 133. Liszt did provide the original version, too. Cf., also, SSB XII for changes Liszt made in the finale of Chopin's Sonata in b.

Ex. 4. From Carl Maria von Weber's Sonata in A♭, Op.
39/iv/87–94 and its "modernization" by Adolph Henselt (as
quoted from the Schlesinger ed. in MMR IV [1874] 149).

The Monthly Musical Record for 1874 gives an extraordinary, mostly
laudatory report, complete with examples, of the changes Henselt
made in an edition of Weber's Sonata in A♭, Op. 39.[74] Some of
these changes add melody, harmony, and richness of sound, but most
pile virtuoso difficulties on what are already virtuoso difficulties (Ex. 4).

Evidently the same sorts of changes and more were improvised,
if not prepared, in public performance. Again, Liszt was one of the
main exponents. Moscheles told how at a Philharmonic Concert in
1840 Liszt "played three of my 'Studies' quite admirably. Faultless in

74. MMR IV (1874) 133–34, 148–50.

the way of execution, but by his powers he has completely meta-morphosed these pieces; they have become more his Studies than mine. With all that[,] they please me and I shouldn't like to hear them played in any other way by him." [75] Thus, another free performer, Paganini, had hardly been right if he thought only Italians took liberties. In 1816, during the two-violin passages of a double-concerto by Kreutzer, "I held strictly note for note to the written text. . . . But in the solo passages I gave free rein to my imagination and played in the Italian manner—in the style that is really natural to me." [76]

With further regard to rhythm and tempo, many such advices favoring freedom have turned up in the present study, but none happened to turn up that argue for a consistent or prevailing tempo. The metronome seems to have been advocated only for setting tempos, not for maintaining them. One reviewer regretted that no metronome marks were supplied in A. G. Ritter's Op. 20 and another disagreed when he came to Op. 21, saying, as has been said so often, that a good musician will sense the right tempo.[77]

With regard to two other aspects of performance practices, the custom of playing solo music from memory was developed by Liszt among others and began to take hold by the mid century, as noted earlier.[78] The matter of taking repeats, especially in "sonata form," is brought up as part of the discussion of form in the next chapter.

75. MOSCHELES II 64. Cf. Schonberg/PIANISTS 166–67 for further instances; also, Prod'homme/BEETHOVEN 125–27 for Berlioz' anguish when Liszt added trills, tremolos, and rubato in Beethoven's Op. 27/2/i.
76. As trans. in Courcy/PAGANINI I 148.
77. NZM XXXV (1851) 258–59, XXXIX (1853) 115.
78. Cf. SSB III; Hanslick/WIEN I 421; Newman/OP. 106.

Romantic Sonata Form: Process, Mold, and Unicum

The Problem

This last, yet most central, chapter in the overview that comprises Part One concentrates on the music itself—that is, on the styles and forms of the Romantic sonata since Beethoven. Its object is an ordered summary and rationale of the most representative and salient traits discovered throughout the survey that comprises Part Two, on individual composers and their sonatas. And as with the Baroque Era and Corelli, or the Classic Era and Haydn, Mozart, and Beethoven, the method of exposition in this sixth chapter has been to focus on the few masters who have exercised the greatest influences, and to draw on their contemporaries only as needed to round out the summary. Four masters serve as the focal points this time—Schubert, Chopin, Schumann, and Brahms (meaning that their sons. are examined here rather than in Part Two, where the extended, separate discussions of each master's sons. are confined to sources, background, tabulations, and circumstances [ssb VII, XII, VIII, and IX, respectively]). Except for Brahms's last works, the sonatas of these composers all fall in the early- or mid-Romantic Era as delimited here (ssb I). Furthermore, they largely fall on the more conservative side of the style dichotomy shortly to be defined, with Liszt's sonatas, in particular, requiring full recognition on the other side. Yet, next to Beethoven's it is their sonatas and not Liszt's isolated masterpieces (ssb X) that exercised the clearest, most demonstrable influences on contemporary and subsequent sonata history, which, all in all, is a conservative facet of Romantic music history, in any case.

In the examination of this music, the approach can no longer be by way of contemporary (19th-c.) concepts, as it was in Chapter II. Nor can it be by way, even, of the relatively few, pertinent, present-day studies that already have been done, fine as some of them are. These studies are acknowledged for valued insights and conclusions where they apply (*infra*),[1] and sometimes are quoted, especially for statistical findings. But as it has been necessary to emphasize more than once before (cf. ssb I), one writer cannot accept and acknowledge the music analysis of another in the way that he might accept and acknowledge another's factual discoveries. Music analysis must still depend to a considerable degree (fortunately!) on firsthand experience with the music, on subjective reactions to it, and on the particular slant being observed.

The starting point in this chapter needs to be, therefore, a restatement of the particular slant and premises that have governed, from its beginning, the present approach to styles and forms in the sonata. In revised wording that still retains the sense of previous statements (cf. scE 114–15), we may recall three essential distinctions in the meaning of the broad term "form." (1) Form may be viewed, dynamically, or in action, as a *generative process*, characterized by a certain corpus of style treatments or traits. Here the most benefit has derived from distinguishing between two processes that, in their theoretical extremes, are diametrically opposed.[2] One is "motivic play," characterized variously by imitative treatment of a significant but fragmentary idea, by relatively fast harmonic rhythm, by irregular or proselike meter, and by constant tonal flux. The other is "phrase grouping," characterized variously by pairings or larger juxtapositions of complete phrases and periods (thematically significant or not), by homophonic textures, by relatively slow harmonic rhythm, by more regular, verselike meter, and by broad tonal plateaus. (2) Form may be viewed, textbook fashion, as a *mold* or standardized design, with all the conveniences of quick reference that such classifications permit and all the dangers of Procrustean analysis and false criteria that they pose. Approaching a form as a mold puts the emphasis on everything that is typical or common practice, if not commonplace. Our best illustration, of course, is textbook "sonata form," itself. The several textbook rondo designs present almost as many conveniences and dangers. (3) Form may be viewed as a *unicum*—that is, as the one and only result of a particular corpus of generative traits and/or a particular set of variants in a mold, if, indeed, it happens to approximate *any* recognized mold. Typically, motivic play leads to a structural result that is monothematic (or monomotivic) and cursive (or open), whereas phrase grouping leads to a structural result that is polythematic and hierarchic (meaning an integration of sections within sections). But approaching a form as a

1. Most of them are cited, too, in the individual composer discussions of Part Two.
2. Cf. Newman/UNDERSTANDING 133–55; scE 113–14.

unicum puts the emphasis on everything that is *a*-typical—in other words, on whatever may distinguish it from other forms.

As an illustration of these three meanings of form within the scope of the present volume, the first movement of Chopin's Sonata in b, Op. 58, may be used. The *mold* that this movement most nearly approximates and that provides the most convenient term of reference is "sonata form," with its standardized subdivisions as convenient reference terms, too—"exposition," "development," and "recapitulation" (beginning at mss. 1, 92, and 151, respectively[3]). Of the two *generative processes* motivic play prevails only in the development section of Op. 58/i (as in most "sonata forms"), and only in its first seventeen measures, at that. Otherwise, phrase grouping prevails. Even when the phrase consists of little more than motivic reiterations, in place or in sequence (mss. 23–26), the phrase grouping prevails. Put differently, when the reiterations of a motive fall into larger rhythmic composites (as happens in one basic kind of sonata theme—e.g., Brahms's Op. 5/i/1–6), the larger composites take precedence in determining the generative process. Finally, Chopin's Op. 58/i qualifies as a *unicum* when all of its peculiarities and departures from textbook norms are brought together. To name but two of these, a peculiarity from the standpoint of its prevailing generative process, phrase grouping, is the rapid harmonic rhythm produced by the block-chords in its main theme and related phrases (e.g., mss. 1–2, 17–19, 21–22). A departure from the mold of "sonata form" is the start of its recapitulation at the second theme (ms. 151), without any return to the first theme.

It is possible and helpful to relate these three meanings of form in music to the main trends in the styles and "forms" of the Romantic sonata—in fact, to one main trend per meaning. From the standpoint of form as a generative process the most important trend was an exaggeration and, at the same time, attenuation or rarefaction of Classic sonata means.[4] Thus, the Romantic motives persisted longer and pervaded more of the structure; the phrases grew lengthier and projected more tellingly; the textures grew fuller and their activity increased; the harmonies became more dissonant, more varied, and more remotely interrelated; the tonal schemes ranged further afield and changed more abruptly. Often this exaggeration occurred at both extremes, as in the wider range, at both ends, of pitch, of tempos, of dynamics, of volume, of expressive freedom. From the standpoint of

3. The ms. nos. given in Chopin/WORKS-m are used here, although they include separate nos. for 2d endings (contrary to the usual practice, here and elsewhere).

4. Mersmann/ROMANTISCHEN, on the son. principle in Romantic chamber music, stresses its attenuation after Beethoven; its loss of, or substitutes for, Classic thematic dualism; and its chief positive contribution as the advance of cyclical unity.

form as a mold the most important trend was the increasing recognition and description of an explicit "sonata form" by theorists and other writers of the 19th century, as has already been discussed in Chapter II. This trend had the levelling effect, at least among the weaker, less imaginative composers, of rigidifying the once fluid form and making it into a stereotype. And from the standpoint of form as a unicum, the most important trend was the growing dichotomy of sonatas by conservatives and absolutists as against those by progressives and programmatists. In general music this dichotomy, affecting both styles and forms, is associated chiefly with the opposition of Brahms and Wagner.[5] In sonata history it came into the open earlier, though not tangibly before the opposition of Brahms and Liszt, whose very different Op. 1 in C and Sonata in b both originated in 1853. That was the year of Brahms's awkward meeting with Liszt, his joyous meeting with the Schumanns, and Schumann's panegyric on his Op. 1, followed in the next years by the counter force of the "New German" school formed by Liszt and his disciples, then followed in turn by Brahms's "Manifesto" of 1860 against those "moderns" (all in SSB IX). The dichotomy was still much in evidence at the era's end, although often clouded by cross influences from both sides in the sonatas of the epigones.

The next three sections of this chapter consider three main, successive style phases in the Romantic sonata—early, high or middle, and late. In those sections, form is viewed as a generative process. The five remaining sections consider the Romantic sonata first for the over-all unity and relationships of its several movements, then for the nature of each of its four main types of movements (as in SCE VI). In those five sections, form is viewed now as a mold and now as a unicum. That there are only three successive style phases, not sharply defined, to distinguish in the Romantic sonata, as compared with five styles, more or less distinct, in the Classic sonata (SCE 119–33), is partly explained by the lack of a clear break between Classic and Romantic styles such as had occurred between Baroque and Classic styles (cf. SSB I). In other words, to the extent that the Romantics did exaggerate rather than alter or renounce the means of the Classics (*supra*), they did not create radically different styles. There is also the fact that the Romantic style phases, especially the second (at the time of the Brahms-Liszt opposition) presented not only one style but rather two opposed styles in that dichotomy or polarity of conservatives and progressives that was mentioned earlier. There had been no precedent for such a dichotomy in the Classic sonata, the nearest to it being either that of

5. Cf. the reappraisal of the Brahms-Wagner dichotomy and its repercussions in Waltershausen/DUALISMUS.

empfindsam versus *galant* or that of chamber versus symphonic. However, neither of these Classic dichotomies was a matter of conservative versus progressive. The former was, rather, a matter of relative aesthetic weight and the latter of different social functions

The early, high, and late style phases of the Romantic sonata were, in effect, its bubbling naive youth, its mature masterful adulthood, and its final, more calculated flowering. They are viewed here as roughly coterminous with the successive overlapping time spans—about 1800–1850, 1840–85, and 1875–1915—that help to mark off our subgroups of composers in Part Two. But the early phase did not last quite through the first time span, its youthful bloom disappearing during the sonata slump of the second quarter-century (ssB II and IV). Yet it lasted long enough to take in the sonatas of some important composers, including Dussek, Hummel, Weber, and Schubert. For our purposes Schumann is included in that first phase, too, at least to the extent of his Op. 11. His subsequent sonatas, like those of Chopin, Liszt, and Brahms (prior to the late Op. 120) are put here in the second or adulthood phase. In the last phase are included the sonatas of Reger, d'Indy, Dale, Nielsen, Medtner, and MacDowell, among other composers of distinction.

The Early-Romantic Style Phase

Although the Romantic tendency simply to exaggerate Classic means did not favor innovational styles, certain treatments did impart more newness than others to the "frühromantischen" or early-Romantic sonata.[6] These are apparent first of all in that element of the generative process requiring attention first, anyway—**melody.** However, one must realize the impracticality of arriving at broad yet meaningful generalizations about Romantic melody, or of reducing it to useful statistics covering its behavior. Throughout the era its variety was far too great to permit such generalizations and statistics. Already the early-Romantic Era tended to promote this great variety, both because of the premium it was coming to place on originality per se (ssB II) and because of the new interest it was beginning to take in past styles as part of the growing historical consciousness (ssB II). The alternative to arriving at generalizations and statistics concerning melodic behavior

6. Egert/FRÜHROMANTIKER and Favre/FRANÇAISE concentrate on son. styles in this period. Cf., also, the illuminating discussions in F. Blume's article on the Romantic Era for MGG (XI 785–845, *passim*), in Einstein/SCHUBERT 76–85 (a comparison of Schubert's sons. with Haydn's, Beethoven's, and, especially, Hummel's and Weber's), and in Werner/PALE (with references to textural and cyclical treatment in sons. by composers of the Classic-Romantic borderland). Much of Chusid/SCHUBERT, on Schubert's instrumental works for larger chamber ensembles, is relevant here, too.

is to single out the few melodic styles that have seemed most distinctive in the course of the present study. Each of these styles has tended to be associated with a particular composer. Each one may have been exhibited to best advantage in that composer's sonatas (or other music) but, in fact, every one of them can be found in the air, so to speak, as part of the musical language then current.

A primary style of melody in the early-Romantic Era was the smooth, songful, contemplative sort, couched in complete, well-defined phrases, that often is associated with Schubert, especially his lieder. As one outstanding example, the opening theme may be quoted from his posthumous Sonata in B♭ (D. 960), which theme also illustrates Schubert's particular fondness for melodies that keep centering on and turning around the initial note (Ex. 5).[7] In later chapters may be seen another such example by Schubert (in G, D. 894; ssb VII) as well as other related, if not quite so ethereal, examples by Pinto (Op. 3/2; ssb XIV), Moscheles (Op. 49; ssb VII), and Hartmann (Op. 83; ssb XV).[8]

The Moscheles' example is a simple, hymnic line that recalls Tovey's concept of "modern" (i.e., Romantic) melody as the "surface" of harmony (as well as of rhythm, form, and instrumentation).[9] In the "Andante sostenuto" from the same Schubert Sonata in B♭, D. 960/ii, the long steady line, decorated by a lilting harmonic accompaniment, supplies a most effective illustration of Tovey's concept (as does the slow movement of Schubert's string Quintet in C). Hartmann's example introduces a folklike element in its compound-metric lilt. A remarkably precocious example by Dussek (in A♭, C. 221; ssb XVII), to be cited more than once again here, points to the warming, sentimentalizing, even effeminizing effect of chromatic inflections in the melody. The same can be said for the chromaticism in the sort of theme that opens Schubert's D. 850/ii, where the gain in these effects seems to be made at the expense of the lofty nobility in Beethoven's more diatonic slow movements.

When there was a consistent rhythmic pattern and the phrase grouping became still more regular and clear, the result was likely to be an out-and-out tune. Such tunes abound in the early-Romantic sonata, especially in the faster movements. Three examples might be cited from their most fertile breeding ground, the rondo finale. These

7. Hanna/SCHUBERT 115–30 concludes, on statistical bases, that this type is third in frequency among Schubert's melodic types, preceded by scalewise and chordal melodies and followed by melodies with larger skips.

8. When specific son. passages are cited as illustrations in the present chap., they are chosen from exx. in other chaps. as often as the latter exx. apply (and as indicated, though only in this chap., by the parenthetical ssb reference).

9. BRITANNICA XV 228.

Ex. 5. The opening of Franz Schubert's Sonata in B♭, D. 960 (facs. of the autograph as reproduced in Kinsky/KOCH Facs. 13; with the kind permission of M. A. Souchay).

are the rollicking tune in Paganini's Op. 3/6 (ssb XVI), the gay tune in Schubert's D. 850, and the ingratiating tune in Schubert's D. 894. When the patterns and phrase grouping became still more regular, as they did all too often in dance and "perpetuum mobile" movements, the risk was great that such obvious syntax would seem banal. Even the greatest Romantics did not get by this risk altogether unscathed, as can be heard, for example, in a waltzlike double-period by Schubert (Ex. 6).

By contrast, one can find many examples of melodic lines that are quite as compelling in their own way, yet much more varied, supple, and, often, subtle in their rhythmic and pitch organization. Such a line, finely drawn by Kuhlau, is quoted later in an eight-measure phrase with a range of a 12th, for flute (ssb XV). If this example still reveals a late-Classic neatness of organization, one might look for more freedom, even abandon, in the more progressive writing of the time

Ex. 6. From the "Scherzo" of Franz Schubert's Sonata in D,
D. 850/iii (after Schubert/WERKE-m X/11).

(looking toward that eventual dichotomy of styles mentioned earlier).
A bold, impassioned example is the opening of Schumann's Sonata in
f♯, Op. 11 (ssb VIII). We shall be seeing that the key of f♯ seemed to
inspire Romantic composers to write very much this sort of theme.
One would be tempted to say that it was really Schumann's precedent
that inspired them so, except that there were already earlier if more
naive precedents, as in the finale of Ries's Op. 26 (ssb VII) and the
opening of Moscheles' Op. 49.

Such anticipations of Schumann's impassioned melody can be
matched by several anticipations of Chopin's ornamental cantilena,
complete with wide expressive leaps, jagged series of chromatic appoggiaturas, and feminine endings. They already occurred in Beethoven's
Opp. 106/iii/28–36 and 109/iii/17–33, and they may be found in
Czerny's Op. 268/ii (ssb VII), Hummel's Op. 81/ii (ssb VIII), Steibelt's
Op. 64/i (ssb XII), and Kalkbrenner's Op. 56 (ssb XII).

With regard to early-Romantic **rhythm**, the exaggeration of Classic
means took the form of doggedly persistent patterns. Thus, in Schubert's D. 784 in a, the pair of somber, strong-weak half-notes repeats
relentlessly in almost every measure, always starting on the first beat
and relieved only by an occasional triplet filler, diminution, or augmentation (as in mss. 219, 270, and 276–77). There is also a persistent

dotted pattern throughout much of the development section. Similar persistence can be found in the driving pattern of two 16th-notes and an 8th-note throughout the first movements of Mendelssohn's Op. 106 in B♭ and Schumann's Op. 11 in f♯. A significant difference can be found between, on the one hand, the heavy emphasis on the downbeat in such works (even in the textural background of Schumann's habitual syncopations[10]) and, on the other hand, the springier, characteristic emphasis on the offbeat in Beethoven's works of similar character and drive (e.g., Ex. 12, from Op. 81a/i, in SCE 132).[11] The Schubert "Scherzo" quoted above and the two examples quoted later from Weber's Op. 24 (SSB VIII) illustrate the downbeat emphasis, too. In his earlier sonatas Schubert, still as prodigal with his means as most other young composers, had preferred to use a variety of rhythmic patterns, although even then he saw to it that each pattern was given a thorough exposure. That treatment can be found, for example, in the first movement of his earliest Sonata in a, D. 537/i, with such typical patterns in 6/8 meter as a dotted figure, a quarter- and 8th-note, two 16th-notes leading into a quarter-note, and a pair of dotted-quarter notes, the chief rhythmic contrasts being devices like hemiola shifts (mss. 97–101) and arpeggiando septimoles (mss. 106 and 108). Fertile rhythmist that he was, Schubert often indulged his marked propensity for dotted groups and for triplets by combining the two figures throughout extended passages (as in D. 575/i/15–33).

The exaggeration of Classic **harmonic means** is evident in an increased range of dissonance, a more frequent alternation of major and minor in the same interval, a freer use of borrowed tones in either mode, a richer application of the dim.-7th, aug.-6th, and other altered chords, and a greater percentage of chord-root progressions by 2ds and 3ds. Illustrations of these harmonic tendencies may be seen, variously, in the three Dussek examples quoted later (SSB XVII), in Schubert's D. 537/i/150–82, and in the modal vacillations and other inflections, extraordinary even for Schubert, by which he brings the first movement of his "Grand Duo" in C, D. 812, to a close (Ex. 7). The dim.-7th chord —as used by Weber and Mendelssohn, for example—seems to have had a special significance for the early-Romantics and their successors, whether as a color harmony, a terrifying climax, a convenient modulatory agent (chiefly through its enharmonic re-interpretations in V_9 chords), a mainstay in passagework, a basic chord in sideslipping,

10. Honsa/SCHUMANN is a recent diss. on syncopation, hemiola, and metric changes in Schumann's instrumental music, including numerous references to, and exx. from, his sons.
11. Cf. Westphal/ROMANTISCHE 189–90.

Ex. 7. From the first movement of Franz Schubert's "Grand

Duo" in C, D. 812 (after Schubert /WERKE-m IX/12).

Ex. 8. From the first movement of Carl Maria von Weber's
Sonata in e, Op. 70 (after Augener's Ed. No. 8470).

chromatic progressions, or a means of achieving the intentionally
ambiguous and noncommittal, hence the mystical (Ex. 8).

Tonality in the sense of key organization comes up further on as a
main structural consideration in the cycle and the separate movements. But it belongs here, too, because the modulations that effect
tonal changes reveal further exaggerations of Classic means in the early-
Romantic sonata. These modulations do not increase the Classic tonal
range significantly, since at least in rare instances nearly the full range
had been explored in the Classic sonata (SCE 137–38).[12] But they do
occur more often—more often, that is, in proportion to the tonal
plateaus, so that they serve not only to attain the tonal landmarks of
the design but to decorate much of the territory in between. Furthermore, a larger proportion of the early-Romantic modulations qualify
as the moderately distant or the remote sort, based on change of mode,
chromatic harmony, and enharmony. And a larger proportion of these
sorts of modulations connect keys a major 3d apart.

We get a striking display of all three trends, by one of the greatest
masters of modulation, in the "Con moto" movement of Schubert's
Sonata in D, D. 850. In the initial 41 measures Schubert flexes his
modulatory muscles by paying effortless, transitory visits to three different keys—first going from the home key of A to the mediant, c♯, and
back, by common chord; then through the ♭VII chord to the lowered
mediant, C♮, and back by common chord and change of mode; and
then through a dim.-7th chord to the lowered supertonic, B♭, and back
through ♭II as a Neapolitan harmony. The next 44, highly syncopated

12. Cf. the statistical conclusions to this effect in Abbott/FORM 323–29, which also
show Schubert to have been more adventuresome than Brahms.

measures (42–85) leave the home key, starting in the subdominant, D, by assumption of key, changing to its subdominant, G, by the same method (ms. 51), then modulating to D (again; ms. 68), to F (ms. 76), and, after a cumulation of chromatic, syncopated chords progressing by roots mostly a 3d apart, back to the home key of A again (ms. 86). Comparable modulations enhance the remaining four-sevenths of this movement.

Along with the songful melody in complete phrases and periods, the most conspicuous difference in the early-Romantic sonata lies in its **textures and sonorities**.[13] This time the exaggeration extends in all directions, as though it were a photographic enlargement. First of all, as we have seen, the pitch range itself expanded both up and down, thanks especially to the expanding range of the rapidly developing piano (ssb V). Schubert and Czerny were among composers who seem to have taken special delight in the new highs and lows, as in the arpeggios reaching up to e^4 in Schubert's D. 959/iv/271–79, or the mystical trill on contra-G♭ in his D. 960/i/8 (*supra*), or the coursing over six octaves, contra-F to f^4, in the "Scherzo" of Czerny's Op. 268 (ssb VII, but the quoted mss. get down only to contra-A).

Secondly, with regard to textural changes, much of the former close-position scoring expanded into open-position scoring. In this way, the close-position Alberti bass, which had been one of the most characteristic earmarks of the Classic style (sce 122, 180–82), did not quite disappear in early-Romantic scoring. Rather, along with some continued use in close position (e.g., Steibelt's Op. 64/i; ssb XII), it expanded on occasion into its open-position equivalent. A well-known though rare instance for Beethoven occurs in his Op. 90/i/55–58, and more frequent instances occur, for example, in Dussek's sonatas (as in C. 221, ssb XVII) and Weber's (as in Op. 49/i/223–28). But much more frequent are many other wide-spaced accompaniments in a considerable variety of chordal dispositions, such as the broken chords in triplets at the start of Schumann's Op. 11 (ssb VIII), the regular arpeggio pattern in Weber's Op. 49/ii/104–12 and the irregular one in Mendelssohn's Op. 6/iv/54–75, the repeated block chords in Hummel's Op. 81/ii/21–27 and the changing ones in his Op. 106/i/217–24, and, of course, the counterpart of the Alberti bass in the Classic Era, which was the Romantic's um-pah-pah-pah or related figure. This last was the most prevalent of all Romantic accompaniments (as in Dussek's C. 221, again, ssb XVII; or Reissiger's Op. 93/i, ssb VIII). The tendency to-

---

13. It is significant that the 6 styles depicted in C. Potter's "Enigma" variations of 1825 differ primarily in their idiomatic piano textures, sonorities, and techniques (as discussed in ssb XIV; QUARTERLY VII [1825] 507–9).

ward open-position scoring also favored wider stretches, such as the 9ths and 10ths in Mendelssohn's Op. 106/ii/66–88, or the four-note, open-position, left-hand chords, which few pianists can reach, in Weber's Op. 39/i/58; and it favored wider skips, such as the cross-hand leaps up to three octaves and more in Schubert's D. 575/i/60–80, and four octaves in Hummel's Op. 81/i/112–26 (cf. ssb VIII).

Thirdly, with regard to textural changes, the sound is richer in the early-Romantic than in the Classic sonata, if only because there are more notes in the scoring and more use of the pedal to multiply them, as it were, by running them together and releasing their upper partials. Four- or five- rather than three-part writing becomes the norm. Sometimes the added parts come in chord doublings, or in octave doublings in either hand, or in melodic lines reinforced by 3ds and 6ths, or in the euphony of a tenor melody with its bass below and arpeggiations above (all of which may be found in Dussek's C. 221, again [ssb XVII], except the last, which is in Moscheles' Op. 49 [ssb VII]). The passagework, especially that for piano, adds to the richness of sound by being more complex, more inflected by foreign tones, and wider-ranged. Among the countless varieties there are broken octaves that outline chords (as in Hummel's Op. 81/i/63–65), chains of first-inversion chords topped by two-note appoggiatura slurs (as in Weber's Op. 24/i, ssb VIII), fleet chromatic fingerwork in close quarters (as in Spohr's Op. 125, ssb XIII, and Weber's "Perpetuum mobile," Op. 24/iv), chordal figuration divided between the hands (in anticipation of Schumann's writing, as in Cramer's Op. 23/3, ssb XIV), and rapid octaves, staccato or legato, in either or both hands (as in Weber's Op. 39/i/124–30).

It was mainly Hummel and Dussek who revealed these new athletic horizons, a fact our several citations have already indicated.[14] They left Clementi behind, to his distress, as Chopin, Thalberg, and Liszt were to leave them and Moscheles behind.[15] Along with minor innovators like Prince Louis Ferdinand (who contributed no extant sons.),[16] Weber and Schumann stood next in line in these trends, bypassing Schubert, whose genius did not happen to include a flair for innovative or especially resourceful piano techniques. But it should be remembered, in any case, that the decided trend toward increasing virtuosity could not be an entirely steady trend. For it was the product not only of the youthful early-Romanticism but of youth itself, and the trend of youth is toward maturity. In other words, within each

14. Cf. the intriguing survey of 19th-century technical advances in pma LIX (1932–33) 45–59 (T. Fielden).
15. Cf. moscheles I 109; II 43–44, 171–72, 203, 220, 221, 252.
16. Cf. mgg VIII 1232–37 (F.-M. Langner).

composer's own sonatas the trend was more likely to be toward less, not greater, virtuosity, as practical experience tempered and channeled the initial animal energies until reaching for the moon became reaching for the obtainable. Like Clementi's sonatas, Weber's and Schumann's became not only more controlled in form but more reasonable to play. It is true that, like Beethoven's late sonatas, Hummel's became more difficult to play, but the new difficulties reflected not so much increased virtuosity as changing styles in a search for new expressive forces. Furthermore, however great the new athletic challenges in the early-Romantic sonata, they never quite add up to the extent and variety of challenges posed by Beethoven's last and most difficult sonatas.

A fourth kind of textural enrichment is the polyphonic activity to be found in the early-Romantic sonata. Nägeli's request for "contrapuntal movements" in 1803 (SCE 26) yielded at least two attempts at actual fugue (by Wölfl, SCE 563–64, and E. T. A. Hoffmann, SSB VIII). But if both this request and its response were unusual there still are many polyphonic passages to report, such as the close, emphatic imitations in the development section of Mendelssohn's Op. 106/i/80–95, or the nearly strict triple counterpoint in the exposition of Schubert's D. 959/i/83–91;[17] or the homage to Mozart's "Jupiter Symphony" finale in the *fugato* coda of Hummel's Op. 20/iii (SSB VIII).

The High-Romantic Style Phase

A near compendium of high-Romantic sonata styles can be found in the unabashed "editorial changes"—the programmatic titles, filled-out textures, "Meistersinger polyphony," and cyclically treated motives —that Wilhelm Rust made without acknowledgment (along with sizable additions up to whole mvts.) in the originally spare, 18th-century sonatas by his grandfather F. W. Rust (SCE 585–87, with ex.; SSB V). Yet these styles do not differ sharply from those of the early-Romantic sonata any more than the latter had from the late-Classic sonata. Rather, the high-Romantic styles reveal that the process of exaggeration was still continuing, and continuing now in relation to the early-Romantic as well as the Classic means. However, the high-Romantic styles do contrast with the early-Romantic in the greater mastery and control that they reveal and in the dichotomy of conservative and progressive that developed within them (*supra*). These several aspects call for separate discussions.

17. But Winkler/SCHUBERT 125–73 and 216–17 concludes that much of the polyphony in Schubert's sons. is of the "latent" or pseudo kind implied by different elements of the texture, cross rhythms, and contrasting sonorities.

With regard to the continuing exaggeration of previous styles, the most evident changes are again in the melody and the texture.[18] The **melody writing** continues to be too varied to permit any generalizations about types beyond describing some of the most prevalent of them again. However, one can now observe a greater breadth and plasticity in much of the melody writing. Extended phrases, especially consequent phrases, had not lacked in the early-Romantic sonata (as in Schubert's D. 960/i/24–35, *supra,* or the last 18 mss. in Mendelssohn's Son. in F/i, for P & Vn, ssb VIII). But now they are cultivated more frequently and knowingly, and, apparently, more deliberately, especially by that past master of artful phrase-and-period syntax, Brahms. Thus, already in the concise exposition of Brahms's Op. 5/i, the first thematic group comprises a double period of three extended phrases each, 6+5+5 and 6+8+8 measures, and the second and closing thematic groups combined comprise a double period of two extended phrases each, 8+9 and 6+10 measures. In this characteristic treatment the composer was achieving his own antidote for the curse of the square, most often four-measure, phrase.

The square phrase was a concomitant of homophonic texture.[19] It challenged, sometimes plagued, imaginative, free spirits of the sonata increasingly, from Mozart and Beethoven to the last of the Romantics. In the Brahms periods just described it shows up only in the subdivisions of the eight-measure phrases. The breadth and plasticity in the other phrases result from skillful extensions that do not simply prolong the cadence but alter the internal rhythmic organization. Schumann thought more often in regular phrases, especially in his earlier sonatas (as in the opening of Op. 11; ssb VIII). But he was no addict of the square phrase. His approach was flexible, as in the fantasy-like period of two phrases, 6+5 measures, that opens Op. 14 (ssb VIII) or the more controlled period of two antecedent phrases and a consequent, 6+6+8 measures, that opens Op. 22 (Ex. 9). In his

18. Schering/NEUROMANTIK compares the "new-" or high-Romantic with early-Romantic music chiefly in terms of society and other arts rather than specific musical traits, but does emphasize the increased pathos, brilliance, musico-historical consciousness, programmatic interest (in instrumental music), and fondness for characteristic means like the much used dim.-7th chord. With particular reference to 2 of our 4 focal composers in this chap., Sturke/BRAHMS explores Brahms's style traits according to early, middle, and late stages of his music (cf. Mitschka/BRAHMS 4–5) and Haase/BRAHMS with special regard to the polyphonic forms and processes in his piano writing; Meister/CHOPIN, Abraham/CHOPIN, Bronarski/CHOPIN, Thomas/CHOPIN, and Walker/CHOPIN all explore style traits in Chopin's piano writing. A new but undated study in Polish, *Studia chopinowskie* by Lew Maze, concentrates on Chopin's Fantasy in f and pieces of similar scope, with only infrequent references to the sons.

19. Cf. Newman/UNDERSTANDING 144–50.

Ex. 9. The opening thematic group in Robert Schumann's
Sonata in g, Op. 22 (after Schumann/WERKE-m VII/iv/22).

three late violin sonatas the flexibility seems to have become more deliberate (as in the opening of Son. 3 in a, SSB VIII).[20]

Chopin showed decidedly the strongest inclination among our four
focal composers to accept and live with the regular four-measure phrase.
Only his Op. 65 (SSB XII) shows an inclination, characteristic of his
last compositions,[21] to experiment with longer and more irregular
phrase lengths. Occasionally his phrases are as obviously regular as
those in Schubert's D. 850/iii quoted above—for example, in the trio
of his "Marche funèbre" (Op. 35/iii), which Bülow found "abominable" [22] but which others, playing it straight and without "interpretation," have found ideal in its simple, unsophisticated purity. Most of
the time Chopin avoided the curse of square phrases, not by defying
the regularity but by disguising it, at either or both ends and/or internally. Thus, in Ex. 10 the first phrase starts on an offbeat, the second
on a downbeat, and the third and fourth on an upbeat.[23] All four
phrases differ in their internal contours and rhythmic organization,
though only slightly between the first and second phrases. Only the
third phrase has two similar subphrases and these differ internally,
too. Only the last phrase has a masculine ending. In the four measures
of Op. 58/i/13–16 Chopin produces a cumulative effect by writing 2
groups of 4 beats, 4 of 2, and one "group" of one beat.

One of the most prevalent types of high-Romantic melody is, again,
the smooth, songful sort. Brahms's Op. 100 starts with the "Meistersinger theme" that appears actually to be based on a song (SSB IX).
Rheinberger exhibits the unusual breadth of his lyricism in the

20. Cf., also, the proselike style of Opp. 105/i/1–11 and 121/i/21–43.
21. Cf. Abraham/CHOPIN 103–4.
22. Cf. Bronarski/CHOPIN II 155.
23. Chopin's own slurs in Ex. 10 go beyond what is meant here but do not
necessarily demarcate phrases.

Ex. 10. From the first movement of Frédéric Chopin's Sonata
in b, Op. 58 (after Chopin/WORKS-m VI 82–83).

"Andante molto" of his Op. 105 (ssb X). Fauré exhibits the unusual
refinement of his lyricism in the "Andante" of his Op. 117 (ssb XIII).
Bennett reveals a gentle, contemplative outlook in the opening of his
Op. 4 (ssb XIV). A more decorative, songful melody may be seen in the
opening movement of Lalo's Sonata for P & Vc (ssb XII). And more
driving yet songful melodies may be seen in the opening movements of
A. G. Ritter's Op. 21 and Hiller's Op. 47 (both ssb X), and of Franck's
Son. in A, Fauré's Op. 13, and Saint-Saëns' Op. 75 (all ssb XIII). Not a
few of the songful melodies are folklike in their simple, reiterated
patterns and their particular scale inflections (as in Grieg's Op. 13/ii,
ssb XV).[24] Others are hymnlike in their simplicity, with one note, one
harmony, and one block chord accompaniment per beat (as in Thalberg's Op. 56/i, ssb XII, and in the trios of several Brahms scherzos—
e.g., the 3d mvts. of Opp. 1, 5, and 34b).

With regard to further aspects of high-Romantic melody, chromaticism continues to abound.[25] Often it occurs as a kind of rhythmic
filler over a relatively diatonic harmony (cf. the quotation from
Chopin's Op. 65/iv in ssb XII). And often it results from borrowed
tones and the alternation of major and minor modes (as in Brahms's Op.
99/iv/1–9). Tovey's concept of melody as the "surface" of harmony
continues to find ample illustration, too, as in the lovely diatonic
middle section in E in Chopin's Op. 58/iii (perhaps the inspiration for
the more chromatic, "Molto più lento" variation in F♯ in Franck's
"Symphonic Variations").

24. Cobbett/CHAMBER I 409–18 (W. W. Cobbett & L. Henry) offers interesting
views on folk elements in chamber music, but unfortunately (and unavoidably, in
the experience of this study) with virtually no concrete evidence nor specific
instances.

25. Cf. Hewitt/DISSERTATIONS item 776 for a study of chromaticism from Beethoven
to Brahms, in progress.

Certain types of high-Romantic melody seem also to require classification by quality, as indefinable as that term still may be in the musical laboratory. Thus, two types seem to be the province almost exclusively of the masters. One is the short, bold, trenchant, dynamic idea—that is, the type that begs for development in a "sonata form." Ideas of that type launch all three piano sonatas by Brahms, all three violin sonatas by Schumann, and Op. 58 by Chopin. The other type is the full-fledged, memorable tune, such as the admirable refrain in the rondo finale of Chopin's Op. 58, called "a sort of war song," by d'Indy, among the themes so "truly resplendent of melodic richness" in this work.[26] On the other hand, one would be tempted to make a melodic type, too, out of the many well-constructed, academically correct themes that are too flat, too naive or innocuous, and often too complete or closed in their own phrase grouping to invite any purposeful continuation in "sonata form" (as seems to be true of many of Reinecke's opening themes, for example). This type, obviously enough, would be the province especially of the second-rate composers. But it is a type that seems to be more conspicuously inadequate in high- than in early- or late-Romantic music, since flat, innocuous themes tend to prevail, anyway, in the early phase of any era (as in Loewe's sons.) and again in the late phase at least in the "creations" of the epigones (as in Sinding's sons.). All of which is tantamount to the truism that sonatas can no more succeed without significant ideas, however these may be defined and typed, than without convincing rhythmic flow, compelling tonal organization, or euphonious, idiomatic scoring. One might even argue that the significant ideas matter exceptionally in the high-Romantic sonata, where actual development of ideas is more often lacking (as in Bennett's Op. 46) than in the high-Classic sonata.

The **harmony and tonality** reveal no clear innovations in the high-Romantic sonata, although both the variety of chords and modulations and the extent of their use seem, on the average, to be proportionally greater. Chopin's fresh, resourceful harmony reveals nearly every imaginable chord type, diatonic or chromatic, and every extension, all the way to a 13th-chord; yet only a surprisingly small percentage of his total chords are altered.[27] Subsequent composers tended to make more constant use of 7th- and 9th-chords (as in Goldmark's Op. 25/ii, ssb IX). The greater co-ordination of dissonance, rhythmic drive, half-step tendencies, and bass-line direction in high-Romantic harmony all help

26. D'Indy/COURS II/1 410 and 407.
27. According to the statistical conclusions in Thomas/CHOPIN 639–68. The first thematic group and bridge in Op. 58/i/1–40 give as concentrated a view of Chopin's harmonic resourcefulness as any comparable section in his sons.

to make the harmonic goals more purposeful, too. A telling example is the broad cadence described in the first twenty-one measures of Brahms's Op. 100, starting and ending in the tonic and emphasizing ii, IV, and ♭II along the way, each approached through its own dominant. The dim.-7th chord continues to occupy a central place in the harmony, in the various ways mentioned earlier.[28] It is inherent right in the opening thematic complex of Liszt's Sonata in b, for example (ssb X), and prevalent in much of the passagework. There is more efficiency, even slickness, in the modulations, near and far. Thus, in thirteen measures Schumann moves easily from e♭ to a♭, to V-of-b = aug.-6/5 in b♭, to b♮ (Op. 14/ii/151–63). In Op. 6/ii, Draeseke simply assumes each dominant chord on an offbeat fortissimo as he slips from D♭ to D and back in three 4-measure units (ssb X).

   Texture and sonority in the high-Romantic sonata show further increases in fullness, polyphonic interest, rhythmic diversity, and idiomatic scoring. Furthermore, the craftsmanship in matters textural is more generally of a professional level. The craftsmanship in the early-Romantic sonata had often betrayed a certain amateurishness, especially in the most progressive sonatas. Impeccable craftsmen like Hummel and Mendelssohn left no doubt of their expertise. Nor did Schubert, except for polyphonic limitations that he apparently recognized and got around artfully enough. But quite apart from an actual amateur like E. T. A. Hoffmann or an occasionally careless composer like Dussek, even such front-rankers as Weber and Schumann revealed shortcomings in their training, such as it was, and their backgrounds as littérateurs-cum-musicians (both ssb VIII). Thus, especially in the first sonata that each completed in his adulthood there are telltale aridities and gaucheries in the bass and filler parts taken by the left hand.[29] In the high-Romantic sonata, the professional composers (including Chopin) rarely reveal such holes in their training, no doubt reflecting the growth and spread of conservatories and the corresponding improvements in teaching (ssb III and IV).

   The greater fullness of texture was soon taken for granted, as we gather from one reviewer, who found Gurlitt's Op. 16 for P solo archaic because of its spare texture.[30] A richly sonorous texture may be observed in the rolled chords of up to ten tones by which the piano states the chorale melody, with a poetic commentary from the cello, in Op. 58/ii by Mendelssohn (ssb VIII). But fullness of texture could be

---

28. Cf. Schering/NEUROMANTIK 58.
29. Cf. the exx. quoted in ssb VIII from Weber's Op. 24/i and Schumann's Op. 11/i; also, Saunders/WEBER 174, 223; Niecks/SCHUMANN 62–64.
30. NZM XLIII (1855) 278.

achieved by polyphonic enlivenment, too, as in the expressive exchanges between partners in Op. 17 for P-duet by Goetz (ssb V). Polyphonic interest of some sort, especially imitative writing, is rarely absent in the sonatas of both Schumann and Brahms [31] And, of course, there are not a few actual fugal movements, like the finale of Brahms's Op. 38 and the "Allegro energico" of Liszt's Sonata in b. Fullness of texture could also be achieved by rhythmic enlivenment—for example, by the dexterous cross rhythms of hemiola in Brahms's Op. 78/i/11–20 or two-against-three in his Op. 100/i/51–74, or by the dotted against the even pattern in Gade's Op. 28/iii (ssb XV), or by the 16th-note syncopations in the passagework of Schumann's Op. 22/i/24–40, or by the isometric pattern, conflicting with the meter of the passagework, in Brahms's Op. 5/v/25–31.[32]

The exaggeration to be noted in high-Romantic texture occurs most conspicuously in the virtuoso piano writing, or what might now be called massive pianism. Alkan's Op. 33/ii, covering almost the whole keyboard at once, provides the extreme example to be expected of that remarkable eccentric (ssb XII). Reubke's Sonata in b♭, with its majestic sonorities and dashing runs in the Lisztian manner, is more representative (ssb X). That such writing was an exaggeration even of early-Romantic piano writing is suggested by the need Liszt and his contemporaries felt to rescore and elaborate on the compositions of Schubert, Weber, and others (as in Liszt's eds. discussed in ssb V and Henselt's version of Weber's Op. 39/iv illustrated in ssb V).[33] Not all the technically advanced writing was of the massive sort. There was, for instance, the light, extremely rapid finger work required by Chopin in Op. 58/ii and iv, or the open-position chordal passagework that often figured in more impassioned music, as in Schumann's Op. 14/i (ssb VIII) or Raff's Op. 14/ii (ssb X).

In the first section of this chapter was noted the **dichotomy of conservative and progressive styles and forms** that developed most sharply in the high-Romantic sonata between Brahms and Liszt. This dichotomy is not to be confused with the functional one of old and new, represented by the 19th-century pedagogic sonatina that never left 18th-century styles as against the full-scale 19th-century sonata that was admired in artistic circles and played in the concert halls (ssb III). Only the latter is concerned in the dichotomy now in question. The

31. Cf. Haase/BRAHMS 78 for an index of numerous polyphonic styles in Brahms's P music. A similar study, concentrating on his chamber music, is in preparation by Donald Pease at the University of North Carolina (as of 1968).

32. Cf. Kempers/ISOMETRISCHE.

33. Recall, too, Liszt's elaboration of music from his own day, including the page from Chopin's Op. 58/iv mentioned in ssb XII.

Ex. 11. From the penultimate statement of element y (cf. ssв X) in Franz Liszt's Sonata in b (after Ed. Peters No. 3601b, p. 315).

actual difference in this instance between conservative and progressive might be elaborated as that between traditional law and logical order versus experimentation and fantasy. The elements and means are essentially the same but they are treated more freely and subjectively, with a compensatory loss in dynamic tension.[34] Thus, the melody tends to unfold continuously, in chain phrases or smaller units rather than in phrase-and-period groupings. The harmony tends toward more exploitation of third relationships, enharmony, and remoter chord progressions (Ex. 11). The passagework depends more on sequence, the ambiguity of the diminished 7th-chord, and continual modulations. The tempo undergoes frequent changes, graduations, and grand pauses. And because these treatments and processes operate in all

34. This conclusion is the gist of the discussion in Mersmann/ROMANTISCHEN. Cf., also, Lang/WESTERN 816–19.

sections of the sonata, not only in development sections, there is a sense of fantasy and improvisation throughout, however tight the logic behind it may be (as it certainly is in Liszt's Sonata in b; cf. ssB X).

One element of the progressive style we are describing was furthered in particular, and has even been called an original (German) contribution.[35] This is the full opening theme that actually proves to be a complex of several separate and separable motives, each capable of independent extension, re-formation, and development. Such a thematic complex was not really without precedent, as in Beethoven's Op. 53/i/1–4. But now it became the fund from which most if not all of the work was drawn.[36] The structural result of planting such a complex seed is a matter of over-all design rather than style (as differentiated earlier). But note may be taken here of the five thematic elements used in Liszt's Sonata in b (ssB X, with structural analysis), the first three of which comprise the initial thematic complex. As discussed in Chapter X, the double-function design that Liszt created out of this complex stands alone at its high level in the 19th-century sonata, with remarkably few imitators and these chiefly among the works of his direct disciples like Viole, Draeseke, and Reubke (all ssB X).

The Late-Romantic Style Phase

In the late-Romantic sonata the **dichotomy of styles and forms** just discussed became both more and less pronounced. It became more so in the sense that it hardened and widened, with the conservatives often becoming epigones, like, say, Dubois (ssB XIII), and the progressives often becoming radicals, like Reger (ssB XI). It became less so in the sense that there were increasing cross influences, new nationalistic influences, and men who do not really fit on either side but fall somewhere in between. Since the epigones were eclectics at bottom, they could respond equally well to influences from either side. Thus, d'Albert's Op. 10 shows some influences of Liszt as well as Brahms (ssB XI). On the other hand, composers like Tchaikovsky and Saint-Saëns, though conservative in their sonata styles, were strong and individual enough to escape the brand of epigonism (ssB XVIII and XIII). Not all the close imitators of Brahms, such as Kiel or W. Berger (ssB X and XI) are necessarily to be written off in that way, either. Nor were all the progressives as abruptly radical as Reger. Composers like Fauré and Sibelius made smoother transitions to the new, different, though

35. MGG XI 813–15 (F. Blume).
36. Reti/BEETHOVEN 166–75 argues, for the most part convincingly, that Op. 53, too, derives entirely from its opening material.

less debatable styles of their later sonatas or sonatinas (SSB XIII and XV).

By his very nature, the epigone offered nothing in his sonatas that could be regarded here as a stylistic change or exaggeration. Rather, he reviewed and often—again, because he was an eclectic—medlied past styles. The further marks of the epigone are high technical competence, untroubled neatness and propriety in the handling of styles and forms, sure practicalness and effectiveness, and a certain initial gloss and excitement that quickly reduce to hollow academicism. A fully representative example, among many such sonatas that still are to be rediscovered on the shelves of the larger dealers, is Op. 9 by Bortkiewicz, written under the strong influence of Chopin's Op. 58 (as described in SSB XVIII).

Without further attempts, then, to dwell on a late-Romantic dichotomy of styles, we may observe some of the relatively fewer changes and exaggerations to be found in this style phase. As before, the **melody** cannot be generalized. One can only point to certain prevalent types. There are simple, lyrical, nicely drawn melodies that could come right out of Mendelssohn except for the late-Romantic tendency to think increasingly in eight-measure phrases (as in the opening of Gernsheim's Op. 12, SSB XI). There are melodies of wider range and broader sweep, such as are in R. Strauss's Op. 6/ii (SSB XI), Sinding's Op. 91/i (SSB XV), Dohnányi's Op. 8/i (SSB XVII), and Glazunov's Op. 74/i (SSB XVIII). There are melodies that unfold in the "endless" Wagnerian manner (as in Medtner's Op. 25/1/ii, SSB XVIII). There are melodies that enter precipitately, with dramatic upward thrusts, as in R. Strauss's Op. 18/iii (SSB XI), Elgar's Op. 82/i (SSB XIV), Dale's Op. 1/i (SSB XIV), and Nicholl's Op. 21/i (SSB XIX). And there are melodies now that not only suggest but actually incorporate folk materials, including the finales of Dvořák's Op. 100 (SSB XVII), Sinding's Op. 73, and Williams' Op. 74 (SSB XIX). This last type only touched the sonata peripherally and infrequently, but does recall at least the atmosphere of nationalism in which many late-Romantic sonatas were created, especially in the "outlying" countries of the sonata.[37]

The **harmony and tonality** in the late-Romantic sonata reveal the most evident changes since the previous style phase. As discussed earlier (SSB I), the present volume stops short of Busoni, J. Haas, Scriabin, Ives, Debussy, and others who were already making frontal attacks on traditional harmony and tonality before World War I. But it still includes among their contemporaries men like Reger, Karg-Elert, Nielsen, and d'Indy who were straining so hard to find new worlds to conquer

37. Cf. SSB IV; Lissa/NATIONALEN.

within the logic of the old that they unintentionally, and probably unwittingly, accomplished almost equivalent attacks. Their ways of straining tradition differ with each composer, as discussed later when each is considered separately. Among others, examples are quoted from Reuss's Op. 27/i, Reger's Opp. 72/i and 89/4/i, and Karg-Elert's Op. 105 (all in ssʙ XI); d'Indy's Op. 63/iii (ssʙ XIII); and Nielsen's Op. 35/i (ssʙ XV). At this point the "strains" may be generalized as increased chromaticism, bigger elisions in standard harmonic progressions, diagonal relations more often and further apart, freer dissonance and voice-leading, and dominant or subdominant relationships two- or three-times removed (V-of-V-of-V, etc.). Gliding in and out of the remotest keys happens so easily and so often that modulation as a means of bridging two structural landmarks almost ceases to exist and the relatively close tonal relationships that still obtain between those landmarks scarcely stand out if at all.

Unfortunately, not all of the late-Romantic strains on harmonic and tonal tradition were quite so enterprising or worthy of respect. In the same style category, a good many other sonatas show advances, hence cannot strictly be called epigonic. But these "advances" tend to strain the good taste rather than the intelligibility of tradition, mostly by making clichés ("barber-shop" harmony) out of the standard altered-chord progressions, by overloading the active chromatic chords with half-step pulls, and by adding 2ds, 6ths, 7ths, and 9ths to diatonic as well as chromatic chords for the sake of piquancy or pungency. By way of illustrations, the three successive examples by Martucci, Longo, and Albéniz in Chapter XVI would be regarded here as stopping just short of sentimentality and triteness in their day, whereas the example by Schytte in Chapter XI would not.

The **texture and scoring** show no distinct advance in the late-Romantic beyond the high-Romantic sonata unless it be in the further exploitation of polyphonic means. An example of the latter is the extraordinary climactic coda of d'Indy's Op. 63/iii, with its culminating apotheosis, triple-forte, in the combination of the two triumphant themes (ssʙ XIII). Otherwise, there was little further to go in the writing for the established instruments. Karg-Elert's Op. 105 and Schäfer's Op. 9 may be more frenetic in their massive pianism and their blood-and-thunder assaults on fading Romanticism, Rachmaninoff may crowd more black notes into his Op. 36/i (ssʙ XVIII), but none could engulf the instrument more than had Alkan's Op. 33 a half-century earlier (ssʙ XII). That some would have liked to is suggested by the increased amount of overthick, unpianistic, quasi-orchestral writing for the piano, as in R. Fuchs' Op. 19/i and Tchaikovsky's Op. 37/i (ssb XI and XVIII; cf. ssb V). Sibelius wrote orchestrally and unpianistically for the piano, too (as in Op. 67/i, ssb XV), but sensitively, not thickly.

The Sonata as a Whole

Thus far, this chapter on "form" has examined the Romantic sonata for its main styles in its early, high, and late phases—that is, for the traits that have governed its behavior as a "generative process." There remains its examination for its main over-all designs—that is, for the designs that appear most often or typically in it throughout the era (form as a "mold"), and for the most noteworthy departures from those designs (form as a "unicum"). First comes the question of the sonata as an organized whole, then the separate consideration of each of its main movement types.

The sonata as a whole, meaning its unity and interrelationships as a cycle of several movements, has received remarkably little attention (cf. sce 133–43), and then chiefly with regard only to thematic inter-relationships in particular sonatas by a particular composer, especially Beethoven.[38] Of course, the **one-movement sonata** raises no problems of cyclical unity, at least not when it is actually no more than a single form. But in the century before Scriabin's later piano sonatas (1907–13) the number of one-movement sonatas of any sort is remarkably small, including chiefly Moscheles' Op. 49, Liszt's "Dante Sonata," Wagner's *Album-Sonate*, Raff's Op. 129, and several examples by Medtner (both before and after Scriabin's; ssb XVIII). These are all simply single "sonata forms" or single, freer, fantasy movements. Liszt's Sonata in b is not a simple "sonata form" but a double-function form, because its several components also serve as the (unseparated) movements of the complete cycle (as discussed and diagramed in some detail in ssb X). Shedlock, Cyril Scott, and others have seen Liszt's work as the single original contribution to form in the 19th-century sonata.[39] Yet it stands alone, with only a few follow-ups, as noted earlier (*supra*), by Liszt's immediate disciples and an occasional later

38. E.g., cf. Misch/EINHEIT and Rosenberg/BEETHOVEN as listed in sce 845 and 854; Reti/BEETHOVEN. Noé/ZYKLISCHEN is a brief survey, from Beethoven on, of interlocking mvts. in a cycle. Richard Crocker has touched briefly but provocatively on whether and how a son. cycle is heard as a whole, comparing its usually substantial length with a hypothetical age-old norm of 5±4 minutes for an immediately digestible "piece" of music (*Current Musicology* V [1967] 50–56); cf., also, Newman/UNDERSTANDING 202–4.

39. Shedlock/SONATA 218–20, 235; Schüz/SONATE; Scott/SUGGESTIONS.

composer (e.g., Liapunov) and none of equivalent importance in solo or duo music.

With regard to the vast majority of **sonatas, in several movements,** only 1 out of the 17 completed, adult sonatas by our 4 focal composers offer any appreciable challenge to the most usual Classic plans of 3 and 4 movements.[40] Of those 4, one is in 2 movements and 3 are in 5 movements. Of the other 43, only 12 are in 3 movements and 31, or about 2½ times as many, are in 4 movements. This last ratio is about the same for the solo and the duo sonatas and seems to apply pretty generally throughout the era. It is no wonder that Brahms joked with his publisher Simrock about cutting his fee by one fourth because he wrote only three movements in Op. 78 (ssB IX). It will be recalled, by contrast (scE 133–34), that the 3-movement sonata had predominated in the Classic Era, with 4- and 2-movement sonatas about tied for second place. The 2-movement sonata appeared much less often in the Romantic Era, mostly only in some sonatinas.

Not a one of the 43 sonatas in 3 and 4 movements departs from what had already been standard solutions to the **order of movements** in the Classic Era (scE 135–36). The first movement is a "sonata form" in a moderate, fast, or very fast tempo and the last most often a rondo or "sonata form." In between is a slower movement, usually in A-B-A design, and, on either side of it, in 4-movement sonatas, a scherzo or dance. Among the but 4 sonatas in fewer or more movements, the one in 2 movements simply deletes the inner slow movement and the 3 in 5 movements simply add another inner movement, whether moderate or scherzo. It is obvious that, at least outwardly and in its largest outlines, the Romantic sonata showed more conformity to norms than the Classic sonata had. This conformity undoubtedly reflects the increased codification and awareness of sonata procedures in the 19th century (ssB II). But when, in 1844, a reviewer objected to the plan S/VF-Sc-Ro in Gurlitt's Op. 3 because it lacked a complete (inner) slow movement,[41] he seems to have been responding mainly to the need that has always been felt in the sonata, for contrast between adjacent movements.

In Chapter III, in connection with the long recitals that became customary during the later 19th century, the greater length of the sonatas themselves was noted. Beethoven's Op. 106, Schubert's D. 959

40. Reference may be made to the tabulations of sons. by Schubert, Schumann, Chopin, and Brahms (ssB VII, VIII, XII, and IX, respectively), which include bibliographic information plus nos., tempos, and keys of mvts., lengths in measures, and, for Schubert and Brahms, approximate performance times.
41. nzm XX (1844) 115–16.

in A, Brahms's Op. 34b in f, and further examples by Raff, Rheinberger, Reger, d'Indy, Dukas, Medtner, Godowsky, and Dale were cited as works ranging from 35 to more than 60 minutes in performance. And there are numerous occasions in the later discussions of these and other individual sonatas when the problem of length must come up again. Among sample comments, in 1822 Rochlitz was complaining about how sonatas seemed to be getting longer and more boring, partly, to be sure, because of more quantity than quality.[42] In 1839 Schumann twice made his celebrated reference to "heavenly length" in Schubert's Symphony in C.[43] In 1918 F. Corder defended Dale's huge Sonata in d against charges of excessive length, insisting that there was nothing wrong with length in itself.[44] And in 1926 Medtner answered friendly criticisms of his sonatas from Rachmaninoff with the remark that "it is *not the length* of musical compositions that creates an impression of boredom, but it is rather the *boredom* that creates the impression of length." [45]

However, there is no question that the average length of sonatas increased in the Romantic Era (if only because of longer phrases, more writing in double-periods, and more modulations to more keys) and that length per se became an increasing consideration in the over-all effect of the sonata. There is, after all, a point of diminishing returns, whether defined by the performer's musical grasp and physical endurance or by the listener's attention span. This point cannot be fixed in any absolute sense, of course, because there are too many variables— the sustaining forces of the music, the caliber of the performer(s), the comprehension and attitude of the listener, the adequacy of the instrument(s), the acoustics of the hall, and even the weather and time of day. Furthermore, the more varied the timbres and any peripheral interests, visual or programmatic, the greater is the length that can be accepted. In these regards and with other considerations being equal, the usual solo or duo settings of the sonata are at the low end of the length-tolerance scale, followed progressively, say, by larger chamber ensembles, orchestral music, oratorio, and opera (with Wagner's uncut operas, lasting five hours or more, often regarded as surpassing absolute tolerance limits).

If an absolute tolerance limit cannot be set for the length of Romantic sonatas, one might venture merely the conclusions of ex-

42. AMZ XXIV (1822) 383; cf. SSB VII.

43. Storck/SCHUMANN 222; Schumann/SCHRIFTEN I 463. Vrieslander/ORGANISCHE considers the problem of length, supporting Schumann's reference on qualitative grounds.

44. MT LIX (1918) 164.

45. Bertensson & Leyda/RACHMANINOFF 246–47; cf. pp. 180 and 276.

perience to the effect that when the Romantic sonata extends beyond about twenty-five minutes the problems of length per se begin to mount rapidly. At the other extreme, or what might be called the shortness tolerance, it is the music much more than the performer or listener that defines the limit. Regarding this limit, one might venture that any Romantic sonata lasting less than about twelve minutes scarcely has time to whip up the kinds of emotions and climaxes in which that genre ordinarily traffics. To appreciate that observation, recall the surprise that still greets the playing of the finale in Chopin's Op. 35, which averages only one minute and thirteen seconds in performance (ssb XII).

Perhaps some comparisons of lengths in the adult, completed sonatas, both solo and duo, by our four focal composers may help to put these observations regarding length on a little more solid ground, although the numbers of measures, which disregard numbers of beats and differences of tempo, can give only an approximate idea of length. The accompanying tabulation includes works on the fringe of the sonata

The Average Number of Measures in the Adult, Completed Sonatas of Four Masters

	First movements/%	Final movements/%	All movements
Schubert	214/27	318/40	805
Schumann	280/36	266/34	777
Chopin	227/30	187/25	746
Brahms	244/30	257/33	806

(Schubert's "Grande Duo," D. 812; Schumann's *Fantasie,* Op. 17, though not his Op. 118/1–3, "for the young"; and Brahms's Op. 34b in f, for 2 Ps) and it makes no distinction between solo and duo. The solos actually run somewhat longer in these and most other master works of the era (except, understandably, for Brahms's Op. 34b), partly because Dussek, Weber, Brahms, Liszt, and others wrote their most monumental, grandiose sonatas for piano alone and partly because Schumann, Brahms, and others wrote their solo rather than their duo sonatas among their earlier works, before experiencing the tendency of most composers in their advancing years toward more conciseness and moderation.

Taking the sonatas of our four focal composers in the chronological order of their composition, we do not find them showing the gradual increase in length that a broader sampling, covering the whole era, would almost certainly show. But putting them all together yields a total average length of 785 measures that is 199 (or a 3d) more than the average of 586 measures for all of Beethoven's standard 32 sonatas for P solo. To be sure, only 34 per cent of these last are in more than 3 movements as against 72 per cent of the Romantic masterworks in question. The average playing time for Beethoven's solo piano sonatas is about 20 minutes, as against 27 for Schubert (about the same as for Weber) and 26 for Brahms.[46] In our tabulation of lengths the outer movements are averaged separately, for these are the ones most likely to pose length problems, especially the finales. As might be expected, Schubert's finales average substantially more measures than his first movements. Otherwise the differences between outer movements are not considerable, allowing for the effect on the average of the short finale in Chopin's Op. 35. With reference only to solo piano sonatas again, the average length of Schubert's first movements exceeds only by a few measures that of Beethoven's, Weber's, and Dussek's.

With regard to **tonality,** the home keys selected by our four focal composers show an even distribution of major and minor as against a ratio of about four-to-one in favor of major in the Classic Era (SCE 137). All of Schumann's full-scale sonatas (excluding Op. 17) and all of Chopin's are in minor keys, but Schubert's and Brahms's numerous sonatas in major as well as minor balance the ratio. The impression gained here has been of a continuing increase in the number of sonatas in minor keys throughout the era, although statistics are lacking to confirm that impression. Not a few Romantic sonatas change to the opposite mode right from the start of the finale, most often to major. While this change is peculiarly absent in the sonatas of our four focal composers, it can be found early and easily in the era, in Dussek's C. 178 in e♭/E♭, Field's Op. 1/3 in c/C, and Weber's Op. 49 in d/D (as well as Beethoven's Opp. 90 in e/E and 111 in c/C); and increasingly often later in the era, as in three of Mendelssohn's six organ sonatas and five of Reger's thirty-one sonatas. (Each of the 4 separate mvts. changes from minor to major in R. Strauss's Op. 5—b/B, E/e/E, f♯/F♯, b/B.) But it is hard to claim the "heroic" or "victorious" turn to a major finale in the minor/major sonata as a particular Romantic innovation[47] in the face of a fair number of major/minor examples, too, starting with Ries's Op. 21 in A/a, Czerny's Op. 7 in A♭/a♭, and Woržischek's Op. 5 in G/g. (R. Fuchs's Op. 19 is in G♭/f♯.)

The actual keys selected by our four composers range only up to four sharps and three flats in major, and three sharps and five flats in minor, with a, C, f, and A being the most frequently used keys, in that order. Thus, in key choice, too, our four composers did not go much

46. These figures are based on averages of recordings and personal experience.
47. As in Egert/FRÜHROMANTIKER 100.

beyond the Classics (sce 137–38). They were also somewhat on the conservative side of their times again, although the key of Pinto's Op. 3/1 in e♭ must have seemed unusual well after it appeared about 1802 (ssb XIV) and that of Woržischek's Op. 20 in b♭ still brought special mention in 1826, as well as its sections in seven sharps.[48] At first, such sections and entire movements supplied the chief instances of keys in the most sharps and flats, especially e♭ and a♭ (as in the entire middle section in a♭ in the 2d mvt., in A♭, in Loewe's Op. 41 in E♭, or a slow mvt. in e♭ in Cramer's Op. 25/1 in E♭, or the Czerny finale in a♭ noted just above).

Regarding favorite keys or key associations, f♯ was cited (*supra*, under early-Romantic melody) as a favorite key for sonatas opening with an impassioned flow. The key of A♭ was used often for opening or inner movements with a more peaceful, gentle flow, perhaps influenced by Beethoven's Op. 26/i, as in that same Op. 41/ii by Loewe, or Spohr's Op. 125/i, or Bennett's Op. 46/i (ssb XIV; cf. sce 564). The key of f seems to have been a favorite for sonatas with a dramatic opening, like Op. 5 by Brahms. But beyond these generalizations and some key associations peculiar to individual composers,[49] no clearer case can be supported here for key associations in the Romantic sonata, especially in view of its remarkably infrequent use of specific programmes (*infra*).

The choice of key for an inner movement is more likely to be determined, of course, less by association with a mood or style than by its relation to the home key. In the adult, completed sonatas of our four focal composers, about 59 per cent have one movement in another key, 34 per cent have two movements in other keys, and the rest have only movements that change the mode of the home key. In order of frequency, the preference is strongest for the submediant major key, then the mediant major, subdominant major, dominant major, submediant minor, change of mode to major, mediant minor, change of mode to minor, subdominant minor, and raised tonic major. Including both mediant and submediant keys, major or minor, more than half of these preferences illustrate the all-important 3d relationships of Romantic tonality. (Schubert's D. 459 emphasizes the submediant major in the development of the first mvt., the trio of the second, the key of the third, and at two structural landmarks in the finale, mss. 46–47 and 61.)

The tonal organization of the sonata cycle has always been a rela-

48. amz XXVIII (1826) 204.
49. L. Aguettant argues such associations in Chopin's music, key by key, in rm/chopin 79–86, though with few references to the sons.

tively passive means of achieving over-all unity, the more so in the Romantic Era, when frequent distant modulations at the local levels of form tended increasingly to obscure the tonal landmarks at the broader levels. Stylistic consistency has also been a passive means of unity, especially as it must depend chiefly on the circumscribed vocabularies and habits of any one musician. For more positive or active means one must look to four methods, all of them consciously intensified throughout the era except the third—interlocking of movements, thematic interrelationships, programmatic continuity, and an over-all curve of dynamic tension. In that order, these methods need separate comments.

Although there were interesting Classic precedents, such as those in Beethoven's Opp. 101 and 110 (sce 141–42), the **interlocking of movements** through their later repetition, partial or complete, within other movements or separate, provides some of the most evident arguments for structural innovations in the Romantic sonata.[50] The need for closer ties between the movements is suggested by the increased efforts to lead one movement into the next without a distinct break, "attacca" (as had already happened throughout Beethoven's Op. 27/i and happens before the "Scherzo" in Brahms's Op. 1 and before the finale in his Op. 5); or without more than a suspensive cadence between adjacent movements (as happens before the finale of Hummel's Op. 20); or without any more than a slowing of the rhythm (as happens before the finale of Mendelssohn's Op. 106).

Actual interlocking may be illustrated by noting a few out of numerous examples. The "Scherzo e Intermezzo" in Schumann's Op. 11 presents an A-B-A design in which the trio or "Intermezzo" contrasts so sharply in tempo, key, and style with the A or "Scherzo" section that the effect is like alternating movements. A similar procedure, in reverse tempos, occurs in Brahms's Op. 100, with the "Andante" and "Vivace" making an A-B-A-B-A-coda ("Vivace"), an example that was imitated numerous times, as we shall see in later chapters. In the finale of Brahms's Op. 78 the violin returns to the middle (slow) movement without a change in the finale tempo (ms. 83), and again in altered rhythms (mss. 93, 106, etc.), all serving to point up thematic interrelationships, too (*infra*). In Brahms's Op. 5, the fourth movement, "Intermezzo (Rückblick)," is indeed a "glance back," at the second, "Andante." In the finale of d'Indy's Op. 63 the return to the theme of the variations in the first movement is not

50. As cited earlier, Noé/ZYKLISCHEN surveys this topic briefly, starting with the statement that it has been grossly neglected by writers.

simply a recollection of an earlier idea but the incorporation of a complete section (newly scored), and with enough force to give an A-B-A sense to the whole sonata. The finale (2d mvt.) in both of Dale's sonatas is a theme-and-variations in which one or more variations each serve as a slow movement, a scherzo, and an actual finale.[51] Such interlocking through variation form seems to have encompassed the entire cycle in one Arthur O'Leary's "Theme in C Minor (with elaborate variations in form of a sonata)." [52] Of course, the most renowned and certainly one of the most successful examples of interlocking movements is Liszt's Sonata in b, cited earlier as a double-function "sonata form" and sonata cycle rather than a single-movement sonata (and described, with chart and exx., in ssb X).

By far the most prevalent and most discussed means of giving positive unity to the several movements of a Romantic sonata cycle was that of **interrelated themes.**[53] This means had ample precedents in both the Baroque and Classic sonata (sbe 78–79, sce 138–40). But in the Romantic sonata (and other music) it was elevated to a veritable credo, espoused by some of the era's finest composers and writers, including d'Indy, who credited its perfection largely to his teacher Franck and viewed the latter partly on that account as the true successor to Beethoven (ssb XIII). And in the music itself it was applied to the nth degree, until every note of the score could be related to an initial source idea. Here was the final, outermost circle in the trinity that had at its center the source or original idea, next the dualism or tension inherent in that idea, and lastly the composition that grew entirely out of it.[54] There were even those well-known varieties, not always clearly distinguishable, in both the nature and the treatment of the source idea, including Berlioz's "idée fixe," Liszt's "thematic transformation," Brahms's "basic motive," Wagner's "leitmotiv," Franck's "cyclical treatment," and Sibelius's "organic evolution of a germ idea."

Naturally, quite that much emphasis on thematic interrelationships did not go unchallenged. Time and again, later, we shall find 19th-century reviewers complaining that excess application of this means reveals lack of invention and produces dullness and cerebral writing.

---

51. In this view, the objection to the variations as topheavy in Dale's Op. 11 (mt LXIV [1923] 480) seems unjustified.

52. mt XXI (1880) 411.

53. Marx/zyklische is a brief, recent survey of this means. If a full study of it is lacking, the reason is not any lack of special studies confined to the works of single composers, especially Romantics (as noted where pertinent, in later chaps.).

54. Mersmann/romantischen.

In the 20th century the validity of the principle itself has been challenged. Thus, Calvocoressi has observed, reasonably enough, that thematic relationships in themselves are no guarantee of either vitality or beauty.[55] Others have even doubted, for example, that any "organic evolution of a germ idea" actually operates in Sibelius's music.[56] But there can be no doubt that a majority of the Romantics embraced the principle of thematic relationships as a creative way out. The masters found fresh worlds to conquer in it. The less imaginative composers welcomed the crutch it held out to them quite as our less imaginative Moderns have welcomed the tone row.

Contemporary with and soon after the many important precedents that, as always, Beethoven had supplied (SCE 139–40), the principle of thematic relationships began to be taken up with a vengeance. Early examples (all discussed in SSB VIII) include L. Berger's Op. 18, based on a six-note turn without letup in all three movements; Loewe's Op. 41, based in all four movements on a motive that Schumann found increasingly tiresome in spite of his own predilection for intensive thematic relationships; and J. E. Leonhard's prize-winning Op. 5, based as relentlessly as Berger's on a weak initial motive and also deplored in that regard by Schumann.

Our four focal composers rank in the order of Schubert, Chopin, Schumann, and Brahms as regards their interest, from least to most, in exploiting thematic relationships. This order almost duplicates the chronology of their first important sonatas. Schubert, like Mozart, Hummel, Dussek, and Weber, seems to have taken only an occasional, incidental interest in such means of unity.[57] There are always the questions of how subtle the relationships might be and how much certain tentative relationships might result merely from a uniformity of melodic style. One can only answer that Schubert was a forthright melodist and that there is no more reason to suspect unrecognizable subtleties in his music than in that of Schumann, Liszt, Brahms, or Reger, whose obviously deliberate uses of thematic relationships seem always to be recognizable, no matter how subtle. Thus, thematic relationships might be argued in Schubert's D. 459 (cf. the 4-note descents in mvt. i/2 and 33, ii/130–31, iii/1–2 and 20–22 and 24–25) or D. 568 (cf. the rising chordal incipits of the outer movements), but the ideas and their locations seem too casual for the resemblances to be more than fortui-

55. Cobbett/CHAMBER II 3 (with regard to d'Indy's music).

56. E.g., cf. Hill/SIBELIUS and Collins/GERM. In Emmanuel/DUKAS 70–71 a curious parallel in thematic relationships between Beethoven's Op. 101 and Franck's Son. in A is described simply to show how unfruitful such analysis can be.

57. Cf. the doubts raised in Einstein/SCHUBERT 130–32.

tous.[58] In the initial themes throughout his last sonata, D. 960, Schubert may seem more consciously to be establishing relationships. Yet, each of these themes grows out of one of his favorite melodic styles, turning around the first note, and in that respect all four movements of the previous sonata, D. 959, could just as well be related to those of D. 960, too.

Chopin's two most important sonatas, Opp. 35 and 58, show subtle but more positive and likely thematic relationships. Op. 35 seems to exploit 3–1–2(–3) of the minor scale, as in its opening theme (cf. mvt. i/9 and 41–44, ii/1–3 and 87–88, iii/3–4, and iv/1), although, admittedly, one could find similar figures in almost any minor piece of the times and there is the question of the "Marche funèbre" having been composed two years before the other movements. But the interrelation of the two themes in the first movement gives some support for the resemblances in the other movements. In Op. 58, Chopin seems to exploit the descending chordal anacrusis and downbeat at the start (as in mvt. i/23–24 and 41–42, ii/6 and 12–13, iii/11–12 and 29, and iv/18–20 and 257).

The thematic interrelationships in Schumann's and Brahms's sonatas are unequivocal and far too consistent to be unpremeditated. Thus, in Schumann's Op. 11, the rarely absent motive of the "Allegro vivace," starting as 1–2–3 in the minor scale, reappears clearly right from the start of each of the other movements, although it is anticipated only indirectly in the two-page "Introduction." The recurring motives in Opp. 14 and 22—5- and 4-note, stepwise descents, respectively—are similarly active as cyclic ties, but less conspicuously and more artfully so. In Schumann's late sonatas, for P & Vn, the relationships become more subtle, but the clear return in the finale of Op. 105 (at ms. 168) to that work's beginning leaves no doubt that Schumann had those relationships much in mind.

Brahms's melodic interrelationships are regarded here as being unsurpassed in the Romantic Era in the musical versatility they reveal, their functional (or structural) value, their subtlety, and their all-pervasiveness. In these respects they go beyond the related treatment in the big sonatas of Liszt (ssb X) and d'Indy (ssb XIII), and are quite the equal of (though not the same as) the leitmotiv complexes woven into Wagner's last operas. Brahms did not interrelate whole themes ordinarily, but "basic motives" or germ cells, characteristically reducible to

58. A letter from Martin Chusid argues for ties between the outer mvts. in D. 821 (not mentioned in Chusid/1824). Cf. fn. 5 in AM XL (1968) 186–95 (M. K. Whaples), with more on such ties, in Schubert's quartets.

from three to five notes.[59] Thus, in Op. 1 he bases every idea on—or, rather, generates every idea out of—the EFGAG in the opening, or its transpositions, inversions, and other recognizable alterations. Similarly, Op. 2 is based on ABC♯F♯, Op. 5 on A♭GD♭, Op. 34b on FGA♭F, Op. 38 on BCB, and so on.[60] One example, from Brahms's Op. 100, should help to illustrate some vicissitudes of a Brahms basic motive (Ex. 12). As this example also suggests, Brahms resorted to permutations of the order of the notes along with other variations of the basic motive in his later works, increasing the subtlety of the process without evident loss to its functional value. Furthermore, he tended to place the clearest references to the basic motives not necessarily in the incipits but at climaxes, principal cadences, and other strategic moments in the structure.[61] And finally, he seems to have used two similar basic motives in his final two sonatas, Op. 120/1 & 2, in order to unite them in a kind of "diptych," to use the term that already has been applied similarly to his pair of quartets Op. 51/1 & 2.[62]

Contrary to what might be expected, or to the literature of the Romantic symphony and, of course, the symphonic poem, no front-rank Romantic sonata was identified with a **programme,** even a vague one, by its composer. An over-all programme would be another means of achieving unity, at least external unity, in the Romantic sonata cycle. But the closest approaches to a programme in the masterworks are only such as the sad story of mental deterioration Weber is supposed to have had in mind when he wrote Op. 70 (ssʙ VIII), or the intimate thoughts of "Klara" that are supposed to be hidden in Schumann's Op. 11 (ssʙ VIII), or what is only possibly Liszt's own identification of his "Dante Sonata" with the *Divine Comedy* (ssʙ X).

A few specific programmes do appear in sonatas of minor significance, such as the descriptions in several early-19th-century "battle sonatas";[63] the gypsy dances, with explanatory inscriptions, in Loewe's *Zigeuner Sonata* (ssʙ VIII); the scenes before and after marriage, complete with quarrel and reunion, in Krug's *Characteristic Tone-Paintings: Three*

59. "Basic motive" is the term coined and discussed helpfully by P. Goetschius in the prefaces to his analytic eds. of Brahms's (and others') symphonies in piano reductions (pub. by Oliver Ditson in the late 1920's).

60. Fisher/ʙʀᴀʜᴍs examines Brahms's Op. 108 in detail, finding it based on 6 melodic and 2 rhythmic elements, all introduced in the opening 2 mss.

61. Cf. these same processes in his "German Requiem," as described, with exx., in ᴍʀ XXIV (1963) 190–94 (W. S. Newman).

62. Hill/ʙʀᴀʜᴍs. Rubinstein's 3d Vn son. starts with quotations from his first and 2d Vn sons. (cf. Cobbett/ᴄʜᴀᴍʙᴇʀ II 311 [W. W. Cobbett]).

63. Cf. sᴄᴇ 141, 769, 808–9; Subirá/ᴀʟʙᴀ 309 (on an ex. by one Calcina); Favre/ ꜰʀᴀɴçᴀɪsᴇ 118 (on an ex. by V. Dourlen, ssʙ XII); and the finale of I. A. Ladurner, cited in ssʙ XII.

Ex. 12. The basic motive in Brahms's Sonata in A, Op. 100, as it appears in (a) i/1–2, (b) i/66–68, (c) ii/1–2, (d) ii/24–25, (e) iii/3–4, (f) iii/91–92.

Grand Sonatas . . . (ssb VIII); "the four ages" in the life of man in Alkan's Op. 33 (ssb XII); "a life's sketch" in Kühmstedt's Op. 36;[64] and Moorish scenes in the *Alhambra-Sonata* by Schulz-Beuthen (ssb X).

In a larger number of sonatas that have programmatic titles and/or inscriptions, including separate movement titles, at most a mood or style is conveyed, and sometimes nothing at all, unless it be a reminder that sonatas with titles get published more readily and sell better than those without (ssb III). Thus, only a mood is conveyed in Dussek's C. 211, "Élégie harmonique," and his title "Le Retour à Paris" has no programmatic bearing on C. 221. Brahms, like MacDowell a half-century later (ssb XIX), began with a bit of verse on occasion (Opp. 1/ii and 5/ii), but again only a mood is conveyed (ssb IX). The same is true with regard to the titles and bits of verse over the four movements of *The Maid of Orleans* by Bennett (ssb XIV).[65] The majority of Medtner's sonatas bear exotic titles over both the cycles and the separate movements, as well as florid inscriptions in the musical text (ssb XVIII), all of which have little or no direct bearing on the content composed by this absolutist-at-heart. One can only conclude that the absence of any significant use of programmes in Romantic sonatas is one more confirmation of the generally conservative view that the Romantics took of the sonata.[66]

The fourth and last means of binding the complete sonata cycle is the creation of an over-all **curve of dynamic tension.** One almost accepts as axiomatic the idea that in the Romantic Era a complete sonata must describe an over-all curve of force. It must, in other

64. ssb X; described, with exx., in nzm XLVII (1857) 78–80.

65. In mw IV (1873) 51 and 68 is a long review of a Son. in a, Op. 4, for P solo (not known here) by one Eugen Grüel, discussing its association with poetry; cf., also, nzm LXXII/1 (1876) 124.

66. It is interesting to note the resistance to programme sons. & titles in moscheles I 220–21, II 38, 176–77, 249. Schumann insisted more than once that his programmes came to him only after he wrote his music (ssb VIII). Eschman/forms 141–42 calls attention to the incongruity of relating an over-all programme to a type of cycle (the son.) in which the first mvt. is so complete within itself.

words, achieve a climax profile that takes in, and therefore unites, all of its movements. It is true that not all Romantics subscribed (or could subscribe?) to this dynamic view of the sonata. Rheinberger, Raff, Kiel, and Medtner were among those who wrote large-scale sonatas that, in spite of episodes of great power, are essentially contemplative and philosophical in their scope, especially so in the absence of orchestral or vocal color. Bennett and Balakirev were among those who made of their sonatas little more in a structural sense than successions of static tableaux. But for those very reasons, quite apart from any other "deficiencies" that might be listed, these men were neither the true representatives nor the surviving masters of the Romantic sonata.

The truly representative masters and most of the other Romantic composers who understood, did subscribe to the idea of one over-all climax profile—in fact, carried it to the broadest, most monumental applications that are known in all music history. Recognizing the special demands of a time art, these composers learned to shape the climax profile to best advantage, discovering, as in drama and literature, that the rise must be maintained almost, if not right, to the very end so that the peak will be followed by little if any anticlimax.[67] And they showed that the peak itself could be pointed, as just before the end of Wagner's *Tristan und Isolde* or of the strikingly similar ending in d'Indy's Op. 63 (ssʙ XIII); or it could be rounded, as in the chorale-like statements of one main theme that crown the finale of Bruckner's "Romantic Symphony" (No. 4) and the canonic episodes that similarly crown Franck's Sonata in A (all of these being gentlemanly predecessors of the orgiastic peaks in Scriabin's sonatas).

In the Classic sonata we found no clear tendency to put the climax or greatest weight in any one movement (sᴄᴇ 142–43). In the Romantic sonata that tendency did appear, especially after the mid-century, when conscious efforts to put the climax in the finale begin to be evident. But the question of where the profile peaks is so complex that it still has to be evaluated largely on subjective grounds. For example, is the climactic movement the movement that is the fastest, the loudest, the widest-ranged on the instrument, the harmonically most intense, the melodically most sustained, or the structurally most complex? It is hardly likely that all or even most of these extremes would obtain in the same movement. Some of them could be influenced by the performer, perhaps enough to relocate the peak.

Furthermore, there were characteristic problems with the outer

67. Muns/ᴄʟɪᴍᴀx is a diss. on the aesthetic nature and history of climax in music, with considerable space devoted to 19th-c. manifestations. Cf., also, Newman/ᴄʟɪᴍᴀx.

movements that could affect, and no doubt were furthered by, the problem of the over-all climax profile. The "sonata form" of the first movement posed the chief academic demands, increasingly so as its textbook definitions were elaborated and rigidified (ssb II). The finale posed the chief structural problems, one main reason apparently being a felt need to alter, intensify, and, unfortunately, overcomplicate the traditionally light, gay rondo sufficiently for it to carry more weight. Only the inner movements could be composed more freely (which undoubtedly explains why Weber and Schubert found them easier to write).[68] Finally, when all these factors are considered, one must still raise the heretical question of whether the over-all climax profile is quite the determinant of artistic worth in a sonata that the Romantics made of it. Enchanting melody, lilting or driving rhythm, euphonious scoring, idiomatic writing, and a few strokes of genius here and there —these still seem to have been the determinants at least for public success. If Brahms succeeded partly because of the climax profile, Chopin, whose battles with the larger forms no experienced musician can fail to recognize, succeeded in spite of it.

As our four focal composers are viewed here, Schubert seems to have been striving for an over-all peak in his sonata finales no more consciously than Haydn, Mozart, or Beethoven had. All three finales in his three great posthumous sonatas are still light and fast, albeit long and complex, rondos. The finale in his D. 784, in a, is one that is shorter and more intensive, but still not enough so to top the dramatic first movement or the symphonic middle movement in aesthetic weight. Chopin might be said to achieve a peak in the finale of his Op. 35 through the sheer surprise created by its shortness and under- rather than overstatement, though not in any more usual sense. The finale in his Op. 58 would be viewed here as about on a par in weight with the other movements except for the sharp edge that its distinctive, compelling refrain and rousing coda give. In each of the finales of Schumann's three main piano sonatas, there is enough added weight of sound, melodic intensity, and cumulative speed to achieve a peak. And in the coda of the finale in his Op. 105 (now after the mid century) there is that telling return to the first movement's beginning that is climactic by its very nature.

Only in Brahms's Op. 34b, the transcription of the piano Quintet in f, does any of his "sonata" finales make quite so decisive a peak, thanks to the internal climaxes and stunning "Presto, non troppo" coda, as, say, the finale of his Symphony 1, in c, with its pointed peak on a syncopated, *fortissimo* dim.-7th chord (ms. 285) and its culmi-

68. Cf. ssb VIII; Költzsch/schubert 9 and fn. 4.

nating coda. But, again, in each of the three piano sonatas (also after the mid-century), and in spite of the increased weight Brahms gives to the slow and scherzo movements, the tempo, drive, and melodic intensity of the finale are sufficient to achieve a clear peak in the over-all profile. Among other of his finale peaks, the fugue in Op. 38 and the interlocking with the previous movement in Op. 78 should be recalled.

At least two composers seem to have been striving for a steady rise in the climax profile throughout their sonata cycles. Hiller's three piano sonatas omit slow movements and generally tend to step up the speed, volume, and other means of excitement from start to finish; and A. G. Ritter does somewhat the same with the increasingly short movements of his organ sonatas (both ssb X).[69] The over-all dynamic plan, increasingly active tonal movement, and even stepped-up time signatures (from 4/4 to 3/4, and so on) become agents of the climactic rises in these sonatas. But no such agents seem to prevail in the majority of sonatas by our four focal composers.[70] As the structural charts in Chapter X should suggest, Liszt's one-movement "Dante Sonata" achieves an over-all climax profile through its tonal curve and the strong return to the tonic, but not necessarily through its dynamic contrasts, which describe, instead, several subclimaxes. His Sonata in b achieves a more compelling profile with its climactic "finale" that recapitulates the opening and its anticlimactic coda of resignation that recalls the thematic elements. His decision to reject a more brief, obvious, brilliant coda he had written earlier for this Sonata (as quoted in ssb X) bears significantly on the climax profile.

The First Fast Movement

There is less of structural consequence to write about in the separate movements of the Romantic than of the Classic sonata. In the first place, as discussed earlier, the Romantics were only expanding, not replacing the Classic structural means. In the second place, they were using fewer designs and, what is more, applying those designs more uniformly, notwithstanding structural experiments by a few of the more adventurous composers. The greater uniformity reflects, of course, the new awareness of form types (or molds), especially "sonata form," as these were now described in detail by the theorists and crystal-

69. Cf. nzm XXXV (1851) 258–59 on this means in Ritter's Op. 20 for P solo.
70. Fellinger/dynamik 71–77 finds dynamics used for structural unity within "sonata forms" by Brahms but not over the whole cycle.

lized in their textbooks (ssb II). The inevitable consequence was an in-creasingly self-conscious, academic approach to "sonata form." As Busoni wrote in 1907, the moment the composers "cross the threshold of the Principal Subject, their attitude becomes stiff and conventional, like that of a man entering some high bureau of officialdom." [71]

No better evidence of at least outer structural uniformity in Ro-mantic sonata designs can be adduced than the fact that every first movement of every adult sonata by our four focal composers adheres more or less closely to what was to become textbook "sonata form." [72] Yet this identification of a mold does not mean that each composer with sufficient imagination could not take sufficient liberties to give a per-sonal stamp to his handling of "sonata form." Changes, additions, and deletions within the design itself, the options of an introduction and a coda, a surprising variety in the tonal courses that could be followed, and unrestricted flexibility in the proportions throughout the design—all these, coupled with the wide choice of melodic, har-monic, rhythmic, and textural styles such as were discussed earlier in this chapter, gave ample latitude, indeed, to the composer and enabled the creation of many a structural unicum in the Romantic sonata.

Starting with the relative **proportions of the three main sections** of "sonata form," and not including any repeats, introductions, or codas, one finds the following percentages in the first movements of our four composers:

Proportions in the First Movements of the Sonatas by Four Masters

	Exposition	Development	Recapitulation
Schubert	38	25	37
Schumann	33	35	32
Chopin	47	28	25
Brahms	38	30	32

Schumann, with about equal proportions, is the only one to show even a slight preponderance in the development section. Schubert and Chopin both show their lesser interest in this section. The low per-centage for Chopin's recapitulations recalls his by-passing of the opening theme in that section of all three adult sonatas (though not in his early Op. 4). The high percentage for Brahms's expositions

71. Busoni/SKETCH 8.
72. Among rare experiments with the scheme of "son. form" before the mid century, the chiastic (or m-n-o-n-m) principle may be noted in Op. 49/i by Weber and in several of Pocci's "son. forms" (ssb VIII).

recalls the extended bridges he customarily erects in that section.[73] Slow introductions were frequent—at least the short type Beethoven used in his Op. 78—in the sonatas of some early Romantics, like those of Ries, causing one reviewer to exclaim, "What sonatas don't have them now!" [74] But they are infrequent in the first movements now in question, there being none in Schubert's or Brahms's, one, of but 4 measures, in Chopin's (Op. 35), and 3, totalling from 7 to 17 per cent of the earlier movements, in Schumann's (Opp. 11, 121, and Son. 3 for P & Vn). On the other hand, all of the first movements but 3 early ones by Schubert (D. 459, 568, 575) and one by Schumann (Op. 11) have at least short codas, ranging from 4 to 20 per cent of the entire movements in Schubert's, 10 to 32 in Schumann's, only 3 to 5 in Chopin's, and 9 to 19 in Brahms's.

By comparison with the proportions in the sonata first movements of the Classic masters (SCE 146–47), these proportions are similar but less variable. Little reason remains in the Romantic Era for arguing a binary rather than a ternary concept of "sonata form" (cf. SCE 143–47), although we have seen that the binary concept survived a little longer in the textbooks (SSB II). The proportions in Liszt's double-function Sonata in b, when it is viewed as a single "sonata form," are 43, 26, 21, and 11 per cent (including the coda), thus already revealing the diminishing order that was to become increasingly common as a means of cumulative intensity in the late-Romantic and Modern sonata (as well as symphony).

A question vitally affecting the proportions in Romantic "sonata form" is that of taking the **repeat of the exposition** when it is called for (a question deferred in our mentions of performance practices in SSB V because of its significance here). The repeat of the second "half" (development and recapitulation) is no longer a question, because it had disappeared by 1800 with but few exceptions (e.g., Schubert's D. 537/i and 664/i). And the repeats in the other movements have never been a matter of any particular doubt. But Weber, Schubert, and Chopin called for a repeat of the exposition in all their sonata first movements, Schumann in all of his but Op. 14 and Sonata 3 for P & Vn, and Brahms in nearly half of his, not including Op. 2 or any of the sonatas for P & Vn and Cl & P. Starting with occasional examples at the outset of the era (e.g., Moscheles' Op. 49 and Loewe's Op. 41),

73. By way of cumulative statistics for first mvts. in P sons. by Haydn, Mozart, Beethoven, Brahms, and Schubert, Abbott/FORM 316–29 gives as the first 6 dispositions of the 3 sections, in descending order of frequency and descending ratios: E(xposition) D(evelopment) R(ecapitulation), ERD, DER, DRE, RED, RDE (none being equal ratios).

74. AMZ XIII (1811) 212.

the repeat was discarded more and more until, at the end of the era, it was all but gone.

H. J. Moser has concluded that the repeat (when called for) is needed on aesthetic grounds—that it contributes to a satisfying but form, AAB (B being the development and recapitulation as one unit); and that it provides a needed re-view of the exposition material.[75] It has a psychologically different effect from the first statement, he adds, because it returns to ideas now familiar. Yet it does not have the same effect as the recapitulation because it is still leaving, not coming back home. There are also occasional facts that throw light on this repeat question. For example, only after Beethoven had several chances to hear his *"Eroica* Symphony" did he decide a repeat was needed, which he then added.[76] A review of Weber's Op. 24 expressed concern about how the first ending of the exposition might lead back to the start for the repeat.[77] The solicitation of sonatas in 1826 by the Swiss publisher Nägeli included the request that there be no repeats.[78] Instead of using repeat signs Albéniz actually wrote out the exposition a second time in his Sonata 4/i (ssb XVI), though not with the elaborations to be found some 125 years earlier in Emanuel Bach's set "mit veränderten Reprisen" (sce 424–26).

All of which information merely helps to confirm that there was considerable awareness of the repeat question at the time. Weber, Schubert, and Chopin may still have been accepting the tradition of the exposition repeat without much question. Yet, all three did make careful distinctions between their first and second endings. And certainly the characteristically long recitals after the mid-century allowed ample time for sonatas to be played with all repeats (ssb III). In short, the available evidence generally suggests that the Romantics knew and meant what they were doing both when they did put the repeat sign in and when they did not.

In the Romantic "sonata form" the **tonal plan** continued to function as a main means of both cohesion and tension. However, to recall a statement made earlier about tonality in the over-all cycle, as the harmonic progressions and passing modulations grew more colorful and remote, especially near the era's end, the broader shifts in the tonality became increasingly dim and ineffectual as structural landmarks. In other words, the tonal plan retained its structural force most clearly on the conservative side of the dichotomy in style and form that

75. Moser/MUSIKÄSTHETIK 99–104.
76. Cf. NOTES XXV (1968) 41 (C. W. Hughes).
77. AMZ XV (1813) 597 (G. M. Weber).
78. Cf. MOSCHELES I 120; ssb IV.

was discussed earlier, including in this respect both Schumann and Chopin as well as Schubert and Brahms among our four focal composers. The nature of the tonal plan as organized by these four composers may be illustrated best by comparing their choice of keys at six tonally strategic landmarks in "sonata form": (1) the second theme of the exposition; (2) the end of the exposition and very start of the development; (3) the areas of the development section, typically up to three, on which the tonality settles long enough to establish a sense of key; (4) the start of the recapitulation; (5) the second theme of the recapitulation; and (6) the coda, in which one harmony other than the tonic is usually emphasized. In the following paragraph the keys in thirty-one of the sonatas by our four composers are compared, not by letter name but by function, as part of a "grand cadence" [79] in the home key. Thus, ♭II means the major key on the lowered-2d step of the home key, vi(en) means the minor key on the submediant step spelled enharmonically, and so on.

True to expectations, the key when the exposition's second theme starts is V in most major sonatas, the exceptions being vi, IV, and vii in one instance each (Brahms's Op. 1, Schubert's D. 575, and his D. 840). It is III in most minor sonatas, the exceptions being v in four instances (Schumann's Op. 14 and Brahms's Opp. 2, 38, and 120/1) and V, VI, and vi(en) in one instance each (Schubert's D. 784 and 537, and Brahms's Op. 34b). The key by which the exposition ends is the same as that of the second theme in most instances, but when it is not it is V and I in two instances each, vi and iii in one instance each. The development starts with a new key in almost two-thirds of the sonatas, the key choices being divided about equally between 14 functions, including abrupt, *sforzando* shifts from V to ♭VI and v to VI (Schubert's D. 850 and Brahms's Op. 2) and starts even on ♭vii and ♯i (Schumann's Op. 22 and Brahms's Op. 99). Schubert and Brahms are exceptional at this point in starting on the tonic in either mode in eight sonatas (Schubert's D. 575, 845, and 894, and Brahms's Opp. 1, 78, 108, and 120/1 & 2). In this way they would seem to be interrupting the arch described by the "grand cadence," and one does sense that interruption (or excess of tonic harmony) in the hearing.

The one or more keys emphasized in the development sections are too variable to generalize except for the prevalence of the third-relationship created by either mediant in either mode, often lowered. One may also note the absence of any tonal plateaus in the development of Chopin's Op. 35/i, which modulates throughout, and the pedal on the dominant that lasts right through the development of

79. Cf. d'Indy/COURS II/1 45 and 286.

Brahms's Op. 108/i. On the other hand, the keys in which the recapitulations begin are almost as uniform as those at the start and end of the movement, being the tonic in the same mode except for the start on IV in three of the earlier, major sonatas by Schubert (D. 459, 537, and 575) and on ♯i (f♯) in Brahms's Op. 120/i in f. The keys used for the start of the second theme in the recapitulation occur about as uniformly in the tonic, two of the exceptions being ♯i again (Schubert's D. 960 and Brahms's Op. 34b). In the codas a good half of the sonatas place some emphasis on the subdominant in either mode, thus continuing, as in the Classic sonata (SCE 158), to counterbalance the usual movement to the dominant or mediant in either mode in the exposition and development.

Even within these relatively straightforward tonal plans in the Romantic masterworks of the sonata, the variety of procedures was far more than enough to give individual distinction in tonality alone to each composer and, in fact, each "sonata form." Only samples of this variety can be cited here. Although Schubert was the earliest of our four composers and although all of them tended toward fewer, broader, more purposeful shifts in their later tonal plans, Schubert was the freest, supplest, and most adventurous in his tonal treatment. Thus, not only could he write such an unorthodox tonal plan as that of D. 575/i in B (I-IV[2d theme]-V:‖i-remote modulations-I-IV [recapitulation]-♭VII[2d theme]-I‖). But just after the opening theme is stated in this movement he could make a startling interruption, *fortissimo,* on ♭II, followed by a 12-measure dance-like episode or aside in ♭VI and IV, prior to the second theme's entry in IV (all of which is paralleled in the keys of the recapitulation). In the wonderfully sure and effective tonal plan of D. 960/i in B♭, with its early excursion to ♭VI and second theme in ♭vi(en), the recapitulation starting in I is anticipated by its own shadow, as it were, triple *piano,* 22 measures earlier (ms. 194), and already in I. Schumann did much less modulating, but, like Chopin and Brahms, also made excursions to either mediant, as in the episode to vi(en), in place of a bridge, in Op. 11/i/107–126. Brahms is the subtlest of the four in the establishment of his key centers. Thus, already in his Op. 1, the second theme, in vi, is approached through its secondary dominant, not its dominant. His uses of borrowed tones and the resultant vacillations between modes on the same tonic frequently give a mercurial quality to the tonality (Ex. 13). The turn to major in the recapitulation of his Op. 5/i is a practice that was adopted also in Weber's Op. 49 and Liszt's Sonata in b, among other works, and increasingly in later Romantic sonatas.

Ex. 13. From the opening of Johannes Brahms's Sonata in
F, Op. 99 (after Brahms/WERKE-m X 124).

Along with tonal organization, the other main cohesive force in
Romantic (as in Classic) "sonata form" was **thematic organization.**[80]
Any other forces that may also have been organized to implement
the structure, such as the contrasting of soft and loud dynamic
markings,[81] or high and low ranges, or thick and thin textures, can
only be regarded as subordinate to the thematic and tonal organization. Thematic organization raises two successive, opposed problems
in Romantic "sonata form." Up to the mid century there was a
problem of under assimilation, and after then an increasing problem
of over assimilation.

As for the problem of under assimilation, it was similar to the
problem remarked above as being on the increase in later Romantic
tonality—that of the trees cutting off the view of the forest. Thus,
the early-Romantic thematic organization often involved closed themes,
like Dussek's and Weber's complete double-periods (SSB XVII and
VIII), or frank tunes, like that in Reissiger's Op. 93/i (SSB VIII), or

80. Mitschka/BRAHMS 318–30 summarizes thematic types and organization in
Brahms's "son. forms," with conclusions that also bear on Romantic styles and
forms in general.
81. Fellinger/DYNAMIK 71–77 charts dynamics profiles in Brahms's "son. forms."
Unusual is Hiller's Op. 78/i, which describes one grand arch from *pianissimo* to
fortissimo and back (SSB X).

melodious passagework, like that in Field's Op. 1/3/i (ssb XIV), any or all of which could be too self-sufficient, too alluring, or too intriguing in itself to be assimilable in the continuous, dynamic flow of "sonata form." [82]

In the face of such self-sufficient thematic elements how did the dualistic principle fare, the principle that figured so basically in the Classic sonata idea (sce 152–54)? The answer is that those elements favored (without insuring) the contrasts implicit in dualism itself but not the larger unity in which it had to be fostered. There was no lack of sharp contrasts in thematic style, mood, and intensity when the composers chose to make them. There are such contrasts within themes, as in the opening of Woržischek's Op. 20 (ssb VII) or Hummel's Op. 81, and between themes, as in Schubert's D. 575/i (at mss. 1 and 30) or Liszt's sonata in b, where the contrasts (as at mss. 25, 105, and 153) are inherent in the motivic complex of the initial idea (ssb X). As it happens, in the majority of their sonatas, the Romantics seem not to have been seeking such diametric, all-inclusive contrasts—no more so than the Classics had. In the Romantic "sonata form"—for example, Schubert's D. 568/i in E♭—when the contrasts do become so all-inclusive (as between mss. 1–8 and 41–48), the problem of under assimilation or of achieving over-all unity emerges in two ways. There is not only the difficulty of relating such unrelated ideas but there are those characteristic tonal digressions for the sake of color (as in mss. 60–67, to D♭) that dissipate the single dynamic trajectory into which all the musical forces ultimately must be drawn.

But, as already implied, the majority of Romantic sonatas bring up, rather, the opposite problem, the one that was to increase later in the era—over assimilation. In the Romantic as in the Classic masterworks, the dualism was achieved usually by contrasts in only one or two aspects of the theme. The second theme was more an expressive variation rather than an antipode of the first, with the sense of contrast heightened more or less by tonal polarity. Such had been true in the first movement of Mozart's K. 576, or Haydn's last Sonata in E♭, or Beethoven's Op. 57. And it was true in Schubert's D. 960 in B♭/i (starting at mss. 1 and 49), where the two ideas have much the same mood, intensity, and steady quarter-note pace but contrast in tonal mode and pitch motion (stepwise vs. chordal). Generally this degree of contrast has been just sufficient to achieve variety without destroying unity, dualism within oneness. It should be noted

82. In Westphal/ROMANTISCHE this argument is used to explain a loss of tension in Romantic "son. form."

that dualism rather than pluralism is ordinarily the right term. The closing idea, which not seldom had been the most distinctive idea in Baroque and Classic design (SCE 154), largely ceased to be a third new and significant idea by the start of the Romantic Era. Brahms offers some of the exceptions, as in Op. 78/i/70–77. But more often this element proves to be only a different facet of either preceding idea, as in his Op. 38/i/83–90 (deriving from the opening theme).

The problem of over assimilation, or excessive oneness, began to appear early in the era, as a concomitant of the overly persistent working of a motive. When a single motive tends to permeate all of the "sonata form's" themes, as does the strong-weak half-note pattern in Schubert's D. 784/i or the two 16th-notes and an 8th-note in Schumann's Op. 11/i, then we have in miniature a kind of cyclical inter-relationship (*supra*). This tendency to efface the dualism through motivic oneness is not the loss of dualism that more often has been charged to Romantic "sonata form," as it still is by Hindemith:[83]

. . . despite the beauty and often even fascination of their thematic invention, [the post-Classics—i.e., early Romantics] fail to reach the heights attained by the Classic masters. They kill one beautiful theme with another, so that sharp thematic contrasts and consequent melodic tension are lacking —a lack which is brought all the more painfully to the attention of the listener by the faulty proportion between a content which is lacking in tension and a form which is of exaggerated duration.

But that charge has been overemphasized, in the sense that it subjects Romantic art to Classic standards. Moreover, it chiefly fits composers too weak to create the variety of germinal and lyrical themes that Schubert and Brahms wrote—that is, composers like Steibelt and Kalkbrenner (SSB XII), who had only one thing (if anything) to say and therefore produced nothing but "Nebenthemen."

In spite of penetrating almost every measure with his basic motive (*supra*), Brahms was too knowing and too terse to fall victim to over assimilation of his thematic materials. However closely his first and second themes may interrelate (as already in Op. 1/i/1–4 and 39–42), they never fail to contrast sufficiently on tonal and expressive grounds to maintain their separate identities. Schumann's Op. 105/i proves to be virtually monothematic, but it maintains a sense of dualistic tension through variety of range, texture, and rhythm. The problem becomes a more serious one in the "sonata forms" of the late-Romantics, when *the motive* tends to dominate all else and when

83. Hindemith/CRAFT 180–81. Cf., also, Carner/SCHUMANN and Parrott/SCHUMANN on the "problem" of Schumann's "son. forms."

the motivic writing becomes discursive, anyway. Once more, outstanding craftsmen like Rheinberger and Medtner come to mind, as well as Rachmaninoff, whose entire Op. 36 leaves the impression of a remarkable fantasy that never really quite its one overworked idea. In his last sonatas Fauré also reduced the dualism of "sonata forms" to different aspects of oneness. The extreme consequence of continuous motivic writing is the virtual elimination of full-fledged themes as tonal and melodic landmarks, leaving nothing but the rise and fall of portentous, modulatory passagework rich in sonority and interwoven motives. Almost that extreme is reached in the late-Romantic sonatas by Dale, Ashton, and Paderewski, at least the last two of which are melodically impoverished, for all their other worths.

One would suppose that so much motivic writing would show up especially in the working out of ideas that is identified with Classic development sections. That kind of working out, the kind one thinks of in the finale of Mozart's "Jupiter Symphony" or the first movement of Beethoven's "*Eroica* Symphony," does survive in the "sonata forms" of Brahms and his numerous late-Romantic imitators and followers—for example, in Brahms's Op. 34b/i/92–160. But the motivic writing in most other late-Romantic sonatas is less often motivic play in the sense of interwoven contrapuntal exchanges than motives reiterated, sequenced, or more freely unfolded in single continuous lines. This process brings Wagner to mind more than either Bach or the Classic masters of development (cf. the Medtner ex. in ssв XVIII). Furthermore, it goes on continuously, as much in the bridges and transitions as in the development section. In fact, in that respect it tends to lessen the significance of the development section. Typically, the latter—again, excepting Brahms's "sonata forms"—is a kaleidoscopic process of transposing the ideas, reharmonizing and recombining them, and unfolding them into further ideas (as in Schubert's D. 894/i and D. 960/i). Occasionally the development is considerably extended (as in Schumann's Op. 11/i), or concentrated on one idea (such as a closing figure, in Schubert's D. 959/i), or enlivened with new material (such as that starting at mss. 126 and 140 in Schubert's 568/i), or spun out in one long line (as in Schubert's D. 784/i), or made rhythmically cumulative (as in Schumann's Op. 14/i).

The Slowest Movement

Only a few comments are needed regarding the other movements of the Romantic sonata, chiefly on their most characteristic designs. These movements often reveal at least as much of interest as the first movements, of course, but their other aspects have been discussed earlier under style phases and related questions of form. Of the slowest movements in the sonatas by our four focal composers, not a single one, surprisingly enough—not even Chopin's "March funèbre"—calls for a tempo that would be rated "very slow" here, or slow enough for the beat to be subdivided. A full 65 per cent are in moderate tempos and the rest in slow tempos. Schumann and Schubert preferred the moderate tempos in most of their sonatas, Chopin the slow tempos. Brahms's preference was about half and half. The movements in question do not include the kind in which Brahms combined moderate and scherzo sections in one design (Op. 100/ii). This design was anticipated in Schumann's Op. 11, Gade's Op. 21, and Reinecke's Op. 167, and followed by Sjögren's Op. 35, Dohnányi's Op. 21, and numerous others.

Two designs predominate in the slowest movements of our four composers, A-B-A (as in Schubert's D. 959 and D. 960) and, especially, A-B-A-B-A (as in his D. 958). Some of the longer examples of these designs are elaborately hierarchic in their sections within sections—for instance, Schubert's D. 850/ii, with each main section but the last in its design, A-B-A'-B'-A/coda, subdividing into its own a-b-a design. Schubert's D. 664/ii and D. 784/ii are monothematic A-B-A designs in which the B section is a free variation or development of the A section. Other sectional designs in these sonatas include A-B-A'-B', as in Brahms's Op. 108/ii, and A-B-A-C-A, as in Schubert's D. 958. The exceptionally complex design A||:B:||:C:||:B'-C':||:A':||:C''-B''-A':||:C''':||:B''':||:C'''':||:A''-C'''':||:A'''-B'''':||coda|| in Schubert's D. 845/ii, presents highly recondite variations in an unpredictable order. Freer variations provide the structural principle in Brahms's Opp. 1/ii and 2/ii, and more formal, regular variations in Schumann's Op. 14/iii (on a theme by Clara Wieck).

If there is any difference in the tonal organization between the first fast movements and these slower movements, it would be in the still greater use of third relationships, as throughout Schubert's tonally extraordinary "Con moto" described earlier (D. 850/ii). With regard to thematic material, the lyrical, complete period or double-period naturally predominates, with the demarcation of the phrases being even more pronounced than in the first movements but not necessarily more regular (as in Chopin's Op. 65/ii, with the first 2 periods having 2+2 and 3+5 measures).

Although the Beethovian type of lofty, serene adagio movement, sustained by rapid harmonic rhythm, was not indigenous to the Romantic solo or duo sonata, the latter was by no means lacking in relatively slow movements of much expressive warmth and sincerity, with undeniable melodic depth, harmonic richness, and textural interest. Several such movements might be cited that would be ranked here among the finest of their sort in the Romantic sonata, including Schubert's "Andante sostenuto" in c♯, D. 960/ii, with its exceptionally broad melodic arch penetrating through the lilting accompaniment in slow harmonic rhythm; Schumann's "Andantino" in C, Op. 22/ii, with its tender, veiled thoughts introduced at melodic and harmonic tangents until they reach a convulsive climax; Chopin's "Largo" in B, Op. 58/iii, with its deliberately paced nocturne style in the outer sections, enclosing the still quieter, dreamlike middle section; Brahms's "Andante" in A♭/D♭, Op. 5/ii, with one of the most sustained climaxes in any of his instrumental slow movements; his "Andante, un poco Adagio" in A♭, Op. 34b/ii, with a melodic arch that is like Schubert's in its projection and accompaniment but even more drawn out, and with searching leaps in the B section, up and down, from 8^{ves} to dim.-10ths, that must have strained the contemporary limits of melodic perception; Brahms's "Adagio" in E♭, Op. 78/ii, with its tearful chromatic line in the B section and with the return of its main theme taken by the violin in 3ds and 6ths against a new, wider accompaniment by the piano; Fauré's "Andante" in d, Op. 13/ii, with its cumulative outpourings of luscious melody and countermelody (Ex. 14); and Strauss's "Improvisation— Andante cantabile" in A♭, Op. 18/ii, with its poetically delicate, wide-ranged filigree floating through the middle section.

The Quicker of the Inner Movements

The scherzo outnumbers by a wide margin any other inner sonata movement on the quick side, throughout the Romantic Era. Furthermore, its style prevails in most such movements not actually entitled "Scherzo." In two-thirds of all the sonatas by our four composers that include quick inner movements, those movements do carry this title. Only about one-fifth of the same movements are entitled "Menuetto" (or some variant). Schubert's several minuets generally preserve the easy-going, neatly measured, Classic dance spirit in their well-defined phrases (as in D. 568/iii or D. 894/iii), although those in D. 840/iii and D. 958/iii are nearer to the fast tempo and steadier, more vigorous quarter-note drive of the scherzo that had largely replaced the minuet by then (as in Loewe's Op. 47/iii, ssв VIII). Schumann did not use the minuet in his sonatas, nor did Chopin in his mature sonatas. Brahms's one use in his sonatas, the "Allegretto quasi

Ex. 14. From the second movement of Fauré's Sonata in A, Op. 13 (after Wier/VIOLIN-m 263).

menuetto" in his Op. 38, serves as the middle, "slowest" movement, too, and is closer to the traditional style.

But there had been some confusion between these terms early in the century and even some equating of the two titles, as in the "Menuetto o scherzo" of Moscheles' Op. 41 or the "Minuet scherzo" in A. Schmitt's Op. 26, both of which are closer to the scherzo style. Decidedly scherzando in style are the "Minuetto" marked "allegro" in Weber's Op. 24 (SSB VIII), the "Menuetto capriciosso" marked "presto assai" in his Op. 39, and the "Menuetto" marked "presto vivace ed energico" in his Op. 70; also, the "Minuetto" marked only "allegretto" in Chopin's early Op. 4.

The sectional design of both the minuet and the scherzo in the Romantic sonata is most often the expected A-B-A or A-trio-*da capo*, each section being a binary design in itself with each "half" enclosed in repeat signs (cf. sce 162). But Schumann's Op. 22/iii and Brahms's Op. 5/iii are among frequent examples of the rondo principle in the scherzo, these having the plans A-B-A-C-A and A-B-A-C-A-B-A, respectively. The scherzo, which could still relate to the idea of a joke in Beethoven's sonatas (as in Op. 24), became exaggerated into something increasingly and variously sinister, driving, virtuosic, impassioned in a suppressed way, grotesque, or elfish during the Romantic Era (as in Chopin's Op. 35, Schumann's Op. 14, Czerny's Op. 268 [ssb VII], Brahms's Op. 99, d'Indy's Op. 63, and Fauré's Op. 13, respectively).

The scherzo in the Romantic, as in the Classic, sonata is likely to be based on a motive rather than a full-fledged theme. Motivic writing engenders some of the chief uses of imitation, most noticeably in the sonatas of some of the less polyphonically minded composers like Weber (e.g., Op. 24/iii, ssb VIII) or Schubert (e.g., D. 575/iii), and even Chopin (in the middle section of Op. 58/ii). The fugal, scherzando section, marked only "Allegro energico," in Liszt's Sonata in b, starts more polyphonically, of course, than the average. In spite of the motivic writing, phrase-and-period syntax that is both clear and regular usually obtains in the Romantic scherzo, chiefly because the motive's reiterations usually group into clear and regular phrases (as in the extreme ex. from Schubert's D. 850/iii quoted earlier).

But not all the syntax in the scherzo is of this sort. Whereas Schubert's D. 959/iii starts with a completely regular double-period of 4+4 & 4+4 measures, the A section of his D. 958/iii is quite the opposite. In fact, it seems to be deliberately problematic. In any case, it must be parsed somewhat subjectively or arbitrarily into three- , four- , five- , and six-measure phrases (if it should be parsed at all), for it presents fascinating conflicts between such usual phrase determinants as metric, weak-beat, and quantitative accents, harmonic suspense and resolution, rhythmic repetition and contrast, melodic repetition and contrast, and steady rhythmic flow interrupted by whole-measure rests! Among many other interesting though less problematic examples of Schubert's extraordinary rhythmic freshness, one might cite D. 960/iii for its use first of seven phrases of 4 measures each, then four of 6, four of 5 (if the last two are really so intended), three of 4, and a final phrase of 6 measures.

The syntax remains regular in Schumann's "Scherzo" in D♭, Op. 14/ii, but the over-all A-B-A design is made complex and hard to follow on first hearing by the many repetitions and variants of the many ideas, and by the many tonal indirections and changes, including the choice of ♯I (D) for the middle section. Besides the combined "slowest"-and-scherzo movements noted earlier, the most frequent alternative to the minuet or scherzo was the sort of tender, wistful movement to be found in Brahms's Op. 108—"Un poco presto e con sentimento," in 2/4 meter. Although not slow and not scherzando, this movement serves a little in each capacity in its central position as a foil for both, more intensive, outer movements.

The Finale

The large majority of finales in the Romantic sonata, fast or very fast, employ the rondo principle, more or less freely. Relatively few of them actually are called "Rondo," and then chiefly in the early-Romantic sonata (as in Schubert's D. 845 and Weber's Op. 24). The other finales are likely to be in "sonata form" (as in Schubert's D. 459 or D. 664), in fugal form (as in Brahms's Op. 38), or in variation form (as in several of Reger's sons. [ssb XI] but none by our 4 focal composers). In connection with the climax profile of the sonata cycle as a whole, the observation was made that the "finale posed the chief structural problem, one main reason apparently being a felt need to alter, intensify, and, unfortunately, overcomplicate the traditionally light, gay rondo sufficiently for it to carry more weight" (supra). The later discussions, in Part Two, include numerous references to this problem of the finale, with regard both to each of our four focal composers and to others as well—for example, the difficulties even Clara Wieck found with Schumann's finales (ssb VIII), or the reviewer (of Op. 17 by A. Krause) who called the finale "that Achilles' heel of modern composers of sonata form" (ssb X), or Wagner's resolve late in life to write one-movement, but not multimovement, symphonies because of the problems the finale still posed.[84]

To get some further idea of the rondo-finale problem, it is necessary to take brief note of specific solutions in representative finales by each of our four composers. In Schubert's D. 537/iii the curiously additive design is A-B-C-D-E-E||A-B-C-D-E-E||A/coda, with the tonal outline being i/I-IV-V up to the first double-bar and v/V-♭VII-I between double-bars. In his later sonatas the designs become simpler but increasingly long, with more substantial subsections, and no letup in the variety of sectional dispositions. In D. 784/iii the design is A(i)→B(VI)-A(i)→ B(III)-C(development)-A(i)-B(I)-A/coda(i). The tonal plans continue to stay close to home, requiring no further mention. In D. 845/iv, the design is A-B-A'-C-A-D-A"-B/coda; in D. 850/iv it is A-B-A'-C-A"/coda; in D. 894/iv it is A-B-A-C-A-B/coda. The outer design of

---

84. Newman/ARTIST 240–41.

the 717-measure finale in D. 958/iv, A-B-A'-B'-A'', is so greatly stretched out, with the first, complex B section alone lasting over 300 measures, that, in spite of Schubert's remarkable genius for extension, no performer can quite hope to hold it together, even playing faster than the "allegro" that is indicated. Still further variants of the rondo principle occur in the designs of D. 959/iv, A-B-A-C-A-B-A/coda (one of Beethoven's favorite dispositions), and 960/iv, A-B-C-A-A-B-C-A/coda.

The outer designs and uncomplicated tonal organization of Schumann's earlier rondo-finales belie the tendency of these movements to sprawl and their themes and sections to run together somewhat inconclusively. The design of Op. 11/iv is A-B-A-B'-A/coda, with the most remote key being VI(en). That of Op. 14/iv falls into more sections (or 2 over-all parts) A-B-C-D-B → A-B-C-D-B/coda. If those designs (unlike Schubert's) seem to have been arrived at empirically, the design of Op. 22/iv—A-B-C-A-B-C-A/coda—seems premeditated in its organizational details and, perhaps as a consequence, somewhat formalistic in its total effect.

The extremely short, *perpetuum mobile* finale in Chopin's Op. 35 is not a rondo, if a rondo's opening idea must appear at least three times, but a balanced A-B-A design based entirely on four-measure phrases (each subdivided into 2+2 mss.) except for measures 17–19, 36–38, and 72–76 (including the final ms.). Chopin's Op. 58/iv is transparently blocked off in its nonstandard rondo design, A-A'-B-C-A-A'-B-C-A-A', but that very transparency helps to reveal the weakness in the design. One can hardly escape the monotony in performance of too many returns to the refrain in the same key (all but once) and too few alterations in its presentation.

Among our four composers, Brahms seems to have been most aware of the finale problem, right from the start (cf. ssb IX).[85] Yet, in the experience of this study, he did not quite solve it, insofar as his sonatas are concerned, until he reached Op. 78 and a more sensitive, more concise, and less pretentious sort of finale. On the other hand, each of the earlier finales discloses decided musical strengths in its separate sections and each, when read in its order of composition, discloses new gains on the problems of structural control. What is the nature of the structural deficiencies? They are not obvious. On the surface the forms look tight and clear. They do not seem to have the diffusion or imbalances that have been ventured above as handicaps in the finales of the other three composers. One can sense deficiencies in Brahms's

---

85. Czesla/BRAHMS is a new diss. (1968) of the finales in Brahms's "chamber" music, including the 3 P sons. (pp. 7–76, with exx.) and Op. 38 (pp. 149–69, with exx.).

earlier finales, both in performance and listening, as problems of under and over assimilation, again. But to pin them down to specific shortcomings, to second-guess a composer who was a finished craftsman right from Op. 1, would take the knowledge and appraisals of another Brahms. One can appreciate the extensive revisions Brahms himself made late in life in the finale (and other movements) of his Trio in B, Op. 8, and still not know what could or should have been done in Opp. 1, 2, and 5 if Brahms had seen fit to return to the problems of their finales, too.

In Op. 1/iv the outer plan of the sections suggests straggling and over repetition of the refrain—A-A-B-A-C-A-D-A-B-A/coda—especially in consideration of the omnipresent basic motive (*supra*). Yet the actual problem would be viewed here rather as under assimilation created by matter-of-fact breaks at the sectional joints, by square-cut rhythms still far from the later Brahmsian rhythmic subtleties, and by uncompromisingly complete presentations of every section, with as yet none of the streamlining and excisions so essential to efficient, compelling form. The same problems seem to exist, although within different and increasingly resourceful plans, in both Opp. 2/iv and 5/v. Op. 2/iv is an elastic "sonata form" enclosed by a slow prelude and postlude. Op. 5/v is a rondo, with fewer sections and more extensions than in Op. 1—A-B→A-C→A→coda.

To the extent that a structural problem does still exist in the magnificent, dramatic finale of Brahms's Op. 34b, it may lie in a certain rhythmic stiffness inherent in the squareness and repetitions of units within the themes themselves and in a type of sectional plan that is more additive than integrated—In/A → B-C → A-B'-C'-A'/coda. In Op. 38/iii the fugal movement falls into a large monothematic A-B-A design, with B being defined by the inversion of the subject and the emphasis on the mediant key. This time, if a finale problem does exist it probably lies not in the structure per se but in a subject that engenders so many single bowings, so much ungrateful "sawing" for the cello (as for all the strings in Beethoven's "Grosse Fuge" for quartet). It should be noted that along with the increasingly laconic style and Spartan excisions in his later sonatas, Brahms gave preference to the simplest rondo designs—for example, A → B → A-C-A/coda in Op. 78/iii and A-B→A-C-A(IV)-A(I)/coda in Op. 100/iii.

Part Two

The Romantic Composers and
Their Sonatas

Chapter VII

Schubert and Other Viennese in Beethoven's Sphere

Vienna as an Early 19th-Century Music Center

The early 19th-century artist in an Austro-German center had to work in a heavy environment of rapid political change. With the harsh treaties codified by the Congress of Vienna in 1814–15 and the Holy Alliance that grew out of them, Europe saw the defeat of Napoleon and the end of more than twenty years of struggle by Austria in coalitions with Prussia, Russia, and other powers against France. From then, starting under the first Austrian emperor, Francis I, and Count Metternich, to beyond the middle of the century, Austria became increasingly autocratic, aggressive, and reactionary, successfully resisting the waves of revolution and liberalism that swept France and other countries in 1830 and again in 1848. In such a continuing atmosphere of international intrigue, political oppression, even terror, it is understandable that the Viennese who were so inclined could and did find one main escape or retreat through music, music that might be at once the most noncommittal and the safest of the arts.

Yet in spite of this international political environment, in spite of the immediate past musical glories of Haydn and Mozart, in spite of the succeeding musical giants that were Beethoven and Schubert, and in spite of the continued guidance of veteran composers and pedagogues like Antonio Salieri (1750–1825) or Simon Sechter (1788–1867) and the continuing patronage of nobles like Archduke Rudolph (1788–1831; cf. scE 524), Vienna tended to fall back to relative provincialism as a music center in the first half of the 19th century.[1] This provincial-

1. Important background information on Vienna and her musical life is found in Weber/WEBER II 395–428; Thayer & Forbes/BEETHOVEN I 150–59 (early 1790's); Schindler & MacArdle/BEETHOVEN 51 and 64–66 (ca. 1800), 135 (early 1800's), 216–17 (1810's), 272 (1820's); Deutsch/SCHUBERT-D xxi–xxix (with maps; ca. 1790–1830); and, above all, except for opera, Hanslick/WIEN I 139–285 (1800–1830) and 289–363 (1830–48). Some of the poetic and musical atmosphere is conveyed in Holmes/RAMBLE 113–70 (1828) and Schumann/SCHRIFTEN I 459–63 (1839).

ism is apparent in limitations of musical taste, requirements, concert life, publishing activities, and journalism. One factor was certainly the growing suspicion of foreigners that the political reactionism fostered. Among two main nationalities under the Austrian heel, the immigrants from Italy suffered from such suspicion notwithstanding Rossini's successes during the second and third decades, but the numerous Czechs who continued to move to Vienna (cf. SCE 545–46), like Woržischek, seem to have felt it less. There were ingrown factors, too. The escape from oppression by way of music and the other arts proved to be more of a pleasurable opiate than a sublimation. If at best Viennese society could still nurture rare masterpieces like Schubert's "Great Symphony in C," if at worst it became positively debauched and dissolute, ordinarily and characteristically it took to the new Biedermeier art,[2] not to mention the *Gemütlichkeit,* of its coffee houses and taverns.

In music, such art was more conducive to the creating of early Viennese waltzes than sonatas. Sonatas did continue to appear in fair number. But the majority of them found a compromise with Biedermeier art, sometimes by introducing those waltzes or other current dances, or by adding variations on familiar tunes, or by exploiting the new preoccupation with virtuosity. Undoubtedly, if Vienna had not continued to be so provincial in her public concert life, she would have given more and earlier encouragement to the serious sort of solo or duo recital on which serious sonatas thrive. To be sure, opera in the theater did not supply the only public opportunities to pay to hear music. Public concerts did occur that included extended, serious instrumental works. But the fact remains that what were easily the most important sonatas by the composers discussed in this chapter, those of Schubert, seem never to have reached public performance. Nor can Schubert's relative obscurity be given as the sole reason. On the one hand, we saw Beethoven's sonatas similarly fail to reach public performance (SCE 528–29); and on the other, we shall see that several of Schubert's sonatas did win favor at the private evening "Schubertiads" that meant so much to him, that four of them got published before his early death (1828, only eighteen months after Beethoven's), and that two of these promptly won enthusiastic reviews as far away as Leipzig.

The underlying theme of the present chapter might be stated as the diametrically opposed influences of Beethoven and Biedermeier art on the early 19th-century sonata in Vienna. With regard to Beethoven, it applies less to his dominating influence on the sonata throughout

2. Cf. BRITANNICA III 600.

the 19th century than to his immediate sphere of personal impressions on other Viennese composers. This theme accounts for more attention here than might otherwise be warranted to three highly competent but hardly great composers—Ries, Czerny, and Moscheles. For in the practical senses of propagating and popularizing his sonatas, these three were the most direct transmitters, more so than several other men, like Wölfl (sce 562–64), Hummel (ssb VIII), and Cramer (ssb XII), who also had at least some direct contact with Vienna and Beethoven. Of course, Schubert in his relative obscurity lived right in the shadow of Beethoven with perhaps never a chance actually to talk with him and scarcely a mention by the other followers. Yet Schubert became no mere transmitter but the most immediate and one of the few real artistic successors to Beethoven. In fact, the chief "problem" of Schubert's sonatas will be seen as that of one's never quite being able to view them independently of Beethoven's, however strong and original they are in their own right.

Peripheral but pertinent to this chapter is the publisher A. Diabelli's clever patriotic venture of 1820–24 that ultimately opposed Beethoven's lofty set of 33 "Diabelli Variations" to the set of 50 single variations by as many different composers, mostly minor Viennese, but including Hummel, Schubert, and Liszt.[3] Here in one project were the conflicting forces of genius and Biedermeier, with a waltz (the theme) at the center. Because the 50 composers provide such a full representation of the Vienna scene, including many met here earlier (sce) or to be met soon, their names should be worth bringing together at this point:[4]

I. Assmayer, C. M. Bocklet, L. E. Czapek, *C. Czernÿ, J. Czernÿ, M. G. v. Dietrichstein, J. Drechsler, E. A. Förster, J. Fraestaedtler, J. Gänsbacher, A. Gelinek, A. Halm, *J. Hoffmann, J. Horzalka, *J. Huglmann, *J. N. Hummel, A. Hüttenbrenner, *F. Kalkbrenner, F. A. Kanne, J. Kerzkowsky, *C. Kreutzer, E. B. Lannoy, M. J. Leidesdorf, *F. Liszt, J. Mayseder, *I. Moscheles, I. F. v. Mosel, *W. A. Mozart fils, J. Panny, H. Payer, J. P. Pixis, *W. Plachy, *G. Rieger, P. J. Riotte, F. Roser, J. Schenk, *F. Schoberlechner, *F. Schubert, S. Sechter, S. R. D. [i.e., Archduke Rudolph], A. Stadler, *J. de Szalay, *W. Tomaschek, M. Umlauff, F. D. Weber, F. Weber, *C. A. v. d. Winkhler, F. Weiss, J. Wittassek, J. H. Worzischek [plus an extended "coda," also by C. Czerny].

3. Cf. Deutsch/schubert-d 348–51 and grove VIII 690–92 (E. Blom), both with further references; also, *Beethovenjahrbuch* I (1908) 28–50 (H. Rietsch).
4. The alphabetic order and spellings of the original Diabelli ed. are followed here. Mod. ed. of 16 of the single vars. (by the composers asterisked in this list): Newman/diabelli-m.

A First Direct Beethoven Transmitter: Ries

No more appropriate link connecting the previous and present volumes, and no more representative, timely opener for our individual composer discussions can be found than **Ferdinand Ries** (1784–1838),[5] best known for his close association with Beethoven (his senior by 14 years). Ries trained right in the Viennese environment and midway in that succession of the sonata's greatest Classic-Romantic masters from Haydn to Brahms. He actually studied piano with Beethoven, from late in 1801 to 1805, while studying theory and composition, on Beethoven's own recommendation, with the aging Albrechtsberger.[6] In fact, the abundant correspondence between the two men, extending from 1802 to 1825, shows Ries to have been the most lasting and one of the closest of all associates in Beethoven's day-to-day work. He was not only the successful student alone entrusted with many performances of Beethoven's music in public.[7] He was also the son in a musical family that had befriended the Beethoven family in Bonn, only to become the recipient himself of Beethoven's unsolicited contributions during early periods of near destitution in Vienna. He was at once Beethoven's confidant, secretary, copyist, and general lackey in countless professional or personal assignments and errands, even in intrigues, much as Schindler was to be all these in Beethoven's final years. He was the idolater of Beethoven's music who eventually became a near colleague as a composer (although Beethoven's request and numerous promises to exchange dedications in new works came to nought[8]). And, finally, he was Beethoven's important editorial and concert agent in London in the years from 1813 to 1824.[9]

As to being an appropriate, representative opener here, Ries was above all a musician à la mode in his day. He excelled as a pianist and

5. The chief biographic sources are Schilling/LEXICON V 747–49, Wegeler's necrologic remarks in Wegeler & Ries/BEETHOVEN v–vii, MOSCHELES I 52, and Fétis/BU VII 255–58 (all contemporary); Thayer & Forbes/BEETHOVEN I 293–96; and Ueberfeldt/RIES (on the years up to 1813, when the closest relations with Beethoven ended).

6. Cf. MacArdle/RIES 23–26; Macfarren/POTTER 45.

7. Wegeler & Ries/BEETHOVEN 115.

8. Cf. Schindler & MacArdle/BEETHOVEN 426–31, including negative appraisals of Ries undoubtedly influenced by Schindler's competitive position as another disciple and biographer of Beethoven.

9. For epistolary samples of these relationships cf. (among many similar indexed references to Ries) Anderson/BEETHOVEN I 62, 76, 87–88, 111–14; II 577; III 1033, 1064, 793–807. Cf., also, SCE 511–32, passim; and Ries's own valued testimonies in Wegeler & Ries/BEETHOVEN 75–77, 88–97, 101–3, 113–19, 123–26.

wrote primarily for the piano, then well on the way to its 19th-century ascendancy; and he wrote the styles of music in the kinds of settings and forms the public then most liked to play and hear (including not only the sons. in review here but much other instrumental music, from one to 8 parts, as well as songs, operas, and oratorios[10]). His talent for satisfying current tastes is the point made most often and emphatically in the numerous reviews of his sonatas, among other works, that Friedrich Rochlitz (and others?) wrote in *Allgemeine musikalische Zeitung* (AMZ) from 1807 to 1823. Especially perceptive now seems the remark that "Herr Ries is for the present time—the present state of music, the present taste, the present way of playing—what Leopold Anton Koželuch was for his time," [11] a generation earlier. That Ries was popular and successful as a composer is evident enough in the rags-to-riches story of his life. The Swiss publisher Nägeli included his piano sonata Op. 141 in the anthology *Die musikalische Ehrenpforte* (1827), which was also meant to, but did not, include works by Schubert, Weber, Mendelssohn, Spohr, Hummel, and Moscheles, among others.[12] Beethoven himself, on one occasion when he was confused as to Ries's whereabouts, addressed a letter to the "celébre compositeur a Londres." [13]

More to the point here, Ries's lifetime successes are evident in the large number of his works that got published, often in competing or successive editions by German, French, and English publishers. The following tabulation of his 54 known sonatas, of which only the first did not get published, should help not only to put them in a needed perspective but, more generally, to illustrate the fashionable titles, settings, instrumental options, programmatic and pedagogic leanings, and journalistic attention given to the sonata in the first quarter of the 19th century. The accessible facts about the earliest editions of the sonatas have been culled from yearbooks throughout the first half-century of (Whistling and) HOFMEISTER, from catalogues of an understandably large collection of Ries's works in London (Cat. ROYAL 283–88), from an early list of his works in HARMONICON II/1 (1824) 60–61 and the full list of his works still to be found in PAZDÍREK XXIV 328–31, and from the more recent information in Egert/FRÜHROMANTIKER

10. Cf. MGG XI 490–94 (R. Sietz).
11. AMZ XIII (1811) 89; cf. SCE 556–58.
12. Cf. Deutsch/SCHUBERT-D 541.
13. Anderson/BEETHOVEN II 763. Barely hinted in the conclusions of Beethoven's later letters to Ries is an envy of his success, security, and domestic joys, including frequent joshing about Beethoven's intention to go to London in order to "kiss your pretty wife" (e.g., Anderson/BEETHOVEN II 954–55, III 1006–7 and 1027).

Ferdinand Ries's Sonatas (grouped by scoring types)

Op./nos.	Keys	Scoring	Latest year (of early pub.)	Sources (of reviews) and/or remarks	Composite numbering
1/1–3	b, C, a	P	1807 (Simrock)	AMZ IX (1806–7) 362–65; Op. 1/1 not pub.	1, 2
5/1–2	Bb, F	P	1828 "	"Sonatine"	5, 6
9/1–2	D, C	P	1811 "	"Deux grandes Sonates"	10, 11
11/1–2	Eb, f	P	1815 "	"Deux grandes Sonates"	13, 14
26	f#	P	1815 "	"Grande Sonate fantaisie intitulée L'Infortunée"	22
45	C	P	1818 "	AMZ XIX (1817) 843–44; "Sonatine"	31
49	Eb	P	1815 "	AMZ XVII (1815) 146–49; Anderson/BEETHOVEN 571; "Le Songe" or "Il Sogno"	—
114	A	P	1823 (Breitkopf)	AMZ XXV (1823) 492	47
141	Ab	P	1827 (Nägeli)		49
175	Ab	P	1835	NZM VII (1837) 127 (Schumann); "Grande Sonate"	52
6	C	P-duet	(Simrock)	"Sonatine"	7
47	Bb	P-duet	1818 (Simrock)	AMZ XIX (1817) 844	(32)
160	A	P-duet	1834	"Grande Sonate"	50
3/1–2	C, A	P + Vn	1811 (Simrock)		3, 4
8/1–2	F, c	P + Vn	1811 "	"Deux grandes Sonates"	8, 9
10	Bb	P & Vn	1811 "	"Grande Sonate"	12
16/1–3	C, Bb, D	P + Vn	1811 "	AMZ XIII (1811) 88–91	15, 16, 17
18	Eb	P + Vn	1811 "	AMZ XIII (1811) 88–91; "Grande Sonate"	18
19	f	P + Vn	1812 "	AMZ XIV (1812) 485; "Grande Sonate"	19
30/1–3	C, a, F	P & Vn	1815	"Sonatines doigtées"	24, 25, 26
38/1–3	e, a, g	P & Vn	1815 (Costallat)		28, 29, 30
59/1–2	D, Bb	P & Vn-or-Fl	1815 (Simrock)	AMZ XVIII (1816) 11 (no. 1, only)	34, 35
69	Eb	P & Vn	1815 (Costallat)	AMZ XIX (1817) 92	36
71	c#	P & Vn	1815 "		37
81/1–2	Eb, d	P ± Vn	1822 (André)	AMZ XXIV (1822) 263; plate no. 4474	40, 41
83	D	P & Vn	1821 (Simrock)	AMZ XXIV (1822) 263; plate no. 1831	42
86/1–3	Eb, D, g	P & Vn-or-Fl	1828 "	"Sonates faciles" (or "non difficiles")	43, 44, 45
20	C	P + Vc	1811 (Simrock)	AMZ XIII (1811) 886; "Grande Sonate"; also pub. for P + Vn	20
21	A/a	P + Vc	1811 "	AMZ XIII (1811) 884–85; "Grande Sonate"; also pub. for P + Hn	21
34	F	P + Vc	1815 (Costallat)	"Grande Sonate"; also pub. for P + Hn	27
125	g	P & Vc-or-Vn	1828 (Kistner)	"Grande Sonate"	48
48	G	P ± Fl	1815 (Simrock)	AMZ XVII (1815) 389–91	33
76/1–2	C, Bb	P ± Fl-or-Vn	1818 "	AMZ XX (1818) 632 (no. 1, only)	38, 39
87	G	P + Fl	1819 "	"Sonatine"	46
169	Eb	P & Fl-or-Cl	1839 (Costallat)	"Sonate sentimentale"	(51)
29	g	P + Cl-or-Vn	1828 (Costallat)		23

122–24 and 159. With regard to composition dates, the 54 sonatas span the years from 1803–6 for Op. 1 [14] to about 1835 for Op. 175, with all but the last three or four originating by 1825. With regard to ap-

14. Egert/FRÜHROMANTIKER 122.

proximate dates of first publication, they span nearly the same years. These approximate dates, which might well be made more exact if and when more of the original publishers' plate numbers could be found, are based here mainly on the *terminus ad quem* of review dates, and only occasionally on the *terminus a quo* of a watermark.[15] In any case, our total of 54 sonatas is likely to be correct or very nearly so, since Ries himself, besides keeping his opus numbers in good order, gave a separate, composite numbering to all of his published sonatas, right from No. 1, Op. 1/2, to No. 52, Op. 175, excluding only the unpublished Op. 1/1 and "Le Songe," Op. 49, which lacks "Sonata" in the titles of some early editions. The tabulation is subdivided according to scoring.

As the tabulation shows, Ries, quite typically for that time, still left about twice as many accompanied or duo as solo and four-hand settings.[16] Yet his whole sonata output is oriented toward his own favorite instrument, anyway.[17] Even the "obligé" accompaniments, which are literally obligatory only when they have lyrical ideas to state, run but poor seconds to the piano parts, whether in the allocation of thematic responsibilities or the relative virtuosity of the many connecting passages (Ex. 15). And the ad libitum parts, during this final bloom of the accompanied setting, sometimes border on the ridiculous. A near virtuoso piano concerto, with scarcely more than intermittent timid peeps from the accompaniment, is how one must describe Op. 76/1, *Sonate pour le Piano avec Accomp.^t de Flute ou Violon ad Libitum dans laquelle se trouve introduit l'Air favori de H. R. Bishop, He is all the World to me.* Only when "l'Air favori" prevails, in the finale, does the piano occasionally accompany and the flute or violin take the lead. The tabulation also reveals Ries's tendency to produce fewer "grande" sonatas and "obligé" accompaniments, and more alternative settings in his later sonatas, suggesting that, unlike Beethoven, he was one more minor master who chose to court success by bowing

15. As in Cat. HIRSCH 348.

16. A brief discussion of some of Ries's earlier solo piano sons. occurs in Egert/FRÜHROMANTIKER 121–24 (superseding the little to be found in Ueberfeldt/RIES 38–62 *passim*). A thorough, comprehensive discussion of both his solo and "accompanied" piano works would make an inviting and not unprofitable dissertation topic. Nearly all of this music is at the Library of Congress, especially in two privately bound collections of 6 and 4 vols. under M22-R56 (solo piano) and M219-R56 (piano and violin), respectively; it is chiefly in Richault editions, which, though probably not as early as those in the foregoing tabulation, included all of Ries's pub. sons. at least through Op. 76.

17. It is interesting to find a Rondo for P+Hn-or-Vc and a "Sextuor" with a variety of accompaniments (including harp, Hn, bassoon, and double-bass) both reviewed at length under the heading merely of "neuste Pianoforte-Compositionen," in CAECILIA VIII (1828) 112–18.

Ex. 15. From Sonata in D, Op. 83/i/7-17, by Ferdinand Ries (after the original Simrock ed. at The University of North Carolina at Chapel Hill).

increasingly to popular tastes. The "Sonatines doigtées" or "Sonates non difficiles" (Opp. 30 and 86) must have been designed quite as much to sell as was that sonata into which he inserted "l'Air favori." And so must the alternative settings, such as the horn and cello parts for Op. 34, which rarely differ except for essential, idiomatic adaptations of range and articulation.

From the same tabulation we see that Ries still stayed within the conservative limit of three sharps and four flats in his choice of keys, with fewer than one out of four sonatas being in minor. Only within a few movements, as in the change of mode to ab in the trio of the "Scherzo" in Op. 175, does he use signatures with more sharps or flats. In Op. 21, his change to the minor mode for the final, fourth movement is quite the opposite of the supposed later Romantic trend (SSB

VI). Moreover, the large majority of the sonatas prove to have the usual three movements in the usual order of F-S-F. An occasional "grande" sonata has four movements, such as Op. 21, just cited, or Op. 9/2 in G in which the order M VF S) VF and even the styles and forms of the movements (with none in "son. form") recall Beethoven's Op. 27/1 in E♭ too closely for comfort. Conversely, some of the later sonatinas have only two moderate or faster movements (as in Op. 45).

A short slow introduction, like that to Beethoven's Op. 78, frequently leads into the fast opening and/or final movements of Ries's sonatas (as in Opp. 11/2/i and 19/i) and may even return in the course of the movement,[18] much in the way that it does in Beethoven's Op. 13/i. Most often the first movement is in "sonata form," the second is free and cursive, and the finale is a rondo, dance (especially a minuet, or a "Polacca" as in Op. 20/iii), or a set of variations on a favorite air (for instance, the set on an "Air russe" in Op. 11/1/iii). The interrelation of movements by similar melodic incipits occurs less often than in Beethoven's sonatas, and only in Ries's more serious sonatas (as in Op. 26/i and ii). The use of a binding programme occurs not at all beyond the general mood implied by "L'Infortunée" or "sentimentale" in the titles of Opp. 26 and 169, respectively. "Le Songe," Op. 49, might be taken as an exception, since it does suggest a dream in its fitful starts and stops, its kaleidoscopic changes of tempo and dynamics, and its alternations of mood. However, Rochlitz, cautiously seeking to interpret this dream section by section, seems to regret the absence of any verbal clue more specific than the "Marcia" inscribed over one section.[19] From the standpoint of our continued semantic approach, one wonders whether Ries actually regarded this piece as one of his sonatas, in spite of "Sonate" in the title of at least the early Simrock edition.[20] Not only did he depart from the usual over-all and separate designs of the sonata in this continuous piece but he gave it no number in his composite numbering of his "fifty-two" sonatas.

"Le Songe" happens to be the only work of Ries that Beethoven mentions specifically in his letters, and with the only unqualified approval he gives to Ries's music. "The Archduke Rudolph plays your works too, my dear Ries, and among these I find 'Il Sogno' particularly

18. It already does this in his first, unpublished son., according to Egert/FRÜH-ROMANTIKER 122.

19. AMZ XVII (1815) 146–49.

20. According to HOFMEISTER 1815 (Whistling), p. 374, but not in any other listing seen here.

delightful."[21] But, paradoxically, "Le Songe" also happens to be the Ries work examined here that reveals the fewest resemblances to Beethoven's music. Such resemblances, including those already noted, occur chiefly in the earlier and more serious sonatas by Ries. They are hardly surprising in view of the close association with Beethoven mentioned above, and of such further intimate contact with his music as transcribing a number of his works, probably with his blessing,[22] and even of composing the lost, final eleven measures to the "Adagio" in Beethoven's Sonata in C, WoO 51/ii.[23]

Ries dedicated Op. 1 with the words "à Louis van Beethoven par son élève," incidentally causing Rochlitz to ask why a German should dedicate a piece to a German, presumably for Germans, in the French language.[24] Rochlitz commented, as he was to do in several later reviews, on the obvious resemblances to Beethoven, without specifically mentioning how remarkably Ries's first published sonata, in C—with its fast scales, double-3rds, 6th-chords, and still other devices of brilliance —recalls Beethoven's Op. 2/3, in the same key. But the flat, inconsequential themes, excessive passagework, and empty tremolo accompaniments that often prevail represent traits that clearly separate Ries's music from Beethoven's, that bring mild yet persistent censure in those later reviews of his music, and that must explain why Rochlitz resorted in this instance to two earthy terms apparently coined for such music by Mozart, "Krabbelsonaten" and "Holzmachern" (freely, "scurry sonatas" and "claptrap players").[25] Beethoven himself was to write Ries of his objections to "mechanical" display pieces in a letter of 1823 that exempts Ries from the criticism a bit too ingenuously.[26]

To be sure, more in the subsequent reviews of Ries's sonatas is favorable than not. Besides the need Rochlitz seems to have felt for treating his successful, well-descended compatriot with respect and caution, there was genuine praise for his undeniable craftsmanship, especially the sure command of form, the advanced harmonic skill, and the fluent

21. April 3, 1816; Anderson/BEETHOVEN II 571 (and fn. 6, in which the editor is unable to identify "Il Sogno").

22. Cf. MacArdle/RIES 34.

23. Cf. G. Weber in CAECILIA XIII (1831) 285.

24. AMZ IX (1806–7) 365. The title page of Op. 16, though not dedicated to Beethoven, still capitalizes on the pupil relationship, and still in French. Only about 4 years later Beethoven himself was to object to the French inscriptions that the publishers used for his Op. 81a (SCE 525).

25. AMZ IX (1806–7) 363–64; our free translations reflect Rochlitz's own expansions of the terms. These terms may well have come from his immediate but frequently undependable recollections; they could not be traced here to previous, post-mortem accounts of Mozart, as by Niemetschek (1798) or Rochlitz himself (AMZ I and IV [1798–99 and 1801–2]).

26. Anderson/BEETHOVEN III 1064.

use of the keyboard. Only when the sameness of style became too apparent and the lighter, dilettante pieces took precedence did the reviews eventually diminish to short notices, with occasional backhanded compliments like the statement hoping Ries would continue to produce such fresh, happy, serious pieces in his second hundred *opera* as were inaugurated by the one under review, his Sonata No. 47, Op. 114, for piano.[27] Less concerned about the feelings of his compatriots, Schumann put an honest finish in 1837 to reviews of Ries's sonatas, in a paragraph about the last one, No. 52 in A♭ for piano solo, that includes this sentence: "Throughout it suffers from all too much mediocrity, and when it occasionally reaches toward the fair heights where we often met this artist earlier, it soon sinks back again as if lead weighted down its wings." [28]

From our present historical viewpoint, in addition to his close associations with Beethoven, his full representation of popular tastes in his day, and his thoroughly typical output of sonatas, Ries is worth noting for the early Romantic traits in his music. The most serious, advanced, and effective examples are found in Opp. 9, 11, and 26 for solo piano, of which the last might best be used for special mention and quotation here, since it remains the most available of all his sonatas.[29] Composed in 1808,[30] *Grande Sonate fantaisie intitulée L'Infortunée*, Op. 26, in f♯, comes nearest in its three-movement cycle, length, dynamic intensity, and keyboard treatment to the "Tempest Sonata," Op. 31/2, in d (1801–2), among Beethoven's works. It reveals a similar use of a return to a slow introduction, and even some thematic resemblances in the first movement, although its middle, slowest movement is shorter, less deliberate, and more suave, and its finale is faster and more dramatic, if somewhat longish for its content. (Ries's three movements total 255, 64, and 429 measures, or 748 in all, as against 228, 103, and 399, or 730 in all, for Beethoven.) Characteristic early Romanticisms in Ries's work are the bold projection of the lyrical ideas, the use of bass/chord or other wide-spaced accompaniments in place of the Alberti bass that still shows up in Beethoven and Schubert, the salon brilliance of passages in broken chords and octaves, and of wide stretches and leaps (all within a total range from FFF♯ to c⁴), and the vivid contrasts of dynamics, moods, tempos, and tessituras, accompanied by copious expressive markings and inscriptions, as well as articulation and accent signs.

27. AMZ XXV (1823) 492.
28. Schumann/SCHRIFTEN I 307.
29. Mod. ed.: TRÉSOR-m XIX.
30. Egert/FRÜHROMANTIKER 124.

Ex. 16. From the finale of *Grande Sonate fantaisie intitulée L'Infortunée,* Op. 26, by Ferdinand Ries (after TRÉSOR-m XIX).

The bold melodic projection of the lyrical theme, over broken chords in open position and slow harmonic rhythm, near the start of Ries's finale (Ex. 16) recalls the same style in main themes of three near successors, all likewise German sonatas in f♯—Hummel's Op. 81/iii, Moscheles' Op. 49 in one movement, and Schumann's Op. 11/i. Besides the command of form, harmony, and keyboard scoring in Op. 26, Ries displays his outstanding craftsmanship in some contrapuntal writing, especially in the middle movement, that certainly surpasses Beethoven's if not Schubert's in grace and felicity. With all these Romanticisms and skills, Ries's music survived longer than Koželuch's had. In fact, in the early 20th century, PAZDÍREK, the comprehensive catalogue of all available published music, still listed nearly all of his sonatas and related works. However, in the last half century publishers have deleted all the sonatas and virtually everything else from their catalogues by this composer once so widely patronized.

A Second Direct Beethoven Transmitter: Czerny

The association of **Carl Czerny** (1791–1857) with Beethoven was as close and durable as that of Ries, although it did not extend back to the Bonn days, nor elicit quite the same respect from Beethoven, nor exercise as much influence on the sonata writing of the younger man (Ries's junior by more than six years).[31] The two disciples must have crossed paths often. Yet they seem not to have developed any warm friendship, for the available letters and reminiscences of Ries make no mention of Czerny and those few of Czerny refer to Ries only to recall reading often at two pianos with him (including an arrangement of Beethoven's "Kreutzer Sonata," Op. 47) and reacting to his playing as being very dexterous and fluent, if not wholly to Beethoven's liking.[32]

As a piano prodigy of about ten and already a Beethoven worshipper, Czerny began his study with Beethoven in Vienna about the same year as Ries, or about 1801.[33] He was an only child, who became the main support of his parents, never married, and rarely travelled. By the time he was fifteen this gentle, kindly soul was well started on his lifetime pursuits of playing, teaching, composing, and writing, as well as studying widely in other cultural fields. He figured in Beethoven's life not only as one of his few bonafide students but as a main performer of his music (along with Ries and Dorothea von Ertmann), as a transcriber of many of his works, as a teacher of his nephew Karl, and as an occasional agent (less so than Ries) in his personal and professional affairs. He is remembered in today's view of the past as a successful Viennese pianist and pedagogue of the early 19th century; as a transmitter of Beethoven's musical ideas and intentions to Liszt, Leschetizky, T. Kullak, and other important pupils who were themselves to become transmitters; as a writer of substance on musical subjects; and, in pianists' circles, of course, as the clever manufacturer of many piano etudes still widely practiced. Much of what he transmitted on the performance of Beethoven's sonatas occurs in his own

31. Ries and Czerny are compared in Schindler & MacArdle/BEETHOVEN 426–27, with little good said about the music of either.

32. Thayer & Forbes/BEETHOVEN I 295; CZERNY 310. The arrangement of Op. 47 is not among the 3 pub. ones by Czerny noted in Kinsky & Halm/BEETHOVEN 112; cf. MacArdle/CZERNYS 132.

33. Czerny's short, valuable autobiography of 1842, trans. in full in CZERNY, is a primary source, much of it included in the chief study to date of the man and his works, which is the unpub. Ph.D. diss. Steger/CZERNY. Other primary sources are Czerny's autobiographic letter of 1824, printed in Schnapp/CZERNY (a letter intended for an unachieved new ed. of the Gerber *lexicon* and remarkable for no mention of Beethoven, especially as Schnapp's statement of a falling out between Czerny and Beethoven at that time cannot be substantiated); the contemporary account in Schilling/LEXICON II 344–46 (as of 1834); and numerous bits of information in several other sources listed in MacArdle/CZERNYS, which is itself an efficient summary of source information about Czerny (and disentanglement from the unrelated Joseph Czerny). Hanslick/TAGEBUCHE 32–40 is a general appreciation of Czerny.

edition of them (Simrock, issued separately, *ca.* 1845–55), and in the final volume of his four-volume *Pianoforte-Schule,* Op. 500 (completed 1839–42 [?], pub. 1842–46 [?] by Diabelli in Vienna).[34] Other of his writings include his annotated translation of Reicha's composition treatise (1832) and his own composition treatise, Op. 600 (written by 1840?),[35] as well as his "Outline of All Music History," Op. 815 (1851).[36]

All of which leads to Czerny's extraordinary output, including operas, masses, requiems, offertories, graduals, symphonies, overtures, concertos, chamber works, stage music, arrangements and editions of other composers, further treatises, essays and plays outside of music, and many other piano pieces besides the sonatas in question! PAZDÍREK (III 661–88) shows a total of 861 opus numbers, many being whole sets of pieces in themselves, plus almost half as many more miscellaneous publications, or an average of over 30 publications, large or small, each year from 1819 to his death in 1857.[37] Such prolificity and its inevitable compromise with low public tastes quite naturally became the target for many a caustic remark. Mendelssohn,[38] Chopin, and Schumann were contemptuous, while recognizing other virtues in Czerny. Chopin, during his Vienna sojourn, 1830–31, wrote his family about "that Viennese specialist in the manufacture of all sorts of musical sweetmeats . . . ," following an earlier report of how Czerny was "happily engaged in arranging some overture or other for eight pianos (sixteen

34. In MGG VII 1186 (H. Haase), "um 1830" is obviously too early for the first Vienna ed.; but in Dale/THREE C's 142, "1839" is just possible for Vols. I–III (only) in a pub. English trans.; John Bishop's preface to Czerny/COMPOSITION states that Czerny sold Op. 500 to Robert Cocks while in London in 1837. The Diabelli plate no. 8212 suggests 1846 (Deutsch/NUMMERN 11–12; cf. HOFMEISTER 1844–51, p. 209) for Vol. IV, rather than the "1842" on p. 23 of Badura-Skoda/ CZERNY (with preface and annotations), which brings together virtually everything Czerny wrote on the performance of Beethoven's music, including portions of the *Erinnerungen,* miscellaneous remarks, a facs. of 89 pp. from Op. 500, and a collation of this last with the sometimes conflicting advices in the Simrock eds. (listed in HOFMEISTER 1844–51, p. 85 [up to Op. 57] and 1852–59, p. 110 [all]). Some of this performance advice in Op. 500 is quoted, and sometimes protested, along with further information about Czerny and Beethoven, in Schindler & MacArdle/BEETHOVEN 397–98, 405–26 *passim.*

35. Reicha & Czerny/COMPOSITION and Czerny/COMPOSITION, as discussed in SSB II. The pedagogic ideas are the likely focus of a Ph.D. diss. on Czerny in progress at Columbia Univ. (as of 1967) by Mrs. Alice Mitchell, whose advices and loan of Steger/CZERNY for the present discussion are gratefully acknowledged.

36. Cf. E. Valentin in NZM CXVIII (1957) 356–57.

37. No one list is complete, but the relatively few gaps in PAZDÍREK can be nearly filled in from the lists in Steger/CZERNY 110–142 (pubs. with op. nos., only), the list of works, both pub. (up to Op. 798) and unpub., in Czerny/COMPOSITION I vii–xiv (cf. Dale/THREE C's 146), and the summary list by categories in Prosniz/ HANDBUCH I 111–16. On Czerny's method for composing 4 pieces at a time, cf. Loesser/PIANOS 362 and Dessauer/FIELD 75–76.

38. Cf. Werner/MENDELSSOHN 168.

hands)." [39] And Schumann reviewed Czerny's "4 brillante Phantasien," Op. 434, in 1838, with the comment, "By all means let him retire and give him a pension; truly, he deserves it and would not [have to] write any more. . . . In a word, he's gotten stale; we've gotten fed up with his things. . . ." [40] Even the more tactful editor of the *Allgemeine musikalische Zeitung* in Leipzig was already cautioning in 1827 about the danger of sacrificing quality and satiating the public by turning out so much, only to go into a much longer discussion of the problem one year later that equated Czerny and the keyboard with Rossini and the opera.[41]

In all that prolificity, Czerny's sonata writing, however commonplace much of it may seem today, stands out as a main part of his most serious composing. He himself acknowledged to Beethoven in 1825 the worthlessness of his " 'Kleinigkeiten,' since I jot them down very rapidly . . . I long to get going in earnest now with [some] larger orchestral things." [42] Particular evidence of his special regard for his sonatas turns up near the start of a letter of 1823 to the Leipzig publisher C. F. Peters:[43]

My solo piano sonatas, however many I plan to write, ought through [one separate] continuous numbering to comprise an entirety [in themselves], in which I want, little by little, to record my artistic views and experiences. Therefore I ask you to consider the 3ième *Sonate,* sent to you, as one item of an over-all series, which I hope to make more and more significant.

This statement makes clear which of his own sonatas Czerny took most seriously. Out of 64 works that could be identified here with "sonate" or "sonatine" in the title—more than Ries's, yet a mere 5 per cent of Czerny's total output as against about 22 per cent for Ries—Czerny assigned a special numbering only to the "sonatas" for solo piano, 11 in all. He did not so distinguish any of the "sonates" or "sonatines" for 4 hands at one piano (about 23 per cent of all his sonatas) or for piano and violin (about 11 per cent), nor, for that matter, any works at all called "sonatines" (about 63 per cent), including those for solo piano.[44]

The 11 solo sonatas in Czerny's special series are No. 1 in A♭, Op. 7,

39. Sydow & Hedley/CHOPIN 82 and 67.
40. Schumann/SCHRIFTEN I 364–65; cf., also, I 236–37.
41. AMZ XXIX (1827) 234 and XXX (1828) 233–38.
42. Thayer & Riemann/BEETHOVEN V 267.
43. Printed in full in La Mara/MUSIKERBRIEFE II 98–101.
44. Thus, at least for the sons., neither the proportions nor the categories can be reconciled with the translator's summary of 1848 in Czerny/COMPOSITION I vi: "Of his [Czerny's] original productions, about one third are written in the strict style, one third in the brilliant style, and the remainder for the purpose of instruction. . . ."

1820; No. 2 in a, Op. 13, 1821; No. 3 in f, Op. 57, 1824; No. 4 in G, Op. 65, 1824; No. 5 in E, Op. 76, 1824; No. 6 in d, Op. 124, 1827; No. 7 in e, Op. 143, 1827 (?); No. 8 in E♭, Op. 144, 1827 (?); No. 9 in b, Op. 145, 1827 (?); No. 10 in B♭, Op. 268, 1831 (?); and No. 11 in D♭, Op. 730, 1843 (?).[45] Czerny uses descriptive titles for his sonatas only infrequently. Each of Nos. 7–9, Opp. 143–145, carries the title "Grande Fantaisie en Forme de Sonate," but for no evident reason in the cycles or music itself; Op. 268 is rightly called "Grande Sonate d'Étude," though for little more reason than most of his sonatas might be; and the lighter sonatas or sonatinas occasionally carry terms like "faciles et brillantes," "militaire," "sentimentale," "pastorale," and even "à la Scarlatti" (a one-movement 4-hand sonatina in f♯, Op. 788) in their titles. The reviewer of Op. 7 actually asks why "grande" does not precede "Sonate" in the title, in view not only of this work's length but its design and its performance difficulties.[46] "Grande" or "grosse" does appear in the subsequent editions of Op. 7 as well as the titles of most of the other "sonatas," though not the "sonatinas."

Czerny's more serious sonatas may be seen in better perspective by comparing them with Ries's. Czerny uses over-all keys up to one more flat and sharp (D♭ and E), and puts a larger proportion, nearly half, of them in minor keys. Instead of the usual three-movement plan, F-S-F, he uses at least four movements in the standard order F-S-Sc-Ro. In Op. 7 he adds a final, fifth movement, "Capriccio fugato," putting it, as with Ries's Op. 21, in the tonic minor (a♭!) except for a Picardy 3ᵈ in the four ending measures. In the four-hand sonata in C minor Op. 10

45. Czerny apparently excluded from this special series his piano "Sonate" Op. 167, which is therefore relegated here to the sonatina group. "Op. 124" was assigned not only to No. 6 in this series but to some string arrangements. Czerny himself supplied pub. years for Opp. 1–85 (in his letter of 1824 printed in Schnapp/CZERNY; 1820 for Op. 7 is confirmed in Weinmann/ARTARIA item 2632, although it had been composed in 1810, according to Egert/FRÜHROMANTIKER 126). Nägeli issued Op. 124 in 1827 in *Die musikalische Ehrenpforte* (with Ries's Op. 141; cf. Deutsch/SCHUBERT-D 541). Conjectures for the years of Opp. 143–45 are based on 1827 for Op. 124, plus a review in 1828 of Op. 144 (AMZ XXX 233–39), the listing of all 3 in HOFMEISTER 1828, p. 585, and the fact of their consecutive op. nos.; for Op. 268, on 1830 for both the performance (Czerny/COMPOSITION I ix) and pub. (MacArdle/CZERNYS 133) of Op. 238; and for Op. 730, on its listing in HOFMEISTER 1843/II, p. 151, plus a review of Op. 601 in 1841 (AMZ XLIII 653).

The relatively brief discussions of Czerny's entire son. output in Steger/CZERNY 78–94 and of the solo piano sons. in Egert/FRÜHROMANTIKER 9 and 125–28 (largely derived from Steger) leave open the need for a fuller, more systematic study. Hasenöhrl/CZERNY, unaware of Steger/CZERNY and unavailable in Egert/FRÜH-ROMANTIKER (cf. p. 125), is a rather superficial diss. of 1927 that provides almost no bibliographic information but mainly facts about the cycles and forms of the sons. (pp. 17–39) and a survey of melodic traits (based on G. Adler and W. Fischer) by mvt. types (pp. 77–103).

46. AMZ XXIV (1822) 382–84.

(1821) he also uses five movements, and in Op. 124 he uses seven movements counting the slow introduction. But Czerny shows little of Ries's
predilection for slow introductions and none for their recurrence
during the movements. His only efforts to give more unity to the cycle
occur with the occasional instruction "attacca" before the finale (as in
Op. 65 or the duet Op. 331) and in the surprising arch effect created
by the return in those last four measures of Op. 7 to the very opening
of the sonata.

Where Ries is strongest, in the command of structural techniques,
Czerny has here seemed weakest. One notes especially how little the
ideas develop and how often the modulations lead to no clear goal in
the initial, "sonata-allegro" movements. The ideas themselves show
Czerny to be even less of a creative melodist than Ries. They are
usually no more than slight melodic fragments reiterated sequentially
or in place. For that matter, Czerny introduces and restates fewer
tangible ideas, devoting even more space to passagework. But his
passagework is quite as idiomatic for the keyboard as Ries's and decidedly more varied and ingenious, in spite of its exploitation of the
piano's highest registers, enough to bear out Beethoven's oft-misquoted
remark, "Czerny gives me too much piccolo." [47] In the scherzos and
rondos, where ingenuity and charm can matter more than original
ideas or development, Czerny is at his best; and even in the relatively
static slow movements—to the surprise of all who know only his etudes
—he can convert the passagework into remarkably Chopinesque
fioriture (Ex. 17). Arthur Loesser pinpoints both the charm and pitfalls
of the passagework that serves Czerny as the chief means of continuity
in his sonatas as well as his etudes:[48]

Rapid, feathery, well-articulated pianistic passage-work, chiefly for the right
hand, was his best product—just what the light, bouncing, leather-covered
little hammer-heads of the Vienna pianos could deliver best. It was a music
without depth, intensity, or wit, but always smooth and pretty and rather
ear-tickling when played fast; it displayed tonal ruffles and ribbons, ruching
and rickrack, in endless variety of patterns and endless monotony of import.
Its low specific gravity made it easy to take, and the Viennese as well as other
Europeans took it in vast quantity.

"From a spirited virtuoso and warm sensitive Romantic in his youth,
Czerny developed over the years into a dry academician." [49] Although
most of his "sonatas" appeared within the first quarter of his output,
the same generalization might already be made within their own en-

47. Thayer & Riemann/BEETHOVEN V 300 fn. 2, said in reference to an arrangement of Beethoven's Op. 133 that proved not to be acceptable.
48. Loesser/PIANOS 145.
49. Georgii/WEBER 4 fn. 1.

Ex. 17. From the "Scherzo" and the slow movement of Carl
Czerny's *Grande Sonate d'Étude,* Op. 268/iii and ii (after Edition
Peters No. 3239).

tirety. His best sonatas—"best" not only for their spirit and warmth
but their contributions to the new Romanticism—are certainly his
first two, No. 1, Op. 7, in A♭ for solo piano and Op. 10 in c for four
hands. Also in both these sonatas, but not in the later ones, distinct
references to Beethoven turn up. Thus, in Op. 7 the restful, almost
hymnlike first movement, "Andante allegro moderato ed espressivo" in
C meter, suggests the opening of Beethoven's Op. 26 or even 110 in
the same key. This is a monothematic movement, except for a new,
rather weak line in the submediant and mediant keys (leading to uneventful sequential modulations) by way of a "development" section. A
difficult "Beethoven trill" decorates the dominant retransition to the
recapitulation. In the fluent, scherzando second movement, "Prestissimo
agitato" in c♯ and 3/4 meter, we get hints, among others, of Beethoven's Opp. 27/1/ii and the "Trio" of the "Scherzo" in his "Sinfonia

eroica," as well as some empty, repeated bass octaves that Beethoven would not have written. In the third movement, "Adagio, espressivo e cantabile" in D♭ and 3/4 meter, the start suggests the chromatic passages, with 32d-note triplets in the bass, of Beethoven's Op. 31/2/ii, but the line is vacuous again. In the "Rondo" fourth movement, "Allegretto" in A♭ and 2/4 meter, we get an introduction that recalls at least the similar function in the finale of Beethoven's first symphony, followed by a polka-like refrain typical of Czerny's freshest melodies, and soon some octaves that already sound like "too much piccolo." As observed earlier, the finale, "Tempo moderato" in 4/4 meter, is a "Capriccio fugato" in the tonic minor with an ending that brings back the sonata's opening idea. Its counterpoint is more scholastic than Ries's, but not unskillful.

Rochlitz's extended review of Op. 7 in 1822 [50] notes difficult but legitimate technical problems, sustained, impassioned, gloomy, sometimes wild content, departures from "the usual form of the sonata" leading to excessive length ("almost any two or three movements, in whatever conceivable order, could suffice well in themselves"), superiority of the first three movements, especially the "Prestissimo agitato," over the final two, and objections to certain dissonances as well as to extremes of range and dynamics. And Liszt, writing hurriedly and belatedly from Paris in 1830 to his onetime master, tells Czerny he has given special study to "your admirable Sonata" (Op. 7) and has played it for various groups of ("at least so-called") connoisseurs with overwhelmingly enthusiastic response, particularly to the "Prestissimo." [51]

But the reviews of Czerny's sonatas did not go on for long and soon began to express more cons than pros.[52] Why becomes clear enough again, if one reads through a later sonata like that in b for piano and violin, Op. 686 (1842, around the time Czerny was writing about "Sonata form"; cf. ssb II). This work is a true duo in four movements, F-S-Sc-Ro, which carefully goes through all the proper motions, modulations, and climaxes, yet advances so perfunctorily with its innocuous themes, square phrases, and empty passages, that it produces a sense only of complete sterility. Even so, as recently as the 1930's, that *Grande Sonate d'Étude,* Op. 268, was played as the required piece for the *prix du concours* by a daylong succession of graduating pianists at the

50. AMZ XXIV 382–84.

51. La Mara/MUSIKERBRIEFE II 209–10; cf. Ramann/LISZT I 488. In a letter to Dionys Pruckner 26 years later, Liszt was still speaking highly of Op. 7 (LISZT LETTERS I 266; but read Op. 7, not 6).

52. E.g., cf. AMZ XXVII (1825) 87–88 on Op. 58, or XXX (1828) 233–39 on Op. 144; also, AMA No. 20 (Nov., 1826) 153 on Op. 65.

Paris Conservatoire, undoubtedly because it exploits every standard, advanced piano technique.[53]

A Third Direct Beethoven Transmitter: Moscheles

Ignaz Moscheles (1794–1870) knew Beethoven neither so well nor so long as Ries or Czerny, and received no instruction from him other than the direct and frequent advices required when he made a piano reduction of *Fidelio* in 1814.[54] On the other hand, Moscheles became at least as active and influential a champion of Beethoven's music, and for a considerably longer time, outliving Beethoven himself by 43 years, Ries by 32, and Czerny by 13. Furthermore, he won greater renown as a pianist than either of his fellow Beethoven worshipers,[55] his importance as a piano pedagogue eventually surpassed Czerny's, and two or three of his sonatas gained at least as wide and lasting acceptance as any by Ries or Czerny.

Moscheles' busy, long career is outlined by his changes of residence from Prague to Vienna in 1808, to London in 1826, and to Leipzig in 1846 (where he joined Mendelssohn at the new Conservatory). This career is recorded in exceptional detail in the perceptive and devoted (but sensitively restrained) biography that his wife published after his death, based largely on his own careful diaries and abundant correspondence.[56] As one of our best firsthand surveys of European musical life in the 19th century, this biography (covering mainly the years from 1815 to 1860) brings us close to the astonishing number of important musicians that Moscheles got to know at home and during his many recital tours or other travels. Included are not only the three masters who seem to have affected him most deeply—Beethoven,

53. Curiously, except for a Sam Fox ed. in 1963 of the 4-hand Son. in G, Op. 50/1, Op. 268 comes nearest of all Czerny's sons. to being a "mod. ed." Edition Peters 3239 is a reprint of it issued in 1909, though no longer in the Peters catalogue. Two other 20th-century, French appreciations of Czerny's piano writing occur in ENCYCLOPÉDIE II/3 2092–93 (Gratia & Duvernoy) and STRAVINSKY 178.

54. Cf. Thayer & Forbes/BEETHOVEN I 584–86. Regarding Schindler's scurrilous, damaging, and entirely unwarranted attempt to discredit Moscheles and his association with Beethoven (19 years after Moscheles' trans. of the first ed. of Schindler's Beethoven biography) cf. Schindler & MacArdle/BEETHOVEN 17, 29, 322, 359–60, 372–74, 391–92.

55. Cf. Hanslick/WIEN I 216–18; Schindler & MacArdle/BEETHOVEN 392 fn. 300; SSB II, III.

56. MOSCHELES (with inadequate index). Worthwhile contemporary views from the outside are added in Schilling/LEXICON V 8–11 and Mendel/LEXIKON VII 176–77. MOSCHELES and still other contemporary sources supply the choice descriptions of Moscheles in Loesser/PIANOS 145, 285–92, 302–3.

Weber, and Mendelssohn[57]—but many others like Albrechtsberger, Salieri, Ries, Czerny, Hummel, Spohr, Cramer, Liszt, Clara and Robert Schumann, Clementi, Chopin, Ferdinand David, A. B. Marx, Paganini, Field, Henriette Sontag, Jenny Lind, Thalberg, Rossini, Ferdinand Hiller, Meyerbeer, Joachim, Wagner, and Anton Rubinstein, quite apart from eminent nonmusicians like Heine and Walter Scott.

The biography shows Moscheles deriving special pleasure from intimate musical sociability, from a tourist's views of the arts in general, and from everything about the piano in particular, especially its performers, music, and continuing improvements as a concert instrument. His generosity and altruism rarely permitted such mistrust as Field and Paganini aroused in him. But for all his active, often historically minded interest in Handel, (Domenico) Scarlatti, Bach "and even older composers," Clementi, and both early and late Beethoven (all furthered by his association with Mendelssohn),[58] and for all his obvious desire to understand, he could never endorse (nor compete with) the younger school of virtuosos like Thalberg and Liszt,[59] and he could only admire, never fully accept, all that he found too modern in the music of Schumann, Chopin, Berlioz, Liszt, and Wagner.[60] Hummel figured in his life somewhat as an older rival, with a similar career.[61] Among Moscheles' many piano students, Mendelssohn and Thalberg should be included for at least a few lessons each.[62]

It was his chronic, lifelong "Beethoven fever," [63] brought on by discovering and playing at *Sonata pathétique* while the little prodigy was still only seven (SCE 513), that helped decide Moscheles' move to Vienna when he was only fourteen. And it was while still in the environment of Beethoven that he wrote all of his solo and most of his duo sonatas. When increasing concert tours eventually took him away from Vienna for good, he turned to writing mostly display pieces for piano like his celebrated "Alexander Variations," Op. 32, or the Concerto in G Minor, Op. 60, and *Concerto pathétique,* Op. 93. After

57. Moscheles' long, close friendship with Mendelssohn (from 1824) is richly documented throughout both MOSCHELES and the many letters in MENDELSSOHN/Moscheles.
58. E.g., cf. MOSCHELES II 23–24, 35–36, 45, 224–25.
59. Cf. MOSCHELES II 43, 203.
60. Cf. MOSCHELES I 295, 316, 319; II 52–53, 172, 213, 219, 228–29, 243, 260, 266, 297–98.
61. See the comparison of Moscheles, Hummel, and W. A. Mozart "the Younger" in AMZ XXII (1828) 369; but see, also, MOSCHELES I 28, 22, 241–42.
62. According to MOSCHELES I 99–100 and 131, though not mentioned in most reference works.
63. MOSCHELES I 4.

about 1840 and decreasing public performances[64] he devoted himself especially to songs and to writing more of those fine etudes, which, as with Czerny and Cramer, are mainly what keep his name alive today. The few sonatas from his later years are all duos that seem to have been written as much to satisfy his love for sociability as his later concert needs.

Out of the 173 published works or sets of pieces that his widow tabulated,[65] Moscheles left only 9 sonatas (5 per cent); besides which should be mentioned an early, three-movement piano sonatina in G, Op. 4 (or Op. 6, 1810); one early, apparently unpublished sonata each for P & Vn and P & Bn, according to the biography;[66] and a "Grande Sonate" in E♭, Op. 35, in four movements, variously arranged in 1815 for P alone, for P & Vn, Vc, Fl, & 2 Hns, and for 4 hands at one and at two pianos, from his sextet Op. 35.[67] The four solo sonatas began with Op. 22 in D (Vienna: Mechetti, between 1811 and 1813), a weak three-movement piece that evidently aroused too little interest to get special mention either in MOSCHELES or contemporary reviews.[68] The next solo sonata in numerical order, *Eine charakteristische Sonate* in B♭, Op. 27 (Vienna: Artaria, 1814), did get mentioned at least in the biography,[69] though only for the occasion its fuller German title commemorated—"Sentiments in Vienna Upon the Return of His Majesty Francis I, Emperor of Austria . . . in the Year 1814." Although the music of this equally banal, square-cut sonata is not other-

64. Cf. MOSCHELES I 221–22.

65. MOSCHELES II 302–11; the list has errors; also, dates are lacking but do appear in several instances in earlier pp. of the biography. One main source for this tabulation seems to have been VERZEICHNISS MOSCHELES, a thematic index of pub. works up to *ca.* 1860. Cf., also, the full list in PAZDÍREK XIX 826–32.

66. MOSCHELES I 13; but these may only be alternative listings, respectively, for the Son. for P & Fl, Op. 44, and the "Grand Duo concertant" for P & Vc-or-Bn, Op. 34.

67. Egert/FRÜHROMANTIKER 139–46 provides a brief discussion, with exx., of the solo sons., including Op. 35; but since Hummel's *Grand Septuor* Op. 74 did not appear until 1816, Op. 35 was not an imitation of it; only later could Moscheles have referred to Op. 35 as "a light youthful effort, not to be compared with Hummel's work" (MOSCHELES I 20). The 1963 diss. Heussner/MOSCHELES (by the authoress, née Schmidt, of the earlier article on Moscheles in MGG IX 617–20) is a more detailed historic and style study that includes unpub. letters and other new biographic information, the chamber works and concertos with piano, as well as all the solo and 4-hand P sons.; the latter are analyzed by mvt. types, with bibl., charts, and exx., on pp. 52–93.

68. Among the scarce copies today, one is listed in Cat. BRUXELLES IV 210 and one is to be found in a "complete" 8-vol. set of Moscheles' solo and chamber piano works (with all sons. through Op. 79) at the Library of Congress (M3.1/M85), pub. in Paris, *ca.* 1835? (cf. MENDELSSOHN/Moscheles 130 on Schlesinger's "complete" ed.; Hopkinson/PARISIAN 113 on Société musicale), by the Société pour la Publication de Musique Classique et Moderne.

69. MOSCHELES I 12.

wise programmatic, its two outer movements carry further inscriptions
—"Expression of Inner Delight Upon the Glorious Return of His
Majesty" and "Rejoicing Over Favored Austria"—and its middle movement is a set of variations on Nägeli's "Freut Euch des Lebens" ("Life
Let Us Cherish"; following by about 7 years Wölfl's variations on the
same theme in his technically difficult sonata "Non plus ultra"; SCE
563).[70]

The third of his four solo examples is Moscheles' *Grosse Sonate* in
E, Op. 41, composed in 1816 (and pub. in Vienna by Steiner not later
than 1819). Dedicated to Beethoven, it is more original, intimate, easy-
going, and free of empty passagework than its predecessors.[71] There is,
however, little contrast or Beethovian development of the ideas in its
four movements (F-"Minuetto o 'Scherzo"-M-"Rondo scherzando"), the
finale being the most ingratiating and convincing of the cycle. The
last of these solo sonatas is the one that has come nearest to surviving
today and the one "thought by [Moscheles] himself and competent
judges to be among his best works"—Op. 49, *Sonate mélancolique*
in f♯ (Offenbach: André, 1822?), the "subject" of which had "occurred
to him [in 1814] while giving a lesson, [and] was worked out with
particular pleasure." [72] This work is one of the surprisingly few one-
movement sonatas of consequence from the 19th century (SSB VI). But
unlike Liszt's Sonata in b, it consists not of several movements within
a movement but a single movement of 247 measures that approximates
"sonata form." The "sonata form" divides asymmetrically, tending to
make it cumulative, with 45 per cent going to the exposition, 25 to
the development, 26 to the recapitulation, and 4 to the coda.

Even though there is that distinctive "subject" (mss. 1–19), an extended bridge (mss. 20–44), a well-prepared second theme (mss. 45–79),
and a chain of four differentiated closing ideas (mss. 80–109), most of
the material in Op. 49 derives from or maintains the "mélancolique"
lyricism of the opening, presaging Moscheles' own composition advice
in 1859 "always to express some one definite thought, be it serious or
gay, cheerful or anxious." [73] Only the start of the closing section, with
its sudden swish of 16th-note scales, achieves enough melodic contrast

70. The Paris ed. cited in the previous fn. omits all of the programmatic inscriptions in Moscheles' Op. 27.
71. A complimentary review is cited in Heussner/MOSCHELES 54.
72. MOSCHELES I 13; cf., also, I 221, II 266 (Liszt's playing of Op. 49 in 1859)
and 304 (but Weinmann/ARTARIA does not list this work). Our pub. year for Op.
49 is based on its André plate no. 4407, as in Deutsch/NUMMERN 6; Heussner/
MOSCHELES 56 cites a Cappi ed. with plate no. 1095 that also falls in 1822, also
high praise of Op. 49 from F. Hiller. Mod. ed.: Newman/THIRTEEN-m 162 (with
preface, pp. 25–26).
73. MOSCHELES II 267.

to contribute any appreciable structural tension. More structural tension obtains through clear tonal organization (basically f♯-A/a-C-a-dominant pedal/f♯-D-F♯), carried out in well-balanced phrases and implemented by skillful, logical harmony. There are also a few strategically located third relationships, such as the almost Wagnerian climax on an F triad (ms. 38) four measures before the cadence in A that prepares the second theme. The regularity of the phrase syntax still weighs heavy, though relief comes in an occasional unsquare phrase (e.g., mss. 17–19), or in progressive shortening of phrase elements for cumulative drives to a tonal goal. The latter procedure (as at mss. 153–62) and some contrapuntal exchanges (mss. 132–38) recall similar techniques used by Beethoven (as in Op. 57/i/110–30 and Op. 28/i/195–206), but also define the limit to which Moscheles actually developed his ideas. The style of this music is somewhat eclectic. Thus, the first theme, descending over broken chords in open position (mss. 1–8), suggests Ries's Op. 26/iii (as noted earlier). The closing section begins in the salon style of the *leggermente* close in Weber's Op. 39/i, and passes from one idea into the next much as Mozart might do in a closing section (e.g., K. 300k/iii/65–90). And the triplet figuration that embellishes the restatement of the second theme (Ex. 18) brings Beethoven to mind again, this time the corresponding passage in Op. 53/i/43–53.

Moscheles' other five sonatas, each of which enjoyed considerable success, are all duos, three with a second *concertante* instrument and two for P-duet. Of the former, the *Grande Sonate concertante* in A, Op. 44, for P & Fl was another early work, published by Artaria in 1818. The *Sonata concertante* in G, Op. 79, for P & Fl-or-Vn, published by Kistner in Leipzig in 1828, won an enthusiastic review in 1830 that preferred it "even" to Op. 44 for its consistent musical significance in all three movements, over and above its dexterous passagework.[74] And the *Sonata* in E, Op. 121, for P & Vc-or-Vn (or P-duet) was a late work, composed in 1850–51 (about the time Moscheles was finding "a wild overgrown forest" in Chopin's cello sonata),[75] and published within a year by Kistner. This last was dedicated to Schumann, who replied with cordial thanks for Moscheles' earlier encouragement and inspiration, in keeping with earlier praise for him (but without any detailed reference to his sons.).[76] It was arranged for violin and so played by Ferdinand David.

74. AMZ XXXII 669–70 (G. W. Fink).
75. MOSCHELES II 172, 213, 215, 218; cf. SSB XII.
76. MOSCHELES I 24–25; Schumann/SCHRIFTEN I 114–15 (1835) and 360–63 (1838) present Schumann's 2 main reviews of Moscheles.

Ex. 18. From Ignaz Moscheles' *Sonate mélancolique,* Op. 49
(after the Société . . . ed. at the Library of Congress).

The *Grande Sonate* in E♭, Op. 47, for P-duet was composed early, in
1819 (not 1816),[77] and published that same ˙ ar by Artaria, with a
dedication to Archduke Rudolph (SCE 524), "who played it in musician-
like style at first sight with him." [78] Mendelssohn, Chopin, Ferdinand
Hiller, and probably Liszt were among those who also played it with
him.[79] The success with Chopin in Paris was so great and so frequent,
including a command repetition of this work in 1839 for the Royal
Family at Saint-Cloud, that it "came at last to be called and only
known by the name of 'La Sonate.' " [80] Finally, Moscheles' *Grande
Sonate symphonique* in b, Op. 112, for four hands, was composed in
Paris in 1845 (this time to be played at court with daughter Emily)
and published by Kistner, among others, in 1846, after the proofs had
been read by Mendelssohn.[81] One reviewer in 1847 welcomed this
revival of the four-hand idiom, with all its valued social intimacies,
and expressed his preference for the final two movements—a "Scherzoso
alla tedesca antica" that is "charming" and "witty," and a finale based

77. Heussner/MOSCHELES 54–55.

78. MOSCHELES I 23, 221.

79. MOSCHELES I 274; II 57–60, 88, 133, 265–66. Cf., also, Schumann/SCHRIFTEN
I 114.

80. MOSCHELES II 60; Heussner/MOSCHELES 55.

81. MOSCHELES II 149, 154; MENDELSSOHN/Moscheles 261, 269; HALLÉ 108. The
work got several passing mentions in RGM about this time.

on the chorale "Lob, Ehr' und Preis"—for they give "a glimpse into the romantic world of the newer tone poem," whereas the two first movements show more skill than youthful fire and reflect the "older period." [82]

Schubert and the Beethovian Standard

Among all who worked in the shadow of Beethoven, and among all his other contemporaries and near successors, too, it was **Franz Schubert** (1797–1828) who, though scarcely acknowledged or mentioned by these others, "understood most clearly and felt most deeply the content and force of Beethoven's music." [83] That generalization suggests that it might have been more appropriate, following our designations of Ries, Czerny, and Moscheles as "Direct Beethoven Transmitters," to head this next section "Schubert, the Prime Beethoven Transmitter." But such a heading would underplay Schubert's originality and genius in his own right, as well as his importance here, along with Brahms, as one of the two Viennese masters of the 19th-century sonata after Beethoven. Furthermore, even without guessing his own future historical eminence, Schubert himself might well have protested such a classification. For, besides being a self-avowed, although shy and distant, "Worshipper and Admirer" of Beethoven,[84] he also tended to belittle himself in those few references to Beethoven that turn up in his letters, hinting at a certain despair if not actual envy.[85]

The relationships between Beethoven and Schubert, both biographic and musical, have received considerable attention.[86] How much the two men actually met and how much notice Beethoven took of Schubert's music, if any, remain moot questions. But there can be no question that Schubert knew much of Beethoven's music well, almost certainly including each sonata about as rapidly as it appeared.[87] Nor

82. NZM XXVI (1847) 41–42 (initialed "1"); echoed in brief in AMZ XLIX (1847) 691–92; cf., also, Heussner/MOSCHELES 57.

83. Frimmel/SCHUBERT 410.

84. Deutsch/SCHUBERT-D 221 and 255. Among numerous corroborations by his friends, cf. Deutsch/SCHUBERT-D 228; Deutsch/SCHUBERT-M 19, 26, 98, 121, 126, 180.

85. E.g., cf. Deutsch/SCHUBERT-D 64, 265, 339; cf., also, the observations of Josef Hüttenbrenner and Josef von Spaun in Deutsch/SCHUBERT-M 76, 77, 128.

86. Kreissle/SCHUBERT I 258–69 already summarizes most of the conflicting evidence for personal relations and meetings; cf., also, Nohl/SCHUBERT, Deutsch/SCHUBERT-M 328. Frimmel/SCHUBERT is a pioneer study of Beethoven's musical influences; Chusid/SCHUBERT-m 98–110 illuminates especially the influences on the "Unfinished Symphony."

87. Cf. Deutsch/SCHUBERT-M 180 (A. Hüttenbrenner), 299 (K. Holz), 363 (J. v. Spaun).

can there be any question that this music clearly influenced his own. The influence is manifest in the frank imitations of the student—for example, throughout Schubert's "Tragic Symphony" in c (1816; D. 417),[88] or the opening theme of the "Allegretto" from his Sonata in e/E for piano (1817; D. 566), which so closely resembles the opening theme of the similarly paced finale in Beethoven's Op. 90, likewise in e/E.[89] And the influence is still manifest in the more confident allusions by the mature composer—for example, in the homage or less conscious respect paid throughout the Sonata in c for piano (1828; D. 958), including at the start (Ex. 19) what must have been a deliberate reference to, as well as an intensified expansion of, the theme in Beethoven's 32 Variations in c (WoO 80).

Schumann, the most important and one of the most ardent champions of Schubert, referred to him in 1838 as the feminine counterpart of Beethoven (much as Picquot had related Boccherini to Haydn, SCE 256).[90] The occasion was a review of the great four-hand Sonata in C (D. 812):

To [any-]one with a measure of feeling and training, Beethoven and Schubert will be [both] related and differentiated on the[ir] very first pages. Schubert is a maidenly character [when] held up alongside the other, much more garrulous, delicate, and spacious; alongside the other, [he is] a child who sports recklessly among the giants. Thus do these symphonic movements relate to those of Beethoven, and [yet?] in their intimacy [they] certainly could not be thought of as [being] other than by Schubert. To be sure, he too introduces his vigorous passages, he too calls up large forces; nevertheless, he keeps relating as woman to man, entreating and persuading where the other commands. But all this [applies] only in contrast to Beethoven; alongside others he is still man enough—in fact, the most daring and freethinking of the newer musicians.

Especially that concluding remark on a seeming bipolarity in Schubert's musical relationships bears significantly on the familiar but not always fruitful question of his historical identification. According to typical evaluations of the later 19th century, Schubert was best, most original, and most "Romantic" in his songs and other smaller pieces; but he was more tied to the past and more circumscribed by form

---

88. Cf. Abraham/SCHUBERT 48–52 (M. Carner).

89. Cf. Vetter/SCHUBERT I 181–82, 186; but this handsome, extended, little-noted study of 1953 fails by overemphasizing the Beethoven reminiscences, too often and on too little basis (cf. DMf VII [1954] 234–35 [H. J. Moser]).

90. Schumann/SCHRIFTEN I 330. On the psychological identification of masculine and feminine traits, mostly in Romantic composers—including "Table 1" showing Schubert as more masculine than Mendelssohn or Schumann, but less so than Chopin, Brahms, or Beethoven, among others—cf. Farnsworth/PHENOMENA.

Ex. 19. From the start of Franz Schubert's Sonata in c, D. 958 (after Schubert/WERKE-m X 204).

problems, without quite being able to amalgamate his exceptional lyricism, in his symphonies, sonatas, and other larger works.[91] More recently Einstein simplified and balanced Schubert's historical identification by labelling him "the Romantic Classic" (as distinguished from Mendelssohn, "the Romantic Classicist").[92] Other recent writers have gone further to reverse the 19th-century view by preferring to consider Schubert primarily as still a Classic.[93] In any case, there can be no doubt that all of these views have so emphasized Schubert in terms of Beethoven and other contemporaries that they have stood in the way of a full view of him in his own right. Put differently, much of the criticism of Schubert that has been negative actually reduces simply to ways in which he was not like Beethoven, although escaping the fate of being too much like Beethoven must have motivated Schubert quite as much as escaping the "Wagner maelstrom" was to worry Verdi and Debussy (ssb I).

91. E.g., cf. Bie/PIANOFORTE 225–30, including "the first musical Romantic" as a designation for Schubert; or, "Schubert" in BRITANNICA XX 103–5 (W. H. Hadow).
92. Einstein/ROMANTIC 89–91, 124–26.
93. E.g., Bücken/SCHUBERT; Vetter/SCHUBERT I 60–72; GROVE VII 570 (M. J. E. Brown).

An Uphill Century for Schubert's Sonatas

Further discussion of Schubert's relation to his environment would mean delving into his music once more and returning to those problems of style and form considered in Chapter VI. In that chapter the sonatas of Schubert, Schumann, Chopin, and Brahms have already served as the main reference points for the over-all consideration of style and form in the Romantic sonata, leaving primarily a recapitulation of the facts, cultivation, and circumstances of Schubert's sonatas to be brought up in the present chapter. But we may stop on the question of historical identification enough longer here to note in particular some changing attitudes toward Schubert's sonatas since his own day. Unlike Haydn, Mozart, Beethoven, and Clementi, who saw most or all of their own sonatas published while they were still alive (SCE 464, 484, 509, 742–45), Schubert saw only about a fifth of his completed sonatas in print (as detailed shortly).[94] And to judge by extant programs, correspondence, and other pertinent documents, none of his sonatas, not even these in print, ever got performed in public while he was alive.[95] But (as also will be detailed shortly) at least five of them did get private performances before enthusiastic groups, some given by Schubert himself, and two of the sonatas published in his lifetime did win attention through substantial, largely favorable reviews.

Yet further interest in Schubert's sonatas developed remarkably little throughout the century after his death. Schumann's general evaluation, only six years after (1834), already shows the slight reservation that was to increase rather than diminish: Though few knew Schubert and then mainly his songs, and though he "may turn out to be even more original in his songs than in his instrumental works, we value these [latter] just as much for [being] thoroughly musical and original in their own right." [96] In a pioneer article of 1862, probably by Selmar Bagge,[97] Schumann's enthusiasm was the starting point. The author had noted little subsequent interest in Schubert's instrumental music, as confirmed by so little evidence of its posthumous influence. He saw

94. All of Schubert's lifetime pubs. are listed in Deutsch/SCHUBERT-D 938–46.
95. All of Schubert's works performed publicly during his lifetime are listed in Deutsch/SCHUBERT-D 934–38. These do include such related types as the String Quartet in a (D. 804), the P Trio in E♭ (D. 929), the Fantasy for Vn & P in C (D. 934), and the String Quartet in G/i (D. 887); cf. Deutsch/SCHUBERT-B 178 for the facs. of a public program in 1828 that included the trio and later quartet.
96. Schumann/SCHRIFTEN I 124, 125.
97. Bagge/SCHUBERT.

Schubert's sonatas as being somewhat interrelated with fantasias, as showing more concern for content than form (with the finales sometimes growing tedious), as imitating orchestral sonorities in their keyboard writing, and as achieving less sustained passion than Beethoven's sonatas. Seven years later (1869), Kreissle, who as yet knew the "Unfinished Symphony" only by hearsay from the "initiated," gave passing mention to a few of Schubert's solo piano sonatas, adding in one instance that it "is impossible to contemplate without emotion and wonder these precious results of quiet honest industry, which, in the majority of instances, were not to be reckoned amongst the artistic treasures of the world until long after Schubert's death." [98] In another early article, written in 1873 on Schubert's solo and duet sonatas, Adolf Bernhard Vogel still noted their neglect as against the popularity of his songs and quoted Schumann's poetic praise of them at some length.[99] Concurring in the praise, Vogel cautioned only that Schubert's inspired outpourings had been those of a youthful idealist who lacked the mature logic of thematic manipulation in which Haydn, Mozart, and Beethoven had excelled.

The well-grounded Swiss writer Arnold Niggli surveyed the available solo sonatas five years later (1878), calling them the least known of Schubert's piano works and virtually unknown in concert.[100] Although their lyricism—so effective in Schubert's smaller vocal and instrumental pieces—could not cope with the "dialectic" such as Niggli had found in Beethoven, the beauties of melody, harmony, sonority, and texture that Schumann had praised must not go unrecognized. In 1895 John Shedlock wrote what now seems like a more balanced view of the sonatas.[101] Yet as late as 1903, Alfred Mello, in a somewhat more detailed article on the piano sonatas, again lauded Schubert as a genius of melody whose incomparable songs as well as his symphonies and chamber music had become well known, but (still) not his sonatas.[102] These last Mello found to be more homophonic than Beethoven's (for Schubert was "no outstanding contrapuntist") and to be blessed with a fine sense of piano sonority, harmony, and melody, although the melody sometimes seemed obscured to him by the excessively long phrases.

98. Kreissle/SCHUBERT I 257–58, 135. It was about this time (1868) that Liszt called Schubert's sons. a "glorious treasure" but did not hesitate to make what he felt were needed changes in them (LISZT LETTERS II 164–65).

99. Vogel/SCHUBERT.

100. Niggli/SCHUBERT.

101. Shedlock/SONATA 198–206. But among Englishmen even George Grove had been markedly unreceptive to the sons. in 1882, as quoted in Brown/SCHUBERT 344–45.

102. Mello/SCHUBERT.

Meanwhile, Schubert's sonatas themselves had not been quite that inaccessible. By the mid-19th century some two-thirds of the completed ones had been made available by publishers in Austria and Germany.[103] From about that time on, nearly half of them became available in England (especially Charles Hallé's ed. for Chappell and E. Pauer's for Augener) and in France (especially in Richault's early, incomplete "Collection complète").[104] Furthermore, we read of Charles Hallé (who had played all the Beethoven sonatas in 1861; SCE 527) playing all of Schubert's published sonatas "repeatedly" in public from 1863 on, in London,[105] and of Charles Alkan venturing to play the whole of Op. 78 in G, D. 894, in Paris in 1875 (only to evoke the familiar complaint of excessive length from the reviewer).[106] However, reservations about the sonatas continued to prevail, even to swell, through the first quarter of the present century. As a sample, here is what the American teacher and author Leland Hall wrote in 1915:

The sonatas are for the most part unsatisfactory as such. In such extended forms there is need of an intellectual command of the science of music, and a sense of great proportions, both of which Schubert lacked. Hence the separate movements, the first and even more often the last, are loose and rambling in structure, and too long for the work as a whole. There is so little cohesion in the group that one may in most cases take the individual movements quite out of it and play them with perfect satisfaction.[107]

In this statement, or more general statements such as Parry had made in 1896 and d'Indy in 1909 about Schubert's lack of formal training, the use of Beethoven as the primary criterion is still implied if not mentioned.[108] Such statements tie in, too, with that other most frequent negative reaction to Schubert's sonatas (and sometimes his other larger instrumental works)—the feeling that the lyricism taken over from his songs became too much of a good thing, not wholly appropriate, especially in its tendencies toward static A-B-A designs, to the tight muscular development of pithy ideas expected in a "true" (for which read Haydn, Mozart, or Beethoven) "sonata form." [109]

103. Cf. the full lists of Schubert's sons. below; also, Brown/SCHUBERT 318–22 for a brief historical survey of Schubert eds. in these countries.
104. For scattered bits of information about these often elusive 19th-c. eds., cf. George Grove in the first ed. of GROVE III (1882) 357–58; Prod'homme/SCHUBERT 495–96, 505–6, 508–10; Brown/SCHUBERT 341–42; PAZDÍREK "S" 399; Cat. ROYAL 316; MGG XII 165, 168–70, 173–74 (K. Hortschansky).
105. GROVE (first ed.) III 358 (G. Grove). Cf., also, Shedlock/SONATA 205.
106. Prod'homme/SCHUBERT 510. Cf., also, Brown/SCHUBERT 324–26; Moser/JOACHIM I 105.
107. Hall/PIANOFORTE 195.
108. Parry/EVOLUTION 287; d'Indy/COURS II/1 402. Cf. Brown/SCHUBERT 195–96.
109. Cf. Salzer/SCHUBERT (especially pp. 98–101 and 124–25) and Adler/SCHUBERT 480.

New Interest Since the Schubertian Centenary

This summary review of a century of relatively negative attitudes and slow cultivation in the history of Schubert's sonatas is needed here not only as a partial background for their understanding but because their full acceptance—such as the question of which if any of them make consistently satisfying cycles throughout—is by no means universal even among today's writers, performers, and listeners.[110] Furthermore, so close was the proximity of time, place, and prevailing idiom that we may never be able quite to dispel that tendency to weigh Schubert in terms of Beethoven. However, a decided improvement in both the quantity and quality of interest in Schubert's sonatas did occur with the flurry of writings around 1928 that marked the centenary of his death.[111] Of major significance, equal in its way to Richard Capell's admirable book on Schubert's songs one year later, was Hans Költzsch's dissertation on Schubert's piano sonatas, published in 1927,[112] which provided both the bibliographic and style-critical foundations for further studies of the sonatas. Among the latter may be singled out the discussion of 1934 in Egert/FRÜHROMANTIKER 71–92 (with considerable exception taken to Költzsch's style-critical conclusions), the survey of 1947 in Abraham/SCHUBERT by Kathleen Dale (Dale/SCHUBERT 129–47), the dissertation of 1961 on the chamber music by Martin Chusid (Chusid/SCHUBERT), the dissertation of 1963 on text and performance problems in the sonatas by J. L. Taggart (Taggart/SCHUBERT), the dissertation of 1965 based on style-statistical analyses by A. L. Hanna (Hanna/SCHUBERT), the chapter of 1966 in Brown/ESSAYS 197–216 on authenticity, order and number of movements, and chronology of the solo piano sonatas, and the series of brief form analyses done in 1967 by Walter Riezler (Riezler/SCHUBERT), including most of the sonatas.[113]

110. Thus, Gillespie/KEYBOARD 204–6 continues to echo 19th-century views; Kirby/KEYBOARD 237–44 does not. In the late 1930's Nadia Boulanger still was doing pioneer work through her lecture-recitals in this country centered around the question of why Schubert's sonatas are not played more.

111. Pertinent samples in special Schubert periodical issues of that year are Souchay/SCHUBERT in ZfMW, Salzer/SCHUBERT in SzMW, Bauer/SCHUBERT in MQ.

112. Költzsch/SCHUBERT; abstract in the reports from the international Schubert congress of 1928 (KONGRESS SCHUBERT 199–208). Cf. Kahl/SCHUBERTSCHRIFTTUMS 95; Abraham/SCHUBERT 6–7.

113. The extensive literature on Schubert is covered exhaustively and systematically for the first century after his death in Kahl/SCHUBERT (cf. Kahl/SCHUBERTSCHRIFTTUMS) and brought up to date as late as 1963 for the more important publications, in MGG XII 174–85 (W. Pfannkuch), with further diss. listed in Schaal/DISSERTATIONEN and Hewitt/DISSERTATIONS. A basic Schubert bibliography appears in Deutsch/SCHUBERT-D 962–65 (with additions in the 1964 German ed., pp. 615–18); cf., also, Abraham/SCHUBERT 255–62 (A. H. King).

Among other more recent studies of Schubert's styles and forms that bear tangentially on his sonatas are Maurice Brown's book of 1954 on his variations (Brown/VARIATIONS), Georg Winkler's dissertation of 1956 on the unjustly maligned or inadequately recognized polyphony in his piano writing (Winkler/SCHUBERT),[114] and Elmer Seidel's dissertation of 1963 on enharmony in his larger forms (Seidel/ENHARMONIK). And, of course, no work on Schubert can proceed today without constant recourse—as already in the present discussion—to those four voluminous, complementary mines of primary information provided over more than a half-century (1913–64) by the late Otto Erich Deutsch, including all discoverable letters and other lifetime documents, posthumous personal recollections, and iconographic matter, richly annotated throughout, plus a critical though abbreviated thematic index.[115] The complete edition of Schubert's music prepared in the late 19th century (pub. 1884–97) by Mandyczewski, Brahms, and others, furnished a largely satisfactory edition of the sonatas, with but few omissions.[116] Undoubtedly, the needed improvements will be made in the sonata volumes of the *Neue Ausgabe* that has been planned by the Internationalen Schubert-Gesellschaft and launched in 1964 with Deutsch's new German edition of the documents and letters.[117] Meanwhile, though each has yet to be completed with a third volume, two two-volume sets of Schubert's solo piano sonatas have appeared recently in excellent critical editions, one prepared in 1958 by Erwin Ratz and one in 1961 by Paul Mies.[118]

Schubert's Sonatas in Toto

The but thirty-one years of Schubert's outwardly uneventful life were brightened chiefly by those wonderful, at times almost nightly, "Schubertiaden" with his numerous artistic friends,[119] at which must have taken place most of whatever performances there were of his sonatas (as mentioned above). During the 17 years from age 15 (1812)

114. Winkler concentrates especially on "latent" polyphony in the sons.; cf. pp. 33, 52–53, 99, 124.

115. Deutsch/SCHUBERT-D, -M, -B, and -I, respectively. Cf. the prefaces to each of these vols.; also, MR XIV (1953) 257–61 (Brown) and Brown/SCHUBERT 347–48.

116. Schubert/WERKE-m VIII, IX, X, XI, and XXI. Cf. the tabulations below; also, Deutsch/COLLECTED and MGG XII 164–74 (including other eds.; [K. Hortschansky]).

117. Cf. NOTES XXII (1966) 698–99 and 1231. At about the same time a complete, unaltered reprint of Schubert/WERKE-m was well under way at low cost from Dover Publications of New York.

118. Ratz/SCHUBERT-m, with preface (cf. the detailed collation of texts in Taggart/SCHUBERT 32–55); Mies/SCHUBERT-m, with prefaces.

119. For sample accounts, cf. Deutsch/SCHUBERT-D 302–4, 571–72, 630–31.

to within 54 days of his death (Nov. 19, 1828) he left a total of 33 extant solo and duo works, complete or incomplete, that were called or have been otherwise identified as "sonatas." These 33 represent scarcely more than 2 per cent of his total known output of 1,515 pieces large and small.[120] Of the 33 sonatas, 20 are unquestionably complete as they stand, 5 may or may not be complete as we now have them, depending upon identification of missing movements as well as certain questions of tonality, and 8 are more or less clearly incomplete (including one, D. 567, that was a first draft of a complete son., D. 568). These last Schubert probably left incomplete for no more or better reason than seems to resolve out of all the theorizing about the why of the "Unfinished Symphony" [121]—nearly as much, in fact, as that about the intended recipient of Beethoven's letter to his "Eternally Beloved" (SCE 518). In short, Schubert seems to have left from 24 to as many as 39 per cent of all his sonatas (or up to 44 per cent of his solo piano sonatas) incomplete simply because he got sidetracked by some other interest. The statistics are more characteristic than not of Schubert's larger forms, including both the symphonies and the quartets.

Of course, with Schubert "incomplete" applies sometimes only in the most literal sense. As we shall see (e.g., Son. in f♯, D. 571, 570), he was satisfied simply to drop some movements at the apparent start of the recapitulation in the first drafts. Furthermore, four of the sonatas that may or may not be complete as they stand raise questions because their presumed or extant first and final movements are not in the same key (D. 15, 17, 23, 968). Such tonal contradictions would be rare but not unprecedented (SCE 138). An example is the solo piano Sonata in A♭/E♭, D. 23, with two manuscript sources seeming to confirm that the final "Allegro" in E♭ does constitute that work's finale.[122] But if this example is valid, why not so regard the sonatas in E/B and C/a, D. 157 and 279, each of which ends with a "Menuetto" in the then frequent manner (SCE 161–62), yet in a new key, without any other finale being known? [123]

Other of Schubert's sonatas have raised questions of completeness and identification because he wrote the movements in separate manu-

120. Cf. the statistics in Deutsch/SCHUBERT-I xvi–xvii.

121. Cf. Abraham/SCHUBERT 63–64 (M. Carner); Brown/SCHUBERT 116–24. But Chusid/SCHUBERT-m 9–10 and 98–110 suggests that Schubert was experiencing an instrumental form crisis, perhaps under new Beethoven influences, during the period when Schubert wrote most of his truly incomplete works, 1817–23.

122. Cf. Költzsch/SCHUBERT 4–5.

123. The autographs give only contradictory hints as to whether an additional mvt. was intended in D. 157 and 279 (cf. Költzsch/SCHUBERT 4; Brown/ESSAYS 200–201).

scripts or someone after him split up the manuscripts (D. 566 and 506), or he left two versions of the work (D. 567), or the several movements were originally published as separate pieces (D. 459).[124] Perhaps some further works not yet recognized as sonatas lie scattered as separate pieces that should be united and admitted to the fold, too. Thus, Schumann insisted in 1838 that the four Impromptus Op. 142 (D. 935; 1827)—in f, A♭, B♭, and f—comprise a sonata in all but the name,[125] and Einstein has agreed enthusiastically.[126] But Brown has disagreed peremptorily,[127] arguing that the key of No. 3 is "an awkward one to square with the others" (in spite of several, more remote relationships in Schubert's unequivocal sonatas) and that "the first piece is certainly not a 'first movement' from any formal point of view" (debatable in any case and hardly tenable in view of the precedents in Beethoven's Opp. 101, 109, and 110, or Schubert's own Op. 164, D. 537). Brown is more inclined to view as the two movements of a projected, unfinished four-hand piano sonata Schubert's two extraordinary, last pieces in that scoring, the "Allegro" in a, D. 947, first published by Diabelli about 1840 as "Lebensstürme," Op. 144, and the Rondo in A, D. 951, written for Artaria and published by that firm only three weeks after Schubert's death, as "Grand Rondeau," Op. 107.[128] A work referred to in 1839 by Schubert's brother Ferdinand as a four-hand Sonata in e♭ of 1828 probably was an error for the *Drei Klavierstücke* for two hands of that year, of which No. 1 is in e♭.[129]

In addition, there are works by Schubert that have suggested sonatas even where no problem of bibliography or original intentions arises. Thus, the cyclic structure and emotional range of three of his greatest "fantasias" have prompted writers, from his own day on, to ask why each is or is not like a sonata. His celebrated, four-movement "Wanderer Fantasy" in C, Op. 15, for P solo (D. 760; 1822) brought a promptly favorable review in Vienna in 1823, but one that seems to puzzle over its freedoms as though, without any specific mention, the then conventional sonata were its measuring stick.[130] Although Schu-

124. A detailed survey of these problems occurs in Taggart,/SCHUBERT 225–62.

125. Schumann/SCHRIFTEN I 371–72.

126. Einstein/SCHUBERT 283–85, with trans. of most of Schumann's review.

127. Brown/SCHUBERT 269–70.

128. Brown/SCHUBERT 286–87 (but with no source for the idea of the projected sonata). Schumann's youthful wonderment over the Rondo, in a letter of Nov. 6, 1829, to Friedrich Wieck, may be read in Schumann/JUGENDBRIEFE 82–83.

129. Cf. Deutsch/SCHUBERT-D 919, 924; Brown/ESSAYS 264–66.

130. Trans. in full in Deutsch/SCHUBERT-D 272–78; still echoed in Kreissle/SCHUBERT II 210. In Hanslick/WIEN I 382, Op. 15 is actually referred to as "Sonate." Cf., also, MT XIII (1868) 318.

mann at the age of eighteen seemed only to rejoice in the freedoms of this work,[131] a century later Marc-André Souchay analyzed it in detail to show that it actually revealed the close-knit logic of the Classic masters, differing from the sonata in its emphasis more on melodic variation than development.[132] The still freer, four-movement Fantasy in C for P & Vn, Op. 159 (D. 934; 1827) brought similarly early and puzzled reactions, although mostly curt and irritated this time.[133] And though the final, great Fantasy in f for P-duet, Op. 103 (D. 940; 1828), seems not to have been reviewed after its early publication in 1829, recently it too has been considered in relation to the sonata, in a perceptive bibliographic and music analysis by Brown.[134]

The converse of all these evaluations in terms of the sonata is found in the few instances where Schubert's bona fide "sonatas" are viewed in orchestral or symphonic terms. Schumann fairly insisted in 1838 that "vierhändige Sonate" on the autograph of what the publisher called "Grand Duo" in C, Op. 140 (D. 812), was a misnomer for "symphony" and that the huge work demanded orchestration,[135] which, indeed, it got from Joachim in 1855. Joachim (and perhaps at least two later orchestraters of this work) probably got the idea from this statement by Schumann,[136] but neither Schumann nor Joachim yet identified the work with the as yet unrecognized problem of the "Gastein Symphony."[137] The possibility, however improbable, has even been raised that the sketches for this symphony may have been used for the solo piano Sonata in D, Op. 53 (D. 850), also placed in Gastein in 1825.[138]

Schubert's Solo Piano Sonatas

Although Schubert left his manuscripts in better order than many another composer, and usually dated them (to the pleasant surprise of

131. Diary entry for August 13, 1828, as reproduced in the 1964 German ed. of Deutsch/SCHUBERT-D, p. 532.

132. Souchay/SCHUBERT. Cf., also, Vetter/SCHUBERT I 289–91; Brown/SCHUBERT 124–25.

133. Trans. in Deutsch/SCHUBERT-D 715–16; cf. p. 767. Cf., also, Cobbett/CHAMBER II 360 (W. Kahl).

134. Brown/ESSAYS 85–100.

135. Schumann/SCHRIFTEN I 329–30, echoed (again) in Kreissle/SCHUBERT II 217–18, endorsed in Tovey/ANALYSIS I 215–18, but protested in Einstein/SCHUBERT 240–42.

136. Cf. Moser/JOACHIM II 82; Brown/SCHUBERT 186–88 (but with an incorrect German title for Schubert's work).

137. As is wrongly stated in Deutsch/SCHUBERT-D 364–65 (but corrected in the 1964 German ed., p. 251) and in Deutsch/SCHUBERT-I 391. The duo was composed in 1824, in any case, and the supposedly lost symphony, D. 849, not until 1825. The recent identification of this symphony with the "Great Symphony in C," D. 944, in Brown/SCHUBERT 354–61 is convincing, and is made more so in ML XL (1959) 341–49.

138. Brown/SCHUBERT 356.

Schubert scholars), he still left enough questions to engender considerable bibliographic interest and speculation. The tabulation of the solo piano sonatas that follows, like that of the ensemble sonatas further below, derives from nearly every item of Schubert bibliography singled out earlier, but especially from Költzsch/SCHUBERT 1–32, Ratz/SCHUBERT, Deutsch/SCHUBERT-I, and Brown/ESSAYS 197–216. In short, our tabulation is hardly the first and is not likely to be the last. The chronology followed here, in spite of uncertainties that remain in the order of Nos. 8, 9, and 15, is the one arrived at most recently, by Brown (1966).[139] The tabulation also shows the uncertainties that remain in the identification and inclusion of several of the movements, as well as the incomplete or complete status of all the sonatas. The opus numbers and the other early series numbers have little or no numerical logic,[140] but are included here because of the frequent reference to them.[141] The number of measures in each movement and each cycle is included for several reasons besides the obvious value of comparing dimensions. Deutsch regretted not being table to include them in his *Thematic Catalogue*,[142] they are lacking in the Schubert/WERKE-m (as is true so often, alas, in the older complete sets), and they give at least a hint of how incomplete the incomplete movements are. Moreover, they are needed for consideration of that familiar problem of "heavenly length" [143] in Schubert's larger instrumental works.[144] And as a help toward the same problem, representative performance times to the nearest minute are given for each of the complete and all the substantial incomplete sonatas.[145]

Some of the circumstances surrounding the individual solo sonatas should be mentioned now (referring to these sons., only for this immediate discussion, by the chronological order number in the leftmost column of our tabulation). What we have listed as Nos. 1 and 2 from 1815, in E/B and C/a, actually followed by some three years several earlier student sonatas[146] (not to mention his early string quartets and symphonies) and already show more spirit and architec-

139. But in the last sentence of Brown/SCHUBERT 199 read "6" for "7" and add the question of the crossed-out "1" as an early series number for D. 566 (Költzsch/SCHUBERT 5, 31–32).

140. Cf. Költzsch/SCHUBERT 31–32.

141. For full bibliographic listings of the first eds. cited here cf. Cat. HIRSCH IV 191–253.

142. Cf. Deutsch/SCHUBERT-I xiv.

143. To use the well-known expression in Schumann/SCHRIFTEN I 463; cf. II 432. Cf., also, Vrieslander/ORGANISCHE.

144. Cf. Mello/SCHUBERT for an early consideration of this problem.

145. The times are those of the fine Austrian pianist Friedrich Wuehrer in his three recorded vols. of Schubert's "complete" P sons. (Vox Box Nos. 9–11).

146. Cf. Költzsch/SCHUBERT 20; Deutsch/SCHUBERT-M 127–28 (J. v. Spaun), 369.

Schubert's Solo Piano Sonatas

Chron. order	Key	Opus no.	Deutsch no(s).	Early series no.	Composed	First edition	Schubert/WERKE-m	Now complete or inc.	Mvts.: tempos or types / Keys: mvt.-by-mvt. / mss.: mvt.-by-mvt.	Performance time in minutes	Remarks
1	E/B♭?		154, 157		1815	*Werke*, 1888	X/1	inc.?	3: F -M -Mi / keys: E -e -B / 563: 251-112-200	17	finale in home key lacking?
2	C/a?		279	1	1815	*Werke*, 1888	X/2	inc.?	3: F -M-Mi / keys: C -F -a / 433: 211-80-142	15	finale in home key lacking?
3	E		459		1816	Klemm, 1843	XI/14	com.	5: F -Sc -S -Sc -F / keys: E -E -C -A -E / 712: 124-231-114-137-106	27	first pub. as *Fünf Klavierstücke*
4	a	164	537	7	1817	Spina, 1852?	X/6	com.	3: F -M -VF / keys: a -E -a / 707: 196-144-367	17	
5	A♭/E♭		557		1817	*Werke*, 1888	X/3	com.?	3: F -M -F / keys: A♭-E♭-E♭ / 328: 99-96-133	23	finale not in home key
6	D♭		567	2	1817	*Werke*, 1897	XXI/9	inc.	3: F -M -F / keys: D♭ -c♯ -D♭ / 545: 238-122-168 (185?)		last 17 (?) mss. of iii completed but lost
7	E♭	122	568	3	1817	Pennauer, 1829	X/7	com.	4: F -M -Mi-F / keys: E♭ -g -E♭ -E♭ / 705: 258-122-102-223	24	revision of D. 567; first pub. title: "Troisième grande Sonate"
8	e		994	(3?)	1817?	Brown/SCHUBERT, 1958		inc.	1: F / key: e / 38: 38		only a fragment

No.	Key	iv = 145/2	D.	1? (4?)	Date	First publication	AGA	com.?	Movements and keys	No.	Remarks
9	e/E	iv = 145/2	566, 506	1? (4?)	1817	piecemeal, 1848–1928	X/4 (i) XI/5/2 (iv)	com.?	4: M-F -Sc -Ro; keys: e -E -Ab -E; 879: 97-227-266-289	16+	first pub. as complete unit: Dale/Schubert-m (1948)
10	f#		571, 570	5	1817	Werke, 1897	XXI/10 & 20	i & iii inc.	3: F -Sc -F; keys: f# -D -f#; 427: 141-112-174		relation of mvts. not certain
11	B	147	575		1817	Diabelli, 1846	X/5	com.	4: F -M-Sc -F; keys: B -E-G -B; 637: 147-82-192-216	21	order originally F-Sc-M-F; first pub. title: "Grande Sonate"
12	C		613, 612		1818	piecemeal, 1870–97	XXI/11, XI/11	i & iii inc.	3: M -S -F?; keys: C -E-C; 297: 121-52-124		inclusion of ii uncertain; tempo of iii missing
13	f		625, 505		1818	Werke, 1897, 1898	XXI/12 (not ii) Rev. XI/5 (ii)	i & iv inc.	4: F -S-Sc -F; keys: f -Db-E -f; 693: 118-22-260-293	19	nearly completed
14	c#		655		1819	Werke, 1897	XXI/13	inc.	1: F; key: c#; 73: 73		only an exposition
15	A	120	664		1819?	J. Czerny, 1829	X/10	com.	3: F -M-F; keys: A -D-A; 424: 133-75-216	22	composing formerly dated 1825
16	a	143	784		1823	Diabelli, 1839	X/8	com.	3: F -M-F; keys: a -F -a; 625: 290-66-269	21	first pub. title: "Grande Sonate . . ."
17	a	42	845	1	1825	Pennauer, 1826	X/9	com.	4: M -M-Sc -Ro; keys: a -C -a -a; 1357: 311-181-316-549	31	first pub. title: "Première grande Sonate"
18	C		840		1825	Whistling, 1862	XXI/14	iii & iv inc.	4: M -M -Mi -Ro; keys: C -c -Ab -C; 897: 318-121-186-272	34	first pub. title: "Reli- quie . . ."
19	D	53	850	2	1825	Artaria, 1826	X/11	com.	4: F -M -Sc -Ro; keys: D -A -D -D; 1007: 267-197-331-212	31	first pub. title: "Seconde grande Sonate"

Schubert's Solo Piano Sonatas (Continued)

Chron. order	Key	Opus no.	Deutsch no(s).	Early series no.	Composed	First edition	Schubert/ WERKE-m	Now complete or inc.	Mvts.: tempos or types Keys: mvt.-by-mvt. mss.: mvt.-by-mvt.	Performance time in minutes	Remarks
20	G	78	894	4	1826	Haslinger, 1827	X/12	com.	4: M -M -Mi -F keys: G -D -b -G 900: 174-181-134-411	29	first pub. title: "Fantasie, Andante, Menuetto und Allegretto"
21	c		958	1	1828	Diabelli, 1838	X/13	com.	4: F -S -Mi-F keys: c -A♭ -E♭ -c 1226: 274-115-120-717	28	D. 958, 959, 960 originally pub. as "Drei grosse Sonaten"
22	A		959	2	1828	Diabelli, 1838	X/14	com.	4: F -M -Sc -Ro keys: A -f♯ -A -A 1136: 360-202-192-382	35	
23	B♭		960	3	1828	Diabelli, 1838	X/15	com.	4: M -M -Sc -F keys: B♭ -c♯ -B♭ -B♭ 1255: 365-138-212-540	32	

tural wisdom than would be expected from even a gifted youth of eighteen (until one remembers that "Erlkönig" was also to be composed in that same year). Furthermore, they already show more skill in polyphony and thematic development than would be expected from a composer commonly taken to be deficient in these very respects. Schubert must have been advancing by leaps and bounds then. No. 1/i, in which he anticipates some of his "Rossini-isms" of 1816–17,[147] is clearly in better tonal and thematic control than its incomplete sketch of only a few days earlier (Schubert/WERKE-m XXI/8). No. 2, composed seven months later, reveals a decidedly more dramatic idea of the sonata. Perhaps its advance in this sense explains why Schubert chose to label it "Sonata I" on the autograph, looking toward a specially numbered series of sonatas, as did Czerny (supra).[148]

With regard to No. 3, the identification of the Fünf Klavierstücke as this Sonata in E is one of several bibliographic discoveries about the Schubert sonatas that Ludwig Scheibler made early in this century, although the confirmation in this instance took longer.[149] Since the second version of the duet Sonata in c, D. 48, consists of five free sections, not movements, and since Schubert wrote no other sonatas with more than four movements, he may not have intended that both scherzos be retained in No. 3. Formerly the year of this work was put as 1817, partly because of the exact recurrence of the last three measures of the first movement in Schubert's song "Elysium," D. 584 (mss. 31–33), dated September, 1817.[150] But the recurrence seems more like a coincidence of prolificity. The advance in tonal resources, keyboard writing, and general craftmanship is again conspicuous in No. 3.

No. 4 in a is the first of nine sonatas (including Son. for P & Vn in A, D. 574), complete or incomplete, that date from Schubert's most prolific sonata year, 1817.[151] A concise, mature, compelling work,[152] it

147. Cf. Abraham/SCHUBERT 19–20, 38 fn., 39–40 (M. Carner).
148. But cf. Költzsch/SCHUBERT 4. Efforts to identify a finale for this work remain in question (cf. Brown/SCHUBERT 56 and Brown/ESSAYS 201).
149. Cf. Költzsch/SCHUBERT 10–11, 169; Brown/SCHUBERT 57. However, the reviewer of the 1843 ed., in AMZ XLVI (1844) 168–69, after objecting to certain eccentricities and signs of carelessness (as in several early reviews of Schubert) already guessed that these 5 pieces might comprise a son.
150. Cf. Költzsch/SCHUBERT 11, 90–91.
151. Cf. the excellent summary in Brown/1817. A division of Schubert's sons. into 3 periods is frequently suggested—in fact, argued at some length in Mason/ SCHUBERT—but the short total span, the bridging of some of the divisions by more recent dating, and certain inconsistencies all tend to make such a division less meaningful.
152. Cf. Truscott/UNITY (arguing warmly, at length, that the organic development in No. 4 is disregarded in Brown/SCHUBERT 60–61).

is, moreover, his earliest sonata to figure rather often in the pianist's repertoire today. The year 1817 has also proved to be the most complex year for bibliographers of Schubert's sonatas. No. 5 is that Sonata in Ab/Eb mentioned earlier for appearing to have a finale not in the original key, but otherwise of lesser musical interest. No. 6 is an incomplete first version, in a different key, of No. 7 in Eb, with further complexities in the inner movements.[153] In this neat, relatively cool sonata, as in the Symphony in Bb, D. 485, one already detects a certain neo-Classicism in Schubert, referring back to Haydn and Mozart more than to Beethoven. Following the mere fragment that is No. 8 in e,[154] No. 9 in e is a bibliographic nightmare in which, besides questions of first and second versions, each movement was first published separately over a period of eighty years before all four movements were issued together—if, indeed, they all do belong together and in the order thus far preferred—twenty years later in Dale/SCHUBERT-m.[155] The music of this sonata is stirring and convincing enough to justify these efforts to put it in final order.[156]

In No. 10 in f♯, still from 1817, the choice and order of movements is even less certain,[157] with the bare possibility added that the isolated "Andante" in A, D. 604, supplies "the missing slow movement." [158] Egert believes the first movement remained unfinished because its ethereal first theme proved unsuitable for sonata treatment.[159] Certainly the exceptional lyricism of this movement's ideas illustrates what Beethoven presumably would have rejected in comparable instrumental forms. Yet Schubert did develop these ideas here in his own way, and effectively. Furthermore, he might be said to have finished this movement in his own way. For, as in several other "unfinished" sonata movements, he seems merely to have stopped for the time being where the recapitulation is expected—in this instance,

153. Cf. Költzsch/SCHUBERT 7–9, 82–94; Truscott/VERSIONS (a detailed comparison); Brown/SCHUBERT 63–64; Ratz/SCHUBERT-m I 55 (facs. of the start in the autograph).

154. First published as a facs. in 1956 (cf. Brown/ESSAYS 205) and as an "edition" in Brown/SCHUBERT 58–59.

155. As usual, the main discoveries come from Scheibler and Költzsch (Költzsch/SCHUBERT 5–7). A further, detailed summary appears in Brown/1817 36–38, with more on the finale in Brown/DISCOVERIES 307–8, and Brown/MANUSCRIPTS 182; cf., also, Taggart/SCHUBERT 239–46 (but with errors and a largely indefensible support for accepting only i and ii in No. 9, à la Op. 90 of Beethoven).

156. Schubert's slight reworking of i is taken to show his own special interest in at least that mvt., in Einstein/SCHUBERT 129–30.

157. Cf. Költzsch/SCHUBERT 9, Brown/1817 40–41, Brown/MANUSCRIPTS 182, Brown/SCHUBERT 64–66. This possibility, offered in Brown/ESSAYS 207, seems more plausible than the categorical identification of D. 604 with No. 19 (Son. in D, D. 850) in Einstein/SCHUBERT 250.

159. Egert/FRÜHROMANTIKER 78–80.

evidently at one of his not untypical returns by way of the sub-dominant, and in the supposed, similarly incomplete finale of this sonata, at the tonic.

No. 11 in B was the last sonata of 1817 (if the lost, final autograph actually dates from the same year as the extant preliminary version[160]). It was only the third unequivocally complete sonata of that year, its bibliographic problems being relatively simple ones. The celebrated virtuoso Thalberg became the dedicatee of this highly sensitive, tightly motivic work when Diabelli published it eighteen years after Schubert died. But whether Thalberg ever played it on any of his many successful recitals could not be learned here. In any case, it got only a half-hearted nine-line review when it appeared, a review that suggests no more than a cursory glance at it.[161]

The two, "incomplete" sonatas of 1818 lack mainly and merely recapitulations again. For the first, No. 12 in C, Scheibler and Költsch once more have supplied the prime conjectures.[162] Brown adds that its supposed "Adagio" was first published alone, probably because it was the only completed movement, and that it apparently belongs with the other two movements not only because it is dated in the same month but because of stylistic consistencies and the fact that Schubert was not writing single pieces at this time.[163] Deutsch first established the association of the "Adagio" in D♭, D. 505, with No. 13 in f,[164] but all four movements have yet to be printed together. Költzsch, Einstein, and Vetter all found in this work, or what Brown dubs "Schubert's appassionata," some vivid recollections of Beethoven's Op. 57 in f that do seem justified especially for the openings, figuration, and sustained drive of the outer movements.[165]

Following another mere fragment, No. 14 in c♯, supposedly came one other sonata from 1819, No. 15 in A, now one of the most played of all Schubert's sonatas. Scheibler left no doubt that "1825" for the composition of this work was an error starting with Schindler,[166] although he provided only a likely, educated guess when

160. Cf. Költzsch/SCHUBERT 9–10, Brown/1817 41–42.
161. AMZ XLII (1848) 531–32.
162. Költzsch/SCHUBERT 11–12.
163. Brown/MANUSCRIPTS 184. The "Andante" in A, D. 604, might fit as well in No. 12 as in No. 10, although the key relationships would be less likely if, conversely, the "Adagio" in E, D. 612, were used in No. 10 rather than No. 12.
164. Cf. Deutsch/SCHUBERT-I 277–78, Brown/RECENT 356–57. The subjective objections in Vetter/SCHUBERT II 293–94 fall before Deutsch's facts.
165. Költzsch/SCHUBERT 94–100, Vetter/SCHUBERT I 284–85, Brown/SCHUBERT 67–68. The recapitulation of the first mvt. and other, briefer missing passages are supplied by the ed. in Ratz/SCHUBERT-m I 70, simply by drawing upon what Schubert had already written.
166. Cf. Deutsch/SCHUBERT-M 323.

he identified it with a sonata composed, during a visit to Steyr in the summer of 1819, for "Pepi" von Koller, who, Schubert wrote his brother Ferdinand, "is very pretty, plays the pianoforte well and is going to sing several of my songs." [167] Miss von Koller's talents may very well account for both the brilliance and the ingratiating tunefulness of this work,[168] which, like No. 7 in E♭, harks back neo-Classically more to Haydn and Mozart than to Beethoven. Its publication in Vienna only a year after Schubert's death brought no printed review that could be found here.

The only gap in Schubert's yearly production of sonatas seems to have occurred in the three years, from 1820 to 1822, preceding the eight solo and two ensemble examples of his last six years, 1823–28, all of which but one (D. 840) qualify as "completed" works. The first of these mature masterpieces was the second of his three fine solo sonatas in a, No. 16. Considering the terse, dramatic thrust of No. 16, one accepts its amended title "Grande Sonate" in the first published edition[169] more readily than the similar titles for most of the other first publications of Schubert's sonatas. Was it the sinewy, lean texture, exceptional concentration on single motives, and unpianistic broken octaves in the first movement, or merely fatigue at the end of a long review, that caused Schumann to brand this highly unified work not one of Schubert's best? [170] To be sure, by then, 1839, Schumann had already spent his superlatives on some of Schubert's greatest works, including several later sonatas, adding "how much we [tend to] judge men and artists always [only] by the best each has done." [171] Schubert, too, thought enough of No. 16 to make more exacting revisions than usual in the autograph.[172]

Schumann did write in glowing terms of No. 17,[173] Schubert's final sonata in a, which was also the first of his three solo sonatas to be published and evidently the best known while he was alive; and it is one of the few sonatas by him that could be found here on public recital programs before the Schubert/werke-m began to

167. Költzsch/schubert 12–13; Deutsch/schubert-d 121, -m 148. Cf. Brown/ schubert 68–69, Brown/essays 210–11.

168. Yet it was called uninspired, without freshness or vitality, in 1862, in Bagge/ schubert 43.

169. Cf. the facs. of the first page of the autograph in mgg XII Tafel 9 with the full pub. title in hirsch IV 241.

170. Schumann/schriften I 399.

171. Schumann/schriften I 125.

172. Cf. Brown/schubert 128, 209–10.

173. Schumann/schriften I 124–25. On the dating of the first ed. of No. 17, cf. Deutsch/schubert-d 507. On Paul Badura-Skoda's discovery of errors in this (and later) eds., cf. Brown/discoveries 309–10.

appear in the 1880's.[174] Said Schumann, along with flowery metaphors and similes that include our Nos. 19 and 20 in D and G, "Most [nearly] related to it [our No. 20 in G] is the one in A minor. The first part [is] so still, so dreamlike; it could move [one] to tears; withal so lightly and simply formed out of two fragments that one must marvel at the magician who knows how to interweave and oppose them so unusually." No fewer than three reviews of No. 17 had already appeared, all favorable, in time for Schubert himself to read them. Representative passages may be quoted from the first, longest, and most knowing of these, a self-conscious, prolix, four-column piece of early 1826, probably written by G. W. Fink.[175]

. . . it moves so freely and originally within its confines, and sometimes so boldly and curiously, that it might not unjustly be called a Fantasy. In that respect it probably can be compared only with the greatest and freest of Beethoven's sonatas. . . . It is easy to see that these [original melodic and harmonic] inventions are often somewhat odd, and that their exposition is even more curious (particularly in the first movement, where for example the principal theme, which is almost dry in itself, is not only intentionally introduced in a dry manner, but often, and clearly of set purpose, repeated in the same way); also, that the composer now and again hardly knew the ins and outs of the sometimes strange harmonies that visited him (even as regards grammatical writing); and there are other things of the sort over which one can hardly refrain from shaking his head a little. But once it has been shaken . . . one cannot after all refrain from accepting it [the son.] with pleasure . . . [In the first mvt. the] predominant expression is a suppressed but sometimes violently erupting passion, alternating with melancholy seriousness. The movement is not short, which is [not?] as one would wish if one would remain in this mood without growing weary of it. . . . [The second mvt.] resembles in its invention, expression and workmanship the andantes with variations in the quartets of J. Haydn's later years; and every one knows that this [comparison] implies no small praise. . . . Restrained passion breaks out hastily and violently in the scherzo; the trio brings again some calm . . . [This mvt.] might be described as Beethovenian, without, be it understood, any attempt to dispute the composer's [Schubert's] originality. [And the finale is] long and technically very well-knit. . . . In order to perform it adequately this Sonata does not so much demand virtuoso playing (as it is commonly understood) as rather a painstaking performance, somewhat like that demanded by the largest sonatas by Beethoven or by Cramer. The instrument, too, should be good, capable of the most diverse modifications of loud and soft as well as of *legato,* sustained tone and accurate damping.

174. E.g., in MT XII (1865) 74 and 317, XV (1872) 413, and XVI (1874) 462, performances of No. 17 are reported in London as being given by Walter Macfarren, Agnes Zimmermann, Clara Schumann, and Charles Hallé, respectively.

175. AMZ XXVIII (1826) 137–40, as trans. in Deutsch/SCHUBERT-D 512–15. For the other two, shorter reviews, from Frankfurt/M in 1826 and Vienna in 1828, cf. Deutsch/SCHUBERT-D 549 and 799–800.

This first review already introduces those perennial questions in Schubert's sonatas of fantasy and strange harmony, which had so often disturbed the early reviewers of Beethoven's sonatas (SCE 511–37, *passim*); of Classic predecessors, especially Beethoven; of precarious length; and of unusual keyboard writing and requirements. The "greatest and freest of Beethoven's sonatas," especially his most recent publications, and his most favored dedicatee (cf. SCE 509, 524) may well have been in Schubert's mind when he dedicated (only) this work, our No. 17, to the same Archduke Rudolph (who, however, is not known to have taken any similar interest in Schubert).[176] Brown mentions in particular another, still more recently published work by Beethoven, the "Diabelli Variations" (1823), for the influence of its fifth variation on the powerful "Scherzo" of No. 17 [177] (which, in turn, seems to have influenced the "Scherzo" of Schubert's own string Quintet in C, D. 956). Regarding length, the problem does hinge primarily on sustaining the interest through sufficient content. But there are absolute considerations, too. As our tabulation shows, No. 17 is one of five solo sonatas by Schubert that last beyond a half-hour in performance—a long time, in any case, for a single instrument of relatively monochrome sonority. With today's streamlined recitals scarcely allowing even for "heavenly length," No. 17 is not heard often.

The performer may not be able to manage such length—whether it is he or the composer who lacks the requisite sense of architecture[178]—but it is the listener who is more likely to object to it. The performer, on the other hand, is more likely to resist playing Schubert's sonatas if and when they fail to provide him with sufficient pianistic interest—original figurations, new technical challenges, unusual sonorities, rich textures, ingenious accompaniments—as is at least hinted in the foregoing and nearly every subsequent 19th-century discussion of them.[179] In a rare reference to the content of his sonatas and to his own playing, Schubert, who also sang and played the violin well enough,[180] confirmed his own preference for the piano as a lyrical instrument:

176. Cf. Deutsch/SCHUBERT-D 439, 693, 873.

177. Brown/SCHUBERT 188–90. For Schubert's contribution to the "other" set of "Diabelli Variations" cf. Newman/DIABELLI-m 21.

178. The conclusion in Vrieslander/ORGANISCHE is that the "epic-lyric breadth" in Schubert's longest sonatas does sustain the interest.

179. For references to these discussions and continued resistance on the same grounds by a prominent recitalist in 1928, cf. Samaroff/SCHUBERT. Cf., also, SSB III and VI on the problem of length.

180. Cf. Deutsch/SCHUBERT-M 18, 179, 209–10, 271, 336–37; 125–26, 145.

What pleased especially were the variations in my new Sonata for two hands [our No. 17], which I performed alone and not without merit, since several people assured me that the keys became singing voices under my hands, which, if true, pleases me greatly, since I cannot endure the accursed chopping in which even distinguished pianoforte players indulge and which delights neither the ear nor the mind.[181]

Could it have been the playing of this sonata that brought forth from one well-meaning but tactless listener the remark, "Schubert, I admire your pianoforte-playing more than your compositions!"?[182] Schumann, himself one of the most resourceful composers for piano in the 19th century, made a special point of the excellence of Schubert's piano writing, yet in a way that stresses its neutral rather than its color values:[183]

Particularly as a composer for the piano has he [stood] out somewhat above others, in certain respects even above Beethoven (as remarkably acutely as the latter otherwise heard, in [spite of] his deafness, through his imagination) —namely therein, that he knows [how to] score more pianistically; that is, everything sounds out so appropriately and inherently from the [very] heart of the piano, whereas with Beethoven, for example, we first have to borrow the tone color from the horn, [or] the oboe, etc.

No. 18 in C is the longest, best known, last, and most significant of Schubert's incomplete sonatas.[184] Schumann reportedly published the "Andante" as a supplement to the *Neue Zeitschrift für Musik* of December 10, 1839,[185] presumably without discussing it. When Whistling first published all that remains of No. 18 in 1862, he mislabelled it "Letzte [last] Sonate" and romantically entitled it "Reliquie" ("Relic"), perhaps remembering that Schumann had used that title when he published posthumously some letters and poems left among Schubert's effects.[186] But the incomplete movements iii and iv do not seem to lack much, and may be further instances of Schubert's breaking off where the continuations by sectional repetition seemed obvious enough, at least to him. To those who have tried their hands

181. Letter of July 25, 1825, to his parents, as trans. in Deutsch/SCHUBERT-D 436. A short analysis of the variations may be found in Brown/VARIATIONS 72–76.

182. Kreissle/SCHUBERT I 132 fn. Franz Schober, in Schubert's circle, also may have objected to this son. (cf. Deutsch/SCHUBERT-D 588–89). For descriptions, sometimes conflicting, of Schubert's piano playing, cf. Deutsch/SCHUBERT-M 37, 146, 176, 180, 189, 194, 282–83, 330.

183. Trans. from Schumann/SCHRIFTEN I 125. The same point is developed in Mello/SCHUBERT.

184. It is analyzed in detail in Truscott/UNFINISHED.

185. Deutsch/SCHUBERT-I 408.

186. NZM X (1839) 37; cf. Schumann/SCHRIFTEN I 460. In a review of the early Whistling ed., in DMZ III (1862) 69–70, C. v. Bruyck deprecated this work and regarded its pub. as quite unnecessary.

at completing the work, including Ernst Krenek in 1921 and Walter Rehberg in 1927,[187] the continuations could not have been that obvious, since the differences are considerable.[188] In any case, No. 18 is almost never played in recital, for all its strengths and charms. Pianists do not like to play incomplete works and find it psychologically difficult to accept completions by others.[189]

No. 19 in D was composed in the but three weeks that Schubert was in Gastein in 1825, hardly leaving time, as Deutsch says, for the supposedly lost "Gastein Symphony," too.[190] It was the second of the three solo sonatas published in Schubert's lifetime (and was designated "Seconde" after his Op. 42 [191]). Curiously, though it was to win as much praise as any Schubert sonata in the 19th century, and though Joseph von Spaun described it as a "most original Sonata for the pianoforte" in his extended obituary of 1829,[192] it got no review in Schubert's two remaining years and none discovered here before Schumann's short paragraph in 1834:[193]

What a different vitality [from that in our No. 17] gushes out of the spirited D major [sonata]—pulse upon pulse, seizing and carrying [us] away! And then an Adagio [actually labelled "Con moto"], wholly in the Schubert manner, [so] compelling, [so] overflowing that he scarcely can bring it to an end. The last movement hardly fits into the whole, and is a bit comical. Who[-ever] tried to take the thing seriously, would make himself [look] very ridiculous. [The impetuous] Florestan calls it a satire on the [antiquated] Pleyel-Vanhal, nightcap style; [the gentle] Eusebius finds grimaces in the strongly contrapuntal passages such as one uses to startle children. It all adds up to humor.

Later writers have varied from moderate to warm enthusiasm for the first movement, whose exceptional brilliance may explain this sonata's dedication to the pianist Karl Maria von Bocklet.[194] They have concurred in the high worth of the second movement, with its astonishing adventures, even to present-day ears, in modulation and syncopation. But they have not concurred on the "Scherzo" (and its curiously Biedermeier waltz refrain in B♭), which Schumann did not mention, nor on the "Rondo" finale.[195]

187. Cf. Deutsch/SCHUBERT-I 407–8, -D 280. Rehberg has also completed the other sons. that are not mere fragments.
188. Cf. Truscott/UNFINISHED 129–37, with a further completion of iii.
189. But in the Wuehrer recordings cited earlier the Krenek completion is used, providing the timing used in our tabulation.
190. Deutsch/SCHUBERT-D 454–55.
191. Cf. Cat. HIRSCH IV 208 and 212.
192. Deutsch/SCHUBERT-D 873.
193. Trans. from Schumann/SCHRIFTEN I 124.
194. Cf. Költzsch/SCHUBERT 113, Einstein/SCHUBERT 249.
195. Einstein/SCHUBERT 250–51 takes particular exception to Schumann's remarks on the finale. The waltz refrain is quoted in SSB VI.

A favorite sonata of most writers on Schubert has always been No. 20 in G. This sonata used to be published with his shorter pieces rather than in collections of his sonatas because, in place of "IV. Sonate" on the title page of the autograph the title given to the original edition—"Fantasie, Andante, Menuetto und Allegretto . . ." —suggested a set of four separate pieces (Ex. 20).[196] Dedicated to his close friend Joseph von Spaun,[197] No. 20 may have been written in response to a request from the Swiss publisher Nägeli[198] and appears to have been one of the sonatas that Schubert himself played for his friends.[199] It was the last of the sonatas to be published and the only one besides our No. 17 to get reviews, three in all, while he was alive. The first review, along with commendations and a slight implication of excessive concentration on a single idea, concluded that this "Fantasy" provided more than "mere dancing-lessons for the fingers," whereas the second review, much briefer, condescended to say that the work is "quite good" and that its separate "pieces . . . are not too difficult, and are attractive; they may thus be recommended for practice"! [200] The third review was another longish, prolix, somewhat moralistic article from Leipzig, presumably by Fink again.[201] Yet it was reasonable, even prescient, in its way. The dangers of imitating so individual a genius as Beethoven were stressed at length— no doubt, to Schubert's consternation if he saw this review published midway between Beethoven's and his own death. A few excerpts here will bring us back to familiar questions in Schubert:

[In the opening "Fantasy" Schubert] uses for his basis an extremely simple, almost too insignificant melodious song, opposes it to a second, also very simple one . . . and he now develops out of both and out of their variants what is after all a closely knit whole. . . . Here and there, perhaps, he plays for playing's sake—with the instrument, too, which is asked, for example, to produce sustained notes and chords, like a string quartet; he repeats too much and becomes altogether too long for that which he intends to offer, and actually does offer. . . . The finale . . . is a fiery, curious and here and there somewhat freakish bravura movement, devised like a great, free rondo. It runs on for twelve pages, as though in a single breath, and hardly allows the player and listener to gasp. . . . But then this movement, presented as it should be, is difficult to play. . . . Not the fingerwork alone—for what daunts

196. Cf. Költzsch/SCHUBERT 18; Deutsch/SCHUBERT-D 627, -I 432–33; also, the facs. accompanying the present discussion as Ex. 20. The holograph is listed as Add. 36738 in Cat. BRITISH MS 145.

197. Cf. Spaun's own description of the circumstances as trans. in Deutsch/SCHUBERT-M 136.

198. Cf. Deutsch/SCHUBERT-D 533–34, 536–37, 541; but Nägeli did not publish it.

199. Cf. Deutsch/SCHUBERT-D 568, 571, 680.

200. From the complete reviews as trans. in Deutsch/SCHUBERT-D 674–75, 685.

201. AMZ XXIX (1827) 877–81; trans. in Deutsch/SCHUBERT-D 693–97.

Ex. 20. The opening of Franz Schubert's Sonata in G, Op. 78 (D. 894; facs. of the autograph Add. 36738 in the British Museum).

the pianoforte players of today in that respect?—but much rather the energy, the differentiation of the parts and the bringing out of the themes or at least of the allusions to them. . . .

Schumann, though he gave only two sentences to No. 20, called it Schubert's "most perfect" sonata "in form and spirit," with everything "organic," although the finale should be avoided by those without "the imagination to solve its riddles." [202]

The final three solo sonatas, Nos. 21–23 in c, A, and B♭, were left in significant sketches, followed by one continuous, exceptionally clean autograph containing all three sonatas on ninety-four pages

202. Schumann/SCHRIFTEN I 124. Cf., also, the high praise for this work in MT XIII (1868) 318.

and raising few textual or bibliographic questions.[203] Schubert seems to have composed all three of these great swan songs of his instrumental music in the incredibly short time of less than four weeks,[204] possibly playing all three for friends on September 27, 1828, only one day (!) after completing them, then already claiming in a letter written but five days later that "I have played [them] with much success in several places. . . ."[205] In the latter, peculiarly anxious document, addressed only forty-eight days before his death to the publisher Probst, he indicated his desire to dedicate all three sonatas to Hummel. However, the almost immediate plans to publish them changed twice[206] and did not materialize for another ten years (1838), or one year after Hummel's death in 1837. By that time Diabelli very wisely sought and got permission to dedicate them to the man most qualified to appreciate them, Schumann.[207]

Yet Schumann reviewed Nos. 21–23 that same year rather briefly and somewhat halfheartedly, mainly disturbed by the sadness of the inscription "very last compositions" not quite accurately inserted by Diabelli.[208] He did write approvingly of a new preference in them for simplicity over brilliance and for continuous melodic unfolding over a succession of different phrases. Such traits seem to explain objections to No. 23 and disadvantageous comparisons when it was played in a varied London concert in 1865:[209]

The Sonata in B flat of Schubert for pianoforte alone was done ample justice to by Mr. Charles Hallé; but the want of marked character in the leading subjects was made still more apparent by its being placed between Beethoven's Quartett in C, and Mozart's Sonata in E Minor, for pianoforte and violin (most exquisitely performed by Mr. Charles Hallé and Herr Joachim), the beauties of which latter composition seemed thoroughly appreciated by the audience.

In 1895, Shedlock still sensed faults in each of the last three sonatas

203. The autograph and its circumstances are described in detail in Kinsky/KOCH 177–79, along with Facs. 13 of the first p. of No. 23 (reproduced in SSB VI). Cf., also, Költzsch/SCHUBERT 19–20; Brown/ESSAYS 214–15. Mod. ed. of the sketches (incomplete): SCHUBERT WERKE-m *Revisionsbericht* 8–45 (not 9–34).

204. Perhaps in response to a general solicitation for compositions of Aug. 10, 1828, from the publisher Brüggemann (Deutsch/SCHUBERT-D 797; cf. pp. 783 and 785, too).

205. Deutsch/SCHUBERT-D 807–8, 810–11 (evidently the only source for Deutsch's surmise, p. 808, about Sept. 27).

206. Cf. Deutsch/SCHUBERT-D 842–44; Költzsch/SCHUBERT 19–20.

207. Diabelli's thank-you note is printed in Schumann/SCHRIFTEN II 415 fn.

208. Schumann/SCHRIFTEN I 330–31. Again, exception is taken by Einstein (Einstein/SCHUBERT 285).

209. MT XII (1865–67) 29.

that he felt counteracted their great beauties, including a weak finale in No. 22 and excessive length in Nos. 21/iv and 23/i and iv.[210] More recently these works have been viewed as magnificent testimonials at once to Schubert's deep involvement with Beethoven, only six to eight years after that late master's last three sonatas had appeared, and to Schubert's ultimate independence of Beethoven gained through full control of his own idiom.[211] And at present if any one sonata were to be rated first among Nos. 21–23—in fact, among all Schubert's sonatas—not only most writers,[212] but most qualified performers and initiated listeners would give the palm to the very last, in B♭—with its almost elegiac first movement, recalling the gentle contemplation of No. 20/i; its serene yet melancholy slow movement, recalling that of the but recently composed Quintet in C, D. 956; its fleet, surprisingly gay "Scherzo"; its less rapid but more brilliant finale, starting melodically and harmonically much as in the finale of Beethoven's then recent quartet in the same key, Op. 130;[213] and with its truly "heavenly length" throughout.

Schubert's Ensemble Sonatas

Schubert's ten ensemble sonatas include only one work published during his own lifetime and have always aroused much less interest than his twenty-three complete or incomplete solo sonatas. Yet those with violin or arpeggione seldom fail to interest musicians who do play or hear them, and the best of those for piano duet rank by general consent among the best in piano duet literature. A tabulation almost like that for the solo sonatas follows (and again, as with the solo sons., the ensemble sons. are referred to only in the subsequent discussion by the chronological numbers in the leftmost column). No. 1 in B♭ is a "Sonate" in one movement for piano trio that Schubert wrote at fifteen, a precocious student piece curiously like (but, of course, no possible source for) the solo piano sonata in the same key Wagner was to publish at eighteen, only twenty years later.[214] It is the earliest extant venture into the sonata by Schubert.[215] No. 2 is another early work, whose five free sections, cul-

210. Shedlock/SONATA 205–6.
211. E.g., cf. Einstein/SCHUBERT 285–88, 290.
212. As in Brown/SCHUBERT 302–4.
213. Close structural parallels between the 2 finales are also discovered in Hill/SCHUBERT. But see further under the duet Son. in C, D. 812, in the following discussion.
214. Cf. SSB IX. Mod. ed. of our No. 1: Orel/SCHUBERT-m, with preface; cf. Orel/SCHUBERT for further background and an analysis of the work.
215. Cf. Deutsch/SCHUBERT-M 127–28 (J. v. Spaun).

Schubert's Ensemble Sonatas

Chron. no.	Scoring	Key	Opus no.	Deutsch no.	Composed	First edition	SCHUBERT/ WERKE-m	Mvts.: tempos or types / Keys: mvt.-by-mvt. / mss.: mvt.-by-mvt.	Remarks
1	P, Vn, Vc	Bb		28	1812	Wiener Philharmonischer, 1923		1: F / key: Bb / 292: 292	
2	P-duet	c/Bb		48	1813	Gotthard, 1871 (first version)	IX/32	5: S/VF-M-F -S -F / keys: c -Bb-Bb -Db-Bb / 584: 213 -76-201-15-79	called "Fantasie," "Sonate," and "Grande Sonate" in early references; v lacking in first of 2 versions
3	P & Vn	D	137/1	384	1816	Diabelli, 1836	VIII/2	3: F -M-VF / keys: D -A-D / 512: 180-87-245	pub. as one of "Drei Sonatinen . . ."
4	"	a	137/2	385	"	"	VIII/3	4: F -M -Mi-F / keys: a -F -d -a / 641: 137-114-80-310	"
5	"	g	137/3	408	"	"	VIII/4	4: F -M-Mi-F / keys: g -Eb-Bb -g / 468: 145-74-100-149	"
6	P & Vn	A	162	574	1817	Diabelli, 1851	VIII/6	4: F -Sc -M-VF / keys: A -E -C -A / 763: 177-216-92-278	pub. as "Duo . . ."
7	P-duet	Bb	30	617	1818	Sauer & Leidesdorf, 1823	IX/2	3: F -M -F / keys: Bb -d -Bb / 473: 170-112-191	pub. as "Grande Sonate"
8	P-duet	C	140	812	1824	Diabelli, 1838	IX/12	4: F -M -Sc -VF / keys: C -Ab -C -C / 1502: 384-250-401-467	pub. as "Grande Duo"
9	P & arpeggione	a/A		821	1824	Gotthard, 1871	VIII/8	3: F -S -F / keys: a -E -A / 682: 205-71-406	alternative parts for Vc or Vn pub. with first ed.
10	P-duet	C/a		968	early?	Werke, 1888	IX/29	2: F -M / keys: C -a / 193: 148-45	called "Sonatine" (Deutsch, SCHUBERT-I 478)

minating in a scholastic, four-voice fugue, make the title "Fantasia" in the second version more appropriate than "Grand Sonnate" in the first version.[216]

Nos. 3–5, in D, a, and g, get progressively more forceful in content but are still generally light enough, though hardly short enough, to explain the publisher's preference for "Sonatine" rather than the original "Sonate" as the title for each.[217] Schubert still used the phrase "with accompaniment for violin" in his title although the violin is at least a full partner here. The more versatile writing for each instrument in No. 6 in A and the richer texture, resulting mainly from the richer piano part,[218] evince the experience Schubert had gained from Nos. 3–5. This time the same publisher changed the title to "Duo" for the first edition. The only contemporary circumstance that seems to be known about Schubert's string sonatas is that No. 9 in a/A was performed for at least one private hearing late in 1824, with Vincenz Schuster playing the arpeggione or violoncello guitar.[219] This rare, six-stringed, bowed instrument, essentially a bass viola da gamba,[220] seems to have come into and gone out of being just in time for Schubert's unique but hastily written sonata,[221] and has since been replaced by the cello when the work is played.

No. 10 in C/a may actually be one of Schubert's earliest piano duets, related curiously to a lost Mass by him or one by his brother Ferdinand that utilizes the materials.[222] No. 7 in B♭ was the one ensemble sonata and the earliest of all those four sonatas (by nearly two-and-half years) that were published in Schubert's lifetime.[223] But no mention of it can be found until Schumann's, in 1834, as one of Schubert's least original works, with only occasional flashes, although a masterpiece under any other composer's name.[224] Finally,

---

216. The autograph of the first version is filed under ML 30 .8b .S35 D. 48 Case at the Library of Congress; this version appears in Ed. Peters 155d, pp. 14–31, lacking the fugue finale.

217. Cf. Deutsch/SCHUBERT-I 174; Cobbett/CHAMBER II 355. Performances of No. 3 (i.e., D. 384), which remains the most popular, are reported in MT XVI (1874) 417, 544.

218. Cf. Cobbett/CHAMBER II 355.

219. Cf. Deutsch/SCHUBERT-D 384 (source?) and -B 50b (not 50a; drawing).

220. Cf. GROVE I 222–23 (G. Hayes), with photograph on Plate 63/3 (VIII, after p. 146); KONGRESS SCHUBERT 136 (E. van der Straeten).

221. Cf. Einstein/SCHUBERT 245. The first ed. was reviewed as merely an "occasional piece" in MW III (1872) 493–94.

222. Cf. Brown/DISCOVERIES 300–303.

223. Cf. Deutsch/SCHUBERT-D 294, 315.

224. Schumann/SCHRIFTEN I 124–25. It got higher praise in MT XIII (1868) 318, and, recently, in Einstein/SCHUBERT 152 and Brown/SCHUBERT 88.

No. 8 in C is the so-called "Grand Duo" on which Schumann was quoted earlier, first for viewing Schubert as Beethoven's feminine counterpart, and second for viewing this work as a potential symphony. Not only its idiom but its elaborate treatment of ideas suggests symphonic thinking.[225] It is, in fact, 145 measures longer than the longest solo sonata, 52 longer than the Quintet in C, but 1,366 shorter than the "Great Symphony" in C. And both in quality and spirit, however unsatisfying may be its duet idiom, it would be placed here on a par with those latter two masterpieces in C. Perhaps, though not a quartet, No. 8 was one of the consequences of a statement Schubert wrote three months earlier. ". . . I want to write another quartet, in fact intend to pave my way towards grand symphony in that manner." [226] The finale of No. 8, by the way, is another that recalls that in Beethoven's Quartet Op. 130. Since Schubert's finale is the earlier of these two and no known biographical circumstances indicate that Beethoven could have known it, one begins to suspect that its ideas and style were then "in the air."

Some Obscure Viennese (Woržischek)

There remain to mention in this chapter, chiefly to round out the picture, a few other contemporaries or followers of Beethoven, but this time primarily men whose sonatas now rest in almost total oblivion however much those sonatas may once have prospered.[227] One such was a composer on the borderline of the Classic and Romantic eras, **Anton Franz Josef Eberl** (1765–1807). This outstanding pianist had studied with Mozart, was mistakenly credited with some of his music, and was compared favorably with Beethoven as a symphonist.[228] In all, he left 16 sonatas—6 for P solo, 2 for P-duet, and 8 accompanied by Vn or Fl—all published between 1792 and 1806.[229] In spite of many flashes of talent and significant advances in piano writing, in chromaticism, and in certain other early Romanticisms,

---

225. An ex. from the first mvt. is quoted in ssb VI.

226. Deutsch/SCHUBERT-D 339; cf. p. 340.

227. Most of these men are represented by one waltz each in the "other" set of "Diabelli Variations," the full contents of which was given at the start of this chapter.

228. Cf. AMZ VII (1804–5) 321–22; Ewens/EBERL 8–9, 14–19; MGG III 1053–55 (R. Haas).

229. A thematic index, without dates or plate nos., appears in Ewens/EBERL 114–22; approximate dates are given in MGG III 1054. The sons. are discussed, with exx., in Ewens/EBERL 21–38 (solo; summarized in Egert/FRÜHROMANTIKER 52–59) and 77–83 (ensemble). Mod. ed. of a Sonatine . . . à l'usage des Commençans in C, Op. 5 (or 6; 1796): Giegling/SOLO-m no. 14.

these sonatas reveal a lack of fundamental training in composition (as Rochlitz concludes in both the first and last of several moderately favorable reviews[230]), a lack that is apparent today especially in the loose, disjointed forms. Perhaps a lack of vitality in the ideas themselves also worked against their more resourceful development.

A more obscure figure was **Philipp Jakob Riotte** (1776–1856), a successful composer for the stage who came to Vienna from Germany in 1808 and moved in the circles of Beethoven, Schubert, the Archduke Rudolph, and Weber, among others.[231] Riotte also left considerable instrumental music, including over two dozen accompanied and solo piano sonatas or sonatinas that were published from about 1805 to 1820.[232] Eleven of the solo type were still represented in PAZDÍREK XXIV 369 early in the present century. As with most composers who have bowed to public taste Riotte devoted his most extended and serious efforts to his first sonatas. The most conspicuous trait in all his sonatas is fluent, salon virtuosity. His writing is more like that of Weber than of Beethoven or Schubert, but it is less original and more square-cut.[233] His dances have a degree of piquancy and charm. His slow movements are short and inconsequential.

Another composer for the stage, as well as a church organist and pedagogue, **Joseph Drechsler** (1782–1852) also moved in the circles of Beethoven (who respected him) and Schubert.[234] Drechsler, who came to Vienna from Prague in 1807, got no sonata reviews discovered here nor did more than one of his three or four solo and accompanied piano sonatas, first published between 1809 and 1812,[235] survive in PAZDÍREK IV 408. Yet his sonatas disclose not only the virtuosity of Riotte's, ranging over the whole keyboard, but more imagination, richer textural interest, and superior craftsmanship.

Joseph Mayseder (1789–1863), a violinist who figured often in the activities of Beethoven and Schubert, among others,[236] published nearly seventy works that exploit the virtuosity of the violin. Two

230. AMZ III (1800–1801) 95–96, IV (1801–2) 592, V (1802–3) 558–60 and 763–66, VII (1804–5) 748–50, XI (1808–9) 159–60, 337–44, and 521–22.

231. Cf. MGG XI 546–49 (F. Goebels).

232. Op. 3 is reviewed in AMZ IX (1806–7) 92–4; Op. 51 is already listed in HOFMEISTER 1818 (Whistling) 38.

233. This general evaluation was already voiced in part in occasional further reviews of Riotte's sons.—e.g., AMZ X (1807–8) 109 and 256.

234. Cf. MGG III 743–44 (A. Orel); Deutsch/SCHUBERT-D 24; Thayer & Forbes/ BEETHOVEN II 864–65.

235. Weinmann/ARTARIA items 1987, 2033, 2236; HOFMEISTER 1815 (Whistling) 301, 350.

236. Cf. MGG VIII 1851–53 (K. Pfannhauser), with further references but no itemized list of works.

of these, Opp. 13 in E♭ and 42 in e (*ca.* 1816 and 1826), bear the title "Grande Sonate concertante pour piano & [or "et"] Violon." [237] They reveal competence in writing, relatively moderate exploitation of both instruments, and banal ideas that are treated without creative spark.

Anton Halm (1789–1872), who established himself as pianist and teacher in Vienna from 1815, knew Beethoven well and must have crossed paths with Schubert several times.[238] He left mainly solo and "accompanied" piano music, including about a dozen sonatas first published between 1819 and 1828 except for two or three that appeared as late as 1848.[239] A teacher of Stephen Heller and Adolph von Henselt, among others, Halm excelled in his etudes and their virtuoso style, again suggestive of Weber. One of his earliest and most played sonatas, Op. 15 in c for solo piano (*ca.* 1820), deserves the "Grande" in its title for its length and technical demands, but its squareness and excessive sequences of weak ideas make it naive and unacceptable today. With its slow introduction and except for a "Scherzo" in place of a middle slow movement, it sounds like a "Warsaw Concerto" popularization of Beethoven's *Grande Sonate pathétique.* In 1837, in a review of Halm's Piano Trio Op. 57, Schumann found the highest intentions combined with utter stylistic and structural ineptness, granting at the same time that "Nature would explode if she were to give forth nothing but Beethovens." [240]

A surprisingly strong composer turns up in the short-lived **Johann Hugo Woržischek** (or Vořišek; 1791–1825), who arrived in Vienna in 1813 after study with W. J. Tomaschek in Prague, won the praise of Beethoven for his set of piano Rhapsodies, studied with Hummel, also knew Schubert and Moscheles, among others, played the piano and violin well, and conducted the Gesellschaft der Musikfreunde from 1818.[241] Although less well known, Woržischek may be ranked with those two other strong Czech-born composers of instrumental music in the early 19th century, J. L. Dussek and W. J. Tomaschek (SSB

237. Both are listed among many other works by Mayseder in Cat. ROYAL 216 and Altmann/KAMMERMUSIK 215 *et passim.* The approximate dates are based mainly on the dates for near op. nos. in Weinmann/ARTARIA items 2361 and 2941. MT XVIII (1877) 351 mentions a performance of Op. 42/ii and iii.

238. Cf. Thayer & Forbes/BEETHOVEN II 629, 975; Deutsch/SCHUBERT-M 280–81, -D as indexed.

239. Cf. MGG V 1375–76 (H. Federhofer); HOFMEISTER 1819 (Whistling) 27 and 35, 1828 (Whistling) 483 and 589. Three solo sons. still appear in PAZDÍREK XI 122.

240. Schumann/SCHRIFTEN I 278.

241. Cf. MAB-m No. 30, pp. vii–ix (B. Štědroň); Thayer & Riemann/BEETHOVEN III 453; GROVE IX 74 (G. Černušak); Deutsch/SCHUBERT-D 452–3, -M 344, 345; AMZ XVIII (1816) 77, 513.

XVII; cf. SCE 774–75). Only two sonatas by Woržischek have been made known thus far, both in good modern editions—Op. 5 in G/g, for P & Vn, originally published by Mechetti in Vienna about 1823, with dedication to Archduke Rudolph, and Op. 20 in b♭, for P solo, published by Pennauer in Vienna about 1825.[242] Some study has been devoted to his smaller piano forms, especially their influence on Schubert's.[243] But little seems to have been devoted to his sonatas beyond descriptive paragraphs in the modern editions, or to any other of his larger works (suggesting a significant dissertation topic).

Woržischek's Op. 5 is an extended work in four movements—S/F-Sc-S-VF—with the "Scherzo" in the submediant key, the "Andante sostenuto" in the tonic key, and the finale, exceptionally, in the tonic minor key. In spite of the length (1,114 mss. in all) the structural control remains clear and telling. The main ideas, mostly lyrical and stepwise, achieve interest through resourceful harmonic support and contrast. Their development—especially in the relatively short development section of i—attains distinction through skillful, well-spaced motivic writing. The piano and violin share in a true duo, although, as generally holds throughout much of the century, the piano part is technically more challenging and adventurous, including leaps and rhythmically capricious figures that anticipate Chopin's writing. Otherwise, the scale and passagework suggest Mendelssohn, occasionally Weber.

Compared with his Op. 5, Woržischek's Op. 20 is structurally tighter and more compact, more dramatic—with frequent suggestions of Beethoven[244]—and more pregnant melodically. Its plan of VF-Sc-VF includes no moderate or slow movement. Not counting the slow movement of Op. 5, Op. 20 is still 37 per cent shorter in total measures. Its technical requirements are just as interesting, though a little more practical. Unusual is the choice of C♯ for the "Scherzo," not so much for being the lowered, enharmonic mediant as simply for the number of sharps and double-sharps it presented to the pianists of the time. From the first movement, about a third of the polyphonic development section, which goes from b♭ to b and back, is illustrated in Ex. 21. The main theme with octave leaps recurs

242. Plate nos. 1221 and 168, respectively, place these works later (Deutsch/NUMMERN 17, 18) than the *ca.* 1820 suggested for both in the 2 mod. eds.: MAB-m No. 30, p. ix and No. 4, p. [5] (L. Kundera), both with prefaces; the reference to AMZ for 1820 in Kahl/LYRISCHE 106 fn. 2 is an error, and the reference to an 1821 ed. of Op. 20/iii could not be verified here.

243. Cf. Kahl/LYRISCHE 99–110, 112–13, 117–19, 122; MAB-m No. 52, pp. xii–xvi.

244. As is emphasized in Kahl/LYRISCHE 106.

Ex. 21. From Op. 20/i by Johann Hugo Woržischek (after
MAB-m No. 4, p. 12).

in ii and is hinted in iii. This theme and the staccato, rising, chordal
motive that follows suggest that Woržischek knew the opening of
Mozart's "Haffner Symphony" and the finale of his Symphony in g,
respectively. A brief review of Op. 20 in 1826 called attention to
the strength and skill of this newly encountered composer, as well
as the work's technical difficulties, including keys up to seven sharps
and five flats.[245] Present-day pianists would do well to consider including this fine work in a general recital.

After arriving in Vienna in 1817, the Czech violinist **Leopold Jansa**
(1795–1875) studied with Woržischek and the older Czech E. A. Förster (SCE 548–49).[246] A prolific, not unskillful composer of light duos,

245. AMZ XXVIII (1826) 204.
246. MGG VI 1716–18 (A. Wirsta).

rondos, and potpourris for his instrument,[247] he is cited here solely for the infrequent scoring of what may have been his only sonata, a "Sonate brillante" in D for unaccompanied violin with the optional accompaniment of a second violin, published by Artaria in 1828.[248]

The piano prodigy **Franz Schoberlechner** (1797–1843), a pupil of Hummel and E. A. Förster, left at least two solo piano sonatas and one for P, Vn-or-Fl.[249] Published between 1820 and 1828, these sonatas approach Hummel's in their piano writing and brilliance, but are otherwise lighter and more modish to a degree that may help explain Beethoven's refusal to endorse Schoberlechner.[250] Op. 45, "Sonate mélancolique," could well have taken at least its title from the recently published Op. 49 by Moscheles. Another violinist was **Georg Hellmesberger** ("der Ältere"; 1800–73), early classmate of Schubert, first in a long, active, family line of Viennese musicians, and teacher of Joachim and Auer, among others. He left a four-movement Sonata in A♭ for P & Vn, published about 1848, that won praise from Alfred Dörffel as a well-knit, conservative, but sensitive work of moderate difficulty.[251]

Last in this chapter may be mentioned the prolific composer **Franz Lachner** (1803–90), who wrote six of his nine solo and ensemble sonatas between 1824 and 1832 while still studying and/or living in Vienna (1822–34), the remaining three being organ sonatas (Opp. 175–77) published late in his Munich years (1876).[252] A member of an important musical family, a versatile talent acknowledged by Beethoven,[253] a close friend of Schubert,[254] a student of Sechter, and an early detractor but eventual supporter of Wagner,[255] Lachner wrote unevenly. The high spots in his later works that might justify his classification in 1922 as a significant "transitional figure between Schubert and Bruckner" [256] are only occasionally to be found amidst the skilled but often dry and insipid writing of the sonatas. In 1835 Schumann deplored at length the inconsistent quality and unsatis-

247. Cf. PAZDÍREK VIII 83–85.

248. The only listing discoverable here was that in Weinmann/ARTARIA item 2950.

249. Cf. MGG XII 1–2 (E. Badura-Skoda); HOFMEISTER 1828, 602 and 506. The sons. do not survive among the works still listed in PAZDÍREK XIII 301.

250. Cf. Thayer & Forbes/BEETHOVEN II 864.

251. NZM XXX (1849) 142–43; cf., also, MGG VI 113–14 (A. Orel).

252. Cf. MGG VIII 29–31 and 34 (A. Wurz), with further references. In the long list of his works in PAZDÍREK IX 24–29, 6 sons. still survive.

253. Cf. Thayer & Riemann/BEETHOVEN V 121; Egert/FRÜHROMANTIKER 146, with further references.

254. Cf. Deutsch/SCHUBERT-M 195–97 et passim.

255. Cf. Newman/WAGNER I 76; II 304–5, 472, 482–84.

256. As quoted in MGG VIII 32.

factory sonority of Lachner's four-hand Sonata in d, Op. 39 (1832).[257]
(In 1842, he found wholly mediocre and conservative the "Grosse
Sonate" for piano solo in F, Op. 20, by Franz's brother in Vienna,
Ignaz Lachner [1807–95] [258]) Already typical of Franz Lachner's style
is *Grande Sonate* in f♯, Op. 2 (1824?), in four movements (F-Sc-Va-F),
with its genuinely Romantic, though saccharine melodiousness, its
fluent handling of new chordal textures and wide-range passages, its
slavish observance of the four-measure phrase, and its profitless exploitation of flat ideas.[259]

257. Schumann/SCHRIFTEN I 92–94; II 382 fn. 124 (crossed out of the original
review).
258. Schumann/SCHRIFTEN II 118–19; echoed in AMZ XLV (1843) 325. Only slightly
more enthusiasm is shown for Ignaz's 4-hand "Preissonate" Op. 33, in AMZ XLVIII
(1846) 660–61. But his Vn sonatinas were liked, as in MMR XX (1890) 57 and 256.
Cf., also, Egert/FRÜHROMANTIKER 148–49.
259. The support of F. Lachner's sons. in Egert/FRÜHROMANTIKER 146–49 is hard
to justify.

Chapter VIII

Weber, Schumann, and Others in Early 19th-Century German Centers

The New Romanticism in Germany

During the first half of the 19th century the separate German states that were to confederate by 1866 still came under pronounced Austrian influence. From the standpoint of the artist much of the reactionism and oppression that beset Austria after the Congress of Vienna (SSB VII) also prevailed in these states. But there were commercial, philosophic, artistic, and other nationalistic and cultural forces that tended to pull the states away from Austria and to unify them around their strongest and largest representative, Prussia. Eight other states also gained definition and strength, especially Bavaria, Württemberg, and Saxony. The same forces help to explain why the German states soon forged ahead of Austria in military might—again, Prussia first and foremost—in scientific progress, in the industrial revolution, and in the related advances of transportation and communication; why they responded more, though not succumbed, to the international waves of revolution, especially in 1848 (as Spohr, Schumann, and Wagner knew so well); and, yes, why they took the lead in both the spirit and the content of the new Romanticism.

Of prime importance as implementers of the new Romanticism in music were several German authors who had been preceded, in part, by Schiller and the aging but still active Goethe—in particular, Wackenroder, Novalis, Tieck, E. T. A. Hoffmann, Heine, and Jean Paul.[1] Their theories, moods, and themes—night, death, indefinable longing, dreams, the world of make-believe—penetrated music even when it took so abstract a form as the sonata. All of these six authors included music among their literary topics and at least three of them played and wrote music, however amateurishly. But in that age of hybrid art

1. Pertinent here among studies of German literature and music are Longyear/SCHILLER, Schoolfield/GERMAN, and Siegel/GERMANY (which gives chief attention to the above names).

and heterogeneous genius, one hardly needs to go outside of the music profession itself to find literary influences and associations. Quite apart from music theorists and writers like Gottfried Weber and A. B. Marx, nearly every one of our main composers in this chapter was active as a man of letters, too. And some of them, like Weber and Mendelssohn, were skilled in the fine arts, as well. Moreover, nearly every one of these men not only wrote for publication but faithfully maintained a prodigious personal correspondence and elaborate diaries, polished so finely and organized so systematically—how paradoxical for such artistically free spirits—that their ultimate purpose could only have been the edification of posterity.

Three music periodicals in particular provided the outlets for the reviews and other articles that our main sonata composers published, all of which already have been cited frequently in the present and even the previous volume. One was the widely respected *Allgemeine musikalische Zeitung* (AMZ), founded in 1798 and originally edited by J. F. Rochlitz, with G. W. Fink and M. Hauptmann among his successors; another was the *Neue Zeitschrift für Musik* (NZM), founded by Schumann in 1834; and the third was Caecilia (CAECILIA), founded in 1824 under the editorship of Gottfried Weber.[2] In the absence of any other survey, early or present-day, of the 19th-century sonata in Germany, we cannot help but take much interest in the opinions, attitudes, and sometimes the music analyses provided in these periodicals, especially those from so great a musical judge as Schumann. All these editors wrote with authority and carried much weight. Furthermore, the editors of AMZ and NZM made it their avowed purposes to pay as much attention as possible to the sonata, especially the piano sonata (SSB II). Their patient attention to nearly everything received from the publishers produced reviews not only of significant new sonatas but of many run-of-the-mill sonatas and of some deficient ones that could only be described as "miserable." No wonder that almost any creative spark was greeted with enthusiasm, sometimes with a degree of enthusiasm impossible to endorse today. The contrast is noteworthy between the more conservative-minded, diplomatic, and didactic reviews in AMZ and the more modern-minded, frank, even sarcastic reviews in NZM, often signed by "Florestan," "Eusebius," or "Raro" as representatives of Schumann's split personality. Undoubtedly, one reason for the collapse of AMZ in 1848 was the growing preference for the more modern views of its competitor in Leipzig, NZM, although after Schumann stopped most of his writing, in the early 1840's, F. Brendel,

---

2. Freystätter/ZEITSCHRIFTEN gives a summary history of each periodical. Plantinga/SCHUMANN, as noted later, is of special value here on NZM.

A. Dörffel, and others tended to write more conservatively and diplomatically for NZM, too.

This chapter is the longest in the present volume because it not only includes four of our most influential and significant composers of 19th-century sonatas—Hummel, Weber, Schumann, and Mendelssohn—but because, in the interest of a balanced perspective (SSB I), it includes so many of those run-of-the-mill composers, or at least all of them encountered here whose sonatas were once popular or reveal some other reason for bringing them to light again. Among other recurring themes in this chapter are the remarkably wide, quick, and potent spread of Beethoven's influence; the remarkably few instances of actual programmatic sonatas, in spite of the close ties between literature and music; and the remarkably persistent output of sonatas published for piano alone or in ensemble, in spite of recurring recognition around 1840 of a low ebb in their quality (SSB II).

South Germany (Hummel)

If Ries made an ideal starter, in the previous chapter, as a direct Beethoven transmitter in Vienna, then **Johann Nepomuk Hummel** (1778–1837) makes an ideal starter here as one of the most important links between the great Classic masters in that city and the new young Romantics throughout much of the rest of Europe. Born near-by in Pressburg (Bratislava) inside the Czech border, Hummel could have been placed at least as appropriately in Vienna, where he lived from 1786 to 1787 and much of the period from 1793 (not 1795) to 1816.[3] He studied and lived with Mozart during that first stay, as a piano prodigy of but eight and nine.[4] And during that longer stay he quickly moved to the top among Viennese pianists, studied counterpoint and composition with Albrechtsberger and Salieri, taught, composed, and published extensively, studied organ with Haydn,[5] and won both Haydn's and Beethoven's friendship and respect.[6]

3. Benyovszky/HUMMEL includes many letters and other documents as well as most of the known biographic information (pp. 16–129; utilized in GROVE IV 406–9 [D. Hume] and MGG VI 927–35 [W. Kahl]). Cf., also, Hummel's autobiographic letter to J. Sonnleithner of May 22, 1826 in La Mara/MUSIKERBRIEFE II 47–51 and the necrology in NZM VII (1837) 153–54, 157–58, 165–66 (C. Montag).

4. Deutsch/MOZART 346, 569–71. Cf. Zimmerschied/HUMMEL.

5. Benyovszky/HUMMEL 49.

6. Cf. Landon & Bartha/HAYDN 451–52; Holmes/RAMBLE 19; Thayer & Forbes/ BEETHOVEN I 230 and 424, II 1044. Although he may have known Schubert's music earlier, Hummel seems not to have met Schubert until he returned to Vienna in 1827 to visit the dying Beethoven, by which time Hummel had published nearly if not all of his own sonatas and Schubert was soon to request, in vain, that his three great, final sons. of 1828 be ded. to Hummel (SSB VII; cf. Deutsch/SCHUBERT-M 28, 137, 148).

Yet it was away from Vienna that Hummel built his chief reputation and exercised his chief influence as pianist and composer, including the composition of Op. 81, his most significant sonata both musically and Romantically. He is placed here in southern Germany merely because of his first station outside of Vienna, in Stuttgart from 1816 to 1819. But between 1788 and 1793, again before 1803,[7] and during many leaves from his final station, in Weimar from 1819 to his death, he made wide concert-tours that took him variously to nearly all the main centers in Germany, England, Scotland, Bohemia, Russia, France, Holland, Belgium, and Poland. He already played for Haydn during a London concert in 1792,[8] and about the same time he studied with Clementi,[9] got to know Clementi's pupil Cramer, and probably came to know Dussek, too.[10] In later years he crossed paths often as pianist and composer with Cramer and Moscheles, being paired with each as a rival at one time or another (as he had been with Beethoven);[11] his music furnished at least early models for that of Weber, Mendelssohn, Schumann, and Chopin, all of whom he knew personally (Schumann through correspondence);[12] and he himself taught Czerny, Ferdinand Hiller, Adolph von Henselt, and probably Thalberg,[13] among others.

Hummel's range of composition was wide, including operas, church music, symphonies, concertos, chamber music, and a long list of the then fashionable variations, rondos, sonatas, studies, potpourris, dances, arrangements, and transcriptions for piano solo or duet.[14] A few of his publications achieved more than a dozen printings in his lifetime, including the still celebrated Septet in d, Op. 74, the still played "Rondo favori" in E♭, Op. 11, the most successful concertos (especially Op. 85 in a),[15] and one of the earlier solo sonatas, Op. 13 in E♭. Moreover, his

7. Cf. Benyovszky/HUMMEL 44; Philip H. Highfill, Jr., provides new information on Hummel in London in 1801, in JAMS IX (1956) 70–71, revealing a fine voice and ability to play the harp, a handsome face (contradicting CZERNY 308), an intellectual brilliance, a literary background, and alcoholic temperance.

8. Cf. Benyovszky/HUMMEL 42–45; Landon & Bartha/HAYDN 269–70.

9. Cf. CZERNY 309. Other evidence could not be found here.

10. Cf. Pohl/MOZART 43, 107, 127, 155.

11. Cf. Schlesinger/CRAMER 43, 47–48, 71, 77–78; MOSCHELES I 22, 241–42, 276.

12. Cf. Saunders/WEBER 79, 121, 125, 159; MENDELSSOHN/Moscheles 66; Werner/ MENDELSSOHN 55; Storck/SCHUMANN 64–68; Schumann/JUGENDBRIEFE 80; Niecks/ SCHUMANN 101, 141–42; Sydow & Hedley/CHOPIN 24, 70, 80.

13. Schilling/LEXICON VI 628; but further evidence for Thalberg is wanting (SSB XII).

14. Cf. the early index reprinted in Benyovszky/HUMMEL 321–28 (the 2d list, pp. 329–44, repeats PAZDÍREK), the undated list in PAZDÍREK XI 750–56, the less complete, undated list by categories in GROVE IV 408–9, and the partially but uncertainly dated list in MGG VI 929–32. In all these, different op. nos. for the same work are identified insufficiently if at all.

15. Mitchell/HUMMEL is a recent diss. on Hummel's concertos.

Ausführliche theoretische-practische Anweisung zum Piano-Forte-Spiel of 1827, first published by Haslinger of Vienna in 1828,[16] circulated widely during the 19th century, leaving its mark especially on the new style of fingering and of playing trills and related ornaments.[17] Among all those works are about 25 sonatas, representing but a small proportion numerically, yet a much larger proportion in terms of relative attention received, both contemporary and posthumous. In the tabulation of Hummel's sonatas that follows, it has been possible to discover more of the earliest editions and actual publication dates, also to equate and consolidate more of the different opus numbers assigned by different publishers to the same work, than in any previous tabulation known here. But much still remains to be done toward a complete, accurate list of Hummel's sonatas. Not included are several transcriptions from other settings to "sonatas," or the converse.

The 25 sonatas by Hummel that could be identified here divide into 9 (or more than a third) solos, 4 (or about a sixth) duets, and 12 (or nearly half) other ensembles. As was so often true then, the solos provide the most serious, extended, and resourceful examples.[18] The ensemble sonatas may have been played at least as much as the solo sonatas during or soon after Hummel's own day,[19] and two of them have been brought back to view by recent new editions.[20] Certainly, for all their skill and sensitivity, these light, graceful, often brilliant

16. Hummel/ANWEISUNG. Among other contemporary eds. was that trans. and pub. by Boosey in London as *A Complete Theoretical and Practical Course of Instruction on the Art of Playing the Piano Forte* (cf. Cat. ROYAL 180). Cf. Bie/PIANOFORTE 211–12.

17. Cf. Bie/PIANOFORTE 211–12, Schonberg/PIANISTS 109–10.

18. The typed, unpub., 62-page diss. on "Johann Nepomuk Hummel als Klavier-componist," completed at Kiel in 1922 by Walter Meyer (Schaal/DISSERTATIONEN item 1614), was no longer obtainable here, but is digested in the relatively brief discussion in Egert/FRÜHROMANTIKER 108–16. Nor could a copy be found of G. Sprock, *L'Interprétation des Sonates de Johann Nepomuk Hummel* (Paris, 1933; cf. RICORDI ENCICLOPEDIA II 444). The solo sons. also figure in a recent comprehensive article on Hummel's instrumental music, Davis/HUMMEL. But a fuller, up-to-date study of the sons. is still much to be desired.

19. E.g., cf. the reports of Hummel P-duet sons. being played in Paris in 1846 and 1850, in RGM XIII, April 5, and XVI, March 10. Op. 81, the solo son. in f♯, was played in public by Moscheles in Vienna for the first time in 1819 (AMZ XXI [1819] 430); another Vienna performance of it, in 1862, is reported in Hanslick/WIEN II 266.

20. Op. 5/3 for P & Va was published by Doblinger in 1960 (P. Doktor) and Op. 50 for P & Fl by Peters in 1965 (Dieter Sonntag). The new diss. Zimmerschied/KAMMERMUSIK (1966) includes descriptions of most of the acc'd sons., mvt. by mvt., with exx. (pp. 63–100); some information on autographs, early eds., and dates (pp. 6–19, with errors); style discussions; historical orientations; and 144 letters and other documents (pp. 327–530).

J. N. Hummel's Sonatas (grouped by scoring types)

Op./no. (alternate)	Key	Scoring	Early ed., year	Reviews, sources, dedications, titles
2/3 (3/3)	C	H-or-P	André, 1793	cf. Op. 2/1–2 *infra*
13	Eb	P	Haslinger, 1803	ded. to Haydn (cf. Landon & Bartha/HAYDN 452); "1ère Sonate"
20 (29)	f	P	Bureau . . . , by 1807	AMZ IX (1806–7) 422; ded. to Magdalene von Kurzbeck; "2ème grande Sonate"
30 (38)	C	P	Artaria, 1808	AMZ XVIII (1816) 250–51; cf. Weinmann/ARTARIA item 2021; "Sonata di bravura"
81	f#	P	Steiner, 1819	AMZ XXI (1819) 430, XXII (1820) 114–16; Schumann/JUGENDBRIEFE 80; Schumann/SCHRIFTEN I 395; "Grosse . . ."
106	D	P	Diabelli, 1824	"Grande Sonate brillante"
[no op.]/1–3	G, Ab, C	P	by 1799? Bermann, by 1828	AMZ II (1799–1800) Intelligenz-Blatt ix; HOFMEISTER 1828 (Whistling), 591, and 1834–38, 129; PAZDÍREK XI 755
1/1–2	?	P-duet	Artaria, 1798?	cf. Weinmann/ARTARIA item 731
51 (50)	Eb	P-duet	Artaria, 1815	"Sonate ou divertissement"
92	Ab	P-duet	Diabelli, *ca.* 1821	AMZ XXXIV (1832) 12–13; "Grande Sonate . . ."
2/1 (3/1)	Bb	H-or-P & Vn-or-Fl & Vc	André, 1793	HARMONICON VI/1 (1828) 108; "âgé de 14 ans"; dedicated to Queen Charlotte; "avec accompagnement de . . ."
2/2 (3/2)	G	H-or-P & Vn-or-Fl	" "	cf. Op. 2/1, *supra;* also, HARMONICON V/1 (1827) 115?
5/1–2 (3/1–2; 12/1–2?)	Bb, F	P & Vn	André, by 1798	AMZ I (1798–99) 157–58; facs. of title p.: Doktor/HUMMEL-m
5/3 (3/3; 12/3? 19)	Eb	P + Va-or-Vn	" "	AMZ I (1798–99) 157–58; AMZ XX (1818) 563–64
25		P & Vn	Richault, by 1828	
28 (30; 60)	G	P & Fl-or-Vn	Breitkopf . . . , by 1815	
37	C?	P & Vn	Richault, by 1828	
37 (54)	C	P & mandolin (or Vc?)	Diabelli, ?	cf. Bone/GUITAR 175–80
50 (61; No. 2)	D	P & Fl-or-Vn	Artaria, 1815	QUARTERLY VIII (1826) 358–59
62 (64; 126?)	A	P & Fl-or-Vn	Artaria, 1815	
104	A	P & Vc; or P & Fl	Boosey, by 1826	HARMONICON IV/1 (1826) 166–67 and V/1 (1827) 243–44; ded. to the Grand Duchess of Russia; "A Grand Sonata"; autograph in the British Museum dated 1824 (Zimmerschied/KAMMER-MUSIK 16)
108	?	P & Vn	Peters, 1826	called "Amusement"; autograph dated 1825; cf. Zimmerschied/KAMMERMUSIK 16–17

works, in two or three movements, were designed primarily to win the public. But from the mid-19th to the mid-20th century—by which time virtually everything but that Rondo in Eb had disappeared from publishers' catalogues—four of the solo sonatas were to be found among Hummel's dozen or so works that continued most generally in print. These four were Opp. 13, 20, 81, and 106.[21] If we add the two other solo sonatas that have opus numbers and at least approximate dates, Opp. 2/3 and 30, we get six very different works, yet six that give a broad view of trends and styles in all of Hummel's sonatas.

Though still an imitative, formative work, Op. 2/3 in C marks well the prodigy, "âgé de 14 ans," who had already studied with two of the greatest Classic masters. There are clear enough hints of Mozart in the feminine, sometimes chromatic cadences as well as the occasional "singing-allegro" style complete with murky and chordal, though little actual Alberti, bass. And there are clear hints of Clementi in the octave-writing and other tendencies to exploit the instrument. There are even foretastes of the brilliant sonata of the same key, opus, and number that Beethoven was to complete but two years later (1795; SCE 509). By contrast, Hummel's Op. 13 in E♭ is a fully mature work of its type—cool, elegant, skillful, straightforward, and effective both as a sonata and as piano writing. The thin texture (though now freed almost entirely of Alberti bass), the artlessly simple themes, and the feminine cadences may still be Mozartean in origin. But all these, plus the keen ear for piano resonance, the increasing technical brilliance, and the dexterous contrapuntal exploits here point even more to Clementi. There is a nod, too, to the more concentrated drive of Beethoven and to the zigzag passagework of the dedicatee, Haydn. Although, in spite of its wide circulation, the reviewers seem not to have noticed this work in Hummel's day, recent writers have found more than enough reason to hope it will be revived in performance.[22]

Published only four years later (1807), Hummel's Op. 20 in f introduces us to an even more striking change of style. It is at once warmer and more poetic in its speech, freer and more irregular in its design, and less disposed to brilliance than his Op. 13. Its improvisatory character ties in with Hummel's reputation as one of the greatest improvisers alongside Beethoven.[23] Hummel seems to be following the similar path taken by Clementi, although for the moment he has moved less in the direction of the new Romanticism than of the outdated *empfindsam* style, what with its tempo changes, frequent turns and related ornaments, deceptive cadences, and foreshortened phrases.

21. E.g., Peters, Heugel, and G. Schirmer still listed them in Hummel collections up to World War II. Nearest to complete eds. of Hummel's piano music were the 12- and 21-vol. collections pub. by Richault and Schlesinger, respectively, in Paris by 1828.

22. E.g., Egert/FRÜHROMANTIKER 110–12; Davis/HUMMEL 169–70. In Einstein/SCHUBERT 79–81, Schubert's "spontaneous" polyphony is contrasted to Hummel's "severe" or learned style, to the advantage of the former.

23. Cf. the contemporary reports in Spohr/AUTOBIOGRAPHY I 191–92 (1814), Holmes/RAMBLE 261–64, Chorley/GERMAN II 5–11, Kaiser/WEBER 90.

Perhaps it was this latter style that brought a short unfavorable review acknowledging the sonata's craftsmanship but finding too little
new—in fact, too little at all—that might justify the effort to master
its difficulties.[24] Objections were also raised to the scoring, which suggested an arrangement rather than original keyboard music, and to
the length, especially of the slow middle movement. But one can only
guess that the reviewer could not quite accept Hummel's new subtlety,
sensitivity, and freedom, for none of these objections seems valid today.
The sonata is the shortest of Hummel's solos described here and the
least difficult athletically if not musically. Moreover, it offers more
actual melodic substance than any of its fellows.

Hummel's Op. 30 in C brought a much more favorable review,[25]
with only the length being deplored again, this time with more reason
(802 mss. in all, including his only slow introduction in a solo son.,
lasting 11 mss.). Above all, this work caters to a public attracted mainly
by pianistic brilliance. In this respect it recalls Beethoven's Op. 2/3
even more than Hummel's Op. 2/3 had anticipated it. Except for its
greater technical exploitations it makes no advance toward Romantic
styles but rather a return to Mozartean manners (including the frequently cited resemblance of Op. 30/i/44–50 to Mozart's K. 300h/i/19–
26).

Certainly the most remarkable advances into the new Romanticism
—whether in harmonic vocabulary, tonal range, pianistic devices,
melodic arabesque, introspective fantasy, or emotional import—occur
in Hummel's "biggest" though not longest sonata, Op. 81 in f♯ (601
mss. in all, as against 836 in Op. 106).[26] In retrospect, the work sounds
somewhat like a style melange of its time. Passages of unmitigated
salon brilliance alternate with moments of new, unabashed and unspoiled drama like those in the contemporary chefs-d'oeuvre of Ries
and Moscheles (also in f♯; ssb VII), or with sections of harmonic
brooding that recall the late sonatas of Beethoven and Schubert, or
with ingenious melodic decoration that anticipates Chopin's delicate
figuration to a surprising degree[27] (Ex. 22).

Soon after its first appearance in 1819, Op. 81 received one of Hummel's most extended and enthusiastic reviews.[28] It was recognized as
bringing the "otherwise strictly defined form" of the sonata to the

24. AMZ IX (1806–7) 422.

25. AMZ XVIII (1816) 250–51.

26. The first mvt. has been recorded by Robert Collett in *The History of Music
in Sound* VIII/5/iv (RCA LM 6146-2 for Oxford University Press, 1958).

27. Cf. the parallels in Davis/HUMMEL *passim* as illustrated variously between
sundry works by Hummel, Beethoven, and Chopin.

28. AMZ XXII (1820) 114–16.

Ex. 22. From the middle movement of Johann Nepomuk Hummel's Sonata in f♯, Op. 81 (after Edition Peters No. 275b, pp. 16–17).

world of fantasy (hardly for the first time, as over two centuries of previous sonata history should show by now), with not a little influence from Weber. The reviewer found it meaningful, noble, spirited, pathetic, skillful, logical, novel, and pianistically resourceful to an extent truly deserving the term "Grosse Sonate" and making it the finest, also the most difficult, among all sonatas to date (!). As a youth of nineteen Schumann's one performance goal was to conquer the difficulties of this "epic, Titanic work," [29] which he later referred to as the one work by Hummel that would survive.[30]

One more decided style change occurs in Hummel's last solo piano sonata, Op. 106 in D. Except for its rather dull, cut-and-dried first

29. Schumann/JUGENDBRIEFE 80.
30. Schumann/SCHRIFTEN 395. Bülow played Op. 81 along with Liszt, Schumann, and Bach, in 1860 (BÜLOW BRIEFE IV 363; cf., also, III 50).

movement, with its etudelike passages in 3ds, this work is not so much a qualitative letdown, as usually stated,[31] but a neo-Classic return to tighter motivic writing, more conservative harmony and passagework, cooler ideas, and no fantasy. The title of the second movement, in this only Hummel solo sonata with four rather than three movements, implies such a return—"Un Scherzo all'antico." Yet the "Alternativo" in particular of this scherzo has all the rhythmic subtlety and contrapuntal life of "Alla danza tedesca" in Beethoven's still later Quartet in B♭, Op. 130 (pub. in 1827 as against 1824 for Hummel's Op. 106).

As different as these six sonatas are, from Op. 2/3 to 106, they do reveal at least five traits tangible enough to set Hummel apart from his contemporaries. But first should be mentioned what are regarded here as his two chief deficiencies. First, Hummel was not a distinguished melodist; and second, he was not especially fresh or original in the subsequent treatment of his ideas. At best his melodic invention, which never extends beyond a double period in the sonatas, is routine, as in Op. 106/iii/1–17. At worst it is decidedly trite, as in Op. 13/iii/35–51. The failing seems to lie more in uncompromising, nonplastic rhythmic organization than in the pitch outlines themselves. Hummel establishes himself more comfortably, as soon as the first, relatively simple statement ends, by hiding his melody behind florid, sometimes rhapsodic variations, at the making of which he was a past master (as in Ex. 22 above). As for the unoriginal treatment, Hummel knew the possibilities and did not addict himself to standardized formulas or designs. Yet those places where one might still expect the most imagination, as in development sections, are characteristically the most meager and uneventful. Nor are there those strokes of genius such as Beethoven's abrupt turn to e in Op. 57/i/79 or Schubert's sudden *fortissimo* dotted pattern in Op. 143 (D. 784)/i/28–29. Perhaps it was a sense of shortcomings in these respects that underlay the excessive belittlement of his own talents by the reportedly sincere and modest Hummel.[32] In any case, fine and successful as his best music was—and it does stand well above the run-of-the-mill of its time in our present historical perspective—those most able to judge, even among his contemporaries, soon came to see its limitations as well as its strengths.[33]

Among the five, more positive traits in Hummel's sonatas, two have already been cited—the delicate, pre-Chopinesque figuration illustrated above and the keen ear for piano resonance (as in the use of 10ths in the bass at Op. 20/i/126–32 and iii/27–34). The latter, evident as

31. E.g., Egert/FRÜHROMANTIKER 116, Davis/HUMMEL 177.
32. Cf. Chorley/GERMAN II 5–6.
33. E.g., cf. Deutsch/SCHUBERT-M 68, Saunders/WEBER 79.

much in his early writing for the five-octave Viennese piano (FF-f³) as in his later, expanded writing over six octaves (FF-e⁴), reflects his contemporary reputation as a front-rank pianist.[34] Pertinent to it is a third trait, a type of wide-roaming passagework comprising rather dissonant stretched figures that anticipate Schumann's writing, and modulating sequentially in broadly spaced phrases (Ex. 23).

Ex. 23. From the opening movement of Johann Nepomuk Hummel's Sonata in f♯, Op. 81 (after Edition Peters No. 275b, pp. 8–9).

A fourth distinctive trait, related to Hummel's high polyphonic skill, is his effective, intermittent reiteration of a kind of roving *cantus firmus* or freer *ostinato*. This idea, in steady half- or quarter-notes, usually provides more melodic distinction than any of his more extended thematic periods. Near the end of Op. 13/i the fullest statement of such a reiterated idea actually bears the label "Alleluia" and does approximate though not exactly duplicate several traditional alleluias (including some now to be found in the *Liber usualis*). In the slow, middle movement of Op. 20 the simple, initial idea spanning an octave in the bass grows and changes considerably. And in the extended coda of the finale the less clear-cut idea abruptly turns into that

34. Cf. CZERNY 308–9; Chorley/GERMAN II 7–8 (including a backhanded tribute from Goethe in Weimar).

ubiquitous theme of the period known best in the finale of Mozart's "Jupiter Symphony." In unmistakable imitation of Mozart, Hummel treats it as a *fugato* subject, too (Ex. 24), later converting it to a dotted pattern. In the first movement of Op. 81, the stentorian, proclamatory opening in octaves returns only as a signpost in the design. But in the finale the idea approaches the St. Anne's tune in another *fugato* treatment.

Ex. 24. From the finale of Johann Nepomuk Hummel's Sonata in f, Op. 20 (after Schirmer's Library Vol. 45, p. 39).

The fifth trait is Hummel's tendency toward additive, sectional, free variation forms in both fast and slow movements. Op. 13 demonstrates in all three movements his ability to employ closed, integrated designs when he chose to, including in the first the "sonata form" that was to become standard in 19th-century textbooks. But already in the last two movements of Op. 20 each section follows the one before more as a new variant than as a diametric contrast or unequivocal return. These variants even seem to carry over to the succeeding movements, imparting a diffuse cyclic unity, as in Op. 30. Sometimes the sectional divisions give way to continuous unfolding, whether in fugal writing or modulatory, sequential passagework, both of which govern the form of Op. 106/iii.

A few more words should be added on Hummel with regard to his lighter, but equally skillful, ensemble sonatas. The two extant duets achieved considerable popularity[35]—the "Sonate ou divertissement," Op. 51, with its "Marcia," "Andante," and "Rondo, con brio"; and the "Grande Sonate" Op. 92, with a "Grave" introduction to its three movements. The responsibilities are fairly equally divided in these duets, as they are in the other ensembles, whether the accompaniments are marked "obligato" or not. The admittedly fine Sonata in A for P & Vc, or P & Fl, Op. 104, won reviews as hyperbolic as the review cited above for Op. 81:

We say at once, and without any reservation, that this is not only one of the most masterly and beautiful compositions by Hummel that ever fell under our notice, but one of the best and most effective works of the kind, by any author, that we ever heard. The design is elegant and original; there is a definable and melodious subject running through every part of it; the modulations, unexpected and scientific as they are, seem natural and as if accomplished without any labour or research; the harmony is the handmaid of the air, and the various passages which dilate the subject, and throw it into different forms, never lose their analogy and connection, while they abound in novel and happy combinations.[36]

The Sonata for P and mandolin, Op. 37, is a reminder that **Hummel** was an expert guitarist as well as pianist.[37]

Minor Composers in South Germany and Switzerland

Other composers of sonatas in south Germany, mainly around Munich and Mannheim, call for only brief mention here. **Franz Danzi** (1763–1826) was a link between the 18th-century Mannheim School, where he was born and trained (under Vogler; SCE 573–75), and the early German Romantic opera, on which he exercised considerable influence, especially as mentor and friend to the 23-year younger Weber.[38] A pupil of Vogler (SCE 573–75), cellist, conductor, writer, and composer of opera, symphony, and chamber music, Danzi moved to Munich in 1783, Stuttgart in 1807 (9 years before Hummel), and Karlsruhe in 1812. While in these three cities he composed some fifty instrumental chamber works, including around sixteen sonatas published in Munich, Leipzig, Paris, Vienna, and Zürich between about 1797 and 1824. These

35. Cf. AMZ XXXIV (1832) 12–13 on Op. 92.
36. HARMONICON IV/1 (1826) 166–67. This review pertains to the Vc version. One year later the same work was reviewed similarly in the same periodical, in the Fl version (HARMONICON V/1 [1827] 243–44, with 2 exx.); the reviewer did not recognize the same work but recalled the earlier review and said the new work was "entitled to still higher consideration"!
37. Cf. Bone/GUITAR 173–80, with exx.
38. Cf. MGG II 1895–1900 (W. Virneisel), with further references.

last are fairly equally divided between scorings for P solo, P-duet, P & Hn-or-Vc, 2 cellos, and P & Vn, plus one unusual setting for two pianos and obligatory violin (Op. 42).[39] The three sonatas by Danzi that could be examined here, all P & Hn-or-Vc, reveal no neglected master, but they do reveal more of a true melodist than Hummel was, and a knowing composer who could write fluently, with sure purpose. The music shows less of the Romantic tendencies than are credited to his operas, and then chiefly in the breadth of his ideas and the new instrumental flare that they incorporate rather than in any special fantasy, harmonic adventure, or textural innovation.[40]

The versatile **Franz (Graf von) Pocci** (1807–76), a kind of E. T. A. Hoffmann in Munich, left two curious piano sonatas, published in 1832–34.[41] The first he called *Sonate fantastique* and the second *Frühlings-Sonate*. Writing as the poetic Eusebius in a review of both works (1835), Schumann railed, in part,[42]

If anyone had hidden the title [page] from me I should have guessed [it was the work of] a composeress, and perhaps have judged thus: Whatever might be your name—Adele, Zuleika—I love you right off, like all who write sonatas! If only you had ended the way you started—for example, in the Spring Sonata, where veritable sweet violets give off their scent on the first page . . . I would never frighten you with words like "tonic," "dominant," or even "counterpoint," for you would laughingly interrupt me and say, "I wrote it just so and cannot do otherwise". . . . Were I your teacher and smart [about it], I would put Bach or Beethoven in your hands often ([but] of Weber, whom you love so much, absolutely nothing), thereby to sharpen your ear and eye, so as to provide a secure foothold for your tender feelings as well as definition and form for your ideas. And then I should know nothing that even the "newest" periodical could say of you that you would not rhyme with "love and beauty."

But at the end of this fanciful paragraph the rude, precipitate Florestan took over to add,

How subtly my Eusebius beats around the bush! Why not [come] right out with it: "The count has a great deal of talent but little training."

---

39. A partial thematic index of Danzi's chamber music, including 4 sons. (and 3 sons. Op. 1 for P & Vn by his wife Margarethe) appears in DTB-m XVI, pp. xxxi–xxxii (H. Riemann). For mod. eds. of 2 sons. for P & Hn-or-Vc, Opp. 28 and 44, cf. Richter/KAMMERMUSIK 187.

40. "Pleasing and fluent" is the burden of 6 mostly short reviews of 6 sons. by Danzi, ranging from moderate to high praise, in AMZ II (1799–1800) 456, VII (1804–5) 505–6, VIII (1805–6) 382–84 (with ex.), XI (1808–9) 192, XII (1809–10) 112, XXI (1819) 204.

41. Cf. MGG X 1363–64 (O. Kaul); Hirschberg/POCCI (mainly an annotated catalogue of his works, plus descriptive comments), especially pp. 43, 46–48, with exx.; Egert/FRÜHROMANTIKER 149–51 (with ex.).

42. Schumann/SCHRIFTEN I 92.

On the basis of this review, quite different from one the year before that dwelt mainly on the "fantastique" in the first sonata,[43] Pocci resolved to attempt no further large works.[44] Both sonatas are in minor, with the finales in relative major. *Sonate fantastique,* in a/C, has four movements, F-M-Mi-F, and *Frühlings-Sonate,* in e/G, has three, F-M-F. Several of the movements aim at arch form through the "m-n-o-n-m" mirror design of their component ideas. Along with harmonic and melodic flashes of interest, and some resourceful piano writing there are, indeed, many vapid and sophomoric pages in Pocci's sonatas.

Probably the most important violinist in south Germany, **Thomas Täglichsbeck** (1799–1867) trained and served in Munich from 1816 to 1827 and served about 125 miles west in Hechingen until 1848, apart from wide concert tours.[45] Not until 1841, while at the latter post, nor until considerable lighter music had appeared from his pen, did Täglichsbeck publish the first, Op. 16 in a,[46] of at least four sonatas for his instrument with piano. This four-movement work was reviewed from a reprint in 1846 as showing solid training but no originality; as going through the motions of the sonata without imparting life, imagination, or fantasy; as concentrating on single motives to the point of exhaustion; and as being not too difficult but not especially grateful for the two instruments.[47] A set of three further sonatas for P & Vn, Op. 30, listed as "progressive . . . preparatory studies for the Beethoven [P & Vn sons.]," appeared in 1859.[48]

In Mannheim, **Gottfried Weber** (1779–1839), remembered today chiefly as a theorist and writer (whose own occasional son. reviews are cited elsewhere in ssb), was also a conductor, composer, and, like Danzi, important mentor and friend, though no relative, of Carl Maria von Weber.[49] About 1810 Simrock published his only known sonata, a solo piano work in C, in two movements (F-In/VF), dedicated to the eight-year younger Carl Maria. In a short witty letter of June 18, 1811, Nikolaus Simrock told Gottfried his sonata "sleeps safe and sound" because "it is too lofty and, seriously, too difficult for dilettantes"; only a very favorable review could save it.[50] Such a review did follow in 1812, by Carl Maria von Weber himself, praising especially the second movement and finding the writing highly efficient in

---

43. AMZ XXXVI (1834) 752.
44. Hirschberg/POCCI 48.
45. Cf. MGG XIII 45–46 (F. Göthel), with further references.
46. Cf. Altmann/KAMMERMUSIK 229.
47. NZM XXV (1846) 127–28 (F. Brendel?), with exx.
48. HOFMEISTER V (1852–59) 65, Altmann/KAMMERMUSIK 229.
49. Cf. GROVE IX 224 (L. Middleton).
50. Altmann/WEBER 491.

its richness, although suggestive more of a quartet transcription, with little opportunity for the pianist to show off except through the (mainly contrapuntal?) meaning itself.[51] Perhaps both the praise and the reservation prompted Simrock to add an optional violin part (for the dilettante?) in what seems to have been only a further edition of this same work.[52] At any rate, the work does reveal the depth and skill, yet not the sterility, that might be expected of a theorist who also composed.

The brilliant pianist **Johann Peter Pixis** (1788–1874) spent his early years in Mannheim and his later years in Baden-Baden.[53] In between, he studied with Albrechtsberger and got to know both Beethoven and Schubert in Vienna,[54] before spending several years in France, England, and Italy. Both Liszt and Schumann found qualities to admire in him.[55] Yet the lexicographer Schilling, comparing his flashy performance with that of Henri Herz, considered him one step short of charlatanism.[56] Crowd-catching display is certainly a conspicuous trait of the one sonata by Pixis that could be examined here, Op. 14 in three movements (F-M-Ro), for piano with "Violon obligé." But pianistic fluency, good craftsmanship, and attractive melodies are among its traits, too.[57] Out of over 150 works by Pixis still listed in PAZDÍREK XXII 392–94, five are solo or ensemble sonatas. As many more were originally published in the same period, from about 1812 to 1832, the last of which, Op. 85 for piano solo, is dedicated to Cramer.[58]

In Switzerland, an unusual composer was the now obscure pianist, teacher, and conductor **Antoine Liste** (1772–1832), who came from Hildesheim in central Germany to study with Albrechtsberger in Vienna, eventually settling, from 1804 on, in Zürich.[59] Among a rela-

---

51. AMZ XIV (1812) 179–80, with ex.; also in Weber/WEBER III 52–53 and Kaiser/WEBER 186–88. In Kaiser/WEBER 530 is also a witty 3-voice canon, dated 1810, presumably addressed by Carl Maria to Gottfried, with the title, "When Weber wrote me that I should play his new sonata in the evening," followed by a text that begins, "I ought to play the sonata, what unspeakable terror! Ah, I tremble like a stone!"; cf. Benedict/WEBER 163.

52. Listed in HOFMEISTER 1828 (Whistling), 512.

53. Cf. MGG X 1317–19 (R. Sietz).

54. According to MGG X 1317. Cf. Schindler & MacArdle/BEETHOVEN 441–42; Deutsch/SCHUBERT-I 302–3.

55. According to MGG X 1318. Cf. Schumann/SCHRIFTEN II 221–22.

56. Schilling/LEXICON V 477.

57. These virtues (except for specifics singled out in the part-writing), plus considerable warmth and depth, are credited to Pixis's 4-mvt. solo P Son. in E♭, Op. 3 (same as Op. 2?) in a long review in AMZ XIV (not XII; 1812) 526–30.

58. Cf. HOFMEISTER (Whistling), 1815, 372; 1828, 500; HOFMEISTER (1829–33) 132.

59. MGG VIII 961–62 (H. P. Schanzlin), with further references; also, Schilling/LEXICON IV 413–14. No confirmation of study with Mozart or solo P sons. Opp. 1 and 12 by Liste (all in Fétis/BU V 317–18) could be found here. A full study of the man and his music should be of value.

tively few works presently known by him are seven sonatas, all published between 1804 and 1815 (with six getting reviews in AMZ as listed below):

2 Sonatas, in E♭ and G, P solo, in Anth. NÄGELI-m Suite 9, (1804). Cf. AMZ VII (1804–5) 284–89, with exx.

"Grande Sonate" in B♭, Op. 2, P-duet, Breitkopf & Härtel, *ca.* 1810. Cf. AMZ XIII (1811) 210–12.

"Grande Sonate" in A, P solo, in Anth. NÄGELI-m Suite 17, (1810); ded. to Beethoven. Cf. AMZ XIII (1811) 210–13.

"Grande Sonate" in ?, Op. 3, P & Bn-or-Vc, Breitkopf & Härtel, *ca.* 1811.

"Sonate" in A, Op. 8, P solo, Breitkopf & Härtel, 1814 or 1815. Cf. AMZ XVII (1815) 836–37.

"Sonate" in E♭, Op. 6, P solo, Breitkopf & Härtel, 1815 at latest. Cf. AMZ XVIII (1816) 96.

Not only Nägeli's proximity in Zürich but his special tastes in the sonata (SCE 26; SSB IV) must help to explain his publication of three of Liste's solo sonatas. For in spite of the better foundation these exhibit, they prove to be as uneven, unpredictable, and spotty as those by Pocci (*supra*). Of most interest both musically and stylistically are such newly Romantic traits as harmonic progressions and modulations that rival Schubert's in boldness and surprise; wide-spaced scoring, sometimes on three contrapuntal planes (which already suffer for want of scoring on three staffs such as F. Pollini first employed, in 1820; cf. SCE 298); naively charming melodies that achieve wide spans through reiterations of short segments; copious dynamics and expressive inscriptions; and some inventive passagework. Our facsimile of a page from Nägeli's enterprise, Ex. 25, illustrates several of these traits as well as a discard of barlines, in a slow introduction by Liste; the double-barline at the end merely precedes an immediate return to A through its secondary dominant, followed by the second half of this introduction. The "Minuetto molto allegro" that is the penultimate movement (iii) in this sonata resembles Carl Maria von Weber's "Invitation to the Dance" rather than a traditional minuet.

Unfortunately, these traits in Liste's music do not offset sufficiently the aimlessness and lack of tonal or thematic unity in the over-all structures; nor the frequent dullness of the left-hand accompaniments, with their routine chordal figures and repeated notes. The first of several rather long and typically wordy reviews (by Rochlitz?) of Liste's sonatas evinces an eagerness to approve and understand the novelty,

Ex. 25. From the opening of Antoine Liste's first Sonata in A (facs. of p. 2 in "Suite" [vol.] 17 of Anth NÄGELI-m at the Library of Congress).

along with a desire to instruct the novice composer in the correction of specific "errors." Some of these errors could have been made by the engraver, for engraver's errors abound in Anth. NÄGELI (as, presumably, near the end of the foregoing example). The subsequent reviews recall and try not to contradict the first review but show increasing discomfort over that formlessness and rambling of the sonatas.

The notable Swiss composer and intellectual **Franz Xaver Schnyder von Wartensee** (1786–1868) should at least be mentioned here, too, although he left little in our field—two early piano sonatas, in C (1814; pub. by Simrock in Bonn) and f (1814–15; not pub.), and, after he moved to Frankfurt/M in 1817, a single sonata for P & Vn (1825; not pub.).[60] The long "Andante" from the first of these may reflect the formalistic influence of Schnyder von Wartensee's friend Nägeli and the Classic influence of his stay in Vienna (1811–12, including acquaintance with Beethoven, Czerny, and Moscheles). It commands

60. Cf. MGG XI 1922–26 (P. O. Schneider), with further bibliography. Mod. ed. of "Andante" from Son. in C for P: Frey & Schuh/SCHWEIZER-m 20.

respect for his sure control of his materials, including intricate metric relationships. The ideas lack distinction.

Weber in Central Germany

Carl Maria von Weber (1786–1826) occupies a special and important historical niche not only as the founder of Romantic German opera but, in our smaller arena, as a significant pioneer of the Romantic piano sonata. If the contributions are not quite analogous and his contribution to the sonata is not, even relatively, quite so outstanding, it is chiefly because his sonatas betray more of the shortcomings of inadequate, largely self-directed training. Furthermore, his sonatas derived more from his operatic and orchestral interests than his operas derived from his pianistic interests, and they faced more competition from contemporary works in their class, including sonatas by Schubert, Hummel, and Dussek, insofar as these sonatas also pioneered Romantic trends. Yet no less an authority than Adolf Bernhard Marx judged in 1824 that Weber's piano compositions, meaning primarily his sonatas, are "next to Beethoven's unquestionably the most important and valuable of the whole newer period, often even surpassing those in grandeur and make-up." [61] Granting that we no longer can accept that dictum, we still have to recognize the genius that could invent such fresh melodies and exploit so imaginatively the sonorities and techniques of the piano that in spite of those undeniable shortcomings at least two of his sonatas continue to attract performers.

The student looking into Weber's music will find all the precise biographic and bibliographic information he is likely to need and much more in two exhaustive, careful, fascinating labors-of-love from the third quarter of the 19th century. Only a few recent corrections or clarifications would have to be added.[62] One of these sources is the three-volume account of his father's life and cultural environment by Max Maria von Weber (1864–66), with extensive incorporation of letters, writings for publication, diaries running from 1810 to death, reviews of his own works, and other autobiographic or contemporary documents.[63] The other, leaning heavily on Max's biography and other

---

61. As quoted in Jähns/WEBER 8. Cf. similar praise by A. Marmontel in 1881, as quoted in Georgii/WEBER 20.

62. Dünnebeil/WEBER is a recent Weber bibliography.

63. Weber/WEBER (unindexed, but cross references occur regularly in Jähns/WEBER, q.v., pp. 9–10). Benedict/WEBER and P. Spitta's original article on Weber, cut considerably in GROVE (5th ed.) VII 195–222, summarize the essentials of Weber/WEBER efficiently, adding a few corrections and extensive independent evaluations. Kaiser/WEBER is a more complete collection of the writings. Among the many

materials made available, is—to translate the long, explicit title—"Carl
Maria von Weber in his Works: Chronological-Thematic Index of His
Collected Compositions Plus an Account of [Those That Are] Incomplete, Lost, Doubtful, and Spurious; With Descriptions of the
Autographs, Indications of the Editions and Arrangements, Critical,
Art-Historical, and Biographic Annotations, Utilizing Weber's Letters
and Diaries, and a Supplement of facsimiles of His Handwriting," by
the vocal pedagogue, composer, and Weber devotee Friedrich Wilhelm
Jähns (1871).[64] In short, this last is an elaborate (and acknowledged)
imitation of Köchel's chronological Mozart index of 1862, augmented
by extended analyses and evaluations of the music.

Weber lived out his relatively short life of not quite forty years so
hectically, so peripatetically, so diversely that it is not easy to find
stable points of reference against which to view his sonatas.[65] His hectic
existence related partly to social behavior that ranged from the giddy
brink of utter moral dissolution, especially while he was enmeshed in
Duke Ludwig's intrigues at Stuttgart, to the comparative peace of
deeply religious convictions, especially in his last years. His peripatetic
existence resulted primarily from the life in the theater, going back to
earliest childhood, and from numerous concert tours as a virtuoso
pianist. It included, among many, more fleeting visits, at least short
residences in Salzburg from 1796 to 1798 and 1801–2 (with brief study
under Michael Haydn), and in Vienna from 1803 to 1804 (with the
Abbé Vogler [SCE 573–75] first exercising his lasting influence on
Weber). Then followed a series of increasingly important posts, all
disturbed in varying degrees by professional frictions and dissatisfactions. These started with Breslau from 1804 to 1806, after which came
Stuttgart from 1807 to 1810, Prague from 1813 to 1816, and finally,
Dresden from 1816, or just before his marriage with Caroline Brandt,
which did bring him unprecedented content and happiness, though
but little abatement in the countless travels. The diversity of Weber's
existence resulted largely from his own versatility. To the excellence
of this appealing, debonair, resourceful artist as composer and pianist
must be added his front rank as a conductor and as an opera director,
also his substantial contributions as a writer on music (including re-

publications that continue to appear on Weber, Saunders/WEBER (1940) remains
the most satisfactory one-vol. survey in English on his life and works. But cf. ML
XLIX (1968) 233–37 (E. Croft-Murray) on Warrack/WEBER (pub. too late to be
incorporated here).

    64. Jähns/WEBER, in which cf. pp. 9–14.
    65. His own autobiographic sketch (printed in Weber/WEBER III [a complete
vol. of his writings], pp. 175–80 and Kaiser/WEBER 3–8) helps to determine the
turning points up to 1818.

views of sons. by G. Weber and Lauska cited in ssв VIII). Less pertinent
here were still other sides of his versatility, such as his belletristic activities outside the realm of music, or his early exploits in painting,
music engraving, and singing (until the accident that damaged his
voice in 1806).

Originating intermittently from his 13th to his 36th year (1799–
1822), at least 14 sonatas—7 solo, one P-duet, and 6 P & Vn—were
composed by Weber.[66] This total, minute and incidental as it was in
terms of his over-all output, includes the four main piano solo sonatas,
written in the decade from 1812 to 1822, that still figure among his
comparatively few works kept alive today. It does not include the still
popular *Grand duo concertant* in E♭, Op. 48, for piano and clarinet
(J. 204), which Weber himself referred to as a "Sonate" in his diary
references to its composition.[67] But it does include an early lost set of
"Drei Sonaten für's Fortepiano" (J. Anh. 16–18 or 20–22). Apparently
Weber listed the set twice, under 1799, in his own published "Werk-
Verzeichniss," [68] perhaps because he submitted it for publication once
in 1800 to Artaria[69] and again, in 1801 to André (both times in vain).
No later record of these boyhood works exists, but they must have been
written with some degree of skill, imagination, and understanding, to
judge by his *Sechs Fugetten* (J. 1–6) already published as Op. 1 in 1798
(with M. Haydn's help?) or, more pertinently, by his Variations Op. 2
of 1800 (J. 7).[70] Op. 2 reveals not only the neat Classic passagework in
scales and arpeggios to be expected of the young man who knew both
Haydns and was a first cousin to the late Mozart. It also reveals the
fast passages in octaves, wide leaps, and 10th-chords that clearly herald
the virtuoso.

Weber's four-hand Sonatina in C Op. 3/1 (J. 9) is another early

66. No explanation could be found here for Weber's single mention, in a letter to
J. Gänsbacher of Dec. 17, 1816 (Nohl/GLUCK & WEBER 210), of having written "up
to now . . . a new sonata in D♭"; no other source discovered here mentions such
a work.

67. Cf. Jähns/WEBER 217, 133; AMZ XX (1818) 442–43 (favorable review by Rochlitz); MT XX (1879) 605 (performance under the title "Sonata").

68. At least, Jähns/WEBER 427–28 seems to give 2 sets of nos. to a single set of
sons. For the "Werk-Verzeichniss," cf. p. 15, item 7; also, Heyer/HISTORICAL 346.

69. Cf. Nohl/GLUCK & WEBER 86–87; Saunders/WEBER 16–17.

70. Facs. of Op. 1 engraved in open score and 4 clefs by Weber himself: Hauss-
wald/WEBER 56–60 (but this is not a first mod. ed., as indicated on pp. 312 and
314; e.g., Op. 1 appears in condensed P score in Augener Ed. 8470, p. 184). Although H. J. Moser's abortive "Gesamtausgabe" of 1926–28 did not get to any
instrumental works, the 2-vol. pub. under H. W. Stolze's editorship in 1857 had
got far enough to include all the extant sons. (cf. Heyer/HISTORICAL 346–47 [with
errors]). Today these are all still readily available in several eds., including Peters
Ed. 188A, 191, and 717A.

work, probably composed in 1801 and first published in 1803.[71] Dedicated to J. P. Schulthesius (sce 302), it is a gracefully melodious, unpretentious piece in one movement of 61 measures, the first of "Six petites Pièces Faciles." [72] Nine years later Weber wrote a whole set of sonatas with pedagogic intentions, this time *Six Sonates progressives pour le pianoforte avec violon obligé*, Op. 10 (also pub. as Op. 13 and Op. 17; J. 99–104).[73] "Dediées aux amateurs," these sonatas are also melodious, fluent, and unpretentious. Their keys do not exceed three sharps or flats, d being the sole minor key. With an average length of only about 250 measures, half of the sonatas have two moderate or quick movements and half add a middle, slow movement. The violin is an independent though not an equal partner in the duo. Obviously Weber knew his market. Instead of risking the sort of fantasy and display that were to characterize the four solo sonatas, he appealed to amateurs with light rondo finales (Sons. 1–4), with a "Tema dell' opera Silvana," and with five movements brightened by nationalistic colors —"Carattere espagnuolo," "Air polonais," "Air russe," "Siciliano," and "Polacca." As he wrote his mentor Gottfried Weber in Darmstadt, the set "cost me more sweat than as many symphonies." [74] Yet André rejected Op. 10 in 1810 (leaving it for Simrock to publish in 1811), on the curious grounds that the pieces "are too good"! [75] Perhaps André's further objections led to the revisions and enrichments made by Moscheles, including a considerable transfer of melodic responsibility to the violin.[76] Unfortunately, delightful as this music is, it still does not offer the violinist enough, as it is published today, to interest him in playing it.

Weber's Four Big Piano Sonatas

The circumstances surrounding each of Weber's four main solo sonatas should be noted before the nature of their music is considered

71. Jähns/WEBER 45–47.
72. "Good in melody, fluent, and correct," wrote Rochlitz of the set, in AMZ VI (1803–4) 252. Weber's Op. 60 for P-duet (1818–19) consists of 8 separate, unrelated character pieces that have been mislabeled "Sonatinas" posthumously (cf. Jähns/WEBER 251–52).
73. Mod. ed. of Czerny's transcription of No. 6 as a P-duet: Zeitlin & Goldberger/DUETS-m 42. The review in AMZ XVII (1815) 609 treats Op. 10 purely as a pedagogic collection.
74. Jähns/WEBER 121.
75. Jähns/WEBER 121–22; Nohl/GLUCK & WEBER 102–3 (with further details).
76. Jähns/WEBER 122. Cf., also, Cobbett/CHAMBER II 570 (W. Altmann and W. W. Cobbett).

here.[77] All four sonatas were first published by Schlesinger in Berlin soon after the completion of each. Jähns could find a complete autograph only for the last one, a partial, early draft for the third, and no autograph for either the first or second. The first "Grosse Sonate" (as each was called in print), Op. 24 in C (J. 138), was composed in Berlin and first published in 1812. Weber finished the popular "Rondo" finale before the other movements, naming it "L'Infatigable," although Charles Alkan's title for it, "Perpetuum mobile," has since been preferred.[78] In some amusing letters Weber tells of practicing the "Rondo" not in C but in C♯ in order to revive "rusty" fingers, and of wanting to agree only too readily when the dedicatee despaired of ever learning this sonata, except that one hardly reacted so to the Grand Duchess Maria Paulowna of Weimar.[79] Czerny, Brahms (*Studien* No. 2), and Tchaikovsky (Ju. 92) were among those who made special arrangements of the "Rondo." [80] Gottfried Weber opened a three-column review of Op. 24 by citing its most distinctive trait as "a wealth of ideas and harmonic richness." [81] He called it a work that would delight the connoisseurs, with both aesthetic and pianistic challenges, a full melodically active texture, and a tight unity except in the second movement, which goes too long without a return of its initial idea.

Weber's second and third sonatas—Op. 39 in A♭ (J. 199), dedicated to Lauska, and Op. 49 in d/D (J. 206), without dedication—were written close together, Op. 39 alternately in Prague and Berlin in early 1814 and in 1816, and Op. 49 in Berlin in late 1816 (in but 20 days). A first performance of each by Weber followed quickly, in 1816 for Op. 39 and 1817 for Op. 49. Rochlitz, whom Weber first met in 1811 and had already known well through correspondence,[82] wrote a long and particularly glowing review covering both sonatas.[83] Before describing

77. A detailed up-to-date study of Weber's sons. is lacking. Nearest to it is still the section pp. 16–27, in the 1914 diss. Georgii/WEBER; 2 other, unpub. diss. of 1914 (Schaal/DISSERTATIONEN items 268 and 2335) include Weber's sons, but have not been available here and are not listed in Dünnebeil/WEBER nor Egert/FRÜH-ROMANTIKER 92–101. This last, as well as Selva/SONATE 172–84, Hall/PIANOFORTE 183–93, and Dale/NINETEENTH 43–53 provide 4 of the chief, more recent summaries of Weber's P sons. Saunders/WEBER 223–25 goes widest of the mark, as viewed here, in the much needed re-evaluation of these sons.
78. Jähns/WEBER 160–61.
79. Weber/WEBER I 359, 361, 372, 377, 382, 384.
80. Czerny's arrangement (cf. Egert/FRÜHROMANTIKER 101) could not be confirmed here.
81. AMZ XV (1813) 595–98. A favorable review of Op. 24 when Moscheles played it in London in 1837 appears in MUSICAL WORLD IV (1836–37) 156.
82. Weber/WEBER I 313. Regarding "modernizations" that both Liszt and Henselt made in Op. 39, cf. SSB V, with ex.
83. AMZ XX (1818) 681–88.

these very different works separately, he noted certain virtues they shared in common. Thus, he rated them among the finest sonatas of the day in their thorough and meaningful exploitation of single ideas, whether through harmonic, figural, or pianistic varianta. He found the works extraordinarily difficult to play at times, but never without justification, being somewhat like Spohr's for the violin in this respect.[84] His most unqualified praise of individual movements went to the "Menuetto capriccio" ("assuredly!" he adds) of Op. 39 and the "Rondo presto" of Op. 49. The latter became known under the title "Allegro di bravura," given to it in what Jähns called "one of the most monstrous" arrangements in the pianist's world, by Czerny.[85] Overjoyed with Rochlitz's review, Weber replied with a letter to him that, understandably, emphasizes the fine perception of the reviewer and the ideal mating of review and composition.[86] In the infrequent performances of Weber's sonatas today Op. 39 is heard most frequently in public, although only Opp. 49 and 70 happen to be available in commercial recordings, the latter with three choices (as of 1967). In the 19th century the performances discovered here show that Op. 49 was in the lead, with Op. 39, then Op. 24, not far behind, and Op. 70 decidedly in the minority.[87] Jähns saw Op. 24 relating to Op. 39 somewhat as *Der Freischütz* to *Euryanthe,* the first opening the door to Romanticism and the second presenting it in full bloom. The last of the four sonatas, Op. 70 in e (J. 287), was composed in the three years from 1819 to 1822, mostly in Dresden and right in the same highly productive period as "Invitation to the Dance" (J. 260), *Der Freischütz* (J. 277), and *Concert-Stück* in f (J. 282). Although dedicated to Rochlitz and published promptly, it received no special reviews or other attention.

To get to the music of Weber's four big solo sonatas, we might first note their average length of 945 measures, or about nine per cent more than in Schubert's completed sonatas. But their average playing time is probably no greater than for Schubert's sonatas, because proportionately more of Weber's movements are fast or faster. Jähns observes that Weber's four "grosse" sonatas constitute his biggest in-

84. In his *Practical Pianoforte School* Charles Hallé put Op. 49/ii and iii in the "very difficult class" (MT XVI [1874] 701).
85. Jähns/WEBER 220.
86. Quoted in full in Jähns/WEBER 214.
87. E.g., cf. AMA No. 22 (Nov. 25, 1826) 169; RGM for Feb. 11, 1838; MT XII (1866) 448 (with Op. 39 called a "somewhat wild . . . composition"), XIII (1868) 446 and 580, XVI (1873) 361, XVII (1876) 500 and 708, XVIII (1877) 245, 277, and 553, XX (1879) 332 and 646, XXI (1880) 87, 173, 303, 306, and 355, XXII (1881) 138–39, XXIII (1882) 668, XXIV (1884) 135 (on neglect of Weber's sons.), etc.; Dent/BUSONI 331.

strumental works, totaling almost as many measures as all of *Euryanthe*.[88] Three of these sonatas are in four movements in typical cycles of F-S-Mi-Ro (Op. 24), F-M-Mi-Ro (Op. 39), or F-Mi-M-VF (Op. 70). Op. 49 is the exception in omitting the minuet. The sonatas are equally divided between major and minor keys. Although change of mode is frequent, including the change to the tonic major throughout the finale of Op. 49, only the moderate or slow movement is in a foreign key and then always a nearly related key. Except for the incipits of Op. 70/i, ii, and perhaps iv, Weber seems not to have tried to unify the cycles through similar thematic materials.[89]

Three of Weber's rondo finales received or acquired titles—"L'Infatigable" or "Perpetuum mobile" in Op. 24 and "Allegro bravura" in Op. 49 (as noted above), and "La Tarantella" in Op. 70—but he supplied no programmes in the four sonatas.[90] Yet, according to his biographer Julius Benedict, who had been his pupil, protégé, and close friend during the last five years, when Weber wrote Op. 70 he had in mind a sad story of gradual mental deterioration, letting up only in the third movement and leading ultimately to "exhaustion and death."[91] Jähns hears Op. 49 as being dominated much of the time by a demonic spirit, and, indeed, it has been dubbed "Demoniac." However, Weber's piano music actually belies such gloom and terror. The same genial temperament that preferred happy endings in *Der Freischütz* and *Euryanthe* also preferred not to dwell too far or long from major keys, pleasant melodies, and gay dance rhythms.

Weber's detailed diaries reveal that he wrote his final movements first, and the initial and slowest movements last.[92] In other words, he seems to have found it easiest to write the fast, light, dancelike movements—the minuets, which are scherzos in all but the name,[93] and the rondos, which all come close to being perpetual-motion finales. And right from the start of the four sonatas, these are unquestionably the most successful movements, the most resourceful in their composition techniques (Ex. 26), yet the freest from intrinsic problems of style and form. The other movements have problems not because they introduce new designs or indulge in excessive fantasy. Actually, Weber seems to have accepted traditional designs without question; when he produced

88. Jähns/WEBER 160; but his total of 4486 mss., or 64 less than in *Euryanthe*, includes all repetitions as well as da capo sections (cf. SSB Preface).

89. Contrary to the statement and exx. in Kroll/WEBER 71–73.

90. He did supply a literal romancer's sort of programme for *Concert-Stück* in f, as quoted in Weber/WEBER II 311–12.

91. Benedict/WEBER 155.

92. Jähns/WEBER 161, 214, 220, and 346; Egert/FRÜHROMANTIKER 94–96.

93. Weber actually referred to Op. 70/ii as "Scherzo" in his diary (Jähns/WEBER 346).

Ex. 26. From the "Minuetto" of Carl Maria von Weber's
Sonata in C, Op. 24 (after Augener's Ed., No. 8470, p. 14).

some tonal or thematic variant that now appears irregular for its day—
like starting the recapitulation in the lowered mediant in Op. 24/i/98,
or returning to only the first phrase and varying it three times in Op.
24/ii/65–84—this variant was as likely to be accidental as intentional.
"Sonata form" approximately like that described soon after in textbooks (ssb II) can be charted readily enough in each of the first movements, and A-B-A or a sort of variation-rondo design in each of the
slowest movements. But the problem within these designs remains that
of any musical form created in the language that was then current—
that is, how best to treat and integrate particular ideas in a particular
time span.

Thus, Op. 24/i fails, as viewed here, because it is not dynamic
enough to sustain interest throughout its 161 measures. Its charming
but naively square-cut thematic units (Ex. 27) and its apparently unpremeditated tonal course occur statically, without effective integration
or compelling direction. To be sure, the proclamatory, descending
arpeggio that opens the sonata recurs just before and during the
development section and, though not at the recapitulation, again in
the coda. But a plain arpeggio, much less one on the ambiguous dim.-
7th chord, lacks sufficient identity to unify the movement. If Beethoven
really did make that remark about *Euryanthe,* that it is "an accumulation of diminished-7th chords, [all serving as] mere escapes," [94] he
could as well have been speaking of the four sonatas, especially this
first movement. The latter happens to show, of course, that back in
1812 Weber had been less touched by Beethoven's methods and struc-

94. Ascribed to Schindler by G. Kaiser, as noted, with doubts, in Kroll/
BEETHOVEN 138–39.

Ex. 27. From the first movement of Carl Maria von Weber's
Sonata in C, Op. 24 (after Augener's Ed., No. 8470, p. 4).

tures in the sonata than any other important young Romantic we shall
meet here. In fact, from the standpoint of Weber's style innovations,
the early friction created between the two men by his juvenile, in-
temperate disparagement of Beethoven's third and fourth symphonies,
published in 1809,[95] could be viewed as a blessing in disguise. But at
the time of *Euryanthe* (1823) Weber was on the best of terms with the
Viennese master.[96] It is only a pity that Beethoven, who sent both his
last piano sonata, Op. 111, and his "Diabelli Variations" to Weber in
Dresden in the summer of 1823, made no comments that have been
preserved on Weber's later sonatas, which he may well have known.
The better documented objections to a lack of melody and structural
organization in *Euryanthe* that come from Schubert, who also seems to
have been on fine personal terms with Weber, must be attributed at
least in part to the German and Italian opera factions then competing
in Vienna.[97]

   Op. 24/ii fails somewhat, as viewed here, not so much because its

95. Cf. Kroll/BEETHOVEN 126–29; also, Schindler & MacArdle/BEETHOVEN 479–83.
   96. Cf. Thayer & Forbes/BEETHOVEN II 863, 871–74. Benedict/WEBER 62 describes
his fine spirited playing of Beethoven's sons. in 1821.
   97. Cf. Jähns/WEBER 368; Deutsch/SCHUBERT-D 294–95, 301, 310, 892.

ideas again fall into square-cut, static units—such units were the norm, then, in slower movements—but because, as Gottfried Weber implied (*supra*), the form straggles. The B section in the ostensible (and intended?) A-B-A' design subdivides into two sections (18+29 mss.), each. long and distinct enough to rank on a par with the A or A' sections (24+25 mss.), so that the total effect is rather the much more additive one of A-B-C-A. Such an extended form is more likely to succeed if it has a recurring, unifying motive, as in Op. 70/iii (a variation-rondo), or if it has a text, as in Agathe's totally additive but cumulative aria "Leise, leise" *(Der Freischütz/ii)*. The aria makes an interesting analogy, for Weber's melodic line in Op. 24/ii, especially in the B section, flows along for all the world like that in one of his more emotional opera arias. One almost feels the lack of a text. Unfortunately, one is helped to feel the lack of a recurring motive, too, by the routine, even stodgy bass-chord accompaniment, which certainly stands out as the most prevalent yet least attractive trait in Weber's piano scoring.

This much mention of problems in Weber's first and slowest movements needs to be countered now with the contention that his four big solo sonatas—again, as viewed here—progress steadily and conspicuously, from one to the next, in the solution of these problems and in greater skill in handling others. Whereas Op. 24 as a whole hardly passes muster in public recital today, Op. 70 is a completely satisfying masterpiece. In other words, the preference we noted in today's record catalogues is endorsed here, although pianists would be well advised and rewarded if they were to atone much more than they have for the apparent neglect of Op. 70 in the 19th century. Certain changes become especially clear when the four sonatas are read consecutively. The texture becomes thinner and more efficient (giving way to but a single line at the start of Op. 70), yet provides greatly increased interest in the left hand. The melodic unity becomes much tighter, being bound more by significant motives than full-fledged themes. The rhythm becomes more supple, as reflected in more irregular phrases in the first movements and in modifications that relieve the squareness of regular phrases in the other movements. The harmonic progressions and the tonal schemes become more purposeful and varied, and more necessary to the direction of the phrases and to the form itself. And, finally, the piano writing becomes if not less demanding then considerably more reasonable, functional, and resourceful, with most of the impractical leaps and stretches discarded (Ex. 28).

It is in all these respects that Op. 70 stands as an unalloyed masterpiece. But, of course, it is in those respects, too, that many a strong

Ex. 28. From the first movement of Carl Maria von Weber's
Sonata in e, Op. 70 (after Augener's Ed., No. 8470, p. 74).

composer has developed and matured—for example, Clementi or
Dussek, to take near contemporaries of Weber. In short, we are brought
back to the view that the striking innovations of style in Weber's Op.
24 were largely the products of inexperience, or at least of efforts to
apply structural principles and keyboard techniques that proved more
and more to be inimical to the sonata. Certainly, some of the most
characteristic writing of the first two sonatas has disappeared entirely
by the last sonata. For example, along with the early problem traits
mentioned above, one thinks of Weber's characteristic groupings by
twos, both in lines descending stepwise (e.g., Op. 39/i/20) and in
appoggiaturas on inverted triads (Ex. 26, *supra*). In 1875, W. H. Riehl
must have been thinking mainly of Opp. 24 and 39 when he cited
Weber's four "grosse . . . Virtuosensonaten, [or] Concertsonaten" as
being so called because "the instrument and its effects control the
ideas and form," whereas the difficulties in Beethoven's "grosse"
sonatas are always made to serve the form and ideas.[98] In this connection we are brought back, also, to that fantasy element so generally
—in fact, too emphatically—ascribed to Weber's sonatas, as in Spitta's
inversion of Beethoven's title (Op. 27/1 and 2) almost to read "Fantasia

98. Riehl/CHARAKTERKÖPFE II 270.

quasi una Sonata." [99] This fantasy exists in a positive sense not in the
inadvertent looseness of Weber's earlier sonata forms nor in any
deliberate freedoms in any of his sonatas. Rather, to the extent that
the term applies at all, the fantasy must be found in the florid abandon
of some of his melodic lines that suggest arias (as cited above); in
orchestral effects like the chordal melody spread over a tremolo bass at
the start of Op. 39 (recalling portions of the glen scene in *Der Freischütz*); in whimsicalities such as can be found in the delicious
"Menuetto capriccio" of the same work (including perilously close
anticipations of "Invitation to the Dance"); and in occasional brooding
in the harmony, as during the retransition of Op. 70/i (mss. 114–132,
partly quoted, for its dim.-7th harmony, in ssʙ VI).

Schumann in Central Germany: Littérateur and Musician

Robert Schumann (1810–56), the very epitome of musical Romanticism, is one of the four 19th-century composers—along with Schubert, Chopin, and Brahms—around whose sonatas our discussion of
Romantic style and form centered in Chapter VI. Hence, at this point
it is mainly the background, circumstances, and historical orientation
of his sonatas that concern us. Schumann is also—along with Mendelssohn, Chopin, Liszt, and Wagner—one of five leading Romantics
born close in time (1809–13) who devoted something less than their
chief or most characteristic efforts to the sonata. Thus, Schumann's
total of at least 15 complete or incomplete works originally or ultimately called sonatas (but not including his late arrangements of
Bach's unaccompanied violin sons. and cello suites), constitutes scarcely
8 per cent of the cycles, sets, and other main items in his total output.
Of these sonatas, the 6 completed solos called "sonata" constitute less
than 10 per cent of his total keyboard output. Furthermore, as discussed presently, these sonatas have commonly been regarded as falling
short of his most representative and successful music.[100]

Whether from a creative, philosophic, or domestic standpoint, the
main dividing line in Schumann's short, productive, emotionally turbulent life of forty-six years was the year 1840.[101] Prior to that year,
starting with his move in 1828 from his birthplace of Zwickau to
Leipzig, the main events had been his surrender to the lures of music

99. GROVE IX 217.
100. E.g., cf. Shedlock/SONATA 207–9; Bie/PIANOFORTE 241–42, 243, 254; Georgii/
KLAVIERMUSIK 323–25; Dale/SCHUMANN 46–47; MGG XII 303 (E. A. Lippman).
101. Up-to-date, efficient summaries of his life, views, and output appear both
in GROVE VII 600–640 (G. Abraham) and MGG XII 272–325 (E. A. Lippman).

and literature after a dutiful but vain try at law school;[102] his auto-didactic progress in these fields, supplemented, on and off up to 1832, by brief, rather disappointing study with Friederich Wieck, then Heinrich Dorn;[103] his shift from a primary goal of virtuoso pianist to that of composer, especially after the permanent injury to his right hand from a misguided practicing venture in mid 1832;[104] his composition of nearly all of his most important piano music (including his three main solo sonatas) and relatively few other works;[105] his founding of the *Neue Zeitschrift für Musik* in 1833 [106] and the large part of his own writing for it; and the five-year courtship of Clara Wieck, with all its frustrations and final culmination in marriage in 1840.[107]

After 1840, in a gradually slowed, less hectic existence, the main events in Schumann's life were his abrupt turn to composing songs, then orchestral, and then chamber music;[108] his fourteen years with Clara, including the growing family, the travels together on her concert tours as far off as the chief Russian centers and Vienna, and the move to Dresden in 1844, followed by the unhappy appointment as musical director at Düsseldorf in 1850;[109] his later outpouring of compositions, now in all directions including opera and other vocal works, more solo piano works (among them the three little sonatas for his daughters, Op. 118), more chamber works (among them the three violin sonatas), and the Bach transcriptions; and, after serious recurring depressions, especially in 1833 and 1844, the final two years of mental collapse starting in 1854.

The literary interests nurtured by his father and his early environment—especially his almost traumatic introduction to the witty, fanciful novels of Jean Paul (Richter) in 1827—figured at least as

---

102. Among significant letters and other contemporary, largely autobiographic evidence, cf. Boetticher/SCHUMANN 245; Storck/SCHUMANN 50–57; Eismann/SCHUMANN I 66–68.

103. Cf. Eismann/SCHUMANN I 62–63, 74–77; Storck/SCHUMANN 64–68, 73–78.

104. Cf. Storck/SCHUMANN 78–79, 128, 195, etc. The exact cause and nature of this injury vary even in the earliest sources. Schumann's own recollection of the date as "about in Oct., 1831" (Eismann/SCHUMANN I 78) does not tally with his letter of Aug. 9, 1832. Niecks/SCHUMANN 102–6 gives a full account of the whole problem.

105. A convenient though incomplete list of other early works appears in Rehberg/SCHUMANN 727. Cf., also, Gertler/SCHUMANN 33–35; Abraham/RESEARCH 70–71; Redlich/SCHUMANN.

106. NZM, first published in 1834. Cf. Storck/SCHUMANN 86–90, 100–101, 119–22; Niecks/SCHUMANN 127–32; and, especially, Plantinga/SCHUMANN 11–34.

107. The first 2 vols. of Litzmann/SCHUMANN are still the main source. Cf., also, Eismann/SCHUMANN I 102–10, 114–24.

108. Cf. Niecks/SCHUMANN 205–9, 216–23; Gertler/SCHUMANN 33, fns. 83 and 84.

109. Chaps. XV–XXI in Niecks/SCHUMANN include essential documents from the decade 1840–50.

much in Schumann's background and youthful aspirations as his more specifically musical interests.[110] In the present study these literary interests matter because they contributed fundamentally to the making of one of the most discerning critics, most representative aestheticians,[111] and most subtle symbolists, if not programmatists, of the Romantic Era. With regard to Schumann as a critic, his reviews of early 19th-century sonatas are quoted and cited often here, the more so as he made a special point of reviewing current piano music,[112] apparently including every sonata that came his way, good or bad. With regard to Schumann as an aesthetician, in Chapters II and III his views were summarized in some detail as they pertained to the sonata's historical contrasts, nationalistic differences, semantic implications, values to the professonal composer, and recent deterioration.

As for Schumann's symbolism and programmatic tendencies, these principles prevailed chiefly before 1840. They touched the piano sonatas much less than the collections of smaller pieces. But, as noted especially under Opp. 11, 17, and 26 below, they did touch them somewhat. How much, is usually debatable, because the piano sonatas offer no symbolic or programmatic associations quite so tangible as those with Jean Paul's novel *Flegeljahre* in Schumann's *Papillons*, Op. 2,[113] or those with the "sphinx"-motive variants of ASCH in his *Carnaval*, Op. 9,[114] or even those with E. T. A. Hoffman's grotesque tales of Kapellmeister Kreisler (*Fantasiestücke in Callot's Manier*) in Schumann's *Kreisleriana*, Op. 16.[115] On the other hand, anyone who recalls

110. Cf. Schumann/JUGENDBRIEFE 9–10, 16–17, 19, etc.; Storck/SCHUMANN 3–15, 20, 44, 128 (where Schumann says he learned more counterpoint from Jean Paul than from his music teacher); Niecks/SCHUMANN 41–45; Jacobs/SCHUMANN; Lippman/SCHUMANN 342–45.

111. Plantinga/SCHUMANN is a new, valuable, detailed study of Schumann's writings in NZM, with emphasis on their critical and aesthetic significance.

112. Cf. his own explicit statement on this policy for NZM, in Storck/SCHUMANN 111; also, Plantinga/SCHUMANN 35–47.

113. Schumann's own table of derivations and parallels for Op. 2 is reproduced in Boetticher/SCHUMANN 611–13, with further information and references. Cf., also, Lippman/SCHUMANN 314–20, 322, 337–38 (in a valuable article on Schumann's application of his own aesthetic views).

114. Cf. Schumann's own mention of the motive in Storck/SCHUMANN 99 and Niecks/SCHUMANN 175–77; also, Dale/SCHUMANN 39–41. Whether Schumann actually developed a much more extensive and subtle "cipher" (concealing CLARA, WIECK, ROBERT, and other related names) than is generally recognized in ASCH, ABEGG (Op. 1), BACH (Op. 60), and GADE (Op. 68/41), is a question that has been debated recently and hotly, especially in MT CVI (1965) 584–91 (E. Sams), 767–71 and 949 (protests, endorsements, and Sams again), CVII (1966) 1050–51 (Sams), CVIII (1967) 131–34 (Sams), and CIX (1968) 25–27 (Sams).

115. But Clara seems to have been hidden in there even more than the Kapellmeister, according to Schumann's own letters (cf. Niecks/SCHUMANN 186–88; also Dale/SCHUMANN 56 and Wörner/SCHUMANN 360).

Schumann's well-known, admittedly Germanic objections to the detailed, literal programme Berlioz prepared for his *Symphonie fantastique* (and to Beethoven's inscriptions in *Sinfonia pastorale*),[116] will not be surprised to discover Schumann declaring in 1838 even about his *Carnaval*,

I need hardly assure you that the putting together of the pieces and the superscriptions came about *after* the composition. . . . For is not music itself always enough and sufficiently expressive? . . . [The titles in *Carnaval* have] no artistic value whatever; the manifold states of the soul alone seem to me of interest.[117]

If Schumann was contradicting somewhat his earlier approach to *Papillons,* his statements were still no single "silly" product of "excessive diffidence," [118] for only six months later he again declared, more generally and in a different context, that the "inscriptions over my pieces always occur to me after I have finished composing the music." [119] In this latter sense there is much less question about Schumann's interest in programme music. As illustrated by numerous reviews cited in the present volume, especially when he was writing as "Eusebius," he did not hesitate to read programmes into completed works, including others', like Beethoven's or Schubert's, as well as his own.[120]

Schumann, Tools and Tabulations

The literature on Schumann is extensive and the sources are still more extensive.[121] But much of what Otto Erich Deutsch and others have done for Mozart and Schubert, or Max Weber and F. W. Jähns for Carl Maria von Weber, by way of pulling all the sources together, has yet to be done and will be a bigger task for Schumann.[122] Most of his own extraordinarily rich writings on music published in his lifetime, especially his articles for the *Neue Zeitschrift*, were first issued in collected form by Schumann himself in 1854, and more recently in

116. Schumann/SCHRIFTEN I 83–85; cf., also, Gertler/SCHUMANN 59–60. A detailed comparison of Schumann and Berlioz in their whole approach to music aesthetics and composition could be very fruitful.
117. From Schumann's letters to Moscheles of Aug. 23 and Sept. 22, 1838, as trans. in Niecks/SCHUMANN 175–76.
118. Rehberg/SCHUMANN 694.
119. Letter to Simonin de Sire of March 15, 1839, as trans. in Storck/SCHUMANN 128. Cf., also, Gertler/SCHUMANN 38–39; Lippman/SCHUMANN 318, 320, 326, 329–30, 332, 335–36.
120. Cf., also, Abraham/SCHUBERT 8–10 (W. Reich).
121. Cf. the selected bibliography in MGG XII 320–25.
122. The status of Schumann research around 1950 is variously summarized in Abraham/RESEARCH, Redlich/SCHUMANN, and Abraham/SCHUMANN v–vi.

1914 in an expanded fifth edition prepared, with excellent prefaces, notes, and indices, by Martin Kreisig.[123] Unfortunately, the two-volume translation into English of much of this material, done by Fanny Raymond Ritter in 1880,[124] and the two recent, smaller collec-tions have proved too unreliable and/or incomplete for use here.[125] Of some 9,000 letters written by and to Schumann, most of them minutely recorded by himself, many have been lost, about 1,000 have been published in various large and small collections, and a smaller number have been translated into English.[126] Of numerous other writings not published by Schumann—diaries, travel records, reports, literary and musical notes—much still remains unpublished.[127] Important steps toward bringing this material to light were taken by Wolfgang Boetticher in his enormous dissertation of 1941 on Schumann's per-sonality and work and his biography of 1942 told through copious letters, writings, and documents, mostly not previously published.[128] Both books are scarce, besides which the dissertation is difficult to use. It lacks an index of works, it suffers from an overrefined organization based on a pompous, rarefied theory of symbolic logic, and it stems from hateful Nazi wartime philosophies, so that every precaution Boetticher observes with each ill-starred *persona non grata* means a precaution to be observed in accepting Boetticher. In English, some of Boetticher's important findings have been digested and incorporated in Gerald Abraham's Schumann *Symposium* of 1952.[129] Recent up-to-date studies of the life and works in German include those by K. H. Wörner and Paula and Walter Rehberg, although the study regarded here as best in English still remains that by Frederick Niecks, published posthumously in 1925.[130] Studies that apply more particularly to Schumann's sonatas are noted further on, where they apply. But the fact can be stated right here that an over-all study of his sonatas is unexpectedly and conspicuously lacking.

The only "complete" edition of Schumann's music is the incom-

123. Schumann/SCHRIFTEN. Cf. Plantinga/SCHUMANN 4–5.
124. Cf. the reviews in MT XVII (1877) 334 and XXI (1880) 621.
125. Cf. JAMS XVIII (1965) 417–19, ML XLVI (1965) 267–68.
126. Cf. Boetticher/SCHUMANN 627–28; MGG XII 321. Schumann/JUGENDBRIEFE, Wasielewski/SCHUMANN, Litzmann/SCHUMANN (with about one-fifth of the letters to Clara), and Storck/SCHUMANN (with errors and omissions) contain much of the correspondence referred to here.
127. Cf. the list in Boetticher/SCHUMANN 623–29.
128. Boetticher/SCHUMANN, Boetticher/SCHRIFTEN. Cf. Abraham/RESEARCH 72–75, Redlich/SCHUMANN, Abraham/SCHUMANN v–vi, Plantinga/SCHUMANN 6–8, Werner/MENDELSSHON 265–66. Eismann/SCHUMANN (1956) is a small, selected assortment of Schumann documents.
129. Abraham/SCHUMANN, including the excellent chap. Dale/SCHUMANN.
130. Wörner/SCHUMANN; Rehberg/SCHUMANN; Niecks/SCHUMANN.

Robert Schumann's Sonatas and Related Works

Op.	Key	Scoring	Composed	First ed.	Dedicatee	Mvts.: tempos or types / Keys: mvt.-by-mvt. / mss.: mvt.-by-mvt.	SCHUMANN/ WERKE-m	Early titles; remarks
11	f♯	P	1833–35	Kistner, 1836	Clara Wieck	4: S/VF-M-Sc -F f♯: -A-f♯ -f♯/F♯ 1145: 419 -45-219-462	VII/ii/11	Pianofortesonate, *Klara zugeeignet von Florestan und Eusebius*; ed. of 1840: "Grande Sonate"; Schumann preferred "1st Sonate"
14	f	P	1835–36	Haslinger, 1836	Ignaz Moscheles	4: F -Sc -Va -VF f: -D♭-f -f/F 982: 249-231-143-359	VII/iii/14	*Concert sans Orchestre* (with no scherzo); 1853 ed. (revised, with scherzo): "Troisième grande Sonate"; dedication meant for Zuccalmaglio
22	g	P	1833–38	Breitkopf, 1839	Henriette Voigt	4: VF-M-Sc-VF g: -C-g -g 778: 317-61-64-336	VII/iv/22	"Deuxième grande Sonate" (with revised finale)
118/1	G	P	1853	Schuberth, 1854	Julie } daughters	4: F -Va-M-Ro G: G-e -C-G 363: 50-40 -64-209	VII/vi/35	*Drei Sonaten für die Jugend*; the 4 mvts. of Op. 118/1 were originally written to be 4 of *Kinderscenen* Op. 15
118/2	D	"	"	"	Elise } daughters	4: F -F -S -VF D: D -b -G-D 410: 127-62-33-188	"	
118/3	C	"	"	"	Marie } daughters	4: F -M-F -VF C: C -F -a -C 413: 105-29-66-213	"	
—	A♭/D♭	P	1830?			F?-S A♭-D♭		only 2 mvts.; cf. Boetticher/SCHUMANN 586 (incipits; repeated in Dale/SCHUMANN 42), 640 (2d mvt.)
—	f	P	1833–37			F-?-F f f *ca.* 180		"Sonate IV"? cf. Schumann/JUGENDBRIEFE 278 (Op. 14 or this work?), Boetticher/SCHUMANN 566 (with exx. that seem to be confused with this son.) and 639 (only fragmentary information)
—	B♭	P	1840			F? B♭ 4 pp.?		"I started a little Sonatina in B♭—very pretty" (Litzmann/SCHUMANN I 386); perhaps the same as the sketch of a son. mvt. in B♭ dated around 1836 in Boetticher/SCHUMANN 639

8	b	P	1831	Friese, 1835	Ernestine von Fricken	F b 206	VII/i/8	*Allegro*; from first mvt. of a projected "Sonate in H-Moll" to be ded. to Moscheles; derived from sketches for Op. 2 and projected variations on a Paganini theme; cf. Schumann/JUGENDBRIEFE 165, Gertler/SCHUMANN 8-9, Abraham/RESEARCH 69, Dale/SCHUMANN 34 and 42-4, HOFMEISTER 1834-38, 187
17	C	P	1836-38	Breitkopf, 1839	Franz Liszt	3: F -F -S C: C -Eb -C 712: 310-260-142	VII/iii/17	*Fantasie*; originally "Grosse Sonate," Op. 12 for proposed Beethoven monument, ded. to Clara; cf. Schumann/JUGENDBRIEFE 278, 281, 302-3; Dale/SCHUMANN 45
26	Bb	P	1839	Mechetti, 1841	Simonin de Sire	5: VF-S -Sc -F -VF Bb: Bb -g -Bb -eb-Bb 1074: 555-25-128-45-321	VII/iv/26	*Faschingsschwank aus Wien*; originally described by Schumann as a "big romantic sonata"; iv pub. separately in 1839; cf. Dale/SCHUMANN 45
105	a	P & Vn	1851	Hofmeister, 1852		3: F -F -F a: a -F -a 501: 209-79-213	V/iii/10	*Sonate für Pianoforte und Violine*
121	d	Vn & P	1851	Breitkopf, 1853	Ferdinand David	4: S/F-VF-M -F d: d -b -G -d/D 813: 295-193-140-185	V/iii/11	*2te Grosse Sonate für Violine und Pianoforte*
—	a	P & Vn	1853	Schott, 1956	Joseph Joachim?	4: S/F-M-Sc -F a: a -d -d -a/A 509: 163-45-135-166		"3. Sonate"; with Schumann's own 2 mvts. added to his 2 mvts. in F-A-E sonate-m; cf. Boetticher/SCHUMANN 638, Melkus/SCHUMANN, Melkus/VIOLINSONATE

plete, somewhat unreliable set of fourteen series in thirty-one volumes prepared by Clara Schumann and Brahms, and published in 1881–93.[131] In 1964 plans were announced for a much needed new edition of the complete works, literary as well as musical, to be published jointly by Breitkopf & Härtel and B. Schott.[132] Undoubtedly a basic aid to this edition, and presumably a part of it, will be the numerous musical sketchbooks and separate fragments left by Schumann but not investigated in detail until Wolfgang Gertler and Werner Schwarz wrote dissertations on his early keyboard music and variation treatment in 1929 and 1932, respectively.[133] Several of these sketches will be seen to throw light on derivations of the sonatas.

Out of Schumann's 15 works included here in the realm of the sonata, 3 are full-scale solo piano sonatas, 3 are diminutive solo piano sonatas, 3 are unfinished, unpublished solo piano sonatas, 3 are works that started as solo piano sonatas but came out differently, and 3 are sonatas for piano and violin. The essential facts about these 15 works are tabulated in that order (pp. 262–63), before some over-all considerations are advanced and the six main sonatas are noted individually.[134] As this tabulation recalls, Schumann's main sonatas fell into two widely separated groups, the three big piano sonatas being composed intermittently during a five-year period before 1840 (1833–38) and the three ensemble sonatas all in single, short spans during his last three years of significant composing (1851–53).[135] There is truth in the frequent generalization that Schumann—somewhat like Brahms (whose main sonatas fell into two similar groups)—began as a romantic and ended if not quite a classicist then at least a realist.[136] The late sonatas sprang forth quickly[137] because by then he had largely resolved or given up his

131. Schumann/WERKE-m. Cf. Heyer/HISTORICAL 297. Many details of the editorial work in this set can be traced in the letters between Brahms and Clara in Litzmann/SCHUMANN III and SCHUMANN-BRAHMS II, especially for 1877 (also, Sept. and Oct., 1892, as a sample of some of the difficulties).

132. NOTES XXII (1965–66) 696–97.

133. Gertler/SCHUMANN (with a preface, pp. 1–13, on the Zwickau sketchbooks) and Schwarz/SCHUMANN. A full list of sketch sources, both for pub. works with op. nos. and unpub. works, appears in Boetticher/SCHUMANN 630–640. Besides the exx. in these studies only a relatively small part of the sketches have been pub. (cf. MGG XII 321).

134. Cf. the convenient tabulation of Schumann's complete works, by categories, in GROVE VII 627–39 (Abraham). First eds. are listed in MGG XII 293–98 and SCHUMANN/-DRUCKE. An up-to-date *catalogue raisonné* is much needed.

135. Nearest to the needed over-all study of Schumann's sons. is an investigation, at once more general and more specific, into his treatment of "sonata form," in the lost diss. Cohen/SCHUMANN (with the conclusions restated in Carner/FORM). In Abraham/SCHUMANN 307 the listing of a similar diss. by W. Schwarz is an error for Schwarz/SCHUMANN.

136. Cf. Gertler/SCHUMANN 42–45.

137. Cf. MGG XII 289, Melkus/VIOLINSONATE 190.

attempts to fuse the literary and the musical. He was now more of a pure musician, concerned primarily with refinements of structure[138] and texture (as in his polyphonic studies centered around Bach). The early sonatas had evolved somewhat erratically and insecurely in the throes of attempting that fusion. Furthermore, the three "sonatas" that came out differently and the three (or more?) that died a-borning evolved in those throes, too.

Schumann's attempts to fuse the literary and musical in his earlier works related closely to his insecurity in trying to master professional composition techniques largely on his own,[139] and to an apparent schizoid personality that manifested itself even more in his youth than in his later years, and that showed up in his art as much as in his mental state.[140] With regard to the latter, the impassioned, perturbed, harsh, precipitate "Florestan" and the gentle, deliberate, dreamy, tactful "Eusebius" constitute the diametric personifications of his schizoid temperament (cf. Ex. 29), with "Master Raro" as the arbitrating superego—the detached, temperate observer.[141]

All these traits of the young composer who struggled and vacillated so much in his sonata composing contributed in turn to the two aspects of his best known sonatas, those for piano solo, that have served most to orient them historically and musically. First, his solo piano sonatas embraced and cultivated Romantic styles more fully and consistently than any other sonatas from the first half of the 19th century that still survive in today's repertoire.[142] And second, in so doing, they posed structural problems, especially problems of extended "sonata form," that account for most of the technical reservations later writers have held about them. But the problems Schumann encountered must be distinguished from the problems many listeners find in accepting his sonatas today (to return to an observation near the start of this Schumann discussion). As noted when Schumann's styles and forms came up for earlier discussion (ssb VI), Schumann had to solve the problems of development and extent with idioms and aesthetic goals that lent themselves more to small, relatively static forms than to the previous, broader dynamic means of Beethoven and his generation.[143]

138. Cf. Boetticher/SCHUMANN 553.

139. E.g., cf. his own words in Storck/SCHUMANN 42–45, 54, 67, 70–71, 73–74.

140. For various slants, all tending to support this view, cf. Gertler/SCHUMANN 16–17, Boetticher/SCHUMANN 255, Redlich/SCHUMANN 145 and 182–83 (with indications that venereal disease was the primary cause of the final mental collapse); Lippman/SCHUMANN 328. For a summary of a century of theorizing about his illnesses cf. NZM CXXI (1960) 188–89 (D. Kerner).

141. Cf. a typical explanation by the composer himself in Schumann/SCHRIFTEN I 60 (1835); also, Lippman/SCHUMANN 340 and MGG XII 277–78.

142. Cf. Rehberg/SCHUMANN 437–38.

143. Cf. Boetticher/SCHUMANN 579–80, 586.

Ex. 29. The opening of Robert Schumann's Sonata in f♯ (facs. of the original Kistner ed. of 1836 [the only extant copy?] at the British Museum).

At best and in his own way he did solve these problems, chiefly by his personal methods of motivic extension and of sectional organization bordering on fantasy. But, almost as with Schubert, all too many listeners today cannot help evaluating even Schumann in terms of Beethovian standards. If they no longer balk at his "failure," like Beethoven's (SCE 16, 117), to comply with *a posteriori* textbook descriptions of "sonata form," they still find it difficult to hear and enjoy Schumann's sonatas on his own Romantic terms.[144]

In any case, Beethoven's music was not the first or strongest influence on Schumann's.[145] From as early as 1827, Schubert's music, in all its available categories, seems to have stood above all other music in that regard, especially during the years Schumann was composing his solo piano sonatas. "Schubert is still my 'one and only' love, the more so as he has everything in common with my one and only Jean Paul," he wrote at 21 (1830).[146] Early, too, were the single, vivid impressions made on him by the virtuosity of Moscheles (in 1819!) and Paganini (1830);[147] the special interest on his part in Hummel's Sonata in f♯, Op. 81;[148] and the highest regard on his part for Chopin and Mendelssohn among contemporaries.[149] Weber's early influence can be surmised, although the evidence is more indirect and Schumann refers to him less than might be expected in view of the common Romantic ground of the two men.[150]

144. The conclusion in Cohen/SCHUMANN (as restated in Carner/FORM) is that Schumann—in his sons., symphonies, concertos, etc.—loosened the tensions of Classic "son. form" and turned to poetic literary stimuli to the point of creating symphonic poems, thus providing "the earliest decisive attempts to make this classic form serve romantic ideals." Similar conclusions are reached in Gertler/SCHUMANN 110–16 and Hohenemser/SCHUMANN 49–50.

145. Boetticher/SCHUMANN 223–90 provides a detailed consideration of Schumann's derivations from, relations with, and influences or comments on 14 musicians and some "Kleinmeister," from Bach to Liszt and Wagner (to be read with the usual cautions). Cf., also, Gertler/SCHUMANN 50–55.

146. Storck/SCHUMANN 44, and cf. 122 and 222; also, Boetticher/SCHUMANN 244–47, Abraham/SCHUMANN 9, Schumann/SCHRIFTEN I 459–64 *et passim*.

147. Cf. MOSCHELES I 24–25; Eismann/SCHUMANN I 13, 58; Niecks/SCHUMANN 37; Storck/SCHUMANN 61, 45. Moscheles' Son. Op. 49 in f♯ was one of the early pieces studied by Schumann (Heussner/MOSCHELES 56).

148. Storck/SCHUMANN 42–43, 64–65.

149. Schumann's celebrated panegyric ("Hats off . . .") on Chopin's Op. 2 appeared in AMZ XXXIII (1831) 805–8, reprinted in Schumann/SCHRIFTEN 5–7. On Mendelssohn, cf. Niecks/SCHUMANN 146–56, including Schumann's statement of 1839, "I regard Mendelssohn as the foremost musician of the day, and take off my hat to him as a master."

150. Cf. Storck/SCHUMANN 65; Gertler/SCHUMANN 4 and 7; Boetticher/SCHUMANN 247.

Schumann's Sonatas for Piano

A typical view of Schumann's three completed sonatas for solo piano finds Op. 11 in f♯, which came first in order both of completion and publication,[151] to be the most satisfying to hear and play, chiefly because it is regarded as the most successful fusion of his literary and musical interests.[152] Especially in the longer, outer movements, Op. 22 is criticized as being somewhat formalistic, and Op. 14 as being both too repetitive in its motivic treatment and too discursive in its designs, in spite of some rare moments and ideas. On the other hand, the *Fantasie* Op. 17 is regarded as being superior to all three "sonatas" in musical value.[153] Schumann himself had only passing remarks to make about his own sonatas. Very early, in 1831, he had written Hummel that "the concerto form seemed to me easier [to compose] than that of the sonata . . . because of its [the concerto's] greater license."[154] Among all his major piano works, "*Kreisleriana* is my favorite," he wrote in 1839,[155] although previously he had pointed twice with some pride to both Opp. 11 and 14.[156] In any case, by 1839–40 he was finding the piano "too limited for my ideas," with the orchestra and the voice opening new horizons.[157] And even before he wrote his own symphonies he was finding both the symphony and sonata had passed their day.[158] These views and a considerable degree of emotional resolution must go far to explain Schumann's reference, already in 1843, to the "immaturity" of his earlier (that is, piano) music, with its reflection "for the most part [of] the stormy scenes of my early life."[159]

151. But "Première" did not appear in the title of the 2d ed. of 1840 (as stated in Dale/SCHUMANN 43); cf. Cat. ROYAL 320, SCHUMANN/-DRUCKE 13, HOFMEISTER 1843, 235. Boal/SCHUMANN is a recent, unpub. diss. on the extant MSS and eds. of this work.

152. E.g., cf. Shedlock/SONATA 208–9 (but with no mention of Op. 14), Georgii/KLAVIERMUSIK 325; Gillespie/KEYBOARD 215. Op. 11 "must be considered as a volume of lyric poems" (Bie/PIANOFORTE 242). Parrott/SCHUMANN, arguing that it "is more useful to appreciate what is Schumannian in Schumann, rather than flog the old sonata-form warhorse," points up positive structural and poetic values in Op. 11.

153. The only over-all discussions of Schumann's piano sons. are those included as relatively brief sections in broader surveys of his entire output for piano, as in Fuller-Maitland/SCHUMANN 23–26 and 31–32, Dale/SCHUMANN 42–48 and 83–84.

154. Storck/SCHUMANN 67.

155. Storck/SCHUMANN 128, Niecks/SCHUMANN 187–88.

156. Niecks/SCHUMANN 111 (1836), Storck/SCHUMANN 112 (1838).

157. According to letters quoted in Gertler/SCHUMANN 33, Niecks/SCHUMANN 205–6, and Storck/SCHUMANN 140.

158. Cf. Gertler/SCHUMANN 56–57; Schumann/SCHRIFTEN I 394–95; SSB II.

159. Storck/SCHUMANN 241. Cf. his reference (after 1850) to his early music as "confused stuff" (Wasielewski/SCHUMANN 121).

Although they originated variously and deviously, growing by fits and starts, three of Schumann's sonatas—presumably, Opp. 11 and 22, and the other Sonata in f, never to be finished—were all in progress at the same time in early 1834, while the Jean Paul influence still dominated and while the *Neue Zeitschrift* as well as the imaginary "Davidsbündler" were getting into full swing.[160] Schumann had wanted to make these sonatas "masterpieces" and, which did not happen, to dedicate them to his mother.[161] Actually, it was "Klara" (publicized then without her surname) who became the dedicatee of Op. 11, from "Florestan and Eusebius," [162] and it was Op. 11 that most closely related to her among Schumann's sonatas. If this was not the "gigantic work" Schumann mentioned as being started in late 1831,[163] at least it is known to have evolved tortuously by way of a reworked "Fandango, Rhapsodie . . ." of 1832 in the first movement, an early song (1828) in the second, and perhaps one of a set of rejected "Burlesken" of 1832 in the third movement, as well as considerable revision of early sketches in the last two movements.[164] As it evolved further, Clara became more and more a part of it until, as Schumann wrote to her in retrospect, it was "one entire heart's cry for you, in which your theme appears in all possible forms." [165] Naturally, Schumann was hurt when Clara did not reply (or could not because of her father) upon receipt of the published score in May, 1836.[166] But she had already played it in 1835 for Mendelssohn, Chopin, and Moscheles, among others.[167] And she played it in Leipzig in August, 1837, when this was the only way she could reveal "my inmost heart" to Schumann, hidden in the audience near the end of the eighteen months in which all correspondence and

160. Cf. GROVE VII 607; Niecks/SCHUMANN 130–32 (with Schumann's own recollections).

161. Schumann/JUGENDBRIEFE 229.

162. "Florestan und Eusebius" became the popular title of this work (Ex. 29, *supra*), which was even listed so in HOFMEISTER 1834–38, 129, prior to the 2d ed. under Schumann's own name in 1840. Cf. Jansen/NEUE 418; Wörner/SCHUMANN 143–44. The first ed. is very rare, the only complete copy known here being that at the British Museum.

163. Niecks/SCHUMANN 178 believes it was, but could Schumann's intention to dedicate it to Moscheles mean that the "gigantic work" was an early plan for Op. 14 instead? Op. 8 in its earlier stages is a possible candidate, too.

164. Cf. Gertler/SCHUMANN 9–10; Boetticher/SCHUMANN 206, 557, 562, 565–66, 630; Abraham/II & III 126, 162–63; GROVE VII 607; Dale/SCHUMANN 43–44; Boal/SCHUMANN; Lippman/SCHUMANN 314.

165. Litzmann/SCHUMANN I 109–10. On the inter-relation of the Spanish "Fandango" and Clara's own "Hexentanz" Op. 5/4 as well as the application of this material throughout Op. 11, cf. Rehberg/SCHUMANN 439–41 and 663–64.

166. Litzmann/SCHUMANN I 109. In 1838 Schumann wrote in a letter to Clara, "So your father calls me phlegmatic? Phlegmatic, and write . . . the Sonata in f♯! Phlegmatic, and your lover!" (Storck/SCHUMANN 190).

167. Litzmann/SCHUMANN I 87–89; MOSCHELES I 319; Boetticher/SCHRIFTEN 103.

personal visits had been forbidden.[168] So much special meaning did this work have for the two lovers that in most of their references they called it simply "the sonata," even after both other sonatas were completed.[169]

Moscheles left his personal reactions to Op. 11 as Clara played it, which should be qualified by his conservatism (SSB VII) and the newness of the sonata manuscript to Clara.[170] He wrote his wife that it seemed "very laboured, difficult, and somewhat intricate, although interesting music." [171] But within a year it was probably more than diplomacy and Schumann's flattering request[172] that won more favorable, though largely generalized and noncommittal, words in Moscheles' published, three-page review of Op. 11.[173] Beginning, "This work is a true sign of the awakening and sprouting Romanticism in our day," Moscheles first dwells, one at a time, on the passing of Beethoven and on the new Romanticism of Mendelssohn, Berlioz, Liszt, Hiller, and Chopin. Then, taking Florestan and Eusebius as the two sides of one mind (without divulging the pseudonym),[174] he only briefly describes each movement, finding the last strained to the point of structural incoherence. Two years later Liszt, the new lion of the piano world, gave his name to a review of Schumann's Opp. 5 (Impromptus), 11, and 14, all in one long article.[175] He called Schumann an exponent of the new school, second in individuality only to Chopin. Of Op. 11 he said that the mysterious title and its poetic associations might seem affected in Paris,[176] the treatment of his ideas in the first movement was serried and inflexible, the deep second movement was unequalled, the third movement was remarkable for its rhythms and harmonies, and the finale—again—suffered from struc-

---

168. Litzmann/SCHUMANN I 116–25 *passim*. Cf. NZM VII (1837) 87 ("Florestan und Eusebius"); also, Niecks/SCHUMANN 195, 196.

169. E.g., Schumann/JUGENDBRIEFE 271, where Clara confirms the reference; Storck/ SCHUMANN 225.

170. Litzmann/SCHUMANN 87.

171. MOSCHELES I 319.

172. Printed in Wasielewski/SCHUMANN 304–5; cf. Jansen/SCHUMANN I 95–97.

173. NZM V (1836) 135–37. Cf. MOSCHELES II 19–20; Niecks/SCHUMANN 179. Op. 11 got no review in the more conservative AMZ.

174. In a footnote the "editor" wrote that his closeness to the "composers" prompted him to get a third party to review this work. On the 2d ed. of Op. 11, under Schumann's own name, cf. Schumann/SCHRIFTEN II 374.

175. RGM No. 46 (Nov. 12, 1837) 488–90; reprinted, with postscript in Wasielewski/ SCHUMANN 274–80. If Liszt did not write this review himself (as argued convincingly in Haraszti/AUTHOR, especially pp. 492 and 501), one still assumes it had his full blessing and reflected his opinions.

176. Schumann had written in 1835 that Berlioz' programme for his *Symphonie fantastique* was appropriate in France but not in Germany (Schumann/SCHRIFTEN I 83–84)!

tural faults in spite of its great originality. Schumann wrote Clara at once of the "long, very just article," [177] and early in 1840, when he and Liszt met often in Leipzig, he reported that Liszt's playing of Op. 11 "moved me strangely. Although his reading differed in many places from my [and Clara's?] own, it was always inspired, and he does not, I imagine, display such tenderness, such boldness, every day." [178] Liszt himself wrote then that he was getting to understand Schumann's music better, and though so far it had brought little applause in public it was sure eventually to take its rightful, important place.[179] Among the few important performances of Op. 11 in the years that followed were those that Hanslick reported by Brahms in 1867 [180] and Anton Rubinstein in 1884 (at which Brahms was conspicuously absent).[181]

The original manuscript of Schumann's Op. 14, completed in June, 1836, contained five movements—F-Sc-Va-Sc-VF—and bore nothing for a title but "Concert" (Ex. 30).[182] At the request of the publisher Haslinger, Schumann consented to the discard of both scherzos and the change, as Haslinger regarded it, from a passé title to one with more current appeal, "Concert sans orchestre." [183] As we shall see, Haslinger's judgment proved wrong in both respects. Moscheles, the dedicatee, wrote Schumann that Op. 14 had more the character of a "grosse Sonate" such as Beethoven or Weber composed than the brilliance one would expect in a concerto, and that the fantasy character of Op. 14 did not lend itself to brilliance, anyway. He added that its dissonances, so subtle and delayed in their resolutions, could only be appreciated by an educated ear. Schumann printed that much of Moscheles' letter, this time prefacing it by saying that the roguish Florestan and Eusebius had published Op. 14 under his

177. Niecks/SCHUMANN 179–81.

178. Storck/SCHUMANN 225.

179. Wasielewski/SCHUMANN 280–81. The immediate reference is to *Carnaval*.

180. Hanslick/WIEN II 438; but this was not the first public performance of Op. 11 (recalling Clara's in Leipzig in 1837 and Hanslick's own mention [p. 299] of a less satisfactory performance in 1863). PADEREWSKI 98 and 309–10 also describes Rubinstein's playing of Op. 11 *ca.* 1884 and Paderewski's own playing of it in 1901.

181. Pleasants/HANSLICK 228–29. On Clara's performance of Op. 11 in London in 1884, see under Op. 22 *infra*.

182. Cf. the description of this MS prepared for the publisher, Add. 37056, in Cat. BRITISH MS 147.

183. Cf. Schumann/SCHRIFTEN II 374 (Kreisig). To Moscheles Schumann tendered the dedication of "a sonata, or rather [a sonata] extended into a concerto for piano alone . . . [when you receive it] you can only wonder at the crazy brainstorms a man can have" (letter of July 30, 1836, printed in Wasielewski/SCHUMANN 304); cf., also, Jansen/SCHUMANN I 81 and 94. The sole mention of Op. 14 in AMZ (in a survey of Schumann's piano music, XLVI [1844] 1, 17, 33) puts it among works described as confused, eccentric, and difficult; on the other hand, Op. 22 is cited only for its return to sonata form.

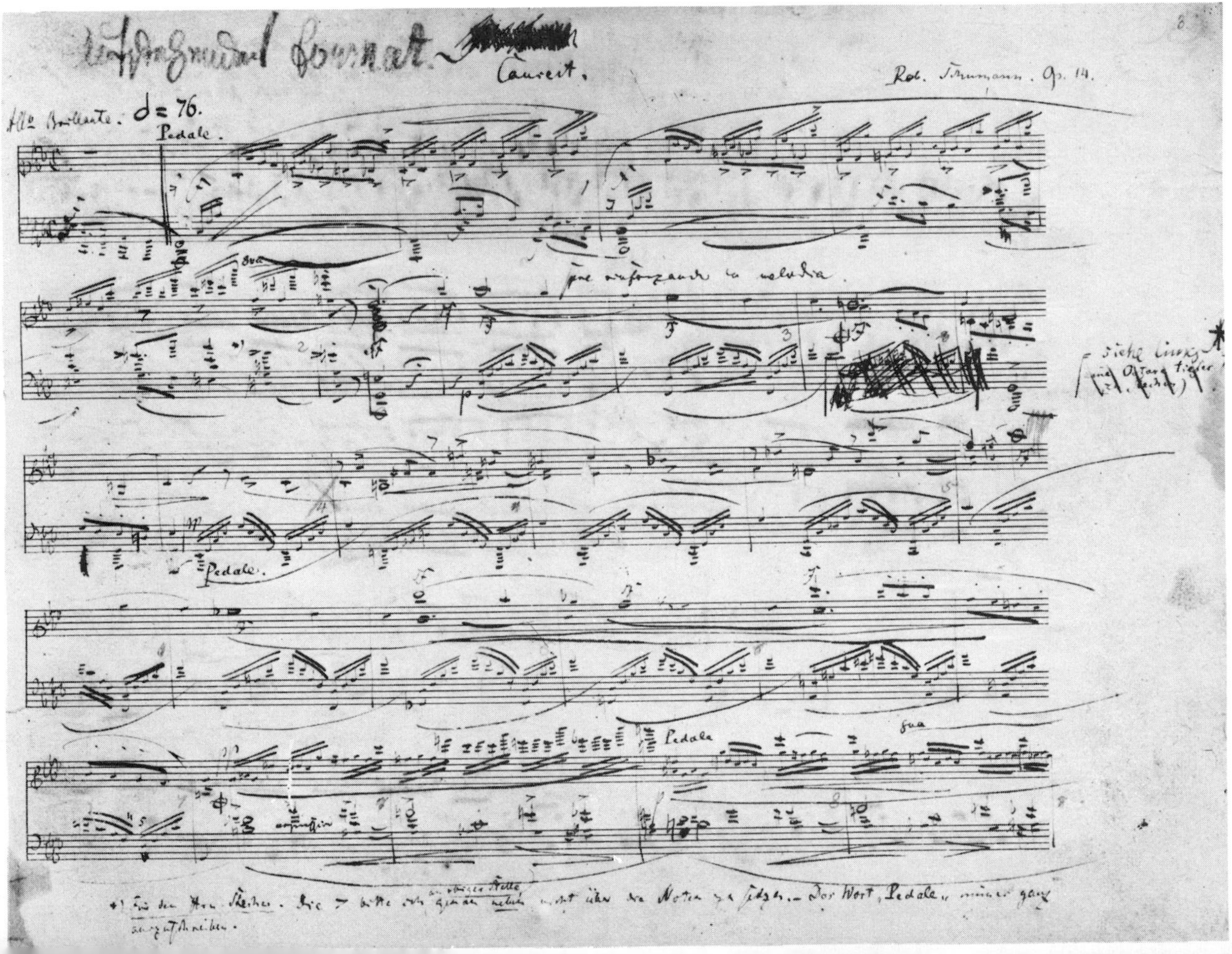
Rob. Schumann. Op. 14.
Pedale

(Schumann's) name.[184] Actually, one reason why musicians have not taken more to Op. 14 may well be that this unjustly neglected masterpiece—this inspired "Sonata appassionata," as it were—lets Florestan's seething, uncompromising passions dominate Eusebius almost completely, much more so than in Op. 11.[185] In his broad review of Opp. 5, 11, and 14, Liszt, the supposed author (SSB X), made even more of "Concerto" as a misnomer for "Sonata," calling attention to implications of ensemble as well as overt brilliance in the word "concerto." [186] But as a "sonata," Liszt found Op. 14 "rich and power-ful," and a reminder that Schumann's works awaited introduction to the French.

These semantic objections must have played their part in the partial restoration of Op. 14's original title to *Troisième grande Sonate* in the second edition of 1853[187] ("Troisième" because in the meantime Op. 22 had appeared as "Deuxième"). There were signifi-cant changes in the music, too, notably the restoration of most of the second scherzo, now as the second movement, plus modifications in the outer movements and deletions in the resourceful "Variazioni" on an "Andantino" by Clara (the only example in Schumann's main sonatas of this important side of his writing).[188] But the new version can hardly be said to have given more voice to Eusebius, who now emerges only tentatively and briefly in the least driving moments of the first and third movements. And there is some question as to whether the restitution of the other scherzo might not have been more in keeping with the whole cycle.[189] Brahms gave the first public performance of Op. 14, in Vienna in 1862, according to Hanslick.[190]

"How little I thought when I published Op. 1 that I should ever reach Op. 22!" wrote Schumann to Clara in 1840.[191] His Op. 22 in g had gone through the longest gestation and most growing pains of his three main solo sonatas. Its first and third movements were fairly well set in 1833 except for a slower, more intense version of the opening idea that had to be rewritten.[192] The ineffably poetic

184. NZM VI (1837) 65.
185. Cf. Rehberg/SCHUMANN 452–54.
186. RGM No. 46 (Nov. 12, 1837) 488–90.
187. Cf. SCHUMANN/DRUCKE 14.
188. Cf. Schwarz/SCHUMANN 43–45, 69; Dale/SCHUMANN 27–28. The changes in Op. 14 are described in Cat. BRITISH MS 147 and both pub. versions are printed in Schumann/WERKE-m VII/iii/14.
189. Cf. Rehberg/SCHUMANN 453. This other, fine scherzo is pub. in Schumann/WERKE-m XIV 48.
190. Hanslick/WIEN II 258.
191. Storck/SCHUMANN 228.
192. Cf. Gertler/SCHUMANN 10–11.

second movement—Eusebius through and through—began as an early song in 1828 and developed into an independent "Andantino" for piano in 1830 before taking its place in the sonata.[193] The original finale, almost completed in 1835,[194] was put aside in 1838 when Clara found it "much too difficult" and Schumann fully concurred, finding it otherwise unsatisfactory, too, "except for some passionate moments." [195] Its successor he himself described as "very simple but intrinsically well suited to the first movement." [196] Gertler is in the minority in suggesting that Op. 22 is less unified than the other two piano sonatas because of its varied and protracted origins.[197] The later finale, which is less choleric or meaningful than the original one, may be a bit slight for the rest of the cycle but does match it well in style and difficulty. Furthermore, there is that same cyclically unifying motive, the stepwise descent heard at the start, that binds, or recurs in, all three piano sonatas, the Concerto in a, and many other Schumann pieces.[198]

Writing to Robert in 1838, Clara was undoubtedly sincere in expressing her pleasure with Op. 22 and the "many happy as well as painful hours" it brought back to her.[199] She reported excellent reactions to it when she introduced it in a recital in Berlin early in 1840.[200] Yet it is noteworthy that neither this nor the other two piano sonatas seem to have figured often in the approximately two thousand recitals she gave throughout much of the rest of the century.[201] It is in the first movement of Op. 22, by the way, that the

193. Cf. Gertler/SCHUMANN 10, with the title "Papillote" for one sketch; Abraham/ II & III 126–27, with ex.; Rehberg/SCHUMANN 477–79, with facs. of sketch. Boetticher/ SCHUMANN 485 finds a characteristic symbol of unsatisfied longing in mss. 8–11 of this mvt.

194. GROVE VII 608.

195. Litzmann/SCHUMANN I 186; Niecks/SCHUMANN 202. This piece is pub. in SCHUMANN/WERKE-m XIV 53.

196. Cf. Boetticher/SCHRIFTEN 139, 221, 230.

197. Gertler/SCHUMANN 70–71.

198. Cf. Rehberg/SCHUMANN 476–77.

199. Litzmann/SCHUMANN I 186, 188.

200. Litzmann/SCHUMANN I 391–93; yet cf. Boetticher/SCHUMANN 322. Schumann had asked her to play as if it were the day before their wedding, but not to "take the sonata too wildly; think of the man who wrote it for you." But previously he had advised against playing the "entire" Son. in recital (Boetticher/SCHRIFTEN 288, 303).

201. Cf. the somewhat incomplete list in Litzmann/SCHUMANN III 615–24, but note that each work is ordinarily listed only the first time it was performed. Clara still played Op. 11 in London in 1884 (MT XXV [1884] 206, with interesting remarks on Schumann's P sons. in London). Performances of Op. 22 prior to 1885 in London are reported in MMR I (1871) 37, XV (1884) 177–78; MT XVIII (1877) 553, XXIII (1882) 382, XXV (1884) 21 (by Pachmann) and 338. None of Op. 14 is reported in that period.

celebrated paradox occurs in the tempo instructions, with "as fast as possible" as the initial, reigning instruction, only to be followed by "faster" and "still faster" in the coda. Much the same occurs in the finale of Op. 14. One can be literal and decry such editorial carelessness. Or, as with the impossibly difficult coda of Op. 17/ii, one can take a transcendental approach; one can throw oneself into the laps of the gods while gambling on superhuman effort!

The three late sonatas Op. 118 that Schumann wrote for his three daughters in June of 1853 are, on the whole, too long to be called sonatinas (as our tabulation shows), too complex to make satisfactory pieces for children (in the manner of *Album for the Young*), and, save for two or three movements, too commonplace and discursive to qualify as significant music.[202] They have never aroused much interest. *Faschingsschwank aus Wien: Fantasiebilder*, Op. 26, has been linked with Schumann's sonatas mainly because he described it in 1839 as "a big romantic sonata" while working on it, but later merely as "a romantic show piece." [203] Although this work does present a tonal cycle of five movements, it scarcely relates to Schumann's main "sonatas" in drive, emotional content, or structural development, even in the finale, which is usually singled out in this connection because of its tangible "sonata form." [204] In all these respects the great *Fantasie* in C, Op. 17, deserves much more to be linked with the sonatas. Furthermore, it started as a sonata in Schumann's mind. At the outset of nearly three years of work on the music and before the original long title underwent numerous changes, this title read, "Obolen auf Beethovens Monument—Ruinen, Trophaen, Palmen—; Grosse Sonate für das Pianoforte; für Beethovens Denkmal." [205] But by early 1838, with the music now revised and completed, the dedication was changed from Clara to Liszt, the mentioned support (by Florestan and Eusebius, again) of a Beethoven monument and the imaginative movement titles were discarded, the mystic quatrain by Schlegel [206] was inscribed over the opening, and the long title including "Grosse Sonate" was replaced simply by "Fantasie." [207]

202. They are discussed briefly in Dale/SCHUMANN 69–70, 71, 73, 83–84. Op. 118/1/ii is discussed for its variations in Schwarz/SCHUMANN 45. Some details and sketches are noted in Boetticher/SCHUMANN 553–54, 571, 636.

203. Jansen/SCHUMANN I 211; cf. Niecks/SCHUMANN 203. The work is described briefly in Gertler/SCHUMANN 71–72, Dale/SCHUMANN 45, Rehberg/SCHUMANN 481–83.

204. The first mvt. is discussed in Schwarz/SCHUMANN 65–66 as a free set of variations.

205. The origins and correspondence are summarized in Niecks/SCHUMANN 188–89, Dale/SCHUMANN 45, GROVE VII 609.

206. Cf. Einstein/SCHUBERT 164–65.

207. On the importance of the fantasy to Schumann cf. Wörner/SCHUMANN 93–96.

Although Schumann did write on one occasion, ". . . sonatas or fantasias (what's in a name!) . . . ,"[208] in all other references discovered here he indicated considerable concern over the best designations not only for his own works (as we have just seen) but for any works that he reviewed in which questions of terminology arose (SSB II; VII, on Schubert). And Op. 17 does stand apart clearly enough from his works actually called "sonata," both in the number, order, and types of its movements and in the freedom and sectional division, greater than usual, of its additive first movement. This is the movement that Schumann described to Clara in 1838 as "certainly the most impassioned I ever wrote—a deep lament for you."[209]

Schumann's Sonatas for Piano and Violin

Of Schumann's three late sonatas for piano and violin, the third was brought to light too recently to be widely known yet and the first two, Opp. 105 and 121, have been valued and played too little, it is felt here. Cobbett's single, redundant paragraph gives (and has undoubtedly furthered) the typical view of the latter:[210]

His mental disease was making further progress, not only affecting his musical thought and fecundity . . . but also embittering his soul. . . . Both sonatas show the disintegration of the fibre of Schumann's musical nature, the uncertainty and vagueness of his thought, the lack of firmness and definite issue and logical clarity in developing musical ideas. There is in general a depressing gloom . . . [only the] allegretto of the first one has something of the old charm.

The persistent minor key, the consistently low, ungrateful range for the violin, and a tendency to assign each instrument what suits the other better, are also usually mentioned as detractions in these works. If there is some truth in each of the charges, they all seem to go too far. The charge of mental deterioration, especially as early as 1851, has been seriously questioned, as noted earlier. In fact, no longer identified with programmatic content or the schizoid opposition of Florestan and Eusebius, these sonatas show, in some ways, more concentration and structural efficiency than the earlier sonatas. (Op. 105 is the only three-movement sonata and the shortest proportionately of all Schumann's sonatas.) And it is more plausible to hear the scoring traits of these late sonatas as premeditated aesthetic

208. Schumann/SCHRIFTEN I 395; but this view is contradicted, for example, on p. 70.
209. Schumann/JUGENDBRIEFE 278.
210. Cobbett/CHAMBER II 386. A more favorable view and brief analyses may be found in Dickinson/SCHUMANN 167–70.

effects by a now very mature, experienced composer than as inadvertent gaucheries.

It is true that Theodor Uhlig's long, contemporary review of Op. 105, in the very periodical Schumann had founded,[211] already found certain faults. But except for a mention of uncharacteristic scoring, these were of a different sort. To paraphrase and synopsize Uhlig's much padded and rarefied disquisition, Schumann is a musical mannerist who strains and stretches harmonic relationships until yesterday's dissonances become today's consonances; for the rest, all three movements reveal formal mastery and Schumann's special torrential drive, lyricism, and a certain (rhythmic?) nibbling ("Knaupeleien"), but also reveal a few commonplaces that betray prolificity and some impersonal writing. Clara first participated in a performance of Op. 105 in 1852 and Op. 121 in 1853.[212] At least Op. 121 was probably done with Joachim, for in September of 1853 he wrote a friend of his joy in playing it with her, adding, "To me it is one of the finest creations of modern times, in the wonderful unity of its feeling and the significance of its themes. It is full of a noble passion—almost harsh and bitter in its expression—and the last movement might almost remind one of a seascape, with its glorious waves of sound." [213] Other performances of these sonatas by the same and other duo teams, including Liszt and Reményi, are reported in the years that followed.[214]

Schumann's "3ᵗᵉ Sonate," in a, for piano and violin consists of the second and fourth movements he wrote for the F[rei]-A[ber]-E[insam] Sonata in a (jointly composed with A. Dietrich and Brahms in Joachim's honor[215]) plus a first and third movement to make a complete cycle of his own, all in but two weeks' time (Ex. 31).[216] Evincing no increased mental deterioration even in late 1853, this work stands close to its two predecessors of 1851 (and to Schumann's newly discovered Violin Concerto in d of 1853) in quality as well as in

211. NZM XXXVII (1852) 117–20; cf. Boetticher/SCHUMANN 358–59.
212. Litzmann/SCHUMANN 620.
213. Joachim/LETTERS 26.
214. Joachim/LETTERS 36, 183, 217, 234, 306, 321, 364; Litzmann/SCHUMANN 95; MT XII (1866) 317, XV (1871) 306, XVIII (1877) 120, XXIII (1882) 602, XXIV (1883) 321; Hanslick/WIEN II 168–69 (in which Schumann's former warmth is missed and excessive gloom is deplored). High regard for both sons. was expressed in MMR XIII (1883) 158 and 189. Op. 121/iii is discussed for its variations in Schwarz/SCHUMANN 48.
215. Mod. ed.: F-A-E SONATE-m.
216. Mod. ed. of complete 3d Son.: Neighbor/SCHUMANN-m. The autograph is listed in Boetticher/SCHUMANN 638 (but read 1853 for 1852); the relationship to the "F-A-E" son. is also guessed in Rehberg/SCHUMANN 362. Melkus/SCHUMANN and Melkus/VIOLINSONATE include circumstances, chronology, and analyses, with exx.

Ex. 31. The opening of Robert Schumann's "3ᵗᵉ Sonate" for piano and violin (facs. of autograph [Ms. 317] at the Bibliothèque nationale).

layout and character. It differs chiefly in having more cheerful moments, more use of the violin's higher registers, and more difficult passagework.

Early Romantics in and around Dresden

We may finish our discussion of early Romantics active in central Germany by proceeding from eastern to western centers with composers of minor importance, at least to the sonata—in other words, composers who require only passing or brief mentions here, for the sake of some degree of completeness. A half dozen of these were in or near Dresden. One was the pianist and organist **August Klengel** (1783–1852), who is remembered as the composer of 24 *Canons et Fugues* (1854) that have been used widely by piano teachers and students. It was much earlier, under the strong influence of his teacher Clementi, who came to Dresden in 1803 and travelled with Klengel over a period of several years,[217] that Klengel wrote his sonatas. These include two sets of three piano sonatas each, Opp. 1 and 2, and another, three-movement sonata Op. 9, as well as fifteen *Leçons ou Sonates faciles et progressives,* Op. 15, all first published between about 1805 and 1818.[218] The lively keyboard techniques and fluency, the harmonic ingenuity, and the textural precision in Opp. 2 and 9 all suggest an overdose of Clementi (cf. SCE 749–59). But the weak ideas, dull accompaniments, and lack of any compelling sense of form do not suggest that master nor explain the respect in which he was held by his young friend Chopin.[219]

The important theorist, composer, and violinist **Moritz Hauptmann** (1792–1868) wrote his sonatas early in his career, too, and while his main center was still Dresden.[220] He left at least ten sonatas or sonatinas, all originally for P & Vn, including three sets of three each, Opp. 5, 10 ("Sonatines"), and 23, plus a single *Sonatine,* Op. 6. These were first published in the decade from about 1825 to 1836, followed by numerous further editions, especially of Op. 10.[221] In Spohr, one of Hauptmann's teachers and closest friends,[222] can be

217. Cf. Unger/CLEMENTI 132–33, 138–39, 142–43, 158–59.
218. Cf. MGG VII 1220–22 (R. Sietz), with further listing of a son. for P & Fl left in MS; AMZ VIII (1805–6) Intelligenz-Blatt for Dec.; HOFMEISTER 1819 (Whistling), 35; Cat. BRUXELLES IV 178–79.
219. Cf. Hedley/CHOPIN 24, 36.
220. Cf. MGG V 1828–35 (M. Ruhnke).
221. Cf. Altmann/KAMMERMUSIK 206. The Peters plate no. for Op. 5 was 1874 (cf. Deutsch/NUMMERN 14) and the set is announced in AMA for July 29, 1826. Among mod. eds. of Op. 10: Peters Ed. 2948.
222. Cf. Spohr/AUTOBIOGRAPHY I 169, II 241.

found the chief influence on the sonatas, rather than in Weber, whom Hauptmann knew during a Vienna stay about 1815, or in Mendelssohn or Schumann, who were close to him later. Joachim, one of Hauptmann's numerous important students, wrote Clara Schumann in 1860 that the King in Hannover had been "charmed" with Hauptmann's compositions and had requested two performances of his Sonata in g, Op. 5/1.[223] Perhaps the King was responding to some early-Romantic touches in Hauptmann's sonatas. In a more limited sense than Schumann, Hauptmann had also come under the spell of Jean Paul. But there are hints, too, of the future theorist, in the almost excessive obligations to structural law and order and to harmonic logic, obligations that later were to block acceptance of Liszt's and Wagner's music. In 1837 Schumann found, in particular, that the three sonatas Op. 23, in spite of their flow and skill, marked a dry, oversimplified retreat from their predecessors into the "primitive [ultra-]classicism of the Haydn-Mozart period." [224] Certainly the same remarks apply at least as much at the more rudimentary level of the three sonatinas Op. 10.

Karl Gottlieb Reissiger (1798–1859), successor to Weber as court opera director in Dresden, was a pianist, singer, and composer, who left well over 200 modish publications, including about 12 sonatas—6 for P & Vn, 2 for P & Vc, and 4 for P solo.[225] These appeared between about 1825 and 1850. What Schumann wrote in 1836 of Reissiger's trios applies here.[226] In essence and in a disarmingly friendly manner he depicted them as glib conversations, as smooth, ingratiating, facile products of an overly prolific composer who imitated Beethoven, Weber, and others unwittingly and betrayed his shallowness the moment he tried anything more independent. A sample of Reissiger's glibness as well as his habit of seeing every phrase right to its relentlessly pedestrian conclusion should bear Schumann out, with interest, and should be taken as a sample of all too much other Philistinism of the sort that aroused his "Davidsbündler" to do battle (Ex. 32). Allowing for differences of tempo and movement styles, this sample is a fair representative of all the sonatas by Reissiger that could be examined here. Yet other reviewers, reporting on these sonatas, must have been less discerning or less honest; for

223. Joachim/LETTERS 193.
224. Schumann/SCHRIFTEN I 276–77.
225. Cf. MGG XI 208–10 (F. Göthel); PAZDÍREK XII 186–93; Altmann/KAMMERMUSIK 222, 262; Egert/FRÜHROMANTIKER 159.
226. Schumann/SCHRIFTEN I 176–77.

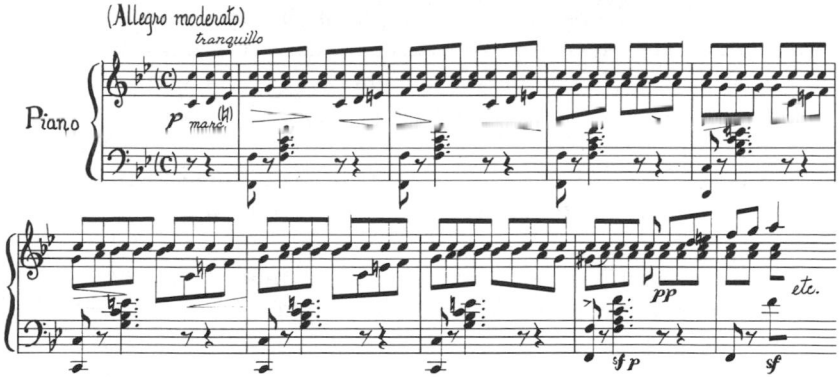

Ex. 32. From the first movement of Karl Gottlieb Reissiger's *Grande Sonate* in B♭, Op. 93 (after the original Schuberth ed. at the Library of Congress).

they all played down the sterility and played up the agreeableness of the music, especially for amateur learners.[227]

Worth mentioning only because of his niche in opera history are at least ten consistently weak, unimaginative sonatas and sonatinas for P solo and P-duet (pub. between about 1815 and 1830) by a more celebrated man linked with Weber, **Heinrich August Marschner** (1795–1861).[228]

Reviewing two piano sonatas in 1835 by a Dresden pianist, one **Wilhelm Christoph Bommer** (1801–43),[229] Schumann hoped the next two might be a little less labored and structurally self-conscious. As with Hauptmann he again objected to a retrogression into the styles of Mozart and Haydn, this time in the "Adagio" of a Sonata in A♭. "Let him wear the periwig whom it fits well; but don't deprive me of the flowing locks of youth, even if they fall somewhat wildly over the brow. So, loosen up, sonata writer, and no falseness!"[230] In a similar vein, in 1838, Schumann reviewed a Sonata Op. 30 for P-duet by **Leopold Schefer** (1784–1862), a Vienna trained composer better known as poet and novelist in Muskau, northeast of Dresden.[231] He

227. Op. 45 (P) is reviewed in AMZ XXXII (1830) 509, Op. 178 (Vn & P) in NZM XXIII (1845) 70 ("E. K."), and Op. 185 (P & Vn) in NZM XXVII (1847) 254 ("E. K."); cf., also, Cobbett/CHAMBER II 287–88 (W. Altmann and W. W. Cobbett).
228. Cf. MGG VIII 1682–88 (V. Köhler); HOFMEISTER 1815 (Whistling) 596, and 1829–33, p. 131. The first mvt. of Son. 6 in A♭, Op. 39, is reprinted in DM II/2 (1903) after p. 241.
229. Cf. Mendel/LEXIKON II 128.
230. Schumann/SCHRIFTEN II 307.
231. Cf. Mendel/LEXIKON IX 88.

found it to be a strong enough example of the past century, written as though Beethoven had not yet existed. "Only in the last movement does a Romantic streak break suddenly and surprisingly into the friendly contentment, somewhat like a cloud shadow across a village sleeping in the moonlight." [232] On the other hand, in 1841 Schumann objected to a *Phantasiesonate* by **Friedrich Wilhelm Klingenberg** (1809–88), violinist and cantor in Görlitz to the east,[233] because he tried to copy Beethoven's "Sonata quasi una fantasia" and to "get free of old routine" without the requisite training or force. "And it is a misfortune when musical villagers suddenly get excited over Parisian fashions—a misfortune that, regrettably, is more common to us in Germany than elsewhere." [234] In 1843, Schumann found little but a student's scholastic efforts in a piano sonata Op. 4 by the Dresden choral director **Adolf Reichel** (1820–96),[235] which he took to be "a first venture into this difficult art form." [236] By contrast, in 1845 a reviewer already found good ideas and treatment in a two-piano sonata Op. 1 by the versatile Chemnitz musician **Adolf Bergt** (1822–62),[237] son of **Christian Gottlob Bergt** (1772–1837), whose own Op. 1 (3 sons. for P & Vn & Vc) had been announced in 1801.[238] The reviewer also mentioned the brilliance, richness, thickness, and difficulty of Adolf's work, as well as some traces of Spohr's influence.[239]

Early Romantics in and around Leipzig (Loewe)

Some of the most interesting early-Romantic sonatas among the more obscure examples now under survey came from that master of the German song ballad, **Karl Loewe** (1796–1869). Trained as a singer and as a pianist (under D. G. Türk; SCE 589–90), Loewe had already written his celebrated "Edward" and "Erlkönig" ballads the year before and in 1819 was still living in his home town of Halle, 25 miles northwest of Leipzig, when he wrote his first of five solo piano sonatas, dating from 1819 to 1847.[240] This first one, *Grande Sonate brillante* in E♭, Op. 41, in four movements (F-M-Sc-F), was

232. Schumann/SCHRIFTEN I 363.
233. Cf. Mendel/LEXIKON VI 99.
234. Schumann/SCHRIFTEN II 10–11.
235. Cf. Riemann/LEXIKON II 1483; Mendel/LEXIKON VIII 282–83.
236. Schumann/SCHRIFTEN II 118.
237. Cf. Mendel/LEXIKON I 557.
238. AMZ IV (1801–2) Intelligenz-Blatt No. 11. Cf. Schilling/LEXICON I 572–74.
239. NZM XXIII (1845) 52–53 ("E. K.").
240. Cf. GROVE V 361–62 (F. Gehring) and MGG VIII 1106–11 (H. Engel; with errors in the son. dates), both with further bibliography.

not published until 1834, when Simrock issued it.[241] Following his
move in 1820 nearly 175 miles northeast to Stettin, Loewe wrote
his second sonata in 1824, *Le Printemps* . . . "a tone poem in sonata
form," in G, Op. 47, This work, in four movements, too (S/T-M-VF-3),
was published in 1835, one year later than Op. 41, by Schlesinger
of Berlin.[242] A further edition of it in 1852 prompted a reviewer
to take note briefly of its lasting favor in spite of its "now" dated
styles of keyboard and programmatic writing.[243] Loewe wrote *Grosse*
Sonate in E, Op. 16, third in order, in 1829, with publication
following in 1830 by Wagenführ of Berlin.[244] Unusual is the optional
part for tenor and soprano in the second of the three movements
(S/F-M-Va) in this sonata, which has been viewed as the most
significant in "content, form, and originality" of all Loewe's sonatas.[245] The fourth of the sonatas, *Grande Sonate élégique* in f,
Op. 32, was another three-movement work (F-Va-VF), composed over
a period of fifteen years—in 1819, 1825, and 1834—and published
by Wagenführ in 1834. This sonata got more reviews than any of
the others—in fact, than any other work by Loewe.[246] Like Weber's Op.
24 (SSB VIII, *supra*), it is dedicated to the Grand Duchess Maria
Paulowna of Weimar, who told Loewe of her pleasure in the work,
rewarded him with a gold snuff-box, and relayed Hummel's praise
of it.[247] Last in order by several years was Loewe's highly programmatic cycle in five movements (VF-M-VF-S-VF), *Zigeuner*-[Gipsy-]*So-*
nate in a, Op. 107, composed in 1847 and published in the same
year by Wilhelm Paul in Dresden.[248]

241. Cf. pp. 17–20 (but read Simrock plate no. 3165, not 5165) in Hirschberg/
LOEWE, a useful though somewhat idolatrous monograph commemorating the 50th
anniversary of Loewe's death, with separate descriptions of 30 instrumental works,
including copious exx. and early reviews or other references to them; cf., also,
Egert/FRÜHROMANTIKER 128–39 (with exx.), 158. A systematic style-critical study of
Loewe's sons. is to be desired. An early review (1835) of Op. 41 appears in
Schumann/SCHRIFTEN I 56–59. Mod. ed. of Op. 41: Newman/THIRTEEN-m 140 (with
preface pp. 23–24 [but read 1835 for 1841]).
    242. Reviewed in Schumann/SCHRIFTEN I 91–92 (1835) and in more generalized
fashion by Rellstab in 1835 (cf. Hirschberg/LOEWE 36).
    243. NZM XXXVII (1852) 182.
    244. There is no chronological reason for Loewe's op. nos. The single review
of Op. 16, in *Berliner musikalische Zeitung* for 1833 (No. 24, p. 97), is quoted in
full in Hirschberg/LOEWE 47. C. Reinecke reprinted this son. in his *Meister des*
Klaviers anth. (Breitkopf & Härtel); mod. ed. of first mvt.: Fischer/SONATE-m 33
(replaced by Schumann's Op. 118/2/i in 1957 reprint).
    245. Hirschberg/LOEWE 40, 47; Egert/FRÜHROMANTIKER 134, 136.
    246. Hirschberg/LOEWE 72. The reviews include Schumann/SCHRIFTEN I 59–60
(1835) 338–39; G. A. Keferstein ("K. Stein") in CAECILIA XVII (1835) 64–65; Rellstab
in 1835 (as in Hirschberg/LOEWE 73).
    247. Hirschberg/LOEWE 75.
    248. Reviewed in AMZ XLIX (1847) 310.

In a letter of June 14, 1829, to the Berlin publisher T. Trautwein (quoted further in ssb II, III, and IV), Loewe already submitted "four grand character sonatas," which he wanted to be published (as a set?) in a single volume, much, he said, as had been done for four sonatas by Dussek.[249] Although he cited these sonatas with titles not used later, presumably "Sonata melancolica" was Op. 32 in an earlier or less complete version, "Sonata pathetica" in E♭ was Op. 41, and "Sonata pastoralis" in G was Op. 47; but "Sonata capricciosa" in C must refer to a work since lost, for not a single one of all Loewe's extant instrumental works happens to be in that key and none of his solo piano works not called "sonata," including "fantasias" and "tone poems," divides into separate movements. In the same letter Loewe pointed to Beethoven's and Weber's sonatas as models of the best[250] and declared he himself was bringing "as little shame to the sonata as to the ballad."

Loewe was justified in claiming that his sonatas were both individual and unusual. Evidence can be found in their means of achieving over-all unity as well as in the details of their separate movements. Loewe put more emphasis on two means of unifying his sonata cycles than did most of his contemporaries. One was the use of a programme and the other the use of recurring motives. The programmes are not simply the moods conveyed by the published titles or the pre-publication titles cited above. Nor can they be the after-thoughts that Schumann insisted his own programmes were (ssb VIII *supra*). Especially in Loewe's *Zigeuner-Sonate* the programme dominates styles and forms, causing an early reviewer to begin by questioning its title, "This sonata (?) consists of five movements," [251] and the scholar Leopold Hirschberg to ask whether "suite," in the absence of a better term, would not at least have been a less confining title.[252] Perhaps growing out of several gypsy numbers in Loewe's oratorio of 1842, *Johann Huss*, the descriptive movements in *Zigeuner-Sonate* begin (to translate) with "Forest Scene" in a, approximately in "sonata form" except that the middle section is new material subtitled "Longing for India" (with reference to gypsy origins). The further movements are entitled "Indian March," an A-B-A design in C with the "B" section marked "Adagio,"; "Dance," in E♭, with tarantella rhythms,

249. La Mara/MUSIKERBRIEFE II 130–32; for the Dussek vol. cf. HOFMEISTER 1815 (Whistling), 352.

250. About the time of Op. 16 Loewe came to know Weber (MGG VIII 1106).

251. AMZ XLIX (1847) 310.

252. Hirschberg/LOEWE 96 (contested in Egert/FRÜHROMANTIKER 139). Hirschberg is surprised that Liszt failed to mention this son. in his [spurious] treatise of 1859 on "The Gypsies and Their Music in Hungary."

and with trios subtitled "Men's Dance With Firebrands" (in g♯), "The Women Dance Around the Forest Grove" (in B♭), and "Festive Dance of the Children" (in B♭); "Evening Worship," in E, when Loewe adds, "They await the moonrise, which they worship as the reflection of the Indian sun temple"; and "Breaking Up Camp in the Morning," in a, a rondo. The musical word-painting is close and frequent throughout this programmatic sonata. It is less close in Loewe's "Spring" Sonata Op. 47, written in his most productive yet saddest period (right after his wife's early death).²⁵³ Op. 47 takes us from sunrise to sunset according to its four, more general titles and an opening six-line verse by Uhland (Ex. 33). This use of verse, the actual "Romance" sung "ad libitum" in Op. 16, and the numerous parallels with his ballads in the more pictorial and expressive sonata movements²⁵⁴ remind us that Loewe was at his best when he was re-creating the ballad style. At other times his music can be trite. Among Schumann's more unfavorable remarks about Op. 47 ²⁵⁵ is the opinion that Beethoven was more selective in his choice of material for the "Sinfonia pastorale," that in "small ways" Loewe's compositions "are often rather pretentious, and that they require us to accept the commonplaces repeated a hundred times over along with the basically good things just because it is a distinguished composer who repeats them."

As for Loewe's use of recurring motives to unify his cycles, his first sonata already provides a clear example. In fact, in this regard Op. 41 occasioned another of Schumann's less favorable reviews, this time signed by the harsh "Florestan." ²⁵⁶ After growing angry with three repetitions of an empty initial motive—"Heavens, thought I while playing ahead, to tell someone four times that you have little to say seems too many to me; and then those philistine ornaments!"— Schumann finds the motive recurring as a second theme. And turning to the second movement, "what do we find?"—the same, again, not only to open the "Andantino" section but in the "Allegro agitato" and the "Adagio non troppo lento" sections that follow. In the "Scherzo," where the motive seems to recur in varied disguises (e.g., mss. 1, 345, 359–60), Schumann overlooks or prefers to disregard it, but not in the finale, where "the fearsome old familiar sounds [again,] *pianissimo* [and] *legatissimo* [mss. 460–61, then] peeps out ubiquitously in round and angular shapes [e.g., mss. 444–45, 470–72, 486–88], and

253. Cf. Hirschberg/LOEWE 31–37; Egert/FRÜHROMANTIKER 131–34.
254. Cf. Hirschberg/LOEWE 97, 99, 42–43, 31–32, *et passim*.
255. Schumann/SCHRIFTEN I 91–92.
256. Schumann/SCHRIFTEN I 56–59.

Ex. 33. From the third movement of Karl Loewe's Sonata in G, "Le Printemps," Op. 47 (after the original Schlesinger ed. at the Library of Congress).

now drawing to a close, in order to make me quite beside myself it tips and taps [as in mss. 649–62]." But as viewed here, Florestan's objections seem excessively harsh. Loewe's ideas tend to be somewhat neutral, anyway. This much repetition and variation of a basic idea, which can be found more or less in all of his sonatas (not to mention Schumann's own sons.), helps it not to pall but to gain in identity. Even in Op. 41, whose only "programme" is its consistent "brillante" style, sufficient variety is achieved through resourceful rhythms, passagework, and keyboard techniques. There is, by the way, considerable affinity between Loewe's and Weber's treatment of the piano, not excluding wide ranges and wide stretches (as in Op. 41/i/37–43). There is also considerable affinity, and sometimes resemblance, between Loewe's themes and those of Beethoven,[257] even including the feel of Beethoven's Op. 57 in Loewe's Op. 32, also in f.[258]

Less significant as programme sonatas were (to translate) *Characteristic Tone-Paintings: Three Grand Sonatas for Piano, Four and Two Hands,* by the pianist **Gustav Krug** (1803–73) in Naumburg,

257. Cf. the exx. in Hirschberg/LOEWE 39 and 41, and 104; Egert/FRÜHROMANTIKER 130 (but the 3d last E probably should be ♮), 136–37.
258. But Op. 32 suggested Weber to Keferstein in CAECELIA XVII (1835) 65.

southwest of Leipzig.[259] Published in 1844 (?), these have titles and
subtitles depicting three crucial aspects of marriage—No. 1, "Love
Awakens": i, "First Meeting"; ii, "Serenade"; iii, "Declaration of
Love"; iv, "The Betrothal." No, 2, "The Engagement": i, "The
Engaged Couple"; ii, "Separation and Reunion"; iii, "Wedding Festivities." No. 3, "Wedlock": i, "The Domestic Quarrel"; ii, "The Wife's
Argument"; iii, "The Husband's Retort"; iv, "Finale." Appropriately,
only No. 3/ii and iii are for two rather than four hands. In a three-
column review of 1845,[260] the writer jests about the wide market this
music is certain to have, wonders whether quite different titles might
not have fit the music just as well, and regards the musical content
as too weak for the extent of these sonatas.

In Leipzig itself, the exceptional flutist (**Gottlieb**) **Heinrich Köhler**
(1765–1833) left some 50 sonatas for his instrument, including a few
trios (P-or-harp & Fl & Vn-or-Va), and about 30 more for P solo or
P-duet.[261] These works were published in the two decades from about
1805 to 1825.[262] A representative sampling of these sonatas confirms
the suspicion that such prolificity could only be identified with that
long line of facile, light, pedagogically oriented, socially pleasing
sonatas that continued throughout the 19th century without ever
coming to firm grips with essential Romantic trends or, for that matter,
with essential music (ssb III).[263] Had he continued to publish for
another decade Köhler might have had the honor of being scorned
by his cocitizen Florestan!

Almost as prolific in sonata writing, the learned Leipzig pianist
and theorist (**Johann Christian**) **Friedrich Schneider** (1786–1853), who
left well over a thousand compositions, composed some fifty sonatas
nearly all in his early years, between 1803 and about 1814, with over
half being published; he wrote only one sonata, in 1831 for cello, after
he moved to Dessau in 1821 and made his chief niche in oratorio.[264]
Most of these sonatas are for solo piano, but there are also a few each
for P-duet and 2 Ps, and for piano with one other instrument (Vn, Fl,

259. Cf. Riemann/LEXIKON I 963; HOFMEISTER IV (1844–51) 70.
260. NZM XXIII (1845) 125–26.
261. Cf. MGG VII 1323–24 (R. Eller). MGG omits the better known, younger Louis
Köhler (ssb XVIII), who appears not to be related to G. H. Köhler and is the only
one of the two in GROVE, Riemann/LEXIKON, and BAKER.
262. Cf. the lists in HOFMEISTER 1815 and 1828 (both Whistling), *passim;* also,
PAZDÍREK VIII 255–56.
263. Such and no more is also the uniform tenor of several short reviews in
AMZ: VIII (1805–6) 192, IX (1806–7) 469–70, XVIII (1816) 448, XX (1818) 214–15.
264. Cf. Mendel/LEXIKON IX 136–38; MGG XI 1900–1904 (M. Wehnert); PAZDÍREK
XIII 287–90; and the careful lists in Lomnitzer/SCHNEIDER 325–32, 339–40, 351–52,
355.

and Vc). Several, especially the earliest, were greeted with decidedly more space and interest than Köhler's sonatas in contemporary reviews, and deserved to be, although Rochlitz obviously went too far in making quite such a protégé of Schneider as a sonata composer.[265] In his last, somewhat tempered review of the sonatas Rochlitz deplored too little public interest in them, blaming it on their "unnecessary" difficulties, their "excessive," "constant" harmonic fullness that tends to obscure the melody, and a certain lack of melodic force, anyway.[266] Actually, although Schneider's later solo sonatas point toward the sort of virtuosity and pathos to be found in Hummel's and Dussek's best sonatas, they remained oriented to the two composers he himself cited as most central to his development, Mozart and, especially, Clementi.[267] In retrospect and by comparison with the sonatas of the leading early Romantics they hardly seem exceptional in their exploitation of the keyboard or their textural fullness. They do reveal considerable skill and surprising freshness in their melodic and harmonic variants, and in some original dispositions of the two-, three-, and four-movement cycles (such as Sc-Ro in Op. 37 in f). Yet their essential conservatism—something Rochlitz might have been little disposed to fault—must be the real reason why Schneider's better-than-average sonatas lost their appeal so soon. As noted earlier (ssb II), Schneider's revised harmony and composition treatise of 1827 (Schneider/ELEMENTS) showed no clear awareness of "sonata form."

The uncommonly gifted but short-lived pianist and composer (**Christian**) **Ludwig** (or **Louis**) **Schunke** (or **Schuncke;** 1810–34) left a *Grosse Sonate* in g, Op. 3, for piano solo, published by Hofmeister of Leipzig in 1834 and dedicated to the warm friend and mentor of his last year, Schumann (who dedicated his *Toccata* Op. 7 to Schunke in the same year).[268] Schunke had already studied with Reicha and met Berlioz, Kalkbrenner, Chopin, and probably Meyerbeer and the young Liszt

265. E.g., AMZ VII (1804–5) 653–57 (heralding the new talent disclosed in Op. 1), VIII (1805–6) 530–36 (enthusiastic, but with cautions about doubtful stretches and harmonies), IX (1806–7) 832–36 (confirming the promise of Op. 1; followed by the score of a "Scherzo" in e by Schneider, *Beilage* No. 2), XII (1809–10) 305–11 (by E. T. A. Hoffmann? maturing talent noted), XIII (1811) 135 (brief only because "previously discussed in such detail"), XIV (1812) 709 (same), XV (1813) 178–79, XVI (1814) 221–27 (by E. T. A. Hoffmann; mainly on P-duet Op. 29, with exx.), XVII (1815) 149–51 (still maturing), XVIII (1816) 382–84 (slight cooling).

266. AMZ XVIII (1816) 383–4. The only recent discussion of Schneider's sons. occurs on pp. 25–40 in the valuable diss. Lomnitzer/SCHNEIDER (mainly on the oratorios), which includes exx., and the autobiography of 1831 (pp. 292–301) by the extraordinarily methodical Schneider.

267 Cf. Lomnitzer/SCHNEIDER 27, 293, 295.

268. Cf. Flinsch/SCHUNKE; MGG XII 325–27 (H. Hopf); AMZ XXVII (1825) 272 and QUARTERLY VII (1825) 312 (both on his playing in Paris).

by March of 1832, when he wrote his father that he had composed "an
entire grand sonata in four movements with a fugue [actually a fugal
coda on the main theme] in the first [opening] allegro [movement]." [269]
In 1835 Schumann wrote a poetic review of this highly Schumannesque
work that also describes Schunke and how they met, and includes the
sentence, "You are a master of your art and I call the sonata your
best work, above all when you [yourself] play it." [270]

Another pianist and Reicha pupil, with a background in Leipzig
and Dresden, **Justus Amadeus LeCerf** (1789–1868) won less enthusiasm
from Schumann for a Sonata in C and a *Sonata quasi fantasia* for piano
solo, published together as Op. 21 by Trautwein of Berlin in 1840
(?).[271] Much the same that the AMZ reviewer wrote in a column-and-a-
half [272] Schumann said in a paragraph and we must reduce to a single,
by now familiar, kind of objection: Beethoven must not have lived in
vain and it was not enough simply to reproduce the successful, well-
balanced styles and forms of a half century back without taking cognizance of all that had happened to composition and the instrument
since then. In 1842, Schumann commended the effort but deplored at
length the inevitable monotony of a prize-winning *Sonata quasi
fantasia*, Op. 5 in f, composed entirely on an initial, unoriginal theme,
by the pianist **Julius Emil Leonhard** (1810–83).[273] Under Mendelssohn's personal influence, Leonhard also wrote two violin sonatas (Op.
10), the second of which was reviewed as skillful but dull.[274] Still less
enthusiastic, the gist of the verdict on a Sonata in D, Op. 15, for violin
and piano by the once popular choral composer **Ruprecht Johannes
Julius Dürrner** (1810–59) was that it was old-fashioned and pedagogic.[275] Published by Peters in 1846 (?), this work may have been composed just after Dürrner left Leipzig for Edinburgh in 1844. More
promise was seen, partly because they were early works, in Sonata in a,
Op. 1, and *Sonate romantique* in E♭, Op. 5, both for P solo, by the
once equally popular pianist, choral director, writer, and teacher
Louis Ehlert (1825–84), who had studied with both Schumann and
Mendelssohn.[276] Published in the later 1840's, these works were praised

269. Flinsch/SCHUNKE 201.
270. Schumann/SCHRIFTEN I 62–64.
271. Schumann/SCHRIFTEN II 10, 11. Cf. Mendel/LEXIKON VI 273–74 and Suppl. 210.
272. AMZ XLII (1840) 824–25 (G. W. Fink?).
273. Schumann/SCHRIFTEN II 79, 80–82. Cf. Mendel/LEXIKON VI 301–3; Riemann/
LEXIKON II 1026.
274. NZM XXIX (1848) 283 (A. Dörffel).
275. NZM XXV (1846) 128. Cf. Riemann/LEXIKON I 431; HOFMEISTER IV (1844–51)
39.
276. NZM XXV (1846) 99, and XXVIII (1849) 16–17; AMZ XLIX (1847) 291–92 (with
exx.). Cf. Mendel/LEXIKON III 327; Riemann/LEXIKON I 452; HOFMEISTER IV (1844–
51) 110.

290   ROMANTIC COMPOSERS AND THEIR SONATAS

mainly for their convincing flow, there being reservations about the force and originality of the ideas. Talent clearly short of genius was seen in the four-movement, motivically interrelated Sonata in a, Op. 17, for P solo, by the important successor to Mendelssohn, Hiller, and Gade as conductor of the Leipzig Gewandhaus concerts (**August Wilhelm) Julius Rietz** (1812–77).[277] This work, published about 1848, and one later one, Sonata in g, Op. 42, for piano and flute, published in 1876,[278] were Rietz's only ventures in the sonata among numerous instrumental compositions.

Other Central German Centers (Spohr)

In the central section of central Germany, **Johann Friedrich Nisle** (1768–at least 1837), able hornist and chamber music composer originally in Rudolstadt, may be mentioned for the novelty of two "Sonates pour le pianoforte et cor de chasse," Op. 6, dedicated to J. F. Reichardt (SCE 597–601) and published in 1805 (?),[279] or five years after Beethoven's similarly scored sonata (SCE 538). In Mühlhausen the organist **Ferdinand Gottfried Baake** (1800–at least 1830) won praise from two reviewers for a *Grosse Sonate* in C, Op. 6, dedicated to both Hummel and Friedrich Schneider (*supra*) and published by Breitkopf & Härtel about 1827.[280] The four movements were regarded as showing considerable individuality, skill, and motivic unity, and considerable challenge for the pianist in the manifold irregularities and variants in the note groupings. And we should not fail to take note of the one music publication by the renowned philosopher **Johann Friedrich Herbart** (1776–1841), a piano Sonata in D, originally published in 1808 and warmly praised for its skill, elevated content, and brilliant piano writing when it was reprinted (for the centennial of his birth?) in 1876.[281]

Ludwig Spohr (1784–1859), who ranked among the most esteemed and renowned Romantics in his own day, is still given considerable space by music historians,[282] especially for his high position in the history of violin playing. But among today's performers he has fallen about as hard as any once great has fallen. Even so, were the topic

277. NZM XXX (1849) 91–92 (A. G. Ritter). Cf. MGG XI 500–502 (F. Göthel).
278. Altmann/KAMMERMUSIK 277. Op. 42 is reviewed briefly as unoriginal but a good exercise, in SMW XXXV (1877) 531.
279. AMZ VIII (1805–6) Intelligenz-Blatt No. 8. Cf. MGG IX 1537–38 (E. Stiefel).
280. CAECILIA VIII (1828) 47–48 (G. Weber?); AMZ XXVIII (1826) 641–44. Cf. Schilling/LEXICON I 366–67.
281. SMW XXXIV (1876) 673–74; MW XI (1880) 377–78. Cf. MGG VI 183–85 (W. Kahl).
282. Cf. MGG XII 1061–77 (F. Göthel), with further bibl.

at hand his 30-odd string quartets, or his 20-odd violin concertos, or his several at least nominally programmatic works, or his numerous oratorios and operas, considerably more space could be justified here than for his 8 listed sonatas.[283] Not only were the sonatas a lesser part of his output quantitatively, but he himself spoke of them less, his contemporaries scarcely seem to have noticed them, they have no programmatic implications, and even the historians since then have rarely seen fit more than to mention them, if they do that. Yet these sonatas do have some bearing on the early-Romantic Era, beyond which Spohr did not advance stylistically. Fortunately we have rich environmental information in Spohr's autobiography.[284] This wonderfully entertaining book happens to tell only a little about the sonatas, but it tells much about his restless, transient concert life of which they were a part (and introduces us elsewhere in the present survey to almost as many sonata notables as we met in MOSCHELES).

Among pertinent landmarks in Spohr's life were his posts in Gotha from 1805 to 1812, in Vienna from 1812 to 1815 (where he knew Beethoven), and in Kassel from 1822 to his death. Six of his sonatas were written for harp and violin so that his first wife, the talented harpist Dorette Scheidler, could appear in concert with him. They date from 1805, the year before the marriage, to 1819,[285] or one year before Dorette had to stop playing harp in public (and fifteen years before her early death). The first was a Sonata in c, not published until 1917 but published again in 1954 [286] and now the only readily available sonata by Spohr. Then followed sonatas in B♭, Op. 16, composed in 1806 and published in 1809; E♭, Op. 113, 1806 and 1840 (?), respectively; A♭, Op. 115, 1809 and 1841;[287] E♭, Op. 114, 1811 and 1841; and A♭, 1819, not published. The only review found here of any of these sonatas is one of Op. 113, *Sonate concertante für Harfe oder Pianoforte und Violine oder Violoncell*.[288] The reviewer recognized this three-movement work (F-S-Ro) as an early one from its styles of melody, ornamentation, and passagework, and the freedom, as yet, from excessive fantasy or "wild Romanticism." He commented on the need to transpose the violin part, which had come about from Spohr's habit of tuning his wife's harp down a half-step (and writing the part

283. Cf. MGG XII 1064–68; GROVE VIII 17–19 (P. David), with a less complete but clearer view of the output.

284. Cf. our listing for Spohr/AUTOBIOGRAPHY.

285. Cf. Spohr/AUTOBIOGRAPHY I 90–96, II 59 and 93–95 (presumably referring to the 1819 Son. in A♭).

286. Zingel/SPOHR–m.

287. Cf. Spohr/AUTOBIOGRAPHY I 127 and 133.

288. NZM XV (1841) 2–3 ("O. L."). Op. 113 is called "Hamburg Sonate" in PAZDÍREK XIII 915, for no apparent reason.

a half-step higher) in order to avoid frequent string breaking and to put the harp in mechanically more convenient keys.[289]

In his later years Spohr left two other sonatas. One is his solo piano Sonata in A♭, Op. 125, in four movements (F-M-Sc-F), composed and first published in 1843, and dedicated to Mendelssohn.[290] A one-paragraph review of 1844 already arrives at an evaluation that still seems right in today's perspective.[291] The first eight measures are enough, says the reviewer, to reveal Spohr's typical chromatic suspensions and harmonic flow in triple meter; the forms are well organized, the harmony offers surprises, but the ideas lack originality; in the sense that it is written unpianistically in quartet style, it is harder to play than Chopin's or Thalberg's music. Nevertheless, nearly two pages in the autobiography referring to notices and congratulatory letters (including one from Mendelssohn, who later played the sonata for Spohr) bear witness to at least a temporary success for this one main work for piano by Spohr.[292] Spohr's final contribution of interest here was an example of his experimental bent (like his "double quartets" or his special harp tuning), a "Sonatine" for piano and voice in B♭, Op. 138, called "An Sie am Klavier," composed in 1848 and published soon after.[293] This work consists of a "Larghetto" introduction of more than one page and an "Allegro vivace" of nearly seven pages. The piano proceeds in regular phrases and characteristic piano passages through a miniature "sonata form" while the voice sings in slower notes along with it, more as an accessory than a leader.

Although the reviewer of Spohr's Op. 125 found the first eight measures typical enough, twelve later measures in the first movement (24–35), from the middle of the bridge to the middle of the second theme, will be more illustrative here (Ex. 34). They show more clearly his somewhat cloying chromaticism, some of that "quartet part-writing," the triple meter, and an undistinguished melody. They also show a hint of Weber in the figuration, in spite of some negative remarks Spohr had made about Weber's music.[294] It is true that the writing in Spohr's sonatas, as in his concertos, is always refined, never cheap and rarely faulty. As with Weber, the shortest movement—the

289. Cf. Spohr/AUTOBIOGRAPHY I 96.
290. It is discussed in Egert/FRÜHROMANTIKER 101–3. One of the more available, further eds. is in RICORDI ARTE-m X 7.
291. AMZ XLVI (1844) 151.
292. Spohr/AUTOBIOGRAPHY II 242–43. Another evidence might be seen in a pub. ed. of each separate mvt. (PAZDÍREK XIII 915).
293. Cf. PAZDÍREK XIII 915.
294. Spohr/AUTOBIOGRAPHY I 109.

Ex. 34. From the first movement of Ludwig Spohr's Sonata in Ab, Op. 125 (after RICORDI ARTE-m X 8).

scherzo—makes the most successful form. But the forms, though well designed outwardly—that is, in the sense of well-proportioned sections —lack inner unity because they lack compulsion. The fault lies partly in the melodic ideas, which are too bland and consistently lyrical to afford the needed identity or contrast. The fault also lies in the melodic treatment, which rarely goes as far as any organic development of the ideas. Unfortunately, the constant chromaticism does little to create a sense of drive. Instead, it combines with the bland melodic lyricism to make for a somewhat effeminate style. In any case, one recalls certain style paradoxes in Spohr's make-up—that in his early years he had found his principal model in Mozart (Hummel being an early favorite, too); that, like Weber, he had shown a certain resistance to Beethoven, though to late Beethoven in this instance; and that he had been one of the first to promote Wagner's operas (producing *The Flying Dutchman* in 1843 and *Tannhäuser* in 1853).[295] The Mozart influence is more apparent in Spohr's fairly conservative, early sonatas, for harp and violin. Not yet encumbered by so much chromaticism, these are not effeminate in character. Furthermore, they do provide

295. Cf. Spohr/AUTOBIOGRAPHY I 12, 109, 188–89, 192; II 245–47, 276–78, 307–8; Newman/WAGNER I 425–26.

some angular and rhythmically pointed ideas that contrast with the lyrical themes and give clearer definition to the forms and cycles (mostly 3-mvt., F-S-F). The violin gets the lion's share of the melodic material, the harp furnishing an accompaniment that is easy, fluent, and straightforward.

In Offenbach, where he took over his father's publishing firm and became one of the first Mozart specialists, **Johann Anton André** (1775–1842) left at least fifty solo or four-hand sonatas or sonatinas, four-hand divertimentos, and four-hand duos (preceded by several acc'd. P sons. in his youth).[296] Published by his own firm between about 1810 and 1825, these piano works are largely light, instructive pieces in two movements (M-Ro), showing decided skill and freshness in the idioms and forms of the Classic sonatina.[297] Thus, except for occasional Romanticisms in the melody, harmony, or scoring, André belongs right back with those other publishers who composed Classic sonatinas, including Clementi, Hofmeister, and Diabelli.[298] In Mainz, the violinist **Joseph Panny** (1794–1838), with a Viennese background, may be mentioned for the novelty of a *Sonate pour le Violon, sur la quatrième Corde, avec accompagnement de grand Orchestre,* published about 1830 by B. Schott's Söhnen in Mainz.[299] A reviewer (J. A. Gleichmann) welcomed this new cultivation of the long neglected G-string, obviously under Paganini's influence, and viewed it as an appropriately pathetic, three-movement work (Recitative-M-Va).[300]

The music writer and scholar **Emil Naumann** (1827–88), grandson of J. G. Naumann in Dresden (sce 592–93) and a pupil of Schnyder von Wartensee in Frankfurt (ssb VIII, *supra*) and Mendelssohn in Leipzig, published a single Sonata in c for piano as his Op. 1, about 1846 while active in Bonn.[301] Two reviewers agreed in calling it an inept, uninspired work.[302] On the other hand, two reviewers from the same periodicals[303] agreed in finding at least some charm and talent in an early work for solo piano published about 1845—Sonata in D, Op. 4, by

296. Cf. mgg I 459–61 (H. Wirth).

297. Among mod. eds.: 6 Sonatinas, P solo, Op. 34, Augener's Ed., No. 8005; 6 Sonatinas, P-duet, Op. 45, Summy-Birchard (1959); Divertimento in a, P-duet, Ed. Peters 6059; Divertimento in F, P-duet, Townsend/DUETS-m 59.

298. Cf. sce 751, 550–51, 566–67; ssb III. According to caecilia XIII (1831) 106–8, with corroboration from both men involved, André's P-duets Opp. 44 and 45 were also, but erroneously, pub. under Diabelli's name.

299. Cf. Schilling/LEXICON V 367–68; Riemann/LEXIKON II 1338.

300. caecilia XIII (1831) 119–20 (as part of a larger review of several of Panny's works, pp. 115–22).

301. Cf. mgg IX 1294–95 (R. Engländer); hofmeister IV (1844–51) 140.

302. nzm XXVI (1847) 166–67 (A. Dörffel) and amz XLIX (1847) 525–26.

303. nzm XXIV (1846) 145–46; amz XLVIII (1846) 609 (starting, "Again a sonata!")

a violinist who had played under Hummel in Weimar and was now resident in Düsseldorf, **Carl Müller** (1818–94).[304]

Mendelssohn in Berlin and Leipzig

(**Jakob Ludwig**) **Felix Mendelssohn** (**Bartholdy;** 1809–47), the most widely celebrated and esteemed composer in the period between Beethoven and Wagner, left at least 19 sonatas (or about 4 per cent) out of a total of some 500 works, large and small, published and unpublished, that are attributed to him (not including arrangements and transcriptions).[305] Among these sonatas, as the following tabulation shows, there are 6 for piano solo, 7 for piano and one other instrument, and six for organ. Not included here are the 9 early works for string orchestra in which the titles "Sinfonia" and "Sonata" are equated.[306] Only 9 of the 19 sonatas were published—which is to say, approved by Mendelssohn for publication—in his lifetime, including the 6 for organ, 2 for piano and cello, one for piano and violin, and one for piano solo. And 4 of the others still have not been published. Furthermore, even those that he did approve for publication seem to have won relatively little interest on the part of Mendelssohn himself, and with the partial exception of the organ sonatas, still less on the part of either his contemporary or subsequent biographers.[307] Next to the ever popular *Elijah,* the violin Concerto in e, the "Scotch" and "Italian" symphonies, "A Midsummer Night's Dream Music," or the "Hebrides" Overture, the sonatas do look small. Yet it hardly would be adequate here to give only passing mention to a body of sonatas that includes, according to all evidence accumulated here,[308] two of the few most popular cello sonatas in the 19th century and what are still the most popular organ sonatas along with J. S. Bach's and "The

304. Cf. Riemann/LEXIKON II 1225; HOFMEISTER IV (1844–51) 140 (but read Op. 4 for Op. 1).

305. For this rough estimate of total works, the approximately 400 items listed in MGG IX 83–85 (E. Werner) are increased by 25 per cent to include unlisted items among some 200 works still unpub. Much needed is a full *catalogue raisonné* of Mendelssohn's works to supersede the long outdated thematic index of 1873 (VERZEICHNISS MENDELSSOHN). A convenient though not complete catalogue is that in Gatti & Basso/LA MUSICA III 310–22, with pub. dates not in GROVE V 699–706 (P. M. Young) or MGG IX 83–85. Cf. Mendelssohn/VERLEGER 353–55.

306. MGG IX 62.

307. Thus, the important recent study Werner/MENDELSSOHN (1963) takes note only of Opp. 6, 45, and 106 (pp. 64–65, 360), and the few words it gives to these 3 sons. are more derogatory than favorable.

308. Cf. the sampling in the final column of the foregoing tabulation; but occasional guessing was necessary where the particular son. was not identified sufficiently or at all.

Mendelssohn's Sonatas

Op.	Key	Scoring	Composed	First ed.	Mendelssohn/ WERKE-m	Early titles; remarks	No. of performances reported in MT, 1860–80
105	E	P	1821	(see remarks)	XI/iii/68	"Sonatina"; facs. of first 2 pp. in Petitpierre/ MENDELSSOHNS 106–7	
4	g	P & Vn	1821	Rieter-Biedermann, 1868	IX/iv/43	ded. to Eduard Rietz cf. Jacob/MENDELSSOHN 54	3
	f	P	1823	Laue, 1825		cf. MGG IX 84	
	D	P & Va	by 1824	"in preparation"		the first ed. of 1941 is overlooked in recent lists	
	c	P & Cl	1824	Sprague-Coleman, 1941			
	Eb		1824			cf. Dahms/MENDELSSOHN 139.	
	d	P & Vn	ca. 1825	Laue, 1826			
6	E	P	1826	Rieter-Biedermann, 1868	XI/i/51		2
106	Bb	P	1827	Simrock, 1834	XI/iii/69		1
28	f#	P	1833		XI/i/56	"Phantasie"; but "Sonate écossaise" in the autograph MS; cf. NOTES XXI (1963–64) 92; ded. to Moscheles	
45	F	P & Vc	1838	Peters, 1953	IX/iv/45		10
58	Bb	P & Vc	1838	Breitkopf, 1839	IX/iv/46		14
65/1	f/F	organ	1841–42	Kistner, 1843	XII/84	ded. to Count Mathieu Wielhorsky announced as "Six Grand Sonatas"; Mendelssohn requested "Sonatas" rather than "Voluntaries" for the title; ded. to F. Schlemmer; Breitkopf & Härtel must have pub. Op. 65 in the same month (Oct., 1845; cf. Edwards/MENDELSSOHN 3–4)	12
65/2	c/C	"	1844	Coventry and Hollier, 1845	"		13
65/3	A	"	1844	"	"		6
65/4	Bb	"	1845	"	"		22
65/5	D	"	1844	"	"		5
65/6	d/D	"	1845	"	"		8

94th Psalm" by Reubke (sbe 271–72; ssb V and X). Indeed, Mendelssohn's organ sonatas of 1845 seem to have been played more in the later 19th century than any other sonatas in any setting except Beethoven's for piano.[309]

The Mendelssohn sources and literature, both first- and secondhand, are abundant but in disarray.[310] As with Schumann, something of what Otto Erich Deutsch did for Handel, Mozart, and Schubert is needed. The letters and other documents, and the music itself all need to be corrected, completed, brought fully to light and together, and reissued in authoritative modern editions.[311] For our purposes, we can only wonder whether the unpublished documents add to the sparse information on all but the organ sonatas. And we can only hope that the edition of Mendelssohn's works newly launched in 1961 will become in fact the needed revised and completed edition, including the six sonatas (and others?) lacking in the original "complete" edition of 1874–77.[312] In any case, not only sufficient documentary details but modern studies of all but the organ sonatas are lacking.[313]

As the foregoing tabulation shows, Mendelssohn wrote about half of his sonatas, including all of those for piano, in the 6 years from age 12 to 18. His main center was still Berlin and he was still under the influence of his teachers Ludwig Berger (with his heritage of Clementi and Field) and Zelter (with his background in the sphere of J. S. Bach).[314] Thanks partly to travels, he was also under the musical influence of early acquaintances like Weber, Hummel, Moscheles, Cherubini, Paganini, Spohr, and Spontini, as well as of Haydn, Mozart,

---

309. Cf. Colin Mason's bracketed comments on Mendelssohn's other chamber music in COBBETT II 135–36.

310. Brief summaries appear in MGG IX 82–83 and 95, and Werner/MENDELSSOHN 493–96.

311. In 1968 Mendelssohn/VERLEGER appeared as Vol. I of a projected complete ed.

312. Cf. Werner/MENDELSSOHN 52. Warm thanks are owing here to Professor Eric Werner, (then) at Hebrew Union School in New York, for his counsel on Mendelssohn and loan of unpub. letters and scores in microfilm. In 1961 the Deutscher Verlag für Musik in Leipzig issued 2 concertos as the initial items in the *Leipziger Ausgabe der Werke Felix Mendelssohn-Bartholdys,* sponsored by the international Felix-Mendelssohn-Gesellschaft. In 1967, Gregg Press in Farnborough (England) announced an unaltered reprint of the original Mendelssohn/WERKE-m.

313. On the organ sons. cf. Edwards/MENDELSSOHN (and further in ZIMG III [1901–2] 337–38 [C. Maclean]); Pearce/MENDELSSOHN (a 79-p. booklet of considerable interest); Mansfield/MENDELSSOHN; Werner/KIRCHENMUSIKER 119–24; Kremer/ORGAN 3–7. Dale/NINETEENTH 71–73 gives 3 pp. to a description of the P sons. (but, curiously, Egert/FRÜHROMANTIKER gives nothing); COBBETT II 134–35 gives nearly 2 cols. to Opp. 4, 45, and 58; and Horton/MENDELSSOHN 15–17 gives 3 pp. to the same works.

314. Cf. Werner/MENDELSSOHN 14–21.

and Beethoven through his studies.[315] Mendelssohn wrote nearly all of his other sonatas in the period after his move to Leipzig and the Gewandhaus orchestra conductorship, in 1835, and including his less satisfactory return to Berlin in 1841. By this period, thanks mainly to further travels, he had become acquainted with nearly every important musician of the time. But by then, too, he was much too firmly established in his own artistic directions to submit to further strong influences. Chopin and Schumann marked the limit of his conservative sympathies, while Berlioz and Liszt were generally beyond or outside the pale.[316] To revert to oft-cited tags, Mendelssohn remained in his later works more the "Romantic Classicist" than the Classicistic Romanticist.[317]

Looking back at the ripe age of eighteen in his short life, Mendelssohn took the view that only with instrumental music had he been successful thus far.[318] Although the nine or more sonatas he had already written, including even the two he had approved for publication, could not have been more than incidental to that view, their styles and forms and the few details of their circumstances that have turned up here help to explain the view. We must start with the fact that the two earliest sonatas, those preserved from his twelfth year, are surely two of history's most remarkable examples of musical precocity. Whatever their shortcomings may be in content, they not only confirm that this "wild, gay lad" [319] was already a master of his craft, but they imply an exceptional degree of confidence. Thus, surrounded by two quick, structurally secure but somewhat prim outer movements, the "Adagio" of Op. 105 in g seems to be a deliberate experiment in a more plastic, free kind of A-B-A design. This sonata was one of his own works, along with Bach fugues and pieces by Mozart and Beethoven, that Mendelssohn says he played, to the delight of Hummel and the Grand Duke at Weimar, during his remarkable visits in 1821 with the much older Goethe.[320] When the first edition of this work appeared in 1868 a London reviewer applauded it quite apart from its precocity, finding less interest only in the weaker slow movement, "as

315. Among numerous references, cf. Selden-Goth/MENDELSSOHN 22 and 31 (on Hummel), 82 (on Weber and others); MOSCHELES I 97–102; MENDELSSOHN/Moscheles 1–4; Mendelssohn/BRIEFE I 5 (on Weber); Lampadius/MENDELSSOHN 183–85 (Jules Benedict on Weber).

316. Cf. Werner/MENDELSSOHN 332, 381.

317. Cf. Einstein/ROMANTIC 124; Werner/MENDELSSOHN 515–21; Enke/MENDELSSOHN (concluding that he was a post- or "manneristic"-Classicist).

318. Letter of Sept. 24, 1827, as quoted in Werner/MENDELSSOHN 74.

319. Werner/MENDELSSOHN 19–20.

320. Selden-Goth/MENDELSSOHN 22. Cf. Werner/MENDELSSOHN 19–21.

might be expected in so juvenile a work." [321] The Sonatina in E, an eight-page piece he put into his sister Fanny's album,[322] gives clearer foretastes of his mature style. In fact, the "Lento" introduction and succeeding "Moderato" respectively anticipate by three years the lyricism and harmonic cumulation, and even the rhythmic regularity of the "Andante" as well as the light fluency of the "Presto" in the much played *Rondo capriccioso* in E, Op. 14. One might go further to say that here was a first germ of the second and third movements of the violin Concerto in e (1838–44).

Information is lacking on two of the next sonatas in our tabulation, those in D and c. Op. 4 in f was written for Mendelssohn's friend and violin teacher, the short-lived Eduard Rietz (older brother of the better known Julius Rietz mentioned earlier in this chapter). The Sonata in E♭ for piano and clarinet reportedly was written for the same clarinetist, Heinrich Bärmann, to whom Weber dedicated several works.[323] Besides their adjacent years of composition[324] and their similar three-movement plans (S/F-S-F; S/F-M-F), these two sonatas have in common some hints of Weber, as in the stepwise descents on two-note groups (e.g., Op. 4/i/19–20 and E♭/i/60–61) or some forthright melodic lines of folklike simplicity (e.g., Op. 4/ii/1–20; E♭/ii/1–10). For the rest, probably because of the violin, the key, and the dedicatee, Op. 4 is a more impassioned, almost rhapsodic, but not ineffective work, with a bit of the drive and purpose Mendelssohn must already have relished in Beethoven's solo piano sonatas in the same key. In 1825, a Berlin reviewer welcomed the absence of "grande," "pathétique," or "mélancholique" in the title (SSB II), remarked on young composers' predilections for F minor, and grew facetious over what he regarded as bold harmonies and other freedoms in Op. 4.[325]

Mendelssohn presumably did not consider Op. 106 to be as worthy of publication as Op. 6, though why is not clear. These two solo piano sonatas, in E and B♭, also composed in adjacent years, make a pair of about equal interest and quality, with somewhat similar four-movement cycles (totalling 703 and 528 measures, respectively). Moreover, they have in common what seems like more than chance resemblances to

321. MT XIII (1867–69) 382.

322. Petitpierre/MENDELSSOHN 100.

323. GROVE V 682, I 439–40.

324. MGG IX 84 gives 1825 as the year Op. 4 was composed, but 1823 is given in all other sources known here, hence is preferred in our tabulation.

325. Trans. in part in Jacob/MENDELSSOHN 48–50 from the Berlin *Allgemeine musikalische Zeitung*. In AMZ XXVII (1825) 531–32 a paragraph of generalized praise is given to this work's naturalness and skill, likening it to, but not equating it with, Mozart's best sons. for P & Vn.

Beethoven's solo piano sonatas Opp. 101 and 106, respectively.[326] Mendelssohn must have had in mind a kind of "hommage à Beethoven" and his Op. 101 when he opened Op. 6 with the same meter, tempo, and mood, and on nearly the identical idea; then, after a second movement in minuet rather than march style, wrote a "Recitativo" that follows Beethoven's movement in key and tempo, and with nearly the same idea, again. Although Mendelssohn's finale is not fugal its ideas resemble those in Beethoven's finale and it, too, returns to an earlier movement (as does the finale of Mendelssohn's Op. 106). Mendelssohn's Op. 106 in B♭ is close enough to Beethoven's Op. 106 in B♭, in certain respects, to make one wonder whether Julius Rietz (editor of Mendelssohn/WERKE-m) could have assigned the nonchronological, posthumous opus number with this resemblance in mind.[327] The opening character, tempo, meter, rhythmic pattern, and melodic outline are all similar, as are the unusual modulation to the submediant through its dominant, the contrapuntally imitative development, and the *diminuendo* ending (except for Beethoven's last two strokes). Other similarities appear in the preludial passages leading to the finale, in cyclical unity through similar incipits (as also in Mendelssohn's Opp. 105 and 6), in Mendelssohn's choice of a "Scherzo" for the second movement, and in this movement's use of the same 2/4 meter and tonic-minor key that Beethoven uses for his trio section, where the elfin style seems almost to be a copy of Mendelssohn in advance! There happens to be ample evidence not only that Mendelssohn knew, played, and modeled after the late as well as the earlier music of Beethoven,[328] but that he knew Op. 106 in particular. About a year before he composed his own Sonata in B♭, he wrote an impish letter to his sister Fanny pretending he was Beethoven and assuring her that "I am sending you my Sonata in B-flat Op. 106 as a present on your birthday. . . ." [329]

In 1834, Schumann, who never ceased treating Mendelssohn as "the

326. Probably taking the cue from Schumann/SCHRIFTEN I 124, Georgii/KLAVIER-MUSIK 307 calls attention to the resemblance of Op. 6 to Beethoven's Op. 101. Bülow, unaware of these early sons., thought it was just as well that Mendelssohn had not competed with Beethoven in the field of the piano son. (BÜLOW BRIEFE III 50).

327. After Op. 72 Mendelssohn's op. nos. were assigned posthumously. They are not necessarily chronological after Op. 80. Cf. Werner/MENDELSSOHN 493–94.

328. E.g., cf. Werner/MENDELSSOHN 25, 83, 107–9, 115–16, 149, 437, *et passim;* Hiller/MENDELSSOHN 214–15.

329. As trans. from a letter of Nov. 8, 1825 in Werner/MENDELSSOHN 108–9 (with parentheses around "Op. 106" that are not in the facs. of the original letter that Dr. Werner kindly made available to this study). Op. 106 is among selected piano works by Mendelssohn scheduled (as of 1967) to appear in "Urtextausgabe" under Dr. Werner's editorship, incorporating changes Mendelssohn made in the autograph.

man to whom I look up as to a high mountain . . . a perfect God," [330] took poetic pleasure in Mendelssohn's effective treatment of the conventional in Op. 6 and already recognized a "reflective sadness" common to its first movement and that of Beethoven's Op. 101, as well as traces of Weber in its finale.[331] As for Op. 106, the same London reviewer quoted above on Op. 105 notes "a large advance, in power of thought and construction," anticipates later writers in liking the "Scherzo" best and, again, the "Andante quasi allegretto" least, and, like Schumann on Op. 6, finds traces of Weber in this finale.[332]

Mendelssohn's Op. 28 in f$\sharp$ was called "Sonate écossaise" on the autograph but its title was changed, presumably by himself, to *Phantasie* for the first edition in 1834.[333] Thus it belongs with the numerous 19th-century sonatas of Beethoven, Schubert, Schumann, Liszt, and others, that raise the question of sonata or fantasy (SSB II). In this instance the fantasy predominates over the sonata in the sense that free passagework predominates over phrase-and-period syntax, or that leading ideas tend to lose themselves in the passagework. However, the ideas do have enough identity to reveal related incipits in the three rather briefly developed movements (M-F-VF, totalling 467 mss.).

Mendelssohn's last nine sonatas, composed between 1838 and 1845, show the mature craftsman who has crystallized his style and no longer experiments so much with the form or seeks to model after his immediate predecessors. The recently published Sonata in F for piano and violin is an effective if not a greatly inspired example.[334] It is on a par with the cello sonata of the same year (1838), Op. 45 in B♭, in quality, import, and length (697 as against 773 mss.). The two works reflect Mendelssohn's new interest in chamber music in preference to solo piano music:

Pianoforte pieces are not exactly the things I write with the greatest pleasure, or even with real success; but I sometimes want a new thing to play, and then if something exactly suitable for the piano happens to come into my head,

330. Letter of April 1, 1836, as trans. in Jansen/SCHUMANN I 87.

331. Schumann/SCHRIFTEN I 123–24 and II 387, fn. 168. Moscheles' enjoyment of Op. 6 is attested in MENDELSSOHN/Moscheles 3–4. A one-col. review in AMZ XXIX (1827) 122–23 commends Mendelssohn's restraint in publishing and the worth of all he did release, especially the freshness, lyricism, expressiveness, and good piano writing in Op. 6.

332. MT XIII (1868) 382 and 387; cf. the similar views on p. 346 after a performance of Op. 106 by Arabella Goddard. An early reference to Op. 106 occurs in AMA No. 29, p. 9 (Jan. 13, 1827).

333. Cf. Dahms/MENDELSSOHN 131; Georgii/KLAVIERMUSIK 309–10. Mendelssohn's reference to a "Schottische Sonate" in his letter of May 25, 1830 (Mendelssohn/BRIEFE I 5) must refer to an early draft of Op. 28; otherwise it is unclear.

334. Mod. ed.: Peters No. 6075 (1953), with facs. from the autograph (our Ex. 35, *infra*) and a brief preface (Y. Menuhin).

even if there are no regular passages in it [i.e., characteristic opportunities for display?], why should I be afraid of writing it down? Then, a very important branch of pianoforte music which I am particularly fond of—trios, quartets, and other things with accompaniment—is quite forgotten now, and I feel greatly the want of something new in that line. I should like to do a little towards this. It was with this idea that I lately wrote the sonata for violin, and the one for cello, and I am thinking next of writing a couple of trios [the Trio in d, Op. 49, was composed in 1839].[335]

Cast in similar designs, both sonatas follow that most standard plan of two quick movements separated by a slower movement, and both still show an interest in cyclic unity through similar incipits. A description of the first movement of the violin Sonata in F should suffice for the numerous, fairly (but never rigidly) standardized uses of "sonata form" in his later sonatas and will bring to light one example of a certain rhythmic monotony or doggedness that seems to constitute the main "problem" of Mendelssohn. The opening theme (similar to systems 3 and 4 in Ex. 35, *infra*) is based on one of Mendelssohn's most characteristic rhythms, ♩ ♩♪ |♩ .[336] The reiterated pattern and its continuation stretch into a 9-measure question phrase by the piano and a 10-measure answer by the violin. The same pattern and its augmentation underlie the simple modulatory bridge (mss. 19–41) to the dominant (by way of its dominant, colored by borrowed tones). The second theme (mss. 42–64) provides contrast through its steadier, quieter course and its modulation (by change of mode) to the lowered submediant, but it recalls the over-all curve of the first theme and presently returns to the pattern, augmented, in the accompaniment. Throughout the closing material (mss. 64–102), which returns to the dominant, the initial pattern and its augmentation prevail again. So do they in the development section (mss. 103–87), which passes through d, g, and E♭ before returning gradually to F by way of V of V of V. By now the pattern, which at best identifies with a rather cut-and-dried melodic figure, wears thin in spite of its elisions and imitations (but without contretemps or other rhythmic relief). Yet it returns fortissimo to initiate and dominate the recapitulation again (mss. 188–266), which remains in the home key, fortunately with a reduction of the opening thematic group by half (from 60 to 30 mss.). The coda (mss. 267–305) begins and climaxes on the initial pattern. Our Ex. 35 includes the last 22 measures, with climactic references to the second theme and to

335. From a typically chatty letter (Aug. 17, 1838, to F. Hiller), as trans. in Hiller/MENDELSSOHN 131–32. Cf., also, Selden-Goth/MENDELSSOHN 278, 281; Mendelssohn/VERLEGER 300–303.

336. E.g., this and very similar patterns predominate in 9 of the 43 nos. in *Elijah*: 11, 14, 20, 22, 34, 38, 39, 41, 43.

Ex. 35. Facs. from the autograph of Felix Mendelssohn's
Sonata in F (1838) for piano and violin (after the frontispiece in
Edition Peters No. 6075, by kind permission of the publisher).

the first theme played fortissimo.[337] It also includes the start of the second movement, in the submediant major key. Throughout this A-B-A design and its extended coda, our pattern, in a more gentle variant, still plays the leading role. In the finale, a deft, sparkling sonata-rondo form in nearly *perpetuum mobile* style, the pattern no longer obtrudes, although Mendelssohn may mean it to be hidden in the steady 16th-note pattern of the refrain.

Mendelssohn was probably indulging in false modesty when he wrote Hiller he was sending him the score of Op. 45 only "because of the lovely cover, and by way of a novelty—otherwise there is not much in it." [338] But there is no question as to the greater musical worth of Op. 58 in D, written about three years later. As viewed here, it ranks with Mendelssohn's finest chamber music. Compared with Op. 45,[339] it well deserves the "Grande" Mendelssohn would not let Kistner add to the title.[340] It opens on a more expansive, idiomatic cello theme, which does not wear thin for that reason even though it supplies the outline for the second theme; its initial motive recurs just as often as in Op. 45; and this motive relates to the incipits of the other three movements, too. Moreover, its harmony is richer and more subtle, with remarkable variety in the use of Mendelssohn's most favored chord, the dim.-7th (as in Op. 58/i/129–30, 191 and 193; or iii/42–44; or iv/1–4, 228–30, 249–53). The generally higher *tessitura* of the cello part and its balance with the piano part make for more telling, grateful sound. In the harmony, melodic development, and texture (as in the 3ds and 6ths of iv/149–50) are frequent anticipations of Brahms. Of special appeal are the scherzo, again (ii), and the juxtaposition in the short "Adagio" (iii) of irregular chorale phrases in the piano with quasi recitative in the cello, so that the A-B-A design consists of chorale, recitative, and a remarkable synthesis of both (as in Ex. 36).

During hectic concert and social activities in England in 1844,

337. The corrections in the neat MS illustrate "the disease" of constant alterations from which he said he suffered chronically (Edwards/MENDELSSOHN 7).

338. Hiller/MENDELSSOHN 135; he similarly disparaged his "Songs Without Words" (cf. Werner/MENDELSSOHN 220; Worbs/MENDELSSOHN 244, fn. 40). As usual, Schumann had only praise for this "latest" work by Mendelssohn, calling it "more refined, more rapturous, . . . more Mozartean than ever" (Schumann/SCHRIFTEN I 398–99; faultily trans. in Jacob/MENDELSSOHN 100–101). Mendelssohn played Opp. 45 and 58 with Julius Rietz (Lampadius/MENDELSSOHN 144; MOSCHELES II 179). Cf., also, Müller-Reuter/LEXIKON 137–38.

339. Cf., also, Dahms/MENDELSSOHN 139–40.

340. Werner/MENDELSSOHN 335. A peripheral explanation for Mendelssohn's restraint in publishing his music is the curiously fastidious argument, with reference to Op. 58 and other new works, in his letter to K. Klingemann of June 12, 1843 (Selden-Goth/MENDELSSOHN 325; SSB IV).

Ex. 36. From the third movement of Felix Mendelssohn's Sonata in D for piano and cello, Op. 58 (after Mendelssohn/ WERKE-m IX/iv/46).

Mendelssohn's impressive playing of Bach and his improvising at the organ brought a commission to write some organ "voluntaries." Although he agreed such a title would "suit" his pieces—"the more so as I do not know what it means precisely," he quipped in flawless English —he preferred to call them "sonatas," and his publisher agreed.[341] They were, in fact, the first consequential organ pieces to bear this title in the 19th century (ssb V). When Coventry and Hollier announced them in 1845, now grown to six from a planned three, the high-flown title was "Mendelssohn's School of Organ-Playing . . . Six Grand

341. Cf. Edwards/MENDELSSOHN 2–4; ZIMG III (1901–2) 337–38 (C. Maclean).

Sonatas for the Organ." But this title was soon reduced to *Six Sonatas for the Organ,* Op. 65. The early comments and reviews were just as high-flown, including Schumann's warm letter about the "intensely poetic new ideas—what a perfect picture they form in every sonata! . . . I . . . think of a St. Cecilia touching the keys; and how delightful that that should be your wife's name! Above all, Nos. 5 and 6 seem to me splendid." [342]

Mendelssohn's preference for "sonata" as the title of his organ pieces probably reflects their somewhat greater size, freedom, and exploitation of the organ as compared with the traditional English "voluntary." [343] In the present survey this majestic music must be regarded as peripheral to the mainstream of sonata history, but central to—in fact, a major landmark in—the special and equally venerable branch of the organ sonata (SBE 56 *et passim;* SCE 89–91 *et passim*). Each "sonata" is a cycle, to be sure, but the cycles, of from two to four movements nearly always in the same key, are highly irregular and foreign to the mainstream of the sonata. In fact, the separate movements seem originally to have been composed as independent organ "studies," of which three of four go back to earlier works; and only after their completion were they grouped, without any premeditated unity, into cycles.[344] More indicative are the forms of the movements, which scarcely ever approach "sonata form," [345] but nearly always are those most encountered in the organist's, especially the church organist's, literature. Among the latter are fugues, chorale fantasias, and variations, and imitative or figural preludes. The chorale, which Mendelssohn cultivated so often in his music, serves even more often and significantly here.[346] The polyphonic styles and mastery at times take us very close to the music of J. S. Bach that Mendelssohn did so much to promote. All of which is hardly conducive to the statements, dualistic opposition, and development of full-fledged themes, the transparent textures, the slow harmonic rhythm, and the broad tonal schemes that we ordinarily identify with the Classic and Romantic sonata.

342. Cf. Edwards/MENDELSSOHN 4–6. For a typical review, cf. AMZ XLVIII (1846) 97–102 (A. G. Ritter). Cf. Mendelssohn/VERLEGER 156–64, *passim,* on the Breitkopf & Härtel ed. in the same year of 1845.
343. Cf. Werner/KIRCHENMUSIKER 119–20; Pearce/MENDELSSOHN 7–9.
344. Werner/KIRCHENMUSIKER 119–20.
345. Cf. Mansfield/MENDELSSOHN 562–63.
346. Cf. Pearce/MENDELSSOHN 43–50 and MT XLII (1901) 798 (Otto Goldschmidt to John Stainer) on chorale identifications; in the latter, on p. 797, are 3 facs. of passages in the autographs of these sons. At least some of these sons. may have been intended for use in the Lutheran service (Mansfield/MENDELSSOHN 564); cf. MT XXII (1881) 589 and Pearce/MENDELSSOHN 5 for their use in English services.

Other Berlin Composers (L. Berger, E. T. A. Hoffmann)

The largest number of German sonata composers in the first half of the 19th century was in Berlin. One of Mendelssohn's principal teachers in that city was **Ludwig Berger** (1777–1839), who brought his special fondness for Mozart, Gluck, and Beethoven to the lessons, as well as his own background of associations with J. G. Naumann, Clementi, Field, Steibelt, Cramer, Klengel, and many others.[347] Although Berger made his mark chiefly as a late, somewhat Romanticized exponent of the "Berlin Liederschule," he also excelled as a pianist and teacher, and left at least eight piano sonatas, all composed relatively early, between 1800 and 1813. These last include two unpublished sonatas composed in 1800, in Eb and G, each in three movements; a three-movement Sonata in c "über die Figur ♪♪♪♪," Op. 18, composed in 1801 but not first published until 1825;[348] a three-movement "Sonate pathétique" in c, composed by 1804, dedicated to Clementi, first published in 1813,[349] then republished by 1815 as Op. 7 in a revised ("nouvelle") edition that left only the second movement unaltered and saw "Grande" added to the title in several reprints; a Sonata in g, Op. 15, for P-duet, composed in 1805 but not published until 1825;[350] a three-movement "Grande Sonate" in F, Op. 9, arranged about 1810 from a trio for two horns and piano[351] and first published in 1818; a two-movement "Grande Sonate" in Eb, Op. 10, composed about 1810 and first published in 1818; and an unpublished, one-movement sonata in G composed in London in 1813.

Berger's Op. 18 (recalling J. E. Leonhard's "Prize Sonata," *supra*) is a highly resourceful, exhaustive, and exhausting essay on its single six-note motive. The plainness of the motive, its recurrence without letup in all three movements, the lack of a break before the second movement, and the choice of c or C for all three movements do lead to monotony in spite of the motivic resourcefulness. Yet some answers

347. The important new study Siebenkäs/BERGER, superseding and encompassing previous studies, includes a biography (pp. 9–32), a main section on the songs, a briefer discussion of the instrumental and choral works (including P sons., pp. 182–89 and 192, with exx.), letters, catalogues of the works (with sons. on pp. 250–51 and 257), and a bibliography. The sons. had previously been discussed in Egert/FRÜHROMANTIKER 104–8, with ex.

348. These first 3 sons. survive together in MSS as "Oeuvre I" (Siebenkäs/BERGER 289, fn. 444), but the pub. Op. 1 is different.

349. Peters plate no. 1112 (cf. Deutsch/NUMMERN 14); hence, probably not late 1814 or early 1815 as in Siebenkäs/BERGER 183 and 250.

350. Cf. Siebenkäs/BERGER 192.

351. Cf. Siebenkäs/BERGER 289, fn. 455.

come to mind when Paul Egert objects that Op. 18 cannot be called a
"sonata" because no movement achieves "sonata form" (presumably
meaning thematic dualism), or when Dieter Siebenkäs finds "no new
aesthetic ideal" in Op. 18, only an artistic exploit in motivic technique.[352] A "sonata form" does exist in the first movement, although
Berger's tonal and dynamic contrasts do more to outline it than his
transformation of the motive by way of a "second theme." In any case,
it is hardly necessary to reargue here the unjustness of disqualifying a
sonata because it lacks any movement in "sonata form" (cf. SCE 16,
117–18). No question of such a lack was raised in Rellstab's unconstrained praise of Op. 18 (along with Opp. 7, 9, and 10), calling it
superior "in depth of invention and meaningful beauty of form" even
to Weber's and Hummel's best sonatas.[353] Also, what now seems like
excessive motivic play must be recalled as one kind of "aesthetic
ideal" in early, post-Beethovian Romanticism, if only because Schubert, Schumann, Mendelssohn, Weber, Hummel, and so many other
early Romantics showed such a predilection for it (SSB VI).

Berger's most original and telling sonata is certainly his *Grande
Sonate pathétique* in c, Op. 7, after which Opp. 9 and 10 suggest
progressive retreats into the demands—mainly for facility, fluency, and
regularity—of public taste. Op. 7 is original in spite of its outward
imitations of Beethoven's Op. 13, imitations not only in the title and
key, but in the recurrence of the slow "Introduzione" during the first
movement and in some thematic resemblances (e.g., cf. Berger's Op.
7/i/28–30 with Beethoven's Op. 13/i/140–43). Op. 7 is original especially in the fresh rhythms and melodies one knows and expects in
Berger's songs—for example, in its rondo, tarantella-like finale
(Ex. 37). Berger's harmony and piano writing are often ingenious and
effective, too. Generally less interesting are his accompaniments and
his efforts to develop his ideas.

The versatile **Ernst Theodor Amadeus Hoffmann** (1776–1822) was
primarily a jurist by profession, a Romantic novelist, poet, and critic
by principal reputation, and a composer by preference.[354] Berlin was
his chief among several centers, although he was active in the now
Polish centers of Plock and Warsaw during the two or three years

---

352. Egert/FRÜHROMANTIKER 105–6; Siebenkäs/BERGER 182–83.

353. As quoted in Egert/FRÜHROMANTIKER 106 from *Ludwig Berger* (Berlin, 1846)
by Ludwig Rellstab, pp. 20–21. Almost as much praise, of a similar nature, is
given to Op. 15 in the only review of a son. by Berger found here, AMZ XXVIII
(1826) 510–11. Many of the other references indexed in the first AMZ "Register"
confuse this and another Ludwig Berger, in south Germany, as MGG I 1691–93
(W. Kahl) still does (cf. Siebenkäs/BERGER 246).

354. Ehinger/HOFFMANN is the main recent study of his life and works (summarized and revised in MGG VI 528–38 [H. Ehinger]).

Ex. 37. From the finale of Ludwig Berger's *Grande Sonate pathétique* in c, Op. 7 (after the Hofmeister ed. at the Library of Congress).

(1803–5) when he is thought to have written most if not all of about eight piano sonatas.[355] None of these sonatas was published in Hoffmann's lifetime, leaving little chance that they could have been known, heard, or discussed much in their day if at all. Only five have survived—in A, f, F, f, and c♯—all but the first being published in 1922 as the first volume in an abortive "complete works" (Hoffmann/WERKE-m I).[356] These sonatas interest us today primarily as coming from the early-Romantic creator of the eccentric, fantastic, and fascinating tales

355. The sons. are discussed at some length in G. Becking's "Vorwort" and "Revisionsbericht" in Hoffmann/WERKE-m I, and more briefly in Kroll/HOFFMANN 536–38, in E. Kroll's review of Hoffmann/WERKE-m I (zfMW V [1922–23] 347–48), and in Ehinger/HOFFMANN 207–9 and 220 (but not in Egert/FRÜHROMANTIKER).

356. Unclear, perhaps overlapping references to other sons., some of which must pertain to one or more of the surviving sons., include a set of 3 sons. in d, f, and C, another set of 3 in similar style (according to Hoffmann's own comment in 1807, but perhaps referring only to a projected set), a Son. in b♭ mentioned in correspondence of 1809 with Nägeli, and another son. sent to Nägeli in 1809. Cf. Becking's preface to Hoffmann/WERKE-m I, Ehinger/HOFFMANN 208, zfMW V (1922–23) 348. Further mod. eds.: Son. in c♯ and Son. in F/ii, pub. by Drei Masken Verlag of Munich in 1921 (G. v. Westerman); Son. (1) in f, Newman/THIRTEEN-m 114, with preface pp. 18–20; Son. in A, Bärenreiter (BA 3420; cf. the Bärenreiter announcements for Mar., 1967, p. 10). Bücken/19. 35–36 includes exx. from Sons. 2 and 3.

that musicians first hear about by way of Schumann's *Kreisleriana*[357] or Offenbach's *Les Contes d'Hoffmann.* But if Hoffmann's opera *Undine,* representing his main forte in music, proves to be disappointingly pale and conservative beside the tales, his sonatas, without benefit of text or programme, prove to be that much more pale and conservative beside *Undine.*[358] Moreover, they have to be characterized as somewhat naive, affected, and gauche.

Probably Hoffmann wrote most or all of his sonatas in response to a general solicitation in 1803 from the Swiss publisher Nägeli. As we have noted on several earlier occasions (e.g., SCE 26; SSB IV, VIII [Liste, *supra*]), Nägeli mainly sought grand, unusual sonatas, strong especially in both counterpoint and virtuosity. However, Nägeli, who had already convinced Hoffmann in 1803 of the "Miserabilität" of a *Grosse Fantasie* he had written, never did accept for publication any of the several sonatas Hoffmann submitted up to 1809.[359] Yet Hoffmann was disposed by background and taste, if not by skill, to comply with Nägeli's requirements. Although in 1814 he criticized one of the strongest sonatas of his former teacher Reichardt as being still in Emanuel Bach's rather than Mozart's or Beethoven's style (SCE 601), his review applies even more to his own sonatas. For Hoffmann seems to have found special fascinations not simply in counterpoint but in a kind of archaic counterpoint that he must have derived in his own amateurish manner from both J. S. and Emanuel Bach by way of another former teacher, C. W. Podbielski (SCE 779). There is much else in his style that is derivative and outmoded, too. The lyrical slow introductions in all but the second of the extant sonatas show the influence of the *Fantaisie* in c, K. 475, by Mozart (after whom Hoffmann changed his third name to Amadeus). The "Scherzo" of the Sonata in c♯ may actually be modelled after Beethoven's Op. 2/1/iii or 10/2/ii. On the other hand, Hoffmann was probably furthering his own concept of the sonata when he virtually repeated the initial, fugal allegros of the first two sonatas as the finales.

In an outline of 1808 for an article "On Sonatas" that never materialized, Hoffmann gives somewhat obscure clues as to what the sonata meant to him:[360]

357. The live model for "Capellmeister Kreisler" was the gifted but eccentric Johann Ludwig Böhner (1787–1860), who himself left 2 P sons. pub. by 1815 and 1849 (cf. GROVE I 788 [G. Grove]; HOFMEISTER 1815 [Whistling] 342; NZM XXX [1849] 14; PAZDÍREK II 836–37).

358. Cf. Georgii/KLAVIERMUSIK 280–81, fn.

359. Cf. Becking's preface in Hoffmann/WERKE-m I. A premature announcement in June, 1808, that Nägeli would "soon" publish 3 of these sons. appeared in AMZ X (1807–8) 590.

360. Trans. in full from Hoffmann/SCHRIFTEN 16.

> Perfection of the pianoforte.—Only beauty
> of harmony, not of tone.—
> Caprice must appear to prevail, and the
> more the highest artistry is thus concealed, the
> more perfect [the sonata will be].
> Greatness of the theorist Haydn.—
> Joy of the cultured man in the
> artistic, etc.

Elsewhere Hoffmann is said to have acknowledged that his sonatas were composed in an old manner and made up largely of a slow introduction and a contrapuntally realized allegro.[361] Musicians today are likely to recognize the flair for the dramatic and lyrical in these sonatas but turn away from the mild, unpianistic virtuosity and from their collapse in clumsy, thick textures, with awkward, purposeless voice-leading.

Franz Lauska (1764–1825), a Czech who had studied in Vienna with Albrechtsberger, settled in Berlin in 1798 to become a successful pianist and teacher (of Meyerbeer among others). In the twenty-five years from around 1796 to 1821 about as many piano sonatas by him were published, including one each with violin and with cello "accompagnement," and one for P-duet.[362] These sonatas immediately reveal the professional, as against the neophyte in Hoffmann's sonatas. They are on a par in competence with Berger's, but lack an equivalent creative spark, or, for that matter, any such dramatic flair as Hoffmann displayed. The very number of Lauska's sonatas rightly implies facility, fluency, popularity, conservatism, and pedagogic values. And such were the traits variously emphasized, deplored, or commended in at least nine contemporary reviews of the sonatas, which do confirm that attention was once paid to them.[363] In addition, one cannot help noting a certain marchlike squareness even after Op. 21 (about 1807) and the introduction of certain Romanticisms in the rhythms, harmony, and accompaniment. Suggestions of Mozart and Clementi were remarked especially in the early reviews. But there are clear hints, too,

---

361. Cf. Becking's preface in Hoffmann/WERKE-m I and Kroll/HOFFMANN 538.

362. Cf. MGG VIII 343–44 (J. Bužga). The 25 years of pub. are suggested by the announcements of his 5th and last son. pubs. (Opp. 9 and 46, respectively) in the "Intelligenz-Blatt" for Sept., 1799, and for Jan., 1822, in AMZ II and XXIV. The sons. are discussed briefly in Egert/FRÜHROMANTIKER 43–47, with exx.

363. AMZ III (1800–1801) 120 (Op. 9; empty), V (1802–3) 562 (P + Vn), VII (1804–5) 642–45 (Op. 19; more favorable), VIII (1805–6) 799–800 (Op. 20; craft improving), XIV (1812) 517–18 (Op. 28, P + Vc; favorable) and 392–93 (Op. 30; skill but not imagination), XVII (1815) 510–11 (Op. 34; exceptional for Lauska in being of more artistic than pedagogic interest) and 631 (Op. 35; of training value), XXV (1823) 850–52 (Op. 45; pedagogically useful and pleasingly conservative, but sterile). In MW XXV (1894) 444, pedagogic values could still be found in a reprint of Op. 20 in B♭, "perhaps 100 years old by now."

of Beethoven (for whom Lauska did some proofreading of scores in
1821 [364]), as in Lauska's own *Sonate pathétique* in c, Op. 43 (about
1820). There are also eerie hints, but hardly the creative strength, of
Weber in Lauska's Sonata in B♭, Op. 41 (1819), dedicated to Weber.[365]
It will be recalled that in 1816 Weber had dedicated his Sonata in A♭,
Op. 39, to Lauska, apparently deriving bits of themes and styles from
Lauska's Sonata in the same key, Op. 24, published in 1809. And still
earlier, in 1812, Weber had reviewed Lauska's *Grande Sonate* in f, Op.
30, saying little more than that it showed how Lauska worked midway
between the most banal and the most lofty composers.[366]

Berlin was only one of several centers in which the concert pianist
and teacher **Aloys Schmitt** (1788–1866) was active.[367] His many modish
works include a substantial number of sonatas for piano alone and
with violin or cello, first published over about a half century from
1813.[368] A reading of one of the most widely circulated of these, the
four-movement *Sonata di bravura per il pianoforte* in C, Op. 26
(1819?), reveals a nonexploratory idiom and only moderate technical
demands in spite of the title and the rapid figuration in the concluding
variations on a theme of Mehul, with their coda in tarantella style.[369]
After a fantasy introduction, the first movement pursues a five-note
motive with considerable melodic and rhythmic variety and ingenuity.
The slow second movement indulges in enharmony and ornamental
passages that point toward Beethoven. Interesting is the title of the
third movement, "Menuetto scherzo," during this period of transition
from the minuet to the scherzo. Actually, the scherzo style prevails. A
reading of a later, much simpler, more routine work by Schmitt, his
Sonata cantante in B♭, Op. 123, for P & Vn (*ca.* 1853), suggests that
he was but another composer who gradually gave in to the deadening
requirements of public taste.[370]

Several other composers active for short or long periods in Berlin
deserve at least a mention for forgotten sonatas that once aroused the
reviewer's ire or enthusiasm, including a couple that Schumann greeted

364. Cf. Anderson/BEETHOVEN II 918–20.
365. Cf. Egert/FRÜHROMANTIKER 45–46.
366. Reprinted from *Zeitung für die elegante Welt* in Weber/WEBER III 71.
367. Cf. MGG XI 1868–69 (R. Sietz).
368. Cf. HOFMEISTER 1815 (Whistling)-1859, *passim*.
369. A review in AMZ XXIII (1821) 283–84 put this son. on a par with Weber's
"three great bravura sonatas" (to date), finding its difficulties chiefly those of
stretches and full texture and giving Schmitt the palm for systematic structure,
but Weber for originality. A short duplicate review in AMZ XXXI (1829) added
nothing. G. W. Fink praised Op. 26 warmly, too, in CAECILIA XV (1833) 272–73.
370. The reviewer of Schmitt's Son. in G, Op. 118, for P & Vn, in NZM XXXVII
(1852) 25–26, tries to rationalize a similar conclusion.

with praise now hard to understand. One of these composers was a pupil of Berger and Zelter and a teacher of Schumann, the successful opera composer and conductor **Heinrich Dorn** (1804–92).[371] Dorn left an early three-movement Sonata in F, Op. 5, for P & Vc-or-Vn (1828?) that Gottfried Weber found genial, melodious, and skillful, though almost too effervescent,[372] and that G. W. Fink (?), citing these same qualities, found "outstanding," with that word not used loosely, he insisted.[373] In an extended review of Dorn's *Grand Sonate* in D, Op. 29, for P-duet (1838 at latest), Schumann wrote guardedly, subjectively, and discursively, mentioning mainly that its size and variety suggested a symphony and that its scherzo had special appeal.[374] Schumann found the *Grande Sonate* in A, Op. 10 (1836?) by the virtuoso pianist **Constantine Decker** (1810–78)[375] to be the typically contrived, unfeeling music of the *Kleinmeister*,[376] but Fink again—no doubt, partly because of the more conservative outlook of AMZ—saw more substance in it.[377] Schumann also found little more than lightness and charm in *Deux Duos en forme de sonates* in A and C, Op. 13, for P+Vn-or-Vc-or-Fl (1837?) by a long favorite song and opera composer, **Friedrich Wilhelm Kücken** (1810–82).[378] But he found much more interesting and original a three-movement piano Sonata in A, Op. 32 (1833 at latest), by an organist and pupil of A. Schmitt, **Heinrich Friedrich Enckhausen** (1799–1885).[379] And, cautioning only about oversimplification, he saw promise of true greatness in *Trois grandes Sonates* in f, A, and Eb, Op. 1 (1838?), by the organist **Daniel Friedrich Eduard Wilsing** (1809–93).[380] Unfortunately, no copy of Wilsing's Op. 1, dedicated to his presumed teacher, L. Berger, has turned up in the present survey, without which no up-to-date view can be added.

371. Cf. MGG III 690–93 (W. Kahl).
372. CAECILIA VIII (1828) 124.
373. AMZ XXX (1828) 598–99.
374. Schumann/SCHRIFTEN I 397–98.
375. Mendel/LEXIKON III 93.
376. Schumann/SCHRIFTEN II 321 (1837); cf., also, I 306 (1837; with similar disdain for Decker's P sonatinas Op. 11). For a later, neutral review, of Decker's Son. for P & Vn, Op. 33, cf. NZM XL (1854) 208.
377. AMZ XL (1838) 160.
378. Schumann/SCHRIFTEN I 275–76 (1837). Cf. HOFMEISTER 1834–38, 89; MGG VII 1850–51 (O. H. Mies); PAZDÍREK VIII 452–59. Four such sons. by Kücken were pub. between 1845 and 1875 (Altmann/KAMMERMUSIK 212).
379. Schumann/SCHRIFTEN II 321 (1837); cf. Plantinga/SCHUMANN 335–38, with exx. An earlier 3-mvt. son. by Enckhausen, Op. 13, was reviewed in AMA for July, 1826, No. 1, p. 4. Cf. Mendel/LEXIKON III 360; BAKER 438.
380. Schumann/SCHRIFTEN I 395–96, including Schumann's fn. added in 1853, indicating this promise had now been achieved (in a choral work). Cf. Riemann/LEXIKON II 2032; HOFMEISTER 1834–38, 131. Strong praise for this set can also be found in about a fifth of a long review by Fink (AMZ XLI [1839] 181–85), the remainder of which inquires into the low state of the son. (cf. SSB II).

Toward the middle of the century in Berlin the renowned pedagogue and pianist **Theodor Kullak** (1818–82), who studied with Czerny and taught H. Bischoff, Moszkowski, and X. Scharwenka, among others, produced two weak piano sonatas along with his large quantity of more successful salon and teaching pieces. His *Grande Sonate* in f♯, Op. 7 (1842?), was reviewed as "a veritable witch piece" with occasional depth but generally more fantasy and display than content.[381] His *Symphonie de Piano, Grande Sonate en quatres parties,* in E♭, Op. 27 (1846?), was reviewed as an unoriginal, largely tedious work with recollections of its dedicatee, Spohr, and the feel more of a symphony reduction than a symphonic creation.[382] The one sonata, Op. 27 in d for piano (1842?), by another of Kullak's teachers, the celebrated opera composer **Carl Otto Nicolai** (1810–49), had fared similarly with the reviewers.[383] So, also, fared the one sonata, Op. 40 in d, for P & Vn (1845?), by the brilliant but short-lived pianist **Alexander Ernst Fesca** (1820–49).[384] And so it was with the only sonata, Op. 16 in e/E (not A; 1846?), by the eminent theorist and writer **Adolf Bernhard Marx** (1795–1866), although the chief reviewer[385] had to ask the reader to decide between his view and a diametrically opposite one in a short (personally biased?) review that praised the work as being strong, varied, heartfelt, and rare for a theorist.[386] On the other hand, a set of *Trois Sonates pour le pianoforte* in E♭, F, and G, Op. 20 (1850 [387]) by one **Karl Lührss** (1824–82) seems to have attracted no reviewer's attention, yet will surprise the researcher looking further into this period. A Mendelssohn pupil and chamber music composer[388] (until a wealthy marriage in 1851 apparently ended the motivation[389]), Lührss struck a style midway between Schubert's and Bruckner's, with straightforward, often dancelike melodies, persistent rhythms, figuration that is essential rather than extrinsic or purely virtuosic, telling modulations, and a sure, deliberate, broad sense of form. Schubert in particular comes to mind in the piano writing (although Lührss' is more pianistic), in the use of the higher registers, in the hints of *Ländler* tunes, and in the major-minor contrasts (Ex. 38).

381. NZM XVIII (1843) 40. Another reviewer objected only to too much Beethoven influence (AMZ XLV [1843] 596–97, with ex.).
382. NZM XXIV (1846) 149–50.
383. NZM XVII (1842) 176. Cf. MGG IX 1446–50 (T.-M. Langner).
384. NZM XXII (1845) 185–86 (with exx.); AMZ XLVII (1845) 740–41. Cf. Riemann/LEXIKON I 500.
385. NZM XXV (184) 37–39, with exx.
386. AMZ XLVIII (1846) 365–66. Regarding Marx's writings on the son. cf. SSB II.
387. Announced in NZM XXXII (1850) 270.
388. A set of 3 sons. for P & Vn, Op. 21, was also announced in 1850, in NZM XXXIII (1850) 225.
389. Riemann/LEXIKON I 1072.

Our last Berliner in this chapter overlaps the Berlin group in the next chapter. The once well-known pianist **(Carl Gottfried) Wilhelm Taubert** (1811–91), a pupil of L. Berger among others, left 8 sonatas that reached publication between about 1832 and 1866 6 for P solo, and one each for P & Vn and P & Vc—along with still more that did not.[390] Florestan, Eusebius, and Raro all have a go at three of the solo sonata publications in three extended, capricious, largely neutral reviews by Schumann, including personified descriptions.[391] The first review begins with Florestan talking: "The first movement of this sonata I regard as the first, the second as the second, and the third as the last—in descending order of beauty." The third review says that

Ex. 38. From the first movement of Sonata in E♭, Op. 20/1,
by Karl Lührss (after the Kistner ed. at the Library of Congress).

Taubert's Op. 35 in e resembles Weber's Op. 70 in e only in that the melancholy of the latter "seems to freeze into hypochondria" in the former. Two other reviews found two other sonatas by Taubert to be mediocre and mechanical.[392] Evidently the folklike quality that made Taubert's lieder so successful, as well as his conservative, Mendelssohnian style, did not serve his sonatas especially well.[393]

390. A detailed list of works, partly dated, follows the long article on his life (up to 1861) in Ledebur/BERLIN 583–92. Taubert also pub. 2 P sonatinas, Op. 44. Cf. PAZDÍREK XIV 41–49; also, Altmann/KAMMERMUSIK 229 and 265.
391. Schumann/SCHRIFTEN I 60–62 (1835, on Op. 20 in c), II 320–21 (1837, on Op. 21/1 & 2 in f & c♯), II 12 (1841, on Op. 35 in e).
392. NZM XLIV (1856) 268 (on Op. 104 in A for P & Vn) and XLVI (1857) 252–53 (on Op. 114 in d for P solo).
393. Cf. MGG XIII 147–49 (R. Sietz).

Other North German Centers

Born in the same year, the cousins **Andreas Jacob Romberg** (1767–1821) and **Bernhard Heinrich Romberg** (1767–1841)—violinist and cellist, respectively—were active in Paris and elsewhere, toured together (including a performance with Beethoven), and settled, on and off, in Hamburg before their sonatas were published.[394] Among his chamber works Andreas left a set of three sonatas for P & Vn in G, B♭, and c, Op. 9 (published in late 1805 or early 1806 [395]), in which the violin is more than the "accompagnement" specified in the title; and a set of three unaccompanied violin "Etudes ou Sonates" in E♭, B♭, and g, Op. 32 (published *ca.* 1813).[396] The sonatas of Op. 9, dedicated to his sister Therese, disclose professional craftsmanship, euphonious scoring, and a disposition for the tuneful that goes well with his use of "Down the burn, and thro' the mead" in the finale of Sonata II. The idiom, including neat scale passages, precise rhythms, thin texture, and Alberti bass, seldom reaches beyond the high- or late-Classic. Living longer, Bernhard got further into the Romantic idiom, but only with a strict sense of stylistic and structural propriety that now seems almost prim. He left about two dozen duos or sonatas, nearly all with or for his instrument, although their considerable popularity resulted in their publication in a variety of arrangements. Thus, the two sets of three "sonatas" each for Vc & P that International Music Company of New York City publishes today—in e, G, and B♭, Op. 38, and B♭, C, and G, Op. 43—were originally published, in 1825 and 1826, respectively,[397] as trios for 2 Vcs & Va and "sonates faciles" for Vc & bass.[398] All cast in the same three-movement plan that Andreas had used, too (F-S-F), these faultless, melodious, friendly, circumscribed "sonatas" remind us how quickly the fresh Romantic idioms could turn into stereotypes. They survive hardily today but—in a class with the "student concertos" of H. Goltermann or the "student trios" of H. Berens—only as "student sonatas."

The versatile musician **Gottlob Schuberth** (1778–1846), father of the publisher Julius, had not yet moved from Magdeburg to Hamburg

---

394. Cf. MGG XI 855–60 (K. Stephenson), with further bibliography.

395. AMZ VIII (1805–6) Intelligenz-Blatt 8 (Jan., 1806).

396. Reviewed with enthusiasm, but only as advanced "Studien," in AMZ XV (1813) 839–40. Op. 32/2 is reproduced in Gates/SOLO 315; cf., also, pp. 152–55.

397. AMZ XXVII and XXVIII (1825 and 1826) Intelligenz-Blatt 5 and 9, respectively.

398. The arrangements for Vc & P appear to go back no further than the 1870's (cf. SMZ XVII [1877] 23).

when three piano sonatas by him were published—two *Sonates faciles,* in C, Op. 1, and F, Op. 2 (both 1825?), and *Grande Sonate agréable,* Op. 3 (1826?). The first was reviewed as appealing and fluent for those not ready for anything more advanced or harmonically daring and dissonant, and the third as not worth the "grande" in its title, either in scope or content.[399] Among several piano sonatas or sonatinas left by the Hamburg cellist **Friedrich Wilhelm Grund** (1791–1874) was a *Grande Sonate* in g, Op. 27, for piano solo (1839?) that had been arranged from a *Trio de salon* for P-duet & Va-or-Vc-or-Hn.[400] A three-movement work of only fourteen pages, the piano version of Op. 27 was dedicated to Marschner. Its first, but only its first, movement won from Schumann in 1839 a "Hats off!" greeting starting like that for Chopin's Op. 2 and Brahms's Op. 1.[401] Today one can only suppose that the Romantic inscriptions and fantasy effect of changing rhythms diverted Schumann from the empty right-hand tremolo, the Alberti and murky bass, and the tawdry ideas, all conveying an emotional drive not unlike that in Suppé's "Overture" to *Poet and Peasant.* A few of the many sonatas and sonatinas for piano solo and duet by the Hamburg piano teacher **Jakob** (or **Jacques**) **Schmitt** (1803–53; brother of A. Schmitt, *supra*),[402] still hold a rightful place as skillful, graceful teaching pieces. Six of his solo sonatas, Opp. 51–56, "à l'usage des elèves avancés," were already reviewed in 1828 as models of the type (SSB III).[403]

In Bremen the talented pianist **Wilhelm Friedrich Riem** (1779–1857) won high praise from friends and reviewers for nearly a dozen sonatas and a half dozen sonatinas for piano.[404] Published between 1804 and 1815,[405] copies of most of these seem to have become very scarce.[406] Especially tantalizing are two long, strongly favorable reviews covering Opp. 1, 4, and 7/1 and 2 and enriched by several Romantically favored examples.[407] In the second review there is only

---

399. AMZ XXVII (1825) 755–56 and XXIX (1827) 99–101. Cf. MGG XII 186 (K. Stephenson).

400. Cf. MGG V 985–86 and 1403 (both K. Stephenson).

401. Schumann/SCHRIFTEN I 455. Cf. Plantinga/SCHUMANN 338–41, with exx.

402. Cf. MGG XII 1868–69 (D. Härtwig); PAZDÍREK XIII 271–72.

403. CAECILIA IX (1828) 193–96 and "Nachschrift" (Heinroth). Cf., also, the review of Op. 26, "aux jeunes amateurs," in AMZ XXVII (1825) 756. Re-eds. of Schmitt's sonatinas were reviewed from time to time throughout the century, as in MMR XV (1885) 160.

404. Cf. MGG XI 479–80 (F. Göthel), with incomplete list.

405. Cf. the Intelligenz-Blatt listings in AMZ VI (1803–4) for Apr., May, Aug., Nov.; VII (1804–5) for Nov.; VIII (1805–6) for June. Cf., also, HOFMEISTER 1815 (Whistling) 374.

406. Cat. BRUXELLES IV 171 lists Opp. 1, 2/1 and 2, 21, and 25.

407. AMZ VI (1803–4) 637–42; VII (1804–5) 438–41.

the significant caution about writing too much too fast. Examination of Riem's three-movement Sonata in b, Op. 25 (F-S-F; 1810?), does reveal a tendency to fall back on formulas—for example, repeated and tremolo chords in the accompanying hand, which weaken the Mendelssohnian sense of sound, flow, and form that otherwise grace this work.

Chapter IX

Brahms and Others in Austria from About 1850 to 1885

Austro-German Ties and Divergencies

In the second half of the 19th century Austro-German artists had to operate in increasingly complex political environments. Austria continued to dominate Germany until the growing rivalry and military power of Prussia forced Austria to withdraw entirely from German affairs in 1866.[1] Beginning in the following year, further lessening of her European influence saw the Dual Monarchy of Austria-Hungary, under Emperor Francis Joseph I, replace Austria's autocratic control of Hungary. The cumbersome relations that ensued between the two rival capitals, Vienna and Budapest, and the racial frictions that grew between German, Polish, Czech, Magyar, and other national groups resident in those capitals generated some of this monarchy's chief political problems right up to World War II.

Meanwhile in Germany, largely through the engineering of the ruthless, conservative Prussian statesman Count von Bismarck, the long-sought unification moved ahead with new speed and soon became a fact, first with the establishment of the North German Confederation in 1866–67 and then with the constitution of the German Empire under former King William of Prussia in 1871. It was this Empire, immediately following Prussia's victory over France, that saw the joining in of the southern German states. At once and throughout the chancellorship (until 1890) of the all-powerful Bismarck, Germany's chief problems became the control of her large, pro-Austrian Catholic population and the containment of her fast-growing, radically liberal Socialist party.

But the political separation of Austria and Germany must not be overemphasized, least of all in the arts. The two countries continued to

1. As we read in Raff/RAFF 177–78, even the composers were discommoded by the Seven Weeks' War of 1866.

be entwined in many ways. First of all, even politically, the separation was not complete. When it came to a showdown, for example, there was the protective alliance against possible Russian attacks that Bismarck set up in 1879 between Germany and Austria-Hungary, soon to be expanded into the Triple Alliance (1882) when Italy joined after concern over French threats. Second, there was always the common language, and third, there were the constant travel and intercourse between the two countries. Thus, Vienna was still the center for some of the greatest German (and other) musicians to move to rather than to be born in (Schubert excepted). Like Beethoven and Bonn, earlier, Brahms in Vienna retained lifelong ties with his home city of Hamburg in north Germany. Indeed, with regard to musical trends in Austria and Germany the ties outweighed the divergencies or bifurcations—more so, in fact, than can be said with regard to literary trends. Among literary trends, for example, Franz Grillparzer's dramas of renunciation and Adalbert Stifter's Biedermeier novels in the new Austrian literary flowering were something quite different from Friedrich Hebbel's tragic social dramas and Otto Ludwig's realistic dramas and novels in the declining literary intellectualism of post-Goethe Germany.

In this and the next chapter the sonata composers in Austria are separated from those in Germany mainly because there are too many of them to fit into a single chapter. Hence, at least this preview, serving as a preface to both chapters, is needed by way of a collective look at both the ties and the divergencies among the Austrian and German composers. The divergencies are represented above all by the polarity of Brahms, the Classic-minded conservative, and Liszt, the patron saint of the "New German" school (SSB VI and X). The ties are represented above all by each of these men and his most direct followers—by Brahms and, for example, Friedrich Kiel or Karl Grädener; by Liszt and, for example, Felix Draeseke or Julius Reubke. It would even be tempting to suggest that the polarity of Brahms and Liszt became the polarity of Vienna, still a relatively provincial center, and Weimar, Liszt's own headquarters for many years. And this suggestion does have a limited justification. But, of course, that polarity had gotten its start all in Germany, perhaps first with Brahms's somewhat unsatisfactory introduction to Liszt in 1853, then with Schumann's sensational, widely debated panegyric that same year on behalf of Brahms's "Op. 1," and with the celebrated "Manifesto" that Brahms cosigned in 1860 against the "New German" school.

In any case, in a day when virtually every important composer but Peter Cornelius wrote at least one or two sonatas, the ties and divergencies among Austrian and German sonata composers were not often so clearly defined. Naturally, there were other lines of influence, too, as well as many cross influences, especially now that more and easier travel became possible by rail. We still meet an occasional composer who had known Beethoven, Weber, or Schubert, and many more who had come under the indirect influence of any or all of these. Particularly numerous were the direct or indirect disciples of Mendelssohn and Schumann—A. G. Ritter, for example, of Mendelssohn, and Ferdinand Hiller of both. They even suggest a tripolarity of Vienna, Weimar, and Leipzig-Dresden-Berlin. Bülow is an interesting instance, not for any sonatas of his own but for his varied performances and changing allegiances, which cut across the Brahms-Liszt polarity.

Three periodicals dominated German musical journalism during the years covered in these next two chapters, although they did not define a polarity of opinion such as the *Allgemeine musikalische Zeitung* and the *Neue Zeitschrift für Musik* had done in the previous half century. One was still the *Neue Zeitschrift für Musik* (NZM), which continued to flourish under its new editors. The second was the *Signale für die Musikalische Welt* (SMW), started in 1842. And the third was the *Musikalische Wochenblatt* (MW), started in 1870. Among incidental trends to bear in mind during these same years are the continuingly high quantities of sonatas published in an increasing number of centers, even though "Op. 1" is often all we get from a particular composer; the rise in general competence of writing; the reduction in that tightly limited number of real masters, though not in near masters like Rheinberger, Raff, Ritter, and Kiel; the almost incredible output of pedagogic, progressively graded sonatinas; and the first signs of Romantic epigones and eclectics.

Brahms: Output, Resources, and Chronology

In the history of the sonata, as we have seen (SSB I), if any one composer is to be placed first in the century and a half since Beethoven it certainly must be **Johannes Brahms** (1833–97). To place Brahms in that perspective is, of course, one of the broader aims of the entire present volume. However, at least a preliminary defense of his preeminence might be made now simply by asking what other front-rank composer in this century and a half has given so much of his attention to problems bearing on the sonata idea, has found those problems so compatible with his own musical nature and methods, and has met with such universal acceptance and appreciation in his solutions to those problems. More than a third of Brahms's music with opus numbers, or nearly a fourth of the total output that he himself allowed to survive in his uncompromising self-criticism,[2] consists of thirty-eight cyclic instrumental works related to the sonata idea.[3] To be sure, with regard to our more specific area of concentration here, Brahms applied the term "sonata" to only twelve, or less than a third, of those cyclic works (or a little more than 7 per cent of the total output he approved). In other words, like most of his contemporaries, he applied "sonata" only to cyclic works in solo or duo scoring. But these alone—nearly every one an acknowledged, much played masterpiece today—suffice to confirm his pre-eminent devotion, aptitude, and success in the problems of the sonata idea.

The chart that follows tabulates the most essential facts about Brahms's twelve sonatas, including the order and lengths of the separate movements for purposes of comparison within his own works and with the sonatas of our other masters.[4] As discussed shortly, the chronological order of the first two sonatas is uncertain, but the lost sonata is included because at one point Brahms did intend that it be published. Op. 34b is included because he meant it to thrive on its own, independently of the piano Quintet in f. But not included in our tabulation are two other items. One is his fine "Scherzo" third movement in c for the four-movement *F-A-E* Sonata in a (P & Vn) that he, Schumann, and Dietrich joined to write for Joachim in 1853.[5] The other is the MS of three movements of a "Sonata" in d for two pianos. Over a period of four years (1854–57), Brahms reworked this "Sonata" with much effort, first into a symphony and then into the Concerto in d, Op. 15, except that he eventually converted the second movement into the second movement or "Funeral March" of the *German Requiem*.[6] Finally, our tabulation cannot show the several early sonatas

2. Cf. Brahms's own statement on this self-criticism, as quoted in Kalbeck/BRAHMS I/1 132–33.

3. Cf. the list of 40 items in Mitschka/BRAHMS 340–41, which includes 2 single pieces, Opp. 79/2 and 81 (Rhapsody in g and *Tragic Overture*) as well as the Piano Trio in A that E. Bücken and K. Hasse first published in 1938, but omits the lost Son. in a for Vn & P (*infra*). If that Trio in A is actually by Brahms (as argued in Mitschka/BRAHMS 355–56, fn. 11), there is still no evidence that Brahms meant it to survive (and it is not counted in our figure of 38).

4. The timings come from outstanding recordings. Tempos vary considerably, of course, from one recording to the next. But even allowing for the slow tempos Brahms is known to have preferred (e.g., cf. Kalbeck/BRAHMS III/1 66, Schauffler/BRAHMS 180–81), what accounts for the 32 minutes allowed for Op. 120/1 in Müller-Reuter/LEXIKON Suppl. 207?

5. Cf. SSB VIII, final pp. on Schumann; also, Dietrich & Widmann/BRAHMS 5; Kalbeck/BRAHMS III/1 13; Evans/BRAHMS III 336; Geiringer/BRAHMS 224. Mod. ed.: F-A-E SONATE-m 19; Brahms/WERKE-m X 88.

6. Cf. the detailed historical summary, with further references, in Müller-Reuter/LEXIKON Suppl. 168–69.

Brahms wrote and eventually destroyed because what remain are only obscure hints (as noted shortly).

The literature on Brahms is extensive and generally well organized.[7] Except for numerous, mostly minor revisions, additions and shifts of perspective that later research and the passing years have brought, Max Kalbeck's monumental, sometimes overly thorough biography and the sixteen volumes of correspondence that he and others edited under the sponsorship early in this century of the Deutsche Brahms Gesellschaft still provide the solid foundation for all subsequent research on Brahms.[8] There is no over-all, systematic, style-critical study of Brahms's sonatas.[9] But there are numerous analytical surveys that include the sonatas, starting with Edwin Evans' academic compilation, *Historical, Descriptive and Analytical Account of the Entire Works . . .* , in four volumes.[10] There are a few studies of individual sonatas, such as that by R. S. Fischer on "motive development" in Op. 108.[11] And there are studies of Brahms's treatment of "sonata form" in his sonatas and related form types, notably the recently completed dissertation, still oriented toward Hugo Riemann, by Arno Mitschka.[12] Brahms oversaw the editing of nearly all the works he approved for publication, including all of the sonatas but the early lost one, and an unusually high proportion of his autographs has survived, leaving comparatively few

7. For an excellent, recent, critical summary of Brahms research and bibliography cf. Grasberger/BRAHMS 445–51. Keller/BRAHMS is a bibliography up to 1912.

8. Kalbeck/BRAHMS and BRAHMS BRIEFWECHSEL. (Schauffler/BRAHMS 27 gives a little evidence that Kalbeck tampered with some of the letters.) Dietrich & Widmann/BRAHMS and May/BRAHMS continue to serve as important, nearly contemporary sources on Brahms's life. Joachim/LETTERS and SCHUMANN-BRAHMS are among significant supplements to the correspondence. Of several later studies of the man and his music that are cited here, Grasberger/BRAHMS and Gál/BRAHMS should be singled out for new information and viewpoints, and Geiringer/BRAHMS as another source of new information and as being still the most rounded, satisfactory text in English. Ehrmann/WEG, another valued source, traces the cultivation of Brahms in other countries (pp. 473–95). Warm thanks are owing to Dr. Karl Geiringer at the University of California in Santa Barbara and Mrs. Geiringer for valued correspondence bearing on the present discussion.

9. Nagel/BRAHMS, first pub. in 1913–14, is essentially a detailed, ms.-by-ms. description of the 3 P sons.

10. Evans/BRAHMS. Among representative surveys of the chamber music, including the duo sons., are Drinker/BRAHMS (chiefly historical), Mason/CHAMBER, Cobbett/CHAMBER I 158–85 (mostly by D. Tovey), and Müller-Reuter/LEXIKON Suppl. 188–208 (mainly factual and bibliographic). Kirby/BRAHMS surveys traits in the 3 solo P sons.

11. Fischer/BRAHMS.

12. Mitschka/BRAHMS comprehends and supersedes the chief previous study of this problem, Urbantschitsch/BRAHMS. A recent, similar, briefer study is Truscott/BRAHMS. Cf., also, Fellinger/DYNAMIK 71–77 and 91–92; Wetschky/KANONTECHNIK (cf. pp. 215–35).

Brahms's Sonatas

Opus	Scoring	Key	Chron. order	Brahms/ werke-m	Composed	First edition	Dedicatee	Mvts.: tempos or types / Keys: mvt.-by-mvt. / mss.: mvt.-by-mvt.	Performance time in minutes	Remarks
1	P	G	3	XIII 1	1852 (ii), 1853	Breitkopf, 1853	Joachim	4: F -M-Sc -VF / C:: C -c -e -C / 957: 270-85-310-292	23	"Andante" composed in 1852; Op. 1 originally listed by Brahms as "Op. 4" (BRAHMS BRIEFWECHSEL V 14)
2	P	f#	2?	XIII 29	1852	Breitkopf, 1853	Clara Schumann	4: F -M -Sc -S/F / f#: -b/B-b -f#/F# / 674: 198-87 -109-280	23	"Nr. 2"
(5)	P & Vn	a	1?		1852?			a		lost (by Liszt?) or destroyed (by Brahms?); rejected for pub. by B. Senff of Leipzig (no Vn sons. wanted)
5	P	f	4	XIII 55	1853	B. Senff, 1854	Ida von Hohenthal	5: F -M -Sc -M-F / f: f -Ab/Db-f -bb-f/F / 1,141: 222-190 -311-53-365	33	"Nr. 3"; ii and iv composed before i, ii, and v
34b	2 Ps	f	5	XI 1	winter, 1863–64	Rieter-Biedermann, 1872	Anna von Hessen	4: F -S -Sc -S/F / f: F -Ab -c -f / 1,371: 301-126-453-491	40	"Sonate für zwei Pianoforte nach dem Quintet"; the dedicatee was the same for both versions
38	P & Vc	e	6	X 96	1862, 1865 (iv)	Simrock, 1866	Josef Gänsbacher	3: F -Mi-F / e: e -a -e / 771: 282-191-298	23	originally in 4 mvts. (F-S-Mi-F), but Brahms discarded the "Adagio"
78	P & Vn	G	7	X 1	1878–79	Simrock, 1880		3: F -S -F / G: G -Eb -g/G / 528: 243-122-163	25	sometimes called the "Regenlied" or "Frühling" son.
99	P & Vc	F	8	X 124	1886	Simrock, 1887		4: VF-S -VF-VF / F: F -F#-f -F / 746: 211-71-320-144	25	"Zweite Sonate"

100	P & Vn	A	9	X 31	1886	Simrock, 1887		3: F -M/VF-F -A A: A -F -A 604: 279-168 -157	19	"Zweite Sonate"
108	P & Vn	d	10	X 57	1886, 1888	Simrock, 1889	Hans von Bülow	4: F -S -F -VF d: d -D -f# -d 757: 264-75-181-337	21	"Dritte Sonate"
120/1	P & Cl-or-Va	f	11	X 153	1894	Simrock, 1895		4: VF-S -M -VF f: f -Ab-Ab -F 663: 236-71 -136-220	20	"Nr. 1"; Brahms arranged the alternative Va part but not the Vn part
120/2	"	Eb	12	X 179	"	"		4: F -VF-M -F Eb: Eb -eb -eb/Eb 649: 173-222-170-84	19	"Nr. 2"; as for No. 1

questions in the *Sämtliche Werke* that Breitkopf & Härtel finally published in twenty-six volumes under E. Mandyczewski's and H. Gál's editorship, between 1926 and 1927.[13] A thematic index by the Brahms biographer Alfred von Ehrmann followed in 1933.[14]

Brahms spaced his sonatas rather evenly throughout his outwardly uneventful creative life. His three solo piano sonatas and the lost sonata for piano and violin came in his "formative" period (up to 1862). They marked the start of his career (1852–53), around the time of his epochal meetings with Joachim, Liszt, and, above all, the Schumanns, and while he was still centered in Hamburg.[15] The Sonata in f for two pianos and the first cello sonata came in the early 1860's, at the start of his "mature" period (1867–75). That is, they came several years after Schumann's death (1856) and Brahms's emotional crisis with Clara, only shortly after the ill-considered "Manifesto" (1860) that Brahms, Joachim, and others signed against the "New German" school headed by Liszt and Wagner,[16] and while Brahms was establishing first ties with Vienna. And his other cello sonata, all three mature violin sonatas, and both clarinet sonatas came during sixteen years (1878–94) of his period of "consummation" (1876–97), well after his decision in 1868 to make his permanent residence in Vienna.

Since Brahms was one of the four composers at the focus of our discussion of Romantic styles and forms in Chapter VI—along with Schubert, Schumann, and Chopin—we are concerned in the present chapter only with the facts, circumstances, historical relationships, and cultivation of his sonatas. Unfortunately, in spite of the extent and relative orderliness of Brahms research, the actual amount of information available, especially on the circumstances of his compositions, is often disappointing. Not a little of the explanation lies in his own secretiveness, his reticence whenever he had occasion to write or speak about his own music, and even a tendency, in his little self-effacing jokes, deliberately to laugh away the facts.[17] We know too little, for example, about just when, where, and why Brahms composed his sonatas, or about any sonatas that he wrote in his student days under the pseudonym "G. W. Marks" and then discarded.[18]

13. Brahms/WERKE-m. The set was reprinted in 1949 (Ann Arbor: J. W. Edwards).

14. Ehrmann/BRAHMS (cf. Ehrmann/WEG). The thematic index by J. Braunstein (New York: Ars Musica, 1956) contains less information except for a few new entries (not on the sons.). Cf., also, Hanslick/MUSIKALISCHES 131–41.

15. The ternary division of Brahms's creative life followed here is that advanced in more detail in Grasberger/BRAHMS 381–83.

16. Cf. Kalbeck/BRAHMS I/2 403–6; Gál/BRAHMS 29–37.

17. Cf. Grasberger/BRAHMS 445–46.

18. Cf. MGG II 208 (R. Gerber). A little light has been thrown on Brahms's own interpretation, teaching, and fingering of his three early piano sonatas in Kross/BRAHMSIANA 132–36.

Brahms's Three Piano Sonatas

Like Schumann about fifteen years before him, Brahms wrote his three published piano sonatas early in his career and his three great violin sonatas, not counting the lost one, much later. The lost sonata, in a, was to have been given the opus number 5 that ultimately went to the solo piano Sonata in f.[19] Apparently Brahms wrote it in 1852 for use on his concert tour in 1853 with Reményi.[20] An exchange of several letters followed suggesting that Liszt may have borrowed or received the manuscript and lost it, possibly around the end of the year while he was in Leipzig. But perhaps only the violin part was referred to then (since Brahms could well have had the piano part in his memory for the tour) and again when Liszt wrote Klindworth that he could get no reply from Reményi. It was only the violin part that Dietrich discovered in Wasielewski's possession in 1872 in a "lengthy and beautifully written manuscript." (Where is that part, now?) Meanwhile, at Schumann's suggestion and after some final polishing, Brahms had offered what presumably was a full score of the work to Barthold Senff of Leipzig, in November, 1853, for publication. But soon he learned that "Senff prints no violin things." Did he then decide to destroy it along with at least two other early violin sonatas, and is that actually why it is lost? It would indeed be interesting to be able to hear this companion to the three solo piano sonatas, each of them so fascinating and "great in spite of its immaturity." [21]

After several letters exchanged in 1853 between himself, Schumann, Joachim, and the publisher Breitkopf & Härtel, Brahms decided to introduce himself with his Sonata in C as Op. 1. "When one first shows one's self," he wrote later to his fellow Hamburg pianist Louise Jappa, "it is to the head and not the heels that one wishes to draw attention." [22] Actually, his Sonata in f♯, finally labeled Op. 2, antedated all but the "Andante" of this work, and the Scherzo in e♭ had come even earlier (1851). In fact, on the title page of the autograph of Op. 1 is written "Vierte Sonate," indicating that at least Op. 2 and two discarded (piano) sonatas had preceded the Sonata in C.[23] Brahms dedi-

19. Scattered bits of information on this work may be found in Kalbeck/BRAHMS I/1 73, 130, and 139; Dietrich & Widmann/BRAHMS 9 and 75 (but read 1853, not 1852); BRAHMS BRIEFWECHSEL V 19 and 23, XIII 5–6; May/BRAHMS I 109, 123, 129, 136, 139, 141, and 149; SCHUMANN-BRAHMS I 2–3; Joachim/LETTERS 29 and 31; LISZT LETTERS I 196.

20. For some details of this tour cf. May/BRAHMS I 94–102, 108–14.

21. May/BRAHMS I 120.

22. As trans. in May/BRAHMS I 137, 70.

23. Ehrmann/WEG 116. Louise Jappa reported hearing Brahms at the age of 11 play a sonata he himself had composed (May/BRAHMS I 70).

cated Op. 1 to "my best friend," [24] the great violinist Joachim, who remained more or less close throughout Brahms's life. But Op. 1 identifies particularly with Robert Schumann, for it was mainly this work by which Brahms introduced himself to the Schumanns on October 1, 1853, as he had to several others in the previous four months, including Joachim, Wasielewski, and Liszt (in the embarrassing meeting at which Brahms is supposed to have fallen asleep when Liszt reciprocated with his Sonata in b).[25] And it was mainly this work that inspired Schumann to herald Brahms before the musical world as "a young blood by whose cradle graces and heroes kept watch," and as a "Minerva [springing forth] fully armed from the head of Jove"—all in the celebrated article "New Paths" that marked a last rare return for Schumann to the *Neue Zeitschrift für Musik* (Oct. 28, 1853).[26] How much that sensational "send-off" tended to antagonize musicians in other camps, especially the "Murls" or anti-Philistines in the Liszt camp, and how much it also acted as a deterrent, both psychologic and artistic, to Brahms himself, are well known and well documented.[27]

In most descriptions and discussions of Brahms's Op. 1, one of the first points to be noted is the similarity of the opening idea to that of Beethoven's Op. 106 in Bb, there being an almost exact duplication of the rhythm for five measures, and at least suggestions of the melodic outlines, as well as the phrase extensions. Usually this similarity is treated as casual or coincidental.[28] However, a fact not previously mentioned in this connection, as with the parallel relation of Mendelssohn's Op. 106 in Bb (ssb VIII), is Brahms's special interest in Beethoven's Op. 106 around the time he wrote Op. 1. In February of 1854 he twice revealed that he had known Franz Wüllner's performance of the Op. 106,[29] and may even have heard this further lifelong friend playing the work several months earlier, before Wüllner first met Brahms officially and heard the latter play his "just

24. BRAHMS BRIEFWECHSEL V 18.

25. Cf. May/BRAHMS I 108–30; MASON MEMORIES 127–31, 141–42 (the most reliable report of the Liszt meeting; too much doubt seems to be cast on this report and the sleep incident in Ehrmann/WEG 31; cf., also, Kalbeck/BRAHMS I/1 85–86 and Gál/BRAHMS 32–33).

26. The original German is in Schumann/SCHRIFTEN II 301–2, and one of many English trans. is in May/BRAHMS I 131–32. Schumann still wrote warmly of Op. 1 in his letters of Nov. 27, 1854, and Jan. 6, 1855 (cf. Kalbeck/BRAHMS I/1 188–89).

27. Cf. BÜLOW BRIEFE II 114–15, 166; May/BRAHMS I 132–37, 142–47; Kalbeck/BRAHMS I/1 123–29, 204–8; Geiringer/BRAHMS 37–38; Gál/BRAHMS 6–8, with a further trans. of the article.

28. E.g., in Murdoch/BRAHMS 209; May/BRAHMS I 137–38. But cf. Geiringer/BRAHMS 207.

29. BRAHMS BRIEFWECHSEL XIV 9, XV 37 (a witty, sparkling document).

completed" Op. 1.[30] In any case, Brahms's clear transformation of the idea in the finale and some probable, subtle but intentional, allusions to it at least in the "Scherzo" suggest that he himself could hardly have been unaware of the similarity to Beethoven's work. Whatever his right to dub Brahms the third "B," Hans von Bülow, who was closest to Brahms in their late years, would have had as much reason to call Brahms's Op. 1 "Beethoven's thirty-third sonata" as he had when he called Brahms's first symphony "Beethoven's tenth." [31] Bülow, as it happened, was the first besides the composer himself to play Brahms's Op. 1—in fact, any Brahms work—in public, when he played the opening movement in Hamburg in 1854, though not the whole work for another thirty years.[32]

Brahms had played music by Beethoven (and Mozart) from at least his tenth year.[33] His playing of Op. 53 in C in public while he was still fifteen was favorably reviewed. And he played Op. 30/2 in c on the tour with Reményi, which included the incident of transposing the piano part up a half-step on the spot because of an out-of-tune instrument (as Beethoven had done for his own horn sonata, Op. 17).[34] Opp. 27/1 in E♭ and 111 in c, as well as the "Eroica" Variations Op. 35, were among the works of Beethoven he most liked to perform in later years.[35] There is a decided kinship with Beethoven in Brahms's use of a pregnant motive rather than a complete theme as the opening idea in Op. 1, and in his development of that motive, both intensive and extensive, which includes fughetta sections and even exceeds what Beethoven did with his motive in Op. 106. Beethovian, too, are Brahms's powerful architectonic sense and his exclusion of anything that is solely virtuosic, ornamental, or extrinsic to the structure in any other way. (Only the absence of virtuosity for its own sake and Brahms's almost phobic aversion to sham, but not any want of inherent grandeur, can explain the omission of "grosse" or "grande" from the titles of all his sonatas.) It is in this architectonic sense more than any other that Minerva sprang "fully armed from the head of Jove." Yet one must qualify the metaphor by recalling that not till later did Brahms find solutions to the problems of the finale that he wrestled with but never quite resolved in all three early

30. Cf. Kalbeck/BRAHMS I/1 104–5; Kämper/WÜLLNER 8, 12, 13. Brahms's teacher Marxsen had taken a special interest in Op. 106 as far back as 1835 (Müller-Reuter/KONZERT LITERATUR Suppl. 138; Kalbeck/BRAHMS I 28).
31. Cf. BÜLOW BRIEFE III 372, 369 (1877); May/BRAHMS II 528–29.
32. Cf. BÜLOW BRIEFE II 183, VII 197; Kalbeck/BRAHMS I/1 156–58; May/BRAHMS I 160; BRAHMS BRIEFWECHSEL IV 151.
33. Cf. May/BRAHMS I 62, 86–87, 98–99.
34. Cf. May/BRAHMS I 99–100; Thayer & Forbes/BEETHOVEN I 526.
35. Cf. Murdoch/BRAHMS 54, 55; Grasberger/BRAHMS 252–54.

sonatas,[36] and that had plagued Beethoven from time to time throughout his cyclic works (SCE 142–43, 164–66).

In most of the foregoing traits—the motivic idea, the exclusion
of extrinsic matter, the problem of the finale—Brahms's Op. 1 already
shows his decided kinship with Schumann, too, especially the Schumann who had written three early piano sonatas of his own. Furthermore, Brahms at once reveals a lyricism, coupled with a new sense
of piano sonority (as in Op. 1/i/39–62), that is more Schumannseque
than Beethovian. Op. 1 was completed, of course, before Brahms
met Schumann but not before he had known and studied Schumann's
music. He may not have been introduced to any of this music by
the relatively conservative Marxsen,[37] but the same Louise Jappa
had sought to interest him in it, especially when the Schumanns
appeared in public in Hamburg "several times" in 1850.[38] If Brahms's
response was severely dampened after he got back, unopened, the
package of compositions he had sent to Robert for comments at
that time, it was greatly aroused by Joachim, Wasielewski, and others
during the tour of 1853, to the point where he experienced a nearly
traumatic awakening to Schumann's poetic genius and could bring
himself to pay the memorable visit.[39]

Like Schumann's three piano sonatas, those of Brahms reveal
scarcely any tangible programmatic influence. Nearest to such an
influence, and taking us perhaps as near as Brahms's sonatas came
to the "New German" school with which he was soon at odds,[40] were
the three poems differently associated with the "Andante" movement
of each sonata (ii in Op. 5). The only other such instances in Brahms's
solo piano music are the poems cited at the head of Ballade in d,
Op. 10/1, and quoted at the head of Intermezzo in E♭, Op. 117/1.[41]
(In his violin sonatas we shall find Brahms making subtler poetic
references through melodic quotations from his own songs.) Op. 1/ii
actually presents as the theme for three free variations "an old

36. E.g., on the finale of Op. 5, cf. SCHUMANN-BRAHMS I 2 and BRAHMS BRIEF-
WECHSEL V 18; cf., also, Schauffler/BRAHMS 357. In DMf XX (1967) 204 a completed
diss. is announced on the finale in Brahms's chamber music, by Werner Czesla in
Bonn.

37. Cf. Kalbeck/BRAHMS I 28, 30, 36.

38. May/BRAHMS I 91–92; Kalbeck/BRAHMS I/1 54–56.

39. Cf. May/BRAHMS I 116, 118, 119; Kalbeck/BRAHMS I/1 100–103, 125 (but something more than "exaggeration" must have prompted Brahms to say later, "I
never learned anything from Schumann but how to play chess"—Brahms, who
played Schumann's Opp. 14 and 17 with such "depth" and "feeling" [according to
Hanslick/WIEN II 258, in 1862]).

40. Cf. Kalbeck/BRAHMS I/1 89.

41. Cf. Evans/BRAHMS IV 29–30, 75; Ehrmann/WEG 116–17; Kalbeck/BRAHMS I/1
212, IV/1 17.

German love song," "Verstohlen geht der Mond auf," complete with words (Ex. 39).[42] Op. 2/ii neither cites nor quotes any verse, but, according to A. Dietrich, Brahms "built up the theme . . . on the words of an old German song 'Mir is leide . . .' "[43] Op. 5/ii quotes a stanza from the poet "Otto Sternau" (A Inkermann) beginning "Der Abend dämmert. . . ."[44]

Op. 2 in f♯ is the earliest (and shortest in number of measures) of Brahms's piano sonatas that survived but not one of the first works he wanted to publish.[45] Its dedication to the "honored Frau Schumann" was preceded by deferential, even timorous inquiries to Joachim, Robert, and Clara herself.[46] As with Opp. 1 and 5, the final page in the autograph of Op. 2 is signed "Kreisler jun." [47] This, or "Johannes Kreisler junior" in full, or even "Jean de Krösel le jeune," was Brahms's early pseudonym among his close friends.[48] Its use in 1852 for Op. 2 recalls that Brahms was already won over to E. T. A. Hoffmann (and Jean Paul) if not yet to Schumann.[49] Schumann wrote enthusiastically to Brahms about Op. 2 on March 20 (?), 1855 (in his last reference found here to any sonatas):

Your second sonata, dear friend, has brought me much closer to you again. You were quite unknown to me; I live in your music, which I can play fairly well at sight, one movement after another. Then do I feel thankful. There never was anything like the opening, the pianissimo, the whole movement. The "Andante" and these variations, and this "Scherzo" that follows, [which is] quite different from the other ["Scherzo" in Op. 1?], and the "Finale" [opened by] the "Sostenuto," the music at the start of the second part, the "Animato," and the ending—in short, [all this is] a new laurel-wreath for that other Johannes.[50]

42. The melody also serves in Brahms's *Deutsche Volkslieder* No. 49 (cf. Ehrmann/ BRAHMS 135; Kalbeck/BRAHMS I/1 52).

43. Dietrich & Widmann/BRAHMS 3–4; cf. Kalbeck/BRAHMS I/1 40, 212–13. Dietrich also said Brahms had in mind "My Heart's in the Highlands" when he wrote the purportedly Scotch-flavored finale of Op. 1.

44. Cf. Kalbeck/BRAHMS I/1 120–22; BRAHMS BRIEFWECHSEL XIV 5, XII 199–200 (on the identity of the obscure poet).

45. Cf. BRAHMS BRIEFWECHSEL V 13–15.

46. Cf. SCHUMANN-BRAHMS I 3, 5; BRAHMS BRIEFWECHSEL V 18.

47. Cf. May/BRAHMS I 95, Brahms/WERKE-m XIII iii and vi. A facs. of the first p. is in DM XII/1 (1912–13) after p. 64.

48. E.g., as in BRAHMS BRIEFWECHSEL IV 1, 2, 4; XIV 8. Cf. Kalbeck/BRAHMS I/1 102–3.

49. Cf. May/BRAHMS I 91. But this early use is not mentioned in Kalbeck/BRAHMS I/1 103, which therefore seems to be mistaken in suggesting that Brahms had Schumann in mind as "Kreisler senior."

50. Trans. from SCHUMANN-BRAHMS I 101–2; Brahms's acknowledgment of these "friendly" remarks a week later (p. 104) and Schumann's specific references leave no doubt that Op. 2 was intended, although some authors have mistaken "second sonata" to mean Op. 1 or the second sonata to be completed.

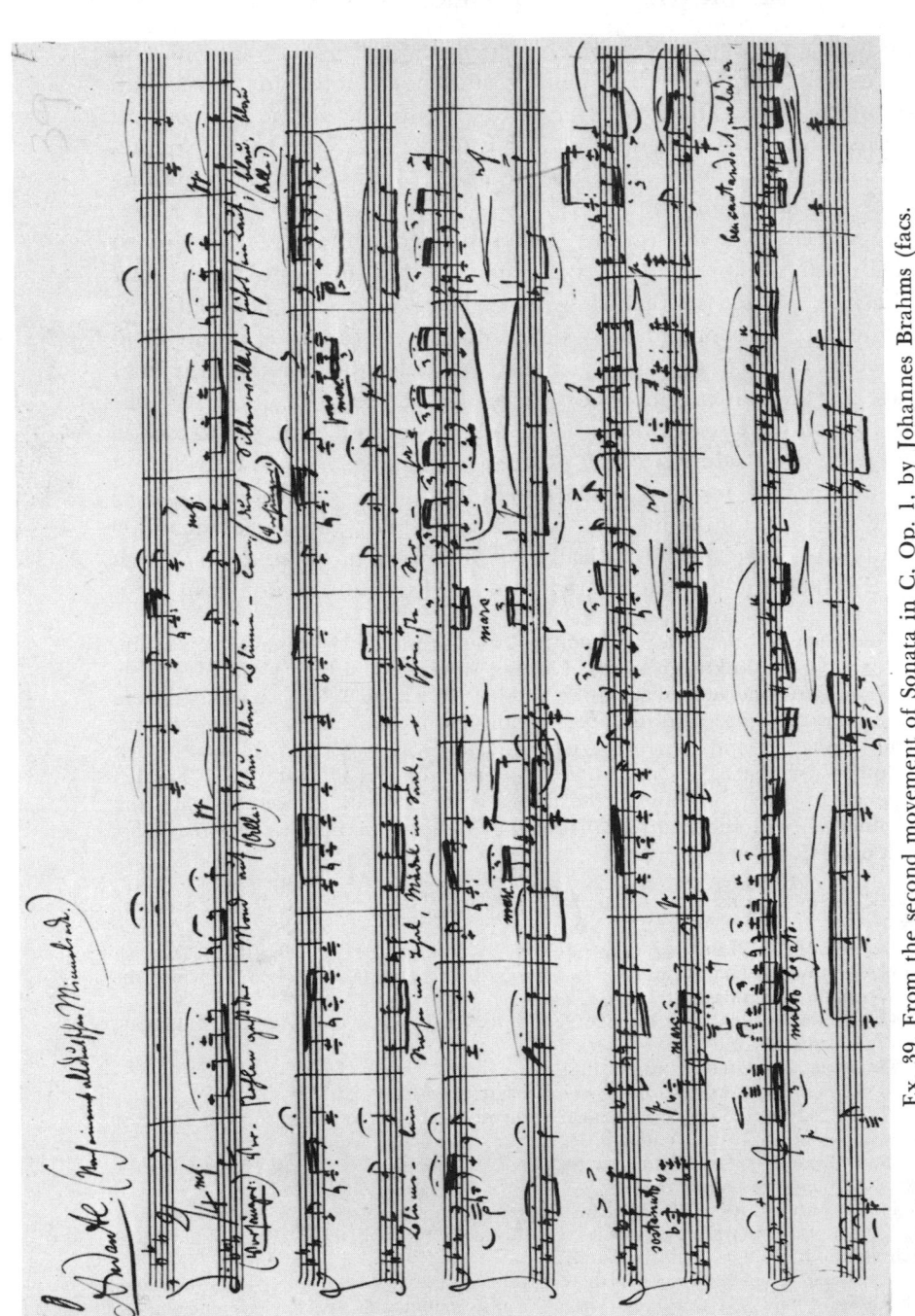

Ex. 39. From the second movement of Sonata in C, Op. 1, by Johannes Brahms (facs. of the autograph at the Österreichische Nationalbibliothek in Vienna).

Schumann had good reason to remark how different Brahms's Op. 2 was from his Op. 1. Even though, or perhaps because, it originated earlier than most of Op. 1 it marks a more frank plunge into Romantic idioms. In fact, although it proves its worth, logic, and practicability with sufficient study, it still must be called the wildest, most bombastic, most declamatory, least playable,[51] and structurally least successful of Brahms's sonatas. Its athletic difficulties and novel harmonies provide the main reasons for believing that not all the hostility vented against Opp. 1, 2, 3, and 4 in the *Süddeutsche Musikzeitung* for 1854 and even in the *Neue Zeitschrift für Musik* for 1855 under Brendel can be charged to the anti-Brahms sentiment that Schumann's "New Paths" aroused.[52] On the other hand, the authors of these diatribes might have recognized a decidedly Lisztian quality in the second theme of Op. 2/i (mss. 10–71) and even a Chopinesque quality in the main theme of the finale.[53] That second theme brings to mind the corresponding theme in Liszt's Sonata in b, in texture, harmony, and import, and even in line. Since both works had been completed recently (except for final polishing?) when the two men first met in June of 1853, there is little likelihood of influences one way or the other, only of a common spirit in the musical air.

However, the theme of the finale, which Kalbeck relates to Liszt and the "New German" school,[54] seems here—with its particular brand of chromaticism, its rhythmic variant, and its Neapolitan approach to an abrupt cadence—to relate more to Chopin's ideas—in fact, to the theme of the finale in Chopin's own Sonata in b. At that initial meeting of Brahms and Liszt, J. J. Raff is supposed to have been the first of many to remark how much Brahms's Scherzo in e♭, Op. 4, suggests Chopin's Scherzo in b♭, Op. 31, only to have Brahms answer that (as yet) "he had never seen or heard any of Chopin's compositions."[55] But Chopin was widely published by then, Brahms was clearly sensitive to motivic relationships from the start (as between the outer movements of all three piano sonatas), he was highly impressionable in his early years—besides the influence of Beethoven's Op. 106 on his Op. 1 (*supra*), it is hard to deny the suggestions of Beethoven's Fifth Symphony in Brahms's Op. 2/iv/110–15—and not only the opening but "Trio II" (mss. 318–30, 354–79) of Op. 4

51. No public performance of Op. 2 was discovered here before Bülow's in 1882 (Ehrmann/BRAHMS 1; BÜLOW BRIEFE VII 112, 141–42).
52. Cf. Kalbeck/BRAHMS I/1 204–8 (but with no other explanation allowed); May/BRAHMS I 147–48.
53. Nagel/BRAHMS 46 finds strong suggestions of Mendelssohn and Schumann, too.
54. Kalbeck/BRAHMS I/1 85–89.
55. MASON MEMORIES 129.

suggest Chopin's Scherzo in b♭ (mss. 1–4 and 65–117, respectively). Both Dietrich and Kalbeck add further evidences that Brahms had not known Chopin's music by 1853.[56] On the other hand, Geiringer has discovered that Marxsen taught Chopin's Polonaise in A♭ to Brahms's brother Fritz in 1853,[57] leaving the question open again. As with Liszt, the thematic relationships may simply have been "in the air." Yet such relationships or derivations seem even closer in Brahms's next sonata, Op. 5 in f, as in the well-known motive of the theme that climaxes so heroically in the first "Andante" (mss. 144–78) and its recollection of the "chorale" theme in the same key of D♭, beginning similarly on a I-6/4 chord, in Chopin's Scherzo in c♯, Op. 39. (Brahms had used a similar motive in the "Trio" of Op. 2/iii.) How greatly Brahms differs from Liszt and Chopin in the disposition and development of his ideas is, of course, quite another matter (ssв VI).

With further regard to Op. 5, this second longest of all Brahms's sonatas, and the only one in five movements, has always been one of his most played sonatas and thrives today, in fact, as one of the favorites in the whole sonata repertoire since Beethoven. It was the only major work written largely during that one month of October, 1853, when Brahms was with the Schumanns (and before Robert's commitment for insanity), although Brahms himself said the two interrelated andante movements originated earlier.[58] But not until Brahms had struggled with the finale another two months did he write B. Senff that Op. 5 was ready for publication.[59] The dedication this time, to a member of the nobility in Leipzig, probably signified nothing more than thanks for hospitality.[60] At first, only the unsurpassed, celestial "Andante espressivo" and the fiery "Scherzo" (ii and iii) were performed in public, as they were initially by Clara in October of 1854 and subsequently by Brahms himself and others, at least as late as 1880.[61] Brahms played the entire sonata in public for the first time, in Vienna in 1863 (not 1862), with Hanslick reacting to the performance as more improvisatory than "clearly and sharply worked out," and to the music as deeply felt and lyrical but "form-

56. Dietrich & Widmann/BRAHMS 6; Kalbeck/BRAHMS I/1 30 and 82–84.

57. Geiringer/BRAHMS 18. Cf. the further discussion of this relationship in the article Siegmund-Schultze/CHOPIN.

58. Kalbeck/BRAHMS I/1 120; May/BRAHMS I 139.

59. Cf. BRAHMS BRIEFWECHSEL V 18 and 28, XIV 5 and 7; SCHUMANN-BRAHMS I 2. Gottschalk/MSS Plate vii is a facs. of the first p. of the autograph.

60. Kalbeck/BRAHMS I/1 139.

61. Cf. SCHUMANN-BRAHMS I 22; BRAHMS BRIEFWECHSEL IV 4; Kalbeck/BRAHMS I/1 120, 196; MT XXI (1880) 462. Brahms had played these 2 mvts. informally during his first month with the Schumanns (cf. Ehrmann/WEG 118).

less in both outer movements." [62] Bülow played the entire Op. 5 on tour in 1884.[63]

As the last of Brahms's solo piano sonatas, Op. 5 does not reveal quite the remarkable advances in craftsmanship and stylistic refinements to be found soon after in Op. 9, *Variations for Pianoforte on a Theme by Robert Schumann*—advances that both Brahms himself and Schumann recognized.[64] But Op. 5 still reveals decided advances over Opp. 1 and 2 in its more reasonable and restrained, yet effective, solutions to the sounds and techniques of the piano, in the greater substance of its ideas and the more logical, satisfying forms into which they are molded (although the finale still presents architectural instabilities to both listener and performer), and, indeed, in a new fusion of Classic ideals and Romantic styles (SSB VI). It is interesting to recall that Wagner was present when Brahms gave that first public performance of all of Op. 5 in Vienna in early 1863, and that Liszt had been among those who heard Brahms play the first "Andante" nine years earlier, at a supper party following the first performance of *Lohengrin* in Leipzig.[65] Regardless of whether either could have influenced the other, Kalbeck is able to quote two passages, one from each of the first two movements (i/39–45 and ii/144–48), that bring Brahms surprisingly close to Wagner's Elsa and Hans Sachs, respectively.[66] These passages, as well as the Chopin resemblance cited above, and some further hints of Schumann (e.g., the left-hand, long-drawn, cello-like line at i/91–117) all rightly suggest that Brahms was fitting more and more comfortably into his 19th-century musical environment. Sternau's verse may be intended to apply to the "Rückblick" as well as the first "Andante," but no over-all programme for the sonata can be guessed safely from this verse, nor any special link with the eventful but somewhat veiled circumstances of Brahms's life in 1853.[67]

Brahms's Ensemble Sonatas

As mentioned earlier, Brahms's Op. 34b, *Sonate* [in f] *für zwei Pianoforte nach dem Quintet, Op. 34,* is included here because the composer

62. Hanslick/WIEN II 258. Clara had evidently played the whole work privately as early as Sept., 1854 (Joachim/LETTERS 77, 105). In Hanslick/CONCERTE 200–201 Anton Door is mistakenly credited with the first public performance, in 1877, of Op. 5 (which is discussed as deriving from Schumann's piano music).
63. BRAHMS BRIEFWECHSEL II 23; MT XXV (1884) 338, 348.
64. SCHUMANN-BRAHMS I 36–37, 53; BRAHMS BRIEFWECHSEL XIV 14.
65. Kalbeck/BRAHMS I/1 117, II/1 34; Mason/MEMORIES 134–35.
66. Kalbeck/BRAHMS I/1 216–17.
67. Cf. Nagel/BRAHMS 76–78.

thought enough of it in its own right to have it published independently of the magnificent Piano Quintet in f. Thus, Brahms wrote Rieter of Rieter-Biedermann on July 22, 1865:

> We might also keep in mind [the possibility] of publishing the work as a "Sonata for Two Pianos." To me and everyone who plays or hears it, it has a special appeal in this form and might indeed be welcomed as an interesting work for two pianos. In any case, I can give you a 4-hand [one-piano] arrangement (but for later publication).[68]

Mainly because the dedicatee kept the manuscript so long ("I'll never lend any manuscript to princesses again!"),[69] publication of the two-piano version did not occur until 1872, seven years after that of the Quintet it had preceded. But in spite of Brahms's special interest, Op. 34b has hardly enjoyed any independent life of its own, partly because two pianos, even more than one piano and even in such an outstanding work, are too monochromatic in their sound to sustain the interest for forty minutes, and because from the start the scoring of Op. 34b seemed to be inadequate to the task. A clue is provided in Brahms's decision by 1871 that the (one-piano) four-hand arrangement of this work would be impractical—in fact, hardly possible—for the work has to be played "with [too] much passion." [70] Henry S. Drinker was alone in concluding that "there is no more glorious or satisfactory work for two pianos." [71] Most pianists who play it are being expedient. They love the Quintet and, having no string quartet at hand, would rather play it on two pianos than not at all.

The genesis of Brahms's Piano Quintet in f has aroused much interest and several investigations, a primary source being the rich correspondence between Brahms, Clara Schumann, Joachim, publishers, and other friends during the decade from 1862.[72] For our

68. BRAHMS BRIEFWECHSEL XIV 114. ·

69. BRAHMS BRIEFWECHSEL XIV 195–6, with references to intervening letters. Princess Anna von Hessen, a good musician and friend of both Clara and Brahms, gave Brahms the autograph of Mozart's Symphony 40 in g in return for the dedication of both Opp. 34 and 34b (Kalbeck/BRAHMS I 61–62). The autograph of Op. 34b is listed in Albrecht/CENSUS 61.

70. BRAHMS BRIEFWECHSEL XIV 196.

71. Drinker/BRAHMS 104.

72. The most thorough account is presumably that by Wilhelm Altmann in a special issue of *Die Musikwelt* pub. in Hamburg in 1921; but it is not in any issue of that periodical from Jan. through Nov. of 1921, and the December issue could not be located here; a summary of the article, loosely trans., appears in the preface to Altmann/BRAHMS-m. Cf., also, the partly complementary, partly contradictory accounts in Nagel/BRAHMS II/1 52–54, 59–62; BRAHMS BRIEFWECHSEL XIV 115–16; Müller-Reuter/LEXIKON Suppl. 191–92; Drinker/BRAHMS 100–104. The bare possibility that Op. 34b could have succeeded rather than preceded Op. 34 (Kalbeck/BRAHMS II/1 59) is completely ruled out by further evidence cited in these accounts (and *infra*).

purposes, it is worth noting that the three settings in the evolution of this work somewhat parallel those in the evolution of Brahms's Piano Concerto in d, Op. 15. In Op. 15, the initial Sonata in d for two pianos called for orchestral treatment, the Symphony in d that followed lacked the piano's incisiveness, and the Concerto in d provided the happy compromise. In Op. 34 the piano again proved to be essential but not self-sufficient. Its original setting in 1862 was a string quintet, about which Clara wrote enthusiastically but Joachim much less so, objecting to a lack of sonority appropriate to the strong ideas.[73] Brahms then heard this and other lacks for himself and decided the work would sound better for two pianos.[74] In fact, he ultimately destroyed the first version,[75] which would have been interesting to see for purposes of comparison. But after completing the new version in the winter of 1863–64 and giving it its first public hearing with Carl Tausig in April, which stirred no interest,[76] Brahms had to conclude that two pianos did not provide the appropriate sonority, either. This time Clara's influence seems to have been paramount, especially when she wrote in July of 1864,

The work is so wonderfully grandiose, interesting throughout in its most ingenious combinations, masterful in every respect, but—it is not a sonata, but [rather] a work whose ideas you might—[in fact, you] must!—strew, as if from a horn of plenty, over the whole orchestra. A multitude of the most beautiful ideas get lost on the piano, [being] recognizable only to the musician [and] not enjoyable to the public. At the first playing I got the feeling of an arranged work . . . please, dear Johannes, follow [my advice] just this one time [and] rearrange the work once more.[77]

The final version that soon followed, to the all but total satisfaction and delight of everyone concerned,[78] completes an object lesson for us in the influence of content and scope on medium, and in the difference between sonata and quintet (or any other designation for a larger chamber ensemble) that was implicit by now in the word "sonata." The actual transfer of responsibilities from two pianos to piano quintet is instructive, too, to any student of scoring. Although only minute changes are made in the content,[79] the scoring changes are considerable (Ex. 40). For instance, the piano part in the Quintet

73. SCHUMANN-BRAHMS I 407–8, 418–19; BRAHMS BRIEFWECHSEL V 324–25, VI 9.

74. Joachim/LETTERS 307; SCHUMANN-BRAHMS I 442.

75. Kalbeck/BRAHMS II/1 53.

76. Cf. Kalbeck/BRAHMS II/1 59–61.

77. SCHUMANN-BRAHMS I 461 (cf. pp. 459, 460). Cf., also, Kalbeck/BRAHMS II/1 59–60 fn. and 62 fn. (indicating H. Levi's influence was strong, too).

78. E.g., cf. BRAHMS BRIEFWECHSEL VII 11–14 (H. Levi); SCHUMANN-BRAHMS I 472–73 and 475–76 (Clara).

79. E.g., Op. 34b/i/83 and 245 are deleted in Op. 34.

Ex. 40. From the first movements of Brahms's Sonata for Two Pianos in f, Op. 34b, and Piano Quintet in f, showing scoring changes and a deleted measure in Op. 34 (after Edition Peters 3662 and 3660).

comes now from "Klavier I" in the Sonata (e.g., i/1–17), now from "Klavier II" (e.g., i/17–22), with the string quartet taking what the other piano part had. At other times, the material is redistributed so that the quartet and piano in the Quintet each get something of both parts in the Sonata (e.g., i/23–32 and 35–38). There are instances where the strings are obviously more expressive (as in the 8ve and 9th leaps of ii/56–65), others where the piano's crisp articulation is more telling (e.g., i/5–11), and still others where only a complete fusion produces the needed orchestral effect (e.g., iii/23–29).

In the same year as he composed the first version of Op. 34, 1862, Brahms wrote the first three movements of what was to be a four-movement sonata for piano and cello. The finale followed in 1865. However, when Sonata in e, Op. 38, appeared in 1866 the "Adagio" that was to be the second movement had been discarded. Brahms seemed to take a whimsical delight in not letting the "Adagio" be seen by Clara or even the dedicatee, Gänsbacher, a conductor, singing teacher, and cellist who had given Brahms valuable Schubert MSS.[80] Schauffler advances tenuous arguments for a theory that this same "Adagio" reappeared as the superb second movement of Brahms's other cello sonata, Op. 99 in F.[81] One of the most solid and eloquent of Romantic cello sonatas, "which throughout is undifficult to play for both instruments," [82] Op. 38 is remarkable, among other virtues, for its powerful fugal finale. Brahms may or may not have been paying homage to J. S. Bach by recalling the subject of "Contrapunctus 13/2 (inversus)" from *Die Kunst der Fuge*, as Wilhelm Altmann has maintained.[83] The two subjects have in common an energetic, initial octave leap downward, with the lower note tied to the first triplet in a sequence of ascending triplets. On possible but less safe grounds, Altmann also suggests that the songful main theme of Brahms's first movement relates to the subject of Bach's "Contrapunctus 3," and that the main idea in Brahms's nostalgic middle movement derives from that main theme in the first movement. Clara was still writing to Brahms in 1890 about the pleasure it gave her to play this sonata (with the cellist Hausmann).[84] It had not been performed publicly until 1874,[85] but numerous performances as far off as London and Peabody Institute in Baltimore (1881) followed soon after.[86]

Op. 78 in G was the first of Brahms's three incomparable, surviving sonatas "für Pianoforte und Violine" (still worded, though now less justifiably, in that pre-Classic order).[87] It was composed in 1878–79 after his longest break between sonatas and near the start of his final or "consummation" period (*supra*). It originated, in fact, right around the time Brahms was consulting Joachim intensively about the violin

80. Kalbeck/BRAHMS I/1 190–93, 13.
81. Schauffler/BRAHMS 56, 378–80.
82. BRAHMS BRIEFWECHSEL IX 45 (to Simrock, Sept. 6, 1865).
83. Altmann/BACH-ZITATE.
84. SCHUMANN-BRAHMS II 408.
85. Ehrmann/BRAHMS 28.
86. E.g., cf. MT XXIII (1881) 99 and 215, XXVII (1886) 82; NZM LXXII/2 (1876) 466 (London) and LXXIII/1 (1877) 193 (Vienna).
87. Including the early lost or destroyed Son., in a, for P & Vn (*supra*) and 2 more sons. in this setting that Brahms is known to have destroyed (Kalbeck/BRAHMS III/1 191; May/BRAHMS II 545), Op. 78 was actually Brahms's 4th son. of its type.

solo writing in his Concerto in D, Op. 77.[88] His concern for the work is suggested by his careful attention to its editorial details while it was in press.[89] Both names that have been given to this sonata—"Regenlied" ("Rain-Song") and, less often, "Frühling" ("Spring")—got their sanction from Brahms himself, as in his remark to Otto Dessoff before publication took place: "You must not complain about the rain. It can be set very well to music, something I have tried to do along with [describing] spring[time] in a violin sonata."[90] Brahms referred, of course, to the first three measures of the finale and their derivation from the start of his song "Regenlied," Op. 59/3, as well as "Nachklang" ("Memories"[91]), Op. 59/4. Previously he had enquired (facetiously?) of his publisher Simrock whether plagiarism could be charged by the publisher of the songs, Rieter-Biedermann, or would the legal maximum of eight measures—that is, a musical period—still hold.[92]

Much has been written about this derivation and its effect on the poignant, exceptionally lyrical quality of the sonata, not only in the finale but throughout the first and parts of the second movements where the initial trochaic pattern of the "Regenlied" becomes a unifying cyclical motive to be reiterated, varied, or recombined almost constantly.[93] Clara could hardly write enough about how deeply this sonata and those uses of the song theme touched her, still recalling its finale in 1890 as the music she always hoped would accompany her to the world beyond.[94] Elisabeth von Herzogenberg, whose highly perceptive comments now mattered at least as much to Brahms as Clara's, wrote similarly, although she implied weariness with reviews that only dwelt on the song derivation.[95] Both women made special mention of the long pedal point near the end of the "Adagio," and both must have relished the interlocking of that movement with the finale through the return to its main theme.

88. Cf. BRAHMS BRIEFWECHSEL VI 158–72; May/BRAHMS II 542.

89. E.g., cf. BRAHMS BRIEFWECHSEL X 133; Fellinger/BRAHMS, with facs. showing changes made in the autograph. Other facs. of the autograph include the first p. of each mvt. in BRAHMS-BILDERBUCH Tafeln X and XI.

90. BRAHMS BRIEFWECHSEL XVI 218.

91. Of springtime? Cf. Kalbeck/BRAHMS III/1 189 and 191–92.

92. BRAHMS BRIEFWECHSEL X 128. In the same letter Brahms jokingly suggests his fee can be reduced by 25 per cent because the sonata is not complete, lacking a fourth mvt.

93. Cf. Kalbeck/BRAHMS II/2 377–80, III/1 189–92; Evans/BRAHMS III 60, 64 (?!); May/BRAHMS II 544; Hollander/BRAHMS.

94. SCHUMANN-BRAHMS II 177–79, 415.

95. BRAHMS BRIEFWECHSEL I 103–4, 120; cf., also, II 259, for her husband's recollection of Op. 78 just after her death in 1892.

But, as Elisabeth von Herzogenberg suggested,[96] the reviewers were not as ready to perceive such subtleties. When Brahms played Op. 78 with the violinist Hellmesberger on November 29, 1879, in Vienna, Hanslick expressed unqualified praise only for the finale. He found the treatment in the first two movements of this wonderfully plastic work less free and original and recommended transfer of the work, more contemplative than passionate, from the concert hall to more intimate, private circles.[97] When Bülow played Op. 78 in London early in 1880 with Madame Norman-Neruda, one reviewer wrote that in spite of their fine performance, the audience turned "with a feeling of relief to the harmonious lucidity and graceful, albeit passionate, melodiousness" in Mozart's Piano Quartet in g, adding:

We do not presume to have formed a definite opinion of Herr Brahms's new work after hearing it once only. We admit that some of its leading "motives" have grown upon us since the performance in question. Still, the general impression produced by the "Sonata" is that of a mind striving to depict in musical language an individual experience scarcely important enough to furnish the material for three movements. The Sonata is, in fact, a reminiscence or paraphrase of the composer's well-known "Regenlied," the contemplative character of which pervades the entire work, while it distinctly interconnects the first and third movements; thus marking a concession on the part of the composer to the "programme" principle generally repudiated by the musicians of his school. The Sonata will, no doubt, soon be repeated at these concerts.[98]

Op. 78 did get performed soon again in London, and often, with increasing favor.[99] But Brahms exhibited his typical depreciation of his own works when he sent the autograph of Op. 78 to the wife of Miller zu Aichholz, recognizing her desire for "stronger paper in which to pack birthday presents for your husband. Should the shape or anything else about this paper not be agreeable to you, I shall be glad to exchange it for other kinds—also from other manufacturers." [100]

96. BRAHMS BRIEFWECHSEL I 120.

97. Hanslick/CONCERTE 257–59; cf. Kalbeck/BRAHMS III/1 228. Müller-Reuter/LEXIKON Suppl. 203 lists three earlier performances that same month that seem to have been more intimate.

98. MT XXI (1880) 125. For other, similar reviews of the same and other concerts, cf. Evans/BRAHMS III 60–61, 64–65.

99. E.g., cf. MT XXI (1880) 192, 234, 288, 296; XXII (1881) 21, 180 (but read 5th performance, not 3d), 184 (Joachim and Hallé), 459; XXIV (1883) 135; XXV (1884) 80, 206 (Clara and Joachim); etc. Other early performances are cited in Kalbeck/BRAHMS III/1 265 and May/BRAHMS II 545.

100. As trans. in Schauffler/BRAHMS 162; cf., also, Kalbeck/BRAHMS III/1 193 fn. For a more cryptic deprecatory sentence about Op. 78 cf. Brahms's remark to

Brahms's second cello sonata, Op. 99 in F, and second violin sonata, Op. 100 in A, make a pair in that they were both written in Thun in that extraordinarily productive month of August in 1886 (along with Piano Trio in c, Op. 101, and songs).[101] Geiringer sees a contrast of "masculine defiance" and "feminine sweetness and tenderness" between them, and a youthful "ardent pathos" in Op. 99 that is exceptional in Brahms's mature writing.[102] The choice of the raised tonic for the key of the slow movement and brief melodic similarities between the main themes of Opp. 99/2 and 38/1 supplied Schauffler's main but tenuous arguments for supposing that here was the discarded slow movement of Op. 38 (*supra*).[103] Again, Brahms sought the reactions of Elisabeth, who replied with much enthusiasm, suggesting only that she would need to hear him play the difficult third movement and that the "quasi-lyrical theme" of the finale might contrast too greatly with the "grand style" of the other movements.[104] She had first heard about the work from the equally enthusiastic Robert Hausmann, the cellist who figured in the early history of the work and its first performances in 1886 with Brahms himself.[105]

The ever popular Sonata in A, Op. 100, for P & Vn, is called the "Thun Sonata" not only for the lovely summer retreat where it was composed but because of the eleven-stanza poem, "Thunersonate von Johannes Brahms," that it inspired Brahms's host and close friend of his last years, Joseph Viktor Widmann, to write.[106] Today it is hard for most of us to relate the sonata to Widmann's flowery, ingenuous programmatic vision in Thun of knights of old and their thrilling, apocalyptic glimpse of a fairy maiden in a passing skiff. Yet, significantly, the poem moved Brahms, who up to his last year

---

Joachim in BRAHMS BRIEFWECHSEL VI 175. Brahms designated no dedicatee for Op. 78, but wrote Elisabeth von Herzogenberg that he almost put her name on it (BRAHMS BRIEFWECHSEL I 105).

101. Cf. Dietrich & Widmann/BRAHMS 121 *et passim;* Kalbeck/BRAHMS IV/1 16–17 and 92; Schauffler/BRAHMS 8–9. The autograph is described in KRAUS/GEIRINGER/ LUITHLEN 55–56.

102. Geiringer/BRAHMS 238–40, including an example of changes Brahms made in the MS of Op. 99 and evidence in the finale that Brahms "could hardly write fast enough." Cf., also, Hanslick/MUSIKALISCHES 149–51 for an earlier similar view (1889), reprinted in Hanslick/TAGEBUCHE 209–10.

103. Schauffler/BRAHMS 378–80.

104. BRAHMS BRIEFWECHSEL II 130–31, 129. Clara was hurt at this time that Brahms was not sending her such things as Op. 99, too (SCHUMANN-BRAHMS II 307–9 [but read "Op. 100, 99" in 2d fn.]; cf., BRAHMS BRIEFWECHSEL II 144).

105. Cf. BRAHMS BRIEFWECHSEL XI 129 fn. 3. A grossly negative review of Op. 99 after the first performance is quoted and trans. in Slonimsky/LEXICON 74.

106. The poem appeared mainly as an appendix to Widmann's *Erinnerungen* (but not in the English trans., Dietrich & Widmann/BRAHMS); it is trans. in May/BRAHMS II 593–94.

was writing for further copies of a private printing issued by Widmann.[107] Less justifiable is the better-known name of "Meistersinger Sonate." In greater measure than the many commentators on this name care to acknowledge,[108] the initial theme does bring Wagner's "Prize Song" clearly to mind by its similarly forthright, downbeat opening on the same (few) notes and by its similar rhythm and lyricism—but only for a moment, and certainly not long enough to validate the charges of plagiarism once heard from the anti-Brahmsites.[109]

More plausible as the source of this theme is the opening of Brahms's own song, "Komm bald," Op. 97/5, composed two years earlier (Ex. 41).[110] But "Komm bald" is only one of at least three probable song derivations in Op. 100, which for this reason and its constant songfulness might well be given still another title, the "Liedersonate." [111] Thus, Op. 100/i/51–54 (the 2d theme) recalls the opening of "Wie Melodien zieht es mir," Op. 105/1,[112] and Op. 100/iii/31–37 and 90–91 hint at measures 1–8 in the fourth song of the same set, "Auf dem Kirchhofe." [113]

After a first reading of the sonata with Joachim at the end of December, 1886, Elisabeth von Herzogenberg wrote Brahms ecstatically that "the whole piece is one veritable caress." [114] Her equally enthusiastic husband raised tiny questions about the juxtaposition in the second movement of the "lovely" andante melody in F with the Grieg-like, "lively-melancholy," scherzando section in d;[115] also, about a need both he and Joachim felt for a new or "second theme" instead of the seemingly abrupt return to the main theme right after the arrival on the dominant in measure 59 of the finale. Actually, Joachim later reported that Brahms told him he "had cut a good deal" out

107. BRAHMS BRIEFWECHSEL VIII 146.
108. E.g., Evans/BRAHMS III 187; Drinker/BRAHMS 70; Mason/BRAHMS.
109. Cf. Kalbeck/BRAHMS IV/1 17–19.
110. The illustration of this derivation in Kalbeck/BRAHMS IV/1 19 has not been taken up by later writers; in III/2 538 a similar theme in Symphony 4 in e/iv/225–33 is noted.
111. Kalbeck/BRAHMS IV/1 17–22. Most of the songs concerned are settings of poems by Brahms's elder friend, Klaus Groth.
112. As illustrated in Kalbeck/BRAHMS IV/1 20. Elisabeth von Herzogenberg spotted this derivation at once (BRAHMS BRIEFWECHSEL II 140).
113. As noted less specifically in BRAHMS BRIEFWECHSEL II 140 fn.
114. BRAHMS BRIEFWECHSEL II 140 (on the confused date of this reading cf. Müller-Reuter/LEXIKON Suppl. 204–5). She had been impatient to see the work and Brahms had kept Simrock waiting while he got her reactions (BRAHMS BRIEFWECHSEL II 131–32, XI 139). Clara recorded her fondness for Op. 100, especially its outer mvts., only in her diary (Litzmann/SCHUMANN III 490).
115. BRAHMS BRIEFWECHSEL II 147 (with reference in fn. 1 to a possible source for the scherzando section in Grieg's Son. in g, Op. 13/ii [1867]).

Ex. 41. The opening themes of Johannes Brahms's "Komm bald," Op. 97/5, for P & voice, and Sonata in A, Op. 100, for P & Vn (after Brahms/WERKE-m XXVI 202 and X 31).

of the finale in the interest of condensation, though apparently not at that same place but in the coda.[116] Brahms had already given a first performance of Op. 100, presumably in its final form, with Josef Hellmesberger on December 2, 1886.[117]

Brahms's Sonata in d, Op. 108, was his third and last sonata for P & Vn and the only one in four movements. It was also the only one of the last six sonatas, from his final or "consummation" period, that bore a dedication—to "his friend Hans von Bülow." Bülow had indeed become a real friend and admirer, the more so with Wagner gone. He received the dedication as if it were an "ennoblement." [118] Brahms started the sonata during that same fruitful summer of 1886 in Thun, but did not complete it until two summers later, probably because it raised weightier creative problems. Again, this late in his career, Brahms participated in the first performance, in Budapest late in 1888, his partner being the Hungarian Jenö Hubay.[119] His performance of Op. 108 in Vienna with Joachim

116. May/BRAHMS II 592.
117. Cf. Kalbeck/BRAHMS IV/1 36–37, 49, 127.
118. BÜLOW BRIEFE VIII 255; cf., also, p. 250 for his praise of the work. Less than 20 years before, Bülow had dismissed Brahms contemptuously (e.g., BÜLOW BRIEFE V 352 fn.).
119. Cf. Kalbeck/BRAHMS IV/1 120; Müller-Reuter/LEXIKON Suppl. 205 (with listings of further early performances).

soon after gave Hanslick the occasion not only to rejoice in the work but to compare all three violin sonatas in subjective terms that today's musicians might still accept.[120] He saw this one as the most brilliant, difficult, passionate, large-scale, and substantial, Op. 100 as an unassuming, easygoing, genial work, but Op. 78 as a loved and trusted friend to whom he was admittedly partial and unable to acknowledge any superior.

Kalbeck finds only one, tentative, though not implausible song derivation in Op. 108—that of the opening of the second movement from "Klage" ("Lament") Op. 105/3. He also finds traces of Schumann, as he had in Op. 100, attributable partly to Brahms's preoccupation with the new Schumann edition around this time, in conjunction with (when not in opposition to) Clara.[121] Op. 108 brought from both Elisabeth von Herzogenberg and Clara some of their most enthusiastic, extensive, and discerning reactions (more perceptive and knowing than Hanslick's).[122] So ardent was Elisabeth's first letter that Brahms replied he would rather take it as a mistake than as hypocrisy, being less suspicious of a previous, franker letter of criticism (on the songs in Opp. 104–6).[123] But Elisabeth protested and Brahms apologized,[124] and Clara repeated her own enthusiasm in her diary,[125] all tending to confirm the genuineness of both women's reactions. Brahms mailed the MS to Elisabeth first, precipitating one of several three-way rounds of caustic, injured, or admonitory remarks centering around Elisabeth's and Clara's competition to get his first attention.[126] Elisabeth expressed particular pleasure in the development section of the first movement, with its rich texture woven around the dominant pedal point; in the simpler coda; in the "Adagio" movement, thankfully free of a contrasting middle section (like that in Op. 100/ii?); in the pianistically graceful, merry, humorous content of the third movement; and in the "compelling drive" of the finale as well as its transition to the second theme through a

120. Hanslick/MUSIKALISCHES 151–55. As early as April 29, 1889, Op. 108 was played in New York, at a reception for Bülow (Salter/AMERICAN 89 fn.).
121. Kalbeck/BRAHMS IV/1 21 and 23. The chief estrangements between Brahms and Clara occurred in 1886–87 and 1891–92 (cf. SCHUMANN-BRAHMS II 306–12, 464–68 and 476–78).
122. BRAHMS BRIEFWECHSEL II 210–13, 215–17, 217–19, 226; SCHUMANN-BRAHMS II 366–70, 395, 541–42.
123. BRAHMS BRIEFWECHSEL II 214 (and 200–209).
124. BRAHMS BRIEFWECHSEL II 219–21.
125. Litzmann/SCHUMANN III 512.
126. BRAHMS BRIEFWECHSEL II 214, 217, 218, 220, 221, 223; SCHUMANN-BRAHMS 362–63, 364, 366.

passing D.[127] She objected (in vain) to the rhythmic difficulty and unsatisfactory violin register in measures 142 to 157 of the finale, and suggested pizzicato for the double-stops in the third movement, which suggestion Brahms did follow starting at measure 119. Although a neuralgic arm prevented her trying Op. 108 at once for herself, Clara wrote of the warmth, depth, over-all melancholy, and consistent interest of the work, singling out the pedal point (again) and the "billows of interwoven harmonies" in the first movement, the frolicking of young lovers, interrupted by "a flash of deeper passion," in the third movement, and (again) the magnificent, impassioned flow of the finale. At 74 (in 1894), after playing the work with Joachim, Clara was still writing, "I love this sonata beyond words, every movement!—who knows whether this is not the last time that I shall [be able to] play it!" [128]

Brahms's last two sonatas, Op. 120/1 in f and 120/2 in E♭, were written for clarinet and piano (the order in the title, or, as it were, "for Piano and Mühlfeld." [129] Richard Mühlfeld, as both clarinetist and person, was closely associated with all four late clarinet works of Brahms—the Trio in a, Op. 114, and the Quintet in b, Op. 115, too.[130] He joined in numerous early performances, private and public, of both sonatas with Brahms, to the latter's great delight during those remarkably peripatetic and universally applauded activities of his third and second last years.[131] Moreover, publication was delayed in 1895 so that Mühlfeld could continue to give some "first" performances abroad.[132] Joachim joined in some of the early performances with Brahms, too, and it must have been partly for these occasions that Brahms himself adapted the clarinet part to viola (chiefly shifting the octave registers).[133] Brahms presented the autographs of Op. 120 to Mühlfeld [134] and perhaps would have dedicated any or all of his late

127. Presumably mss. 37–39, although her mention of a Vn entry in the 3d measure would then have to be an error for piano entry (BRAHMS BRIEFWECHSEL II 212–13).

128. SCHUMANN-BRAHMS II 542.

129. Drinker/BRAHMS 61.

130. Hanslick/FÜNF 312–13.

131. Cf. May/BRAHMS II 643–47; Kalbeck/BRAHMS IV/2 358–66, 368; BRAHMS BRIEFWECHSEL XII 155, 156, 162.

132. Cf. Kalbeck/BRAHMS IV/2 393–94.

133. Cf. BRAHMS BRIEFWECHSEL VI 280 (but the letter is wrongly dated 1892 instead of 1894), 293, 296, 298–99, and XII 165–68, 172–75, 178; as with P-duet and other arrangements of earlier sons. (cf. XII 150–51!), Brahms asked Simrock to have an alternative part prepared for Vn, which Simrock was not to pub. until after the clarinet original had appeared (with only his Va alternative). Cf., also, Cobbett/CHAMBER I 182 (Tovey).

134. May/BRAHMS II 644. The autograph of Op. 120/1 is described in KRAUS/GEIRINGER/LUITHLEN 89.

clarinet works to him had he not come to feel increasingly that a dedication implied more satisfaction with a work than his ever severe self-criticism would allow.[135]

In several senses the two clarinet sonatas helped to round out the Indian summer of Brahms in the 1890's. He meant them to be his last compositions for the public,[136] although he did add the *Four Serious Songs* and *Eleven Chorale Preludes for Organ* in 1896. Furthermore, the sonatas provided the occasions for some of his final and most heart-warming meetings with two of his closest and most lasting friends, Clara and Joachim, both of whom he had originally met soon after completing his first surviving work (Sonata in f♯, Op. 42), more than forty-two years earlier. Elisabeth von Herzogenberg was no longer alive to record her excitement in the music,[137] but Clara was still able to provide what seems to have been one of Brahms's main incentives to composition. Although too deaf by now to hear much other than "chaos" when Brahms and Mühlfeld played both sonatas four times for her in five days, she was still able to read, play over, and express her love for them.[138]

There is also a sense of Indian summer in the music itself of Op. 120—in its sweet mellow resignation, which pervades not only such a gentle nostalgic movement as Op. 120/1/ii but the stronger allegro movements as well. It is sometimes suggested that the two sonatas reflect a late decline in Brahms's creative powers.[139] They certainly show no lessening of craftsmanship or structural control. Together, as implied by their single opus number, they make a remarkable pair. They complement each other by contrasting decidedly in their keys, moods, and aesthetic depths. Yet over all they reveal not only that pervading sense of sweet mellow resignation but some striking common melodic bonds. In fact, right from their opening themes, so idiomatically suited to the clarinet tone and cantabile style, the two sonatas might well be linked under the heading "Diptych" that William G. Hill has proposed with good and similar reason for the pair of string quartets in Brahms's Op. 51.[140] Among all Brahms's many uses of cyclical relationships and free variation techniques there are few as subtle, flexible, or rewarding as those within and between the two

135. Cf. BRAHMS BRIEFWECHSEL I 105.
136. Cf. BRAHMS BRIEFWECHSEL XII 151.
137. There is no reasonable support for calling the sons. of Op. 120 "obituary poems" for her, as in Richard Specht's *Johannes Brahms* (London: J. M. Dent, 1930, p. 327).
138. Litzmann/SCHUMANN III 589–90. Cf., also, May/BRAHMS II 649–50; SCHUMANN-BRAHMS II 563–71, 583.
139. E.g., Schauffler/BRAHMS 381–82.
140. MR XIII (1952) 110–24.

sonatas of Op. 120. Rather than any decline of creative powers in
Op. 120, perhaps one might speak of increasing caution in the treatment of the ideas. Peter Latham has argued persuasively his thesis
that as Brahms matured he proved not to be the prophet Schumann
saw in him. Instead, partly because of the Classical orientation that
had started with Marxsen and partly because of his personal background and character he learned more and more to do only what was
safe and sure.[141] His unwillingness to take chances, reflected somewhat
in that severe self-criticism, may explain at once the perfection of his
music, the leading position he has held in the history of the sonata
since Beethoven, and yet the limitation that gives pause to Bülow's
claim for him as the "third B."

Other Composers in Austria

Brahms had no serious competitor in Vienna in the field of the
sonata. The most likely one, the great symphonist Anton Bruckner
(1824–96), came no closer than his fine String Quintet in F (1879)
except for his earlier, incomplete String Quartet in c and three rather
dramatic first movements to prospective piano solo sonatas in F, f,
and g, all student works of 1861–63.[142] We are left, then, with
scarcely more than a dozen, largely forgotten composers of sonatas in
Austria, as a postscript to our discussion of Brahms. One was the
pianist, organist, and singer (**Friedrich**) **Robert Volkmann** (1815–83),
in whose early music both Brahms and Bülow saw much promise.[143]
Volkmann actually lived in Budapest most of his life (where we shall
meet him as a teacher; ssb XVII) and in Vienna only four years, from
1854.[144] But much of his music was published and made its chief mark
there. Certain of his piano trios, string quartets, and symphonies won
particular favor and occasionally are still played. In our more limited
field of works called "sonata," he left only one substantial example,
a solo piano Sonata in c, Op. 12, and three sonatinas (2 for P & Vn
and one for P-duet).[145] Op. 12, published by Kistner in Leipzig in

141. Latham/BRAHMS 93–96, 168–69, 173.
142. Cf. MGG II 364 (F. Blume). The son. mvts. have yet to be pub., but are
described, with exx., in Böttcher/BRUCKNER.
143. E.g., SCHUMANN-BRAHMS I 174 (1856); BÜLOW BRIEFE II 67, III 76–79.
144. Cf. MGG XIII 1921–23 (R. Sietz), with further references; also, La Mara/
MUSIKERBRIEFE II 292.
145. Cf. the undated lists in PAZDÍREK XIV 290–93 and GROVE IX 68–69 (Grove).
Op. 12 was reviewed in NZM LV (1861) 47 (with ex.) as a work to be more respected
than loved, and not especially "new." His 2 sonatinas Opp. 60 and 61 are reviewed
similarly in MW II (1870) 4.

1854 or 1855, is a three-movement sonata (M-VF-M/VF) that falls stylistically midway between the piano works of Mendelssohn and Schumann, which must already have affected Volkmann while he was still studying in Leipzig in the late 1830's. The ideas, piano writing, and rhythms all suggest these influences. But the unusual, yet convincing alternation of 6/8 and 2/8 meter in the "Prestissimo" middle movement suggest Hungarian influences while he was in Pest. The total effect is one of songful, flowing music, solidly albeit somewhat conservatively grounded, and interesting enough in content without disclosing any conspicuous originality.

The concert pianist **Carl Evers** (1819–75) studied with Karl Krebs, started to compose under Mendelssohn's influence, and met Chopin before he settled in Graz in 1841 and Vienna in 1872.[146] Between about 1842 and 1860, at least eight sonatas by him were published, mainly by Schlesinger of Berlin, and reviewed widely, including six for P solo, one for P & Vn, and one for P-duet.[147] The third solo sonata, Op. 22 in d, appeared early enough to receive one of Schumann's last and more devastating reviews, in 1844.[148] In brief, Schumann said that favorable Vienna reviews of Evers' sonatas needed to be cut down to size, for, like a talented dilettante, Evers, the professional, produced felicitous ideas here and there, but with a tasteless confusion of Classic and more recent styles and no larger sense of organization. Slightly more favorable reviews of later sonatas by Evers suggest that at least the more academic aspects of his composing may have improved,[149] but they hardly inspire any protracted search for the sonatas themselves, none of which have turned up in European or American libraries during the present study.

Only passing mention needs to be given to a well reviewed piano sonata (Op. 2, *ca.* 1854) dedicated to Schumann by one of his correspondents, **Carl Debrois van Bruyck** (1828–1902), who was active west of Vienna in Waidhofen;[150] or to the four somewhat academic solo piano sonatas, published in the 1850's, by Bruyck's teacher and

146. Cf. GROVE II 982 (W. Carr).

147. Cf. PAZDÍREK V 181–82.

148. Schumann/SCHRIFTEN II 346–47. An equally negative review of the same work (with revealing exx.) and a more guarded review of Evers' first son. appear in AMZ XLVI (1844) 732–33 and XLV (1843) 453–55, respectively.

149. E.g., AMZ XLVII (1845) 39–42 (on Sons. 1–3, other works, and biography) and XLVIII (1846) 598; NZM XXIII (1845) 201–2, XL (1854) 158 and 197; MW V (1874) 426–27 (A. W. Ambros). Hanslick's review of Evers' recital of his own sons. and related works in Vienna in 1855 (Hanslick/WIEN II 86–87) largely repeats the substance of the NZM reviews, without acknowledgment.

150. Cf. Riemann/LEXIKON I 242; NZM XL (1854) 209.

Brahms's occasional friend, the pianist **Johann Rufinatscha** (1812–93);[151] or to the two solo piano sonatas (Op. 6 in d, 1858, and Op. 10 in E, 1861) and the duo sonata for P & Vn (Op. 30 in e, 1871) by Brahms's longtime friend, **Franz Wüllner** (1832–1902);[152] or to two sonatas, Opp. 1 and 3 (1872 and 1874) by the Vienna-trained, widely stationed pianist and violinist **Eduard Rappoldi** (1831–1903);[153] or to two sonatas each for P & Vn and P & Vc, published between 1872 and 1881, by the Vienna pianist and teacher **Julius Zellner** (1832–1900);[154] or to the two sonatas each for P & Vc and P & Vn (plus some sonatinas) by Rheinberger's pupil in Graz, **Ferdinand Thieriot** (1838–1919), published between 1868 and 1892;[155] or to the six fairly purposeful, spare duo sonatas, three each for P & Vn and P & Vc, published between 1882 and 1897, by Brahms's close friend **Heinrich von Herzogenberg** (1843–1900).[156]

But there is more interest in the sonatas of two other men who were friends of Brahms and of each other, the pianist **Ignaz Brüll** (1846–1907) and the violinist **Karl Goldmark** (1830–1915). Among seven sonatas by Brüll published between 1871 and 1906, four are for Vn & P, one is for Vc & P,[157] one for 2 Ps, and one for solo P.[158] The last,

151. Cf. MGG XI 1080 (W. Senn); PAZDÍREK XII 681; and the mostly laudatory review of Op. 7 in C, with exx., in NZM XLV (1856) 234–35.

152. Cf. the monograph Kämper/WÜLLNER, including descriptions of the sons. (pp. 72–74) and full lists of Wüllner's works (pp. 142–59). Cf., also, GROVE IX 373–74 (M. Friedländer); BRAHMS BRIEFWECHSEL XV 192–94 (dated list of Wüllner's works); PAZDÍREK XV 572–74. Op. 6 is reviewed with qualified praise in NZM LIV (1861) 79, 80; and Op. 30 similarly in MW III (1872) 439 (G. H. Witte).

153. Cf. GROVE VII 49 (E. Blom); Altmann/KAMMERMUSIK 221; MW XI (1880) 394 (mild pros and cons in Op. 3).

154. Cf. BAKER 1841; Altmann/KAMMERMUSIK 233 and 266; PAZDÍREK XV 345 (including sonatinas for P solo and P-duet; cf. SMW XLI [1887] 643). Praise for the charm, melodic interest, and good scoring in Zellner's sons. is expressed in MW XI (1880) 589–90; Cobbett/CHAMBER II 596.

155. Cf. Riemann/LEXIKON II 1836–37; PAZDÍREK XIV 132; Altmann/KAMMERMUSIK 229 and 265; MW XI (1880) 322 (finding Op. 24 consistently interesting).

156. Cf. MGG VI 302–6 (dated but incomplete list; W. Kahl) Altmann/KAMMERMUSIK 207, 258; Cobbett/CHAMBER I 553–54 (W. Altmann & W. W. Cobbett); Shand/VIOLIN 67–72 (for exx.); MT XXV (1883) 33 and XXVII (1886) 273 (for early performances abroad, the latter by Joachim). Only 2, noncommittal references, to one son., Op. 52 for P & Vc, occur in the correspondence with Brahms (BRAHMS BRIEFWECHSEL II 128 and 151).

157. A review of this first son., Op. 9, stresses the diversity of influences it reveals (including Italian and Hungarian), hints at superficiality, and grants but faint praise (NZM LXVIII/1 [1872] 139).

158. Cf. MGG II 386–88 (H. Wirth); PAZDÍREK II 1154–57; Altmann/KAMMERMUSIK 197, 254, 286. Son. 2 for P & Vn, Op. 60 in a, is reviewed as light, fluent, and not especially attractive (SMW XLVIII [1890] 899). The Son. for 2 Ps (F-Sc-M-F) is reviewed as skillful, sonorous, and often trivial, in MW XII (1881) 411.

Op. 73 in d (1894), seems to have enjoyed the most popularity. Its first movement suffers a bit from the hollowness and sentimentality of Grieg's larger forms (ssв XV). In fact, the widely-spaced, chordal outline and the strategic aug.-6/5 chord of its opening theme recall some Grieg introductories. Though Brüll's ability to develop his ideas is greater than Grieg's, he, too, shows up best in lighter forms, as in the second movement, where a bright scherzando section in 2/4 meter, a lilting "dolce cantando" section in 6/8, and an "Andante con moto" section in 3/8 follow in an extended rondo design, A-B-A-C-A-B-A/ coda. An independent "Andante" and a toccata-like "Allegro moderato" comprise the two movements that complete this well-made but dated and seldom distinctive work.

Goldmark left about ten instrumental chamber works along with his much better known operas, including a Sonata in D/b, Op. 25, for P & Vn (1875) and a Sonata in F, Op. 39, for P & Vc (1893).[159] The two sonatas are unequal works. Instead of the smooth polish and control of Brüll's training they reveal at once the originality and roughnesses of the largely self-taught composer. Their ideas are frequently fresh and unexpected, especially their rhythms and chromatic harmony (pointing to Goldmark's love of Wagner's music; Ex. 42). But the development of ideas so necessary to full-scale sonata forms is characteristically stiff, naive, or nonexistent. Both sonatas are in three movements (F-S-VF and M-M-F). The violin sonata, with its infrequent tonal scheme of D-f♯-b, is somewhat larger, more serious, and more effective than the cello sonata.[160] The finales are the weakest movements of both sonatas. It should go without saying that whatever spark can still be heard in either Brüll's or Goldmark's sonatas will disappear entirely if they are exposed to comparison with any of Brahms's sonatas and their incalculably greater genius and mastery. In all his vast extant correspondence Brahms scarcely ever strained either his kindness or integrity by attempting to comment on the music of such good friends.

As a matter of curiosity, mention should be added of the four piano sonatas left unfinished in MSS by **Hugo Wolf** (1860–1903).[161] They

159. Cf. мcc V 481–84 (W. Pfannkuch); Altmann/каммеrmusik 204 and 256. Altmann/goldmark (with many exx.) is a survey of the chamber music (but Op. 39 is overlooked). A performance of Op. 25 is reported in nzm LXXII/2 (1876) 423.
160. A review of Op. 25 in mw X (1879) 519 rates it below Goldmark's operatic and orchestral music, but finds it not without some attractive details; the form is seen as the chief weakness (yet as the chief point of originality, in smw XXIII [1875] 674). Cf., also, Hanslick/concerte 306.
161. Cf. Walker/wolf 15, 35–39, 463–64; grove IX 331, 338, 343 (F. Walker).

Ex. 42. From the middle movement of Karl Goldmark's Sonata in D/b, Op. 25, for P & Vn (after the original Schott ed. of 1875).

were composed too early to be musically significant, when he was but fifteen and sixteen (during his influential exposure to Wagner and before his unhappy meeting with Brahms). But they are worth noting as early stormy efforts of the great Viennese, late-Romantic song composer.[162]

162. A letter from Dr. Ferdinand Wernigg of the Wiener Stadtbibliothek suggests that they will be included (as of 1969) in the "Jugendwerke" to be pub. as part of the new "Hugo Wolf-Gesamtausgabe."

Chapter X

Liszt and Others in Germany from About 1850 to 1885

South Germany (Rheinberger) and Switzerland

Applicable here, too, is the preface to the previous chapter on Austro-German ties and divergencies in the second half of the 19th century. The most important sonata composer in south Germany during this period was the organist, composer, and teacher **Joseph Gabriel Rheinberger** (1839–1901). An organ prodigy, Rheinberger was thoroughly grounded in Classic music under such teachers as J. J. Maier and F. Lachner (ssb VII).[1] In Munich, where he spent his entire life from the age of twelve, he composed prolifically in nearly every category,[2] won international recognition as a teacher, especially of counterpoint (drawing students, like G. S. Chadwick and H. W. Parker, from as far off as the United States), and received many honors. A total of 29 sonatas by him was published, all in his last 33 years (1868–1901), including 20 for organ, 4 for P solo, one for P-duet, 2 for P & Vn, and one each for P & Vc and P & Hn. The organ sonatas have benefited from studies by several writers.[3] The piano and chamber sonatas deserve but have yet to receive comparable attention.[4] Those who dis-

1. Cf. MGG XI 377–81 (A. Würz), with further references.
2. Cf. PAZDÍREK XII 252–63.
3. Grace/RHEINBERGER is the chief survey. Harvey Grace also prepared a new ed. of the organ sons. for Novello (ca. 1934–56; Cat. NYPL XXV 535) and wrote the full article on Rheinberger for the 3d and 4th eds. of GROVE (IV 378–82), shortened in the 5th ed. (VII 145–48). A facs. of the opening of the autograph of organ Son. 16 in g♯ appears in MGG XI 377 and all of the first mvt. of this son. is pub. in Giegling/SOLO-m no. 17.
4. The P sons. are briefly noted in Georgii/KLAVIERMUSIK 581–82 (Op. 122, P-duet), merely cited in Kirby/KEYBOARD 349 (with p. 350 largely devoted to the organ sons.), and disregarded (in the absence of any reference at all to Rheinberger) in Shedlock/SONATA and Dale/NINETEENTH. The chamber sons. have fared still less well. Exceptional are the 2 short (but enthusiastic) paragraphs on the 2 Vn sons. in Cobbett/CHAMBER II 293–94 (W. Altmann). Rheinberger gets no mention, for example, in Müller-Reuter/LEXIKON, which does give good space to Raff, Reinicke,

miss Rheinberger as the composer merely of teaching pieces that once enjoyed wide use, or because he has all but disappeared from publishers' catalogues are in for a surprise if they start reading into his sonatas. For nearly every one of these is a broadly conceived, serious, masterfully executed work, with many movements of decided musical interest.

In 1925 Harvey Grace ranked Rheinberger's organ music, especially the sonatas, as "second in importance only to Bach's organ music." [5] If his evaluation now seems too categorical and also somewhat confining, it should at least be acceptable to rank the sonatas on a par with the best German organ examples of the 19th century, including those of Mendelssohn, Reubke, and Merkel. Had Rheinberger lived longer he probably would have added organ sonatas in Bb, c#, Gb, and E, since each of the twenty he did complete is in a different key and only those four keys are needed to complete the cycle. In over-all plan, these organ sonatas are more like the piano and duo sonatas of the 19th century than Mendelssohn's, although seventeen of Rheinberger's have fugues. Unlike most German organ sonatas, none of them centers around a chorale. The most frequent plan is the three-movement one, F-S-F, with or without introductions to the fast movements. Various four-movement plans occur, too. The first movement is usually a "sonata form," but a relatively free one in which the development and recapitulation tend to be shortened in favor of an extended, revelatory coda or apotheosis. The middle movement is most often a gentle foil for the outer movements, as suggested by titles like "Intermezzo," "Idyll," "Provençalisch," "Pastorale," or "Cantilene." The finale usually consists of one of the aforementioned fugues, single or double, with or without introduction; but sometimes it is the first movement in which the fugue occurs. A notable factor in the success of Rheinberger's fugues is the careful, effective design of his subjects, both melodic and rhythmic (as in Son. 13 in Eb, Op. 161/iv). Rheinberger shows relatively little interest in exploiting the traditional contrapuntal devices, although one never doubts his ability to use them.

Rheinberger's other sonatas are less free in their over-all plans and, naturally, less polyphonically disposed than his organ sonatas. But, as viewed here (contrary to Harvey Grace), they are not musically less significant. Both the excellences and shortcomings of his sonatas are

---

Draeseke, and Gernsheim. The string sons. were performed often in Rheinberger's own day (although not so often as his once ubiquitous organ sons.); e.g., cf. NZM LXXII/1 (1876) 8 and 104, LXXII/2 345, and LXXIII/1 (1877) 214 (Pittsburgh, Pa.); MT XVII (1876) 697, XVIII (1877) 553, XXV (1884) 82–83; SMZ XVI (1876) 4, 22.

5. Grace/RHEINBERGER v, 125–27. A similar evaluation was arrived at independently by A. Farmer in MT LXXVIII (1937) 538–39. Cf., also, Sandberger/AUFSÄTZE 325–26.

common, more or less, to all of them. The excellences include a seemingly inexhaustible fund of musical ideas, sometimes very distinctive ideas; a complete command of compositional techniques, whether melodic, rhythmic, harmonic, textural, or instrumental; an exceptional versatility and resourcefulness in the use of these techniques; and a broad, unfailing sense of musical architecture. The sense of architecture is most apparent in the "sonata forms," where the long-range opposition of large sections and the steady, deliberate pursuit of a principal motive or thematic element seem to lead gradually but surely to that apotheosis in the coda. In this aspect, Rheinberger's sonatas at once bring Bruckner's symphonic "sonata forms" to mind.[6] A fine example is the first movement of Sonata in E♭, Op. 77, for P & Vn, a telling work that duo teams overlook in their searches for worthwhile Romantic alternatives to the sonatas of Brahms, Franck, and Fauré.

What are the shortcomings of Rheinberger's sonatas that may account for their virtual oblivion today, except for a few isolated movements in the organ sonatas? As viewed here, the problem is not one of unoriginality, although unoriginality is blamed in most references to Rheinberger today.[7] A movement like the "Scherzo" in G♭ from his Sonata 3 in E♭, Op. 135, for piano reveals much of the tonal color, rhythmic ingenuity, melodic freshness, and structural purpose that can be found in the "Scherzo" from Bruckner's Fourth Symphony. But that analogy suggests one of the problems of Rheinberger's sonatas. Bruckner's deliberately paced development of ideas serves well when enhanced by the contrasts of orchestral colors, but would serve less well, especially in the even larger forms, if the color contrasts were limited to the piano alone or to the piano with one other instrument. Furthermore, it is in Rheinberger's nature to be not only deliberate but more reflective and contemplative than dynamic and agitated. Even his fine themes tend to be serene and optimistic rather than troubled and portentous. If we add to these traits the fact that—in

6. But Anton in Vienna seems to have been no relation of one "Herrn Franz Bruckner, Kgl. Kammermusiker in München," to whom Rheinberger's 2d Vn son., Op. 105, is ded. In a lengthy review of Symphonische Sonate for P, Op. 47, in MW II (1871) 389–91 and 406–7, A. Maczewski discusses the differences between the symphony and son. (cf. SSB II) and finds the long development in i explains "Symphonische" and the "Tarantella" finale explains "Sonate" in the title. Strongly favorable reviews of Rheinberger's Romantische Sonate in f♯, Op. 184, occur in MW XXVIII (1897) 561 (L. Bödecker) and SMW LV (1897) 243.

7. E.g., cf. MGG XI 380–81. The provocative evaluation of Rheinberger in Sandberger/AUFSÄTZE 320–30 puts more emphasis than seems justified here on Bach, middle Beethoven, and Mendelssohn as the main points of departure and of Romantic limitations in Rheinberger's music.

spite of frequent titles for his sonatas like "Fantasie," "Pastoral," "Romantische," or "Sinfonische"—Rheinberger showed no special interest either in programme music or German literature, we are forced to conclude that in a Romantic sense he qualifies somewhat as an anti-sonata composer. Finally, some acknowledgment must be made of infrequent saccharinities, especially chromaticisms, in Rheinberger's melody and/or harmony that (to recall a trait not unfamiliar in Mendelssohn) can extend beyond the borderline of sentiment into sentimentality (as in that same P son., Op. 135/iii/24–30 and 43–48). On the other hand, Rheinberger can keep such moments under control and create slow movements with uncommonly long, expressive, purposeful lines, couched in harmony far more adventuresome than writers generally have credited to him—harmony, in fact, that at times seems to anticipate or parallel Fauré's. A representative illustration is the "Andante molto" from his Sonata 2 for P & Vn in e, Op. 105, from which an extract can give only a hint (Ex. 43).[8]

One of Rheinberger's few cocitizens in Munich who won any attention with their sonatas was Wagner's sometime friend **Robert von Hornstein** (1833–90), who left one published sonata each for Vn & P, P-duet, and P solo, in the 1870's.[9] The first of these, Op. 7, is reviewed as pleasingly constructed but anachronistic in its rococo figuration, and as somewhat lacking in the development or contrapuntal interest expected in a sonata.[10] Another cocitizen, at least during parts of his peregrinatory career, was the versatile conductor and composer **Bernhard Scholz** (1835–1916), who left 9 published sonatas in the 62 years from 1850 to 1912—4 each for Vn & P and Vc & P, and one, Op. 28 in B (1868 or 1869), for P solo.[11] An examination of Op. 28, "friendlily dedicated to his teacher Ernst Pauer," confirms the verdict of much skill but weak ideas on the part of this active champion of Brahms, musical conservative, and cosigner of the anti-Liszt-Wagner "Manifesto."[12] The most effective of Scholz's four movements (F-Sc-Va-F) are the last two, an "Adagio molto" theme with seven variations and a fugal finale à la Beethoven of Op. 101. And a third cocitizen for a while as well as a pupil of Rheinberger was the esteemed pianist and teacher **Luise Adolpha Le Beau** (1850–1927), one of the few women

---

8. In MW X (1879) 421 a review of Op. 105 offers warm praise for all mvts. apart from a slight letdown noted in the finale; cf., also, SMW XXXVII (1879) 82–83.

9. Cf. Mendel/LEXIKON V 306; Riemann/LEXIKON I 783–84; PAZDÍREK VII 672–3.

10. NZM LXVIII/2 (1872) 377; MW III (1872) 537.

11. Cf. MGG XII 36–39 (R. Sietz, with further references); Altmann/KAMMERMUSIK 225 and 263.

12. Cf. Cobbett/CHAMBER II 343 (W. Altmann); MW I (1870) 102 (on Op. 28); NZM LXXIX (1879) 185–86 and NZM IV/3/2 (Feb. 1, 1883) 2 (both on Op. 55); MW XXXIII (1902) 201 (on Op. 81); DM XI/4 (1911–12) 382 (E. Thilo on Op. 94).

Ex. 43. From the second movement of Joseph Rheinberger's
Sonata in e, for P & Vn, Op. 105 (after the Kistner ed. [1893?]
Op. 105a, in e♭, for Cl & P).

who find a place in the present survey.[13] Along with three sonatinas
for P solo, Op. 13, this lady wrote three sonatas that were published—
Op. 8 in a (*ca.* 1879) for P solo, Op. 10 in c (1882) for Vn & P, and
Op. 17 in D (1883) for Vc & P.[14]

North of Munich in Lemberg the pianist and successful composer
of light piano works **Joseph Christoph Kessler** (actually **Kötzler**;

13. A midway biographical account appeared in NMZ VII (1886) 53–54. Cf., also,
Riemann/LEXIKON I 1010; Elson/WOMAN 164–65.
14. Cf. Altmann/KAMMERMUSIK 213 and 260, PAZDÍREK IX 230; and, on Op. 17:
NMZ V (1884) 54 (commending the Vc treatment and melody), NZM LXXX/2
(1884) 498 (W. Irgang questioning some structural details and so many modulations
in the finale; also, whether Vn is better for the Vc part), and MW XIV (1883) 445
(short and favorable).

1800–1872) dedicated his only sonata, Op. 47 in E♭ for piano (1852?), "to the memory of his dear friend F. Chopin." [15] Except for a few reminiscences of his Polish (and Czech?) background, especially in the middle two of its four movements (F-S-Sc-Ro), this work was reviewed at length by Bülow as competent but somewhat static and still oriented to Hummel's style, with less charm and pianistic significance than Kessler's Etudes Op. 20.[16]

Elsewhere in south Germany the sonatas of three composers in or near Stuttgart call for only the briefest mentions. The pianist and teacher **Wilhelm Speidel** (1826–99), trained and employed in Munich before moving to Stuttgart in 1857, left one published sonata each for P & Vc and P & Vn, Opp. 10 and 61, in 1855 and 1879, respectively,[17] and two published sonatas for P solo, Op. 46 (1872?).[18] The last were reviewed as generally competent, again, but lacking in depth or inspiration.[19] As the author of the first significant monograph on the sonata's history (1846; sbe 11 and ssb II), the Stuttgart organist and choral conductor **Immanuel Gottlob Friedrich Faisst** (1823–94) should at least be named here for an organ Sonata in E published posthumously.[20] And the highly esteemed organist in nearby Esslingen, **Christian Fink** (1822–1911), may be noted for at least five organ sonatas and four piano sonatas or sonatinas, published between about 1856 and 1898.[21] Several reviews acknowledge charm and skill in Fink's sonatas but sometimes find them inconsequential.[22]

The only mid-Romantic name in Switzerland to mention here is that of the gifted, versatile, short-lived musician **Hermann Goetz** (1840–76), who had been close to Bülow and Brahms before moving to Zürich in his last years.[23] To our genre Goetz contributed only two

15. Cf. Mendel/LEXIKON VI 37; Riemann/LEXIKON I 876; Sydow & Hedley/CHOPIN 35, 36, 173. Chopin ded. the original German ed. of his *24 Préludes* to Kessler.

16. NZM XXXVI (1852) 233–35, with exx. (reproduced only in part in BÜLOW BRIEFE III 49–50).

17. Cf. Altmann/KAMMERMUSIK 264 and 228 (but Op. 10 was originally for P & Vc, and in D, not d). In MW XIII (1882) 130, Op. 61 is reviewed as "a big sonata with little content"; cf., also, SMW XXXVIII (1880) 546.

18. Cf. Mendel/LEXIKON IX 350–51; Riemann/LEXIKON II 1735. Op. 111 by Speidel (1898?) is a "Suite (Quasi-Sonate)" pub. in 5 separate pieces or mvts. (cf. MW XXX [1899] 196).

19. NMZ LXVIII/2 (1872) 405–6.

20. Composed before 1876? (cf. NZM LXXII/1 [1876] 432; SMZ XVI [1876] 175). Cf., also, MGG III 1735–37 (R. Sietz).

21. Cf. Mendel/LEXIKON III 530–31; Riemann/LEXIKON I 509; PAZDÍREK V 352–53; Kremer/ORGAN 184.

22. NZM XLV (1856) 253–54, XLVII (1857) 166–67, LV (1861) 93 and 208, XL/2 286.

23. Cf. MGG V 470–73 (W. Kahl), with further bibliography.

sonatinas for P, Op. 8 (first pub. in 1869), and a Sonata in g for P-duet, Op. 17 (composed in 1865–66 and first pub. posthumously, by Kistner in 1878, plate no. 5048). But these are three fluent, fresh works of exceptional melodic and harmonic interest.[24] Some enterprising publisher seeking to enrich the piano literature at junior solo and moderately advanced levels would do well to rediscover and reprint all three, especially Op. 17. The latter, in three movements (S/VF-S-F), has a Mendelssohnian flavor and achieves depth through meaningful themes, expressive harmony, and contrapuntal exchanges between the parts.[25]

Liszt in Central Germany

We reach another main landmark, in the sonatas of **Franz** (or **Ferencz**) **Liszt** (1811–86), one of the half-dozen most influential musicians of the 19th century, after Beethoven. Liszt is not known to have composed more than eight sonatas, out of a total of some 1,420 single works, large or small,[26] and only three of these have survived. Moreover, he composed all eight before the midpoint in his career (about 1855). Yet the two solo piano sonatas that won fame, especially his last sonata, in b, are so unusual as to be without significant precedent or consequent at least in solo piano music, and at the same time so generally enjoyed and esteemed by performers and listeners alike as to rank among the most successful piano sonatas of the Romantic Era.

In spite of their importance, Liszt's surviving sonatas have yet to be treated to a full study that will pull together the scattered bits of information about their background, genesis, and further circumstances, and one that will provide more detailed style-critical analyses than the numerous summary statements now to be found on the thematic elements and peculiar structure of the Sonata in b. This need only reflects in a small way the much larger need to purge, desentimentalize, correct, restore, fill out, and, at last, co-ordinate the whole

---

24. Cf. the enthusiastic reviews in NZM LIX/2 (1873) 400 and MMR VIII (1878) 12 and XIV (1884) 154 (all on Op. 8); MW IX (1878) 542–43 and XIII (1882) 581 (both on Op. 17); also, Georgii/KLAVIERMUSIK 577–78, with ex. (calling Op. 17 "the most beautiful four-hand sonata in the past century after Schubert"); and Ganzer & Kusche/VIERHÄNDIG 71–72.

25. Opp. 8 and 17 were most recently listed in the Augener and Kistner cats., respectively. Mod. ed. of Op. 8/2/ii and iii: Frey/SONATINA-m 42. Cf. SSB V for an ex. from Op. 17/i.

26. This total roughly combines the 1,321 works added up in Beaufort/LISZT with the 95 lost works listed in Schnapp/LISZT. The totals of 673 items in Raabe/LISZT II 242–361 and 768 items in GROVE V 264–314 (H. Searle) often include several sublistings per item.

vast but often erratic literature pertaining to Liszt.[27] The starting point for such improvements would have to be fundamental publications like Lina Ramann's detailed, nearly contemporary study of the man and his works and La Mara's collections of his letters.[28] Revision and completion of the collected edition of Liszt's works, started in 1907, is another goal.[29] Humphrey Searle has provided a balanced, recent overview of Liszt's music (Searle/LISZT), with new light on the remarkable significance of the late works for the 20th century.

Liszt composed six of his eight sonatas for P solo, one for P-duet, and one for Vn & P. Of the five lost sonatas, three were little three-movement works, apparently not unadventurous in style, yet composed while the young prodigy was still only thirteen (1825); a fourth was the P-duet, composed in the same year; and the fifth was only the start of a projected Sonata in c, dating at latest from early 1835.[30] Earliest of the three surviving sonatas is the "Duo (Sonate)" in c♯ for Vn & P, composed in 1832–35 (presumably in Paris) but not published until 1964, after the pianist Eugene List had called the MS to the attention of its editor, Tibor Serly.[31] This is a full-scale work in four

27. Haraszti/LISZT summarizes the most serious needs and problems in Liszt research and evaluates some of the contributions. A detailed, up-to-date bibliography is itself a need. The bibliography in GROVE V 262–63 stops short of special studies; that in MGG VIII 986–88 (H. Engel) includes these, but only in limited number. Cat. NYPL XVII 445–84 is helpful. L. Koch's exhaustive bibliography (cf. Searle/LISZT 196) extends only to 1936.

28. Ramann/LISZT, LISZT LETTERS, "LISZT" SCHRIFTEN; on the letters, cf. ML XLVIII (1967) 148–50. Raabe/LISZT (currently being revised by Felix Raabe) made important advances in 1931 (but cf. Haraszti/LISZT 126–28), especially toward the co-ordination of resources and a more accurate cat. of Liszt's works (utilized in summary form, with revisions by H. Searle, for GROVE V 264–314). The authenticity of every writing attributed to Liszt other than letters, including the 7 vols. in "LISZT" SCHRIFTEN, is challenged convincingly in Haraszti/LISZT 130–35 and Haraszti/AUTHOR. The Liszt specialist Emile Haraszti did not live to complete his long projected, over-all study; but new advances are to be expected in the biographic study that is now in progress (1967) by Edward Waters of the Library of Congress.

29. Liszt/WERKE-m.

30. These 5 sons. are nos. 5, 6, 7, 10, and 19, respectively, in Schnapp/LISZT. This study provides all known details, including the incident in which the youngster fooled the 51-year-old French violinist Pierre Rode into thinking no. 5 (Liszt's earliest son.) was by Beethoven, and a facs. (after p. 128) of the first 14 mss. of this son. (in f) as recalled and written down by Liszt in 1881 for Miss Ramann; also, the incipit of no. 19 (in c).

31. Serly/LISZT-m, with quadrilingual preface. Cf., also, Serly's article in *The New York Times* for Sunday, Feb. 14, 1960, X 9, following the first performance of this work on Feb. 5 at the Library of Congress, by List and his wife, the violinist Carroll Glenn; Newman/LISZT (review); Searle/LISZT 34. Chopin's Mazurka in c♯, Op. 6/2 (B. 60), on which Liszt's Vn Son. in c♯ is based, was composed in Vienna in "late 1830," but a *terminus a quo* for Liszt's son. would be his first hearing of Chopin on Feb. 26, 1832 (Hedley/CHOPIN 47–48), or, more likely the first pub. of the Mazurka in c♯ in Dec., 1832 (Leipzig), or even the first Paris ed. in Nov., 1833

movements (totalling 628 mss.), the "one-movement" Sonata in b being 22 per cent longer (760 mss.) and the one-movement "Dante Sonata" 40 per cent shorter (376 mss.). Its 81-page score (47 pp. in print) was left in an unpolished state, requiring a little deciphering, filling in, choosing of alternatives, and even some pruning on Serly's part (and still leaving much to be desired). As it now stands, the work, composed before Liszt was 24, is still immature enough to suggest that it is not likely to win general acceptance on its musical merits alone. But it is fascinating as a major example of one of the most Romantic Romantics in the making and, especially, of the three epochal, though very different and still unassimilated, impressions made upon Liszt in Paris by his first acquaintance with the playing and/or music of Paganini in 1831, Chopin in 1832, and Berlioz in 1832.[32]

Liszt sketched "Une Fantaisie (quasi sonate [,] après une lecture de Dante" in 1837 (during his least productive years as a composer), performed it for the first time in 1839, revised it in 1849,[33] and finally saw it published by Schott in 1858 as the seventh and last piece in his second set of *Années de pèlerinage.*[34] The last part of the title is said to have been taken from Victor Hugo's 32-line poem "Après une lecture de Dante." [35] There can be no doubt that Liszt had known Hugo personally and had warmly admired his works for nearly ten years;[36] nor, for that matter, that Liszt had taken a strong, Romantically oriented interest in Dante, thanks to the Countess d'Agoult,

(Brown/CHOPIN 60–61 and 24–25). A *terminus ad quem* might well be Liszt's departure from Paris for Switzerland in 1835. Liszt's 3 surviving sons. are nos. 461, 10b7, and 21 in Raabe/LISZT II and nos. 127, 161, and 178 in Searle's cat. for GROVE. The last 2 appear in Liszt/WERKE-m II/vi/96 and II/viii/103.

32. Cf. Ramann/LISZT I 161–75, 216–33, 185–92, 205–12; Haraszti/LISZT 36–37; Hedley/CHOPIN 48–51; "Liszt" & Waters/CHOPIN 5–16. Immediate by-products were Liszt's P transcriptions of works by Paganini and Berlioz (Searle nos. 420 and 470) as well as the son. under discussion.

33. Cf. LISZT-RAFF 286.

34. Cf. Raabe/LISZT II 246; Raff/RAFF 137 (on Schott as a procrastinative pub.). The title is given here as on the facs. of the title p. in Bory/LISZT 90; it usually is cited in reverse order ("Après . . . Fantaisie . . ."). The wording "Fantaisie quasi sonate" seems to have been a deliberate reversal of Beethoven's titles in Op. 27/1 and 2, much as with Weber's sons. as Spitta described them (SSB VIII). The endless variants of the title have even included "After a Lecture by Dante"! (as cited in Sitwell/LISZT 71 fn.). The autograph, with all of at least the 2d set of *Années*, is now in the Soviet Union, according to information from Professor J. Milstein, kindly relayed by Miss Erna F. Novikova of the State Gnesin Music-Pedagogical Institute in Moscow.

35. As (first?) suggested in Sitwell/LISZT 65–66 and repeated in Searle/LISZT 32 and Dale/NINETEENTH 90–91, but not in Grew/LISZT (an article that seeks to relate Liszt's work to the *Divine Comedy* in particular).

36. E.g., cf. Ramann/LISZT I 137; LISZT LETTERS 7, 8; Haraszti/Paris 10–11.

Delacroix, and others.[37] However, the conclusion here would be that he added the last part of the title later. If not, there would be good reason to question that he derived it at all from Hugo's poem. For the poem bears the date August 6, 1837, the collection in which it appears (*Les Voix intérieures,* no. 27) could not have been published until some time after that date in 1837, and Liszt was already sketching the "Dante Sonata" in October at Lake Como in Italy, well removed from Paris with the Countess d'Agoult.[38] The question is an interesting one, because if Hugo's poem did provide the inspiration for the "Dante Sonata" then we know at least that Liszt was describing either the sharp contrasts of the *Divine Comedy* or, less likely, Hugo's analogy between the afterlife and life on earth. Otherwise we cannot even be certain, as we can unequivocally with his "Dante Symphony" completed two decades later (Searle no. 109),[39] that the *Divine Comedy* was the Dante poem Liszt had in mind in 1837.[40] An anonymous, literal prose translation of the Hugo poem follows:

When the poet paints hell, he paints his own life.
His life, a fleeing shadow pursued by spectres;
A mysterious forest where his terrified feet
Wander, stumbling astray from the well-worn paths;
A dark journey, obstructed by strange encounters;
A spiral with vague boundaries and enormous depths,
Whose hideous circles go forever onward
Into a gloom where there moves the vague and living hell!
This stair is lost in the obscure mist;
At the base of each step a wretched figure sits,
And one sees pass by with a slight sound
White teeth grinding in the dark night.
One sees visions, dreams, illusions there;
The eyes that sorrow turns to bitter tears;
Love, as a couple embracing, sad and still ardent,
Who pass in a whirlwind with a wound in their sides;
In one corner, the impious sisters, vengeance and hunger,
Crouch side by side over a skull they have gnawed;
Then pale want, with her impoverished smile;
Ambition, pride nourished upon itself,
And shameless lust, and infamous avarice,
All the leaden cloaks with which the soul can be weighed down,
Farther on, cowardice, fear, and treason

37. Cf. Haraszti/LISZT 136.
38. Ramann/LISZT I 460; LISZT LETTERS I 20–21. "LISZT" SCHRIFTEN II 173–75 describes the couple's idyllic environment and reminders of Dante and his *Divine Comedy* at that time.
39. Cf. Ramann/LISZT II/2 17–22.
40. In 1849 Liszt did refer to his "Dante Son." parenthetically as "Prologomènes zu Dantes Göttlicher Comödie" (LISZT-RAFF 287).

Offering keys for sale and tasting poison;
And then, lower still in the very depths of the gulf,
The grimacing mask of suffering hatred!
Yes, that is life, O inspired poet!
And its murky way beset with barriers,
And, so that nothing may be lacking in this narrow path,
You show us forever standing to your right
The genius with the calm brow and radiant eyes,
Vergil unperturbed saying: "Let us go on."

Liszt played the "Dante Sonata" for the first time, in its original form, in Vienna during his sensationally successful concerts there in late 1839.[41] The particular recital seems to have been one of Liszt's innovational "musical soliloquies," given entirely by himself at the piano (SSB III).[42] Although the "Dante Sonata" has become increasingly popular in recent years, no further performance of this athletically difficult work turned up in the present study (nor reviews after its publication in 1858) prior to a London (memorial?) piano recital in 1887 played by Liszt's pupil Walter Bache.[43] Busoni, one of Liszt's most important successors and champions, is reported to have played the work with "crystalline and unforgettable purity" early in this century.[44] After Bache's recital, made up almost entirely of Liszt's works, the reviewer for *The Musical Times* wrote,

The most conspicuous of Liszt's works was a so-called Fantasia *quasi* Sonate, "Après une Lecture de Dante." This is a most extraordinary composition, of which it is absolutely impossible to form any idea at first hearing. Three themes were quoted in the programme, of which the first evidently represented the "Inferno," and the last the "Paradiso," but beyond this we could not trace any definite meaning in the constant progression of discords of which the piece is made up.

Bache seems not to have studied this work formally with Liszt,[45] but some specific identifications with the *Divine Comedy* would be confirmed if we could know that two passages from "Inferno" pencilled into Bache's score (which he purchased in 1883) were actually suggested by the master.[46] These consist of (1) a few lines from near the start of Canto iii ("Here sighs . . ." to ". . . sand that in the

41. Cf. Ramann/LISZT II/1 14 and 17 (preceded by accounts of Liszt's brilliant Vienna recitals of 1838, in I 484–500); also, Loesser/PIANOS 366–74, Schonberg/PIANISTS 151–71, Pleasants/HANSLICK 107–110, for the extremes of Liszt's successes as pianist. The "Dante Sonata" is reported merely as "Fragment nach Dante" in AMZ XLII (1840) 92.
42. Cf. LISZT LETTERS I 31–33; Loesser/PIANOS 368, 371; SSB III.
43. MT XXVIII (1886) 154; cf. MT CVIII (1967) 342.
44. Cernikoff/HUMOUR 91. Cf. BUSONI-Frau 50.
45. Cf. Bache/BACHE 309 and 312.
46. Discussed at length in Grew/LISZT.

whirlwind flies," in Cary's trans. of the *Divine Comedy*), inserted plausibly enough at the start of the second theme (ms. 35; see the chart in the next section of this chap.); (2) the first and last of the opening lines of Canto xxxiv (not xxxix! from *"Vexilla regis . . ."* to "The creature eminent in beauty once"), inserted equally plausibly at the return to the initial theme (ms. 115); (3) but also the last same lines inserted, much less plausibly, at the start of the third theme (ms. 103). Eva Mary Grew views that third theme, in broad whole-notes, as Liszt's setting of the first half of the *Tonus peregrinus*[47] and rationalizes what would be an incongruous reference to the psalm of deliverance as Liszt's subtle, parodic hint of blasphemy that yet promises salvation.[48] Programmatic associations certainly abound in Liszt's instrumental music—associations of mood, that is, rather than literalities[49]—but not such subtleties as Miss Grew suggests. Moreover, it is odd that those pencilled insertions come only from "Inferno" and make no better allowance, contrary to the "Dante Symphony" (with its "Purgatorio" and "Magnificat" sections) for the "Purgatorio" and "Paradiso" of the *Divine Comedy*. If our imaginations are to have free rein, we might well relate the transformations of the "infernal" second theme (as they start at mss. 124 and 151) to "Purgatorio," and the contrasting guises of the exalted third theme (as they start at mss. 103, 136, 203, and 309) to "Paradiso." The piano is felt by Searle (but not here) to be inadequate to the expressive range of this piece, with the "far clearer and more incisive" solution being something like Constant Lambert's transcription for piano and orchestra done for a Sadler's Wells ballet called "Dante Sonata." [50]

Except for having jotted down the theme of its "Adagio" in 1849,[51] Liszt wrote his Sonata in b in 1852–53, some five years after much of his public recitaling had ended and his residence in Weimar had begun with the Princess Carolyne von Sayn-Wittgenstein.[52] This work marked the end of much of his important writing for piano. As he himself remarked just after Breitkopf & Härtel published it in 1854, "I shall have done for the present with the piano, in order to devote myself

47. Cf. the ex. in GROVE VI 955. Pirro heard the related succession of major triads near the end (mss. 364–68), over a whole-step descent in the bass, as a reference (hardly exact!) to the opening of Palestrina's much Romanticized "Stabat Mater" (Haraszti/LISZT 32).

48. Grew/LISZT 37–39.

49. Cf. Ramann/LISZT I 196–202.

50. Searle/LISZT 32.

51. According to a letter received from Mr. Arthur Hedley of London, referring to an autograph notebook in his possession.

52. Cf. Ramann/LISZT II/1 178 and II/2 28–35.

exclusively to orchestral compositions. . . ." [53] Liszt gave the sonata its first performances, for private hearings as early as May, 1853, including the somewhat unsatisfactory meeting with Brahms the next month (SSB IX).[54] As evidence of his special regard for it, he is said to have played its expressive parts "with extreme pathos" and to have written "Für die Murlbibliothek" on the autograph,[55] meaning appropriate for his clique known as "The Society of Murls" and devoted to the advancement of the "New German" school against the Philistines.

Liszt dedicated his Sonata in b to Schumann in return for the latter's dedication of his great Fantasie in C, Op. 17, to Liszt fifteen years earlier (SSB VIII).[56] The two 19th-century masterpieces, which stand almost alone in the heat and inspiration of their full-bloomed Romanticisms, might well be illuminated by a comparative study. But the dedication caused some embarrassment to Robert and Clara, who, with Brahms, represented the opposition to the Liszt school and felt a growing antagonism toward Liszt himself as well as doubts regarding his sincerity.[57] Of course, Wagner, being on the Liszt side musically as well as politically,[58] was entirely disposed to enjoy the Sonata in b when Liszt's pupil Karl Klindworth played it to him in London the following year (probably at Liszt's own behest):[59]

The sonata is beautiful beyond all belief; huge, lovable, profound, and exalted,—stately, the way you are. I have been stirred to the depths [of my soul] by it, and all the misery of London is suddenly forgotten. More I shall not [attempt to] say to you right after the hearing; but I am as filled with what I [do] tell you as any man could be. . . . Klindworth amazed me by his playing; no lesser [pianist] would dare to play your work for me the first time. Truly, truly, he is of your calibre—that's wonderful!
   Good night—many thanks for this pleasure at last revealed!

53. LISZT LETTERS 186–87.
   54. Cf. MASON MEMORIES 123, 125, 129–30; LISZT/Marie 68.
   55. MASON MEMORIES 159. In NOTES XXI (1963–64) 83–93, the autograph was listed among important works in the "ROLF archives" to be made available in facs. under restricted conditions. Since then the MS has been withdrawn from public view. One only hopes it "surfaces" again soon and does become available for inspection.
   56. Cf. LISZT LETTERS I 33 (1839, to Schumann) and 308 (1854, to Wasielewski); Ramann/LISZT II/1 72–74; SSB Frontispiece.
   57. Cf. Kalbeck/BRAHMS I/1 85. Brahms referred to Liszt's Son. in b slightingly (SCHUMANN-BRAHMS I 19 [1854]).
   58. Further mention of his relation to Liszt occurs in the discussion of his own sons. later in this chap.
   59. Trans. from WAGNER-LISZT 69 (cf. pp. 58, 60, 63, 65); cf., also, LISZT LETTERS I 194.

The pianist, pedagogue, and writer Louis Köhler (ssʙ XVIII), to whom Liszt had sent his Sonata in b soon after publication,[60] wrote a long, early review as enthusiastic and nonspecific as Wagner's letter.[61] He started by declaring that the work would stand comparison with the best sonatas of all time, although only music lovers in tune with and equal to the spirit of the current times would appreciate it.

The idea has spread only too widely [that] even as a composer Liszt is merely a virtuoso, to the extent that he composes purely in the sense of a glorification of execution, but not [by] applying the same to the service of a higher ideal. The fact that strange themes lie at the basis of many of his works, as also that a considerable technical capability is required for their performance, appears to be at the root of a superstition that already would be contradicted simply by the original manner, by the how in the manipulation of those strange themes.[62]

Köhler accepted "sonata" as a title for this free work although its form (to be discussed shortly) was more than he could fathom, so that he had to end by saying,

I feel I probably have spoken a lot and said nothing. I confess what concerned me actually was only an unburdening of my heart, which overflows from the fresh impression of this sonata.

A very different review greeted Liszt's Sonata in b when Bülow, who had moved to Weimar to study with Liszt in 1851,[63] played it for the first time in public in Berlin in early 1857. From the public's standpoint the work immediately "took fire." [64] But Gustav Engel, reviewer for the *Spener'sche Zeitung,* noting its "very long" one-movement form and the revealing character of its opening theme, wrote among other "impersonal" observations,[65]

The structure rests on harmonic and rhythmic extravagances that no longer have anything to do with beauty; even the first theme is to be condemned as decidedly inartistic; yet, what faces us in the course of the development is surely much worse. Often it becomes impossible to speak of intelligent harmonic unity; we are expected to take pleasure in the arbitrary juxtaposition of keys; the melodies, which appear here and there, have such an affected character that all attractiveness is ruled out; [etc.]

Only the manifold transformation of piano figurations and Bülow's

60. ʟɪsᴢᴛ ʟᴇᴛᴛᴇʀs I 186.
61. ɴᴢᴍ XLI (1854) 70–72.
62. In the unequalled firsthand description of Liszt as teacher and person in Fay/ɢᴇʀᴍᴀɴʏ 205–75, a similar protest and defense can be found (pp. 236–37) with regard to his prevailing reputation only as a virtuoso.
63. ʙüʟᴏᴡ ʙʀɪᴇꜰᴇ I 343.
64. ʙüʟᴏᴡ ʙʀɪᴇꜰᴇ IV 63–64. Cf. Raabe/ʟɪsᴢᴛ II 250. Bülow became Liszt's son-in-law in the same year (1857).
65. Trans. from the complete transcript in ʙüʟᴏᴡ ʙʀɪᴇꜰᴇ IV 58, 65–66.

performance were approved by the reviewer. Bülow answered with a letter vigorously protesting the unfair judgment based on one hearing (not true, replied the reviewer) and reminiscent of the treatment Wagner got, and he kept the issue alive in letters to others.[66] In 1859 Liszt himself referred to A. H. Dietrich's playing of the "Invitation to Hissing and Stamping," "as [the critic Otto] Gumprecht designates that work of ill odour—my Sonata." [67] And it is not too surprising to find this music getting at least as hostile a reception from both Hanslick in 1881 (when Bülow played in Vienna) and *The Musical Times* critic in 1882 (in an earlier London recital by the same Walter Bache, *supra*).[68] Yet its performances multiplied steadily from the time of its publication and it became increasingly popular wherever there were performers equal to its physical and architectural difficulties and to the sufficient projection of its wide-ranging, freighted emotional content.[69]

Liszt's Styles and Forms

Liszt's three extant sonatas advance conspicuously from one to the next in their styles and forms. The violin sonata reaches toward the future boldly but naively and ineptly, with still some dependence on the traditional four-movement cycle and its individual forms. The "Dante Sonata" evinces much more control over its new resources and presents them in a free, apparently intuitive form in one movement. And the Sonata in b shows the mature master in complete and, apparently, fully conscious control of both styles and forms as he contrives a free form that is at once a one-movement "sonata form" and a four-movement sonata cycle. The three sonatas call for individual discussions in more detail.

The four movements of Liszt's "Duo (Sonate)" are all, tiresomely enough, in c♯. Furthermore, all of them begin (and iii ends) on the dominant of that key. The opening "Moderato" bows to "sonata form" only to the extent of contrasting sections, of developmental passages like the fugato starting in b♭ (mss. 65–90), and of the return to the

66. BÜLOW BRIEFE IV 66–68, 73, 74–75, 87; cf., also, pp. 366, 368–69.
67. LISZT LETTERS I 389.
68. Slonimsky/LEXICON 116 (the deleted passage may be seen in Kapp/LISZT 506); MT XXIII (1882) 663–64.
69. For a few of numerous other 19th-c. performances of Liszt's Son. in b, cf. BÜLOW BRIEFE IV 279 and 362 (Berlin, 1860); Müller-Reuter/LEXIKON 424–25 (Bülow in Leipzig, 1860); LISZT/Marie 138 (Vienna, 1869); NZM LXXII/1 18 (Rome, 1875); MT XXII (1881) 138–39 (London, 1881); MASON MEMORIES 270 (both Arthur Friedheim and Richard Burmeister, New York, about 1900); Friedheim/LISZT 5, 136, 139, 140, 141, 181, 188, 199, 213, 243, 311–12, 319; BUSONI-Frau 186, 200.

introductory idea in the tonic key, near the end (mss. 170–82). The second movement, called "Tema con Variazioni," actually consists of one continuous, extended, fantasy variation. The third, "Allegretto," has the requisite dance rhythms and harmonic caprice, if not quite the tightly closed form, to qualify as a 19th-century scherzo movement. And the finale, "Allegro con brio," might qualify similarly as a rondo. The prime fact about this cycle is its derivation of all thematic material—indeed, its utter, unabashed derivation, *ad taedium*—from Chopin's Mazurka in the same key, Op. 6/2. At best only an average, unpretentious example of Chopin's art, this Mazurka presents an introduction that merely embellishes a dominant drone, followed by three thematic periods, all in c♯ except for the "C" theme on the mediant harmony. These elements are disposed as follows:

In-||:A:||:BA:||C-In-||:A:||.

If Chopin really did complain about Liszt's borrowings from his music, as he is made to do so grossly and untypically in the fraudulent letters to Delfina Potocka,[70] then he surely must have had in mind more subtle derivations than those throughout this sonata. In this instance, Liszt used any and all of the Mazurka themes at random, sometimes intact and complete with Chopin's accompaniment. Thus, his first movement opens with Chopin's introduction almost note for note (mss. 1–10), then treats the "A" theme improvisatorily (mss. 11–40), cadencing on a return to the introduction in the subtonic key (B) plus another reference to "A" (mss. 41–52). The introduction and return to "A" recur, "poco tranquillo" and altered, in D (mss. 53–64), followed by that fugato on "A" in b♭ (mss. 69–90), next an episode freely derived from "B" (mss. 90–137), then a section based on "C" (mss. 137–51), another derived from "B" (mss. 152–60), another from "C" (mss. 160–69), and finally the return to the introduction. The "Tema" of the second movement is no less than the complete Mazurka minus the introduction and last return, arranged simply for violin and piano. The fantasy variation takes up the several themes at random again. More of the same occurs in the other two movements, with even the abstracted version of "C" in the finale (mss. 35–60) providing no satisfactory escape from the source themes. The monotony is compounded by the lack of potential development in these light dance themes, at least as they revealed themselves to the young Liszt.

The most significant musical traits in Liszt's violin sonata are its

70. E.g., cf. pp. 180–81 in *The Life and Death of Chopin* by C. Wierzynski (New York, 1949). On those letters, cf. Sydow & Hedley/CHOPIN 377–87. Warm thanks are owing to Mr. Arthur Hedley of London for further information by correspondence.

advanced technical figuration and its experimental harmony and tonality. Even in this early work scarcely a trace remains of Liszt's Vienna background, whether it be the formal instruction he got from Czerny and Salieri or the inspiration he found, above all, in the music of Beethoven, Schubert, and Weber.[71] One would have to observe that the new technical figurations pose unreasonable difficulties, especially for the piano that Liszt already knew so well. Unreasonable difficulties were characteristic, too, of the early writing of Weber, Schumann, Brahms, Alkan, and even Mendelssohn, before these men refined their styles (but not of Beethoven, whose trend in technical requirements was much the opposite). Also, one would have to recall that Liszt's experiments with harmony and tonality at this point, as with uncontrolled musical forms, showed him to be striking out boldly but blindly. To repeat what a critic was still to observe in 1840, ". . . the pianist has arrived, but the composer is perhaps delayed. . . ." [72] Yet, the technical figurations confirm the enormous influence of Chopin and Paganini on Liszt in the early 1830's (as in the obvious parallels with Chopin's Etudes in G♭ and E, Op. 10/5 and 3, in Ex. 44). And both the chromatic and enharmonic harmony and the wide-ranging tonality (as throughout iii) suggest the impression made by Berlioz' *Symphonie fantastique,* which Liszt was currently arranging for piano solo (Searle no. 470). Moreover, in all these traits we get remarkable previews of the Liszt to come. The piano's descending line in octaves near the start of the first movement naively anticipates the stentorian descents in both of the solo piano sonatas. The octaves and chords in the finale (as at mss. 102–8 and 147–62) point the way to many a bravura passage in these same sonatas (and in much other later piano music by Liszt). And the several areas of little or nothing but dom.- and dim.-7th harmonies (as in i/90–126) already create periods of amorphous tonality that were eventually to take Liszt to the very brink of atonality.

Liszt's "Dante Sonata" reveals major strides beyond the violin sonata toward the full control of styles and forms. The three main melodic ideas, however they might bear on Dante (*supra*), are now essentially Liszt's own and are germinant enough to lend themselves to Liszt's development and transformations of them. The piano figurations, harmony, and modulations all show considerably greater assurance and reason in their handling. And the form, if it does not show the same (conscious?) reason, *has* reason, especially in its stunning contrasts and the heights and depths of its climax structure. Liszt himself objected to standardized methods and structural formulas. In a letter to Louis

71. Cf. CZERNY 314–16; MGG VIII 965–66; LISZT LETTERS II 161, 164.
72. As trans. in "Liszt" & Waters/CHOPIN 10.

Ex. 44. From the second movement of Franz Liszt's "Duo (Sonate)" for Vn & P (after Serly/LISZT-m 29, used with the kind permission of, and copyrighted in 1957 and 1964 by, Southern Music Publishing Co.).

Köhler, written July 9, 1856, just after the "Dante Symphony" was finished, Liszt remarked,[73]

. . . [My works] are for me the necessary developments of my inner experiences, which have brought me to the conviction that *invention* and *feeling* are not so entirely *evil* in Art. Certainly you very rightly observe that the *forms* (which are too often changed by respectable people into *formulas*) "First Subject, Middle Subject, After Subject, etc., may very much grow into a habit, because they must be so thoroughly natural, primitive, and very easily intelligible." Without making the slightest objection to this opinion, I only beg for permission to be allowed to decide upon the forms by the contents, and even should this permission be withheld from me from the side of

73. As trans. in LISZT LETTERS I 273–74. Cf., also, Haraszti/LISZT 34–35.

the most commendable criticism, I shall none the less go on in my own modest way quite cheerfully. After all, in the end it comes principally to this—*what* the ideas are, and *how* they are carried out and worked up—and that leads us always back to the *feeling* and *invention,* if we would not scramble and struggle in the rut of a mere trade.

Perhaps the reviewer's failure to discover the clear landmarks of "sonata form" helps to explain the puzzled review of the "Dante Sonata" cited earlier. If the one-movement work is not only a "Fantaisie quasi sonate" but a "Sonate quasi fantaisie," it is so in the most general sense of thematic pluralism, contrast, and development, and of tonal movement and opposition (mainly between the tonic, d/D, and the raised mediant, F♯). Perhaps the audible form of this free, sectional work can be clarified by visual means—that is, by a chart scaled to the measure numbers, showing themes, keys, tempo changes, and dynamic contrasts. "I," "II," and "III" refer to the variants as well as the original versions of the main themes. The repeated "xxx" after any of these indicates its extension or development. The arrow pointing to the same or a different key center means an area of tonal flux. The symbols for increase (+) and decrease (−) of tempo and dynamic level apply to passages of at least six measures.

By comparison with the "Dante Sonata," Liszt's Sonata in b reveals its consummate mastery of composition in several tangible ways, as well as in those intangible aspects of the *Gestalt* that exercise their influence subjectively even if they still resist codification. The melodic ideas are more significant in themselves, more fruitful for development, and more susceptible to plastic transformation (or thematic "metamorphosis," to use the term usually linked with Liszt).[74] And, indeed, we do find more actual development and more frequent and subtle transformations, the latter perhaps stimulated by Liszt's transcription of Schubert's "Wanderer Fantasia" a year or so earlier (Searle no. 366).[75] Even the passagework and figural accompaniments in the Sonata in b derive from the main ideas. Moreover, this writing now exploits the piano tone and technical idiom to their every best advantage. Yet, for all the difficulties it poses, the writing still stops short of virtuosity for its own sake or physical impracticalities. The harmony and tonality continue to look forward (as at the remarkable embellishment of the

74. Liszt may have been influenced not only by the choice of key (cf. Walker/ CHOPIN 251) but by the opening theme of Chopin's Sonata in b, Op. 58, from the finale of which Liszt copied and "revised" a page in his own hand (SSB XII). In *Music and Musicians* for Feb., 1963, p. 10, Arthur Hedley ("Chopin: A False Tradition?") takes a dim view of this "revision" by Liszt.

75. In the preface to his recent ed. of the latter (Vienna: Universal, 1965), Paul Badura-Skoda sees in it a perhaps unwitting discovery of the double-function form about to be described here in Liszt's Son. in b.

Franz Liszt's "Dante Sonata"

Ms. nos.	10	20	30	40	50	60	70	80	90	100	110	120	130	140	150	160	170
Themes	I	XXXXXX(II)	II		II		XXXXXXXXXX(I)			III	I	II	III		II		X
Keys			→d				→f♯			F♯		→F♯			→F♯		
Tempos	M	+	-+	-VF				+			M	M	M		-	S+ + + + +
Dynamics	f	ff,P > P			mf		ff			fff	ff	[PPP]	PP		P	PPP	P ff

Ms. nos.	180	190	200	210	220	230	240	250	260	270	280	290	300	310	320	330	340	350	360	370	376
Themes	I	XXXX	IIXXXXIIXXXXXX		XXXXXX		XXXXXXXX¹III,III			II	(I) III		XXIII		IXX	IIXX	IIXXX	IIXXX XXXXXXX(III,I)
Keys								→B,G		→d	D		D		→D			
Tempos	F		++	+						-[S]	M	M	+F		-	VF	+	-	M
Dynamics	PP	P		ff	fff	fff	fff			PP P	PPP	PP	fff	fff		ff	ff	P	ff	fff

dominant harmony in F♯, mss. 415–31, a page before the fugue in b♭), at the same time achieving a new clarity, logic, and breadth. Above all, Liszt seems to have gained conscious control of his form, and a highly complex, innovative form, at that, lasting nearly twice as long as the "Dante Sonata" in performance (29 as against 16 minutes in the fine new recordings by Alfred Brendel, Vox PL 12–150).

The idea of "conscious control" is worth stressing, if only because the fact of such control would bolster attempts at systematic analysis of the Sonata in b. Obviously Liszt could no more have been unconscious of the broad sectional interrelationships than of the ingenious thematic transformations in this work. If circumstantial evidence is needed, he gives it by his own explanation of similar relationships in his Piano Concerto in E♭ (Searle no. 124), revised around this same time.[76] Furthermore, in spite of his objection to structural formulas, quoted earlier, Liszt apparently was receptive to analyses of his larger forms, including an analysis of the Sonata in b left with him in 1859 by Peter Cornelius.[77] The chief problem Liszt gives to the music analysts is to discover quite how he could have his cake and eat it, too—that is, how he could so unify a four-movement cycle that at the same time its separate movements interrelate like the components of one huge "sonata form." Although his contemporaries (as quoted above) may not have perceived this double function, many subsequent writers on Liszt have at least hinted at it. But, as implied earlier—and curiously enough in view of its wide renown—writers seem generally to have preferred to discuss the Sonata in b only briefly, sketchily, or subjectively, rather than attempt to pin down the specific divisions that define the double function.[78] Perhaps these writers have regarded it as too free for systematic analysis. The work does seem free in the sense of being unconstrained by squareness or artificial symmetry. But it is not free in the sense of being loose-jointed or aimless. From its smallest to its largest elements, it shows every sign of much stylistic refinement and much attention to tight structural relationships.[79]

Although there is hardly space for the needed detailed analysis here, it should be possible, after first illustrating the main thematic ele-

76. Cf. LISZT LETTERS I 330–32.
77. Cited in LISZT LETTERS I 389, but not preserved in the published writings of Cornelius.
78. E.g., cf. Searle/LISZT 59–61, Dale/NINETEENTH 92–94, and Cortot/INTERPRÉTATION 152–57, respectively. The "hermeneutic study" Schmitz/LISZT is brief and peripheral only. Georgii/KLAVIERMUSIK 382–85 ventures somewhat more detail, though also without any exact delimitations. Egert/LISZT 678–82 provides the most detailed analysis of the "Son. form" but refers to the cycle only in more general terms and without recognition of a "scherzando movement" in the fugue.
79. For more on Liszt's concern with form cf. Kapp/LISZT 120–21.

mcnts in Liszt's Sonata in b, at least to chart the course of this work
(scaled, again, to ms. nos.) so as to provide a concurrent view of the
restatements and interplay of these elements, the principal tonal,
tempo, and metric changes, and, over all, the two structural functions
or interpretations, one being the complete cycle and the other the
single movement. As an essential adjunct to the chart, Ex. 45 illustrates at least the start of the five thematic elements—here labeled v,
w, x, y, z—at the first occurrence of each (as keyed by its ms. no.). But

Ex. 45. Five thematic elements in Franz Liszt's Sonata in b as
each first occurs (at the indicated ms. no.).

it shows none of the transformations of these elements, which abound
especially in the recurrences of elements w and x. The accompanying
chart uses abbreviations from the list at the start of this volume; also,
M., T., S., and K. for main theme, transition, second theme, and closing theme; the arrow, again, for tonal flux; and the symbols v, w, x,
y, and z, for the thematic elements and their transformations (with
the horizontal spaces indicating thematic extension and the symbols
w/x or x/w meaning the interplay of two elements). "Sonatina form"
refers to "Sonata form" in which a simple retransition ("T.") replaces
the development section. But, as always, one must recall the danger of
making Procrustean beds out of such classifications (scᴇ 114–19).

Franz Liszt's Sonata in B Minor

Ms. nos.	25	50	75	100	125	150	175	200	225	250	275	300	325	350	375	400	425	450	475	500	525	550	575	600	625	650	675	700	725	750	760
One-mvt. "sonata form"	Exposition: M. T.			S.		K.					Development (sectional):	Coda	new (z)					fugue (w/x)			Recapitulation: M. T.			S. K.			Coda (return of all themes)				
Four-mvt. cycle	i (incomplete "sonatina form"): Exposition M. T.			S.		K.		Recapitulation T. M.		K.			ii (A-B-A slow mvt.): Coda||"A" "B"		T."A"		Coda||fugue	iii (scherzando fugue):		iv (finale: incomplete "sonatina form"):	M. T.			S. K.			Coda (return of all cyclic themes)				
Main tempos and meters	S/F ¢, ¢				3 ¢ / 2								S 3 / 4					F ¢			(F) (¢)			3 ¢ / 2			VF	F /S 3 3 / 2, 4 ¢	F	S	
Main tonal centers	→b				D		D		D		(B/b) ——→		F#					bb		——→b				B B			B				
Main thematic elements (see Ex. 45)	vw/x vw		v	y	v	xx	wxw			wx	vwy	x/w z	x	y	z		zv	w/x		w		w/xvw &w		xy		w	vw	·rz	xwv		

As the lowest rank of the chart suggests, Liszt assigns much of the responsibility for thematic interest and continuity to elements x and (especially) w. The presence of these elements might be heard even in such reductions as the steady repeated notes (suggesting x) that continue over elements v and y at measures 81 to 113, or the tender leaps down and up (suggesting w) during the unfolding "slow movement" (mss. 356–59). Element w represents a Lisztian melodic type that crops up in other of his works, too.[80] The descending scale that constitutes element v has a (pre-)Wagnerian quality (as in the "Treaty Motive" from the *Ring*) and has been traced to various Central European and Near Eastern cultures.[81] It serves mainly as an initiator and terminator of sections and, indeed, of the whole sonata. Elements y and z are relatively static, tending to repeat almost intact rather than germinate significant development or transformation. They unfold into extended melodies where a "second theme" for the "sonata form" and a main theme for the slow movement are needed. (The latter and its harmonization bring us close to César Franck for a moment.) All these distinctive thematic elements, along with their various transformations and rich harmonic supports (particularly when element y occurs), must be recognized as main factors in the remarkable individuality of Liszt's Sonata in b.

The double structural function in this work results largely from three innovations and makes three modest, corollarial compromises. One innovation is the construction of the entire, continuous "cycle" primarily out of the same thematic elements. Of course, the interrelating of some or all sonata movements by the use of the same or similar themes or incipits goes back as far as the origins of the sonata (SBE 78–79; SCE 138–40). But the innovation here is the nearly total dependence in all movements on the same basic set of contrasted ideas.[82] A second innovation is the construction of the sectional development in the "sonata form" out of the slow and scherzando movements of the "cycle," the latter being a rare instance of fugue in Liszt's piano music. And the third is to make the finale of the "cycle" out of the recapitulation of the exposition in the "sonata form." One compromise, then, is the fact that the finale has nothing thematically new to say, although changes in the figuration, harmony, tonality, and succession of ideas, plus the culmination and release in the coda that follows, all seem to satisfy this need for performers and listeners. In this connection it is

80. Cf. Searle/LISZT 57, 59, 78–79 ("Faust Symphony").
81. Cf. Gárdonyi/LISZT 95; Szelényi/LISZT 313–15.
82. Extremes like L. Berger's entire Son. Op. 18 on a single 6-note motive (SSB VIII) are not considered here. The effort in Egert/LISZT 674–75 to relate *all* of the thematic elements in Liszt's Son. in b to the first of them is strained and unconvincing.

Ex. 46. Franz Liszt's original ending for his Sonata in b (as first printed in Liszt/WERKE-m II/viii/vi).

worth noting how unsatisfying is the brilliant but perfunctory ending of 25 measures that Liszt originally wrote (Ex. 46) before crossing it out and replacing it with the ending of 50 measures (from "Andante sostenuto") that we now know. A second compromise might be seen in the two relatively stationary tonal centers, F♯ and b♭, instead of the expected modulations in the development section. Again a compensation may be found, this time in the considerable tonal flux throughout the rest of the sonata. And a third compromise might be seen in certain irregularities in the form types, such as the new theme (y) that opens the development section, or the shortened recapitulation of the "sonata form," or the start of that recapitulation at a point beyond where the exposition started, or the incomplete "sonatina forms" in the outer movements of the cycle. But these instances are compromises only in that Procrustean sense, none of them being irregularities outside of textbooks in the 19th century.

At the start of this discussion of Liszt, his Sonata in b was stated to be without significant precedent or consequent in solo piano music. There were significant successors, to be sure, in his own orchestral works and in a few later orchestral and chamber works by Richard Strauss, Sibelius, Schoenberg, and others.[83] But in piano music, the relatively few one-movement sonatas that preceded Liszt's, like those of Moscheles and Dussek, or succeeded it, like those of Scriabin and his closest followers, are single "sonata forms" and nothing more. To some extent Liszt anticipated his own form in the Sonata in b (and its w thematic element) when he wrote his less important *Grosses Konzertsolo* for piano in 1849 (?; Searle no. 176), which might even be called a preparatory study.[84] And we shall be coming to occasional direct imitations, including those of more or less forgotten students (F. Draeseke, R. Viole, and J. Reubke, all later in this chap.) and those of Dale and Liapunov (SSB XIV and XVIII). Cyril Scott not only adapted the form in his sonatas but wrote about it in 1917 as the "logical" way out for the sonata.[85] But these efforts bore no special fruit and can hardly be called "significant consequents" of a work so important and widely played as Liszt's Sonata in b.

Other Central German Composers (Wagner, Raff, Draeseke, Ritter, Hiller)

The great music dramatist **Richard Wagner** (1813–83) wrote at least five sonatas, all for one piano, during his lifetime.[86] These represent but a minute, purely incidental part of his enormous output of music, poetry, and prose, and of his enormous industry as composer, writer, conductor, and controversial man of the world. Four of the sonatas, including two that are lost, were student works all completed in Leipzig by his eighteenth year, and the other is a somewhat perfunctory piece written in 1853 during his exile in Zürich. On their musical merits these sonatas would justify no more than a brief, though respectful mention here. But as historical insights into the making and

---

83. Cf. Hans Engel's diagram of Liszt's *Les Préludes* in MGG VIII 983–84. Cf., also, Austin/20th 136, 214; LISZT-BARTÓK 1961, pp. 279–80 (Searle).

84. Cf. Searle/LISZT 57–58; Ramann/LISZT II/2 345–46. It is in Liszt/WERKE-m II/viii/47.

85. Scott/SUGGESTIONS. The same conclusion, in more flowery words, had been reached in 1903 in Schüz/SONATE. Cf., also, Shedlock/SONATA 218–20.

86. Much of the section on Wagner that follows appeared originally under the title "Wagner's Sonatas" in Boston University's *Studies in Romanticism* VII (1968) 129–39.

aesthetic views of one of the most influential musicians of all time—
and of an author whose opinions on instrumental music are cited
several times in the present volume—they justify a discussion sufficient
at least to graze the more general subject of Wagner and Wagnerism.

Wagner follows Liszt appropriately here because, whatever their
differences, their music and tastes in the "New German" school still
had many points in common; because they still were each other's best
male friends throughout much of their careers, including the period
when each wrote his main sonata; and because they were frequently
close geographically, too, as in 1849 when the "revolutionary" fled
from Dresden to Liszt's haven in Weimar, or in 1853 when Liszt visited
Wagner in Zürich.[87] The practical benefits of this relationship flowed
almost exclusively in Wagner's direction. The musical benefits may
have flowed both ways but are less easily decided. Of course, the musical superiority of Liszt's Sonata in b over Wagner's little one-movement
Album-Sonate in A♭ is so manifest as to make any comparison absurd
except for this question of influences.

Furthermore, there cannot be any question of influences either way
so far as these sonatas themselves are concerned. Wagner did not hear
Liszt's Sonata in b until he wrote his warm letter to Liszt about it in
1855 (as quoted under Liszt, *supra*); and Liszt, if he knew Wagner's
Album-Sonate at all, could not have seen or heard it until he reached
Zürich in July of 1853, about five months after he had finished his own
sonata (Feb. 2, 1853, is the date on the autograph), but less than a
month after Wagner finished his. It is true that Liszt had conducted
and/or known important music of Wagner by 1852, including *Rienzi,
The Flying Dutchman, Tannhäuser,* and *Lohengrin,* and that he did
much of his most serious and large-scale composing from that year
on. On the other hand he had completed no less significant a work than
the "Dante Sonata" by 1839, before he knew Wagner or his music at
all (granted that he had yet to make substantial revisions in this work).
And it is much easier to find specific antecedents of Liszt's Sonata in
b in his own "Dante Sonata" and *Grosses Konzertsolo* than in anything
he might yet have known by Wagner. Conversely, much the same applies to Wagner's *Album-Sonate,* which relates more specifically to his
own music, both previous and concurrent, than to anything he might
have got from Liszt, including Liszt's magnificent use of the piano.
Yet, had the chronology permitted, it would not be hard to believe

87. All these aspects of their friendship are richly, if not always completely or
quite accurately documented in their extensive correspondence (WAGNER-LISZT). Much
further light on the ins and outs of the relationship is given in Newman/WAGNER
I 277–78, 348–49, 454–55, 494–95; II 191–217, 301, 382–87 (up to 1853).

that the influences could have flowed either way between these two sonatas. As far apart as they are in size, architecture, and technical requirements, they do share the general spirit and styles of the "New German" school, and of two composers who had long found a common interest, for example, in the music of Berlioz.[88]

The critical literature on Wagner, both strong and weak, is today almost incalculable in quantity, being considerably greater than that on any other figure in music history.[89] Here there is occasion to refer only to the standard major biographies and edition of his prose writings,[90] along with a few special aids (cited where they apply) and three studies that deal especially with the sonatas. These last include a descriptive article of 1904 on Wagner's piano works by the writer, pianist, and teacher Rudolf Breithaupt;[91] a twenty-page pamphlet of 1961 by granddaughter Friedelind Wagner, accompanying Bruce Hungerford's excellent recording of the extant "Complete Piano Works";[92] and a style study of 1963 on Wagner's student works, by the veteran Wagner specialist Otto Daube.[93]

We learn all we know about the two lost, earliest sonatas by Wagner from Wagner himself. By the age of sixteen (1829?), when he already had become absorbed in Beethoven, Mozart, Weber, and E. T. A. Hoffmann, "I had composed a first Sonata[,] in D minor." [94] And around the age of seventeen (?; 1830), when he had determined on a course of "serious musical study," he wrote, but later had "no clear recollection" of, "an Overture in C major (6/8 time) and a four-hand Sonata in B-flat major, which last I practiced with my sister Ottilie, and, since it pleased us both, arranged for orchestra. . . ." [95] One assumes this early music was conspicuously untutored, both because of the amusing stories of the time Wagner told on himself and because his first successful learning did not start until his brief but productive

---

88. Cf. Newman/WAGNER I 322–23, II 214 and 301, etc.

89. For example, it is about double that for Beethoven, Wagner's nearest competitor, in the *British Museum General Catalogue of Printed Books*, 263 vols. (London, 1961–66). In Cat. NYPL the important special Beethoven collections account for about as many books on Beethoven as Wagner.

90. WAGNER LEBEN, WAGNER PROSE (including "Autobiographic Sketch" in I 1–19). Newman/WAGNER. The many collections of his letters have yet to be brought together in a revised, up-to-date ed.

91. Breithaupt/WAGNER, with many exx.

92. Festival Masterclasses, Inc., LO8p (2 discs). Warm thanks are owing to Miss Wagner for letters contributing to the present discussion. Vox has also issued a recording of the complete piano works (VOX-2022 and SVOX-52022).

93. Daube/WAGNER, with many exx.

94. WAGNER LEBEN 37–45, especially pp. 44–45.

95. Trans. from WAGNER LEBEN 66.

half year at the age of eighteen (1831–32) under Theodor Weinlig.[96]

Wagner's earliest extant sonata is a solo *Sonate für das Pianoforte* in B♭, composed probably late in 1831, dedicated to Weinlig, and published at Weinlig's suggestion by Breitkopf & Härtel in the spring of 1832 (Ex. 47).[97] Wagner had chafed under Weinlig's contrapuntal discipline, including the laborious writing of "the most intricate" fugues and canons, and now, as he recalled,

> In order to bring me, however, fully within his friendly, calming authority, he had requested a sonata [from me] at the same time, which I, as evidence of my friendship for him, was supposed to construct according to the most insipid harmonic and thematic principles, [and as] the model for which he recommended to me one of the most childlike Pleyel sonatas. Those who knew my but recently composed overtures [including an experimental piece whose public performance was a fiasco as related in WAGNER LEBEN 66–69] surely must have been astonished that I could bring myself to write this required sonata, which is still being circulated today in a new reprinting through an indiscretion of the Breitkopf und Härtel music firm. In order to reward me for my temperance [after recent liquor sprees, as related in WAGNER LEBEN 58–60], none other than Weinlich himself took pleasure in getting my sorry work into print through that [same] publishing firm. From now on he let me do as I pleased.[98]

96. WAGNER LEBEN 66–69, 66–68; WAGNER PROSE I 6–7; Newman/WAGNER I 76–78, 84–86.

97. A facs. of the title page is in Daube/WAGNER 133 and in Panofsky/WAGNER 11. The pub. reissued the "Menuetto" separately (PAZDÍREK XV 68). The printed ed. does not differ from the autograph in "The Burrell Collection" at Curtis Institute of Music (cf. Burk/WAGNER 453). There is no basis in the first ed. itself for occasional listings of this work as Op. 1 (or Wagner's Son. in A as Op. 2).

98. WAGNER LEBEN 71; Breitkopf & Härtel's reprint in 1862 (plate no. 10433) probably was issued to capitalize on Wagner's newly won fame (Newman/WAGNER I 86). The foregoing trans. may be compared with that in the "authorized translation" of 1931 (pp. 68–69; cf. WAGNER LEBEN in SSB Bibliography) as but an average sample of all too many trans. that have proved too loose or inaccurate for use here. (The German itself is incorrectly quoted in Daube/WAGNER 132–33.) The original German (in which "zu erstaunen" seems to be an error for "zu schreiben") reads as follows: "Um mich aber vollständig in seine freundlich beruhigende Gewalt zu bekommen, hatte er zu gleicher Zeit eine Sonate verlangt, welche ich, als Beweis meiner Freundschaft für ihn, auf den nüchternsten harmonischen und thematischen Verhältnissen aufbauen sollte, zu deren Modell er mir eine der kindlichsten *Pleyel*-schen Sonaten empfahl. Wer meine noch vor kurzem verfaßten Ouvertüren kannte, mußte gewiß erstaunt sein, daß ich es über mich vermochte, diese verlangte Sonate, wie sie gegenwärtig noch durch eine Indiskretion der Breitkopf- und Härtelschen Musikhandlung zum erneuten Abdruck befördert worden ist, zu erstaunen: um mich für meine Enthaltsamkeit zu belohnen, machte sich *Weinlich* nämlich die Freude, mein dürftiges Werk durch jene Verlagshandlung zum Druck zu befördern. Von nun an erlaubte er mir alles."

The "authorized translation" reads:

"In order to keep me strictly under his calming and friendly influence, he had at the same time given me a sonata to write which, as a proof of my friendship

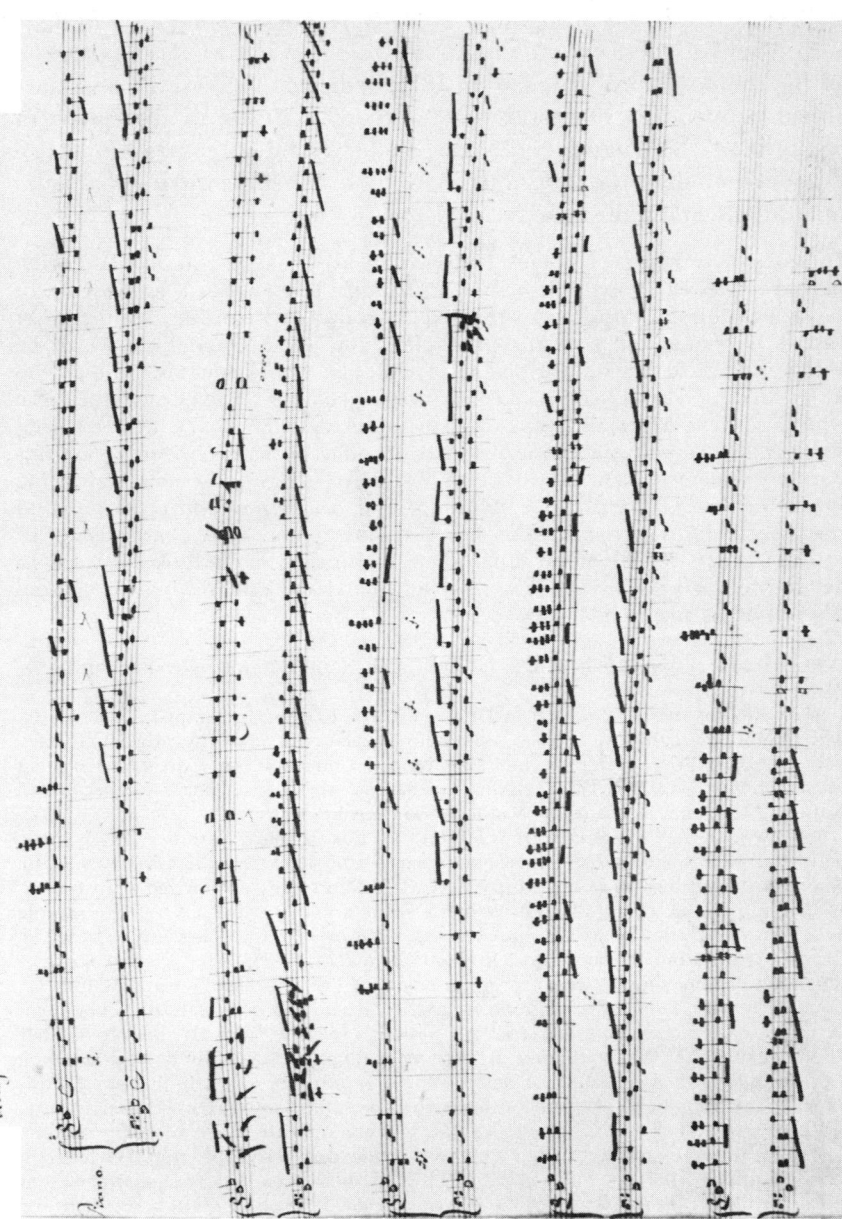

Ex. 47. From the opening of Richard Wagner's Sonata in B♭ (facs. of the autograph in "The Burrell Collection" at Curtis Institute of Music in Philadelphia).

Earlier, in 1842 (?), Wagner had recalled the circumstances a bit differently: "At this epoch I first acquired an intimate love and knowledge of Mozart. I composed a Sonata, in which I freed myself from all buckram, and strove for a natural, unforced style of composition. This extremely simple and modest work was published by Breitkopf und Härtel." [99] Wagner told the Londoner Edward Dannreuther in 1877 that Weinlig's teaching procedure had been to have him follow the number, the relative length, and even the character of the themes, modulations, and sections in some model piece, usually by Mozart.[100] In this instance it would be interesting to discover which of the many Pleyel sonatas then in print (SCE 551) could have been the model.[101]

Heinrich Dorn, Schumann's onetime teacher (SSB VIII), described the Sonata in B♭ as sterile and unpromising, and said Wagner had showed it to him at the time of its writing,[102] but probably had in mind an earlier piece, perhaps Wagner's four-hand Sonata in B♭.[103] Stephen Heller probably did mean the solo Sonata in B♭ when he wrote to Charles Hallé in 1874,[104]

> Wagner's sonata is idiotic. One is all the more astonished at the immense transformation of the man. When can he have written this frippery? One would say that he had not yet known, I won't say Beethoven, but not even one sonata by Hummel, Dussek, nor even Kalkbrenner, who has produced fine examples of this type. At least, this last knew his piano.

The solo Sonata in B♭ is a competent work, showing a more solid grounding than is popularly credited to Wagner. It is carefully worked out, surprisingly deliberate in its pace for a young man so full of passions, ambitions, and hectic experiences, and not without some strengths in its ideas, development, and structures. Its four movements (F-S-Mi-VF) indicate that Wagner knew very well what was expected in each. But this work does suggest Classic models and reveals none

---

for him, I had to build up on strictly harmonic and thematic lines, for which he recommended me a very early and childlike sonata by Pleyel as a model.

"Those who had only recently heard my Overture must, indeed, have wondered how I ever wrote this sonata, which has been published through the indiscretion of Messrs. Breitkopf and Härtel (to reward me for my abstemiousness Weinlich induced them to publish this poor composition). From that moment he gave me a free hand."

99. As trans. in WAGNER PROSE I 7; cf. Daube/WAGNER 133 for the German.

100. GROVE, first ed., IV 347.

101. Dr. Rita Benton at the University of Iowa, currently (as of 1967) working on a study of Pleyel, kindly looked for such a model throughout her large collection of Pleyel materials but found none that could have served literally and consistently.

102. Ellis/WAGNER IV 451–53; cf., also, I 124–26. For further discussions of this work cf. Breithaupt/WAGNER 114–17; Daube/WAGNER 132–38.

103. Cf. Newman/WAGNER I 76–77.

104. HALLÉ 300.

of the anticipations of his future styles that are to be found in the work he himself mentions next, and with considerable pride,[105] which is his much more interesting, multisectional "Phantasie fürs Klavier in fis-moll" (or "Fantasie für das Pianoforte" in the autograph).[106]

Curiously, not until forty-five years later did Wagner or any of his contemporaries leave any reference to his other early extant sonata, "Grosse Sonate für Klavier" in A. Then he expressed interest in seeing it again but not in having it published, after Cosima's efforts led to the return of the autograph to him.[107] Also reported to be composed in late 1831, this work was first described by Breithaupt, who saw it as a "middle stage" in Wagner's piano development and "much less interesting and attractive than the Phantasie." [108] But it was not printed until Daube supervised its publication by Hans Gerig of Köln in 1960.[109] Like Sonata in B♭ (totaling 848 mss.), Sonata in A (totaling 746 mss.) is a full-scale work in four movements, although its third movement consists of an introduction and a free forty-measure fugue[110] rather than a minuet and trio. Both works by the future master of the leitmotiv concentrate tightly on single motives. But whereas Sonata in B♭ exhibits a veiled relationship between (only) its two inner movements that may well have been fortuitous, Sonata in A exhibits a more obvious relationship, marked by a repeated-note motive stated clearly enough at or near the start of all four movements to leave no doubt of its premeditated use. Sonata in A still makes some use of murky, Alberti, and other more elementary bass types. Otherwise, if it also had a model it must have been not anything by Mozart or Pleyel but one of Beethoven's later works—or rather any of Beethoven's later works, for with Weinlig's carte blanche to compose as he pleased, Wagner was not likely to restrict himself to matching one model. The ideas and styles of both the introduction and the fugue,[111] for example, recall

---

105. WAGNER LEBEN 71–72.

106. Cf. Breithaupt/WAGNER 120–26; Daube/WAGNER 149–68, with many exx. and facs. of 3 pp. in the autograph.

107. As documented in some detail on pp. 2 and 3 of Friedelind Wagner's (unpaginated) pamphlet cited earlier.

108. Breithaupt/WAGNER 113, 126–30. Breithaupt seems to have been unaware of the fugal third movement.

109. A complete photograph of this ed., reduced in size, appears in Daube/WAGNER 230–57, with discussion 140–48.

110. Cf. Daube/WAGNER 144–47, with extracts from Weinlig's "Anleitung zur Fuge."

111. The fugue may or may not have been written before Weinlig's farewell prediction that Wagner "probably never will write [any more] fugues and canons" (WAGNER LEBEN 70). This prediction gives at least tentative circumstantial evidence for dating Sonata in A around the end of 1831.

those in the finale of Beethoven's Op. 101 in A, whereas those of the first two movements recall passages in the first movement of the *"Eroica* Symphony" and the slow movement of Op. 106 in B♭, respectively. Only the finale, in its brilliant, more coarsely melodious manner, seems to give any foretaste of the Wagner to come—of *Rienzi,* in particular, nearly ten years later. For the rest, Sonata in A reveals new character and drive but does not have the recitative, the free sections, the sinister use of the "chalumeau" register, the clipped rhythms that open "Siegfried's Funeral March," or the abundant chromaticism that are all anticipated in the "Phantasie" in f♯.

As indicated above, Wagner wrote his *Album-Sonate* in A♭ nearly twenty-two years later, while he was a political exile in Zürich.[112] Its fuller title, "Eine Sonate für das Album von Frau M. W.[,] componirt im Jahre 1853," appears on the cover of the first edition, published with an improved coda in 1878 and after characteristic financial pressures had forced Wagner to sell the work to Schott in 1877.[113] This title reminds us that Wagner wrote the sonata and presented it to Mathilde Wesendonk as his "first composition since the completion of *Lohengrin* (6 years ago!)" and as an apparently unsolicited way of discharging one of his numerous recent debts to her generous, tolerant husband Otto.[114] In spite of the growing attachment between her and Wagner, Mathilde was able to write a warm, grateful letter to his wife Minna, rejoicing in "the glorious work" even though Mathilde was "capable of reproducing only the slightest shadow of it" by her own playing.[115] She was puzzled by the inscription on the first page of music in the autograph (only; cf. Ex. 48 below), "Wisst Ihr wie das wird?" ("Do you know what will come of it?"), which enigmatic phrase could have referred to anything from concern over his slowed down com-

---

112. A facs. of the title page of the autograph appears in Panofsky/WAGNER 49.
113. Plate no. 22431. Cf. Ellis/WAGNER IV 450; Newman/WAGNER IV 610. Schott pub. E. Singer's transcription for Vn & orchestra in the same year (HOFMEISTER 1878, p. 311) and K. Müller-Berghaus's orchestral transcription of the piece within 2 years (HOFMEISTER VIII [1874–79] 605). English sources often erroneously refer to this work as being in E♭ instead of A♭, as in Newman/MAN 454 and GROVE IX 123 (P. M. Young). Was the "Skizze zu einer Sonate f. Pfte." listed in 1877 (HOF-MEISTER 1877, p. 280) simply a preliminary announcement by Schott of the *Album-Sonate* (cf. fn. 117, *infra*)?
114. The transmittal letter to Otto, June 20, 1853, is in WAGNER-WESENDONK 4. Nearly 25 years later he explained the debt differently (in a letter in his curious French, quoted in Friedelind Wagner's pamphlet, p. 5, cited earlier): "Don't look for too many unmentionable motivations ["choses indicibles"] in the Album Sonata. I promised it to a young woman who was very kind to me, in return for a beautiful sofa cushion that she gave as a present to me."
115. July 4, 1853; trans. in Burk/WAGNER 362–63.

posing to hints of impending crisis in the Wagner-Wesendonk quadrangle.[116]

The Musical Times of London ended a short, pleasantly favorable review of Wagner's *Album-Sonate,* regarded there as more of a "sonatina," with the sentence, "No person hearing this unambitious trifle would believe that Herr Wagner is its composer; but everybody must feel that it is the holiday-work of an artist." [117] Today, the stamp of Wagner, however attenuated, seems unmistakable in this work, even though it fails to appear in his two early extant sonatas. But the reminders are less of *Das Rheingold,* nearing completion in 1853, than of *Tristan und Isolde,* still a few years off, as in the anticipations of main themes from both the "Love's Death" and "Prelude," respectively, in the first eight measures of the sonata (Ex. 48).[118] The sonata's one-movement form reveals nothing of the double function in Liszt's Sonata in b. However, contrary to earlier statements,[119] this work does acknowledge "sonata form," at least a chiastic "sonata form" in which the order of the recapitulation is reversed. In the exposition the first thematic group in A♭ leads to a second thematic group in the mediant, C (from ms. 39), followed by a closing idea in that key. The development (from ms. 75), vacillating between the tonic and submediant, f, rises to a climax (on a dim.-7th chord, mss. 136–44) in a sequential manner anticipating the lovers' reunions in both the second and third acts of *Tristan und Isolde.* After a cadence in c (mss. 149–51) the recapitulation begins (ms. 158) with the second thematic group, hovering around rather than in A♭ by means of Wagner's characteristic deceptive cadences, then proceeds to the closing theme, now mainly in the dominant, E♭ (from ms. 195). Only at this point does the first theme return, in the tonic (from ms. 206), after which a coda (from ms. 230), largely on a tonic pedal-point, completes the piece.

The piano writing in this work is not especially resourceful, but it lies and sounds well, especially for a disinterested and professed nonpianist like Wagner.[120] The strongest traits are the developments of

116. Cf. Ellis/WAGNER IV 448–50; Newman/WAGNER II 508–9, 524–27, *et passim.* WAGNER LEBEN avoids saying much at all about the Wesendonks and omits all mention of the *Album-Son.*
117. MT XIX (1878) 84; on p. 33 the new pub. from Schott had been announced as "a Sketch for a Pianoforte Sonata"; a performance of the work is cited in XXI (1880) 247. It is discussed in Ellis/WAGNER IV 448–50; Breithaupt/WAGNER 130–34; Newman/MAN 284.
118. Cf. Breithaupt/WAGNER 131 for other anticipations.
119. Ellis/WAGNER IV 448–50; Breithaupt/WAGNER 130.
120. ". . . in my whole life I have never learned to play the piano properly" (WAGNER PROSE I 4). But he played at the piano, nonetheless, including Beethoven sons. for Mathilde Wesendonk. Cf. Breithaupt/WAGNER 109–12; Daube/WAGNER 17.

Ex. 48. From the opening of Richard Wagner's *Album-Sonate* in A♭ (facs. of the autograph in the Wahnfried Archive at Bayreuth, kindly provided by Miss Friedelind Wagner).

ideas, in leitmotiv fashion, the sure control of modulations and tonal directions, the effortless, slick passing from one section to the next, and, in fact, the mastery of form as a whole. The music is at its weakest in its thematic ideas, particularly the second theme with its sentimental chromaticism. All these observations recall Ernest Newman's conclusion that for all his reputation as a music dramatist Wagner was an instrumental symphonist at heart, but that his dilemma in this regard was his inability to find inspiration without a poetic programme (which his *Album-Sonate* does lack).[121]

As a matter of curiosity, mention may be made here of two weak (incomplete?) sonatas for piano, dating from not before 1862, by the philosopher **Friederich Nietzsche** (1844–1900). Still in his youth, Nietzsche had yet to become the champion and ultimate opponent of Wagner. Recently an edition of his music was projected that was to include these sonatas.[122]

The once immensely popular composer (**Joseph**) **Joachim Raff** (1822–82) also fits in here most appropriately with Liszt. In fact, in Weimar from 1850 to 1856 Raff actually dedicated all his best efforts to Liszt—as friend, copyist, orchestrator, and secretary—after which he finally had to leave to preserve his own individuality.[123] Like Liszt and Wagner, Raff, too, became identified with the "New German" school, although his continual efforts to combine the best from the past made him increasingly Classic-minded in later years and contributed to his eventual reputation as an eclectic solitary among his contemporaries and but an epigone to his successors.[124] A largely self-taught composer born in Switzerland of a Swabian family, Raff made his first mark with a series of piano pieces that Breitkopf & Härtel started to publish in 1844 on Mendelssohn's recommendation.[125] By the end of his life, spent largely in Wiesbaden after the departure from Liszt, he had composed some 250 works, in virtually all instrumental and vocal categories, and almost as many more transcriptions of other composers' works. Eleven of the original works are sonatas or "sonatilles" pub-

121. Newman/ARTIST 265–84, *passim*. Cf., also, WAGNER PROSE VI 187–91. W. Cobbett writes at some length of a sympathetic but poorly informed view of chamber music on Wagner's part (Cobbett/CHAMBER II 562–63 and I 257).

122. This information comes from an unpub. article (as of 1964) on Nietzsche's music by Andres Briner at the University of Pennsylvania in Philadelphia. Cf., also, Love/NIETZSCHE 27; MGG IX 1521–26 (H. G. Hoke).

123. Cf. pp. 90–113 in Raff/RAFF, the chief account of the man and his music, by his daughter. Cf., also, Mendel/LEXIKON VIII 225–29.

124. Cf. MGG X 1863 (R. Sietz); MASON MEMORIES 133–34, 161–64.

125. Cf. Raff/RAFF 32–33.

lished between about 1850 and 1873, including 5 for P solo, 5 for P &
Vn, and one for P & Vc,[126] as follows:

Grande Sonate in e♭, Op. 14, P. solo; composed in Zürich late in 1845
(Raff/RAFF 34) and first pub by Breitkopf & Härtel not later than 1851
(HOFMEISTER I [1844–51] 148).

Trois Sonatilles, in a, G, and C, Op. 99, P solo; first pub. by J. Schubert
not later than 1880 (Altmann/KAMMERMUSIK 221).

Fantasie-Sonate in d, Op. 168, P solo; pub. by C. F. W. Siegel, 1872
(HOFMEISTER 1872, p. 137).

Grosse Sonate für Pianoforte & Violine in e, Op. 73, composed in Weimar
by April, 1854 (cf. Raff/RAFF 137) and first pub. by J. Schuberth in 1859
(plate no. 2444); ded. to Ferdinand Laub.

Zweite grosse Sonate für Pianoforte und Violine in A, Op. 78, composed
by 1858 (Mendel/LEXIKON VIII 228) and first pub. by J. Schuberth in 1861
(Müller-Reuter/LEXIKON 425); ded. to Joseph Hellmesberger.

Dritte grosse Sonate für Pianoforte und Violine in D, Op. 128, composed
between 1860 and 1865 (before the Austro-Prussian War of 1866; Raff/RAFF
177–78) and first pub. by J. Schuberth in 1867 (HOFMEISTER 1867, p. 26); ded.
to Ferdinand David.

*Vierte grosse Sonate (chromatische Sonate in einem Satze) für Pianoforte
und Violine* in g, Op. 129; composed between 1866 and 1869 (Raff/RAFF
177–78) and first pub. by J. Schuberth in 1867 (plate no. 4301); ded. to Henri
Vieuxtemps.

Fünfte grosse Sonate für Pianoforte und Violine in c, Op. 145; composed
in 1869 and first pub. by J. Schuberth in 1869 (Müller-Reuter/LEXIKON 427);
ded. to Hubert Léonard.

Sonate für Pianoforte und Violoncello in D, Op. 183; composed in 1873
and first pub. by C. F. W. Siegel in 1873 (Müller-Reuter/LEXIKON 427; Raff/
RAFF 271).

Raff's sonatas suggest a comparison with Rheinberger's (*supra*), not
only because both men were masters of their craft whose music has
slipped into almost total oblivion but because this music seems to have
slipped thus for similar reasons. Of the two men as musical personalities, Raff is the more compelling and excitable (Ex. 49). And he
could be quite as original as Rheinberger, as in the changing meters of
Op. 73/ii[127] or the one-movement design, starting with a recitative, in
Op. 129. Yet Raff, too—to put it bluntly—had a like problem of being
long-winded and, perhaps in a more uncritical sense than with Rheinberger, of not knowing when to stop.[128] And he, too, could write senti-

126. Cf. the full list in Raff/RAFF 267–86, which is chronological (but not dated)
by categories and supersedes the index by A. Schäfer made in 1888 (cf. p. 267, fn.).
Cf., also, PAZDÍREK XII 15–25; Cat. NYPL XXV 205.

127. Liszt's remarkable sightreading of this scherzando mvt. is described in MASON
MEMORIES 142–44; cf., also, Cobbett/CHAMBER II 267 (W. Altmann).

128. Müller-Reuter/LEXIKON 424–27 gives durations from 16 minutes (Op. 129
in one mvt.) to 38 minutes (Op. 78) among the 6 string sons.

Ex. 49. From the second movement of Joachim Raff's Sonata in e♭, Op. 14 (after the Breitkopf & Härtel re-ed. of *ca.* 1880 at the Library of Congress).

mental as well as strong themes, again more indiscriminately than Rheinberger—as sentimental, in fact, but also as well constructed (e.g., the theme of the vars. in Op. 78/ii) as the little "Cavatina" in D, Op. 85/3 for Vn & P, which alone keeps today's performers aware that Raff ever lived.[129] In a shrewd series of analytic articles published in 1875, three English writers came to much the same conclusions about six of Raff's symphonies, then enjoying much recognition.[130] They thought highly of the composer's comprehensive skills, his musical individuality, his idiomatic instrumental writing,[131] his development techniques, and the suitability of his themes to such development, but similarly found him to be the uncritical victim of his own prolificity (occasioned partly by lifelong financial needs).[132] Perhaps what we assume to have been the more leisurely pace of the 19th-century musician helps to explain how in Raff's day such lengthy, discursive sonatas as he wrote could win more favor than disfavor in reviews, as well as many performances, near and far.[133] Pertinent here are

129. Cf. Raff/RAFF 159.

130. Prout *et al.*/RAFF, with many exx. and a table (p. 33) of comparative symphony lengths, increasing from Mozart to Raff.

131. In 1846 Liszt had begged Raff "only to make your works as playable as possible, and to avoid carefully the wretched, abominable, monstrous Liszt piano style" (LISZT-RAFF 116).

132. In 1878 Raff wrote Bülow he could not answer a question about Op. 145 (1869) because he had no copy on hand and never remembered anything but what he was composing currently (La Mara/MUSIKERBRIEFE II 318–19). Liszt had warned Raff of the dangers of such prolificity (LISZT-RAFF 116).

133. The peak of their popularity seems to have been reached in the 1870's (cf. Raff/RAFF 198–99). Early performances are cited in Müller-Reuter/LEXIKON 424–27. For samples of other performances while Raff was alive, cf. NZM CXXII/1 (1876) 92, 157, 215, (2), CXXII/2 (1876) 327, CXXIII/1 107, 140, 141, 212, 240, 274; MT

excerpts from W. W. Cobbett's nostalgic recollections of Raff, following a page by Wilhelm Altmann on three of Raff's violin sonatas:[134]

. . . I am an admirer, though not a worshipper, of Raff, whose reputation has always suffered through his deplorable lack of the faculty of self criticism. He composed at rare intervals music which alternates between extreme brilliance and sentimental tenderness, but he also poured out incessantly masses of pot-boilers with which, unfortunately, his name is only too often associated. I would not willingly be without his sonatas for piano and violin; they are not severely classical, but they are delightfully written for the violin. (After all, we fiddlers must be allowed sometimes to revel in the purely violinistic element.) [Sarasate enjoyed Raff and played his music frequently] . . . whenever he introduced into his programmes such works as the sonatas, the suite, and the *Fée d'amour,* he was rapturously applauded by the public. [Raff was] . . . a master musician, with real insight into the inner life of the violin.

Two other men in Weimar and Liszt's circle may be noted here for sonatas now forgotten but not without musical merits. One was the virtuoso organist and theorist **Johann Gottlieb Töpfer** (1791–1870), who left at least two sonatas for organ, one for P solo, and one for P & Fl, all published between about 1840 and 1865.[135] The other was the virtuoso pianist and organist, and student of Liszt, **Alexander Winterberger** (1834–1914), who left a piano sonata as Op. 1 (1857?) and at least six piano sonatinas.[136]

Many of the sonatas or sonatinas not yet mentioned from Leipzig in the mid-Romantic Era were of the light pedagogic sort (ssb III), in several instances by men now remembered only as theorists. The influential if somewhat circumscribed theorist **Salomon Jadassohn** (1831–1902), who had studied piano with Liszt and responded warmly to Wagner's *Lohengrin* before settling in Leipzig,[137] left one sonata for P & Vn in g, Op. 5 (1857), and one for P solo in A, Op. 14 (1858?),

---

XVII (1876) 461 ("The second movement [of Op. 183], marked 'Vivace,' is a perfect gem."), XX (1879) 225, XXII (1880) 43; smz XVI (1876) 45, 48, 54. Among early reviews are dmz III (1862) 46 (objecting to the exhaustive extension of weak, unoriginal motives in Op. 78, except in the "Scherzo" mvt.), Hanslick/wien II 428–29 (1867; except for a similar reservation, general praise for Op. 78), mw I (1870) 6–7 (about the same for Op. 145), mw VI (1875) 552 (on specific pros and cons in Op. 183).

134. Cobbett/chamber II 267–68.

135. Cf. mgg XIII 450–52 (R. Sietz); pazdírek XIV 227; hofmeister *passim;* Mendel/lexikon X 204–7; nzm XXXVII (1852) 90–91 (qualified review of organ Son. in d) and LXXII/1 (1876) 166 (performance of same).

136. Cf. Mendel/lexikon XI 380; Riemann/lexikon II 2036 (with further bibliography); pazdírek XV 465–69; nzm XLVIII (1858) 39–40 (reviewing Op. 1 as betraying inexperience); mw XI (1880) 608–9 (reviewing the "instructive Sonatina" Op. 46 merely as being more difficult than its title suggests) and XXIV (1893) 419 (on more sonatinas for P, Op. 93, reviewed as simple but highly musical).

137. Cf. mgg VI 1647–51 (G. Feder).

among many published works.[138] Op. 5, in four movements (F-M-M-F), is reviewed at length as skillful, light, fluent, without warmth, sometimes trite (especially the finale), and consistent with Jadassohn's training in the environment of Mendelssohn and Hauptmann.[139] A widely known father and two lesser known sons in the Leipzig area— **Heinrich Wohlfahrt** (1797–1883), **Franz Wohlfahrt** (1833–84), and **Robert Wohlfahrt** (?–?) [140]—all left instructive sonatinas for piano solo or duet, and Franz left some for Vn & P, too.[141] Dating from the late 1850's to early 1880's, these works seem to have thrived in their day.[142]

Of a more serious nature were two sonatas by the erstwhile soldier **Franz von Holstein** (1826–78), who made his mark chiefly as an opera composer, poet, and music benefactor in Leipzig.[143] One is for P solo in c, Op. 28 (1871?), and the other for P & Vn in F, Op. 40 (1899, posthumous). Op. 28, in three movements (F-M-VF), was reviewed as showing skill and vitality, but with some passages that offer only technical display and others that sound more like the reduction of an orchestral work.[144] A Czech product of the Leipzig Conservatory, the teacher **Edmund Uhl** (1853–?), left an unpublished four-movement Sonata in F for P & Vn that achieved some success through performances,[145] and a published four-movement Sonata in G, Op. 5, for P & Vc, (1889; F-S-Sc-VF) that earned approval from reviewers for its musical solidity, freshness, and sonority, though not for a certain unoriginal conservatism.[146] Even the important pioneer musicologist and sometime Leipzig resident (**Karl Wilhelm Julius**) **Hugo Riemann** (1849–1919) contributed his bit, à la mode, to sonata literature as one facet of his all-embracing industry.[147] That "bit" includes a piano Sonata in G, Op. 5 (1872), a Sonata in b, Op. 11, for Vn & P (1875), and a Sonatina in G "without octave stretches," Op. 49, for P-duet (1887), as well as several other sonatinas.[148] We may also note that the

138. Cf. PAZDÍREK VIII 60–64.

139. NZM XLVI (1857) 274–75 (A. v. Dommer). Op. 14 is similarly but only briefly reviewed in NZM LI (1859) 135.

140. Mendel/LEXIKON XI 399–400; Schuberth/LEXIKON 638; BAKER 1809.

141. Cf. PAZDÍREK XV 503–11; Altmann/KAMMERMUSIK 174, 179, 232, 307.

142. Brief, typical reviews of Heinrich's sonatinas occur in NZM LVI (1862) 59 and LXI/2 (1865) 343; DM VIII/3 (1908–9) 365–66.

143. Cf. Riemann/LEXIKON I 776; PAZDÍREK VII 643–45.

144. MW III (1872) 118, 132–33. Op. 28 was played at a memorial concert for Holstein (MT XIX [1878] 502).

145. Cf. NZM LXXII/1 (1876) 244, LXXII/2 (1876) 291, LXXIII/1 (1877) 261; SMZ XVII (1877) 120.

146. Cf. NZM LXXXV/2 (1889) 593; SMW LIX (1889) 931; MW XX (1889) 575; NMZ XI/6 (1890) p. 1 of Beilage.

147. Cf. MGG XI 480–85 (H. C. Wolff).

148. Cf. PAZDÍREK XII 323–26; Egert/FRÜHROMANTIKER 159; Altmann/KAMMERMUSIK 223 and 304. The child Reger valued the sonatinas (Stein/REGER 9). Op. 49 is reviewed favorably in SMW LIX (1887) 931.

organist and theorist, **Ernst Friedrich Eduard Richter** (1808–79), another product of the Mendelssohn environment, left four published sonatas between 1861 and 1869, including two for P solo and one each for P & Vn and P & Vc.[149]

The once renowned pianist, director, and pedagogue, **Carl (Heinrich Carsten) Reinecke** (1824–1910) won the respect of Mendelssohn, Schumann, and Liszt, toured widely, and served in several other centers besides Leipzig.[150] His enormous list of publications includes at least four sonatas that were well known in their day—Op. 42 in a (not A) for P & Vc (1855), Op. 116 in e for P & Vn (1872), Op. 167 in e ("Undine") for Fl & P (1882),[151] Op. 179 in c for P left hand alone (1884?)[152]—along with others for organ[153] and for 2 P's, and about ten sets of sonatinas for P solo.[154] As a sample, Op. 167 is a large work in three movements (F-VF-M/VF), with a slower middle section in the second movement. The music is skillful, idiomatic, up-to-date harmonically without being experimental, weak in its melodic ideas, and, as the general consensus seems to be, unable to compete with that of Schumann and Brahms, which it often approximates.[155] Regarding Op. 116, one reviewer noted how the last two movements failed to "go" in spite of all the caloric Italian inscriptions.[156] Another who won the respect of Mendelssohn, Schumann, and Liszt, among others, was the organist **Theodor Kirchner** (1823–1903), whose charming music would receive more attention here had he contributed more to our topic than his five delicate, sensitive, Schumannesque sonatinas Op. 70 (1883?).[157]

In Dresden the fine organist **Gustav Merkel** (1827–85), a protégé at one time of both Friedrich Wieck and Schumann, left nine organ sonatas that put him in the 19th-century company of Mendelssohn,

149. Cf. PAZDÍREK XII 305–8; Altmann/KAMMERMUSIK 223 and 262; MGG XI 451–52 (B. Stockmann); also, NZM LXXII/2 (1876) 510 for a performance of P Son. in E♭, Op. 33.

150. Cf. MGG XI 187–92 (R. Sietz), with further bibliography.

151. Reviewed fancifully at length as a programme son. in MUSIC IV (1893) 151–59 (E. V. Eastman).

152. Mod. ed. of Op. 179/ii ("Andante"): Ruthardt/LINKE-m 28. Cf. NMZ XVIII (1885) Beilage 2, p. 2, on Op. 179.

153. Cf. the review of Op. 284 in DM IX/1 (1909–10) 122 (E. S. v. Carolsfeld).

154. Cf. PAZDÍREK XII 135–59. A typically favorable review is in MW IX (1878) 639. Bibliographic details on 5 duo sons. are given in Müller-Reuter/LEXIKON 544–46.

155. Cf. the evaluations of Reinecke in Cobbett/CHAMBER II 286–87 (W. Altmann) and MGG XI 190–91.

156. NZM LXIX (1873), 50. Sample performances of Op. 116 are listed in NZM LXXII/1 (1875) 92, 156, and 211, all in Leipzig. Exx. from Op. 116 are included in Shand/VIOLIN 30–32. One of Reinecke's best and last sons., Op. 238 in G for P & Vc (cf. SMW LVI [1898] 321–22) seems not to have circulated widely.

157. Cf. MGG VII 943–47 (R. Sietz); DM VI/1 (1906–7) 115 (A. Göttmann). Mod. ed. of No. 3 in C: Frey/SONATINA-m 59.

Rheinberger, and Reubke, although they are rarely heard any more.[158] These sonatas (and some piano sonatinas by Merkel) were originally published between 1858 and 1886.[159] The first, Op. 30 in d, which alone is designated for "vier Händen und Doppel-Pedal," won its composer a prize when he first came to Dresden in 1858. Like most of their 19th-century companions, Merkel's organ sonatas take their starting point from J. S. Bach in their tendency toward contrapuntal forms and chorale treatment. And like these companion works, they make masterful use of the Romantic organ, yet show a decidedly more conservative harmonic style than that in the contemporary sonatas for piano alone or in duos. All nine of Merkel's sonatas are in three movements. The first movement is essentially preludial at moderate to fast tempos. It may tend to approach "sonata form," although the second theme may not provide the traditional contrast and the development is likely to be imitative, or even fugal. In Sonata 6, the first movement concentrates on the chorale melody "Aus tiefer Noth." [160] The middle movement, in slow to moderate tempos, is likely to be a spun out, free discourse, often between two ideas in aria style. And the finale, in moderate fast tempos, is an introduction and massive fugue (as in Son. 2), a contrapuntally imitative piece (as in Son. 9), or an introduction and "Passacaglia" (in Bach's sense; Son. 8).[161] Three other worthwhile organ sonatas were composed by **Karl Müller-Hartung** (1834–1908), presumably after he left Dresden in 1859 for Eisenach;[162] they were published in 1864. In a detailed, laudatory review they are described as cyclic chorale fantasias, with up-to-date harmony, brilliant use of the instrument, and a virtuoso command of imitative and fugal counterpoint.[163]

The most prominent Dresden composer at this time was the theorist and the champion of the "New German" school, **Felix Draeseke** (1835–1913).[164] Draeseke was close to Bülow as well as to Liszt and Wagner, and a pupil of Mendelssohn's friend and editor Julius Rietz (SSB VIII). Draeseke's sonatas (and their pub. years) include Op. 6 in c♯/E for P solo (1870; ded. to Bülow);[165] Op. 38 in B♭ for Cl & P (1888); Op.

158. Cf. MGG IX 126–27 (K.-E. Bergunder), with further bibliography.

159. Individual titles, keys, and dates are listed in Cat. NYPL XIX 86. Novello pub. at least the first 7 in a set (MT XXI [1880] 421).

160. Mod. ed.: Edition Peters H38.

161. Cf., also, Frotscher/ORGELSPIEL II 1173–74.

162. Cf. Mendel/LEXIKON VII 194; Riemann/LEXIKON II 1227.

163. NZM LX/2 (1864) 285–86. Cf., also, Frotscher/ORGELSPIEL II 1209.

164. Cf. MGG III 728–34 (H. Stephani), with further bibliography and a dated list of works. The only extended study is the recent diss., Krueck/DRAESEKE, on his symphonies (including biographical orientation).

165. HOFMEISTER XIX (1870) 59.

51 in D for Vc & P (1892);[166] and two for Hermann Ritter's short-lived, large viola alta (SSB V) and P, of which one, (Op. 56?) in c, was composed in 1892 and first published posthumously and privately by the onetime Draeseke Gesellschaft in 1935,[167] and the other, in F, was composed in 1901–2 but remains in MS.[168]

Composed between 1862 and 1867, Op. 6, *Sonata quasi fantasia*, is the remarkable inauguration of Draeseke's five sonatas, revealing the fiery though not wholly co-ordinated impetuosity of the young musical radical.[169] In the first of its three movements, "Introduzione e Marcia funebre," the "Marcia" follows the virtuosic and rhythmic abandon of the introduction with a clear enough ternary design (A-B-A-coda). The second movement, "Intermezzo (Valse-Scherzo)," in D♭, has the swing of the waltz, the speed ("Presto"), light texture, and friskiness of the scherzo, and the frequent returns to the main idea of a rondo. And the long finale, "Allegro con brio," begins as the first movement does and never quite gets away from that movement because its other ideas relate to it, too, and because it continues throughout as a fantasy. Although the broad tonal directions, including the turn to E in the finale, border on the oversimple in this work, there is considerable harmonic and chromatic indirection, including flitting in and out of the key in a manner pointing to Richard Strauss a generation later (Ex. 50). Draeseke's sonorous, expansive, advanced piano writing and his occasional sweet lyricism (as in the B section of the "Marcia") suggest the strong influence of Liszt. But the actual content, especially the quality of the main themes, falls somewhat short of the aims and promise in this music.

Another composer of the "New German" school under Liszt's influence, and a man who had studied with Moscheles and Hauptmann, and had known Brahms, was **Heinrich Schulz-Beuthen** (1838–1915), who left a "light" sonata, Op. 5/1, for P-duet (1874); "Three Piano Pieces: Cycle in Sonata Form," Op. 23, for P solo (1876); *Alhambra-Sonate* in f♯, Op. 34, for P solo (1883?); and "Heroische oder Akropolis Sonate" in c, for P solo (composed in 1878–84 but not pub.).[170] Char-

166. Reviewed as a deeply felt, structurally convincing work, in MW XXV (1894) 162.
167. Altmann/KAMMERMUSIK 247.
168. Müller-Reuter/LEXIKON 509–11 gives bibliographic details about the duo sons. Among the few reviews (or mentions of performances) discovered here are NZM XCIX (1903) 77 (on the fiery spirit and difficulty of Op. 6), SMW XLVIII (1888) 42 (on the charm and individuality of Op. 38), and SMW LII (1892) 818 (on the difficulty and unequal quality of Op. 51). A full study of Draeseke's sons. should be rewarding.
169. It is compared with J. Reubke's Son. in b♭ in Georgii/KLAVIERMUSIK 422.
170. Cf. pp. 25, 67–68 and 79–80 in Zosel/SCHULZ-BEUTHEN (a short diss. on the man and his works; but on p. 67 the "Symphonic Concerto" for P & orchestra should

Ex. 50. From the second movement of Felix Draeseke's Sonata in c♯/E, Op. 6 (after the original Rózsavölgyi ed. at the Library of Congress).

acteristic of Schulz-Beuthen's music, the last two have programmatic inscriptions, although only Op. 34, regarded as one of his best works, departs from standard sonata forms to depict its programme. This "sonata" has six movements, perhaps better called scenes, in the distantly related keys of F♯, B♭, F♯, C/E♭, E, F♯, and with the subtitles "On the Way to the Alhambra," "Procession by the Church of Our Lady," "Entrance into the Alhambra," "The Abencerrages [family of Moors] (Tournament)," "In the Garden Xeneralife [summer palace] (Love Scene)," and "Retrospections." The trills and other rich ornamentation, the fantasy style, the free rhythms, and the full active texture suggest, especially in the first and fifth movements, that the composer successfully achieved the goal stated in his "preface to this 'Fantasie-Sonate' "—to capture the feel, style, and atmosphere of Arabian music without actually quoting specific themes. The music also depicts the subject matter of its titles, especially the massacre at the end of the fourth movement. Today it sounds like a more developed, refined, genuine, and ingenuous version of *In a Persian Market* by "Albert W. Ketèlbey."

Somewhat less significant though not uninteresting are the three published sonatas of Draeseke's younger but more conservative contemporary in Dresden, the highly rated pianist, teacher and director **Jean Louis Nicodé** (1853–1919).[171] One of these is Op. 19 in f for P solo (pub. in 1879) and the other two are Opp. 23 in b and 25 in G for

---

not be grouped with the solo sons.); MGG XII 254 (R. Sietz, with same error); MW XV (1884) 409–10 (detailed, enthusiastic review of Op. 34).

171. Cf. MGG IX 1445–46 (R. Sietz).

Vc & P (first pub. in 1890 and 1882, respectively).[172] All three sonatas are foretastes of the epigonic works we shall be finding often in every country throughout the last decades of the Romantic Era. The styles are derivative. The level of craftsmanship is high, including the know ing treatment of the instruments, which is always telling but reasonable; the command of harmony and counterpoint, which never advances beyond anything that might occur (more imaginatively) in Schumann; and the control of form in the standard three- and four-movement cycles, which now borders on formalism. As effective as the music sounds, and as effectively as it is put together, one finds it difficult to accept either Nicodé's lyrical melody or his impassioned development at face value.

Dresden had its share of "instructive sonatina" composers, too, among them two prolific piano teachers who held their own corner on the pedagogic market for a time. One of these last was **Fritz Spindler** (1817–1905), whose more than 400 opus numbers (about half of Czerny's output) included three sets of ten sonatinas each, a one-movement piano sonata or "sonata form" (Op. 83), and a horn sonata (Op. 347), among other such works published in the 1850's–1870's.[173] The other was **(Carl) Heinrich Döring** (1834–1916), who had trained at the Leipzig Conservatory and mainly in the 1870's left, along with much other music and some related publications, a considerable number of widely used sonatinas. These were reviewed repeatedly as pleasing, skillful, and pedagogically valuable when not too complex.[174]

Lastly among sonatas from Dresden, it would be interesting to see the three published for P solo between 1852 and 1857—Opp. 1 in E, 2 in f$\sharp$, and 5 in c (all pubs. of Breitkopf & Härtel)—by Schumann's onetime pupil **Karl Ritter** (1830–?). But these could not be found here. Indeed, nearly all we know about them, or, for that matter, about Ritter, who spent his later life in Venice, comes from Bülow's unusually long review of 1858 on these and two other publications by Ritter, the gist of which is that the young man showed real promise and would bear watching (as Schumann had written Hiller 9 years earlier, though with some misgivings as to Ritter's continued progress).[175] Bülow

172. Cf. Altmann/KAMMERMUSIK 261. Op. 25 is reviewed favorably in MMR XV (1875) 249.
173. Cf. Mendel/LEXIKON IX 373; Riemann/LEXIKON II 1738; PAZDÍREK XIII 892–904; NZM XLVI (1857) 253 (facetious review of Op. 83, by A. v. Dommer).
174. Cf. Mendel/LEXIKON III 195; Riemann/LEXIKON I 412; PAZDÍREK IV 302–7; MW VI (1875) 541, VII (1876) 696, VIII (1877) 465, X (1879) 300, XI (1880) 608; NZM LXXIII/1 (1877) 265–66.
175. NZM XLVIII (1858) 101–5. Cf. Wasielewski/SCHUMANN 369–70 (not 416); HOFMEISTER V (1852–59) 203; Schumann/SCHRIFTEN II 550. Ritter is not listed in any biographic dictionary used here.

emphasized the consistent force of Ritter's ideas, his inner sense of form, the nobility and depth of the music, and its origins in Beethoven's late sonatas.

In Magdeburg, well northwest of Dresden, another, better known composer with the same surname was the organist and writer on organ music **August Gottfried Ritter** (1811–85).[176] A student of J. N. Hummel and Mendelssohn's teacher Ludwig Berger, among others, this Ritter left a total of eight sonatas, including Opp. 11 in d, 19 in e, 23 in a, and 31 in A for organ, and Opp. 12 in B♭, 18 in D, 20 in D, and 21 in b for P solo, all published between about 1849 and 1858.[177] Each of these is a superior work, even Opp. 12 and 18, entitled "Instructive Sonatas in Preparation for Larger Works." And all were uniformly and warmly welcomed when they first appeared, for their sincerity, depth of content, natural flow, over-all unity, and expert writing.[178] Furthermore, all of them might be nearly as warmly welcomed if they were to be revived today. Indeed, one wonders whether it was not the mere caprice of fate quite as much as the allegedly right judgment of time and posterity that catapulted, say, Mendelssohn into one of the highest niches occupied by Romantic composers and left Ritter almost without any composer's niche. The comparison is not actually so idle, for Ritter, only two years younger and stemming from one of the same teachers, has much in common with Mendelssohn in their musical styles, including the sureness of form from the most local to the broadest levels, the frank lyrical melodies clearly projected against thin, transparent, accurate, idiomatic textures, the deft scherzando movements, the climactic uses of dim.-7th chords, and even a similar tendency toward rhythmic flatness and predictability. In some respects, especially enharmony and related harmonic resources, Ritter went beyond Mendelssohn. But in spite of their closeness in age, the precocious Mendelssohn led the way; and history focuses more on leaders than followers.

---

176. Cf. MGG XI 565–67 (P. Schmidt), with further bibliography (but an inadequate list of works).

177. Cf. HOFMEISTER IV (1844–51) 150 and 215, V (1852–59) 203 and 293.

178. E.g., NZM XXX (1849) 185–86 (G. Siebeck, comparing Op. 11, with exx., to the disadvantage of a *Phantasie-Sonate* for organ by Adolph Hesse), XXXII (1850) 213–14 (E. Bernsdorf discussing Op. 12 as preparation for the spirit as well as the fingerwork of the Classics), XXXII (1850) 91–92 and XXXIII (1850) 97–98 (calling Op. 19 a model of its type since Bach), XXXV (1851) 258–59 (on Op. 20, its freedom from eclecticism, its resemblance to Beethoven's Op. 28, and its increasing tonal enterprise in ii and iii), XXXIX (1853) 114–15 (E. Klitzsch on Op. 21), and XLIII (1855) 155–56 (L. Kindscher on Op. 23 as a landmark in the trend initiated by Mendelssohn).

Sample performances of Ritter's sons. are cited in NZM XXXII (1850) 91, LXXII/1 (1876) 225 and 244, LXXII/2 (1876) 475.

One sample of Ritter's writing might be quoted here from his piano Sonata in b, Op. 21 (Ex. 51), whose more driving sections recall, for example, Mendelssohn's *Capriccio brillant* for P and orchestra, Op. 22 (first pub. in 1832). In this sonata, as in Ritter's Op. 20, there are three movements—an extended "sonata-allegro" form, a scherzando ternary design marked "Träumerisch," and an expressive rondo finale. The unity of mood and style is furthered by clear cyclic links. By contrast, the organ sonatas, which include indications for Ritter's fine art of

Ex. 51. From the first movement of August Gottfried Ritter's Sonata in b, Op. 21 (after the original Breitkopf & Härtel ed. of 1853).

registration, are cast in more and shorter movements and these, in turn, are freer in all respects, often connected without breaks, more contrapuntal, and even more closely bound by related themes (but not chorale melodies).[179]

A more detailed survey of the organ sonata in this period would include the once popular examples by A. G. Ritter's organ pupil **Rudolf Palme** (1834–1909), also of Magdeburg;[180] by the organist near

179. Cf. Frotscher/ORGELSPIEL II 1164–65.
180. Cf. Riemann/LEXIKON II 1335–36; HOFMEISTER IX (1880–85) 474; NZM LXXI/1 (1876) 165–66; MT XXII (1881) 376.

Kassel **Wilhelm Valentin Volckmar** (1812–87), recently dubbed the "Czerny of the organ" for his prolificity, banality, and stereotypes;[181] by **Friedrich Kühmstedt** (1809–58) in Eisenach, who also aroused interest with his *Grosse Sonate* (*ein Lebensbild*) in g, Op. 36, for P solo (1857?), cited earlier for its programmatic implications (SSB VI);[182] and by his Dutch contemporary in Elberfeld (north of Köln), the organist **Jan Albert van Eyken** (or **Eijken;** 1823–68).[183]

From the pianist **Julius Otto Grimm** (1827–1903) in Münster, best known for his close friendship with Brahms, we have just one sonata, Op. 14 in A, for P & Vn, composed in 1854 and published in 1869.[184] Grimm's individual style plus the value he placed on comments from his younger friend (by 6 years) should make this scarce work interesting to see and hear.

In Köln from 1850 on lived one of the most representative and diversely active of Romantic musicians, although a man who gave but a small part of his attention to the sonata, **Ferdinand Hiller** (1811–85).[185] Trained by Hummel among others, Hiller was more disposed by nature to the Classics (he was a pioneer in his Parisian performances of Bach and Beethoven) than to the "New German" school. Yet his career brought him close to musicians of all tastes, including Moscheles and, especially, Mendelssohn, Schubert, and Beethoven while they were still alive in Vienna, Schumann, Brahms, Chopin, Liszt, Wagner (before Hiller turned against him), Berlioz, and even Verdi.

Hiller wrote at least seven sonatas, including an early one in a, for P solo, that remains in MS and another labeled Op. 2, for Vn & P;[186] three mature sonatas for P solo[187]—Op. 47 in a (pub. in 1853), Op. 59 in A♭ (composed probably in 1851–53, pub. in 1861), and Op. 78 in g

181. Cf. MGG XIII 1917 (R. Sietz); NZM LXV/2 (1869) 294 (A. W. Gottschalg); Kremer/ORGAN 228–29 (list of 44 sons., etc.).

182. Cf. Mendel/LEXIKON VI 177–78; MGG VII 1854–55 (G. Kraft); NZM XL (1854) 273 and 274, XLV (1856) 174, XLVII (1857) 78–80 (on Op. 36, with exx.); Frotscher/ORGELSPIEL II 1190; Kremer/ORGAN 198 (list of 4 sons.).

183. Cf. Mendel/LEXIKON III 445–46; Riemann/LEXIKON I 455; NZM XL (1854) 273 (somewhat negative on Son. 1, Op. 13, for organ), XLV (1856) 174 (more favorable on Son. 2, Op. 15), LV (1861) 18 (on 2 P sonatinas, Op. 3); Reeser/NEDERLANDSE 109–111; Frotscher/ORGELSPIEL II 1234, 1235; Kremer/ORGAN 181 (list of 4 sons.).

184. Cf. MGG V 930–32 (R. Sietz), with further references; Altmann/KAMMERMUSIK 205.

185. Efficient biographic summaries appear in Hering/HILLER (a diss. on his P music), pp. 7–15; MGG VI 399–409 (R. Sietz), with further bibliography; and Sietz/HILLER (an annotated collection of previously unpub. letters to and from Hiller, valuable for many insights into the era) I 1–3 (first years).

186. Hering/HILLER 17–18.

187. The 3 P solo sons. are discussed in Hering/HILLER 32–37, with exx. Cf. HOFMEISTER V (1852–59) 156 and HOFMEISTER 1861, p. 68. Hiller also left 2 sets of "easy sonatinas" for P solo (Hering/HILLER 55–56, with ex.).

(pub. probably in 1855); and two mature sonatas for P & Vc—Op. 22 in E (pub. in 1872) [188] and Op. 172 in a (pub. in 1878).[189]

Hiller's three piano sonatas all lack inner slow movements. Nearest to slow are the opening section[190] and opening movement of Opp. 47 and 59, respectively, both in moderate tempo. Starting in that tempo contributes to an apparently calculated increase of tempo and excitement from that moment right to the brilliant codas in the finales of each sonata. The same increase can be noted in Op. 78, although the plan differs markedly from that in Opp. 47 and 59. Opp. 47 and 59 employ a free "sonata form" in their first main movements and still freer, cursive forms in their finales (with no middle, scherzando movement in Op. 47). Op. 78, which dispenses with the improvisatory moments to be found in the two previous sonatas, starts with an exceptional movement that (almost like *Le Djinns* by Franck) describes a single broad dynamic curve, from *pianissimo,* "Andante agitato," to *fortissimo,* "Più vivace," and back. Then, without pauses, follow a "Scherzo" in ternary design, marked "Vivace," and a finale, "Allegro energico e con fuoco," that supplies a complete "sonata form."

At most, Hiller's compositions, even his major vocal works, achieved no conspicuous popularity. Nor have any reviews or other records turned up here that would alter this statement for the sonatas. Yet these last, especially Opp. 47 and 78, are not lacking in melodic appeal, musical conviction and freshness, rhythmic and harmonic ingenuities, or telling uses of the keyboard. Their keyboard writing is a kind of cross between the thin, precise Mendelssohnian texture we found in A. G. Ritter's sonatas and more subtle Schumannesque touches (as in Ex. 52). Perhaps the chief drawbacks in Hiller's sonatas are this sort of eclecticism and a certain tentativeness about the forms. The anticipations and build-ups promise much, but what they arrive at—in other words, the substance we have been led to expect—often disappoints. Or put still differently, Hiller had a greater gift for creating interesting crescendos and passagework than for the creation of strong ideas or for developing them. Even so, a capable pianist might revive one of the sonatas today with fair hope of a real artistic success.

The choral and orchestral director **Albert Hermann Dietrich** (1829–

188. HOFMEISTER 1872, p. 77. Actually, this is the only son. (or concerto) listed in Cobbett/CHAMBER I 555 (R. Felber); the paragraph on a "Violin Sonata in D," Op. 122, by Hiller probably refers inaccurately to his Concerto for Vn, Op. 152. A Leipzig performance of Op. 22 is listed in NZM LXXIII/1 (1877) 140. Hiller reported a performance of Op. 22 (?) in Leipzig in 1875 in which he participated (Sietz/HILLER III 179).

189. Altmann/KAMMERMUSIK 258.

190. Hering/HILLER 32–34 makes too much of this short tonally dependent section by counting it as an independent mvt.

Ex. 52. From the first movement (second theme) of Ferdinand Hiller's Sonata in a, Op. 47 (after the original J. Schuberth ed. of 1853).

1908) is mentioned in the present volume chiefly as the pupil of Schumann and longtime friend of Brahms who joined with those two men in Düsseldorf to write the *F-A-E* Sonata in a, in 1853, as a salute to Joachim.[191] Dietrich's share, the first movement, does not quite stand up with the others', partly because it pursues the "F-A-E" theme too doggedly. A Sonata in G, Op. 19, for P-duet, published in 1870,[192] after Dietrich moved to Oldenburg in northernmost Germany, was reviewed as being agreeable and unpretentious, with perhaps too much recollection of the Classic masters and some structural inadequacies.[193] Dietrich's Sonata in C, Op. 15, for P & Vc, was likewise published in that year. In Barmen, near Düsseldorf, the well-reputed piano pedagog **Anton Krause** (1834–1907) left about thirty "instructive" sonatinas or sonatas in some twelve sets published in the 1860's and 1870's.[194] They are scored for P solo, P-duet, 2 Ps, and P & Vn.[195] These received numer-

191. Cf. our last pp. on Schumann (ssb VIII) and the first pp. on Brahms (ssb IX).
192. Altmann/KAMMERMUSIK 298.
193. NZM LXIX/2 (1873) 418.
194. Cf. Riemann/LEXIKON I 949; HOFMEISTER VI–VIII (1860–79) *passim.*
195. Cf. PAZDÍREK VIII 354–55.

ous approving reviews, aside from occasional reservations about dryness or gaucheries, and evidently sold widely and well.[196]

North German Composers (Kiel, Reubke, Gradener)

Except for Gustav Flügel in Stettin, all our North German composers were concentrated in Berlin and Hamburg. Berlin, especially, harbored several figures of minor interest including products of Mendelssohn, Schumann, and the Leipzig Conservatory, and the opposing influences of Brahms and Liszt. The esteemed but somewhat withdrawn teacher of piano and composition **Friedrich Kiel** (1821–85) left among many other works six duo sonatas (4 for P & Vn, one for P & Va, and one for P & Vc) and two sonatinas for P-duet (Op. 6) [197] that were all published between 1850 and 1876 (chiefly in the 1860's).[198] These works disclose another master of his craft who came remarkably close to ranking with the recognized greats. But like Rheinberger versus Bruckner, or Raff versus Mendelssohn, Kiel came too close to the Brahms he admired so much, to stand independently or to withstand the competition. In the resourcefulness and conduct of his polyphony, his harmony, and his texture and scoring, and in both his tonal and his thematic unfolding and development of these techniques toward broad, serious, highly organized forms, Kiel ranked second to none. But he indicated no interest in the "New German" school or other new trends. And in the vitality of his ideas, in the imagination and flexibility of their treatment, and occasionally in that important virtue of conciseness where prolixity threatens—one of the virtues that Brahms appreciated so fully—he must be ranked below the greats. The temptation here would be to ascribe these relative weaknesses to Kiel's solitary, retiring nature, except that Brahms could be solitary and retiring in his own way, too.

Representative is Kiel's *Vierte Sonate für Pianoforte und Violine,* Op. 51 in e (1868).[199] Its movement, "Allegro maestoso," is a powerful,

196. E.g., NZM LIV (1861) 147, LXIII/1 (1867) 166–67 (on Op. 17, a more substantial, 3-mvt. Son. in E for 2 Ps), LXIX/1 (1873) 103, LXIX/2 (1873) 391, LXXIX/1 (1883) 280 (2d ed. of Op. 17); MW III (1872) 603, V (1874) 429. Cf. the biography in MW XXXV (1904) 816–17.

197. Cf. DM VIII/4 (1908–9) 242 (H. Wetzel).

198. Cf. MGG VII 880–83 (R. Sietz), with detailed, dated list of works and further bibliography. The Library of Congress also has the MS of an unpub. Son. in A for P & Vn, labeled Op. 2. In 1880 Kiel recalled writing 4 P sons. before his 21st year (La Mara/MUSIKERBRIEFE II 314).

199. Among reviews of his sons. are those in NZM LVIII (1863) 199–200 (on the skills, especially in thematic development, and on a certain unusualness in Op. 16

fully developed "sonata form" in which motivic reiteration and evolution provide the chief means of structural prolongation. In the absence of independent thematic distinction (but not lyricism) they and the Schubertian modulations in the development section also provide the chief interest. As in Brahms's duo sonatas, the range, idioms, and techniques of the piano are challenged more than those of the violin. The second movement, "Adagio con gran espressione," approaches the loftiness, sincerity, and style of a Beethoven adagio—in fact, it scarcely goes further in style, apart from some wider modulations and some chromatic figuration. The third movement, "Allegro ma non troppo," is a neatly defined scherzo, effective without any striking originality. And the finale, "Allegro agitato," is another complete "sonata form," this time in a more fluent and nearly *perpetuum mobile* style. Its most conspicuous feature is its start at a tonal tangent (Ex. 53).

Another somewhat withdrawn piano teacher in Berlin, more obscure but scarcely less interesting, was Liszt's sometime pupil **Rudolf Viole** (1825–67).[200] Viole left a total of eleven sonatas, all for piano solo. These consisted of an Op. 1 in bb, dedicated to Bülow and published in 1855, and a series of ten more sonatas, Opp. 21–30, published between about 1866 and 1871 (posthumous), singly dedicated to Tausig, Wagner, and Liszt, among others, and perhaps originally intended to cover the keys systematically (C, a, F, d, b, d, E, f, f♯, Eb, respectively). Of first importance was Op. 1, which followed Liszt's Sonata in b by only three years and reportedly followed its style and form, too, in a naively exaggerated way. Bülow gave extravagant endorsement to it in a long review[201] that anticipates curiously the bewildered yet defensive reviews of recent years greeting each new, *avante-garde* sonata of a Pierre Boulez or a Hans Werner Henze.[202] Salient portions of Bülow's wordy, repetitive, sometimes almost incomprehensible comments may be translated here:

---

in d for P & Vn), LXI/2 (1865) 277–78 (H. Zopff on the skills, yet the conservative adherence to Beethoven and Schumann styles, in Opp. 35/1 & 2, in d and F, for P & Vn; with several exx.), LXIX/1 (1869) 197–98 (on the continuing superiority and specific delights in Opp. 51 and 52 [in a for P & Vc]), and LXXIII/1 (1877) 133 and 146–47 (A. Maczewski, similarly on Op. 67 in g for P & Va). A performance of Op. 51 is cited in MW I (1870) 459. Cobbett/CHAMBER II 51–52 (W. Altmann) gives more praise and space than usual to sons. so nearly forgotten as Kiel's. A detailed study of Kiel's sons. is clearly needed.

200. The helpful, one-column summary in MGG XIII 1691 (R. Sietz), plus the reviews noted below, and the good list of works in PAZDÍREK XIV 248, have provided all the information available here, since it has not been possible to locate any of Viole's sons. themselves in the foreign and U.S. libraries approached for this purpose.

201. NZM XLV (1856) 21–23; also in BÜLOW BRIEFE III 140–44.

202. E.g., NOTES VIII (1950–51) 135 (W. S. Newman on Boulez's 2d P Son.).

Ex. 53. From the finale of Friedrich Kiel's Sonata in e, Op. 51, for P & Vn (after the original Simrock ed.).

A surprising, unsuspected music publisher in Weimar, who dresses up the first fruits of a composer still unknown with an elegance à la Breitkopf & Härtel—what critical raven might not scent out the "future" there! And in fact, a mere try at the sonata . . . a single glance at the first page suffices to confirm this [first impression]. Here, indeed, is music-of-the-future, in the superlative, [the] music-of-the-future of [the] music-of-the-future, [the] music-of-the-future to the third power, against which perhaps musicians-of-the-future themselves would protest if they were so timid as to believe themselves compromised through certain extravagances and eccentricities and were otherwise misled, through [concern for] tangible formalities, into myopic, unreasonable disregard of the heart and soul of an individuality. For many it may well be no small sacrifice to entrust themselves but superficially with a sonata in one movement lasting thirty-one closely engraved pages, [a work] that, at least *a [prima] vista,* poses many riddles to solve, many obstacles to overcome, no less to the eye of the reader than to the hand of the player. . . . It is evident that the composer wants to create a new musical speech. . . . [But] in the practical realization of this recognition [of such a need] he goes, in part much too far and, in part, in a false direction. . . . The choice of such a work [Liszt's] for a model was perhaps more of a foolhardy escapade than a voyage of discovery on his own. . . . [He seems to] have wanted to get an abstract design out of Liszt's very well patterned "yet" free form. . . . The structural composition of Viole shows along with many aberrations many logical, correct principles. Where construction is concerned a considerable know-how is at his command. A lively talent for [new] combinations is undeniable in the thematic development. The exploitation of the four-measure, main motive [theme?] (which was given by Franz Liszt to the composer to work out) is seldom halting and stagnant and has also surprised us all the more agreeably by its rhythmic variety, since this last means is so frequently neglected by the German composers working in increasingly inexcusable ignorance of the Berlioz disclosures in this sphere. [Etc.]

Four reviews by other writers describe the first six in Viole's cycle of ten sonatas.[203] They tell us of a planned increase in complexity of form, treatment, harmonic richness and exploration, and technical difficulty, from one sonata to the next, all within a constant three-movement cycle but with no obligation to repeat the forms in the single movements. They also tell of an individual, subjective style that stands apart in its time and grows in freshness, subjectivity, and flexibility from one sonata to the next. Obviously, a search for this music and, if it is found, a modern study of it are warranted, perhaps to be followed by a reprinting of at least some of it.

Besides Draeseke (supra) and Viole, a third Liszt pupil who wrote under the direct influence of the Sonata in b was the extraordinarily gifted but unhappily short-lived composer **Julius Reubke** (1834–58).[204] It was just after his five years of study and teaching in Berlin and while Reubke was working with Liszt in Weimar—that is, during the winter of 1856–57 or but one year before his death at twenty-four—that he wrote his only two sonatas. One of these was the now scarce and unjustly forgotten Grosse Sonate in b♭ for piano solo, dedicated to Liszt; and the other, which became much better known and is still often played, Der 94. Psalm, grosse Sonate für Orgel in c, dedicated to the important Leipzig teacher and conductor Carl Riedel. Both of these sonatas were originally published posthumously, through the efforts of Julius's brother Otto, in 1871, by J. Schuberth of Leipzig.[205] Harmonically and melodically Reubke's piano sonata smacks strongly of Liszt's Sonata in b. In expressive range and technical exploitation of the keyboard it goes even a bit further. Structurally, including the unifying motives and the less tangible double functions of cycle and form (now 3 mvts., F-S-VF, in one), it is similar though not identical to Liszt's sonata. In all these respects, it comes still closer than Draeseke's Op. 6 to Liszt's Sonata in b; and it is on a par in quality with Draescke's sonata.[206] Reubke's greatest talent appears in his impressively sonorous use of the piano, especially his dramatic rhapsodic

203. nzm LXII/2 (1866) 439–40 (Opp. 21 and 22), LXIII/1 (1867) 189–90 (Op. 23), LXIV/2 (1868) 237–38 (Opp. 24 and 25), LXV/2 (1869) 237–38 (Opp. 25, again, and 26).

204. Cf. mgg XI 326–28 (T.-M. Langner), with further bibliography.

205. hofmeister XX (1871) 143–44. Mod. eds.: Son. in b♭ ed. by A. Stradal and pub. in 1925 and 1940 by J. Cotta in Stuttgart (along with Stradal's P transcription of the organ son.); Son. in c, cf. mgg XI 328.

206. Cf., also, Georgii/klaviermusik 421–22.

Ex. 54. From the opening section of Julius Reubke's Sonata
in b♭ (after the J. Cotta reprint of 1940).

thrusts, his ingenious runs, and his stentorian chords (Ex. 54). As with
Hiller and other near greats, this talent seems somewhat less noteworthy when these anticipatory, harmonically active passages at last
arrive at a tonic and a melodic moment of truth (as at ms. 53 in E).
There also is an uncomfortably close resemblance, both melodic and
rhythmic, between Reubke's main motive and the "w" thematic element in Liszt's Sonata in b (*supra*), although one soon discovers how
much that motive was common property in the 19th century.

Reubke's popular organ sonata divides into three movements,
S/F-S-F, the finale being a big, contrapuntally rich fugue. The avoidance of a complete break between these movements and their unification through thematic transformation leave no doubt, again, that

Liszt's forms were much in mind. But there is no longer a double function, the music is more personal and subjective, and it is written in an intensely chromatic idiom that now suggests Franck more than Liszt. The sonorities, challenging the resources of the largest organs, and the figuration, challenging the most advanced pedal and manual techniques, are main strengths again. The more extended themes have somewhat firmer character in this work than in Reubke's Sonata in b♭. In the title reference to the 94th Psalm and in the specification of particular verses in the original edition, a programme is implied in this landmark of organ literature. But the exact association of the verses with the music has to be guessed at, as it has been by Harvey Grace.[207]

Woldemar Bargiel (1828–97), the disciple and brother-in-law of Schumann, studied under Mendelssohn and other of our notables here, then became a successful teacher himself in Berlin and elsewhere.[208] He left three sonatas among numerous other publications, one for P & Vn in f, Op. 10, first published in 1858,[209] one for P-duet in G, Op. 23, first published in 1864,[210] and one for P solo in C, Op. 34, first published in 1867.[211] These standardized, three-movement works confirm Bargiel's excellent composition training and also his keen understanding of both the piano and violin idioms. At the same time, alongside the much more progressive, imaginative products of a Reubke they reveal a more limited talent and circumscribed personality. In fact, they sound not only conservative but faintly scholastic. All the nicely turned phrases, fetching rhythms, and adroit polyphonic diversions, even the fairly advanced uses of the instruments, fit too patly to leave any real artistic challenge to the performer or listener. One finds it hard to take seriously such an inscription as the "ma con passione" that follows "Allegro moderato" at the start of Op. 34. Pertinent is Riemann's observation that with Bargiel "the Romantic school took a firm foothold for the first time in the circles of the academicians." [212]

Although their style is more complex, a similar evaluation must be made of the sonatas by the brilliant pianist and respected teacher

207. GROVE VII 134–35.
208. Cf. MGG I 1267–69 (A. Adrio).
209. Altmann/KAMMERMUSIK 193. Among later eds.: Wier/VIOLIN-m 65.
210. Altmann/KAMMERMUSIK 296.
211. Breitkopf & Härtel plate no. 11357. A performance of this work (in "A Dur"!) in Pittsburgh in 1877 is listed in NZM LXXIII/1 (1877) 64.
212. MGG I 1268. A brief appreciation of Op. 10 may be read in Cobbett/CHAMBER I 58 (W. Altmann), to be weighed against a report of it in MT XVI (1874) 449 as "abounding with passages of extreme beauty . . . [yet] wearisome in length, the last movement especially not having sufficient interest to rivet the attention of the listener throughout."

Xaver Scharwenka (1850–1924). Xaver was the younger and more successful of the two well-known brothers trained in Theodor Kullak's Neue Akademie der Tonkunst in Berlin.[213] His output[214] includes four solo and duo sonatas (and two piano sonatinas, Op. 52)—Opp. 6 in c♯ and 36 in E♭ (first pub. in 1871 and 1878 [215]) for P solo, Op. 2 in d for P & Vn (1872), and Op. 46a in e for P & Vc (1879).[216] In both solo sonatas, but not in the duos,[217] a scherzando is inserted before the middle of the usual three movements (F-S-F).[218] As a more mature sample than his Op. 6, Xaver's Op. 36 differs from Bargiel's Op. 34 in its more advanced harmony, its more chromatic, active inner voices, and its rather abrupt, truncated, rhythmically precious phrases. Since the themes and underlying harmony are essentially diatonic, the chromaticism serves mainly to create the activity in those inner voices. Its effect borders on the sentimental and detracts from the genuineness of highly competent writing as well as resourceful, pleasurable pianism.[219]

Two longtime Berliners, both pianists still writing in the Mendelssohnian manner, achieved considerable recognition in their day as composers, enough to insure them of substantial space in present-day music dictionaries, although their music is now all but forgotten. **Eduard Franck** (1817–93), who actually studied with Mendelssohn and was close to Schumann, Sterndale Bennett, and Ferdinand Hiller, is credited with 2 sonatas for Vn & P, 2 for Vc & P, and 9 for P solo published between 1846 and 1882.[220] A certain lack of originality in spite of secure compositional techniques is reported in one of the violin sonatas (Op. 19) and one of the cello sonatas (Op. 42),[221] and proves to characterize Franck's six piano sonatas Op. 40 and three piano sonatas Op. 44 as well.[222] **Heinrich Karl Johann Hofmann** (1842–1902), a

213. Cf. MGG XI 1602–6 (R. Sietz); H. Schonberg in *The New York Times* for Dec. 15, 1968, p. D27. Philipp Scharwenka is noted in SSB XI.

214. Cf. PAZDÍREK XIII 176–79. His prolificity is frowned upon in NZM LXXII/2 (1876) 305–6.

215. HOFMEISTER XX (1871) 155 and XXVII (1878) 267.

216. Altmann/KAMMERMUSIK 225 and 263.

217. Cf. Cobbett/CHAMBER II 332. Op. 2 was reviewed as a promising fluent, easy student work, showing a bit too much of Mendelssohn's influence, in NZM LXIX/1 (1873) 31. A performance of Op. 46a is listed in MT XXI (1880) 192.

218. Two reviews of Op. 6 offered moderate praise for both the writing skills and idiomatic keyboard treatment (MW III [1872] 470 [W. Freudenberg] and NZM LXIX/2 [1873] 361).

219. Yet it is praised for its noble themes as well as its skill in SMW XXXVI (1878) 580.

220. Cf. MGG IV 653–56 (F. Feldmann) with dated list (including 2 more Vn sons., one left in MS in 1861 and one, Op. 60, not pub. until 1910).

221. Cobbett/CHAMBER I 429 (W. Altmann) and NZM LXXIX/1 (1883), respectively.

222. Cf. NMZ V (1884) 54.

pupil of Theodor Kullak, is credited with but one full-scale sonata, Op. 67 in f, for Vn & P (1883), along with three diminutive sonatas for P-duet (Op. 86; 1887).[223] Similarly, the three movements of Op. 67 (VF-M-VF) are melodious, flowing, well-constructed applications of the standard forms, but routine in their stock accompaniments and chord progressions and in their predictably regular phrases.[224]

Further exploration of sonatas from Berlin in this period might include an Op. 1 in G for P-duet (1853?) by a teacher, director, and composer named **Ludwig Hoffmann** (1830–at least 1870), for this work was greeted by a seasoned reviewer as far above the usual Op. 1 in maturity, skill, depth, and keyboard treatment.[225] A Sonata in a, Op. 14, for P & Vn, and another in E, Op. 15, for P solo (both pub. in 1869) by the piano teacher **Constantin Bürgel** (1837–1909) won full-length, favorable reviews emphasizing his natural talent and almost unbridled passion in Op. 14.[226] A *Sonate in einem Satze* in A, Op. 2 (1863), by Bülow's pupil **Wilhelm Fritze** (1842–81), received similar praise, especially for its thematic development and harmony.[227] Several of the sonatas for Vn & P and Vc & P by "one of Germany's greatest women composers," **Emilie Meyer** (1812–83),[228] were published between 1863 and 1883. For these, prior to a more impartial estimate after her death, she received reviews that were variously chivalrous, cavalier, and facetious in their references to her high-minded goals, her dependence on Beethoven and other Classic models by way of her teacher Karl Loewe (ssb VIII), her feminine limitations not quite equal to the challenge of sonatas and symphonies, and her poetic inclinations.[229] The teacher **Leopold Amandus Leidgebel** (1816–86), a pupil of A. B. Marx, left a "third" Sonata for Vn & P, Op. 33 in E (1871) [230] that one reviewer commended highly for having the plasticity of Beethoven and

223. Cf. MGG VI 557–60 (T.-M. Langner), with full, dated list of works.

224. Like conclusions are reached in MW XVIII (1887) 434; but there is only approval in the short review in NZM LXXX/2 (1884) 343.

225. NZM XXXIX (1853) 186 (E. Klitzsch). Cf. Mendel/LEXIKON V 263–64.

226. MW I (1870) 210 (F. Stade on both sons.) and III (1872) 662–63 (C. Fuchs on Op. 15, with exx.). Cf., also, Riemann/LEXIKON I 248; Altmann/KAMMERMUSIK 198; NZM LXXII/2 (1876) 309 and 401 (on performances of, presumably, Op. 14).

227. NZM LVIII (1860) 189. Cf. NZM LXXII/1 (1876) 205, which also mentions a Son. in d, Op. 6, for Vn & P (1867); Riemann/LEXIKON I 543.

228. Cf. Ledebur/TONKÜNSTLER 357–58; Elson/WOMAN 161–62; Altmann/KAMMERMUSIK 215 and 260.

229. NZM LXIII/1 (1867) 181–82 (H. Zopff on Opp. 17 and 18), LXV/1 (1869) 215 (on Op. 21), LXIX/2 (1873) 387 (A. Winterberger on Op. 40), LXXX/2 (1884) 544–45 (posthumously on Op. 47). Cf. SSB III.

230. Altmann/KAMMERMUSIK 213. Cf. Schuberth/LEXIKON 310–11. HOFMEISTER VIII (1874–79) 321 also lists a Son. for P solo, Op. 40.

Schubert plus the Romantic warmth and poetry of Weber and Schumann.[231] And there were six duo sonatas—4 for Vc & P, one for Vn & P, and one for harp & P—by the popular harpist **Ferdinand Hummel** (1855–1928),[232] all of which but the harp sonata (1912) were early works published between 1877 and 1885 and generally reviewed as unoriginal and in a salon style inappropriate to the sonata.[233]

The most successful composer of "instructive sonatinas" in Berlin at this time was the pianist and teacher **Albert Loeschhorn** (1819–1905), several sets by whom, all oriented largely to Classic masters, appeared in the 1870's.[234]

Also waiting to be explored in the present day are the 5 sonatas and one Sonatine for P solo and the Sonata in E, Op. 83, for organ by the organist **Gustav Flügel** (1812–1900) in Stettin (inside the Polish border north of Berlin).[235] These works were published between about 1845 and 1881. Curiosity is aroused in his now scarce piano sonatas by five lengthy, interrelated, increasingly enthusiastic reviews by at least three different reviewers.[236] For example, the fourth piano sonata, Op. 20 in c, is viewed by no less a critic than Alfred Dörffel as arriving at the universality of an imminent master. And the fifth, Op. 36 in C, with its opening inscription (from Goethe), "Oh! Who [could] bring back the beautiful days, the lovely time!" is viewed by Emanuel Klitzsch as an essay in idyllic poetry.

In Hamburg, one of the best known composers in the later 19th century was **Cornelius Gurlitt** (1820–1901), who was actually there only after 1879 and after considerable activity elsewhere that had included close associations with the Schumanns, Carl Reinecke (*supra*), and Niels Gade (SSB XIII).[237] Gurlitt is of only minor interest here because his relatively few attempts at writing serious full-size sonatas,

---

231. MW III (1872) 614.

232. Cf. MGG VI 921–24 (T.-M. Langner).

233. E.g., MW X (1879) 366 (on Op. 9) XI (1880) 537 (on Opp. 2 and 12), XIII (1882) 555–56 (favorable on Op. 24, ded. to Joachim, "though a Joachim is not always on hand" to play the difficult coda of its finale). SMW XXXIX (1881) 1107 is also favorable on Op. 24, in a cautious way.

234. Cf. MGG VIII 1105 (K. Hahn); PAZDÍREK IX 579; MW II (1879) 314; MMR XX (1890) 274.

235. Cf. Mendel/LEXIKON III 578–79; Riemann/LEXIKON I 521; PAZDÍREK V 420–22. The Sonatine (Op. 54 in C) is briefly and favorably reviewed in NZM LI (1859) 209. On Flügel's fine organ music other than Op. 83 cf. Frotscher/ORGELSPIEL II 1172–73.

236. NZM XXIII (1845) 177–79 (on Op. 7, with exx.), XXIV (1846) 145 (on Op. 4), XXV (1846) 14 (on Op. 13), XXVIII (1848) 245–46 (A. Dörffel on Op. 20), XLI (1854) 77–78 (E. Klitzsch on Op. 36). No copies of these sons. turned up in the present study.

237. Cf. MGG V 1127–28, 1131 (W. Gurlitt).

from about 1844 to 1859,[238] gave way to the production of many, much more successful, pedagogic sonatinas over the next two decades. Apparently the several reviewers discouraged him from those serious works by making only incidental mentions of their good workmanship while deploring their derivative, even archaic styles, old-fashionedly thin textures, and frequent arid sections.[239] But, ironically for the state of pedagogy, they made more of the workmanship (which does stand high) while finding only slight reasons to deplore these same shortcomings when they came to writing their seemingly endless flow of repetitive short reviews that followed the seemingly endless flow of Gurlitt's sonatinas—in sets for P solo (including even a "Fugen Sonate," Op. 99), P-duet, P & Vn, and P & Vc—that the publishers were willing to keep publishing.[240]

There is more musical interest for us in the one solo and three duo sonatas by the cellist and conductor **Karl Grädener** (1812–83), who settled in Hamburg in 1848.[241] These include Op. 11 in d (not D) for P & Vn (pub. in 1853),[242] Op. 28 in c for P solo (1862?), Op. 59 in C for P & Vc (1873), and Op. 68 in B♭ for P & Cl.[243] A strong example of these is the solo sonata in three movements (VF-S-Sc), which has the bravura dash and octave scoring of Brahms's Op. 2 in f♯, and clearly recalls Brahms, too, in its motivic development and rich textures (especially its 3ds and 6ths; Ex. 55). Grädener's writing differs from that of Brahms (who reportedly acknowledged the high quality of his music) chiefly by being a bit more discursive, somewhat more direct and simple in harmony, and a little weaker in the character of its ideas.[244]

238. Cf. Altmann/KAMMERMUSIK 205 (but Op. 3 was pub. not later than 1844); HOFMEISTER V (1852–59) 151.

239. E.g., cf. NMZ XX (1844) 115–16 and XXVII (1847) 135–36 (both on Op. 3 for P & Vn-or-Vc), XXVIII (1848) 253 (on Op. 4 for P & Vn), XLIII (1855) 278–79 (with ex.) and LIV (1861) 50 (both on Op. 16 for P solo), XLIX (1858) 49–50 (R. Viole [supra] on Op. 20 for P solo); MW I (1870) 564 (on Op. 21).

240. Cf. PAZDÍREK VI 679–87. Sample reviews: NZM LXXII/1 (1876) 106, with ex. (arguing that even in a sonatina one expects 19th-c. styles, not 18th-c.); MW VI (1875) 291, X (1879) 325; MMR XII (1882) 160–61 and 208, XIII (1883) 69, XVII (1887) 65, XX (1890) 82, etc.

241. Cf. MGG V 659–61 (K. Stephenson), with errors in the list of works.

242. Altmann/KAMMERMUSIK 205 also lists 2 sonatinas for Vn & P, Op. 41 (reviewed in NZM LVI [1856] 219 and further described by Wilhelm Altmann in Cobbett/CHAMBER I 485).

243. Op. 68 is listed only in PAZDÍREK VI 486.

244. E. Klitzsch's favorable review of this work (NZM LVI [1862] 218–19) does not mention Brahms but commends Grädener for freeing himself from an earlier influence of Schumann. Liszt, understandably, did not take much pleasure in Op. 28 when Grädener visited him in Weimar in 1855 (letter of May 7, 1855, in LISZT/ Amie 15).

Ex. 55. From the first movement of Karl Grädener's Sonata
in c, Op. 28 (after the 2d revised ed. of F. Schuberth in 1878).

This chapter may be completed with the naming of two other prolific
and, evidently, successful composers of light, educational sonatinas in
Hamburg—**Albert Biehl** (1833–at least 1892?) [245] and **Louis Bödecker**
(1845–99).[246]

245. Cf. Schuberth/LEXIKON 58; PAZDÍREK II 670–74; MW X (1879) 300 and 325, XI
(1880) 562, XIV (1883) 508.
246. Cf. Riemann/LEXIKON I 192; PAZDÍREK II 829; MW XI (1880) 608.

Late Romantics in Austria, Germany, and Switzerland

Quantity and Quality

This chapter brings to an end our account of Romantic sonata composers in Austrian, German, and Swiss centers. It covers about a generation, from around 1885 to 1915 or the start of World War I (1914). As for the political environment in, for, or against which these composers operated, it was largely an extension of that summarized at the start of Chapter IX. The Austro-Hungarian Monarchy had to cope with growing nationalistic forces and to struggle against increasing ethnic frictions that embittered the Balkan and Slavic states, especially Serbia, and ultimately led to the start of World War I. In Germany the autocratic, one-man rule, from 1888, of Emperor William II, King of Prussia, favored notable growth in economic prosperity, military and naval power, and social reforms, all falsely pointing to German invincibility when war broke out.

Throughout this late-Romantic phase the quantity of sonata production continued surprisingly high. If that production takes proportionately less space here, permitting both Austrian and German activities to fit into one chapter, the reason is simply the historiographic tendency to pay less attention to epigones than pioneers. Not a few composers who once made appreciable marks with their sonatas can get only bare mentions here, and only for the sake of a more rounded view. In the same period the quality of production continued surprisingly high, too. In fact, it may have been generally and relatively higher than in our two previous phases of the Romantic Era. One explanation might be the greater sophistication, through accumulated experience, of composer, performer, and listener alike, tending either to scare off or to indoctrinate more of those rank novitiates who had previously dared to see their untutored sonatas in print. Even so, there

Marteau in Frankfurt/M. On the same program was Ludwig Thuille's Sonata in e, Op. 30, for P & Vn (*supra*), which proved to serve as but a weak foil to Op. 72. And sitting in front were two recognized critics from Munich who would have reacted still more venomously had they realized that behind Reger's genial performance and music were some bitter slashes aimed back at them in the music itself, perhaps inspired by the parodying of his critics that Strauss had introduced into *Ein Heldenleben* in Frankfurt/M five years earlier.

Actually, Reger, piqued by growing hostility to his "new music" and "progress," [88] had courted the controversy over Op. 72. His first idea had been to dedicate the work to "The German critics," but neither this dedication nor his inscription "To Many" in the autograph got past the publisher into print.[89] However, "many" must have recognized the musical motives that spell out "sheep" and "monkeys," which, like B-a-c-h in the third movement (ms. 33), are skillfully interwoven into all four, especially the outer, movements (Ex. 62; with S for *Es* or E♭ and *b* for B♭, as usual).[90] Reger himself was especially fond of this bold yet heartfelt work. After that early performance he wrote, "I am certainly not arrogant, but this much still becomes clear to me, that in Frankfurt my Op. 72 was in every respect the best work." Moreover, three weeks later he concluded, ". . . if one looks more closely, there is nothing simpler or clearer than my Op. 72; and it is a truly grievous sign of the colossal depths of the 'current' musical intelligence when one can write about the 'total perversity,' incurable sickness, [and] nerve-killing unnaturalness of my Op. 72." [91]

Today, one can certainly agree that Reger's later sonatas (and other music) continued to be logical and purposeful as regards the forms, even in their complex fantasy, and also the over-all key relationships of the cycles. Both the forms and key choices are traditional and surprisingly straightforward (a fact already surmisable from the foregoing chart of movements and keys), although his "sonata forms" become increasingly asymmetrical, elastic, dualistic, and expressively refined, with a seamless flow like that of Wagner or Bruckner.[92] But the harmony, especially the voice-leading and more local or transitory modulations, do make for a problem—in fact, *the* problem as well as the most

88. Cf. Bagier/REGER 64–65.

89. Cf. Stein/VERZEICHNIS 136.

90. The motives are not so identified in the printed ed., but a letter from Reger of Nov. 1, 1903, first pub. in Heger/REGER, leaves no doubt as to his intentions.

91. Both letters, June 16 and July 25, 1904, to K. Straube, are quoted in Stein/REGER 105. In DM III/4 (1903–4) 463, W. Altmann wrote of the "cacophony" in Op. 72. Much more sympathetic are the reviews of Opp. 72 and 78 in NZM CI (1905) 866 and of Op. 78 in DM IV/4 (1904–5) 287 (H. Schlemüller).

92. Cf. Denecke/REGER.

Ex. 62. From the final climax of the development section in the first movement of Max Reger's Sonata in C, Op. 72 (after Reger/WERKE-m XIX 113).

conspicuous style determinant—in Reger's music. In 1920 one of Reger's students, the theorist, and composer Hermann Grabner, wrote a useful monograph on Reger's harmony, starting with the fact that Reger repeatedly insisted on the complete logic and "legality" of his harmony, then going on to expound five basic laws formulated by Reger to comprehend all (late-Romantic) harmonic behavior.[93] Briefly and in slightly modernized terms: (1) all harmonic activity, even the most remote, goes back to the three primary triads—I, V, and IV—and to nothing else. Contrary to implications in Baroque thorough bass, ii, iii, vi, and vii are not independent chords but merely substitutes (having 2 notes in common) for IV, I or V, I or IV, and V, respectively. Even alterations like B-D♭-F-A (or -A♭) for V in C are included within what then becomes a very wide and flexible orbit. (2) Extending the first law, a chord (or incipient 2-note chord) functions as I, IV, or V (regardless of chromatic alterations) when it bears a third-relationship (of roots) to any of these. Thus, the progression from A♭-C-E♭ to C-E-G can sound like a plagal cadence, and Reger's much cultivated Nea-

93. Grabner/REGER 1–12; written, of course, in full cognizance of Reger's own *Beiträge zur Modulationslehre* (1903 and later eds.).

politan-6th triad like iv. (3) The primary triads can be extended without modulating to encompass—parenthetically, as it were—the V-of-V and IV-of-IV. For example, a tonic triad on E will relate to the triads on B and F♯ and on A and D. One curious concomitant of this law is Reger's idea that the V-of-V may progress directly to the tonic in slow music but only after a pause in faster music. (4) Any chord may connect with any chord, except that obscure progressions may require the clarification of an intervening chord. But Reger is less likely than the listener to feel any clarification is needed, or he may supply no more than a chromatic inflection in a quick modulation attenuated to a unison passage. And finally, (5) Enharmony, including all spellings of each dim.-7th chord, may serve to bring foreign keys within the orbit of the home key.

All of which rationale seems logical and traditional enough except for oddities like that pause in faster music between V-of-V and I, or loopholes like that question of when a clarifying interpolation is needed. But one must grant that such exceptions, along with abrupt, rhythmically truncated modulations, persistent chromaticism, and angular voice-leading, can bring even a relatively short and spare piece like the piano Sonatina in a, Op. 89/4, momentarily to the edge of atonality (Ex. 63).[94] And taking a larger tonal view, one must grant a certain over-all effect, even in so rich and subjective a work as the cello Sonata in a/A, Op. 116, of monotonality, not relieved by the more specific effect of a chromatic whine in much of the cello line. But these "problems" and the fault of writing (and publishing) more than could be kept under good qualitative control, should not impede a renaissance, or at least re-evaluation, of Reger's music outside as well as inside Germany. For, sticking to the sonatas, there is much of musical wonderment, glory, and soul to be heard yet in this composer so prodigal with his talents—in the deft, muted, triple-*piano*, flawlessly formed, scherzando "Presto" of that same cello sonata, for example; or the sections of driving, soaring passion in the first movement, especially, of the ninth and last violin sonata, Op. 139; or the profoundly expressive slow movement of the third and last clarinet sonata, Op. 107;[95] or the astute recollections of Bach in the "chaconne" finale in

94. On Reger's modulations and approaches to atonality, cf. Truscott/REGER (with reply by E. Wellesz); also, Austin/20th 144–47. Even the 4 sonatinas Op. 89 got mixed reactions, favorable to nos. 1 and 2 and unfavorable to nos. 3 and 4 in DM V/3 (1905–6) 107 (H. Teibler) and VIII/3 (1908–9) 104–5 (W. Niemann), respectively. The 2 Vn sonatinas Op. 103B are similarly subtle and beyond the range of "house music" (cf. their review in DM X/3 [1910–11] 313), which is also how W. Altmann viewed Op. 122 (DM XI/2 [1911–12] 168).

95. Cf. the review in DM IX/4 (1909–10) 250 (W. Altmann).

the last of each set of unaccompanied violin sonatas,[96] and the stunning fugue that caps the second organ sonata, Op. 60 (whose first 2 mvts. are called "Improvisation" and "Invokation").[97]

Next to Reger the most important composer of sonatas (and other music) in Leipzig was one of his close friends and immediate disciples, **Sigfrid Karg-Elert** (1877–1933).[98] This harmonium virtuoso, belated organist, and generally versatile musician left some 27 sonatas and sonatinas, 20 of them published (between 1905 and 1929),[99] among a large number of varied works ranging from small piano pieces and songs to substantial solo, chamber, orchestral, and choral works. There are 2 sonatas and 3 sonatinas for "Kunstharmonium," which to Karg-Elert meant not only the special (reed) harmonium on which he ex-

Ex. 63. From the opening page of the first movement in Max Reger's Sonatina in a, Op. 89/4 (after Reger/WERKE-m XI–65).

celled but the (pipe) organ when played on the manuals only, for intimate music;[100] one free but not short "Sonatina" for the organ using pedal board, too; 5 sonatas and 3 sonatinas for P solo, "Sonata Carla Madonna" and "Sonata esaltata" in MS; 7 sonatas for 6 different, unaccompanied orchestral instruments, including Vn, Va, Cl (2), Fl ("Sonata appassionata"), saxophone, and Bn; and 7 duos, in-

96. On these sons. cf. Gates/SOLO 197–208, with exx.
97. On this son. (generally preferred to the first organ son.) cf. Brennecke/REGER 390–91; on its fugue, in particular, cf. pp. 184–85 in a diss. on Reger's fugues by one of his students, Gatscher/REGER.
98. MGG VII 682–88 (R. Sietz), with dated list of works and further references.
99. The first and last sons. left in MSS, for oboe and P and Vn & organ, respectively, are dated 1898 and 1927.
100. Cf. GROVE IV 74 (A. J. Hipkins), 703 (H. Grace), 870–71 (E. Blom); Sceats/KARG-ELERT 9.

cluding P & Vn (2), P & Vc, Fl & P, Ob & P, Cl & P ("Sonata quasi fantasia"), and Vn & organ ("Sonata quasi canzona"). Although Karg-Elert made his chief mark with his organ music, the sonatas he wrote for harmonium and organ were too early to be fully representative of his mature styles and forms, the latest being composed in 1912.[101] The published duo sonatas were similarly too early to be fully representative, only the MS duos being later.[102] All in all, as a sonata composer Karg-Elert seems to have offered most in his piano music. But only the needed full study of his sonatas, including the unpublished MSS, can confirm or correct that opinion. And such a study ought to be made before he slips entirely into the oblivion that now hides not a few other significant late Romantics.[103]

Karg-Elert's mature, boldly experimental music is said to combine the virtuosic splash of Liszt (by way of A. Reisenauer's instruction), the precise craftsmanship of Reinecke (another of his instructors), the artistic folk treatment of Grieg (a warm supporter), and the polyphonic breadth of Reger.[104] His style might best be explained further through an examination of one of his most mature, developed, phrenetic works, *Dritte Sonate* (*Patetica*) in c♯, Op. 105, for P solo, composed in 1920[105] and first published in 1922. This is a big, one-movement sonata of 570 measures in 37 pages—big in length, emotional range, and pianistic demands. Its emotional and dynamic programme is indicated not only by "Patetica" in the title but by a Brahman wisdom inscribed at the start: "Death is life; life death. Out of the night the dawn. Out of the twilight the night. And the full circle is completed." Abundant advices—a few in Italian, most in German—and dynamic as well as articulation signs and footnotes add much detail, not unlike that in Scriabin's sonatas, to the emotional program: for example, "striding solemnly," "like muted horns," and triple *piano* at

101. Descriptions of these works occur in Sceats/KARG-ELERT 9, 10, 12–13, 18; Frotscher/ORGELSPIEL II 1248. A short favorable review of Sonatinas in G and a, Op. 14/1 and 3, for harmonium, occurs in DM VIII/4 (1908–9) 315. Mr. Stephen E. Young is completing a Ph.D. diss. on Karg-Elert's organ works, at the University of N.C. as of this writing (1968).

102. But even Op. 71 in A, for P & Vc, although composed as early as 1907, was already being criticized for "unprecedentedly many rhythmic and harmonic sophistries" (DM IX/4 [1909–10] 186); it is viewed more kindly in MW XLI (1910) 378 and in Cobbett/CHAMBER II 47–48 (R. Felber). Op. 88 is reviewed favorably as a demanding work, modern yet still related to Bach's unaccompanied Vn sons. (DM XI/2 [1911–12] 203 [W. Altmann]).

103. Even now (1967), whereas a few works by Reger are still available on recordings, not a single work by Karg-Elert is listed in the standard catalogues.

104. MGG VII 686.

105. According to MGG VII 684, although "[28/9. 1914]" appears beside his name in the pub. score.

the start; elsewhere, "suddenly very violent," "sinister stirring" and "secretive, spooky," "lingering and musing, still calmer, longingly"; and near the end, a quadruple-*forte* climax, followed by a quintuple-*piano* ending.

This sonata is multisectional in form, too much so to suggest any kind of standard sonata cycle, or any double function of cycle within single form such as Liszt created. Yet there is unity in the return at the end to the hushed, mystical opening, in keeping with the full circle of that Brahman wisdom; in the consistently rhapsodic style, implemented by the many contrasting sections, meter changes, and wide-ranging, idiomatic, proselike figurations (including a Schumann-esque section on one staff, mss. 450–93); and in the over-all tonal course, which touches simply and traditionally enough on c♯, E, A, A♭ (V of c♯), c♯, b♭, c♯, A♭, A, e♭, b♭, a, C♯, and c♯, among main keys. The many sections are based variously, often in contrapuntal combinations, on no fewer than fifteen identifiable motives. (Indeed, the motives have been enumerated in the printed score, presumably by the composer, not only for the first entry of each but at the resumption of each after it has been discontinued for a while.) Motive no. 14 (introduced on p. 12) is the opening of a chorale set by Bach, "Straf' mich nicht in deinem Zorn" ("Punish me not in Thy wrath"), which motive figures significantly in the return to calm and the air of sweet resignation near the end.

In spite of such structural freedom and his disregard for the traditional designs and cycles that Reger preserved so faithfully, Karg-Elert was still like Reger in making his chief advances (and arousing his main opposition) through his harmony. He, too, stretched and extended traditional principles, on occasion, to the very brink of atonality. But his method was not so much one of increasingly remote interpretations of chord relations as of increasingly oblique rather than vertical relations of both chord and foreign tones.[106] By such means and a fair amount of harmonic and melodic chromaticism he produces passages with parallel 4ths and 5ths or suggestions of linear counterpoint that seem to embrace the very styles of the three "radical leftists"—Schoenberg, Debussy, and Scriabin—with whom he decided not to join during his creative crisis of about 1915.[107] Yet, though he strained traditional harmonic limits as much as Reger had, and more than Schoenberg in *Verklärte Nacht,* the results now seem more dated, with tendencies not unlike MacDowell's toward a cloying of the appetite in

---

106. Hasse/KARG-ELERT is a helpful study of the harmonic style in the light of Karg-Elert's own notable writings on harmony.
107. Cf. MGG VII 686.

Ex. 64. From a late section (mss. 401–8) of Sigfrid Karg-
Elert's *Dritte Sonate* (*Patetica*) in c♯, Op. 105 (after the original
Simrock ed. of 1922, recopyrighted in 1950, and used by kind
permission of the pub. and Associated Music Pubs., Inc., sole
agents for the U.S.A.).

sweet melodious phrases and the abetting of bombast in those more
phrenetic moments (Ex. 64).

The published sonatas of a few other composers in and near Leipzig
have already disappeared from view. Another expert on the harmonium, **August Reinhard** (1831–1912) in Ballenstedt to the northwest,
left three sonatinas, Op. 38, and two sonatas, Opp. 84 and 85 (both
pub. in 1903–4) for his instrument. The latter were greeted as skillful,
effective pieces for that instrument.[108] Another organist, at the Thomas-
kirche in Leipzig, was **Carl Piutti** (1846–1902), composer of three
organ sonatas published between 1875 and 1896.[109] The first of these—
"The Wedding: a cycle of four pieces in the form of a sonata"—proved
disappointingly commonplace to one reviewer, who had hoped for a
symphonic poem for organ with further inscriptions elucidating the
title.[110] Still another organist was the pupil of Draeseke and Schulz-

108. DM II/3 (1903) 449 and 451 (M. Puttmann), and III/3 (1903–4) 51 (A. Göttmann).

109. Cf. Riemann/LEXIKON II 1399; Kremer/ORGAN 214.

110. MW VI (1875) 224, with exx.

Beuthen, **Paul Claussnitzer** (1867–1924), whose organ *Choral-Sonate zur Totenfeier* in c, Op. 30, was published in 1912.[111]

A theory instructor at the Leipzig Conservatory, **Gustav Ernst Schreck** (1849–1918), was hailed for his highly competent, if somewhat academic, contribution to the limited literature of sonatas for Ob & P (Op. 13, 1889?).[112] He also left a Sonata for Bn & P, Op. 9. The largely self-taught composer and protégé of Grieg, **Robert Hermann** (1869–1912), left one published sonata, Op. 13 in c♯ for P & Vn, which was reviewed as being exceptionally and consistently original and attractive, sometimes rising to unexpected expressive heights.[113]

Once successful composers of light pedagogic and diversionary sonatas or sonatinas in Leipzig still deserve a mention, including **Albert Karl Tottmann** (1837–1917);[114] **Wilhelm Moritz Vogel** (1849–1922) for several sets;[115] the better known author and pianist **Walter Niemann** (1876–1953), for some two-dozen pleasant, innocuous short sonatas or sonatinas mostly bearing titles of nature, folklore, poetry, or romance;[116] the chamber music specialist **Fritz von Bose** (1865–at least 1929) for three sets of piano sonatinas;[117] the violinist **Richard Hofmann** (1844–1918), for about two-dozen more sonatinas, scored variously for P solo, P-duet, Vn & P, Va & P, Vc & P, Ob & P, and Cl & P;[118] and the important cellist **Julius Klengel** (1859–1933), for two sets of three sonatinas each as well as a sonata for his instrument.[119]

In Dresden only minor composers of sonatas are to be found at the end of the Romantic Era. Four organ sonatas by **Friedrich Oskar Wermann** (1840–1906), pupil of Merkel and Wieck, were published in the two decades from about 1885 to 1905,[120] and at least eleven of fourteen others by the organist **Ernst Hans Fährmann** (1860–1940), pupil of J. L. Nicodé, appeared, plus a solo piano sonata, Op. 6,

---

111. Cf. Riemann/LEXIKON I 324–25. Op. 30 is damned with faint praise in DM XII/2 (1912–13) 364 (E. Schnorr).

112. NZM LXXXV/2 (1889) 425 and MW XXI (1890) 490. Cf. MGG XII 69–70 (G. Hempel).

113. DM V/4 (1905–6) 177 (W. Altmann). Cf. Riemann/LEXIKON I 742.

114. Cf. Riemann/LEXIKON II 1871; PAZDÍREK XIV 257; SMW XL (1882) 819 (praising Op. 32 for Vn open strings & P!).

115. Cf. Riemann/LEXIKON II 1955; PAZDÍREK XIV 269.

116. Cf. MGG IX 1517–21 (R. Sietz); DM XII/4 (1912–13) 317 (R. H. Stein on Op. 24), XV/2 (1915) 616 (on Opp. 60, 75, and 83).

117. Cf. Riemann/LEXIKON I 209; DM XII/2 (1912–13) 42 (Jenö Kerntler).

118. Cf. Riemann/LEXIKON I 770–71; PAZDÍREK VII 599–605.

119. Cf. MGG VII 1222–23, 1225 (R. Eller); Cobbett/CHAMBER II 53 (H. Leichtentritt); DM X/4 (1910–11) 374 (H. Schlemüller).

120. Cf. Riemann/LEXIKON II 2013–14; Kremer/ORGAN 230; MW XXX (1899) 642 (on Son. 3 as an improvement over 1 and 2, but still weak in ideas and development).

in the nearly three decades from 1891 to about 1918.[121] Fährmann's later organ sonatas were welcomed as resourceful, harmonically clever, eclectic pieces.[122] And there was a spate of weak to fair sonatas for cello and piano, including Op. 27 in D (1891) by Swiss-born **Albert Fuchs** (1858–1910), who also wrote a prize-winning Sonata in f, Op. 11 (1887), for P solo and three sonatinas for P & Vn, Op. 36 (1898);[123] Op. 4 in f♯ (1887) by the organist **Maximilian Heidrich** (1864–1909; father of the infamous Nazi SS officer), who had known Liszt in Weimar and also left a Sonata in g, Op. 12 (1888) for P & Vn and a big, impassioned, traditional "Phantasie-Sonate" in D, Op. 70 (1914, posthumous) for P solo;[124] Opp. 10 in D and 15 in A (1898 and 1910) by an English pianist and pupil of Draeseke among others, **Percy Sherwood** (1866–1939), who also left a Sonata in F, Op. 12, for P & Vn (1907), two sonatinas, Op. 22, for P solo (1913?), and an unpublished Sonata for 2 Ps;[125] Op. 18 in C (1908) by another Draeseke pupil, **Leland A. Cossart** (1877–?), who also left a Sonata in D, Op. 27, for P & Vn (1913);[126] and Op. 23 in b (1908) by still another Draeseke pupil, the pianist **Theodor Blumer** (1882–1964), who also left sonatas for P & Vn (Opp. 33 in d [1914] and 43 in c [1920]) and P & Fl (Op. 61 in D [1928]).[127] The violinist and choral conductor **Reinhold Becker** (1842–1924) may be added, too, for one highly commended, difficult Sonata in g for P & Vn, Op. 150 (1911).[128]

In Magdeburg to the northwest, there is only the successful choral composer and conductor **(Wenzel) Josef Krug (Krug-Waldsee;** 1858–1915) to mention, and only one sonata by him to list—a conventional,

121. Cf. Riemann/LEXIKON I 484; Kremer/ORGAN 182–83.

122. E.g., DM III/2 (1903–4) 116 (K. Straube), VI/4 (1906–7) 308, X/1 (1910–11) 375 (E. S. v. Carolsfeld), XIII/3 (1913–14) 176 (E. Schnorr); NZM CIV (1904) 620; MW XXXVII (1906) 44a, XLI (1910) 176.

123. Cf. MGG IV 1072–74 (A. Berner); MW XXVII (1896) 178 (praising Op. 11 and, especially, Op. 27 for its fantasy-ballade style, varied rhythms, and rich harmony).

124. Cf. Riemann/LEXIKON I 728; DM III/2 (1903–4) 52 (H. Schlemüller on Op. 4 as skillful but not distinctive).

125. Cf. GROVE VII 759–60 (J. A. Fuller-Maitland); Altmann/KAMMERMUSIK 227 and 264; MW XXX (1899) 494 and SMW LVII (1899) 354 (with praise and reservations for Op. 10); MW XL (1909–10) 539 (Max Unger on Op. 15 as a large-scale, Brahmsian work); DM XIII/2 (1913–14) 165 (A. Nadel on Op. 22/1 & 2).

126. Cf. Riemann/LEXIKON I 347; Altmann/KAMMERMUSIK 199 and 254; Cobbett/CHAMBER I 303; DM VIII/2 (1908–9) 284, with limited praise for Op. 18, and XIII/3 (1913–14) 106 (with more praise for Op. 27).

127. Cf. Riemann/LEXIKON I 289; BAKER Suppl. 15; Altmann/KAMMERMUSIK 196, 253, and 272; DM VIII/2 (1908–9) 284 (A. Laser decrying Op. 23 as alternately bombastic and trivial) and XIII/4 (1913–14) 230 (W. Altmann approving Op. 33 except for its length).

128. Cf. Riemann/LEXIKON I 132; DM XI/1 (1911–12) 236 (W. Altmann); Cobbett/CHAMBER I 80 (W. Altmann).

trite work in c, Op. 38 (1905), in four movements (F-S-M-VF), its only distinction being good contrapuntal interest.[129] In Kassel, southwest of Magdeburg, **Richard Franck** (1858–1938), who had studied with his father Eduard in Berlin (SSB X), rose to no significant creative heights in his four well-schooled, generally light, pleasant duo sonatas, two each for P & Vn and P & Vc (1890–1903).[130] In Marburg, farther southwest, **Gustav Jenner** (1865–1920), Brahms's biographer and only composition student (during most of 1888–1895), was active after 1900. His two published sonatas—for P & Cl in G, Op. 5 (1900), and P & Vn in a, Op. 8 (1905)—are reported to be able works dominated by his teacher's influence.[131] Also in Marburg and under Brahms's strong influence (as well as Schumann's) was the violinist **Richard Barth** (1850–1923), whose three sonatas for P & Vn were published between 1899 and 1915.[132]

Among minor composers in Köln, **Ewald Strässer** (1867–1933) stands out, although his published works include only one sonata, actually a *Kleine Sonate* in f♯, Op. 54, for P solo.[133] This is a rather objective, melodious, pleasant, readily playable work in three short movements (F-S-F). It presents a stylistic melange in that it follows traditional paths and molds except for repeated, momentary digressions into harmonic progressions and relationships about as remote and abrupt as Reger's. In the middle movement the melodic and harmonic flavor is a kind of synthesis of Johann and Richard Strauss. The piano pedagog and writer **Otto Adolf Klauwell** (1851–1917) may be noted, too, in Köln, not especially for his violin sonata (Op. 6 in c, 1874)[134] and two piano sonatinas that had appeared but for his contribution of 1899 to the very few books on sonata history published in the 19th century.[135]

A U.S. expatriate to Germany, the conductor **Frank L. Limbert** (1866–1938), was studying in Frankfurt/M or Berlin when one sonata each appeared for P & Vn (Op. 4 in A, 1890) and P & Va (Op. 7

129. Cf. MGG VII 1835–36 (R. Schaal); NZM CI (1905) 543; DM V/2 (1905–6) 336 (W. Fischer).
130. Cf. Riemann/LEXIKON I 534; Altmann/KAMMERMUSIK 203 and 256; Cobbett/CHAMBER I 429 (W. Altmann); DM II/1 (1902–3) 208 and 210 (H. Schlemüller), II/2 (1902–3) 39 and 43 (W. Altmann), III/1 (1903–4) 135 (H. Schlemüller) and 287 (W. Altmann); MW XXV (1904) 324 (E. Segnitz).
131. Cf. MGG VI 1881–83 (R. Schaal); Cobbett/CHAMBER II 35 (W. W. Cobbett). Kohleick/JENNER is a study of the man and his music in relation to Brahms, including comments, with exx., on the sons. (pp. 58–61).
132. Cf. Riemann/LEXIKON I 114; Cobbett/CHAMBER I 60 (W. W. Cobbett). Op. 14 is reviewed in SMW LVIII (1900) 355 as a solid, resourceful work.
133. Cf. MGG XII 1433–34 (J. Schwermer), with further bibliography.
134. Reviewed favorably in SMW XXXIII (1875) 402.
135. Cf. Riemann/LEXIKON I 900; SBE 11–12.

in c, 1892).[136] The first was reviewed as large but empty and the second as revealing individualities (such as 5-beat meter in the finale) but as being severe, brooding, and still well short of a masterpiece.[137] Also in Frankfurt/M, a student of Raff and Liszt, **Anton Urspruch** (1850–1907), left one published sonata each for P & Vn (Op. 28 in d, 1894) and P & Vc (Op. 29 in D, 1894), following his debut in print with a *Sonata quasi fantasia* in D, Op. 1, for P-duet.[138] Op. 29 was reviewed as a convincing, effective work in which counterpoint is the essential and omnipresent means both in the presentation and development of its ideas.[139] In Wiesbaden, west of Frankfurt/M, the pianist **Nicolai von Wilm** (1834–1911) showed much composition know-how (as well any such prolific composer might) in at least a half-dozen conservative yet fresh and attractive sonatas published between about 1883 and 1899. These include two for P & Vn, one for P & Vc, and three delightful sonatinas for P solo that once were in the hands of many students.[140]

Finally, in central Germany, the important late-Romantic German **Hans Pfitzner** (1869–1949) was still a student in the Frankfurt/M Conservatory when he wrote the first of his two published sonatas, both duos.[141] This first one is Op. 1 in f♯, published in 1892. It is a long work (1,180 mss. in all), cast in the usual four movements (F-S-VF-F) and standard designs (all but ii, in binary design, being "son.-allegro" forms). Although its fluency and lyricism trace back directly to Mendelssohn, it has enough harmonic and chromatic enrichment and enough melodic and rhythmic originality to stand on its own. In fact, cellists who do not know this work (and how many musicians know Pfitzner's music outside of Germany?) are missing a remarkably expressive, potent addition to today's concert repertoire.

Pfitzner's other sonata, Op. 27 in e/E, for Vn & P, was started about 1918, during his last year in Strasbourg, and completed that year, but not published until 1922. By now Pfitzner was already becoming involved in the controversies, bitterness, disappointments,

136. Cf. Riemann/LEXIKON I 1043; Altmann/KAMMERMUSIK 214 and 248.
137. MW XXI (1890) 427, XXVIII (1897) 194; SMW XLIV (1892) 690–91.
138. Cf. MGG XIII 1180–81 (T. Kircher-Urspruch).
139. SMW LIV (1893) 850; MW XXVI (1895) 567.
140. Cf. GROVE IX 310 (J. A. Fuller-Maitland); Altmann/KAMMERMUSIK 232 and 266; MW XIV (1883) 520 (on the 3 sonatinas). The P "Sonate" in f, reported favorably in NZM LXXIII/1 (1877) 210, must be the 4-mvt. "Fantasie" in that key listed in HOFMEISTER X (1886–91) 875. Wilm's "Duo" for Vn & harp (Op. 156, 1898) is called a son. in BAKER 1802.
141. Cf. MGG X 1170–80 (W. Mohr), with full dated list and further references. The 2 sons. are analyzed in detail in the excellent recent diss. Henderson/PFITZNER (on the man and his instrumental works), pp. 154–73 and 239–56, respectively; cf., also, pp. 3, 12, 19, 65, and 66–67; and Cobbett/CHAMBER II 216–17 (R. Felber).

enmities, and tragedies that were to hang with increasing heaviness over his long career. Even though he was no conscious programmatist in his chamber music, he may have been reflecting some of his uncertainties at this point, in Op. 27—especially the conflict of the artist's need to advance and his own increasing conservatism, if not reactionism, as stated in his belated, sharp, chauvinistic reply of 1917 (*Futuristengefahr*) to Busoni's celebrated *Entwurf . . .* of 1909.[142] At any rate, Op. 27, a three-movement cycle (F-S-VF) of 654 measures, is viewed here as a curiously unequal, often ineffectual work—hardly a primary item in Pfitzner's total output. Its considerable technical demands for both instruments are on a par with those of Op. 1. But except for its finale, which is its most successful movement, anyway, it lacks the melodic strength and tonal purposefulness of the earlier work.[143] More disturbing is the harmonic idiom, which varies from conventional, occasionally banal, progressions to empirical progressions that too often seem to turn back on themselves without any expressive accomplishment or even the more abstruse paper logic of Reger's harmony. At best, this harmony reminds us of Pfitzner's strong devotion to Wagner's music (Ex. 65).

Composers of Exceptional Skill in North Germany

Among surprisingly many composers of real stature active in Berlin around the turn of this century, the most significant and influential man, the eminent pianist **Ferrucio Benvenuto Busoni** (1866–1924), can get only tangential mention here. It is not that his three early sonatas (1883–98) and six later duo sonatinas (1910–20) represent so small a part of his output, but that the latter in particular mark a conscious break with the past and striving toward the future.[144] In other words, among the borderlanders this fine, idealistic humanitarian musician belongs in spirit if not in style more with contemporary early-Moderns, like Debussy, Schoenberg, Scriabin, and Joseph Haas, than with contemporary late-Romantics, like Strauss, Reger, Pfitzner, and Karg-Elert. Even his Second Sonata for P & Vn, Op. 36a in e (composed in 1898, first pub. in 1901), has sections that anticipate his break with traditional tonality. In fact, this powerful, lyrical, deeply expressive, highly Romantic, often rhapsodic duo in four move-

142. Cf. Henderson/PFITZNER 14–17.
143. In Abendroth/PFITZNER the composer refers several times with pride to Op. 1 (e.g., pp. 187–88, 193, 210, 215) but never to Op. 27.
144. Cf. Dent/BUSONI 116, 167, 181, 211, 305–6; MGG II 520–27 (H. Wirth), especially 527; Austin/20th 110–15; BUSONI-Frau 103, 252, 260, 357.

Ex. 65. From the close of the first movement in Hans
Pfitzner's Sonata in e/E, Op. 27 (after the original ed. of 1922,
by kind permission of C. F. Peters Corp. in New York).

ments (S-VF-M-Va) was the earliest of his works that he continued to
acknowledge in his later years.[145]

No such break with the past can be found in the highly competent
sonatas of the long active pianist **Friedrich Gernsheim** (1839–1916),
who taught and conducted in Berlin during most of the second half
of his life.[146] Gernsheim's sonatas figure importantly in his chamber
music, which figures importantly in his total choral and instrumental
output. Six of them were published, over a span of 51 years, including
Op. 1 in f (1863) for P solo; Opp. 4 in c (1864), 50 in C (1885), 64
in F (1899), and 85 in G (1912) for P & Vn; and Op. 12 in d
(1868) for P & Vc.[147] Unpublished are another violin sonata and
three more piano sonatas from his student years, and another, late
cello sonata, Op. 79 in e (1906).[148]

A good clue to Gernsheim's style comes from the names of the no-

145. BUSONI-Frau 103.
146. Cf. MGG IV 1821–24 (W. Kahl), with dated list and further references.
147. For bibliographic details on Opp. 4 (dated 1864), 12, 50, and 64, cf. Mueller-
Reuter/LEXIKON 593–94.
148. This last must be the same work that is (wrongly?) listed as Op. 87 in MGG
IV 1823. Cf. Mueller-Reuter/LEXIKON 594.

table musicians who figured most significantly in his background and environment, whether directly or indirectly. These include Spohr by way of an early theory teacher, Ernst Pauer, Moscheles, and Ferdinand Hiller as piano teachers, the last and Hauptmann as further theory teachers, and Brahms and Max Bruch as close friends. In short, Gernsheim was a traditionalist. The sum of these influences on his sonatas is the distinct impress of Mendelssohn and Schumann, as the reviewers of the earlier sonatas usually noted, along with praise for his mastery of forms, writing techniques, and smooth flow but some hint of a lack of originality.[149] Op. 12 affords a thoroughly convincing illustration (Ex. 66). One reviewer, describing Op. 12 as a pleasant though not

Ex. 66. From the opening of Friedrich Gernsheim's Sonata in d, Op. 12 (after the original B. Schott ed. of 1868).

outstanding work, was grateful that it is, *"mirabile dictu,* not afflicted with the over-elaborations, and undue prolongation of trite themes, which too often form the leading characteristics of the school to which it belongs."[150]

But Gernsheim proved to be more than an efficient sponge and

149. E.g., cf. nzm LVIII/1 (1863) 189 on Op. 1 and LXI (1865) 117–18 on Op. 4 (viewed as more of a sonatina in its facileness and minimal development). A study of Gernsheim's sons. is in order. A paragraph on Opp. 50 and 85 appears in Cobbett/CHAMBER I 458 (W. Altmann); cf., also, DM XII/1 (1912–13) 299 (W. Altmann).
150. MT XXIV (1883) 135–36.

transmitter of past styles. To be sure, he never became a radical, thus perhaps heeding the advice on his Op. 1 that his 69-year-old teacher Moscheles had written to him in 1863:

May God keep you safely on the middle road and prevent you from getting into the labyrinth of the futurists [*Zukunfstjäger*]. You incline toward the romantic school. In the exclusiveness of that tendency lies a certain danger. The classical masters (even as far back as Bach) have their romanticism, too, but thanks to their clear motives and formally and artistically suitable developments this is always kept within the bounds of the beautiful. The romantics tend toward brooding, hypochondria, indeed despair of the world (*Weltschmerz*). Your sonata has much of that color. I wish I were able to counter such moods with a small bottle or a good sermon, or artistically speaking a little Bach ointment, Haydn salt, Beethoven steel drops and Mendelssohn heart medicine.[151]

Yet his later sonatas show increasing perfection and subtlety in overall form, rhythmic construction, idiomatic instrumental writing, and harmonic color that give them many passages and whole movements of rare distinction. For example, Op. 50, with its trenchant themes in three well-contrasted movements (F-S-VF), makes a steady, compelling, well-developed and somewhat Brahmsian chamber work (lasting about 23 minutes) that any enterprising duo team might profitably add to its recital repertoire.

Philipp Scharwenka (1847–1917), older and not quite so successful brother of Xaver (ssʙ X), may be credited with at least 7 published sonatas—3 for P solo, in A, f♯, and g, Op. 61/1-3 (1886), "in smaller form"; 2 for P & Vn, Opp. 110 in b (1900) and 114 in e (1904); one for P & Va, Op. 106 in g (1899); and one for P & Vc, Op. 116 in g (1910).[152] As compared with his brother in their sonatas, Philipp tended to create more extended, serious, developed forms, often somber in character, with broader themes, increased polyphonic interest, and more resourceful, piquant rhythms.[153] Even the "smaller" piano sonatas, although lighter in character, are full-scale cycles with considerable development and variety. But for all their weight and academic worth, none of Philipp's sonatas is likely to be revived in the concert hall. Their themes and outworn, unenterprising, Mendelssohnian har-

151. As trans. and kindly supplied by Professor Alexander L. Ringer at the University of Illinois from an article on correspondence between Max Bruch and Gernsheim, in the forthcoming Lloyd Hibberd Memorial Volume.

152. Cf. mgg XI 1602-3, 1606 (R. Sietz); Altmann/ᴋᴀᴍᴍᴇʀᴍᴜsɪᴋ 224, 250, 263.

153. Wetzel/sᴄʜᴀʀᴡᴇɴᴋᴀ is a short article, with exx., on Philipp's chamber music. Cf., also, mgg XI 1603; Cobbett/ᴄʜᴀᴍʙᴇʀ II 332 (W. Altmann); and Shand/ᴠɪᴏʟɪɴ 93–95, with exx. Op. 114 is reviewed as well proportioned even though the first mvt. is as long as the combined (and interconnected) "Andante" and finale, in ᴍᴡ XXXVII (1906) 868a; Op. 116 is reviewed as a 3-mvt. fantasy rather than a standard form, in ᴅᴍ IX/4 (1909–10) 379.

monic idiom rarely sound fresh even when they do not descend into the trite.

Nor is there likely to be a revival of interest in the published sonatas by the fine pianist **Wilhelm Berger** (1861–1911), although there is more musical justification.[154] Berger was a traditionalist in his language, too, but his music rises above the trite and achieves a more compelling drive than Scharwenka's. His published sonatas include Op. 76 in B, for P solo (1899); Opp. 7 in A (1882), 29 in F (1888), and 70 in g (1898), for P & Vn; and Op. 28 in d for P & Vc (1930, posthumous).[155] The main influence on Berger is clearly that of Brahms—too clearly, in fact, because in spite of Berger's unquestioned mastery of his art and in spite of a few Wagnerisms in the harmony and of some other lesser influences, he provides another example, like Friedrich Kiel or Karl Grädener (both ssb X), of a style too close for independent distinction and not quite strong enough to compete on equal terms. His piano sonata, for instance, is a big, technically demanding, three-movement work (F-S-M) that immediately recalls the fire of Brahms's early piano sonatas (Ex. 67), but its ideas lack quite the vitality (especially in the last two movements) and its structural rhythm quite the organizational genius of the Viennese master's writing.[156]

A Sonata in d, Op. 82, for P & Vn (1908), as well as an early Sonata in A, Op. 2 (1888), and "Three Sonatinas," in c, F, and e, Op. 38 (1917) for P solo, figure at the not inconsequential fringe of the notable choral output by **Hugo Kaun** (1863–1932).[157] Kaun had studied with Friedrich Kiel (ssb X), among others, before spending fifteen valued years in Milwaukee and Chicago and settling in Berlin in 1902. Op. 82, which reportedly replaced a violin sonata withdrawn from publication about eighteen years earlier,[158] is a warmer, freer, more personal

154. Cf. mgg I 1693–95 (W. Kahl).

155. Cf. Altmann/kammermusik 195, 233. The Vn sonatas are endorsed highly by Wilhelm Altmann in Cobbett/chamber I 122 and greeted with increasing enthusiasm in their successive reviews—e.g., smw IV (1882) 371 (Op. 7 regarded as unequal and harmonically disturbing but interesting and lively, anyway); mw XIII (1882) 555 and 556 (Op. 7 described as a pleasant Mendelssohnian miniature), XXI (1890) 411 (Op. 29 remarked for its contrapuntal skill and almost excessive working of themes); dm II/1 (1902–3) 359 and 361 (W. Altmann in praise of Op. 70). Cf., also, Shand/violin 82–88, with exx.

156. Yet these very traits are warmly praised in mw XXXII (1901) 54 (E. Segnitz). Less enthusiastic is smw LVII (1899) 435.

157. Cf. mgg VII 761–65 (R. Schaal), with dated list and further references; also, Schaal/kaun (on the man and his works), especially pp. 24–25, 29, 88–90, 102–3, with exx.

158. According to Cobbett/chamber II 49 (W. Altmann); but could Altmann have been thinking of Op. 2 cited above?

work than Gernsheim's Op. 50, and hence somewhat dated. In four movements (F-Sc-M-F), it is marked by expressive, well-defined themes, pungent harmony, fertile rhythms, and an advanced but not frilly use of the instruments. It deserves to be played again.

Another pupil of Kiel, as well as of Rheinberger in Munich and, less formally, Brahms in Vienna, was the pianist **Robert Kahn** (1865–1951).[159] Kahn's MS and published sonatas are all duos, including Opp. 5 in g (1886), 26 in a (1897), and 50 in E (1907) for P & Vn; and Opp. 37 in F (1903) and 56 in d (1911) for P & Vc.[160] Kahn was another traditionalist developing along the paths started by Mendelssohn, Schumann, and Brahms. His surprisingly mature and ener-

Ex. 67. From the opening of Wilhelm Berger's Sonata in B, Op. 76 (after the original Otto Forberg ed. of 1899).

getic Op. 5 is a three-movement work (F-S-VF) recalling the symphonic breadth and development of Rheinberger. Op. 26 continues the promise of Op. 5 [161] and Op. 50 becomes, according to Wilhelm Altmann in 1910, "the most valuable of the violin sonatas composed since Brahms and one of the best works by Robert Kahn." [162] The honor might be contested on behalf of Robert Fuchs, Strauss, Reger, and Wilhelm

159. Cf. MGG VII 427–29 (R. Schaal), with further references.

160. Cf. Altmann/KAMMERMUSIK 210 and 258. These sons. are described briefly in Altmann/KAHN 354, 355–57. Cf., also, Shand/VIOLIN 77–82, with exx.

161. In MW XXIX (1896) 27 and SMW LVI (1898) 33–34 only the degree of inspiration in Op. 26 is questioned.

162. Altmann/KAHN 356. He had made the same statement in DM VII/2 (1907–8) 228, and made it again in Cobbett/CHAMBER II 45–46 (W. Altmann).

Berger, as well as Fauré, Saint-Saëns, and a very few other non-Germans, but remarkably few in all. Intimacy, artistic optimism, precise, resourceful writing, and intelligent scoring characterize Op. 50. The "Andante sostenuto" of the short first movement gives way twice to a "Presto" section but reappears to end both this movement and the finale. Between these outer movements is a well-developed scherzo movement. Both of Kahn's cello sonatas are significant duos, too.[163]

The fine pianist **Conrad Ansorge** (1862–1930) was one of Liszt's last students, in Weimar and Rome.[164] A Sonata in d, Op. 24 (1909), for P & Vc, and three solo piano sonatas—Opp. 1 in f (1884?), 21 in e (1905), and 23 in A (1908)—are among his few published works.[165] The Lisztian touch is evident at once in the stentorian, heroic, elegiac quality of Op. 1, in its taxing but not empty virtuosity, and in the structural freedom and variety of its three movements (F-S-F), including a brilliant fugal introduction to the finale based on the main theme of the first movement. By contrast the last of Ansorge's three piano sonatas takes a quite different turn. It exhibits all the subtle poetry remarked in his piano playing.[166] Moreover, it leaves Liszt and goes back to the Beethoven, Schubert, and Schumann he so loved to play, too—in particular, it would seem, to the Beethoven of Op. 101. But, Ansorge was no mere epigone. This work throws new light on past styles with a surprising freshness and individuality. If the harmony is traditional, the mercurial modulations and melody are not. And the structural methods make a refreshing departure from textbook sonata designs. Thus, the first movement is monothematic and freely sectional, each section starting with the governing idea and going off most often in its own, different direction, rhythmically and melodically as well as tonally. Some capable, enterprising, musicianly pianist is likely to rediscover this work and find it as rewarding and refined as late Clementi or any other composer still mainly cultivated as a cult.

The near centenarian **Ernst Eduard Taubert** (1838–1934; apparently not closely related to K. G. W. Taubert, ssb VIII) was another student of Kiel, also of Albert Dietrich.[167] To his credit among relatively few publications are only a Sonatina in A, Op. 11 (1870) for P & Vn and a *Fantasie-Sonate* in i, Op. 68 (1905), for P solo, although he also left a Sonata in d for Vn & P (1922) in MS. Op. 68 may be slightly too pat, too near to glibness, to be revivable in concert today. But it should

163. Cf. Altmann/KAHN 375; DM XI/2 (1911–12) 168 (H. Schlemüller).
164. Cf. MGG I 508–9 (Karl Laux).
165. Generally enthusiastic reviews of Op. 1 occur in NZM LXXX/2 (1884) 536–37 and LXXXIII/1 (1887) 218; also, MW XVII (1886) 102–3.
166. Cf. MGG I 507–8.
167. Cf. Riemann/LEXIKON II 1815; BAKER 1620.

make an ideal work for a student looking toward, though not quite yet ready for, the freer, bigger sonatas of Schumann, Chopin, and Brahms. Consisting of three interconnected movements (S/F-M-Va), it employs only established harmonic, structural, and keyboard techniques to move smoothly, comfortably, and surely to its clear-cut goals. If Taubert was not deliberately addressing himself to students in this work, then it brands him as the epigone Ansorge rose above being.[168]

Trained in Leipzig and related to his namesake by style though not by blood, **Georg (Alfred) Schumann** (1866–1952) was a successful director, chamber music participant, and composer who lived in Berlin after 1899.[169] Among his published works are three duo sonatas—two for P & Vn (Op. 12 in c♯, 1896; Op. 55 in d, 1912) and one for P & Vc (Op. 19 in e, 1898)—of which Op. 55 is much the most interesting.[170] This last, in three thematically related movements (F-S-VF), provides good tastes of the poetry, drama, occasional folk elements, large scope, and broad practical musical experience in Georg Schumann's writing. Of special appeal is the funeral-march coda to the finale. (Georg's brother in Eisenach, **Camillo Schumann** [1872–1946], won little success with five organ sons. and numerous duo sons., mostly unpub.[171])

A prolific, able, impassioned composer was the conductor and teacher **Waldemar von Baussnern** (1866–1931), who held posts in Mannheim, Dresden, Köln, Weimar, and Frankfurt/M between his first and last years in Berlin.[172] Out of at least nine sonatas or sonatinas composed by Baussnern, the only one to be published besides three piano sonatinas is his *Sonata eroica* in c♯ for P solo (1910). But this hot-blooded, multifaceted, sonorous, thoroughly pianistic work[173] is more than enough to arouse one's curiosity about the several ensemble sonatas still in MS, including a set of "Drei Triosonaten" for 2 Vns and P, 2 sonatas for Vn & P (one of them called "Ungarische" and one dated 1916), as well as one more for Vc & P (1896). *Sonata eroica* is a big work (41 pp.) in three movements (F-S-VF). Its rather improvisatory

---

168. Op. 68 is highly commended, without any such pedagogic reservation, in DM VI/4 (1906–7) 48 (A. Laser).
169. Cf. GROVE VII 602–3 (J. A. Fuller-Maitland) and MGG XII 270–71 (T.-M. Langner), with further references but no list of works.
170. Cf. Altmann/KAMMERMUSIK 226 and 264; Cobbett/CHAMBER II 367–68 (W. Altmann). Favorable reviews of each may be seen in SMW LV (1897) 114 (Op. 127); MW XXVIII (1897) 561 (Op. 12) and XXXII (1901) 603–4 (E. Segnitz, Op. 55); DM XII/2 (1912–13) 42 (W. Altmann, Op. 19); SMW LVIII (1900) 723 (Op. 19).
171. Cf. Riemann/LEXIKON II 1668; BAKER 1473. An organ son. is reviewed with no enthusiasm in MW XLI (1910) 330.
172. Cf. MGG I 1423–24 (G. F. Wehle), with full list of pub. and unpub. works.
173. The curt negative review of it in DM X/2 (1910–11) 296 (A. Leitzmann) makes no sense here.

charactcr, furthered by frequent tempo gradations, may relate to
Baussnern's improvisational skill as a student but belies his well-or-
ganized, standard forms. Although the rich harmony and tonal third-
relationships were standard, too, by then—for Baussnern was not an
innovator—his ideas and their treatment are individual enough to
keep his music barely clear of melodic and harmonic clichés and to
make it, for the most part, ring true (Ex. 68).

Ex. 68. From the second theme in the first movement of
Waldemar von Baussnern's *Sonata eroica* in c♯ (after the original
ed. of 1910).

The renowned Berlin teacher **Paul Juon** (1872–1940) retained his
Russian background under Arensky and Taneyev, including Slavic folk
influences, even after further study with Bargiel in Berlin and after his
permanent move to that city in 1897.[174] This background contributed
to Juon's remaining more on the Romantic than the Modern side of
the border line and shows up in the sonatas—for example, in the
"Romanze" in minor introduced as variation "V" in the middle movement of Op. 7, as well as the main theme announced at once in the
finale. Brahm's marked influence seems to have contributed, too. There
are at least 8 duo sonatas and one piano sonatina by Juon, spread over
the years from 1898 to 1930 and nearly all published. The duos include 2 for Vc & P, 3 for Vn & P, one for Va & P plus another for
Cl-or-Va & P, and one for Fl & P.[175] One of the most attractive and
most played of those duos, in spite of the relative inexperience it

174. Cf. MGG VII 389–93 (T.-M. Langner), with dated list of works and further
references; GROVE IV 676–77 (E. Evans).
175. Cf. Cobbett/CHAMBER II 43 (E. Evans) and 44 (W. W. Cobbett) for 2 concurring, largely favorable paragraphs on the duo sons.

betrays in problems of tight form, is Juon's first sonata, that same Op. 7 for Vn & P (1898). All three movements (M/F-Va-VF) achieve a plasticity, sometimes even a proselike quality, in the rhythm, furthered in the first movement by the 6/1 meter, and in all movements by the frequently wide and free roaming of the melodic lines. The harmony is traditional—in fact, conspicuously diatonic (partly in keeping with the folk element). But the texture is much thicker than that economical sort, with its many open fifths, that Juon tended to cultivate in his later years.[176]

The restless, roving composer of opera and other types of music, **Paul Graener** (1872–1944), left two published duo sonatas, Opp. 56 in C, for Vn & P (1914?), and 101 in f, for Vc & P (1935).[177] These reveal Graener's decided yet unclassifiable individuality of style—the lyricism, tenderness, sadness, mysticism, and even Impressionism, expressed in late-Romantic harmony that lies somewhere between that of Strauss, Reger, and Pfitzner. Op. 56 is an improvisatory, brooding work in one extended movement of three sections.[178] The organist and conductor **Martin Grabert** (1868–1951) may be mentioned for his contribution to the sonata for Ob & P (Op. 51, 1921).[179]

Further in Berlin, organ sonatas of no lasting consequence came from the virtuoso organists **Otto Dienel** (1839–1905),[180] **Heinrich Reimann** (1850–1906),[181] **Max Gulbins** (1862–1932);[182] and **Ludwig Neuhoff** (1859–1909).[183]

Among still other, less remembered Berliners, **Theodor Kewitsch** (1834–1903) wrote an *Erste Sonate für Pianoforte und eine Singstimme*

---

176. A review of Op. 7, pointing to some of these same traits, appears in smw LX (1902) 765.

177. Cf. mgg V 663–66 (L. K. Mayer). The first ed. of Op. 56 did not get into hofmeister.

178. It is reviewed, somewhat confusedly, with mention of a lack of structural development, in dm XV/1 (1915) 294–95 (M. Broesike-Schoen) and noted briefly in Cobbett/chamber I 486 (H. Leichtentritt).

179. Cf. mgg V 614–15 (H. Becker) and the review in dm XV/1 (1915) 456 (describing it as well suited to the Ob but not interesting to the pianist and unexceptional as music).

180. Cf. Riemann/lexikon I 401; mt XXIII (1882) 403, XXVII (1885) 42, 358, and 364; mw XXIX (1898) 43 (reviewing the 3 mvts. of "Christmas Sonata," No. 4, as not developed enough); mt XXXIV (1893) 295–96 (more favorable on No. 4).

181. Cf. mgg XI 169–71 (T.-M. Langner); mw XXI (1890) 393 (with praise for good workmanship in the 3 mvts. of Op. 10 in d—a chorale prelude, passacaglia, and fugue); Frotscher/orgelspiel II 1216.

182. Cf. Riemann/lexikon I 677; baker 627; smw LVIII (1900) 883 (praise for the polyphony and scoring in Op. 4); dm II/2 (1903) 39, 40–41 (K. Straube, reviewing Opp. 4, 18, and 19 as trivial reversions to the Mendelssohn style); nzm CI (1905) 163 (originality of rhythm and harmony in Op. 28).

183. Cf. Riemann/lexikon II 1261; mw XXXI (1900) 121–22 (praise for "Phantasie-Sonate" in f, Op. 21); Kremer/organ 210.

(Op. 61, *ca.* 1890), with successive texts by Goethe, Tieck, and Rückert for the three movements. The work was considered interesting as an experiment but not as music.[184] The Berlin-trained conductor **Fritz Kauffmann** (1855–1934) wrote two piano sonatas, of which the second was reviewed as a worthy product of the instruction he had received from Kiel.[185] Another Kiel student and conductor, also a pupil of Liszt, **Max Puchat** (1859–1919) left at least one sonata each for P solo and for P & Vn, the latter being reviewed as a difficult but fluent and well constructed work.[186] And another Kiel student, **Eduard Behm** (1862–1946), was reported to recall Grieg in the first of his three violin sonatas.[187] The choral conductor and composer **Karl Kämpf** (1874–1950) left one published sonata each for P & Vn and P & Vc in 1904 and 1920, of which the first (Op. 23 in e) was applauded for its harmonic interest.[188] The Dutch conductor in Berlin and one of our few woman composers, **Elisabeth Kuyper** (1877 to at least 1965?), left two or more violin sonatas, one of which was published (Son. in A, 1902) and reviewed as being more interesting for its sonority than its content.[189]

Carl Bohm (1844–1920) and **Gustav Lazarus** (1861–1920) were among Berliners who wrote sonatinas.[190] **Alban Förster** (1849–1916) in Neustrelitz, north of Berlin, was another.[191] In Hamburg, to the west, the song composer **Hans Hermanns** (1879–?) [192] left an expressive, excellently scored, thoroughly convincing Sonata in b, for P solo, that is unhackneyed and was not published until 1935,[193] yet retains clear and firm ties with late-Romantic melody and harmony. In Bremen the violinist and conductor **Paul Scheinpflug** (1875–1937) left a Sonata in F, Op. 13, for Vn & P (1908) that was reviewed as a broad, substantial, appealing work, with some Brahmsian flavor but no artificialities.[194]

184. NZM LXXXVI/2 (1890) 538 (A. Naubert). Cf. Riemann/LEXIKON I 877.

185. MW XVI (1885) 102 (P. Mirsch). Cf. Riemann/LEXIKON I 868; BAKER 812.

186. MW XXX (1899) 522; SMW LVI (1898) 673–74. The P-solo son., Op. 3 in b♭, is reviewed as attractive, bold, and promising, in SMW XLIV (1886) 103. Cf. Riemann/LEXIKON I 140.

187. DM II/3 (1902–3) 46, 47. Cf. Riemann/LEXIKON I 140.

188. NZM C (1904) 819. Cf. Riemann/LEXIKON I 848; BAKER 804; Altmann/KAMMERMUSIK 210 and 258.

189. MW XXV (1904) 324 (E. Segnitz); cf., also, NZM XCIX (1903) 372, SMW LXI (1903) 138 and 142 (W. Altmann, with praise). Cf. Riemann/LEXIKON I 976; BAKER 889 (not in Suppl.).

190. Cf. Riemann/LEXIKON I 197 and 1009; NZM IV (1883) Beilage I, p. 4; MW XXXI (1900) 117.

191. Cf. Riemann/LEXIKON I 521; MW XI (1879) 11, XIII (1882) 390; XXVIII (1897) 99.

192. Cf. Riemann/LEXIKON I 742; but he is in no other standard dictionary.

193. Breitkopf & Härtel in Leipzig.

194. DM VIII/3 (1908–9) 173 (W. Altmann); MW XLI (1910) 378. Cf. BAKER 1431–32.

Chapter XII

Chopin and Others in France and the Low Countries up to About 1885

Revolutions, Monarchies, Republics, and Sonatas

The sociopolitical background against which the sonata flourished intermittently in 19th-century France begins with the rise and fall of the spectacular Napoleonic empire (1803–15) that had grown out of the French Revolution (1789–99). It continues with the further, familiar alternations of monarchies and republics that occurred throughout much of the century. After Napoleon Bonaparte there was the monarchic period defined by the interludial reigns (1814–30) of the brothers Louis XVIII and Charles X and the shift, with the second revolution and its wider, European repercussions (1830), to the Orléans monarchy during the reign (1830–48) of Citizen King Louis Philippe. Then, with the third revolution and its even wider repercussions (1848), came the brief Second Republic (1848–51) and from it the Second Empire (1851–70), under Napoleon III. The Franco-Prussian War of 1870–71, largely resulting from the government's suspicion and jealousy of Prussia's growing power, brought not only disastrous defeat, including the loss of Alsace and Lorraine to Germany (and some second thoughts to the more pro-German artists like Franck and d'Indy), but the establishment of the Third Republic (1870–1940), with its National Assembly, eventual constitution (1875), and more lasting control, beyond music's Romantic Era. Meanwhile, the most essential events in the Low Countries were their subjugation by the French during the French Revolution, their union in the Kingdom of the Netherlands (to Belgium's disadvantage) under terms of the Congress of Vienna in 1815, and their continuation as separate, independent kingdoms after Belgium's successful revolt during the revolutions of 1830.

Apparently more by consequence than by accident, France's musical developments, especially as viewed in this and the next chapter on the sonata in Romantic France, virtually coincided with those sociopolitical developments. Up to about 1830 and the second revolution we still are in a borderland of late-Classic and early-Romantic styles, with several composers of minor significance to sonata history, like Adam, Boieldieu, Steibelt, or Kalkbrenner, but none, to be sure, approaching their near contemporaries Clementi, Beethoven, Schubert, or Weber. Between the second and third revolutions we are in the period, almost to the year, of Chopin's active career in France (1831–48), which also comprehends the chief sonata output of other outstanding pianists in Paris, like Thalberg, Heller, and Alkan (but not Liszt, who left Paris in 1835, well before he wrote his mature sonatas; ssb X). Between the third revolution and the Franco-Prussian War (1848–71) the sonata reached its conspicuously lowest ebb in France. However, as we shall see in Chapter XIII, right from the start of the Third Republic (almost coinciding with the establishment of the Societé Nationale de Musique in 1871), it was soon to rise again, and, indeed, to attain its most important and extensive cultivation in France during the Romantic Era.

Austria and Germany are rightly thought of as the prime contributors to 19th-century instrumental music, both in quality and quantity. But the mere fact of so much going on with the sonata in France and the Low Countries will surprise those who think of these regions, especially France, as being almost as completely absorbed in opera as Italy at that time. There are over eighty composers at least to mention in these next two chapters, including thirteen who call for more or less extended discussions (though none of these in the Low Countries). It is true that, as the French author Georges Servières already noted in 1901,[1] John South Shedlock's book of 1895 on the piano sonata (Shedlock/sonata) mentions not a single "French piano sonata" in any period. But in Shedlock's defense we should recall that (1) from Mozart's time up to about 1870 most of the more important sonata activity in France came from immigrants like Steibelt, Kalkbrenner, Chopin, and Heller in the 19th century,[2] whom Servières presumably identified rather by their nationality than (as here) by their place of chief residence; (2) even the French had not yet brought back to light their own relatively obscure contributions to the sonata in the earlier 19th century; and (3) the period after 1870 not only was too "modern" and recent for Shedlock's survey in 1895 but, like all previous periods of sonata history in France except the late-Classic and early-Romantic, the main emphasis was placed, contrary to Shedlock's, on the ensemble rather than the solo sonata.

It took the French scholar Georges Favre in the 1940's to rediscover

1. In the Brussels *Guide musical* XLVII (1901) 99–101.
2. Cf. sce 626 and 648–49 on the 18th c.

the native French contributions to the sonata in the period between the first two revolutions.[3] These contributions were furthered considerably, it should be observed, by opera composers who started as pianists, such as Méhul, Boieldieu, and Hérold. They were not furthered especially by the curriculum itself of the important Paris Conservatoire, which, in spite of its rebirth during the French Revolution (1795), was to become increasingly academic and, indeed, "conservative."[4] The ever-increasing Chopin research has helped to illuminate lesser composers active in Chopin's sphere. And now perhaps Favre or some other scholar will go on to rediscover further sonata (and other instrumental) activities during the Second Empire, when they seem to have been at such a low ebb. However, one must remember that some of the most important composers in 19th-century France took little or no interest in the sonata, including Auber, Meyerbeer, Berlioz, Bizet, and Gounod. Opera did predominate, and by a generous margin, over all other musical interests.[5]

Moreover, although Paris publishers like Leduc, Pleyel, Imbault, Lemoine, Richault, Cotelle, and Schlesinger were supplying the French public with music of the Classic masters early in the century, including their more popular sonatas,[6] actual performances of sonatas by Clementi, Haydn, and Mozart seem to have been rare, and by Beethoven almost nonexistent prior to the second revolution.[7] In other words, public performances in themselves could have provided but little incentive to the composition of sonatas in early-Romantic France. For example, although early 19th-century French treatises had already recognized the sonata's preeminence among types of piano compositions,[8] an entertaining German description of foreign and native pianists congregated in Paris and their performances in 1825 makes not one reference to sonatas.[9] And Fétis' brief but comprehensive account of the current Paris scene, published right in the year of the second

3. Favre/FRANÇAISE. Saint-Foix/PIANISTES had paved the way by rediscovering the French pianists and their contributions in the previous generation. Cf., also, Gil-Marchex/FRANÇAIS.

4. Cf. Harding/SAINT-SAËNS 34–41.

5. An excellent summary account of 19th-c. French music may be found under "Paris" (which is nearly tantamount to France in 19th-c. art) in MGG X 773–83 (G. Ferchault). Cf., also, Saint-Saëns' own description in 1900 of opera's dominance in Paris around 1860, as trans. in Cooper/FRENCH 9.

6. Cf. Favre/FRANÇAISE 80–81, 103–4.

7. Cf. Schrade/BEETHOVEN 4–38, including information on Haydn and Mozart, and further references on p. 253. To be sure, the public performance of Beethoven sons. anywhere was almost nonexistent while he was still alive (SCE 528–29; SSB XIX).

8. Cf. Favre/FRANÇAISE 127–28; also, SSB II on Reicha.

9. Trans. in QUARTERLY VIII (1825) 310–13.

rcvolution, makes no specific mention of sonatas either, but does say in reference to symphonies and chamber music that "nature struggled in vain to give birth to a Haydn or a Beethoven in France." [10] Beethoven's influence and both the awareness and public acceptance of the sonata certainly increased during Chopin's time, although public performances of sonatas, especially of solo as against duo sonatas or as against lighter solos (potpourris, etc.), were still infrequent. There were such performances of Thalberg's only sonata but none that could be found here of Chopin's own two main solo sonatas during his lifetime, not by himself or by close sympathizers like Liszt or Clara Schumann. Moreover, in a journal like the *Revue et gazette musicale de Paris* (RGM) we still find skepticism about the validity of absolute or purely instrumental music, as in the continued reiteration, after a full century, of the celebrated quip attributed to Fontenelle, "Sonate, que me veux-tu?" (cf. SBE 353; SCE 36–37; SSB II). And, as in the contemporary German periodicals, we still find gloom over the low state of the current sonata and premature assumptions of its early demise (SSB II). Not until the Third Republic was well under way and the finest examples of Franck, Saint-Saëns, and Fauré were published, as discussed in our next chapter, did the sonata come fully into its own in Romantic France.

Paris Residents in the Classic-Romantic Borderland (Steibelt)

Early Romantic traits began to permeate the sonata in France during the last phase of the Classic Era. They can be found in several borderland composers in our previous volume quite as Classic traits persist in several borderland composers about to be met here. Examples are the theatricalism of Johann Edelmann's and Etienne-Nicolas Méhul's sonatas (SCE 650–51 and 668–72), or the "style dramatique" and the pre-Chopinesque cantilena of Johann Ludwig Adam (SCE 655–58). On the other hand, some "Classic" composers who lived well into the Romantic Era as defined here—for example, Rodolphe Kreutzer (SCE 668) or Matthieu-Frédéric Blasius (SCE 678)—showed no ear or inclination for the newer trends.

Among further borderland composers, not mentioned in our previous volume, was one of the most successful leaders of French comic opera, **François-Adrien Boieldieu** (1775–1834). All of some seventeen sonatas identified as his, including seven now lost, were early works published in Paris between 1795, or the year that he left Rouen for Paris, and

10. Fétis/CURIOSITÉS 137–68, especially p. 145.

1803, the year he left Paris for Russia.[11] In other words, these works appeared around the time Boieldieu was teaching piano at the Conservatoire[12] and before he became completely engrossed in opera. They include 9 sonatas for P solo, 4 for P and 2 for harp with optional or obligatory Vn, and one apparently for harp solo.[13] Two were arranged from harp "duos." The sonatas are in two or three movements each, the rondo finale being the one consistent movement in the cycles.

A reading of Boieldieu's sonatas reveals little more than historical interest. We are reminded that opera composers do not necessarily make instrumental composers. The transparent, forthright melodies, which bring the light opera aria to the piano and constitute the most evident Romanticism in this music, rise above the obvious only occasionally to become charming (as in "Rondeau: Allegretto doloroso," Op. 4/2/iii). The texture grows from thin to richer between Opp. 1 and 6, even including 3ds and 6ths (as in Op. 4/2/i/109–17). But the most that can be said for the writing is that it anticipates the scoring and rhythmic mannerisms of Weber occasionally (ssB VIII) and that it is convenient for the pianist; it usually offers only the dullest, primitive, chordal accompaniments. Although the melody introduces chromatic passing tones, the harmony remains diatonic, rudimentary, and sometimes gauche in its voice-leading (Op. 4/2/ii/4–5). Least acceptable are the straggly, poorly integrated sectional forms, which are always too long for their content (with 7 of the solo sons. ranging from totals of 449 to 665 mss.). The continuous diet of square-cut, melodious phrases and periods, without benefit of significant development, are barely tolerable in the lightest movements, and not tolerable in the principal, initial allegro movements. Boieldieu's sonatas got no French reviews, but the first three of them, Op. 1 for P solo, got a German review that treated them as pleasant, good study material for the fingers, too long, lacking in consequential slow music, and unexceptional.[14]

A less remembered but more capable sonata composer among the borderlanders was the Austrian pianist and teacher **Ignaz Anton (Franz Joseph) Ladurner** (1766–1839), who trained in Munich before settling

11. Cf. Favre/BOIELDIEU (the most thorough study of the man and his music) I 79–81, 302–3 (list of sons.), but add *Grand Sonata for the Piano Forte* [in E♭], *Arranged From the Celebrated Duett* (London: Preston, *ca.* 1800; cf. Cat. ROYAL 67); also, Favre/FRANÇAISE 82–83 (which gives 1795, not 1796, for Boieldieu's arrival in Paris).

12. Cf. Favre/BOIELDIEU I 103–4.

13. Mod. ed. of 6 selected sons. for P solo: Favre/BOIELDIEU-m, with extended preface (repeated in Favre/FRANÇAISE 82–97 and 166, with generous exx.). The sons. were first explored in Saint-Foix/PIANISTES VII 102–10.

14. AMZ IV (1801–2) 226–27. It has not been possible here to concur in Favre's high opinions of Boieldieu's sons. (as in MGG I 70).

in Paris in 1788.[15] Between about 1792 and 1805 at least 31 sonatas by Ladurner were published, singly and in sets of 3 each, including 5 sets for P solo, 4 sets and a single for P with Vn and sometimes Vc, and 3 singles for P-duet.[16] The successive sonatas, made up of two to five movements, display increasing virtuosity and exploitation of the instruments, starting with idioms and passages that recall Clementi and culminating with some ideas and figurations not unlike Weber's. Moreover, Ladurner's sonatas display an increasingly imaginative variety of styles and forms. There is even a "battle" finale—"Charge du Cavallerie ou *la* passage du Rhin"—complete with pedal effects and other literalities. Like Boieldieu's movements, Ladurner's sometimes straggle with too many sections and suffer from dull accompaniments, too. But Ladurner has the requisite skill and interest in his themes, harmony, rhythm, and texture to keep the movements alive. And there is some depth and poetry in his slow movements and frequent slow introductions (Ex. 69), as implied by his abundant editorial advices. There is also depth in the richly ornamented passages, in the expressive, rather frequent cadenzas for which he pauses, and in the interplay of the piano and the independent, essential violin parts. (The latter are sometimes cued into the upper staff of the piano score, as in the original ed. of Ex. 69, suggesting that the indicated freedom of performance raised ensemble problems.) Perhaps the most consistent trait of Ladurner's sonatas other than their frequent, but no longer invariable, use of a rondo finale is their tendency toward monothematic writing, evident in derivations of the "contrasting" themes from the main themes, and in the similar incipits for two or more movements in a cycle. Another Austrian in Paris (from 1810) was the organist **Sigismund Ritter von Neukomm** (1778–1858), who left three published sonatas, for P solo and P ± Vn, between 1814 and 1828.[17]

In spite of his new views on the phrase and other aspects of structural rhythm, the few solo and accompanied piano sonatas published (*ca.* 1805–15) in the name of **Jérôme-Joseph de Momigny** (1762–1842) prove in all their skill and charm to be no later in style, no more pianistically challenging, and no more elastically expressive than the most advanced

15. Cf. MGG VIII 51–53 (M. Briquet), with list of sons. (partly dated but not fully reconciled); Schilling/LEXICON IV 296–98 (G. W. Fink).

16. Saint-Foix/PIANISTES VIII (1926–27) 13–20 describes Opp. 2 for P-duet, 4 for P solo, and 5 (a set) for P + Vn. Studeny/VIOLINSONATE 12 describes Op. 7 (another set) for P + Vn. Some of Ladurner's sons. seem to be lost.

17. Cf. MGG IX 1394–96 (H. Jancik); HOFMEISTER 1828 (Whistling), 498 and 599; Cat. NYPL XX 626 and 627; AMZ XVIII (1816) 127 and 15 (repeated on 199), reviewing Opp. 14 and 30 as Haydnesque, with only a little that is new or original.

Ex. 69. From the opening of Ignaz Anton Ladurner's Sonata
in a/A, Op. 5/2 (after the original Pleyel ed. of *ca.* 1797).

of Clementi's familiar high-Classic sonatinas.[18] The several solo, four-
hand, and accompanied piano sonatas by another, younger theorist
and a onetime pupil of Boieldieu, **Victor Dourlen** (1780–1864), were
also published in the early 1800's and reportedly are of interest, including a "battle" sonata, *Bataille de Marengo, Sonate militaire pour
le Piano-Forte,* Op. 2.[19] Several solo sonatas published between 1802
and 1819 were left by the brilliant pianist **Louis-Barthélemi Pradher**
(or **Pradére**; 1781–1843), who succeeded Hyacinthe Jadin (sce 672–73)
as "Professeur de piano au Conservatoire." [20]

18. Cf. MGG IX 448 (A. Palm); HOFMEISTER 1815 (Whistling), 309 and 368. Favre/
FRANÇAISE 127–28 and 131–32 quotes Momigny's high artistic opinions of the son.
19. Cf. MGG III 715–17 (G. Favre); Favre/FRANÇAISE 118–19; HOFMEISTER 1815
(Whistling), 301, 324, and 349.
20. Cf. Fétis/BU VII 110–11; Favre/FRANÇAISE 118 (with the death date [inverted
to?] 1834).

We need to observe one more of those composers on the borderland between Classic and Romantic styles in France. He was the most celebrated pianist among them and the composer of the most, the best known, and the most widely published sonatas, **Daniel Gottlieb Steibelt** (1765–1823). Steibelt flourished in Paris from 1790 to 1796 and during two further, briefer stays. These stays were preceded, separated, and followed by shorter or longer stays in most of the other main centers of music in Europe during the ups and downs that beset his troubled, itinerant life.[21] Born in Berlin in a family of keyboard instrument makers, Steibelt, an eventual progressive in his styles, had received some of his chief training from the conservative theorist Kirnberger (SCE 440–43).[22] HOFMEISTER (Whistling) for 1815 lists the publication of no less than 262 sonatas by Steibelt, not including a few duplications already noted in that surprisingly careful source.[23] One supposes there were actually many more duplications in the total, not only because of Steibelt's notoriously unscrupulous dealings with publishers[24] but because pirated reprints were common, anyway, in that day of no effective copyrights, and because the same sonatas often reappeared in different settings—as solos and as duets (with "accompaniments"), for example. To arrive at a more accurate list one would have to locate all or most of the publications, which originally appeared between 1788 [25] and about 1808 (when Steibelt was last active in Paris),[26] then eliminate duplications by preparing a thematic index (a task that would justify itself chiefly in a sociological study of musical popularity). But a total of at least 150 different sonatas seems not unlikely.[27] The

21. The chief study of the man and his music (but with no list of works) is the diss. Müller/STEIBELT. Cf., also, MGG XII 1222–26 (R. Sietz), with further references (but also no detailed list of works). Some idea of Steibelt's international, lifetime popularity may be had from the big space allotted to him in Schilling/LEXICON VI 475–78, and still in Mendel/LEXIKON IX 413–16, Fétis/BU VIII 119–22, and GROVE first ed. III 699–707 (!), with detailed but undated list of works (J. H. Mee). It is also significant that Steibelt was among the "notables" represented in Anth. NÄGELI-m, with 2 sons. in "Suite" 4 (SSB IV).

22. Cf. Müller/STEIBELT 7–9, 10, 12–14.

23. Pp. 294–95, 315–17, 321, 335, and 378–82, including many references to AMZ reviews. These reviews range from moderate enthusiasm at the start (e.g., AMZ II [1799–1800] 680–82, on 2 solo and 2 4-hand sons.) to weary disparagement in several later instances (as noted, *infra*, under Op. 64). The fact that Steibelt was a German neither active nor interested in Germany did not help his reception in the German periodicals.

24. Cf. GROVE first ed. III 700 and 703; Loesser/PIANOS 178–79.

25. Cf. Müller/STEIBELT 21.

26. The highest op. no. in the sons. is 91 and Op. 84 was reviewed in 1811, probably several years late (AMZ XIII [1811] 332; cf. Müller/STEIBELT 90–92). The Library of Congress and British Museum (BUCEM II 975–76) both have many Steibelt sons.

27. Müller/STEIBELT 90 guesses "well over 100."

1828 edition of HOFMEISTER (Whistling) lists numerous further editions of Steibelt's sonatas, which can only mean more duplications. Thereafter the Steibelt entries abruptly cease. By the turn of this century even PAZDÍREK (XIII 995–98) lists no more than a few of the sonatas.

The listings of Steibelt's sonatas recall typical titles met in our previous volume. These listings stand apart from those of his many other modish pieces (mostly without op. nos.), such as "Etude," "Rondeau turc," "Fantaisie militaire," "La grande Marche de Bonaparte en Italie," "Le Retour de la Cavall. russe a Petersburg," or "Combat naval." Thus, one finds "Six grandes Sonates dédiées à la Reine de Prusse" (Op. 27), or "Trois Sonates faciles avec flutes ou violons" (Op. 42), or "Sonate périodique" (that is, a periodical pub.). About 43 per cent of Steibelt's sonatas are designated for P solo, 33 for P with Vn accompaniment, 11 for P with Fl accompaniment, 10 for P with Vn and Vc accompaniments, and 3 for P-duet or 2 Ps. The accompaniments in the duo sonatas, whether designated optional or obligatory, are generally inconsequential and dispensable.[28] Except for some later sonatas in three, and a very few in four, movements, most of his sonatas are in two movements, in the same key and with a rondo finale, probably because the needed depth in a middle, slow movement was inimical to his rather superficial artistry.[29] Primary-triad harmony and homophonic textures prevail, with the left hand relegated to empty chordal accompaniments or, at most, some doubling of and sharing with the right hand. Scales, triplets, broken octaves, 3ds and 6ths, and a few, more original figures, provide the passagework. Except for occasional dotted and march rhythms,[30] Steibelt tends to write lyrical, rather neutral themes that do not afford distinct contrasts. Mozart comes to mind when the idea is chromatic and ends in a feminine rhythm. There are considerable transposition and redisposition of the themes but almost no development of them. The forms are loosely sectional.

Yet, in spite of this summary of unpromising style traits, there are distinct pleasures in Steibelt's few best solo sonatas. If there is no significant, dynamic drive in them, nor the structural solidity commanded by his near contemporary Hummel (SSB VIII), there is still a youthful, early-Romantic bloom and a degree of elegance, grace, and

28. Müller/STEIBELT 90–102 provides the only substantial discussion of these sons. (following 17 pp. on the other main category of Steibelt's output, his etudes).

29. Cf. the remarks on his polished playing in AMZ II (1799–1800) 399; also, GROVE first ed. III 703–4.

30. Both are inherent in Steibelt's unnumbered Son. in F "In which are Introduced the favorite Airs of *If a Body Meet a Body* [ii] and *Sir David Hunter Blair* [iii]."

refinement in the nicely shaped melodies (recalling the virtues of his own refined playing). The figurations become richer and more ingenious, to the point of anticipating Chopin's in a slight way. And the music balances and sounds well on the piano. In these respects, although Steibelt himself is supposed to have preferred his *Grande Sonate martiale,* Op. 82 in D,[31] our own preference today is likely to be for the three-movement *Grande Sonate* in E♭ (F-S-Ro), Op. 45 (1801?), "dédiée à Madame Bonaparte," [32] or, above all, for the more virtuosic, four-movement *Grande Sonate* in G (F-Mi-S-Ro), Op. 64 (1806? Ex. 70).[33] Even the "Adagio fantaisie" from Op. 64, in the submediant key,

Ex. 70. From the opening of Daniel Steibelt's Sonata in G, Op. 64 (after THÉSOR-m XX).

is more expressive and Beethovian than one might expect, especially when one recalls Steibelt's unhappy encounters with Beethoven in 1800.[34]

A curiosity is *A favorite Sonata for the Piano Forte or Harpsichord, called The Coquette, Composed* [in 1787] *for the late Queen Marie Antoinette of France by Hermann and Steibelt* (and pub. *ca.* 1795 by Longman and Broderip of London). **Johann David Hermann** (*ca.* 1760–1846) was a virtuoso German pianist who left some published accompanied sonatas of his own and gave lessons to Marie Antoinette

31. Müller/STEIBELT 99.

32. Reviewed in AMZ IV (1801–2) 383–84, with more than usual praise for the work and some jesting about the dedicatee's ability to play it.

33. Reviewed at length in AMZ VIII (1805–6) 305–12, with each mvt. separately deplored for its emptiness and its commonplaces; reprinted in TRÉSOR-m XX and RICORDI ARTE-m VI 19. A Son. in E♭ for P solo by Steibelt is reprinted in Méreaux/CLAVECINISTES-m III no. 162.

34. Cf. Thayer & Forbes/BEETHOVEN I 257.

and King Louis XVI himself.[35] In 1787, to settle their rivalry, he and Steibelt composed the first and second movements, respectively, of this two-movement sonata, both on the same tune, "La Coquette." That Steibelt deserved his victory is evident at once from the much fresher music in his rondo finale, which seems to anticipate the 2/4 meter and rhythm of the mid-19th-century German polka.

Further Predecessors of Chopin in Paris (Kalkbrenner)

The brilliant pianist and renowned French opera composer **Louis-Joseph-Ferdinand Hérold** (1791–1833) was the musical product of several sonata composers met in our previous volume, including his Alsatian father F.-J. Hérold, J.-L. Adam, and Méhul (SCE 655–59, 668–72).[36] Early in his short career, between 1810 and about 1817, he produced eight solo and two accompanied piano sonatas, some of them published then and some only posthumously. Starting with a prize-winning Op. 1 at the Conservatoire (ded. to Adam), these are described as generally tasteful but unequal works, with arid sections relieved by flashes of real talent. Precision and grace in the melody and harmony, clarity and smooth flow, and disinterest in pure display are some of their most characteristic traits. Among progressive influences to be noted are those of Boieldieu, Beethoven, and Rossini.

One of the most capable musicians among the earlier 19th-century Parisians was the pianist and organist **Alexandre-Pierre-François Boëly** (1787–1858).[37] Preferring to study with Ladurner rather than the French teachers at the Conservatoire, Boëly received an exceptionally thorough grounding that laid the foundation for his increasing devotion to past styles and made him more interesting to us for his artistic assimilations than for any pronounced Romanticisms. During the first decade of the century, although not performed publicly, Beethoven's sonatas up to Op. 30 were making rapidly growing impressions on French musical life.[38] These impressions are clearly evident, along with considerable musical perception of his own, in Boëly's two piano sonatas Op. 1 (ded. to Ladurner), both in three movements (VF-S-VF and F-Sc-Ro) and published, like Hérold's Op. 1, in 1810. Following a

35. Cf. Müller/STEIBELT 23; MGG VI 222 (J. Vigué); BUCEM I 478 and II 975; WOLFE, item 3674.

36. Cf. MGG VI 250–59 (M. Briquet), with dated list of works; Favre/FRANÇAISE 97–102 (with exx.), 166; Saint-Foix/PIANISTES IX (1927–28) 321–32.

37. Cf. MGG II 44–45 (G. Favre); GROVE I 783–84 (M. L. Pereyra); Favre/FRANÇAISE 102–12, with exx. New biographic information appears in RECHERCHES V (1965) 51–69 (N. Dufourcq).

38. Favre/FRANÇAISE 103–4 cites specific notices and descriptions in French journals.

series of additional pieces that return rather to the style of J. S. Bach, Boëly produced his only other sonata, described as an outstanding, four-movement P-duet in f (F-S-Mi-"Giga"), Op. 17,[39] showing even more depth and closer affinity with Beethoven.[40]

The next major German pianist in Paris after Steibelt was **Friedrich (Wilhelm) Kalkbrenner** (1785–1849), who was younger by twenty years. Kalkbrenner's similarly itinerant life took him to Paris from 1799 to 1803 (where his training under Adam culminated in a first prize from the Conservatoire), again from 1806 to 1814, and finally from 1824 on.[41] However, Steibelt and Kalkbrenner seem not to have been in Paris at the same time. Following the start his father had given him (sce 579) and during his earlier travels, Kalkbrenner profited from the counsel, whether through lessons or less formal advice, of Beethoven, Haydn, Albrechtsberger, and Clementi. Later he attributed his clear, neat, dexterous, facile playing largely to the influence in London of Clementi and Cramer.[42] Although subsequently he also came to know Chopin, Liszt, and both Schumanns, their influence reportedly did not affect his somewhat older style of playing and seems not to have left any conspicuous mark in his music.

There are records of at least 18 published sonatas by Kalkbrenner, which first appeared between about 1810 and 1826 except for Op. 177 in 1845 (interrupting his last two decades of publishing nothing else but fantasias, rondos, and potpourris). Among these, 13 are for P solo, 3 for P-duet, and 2 for P with accompaniment. Because existing lists are incomplete, have conflicting opus numbers and other discrepancies, and lack dates, an attempt seems warranted to piece together the opus number(s), key, year (with "t. a. q." meaning only a *terminus ad quem*), first or early edition, and contemporary comments, insofar as any or all of these have turned up in HOFMEISTER (up to 1851), PAZDÍREK VIII 20–25, contemporary reviews, lists of plate numbers, the "Intelligenz-Blatt" entries in AMZ, and a few chance sources. The sonatas for P solo are listed first.

39. Based only on the chronology of Boëly's other works, a rough date might be 1825 for the composition, with 1855 (cf. Saint-Foix/PIANISTES IX [1927–28] 329) as the publication year of Op. 17.
40. The exx. in Favre/FRANÇAISE 109–10 are convincing.
41. Cf. MGG VII 445–53 (R. Sietz), with further references and a detailed but undated list of works.
42. Regarding this playing, cf. HALLÉ 213–15 and 221 (much of it quoted in Schonberg/PIANISTS 112–13).

Friedrich Kalkbrenner's Sonatas

Op. 1/1-3, P solo· f, C, and C; Paris. Sieber, t. a. q. 1815. A likely *terminus a quo* is Kalkbrenner's arrival in Paris in 1806. Reviewed in AMA No. 40 (Mar. 31, 1827) 373.

Op. 4/1-3, P solo; g, C, and a; Paris: Sieber, t. a. q. 1815.

Op. 13, P solo; g; Paris: Nadermann, t. a. q. 1815.

Op. 28, P solo; F; Paris: Pleyel, 1819. Ded. to Cramer. Reviewed with praise for its vitality and superior texture, including polyphonic interest, in AMZ XXI (1819) 643–44 (cf. Intelligenz-Blatt for Apr. 3); also, in AMA No. 37 (Mar. 10, 1827) 351. "Grande" in title.

Op. 35, P solo; A; Paris: Leduc (plate no. 1193), t. a. q. 1828. "Grande" in title.

Op. 42 (and 40), *Piano Forte Sonata for the left hand (obligato)*; A♭; London: Clementi, t. a. q. 1818. This son. is not for left hand *alone* (as assumed in MGG VII 452, where it is called a "unicum" for its day, as a first) but simply puts the main melodic responsibilities in that hand (as "obligato" implies in the title, or "principale" in the title of the early French and German eds., *Sonate pour la Main gauche principale*; cf. HOFMEISTER XVI [1919–23] 180). Reviewed in QUARTERLY I (1818) 534–35 as excellent training for the left hand, with almost too much neglect of the right hand and a gratifying avoidance of radical key relationships.

Op. 48, P solo; a; Paris: Pleyel, t. a. q. 1828. "Grande" in title.

Op. 56, P solo; f; Paris: Pleyel, t. a. q. 1824 (based on plate no. 67 of Probst ed. in Leipzig). Ded. "to the memory of Haydn."

Op. 177, P solo; A♭; Leipzig: Hofmeister, 1845? "Grande Sonate brillante." Reviewed in AMZ XLII (1845) 888 as a late work that still stands out for its skill, clarity and freshness; but in NZM XXIII (1845) 177 (not by Schumann) as a product of prolificity, still in the modish style now outmoded, and more appropriately called "Souvenir," "Bonbon," or "Fleur."

Op. 3, P-duet; C; Paris: Sieber, t. a. q. 1815.

Op. 76 (and 79), P-duet; F; London: Clementi, 1826? "Grande" in title. "Op. 79" assigned to the "revised" Kistner ed., t. a. q. 1833 (HOFMEISTER 1829–33, 113). Reviewed, with ex., in QUARTERLY VIII (1826) 241–42 as Kalkbrenner's best duet, tight in its form and enhanced by its contrapuntal exchanges, including double counterpoint.

Op. 80, P-duet; B♭; Leipzig: Breitkopf & Härtel, 1826 (AMZ XXVIII [1826] Intelligenz-Blatt for April 6). "Grande" in title.

Op. 22 (or 27, Sieber?), P & Vn-or-Fl; E; Paris: Carli (plate no. 568), t. a. q. 1828. "Grande" in title.

Op. 39, P & Fl-or-Vn ± Vc; B♭; Leipzig: Breitkopf & Härtel, 1826 (AMZ XXVIII [1826] Intelligenz-Blatt for April 6).

Kalkbrenner's piano music has been deplored undeservedly, if one has in mind his best sonatas and etudes. Partly responsible are those many cheap fantasias and potpourris, and partly the stories that have survived about his relationships with his contemporaries. The well-known story of Chopin turning down Kalkbrenner's proffered three years of lessons has probably been played up too much in Chopin's favor.[43] Liszt's peremptory refusal to listen to Wilhelm von Lenz's performance of Kalkbrenner's *Sonate pour la Main gauche principale* (cf. Op. 42, *supra*), presumably on the grounds that it was display purely for display's sake, seems a little unjustified, too.[44] No wonder Kalkbrenner gets such a quick, contemptuous dismissal from a late-19th-century writer like Oscar Bie.[45] But his own contemporaries knew better. After all, Chopin did dedicate his Concerto in e to Kalkbrenner and share in concerts with him, including some of those curious pieces for as many as six pianists.[46] Moscheles, who might be considered a rival, seems to have respected him highly.[47] And Schumann, ever honest, wrote that he was no "great worshipper" of Kalkbrenner but in his earlier years had enjoyed the "first, lively, truly musical sonatas" of Kalkbrenner's youth and, until genuine Romanticism passed him by, continued to enjoy the music of "one of the most skilled, masterly piano composers for finger and hand. . . ."[48]

The fact is that Kalkbrenner was a solidly grounded, resourceful musician. Although Steibelt's sonatas seem to have had still more of a following, Kalkbrenner's show him to be a much better, though only a slightly more Romanticized edition of Steibelt. In one of his best, most circulated, and most representative sonatas, Op. 56 in three movements (F-M-Ro), the melodic interest is about on a par with Steibelt's, often achieving an expressive cantilena that is a step closer to Chopin's style; the harmony is still relatively simple, although greatly intensified by

43. Cf. Schonberg/PIANISTS 113; Sydow & Hedley/CHOPIN 93–99, 115–16; Hedley/CHOPIN 44–46.

44. Cf. Ramann/LISZT I 169.

45. Bie/PIANOFORTE 192, 218. The evaluation in Georgii/KLAVIERMUSIK 271–72 has seemed more balanced here.

46. Cf. Hedley/CHOPIN 46–47.

47. MOSCHELES I 58–59, 77; II 58.

48. Schumann/SCHRIFTEN I 155–56.

Ex. 71. From the second theme in the first movement of
Friedrich Kalkbrenner's Sonata in f, Op. 56 (after the Probst ed.
of 1824 [?] at the Library of Congress).

the more skillfully placed appoggiaturas; the voice-leading reveals the
expert craftsman, one who can summon polyphonic entries when they
are needed; and the sense of good piano sound is at least as acute (Ex.
71) . The chief shortcomings are, alas, similar to Steibelt's, too. For all
his solid grounding, Kalkbrenner has little sense of architecture. His
forms are static, not dynamic. The cantilena themes are too similar to
each other to have independent character and to serve as landmarks.
Nor do they undergo any development. The passagework, including
some new figurations, delights the ear but fails to relate to or derive
from the themes and meanders from one irrelevant key in the total
scheme to another. In short and at best, one is hypnotized mildly without being drawn, driven, or, in fact, moved.

An exceptionally strong and intriguing composer and the principal
contributor to chamber music in France before Chopin's arrival was
the pianist (**André**) **Georges** (**Louis**) **Onslow** (1784–1853), of noble,
Anglo-French descent. An amateur in the best sense, Onslow had
studied with Hüllmandel, Dussek, and Cramer before settling in his
scenic home province of Auvergne, after which he studied composition
with Reicha, took up the cello as a part of his special interest in
chamber music, and came up to Paris only part of each year to try his

new works.[49] All of the 9 known sonatas by him were composed early, before 1821 or well before his hunting accident of 1829 that he set in oft-cited programme music known as the "Bullet Quintet," and before the composition of most of those many other larger chamber ensembles that represent his chief contribution. These sonatas, which must have enjoyed wide popularity to judge by their numerous re-editions from several publishers,[50] included one (not 3) for P solo, 2 for P-duet, 3 for P & Vn, and 3 for P & Vc. Since the information has not been brought together previously,[51] there follows a list of those sonatas along with the key, the first or one early publisher, at least a *terminus ad quem* (t. a. q.), and any contemporary reviews that have turned up here. Not included are Onslow's 3 similarly constructed "Duos" for P & Vn, Opp. 15, 29, and 31 (t. a. q. 1828).

Georges Onslow's Sonatas

Op. 2, "Grande Sonate," P solo; c; Paris: Pleyel, 1807 ("13 Rue Neuve . . . Trésor public"; cf. Hopkinson/PARISIAN 99). Reviewed in AMZ XX (1818) 702–4 as the work of an unknown who must be a German (!) by virtue of the originality, skill, excellent advanced piano writing, and pathetic quality (including much use of the dim.-7th chord).

Op. 7, "Grande Sonate," P-duet; e; Paris: Pleyel, t. a. q. 1815 (HOFMEISTER 1815 [Whistling], 332).

Op. 22, P-duet; f; Leipzig: Breitkopf & Härtel, t. a. q. 1820 (AMZ XXII [1820] Intelligenz-Blatt for Jan.). Reviewed in RGM for Apr. 1, 1838, with high praise for the dramatic and pathetic character, the rich harmony with all its surprises, and the effective modulations. In a similar review in AMZ XXVII (1825) 641–44, Op. 22 is called one of the best, well-distributed 4-hand works since Mozart's 2-piano Son. in F.

Op. 11/1–3, P & Vn; D, E♭, and f; Paris: Pleyel, t. a. q. 1818 (HOFMEISTER 1818 [Whistling], 28).

Op. 16, 1–3, P & Vc-or-Va; F, c, A; Leipzig: Breitkopf & Härtel, t. a. q. 1821 (AMZ XXIII [1821] Intelligenz-Blatt for Jan.). Reviewed at length in AMZ XXIII (1821) 185 as showing unusual progress (much as had been true of Haydn), surprising originality and harmonic depth (recalling Beethoven), delicate, ingenious scoring, and full partnership of the two instruments.

49. Cf. MGG IX 1937–40 (B. Schwarz), with further bibliography but no detailed list of works.
50. Fétis/CURIOSITÉS 145 attributes Onslow's exceptional success in chamber music to the social position that freed him from financial worries.
51. A study of Onslow's sonatas would make an excellent thesis topic.

Such recent evaluations of Onslow's music as there are tend to support the reviews just cited with regard to his craftsmanship (especially in creating polyphonic interest), his harmonic ingenuity, and his Beethovian pathos; but they do not agree that he was genuinely original.[52] All of which applies well enough to an early work like Op. 2 but not to the outstanding P-duet Op. 22, which proves to be another sleeper like that, Op. 17, of Hermann Goetz a generation later (ssb X).[53] The originality—particularly the harmonic diversions and unexpected modulations, the fresh ideas, and the clever, often contrapuntal distribution of parts—is apparent on every page. In Onslow's emphasis on the dim.-7th chord and its manifold treatment lies a kinship with Mendelssohn, Spohr, and sometimes Weber. Beethoven and further German orientation is suggested rather by ascending harmonic sequences driving to dramatic peaks, by the dignified pace of the slow movement, and by the witty turns in the minuet (of this 4-mvt. cycle, typical for Onslow—F-Mi-S-F). Mendelssohn comes to mind again in the scales, broken chords, and oscillating figures that supply the passagework, especially in the fluent finale in 6/8 meter. There may be a certain artificiality, self-consciousness, or posing in this music, too, which recalls Spohr more than Onslow's other contemporaries. Or one can hear those declamatory chords, the calculated pauses, and the sharp sudden contrasts as part of the unspoiled naivety that characterizes the early 19th-century Romanticism (as in Ex. 72, although the deliberate pace of Onslow's music makes it difficult to quote an example with more than two or three characteristic traits at any one time).

Such other sonatas dating before Chopin's arrival as might be mentioned here would be of no more importance, say, than the several tasteful but decidedly academic sonatas for oboe and unfigured bass to be found in the *Grande Méthode complète pour le Hautbois* (before 1828) by the then celebrated Parisian oboist, **Henri Brod** (1799–1839).[54] In the Alsatian capital of Strasbourg there is only the violinist **Conrad Mathias Berg** (1785–1852), a product of the Paris Conservatoire, to point to, and a couple of sonatas for P solo, of which the second was described as routine but capable of pleasing the amateurs.[55]

52. E.g., Favre/FRANÇAISE 119; Cobbett/CHAMBER II 195–200 (H. Woollett and W. Cobbett); MGG IX 1939–40.

53. Georgii/KLAVIERMUSIK 565 puts Onslow's Op. 22 on a par with J. N. Hummel's Op. 92 (ssb VIII) and second in their day only to Schubert's P-duets.

54. Cf. Fétis/BU II 78–79; HOFMEISTER 1828 (Whistling), 313. There have been numerous re-eds., as by Lemoine in Paris.

55. Cf. Riemann/LEXIKON I 154; CAECILIA X (1829) 167, 172–74.

Ex. 72. From the first movement of Georges Onslow's Sonata in f, Op. 22 (after the Schlesinger re-ed. in Paris of *ca.* 1834 [plate no. 1625]).

Chopin's Niche

The great Polish-French genius of the piano, **Frédéric François** (or **Fryderyk Franciszek**) **Chopin** (1810–49) brings us to the fourth of those four main composers who figured at the center of our Chapter VI on styles and forms. As with our separate discussions of Schubert, Schumann, and Brahms (SSB VII, VIII, and IX), we limit our concern in this chapter to the circumstances, background, and effect of Chopin's sonatas. (The exception is his early Op. 4, whose music was not representative enough for Chapter VI but does have historical interest for us now.) Chopin left fewer sonatas than these other men, only four. And his sonatas have long been viewed, especially in matters of form, as being even less representative of his special genius[56] than Schubert's and Schumann's of theirs. Yet two of his solo sonatas, the mature ones, continue to retain their popularity as few other Romantic sonatas do—more so than any by Schumann, and as much as the few most successful sonatas by Schubert, Brahms, and Liszt. In fact, their popularity is consistent with that of all Chopin's music, which in its apparently greater artistic truth, more than holds its own while the piano music of every important contemporary, especially Mendelssohn, has lost ground markedly.[57] Not many pianists, even in today's world of hectic musical changes, will deny in these sonatas, as in his other music, their unsurpassed melody and poetic lyricism, drama, spontaneity, warmth, drive, resourcefulness of figurations, sonorities, and sense of good structural timing.

The information about Chopin and his music has kept pace with this devotion to it, continuing, if anything, at an increasing rate, too. One example is the compact, efficient, sympathetic little book by Arthur Hedley,[58] a leading Chopin specialist, which during the past twenty years has proven to be the best biography and general interpretation in English and a model of its sort in any language. Excellent, too, are the annotated, chronological thematic index by Maurice J. E. Brown;[59] the three chronological volumes of letters, by, to, and about Chopin, edited (in French) by another leading specialist, the late Bronislas Édouard Sydow (completed by his successors);[60] Hedley's

56. E.g., Hanslick/WIEN II 323–24 (but read Op. 35 for Op. 4!); Bie/PIANOFORTE 262–63; Dale/NINETEENTH 74–78; Jachimecki/CHOPIN 197.
57. By comparison, the new and renewed interest in Liszt must still be recognized primarily as a cult rather than a general trend.
58. Hedley/CHOPIN; cf. pp. v, 2, 68, and 92 regarding Niecks's standard biography.
59. Brown/CHOPIN; cf. the review in PQ XXXIII (fall 1960) 24 and 26 (W. S. Newman).
60. Sydow/CHOPIN.

annotated English translation of these letters, revised, augmented by
a few letters not previously published, and reduced by the deletion of
many items "of little interest or importance";[61] three fascinating,
largely pictorial collections of documents;[62] and Sydow's thorough
bibliography listing 11,527 (!) items of Chopin literature (hopefully to
be brought up to date soon again).[63] The sesquicentennial in 1959–60
of Chopin's birth has stimulated further research and writing, in
special issues of periodicals[64] and in such major events as the inauguration of a *Chopin Jahrbuch* by the International Chopin Society (Warsaw, 1956) and "The First International Musicological Congress Devoted to the Works of Frederick Chopin" (Warsaw, 1960), each with its
substantial publication of more or less significant papers.[65] Unfortunately, an increasing amount of this material has appeared only in
Polish—or in Russian, Czech, or Hungarian—meaning that it is closed
to all but a very few Westerners until it is translated or paraphrased.

However, even including all of this material, the actual information
about the circumstances of Chopin's sonatas does not add up to much.
As with Schubert, it is less than it is for Schumann and Brahms. Not
only was Chopin as reticent with regard to his own sonatas as each
of these other three, but he did nothing to generate stories about them.
He inscribed no verse over a movement as Brahms was to do, he gave
no programmatic title (other than "Marche funèbre" over Op. 35/iii)[66]
as Liszt was to do, he hinted at no cryptic meanings such as Schumann
did, and he associated no colorful biographic episodes when he did
refer to his sonatas. To be sure, we are better off when we come to the
music itself. The new "Polish Complete Edition," which began to
appear in 1949, has brought us a big step closer to the ideal edition.[67]

61. Sydow & Hedley/CHOPIN; cf. pp. vii–xi; also, with regard to the hotly contested "Letters to Delfina Potocka," now "officially" declared to be "spurious," cf.
pp. 377–87 (also, DMf XV [1962] 341–53 [Z. Lissa]).

62. Bory/CHOPIN; Kobylańska/CHOPIN (Polish years, through 1830, exclusively);
and Czekaj/CHOPIN (including chronological lists of works and of all main concerts
in which Chopin played).

63. Sydow/BIBLIOGRAPHIE (with Suppl.).

64. E.g., MUSICA XIV/3 (Mar., 1960).

65. CHOPIN JAHRBUCH (only 2 issues up to 1967); CONGRESS CHOPIN. Cf. the summary
of Chopin research in SMZ CIV (1964) 224–31 (W. Poźniak).

66. Cf. Hedley/CHOPIN 133–34; also, Sydow & Hedley/CHOPIN 99 (for Chopin's
ridicule of Schumann's programmatic interpretations).

67. Chopin/WORKS-m; cf. Newman/CHOPIN. The forerunners of this ed., including
the earliest "complete" ed., from England (cf., further, ML XXXIX [1958] 363–71
[M. J. E. Brown]), and the Breitkopf & Härtel "First Critically Revised Complete
Edition" (1878–80), are summarized in Brown/CHOPIN 173–77; also, in RAM XXII
(1949) 336–38 (R. Caporali) and MT XCVII (1956) 575–77 (F. Merrick).

And certain MSS have appeared in facsimiles, as noted shortly.[68] But we are not better off with respect to significant interpretative and analytic literature on the sonatas. There is no separate systematic study of them, although there are a very few, brief articles that will also be noted shortly on the individual sonatas. Most helpful are the general style studies and surveys, including primarily, those of Hugo Leichtentritt, Paul Egert, Gerald Abraham, and Ludwik Bronarski.[69]

Chopin's four sonatas, three for P solo and one for P & Vc, spanned nearly the whole of his short career, from 1827 to 1846, and identify with rather clear stages in that career. They originated at shorter and shorter intervals. Op. 4 in c, for P solo (B. [for Brown/CHOPIN no.] 23), was composed in 1827 and/or 1828,[70] around the middle of his three-year course under Joseph Elsner at the Warsaw Conservatoire.[71] Chopin could have written still earlier sonatas as exercises,[72] but none have come down to us.[73] The next sonata was the one that has always been best known, Op. 35 in b♭, for P solo (B. 114 and 128). Except for its celebrated "Marche funèbre," which had been composed separately in 1837, Op. 35 was not written until 1839—that is, not until more than a decade after Op. 4 or nearly a decade after the year that saw Chopin's last concerts in Warsaw, his seven months of indecision during his second visit to Vienna, and his further travels through various centers that ended with his move to Paris in the fall of 1831. This work, Op. 35, identifies with Chopin's first happy, productive summer at Nohant with George Sand.[74] By contrast, Op. 58 in b, for P solo (B. 155) originated in 1844, five years later, during the last happy, relatively untroubled summer at Nohant with George Sand. And Op. 65 in g, for P & Vc (B. 160), originated fitfully over the next two years, 1845–46, during the crisis that was to culminate in the final break with George Sand in 1847.

68. One should not overlook, of course, the representative pp. reproduced in facs. from the best available sources in each vol. of Chopin/WORKS-m.

69. Leichtentritt/CHOPIN, especially II 210–66; Egert/CHOPIN; Abraham/CHOPIN; Bronarski/CHOPIN. Cf., also, RM/CHOPIN; Meister/CHOPIN (especially on the background); the chaps. by P. Gould and A. Walker in Walker/CHOPIN; and Jachimecki/CHOPIN 197–205.

70. Sydow/CHOPIN I xxxiv (as well as Sydow & Hedley/CHOPIN xiv) and Czekaj/CHOPIN give "1827"; Brown/CHOPIN 22–23 gives "early 1828," undoubtedly because of the "1828" on the autograph (as confirmed in Kinsky/KOCH 214), although this could be only a completion date.

71. Cf. Hedley/CHOPIN 15–16.

72. Cf. Hedley/CHOPIN 16.

73. In Czekaj/CHOPIN 66–67, several lost works are included in the listing of his earliest compositions, but no sons.

74. Cf. Hedley/CHOPIN 84.

Chopin's Sonatas

Opus	Brown/ CHOPIN	Key	Scoring	Composed	Probable first ed.	Chopin/ works-m	Dedicatee	Mvts.: tempos or types Keys: mvt.-by-mvt. mss.: mvt.-by-mvt.	Early titles; remarks
4	23	c	P	1827–28	Haslinger, 1851	VI 15	Josef Elsner	4: F- Mi- S- VF c: c- Eb-Ab- c 818: 249-128-42-399	"Sonata" on the MS; "Grande Sonate" in the first ed. (without the ded.); original "Op. 3" changed to Op. 4 because another Op. 3 (B. 41) had appeared in the meantime
35	114, 128	bb	P	1837 (iii), 1839 (i, ii, & iv)	Breitkopf, 1840	VI 54	none	4: S/F- Sc- S- VF bb: bb- eb-bb-bb 690: 242-288-85-75	"Sonate" in the first ed.; referred to as Chopin's "first sonata" (i.e., first to be pub.), or, especially, as his "Funeral March Sonata," for iii, which originated (but was not pub.) 2 years before the other mvts.
58	155	b	P	1844	Breitkopf, 1845	VI 79	Countess E. de Perthuis	4: F- Sc- S- VF b: b/B- Eb- B-b/B 826: 204-216-120-286	"Sonate" in the autograph and the first ed.; a page copied in Liszt's own hand contains changes in the finale probably made for a student (cf. Bory/CHOPIN 166)
65	160	g	P & Vc	1845–46	Brandus (Paris), 1847	XVI 95	Auguste Franchomme	4: F- Sc- S- F g: g- d-Bb-g/G 721: 236-259-27-199	"Sonate" in the (incomplete) autograph and the first ed.; also pub. in 1847 in Ferdinand David's arrangement for P & Vn

Most of the foregoing information is incorporated briefly in the adjoining chart, which lists the outer circumstances and facts of Chopin's sonatas and can serve for comparisons with the details in the sonata charts for our other main composers. With further regard to the circumstances, Chopin offered Op. 4 (originally as Op. "3") to Haslinger of Vienna in 1828, hoping that it would be published along with his Variations Op. 2 (which did appear early in 1830) and asking that it be dedicated to his esteemed teacher Elsner.[75] But probably fear that so difficult a work by a virtual unknown would not sell kept Haslinger from engraving Op. 4 until 1839, by which time Chopin's high reputation was international. Even then Haslinger must only have circulated some proofs to test the work's potential market, apparently without informing Chopin directly.[76] When he did send the proofs to Chopin in 1841 and indicate his desire, at last, to publish the work, Chopin refused permission, ostensibly because "it needed considerable alteration," but more accurately because he regarded the proposal as an exploitation of something that "I gave him for nothing in Vienna twelve years ago." [77] Undoubtedly this refusal caused Tobias Haslinger's son and successor Karl to defer actual publication until 1851 (without the dedication and now as Op. 4), two years after Chopin's death.

No reviews and no reports of 19th-century performances of Chopin's Op. 4, not even by Chopin himself, have turned up here. Nor is the work played today much more than as a historical curiosity. As evidence of its relative unpopularity, in the latest issue of the *Schwann Long Playing Record Catalog* (July, 1967) there is only one listing for it as against thirteen each for Opp. 35 and 58, and three for Op. 65. The discussions of Op. 4 are few, too, and then largely deprecatory. Says Gerald Abraham, ". . . the whole Sonata is so evidently a student-exercise that it is difficult to understand why Chopin should have sent it to a publisher. . . . Even the piano-writing is extraordinarily dull and conservative; perhaps because the young composer felt that any suggestion of virtuosity was incompatible with pseudo-classical sonata-composition." [78] Agreeing that the "intrinsic musical worth of the Sonata may be extremely slight," Kathleen Dale does acknowledge

75. Cf. Sydow & Hedley/CHOPIN 14, 66; Hedley/CHOPIN 22, 37. The autograph and its circumstances are described in Kinsky/KOCH 214–15 and Chopin/WORKS-m VI 125; facs. of its first p. of music are in Bory/CHOPIN 57 and Kobylańska/CHOPIN 125.

76. Cf. Sydow & Hedley/CHOPIN 182; Brown/CHOPIN 182. Haslinger's plate no.. 8147, is included incorrectly under 1840 in Deutsch/NUMMERN 25.

77. Cf. Sydow & Hedley/CHOPIN 203 and 254.

78. Abraham/CHOPIN 14–16.

its historical value for style comparisons with its two successors and, contrary to Abraham, asserts that at least the first movement "is undeniably attractive on account of the interesting part-writing and the decoratively beautiful passage-work of which it largely consists." [79]

It is true that Chopin may have been driven into a more academic stance by the very title "sonata." One still senses that stance at least in the opening movements of the three later sonatas, too. And there is already more of the eventual Chopin style in his Variations Op. 2 than in Op. 4. However, when heard in the context of its own decade and *not* that of Chopin's later, unique style development, it has seemed here to stand up well in most respects. It can hardly compete, of course, with the last, most mature sonatas by Beethoven and Schubert from that same decade. But it reveals at once a more solid craftsmanship than is generally credited to Chopin, and, like the record of his formal training, it should help, as Arthur Hedley says, to "dispose of the legend of a Chopin self-taught and ignorant of basic principles." [80] The voice-leading is precise and fluent, the counterpoint is unforced and fully adequate to the need, the motivic play is both consistent and persistent, the command of chromatic harmony is already considerable (Ex. 73), and the rhythm benefits from occasional cross accents and syncopations (as in the second section of the "Minuetto," mss. 17–32) as well as the successful introduction of 5/4 meter in the "Larghetto" movement. Moreover, it is not surprising to find the piano scoring, even in this early work, above average in sonority and resourceful figurations, in spite of somewhat fuller, more regularized part-writing than Chopin later used.

What, then, limits the interest and appeal of Op. 4? First, perhaps, is its lack of full-fledged, attractive themes. Except for one rather neutral theme in each of the last two movements, the music is taken up with recurring motives and passagework. The lack is particularly noticeable in the opening movement, where there is no real contrasting idea, hence none of the dualism or pluralism expected in "sonata form." A second limitation is the uncompromising treatment of the motives. Literal repetition, most often by twos, tends to make the motive wear thin rather soon. Third, in spite of the adroit chromatic modulations there is no simple over-all tonal scheme in the longer movements that gives purpose and direction to what otherwise can be only perfunctory designs. Too often the modulations lead nowhere, achieving no more than color contrasts in their vacillations. And fi-

79. Dale/NINETEENTH 74–78.
80. Hedley/CHOPIN 15.

Ex. 73. From the first movement of Frédéric Chopin's Sonata
in c, Op. 4 (after Chopin/werke-m VI 20–21).

nally, there is that academic stance, reflecting not only the early-Romantic attitude in general toward the sonata (ssb II) but Chopin's own
last concessions to formal training, already being complicated and
diffused by the medley of new influences, past and present, that were
beginning to impress him from all sides.

Those influences on the young Chopin, in Warsaw alone, were
manifold.[81] But like the young Mozart, he had a rare "talent for
appropriating what was congenial and rejecting whatever was opposed
to his nature." [82] The music of Mozart himself and J. S. Bach—always
his two favorite masters—had been inculcated from his earliest training, under Adalbert Zywny.[83] Ludwik Bronarski relates the motivic
writing of Op. 4 to Bach—specifically, the opening to the start of
Bach's Two-Part Invention in the same key,[84] which seems here like
an example of precarious melodic identification. So does Bronarski's

81. Besides the studies to be cited below, all of "Section II" in congress chopin
concentrates on influences on Chopin's style.
82. sce 498–99, as quoted from A. Einstein.
83. Cf. Hedley/chopin 10; Meister/chopin 25–27; chopin jahrbuch 177–207
(F. Zagiba on Mozart's influence). In rm/chopin 100–107, Wanda Landowska argues,
mostly subjectively, for the influence of the Rococo French clavecinists on Chopin's
piano writing.
84. Bronarski/chopin II 48–49, with exx.

parallel between the openings of the finale and of Schubert's "Wanderer Fantasy" in C (D. 760).[85] As with the Bach instance, the rhythmic parallel is only superficial, not to mention the unlikelihood of Chopin's knowing Schubert's work so soon after its first publication in 1823. For that matter, Chopin never spoke of Schubert in his published letters, although he certainly got to know some of the songs and perhaps the impromptus after he got to Paris.[86] And Bronarski's parallel between the short chromatic rise in Chopin's Op. 4/i/9 (etc.) and Beethoven's Op. 13/i/8 (etc.) seems too tenuous to accept.[87] Chopin clearly had more exposure to Beethoven, right from the start.[88] But his sympathies for Beethoven's music remained so restricted that in his last years he could still thank Charles Hallé for the first pleasing performance of a sonata that "had always appeared to him vulgar," Beethoven's Op. 30/3.[89]

The influence of living performers and composers on the young Chopin is easier to demonstrate. It is possible that Hummel's several recitals in Warsaw in 1828, of great interest to Chopin,[90] occurred in time to leave their mark on Op. 4. In any case, we have seen that Hummel's Op. 81 in f♯, which had been circulating for nine years and which so impressed Schumann about this time, contains remarkable anticipations of Chopin's later figurations (ssb VIII)—more remarkable, in fact, than can yet be found in Chopin's own Op. 4 (though not in his Variations Op. 2 or the two concertos). Other strong impressions on Chopin while he was still in Warsaw, notably the "shock" of Paganini,[91] did occur too late to apply to Op. 4.

85. Bronarski/CHOPIN II 49–51, with exx.

86. Cf. Hedley/CHOPIN 54, 156; Sydow & Hedley/CHOPIN 177.

87. Bronarski/CHOPIN II 51–54, with exx. (including further instances of this same motive in other Beethoven and Chopin works, as also advanced, equally tenuously, in Leichtentritt/CHOPIN I 117–20, 175–76, and II 146).

88. Cf. Hedley/CHOPIN 10; also, pp. 54 and 125–26. A short article by H. Opienski relating Chopin's to Beethoven's sons. is listed under nos. 3060, 3346, and 4905 in Sydow/BIBLIOGRAPHIE.

89. HALLÉ 35. Op. 31/3 seems more likely, although Op. 30/3 (with Vn) could have been intended, still in keeping with the custom of mentioning only the pianist in a duo. But as one proof of earlier enthusiasm for Beethoven on Chopin's part, cf. Sydow & Hedley/CHOPIN 36. Wessely/CHOPIN argues (though to excess, it is felt here) that the interval of the 3d binds all 4 mvts. in Chopin's Op. 35, which trait plus the layout of the development in i and the character of the trio in iii reveal unsuspecting links with Beethoven.

90. Cf. Kobylańska/CHOPIN 153, 279, 149.

91. Cf. Kobylańska/CHOPIN 156; Hedley/CHOPIN 20.

Chopin's Mature Sonatas

By the time he completed Op. 35 in 1839, many further composers had entered into Chopin's circle of interinfluences. These included some of the most significant younger Romantics—Liszt (whose relationship was discussed in ssb X), Mendelssohn, Berlioz, Bellini (whose alleged influence contradicts chronological facts[92]), and both Schumanns (with Robert's early panegyric on Op. 2 [93] being another "Hats off!" article and a major pathbreaker for Chopin). Lesser figures, like Moscheles and John Field, passed in and out of that circle, too. But well before 1839 Chopin had arrived so completely at his own individual style that there could no longer be any question of pronounced influences from others, only more subtle, slower changes reflecting his own inner growth.

After Op. 35 appeared in 1840, it was sometimes referred to as Chopin's "first sonata," [94] since, of course, it was the first of all his sonatas to be published. More often it was referred to as the "Funeral March Sonata" or in similar wording, as by Chopin himself in 1847.[95] Although the "Marche funèbre" in b♭ had originated earlier as an independent piece and may well have been introduced as such by Chopin himself,[96] it did not come out in print before he incorporated it as the slow movement of the complete, four-movement sonata in the same key.[97] But upon the news of Chopin's death, it did come out separately, in three different editions.[98] It had already been orchestrated for Chopin's own funeral,[99] and even earlier by Franchomme, apparently along with the rest of Op. 35.[100] Moreover, it

92. Cf. Hedley/CHOPIN 58–59, 136.
93. AMZ XXXIII (1831) 805–8 and Schumann/SCHRIFTEN I 5–7.
94. E.g., "Liszt" & Waters/CHOPIN 37; Fay/GERMANY 194.
95. Sydow & Hedley/CHOPIN 290.
96. Cf. Sydow & Hedley/CHOPIN 181.
97. For facs. of the title p. of the first printed ed. and of a MS of the first p. of the "March," stated to be in Julian Fontana's handwriting, cf. Bory/CHOPIN 146. But the latter seems to be in still some other hand than Fontana's, to judge by a surer ex. of Fontana's hand (remarkably like Chopin's) as reproduced in Winternitz/AUTOGRAPHS II Plate 109 (misattributed to Chopin himself; cf. Brown/CHOPIN 73 and Hedley/AUTOGRAPH 476). The 2 facs., showing the opening p. of each outer mvt., in the front matter of Chopin/WORKS-m VI are stated in the caption to be from the autograph, but Chopin's autograph has disappeared and these seem to be in the same (unidentified) hand as the "March." On Chopin's firm price for the pub. of Op. 35 cf. Sydow & Hedley/CHOPIN 188–89.
98. Brown/CHOPIN 111.
99. Sydow/CHOPIN I liv.
100. Sydow & Hedley/CHOPIN 290.

was to continue to be arranged and played separately,[101] as *the* standard funeral march, for longer than can be predicted here.[102]

But taking Op. 35 as a complete cycle, it is not the penultimate "Marche funèbre" but the short, 75-measure finale, "Presto, non tanto," that has raised the most questions. The shortness itself raises the first question, for its average duration up to the last three measures, which are usually played more freely, is only about one minute and thirteen seconds,[103] as against a total of about twenty minutes for the other three movements. Musicians expect fleet scherzos now and then that go by that quickly, but in a finale the brevity, especially right after such a relatively long movement (about 9 minutes) seems disproportionate. Even so, in the more than a century-and-a-quarter since Chopin completed Op. 35 the attitude toward this "disproportion" has generally changed from dismay to unqualified endorsements,[104] and from calling the finale "a sphinx with a mocking smile" [105] to calling it "one of the most remarkable movements in the entire history of the piano sonata, and at the same time, a tone-poem as compelling in effect as it is simple in the musical means it employs." [106]

Chopin himself took first note of the short finale and its unusual scoring, all in octaves, when he wrote to Julian Fontana, his compatriot, friend, and general factotum,

At present I am writing a Sonata in B-flat minor in which will be found the march that you know. This sonata contains an allegro, a scherzo in B-flat, the march, and a short finale—three pages, perhaps, in my notation. After the march the left hand babbles in unison [at the octave] with the right.[107]

Did Chopin add "non tanto" to the "Presto" over the finale, an instruction rarely believed or observed by performers,[108] because he feared he had made the movement all too short? Schumann expressed puzzlement when he came to this movement, near the end of full review that deserves almost complete translation here, as much for its early, contemporary view as its sympathetic perception:[109]

101. E.g., MT XIII (1867–69) 526, XVIII (1878) 509, and XX (1879) 327—all for organ; Habets/BORODIN 108, on Liszt's arrangement for P, Vc, and organ.

102. It was played, for example, at President Kennedy's funeral.

103. In Walker/CHOPIN 248, Alan Walker tabulates recorded performances by Horowitz, Rachmaninoff, Arthur Rubinstein, and Cortot.

104. Walker/CHOPIN 158–61 (P. Gould) and 239–50 (A. Walker).

105. Schumann/SCHRIFTEN II 14–15; cf. *infra.*

106. Dale/NINETEENTH 78.

107. Letter of Aug. 8, 1839, from Nohant, trans. from Sydow/CHOPIN II 348.

108. Walker/CHOPIN 248: "It is a mistake to take it too slowly." A half-note at a metronome speed of at least 108 is urged by Walker.

109. NZM (1841) 38–39 and Schumann/SCHRIFTEN II 12–15. An illuminating evaluation of this review, including the question of a satisfactory cycle, occurs in

To look at the first measures of the . . . sonata and still not be sure who it is by, would be unworthy of a connoisseur. Only Chopin starts so and only he ends so, with dissonances through dissonances in dissonances. And yet, how much beauty this piece contains. What he called "Sonata" might better be called a caprice, or even a wantonness [in] that he brought together four of his wildest offspring [,] perhaps in order to smuggle them under this name into a place where they otherwise might not fit. One imagines some cantor, for example, coming from the country into a music center in order to buy some good music; he is shown the newest [things]; he will have none [of them]; finally a sly fox shows him a "Sonata"; "yes," he says happily, "that is for me [,] and a piece still from the good old days"; and he buys and gets it. Arriving home he goes at the piece—but I would have to be very wrong if, before he even gets painstakingly through the first page, he will not swear by all the holy musical ghosts that this [is] no ordinary sonata style but actually godless [trash]. Yet, Chopin has still accomplished what he wanted; he finds himself in the cantor's home, and who knows whether in that very home, perhaps years later, a romantic [-ally inclined] grandson will be born and raised, will dust off and play the sonata, and will think to himself, "The man was not so wrong after all."

With all this, a half judgment has already been offered. Chopin no longer writes anything that could be found as well in [the works of] others; he remains true to himself and has reason to.

It is regrettable that most pianists, even the cultivated ones, cannot see and judge beyond anything they can master with their own fingers. Instead of first glancing over such a difficult piece, they twist and bore (their way) through it, measure by measure; and then when scarcely more than the roughest formal relationships become evident, they put it aside and call it "bizarre, confused etc." Chopin in particular (somewhat like Jean Paul) has his decorative asides and parentheses, over which one should not stop too long at the first reading in order not to lose the continuity. Such places one finds on almost every page in the sonata, and Chopin's often arbitrary and wild chord writing make the detection [of the musical goals] still more difficult. To be sure, he does not like to enharmonize, if I may call it that, and so one often gets measures and keys in ten or more sharps, which [extremes] we can tolerate only in the most exceptional cases. Often he is justified, but often he confuses without reason and, as stated, alienates a good part of the public in this way, who, that is, do not care to be fooled all the time and to be driven into a corner. Thus, the sonata has a signature of five flats, or B-flat minor, a key that certainly cannot boast any special popularity. The beginning goes thus: [The opening four measures are quoted.]

After this typically Chopinesque beginning follows one of those stormy passionate phrases such as we already know by Chopin. One has to hear it played frequently and well. But this first part of the work also brings beautiful melody; indeed, it seems as if the Polish national flavor that inhered in most of the earlier Chopin melodies vanishes more and more with time, [and]

Bronarski/CHOPIN II 101–11, along with a reference (p. 103, fn.) to a 25-page article in Polish on Chopin's four sonatas, Opieński/CHOPIN, which proves to consist of a comprehensive recapitulation of previous comments on them (from Schumann's to Leichtentritt's) plus traditional form analyses especially of Opp. 35 and 58.

as if even he sometimes turned (beyond Germany) towards Italy. One knows that Bellini and Chopin were friends, that they often told each other of their compositions, [and] probably were not without artistic influence on each other. However, as suggested, it is only a slight leaning toward the southern manner. As soon as the melody ends, the whole [barbarian tribe of] Sarmatae flashes forth again in its relentless originality and tumult. At least, Bellini never dared to write and never could write a crisscross chord pattern such as we find at the end of the first theme in the second part [undoubtedly mss. 138–53]. And similarly, the entire movement ends [but] little in Italian fashion, which reminds me of Liszt's pertinent remark. He once said, Rossini and his compatriots always ended with a "vôtre tres humble serviteur," but not so Chopin, whose finales express rather the opposite.

The second movement is only the continuation of this mood, daring, sophisticated, fantastic, [with] the trio delicate, dreamy, entirely in Chopin's manner: [that is,] a Scherzo only in name, as with many of Beethoven's [scherzos]. Still more somber, a *Marcia funebre* follows, which even has something repulsive [about it]; an adagio in its place, perhaps in D♭, would have had a far more beautiful effect. What we get in the final movement under the title "Finale" seems more like a mockery than any [sort of] music. And yet, one has to admit, even from this unmelodic and joyless movement a peculiar, frightful spirit touches us, which holds down with an iron fist those who would like to revolt against it, so that we listen as if spellbound and without complaint to the very end, yet also without praise, for *music* it is not. Thus the sonata ends as it began, puzzling, like a sphinx with mocking smile.

In part, this review may have been intended alternately to counter, parody, and second a still more puzzled, rhetorical review of Op. 35 (in over 4 columns; by G. W. Fink?), in which the unity of the cycle, the harmony, and the modulations also seem to have been the main stumbling blocks.[110] Liszt is credited with writing in 1851 that Chopin shows "more determination than inspiration" in his concertos and sonatas, in the face of their Classical architectural disciplines and requirements; yet also with writing a paragraph of the highest poetic praise on the "Marche funèbre." [111] Hanslick seems to have remembered Schumann's remarks when he described a performance by Tausig in 1864 of Chopin's Op. 35 (still a novelty in Vienna).[112] He, too, questioned the binding of four such different pieces under the title "sonata" and whether Chopin was at home in this larger form. Yet he, too, found much to like in the work, including the finale, "which can hardly create any other impression than that of astonishment." Tausig himself reportedly described the "very peculiar" finale as "the ghost of the departed wandering about" after the "Marche funèbre," and subsequently, only two weeks before his own death in 1871, as

110. AMZ XLII (1840) 569–73.
111. "Liszt" & Waters/CHOPIN 35–38.
112. Hanslick/WIEN II 323–24.

"the wind blowing over my grave." [113] Later in the century, Frederick Niecks, William Henry Hadow, and Oscar Bie were still raising the same questions and doubts about Op. 35.[114] Only in recent decades have writers come to view it as a highly successful, unified cycle.[115] At any rate, long familiarity with the movements associated as they are would hardly permit us to take any other view of Op. 35 today.

The single report found here of Chopin's own performance of Op. 35 was that written when Moscheles visited him in Paris just after it was completed, in October, 1839 [116] (and just before the two men made such a hit as a duo team in "La Sonate," Op. 47, by Moscheles; ssb VII). Only after hearing Chopin, says Moscheles, "did I now for the first time understand his music, and all the raptures of the lady world become intelligible." In the decades following its publication nearly every renowned pianist, as well as many a lesser known one, seems to have included Op. 35 in his or her concert repertoire, including Bülow, Liszt, Tausig, Walter Bache, Busoni, Anton Rubinstein, and Pachmann.[117]

Chopin's known correspondence on Op. 58 merely confirms the times of its composition, sale, and publication in 1844–45,[118] without even the brief comments he left on Op. 35. But we do have an exceptionally clear facsimile of his autograph.[119] There is also a copy of a page from the finale in Liszt's own hand that includes changes presumably made by him for himself or one of his students.[120] These changes neither add nor subtract measures but enrich the right hand and reduce the left hand to 8th-notes, first in quintuplets, then in octaves and chords, producing a more incisive, stentorian, and less fluid effect.

From the start Op. 58 raised fewer questions of unity and form than Op. 35 did. Moreover, it presented nothing like the latter's march

113. Fay/GERMANY 194.
114. Niecks/CHOPIN II 246–49, with further references; Hadow/MODERN II 155–57; Bie/PIANOFORTE 262–63. The perplexity over the finale had more specific by-products, too, such as a full harmonization of it accompanying the article Stade/CHOPIN.
115. E.g., Georgii/KLAVIERMUSIK 352–53 and further pubs. as cited above.
116. MOSCHELES II 52–53. In Sydow/CHOPIN II xliii the date is pinpointed at Oct. 29.
117. For sample reports of 7 years in one Chopin center like London, alone, cf. MT XVII (1876) 500, XVIII (1877) 241 and 277, XX (1879) 262, XXI (1880) 606–7, XXII (1881) 302, XXIV (1883) 660. Also, cf. Habets/BORODIN 126 (on Liszt and the march); Pleasants/HANSLICK 228 (on Rubinstein in 1884); Dent/BUSONI 85.
118. Sydow & Hedley/CHOPIN 240, 245, 250, 254.
119. CHOPIN/facs.-m, with preface.
120. Bory/CHOPIN 166 has a facs. of Chopin's title p. and the page in Liszt's hand showing changes in mss. 207–53 of Chopin's finale. Cf. Walker/CHOPIN 251 and ssb X (Liszt) on Chopin's possible influence on Liszt's Son. in b.

or short finale to bring it special notoriety. One of its first main reviews, in 1846, called Op. 58 a distinctly superior work, citing especially its mastery of form and rich figuration.[121] Only some harmonic details of voice-leading and spelling were questioned, as they had been in the opening and other passages of Op. 35. Another early review (apparently marking a near capitulation on the part of Franz Brendel, who for long had been conspicuously hostile to Chopin)[122] asserted that no composer was entirely free of problems; that, in fact, the reviewer had been no Chopin worshipper and had repeatedly charged him with the same (harmonic?) peculiarities; but that without these peculiarities Chopin would not be Chopin and "in spite" of them Op. 58 "is and remains one of the most significant publications of the present." [123] When Pachmann played the work in London in 1883 a reviewer did find it "unequal in itself," with problems in the development section of the first movement, yet well designed to show off the performer in his "most favourable light." [124] A lack of genuine development of its ideas was Vincent d'Indy's chief reservation about Op. 58 when he preferred to analyze it alone among all four of Chopin's sonatas because of the high quality of its themes.[125] Today, as with Op. 35, several writers give unqualified endorsement to the form and content of Op. 58 as one of Chopin's finest, most mature works,[126] although most recitalists will confess to doubts about ever quite projecting a completely satisfying, purposeful form when either outer movement is played (cf. ssb VI), for all the unquestioned beauty of the themes.[127]

No report could be found here of Chopin playing Op. 58 himself. It may well have been too much for his frail body by then.[128] But there are again increasing reports, throughout the century, of performances by other pianists.[129] The work must have taken hold quickly. Scarcely six months after its publication in mid 1845 we find a deferential letter to Chopin from Kalkbrenner begging instruction for "my son Arthur [, who] makes so bold as to want to play your fine Sonata

121. AMZ XLVIII (1846) 74–75.
122. Cf. Jachimecki/CHOPIN 151, 204.
123. NZM XXIII (1845) 89–90.
124. MT XXV (1884) 21.
125. D'Indy/COURS II/1 407–10.
126. E.g., Hedley/CHOPIN 91; Jachimecki/CHOPIN 202–5.
127. Cf., also, Walker/CHOPIN 254.
128. Cf. Hedley/CHOPIN 106–7.
129. For sample reports in one 7-year period of performances as far off as Moscow and New York, cf. NZM LXXII/1 (1876) 234, LXXII/2 (1876) 498 and 510, LXIII/1 (1877) 230; MT XVIII (1878) 282, XXI (1880) 249, XXIII (1882) 662, XXIV (1882) 17, XXV (1884) 21.

in B minor. . . ." [130] It is surprising to find no record of Clara Schumann playing either this work or Op. 35, considering that she did play both of Chopin's concertos and much other music by him.[131] Among special mentions of Op. 58 is the candid description by the American pianist Amy Fay of her nervous trial of this work for Liszt in 1873 and of his masterful playing of its last three movements for her at the end of the lesson.[132] And Arthur Friedheim recalls one of Anton Rubinstein's characteristically gargantuan recitals in which all twenty-five minutes or thereabouts of Op. 58 served as the first encore![133]

There are numerous references to his last sonata, Op. 65, in Chopin's late correspondence, partly because of the involvement of its dedicatee, Auguste Franchomme, a fine cellist, a close friend in Chopin's last years, and an advisor to him in writing for the cello.[134] By mid December of 1845 Chopin was hoping to finish Op. 65—in fact, was already trying it out with Franchomme ("it goes very well") and wondering whether it could not yet be printed that year.[135] However, ten troubled months later (Oct., 1846) he still had to write, "Sometimes I am satisfied with my 'cello sonata, sometimes not. I throw it aside and then take it up again." [136] Then, in April of 1847 he reported playing it with Franchomme for Delfina Potocka ("you know how fond I am of her"); and in June he announced, besides another performance with Franchomme of Op. 65, its imminent publication (by Brandus in Paris) and its sale (the last work he himself sold) to Breitkopf & Härtel.[137]

We learn of another performance of Op. 65 by Chopin and Franchomme from Charles Hallé in which the ailing Chopin began in great pain but "warmed to his work" and improved, "the spirit having

130. Sydow & Hedley/CHOPIN 260–61.
131. Neither son. is in the repertoire listed in Litzmann/SCHUMANN III 613–24.
132. Fay/GERMANY 211–14.
133. Friedheim/LISZT 195.
134. Cf. RDM XXXVIII (1956) 168–70 (M. Debrun).
135. Sydow & Hedley/CHOPIN 258, 259.
136. Sydow & Hedley/CHOPIN 270.
137. Sydow & Hedley/CHOPIN 276, 288–89, 290, 291. Sydow/CHOPIN I xlviii reports another performance of Op. 65 by the same team. Brandus announced "immediate" pub. of Op. 65 in Oct., 1847 (Brown/CHOPIN 155), but the first advertisement of its availability does not seem to have appeared in RGM until Jan. 30, 1848 (or the same month that the Breitkopf & Härtel ed. appeared). A fragment of the autograph, dated May 23, 1846, is reported in Brown/CHOPIN Suppl. no. 160. Only such fragments of the autograph and sketches (cf. MMR LXXXV [1955] 62 [M. J. E. Brown]) seem to be extant; a facs. of the first p. of the autograph is in Bory/CHOPIN 173 (along with a facs. of the title p. of the original Brandus ed., including the ded.); the facs. of a sketch is in CONGRESS CHOPIN 336.

mastered the flesh." [138] There are reports of Walter Bache playing it with Franchomme (and others), too, in 1864;[139] and of Liszt playing it with some unidentified cellist in 1877.[140] And as with Opp. 35 and 58, the performances of Op. 65 multiplied rapidly during the last third of the century.[141]

Yet, Op. 65 has never won the general acceptance that Opp. 35 and 58 have won. Certain objections were raised from the start. Those from forerunners like Moscheles simply represented, of course, the conservative view of Chopin: "I often find passages [in Op. 65] which sound to me like some one preluding on the piano, the player knocking at the door of every key and clef to find if any melodious sounds are at home. . . . I find it a wild overgrown forest, into which only an occasional sunbeam penetrates." [142] But the objections require more notice when a contemporary reviewer writes of a deterioration in Op. 65 in the quality of Chopin's themes and a harmonic distortion of their cantabile style, in spite of the use of so songful an instrument as the cello.[143] In 1858 Hanslick criticized not only the themes but a lack of aptitude for handling the larger forms and for the polyphony expected in a duo.[144] In 1888 Niecks found nothing at all to redeem the work.[145] More recently A. Eaglefield Hull recognized "many beauties" in the work that "atone" for its structural weaknesses and an excess of ideas.[146]

As viewed here, Chopin's cello sonata has been misunderstood and wronged by these objections.[147] The reason it still is not much played lies neither in them nor in any failure, as is sometimes said, to give the cello an equal share of the musical interest. It lies rather in two kinds of difficulties that remove the work from the realm of social chamber music and restrict it to performance by advanced artists. The first difficulty is the piano part. Unless the pianist is able to put this part in suitable perspective by tossing off its many tricky passages easily and deftly, it will give, like Chopin's early Trio in g, more the effect

138. HALLÉ 36; also quoted, almost in full, in Cobbett/CHAMBER I 276 (A. E. Hull and W. W. Cobbett).

139. Bache/BACHE 173, 162.

140. Habets/BORODIN 132.

141. Sample performances over a period of 14 years may be found in MT XV (1872) 437, XX (1878–79) 146 and 621, XXI (1880) 233, XXVII (1886) 141 and 417; NZM LXXII (1876) 466.

142. MOSCHELES II 172, 213.

143. AMZ L (1848) 214–15.

144. Hanslick/WIEN II 167.

145. Niecks/CHOPIN II 250–51.

146. Cobbett/CHAMBER I 276; but one known instance does not justify the generalization that Chopin omitted the first mvt. when he played Op. 65 in public.

147. Cf. the recent and, from our standpoint, enlightened appraisals of Op. 65 in Jachimecki/CHOPIN 235–37 and Walker/CHOPIN 165–68 (P. Gould).

Ex. 74. From the finale of Frédéric Chopin's Sonata in g, Op. 65 (after Chopin/WERKE-m XVI 125).

of a weakly accompanied piano concerto. The second difficulty is the almost Schumannesque subtlety both of phrase syntax and harmony. Unless the performers fully perceive and adapt to the irregular exchanges between the instruments and the mercurial chromaticisms (Ex. 74), their playing will sound pasty and gauche. For the rest, performers able to meet the challenges will find all the thematic and polyphonic interest, all the structural unity and contrast (in this markedly cyclical work), and all the pleasure of sound needed to make Op. 65 an attractive, compelling duo. In its own way it reveals many of the traits—especially the melody, phrase syntax, rhythms, and harmony—that made Chopin one of the most influential of all 19th-century composers, whether we are thinking of Liszt (SSB X), Wagner, Brahms (SSB IX), Franck, Fauré, and lesser contemporaries, or Rachmaninoff, Scriabin, Debussy, Ravel, and even Prokofiev, among more recent composers.[148]

Pianists in Chopin's Sphere (Thalberg, Heller, Alkan)

During and right after the hegemony of Chopinism several other fine pianists in Paris wrote almost exclusively for piano, too, although

148. Cf. the helpful discussions of Chopin's influences in RM/CHOPIN 30–34 (K. Szymanowski) and 111–15 (S. Lobaczewska); Walker/CHOPIN 258–76 (P. Badura-Skoda).

working rather independently of each other. Chopin was fully aware
of one of his two most celebrated peers among pianists, **Sigismond
Thalberg** (1812 [149]–71), though he liked him personally no better than
the other, Liszt, and had less good to say about him as a pianist.[150] If
Thalberg is hidden in the darker historical shadows of Chopin and
Liszt today, he did rank on equal terms with them in the 1830's and
1840's, certainly as a pianist—contrary to some reports, his much publicized contests with Liszt did not end in any decisive defeat—and, at
least within the range of his many published fantasies and other
potpourris, as a composer.[151] Thalberg's justification for appearing in
these pages is but one work—his only one of the sort, in fact—*Grande
Sonate pour le Piano,* Op. 56 in c, published by Schlesinger of Paris in
1844 and about the same time by Breitkopf & Härtel (plate no. 7182).[152]
Op. 56 is a large, technically advanced work made up of four movements in forty-five pages (F-Sc-M-VF). Although its themes, motivic
concentration, handling of texture, and keyboard writing are above
average,[153] and although it apparently had enjoyed real popularity for
a short time,[154] the sonata is not one that could be revived successfully
today. Yet it does hold interest at least to the extent that its chief traits
help to confirm what we know about Thalberg's training and
playing.[155]

Thus, Op. 56 reveals a neatness, objectivity, and economy of means
about Thalberg's writing that tallies with his instruction by Sechter
in Vienna, his reported lessons under Moscheles and Hummel,[156] his

149. MGG XIII 273–75 (R. Sietz) and most other sources still do not take
cognizance of the birth certificate discovered and first reported early in this
century (as noted in BAKER vii and 1635; cf., also, GROVE Suppl. 436). This certificate
discredits the Romantic accounts (cf. Loesser/PIANOS 371) of Thalberg as the
natural son of mixed nobility (though it does not quite clarify his Frankfurt/M
parentage) and of the poetic derivations of his name.

150. Cf. Sydow & Hedley/CHOPIN 76, 135, 214, 218.

151. See the contemporary comparisons in Schumann/SCHRIFTEN I 480–81; by
Chopin's pupil Joseph Filtsch in Sydow & Hedley/CHOPIN 217; and by Mendelssohn
(as trans. in Schonberg/PIANISTS 174); also, the colorful accounts of Thalberg in
Loesser/PIANOS 371–74 and Schonberg/PIANISTS 172–78.

152. Mühsam/THALBERG, an unpub. diss. on the piano music, includes a detailed
description of Op. 56 that emphasizes "son. form" (pp. 51–65; with exx.), a short
biography that does not correct long-standing errors (pp. 17–26), and an undated,
unreconciled list of works by op. nos. (pp. 175–77).

153. In 1839 Schumann had described Thalberg as having "no invention except
in technique" (Storck/SCHUMANN 130).

154. Passing mentions of the publication of Op. 56 and Thalberg's performances
of it are numerous in issues of RGM for 1844–46 (and in 2 articles on it noted below).

155. Among contemporary descriptions of his playing, cf. Schumann/SCHRIFTEN
I 233 and 410, II 19–20; Sydow & Hedley/CHOPIN 76; MOSCHELES II 12–13, 49, 61,
210.

156. More and better biographical information is needed. Schilling/LEXICON

known predilection for the Classics (on those relatively few occasions when he was not playing his own show pieces),[157] and his impassive, immobile posture at the piano. Op. 56 also reveals some of those quasi three-hand settings so widely remarked in his playing,[158] in which the theme "sings" in the middle of the texture while arpeggios, chords, or other devices accompany both below and above (as at the start and, especially, at the return in 8ves in the "Andante," though without the 3-staff scoring he sometimes used elsewhere). One might even say that Op. 56 reveals a certain elegance and dignity, in the many virtuoso passages as well as the simpler ones, that recall Thalberg's impeccable dress and polished manners.

With further regard to those passages themselves, their wide stretches (often encompassing 10ths) and the way they course up and down over the whole keyboard, bring to mind, like much else in Thalberg's sonata, his last teacher, Kalkbrenner, and both the style traits and the pros and cons of the latter's own Sonata with the same opus number (*supra*). Although they are less free and spontaneous, those passages bring Chopin to mind, too. And still more indicative of Thalberg's close relationship to Chopin[159] are certain hymnic melodies with block chord accompaniments and free tonal transpositions to the next scale degree either way. Thus, Ex. 75, the second theme of Thalberg's first movement, might be compared with the middle section of Chopin's Nocturne in g, Op. 37/1.

As with Kalkbrenner's Op. 56, the chief shortcoming of Thalberg's Op. 56, for all its fine lines and suave brilliance, is its tendency to wander on and on without a clear sense of direction at the higher architectural levels. However, contemporary criticisms did not touch on this aspect. One reviewer, acknowledging the telling sound, the objective style, the suggestions of Chopin, and the significance of "a first sonata by a first virtuoso," expressed dissatisfaction mainly with the content itself and Thalberg's failure to advance beyond the styles of

VI 628 seems to be the prime source for Hummel (SSB VIII), and MOSCHELES I 131 and II 12–13 for Moscheles. Thalberg is usually said to have studied with Hummel and Sechter in Vienna. Mrs. Moscheles twice places the lessons with Moscheles in London and says they ended in 1826 (Thalberg remained a close friend of Moscheles). Neither Moscheles nor Hummel is reported to have been in Vienna within several years of 1826. It is more possible that Thalberg could have studied with one or both in London, if at all.

157. Performances by him of Beethoven, Dussek, and Chopin are mentioned in Schumann/SCHRIFTEN I 392; of Bach, Mozart, and Moscheles in MOSCHELES II 8, 26, and 210; and of Beethoven and Mendelssohn in Schonberg/PIANISTS 177. Did he perform in public the Schubert Sonata in B (D. 575) that Diabelli pub. posthumously and ded. to him in 1846 (SSB VII)?

158. Cf. MOSCHELES II 12–13.

159. A relationship already noted in Schumann/SCHRIFTEN I 304.

Ex. 75. From the first movement of Sigismond Thalberg's
Sonata in c, Op. 56 (after the early Breitkopf & Härtel ed.).

Beethoven.[160] Neither objection seems quite justified. Another, more
verbose reviewer, in Paris, saw only good in the work—in its themes,
rhythms, modulations, nobility of style, texture (with the melody in
the middle), and figurations.[161]

Born in Hungary of Bohemian parents, trained in Vienna, **Stephen
Heller** (1813–88) moved to Paris permanently in 1838. In Vienna he
had studied with Anton Halm (ssb VII), been introduced to both Beethoven and Schubert, and made his debut as a piano prodigy.[162] Meanwhile, he had come under the influence of Schumann and Chopin,
among others, and when expected lessons with Kalkbrenner could not
follow upon his arrival in Paris, Heller apparently was glad enough to
give up the idea of a virtuoso's career in favor of composing and be-

160. nzm XXII (1845) 39–40 (C. d. Jüngste).

161. rgm for March 3, 1845, pp. 68–69 (M. Maurel); an answer to this review in
rgm for March 8, 1846, pp. 77–78 (H. Blanchard) takes exception to certain
statements but is at least as poetic and enthusiastic about Op. 56 itself.

162. Booth/heller is a recent diss. especially helpful for its full biography and
documents (pp. 8–61) and description of selected works (pp. 86–184); its list of
works (pp. 240–45) is partially dated. Cf., also, mgg VI 100–104 (R. Sietz) and grove
IV 226–29 (R. Gorer), with further references. On Heller's birth year, cf. grove
Suppl. 218; Booth/heller 8–10. Heller's autobiographic summary in hallé 317–22 is
pertinent here.

coming something of a recluse.[163] As for his compositions, he wrote more than 150 that were published, nearly all for P solo and ranging from single short pieces to five cyclic sonatas and three late sonatinas (Opp 146, 147, and 149; pub. in 1878–79).[164]

Four of Heller's five sonatas were numbered in series, beginning with Op. 9, a four-movement work (S-Sc-M-F) in d (not D) that originated between about 1835, when Schumann brought Heller into his imaginary "Davidsbündler," [165] and about 1838, before publication took place in Leipzig.[166] Schumann, strengthening Heller's confidence to continue composing, reviewed and praised Op. 9 as an imaginative, personal, unorthodox work that would shock the traditionalists and that produces some clever new resource every time it seems about to falter.[167] Sonata 2, Op. 65 in b, was published in Leipzig about 1846 (Friedrich Hofmeister, plate no. 4150). It was reviewed in 1849 as a basic, purely musical creation, full of contrast and tragic import, and quite isolated from the salon style that was making Heller a favorite of the dilettantes.[168] Sonata 3, Op. 88 in C, was first published by Breitkopf & Härtel in 1856. It is a cyclically interrelated, four-movement work (F-Sc-M-VF) suggesting some influences from Weber's piano writing and ending with a witty "Allegro umeristico e molto vivace." [169] Although no separate review of it has turned up here, it was cited in 1878 as "the greatest favourite of all his works in this fashion, because of the well sustained power in each movement, and its vigour as a whole." [170] And Sonata 4, Op. 143 in b♭, was first published by Breitkopf & Härtel in 1878, with the reviewer calling it "the most masterly of all, as well for the worth of the separate movements as for the homophonous character of the whole, so that it appears to be like the pursuit of one idea in its various phases, not so erratic, as more or less connected, with just such divergencies as would help to make

---

163. Cf. his description of himself in Joachim/LETTERS 355.
164. Op. 149 is favorably reviewed in MW XIV (1883) 508.
165. MGG VI 101.
166. A study of Heller's sons. is lacking. Booth/HELLER 128–38 describes Opp. 88 and 143, with exx.; cf., also, the summaries of Heller's style traits on pp. 85 and 181–83.
167. Schumann/SCHRIFTEN I 453–55. In MMR VIII (1878) 91, Op. 9 is recalled as a "well-known" work, "elaborate in form, yet lacking in melody."
168. NZM XXXI (1849) 281–82 (with ex.). In MMR VIII (1878) 91, Op. 65 is recalled as a "well-known" work of "dignified, yet somewhat uneven and sombre character."
169. Cf. Booth/HELLER 128–34.
170. MMR VIII (1878) 91; but the next sentence, on Schumann, confuses Heller's Opp. 88 and 9. Shedlock/SONATA 235–36 refers negatively to Op. 88.

the expression elegant and eloquent." [171] Charles Hallé, one of Heller's closest friends, seems to have done much to popularize this last work in England;[172] Heller's fifth sonata, not in the numbered series of four, is his *Es ist bestimmt in Gottes Rath [God Has Decreed It], Volkslied von Felix Mendelssohn-Bartholdy,*[173] *Fantasie in Form einer Sonate,* Op. 69 in D, published about 1847 by Bote et Bock. In this work the main themes of all four movements (S/F-Sc-S-F) derive freely from Mendelssohn's tune, which is stated almost literally at the start.

As surveyed today, Op. 65 represents Heller's sonatas at their best— that is, in their most enterprising and original writing. It is a serious, intense, relatively free work in four motivically interrelated movements totalling thirty pages. The first movement, in 3/4 meter, is marked "Fiery, and with potent expression" (as trans. from the German Heller preferred to use); the second, in 2/4 and in the tonic major key, is headed "Ballade," with the mark "Moderato"; the third, in 3/4 and in the submediant key, is headed "Intermezzo," "Moderately fast"; and the last, in "C" meter and in the home key of b again, is headed "Epilog" and marked "Animated to the extreme, and with appropriate expression" (Ex. 76). Those who know only Heller's etudes, preludes, or other short teaching pieces that have served so many young students so well, would scarcely recognize his much freer and, of course, more advanced writing in Op. 65. The outer movements sustain considerable intensity through successive climaxes of motives reiterated and advanced sequentially. Gentle, poetic contrasts are achieved in all movements through abrupt dynamic reductions, manifold rhythmic transformations, and a wealth of editorial detail, from articulation, pedal, and swell signs to copious inscriptions, including an initial footnote authorizing the performer to read more into Heller's tempo indications.

The more poetic aspects of Heller's sonatas have hardly borne out the prediction of Fétis that a "day will come when the influences of the clique will have passed, permitting [one] to judge the true merit of things; then one will realize, without any doubt, that Heller, even more than Chopin, is the modern poet of the piano." [174] But intimate, sensitive episodes do enhance his music, along with other original turns in the harmony and phrase syntax such as one encounters in the music of a composer who has had to fill in much of his own training. In these traits Heller's sonatas bring to mind the music of two of his

171. MMR VIII (1878) 91.
172. Cf. HALLÉ 171, 241.
173. I.e., Mendelssohn's "Volkslied," Op. 47/4 (Mendelssohn/WERKE-m XIX/145 82).
174. Fétis/BU IV 288.

Ex. 76. From the finale of Stephen Heller's Sonata in b, Op. 65 (after the original ed. of Friedrich Hofmeister).

Paris friends—Liszt to a small degree and Berlioz, a close friend,[175] to a greater degree. There is much less influence of Chopin than might be expected, considering Heller's devotion to Chopin and references to him in his music titles.[176] On the other hand, Heller, never really a modernist, does recall in his sonatas the sonatas of his contemporaries August Gottfried Ritter and Ferdinand Hiller (both ssb X), especially their Mendelssohnian traits,[177] including much dependence on the dim.-7th chord. In other respects Heller's sonatas are curiously lacking, or curiously ascetic, if a more positive view is preferred. In spite of their poetic episodes they reveal little lyricism—in fact, little outright melody. In spite of their harmonic color they reveal relatively little tonal movement or the tension of strong modulations—in fact, they suffer from a certain tonal monotony. In spite of their motivic reiterations and rhythmic changes, or perhaps because of these, they show little interest in polyphonic activity. And in spite of Heller's early pianistic achievements, they show little interest in exploiting the ranges

175. Cf. the high esteem for Heller expressed in BERLIOZ MEMOIRS 510.
176. Cf. GROVE IV 227–29 (including Opp. 71 and 154).
177. But in Selden-Goth/MENDELSSOHN 245, Mendelssohn pairs Heller with Berlioz in a protest against then recent music.

and diverse figurations of the keyboard. Indeed, Heller's tendency to write largely in chords and octaves is seen here as one of the main deterrents to a possible revival of sonatas that remain intriguing both despite and because of those other "lacks."

Even more of a recluse in the Chopin era, as well as an eccentric, was the native Parisian **Charles-Valentin (Morhange) Alkan** (1813–88).[178] Like Heller, Alkan began his career as a virtuoso prodigy but turned almost entirely to teaching and composing in the 1830's, with a substantial number of publications following, which are nearly all for P solo. He, too, knew Chopin[179] and Liszt, winning their respect as well as that of such other notables as Anton Rubinstein, César Franck, and Bülow.[180] His music has always seemed too difficult and experimental to win general popularity. But as often as it has been vehemently decried and dismissed it has been revived with enthusiasm, usually as a cult, winning such tributes to Alkan as Busoni's placing him on a par with Chopin, Schumann, and Brahms among "the greatest of the post-Beethoven piano composers." [181]

Three sonatas by Alkan were published—Op. 33 in b/g♯, a "Grande Sonate" for P solo sometimes called "Les quatres Âges," published by Joubert of Paris in late 1847 or early 1848;[182] Op. 47 in E (not e), a "Grande Sonate de concert" for P & Vc-or-Va, consisting of four movements (VF-VF-S-VF) that keep the piano busier than the cello, published by Costallat of Paris in 1858,[183] and described as "long and dull";[184] and Op. 61 in a, which is a thinner, lighter "Sonatine" for P solo, in four very-fast movements totalling thirty-five pages (iii being

178. Most of the known biographical information is recapitulated on pp. 1–3 of a 58-p. undergraduate study of Alkan's music done at Harvard University, Bloch/ALKAN (with bibliography, undated list of works, and many exx.). It is summarized again, more briefly (along with information about Alkan's birth certificate and the false addition of "Henri" to his name, and with mention of a book on Alkan [in progress]), in the preface (pp. v-xx, with style and performance comments) to a recent anthology of selected works for P solo by Alkan, Lewenthal/ALKAN-m. Cf., also, GROVE I 111–13 (H. Searle); MGG IX 579–80 (under "Morhange-Alkan"; R. Sietz). Warm thanks are owing to Mr. Joseph Bloch and Mr. Raymond Lewenthal for further information by correspondence.

179. Cf. Hedley/CHOPIN 54–55; Sydow & Hedley/CHOPIN 375; Bellamann/ALKAN 252.

180. Cf. BÜLOW BRIEFE III 180–85; Sietz/HILLER 121.

181. Bloch/ALKAN 3. Most recently in this country, Raymond Lewenthal's ed. (Lewenthal/ALKAN-m), recitals, and recording (Vic. LM-2815) of Alkan's music have aroused new interest.

182. It is not in HOFMEISTER but is advertised, from Feb. 13 on, in several issues of RGM for 1848. It is described and discussed, with exx., in Bloch/ALKAN 26–37 and 38, and described in Bellamann/ALKAN 255–56. The 2d mvt., "Quasi-Faust," is reprinted in Lewenthal/ALKAN-m 14 (with preface, pp. xviii–xx).

183. Cf. Altmann/KAMMERMUSIK 245 and 251.

184. Bloch/ALKAN 40.

a "Scherzo-Minuetto"), published posthumously by Costallat about 1900, and described variously as "classic" in its "purity of form" and "as what a piano sonata by Berlioz might have been like." [185]

When Alkan's music has been played at all it is his etudes that have received most attention, including Op. 39/4–7 and 8–10, which respectively make up an enormous solo "Symphonie" and solo "Concerto" (both played by Egon Petri in 1938).[186] Of the sonatas, the only one that has received appreciable attention, though no performances discovered here, is Op. 33, and that chiefly because of its programme. (A biblical quotation over the "Adagio" 3d mvt. is all the "programme" to be found in Op. 47.) The four movements of Op. 33, approaching Scriabin in their colorful, abundant inscriptions, bear the following headings, starting instructions, and internal advices that are worth quoting (excluding standard tempo and dynamic indications). Thus, we find in i, in b/B: "20 Ans; très vite; décidément . . . gaiement . . . ridendo [laughing] . . . palpitant . . . avec bonheur . . . bravement avec enthousiasme . . . valeureusement"; ii, in d$\sharp$/F$\sharp$: "30 Ans, Quasi-Faust; assez vite; sataniquement . . . Le Diable [identifying a chordal, climactic theme] . . . avec candeur . . . passionément . . . avec désespoir . . . déchirant . . . Diabolique . . . Le Seigneur [the Lord God; identifying another chordal, climactic theme] . . . avec délices"; iii, in G: "40 Ans, Un heureux Ménage; lentement; très lié, avec tendreuse et quiétude . . . Les enfans [identifying a characteristic double-note figure] . . . amoureusement . . . (10 heures [identifying 10 gonglike strokes]) . . . La prière [identifying a chordal, hymnic theme]"; and iv, in g$\sharp$: "50 Ans, Promethée enchâiné [with 3 extracts —lines 750–54, 1051, and 1091—from Aeschylus' *Prometheus*]; extrèmement lent." The only other programmatic help comes in a preface by Alkan that deserves translation almost in full, although it seems to understate the importance he attached to programme music in general:

Many things have been said and written on the limits of musical expression. Without adopting this or that rule, without seeking to resolve any of the far-reaching questions stirred up by this or that system, I shall tell why I have given similar titles to these four movements and sometimes used quite unusual terms.

It is not imitative music that is concerned here; still less music seeking its true justification, [or] the explanation for its effect, [or] its worth in an extramusical environment. The first movement is a Scherzo; the second an Allegro; the third and the fourth [movements] are an Andante and a Largo;

185. Bellamann/ALKAN 261; Searle/ALKAN 277. The Library of Congress has a copy of this scarce work, which is not listed in HOFMEISTER.
186. Cf. Bloch/ALKAN 3; Lewenthal/ALKAN-m xi–xiv, 27.

Ex. 77. From the second movement of Charles-Valentin
Alkan's Sonata in b/g♯, Op. 33 (after the original Joubert ed. of
1847 or 1848).

but each one of them corresponds in my mind to a given moment of existence,
to a particular kind of thought, [or] of imagination. Why shouldn't I indicate
this? The musical element will always remain, and the expression can only
improve in this way; the performer, without in any way giving up his individual feeling, is inspired by the same idea as the composer; such a name
and [/or] such a thing seem to run aground [when] taken in a material [and
literal?] sense [but] work perfectly in the realm of the intellectual. . . .

Alkan's work is long, 1,121 measures in 50 pages lasting well over a
half hour, yet not too long for its musical interest, which has seemed
stronger here than is usually acknowledged. If there were nothing else
to further it, the interest would be sustained by the long, well-drawn,
diatonic, melodic lines in each movement, with their accurate, choice,
sometimes chromatic harmonic support, and the resourceful piano
writing, with its excellent textural interest, variety and range of color,
and euphonious scoring (except in Alkan's fullest, most bombastic
chordal writing). Moreover, the technical difficulties that are always
cited in Alkan's piano music, such as his characteristic full chordal
climax, "The Lord God [Supreme]," late in the second movement (Ex.

77), and its equally characteristic continuation up to the edge of physical endurance, are not insurmountable. The athletic problems are certainly no greater than those in Liszt's Sonata in b, though they may be a little more uncompromising. And when the difficulties do get almost unmanageable, as in the seven-voice fughetta that leads into Ex. 77, Alkan is careful to supply a "Facilité" brace.

Op. 33 makes a satisfying cycle apart from its programme, even though the movements differ considerably in their lengths—525, 332, 192, and 72 measures—, even though the last two movements are both mostly on the slow quiet side, and even though the tonal scheme is open and unusual (b/B-d♯/F♯-G-g♯). But the tonal scheme might be said to give unity in the sense of a "grand cadence" (ssʙ VI). And there is the unity of thematic interrelationships in all four movements, about as much and as varied as can be found nearly twenty years earlier in Berlioz' *Symphonie fantastique; épisode de la vie d'un artiste* (a work that seems to have left its deep mark on the programme, melody, harmony, scoring, and intensity of Alkan's Op. 33).

The forms of the separate movements, if naively deliberate at times and at best not a conspicuous means of dynamic tension in themselves, are clear and balanced enough at least not to interfere with the progress of the music. The scherzo first movement is a fluent thinly scored piece in simple A-B-A design, with the B or trio section being an excellent melody for all its ingenuous simplicity. The satanic second movement, more accurately a battle with God triumphing over the Devil, is the biggest movement in design (approximately "sonata form" with coda), emotional range, and technical challenges. The climaxes are obviously meant to be both visually and aurally phrenetic and soul shattering. As an ideal foil for all this excitement, the third movement is a sweetly melodious piece in A-B-A design, not too far removed from a Mendelssohn "Song Without Words." And the short brooding finale, a kind of free rondo, could pass for one of Liszt's "Harmonies poétiques et religieuses" in advance of Liszt himself. Its treatment of Man at "50 Ans" by the approximately 33-year-old Alkan may not quite anticipate maturity to the extent that "Thanatopsis" does, by the 16-year-old William Cullen Bryant. But it provides some of the maturest moments not only of this sonata but in all of Alkan's music explored here.

Among other, more obscure composers active in Chopin's sphere should be mentioned the pianist **Louis (Trouillon-) Lacombe** (1818–84), who trained in Paris, then in Vienna under Czerny and Sechter, before returning to Paris in 1839 to give his full time to composition.[187]

187. Cf. ᴍɢɢ VIII 38–39 (G. Ferchault), with further references but no sons. in the partial list of works.

Lacombe's Op. 1 is a *Sonate fantastique* in f, published by Artaria in Vienna in 1839 [188] and reviewed by Schumann as promising in its best moments of virtuosity and quasi-orchestral writing.[189] To judge by a later, weak, perfunctory *Sonate de salon,* Op. 33 in e, composed about 1850, the promise did not materialize.[190] **Camille-Marie Stamaty** (1811–70) was a pianist of Italian and Greek descent who studied with Kalkbrenner and taught Gottschalk and Saint-Saëns, among others.[191] The first of two published piano sonatas by him, Opp. 8 in f and 20 in c, was reviewed flamboyantly in 1843 as a consistently outstanding example, especially in its melodies and advanced piano writing, of a new renaissance of the sonata after a century of its supremacy and decline! [192] The Czech pianist **Sigmund Goldschmidt** (1815–77), a pupil of Tomaschek (ssb XVII), was in Paris from 1845 to 1849, around the time when his two piano sonatas, Opp. 5 (or 6) in f and 8 in d, were published by Schuberth in Hamburg. These were reviewed (in 1846) as fluent, skillful, significant works in which the composer courageously renounced his virtuosic tendencies.[193]

A Low Ebb Early in the Mid Period, 1850–1885

Both qualitatively (with rare exceptions to be noted below) and quantitatively the sonata output reached a low ebb in France around the middle of the Romantic Era. Most of the composers were not native Frenchmen. Most of them can get only brief mentions, and then primarily for the usual reason of filling in the historical picture. Thus, there was the celebrated harpist from Boulogne-sur-Mer, **Dieudonné-Joseph-Guillaume-Félix Godefroid** (1818–97), who prospered in Paris and during wide concert tours abroad.[194] His *Sonate dramatique* in c, Op. 45, and a *2me Sonate* in g, Op. 53, figured among his many elegant salon and recital pieces for P solo (along with many others for harp), and were published in the mid 1850's by Heugel of Paris and Schott of Mainz. There was the Bohemian virtuoso who lived mostly in Paris, **Karl Wehle (Wehli; 1825–83).** A pupil of Moscheles and Theodor

188. Weinmann/ARTARIA item 3124.
189. Schumann/SCHRIFTEN I 452–53.
190. No lifetime ed. was found here, only an ed. pub. posthumously, about 1895, by Émile Gillet in Paris (as part of an effort to revive interest in Lacombe? cf. MGG VIII 39; Hopkinson/PARISIAN 46).
191. MGG XII 1148–49 (J. Vigué).
192. RGM for Dec. 10, 1843, pp. 419–20.
193. NZM XXV (1846) 13–14. Cf. Riemann/LEXIKON I 629.
194. Cf. MGG V 395–97 (F. Vernillat).

Kullak, Wehle left a *Grande Sonate* in four movements (F-Sc-M-VF) for
P solo, Op. 38 in c, published by Schlesinger in Berlin (1856?) and reviewed as superior rather than trivial salon music, in which, however,
virtuosity predominates over expressive values.[195] Another Bohemian
in Paris, **Julius Schulhoff** (1825–98), was given encouragement by
Chopin.[196] He left one published sonata, Op. 37 in f, for P solo (*ca.*
1855), which proves to bear the strong mark of Chopin divested of his
genius. The first of its three movements clearly recalls Chopin's Etude
in f, Op. 10/9, the second his Etude in c♯, Op. 25, and the third less
specifically the opening movement of his Sonata in b♭, Op. 35. And
there was the German cellist, **Berthold Damcke** (1812–75), who left
four published sonatas after settling in Paris in 1859—Op. 43 in D, for
P & Vc (1861), recommended by Heller in a letter to Joachim as "far
above the *veillée* [nocturnal diversions]" that the Parisians were accepting;[197] and Opp. 44 in D (1861) and 55 in f (1876 [2d ed.?]), as
well as a "Sonatine sur les cinq notes de la gamme" in C, all for P-duet.
Op. 44, in four movements (F-Sc-M-F), was reviewed as a work too long
for its content and idiom, and therefore not likely to succeed in spite
of many good things, especially its fugal climax in the finale.[198] Damcke
and Berlioz had a high regard for each other.[199]

Furthermore, there was the Norwegian born pianist **Thomas Dyke
Acland Tellefsen** (1823–74), who studied with Kalkbrenner and Chopin
before Richault in Paris published five sonatas by him, in the 1850's—
two for P solo, one each for P & Vn and P & Vc, and one for P &
Vn-or-Vc.[200] And there was the piano virtuoso of worldwide fame,
Henri Herz (1806?–88) who, unfortunately, is remembered today for
little else than Schumann's sarcastic remarks about "him and [Franz]
Hünten," whom the musical world "already has long recognized as
masters (and business men, too). . . ."[201] Amongst his myriad potpourris, fantasias, variations, and other salon diversions, nearly all for
piano,[202] is a *Grande Sonate di bravura,* Op. 200 in E (1860?), reviewed
at length and facetiously as being not appreciably different from his
other works in its passages, its melodic resemblances to the music of

195. NZM XLV (1856) 279 (E. Klitzsch). Cf. Riemann/LEXIKON II 2000; Fétis/BU
Suppl. II 665–66.
196. Cf. Fétis/BU VII 519; MGG XII 237–38 (R. Quoika).
197. Joachim/LETTERS 251.
198. MW IV (1873) 533–34 (G. H. Witte).
199. Cf. Berlioz/MEMOIRS 440–41, 529.
200. Cf. MGG XIII 212 (O. Gurvin), with a further reference; also, Sydow/CHOPIN
III 386.
201. Schumann/SCHRIFTEN I 284 *et passim.* The amused contempt of Mendelssohn
and Moscheles is suggested in MOSCHELES I 292–93.
202. Cf. PAZDÍREK VII 454–66.

Liszt and others, and its sentimental slow movement.[203] One might add, though, that the passagework is well scored and intriguing to work out, and that Herz knew his "business" as a professional should.

The two duo sonatas of a better known composer in Paris, the cellist and violinist of Spanish descent (**Victor Antoine**) **Édouard Lalo** (1823–92), have somewhat more interest.[204] The first, Op. 12 in D, for P & Vn (composed in 1854 and first pub. in 1855 [205]), is a relatively conservative work in three movements (F-Va-Ro).[206] Yet its precise, transparent texture, its frank forthright melodies, characterized throughout by frequent octave leaps, and its constant attention to rhythmic detail still make it a delight to play. The rondo is a virtual *perpetuum mobile*. Lalo's other sonata is for P & Vc, in a (not A; without op. no., composed in the 1850's; first pub. by Hartman of Paris between 1869 and 1881, then by Heugel of Paris *ca.* 1892 [207]). Although not a late work, it already reveals conspicuous advances in melodic depth and character, in harmonic range and subtlety, in structural freedom, and in the exploitation of technical resources (Ex. 78). In its three movements (M/F-M-F) are foretastes not only of Lalo's own familiar *Symphonie espagnole* (1875) but of music by Fauré, Debussy, and Ravel.

The short-lived, native French composer **Alexis de Castillon** (1838–73), bred on Bach, Beethoven, and the German Romantics and directly influenced by Franck, ranks with his friends Lalo and Saint-Saëns among the pioneers in France of absolute chamber music during the second half of the 19th century.[208] Except for some early (lost?) sonatas in which, says d'Indy, he was required by a weak teacher to make no modulations throughout,[209] Castillon wrote only one sonata, Op. 6 in C, for P & Vn (pub. by Heugel in 1872).[210] He wrote this sonata around 1870, during the much better instruction he got from Franck. Although it still betrays inexperience in the development and tonal organization of his ideas, Op. 6 is interesting especially for the structural freedoms in its four movements (In/F-Sc-M-VF). In the first movement an introduction anticipates a lovely, songful theme, followed by a weaker

203. DMZ II (1861) 229–30, with exx.

204. Cf. RM/LALO (with list of works and composition dates, pp. 123–24, by P. Lalo); Tiersot/LALO (life, works, and letters); MGG VIII 106–8 (G. Ferchault). Both sons. are described in Cobbett/CHAMBER II 88–89 (F. Schmitt).

205. Tiersot/LALO 12, 27.

206. Exx. are quoted in Shand/VIOLIN 247–48.

207. Cf. Tiersot/LALO 12, 27 (regarding another Vc son., which became an orchestral piece); Fétis/BU Suppl. II 68 and Hopkinson/PARISIAN 56; Cat. NYPL XVI 740.

208. Cf. MGG II 901–4 (A. Gauthier).

209. MGG II 902; cf. d'Indy/COURS I/1 427.

210. Op. 6 is described in some detail, with exx., in both Selva/SONATE 235–38 and Cobbett/CHAMBER I 233–34 (V. d'Indy).

Ex. 78. From the start of the development section in the first movement of Sonata in a, by Édouard Lalo (after the Heugel ed. in the New York Public Library at Lincoln Center).

second theme, a development of the first theme, a partial recapitulation in which that theme is restored to interest in a fughetta in A♭, and a coda that prepares for the scherzo. The latter, in G, reaches a melodic high point in the trio section. The third movement presents a poignant theme in a, with inspired rises and falls that anticipate similar passages in the violin sonatas of both Franck and Fauré. The finale, an extended free "sonata form," dwells too long on, and exploits too much, the vigorous, rhythmically clipped theme with which it opens. A brilliant coda closes the work. Castillon's preference for the deliberately paced, drawn out development of a single idea recalls Rheinberger's approach to form (ssB X).

Among other sonata composers in this period, the cosmopolitan **Louis-Théodore Gouvy** (1819–98), born in Saarbrücken of French descent, was a musician of independent means who was close to Chopin, Berlioz, and Hallé, among others.[211] His several fluent, skillful, rather routine sonatas do not show any later trends in style and form, however, than can be found in Mendelssohn's music. These sonatas include one example each for P & Vn and P & Cl, one for 2 P's, and three for

211. Cf. MGG V 605–7 (E. Haraszti), with inadequate list of works.

P-duet, all published between 1862 and 1880.[212] Somewhat similar, a little less dynamic, a little more square-cut and pedagogic in character, are the several sonatas by the Paris-born violinist and much published composer **Benjamin (Louis Paul) Godard** (1849–95). These include four for P & Vn, one for P & Vc, and two for P solo, all published between 1867 and 1887.[213] The fourth for violin, Op. 12 in A♭ (1880), apparently was the most played of the sonatas. It was reviewed with more praise for its skill than its content, and for its inner, lighter movements than its outer movements.[214] The second piano solo, Op. 94 in f (*ca.* 1885), is a standard sort of sonata in three movements (F-S-Sc) whereas the first solo, "Sonate fantastique" in C, Op. 63 (*ca.* 1880 [215]), is more of a four-movement suite distinguished chiefly by its programmatic titles over each movement—"The forest demons," "The goblins," "The love fairy," and "The ocean spirits" (the last with three stanzas of verse by Godard). But the facile music sounds more like a suite of four character pieces than a sonata. Its regularly paired or repeated phrases, its stock harmonies, and its run-of-the-mill themes (well short of its composer's ever favorite "Berceuse" from *Jocelyn*), preclude more serious attention.

The virtuoso, French-born pianist **Georges-Jean Pfeiffer** (1835–1908), pupil of Kalkbrenner and Damcke, among others, left one published sonata each for P & Vn (Op. 66 in e, 1879), P & Vc (Op. 28 in c, 1868), and 2 Ps (Op. 65 in ?, 1879).[216] Op. 66 was reviewed as an interesting work, more for its rhythms than its melodies or any special originality.[217] The popular German pianist and associate of Johann Baptist Cramer, **Jacob Rosenhain** (1813–94), left 3 sonatas for P & Vc (Opp. 38 in E, 53 in C, and 98 in d) and 3 more for P solo (Opp. 12 in c, 44 in f, and 74 in D), all first published between about 1847 and 1886.[218] Following Schumann's friendly, favorable reception of Rosenhain's early Piano Trio Op. 2 in 1836,[219] Rosenhain's Op. 38 (dedicated to Mendelssohn) was reviewed as a light, piquant, German-flavored "dish

---

212. Cf. Altmann/KAMMERMUSIK 204, 281, 288, 299; Cobbett/CHAMBER I 483–85 (W. Altmann), especially on Op. 61 in g, for P & Vn (1876); cf., also, the short reviews (to the same effect) of Op. 61 in SMW XXXV (1877) 708 and MW XI (1880) 250.

213. Cf. MGG V 389–91 (E. Haraszti), with inadequate list.

214. MW XII (1881) 594; NZM LXXVIII/2 (1882) 256.

215. The year is based on the approximate time the pub. J. Hamelle succeeded J. Maho (Hopkinson/PARISIAN 85 and 55).

216. Cf. Fétis/BU Suppl. II 331; MGG X 1167 (G. Ferchault), with inadequate list of works; Altmann/KAMMERMUSIK 220, 262, 289.

217. SMW XXXVIII (1880) 180.

218. Cf. GROVE VII 235–36 (G. Grove); MGG XI 912–13 (R. Sietz); Altmann/KAMMERMUSIK 263; HOFMEISTER IV (1844–51) 152, V (1852–59) 204, 1886 p. 243.

219. Schumann/SCHRIFTEN I 168–69.

for the Paris salon world," [220] and his four-movement solo Sonata Op. 44 (dedicated to Fétis) as a skillful, unoriginal work with some rhythmic ambiguity.[221]

A Few Minor Composers in Belgium and Holland

There is curiously little even to mention by way of sonatas in Belgium and Holland up to 1885. Not one Belgian example is singled out in the fine survey Closson & Borren/BELGIQUE (pp. 237–61) and only a very few, obscure Dutch examples are cited in the similarly fine survey Reeser/NEDERLANDSE (pp. 13–184). Belgium's chief name in Romantic sonata history, César Franck, is shortly to be discussed not in this section but among Parisian residents who contributed late in the era. Other, relatively important composers like Albert Grisar, Peter Benoit, François-Joseph Fétis, and François Auguste Gevaert (the last two remembered only as scholars) showed little or no interest in the sonata. Moreover, as had already been implied by Gossec and Grétry (two late-Classic Belgians who also had shown little interest in the sonata; SCE 608), Belgium had hardly provided the soil for any sort of present or future artistic greatness so long as she remained "occupied" (up to 1831).[222]

The only generally recognized name among four composers in Brussels or Liège that are to be mentioned now is that of the widely travelled virtuoso **Henri Vieuxtemps** (1820–81). Vieuxtemps' leadership in French violin playing reflected the influences of Charles de Bériot (another Belgian not interested in the sonata), Paganini, and, indirectly, Viotti.[223] Two duo sonatas are among his nearly ninety publications, mostly effective display pieces. Those two are Opp. 12 in D, for P & Vn (1844), and 36 in B♭, for P & Va (1863), plus an "Allegro et Scherzo" in B♭ from an unfinished sonata (1884, posthumous).[224] The sonatas have never had the success of Vieuxtemps' violin concertos[225] and unfortunately, they lack both the substance and the imagination that might justify further discussion here.[226] In all three movements (F-M-F) of Op. 36, for example, although the treatment of the instruments is knowing, the themes are flat.

The dozen-or-so publications of another Belgian violinist and student

220. NZM XXVII (1847) 136.
221. NZM XXXIII (1850) 174.
222. Cf. Closson & Borren/BELGIQUE 237–39.
223. Cf. MGG XIII 1613–16 (B. Schwarz).
224. Cf. Altmann/KAMMERMUSIK 230 and 250; PAZDÍREK XIV 212–14.
225. Cf. Closson & Borren/BELGIQUE 243.
226. Cf., also, Cobbett/CHAMBER II 536 (W. W. Cobbett).

of Bériot, **Lambert-Joseph Meerts** (1800–63), include four "Sonatinen" for 2 Vns (*ca.* 1865, posthumous?) that were reviewed as good teaching material.[227] Among a larger number of publications the pianist **Philippe-Bartholomé Rüfer** left a Sonata in g, for P & Vn (1861), reviewed as promising for an Op. 1 in spite of certain naive, weak, or overly repetitive sections;[228] and an organ sonata, Op. 16, also in g (1875 at latest) .[229] Three more organ sonatas, entitled "Pontificale" (in d), "O Filii" (in e), and "Pascale" (in a), were left by the capable Brussels organist **Jacques-Nicolas Lemmens** (1823–81), who is credited with building up the Belgian and French schools of organ music in the second half of the 19th century.[230] All first published in 1876, these sonatas were welcomed for rejecting the light French style in favor of the solid, though somewhat academic, German style, especially in the one or two fugues of each sonata.[231]

In Holland, although there was no 19th-century composer of Franck's stature, we again find little or no interest on the part of the relatively important composers. There seem to be no sonatas left by Johannes Bernardus van Bree (although a Sonata in C, for P-duet, by his scarcely known son **Herman J. van Bree** [1836–85] was pub. in 1863 [232]), or by Richard Hol, or by Johannes Verhulst. But the absence of sonatas is not surprising in a country where even Beethoven's sonatas seem to have been but rarely performed as late as the middle of the century.[233] Among works by seven composers in Holland to be mentioned here, a competent, Germanic "Fantasie-Sonate" in B♭, for organ (1849), was left in MS by the organist **Johannes Gijsbertus Bastiaans** (1812–75), a pupil of Mendelssohn among others. Consisting of four movements (F-S-Sc-VF/fugue), this work is based throughout on the Dutch national song "Wien Neêrlands bloed." [234] A "Sonate-Symphonie" in c, Op. 21, for P solo, by **Edouard de Hartog** (1829–1909), was composed before his return from Germany and France to The Hague and published by

---

227. NZM LXI/2 (1865) 275. Cf. Fétis/BU VI 52–54; PAZDÍREK X 386; MGG VIII 1895 (A. Wirsta).
228. NZM LXVI/2 (1870) 369–71, with several generous exx. Cf. Fétis/BU Suppl. II 460–61; BAKER 1388–89.
229. Cf. Frotscher/ORGELSPIEL II 1206.
230. Cf. Fétis/BU V 267–68 and Suppl. II 97–98; Closson & Borren/BELGIQUE 243–44; MGG VIII 606–7 (A. Van der Linden); PAZDÍREK IX 335–36.
231. MT XVII (1876) 564 (also p. 443); but cf. Frotscher/ORGELSPIEL II 1235, where French traits are seen.
232. Altmann/KAMMERMUSIK 297. Cf. Keller & Kruseman/MUZIEKLEXICON I 77; NZM LIX (1863) 90 (reviewed as a trivial work).
233. Cf. Reeser/NEDERLANDSE 31, 34, 46, 86.
234. Cf. Reeser/NEDERLANDSE 104–8, with 2 exx.; GROVE I 494 (H. Antcliffe; could the reference to another Dutch national song be an error or pertain to another organ son. by Bastiaans?) and VI 21.

Meyer in Braunschweig by 1849.[235] A four-movement work (F-M-Sc-VF) with the subtitle "Poésies musicales et la Calabraise," it was reviewed as having some good and some less good, with no significance in the title's addition of the word "Symphonie."[236] No descriptive information has turned up here regarding the only sonata known by the esteemed keyboardist, conductor, and song composer **Willem Frederik Gerard Nicolai** (1829–96), Op. 4 in E, for P & Vc, first published in 1859.[237]

A Sonata in g, Op. 11, for P & Vn, by the pianist **Oskar Raif** (1847–99), was published in 1878, well after he had settled in Berlin.[238] It is a somewhat diminutive work in three movements (VF-M-VF) that might better have been called a sonatina.[239] A prize-winning Sonata in d, Op. 15, for P & Vc, by the organist **Georg Hendrik Witte** (1843–1929), appeared in 1882.[240] Two duo sonatas—Opp. 3, in D, for P & Vn, and 4, in c, for P & Vc—by the late conductor and author **Wouter Hutschenruyter** (the grandson; 1859–1943), were both published in 1883.[241] And a Sonata in f, Op. 4, by the violinist and conductor **Willem Kes** (1856–1934) was published in 1884, before he left for a series of posts in other countries.[242] Among orchestral transcriptions by Kes is that of Brahms's Sonata in C, Op. 1, for P solo.

235. Cf. Fétis/BU IV 232–33 and Suppl. 451–52; Riemann/LEXIKON I 712; Reeser/ NEDERLANDSE 173–75; HOFMEISTER 1844–51 119.

236. RGM for Dec. 30, 1849, 415.

237. Cf. Riemann/LEXIKON II 1267; Reeser/NEDERLANDSE 170–73; Altmann/KAMMER-MUSIK 261.

238. Cf. Riemann/LEXIKON II 1463.

239. Cf. Shand/VIOLIN 73–75, with exx.

240. Cf. BAKER 1808; Cobbett/CHAMBER II 588–89; Altmann/KAMMERMUSIK 266 (also p. 307, on a Sonatine in C, Op. 8, for P-duet).

241. Cf. Keller & Kruseman/MUZIEKLEXICON I 300; BAKER 753; MT XXIV (1883) 168 and 407. Among Hutschenruyter's books is one on Beethoven's sons. (SCE 508 and 834).

242. Cf. MGG VII 862–63 (E. Reeser); MT XXV (1884) 563.

Chapter XIII

A Peak in Late-Romantic France and the Low Countries

The Third Republic and Chamber Music

As noted early in the first of these two chapters on the Romantic sonata in France, the most important and extensive fruition came relatively late in the era (as had been true in the Baroque but not the Classic Era). It came during about the first half-century (1870–1920) of France's Third Republic (1870–1940). The Third Republic demonstrated its unprecedented durability by withstanding such strains as growing, worldwide imperialism, renewed conflicts of church and state, the rise and fall of Boulangism, the Panama Canal scandal, and "l'affaire Dreyfus." The new, positive interest in chamber music demonstrated its unexpected vitality by withstanding innumerable conflicts of art, temperament, and background, including those of national and international (meaning mainly Wagnerian) tastes, and by surviving right to the present day.[1] Now, however, although one can point to particular involvements in sociopolitical events by a Saint-Saëns or a d'Indy,[2] the relationships between those events and the broader, concurrent trends in music became less tangible.

César Franck, Camille Saint-Saëns, and Gabriel Fauré comprise the notable triumvirate who did most to elevate instrumental music in late-Romantic France, including the creation of symphonies, concertos, and larger chamber ensembles as well as duo sonatas. (Curiously, although all three excelled as pianists and organists, they did not extend their main interests to the solo sonata; nor did many of their students and other more immediate followers do so, the two chief exceptions being Dukas and d'Indy.) This triumvirate, with their contemporaries and followers, also marked the first time in about a century that most

1. Cf. the recent study based on musical criticism, Eckart-Bäcker/FRANKREICH, especially pp. 184–86.
2. E.g., cf. Harding/SAINT-SAËNS 108–9; Vallas/D'INDY I 69–77, 131, 260.

of the sonata activity was carried on by natives rather than immigrants. Moreover, all of the important native composers were trained in their own country rather than in Germany. (Even Franck, with his German and Belgian ancestry, was French trained and oriented.) And it was this whole group who made of the sonata a more developed or "symphonic" form than any earlier sonata composers in France had. Granted that along with the influences of Chopin and Berlioz those of the chief Romantic Germans—Mendelssohn, Schumann, Brahms, Liszt, and Wagner—were now paramount, the group still succeeded in disproving if not quite dispelling an age-old assumption that the French have always been too dance-minded by nature to think symphonically or in other than simple, square-cut, binary, ternary, and rondeau designs.[3] All of these considerations, plus some others less pertinent to the sonata, may help to explain the more-than-average literary attention that has been paid to fin-de-siècle music in France, by men like G. Jean-Aubry, Paul Landormy, Maurice Emmanuel, Léon Vallas, Norman Demuth, Martin Cooper, Edward Lockspeiser, and James Harding.[4]

A major aid to the advancement of French chamber music can be found in the concerts and related activities sponsored by various music societies, new and revived, of which the most important was the Société Nationale de Musique, founded in 1871 (even before the final indignities of the Franco-Prussian war had been heaped upon the French) by Saint-Saëns and Romain Bussine.[5] Frictions and dissatisfactions within this group—especially between Saint-Saëns and the followers of Franck, who were quite as devoted and numerous as those of Rheinberger in Germany—led to offshoots like the Société Musicale Indépendante, founded in 1909. The increasingly conservative Conservatoire in Paris continued to sponsor its own Société des Concerts, and there were several other outlets for chamber music, including even d'Indy's "Société Schola Cantorum" as its functions widened.[6] The composers themselves often joined in the initial performances of their works. But certain other musicians are remembered still more for first or early performances of the new sonatas. Thus, Edouard Risler and Blanche Selva each made strongly favorable impressions with what must have been outstanding performances of both the Dukas and the d'Indy piano sonatas. Above all, the Belgian violinist Eugène Ysaÿe did much to popularize the Franck, Lekeu, and several other violin sonatas that we shall find were dedicated to him.

3. On some of the background for this assumption cf. SCE 605.
4. See these names in the Bibliography.
5. Cf. Landormy/FRANÇAISE 7–13; Vallas/FRANCK 190–94.
6. Cf. Cooper/FRENCH 10; Demuth/D'INDY 14–20.

As in Chapter XI, on the late-Romantic sonata in Austro-Germany, the problem arises in this chapter of drawing some line between late-Romantic and early-Modern composers (including not a few octogenarians who lived deep into the present century). Debussy, Bréville, Ropartz and his pupil Thirion, Désiré Pâque, and Delius are among those excluded here because they seem to have looked ahead more than behind. (None of the slightly more active crop of Belgian and Dutch composers introduced in this chapter raises the problem.) But again the decisions have had to depend as much on subjective reactions as on any purely theoretical distinctions or hard-and-fast boundary. In general, those who continued to depend on tonality as a main cohesive factor in their forms (even though, like d'Indy, they may have exploited traditional harmony to a point almost beyond recognition) are retained, whereas those who tended to upset or defy tonal relationships (even though, as in Delius' lush harmony, the immediate chord progressions may still exhibit established functions) are excluded. And the same might be generalized with regard to those who still preferred complex lyrical melodies, extended or "endlessly" unfolding phrase-and-period syntax, expansive forms, and opulent textures as against those who leaned toward squarer melodies or tunes, more punctuated if not simpler syntax, concise forms, and thinner textures.

Franck, Saint-Saëns, and Fauré

Although their birth years—1822, 1835, and 1845—do not make Franck, Saint-Saëns, and Fauré exact contemporaries, these three front-rank instrumental composers in late-Romantic France were too close in their interests and milieu not to be interrelated in one section here. All three were expert pianists and organists, yet, oddly enough, left only duo sonatas that are remembered today. How they related and differed in these sonatas may be clarified in a comparison of one representative work by each to follow shortly. The important Belgian-born composer and organist **César (-Auguste) Franck** (1822–90) maintains a significant niche in sonata history for only one work, his Sonata in A for P & Vn. But that work, composed in 1886—that is, late in his career, like his other few masterpieces, including the Symphony, *Variations symphoniques,* Quintet, Quartet, and *Les Béatitudes*—continues to be one of the most popular duos of all chamber music. The lateness of his masterpieces and influence explains why Franck is grouped here with the late-Romantics in spite of his life dates. He had studied composition with Reicha, among other teachers at the Paris Conservatoire, back in the 1830's. Drawn ever closer to this interest, he had abandoned the career of a concert piano virtuoso that his opportunistic father preferred for him, made his first mark as a composer with his four piano trios Opp. 1 and 2 (attracting the attention of Liszt and others), and started teaching in Paris, all by 1844, or his 22d year.[7] Two early piano sonatas by Franck are extant in his autographs. The first, composed while he was still in Liège, "âgé de 13 Ans" (end of 1835), was dedicated to his younger brother, the violinist Joseph, and given the pre-opus number 10.[8] This "Grande Sonate pour le Piano-Forte" consists of three movements (I/F-S → Ro) in ten handsomely written pages (recalling Franck's ability at drawing, too). It is correct and talented, but juvenile, music, with a flair, already, for chromaticism and modulations in the first movement and a knowledge of keyboard technique in spite of the most banal accompaniments. Except for anticipating the opening style of the *Variations symphoniques* in the slow movement, it suggests Mozart, Hummel, and occasionally Beethoven as the chief influences on the youngster's melodies and passagework. A sense of form is not yet developed. From not much later[9] comes the autograph of a "Deuxième Sonate" for P solo, which is reported to give a foretaste of Franck's cyclical procedures.[10] Perhaps this was still the same sonata Liszt mentioned receiving from Franck in 1853, at a time when he was continuing to enjoy Franck's trios.[11] If not, then Liszt may have received and lost a third, newer sonata (in the same year he may have lost part of Brahms's early Vn son. [SSB IX]), for no further sonata by Franck is extant prior to the main one.[12]

That main one, the Sonata in A for P & Vn, seems to have been written without delay in the fall of 1886 [13] and without anyone else hearing about it until it was completed, unless this work possibly could have been the greatly belated accomplishment of a violin sonata Franck had promised to write for Bülow's wife twenty-eight years earlier (be-

7. Cf. d'Indy/FRANCK 31–36, 114–15, 110–12; Vallas/FRANCK 19–22, 24–25, 39–40, 42–43, 46–58, 87; Emmanuel/FRANCK 20–27; BÜLOW BRIEFE I 494, II 183, IV 64. Vallas/FRANCK provides one of the most up-to-date, reliable biographies of Franck. For a full bibliography cf. Borren/FRANCK 127–41 (also, pp. 13–14).

8. It is discussed, with exx., in Tiersot/FRANCK 109–11. In Vallas/FRANCK 22–23 the trans. leaves the impression that this work was "published by the composer"; the original French is less ambiguous, and no evidence could be found here of such a pub. The autograph is MS 8546 in the Bibliotèque nationale.

9. Before 1841, in any case (MGG IV 644 [W. Mohr]).

10. Tiersot/FRANCK 112.

11. Cf. Vallas/FRANCK 108–9; MASON MEMORIES 122–23.

12. D'Indy/COURS II/1 423 is not followed here in the consideration of *Grande Pièce symphonique*, in f♯ (1861), as another "Sonate" by Franck.

13. The exact dates for each mvt. are quoted from the autograph in Ysaÿe/YSAŸE 164. Further details about the early circumstances of this son. are taken here primarily from Ysaÿe/YSAŸE 163–68 and Vallas/FRANCK 195–200.

fore she left Bülow for Wagner).[14] Nor could any confirmation be found here to the effect that the Sonata in A had been intended originally for cello, as has been asserted.[15] The cello is not mentioned in the autograph[16] nor in the first edition, which Hamelle of Paris published promptly that same year of 1886.[17] On the other hand, contrary to another assertion,[18] the Sonata in A may not have been written expressly for its dedicatee, the renowned violinist and Franck's younger compatriot Eugène Ysaÿe.[19] However, Ysaÿe, who was presented with the autograph on his wedding day,[20] at once and unquestionably became the performer identified above all others with the work and the one who did most to start it on its great popularity. Thus, among reports of its early performances and growing successes (including the late afternoon when increasing darkness compelled Ysaÿe to complete its performance from memory[21]), we read how Ysaÿe and the pianist Raoul Pugno[22] "carried the Sonata round the world like a torch and gave to Franck, that misunderstood, unrecognized saint, one of the few earthly joys he knew before regaining paradise." [23] We also read that Franck welcomed and acceded to some different concepts from his own in Ysaÿe's playing, including a faster tempo at the start.[24]

Franck's Sonata in A consists of four movements (705 mss. in all;

14. Cf. Vallas/FRANCK 122–23, 195.

15. Cf. the unsigned jacket notes for the Allegro recording No. 110, with reference to unidentified information from the cellist J. A. Delsart and the harpist Carlos Salzedo. One origin for this supposition may be Franck's unrealized hope, expressed about nine weeks before he died, to write a Vc son. (cf. Vallas/230, deleting further [erroneous?] information in the original French ed., p. 289).

16. The autograph was examined for the present study when it was on display in 1963 in Seattle for the annual meeting of the American Musicological Society. Like Liszt's Son. in b (SSB X), it was to have become available under limited conditions, in facs., as part of the "ROLF archives" (cf. NOTES XXI [1963–64] 83–93, especially 91) but has since been withdrawn from public view. Early information on the autograph appears in Ysaÿe/YSAŸE 164.

17. On the title page (facs. in Ysaÿe/YSAŸE opposite p. 44) is "Sonate pour Piano et Violon" and not ". . . Violon ou Violoncelle" as in the subsequent dual-purpose ed. arranged by J. A. Delsart and pub. ca. 1906 by Hamelle (not 1886, as in Cat. NYPL XI 566; cf. Altmann/KAMMERMUSIK 256, PAZDÍREK IV 162 and V 498, Weigl/ VIOLONCELL 97). Regarding Franck's unkept promise to transcribe his Son. in A for 2 Ps, cf. Vallas/FRANCK 250.

18. E.g., cf. Cobbett/CHAMBER I 424 (V. d'Indy).

19. Cf. Ysaÿe/YSAŸE 164–65 (in spite of the statement on p. 159 and Franck's immediate concern with the dedication on p. 165).

20. Cf. Vallas/FRANCK 195.

21. Ysaÿe/YSAŸE 165–66. In Cobbett/CHAMBER I 425–26, d'Indy amplifies the story.

22. The first mvt. of a "Grande Sonate" in d for P solo by Pugno (1852–1914) is noted favorably in MERCURE II/1 (1906) 531–32. This work (a copy of which is at the Boston Public Library) proves to be grandiose, stilted, and watery.

23. Ysaÿe/YSAŸE 167.

24. Ysaÿe/YSAŸE 167; Vallas/FRANCK 199–200.

M-VF-S-F, as interpreted here) lasting a total of about twenty-eight minutes—(i) "Allegretto ben moderato" in A, in 9/8 meter, which presents a miniature "sonata form"; (ii) "Allegro" in the minor subdominant (d), in 4/4 meter, which presents a more complete "sonata form"; (iii) "Ben moderato," primarily in f♯, in alla breve meter, a cursive, modulatory fantasy, quasi recitative at the start; and (iv) "Allegretto poco mosso," in A, in alla breve meter, a free sonata-rondo form with themes stated canonically between the two instruments and with a development section at the middle that returns to earlier movements.[25] By far the most attention to the construction of this work has focused on its cyclical organization. Taking the lead as the former, idolatrous, longtime student, Vincent d'Indy all but credits Franck with inventing the principle of evolving a complete cycle out of a few recurring, often altered motives or "cellules." [26] Indeed, this "contribution" seems to become the main support for d'Indy's equation of Franck with Beethoven, or, rather, for sanctifying him as the true successor to Beethoven, among the world's greatest composers.[27]

However, three observations need to be made on Franck's cyclical treatment, the first two recalling our broader discussion of such treatment in Chapter VI. For one thing, it would be historically absurd to call Franck the inventor of cyclical treatment. Franck was simply one of its important cultivators in a line that goes back, for example, to Palestrina and the cantus firmus Mass, or Frescobaldi and the variation ricercar, or Bach and the *Musicalisches Opfer*. Beethoven set still more of a precedent than d'Indy allows, whether in an early sonata like Op. 2/3 (sce 139–40, with ex.) or throughout the late quartet triptych Opp. 130–32 (and Op. 133), with its recurring motive. And especially in Franck's own century, Liszt surely gave much more in his own Sonata in b than he could have received from Franck's early trios. Moreover, the main applications of Berlioz's "idée fixe," Brahms's "basic motive," Wagner's leitmotif, and Bruckner's chorale evolution all antedated or paralleled the (late) masterpieces of Franck in which

25. Among numerous analyses of this work, all relatively brief and largely centered around its cyclical treatment, those of d'Indy (d'Indy/FRANCK 169–71, d'Indy/COURS II/1 422/26, Cobbett/CHAMBER I 424–26) have been most cited, partly because of his close relation to his teacher. Selva/SONATE 227–31, as usual, follows d'Indy, *her* teacher, to the letter. Emmanuel/FRANCK 63–71 is essentially the same, too. Emmanuel/DUKAS 70–71 draws a striking parallel between Franck's 4-mvt. cycle and that of Beethoven's Op. 101 merely to argue that such tectonic analyses are purely external and fail to reveal the important (actually, more local) internal differences.

26. Franck's position as "inventor" of this principle is discussed at some length, though without sufficient historical reinforcement or significant conclusions, in Demuth/FRANCK 53–58.

27. E.g., d'Indy/COURS II/1 421–22; cf. GROVE IV 470 (L. Vallas).

cyclical treatment prevails. Certainly Franck, whose devotion to German as well as French music so embittered Saint-Saëns and the other more nationalist minded members of the Société Nationale de Musique,[28] knew these precedents well. As a second observation, it is doubtful that cyclical treatment makes that much difference in the strength and conscious or even unconscious enjoyment of Franck's music. As M. D. Calvocoressi has emphasized with regard to d'Indy's own cyclical treatment,[29] ". . . a theme or melody must stand or fall quite apart from the fact that its 'skeleton' is that of another heard before or to be heard further; and the aesthetic value of a development is not determined by the origin of its materials." As our third observation, one learns that Franck himself neither taught nor advocated the application of the cyclical principle.[30] Naturally, this is not to suggest that he was not deliberately and consciously exploiting the unifying and cumulative values of recalling ideas from the earlier movements as he composed the succeeding movements of his Sonata in A. But it may well be that he never quite thought of this work as deriving entirely and climactically from three "cellules," as d'Indy (and, of course, Blanche Selva) would have it, all too categorically.[31] Perhaps d'Indy was only transferring to his teacher the highly systematized principles of generation and unity he was currently and unequivocally evolving for his own Sonata in e (*infra*).

To get closer than cyclical relationships are likely to bring us to the salient style traits, including the chief strengths and pleasures of Franck's Sonata in A, it may help to compare this work with the most representative violin sonata by each of his two most important near-contemporaries in French instrumental music—that is, by Saint-Saëns and Fauré, who come up next in this chapter, anyway. Between Saint-Saëns' two violin sonatas, Opp. 75 in d/D (1885) and 102 in E♭ (1896), the former is chosen for comparison, not only because it appeared nearer in time (only one year earlier) but because it is nearer in spirit as the more compelling and impetuous of the two[32] (although neither

28. Cf. Saint-Saëns/ESSAYS 45–49; Vallas/FRANCK 166–67, 191–95; Gatti & Basso/ LA MUSICA II 473 (Dufourcq); Harding/SAINT-SAËNS 154.

29. Cobbett/CHAMBER II 3; cf., also, the similar objections in Cortot/FRANÇAISE II 147.

30. According to Breville, as cited in Demuth/FRANCK 55.

31. E.g., d'Indy/COURS II/1 423–26. The "x" *cellule,* most prevalent and most seminal of the 3 cellules, is found in the rise and fall of a 3d, as first in the first 3 notes of the Vn, in i/5; "y" is found in the inverted cambiata as initially defined (sooner than d'Indy says) by the first 4 notes of the Vn in i/19; but "z" is not found (weakening d'Indy's approach) until the middle of the 3d mvt., in the rise and fall of both a 4th and a 5th that the Vn first plays in iii/59–60. Cf., also, Vallas/FRANCK 198–99.

32. It is much preferred in Servières/SAINT-SAËNS 109–11.

is played any more than any other Saint-Saëns chamber works today). Between Fauré's two violin sonatas, Opp. 13 in A (1877) and 108 in e (1917), it is the former again that is chosen, both because it appeared nearer in time and because it has been much the more successful of the two with the public (if not necessarily with the connoisseurs[33]). Like Franck's Sonata in A, both Saint-Saëns' Op. 75 and Fauré's Op. 13 fall into familiar but not identical, four-movement plans—F-S-F-VF and VF-M-VF-VF, respectively (although actually, in Saint-Saëns' Son., as in his Symphony No. 3 of the following year, 2 pairs of mvts. are indicated, with each pair separated only by a transition[34]). They last a little less long—21 minutes (948 mss.) and 26 (1,161 mss.), respectively. Neither Saint-Saëns nor Fauré happens to have showed as much interest in cyclical relationships, even though as masters, like Franck, of variation techniques both men could hardly have been unaware of the fullest possibilities. Saint-Saëns does return to the second theme of his first movement (mss. 76–83) in the coda of his finale (mss. 144–79, 210–16, plus more in the bass), and it is not hard to hear him making other, more subtle interconnections, here and there.[35]

Comparing the three violin sonatas produces no striking new conclusions but does help to confirm and sharpen familiar observations about their composers' styles. Franck's sonata reveals less of the broad symphonist in the Classic and Brahmsian architectural sense than either of the other sonatas. The differences show up especially in tonality and syntax. The tonal outlines created by Saint-Saëns and Fauré suggest premeditated organization whereas Franck's outline seems more haphazard—more like the consequence than the cause of the harmonic color that figures so prominently in Franck's style. In other words, Franck seems to modulate to new keys more for their surprise value than their larger function in any "grand cadence." Thus, to compare the tonal outlines in the most developed form of each sonata (with Roman numerals indicating the functions of the most essential key areas), Franck's finale is outlined by I-vi-V||-♭ii-♮III-I,[36] Saint-Saëns' opening movement by i-III-i||iv/IV/-iv-i, and Fauré's opening movement by I-V||-I-iii-vi/VI-I. With regard to syntax, Saint-Saëns and Fauré both achieve a dynamic structural rhythm through

---

33. Thus, Cobbett/CHAMBER I 390 (F. Schmitt) finds Op. 108 to be "irritating" at times because of tonal, harmonic, and motivic redundancies, whereas Koechlin/ FAURÉ 43–44 prefers it as confirming "Fauré's evolution toward an ever greater purity."

34. The 4 mvts. of the 2 pairs are referred to here simply as i, ii, iii, and iv.

35. On Fauré, cf. Suckling/FAURÉ 94; also, infra.

36. But cf. d'Indy's defense in 1919 of this plan, in Vallas/SAINT-SAËNS 83, and Saint-Saëns' reply, pp. 86–87.

flexibility of phrase lengths. Often their phrases evolve cumulatively by growing progressively shorter, as in the succession at the start of Saint-Saëns/i: 4-4-4-2-2-2-1-1-1 (etc., with the squareness of the 4-ms. phrases relieved by meter changes); or they spin out after starting regularly, as at the start of Fauré/i: 4+4 & 4+10. Fauré gives more of a sense of spinning out, anyway, because, as in the example just cited, the consequent is more likely to contrast with the antecedent than to parallel it (in Saint-Saëns' manner). Remarkably plastic in effect are the irregular phrase lengths in the scherzo movement of each—the six-measure overlapping phrases at the start of Saint-Saëns/iii and the sharply defined three-measure phrases at the start of Fauré/iii. By contrast, Franck's phrases are most often regular in length, even in much of the recitative of iii and the canonic treatment of iv. His most frequent syntactic method is the familiar, relatively static one of two short units followed by a long unit, as in the second theme of i (e.g., 2+2+4 in mss. 32–39) or the main theme of ii (e.g., 2+2+6 in mss. 138–47). Single, long-drawn-out phrases do not occur in Franck's Sonata in A.

If Franck's is the least dynamic of the three sonatas in its tonal and syntactic organization (and in spite of its cyclical relationships), its strong appeal and success must be credited to other factors, especially its melody, harmony, and rhythmic flow.[37] Sometimes his melody barely outlines the chords (as in most of i/1–31) or traces the surface (as in i/108–17) of his luscious chromatic harmony, often toying with the minor and major 3d or 2d in the process[38] (as in iii/11–13 and 17–21); and sometimes it qualifies as an independent, songful tune (as in two main themes of iv, starting at mss. 1 and 87). At all times his melodies tend to divide into clear, relatively short units, in keeping with his regular, relatively short phrases. By contrast, the melodies of both other composers tend to give rise to, and do not rise out of, the harmony. That is, they possess sufficient intervallic and rhythmic character to be at least identifiable without harmonic qualifications and interpretations. Beyond that starting point the melodies of Saint-Saëns and Fauré differ considerably in the sonatas in question. (One must take care to delimit references to Saint-Saëns' style traits to the work or even the movement "in question," for the craft of that past master was as eclectic as it was skillful, with almost any established trait being fair game for a particular work. Witness how florid, eventually rhapsodic, the lines become during the slow movement of the same sonata "in question.") In their more developed, fast

37. Colles/FRANCK finds certain ineptitudes for "son. form" on Franck's part.
38. Cf. Colles/FRANCK 207.

movements, Saint-Saëns gives preference to narrow-ranged, technically convenient motives that violate no traditional precepts for a "good" melody yet are distinctive enough to invite development and expansion, whereas Fauré prefers wide-ranged, full-fledged, themes that are intimately bound up with their supporting harmony, yet have melodic significance in their own right. Although Fauré's themes stretch hand and ear with their frequent intervals of a 4th and larger, most of them are so essentially lyrical that they tend to flow from one to the next without sharp contrasts. In the slow movements of these particular sonatas, Fauré, as well as Saint-Saëns, prefers to deal in motives. Fauré and Franck have in common their surging, continuous, lyrical flow, which one thinks of as almost too Romantic, too heated for the more Classically oriented Saint-Saëns. That flow may be attributed not only to the compelling lines and harmony but to the rhythmic impetus of rocking, triplet, syncopated, or other motoric figures in the accompaniment. Their melodic styles and differences may at least be hinted by quoting from the first occurrence of the second theme in the first fast movement by each of our three composers (Ex. 79a, b, c).

With regard to their most characteristic harmony, all three composers indulge expertly in what might be called chromatic and enharmonic evolution, one or more voices at a time, from one chord to the next. But Saint-Saëns does this least and does it around a traditional harmonic framework—in fact, largely around a framework of primary triads. Fauré's harmony is at once more active, with a variety of resolved and unresolved 7th-chords and accented dissonances; and it is more colorful, with emphasis not only on the Neapolitan-6th chord but on the lowered mediant and submediant. And Franck's harmony, while stabilized by long bass tones, is made still more colorful and active through the introduction of frequent and varied 9th-chords treated as consonances, through an extreme use of chromatic voice-leading, through one new, unexpected, often dramatic, resolution or deceptive cadence after another, and through resourceful exploitations of the various aug.-6th chords and the dim.-7th chord. The fughetta in the development section of Saint-Saëns' first movement, Franck's canonic finale, and Fauré's nonacademic but frequent melodic duets and exchanges between piano and violin supply only part of the evidence for the polyphonic abilities and interests of all three composers.[39] But in keeping with their

39. Regarding Saint-Saëns' disparagement and d'Indy's defense of Franck's canonic and fugal techniques, in 1919, cf. Vallas/FRANCK 269; Vallas/SAINT-SAËNS 83 and 87; Harding/SAINT-SAËNS 218–20.

Ex. 79. From the first movements of (a) César Franck's Sonata in A, (b) Gabriel Fauré's Sonata in A, Op. 13 (after Wier/ VIOLIN-m 42 and 251, respectively), and (c) Camille Saint-Saëns' Sonata in d, Op. 75 (after the early Durand ed., p. 4).

harmonic differences, Saint-Saëns produces the thinnest, most precise, and most conveniently playable texture, not only in the very light, rapid finale, which is almost a *perpetuum mobile* (or "grand exercise de concert"[40]), but in the other movements as well. Fauré's texture is fuller and causes each player to make wider stretches and leaps, and more shifts of position about his instrument. Franck's texture is still fuller, similarly difficult in its position shifts, but much freer in its doublings and its addition and subtraction of voices, and too often unimaginative in the piano bass. One should add that the total effect of all three styles of texture, as different as they are, is almost invariably that of clear, telling sonority.

The second in our trio of important French instrumental composers, **(Charles-) Camille Saint-Saëns** (1835–1921), composed at least ten sonatas, all duos, during his long life.[41] The first of these originated when he was only about six, as but one instance of his extraordinary precocity, and the last three as his last compositions, in his eighty-sixth or final year. Saint-Saëns' thorough training seems to have come as much from his own early curiosity and meticulous, self-guided

40. Selva/SONATE 235.

41. Harding/SAINT-SAËNS is a recent book (1965) on his life and artistic environment, based partly on newly explored sources and supplemented with a dated (somewhat careless) list of nearly all but the earliest works. Bonnerot/SAINT-SAËNS (1922) continues to be valuable, too. Cf., also, MGG XI 1272–84 (M. Briquet), with full bibliography and dated list of works.

study of past music (and other arts) as from Stamaty (ssʙ XII), Halévy, Boëly (ssʙ XII), and very few other teachers.[42] This training led to an increasingly successful and honored career as a prolific composer in virtually all genres; as a touring concert pianist right to his last year, expert enough to be ranked with Liszt by Liszt himself, to amaze Wagner, yet to be judged responsibly as lacking in "poetic intensity and fervour";[43] as an equally capable organist; and as an author.[44] But his life was not without the personal tragedies, loneliness, and professional frictions that should help to explain a growing, outspoken bitterness in his later years. Much of the friction related to the Société Nationale de Musique that he himself and Romain Bussine founded in 1871, and to questions of its national or international goals.[45] Saint-Saëns felt a special personal and artistic kinship with Liszt and with his own most important student, Fauré, among outstanding near contemporaries. The same cannot be said of his feelings for Franck, d'Indy, Massenet, and Debussy. Perhaps the most pertinent observation to add here is one of surprise at the extent to which all of the darker side of Saint-Saëns' life is excluded from his music.

Those ten sonatas by Saint-Saëns include five for P & Vn, two for P & Vc, and one each for P & Ob, P & Cl, and P & Bn. The first three for P & Vn remained in MS, including a very early "Sonata à Bessens" (*ca.* 1841), another youthful work from about 1850, and a Sonata in d placed in 1876.[46] The last was played in London in 1876 with the composer at the piano during one of his many periods of crowded touring,[47] but must have been discarded by him within a few years because in 1885 Op. 75, also in d, was published as the "1ère Sonate" for P & Vn. Op. 75 (discussed previously in connection with Franck) was composed early in 1885 for the violinist Pierre Marsick in recognition of a full, triumphal tour the two men had just completed in Switzerland.[48] The other or "2me" sonata published for P & Vn is Op. 102 in E♭, a colder, more abstract, more subtle, and

42. Cf. Harding/saint-saëns 13–16, 18–20, 23–24, 26–27, 31–39.
43. Cf. Harding/saint-saëns 223, 83–84; grove VII 366 (M. D. Calvocoressi).
44. Saint-Saëns/essays is the collection of his writings that applies most here.
45. Cf. Harding/saint-saëns 109–11, 113–14, 154, 173–74.
46. Cf. mgg XI 1278. Presumably "Bessens" is a misspelling of (Antoine) Bessems, the violinist who played with Saint-Saëns at the time (Bonnerot/saint-saëns 17). The second of these sons. seems to have been only an incomplete sketch done during the study with Halévy (Bonnerot/saint-saëns 25).
47. Cf. Bonnerot/saint-saëns 79–80.
48. Bonnerot/saint-saëns 118. According to Harding/saint-saëns 201, the opening theme of Op. 75 had a special appeal for Marcel Proust, in whose novel *À la Recherche du temps perdu* it figures as Vinteuil's celebrated "little phrase"; cf., also, A. Coeuroy in rm IV/3 (Jan., 1923) 199–201, 203–4 (but with reference to a Fauré son.), 208–12; also, Lockspeiser/fauré (with Fauré suggested).

more polyphonic work. It was composed at least in part on tour in Cairo in 1896, then first played in Paris soon after, by Saint-Saëns and Sarasate, during the composer's fiftieth-anniversary recital,[49] and published there before the year was ended with a dedication "a Monsieur et Madame L. Carembat." [50]

The first of Saint-Saëns' two cello sonatas, Op. 32 in c and in only three movements (F-M-F), was composed in 1872 in the throes of grief and emptiness following the death of the great-aunt who had cared for him from infancy.[51] More specifically it is reported to have grown out of some organ improvising that actually supplied, "note-for-note, the first and last pages" of the sonata score.[52] Publication and a (first?) performance, with the composer at the piano, occurred a year later, with an extraordinary number of performances of Op. 32 following in the next few years.[53] In 1905 after retreating southeast to Biskra from a bad winter in Algiers, Saint-Saëns wrote his other, more difficult, less known "2e" cello sonata, Op. 123 in F. Published that same year and dedicated to Jules Griset, it was composed, we are told,[54] between walks to visit with "three gazelles who had become friends" with Saint-Saëns, the lifelong lover of animals. Perhaps its warmly Romantic slow movement relates to this association. The three sonatas from his last year, 1921—Opp. 166 in D for Ob & P, 167 in E♭ for Cl & P, and 168 in G for Bn & P—are all relatively short, lean, spare, muscular, economical, technically easier works reflecting great compositional maturity and wisdom, plus a fondness for and keen awareness of the instrumental idioms and a late preoccupation with Rameau and other earlier French composers. They were sketched in Algiers, completed in Paris, and published in the same year with dedications, respectively, to Louis Bas, Auguste Perrier, and Léon Letelier.[55]

The two of Saint-Saëns' seven published sonatas that seem most nearly to get past his barrier of objectivity into his emotional self are the first cello sonata (Op. 32), the one identified with his great-aunt's death, and the clarinet sonata (Op. 167), shortly preceding his own death.[56] These two works and the "first" violin sonata (Op. 75) are

49. Bonnerot/SAINT-SAËNS 161, 162.
50. A review in SMW LIV (1896) 945 calls Op. 102 a fine challenge to the enterprising, although a bit harsh in its polyphony and "baroque" (i.e., extravagant).
51. Harding/SAINT-SAËNS 124.
52. Bonnerot/SAINT-SAËNS 69.
53. As samples for but 18 months, cf. NZM LXXII/1 (1876) 224, 238, 249; LXXII/2 (1876) 300, 310, 436; LXXIII/1 (1877) 30, 52, 63, 73, 116, 249, 274.
54. Bonnerot/SAINT-SAËNS 182.
55. Bonnerot/SAINT-SAËNS 215.
56. Useful descriptions of the 7 sons. occur in Servières/SAINT-SAËNS 108–11, 115–16, and 117–18; Cobbett/CHAMBER II 322–23 (E. Baumann; string sons. only).

regarded here as the strongest of the sonatas and the ones most likely to succeed if Saint-Saëns' music is given another chance. During his lifetime, his first published sonata, Op. 32, won the most interest (as suggested above), with the interest in the later sonatas, as in his other music, tending to diminish in keeping with his changing popular image from modernist to conservative. Today (in 1967) all seven sonatas still appear in the Durand catalogues, but perhaps more indicative of public taste is the fact that only two of them are currently available in recordings—Opp. 75 and 167, as it happens.[57]

The important point is that except for two or three concertos, one symphony, and *Le Carnaval des Animaux*, Saint-Saëns is scarcely heard or played at all, anymore. He has toppled from his deserved eminence as one of the most universally skilled and talented composers. And the most tangible reason is that changing image, or, rather, the fact that Saint-Saëns stood still while the musical world passed by him. Or one might give as the reason that prevailing sense in his music of objectivity and abstract perfection, traits of which were noted in our comparison of representative violin sonatas by him, Franck, and Fauré (*supra*, including Ex. 79c). But the objectivity is only a corollary of the conservatism. Composing more than eighty of his eighty-six years, Saint-Saëns had an almost unprecedentedly long time to stand still. Far from keeping abreast of Debussy or even d'Indy, he barely kept up with Liszt, Berlioz, Wagner, and Fauré in his tastes,[58] and advanced not even that far in practice. In spite of the vast, comprehensive resources at his command and both his ability and his inclination to choose among them eclectically, the range of his "practice" might be represented realistically by his inclination in 1874 to write Variations for 2 Ps on the "Trio" in Beethoven's Sonata in E♭, Op. 31/3/iii, or in 1908 to transcribe Chopin's Sonata in b♭, Op. 35, for 2 Ps. But, of course, conservatism in itself is no more of a fault than it is a virtue in art. In the long appraisal of Saint-Saëns' sonatas one cannot deny the exceptional force and worth of his best melodies, developments, and forms, as may at least be suggested in part by one illustration from the remarkably simple yet poignant slow movement of his clarinet sonata, a movement in steady, fateful 3/2 meter that might have come right out of Bach's "St. Matthew Passion" (Ex. 80).

The third of our three outstanding instrumental composers in late-Romantic France, the organist **Gabriel-Urbain Fauré** (1845–1924), was

---

57. Cf. the laudatory review by I. Kolodin of a further recording of Op. 75, by Jascha Heifetz and Brooks Smith, in the *Saturday Review* for Oct. 28, 1967, pp. 58–59.

58. Cf. Harding/SAINT-SAËNS 148–49, 151, 53–55, 83–84, 144–46.

the least universal of the three, in several senses.[59] He touched on most branches of composition yet wrote fewer works—only about one hundred that he allowed to stand—and excelled in fewer branches, primarily chamber music and songs. By way of Saint-Saens and other teachers he received a thorough introduction to the great masters of the past, up to and including Wagner and Liszt, yet underwent the least direct influence from any of their styles, whether it be the rhetorical drama of the last two, the "singing allegro" of Mozart, the fugal writing of Bach, or even the Romantic mannerisms of the salon and the virtuoso that Franck and Saint-Saëns themselves could assume

Ex. 80. From the third movement of Camille Saint-Saëns' Sonata in E♭, Op. 167 (after the original Durand ed., with the kind permission of Elkan-Vogel Co. in Philadelphia).

so well when they chose to. In fact, if Fauré, the teacher of Ravel, Koechlin, Roger-Ducasse, and Florent Schmitt, may be called the most French of our three instrumental masters,[60] he also may be called, like Chopin, one of the most individual of stylists—precious, restrained, refined, poetic, and subtle.

59. Suckling/FAURÉ (1946) is one of the most recent and helpful studies of the man and his music; Vuillermoz/FAURÉ (by an important student; 1960) skirts factual details in favor of viewpoints and philosophies (with considerable insight); cf., also, the article by Fauré's son Philippe Fauré-Fremiet in MGG III 1867–80, digesting his book of 1929 (Fauré-Fremiet/FAURÉ).
60. Cf. Roger-Ducasse/FAURÉ 79.

Fauré left only four sonatas, two each for Vn & P and Vc & P. Both temporally and stylistically they divide into one early work and three late works. In other words, one sonata was composed in 1876 at the end of his "first period," [61] following his service in Rennes, in the army, and at the Swiss wartime retreat of the École Niedermeyer; and the other three sonatas appeared in 1916–21 or forty and more years later, near the end of his "fourth" or "last period" and well after his advances both to the post of chief organist at the Madeleine in Paris in 1896 and to the directorship of the Paris Conservatoire in 1905.

That first sonata was the one in A, Op. 13, for Vn & P, which figures among the most successful of all his works (and was the choice, *supra*, for our comparison with one Vn son. each by Franck and Saint-Saëns). It was composed on "vacation" in the home of two longtime friends, Camille Clerc and wife, and tried over, as it grew, with the Belgian violinist Hubert Léonard.[62] Because the Paris publishers were afraid to invest in its printing, Fauré had to be content with all honor and no pay whatsoever in a contract for publication engineered by Clerc with Breitkopf & Härtel of Leipzig (1877).[63] Fauré dedicated Op. 13 to Paul Viardot, son of the influential singer and brother of the girl to whom he now became engaged after a long ardent courtship, although the breaking off of that engagement was soon to follow, leaving a wound that never quite healed. A (first?) performance in Paris on April 29, 1877,[64] followed by a more conspicuous one at the Trocadéro in 1878, got the Sonata in A off to a slow start with the public. Perhaps its progress was hindered by an early, negative review from Germany that found harmonic and modulatory eccentricities intolerable to the structure, and, notwithstanding signs of talent, predicted that only firm willpower and good nerves could get a person through the work.[65] But by the same token its progress should have been furthered by a laudatory announcement, headed simply "Une Sonate," that Saint-Saëns wrote for the *Journal de musique* of April 7 (not May 22), 1877 (p. 3), possibly in answer to the German review:[66]

It is outside the theater that one of the most interesting works of our times is revealed, a simple and modest sonata for piano and violin. . . . A

61. According to his son's division of his life into 4 periods (MGG III 1268–70).
62. Cf. Rostand/FAURÉ 54–55; Suckling/FAURÉ 15–17; Servières/FAURÉ 62.
63. Cf. Fauré-Fremiet/FAURÉ 46–47. The year of pub. is wrongly given as 1876 in most sources (and as 1878 in MGG) but should be 1877, as in HOFMEISTER 1877 66 and NZM LXXI (1877) 143.
64. This early performance, reported in NZM LXXIII/1 (1877) 214, is overlooked by all authors consulted here.
65. SMW XXXV (1877) 449.
66. Trans. from the quotation (including italics) in Servières/FAURÉ 60. Cf., also, Vuillermoz/FAURÉ 72–74.

repertoire of French instrumental music is developing [that is] capable of contesting to advantage in a closed field where, for a long time, the German school had no rival. The appearance of the sonata by Fauré has revealed to us a new champion, *perhaps the most formidable of all, for he combines with u profound musical knowledge a great melodic wealth* and a kind of unconscious naivety that is the most irresistible of forces. One finds in this sonata the most alluring delicacy, novelty of forms, resourcefulness of modulations and unusual sonorities, [and] use of the most unanticipated rhythms; above all that [allure] hovers a charm that envelops the entire work and makes the most unexpected adventures acceptable, like something entirely natural, to the crowd of ordinary listeners.

In spite of the differences noted in our comparison offered earlier, Fauré's individuality of style does bring Franck's to mind at times, especially in the realm of harmonic color displayed by both sonatas in A. As Koechlin has so aptly put it,[67]

Without knowing the facts one would say that it [Fauré's Son. in A] was inspired by the much [actually only one decade] later work of César Franck. Indeed, the vehemence of the Allegro does show some affinity at times with Franck's second movement [as may be sensed even in our Ex. 79a and b, *supra*]. But render unto Gabriel, and not unto "César," that which is Gabriel's.

Another individual stylist, Richard Strauss, took an understandable interest in Fauré's Sonata in A.[68] One suspects that d'Indy would have expressed more interest, too, and not dismissed it so politely but briefly were he not transferring to the onetime pupil some of the antagonism still felt between Saint-Saëns and himself.[69] But one looks in vain for any demonstrable affinity between this or any other sonata by Fauré and any of Saint-Saëns' sonatas.

Fauré's last three sonatas, composed during the deafness and sadly failing health of the septuagenarian's last period,[70] include Op. 108 in e/E, for Vn & P, composed in 1916, published in 1917, and dedicated to Queen Elizabeth of Belgium;[71] Op. 109 in d/D, for Vc & P, composed in 1917, published in 1918, and dedicated to the cellist Louis Hasselmans; and Op. 117 in g, for Vc & P, composed in 1921, published in 1922, and dedicated to the Alsatian-American composer Charles Martin Loeffler. All three works are available in print (Durand), but only Op.

67. Koechlin/FAURÉ 41.
68. BÜLOW-STRAUSS 20, referring to a program of chamber music planned for Jan., 1886.
69. D'Indy/COURS II/1 428, repeated, as usual, in Selva/SONATE 238–40.
70. Cf. Fauré-Fremiet/FAURÉ 110, 117; Fauré/LETTRES 229–35 and 269–70 (reporting progress on each son.).
71. The autograph was on view in 1963 (cf. NOTES XXI [1963–64] 91 and read Op. 108) but has since been withdrawn.

108 among them is available in current recordings, and none of them gets the performances that they all deserve and that are certain to be welcomed.[72] All three are three-movement cycles (F-M-VF and F-M-F), lacking the scherzo of the first sonata.[73] Furthermore, all three have in common the spareness, and preciseness, if not cerebralism, and the reduced, or at least refined, technical demands that we have found in the very late sonatas of Saint-Saëns and not a few others. They no longer reveal the opulent Romanticism of the first sonata, with its melodic expansiveness, its harmonic color for color's sake, and its communion with Mendelssohn, Schumann, and Chopin, in whom Fauré had been so thoroughly steeped. Instead we find a remarkable turn to intensive exploitation of single motives in a persistent manner that does tend at times to become cerebral and even crotchety.

Thus, in the second of the two violin sonatas, Op. 108, the motive announced at once may well have been intended to underlie the entire work, although Fauré is usually not credited with much interest in cyclical treatment.[74] There are climactic measures in the second and third movements (e.g., ii/61–63 and iii/43–45), where references to the initial motive could hardly be other than deliberate. But deliberate or not, a cyclical effect exists, and it becomes far more pervasive, sometimes to the point of irritation and/or monotony,[75] than the more obvious relationships that d'Indy so pointedly exalted in Franck's Sonata in A (supra). In spite of its free, plastic treatment, the initial motive is identified melodically in its reiterations by the play with the intervals of a 2d and 3d around a focal tone, and rhythmically by the syncopations in which these intervals share. Although the violin spins out long, finely drawn lines much of the time, one senses that these lines derive from or sing above the motivic reiterations.[76] If there is monotony now and then, it owes in part to the literally monotonal effect of returning so often to the focal tones of the motive (as during the curious enharmonic oscillation between the E and f triads in ii/24–33) and partly to the monothematic effect of a "sonata allegro" form in which sharp contrasts of ideas reduce to different facets of one idea.

72. Cf. the "Discographie" in Fauré-Fremiet/FAURÉ 229–31.

73. Favre/FAURÉ is a full style-critical diss. on the chamber music, though without separate or considerable mention of the sons. Koechlin/FAURÉ, Servières/FAURÉ, Cobbett/CHAMBER I 386–87 and 390–91 (F. Schmitt), Rostand/FAURÉ, and Vuillermoz/FAURÉ 166–68 and 175–78 all include brief descriptions of each son.

74. E.g., cf. Suckling/FAURÉ 94.

75. As remarked, though only in the outer mvts., by Florent Schmitt in Cobbett/CHAMBER I 390.

76. In Fauré-Fremiet/FAURÉ 157–58 it is suggested that Op. 108 will succeed if the "prudent" approach is replaced by the warm lyricism of an Ysaÿe (who never played it).

Ex. 81. From the start of the middle movement in Gabriel
Fauré's Sonata in g, Op. 117 (after the Durand ed., by kind
permission of Elkan-Vogel Co. in Philadelphia).

If there is irritation it may come from the extra emphasis given to
those focal tones by the almost jerky syncopations.

To these traits may be added one other that probably bears on the
apparent resistance to Fauré's late sonatas in spite of all the respect
in which they are held. That is the thin, meticulous texture, in which
the dissonances—no more than those that had been cloaked in the
richer sound of his earlier music—now stand out, more bare and harsh.
In the absence of fuller sound, Fauré sometimes resorts to canonic
treatment, not, as Franck does, to provide structural extension, but as
a means of structural enrichment (e.g., Op. 108/i/8–11 and ii/20–23).
The two cello sonatas, which are similar in character and style, are
smoother in their rhythmic flow than Op. 108 is, not so dogged in their

motivic unifications (allowing for clearer contrasts), and somewhat less demanding on the pianist, relegating his part to that of simple accompaniment more of the time. Op. 109 tends to be a little more poetic, free, and troubled, and Op. 117 a little more contrived, especially in the finale. But the relative simplicity of these two works should not belie their worthwhile substance, expressive intensity, or structural tightness. The slow movements of all three late sonatas are masterpieces of affecting, simple melody, including Op. 117/ii, which starts as though recalling Fauré's own *Élégie* for Vc & P of 1883 (Ex. 81).

Followers of Franck (Dukas, d'Indy)

Although the notable composer and teacher **Paul Dukas** (1865–1935) received no formal instruction from Franck, his one sonata shows the clear influence of that master's musical language. Moreover, Dukas' sonata has much in common with the main sonata, which appeared only seven years later, by his longtime friend [77] and Franck's most illustrious and proclaimed pupil, **(Paul-Marie-Théodore-) Vincent d'Indy** (1851–1931). Hence, Dukas and d'Indy, the two chief contributors to the sonata in France at the end of the Romantic Era, are paired here as followers of Franck and by way of a sequel to our trilogic section on Franck, Saint-Saëns, and Fauré.

Dukas' Sonata in eb, for P solo, was composed in 1899–1900 and published in 1901 by Durand in Paris.[78] It was dedicated to Saint-Saëns even though the latter seems never to have acknowledged receiving the work.[79] Its first performance, by Edouard Risler at the Salle Pleyel on May 10, 1901, was generally well received, especially in the review by Lalo's son Pierre, published two weeks later.[80] Dukas' immediate, grateful, personal reply[81] reveals chiefly the almost phobic concern for maintaining high standards and eliminating weaknesses that kept him from putting his stamp of approval on more than about a dozen works during his lifetime (including the Symphony in C, the

77. Cf. Vallas/D'INDY II 43–44.
78. Cf. pp. 23–25 in Favre/DUKAS, the chief and most recent study of the man and his works; also, MGG III 914–18 (G. Favre; but the year of pub. should read 1901, not 1906).
79. Cortot/FRANÇAISE I 234–35.
80. In the newspaper *Temps*, pub. May 23 (dated May 24); quoted almost in full in Favre/DUKAS 24–25. On Feb. 3, in the Brussels *Guide musical* XLVII (1901) 99–101, G. Servières had already reviewed the pub. work, under the heading "The Renaissance of the Piano Sonata," as skillful, with derivations from Franck and d'Indy and with more virtuosity than sentiment or melody.
81. Letter of May 24, 1901, printed in Pincherle/MUSICIENS 228–29.

P Variations on a Rameau theme, and, of course, "The Sorcerer's Apprentice," among other instrumental works). Several weeks earlier, after Dukas' Sonata in e♭ had appeared in print, his onetime classmate Debussy had written some perceptive comments on it, praising especially its tonal organization and emotional control and citing especially its last two movements.[82] But several weeks after Pierre Lalo's review appeared, Debussy added, in the guise of "Monsieur Croche the dilettante hater," that Lalo should not have gone quite so far as to sacrifice Schumann and Chopin on the altar of Dukas, or to relate Dukas to Beethoven, with which comparison Debussy says he himself would have been "only mildly flattered," since Beethoven's sonatas, especially the later ones, "are very badly scored for piano," like "orchestral transcriptions . . . lacking a third hand. . . ."[83] We can return to the music of Dukas' Sonata in e♭ after summarizing what d'Indy contributed.

Although d'Indy gave much attention to the sonata in the writings, lectures, and teaching that occupied him during a good part of his long, distinguished career, he actually composed only five sonatas among the 118 orchestral, chamber, piano, dramatic, church, and other choral works that are known by him.[84] The earliest of these was a presumably weak, inexperienced work, for P solo, composed in about his 19th year (1870) and since unexplored (and lost?).[85] The second is a *Petite Sonate dans la forme classique*, Op. 9, for P solo, composed and published (by Hamelle) in 1880—a four-movement work (F-M-Sc-VF) that is reported to be scholastic, unimaginative, and rudimentary, with some suggestions of Mendelssohn and Chopin (mainly in iv) but remarkably few evidences (mainly in ii and iii) that by now d'Indy had been with Franck seven years, become an ardent Wagnerian, and composed the trilogy of symphonic overtures known as *Wallenstein*.[86]

The third sonata we have from d'Indy is that for Vn & P, Op. 59 in C, composed in 1903–04, published in 1905, and first performed, with

82. DEBUSSY CROCHE 47–49, from *La Revue blanche* for Apr. 15, 1901 (cf. Lockspeiser/DEBUSSY I 63–64 and II 282).

83. DEBUSSY CROCHE 9–10.

84. Vallas/D'INDY (efficiently digested by Vallas in GROVE IV 467–77) is the chief study of the man and his works, with a full list of the compositions (II 355–66) as well as writings and lectures (II 369–76, including 3 items specifically on the son. and several others in which the son. is central). D'Indy/COURS II/1 153–433 is d'Indy's main, highly individualized, historical and stylistic discussion of the son. (to which numerous references are made in SBE, SCE, and SSB).

85. Cf. Vallas/D'INDY I 62, II 357; Cortot/FRANÇAISE II 117.

86. Cf. Cortot/FRANÇAISE II 117–20; Vallas/D'INDY I 256–57, II 165 and 357 (with a speculation that Op. 9 might be a reworking of the [lost?] son. from 1870).

much success, by d'Indy and the violinist Armand Parent on February 3, 1905.[87] Almost never heard since its debut performances, Op. 59 is a mature, lyrical, but overly intellectualized work in the standard four movements (F-Sc-S-F), cyclically bound by three "cellules," extended by skillful variation techniques, and enhanced by a folklike melody (in the trio of ii) such as had come to interest d'Indy greatly.[88] The fourth of the five sonatas, Op. 63 in e/E, for P solo (1908), is d'Indy's most important one, about to be discussed. And the last is Op. 84 in D, for Vc & P, composed in 1924–25, published in 1926, and first played in 1926, by d'Indy and the cellist Edwige Bergeron.[89] This work, one example of d'Indy's late, extraordinary, nationalistic turn to much simpler, neo-French-Baroque styles and to full themes rather than cellules, is virtually a suite, with its four movements entitled "Entrée," "Gavotte en rondeau," "Air," and "Gigue." [90]

D'Indy's *Sonate* in e/E, Op. 63, was composed in 1907, at the start of the third of his four main periods.[91] It was published in 1908, and already introduced, with much acclaim, on January 25 of that year by its dedicatee and the one pianist most identified with it, Blanche Selva.[92] The seriousness with which both the dignified master and his devoted followers approached this one piano sonata paved a broad highway for that acclaim. Yet remarkably few pianists have followed Selva in playing it. Why so few have played either it or Dukas' Sonata in e♭ brings us to a comparison and a further discussion of these two works.[93] The

87. Vallas/D'INDY II 194–95 (with further details on the circumstances of the composing). Cf., also, MERCURE II (Jan.–June, 1906) 280 and 529.

88. Cf. Vallas/D'INDY II 59, 131 (on the origins in 1896 of the [un-]"inspired" main cellule), 138, 194–97 (mentioning influences not only by Franck but by d'Indy's artistic arch rival Debussy), and 363. Op. 59 is described, with exx., in Cobbett/CHAMBER II 6–7 (M. D. Calvocoressi) and was analyzed by 2 of d'Indy's disciples at his Schola cantorum, especially for its cyclical principles—Albert Groz in 1908 (in detail; cf. Vallas/D'INDY II 196) and Blanche Selva in 1913 (Selva/SONATE 259–63).

89. Cf. Vallas/D'INDY II 201–2, 364; Cobbett/CHAMBER II 8.

90. The first mvt. of d'Indy's chamber Suite in A, Op. 91 (pub. in 1930), is called, in the manner of the early suite, "Entrée en Sonate" (cf. Vallas/D'INDY II 202–3).

91. Cf. Vallas/D'INDY II 171 and 198.

92. Vallas/D'INDY II 171.

93. Most of the rare performances of each work have occurred in France, including one of d'Indy's Op. 63 by E. Risler that is praised in Vallas/D'INDY II 175. The performances of Op. 63 by the present author, in about 3 dozen centers between 1941 and 1965, are the only ones in this country known here (not including an informal "reading" about 1935 by the fine pianist Bruce Simonds at Yale University). An Australian recording of Op. 63 (WG-A-2325, with a facs., on the jacket, of the first page of the autograph score) was made by the Australian pianist Raymond Lambert not later than 1965. Demuth/FRENCH 69 mentions performances of the Dukas Son. in e♭ by the French pianist Lélia Gousseau. A probable first

most obvious answer to that question and the most obvious trait common to both works is excessive length, that recurring problem in the larger forms of Romantic music, especially Romantic piano music (ssʙ VI). The three movements (Va-VF-M/F) of d'Indy's Op 63 contain 815 measures (252+204+359) in 40 crowded pages and last nearly 38 minutes in all. The four movements (F-S-VF-S/F) of Dukas' Sonata in e♭ contain 1,502 measures (247+181+565+509) in 55 similarly crowded pages and last about 65 minutes in all! The problem exists primarily in the finales (nearly 18 and 28 minutes, respectively), each of which takes up more than 40 per cent of its cycle (as does the finale of Beethoven's Op. 106). There are arid sections in both finales and a sense, especially in d'Indy's finale, that every last detail of textbook "sonata form" must be seen through in full before the coda can begin.[94] Moreover, even if the other movements in both sonatas do not seem too long for their contents, they still help to approach both the performer's and the listener's limits of *Sitzfleisch* endurance. One never can forget that the point of diminishing returns in the length of piano pieces comes well before that of ensemble pieces enhanced by distinct contrasts of timbre.

But these chefs d'oeuvre by d'Indy and Dukas share not only their exceptional lengths and exceptional setting (since no consequential sons. for P solo were left by their chief contemporaries, Franck, Saint-Saëns, and Fauré); they also share certain more positive values by which they stand out at the end of the era.[95] First is the high and serious aesthetic

---

performance of it in this country, at Town Hall in New York on Feb. 29, 1952, brought from reviewer Harold C. Schonberg of *The New York Times* (Mar. 1, 1952, p. 8, col. 8) the opinion that "the work is as empty as can be found in the repertoire," although the possibility that a different performance might have done more for the work was acknowledged.

94. One contemporary reviewer said Op. 63 was stretched to the point of bursting the son.'s framework (Vallas/ᴅ'ɪɴᴅʏ II 176).

95. They invite a detailed comparison; they are similarly paired in Demuth/ꜰʀᴇɴᴄʜ 68 and Salazar/ᴛʀᴇɴᴅs 111–12 and 136 (where they are seen as "the most serious achievement[s] in this form in France and in the music of Latin countries" since Liszt's Son. in b). Dukas' Son. in e♭ is outlined, with overemphasis on cyclical relationships, in d'Indy/ᴄᴏᴜʀs II/1 431–33, and a little more fully, with objections only to some impractical, quasi-orchestral scoring, in Selva/ꜱᴏɴᴀᴛᴇ 244–48; it is described more subjectively (and more illuminatingly in these instances) in Emmanuel/ᴅᴜᴋᴀs 72–76 and, especially, Cortot/ꜰʀᴀɴçᴀɪsᴇ I 218–35 (with objections to statements by d'Indy and Selva and references to comments by others), and in Favre/ᴅᴜᴋᴀs 58–69 (with further references to comments by others). D'Indy's Op. 63 is analyzed by the composer himself (with apologies) in d'Indy/ᴄᴏᴜʀs II/1 428–31, more briefly (but with almost religious fervor) in Selva/ꜱᴏɴᴀᴛᴇ 263–67, and in exhaustive detail in an article by Albert Groz pub. in 1908 soon after Op. 63 appeared (cf. Selva/ꜱᴏɴᴀᴛᴇ 254), in all instances with emphasis on the cyclical principles. It is discussed as a kind of magnificent failure, because of its intellectuality, in Cortot/ꜰʀᴀɴçᴀɪsᴇ II 141–48; as a potential success in spite of the

Ex. 82. From the development section in the first movement of Paul Dukas' Sonata in e♭ (after the Durand ed., p. 8).

aim of the two works. They are lengthy because, as the polish and perfection of every notational and editorial detail alone would suggest, each is intended to be a monumental, all-encompassing, and indefectible experience in the loftiest reaches of the sonata idea. Neither score gives any outward hint of a programme for that experience, yet one guesses that nothing less than life itself must be the subject of each.[96] Dukas was a programmatist at heart, and so was d'Indy in spite of his avowed absolutism.[97] Second, as suggested earlier, both works show unmistakable influences of Franck, especially in their chromatic harmony, in their use of enharmonic modulations for surprise and color values, in certain specific melodic fragments, and in the canonic treatments of main ideas. Ex. 82 crowds in a little of each of these traits, including a melodic idea at the change of key that is reminiscent less of the actual pitch outline than of a kind of idea often used by Franck (as in the "Choral" theme of *Prélude, choral, et fugue,* or the measures just

---

intellectuality, given the right performers, in Vallas/D'INDY II 171–76; and as a supreme masterwork, in which the intellectuality has been unjustly censured, in Demuth/D'INDY 72–81.

96. Selva/SONATE 247 and 266 sees "a sort of underground cavern full of mysterious horror" in Dukas' 3d mvt., and a victory of Good over Evil in d'Indy's finale (cf. Cortot/FRANÇAISE II 144).

97. Cf. GROVE IV 472–73.

before the development section of Symphony in d/i). D'Indy's "y" cellule (as in i/64–66) is a saccharine bit that, even without its harmony, almost exudes another melodic style of Franck (as in Son. in A/iii/11–13). (As regards their syntax and larger structural considerations, and except for d'Indy's preoccupation with cyclical principles, the two works do not show the influence of Franck.)

Third, the Dukas and d'Indy piano sonatas have in common their essential broad lyricism, including most of the textural dispositions in which the melody is set. In fact, the scores often look alike, as in sections with the melody in octaves supported by arpeggiated figures in triplets, or with the left hand crossing back and forth over a central right-hand accompaniment figure to supply both bass and soprano melody line, or with the filler being a "Beethoven trill." Fourth, and more specifically, both finales rise to unusually powerful climaxes and both begin with a slow, free introduction. Indeed, d'Indy's introduction is so much like Dukas'—in the stentorian, Lisztian octaves and chords of the first measures, in the rising arpeggiated cadenzas into which those octaves and chords dissolve, and in the unmeasured measures—that he must have taken it, at least unconsciously, as his model. (Curiously, Dukas, in turn, seems to refer deliberately to the similarly free introduction in the finale of Beethoven's Op. 106.)

But the differences between d'Indy's and Dukas' sonatas become at least as revealing as the likenesses. These differences might be explained largely by two considerations, both in d'Indy's favor. At 56, in 1907, d'Indy was more experienced than Dukas at the midpoint in his career, in 1899–1900. D'Indy had composed more and he had gotten around more in the musical world (with Liszt, Wagner, and Brahms being among those he had known).[98] Moreover, as judged here, d'Indy was the more gifted composer, with more to say and more imagination with which to say it. Hence, as a first difference, we find d'Indy's Op. 63, long as it is, to be more concentrated and intense than Dukas' Sonata in e♭. In effect, d'Indy compresses Dukas' 65 minutes into 38. As one result, we get something like the richly scored second variation or the extraordinarily expressive conclusion in d'Indy's first movement, which, as in many a page of Reger's later music, may sound almost atonal at first in the chromatic, dissonant extremes to which it extends traditional harmony. A second, related difference is the greater sense of direction in d'Indy's music, which always aims for and reaches structural goals, where Dukas', for all its broad melodic arches and its fine craftsmanship in textural details, often seems to be rambling. Contributing to the sense of rambling by Dukas is a device used so often

98. Cf. Vallas/D'INDY II 171–72.

in his outer movements that it becomes a mannerism—that is, the extension of an idea by cumulative harmonic sequence (as at the start of Ex. 82, *supra*).

As a third difference, we find d'Indy's greater imagination bearing fruit in more distinctive and more sharply contrasted themes, more resourceful, often contrapuntal dispositions of the texture, and more varied and ingenious solutions to the problems of form. Where Dukas' expanded solution to over-all design is still the standard one of the usual four movements in the usual cycle,[99] d'Indy works out a highly original three-movement cycle. His first movement includes a slow, free introduction, an extended theme and four markedly different variations, each ending with a clear, unifying return to the "y" cellule and

Ex. 83. From the climax in the finale of Vincent d'Indy's Sonata in e/E, Op. 63 (after the Durand ed., p. 39).

the fourth dissolving into some dynamic fantasying around the main ideas, then that expressive conclusion, in which the theme returns in the tonic major key. The second movement is a five-part scherzo (A-B-A-C-A-coda) cast effectively in 5/4 meter. It is difficult to play because of its maximum use of the peculiarly French device of superimposed hands. And the greater concentration makes d'Indy's work generally more difficult to play. But contrary to some statements,[100] neither work is unreasonably difficult. Neither has quite the virtuoso problems of Liszt's Sonata in b nor the intricacies of Beethoven's Op.

99. The emphasis in Cortot/FRANÇAISE I 217 on Dukas' Son. in e♭ as one of France's main returns to Beethoven in piano music seems to mean no more than that Dukas followed standard Classic procedures and techniques; cf., also, p. 235.
100. Cf. Vallas/D'INDY II 172 and 175; Demuth/FRENCH 69–71.

106. D'Indy's finale opens with an introduction that returns to that of the first movement except for being freer. The exhaustive "sonata form" follows, based mainly on new themes, but with a return to the "x" cellule or main theme of the first movement, so labeled, just before the recapitulation, and finally one of the grandest climactic codas in all piano literature. This last, which more than makes up for those arid sections before it, is more telling than Dukas' climactic coda. In the first place, it reaches a clearer goal again, peaking on the biggest, most chorale-like statement of the "x" theme, with the main "sonata allegro" theme joining below its last two phrases (Ex. 83). And secondly, like a veritable "Liebestod" (the parallel, even to the line and harmony, is striking), it relaxes courageously on the last page into a quiet, gentle, sublimatory end.

Dukas showed only casual and occasional interest in cyclical relationships. But a word should be added about d'Indy's cyclical methods, his intellectuality, and his intransigent nature (including even the excessive moral principles and the hateful social prejudices), as any or all of these may have affected his masterpiece Op. 63. As noted earlier (also in ssb VI), d'Indy himself and his followers made much of his avowed creation of Op. 63 out of three germinating (contrapuntally related) "cellules," "x," "y," and "z," in that order of importance. But in this work the musician governs the theorist, the cellules never get in the way of the musical flow, and, moreover, the final climactic return to "x" achieves positive values as stunning as the complete chorale statements in the finales of Bruckner's last symphonies. If the intellectuality obstructs the musical flow at all it may be in those sections where the ultrachromatic harmony becomes most recherché and esoteric. But more likely, as an obstruction to the work, is the intransigent nature that would yield in no detail of that "sonata allegro" finale, to the point where the listener feels he cannot tolerate one more repetition of the trill bridge theme or the lyrical second theme to which it leads.

Minor Composers in Late-Romantic France

Alongside and often associated with the important composers we have been considering, most of some 30 others yet to be noted can get only passing recognition. The violinist **Paul Viardot** (1857–1941), son of the important singer Pauline Viardot-Garcia and dedicatee of Fauré's Op. 13 (*supra*), himself left three sonatas for P & Vn (pub. in 1883, ?, and 1931) and one for Vc & P (1928), the earliest of which (Op. 5 in G; 3 mvts.), was reviewed as showing little of consequence beyond too self-conscious an effort to be original.[101] A contemporary and a more facile, less imaginative version of Saint-Saëns, **Charles-Henri-René Boisdeffre** (1838–1906), left three more duo sonatas (one for P & Cl-or-Vn and 2 for P & Vn, pub. between 1875 and *ca.* 1910), among the nearly twenty chamber works that comprise his chief contribution.[102] One of the many forgotten winners of the Grand Prix de Rome from the Paris Conservatoire (in 1870), **Charles-Édouard Lefebvre** (1843–1917) left a conventional but skillful Sonata for Vc & P, Op. 98 in a (pub. in 1896) that won a good response, especially for its slow movement.[103] And the composer and conductor who presided in 1916 over the Société française de musique de chambre, **(Paul-Alexandre-) Camille Chevillard** (1859–1923), left two duo sonatas, Opp. 8 in g, for P & Vn (pub. in 1894), and 15 in B♭, for P & Vc (pub. in 1897).[104] These last are big works, superior in their originality and workmanship, and variously incisive, poetic, dramatic, and lyrical. Franck's influence is felt, though not oppressively, in their chromatic harmony, especially when there are successive unresolved 9th chords, and in both their syntax and their cyclical relationships. Each of the three-movement works derives almost entirely, and sometimes excessively, from its initial motive. Op. 8 is freer, more complex, and more changeable than Op. 15, with chromaticism that at times brings us even closer than d'Indy does to Reger's tonal amorphousness, with a fantasy slow movement, and with a "Mouv^t de Polonaise, brillant et très rhythmé" that makes a stunning finale.

Better known than Chevillard, though less deserving of renown as viewed here, was the short-lived composer **(Jean-Joseph-Nicolas-) Guillaume Lekeu** (1870–94).[105] As to the question of whether Lekeu should be grouped with (Walloon-) Belgian or French composers,[106] we resolve it here, as usual, by placing him where he was most active, in Paris. There he entered the University in 1888, started the study with his compatriot Franck in late 1889 that lasted until the latter's death a year later, then went to d'Indy for further study.[107] His late start at 19 and early death at 24 left him but few years for serious study,

---

101. MW XVIII (1887) 466–67. Cf. GROVE VIII 763 (F. A. Marshall); Altmann/ KAMMERMUSIK 230.

102. Cf. Cobbett/CHAMBER I 143 (A. Piriou & W. W. Cobbett); BAKER 175; MDC IV (1906) xxxiv.

103. MDC IV (1906) xxxviii. Cf. MGG VIII 464–65 (G. Ferchault).

104. Cf. GROVE II 205–6 (G. Ferrari & M. L. Pereyra); BAKER 284; Cobbett/CHAMBER I 274 (W. J. Mitson).

105. Cf. MGG VIII 594–95 (A. Van der Linden), with further references; Sonneck/ LEKEU (including much of the information available on the sons.).

106. Cf. Sonneck/LEKEU 111–13.

107. Cf. Sonneck/LEKEU 116–19, 136.

yet he managed to complete nearly 20 main works during that time and to get to various stages of completion in perhaps 40 more.[108]

Three sonatas figure in that output of Lekeu. One is the *Sonate pour piano* in g, composed in April, 1891, according to an inscription at the end of its printed score, which was published posthumously in 1900 (?) by E. Baudoux in Paris, predecessor to Rouart, Lerolle.[109] About the genesis of this work we have only two bits of unconfirmed information, supplied by Marcel Obran with the publication in the *Courrier musical* for 1910 of a few letters by Lekeu, but evidently based on letters or portions not yet published:[110]

A *Suite* for piano was published after his death under the title of Sonata. He did not consider it more than a study in composition; but it is a study of real beauty. The fugue remains a monumental example of the genre. [And quoting a reference to this work in an unpub. letter by Lekeu:] "This passage I should not to-day write again, but the fugue is *bien*."

Actually, "Suite" does seem like the more appropriate title, although no standard title applies in its textbook sense. The work is relatively short (19 pp.) and contains five movements—"Très modéré," one page, chordal and preludial; a 7-page fugue in the home key, without heading or tempo indication (probably andante); a 4-page fugue in the relative minor (b) of the major dominant key, again without initial markings (probably andante); "Dans un mouvement plus lent," 4 pages, in the home key, improvisatory, climactic, largely contrapuntal, and based on the single idea that prevails in all five movements; and a somewhat similar, 3-page conclusion, in the tonic major key, with no initial marking other than a return to the quarter-note beat "du Prélude." "Sonata" might have seemed more appropriate as a title if this work had been scored for organ and designated for church use.

Lekeu's other two sonatas are duos. One, for Vc & P in F, was composed as far as he got with it in 1888, completed by d'Indy for publication by Rouart, Lerolle in 1910, but not actually published until 1923. It is reportedly a weak and amateurish work (as well it might be at the start of Lekeu's serious study), with no acknowledgment by either Lekeu or d'Indy of its borrowing in the outer movements, note for

108. Cf. Sonneck/LEKEU 119–20, with a dated list of main works.
109. The pub. dates of all 3 sons. are given variously. The Baudoux plate no. for the P Son. is 601 and the address 37 Boulevard Haussmann (cf. Hopkinson/PARISIAN 7).
110. As trans. in Sonneck/LEKEU 130. A first collection of Lekeu's interesting letters was pub. in the *Courrier musical* for 1906, ed. by de Stoecklin; they are trans. in part in Sonneck/LEKEU, *passim*, and in Abraham/LEKEU; cf., also, Closson & Borren/BELGIQUE 274–75. Another set of Lekeu's letters, to Octave Maus, is pub. in Van der Linden/LEKEU.

note, of a main theme from the first movement of Liszt's "Faust Symphony."[111] The other duo is Lekeu's best known and most successful work, the Sonata for Vn & P in G, composed in 1892 and published by E. Baudoux in 1894 but posthumously.[112] The success was insured when its eventual dedicatee, Eugène Ysaÿe, undoubtedly recalling his close association and success with the violin sonata of another compatriot, Franck (*supra*), suggested to Lekeu that he write such a work, in February, 1892.[113] Lekeu completed it, "at great pains" and "fatigued" by the effort, apparently in July, well before Ysaÿe's first of several private performances of it, in November, 1892, with Lekeu, and his first public performance of it, with a Madame Theroine, at one of Octave Maus's "Cercle des XX" concerts in Brussels, March 7, 1893.[114] Thenceforth, for a while, the work was performed widely.[115]

The most frequent evaluation of Lekeu's music might be summed up as an acknowledgment of much promise, a recognition of some gaucheries and inexperience, and regrets that the composer did not live to fulfill the promise.[116] After a rereading of his two completed sonatas the temptation here has been to ask whether even the "much promise" does not need re-evaluation.[117] It is possible that a good part of the exceptional interest shown in Lekeu ever since his early death has grown primarily out of the patriotic Ysaÿe's masterful projections of the violin Sonata, the desire to point to a worthy Belgian successor to Franck, and the popular fascination with the tragic spectacle of such an ingenuously eager, willing composer, who could be affected almost traumatically as he discovered Beethoven, Wagner, and Franck, or when Ysaÿe played his own sonata,[118] yet had to die before he could realize his "promise"? Otherwise, even allowing for our vast changes of taste today, it is hard to understand earlier statements such as that of Sonneck in 1919, ". . . every unbiased critic will have to admit that of violin sonatas composed since Brahms and Franck, Lekeu's is inferior to none."[119] In the experience of this study Lekeu is not entitled

111. Cf. Weigl/VIOLONCELL 77; Sonneck/LEKEU 120, 121.

112. The date of first pub., which is lacking in HOFMEISTER and generally given incorrectly (cf. Sonneck/LEKEU 120 and 140), is correct in Altmann/KAMMERMUSIK 213 and specified as September 1894 in Selva/SONATA 240. A memorial engraving for that ed. is reproduced in Closson & Borren/BELGIQUE 283. Rouart, Lerolle reprinted the work in 1907 and 1934.

113. Cf. Sonneck/LEKEU 137; Ysaÿe/YSAŸE 184–86.

114. Ysaÿe/YSAŸE 185–86 and Van der Linden/LEKEU 158.

115. Cf. Sonneck/LEKEU 140–41. No standard recording is pub. as of 1967.

116. Cf. the sample evaluations quoted in Sonneck/LEKEU 109–11.

117. Cf. GROVE V 124 (M. Kufferath).

118. Cf. Cobbett/CHAMBER II 95 (G. Systermans); Abraham/LEKEU 62–63, 85–86, and 108–; Ysaÿe/YSAŸE 185–86.

119. Sonneck/LEKEU 140.

to compete with Strauss (at the same age!), Reger, Fauré, Saint-Saëns, and the other main composers we have been discussing. Apparently Franck was too near the end of his own years when Lekeu came to him to leave any significant comments. But it is interesting that for all of their sympathy with "the lad" and their tendency then to speak in strong terms, two of the contemporary musicians best qualified to judge, d'Indy and Dukas, wrote only in the most guarded terms of Lekeu's talent.[120] Nor, after its first performance, did the several reviewers praise the violin Sonata without distinct reservations about its skill and content.[121]

To be sure, Lekeu's violin Sonata has given many a musician real pleasure. Milhaud writes, for example, "How many times did we play together Lekeu's Sonata, which filled us with such enthusiasm in those days!" (around 1910).[122] And this work, now in the standard three-movement plan (In/F-S-F), does show improvements, as in its expressive use of the violin or several sections of melody and harmony that surge warmly; and it does show more "promise" than the piano "Sonata," which at best can be said to reveal competence in the *fugue d'école*. But further experience with the violin Sonata suggests that Lekeu's own several references to his struggles in composition and, in particular, to his dissatisfaction with that work after its completion were not simply reports of typical creative growth but included genuine and justifiable misgivings as to the actual significance of his talent.[123] Today the more curious harmonies and irregular textures (especially the voice-leading in the pedestrian piano writing) do not sound like gropings toward new styles but like the unlearned crudities of an average student who got a late start.[124] More serious is the sense one now gets that the work is based on one (not very substantial or prepossessing) idea not only in the interest of cyclical relationships but because no other ideas could be found; and that the work is free not only in the interest of Romantic abandon but because better structural solutions could not be found. The germinal idea, incidentally, happens to get uncomfortably close to that in the piano Sonata and in other works by Lekeu, too.[125]

---

120. Cf. Dukas/ÉCRITS 176–78; d'Indy/COURS II/2 270 and III 354; d'Indy/FRANCK 254; also, the negative evaluation in Selva/SONATE 240–42.
121. Cf. Van der Linden/LEKEU 163–64; Sonneck/LEKEU 111; also, MERCURE II (Jan.–June, 1906) 472 and 529.
122. Milhaud/NOTES 23.
123. Cf. Sonneck/LEKEU 140–41, 146, 147.
124. MacDowell was amused over the "queerness" of the Vn Son. (Gilman/MACDOWELL 75).
125. Cf. Cobbett/CHAMBER II 95.

Gabriel (Henri-Constant-) Pierné (1863–1937), a student of and successor to Franck as organist and the esteemed composer of the oratorio *La Croisade des Enfants,* left three published sonatas—Op. 36 in d, for Vn & P (pub. in 1901), the only one that has been played more than a few times; Op. 46 in f♯, for Vc & P (composed in 1922 and pub. in 1923); and Op. 48 in C, a "Sonata da camera" for Fl, Vc, and P.[126] Op. 46 is a free but well-balanced form in one movement that includes all the characteristic styles and tempos of the complete sonata cycle. Although not otherwise innovational, both of Pierné's duos achieve real musical distinction in their expressive warmth, resourceful harmony (nearer to Fauré's than Franck's), melodic grace, rhythmic variety, and light but telling sonority, all with surprising economy of means.

Four other, interassociated organists in Paris of high repute and influence made worthy if not numerous contributions to the sonata. **Charles-Marie (-Jean-Albert) Widor** (1844–1937), another successor to Franck and a productive composer in all branches, left three sonatas, two for Vn & P and one for Vc & P, that were published in the first decade of this century.[127] Although these duos have not attracted the interest of his important, variform "Symphonies" for organ, they too show, much as in Saint-Saëns, an expert craftsman, an eclectic able to draw at will on the past as far back as Bach, and a creative musician both subtle and imaginative.[128] The blind organist **Louis Vierne** (1870–1937), a pupil of both Franck and Widor, left two more duo sonatas published about the same time, one each for P & Vn (Op. 23 in g, 1908) and P & Vc (Op. 27 in b, 1911).[129] These duos are similar in style and skill to Pierné's, including the suggestions of Fauré's harmony. Ysaÿe, who introduced the four-movement violin Sonata (F-M-M-In/VF) with Pugno in 1908, won success with it, writing Vierne that this work (composed during a period of severe personal troubles for Vierne) was much the best work of its sort after Franck's.[130] The cello Sonata, a somewhat freer work in three movements (S/F-VS-F) also composed in a difficult period, has been rated similarly high in quality and idiomatic treatment among the fewer examples of its time, place, and type,[131] although one German critic, after describing the cello part as masculinely energetic and the piano part as femininely

126. Cf. MGG X 1257–61 (G. Ferchault); Cobbett/CHAMBER II 222–23 (A. Piriou & W. W. Cobbett); MERCURE II (Jan.–June, 1906) 529.

127. Altmann/KAMMERMUSIK 231 and 266.

128. Cf. GROVE IX 284–85 (H. Grace); Cobbett/CHAMBER II 580–81 (A. Piriou).

129. Cf. MGG XIII 1612–13 (F. Raugel); Gavoty/VIERNE, a full study of the man and his works, with detailed list of works (pp. 298–312) and discussion of the sons. (pp. 269–71).

130. Gavoty/VIERNE 91, 99–101, 113.

131. Gavoty/VIERNE 269–70, 110–11.

delicate, found only the first movement not to be somewhat weak and dry.[132]

The prolific composer **Felix-Alexandre Guilmant** (1837–1911), a student, like Widor, of Jacques Nicolas Lemmens in Brussels and a cofounder with d'Indy of the Schola cantorum, left eight organ sonatas published between 1874 and 1907.[133] Although the harmony is more traditional and the texture heavier and simpler, these sonatas (with "Suite" as an alternate title in No. 7 and "Symphonie" in No. 8) are like Widor's "Symphonies" in their splendorous orchestral, highly idiomatic uses of the instrument, and their variform cycles. Guilmant's sonatas have three to five movements, including examples of the prelude, chorale and fugue, scherzo, march, minuet, recitative, and "sonata form." **Francois-Clement-Théodore Dubois** (1837–1924), a successor to Saint-Saëns and renowned teacher at the Paris Conservatoire, included three sonatas among his many works in all main categories of music.[134] Two are duos, Sonata in A for Vn & P (1900), a light but appealing work that Ysaÿe and Pugno enjoyed playing,[135] and Sonata in D for Vc & P (1905). The other is Sonata in a, for P solo (1908), a highly effective cycle of three movements (F-S-S/VF) that is epigonic in its conservatism, neat and convenient brilliance, and unabashed eclecticism. Typical are the dramatic opening measures (Ex. 84) that soon peter out and the clear reminders of Schubert, Wagner, Tchaikovsky, Grieg, and others as one reads from theme to theme. One is not surprised to learn that Dubois was close at one time or another to Franck, Liszt, Fauré, Ambroise Thomas, Saint-Saëns, Delibes, and numerous other contemporaries.

Albéric Magnard (1865–1914) was a pupil of d'Indy, a member of his circle early in this century, and a Wagner enthusiast though not an imitator.[136] Two of the five valued chamber works in his small (sadly interrupted) output are four-movement duo sonatas—Op. 13 in G, for Vn & P (1903; ded. to Ysaÿe) and Op. 20 in A, for Vc & P (1911). These do not lack melodic invention or emotional excitement, nor go beyond their time in free forms or styles. But they stand apart by virtue of their abstraction and aloofness from popular taste, as manifested especially in somewhat severe, harsh textures, with frequent accented, unprepared dissonances and a somewhat stark, unidiomatic

132. DM XI/2 (1911–12) 301–2.
133. Cf. MGG V 1099–1101 (F. Raugel), with further references; Dufourcq/FRANÇAISE 172–78; Frotscher/ORGELSPIEL II 1213–14; Kremer/ORGAN 187–88.
134. Cf. MGG III 838–41 (F. Raugel), with dated list; Altmann/KAMMERMUSIK 201 and 255.
135. Cobbett/CHAMBER I 399 (W. W. Cobbett).
136. Cf. MGG VIII 1481–82 (G. Ferchault), with further references.

Ex. 84. From the opening of Théodore Dubois' Sonata in a
(after the original Heugel ed. of 1908).

treatment of the piano.[137] A Franck pupil and another Wagnerian, the
Austrian-born violinist **Sylvio Lazzari** (1857–1944) left a single sonata
among numerous works, Op. 24 in E, for Vn & P (1894).[138] This three-
movement work (F-S-VF), successfully introduced by Ysaÿe, is strongly
reminiscent of Franck's styles and cyclical treatment. But it has enough
individuality of melody, harmony, and instrumental technique to be
interesting in its own right.[139] **Gustave (Marie Victor Fernand) Samazeuilh** (1877–?), a student of Chausson and d'Indy, a friend of Richard
Strauss, and a protégé of Fauré and Dukas, left among relatively few
works one sonata each for P solo (1903;?) and Vn & P (1904, in b/B).[140]
The latter is described as being close to Franck in idiom, with some
fine themes, but labored and often suffocatingly thick in texture.[141]

137. Cf. the slightly different reactions in Selva/SONATE 277–83 (with exx.);
MERCURE I (1905) 141 and II (Jan.–June, 1906) 31 and 529; Cobbett/CHAMBER II
109–10 (M. Labey).
138. Cf. MGG VIII 403–4 (G. Ferchault).
139. It is described, with 11 generous exx., in Cobbett/CHAMBER II 91–93 (H.
Woollett & W. W. Cobbett).
140. Cf. MGG XI 1331 (R. Dumesnil), but the P son. could not be confirmed in
HOFMEISTER, PAZDÍREK, early Durand cats., nor other sources available here.
141. Cf. MW XXXVI (1905) 407, 408; MERCURE II (Jan.–June, 1906) 426; Cobbett/
CHAMBER II 326–27 (F. Schmitt & W. W. Cobbett).

The four duo sonatas by the Languedocian composer **Paul Lacombe** (1837–1927) include three for Vn & P and one for Vc & P, all published between 1868 and 1902 in Paris.[142] These works, which show the Classical orientation to be expected of a devoted pupil of Bizet and warm admirer of Saint-Saëns, were uniformly praised for their skill and their charm when they appeared.[143] But today they seem rather flat, light, and inconsequential, probably reflecting both the prolificity of Lacombe and his continuing orientation toward Mendelssohn, Schumann, and Chopin. The Polish-born pianist **Sigismund (Denis Antoni) Stojowski** (1869 [not 1870]–1946) studied with Delibes and Massenet in Paris and with Paderewski before emigrating from Paris to the United States in 1906.[144] His three duo sonatas—two for Vn & P, one for Vc & P, published between 1894 and 1912—are melodious, transparent, and flowing enough to have immediate appeal.[145] But as heard here they suffer from rhythms and phrases that incessantly reinforce the barline and harmonic progressions that convert Fauré's idiom into clichés.

Much broader is the musical outlook in the one sonata by **Georges-Martin Witkowski** (1867–1943), a pupil of d'Indy who established his own Schola cantorum in Lyons in 1924.[146] As with d'Indy's Op. 63, Witkowski's Op. 16 in g, for Vn & P, was composed in 1907 and published a year later by Durand (ded. to the violinist Jacques Thibaud). It is a big, impassioned, soaring work, almost as long as d'Indy's, close to the latter in idiom, and even more thoroughly based on a progenitor theme and cyclical principles. The first of its but two movements is a large "sonata form" and the second a set of five variations in E, of which the last returns to g and serves as a finale. The skill and musicality of this work are impressive. Blanche Selva finds it overly complex in its cyclical derivations and too orchestrally conceived for its setting.[147] Although the writing has not seemed that orchestral as viewed here, the progenitor theme does seem to be overdone, the more so as it is lacking somewhat in inherent vitality.

142. Cf. MGG VIII 39–40 (G. Ferchault); GROVE V 8–9 (M. L. Pereyra); Cobbett/CHAMBER II 87 (L. Moulin).

143. E.g., MW XXXIV (1903) 163 (E. Segnitz) and NZM LXVI/2 (1870) 311, both on Op. 8 in a, for Vn & P; MW XI (1880) 359, on Op. 17 in f, for Vn & P; MW XXXI (1900) 619, 620 (E. Segnitz), on Op. 98 in G, for Vn & P.

144. Cf. MGG XII 1392 (J. Ekiert). BAKER 1576; Cobbett/CHAMBER II 459 (E. Evans).

145. Cf. the review of Op. 37 in E (not e), for Vn & P, in DM XII/3 (1912–13) 107.

146. Cf. Boucher/WITKOWSKI, especially pp. 198, 202, 207; GROVE IX (M. L. Pereyra) 324.

147. Selva/SONATE 252–58, with outline analysis and exx. Cf., also, Cobbett/CHAMBER II 588 (A. Piriou).

A negative review of a Sonata in f♯ (not f), for P solo, by d'Indy's pupil **Antoine Mariotte** (1875–1944) appears to reflect not on the composer but on the reviewer, who seems not to have understood either the idiom or the independent ideas and uncompromising style of Mariotte.[148] But a negative review of Sonata in b, for Vc and P (1907, not 1902) by the Belgian in Paris **Louis Delune** (1876–1940) seems justified in crediting the three-movement work (F-S-Ro) with little more than satisfactory workmanship.[149] Two duo sonatas, one each for Vn & P and Vc & P (1907 and 1910), by **Albert Bertelin** (1872–1951), pupil of Dubois, Widor, and Pugno, are described as solid in construction, cyclical in Franck's manner, and conservative.[150] Two women composers of published sonatas may be noted in late-Romantic France. The Countess **Armande de Polignac** (1876–1962), although a student of both Fauré and d'Indy, fared less well than the other, for the second of her two sonatas for Vn & P (1902 and 1911) was branded a dull and affected work.[151] But the much better known pianist and composer **Cécile (-Louise-Stéphanie) Chaminade** (1857–1944), a pupil of Godard and others, left a Sonata in c, Op. 21 for P solo (1895; ded. to Mozskowski) that, both in its ideas and their development, rises a shade above "the level of agreeable drawing-room music" usually regarded as the upper limit of her art.[152] Chaminade's Op. 21 is a concise cycle of the traditional three movements (VF-M-F), well scored in idioms no later than Mendelssohn's. Of the same ilk are at least two sonatas (especially Son. in C) and three sonatinas for P solo, and one Sonatina for P-duet, all published in the later 19th century, by the pianist, prolific composer, and longtime teacher at the Paris Conservatoire, **Theodore Lack** (1846–1921);[153] also, three duo sonatas by Dubois' pupil **Jules Mouquet** (1867–1946), one each for Vn & P, Vc & P, and Fl & P ("La Flûte de Pan"), published between 1906 and 1912.[154] A "Sonate pour piano en 4 parties" (sold together and separately; *ca.* 1907) by a follower of Franck and pupil of d'Indy, **Marcel Labey** (1875–?) retains the har-

148. DM VI/4 (1906–7) 306 (A. Leitzmann). Cf. MGG VIII 1660 (G. Ferchault); GROVE V 581–82 (F. Raugel).

149. DM VI/4 (1906–7) 373 (A. Laser). Cf. BAKER 369; Closson & Borren/BELGIQUE 258–59; Cobbett/CHAMBER I 323 (G. Systermans), with wrong dates and a reference, also, to a Son. in d, for Vn & P (actually 1907, too).

150. Cobbett/CHAMBER I 124 (A. Piriou). Cf. Riemann/LEXIKON I 163; LAROUSSE I 102.

151. DM X/4 (1910) 376 (W. Altmann). Cf. BAKER 1262 and Suppl. 104; Altmann/KAMMERMUSIK 221.

152. As in GROVE II 156–57 (G. Ferrari). Cf. Elson/WOMAN 174–77.

153. Cf. BAKER 894; PAZDÍREK IX 33–38; Altmann/KAMMERMUSIK 288; Westerby/PIANOFORTE 186.

154. Cf. BAKER 1122; Altmann/KAMMERMUSIK 217, 261, 277; DM XIII/3 (1912–13) 107 (W. Altmann).

monic idiom of his mentors and the standard designs but adopts a clipped, neat, chordal, and less pianistic texture and a continuously jerky alternation of triplet, duplet, and dotted rhythms that produces an almost flippant, dancelike distortion of d'Indy's style. Three duo sonatas—two for Vn & P and one for Va & P (1901–24)—resort to this style at times, but in a more folklike manner.[155]

The American-born composer **Swan Hennessy** (1866–1929) studied in England and Germany, spent most of his adult years in Paris, but paid allegiance chiefly to his Irish descent in his light, contrived "Sonata in Irish Style" for Vn & P (Op. 14 in F, 1905) and his freer, three-movement *Sonatine celtique* for Va & P (Op. 62 in E♭, 1925).[156] The Alsatian organist **Marie-Joseph Erb** (1858–1944), who studied with Saint-Saëns among others before returning to Strasbourg, left a pleasing, readily playable organ sonata in Franck's idiom and three sonatas for Vn & P, all published between 1901 and 1931, during his increasing interest in chamber music.[157]

Some Belgian and Dutch Composers in the Late-Romantic Era

The exceptionally small contribution to the sonata that we found in Belgium midway in the Romantic Era (ssb XII, near the end) was only slightly bettered by the end of the century. However, it must be remembered that here two of the best known Belgian contributors, Franck and Lekeu, have already been put where they resided, in Paris (*supra*), and another, the peripatetic Désiré Pâque (1867–1939), is put with the Moderns because, although his honeyed, Franckian chord progressions belie the fact, he deliberately cultivated his own brand of "atonalité." [158] Certain others are noted here only for the earlier works they wrote before they turned to participate in newer trends. The best known name is that of the leading Belgian violinist, **Eugène Ysaÿe** (1858–1931), who studied with Wieniawski and Vieuxtemps, and whom we have already met, sometimes with the pianist Raoul Pugno, doing yeoman's service for the violin sonatas of Franck, Lekeu, and numerous other composers.[159] Among more than two dozen published works by Ysaÿe are a set of six sonatas for unaccompanied Vn, Op. 27 (1924), and

155. Cf. Cobbett/CHAMBER II 84 (A. Piriou); MGG VIII 12–13 (F. Raugel); MERCURE I (1905) 306, on Labey's Son. for Va & P in C (1904).
156. Cf. Cobbett/CHAMBER I 550–52 (H. Woollett), with several errors and with exx. from Op. 62; MGG VI 152–53 (G. Ferchault), with dated list of works, including 2 other duo sonatinas (both 1929) but not an earlier *Sonatine*, Op. 43 (cf. DM XII/2 [1912–13] 108 [R. H. Stein]) nor Op. 14; HOFMEISTER 1905, 76.
157. Cf. MGG III 1464–65 (J. Feschotte); DM XI/2 (1911–12) 168 (E. Schnorr von Carolsfeld).
158. Cf. MGG X 739–40 (A. Van der Linden); Closson & Borren/BELGIQUE 280.
159. Cf. BAKER 1832–33.

a single Sonata for unaccompanied Vc, Op. 28 in c (1924).[160] The six sonatas of Op. 27 are dedicated respectively to Szigeti, Thibaud, Enesco, Kreisler, Crickboom, and Quiroga. Inspired by hearing Joseph Szigeti play one of Bach's unaccompanied "sonatas," Ysaÿe makes references to the latter in Op. 27 (including a fugal section in Son. 1/ii and direct quotations from the "Preludio" of Bach's Partita in E, in Son. 2/i). For the rest, these are light, fanciful, short but multimovement works that exploit all the standard resources of the virtuoso, ostensibly in the national and technical styles and with movement titles appropriate to their dedicatees. But although their dominant, chromatic harmonies and frequent crescendo passages are often portentous, nothing significant is ever attained in these sonatas.

The best known of the few other Belgian sonata composers is the organist and prolific composer **Joseph (-Marie-Alphonse-Nicolas) Jongen** (1873–1953), who came to know Richard Strauss, d'Indy, Fauré, and Chausson, along with other composers.[161] Among Jongen's many chamber works (his favorite medium) are at least eight sonatas in varied scorings, including two for Vn & P and one each for Vc & P, Fl & P, Vn & Vc ("Sonate-duo"), P solo "Sonatine," organ, and unaccompanied Vn (all pub. between 1903 and 1938). A sampling of Jongen's earlier, published sonatas (before his style changed somewhat in keeping with newer trends) reveals a knowing craftsman, sure of his form and writing techniques, thoroughly conversant with but not overwhelmed by Franck's idiom, and generally on the conservative side of his contemporaries. There is also sensitivity, delicate passagework, and fire in the music. Yet it fails for the most part to achieve real creative distinction. The ideas are a little plain, the motives are worked somewhat too hard and even mechanically, the phrase syntax tends to be too predictable, and the piano writing is routine.[162] The composer **Victor Vreuls** (1876–1944) left Belgium in 1901 to study with d'Indy, then taught at the Schola cantorum, and later became director of the Luxembourg Conservatory (up to 1926).[163] His chamber works include three published duo sonatas, two for Vn & P (1901 and 1919) and one for

160. Cf. the list of works and description of Op. 27 in Ysaÿe/YSAÿE 244–45 and 222–25; also, Closson & Borren/BELGIQUE 261 (dismissing his music except for its technical treatment of the Vn).

161. Cf. MGG VII 169–73 (A. Van der Linden); Closson & Borren/BELGIQUE 276; Cobbett/CHAMBER II 39–40 (G. Systermans & W. W. Cobbett); Cat. BELGISCH V.

162. But except for the piano writing, these objections were not raised in contemporary reviews seen here, as in MERCURE II (Jan.–June, 1906) 168 (on Op. 27 in D, for Vn & P); DM X/3 (1910–11) 31 (W. Altmann on Op. 34 in E, for Vn & P); DM XII/4 (1912–13) 177 (H. Schlemüller on Op. 39 in c, for Vc & P).

163. Cf. GROVE IX 78 (E. Blom); Closson & Borren/BELGIQUE 276; Cobbett/CHAMBER II 560 (G. Systermans and W. W. Cobbett); MERCURE II (Jan.–June, 1906) 268–69.

Vc & P (1923). The first of these, dedicated to Ysaÿe and composed before Vreuls, too, became interested in newer trends, is an extended, serious, individualized, energetic, and convincing work in three movements (F-S-F) that also shows the clear influence but not the domination of Franck.

More briefly in Belgium may be mentioned a composer of "deeply lyrical, often dramatic oratorios," **Joseph Ryelandt** (1870–1965), who is credited with at least 21 sonatas—11 for P solo, 7 for Vn & P, and 3 for Vc & P, from all of which at least 4 were published, between 1897 and 1912.[164] **Raymond Moulaert** (1875–1962) left a Sonata for P solo (1917), a *Sonate en forme de passacaille* for P & Vc (1942), and a prizewinning Sonata in d for organ (1906), the last regarded as Franckian in flavor, fluent, well constructed, and conventional.[165] And **Nicolas Daneau** (1866–1944) should at least be named for his *Suite en forme de sonate* in d, for Vn & P (1912), reviewed as a concise work, accessible and likely to appeal to amateurs.[166]

The Dutch interest in the sonata was a little more. One of the better known composers was the organist **Samuel de Lange, Jr.** (1840–1911), who left at least 16 published sonatas—8 for his instrument (1870–1903), 4 for P & Vn (1875–96), 2 for P & Vc (1883 and 1899), and one each for P solo (1892) and P-duet (1881).[167] These works, several of which seem to have circulated rather widely for a time, were greeted by reviewers as skillful, derivative (mostly from Mendelssohn), and sometimes dry.[168] Only occasionally does one find in them a distinctive musical personality. Thus, in de Lange's Op. 63 in c, for P solo, the scoring is unquestionably Mendelssohnian, but there is some individuality in the bold rhythms, and in the modulations when they approach the new key with deceptive cadences and with dissonant harmonies that grow out of diagonal relationships (as in Op. 63/i/88–103). The use of "The Star-Spangled Banner" as a theme for variations in the third (final) movement of his organ Sonata 4 in D, Op. 28 (1879), may reflect its dedication to the outstanding American organist

164. MGG XI 1205–6 (M. Boereboom); cf. BAKER Suppl. 113.

165. DM VIII/1 298 (E. Schnorr von Carolsfeld). Cf. MGG IX 672–73 (A. Van der Linden); Cat. BELGISCH VIII; Closson & Borren/BELGIQUE 289.

166. DM XII/4 (1912–13) 318 (W. Altmann). Cf. BAKER 347.

167. Cf. Kremer/ORGAN 200–201; Altmann/KAMMERMUSIK 213, 259, 302; MGG VIII 185–86 (A. Annegarn); Reeser/NEDERLANDSE 176. **Samuel de Lange, Sr.** (1811–84), esteemed by Brahms, had also left several concert organ sons. (cf. MGG VIII 185; MW XVIII [1887] 352 [about the 4th organ son. and its marchlike fugal finale]).

168. E.g., cf. MW XII (1881) 162 (on the first Vn son., Op. 19 in G, 1875); MW XVI (1885) 218–19 (on the P-duet, Op. 33 in e, with objections to the length of the fugue, 7 pp., in the first mvt.); MW XXXIV (1903) 740 and 741 (G. Riemenschneider on the 8th organ son., finding the finale uninteresting).

Clarence Eddy.[169] Similarly numerous, conservative, and unoriginal are the at least fifteen sonatas by the conductor, editor, and prolific composer **Julius Röntgen** (1855–1933), who studied with Reinecke, Hauptmann, and Franz Lachner, met Liszt, and knew Brahms and Grieg well.[170] These sonatas, of which about eight were published (between 1873 and 1922), are scored variously for P & Vn, P & Va, P & Vc, P & Ob, unaccompanied Vn, and P solo. Numerous reviews, although more favorable in later years, largely concur on the competence, the influence of Mendelssohn, Schumann, and eventually Brahms, and the rather weak creative spark that Röntgen's sonatas reveal.[171]

The sensitive, enterprising pianist **Dirk Schäfer** (1873–1931), a pupil of Max Pauer, also turned to the past for the styles and forms in the six sonatas (1901–18) that figure among his relatively few works.[172] These include four for Vn & P, one for Vc & P, and one, *Sonate inaugurale*, Op. 9 in b♭ (pub. in 1913), for P solo. Schäfer's first two violin sonatas were well received.[173] Op. 9, which became the best known of his sonatas because of his own telling performances of it and because of its slightly programmatic title and character, was reviewed as an example of "the most modern trends," [174] although today it conveys the same sense of post Mendelssohn, Schumann, Brahms, and Wagner that the reviewers had noted in Schäfer's earlier sonatas and that dates his music to the extent of making its revival unlikely. Yet there is much skill in these well organized, smoothly flowing, richly if not too thickly scored sonatas, with their Wagnerian polyphony, their extremes of range and dynamics, and their copious editorial advices. The "inaugural" or fanfare character of Op. 9, which is also present

169. Kremer/ORGAN 74–75.

170. Cf. MGG XI 613–15 (J. H. v. d. Meer); Reeser/NEDERLANDSE 242–45; PAZDÍREK XII 439–41; Altmann/KAMMERMUSIK 223 and 263; Cobbett/CHAMBER II 301 (H. Antcliffe).

171. E.g., cf. NZM LXIX/1 (1873) 190–91 (on Opp. 1 for P & Vn and 2 for P solo); MW IV (1873) 146–47 (on Op. 2) and VI (1875) 627–28 (on Op. 1, with ex.); MMR V (1875) 173–74 (on Opp. 1 and 2); NZM LXXXI/2 (1885) 418 (E. Klitzsch on Op. 20 for P & Vn); DM VI/1 (1906–7) 231 (W. Altmann on Op. 40 for P & Vn); NZM CI (1905) 338 (on Op. 40) and XCIX (1903) 372 (on Op. 41); SMW LXI (1903) 789 (on Op. 41 for P & Vc); MW XXXV (1904) 324 (on Op. 41); DM III/1 (1903–4) 135 (H. Schlemüller on Op. 41); DM X/2 (1910–11) 43 (H. Schlemüller on Op. 56). Westerly/PIANOFORTE 169 and 186 has praise for Opp. 2 and 10 for P solo.

172. Cf. MGG XI 1530–31 (E. Reeser); Keller & Kruseman/MUZIEKLEXICON II 680; Reeser/NEDERLANDSE 253–55, with 2 exx. from Op. 9; Cobbett/CHAMBER II 330–31 (W. Landré and W. W. Cobbett, rating Schäfer's Vn sons. at the top of the Dutch output); Altmann/KAMMERMUSIK 224, 263.

173. E.g., on Op. 4, cf. MW XXXIII (1902) 599 (E. Segnitz) and DM II/1 (1902–3) 359 and 361 (W. Altmann); on Op. 6, cf. NZM C (1904) 819, MW XXXVI (1905) 367 (E. Segnitz), and DM IV/4 203–4 (W. Altmann).

174. DM XIII/2 (1913–14) 229 (C. Rorich).

to some extent in Schäfer's other sonatas examined here, gives to all of Op. 9 an atmosphere somewhere between the final entry of Wagner's "Meistersinger" and Elgar's "Pomp and Circumstance" marches. It persists not only in the outer movements—"Allegro marziale" and "Moderato, maestoso," both on the threshold of bombast (Ex. 85)—but in the middle movement, "Improvisata," with three initial instructions, "Adagio, con molto espressione," "sempre dolce e sostenuto," and "p[iano] maestosamente."

The Dutch conductor **Dirk Fock** (or **Foch**; 1886–   ) may be noted for a single, competent, relatively short sonata in four movements (F-Sc-S-Ro), Op. 1 in a, for P solo, that skirts the styles of Brahms's

Ex. 85. From the opening of Dirk Schäfer's *Sonate inaugurale,* Op. 9 (after the A. A. Noske ed. of 1913).

early piano sonatas too closely for comfort, yet without his flashes of genius. Another conductor, **Kor Kuiler** (1877–1951), left a Sonata in d, for P solo (pub. in 1899), and a Sonata in g, for Vn & P (pub. in 1902), which are conservative works of the sort we have been noting in Holland, but not without melodic character and harmonic interest.[175] Likewise conventional but not without appeal are the two duo sonatas by the organist and teacher **Jan Willem Kirsbergen** (1857–1937), Op. 4 in d, for Vn & P (pub. in 1901), and Op. 7 in F, for Vc & P (not pub. until 1928).[176] A Sonata in E♭, for P-duet (pub. in 1902), by the pianist **Louis Coenen** (son of Frans; 1856–1905) was reviewed as being skillful

175. Cf. Reeser/NEDERLANDSE 241–42 (with ex. from the Son. in d); also, GROVE IV 868 (H. Antcliffe) and Altmann/KAMMERMUSIK 212.

176. Cf. Keller & Kruseman/MUZIEKLEXICON I 334 and II 185; DM II/1 (1902–3) 359 and 361 (W. Altmann praising Op. 4); Altmann/KAMMERMUSIK 211 and 259.

enough but somewhat academic and unpianistic.[177] And the second of two duo sonatas (Op. 23 in F, Vn & P, 1905) by the pianist **Gerard H. G. von Brucken-Fock** (1859–1935) was reviewed as "spiritually barren." [178]

177. MW XXXV (1904) 902 (E. Segnitz) and DM II/2 (1902–3) 197 and 201 (R. M. Breithaupt). Cf. Keller & Kruseman/MUZIEKLEXICON I 119; Altmann/KAMMERMUSIK 297.

178. DM VIII/1 (1908–9) 367 (W. Altmann). Cf. GROVE III 177 (H. Antcliffe); Reeser/NEDERLANDSE 245–46.

Chapter XIV

Great Britain, from Cramer to Elgar

The Sonata's Changing Status

England, the almost exclusive representative of Great Britain in the present volume, enjoyed a degree of sociopolitical equilibrium throughout music's Romantic Era that seemed to provide at least outward inducements to artistic endeavor. It is true that reaction and suppression prevailed up to about 1830, relating to the fear of the Napoleonic conquests and lasting while the Tories still held sway. And there were the growing pains of the continuing industrial revolution, with its rising working classes and trends toward socialism; of an increased population and new agricultural problems; and of expanding imperial colonialism with its trade rivalries and an endless succession of relatively minor territorial wars. But from the return to power of the Whigs in 1830 and the passage of the Reform Bill in 1832, which opened the long road to universal suffrage (shared by Dame Ethel Smyth, *infra*) nearly a century later, England became the freest state in Europe. Even so, as is all too well known, that country achieved little in its own right of significance to music, least of all instrumental music,[1] throughout the short reigns, from 1820 to 1830, of George IV and, from 1830 to 1837, of William IV, and through more than half of the long, 64-year reign, from 1837 to 1901, of Queen Victoria. In spite of great and influential literary figures like Wordsworth, Coleridge, Scott, Keats, Shelley, Byron, Dickens, Thackeray, the Brontë sisters, and both Brownings, in spite of important writers and thinkers in related fields, like Darwin, Spencer, Huxley, Carlyle, Mill, and Macauley, and in spite of some distinguished painters like Blake, Constable, Turner, and Rosetti, neither the reigns immediately preceding nor the early Victorian reign produced more than two, isolated, little known figures, Pinto and Bennett, whose sonatas can even be mentioned in the same breath with those of Clementi, the notable

---

1. Cf. Walker/ENGLAND 311 *et passim*.

London resident (sce 739–59), or Mendelssohn, the favorite London visitor (ssb VIII).

The limited contributions to the sonata before the last quarter of the 19th century should not be taken as evidence for any, more general lack of musical activities in London. Cramer, Field, and Pinto are the only early names of any consequence we shall be meeting here. (Among other notable pianist-composers resident in London at one time or another, we meet Wölfl in Vienna [sce 562–64], Dussek in Prague [ssb XVII], and Kalkbrenner in Paris [ssb XII].) But the records of musicians active in London at the time reads more like a cross section of all Europe. In 1815, for example, Camille Pleyel (son of Ignaz; sce 551) wrote to his family in Paris of his meetings with Cramer, Kalkbrenner, Ries, Cherubini (sce 300–301), Clementi, Viotti (sce 675–80), Hüllmandel (sce 652–56), Sor (sce 663–64), and many others.[2] In 1822, Moscheles, who met several of the same musicians and others, recorded some of the London concert life in his diaries, including the performance of considerable music by Handel, Mozart, Beethoven, and Rossini.[3] In 1825, a valuable article on the current "state of music in London" showed that the usual prominence was being given to opera, song, and other vocal music, but confirmed that instrumental music was getting its performances, too.[4] Another, like report, this time relayed to Leipzig, in 1823, includes mention of such instrumental music being played in London as a sonata for "viola" (Vn?) by Corelli, Hummel's Sonata Op. 92 for P-duet (ssb VIII), and a Mozart piano concerto.[5]

Yet even at that time the low state of composition in England was generally recognized—especially instrumental composition, as noted above. In 1830, Fétis in Paris, after describing the prevalent opera and choral music in London and the excellence of Moscheles and Cramer among "professors" of instrumental music, concluded that music was dead there because the English could not understand and appreciate it.[6] Seven years later (1837) Schumann still saw England's only musical hope as being composers like Field, Onslow, Potter, Bishop, and, above all, Bennett.[7] Fétis did not even mention the sonata

2. The letters are trans. in Benton/LONDON.
3. MOSCHELES I 64–90.
4. QUARTERLY VII (1825) 186–211, with references to instrumental music on pp. 201–3, 205–6. Henry George Farmer's article on "British Musicians a Century Ago," first pub. in ML XII (1931) 384–92 and reprinted in 1966 with slight changes as the "Introduction" to SAINSBURY I vii–xvi, provides a similarly valuable survey.
5. AMZ XXV (1823) 561 and 615. The Corelli work may have been a son. arranged for Vc & double-bass by R. Lindley and played by him with D. Dragonetti as a stunt at a Philharmonic Society program in 1823 (Temperley/CORRESPONDENCE).
6. Fétis/CURIOSITÉS 176–95, 207–21, 230–71 (especially from 260).
7. Schumann/SCHRIFTEN I 245–47.

itself in England. And to make matters worse, English reviewers anticipated Schumann's dismal outlook of 1839 (ssb II) by already calling the
sonata outmoded as much as fifteen years earlier.[8] Hence, unusual was
the piano sonata Frederick Hallé wrote for his son Charles to play at
the Concordia Society concerts in 1823.[9]

From the late 1840's on, especially after 1870, the status of the sonata
began a marked rise in England. This rise was part both of the more
general musical renaissance that Frank Howes has recently traced [10] and
of the more specific return to instrumental chamber music. Although
they were bounded by the "splendid isolation" of the later Victorian
period and their sonatas proved to be less significant, Parry, Stanford,
and Elgar comprised a trio that gave yeoman's service to the cause of
British chamber music,[11] contemporary with Franck, Saint-Saëns, and
Fauré during the similar French renaissance (ssb XIII), and with
Hartmann, Gade, and Grieg during a corresponding Scandinavian
renaissance (ssb XV). Among concomitants in this newly fired British
cause was the growing number of appropriate concerts sponsored
variously by the Royal Academy of Music, the Royal College of Music,[12]
the Philharmonic Society, and the groups behind the various series of
Promenade, Crystal Palace, and Popular Concerts.[13] There was also a
growing number of devoted chamber and solo performers, including
the pianists Charles Hallé, Walter Macfarren, Emil Pauer, and two
very active women champions, Arabella Goddard (Mrs. J. W. Davison)
and Agnes Zimmermann, as well as the violinist Wilma Maria Francisca
Neruda (later Lady Hallé) and the cellist Alfredo Carlo Piatti. Interest
in serious chamber music had begun to develop as far back as the
start of "Dando's Quartett Concerts" in 1836, as evidenced in several
daily or weekly newspapers and the important periodical *The Musical
World* (1836–91). But this interest got little attention before around
1870 in the pages of the thriving, illustrious London periodical often

8. QUARTERLY VII (1825) 104 and HARMONICON X/1 (1832) 256. In Temperley/
DOMESTIC 37–38, Nicholas Temperley (whose researches and personal advices on
early 19th-c. music in England have been utilized gratefully here, including the
information designated as Temperley/CORRESPONDENCE) describes the almost total
disappearance of the son. in England in the 1820's, 1830's, and 1840's. Cf., also,
George Hogarth's negative view in 1835, as quoted in Howes/ENGLISH 35.
9. HALLÉ 4. In 1827 a London Review of Cramer's "Last Sonata," Op. 74, begins
"A sonata is indeed a rarity! The title has remained dormant for many a long
year . . ." (HARMONICON V/1 [1827] 228 [W. Ayrton]).
10. Howes/ENGLISH; cf. p. 20, where the approximate year of 1880 is preferred as
the starting point. Cf., also, Walker/ENGLAND 316–40.
11. The three pioneers of the more general British musical renaissance are given
in Howes/ENGLISH 23–24 as Mackenzie, Parry, and Stanford.
12. Cf. Howes/ENGLISH 24, 60; O'Leary/BENNETT 124.
13. Cf. Howes/ENGLISH 44–48, *et passim.*

cited here, *The Musical Times* (MT; from 1844), which, in any case, was then becoming more sophisticated, scholarly, and cosmopolitan. (Although *The Quarterly Musical Magazine* and *The Harmonicon,* two other main predecessors of *The Musical Times,* had been surprisingly urbane, witty, and knowing in their own ways, neither periodical had evinced much interest in chamber music beyond an occasional review of a new publication, English or foreign.) In the later 19th century increasing interest of a still more serious, even scholarly sort is reflected in several papers to be cited here from the *Proceedings of the Royal Musical Association* (PMA; from 1874) and in the activities that led eventually to the important *Cyclopedic Survey of Chamber Music* (Cobbett/CHAMBER; originally pub. in 1929), edited by that inveterate avocational enthusiast and promoter Walter Willson Cobbett (1847–1937), who naturally gave extra space to his fellow countrymen.

As noted early in Chapter XIII, Frederick Delius (1862–1934), the French resident born in England of German parents, belongs tonally with the Moderns in spite of all the Romantic sentiment in his music. There were other late-Romantics—among them, Rutland Boughton (1878–   ), Frederick Charles Nicholls (1871–?), Arthur Somervell (1863–1937), and Harry Farjeon (1878–   )—who adhered thoroughly to Romantic styles yet produced their sonatas so late (after World War I) that these must be regarded rather as anachronisms of the Modern Era.

The Classic-Romantic Borderland in London
(Cramer, Field, and Pinto)

The celebrated pianist **Johann Baptist Cramer** (1771–1858) is the most appropriate of the three main early composers with whom to begin our chapter on the Romantic sonata in England.[14] Although born in Germany, as the son of the brilliant violinist Wilhelm Cramer in Mannheim (SCE 722–23), J. B. Cramer was brought to London at about the age of three,[15] where during much of his life he became almost as influential in performance, teaching, and music publishing as the even

14. The valuable, thorough diss. Schlesinger/CRAMER remains (since 1925) the one chief study of his life, environment, piano career, and sons. (but not other works); as with Unger/CLEMENTI (cf. SCE 738), even some of the main biographic findings in this study have yet to be incorporated in present-day music dictionaries, only partially excepting MGG II 1762–66 (W. Kahl). The prolix but informative article of 1824 on Cramer in SAINSBURY I 180–85, not known to Schlesinger, was probably based on firsthand information (cf. I xvi). On Cramer as performer cf. Schonberg/PIANISTS 60–63.

15. Schlesinger/CRAMER 13 and 138.

more renowned, respected, and versatile teacher with whom he studied in 1783, Clementi (SCE 738–59). Furthermore, he became an important link with the past, not only through Clementi but as a main Beethoven transmitter, along with Hummel, Ries, Moscheles, and Czerny (SSB VII and VIII), all four of whom he knew personally though differently as friends, rivals, and fellow professionals.[16] Ries begrudgingly acknowledged that the one pianist Beethoven "praised as outstanding" was Cramer.[17] Beethoven, to whom Cramer may first have been introduced by Haydn, is also known to have had a high regard for Cramer's excellent etudes, preferring them to Czerny's (and perhaps deriving the main theme of Op. 26/iv from one of them; cf. SCE 516–17).[18] Cramer's own performances of Beethoven's sonatas (only in private circles?) undoubtedly did much to introduce them in London.[19] Before his long life was ended, including prolonged visits to Vienna, Paris, and other centers, Cramer also became something of a link with the then present and future, for he got to know personally, though not keep up with, Wölfl (SCE 562–64), Dussek, Kalkbrenner, Liszt, and possibly Chopin.[20]

In the more than four decades, from Op. 1 in about 1788 [21] to "Sechs leichte Sonatinen" (without op. no.) in 1830, around 120 different sonatas or sonatinas by Cramer were published in sets or singly in London, Paris, Vienna, Leipzig, and other centers, of which about 65 per cent, especially the later sonatas, appeared originally as P solos and the rest with accompaniments (P & Vn-or-Fl, etc.).[22] A thematic index would have to be prepared, assuming that all or most of the music could still be found,[23] in order to eliminate reprints and other duplica-

16. Cf. Schlesinger/CRAMER 167, 36–37, 64, 68–69, 74, 46, 47, 77–78. Among Cramer's son. dedicatees are Clementi (Op. 7), Haydn (Op. 22), Wölfl (Op. 36), Ries (Op. 62), Hummel (Op. 63), and Moscheles (Op. 69).

17. Wegeler & Ries/BEETHOVEN 99–100; Thayer & Forbes/BEETHOVEN I 208–11; Schindler & MacArdle/BEETHOVEN 120–21. Cf. Schlesinger/CRAMER 43–49.

18. Cf. Schindler & MacArdle/BEETHOVEN 379, 394. No comment by Beethoven on Cramer's son. is known. He could also have derived a passage like Op. 57/iii/50–57 from Cramer's Study in f, Op. 30/16 (Temperley/CORRESPONDENCE).

19. Cf. Schlesinger/CRAMER 47–48.

20. Cf. Schlesinger/CRAMER 51, 64–65, 71–72, 87, 152–53; Craw/DUSSEK 133–34, 445.

21. BUCEM I 237.

22. Schlesinger/CRAMER 93–94 gives the total that previous writers had given of 105 sons., and identifies "about 70" of these in a dated list (with some years being too late); cf. pp. 58–77 for more on dates, with mentions of numerous reviews, especially in AMZ and HARMONICON. The list in SAINSBURY I 184–85, totalling 109 sons., stops at 1823 and is the same as that in HARMONICON I/1 (1823) 181. It often does not mention the accompaniments, but if it was submitted or approved by Cramer it presumably would be free of duplications.

23. As early as 1880, S. Bagge remarked how hard it had become to obtain Cramer's sons. (Bagge/SONATE 222–23).

tions, reconcile conflicting opus numbers, and provide a reasonably accurate, consolidated catalogue of these sonatas.[24] But Cramer's sonatas are too nearly forgotten and of too little interest, except as examples of a widespread, short-lived taste in the early Romantic Era, to justify such a catalogue. In any case, a sufficient idea of the scorings, titles, and publishers may be had from similar catalogues offered here, including those of Clementi (SCE 740–45),[25] Ries (SSB VII), and Hummel (SSB VIII).

Cramer's titles include modifiers like "grande" and "easy" only infrequently and a few vaguely programmatic designations like "La Parodie," Op. 43 (or 50) in B♭ (1809?);[26] "Le Retour à Londres," Op. 62 in E (1818);[27] "L'Ultima," Op. 53 in a (1815);[28] "Les Suivantes," Op. 59/1–3 in C, B♭, and e (1817–18);[29] "Les Souvenirs," Op. 63 in d (1824 at latest);[30] and "Amicitia," arranged for P ± Vn-or-Fl from

24. Sizable collections of them can be found at the British Museum (of which a few appear in BUCEM I 237), the Royal College of Music (cf. Cat. ROYAL 95–96), and the Library of Congress; cf., also, Eitner/QL III 94–95. The list in PAZDÍREK III 589–93 is extensive but neither complete nor consolidated. Help toward a consolidated list would come from the many reviews and Intelligenz-Blatt entries in AMZ up to Vol. XXXII (1830). A thematic index of Cramer's sons. is actually projected as part of a diss. in progress by Jerald Graue at the University of Illinois (as of spring, 1968), on the English pianoforte school at the turn of the century.

25. The much needed thematic index of Clementi's sonatas has been completed (1964), by Alan Tyson, and published by Schneider of Tutzing in 1967.

26. The Johann Traeg ed. (1809? plate no. 454; one of 3 eds. of Op. 43 listed in Cat. NYPL VIII 190–91) has an inscription that reads (in French), "This piece provides a parody of a sonata composed by another celebrated author." Dussek's Op. 24 in the same key (C. 96) is stated (and seems) to be the parodied work, in a catalogue of J. B. Cramer & Co. dated 1851 (Temperley/CORRESPONDENCE). The suggestion in Schlesinger/CRAMER 164 that Haydn is that "author" has more biographic than stylistic justification. In any case, the "parody" seems not to be a caricature and does not depart from Cramer's typical sons. in style or form.

27. AMZ XX (1818) 449–51 could find no reason or musical clarification for the title. But Op. 62 appeared in time for Cramer's own return to London after continental travels (Schlesinger/CRAMER 64 and 67). Temperley/CORRESPONDENCE detects possible "street noises" in the first mvt. The title recalls Dussek's celebrated Son. in A♭ of 1807, "Le Retour à Paris" (C. 221), and Cramer's own later set of vars. Op. 85, "Le Retour à Vienne," (Weinmann/ARTARIA item 3102).

28. In AMZ XVII (1815) 473–75, the reviewer hopes Op. 53 actually will not be Cramer's last son.

29. Probably the title simply means (the first of what were to be several) additions to "L'Ultima," and not a turn to a deeper style (as guessed in Egert/FRÜH-ROMANTIKER 64).

30. AMZ XXVI (1824) 96–98 suggests that "souvenirs" means recollections of pleasant associations with Hummel, dedicatee of Op. 63; cf. Schlesinger/CRAMER 167. This outstanding work among Cramer's sons. (cf. Egert/FRÜHROMANTIKER 70) is probably the Son. in d praised by Moscheles, which would put its year of composition, if not pub., back in 1821 (MOSCHELES I 51–52).

Cramer's Quintet in E, Op. 69.[31] Not only these titles but somewhat more character and inclination toward Romantic trends account for the special popularity and more-than-average reprintings of the works just cited, among all Cramer's sonatas during his lifetime.[32] Today, however, not one of them happens to be among the few sonatas by Cramer that can be found in "old master" collections.[33]

Nearly all of Cramer's sonatas adhere to the standard plan of three movements (mainly F-S-Ro and F-M-Ro) or the plan still used in many lighter works of two movements, without the middle, slowest movement.[34] The home keys do not exceed four flats or sharps, with major keys predominating over minor by a ratio of about three to one. In the first movements, occasionally prepared by a slow introduction, "sonata form" prevails, insofar as there is any clear dualism or pluralism of main ideas. The middle movements fall chiefly into A-B-A and variation forms, and the finales into rondos. Except for the transcribed "Amicitia" (supra), the accompanied sonatas tend to be Cramer's lightest sonatas. Their accompaniments, whether indicated as optional or obligatory, are usually dispensable with regard to thematic continuity if not texture. From "L'Ultima" on,[35] most of the last few sonatas mark a conspicuous and probably a consciously motivated turn to a richer, more compelling, more emotionally involved style of writing.[36] Whereas, Haydn, Mozart, Clementi, and only the earliest Beethoven sonatas are the clear influences in Cramer's previous sonatas,[37] an awareness of the increasing pathos and agitation in the Beethoven of Opp. 13 to 31 is evident in the later sonatas. Early-Romantic traits show up in an increase of tonal tension, including a more chromatic harmonic style, a variety of more sharply defined

31. The "Amicitia" undoubtedly refers to Cramer's friendship with Moscheles, the dedicatee. Cf. MOSCHELES I 64–65.

32. Cf. Egert/FRÜHROMANTIKER 64, 69–70, 153–54; HOFMEISTER 1828 (Whistling) 582–84.

33. Op. 6/1 in D (ca. 1792) is in Méreaux/CLAVECINISTES-m III no. 164. The same plus Opp. 6/3 in F and 8/2 in G (ca. 1795) are in TRÉSOR-m XX. A few of Cramer's sons. and separate mvts. were pub. in one vol. by Steingräber in 1898 (R. Kleinmichel). Op. 23/3 in a (1799) is in "Fascicolo VIII" of B. Cesi's Biblioteca del pianista . . . autori classici (G. Ricordi). In Anth. NÄGELI II (1803) are 3 sons., in D, G, and F without op. no.; these are not mentioned in Schlesinger/CRAMER.

34. Schlesinger/CRAMER 102–33 is a style-critical discussion of the sons., with 162 exx. (up to 16 mss. each). Egert/FRÜHROMANTIKER 63–70, with exx., largely derives from the foregoing. Cf., also, Georgii/KLAVIERMUSIK 272–73.

35. Cf. Exx. 18, 20, 22, 48, 78, and 119 in the back of Schlesinger/CRAMER, all quoted from "L'Ultima."

36. Cf. Schlesinger/CRAMER 102–3; Egert/FRÜHROMANTIKER 69–70.

37. On Mozart's influence, cf. Temperley/MOZART 313.

rhythms, a more florid kind of melodic line, and some measures in the manner of recitatives.

But even with these changes in mind, one has to conclude that Cramer's sonatas are at their best in the skill at which he excelled right from the start and for which alone, as with Czerny, he is still remembered today. That skill is the writing of ingenious, cleanly scored, euphonious passagework such as is well known to pianists who play his etudes. In a sense, the passagework is more progressive than the changes noted in Cramer's last sonatas. It not only paves one way to the piano virtuosity of the 19th century but in its open-position, arpeggiando dispositions it supplants the Alberti, murky, and related basses of the Classic Era (SCE 122) with fuller, more liquescent accompaniments and

Ex. 86. From near the opening of Johann Baptist Cramer's Sonata in a, Op. 23/3 (after B. Cesi's ed. for G. Ricordi, *ca.* 1900).

textures such as might grace a lyrical piece by Schumann.[38] Ex. 86 comes from a sonata in which texture and passagework rather than any distinctive melodies or tunes supply the entire and not inconsiderable interest of the outer movements.

More often Cramer does employ more tangible themes. Although his ability to construct themes, textures, and forms is always at least adequate and although his themes reveal somewhat more character and undergo a more organic sort of development in the later sonatas, at best they, their attendant harmony, and their treatment are less than inspired or original. (From the standpoint of unoriginality it is not surprising to learn that Cramer twice plagiarized his teacher's sonatas.[39]) The lack of melodic invention shows up especially in the

38. Temperley/MENDELSSOHN 226 quotes the finale of Op. 59 in G (*ca.* 1817) as an entire mvt. "that might well have been writen by Mendelssohn."
39. Cf. Schlesinger/CRAMER 66 and 157; SCE 748.

slowest movements (as in ii in the work just quoted). The themes used in the sets of variations are likely to be tuneful, sometimes folklike, enough to have melodic identities (as in Anth. NÄGELI II/2/iii). Many of the main themes in the rondos and even in the first movements in "sonata form" are likely to be of this sort, although in the latter they only occasionally seem to lend themselves to the expected extensions and developments (as in Op. 25/1/i in E♭ [1802], an ingenuous, gay mvt. of considerable charm). Actually, three of Cramer's sets of sonatas incorporate "popular airs." [40] Yet it is undoubtedly the melodic deficiencies of Cramer's sonatas that brought a quick dismissal of them from Bie, a description of Cramer as a mere "sonata-maker" (along with Steibelt and Wölfl) from Shedlock, and a frequently neutral or even negative reception from the reviewers until several of the later sonatas brought more favorable responses.[41]

Another important pupil of Clementi, also widely celebrated in his day, was the Irish-born pianist **John Field** (1782–1837).[42] In 1802 Field travelled to Russia with his teacher, remaining, after Clementi left in 1803, to spend the rest of his life in St. Petersburg and Moscow except for some less successful tours in West Europe during his last years.[43] Field's relatively small output—7 concertos, 3 piano quintets, about 60

40. Cf. HARMONICON I/1 (1823) 181.
41. Bie/PIANOFORTE 210–11; Shedlock/SONATA 192–94. Shedlock adds that no son. by Cramer was ever played at the Popular Concerts (from 1859) in London (although Cramer had played often at the earlier "professional Concerts [MGG II 1762]). Many of the German and English reviews are summarized in Schlesinger/ CRAMER 102–34 and 176, *passim*. For samples of some of these and others, cf. AMZ II (1799–1800) 67 (on the superfluity of the Vn & Vc in Op. 19), V (1802–3) 359–60 (favorable on Op. 27), V 606 (on Op. 28 as correct but sometimes dull), V 176 and 606 (on Op. 29 as uneven in quality), V 606–7 (more pros than cons in Op. 30), V 607 (on facile brilliance but melodic lacks in Op. 31), V 607–8 (on Op. 33 as best for exercises), XII (1809–10) 773–76 (on stylistic though not musical excellence in an unidentified son.), XIII (1811) 32 (neutral on Op. 41), XII (1809–10) 902–3 (mildly favorable on Op. 44), XXIII (1821) 528 (mildly negative on "La Parodie"), XXVII (1825) 596 (similar on Op. 47), XVII (1815) 473–75 (on "L'Ultima" as one of Cramer's best sons.), XX (1818) 449–51 (similar on "Le Retour à Londres"), XXVI (1824) 96–98 (similar on "Les Souvenirs"); CAECILIA V (1825) 40 (on Op. 48 as good teaching material); HARMONICON III/1 (1825) 61–62 and QUARTERLY VIII (1826) 64–66 (both with praise for "Amicitia" and 2 exx.); HARMONICON V/1 (1827) 228 (qualified praise of Op. 74, with a 16-ms. ex. from ii).
42. Cf. GROVE III 85–87 (E. Dannreuther); MGG IV 169–72 (W. Kahl, with further references). Dessauer/FIELD is a Ph.D. diss. of 1911 that contributes more on the biography than on the music. In Hopkinson/FIELD vii the supposition that Field's popularity between 1815 and 1835, which did reach surprising heights, "exceeded that of contemporaries such as Clementi, Cramer, Dussek, Hummel and Steibelt" does not tally with findings here; for example, at least as many concurrent eds. of a single pub. and considerably more reviews can be found for the more successful works of each of the others.
43. Negative reactions by both Moscheles and Chopin, in 1831 and 1832, are reported in MOSCHELES I 251 and Hedley/CHOPIN 55.

piano picccs, and a very few songs, according to Cecil Hopkinson's outstanding thematic *catalogue raisonée* (Hopkinson/FIELD)—includes 4 sonatas, all for P solo, of which 3 were published a year before the move to Russia and one later. The three early sonatas, in E♭, A, and c/C, were his only works to which Field himself assigned an opus number, Op. 1/1–3. First appearing in 1801 and dedicated to Clementi, they actually comprised his eighth publication, with no fewer than a dozen reprints or new editions of the set following during the century, and as many more of single sonatas or even single movements.[44] Field's other, fourth sonata, in B, was first published about 1813 by Dalmas in St. Petersburg, with about a dozen reprints or new editions following again, all by 1830 and mostly German.[45]

Field's four sonatas, especially the first three, have little of the musical, pianistic, or pre-Chopin interest that has rightly drawn so much attention to his nocturnes and piano concertos.[46] All four are in only two movements, mostly F-Ro, with no slow movements or key contrasts.[47] In Op. 1 the first sonata is decidedly the best. It is compact and fluent, and it is melodically fresh to an extent rarely found in Cramer. The harmony reveals some surprises, including alternations of major and minor through the use of borrowed tones and a modulation, by change of mode, to the lowered mediant (i/72–75). Of special delight is the rondo, which is based on the schottische dance (or "German polka") in 2/4 meter and might well have been in Chopin's mind when he wrote the first of his three "Écossaises" in 1826. The other two sonatas in Field's Op. 1 come closer to deserving the early review of all three that charged Field with a lack of poetry and with deriving not the seed but the chaff of his master's style, including "dry melody, [and] harsh harmonic progressions and transitions, along with many stretches of 9ths and 10ths in both hands." [48]

44. Cf. Hopkinson/FIELD 13–16, with incipits of each mvt. Mod. ed. of all 3 sons. separately: Augener in London, 1939–40.

45. Cf. Hopkinson/FIELD. The correspondence following Tyson/FIELD (ML XLVIII [1967] 99) suggests that Hopkinson's "c. 1812" might be a year of two too early for the original Dalmas ed. There is no mod. ed. of this son. (as of 1967).

46. As with Cramer's sons., no son. by Field was ever performed at the London Popular Concerts (Shedlock/SONATA 229). Relatively brief discussions of the sons. occur in Dessauer/FIELD 83–89 (with exx.); Blom/FIELD 237; Egert/FRÜHROMANTIKER 116–20 (following Dessauer almost verbatim; with exx.); Georgii/KLAVIERMUSIK 261. A diss. on Field's piano music by William Perryman was reported to be in progress at Indiana University in JAMS XIX (1966) 391.

47. Hibbard/FIELD is an attempt—far-fetched and unsuccessful, as viewed here—to find intended slow mvts. and suitable key contrasts in 4 Romances (Hopkinson/FIELD 24A[r] in E♭, 25A[r] in c, 26A[n], and 46B[e] in e, respectively); both the historical and the bibliographical premises are inaccurate.

48. AMZ V (1802–3) 490–91; but the quoted ex. from Op. 1/1/ii/1–3 showing

There are moments of some local interest in Op. 1/2 and 3, such as the *fortissimo* climax marked "con fuoco" (unusual for Field at any time) in the lengthy development section of Op. 1/3/i (Ex. 87). But the ideas and textures, especially the triadic themes set in slow harmonic rhythm in Sonata 2, generally do prove to be weak and, what is more detrimental to the over-all effect, the forms straggle helplessly for want of adequate tonal organization and thematic development and because they last too long for their slight content, anyway. Field's fourth sonata is no masterpiece but shows more maturity. The first movement brings us near to his nocturnes in form and mood (evoking the title

Ex. 87. From the first movement of Sonata in c/C, Op. 1/3, by John Field (after the Augener reprint of 1940).

of "Spring Sonata" from Dessauer[49]). The second movement is an ingratiating rondo.

In the realm of the early-19th-century sonata in England, the most remarkable yet least known of our three composers was certainly the precocious, short-lived violinist and pianist **George Frederick Pinto (Sanders or Saunders; 1785–1806)**.[50] Pinto was close to Field as a fellow violin student of Haydn's impresario Johann Peter Salomon, who sponsored a benefit in 1800 that included an unidentified " 'So-

---

leaps of staccato 10ths in the bass posed no unusual problem for pianists of the time.

49. Dessauer/FIELD 88–89.

50. Cf. Temperley/PINTO, with revision of the birth year and other details in MGG X 1286–87 (N. M. Temperley). A "Memoir" possibly by Pinto's mother was first pub. in 1807 and revised in HARMONICON VI/1 (1828) 215–16, with further ancestral and biographic details.

nata Concertante, Piano Forte and Violin' [played] by 'Master Field and Master Pinto.' " [51] Although no factual evidence is at hand, it would be hard to believe, from his music and environment, that Pinto did not also come under at least the indirect influence of Cramer. Credit for bringing Pinto's sonatas back to light goes to the Cambridge scholar Nicholas Temperley and his valued studies on instrumental music in England in the first half of the 19th century.[52]

Along with about three dozen other works—Vn-duets, smaller P solos, and songs—by Pinto, there were at least a dozen of those sonatas, eight for P solo and four for P & Vn, published originally (and but once) between 1802 and 1807 except for an incomplete P solo in G in an autograph MS of 1803 entitled "Sonata for Scotland." [53] The solo sonatas include Op. 3/1-2, in e♭ and A (ded. to a "Miss Griffith" and "Printed for the Author" in 1802 or 1803);[54] A Grand Sonata [in c], "Inscribed to his Friend John Field" (and pub. in 1803 by Birchall);[55] Op. 4/1-3, in G, B♭, and C (pub. in 1804 or 1805 by Turnbull), "in which are Introduced Marches, Quick Steps, Waltzes, and Scotch Airs"—a set described as less serious and significant;[56] and a "Fantasia & Sonata" in c that was published posthumously (ca. 1807) by (or for?) Pinto's mother, "Mrs. Sanders." The last was edited by the early champion of J. S. Bach's works, **Samuel Wesley** (1766–1837; himself the composer of nearly 2 dozen skillful sons., more solo than accompanied and mostly pub., between 1777 and ca. 1812 [57]); it was supplied with "an inappropriate C major conclusion" by Joseph Wölfl (then in London; scE 562–64); and it is described as an "unequal" work, in five (four?) interconnected movements, all in minor keys (S-F-fugue-S/F

51. As cited in Temperley/PINTO 265.
52. Besides Temperley/PINTO, cf. Temperley/ENGLISH, Temperley/MOZART, Temperley/HANDEL. Warm thanks are owing to Dr. Otto Albrecht for calling attention here to Pinto's Op. 3 and for supplying a copy from the Library of the University of Pennsylvania; and to Dr. Temperley for further information and help by correspondence.
53. Cf. the cat. in Temperley/PINTO 266, 269, and 270, including locations of the rare extant copies.
54. Mod. ed. of Op. 3/1: Temperley/PINTO-m. On W. S. Bennett's reprinting and performance of Op. 3/2 in 1841 cf. Bennett/BENNETT 110. For extracts from Op. 3/1, cf. Temperley/MOZART 312 (Op. 3/1/iii) and Temperley/PINTO 267–68 (Op. 3/2/i and ii).
55. The "Rondo" refrain of this son. (not Op. 4) is quoted in Temperley/HANDEL 171–72. Mod. eds. of this son. and Op. 3/2 have been prepared for pub. (Stainer & Bell) by Dr. Temperley.
56. Temperley/PINTO 269. The "Rondo" of Son. 2 is quoted in Temperley/PINTO 268.
57. Cf. GROVE IX 262–65 (W. H. Hadow); BUCEM II 1069; Shedlock/SONATA 229–30. Besides Wesley's battle son. pub. ca. 1812, "The Siege of Badajoz," there is a "fine" 3-mvt. Son. in d, for P solo (1808), of which the middle mvt. is a "Fugue on a Subject of Salomon's" (Temperley/CORRESPONDENCE).

[separately titled "Sonata"]).[58] Pinto's accompanied sonatas include a set of three, in g, A, and B♭, again published by his mother around the time of or soon after his early death—a set described as having essential violin parts and as being outstanding in quality except for weak slow movements in Sonatas 2 and 3; and a single Sonata in A, in the slow movement of which "is introduced the Air of 'Logie o' Buchan' " (ed. by Wesley and pub. by Pinto's mother)—a work described as undistinguished, with the accompaniment (Fl-or-Vn) incomplete in the rondo finale.[59]

Temperley regards the two sonatas of Op. 3 and the Sonata in c dedicated to Field as Pinto's "greatest achievement." [60] Among these the one that presumably came first, Op. 3/1 in e♭, is regarded here as the consistently best. But except for their standard, over-all, three-movement plans (F-S-Ro) and their general keyboard idioms in the current language of Clementi, Cramer, and Dussek, the three sonatas differ so greatly and, in their unpretentious manner, cover such a wide range of musical thinking and feeling that one finds it hard to ascribe them to a single composer, much less to a boy who could have been only sixteen or seventeen when he wrote them. Op. 3/1 is a compact work of 523 measures (179+82+262), lasting about seventeen minutes in performance. In several ways it brings to mind Beethoven's early sonatas, especially his similarly proportioned Op. 13. Beethoven's Opp. 2, 7, 10, and 13 had first appeared in Vienna between 1796 and 1799 (cf. SCE 509), though not in London until much later.[61] Pinto's performances and travels are not reported to have taken him further than Paris.[62] But these works possibly could have become known to Pinto almost as soon as they appeared, through important transient or resident transmitters in London like Clementi, Cramer, and Dussek. It is not that Pinto offers any specific melodic reminders of Beethoven. Nearest to such are the similarities between the finales of Pinto's Op. 3/1 and Beethoven's Op. 10/1, as well as of Pinto's Sonata in c and Beethoven's Op. 13. Nor does he take over any specific structural devices, such as the recurrence of the introduction in Beethoven's Op. 13/i (SCE 136) that Ries (SSB VII) and others expropriated. But on a somewhat lower and more naive plane of drama, intensity, melodic inspiration, and pianism, the three movements of Pinto's Op. 3/1 recall the moods, drive, frank songfulness, textural styles, cumulative syntax and dissective development, dynamic con-

58. Temperley/PINTO 269.
59. Temperley/PINTO 269.
60. Temperley/PINTO 267.
61. Cf. Tyson/BEETHOVEN 26–27.
62. HARMONICON VI/1 (1828) 216.

Ex. 88. From the retransition in the first movement of Georges Frederick Pinto's Sonata in A, Op. 3/2 (after the original ed., "Printed for the Author," at the University of Pennsylvania in Philadelphia).

trasts, harmonic surprises, syncopations and sforzandos, and even the sense of structural inevitability or "fatalism" all manifested variously and consummately in the respective movements of Beethoven's Op. 13.

By comparison, Pinto's Op. 3/2 in A is ruminative and gentle; and his Sonata in c is a turbulent "pathétique" work, with wider extremes and some brooding, at times recalling its dedicatee's (Field's) weaker Sonata in c, Op. 1/3, that had been published only recently (1801). Op. 3/2 in particular, as Temperley notes,[63] is remarkably Schubertian. It is more so, in fact, than Op. 3/1 is Beethovian, yet now, of course, with no possibility of Schubert's influence (ssв VII). Along with the tenderly expressive slow movement in D, starting at a tonal tangent (from V-of-I to V-of-IV), the outer movements contain melodies, rhythms, and parenthetical modulations, so to speak, that might well convince any trained musician he is hearing Schubert's own piano music (Ex. 88). The first movement of Pinto's accompanied Sonata in g is also Schubertian, recalling especially the style and even the main theme of Schubert's Op. 137/1/i in D.

Pinto did arouse interest and win some warm praise while he was alive,[64] and occasional editions and organ arrangements of his sonatas

63. Temperley/PINTO 267.
64. Temperley/PINTO 266.

appeared later in the century, indicating that he and they were not entirely forgotten.[65] Although the apparent deterioration in his "later" sonatas and dissipation in his last years[66] did not augur well for a continuingly distinguished future, he belongs with Schunke, Reubke, and Lekeu (ssb VIII, X, and XIII) among the precious few in which so much promise had been seen before they were cut off in their early twenties. One is inclined to agree with Temperley that Pinto's music is indeed "a bright light in a dark hour of English music." [67]

The London pianist and composer **(Philip) Cipriani (Hambly) Potter** (1792–1871) was competent enough as a composer, as both Beethoven in 1818 and Wagner in 1855 found reason to observe,[68] but is more interesting here for the curiosity of his modish, empty, largely derivative piano music, and more notable for his performances and promotion during his long life in London of the continental masters from Bach to Schumann and Brahms.[69] Potter had been a student of Wölfl, Thomas Attwood (Mozart's pupil), and William Crotch (who himself had left 3 pub. sons. for P-or-H solo in London *ca.* 1794 [70]) before he went first to Beethoven for instruction in Vienna in 1817 and then, because Beethoven would give only informal advice, to Emanuel Alois Förster (sce 548–49).[71] Among numerous works left by Potter are at least six sonatas, all published rather early in his life, between 1817 and about 1825, plus others left in MS.[72] Of the six, Opp. 1/1–2 in C and ? (1817), 3 in D (1818?), and 4 in e (1819?) are for P solo, whereas Op. 6 is a "Grand Duo" in F for 2 Ps (1821; described in 1884 as "a noble work which has been many times played, and is very admirable for displaying the skill of the executants as much as for the interest of its ideas"),[73] and Op. 13 is a 4-movement *Sonata di bravura concertante* in E♭ (S-F-Va-F), for P and Hn(-or-Bn-or-Vc; 1825?), ded. to "le fameux Cor, Monsieur Puzzi." [74]

A good idea of Potter's compositional influences and tastes can be

---

65. E.g., cf. Temperley/PINTO 267; also, MT XV (1872) 644, XX (1879) 389, XXIV (1883) 405 and 468.

66. Cf. SAINSBURY II 294 (with wrong year of death).

67. Temperley/PINTO 265 and 270.

68. Anderson/BEETHOVEN II 759; Macfarren/POTTER 45–46; WAGNER LEBEN 606; Newman/WAGNER II 458 and 473.

69. Macfarren/POTTER (by Potter's pupil) is the main biographic account; cf., further, GROVE VI 895–96 (W. H. Hadow); MGG X 1523–24 (J. M. Allan), with further bibliography. Mr. Philip H. Peter of Mt. Prospect, Ill., is doing a diss. on Potter (as of early 1969).

70. BUCEM I 241.

71. Macfarren/POTTER 45; SAINSBURY II 304–5.

72. Cf. SAINSBURY II 305; HOFMEISTER 1828 (Whistling), 502, 517, 599.

73. Macfarren/POTTER 49.

74. Temperley/CORRESPONDENCE.

had from his piano piece, nearly 75 years in advance of Elgar's orchestral work, called *The Enigma, Variations and Fantasia on a Favorite
Irish Air* (London: Boosey, 1825). With more or less confidence and
some surprising pinpointing of specific traits, a contemporary reviewer
identified the "Introduzione" as being in the style of Moscheles; Variations 1–5, respectively, as being in the styles of Ries, Kalkbrenner,
Cramer, Rossini (even though the reviewer knew no piano music by
him), and Beethoven (or Moscheles again); and the concluding "Fantasia" as being a medley of all these styles.[75] Although the identifying
traits, mostly individual keyboard techniques, are tangible enough
when the reviewer singles them out, today's students of the Romantic Era might find it hard to relate each of them so confidently to
but one name, for they all seem to have been in the *frühromantische* air
(cf. ssb VI). More conspicuous today is Potter's own approach to keyboard music, which not only provides the vehicle for introducing
these traits but dominates (and constitutes nearly all that needs to be
said about) most if not all of his sonatas, too. His Op. 1, reportedly
deriving from Haydn and Clementi,[76] presumably reveals a more
modest, established idiom. But from Op. 3 on,[77] confirming his recognized gifts as a piano virtuoso, Potter wrote little else in his piano
music besides alternations of free, inconsequential thematic bits, usually highly ornamented, and still freer, emptier, but fairly difficult
runs and cadenzas, all amidst copious editing and even some footnoted
instructions. Whether the title is "Enigma," "Sonata di bravura," or
simply "Sonata," the procedure is essentially the same, there being
no use of established forms other than the variation principle.

Among a few other, more obscure composers of sonatas in early
19th-century England, mention might be added of the London organist **William Crouch** (*ca.* 1775–*ca.* 1835), for at least 23 sonatas for H-
or-P, published (*ca.* 1775–*ca.* 1800) as Opp. 1, 4, 6, 7, and 9, and
presumably oriented toward the past;[78] the oratorio and opera composer **Matthew Peter King** (1773–1823), for several solo and accompanied piano sonatas published between about 1785 and 1820, the
latest being a programmatic, Handelian work in four movements all
in D, with the title "The Coronation [of George IV?]: A Grand Sonata
Sinfonia for Piano Forte";[79] the pianist and singer **Maria Hester
Parke** (1775–1822), for several more solo and accompanied piano

75. QUARTERLY VII (1825) 507–9.
76. Shedlock/SONATA 230.
77. Cf. the review of Op. 3 in AMZ XXI (1819) 64 and the more general survey
of Potter's earlier works, including sons., in QUARTERLY V (1823) 376–80.
78. Temperley/CORRESPONDENCE; cf. BROWN & STRATTON 109 and BUCEM I 242.
79. Temperley/CORRESPONDENCE; cf. BROWN & STRATTON 231 and BUCEM I 570.

sonatas, including "Two Grand Sonatas" for P solo, Op. 2 in C and F (*ca.* 1805), each in three movements (F-S-Ro), with distinct recollections of Mozart;[80] and the Aberdeen organist **John Ross** (1763–1837), for more than twenty solo and accompanied piano sonatas published about 1795 to 1815, including several with "favorite Scots and Irish airs" and one "with an Introductory Prelude." [81] And mention might be made, too, of the teacher **James Fisin** (1755–1847), pupil of Burney, for two sets of accompanied sonatas, Op. 10 published in 1801 and Op. 12, dedicated to "Mrs. Burney," about 1806;[82] the opera composer **Henry Rowley Bishop** (1786–1855), for a reported Sonata for P & Vn of 1807 not currently locatable;[83] the pianist **Charles Neate** (1784–1877), a piano student of Field, a cellist, and an acquaintance of Beethoven, for two sonatas for P solo (Op. 1 in c, 1808; Op. 2 in d, *ca.* 1822) and a lost sonata for P & Vc;[84] the organist **John (Freckleton) Burrowes** (1787–1852), for an accompanied sonata (P & Vc), published as Op. 7 about 1810;[85] and **George Eugene Griffin** (1781–1863) for at least five sonatas, including two for P solo (Opp. 2 in E♭ [1810?] and 7 in E [1811?]).[86]

There was also a teacher of violin and piano in Bristol, **Thomas Howell** (1783–?), who left a more elementary publication, *Six Progressive Sonatinas for the Pianoforte*, that was well received in 1818 for its musicality and training values.[87] There was the keyboardist **Charles Wesley** (1757–1834), whose one published sonata, for P solo (*ca.* 1820), is a three-movement work ("Preludio," "Aria" with one variation, "Giga") that reflects an early interest in J. S. Bach similar to his brother-and-student Samuel's (*supra*).[88] And there was one **Charles Ambrose** (?–?), perhaps the ballad composer and professor in Chelmsford that Sainsbury lists without first name, whose published set of three solo piano sonatas, in E, E♭, and E, were twice reviewed in 1825 as pleasant, well-written study material in the outmoded style of Dussek or even Koželuch (SCE 556–58), with the best movement being the variations in Sonata 2 on the Irish song, "My Love's Like the Red, Red Rose." [89] Another was the precocious pianist **Pio Cian-**

80. Temperley/CORRESPONDENCE; cf. BROWN & STRATTON 308 and BUCEM II 762.
81. Temperley/CORRESPONDENCE; cf. BROWN & STRATTON 355 and BUCEM II 902.
82. Cf. GROVE III 147 (R. Gorer).
83. Temperley/CORRESPONDENCE, citing R. Northcott's biography of Bishop (London, 1920), pp. 149–58.
84. Cf. GROVE VI 40 (M. K. Ward).
85. Cf. GROVE I 1032 (W. H. Hadow).
86. Temperley/CORRESPONDENCE.
87. QUARTERLY I (1818) 382–83. Cf. SAINSBURY I 879.
88. Temperley/CORRESPONDENCE.
89. HARMONICON III/1 (1825) 139; QUARTERLY VII (1825) 104–5. Cf. SAINSBURY I 17.

chettini (1799–1851), London-born "son of F. Cianchettini, of Rome, and Veronica [sister of J. L.] Dussek" [90] (herself the composer of 3 sons. for P solo, Op. 6 [pub. *ca.* 1812] that "introduce popular tunes by Mozart and others" [91]). Pio left a published work, Op. 26 in e, called "Le Delire: Grande Sonate," for P+Vn, which a reviewer in 1832 found effective and Beethovian, but too difficult to be popular, especially with its use of the "demisemidemisemiquaver" (128th-note):

> To pronounce the word, without taking breath in the midst of it, demands the lungs of a diver:—to play the note in time requires a finger as nimble as the Eclipse, or Flying Childers; and such lungs and such fingers are not so common as tubercles and chalk-stones, we can venture to assure the composer of this *Grande Sonate*.[92]

Still in the same decade, a Scottish piano pupil of Potter and eventual teacher at the Royal Academy in London, **Frederick Brown Jewson** (1823–91), left a solo Sonata in E, published in 1838 as Op. 1, that is described as a commonplace, although pianistically grandiose work in four movements.[93] In the final decade of the first half-century, mention may be made of the leading Victorian music critic, **James William Davison** (1813–85), for two missing sonatas for P solo, both in E, and published in 1842—Opp. 6, (perhaps called) "Fioretta," and 7, "Phantasmion";[94] the violinist and organist **Henry John Westrop** (1812–79), for two published duo sonatas, in B♭ (posthumous), for P & Vn, and in F, Op. 6, for P+Fl (4 mvts., F-S-Sc-F), both played for the Society of British Musicians, in 1844 and 1845, respectively;[95] the pianist and organist **Charles Edward Horsley** (1822–76), a pupil variously of his father (**William Horsley,** who himself had left 3 sons., for P solo, between about 1812–17 [96]), Moscheles, Hauptmann, and Mendelssohn, for five duo sonatas—Op. 3 in A (pub. in 1843; ded. to Mendelssohn)[97] and two other, unpublished duos for P & Vc, in G and E♭ (played for the Society of British Musicians in 1847 and 1848),[98] Op. 9 in a, for P & Fl (pub. in 1846), and Op. 14 in F, for

90. SAINSBURY I 153–54. Cf. Craw/DUSSEK 15 and 102.

91. Temperley/CORRESPONDENCE.

92. HARMONICON X/1 (1832) 256. Another passage from this review is quoted in SSB II.

93. MUSICAL WORLD XI (1839) 59.

94. Cf. MUSICAL WORLD XVII (1842) 80, 216, 8. Temperley/CORRESPONDENCE refers to a limerick written a little later: "There was a J. W. D./ Who sought a composer to be;/ But his muse wouldn't budge,/ So he set up as judge/ Over better composers than he."

95. MUSICAL WORLD XIX (1844) 110 and XXI (1845) 9. Cf. BROWN & STRATTON 442, referring also to a (MS?) Son. for P & Va.

96. Mod. ed.: Son. 2 in F (1814), Smart/EIGHTEENTH-m 85.

97. Reviewed as songful, pleasant music for the home in NZM XIX (1843) 42–43.

98. MUSICAL WORLD XXII (1847) 658 and XXIII (1848) 648.

P & Vn (1848);[99] and one **John James Haite** (?–1874), for a not otherwise identified sonata played at the Society of British Musicians in 1847.[100]

The Sonata in England from about 1850 to 1885 (Bennett)

The most successful and notable sonata composer in mid-Romantic England was the pianist, violinist, and conductor **William Sterndale Bennett** (1816–75), who studied with William Crotch and Cipriani Potter, became a close friend of Mendelssohn and Schumann in the later 1830's, and devoted much of his time to the Royal Academy of Music and the London Philharmonic Society in his later years.[101] Within his rather small life's output of some 65 piano, chamber, orchestral, and choral works Bennett wrote four sonatas that were published, between 1838 and 1876, three of them for P solo and one for P & Vc.[102] Op. 13 in f, for P solo, was composed in 1836–37, mostly while Bennett was enjoying music and the frequent company of Mendelssohn and Schumann in Leipzig for several months.[103] It was, in fact, dedicated to Mendelssohn on his wedding day and published by Kistner in Leipzig in 1838. Op. 32 in A, for P & Vc, was composed for and dedicated to the then leading cellist in London, Alfredo Piatti, but not completed until the very moment of its first performance in 1852, which was successful in spite of no rehearsal; Op. 32 was also published by Kistner, in 1853.[104] Op. 46 in A♭ originally bore a bilingual title that reads in full, *Die Jungfrau von Orleans (Schiller), The Maid of Orleans, Sonata for the Pianoforte, Composed Expressly for and Dedicated to Madame Arabella Goddard*

99. A performance of 2 mvts. of Op. 14 in 1875 is reported in MT XVII (1875) 58. For more on Horsley cf. MGG VI 764–68 (N. M. Temperley).

100. MUSICAL WORLD XXII (1847) 658.

101. Cf. MGG I 1661–63 (W. Kahl), with partly dated list of works; GROVE I 625–28 (H. C. Colles). Among numerous first-hand accounts and memoirs, considerable background information may be found in MT XVII (1875) 7–9 (obituary by H. C. Lunn); O'Leary/BENNETT; MT XLIV (1903) 306–9, 379–81, 523–27 (F. G. Edwards); Stanford/BENNETT; MT LVII (1916) 233–35 (F. Corder), 362–63 (L. N. Parker), 456–57 (K. C. Field); also, in Bache/BACHE *passim* (in connection with Bennett's pupil F. E. Bache). Most important is his son's detailed, fascinating biography, Bennett/BENNETT, which throws much light on contemporary English musical life and gives the circumstances of (though no commentaries on) the sons. by Bennett.

102. All of these sons. are listed in Cat. ROYAL 50. The "Notturno" in B reproduced in AMZ XLII (1840) as "Beilage No. 2 [actually 3]" affords a remarkable facs. of Bennett's handwriting.

103. Cf. Bennett/BENNETT 60, 61, 456.

104. Cf. Bennett/BENNETT 194, 211–12; MT XLIV (1903) 526. The early pub. by (Benjamin or Joseph?) Williams in London that is listed in MGG I 1662 could not be confirmed here.

(celebrated pianist, and pupil and wife of Bennett's friend J. W. Davison). One of the last, if not the last, of Bennett's compositions, following several years of no works for piano,[105] Op. 46 was started in 1869 but composed mostly "at the seaside" in the summer and fall of 1872,[106] and published first in London by Lamborn Cock not later than July, 1873, then posthumously by Kistner early in 1876.[107] Bennett's charming "Sonatine" in C for P solo, also published posthumously in 1876 by Kistner, was composed in 1871 for his grandson.[108]

Bennett's Op. 13 has four movements, F-Sc-M-VF, all in the same key, with a change of mode only in one movement (from f to F in iii). The shorter, inner movements are more appealing and original than either the long, Mendelssohnian first movement or the "weak" finale.[109] Schumann never got to the review that he promised to do of this "excellent" work in 1837,[110] although he had recently lauded Bennett's poetic compositions as significant redemptions for England's disappointing contributions to music,[111] and thought enough of Bennett at that time to dedicate his *Études symphoniques,* Op. 13, to him. Bennett's Op. 32, one of the few noteworthy cello sonatas from England at the time, again puts all movements in the same key, without even a change of mode. The ingratiating first movement, framed by a slow introduction that returns as a coda, succeeds well enough, but the other two movements suffer from the tonal monotony, especially as their harmonic progressions tend to be repetitious anyway.[112] Whereas Opp. 13 and 32 are scarcely mentioned in 19th-century sources seen here,[113] Bennett's Op. 46 is mentioned often, including references to more performances than can be credited to any other English sonata discussed in the present volume.[114] Undoubtedly, as we have seen in other sonatas

105. Stanford/BENNETT 657.

106. Bennett/BENNETT 390, 418, 423, 442; O'Leary/BENNETT 135.

107. Cf. MMR III (1873) 104–5; HOFMEISTER 1876, p. 22; NZM LXXII/1 (1876) 83.

108. Bennett/BENNETT 442, 460; MT XLIV (1903) 526; NZM LXXII/2 (1876) 283.

109. This opinion is also expressed in Shedlock/SONATA 231 and Bush/BENNETT 91–92.

110. Schumann/SCHRIFTEN I 308 (cf. II 410); he must have known Op. 13 in MS, meaning to review it when it got pub. in 1838.

111. Schumann/SCHRIFTEN I 245–47. Recall the introduction to the present chap. Cf., also, Spink/BENNETT.

112. Cf. Cobbett/CHAMBER I 118 (F. Corder).

113. Two performances of Op. 32 are noted in MT XV (1871) 142, one with Walter Macfarren at the piano; another (in Berlin) is noted in NZM LXXIII/1 (1877) 172.

114. E.g., cf. MT XVI (1874) 359 (played by Franklin Taylor at Crystal Palace in Dec., 1873; first public performance?), 367, 427, 519, 544, 723; XVII (1875–76) 58 (called "Joan of Arc"), 114, 671; XVIII (1877) 20, 138; XIX (1878) 40 (played by the dedicatee), 685; XXI (1880) 91; XXII (1881) 378, 430; XXIV (1882) 21; XV (1884) 338 (played by Bülow, whom Bennett had known).

with programmatic titles (cf. ssв IV), the popularity of Op. 46 was stimulated by the attraction of such a title plus more specific programmatic associations. Moreover, although Op. 46 stands well on its purely musical merits, in this instance the content does justify the emphasis on programmatic considerations that the initial reviewers and subsequent writers have made, as is already apparent in sentences extracted from the first (?) review:[115]

A new work by Sir W. Sterndale Bennett—unquestionably the greatest of living English composers—cannot be otherwise than in the highest degree welcome. As a sonata *per se* the work before us quite comes up to any anticipations we might have formed on being told that Sir W. Sterndale Bennett was about to issue a new sonata. It is additionally welcome, because in great measure it bears out the fact, so often maintained in these columns, that since Beethoven the greatest musical composers have relied upon a "poetic basis" for their inspirations. . . . The idea that his [Bennett's] choice of subject is governed by its compressibility into some fixed form is altogether to be scouted. . . . The subject of Joan of Arc is an admirable one for musical portrayal, though it treats of one of the blackest pages of English history. One may feel some regret that England's disgrace should thus be perpetuated by music, but the beauty and interest of Bennett's work fully atone for any such regret. . . . Curiously enough . . . [Moscheles' overture on the same subject] was played under its composer's direction at a concert of the Philharmonic Society, in 1835, at which Bennett, then a youth of about seventeen, came forward with his piano concerto in E flat.[116] Can it be that it was then that he was first struck with the idea of composing a sonata on the same subject, and that so many years have gone to maturing it? . . .

Bennett's Op. 46 falls in four contrasting movements totalling 36 pages in print, each headed and influenced by its own line or two, quoted in both German and English, from *Die Jungfrau von Orleans* by Schiller. The first movement, an "Andante pastorale" in A♭ that shifts frequently and freely between 12/8, 9/8, and 6/8 meter, is a songful, tender, almost childlike piece with the title "In the Fields" and the inscription (from Act iv, Scene 1) "In innocence I led my sheep/ Adown the mountain's silent steep." The second and longest movement, "Allegro marziale" in a♭ (with enharmonically related sections in b, B, and E) and in C meter, is a dramatic yet subtle piece faintly suggestive of the "Marche au supplice" in Berlioz' *Symphonie fantastique,* with the almost identical but different title "In the Field" and the inscription (Prologue/4) "The clanging trumpets sound, the chargers rear,/ And the loud war cry thunders in mine ear." The third move-

---

115. MMR III (1873) 104–5. Cf., also, MT XVI (1874) 391 (a similar, laudatory review); Statham/BENNETT 134; Shedlock/SONATA 231–32; Bie/PIANOFORTE 279; Westerby/PIANOFORTE 127 and 130–31; Bush/BENNETT 96–97.
116. Cf. MOSCHELES I 313–14.

ment, "Adagio patetico" in E and in 3/8 meter, is a poignant but gentle prayer and lament with the title "In Prison" and the inscription (v/2) "Hear me O God in mine extremity,/ In fervent supplication up to thee;/ Up to thy heaven above, I send my Soul." And the finale, "Molto di passione" in A♭ and in ¢ meter, presents an extended, rapid, naively impetuous yet hushed piece, almost a *perpetuum mobile*, with merely "The End" as the title and "Brief is the sorrow, endless is the joy" as the inscription (v/14). No further verbal guides to the subject of the programme occur except "alla Tromba" once in the course of the martial movement and one more inscription—"When on my native hills I drove my herd/ Then was I happy as in Paradise" (iv/9)—at a "semplice," "limpido," pianissimo section of "In Prison."

Although Bennett is able to create songful, fresh, unspoiled melodies that flow freely and spontaneously (Ex. 89), the separate movements produce the over-all effects not of standard, dynamic sonata forms but of miniature tone poems for the piano, or even of musical tableaux. Their only real structural principle is that of the rondo, but even this principle is applied so loosely, if not indifferently, that it seems more aimless than organized. Similarly and pertinently, the harmonic progressions are often interesting and generally compelling enough in themselves, but the over-all tonal movement is largely without significant direction, although there is now at least the key contrast in one inner movement that lacks in Bennett's earlier sonatas. Furthermore, there is pleasure in the euphony of Bennett's piano textures but eventual monotony in the rudimentary, stereotyped nature of his accompaniments. Finally, Bennett's artistic scope is narrow. He was a conservative who, failing to keep up with his contemporaries, never got beyond *frühromantische* music. And he was at his best in his simplest, most gentle, and most delicate writing, short of letting it become sickly sweet. His occasional attempts to write with passion and drama do seem naive. In all these respects, except for his earliest works,[117] his style is less like Mendelssohn's, in spite of frequent statements to the contrary, and more like that of Spohr, whom he met and admired,[118] with some hints, too, of the styles of Mozart, Hummel, and Dussek, whose music had made deep impressions on him,[119] and of Moscheles, who took an understandable liking to Bennett's music.[120]

117. Cf. MENDELSSOHN/Moscheles 170–71.
118. Cf. Bennett/BENNETT 116–22, 213–15, 451–53; MT LVII (1916) 233–34 (a somewhat negative reappraisal of Bennett's music by F. Corder); Stanford/BENNETT 638.
119. Cf. Bennett/BENNETT 21–26, 39; Temperley/MOZART 315–17; Temperley/MENDELSSOHN 229–32.
120. Cf. MOSCHELES I 314, II 49. But one would never discover in Bennett's music

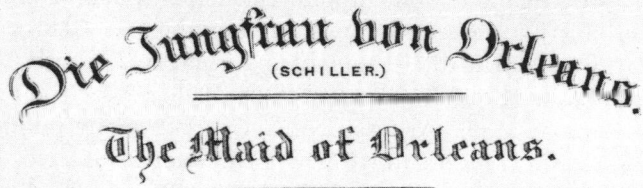

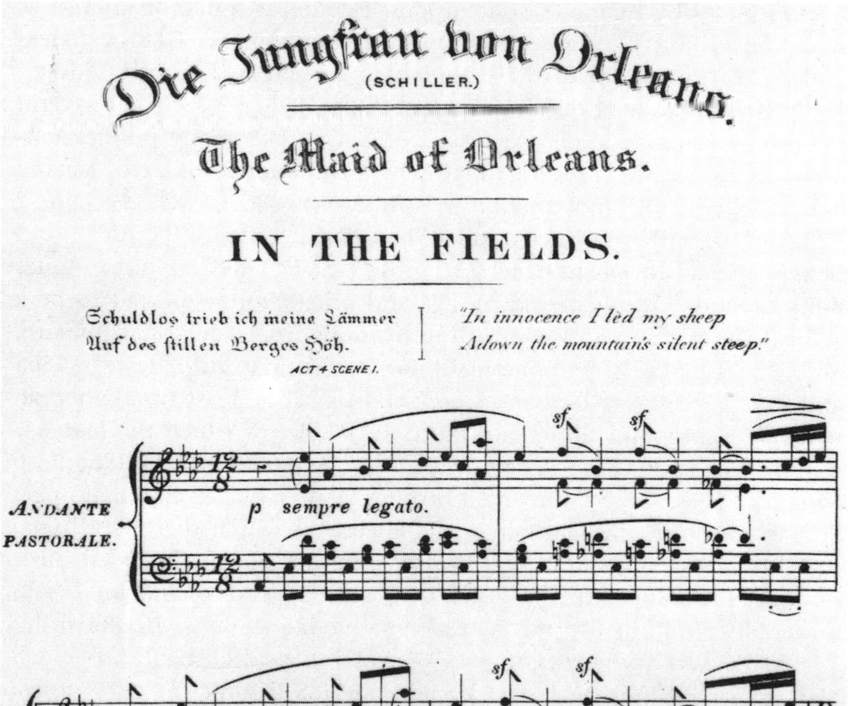
Die Jungfrau von Orleans.
(SCHILLER.)
The Maid of Orleans.
IN THE FIELDS.
Schuldlos trieb ich meine Lämmer
Auf des stillen Berges Höh.
ACT 4 SCENE I.
"In innocence I led my sheep
Adown the mountain's silent steep."
ANDANTE PASTORALE.
p sempre legato.
sf
sempre legato.
espress: cres: dim:
cres: dim:
W. STERNDALE BENNETT. Op. 46. "THE MAID OF ORLEANS."
(J.B.C&Co A.567)

Ex. 89. From the opening of William Sterndale Bennett's Sonata in A♭, Op. 46, "The Maid of Orleans" (facs. of the J. B. Cramer reprint, *ca.* 1905).

No sonatas by Bennett's contemporaries offer as much of interest as his. The productive, respected composer and theorist **George (Alexander) Macfarren** (1813–87) [121] and his younger, less known brother, the pianist **Walter (Cecil) Macfarren** (1826–1905),[122] each left several sonatas in print or MS.[123] At least five of George's many publications are sonatas—one in C for organ (1872?);[124] three for P solo, No. 1 being a Beethovian, four-movement work in E♭ (F-S-Sc-F; 1842),[125] No. 2 being in A, with the inscription "Ma Cousine" (1843),[126] and No. 3 being a four-movement work in g (F-M-Sc-F), dedicated to Agnes Zimmermann (*infra*), played by her and others, and reported to be a skillful if not inspired work, with derivations from Weber, Schumann, and Mendelssohn;[127] and one in B♭ for P & Fl (first pub. between 1865 and 1871).[128] But performances are reported of at least four other sonatas by George, including two more for P solo, of which the first was written for Agnes Zimmermann and first played by her in 1866;[129] a Sonata in C for P & Vn, in which brother Walter played the piano part at least twice;[130] and another organ sonata, in which there is a fugue based on "Rule Britannia." [131] Walter's smaller output included three published sonatinas for P solo (in C, g, and D), two sonatas for P solo played in 1845 (in c♯ and A, the first having 4 mvts. in the order F-Sc-M-VF and in the keys of c♯-E-A♭-c♯),[132] three duo sonatas of which two are for P & Vn (in F and D) and one for P & Vc (in e),[133] and a Sonata in e for P-duet performed in 1850.[134] Subsequent reviews of the

---

that he, too, was one of the many Romantics fascinated by Beethoven's Op. 106, in this instance by way of Potter and before Bennett met Mendelssohn (SSB VIII; cf. Bennett/BENNETT 33–34 and 400).

121. Cf. GROVE V 468–69 (W. H. Hadow) and MGG VIII 1385–88 (R. A. Harman), with further bibliography. Macfarren/POTTER includes recollections of his training under Potter.

122. Cf. GROVE V 469 (W. H. Hadow).

123. The pub. sons. of each are listed in PAZDÍREK X 26 and 29.

124. MT XV (1873) 743 and XVIII (1878) 359.

125. Reviewed in MUSICAL WORLD XVIII (1843) 102 and XIX (1844) 54; played in the same years.

126. Played in 1843, as noted in MUSICAL WORLD XVIII (1843) 122 and 134.

127. Shedlock/SONATA 230–31; MT XX (1879) 185, XXI (1880) 308, XXII (1881) 105, and XIV (1884) 386; NZM LXXI (1876) 70.

128. Temperley/CORRESPONDENCE.

129. MT XII (1866) 339.

130. MT XV (1871) 108 and 340.

131. MT XXII (1881) 197. MT XVII (1876) 251 advertises George's pamphlet "On the Structure of a Sonata."

132. MUSICAL WORLD XX (1845) 86, 583.

133. The sons. in D and e were played at the Society of British Musicians in 1848 and 1846, respectively (MUSICAL WORLD XXIII [1848] 685 and XXI [1846] 533). All 3 duos were pub. in 1876. At least Sonata in e had appeared earlier, *ca.* 1860.

134. MUSICAL WORLD XXV (1850) 27, 147.

duos mention "charmingly harmonized" themes, "happy modulations," "striking" tonal schemes, effective scoring, and good audience response.[135]

The composer, writer, and teacher (Charles) Hubert (Hastings) Parry (1848–1918) is generally regarded as "the most powerful influence in English musical life" and (with C. V. Stanford, *infra*) the most effective leader of its renaissance during the late 19th and early 20th centuries.[136] He already has been cited in the present volume for his stimulating though no longer widely accepted ideas on musical evolution (Parry/EVOLUTION) and for numerous contributions to GROVE.[137] As a composer, trained primarily by Bennett, G. A. Macfarren, H. H. Piersen, and Edward Dannreuther, Parry made his chief mark in choral music. But Dannreuther had directed his early interests (about 1876–83) chiefly to chamber music.[138] Among Parry's chamber works are the six solo and duo sonatas that constitute but an inconspicuous part of his large, rounded output of published and unpublished music.[139] Three of the sonatas were not published—Op. 20 in f, for P-duet, composed in 1865, Op. 75 in b, a one-movement "Fantasie-Sonata" for P & Vn, composed in 1878, and Op. 103 in D, for P & Vn, composed by or in 1889. The three that did appear in print include two for P solo —Op. 71 in F, composed and published in 1877,[140] and Op. 79 in A, published in 1878—and one for P & Vc, Op. 85 in A, composed about 1880 and published in 1883.[141]

H. C. Colles concludes that Parry's chamber works must be regarded "rather as evidences of abilities never wholly fulfilled than achievements in themselves" and quotes Parry on his own cello sonata (Op. 85) to the effect that "it all sprawls and is too long and indefinite." [142] Except for performances sponsored by Dannreuther,[143] the sonatas seem

135. MT XV (1871) 142 (Son. in F played by the composer and M. Sainton), XVI (1874) 712 (review of Son. in e, played by the composer and "Sig. Pezze") and 657 (Son. in F pub.), XVII (1876) 379 (3 sons. pub. by Novello), 515 and 558 (Son. in D, with the composer at the P), and 696 (Son. in e pub.), XVIII (1877) 185 (Son. in D reviewed), XXI (1880) 141 (Son. in F played), XXVII (1886) 480 (Son. in D played); MMR VI (1876) 95 (Son. in D reviewed).
136. Cf. GROVE VI 561–65 (J. A. Fuller-Maitland) and WESTRUP & HARRISON 484; also, MGG X 836–39 (J. M. Allan & H. F. Redlich), with further bibliography. Graves/PARRY is a full biography (with only incidental mentions of the sons.).
137. Cf. Graves/PARRY I 224, II 237.
138. Cobbett/CHAMBER II 207–11 (H. C. Colles) discusses Parry's chamber music at length, though mostly in broad terms.
139. The fullest and most specific list is that prepared by Emily Daymond for GROVE 3d ed. (and 4th) IV 57–63.
140. Cf. Graves/PARRY I 169.
141. Cf. Graves/PARRY 207, 208. Fuller-Maitland/PARRY 31 describes Op. 85 briefly.
142. Cobbett/CHAMBER II 209–10.
143. Dannreuther played the P part in performances of Op. 85 reported in MT XXII (1881) 302 and XXVII (1885) 20.

Ex. 90. From the start of Hubert Parry's Sonata 2 in A, Op. 79 (after the Augener reprint, plate no. 10775).

not to have been played to any appreciable extent. The abiding influence of Schumann and Brahms pervades the two piano sonatas. Shedlock finds Stephen Heller's stamp in them, too.[144] Apart from a Schumannesque opening in the second one that promises better (Ex. 90), these are competent, conservative works at best, circumscribed by flat, occasionally sentimental ideas, couched in piano writing that is practical and convenient but colorless, and developed in a Teutonically academic manner. Both sonatas follow usual four-movement plans (F-Sc-M-Ro and F-S-Sc-Ro), in which their scherzos make the most successful forms.

Further exploration of the sonata in England during the period from 1850 to 1885 would lead to such obscure and forgotten composers as the Austrian pianist and pedagogue **Ernst Pauer** (1826–1905), who had studied with W. A. Mozart "the Younger" (sce 567–68) before living in London from 1851 to 1896 and before composing one competent, Mendelssohnian sonata each for P solo (Op. 22 in f, pub. *ca.* 1847), P & Vc (Op. 45 in A, pub. in 1855), and P & Vn (Op. 46 in a, pub. in 1856), as well as some elementary, Mozartean sonatinas for P solo.[145] From

144. Shedlock/SONATA 233. Fuller-Maitland/PARRY 25 finds Weber in Op. 79/ii and an anticipation of the canon of Franck's Sonata in A/iv in Op. 79/iv.
145. Cf. GROVE VI 595 (A. J. Hipkins); Altmann/KAMMERMUSIK 262 and 220; MMR

the same decade around the mid century may be noted two "modest but distinguished" sonatinas for Ob & P in g/B♭ and G (No. 1 dated 1848; both pub. posthumously in 1890) by the church composer **Thomas Attwood Walmisley** (1814–56);[146] thirteen sonatas, not further identified, by the "amateur" composer trained in Rome and often resident in Germany, **John Lodge Ellerton** (1801–73);[147] two academically correct sonatas suggesting Mendelssohn and Beethoven, Opp. 1 in f and 7 in E, for P solo, by the London organist **Henry Wylde** (1822–90), who seems himself to have given performances of them in 1846 and 1850, respectively;[148] and both solo and duo sonatas by two women composers, **Caroline Orger (Reinagle**; 1818–92; possibly a niece-by-marriage of A. Reinagle in the United States, SCE 806–7) and the pianist **Kate Fanny Loder** (1825–1904).[149]

Furthermore, the German-born pupil of Hummel and Weber, **Julius Benedict** (1804–85), lived in London from 1835 on, where besides operas and other works he left two pleasant, inconsequential sonatas for P & Vn (Op. 1 in d; Op. 80 in E, pub. in 1870).[150] An otherwise unidentified (German?) composer of chamber music, **Joseph Street** (?–?) left at least 6 sonatas for P solo, 2 for P & Vn, and one for P & Vc ("Sonate quasi Fantaisie" in G) that were published in Germany during the approximately 15 years that he was in London (1860–75).[151] The outstanding German-born pianist **Agnes Zimmermann** (1847–1925), who had studied with Potter, Pauer, Stegall, and G. Macfarren, not only introduced the sonatas of many others, from Mozart to Brahms, but herself left four Mendelssohnian duo sonatas, all published between 1868 and 1879 and warmly praised for their "invention," instrumental handling, and "individuality"—Opp. 16 in d (1868; ded. to Joachim), 21 in a (1875), and 23 in g (1879) for P & Vn, and Op. 17 in g (1872) for P & Vc.[152]

XV (1885) 57 and XX (1890) 130 (short favorable reviews of the sonatinas); SCE 15 and 116 (on Pauer's eds. and textbook).

146. Temperley/CORRESPONDENCE; cf. MT XCVII (1956) 636–39 (N. Temperley).

147. Cf. BROWN & STRATTON 137.

148. MUSICAL WORLD XXI (1846) 335; Temperley/CORRESPONDENCE.

149. Temperley/CORRESPONDENCE; MUSICAL WORLD XXI (1848) 655; BROWN & STRATTON 304, 252–53.

150. GROVE I 618–19 (H. S. Edwards). Cf. Altmann/KAMMERMUSIK 195; La Mara/MUSIKERBRIEFE II 177 and 179.

151. Cf. PAZDÍREK XIII 1140; Altmann/KAMMERMUSIK 228 and 265; MT XIII (1868) 573 (generally favorable review of 2 duos); Cobbett/CHAMBER II 467 (W. W. Cobbett).

152. Cf. GROVE IX 418 (G. Grove); MT LXVII (1926) 28–29 (Arbuthnot); Elson/WOMAN 145 and 239. On Op. 16, cf. Joachim/LETTERS 377; MT XIII (1868–69) 586, 622, and 645 (favorable review); XV (1871) 95 and 613; XVII (1876) 254; XVIII (1877) 311. On Op. 21, cf. MT XVI (1874) 513 and XVII (1875) 215; XX (1879) 605;

One **Charles Gardner** (1836–?), a pupil of Pauer and Macfarren, among others, left a Sonata in A, for P solo (pub. in 1871?), that was well received when he played it.[153] The Dutch-born violinist and editor for Novello, **Berthold Tours** (1838–97), moved to London in 1861, where his single contribution to the genre pursued here—a Sonatina in G, for P solo (pub. in 1871)—was reviewed as a charming, melodious, expressive work, superior to the usual children's teaching pieces with that title.[154] The pianist **William Henry Holmes** (1812–85) contributed to the sonata indirectly as a teacher of Bennett and the Macfarren brothers, among others, but also composed at least one Sonata for P & Vn himself that was performed though not published.[155] One **Charles Henry Shepherd** (1847–86), a student at the Royal Academy of Music in London and later an organist at St. Thomas's Church, Newcastle-on-Tyne, left a Sonata for P solo that was dedicated to G. A. Macfarren, published by Augener in 1871, and reviewed with some praise for the skill and some censure of the ideas.[156] The organist, teacher, conductor, and writer **Henry Hiles** (1826–1904) won a prize in 1868 from the "College of Organists" for his Sonata in g for organ, published in that year.[157] At fourteen the pianist and "Sterndale Bennett Scholar" at the Royal Academy of Music, **Charleton (Templeman) Speer** (1859–1921), dedicated to his teacher G. A. Macfarren his only known sonata, in G for P solo, whose publication by Novello in 1875 brought strongly favorable reviews for its skill, propriety, and musical fluency, "without any allowance on the score of years."[158] The operetta composer **Julian Edwards** (1855–1910) saw his Sonata in D, for P solo, published in 1876 before he emigrated to the United States (1888).[159] One **Robert Hainworth** (?–?) left three organ sonatas that were published between 1872 and 1876 and reviewed as weak, unidiomatic, and rhythmically imprecise works in spite of prizes awarded earlier for two of them by the

XXIV (1883) 321 (favorable report); XXVII (1886) 141. On Op. 23, cf. MT XX (1879) 313 (favorable review) and 443; XXI (1879) 28 (favorable report from Berlin); XXIV (1883) 206. On Op. 17, cf. MT XV (1871) 115. If the reference to a Son. for P solo, Op. 22, is correct in GROVE IX 418 the work seems not have been pub.; the "Sonata" for Vn, Vc, & P was actually a "Suite." The dates of pub. in Cobbett/CHAMBER II 598 and Altmann/KAMMERMUSIK 233 are mostly incorrect.
    153. MT XV (1871) 141 and XVIII (1878) 336. Cf. PAZDÍREK VI 80.
    154. Cf. MGG XIII 595 (B. Ramsey); MT XV (1871) 243.
    155. Cf. GROVE IV 327–28 (G. Grove); MT XV (1872) 622 and 690.
    156. MT XV (1871–72) 217 and 509.
    157. MT XIII (1868) 556 and XV (1871) 158. Cf. GROVE IV 277 (A. Chitty).
    158. MT XVII (1875) 60, 62, 117, 282 (with excerpts from 2 other reviews). Cf. GROVE VIII 3 (G. S. K. Butterworth).
    159. It is reviewed as a careful work, with poor ideas, poorly developed, in MT XVII (1875–76) 533 (cf. p. 446). Cf. BAKER 423.

"College of Organists." [160] Six more organ sonatas (1876) and three sonatas for Fl & P (1883) were left by the gifted organist, violinist, clarinetist, conductor, and much published composer (James) Hamilton (Smee) Clarke (1840–1912),[161] The theorist Henry Charles Banister (1831–97) left two unpublished sonatas for P solo, in f and f♯, that were both reported with praise after recitals of new music in 1874 and 1875.[162] The organist Charles Joseph Frost (1848–1918) left one long, favorably reviewed sonata (in A, 1876) and one sonatina for his instrument and seven sonatinas for P solo, all published, plus at least one more organ sonata (in A♭, 1877), in MS.[163] The Dutch-born organist Edouard Silas (1827–1909) left at least one sonata for P solo and twelve organ sonatas of which only the last organ sonata, Op. 82 in F, was published (1873 and later), in its entirety and in extracts.[164] Another among "all those obscure English organists," [165] Francis Edward Gladstone (1845–1925), left a Sonata in a, for organ (pub. in 1879), that was described as being skillful and well scored but unoriginal.[166]

The German-born organist and conductor Wilhelm Meyer Lutz (1822?–1903), in England from 1848, left a Sonata for P & Vn, Op. 23 (pub. by André in Offenbach/M in 1874) that was reviewed as an essentially empty work.[167] Another born in Germany, the pianist and writer Ferdinand Christian Wilhelm Praeger (1815–91), was a protégé of both Hummel and Schumann before moving to London in 1834 and left four published sonatas—one for P & Vn and three for P solo (a, C, and E)—of which the first (1889) fared only slightly better with the reviewers.[168] The esteemed organist and theorist Frederick Arthur Gore Ouseley (1825–89) left a Sonata in C and a "Second Sonata" for organ that seemed to have enjoyed a number of performances following their respective publications in 1879 and 1883.[169] The fine organist Walter Battison Haynes (1859–1900) composed a Sonata for Vn & P (MS only?)

160. MT XII (1866) 460, XV (1872) 158 and 630 (review), XIX (1878) 301 and 453 (review); PAZDÍREK VII 97.

161. Cf. MT XVII (1876) 637; PAZDÍREK III 362–63; Altmann/KAMMERMUSIK 272; GROVE II 330 (H. G. Farmer).

162. MT XVI (1874) 583, XVII (1875) 13. Cf. GROVE I 400 (J. A. Fuller-Maitland).

163. MT XVII (1876) 685, XVIII (1877) 281 and 297; PAZDÍREK V 570–71. Cf. BAKER 516.

164. MT XV (1873) 743, XVIII (1878) 359, XX (1879) 499, XXI (1880) 645; NZM LXXII/2 (1876) 354. Cf. GROVE VII 790–91 (G. Grove).

165. Cf. GROVE I vi (E. Blom).

166. MT XX (1879) 547; XXI (1880) 137. Cf. GROVE III 655 (F. G. Rendall).

167. MW XI (1880) 203. Cf. GROVE V 449 (G. Grove).

168. SMW XLVII (1889) 737–38; MW XXI (1890) 127. Cf. GROVE VI 904 (G. Grove); PAZDÍREK XI 511.

169. MT XVIII (1877) 554, XXII (1881) 471, XXIV (1883) 638, XXV (1884) 353. Cf. GROVE VI 467–68 (H. W. Shaw); MGG X 491–93 (R. A. Harman).

and a Sonata for organ in d, Op. 11, while studying in Leipzig, Op. 11 being published in 1883 and welcomed for its free fantasy, originality, high artistry, and unusual "Scherzoso."[170] The pianist and conductor **Charles Swinnerton Heap** (1847–1900), an eventual pupil of Bennett whose "Mendelssohn scholarship" in 1865–66 had brought instruction in Leipzig from Moscheles, Hauptmann, Richter, and Reinecke, left a Sonata in B♭, for P & Cl (pub. in 1880?), and a Sonata in d, for P & Vn (pub. in 1884?), the latter being reviewed favorably for its good ideas, contrasts, and scoring.[171] Another organist and a pupil of Potter, **Charles Edward Stephens** (1821–92), composed a "Sonata piacevole," for P & Fl, that was published in 1883 and performed at least twice in public,[172] and a Sonata for P solo, Op. 8 in A♭ (pub. in 1866). One **J. Conway Brown** won "ten guineas and a gold medal" in 1882 for a Sonata in E, for P & Vn, that Novello published in 1884.[173] And in Edinburgh, the respected organist and pedagogue **Herbert (Stanley) Oakeley** (1830–1903) left a four-movement Sonata in A, for P solo (presumably pub., *ca.* 1873) that was reviewed as a generally weak work, especially in its outer movements.[174]

England in the Late-Romantic Era (Stanford, Dale)

Right through World War I England continued to produce sonatas in surprising abundance, yet still without making a major contribution to that literature. Most important in this last group, although more so because of their general importance to music than the actual sonatas they left, were Stanford and Elgar. Both men were near contemporaries of Parry (*supra*) and figured similarly in the "renaissance of English music," but belong in a later grouping here because they wrote some of their sonatas much later. Born in Dublin, **Charles Villiers Stanford** (1852–1924) moved to England at the age of eighteen, studied with Reinecke and Kiel in Germany (ssb X) in the mid 1870's, came under the strong influences of Schumann's and Brahms's music, and gave his time to being a respected organist, teacher, and conductor as well as a prolific composer in all main branches of music.[175] Thirteen sonatas

170. mw XVIII (1887) 351, 352. Cf. grove IV 211 (F. G. Edwards).
171. mt XXI (1880) 141 and 626, XXIV (1883) 551, XXV (1884) 208 (review), XVII (1886) 283. Cf. grove IV 593 (W. B. Squire). The Son. for P solo cited in baker 681 could not be confirmed here.
172. mt XXIV (1883) 638, XXV (1884) 33, XXVII (1886) 480. Cf. grove VIII 79 (W. H. Hadow).
173. mt XXIII (1882) 450, XXV (1884) 596 and 670.
174. mmr III (1873) 148. Cf. grove VI 142 (W. H. Hadow).
175. Cf. grove VIII 45–55 (S. Goddard and B. D. Banner) and mgg XII 1172–84 (F. Hudson), each with a fully dated list of works (but with gaps and several errors,

by Stanford are known, dating from his student to his last years. Five of these are duos, including two each for P & Vc and P & Vn, and one for Cl-or-Va & P; two late works (Op. 165) also call for two performers but are not true duos, for they are designated, exceptionally, "for violin solo with pianoforte accompaniment" and are aimed rather at the style of the Baroque "solo" sonata;[176] and six are solos, of which one is for piano and five are late works for organ. Out of all thirteen sonatas nine have been published, including Op. 9 in A for P & Vc (1879; composed by 1877; ded. to the cellist R. Hausman)[177] and Op. 39 in D for P & Vc (1893; ded. to the cellist A. Piatti);[178] Op. 11 in D, for P & Vn (1880; ded. to the violinist L. Straus);[179] Op. 129 in F for Cl(-or-Va) & P (1918; composed in 1911; ded. to O. W. Street and C. Draper); and the five organ sonatas—Op. 149 in F, No. 1 (1917; ded. to A. Gray); Op. 151 in g/G, No. 2, "Eroica" (1919; ded. to C. M. Widor; i and iii called "Rheims" and "Verdun, 1916"); Op. 152 in d, No. 3, "Britannica" (1918; ded. to W. Parratt); Op. 153 in c/C, No. 4, "Celtica" (1920; ded. to H. Darke; iii called "St. Patrick's Breastplate"); Op. 159 in A, No. 5, "quasi una fantasia" (1921).[180]

Contemporary reviewers greeted especially Stanford's earlier sonatas with unqualified praise. Thus, with a "welcome [for] this Sonata, [simply] because it is a Sonata, and before looking at a single bar," and with "special commendation in the present instance" for a new contribution to the "strangely neglected" cello repertoire, the reviewer in the London *Musical Times* describes Op. 9 movement by movement (M/F-F-S-F), incorporating thirteen music examples, and concludes that it "is a more than creditable addition to high-class English music, and an honour to its composer." [181] In 1884, when Agnes Zimmermann introduced Stanford's "new [MS] Sonata, which is in the unusual key of D flat" (Op. 20 for P solo; unpub.), the reviewer in the same periodical had "no hesitation in characterising it as one of the most important compositions for piano solo produced within the present genera-

as also in Altmann/KAMMERMUSIK and in the cat. Hudson/STANFORD). Greene/STANFORD is the chief account of the man and his music.

176. At least one of these 2 sons., Op. 165/2, was commissioned by the British chamber music promoter W. W. Cobbett and played in London on May 7, 1919; cf. Cobbett/CHAMBER II 453 (T. F. Dunhill) and 454 (W. W. Cobbett); MT LX (1919) 306 (reporting Op. 165/2 as "characteristic of the composer in merit, while tending to an unusually simple style").

177. Cf. NZM LXXIII/1 (1877) 222 (played in London); MT XX (1879) 150, 157, 321.

178. Played by Fanny Davies and Piatti in 1886, Op. 39 is described in Fuller-Maitland/PARRY 34.

179. Cf. MT XXI (1880) 631, XXIV (1883) 147, 206, and 265.

180. These 5 sons. are described briefly in Fuller-Maitland/PARRY 102–3.

181. MT XX (1879) 150 and 157.

tion." [182] He had started by deploring the poor attendance and such "indifference on the part of the public to the claims of native art," for "We have three or four young composers whose collective ability is at least equal to that of the same number of leading German living musicians, whose utterances always awaken interest and expectation." Referring to analyses of all but the finale in the program notes, the reviewer merely summarized the three movements (S/F-F-F). Friendly but matter-of-fact approval rather than unqualified praise characterizes the short review in 1917 of the first organ sonata as a work in three movements (F-Mi-F), "of moderate length, straightforward in character, admirably suited to the instrument, and not difficult" [183] (a comment that more or less fits all of Stanford's sonatas seen here).

In a longish, ruminative article for *Cobbett's Cyclopedic Survey of Chamber Music,* T. F. Dunhill emphasizes that Stanford was a pioneer in the "revival" of English chamber music, furthered chiefly by his own students—including Vaughan Williams, Frank Bridge, Rutland Boughton, John Ireland, and Herbert Howells (as well as Dunhill himself).[184] But Dunhill concludes that Stanford in his devotion to this branch of music clung too uncompromisingly to German tradition, especially the precedent of Brahms (as might be expected of Kiel's student), and approached the composition of it almost too reverently and circumspectly to achieve the originality, sparkle, and human warmth such as have made his songs more popular. And hoping (evidently in vain) that the best of Stanford's chamber music might not drown with the weakest—"as has happened in the case of other prolific composers like Raff, or Jensen, or even Saint-Saëns"—Dunhill singled out Stanford's piano Quintet in d, the piano Trio in E♭, the cello Sonata in d (Op. 39), and the middle movement of the clarinet Sonata in F (Op. 129) as most deserving of continued or renewed attention. Others have concluded that Stanford was at his best, anyway, in shorter forms and in the more local writing techniques, and that "the vision becomes clouded" in the larger works.[185]

Here we may take Op. 129 as thoroughly representative of Stanford's published duo sonatas and as his sonata most likely to survive, if only because of its need in the relatively limited literature of both the clarinet and the viola. In this work the stamp of Brahms's two clarinet

182. MT XXV (1884) 147 (with mention of another performance 12 days later); much of the review is quoted in Shedlock/SONATA 233–34. Cf. also, Fuller-Maitland/PARRY 24.

183. MT LVIII (1917) 549.

184. Cobbett/CHAMBER II 451–54 (with an addition by W. W. Cobbett). The substance of this article is repeated in Greene/STANFORD 224–30.

185. Cf. GROVE VIII 46.

Ex. 91. The retransition to the recapitulation in the first movement of Charles Villiers Stanford's Sonata in F, Op. 129 (after the original ed. of 1918, by kind permission of Stainer & Bell, Ltd., copyright holders).

sonatas stands clear from the start, whether in the 3ds and 6ths of the precise texture, the grouping and nature of the rhythmic incises, the arpeggiated writing for both instruments, or the chordally oriented ideas themselves. But Stanford's highly skillful writing is sparer than Brahms's (Ex. 91), sometimes almost antiseptically spare. It also poses fewer technical demands on the performer, while still presupposing an advanced command of each instrument. The closely interrelated themes in the three movements of Op. 129 (F-S-F) are well-conceived as kernels for sonata treatment, but not especially attractive or warm in their own right. The one conspicuous exception, as might be expected from the composer of the successful "Irish Rhapsodies" for orchestra, is the tender Irish lament called "Caoine," which enters at the turn to major in the middle movement in d, marked "Adagio (quasi fantasia)."

In 1898 England's most celebrated Romantic composer, **Edward (William) Elgar** (1857–1934), wrote his Novello agent August Jaeger that "you are wrong in thinking I don't like some 'forms' of music—anything 'genuine' and natural pleases me—the stuff I hate and which I know is ruining any chance for good music in England is stuff like Stanford's which is neither fish, flesh, fowl, nor good red-herring!" [186]

186. ELGAR-Nimrod 30–31.

Elgar's relations with Stanford did improve a little from time to time.[187] But there were frictions between Parry, Stanford, and Elgar, as within the similarly close trio of near contemporaries in France—Franck, Saint-Saëns, and Fauré (ssb XIII)—and, to quote Percy Young, "Considering their respective temperaments it is surprising that Elgar and Stanford did not collide more often." [188] At any rate, although he was similarly productive in all main branches of music, Elgar paid less attention to the sonata than either Parry or Stanford, and wrote only two significant examples, one for organ and one for P & Vn.[189] A so-called organ "Sonata No. 2," Op. 87a (pub. in 1933), is Ivor Atkins' arrangement of Elgar's *Severn Suite for Brass Band,* completed in 1930.[190] A "Sonatina, Op. 1 [!]," composed for his niece May Grafton and published by Keith Prowse in 1931 (not 1932), proves to be a purely pedagogic piece of seven pages in two movements (M-F), too elementary to be pertinent here. The MS of an early violin sonata, Op. 9, was destroyed by the composer himself.[191]

Elgar wrote his Sonata in G for organ, Op. 28, mostly in June of 1895 during a hectic year of composition, rehearsals, and performances.[192] It was performed first on July 8 by Hugh Blair at the Worcester Cathedral for a congress of American organists; then published by Breitkopf & Härtel in the following year, with a dedication to Swinnerton Heap (*supra*). Elgar described Op. 28 as a "big" work.[193] It meets that description in the sense of four movements occupying thirty-three pages but not in greatness, for it is no more than a highly competent, routine work. Its movements (F-F-M-VF) fall into standardized though asymmetrical designs, "sonata form" in the outer and A-B-A in the inner movements. Although the texture is frequently contrapuntal, there is no preludial, fugal, or chorale movement and no titles that might suggest the frequent association of the organ sonata with the church. There is considerable chromaticism, but mostly in melodic passing tones supported by diatonic, conventional harmony. The ideas themselves are not distinguished and suffer from pedestrian rhythms in the phrases.

Elgar's Sonata in e, Op. 82, for Vn & P, was composed during a

187. Cf. ELGAR-Nimrod 10, 31, 76, 111, 197, 212; Young/ELGAR 119–20, 92–94, 126; Greene/STANFORD 149–59.

188. ELGAR-Nimrod 289.

189. The chief recent studies of the man and his music are Reed/ELGAR, Young/ELGAR, and McVeagh/ELGAR. Additional facts on the sons. may be gleaned from the letters in ELGAR-Nimrod and Elgar/LETTERS.

190. Young/ELGAR 415.

191. Cf. MT LX (1919) 162; Young/ELGAR 405.

192. Cf. Young/ELGAR 73, 406.

193. ELGAR-Nimrod 5.

burst of three master chamber works in 1918 that included the string Quartet in e, Op. 83, and the piano Quintet in a, Op. 84. Begun while the composer was convalescing from a minor operation in March, it was completed in September, the background of those six months being a delightful stay in the country, far from the continuing rages of World War I.[194] It was dedicated to an old friend, Mrs. Marie Joshua, whose death four days before its completion explains the turn to a gentle, retrospective, almost elegiac section, marked "molto più lento," on the second last page.[195] Publication by Novello followed in 1919, with the first of two early, warmly welcomed performances occurring on March 21.[196] Among further performances of Op. 82 during Elgar's lifetime were those by Thibaud and Cortot in 1922 and one in which the enterprising English pianist Harriet Cohen participated in 1933.[197] The work is in three movements (F-M-F) of moderate length, comprising asymmetrical "sonata forms" in the outer movements again, and an A-B-A design in the middle "Romance."[198] The first movement is direct and moderately intense as well as compelling (Ex. 92). The second seems curiously un-Elgarian in its A section, if one has in mind the Elgar of the violin Concerto in b, *The Dream of Gerontius,* the ever-popular "Pomp and Circumstance" March in D, or even the greater intimacies of the "Enigma Variations." This section is at once gossamer in its texture, mysterious in a flippant way, and quasi-Spanish in the vamp that supplies bits of its accompaniment. Perhaps here was the "wood magic" that his wife reported to be coming from Elgar's room during that summer of 1918.[199] As with the organ sonata, the finale is the most original and convincing movement. But this whole sonata is more alive and appealing than the organ sonata. The violin rather than the keyboard was Elgar's own main instrument. Although the keyboard writing is anything but resourceful in either work and the harmony is only a little more enterprising in the later one, the violin seems to have stimulated the bolder, more potent ideas and the more effective idiomatic passagework that help to make this work go. The short time span of but one generation has canceled H. C. Colles's

194. Circumstances of the composition are related in Reed/ELGAR 121–22, Young/ELGAR 192, and Elgar/LETTERS 245–46.

195. Young/ELGAR 192.

196. Cf. MT LX (1919) 71, 179, 245; Reed/ELGAR 127 (W. H. Reed himself being the violinist); Young/ELGAR 198.

197. Elgar/LETTERS 277 and 312.

198. Op. 82 is described briefly in MT LX (1919) 163–64 (with 5 exx.); Cobbett/CHAMBER I 373–74 (W. H. Reed; with 8 exx.) and 377 (W. W. Cobbett); Reed/ELGAR 125 and 148–49; McVeagh/ELGAR 179–80; Young/ELGAR 349–50; Shand/VIOLIN 203–6 (with 7 exx.).

199. Young/ELGAR 192.

Ex. 92. From the opening of Edward Elgar's Sonata in e, Op. 82 (after the original ed. of 1919, by kind permission of H. W. Gray, U.S. agents for Novello & Co. in London).

remark that "in England at any rate all his [Elgar's] major works are regularly given." [200] But if there is to be a revival of Elgar's best works, Op. 82 deserves at least a chance to be tried.

Among numerous minor contemporaries of Parry, Stanford, and Elgar, **Algernon (Bennett Langton) Ashton** (1859–1937) trained under Moscheles, Reinecke, and Raff, among other Germans, and wrote music in most of the main categories.[201] After his return to England as a young man, some 160 of his many more works achieved publication, although most that did so appeared and won favor in Leipzig rather than London. These include 9 sonatas published between 1881 and 1899 (following MS duo sons. that date back to at least 1876 [202]), 4 being for P & Vn, 4 for P & Vc, and one for P & Va. Ashton's publications also include 7 of 24 sonatas for P solo that he wrote in all major and minor keys, these 7 being published between 1899 and 1925.[203] Ashton's published sonatas were generally praised for their skill, ideas, and serious purpose, although the later reviews hint at prolixity and less con-

200. GROVE 4th ed. Suppl. 196.
201. Cf. GROVE I 240–41 (F. G. Edwards); MGG I 749–50 (G. Abraham).
202. Cf. NZM LXXII/2 (1876) 475.
203. Cf. Altmann/KAMMERMUSIK 192, 245, 251. Most of the duo and all of the solo sons. are at the Library of Congress.

sequential ideas.[204] The early and late samples examined here show no pronounced changes of style.[205] They follow standard designs and plans, and adhere to traditional harmony. And they abound and excel in continuous figural writing fluent enough to be almost glib, were it not for the pointed harmony and sonorous use of the keyboard. In a somewhat flat, less imaginative manner the solo sonatas bring to mind the frequently continuous figural writing, the keyboard scoring, and the chromatic harmony of Medtner and Rachmaninoff. Ashton is at his weakest when he must stop the figural writing long enough to commit himself to a tangible idea.

A composer of exceptional craftsmanship, polish, and sensitivity was **Benjamin (James) Dale** (1885–1943), who stemmed from German training only indirectly through Frederick Corder, a pupil of F. Hiller, at the Royal Academy of Music in London.[206] Corder once claimed "that Dale had then written 'fewer and better works than any English composer of his generation' "; and Edwin Evans wrote in 1929 that Dale's first and best known publication, his Sonata in d for P solo, was "still regarded as one of the outstanding works of the English neo-romantics." [207] This publication was still a student work, composed in his late teens (1902–5), dedicated to York Bowen (*infra*) and first played by him in 1905, and published by both Charles Avison in London and Breitkopf & Härtel in Leipzig in 1906, as Op. 1.[208] Dale's only other sonata was Op. 11 in E, for P & Vn, composed in 1921–22 and first performed in 1922 after his partial recuperation from four years of war internment in Germany, then published by Augener in 1923.[209] The two sonatas follow the same unusual plan of an extended "sonata form" followed by an even more extended set of variations in which

---

204. E.g., cf. MT XXX (1889) 616 (on Op. 38 in E, for P & Vn; also praised in Cobbett/CHAMBER I 27 [A. Mann] as against Op. 86 in c; described, with 7 exx., in Shand/VIOLIN 206–9); MT XXXIV (1893) 613 (on Op. 75 in G, for P & Vc); SMW LIV (1896) 290 (on Op. 86 in c, for P & Vn); MW XXXII (1901) 612 (on Opp. 115 in a and 128 in B♭, for P & Vc); MW XXXII (1901) 165 and DM III/1 (1903–4) 439 (both on Op. 101 in e♭, for P solo). Cf., also, MT XXVII (1885) 33 (performance of Op. 3 D, for P & Vn).

205. W. W. Harrison describes and illustrates 2 Vn sons. in STRAD XXVII (1916–17) 135–36 (Op. 86) and 163–65 (Op. 99), and 3 Vc sons. in STRAD XXVIII (1917–18) 125–27 (Op. 75), 151–52 (Op. 115), and 181–82 (Op. 128).

206. Cf. GROVE II 578–80 (E. Evans, H. C. Colles, and W. H. Stock); MGG II 1871–73 (H. F. Redlich).

207. GROVE II 579; Cobbett/CHAMBER I 310; cf., also, MGG II 1872.

208. Cf. MT LIX (1918) 164 on the problem of getting such a big work published. No English review of either the first performance or first ed. has turned up here.

209. In MT LXV (1923) 480, Op. 11 is reviewed as charming, solid, and free of shock, but unbalanced by its overly imposing set of variations.

are embodied among other variations a slow movement, a scherzo, and a finale.[210] Whereas Dale's huge Op. 1 (totalling 1,246, or 317+929, mss. in 62 pp., and lasting nearly an hour) discloses all the exuberance and energy, plus even some of the splash, of youth, his somewhat shorter Op. 11 tends to be more refined and emotionally controlled. Yet Op. 11, with its parallel 5ths and chord strands, does not lag harmonically behind at least the less daring trends in the early 1920's. By contrast, as Corder wrote in 1918 (while revealing his own tastes), Dale's Op. 1 still manifested "not the faintest tendency to extravagance, or what is called modernism—that foolish and offensive employment of discords as concords which the younger French writers affect." [211]

But Op. 1 was not really conservative, either, for its day. Both its harmony and its unusual and flexible form were new enough to puzzle a main German reviewer.[212] In its less sentimental, obvious passages Op. 1 leaves not so much the impression of Reger (ssb XI) that H. F. Redlich finds in Dale's music[213] as of the similarly precocious Richard Strauss (ssb XI), especially in its near surfeit of continuous, bold, upward thrusts, appoggiaturas, anticipations, and passing tones (Ex. 93). There are also passages, such as the sequential crescendo in measures 85–96 of the first movement, that leave the impression of Liszt and add interest to Norman Demuth's ranking of Dale's Op. 1 on a par with Liszt's Sonata in b "for resource and design." [214] Dale's precocious chef-d'oeuvre does rank high in the late Romantic sonata and could be revived successfully by a capable pianist playing for an audience sympathetic to that period and genre. Its sustained drive during the passagework is generally convincing and exciting. Its piano writing is rich and balanced in sound, often polyphonically active, remarkably varied, decidedly idiomatic, and, though nearly as difficult as Liszt's, similarly practical to play. Its two out-and-out melodies, the second theme of the first movement and the theme of the variations, are well drawn and well drawn out. And its forms, even on such a large scale, already show a developed sense of broad organization and creative flexibility, including the asymmetrical "sonata form" and the seven-variations-and-finale, headed "Slow Movement [vars. I–IV], Scherzo [V–VII] and Finale."

210. Op. 1 was analyzed authoritatively by Corder, with frequent superlatives injected, in MT LIX (1918) 164–67 (including 14 exx.), immediately after Dale's despondent return from internment. Op. 11 is described, with 2 exx., in Cobbett/CHAMBER I 312–13 (E. Evans).

211. MT LIX (1918) 165.

212. DM VI/4 (1906–7) 306 (A. Leitzmann).

213. MGG II 1872.

214. Demuth/TRENDS 121–22.

Ex. 93. From the first bridge in Benjamin J. Dale's Sonata in
d, Op. 1 (after the original Charles Avison ed. of 1906).

Already forgotten from late-Romantic England are three early duo
sonatas in MS and a "promising," published, four-movement Sonata in
g, for P solo (1886?), by the esteemed writer on the sonata and other
music, **William Henry Hadow** (1859–1937);[215] the two published,
Mendelssohnian sonatas, for Fl & P (1883) and P solo (Op. 45 in e;
1886), by the successful, German-trained pianist **John Francis Barnett**
(1837–1916);[216] and five early, more-or-less Brahmsian sonatas of little
musical significance, by "the most remarkable and original woman
composer in the history of music," [217] that redoubtable and, at her
best, more than competent **Ethel (Mary) Smyth** (1858–1944).[218] These

215. Cf. MGG V 1219–23 (R. A. Harman); MMR XV (1885) 233 (favorable review of
Son. in g♯). The MS duos, cited in GROVE IV 10 and BAKER II 636, seem now to be
lost.
216. Cf. MMR XVI (1886) 88 (review of Op. 45 as "melodious and elegant");
GROVE I 442–43 (E. F. Rimbault); Cobbett/CHAMBER I 59 (W. W. Cobbett). The
autograph of an unpub. 4-mvt. Son. in c (VF-Va-Mi-F), for P solo (ca. 1820), by
Barnett's father John (1802–90) is in the Boston Public Library (according to Mr.
N. K. Moran of the Rare Book Dept.).
217. In the words of George Henschel, as quoted in St. John/SMYTH 43. A similar
evaluation is made by Ernest Newman in his "Introduction," p. xi, to SMYTH MEMOIRS.
218. Cf. SMYTH MEMOIRS; St John/SMYTH (with a full list of works, pp. 305–8, and
a "critical study" of the music, by K. Dale, pp. 288–304).

last include two sonatas and most of a third for P solo, all generally
unpianistic student works left in MSS dated 1877;[219] and two duos in
a, both published by Peters in Leipzig in 1887, one each for P & Vc
(Op. 5; first performed in London in 1926 [220]) and P & Vn (Op. 7). Op.
7 was reviewed by the same Eduard Bernsdorf who railed for so long
against Grieg (ssb XV), as "corrupt and tasteless to a shocking degree
scarcely believable from a woman";[221] and it was rejected by Joachim
for his own performances as "unnatural, farfetched, overwrought, and
not good as to sound." [222]

A London pianist of Spanish descent, **Emanuel Abraham Aguilar**
(1824–1904) left among "much chamber music" three sonatas for P
solo, of which one, in C, was published and two, in a and e, were
played by him in 1888, bringing such noncommittal reactions as
"meritorious" and "not of the most advanced school." [223] The Italian-
born pianist **Carlo Albanesi** (1856–1920), a student of his father Luigi
before he prospered in London (from 1882), left six sonatas for P solo.
The five of these that were published (1894–1913) reveal undistinguished, sometimes trite themes, extended and developed with the
typically professional know-how of the epigone, supported by traditional, chromatic harmony, spiced with added dissonances, weighted
with full textures, and enhanced by varied, idiomatic uses of the keyboard.[224] Even the venerated, self-taught theorist, writer, and pedagogue
Ebenezer Prout (1835–1909) had a try at composing sonatas, among
other chamber works, his three published examples being Op. 4 for
organ (ca. 1875), Op. 17 in A, for Fl & P (1882), and Op. 26 in D, for
Cl-or-Va & P (1890). These were politely damned with the usual
theorist's curse of much skill and little imagination.[225] On the other
hand, the organist **William Henry Speer** (1863–1937), a pupil of Stanford and others (and a cousin of C. T. Speer, *supra*), won praise for the
content but not the form of two Brahmsian sonatas in D, both pub-

---

219. The delectable smyth memoirs 192, 195, 197–98, 205 describe and partly disparage these 3 sons.; cf., also, Dale/smyth 332–35 (with an ex. from the rondo finale
of the first son., in C).
220. grove VII 860 (K. Dale).
221. smw XLV (1887) 1030.
222. Joachim's letter is trans. in full in smyth memoirs 407. Cf. this same source,
pp. 396, 398–99; also, St John/smyth 54–55, 183 (a more favorable reaction in 1923),
292 (K. Dale's evaluation); Cobbett/chamber II 433–34 (a description of Op. 7 by
K. Eggar).
223. mt XXIX (1888) 356. Cf. baker 12; pazdírek I 95.
224. Cf. grove I 87 (E. Blom); mt XXXV (1894) 689 (S. Lucas in a review of Son.
1 in Ab) and L (1909) 792 (review of Son. 5 in E).
225. Cf. Cobbett/chamber II 244–45 (A. Mann and W. W. Cobbett); mmr XX
(1890) 113–14 (on Op. 26); grove VI 951 (W. H. Hadow); mgg X 1661–62 (R. A.
Harman).

lished by Breitkopf & Härtel in 1893 (Opp. 2 for P solo and 4 for P & Vn).[226]

The gifted but short-lived pianist **William (Yeates) Hurlstone** (1876–1906), a pupil of Stanford and Ashton, left three duo sonatas that were published, two of them posthumously in 1909. The first of these, for P & Vn in d (1897), is described as "technically interesting if not characteristic," the second, for P & Vc in D, as "a fine work," and the third, exceptionally for Bn & P, as outstanding in scoring, originality of treatment, and melodic appeal.[227] An erstwhile businessman (though no Charles Ives!), **Ernest Austin** (1874–1947) indulged his primary musical inclinations by composing "14 sonatinas on English folksongs for children" (pub. *ca.* 1910–30) but also left a "Lyric Sonata" for P & Vn in D, Op. 70 (pub. in 1925) and at least two sonatas for P solo, of which the second, Op. 31 in b♭ (pub. in 1907), runs on anemically, like casual dinner music, with its chief harmonic "surprise" being an occasional reference to the major triad on the lowered submediant degree.[228] The fine pianist **Oscar Beringer** (1844–1922), born and trained in Germany, also left piano sonatinas of interest to children, of which at least six appeared in full or in part in 1903, including two with programmatic title ("pastorale" and "marziale").[229]

The London violinist **Arthur Hinton** (1869–1941) probably was studying with Rheinberger in Munich before he wrote the earliest of several chamber works and his only sonata, in B♭ for P & Vn, first published by Breitkopf & Härtel in 1893 (not 1903). This is a lyrical, fluent, well-scored work in three free movements (F-M-VF) that employ traditional harmony and recall Rheinberger's deliberate treatment of single ideas (ssb X), but sacrifice broad tonal organization to a process of almost constant chromatic modulation.[230] Another violinist, the Italian-born **Alberto Randegger, Jr.** (1880–1918), introduced his own "well-written, effective," virtuosic Sonata in e, Op. 15, for Vn & P, published by Novello in 1903.[231]

---

226. MT XXXIV (1893) 361 and 426; Cobbett/CHAMBER II 445. Cf. GROVE VIII 3–4 (G. S. K. Butterworth).

227. Cobbett/CHAMBER I 583–85 (R. H. Walthew) and II 454. Cf. GROVE IV 417 (W. W. Cobbett), with faulty list of works (including a "Sonata" for Cl & P that is actually a Suite); MGG VI 977–78 (R. Nettel); Altmann/KAMMERMUSIK 209, 258, 283.

228. Cf. BAKER 59–60.

229. Favorable reviews of the latter 2 are found in MW XXXV (1904) 660 (M. Puttmann) and DM III/4 (1903–4) 392 (R. Kursch). Cf., also, PAZDÍREK II 562–63; GROVE I 643–44 (W. B. Squire). For an extraordinary son. recital played by Beringer in 1881 cf. SSB III.

230. Cf. MT XXXIV (1893) 426 (with praise except for the modulations); Cobbett/CHAMBER I 562 (H. W. Richards); GROVE IV 292 (J. A. Fuller-Maitland).

231. MT XLIV (1903) 802; Cobbett/CHAMBER II 268 (W. W. Cobbett); BAKER 1306.

598   ROMANTIC COMPOSERS AND THEIR SONATAS

Called "perhaps the most grievously neglected British composer of
his generation," [232] the pianist, theorist, and pedagogue **John Black-
wood McEwen** (1868–1948) trained first in his homeland of Scotland
and then under Corder, Prout, and others after moving to London. Six
of his sonatas, for P & Vn(-or Va in No. 2 in f), were published by
Oxford between 1913 and 1929, and two, for P solo in e and a, in 1903
and 1918.[233] The violin sonatas disclose notable originality and variety
in their styles, individual forms, and cyclic plans.[234] Thus, No. 2,
which seems to have been the most successful, constitutes a single movement divided into three sections (M-In/S-VF), the last being barred
according to rhythmic units rather than metric groupings. No. 4 is
called "A Little Sonata" with reference mainly to the lightness of its
content rather than shortness or technical ease. No. 5 is a still freer
work, in two movements. The first piano sonata is a large-scale, highly
charged, profusely edited work of four movements (F-S-VF[Sc]-S/VF)
filling 41 pages,[235] in the general class of its contemporaries in e and d
by d'Indy (ssв XIII) and Dale (*supra*). The ideas are a little less worthy
in themselves and the extensive use of both bare and filled-in octaves
in the thematically interrelated, outer movements makes somewhat
heavy-handed piano writing. But the rich, often subtle harmony, the
imaginative rhythmic treatment, and the over-all sense of form raise
this sonata well above many like-purposed works of the late-Romantic
era. Thus, the one Sonata for P solo, Op. 72 in f (pub. in 1923), by
the brilliant pianist (**Edwin**) **York Bowen** (1884–1961)[236] is a similarly large-scaled work, in three movements (M/F-M-VF), but by
contrast it seems bombastic, free with a vengeance in its tempo changes,
self-conscious in its rhythmic diversity, over-edited, even more heavy-
handed, and more epigonic in its sentimentality and in its pseudo-
Modern dissonances forced onto more conventional harmony. Another
pupil of Corder, Bowen also left at least four published duo sonatas
with more or less of the same traits, including two for P & Va, Opp.
18 in c[237] and 22 in F (1907 and 1912), one for P & Vc, Op. 64 in
A (1923), and one for P & Vn, Op. 112 in e (1946).[238]

232. GROVE V 466–68 (E. Blom).
233. Cf. MGG VIII 1383–85 (J. M. Allan).
234. Sons. 2, 4, and 5 are described in Cobbett/CHAMBER II 107–8 (S. Dyke and
W. W. Cobbett).
235. It is praised highly and described in some detail in MT XLVI (1905) 31–32.
236. Cf. GROVE I 856 (G. S. K. Butterworth).
237. A favorable review appears in MT XLVI (1905) 403, following the first performance of Op. 18 by Lionel Tertis.
238. All but Op. 112 are listed in Altmann/KAMMERMUSIK 246 and 253, and described briefly in Cobbett/CHAMBER I 157 (T. F. Dunhill).

The pianist and prolific composer of opera, orchestra, and chamber music **Josef Holbrooke** (1878–1958) left four published duo sonatas, three for Vn & P (Op. 6, "Sonatina," 1907; Op. 59 in F, 1918; Op. 83, "Oriental," 1926) and one for Vc & P (Op. 19 in g, "Fantasic-Sonate," 1914).[239] In Op. 83 the piano serves more as an accompaniment than a duo participant. In Op. 19 the "Fantasie" pertains to a chain of sections (VF-S-VF) rather than complete movements. The conventional harmony, rather thick texture, and unprepossessing themes in Holbrooke's sonatas do not account for the considerable interest other music by him has aroused from time to time.

The pianist and author on chamber music **Thomas Frederick Dunhill** (1877–1946) himself left two published sonatas for P & Vn, Opp. 27 in d (1911) and 50 in F (1920). These are described as the freest and most intimate of a group of chamber works that is notable for "melodic invention, felicity in statement, and logic in design," and for being "as companionable, healthy, and English as the South Downs on a sunny day." [240] At least five published sonatas—Opp. 4 in F, for P & Vc (1910), 16 in Bb, for P & Cl-or-Vn-or-Va (1912), 29 in C, for Vn alone ("eroica," 1913), and 30 in D for Vc alone (1914), as well as a Sonata for 2 cellos alone (1913)—may also be credited to the important writer, pianist, and teacher **Donald Francis Tovey** (1875–1940). These constitute about a fourth of a chamber music output understandably distinguished by high skill and intellectual grasp right from Op. 1, clear orientation toward the great German masters, some affinities with Reger's chamber music, and tangible individuality of its own.[241] And four published duo sonatas, including two for P & Vn (Opp. 8 in a, 1898, and 44 in Eb, 1930), and one each for P & Va (Op. 29 in C, 1912) and P & Vc (Op. 41 in f, 1928), may be credited to the esteemed music historian **Ernest Walker** (1870–1949).[242] These, too, are German oriented, skillful, and musical, though freer and more impetuous and less intellectual than Tovey's sonatas. Moreover, in Op. 41 the essentially traditional harmony is extended to some remote, chromatic relationships suggesting Reger again.

Brief mentions may be added of published organ sonatas by some

239. Cf. GROVE IV 320–21 (H. C. Colles); MGG VI 613–15 (A. J. B. Hutchings); Altmann/KAMMERMUSIK 208, 258; Cobbett/CHAMBER I 565–66 (R. W. Walthew).

240. Cobbett/CHAMBER I 345–47 (M. M. Scott), with further details on the sons. Cf. GROVE II 804–5 (G. S. K. Butterworth and H. C. Colles).

241. Cobbett/CHAMBER II 515–16 (E. Walker). Cf. GROVE VIII 524–25 (H. C. Colles); MGG XIII 598–600 (H. F. Redlich).

242. Cf. GROVE IX 141–43 (I. Keys); Cobbett/CHAMBER II 565 (H. C. Colles).

of the many once recognized organists active in late-Romantic England,[243] including **Edward Henry Thorne** (1834–1916; Son. in f,
1912),[244] **William Thomas Best** (1826–97; Sons. in G, 1862, and d,
1887),[245] **Bertram Luard Selby** (or **Luard-Selby;** 1853–1918; Son. in
D, 1881; "Fantasia Sonata" on "Dies Irae," 1891; Son. 3, 1913; as
well as Op. 21 in b, for P & Vn, 1885),[246] **William Joseph Westbrook**
(1831–94; 2 sons., 1882 and *ca.* 1895),[247] **Charles Harford Lloyd**
(1849–1919; Son. in d, 1886),[248] **Alan Gray** (1855–1935; 4 superior
sons., 1890, as well as a Son. for P & Vn, 1900),[249] **John Ebenezer West**
(1863–1929; E. Prout's nephew and pupil; 3 sons.: "Allegro maestoso,"
"Allegro pomposo," "Andante religioso"),[250] **Percy Carter Buck** (1871–
1947; Opp. 3 in E♭, 1897, 9 in D, 1902, and 12 in B♭, 1905, as well
as Op. 21 for P & Vn),[251] **Albert Lister Peace** (1844–1912; 3 "Sonate
da camera" for organ, 1891–97 [?]),[252] **William Wolstenholme** (1865–
1931; Son. in F, 1901, and Son. in D "in the Style of Handel," 1904,
as well as Son. in G for P & Vn, 1903),[253] and one **Bernard Ramsey**
(1873–?; Nos. 1 in d, 2 in b, 1906?).[254]

   In Ireland almost no attention was paid to the sonata for nearly a
century after Philip Cogan's last publications around 1805 (sce 770–
71).[255] The ill-fated Union established in 1800 hardly favored such an

   243. Cf. Frotscher/ORGELSPIEL II 1230–33.
   244. A favorable review appears in MT LIII (1912) 455. Two performances of a Son.
in F, for P & Vn, in MS, are reported in MT XVII (1875) 22 and 82. Cf. GROVE VIII
435 (W. B. Squire).
   245. The year 1862 comes from Temperley/CORRESPONDENCE. A strongly favorable
review of Son. in d and a separate printing of its "Romanza" mvt. in D appear in
MMR XVIII (1887) 16 and 227–30. Cf., also, MT XV (1871) 158; GROVE I 695–97 (W. H.
Hadow & H. C. Colles).
   246. Cf. MT XXII (1881) 592 and XXXIII (1891) 45 (favorable review of the 2d
son.); Altmann/KAMMERMUSIK 227; GROVE V 412–13 (J. A. Fuller-Maitland); Kremer/
ORGAN 222.
   247. Cf. MT XXIII (1882) 423; GROVE IX 268 (G. Grove); Kremer/ORGAN 230.
   248. Cf. MT XXVII (1886) 172, 438; GROVE V 347 (J. A. Fuller-Maitland & H. C.
Colles); MGG VIII 1065–66 (S. Sadie).
   249. Cf. MT XXXI (1890) 613 (mostly favorable review); GROVE III 765 (J. A. Fuller-
Maitland); MGG V 727 (N. Fortune).
   250. Cf. MT XXXVI (1895) 675–76 (Son. 1 approved "for recitals or church voluntaries"); GROVE IX 268 (H. C. Colles).
   251. Favorably reviewed, respectively, in MW XLIII (1802) 538 and XLVI (1905)
401. Cf. GROVE I 993 (H. C. Colles).
   252. Cf. MW XXIX (1898) 43 (unfavorable review of No. 2); GROVE VI 602 (J.
Hullah); Kremer/ORGAN 212.
   253. Cf. MT LXXII (1931) 799 (praise for Son. in F by F. H. Wood); Kremer/ORGAN
232; GROVE IX 352 (H. Grace), with reference to 2 worthy unpub. sons., for organ
and for P solo.
   254. Cf. MW XXXVII (1906) 43 and XXXVIII (1907) 1047 (high praise for No. 2);
Kremer/ORGAN 215.
   255. Warm thanks are owing here for information by correspondence from Pro-

interest, there being no more significant contributor than the German-born inventor of the piano-training device known as the "Chiroplast," **Johann Bernhard Logier** (1777–1846) in Dublin, who left several light, unaccompanied, solo, and four-hand piano sonatas in salon style, in the decade from about 1815 to 1825.[256] Efforts to explore the sonata in later-19th-century Dublin might start with the two examples for organ, both in d, and the Sonatina for P solo, by the English-born organist **James C. Culwick** (1845–1907);[257] and the sonatas for P & Vn (1904, 1907, 1913) as well as the prizewinning Sonata in D, Op. 43, for P & Vc (1900?) by the Italian-born pianist **Michele Esposito** (1855–1929).[258]

---

fessors Aloys Fleischmann of the Music Dept. at University College in Cork and Brian Boydell at the University of Dublin. Cf., also, Hogan/ANGLO-IRISH 145–55.

256. Cf. MGG VIII 1121–24 (G. Pugner); HOFMEISTER 1828 (Whistling), 460, 493, 542, 595.

257. Cf. BAKER 337; PAZDÍREK III 639; MMR XII (1882) 184 (negative review of the Sonatina).

258. Cf. MW XXXIII (1901) 12–13 (rather negative review of Op. 43); Altmann/ KAMMERMUSIK 202 and 255; GROVE II 973 (L. M. L. Dix); MGG III 1537–38 (C. Jachino).

Chapter XV

Scandinavia, from Kuhlau to Nielsen

Relationships Musical and Political

This chapter on the sonata in Scandinavia follows that on the sonata in Great Britain not only because the two regions share geographically in lying to the north of the sonata's other main regions. They also enjoyed considerable artistic interchange throughout the Romantic Era. And especially in their instrumental music they revealed a common heritage from predominantly German training and influences. Two of the main countries of Scandinavia enjoyed good enough political relationships with England, too—Sweden, the conspicuous neutral, and Norway, her longtime recalcitrant dependency. The same can be said for Russia's autonomous little neighbor Finland. Finland is assigned her occasional classification as Scandinavian here both because of her extensive derivations from Swedish culture and because her one composer of appreciable consequence to the Romantic sonata, Sibelius, had some artistic ties with Norway through his affinity to Grieg, not to mention some of that German (and Austrian) training and some good rapport with the British musical world. The same cannot be said for the political relations between Denmark, the other main Scandinavian country, and England. Whereas Sweden had sided with England at the heart of the opposition to Napoleon's vast, terrifying conquests, Denmark had actually lent support to the Napoleonic forces, thus both answering and causing some aggressive acts by the British during the earlier 19th century.

As in France and England, the sonata in the Scandinavian countries enjoyed some cultivation early in the 19th century, still influenced largely by Classic trends (scE 790–800), but it hardly came into its own until later in the century. Then a third triumvirate may be pointed to as roughly paralleling that of Franck, Saint-Saëns, and Fauré in France and that of Parry, Stanford, and Elgar in England (ssB XIII and XIV). This consisted of Hartmann, Gade, and Grieg.

Although there were decided ups and downs in the political relationships even between the Scandinavian countries themselves, there was no corresponding loss of sympathy or collaboration in the friendly three-way relationships between these two Danes and one Norwegian who did most to advance the cause of Scandinavian music per se. A succeeding Scandinavian triumvirate, from our viewpoint, consisted of Nielsen, Sjögren, and Sibelius, roughly concurrent with d'Indy and Dukas in France, and Dale and McEwen in England at the era's end.

Early 19th-Century Composers in Scandinavian Centers (Kuhlau)

The first composer to be met in this chapter was a Danish citizen who had been born and trained in Germany. The pianist and flutist **Friedrich Daniel Rudolph Kuhlau** (1786–1832) studied in Hamburg with a pupil of Emanuel Bach before establishing himself in Copenhagen in 1811.[1] He became an ardent champion of Beethoven, whom he met in Vienna in 1825 during a merry evening of inebriation and punnic canons.[2] Although Kuhlau made his chief contribution historically as a cofounder of national Danish opera (with his compatriot **Christoph Ernst Friedrich Weyse** [1774–1842], who also left at least 5 pub. sons., in the 1820's, for P solo and for 2 Bns [3]), he is remembered by today's performers, when he is remembered at all, for certain of his numerous sonatas and sonatinas, of which there is a total of at least 55.[4] First published in the 18 years from 1810 to 1828,[5] these last divide into 12 sonatas (mostly "grandes") and 19 sonatinas (or "sonates faciles") for P solo, 7 sonatinas for P-duet, 6 sonatas for P & Fl (not including the "Solos" Op. 57 or the "Duos" Op. 110), and 6 sonatas and 5 sonatinas for P & Vn (not including the Fl sons. that were pub. also for P & Vn).

Kuhlau's sonatinas for P solo and P-duet and a few of his flute sonatas are the ones that still survive. The latter account for his somewhat extravagant, posthumous sobriquet, "The Beethoven of the

---

1. Cf. Schilling/LEXICON IV 252–54; GROVE IV 866 (J. Hullah); MGG VII 1874–78 (R. Seitz), with full list of works and further references.

2. Cf. Thayer & Forbes/BEETHOVEN II 958–59, 971.

3. Cf. MGG XIV 543–45 (S. Lunn), but with no mention of the sons.; GROVE IX 272 (J. Horton); HOFMEISTER 1828 (Whistling), 606; Cat. NYPL XXXIII 315; AMZ II (1799–1800) 151 (indicating that P sons. 1 and 2 [described as "very fine," especially the "brilliant" No. 1 in E] had already appeared in 1799 in a mixed collection of Weyse's songs and piano pieces).

4. Further, not wholly reconciled lists may be found in HOFMEISTER 1828 (Whistling), *passim;* PAZDÍREK VIII 487–93.

5. Based on Intelligenz-Blatt entries in AMZ XII–XXX.

Flute," [6] and put him on a par with Reicha, his contemporary (SCE 564–65). His violin and flute parts, when not marked "ad libitum," share equally with the piano parts in genuine duets. His full-scale sonatas differ from his sonatinas not only in being more advanced in their instrumental techniques, longer, larger in number of move- ments (mostly 3 or 4 rather than 2 or 3), more sustained and devel- oped in their ideas, fuller in texture, and more serious in import, but also in a sense distinguished earlier (SSB III)—that is, in keeping abreast of current styles rather than exuding the atmosphere of the piano studio by what was already a neo-Classic return to the outstand- ing sonatinas of Clementi (SCE 751). For example, the sonatas gener- ally employ newer, more active textures than those of the "singing- allegro" style with Alberti or similar basses (SCE 122, 126) that still prevail in many of the sonatinas. And the sonatas more often include sets of variations on popular tunes of the day (e.g., on a Danish air, in Op. 64/ii, for P & Vn-or-Fl). Exceptional are the three finales in the solo sonatinas Op. 60/1–3, each a set of variations on a different tune by Rossini.

But even the sonatas by Kuhlau were relatively conservative in their day, with few departures from established styles or forms. Already this fact was implied in a review of his Op. 8, "Grande Sonate" in a, for P solo (pub. in 1814?).[7] The reviewer emphasized in consider- able detail not only the convincing melodies, the effective passage- work, and the contrapuntal interest, but the correctness and propriety of whatever Kuhlau did, qualifying his praise merely by adding that, of course, Kuhlau could only compose within his limitations. Although the fresh melodies and compelling harmony in Kuhlau's sonatas fre- quently take unexpected, sometimes bold turns (Ex. 94), Kuhlau was no Weber or Schumann in the advance of musical Romanticism.[8] The gist of the many, progressively brief reviews of his sonatas and sona- tinas is that in spite of his prolificity he continued to put out works of noteworthy skill, variety, and interest within acceptable tastes and idioms and reasonable technical limits, there being mild objections only to excessive passagework (mostly scales) and overly prolonged endings.[9]

6. Cf. Cobbett/CHAMBER II 81–82 (H. M. Fitzgibbon).
7. AMZ XVII (1815) 179–83, with 14 mss. quoted from the start of i.
8. Brahms wrote to Joachim in 1854 that he wanted to learn flute so that he could "accompany" Clara, but that Kuhlau's (Fl?) sons. "bore her" (Joachim/ LETTERS 78).
9. Other representative reviews include AMZ XV (1813) 79–80 (on Op. 5 for P solo, likening Kuhlau to Cramer) and 449–50 (on an unidentified son. "facile" for P & Vn), XXIII (1821) 410–12 (on Op. 26/1–2 for P solo, likening Kuhlau to Haydn

Ex. 94. From the finale of Friedrich Kuhlau's *Grande Sonate concertate pour piano et flûte,* Op. 85 in a (after the original Schott ed. of 1827; plate no. 2684).

The brilliant pianist **(Heinrich) Rudolf Willmers** (1821–78) was born in Copenhagen if not in Berlin,[10] studied with Hummel and others, toured widely, and settled in Vienna in 1866. His sonatas include Op. 11 for P & Vn, a Sonata in B♭ for P solo, and a "Sonate héroique," Op. 33 for P solo that was reviewed in 1846 as a distasteful example of the "contemporary fad of virtuosity." [11]

Several composers were writing sonatas in Sweden, meaning Stockholm and Uppsala almost exclusively, while Kuhlau was in Copenhagen.[12] Some of these wrote in the borderland between Classic and Romantic styles, like Olaf Åhlström (SCE 800) or the important, versatile historian, poet, philosopher, and composer **Erik Gustaf Geijer** (1783–1847). Although Geijer made his musical mark primarily with

and Beethoven) and 672 (on Op. 20/1–3, the well-known Sonatinas for P solo), XXIV (1822) 215–16 (on Op. 33 for P+Vn) and 279–80 (on Op. 30 for P solo), XXV (1823) 596 (on Op. 34 for P solo) and 795 (on 3 "Grandes Sonates brillantes" for P solo), XXVIII (1826) 272 (on Op. 64 for P & Fl [Vn, originally]), XXXI (1829) 388 (on Op. 85 for P & Fl as one of Kuhlau's best sons.); CAECILIA XI (1829) 229–30 (I. X. Seyfried, similarly on Op. 85); AMA No. 6 (Aug. 5, 1826) 42 (on Op. 69 for P & Fl).

10. Cf. Fétis/BU VIII 475; BAKER 1801.

11. NZM XXV (1846) 108–9. Cf. PAZDÍREK XV 421–22.

12. It is again (cf. SCE 794) a pleasure to thank Professor Ingmar Bengtsson at the University of Uppsala for specific information, counsel, and further leads on the sonata in Sweden.

songs, he also left at least eight solo and duo sonatas, including one for P solo, in g/G (1810), and two for P-duet, in E♭/c and f (both 1819); four for P & Vn, in g/G, F/g, d/F, and A♭/E♭ (1819, 1830?, *ca*. 1832, 1840 [called "Sonatina"]); and one "Sonatina" for P & Vc, in F/a (1838–39).[13] Among these only the P-duet in f was or has been published (Stockholm: C. Müller, 1820), the rest being MSS in the Uppsala Universitetsbibliotek. But the melodic and harmonic appeal of that work[14] plus the interest in Geijer's songs and in his significant influence on Swedish cultural life in general would seem to warrant a study of his sonatas in MSS as well. Their style recalls that of Beethoven (up to Op. 22) and Mendelssohn. The movement types and proportions of his sonata cycles, ranging from two to four movements, appear to be standard enough. Furthermore, there are subtle but unmistakable similarities between the incipits of the movements in each cycle. Yet, as the foregoing listing suggests, the cycles are exceptional for their defiance or disregard of tonal unity. Apart from the printed sonata and two others in which only the mode changes, Geijer put each finale in a key other than that of the opening movement. Most striking in this respect is the second violin sonata, in which the successive keys of the four movements are F, B♭, b♭, and g.

Further exploration of the sonata in Sweden in the first half of the 19th century would bring us to composers some of whom are now little remembered even in that country. The once esteemed theorist, teacher, and folklorist **Erik Drake** (1788–1870) left an example in MS for P & Vn (1816) in which there are four movements (S/F-S-Mi-VF) that again defy tonal unity (E♭, B♭, g, B♭) while interrelating thematically.[15] Drake's melodic style has been likened to Spohr's and Rossini's.[16] A friend of Drake, the obscure, roving cellist and pianist **Carl Schwencke** (1797–at least 1870) was born in a musical family in Hamburg in Emanuel Bach's sphere and spent several years in Sweden, presumably some or all of the years from 1815 to 1819, when he wrote at least 10 sonatas—6 for P solo, 3 for P-duet, and one for P & Vn.[17]

---

13. Cf. SOHLMANS II 512–15 (Törnblom); GROVE III 588–89 (K. Dale); MGG IV 1615–16 (R. Engländer). In general reference works Geijer's musical activities are scarcely mentioned.

14. The judgment is based on incipits and related information kindly supplied by Professor Bengtsson and his students.

15. The MS, in the Musikaliska akademiens Bibliotek (Nybrokajen, Stockholm), lacks the Vn part. Cf. GROVE II 762–63 (K. Dale); MGG III 742–43 (M. Tegen); SOHLMANS I 1180–81 (Å. Vretblad); Nisser/SVENSK 109.

16. GROVE II 763.

17. Cf. MGG XII 401 and 403–5 (P. Schmidt), with further references and a full, undated list of works. Beethoven's canon on this Schwencke's name dates from 1824 (Thayer & Forbes/BEETHOVEN 923, 928).

In any case, these are all to be found in a special "Schwenckesam-longen" at the Musikaliska akademiens Bibliotek. And about half of them plus at least two others (for P & V-or-Vc and for P-duet) were published by Breitkopf & Härtel in Leipzig or Lemoine in Paris.[18] Schwencke's works are described as ranging from light, often charming diversions to pieces of considerable force and originality, with Romanticisms that point ahead to Grieg.[19] Evidently his sonatas, being early works, fall more into the former category.

The gifted but short-lived flutist **Frans Frederik Edward Brendler** (1800–31) left a three-movement "Sonatine" in C (F-S-Sc), for P-duet, that was published by Eberling in Stockholm in 1830.[20] Its melodic styles recall Kuhlau's (rather than Spohr's, as has been suggested of Brendler's more Romantically tinged works). Ranked with his friend Geijer as a song composer, **Adolf Fredrik Lindblad** (1801–78) left a Sonata in A/D, for P solo, in a MS dated 1828 that extends to 409 measures, yet may not be complete, since there are only two movements (F-M) and no return to the home key.[21] Lindblad, who worshipped Beethoven, studied with Zelter, and knew both Weber and Mendelssohn, reveals themes and harmonies much like Mendelssohn's. Variously like Clementi's and Mendelssohn's sonatas in style are two four-movement sonatas for P solo by one **Carl Ludvig Lithander** (1773–1843).[22] One of them, in C (F-M-Sc-Ro/Va), was dedicated to and published by Clementi in London (before 1832). Exceptionally, three variations on a Swedish air conclude its rondo finale whereas an "Adagio espressivo" concludes that of Lithander's other sonata, Op. 15, all in f♯/F♯ (F-S-Mi-Ro/S; composed in 1822 and pub. by Böhme in Hamburg).[23] The violinist and conductor **Johan Frederik Berwald** (1787–1861), member of an important Swedish family of musicians, left two sonatas for P & Vn, one in E♭, in three movement (F-M-Ro), composed in 1812 and published in 1816 by Breitkopf & Härtel, and the other finished only to the end of one fast movement, in f (before 1832).[24] His more important cousin, **Franz Adolf Berwald** (1796–1868), who is now ranked as Sweden's greatest 19th-century instrumental composer, left one sonata each for P & Vn (Op. 6 in E♭; 1858) and P & Vc

18. Cf. HOFMEISTER 1828 (Whistling) 506, 558, 602.

19. MGG XII 405.

20. Cf. GROVE V 926 (K. Dale).

21. Cf. MGG VIII 888–89 (A. Melander), with mention of 3 Vn sons., one of which is listed in Nisser/SVENSK 174.

22. He is not listed in any encyclopedia consulted here.

23. Op. 15 is listed in HOFMEISTER 1828 (Whistling), 595.

24. Cf. GROVE I 690–91 (M. L. Pereyra).

("Duo" Op. 7 in B♭; 1859), which do not have the importance of his forward-looking symphonies and larger chamber ensembles.[25]

Hartmann, Gade, Grieg, and Other Mid-Romantic Scandinavians

All three Scandinavians in the later-19th-century triumvirate mentioned at the start of this chapter demonstrated at least peripheral interest in the sonata.[26] The earliest of these was the organist, teacher, and best known member in a prominent family of German-Danish musicians, **Johann Peter Emil(ius) Hartmann** (1805–1900).[27] Throughout his long, outwardly uneventful life, Hartmann left many compositions, in nearly every category of music. Most of these achieved publication, over a span of more than a half-century, including at least three solo and three duo sonatas that appeared chiefly around the start and around the end of that span. There are three sonatas for P & Vn—Op. 8 ("Grande Sonate concertante") in g, composed in 1826 (?[28]), dedicated to Spohr, and published in 1837 by Kistner in Leipzig; Op. 39 in C, published in 1846 by Schuberth in Hamburg; and Op. 83 in g, published in 1888 (not 1886) by Hansen in Copenhagen. There are two sonatas for P solo—Op. 34 in F ("awarded second prize"), published not later than 1842 by Schuberth, and Op. 80 in a, published in 1885 by Hansen.[29] And there is one organ sonata, Op. 58 in g, composed in 1855 (?[30]) and published in 1888 by Hansen.

In 1837 Schumann reviewed Hartmann's Op. 8 favorably, especially for its natural flow, its cumulative interest, its craftsmanship, and its development of ideas, although he found the "Andante" too long and the first of the four movements (F-M-Sc-F) still oriented toward Hummel and Classic styles.[31] In 1842, he wrote even more favorably on Op.

25. Cf. GROVE I 691–92 (M. L. Pereyra); Cobbett/CHAMBER I 125 (G. Jeanson); Layton/BERWALD (a full survey of the man and his works), pp. 84, 181; Altmann/KAMMERMUSIK 195 and 253. A complete ed. of his works is currently (1967) being ed. by Ingmar Bengtsson and others for pub. by Bärenreiter.

26. Cf. the valuable discussion of "Grieg's relationship to N. W. Gade and J. P. E. Hartmann" in Schjelderup-Ebbe/GRIEG 149–66.

27. Cf. MGG V 1748–53 (N. Schiørring), with further references and dated list of works; also, Hammerich/HARTMANN. A Son. in F, Op. 17, by Hartmann's son Emil (1836–98; cf. MGG V 1752–53) is reviewed as a contrived work with some interesting spots, in MW XI (1880) 608.

28. MGG V 1750.

29. The Library of Congress also has a Sonatina Op. 48, for P solo, by Hartmann, pub. by Hansen. Cf. PAZDÍREK VII 181–83. Among early (unpub. student?) works cited in Hammerich/HARTMANN 459 are a Son. Op. 1, for P & Fl, and a Sonatine Op. 4, for P-duet.

30. MGG V 1750.

31. Schumann/SCHRIFTEN I 277. Praise from a contemporary Berlin review is quoted in Hammerich/HARTMANN 461.

Ex. 95. From the "Andantino" of Johann Peter Emil Hartmann's Sonata in g, Op. 83 (after the Hansen ed. of 1888).

34 as the work that should have been ranked first among "three prize
sonatas" by C. Vollweiler,[32] J. C. Leonhard, and Hartmann, declaring
the four movements (F-M-Sc-F) to be characterized by genuine artistry,
by masterly harmony and form, including interrelated themes, and by
the poetry of its inner movements as well as the strong, orchestral
coloring of its finale.[33] And in 1846 a successor to Schumann wrote
similarly on Hartmann's Op. 39.[34] A reading of Hartmann's last sonatas
suggests that his styles and forms underwent little if any change over
the near half-century, in spite of his late interest in Brahms and
Wagner. In the four interconnected movements (F-M-VF-Ro) of Op.
83, for example, the harmony still proves to be secure, uncomplicated,
and entirely traditional, the texture still proves to be precise and
rather thin, and the phrase syntax once more reveals Hartmann's own
manner of continuous unfolding through the constant but rhythmically
plastic reiteration and development of an idea (as in the extension of
the opening theme over the first two pages). Unless it be in the

32. Cf. MGG XIV 1 (R. Seitz).
33. Schumann/SCHRIFTEN II 79 and 82–83. An ex. from Op. 34/i is quoted in
Bücken/19. 291 and related to the styles of Spohr, who as one of the judges, had
also wanted Op. 34 to get first prize. Cf., further, Hammerich/HARTMANN 462, 464,
and 467; but the title of the work indicates Hartmann had won 2d, not 3d,
prize.
34. NZM XXV (1846) 176–77.

"Andantino" (Ex. 95) or the "Rondo" refrain, Op. 83, like his early sonatas, shows little of the interest in Danish folk music that Hartmann is reported to have shown in some of his other music.[35]

More renowned in his day though scarcely better remembered today than his colleague Hartmann, the violinist and composer **Niels Wilhelm Gade** (1817–90) was the strongest force in Danish music between Kuhlau and Weyse (*supra*) and Nielsen (*infra*).[36] Gade spent five years (1843–48) in Leipzig and brief Italian travels, assisting and succeeding Mendelssohn as conductor at the Gewandhaus concerts and also enjoying the warm friendship of Schumann. Otherwise he spent nearly all of his life in Copenhagen. Another prolific composer in every main branch of music, Gade left four published sonatas—Op. 28 in e (not c), for P solo (pub. by Hansen in 1840 and, with revisions, by Breitkopf & Härtel in 1854); and Opp. 6 in A, 21 in d, and 59 in B♭, for P & Vn (pub. by Breitkopf & Härtel in 1843, 1850, and 1887).[37] The piano sonata was dedicated to Liszt and the first and second violin sonatas were dedicated to Clara and Robert Schumann, respectively.

Of Gade's four sonatas, Opp. 28 for P solo and 21 for P & Vn seem to have aroused the most interest among performers.[38] But even these aroused much less interest than his symphonies or more nationalistic music and got little notice from the reviewers.[39] Yet both sonatas are convincing, well realized cycles, not suffocated by overly specific recollections of Mendelssohn's writing, as is sometimes charged,[40] but, it is true, largely confined to the range of Mendelssohn's musical language. Opp. 21 and 28 have much in common in this respect and in the general plan and emotional content of their relatively short, three-movement, thematically interrelated cycles. Op. 21 differs chiefly in having brief slow introductions in the outer movements and an alternation of S-VF in its middle movement that anticipates Op. 100/ii by Brahms. Historically Op. 28 is Gade's most noteworthy sonata, by virtue of its direct, demonstrable influence on Grieg's only piano sonata (*infra*), also in e. And Op. 28 is somewhat stronger than Op. 21, by virtue of a little

35. Hammerich/HARTMANN 466 *et passim*.

36. Cf. MGG IV 1223–28 (N. Schiørring), with further references and a (somewhat inaccurately) dated list of works.

37. In Shand/VIOLIN 122–30, 13 exx. from all 3 Vn sons. are quoted. Bücken/19. 293 gives an ex. from Op. 21/ii. The pub. years are too early in MGG IV 1226.

38. E.g., performances of Op. 21 are reported in MT XIII (1868) 446 and XVI (1874) 512; NZM LXXII/1 (1876) 79 and 146, LXXII/2 523, LXXIII/1 52, 53, and 116; and SMZ VI (1876) 29.

39. E.g., the only review of Op. 21 found here in English or German periodicals was that in MMR XIII (1883) 70–71, which greets cordially the lyricism, charm, and "adequate" development of its ideas. Neither Op. 21 nor Op. 28 is currently pub. or recorded (as of late 1967).

40. Cf. Cobbett/CHAMBER I 440–41 (W. W. Cobbett); BAKER 526.

more intensity and imagination in the former's ideas and their development. Moreover, Op. 21 is less satisfying to the pianist because it
hardly qualifies as a true duo; the piano rarely takes the lead or even
engages the violin antiphonally.

With further regard to Gade's Op. 28, the harmonic color and
melodic lyricism reveal a more Romantic spirit than can be found in
Hartmann's sonatas. The themes are not of outstanding interest in
themselves, but the concentrated yet unhurried extensions and symphonic development of them, especially of the initial theme in each
movement (VF-M-F), and the clear, purposeful tonal logic result in
surprising structural breadth and solidity.[41] The conciseness of the

Ex. 96. From the third movement of Niels Gade's Sonata in
e, Op. 28 (after the Breitkopf-Härtel reprint of about 1890
[V. A. 2299]).

forms, the superior, imaginative treatment of the main rhythms, and
the fluent, eminently practical and reasonable scoring for keyboard
lend further conviction to the music (Ex. 96) and compensate partially
for the absence of individual master strokes and flights of inspiration
such as occurred to Grieg at his best.

This mention of the Norwegian **Edvard (Hagerup) Grieg** (1843–
1907) brings us to the most successful, representative, and renowned of
all Scandinavian composers.[42] Trained early in piano by his talented
mother in their home town of Bergen, and encouraged by the cele-

41. Similar traits already evident in Op. 6 probably account for a reviewer's
observation that "harmonic masses prevail rather than melodic design" (MMR XVI
[1886] 184).

42. From the considerable literature on Grieg, the studies of both the man and

brated Norwegian violinist Ole Bull, Grieg, like Gade, spent several years in Leipzig (1858–62), where he drank in the music of the late Mendelssohn, Schumann, and Chopin, along with other music as up-to-date as Wagner's *Tannhäuser,* but chafed under (and never quite forgave) the more conservative, pedantic aspects of his instruction.[43] Further influences were exercised on him by the music and counsel of both Gade and Hartmann in Copenhagen;[44] by the ardent Norwegian nationalism of Ole Bull and the short-lived composer Rikard Nordraak (1842–66);[45] by Grieg's marriage in 1867 to the fine singer (and his first cousin) Nina Hagerup;[46] and by his two memorable meetings with Liszt in Rome (1870).[47]

Grieg's output, which amounts to 74 opus numbers and a few other works, is neither so large nor so comprehensive as that of Hartmann or Gade. Along with the many sets of intimate songs and piano pieces in which he excelled, as well as the four suites for orchestra and/or piano that did much to win him fame, there are only 8 full cycles of the sonata type, including the familiar piano Concerto in a, the 2 string quartets, and 5 actual "sonatas." [48] Of the last, 3 are for P & Vn, one is for P & Vc, and one is for P solo. He wrote the solo and first two violin sonatas near the end of the formative years just summarized, and the other two sonatas about two decades later in the thick of a career defined variously by idyllic composing at "Troldhaugen" near Bergen in spite of his increasing sterile periods, by strenuous, annual, wide-ranging concert tours in spite of his chronic, increasing ill health, and by ever new honors and recognition in spite of his increasing expressions of artistic credos, broad liberalism, and political differences that created no little friction.[49]

his music that have proved to be most helpful and dependable here are Monrad-Johansen/GRIEG and Schjelderup-Ebbe/GRIEG (on the early years). Significant information and views are also to be found in Finck/GRIEG (in spite of its idolatry), Rokseth/GRIEG (with 60 intriguing photographic plates), and the "symposium" Abraham/GRIEG. Further sources are listed in the 2 chief encyclopedia articles, GROVE III 798–811 (J. Horton), with a detailed, classified "Catalogue of Works," and MGG V 896–908 (W. Kahl). *Die Sonate von Grieg* by Wera von Landesen (Nürnberg: J. L. Schrag, 1944) is an irrelevant book of fiction (cf. pp. 44, 95).

43. A main source on Grieg's background up to about 1862 is his own autobiographic article of 1903, "My First Success," which has been reprinted several times (as in Grieg/VERZEICHNIS) or drawn upon at length, as it has, with further material added, in Schjelderup-Ebbe/GRIEG 17–67, 357, *et passim.*

44. Cf. Schjelderup-Ebbe/GRIEG 149–63.

45. Cf. Monrad-Johansen/GRIEG 61–69; Schjelderup-Ebbe/GRIEG 164–66, 212–25.

46. Cf. Monrad-Johansen/GRIEG 56–60, 78, 98–99.

47. Cf. Monrad-Johansen/GRIEG 115, 122–27; Finck/GRIEG 47–57.

48. There had also been 2 student cycles—a lost string quartet in d (1861?) and a "Sinfonie" in c "never to be performed" (1863–64); cf. Schjelderup-Ebbe/GRIEG 351, 352. Grieg's 2d-P parts to 5 Mozart sons. are noted in SCE 500.

49. Cf. Monrad-Johansen/GRIEG 255–70 and 351–73.

The first sonata Grieg is known to have written, not excluding student exercises,[50] is Op. 7 in e, for P solo, composed in Rungsted, near Copenhagen, in June of 1865, dedicated to Gade, published first by Breitkopf & Härtel in June of 1866[51] and next, with revisions, by Peters in 1887.[52] In an interview of 1893, published in English in 1904, Grieg recalled how

. . . within eleven days I had composed my sonata for the pianoforte, and very soon after my first sonata for the violin. I took them both to Gade, who was living out at Klampenborg. He glanced through them with satisfaction, nodded, tapped me on the shoulder, and said, "That's very nice indeed. Now we'll go over them carefully and look into all the seams." So we climbed a small steep staircase to Gade's studio, where he sat down at the grand pianoforte and played with absolute inspiration. I had often been told that when Gade was inspired, he drank copious draughts of water. That day the Professor emptied four large water-bottles.[53]

On November 20, 1865, during his final illness, Nordraak entered in his diary, "Grieg's letter [received] yesterday described his performance of his piano sonata and his sonata for piano and violin [Op. 8] at the evening entertainment in the Gewandhaus in Leipzig. A tremendous success. Encored. . . ."[54] In his own country less than a year later, Grieg also fared well with Opp. 7 and 8. An early review of Grieg's music up to that time found the ideas in Op. 7 to be fresher, with less of Gade's influence, but the structure of Op. 8 to be sounder; soon after, the further performances of both works aroused "great rejoicings."[55] Only a few reports of other performances of Op. 7 during the next few years have turned up in the present study.[56] Perhaps dissatisfaction with both the substance and form of the finale discouraged more performances, for Grieg's revisions of Op. 7 largely concerned that movement, especially the reduction of its length.[57] The fast tempo at which Grieg reportedly played the finale (and that of

50. These last are catalogued in careful detail, along with all his other compositions written before 1867, in Schjelderup-Ebbe/GRIEG 348–56.

51. HOFMEISTER Monatsbericht 1866, p. 93.

52. The circumstances of Op. 7 are reported in Finck/GRIEG 39; Monrad-Johansen/GRIEG 71, 81, 92–93, 281; Schjelderup-Ebbe/GRIEG 151, 234, 311–13.

53. As trans. in Finck/GRIEG 39 (cf. p. 306); cf., also, Schjelderup-Ebbe/GRIEG 244.

54. As trans. in Monrad-Johansen/GRIEG 81.

55. Monrad-Johansen/GRIEG 92–93; Schjelderup-Ebbe/GRIEG 311–13. In 2 reviews, in MMR XIII (1883) 182 and XV (1885) 137, Op. 7 is described as being less rich in "invention and constructive skill" than Op. 13, possessed of a "strong national flavour," and "a pleasing and wholesome (because healthy) work."

56. E.g., NZM LXXIII/1 (1877) 126 (Barmen, near Düsseldorf); MT XVIII (1878) 164 (London), XXI (1880) 303 (Syracuse, N.Y.), XXVII (1885) 20 (London); ML XLIX (1968) 25 (Köln, 1878, finale only).

57. Cf. MGG V 905.

Op. 8) [58] may relate to problems in it, too. But unfortunately that movement still remains an artistic obstacle to most performers. [59] Op. 7 reveals the likely influence of Gade's Op. 28 (in spite of the early review just noted), not only in the choice of over-all key, but in the number, order, and tempos of the four movements (F-M-Mi-VF in Grieg's work), and the textural styles, character, and even thematic types of the first two movements in particular. To be sure, Grieg does not develop single ideas symphonically as Gade does in Op. 28. But he creates ideas in Op. 7 that are more original, he creates more of them, he breaks up his movements into shorter sections, and he achieves his own kind of drive and drama through sharper, more imaginative contrasts. [60]

As we just learned from Grieg himself, Op. 8 in F, for P & Vn, was composed "very soon after" Op. 7 (1865), also in Rungsted. Another four-movement cycle (F-M-F-VF), it was dedicated to the Bergen violinist August Fries and published first by Peters in February, 1866. [61] This was the work that led to the two memorable meetings with Liszt in Rome. At the end of 1868 Liszt had written Grieg, out of the blue and without any direct advance on Grieg's part, [62] to congratulate him on the talent and promise revealed in Op. 8 and to encourage a visit in Weimar should Grieg be getting to Germany. [63] Actually, this unexpected support from so great a celebrity clinched the Norwegian government subsidy Grieg had been seeking for a return visit to Rome, where he called on Liszt in early February (?), 1870, and "soon after," on February 17. As related in two detailed letters to his parents (Feb. 17 and Apr. 9, 1870) and a travel report to his government, [64] Grieg played "my last violin sonata" (i.e., Op. 13 in G, pub. in 1869; *infra*) with trepidation, Liszt joining in with the violin part "higher up on the piano in octaves" and applauding it all "so copiously," including the violin's first entry on "a little baroque but national passage," that "I felt the most singular thankfulness streaming through me." Then, to hear Op. 13 a second time, Liszt

58. Cf. Schjelderup-Ebbe/GRIEG 313.
59. Cf. Schjelderup-Ebbe/GRIEG 243; Monrad-Johansen/GRIEG 73.
60. Schjelderup-Ebbe/GRIEG 240–42 also finds close parallels between Op. 7/iii and a piece by Hartmann, "Vikingefruens Dröm" ("The Viking Woman's Dream").
61. The further circumstances of Op. 8 are related in Finck/GRIEG 47–55; Monrad-Johansen/GRIEG 81, 92, 93, 286; Schjelderup-Ebbe/GRIEG 244–45, 312, 313.
62. However, contrary to Finck/GRIEG 47–49, Monrad-Johansen/GRIEG 115–16 shows that Liszt's letter was not entirely spontaneous.
63. A facs. of the original letter, in French, appears in Plates XII and XIII of Rokseth/GRIEG; it is trans. into English in LISZT LETTERS 168–69 and in Finck/GRIEG 47.
64. All three, affording fine samples of Grieg's superior literary talents, are trans. nearly in full in Monrad-Johansen/GRIEG 122–28.

played the whole affair, lock, stock and barrel, violin, piano, nay more, for he played with more fullness and breadth. The violin was given its due right in the middle of the piano part, he was literally all over the whole piano at the same time, without a note being missed. And how, then, did he play? With majesty, beauty, genius beyond compare in interpretation. I believe I laughed, like an idiot. . . . The day after the visit I have just described for you, the Italians Sgambati [pupil of Liszt] and Pinelli (pupil of Joachim) [65] played my first violin sonata [Op. 8] at a matinee where the whole fashionable world was present. Liszt came in the middle of the concert, just before my sonata, and that was well. For I do not put down the applause the sonata received to my own account. The thing is that when Liszt claps they all clap—each louder than the other.[66]

This Sgambati-Pinelli performance and the two earlier performances of Op. 8 in conjunction with Op. 7 marked only the beginning of enough performances of Op. 8 to suggest that it remained Grieg's most popular sonata, near and far, during his lifetime.[67] The undeniable worth and charm of Op. 8 supply reason enough for this popularity. But one learns with interest that its dedicatee Gade, whose influence on Op. 8 Grieg himself acknowledged, seems to have liked it partly because it was still free of the nationalistic flavors he was to object to in Op. 13.[68] On the other hand, the first Norwegian critic to review Op. 8 did find such flavors, at least in a backhanded way when, in September, 1866, he wrote, "I cannot deny that there are a few rather ugly [dissonantly experimental?] measures in the first movement (in cadential progressions [as in the start of the two 'Andante' sections?]) at the very places where he [Grieg] wants to strike the national chords." [69] And twenty-two years later a critic for the *Musical Times* of London was still writing that

Norway has no musical forms apart from simple melodies, and the Norwegian working on the higher lines of art must borrow his models. But he can fuse into his productions more or less of the national musical dialect and feeling, and this is precisely what Grieg does. The Sonata in F is a remarkable illustration of the fact.[70]

65. Cf. RICORDI ENCICLOPEDIA III 443.
66. As trans. in Monrad-Johansen/GRIEG 125.
67. Sample performances during the decade 1876–86, when Grieg's popularity was at a peak, are reported in NZM LXXII/2 (1876) 381 (Leipzig) and 498 (St. Petersburg), LXXIII/1 (1877) 72 (Leipzig), 140 (Brussels), 249 (Zwickau); MT XXI (1880) 138 (London), XXIII (1882) 83 (London), XXIV (1883) 159 (Leipzig), XXVII (1886) 147 (London) and 210 (Birmingham). Among numerous reports of performances of Grieg's Vn sons. that do not specify the key or op. no., one guesses that most also refer to Op. 8.
68. Cf. Schjelderup-Ebbe/GRIEG 244.
69. As trans. in Schjelderup-Ebbe/GRIEG 312.
70. MT XXIX (1888) 75. Cf., also, the more specific Norwegian imagery culled up by Niecks, as quoted at length in Finck/GRIEG 193–95.

The sonata Grieg showed Liszt in 1870 was his second for P & Vn. This work, Op. 13 in G, had been composed in three weeks of July, 1867, in the Norwegian capital of Christiana (Oslo) soon after the newly married couple moved there from Denmark.[71] The dedicatee was Grieg's friend, the violinist, conductor, composer, and fellow country-man Johan Svendsen, who may have joined in the first performance.[72] And the first publisher was Breitkopf & Härtel in 1869. It was after the first performance of this work that, as Grieg reported in a letter of 1905, "Gade came to the artist's room and said: 'No, Grieg, the next sonata you must not make as Norwegian.' I had at that moment tasted blood and answered: 'Yes, professor, the next one is going to be even worse.' (However, that was not the case, as you know.)"[73] We have just noted how Liszt spotted a nationalistic flavor in Op. 13, too, though more approvingly. In the years since then, several writers have described Op. 13 as Grieg's most nationalistic sonata, and some, indeed, as one of the most nationalistic of all his works.[74] Unquestionably, there are pronounced folklike elements in each of the three move-ments (S/VF-M-VF), especially rhythms in this so-called "Dance So-nata"[75] that define the oddly similar main themes of the outer move-ments[76] and characteristic scale inflections, including the lowered 7th and 2d, that also pervade the more lyrical themes (Ex. 97). But in spite of these traits and all the varied Norwegian imagery that they have inspired in writings on Op. 13,[77] the fact remains that no tangible or specific Norwegian source could be discovered here for any of the ideas in this work. Before World War I other writers already were an-ticipating more recent, ethnomusicological debates by asking whether Grieg's music was really a case of Grieg becoming more Norwegian or Norway becoming more "Griegian."[78] If such a question applies to Grieg's music in general, it certainly applies to his five sonatas in particular, which all reveal every trait in abundance that can be

71. A few circumstances of Op. 13 are reported in Monrad-Johansen/GRIEG 99. A facs. of the first page of the autograph appears as Plate X in Rokseth/GRIEG.

72. GROVE III 800; Monrad-Johansen/GRIEG 101.

73. As trans. in Schjelderup-Ebbe/GRIEG 244.

74. E.g., cf. MMR XIII (1882) 182; Cobbett/CHAMBER I 497 (M. M. Ulfrstad); Monrad-Johansen/GRIEG 99–100; Finck/GRIEG 195.

75. Cobbett/CHAMBER I 497.

76. Frank/GRIEG 35 and 39 sees the thematic similarity as a main fault of Op. 13. Although this particular similarity may confuse the hearer by falling somewhere between clear identity and subtle derivation, such an argument could not be valid per se without ruling out many cyclically interrelated works that have won almost universal approval.

77. E.g., cf. Monrad-Johansen/GRIEG 99–100; Finck/GRIEG 195.

78. Cf. Gilman/NATURE 171–74.

Ex. 97. From the middle movement of Edvard Grieg's Sonata in G, Op. 13 (after the Breitkopf & Härtel reprint of *ca.* 1887; plate no. 17877).

classified as "Griegian," but nothing more tangible that can be called "Norwegian" than their allegedly indigenous flavors.

Grieg dedicated some of his Norwegian songs to Ole Bull—Op. 17, appropriately enough[79]—but not any of his violin sonatas, not even the more nationalistic Op. 13. Nor does that colorful but circumscribed, conservatively oriented violinist seem to have participated in performances of Op. 13 (or any other Grieg sonata). For that matter, 19th-century violinists in general seem not to have chosen often to play this sonata in recital.[80] They may have felt that in spite of the nationalistic appeal, it was not feasible to appropriate folk elements to full sonata treatment, although such a view is belied by Grieg's skill in accomplishing just that.[81]

Grieg composed his Sonata in a, Op. 36 for P & Vc, in Bergen in 1883 at a time when he was reducing his activities mainly to composition and concert tours. He dedicated it to his elder brother John, a

79. Cf. Schjelderup-Ebbe/GRIEG 91–95.
80. Representative performances in a peak decade are reported in SMZ XVI (1876) 175 (Basel, with Grieg himself); NZM LXXII/2 (1876) 466 (London), LXXIII/1 (1877) 173 (Brussels); MT XXII (1881) 204 (Birmingham), XXVII (1885) 33 (London).
81. Cf. Monrad-Johansen/GRIEG 99–100.

cellist who played it and other works with Edvard, and he saw its first publication by Peters in the same year of 1883.[82] Two decades later, Grieg wrote that he himself did not rate this work "very highly, because it does not betoken any forward step in my development"; and taking his cue from this statement, the author Monrad-Johansen finds in it less of richness, charm, and contrast, and more of mannered devices aimed at routine writing and sure effect.[83] But others, seconded here, have regarded Op. 36 as one of Grieg's best sounding, most rewarding sonatas.[84] Grieg certainly did not hesitate to play Op. 36 a number of times, including its first performance, on October 22, 1883, in Dresden, with the important cellist Friedrich Grützmacher; a performance soon after with the equally recognized Julius Klengel (SSB XI) in Leipzig; and two performances with his brother two years later in Christiana.[85] Otherwise, relatively few performances of the work during Grieg's lifetime have been discovered here.[86] Perhaps some impediments to its success were created by one of the numerous, almost incomprehensible diatribes on his music that appeared in the *Signale für die musikalische Welt* of Leipzig (SMW). In this instance (Oct. 27, 1883), the reviewer (E. Bernsdorf), who had previously railed against both Opp. 8 and 13, complained of the ridiculous Scandinavianism, empty content, and unskilled development and form, yet acknowledged the enthusiastic reception given to Op. 36.[87]

Grieg composed his fifth sonata, Op. 45 in c, for P & Vn, in the winter of 1886–87, completing it on January 21 and dedicating it to the German painter Franz von Lenbach.[88] This so-called "Tragic Sonata," published by Peters in 1887, came on the heels of the third set of *Lyric Pieces* for P solo and the "Travel" songs, which had broken nearly two years of unproductivity.[89] In 1900 Grieg was to write his valued friend and cousin, the esteemed author Bjørnson, that his three violin sonatas "belong to my best works and represent [main] periods of [my] develop-

82. Some circumstances of Op. 36 are related in Monrad-Johansen/GRIEG 242–44, 247–48, 271. The autograph is listed in NOTES XXI (1963–64) 91 but has been withdrawn from public access.

83. Monrad-Johansen/GRIEG 242–43.

84. E.g., Finck/GRIEG 197; Cobbett/CHAMBER I 497–98; Dunhill/CHAMBER 181–82.

85. Monrad-Johansen/GRIEG 247 and 271.

86. E.g., in London 3 are reported during the first 3 years of its existence, in MT XXV (1883) 33 and 701, XXVII (1886) 336–37 (with only moderate approval of the music).

87. SMW XLI (1883) 996. Cf. SMW XXXV (1878) 1046 and XXXVI (1879) 406; also, Monrad-Johansen/GRIEG 248 and 217–19 (with the 1883 and 1878 reviews quoted in full in the original German).

88. Some circumstances of Op. 45 are related in Monrad-Johansen/GRIEG 278–81; Finck/GRIEG 112 and 196–97.

89. Monrad-Johansen/GRIEG 275–78.

ment; the first, naive, rich in models; the second, national, and the third with the wider horizons." [90] As the last and, by consensus, best of his sonata-type works, Op. 45 seems to fulfill a revealing vow uttered shortly before—"I will fight my way through the great [large?] forms, cost what it may." [91] To be sure, Bernsdorf, in still another *Signale* diatribe, attacked mainly this very question of large form after Grieg and the fine Russian violinist Adolf Brodsky played Op. 45 for the first time, with much success, in Leipzig on December 10.[92] But most other commentators, from early to recent, have agreed that Grieg met the problem successfully in Op. 45—achieving greater simplicity, development, and breadth, in fact, than in any of its four predecessors. Thus, a Parisian critic wrote in 1890, "This brilliant composition [Op. 45] seems to dispose completely of the reproach that has been levelled against Grieg, that he is not the man for works that require a long breath." [93] Tchaikovsky was understandably "enchanted" with the immediately popular work, and the critics Lawrence Gilman and Ernest Closson found grandeur, heroism, and greatness in it, to a degree Closson considered unsurpassed." [94]

In the year (1887) that Peters published Op. 45, this firm, which already controlled Opp. 8 and 36, also bought the publishing rights to Opp. 7 and 13, and by 1889, confirming Grieg's increasingly wide popularity and importance, had bought the rights to every one of his works then completed.[95] As of 1967 all five sonatas still appear in the Peters catalogues and all but Op. 7 are available in recordings.[96] However, time has scarcely borne out Henry Finck's prognostication—"In the concert halls of the future it is safe to predict that no music of this [chamber] class will be played more frequently than his superb string quartet and his no less admirable sonatas for piano and violin." [97] In spite of both the publications and this prognostication, interest in Grieg has declined conspicuously in the 20th century, especially in the last generation. What explains the decline? Or more to our specific purpose, what strengths and weaknesses stand out today in Grieg's sonatas?

90. As trans. in Schjelderup-Ebbe/GRIEG 245.

91. Monrad-Johansen/GRIEG 278.

92. SMW XLV (1887) 1127; cf. Monrad-Johansen/GRIEG 280–81, with the pertinent section quoted in the original German.

93. As trans. from *Le Matin* of Jan. 4, in Monrad-Johansen/GRIEG 279.

94. As quoted in Finck/GRIEG 112 and 196–97. Cf., also, MT XXIX (1888) 91.

95. Monrad-Johansen/GRIEG 281.

96. A notable recent release is the reissue of Op. 45 as played by Kreisler and Rachmaninoff (along with Schubert's "Duo" Sonata in A, D. 574; RCA Victor LCT 1128).

97. Finck/GRIEG 193. Although he is idolatrous and on the defensive, Finck writes significantly on "Grieg's Rank as a Composer" (pp. 225–45).

The broad answer regarding the decline would have to be simply this: Whereas Grieg's music spells the essence of Romanticism in full bloom, it is precisely his newly self-conscious, slightly mannered, yet still highly emotive phase of Romanticism that the Modern Era has rejected most uncompromisingly. But such a broad answer must not be allowed to blur either the strengths or the weaknesses of Grieg's particular style, for he did develop a particular style—too particular or "Norwegian," some have said (*infra*)—that is almost instantly recognized by seasoned musicians. First among his strengths must be put his superiority as an original, fecund melodist, a superiority, as Finck argues with some reason,[98] that can outweigh a number of more pedantic but less favorable considerations. A sample of Grieg's best melody writing is provided in the A sections of the ternary middle movement in Op. 45, marked "Allegretto espressivo alla Romanza." The piano begins alone with a homophonic double-period extended in its final phrase from a square design of 32 measures to a more plastic one of 45 measures. Thereupon, the violin overlaps by one measure to repeat the 45 measures of melody almost exactly, with the piano now supplying only the purely chordal accompaniment. Notable in this double-period is the folklike simplicity yet sustained interest of the melodic line as it unfolds intensively rather than extensively. Entirely diatonic, largely stepwise, and rather narrow-ranged (not exceeding a 12th until the final octave transplant), the line might have served in one of Grieg's most expressive songs. It achieves breadth of contour by describing only two arcs over-all and by falling into two nearly parallel periods. It achieves rhythmic plasticity by alternating feminine and masculine endings in the phrase members and by reiterating phrase members climactically to extend the cadence 13 measures in the last, 21-measure "phrase." Stamped with Grieg's name are the 8-7-5 and 6-5-3 progressions in the melody (as in mss. 6–7 and 11–12) and the dissonant, chromatic passing or neighboring tones in the harmony. It is the harmony that foretells MacDowell's style (ssв XVII) and frequently edges Grieg's warm sentiment perilously close to sentimentality. Although this harmony is rarely quite so experimental and dissonant in his sonatas (e.g., Op. 7/i/92–105 and iv/178–86) as it is in his songs and smaller piano pieces,[99] it sometimes brings to mind the harmony of Fauré, his near contemporary, admirer, and opposite

98. Finck/GRIEG 235–40.
99. Cf. Finck/GRIEG 213–18; Schjelderup-Ebbe/GRIEG *passim* (on the evolution of Grieg's early harmonic style); Fischer/GRIEG (on harmony in Grieg's songs, including anticipations of Debussy); and Dale/GRIEG 68–70.

Ex. 98. From the first movement of Edvard Grieg's Sonata in
c, Op. 45 (after the original Peters ed. of 1887).

number in France,[100] as in the turn to the lowered submediant chord
(mss. 27–28 and 71–72) in the double-period just described.

Along with his melodic strength and the concomitant strengths in
his rhythm and harmony, Grieg's scoring stands out. The sound is
almost always clear, telling, and well suited to its instrument. Occasionally a passage will fail to come off, though for reasons of technique
as much as of sonority. Thus, at the fortissimo, most climactic statement of the main theme in both the exposition and recapitulation of
Op. 45/i, the piano line fails to project as it should and as it looks, in
the score, as though it would (Ex. 98). Unfortunately, the distribution
of octaves and single notes in the right hand denies more than a weak
application of strength to the melody, and the lower, thicker chords
by which the left hand accompanies on the afterbeats interfere further,
especially if the accents on those chords are observed. More often, being
the fine pianist that he was,[101] Grieg can be counted on to write well,
if not very resourcefully, for piano. And in general, performers find his
music grateful to play and not more than moderately difficult, for, as

100. Cf. Monrad-Johansen/GRIEG 354.
101. Cf. the high praise by Hanslick and others for his "tender," "elegant,"
"flawless" playing as quoted in Finck/GRIEG 109–11.

Schjelderup-Ebbe says,[102] he addressed his music primarily to the "skilled amateur." In any case, Grieg eschewed virtuosity for its own sake, in his sonatas (and even his Concerto in a) as well as his smaller pieces. With his solid Leipzig training in harmony and counterpoint, however scholastic in retrospect, he kept as his main goal the ideal projection and treatment of the musical idea.

Finck considers at some length four "faults" attributed to Grieg by his contemporaries, especially by his German critics[103]—a lack of "logical development" in his music; an inability to "write operas, oratorios, and symphonies"; "too much of the 'Norwegian' idiom"; and more popularity than is commensurate with greatness. Only the first "fault" needs to be considered here, along with one other evaluation, pertaining to Grieg's stature. Regarding his ability to develop the musical ideas in his sonatas, there was little disagreement among earlier writers that at the outset, in Op. 7, he did too little with too much.[104] But Finck sought to rationalize the virtues of fertility[105] and later writers have regarded at least the first three movements as tighter and more logical than was previously supposed.[106] Granted that Op. 7 does offer enough interest, flow, and order to make a generally successful sonata, it is still but the first of five sonatas that show a composer's typical progress toward doing more with less, culminating in the exceptional economy and concentration of ideas in Op. 45. Grieg clearly recognized the problem of large form—that is, "sonata form"—from the start. The question is how successfully he was able to meet it. And if any "fault" does exist in his best large forms it lies, as viewed here, not in the over-all plan—these forms gratify the listener with their logic and freedom from prolixity—but at the more local level of phrase syntax. Even in Op. 45, especially in its fast, outer movements, the syntax must be described as mechanical. Thus, the first movement starts right off with phrases and shorter units of $3+3$, $2+2$, $1+1$, $1+1$, and 8 measures. Obviously, there is no failure to recognize the problem at this level, either. Grieg knew the dangers of oversquareness, but in his efforts to escape them he merely fell into another kind of pernicious symmetry. One finds the proof in his consistent need to make every consequent phrase rhyme, as it were, often by filling it out with rests or with those inevitable afterbeat patterns in his music (e.g., Op. 45/i/55–58). As with

102. Schjelderup-Ebbe/GRIEG 338.
103. Finck/GRIEG 227–45.
104. Typical views are summarized in Finck/GRIEG 229–30. Cf., also, Dale/GRIEG 57–58 and Einstein/ROMANTIC 321.
105. Finck/GRIEG 230–32.
106. Monrad-Johansen/GRIEG 71–73; Schjelderup-Ebbe/GRIEG 234–43.

his contemporary and "warm friend" [107] Tchaikovsky, or even Scriabin later, the methodologist superseded the musician in matters of phrase syntax.

Finally, Grieg's five interesting sonatas, as viewed here, fail to qualify as ideal Romantic masterpieces because his own stature as an artist was limited. To say that he was essentially a miniaturist is not quite sufficient because he fell short not only in the structural means of his larger forms (the phrase syntax just discussed) but in the expressive range. He had the fertility of ideas (when he was not in one of those sterile periods) but not the variety nor depth of imagination essential to a great composer. Thus, the comparison made with Fauré had to stop with certain harmonic traits, for—again, as viewed here—Fauré outclassed Grieg not only in the suppleness of his phrase syntax but in the variety and depth of his imagination. Nothing illustrates Grieg's limitations more graphically in the sonatas than the recurrences in each of similar, if not the same, melodic extensions, accompaniment styles, harmonic formulas, and climactic devices. Opp. 36 and 45 are remarkably similar throughout in feel and purpose. Moreover, there is an almost embarrassing similarity between the styles and even several of the ideas (not necessarily the corresponding ideas) in the three movements of the Concerto in a, Op. 16, and those of the cello sonata in the same key.[108] It should be added that once more Grieg recognized the problem. He appears to have been acknowledging his limitations honestly enough, not in false modesty, when he vowed to "fight my way through the great forms" (*supra*) or when he wrote in 1903, "I cannot understand it. So many creative spirits far more important than I do not get the sympathy I meet everywhere." [109]

Among other composers of sonatas in Scandinavian countries during the period of Hartmann, Gade, and Grieg, may be mentioned "Denmark's most important Romantic song composer," **Peter Arnold Heise** (1830–79), for five relatively early sonatas (*ca.* 1859–69)—two for P solo, two for P & Vn, and one for P & Vc.[110] Only the last, "Sonata quasi fantasia" in a (1869), was published, posthumously by Hansen, in 1902, followed by a review that dismissed it as insignificant.[111] A member of a musically active, Danish family, a longtime friend of

107. Cf. Monrad-Johansen/GRIEG 361–63.
108. Cf., also, Monrad-Johansen/GRIEG 303–4, on the similarity between Op. 8 and the String Quartet in F.
109. Monrad-Johansen/GRIEG 259–60; Grieg's own remarks on pp. 261, 293, and 301 (among others) are pertinent, too.
110. MGG VI 89–91 (N. Schiørring).
111. SMW LXI (1903) 187.

Grieg, and an organist, **Gottfred Matthison-Hansen** (1832–1909) left
two duo sonatas published in 1877 by Breitkopf & Härtel that remain
to be re-explored—Opp. 11 (not 10) in f, for P & Vn, and 16 in F, for
P & Vc.[112] **Erik Anthon Valdemar Siboni** (1828–92), a highly regarded
organist and singing coach of Italian descent whose teachers included
Hartmann in Copenhagen and Moscheles and Hauptmann in Leipzig, left at least two published sonatas each for P solo and P-duet, as
well as two or more each for P & Vn and P & Vc that apparently remained unpublished.[113] In Stockholm the German-born pianist (**Johan**)
Herman Berens (1826–80) left, along with two sonatas for P-duet and
six "Kunder-Sonaten" for P solo, two other published sonatas—Op. 5
for P & Vn (1847), reviewed as a promising but inconsistent work in
four movements (F-M-Sc-F) with inadequate development in the first
movement and meaningless brilliance in the finale, and Op. 60, for P
solo (1862), a prize-winning work reviewed as a return to propriety,
moderation, and tradition.[114] Another Stockholm composer and pupil
of Moscheles and Hauptmann among others, the pianist (**Frederick
Vilhelm**) **Ludwig Norman** (1831–85) was a protégé of Jenny Lind and
Schumann, successor to the important instrumental composer F. A.
Berwald (*supra*), and the composer of several sonatas and other chamber music, as well as more large-scale works. At least three duo sonatas
were published—one each for P & Vn (Op. 3 in d; 1852), P & Va (Op.
32 in g; 1875), and P & Vc (Op. 28 in D; 1876)—a sample evaluation
being that these are "underrated," although it is skill more than imagination or originality that makes them deserving.[115] Worth investigating,
too, might be the canonic "Grand Sonata" for P solo, Op. 2 (1869), by
the church music authority, influential teacher in Stockholm, and expert polyphonist **Johan Lindegren** (1842–1908).[116]

The Late-Romantic Sonata in Scandinavia (Nielsen, Sjögren, Sibelius)

During the *fin-de-siècle* generation after Hartmann, Gade, and Grieg
had flourished, the sonata enjoyed a new rise of interest in all three
main Scandinavian countries, Denmark, Norway, and Sweden. This
rise paralleled the more general rise of interest in chamber and orches-

---

112. Cf. Altmann/KAMMERMUSIK 215, 260; MGG VIII 1816–19 (G. Hahne).
113. Cf. GROVE VII 781 (J. A. Fuller-Maitland); MGG XII 662–63 (N. Schiørring);
PAZDÍREK XIII 630; Altmann/KAMMERMUSIK 306.
114. NZM XXVI (1847) 220–21 and LVI (1862) 199. Cf. GROVE I 634 (K. Dale);
PAZDÍREK II 534–35; Altmann/KAMMERMUSIK 195 (but read 1847, not 1848) and 296.
115. Cobbett/CHAMBER II 191 (G. Jeanson). Cf. GROVE VI 104–5 (Sinclair & K.
Dale); MGG IX 1572–74 (L. E. Sanner).
116. Cf. SOHLMANS III 642 (I. Stare); MGG VIII 890 (A. Helmer).

tral music already noted here in France, England, and other countries that had been coming increasingly under the influences of German teachers and composers (shortly before newer turns to French influences). Before taking note of Denmark's Nielsen, we may stop more briefly on two minor Danish composers, Bendix and Glass. Like several of the other Danes to be mentioned, the pianist **Victor Emanuel Bendix** (1851–1926) was a pupil of Gade.[117] His one sonata is Op. 26 in g, for P solo, published by Breitkopf & Härtel in 1901.[118] This is a long work of 46 pages in four movements (F-Sc-Va-VF), yet no typically grandiloquent product of an epigone. Instead it is marked by poeti-

Ex. 99. The start of the second movement in Victor Emanuel Bendix's Sonata in g, Op. 26 (after the original Breitkopf & Härtel ed. of 1901).

cally sensitive and nicely contrasted moods, created chiefly by Bendix's subtly variegated, chromatic harmony, with still a hint of the idiosyncratic harmonic colors and scale intervals in Grieg's writing. Exceptional harmonic ingenuity may be heard, for example, in the development of the first movement, the coda of the second, and the "Adagio" variation of the third. The sense of a broad dynamic structure is defeated somewhat in the first movement by extended, freely motivic sections that tend to unfold without clear directions. Bendix showed himself not to be weak but not to be distinctive, either, as a melodist.

117. Cf. Riemann/LEXIKON I 148; GROVE I 616–617 (E. V. d. Straeten).
118. Largely favorable reviews appear in NZM XCI (1903) 247 and MW XXXIV (1903) 40 (E. Segnitz).

He is most distinctive when he is creating a mood such as that of troubled gaiety in the "Intermezzo scherzando" of Op. 26 (Ex. 99).

The pianist **Louis Christian August Glass** (1864–1936), another sometime pupil of Gade, left four published sonatas—Opp. 7 in E♭ (1895) and 29 in C (1909) for P & Vn, and Opp. 6 in E (1892) and 25 in A♭ (1898) for P solo.[119] Except for the slighter, lighter, and more intimate Op. 29,[120] Glass's sonatas do not reveal the values found in his later works.[121] Although one reviewer of Op. 25, inverting Mattheson's remarks of 1739 (cf. SBE 26), was glad to find a sonata that could still move the heart as well as the fingers,[122] and although this work includes some chromatic and recherché harmony (as in the bridge of i), its four competently written movements (F-Sc-S-M), with their rather ordinary themes and some rather thick scoring, do bring us once more to the somewhat sterile and academic atmosphere of the epigone.

Still another pupil of Gade and a violinist, **Carl (August) Nielsen** (1865–1931) is being viewed increasingly today as one of the most significant composers among Danish Romantics and one of the most original on the threshold of Danish Modern music.[123] Nielsen's considerable, rounded output includes only two published sonatas, both duos for Vn & P,[124] among fourteen instrumental chamber works. But these two sonatas make up in outstanding quality and interest for any neglect in quantity. One is Op. 9 in A, composed in 1895, dedicated to the violinist Henri Marteau, and first performed and published in 1896 (both sonatas have been kept in print by Hansen). The other is Op. 35, in no one key (*infra*), composed in 1912,[125] first performed in 1913, and first published in 1919.

Nielsen's Opp. 9 and 35 have in common their three-movement cycles (F-M-F and F-VS-F), with about the same wide but not extreme ranges of expressive intensity and nearly the same over-all lengths (22 and 20 minutes).[126] Furthermore, they share their clear, orthodox "sonata

119. Cf. MGG V 239–40 (N. Schiørring), including the listing of a Son. in F, Op. 5, for P & Vc, in MS (1889).

120. Cf. the review by W. Altmann in DM X/2 (1910–11) 243.

121. A review of Op. 7 in SMW LIII (1895) 946 finds too much modulation and striving for effect.

122. MW XXXI (1899) 2.

123. Simpson/NIELSEN is a main account of the man (by T. Meyer) and his works (not only the symphonies). Cf., also, GROVE VI 85–88 (K. Jeppesen); MGG IX 1514–17 (N. Schiørring).

124. Items 20 and 64 in the full catalogue Fog/NIELSEN; item 3b) is an early, unpub. Son. "Nr. 1" for Vn & P, in G (1891–92; or 1892–93, as in Simpson/NIELSEN 187).

125. Cf. Simpson/NIELSEN 199; Balzer/NIELSEN 12–13 (T. Nielsen).

126. These sons. are described in Simpson/NIELSEN 149–50; in the symposium Balzer/NIELSEN 26–27 and 36–37 (P. Hamburger), 59–60 (A. Skjold-Rasmussen); and

forms" and A-B-A designs in the first and second movements, respectively; their fresh, inventive main ideas and warm, lyrical, persuasive contrasting themes (with the rising 4th being a basic interval in nearly all of Nielsen's themes known here); their clear but pliably irregular phrase syntax; their varied, frequently precious rhythms; and their well-balanced sound, with no special exploitation of instrumental display, color, or techniques, and with more understanding shown in the violin treatment than in the somewhat pedestrian, often chordal piano writing. One also notes the unfamiliar, piquant, though not programmatic inscriptions in both sonatas, such as "Allegro glorioso" and "agitato et adirato [angry]" in Op. 9/i, "Allegro piacevole e giovanile [agreeable and youthful]" in Op. 9/iii, and "Allegro con tiepidezza [with lukewarmth]" in Op. 35/i.

The parallel in the designs of Nielsen's sonatas breaks down in the finale of Op. 35, which is a decidedly freer adaptation of "sonata form" than its counterpart in Op. 9. Moreover, in Op. 35 there is the Modern tendency to develop each main idea as soon as it is introduced, leaving less reason for the traditional development section. But Nielsen's innovations pertain less to design or the other traits previously mentioned—there is actually a neo-Classic feel in the structural aspects of his music—than to harmony and tonality. In Op. 9 the broad tonal relationships are still simple and traditional, although their effect may be overshadowed somewhat by the newly bold dissonance in the harmony. This dissonance is largely explained by the diagonal harmonic relationships between the two instruments, which the listener absorbs readily enough as vertical relationships thanks to the integrity of the lines and the more conventional harmony within each part. By the time of Op. 35 Nielsen had advanced, liberated, and consolidated both his harmonic and his tonal language. The diagonal relationships sometimes border on polytonality in this sensitive thoroughbred work (Ex. 100), although at climaxes and other strategic moments they usually converge, briefly and with a clear focus, in harmonic oneness (e.g., Op. 35/i/43–47 and 74–78). In this converging, Nielsen anticipates the early polytonality of Milhaud. And when he stretches the diagonal relationships he can sound quite as recondite as Reger, with less chromaticism and less straining of traditional chord relationships, yet quite as much foundation in traditional harmony.[127]

---

in Dolleris/NIELSEN 39–42 and 183–89 (along with extracts from reviews). Op. 35 is described in Cobbett/CHAMBER II 189–90 (R. Simonsen), beginning with the assertion that it is "one of the weightiest chamber works of late years"; it is seen as the start of a compositional crisis for Nielsen in MT CVI (1965) 426–27.

127. Simpson/NIELSEN 35–36 and 145 offers further comparisons with Reger.

Ex. 100. From the start of the development section in the first movement of Carl Nielsen's Sonata Op. 35 (after the first ed. of 1919, by kind permission of Wilhelm Hansen Musik-Forlag, copyright owners in Copenhagen).

If there is a real challenge to tradition in Nielsen's Op. 35, it is at the tonal level.[128] Although key signatures still appear, the tonal center is often amorphous. In the second movement the two sharps do establish the key of b, at least at the main joints in the A-B-A design. But in the first movement the two flats can only mean the Lydian mode on Eb when they mean anything at all. In the last movement the two flats establish Bb at the start and the return, but in a stunning 52-measure coda the tone Bb proves to be not a tonic but a lowered-7th step that persists until it rises to C and a triple-*piano* cadence in the Mixolydian mode on that tone. Thus, the tonality of this work is not closed but open-ended, and most of the sense of key one gets derives not from one stable, clearly established tonality but from transient tonal centers.[129]

In Denmark mention should also be given to the organist **Otto (Valdemar) Malling** (1848–1915), pupil of both Hartmann and Gade, for a charming, light-hearted, three-movement Sonata in g (F-M-F),

128. Dolleris/NIELSEN 183–89 discusses the tonal aspects in some detail.
129. Cf. Jeppesen/NIELSEN 173–74.

Op. 57, for P & Vn (pub. in 1895); [130] the organist **Johann Adam Kry-gell** (1835–1915), for a "Sonata appassionata," Op. 57 in F$\sharp$, for organ (1904); [131] the violinist **Georg Höeberg** (1872–1950), for a rhythmically interesting, cyclical, three-movement Sonata (F Sc/M F) in G, Op. 1, for P & Vn (pub. in 1905); [132] the fine pianist **Roger Henrichsen** (1876–1926), for a three-movement, Brahmsian Sonata in F (F-S-VF), Op. 10, for P solo (pub. in 1912), a pianistically fluent work with considerable Romantic drive and lyricism;[133] the violinist **Fini Valdemar Henriques** (1867–1940), for a once popular Sonata in g, Op. 10, for Vn & P (pub. in 1893, revised later); [134] the organist and pupil of both Hartmann and Gade, **Gustaf Helsted** (1857–1924), for two published sonatas for P & Vn, Opp. 13 in A (1908) and 20 in G (1899); [135] and **Christian Barnekow** (1837–1913), for one more Sonata for P & Vn, Op. 23 in F (pub. in 1907), whose first movement still "breathes the spirit of Schumann and Gade." [136]

Norway's most notable Romantic composer after Grieg was certainly the Leipzig-trained violinist **Christian August Sinding** (1856–1941), whose teachers included Reinecke and Jadassohn.[137] Sinding's large and rounded list of publications, in which both the piano and violin figure importantly, includes more than thirty chamber works, large and small. Among these last, excluding two early discarded MSS played in 1879,[138] are five sonatas, Op. 91 in b (not g), for P solo (1909), and Opp. 12 in C (1892, not 1894), 27 in E (1895), 73 in F (1905), and 99 in d ("im alten Stil"; 1909) for Vn & P. Although these sonatas are forgotten today, at least Op. 99 enjoyed some popularity in its day— a work that is more of a suite, with its five short, colorful (nationalistic?), relatively static movements ("Praeludium," "Andante," "Menuett," "Intermezzo" in 5/4 and 7/4 meter, and "Finale").[139] Sinding's other sonatas are all more broadly conceived works and all in the usual

---

130. Cf. BAKER 1018. The work gets qualified praise as pleasant amateur music in SMW LIII (1895) 930 and LXI (1903) 126; MW XXVIII (1897) 584; Cobbett/ CHAMBER II 111 (W. W. Cobbett).

131. Cf. BAKER 880; MW XXXVI (1905) 143 (qualified approval).

132. Cf. BAKER 722; DM IV/4 (1904–5) 205 (W. Altmann).

133. Cf. Riemann/LEXIKON I 737.

134. Cf. MGG VI 161–62 (N. Schiørring); MW XXV (1894) 545 (approving all but an excess of motivic treatment).

135. Cf. BAKER 690; DM X/3 (1910–11) 184 (W. Altmann, praising the ideas, development, and scoring of Op. 13).

136. DM XI/3 (1911–12) 178 (W. Altmann). Cf. GROVE I 441 (H. C. Colles).

137. Cf. MGG XII 726–28 (O. Gurvin), with dated list of works.

138. MGG XII 726 (a son. for Vn & P and a son. mvt. for P solo).

139. The Vn sons. are described briefly in Cobbett/CHAMBER II 421–22 (M. M. Ulfrstad) and Shand/VIOLIN 147–50 (with exx. from Op. 27). Op. 99 is reviewed favorably in DM X/2 (1910–11) 242–43 (W. Altmann).

Ex. 101. From the opening-theme section of Christian Sinding's Sonata in b, Op. 91 (after the original Hansen ed. of 1909).

three-movement plan (F-M-F or F-M-VF). In Op. 73, the main theme of the finale is actually based on a Norwegian national dance, the "Springer." [140] Op. 73 is generally more chromatic, poetic, and sensitive than Op. 27, the style of which is as close to Richard Strauss's as to that of Wagner, of whom he was a staunch admirer. Also, at least in the first movement, there are passages that will sound familiar to anyone who knows Sinding's most popular piece, *Frühlingsrauschen,* Op. 32/3, for P solo, with its bold, sonorous dash, its cascades of arpeggio figures, and its protracted, sequential, climactic ascents to heroic peaks. The other two movements of Op. 27 are slightly thinner in texture but no less compelling (and traditional) in their harmony, nor any less songful in their attractive melodies.

Sinding's Op. 91 still recalls *Frühlingsrauschen* in its first movement, too. The almost constant modulation in that movement, chiefly through enharmonic re-interpretations of augmented and diminished chords, blurs the outlines of an entirely standardized "sonata form." Furthermore, it explains a reviewer's inability to find anything more than "swimming fantasies" in the outer movements[141] and it illustrates another product of Sinding's strong attraction to Wagner's music (Ex.

140. Cobbett/CHAMBER II 422.
141. DM IX/4 (1909–10) 50 (A. Leitzmann).

101). In the somber opening theme,[142] with its descending 5th and inner pedal, one finds a kinship with melodies by Sibelius. But here Sinding's undeniable melodic strength and originality are limited largely and somewhat tiresomely to this type of theme and to lines that outline scales in steady quarter- and 8th notes (as in both remaining movements). The resultant continuous, impelling flow, in conventional harmony and in textures that are idiomatic but almost too full, is, in fact, one of the most pronounced traits in all of Sinding's sonatas.

In Sweden the most important of the late Romantics was the organist (**Johan Gustaf**) **Emil Sjögren** (1853–1918), whose background included composition studies under Kiel in Berlin (ssb X) in 1879–80 and opportunities to know the music of Franck and Saint-Saëns in Paris in 1885.[143] Between 1886 and 1914 eight sonatas by Sjögren were published. Two are for P solo—Opp. 35 in e (1903, not 1902) and 44 in A (1905). Five are for Vn & P—Opp. 19 in g (1886), 24 in e (1889), 32 in g (1901), 47 in b (1908), and 61 in a (1913). And one is for Vc & P, Op. 58 in A (1914). The first two of the violin sonatas, especially the second, in e, were Sjögren's most successful and are now regarded as his best chamber works in a somewhat circumscribed output otherwise noted chiefly for its songs and shorter piano pieces.[144] These sonatas are made distinctive mainly by their tender, fresh, songful melodies and the choice, precise harmony that supports them rather than by any innovations in tonality and design, or, for that matter, by any conspicuous ability to develop the ideas or control the broad outlines of the larger designs.

The better-known of Sjögren's two piano sonatas, Op. 35, is a case in point, too. A relatively short work of twenty pages, it approximates his more usual four-movement plan by the not infrequent method of alternating andante and scherzando sections in a middle movement between two fast movements.[145] Although the duple and triple meters

142. Mss. 3–6 of Ex. 101 illustrate its first half in another key.

143. Cf. GROVE VII 827 (D. Hume & K. Dale); MGG XII 742–44 (A. Helmer), with partial, dated list of works, including a re-ed. in 1957 of the complete Vn sons. A study of Swedish instrumental music in the 19th-c., by Bo Wallner, is reportedly nearing completion as of this writing.

144. Cf. Cobbett/CHAMBER II 423–24 (G. Jeanson & W. W. Cobbett). But the later Vn sons. were generally greeted with enthusiasm, too, when they first appeared. On Op. 32, cf. DM I/1 (1901) 424 (W. Altmann); MW XXXIII (1902) 600 (E. Segnitz); SMW LXI (1903) 189 (less favorable). On Op. 47, cf. DM VIII/1 (1908–9) 367 (W. Altmann). There was also approval of the Vc son., Op. 58, in DM XII/2 (1912–13) 363 (H. Schlemüller). The 5 Vn sons. are described, with 10 exx., in Shand/VIOLIN 152–57. Mod. ed. of the 5 Vn sons.: SJÖGREN-m. with preface.

145. In a favorable review that questions only the (already!) slightly dated Scandinavian style, H. Teibler actually writes (erroneously) of "four concise movements" (DM III/3 [1903–4] 372). Op. 44 was reviewed as a somewhat lighter work, of value to the amateur and student (DM V/4 [1905–6] 326).

are reversed, there is an awareness of Brahms's Op. 100/ii in this double-purpose movement, in all probability by way of Kiel. One well-pleased reviewer likened the style of Op. 35 to that in the piano works of Brahms and Reger.[146] But his reference is mainly to Sjögren's harmonic style and today this style might more accurately be likened to that of Grieg (*supra*), including even the occasional hints of Franck or Fauré (ssb XIII), as in a succession of tonics that descend by whole-steps (Ex. 102). In other respects, too, Op. 35 recalls Grieg—in fact, at least the styles and occasionally the ideas of Grieg's own piano Sonata in e, Op. 7, published 37 years earlier.[147] The melodic ideas have similar popular appeal, though a little less distinction and originality. The

Ex. 102. The subordinate theme near the start of Emil Sjögren's Sonata in e, Op. 35 (after the original Hansen ed. of 1903).

texture is similar in its moderate chordal fullness, its but moderate challenges to the pianist, its shifts of range as means of color contrasts, and its occasional uncomplicated dialog and imitations. The association of dance and other type melodies with nationalistic influences is similar (as in the subordinate theme of Op. 35/iii), but with still less possibility of pointing to specific derivations. And the aesthetic scope is similar. Like Grieg, Sjögren was a gifted musician within narrow confines. In particular, he was even less of an architectonic composer at heart (or by training), with even less inclination (or ability) to develop his ideas in the Teutonically Classic sense and still more inclination than Grieg showed to resort to fantasy, excessive sequence, and

146. mw XXXVII (1906) 205.
147. E.g., there is a certain kinship between Ex. 102 and Grieg's Op. 7/i/94 ff.

matching pairs of square-half-phrases as the structural outs in his larger forms.

Though largely self-taught in composition, the pianist **Karl Wilhelm Eugen Stenhammar** (1871–1927) did get some early training with Sjögren.[148] Following an early, unpublished Sonata in g, for P solo (1890), he left two published sonatas, Op. 12 in A♭, for P solo (1897), and Op. 19 in a/A (not C), for P & Vn (1904). The first movement of Op. 12 alternates a chorale-like section, "Moderato, quasi Andante," with a more agitated, dynamically cumulative section marked "Allegretto animato," somewhat in the manner of Beethoven's Op. 27/1/i (sce 517). Then, after a light scherzando movement in the mediant key and ¢ meter, marked "Molto vivace" (and "Presto" over its "Trio" in 3/4 meter), there follows a free allegro finale in "sonata form," with a slow introduction that recalls the opening chorale idea. Op. 19, described approvingly as something of an idyll,[149] follows a simpler, more straightforward three-movement plan (F-M-F). Although Stenhammar's sonatas have been dismissed as inconsequential[150] and do tend to discourage performance with their Mendelssohnian and Brahmsian harmony and other traits that were archaic at the turn of this century, they actually reveal unexpected harmonic and melodic depths, considerable imagination in the scoring and disposition of ideas, and a broad, unconstrained command of form.

Other late-Romantic sonatas in Sweden that might repay further investigation include an Op. 1 in a, for P & Vn (pub. in 1893), by the Stockholm composer **Bror Beckman** (1866–1929); [151] Op. 19 in d, for P solo (pub. in 1899), by the organist and devotee of Franck and Widor **Gustaf Wilhelm Hägg** (1867–1925);[152] two light, charming works suggesting Grieg, in e and G, for P & Vn (composed in 1887 and 1910, and pub. in 1901 and 1916), by the pianist and prominent Swedish nationalist **Wilhelm Peterson-Berger** (1867–1942), noted mainly for his songs and operas;[153] Op. 7 in D♭, for P solo (1908?), by the Spanish-

148. Cf. GROVE VIII 75–76 (Sinclair & K. Dale) and MGG XII 1255–57 (B. Wallner), both with incomplete lists of works and further bibliography; also, SOHLMANS IV 915–22 (B. Wallner, with a more detailed survey).

149. Cobbett/CHAMBER II 455–56 (S. Broman & W. W. Cobbett). Cf., also, Shand/VIOLIN 165–67, with 5 exx.

150. MGG XII 1255. In NZM C (1904) 818, Op. 19 was reviewed with praise and as a work relatively little colored by nationalism (somewhat contrary to B. Wallner in SOHLMANS IV 918).

151. The names in this paragraph have been suggested as being of possible interest by Professor Ingmar Bengtsson of Uppsala Universitet.

152. Cf. SOHLMANS II 1210–11 (G. Percy); GROVE IV 14 (K. Dale). Op. 19 (especially its "Intermezzo") is praised in MW XXX (1899) 587.

153. Cf. MGG X 1123–24 (B. Carlberg); Shand/VIOLIN 157–62, with brief descriptions and 12 exx.; Cobbett/CHAMBER II 215 (W. W. Cobbett).

born organist and pupil of Stenhammar among others, **Olallo Juan Magnus Morales** (1874–1957);[154] and Op. 7 in e, for P & Vn (pub. in 1911), by the complex harmonist, under Wagner's and Reger's influence, **Edvin Kallstenius** (1881–   ).[155] The "Sonata à la legenda" for Vn & P, Op. 7 in C (1919), by Harold Leonard Fryklöf (1882–1919) and most of the numerous solo and duo sonatas (largely unpub.) by Ivar Henning Mankell (1868–1930) are a little late and too progressive in their harmonic and tonal styles to be grouped with the sonatas of our other late-Romantics.[156]

As suggested at the start of this chapter, the renowned Finnish master **Jean Sibelius** (1865–1957) might best be grouped with our Scandinavian, especially our Swedish composers. His early training was followed similarly by German training and by study in Austria under Fuchs and Goldmark (ssb XI and IX).[157] Along with his many orchestral, accompanied and unaccompanied choral, and incidental stage works, and his many smaller pieces for piano, for solo voice and piano, and for nearly every other setting he employed, he left but little in the category of chamber music.[158] Besides only one mature, large-scale work, the string Quartet "Voces intimae," there was one duo "Sonatine," Op. 80 in E, for Vn & P (composed in 1915 and pub. by Hansen in 1921). Two earlier "sonatas" in the same scoring were left unpublished (1883, 1886 in F).[159] For P solo there were also the Sonata in F (composed in 1893 and pub. by Breitkopf & Härtel in 1906) and three later "sonatines," Op. 67/1–3, in f♯ (not A, as on the printed cover!), E, and b♭ (composed and pub. in 1912). Thus, Sibelius left a total of four published sonatinas and one published sonata.

Although all five works are slight, especially in texture and expressive weight, they bear the unmistakable stamp of the master. In fact, partially excepting the less subtle and experienced Op. 12, they may be called miniature Sibelius masterpieces. Yet they have received re-

154. Cf. sohlmans III 987–88 (G. Percy); mgg IX 563–64 (A. Helmer), calling Op. 7 Brahmsian. Yet, Op. 7 was reviewed as another of "the many modern sonatas" that lack form and thematic development (dm IX/4 [1909–10] 109 [A. Leitzmann]).

155. Cf. mgg VII 459–61 (L. Reimers); Cobbett/chamber II 46; dm XI/1 (1911–12) 235 (W. Altmann, with praise for the poetic slow mvt. but not for harmonic excesses in the outer mvts.).

156. Cf. grove III 510–11 (K. Dale); mgg VIII 1585–87 (I. Bengtsson); stfmf XXIII (1941) 5–33 (I. Bengtsson), with full, dated cat. of Mankell's MS and pub. works.

157. For more exact biographical information than that in grove VII 772–81 (E. Blom) and mgg XII 652–62 (N.-E. Ringbom), cf. the "Persönlichkeit" section in Tanzberger/sibelius 14–69 and the additional studies singled out in the "Introduction" (especially p. ix) of the valuable bibliography Blum/sibelius.

158. Cf. the "Werkverzeichnis" of pub. works and MSS, with and without op. nos., in Tanzberger/sibelius 265–89.

159. Cf. Blum/sibelius item 42.

markably little attention by either writers or performers.[160] Even including Op. 12, when they first appeared their striking originality and
independence seem to have puzzled or at least put off the reviewers.[161]
And in recent studies their peripheral position in Sibelius' total output
seems to have discouraged anything more than a few brief discussions
of them.[162]

Sibelius' one so-called "Sonata," Op. 12, makes a publication of
twenty-five pages, a fifth longer than Op. 80 and over two-and-a-half
times the lengths of Op. 67/1–3. All these works divide clearly into
three movements, with two quick movements enclosing a slower movement, except Op. 67/3, in which the second of the but two movements
accelerates from an "Andante" to an "Allegretto" section on the same
theme. The fast movements Opp. 67/3/i and 80/i and iii have brief,
slower introductions. Whereas the middle movements of Opp. 12 and
80 are in contrasting keys—subdominant minor and dominant major,
respectively—all movements are in the same key in each sonatina of
Op. 67. Except for Op. 67/1, each of these works reveals more or less
clear thematic relationships between its movements. "Sonata form"
seems still to be a conscious guiding principle in the outer movements
of Op. 12 in F, although the emphasis on the key of the raised 2d (g♯)
in the development sections of both movements and the choice of the
subdominant key (B♭) for the subordinate theme in the exposition of
the first movement tend to contradict that principle. A freer "sonata
form" seems to be intentional, also, in Op. 80/i, but hints of that principle seem more coincidental than intentional in Op. 67/1/i and 3/i.
The rondo principle operates more or less in Opp. 12/ii and all the
sonatina finales. Op. 67/2/i suggests an invention. The middle movements of the three three-movement sonatinas are all free, open forms
that unfold continuously.

However, the real interest in Sibelius' forms lies not in discovering
standardized designs that happen at least to be hinted in some of the
movements but in the seemingly intuitive, independent process out of
which all these forms grow. It was Cecil Gray, echoed by later writers,

160. Op. 80 was played at the first German Sibelius festival in Lübeck, in 1958
(Tanzberger/SIBELIUS 243).

161. E.g., DM VI/4 (1906–7) 305 (A. Leitzmann, reporting the originality as incompatible with "rigid sonata form" and the ideas weak except in ii); DM XII/4
(1912–13) 108 (A. Leitzmann, reviewing Op. 67/1–3 as dull and unimportant); SMW
LXXXII (1924) 1942 (Op. 80 reviewed in 2 sentences as Nordic, less characteristic
of Sibelius than his large, orchestral fantasias, not too difficult, and effective).

162. Cf. Abraham/SIBELIUS 96 (Op. 80, by S. Goddard), 98–100 and 101–3 (Opp.
12 and 67/1–3, by E. Blom); Tanzberger/SIBELIUS 242–43 (Op. 80) and 245 (one
sentence on Opp. 12 and 67/1–3). More on the P sons. is cited in Blum/SIBELIUS
item 52. Cobbett/CHAMBER II 416–19 (E. Blom) discusses only the string quartet.

who found the main generative process in Sibelius' symphonies, especially No. 4, to be the "organic evolution of a germ idea." [163] But that view, which sees the form as beginning only with thematic fragments and culminating with their ultimate synthesis in a grand theme (a process ascribed to Bruckner's symphonies, too) has rightly been challenged in Sibelius[164] and fails to apply in the sonatinas, in any case. In the latter the generative process is one of simple syntactic extensions. A main idea is likely to be toyed with and restated piecemeal through imaginative, rhythmically free, unpredictable reiterations, variations, or rondo-like recurrences of its most salient motives. Actually, this process, plus thin, precise textures sometimes attenuated to

Ex. 103. From the middle movement of Sonatina in f♯, Op. 67/1, by Jean Sibelius (after the original Breitkopf & Härtel ed. of 1912).

the point of monophony, plus persistent accompaniment figures in the manner of an *ostinato,* plus scoring that disappoints the keyboardist (especially in the unidiomatic accompaniments) but does evoke orchestral colors, plus harmonic progressions that are constantly fresh without being tonally disruptive—all these traits, which too often produce mere platitudes in Sibelius' other piano music, make his sonatinas sound not only like miniature masterpieces but like miniature Sibelius symphonies. Unfortunately, in the one example that can be allowed, only hints and only some of these traits can be illustrated (Ex. 103, including faint reminders of stentorian brass passages in Symphony 4 in a, completed about a year earlier [1910–11]).

163. As in Gray/SIBELIUS 142–43; Tovey/ANALYSIS II 121–22. The quoted expression is a composite of several similar descriptions (cf. Newman/TREND 124–35).
164. As in Hill/SIBELIUS; Collins/GERM.

Finally in this chapter, passing mention may be given to three Finnish contemporaries of Sibelius. The internationally successful, German-trained pianist **Selim Palmgren** (1878–1951), whose teachers included Busoni and whose piano works included the pedagogically popular "May Night," composed in 1900 a three-movement, pseudo-Modern, harmonically mawkish, melodically sterile, texturally thick, rhythmically free, and structurally traditional Sonata in d, Op. 11, for P solo (pub. in 1927 by Augener).[165] The theorist and conductor **Erkki Gustaf Melartin** (1875–1937), a pupil of Robert Fuchs in Vienna, left in print four sonatinas for P solo, Op. 84 (1919) and Sonata in E, Op. 10, for P & Vn (1909), described as a warm, melancholy, original concert work, although somewhat prolix.[166] And the conductor **Toivo Kuula** (1883–1918), who completed his training in Bologna, Leipzig, and Paris, left a youthful Sonata in e, Op. 1, for P & Vn (1909), which is described in similar terms.[167]

165. Cf. MGG X 714–15 (N.-E. Ringbom).

166. DM X/4 (1910–11) 247 (W. Altmann). Cf. MGG IX 7–8 (N.-E. Ringbom), with reference to two other duo sons., as well; Cobbett/CHAMBER II 127.

167. DM X/4 (1910–11) 247 (W. Altmann). Cf. MGG VII 1924–25 (N.-E. Ringbom); Cobbett/CHAMBER II 83–84 (E. Blom).

Chapter XVI

A Low Ebb in Italy, Spain, and Portugal

Circumstances and Sources

That this is the shortest of our thirteen regional chapters reflects the low ebb of the sonata not only in Spain and Portugal during the Romantic Era, but in Italy, which for so long had been a main fountainhead of independent instrumental music. After Turini in Italy and Soler in Spain (SCE 295–97 and 279–85), there are only sporadic, average products to report, at best, and scarcely more even with the instrumental renaissance of the 1870's that touched these countries as well as most of the rest of Europe. It would be tempting to blame the low ebb on the political distresses of foreign rule, civil disruptions, and scattered revolutionary movements. These distresses plagued both Spain and Portugal, with their persistently unstable monarchies, and Italy, which still remained largely a "geographical expression" until the Risorgimento. Valiantly guided by Cavour, Garibaldi, and others, the Risorgimento finally led to full unification in 1870 (the same year unification obtained in Germany) as well as emancipation, under Victor Emmanuel II, from the rival French and Austrian controls. However, the political problems did not stop important music in other categories from appearing in these countries, notably Italian opera and its Iberian counterparts. One has to assume that Bellini, Verdi, Puccini, Manuel Garcia (Sr.) and nearly all of the other most successful composers saw nothing to attract them in the sonata.[1] Men of this sort who did respond to it, including Paganini, Rossini, and Albéniz, did so only more or less incidentally within their total outputs. Furthermore, even when that instrumental renaissance occurred in Italy during the later 19th century, only two of its three main champions wrote sonatas— that is, Martucci and Bossi but not Sgambati, as against all three in the contemporary triumvirates we have already noted in France, England, and Scandinavia (early in Chaps. XIII, XIV, and XV).

1. Cf. MGG VI 1533–34, 1542, 1543, 1546 (M. Mila); XII 1006–7 (J. Subirá); X 1485 (J. d. Freitas Branco).

During travels of 1853 Moscheles found almost no evidence of creative musical distinction, pianistic or otherwise, in Italy.[2] In Venice, "I find on all sides shallowness and mediocrity. . . . The only good music . . . is that of the Austrian military band"; the music of Moscheles himself was regarded as "too serious" to play there. At the Milan Conservatory, "of Beethoven or Mendelssohn they know absolutely nothing." While in Paris in 1860 Moscheles reported Rossini's joy in the Classic masters (including Clementi and his sonatas) and in Weber, but not in the current Italian music.[3] At any rate, a curious unawareness of the "sonata" in full bloom, as it had matured in their own and other countries, becomes apparent in the reversion by Paganini, Rossini, and others to the earlier, looser meaning merely of "soundpiece." (In such a sense, even Verdi might qualify as a "sonata" composer, with his "Suona la tromba" ["Sound the trumpet"] for male chorus and P-or-orchestra, dated 1848). And we get more evidence of the little interest in the sonata in 19th-century Italy from the fact that most of the sonatas by Italians were either composed while they were residing in foreign, more receptive regions, or at least published in those regions (especially London, Paris, and Leipzig). Furthermore, during the Italian instrumental renaissance the single strongest influence was not an Italian, but a resident foreigner in Rome, Liszt.[4]

The studies are lacking that might turn up further and more significant instrumental activities in Italy, Spain, and Portugal during the Romantic Era. There is one reference work from each country that frequently contributes specific details of value—Schmidl/DIZIONARIO (by Carlo Schmidl, himself variously involved in late-19th-c. Italian music), DICCIONARIO LABOR, and DICCIONARIO PORTUGUEZES. Otherwise the sources are too often poor or nonexistent. For example, except where the publications occurred in foreign centers, precise dating of printed sonatas, such as those issued by Ricordi in Milan or Unión Musical Español in Madrid, is generally not yet possible.

Italy in the First Half-Century (Paganini and Rossini)

The two most important musicians who wrote sonatas in early 19th-century Italy were certainly the warm friends Paganini and Rossini, although those sonatas contributed only incidentally to Paganini's importance and not at all to Rossini's. The legendary master violinist **Nicolò** (or **Niccolò**) **Paganini** (1782–1840) wrote at least 51 solo and

2. MOSCHELES II 234–40.
3. MOSCHELES II 270–79.
4. Cf. De Angelis/ROMA *passim.*

ensemble "sonatas," so called, over the years from his earliest training with his father in Genoa,[5] through his rising fame in Lucca and other Italian centers, to his sensational concert triumphs (from 1828) in Austrian, German, French, and British centers, and his final years of failing health in Italy and France.[6] Of 50 "sonatas" that have been identified in the best but still somewhat unresolved lists of Paganini's compositions[7] some were written as diversional music for the amateur and some for his own electrifying, virtuosic performances, on both the violin and the guitar (which interest derived from mandolin instruction that his father had given to him).[8] No fewer than 32 of the 50 sonatas (64 per cent) are scored for violin and guitar, with the violin being the solo instrument in most, the guitar in a few, and the two instruments being partners in a few. Of these 32, 2 sets of 6 each were composed about 1802–9 and first published by G. Ricordi in 1820 (Paganini's only sons. pub. in his lifetime); 3 sets of 6 each, referred to by the collective title "Centone [medley?] di Sonate" added in another hand, were composed after 1828 and appeared only posthumously, chiefly piecemeal and in arrangements for Vn & P until W. Zimmermann of Frankfurt/M published all 3 sets in their original version in 1955–56;[9] and 2 or 3 separate sonatas for violin and guitar appeared only posthumously, including a delightful duet in A, called "Sonata concertata" (composed in 1804 [10]), and a long "Grande Suonata" in A, in which the guitar dominates entirely.[11]

5. "Even before I was eight years old, I wrote a sonata under the supervision of my father, but it is no longer in existence, having been torn up like numerous other experimental works of the same kind" (from Paganini's autobiographical sketch for J. Schottky, as trans. in Courcy/PAGANINI II 369).

6. Courcy/PAGANINI (outlined in Courcy/CHRONOLOGY) has proved to be much the fullest and most authoritative biographical and documentary source (only) since it was added in 1957 to the considerable, recently mushrooming literature on Paganini, although it still does not contain some of the information on the sons. to be found in the voluminous documentary study Codignola/PAGANINI (1935). Vyborny/PAGANINI surveys that literature up to 1964, including serious flaws that still persist from early sources, in GROVE VI 488–94 (E. Blom), and even in Courcy's article, especially in the music listings, for MGG X 627–33; cf., also, Codignola/PAGANINI 75–76. The most accurate, up-to-date encyclopedic article as of this writing (1968) is that by Pietro Berri in Gatti & Basso/LA MUSICA III 679–91, including recent bibliography.

7. Codignola/PAGANINI 653–55 (pub.) and 655–63 (unpub.), including descriptive comments by A. A. Bachmann, A. Bonaventura, and others; Courcy/PAGANINI II 373–88; Gatti & Basso/LA MUSICA III 687–91. The last 2 lists give the most recent as well as the earliest eds., but cannot be fully reconciled with PAZDÍREK XI 31–32.

8. Cf. Bone/GUITAR 262–74.

9. A recording of the first set is reviewed informatively by A. Mell in MQ XLVI (1960) 557–59.

10. Cf. Courcy/CHRONOLOGY 14; Codignola/PAGANINI 212.

11. A recording (Mace SM-9025) of these 2 sons. and another duet by Paganini,

Four more of Paganini's 50 identified "sonatas" are "Sonatines" for guitar alone.[12] Another, composed by 1834, is scored "per la grande viola," with guitar accompaniment.[13] And the remainder are scored for violin with various accompaniments, including one "a violino scordato" accompanied by 2 other violins (probably composed about 1802–6),[14] 3 with P as accompaniment (composed between 1825 and at least 1831),[15] and 9 with orchestral accompaniments.[16]

By their descriptive titles alone the separate sonatas in the category last cited—that is, for Vn with various accompaniments—would reveal that Paganini used the word sonata not with any standardized plan or designs in mind but merely in its earlier, generic sense of a relatively extended instrumental piece, often, though not always, in only one sectional movement. If his use of the word connotes any one principle it is that of variation form rather than "sonata form." Several of those titles actually specify variations in subtitles. A "Sonata a preghièra [prayer]" is subtitled (and trans.) "Introduction and Variations on the theme 'From Thy Star-Studded Throne' in Rossini's Moïse." [17] A "Sonata Amorosa Galante" includes in its title, as given on a London poster of 1831, the facts of both the variation form and one of the composer's most frequent virtuoso stunts—"with Variations on a Tema by Rossini, composed expressly and performed on a SINGLE STRING, (the Fourth,) by Signor PAGANINI, with Piano-Forte Accompaniment." [18] Haydn's "Austrian National Hymn," Weigl's opera L'Amor marinaro, and Mozart's Marriage of Figaro were among other sources of themes for Paganini's variation "sonatas." [19] The sections in such

identified only as "Sonata Opus Posthumous," is reviewed in The New York Times music section for Feb. 20, 1966.

12. Cf. Courcy/PAGANINI II 385.

13. Cf. Courcy/PAGANINI II 382; Codignola/PAGANINI 379, 657.

14. Facs. of the autograph of the first and last pp. are pub. in Berri/PAGANINI 48–49. Cf. Courcy/PAGANINI I 64 and II 283.

15. Cf. Gatti & Basso/LA MUSICA III 689 and Courcy/PAGANINI II 379–80 (but "Sonata movimento perpetuo" is indicated here with chamber accompaniment; no accompaniment is shown in the facs. of the last autograph p. in Codignola/PAGANINI 142), 381, 382.

16. Cf. Gatti & Basso/LA MUSICA III 687–88.

17. Codignola/PAGANINI 265, 381; Courcy/PAGANINI II 377. The work, also known as "Moses Fantasy," was composed presumably in 1818 or 1819 after the first performance of Rossini's Mosè in Egitto in Naples in 1818, although the title Moïse en Egypte was not used until the first Paris performance in 1827.

18. Facs. of this and another Paganini poster of 1831 (including 2 more, similar sons.) appear as Plate 3 in Spivacke/PAGANINIANA. Cf., also, Gatti & Basso/LA MUSICA III 685; Courcy/PAGANINI II 381.

19. Cf. Codignola/PAGANINI 265; Courcy/PAGANINI II 380 and 382. Some of the titles were occasional, like "Sonata Napoleone," named for Paganini's performance of it on the Emperor's birthday in 1807. A facs. of the opening in the autograph

sonatas consist typically of an introduction in slow-to-moderate tempo, the theme-and-variations, and a brilliant final variation or coda. These "sonatas" do not differ tangibly from other variation works similarly scored by Paganini that happen not to include "sonata" in their titles.[20] Mainly, such variation works supplied the display pieces, including the "secret" techniques,[21] that enraptured audiences whenever and wherever he played them, at home and abroad, and inspired Schumann, Chopin, Liszt, Berlioz, and other important musicians to write verbal tributes, musical homages, and/or transcriptions adapted to their own instrumental tastes. Moscheles' lavish praise and exceptional interest were characteristic, as also, however, were certain reservations after increased exposure to Paganini's playing and compositions:

Suffice it to say, my admiration of this phenomenon, equally endowed by nature and art, was boundless. Now, however, after hearing him frequently, all this is changed; in every one of his compositions I discover *the same* effects, which betrays a poverty of invention; I also find both his style and manner of playing monotonous. His concertos are beautiful, and have even their grand moments; but they remind me of a brilliant firework on a summer's eve, one flash succeeding the other—effective, admirable—but always the same. His 'Sonata Militaire,' and other pieces, have a southern glow about them, but this hero of the violin cannot dispense with the roll of the drum; and completely as he may annihilate his less showy colleagues, I long for a little of Spohr's earnestness, Baillot's power, and even Mayseder's piquancy.[22]

Although variation forms occur in the sonatas of Paganini's Opp. 2 and 3, too, in general those sonatas and the "Centone di Sonate" for Vn & guitar come closer to the then established idea of the sonata, at least in its lighter forms and sometimes to an extent that belies Cobbett's peremptory dismissal of Paganini's compositions as "not real chamber music." [23] The most frequent plan of these duo sonatas is that of a songful slow or moderate movement followed by a simple binary, ternary, or rondo design in quick tempo. The feeling of a sonatina rather than a sonata is conveyed by the brevity of the movements, the lightness of texture, and the lack of any significant develop-

of the latter appears in Codignola/PAGANINI 78, and of "Suonati con variazioni," in Gatti & Basso/LA MUSICA III 686.

20. E.g., those listed in Courcy/PAGANINI II 375–76; on pp. 272 and 276 the 3 *"grandiossissime* sonatas with variations," "just composed" by Paganini, according to 2 letters he wrote in 1838, are believed to include a "Balletto Campestre" without "sonata" in the title.

21. Probably extended uses of harmonics (cf. W. Kirkendale in JAMS XVIII [1965] 394–407).

22. MOSCHELES I 251–57; cf. pp. 272 and 293. Cf., also, the contemporary reports from Vienna and Paris in praise of Paganini's wondrous effects in the same "suonata militare," as quoted in Codignola/PAGANINI 64, 66–69.

23. Cobbett/CHAMBER II 205–6 (W. W. Cobbett).

Ex. 104. From the second (final) movement of Nicolò Paganini's Sonata in e, Op. 3/6 (after the reprinting by the International Music Co., 1943).

ment of materials. As for the nature of the ideas and their treatment, Paganini's well-known violin caprices Op. 1 and his closeness to Rossini are safe clues. Clear-cut melodies and figures, organized into regular, well-defined phrases, prevail. Nor are these ideas without idiomatic refinements, some originality, and the support of appropriate well-balanced accompaniments. An illustration may be provided from the duo best known in print (Ex. 104).

Paganini undoubtedly knew another popular Italian guitarist, seven years his senior, **Antonio Maria Nava** (1775–1828), who was also the author of a guitar method (1812) as well as a vocalist.[24] Between about 1810 and 1825 Nava published numerous sonatinas and sonatas, singly and in sets, for guitar solo, as well as numerous duets for two guitars or guitar and violin that are similarly light and similarly oriented to the variation principle.[25]

Our justification for including here the major Italian opera composer **Gioacchino (Antonio) Rossini** (1792–1868) is no more than the generic title "Sonate a quattro" applied to his earliest known compositions.

24. Cf. Bone/GUITAR 257–58.

25. The only son. that survives in PAZDÍREK XI 45 is a "Sonatine" for guitar. But cf. HOFMEISTER 1815 (Whistling), 258, and 1828 (Whistling), 410–11. Weinmann/ ARTARIA item 2194, dated 1811, is a "Sonata sentimentale" for guitar.

The set in question comprises six three-movement cycles composed in his twelfth year (1804) for a hospitable friend Agostino Triossi and scored for 2 Vns, Vc, & double-bass. In this original version, it was not made known nor published until recently, in 1954.[26] But five of the quartets (minus No. 3 [27]) appeared in other scorings, perhaps neither made nor sponsored by Rossini himself, including standard string quartets (first pub. in 1826) and, most successfully, as wind quartets (Fl, Cl, Hn, Bn; first pub. in 1828–29).[28] The original set, in other words, contained the only quartets Rossini is known to have written.[29]

Each of Rossini's six "Sonate" is in a major key of no more than three sharps or flats and contains three movements in the order F-M-F (except that Son. 1/i is "Moderato"). Three of the middle movements are in minor keys and two get as far afield tonally as the lowered submediant (Son. 1) and lowered mediant (Son. 6). The first movements fall short of anticipating textbook "sonata form" by providing no dualistic contrast beyond successions of like ideas and no development beyond mere transpositions of thematic elements.[30] Four of the middle movements return sooner or later to their openings and two do not. Four of the finales are rondos, one (Son. 3) is a naively virtuosic set of variations and one (Son. 6), marked "Tempesta," is a fantasy that anticipates distantly but significantly the "Overture," especially the storm, in *William Tell*. The Mozartean, clearly phrased tunes, the triplets and dotted patterns, the telling scoring, the prevailing gaiety, and the harmonic progressions that amount to continuous cadential formulas all anticipate later Rossini styles, too, especially the *buffa* styles of *The Barber of Seville*. In these respects Rossini was undeniably precocious (cf. SCE 289–90). As "sonatas," these early quartets, for all their brightness and Classic charm, suffer, understandably enough, from sameness of style (the compound meter in the finale of Son. 1 differs little in effect from the 4/4 meter with triplets in the first mvt.). Those successions of like ideas straggle, without thematic interrelations or development, and the lack of adequate key contrast precludes tonal tension, particularly in the first movements.

26. Rossini/SONATE-m, with a helpful preface by A. Bonaccorsi and a facs. of an autobiographical note by Rossini. Cf., also, MGG XI 948–74 (F. Lippmann), especially 957, 967, 970–71 (other versions and eds.), and 973. The original MS is in the Library of Congress.

27. No. 3 is the "ignota 'Sonata'" discovered by A. Casella in 1942 (MGG XI 973) and ed. by him for pub. in 1951 (Milan: Carisch).

28. Cf. MGG XI 970–71.

29. This fact was not realized by earlier writers, as in the primary documentary study Radiciotti/ROSSINI I 45–46 and in Cobbett/CHAMBER II 305–6 (E. Blom & W. W. Cobbett); nor in the jacket notes for the Dover recording HCR-5214 (wind version).

30. The styles and forms are not viewed here quite as they are by A. Bonaccorsi in Rossini/SONATE-m ix.

Although Vincenzo Bellini wrote no sonatas along with his "Sinfonie" and other early instrumental music, the other member besides Rossini in the illustrious trio of Italian opera composers, **Gaetano Donizetti** (1797–1848), did do so. In fact, in Donizetti's vast and varied output no fewer than twelve sonatas have survived.[31] All twelve survived only in MSS (all autographs but one) and, to judge from the years 1819 or 1820 on seven of the MSS, most or all originated as student works. Eight are P-duets and four are duos, one each for P & Vn, P & Fl, P & Ob, and P & Vc. Very little is known about the circumstances of Donizetti's instrumental music.[32] The only information about his sonatas consists of a few dedications and a few capricious titles or inscriptions in the MSS, the latter including (in trans.) "The Usual Sonata," "One of the More Freakish," and "Captain Battle." Unfortunately, the only one of these sonatas that has been made available through a modern edition proves to be too commonplace, inconsequential, and derivative (from Mozart and his contemporaries) to stimulate exploration of the other eleven sonatas. It is a "Suonata per Oboe, e Pianoforte di G. D. all'Amico Severino degl'Antonj . . ." in F.[33] Two annotations in the autograph suggest orchestration of the work was planned. The first of the two short movements is, as with Rossini, a succession of similar, clearly phrased melodies, undeveloped, only slightly interrelated, and accompanied by nothing but the most elementary, routine basses. The finale, an "Allegro" in 6/8 meter, is similar in style and principle except for its rondo design.

In 1817 a set of *Dodici Sonate di stile fugato pel pianoforte,* perhaps meant for organ as well as P solo, was published in Lucca as one of the numerous vocal and instrumental works, mostly sacred, by the canon of the cathedral, **Marco Santucci** (1762–1843).[34] This scarce music awaits present-day exploration but presumably reflects Santucci's preoccupation with past styles. Scarcely less obscure are the five sonatas for P solo, published between 1844 and 1859, by an early Chopin editor for Ricordi and the pianist whom Ferdinand Hiller regarded as Italy's best at the time, **Stefano Golinelli** (1818–91).[35] Golinelli's music is reported

31. Cf. Gatti & Basso/LA MUSICA II 258–83 (G. Barblan), especially pp. 277 and 288; Zavadini/DONIZETTI 16–18; Weinstock/DONIZETTI 385, 387.

32. Cf. Weinstock/DONIZETTI 18, 22, 23.

33. Mod. ed.: Peters Nr. 5919 (1966), ed. and prefaced by R. Meylan.

34. The place and date are given with the listing of the MS (autograph?) in Cat. BOLOGNA IV 64. Ricordi in Milan pub. the set, for P solo, between 1820 and 1828 (HOFMEISTER 1828 [Whistling], 601). On Santucci, cf. MGG XI 1386–87 (A. Bonaccorsi).

35. Cf. RICORDI ENCICLOPEDIA II 333–34; Sietz/HILLER I 51; HOFMEISTER 1844–51, 115–16, and 1852–59, 158; PAZDÍREK VI 369–70. Ricordi pub. all but Son. 4 (Breitkopf & Härtel), and repub. Sons. 2, 3, and 5 in the now scarce RICORDI ARTE-m XVII and XIX (among the 73 pieces by Golinelli that fill Vols. XVII–XX!).

to be "distinguished by elegance and grace of form, refinement of style, and originality of splendid melodies that exist in great profusion," and is regarded as unjustly forgotten today.[36] We may add that his music proves also to be worth investigating for the great breadth of its melodies, for its ingenious passagework, and for its expert piano scoring apart from some octave excesses and wide spacing that sometimes dangerously attenuate the sonorities.

Italy in the Later Romantic Era (Martucci)

The most important sonata composer in late-Romantic Italy and a pioneer in the renaissance of Italian instrumental music, **Giuseppe Martucci** (1856–1909) excelled also as a pianist, encouraged early by the support of both Liszt and Rubinstein; as an editor (like Golinelli, of Ricordi's early ed. of Chopin); and as a conductor.[37] Among a variety of instrumental (and a few vocal) works, four sonatas by Martucci were published, all in the decade 1874–84, including Op. 22 in G, for P & Vn (Ricordi, 1874); Opp. 34 in E and 41/1 ("Sonate facile"), for P solo (Ricordi, 1875 and ?); and Op. 52 in f♯, for Vc & P (Kistner in Leipzig, 1884). The last may well have been played on the recital tours in which he joined with the celebrated cellist Piatti in 1877–78. An organ sonata in D, dated 1879, was left in MS.

Opp. 34 and 52 are Martucci's most interesting, and apparently his most successful, sonatas.[38] Both sonatas are serious, substantial works in four movements, in the order F-Sc-M-F. Both are rich in texture and harmony, both show refined craftsmanship, including expert scoring and continual polyphonic interest, and both show a large, well-grounded view of the standard forms. Obviously Martucci was no descendant of Paganini or Rossini, but derived from Austro-German models. Brahms in particular comes to mind, although occasionally Mendelssohn is suggested, as in the more chromatic harmonic progressions that support the opening theme in Op. 34/i, or Chopin, as in the figural accompaniment in the middle section of Op. 34/iii. Indeed, it is the uncomfortably close resemblance to Brahms's music along with generally unprepossessing themes, sentimental chromaticism from time to time, and some moments when the textural fullness seems excessive (as in the start of Op. 34/iii) that make any appreciable revival of

36. Schmidl/DIZIONARIO I 644.
37. Cf. MGG VIII 1732–33 (D. Di Chiera); RICORDI ENCICLOPEDIA III 116–17.
38. Op. 34 was reprinted in Ricordi's 6-vol. ed. (II 112) of Martucci's *Composizioni* for P solo (plate nos. 95491–96). Op. 52 (but not Op. 22) is described, with 4 exx., at the end of an extended discussion of his main chamber works in Cobbett/CHAMBER II 117–22 (G. Cesari).

Ex. 105. From the opening of the third movement in Giuseppe Martucci's Sonata in f♯, Op. 52 (after the original Kistner ed. of 1884).

Martucci's worthy sonatas unlikely today. Compared with Parry's similar sonatas in England, from the same decade (SSB XIV), Martucci's seem a little more fluent, expressive, and compelling. Never do they reveal quite the creative flashes of a Franck or a Fauré at his best, but they do have their special moments, as in the fresh marchlike rhythm of the opening theme in Op. 34/iv, or the exceptionally warm melody in the short "Intermezzo" of Op. 52 (Ex. 105).

Another important pioneer of the late-Romantic renaissance in Italian instrumental music, Giovanni Sgambati (1841–1914), left only larger ensembles among cyclic works, not sonatas nor their equivalents. For the rest, the few names are mostly obscure today. The concert violinist **Antonio Bazzini** (1818–97) settled in Brescia in 1864 and Milan in 1873 after wide concert tours originally encouraged by Paganini.[39] Two of his several more important instrumental publications were *Trois Morceaux en forme de Sonate,* in E♭ (Ricordi, 1866), and Sonata in e, Op. 55 (Ricordi, 1872), both for P & Vn.[40] The music writer and publisher Carlo Schmidl found Bazzini's music to be distinguished by lightness and grace of melody, nobility of style, and

39. Cf. Schmidl/DIZIONARIO I 132; RICORDI ENCICLOPEDIA I 210.
40. Altmann/KAMMERMUSIK 194.

precise, rich harmony." [41] He found somewhat similar distinction in the music of the pianist **Carlo Rossaro** (1828–78) in Torino, whose publications include a Sonata in d, Op. 28, for P-duet (Ricordi, 1864) and a posthumous Sonata for Vc & P (Ricordi, 1879?).[42]

Among organists, **Filippo Capocci** (1840–1911) in Rome left six full-scale organ sonatas published between about 1878 and 1908 and both widely and highly regarded in their day.[43] Among nearly 300 publications, mostly for piano, by the pianist **Polibio Fumagalli** in Milan (1830–1901 [44]), there are one "sonata movement" each for organ and for P solo, Opp. 225 and 226; a "Capriccio alla sonata," Op. 230, and three other sonatas for organ, Opp. 269, 290, and 292; and "Giubilo, Sonata brillante alla marcia," Op. 237, for P-duet, all published between about 1880 and 1893.[45] Somewhat stronger and more successful are the four published sonatas within the large, rounded output by the chief organist of his day, another significant contributor to the instrumental renaissance, and a successor to Martucci in Bologna, **Marco Enrico Bossi** (1861–1925).[46] Two of these sonatas are for organ, Opp. 60 in D (Ricordi, *ca.* 1890) and 71 in f (Cocks, 1894), and two are for Vn & P, Opp. 82 in e (Breitkopf & Härtel, 1893) and 117 in C (Kistner, 1899).[47] Cast in the standard cycles of three and four movements and aligned less with newer trends than some of Bossi's other music, these sonatas suggest German models again, including Brahms's music, in their ideas and solid treatment, but are not without some melodic and harmonic originality and strengths of their own.[48] In October of 1893 Bossi sent what is probably his best sonata, Op. 82, to Verdi for criticism and, hopefully, a stamp of approval, receiving a somewhat enigmatic, cautious reply, most of which follows:[49]

I have admired your work with Boïto (who was here), especially the beginning of the first movement, a most beautiful and powerful phrase; and if

41. Schmidl/DIZIONARIO I 132.

42. Schmidl/DIZIONARIO II 398; Altmann/KAMMERMUSIK 304 and 263.

43. Cf. Schmidl/DIZIONARIO I 289; Kremer/ORGAN 175–76; PAZDÍREK III 79; SMW XLIV (1886) 371 (praise for contrapuntal skill and flow but not for the handling of large form nor for imagination in Son. 1); MMR XVI (1886) 233 (review of Son. 3 as striking in harmony and modulations, but more of a "Suite de pièces" than a unified son.).

44. GROVE III 524 (A. Chitty); BAKER 520 gives 1891; other sources give 1900.

45. Cf. Schmidl/DIZIONARIO I 574; PAZDÍREK V 608–12; Kremer/ORGAN 185; MMR XVII (1887) 178 (review of Op. 269 [3 mvts., in D] as fluent and musical but not very original). On Fumagalli's piano virtuosity, cf. MOSCHELES II 236, 239.

46. Cf. MGG II 149–51 (L. Bossi); Schmidl/DIZIONARIO I 229–30.

47. Cf. Kremer/ORGAN 173; Altmann/KAMMERMUSIK 196.

48. The Vn sons. are described, with exx., in Cobbett/CHAMBER I 153–54 (G. Cesari) and Shand/VIOLIN 189–91.

49. As trans. in Cobbett/CHAMBER I 153. The original and a further exchange from June, 1895, that recalls Op. 82 may be seen in Verdi/COPIALETTERE 400–401.

I said that the composition in general appears to me to be too much based on dissonance, you might answer: "Why not? dissonance and consonance are both essential elements in music; I give the preference to the former." And you would be right. On the other hand, why should I be wrong?

Was the "dissonance" the harmonic support, with 9th chords, of the second theme in the first movement? If so, it hardly seems shocking in relation to other music of its day or, for that matter, to Verdi's own late music.

Brief mention may be added of some pianists who composed duo sonatas, including the Martucci pupil and (now disfavored) Bach editor **Bruno Mugellini** (1871–1912), for a Sonata in g, for Vc & P, first published by Rieter-Biedermann of Leipzig in 1899 (not 1898 or 1908);[50] another Martucci pupil, **Guido Alberto Fano** (1875–1961), for a Sonata in d, Op. 7, that won a prize from the Società del Quartetto di Milano in 1898, appeared in Leipzig in 1905 (Breitkopf & Härtel), and brought an unfavorable review soon after in the German press;[51] and the Sgambati pupil **Giuseppe Cristiani** (1865–1933), founder of the "Quintetto romano," for a Sonata in g, for P & Vn, published by Jurgenson of Moscow in 1907 and reviewed more favorably in the German press.[52]

Among three other late-Romantics in Italy who wrote sonatas (most still awaiting investigation) was the cellist **Luigi Abbiate** (1866–1933), who spent many years in Paris, St. Petersburg, and Monaco as well as in Italian centers.[53] His sonatas include one in g, for P & Vc (year?), and at least five for P solo, composed by 1914 but, like one other—Op. 57 in Bb, for P & Vn—not published until his last years, mostly by Hayet in Paris (1925–32).[54] These are physically imposing works of three and four movements, characterized by more passagework than melody, post-Brahmsian and -Franckian harmony, almost continuous modulation and frequent metric changes (with double-bars to define numerous little sections), and thick textures. The priest **Giovanni Pagella** (1872–1944), who also spent some time in Paris, left at least five sonatas, four of them published—Op. 110 in D, for P & Vn (1914); three for organ (Nos. 2 in 1910 and 3 in 1922); and one for P solo (year?).[55] The

---

50. Cf. Schmidl/DIZIONARIO II 145; HOFMEISTER 1899, 118.

51. Schmidl/DIZIONARIO I 519 and MGG III 1761–62 (R. Allorto; with mentions, also, of a "Fantasia" Vn. Son. [in MS] arranged by Fano from a P son. by him, of a P Sonatina, Op. 5, pub. in 1906, and of another Son. for P solo, in E, pub. by Ricordi in 1920); DM V/2 (1905–6) 260 (A. Laser).

52. DM IX/1 (1909–10) 123 (W. Altmann). Cf. Schmidl/DIZIONARIO I 389 and Suppl. 225.

53. Cf. Schmidl/DIZIONARIO I 5 and Suppl. 2.

54. All of the last 6 sons. are in the Library of Congress.

55. Schmidl/DIZIONARIO II 212 and Suppl. 583; DICCIONARIO LABOR 1702; HOFMEISTER

Neapolitan pianist **Alessandro Longo** (1864–1945), best known for his eleven-volume edition of Domenico Scarlatti's sonatas (Ricordi, 1906; sce 265, 266, 840), left seven sonatas for P solo—Opp. 32 in c, 36 in B, 63 in C, 66 in a, 67 in G, 70 in f, and 72 in A♭. These were all published as a one-volume set, as a "deluxe bound" one-volume set, and separately, by Kistner of Leipzig in 1912, following their individual, successive issues by various other publishers over the previous seven years or so.[56] They follow the standard three- and four-movement plans, with occasional slow introductions in the outer movements, fugal finales in Opp. 32 and 67, and cyclical relationships in every sonata. Longo's writing shows much variety, skill, and experience, although

Ex. 106. From the opening of Alessandro Longo's Sonata in C, Op. 63 (after the Kistner ed. of 1912).

his styles, this late, never go beyond the orbit described by Mendelssohn and Brahms. This limitation and his inability to be either real or urgent in his ideas and their development make him another epigone (Ex. 106).

Two Italian sonata composers of the late-Romantic Era were noted in Chapter XIV, Carlo Albanesi in London and the man to whom he dedicated his last piano sonata, Michele Esposito in Dublin. The

---

1910, 132, and 191; Kremer/organ 211. A short, sympathetic review of Op. 110 as a melodious, sweet work, at times rhythmically piquant, appears in dm XIII/4 (1913–14) 331 (W. Dahms).

56. Cf. mgg VIII 1189–90 (A. Mondolfi); pazdírek IX 621; dm XII/4 (1912–13) 251–52 (R. H. Stein), a favorable, one-column review of the set as skillful, though not very original, music throughout. Each separate Kistner ed. includes the thematic index of all mvts. of all 7 sons. The complete set is in the Library of Congress.

sonatas of three others appeared too late in the 20th century to be included here, even though their orientation to the Romantic Era remains unmistakable—the pianist Amilcare Zanella (1873–1949), the scholar Fernando Liuzzi (1884–1940), and, more important, Léone Sinigaglia (1868–1944), whose other chamber music dates back as much as a generation earlier, almost to that late-Romantic renaissance of Italian instrumental music.

Spain and Portugal (Albéniz)

Strongly influenced at first by such Italians formerly on her soil as Boccherini and Brunetti (scE 247–58), Spain fostered several consequential instrumentalists and instrumental ensembles of her own throughout the 19th century,[57] including, among violinists, the precocious, short-lived composer Juan Crisóstomo de Arriyaga (1806–26), Jesús de Monasterio (1836–1903), and, of course, Pablo de Sarasate (1844–1908; mostly away from Spain); among cellists, Victor Mirecki and, ultimately, Pablo Casals (1876–   ); among pianists, Pedro Albéniz (1795–1855), Pedro Tintorer (1814–91), and Juan Bautista Pujol (1835–98); and, among organists, Olallo Morales (in Sweden; ssB XV). But after the heyday of the guitarists, especially Fernando Sor (1778–1839), whose sonatas appeared up to the early 1830's (scE 663–64), almost no sonatas by Spanish composers, whether published in or out of Spain, can be found until around the end of the century. Composers like Manuel Garcia (Sr.) and his successors were too greatly preoccupied with folk, national, and theatrical music (including the *tonadilla* and revised zarzuella). At last, two of the most successful composers, Isaac Albéniz and Joaquín Turina, showed at least a side interest in our genre.

One of Spain's finest pianists and a popular idol among Spanish composers before Falla, **Isaac Albéniz** (1860–1909) spent the first half of his adventuresome career (from the age of four!) largely as a recitalist, touring as far away as South and North America; he did not start his increasing shift toward serious composition until almost his mid twenties.[58] Jadassohn and Reinecke in Leipzig (ssB X) had been among his several teachers. And the sonatas of Haydn, Mozart, and Beethoven,

57. Cf. mgg XII 1006–7 (J. Subirá); Subirá/historia 655–79; Subirá & Cherbuliez/musikgeschichte 129–33; Chase/spain 150–59.

58. Laplane/albéniz is the most recent and helpful study, including the man, his music, the chief style traits, and the best critical, chronological list of his works, though incomplete, that could be assembled; it does not, however, contain much of the documentary evidence to be found in Collet/albéniz (including pp. 50–51 and 97 on the sons.).

the concertos of the last two plus Weber, Mendelssohn, Chopin, Moscheles, Schumann, Rubinstein, Liszt, and Grieg, and pieces by Bach, Handel, Rameau, Couperin, D. Scarlatti, Schubert, Dussek, and others (including himself) had been among the experiences to which he exposed himself through recitals up to his 20th year.[59] But more influential on the new seriousness and eventual nationalism in Albéniz's composing seem to have been his few days (only) in August, 1880, and his study in Barcelona in the summer and fall of 1885 (only?) with one of the most ardent, loyal, versatile and respected champions of Spanish music, Felipe Pedrell (1841–1922).[60]

Albéniz's sonatas consist of five, all for P solo. Information about them is scant, at best, beyond the indication that he wrote them early in his shift to more serious composition, probably between 1883 and 1886 [61] and perhaps mostly during his study with Pedrell in 1885. Of Sonata 1, Op. 28, only the printed "Scherzo" can be found today (as pub. separately by Zozaya in Madrid [?], in 1883 [?]). Of Sonata 2 nothing seems to be known. Sonatas 3 (Op. 68 in A♭), 4 (Op. 72 in A), and 5 (Op. 82 in G♭) were all first published in 1887 (?) by Romero in Madrid and subsequently taken over or reprinted by Unión Musical Español.[62] Each of the last three is dedicated to a "beloved" friend— respectively, "the celebrated pianist" Manuel Guervós (3 years younger than Albéniz), "my" onetime "master [actually, sponsor]" Count Guillermo Morphy (himself the composer of a Son. for P & Vn, not accessible here), and "the eminent artist [a Catalan pianist]" Carlos Gumersindo Vidiella.[63] These three sonatas are of moderate length (20–27 pp.), in three or four movements. The outer movements are all fast and the inner movements moderate to fast, never slow. The first movements are progressively freer "sonata forms," with a rare written-out repetition of the exposition in Sonata 4 and both the most development and the widest tonal ranges in Sonata 5. With regard to inner movements, Sonata 3 has an "Andante" in the minor supertonic key, Sonata 4 has both a "Scherzino" in the dominant and a "Minuetto" in the subdominant keys, each with its trio, and Sonata 5 has both a "Minuetto del gallo" in the minor enharmonic-dominant and a "Reverie et al-

59. Laplane/ALBÉNIZ 39. Brahms is conspicuously absent, although his late pieces for P solo had yet to appear.

60. Cf. Laplane/ALBÉNIZ 35–47, 216, 217.

61. Based on the meager pub. facts in Laplane/ALBÉNIZ 140 and 192–97. No discussion of them is known here.

62. Plate nos. A. R. 6962, 7007, 7085; cf. Cat. NYPL I 186, but the pub. occurred before "189-," to judge by near plate nos. in Albéniz's output that can be dated more accurately.

63. Cf. DICCIONARIO LABOR I 1171, II 1571 and 2225; Laplane/ALBÉNIZ 32–33 (on Morphy).

legro" in the major lowered-submediant key (with no apparent reasons for either the "cock" or the "lively" in the titles).

Extracts have been published from two reviews of Madrid recitals in 1887 at which Albéniz played at least Nos. 3 and 4 among his sonatas.[64] Besides the playing itself, the brilliance of Sonata 3/iii and the working out, second theme, and delicacy of Sonata 4/i were extolled. But finding the refrain in Sonata 4/iv unprepossessing and too often repeated, one critic saw the artist, for all his fine imagination and intuition, as still needing a structural discipline denied to him thus far by his turbulent life. The author Henri Collet concurred in the latter view, finding Albéniz's sonatas "spineless," lacking in originality and skill, and without plan in No. 5 except for its "Minuetto del gallo." [65]

But these objections have seemed too strong here, if they are deserved at all. Perhaps they partly reflect the hearer's surprise at coming on most of the familiar traits and mannerisms of Albéniz's style without so much as a hint of the popular Spanish rhythms and melodic elements that were to be introduced so profusely and effectively throughout the four-volume *Iberia* suite (1906–9). When Albéniz composed his sonatas he was not yet quite ready to put the nationalistic ideals of Liszt and Pedrell into practice. But those sonatas show his compositional skills to have been more developed by the mid 1880's and more grounded in the earlier masterworks of the 19th century than is generally acknowledged. Their craftsmanship in harmony, scoring, and voice-leading is beyond reproach. And they already exhibit some of Albéniz's favorite devices, like the chordal elaborations by two-note figures (e.g., Son. 4/ii/23–26) that contribute to several recollections of Weber's piano writing; or the accented dissonances through skips and chromatic passing-tones (e.g., Son. 5/i/85–88), with something of the piquancy of Godowsky's writing; or the allocation of songful melodies to the tenor register in the middle of the texture (e.g., Son. 3/iii/21–32); or the exploitation of advanced piano techniques (as in the finale of Son. 4, which includes all of the foregoing plus wide leaps and frequent double-note passages), although the sonatas are less hard to play in these respects than the frequently more congested, complex passages in the twelve *Iberia* "scenes." Furthermore, the best melodies in the sonatas, although never quite so compelling or characterful as those in *Iberia,* are not without their own good directional and linear qualities, as in the second theme from Sonata 5/i, with its frequent enharmonic modulations (Ex. 107).

64. Collet/ALBÉNIZ 50–51.
65. Collet/ALBÉNIZ 97.

Ex. 107. From the first movement of Sonata 5, in G♭, by Isaac Albéniz (after the ed. of Unión Musical Español, in the 1890's).

As for Albéniz's control of form, his sonatas employ the same sectional forms to be found in *Iberia,* including both simple A-B-A forms (Son. 3/ii) and more elaborate "sonata forms" (Son. 5/i). The sonatas show moderate ability to develop ideas (Son. 5/i) but more inclination toward rondo designs. The forms in *Iberia* are tighter, better planned, and more pointed toward their climaxes and returns. But even when the enharmonic changes create the widest tonal ranges, the sonata movements show at least an adequate awareness and logic of structure.

The other chief Spanish composer to present, **Joaquin Turina** (1882–1949), would be generally too late for our consideration here except that the best known of his five published sonatas (among a considerable variety and number of other works) appeared early in his career, in 1910 (not 1909).[66] This was the *Sonate romantique sur un thème espagnol,* Op. 3 (?) in c/C, for P solo, composed in 1909 "in memory of Isaac Albéniz," and published by E. Demcts (transferred to Max Eschig) in Paris. Another piano work, *Sonata fantasia,* Op. 59, did not appear until 1930, in Madrid, nor a guitar work, Sonata in d, Op. 61, until 1932, in London. And two sonatas for violin and piano, Opp. 51 in d/D and 82, freely in C ("Sonata española"), did not appear until 1930 and

66. Cf. MGG XIII 992–94 (M. Querol), with full dated list of works and further bibliography.

1934, in Paris.[67] But Turina's early and late sonatas are generally similar in styles and forms. In fact, the last of them shows little advance or contrast as compared with the first. Opp. 3 and 82 have almost identical plans in the order, type, forms, and thematic interrelation ships of their movements—In/Va-VF-S/F. Both of their middle movements alternate scherzando with slower sections. And both works exhibit much the same ideas, texture, and harmony in their corresponding movements, aside from a little modernization through added dissonance and tonal freedom in the later work.

Turina's sonatas also show little qualitative or stylistic evidence of the composer's extended period of study under d'Indy in Paris (1905–14). They reveal considerable experience in composition. Their scoring is full, well balanced, and idiomatic enough. Their melodic and rhythmic ideas offer the expected allure as Spanish music, within any one group of phrases and periods. But in all these respects they hardly rise above the ordinary. And measured against the prevailing sonata idea of his time Turina's sonatas as aesthetic wholes do not offer the expected development of materials, compelling dynamism, or broad architecture. Instead one gets that more static feeling, typical in much Spanish music, of forever marking time or of always anticipating some sustained, developed section but never arriving at it.[68]

Further exploration into what little might turn up in the way of late 19th-century sonatas in Spain could start with four obscure names mentioned only in passing by the important Spanish music historian José Subíra[69]—**Marcial del Aldalid** (1827–81), for two sonatas for Vn & P; **Martín Sánchez Allú** (?–?), for another of the same; the Cuban-born **Nicolás Espadero** (?–?), for all or most of two sonatas (for P solo?); and **Vicente Zurrón** (1871–1915), for another for piano and a Sonata for P & Vc. No publication of any of these sonatas is known here.

In Portugal the one name to include here is that of the early 19th-century pianist and founder of a "Philharmonic Society" in Lisbon, **João Domingos Bomtempo** (1775–1842), who did his final training in Paris and came under Clementi's influence both there and in London.[70] Between about 1805 and 1816, at least four sonatas for P solo and seven for P ± Vn by Bomtempo were published, all where the markets for

67. PAZDÍREK XIV 374 also lists 3 "Sonatine ad uso dei principianti, canto."
68. In a rather more complimentary fashion Cobbett/CHAMBER II 522–24 (P. G. Morales & W. W. Cobbett) seems to come to similar conclusions about other chamber music by Turina.
69. Subíra/HISTORIA 663 and 665; cf., also, Subíra & Cherbuliez/MUSIKGESCHICHTE 127, 130, 153.
70. The detailed article in DICCIONARIO PORTUGUEZES I 108–63 includes citations from numerous contemporary documents and an undated list of works.

the solo and accompanied settings were best—that is, in Paris (Opp. 1, 5, and 9/1–2 for P solo, and 9/3 for P ± Vn) or London (Opp. 13, 15/1–2, and 18/1–3 for P ± Vn).[71] Knowing of Clementi's direct influence, one is not surprised to find Bomtempo's sonatas still firmly planted in the high-Classic style of Haydn and Clementi. But they have melodic freshness of their own, besides being skillfull, light, well formed works in two or three movements, with the fluent, sometimes brilliant passagework that would be expected of a professional pianist.

71. Cf. DICCIONARIO PORTUGUEZES I 112, 116–17, 119, 122, 123, 159; HOFMEISTER 1815 (Whistling), 342, and 1828 (Whistling), 580. In his "Introduction" of 1963 to PORTUGALIAE-m VIII (a score of Bomtempo's Sinfonia Op. 11/1 in E♭, giving a good ex. of his style), F. de Sousa mentions a full cat. of Bomtempo's works in preparation by J.-P. Sarrautte.

Chapter XVII

Composers in Czechoslovakia, Poland, and Hungary

On Fanning Out from the Austro-German Epicenter

Our remaining three chapters on the composers and their sonatas take us increasingly far, musically as well as geographically, from the prime centers of the Romantic sonata, in Austro-Germany. Brief orientations introduce each country as we fan out, first eastward, to three East European countries, then to Russia, and finally westward, to the Americas. Here it is necessary only to make a few broader generalizations about these remoter cultivations, especially those to the east.

In our previous two volumes the same outlying countries were noted chiefly for their emigrants (mostly the Czechs in Austro-Germany and London), somewhat for their immigrants (mostly Italians), and only slightly for natives or longtime residents. In this final volume it is possible to report native schools of the sonata developing more or less significantly, though slowly, in each country. The immigrants are now few. But, to be sure, the only real front-rankers of the sonata in these countries still have had to be treated here as emigrants—Chopin from Poland and Liszt from Hungary (SSB XII and X), not to mention the numerous less important emigrants from each country. Even Dussek, the important, precocious Romantic who comes first in these final chapters, can be identified with his native land, Czechoslovakia, only by virtue of his training. He, too, was an emigrant, although one who roved too much to be identified with any other one locale, either.

The historical, 19th-century pattern of the sonata continued to operate about as in the other outlying countries—that is, starting with a fair amount of late-Classic activity that carried over into the early-Romantic efforts, followed by a low ebb in the generation from about 1835, and then, around 1870, by a rather conspicuous rise, if not renaissance, of solo and duo sonatas (along with other instrumental chamber music). Furthermore, especially during that rise, Germany continued to operate as the epicenter of the sonata (and much else in music). And the conflict between German and growing nationalistic influences in each country continued to affect the course of the sonata in one direction or the other, with efforts toward a 19th-century "vermischter Geschmack" (SBE 32) being only rarely successful. Evidence both for the growing schools of the sonata in these outlying countries and for their strong German affiliations can be seen in the increasing production of their sonatas by German publishers (e.g., Dvořák's sons. pub. by Simrock in Berlin at Brahms's urging) or by publishers that established branches in German centers (e.g., numerous Russian sons. pub. by Russian firms like Jurgenson, Belaieff, and Zimmermann). Moreover, the same sonatas were duly reviewed in the German periodicals.

As in the other outlying countries, the sonata generally took a fourth place to nationalistic opera, song, and programme music. Something as specialized as the sonata could be counted on to thrive only in the largest centers and usually in the spheres of their music conservatories or chamber music societies. For our purposes, Czechoslovakia was Prague, Poland was Warsaw, Hungary was Budapest, and Russia was the somewhat interrelated pair of centers, St. Petersburg and Moscow. We shall be coming to a modest, growing literature on the activities at these centers and to a fairly solid literature on the most important composers. But much of that literature remains in the language of the country (accessible here only to the extent that translation services were practical). And in any case, all too little of it pays attention to the sonatas of the times.

Turning to Czechoslovakia as the first of our outlying countries, we find the 19th-century sonata developing as part and parcel of a growing spirit of nationalism, a new economic prosperity, and a rising educated middle class. The chief frictions that beset this proud, tradition-minded, often troubled country were still those that had long plagued and would continue to plague the effort to unite Bohemian, Moravian, and Teutonic peoples. But these frictions did little to stem the musical activities in Prague that flourished especially from the time of Mozart.[1]

Dussek and Other Early Czech Romantics

In spite of his early life dates, the notable Czech pianist and composer **Jan Ladislav Dussek (Dussik, Dusík,** etc.; **1760–1812)** was

1. Helpful background summaries may be found in MGG X 1584–94 (J. Bužga); MGG IV 154–55 (P. Nettl); MGG XIII 888–96 (V. Lébl); Helfert & Steinhard, including a (somewhat careless) cat. of instrumental compositions, pp. 252–98; Newmarch/CZECHOSLOVAKIA 42, 55, et passim; Buchner/LISZT passim; Cobbett/CHAMBER I 306–9 (R. Newmarch).

deferred to the present volume (cf. SCE 5, 774) because of significant pre-Romanticisms in his musical style and piano writing. His sonatas actually antedate those of Schubert, Ries, Moscheles, Hummel, and Cramer, among other *Frühromantiker* who excelled at the keyboard. Moreover, as noted above, Dussek is put in his homeland here simply because he resided in too many other countries to be identified with any one of them in particular. This rather loose-living but ingratiating, well-informed, multilingual cosmopolitan left Bohemia after completing his education in Prague in 1778, apparently returning to Prague only once, in 1802. More specifically, among other places, he played, visited, or resided from 1778 to 1782 in Mechelen (Belgium), The Hague, and Hamburg (where Emanuel Bach is said to have counseled or actually taught him); from 1783 to 1784 in St. Petersburg and Lithuania; from 1784 to 1786 in cities throughout Germany; from 1786 to 1789 in Paris and Milan; from 1789 to 1799 in London (that is, until his father-in-law and he saw their publishing firm, Corri, Dussek & Co., fail); from 1800 to 1807 in Hamburg, Berlin, and numerous other European centers, serving for three of those years as *Kapellmeister* and companion to the gifted Prince Louis Ferdinand; and from 1807 to 1812 in Paris.[2] Haydn, Clementi, Cramer, Field, Spohr, and Pleyel were among the important musicians whom Dussek knew.[3]

In an order that generally decreases in both quantity and historical importance as it increases in size of ensemble, Dussek's nearly 300 works consist of many solos for piano plus a few for harp, duos for piano and another instrument, larger chamber ensembles that are mostly piano trios, concertos mainly for piano and orchestra, and a scattering of assorted vocal works.[4] Approximately 139, or nearly half of these works (not subtracting some 14 duplications or recombinations in other set-

2. The recent, valuable diss. Craw/DUSSEK brings together and augments the biographical information previously pub., reproduces all available letters by Dussek in the original language and in English trans. where needed, and provides an extended thematic catalogue that is the fullest record of Dussek's works.

3. Cf. Landon & Bartha/HAYDN 257, 278–79, 497–99, 547; Unger/CLEMENTI 23, 72, 81, 85, 88, 106–7, 143–44; Schlesinger/CRAMER 36, 53, 75; Dessauer/FIELD 5; Spohr/ AUTOBIOGRAPHY 19, 79, 86–88; MMR XC (1960) 17 (S. V. Klíma).

4. The "nearly 300" is based on the tabulations in Craw/DUSSEK 207. Racek's estimate of "about 450 works," in MAB-m XLVI xxvi, appears to include a good many duplications. The thematic index in Craw/DUSSEK 210–394 lists, where possible, full titles, dates of composition and pub., first and later eds., locations of MSS, first performances, and references to early reviews; it is followed (pp. 395–426) by separate indexes of op. nos., titles, and pubs. The "C." (Craw) nos. in the index, which are meant to be chronological, are adopted here rather than the then typically inconsistent, duplicative, and conflicting op. nos. (cf. SCE 78–79; BUCEM I 300–303; PAZDÍREK IV 506–11; HOFMEISTER 1828 [Whistling], *passim* [cf. p. 1255]). A concordance of Dussek's most published sons. appears later in the present discussion.

tings) arc cxamples of our genre, about 121 of them being called "sonatas" and 18 "sonatinas." [5] All of these were originally published over the 30 years from 1782 to 1812, rather evenly spaced and mostly in sets of 2 to 6 sonatas each, with the last, unfinished set of 2 being posthumous. And most were reprinted at least once and sometimes as many as ten times (e.g., C. 96). By scoring types, the 139 include approximately 35 sonatas and 12 sonatinas for P solo, 11 sonatas for P-duet, 2 sonatas for harp & Vn, one sonata and 6 sonatinas for harp alone, 65 sonatas for P & Vn, and 8 sonatas for P & Fl.

Dussek's scorings are often not that exact, since they may vary in different editions, with the main instrument changed (e.g., harp to P, in C. 147 and 148) or made optional (e.g., harp-or-P, C. 160–65) and the accompanying instruments, if any, added (e.g., Vn, Vc, and drums in C. 152) or deleted (e.g., the Fl in C. 88–93). The accompaniments are predominantly optional and subordinate in the earlier sonatas, and they are obligatory, making true duos, in the later ones. But not all the duos are limited to two players. Several of the earlier ones (e.g., C. 11–13, 30–32, and 141–43) mention the optional use of a "basse" in their titles, meaning a cello that largely doubles the pianist's left hand, whether or not a separate part was actually printed (cf. SCE 101). In *A Favorite Sonata for the Michrocordon, or Piano Forte, with Drum and Triangle (ad Libitum)* . . . , *Op. 45* (C. 182; *ca.* 1800), no additional parts were printed because the instrument intended was a small upright piano then made by Longman, Clementi and Company, with drum and triangle attachments to be introduced at will by the one performer.

Numerous other profuse titles of Dussek's sonatas add further sidelights and flavor to our knowledge of them. Thus, his alertness both as a champion of several piano construction innovations[6] and as a connoisseur of public taste is reflected in the title of his Op. 25 (C. 126–28), published by his own firm in London in 1795, *Three Sonatas for the Piano Forte, And also arranged for the Piano Forte with additional Keys, in which are introduced The Fife Hunt, A Scotch Reel, and the National Air of Rule Brittania, as Rondos, with an Accompaniment for a Violin or Flute Dedicated to the Right Honorable Lady Elizabeth Montagu.* Dussek's timely composition of programmatic *pièces d'occasion* is reflected in one of those late-18th-century battle sonatas (C. 152; cf. SCE 141), also published by Corri, Dussek & Co., *The Naval Battle*

5. These figures do not include works like "La Chasse" for P solo (C. 146), which is sometimes listed as a "sonata" (as in Craw/DUSSEK 415) but was not so called in Dussek's time; or Concerto for P and orchestra, Op. 22 (C. 97), the solo part of which was pub. as "Grande Sonate pour le Piano-Forte," Op. 40, by Artaria (Craw/DUSSEK 267). Cf., also, C. 264, 170, 98, 144, 186, 234, 243, 106–17, 214.
6. Cf. Craw/DUSSEK 53–54, 75, 171, and the listings for C. 96, 126–28, 132–34.

and Total Defeat of the Grand Dutch Fleet by Admiral Duncan on the 11th. of October 1797[,] A Characteristic Sonata for the Piano-Forte Composed and Dedicated to Viscount Duncan. His equally timely composition of more penetrating but nonliteral programme music is suggested by the title of a work commemorating a severe personal loss to him through war, *Élégie Harmonique Sur la Mort de Son Altesse Royale, le Prince Louis Ferdinand de Prusse, En forme de Sonate pour le Piano Forte, Composée et Dediée A son Altesse le Prince de Lobko-vitz, Duc de Raudnitz . . . Op. 61* (C. 211; pub. by Pleyel of Paris in 1807).[7] On the other hand, Dussek's use of programmatic titles that lack similarly obvious associations or appear to be topical at most, if not merely nominal, is revealed in *L'Invocation, Grande Sonate Pour le Piano Forté . . . Op. 77* (C. 259; pub. in 1812), wherein, one writer suggests, Dussek could have been invoking thoughts of approaching death;[8] or *The Farewell[,] A New Grand Sonata, for the Piano Forte Composed and Inscribed to his Friend Muzio Clementi . . . Op. 44* (C. 178; pub. by Longman, Clementi in London in 1800), which is a generally gay work that hardly suggests the pangs of leaving London, unless in its *grave* "Introduzione" in e♭; or *Le Retour à Paris[,] Sonate Pour Le Piano Forté . . . Op. 64* (C. 221; pub. by Pleyel, presumably in late 1807). This last title is supposed merely to mark the time when Dussek returned to Paris, in 1807. It was the butt of one critic's joshing, who suggested that it could just as well have been "le départ pour Petersbourg." [9] Furthermore, this same Op. 64 (or 70, or 71, or 77, according to other eds.) was also the Op. 71 on which English publishers bestowed the title, first in 1810, "Plus ultra en opposition à celle de Joseph Wölffl intitulée Non plus ultra" (that is, Wölfl's Son. in F, Op. 41), thus archly (and rightly) claiming even greater technical difficulty for Dussek's work.[10]

Although the study has yet to appear, even in the Czech language, that will explore the styles and forms of Dussek's sonatas in sufficiently full and systematic detail,[11] at least two doctoral dissertations and a number of brief discussions and surveys have come from writers attracted to those sonatas over the last century, including Prout in 1877, Shedlock in 1895, F. L. Schiffer in 1914, Blom in 1927–28, Egert in 1929, R. Felder and Cobbett in 1929, Georgii in 1950, K. Krafka in 1950, and V. J. Sýkora in 1960.[12] The reception of Dussek's sonatas

7. Cf. Craw/DUSSEK 151–53; Shedlock/SONATA 144–45.
8. MAB-m LXIII xi (J. Racek & V. J. Sýkora).
9. AMZ XII (1809–10) 842.
10. Cf. SCE 563 and MAB-m XLVI xxvi; also, Shedlock/SONATA 149 and Craw/DUSSEK 163 and 353.
11. Cf. Craw/DUSSEK 1–6 and 477–89 (bibliographies); MAB-m XLVI xxxviii–xxxix (J. Racek).
12. Prout/DUSSEK; Shedlock/SONATA 142–52; Schiffer/DUSSEK, a pub. Ph.D. diss.

seems to have been consistently enthusiastic, right from the start, if one is to judge from fifteen or more reviews that followed original editions, the majority of them being in the Leipzig *Allgemeine musikalische Zeitung*.[13] The recurring theme in these reviews is steadily increasing praise for the originality, expressiveness, and appropriateness to the piano idiom of most of the melody, harmony, and scoring. Sometimes questioned are varying degrees of fantasy in the treatment and certain more local licenses (specific references are made in nearly every review to accented passing notes and to harmonic and tonal progressions that seemed audacious in their voice leading and remoteness). The most extended and effusive among the reviews was the nine-column discussion (by Rochlitz?) of C. 221, as Op. 70, "Le Retour à Paris," in AMZ for October 3, 1810. Along with detailed analyses of select passages (and references to 24 music exx. in the 4 extra pp. of "Beilage VIII") one finds sentences like the following:

> It is all one [grand] inspiration, one outpouring. Lofty seriousness and subjective moodiness [*sentimentale Laune*], both arising out of a profound soul, overwhelmed perhaps by extraordinary circumstances, [yet] surrounded, as it were, by a romantic twilight—[such] are the elements of this admirable sonata. It is a product of genius such as seldom occurs; [it is] one of the most characterful [of] musical poems, which will retain its value as long as music provides good pianos and accomplished pianists.

Although Breitkopf & Härtel issued Dussek's so-called *Oeuvres complètes pour le pianoforte,* in twelve volumes, between 1813 and 1817,[14] actually including 19 of his sonatas for P solo, 27 for P with accompaniment, and 3 for P-duet, relatively little interest can be found in Dussek's music in the half century after his death. Some of the early publications stayed in print,[15] but almost no new editions appeared

on both the sons. and concertos that suffers chiefly from a lack of either dates of any clear chronology, permitting faulty conclusions on influences (kindly supplied in an approximate trans. by Professor H. A. Craw of Loma Linda University; cf. Craw/DUSSEK 1–2); Blom/DUSSEK (cf. Newman/K. 457); Egert/FRÜHROMANTIKER 34–42; Cobbett/CHAMBER I 351–52 (R. Felber & W. W. Cobbett, on C. 240 and 241); Georgii/KLAVIERMUSIK 262–63; Krafka/DUSÍKA, an unpub. Ph.D. diss. on Romanticisms in Dussek's sons., kindly made available by Professor Craw in a digest trans. prepared for him by S. V. Klíma of Prague (himself the author of a still unpub. "life and works" of Dussek, according to MAB-m LIX x; cf. Craw/DUSSEK ii, 2, 481, 486); MAB-m XLVI xxx–xxxii (V. J. Sýkora).

13. E.g., AMZ XII (1809–10) 540–44 (on C. 149–51), II (1799–1800) 67 and XI (1808–9) 73–75 (both on C. 166–68), XVII (1815) 156 (on C. 207), XII (1809–10) 841–49 (on C. 221) and 15–16 (on C. 230–32), XIII (1811) 555–61 (on C. 240–42) and 880–82 (on C. 247), XIV (1812) 581–82 (on C. 259), and XV (1813) 251–53 (on C. 260 and 261). For reviews in other periodicals cf. the listings in Craw/DUSSEK for C. 5–7, 71–73, 79–81, 207, 230–32.

14. Cf. AMZ XV (1813) Intelligenz-Blatt IV 21–23 (with a useful contemporary evaluation); HOFMEISTER 1828 (Whistling), 1150; Craw/DUSSEK 201 and 418 (with other, smaller collections listed on pp. 419–20); MAB-m LIX x–xi.

15. E.g., cf. HOFMEISTER 1844, pp. 22, 31, 83, 156–57.

during that time. And it is noteworthy that Dussek's name appears not at all in the available letters of Beethoven, Mendelssohn, either of the Schumanns, or Chopin, nor in the memoirs of Moscheles, and only twice, quite incidentally, in the journalism of Robert Schumann.[16] For the historical moment the music world was already making passé even the precocious Romanticisms of Dussek.[17] But starting in the 1860's a revival of interest in his sonatas was manifested by new editions, including a two-volume collection of 32 sonatas that both Breitkopf & Härtel and Litolff published in 1868–73,[18] and by numerous performances of certain favorites, especially in London.[19] Today, over and above a fair number of further editions of single sonatas by Dussek, the series *Musica antiqua bohemica* in Prague has been enriched by "the first complete Czech edition of Dusík's piano sonatas," in 4 volumes— actually, 23 of the approximately 47 solo sonatas or sonatinas plus 6 that originally had violin accompaniments.[20] Perhaps the easier availability of the sonatas will stimulate more than the few performances they have been getting, which are mainly limited to the same three or four sonatas for P solo and are mainly esoteric.[21] The following partial concordance will help to clarify references in the ensuing discussion, which for reasons both of musical interest and the reader's convenience are largely confined to the works most often published and currently available:

16. Schumann/SCHRIFTEN I 392 and II 286.

17. As early as 1825 his sons. were called "outmoded" (HARMONICON III/1 [1825] 139).

18. Cf. Craw/DUSSEK 419–20; also, the issue of separate mvts. in various arrangements—e.g., as advertised in MT XII (1865) 124 and 152, or XVIII (1877–78) 395 and 509, or XXII (1881) 97.

19. E.g., C. 259 ("L'Invocation") in MT XII (1865) 8 (which was "listened to with a breathless attention speaking volumes for the taste of a popular audience") and 339, XV (1871) 46; C. 151 (Op. 35/3 in c) in MT XIII (1867) 105, XV (1872) 420; C. 240 (Op. 69/1 in B♭) in MT XV (1871–72) 121, 436, and 500, XVI (1874) 544, XVII (1876) 443, XXI (1879) 38, XXIV (1883) 269; C. 96 (Op. 24 in B♭) in MT XVI (1874) 544. Numerous other references to performances of Dussek's sonatas do not specify the particular work sufficiently if at all, as in MT XIII (1869) 679, XV (1872) 404, XVI (1874) 582, XVIII (1878) 228, XIX (1878) 685, XXI (1880) 363, XXII (1881) 363.

20. MAB-m XLVI (cf. p. xxx), LIII, LIX, and LXIII, with prefaces by J. Racek & V. J. Sýkora (and confusions that illustrate the need for a thematic index like that in Craw/DUSSEK, as in the equating of C. 96 and C. 98 because each was pub. as Op. 23 at one time). A concordance with the C. nos. appears in Craw/DUSSEK 420, to which should be added the 8 more Dussek sons. and one duplication pub. in MAB-m, as listed in the concordance that follows here, along with 4 sons. in the recent mod. eds. Zeitlin & Goldberger/DUSSEK-m and Madden & Rees/DUSSEK-m, and 8 of the sons. reprinted in 3 of the "old masters" collections.

21. Among the few recordings of Dussek's music (cf. Craw/DUSSEK 488–89) should be noted that of 3 sons. for P solo (including C. 211, "Élégie harmonique") and one son. for P-duet, played by H. Hermanns & R. Stonebridge, SFM 1002 (reviewed by P. H. Lang in MQ XLVI [1960] 118–20).

A Concordance of 42 Selected Sonatas by J. L. Dussek

Craw/ DUSSEK no.	Op(p). no. (if any)	Key	Original scoring	Sometime name &/or dedicatee	Probable first ed.	Movement plan	MAB-m vol./no.	Other collections
43	5/3	A♭	P	Mme. de Mongeroult	1788	F-Ro	LXIII/29	
57	9/1	B♭	P & Vn		ca. 1789	F-Ro	XLVI/1	
58	9/2	C	"		"	F-S-VF	XLVI/2	
59	9/3	D	"		"	F-VF	XLVI/3	
60	10/1	A	P & Vn		ca. 1789	F-S-Ro	XLVI/4	
61	10/2	g	"		"	S-F	XLVI/5	
62	10/3	E♭	"		"	F-VF	XLVI/6	
80	18/2	a	P & Fl		1792	F-Ro	XLVI/7	
92	19/5; 20/5	C	P & Fl	"Sonatina"	1793	F-Ro		Tagliapietra/ANTOLOGIA-m XIV
96	24	B♭	P	Mrs. Chinnery	1793	F-F	LIII/8	
102	26	F	2 Ps	"Duetto"	1794	F-S-Ro	LIII/9	Madden & Rees/DUSSEK-m
127	25	D	P & Vn-or-Fl	Lady Montagu	1795	S/VF-S-Ro	LIII/10	"
133	31/2	D	P & Vn-or-Fl & Vc	Misses Wheler	ca. 1795	F-S-F		"
149	35/1	B♭	P	Clementi	1797	F-F	LIII/11	TRÉSOR-m XVIII
150	35/2	G	"	"	"	F-Ro	LIII/12	"
151	35/3	c	"	"	"	F-S-VF/VF	LIII/13	"
160		C	harp	Mme. Krumpholtz	1799	M-F	XXII/1	
161		F	"	"	"	M-F	XXII/2	
162		G	"	"	"	M-F	XXII/3	
163		B♭	"	"	"	S-F	XXII/4	
164		F	"	"	"	S-F	XXII/5	
165		E♭	"	"	"	S-Mi	XXII/6	
166	39/1	G	P	Mrs. Apreece	1799	F-M	LIII/14	
167	39/2	C	"	"	"	F-M-Ro	LIII/15	
168	39/3	B♭	"	"	"	F-Ro	LIII/16	

177	43	A	P	Mrs. Bartolozzi	1800	F-Ro	LIX/17	
178	44	eb/Eb	P	"The Farewell"; Clementi	1800	S/F-S-Mi-Ro	LIX/18	
179	45/1	Bb	P		ca. 1800	F-S-Ro	LIX/19	
180	45/2	G	"		"	S/F-Ro	LIX/20	
181	45/3	D	"			F-S-Ro	LIX/21	
184	47/1	D	P	Mrs. Marshall	1801	F-S-Ro	LIX/22	
185	47/2	G	"	"	"	F-Ro	LIX/23	
211	61	f#	P	"Élégie harmonique"; Prince Lobkovitz	1807	S/F-VF	LXIII/24 XX/2	RICORDI ARTE-m VI; Tagliapietra ANTOLOGIA-m XIV
221	64; 70; 71; 77	Ab	P	"Le Retour à Paris", or "Plus ultra"; Princesse de Benevent	1807	F-VS-Mi-Sc	LXIII/26	TRÉSOR-m XVIII; RICORDI ARTE-m VI
230	67/1; 66/1	C	P-duet	"Sonates progressives"; Mademoiselle Talleyrand	1809	M-Ro		Zeitlin & Goldberger/ DUSSEK-m
231	67/2; 66/2	F	"		"	F-Ro		"
232	67/3; 66/3	Bb	"		"	F-Polonaise		"
240	69/1; 72/1	Bb	P+Vn	Duchess of Courlande	1811	F-S-Ro	XL/1	
241	69/2; 72/2	G	"	"	"	F-Ro	XL/2	
242	69/3; 72/3	D	P		"	F-S-F	LXIII/25	
247	75	Eb	P	"Grande Sonate"; Countess de Périgord	1811	F-M-Ro	LXIII/27	
259	77	f	P	"L'Invocation"; Mademoiselle Ouvrard	1812	F-Mi-S-Ro	LXIII/28	

More than half of Dussek's sonatas are in two movements, with but few of the movements being slow (e.g., S-F in C. 61 in g) and F-Ro being the most frequent plan. Nearly all of the remaining sonatas are in three movements, with F-S-Ro being the most frequent plan and F-M-Ro the next most. The three remaining sonatas, all relatively late works, have four movements with similar plans (C. 178, 221, and 259), including fast outer movements (a "sonata form" and a rondo in each) and both a slow movement and a minuet as inner movements. Major keys, up to two sharps and three flats, are in the great majority, with but a few keys having as many as four flats or three sharps, major or minor, although one of the several slow introductions, that to C. 178 in E♭, is in the tonic minor, hence in six flats. The outer movements change mode from E to e in C. 62, and, more in keeping with later Romantic predilections, from c to C in C. 151. For the inner movement in another key, in the sonatas of three and four movements, the subdominant is Dussek's choice more than half the time. More remote keys, like the lowered submediant major spelled enharmonically (e.g., B in C. 178 in e♭/E♭, or E in C. 222 in A♭), are occasional choices. All three movements remain in f♯ in "Élégie harmonique" (C. 211). In most of his sonatas, Dussek seems almost deliberately to avoid cyclical ties, for he generally contrasts both the styles and melodic directions of the main ideas in successive movements and even between slow introductions and what follows. Nearest to interrelated themes are the similarly contoured, mostly dotted, incipits in all four movements of "The Farewell" (C. 178), the syncopated figures in both the introduction and finale of "Élégie harmonique" (C. 211), and the stepwise descents that stand out in the initial themes of the first three in the four movements (F-VS-Mi-Sc) of "Le Retour à Paris" (C. 221).

Dussek's best sonatas are regarded here as close to the best of their day, including those of Clementi, Beethoven, Schubert, and Weber—a view that may well surprise all but the relative few who have had the opportunity to explore or re-explore for themselves. Moreover, in addition to their purely musical strengths, Dussek's sonatas prove to be remarkable in two other ways. One is their early exploitation of the newly popular "forte piano," an exploitation scarcely surpassed in Clementi's piano music. The other is their historical precocity. As noted earlier, their several innovational styles often go beyond Dussek's environment of high-Classicism and well into that of unequivocal, sometimes fully bloomed, Romanticism. All these traits can be found scattered throughout the sonatas (and concertos) that he produced for thirty years. But it is noteworthy that not until his later years did he write what generally (and here) are regarded as his finest sonatas—

that is, his solo sonatas that have special titles and at least slight programmatic associations, including C. 178, 211, 221, and 259.[22] In other words, although he, too, wrote timely *pièces d'occasion*, variations on favorite tunes, *tours de force*, and other pieces that show full awareness of the public pulse, he did not, as more than one contemporary reviewer noted,[23] make any of the increasing concessions to popular taste that were made so often by his less worthy contemporaries. Far from it! A fine late sonata like his "Le Retour à Paris" must have scared off not a few potential performers and purchasers with its bristling technical problems and its novel harmonic treatment.

Throughout Dussek's sonatas the respective movements tend to fall into the same few over-all designs, especially into clear previews of textbook "sonata form" in the first movements, A-B-A plans when there are slow movements, minuets with trios when there are inner dances, and the rondo principle in the finales. Some of the most convincing first movements achieve a sense of cumulative structure by being asymmetrical, with a shortened recapitulation. Thus, C. 211/i drops by almost half from an exposition of 60 measures (not including the 52 mss. of slow introduction) to a recapitulation of 31 measures, and C. 221 by over two-fifths from 103 to 64 measures. Yet at the more local levels of phrases and periods there is seldom the sense of tight organization or quite the concentrated, relentless drive one identifies with Beethoven. It is not simply the considerable length of Dussek's first movements, which averages about 206 measures as against 209 in Beethoven's solo piano sonatas and 201 in both Weber's and Schubert's. Nor, with slight reservations for C. 211/i, are Dussek's first movements discursive in the sense of Clementi's later examples, with their personalized digressions that probe a single idea fascinatingly yet gratuitously (SCE 750–51). Instead, in keeping with the first movements in the sonatas by Schubert, Weber, and other early-Romantics, Dussek's first movements reveal a preference for phrase-and-period units that are more rounded and more complete in themselves, causing the forms to seem more spacious and deliberate, and hence less dynamic and compelling.

Dussek in particular thinks most characteristically in complete, often parallel double-periods (e.g., C. 167/i/130–45: 4+4 and 4+4). When the second period parallels the first it is usually an extrinsically elaborated variation (as in the same ex. or C. 259/iv/1–16). Sometimes the

22. Fétis/BU III 96 lists only C. 178 and 221 among these 4, along with C. 57–62, 71–73, and 149–51, as the sons. Dussek himself preferred.

23. E.g., in AMZ XIII (1811) 880–82, on C. 247, noting that Dussek was no "Vielschreiber."

double-period is lengthened considerably by one or more cadence extensions—for example, by three such extensions, including prolonging of the cadential tonic-6/4 triad and of deceptive cadences on both the major and the minor subdominant triads at the end of the exposition in C. 181/i/44–80 (4+4 and 4+25 [11+6+8]; cf., also, the charming extension of the single period in mss. 31–44 [4+10]). To be sure, such procedures and other freedoms, especially in the later works, generally preclude the danger of monotony in so much use of the double-period. But one should note that phrase-and-period units of one sort or another predominate in all of Dussek's movement types and can even occur not only in every distinct theme of the "sonata-allegro" exposition but in the development section as well (as in C. 242/i). On the other hand, Dussek certainly understood the values of "chain-phrases" (to use Percy Goetschius' term), whether in sequential passage-work and modulatory bridges (e.g., C. 247/i/22–38) or actual development of ideas (e.g., C. 80/i/100–146). However, only infrequently and in his later works did Dussek achieve the same imagination and suppleness in the development of his ideas (e.g., C. 259/i/71–111) that he seems to have achieved more intuitively, from the start, in his phrase-and-period structures.

Dussek's most frequent method in the A-B-A designs of his slow movements is to put the B section in the tonic minor mode and to vary the A section when it returns (e.g., C. 181/ii in G/g). His change to the minor mode in C. 259/iii in Db is enharmonic. Among his rare slow movements that begin and end in the minor mode, one that mirrors the same plan is C. 58/ii in a, with the B section in the relative major. The "slow" movement in C. 166 changes not only the mode in the B section, from G to g, but the tempo, from moderate to fast. The variation of the return consists of extrinsic elaborations, as it does when a repeated period is varied (which happens about as often in Dussek's slow as in his fast mvts.). These elaborations constitute Dussek's main use of variation technique in his sonatas. Unlike his other piano music, none of his more important sonatas and but three of the less known ones contain actual sets of variations (including C. 65/ii on "God Save the King"). A larger, rondo form results, A-B-A-C-A, when Dussek inserts another contrasting, minor section in the slowest movement, namely in the subdominant minor key in C. 247/ii in Bb. C. 611 is a slow first movement in so-called "sonatina form"—that is, with only a retransition rather than a development section. C. 178/ii is a grand "sonata form" of symphonic breadth and character, with a full, intensive development section.

As with Weber, Dussek's short dances provide some of his most concentrated, structurally convincing movements. Only in his three, relatively late sonatas in four movements is a dance included as an inner movement, and in each instance this is marked "Tempo di minuetto." However, in C. 178 the qualification ". . . più tosto allegro" is added, and in C. 221 ". . . scherzo quasi allegro." In these two movements both the faster tempo and the persistent, driving quarter-notes in 3/4 meter suggest a scherzo rather than a minuet. In Dussek's two- and three-movement sonatas there are also five minuets used as finales, all more in the character of a minuet, including one with a different title, "Minuetto, Tempo di ballo" (C. 91/ii). Other finales include a "Polonaise" (C. 232/ii), a "Finale chasse, Allegro scherzo" in 6/8 meter (C. 242/iii) that groups with several other quasi tarantellas not so entitled (e.g., C. 62/ii), and a few pieces in the style of the German polka, of which C. 221/iv is a delicious masterpiece (entitled "Scherzo, Allegro con spirito"). But even in most of these finales as well as the large majority of pieces actually called "Rondo," the rondo principle prevails. And already we find the fetching refrains, the devious retransitions, the emphasis on the middle episode, the choice of the opposite mode for one episode, and other traits that distinguish Beethoven's rondos. However, Dussek usually employed the "second rondo form" (Goetschius' term, again)—for example, A-B-A-C-A-coda in C. 150/ii and 247/iii—rather than the more integrated "third rondo form," A-B-A-C-A-B'-A-coda, as in C. 211/ii and as used more often by Beethoven (e.g., Op. 13/iii).

Dussek's treatment of harmony and tonality, which aroused the most specific comments and questions on the part of his contemporary reviewers (*supra*), still stands out today, along with his piano writing, as one of his most significant contributions. The composer proved early that he knew the rules of conventional harmony (e.g., C. 57/i or 96/i) and that he could manage well enough with little more than the primary triads (e.g., C. 59/ii). But he also proved early and thereafter that he could think for himself, as in occasional parallel 5ths and 8ves that he seems to have approved between outer voices (e.g., C. 151/ii/10 and 59/ii/2) and in frequently bold, academically unauthorized dissonances. As for the latter, one might cite at random the long, chromatic, accented passing tones in the opening theme of C. 59, the cross-relation and the long appoggiatura on the minor-9th in C. 62/ii/66–68, the combined cross-relation and appoggiatura that is reiterated in C. 178/iv/101–3, the conflict of major and minor 7ths over a four-measure dominant pedal in C. 179/iii/51–54, the successive accented 7ths in C. 247/i/195–96, or the biting 7ths and 9ths that contribute to the striking sonorities in C. 181/ii/21–24 (Ex. 108). Apart from such dissonance, the harmony frequently produces new telling effects for its day through imaginative chord choices, as in the major-minor alternations in the refrain of C. 247/iii or the expressive chromaticism of C. 178/ii, with, for example, the stunning use of the Neapolitan chord at measure 12. Lowered-7ths provide unexpected modal inflections in C. 184/ii/6–7.

Telling and new for their time, too, are the numerous remote modulations or assumptions of key, which began to appear early in Dussek's sonatas. In the development section of C. 96/i, enharmony and deceptive resolutions over a bass that ascends chromatically provide the means for a wide Haydnesque excursion that proves to be no more than a long way around from the dominant to the tonic key. In C. 178/i/106–17 (cf. Ex. 109, *infra,* starting at ms. 116), after the exposition closes on the dominant, B♭, the development at once assumes the

Ex. 108. From the middle movement of Sonata in D, C. 181, by Jan Ladislav Dussek (after MAB-m LIX 102).

dominant of E, without modulation, only to return almost as abruptly to E♭ eleven measures later by letting the dim.-7th chord on C𝄪 stand for the restored dominant (-9th) harmony on B♭. Similarly, the development section of C. 149/i returns from F to B♭ after episodes in D♭, G♭, B, e♭, and b♭; the exposition of C. 221/i detours into e♭, B, and e♭ (mss. 45–61) before the subordinate theme begins in the dominant key, E♭ (as in Ex. 110, *infra*); and one 16-measure portion (mss. 87–102) of the development section in C. 259/i passes rapidly from c to f, b♭, e♭, c♯, b, a, g, and back to the home key of f. An extraordinary opening at a tonal tangent occurs when C. 221/iii, "Tempo di menuetto; scherzo quasi allegro," begins in f♯ and, by reinterpreting the dim.-7th chord on that tonic as V_9-of-ii in A♭, drives forcefully to a full cadence in the latter, home key (mss. 1–20).

Naturally, there are interinfluences between Dussek's harmonic treatment and his writing for piano. Both traits relate in turn to his own superior performance at the keyboard, whether as a virtuoso or a sensitive musician, and to his position, along with Clementi and Mozart, as a pioneer composer in the exploitation of the piano, whether as a developer of new technical idioms, sonorities, and pedal effects,[24] or as an advocate of wider ranges (cf. C. 127/iii/92–111), better action, and other construction advances.[25] Dussek's textures are predominantly homophonic, with accompaniment styles ranging from high-Classic to high-Romantic. Repeated notes or chords, murky bass, broken chords in 8th-notes and triplets, Alberti bass, and similar standard Classic devices abound, for example, throughout C. 57, whereas wider chord arpeggiations, bass-chord ("um-pah") techniques, and some less stereo-typed figures characteristic of Romantic styles prevail throughout C. 221. One has to acknowledge that an excess of the stereotyped accom-paniment figures representing either or both eras (as in much of C. 179 and 184) tends to weaken the textural interest all too often in Dussek's sonatas. Occasionally the harmonic rhythm is so slow—deliberately slow throughout much of C. 242?—that such solutions seem almost unavoidable.

Yet the textural solutions are generally so resourceful and happy in Dussek's finest sonatas, including C. 221, that one can only accuse him of not trying hard enough or, at least, not feeling the need for anything more enterprising in his somewhat more routine sonatas. At best his passagework and figuration anticipate some of the fine piano writing of the 19th century—for example, the exchange of appoggiatura figures, the arpeggiated chords, the broken 10ths, the double-notes, and the other figures in his C. 211/i/129–61. The technical difficulties mount conspicuously from C. 147 on, with easier sonatas occurring thereafter only infrequently, and new idiomatic problems on the increase, like trills and melodies in the same hand (C. 150/i/198–203), a dialog made by the left hand crossing high and low while the right supplies figural harmony (C. 181/i/44–46; but cf. Beethoven's similar technique 5 years earlier, in Op. 2/2/i/131–59), or tricky passages involving double-notes (C. 259/i/104–11). There also are several movements that display excep-tional contrapuntal ingenuity on Dussek's part, including one that sounds at times like a two-part invention (C. 180/i), another that is a "Tempo di minuetto con moto; Canone alla seconda" (alternately "grave" and "acuta"; C. 259/ii), and a few with motivic exchanges in their development sections that also reveal exceptional rhythmic inge-nuity (Ex. 109).

24. According to information kindly supplied by Professor Craw, specific pedal indications in Dussek's scores appeared at least as early as *ca.* 1799 ("Military Concerto," Op. 40); cf., also, MAB-m LIX xi; Schiffer/DUSSEK 51–52; Egert/FRÜH-ROMANTIKER 37–38).

25. Cf. Schiffer/DUSSEK 51–52; Craw/DUSSEK 53–54, 75, 175, 445–72 (*passim*).

Ex. 109. From the first movement of Jan Ladislav Dussek's Sonata in e♭/E♭, C. 178 (after MAB-m LIX 25).

Dussek is as fertile and resourceful if not quite so innovational or distinguished, in his melody writing as in his harmonic treatment and keyboard writing. Indeed, his melodic "fecundity" has been viewed as an embarrassment of riches,[26] sometimes providing more than is needed or assimilable in his "sonata forms." Only in the most intense and mature examples does a clear dualistic opposition of themes obtain (e.g., 211/i). Although a movement as nearly monothematic as C. 259/i is an exception, "sonata forms" with a pluralism of similar, not distinctly contrasted, themes are not rare (e.g., C. 127/i). The main ideas range from the concise motives of C. 96/i to the cantilena of the full-fledged themes in C. 221/i. Dotted and syncopated ideas are frequent (as in C. 149/i/1–18 and C. 211/i/53–74). Dussek implied that performers were still improvising ornamentation in slow melodic passages when he inscribed "senza ornamenti" over the start of C. 211. But he himself generally built up such lavish ornamentation and filigrees in the lines of his more serious slow movements, including the sort of rhythmic complexities introduced later in Beethoven's string quartets, that little or no opportunity remained for improvisation (as was already true in C. 60/ii and became still more so in mvts. like C. 259/iii). In his rondo finales, Dussek invented frank tunes of varying

---

26. As by G. A. Macfarren, quoted in Shedlock/SONATA 151–52.

originality, among the most distinctive being the pre-Chopinesque refrains in C. 222/iv and 259/iv.

One long example—in fact, the longest in this three-volume history—
should help to illustrate not only some of the syntactic variation,
harmonic, textural, pianistic, melodic, and rhythmic traits observed
thus far in Dussek's sonatas but also what astonishingly precocious
Romanticisms these traits often produce (Ex. 110). This example comes
from the sonata regarded here as Dussek's best, C. 221—more specifically, from the exposition of the first movement, beginning at measure
62 with the start of the third theme (or *the* "subordinate" theme, in
that the 2d theme, starting at ms. 25, is still in the home key of A♭) and
extending through its varied repetition, a closing idea, and dissolution
in passagework, almost to the double-bar.

One's first impulse after reading such an excerpt from Dussek is to
call him a master eclectic, almost in league with our late-Romantic
epigones (cf. the start of ssb XI). However, one would have to realize
that chronologically Dussek could only be an eclectic-before-the-fact, a
Shakespeare who depends on "so many familiar quotations." When he
does choose from the (immediate) past, he does so primarily from
Haydn (as in C. 58/iii or C. 151/iii) and Mozart (as in C. 96/i). But
even then he produces something new or different—namely, the exaggeration of high-Classicism that was to become one characteristic of
early-Romantic music (ssb VI). In less basic ways he also derives from
Clementi, as in the triplets, octaves, and broken-octaves of C. 57/i, or
the mood in C. 211/i that recalls the pathos of "Didone abbandonata"
(sce 749). But he shows remarkably little trace of Emanuel Bach, who,
if he actually taught Dussek at one time, left none of the tangible
influences that mark other of Bach's students so clearly (sce 123), unless
one searches for the consequences in isolated passages and cadence extensions like those in C. 62/i/144–55 or C. 151/i/78–83.

Nor can substantial evidence be found for clear interinfluences between Dussek and his greatest contemporary, Beethoven. If anything,
the influences seem to have acted on Beethoven, although the chief
discussions of this possibility tread shaky ground, chronologically as
well as musically, by emphasizing possible influences of Dussek's C. 151
on Beethoven's Op. 13 in the same key.[27] More plausible might be the
influences of C. 62/ii on Op. 109/ii in the same key, tempo, and
meter; or C. 184/i on Op. 79/i, with similar ideas, treatment, and
meter. Still more plausible on internal musical grounds are Dussek's
possible influences on another great, near contemporary, Schubert—for
example, the sense of gentle flow, folklike simplicity, and *Gemüt-*

27. E.g., as in Blom/DUSSEK 708–9; cf. Newman/K. 457.

Ex. 110. From the first movement of Jan Ladislav Dussek's Sonata in A♭, C. 221 (after MAB-M LXIII 45–47).

lichkeit in C. 166/ii or 179/i, which movements immediately bring certain of Schubert's impromptus and songs to mind; or the grandeur and drama of C. 178/ii in advance of the first movement of the "Unfinished Symphony"; or the peaceful, resigned, marchlike quality of C. 247/ii in advance of the "Great" Symphony in C/ii and the final "Ballet Music" from *Rosamunde*.

Returning to our Ex. 110 for anticipations of more mature Romanticisms, one can hardly help but say "Brahms" over the first eight measures, with the melody in rich 3ds and 6ths and, especially, the turn to the major key on the lowered-submediant degree (mss. 66–67). And one can hardly help saying "Weber" over the Alberti bass in open position, as it were (mss. 70–72), and the later line that descends by twos and dotted patterns above a bass-chord accompaniment (mss. 78–81); or "Hummel" and like virtuosos over the passagework that follows. Moreover, in other Dussek passages we find anticipations of Schumann (cf. C. 178/iv/90–97 with Op. 22/i/148–63, respectively), Rossini (cf. C. 59/ii/12–20 and the "Overture" to *The Barber of Seville*), Mendelssohn (cf. C. 211/ii and the Scherzo in b of 1829 or similarly deft scherzos), and Chopin (as suggested by the German-polka refrain in C. 259/iv or the *fioriture* in C. 221/ii). Anticipations of later Czech styles and composers, especially Smetana and Dvořák, also have been observed in Dussek's sonatas.[28] These include folklike themes and settings such as those in C. 127/iii/61–68 (starting with a refreshing turn to the subdominant) and C. 133/iii/1–24 (starting with a dominant harmony over a tonic drone bass).

In conclusion, Dussek's best sonatas are regarded here as being not only outstanding in quality but the most precociously Romantic sonatas, especially in harmony and keyboard writing, at the outset of the new era. If their quality does not quite match that of Beethoven's and Schubert's best sonatas, the reasons advanced here would be less, though far from little, melodic distinction in Dussek's sonatas; a less dynamic, concentrated approach to form, owing partly to the prevalence of complete double-periods; and somewhat less warmth and intimacy, except in his most expressive movements, for Dussek's variety of styles is so pronounced that it often suggests deliberate, conscious experimentation rather than subjective "inspiration."

Of considerably less significance to the sonata was Dussek's fellow countryman, onetime acquaintance, and junior by fourteen years, **Wenzel Johann Tomaschek (Václav Jan Tomášek; 1774–1850).**[29]

---

28. Cf. MAB-m XLVI xxviii and xxxi, LIII ix–x, LIX ix–x, and LXIII x–xi.

29. The order of Wenzel Johann is reversed in most sources. Thompson/ TOMASCHEK is the principal study of the man and his piano works, including a

Largely a self-taught musician, Tomaschek forwent a concert career as pianist to devote his full time to composition, creating prolifically in all categories, and to teaching, in which he stood highest among early 19th-century Czechs.[30] He idolized Mozart (but did not meet him) during that composer's last visits and operatic productions in Prague.[31] In the same city in 1798 he was greatly moved, at first even disturbed, by hearing the music and performance of Beethoven, whom he met then, as he did again in 1808 and 1814 in Vienna.[32] And in the same city he admired the music and performance of Spohr and Hummel, and met them,[33] as well as Vogler, Forkel, the Koželuch cousins, and the aging Goethe (1822).[34] He also met Clementi and Moscheles, but whether he knew Schubert in Vienna can be only a guess. His students included the gifted composer Woržischek (ssb VII) and the noted critic Eduard Hanslick. In spite of the visits to Vienna and a few lesser centers, Tomaschek was one Czech who stayed mostly at home.

Among some 110 solo piano works by Tomaschek are his only known sonatas—five in all, first published approximately in the 11 years from 1805 to 1816 (overlapping Dussek's late sonatas). These include Opp. 10 in B♭ (in Anth. NÄGELI-m XIV), 14 in C, 15 in G, 21 in F, and 48 in A (Hofmeister in Leipzig, plate no. 418), with "Grande" in the title of all but Opp. 10 and 48.[35] All are four-movement cycles with fast outer movements and, in between, the usual slow or moderate movement and the usual minuet or scherzo, or vice-versa. All but Op. 10 have slow introductions and all but Op. 15 have rondo finales.

If Dussek did exercise some of the strongest influences on Tomaschek, as has been asserted,[36] he seems to have done so, at least in the latter's sonatas, chiefly in the realm of tonal relationships and struc-

---

bibliography (pp. 234–42) with a brief undated list of the eds. used (pp. 239–42). Tomaschek's only opportunity to know Dussek was in Oct. and Nov. of 1802, not in 1804 as wrongly recalled by Tomaschek himself (and repeated in Thompson/ TOMASCHEK 84–86); cf. Craw/DUSSEK 124–30 and 458.

30. Cf. MGG XIII 469–72 (J. Bužga); Buchner/LISZT 42–43.

31. Cf. Thompson/TOMASCHEK 71–72.

32. Cf. Thompson/TOMASCHEK 78–79, 90; Nettl/DOCUMENTS 162–63, 178–85; TOMASCHEK (extracts from his autobiographic sketch of 1845–50) 251–61, passim (pp. 245–47 concern a visit in 1808 to Haydn in his dotage).

33. Cf. TOMASCHEK 247–48 and 261–62.

34. Cf. Thompson/TOMASCHEK 81–84, 94–95.

35. A "Sonatine" listed in MGG XIII 471 may or may not be a reprint of one of these. The 5 sons., especially Opp. 10 and 15, are described in Thompson/TOMA- SCHEK 111–49 (with copious exx.). Mod. ed.: only Op. 21/i, Giegling/SOLO-m 98 (cf. p. 18); Op. 21 is regarded here, unfortunately, as Tomaschek's weakest and least characteristic son.

36. Thompson/TOMASCHEK 84–86.

Ex. 111. From the first movement of Sonata in A, Op. 48, by Wenzel Johann Tomaschek (after the original Hofmeister ed. at the Library of Congress).

tural methods. His pianistic flare, which Tomaschek could have observed in person only during Dussek's one relatively brief return to Prague in 1802 (*supra*), and his extraordinary variety of keyboard styles did not carry over to Tomaschek's sonatas. More specifically, the influences that might be discovered on the younger Czech's sonatas can be found primarily in such traits as a similar fondness for modulations to moderately or distantly related keys by change of mode and enharmony, or for progressing by complete, relatively static double-periods, especially the parallel kind in which the second period is an elaboration of the first, or for creating driving scherzos and tuneful rondo finales. As for keyboard treatment, Tomaschek's writing fits and sometimes challenges the hand well enough, but it does little of what Dussek's does to display the virtues and capabilities of piano techniques and sounds. In fact, Tomaschek's most characteristic keyboard treatment is a close-position three- and four-part texture in the center of the keyboard, with the hands interplaying in rather intricate dotted and related rhythms (Ex. 111).

Tomaschek's sonatas cannot quite claim the pre-Schubertian charm and Romanticisms that have been regarded as significant in his "Eglogues," "Rapsodies," "Ditirambi," and other shorter piano pieces (composed from 1807 on).[37] One must acknowledge the somewhat static form and the limits in both the texture and the piano idiom, as well as a certain predisposition toward conservatism and the high-Classic styles.[38] Also, one must acknowledge ideas that are well drawn and harmony that is appropriate without either being distinctive. There is little actual development of the ideas, most of which are too broadly and conjunctly outlined to provide kernels for development, anyway. Nor is there any of the experimenting with harmonic dissonance to be found in Dussek's music. Nor are there, for that matter, the generalized programmatic associations that seem to have given rise to Dussek's finest sonatas. All these considerations help to explain why Tomaschek's sonatas have never aroused the enthusiasm, in relation to either his own or other works, that Dussek's and even Woržischek's sonatas have.[39]

Another Czech who wrote in Mozart's shadow and had contacts with Beethoven was the dilettante pianist and professional jurist in Prague, **Johann Nepomuk Kanka** (1772–1865).[40] His two sonatas for P solo, in G and b♭, are preserved in MSS that await exploration in Prague. Tomaschek's pupil, the brilliant, widely-traveled concert pianist **Alexander Dreyschock** (1818–69) wrote at least three sonatas for P solo, presumably in the salon, virtuoso style of Kalkbrenner and Thalberg.[41] One of the sonatas by this "Hannibal of the octaves" (in Mendelssohn's words), "with two right hands" (in Cramer's words), was that in d, published as Op. 30 (Schott, *ca.* 1845); one was played in Paris in March, 1843; and the finale of one (his "third" son., in E♭) was played in Prague in 1847.[42] The Czech violinist **Johann Wenzel Kalliwoda** (1801–66) should get at least a mention here because of the interest and best moments in his symphonies, although his only two known sonatas are late works written while he was still in Donaueschingen, in southwest Germany—Opp. 135 in g, for P-duet (1845), and 176 in E♭, for P solo (1851)—and although the second of these, Op. 176, got reviewed as a formalistic, artistically worthless piece.[43] Another jurist

37. Cf. Kahl/LYRISCHE; Thompson/TOMASCHEK 89; SSB II.

38. Cf. Thompson/TOMASCHEK 222–23.

39. Cf. the early reviews in AMZ VIII (1805–6) 261–63 (praise for the ideas and treatment in Op. 10, but not the texture), XII (1809–10) 94–96 (mixed reactions to Op. 14).

40. Cf. MGG VII 511–12 (P. Nettl), with further bibl., including an unpub. Czech diss. of 1956; Thayer & Forbes/BEETHOVEN I 183–84 and 590–91; Anderson/BEETHOVEN *passim.*

41. Cf. MGG III 819–21 (W. Kahl).

42. Cf. MGG III 819–21; HOFMEISTER 1844–51, p. 108; Buchner/LISZT 43–44.

43. NZM XXXV (1851) 137–38. Cf. MGG VII 454–59 (W. Kramolisch); Altmann/KAMMERMUSIK 301.

by profession, yet also a onetime director of the Prague Conservatory, a friend of Wagner, and another pupil of Tomaschek, the pianist **Johann Friedrich Kittl** (1806–68) left a further published P-duet, Op. 27 in f (1847), that brought a similarly negative review.[44]

Smetana, Dvořák, and Other Later Czech Romantics

As compared with the obscure composers just mentioned, the major Czech composer **Friedrich Smetana** (1824–84) left two unpublished sonatas that, although not made known until recently, prove to have considerable interest and musical value.[45] Both sonatas were composed in the later 1840's, while he was still a young man, and during the least troubled years of his troubled career. One is a Sonata in g, for P solo, composed in 1846 but not published until as recently as 1949, only after a public appeal in 1944 recovered two opening pages of the MS that were missing since 1892.[46] The other is a Sonata in e, for 8 hands at 2 Ps, a rare example of this setting, composed in 1849, first published in 1906 as part of a not-quite-complete "complete" edition of Smetana's piano music, and republished in 1938.[47] These two sonatas remained unpublished because by 1879, when his successes in opera, orchestral, and chamber music would have insured publication of anything he wrote, Smetana was insisting that he had no piano works worthy of publication.[48] On the other hand, a third contribution, a Sonatina for P & Vn in d, Op. 27, did get published about a year earlier (*ca.* 1878, by F. A. Urbánek in Prague),[49] yet still remains unknown (and could not be found here).

Both of Smetana's piano sonatas reflect the circumstances of their origins. The solo sonata was composed between July and October of 1846 during his fourth and last year of study with the Romantic Czech pianist **Joseph Proksch** (1794–1864; himself the composer of at least one Sonata for P & Vn and a "Skalen-Sonate" for 4 Ps[!]).[50] In that year

44. NZM XXVI (1847) 41–42. Cf. MGG VII 973–74 (R. Quoika); Altmann/KAMMER-MUSIK 301.

45. Cf. GROVE VII 843–49 (G. Černušak) and MGG XII 774–87 (K. Honolka), each with further bibliography and a dated (but not quite complete) list of works; also, Newmarch/CZECHOSLOVAKIA 54–102.

46. Řepková/SMETANA-m, with valuable preface (in Czech) by M. Očadlík.

47. Kuhlmann/SMETANA-m, with "Explanatory Note." Another son. in the same setting, dated 1851, was left unfinished, according to Helfert/SMETANAS 177.

48. Kuhlmann/SMETANA-m "Explanatory Note."

49. According to Cobbett/CHAMBER II 425 (R. Newmarch & W. W. Cobbett); but no other reference to this work has turned up here.

50. Cf. MGG X 1653–54 (R. Quoika); Buchner/LISZT 47–48, 116–17; NZM LXXII/2 (1876) 318 (performance of the "Skalen-Sonate").

Smetana was deliberately experimenting with musical forms (thus, with "sonata form" in March) as part of a larger, planned exploration of the whole field of composition.[51] Whether he himself ever actually performed this work is not known. But this man, who was soon to gain distinction as a Chopin interpreter, could already derive influences, ideas, and styles from his own direct, youthful experiences and successes as a brilliant performer of Liszt, Thalberg, and Henselt.[52] And he undoubtedly derived more far-reaching and even more immediate influences on his Sonata in g (as well as his later music) from the sensational Prague visits in January, March, and April of that same year (1846) by Liszt as virtuoso and composer and Berlioz as composer and conductor (mainly of *Romeo and Juliet*).[53]

In any case, the Sonata in g, without any programmatic titles or other associations, reveals more daring, freedom, and striking originality in certain respects than *The Bartered Bride, The Moldau,* the Quartet "Aus meinem Leben," or any other of the recognized masterworks that were to be composed later, in the 1860's and 1870's, by Smetana. In its outward aspects the work offers no surprises. It is cast in the usual four movements (F-S-Sc-VF), with the opening idea—a stepwise descent and ascent within a 3d—undergoing "thematic metamorphosis" or recurring as an "idée fixe" throughout the first movement and in portions of each of the other three movements. Moreover, in these movements the over-all designs, although not conspicuous as such, are the standard ones of "sonata form," A-B-A, A-B-A, and rondo, respectively. But what does seem more conspicuous and less standard is the over-all style of progression. This style is a continuous unfolding through constant yet rhythmically plastic reiterations of a pattern. The pattern goes through frequent slight and more radical mutations, it depends on purposeful, choice, though not unusual harmonies (such as Dussek used) to move in slow harmonic rhythm toward changing tonal goals, near or far, and it lends itself well to the exploitation of varied techniques, ranges, and sonorities on the piano. In all these respects Smetana not only reflected the vivid impressions that Liszt's and Berlioz's music made on him but anticipated no other composer more than the Sibelius of the piano sonatinas noted earlier (end of ssb XV). At the same time, Smetana showed himself

51. According to M. Očadlík's preface in Řepková/SMETANA-m. Cf. pp. 64–93 (though with no special reference to the Son. in g) in the chief study of Smetana's development, Helfert/SMETANAS.

52. Cf. GROVE VII 843; BAKER 1527.

53. Cf. Ramann/LISZT II/1 270–71 and footnote 2 (giving the programs of 10 concerts just played by Liszt in Vienna); Barzun/BERLIOZ I 476 and 478; Buchner/LISZT, especially pp. 87–103 (with details on Berlioz, too).

Ex. 112. From the second movement of Sonata in g, by Friedrich Smetana (after the original ed. of 1949, by kind permission of the publisher Melantrich in Prague).

well able to depart from or broaden his over-all style of progression long enough to mold an expressive line such as would do honor to his later reputation as a fine melodist. Our Ex. 112, from the slow movement, includes a phrase with a reference to the "idée fixe" (bracketed here), approached and quitted by abrupt, remote modulations.

Whereas his Sonata in g originated as an advanced composition exercise, Smetana's Sonata in e supposedly originated as a pedagogic work, designed for use at the private music school that Liszt had encouraged him to open in Prague in 1848.[54] At any rate, it is a more regularized work, closer in phrase syntax, clarity of design, and straightforward scoring to his later comparable instrumental works or, for example, to those of Grieg. (Indeed, there are faint melodic anticipations of Grieg's sonata in the same key, Op. 7 [ssb XV].) Its chief structural distinction is the fact that it is in one movement, although that movement is simply textbook "sonata form" extended to 490 measures. The work can be made to sound well and structurally con-

54. Kuhlmann/SMETANA-m "Explanatory Note."

vincing by four moderately advanced students properly coached in their ensemble and artistry.

Between the contributions of Smetana and Dvořák appeared such works as a thoroughly competent but nondistinctive Sonata in C for P & Vc, Op. 58 (pub. in 1853), by Tomaschek's onetime piano student and Liszt's friend in song, **Joseph Dessauer** (1798–1876);[55] a favorably received Sonatina and two Sonatas, Opp. 9–11 (1863–67), in A, D, and f, respectively, by Smetana's student, the important pedagogue **Josef Jiranék** (1855–1940);[56] and a Mendelssohnian "Sonatine instruktiv" in d (1884; composed *ca.* 1869), Op. 27, for P & Vn, along with a Sonata in B♭, Op. 28 (1887), for P-duet, by the successful opera composer **Zdenko Fibich** (1850–1900).[57]

A half generation younger than Smetana, the other of the two most important Czech Romantics in music, **Antonin Dvořák** (1841–1904), also left two contributions to our genre that are only on the fringe of a large output, yet have real musical interest. But unlike Smetana Dvořák made these contributions chiefly late in his life, well after he had profited from the support of Liszt, Brahms, and Bülow, and had won international recognition. Also, Dvořák, being mainly a violinist insofar as he performed and certainly not being the pianist that Smetana was, preferred to write his sonatas in duo rather than solo-piano settings.[58]

Dvořák did write two other, complete sonatas earlier in his life. One, written at the age of 32 (1873), was a three-movement duo in a, for Vn & P, actually played in 1875 but destroyed by the composer.[59] The other, written two years earlier, was a one-movement duo in f, for Vc & P (designated Op. 10), which was also destroyed by the composer, although the cello part remains.[60] Furthermore, all in 1893

---

55. NZM XXXIX (1853) 203–4. Cf. Mendel/LEXIKON III 121–22; Buchner/LISZT 60; LISZT LETTERS I 418 and II 502.

56. NZM LX (1864) 155; HOFMEISTER *Monatsbericht* for Dec. 1863, p. 235, Sept.–Oct. 1865, p. 158, Sept. 1867, p. 146. Cf. GROVE IV 642 (G. Černušak).

57. Cf. MGG IV 153–55 (P. Nettl); Helfert & Steinhard 254 and 269 (with further [MS?] sons., including errors); Newmarch/CZECHOSLOVAKIA 104–24.

58. Within the extensive literature on Dvořák the most recent, authoritative, and up-to-date studies that pertain here are Šourek/DVOŘÁK on the chamber music (cf., also, Šourek's remarks in Cobbett/CHAMBER I 365 and 369–70), DVOŘÁK LETTERS, Clapham/DVOŘÁK on the life (brief) and works (by categories), and Burghauser/DVOŘÁK, a trilingual thematic index, bibliography, biographic chronology, and general documentary summary. Cf., also, Newmarch/CZECHOSLOVAKIA 125–75.

59. Cf. Burghauser/DVOŘÁK 123–24 (item 33, with further [Czech] references), 67 ("DAnn"), but not the list of destroyed works on pp. 616–17; Clapham/DVOŘÁK 190 and 219.

60. Cf. Burghauser/DVOŘÁK 106 (item 20, with incipit and further [Czech] references) and 617; Clapham/DVOŘÁK 189 (cf. pp. 162–63) and 219; Šourek/DVOŘÁK 14.

Dvořák started sketches for another Sonata for Vc & P, a Sonatina for the same, and a Sonata in f for P solo.[61] But it was still two other works that comprised the only two contributions to our genre completed by him and allowed to survive, both being duos for Vn & P. One is Op. 57 in F, a three-movement, 20-minute, noncyclical sonata (F-S-VF) composed in Prague while Dvořák was working on his violin Concerto in a, tried out with success in Berlin by the composer and Joachim, first published by Simrock, and first performed publicly in Chrudim (east of Prague), all in 1880.[62] The other is a Sonatina in G, Op. 100, a four-movement but shorter work (F-S-Sc-F) that was composed in two weeks late in 1893 during his first stay in New York and soon after two larger chamber works and the "New World Symphony" had been completed.[63] Published in 1894 by Simrock, this Sonatina was "dedicated to my children . . . on the occasion of completing my hundredth work" and welcomed by 15-year-old Otilie, his eldest surviving child, as "delightful," although Dvořák wrote Simrock suggesting that adults could enjoy it, too.[64]

Both of Dvořák's contributions, if not quite the equals of his greatest masterpieces in originality, strength, or melodic and harmonic sensitivity, deserve to be kept alive in chamber music literature. Op. 57 has less of a chance because, as we have seen happen so often, it approaches too closely the musical ideas, textures, and development techniques of his staunch supporter and friend Brahms[65] to stand on its own merits. Whether during the flexible, tonally extended applications of "sonata form" in the first movement, or the expressive, broadly drawn lines of the ternary, A-B-A design in the middle movement, or the more curt, clipped themes of the sonata-rondo-form finale, almost every passage brings some idea or style from Brahms's chamber music to mind. There are even hints of contemporary or future Brahms works that Dvořák could not yet have known, such as the descending triplets in Dvořák's opening, main theme, suggesting those in the bridge to the second theme of Brahms's piano Trio in C, Op. 87/i. And in this work Dvořák shows that he, like Brahms, enjoyed a dis-

61. Cf. Burghauser/DVOŘÁK 352 and 354 (items 419, 428, and 426, respectively).

62. Cf. Burghauser/DVOŘÁK 497–98, 500, 216 (item 106), with further (Czech) bibliography; Clapham/DVOŘÁK 193–95; Šourek/DVOŘÁK 169–72 (description, with exx.); DVOŘÁK LETTERS 54, 56; MT XXVII (1885) 147, 162 (early English performances).

63. Cf. Burghauser/DVOŘÁK 563, 311–12 (item 183), with further (Czech) bibliography; Clapham/DVOŘÁK 209–10, 31–32 (sketches); Šourek/DVOŘÁK 172–78 (description); DVOŘÁK LETTERS 176, 178. Opp. 57 and 100 are reprinted in Dvořák/WERKE-m IV/1, among other mod. eds.

64. Clapham/DVOŘÁK 209, 8–9; Šourek/DVOŘÁK 172. To make this his "hundredth" work, Dvořák assigned "Op. 100" before it was quite due.

65. Cf. Clapham/DVOŘÁK 9, 13, 23.

tinct heritage from Schumann—for example, in the octave leaps (with the two instruments in contretemps) in Op. 57/i/83–95, which recall the "Scherzo" of Schumann's Symphony in d. Dvořák's piano writing is appropriate but not especially resourceful.

Dvořák's Op. 100 is in quite another style, immediately suggesting the freshness and originality, as well as some specific ideas, in the "New World Symphony" and other of his works composed in this country. To be sure, the "sonata forms" in the outer movements and A-B-A designs in the inner movements are standard again and they are exceptionally clear, as is the simpler texture, in keeping with music for children. But the freshness and originality lie less in these aspects than in the frank melodies, with their modal flavors, dancelike rhythms, and elementary yet fully appropriate harmonies. Thus, the violin and its accompaniment open on a gay theme that recalls the rising contour, dotted pattern, and single tonic major chord on which "Oh, My Darling Clementine" opens. The second theme starts in the submediant minor key with the scale pattern 8-7-5 and the lowered 7th sometimes associated with Grieg's and with American Indian music.[66] The "Larghetto" movement, in the tonic minor key, starts with a melancholy theme jotted down a few months earlier by Dvořák as he was shown the Minnehaha Falls near St. Paul, Minnesota, perhaps while longing for his family and homeland. The special appeal of this movement and this theme with its emphasis on the Indian minor 3d, 3-1, prompted Simrock to publish it separately, with such unauthorized titles as "Indian Lament," "Indian Conzonetta," and "Indian Lullaby." [67] After a bright "Scherzo" the finale announces its character with a piquant idea and syncopations that provide some of those specific recollections of the "New World Symphony" (Ex. 113). Highly characteristic of Dvořák's style, too, is the lyrical, syncopated, rising theme of the "Molto tranquillo section" in E, and the approach to it through an alternation of the tonic and mediant triads in e.

The esteemed Prague organist **Joseph Bohuslav Foerster** (1859–1951) revealed both his devotion to Dvořák and Mahler and his conservative orientation in his sonatas (as well as his other music). These include three duos for Vn & P and two for Vc & P, published over nearly a half century (1898–1943).[68] A full half-century (1891–1941) spans the composition dates of three sonatas and six sonatinas left by a similarly important but quite different conservative, the Dvořák

66. Chapham/DVOŘÁK 210 likens it to a "well-known Moravian folk-song."
67. Cf. Clapham/DVOŘÁK 209.
68. Cf. GROVE III 178–79 (G. Černušak), with dated cat.; MGG IV 455–57 (P. Nettl); Helfert & Steinhard 67–72; Newmarch/CZECHOSLOVAKIA 182–91.

Ex. 113. From Antonín Dvořák's Sonatina in G, Op. 100/iv (after the original Simrock ed.).

student and further Brahms protégé **Vitězslav Novák** (1870–1949). Novák took for his models, as his style and control developed, first Mendelssohn, then Schumann, Grieg, Berlioz, Liszt, Brahms, and eventually Smetana and Dvořák in their more nationalistic guises.[69] He started at twenty-one with a Sonata in d, for P & Vn, which was not published until 1920.[70] In 1900, he followed with his single example that achieved any success, "Sonata eroica" for P solo, Op. 24 in f, first published in 1905 and again in 1951. A laudatory review greeted this work, ascribing to it some of that heroic element to be found in Bruckner's third and Beethoven's third and ninth symphonies.[71] At least the comparison with Bruckner seems appropriate today, not only in the sense of the heroic, achieved mainly by broad melodic arches moving in slow harmonic rhythm, but in the more personal and local flavors of the melody, in the dramatic tonal surprises in spite of traditional harmony, in the orchestral sonorities implicit in full piano writing that seems more like a transcription than an original, and in the persistent rhythmic patterns of both of the well-planned, freely

69. Cf. GROVE VI 130–33 (G. Černušak) and MGG IX 1723–27 (J. Bužga), both with dated cats. and further bibliography; Helfert & Steinhard 72–79; Newmarch/CZECHOSLOVAKIA 195–201.

70. Altmann/KAMMERMUSIK 219. It is mentioned as an "acceptable" work, only as an afterthought, in Cobbett/CHAMBER II 192 (W. W. Cobbett).

71. NZM CI (1905) 543.

and emotively paced, closely edited movements (F-S/F/S). Novák's set of *Sechs Sonatinen,* Op. 54, for P solo were published originally about 1915 [72] and again in 1951. But a Sonata for Vc & P, composed by him in 1941, apparently still remains in MS.

Novák's two chief contemporaries among Czech pioneers of the 20th century, Josef Suk and Otakar Ostrčil,[73] did not happen to leave any consequential sonatas. But several other late-Romantics of less renown and success in Czechoslovakia did,[74] including, for example, a violinist and biographer of Smetana, **Karl Navrátil** (1867–1936), who left one sonata each for P & Vn (Op. 20 in d; 1894) and P & Vc (Op. 24 in d; 1903). Op. 20 was reviewed as Brahmsian, skillful for an "amateur," "but very physiognomelióse." [75] The violinist **Johann Sluničko** (1852–1923) left five or more sonatas for P & Vn published between 1904 and 1913, at least two of which brought warm praise for fine workmanship and attractive themes still in the style of Gade and Grieg.[76] By contrast, Dvořák's last student, **Rudolf Karel** (1880–1945), left two impassioned, rhapsodic sonatas. Op. 14 in c (although the finale begins in f) is a four-movement work (M-S-Sc-F) for P solo (composed in 1910, pub. in 1921); and Op. 17 in d is a one-movement, largely polyphonic work for Vn & P (composed in 1912, pub. in 1913). Both sonatas suggest Reger in their chromatic, recherché harmony and remote tonal relationships, hence aroused the expected discomfort and puzzlement among reviewers.[77]

Composers in Poland (Paderewski)

Aside from Chopin, whose main sonatas originated in France (and are so identified in ssb XII), there is no front-rank composer to bring up in connection with the Romantic sonata in Poland. In fact, in the politically and socially unfavorable environment of the early 19th century[78] there are almost no sonata composers to mention, and even by the end of the century there are few who survive today beyond the ken of Polish specialists. As one example from the start of the era,

72. DM XV/2 (1915) 616.
73. Cf. Helfert & Steinhard 72.
74. Cf. the lists in Helfert & Steinhard, especially pp. 254–55 and 269–72, although many of the names would have to be put here with the Moderns.
75. NZM XCIX (1903) 596.
76. DM III/4 (1903–4) 463 (W. Altmann on Op. 51 in c); DM VI/4 (1906–7) 239 (W. Altmann on Op. 60 in A). Cf. Riemann/LEXIKON II 1715; Altmann/KAMMER-MUSIK 227.
77. E.g., DM XIII/2 (1913–14) 231 (W. Dahms on Op. 14). Cf. MGG VII 680–82 (J. Bužga); Cobbett/CHAMBER II 47 (R. Veselý); Helfert & Steinhard 97–99.
78. Cf. Lissa/POLISH 104–13 (part of a helpful survey of Polish music).

Chopin's versatile teacher in Warsaw, **Joseph Xaver Elsner** (1768 [BAKER]–1854), left a "Grande Sonate" for P+V+Vc, Op. 2 (1798); three "Sonaten" for P & Vn, published separately as Op. 10/1–3 (1805–7); and a "Sonate" for P-duet, Op. 16 (between 1820 and 1828) [79] Elsner's Op. 10/1 and 3 were reviewed as light if not really easy pieces good for fun and practice (including a "Polonaise" as the last variation in Op. 10/3/ii).[80] As another early example, Haydn's pupil and friend, the pianist **Franciszek Lessel** (1779–1838), left at least one set of three sonatas, Op. 2, dedicated to Haydn, and a "Grande Sonate," Op. 6, all for P solo. These sonatas were published (shortly?) before 1815 and presumably bear out the popularity of some of Lessel's music in his day as well as the present small consensus to the effect that his music is Haydnesque, includes some Polish national elements, and is above average in quality.[81] Among the few others who were successful in Poland at the era's start—for example, Karol Kurpiński and Karol Lipiński[82]—none were noted here who left sonatas.

About a half-century later, the pianist and teacher **Władysław Żeleński** (1837–1921) left three sonatas for P solo (Opp. 3, 5, and 20) and two for P & Vn (Opp. 30 and 67), all published between about 1850 and 1885.[83] Representative is Op. 20, a musicianly, fluent, well-knit work in four movements (F-Va-Sc-F) that shows Żeleński still living in the world of Schumann and Mendelssohn. The celebrated, widely travelled pianist **Joseph Wieniawski** (1837–1912) was the brother of the even more celebrated violinist Henryk, who figures here only as the joint author with Joseph of an "Allegro de sonate" in g, Op. 2, composed when they were thirteen and eleven years old, published in 1854, and reprinted in 1898. Joseph himself left three published sonatas regarded as traditional and not the equal of Henryk's music—Opp. 22 in b, for P solo (*ca.* 1865?), 24 in d, for P & Vn (1869), and 26 in E, for P & Vc (1878).[84]

Although neither the symphonist Zygmunt Noskowski (1846–1909)[85]

79. Cf. MGG III 1313–16 (W. Kahl).

80. AMZ VIII (1805–6) 144 and IX (1806–7) 660.

81. Cf. MGG VIII 667–69 (J. Morawski), with errors; Lissa/POLISH 106; HOFMEISTER 1815 (Whistling), 365–66.

82. Cf. Lissa/POLISH 105–6.

83. Cf. GROVE IX 407–8 (C. R. Halski); Lissa/POLISH 120–21; HOFMEISTER 1852–55, 231 (Op. 5); NZM LXXII (1876) 488 and LVI/1 (1880) 98 (high praise by R. Musiol of Op. 20 for its ideas, concentration, and skill; with ex.); Cat. NYPL XXXIII 688 (Op. 30).

84. Cf. DM VIII/1 (1908–9) 235 (negative review of Op. 22 by A. Leitzmann); NZM LXXXI/1 (1885) 3–4 (viewing Op. 24 more as an effective virtuoso concerto); MGG XIV 627–33 (B. Schwarz & R. Sietz); Altmann/KAMMERMUSIK 232 and 266; PAZDÍREK XV 395–96.

85. Cf. MGG IX 1595 (A. Sutkowski) and Lissa/POLISH 121.

nor the chamber composer Gustaw Roguski (1839–1921)[86] left published sonatas, the gifted, short-lived pianist **Antoni Stolpe** (1851–72), a pupil of Elsner and Kiel, left a Sonata for P & Vn and two sonatas for P solo (all *ca.* 1870?). One of the latter, in d, was played often by the pianist Joseph Wieniawski (*supra*) and has been called "remarkable for its stylistic maturity." [87] Another who also died young is the Count and onetime piano student of Liszt, **Władisław Tarnowski** (1841–78). He is credited with a "Grande Sonate" for P solo, Op. 10 (1875?), and a "Fantaisie quasi sonate" on "some themes from an unpublished opera," for P & Vn (1870), both reviewed with extreme mockery as "crass dilletantism." [88] The pianist **Anastazy Wilhelm Dreszer** (1845–1907) wrote a "Sonata appassionata" that appeared as his Op. 1 in 1865 or 1866, before he moved to Halle (in east Germany), and a "Zweite grosse Sonate" published as his Op. 13 in 1879 (?). The latter would be interesting to see, if only to evaluate the reviewer who faulted it for depending in all three movements on the "swan motive" in *Lohengrin,* for inconsistencies of texture and keyboard idiom, for poor development of ideas, and for unclear, arbitrary tonality and forms![89]

Throughout his long distinguished musical and political career, the world-renowned pianist **Ignace Jan Paderewski** (1860–1941) held composition as his foremost goal.[90] His musical training, especially in the years from 1882 to 1889, included graduation from the Warsaw Conservatory, composition study in Berlin under Kiel and with Rubinstein's encouragement,[91] and the oft-cited study in piano with Leschetizky in Vienna.[92] Among only about 35 published works or sets of pieces by Paderewski, including the opera *Manru,* the Symphony in b, and the Concerto in a, as well as solos and duos with piano, there are two sonatas. One is Op. 13 in a, for Vn & P, dedicated to Sarasate, composed and first played in Vienna in 1885, and published by Bote & G. Bock of Berlin in 1886. After hearing this work in 1885,

86. Cf. GROVE VII 207–8 (C. R. Halski).

87. Lissa/POLISH 122; a mod. ed. was pub. in Krakow in 1957. Cf. MGG XII 1396–97 (J. Ekiert), with reference to an article (in Polish) on the Son. in d, by S. Goldchowski.

88. MW VI (1875) 513; PAZDÍREK XIV 36; Altmann/KAMMERMUSIK 229. Cf. GROVE VIII 310 (C. R. Halski).

89. MW X (1879) 366. Cf. GROVE II 767 (C. R. Halski).

90. E.g., cf. pp. 36, 112, 268, and 327 in PADEREWSKI (a fascinating *fin-de-siècle* view of musical Europe and America). Cf., also, MGG X 561–64 (J. Ekiert), with list of works and further bibliography.

91. Cf. PADEREWSKI 59–60, 63–64, 95–97, 108–21.

92. Cf. PADEREWSKI 83–88.

Brahms reportedly said, "Well, Paderewski, it is very effective, very fine, but it is not chamber music; it is a concert Sonata," which criticism Paderewski says he valued.[93] Another commentator found its finale alternately "turbulent" and "tender," but too little developed, and its preceding "Intermezzo" a "charming," "skillful," "felicitous" piece that is the "best" of its three movements.[94] Paderewski's other example is his Op. 21 in e♭, for P solo, composed and first played by him in 1903 at his Châlet de Riond-Bosson on Lake Geneva, performed publicly (by him?) that winter in Boston, and issued by the same (and then his only) publisher in 1906 (?).[95]

Paderewski himself regarded Op. 21 as "one of my most important and best works. But it is extremely difficult and for that reason will never be very popular." [96] As more of a tone poet than a virtuoso he exaggerated these difficulties, which now seem quite legitimate in such good piano scoring, and only moderate in relation to those of Brahms's, Liszt's, and Chopin's solo sonatas. However, Op. 21 is as large as these sonatas in scope, for its three movements occupy 49 pages of printed score. Daniel Gregory Mason found it and the Symphony in b, from the same period, to be Wagnerian in character.[97] Chopin-esque seems more appropriate to describe its prevailing style,[98] unless one thinks not so much of idiom, melody, or tonality as of continuous drive. And one cannot but feel that this drive, like that in Ashton's (ssb XIV) or other epigonic sonatas of the time, becomes essential partly to mask the late-Romantic composer's increasing inability or hesitation to commit himself to frank, clear-cut themes (ssb VI). Yet without such themes the drive sacrifices its main structural landmarks. In his opening movement Paderewski commits himself only to short ideas that scarcely interrupt the drive, for they merge both melodically and harmonically with the passagework, generally evading strong references to the tonic chord. Even in the more sectionalized, lyrical, moderate-paced middle movement in broad A-B-A design, "Andante ma non troppo," the one complete thematic period (mss. 34–49) is less a distinctive melody than a melodic and tonal climax stated and restated. In these respects, Paderewski's finale, "Allegro vivace," seems to be the most successful of the movements. Its design may be outlined

93. PADEREWSKI 91; cf., also, p. 97.
94. Cobbett II 205 (Adolph Mann).
95. Cf. Johns/REMINISCENCES 103.
96. PADEREWSKI 326.
97. Mason/MUSIC 168.
98. Such was the opinion, too, of H. Wetzel, reviewing its pub. in DM VII/4 (1907–8) 312, with special praise for the fluency, clarity, and structural control.

as toccata-fugue-toccata-coda. The toccata thrives on steady drive and melodic bits, and the fugue, based on a vigorous subject in two-part writing (Ex. 114), shows the devoted composer's noble command of the keyboard and his superior craftsmanship at their best.

The Warsaw conductor **Gregor Fitelberg** (1879–1953; father of Jerzy) won the Paderewski composition prize in Leipzig in 1896 for a Sonata for P & Vn, Op. 2, composed in 1894 but never published (in spite of the announcement on the jacket of Op. 12).[99] Fitelberg's Op. 12 is another Sonata for P & Vn, in F, composed in 1901, published in 1905, and described as an original, un-Germanic work in three concise movements, the middle of which is an "Intermezzo" interesting for its unusual metric organization.[100] About the same time, the

Ex. 114. From the finale of Ignace Jan Paderewski's Sonata in e♭ (after the original Bote & G. Bock ed., plate no. 15915).

German-trained organist **Mieczysław Surzyński** (1860–1924) left for his instrument a Sonata in three movements (F-M-fugue), Op. 34 in d, published in 1904 and reviewed as an original, bold, impassioned, and skillful work.[101] Three early sonatas—two for P solo, in c and f♯, and one for P & Vn, in a—were composed in 1902–3 by the important pupil of G. Fitelberg, **Ludomir Różycki** (1884–1953), before he went from Warsaw to Berlin in 1904 for further study.[102] In the latter center

99. Cf. MGG IV 281–82 (Z. Lissa); Altmann/KAMMERMUSIK 202.
100. DM VI/1 (1906–7) 171 (W. Altmann). GROVE III 148 (K. Geiringer) also lists a "Sonatina for 2 vns." (unpub.?).
101. NZM C (1904) 620; MW XXXVI (1905) 143 (G. Riemenschneider). Cf. MGG XII 1759–60 (H. Feicht).
102. Cf. GROVE VII 287–90 (C. R. Halski).

he also wrote a Sonata for Vc & P, Op. 10 in a (1906, pub. in 1912),[103] presumably already showing the influence of R. Strauss.

In the Lower Silesian center of Breslau (Wroclaw) as well as other sometime Polish centers under Prussian control throughout the Romantic Era (and until the end of World War II), several obscure sonata composers of German descent were active. Thus, in Breslau may be noted the organist and conductor **Adolph Hesse** (1809–63), a pupil of Hummel and Spohr among others, for a Sonata in Ab, Op. 42, for P-duet, and a *Phantasie-Sonate*, Op. 83 (1848?), for organ. The latter was reviewed as being well worked out though somewhat loose structurally and sentimental for church styles.[104] A Breslau hornist and writer, **Heinrich Gottwald** (1821–76) offered as his Op. 1 (1856?) another *Sonate fantastique,* this time for P solo, eliciting a reviewer's description of it as a three-movement, thematically interrelated cycle showing superior craftsmanship, harmonic interest, and imagination, as well as some hints of Schumann, Brahms, and Liszt.[105] After receiving Op. 1 from Gottwald, Bülow replied belatedly (Jan. 31, 1867), praising it warmly and copiously, though nonspecifically, for its "noble, pregnant, original content" and impressive structural mastery.[106] In spite of numerous performances of his chamber music, the Breslau composer **Paul Caro** (1859–1914) received only unfavorable reviews for his three published sonatas—Opp. 2 in F, for P & Vn (pub. 1883), 41 in f♯, for P solo (composed in 1886, pub. in 1911), and 42 in d, for P & Vc (pub. in 1911).[107] Two more organ sonatas, Opp. 33 in A (1902?) and 62 in D (1910), were composed by the Breslau conductor **Georg Riemenschneider** (1848–1913).[108] The first was reviewed as a highly musical, artful work in the vein of Schumann.[109]

Two other Polish centers formerly under Prussian control are represented by one obscure composer each here. In Danzig (Gdansk) the organist and pianist **Friedrich Wilhelm Markull** (1816–87) left three three-movement sonatas for P-duet, Opp. 75–77 in a, D, and Eb, that appeared in 1860–61 and brought favorable reactions for their (tradi-

103. Altmann/KAMMERMUSIK 263. The faulty listing in MGG XI 1033–34 (Z. Lissa) adds 1928 as the pub. year.
104. NZM XXX (1849) 184–86 (G. Siebeck). Cf. GROVE IV 263–64 (G. Grove); Mendel/LEXIKON V 223; PAZDÍREK VII 484.
105. NZM XLVIII (1858) 80 (R. Viole). Cf. Mendel/LEXIKON IV 310–11 and Suppl. 131.
106. BÜLOW BRIEFE IV 68–72.
107. NZM LXXXI/2 (1885) 407 (E. Klitzsch sees no hope in Op. 2); DM X/4 (1910–11) 246–47 (R. Cahn-Speyer calls Op. 41 ineffectual); DM X/4 189 (H. Schlemüller deplores the P part as inadequate). Cf. Riemann/LEXIKON I 280 and 12th ed. I 279.
108. Cf. Riemann/LEXIKON II 1517; Kremer/ORGAN 218.
109. MW XXXIV (1903) 379 (H. Schöne); DM III/2 (1903–04) 275 (K. Straube).

tional) artistic ideas and treatment, clear forms, and pedagogic values.[110] In Sorau (Żary) the cantor **Hermann Franke** (1834–1919) left two sets of sonatinas for P solo, Opp. 28 and 50, and a three-movement Sonata for P & Vc in g, Op. 69 (pub. in 1877), that was criticized negatively in 1882 not only for some lack of structural balance in the outer movements but for adhering to the traditional three-movement cycle and standard forms, by then "long since canonized" and "archaic." [111]

Composers in Hungary (Dohnányi)

Throughout music's Romantic Era the political struggle for nationalistic (Magyar) identity in Hungary and the alternate joining and clashing with Austria, even after Hungary's Revolution of 1848 and pseudo "independence" in 1867–68, are reflected in Hungary's music. There were both Germanic and nationalistic trends, sometimes clearly opposed, sometimes combined, although when they were combined, by a self-conscious process of Romantic "westernization," to produce several sonatas "in Hungarian style," the results were generally rather pale.[112] In the earlier 19th century, during the heyday of the Hungarian "Verbunkos" dance,[113] the interest in the sonata was even rarer than in Poland, with only a Liszt *in absentia*. (It was not until 1875 that Liszt figured in the founding of the Academy of Music in Budapest.) And again some of the composers whose names still stand out did not happen to write sonatas or, in their nationalistic zeal, actually resisted such Germanisms or other foreignisms—for example, the founder of Hungarian national opera, Franz Erkel, or the increasingly nationalistic Mihály Mosonyi, or the esteemed scholar, writer, and composer Gábor Mátray, or, later, the violinist Eduard Reményi and the Liszt follower Károl Aggházy. Furthermore, several composers who reportedly did write sonatas or works of a similar sort left no further traces of themselves or their sonatas that have turned up here, including Kálmán Simonffy (1832–81), Károly Huber (1828–85), and Imre Székely (1823–87).[114]

110. nzm LVI (1862) 163. Cf. grove V 582 (H. S. Oakeley).
111. mw XIII (1882) 555–57 (C. Kipke). Cf. Riemann/lexikon I 535.
112. Cf. the summaries of Romantic trends in Szabolcsi/ungarischen 75–87 and mgg XIII 1076–80 (Z. Gardonyi). Bartók/ungheria and the documentary pictorial study Keresztury/magyar have also proved helpful. Warm thanks for personal communications on the son. in Hungary are owing to Dr. Elod J. Juhász and the late Dr. József Gát, both at Budapest Academy of Music, and to Professor Béla Böszörmenyi-Nagy of Boston University.
113. Cf. mgg XIII 1076 and 1419–20 (B. Rajeczky). Szabolcsi/ungarischen 54–66.
114. Cf. Szabolcsi/ungarischen 69 and 82.

Although music by both Haydn and Beethoven became known as early as 1800 in Hungary,[115] no sonatas are listed among the works by two pioneers of instrumental chamber music in that country, Antal György Csérmak (1774–1822) and Márk Rózsavölgyi[116] In fact, the first 19th-century examples known here to have been published did not appear until 1857 and 1860. These are two sonatas for P & Vn, Opp. 7 in g and 10 in d, by a capable violinist of German descent, **August von Adelburg** (1830–73).[117] Op. 7 was called overly simplified and repetitive, with inadequate development of its ideas and exploitation of the instruments.[118] Previously, in 1851, an unpublished Sonata for P solo had been written during the Viennese training of the Hungarian composer and engineer **Julius Beliczay** (1835–93), who in 1887 also wrote a "Sonata quasi fantaisie" for P solo, Op. 10 (never pub.?).[119] Two (unpublished?) sonatas dating from 1861, one for P solo, Op. 4, and the other for P & Vn, in E♭, were left by an influential pro-German composer and early Wagnerite in Hungary, **Ödon von Mihalovich** (1842–1929).[120] More nationalistically inclined, the pianist **Henri Gobbi** (1842–1920) dedicated a "first" *Grande Sonate dans le style hongrois,* Op. 13 in E (pub. *ca.* 1872), to his teacher Liszt.[121] Another of Gobbi's teachers was the distinguished German composer in Budapest, Robert Volkmann, whom we have noted earlier, during his four-year stay in Vienna (ssb IX). Further investigation into this period might also include a *Sonate romantique* for P & Vn, Op. 22 in D (1871), by the celebrated violinist **Jenö Hubay (Eugene Huber;** 1858–1937), whose music recalls his teacher Vieuxtemps (ssb XII);[122] a Sonata in E, for P solo (pub. by 1885), by the pianist **Coloman Chovan** (1852–?), reviewed as difficult and clumsy to play, and not worth the effort, anyway;[123] and an unpublished Sonata for P & Vn by the eminent, international conductor **Arthur Nikisch** (1855–1922).[124]

A prolific, able, though not outstanding sonata composer was the pianist **Emánuel Moór** (1863–1931), chiefly remembered for his in-

115. mgg XIII 1076.
116. Cf. grove II 555–56 (J. S. Weissmann); mgg XI 1030–31 (Z. Gárdonyi).
117. Cf. grove I 57–58 (J. S. Weissmann).
118. nzm XLVI (1857) 273–74. But cf. Cobbett/chamber I 3 on his chamber style.
119. Cf. grove I 601–2 (J. S. Weissmann).
120. Cf. grove V 748–49 (J. S. Weissmann); mgg IX 284–86 (J. Ujfalussy).
121. Cf. Riemann/lexikon I 622; Szabolcsi/ungarischen 82; hofmeister 1868–73, 154.
122. Cf. mgg VI 804–6 (H. Haase); Cobbett/chamber I 575 (W. W. Cobbett); Szabolcsi/ungarischen 85.
123. mw XVI (1885) 236. Cf. pazdírek III 308; Riemann/lexikon I 317, with mention of a Son. for P-duet, Op. 22.
124. Cf. baker 1162–63; mgg IX 1531–33 (M. Schuler).

vention of the rather bulky "Duplex Coupler" piano.[125] Some 25 sonatas were composed by Moór, including 12 for P & Vn, 7 for Vc & P, 3 for P solo, 2 for harp solo, and one for 4 harps, but apparently none was created especially for the 2-manual piano. Some 12 to 14 of these were published, between 1889 and about 1913, including 7 for P & Vn, 4 for Vc & P, possibly 2 for P, and possibly the one for 4 harps.[126] A sampling of the published sonatas reveals the usual standardized cycles of three and four movements, although the forms of these movements, especially in the later sonatas, prove to be either less usual, freer applications of standardized forms (as in the 3 mvts., F-S-F, of Op. 76 in a/A, for Vc & P; pub. in 1909) or so open, cursive, and free in sectional organization and tempo as not to relate readily to any standardized forms (e.g., the 4 mvts., M-F-S-VF, of Op. 60 in c♯, for P solo; pub. in 1906). Moór's themes, which tend to unfold at some length by winding around their starting notes, are not particularly compelling or original. Moreover, their reiterations and development seem somewhat perfunctory. There is more interest in the warm but traditional harmony, with its occasionally chromatic, enharmonic, and diagonal relationships (Ex. 115), and in the sonorous wide-ranging textures, although these textures, consistent with a degree of bombast in this music, soon confront the pianist with too much writing in octaves, plain or filled.

The one-armed pianist **Géza Zichy** (1849–1924), a pupil of Liszt and Volkmann, wrote a piano Sonata in G, in three movements (F-M-VF), for left hand alone, that was published by D. Rahter of Leipzig in 1887.[127] It proves to be a melodious, unoriginal work in conventional, light opera style, mildly interesting only as a keyboard scoring problem.[128] The pianist **Kornél Ábrányi** ("the Elder"; 1822–1903) was a pupil variously of Chopin, Kalkbrenner, and Mosonyi, and a devoted nationalist, who founded what was reportedly the first Hungarian music periodical in 1860, who helped to establish the Academy of Music in Budapest in 1875, and who sought to amalgamate Western European and Hungarian styles.[129] Presumed products of the amalgamation (but not seen here) are his *Sonate im ungarischen Style,* Op. 84, and *Ungarische Millenium-Sonate,* Op. 103, both for P solo and published in Budapest (*ca.* 1891 and 1896).[130] **Árpád Szendy** (1863–1922),

125. Cf. MGG IX 542–44 (P. P. Hoffer); ML III (1922) 29–48 (D. Tovey).
126. Cf. GROVE V 863–64 (J. S. Weissmann); Altmann/KAMMERMUSIK 216 and 261; PAZDÍREK X 779; Cobbett/CHAMBER II 147–48 (Adolph Mann).
127. Cf. GROVE IX 414–15 (J. S. Weissmann); HOFMEISTER 1887, 373.
128. In MW XXI (1890) 505 it is called folklike, slick, and skillful in its scoring.
129. Cf. GROVE I 15–17 (J. S. Weissmann); Szabolcsi/UNGARISCHEN 82.
130. Cf. HOFMEISTER X (1886–91) 2 and XI (1892–97) 1 (but neither is in the annual vols.).

Ex. 115. From the second theme of the first movement in Emanuel Moór's Sonata in c♯, Op. 60 (after the C. F. W. Siegel ed., plate no. 14482).

a pupil of Liszt, a fine pianist and teacher, and a respected editor of musical masterpieces, left two sonatas for P solo—one in b, composed about 1896 as his Op. 1 but apparently not published, and one in D, composed about 1904 and published by 1908.[131]

A more successful composer at one time, the concert pianist and conductor **Jakab Gyula Major** (1858–1925) left two sonatinas and two sonatas for Vn & P and five sonatinas and two sonatas for P solo, all composed and published between about 1882 and 1909.[132] The first of Major's two solo sonatas, Op. 35 in A (1896), is another "Hungarian Sonata." This and his later solo sonata, Op. 68 in e/E (1909; in 3 mvts., F-M-F), evince good training under Volkmann and Erkel but still cling to the Mendelssohn idiom except for more octave writing, and seem sterile in their trite ideas, conventional harmony, and excessive motivic reiterations. A distinguished writer and teacher at both the Fodor Conservatory and the Academy in Budapest, **Albert Síklos**

131. HOFMEISTER 1904–8, 784 (not in the annual vols.). Cf. GROVE VIII 268–69 (J. S. Weissmann).

132. Cf. GROVE V 524–26 (J. S. Weissmann); MGG VIII 1536–38 (J. Ujfalussy); Altmann/KAMMERMUSIK 214 and 260 (Op. 57 in g alternatively for Vc & P).

(1878–1942) remained a traditionalist, too, in his compositions, in spite of a declared interest in some newer Hungarian idiom that would be neither German nor French in origin, and in spite of such incipient anti-Romantics within his sphere as the young Bartók and Kodály.[133] Three of Síklos's four sonatas have remained unpublished, including one each for P solo (1898; in B♭), Vn & P (1902; in A♭), and Vc & P (before 1910; in f). The fourth, for Hn & P, was composed and published in Budapest in 1920.[134]

Among further sonatas for P & Vn, one by a winner of the "Liszt prize" and friend of Liszt in the early 1880's, **János Végh** (1845–1918), was published in Budapest about 1900.[135] Another, Op. 26 in D, by the blind, pro-Hungarian pianist and teacher **Attila Horváth** (1862–1920), was published in 1902.[136] Still another, a conservative, solid, Brahmsian work in e (3 mvts., F-Sc-F), was published in 1902, being the work of **Hans Koessler** (1853–1926). Koessler was the German-born organist who, after study with Rheinberger in Munich and some choir conducting in Köln, moved to Budapest, eventually succeeding Volkmann and becoming one of the teachers of Dohnányi, Bartok, and Kodály.[137]

Probably the best known—or, rather, least forgotten—of all these sonatas from Hungary are the two full-blooded, unabashedly Romantic examples by the important, late-Romantic composer, pianist, conductor, and teacher **Ernst (Ernö) von Dohnányi** (1877–1960).[138] Dohnányi had already done much before he wrote his first duo sonata. He had written early "pianoforte sonatas" and other boyhood works (by the age of 16),[139] won Brahms's support (in 1896?) for his piano

133. Cf. GROVE VIII 788–90 (J. S. Weissmann); MGG XII 690–91 (J. Ujfalussy).

134. The only reference to its pub. known here is that in MGG XII 690.

135. Cf. Riemann/LEXIKON II 1915; Szabolcsi/UNGARISCHEN 85; Altmann/KAMMER-MUSIK 230; Keresztury/MAGYAR 238 (facs. of printed cover).

136. Cf. Riemann/LEXIKON I 784; Szabolcsi/UNGARISCHEN 82; Altmann/KAMMER-MUSIK 209.

137. Cf. GROVE IV 813 (J. S. Weissmann), with a listing, also, of a (MS?) Son. for Vc & P, by Koessler; MGG VII 1390–92 (R. Sietz); Cobbett/CHAMBER II 68 (W. Altmann); MW XXXIV (1903) 40–41 (E. Segnitz praising the force, intensity, and beauty of Son. in e).

138. Cf. GROVE II 722–23 (J. A. Fuller-Maitland & E. Blom); MGG III 624–27 (E. Haraszti). A full study of the man and his music has yet to appear. Rueth/DOHNÁNYI is a documentary M.A. thesis on his last 11 years (1949–60, at Florida State University in Tallahassee), introduced by a helpful chapter (pp. 11–24) on his life up to then; supplemented by an abbreviated cat. of works (pp. 205–12), a bibliography (almost entirely of recent articles in English), and other aids; and fortified (cf. pp. 4–7) by access to an as yet unpub. biography up to 1953 that has been prepared by his widow Ilona (Helen). Warm thanks are owing to Mr. James F. Jones, former Music Cataloger and Music Librarian at Florida State University, for further information on the Dohnányi materials.

139. GROVE II 722.

Quintet in c, Op. 1 (1895), even before graduating from the Budapest Academy (in 1897), done a little postgraduate piano study with the Brahms disciple Eugen d'Albert (in 1897; ssʙ XI), embarked on a brilliant wide-ranging concert career (though not reaching the United States until late 1900),[140] and composed several more large-scale works. His first duo is Op. 8 in bb/Bb, for Vc & P, composed in 1899, originally played by the composer and Ludwig Lebell (its dedicatee) in London that same year,[141] and first published by B. Schott in Mainz in 1903. The other duo is Op. 21 in c♯, for P & Vn, composed in 1912, originally played by the composer and Karl Klingler in Berlin that same year,[142] and first published a year later by Simrock in Bonn.

Both of Dohnányi's sonatas are decidedly Brahmsian in flavor and method. Even Op. 21 still preceded by 13–14 years his more independent and most characteristic, successful works, especially the "Variations on a Nursery Song" and the *Ruralia hungarica* in several settings. Between the two sonatas, Op. 8 is preferred here as the more spontaneous, thematically significant work.[143] It is a kind of exaggeration of Brahms's duo sonatas, not in length but in scope of emotions and in range of styles, whether richness and mellowness of sonority, surprise and color of harmony, or sweep and breadth of melody (Ex. 116). In these last respects, Op. 8 brings to mind Dohnányi's *Four Rhapsodies* for P solo, Op. 11, which first appeared two years later (1905). It treats the four-movement cycle freshly, with a first movement in a surging "sonata form" that recapitulates in the tonic major; a deft, rhythmically compelling "Scherzo" and "Trio" in the minor submediant key (g); a cursive, lyrical, harmonically opulent "Adagio non troppo" in the raised subdominant key (E), leading directly, like an introduction, into the finale; and the finale itself, which is a "Tema con Variazioni" that returns in its several variations to main ideas from the previous movements (as had been done in Brahms's Quartet in the same key, Op. 67/iv). Op. 21 is also a warm, impassioned work, even more Brahmsian albeit rather more controlled, calculated, and concentrated, in its themes as well as its textures and forms. It is constructed in three thematically interrelated movements, with a first

140. Rueth/DOHNÁNYI 13–14, contrary to "1898–99" in previous reports.
141. Cf. Rueth/DOHNÁNYI 205, 242 (recording).
142. Cf. Rueth/DOHNÁNYI 205, 214, and 220 (2 late U.S. performances), 242 (recording).
143. The 2 sons. are described enthusiastically in D. F. Tovey's article in Cobbett/CHAMBER I 327–31. Op. 8 is reviewed by H. Schlemüller in DM III/3 (1903–4) 373 as "one of the most important sonatas since Brahms," and Op. 21 by W. Altmann in DM XII/4 (1912–13) 175–76 as a convincing, unlabored example of how to create a whole work out of a single idea.

Ex. 116. From the second theme in the first movement of
Ernst von Dohnányi's Sonata in b♭/B♭, Op. 8 (after the original
B. Schott ed.).

movement in a tight "sonata form" that rarely loses sight of its opening
theme; a second movement, in the subdominant key, that alternates a
songful section in duple meter with a scherzando section in triple
meter, somewhat in the manner of Brahms's Op. 100/ii; and a finale,
"Vivace assai," in which a free rondo culminates in a return to the
sonata's opening and an ending of quiet, peaceful resignation.

Other sonatas for P & Vn contemporary with Dohnányi's include
Op. 3 in D (1906), reportedly an ingratiating, traditional work in three
movements, by a violin student of Hubay in Budapest, **Petar Stojanović**
(1877–1957);[144] Op. 10 in a (1908), welcomed as a colorful, brilliant,
large-scale work, and No. 2 in f♯ (1930; unpub.?), as well as a "Sonata
appassionata," Op. 13 for P solo (unpub.?), by the pianist and teacher
Ákos Buttkay (1871–1935);[145] a "Concert Sonata in Hungarian Style"
(composed in 1906 and pub. in 1909), by the cosmopolitan pianist
Theodor Szántó (1877–1934), who had studied with R. Fuchs, H. Koessler, and Busoni, among others;[146] and Opp. 9 in D (1912) and 11 in f♯

144. DM VI/4 (1906–7) 372 (W. Altmann). Cf. MGG XII 1391–92 (S. Djurić-Klajn).
145. DM VIII/2 (1908–9) 44 (W. Altmann). Cf. GROVE I 1051–52 (J. S. Weissmann).
146. Cf. MGG XIII 20–21 (F. Bónis); Altmann/KAMMERMUSIK 229.

(1918, not 1919) by the versatile pianist, teacher, and multi-prize-winning composer **Leo Weiner** (1885–1960).[147] Weiner's sonatas are both adroit, lyrical, emotionally charged works in large, thematically interrelated cycles (Op. 21/iv begins with kaleidoscopic references to the earlier mvts., as in the finale of Beethoven's Ninth Symphony). The structural methods of Brahms and, especially, the idiom of Franck are still in evidence.

Note may also be taken here of a "founder of the Rumanian instrumental school," **George Stephănescu** (1843–1925) in Bucharest, who composed two conventional (unpub.?) sonatas in 1863, one for Vc & P and one for P solo.[148]

147. Cf. MGG XIV 402–7 (F. Bónis); Szabolcsi/UNGARISCHEN 86.
148. MGG XII 1263–64 (V. Tomescu).

Chapter XVIII

Composers in Russia

From the Classic-Romantic Overlap to about 1850 (Aliabiev)

Along with the introductory remarks in the preceding chapter, a few, more specific ones are needed here. As in Poland and Hungary there was little concern with the sonata in Russia during the first half of the 19th century.[1] The relatively few examples that did originate there during the overlap of the Classic and Romantic eras were largely the contributions of visitors-in-residence—for example, J. W. Hässler (SCE 579–81),[2] Cimarosa (SCE 302–4), Sarti (SCE 229–31), Viotti (SCE 675–78), Field (SSB XIV), and a Pole who had studied with Albrechtsberger in Vienna, G. Tepper von Ferguson.[3] Of contributions by their native Russian contemporaries, mention can be made here only of some obscure sonatas, explored but little, if at all, including several for strings by I. E. Khandochkine (SCE 779);[4] five for keyboard solo (and three for keyboard + Vn, now lost) among the MSS left in the 1780's by Galuppi's pupil, the church and opera composer **Dmitri Stepanovitch**

1. Surveys that have provided helpful background material here are Asaf'ev/RUSSIAN 134–268 (especially 209–55); MGG XI 1156–68 (K. Laux); Cobbett/CHAMBER II 312–19 (N. Findeisen, L. Sabaneiev, & W. W. Cobbett); Seaman/RUSSIAN 114–27; and the studies of L. N. Raaben and of A. D. Alekseev (Alekseev/FORTEPIANNAIA) as partly trans., paraphrased, or summarized in Seaman/AMATEUR, Seaman/CHAMBER, and Seaman/PIANO. Warm thanks are owing to Miss Erna F. Novikova of the State Gnesin Musical Pedagogical Institute in Moscow for valued scores and information by correspondence, and for her trans. and supplementing of a valued, detailed critique of this chap. (Alekseev & Novikova) prepared by Professor A. D. Alekseev, author of Alekseev/FORTEPIANNAIA and of a new "History of Pianoforte Art" (Moscow, 1967; in Russian), among other studies.

2. Seaman/CHAMBER 329 mentions 3 Sons. by Hässler for P & Vn & Vc, pub. in 1799.

3. His *Grande Sonate* in c, Op. 8 (St. Petersburg, 1802), for P solo—a 4-mvt. work (F-M-Mi-Ro) with hints of Beethoven's Op. 13—is reprinted in Smart/EIGHTEENTH-m 106, with preface on p. 2.

4. Cf. Asaf'ev/RUSSIAN 140, 141, 306 (under "Handoshkin"); Seaman/RUSSIAN 82–83.

Bortniansky (1751–1825);[5] a Piano Sonata in d (F-S-M; [pub.?] 1794) with variations in the finale on a Russian folk theme, by the violinist **Lev Stepanovich Gurilëv** (1770–1844);[6] some sonatas for P & Vn, including one published in 1795 by Gerstenberg in St. Petersburg, by the esteemed violinist **(August) Ferdinand Titz (Tietz;** 1742–1810);[7] and a Sonata for Vc & P (1802) as well as some folklike sonatas for P solo, including a lost "Grand Sonata on Russian Themes" published in 1806, by **Ivan Prach (Johann Gottfried Pratsch;** ?–1818).[8]

Although the sonata happens not to have taken any firm hold in early 19th-century Russia, society under the successive czarist regimes, especially in St. Petersburg (now Leningrad) was becoming increasingly favorable to the cultivation of such music. Even the institution of serfdom, which bound not a few musicians and continued right through the retreat of Napoleon in 1812–13, the "Decembrist Uprising" of 1825, and the Crimean War in 1854–56, seems not to have blocked musical progress.[9] From the turn of the century at least the vocal music of Haydn, Mozart, and Beethoven, as well as nearly all their important contemporaries, began to be played.[10] Orchestral and chamber groups were formed, both professional and amateur, and concert series, both private and public, were instituted by new societies and schools.[11] At the same time, the number, proportion, and caliber of native composers increased. Their efforts as regards instrumental music were devoted at first to transcriptions of, and variations on, the popular folk, national, and opera songs and dances, then to suites, symphonies, quartets, and the infrequent sonatas.[12] As in other outlying regions of the sonata the German influence was strong, whether it was accepted or resisted in favor of nationalistic elements.

Mikhail Ivanovitch Glinka (1804–57) was one who did turn to the sonata in this period, although what he left is only the MS of an

5. Cf. Seaman/CHAMBER 330, with reference to N. F. Findeisen's study of Bortniansky; Seaman/PIANO 179, with ex. from a Son. in F purportedly showing Ukrainian folk influences; Alekseev/FORTEPIANNAIA 24–26, with further exx.; Asaf'ev/RUSSIAN 140 (naming clavichord as the intended instrument), 141; also, GROVE I 827 (A. Loewenberg).
6. Cf. Seaman/PIANO 180–82, including reference to a mod. ed.; Alekseev/FORTE-PIANNAIA 33–34, with ex. from first mvt.; VODARSKY-SHIRAEFF 52; Alekseev & Novikova.
7. Cf. Seaman/CHAMBER 328–29; MGG XIII 411 (A. Weinmann).
8. Cf. Seaman/PIANO 179 fn.; Alekseev/FORTEPIANNAIA 26, with ex. from slow mvt. of Son. in C. (pub. in 1887); MGG X 1601–2 (G. Waldmann); Alekseev & Novikova.
9. Cf. Asaf'ev/RUSSIAN 137–38.
10. Cf. Asaf'ev/RUSSIAN 136–37.
11. Cf. Seaman/AMATEUR and Seaman/CHAMBER.
12. Cf. Asaf'ev/RUSSIAN 137–40.

"Allegro" and an incomplete "Larghetto ma non troppo" of a projected Sonata in d, for P & Va.[13] In his own words,

> It was about this time [1825] that I wrote the first allegro of a D minor sonata for piano and viola; this composition was more tightly constructed than the others, and I performed it with Böhm and [with] Liglya, in the latter instance playing the viola myself. I wrote the adagio later [1828], but did not get around to the rondo (I recently used its Russian-style motif in a children's polka). . . . I stayed with Melgunov [in Moscow in 1828] only until May 9 (his name day), but in those few days I wrote the adagio (B [Bb] Major) for the D minor *Sonata* and I recall that I had some fairly clever counterpoint in this number.[14]

Glinka's Sonata is worth noting mainly because it was composed not only by the future leader of Russian national opera but by the man with whom truly Russian music is said to begin. However, its music is not yet more than that of a talented student still writing in a post-Mozartean idiom complete with feminine endings, chromatic melody, and late-Classic accompaniments. Even so, its appropriate scoring, which could be expected from a good pianist who could also play the violin, its good counterpoint, as claimed by Glinka himself, and some freshness in its themes and figures all suggest more promise for "absolute" chamber music, still five to eight years before his "serious" training with S. W. Dehn in Berlin (1833–34), than most writers have seen in his early instrumental works.[15]

Of more musical substance is the Sonata in e, for P & Vn, left in MS (*ca.* 1827?), among other pioneer chamber works of significance, by the talented Moscow composer **Alexander Alexandrovitch Aliabiev** (1787–1851).[16] In three movements, it proves to be another post-Mozartean work, more broadly conceived but on a par otherwise with, say, Kuhlau's flute sonatas (SSB XV) in general idiom and style, including quality and types of themes, textural, especially contrapuntal, interest, equal responsibility of the two parts, conservative harmony, and pat

---

13. Mod. eds. appeared in 1932 (Altman/KAMMERMUSIK 247) and 1958 (Glinka/ WORKS-m IV 3; with preface, in Russian). Cf. MGG V 261–67 (G. Abraham); Seaman/ RUSSIAN 191–92.

14. Glinka/MEMOIRS 32, 41–42.

15. E.g., cf. Cobbett/CHAMBER I 472–73 (L. Sabaneiev).

16. Mod. ed.: State Music Pub. in Moscow, 1951. It is discussed, with an ex. from the opening of each mvt., in Seaman/CHAMBER 331 and 335–36. Cf. BAKER 23 and Suppl. 3. I am indebted to Miss Carol Greene at the University of Indiana for valued help with Aliabiev, including copies of pertinent sections from L. N. Raaben's book on Russian instrumental ensemble music (Moscow, 1961; pp. 94–96 as trans. by M. H. Brown) and from her own forthcoming study of Aliabiev's chamber music, as well as a copy of Aliabiev's Son. in Ab, for P solo. Dobrokhotov/ ALIABIEV is a new book (in Russian) on the man and his music, with many exx. (Moscow, 1966).

skill. The first movement, "Allegro con brio," is a well-balanced "sonata form." The second movement, "Adagio cantabile," is an A-B-A design based on expressive, nicely drawn lines. And the finale is a vivacious rondo design, marked "Allegretto scherzando." Aliabiev also left in MS a one-movement Sonata in A♭, for P solo.[17] This is a different sort of work, in "sonata form" but without the associated dynamism or tensions. The themes are all lyrical, without contrast, development, or integration in the passagework. But the themes are attractive, and the scoring for piano is neat and clear. The style gives support to the possibility that Aliabiev studied with Field while the latter was in Moscow.[18]

Among others who produced sonatas before 1850, the German contrabassist and pianist **Ludwig (Louis) Schuberth** (1806–50) was in Riga and Königsberg (now Kaliningrad) while his four or more published sonatas appeared (*ca.* 1835–45) and before he moved to St. Petersburg.[19] A pupil of Weber and a brief obstacle to Wagner's career,[20] Schuberth fared poorly in two reviews that Schumann wrote in 1837.[21] One review heaped recondite sarcasm and scorn on *Souvenir à Beethoven: Grande Fantaisie en forme d'une sonate,* Op. 30, for P solo, finding only desecration of the "honored" master. The other review deplored his haste and superficial talent in *Sonate* ("L'Espérance"), Op. 25 in C, for P solo. Yet Wagner did speak of Schuberth as "a very capable musician." [22] Schuberth's other published sonatas include Op. 36 in B♭, for P-duet, and some sonatinas for P & Vn, Op. 37.[23]

The pianist **Iosif Iosifovitch Genishta** (1795–1853), a pupil of both Hässler and Field and an early performer of Beethoven, left at least four sonatas, published between about 1837 and 1847—two each for P solo and for P & Vc.[24] Schumann reviewed one of each with pleasure, in 1837 and 1841,[25] finding Op. 7 in A ("Grand Sonate" for P & Vc-or-Vn) to be a transparent, lyrical "musical still life" appropriate

17. Mod. ed.: p. 85 in an anth. of Russian piano music ed. by A. Natanson & A. A. Nikolayev (Moscow, 1956).
18. Perhaps around 1811, according to information in B. Dobrokhotov's book on Aliabiev as supplied by Miss Greene. Aliabiev's piano Quintet in E♭, recorded on Westminster XWN 18679, is another post-Mozartean work.
19. Cf. MGG XII 186–88 (K. Stephenson); GROVE VII 593 (W. B. Squire).
20. Cf. Newman/WAGNER I 198, 201, 212–13.
21. Schumann/SCHRIFTEN I 302–3, 307. Cf. HOFMEISTER 1834–38, p. 130.
22. MGG XII 187.
23. Cf. Altmann/KAMMERMUSIK 226; HOFMEISTER 1844–51, p. 78.
24. Cf. Alekseev/FORTEPIANNAIA 74–76, with 2 exx. from Op. 9 in f; Seaman/PIANO 192, with ex.; HOFMEISTER 1834–38, p. 129, and 1844–51, pp. 115 and 49; PAZDÍREK VI 156.
25. Schumann/SCHRIFTEN I 275 and 277, II 11–12. Nikolaiev/TCHAIKOVSKY 195 emphasizes the developed pianism, lyricism, and strong finales in Genishta's sons.

for cello rather than violin, and Op. 9 in f/F (P solo) to be similarly skillful and transparent, with the first two of the three movements (F-S-VF) being "very well rounded" and the finale the best of all, suggesting the influence of Beethoven's Op. 57 (iii?). Genishta's other two sonatas are Opp. 12 in C for P solo and 13 in D for P & Vc. Uninvestigated are at least three sonatas for P solo, published between about 1844 and 1852, by the conductor and valued friend of Wagner, **Louis Alexander Balthasar Schindelmeisser** (1811–64), who moved about so much he can only be put where he was born, Königsberg.[26] Schindelmeisser's sonatas are Opp. 8 in F, entitled "Sonate héroique," 23 in g, and 40 (or 31? or both?) in D.

From about 1850 to 1910 (A. Rubinstein, Tchaikovsky, Rachmaninoff, Medtner, Liapunov)

Although a number of important musicians continued to show little or no interest in composing sonatas during the later Romantic Era in Russia—including Dargomyzhsky, Borodin, Rimsky-Korsakov, Tanayev, Arensky, and Glière—the cultivation of the sonata advanced greatly during that time. The conservatories founded in St. Petersburg by Anton Rubinstein in 1862 and in Moscow by his brother Nicholas in 1866 proved to be fruitful breeding grounds. One of the pivotal Romantics in musical Russia, one of the greatest pianists of the later 19th century, and, more specifically here, one of the most notable Romantic performers of piano sonatas (especially Beethoven's), was **Anton Grigorievitch Rubinstein** (1829–94). Rubinstein was also a major force in music education, a promoter of past music, an active conductor, and a prolific, wide-ranging, once successful composer.[27] Among nearly 150 publications, chiefly in Germany, there are 11 sonatas by Rubinstein. These originally appeared between 1855 and 1878, none with special titles. For P solo there are Opp. 12 in e (1855), 20 in c (1855), 41 in F (1857), and 100 in a (1878). For Vn & P there are Opp. 13 in G (1856), 19 in a (1855), and 98 in b (1878). For Vc & P there are Opp. 18 in D (1855) and 39 in G (1857). For Va & P there is Op. 49 in f (1857), and for P-duet Op. 89 in D (1871).[28]

26. Cf. MGG XI 1726–28 (K. Rönnau); HOFMEISTER 1844–51, p. 153 and 1852–59, p. 207; PAZDÍREK XII 218.

27. Cf. GROVE VII 295–97 (author unknown according to p. 298 fn., but given as F. Corder in Maclean/RUBINSTEIN 131) and Suppl. 383, with undated list of works; MGG XI 1043–47 (G. Waldmann), with further bibl.; Rubinstein/ERINNERUNGEN, especially pp. 15–17, 21–22, 25, 27, 31, 33–34, 50–51, 66–68, 105–120 (including the itemized programs of his celebrated "seven historical concerts"); Maclean/RUBINSTEIN, with bibliographic information (pp. 143 and 146–47).

28. The foregoing dates derive from Altmann/KAMMERMUSIK and the cumulative

For a man who contributed so much to music education in Russia,[29] Rubinstein showed little interest in furthering Russian nationalism, least of all in his entirely unprogrammatic sonatas. In fact, after coming under Chopin's and Liszt's influence in Paris, after finishing his training under Dehn and others in Berlin, after speaking and writing in German much of the time, and after travelling and/or living in several other European centers and in the United States, he made clear that he saw himself as a cosmopolitan.[30] Furthermore, he recognized and defended himself as a conservative in musical styles:[31]

It is remarkable how criticism operates more strictly and harshly in music than in the other arts—for example, when Raphael leans upon Perugino, Leonardo, or Fra Bartolommeo before he arrives at his own style, or a present-day painter on Meissonier or Lenbach, then it [the derivation] is merely noted—but the minute a musician leans in his style upon Schumann, Chopin, Mendelssohn, Wagner, [or] Liszt, he is harshly reproached for it [the derivation] and it is cited as [evidence for] a lack of originality—which [inequity] leads the [musical] young to the quest for originality [for its own sake], and how often to the unbeautiful!

Together, Rubinstein's cosmopolitanism and conservatism help to explain the neutralism or what might be called excessive universalism of his style. And that style probably explains the extinction of his sonatas more than a half-century ago, beyond reasonable hope of revival. Yet the sonatas, including some duos regarded as his best chamber music,[32] have numerous pages of real musical distinction and interest (as might be expected from the composer of three works still heard on occasion, piano Concerto 4 in d, "Melody in F," and *Kammenoi Ostrow*). In any case, these sonatas must have appealed to public tastes, for during his later years at least certain of the duos were performed almost as often and widely as Brahms's, Rheinberger's, Raff's, or Grieg's most successful sonatas.[33]

---

and annual vols. of HOFMEISTER. The helpful lists of A. Rubinstein's works compiled by O. E. Albrecht in Bowen/RUBINSTEIN 375–90 are not dated.

29. Cf. Maclean/RUBINSTEIN 141–42.

30. Rubinstein/GEDANKENKORB 86. Preferring the term internationalist, Alekseev & Novikova remark that Rubinstein did exhibit national and folk interest in some (other) of his compositions.

31. Trans. from Rubinstein/GEDANKENKORB 69.

32. Cf. Cobbett/CHAMBER II 309–11 (L. Sabaneiev & W. W. Cobbett); Nikolaiev/TCHAIKOVSKY 196 (calling Rubinstein's sons. Russia's best mid-19th-c. instrumental music). The 3 Vn sons. are described, with 11 exx., in Shand/VIOLIN 193–99.

33. Thus, for duo performances during the 15 years 1871–86 cf., on Op. 13: MT XV (1871) 319 (or Op. 19? London), NZM LXXII/2 (1876) 485 (Hildesheim and Leipzig) and LXXIII/1 (1877) 140 (Leipzig) and 193 (Prague), MT XVIII (1878) 369 (London) and XX (1879) 329 (Birmingham) and XXIV (1883) 324 (London); on Op. 18: MT XV (1871) 109 (London), NZM LXXII/1 (1876) 203 (Kiev) and LXXII/

Rubinstein's sonatas were not innovational in their day, in the sense of new language or form. Nothing more innovative happens than the quotation of themes from the first two of the three violin sonatas at the start of the last. Otherwise, they seldom depart from the three- and four-movement cycles and their respective designs as standardized by then. Yet within their own range they do reveal fairly steady advances from the more imitative and formalistic Op. 12 to the more independent and free Op. 100. In an extended, increasingly laudatory article of 1858 on all eight sonatas published by then, one "C. Petersen" emphasized this creative evolution.[34] He viewed Op. 12 as being Beethovian and somewhat scholastic, Op. 13 as "almost slavishly" Mendelssohnian, both Opp. 18 and 19 as still related to but freer of the same models and distinctive in scoring, both Opp. 20 and 49 as Schumannesque in their more imaginative, poetic ideas and treatment, and Op. 39 as a sequel to Op. 18 except for its added, spirited "Scherzo." Quoting twenty-six examples in all, Petersen singled out Op. 41 as a masterwork and its first movement, "Allegro risoluto con fuoco," as a "consummation" of "sonata form" since Beethoven, notable for its thematic architecture, transformations, and recombinations. He characterized the second movement, an "Allegretto con moto" in A-B-A design, as gloomy and more repressed; the third movement, a similarly tripartite "Andante," as filled with "grief, lamentation, and longing"; and the finale, an "Allegro vivace" in "sonata form" beginning in the tonic minor mode, as freely but firmly organized and triumphant in its ending.

Of course, from our later vantage point, later by more than a century, we can look not only for derivations but for anticipations—anticipations of works not yet born when Petersen wrote on Rubinstein's sonatas. Thus, in key, meter, texture, parts of the tonal schemes, and certain figures or ideas, the first movements of Rubinstein's Opp. 12 and 13 anticipate those of Grieg's Op. 7 and Brahms's Op. 78,

---

2 (1876) 475 (Leipzig) and LXXIII/1 (1877) 138 (Bremen), MT XVII (1877) 697 (London) and XX (1878–79) 23, 81, and 646 (all London) and XXII (1880–81) 40 (Birmingham) and 652 (London) and XXIII (1882) 328 (Birmingham) and XXIV (1883) 193 (London) and XXV (1884) 147 and 338 (both London); on Op. 19: NZM LXXII/1 (1876) 57–58 (Strasbourg) and 136 (Dresden) and LXXII/2 454 (Mainz) and LXXIII/1 (1877) 53 (Vienna) and 116 (Graz), SMZ XVII (1877) 39 (Geneva), MT XXI (1880) 84 (London); on Op. 39: NZM LXXII/1 (1876) 224 (Moscow) and LXXIII/1 (1877) 192 (Copenhagen), MT XXI (1880) 239 (London) and XXIV (1883) 346 (or Op. 13? Salisbury); Op. 49: MT XXI (1880) 303 (Baden-Baden); plus numerous book references, such as that in Bowen/RUBINSTEIN 221 on the playing of Op. 89 in St. Petersburg in 1870 by the 2 brothers, Anton and Nicholas, or Hanslick/WIEN II 135 (Op. 18 in 1857) and 187 (Op. 49 in 1859; negative reaction); plus numerous references in which the exact son. is not specified.
34. NZM XLIX (1858) 137–38, 143–44, 151–54, 163–66.

Ex. 117. From the opening of Anton Grigorievitch Rubinstein's Sonata in f, Op. 49 (after an ed. of 1960 by State Music
Publishers in Moscow).

respectively (pub. 10 and 24 years later). To be sure, Rubinstein's
early works lack the force and directness of Grieg's early work or
Brahms's more mature work, especially as regards melody. But some of
that force and directness did develop in the course of the style evolution just described, especially in the two works with middle opus
numbers written concurrently in 1855,[35] one being the Op. 41 for P
solo that was rightly singled out by Petersen and the other being Op.
49, Rubinstein's one contribution to viola literature (Ex. 117).

Unfortunately, although Rubinstein's later works continued to
evolve stylistically, they show a decline in their quality of workmanship, especially in details of texture and keyboard scoring, to the point
where most present-day performers would be likely to reject them on
that account alone. To be sure, in his previous sonatas Rubinstein had
never excelled in harmony or polyphony, and in his previous scoring
for keyboard he can merely be said at best to have scored idiomatically,
and hardly with the resourcefulness to be expected from so great a
pianist. But now, at worst and by the time of his last sonata, Op. 100

35. Cf. Rubinstein's letter of June 25, 1855, to Liszt, as trans. in the preface to
the Moscow reprint of Op. 49 in 1960. Barenboim/RUBINSTEIN 129 attributes to
Rubinstein a combination of the lyric (under Glinka's influence) and the dramatic
heroic.

for P solo, he was writing in a routine, pasty fashion that could only discourage performers. In the course of those later works critical opinion began to waver and sometimes turn against him correspondingly.[36]

Like Glinka before him, the important programmatist and contributor to Russian national opera, **Modest Petrovitch Mussorgsky** (1839–81), also tried his hand at the sonata only in his student days and without any example being published in his lifetime.[37] Exposed especially to Beethoven and Schumann and taught from his eighteenth year by the two-year-older Balakirev,[38] this second youngest of the "mighty five" actually wrote at least four sonatas in the four years from 1858 to 1862, only one of which has survived. All four were for piano and all but one (in f♯) figure among the thirty-five piano works credited to Mussorgsky in his collected works.[39] Three of them, in E♭ (1858), f♯ (1858), and D (1862), all for P solo, were lost or destroyed.[40] The remaining example is an incomplete, projected four-movement Sonata in C, for P-duet, composed in 1860 [41] and published at least twice in the present century.[42] Planned to consist of an "Allegro assai" in C, an "Andante" in D♭, a "Scherzo" in F, and an "Allegro con brio" in C, this work actually only contains the first movement and a "Scherzo" in c. It reads like the convenient reduction that its subtitle in the MS suggests, "A symphonic exercise for orchestra." [43] But it does not lack tiny hints of the freshness of melody and key contrast that were to distinguish *Boris Godunov* and *Pictures at an Exhibition*. The first movement concentrates on a single motive—too greatly for too long, in fact—suggesting a cursive prelude more than any hierarchic

36. In SMW XXXV (1877) 1041–42 Op. 98 is praised as a huge, late-Beethovian, instrumental drama, free but controlled. In SMW XXXVI (1878) 945–46 Op. 100 is praised for its youthful freshness; but in MMR VIII (1878) 27–28 it is (more justly) called an *"improvisata"* hastily done, with a finale that is a "dreary wilderness." Probably this Op. 100 was meant when a writer said in MT LXIV (1923) 480 that "the best Sonata of Rubinstein is ruined by the set of variations [3d mvt.?] which, good enough in themselves, contrive utterly to spoil the proportions of the work."

37. MUSORGSKY READER, Riesemann/MOUSSORGSKY, and Calvocoressi/MUSSORGSKY supply the factual information used in this paragraph.

38. Cf. MUSORGSKY READER 4–6.

39. Musorgsky/WERKE-m VIII; from this vol. comes the list of piano works in MUSORGSKY READER 434–37.

40. Cf. MUSORGSKY READER 6, 9, 11 (with 3 incipits from Son. in E♭, 12, 40–41; pp. 40–41 seem to contradict the possible identification of Son. in D with the "andante" and "allegro finale" also mentioned (as suggested in Riesemann/MOUSSORGSKY 69).

41. Cf. MUSORGSKY READER 25, 30, 33, 34.

42. Musorgsky/WERKE-m VIII no. 9; Balogh/DUETS-m 104.

43. If the symphony was to be in D, the keys specified in MUSORGSKY READER 30 and 435 are not equivalents by transposition. Cf., also, Riesemann/MOUSSORGSKY 42–43; Calvocoressi/MUSSORGSKY 11, 167–70 (with exx.).

sonata design. Except for its lyrical trio section in 3/4 meter, the "Scherzo," in 2/4 meter, is a gay hopak in style.

Pleasing conservative styles and a degree of virtuosity are ascribed to four published sonatas by the German born and trained organist in St. Petersburg, **Heinrich Franz Daniel Stiehl** (1829–86). These include a prize-winning work, Op. 37 in a, for P & Vc (1861);[44] Op. 38 in D, for P solo (1863); a "Fantasia quasi sonata" in B♭, Op. 68, also for P solo (1876); and Op. 100 in B♭, for P & Vn (1873).[45] Talent without sufficient melodic distinction or structural control was seen in a Sonata in b, Op. 2, for P & Vc, composed (and pub. in 1863) during his Leipzig training by an eventual director of the St. Petersburg Conservatory, **Mikhail Asanchevsky** (1838–81).[46] Not explored in the present day are several sonatas for P solo, P & Vn, and P & Vc by the successful violinist and nationalist **Nikolai Jakovlevitch Afanassiev** (1821 or 1820–98), reportedly left about the same period but apparently not published.[47]

Among works produced around the same time in Königsberg should be mentioned the approximately fifteen sets or single issues of pedagogic sonatinas for P solo or P-duet by the German-born pianist, teacher, and writer on music **(Christian) Louis (Heinrich) Köhler** (1820–86). Originally published between about 1855 and 1876 (starting at Op. 33 and ending at Op. 285), these generally dry, outmoded, two-movement works appear to have won more endorsement in pedagogic than in reviewers' circles.[48] Although largely self-taught, the once esteemed pianist and composer **Adolf Jensen** (1837–79) did study briefly with Köhler, and moved variously in the circles of Gade, Hartmann, Liszt, Bülow, Wagner, Rubinstein, Clara Schumann, and Brahms! [49] (Adolf was the brother of the violinist **Gustav Jensen** [1843–95] in Köln, himself the composer of a Son. in G, ⊙p. 14, pub. in 1883, and 2 well regarded sons. for P & Vc, Op. 12 in g, a prize-winning work pub. in 1882, and Op. 26 in a, pub. in 1889.[50]) Adolf's one sonata,

---

44. Op. 37 is reviewed favorably in NZM LX (1864) 112. Cf. MGG XII 1297–98 (G. Karstädt).

45. The pub. dates come from the annual vols. of HOFMEISTER.

46. NZM LIX (1863) 12. Cf. GROVE I 238–39 (E. Dannreuther).

47. Alekseev & Novikova. Cf. GROVE I 65–66 (M. Montagu-Nathan).

48. E.g., cf. NZM LII (1860) 165–66 (collective negative view), LX/2 (1864) 337 (P-duet), LXVIII/1 (1872) 87 ("Sonaten-Studien"), LXIX/2 (1873) 294 (more favorable, ranking Köhler with Clementi and Kuhlau); MMR II (1872) 135 (preferring Clementi and Kuhlau). Cf., also MGG VII 1321–23 (E. Kroll).

49. Cf. MGG VII 1–5 (R. Sietz), with undated list of works and further bibliography.

50. Cf. BAKER 781; Altmann/KAMMERMUSIK 209, 258; Cobbett/CHAMBER II 35 (R. Felber, on Op. 12); MMR XX (1890) 16 (on Op. 26).

Op. 25 in f♯, for P solo (ded. to Brahms, pub. in 1864), is a four-movement work (F-M-Sc-VF) revealing superior craftsmanship, an adequate but not distinctive sense of melody, and strong ties with the language and idiom, though not the structural methods, of Mendelssohn. Adolf's prevailing method of writing in closed periods, typically marked off by rests and often subdivided into repeated phrases and phrase members, seems more appropriate to his sectionalized inner movements than to the "sonata forms" of his outer movements, where a more dynamic, continuous, cumulative flow is essential to the broader designs.

Like Glinka and Mussorgsky, the immensely popular Russian composer **Peter Ilyitch Tchaikovsky** (1840–93) cannot be met squarely here because his contribution to the sonata is so incidental to, and unrepresentative of, his total output.[51] That contribution consists of two works, both for P solo.[52] The Sonata in c♯ was composed in 1865, the year Tchaikovsky finished his studies at the St. Petersburg Conservatory, under A. Rubinstein and others. It was not published until 1901, posthumously, by his lifelong friend, benefactor, and publisher P. I. Jurgenson in Moscow.[53] The work is cast in four movements (F-M-Sc-VF) that add up to 49 pages in the original edition. Particularly in the first movement, the forthrightness of the melodic material, the shapes of certain specific ideas, the rightness of the harmony, the dependence on phrase repetition in the syntax and sequence in the development of ideas, and a very few dramatic contrasts all foretoken in a small way the Tchaikovsky of the last three symphonies. But the piano writing is unresourceful and the last three movements offer neither significance nor urgency, including the "Scherzo," which Tchaikovsky adapted to better advantage when he transposed it from c♯ to c and orchestrated it in his Symphony 1.[54] In short, his Sonata in c♯ was hardly the success that its exact contemporary was by the three-year-younger Grieg (Op. 7 in e).

51. The full documentary biography Tchaikovsky/TSCHAIKOWSKY by his younger brother Modest remains the most important source, supplemented by Peter Ilyitch's diaries and correspondence (cf. M. D. Calvocoressi's summary at the end, p. 342, of R. Newmarch's extended article in GROVE V 327–50; and BAKER 1626–27).

52. A study of these 2 sons. by S. Frolowa, pub. in Russian in 1955, is listed in Kirby/KEYBOARD 487.

53. It was later assigned the posthumous op. no. 80, as in Abraham/TCHAIKOVSKY 245 and MGG XIII 864 (D. Lloyd-Jones). It is not listed in the thematic index of 1897, Jurgenson/TSCHAÏKOWSKY, nor in Tchaikovsky/TSCHAIKOWSKY I 106 and II 825, but it is reprinted in Tchaikovsky/WORKS-m LI A no. 2. It is discussed briefly in Weinstock/TCHAIKOVSKY 41, in Stein/TSCHAIKOWSKIJ 460–61 (as containing anticipations of Symphony 6, "Pathétique"), and in Abraham/TCHAIKOVSKY 40, 115, and, especially, 120–21.

54. Cf. Abraham/TCHAIKOVSKY 40.

Ex. 118. From the first movement of Peter Ilyitch Tchaikovsky's Sonata in G, Op. 37 (after a D. Rahter re-ed. of 1889,
plate no. 2534, "revised by the composer").

Tchaikovsky's other piano sonata, Op. 37 [55] in G, is only slightly better known. Composed in March and April of 1878 during stays at Lake
Geneva and in the Ukraine, it was dedicated to Karl Klindworth, first
published by Jurgenson in 1879, and already introduced to the public
that same year by one of Tchaikovsky's most valued and influential
friends Nicholas Rubinstein.[56] Tchaikovsky had written Rubinstein
after a prehearing of Op. 37 that the performance "was one of the
finest moments of my life." [57] But Op. 37 has provided no match in
quality or popularity for the violin Concerto in D, composed in the
same year, or for the piano Concerto in b♭, completed three years
earlier.[58] Its chief problem is the elephantine, ungrateful thickness of

55. Or Op. 37a, because of *The Seasons* for P solo, Op. 37b.
56. Tchaikovsky/TSCHAIKOWSKY I 484, 504, 538. Among mod. eds.: Tchaikovsky/
WORKS-m LII no. 5; Rahter in London, 1959.
57. Tchaikovsky/TSCHAIKOWSKY II 70. Op. 37 has been recorded on Monitor MC
2034 by S. Richter. According to Alekseev & Novikova, it is performed "often" today
(1968) by Soviet pianists, notably by K. N. Igumnov. The only performances of Op.
37 in America that are known here are about a dozen in the 1940's by the present
author.
58. Op. 37 is discussed briefly in Weinstock/TCHAIKOVSKY 180–81, 184, and 218
(with some further details on its origins); Stein/TSCHAIKOWSKIJ 458–59 (negative

its piano writing. Its first movement in particular progresses almost
entirely from complete handful to complete handful (Ex. 118). Otherwise, although its thematic material does not come up to Tchaikovsky's
outstanding best, the work does provide enough attractive ideas,
enough excitement at its peaks, and enough samples of his mature,
easily recognized styles and procedures that, had he rescored it for
orchestra, it would have made an acceptable Tchaikovsky symphony.
In any case, it flows more convincingly and can be brought back to
life more successfully than his other main sonata-type venture with
piano, the Trio in a, composed four years later (1882).[59]

In the first movement of Op. 37, the phrase syntax discloses Tchaikovsky's characteristically mechanical but effective asymmetry needed
for a sense of flow and goal in "sonata form" and largely lacking in his
earlier piano sonata.[60] A case in point is the cumulative effect of
progressively shortened phrase members in our foregoing example
from the development section. This example also gives some indication
of the considerable modulatory activity in the movement. The second
movement, "Andante non troppo quasi moderato," is a kind of rondo-
variation design in which Tchaikovsky, like Verdi, reveals some of the
elemental reserve strengths upon which he can draw to enhance and
"pull off" essentially obvious, even insipid themes. The third movement, a "Scherzo" in A-B-A and a *perpetuum mobile,* anticipates the
third movement of the *"Pathétique* Symphony" in its busyness and
quick shifts of range. By contrast, the finale, a rondo and near
perpetuum mobile marked "Allegro vivace," anticipates the finale of
the same Symphony 6 and harks back to the first movement of
Symphony 4 in its more lyrical, impassioned themes and their stepwise descents. The feel of a Russian folksong lies in its first subordinate, scherzando idea, in e.

In the interest of a rounded view, mentions may be inserted here of
several, more obscure works. One of these, *Fantasie in Form einer*

---

view); Asaf'ev/RUSSIAN (laudatory view, calling it "the first important Russian
sonata for the piano of the concert chamber type . . ."); Abraham/TCHAIKOVSKY
121–22; Dale/NINETEENTH 69, 95 (negative view).

59. Alekseev & Novikova (citing corroborative views in Nikolaiev/TCHAIKOVSKY
201, Al'shvang/TCHAIKOVSKY 567, and A. D. Alekseev's own recent "History of Pianoforte Art" (Moscow, 1967) II 269 would have preferred a higher evaluation of Op.
37 (and the Trio), emphasizing its significance as "an important landmark in the
development of the Russian sonata," its combination, essential to the sonata idea,
of the brooding and introspective ("lyrico-psychological") with the popular and
nationalistic (or "genre"), and the similarity, as regards this combination, to the
Concerto in b♭ and the Fourth Symphony.

60. Cf. his own recognition in 1878 of limitations in his control of musical form,
as quoted and trans. in Abraham/STUDIES 342–43.

Sonate for P solo, Op. 5 in b♭ (pub. by Leuckart of Leipzig in 1873),
proves to be an academic yet telling work in four movements (F-M-Sc-F)
by a German pupil of Robert Franz on military duty in Königsberg,
August Friedrich Saran (1836–1922).[61] There are *Drei Sonaten* for P
solo, Op. 9 in G, C, and C (pub. in 1872), and a Sonata in F, Op. 22,
for Vn & P (ded. to Reinecke, pub. in 1893) by the Moscow organist
Johannes Bartz (1848–1933).[62] There is a "Fantaisie-Sonate pour le
piano" in A♭, published in 1877 and highly praised for its technical
and musical worth, by one **"M. de Schoulepnikow,"** otherwise un-
identifiable here.[63] There is a Sonata in g, Op. 7 for P & Vn (pub. in
1882), reviewed as pedantic and conservative, by the violinist, organist,
and teacher in St. Petersburg, **Joseph Hunke** (or **Gunke;** 1801–83).[64]
And there is a set of two well-liked Sonatinas for P solo, Op. 46 (pub.
in 1881), by the Leipzig-trained composer **Robert Schwalm** (1845–
1912) in Königsberg.[65]

One rediscovers a fresh, short, compelling, harmonically deft Op. 1
in three movements (F-Va-Sc), for P solo (pub. in 1886), by the talented
Latvian pupil of Rimsky-Korsakov and teacher at the St. Petersburg
Conservatory, **Joseph Wihtol** (or **Vitol;** 1863–1948).[66] One comes on a
Sonata for P & Vn in A, Op. 8 (pub. in 1887), a lyrical but somewhat
cerebral work that was rescored fifteen years later as an orchestral
"Sinfonietta," by another pupil of Rimsky-Korsakov and the composer
of the popular "Caucasian Sketches," **Mikhail Mikhailovitch Ippolitov-
Ivanov** (1859–1935).[67] There is a Sonata in G for P & Vn, Op. 52 (pub.
in 1892), by the influential, Czech-trained conductor in St. Petersburg,
Eduard Nápravník (1839–1916).[68] And there can be found an epigonic,
chromatic, pedagogic, but not unskillful *Sonate en trois parties,* Op. 10
in c (ded. to Arensky and pub. in 1894), as well as a Sonata in F, Op. 27
(ded. to Rachmaninoff and pub. in 1910) by the pianist and teacher at
the Moscow Conservatory, **Heinrich Albertovitch Pachulski** (1859–
1921).[69]

61. Cf. Riemann/LEXIKON II 1590.
62. Cf. Riemann/LEXIKON 12th ed. I 108; MW IV (1873) 157 (viewing Op. 9 as
easy enough but too recondite for teaching purposes).
63. Cf. HOFMEISTER XXVI (1877), 236; MW XII (1881) 464.
64. MW XVI (1885) 483. Cf. Riemann/LEXIKON I 678.
65. MW XXI (1890) 214. Cf. Riemann/LEXIKON II 1674.
66. Cf. MGG XIV 638 (D. Lehmann). The listing of P sons. Opp. 30, 32, 33, and
41 in GROVE IX 291 (K. D. Hurst) seems to be in error.
67. Cf. SMW XLVI (1888) 434; Cobbett/CHAMBER II 20 (L. Sabaneiev); MGG VI
1396–99 (M. Montagu-Nathan).
68. Cf. MGG IX 1262–64 (G. Waldmann); Cobbett/CHAMBER II 187 (L. Sabaneiev
& W. W. Cobbett).
69. GROVE VI 479 (E. Blom).

Somewhat more attention has been paid to the two sonatas, both for P solo, by the versatile, highly respected musician **Aleksandr Konstantinovitch Glazunov** (1865–1936).[70] Glazunov wrote both of these sonatas, Opp. 74 in b♭/B♭ and 75 in e, in 1901 while he was still teaching composition at the St. Petersburg Conservatory. He dedicated the first of them to the wife of his most important teacher, Rimsky-Korsakov.[71] His elder friend and chief publisher, M. P. Belaiev, issued them soon after, in 1901 and 1902, and, most recently, in 1960, State Music Publishers in Moscow reprinted them. Both sonatas have three movements, fast outer movements whose main ideas interrelate, first movements that adhere to the usual "sonata form," and middle movements in A-B-A designs. Op. 74/ii is an "Andante" with a richly ornamented reprise, whereas Op. 75/ii is a "Scherzo" in 9/8 meter whose steady 16th-note patterns produce a near *perpetuum mobile.* Op. 74/iii is another near *perpetuum mobile,* in which the square phrases and change to the major mode impart a carefree, light effect, making a disappointing finale after the surging lyricism of the previous two movements.[72] Op. 75/iii makes a more impressive and original finale, consisting of an energetic preludial section, a short, equally energetic fugue on the same idea, and a restful chorale-like section in the tonic major key (E) that rises to a brilliant ending.[73]

Glazunov came under the strong influence of Liszt, Wagner, and Tchaikovsky, and, perhaps because of his technical mastery though hardly his style, he was even dubbed the "Russian Brahms." Yet the most apparent model for his Op. 74, apart from the greater polyphonic interest, is Chopin's music, especially in the first movement, where the cantilena of the subordinate theme (Ex. 119) recalls that in Chopin's Op. 58/i. And the most apparent model for Op. 75, apart from the fuller chordal writing, is Mendelssohn's music, as in that impressive finale, which recalls Mendelssohn's Fugue in e in Op. 35/1 and *its* similar choral-like ending in E.

When one first encounters Glazunov's sonatas, their technical mastery, melting lyricism, and good use of the piano make an excellent impression, explaining some enthusiastic statements about them.[74] But that impression gradually palls as one discovers no relief from the

70. Cf. MGG V 241–47 (H. Gunther).
71. During study with Rimsky-Korsakov, Glazunov had written 6 early sons. (Alekseev & Novikova).
72. But Alekseev & Novikova see it as the optimistic resolution through rejuvenation of the conflict of dramatic and lyrical in i and ii.
73. V. V. Stasov (as quoted in Yuzhak/GLAZUNOV 40) considered Op. 75, especially iii, to be Glazunov's greatest work.
74. E.g., Asaf'ev/RUSSIAN 220 and 235; Georgii/KLAVIERMUSIK 501.

chromatic double-appoggiaturas that infest nearly all of the melody and passagework, or from the lyricism that cloys to the point of seeming hollow and sentimental, or from the tonal changes and emotional climaxes that keep recurring without falling into any commanding, over-all order, or, for that matter, from a style that persists without sufficient compromise and contrast, and, above all, without those bold flashes and new insights that characterize genius. It is interesting to find Gerald Abraham reaching similar conclusions about the symphonies of Glazunov, whom he rightly brands as an epigone; and it is

Ex. 119. From the recapitulation of the first movement in the Sonata in b♭/B♭, Op. 74, by Aleksandr Konstantinovitch Glazunov (after the original Belaiev ed. of 1901).

worth quoting him, because Glazunov's kind of pseudo, impassioned lyricism became all too prevalent in his day:[75]

A Glazunov symphony is just an uninterrupted flow of melodious ideas, laid out according to the classical or neo-romantic (Lisztian) forms, lusciously harmonized and beautifully orchestrated. But nothing ever happens to these ideas. The flow of music never gets anywhere. Climaxes are arranged; the current rises and falls; there are delightful touches of orchestration (such

75. Abraham/RUSSIAN 235 and 240. In an early review of both sons. (SMW LX [1902] 682), Glazunov is regarded as more able to create in smaller forms. But Alekseev & Novikova defend his handling of the large forms, citing the opinions of Ossofski/GLAZUNOV 42, Rimsky-Korsakov (in Yuzhak/GLAZUNOV 40), and Taneyev (in Glazunov/MUSICIANS 228: "I cannot help but rejoice that you implement so energetically the renaissance of the piano sonata, [which had been] supplanted temporarily by small piano forms. The greater forms have not yet outlived their times, and probably even our grandsons will not exhaust all the content that can be expressed in these forms.")

as the deliciously sugary trio of the fourth symphony) and endless—and effortless—technical skill. Melodious phrases are beautifully interwoven, ingeniously transformed. But there is no growth, not even a sense of direction.

A stylistic affinity with Glazunov's two sonatas can be heard in the three published sonatas, one for Vc & P and two for P solo, by the world-renowned pianist **Sergey Vassilievitch Rachmaninoff** (1873–1943).[76] Rachmaninoff's sonatas show similar influences of Chopin, Liszt, and Tchaikovsky,[77] over and above the solid training the younger man got from Arensky and the distinguished Taneyev. But his sonatas are regarded here as being superior to Glazunov's—mainly, as being more genuinely musical and, in spite of their equally impassioned lyricism, freer of sentimentality. They show broader, more positive approaches to form, fresher, better contrasted funds of melody and rhythm, supported by equally expressive, chromatic harmony, and still more varied, advanced treatments of the keyboard.[78]

Rachmaninoff composed the first of these three works, Op. 19 in g/G, for Vc & P, in the summer of 1901, just after completing one of the most popular of all piano concertos, his No. 2 in c. He dedicated Op. 19 to the cellist Anatoli Brandukov and gave it its first performance with him that same year, with publication following the next year (1902) by his chief publisher, Gutheil in Moscow.[79] Since then, Op. 19 has enjoyed the majority of the relatively few performances Rachmaninoff's sonatas have been given, whether in public or on recordings.[80] Like every other cyclic instrumental work by him, Op. 19 lies primarily in minor keys, but, unlike his other sonatas and his concertos, it falls into four rather than three movements, in the order S/F-Sc-M-F.[81] Its predominant mood is that of sweet, gentle, probing, melancholy, with hints, too, of the composer's characteristic self-effacement as well as the insecurity and despondency he had just

76. The chief source used here on the man and his music has been the detailed, objective study Bertensson & Leyda/RACHMANINOFF. Cf., also, MGG X 1839–44 (G. Abraham); Reither/RACHMANINOFF (on recent research and recordings).
77. On Tchaikovsky's influence, cf. MQ XXX (1944) 177 (A. & K. Swan).
78. Cf. Rachmaninoff's own, early, negative report on Glazunov's musicianship, in Bertensson & Leyda/RACHMANINOFF 73.
79. All 3 of his sons. have been pub. more recently by both Boosey & Hawkes in London and International in New York.
80. Public performances by Lamond, Casals, and Schuster are cited in Bertensson & Leyda/RACHMANINOFF 154, 219, 378; 3 recordings are cited on p. 430, as against one each (sponsored by The Rachmaninoff Society) for the 2 P sons., on pp. 431 and 432.
81. Op. 19 is described briefly (and rated among Rachmaninoff's best works) in Cobbett/CHAMBER II 264–65 (L. Sabaneiev). Yasser/RACHMANINOFF is a general discussion of Rachmaninoff's style in the light of 20th-c. trends (as of 1951).

battled.[82] If the mood seems almost too consistent throughout the work, one has to attribute it to the free recurrences of the opening theme in all movements as a cyclical tie, to that emphasis on the minor mode, and to the nature not only of the man but of the cello and its warm invitation to concentrate on songful melodies in the tenor range. Following a tenuous page of introduction, strangely reminiscent of the opening in Franck's Sonata in A, the melodies prove at once to be of a high order, with their ensuing development already confirming their composer's structural mastery. The cello gets the lion's share of the melodic material. But the piano is much the more active and technically burdened instrument, so that, in spite of Rachmaninoff's own caution that Op. 19 "is not for cello with piano accompaniment, but for two instruments in equal balance," [83] almost another Rachmaninoff is needed (as in his other sonatas) to keep the part in balance, not to mention toss it off with appropriate insouciance and *élan*.

Rachmaninoff's second sonata was his first for P solo, Op. 28 in d, a favorite key of this "d-minor composer." [84] He composed it in early 1907, partly in Moscow and partly while adjusting to the strangeness of Dresden, while he was still occupied with the Second Symphony in e.[85] In a letter of May 14 the generally secretive composer bared the creative process to the extent of revealing agonies and doubts, plus even the fact of programmatic inspirations, although these last are not identified in the score (2 years before his best known programme work, *The Isle of the Dead*):[86]

Now I'm completing a piano sonata. Yesterday I finished writing the second movement. Only the last movement is left to do, but I don't know if I can finish it before going to Paris. Probably not. This work is *not* a secret. . . . Two days ago I played the sonata for [Oskar von] Riesemann, and he *doesn't* seem to like it. Generally I've begun to notice that no matter what I write lately nobody likes it. And I myself often wonder; maybe it *is* all nonsense. The sonata is certainly wild and interminable. I think it takes about 45 [actually 40] minutes. I was lured into this length by its guiding idea. This is—three contrasting types from a literary work [Faust, Gretchen, and Mephistopheles, as in Liszt's "Faust Symphony," according to Bertensson & Leyda/ RACHMANINOFF 153]. Of course no program will be indicated, though I begin

82. Cf. Bertensson & Leyda/RACHMANINOFF 75–96 *passim*.
83. Bertensson & Leyda/RACHMANINOFF 378.
84. MGG X 1843.
85. Cf. Bertensson & Leyda/RACHMANINOFF 131–45, *passim*, and the informative notes on the jacket of M-G-M recording E3247, of Op. 28 (E. Cole). Both P sons. are discussed briefly in Asaf'ev/RUSSIAN 254 and 320 as broadly conceived works with "well-moulded" material, though somewhat hampered by diffusion, rhetoric, and massive virtuosity, and not quite the equals of Tchaikovsky's Sonata in G (contrary to the view held here).
86. As trans. in Bertensson & Leyda/RACHMANINOFF 138.

to think that the sonata would be clearer if the program were revealed. Nobody will ever play this composition, it's too difficult and long and possibly—and this is the most important—too dubious musically. At one time I wanted to make a symphony of this sonata, but this seemed impossible because of the purely pianistic style in which it is written.

Without any dedicatee, Op. 28 was published by Gutheil in June of 1908.[87] It was first played in public in an all-Rachmaninoff concert in Moscow in October, with the critic reacting to it as being overly complex and hence somewhat dry.[88] The pianist was K. N. Igumnov, who was to play it again and had advised on revisions the composer felt were needed before publication—not in vain, as Igumnov later recalled:[89]

. . . it was apparent that the most essential part of my comments had been taken into consideration by the author. A considerable part of the recapitulation in the first movement had been recomposed, shortening it by more than 50 bars; some cuts had been made in the finale, mostly in the recapitulation, about 60 bars. Changes of treatment were made only in the finale, mostly in the recapitulation. The second movement was unchanged.

Rachmaninoff himself "usually" played Op. 28 on the solo recitals during his first American tour, in 1908–9.[90]

Op. 28 has much to commend it, including the deep serenity of its middle, "Lento" movement and its numerous clear anticipations, both melodic and figural, of the Third Concerto (also in the key of d), which Rachmaninoff introduced on that same tour. But Op. 28 does seem overly complex, at least in its outer movements. The outer movements not only present problematic sonata-rondo designs[91] but their sections themselves are too subtly demarcated to define those designs. Moreover, these sections relate closely in their general style, which, unlike the consistent style in the cello sonata, grows oppressive with its heavier moods, sonorities, and technical requirements. And the sections in Op. 28 lack quite the melodic individualities and contrasts to be found in the Third Concerto. In short, the fears Rachmaninoff

87. Bertensson & Leyda/RACHMANINOFF 413.
88. Cf. Bertensson & Leyda/RACHMANINOFF 152–53.
89. As trans. in Bertensson & Leyda/RACHMANINOFF 152; cf. pp. 136–37, 141, 145.
90. Bertensson & Leyda/RACHMANINOFF 160.
91. However, Bertenssen & Leyda/RACHMANINOFF 132–33 seems to err in connecting Op. 28 with Rachmaninoff's guarded inquiry as to how rondo plans were defined in textbooks, and in Beethoven's sons. This curious inquiry, so naive for such an expert craftsman, dates from Dec. 10, 1906, before Op. 28 was begun but during the much greater troubles Rachmaninoff was having with Symphony 2 (cf. pp. 136–37, 141, 145). In any case, as they turned out, no mvts. in either work quite tally with the nonstandardized design he asked about in general terms.

expressed about Op. 28's worth and success (*supra*) cannot be dismissed entirely as mere evidences of his emotional insecurity.

Rachmaninoff's last sonata and second for P solo, Op. 36 in b♭, was composed in 1913, partly in Rome. It was played by him (in its first public performance?) in St. Petersburg in November, dedicated to Matvei Pressman (fellow pupil of N. Zverev in the 1880's), published by Gutheil in 1914, extensively revised by the composer in the summer of 1931, and published in its revised form by Gutheil (in Paris) in that year.[92] It should be instructive to compare the two versions. When Rachmaninoff played the original version, a St. Petersburg critic, who preferred the moderns (Scriabin, Debussy, Stravinsky), anyway, reported that the audience received it coolly and that he found it devoid of "interesting or profound ideas," although not without "some fresh and, for Rachmaninoff, rather unusual harmonies and counterpoint. In certain passages of the central movement the composer shows an excellent inventive capacity for variations." [93] Rachmaninoff himself is quoted as remarking in 1931, presumably still about the original version, that "so many voices [in it] are moving simultaneously, and it is too long. Chopin's Sonata [in b♭, which Rachmaninoff's Op. 36 resembles near the start] lasts nineteen minutes, and all has been said." [94] In the later version, says one commentator, "the work is much tightened and shortened and certain important simplifications of executional problems are introduced." [95] After Rachmaninoff's death Olin Downes wrote in *The New York Times* (March 26, 1944), "It can now be told that when he played Rachmaninoff's piano sonata [Op. 36] published in two versions, years apart, Mr. [Vladimir] Horowitz, after long and scrupulous study, combined the two versions in a way which earned him the very sincere thanks and musician's esteem of the composer." [96]

Certainly, Rachmaninoff's Op. 36 in its second version is structurally more compressed and concentrated and harmonically if not tonally more daring than his Op. 19 or, especially, his Op. 28. Because it never loses sight for long, in any of its three movements, of its main idea (anticipated in the initial "veloce" descent and first stated in mss. 3–4, as in Ex. 120); because there are no full breaks between movements; and because all three movements have in common a sense

---

92. Cf. Bertensson & Leyda/RACHMANINOFF 184, 186–87, 276–77, 415 (the mention of "Tair" as pub. could not be confirmed here for the revision; cf. Cat. NYPL XXV 225).

93. As trans. in Bertensson & Leyda/RACHMANINOFF 186–87.

94. Bertensson & Leyda/RACHMANINOFF 276–77.

95. From the unsigned jacket notes for M-G-M recording E3248.

96. According to a letter received from Mr. Horowitz, dated July 18, 1968, no score exists of the combined version, which he has played as recently as 1968.

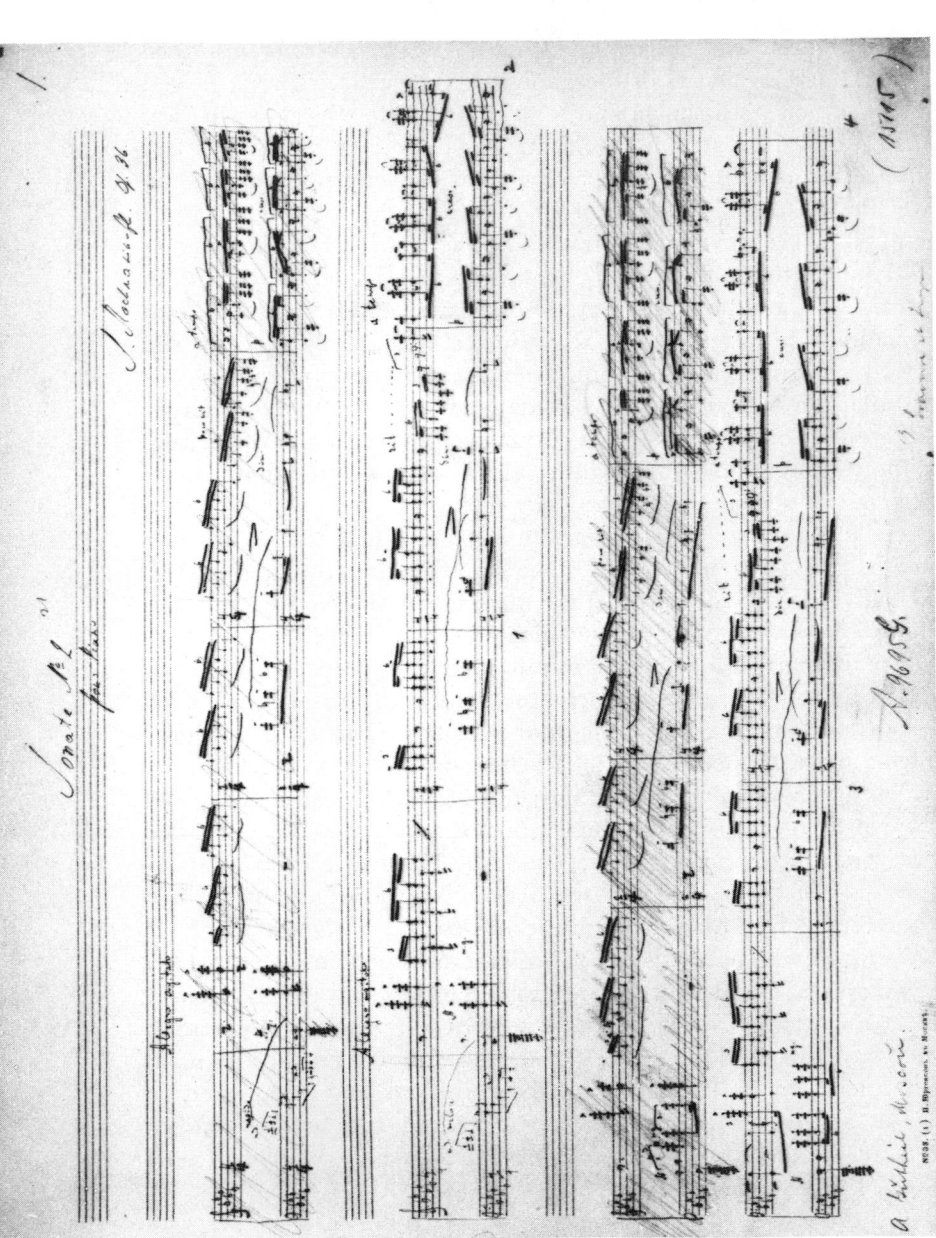

Ex. 120. From the opening of Sergey Vassilievitch Rachmaninoff's Sonata in b♭, Op. 36 (facs. of the first autograph version of 1913, reproduced with the kind permission of Madame E. N. Alekseeva, Di-

of fantasy, Op. 36 gives the impression on first hearing of being a free one-movement work. Its most vital structural principle is not that of sectional design nor motivic development but of variation through irregular restatements freely altered in melody, rhythm, harmony, and figuration. It is these free restatements that create the sense of fantasy. Only in the sequential ascents and descents of Rachmaninoff's artfully prolonged climactic curves is the syntax somewhat more regular. A fairly standard "sonata form" does underlie the first movement, but the middle movement, after an A-B-A treatment of two characteristically mournful themes based on stepwise descents, rises to a climax, then devotes its second half to more fantasy on the two main themes of the first movement. And the finale, introduced by nearly the same Franckian phrase that introduces the middle movement, gives us a scherzando "sonata form" that skips any trace of the recapitulation and goes right on to a brilliant coda with more references to the opening movement. Op. 36 is a rich, unusual, advanced, genuine work.[97] If reasons must be found for the rarity of its performances they may well be, first, the keyboard difficulties almost equal to those in the Third Concerto, without equally trenchant and varied ideas; and second, the degree of fantasy, which makes especially the finale hard to pull together, with its structural and motivic rhythms that are divergent enough to suggest the influence of Scriabin's later sonatas. Rachmaninoff was neither a Modern nor a modernist by nature. Such rhythms and some oblique, chromatic harmonic relationships (like those at the return in the first mvt., but never as extreme as the soloist's astonishing entry in the middle mvt. of the Third Concerto) marked the forward limits for that noniconoclastic, completely sincere musician.

A lifelong friend of Rachmaninoff, younger by seven years, **Nikolai Karlovitch Medtner** (1880–1951) likewise trained under Arensky and Taneyev, among others, excelled as a pianist, and pursued his career primarily in Moscow until he emigrated (to Berlin in 1921, Paris in 1925, and England in 1936).[98] However, unlike Rachmaninoff and notwithstanding considerable touring as a concert pianist in his own

97. Unendorsed here are the peculiarly opinionated, unprescient dismissals of Rachmaninoff (and Scriabin) by E. Blom in GROVE VII 27 and in Holt/TRIBUTE 75–76.

98. The principal, though brief, study of the man and his music is Holt/MEDTNER; followed by Holt/TRIBUTE (with an undated, careless list of works), which is a posthumous anth. of eulogistic articles, mostly short, on various aspects of Medtner's artistry and music, including emphasis on his sons. in Yasser/MEDTNER, Raybould/MEDTNER, and Ilyin/MEDTNER. Cf., also GROVE V 648–52 (E. Blom), with faulty list of works; MGG VIII 1893–94 (H. Lindlar), with inadequate list of works.

right, Medtner gave priority to composing over performing.[99] At the same time he seems to have compensated for this subordinating of the recitalist in him by writing more than half of his music for piano solo and the rest for piano and one more instrument (including about 100 songs), or piano and a group of other instruments (including a quintet and three concertos). Central in his more than 60 opus numbers, some subdivided, are 18 sonatas in one or more movements, originally published between 1904 and 1939, including 14 for P solo, 3 for Vn & P, and one for voice & P. The following chart of Medtner's 18 sonatas, in order of opus numbers and chronology, includes key, further title if any, scoring, probable or confirmed year(s) of composition, original publisher and year, volume and inclusive pages (plus total pp.) in the "Complete Works" (Medtner/WORKS-m, a set that began to appear in 1959), and number, tempo or type, and order of movement(s):[100]

In the following chart, the lengths in pages, from 9 to 85, and the number of movements, from one to 4, alone give some idea of the variety of approach and design in Medtner's sonatas.[101] Obviously Medtner was no slave to stereotypes. Even within the different move-ment plans there is little that can be generalized safely about his approaches or designs. The one-movement sonatas include some of the most developed and extended as well as the simplest and shortest designs (e.g., Opp. 25/2 and 11/2, respectively); and so do the multi-movement sonatas (e.g., Opp. 44 and 25/1). Moreover, the line between the ten one-movement sonatas, which type Medtner seems to have followed Scriabin in preferring, and the eight multimovement sonatas is not clear. Only Opp. 30 and 53/2 are unequivocal single movements without substantial changes of mood, tempo, or style.[102] The three sonatas of Op. 11, published separately in three successive years, qualify similarly, but originally they may have been intended to comprise the three movements of one sonata, and might still be so understood, if not tonally then in order of tempos and moods (first a gentle "Allegro non troppo," then a slower "Andante molto espressivo," and last a more

99. Cf. Holt/TRIBUTE 18–20 (by his wife Anna).

100. The dates of composition and pub. and the titles given in the valuable pref-aces (in Russian) to the separate vols. of Medtner/WORKS-m are preferred here to those in earlier sources when the information differs.

101. There are several brief discussions and passing descriptions of one or more sons. by Medtner, as cited here when and where they apply. Ilyin/MEDTNER is of interest on Medtner's use of "sonata form" in his sons. and other works. But a thorough, comprehensive study of his sons., which is certainly warranted in any case by the interest they have aroused, seems not yet to have been done either in the Soviet Union or abroad.

102. On this subject cf. Swan/MEDTNER 51–52; Truscott/MEDTNER, which is pri-marily an analysis of Op. 22.

Op./no.	Key	Further title	Scoring	Composed	First pub., year	Medtner/ works-m (pp.)	No. of mvts.: by types
5	f		P	1902–3; later revised	Belaiev, 1904 (1955, rev.)	I/98–142 (45)	4: F-F-S-F
11/1	Ab	⎰ "Sonaten-	P	1904–6	Jurgenson, 1906	I/216–30 (15)	1: F
11/2	d	⎱ Triade" (no. 2 =	"	1904–6	Jurgenson, 1907	I/231–39 (9)	1: M
11/3	C	"élégie")	"	1907–8	Jurgenson, 1908	I/240–50 (11)	1: F
21	b		Vn & P	1909–10	Édition Russe, 1910	VII/26–68 (43)	3: M-F-M
22	g		P	1909–10?	Édition Russe, 1910	II/46–72 (27)	1: F(M)F
25/1	c	"Fairy Tale-"	P	1910–11?	Édition Russe, 1911	II/101–20 (20)	3: F-M-F
25/2	e		"	1911	Édition Russe, 1912	II/121–81 (61)	1: M/F
27	F#	"-ballade"	P	1912–14?	Édition Russe, 1913–14	II/202–43 (42)	2: F-In/F
30	a		P	1914–15?	Édition Russe, 1917	II/244–70 (27)	1: F
38/1	a	"-reminiscenza"	P	1918?	Zimmermann, 1922	III/65–85 (21)	1: F
39/5	c	"-tragica"	P	1920?	Zimmermann, 1923	III/170–89 (20)	1: F
41	C	"-vocalise"	Voice & P	1922–23?	Zimmermann, 1924	VI/97–116 (20)	1: In/F
44	G		Vn & P	1926	Zimmermann, 1928	VII/93–177 (85)	3: In/F-In/√a-In/Ro
53/1	bb	"Romantische-"	P	1931–32?	Zimmermann, 1933	IV/99–146 (48)	4: M-Sc-M-⌐
53/2	f	"-orageuse" (or "-minacciosa")	"	"	"	IV/147–83 (37)	1: F
56	G	"-idylle; Pastorale"	P	1937?	Novello, 1935	IV/242–61 (20)	2: F-F
57	e	"-epica"	Vn & P	1938	Novello, 1939	VII/178–260 (83)	4: In/F-Sc-L-VF

driving "Allegro moderato, con passione innocente"). Apparently, each one of these three pieces won its independence by falling into a "sonata form" of its own, almost in spite of the composer.[103]

As for Medtner's Opp. 38/1 and 39/5, these are not wholly independent, single-movement sonatas. More accurately, each is a single movement within a five-movement, thematically interrelated suite.[104] Medtner's other "one-movement" sonatas are actually something more than that. Thus, Op. 22 acquires an incipient slower movement by incorporating an "Interludium" ("Andante lugubre") into the development section of its elaborate, allegro "sonata form." Op. 25/2 (ded. to Rachmaninoff) frames a huge, complete "sonata form" with an extended "Introduzione" and an even more extended coda. On the other hand, whereas Medtner's single-movement sonatas tend to add additional, incipient movements, his multimovement sonatas tend to fuse into one long, fantasy movement. In Op. 53/1, for example, the four movements tend to fuse because they all come back to the same opening idea, they run on from one to the next, *attacca,* and much of their separate identities of tempo and mood tend to be neutralized or camouflaged by the internal contrasts of tempo and mood that each movement reveals. (In all these respects, as well as the key, year of composition, and even the very notes of the cyclical idea, Op. 53/1 is curiously like the revision of Rachmaninoff's Op. 36.)

Taneyev is supposed to have said that his important pupil "was born with sonata form." [105] Others have called Medtner "the Russian Brahms." [106] Although each of these remarks has some justification if it suggests Medtner's exceptional command of structural techniques, both of them are misleading. Medtner did show a decided predilection for "sonata form," employing other standardized designs—such as the scherzo, theme-and-variations, and rondo in the last two violin sonatas (Opp. 57/ii and 44/ii and iii)—much less often. But Medtner's "sonata forms" are as free of standardization and as variable as his sonata cycles. For instance, each of those two one-movement sonatas that belong to five-movement suites is an irregular "sonata form." Op. 38/1, which is preludial in character, repeats not its whole exposition but only its second theme. Op. 39/5, which is episodic in character, omits its second theme in its recapitulation. Other of the sonatas, in spite of the frequent instruction "sempre al rigore di tempo," give way to free sections, often labelled "cadenza," in the course or at the end of move-

103. Cf. GROVE V 650.
104. Cf. Truscott/MEDTNER 114.
105. Holt/TRIBUTE 18.
106. Cf. Holt/TRIBUTE 86 (G. Abraham); Yasser/MEDTNER 48–49.

ments (as before the indicated "Coda" of Op. 53/2 or near the ends of Opp. 21/i and 22).

Yet the point should be made that Medtner's freedoms and substantial variants of textbook form cannot be attributed to programmatic influences. One must not try to interpret literally the titles that head more than half of his sonatas (as on our tabulation, *supra*), or the titles that appear over some of the separate movements (e.g., "Meditazione" over Op. 53/1/iii), or Tutchev's desolate poem about the night wind under the title of Op. 25/2,[107] or even the interpretative instructions couched in Medtner's rich editorial vocabulary (reminiscent of, but not so wild as, Scriabin's)—for instance, "Canterellando; con fluidezza" (at the start of Op. 21), "L'istesso tempo (ma con entusiasmo)" (after an "appassionato crescendo" in Op. 53/2!), "carezzando," "sognando," "pieghevole," "sussurrando," "stentato," "sfrenetamente," "vertiginoso," "svegliando," or "fastosamente." Such titles and advices in Medtner's sonatas not only have no literal programmatic significance. They often seem not even to convey any compelling or immediate emotional message. They are more like philosophical commentaries on the designated emotions.[108] Medtner was an absolutist par excellence. Only he dared to write an extended "sonata form," the difficult, neglected *Sonate-vocalise,* Op. 41, in which, except for an introduction that sets a verse by Goethe, the voice serves purely as an instrument, singing nothing but vowels (chiefly "a," Medtner explains in a preface).[109] Even the archaic movement titles in Op. 21—"Canzona," "Danza," and "Ditirambo"—have only stylistic rather than programmatic significance.[110]

Medtner's sonatas, most of which he himself introduced to the public, did not arouse exceptional enthusiasm at the start.[111] Opp. 21 and 22 achieved a certain popularity after they appeared.[112] But not until his last years did his music win ardent champions, who, governed by special tastes, formed something of a cult (well represented by the

107. Cf. Holt/TRIBUTE 127–28 (K. S. Sorabji) and 205 (K. Klimov).

108. Medtner's sons., like Rheinberger's, might have benefited from more instrumental color, perhaps explaining why Medtner thought of orchestrating Opp. 25/2 and 57 (Raybould/MEDTNER 142).

109. Cf. Holt/TRIBUTE 38–40 (E. Newman) and 44–45 (M. Ritchie); Yasser/MEDTNER 52–53.

110. Brief, nonspecific descriptions of Medtner's first 2 Vn sons. occur in Cobbett/CHAMBER II 126–27 (L. Sabaneiev & W. W. Cobbett).

111. Op. 5 was reviewed but briefly, and with reservations about its content, in NZM CI (1905) 543 and MW XXXVII (1906) 64 (E. Segnitz). Op. 5 is described in Ilyin/MEDTNER 186–88. Cf., also, Yasser/MEDTNER 46–48. The prefaces to the pertinent vols. in Medtner/WORKS-m include information about first performances.

112. Cf. Holt/MEDTNER 141 (L. Collingwood).

contributors to Holt/TRIBUTE). Since his death, interest in Medtner's music has slipped badly and for the most part undeservedly. Today (as of 1968) his sonatas and other music rarely get performed and not a piece by him appears in the standard recording catalogues (in spite of the support The Maharajah of Mysore gave in 1950–51 to the recording of many of his works).[113] As viewed here, Medtner's sonatas have somewhat the same strengths and failings as those of another neglected master before him, Rheinberger (SSB X). The identifications of Medtner with "sonata form" and Brahms (*supra*) do have significance if they pertain to his extraordinary ability, like Rheinberger's, to evolve, transform, develop, and permute an idea (as already in Op. 5/i).[114]

Ex. 121. From the second movement of Nikolai Karlovitch Medtner's "Fairy Tale-Sonata" in c, Op. 25/1 (after the original Édition Russe).

This ability may well be his greatest, though hardly his only, strength. He is an expert, enterprising, fluent contrapuntist. Although he does not expand the traditional vocabulary or range of mid-19th-century harmony, he does apply his harmony in newly sensitive and fresh ways (as in the end of Op. 11/1 or the diagonal relationships, passing dissonances, and pungent cross relationships of Op. 25/1/19–26). He evolves similarly fresh rhythmic patterns that are both supple and subtle in their alternate support and defiance of the prevailing meter (as in Op. 30, mss. 17–29).[115] He does not exploit virtuosity for its own sake, but he does write with considerable variety, ingenuity, and, of course,

113. Cf. Holt/TRIBUTE 20–21 and 237–38 (including Opp. 22, 27, and 41).
114. Cf. the description of style traits in Yasser/MEDTNER.
115. Cf. Yasser/MEDTNER 51–52.

sympathetic understanding, for the piano in particular. And it is important to note that, when he chooses, he can create an expressive, distinctive melody, well planned and well spun out (Ex. 121).[116]

The "failings" that Medtner shares with Rheinberger are failings only while we insist that ideal "sonata form" must reflect Beethoven's example in logic, tightness, and dynamism. According to that example, Medtner's forms, especially those with almost constant developments of main ideas, are too prolix to be called "tight" (the "heavenly length" problem, again; ssb VI), too free to be called "logical," and too philosophical and homogeneous (or devoid of dramatic contrast) to be called "dynamic." [117] Although Rachmaninoff and Medtner expressed high mutual admiration for each other's music, Rachmaninoff found the development sections too long in Medtner's "sonata forms." [118] Medtner's answer on one occasion was that "it is *not the length* of musical compositions that creates an impression of boredom, but it is rather the *boredom* that creates the impression of length." [119] But this overly pat remark merely raises the chicken-or-the-egg question. We still have to account for the boredom when it does occur. As viewed here, a primary cause is found in Medtner's frequent selection of ideas—usually motives rather than themes—that are too bland to justify extensive developments. In other words, in at least some of his sonatas Medtner did not choose to write distinctive melodies, and even his most ingenious, resourceful development is not quite enough in itself to carry the music.

By way of contrast to the sonatas of Glazunov, Rachmaninoff, and Medtner, there could hardly be an example more different from the same period than the one main Sonata by **Mily Alexeyevich Balakirev** (1837 [new style]–1910). Another fine pianist, who had studied with a pupil of Field, Balakirev fed early on the inspiration and encouragement of Glinka, became thoroughly versed in all the main European masters from Mozart to Chopin and Liszt, and, among many other musical activities, organized that concert of Russian music in 1867 that brought from the writer Stasov the label "The Mighty Handful" (a term later transmuted to "The Five").[120] In addition to an unfinished Sonata in D and a weak Sonatina in G called "Esquisses"

116. Cf. Holt/TRIBUTE 155 (C. Glover) on Medtner's melody.
117. Cf. the somewhat similar appraisal of Medtner's forms in Asaf'ev/RUSSIAN 253.
118. Bertensson & Leyda/RACHMANINOFF 180 and 276.
119. Bertensson & Leyda/RACHMANINOFF 246–47.
120. Cf. the biographical section (Chaps. 1–11) in Garden/BALAKIREV, a recent study in English (1967) of the man and his music that supersedes previous studies and includes an unannotated "Catalogue of Works" (pp. 330–39) and a full "Bibliography" (pp. 321–25).

(1909), both for P solo, Balakirev completed his main work of this
type, Sonata in b♭, for P solo, only after seeing it through three versions, two at the start and one almost a half century later, near the
end of his career.[121] The earliest version, dating from 1855 (as Op.
3?), got to the end of four movements, with a scherzo that relates to
his Octet, Op. 3, and a fugal epilogue still in the planning stage.
The second version, labelled Op. 5 and probably dating from 1856–
57, got as far as three completed movements, beginning with a movement in contrasting sections labelled "Andante," "Allegro assai fe-
roce," and "Maestoso"; followed by a "Mazurka," and stopping with
an "Andante" revised from the earliest version and dedicated to
Cui.[122] The third version was completed in 1905, dedicated to his
disciple Liapunov, published without opus number in 1906 by Zimmermann in Leipzig,[123] and already performed in public that same
year as far west as Paris.[124] The second of its four movements,
"Mazurka" in D, was a revision, already published separately in
1900, of the corresponding movement in the second version.

The fact that Balakirev's Sonata in b♭ is so different from other
sonatas of the time may explain at least in part two reviews that
deplored both its content and its treatment when it appeared.[125]
The first movement is unusual for its intended synthesis of "sonata
form" and fugal sections (perhaps at last realizing the "fugal epilogue" that had been planned for the earliest version). The "synthesis"
does appear clearly enough on paper. But it does not produce a new,
more dynamic form, since the sections simply alternate and repeat,
in the same or another key, without any appreciable development.
Instead, the effect is the rather static, oriental one of viewing the
same material repeatedly or merely from different angles, somewhat
as in "The Young Prince and the Young Princess" from Rimsky-
Korsakov's *Scheherazade*. But if the music is not compelling, if it
lacks the elemental, exhibitionistic drive of Balakirev's *Islamey*, or
quite the forthright lyricism of "The Lark" that he transcribed so

121. Cf. Garden/BALAKIREV 35, 36, 147–48, 237–43 (including genesis and analysis), 311, 315, 317, 333–34; Liapunova & Yazovitskaya/BALAKIREV 574 (with references to further documentary information about the sons. in this new, 1967, documentary chronology); Abraham/RUSSIAN 205–15 (description and evaluation of Son.
in b♭).
122. This 2d version was first pub. in Balakirev/WORKS-m I/2 in 1951, but neither
the first nor the 3d version has (yet?) appeared in that set.
123. Cf. Cat. NYPL II 467.
124. Garden/BALAKIREV 153 and 156 (fn. 36).
125. DM VI/4 (1906–7) 306 (A. Leitzmann) and MERCURE II (Jan.-June, 1906) 263.
Asaf'ev/RUSSIAN 231 qualifies it as a "highly interesting" but "contemplative," even
"cerebral" work.

successfully from a Glinka song, it is still pleasant and intriguing music. It offers smooth counterpoint in the fugal sections, wide-spaced, euphonious, Chopinesque figurations in the more homophonic sections, and satisfying if thoroughly traditional harmony. The second movement, which is the "Mazurka" in D, in A-B-A design, could almost be mistaken for one of Chopin's, by this former devoted performer of Chopin's music. The third movement, an innocuous, cursive, tonally transitional "Intermezzo," brings more recollections of Chopin's writing and Rimsky-Korsakov's manner. And the sectional, more virtuosic "Finale," which returns to Balakirev's favorite key of $b\flat$[126] and confirms casual cyclical relationships in this 34-page work, reminds us of his strong Russian nationalism by introducing square-cut, rhythmically clipped tunes that smack a bit of the barbaric "Polovtzian Dances" from Borodin's *Prince Igor*.

One can accept the evaluation of Balakirev's Sonata in $b\flat$ as one of his best piano compositions, as one of his few noteworthy compositions that are not programmatic, and even as the best sonata (out of but few, incidental sons.!) to come from any of "The Five." [127] But to imply that it is a masterpiece of the Russian Romantic sonata[128] would be regarded here as too high an evaluation. Quite apart from its disregard for dynamic organization as the most inviolable principle in the tradition of the Romantic sonata,[129] it does not offer the high or fresh quality either of ideas or of treatment that might justify that evaluation.

Two Russian piano sonatas of more than average interest remain to be mentioned, both of them epigonic works evincing advanced writing skills, expert knowledge of the keyboard, and undeniable musicality if not originality. One of them, published in 1908 by Zimmermann in Leipzig, is Op. 27 in f, composed by the pianist **Sergey Mikhailovitch Liapunov** (1859–1924).[130] Liapunov had studied with Klindworth (to whom Op. 27 is ded.), Tchaikovsky, and Taneyev before becoming "of Balakirev's pupils the one who was most intimately associated with him personally and who followed most closely in his footsteps as a composer." [131] But of that last association there is

126. Cf. Davis/LYAPUNOV 187–88. Both "The Lark" and *Islamey*'s opening are also in $b\flat$.
127. Cf. Abraham/RUSSIAN 206, 212–15; Garden/BALAKIREV 147, 237, 243, 317.
128. As in Garden/BALAKIREV 147 *et passim*.
129. Abraham/RUSSIAN 206–8 argues that this Son. sounds at first like a suite.
130. Cf. GROVE V 158–59 (E. Blom); he is overlooked in MGG. Op. 27 is described (pp. 196–98, with exx.) in a comprehensive discussion of his P music, Davis/LYAPUNOV (with dated list of P works and deds.). It is evaluated briefly and neutrally in Asaf'ev/RUSSIAN 234.
131. Abraham/RUSSIAN 206.

scarcely a trace in this highly developed and organized work beyond the most standard ingredients common to the musical language then current. Rather is there clear evidence of Liapunov's love for Liszt's, Chopin's, and a bit of Wagner's music[132] (as in the second theme, "Cantabile ed espressivo" on p. 5, which has something of all 3 masters in it; cf. *infra*).

Indeed, Liapunov's Op. 27 is one of the few consequential works modeled directly after Liszt's Sonata in b (ssb VI and X).[133] It begins, in the first 4 of its 31 pages,[134] with an exposition that moves from f to A♭ as it presents virtually all of the material to be restated, developed, and transformed in the remainder of the work. There follow 3 sections in 19 pages that can be viewed, much as in Liszt's

Ex. 122. From Sergey Mikhailovitch Liapunov's Sonata in f,
Op. 27 (after the original Zimmermann ed.).

double-function design, either as one huge, sectional excursion, all in foreign keys, that comprises the "development section" in a grand, complete one-movement "sonata form"; or as, respectively, the development section of a first movement (emphasizing the key centers of b, c♯, e♭, and B♭, but not followed by a return to f or a recapitulation section), a slower, second movement ("Andante sostenuto e molto espressivo," an A-B-A design in E/e/E), and a third, "scherzo" movement ("Allegro vivo" in g♯). There remain 8 pages, in f/F, that serve either as the recapitulation and coda of a one-movement design

132. Cf. Davis/LYAPUNOV 191–92 (but p. 204 unjustly contradicts p. 196).
133. It was an inability to recognize this form and its derivation that provoked the negative review of Op. 27 as a "Phantasie," not a son. (MW VIII/3 [1908–9] 365 [A. Leitzmann]).
134. Or 45 pp. in the reprint of 1951: Liapunov/PIANO-m I 88.

or the finale and coda of a 4-movement cycle. Even Liapunov's coda is modelled after Liszt's, being a similar peaceful resignation in andante tempo.

A sample of Liapunov's epigonic style may be quoted from the second theme (cited above) as it undergoes polyphonic extensions in the first development section (Ex. 122). Op. 27 is a telling work that reveals considerably more order and purpose and considerably less saccharinity than Glazunov's sonatas. Yet if it does not quite deserve to be kept alive, either, the problems lie in the same directions—excessive, insufficiently imaginative working of ideas that are not quite that important, to the point where the listener no longer can or wants to keep track of the elaborate design. Very different—in fact, sounding throughout like the Russian folk music he had formerly collected—is Liapunov's pointed, straightforward, three-movement Sonatina in D♭, Op. 65, for P solo, composed in 1917 and first published in 1922 in Moscow.[135]

Our example from Liapunov's Op. 27 can serve about as well to illustrate the other epigonic piano sonata awaiting mention. This is Op. 9 in B (pub. by Rahter in Leipzig in 1909), by the pianist **Sergei Eduardovitch Bortkiewicz** (1877–1952), a pupil of Liadov and Jadassohn.[136] Again, the main influences are Chopin's and Liszt's music, as is all too clear in the parallel between the second theme of the first movement and that in Chopin's Op. 58, or the main themes in the finales of both works. Now, in the three separate, thematically unrelated movements of Op. 9, there is no question of tight, convincing forms. Nothing more irregular happens than keeping the second theme in the tonic key in the exposition of the first movement's "sonata form" and putting that much of the recapitulation in the subdominant key. But this time the epigonic style is too epigonic. One can no longer take it at face value, if it ever could be so taken.[137] Unwittingly (surely!), the composer only plays at being soldier in the stern passages and only parodies love-making in the lyrical ones. A Sonata in g, Op. 26 for Vn & P, by Bortkiewicz (pub. in 1924), has not been available here.[138]

Among further piano sonatas, passing mention can be given to Op. 10 in G (1905?), a two-movement work (F-Va) by violist **Vassily Andreyevitch Zolotarev** (1873–1964), who had been a pupil of Bala-

---

135. Reprinted in Liapunov/PIANO-m II 126. Cf. Davis/LYAPUNOV 202–3, 204–5, with exx.

136. Cf. GROVE I 827 (H. J. Kalcsik); BAKER 186.

137. Such was a typical reaction when the present author sought to revive Op. 9 in U.S. recitals of 1946.

138. Listed in Altmann/KAMMERMUSIK 196.

732   ROMANTIC COMPOSERS AND THEIR SONATAS

kirev, Liadov, and Rimsky-Korsakov;[139] and to Op. 4 in G♭, (1907),
praised for its power, warmth, and phantasy, by another pupil of
Balakirev and Rimsky-Korsakov, **Semion Alekseyevich Barmotin**
(1877–?).[140]

Several composers wrote sonatas for Vn & P during the same period
that also should get passing mention here, although not more, for
these sonatas, like those for viola and those for cello were preceded
by no Russian masterpieces such as might have stimulated stronger
works.[141] Balakirev's pupil and another member of "The Five," **César
Antonovitch Cui** (1835–1918) left an example published late in his
life, Op. 84 in D (1911). Originally reviewed as a "pleasing" work,
it now seems no better than would be expected of a generally reactionary, colorless, inadequately trained composer more recognized
for his (conservative) nationalism than any special artistic heights.[142]
The Moscow pianist **Alexander Fedorovitch Goedicke** (1877–1957)
left a two-movement Sonata in A, Op. 10 (pub. in 1901), that is not
one of his more challenging, substantial works but has been commended to amateurs for its charm.[143] The Polish-born composer
Witold Maliszewski (1873–1939), saw his Op. 1 in G published in
Leipzig (1902) after he had settled in St. Petersburg—a three-movement
work (F-S-Va) welcomed at the time for its lyricism, strength, and
treatment of each variation in the finale as an independent piece (as
in Tchaikovsky's piano Trio).[144]

The pianist **Alexander Gustav Adolfovitch Winkler** (1865–1935)
left a Sonata in c, Op. 10, for Va & P (pub. in 1902) that was reviewed
as a fresh, cheerful, skillful work, although it no longer stands out
today.[145] Winkler also left one sonata each for Vc & P, completed
by Glazunov (Op. 19 in d, 1936), and Vn & P (Op. 20 in C, 1930).[146]

139. It is unfavorably reviewed in NZM CI (1905) 543–44 and DM V/1 (1905–6) 335
(A. Göttmann). Cf. BAKER 1852 (with reference to 2 later sons., as well) and Suppl.
143; Cobbett/CHAMBER II 598 (L. Sabaneiev & W. W. Cobbett), but not on the sons.
140. DM VIII/1 (1908–9) 116 (A. Leitzmann). Cf. VODARSKY-SHIRAEFF 18–19; Cob-
bett/CHAMBER I 59, for the listing of a Son. in a, Op. 14, for Vn & P.
141. Cf. Asaf'ev/RUSSIAN 229.
142. Cf. DM XI/3 (1911–12) 105 (W. Altmann); Cobbett/CHAMBER I 305 (V. N.
Belaiev & W. W. Cobbett); Asaf'ev/RUSSIAN 219; MGG II 1818–22 (G. Abraham).
143. Cf. BAKER 579 and Suppl. 48; Cobbett/CHAMBER 474 (V. M. Belaiev & W. W.
Cobbett); Asaf'ev/RUSSIAN 260–61 (incl. reference to a Son. in D, Op. 18, for P solo,
pub. in Berlin).
144. NZM C (1904) 819; DM IV/3 (1904–5) 207 (W. Altmann). Cf. MGG VIII 1551–
52 (Z. Lissa); Cobbett/CHAMBER II 110 (L. Sabaneiev & W. W. Cobbett), without
evaluation of Op. 1.
145. MW XXXVI (1905) 306 (E. Segnitz); NZM C (1904) 819. Cf. Cobbett/CHAM-
BER II 587–88 (L. Sabaneiev & W. W. Cobbett); Asaf'ev/RUSSIAN 229; MGG XIV 711–
12 (M. Goldstein).
146. MGG XIV 712.

The pianist of French descent, **Georgy Lvovitch Catoire** (1861–1926), left two published violin sonatas of some substance, depth, and skill, Opp. 15 in b (1904) and 20 ("Poème"; 1910).[147] Rimsky-Korsakov's pupil **Ivan Ivanovitch Kryzhanovsky** (1867–1924) left one published sonata each for Vc & P (Op. 2 in g [not G], 1903) and Vn & P (Op. 4 in e, 1906), the former receiving qualified praise for somewhat undisciplined spontaneity.[148] Another pupil of Balakirev and Rimsky-Korsakov, **Fyodor Stepanovitch Akimenko** (1876–1945) was the composer of four published sonatas—Opp. 32 and 38b for Vn & P, in d and G (1905 and 1911), Opp. 37 for Vc & P, in D (1908?), and 44 ("Sonate fantastique") for P solo (1910). Op. 32 was greeted as having more harmonic than melodic interest, although Cobbett later called it Akimenko's best chamber work.[149] And the pianist **Leonid Vladimirovitch Nikolayev** (1878–1942), a pupil of Taneyev and Ipollitov-Ivanov, left two sonatas, Opp. 7 in D, for P solo (pub.?), and 11 in g, for Vn & P (pub. in 1908). The latter has been described as competent but not distinctive.[150]

147. Cf. Cobbett/CHAMBER I 236–37 (V. M. Belaiev); BAKER 267–68; Cat. NYPL V 538; HOFMEISTER 1910, p. 27; DM X/1 (1910–11) 244.
148. MW XXXV (1904) 923 (E. Segnitz); DM III/4 (1903–4) 64 (H. Schlemüller). Cf. GROVE IV 861 (M. D. Calvocoressi); Asaf'ev/RUSSIAN 229.
149. DM VIII/3 (1908–9) 174 (W. Altmann); Cobbett/CHAMBER I 4 (V. M. Belaiev). Cf. VODARSKY-SHIRAEFF 11; GROVE I 80 (R. Newmarch).
150. DM IX/1 (1909–10). Cf. Cobbett/CHAMBER II 189; MGG IX 1533 (D. Lehmann); VODARSKY-SHIRAEFF 94 (including a MS Son. in g, Op. 22, for Vc & P).

Chapter XIX

The Americas Under European Guidance

U.S. Circumstances and Output

During the 19th century, in a land that still had been facing colonial struggles and reapportionments while Bach and Handel flourished, that had not attained its Constitution as an independent, unified country until the period of Haydn's and Mozart's greatest masterworks, and that was entering only its second half-century as the United States of America while Mendelssohn, Chopin, and Schumann were at their creative peaks, one could hardly expect to discover significant contributions to so specialized a genre as the sonata. Yet the familiar apology—familiar throughout the arts—that the country was still too young to do better can be both unwarranted and misleading here. It can be unwarranted because, at least after the Civil War (1861–65), the quality of the American sonata output, especially of the duo sonatas, was generally competent by anybody's standards, if not better. It can be misleading because, from before the start of the century, there was more awareness of current European trends, more interest in the sonata idea, and more actual publication of sonatas than has yet been noted or supposed. To be sure, we shall be encountering a conspicuous gap in production during slightly more than the second quarter of the century. But this gap only paralleled the low ebb of sonata production already noted at the time in the most active European countries (ssb II). And after the Civil War there was, proportionally, quite as sharp a rise of interest in the sonata (and other chamber music) as in those other countries, followed by a further spurt of interest during the wave of international good will, labor harmony, and capitalist prosperity that were enjoyed after the Spanish-American War (1898).

In any case, to temper our evaluations of the American sonata up to World War I with an apology for the country's newness would mean confusing the intended critical uniformity in the present volume by introducing a double standard. Schubert, Schumann, Chopin, and Brahms still can and should serve as our artistic points of reference. Furthermore, our composers themselves probably would have been the first to expect, even demand, comparison by European standards. In fact, if there was any one problem that beset the American sonata (and other absolute music) during the Romantic Era it was not so much the lack of a two-century tradition per se as the nearly total dependence on European traditions and practices. In particular, the dependence was on German traditions and practices, thus illustrating, at least as consistently as any other country we have visited, a recurring theme of *The Sonata Since Beethoven*. Only occasionally were there derivations from the English, especially at the start (as with A. Reinagle, J. Hewitt, and B. Carr),[1] or from the French, all toward the end of the era (as with D. G. Mason's study under d'Indy).

Some of the German influence came by way of composers born, trained, and even already established in Germany before emigrating to the United States (e.g., O. Singer). But most often—in fact, to a surprising degree—it came by way of American-born composers who followed *the* favorite course if they wanted to succeed in serious music, which was to go to Germany for their several years of advanced training. A relatively few American-born composers of some success stayed home and got their German training at second hand—for example, E. R. Kroeger in St. Louis. But most of the better known Americans went where the Germans themselves went—to Leipzig and the successors of Mendelssohn, especially Hauptmann, E. F. Richter, Jadassohn, and Reinecke; to Weimar for summer study with Liszt; to Munich and Rheinberger; to Berlin and Kiel; and to Dresden or several other German centers.[2] Generally these Americans held their own well abroad,[3] not a few making sufficient reputations before returning to get one or more sonatas published by the more receptive German firms. Our most celebrated American example was, of course, MacDowell, who was at least as Germanic as the rest of them, for all the discussions of his Americanism.

Both the German or Austro-German orientation and the U.S. alertness to foreign trends are already illustrated at the start of the era

1. On Reinagle and Hewitt cf. SCE 806–9. A new, complete ed. of Reinagle's 4 Sons. for P solo was first announced by Da Capo Press in 1964 and later expected to appear in early 1969.

2. MASON MEMORIES, Fay/GERMANY, and Mannes/MUSIC are among the most entertaining and informative of numerous memoirs of such study throughout the century, though mostly pertaining to performance rather than composition.

3. In 1863 a Sandusky newspaper reported that the "best musical talent at the [Leipzig] conservatory was said to be American . . ." (DWIGHT'S XXIII–XXIV [1863–64] 255).

by the remarkable number of current European hits being published in this country, including one or more sonatas by Beethoven, Clementi, Cramer, Dussek, Edelmann, Gyrowetz, Haydn, Hook, Kočžwara, Koželuch, Mozart, Nicolai, Pleyel, Steibelt, Türk, Vanhal, and Wölfl! [4] That Beethoven's sonatas may have aroused interest here earlier than hitherto supposed is suggested by a public performance of his Op. 26 in Boston by Hewitt's daughter Sophia in 1819.[5] Indeed, we have here the earliest known public performance not only of this work in this country but of any Beethoven sonata for P solo that was clearly identified, anywhere, throughout his lifetime.[6] Beethoven sonatas were played increasingly in public from the middle of the century, especially in New York and including a total of five complete series of the "thirty-two" as early as 1863 (only 2 years after the feat had first been accomplished in Europe) and 1874.[7] Corresponding interest is reflected in U.S. articles on his early and late sonatas, not excluding the usual programmes offered for the "Moonlight Sonata." [8] One New York layman asked the editor of the *Musical World and New York Musical Times* for December 25, 1852 (pp. 1–2), what it means to " 'comprehend,' 'appreciate,' 'understand,' 'feel,' and perhaps do many other things with . . . a Sonata of the great Beethoven. . . . What is the *pith* and *substance* of all this, divested of the hazy transcendentalism which surrounds it?" Replied the editor, "No un-professional person ordinarily *comprehends* . . . such music. . . . But every person may *appreciate* and keenly enjoy such music (as far as the sensuous effect goes). . . ."

That sort of interest was also found, though to a much lesser degree, in the sonatas of others—for example, Onslow, Clementi, Hauptmann, and Mendelssohn.[9] And there were further remarkably early performances of European masterworks, such as that in 1855 of Brahms's Trio in B, Op. 8, for the first time anywhere, and of his duo Op. 108 at a New York concert honoring Bülow, even before its publication took place.[10] But with all these evidences one must not lose perspec-

4. Cf. WOLFE I x, and *passim;* also, SCE 804–5 (for sons. in Thomas Jefferson's library).

5. The discovery of this information in the *Columbian Centinel* of Boston for Feb. 27, 1819, was reported recently in Horton/PIANO 15–20, 58.

6. Cf. SCE 528–29 (but without knowledge of the U.S. performance).

7. Cf. GROVE Am. Suppl. 407; Horton/PIANO 58–59; SCE 527.

8. E.g., DWIGHT's X (1856) 102, 119; XI (1857) 35–36; XII (1857) 265, 274, 282, 289, 287–98; XIII (1858) 12 ("Liszt" on the "Moonlight"); XVI (1860) 346–47 (Anne Brewster on the "Moonlight").

9. As in DWIGHT's II (1852) 2, IX (1856) 179, and XXIII–XXIV (1863–64) 6, 11, 278–79, 286–87, 376.

10. Cf. GOTTSCHALK/Notes xxxiv; Salter/AMERICAN 89; SSB IX.

tive and forget that in the total musical picture neither the sonata nor other serious independent instrumental music was any match for opera, oratorio, or light social music—certainly no more so in the United States than in Europe. A few composers of real importance, like Charles Martin Loeffler, left no sonatas at all.

Moreover, we get here the same kind of doubts expressed about the sonata's survival as we have seen in Europe (SSB II). In 1852, near the end of that conspicuous production gap, a writer for *Dwight's Journal,* noting the prevalence of capriccios, romances, sketches, and other light music for piano, asked, "Where is now the Sonata, that finished, elegant composition with its three or four varied movements, each complete in well ordered beauty? . . . This form . . . is . . . now almost extinct. . . ." [11] Within a year the same periodical took a more optimistic view, although still not quite seeing an end to the gap: "Sonatas of the old solid construction are welcome revivals at the present day, not only from Spohr, Mendelssohn, and Thalberg, but from younger pens desirous to identify themselves with music at any rate, even should the wish rather than the accomplishment be discerned. . . ." [12] Yet the Beethoven sonatas themselves, for all "their rank in history and their value in the souls of all true music-lovers," were said to be "surpassed [by the music of] a young man, an American [Gottschalk]." [13]

To the end of the century the prognosis for the sonata in the United States remained doubtful. In 1884 Willard Burr (*infra*) commented at the Cleveland meeting of the Music Teachers National Association on how important foreign publication continued to be to serious American music. Publication in America, he said, "not only gives little or no surety of success, but is it not rather in most cases a guarantee that they [the American works] do not possess any real value?" [14] In an extended article on music in this country (occasioned in 1890 by the 2d ed. of F. L. Ritter's *Music in America*), the Vienna critic Hanslick found very little at all to mention in the way of instrumental music.[15] In 1891 the American critic H. T. Finck was still advising against writing sonatas, both because "sonata form is too complicated and artificial to contain the new ideas of our time" and because it was too difficult to win acceptance of sonatas, whether by publishers, purchasers, performers, or audiences.[16] When, at last,

---

11. DWIGHT'S I (1852) 67.
12. DWIGHT'S II (1853) 124.
13. DWIGHT'S II (1853) 158.
14. Quoted in Salter/MTNA 19–20.
15. Hanslick/TAGEBUCHE 58–91, especially 62 and 79.
16. In "What Shall I Compose?" *Etude* IX (1891) 166.

David and Clara Mannes began their recitals of sonatas for violin and piano in the early 1900's they felt even that late that they were starting something new.[17] Spreading their repertoire from the early Italian masters to Brahms and Franck, and their touring radius from New York, Boston, and Philadelphia as far north as Bangor, as far west as Kansas City, and as far south as St. Louis they were the inspiration for several further recital pairs with the same aim.

One category of vital stimulants and standard-raisers in 19th-century American music was the succession of epochal concert series by the great performers of the age, starting with Jenny Lind's U.S. debut in 1850,[18] and followed by Gottschalk's in 1853,[19] Anton Rubinstein's in 1872,[20] Bülow's in 1875,[21] Josef Hofmann's in 1887,[22] and Paderewski's in 1891,[23] among others.[24] The incomparable Gottschalk, who left no examples of his own, occasionaly played a Mozart or Beethoven sonata or sonata movement, especially in New York, and his successors did increasingly more for our genre. Another important stimulant occurred in the prolonged visits of notable European composers, especially Dvořák's tour of duty as "artistic director" at New York's National Conservatory from 1892 to 1895 (SSB XVIII).

At first it was mainly the three big eastern centers—New York, Philadelphia, and Boston—that provided the properly hightoned environment for such music.[25] New York and Boston, with its "Boston Classicists" (including Paine, Chadwick, Foote, Parker, Beach, Hill, and D. G. Mason),[26] continued to be important. But the horizons soon spread to include Chicago, Cincinnati, St. Louis, Kansas City, Minneapolis, and many another center farther west. A significant year to note is 1867, when no fewer than five of America's leading conserv-

17. Mannes/MUSIC 196–97, 282.
18. Cf. BAKER 957.
19. Cf. GOTTSCHALK/Notes xxv–xxxix (including debut program).
20. Cf. Loesser/PIANOS 515–18; Schonberg/PIANISTS 259–61.
21. Cf. Loesser/PIANOS 531–32.
22. Cf. Schonberg/PIANISTS 358–62.
23. Cf. PADEREWSKI 189–228, including programs; Schonberg/PIANISTS 289–90.
24. In addition to the pp. just cited, GOTTSCHALK/Notes 39–320 (1862–65), PADE-REWSKI 247–66 (1892–93?), Mannes/MUSIC passim, Dent/BUSONI 97–98 (1891–94) and 190–95 (1910–11), and DAMROSCH/Life passim are among vivid recollections of American concert life during the Romantic Era. Cf., also, Lang/AMERICA 109–27 (N. Slonimsky); Salter/MTNA; Salter/AMERICAN; GROVE Am. Suppl. 12–16, 30–37, and 80–87.
25. For some useful surveys of American instrumental musical life by cities, cf. ART OF MUSIC IV 181–205; Howard/AMERICAN 150–58; Wolverton/KEYBOARD 171–77, 209–20, 289–92, 379–430 passim (all mainly on keyboard activities). Two foreign periodicals that regularly reported U.S. son. performances, city by city, were NZM and MT.
26. Cf. Chase/AMERICA 365–82.

atories were established, two in Boston and one each in Cincinnati, Oberlin, and Chicago.[27]

There follow two tabulations, one of about 160 published sonatas and the other of about 70 unpublished sonatas produced between 1001 and 1915 by residents in the United States. The published sonatas are listed in the chronological order of their (presumed) first editions, the unpublished ones only in the order of their composers' birth years, since the dates (in the rightmost column) that are known for these MSS are few. Although such tabular summaries of a country's output have been avoided earlier in the present volume (partly in the interest of maintaining a prose continuity), they can be helpful here in providing a collective view of an output that is interesting more often as one facet of 19th-century Americana than as music significant enough to merit individual discussions of more than a relatively few selected examples. Except for publications up to 1820, brought to light in WOLFE and Wolverton/KEYBOARD, our tabulations can hardly be said to approach completeness, least of all with regard to the MSS. Until Wolfe's thorough bibliography of the publications can be extended to later years and until more explorations of surviving MSS can be made, we must be content with the few, more general surveys and with the gradual improvement of information during the 19th century that results from a gradual increase of copyright entries since the first U.S. law protecting music was enacted in 1831.[28] Surely, the extraordinary gap in sonata production that now appears to exist from 1821 to 1856 will be filled in, at least in part, as our information for the period improves. For the years following, the chief help comes from the actual holdings at the Library of Congress (LC in the "References" cols.), the New York Public Library (including some not in Cat. NYPL), the Boston Public Library, and the special collection of the present author, as well as Horton/PIANO, Kremer/ORGAN and Sloan/VIOLIN (2 diss. and a thesis), and the numerous though mostly nonspecific listings in GROVE Am. Suppl.[29]

27. Cf. ART OF MUSIC IV 247–59.

28. Cf. Lang/AMERICA 285–86 (R. Burton); Sonneck/SUUM 91–93; Salter/AMERICAN 13–14. Occasionally, MS as well as pub. sons. turn up in the old U.S. copyright cats., thanks often to the naive vanity that prompted even (or especially) some of the weakest composers to copyright their frequently eccentric products. But all music listings are harder to dig out before 1891, when music began to be listed separately (and protected internationally), and 1906, when the present "Music" cat. of the U.S. Copyright Office began.

29. Our short titles for these and a few other sources are further shortened in the "Reference" cols. of the tabulation, but should be immediately identifiable in the Bibliography of SSB. The "References" merely document information about the particular work(s) to which they pertain. One should not overlook BIO.-BIBL. U.S.

In the tabulations that follow, the composer's national origin is given when known, as well as his or her first or main U.S. post and current residence at the time any sonatas were published. The tabulations include sonatas composed by U.S. residents while temporarily abroad (e.g., L. A. Coerne and H. A. Brockway), but not those composed after actual emigration, such as three by the New York-born resident in Berlin, **William Humphreys Dayas** (1863–1903),[30] nor those composed by foreigners before they became U.S. residents, such as Julian Edwards (ssb XIV), Felix Borowski (*infra*), **Hermann Spielter** (1860–1925),[31] and the world-famous pianist Josef Hofmann (1876–1957).[32] The tabulations also omit MSS that eventually achieved publication, sometime after 1915. Among those omitted sonatas are four of the five left by John Powell, which get notice in any case when his name comes up later here; a songful, flowing, orthodox four-movement Sonata in D, Op. 8 (F-VF-S-F), composed in 1891 during composition study in Berlin with Max Bruch, by the Chicago organist **Rossetter Gleason Cole** (1866–1952); [33] and eight of the nine completed sonatas left by Charles Ives,[34] which do not get notice, since they exceed the scope of the present volume by belonging with Scriabin's, Debussy's, Busoni's, and other significant innovational sonatas of the Modern Era.

To the extent that they are representative, the following tabulations provide some statistics worth noting. The approximately 110 different composers of the 230 published and unpublished sonatas represent at least 12 national origins, with 14 per cent of unknown origin and most of the rest born in 3 countries—a surprising 55 per cent in the United States and only 14 and 10 per cent in Germany and England,

---

as a valuable guide to further literature on all but the most obscure of the composers in the tabulations.

30. Cf. BAKER 356; GROVE Am. Suppl. 183; Kremer/ORGAN 178 (listing Son. 1, Op. 5 in F, for organ); SMW XLVI (1888) 501 (reviewing Son. 2 for organ, Op. 7 in C, as musically interesting but too difficult and somewhat contrived); SMW LVI (1898) 977–78 (reviewing Op. 11 in D, for Vn & P, as promising but still in Dayas' *Sturm und Drang* period and not distinguished by either originality or development of ideas).

31. Cf. BAKER 1546; Altmann/KAMMERMUSIK 264 (Op. 14 in D, for Vn & P, pub. in 1889).

32. Cf. BAKER 724–25. In SMW LI (1893) 691 a reviewer found ideas that are good but in need of more Classic discipline in the score of Hofmann's Op. 21 in F for P solo (Hainauer, 1893). And in MT XLVI (1905) 262 a reviewer found modern trends, earnest purpose, and brilliance in a performance of this work or possibly Op. 24 (unpub.) for P solo.

33. Played (first?) in 1897 (Sloan/VIOLIN 147); not pub. until 1917 (A. P. Schmidt). Cf. BAKER 4th ed. 220.

34. Kirkpatrick/IVES 70–92, 96.

respectively. The trend, of course, was toward proportionately more U.S.-born composers as the era advanced. In this country the 110 composers lived primarily in 4 out of about 30 cities, including 32 per cent in New York, 25 per cent in Boston, and 9 per cent each in Philadelphia and Chicago. Approximately 72 per cent of the published editions of the sonatas appeared in the United States and 26 per cent in Germany, with the trend this time being toward the latter as the era advanced. As for scoring, nearly 48 per cent are set for P solo, but that figure is swollen unjustly by several sets of from two to six sonatinas. Next come about 31 per cent for Vn & P, 16 for organ, 3 for Vc & P, and 2 for 3 other settings.

Immigrants Before the Gap of 1821–56

From our tabulations certain of the sonatas may be singled out, in roughly chronological order, for further discussion. The sonatas prior to the conspicuous hiatus of 1821–56 are all by foreign-born composers, all in the programmatic (mostly battle) or pedagogic categories, and all in the jargon of mid-Classic music. Ten of them figure among the totals of thirteen published sonatas each (all P solo; 1796–1815) that are known by two English-born performers, publishers, and composers. Flourishing a half generation later than Reinagle and Taylor (SCE 806–8), these are the two who dominated musical life from the early 1790's on in New York and Philadelphia, respectively—that is, James Hewitt (1770–1827) [35] and **Benjamin Carr** (1768–1831).[36] Except for less consistent, two-movement plans and more advanced technical requirements (including a right-hand, upward glissando in 6ths!), Carr's sonatas are like Hewitt's. They reveal much the same naive squareness of ideas and phrases that follow additively without any development or structural integration, and the same accompaniments, whether Alberti, chordal, or repeated-note. **Francisco Masi** (?–1853?) provided another similarly virtuosic battle sonata, complete with programmatic inscriptions, in *The Battles of Lake Champlain and Plattsburg, a Grand Sonata.*[37]

The Czech-born **Anthony Philip Heinrich** (1781–1861) wrote his only contribution, "La Buona Mattina, Sonata for the Pianoforte," as

---

35. SCE 808–9. Cf. Wolverton/KEYBOARD 221–43, 469–73 (facs. of Op. 5/2, complete).

36. Cf. Wolverton/KEYBOARD 293–324 (including a facs. of p. 5 in "The Siege of Tripoli, an Historical Naval Sonata," p. 311, a description of Carr's sons., pp. 310 and 312–14, and a list of P works, pp. 317–24) and 474–76 (facs. of Carr's Son. 6 in B♭, pub. in 1796).

37. Cf. Wolverton/KEYBOARD 185–88, including a facs. of p. 4 and list of P works.

Some Published Sonatas by U.S. Residents, in Order of First Editions (1801–1915)

Composer	Born-died	Natl. / arrived / 1st U.S. post / res. at pub.	Title, op., &/or key	Scoring	References	Publisher, year
James Hewitt	1770–1827	Eng. 1792 / New York / same	"4th of July"	P solo	WOLFE 3697; Wolverton 229–30	J. Hewitt, 1801
Benjamin Carr	1768–1831	Eng. 1793 / Philadelphia / same	"The Siege of Tripoli . . ."	P solo	WOLFE 1653–54; Wolverton 310–12	J. Carr, etc., 1804–5
J. Hewitt		New York	"to Miss M. Mount"	P solo	WOLFE 3781; Wolverton 236	J. Hewitt, 1809
B. Carr		Philadelphia	*Six Progressive Sonatinas* . . .	P solo	WOLFE 1657; Wolverton 313–14	J. Carr, 1812?
J. Hewitt		Boston	"Military"	P solo	WOLFE 3743; Wolverton 240	? (U.S.), 1813–15
Francisco Masi	?–1853?	Italy 1807 / Boston / same	"Battles of Lake Champlain and Plattsburg"	P solo	WOLFE 5622; Wolverton 185–88	F. Masi, 1814
John F. W. Pchellas	?–? (U.S., 1815?–35)	1815? / ? / ?	"Peace of 1815"	P-or-harp solo	WOLFE 6864	J. Hewitt, 1815?
Stefano Cristiani	1768?–ca. 1825?	Italy 1818? / Philadelphia? / same	to the Misses Izard & Deas	P-duet	WOLFE 2215	"author," 1819?
S. Cristiani			"to Miss Adele Sigoine"	harp-or-P solo	WOLFE 2214	G. E. Blake, 1820?
Peter K. Moran	?–1831	Ireland 1817 / New York / same	*Petit Sonata*	P ± Fl	WOLFE 6121; Wolverton 243–47	W. Dubois, 1820
Anthony Philip Heinrich	1781–1861	Bohemia 1818 / Philadelphia / Lexington, Ky.	"La buona Mattina"	P solo	WOLFE 3592	Bacon & Hart, 1820
J. F. W. Pchellas		Philadelphia by 1820?	3, "to Miss Mary Maden"	P & Vn	WOLFE 6863	"author," 1820
Jan Nepomucene Pychowski	1818–1900	Bohemia 1850 / New York / same	"Grande . . . ," Op. 8 in a	P & Vn	Sloan 25–32	J. Schuberth, 1857
Karl Merz	1836–90	Germ. 1854 / Philadelphia	"L'Inquiétude," Op. 50	P solo	LC; Howe 399–401	Russell, 1864
Caryl Florio (William James Robjohn)	1843–1920	Eng. 1857 / New York / touring	2, in A & B♭	P solo	Horton 195; Teal & Brown 41	C. J. Whitney, 1866

Name	Dates	Origin / Place	Year / Place	Work	Medium	Reference	Publisher
Dudley Buck	1839–1909	U.S. / Hartford	1862 / Brooklyn	Son. 1, Op. 22 in E♭	organ	Howe 683; Kremer 174	Beer & Schirmer, 1866
Whitney Eugene Thayer	1838–89	U.S. / Boston	1862 / Berlin	Sons. 1–4, Opp. 1, 4, 5, 8, in F, d, C, d	organ	Am. Suppl. 381; Kremer 225	Bote & Bock, 1865
Stephen Albert Emery	1841–91	U.S. / Portland, Me.	1864 / Boston	"Sonatella" 1 & 2, Opp. 9 & 11	P solo	Horton 193; Am. Suppl. 198	Henry Tolman, 1866 & 1867
Louis Falk	1848–1925	Germ. / Rochester	1859 / Chicago	Op. 7	P solo	LC; Am. Suppl. 39	author, 1867
Otto Singer	1833–94	Germ. / New York	1867 / same	"Grosses Duo . . . ," Op. 3	Vn & P	Sloan 39–44; Howe 444–46	J. Schuberth, 1864
Smith Newell Penfield	1837–1920	U.S. / Rochester?	1869? / same	"Poem of Life," Op. 10	P solo	Horton 194; Am. Suppl. 324–25	Root & Cady, 1870
G. R. Paine	?–?	? / ?	? / Portland, Me.?	2, in C & B♭	P solo	LC	Stockbridge, 1870 & 1871
Hugh Archibald Clarke	1839–1927	Canada / Philadelphia	1859 / same	"Three Easy . . ."	P solo	Horton 193	W. H. Boner, 1872
Richard Zeckwer	1850–1922	Germ. / Philadelphia	1870 / same	2 Sonatinas	P solo	LC; BAKER 1840	G. André, 1875
George Matzka	1825–83	Germ. / New York	1852 / same	Son. in D	Vn & P	Sloan 33–39	E. Schuberth (New York), 1876
D. Buck			Brooklyn	Son. 2, Op. 77 in g	organ	Kremer 174; Howe 683	G. Schirmer, 1877
Albert Rowse	?–?		? / New York? ? / ?	"Ariel"	P solo	LC	Pond, 1879
Walter Russell Johnston	?–?		? / New York? ? / ?	one Son.	P solo	LC	E. Schuberth, 1879
Henry Morton Dunham	1853–1929	U.S. / Brockton, Mass.	1870 / Boston?	Op. 10 in g	organ	Am. Suppl. 192; Kremer 180; Salter/MTNA 11	A. P. Schmidt, 1882
Minnie Koch	?–?		? / Philadelphia? ? / ?	one Son.	P solo	LC	J. J. Hood, 1884
Henry Maylath	1827–83	Aust. / New York	1867 / same	6 "Sonatines," Op. 301	P solo	LC; BAKER 1053	Grand Conservatory, 1884
Charles Fradel	1821–88	Aust. / New York	1861 / same	6 "Sonatines," Op. 505	P solo	Horton 66–77, 193–94, 202; LC	Grand Conservatory, 1884 & 1885

Some Published Sonatas by U.S. Residents, in Order of First Editions (1801–1915) (Cont.)

Composer	Born-died	Natl. / arrived	1st U.S. post / res. at pub.	Title, op., &/or key	Scoring	References	Publisher, year
Preston Ware Orem	1865–1938	U.S. /	Philadelphia /	Son. in f	P solo	Horton 194; Am. Suppl. 317	F. A. North, 1885
Abram Kimmell	?–?	1885? /	same /	5 Sonatinas, Opp. 65–69	P solo	LC	author, 1885
H. Maylath		? /	Kansas City, Kan.	6(?) Sonatinas, Op. 151	P solo	LC	Grand Conservatory, 1885
Carl Venth	1860–1938	Germ. / 1880	New York / same	2 Sonatinas, Opp. 17, 18	P solo	LC; BAKER 1696–97	J. O. von Prochazka, 1885, 1886
H. Maylath			New York	Sonatina	P solo	LC	Grand Conservatory, 1886
William F. Sudds	1843–1920	Eng. /	Boston?	3 Sons., in F, A, c	P solo	Horton 195; BAKER 1598	F. A. Shaw, 1886
C. Fradel		"early" /	New York?	6 Sonatinas Op. 511 & 3 Op. 523	P solo	Horton 194; LC	Grand Conservatory, 1887
Henry Stephen Cutler	1825–1902	U.S. / 1852	Boston / ?	Son. in c	organ	Kremer 177	Oliver Ditson, 1887
William E. Ashmall	1860–1927	Eng. / ?	New York / same	2 Sonatinas, Op. 49	P solo	LC; Am. Suppl. 53	author, 1887
Frank L. Eyer	?–?	? / ?	? / ?	Sonatina in F, Op. 1/1	P solo	LC; Horton 193	John Church, 1887
Bruno Oscar Klein	1858–1911	Germ. / 1878	U.S. tours / New York	Op. 10 in G	P & Vn	Satter/MTNA 32; Am. Suppl. 262	Hofmeister, 1887
Horace Wadham Nicholl	1848–1922	Eng. / 1871	Pittsburgh / New York	Op. 13 in A	Vc & P	Am. Suppl. 311; Cat. NYPL XX 711	Rahter, 1888
Hugo Kaun	1863–1932	Germ. / 1887	Milwaukee / same	Op. 2 in A	P solo	SSB XI	Kaun (Berlin), 1888
George Philipp	?–?	? / ?	? / ?	Sonatina in C	P solo	Horton 194; LC	A. P. Schmidt, 1889
George Elbridge Whiting	1840–1923	U.S. / 1867	Hartford / Boston	"Grand" Son., Op. 25	organ	BAKER 1789–90; Kremer 230–31	A. P. Schmidt, 1890

Name	Dates	Origin/Year	/ Location	Work	Medium	Reference	Publisher, Year
Arthur Foote	1853–1937	U.S. 1874	/ Boston	Op. 20 in g	P & Vn	Sloan 79–84; Shand 220–22	A. P. Schmidt, 1890
Carl Christian Müller	1831–1914	Germ. 1854	/ New York same	Op. 47/1 & 2 in f & b	organ	Kremer 209; Am. Suppl. 301	Kistner, 1890
H. M. Dunham		1854	/ same	Op. 16 in F	organ	Kremer 181	A. P. Schmidt, 1891
Lottie H. Taft	?–?	? / ?	Boston	"La Belle," Op. 4	P solo	LC	Broser & Schlam, 1892
Clara Kathleen Rogers	1844–1931	Eng. ?	/ San Francisco?	Op. 25 in d	Vn & P	Sloan 55–58	A. P. Schmidt, 1893
Edward (Alexander) MacDowell	1861–1908	US. 1871	/ New York Boston	"Tragica," Op. 45 in g/G	P solo	Gilman 36–37; Sonneck/SUUM 35	Breitkopf, 1893
J. B. Schmalz	?–?	1888	/ same ?	"Homesick," Sonatina	P solo	LC	Schwankovsky, 1894
Howard A. Brockway	1870–1951	? / Detroit? U.S. 1895	/ New York Berlin	Op. 9 in g	Vn & P	Mannes 111; Am. Suppl. 143–44; ART OF MUSIC IV 383	Schlesinger, 1894
Leo Rich Lewis	1865–1945	U.S. 1892	/ Boston same	Op. 3 in A	P & Vn	Sloan 129–136	H. B. Stevens, 1894
E. (A.) MacDowell			Boston	"Eroica," Op. 50 in g	P solo		Breitkopf, 1895
Alfred Monson	?–?	? / ?	Boston?	2 Sonatinas	P solo	LC	E. E. Tuette, 1895
Frederick Newell Shackley	1868–?	? / ?	/ Boston	Sonatina in C	P solo	Am. Suppl. 63; LC	Wood, 1895
Rubin Goldmark	1872–1936	U.S. 1891	/ New York same	Op. 4 in G	P & Vn	Am. Suppl. 122; Cobbett I 476–77	Breitkopf, 1896
Ernest Richard Kroeger	1862–1934	U.S. 1887	/ St. Louis same	Op. 32 in f#	Vn & P	Am. Suppl. 266; Sloan 109–114	Breitkopf, 1896
C. C. Müller			New York	Op. 61 in A	P & Vn	Am. Suppl. 301	Breitkopf, 1897
Carl Adolph Preyer	1863–1947	Germ. 1881	/ Newark Lawrence, Kan.	Son. 1 in c#, Op. 33	P solo	Gloyne 15, 25–26	Breitkopf, 1899
E. R. Kroeger			St. Louis	Op. 40 in Db	P solo	Am. Suppl. 266	Breitkopf, 1899

Some Published Sonatas by U.S. Residents, in Order of First Editions (1801–1915) (Cont.)

Composer	Born-died	Natl. / arrived	1st U.S. post / res. at pub.	Title, op., &/or key	Scoring	References	Publisher, year
Amy Marcy Beach	1867–1944	U.S. / 1883	Boston / same	Op. 34 in a	Vn & P	Shand 224–27; Cobbett I 79	A. P. Schmidt, 1899
Walter (Johannes) Damrosch	1862–1950	Germ. / 1885	New York / same	"At Fox Meadow," Op. 6 in G	Vn & P	Sloan 121–29	John Church, 1899
Herbert James Wrightson	1869–1949	Eng. / 1897	Philadelphia / Chicago?	Son. 3 in F, Op. 45	organ	BAKER 1825; Kremer 233	Clayton F. Summy, 1899
E. (A.) MacDowell			New York	"Norse," Op. 57 in d/D	P solo	Eagle passim	A. P. Schmidt, 1900
C. C. Müller			New York	Son. 3, Op. 57 in d	organ	Kremer 209	Breitkopf, 1900
Camille W. Zeckwer	1875–1924	U.S. / 1895?	Philadelphia / same	Son. 2, Op. 7 in D	Vn & P	Am. Suppl. 410	Breitkopf, 1900
Frederick Shepherd Converse	1871–1940	U.S. / 1898	Boston / same	Op. 1 in A	Vn & P	Shand 222–24	Boston Music, 1900
H. W. Nicholl			abroad?	"Symphonische Sonate," Op. 42 in a	organ	Sloan 58–59; Kremer 210	Peters, 1901
E. (A.) MacDowell			New York	"Keltic," Op. 59 in e	P solo	Eagle passim	A. P. Schmidt, 1901
Ralph Layman Baldwin	1872–	U.S.? / ?	? / Boston?	Op. 10 in c	organ	Kremer 168	G. Schirmer, 1901
Louis Adolphe Coerne	1870–1922	U.S. / 1894	Buffalo / Leipzig?	"Schwedische" Son., Op. 60 in a	Vn & P	Elson/AMERICAN 201–4	Hofmeister, 1901
William Henry Berwald	(1864–1948)	Germ. / 1892	Syracuse / same	Opp. 20 in B♭ & 21 in F	Vc & P, Vn & P	Am. Suppl. 131; Altmann 195, 253	Breitkopf, 1901
John Victor Bergquist	1877–1935	U.S. / 1895	Minneapolis / same	Son. in c	organ	Am. Suppl. 67; Kremer 170	Schlesinger, 1902
Henry Schoenefeld	1857–1936	U.S. / 1879	Chicago / same	Son. "quasi fantasia," Op. 53 in g	P & Vn	Sloan 85–92; Am. Suppl. 433–34	Simrock, 1903
Harry Newton Redman	1869–1958	U.S. / 1897	Boston / same	Op. 16 in c	Vn & P	Cobbett II 277; BAKER 1316	White-Smith, 1903

Name	Dates	Origin / date / place / place	Work	Medium	Reference	Publisher
Henry Holden Huss	1862–1953	U.S. 1885 / New York / same	Op. 19 in g	Vn & P	Sloan 114–21; Shand 228–30	G. Schirmer, 1903
Felix Borowski	1872–1956	Eng. 1897 / Chicago / same	Son. 1 in A	organ	Am. Suppl. 139; Kremer 172	Laudy, 1904
B. O. Klein		New York	Op. 31 in b	Vn & P	Sloan 92–98	Simrock, 1904
Louis Campbell-Tipton	1877–1921	U.S. 1900 / Chicago / same	Son. "Heroic" in c♯	P solo	Am. Suppl. 152; ART OF MUSIC IV 423	Wa-Wan Press, 1904
Louis Victor Saar	1868–1937	Holland 1894 / New York / same	Op. 44 in G	Vn & P	Cobbett II 320; Am. Suppl. 346	Kistner 1904
Frank Edwin Ward	1872–1953	U.S. 1902 / New York / same	Son. 2, Op. 9 in G	Vn & P	Am. Suppl. 399; ART OF MUSIC IV 393	Breitkopf (New York), 1904
William Henry Pommer	1851–1937	U.S. ? / ? / St. Louis	Op. 17 in a	P & Vn	Sloan 71–73	Rahter, 1905
W. H. Berwald		Syracuse	Op. 32 in c	Vn & P	Am. Suppl. 131; DM V/3 (1905–6) 171	Bosworth, 1905
H. N. Redman		Boston	Op. 17 in D	Vn & P	Cobbett II 277	White-Smith, 1905
F. Borowski		Chicago	Son. 2 in C	organ	Am. Suppl. 139; Kremer 172	Laudy, 1906
A. I. Earle	?–?	? / ? / Lawrence, Mass.?	Sonatina, Op. 15	P solo	LC	author, 1906
Frank Lynes	1858–1913	U.S. 1885 / Boston / same	Op. 49 in C	organ	BAKER 997; Kremer 203	A. P. Schmidt, 1907
Alexander Stewart Thompson	1859–?	? / ? / ?	Op. 21/1 in A	P solo	LC; Am. Suppl. 172, 381	Breitkopf, 1907
Mark Andrews	1875–1939	Eng. 1902 / Montclair, N.J.	Op. 17 in a	organ	Kremer 166; ASCAP 16	G. Schirmer, 1908
Percy Goetschius	1853–1943	U.S. 1890 / Syracuse / New York	Op. 15 in b/B	P solo	Am. Suppl. 221	G. Schirmer, 1908
H. M. Dunham		Boston	Op. 22 in d	organ	Kremer 180–81	A. P. Schmidt, 1908
Horatio William Parker	1863–1919	U.S. ? / Boston / New Haven	Op. 65 in e♭/E♭	organ	BAKER 1208–9; Kremer 211–12	G. Schirmer, 1908

Some Published Sonatas by U.S. Residents, in Order of First Editions (1801–1915) (Cont.)

Composer	Born-died	Natl. / 1st U.S. post arrived / res. at pub.	Title, op., &/or key	Scoring	References	Publisher, year
James Hotchkiss Rogers	1857–1940	U.S. / Cleveland 1883 / same	Son. in e	organ	Kremer 219; Am. Suppl. 342–43	G. Schirmer, 1910
W. E. Thayer		/ Boston	"Concert" Son. 5, Op. 45 in c	organ	Kremer 225	G. Schirmer, 1911
Arthur Shepherd	1880–1958	U.S. / Salt Lake City 1897 / Boston	Op. 4 in f	P solo	MQ XXXVI (1950) 159–79; ART OF MUSIC IV 418–19	G. Schirmer, 1911
Charles Frederick Dennée	1863–1946	U.S. / Boston 1883 / same	4 Sonatinas, Op. 36	P solo	LC; Am. Suppl. 187–88	A. P. Schmidt, 1911
Clara Anna Korn	1866–1940	Germ. / New York 1893 / same	"Nautical," Op. 14	P solo	Am. Suppl. 264; LC	Essex Music, 1911
Joseph Henius	ca. 1880–1912	? / New York ? / ?	Op. 9	Vn & P	ART OF MUSIC IV 393	Gray, 1911
Sigismund Stojowski	1869–1946	Poland / New York 1906 / same	Op. 37 in E	Vn & P	SSB XIII	Heugel, 1912
Mary Edwina Walker	?–?	? / ? ? / ?	Sonatina, Op. 7	P solo	LC	Willis, 1912
Julia Mary Canfield	?–?	? / ? ? / ?	Sonatina	P solo	LC	Willis, 1912
M. A. Andrews		? / ?	Son. 2, Op. 34 in c	organ	Kremer 166	H. W. Gray, 1912
Adolf Gerhard Brune	1870–1935	Germ. / Peoria, Ill. 1889 / Chicago	Op. 33 in d	P & Vn	Am. Suppl. 146; DM XII/1 (1912–13) 172	Schott, 1912
James A. Bliss	?–?	? / ? ? / Minneapolis?	Son. in C	P solo	LC	J. E. Frank, 1912
René Louis Becker	1882–1956	Alsace / St. Louis 1904 / same?	Opp. 40 in g, 41 in F, 43 in E	organ	Am. Suppl. 128; Kremer 170	G. Schirmer, 1912, 1912, 1913
John Alden Carpenter	1876–1951	U.S. / Chicago 1897 / same	Son. in G	Vn & P	Shand 236–37; Cobbett I 227	G. Schirmer, 1913

Name	Dates	Origin / Place	Work	Medium	Reference	Publisher
Heniot Lévy	1879–1946	Poland / Chicago / 1900 / same	Op. 6 in c	Vn & P	Am. Suppl. 270; DM XIII/1 (1913–14) 297	Ries & Erler, 1913
Daniel Gregory Mason	1873–1953	U.S. / New York / 1910 / same	Op. 5 in g/G	Vn & P	Mason/MUSIC 56–57, 163, 165, 170, 296–97	G. Schirmer, 1913
Harry Benjamin Jepson	1870–1952	U.S. / New Haven / 1895 / same	Son. in g	organ	Kremer 194	H. W. Gray, 1913
Frederic(k) Ayres (Johnson)	1876–1926	U.S. / Colorado Springs / 1900? / same	Op. 15 in d	Vn & P	Cobbett I 49; Upton/AYRES 40, 47–48, 58	Stahl, 1914
Pauline Hospes	?–?	? / ? / ? / Chicago?	Op. 2	P solo	LC	Wilcox, 1914
Mortimer Wilson	1876–1932	U.S. / Atlanta / 1911 / same	Opp. 16 in E & 14 in D	Vn & P	BAKER 1802–3	Boston Music, 1914, 1915
Charles Wakefield Cadman	1881–1946	U.S. / Pittsburgh / 1908 / Los Angeles	Op. 58 in A	P solo	Am. Suppl. 150	White-Smith, 1915

Some Unpublished Sonatas by U.S. Residents Listed in Order of Birth (1825–1882)

Composer	Born-died	Natl., main U.S. post (from)	Title, op., &/or key	Scoring	References	Year (when known)
George Frederick Bristow	1825–98	U.S., New York (1836!)	Op. 12 in G	Vn & P	at NYPL; Roger/BRISTOW 80–81, 143–44, 159–60	before 1850
John Knowles Paine	1839–1906	U.S., Boston (1862)	"Fantasia" Son. in d	organ	DWIGHT's XXIII (1863–64) 163	1863?
"	"	"	Op. 24 in b	P & Vn	Boston Public Library; Sloan 44–50	1875
Hugh Archibald Clarke	1839–1927	Canada, Philadelphia (1859)	2 Sons.	Vn & P	Sloan 147; Am. Suppl. 164	
Adolph Kölling	1840–?	Germ., Poughkeepsie (1872)	Sons. in c & C	P solo	Howe 668	
"	"	"	Son. in B(b?)	P & Vn	Howe 668; cf. Sloan 50–55	
Calixa Lavallée	1842–91	Canada, Boston (1882?)	?	Vn & P	Am. Suppl. 269	
Caryl Florio	1843–1920	Eng., New York (1857)	4 Sons.	Vn & P	Am. Suppl. 206	1879?
Isaac Van Vleck Flagler	1844–1909	U.S., Auburn, N.Y. (1878?)	Son. in G	organ	MT XXI (1880) 138, 244; BAKER 486	
Clara Kathleen Rogers	1844–1931	Eng., Boston (1874)	?	Vc & P	Sloan 55–58	by 1890
William Wallace Gilchrist	1846–1916	U.S., Philadelphia (1874)	?	organ	Salter/MTNA 31	ca. 1890?
Horace Wadham Nicholl	1848–1922	Eng., Farmington, Conn. (1888)	Op. 21 in D	Vn & P	Sloan 58–64; Cat. NYPL, XX–711	
Richard Zeckwer	1850–1922	Germ., Philadelphia (1870)	"several" sons.	P solo	MUSIC IV (1893) 48–49	1893
"	"	"	one Son.	Vn & P	"	
Louis Philipp Maas	1852–89	Germ., Boston (1880)	3 "important" Sons.	P solo or Vn & P	Howe 127–29; Am. Suppl. 277	after 1880?
Willard Burr	1852–1915	U.S., Boston (1880)	"Grand" Son., Op. 18 in Bb	P & Vn	Sloan 74–79; Am. Suppl. 54	after 1880?
Arthur Foote	1853–1937	U.S., Boston (1878)	Op. 76	Vc & P	Am. Suppl. 207–8	
Alfred Dudley Turner	1854–88	U.S., Boston (ca. 1870?)	2 Sons., in d & c	Vn & P	BAKER 1669; Sloan 153	ca. 1910?
Martinus Van Gelder	1854–1910?	U.S., Philadelphia (by 1893)	one "fine" Son.	Vn & P	MUSIC IV (1893) 51; Keller & Kruseman I 229	1893?
Helen Hopekirk	1856–1945	Scotland, Boston (1887)	2 Sons., in e & D	Vn & P	Am. Suppl. 245	
Henry Schoenefeld	1857–1936	U.S., Los Angeles (1904)	Op. 70	Vc & P	Am. Suppl. 354	
Edgar Stillman Kelley	1857–1944	U.S., San Francisco (1880)		P solo	New York Times Jan. 26, 1969 (H. Schonberg)	ca. 1878
Carl Venth	1860–1938	Germ., New York (1880)	one Son.	P solo	Am. Suppl. 396	
"	"	"	3 Sons.	Vn & P		
Harrison Major Wild	1861–1929	U.S., Chicago (1876)	one Son.	organ	Howe 252–53; MT XXII (1881) 649	1881?
Arthur Battelle Whiting	1861–1936	U.S., Boston (1885)	one Son.	Vn & P	Am. Suppl. 403–4; Sloan 153	ca. 1891
Edmund Severn	1862–1942	Eng., Hartford (1890?)	one Son.	Vn & P	Am. Suppl. 359	
Henry Holden Huss	1862–1953	U.S., New York (1885)	Op. 24	Vc & P	Am. Suppl. 248–49; GROVE IV 418	ca. 1910?
Carl Adolph Preyer	1863–1947	Germ., Lawrence, Kan. (1891)	Son. 2, in f	P solo	Gloyne 34, 88	1909

Name	Dates	Place (year)	Works	Medium	References	Date
Charles Frederick Dennée	1863–1946	U.S., Boston (1883)	2 Sons.	Vn & P	Howe 624, 626; Sloan 147	1885 & 1910
Winton James Baltzell	1864–1928	U.S., New York (1907)	one Son.	Vn & P	Hughes/AMERICAN 275–78; Sloan 146	before 1900
Harvey Worthington Loomis	1865–1930	U.S., New York (after 1893)	one Son.	P solo	Am. Suppl. 274	before 1900
"	"	"	one Son. + one "Lyric Finale"	Vn & P	Hughes/AMERICAN 84–85	
Edward Benjamin Scheve	1865–1924	Germ., Rochester (1888)	Son. in c	Vn & P	Am. Suppl. 352	
"	"	"	Son. in E♭	organ	"	
Maurice Arnold (Strothotte)	1865–1937	U.S., New York (by 1894)	Son. in e	P solo	ART OF MUSIC IV 433; Hughes/AMERICAN 136	ca. 885
"	"	"	one Son.			
Clara Anna Korn	1866–1940	Germ., New York (1893)	one Son.	Vn & P	Hughes/AMERICAN 139; Sloan 146	before 1900
William Edwin Hoesche	1867–1929	U.S., New Haven (1897?)	one Son.	Vn & P	Sloan 150; Am. Suppl. 264	
Henry Kimball Hadley	1871–1937	U.S., Garden City (1895)	one Son.	Vn & P	Sloan 148; Hughes/AMERICAN 500–502	
Percy Lee Atherton	1871–1944	U.S., Boston (by 1915)	2 Sons.	Vn & P	BAKER 635–36; Salter/AMERICAN 97	ca. 896
Edward Burlingame Hill	1872–1960	U.S., Boston (1894)	3 Sons.: in f♯, in E ("The Light that Failed"), "Patriotica"	P solo	Am. Suppl. 118 ART OF MUSIC IV 388–89	before 1896
Frank Edwin Ward	1872–1953	U.S., New York (1902)	Son. 1, in e	Vn & P	Am. Suppl. 399	before 1904
"	"	"	Sons. 1 (Op. 15) & 2, in f & d	organ	"	
Thomas Carl Whitmer	1873–1959	U.S., Columbia, Mo. (1899)	"Athenian" Son. in d	Vn & P	Am. Suppl. 404	"given many times", 1894–1908
Charles Edward Ives	1874–1954	U.S., New York (1899)	"Pre-First Violin Sonata"	Vn & P	Kirkpatrick/IVES item I.C.2	
Camille W. Zeckwer	1875–1924	U.S., Philadelphia (1895?)	(Son. 1), Op. 2	Vn & P	Am. Suppl. 410	before 1900
Frederic(k) Ayres (Johnson)	1876–1926	U.S., Colorado Springs (1900?)	Op. 16	P solo	ART OF MUSIC IV 417	by 915
"	"	"	Op. 17	Vc & P		
John Victor Bergquist	1877–1935	U.S., Minneapolis (1895)	2 Sons.	organ	Am. Suppl. 67	
Mabel Wheeler Daniels	1879–	U.S., Boston (1911)	one Son.	Vn & P	Sloan 147; BAKER 347	
Heniot Lévy	1879–1946	Poland, Chicago (1900)	Op. 12 in a	Vc & P	BAKER 947	
John Powell	1882–1963	U.S., Richmond (1912)	Sons. "psychologique" & "teutonica"	P solo	ART OF MUSIC IV 431–32; MGG X 1532	1912 & 1914

one among 46 miscellaneous songs and instrumental pieces that he had started to compose in 1818 and that were published in Philadelphia in 1820 with the collective title *The Dawning of Music in Kentucky, or the Pleasures of Harmony in the Solitudes of Nature, Opera Prima.*[38] Heinrich had worked his way to Kentucky after failure as a merchant in Philadelphia. Except for uncertain abilities as a pianist and violinist, his formal musical training, especially in theory and composition, his colorful, checkered career as "Father Heinrich," and some real successes at home and abroad still lay far ahead. The Sonata's dedication is a clue in itself to the musical mumbo jumbo that follows:

> Especially dedicated to the VIRTUOSOS of the United States: not as a NON PLUS ULTRA or NOLI ME TANGERE but as a "firstling" in its kind from the BACKWOODS and as a small Morning's Entertainment or "BUONA MATTINA" in addition to the SERENADE or "BUONA NOTTE," already presented to them [item 3 in the collection] by their most humble— . . .

First comes a two-page introduction in D, alla breve and "Alla maniera giusta," that consists of a separate, unexplained soprano part in coloratura operatic style, with an elaborate free accompaniment and with a dedicatory text in Italian beginning "Accettate gli Ossequi d'un povero Figlio d'Orfeo. . . ." Next comes an "Allegro di molto" in D, in 3/4 meter, that suggests a degree of musical imagination and pianistic flare in spite of being nothing but a clumsily written hodgepodge of opera and concerto impressions, mostly expressive melodic bits and cumbersome passagework treated sequentially and bombastic cadences.[39] Then follows an "Andante piu tosto Adagio" in d, 3/4 meter, that does the same more rhapsodically but still without any real melodic commitment, leading into a "Finale all Polacca" in Bb, 3/4 meter, that imparts a slight sense of theme and structure, if only because it divides into small repeated sections. The work closes with one more, perorative line of Italian text, though no separate soprano part this time: "Cari Amicivi auguro sempre felicissimi giorni Addio."

---

38. It is the 4th work in the collection as itemized on p. 261 of Upton/HEINRICH (a thorough, appropriately extravagant study of the man and his music); on p. 260 appears Heinrich's advertised proposal for this collection (1819), on p. 226 his recollection of it 36 years later, and on pp. 44–54 Upton's discussion of it, including (pp. 52–53) facs. of the first 2 pp. in the printed finale. Cf., also, Wolverton/KEYBOARD 420–29.

39. One wishes there were more reason to believe that the high praise of this Son. in Upton/HEINRICH 47 was written with tongue in cheek, although the concession that the "amateur is betrayed" suggests the contrary.

The Generation before MacDowell (Buck, Paine, Foote)

After the gap in sonata production, we may note first the one sonata of another Bohemian by birth and a pupil of Tomaschek, **Jan Nepomucene Pychowski** (1818–1900). His Op. 8 in a, for P & Vn, is a competent, lyrical, relatively free work in three movements (F-M-Sc), with pleasing ideas, traditional harmony, some distant modulations, and moderate exploitation as well as equal sharing of the two instruments (including some imitative exchanges).[40] The Sonata in B♭ for P solo by the English-born organist **Caryl Florio** (pseudonym for **William James Robjohn;** 1843–1920 [41]) is a rather fresh work unusual for its three-movement plan, M-Mi-Ro; its rondo finale, in which a chorale-like "Intermezzo—Larghetto, solennelle" serves both as one episode and a coda; and for the unhackneyed rhythmic structure of its phrases and scale passages in the 6/4 meter of its first movement. Florio's forms tend to be static and additive and the idiom to be a kind of extension of Classic styles (including considerable Alberti bass and repeated-note accompaniments).

A more renowned organist and composer of church music was **Dudley Buck** (1839–1909), an American by birth who set the pattern of foreign training by studying in both Germany and France.[42] Buck's "Second Sonata" for organ, Op. 77 in g, is dedicated to another fine American organist, Clarence Eddy. It is the first U.S. work introduced here that speaks in the Romantic idiom and the first that displays professional writing skills needing no apologies. That Mendelssohn is the primary style influence is not surprising for one who studied in Leipzig with Moscheles, Hauptmann, and Rietz.[43] The first of the three movements, "Allegro moderato ma energico," is a "sonata form"; the second, "Adagio molto espressivo," is an A-B-A design with an extended, florid, retrospective coda; and the finale, "Allegro vivace non troppo," is a driving rondo that was sure to please the crowd,[44] although it includes no section quite so surefire as the fughetta on "Hail, Columbia!" in the finale of Buck's first Sonata for organ. Buck's music is fluent, harmonically resourceful, and expressive (Ex. 123), although its themes usually lack distinction and too often border on the sentimental because of chromatic subdivisions of the line.

40. Cf. Sloan/VIOLIN 25–32, with exx.
41. Cf. GROVE Am. Suppl. 206, including reference to 4 (unpub.) Vn sons.
42. Cf. Howe/AMERICA 679–84.
43. GROVE I 992–93 (R. Aldrich).
44. Op. 77 was played at the 10th annual meeting of the Music Teachers National Association, in Boston in 1886 (MT XXVII [1886] 54; Salter/MTNA 25).

Ex. 123. From the return in the middle movement of Dudley
Buck's Sonata in g, Op. 77 (after the G. Schirmer ed. of 1877).

The pianist **Stephen Albert Emery** (1841–91) reveals almost the same
German training in his ingratiating "Erste Sonatella," Op. 9 in A, and
his more driving, scherzando "Zweite Sonatella," Op. 11 in c. Each
piece is a skillful, one-movement, near *perpetuum mobile* in "sonata
form" that might have come right out of Mendelssohn's *Songs Without
Words*. Still another American-born pianist (also, organist) with the
same German training and the same professional, resourceful command of the Mendelssohnian idiom and of the instrument was **Smith
Newell Penfield** (1837–1920). Penfield's *Poem of Life, Four Characteristic Pieces in the Form of a Sonata,* adequately suggests the nature of
its four separately published movements by their effusive titles alone—
"Parnassus" ("Allegro moderato," E♭, 4/4; starting with full, rolled
chords), "The Vale of Romance" ("Adagio," c, 3/4; starting with
rising, chromatic, dotted patterns), "The Cascade of Pleasure" ("Scherzo
and Trio, Allegretto," C, 2/4), and "The Stream of Time" ("Rondo,
Allegro brillante," E♭, 6/8).

Of two German-born composers of violin sonatas in New York, **Otto
Singer** (1833–94) had studied with Moscheles, Hauptmann, and Liszt,
among others, before coming here in 1867,[45] two years before the pub-

45. Howe/AMERICA 444 mentions a Son. for P solo composed while he was still
in Leipzig.

lication of his *Grosses Duo (in Sonatenform) in einem Satze*, Op. 3 in
c.[46] This last is a grandiose, somewhat repetitious and hollow movement of eighteen pages. The thick, chordal piano part, with its Lisztian
arpeggios, tremolo, and sequential climaxes puts the less idiomatic,
simpler violin part in the shade. The other German, **George Matzka**
(1825–83), was a stringsman, as might be guessed from the more
idiomatic, though not virtuosic, violin part in his Sonata in D of
1876.[47] This work, in three movements (F-Ro-VF), is more conventional,
concentrated, and straightforward in form and style.

Continuing to draw from our tabulations (*supra*), we find only elementary pedagogic material, although of a generally appealing, graceful sort, in the "easy sonatas" and sonatinas for P solo by several

Ex. 124. From the start of an unpublished Sonata in D, Op.
21, by Horace Wadham Nicholl (after the autograph at the New
York Public Library).

esteemed teachers, including **Hugh Archibald Clarke** (1839–1927),
Henry Maylath (1827–83), **Charles Fradel** (1821–88), **Carl Venth**
(1860–1938), and **William F. Sudds** (1843–1920). But somewhat more
advanced in purpose and content is the Sonata in f, for P solo, by the
Philadelphia teacher **Preston Ware Orem** (1865–1938). This work,
another example of the fluent Mendelssohnian idiom, may be incomplete, for it contains only a driving first movement in f, curious
for its square, clipped phrase rhythms, and a songful "Andante quasi
allegretto" in B♭. The unpublished piano sonata has not been found
here that **Edgar Stillman Kelley** (1857–1944) wrote during study in
Stuttgart (*ca.* 1878?) and played for Liszt, never to forget how Liszt
played much of it right back to him from aural memory.[48] We shall

46. Cf. Sloan/VIOLIN 39–44, with exx.
47. Cf. Sloan/VIOLIN 33–39, with exx.; BAKER Suppl. 85.
48. Cf. H. Schonberg's column in *The New York Times* for Jan. 26, 1969.

have to leave without further mention the "Homesick Sonatina" by one J. B. Schmalz, on our tabulation.

Several MS sonatas for Vn & P from the later 19th century deserve serious mention. The unpublished, 32-page Sonata in D, Op. 21, for Vn & P, by the English-born organist **Horace Wadham Nicholl** (1848–1922) [49] is an impassioned, energetic, virtuosic, often florid work, intriguing for its rhythmic diversity and ingenuity as well as for some rapid, remote modulations and some melodic chromaticism that occasionally challenge its tonal stability.[50] The bold rising leaps by which the first of its three movements opens (F-S-F) brings Richard Strauss's instrumental openings to mind (Ex. 124). By contrast, the unpublished, 29-page Sonata in G, Op. 12 (before 1850?), by the New York violinist and organist **George Frederick Bristow** (1825–98) is less sophisticated

Ex. 125. From the recapitulation, second theme, in the first movement of George Frederick Bristow's Sonata in G, Op. 12 (after the MS at the New York Public Library).

in its songlike charm and Weberian brilliance, yet not without freshness and originality in its figuration and in the well-contrasted styles of its three movements (M/F-M-Ro).[51] The violin often doubles one or another element in the piano part (Ex. 125).

Among further unpublished sonatas for Vn & P, Op. 24, in b, by one of the most influential American organists, composers, and music educators of the 19th century, **John Knowles Paine** (1839–1906), was composed in 1875, after his training in Berlin and in the same year that he assumed the first American professorship of music, at Harvard Uni-

49. Cf. BAKER 1157.

50. Cf. Sloan/VIOLIN 58–64, with exx. High praise for Nicholl's fugal mastery in his "Symphonische Sonate" for organ, Op. 42 in a, is voiced in MT XLII (1901) 748.

51. Cf. its description on pp. 80–81, 143–44, 159–60, and 190 (item 18), of Rogers/BRISTOW, a valuable recent diss. on the man, his environment, and his music.

Ex. 126. From the start of the finale of John Knowles Paine's Sonata in b, Op. 24 (after the autography, dated 1875, at the Boston Public Library).

versity.[52] This duo and the earlier Fantasia Sonata in d, for organ, also unpublished,[53] were Paine's only ventures in the sonata. Op. 24 is an extended work (46 pp. of MS) in three movements, including an "Allegro con fuoco" in "sonata form," a "Larghetto" in the relative major key and in rondo design, and a canonic, cursive, monothematic finale, "Allegro vivace," back in the home key of b/B (Ex. 126). In the first movement the style is plain and direct in harmony, melody, and texture, and the main idea is amply reiterated and developed, all making for telling, sincere music when the effect is not a bit cut-and-dried. The second movement is more ornate, graceful, and melodically flowing. And the finale reveals the fluent drive of Mendelssohn as its canonic motive recurs in varied guises. Another Bostonian, the Ohio-born, German-trained composer and writer **Willard Burr** (1852–1915), left a MS duo, "Grand Sonata" in b♭, in which the three movements (F-M-F) are interrelated in all their elements by a triplet motive that prevails in the opening theme.[54] The development of materials is con-

52. Cf. BAKER 1199, with further bibliography; Sloan/VIOLIN 44–50 (with exx.); Salter/AMERICAN 22 (Op. 24, played in New York in 1885 for the Music Teachers National Association).

53. Played by Paine himself in 1863 (DWIGHT's XXIII [1863–64] 143).

54. Cf. Sloan/VIOLIN 74–79, with exx. The MS is at the Library of Congress.

siderable, the harmony is rich, the tonal range is wide (especially in the flat keys), and the melodic lines are active, although more through somewhat empty scale and chord figures than truly inventive patterns.

Among published sonatas of the later 19th century for Vn & P should be noted Op. 20 in g by still another Bostonian, **Arthur Foote** (1853–1937), one of Paine's several notable students and himself a fine pianist and organist.[55] This work is cast in four movements, VF-M-S-VF, with a light, *perpetuum mobile* B section, "Allegretto grazioso," following a songful A section, "Alla Siciliana," in the A-B-A design of the second movement. The ideas, harmony, and treatment are conservative but not dull. Also in Boston lived the English-born, German-trained soprano, teacher, pianist, and composer **Clara Kathleen Rogers** (1844–1931). She first performed her so-called "Sonata dramatico" in public in 1888 with Loeffler as the violinist.[56] It is a three-movement work, F-M-F, that is like Foote's in being conservative in all respects, apart from a few remote modulations, yet not without musical, especially melodic, appeal.

More abreast of the times in Europe is the duo, Op. 3 in A, that the American-born composer and educator **Leo Rich Lewis** (1865–1945) wrote during or just after his training under Rheinberger in Munich (1889–92). That training helps to explain the resourceful harmony and the imaginative, concentrated development of ideas, particularly their contrapuntal imitative treatment, in all three movements (F-S-VF).[57] In warmth and rhythmic urge Lewis came closer to Brahms than to his teacher. There is a Sonata in b, Op. 4, for P & Vn, by the Vienna-trained student of R. Fuchs, **Rubin Goldmark** (1872–1932; nephew of Karl), who later became identified with the Juilliard School in New York. It is described as "romantic in content and classical in form, and [it] exhibits vigorous inventiveness," yet is still "in the formative stage."[58]

The Four Sonatas by MacDowell

From the standpoints of high contemporary praise, wide international endorsement, and persistent success as publications, the four

---

55. Cf. Sloan/VIOLIN 79–84, with exx.; BAKER 494–95, with further bibliography; GROVE Am. Suppl. 207–8 (listing an unpub. Son. for Vc & P, Op. 76, not seen here). Op. 20 is reviewed in SMW L (1892) 23 as a delightful if not very original work that avoids "foolhardy problems."

56. Cf. Sloan/VIOLIN 55–58, with exx.; BAKER 1359.

57. Cf. Sloan/VIOLIN 129–36, with generous exx.; BAKER 948.

58. Cobbett/CHAMBER I 476–77 (A. Shepherd); but SMW LIX (1901) 948 finds it lacking in both originality and energy. Cf. BAKER 583–84.

piano sonatas by **Edward (Alexander) MacDowell** (1861–1908) easily outrank any other U.S. sonatas produced before World War I.[59] Furthermore, apart from the recent, mainly historical interest in Reinagle's sonatas (*supra*) and the belated interest in Ives's sonatas (and his other music) that has developed only in the last generation, Mac-Dowell's sonatas are the sole examples from that whole century-and-a-quarter that have survived, whether in print, recordings, or public performance. In fact, they seem even to have won some new interest in recent years.[60] To be sure, we can no longer accept the numerous extreme statements that his contemporaries made (speaking volumes for themselves, too) about the greatness of his sonatas, of which the following is but one sample:

> If there is anything in the literature of the piano since the death of Beethoven which, for combined passion, dignity, breadth of style, weight of momentum, and irresistible plangency of emotion, [that] is comparable to the four sonatas . . . [of MacDowell], I do not know of it. And I write these words with a perfectly definite consciousness of all that they may be held to imply.[61]

Nor, for that matter, need we accept the complete reversal of the critical pendulum, within two decades, as in the following disconnected remarks by Paul Rosenfeld:

> . . . as late as the Tragic and Heroic sonatas, [MacDowell continued to be] a mere sectary of the grandiose German romantics. . . . We cannot avoid hearing a reminiscence of the pompous Meistersinger march in the slow movement of the Celtic sonata. . . . The echoes are not only Wagnerian; the theme of the finale of the Celtic sonata has a strong resemblance to that of The Hall of the Mountain King in Grieg's Peer Gynt Suite. And to the end, MacDowell shared his school's narrowness of artistic vision, embracing little outside the confines of homophonic music. He was badly equipped in polyphonic technique; and where, as in a passage of the last movement of

59. A main source on the man and his music, in spite of what now seem like much inflated evaluations, is Gilman/MACDOWELL. A helpful style study of the sons., prefaced by their artistic and historical orientation, is Eagle/MACDOWELL (an M.A. thesis of 1952). Of value as shorter surveys of MacDowell that emphasize the sons. are the separate sections or chaps. in Hughes/AMERICAN 34–57, Howard/AMERICAN 323–44, and, especially for their superior examinations of his aesthetic posture and its up-to-date perspective, Chase/AMERICA 346–64 and Austin/20th 54–56.

60. For 2 recent articles intended to revive interest, cf. Kaiserman/MACDOWELL (on Opp. 59 and 50) and Lowens/MACDOWELL (including listings of recordings of Opp. 45, 50, and 59 in "A Selective Discography" [with M. L. Morgan]).

61. Gilman/MACDOWELL 161. ("Plangency" is a favorite word in MacDowell criticism.) Cf., also, Eagle/MACDOWELL 12–14 (citing W. S. B. Matthews, H. T. Finck, A. Seidl, J. Massenet, J. Huneker, W. Mason, and H. E. Krehbiel); Hughes/AMERICAN 52.

the Norse sonata, he attempted canonic imitation, we find him essaying it clumsily, and with all the obsessive rapture of a child in possession of a new and dazzling toy. . . . He never attained real facility in moving his ideas, or in moving himself through them . . . whether we wander in the Guinevere section of the Sonata Eroica, or in the Old-Fashioned Garden of the New England Idylls, we are never far from the little old rendezvous. . . . The feelings entertained about life by him seem to have remained uncertain; and while fumbling for them he seems regularly to have succumbed to "nice" and "respectable" emotions, conventional, accepted by and welcome to, the best people. It is shocking to find how full of vague poesy he is. Where his great romantic brethren, Brahms, Wagner, and Debussy, are direct and sensitive, clearly and tellingly expressive, MacDowell minces and simpers, maidenly and ruffled. He is nothing if not a daughter of the American Revolution. . . .[62]

We must recognize such extreme judgments as the norm rather than the exception in a late-Romantic environment that found MacDowell himself giving vent, for example, to a severe deprecation of Mozart's piano sonatas. They are, he said, "entirely unworthy of . . . any composer with pretensions to anything beyond mediocrity. They are written in a style of flashy harpsichord virtuosity such as Liszt never descended to, even in those of his works at which so many persons are accustomed to sneer." [63] In short, MacDowell's four sonatas must be viewed in moderation here, as containing some of the best music by a gifted U.S. composer of limited aesthetic range.

MacDowell's four piano sonatas and two piano concertos are his only complete works of the sonata type within a modest output of about 100 works that consists mostly of solo piano pieces, solo songs, and part songs.[64] With regard to their circumstances, he composed the first two of his sonatas during his Boston years (1888–96) and the other two during his lucid New York years (1896–1905). More specifically, he composed all four during approximately the eight years from 1892 to 1900, or during approximately the last two-fifths of his over-all, 24-year creative life (1879–1903).[65] And he saw all four first published within a span also of eight years, 1893 to 1901.[66] He himself introduced "Sonata tragica," Op. 45 in g/G, to the public, first playing the third movement in Boston in 1892, the year before publication, and the whole sonata in that city in 1893. A critic wrote, "One feels genius in it

62. Rosenfeld/AMERICAN 40–46 passim.
63. MacDowell/ESSAYS 194; cf., also, pp. 193, 200, 239, and 253, as well as SCE 500.
64. Cf. Sonneck/SUUM 87 ("MacDowell Versus MacDowell: A Study in First Editions and Revisions"); Gillman/MACDOWELL 92–93.
65. The available information on MacDowell's composition dates is generally vague.
66. The complex pub. details of the first eds. and some later printings are unraveled in Sonneck/MACDOWELL 35, 38, 41, 42.

throughout. . . . The composer played it superbly, magnificently." [67]
Among others who soon performed it, too, was the American pianist
William Mason, who first played Op. 45 at a summer colony (by
1894)—in fact, played it almost daily throughout the season, completely winning over his audiences (more so than when he later played
Op. 50 in a similar experiment).[68] Most early reactions to this work
were highly favorable; but some found too conscious an obligation to
"sonata form" in MacDowell's first such effort.[69] And one early review
of the original Breitkopf & Härtel edition of "Sonata tragica" found
excesses, especially in the contrasts and chromaticism, even allowing
for the dramatic implications of the title.[70] That title has been related
to MacDowell's "memory of his grief over the death of his master
Raff," [71] although without further programme, dedication, or other
evidence and although Raff had died a full decade earlier (ssb X),
shortly after MacDowell's two years of studies with him in Frankfurt.
But, apparently some time before 1900, MacDowell's wife explained
the programme without mentioning Raff, as simply a desire

to heighten the darkness of tragedy by making it follow closely on the heels
of triumph. Therefore, he attempted to make the last movement a steadily
progressive triumph, which, at its climax, is utterly broken and shattered.
In doing this he has tried to epitomize the whole work. While in the other
movements he aimed at expressing tragic details, in the last he has tried to
generalize; thinking that the most poignant tragedy is that of catastrophe
in the hour of triumph.[72]

MacDowell's "Sonata eroica," Op. 50 [73] in g, was composed, presumably, in 1894–95 (i.e., between the pub. of Opp. 45 and 50). The composer deplored his own first performance of it in Boston (in 1895?),
although his wife and others "thought he did it wonderfully" and it
soon won new (though less) interest, as a "noble," freer, and "lovelier,"
if less "dynamic," work than Op. 45.[74] This time he did supply a dedication, a subtitle, and a programme. He dedicated Op. 50 to William

67. Cf. Gilman/MACDOWELL 36–37, 69, 147–50 (including a facs. of Op. 45/iii/1–7
in MS).
68. MASON MEMORIES 255–56; cf. [nephew Daniel Gregory] Mason/MUSIC 53; MUSIC
IX (1895–96) 429–31 (W. S. B. Mathews on the pedagogical values of Op. 45).
69. Several reactions are cited in Eagle/MACDOWELL 22–24.
70. SMW LIV (1896) 194.
71. Gilman/MACDOWELL 148. Cf. Eagle/MACDOWELL 20–22 for follow-ups of this
interpretation.
72. Quoted in Hughes/AMERICAN 53–54. An emotional 4-line poem by Philip
Becker Goetz, headed "MacDowell's Sonata Tragica," appears, isolated, in MUSIC
XI (1896–97) 503.
73. Originally it was to be Op. 49 (Sonneck/MACDOWELL 38).
74. Gilman/MACDOWELL 92, 152–53; Eagle/MACDOWELL 25; MASON MEMORIES 256;
MUSIC X (1896) 309–10 (W. S. B. Mathews on W. Mason and Op. 50).

Mason, perhaps rewarding Mason's share in popularizing Op. 45. When Op. 50 appeared (Nov., 1895), he wrote Mason that there were parts "of the sonata I am fond of and parts of it I have felt deeply, though I am afraid they—the feelings—are not fully expressed." [75] The subtitle of Op. 50 is "Flos regum Arthurus" ("The Flowering of Arthur's Princes" or more freely, "The Heyday of the Round Table") and his elaboration of it appeared not in any further inscriptions nor in the separate movement titles but in a later commentary (written for Gilman?):

> While not exactly [literal?] programme music, I had in mind the Arthurian legend when writing this work. The first movement typifies the coming of Arthur. The scherzo [an "interruption" or "aside" that might have been omitted, MacDowell confessed still later, in New York] was suggested by a picture of Doré showing [in Tennyson's *Guinevere*] a knight in the woods surrounded by elves. The third movement was suggested by my idea of Guinevere. That following represents the passing of Arthur.[76]

None of the implied programmes in this or MacDowell's other three sonatas happens to raise directly the fuzzy question of American music versus American composer,[77] analogous to the question of nationalism in Grieg's music (ssb XV). But they do raise the equally fuzzy question in MacDowell's aesthetic of sound per se versus sound as but one access to the poetic idea.[78] Whether MacDowell was or was not a programmatist at heart, it is hard to believe that the actual composition of his sonatas was not guided by considerations primarily musical.

MacDowell's "impulse to write" his "Third Sonata," Op. 57 in d, "was enhanced," according to his wife's later recollection,[79] "by the close friendship which existed between him and Edvard Grieg. They never saw each other, but they corresponded constantly." Grieg accepted MacDowell's proffered dedication in a charming letter in his own "bad English," [80] the date of which, Oct. 10, 1899, at least suggests about when the composition had been completed. The Nordic, colorful, eight-line poem at the head of Op. 57 provides another link with Grieg. Furthermore, this poem's publication in 1903, slightly extended, under the title "Norse Sonata" in a collection of *Verses by Edward MacDowell* [81] probably explains the title by which Op. 57 is generally

75. More of the letter is quoted in Mason/MUSIC 53.
76. As quoted in the course of Gilman/MACDOWELL 150–53.
77. Cf. Howard/AMERICAN 323, 326–27; Chase/AMERICA 354–56; Lowens/MACDOWELL 62, 69; Eagle/MACDOWELL 6–11 (various sources quoted); Gilman/MACDOWELL 83–85.
78. Cf. the illuminating discussion in Chase/AMERICA 356–59; also, Howard/AMERICAN 328–29; and the composer's own words in MacDowell/ESSAYS 254–73.
79. MacDowell/MACDOWELL 19.
80. A facs. of the original and a printed version are both given in Gilman/MACDOWELL 72–73.
81. Cf. Sonneck/MACDOWELL 41–42.

known. But as in his other three sonatas, nothing in the music of Op. 57, notwithstanding efforts to find a Nordic programme,[82] keeps Mac-Dowell's four sonata titles from being completely interchangeable. Yet Op. 57 seems to have posed more problems for MacDowell's contemporaries (and interested its own composer less[83]) than the other three sonatas (and is today the only one not recorded and the only one so rarely played). Although one German reviewer praised it along with Op. 59 as "tone poems in the highest sense," [84] the American organist and writer W. S. B. Mathews balked when he came to Op. 57, finding it incomprehensible and intolerable.[85] He discussed at length how MacDowell achieved his primary goal, originality, only through tonality "so vague as to leave all accidentals alike probable or improbable, according to the weird fancy of the player"; through rhythm, of which there is a "total absence" in the senses of pulsation, flow, and symmetry; through "fundamental harmonies" that are "unusual and forced"; and through "almost universal dissonances."

MacDowell composed his "Fourth Sonata (Keltic)," Op. 59 in e, presumably in 1900 (between the pubs. of Opp. 57 and 59). Originally he had sought to dedicate it to "Fiona Macleod," a pseudonym (as he did not then realize) for the Mr. and Mrs. William Sharp whose joint collection of stories and sketches, *Lyra Celtica* (1896), seems to have been the literary "inspiration" for Op. 59. Perhaps MacDowell's own Scotch-Irish ancestry had a bearing, too. At any rate, when Mr. Sharp's delighted acceptance failed to reach him[86] MacDowell decided to dedicate this work, too, to Grieg. However, this time the initial bit of verse does not relate nationalistically to the dedicatee:

> Who minds now Keltic tales of yore,
> Dark Druid rhymes that thrall,
> Deirdre's song and wizard lore
> of great Cuchullin's fall.

Following this quatrain in the 1903 collection of *Verses by Edward MacDowell* is a 22-line poem on the majestic death of Cuchillin (beginning "Cuchullin fought and fought in vain"). MacDowell wrote Gilman that the longer poem did not "entirely fit the music [only the coda of the finale, surmises Gilman]," that it might yet underlie "another musical form [a symphonic poem never started, surmises Gil-

82. E.g., Gilman/MACDOWELL 153–54; MUSIC XIX (1900–1901) 411 (W. S. B. Mathews). Cf. Eagle/MACDOWELL 26–27.

83. Gilman/MACDOWELL 71.

84. MW XXXIII (1902) 686 (E. Segnitz).

85. MUSIC XIX (1900–1901) 410–12.

86. Neither he nor MacDowell lived to learn that it probably got sidetracked, according to MacDowell/MACDOWELL 20.

man]," that it still could implement an "understanding of the *stimmung* of the sonata," and that in any case, "as with my 3d Sonata, the music is more a commentary [or " 'bardic' rhapsody," he said elsewhere] on the subject than an actual depiction of it [Beethoven's "more through feeling than tone painting," again; scᴇ 525]." [87]

The first two of MacDowell's four sonatas begin with separate, slow introductions and have four movements, with scherzando types in second place—S/F-VF-S-VF and S/F-Sc-S-VF. The last two have only three movements, both M-M-F, leaving out the scherzando types (such as had given MacDowell doubts in Op. 50). In length the sonatas are average for the time—854, 843, 478, and 579 measures, respectively. All four sonatas are in minor keys except for characteristically Romantic shifts to the tonic major mode in Opp. 45/iv and 57/iii. Apart from Op. 50/ii in the minor key on the mediant (b♭), the inner movements are all in nearly-related keys. Thematic ties, more or less subtle, largely interrelate the contrasting ideas within a movement (e.g., the introduction and main theme in Op. 50/i or the main and subordinate themes in Op. 59/iii) and all the movements of each sonata. By these internal and over-all relationships, MacDowell was putting into practice two of his own quoted dicta, about "sonata form" and form in general:

> If the composer's ideas do not imperatively demand treatment in . . . ["sonata form"]—that is, if his first theme is not actually dependent upon his second and side themes for its poetic fulfillment—he has not composed a sonata movement, but a potpourri, which the form only aggravates.[88]
>
> Form should be a synonym for *coherence*. No idea, whether great or small, can find utterance without form, but that form will be inherent to the idea, and there will be as many forms as there are adequately expressed ideas. In the musical idea, *per se*, analysis will reveal form.[89]

Although, from one to the next, MacDowell's sonatas get somewhat freer in tempo, thicker in texture, and more smoothed over at the joints, they still adhere throughout to the standardized designs—in fact, to but two of them, "sonata form" (with only such variants as the omission of nearly all but the main theme in the recapitulation of Op. 45/iv) and the A-B-A design. Neither in form nor in style was MacDowell an experimenter or innovator in his day.

With regard to chief style traits, MacDowell reveals a severely limited but markedly individual group of solutions to specific situations in his four sonatas, with mood, tempo, and major or minor

---

87. Cf. Gilman/ᴍᴀᴄᴅᴏᴡᴇʟʟ 151–61 (including a facs. of the autograph of Op. 59/i, last page).
88. As quoted in Gilman/ᴍᴀᴄᴅᴏᴡᴇʟʟ 147.
89. MacDowell/ᴇssᴀʏs 264.

mode being main determinants (or main consequents, depending on one's point of view). In these senses any one sonata could do for them all, with Op. 45 being no worse for being first and slightly more restrained and Op. 59 no better for being last, slightly more bombastic, and MacDowell's own favorite.[90] Their enjoyment is limited only by the style limitations and their rapidly cloying effect, and it is only impeded, not helped, by those superimposed programmes, especially today, when musicians tend to reject both the fact and the nature of such idyllic and chimerical associations. For that matter, at least as regards styles rather than forms, the sonatas disclose little new to all who know such favorite piano pieces as "From a Wandering Iceberg" and "From Uncle Remus" (cf. the first 2 themes in Op. 59), or "Scotch Poem" and "Told at Sunset" (cf. Op. 50/i and iii).

Turning first to MacDowell's melodies, we find these typically to be wide-ranged, particularly in the slowest sections or movements and in the gayest or most energetic themes, where they may roam over more than half of the keyboard (e.g., Opp. 50/iii, throughout, and 57/i/44–66). Their range tends to be narrower, not surprisingly, in themes of "simple tenderness" like that in Op. 59/ii (recall "To a Wild Rose") or in "swift," crisp themes like that in Op. 59/iii (recall "In Autumn"). More than anything else, what seems to give MacDowell's themes their special modal or American Indian flavor, along with the inevitable lowered-7th step, is their centering around leaps or gaps in the underlying scale—for example, mostly around 3–1 in the introduction to Op. 45/i, or 5–3 in the second theme, "simply, yet with pathos," in Op. 50/i. Certain frequent rhythmic patterns add individuality to MacDowell's melodies, too, including ♩ ♪♩ in both 3/4 and 4/4 meter (e.g., the main themes of Op. 45/i and iv) or ♫♩ and, simply, ♫♪ as a triplet or compound pulse, often an upbeat (e.g., Op. 57/iii). Frequent, too, are Scotch snaps (e.g., Op. 57/i/44–62), strategically located syncopations (e.g., Opp. 45/iii/5 or 59/ii/20), and the amplified pulse created by afterbeat accompaniments (e.g., the "Maestoso," triple forte, "grandioso" return near the end of Op. 45).

MacDowell's harmonic vocabulary, chromaticism, use of dissonance, and tonal range are all considerable, yet all more conservative, law-abiding, and metrically controlled than the early reports of them would suggest. Again, it is a few specific treatments or devices that impart the special flavor, most of which are well-known in, for example, "To a Water-lily." Those "unusual and forced" uses of "fundamental harmonies" that W. S. B. Mathews found (*supra*) might refer to such

90. He put Op. 50 second and also had a special fondness for Op. 45/iii (Gilman/ MACDOWELL 71).

harmless passages as that in Op. 57/i/19–23, where each 7th or 9th chord resolves into another 7th or 9th chord, and Op. 57/i/40–43, where, mainly, chromatic and diatonic appoggiaturas over a pedal bass disguise but do not invalidate a simple I_4^6-IV-ii-I_4^6-V-I progression. A characteristic procedure of MacDowell, and one that carries him perilously close to the brink of sentimentality, is the opposition of "fundamental harmonies" to a melodic line that descends chromatically from its peak, as in Ex. 127. Also characteristic and near to sentimentality in that example are the several major-7th dissonances, occurring both as passing notes and as untied suspensions. By such innocent means MacDowell achieved his most tender moments of poetic

Ex. 127. From the third movement of Edward MacDowell's "Sonata eroica," Op. 50 in g (after the revised Schirmer ed. of 1924).

yearning (as in Op. 50/i/121) as well as his most naughtily dissonant climaxes (as at the quadruple forte near the end of Op. 59).

MacDowell's writing for piano shows all the variety and the understanding of the instrument that can be expected of a pianist fine enough to win Liszt's own warm praise.[91] One may find writing that is heavy and chordal (Op. 59/i/16–23), thin and scherzando or fleet (Op. 50/ii), intricate in the changing figures of its passagework (Op. 59/i/84–99), purely homophonic (Op. 57/i/10–40), or moderately polyphonic and more often and successfully so than writers have generally granted [92] (e.g., the telling, concurrent lines in Opp. 45/iii/32–61 and 50/iii/57–69; or the motivic play in Op. 45/i/185–93). Yet all these traits also are typed in MacDowell's sonatas (and other piano music),

91. Cf. the reports collected in Gilman/MACDOWELL 16–19, 85–92.
92. Recall P. Rosenfeld's criticism, *supra*.

and recur often enough to become further identification tags of his style.

MacDowell's individuality is as marked, in fact, as that of the composer he most closely resembles in style, Grieg (SSB XV).[93] Though Grieg was older by eighteen years, the two men shared about the same stage of development in the language of music. Furthermore, they are often similar in more specific ways, as in their modal treatments of the scale, their problematical positions as musical nationalists, their limited range of output, and, indeed, their limited artistic scope, including the dependence of each on a few characteristic solutions to certain recurring musical situations. Most of these similarities apply to their respective sonatas, although the latter reveal no resemblances quite so close as those between the first lyrical piano themes in their respective Concertos in e and d. Coming half a generation later, MacDowell proved to be a kind of exaggeration of Grieg (and in this sense a little closer to Rachmaninoff [94]). Not necessarily did he hover still closer on that brink of sentimentality. (As always, of course, one must be both willing and able to hear each work on its own terms and in its own milieu.) But he did strive for still wider emotional extremes (including greater extremes in the dynamic indications, insofar as Mrs. MacDowell's revisions and amplifications in all 4 sons. of his somewhat careless and inadequate editorial markings are authentic[95]). But apart from the extremes, which are likely to reflect less in MacDowell's favor, MacDowell must be acknowledged as Grieg's superior in two respects. He handled the larger forms more naturally and more flexibly, mainly because he handled phrase-and-period syntax more naturally and more flexibly.[96] And he scored more interestingly and more knowingly for what was to him a "cold" yet favorite instrument, the piano.[97] Indeed, whatever his limitations, performers are likely to return to one or another of his sonatas again and again, perhaps more than to Grieg's Op. 7, for several compelling reasons. The sonatas abound in frank songful melody, in opportunities to emote with judicious abandon, and in piano writing that makes good sounds and pleasurable technical challenges (Ex. 128). Furthermore, the forms are invariably timed right and last only long enough to state their messages and achieve their goals.

93. Their styles are compared in Howard/AMERICAN 325–26.

94. But in Bertennson & Leyda/RACHMANINOFF, Rachmaninoff is quoted as disliking MacDowell's Concerto (in d?) when Carreño played it in 1906.

95. Cf. her preface to the G. Schirmer re-editions of Opp. 45 and 50 in 1922 and 1924; also, MacDowell/MACDOWELL 20–21.

96. Service/CADENCE 43–62 finds the structural landmarks clearly defined, largely owing to traditional harmony and clear phrase structure.

97. Cf. his own words to a friend as quoted in Eagle/MACDOWELL 3.

Ex. 128. From the opening of Edward MacDowell's "Sonata tragica" in g/G, Op. 45 (facs. of the autograph, with the kind permission and co-operation of the Butler Library at Columbia University).

MacDowell's Contemporaries and Successors

Among some contemporaries and successors to MacDowell in the field of the piano sonata, the active St. Louis pianist, organist, and teacher **Ernest Richard Kroeger** (1862–1934) left a three-movement example, Op. 40 in D♭ (F-S-VF), that shows good compositional training but utterly banal content. The same reaction greeted his Sonata for Vn & P, Op. 32 in f♯, which has a similar movement plan.[98] The equally active Kansas pianist **Carl Adolph Preyer** (1863–1947), born and trained in Germany, left three completed examples. Op. 33 in c♯ is a four-movement work (F-M-Sc-VF), well reviewed when he first played it in Cincinnati in 1899.[99] Op. 50 in f, less highly regarded by Preyer himself, has a similar cycle, of which only the third movement was published ("The Brook-Nymphs").[100] "Sonata No. 4," in E♭ (without op. no. and preceded by an incomplete Son. in F), won a prize in 1939 from the National Federation of Music Clubs and was published posthumously by Carl Fischer in 1949. In spite of its outdated idiom and slightly pedagogical flavor, this three-movement, "highest fulfillment" of "Preyer's gifts" (VF-S-Sc) is still fresh in its clean pianistic scoring, its imaginative rhythm and harmony, and some genuine melody (including references to a cheer and the alma mater song of the University of Kansas).[101]

Other late piano examples include *Sonata Heroic* in c♯, by the German-trained Chicagoan **Louis Campbell-Tipton** (1877–1921). This is an effective, 22-page, one-movement "sonata form" in the epigonic grand manner, with a stentorian main theme that reportedly depicts the "Hero" and a tender, expressive subordinate theme that reportedly depicts the "Ideal." [102] The Sonata in B♭, Op. 15 for P solo, by **Percy Goetschius** (1853–1943) reveals that this long-lived, successful teacher and writer of theory texts could have done well, too, by continuing as a composer. Although not published until 1908, Op. 15 is the same sonata[103] that the young man from New Jersey showed to both Liszt

98. MW XXVIII (1897) 670. Cf. Sloan/VIOLIN 109–14; GROVE Am. Suppl. 266; ART OF MUSIC IV 380.

99. Cf. pp. 25–26 in the interesting and thorough, albeit somewhat idolatrous, monograph on the man and his music, Gloyne/PREYER, including full list of works (pp. 87–91).

100. Gloyne/PREYER 34, 49–50,.88.

101. Gloyne/PREYER 47–48, 78–82 (detailed description).

102. No such identifications appear in the score, but cf. ART OF MUSIC IV 422–24. Cf., also, GROVE Am. Suppl. 152.

103. According to information kindly contributed (along with the score itself) by the late Arthur Shepherd of Cleveland. Cf., also, Shepherd/GOETSCHIUS, especially pp. 309–10; BAKER 580–81; MGG V 458 (N. Broder), listing a few compositions as well as texts.

(hence, by 1886) and Brahms while he was a student, then a teacher, in Germany. As he was to recall proudly, Liszt suggested a textural change, then kissed him on the cheek; and Brahms read it all the way through, making only one comment, "Chopin," after a particular passage. But Beethoven, Schumann, and Brahms himself are still more in evidence in this knowing, warm, rich, well scored, frankly melodious, moderately free work of three movements (F-S-VF).

The three organ sonatas by the Chicago violinist **Felix Borowski** (1872–1956) include No. 3 in d (pub. by A. P. Schmidt in 1924) and were preceded by *Grande Sonate russe* for P solo, which was reportedly liked by Grieg and had been composed and published (by Lowdy of London in 1896) before Borowski left England.[104] The Sonata in e♭/E♭, Op. 65 for organ, by the eminent composer of the oratorio *Hora Novissima,* **Horatio William Parker** (1863–1919), reveals in its concentrated motivic development the influence of his teacher Rheinberger.[105] Its four traditional, well-constructed movements include an "Allegro moderato" in "sonata form"; an "Andante" in B, in A-B-A design; an "Allegretto" in b♭, in A-B-A design; and a "Fugue."

The Richmond pianist **John Powell** (1882–1963), who studied in Vienna with Leschetizky and Karl Navrátil (ssb XVII), left three sonatas for P solo and two for Vn & P, all composed between 1908 and 1928.[106] The piano sonatas are further titled "Psychologique" (Op. 15), "Noble" (Op. 21, pub. by G. Schirmer in 1921), and "Teutonica" (Op. 24), and the first violin work is called "Sonata Virginianesque" (pub. by G. Schirmer in 1919). But the music does not bear out the interest promised in these titles and by the success of Powell's *Rapsody Nègre*. It is dull and unidiomatic in its scoring, academic in its approach to form, and indifferent in melodic and harmonic material except for its use of Negro and folk ideas.

Further late violin sonatas include Op. 34 in a (1899) by the Boston pianist Mrs. **Amy Marcy Cheney Beach** (1867–1944), a conservative, Brahmsian, four-movement work (F-Sc-S-VF) of real warmth, charm, structural skill, and imagination. This work was once widely played.[107] Op. 6 in G, "At Fox Meadow," by the German-born, New York conductor **Walter (Johannes) Damrosch** (1862–1930),[108] is a three-move-

104. Cf. BAKER 185; Cat. NYPL IV 372; Kremer/ORGAN 172.
105. Cf. BAKER 1208–9, with further bibliography.
106. Cf. MGG X 1532 (N. Broder); Mason/MUSIC 298–99; ART OF MUSIC IV 431–32.
107. Cf. BAKER 104; Goetschius/BEACH 17 (facs. of first p. of the autograph), 46, 83, 110–19 (numerous laudatory reviews); Cobbett/CHAMBER I 79 (A. Shepherd); Shand/VIOLIN 224–27 (with exx.); MUSIC XI (1896–97) 473–74 (collected, laudatory reviews of performances prior to pub.).
108. Cf. Sloan/VIOLIN 121–29, with exx.

ment work (F-M-F) that begins by pleasing with its warm melodies and good scoring and ends by glutting with its excessive, uncontrolled sweetness and passion (recalling Glazunov's sons., ssв XVIII). Nor is one persuaded in Damrosch's favor by such near plagiarisms as the start of the second movement, which gets uncomfortably close—hardly by accident!—to that in Brahms's Concerto in B♭. The Op. 1 in A (1900) by the esteemed Bostonian who studied with Rheinberger in Munich, **Frederick Shepherd Converse** (1871–1940), is an innocuous, four-movement work (F-M-Mi-F) still betraying the student.[109] Later a Sonata by him for Vc & P was published (1922), this time a rhapsodic, warm work in two movements (S-F). And still later a Sonata in a, for P solo, appeared (1937), a similarly convincing work in three movements (F-S-F) that differs only in coming but slightly more to grips, and somewhat uneasily, with newer directions in harmony, tonality, and independent dissonance.

The prizewinning "Sonate (*quasi Fantasia*)," Op. 53 in g, for P & Vn, by the Chicago pianist **Henry Schoenefeld** (1857–1936) confirms his good German training in title, publisher, as well as writing skills. But it is his pioneer interest in Negro music that shows through the content, including lively syncopations, folklike melodies, dramatic contrasts, and colorful scoring.[110] By contrast, the two violin sonatas of the Boston teacher **Harry Newton Redman** (1869–1958) are more restrained and melodically direct.[111] The one published Sonata, Op. 19 in g, for Vn & P, by the New York pianist and pupil of Rheinberger in Munich, **Henry Holden Huss** (1862–1953), is also a transparent work, in spite of some fresh approaches to harmony and rhythm (especially in both the "Andante" and scherzando sections of ii).[112] It would be still more interesting if the writing for both instruments were not somewhat pedestrian.

The German-born, New York pianist **Bruno Oscar Klein** (1858–1911) was another Rheinberger composition student in Munich (1876–77?), just before emigrating to America.[113] Of two published sonatas by him for Vn & P, Op. 10 in G (Hofmeister in Leipzig, 1887) is a four-movement work (F-M-F-F) reviewed as skillful and knowing, though "unoriginal";[114] and Op. 31 in b (Simrock in Berlin, 1904; ded. to Ysaÿe)

---

109. Cf. BAKER 313–14; Cobbett/CHAMBER 301 (A. Shepherd); Shand/VIOLIN 222–24 (with exx.).
110. Cf. Sloan/VIOLIN 85–92, with exx.; GROVE Am. Suppl. 354; ART OF MUSIC IV 433–34.
111. Cf. BAKER 1316; Cobbett/CHAMBER II 277 (A. L. Goldberg).
112. Cf. GROVE IV 418 and Am. Suppl. 248–49; Sloan/VIOLIN 114–21, with exx.; Shand/VIOLIN 228–30. At least 3 later duo sons. remain in MS.
113. Cf. BAKER 4th ed. 589–90.
114. MW XX (1889) 419.

is a somewhat more brilliant, chromatic, unidiomatic work in three
well integrated movements, still reflecting Schumann and Brahms but
also showing the rhythmic, melodic, and harmonic influence of
Dvořák's music after his directorship at the National Conservatory in
New York.[115] Like Klein, the Dutch-born composer **Louis Victor
(Franz) Saar** (1868–1937) had studied with Rheinberger (as well as
Brahms during a winter in Vienna) and he taught at the National
Conservatory in New York. His one published Sonata, Op. 44 in G,
for Vn & P (pub. by Siegel in Leipzig, 1904) was reviewed as evidence
that Americans still depended on German training and as a feminine
counterpart to Dirk Schäfer's Op. 6 of the same year and scoring (SSB
XIII).[116] Another traditional work is the three-movement Sonata in a
(F-S-VF), Op. 17 (pub. by Rahter in Hamburg, 1905), by the St. Louis
organist and teacher **William Henry Pommer** (1851–1937), who had
enjoyed training under Reinecke, Richter, and Bruckner, among
others.[117]

The one Sonata by the important Chicago composer **John Alden
Carpenter** (1876–1951) is somewhat ungrateful to play for both violinist
and pianist, especially in the first of its four unorthodox, free movements (S-F-S-VF).[118] The compositional skill is considerable and both
the melody and harmony are enterprising. But there is little of the
distinction or character to be found in Carpenter's later, more successful works. The two mature sonatas by the equally important American
composer, author, and longtime professor of music at Columbia University, **Daniel Gregory Mason** (1873–1953), are characteristic of the
conservatism, exceptional craftsmanship, and scholarly reflection in
his music. Op. 5 in g, for Vn & P, was composed in 1907–8 and
published in 1913 by G. Schirmer. It won considerable approval—from
Paderewski and John Powell, among others[119]—but gave the composer
some doubts about its final worth. Broad melodic arches, plastic
rhythm, concentrated motivic play, good scoring, harmonic warmth,
and a strong Brahmsian flavor (with no sign of Mason's post-American
study under d'Indy) are the predominant traits in all three movements (F-M-VF[Ro]). Op. 14 in c, for Cl-(or-Vn) & P, was composed in

115. Cf. Sloan/VIOLIN 92–98, with exx.
116. MW XXXVIII (1907) 280 and NZM C (1904) 819. Cf. GROVE Am. Suppl. 346
(with mention of a Vc son. and a Hn son., too); BAKER 1394; Cobbett/CHAMBER II
320 (A. L. Goldberg).
117. BAKER 4th ed. 856; cf. Sloan/VIOLIN 71–73, with exx.
118. Cf. BAKER 253–54; Shand/VIOLIN 236–37, with exx.; Cobbett/CHAMBER I 227
(C. Engel).
119. Cf. Mason/MUSIC 165, 170–71, 296–97; also, pp. 56–57 on Paderewski's pleasure
in hearing Mason play his early Son. in B♭ for P solo. Cf., further, Shand/VIOLIN
230–32, with exx.; ART OF MUSIC IV 386; SSB V (ex. from Op. 5/i).

1912 and 1915 and was published in 1920 after it had become both an immediate occasion for founding (in 1919–20) and a first product of the Society for the Publication of American Music.[120] Dedicated to another of S.P.A.M.'s founders, the late educator, composer, and clarinetist B. C. Tuthill, Op. 14 is likewise a Brahmsian, three-movement work (M-VF-F).[121]

A student of E. S. Kelley and A. Foote, **Frederic Ayres (Johnson;** 1876–1926) left one published Sonata, Op. 15 in d, which, appearing in 1914, marks "the culmination of Ayres' earlier, more tentative period." [122] Its two movements, a slow, gentle, expressive opening and a rushing, rollicking, rondo finale, are distinguished by intensive, unsuppressed lyricism. Ayres also left one sonata each in MS for P solo (Op. 16), and for Vc & P (Op. 17, a free fantasy ded. to Pablo Casals), both by 1915, and a technically difficult "Second Violin Sonata," in b, one of his last MSS.[123] There is one published Sonata, Op. 6 in c, for Vn & P, by the Polish-born, Chicago pianist **Heniot Lévy** (1879–1946), who had studied composition with Max Bruch in Berlin. It was reviewed as a strong, concentrated, traditional work of four movements.[124] The two published violin sonatas on our tabulations (*supra*) by the American organist **Mortimer Wilson** (1876–1932) reflect his training under Reger in Leipzig, with their mercurial harmonic chromaticism, thorny technical problems, and complex rhythms.[125] Wilson's 11-page "Sonatilla" in C, Op. 52 for P solo (1919), is consistent in style with its predecessors but in a diminutive, simpler, effective projection of that style throughout its four short movements (F-Sc-M-F).

Trained in Pittsburgh, **Charles Wakefield Cadman** (1881–1946) became identified especially with American Indian music.[126] In fact, the flavor of that music, including its modal inflections and primitive rhythms, shows through even in both of his published sonatas—Op. 58 in A, for P solo (1915) and Sonata in G, for Vn & P (1932). Yet, in defiance of verses inscribed before each movement, a firm note at the start of Op. 58 insists that "No Indian or Negro themes are used in this work." Both works have the three-movement plan F-S-F. Both are somewhat rhapsodic and the second in particular stretches the tonal relationships. But this music is not innovational; nor does it come to

120. Cf. Mason/MUSIC 186–87.
121. Cf. Cobbett/CHAMBER II 123 (A. Shepherd).
122. Upton/AYRES 40, 47–48 (with exx.). Cf., also, Cobbett/CHAMBER I 49 (A. Shepherd); BAKER 62.
123. Cf. Upton/AYRES 49, 57, 59. But the P Son. is listed only in ART OF MUSIC IV 417.
124. DM XIII/1 (1913) 297 (W. Altmann). Cf. BAKER 947.
125. Cf. BAKER 1802–3; Cobbett/CHAMBER II 586 (A. L. Goldberg).
126. Cf. BAKER 239; Cobbett/CHAMBER I 224 (A. L. Goldberg).

grips with the sonata idea in any consequential manner—that is, by building the structures out of the development of basic ideas. The ideas themselves are songful bits that do not seem to invite development.

The Latin-American Sonata in the Romantic Era

No sonatas have turned up here by residents in Canada during the Romantic Era.[127] And those by residents in Latin-American countries are too few, too obscure, too often unpublished, and too inconsequential to justify much more than passing mention in one approximately chronological order (rather than chronologically by countries). Only passing mention is all that is given to these same works in the principal over-all encyclopedia of Latin-American music, Mayer-Serra/LATINOAMERICA.[128] Not until after our approximate limit here of World War I did a substantial rise begin in the Latin American cultivation of the sonata. It should be noted that even before then the primary influences and training were Italian and French rather than German.

The Cuban pianist **Nicolás Ruiz Espadero** (1832–90), influenced and praised by Gottschalk, is credited with a *Gran Sonata* for P solo in MS.[129] The Brazilian **Flavio Elisio** (actually **Alfredo d'Escragnello Taunay;** 1843–99) left a Sonata in e♭, for P solo, presumably Chopinesque and in MS.[130] The pianist and "grand old man of Argentine music" **Alberto Williams** (1862–1952) left a total of six sonatas, composed between 1905 and 1917 and published between about 1920 and 1923 by Gurina in Buenos Aires.[131] Five are duos, including Opp. 49 in a, 51 in d, and 53 in D, for Vn & P; Op. 48 in e, for Fl & P; and Op. 52 in D, for Vc & P. These fully competent examples of "musica culta" recall his study with Franck both in their harmonic style and cyclical treatment. Williams' Op. 74, *Primera Sonata Argentina* for P solo, is, as its title suggests, closer to his interest in native rhythms and melodies. In fact, an initial inscription tells us, "This Sonata is inspired by motives of Argentine dances and popular songs." Its four movements

127. Cf. MacMillan/CANADA 114–18; Kallmann/CANADA, especially pp. 235–55.
128. Chase/LATIN AMERICA is a valuable guide to further literature and orientation.
129. Mayer-Serra/LATINOAMERICA II 864–65.
130. Mayer-Serra/LATINOAMERICA I 342.
131. Cf. GROVE IX 302–3 (N. Fraser); Slonimsky/WILLIAMS; COMPOSITORES II 136–55 (full list of works with composition years), especially 141, 147, 154; Cat. NYPL XXXIII 421 (with pub. years approximated).

are labeled "Rumores de la Pampa," "Vidalita," "Malambo," and "Gauchos alegres" (Ex. 129).

In 1895 the Italian-, German-, and French-trained Brazilian, **Alberto Nepomuceno** (1864–1920), performed an early Sonata for P solo of his own composing.[132] Another Brazilian, trained in France and Germany, **Sylvio Deolindo Frões** (1865–?), is credited with sonatas for both P solo and Vn & P.[133] An Argentine violinist, **Ricardo Rodríguez** (1877–?), was training under d'Indy when he wrote an early Sonata in e, for P solo, followed by a later Sonatina for P solo and a still later, prize-winning Sonata for Vn & P (1943).[134] The home-trained Chilean violinist **Pédro Humberto Allende** (1885–1959) left four early, unpublished sonatas composed between 1906 and 1915, all for P solo.[135]

Ex. 129. From the opening of the finale in Alberto Williams' *Primera Sonata Argentina,* Op. 74 in c♯/D♭ (after the Gurina ed., *ca.* 1923).

The Costa Rican composer **Julio Fonseca** (1885–1950) studied in Milan before writing an unpublished Sonata in B for Vn & P.[136] And the Argentine conductor **Celestino Piaggio** (1886–1931) studied under d'Indy before writing a Sonata in c♯, for P solo (pub. in Buenos Aires not before 1913).[137] This work occasionally recalls the chromatic harmony and lyricism of d'Indy, but it more generally employs the traditional harmony, the regular phrase syntax, and the technically convenient figurations that mark the epigonic Romantic rather than the incipient Modern.

132. Mayer-Serra/LATINOAMERICA II 680–82. Cf. BAKER 1152.
133. Mayer-Serra/LATINOAMERICA I 315.
134. Mayer-Serra/LATINOAMERICA II 845.
135. Mayer-Serra/LATINOAMERICA 25–31, with dated, full list of works.
136. Mayer-Serra/LATINOAMERICA I 386–88.
137. Cf. Mayer-Serra/LATINOAMERICA II 775.

Bibliography

Note: All the short-title references in the footnotes and main body of the present book, as well as some initials used only in this Bibliography to represent the most cited periodicals, will be found in the one alphabetical listing that follows. References with a lower-case "-m" at the end indicate sources made up primarily of music. Articles in GROVE and MGG and single volumes in the various "Denkmäler" series do not have separate entries in the Bibliography, but their authors or editors are cited where the first references occur during any one discussion in the text.

Abbott/FORM William W. Abbott, Jr., "Certain Aspects of the Sonata-Allegro Form in Piano Sonatas of the 18th and 19th Centuries," unpublished Ph.D. diss., Indiana University, 1956.

Abendroth/PFITZNER Walter Abendroth (ed.), *Hans Pfitzner: Reden, Schriften, Briefe.* Berlin: Hermann Luchterhand, 1955.

Abraham/CHOPIN Gerald Abraham, *Chopin's Musical Style,* corrected ed. (first pub. in 1939). London: Oxford University Press, 1960.

Abraham/GRIEG ——— (ed.), *Grieg: A Symposium.* Norman: University of Oklahoma Press, 1950 (first pub. in England, in 1948).

Abraham/LEKEU Pat Abraham (trans.), "Lekeu in His Letters," MMR LXXVI (1946) 62–64, 85–89, 107–11.

Abraham/RESEARCH Gerald Abraham, "Modern Research on Schumann," PMA LXXV (1948–49) 65–75.

Abraham/RUSSIAN ———, *On Russian Music.* London: William Reeves, [1939].

Abraham/SCHUBERT ——— (ed.), *The Music of Schubert.* New York: W. W. Norton, 1947.

Abraham/SCHUMANN ———, *Schumann: A Symposium.* London: Oxford University Press, 1952.

Abraham/SIBELIUS ———, *Sibelius: A Symposium.* London: Lindsay Drummond, 1947.

Abraham/STUDIES   Gerald Abraham, *Studies in Russian Music*. London: William Reeves, [1935].

Abraham/TCHAIKOVSKY   —— (ed.), *The Music of Tchaikovsky,* including Chap. 6 on "The Piano Music," by A. E. F. Dickinson. New York: W. W. Norton, 1946.

Abraham/II & III   Gerald Abraham, "Schumann's Op. II and III," MMR LXXVI (1946) 123–27, 162–64, 222.

Adler/SCHUBERT   Guido Adler, "Schubert and the Viennese Classic School," MQ XIV (1928) 473–94.

AdMZ   *Allgemeine deutsche Musikzeitung* (*Allgemeine Musikzeitung* from 1883). 1874–1943.

AfMW   *Archiv für Musikwissenschaft*. 1918–27, 1952——.

Albrecht/CENSUS   Otto E. Albrecht, *A Census of Autograph Music Manuscripts of European Composers in American Libraries*. Philadelphia: University of Pennsylvania Press, 1953. A suppl. is in progress as of 1969.

Alekseev/FORTEPIANNAIA   Aleksandr Dmitrievich Alekseev, *Russkaia fortepiannaia muzyka ot istokov do vershin tvorchestva* ("Russian Piano Music from the Origins to the Peak"). Moscow: Izd-vo Akademii nauk SSSR, 1963.

Alekseev & Novikova   Unpub. critique of SSB XVIII kindly prepared in 1968 by Professor Aleksandr Dmietrivich Alekseev and trans. and suppl. by Miss Erna F. Novikova, both of Moscow.

Allen/PHILOSOPHIES   Warren Dwight Allen, *Philosophies of Music History*. New York: American Book Co., 1939.

Al'shvang/TCHAIKOVSKY   Arnold Al'shvang, *Peter Ilyitch Tchaikovsky*. Moscow, 1951. References are cited here by way of Alekseev & Novikova.

Altmann/BACH-ZITATE   Wilhelm Altmann, "Bach-Zitate in der Violoncello-Sonate Op. 38 von Brahms," DM XII/1 (1912–13) 84–85.

Altmann/BRAHMS-m   —— (ed.), *Johannes Brahms: Quintet F moll für Pianoforte, 2 Violinen, Viola und Violoncell, Op. 34*. Leipzig: Ernst Eulenberg, [preface dated 1926].

Altmann/GOLDMARK   Wilhelm Altmann, "Karl Goldmark's Kammermusik," DM XIV/2 (1914–15) 209–21, 255–66.

Altmann/KAHN   ——, "Robert Kahn," DM IX/4 (1909–10) 532–63.

Altmann/KAMMERMUSIK   ——, *Kammermusik-Katalog*, 6th ed. (to Aug., 1944). Leipzig: Friedrich Hofmeister, 1945. Cf. Richter/KAMMERMUSIK.

Altmann/WEBER   ——, "Aus Gottfried Weber's brieflichem Nachlass," SIMG X (1908–9) 477–504.

AM   *Acta musicologica*. 1928——.

AMA   *Allgemeiner musikalischer Anzeiger* (Frankfurt/M). Nos. 1–52, 1826–27.

AMZ   *Allgemeine musikalische Zeitung.* 3 series: 1798–1848, 1863–65, 1866–82. The editors (and authors of most of the unsigned reviews) for the first series were J. F. Rochlitz until 1827, G. W. Fink until 1841, C. F. Becker in 1842, M. Hauptmann until 1846, and J. C. Lobe to the end. Cf. Mendel/ LEXIKON XI 453, 459; Freystätter/ZEITSCHRIFTEN 32–34; GROVE VI 669; Hedler/TÜRK 16–17; Haupt/ MÜLLER 13–14; MOSCHELES II 199. A reprint of the complete set was announced by Frits Knuf (Hilversum, Holland) in 1967.

Anderson/BEETHOVEN   Emily Anderson (ed. & trans.), *The Letters of Beethoven,* 3 vols. London: Macmillan, 1961.

Anth. NÄGELI-m   Johann (Hans) Georg Nägeli (ed.), *Repertoire des clavecinistes,* 26 sons. (and other pieces) in 17 "Suites" (vols.). Zürich: Nägeli, 1803–10. Cf. AMZ V (1802–3) 579–80 and Intelligenz-Blatt 97–100; HIRSCH MUSIKBIBLIOTHEK IV item 1012; Heyer/ HISTORICAL 278; MGG IX 1245–48 (Schanzlin & Walter) and VIII 961 (H. P. Schanzlin); SCE 26; SSB IV.

Apel/DICTIONARY   Willi Apel, *Harvard Dictionary of Music.* Cambridge: Harvard University Press, 1944.

ART OF MUSIC   Daniel Gregory Mason (ed.), *The Art of Music, a Comprehensive Library of Information for Music Lovers and Musicians,* 14 vols. New York: National Society of Music, 1915–17.

Asaf'ev/RUSSIAN   Boris Asaf'ev (or Igor' Glebov, pseudonym), *Russian Music, from the Beginning of the Nineteenth Century,* trans. from the original Russian ed. (Moscow, 1930) by A. J. Swan. Ann Arbor: J. W. Edwards (for the American Council of Learned Societies), 1953.

ASCAP   *The ASCAP Biographical Dictionary of Composers, Authors, and Publishers,* 3d ed. (first ed. in 1948), compiled and ed. by The Lynn Farnol Group. New York: The American Society of Composers, Authors and Publishers, 1966.

Austin/20th   William W. Austin, *Music in the 20th Century, from Debussy through Stravinsky.* New York: W. W. Norton, 1966.

Bache/BACHE   Constance Bache, *Brother Musicians: Reminiscences of Edward and Walter Bache.* London: Methuen, 1901.

Bachmann/VIOLINISTES   Alberto Bachmann, *Les grands Violinistes du passé* (including many thematic identifications). Paris: Librairie Fischbacher, 1913.

Badura-Skoda/CZERNY   Paul Badura-Skoda (ed.), *Carl Czerny: Über den richtigen Vortrag der sämtlichen beethoven'schen Klavierwerke.* Vienna: Universal, 1963.

Bagge/SCHUBERT — [Selmar Bagge?], "Franz Schubert als Claviercomponist," DMZ III (1862) 1–3, 25–28, 33–34, 41–43. The promised continuation never appeared, but the son. section seems to be complete.

Bagge/SONATA — Selmar Bagge, "Die geschichtliche Entwickelung der Sonate," in Waldersee/VORTRÄGE II 203–24.

Bagier/REGER — Guido Bagier, *Max Reger*. Stuttgart: Deutsche Verlags-Anstalt, 1923.

BAKER — Nicolas Slonimsky (ed.), *Baker's Biographical Dictionary of Musicians*, 5th ed.; plus *1965 Supplement*. New York: G. Schirmer, 1958. The 5th ed. is intended except when the 4th ed. of 1940 is specified.

Balakirev/PIANO-m — Mily Alexeyevitch Balakirev, *Complete Piano Works*, ed. by K. S. Sorokin, 3 vols. in 5 parts. Moscow: State Music Publishers, 1949–54. Cf. Gardner/BALAKIREV 325.

Balogh/DUETS-m — Erno Balogh (ed.), *Eighteen Piano Duets . . .* , including Mussorgsky's Son. in C. New York: G. Schirmer (Library Vol. 1764), 1953.

Balzer/NIELSEN — Jürgen Balzer (ed.), *Carl Nielsen: Centenary Essays*. London: Dennis Dobson, 1966.

Barenboim/RUBINSTEIN — L. A. Barenboim, *Anton Grigorievitch Rubinstein*. Leningrad, 1954. References are used here by way of Alekseev & Novikova.

Barker/REGER — John Wesley Barker, "Reger's Organ Music—3," MT CIX (1968) 170–73.

Bartók/UNGHERIA — Béla Bartók, "Della Musica moderna in Ungheria," PIANOFORTE II (1921) 193–97.

Barzun/BERLIOZ — Jacques Barzun, *Berlioz and the Romantic Century*, 2 vols. Boston: Little, Brown, 1950.

Bauer/SCHUBERT-m — Adolf Bauer, "Scherzo aus der Klaviersonate E-moll (Juny 1817 [D. 566]) von Franz Schubert," with mod. ed. of the complete "Scherzo" and facs. of the holograph of its "Trio," in DM XXI (1928–29) 13–16 and suppls. after pp. 16 and 48.

Beaufort/LISZT — Raphaël Ledos de Beaufort, *Franz Liszt: The Story of His Life, to Which Are Added Franz Liszt in Rome by Nadine Helbig*. Boston: Oliver Ditson, 1887 [and 1910].

Becker/CLAVIERSONATE — Carl Ferdinand Becker, "Die Claviersonate in Deutschland," NZM VII (1837) 25–26, 29–30, 33–34. Revised, with exx. added, in Becker/HAUSMUSIK 33–39.

Becker/HAUSMUSIK — ———, *Die Hausmusik in Deutschland in dem 16., 17. und 18. Jahrhundert. . . .* Leipzig: Fest'sche Verlagsbuchhandlung, 1840. Cf. Becker/CLAVIERSONATE.

Bellamann/ALKAN — Henry H. Bellamann, "The Piano Works of C. V. Alkan," MQ X (1924) 251–62.

Benedict/WEBER — Julius Benedict, *Weber,* 3d ed. London: S. Low, Marston, Searle, & Rivington, 1889.

Bennett/BENNETT — James Robert Sterndale Bennett, *The Life of William Sterndale Bennett, by His Son.* . . . Cambridge [England]: University Press, 1907.

Benton/LONDON — Rita Benton, "London Music in 1815, as Seen by Camille Pleyel," ML XLVII (1966) 34–47.

Benyovszky/HUMMEL — Karl Benyovszky, *J. N. Hummel: Der Mensch und Künstler.* Bratislava: Eos-Verlag, 1934. ("English resumé" on pp. 381–84.)

BERLIOZ MEMOIRS — *Memoirs of Hector Berlioz, from 1803 to 1865, Comprising His Travels in Germany, Italy, Russia, and England* (written between 1848 and 1865 and first pub. in 1870), trans. by Rachel and Eleanor Holmes and revised, with annotations, by Ernest Newman. New York: Alfred A. Knopf, 1932.

Berri/PAGANINI — Pietro Berri, *Paganini: Documenti e testimonianze.* Genoa: Sigla Effe, 1962.

Bertensson & Leyda/RACHMANINOFF — Sergei Bertensson & Jay Leyda, *Sergei Rachmaninoff: A Lifetime in Music,* "with the assistance of [Rachmaninoff's sister-in-law] Sophia Satina." New York: New York University Press, 1956. Cf. J. Yasser's review in NOTES XIII (1956) 643–44; Reither/RACHMANINOFF 36.

Bie/PIANOFORTE — Oscar Bie, *A History of the Pianoforte and Pianoforte Players,* trans. and revised [in 1899] from the original German ed. of 1898 by E. E. Kellett and E. W. Naylor, with a Foreword to the Da Capo reprint by Aube Tzerko. New York: Da Capo Press, 1966.

BIO-BIBL. U.S. — *Bio-Bibliographical Index of Musicians in the United States of America Since Colonial Times,* prepared by the District of Columbia Historical Survey; 2d (unrevised) ed. (originally pub. in 1941). Washington, D.C.: Pan American Union, 1956.

Bloch/ALKAN — Joseph Bloch, *Charles-Valentin Alkan,* an undergraduate study done at Harvard University. (Indianapolis: privately printed for the author, 1941.)

Blom/DUSSEK — Eric Blom, "The Prophecies of Dussek," MO LI (1927–28) 271–73, 385–86, 495–96, 602, 807–8, 990–91, 1080–81; reprinted in Blom's *Classics Major and Minor* (London: J. M. Dent, 1958) 88–117. Cf. Newman/K. 457.

Blom/FIELD — ———, "John Field," CHESTERIAN XI (1930) 201–7, 233–39.

Blum/SIBELIUS — Fred Blum, *Jean Sibelius: An International Bibliog-*

raphy on the Occasion of the Centennial Celebrations, 1965. Detroit: Information Service, 1965.

Boal/SCHUMANN

Dean Elmer Boal, "A Comparative Study of Existing Manuscripts and Editions of the Robert Schumann Sonata in F Sharp Minor, Op. 11 for Piano," unpub. Ph.D. diss., University of Colorado, 1959.

Böttcher/BRUCKNER

Lukas Böttcher, "Unbekannte Klavierwerke von Anton Bruckner," MUSIKLEBEN II (1949) 236–37.

Boetticher/SCHRIFTEN

Wolfgang Boetticher, *Robert Schumann in seinen Schriften und Briefen*. Berlin: Bernhard Hahnefeld, 1942.

Boetticher/SCHUMANN

———, *Robert Schumann: Einführung in Persönlichkeit und Werk*. Berlin: Bernhard Hahnefeld, 1941. Cf. Abraham/RESEARCH 72–75; Redlich/SCHUMANN; Abraham/SCHUMANN v–vi, 1–11 (W. Reich); Werner/MENDELSSOHN 265–66.

Bone/GUITAR

Philip J. Bone, *The Guitar and Mandolin*, 2d, "enlarged" ed. (first pub. in 1914). London: Schott, 1954.

Bonnerot/SAINT-SAËNS

Jean Bonnerot, *C. Saint-Saëns (1835–1921): Sa Vie et son œuvre*, 2d, revised ed. (originally pub. in 1914). Paris: A. Durand et fils, 1922.

Booth/HELLER

Ronald E. Booth, Jr., "The Life and Music of Stephen Heller," unpub. Ph.D. diss., University of Iowa, 1967.

Borren/FRANCK

Charles van den Borren, *César Franck*. Brussels: La Renaissance du Livre, 1950.

Bory/CHOPIN

Robert Bory, *La Vie de Frédéric Chopin par l'image*. Paris: Horizons de France, [1951].

Bory/LISZT

———, *La Vie de Franz Liszt par l'image*, with a biographical introduction by Alfred Cortot. Geneva: Éditions du Journal de Genève, 1936.

Boucher/WITKOWSKI

Maurice Boucher, "G.-M. Witkowski," RM VII/5 (Mar. 1, 1926) 193–223.

Bowen/RUBINSTEIN

Catherine Drinker Bowen, *"Free Artist": The Story of Anton and Nicholas Rubinstein*, with lists of Anton's works on pp. 375–90, by op. nos. and types, compiled by O. E. Albrecht. New York: Random House, 1939.

Boyer/BEETHOVEN

Jean Boyer. *Le "Romantisme" de Beethoven*. Paris: H. Didier, 1938.

BRAHMS-BILDERBUCH

Max Kalbeck (ed.), *Ein Brahms-Bilderbuch*, issued by Viktor von Miller zu Aichholz. Vienna: R. Lechner, 1905.

BRAHMS BRIEFWECHSEL

M. Kalbeck, W. Altmann, A. Moser, L. Schmidt, J. Röntgen, E. Wolff, and C. Krebs (eds.), *Johannes Brahms Briefwechsel*, first to 3d eds., 16 vols. Berlin:

Deutsche Brahms-Gesellschaft, 1908–22. Vols. I & II contain correspondence with the Herzogenbergs; III with Reinthaler, Bruch, Deiters, Heimsoeth, Reinecke, Rudorff, and the Scholzes; IV, Grimm; V and VI, Joachim; VII, Levi, Gernsheim, the Hechts, and the Fellingers; VIII, Widmann, the Detters, and Schubring; IX–XII, Simrock; XIII, Engelmann; XIV, Breitkopf, Senff, Rieter-Biedermann, Peters, Fritzsch, and Lienau; XV, Wüllner; XVI, Spitta and Dessoff. To keep the references consistent, the English trans. of Vols. I and II by Hannah Bryant (London: John Murray, 1909) is not cited in SSB. For Brahms's correspondence with the Schumanns, see SCHUMANN-BRAHMS.

Brahms/WERKE-m   Eusebius Mandyczewski and Hans Gál (eds.), *Johannes Brahms sämtliche Werke,* 26 vols. Leipzig: Breitkopf & Härtel, [1926–27]. Cf. Heyer/HISTORICAL 39–40.

Breithaupt/WAGNER   Rudolf M. Breithaupt, "Richard Wagners Klaviermusik," DM III/4 (1903–4) 108–34. Cf. Daube/WAGNER vi–vii.

Brendel/GESCHICHTE   Franz Brendel, *Geschichte der Musik in Italien, Deutschland und Frankreich . . . ,* 2d ed. (1st ed. in 1852), 2 vols. in one. Leipzig: Heinrich Matthes, 1855.

Brennecke/REGER   Ernest Brennecke, "The Two Reger-Legends," MQ VIII (1922) 384–96.

BRITANNICA   *Encyclopaedia Britannica,* 24 vols. Chicago: William Benton, 1963.

Bronarski/CHOPIN   Ludwik Bronarski, *Études sur Chopin,* 2 vols. (2d ed. of Vol. II, originally pub. in 1944). Lausanne: La Concorde, 1947 and 1946.

Brown/CHOPIN   Maurice J. E. Brown, *Chopin: An Index of His Works in Chronological Order.* New York: St Martin's Press, 1960. Cf. "Corrections and Additions" in MT CVI (1960) 28–30; review in PQ XXXIII (fall, 1960) 24, 26 (W. S. Newman).

Brown/DISCOVERIES   ———, "Schubert: Discoveries of the Last Decade," MQ XLVII (1961) 293–314.

Brown/ESSAYS   ———, *Essays on Schubert,* including "Towards an Edition of the Pianoforte Sonatas," pp. 197–216. New York: St Martin's Press, 1966. Cf. the reviews in ML XLVII (1966) 274–75 (M. Tilmouth); JAMS XX (1967) 505–7 (M. Chusid).

Brown/MANUSCRIPTS   ———, "Schubert's Manuscripts: Some Chronological Issues," MR XIX (1958) 180–85.

Brown/RECENT   ———, "Recent Schubert Discoveries," ML XXXII (1951) 349–61.

Brown/SCHUBERT ————, *Schubert: A Critical Biography*. New York: St Martin's Press, 1958. Cf. the reviews in JAMS XII (1959) 252–54 (D. Mintz): MQ XLVI (1960) 95–102 (K. Wolff).

Brown/TONES Calvin S. Brown, *Tones into Words, Musical Compositions as Subjects of Poetry*. Athens: University of Georgia Press, 1953.

Brown/VARIATIONS Maurice J. E. Brown, *Schubert's Variations*. New York: St Martin's Press, 1954.

Brown/1817 ————, "An Introduction to Schubert's Sonatas of 1817," MR XII (1951) 35–44.

BROWN & STRATTON James D. Brown & Stephen S. Stratton, *British Musical Biography: A Dictionary of Musical Artists, Authors and Composers Born in Britain and Its Colonies*. Birmingham: S. S. Stratton, 1897.

BUCEM Edith B. Schnapper (ed.), *The British Union Catalogue of Early Music*, printed before 1801; 2 vols. London: Butterworth, 1957.

Buchner/LISZT Alexander Buchner, *Franz Liszt in Böhmen*. Prague: Artia, 1962.

Bücken/SCHUBERT Ernst Bücken, "Schubert und die Klassik," KONGRESS SCHUBERT 47–53.

Bücken/19. ————, *Die Musik des 19. Jahrhunderts bis zur Moderne*. Potsdam: Akademische Verlagsgesellschaft Athenaion, 1932.

BÜLOW BRIEFE Marie von Bülow (ed.), *Hans von Bülow: Briefe und Schriften, from 1841–94*, 8 vols. Leipzig: Breitkopf & Härtel, 1895–1908.

BÜLOW-STRAUSS Willi Schuh and Franz Trenner (eds.), *Hans von Bülow and Richard Strauss: Correspondence*, trans. by Anthony Gishford (from the original ed. of 1953). London: Boosey & Hawkes, 1955.

Bundi/HUBER Gian Bundi, *Hans Huber: Die Persönlichkeit nach Briefen und Erinnerung*. Basel: Helbing & Lichtenhahn, 1925.

Burghauser/DVOŘÁK Jarmil Burghauser, *Antonín Dvořák: Thematic Catalogue, Bibliography, Survey of Life and Work* (in Czech, German, and English). Prague: Artia, 1960.

Burk/WAGNER John N. Burk (ed.), *Letters of Richard Wagner: The Burrell Collection*, in Eng. trans. New York: Macmillan, 1950.

Bush/BENNETT Geoffrey Bush, "Sterndale Bennett: The Solo Piano Works," PMA XCI (1964–65) 85–97.

BUSONI-Frau Ferruccio Benvenuto Busoni, *Briefe an seine Frau*. Zürich: Rotapfel, 1935.

Busoni/SKETCH ————, *Sketch of a New Esthetic of Music*, trans.

784   BIBLIOGRAPHY

                (from the original German of 1907) by T. Baker. New York: G. Schirmer, 1911.

BZMW   *Beiträge zur Musikwissenschaft.* 1959————.

CAECILIA   *Caecilia, eine Zeitschrift für die musikalische Welt.* 1824–48. Cf. Freystätter/ZEITSCHRIFTEN 41–46.

Calvocoressi/MUSSORGSKY   Michael D. Calvocoressi, *Mussorgsky,* completed by G. Abraham. London: J. M. Dent, 1946.

Carner/FORM   Mosco Carner, "Some Observations on Schumann's Sonata Form," MT LXXVI (1935) 884–86. Cf. Cohen/SCHUMANN, of which this article restates and ramifies the conclusions.

CASTIL-BLAZE   François-Henri-Joseph Blaze, *Dictionnaire de musique moderne,* 2d ed. (first ed. in 1821), 2 vols. Paris: Au Magazin de Musique de la Lyre Moderne, 1825.

Cat. BELGISCH   *Catalogus van Werken van Belgische Componisten,* 20 vols. up to 1957. Brussels: Belgisch Centrum voor Muziekdocumentatie (Cebedem), 1954————.

Cat. BOLOGNA   *Catalogo della Biblioteca del Liceo musicale di Bologna,* 5 vols. Bologna: Libreria Romagnoli dall'Acqua, 1890–1905, 1943. Reprint of vols. I–IV, with corrections by Napoleone Fanti, Oscar Mischiati, and Luigi Ferdinando Tagliavini; Bologna: Arnaldo Forni Editore, 1961.

Cat. BRITISH MS   Augustus Hughes-Hughes (ed.), *Catalogue of Manuscript Music in the British Museum, Vol. III: Instrumental Music, Treatises, etc.* London: British Museum, 1909.

Cat. BRUXELLES   Alfred Wotquenne (ed.), *Catalogue de la Bibliothèque du Conservatoire royal de musique de Bruxelles,* 4 vols. Brussels: J. J. Coosemans, 1898, 1902, 1908, 1912.

Cat. HIRSCH   A. Hyatt King and Charles Humphries (eds.), *Music in the Hirsch Library,* Part 53 of *Catalogue of Printed Music in the British Museum.* London: Trustees of the British Museum, 1951.

Cat. HIRSCH IV   Kathi Meyer and Paul Hirsch (eds.), *Katalog der Musikbibliothek Paul Hirsch,* Vol. IV. Cambridge (England): University Press, 1947.

Cat. NYPL   *The New York Public Library Reference Department: Dictionary Catalog of the Music Collection,* 33 vols. and Suppl. I. Boston: G. K. Hall, 1964–67.

Cat. ROYAL   *Catalogue of Printed Music in the Library of the Royal College of Music,* edited by W. Barclay Squire. London: Novello, 1909.

Cernikoff/HUMOUR   Vladimir Cernikoff, *Humour and Harmony.* London: Arthur Baker, 1936.

Chase/AMERICA — Gilbert Chase, *America's Music, from the Pilgrims to the Present,* revised 2d ed. (originally pub. in 1955). New York: McGraw-Hill, 1966.

Chase/LATIN AMERICA — ————, *A Guide to the Music of Latin America,* 2d ed., revised and enlarged (originally pub. in 1945). Washington: The Pan American Union and the Library of Congress, 1962.

Chase/SPAIN — ————, *The Music of Spain,* 2d ed. (first ed. pub. in 1941). New York: Dover, 1959.

CHESTERIAN — *The Chesterian.* 1915–19, 1919–40, 1947–62.

CHOPIN/facs.–m — *Fryderyk Chopin: Sonata h–moll,* facs. of autograph by way of photographs at the National Library in Warsaw (where the autograph has since been returned), with preface. Krakow: Polskie Wydawnictwo Muzyczne, 1954.

CHOPIN JAHRBUCH — Franz Zagiba (ed.), *Chopin Jahrbuch,* 2 issues to date (1967). Vienna: International Chopin Society, 1956 and 1963. Cf. DMF X (1957) 442–43 (R. Seitz) and NOTES XXI (1963–64) 379–80 (A. Loesser), respectively.

Chopin/WORKS–m — I. J. Paderewski, L. Bronarski, and J. Turczyński (eds.), *Fryderyk Chopin: Complete Works,* 27 vols. (including orchestral parts), variously 1st, 2d, or 3d ed. Warsaw: Fryderyk Chopin Institute, 1949–at least 1962. Cf. Newman/CHOPIN. The pagination of the "Critical Commentary" at the end of each vol. varies slightly depending on the language (English, in the present reference).

Chorley/GERMAN — Henry F. Chorley, *Modern German Music, Recollections and Criticisms,* 2 vols. London: Smith, Elder, 1854. Cf. Chorley/RECOLLECTIONS v-xxii (E. Newman).

Chorley/RECOLLECTIONS — ————, *Thirty Years' Musical Recollections,* ed. (from the original ed. of 1862) with an introduction by Ernest Newman. New York: Alfred Knopf, 1926.

Churgin/SONATA — Bathia Churgin, "Francesco Galeazzi's Description (1796) of Sonata Form," JAMS XXI (1968) 181–99.

Chusid/SCHUBERT — Martin Chusid, "The Chamber Music of Franz Schubert," unpub. Ph.D. diss., University of California at Berkeley, 1961.

Chusid/SCHUBERT–m — ———— (ed.), *Franz Schubert: Symphony in B Minor ("Unfinished"),* with articles on "The Historical Background" (pp. 1–11) and "Beethoven and the Unfinished" (pp. 98–110), as well as studies and comments by O. E. Deutsch and others. New York: W. W. Norton, 1968.

Chusid/1824 — Martin Chusid, "Schubert's Cyclic Compositions of 1824," AM XXXVI (1964) 37–45.

Clapham/DVOŘÁK — John Clapham, *Antonin Dvořák, Musician and Craftsman*. London: Faber and Faber, 1966.

Closson & Borren/BELGIQUE — Ernest Closson and Charles van den Borren (eds.), *La Musique en Belgique du Moyen Age a nos jours*. Brussels: La Renaissance du Livre, 1950.

Cobbett/CHAMBER — Walter Willson Cobbett (ed.), *Cobbett's Cyclopedic Survey of Chamber Music*, 2 vols. reprinted from the original ed. of 1929, with suppl. prepared by Colin Mason. London: Oxford University Press, 1963. (I ix: " . . . with rare exceptions, M.S. works are ignored.")

Codignola/PAGANINI — Arturo Codignola, *Paganini intimo*. Genoa: A cura del municipio, 1935.

Cohen/SCHUMANN — Mosco Cohen [later, Mosco Carner], "Studien zur Sonatenform bei Robert Schumann," unpub. Ph.D. diss., University of Vienna, 1928. Cf. Carner/FORM. The Vienna copy was reportedly "destroyed during World War II."

Colles/FRANCK — Henry Cope Colles, "César Franck and the Sonata," MT LVI (1915) 206–9.

Collet/ALBÉNIZ — Henri Collet, *Albéniz et Granados*, 2d ed. (originally pub. in 1925). Paris: Librairie Plon, 1948.

Collins/GERM — M. Stuart Collins, "Germ Motives and Guff," MR XXIII (1962) 238–43.

COMPOSITORES — *Compositores de América, Datos biográficos y catálogos de sus obras*. Washington: Pan American Union, 1955—— (8 vols. to 1962) .

CONGRESS CHOPIN — Zofia Lissa (ed.), *The Book of the First International Musicological Congress Devoted to the Works of Frederick Chopin, Warszawa, 16th-22nd February 1960*. Warsaw: Polish Scientific Publishers, 1963. Cf. ML XLV (1964) 268–70 (review by M. J. E. Brown).

Cooper/FRENCH — Martin Cooper, *French Music, from the Death of Berlioz to the Death of Fauré*. London: Oxford University Press, 1961 (first pub. in 1951).

Cortot/FRANÇAISE — Alfred Cortot, *La Musique française de piano*, 3 series (vols.), 5th ed. (originally pub. 1930–44 except for separate pubs. of I as articles in RM). Paris: Presses universitaires de France, 1948. (Also pub. in English trans. [London: Oxford, 1932], not used here.)

Cortot/INTERPRÉTATION — ——, *Cours d'Interprétation*, ed. by Jeanne Thieffry. Paris: Librarie musicale R. Legouix, 1934.

Courcy/CHRONOLOGY — Geraldine de Courcy, *Chronology of Nicolo Paganini's Life,* with parallel trans. into German by H. Dünnebeil. Wiesbaden: Rud. Erdmann, 1962 (copyright 1961).

Courcy/PAGANINI ———, *Paganini, the Genoese,* 2 vols. Norman: University of Oklahoma Press, 1957.

Craw/DUSSEK Howard Allen Craw, "A Biography and Thematic Catalog of the Works of Dussek (1760–1812)," unpub. Ph.D. diss., University of Southern California, 1964.

Czekaj/CHOPIN Kazimierz Czekaj, *Guide Chopin illustré,* trans. (from Polish mainly into French) by J. Bourilly and J. Kasińska. Warsaw: Société "Frédéric Chopin," 1960.

CZERNY Carl Czerny, "Recollections from My Life," trans. from "Erinnerungen aus meinen Leben" by Ernest Sanders, MQ XLII (1956) 302–17.

Czerny/COMPOSITION ———, *School of Practical Composition,* trans. from the original German of about 1840 (pub. by Simrock of Bonn in 1849–50 as *Die Schule der praktischen Tonsetzkunst* [cf. Newman/CZERNY]) by John Bishop (with author's "Memoir" and list of works both pub. [up to Op. 798] and unpub.), 3 vols. London: Robert Cocks, [preface dated 1848].

Czesla/BRAHMS Werner Czesla, *Studien zum Finale in der Kammermusik von Johannes Brahms* (Ph.D. diss., 1966). Bonn: Rheinische Friedrich-Wilhelms-Universität, 1968.

DA *Der Auftakt, Musikblätter für die tschechoslowakische Republik* [in Prague]. 1921–23.

Dahms/MENDELSSOHN Walter Dahms, *Mendelssohn.* Berlin: Schuster & Loeffler, [1919].

Dale/GRIEG Kathleen Dale, "The Piano Music [of Grieg]," in Abraham/GRIEG 45–70.

Dale/NINETEENTH ———, *Nineteenth-Century Piano Music.* New York: Oxford University Press, 1954.

Dale/SCHUBERT ———, "The Piano Music [of Schubert]," in Abraham/SCHUBERT 111–48.

Dale/SCHUBERT-m ——— (ed.), *Schubert: Sonata in E Minor* (D. 566 and 506, plus Adagio in D♭ and same transposed to E). London: British & Continental Music Agencies, 1948.

Dale/SCHUMANN Kathleen Dale, "The Piano Music [of Schumann]," in Abraham/SCHUMANN 12–97.

Dale/SMYTH ———, "Ethyl Smyth's Prentice Work," ML XXX (1949) 329–36.

Dale/THREE C'S ———, "The Three C's: Pioneers of Pianoforte Playing," MR VI (1945) 138–48.

DAMROSCH/Life Walter Damrosch, *My Musical Life.* New York: Charles Scribner's Sons, 1930.

Dannreuther/   Edward Dannreuther, *The Romantic Period* (Vol.
ROMANTIC   VI in *The Oxford History of Music*), 2d ed. (origi-
                      nally pub. in 1905). London: Humphrey Milford,
                      1931.

Daube/WAGNER   Otto Daube, *"Ich schreibe keine Symphonien mehr":
                      Richard Wagners Lehrjahre nach den erhaltenen
                      Dokumenten.* Köln: Hans Gerig, 1960.

Davis/HUMMEL   Richard Davis, "The Music of J. N. Hummel, Its
                      Derivations and Development," MR XXVI (1965)
                      169–91.

Davis/LYAPUNOV   ———, "Sergei Lyapunov (1859–1924); the Piano
                      Works: A Short Appreciation," MR XXI (1960) 186–
                      206.

DDT-m   *Denkmäler deutscher Tonkunst,* erste Folge, 65 vols.,
                      1892–1931.

De Angelis/ROMA   Alberto De Angelis, *La Musica a Roma nel secolo
                      XIX.* Rome: Giovanni Bardi, 1935.

DEBUSSY CROCHE   Lawrence Gilman (ed.), *Monsieur Croche, the Dilet-
                      tante Hater, from the French of Claude Debussy*
                      (articles written in 1901–14, collected and abridged
                      by the author, and first pub. in collected form in
                      1921; cf. Gilman's Foreword and Lockspeiser/DEBUSSY
                      II 282–84). New York: Lear, 1948.

Del Mar/STRAUSS   Norman Del Mar, *Richard Strauss: A Critical Com-
                      mentary on His Life and Works,* Vol. I of two
                      projected vols. London: Barrie and Rockliff, 1962.

Demuth/FRANCK   Norman Demuth, *César Franck.* London: Dennis
                      Dobson, 1949.

Demuth/FRENCH   ———, *French Piano Music.* London: Museum
                      Press, 1959.

Demuth/D'INDY   ———, *Vincent d'Indy, 1851–1931: Champion of
                      Classicism.* London: Rockliff, 1951.

Demuth/TRENDS   ———, *Musical Trends in the 20th Century.* Lon-
                      don: Rockliff, 1952.

Denecke/REGER   Heinz Ludwig Denecke, "Max Regers Sonatenform
                      in ihrer Entwicklung," in FESTSCHRIFT STEIN 26–32.

Dent/BUSONI   Edward J. Dent, *Ferruccio Busoni: A Biography.*
                      London: Oxford University Press, 1933.

Dessauer/FIELD   Heinrich Dessauer, *John Field: sein Leben und seine
                      Werke* (Ph.D. diss., Universität Leipzig, 1911).
                      Langensalza: Hermann Beyer, 1912.

Deutsch/COLLECTED   Otto Erich Deutsch, "Schubert: The Collected
                      Works," ML XXXII (1951) 226–34.

Deutsch/MOZART   ———, *Mozart: A Documentary Biography,* trans. by
                      Eric Blom, Peter Branscombe, and Jeremy Noble.
                      Stanford: Stanford University Press, 1965.

Deutsch/NUMMERN ———, *Musikverlags Nummern,* 2d revised and first German ed. Berlin: Merseburger, 1961. Cf. SCE 824.

Deutsch/SCHUBERT-B ——— (ed.), *Franz Schubert: Sein Leben in Bildern.* Munich: Georg Müller, 1913. Cf. Deutsch/SCHUBERT-M V.

Deutsch/SCHUBERT-D Otto Erich Deutsch, *The Schubert Reader: A Life of Franz Schubert in Letters and Documents,* trans. by Eric Blom. New York: W. W. Norton, 1947. Revised from the original German ed. of 1914. A very few new changes and additions appear in the German ed. of 1964 pub. as "Serie VIII: Supplement·Band 5" in the *Neue Ausgabe* of the Internationalen Schubert-Gesellschaft. Cf., also, Deutsch/SCHUBERT-M V.

Deutsch/SCHUBERT-I ——— (ed., with Donald R. Wakeling), *Schubert: Thematic Catalogue of All His Works in Chronological Order.* London: J. M. Dent, 1951. Cf. Deutsch/SCHUBERT-M V.

Deutsch/SCHUBERT-M ———, *Schubert: Memoirs by His Friends* (cf. p. v herein). New York: Macmillan, 1958.

DICCIONARIO LABOR Joaquín Pena and Higinio Anglés, *Diccionario de la música labor,* 2 vols. Barcelona: Editorial Labor, 1954.

DICCIONARIO PORTUGUEZES Ernesto Vieira, *Diccionario biographico de musicos portuguezes,* 2 vols. Lisbon: Mattos Moreira & Pinheiro, 1900.

Dickinson/SCHUMANN Alan Edgar Frederic Dickinson, "The Chamber Music [of Schumann]," in Abraham/SCHUMANN 138–75.

Dietrich & Widmann/BRAHMS Albert Dietrich and Josef Viktor Widmann, *Recollections of Johannes Brahms,* trans. by Dora A. Hecht (from two separate, complementary accounts, both originally pub. in 1898). London: Seeley, 1899.

DM *Die Musik.* 1901–41.

DMf *Die Musikforschung.* 1948———.

DMZ *Deutsche Musiz-Zeitung* (ed. by Selmar Bagge). 1860–62.

Dobrokhotov/ALIABIEV B. Dobrokhotov, *Alexander Aliabiev.* Moscow: Izdatel'stvo, 1966.

Dolleris/NIELSEN Ludvig Dolleris, *Carl Nielsen en Musikografi,* with 300 exx. Odense (Denmark): Fyns Boghandel, 1949.

DOMMER & KOCH Arrey von Dommer, *H. Ch. Koch's Musikalisches Lexikon* [originally pub. in 1802], *zweite durchaus umgearbeitete und vermehrte Auflage.* Heidelberg: J. C. B. Mohr, 1865.

Drinker/BRAHMS Henry S. Drinker, Jr., *The Chamber Music of Johannes Brahms.* Philadelphia: Elkan-Vogel, 1932.

DTB-m — *Denkmäler der Tonkunst in Bayern* (DDT-m, zweite Folge), 36 vols., 1900–31.

DTÖ-m — *Denkmäler der Tonkunst in Österreich*. 1894———.

Dubitzky/STRAUSS — Franz Dubitzky, "Richard Strauss' Kammermusik," DM XIII/3 (1913–14) 289–96.

Dünnebeil/WEBER — Hans Dünnebeil, *Schrifttum über Carl Maria von Weber,* 4th ed. Berlin: Bote & Bock, 1957.

Dufourcq/FRANÇAISE — Norbert Dufourcq, *La Musique d'orgue française de Jehan Titelouze a Jehan Alain,* 2d ed. (first pub. in 1941). Paris: Librairie Floury, 1949.

Dukas/ÉCRITS — Gustave Samazeuilh (ed.), *Les Écrits de Paul Dukas sur la musique.* Paris: Société d'Éditions françaises et internationales, 1948.

Dunhill/CHAMBER — Thomas F. Dunhill, *Chamber Music: A Treatise for Students,* 2d reprint. London: Macmillan, 1938 (originally pub. in 1913).

DVOŘÁK LETTERS — Otakar Šourek (ed.), *Antonín Dvořák: Letters and Reminiscences,* trans. (from the original Czech ed. of 1938, 9th ed. in 1951) by R. F. Samsour. Prague: Artia, 1954.

Dvořák/WERKE-m — ———, *Antonín Dvořák: Kritische Gesamtausgabe, nach Originalquellen zum Druck vorbereitet von der Kommission für die Herausgabe der Werke. . . .* Prague: Artia, 1956———. Cf. Heyer/HISTORICAL 92–93; Clapham/DVOŘÁK 319.

DWIGHT'S — *Dwight's Journal of Music, a Paper of Art and Literature.* 1852–81.

Eagle/MAC DOWELL — Nancy Eagle, "The Pianoforte Sonatas of Edward A. MacDowell, a Style-Critical Study," unpub. M.A. thesis, The University of North Carolina at Chapel Hill, 1952.

Eckart-Bäcker/ FRANKREICH — Ursula Eckart-Bäcker, *Frankreichs Musik zwischen Romantik und Moderne: Die Zeit im Spiegel der Kritik.* Regensburg: Gustav Bosse, 1965.

Edwards/MENDELSSOHN — F. G. Edwards, "Mendelssohn's Organ Sonatas," PMA XXI (1894–95) 1–16. Reprinted with deletions and additions (including facs. of three passages in the autographs) in MT XLII (1901) 794–98. Cf. ZIMG III (1901–2) 337–38 (C. Maclean).

Egert/CHOPIN — Paul Egert, *Friedrich Chopin.* Potsdam: Akademische Verlagsgesellschaft Athenaion, 1936.

Egert/FRÜHROMANTIKER — ———, *Die Klaviersonate der Frühromantiker* (Vol. I [diss., 1929] of "Die Klaviersonate im Zeitalter der Romantik," not published to date, but cf. p. 46, fn. 5). Berlin: R. Niedermayr, 1934.

Egert/LISZT — ———, "Die Klaviersonate in H-Moll von Franz Liszt," DM XXVIII/2 (1936) 673–82.

Ehrmann/BRAHMS — Alfred von Ehrmann, *Johannes Brahms: Thematisches Verzeichnis seiner Werke.* Leipzig: Breitkopf & Härtel, 1933.

Ehrmann/WEG — ———, *Johannes Brahms: Weg, Werk und Welt.* Leipzig: Breitkopf & Härtel, 1933.

Einstein/ROMANTIC — Alfred Einstein, *Music in the Romantic Era.* New York: W. W. Norton, 1947.

Einstein/SCHUBERT — ———, *Schubert: A Musical Portrait.* New York: Oxford University Press, 1951.

Eismann/SCHUMANN — Georg Eismann (ed.), *Robert Schumann: Ein Quellenwerk über sein Leben und Schaffen,* 2 vols. Leipzig: Breitkopf & Härtel, 1956. (A 2d ed. appeared in 1964.)

EITNER MISCELLANEA — Hermann Springer, Max Schneider, and Werner Wolffheim, *Miscellanea musicae bio-bibliographica* [1904–13] . . . *als Nachträge und Verbesserungen zu Eitners Quellenlexikon,* 2d ed. New York: Musurgia, 1947.

Eitner/QL — Robert Eitner, *Biographisch-bibliographisches Quellenlexikon der Musiker und Musikgelehrten . . . ,* 10 vols. Leipzig: Breitkopf und Härtel, 1899–1904.

Eitner/SONATE — ———, "Die Sonate, Vorstudien zur Entstehung der Form," MfMg XX (1888) 163–70 and 179–85.

Elgar/LETTERS — *Letters of Edward Elgar and Other Writings,* selected, ed., and annotated by P. M. Young. London: Geoffrey Bles, 1956.

ELGAR-Nimrod — Percy M. Young (ed.), *Letters to Nimrod* [Elgar's trans. of Jaeger]: *Edward Elgar to August Jaeger, 1897–1908.* London: Dennis Dobson, 1965.

Ellis/WAGNER — William Ashton Ellis, *Life of Richard Wagner,* 6 vols. London: Kegan Paul, Trench, Trübner, 1900–1908. Vols. I–III are revisions of C. F. Glasenapp's *Das Leben Richard Wagner's* (Vols. I–III, 1894–99).

Elson/AMERICAN — Louis C. Elson, *The History of American Music,* 2d ed. (revision of original ed. of 1904). New York: Macmillan, 1915.

Elson/WOMAN — Arthur Elson, *Woman's Work in Music.* Boston: L. C. Page, [1913].

Emmanuel/DUKAS — Maurice Emmanuel, "La Musique de Piano de Paul Dukas," RM XVII/166 (May–June, 1936; *Paul Dukas: Numéro spécial*) 69–78.

Emmanuel/FRANCK — ———, *César Franck, Étude critique.* Paris: Henri Laurens, 1930.

ENCYCLOPÉDIE — *Encyclopédie de la musique et dictionnaire du conservatoire,* 11 vols. Paris: Delagrave, 1913–31.

Engel/GESELLSCHAFT — Hans Engel, *Musik und Gesellschaft, Bausteine zu einer Musiksoziologie.* Berlin: Max Hesse, 1960.

Engel/ROMANTISCHEN — ———, "Die Grenzen der romantischen Epoche und der Fall Mendelssohn," in *Festschrift Otto Erich Deutsch* (Kassel: Bärenreiter, 1963) 259–72.

Enke/MENDELSSOHN — Heinz Enke, "Mendelssohn und der Manierismus," NZM CXXV (1964) 3–5.

Eschman/FORMS — Karl Eschman, *Changing Forms in Modern Music*. Boston: E. C. Schirmer, 1945.

ESCUDIER — Marie & Léon Escudier, *Dictionnaire de musique*, 2 vols. in one. Paris: Bureau Central de Musique, 1844.

Evans/BRAHMS — Edwin Evans, *Historical, Descriptive and Analytical Account of the Entire Works of Johannes Brahms*, 4 vols.: I, *Handbook to* [the] *Vocal Works*; II, . . . *Chamber & Orchestral Music* through Op. 67; III, . . . *Chamber & Orchestral Music* from Op. 68 to the end; IV, . . . *Pianoforte Works*. London: William Reeves, [1912, 1933, 1935, 1936].

Ewens/EBERL — Franz Josef Ewens, *Anton Eberl: Ein Beitrag zur Musikgeschichte in Wien um 1800* (Ph.D. diss., Köln, 1923). Dresden: Wilhelm Limpert, 1927.

F-A-E SONATE-m — Erich Valentin and Otto Kobin (eds.), F[*rei*]-A[*ber*]-E[*insam*]; "in anticipation of the arrival of the revered and beloved friend Joseph Joachim, this sonata was composed by Robert Schumann [mvts. ii and iv], Albert Dietrich [i] and Johannes Brahms [iii]." Magdeburg: Heinrichshofen, 1935; reprinted by C. F. Peters in New York, 1953.

Faisst/CLAVIERSONATE — Imanuel Faisst, "Beiträge zur Geschichte der Claviersonate von ihrem ersten Auftreten bis auf C. P. Emanuel Bach" (Berlin, 1845), reprinted from CAECILIA XXV (1846) 129–58 and 201–31, XXVI (1847) 1–28 and 73–83, in NBJ I (1924) 7–85.

Farnsworth/PHENOMENA — Paul R. Farnsworth, "Masculinity and Femininity of Musical Phenomena," JAAC IX (1950–51) 257–62.

Farnsworth/TASTE — ———, *Musical Taste: Its Measurement and Cultural Nature*. Stanford: Stanford University Press, 1950.

FASQUELLE — François Michel and others (eds.), *Encyclopédie de la musique*, 3 vols. Paris: Fasquelle, 1958–61.

Fauré/LETTRES — Philippe Fauré-Fremiet (ed.), *Gabriel Fauré: Lettres intimes* (extracts to his wife, 1885–1924). Paris: La Colombe, 1951.

Fauré-Fremiet/FAURÉ — Philippe Fauré-Fremiet, *Gabriel Fauré* (originally pub. in 1929), plus "Réflexions sur la confiance Fauréenne" (after 1945) and "Notes sur l'interprétation des œuvres" (1950). Paris: Albin Michel, 1957.

Favre/BOIELDIEU — Georges Favre, *Boieldieu: Sa Vie—son œuvre,* 2 vols. Paris: Librairie E. Droz, 1944 and 1945.

Favre/BOIELDIEU-m — ———— (ed.), *Adrien Boieldieu:* (6) *Sonates pour le piano-forte,* 2 vols., with preface (repeated in Favre/FRANÇAISE) and facs. of title pages of Opp. 4 and 6. Paris: Librairie E. Droz, 1944, and Librairie Fischbacher, 1947.

Favre/DUKAS — Georges Favre, *Paul Dukas, sa vie et son œuvre.* Paris: La Colombe, [1948].

Favre/FAURÉ — Max Favre, *Gabriel Fauré's Kammermusik* (diss., prefaced in 1947). Zürich: Max Niehan, 1948.

Favre/FRANÇAISE — Georges Favre, *La Musique française de piano avant 1830.* Paris: Didier, 1953. Cf. Gil-Marchex/FRANÇAIS 171–76 (evaluation and additions).

Fay/GERMANY — Amy Fay, *Music-Study in Germany in the Nineteenth Century* [1869–75], with a new introduction by Frances Dillon. New York: Dover, 1965 (reprinted from the original ed. of 1880, in Chicago).

Fellinger/BRAHMS — Imogen Fellinger, "Brahms' Sonate für Pianoforte und Violine Op. 78," DMf XVIII (1965) 11–24.

Fellinger/DYNAMIK — ————, *Über die Dynamik in der Musik von Johannes Brahms.* Berlin: Max Hesse, 1961.

Fellinger/MUSIKBIBLIOGRAPHIE — ————, "Musikbibliographie des 19. Jahrhunderts im Forschungsunternehmen der Fritz Thyssen Stiftung," DMf XIX (1966) 172–76.

FESTSCHRIFT SANDBERGER — *Festschrift zum 50. Geburtstag Adolf Sandberger, überreicht von seinen Schülern.* Munich: Hof-Musik-Verlag, 1918.

FESTSCHRIFT STEIN — Hans Hoffmann and Franz Rühlmann (eds.), *Festschrift Fritz Stein zum 60. Geburtstag.* Braunschweig: Litolff, 1939.

Fétis/BU — François-Joseph Fétis, *Biographie universelle des musiciens . . . ,* 2d ed., 8 vols.; suppl., 2 vols. Paris: Firman-Didot, 1860–65; 1878–80.

Fétis/CURIOSITÉS — ————, *Curiosités historiques de la musique, complément nécessaire de La Musique mise a la portée de tout le monde.* Paris: Janet et Cotelle, 1830.

Fétis/MUSIQUE — ————, *La Musique mise a la portée de tout le monde.* Paris: Alexandre Mesnier, 1830.

Finck/GRIEG — Henry T. Finck, *Grieg and His Music,* 2d. revised ed. New York: John Lane, 1909. Cf. Frank/GRIEG 36.

Fischer/BRAHMS — Richard Shaw Fischer, "Brahms' Technique of Motive Development in His Sonata in D Minor, Opus 108 for Piano and Violin," unpub. D.M.A. "Paper," University of Arizona, 1964.

Fischer/GRIEG — Kurt von Fischer, *Griegs Harmonik und die nordländische Folklore.* Bern: Paul Haupt, 1938.

Fischer/SONATE-m

Hans Fischer (ed.), *Die Sonate,* vol. 18 in *Musikalische Formen in historischen Reihen.* Berlin: Chr. Friedrich Vieweg (1937). References are made to this first ed. rather than the radically altered 2d ed. (Wolfenbüttel: Möseler, 1957).

Flinsch/SCHUNKE

Erich Flinsch, "Ludwig Schunke, Schumanns Freund und Mitbegründer der Neuen Zeitschrift für Musik," NZM CXXI (1960) 199–203.

Fog/NIELSEN

Dan Fog, *Carl Nielsen, Kompositioner: En Bibliografi.* Copenhagen: Nyt Nordisk, 1965.

Frank/GRIEG

Alan Frank, "The Chamber Music [of Grieg]," in Abraham/GRIEG 32–44.

Frey & Schuh/SCHWEIZER-m

Walter Frey and Willi Schuh (eds.), *Schweizer Klaviermusik aus der Zeit der Klassik und Romantik* (including pieces by Nägeli, Schnyder von Wartensee, and Fröhlich). Zürich: Hug, 1937.

Frey/SONATINA-m

Martin Frey (ed.), *The New Sonatina Book.* London: Schott, 1936.

Freystätter/ZEITSCHRIFTEN

Wilhelm Freystätter, *Die musikalischen Zeitschriften.* Munich: Theodor Riedel, 1884.

Friedheim/LISZT

Arthur Friedheim, *Life and Liszt: The Recollections of a Concert Pianist.* New York: Taplinger, 1961.

Frimmel/SCHUBERT

Theodor Frimmel, "Beethoven und Schubert," DM XVII/6 (1924–25) 401–16.

Frotscher/ORGELSPIEL

Gotthold Frotscher, *Geschichte des Orgelspiels und der Orgelkomposition,* 2 vols. Berlin-Schöneberg: Max Hesses Verlag, 1935–36; reprinted unaltered by Merseburger of Berlin, 1959.

Fuchs/CRITIQUE

Julius Fuchs, *A Critique of Musical Compositions;* Vol. I, *From Bach to the Present Time,* with "Preface" in French, English, and German. Leipzig: Friedrich Hofmeister, 1898.

Fuller-Maitland/PARRY

John Alexander Fuller-Maitland, *The Music of Parry and Stanford, An Essay in Comparative Criticism.* Cambridge: W. Heffer & Sons, 1934.

Fuller-Maitland/SCHUMANN

————, *Schumann's Pianoforte Works.* London: Oxford University Press, 1927.

Gál/BRAHMS

Hans Gál, *Johannes Brahms, His Work and Personality,* trans. by Joseph Stein from the original German of 1961. New York: Alfred A. Knopf, 1963.

Ganzer & Kusche/VIERHÄNDIG

Karl Ganzer and Ludwig Kusche, *Vierhändig.* Munich: Ernst Heimeran, 1937.

Garden/BALAKIREV

Edward Garden, *Balakirev: A Critical Study of His Life and Music.* London: Faber and Faber, 1967. Cf. the reviews by D. Brown in ML XLIX (1968) 167–69 and B. Schwarz in NOTES XXV (1968–69) 30–31.

Gárdonyi/LISZT	Zoltán Gárdonyi, *Le Style hongrois de François Liszt* (in Hungarian and French). Budapest: Magyar Nemzeti Múzeum, 1936.
Gáscue/SONATA	Francisco Gáscue, *Historia de la Sonata*. San Sebastian: Palacio de Bellas Artes, 1910.
GASSNER	Ferdinand Simon Gassner (ed.), [Schilling's] *Universal-Lexikon der Tonkunst, neue Hand-Ausgabe in einem Bande*. Stuttgart: Franz Köhler, 1849.
Gates/SOLO	Willis Cowan Gates, "The Literature for Unaccompanied Solo Violin," unpub. Ph.D. diss., The University of North Carolina at Chapel Hill, 1949.
Gatscher/REGER	Emanuel Gatscher, *Die Fugentechnik Max Regers* (Ph.D. diss., Bonn, 1924; Schaal/DISSERTATIONEN no. 663). Stuttgart: J. Engelhorn, 1925.
Gatti & Basso/ LA MUSICA	Guido M. Gatti and Alberto Basso (eds.), *La Musica: Parte prima, Enciclopedia storica*, 4 vols. Torino: Unione tipografico, 1966.
Geiringer/BRAHMS	Karl Geiringer, *Brahms: His Life and Work*, 2d ed. (first ed. pub. in German in 1934). New York: Oxford, 1947; reprinted as a paperback by Doubleday in 1961.
Georgii/KLAVIERMUSIK	Walter Georgii, *Klaviermusik*, 2d ed. Zürich: Atlantis-Verlag, 1950.
Georgii/WEBER	———, *Karl Maria von Weber als Klavierkomponist* (Ph.D. diss., Halle). Leipzig: Breitkopf & Härtel, 1914.
Gertler/SCHUMANN	Wolfgang Gertler, *Robert Schumann in seinen frühen Klavierwerken* (diss., Freiburg im Breisgau, 1929). Berlin: Georg Kallmeyer, 1931. Cf. Abraham/ RESEARCH 66–69.
Giegling/SOLO-m	Franz Giegling (ed.), *The Solo Sonata* (in the *Anthology of Music* series), with extended Preface. Köln: Arno Volk, 1960. Cf. NOTES XIX (1961–62) 685–87 (review by W. S. Newman).
Gillespie/KEYBOARD	John Gillespie, *Five Centuries of Keyboard Music*. Belmont (Calif.): Wadsworth, 1965.
Gilman/MACDOWELL	Lawrence Gilman, *Edward MacDowell: A Study* (revised in 1908 from a "monograph" of 1905). New York: Dodd, Mead, 1931.
Gilman/NATURE	———, *Nature in Music, and Other Studies in the Tone-Poetry of Today*. New York: John Lane, 1914.
Gil-Marchex/FRANÇAIS	Henri Gil-Marchex, "Le Language pianistique des compositeurs français," RM No. 226 (1955) 163–87.
Glazunov/MUSICIANS	Alexandr Konstantinovitch Glazunov, *Musicians, Correspondence, Reminiscences* (in Russian). Moscow, 1958. References are cited here by way of Alekseev & Novikova.

Glinka/MEMOIRS   Mikhail Ivanovitch Glinka, *Memoirs*, written in 1854–55 and trans. from the Russian by R. B. Mudge. Norman: University of Oklahoma, 1963.

Glinka/WORKS-m   ———, *Polnoe sobranie sochinenil*, 16 vols. to date (1968). Moscow: Muzykal'nve Izdatel'stvo, 1955———.

Gloyne/PREYER   Howard F. Gloyne, *Carl A. Preyer: The Life of a Kansas Musician*. Lawrence: University of Kansas, 1949.

Goetschius/BEACH   Percy Goetschius, *Mrs. H. H. A. Beach, Analytical Sketch*. Boston: Arthur P. Schmidt, 1906.

Goldschmidt/SONATENFORM   Hugo Goldschmidt, "Die Entwicklung der Sonatenform," *Allgemeine Musik-Zeitung* XXIX (1902) 93–95, 109–11, 129–32.

Gollmick/TERMINOLOGIE   Carl Gollmick, *Kritische Terminologie für Musiker und Musikfreunde*. Frankfurt/M: Lauten, 1833.

Gottschalk/MSS   Paul Gottschalk (ed.), *A Collection of Original Manuscripts of the World's Greatest Composers* (in facs.). Berlin: pub. by the editor, 1930.

GOTTSCHALK/Notes   Louis Moreau Gottschalk, *Notes of a Pianist*, ed. by Jeanne Behrend. New York: Alfred A. Knopf, 1964. Cf. JAMS XVIII (1965) 259–62 (H. E. Johnson).

Grabner/REGER   Hermann Grabner, *Regers Harmonik*, 2d ed. (originally pub. in 1920). Wiesbaden: Breitkopf & Härtel, 1961.

Grace/RHEINBERGER   Harvey Grace, *The Organ Works of Rheinberger*. London: Novello, [1925].

Grasberger/BRAHMS   Franz Grasberger, *Johannes Brahms: Variationen um sein Wesen*. Vienna: Paul Kaltschmid, 1952.

Grasberger & Hadamowsky/STRAUSS   Franz Grasberger and Franz Hadamowsky, *Richard-Strauss-Ausstellung zum 100. Geburtstag*. Vienna: Österreichische Nationalbibliothek, 1964.

Graves/PARRY   Charles L. Graves, *Hubert Parry: His Life and Works*, 2 vols. London: Macmillan, 1926.

Gray/SIBELIUS   Cecil Gray, *Sibelius: The Symphonies*. London: Oxford University Press, 1935.

Greene/STANFORD   Harry Plunket Greene, *Charles Villiers Stanford*. London: Edward Arnold, 1935.

Grew/LISZT   Eva Mary Grew, "Liszt's Dante Sonata," CHESTERIAN XXI (1940) 33–40.

Grieg/VERZEICHNIS   Edvard Grieg, *Verzeichnis seiner Werke mit Einleitung: Mein erster Erfolg*. Leipzig: C. F. Peters, [1910].

GROVE   Eric Blom (ed.), *Grove's Dictionary of Music and Musicians*, 5th ed., 9 vols. and Suppl. New York: St Martin's Press, 1954, 1961. References are to this ed. unless an earlier ed. is specified. Am. Suppl. refers to 1935 reprint of 2d ed. (1928) of *American*

Supplement. Cf. MMR LXXVI (1946) 99–102, 132–34 (A. H. King); PQ No. 31 (spring, 1960) 25–27 and No. 36 (summer, 1961) 28 (W. S. Newman).

Haase/BRAHMS

Rudolf Haase, "Studien zum kontrapunktischen Klaviersatz von Johannes Brahms," unpub. Ph.D. diss., Universität Köln, 1951.

Habets/BORODIN

Alfred Habets, *Borodin and Liszt* (through Borodin's letters), trans. (from the original French ed. of 1893) by Rosa Newmarch. London: Digby, Long, [1895].

Hadow/MODERN

William Henry Hadow, *Studies in Modern Music,* Series I and II in 2 vols., 12th ed. (originally pub. in London in 1892 and 1895). New York: Macmillan, [*ca.* 1925 and later].

Hagenbucher/FUCHS

Franz Hagenbucher, "Die Original-Klavierwerke zu zwei und vier Händen von Robert Fuchs," unpub. Ph.D. diss., Universität Wien, 1940.

Hall/PIANOFORTE

Leland Hall, *Pianoforte and Chamber Music,* Vol. VII in *The Art of Music.* New York: The National Society of Music, 1915.

HALLÉ

C. E. and Marie Hallé (eds.), *Life and Letters of Sir Charles Hallé.* London: Smith, Elder, 1896.

Halm/KULTUREN

August Halm, *Von zwei Kulturen der Musik.* Munich: Georg Müller, 1913.

Hammerich/HARTMANN

Angul Hammerich, "J. P. E. Hartmann," trans. from the original Danish (1900) into German by L. Freifrau von Liliencron, SIMG II (1900–1901) 455–76.

Hanna/SCHUBERT

Albert Lyle Hanna, "A Statistical Analysis of Some Style Elements in the Solo Piano Sonatas of Franz Schubert," unpub. Ph.D. diss., University of Indiana, 1965.

Hanslick/CONCERTE

Eduard Hanslick, *Concerte, Componisten und Virtuosen der letzten fünfzehn Jahre, 1870–1885,* 2d ed. Berlin: Allgemeiner Verein für Deutsche Litteratur, 1886.

Hanslick/FÜNF

———, *Fünf Jahre Musik* (Vol. VII of *Modernen Oper*). Berlin: Allgemeiner Verein für Deutsche Litteratur, 1896.

Hanslick/MUSIKALISCHES

———, *Musikalisches und Litterarisches* (Vol. V of *Modernen Oper*). Berlin: Allgemeiner Verein für Deutsche Litteratur, 1890.

Hanslick/TAGEBUCHE

———, *Aus dem Tagebuche eines Musikers* (Vol. VI of *Modernen Oper*). Berlin: Allgemeiner Verein für Deutsche Litteratur, 1892.

Hanslick/WIEN

———, *Geschichte des Concertwesens in Wien,* 2 vols. Vienna: Wilhelm Braumüller, 1869–70.

Haraszti/AUTHOR   Emile Haraszti, "Franz Liszt: Author Despite Himself," trans. by John A. Gutman, MQ XXXIII (1947) 490–516.

Haraszti/LISZT   ———, "Le Problème Liszt," AM IX (1937) 123–36 and X (1938) 32–46.

Haraszti/PARIS   ———, "Liszt à Paris: Quelques documents inédits," RM XVII (1936) no. 165, 240–58, and no. 167, 5–16.

Harding/SAINT-SAËNS   James Harding, Saint-Saëns and His Circle. London: Chapman & Hall, 1965.

HARMONICON   The Harmonicon. 1823–33.

Hasenöhrl/CZERNY   Franz Hasenöhrl, "Karl Czernys solistische Klavierwerke," unpub. Ph.D. diss., Universität Wien, 1927.

Hasse/KARG-ELERT   Karl Hasse, "Drei neue musiktheoretische Lehrbücher; I: Siegfried Karg-Elert, 'Polaristische Klang- und Tonalitätslehre,' " NZM C/1 (1933) 336–45.

Hastings/TASTE   Thomas Hastings, Dissertation on Musical Taste. . . . Albany: Websters and Skinners, 1822.

Haupt/MÜLLER   Günther Haupt, August Eberhard Müllers Leben und Klavierwerke. Leipzig: Breitkopf & Härtel, 1926.

Hausswald/WEBER   Günter Hausswald (ed.), Carl Maria von Weber: Eine Gedenkschrift (on the 125th anniversary of his death). Dresden: VVV Dresdner Verlag, 1951.

Hedler/TÜRK   Gretchen Emilie Hedler (Thieme), Daniel Gottlob Türk (1750–1813). Leipzig: Robert Noske, 1936.

Hedley/AUTOGRAPH   Arthur Hedley, "Some Observations on the Autograph Sources of Chopin's Works," CONGRESS CHOPIN 474–77.

Hedley/CHOPIN   ———, Chopin. London: J. M. Dent, 1947.

Heger/REGER   Erich Heger, "Max Reger: Brücke zwischen den Jahrhunderten," MUSICA VII (1953) 168–70.

Helfert/SMETANAS   Vladimír Helfert, Die schöpferische Entwicklung Friedrich Smetanas, trans. (into German from the original Czech ed. of 1924) by B. Liehm. Leipzig: Breitkopf & Härtel, 1956.

Helfert & Steinhard   Vladimír Helfert and Erich Steinhard, Histoire de la musique tschécoslovaque. Prague: Orbis, 1936.

Henderson/PFITZNER   Donald Gene Henderson, "Hans Pfitzner: The Composer and His Instrumental Works," unpub. Ph.D. diss., University of Michigan, 1963.

Hering/HILLER   Hans Hering, Die Klavierwerke F. v. Hillers (Ph.D. diss., Universität Köln). Düsseldorf: Otto Fritz, 1928.

Heussner/MOSCHELES   Ingeborg Heussner, "Ignaz Moscheles in seinen Klavier-Sonaten, -Kammermusikwerken, und -Konzerten," unpub. Ph.D. diss., Universität Marburg/Lahn, 1963.

Hewitt/DISSERTATIONS   Helen Hewitt, Doctoral Dissertations in Musicology,

4th ed. Philadelphia: American Musicological Society, 1965.

Heyer/HISTORICAL   Anna Harriet Heyer, *Historical Sets, Collected Editions and Monuments of Music.* Chicago. American Library Association, 1957.

Hibbard/FIELD   Trevor Davies Hibbard, "The Slow Movements of the Sonatas of John Field," MR XXII (1961) 89–93.

Hill/BRAHMS   William G. Hill, "Brahms' op. 51—a Diptych," MR XIII (1952) 110–24.

Hill/SCHUBERT   ———, "The Genesis of Schubert's Posthumous Sonata in B flat Major," MR XII (1951) 269–78.

Hill/SIBELIUS   ———, "Some Aspects of Form in the Symphonies of Sibelius," MR X (1949) 165–82.

Hiller/MENDELSSOHN   Ferdinand Hiller, *Mendelssohn: Letters and Recollections,* trans. from the German (Köln, 1774) by M. E. von Glehn, 2d ed. London: Macmillan, 1874.

Hindemith/CRAFT   Paul Hindemith, *The Craft of Musical Composition;* Book I, Theoretical Part, trans. by Arthur Mendel (from the original German ed. of 1937). New York: Associated Music Publishers, 1942.

Hirschberg/LOEWE   Leopold Hirschberg, *Carl Loewes Instrumentalwerke.* Hildburghausen: F. W. Gadow, 1919.

Hirschberg/POCCI   ———, "Franz Pocci," ZFMW I (1918–19) 40–70.

Hoffmann/REGER   Hans Hoffmann, "Zu Max Regers Sonate Op. 72 für Violine und Klavier in C dur," REGER-GESELLSCHAFT X (June, 1933) 1–7.

Hoffmann/SCHRIFTEN   Ernst Theodor Amadeus Hoffmann, *Schriften zur Musik,* ed. by Friedrich Schnapp. Munich: Winkler, 1963.

Hoffmann/WERKE-m   Gustav Becking (ed.), *E. Th. A. Hoffmann: Musikalische Werke,* 3 vols. (inc.). Leipzig: C. F. W. Siegel in conjunction with Fr. Kistner, [1922–27]. Cf. ZFMW V (1922–23) 347–48 (Kroll).

HOFMEISTER   Friedrich Hofmeister (ed.; and successors), *Musikalischer-literarischer Monatsbericht, Handbuch der musikalischen Literatur, Verzeichnis* or *Jahresverzeichnis,* and related titles. Leipzig: Friedrich Hofmeister, from 1829; preceded by Carl Friedrich Whistling's *Handbuch der musikalischen Litteratur* for 1815 (with suppl. of 1818–19) and 1828 (cumulative). Cf. MGG VI 576–77 (Virneisel); Hopkinson/FIELD 173.

Hogan/ANGLO-IRISH   Ita Margaret Hogan, *Anglo-Irish Music, 1780–1830.* Cork: Cork University Press, 1966.

Hohenemser/SCHUMANN   Richard Hohenemser, "Formale Eigentümlichkeiten in Robert Schumanns Klaviermusik," in FESTSCHRIFT SANDBERGER 21–50.

Hollander/BRAHMS — Hans Hollander, "Der melodische Aufbau in Brahms' 'Regenlied'-Sonate," NZM CXXV (1964) 5–7.

Holmes/RAMBLE — [Edward Holmes], *A Ramble Among the Musicians of Germany . . . by a Musical Professor*. London: Hunt and Clarke, 1828.

Holt/MEDTNER — Richard Holt, *Medtner and His Music, a Tribute to a Great Russian Composer,* ed. by Fred Smith. London: Rimington, Van Wyck, 1948.

Holt/TRIBUTE — ——— (ed.), *Nicolas Medtner (1879–1951): A Tribute to his Art and Personality.* London: Dennis Dobson, 1955. (A symposium of 38 items by 32 authors, including Medtner himself.)

Honsa/SCHUMANN — Melitta Honsa, *Synkope, Hemiole und Taktwechsel in den Instrumentalwerken Robert Schumanns* (Ph.D. diss., Leopold-Franzens-Universität zu Innsbruck). Innsbruck: pub. by the author, 1965.

Hopkinson/FIELD — Cecil Hopkinson, *A Bibliographical Thematic Catalogue of the Works of John Field, 1782–1837.* London: Printed [by Harding & Curtis] for the author, 1961.

Hopkinson/PARISIAN — ———, *A Dictionary of Parisian Music Publishers, 1700–1950.* London: Printed for the author, 1954.

Horton/MENDELSSOHN — John Horton, *The Chamber Music of Mendelssohn.* London: Oxford, 1946.

Horton/PIANO — Charles Allison Horton, "Serious Art and Concert Music for Piano in America in the 100 Years from Alexander Reinagle to Edward MacDowell," unpub. Ph.D. diss., The University of North Carolina at Chapel Hill, 1965.

Howard/AMERICAN — John Tasker Howard, *Our American Music, a Comprehensive History from 1620 to the Present,* 4th ed. (originally pub. in 1929). New York: Thomas Y. Crowell, 1965.

Howe/AMERICA — Granville L. Howe (ed.), *A Hundred Years of Music in America.* Chicago: G. L. Howe, 1889.

Howe/PAINE — M. A. De Wolfe Howe, "John Knowles Paine," MQ XXV (1939) 257–67.

Howes/ENGLISH — Frank Howes, *The English Musical Renaissance.* New York: Stein and Day, 1966.

Hudson/STANFORD — Frederick Hudson, "A Catalogue of the Works of Charles Villiers Stanford (1852–1924)," MR XXV (1964) 44–57. Cf. the sequel, "C. V. Stanford: Nova Bibliographica," in MT CIV (1964) 728–33.

Hughes/AMERICAN — Rupert Hughes, *American Composers,* 2d ed. (originally pub. in 1900) with new chaps. by Arthur Elson. Boston: The Page Co., 1914 (11th impression, 1921).

Hughes/INSTRUMENTAL   David Hughes (ed.), *Instrumental Music: A Conference at Isham Memorial Library, May 4, 1957.* Cambridge: Harvard University Press, 1959.

Hummel/ANWEISUNG   Johann Nepomuk Hummel, *Ausführliche theore tisch-practische Anweisung zum Piano-Forte-Spiel,* 2d ed. (first pub. in London in English in 1827; cf. Cat. NYPL XIV 663). Vienna: Haslinger, 1828.

Humphries & Smith/ PUBLISHING   Charles Humphries and William C. Smith, *Music Publishing in the British Isles.* London: Cassell, 1954.

Ilyin/MEDTNER   Ivan Ilyin, "Sonata Form in Medtner," in Holt/ MEDTNER 180–88.

d'Indy/COURS   Vincent d'Indy, *Cours de composition musicale,* with collaboration of A. Sérieyx and De Lyoncourt, 3 vols. (2 parts in Vol. II). Paris: Durand, 1909–50. Cf. Demuth/D'INDY 22–41.

d'Indy/FRANCK   ———, *César Franck,* trans. from the original French of 1906 by Rosa Newmarch and reprinted from the first English ed. of 1909 (not 1910). New York: Dover, 1965.

JAAC   *Journal of Aesthetics and Art Criticism.* 1942———.

Jachimecki/CHOPIN   Zdzislaw Jachimecki, *Chopin: La Vita e le opere,* trans. and revised from the final Polish version of 1949 by Wiarosław Sandelewski, in 1959. Milan: G. Ricordi, 1962.

Jacob/MENDELSSOHN   Heinrich Eduard Jacob, *Felix Mendelssohn and His Times,* trans. from the German (Frankfurt, 1959) by Richard and Clara Winston. London: Barrie and Rockliff, 1963.

Jacobs/SCHUMANN   Robert L. Jacobs, "Schumann and Jean Paul," ML XXX (1949) 250–58.

Jähns/WEBER   Friedrich Wilhelm Jähns, *Carl Maria von Weber in seinen Werken; chronologisch-thematisches Verzeichniss seiner sämmtlichen Compositionen. . . .* Berlin: Schlesinger, 1871.

JAMS   *Journal of the American Musicological Society.* 1948———.

Jansen/NEUE   Gustav Jansen, *Robert Schumanns Briefe: Neue Folge,* 2d ed. Leipzig: Breitkopf und Härtel, 1904.

Jansen/SCHUMANN   ——— (ed.), *The Life of Robert Schumann Told in His Letters,* trans. by May Herbert (from *Briefe von Robert Schumann: Neue Folge,* 1886), 2 vols. London: R. Bentley, 1890.

Jarociński/POLISH   Stefan Jarociński (ed.), *Polish Music.* Warsaw: Polish Scientific Publishers, 1965.

Jean-Aubry/FRANÇAISE   Georges Jean-Aubry, *La Musique française d'au-*

jourd'hui, with a preface by Gabriel Fauré. Paris: Perrin, 1916.

Jeppesen/NIELSEN — Knud Jeppesen, "Carl Nielsen, a Danish Composer," MR VII (1946) 170–77.

Jiránek/LISZT — Jaroslav Jiránek, "Liszt und Smetana: ein Beitrag zur Genesis und eine vergleichende Betrachtung ihres Klavierstils," in LISZT-BARTÓK 1961 139–92.

JMP — *Jahrbuch der Musikbibliothek Peters.* 1894———.

Joachim/LETTERS — Nora Bickley (ed. and trans.), *Letters from and to Joseph Joachim,* with a preface by J. A. Fuller-Maitland. London: Macmillan, 1914.

Johns/REMINISCENCES — Clayton Johns, *Reminiscences of a Musician.* Cambridge, [Mass.]: Washburn & Thomas, 1929.

JRME — *Journal of Research in Music Education.* 1952———.

Jurgenson/ TSCHAÏKOWSKY — Boris Jurgenson, *Catalogue thématique des œuvres de P. Tschaïkowsky,* facs. reprint of original Moscow ed. of 1897. New York: Am-Rus, [1941].

Kämper/WÜLLNER — Dietrich Kämper, *Franz Wüllner: Leben, Wirken und kompositorisches Schaffen.* Köln: Arno Volk-Verlag, 1963.

Kahl/LYRISCHE — Willi Kahl, "Das lyrische Klavierstück Schuberts und seiner Vorgänger [especially W. J. Tomaschek and J. H. Woržischek] seit 1810," AfMW III (1921) 54–82 and 99–122.

Kahl/SCHUBERT — ———, *Verzeichnis des Schrifttums über Franz Schubert, 1828–1928.* Regensburg: Gustav Bosse, 1938.

Kahl/ SCHUBERTSCHRIFTTUMS — ———, "Wege des Schubertschrifttums," ZMW XI (1928–29) 79–95.

Kaiser/WEBER — Georg Kaiser, *Sämtliche Schriften von Carl Maria von Weber.* Berlin: Schuster & Loeffler, 1908.

Kaiserman/MACDOWELL — David Kaiserman, "Edward MacDowell—The Celtic and Eroica Piano Sonatas," in *Music Journal* XXIV/ 2 (Feb., 1966) 51 and 58.

Kalbeck/BRAHMS — Max Kalbeck, *Johannes Brahms,* first to 4th eds., 4 books in 8 vols. Berlin: Deutsche Brahms-Gesellschaft, 1912–21.

Kallmann/CANADA — Helmut Kallmann, *A History of Music in Canada, 1534–1914.* Toronto: University of Toronto Press, 1960.

Kański/VIRTUOSI — Józef Kański, "Eminent [Polish] Virtuosi of the XIX and XX Centuries," in Jarociński/POLISH 128–53.

Kapp/LISZT — Julius Kapp, *Franz Liszt.* Berlin: Schuster & Loeffler, 1909.

Keller/BRAHMS — Otto Keller, "Johannes Brahms-Literatur," DM XII/ 1 (1912–13) 86–101.

Keller & Kruseman/ MUZIEKLEXICON
Gerard Keller and J. Philip Kruseman, *Geïllustreerd Muzieklexicon*, 2 vols. and Suppl. The Hague: J. Philip Kruseman, 1932 and 1949.

Kempers/ISOMETRISCHE
Karel Philippus Bernet Kempers, "Isometrische Begriffe und die Musik des 19. Jahrhunderts," in *Festschrift Friedrich Blume zum 70. Geburtstag* (Kassel: Bärenreiter, 1963) 34–49.

Keresztury/MAGYAR
Dezsö Keresztury, Jenö Vécsey, and Zoltán Falvy (eds.), *A Magyar zenetörténet Képeskönyve*. Budapest: Magvetö Könyvkiadó, 1960. A valuable pictorial and documentary history of Hungarian music.

Kinsky & Halm/ BEETHOVEN
Georg Kinsky, *Das Werk Beethovens, thematisch-bibliographisches Verzeichnis seiner sämtlichen vollendeten Kompositionen*, completed by Hans Halm. Munich: G. Henle Verlag, 1955.

Kinsky/KOCH
————, *Katalog der Musikautographen-Sammlung Louis Koch, . . . von Scarlatti bis Stravinsky* (completed by M. A. Souchay). Stuttgart: Hoffmannsche Buchdruckerei Felix Krais, 1953.

Kirby/BRAHMS
Frank E. Kirby, "Brahms and the Piano Sonata," in PISK ESSAYS 163–80.

Kirby/KEYBOARD
————, *A Short History of Keyboard Music*. New York: The Free Press, 1966.

Kirkpatrick/IVES
John Kirkpatrick (ed.), *A Temporary Mimeographed Catalogue of the Music Manuscripts of Charles Edward Ives, 1874–1954, given by Mrs. Ives to the Library of the Yale School of Music, September, 1955*. New Haven: Yale School of Music, 1960.

Klauwell/ÄSTHETISCHE
Otto Klauwell, "Die ästhetische Bedeutung der Sonatenform" (1897), in O. Klauwell's *Studien und Erinnerungen, gesammelte Aufsätze über Musik* (Langensalza: Hermann Beyer, 1906) 44–55.

Klauwell/SONATE
————, *Geschichte der Sonate*. Leipzig: H. vom Ende's Verlag, [1899].

Knepler/XIX.
Georg Knepler, *Musikgeschichte des 19. Jahrhunderts*, 2 vols. Berlin: Henschelverlag, 1961. A 3d vol., on Slavic countries, is in progress. Cf. Lissa in BZMW VIII (1966) 68–73; R. Longyear in JAMS XVIII (1965) 419–21.

Kobylańska/CHOPIN
Krystyna Kobylańska, *Chopin in His Own Land; Documents and Souvenirs* (with English text). Krakow: Polish Music Publications, 1955.

Koechlin/FAURÉ
Charles Koechlin, *Gabriel Fauré (1845–1924)*, trans. (from the original French ed. of 1927) by Leslie Orry (with minor additions). London: Dennis Dobson, 1945.

Költzsch/SCHUBERT
Hans Költzsch, *Franz Schubert in seinen Klaviersonaten* (Ph.D. diss., Erlangen, 1926). Leipzig: Breit-

kopf & Härtel, 1927. Cf. the abstract in KONGRESS SCHUBERT 199–208 and the review in DM XXI (1928–29) 50–51 (E. Bücken).

Kohleick/JENNER   Werner Kohleick, *Gustav Jenner (1865–1920)*: *Ein Beitrag zur Brahmsfolge.* Würzburg: K. Triltsch, 1943.

KONGRESS SCHUBERT   *Bericht über den internationalen Kongress für Schubertforschung, Wien 25. bis 29. November, 1928.* Augsburg: Benno Filser, 1929.

Krafka/DUSSEK   Karel Krafka, "Romantické Prvky v klavírních sonatách Jana Ladislava Dusíka" ("Romantic Elements in the Piano Sonatas of Jan Ladislav Dussek"), unpub. Ph.D. diss., University of Brno, 1950 (available only indirectly to the present study; cf. SSB XVII and Craw/DUSSEK 2).

KRAUS/GEIRINGER/
LUITHLEN   H. Kraus, K. Geiringer, and V. Luithlen (eds.), *J. Brahms Zentenar-Ausstellung der Gesellschaft der Musikfreunde in Wien, beschreibendes Verzeichnis.* [Vienna: Gesellschaft der Musikfreunde, 1934].

Krause/STRAUSS   Ernst Krause, *Richard Strauss, the Man and His Work,* trans. by John Coombs from the 3d German ed. of 1963 (the first ed. appeared in 1955). London: Collett's, 1964.

Kreissle/SCHUBERT   Heinrich Kreissle von Hellborn, *The Life of Franz Schubert,* trans. by A. D. Coleridge, with an Appendix by George Grove, 2 vols. London: Longmans, Green, 1869. Cf. Brown/ESSAYS 170–84.

Kremer/ORGAN   Rudolph Joseph Kremer, "The Organ Sonata Since 1845," unpub. Ph.D. diss., Washington University (St. Louis), 1963.

Kretzschmar/AUFSÄTZE   Hermann Kretzschmar, *Gesammelte Aufsätze über Musik . . .* , 2 vols. Leipzig: Breitkopf & Härtel and C. F. Peters, 1910 and 1911.

Kroll/BEETHOVEN   Erwin Kroll, "Carl Maria von Weber und Beethoven," NBJ VI (1935) 124–40.

Kroll/HOFFMANN   ———, "Über den Musiker E. T. A. Hoffmann," ZfMW IV (1921–22) 530–52.

Kroll/WEBER   ———, *Carl Maria von Weber.* Potsdam: Akademische Verlagsgesellschaft Athenaion, 1934.

Kross/BRAHMSIANA   Siegfried Kross, "Brahmsiana: Der Nachlass der Schwestern Völckers," DMf XVII (1964) 110–51.

Krueck/DRAESEKE   Alan Henry Krueck, *The Symphonies of Felix Draeseke* (Ph.D. diss., University of Zürich, 1966). Roscoe, (Pa.): Roscoe Ledger, 1967.

Kuhlmann/
SMETANA-m   Georg Kuhlmann (ed.), *Friedrich Smetana*: *Sonata in One Movement for Two Pianos (Eight Hands),* with preface. London: Hinrichsen, 1938.

La Mara/
MUSIKERBRIEFE

La Mara (Marie Lipsius; ed.), *Musikerbriefe aus fünf Jahrhunderten,* 2 vols. Leipzig: Breitkopf & Härtel, ["Vorrede" dated 1886].

Lampadius/
MENDELSSOHN

Wilhelm Adolf Lampadius, *Memoirs of Felix Mendelssohn Bartholdy,* trans. from the German (Leipzig, 1848) by W. L. Gage. Boston: Ditson, 1865.

Landon & Bartha/
HAYDN

H. C. Robbins Landon and Dénes Bartha, *Joseph Haydn: Gesammelte Briefe und Aufzeichnungen.* Kassel: Bärenreiter, 1965. Cf. K. Geiringer in JAMS XIX (1966) 251–54.

Landormy/FRANÇAISE

Paul Landormy, *La Musique française de Franck à Debussy.* [*Paris*]: Gallimard, 1943.

Lang/AMERICA

Paul Henry Lang (ed.), *One Hundred Years of Music in America.* New York: G. Schirmer, 1961.

Lang/WESTERN

Paul Henry Lang, *Music in Western Civilization.* New York: W. W. Norton, 1941.

Laplane/ALBENIZ

Gabriel Laplane, *Albeniz: sa vie, son œuvre.* Paris: Milieu du Monde, [1957].

LAROUSSE

Norbert Dufourcq, Félix Raugel, and Armand Machabey (eds.), *Larousse de la musique,* 2 vols. Paris: Librairie Larousse, 1957.

Latham/BRAHMS

Peter Latham, *Brahms.* London: J. M. Dent, 1948.

Layton/BERWALD

Robert Layton, *Franz Berwald,* with a Foreword by Gerald Abraham. London: Anthony Blond, 1959.

LC MUSIC

The Library of Congress, Division of Music, [report for] *1929–30.* Washington: United States Government Printing Office, 1931.

Ledebur/BERLIN

Carl Freiherr von Ledebur, *Tonkünstler-Lexicon Berlin's, von den ältesten Zeiten bis auf die Gegenwart.* Berlin: Ludwig Rauh, 1861.

Leichtentritt/
CHOPIN

Hugo Leichtentritt, *Analyse der Chopin'schen Klavierwerke,* 2 vols. Berlin: Max Hesse, 1921 and 1922.

Lewenthal/ALKAN-m

Raymond Lewenthal (ed.), *The Piano Music of Alkan,* with prefaces. New York: G. Schirmer, 1964. Cf. MT CVI (1965) 620 (F. Dawes).

Lewinski/FORM

Wolf-Eberhard von Lewinski, "Fuge und Sonate—die Form von Morgen," MUSICA XX (1966) 201–2.

Liapunov/PIANO-m

Sergey Mikhailovitch Liapunov, *Complete Piano Works,* 2 vols. Moscow: State Music Publishers, 1950–51.

Liapunova & Yazo-
vitskaya/BALAKIREV

A. S. Liapunova & E. E. Yazovitskaya, *Balakirev: A* [documentary] *Chronology of His Life and Works* (in Russian). Leningrad: State Music Publishers, 1967.

LICHTENTHAL

Peter Lichtenthal, *Dizionario e bibliografia della musica,* 2 vols. Milan: Antonio Fontana, 1826.

Lippman/SCHUMANN — Edward A. Lippman, "Theory and Practice in Schumann's Aesthetics," JAMS XVII (1964) 310–45.

Lissa/NATIONALEN — Zofia Lissa, "Über den nationalen Stil," BZMW VI (1964) 187–214.

Lissa/POLISH — ————, "Polish Romanticism and Neo-Romanticism," in Jaronciński/POLISH 104–27.

LISTENER — Felix Aprahamian (ed.), *Essays on Music: An Anthology From "The Listener."* London: Cassell, 1967.

LISZT/Amie — La Mara (Marie Lipsius, ed.), *Lettres de Franz Liszt à une Amie* (almost identical with LISZT BRIEFE III). Paris: Costallat, 1894.

LISZT-BARTÓK 1961 — Zoltán Kodály (ed.), *Studia musicologica, Academiae Scientiarum Hungaricae: Liszt-Bartók*, Vol. 5, report of the Second International Musicological Conference, 1961. Budapest: Akadémiai Kiadó, 1963.

LISZT BRIEFE — La Mara (Marie Lipsius, ed.), *F. Liszt's Briefe*, 8 vols. Leipzig: Breitkopf & Härtel, 1893–1904.

LISZT LETTERS — La Mara (Marie Lipsius, ed.), *Letters of Franz Liszt*, trans. (from the early vols. of LISZT BRIEFE?), by Constance Bache, 2 vols. London: H. Grevel, 1894.

LISZT/Marie — Howard E. Hugo (trans. & ed.), *The Letters of Franz Liszt to Marie Sayn-Wittgenstein*, with "Foreword." Cambridge: Harvard University Press, 1953.

LISZT-RAFF — Helene Raff (ed.), "Franz Liszt und Joachim Raff im Spiegel ihrer Briefe," DM I/1 (1901) 36–44, 113–23, 285–93, 387–404, 499–505; I/2 (1902) 688–95, 861–71, 977–86, I/3 (1902) 1161–72, 1272–86, 1423–41.

"LISZT" SCHRIFTEN — Lina Ramann (ed. & trans. [from French to German]), *Gesammelte Schriften von Franz Liszt,* 6 books in 7 vols. Leipzig: Breitkopf und Härtel, 1880–83. Cf. Ramann/LISZT II/2 112–26; but quotation marks in our short title acknowledge the strong evidence against Liszt's authorship of all these writings (cf. Haraszti/LISZT 130–35; Haraszti/AUTHOR).

"Liszt" & Waters/CHOPIN — Franz Liszt (?), *Frederic Chopin*, trans., with an Introduction by Edward N. Waters. New York: Macmillan, 1963. Cf. NOTES XXII (1965–66) 855–61 (commentary by C. Cooke).

Liszt/WERKE-m — Peter Raabe (and others, eds.), *Franz Liszts musikalische Werke*, 34 vols. (to date). Leipzig: Breitkopf & Härtel, 1907 [1856?]–1936. Cf. Heyer/HISTORICAL 171. Reprinted in 1966 by Gregg Press (Westmead, England); cf. MT CVIII (1967) 352.

Litzmann/SCHUMANN — Berthold Litzmann, *Clara Schumann: Ein Künstlerleben nach Tagebüchern und Briefen,* 3 vols. Leipzig: Breitkopf & Härtel, 1902–8.

Lochner/KREISLER — Louis P. Lochner, *Fritz Kreisler* New York: Macmillan, 1950. Cf. BAKER 869.

Lockspeiser/DEBUSSY — Edward Lockspeiser, *Debussy: His Life and Mind,* 2 vols. (1862–1902 and 1902–18). London: Cassell, 1962 and 1965.

Lockspeiser/FAURÉ — ———, "Gabriel Fauré and Marcel Proust," in LISTENER 111–14.

Loesser/PIANOS — Arthur Loesser, *Men, Women and Pianos.* New York: Simon and Schuster, 1954.

Lomnitzer/SCHNEIDER — Helmut Lomnitzer, *Das musikalische Werk Friedrich Schneiders (1786–1853), insbesondere die Oratorien* (Ph.D. diss.). Marburg: Universität Marburg, 1961.

Longyear/SCHILLER — Rey M. Longyear, *Schiller and Music.* ("Germanic Languages and Literatures Series," No. 54.) Chapel Hill: The University of North Carolina Press, 1966.

LOUIS FERDINAND-m — Hermann Kretzschmar (ed.), *Prinz Louis Ferdinand Werke,* with preface pp. i–ii; 8 vols. Leipzig: Breitkopf & Härtel, [1915–17 and 1926].

Love/NIETZSCHE — Frederick R. Love, *Young Nietzsche and the Wagnerian Experience.* ("Germanic Languages and Literatures Series," No. 39.) Chapel Hill: The University of North Carolina Press, 1963.

Lowens/AMERICA — Irving Lowens, *Music and Musicians in Early America.* New York: W. W. Norton, 1964.

Lowens/MACDOWELL — ———, "Edward MacDowell" (10th article in "The Great American Composers Series"), in *HiFi/Stereo Review* XIX/6 (Dec., 1967) 61–72.

MAB-m — Jan Racek (ed.), *Musica antiqua bohemica,* 67 vols. up to 1966. Prague: Artia, 1924———.

MacArdle/CZERNYS — Donald W. MacArdle, "Beethoven and the Czernys," MMR LXXXVIII (1958) 124–35.

MacArdle/RIES — ———, "Beethoven and Ferdinand Ries," ML XLVI (1965) 23–34.

MacDowell/ESSAYS — Edward MacDowell, *Critical and Historical Essays: Lectures Delivered at Columbia University,* ed. by W. J. Baltzell. Boston: Arther P. Schmidt, 1912

MacDowell/MACDOWELL — Marian MacDowell, *Random Notes on Edward MacDowell and His Music.* Boston: Arthur P. Schmidt, 1950.

Macfarren/POTTER — George Alexander Macfarren, "Cipriani Potter: His Life and Work," PMA X (1883–84) 41–55.

Maclean/RUBINSTEIN   Charles Maclean, "Rubinstein as Composer for the
                            Pianoforte, PMA XXXIX (1912–1913) 129–51.

MacMillan/CANADA   Ernest MacMillan (ed.), *Music in Canada*. Toronto:
                            University of Toronto Press, 1955.

McVeagh/ELGAR   Diana M. McVeagh, *Edward Elgar: His Life and
                            Music*. London: J. M. Dent, 1955.

Madden & Rees/   Mary Madden & Olive Rees (eds.), *J. L. Dussek:
   DUSSEK-m   Sonata in F Major, Op. 26, for Two Pianofortes*
                            (C. 102). London: Schott, 1957.

Mahaim/BEETHOVEN   Ivan Mahaim, *Beethoven: Naissance et Renaissance
                            des Derniers Quatuors*, 2 vols. Paris: Desclée De
                            Brouwer, 1964.

Mannes/MUSIC   David Mannes, *Music Is My Faith, An Autobiog-
                            raphy*. New York: W. W. Norton, 1938.

Mansfield/   Orlando A. Mansfield, "Some Characteristics and
   MENDELSSOHN   Peculiarities of Mendelssohn's Organ Sonatas," MQ
                            III (1917) 562–76.

Marteau/REGER   Henri Marteau, "Meine Erinnerungen an Max
                            Reger," DA III/3 (1923) 69–78.

Marx/LEHRE   Adolph Bernhard Marx, *Die Lehre von der musi-
                            kalischen Komposition*, 1st ed., 4 vols. Leipzig:
                            Breitkopf & Härtel, 1837, 1838, 1845, 1847, respec-
                            tively. Cf. Newman/THEORISTS; SSB II.

Marx/ZYKLISCHE   Karl Marx, "Über die zyklische Sonatenform—Zu
                            dem Aufsatz von Gunther von Noé," NZM CXXV
                            (1964) 142–46. Concerns thematic interrelationships;
                            cf. Noé/ZYKLISCHEN.

Mason/BRAHMS   Colin Mason, "Brahms' Piano Sonatas," MR V (1944)
                            112–18.

Mason/CHAMBER   Daniel Gregory Mason, *The Chamber Music of
                            Brahms*. New York: Macmillan, 1933.

Mason/LETTERS   Lowell Mason, *Musical Letters From Abroad* (1852–
                            53), facs. of the original ed. of 1854, with a new in-
                            troduction by Elwyn A. Wienandt. New York: Da
                            Capo, 1967.

MASON MEMORIES   William Mason, *Memories of a Musical Life*. New
                            York: Century, 1902.

Mason/MUSIC   Daniel Gregory Mason, *Music in My Time, and
                            Other Reminiscences*. New York: Macmillan, 1938.

Mason/SCHUBERT   Colin Mason, "An Aspect of Schubert's Piano So-
                            natas," MMR LXXVI (1946) 152–57.

May/BRAHMS   Florence May, *The Life of Johannes Brahms*, 2d
                            revised ed. (originally pub. in 1905) with Introduc-
                            tion by Ralph Hill, 2 vols. London: William Reeves,
                            [1948].

Mayer-Serra/   Otto Mayer-Serra, *Música y músicos de Latino-
   LATINOAMERICA   américa*. Mexico City: Editorial Atlante, 1947.

Mdc — *La Musique de chambre.* (Paris: Salons Pleyel). 1893–1903 (10 vols.).

Medtner/WORKS–m — Nikolai Karlovitch Medtner, *Complete Works,* 7 vols. to date (with informative prefaces, in Russian) Moscow: State Music Publishers, 1959——.

Meister/CHOPIN — Edith Meister, *Stilelemente und die geschichtliche Grundlage der Klavierwerke Friedrich Chopins* (Ph.D. diss. at the Hansischen Universität in Hamburg, 1935). Hamburg: Carl Holler, 1936.

Melkus/SCHUMANN — Eduard Melkus, "Zur Revision unseres Schumann-Bildes" and "Schumanns letzte Werke" in ÖMZ XV (1960) 182–90 and 565–71.

Melkus/VIOLINSONATE — ——, "Eine vollständige 3. Violinsonate Schumanns," NZM CXXI (1960) 190–95.

Mello/SCHUBERT — Alfred Mello, "Franz Schuberts Klaviersonaten," NMZ XXIV (1903) 258–60, 274–75, 282–83, 294–95.

Mendel/LEXIKON — Hermann Mendel, *Musikalisches Conversations-Lexikon,* 11 vols. and "Ergänzungsband," completed from M-Z by August Reissmann. Berlin: L. Heimann, pub. from Vol. II by Robert Oppenheim, 1870–83.

Mendelssohn/BRIEFE — Paul and Carl Mendelssohn Bartholdy (eds.), *Briefe aus den Jahren 1830 bis 1847 von Felix Mendelssohn Bartholdy,* 5th ed., 2 vols. Leipzig: Hermann Mendelssohn, 1882.

MENDELSSOHN/Moscheles — Felix Moscheles (ed. and trans.), *Letters of Felix Mendelssohn to Ignaz and Charles Moscheles.* Boston: Ticknor, 1888.

Mendelssohn/VERLEGER — Felix Mendelssohn Bartholdy, *Briefe an deutsche Verleger,* compiled and ed. by R. Elvers (Vol. I of projected complete letters). Berlin: Walter de Gruyter, 1968.

Mendelssohn/WERKE-m — Julius Rietz (ed.), *Felix Mendelssohn Bartholdy's Werke; kritische durchgesehene Ausgabe,* 19 series in 37 vols. Leipzig: Breitkopf & Härtel, 1874–77.

MÉNESTREL — *Le Ménestrel.* 1833–1940.

MERCURE — *Le Mercure musical.* 1905–6.

Méreaux/CLAVECINISTES-m — Amédée Méreaux (ed.), *Les Clavecinistes de 1637 à 1790,* 4 vols. (I–III, music; IV, text). Paris: Heugel, 1867. Cf. Cat. NYPL XIX 81.

Mersmann/KAMMERMUSIK — Hans Mersmann, *Die Kammermusik,* 4 vols. (of which III is *Deutsche Romantik* and IV is *Europäische Kammermusik des XIX. und XX. Jahrhunderts*). Leipzig: Breitkopf & Härtel, 1930.

Mersmann/ROMANTISCHEN — ——, "Sonatenformen in der romantischen Kammermusik," pp. 112–17 in *Festschrift für Johannes*

Wolf zu seinen sechzigsten Geburtstage (Berlin: Breslauer, 1929).

MfMg   *Monatshefte für Musikgeschichte.* 1869–1905.

MGG   Friedrich Blume (ed.), *Die Musik in Geschichte und Gegenwart,* 13 vols. up to this writing (through "Volk-"). Kassel: Bärenreiter-Verlag, 1949———. Cf. NOTES XXIV (1967–68) 217–44 (F. Blume, trans. by J. Godwin).

Michel/SONATE   Henri Michel, *La Sonate pour clavier avant Beethoven.* Amiens: Yvert & Tellier, 1907.

Mies/SCHUBERT-m   Paul Mies (ed.), *Franz Schubert: Klaviersonaten,* 2 vols., with prefaces on texts (11 complete sons., lacking D. 459; with Vol. III, "the Fantasias and the fragments or unfinished sonatas," in progress as of 1966). Munich and Duisburg: G. Henle, 1961.

Milhaud/NOTES   Darius Milhaud, *Notes Without Music, an Aubiography,* trans. by D. Evans (from the original French ed. of 1949) and ed. by R. H. Myers. London: Dennis Dobson, 1952.

Mitchell/HUMMEL   Francis Humphries Mitchell, "The Piano Concertos of Johann Nepomuk Hummel," unpub. Ph.D. diss. Northwestern University, 1957.

Mitschka/BRAHMS   Arno Mitschka, *Der Sonatensatz in den Werken von Johannes Brahms,* (Ph.D. diss. [started in Breslau "several years" before World War II], Johannes-Gutenberg-Universität, Mainz). Gütersloh: pub. by the author, 1961.

ML   *Music and Letters.* 1920———.

MMM   *Monatschrift für moderne Musik.* 1919———.

MMR   *Monthly Musical Record.* 1871———.

MO   *Musical Opinion and Music Trade Review.* 1877———. (The title was later reduced to *Musical Opinion.*)

Monrad-Johansen/GRIEG   David Monrad-Johansen, *Edvard Grieg,* trans. from the original Norwegian of 1934 into English in 1938 by Madge Robertson. New York: Tudor, 1945. Cf. Schjelderup-Ebbe/GRIEG 333–34 *et passim.*

MOSCHELES   Charlotte Moscheles, *Life of Moscheles, With Selections From His Diaries and Correspondence,* trans. (from the original German ed., Leipzig, 1872) by A. D. Coleridge, 2 vols. London: Hurst and Blackett, 1873. (The same trans. appeared as *Recent Music and Musicians . . . ,* in New York in 1874.) Cf. the review in MT XVI (1874) 862–63.

Moser/MUSIKÄSTHETIK   Hans Joachim Moser, *Musikästhetik.* Berlin: Walter de Gruyter, 1953.

Moser/JOACHIM   Andreas Moser, *Joseph Joachim: Ein Lebensbild,* 2d ed. in 2 vols. (revised from the first ed. of 1898). Berlin: Deutsche Brahms-Gesellschaft, 1908 and 1910.

Moser/LEXIKON   Hans Joachim Moser, *Musik Lexikon,* 4th ed., 2 vols. plus *Nachtrag* (1958) and *Ergänzungsband* (1963). Berlin: Max Hesse, 1955.

MOZART-JAHRBUCH   *Mozart-Jahrbuch.* Salzburg: Internationale Stiftung Mozarteum, 1950———.

          The Musical Quarterly. 1915———.

MR   *The Music Review.* 1940———.

MT   *The Musical Times.* 1844———.

Mühsam/THALBERG   Gerd Mühsam, "Sigismund Thalberg als Klavierkomponist," unpub. Ph.D. diss., Universität Wien, 1937.

Müller/STEIBELT   Gottfried Müller, *Daniel Steibelt: sein Leben und seine Klavierwerke (Etüden und Sonaten;* Ph.D. diss., Greifswald, 1932). Leipzig: Heitz, 1933.

Müller-Reuter/LEXIKON   Theodor Müller-Reuter, *Lexikon der deutschen Konzertliteratur,* 2 vols. (Vol. II is *Nachtrag* or suppl.). Leipzig: C. F. Kahnt, 1909 and 1921.

Mueller von Asow/   Erich H. Mueller von Asow, *Richard Strauss:*
STRAUSS   *Thematisches Verzeichnis,* 2 vols. to date; 3d vol. in progress as of 1967, ed. by Alfons Ott and Franz Trenner. Vienna: L. Doblinger, 1959, 1962———.

Muns/CLIMAX   George E. Muns, Jr., "Climax in Music," unpub. Ph.D. diss., The University of North Carolina at Chapel Hill, 1955.

Murdoch/BRAHMS   William Murdoch, *Brahms, With an Analytical Study of the Complete Pianoforte Works.* London: Rich & Cowan, 1938 (first pub. 1933).

MUSIC   *Music.* (Chicago) 1891–1902.

MUSICA   *Musica.* 1947———.

MUSICAL WORLD   *The Musical World, a Weekly Record of Musical Science, Literature, and Intelligence.* 1836–91.

MUSIKLEBEN   *Das Musikleben.* 1948———.

MUSORGSKY READER   Jay Leyda & Sergei Bertensson (eds.), *The Musorgsky Reader: A Life of Modeste Petrovich Musorgsky in Letters and Documents,* largely trans. from A. Rimsky-Korsakov's Russian ed. of 1932. New York: W. W. Norton, 1947. Cf. BAKER 1141.

Musorgsky/WERKE-m   Paul Lamm (ed.), *Modest Petrovich Musorgsky Sämtliche Werke,* 8 series in 25 vols. Vienna [and Moscow]: Universal, 1928–39. Cf. MUSORGSKY READER 424–37.

MW   *Musikalisches Wochenblatt.* 1870–1910.

Nagel/BRAHMS   Willibald Nagel, *Die Klaviersonaten von Joh. Brahms; technische-ästhetische Analysen.* Stuttgart: Carl Grüninger, 1915. Originally pub. in NZM XXXIV (1913) and XXXV (1914), *passim.*

NBJ   *Neues Beethoven-Jahrbuch,* 10 vols. 1924–42.

Nef/HISTORY   Karl Nef, *An Outline of the History of Music,* trans. and enlarged from the 2d German ed. of 1930 (originally pub. in 1920) and the 2d French ed. of 1931 by Carl F. Pfatteicher. New York: Columbia University Press, 1935.

Neighbour/SCHUMANN-m   Oliver Neighbour (ed.), *R. Schumann: Sonata No. 3 in A minor for Violin and Piano.* London: Schott, 1956.

Neighbour & Tyson/ENGLISH   Oliver Neighbour and Alan Tyson, *English Music Publishers' Plate Numbers in the First Half of the Nineteenth Century.* London: Faber and Faber, 1965. Cf. MT CVI (1965) 521 and 683.

Nettl/DOCUMENTS   Paul Nettl, *The Book of Musical Documents.* New York: Philosophical Library, 1948.

Newman/ACCOMPANIED   William S. Newman, "Concerning the Accompanied Clavier Sonata," MQ XXXIII (1947) 327–49.

Newman/ARTIST   Ernest Newman, *Wagner as Man and Artist,* 2d ed. (first pub. in 1924; first ed. pub. in 1914). New York: Random House, 1960.

Newman/CHOPIN   William S. Newman, "Fryderyk Chopin: Complete Works [Warsaw: Fryderyk Chopin Institute, 1949–at least 1962]," review in PQ No. 30 (winter 1959–60) 15, 17, and 19–21.

Newman/CLIMAX   ———, "The Climax of Music," *The University of North Carolina Extension Bulletin* XXXI/3 (Jan., 1952) 22–40; abridged in MR XIII (1952) 283–93.

Newman/CZERNY   ———, "About Carl Czerny's Op. 600 and the 'First' Description of 'Sonata Form,'" JAMS XX (1967) 513–15. Cf. Newman/THEORISTS; SSB II.

Newman/DIABELLI-m   ——— (ed.), *Diabelli Variations: 16 Contemporaries of Beethoven on a Waltz Tune* (with preface). Evanston (Ill.): Summy-Birchard, 1958.

Newman/K. 457   William S. Newman, "K. 457 and op. 13—Two Related Masterpieces in C minor," MR XXVIII (1967) 38–44; reprinted with slight changes from PQ XV (fall 1966) 11–15.

Newman/LISZT   ———, "Franz Liszt's Newly Discovered Duo (Sonate) for Violin and Piano," PQ XIII/50 (winter 1964–65) 25–26.

Newman/OP. 106   ———, "Some 19th-Century Consequences of Beethoven's 'Hammerklavier' Sonata, Op. 106," scheduled to be pub. serially in PQ nos. 67 and 68 (spring and summer, 1969).

Newman/THEORISTS ———, "The Recognition of Sonata Form by Theorists of the 18th and 19th Centuries," PAPERS AMS 1941 (printed 1946) 21–29. Cf. Newman/CZERNY; SSB II.

Newman/THIRTEEN-m ——— (ed.), *Thirteen Keyboard Sonatas of the 18th and 19th Centuries* (by Barrière, Platti, D. Alberti, G. Benda, Agrell, Neefe, Blasco de Nebra, Dittersdorf, Wölfl, E. T. A. Hoffmann, Reichardt, K. Loewe, and Moscheles). Chapel Hill: The University of North Carolina Press, 1947.

Newman/TREND William S. Newman, "The Present Trend of the Sonata Idea," unpub. Ph.D. diss., Western Reserve University, 1939.

Newman/UNDERSTANDING ———, *Understanding Music,* first pub. in 1953, 2d ed. in 1961, with revisions in Colophon paperback. New York: Harper & Row, 1967.

Newman/WAGNER Ernest Newman, *The Life of Richard Wagner,* 4 vols. New York: Alfred A. Knopf, 1933, 1937, 1941, 1946.

Newmarch/ Rosa Newmarch, *The Music of Czechoslovakia.* Lon-
CZECHOSLOVAKIA don: Oxford, 1942.

Nicolescu/SONATA Mircea Nicolescu, *Sonata: Natura, originea și evoluția ei.* [Bucharest:] Editura Muzicală, 1962.

Niecks/CHOPIN Frederick Niecks, *Friedrich Chopin als Musiker,* revised by the author and trans. from the original English ed. of 1888 by W. Langhans, 2 vols. Leipzig: F. E. C. Leuckart, 1890.

Niecks/SCHUMANN ———, *Robert Schumann.* New York: E. P. Dutton, 1925.

Niggli/SCHUBERT [Arnold Niggli], "Franz Schuberts Klaviersonaten zu 2 Händen," SMZ XVIII (1878) 21–22, 29–31, 37–38, 45–47. The authorship comes from Kahl/SCHUBERT item 374.

Nikolaiev/ Aleksandr Aleksandrovich Nikolaiev, *The Piano-
TCHAIKOVSKY forte Heritage of Tchaikovsky* (in Russian). Moscow, 1958. References are cited here by way of Alekseev & Novikova.

Nisser/SVENSK Carl Nisser, *Svensk Instrumentalkomposition 1770–1830, Nominalkatalog.* Stockholm: Gothia, 1943.

NMZ *Neue Musik-Zeitung.* 1880–1928.

Noé/ZYKLISCHEN Günther von Noé, "Der Strukturwandel der zyklischen Sonatenform," NZM CXXV (1964) 55–62. Concerns interlocking of mvts.; cf. Marx/ZYKLISCHE.

Nohl/GLUCK & WEBER Ludwig Nohl (ed.), *Lettres de Gluck et de Weber,* trans. by Guy de Charnacé. Paris: Henri Plon, 1870.

Nohl/SCHUBERT Walter Nohl, "Beethoven's and Schubert's Personal Relations," MQ XIV (1928) 553–62.

814   BIBLIOGRAPHY

Nohl/SYMPHONY   Ludwig Nohl, "The Father of the Symphony," MT
                        XXI (1880) 491–92, 539–40, 597–98; XXII (1881)
                        14–15, 72–73, 121–23.

NOTES   *Music Library Association Notes,* Second Series.
                        1943———.

NZM   Robert Schumann and successors (eds.), *Neue Zeit-
                        schrift für Musik.* 1834——— (with various names and
                        affiliations after 1858; cf. Freystätter/ZEITSCHRIFTEN
                        57–58 [with errors] and GROVE VI 651).

ÖMZ   *Österreichische Musikzeitschrift.* 1946———.

O'Leary/BENNETT   Arthur O'Leary, "Sir William Sterndale Bennett: A
                        Brief Review of His Life and Works," PMA VIII
                        (1881–82) 123–45.

Opieński/CHOPIN   Henryk Opieński, "Sonaty Chopina, ich oceny i ich
                        wartość konstrukcyjna" ("Chopin's Sonatas, Their
                        Understanding and Their Structural Principles"),
                        in *Kwartalnik Muzyczny* I/1 and 2 (1928–29) 59–72
                        and 152–62. Cf. Sydow/BIBLIOGRAPHIE item 3347;
                        Bronarski/CHOPIN II 103.

Orel/SCHUBERT   Alfred Orel, "Franz Schuberts 'Sonate' für Klavier,
                        Violine und Violoncell aus dem Jahre 1812," zfMW
                        V (1922–23) 209–18.

Orel/SCHUBERT-m   ——— (ed.), *Franz Schubert: Sonate für Klavier,
                        Violine u. Violoncell,* D. 28. Vienna: Wiener Phil-
                        harmonischer Verlag, 1923.

Ossofski/GLAZUNOV   Alexandr Vyacheslavovich Ossofski, *Aleksandr Kon-
                        stantinovitch Glazunov.* Leningrad (?), 1907.

PADEREWSKI   Ignace Jan Paderewski and Mary Lawton, *The
                        Paderewski Memoirs* (up to 1914). New York:
                        Charles Scribner, 1938.

Panofsky/WAGNER   Walter Panofsky, *Wagner: A Pictorial Biography.*
                        New York: Viking Press, 1963.

Parrott/SCHUMANN   Ian Parrott, "A Plea for Schumann's Op. 11," ML
                        XXXIII (1952) 55–58.

Parry/EVOLUTION   C. Hubert H. Parry, *The Evolution of the Art of
                        Music* (originally pub. in this form in 1896). New
                        York: D. Appleton, 1916.

Parry/STYLE   Charles Hubert Hastings Parry, *Style in Musical Art.*
                        London: Macmillan, 1911, reprinted in 1924.

PAZDÍREK   Franz Pazdírek, *Universal-Handbuch der Musik-
                        literatur aller Zeiten und Völker,* 34 vols. Vienna:
                        Pazdírek, [1904–10]. Cf. MGG X 981–82 (Výborný).
                        Limited to publications procurable at the time the
                        set was prepared. Vol. nos. differ with the binding
                        of this set, and occasionally conflict in the present

	study; but the pagination and alphabetization remain consistent. A reprint of the complete set was announced by Frits Knuf (Hilversum, Holland) in 1967.
Pearce/MENDELSSOHN	Charles William Pearce, *Mendelssohn's Organ Sonatas Technically and Critically Discussed.* London: Vincent Music, [*ca.* 1902].
Petitpierre/ MENDELSSOHNS	Jacques Petitpierre, *The Romance of the Mendelssohns,* trans. from the French (Paris, 1937) by G. Micholet-Coté. London: Dennis Dobson, 1947.
PIANOFORTE	*Il Pianoforte.* 1920–27.
Pincherle/MUSICIENS	Marc Pincherle (ed.), *Musiciens peints par eux-mêmes, Lettres de compositeurs écrites en français (1771–1910).* Paris: Pierre Cornau, 1939.
PISK ESSAYS	John Glowacki (ed.), *Paul A. Pisk: Essays in His Honor.* Austin: University of Texas Press, 1967.
Plantinga/SCHUMANN	Leon B. Plantinga, "The Musical Criticism of Robert Schumann in the *Neue Zeitschrift für Musik, 1834–44,*" unpub. Ph.D. diss., Yale University, 1964. Since its use in SSB this diss. was pub. by Yale University Press (late 1967); cf. the review by J. A. Westrup in ML XLIX (1968) 182–83 and by P. H. Lang in MQ LIV (1968) 361–75.
Pleasants/HANSLICK	Henry Pleasants (trans. and ed.), *Eduard Hanslick: Music Criticisms, 1846–99.* Baltimore: Penguin Books, 1950.
PMA	*Proceedings of the (Royal) Musical Association.* 1874——.
Pohl/MOZART	Carl Ferdinand Pohl, *Mozart und Haydn in London,* 2 vols. Vienna: Carl Gerold's Sohn, 1867.
PORTUGALIAE-m	*Portugaliae Musica, Série A* (and B), 10 vols. up to 1967. Lisbon: Fundação Calouste Gulbenkian, 1965——.
Pougin/SONATE	Arthur Pougin, "Courte Monographie de la sonate," MÉNESTREL LXVII (1901) 275–76, 282–83, 293.
PQ	*The Piano Quarterly* (founded as *Piano Quarterly Newsletter*). 1952——.
Prod'homme/ BEETHOVEN	Jacques-Gabriel Prod'homme, *Les Sonates pour Piano de Beethoven.* Paris: Delagrave, 1937.
Prod'homme/SCHUBERT	——, "Schubert's Works in France," MQ XIV (1928) 495–514; also pub. in KONGRESS SCHUBERT 87–110 as "Les Œuvres de Schubert en France."
Prosniz/HANDBUCH	Adolf Prosniz, *Handbuch der Klavier-Literatur,* 2 vols. (1450–1830, 1830–1904). Leipzig: L. Doblinger, 1908 (2d ed.), 1907.
Prout/DUSSEK	Ebenezer Prout, "Dussek's Piano Sonatas," MT XVIII (1877) 422–24, 468–70.

816

BIBLIOGRAPHY

Prout *et al.*/RAFF — Ebenezer Prout, John South Shedlock, and Charles Ainslee Barry, "Raff's Symphonies," MMR V (1875) 32–33, 46–49, 61–64, 77–80, 93–95, 109–11, 121–23, 133–35, 147–49, with many exx.

QUARTERLY — *The Quarterly Musical Magazine and Review.* 1818–28.

Raabe/LISZT — Peter Raabe, *Franz Liszt: Leben und Schaffen,* 2 vols. Stuttgart: J. B. Cotta, 1931. A revision by Felix Raabe (son) was in progress in 1967.

Radiciotti/ROSSINI — Giuseppe Radiciotti, *Gioacchino Rossini: Vita documentata, opere ed influenza su l'arte,* 3 vols. Tivoli: Majella di A. Chicca, 1927–29.

Raff/RAFF — Helene Raff, *Joachim Raff: Ein Lebensbild* (completed in 1922). Regensburg: Gustav Bosse, 1925.

RaM — *Rassegna musicale.* 1928–62.

Ramann/LISZT — Lina Ramann, *Franz Liszt als Künstler und Mensch,* 2 books in 3 vols. Leipzig: Breitkopf & Härtel, 1880, 1887, and 1894.

Ratz/SCHUBERT — Erwin Ratz, "Zur Chronologie der Klaviersonaten Franz Schuberts," SMZ LXXXIX (1949) 1–5; reprinted in ÖMZ V (1950) 7–14.

Ratz/SCHUBERT-m — —— (ed.), *Franz Schubert: Klaviersonaten nach den Autographen und Erstdrucken,* with preface; 2 vols. (including 12 complete sons. plus D. 625 and D. 840; with 8 more incomplete sons. expected in a suppl. vol.). Vienna: Universal, 1958. Cf. the detailed check of the text in Taggart/SCHUBERT 32–55; also, the review by H. Ferguson in ML XLVIII (1967) 406.

Raybould/MEDTNER — Clarence Raybould, "A Monograph on Medtner," in Holt/MEDTNER 133–40.

RBdM — *Revue belge de musicologie.* 1946——.

RdM — *Revue de musicologie* (founded as *Bulletin de la Société française de musicologie*). 1917——.

RECHERCHES — *"Recherches," sur la Musique française classique.* 1960——.

Redlich/SCHUMANN — Hans Ferdinand Redlich, "Schumann Discoveries," MMR LXXX (1950) 143–47, 182–84, 261–65 ("A Postscript"); LXXXI (1951) 14–16 ("A Postscript").

Reed/ELGAR — William Henry Reed, *Elgar.* London: J. M. Dent, 1939.

Refardt/HUBER — Edgar Refardt, *Hans Huber: Leben und Werk eines schweizer Musikers.* Zürich: Atlantis, 1944.

Reeser/NEDERLANDSE — Eduard Reeser, *Een Eeuw nederlandse Musiek.* Amsterdam: N. V. Em. Querido, 1950.

REGER BRIEFE — Ottmar Schreiber (ed.), *Max Reger: Briefe zwischen der Arbeit*. Bonn: Ferdinand Dümmler, 1956.

REGER GEDENKSCHRIFT — Ottmar Schreiber & Gerd Sievers (eds.), *Max Reger, zum 50. Todestag am 11, Mai 1966; Eine Gedenkschrift*. Bonn: Ferd. Dümmler, 1966.

REGER-GEORG II — Hedwig and E. H. Mueller von Asow (eds.), *Max Reger: Briefwechsel mit Herzog Georg II von Sachsen-Meiningen*. Weimar: Hermann Böhlaus Nachfolger, 1949.

REGER-GESELLSCHAFT — *Mitteilungen der Max Reger-Gesellschaft*, 17 issues. Stuttgart: J. Engelhorn, 1921–41. Cf. Stein/VERZEICHNIS 574–76.

Reger/WERKE-m — Max Reger: *Sämtliche Werke*, in co-operation with the Max-Reger-Institut; 35 vols. projected. Wiesbaden: Breitkopf & Härtel, 1954——.

Rehberg/BRAHMS — Walter and Paula Rehberg, *Johannes Brahms: Sein Leben und Werk*. Zürich: Artemis, 1947.

Rehberg/SCHUMANN — Paula and Walter Rehberg, *Robert Schumann: Sein Leben und sein Werk*. Zürich: Artemis, 1954.

Reicha & Czerny/COMPOSITION — Anton Reicha, *Vollständiges Lehrbuch der musikalischen Composition*, trans. (with both French and German texts) and annotated (cf. Vol. I, p. 4) by Carl Czerny; Vol. I being Reicha's *Cour de composition musicale* (Paris: Gambaro, 1816), II his *Traité de melodie* (Paris: author, 1814), and III and IV his *Traité de haute composition musicale* (Paris: Costellat, 1824–26). Vienna: Diabelli, [1832; plate no. 4170 and dated preface]. Cf. MGG XI 148 (J. Bužga); Cat. NYPL XXV 412; Newman/CZERNY.

Reither/RACHMANINOFF — Joseph Reither, "Chronicle of Exile [of Rachmaninoff]," TEMPO XXII (winter 1951–52) 29–36.

Řepková/SMETANA — Vera Řepková (ed.), *Bedřich Smetana: Sonáta pro klavir na dvě ruce,* with preface by Mirko Očadlík. Prague: Melantrich, 1949.

Reti/BEETHOVEN — Rudolph Reti, *Thematic Patterns in Sonatas of Beethoven*, ed. by Deryck Cooke. New York: Macmillan, 1967.

RGM — *Revue et gazette musicale de Paris*. 1834–80 (with changes of title). Cf. GROVE VI 647.

Richter/KAMMERMUSIK — Johannes Friedrich Richter, *Kammermusik-Katalog, Verzeichnis der von 1944 bis 1958 veröffentlichten Werke für Kammermusik und für Klavier vier- und sechshändig sowie für zwei und mehr Klaviere*. Leipzig: Friedrich Hofmeister, 1960. Cf. Altmann/KAMMERMUSIK.

RICORDI ARTE-m — *L'Arte antica e moderna, scelta di composizioni per pianoforte*, 21 vols. Milan: G. Ricordi, [ca. 1878-ca.

1910]. "Mostly derived from" TRÈSOR-m; cf. Cat. BOLOGNA IV 180.

RICORDI ENCICLOPEDIA — *Enciclopedia della musica,* 4 vols. Milano: G. Ricordi, 1963–64.

Riehl/CHARAKTERKÖPFE — Wilhelm Heinrich von Riehl, *Musikalische Charakterköpfe,* 4th ed. (first pub. in 1853–61), 2 vols. Stuttgart: J. G. Cotta, 1868 and 1875.

Riemann/LEXIKON — Alfred Einstein (ed.), *Hugo Riemann's Musik Lexikon,* 11th ed., 2 vols. Berlin: Max Hesses Verlag, 1929. This ed. is used unless the 12th ed. (Mainz: B. Schott, 1959——) is specified.

Riesemann/MOUSSORGSKY — Oskar van Riesemann, *Moussorgsky,* trans. from the original German ed. of 1925 by P. England. New York: Alfred A. Knopf, 1929.

Riezler/SCHUBERT — Walter Riezler, *Schuberts Instrumentalmusik; Werkanalysen.* Zürich: Atlantis, 1967.

Rimbault/PIANOFORTE — Edward F. Rimbault, *The Pianoforte, Its Origin, Progress, and Construction* . . . (with music exx., pp. 237–368). London: Robert Cocks, 1860.

Ritzel/SONATENFORM — Fred Ritzel, *Die Entwicklung der "Sonatenform" im musiktheoretischen Schrifttum des 18. und 19. Jahrhunderts* (Ph.D. diss.). Wiesbaden: Breitkopf & Härtel, 1968.

RM — *La Revue musicale* (founded by H. Prunières). 1920——.

RM/CHOPIN — *Chopin: Numéro spécial* (an anthology of historical and analytical articles). RM XII/121 (Dec., 1931). Cf. Sydow/BIBLIOGRAPHIE no. 7779.

RM/FRANCK — Three articles on César Franck, by Julien Tiersot, Henri Duparc, and André Schaeffner, in RM IV/2 (Dec. 1, 1922) 97–154.

RM/LALO — Three articles on Édouard Lalo—by Paul Dukas, Adolphe Jullien, and Pierre Lalo, in RM IV/5 (March 1, 1923) 97–124.

Rösner/REGER — Helmut Rösner, "Max Regers Violinsonate Op. 72, Entwurf und endgültige Gestalt," in REGER GEDENKSCHRIFT 169–88.

Roger-Ducasse/FAURÉ — Jean-Jules Aimable Roger-Ducasse, "[Gabriel Fauré:] La Musique de chambre," RM II (Oct., 1922, *Fauré: Numéro spécial*) 60–79.

Rogers/BRISTOW — Delmar D. Rogers, "Nineteenth-Century Music in New York City as Reflected in the Career of George Frederick Bristow," unpub. Ph.D. diss., University of Michigan, 1967.

Rokseth/GRIEG — Yvonne Rokseth, *Grieg.* Paris: Rieder, 1933.

Rosenfeld/AMERICAN — Paul Rosenfeld, *An Hour with American Music.* Philadelphia: J. P. Lippincott, 1929.

Rossini/SONATE-m

Cioacchino Rossini, *Sei Sonate a quattro,* ed. by L. Liviabella, with "Prefazione" by A. Bonaccorsi; Vol. I in *Quaderni Rossiniani.* Pesaro: Fondazione Rossini, 1954.

Rostand/FAURÉ

Claude Rostand, *L'Œuvre de Fauré,* 5th ed. Paris: L. B. Janin, 1945.

Rubinstein/
ERINNERUNGEN

Anton Rubinstein, *Erinnerungen aus fünfzig* Jahren, trans. into German from the original Russian ed. of 1892 by E. Kretschmann, 2d ed. Leipzig: Bartholf Senff, 1895. The English trans. by A. Delano (1903) was not used here.

Rubinstein/
GEDANKENKORB

Anton Rubinstein's Gedankenkorb, with foreword by H. Wolff, 2d ed. Leipzig: Bartholf Senff, 1897.

Rueth/DOHNÁNYI

Marion Ursula Rueth, "The Tallahassee Years of Ernst von Dohnányi," photoduplication of typed M.A. thesis, Florida State University, 1962.

Ruthardt/LINKE-m

Adolf Ruthardt (ed.), *Album für die linke Hand für Pianoforte.* Leipzig: C. F. Peters No. 2716, [1894?].

SAINSBURY

[John S. Sainsbury], *A Dictionary of Musicians From the Earliest Times* (originally pub. in London in 1824 [not 1825] in 2 vols.), with Introduction by the late H. G. Farmer (ed. version of ML XII [1931] 384–92), 2 vols. New York: Da Capo, 1966. Cf. V. Duckles' review in NOTES XXIII (1967) 737–39.

Saint-Foix/PIANISTES

Georges de Saint-Foix, "Les premiers Pianistes parisiens," RM III (Aug., 1922) 121–36 and Suppl.: "Jean Schobert," IV (April, 1923) 193–205 and Suppl.: "Nicolas-Joseph Hüllmandel," V (June, 1924) 187–98 and Suppl.: "Edelmann (Jean-Frédéric)" and "Rigel (Henri-Joseph)," VI (June, 1925) 209–15: "Jean-Louis Adam," VI (Aug., 1925) 105–9: "Les Frères Jadin," VII (Nov., 1925) 43–46: "Les six Sonates de Méhul," VII (Feb., 1926) 102–10: "Boieldieu," VIII (Nov., 1926) 13–20: "Ignace-Antoine Ladurner," IX (Aug., 1928) 321–32: "A. P. F. Boëly."

St John/SMYTH

Christopher St John, *Ethyl Smyth, a Biography,* with additional chaps. by V. Sackville-West and K. Dale. London: Longmans, Green, 1959.

Saint-Saëns/ESSAYS

Camille Saint-Saëns, *Outspoken Essays on Music,* trans. by Fred Rothwell. London: Kegan Paul, Trench, Trubner, 1922.

Salazar/TRENDS

Adolfo Salazar, *Music in Our Time; Trends in Music Since the Romantic Era,* trans. from *Música moderna* (Buenos Aires, 1944) by Isabel Pope. New York: W. W. Norton, 1946.

Salter/AMERICAN   Sumner Salter, "Early Encouragements to American Composers," MQ XVIII (1932) 76–105.

Salter/MTNA   ———, "The Music Teachers' National Association in Its Early Relation to American Composers," *Proceedings for 1932* of the Music Teachers National Association 9–34.

Salzer/SCHUBERT   Felix Salzer, "Die Sonatenform bei Franz Schubert" (extract from unpub. Ph.D. diss., Vienna, 1926), SZMW XV (1928) 86–125.

Samaroff/SCHUBERT   Olga Samaroff (*née* Hickenlooper), "The Piano Music of Schubert," MQ XIV (1928) 596–609.

Sandberger/AUFSÄTZE   Adolf Sandberger, *Ausgewählte Aufsätze zur Musikgeschichte,* 3 vols. Munich: Drei Masken, 1921, 1924, 1934.

Saunders/WEBER   William Saunders, *Weber.* New York: E. P. Dutton, 1940.

SBE   William S. Newman, *The Sonata in the Baroque Era,* vol. I in *A History of the Sonata Idea.* Chapel Hill: The University of North Carolina Press, 1959; revised 2d ed., 1966. References in this vol. are to the 2d ed.

SCE   ———, *The Sonata in the Classic Era,* vol. II in *A History of the Sonata Idea.* Chapel Hill: The University of North Carolina Press, 1963.

Sceats/KARG-ELERT   Godfrey Sceats, *The Organ Works of Karg-Elert,* 2d ed. (originally pub. in 1940). New York: Peters, 1950.

Schaal/DISSERTATIONEN   Richard Schaal, *Verzeichnis deutschsprachiger musikwissenschaftlicher Dissertationen 1861–1960.* Kassel: Bärenreiter, 1963.

Schaal/KAUN   ———, *Hugo Kaun (1863–1932): Leben und Werk.* Regensburg: Josef Habbel, [1948].

Schaal/LOKALGESCHICHTS   ———, *Das Schrifttum zur musikalischen Lokalgeschichts-Forschung.* Kassel: Bärenreiter, 1947.

Schauffler/BRAHMS   Robert Haven Schauffler, *The Unknown Brahms: His Life, Character and Works; Based on New Material.* New York: Crown, 1940 (first pub. 1933).

Schering/NEUROMANTIK   Arnold Schering, "Aus den Jugendjahren der musikalischen Neuromantik," JMP XXIV (1917) 45–63.

Schiffer/DUSSEK   Leo Schiffer, *Johann Ladislau Dussek, seine Sonaten und seine Konzerte* (Ph.D. diss., University of Munich). Leipzig: Robert Noske, 1914 (available only indirectly to the present study; cf. SSB XVII and Craw/DUSSEK 1–2).

Schilling/LEXICON   Gustav Schilling (ed.), *Encyclopädie der gesammten musikalischen Wissenschaften oder Universal-Lexi-*

con der Tonkunst, 6 vols. Stuttgart: F. H. Köhler, 1835–38. *Supplementband,* 1842. Cf. GASSNER.

Schindler & MacArdle/
BEETHOVEN

Anton Felix Schindler, *Beethoven as I Knew Him,* trans. by Constance S Jolly and annotated by Donald W. MacArdle from the 3d ed. of 1860, 2 vols. in one. Chapel Hill: The University of North Carolina Press, 1966. Cf. MT. CVIII (1967) 40–41 (J. Kerman).

Schjelderup-Ebbe/
GRIEG

Dag Schjelderup-Ebbe, *Edvard Grieg* [and his early works:] *1858–1867, with special reference to the evolution of his harmonic style.* Oslo: Universitetsforlaget, 1964.

Schlesinger/CRAMER

Thea Schlesinger, *Johann Baptist Cramer und seine Klaviersonaten* (Ph.D. diss. [completed in 1925], Ludwig-Maximilians-Universität in Munich). Munich: Knorr & Hirth, 1928.

Schmidl/DIZIONARIO

Carlo Schmidl, *Dizionario universale dei musicisti,* 2 vols. and "Supplemento." Milan: Sonzogno, 1926 and 1938.

Schmitz/LISZT

Eugen Schmitz, "Liszts H-moll Sonate: eine hermeneutische Studie," ADMZ XXXI (1904) 451–53, 470–71.

Schnapp/CZERNY

Friedrich Schnapp, "Ein autobiographischer Brief Carl Czernys aus dem Jahre 1824," NZM CVIII (1941) 89–96.

Schnapp/LISZT

————, "Verschollene Kompositionen Franz Liszts," in *Festschrift zu Peter Raabes 70. Geburtstag* (Leipzig: C. F. Peters, 1942) 119–53.

Schneider/ELEMENTS

Frederick [Johann Christian Friedrich] Schneider, *The Elements of Musical Harmony and Composition,* trans. (by?) from the 2d, revised ed. of *Elementarbuch der Harmonie und Tonsetzkunst* (Leipzig: Peters, 1827; originally 1820). London: Clementi, 1828.

Schonberg/PIANISTS

Harold C. Schonberg, *The Great Pianists.* New York: Simon and Schuster, 1963.

Schoolfield/GERMAN

George C. Schoolfield, *The Figure of the Musician in German Literature.* Chapel Hill: The University of North Carolina Press, 1956.

Schrade/BEETHOVEN

Leo Schrade, *Beethoven in France, the Growth of an Idea.* New Haven: Yale University Press, 1942.

SCHUBERT WERKE-m

Franz Schubert's Werke, 21 Series (including suppl.) in 39 vols. (or 41 in the 1928 reprint), plus *Revisionsbericht.* Leipzig: Breitkopf & Härtel, 1884–97. Reprinted unaltered in 1964, in 19 vols., by Dover Publications, New York. Cf. Deutsch/COLLECTED.

Schuberth/LEXIKON

Julius Schuberth's Musikalisches Conversations-

Lexicon, 11th ed., ed. by Emil Breslauer. Leipzig: J. Schuberth, 1892.

Schüz/SONATE

Alfred Schüz, "Die Sonate der Zukunft," NMZ XXIV (1903) 4, 34–35, 58–59, 70–71.

SCHUMANN-BRAHMS

Berthold Litzmann (ed., "im Auftrage von Marie Schumann"), *Clara Schumann* [and] *Johannes Brahms: Briefe aus den Jahren 1853–1896,* 2 vols. Leipzig: Breitkopf & Härtel, 1927. Primarily because it is abridged, the trans. of this collection that appeared in the same year (New York: Longmans, Green) is not referred to in SSB.

SCHUMANN/-DRUCKE

Erst- und Frühdrucke von Robert Schumann in der Musikbibliothek Leipzig, prepared by Ferdinand Hirsch and Ellen Roeser. Leipzig: Musikbibliothek, 1960.

Schumann/ JUGENDBRIEFE

Robert Schumann, *Jugendbriefe, nach den Originalen mitgetheilt von Clara Schumann,* 2d ed. Leipzig: Breitkopf und Härtel, 1886.

Schumann/SCHRIFTEN

Martin Kreisig (ed.), *Gesammelte Schriften über Musik und Musiker von Robert Schumann,* 5th ed., 2 vols. Leipzig: Breitkopf & Härtel, 1914. (No English trans. proved adequate for reference here and none is complete; cf. SSB VIII; ML XLVI [1965] 267–68 [Westrup]; JAMS XVIII [1965] 417–19 [Plantinga].)

Schumann/WERKE-m

Clara Schumann (and Johannes Brahms; eds.), *Robert Schumann's Werke,* 14 series in 31 vols. Leipzig: Breitkopf & Härtel, 1881–93. Cf. Heyer/ HISTORICAL 297; Litzmann/SCHUMANN 359–61.

Schwarz/SCHUMANN

Werner Schwarz, *Robert Schumann und die Variation, mit besonderer Berücksichtigung der Klavierwerke.* Kassel: Bärenreiter, 1932.

SCHWEIZER LEXIKON

Edgar Refardt, Willi Schuh, and Hans Ehinger (eds.), *Schweizer Musiker Lexikon.* Zürich: Atlantis, 1939.

Scott/SUGGESTIONS

Cyril Scott, "Suggestions for a More Logical Sonata Form," MR XLVII (1917) 104–5.

Seaman/AMATEUR

Gerald Seaman, "Amateur Music-Making in Russia," ML XLVII (1966) 249–59. But cf. MR XXVIII (1967) 78–82 for M. H. Brown's and C. Greene's charges of plagiarism (mere translation) from L. N. Raaben's book on Russian instrumental ensemble music (Moscow, 1961).

Seaman/CHAMBER

———, "The First Russian Chamber Music," MR XXVI (1965) 326–37. But cf. MR XXVIII (1967) 78–82 and 256 for M. H. Brown's and C. Greene's charges of plagiarism (mere translation) from L. N.

Raaben's book on Russian instrumental ensemble music (Moscow, 1961); with replies by Seaman.

Seaman/PIANO ————, "The Rise of Russian Piano Music," MR XXVII (1066) 177 93. But cf. MR XXVIII (1907) 80–82 and 256 for M. H. Brown's charges of plagiarism (mere translation) from Alekseev/FORTEPIAN-NAIA; with reply by Seaman.

Seaman/RUSSIAN ————, History of Russian Music ("an amplification of a doctoral thesis completed in 1961"), Vol. I, "From Its Origins to Dargomyzhsky." New York: Frederick A. Praeger, 1967.

Sear/SPOOK H. G. Sear, "The Spook Sonata" (by Strindberg), MMR LXXXVI (1956) 94–97.

Searle/ALKAN Humphrey Searle, "A Plea for Alkan," ML XVIII (1937) 276–79.

Searle/LISZT ————, The Music of Liszt. London: Williams & Norgate, 1954. The 2d, revised ed. (New York: Dover, 1966) was not used here.

Seidel/ENHARMONIK Elmar Seidel, Die Enharmonik in den harmonischen Grossformen Franz Schuberts (Ph.D. diss. 1962). Frankfurt am Main: Johann Wolfgang Goethe-Universität, 1963.

Selden-Goth/MENDELSSOHN Gisella Selden-Goth (ed.), Felix Mendelssohn: Letters. London: Paul Elek, 1946.

Selva/SONATE Blanche Selva, La Sonate. Paris: Rouart, Lerolle, 1913.

Serly/LISZT-m Tibor Serly (ed.), Franz Liszt: Duo (Sonate) for Violin and Piano. New York: Southern Music, 1964.

Service/CADENCE Alfred Roy Service, "A Study of the Cadence as a Factor in Musical Intelligibility in Selected Piano Sonatas by American Composers," unpub. Ph.D. diss., State University of Iowa, 1958.

Servières/FAURÉ Georges Servières, Gabriel Fauré, étude critique. Paris: Henri Laurens, 1930.

Servières/SAINT-SAËNS ————, Saint-Saëns. Paris: Librairie Félix Alcan, 1923.

Shand/VIOLIN David Austin Shand, "The Sonata for Violin and Piano from Schumann to Debussy (1851–1917)," unpub. Ph.D. diss. (with many exx.), Boston University, 1948.

Shaw/LONDON Bernard Shaw, Music in London 1890–94, weekly criticisms contributed to The World, originally issued as an anthology in 1932; 3 vols. London: Constable, 1949.

Shedlock/SONATA John South Shedlock, The Pianoforte Sonata: Its Origin and Development (reprinted from the original ed., London, 1895), with a new Foreword by

W. S. Newman. New York: Da Capo Press, 1964. Cf. Kretzschmar/AUFSÄTZE I 61–63; NOTES XVII (1965–66) 912 (K. Speer).

Shepherd/GOETSCHIUS   Arthur Shepherd, "'Papa' Goetschius in Retrospect," MQ XXX (1944) 307–18.

Siebenkäs/BERGER   Dieter Siebenkäs, *Ludwig Berger: Sein Leben und seine Werke unter besonderer Berücksichtigung seines Liedschaffens.* Berlin: Merseburger, 1963.

Siegel/GERMANY   Linda Siegel, "The Influence of Romantic Literature on Romantic Music in Germany During the First Half of the Nineteenth Century," unpub. Ph.D. diss., Boston University, 1964.

Siegmund-Schultze/CHOPIN   Walther Siegmund-Schultze, "Chopin und Brahms," CONGRESS CHOPIN 388–95.

Sietz/HILLER   Reinhold Sietz, *Aus Ferdinand Hillers Briefwechsel (1826–61, 1862–69, 1870–75,* [to date]): *Beiträge zu einer Biographie Ferdinand Hillers,* 3 vols. (to date), Nos. 28, 48, and 56 in *Beiträge zur Rheinischen Musikgeschichte.* Köln: Arno Volk-Verlag, 1958, 1961, and 1964.

SIMG   *Sammelbände der Internationalen Musikgesellschaft.* 1900–1914.

Simpson/NIELSEN   Robert Simpson, *Carl Nielsen, Symphonist,* with a biographical appendix by Torben Meyer. London: J. M. Dent, 1952.

Sitwell/LISZT   Sacheverell Sitwell, *Liszt,* with "minor corrections" of the revised ed. in 1955 of the original ed. in 1934 (London). New York: Dover, 1967.

SJÖGREN-m   Emil Sjögren, *Cinq Sonates pour violon et piano,* with preface by Berta Sjögren. Stockholm: Edition Suecia, 1957 [copyright 1917 and 1945 by C. F. Peters].

Sloan/VIOLIN   Frances Sloan, "A Historical Survey of Violin Literature in America from the Colonial Period to 1880 (Composers' Birth-Date)," unpub. M.A. thesis, The University of North Carolina at Chapel Hill, 1950.

Slonimsky/LEXICON   Nicolas Slonimsky, *Lexicon of Musical Invective,* 2d ed. New York: Coleman-Ross, 1965.

Slonimsky/WILLIAMS   ———, "Alberto Williams: the Father of Argentinian Music," *Musical America* LXII/1 (Jan. 10, 1942) 11 and 37.

Smart/EIGHTEENTH-m   James R. Smart (ed.), (10) *Keyboard Sonatas of the Eighteenth* [and early 19th] *Century,* with brief prefaces. New York: G. Schirmer, 1967. Cf. NOTES XXV (1968–69) 133–34 (review by W. S. Newman).

Smith/FRIEDBERG   Julia Smith, *Master Pianist: The Career and Teaching of Carl Friedberg.* New York: Philosophical Library, 1963.

SMW — *Signale für die musikalische Welt.* 1842–1941.

SMYTH MEMOIRS — Ethel Symth, *Impressions That Remained: Memoirs* (up to 1892; first pub. in 1919), with an "Introduction" by E. Newman. New York: Alfred A. Knopf, 1946.

SMZ — *Schweizerische Musikzeitung.* 1861————.

SOHLMANS — *Sohlmans Musiklexikon,* 4 vols. Stockholm: Sohlmans Förlag, 1951–52.

Sonneck/LEKEU — Oscar George Theodore Sonneck, "Guillaume Lekeu (1870–1894)," MQ V (1919) 109–47. Reprinted in Sonneck/MISCELLANEOUS 190–240.

Sonneck/MAC DOWELL — ————, *Library of Congress Catalogue of First Editions of Edward MacDowell.* Washington: Government Printing Office, 1917.

Sonneck/MISCELLANEOUS — ————, *Miscellaneous Studies in the History of Music.* New York: Macmillan, 1921.

Sonneck/SUUM — ————, *Suum Cuique: Essays in Music.* New York: G. Schirmer, 1916.

Souchay/SCHUBERT — Marc-André Souchay, "Schubert als Klassiker der Form," zfMW XI (1928–29) 141–55.

Soullier/DICTIONNAIRE — Charles Simon Pascal Soullier, *Nouveau dictionnaire de musique illustré.* . . . Paris: E. Bazault, 1855. Cf. Cat. NYPL XXIX 287.

Šourek/DVOŘÁK — Otakar Šourek, *The Chamber Music of Antonín Dvořák,* trans. (from the original Czech ed. of 1943 and its 2d ed. of 1949) by R. F. Samsour. Prague: Artia, [1956].

Specht/STRAUSS — Richard Specht, *Richard Strauss und sein Werk,* 2 vols. Zürich: E. P. Tal, 1921.

Spink/BENNETT — Gerald W. Spink, "Schumann and Sterndale Bennett," MT CV (1964) 419–21.

Spivacke/PAGANINIANA — Harold Spivacke, "Paganiniana," in *The Library of Congress Quarterly Journal of Current Acquisitions* II/2 (Feb., 1945).

Spohr/AUTOBIOGRAPHY — *Louis Spohr's Autobiography,* started by him in 1847 (cf. Vol. II, p. 285) and brought up to 1838, the remainder being completed posthumously by his family; trans. from the German in 1864, 2 vols. London: Longman, Roberts, & Green, 1865. Cf. GROVE VIII 16–17 (P. David). About a third of the original German ed. (Kassel, 1860–61), all from the journeys, has been retrans. by Henry Pleasants as *The Musical Journeys of Louis Spohr* (Norman: University of Oklahoma Press, 1961). Bärenreiter in Kassel pub. a facs. of the original German ed. in 1954. All references in SSB are to the English trans. of 1865.

SSB　　　　　William S. Newman, *The Sonata Since Beethoven* (for cross references within the present vol.).

Stade/CHOPIN　　Friedrich Stade, "Die Harmonische Grundlage des letzten Satzes der B moll-Sonate von Chopin" (complete with full harmonization), MW XXXV (1904) 87–89 and "Musikbeilage."

Stanford/BENNETT　Sir Charles Villiers Stanford, "William Sterndale Bennett, 1816–1875," MQ II (1916) 628–57.

Statham/BENNETT　Henry Heathcote Statham, "Sterndale Bennett's Pianoforte Music," MT XIX (1878) 130–34, with exx.

Steger/CZERNY　Hellmuth Steger, "Beiträge zu Karl Czerny's Leben und Schaffen," unpub. Ph.D. diss., Ludwig-Maximilians-Universität, Munich, 1924.

Stein/REGER　　Fritz Stein, *Max Reger*. Potsdam: Akademische Verlagsgesellschaft Athenaion, 1939.

Stein/TSCHAIKOWSKIJ　Richard H. Stein, *Tschaikowskij*. Stuttgart: Deutsche Verlags-Anstalt, 1927.

Stein/VERZEICHNIS　Fritz Stein, *Thematisches Verzeichnis der im Druck erschienenen Werke von Max Reger*. Leipzig: Breitkopf & Härtel, 1953.

Steinitzer/KLAVIER　Max Steinitzer, "Richard Strauss' Werke für Klavier," DM XXIV/1 (1931–32) 105–9.

Steinitzer/STRAUSS　———, *Richard Strauss*. Berlin: Schuster & Loeffler, 1911.

STfMF　　　　*Svensk Tidskrift för Musikforskning.* 1919———.

Stockmeier/ORGELSONATE　Wolfgang Stockmeier, *Die deutsche Orgelsonate der Gegenwart* (Ph.D. diss., 1957). Köln: Universität Köln, 1958.

Storck/SCHUMANN　Karl Storck (ed.), *The Letters of Robert Schumann*, trans. by Hannah Bryant (from the original German selections and excerpts pub. in 1896). London: John Murray, 1907.

STRAD　　　　*The Strad.* 1891———.

STRAVINSKY　　Igor Stravinsky, *An Autobiography, trans. of Chroniques de ma vie,* Paris, 1935. New York: Simon and Schuster, 1936.

Studeny/VIOLINSONATE　Bruno Studeny, *Beiträge zur Geschichte der Violinsonate im 18. Jahrhundert*. Munich: Wunderhorn-Verlag, 1911.

Sturke/BRAHMS　Auguste Sturke, *Der Stil in Johannes Brahms' Werken* (Ph.D. diss., Universität Hamburg). Würzburg: Konrad Triltsch, 1932.

Subirá/ALBA　　José Subirá, *La Música en la casa de Alba*. Madrid: Sucesores de Rivadeneyra, 1927.

Subirá/HISTORIA　———, *Historia de la música española e hispanoamericana*. Barcelona: Salvat Editores, 1953.

Subirá & Cherbuliez/ MUSIKGESCHICHTE | José Subirá and Antoine-E. Cherbuliez, *Musikgeschichte von Spanien, Portugal, Lateinamerika.* Zürich: Pan-Verlag, [1957]. Pp. 1–200 (up to Latin America) are "freely translated" from Subirá/HISTORIA.

Swan/MEDTNER | Alfred J. Swan, "Medtner and the Music of Our Times," ML VIII (1927) 46–54.

Sydow/ BIBLIOGRAPHIE | Bronislas Édouard Sydow, *Bibliographie de F. F. Chopin* (completed in 1947). Warsaw: Nakł. Tow. Naukowego Warszawskiego, 1949. *Supplement.* Warsaw: Państwowe Wydawn. Naukowe, 1954.

Sydow/CHOPIN | B. E. Sydow, S. and D. Chainaye, and I. Sydow (eds.), *Correspondence de Frédéric Chopin,* 3 vols. (covering 1816–49). Paris: Richard-Masse, [1953–60].

Sydow & Hedley/ CHOPIN | Bronislaw Edward Sydow and Arthur Hedley (eds.), *Selected Correspondence of Fryderyk Chopin.* New York: McGraw-Hill, 1963.

Szabolcsi/UNGARISCHEN | Bence Szabolcsi, *Geschichte der ungarischen Musik,* trans. (into German from the original Hungarian ed. of 1947 [cf. Cat. NYPL XXX 401]) by I. Frommer & G. Knepler. Budapest: Corvina, 1964.

Szelényi/LISZT | Istvan Szelényi, "Der unbekannte Liszt," in LISZT-BARTÓK 1961, 311–31.

SZMW | *Studien zur Musikwissenschaft, Beihefte* of DTÖ-m, 1913–34, 1955——.

Taggart/SCHUBERT | James Leland Taggart, "Franz Schubert's Piano Sonatas: A Study of Performance Problems," unpub. Ph.D. diss., State University of Iowa, 1963.

Tagliapietra/ ANTOLOGIA–m | Gino Tagliapietra (ed.), *Antologia di musica antica e moderna,* 18 vols. Milan: G. Ricordi, 1931.

Tanzberger/SIBELIUS | Ernst Tanzberger, *Jean Sibelius: Eine Monographie, mit einem Werkverzeichnis.* Wiesbaden: Breitkopf & Härtel, 1962.

Tchaikovsky/ TSCHAIKOWSKY | Modest Tchaikovsky, *Das Leben Peter Iljitsch Tchaikowsky's,* trans. into German from the original Russian ed. of 1900–1902 by P. Juon, 2 vols. Moscow: P. Jurgenson, [1900?] and 1903 (not 1902). Cf. Abraham/TCHAIKOVSKY 241; BAKER 1626.

Tchaikovsky/WORKS–m | *Peter Ilyitch Tchaikovsky: Complete Works* (transliteration), 78 vols. up to 1955. Moscow: State Music Publishers, 1940——. Cf. Heyer/HISTORICAL 318–20.

Teal & Brown/ MICHIGAN | Mary D. Teal & Lawrence W. Brown, *The Effect of the Civil War on Music in Michigan.* Lansing: Michigan Civil War Centennial Observance Commission, 1965.

Temperley/
CORRESPONDENCE

Unpub. information pertinent to ssb XIV (also III-V), kindly supplied by Professor Nicholas Temperley (at the University of Illinois as of 1968) between 1964 and 1968 and founded largely on material in his unpub. Ph.D. diss. (Cambridge, 1959), "Instrumental Music in England, 1800–1850."

Temperley/DOMESTIC

Nicholas Mark Temperley, "Domestic Music in England, 1800–1860," PMA LXXXV (1958–59) 31–47.

Temperley/HANDEL

————, "Handel's Influence on English Music," MMR XC (1960) 163–74.

Temperley/
MENDELSSOHN

————, "Mendelssohn's Influence on English Music," ML XLIII (1962) 224–33.

Temperley/ MOZART

————, "Mozart's Influence on English Music," ML XLII (1961) 307–18.

Temperley/PINTO

————, "George Frederick Pinto," MT CVI (1965) 265–70; with pertinent correspondence following on pp. 446 and 523–24.

Temperley/PINTO–m

———— (ed.), *George Frederick Pinto: Sonata in E♭ Minor* (Op. 3/1 for P solo). London: Stainer & Bell, 1963.

TEMPO

Tempo: A Quarterly Review of Modern Music. 1948————.

Thayer & Forbes/
BEETHOVEN

[Alexander Wheelock] *Thayer's Life of Beethoven,* revised and edited by Elliot Forbes, 2 vols. Princeton: Princeton University Press, 1964.

Thayer & Riemann/
BEETHOVEN

Alexander Wheelock Thayer, *Ludwig van Beethovens Leben,* revised by Hugo Riemann from the German trans. by H. Dieters, 5 vols. Leipzig: Breitkopf & Härtel, 1917–23.

Thomas/CHOPIN

Betty Jean Thomas, "Harmonic Materials and Treatment of Dissonance in the Pianoforte Music of Frederick Chopin," unpub. Ph.D. diss., University of Rochester, 1963.

Thompson/
TOMASCHEK

Verne Waldo Thompson, *Wenzel Johann Tomaschek: His Predecessors, His Life, His Piano Works* (Ph.D. diss., Eastman School of Music, 1955). Rochester: University of Rochester Press (Microcard), 1957.

Tiersot/FRANCK

Julien Tiersot, "Les Œuvres inédites de César Franck," in RM/FRANCK 97–138.

Tiersot/LALO

————, "Édouard Lalo," trans. by F. Martens, MQ XI (1925) 8–35.

TOMASCHEK

"Excerpts From the Memoirs of J. W. Tomaschek," trans. from the German original in the Prague periodical *Libussa* IV (1845–50) by Abram Loft, MQ XXXII (1946) 244–64. Cf. Craw/DUSSEK 128; Thompson/TOMASCHEK 100–104.

Tovey/ANALYSIS   Donald Francis Tovey, *Essays in Musical Analysis,* 7 vols. London: Oxford University Press, 1936–44.

Townsend/DUETS–m   Douglas Townsend (ed.), *Piano Duets of the Classical Period for One Piano, Four Hands.* Bryn Mawr: Theodore Presser, 1956

TRÉSOR–m   *Le Trésor des pianistes,* 20 vols. Paris: Aristide and Louise Farrenc, 1861–72. For contents cf. GROVE 2d ed. V 148–49; Heyer/HISTORICAL 110–11 (but with a different grouping, in 23 vols.).

Truscott/BRAHMS   Harold Truscott, "Brahms and Sonata Style," MR XXV (1964) 186–201.

Truscott/MEDTNER   ———, "Medtner's Sonata in G Minor, Op. 22," MR XXII (1961) 112–23.

Truscott/REGER   ———, "Max Reger," MR XVII (1956) 134–52; with reply by E. Wellesz, p. 272.

Truscott/UNFINISHED   ———, "Schubert's Unfinished Piano Sonata in C Major (1825)," MR XVIII (1957) 114–37.

Truscott/UNITY   ———, "Organic Unity in Schubert's Early Sonata Music," MMR LXXXIX (1959) 62–66; with follow-up by Robert L. Jacobs on p. 114.

Truscott/VERSIONS   ———, "The Two Versions of Schubert's Op. 122," MR XIV (1953) 89–106.

Tuthill/CLARINET   Burnet C. Tuthill, "The Sonatas for Clarinet and Piano," JRME XIV (1966) 197–212.

Tyson/BEETHOVEN   Alan Tyson, *The Authentic English Editions of Beethoven.* London: Faber and Faber, 1963.

Tyson/FIELD   ———, "John Field's Earliest Compositions," ML XLVII (1966) 239–48; followed by correspondence with Nicholas Temperley in ML XLVIII (1967) 97–99.

Ueberfeldt/RIES   Ludwig Ueberfeldt, *Ferdinand Ries' Jugendentwicklung* (Ph.D. diss.). Bonn: Paul Roft, 1915.

Unger/CLEMENTI   Max Unger, *Muzio Clementis Leben.* Langensalza: Hermann Beyer & Söhne, 1913.

Upton/AYRES   William Treat Upton, "Frederic Ayres (1876–1926)," MQ XVIII (1932) 39–59.

Urbantschitsch/BRAHMS   Viktor Urbantschitsch, "Die Entwicklung der Sonatenform bei Brahms," SZMW XIV (1927) 264–85.

Vallas/FRANCK   Léon Vallas, *César Franck,* trans. from the original French ed. of 1950 by Hubert Foss. New York: Oxford University Press, 1951.

Vallas/D'INDY   ———, *Vincent d' Indy,* 2 vols. (*La Jeunesse* [1851–86] and *La Maturité*[,] *La Viellesse* [*1886–1931*]). Paris: Albin Michel, 1946 and 1950.

Vallas/SAINT-SAËNS   ———, "Une Discussion Saint-Saëns et d'Indy," RM XXIII/205 (1947) 79–87.

Van der Linden/ LEKEU   Albert Van der Linden (ed.), "Lettres de Guillaume Lekeu à Octave Maus (1892–93)," RBdM III (1949) 155–64.

Verdi/ COPIALETTERE   Gaetano Cesari e Alessandro Luzio (eds.), *I Copialettere di Giuseppe Verdi.* Milan: Stucchi Ceretti, 1913.

VERZEICHNISS MENDELSSOHN   *Thematisches Verzeichniss im Druck erschienener Compositionen von Felix Mendelssohn Bartholdy,* newly augmented (2d) ed. Leipzig: Breitkopf & Härtel, [1873]. Cf. Mendelssohn/VERLEGER 353–55.

VERZEICHNISS MOSCHELES   *Thematisches Verzeichniss im Druck erschienener Compositionen von Ignaz Moscheles.* Leipzig: Fr. Kistner, [1861?]; reprinted in London in 1966 (Stephen Austin for H. Baron).

Vetter/SCHUBERT   Walther Vetter, *Der Klassiker Schubert,* 2 vols. Leipzig: C. F. Peters, 1953. Cf. DMf VII (1954) 234–35 (H. J. Moser).

VODARSKY-SHIRAEFF   Alexandria Vodarsky-Shiraeff, *Russian Composers and Musicians: A Biographical Dictionary.* New York: H. W. Wilson, 1940.

Vogel/SCHUBERT   Adolf Bernhard Vogel, "Franz Schubert's Kammermusik-Werke: I. Sonaten für das Klavier allein; II. Vierhändige Clavierwerke," NZM LXIX/2 (1873) 493–95, 505–7.

Vrieslander/ ORGANISCHE   Otto Vrieslander, "Das Organische in Schubert's 'himmlischer Länge,'" in KONGRESS SCHUBERT 219–31.

Vuillermoz/FAURÉ   Emile Vuillermoz, *Gabriel Fauré.* Paris: Flammarion, 1960.

Vyborny/PAGANINI   Zdenek Vyborny, "Der 'Fall Paganini,'" DMf XVII (1964) 156–62.

WAGNER LEBEN   Richard Wagner, *Mein Leben,* "first authentic publication." Munich: Paul List, 1963. Written between 1865 and 1880 (cf. M. Gregor-Dellin's "Nachwort," pp. 895–912). The "authorized translation" pub. by Dodd, Mead of New York in 1931 proved not to be accurate enough for use here.

WAGNER-LISZT   *Briefwechsel zwischen Wagner und Liszt,* 2 vols. (through 1861). Leipzig: Breitkopf und Härtel, 1887. All references in the present vol. are to this original ed. rather than Francis Heuffer's trans. (New York, 1889) or later, more complete eds.

WAGNER PROSE   *Richard Wagner's Prose Works,* trans. by William Ashton Ellis, 8 vols. London: Kegan Paul, Trench, Trübner, 1893–99.

WAGNER-WESENDONK   Wolfgang Golther (ed.), *Richard Wagner an Mathilde Wesendonk[,] Tagebuchblätter und Briefe[,] 1853–1871*, first pub. in 1908. Leipzig: Breitkopf & Härtel, 1912?

Waldersee/VORTRÄGE   Paul Graf Waldersee (ed.), *Sammlung musikalischer Vorträge*, 5 vols. Leipzig: Breitkopf & Härtel, 1879–84.

Walker/CHOPIN   Alan Walker (ed.), *Frédéric Chopin: Profiles of the Man and the Musician*, including a chapter (pp. 144–69) by Peter Gould on the "Concertos and Sonatas" and a chapter (pp. 227–57) by Alan Walker on "Chopin and Musical Structure: An Analytical Approach." London: Barrie & Rockliff, 1966.

Walker/ENGLAND   Ernest Walker, *A History of Music in England* (first pub. in 1907), 3d ed., revised and enlarged by J. A. Westrup. Oxford: Clarendon Press, 1952.

Walker/WOLF   Frank Walker, *Hugo Wolf: A Biography*. London: J. M. Dent, 1951.

Waltershausen/DUALISMUS   Hermann Wolfgang Sartorius Freiherr von Waltershausen, "Der stilistische Dualismus in der Musik des 19. Jahrhunderts," pp. 202–6 in *Festschrift für Guido Adler zum 75. Geburtstag*. Vienna: Universal, 1930.

Warrack/WEBER   John Warrack, *Carl Maria von Weber*. London: Hamish Hamilton, 1968. Pub. too late to be incorporated in SSB; cf. ML XLIX (1968) 233–37 (E. Croft-Murray).

Wasielewski/SCHUMANN   Joseph Wilhelm von Wasielewski, *Robert Schumann*, 2d revised ed. Dresden: Rudolf Kuntze, 1869.

Weber/WEBER   Max Maria von Weber, *Carl Maria von Weber: ein Lebensbild*, 3 vols. Leipzig: Ernst Keil, 1864–66.

Wegeler & Ries/BEETHOVEN   Franz Gerhard Wegeler and Ferdinand Ries, *Biographische Notizen über Beethoven*. Koblenz: K. Bädeker, 1838.

Weigl/VIOLONCELL   Bruno Weigl, *Handbuch der Violoncell-Literatur*, 3d ed. Vienna: Universal-Edition, 1929.

Weinmann/ARTARIA   Alexander Weinmann, *Vollständiges Verlagsverzeichniss Artaria & Comp*. Vienna: Ludwig Krenn, 1952.

Weinstock/DONIZETTI   Herbert Weinstock, *Donizetti and the World of Opera in Italy, Paris, and Vienna in the First Half of the Nineteenth Century*. New York: Pantheon, 1963.

Weinstock/TCHAIKOVSKY   Herbert Weinstock, *Tchaikovsky*. New York: Alfred A. Knopf, 1943.

Werner/KIRCHENMUSIKER   Rudolf Werner, *Felix Mendelssohn Bartholdy als Kirchenmusiker*. Frankfurt: Selbstverlag des Verfassers, 1930.

Werner/MENDELSSOHN — Eric Werner, *Mendelssohn: A New Image of the Composer and His Age,* trans. from the German by Dika Newlin. New York: Macmillan, 1963.

Werner/PALE — ———, "Instrumental Music Outside the Pale of Classicism and Romanticism," in Hughes/INSTRUMENTAL 57–69 (with discussion).

Wessely/CHOPIN — Othmar Wessely, "Chopins B-moll-Sonate," ÖMZ IV (1949) 283–86.

Westerby/PIANOFORTE — Herbert Westerby, *The History of Pianoforte Music.* London: Kegan Paul, Trench, Trubner, 1924.

Westphal/MODERNEN — Kurt Westphal, "Die Sonate als Formproblem der modernen Musik," MMM XI (1929) 160–63.

Westphal/ROMANTISCHE — ———, "Die romantische Sonate als Formproblem," SMZ LXXIV (1934) 45–49, 117–22, 189–92.

WESTRUP & HARRISON — Jack A. Westrup and F. L. Harrison, *The New College Encyclopedia of Music* (first pub. in London in 1959). New York: W. W. Norton, 1960.

Westrup/SCHUBERT — Jack Allan Westrup, "The Chamber Music [of Schubert]," in Abraham/SCHUBERT 88–110.

Wetschky/KANONTECHNIK — Jürgen Wetschky, *Die Kanontechnik in der Instrumentalmusik von Johannes Brahms.* Regensburg: Gustav Bosse, 1967.

Wetzel/SCHARWENKA — Hermann Wetzel, "Philipp Scharwenka's Kammermusik," DM X/4 (1910–11) 27–35.

Wiberg/MUSIKHANDELNS — Albert Wiberg, *Den svenska Musikhandelns historia.* Stockholm: Victor Petterson, 1955.

Wier/VIOLIN–m — Albert E. Wier (ed.), [11] *Modern Sonatas for Violin* [and Piano], by Bargiel, Brahms (Opp. 78 and 100), Fauré (Op. 13), Franck, Grieg (Op. 45), Pâque, Rheinberger (Op. 77), Rubinstein (Op. 13), Schumann (Op. 121), R. Strauss. New York: Harcourt, Brace, 1935.

Winkler/SCHUBERT — Georg Winkler, "Das Problem der Polyphonie im Klavierschaffen Franz Schuberts," unpub. Ph.D. diss., Universität Wien, 1956.

Winternitz/AUTOGRAPHS — Emanuel Winternitz, *Musical Autographs from Monteverdi to Hindemith,* 2 vols. (corrected repub. of the original 1955 ed.) New York: Dover, 1965.

Wörner/SCHUMANN — Heinrich Wörner, *Robert Schumann.* Zürich: Atlantis, 1949. Cf. Redlich/SCHUMANN 146–47, 182–84.

WOLFE — Richard J. Wolfe, *Secular Music in America, 1801–1825: A Bibliography,* with an "Introduction" by C. S. Smith; 3 vols. New York: New York Public Library, 1964.

Wolverton/KEYBOARD — Byron Adams Wolverton, "Keyboard Music and Musicians in the Colonies and United States of

America Before 1830," unpub. Ph.D. diss., University of Indiana, 1966.

Worbs/MENDELSSOHN — Hans Christoph Worbs, *Felix Mendelssohn Bartholdy*. Leipzig: Koehler & Amelang, 1958.

Yasser/MEDTNER — Joseph Yasser, "The Art of Nicolas Medtner," in Holt/MEDTNER 46–65.

Yasser/RACHMANINOFF — ———, "Progressive Tendencies in Rachmaninoff's Music," TEMPO XXII (winter, 1951–52) 11–25.

Young/ELGAR — Percy M. Young, *Elgar, O. M.* [Order of Merit]: *A Study of a Musician*. London: Collins, 1955.

Ysaÿe/YSAÿE — Antoine Ysaÿe and Bertram Ratcliffe, *Ysaÿe: His Life, Work and Influence*, with a Preface by Yehudi Menuhin. London: William Heinemann, 1947. References in SSB are to this rather than the revised Fr. ed. (Brussels, 1948); cf. BAKER 1833.

Yuzhak/GLAZUNOV — K. I. Yuzhak, *Pianoforte Sonatas by A. K. Glazunov* (in Russian). Moscow, 1962.

Zavadini/DONIZETTI — Guido Zavadini, *Donizetti: Vita, musiche, epistolario*. Bergamo: Istituto Italiano d'Arti Grafiche, 1948.

Zeitlin & Goldberger/DUSSEK-m — Poldi Zeitlin & David Goldberger (eds.), *Jan Ladislaus Dussek: Sonatas for One Piano, Four Hands, Op. 67/1–3* (C. 230–32). Philadelphia: Elkan-Vogel, 1961.

zfMW — *Zeitschrift für Musikwissenschaft*. 1918–35. Superseded by AFMF.

ZIMG — *Zeitschrift der internationalen Musikgesellschaft*. 1900–1914.

Zimmerschied/HUMMEL — Dieter Zimmerschied, "Mozartiana aus dem Nachlass von J. N. Hummel," MOZART-JAHRBUCH 1964, 142–50.

Zimmerschied/KAMMERMUSIK — ———, *Die Kammermusik Johann Nepomuk Hummels* (Ph.D. diss.). Mainz: Johannes Gutenberg-Universität, 1966.

Zingel/SPOHR — Hans Joachim Zingel (ed.), *Louis Spohr: Sonate c-moll für Violine und Harfe*. Kassel: Bärenreiter, 1954.

Zosel/SCHULZ-BEUTHEN — Alois Zosel, *Heinrich Schulz-Beuthen (1838–1915): Leben und Werke* (Ph.D. diss., Universität Leipzig, 1931). Würzburg: K. Triltsch, 1931.

Index

Note: The Index includes every name, place, or other proper noun at least when and if it gets more than passing mention. It also includes other subjects or topics when they are discussed in their own right and can be listed in terms under which the reader might be expected to look. In the longer Index entries the page numbers in italics distinguish the main discussions. The page numbers in quotation marks refer to statements quoted verbatim from the persons indexed (on the topics added in parentheses).